McKinney's® New York Rules of Court: KeyRules

2021 Edition

Volume IIIA - Local Civil

THOMSON REUTERS®

Mat #42622888

ISBN: 978-1-539-21304-8

PREFACE

McKinney's® New York Rules of Court: KeyRules provides the practitioner with a comprehensive "single source" procedural guide for civil practice in state courts, combining applicable provisions of both statewide and local rules of civil procedure with relevant analytical materials.

This book consists of outlines of the applicable rules of practice, timing requirements, filing and service requirements, format requirements, hearing requirements, checklists, and other pertinent documents related to pleadings, motions, requests, notices, and applications in selected New York courts.

The selected New York courts include the following: Bronx County (12th Jud. Dist.), Kings County (2nd Jud. Dist.), Nassau County (10th Jud. Dist.), New York County (1st Jud. Dist.), and Queens County (11th Jud. Dist.).

THE PUBLISHER

October 2020

CONTACT US

What's New

In order to accommodate the growth of this product, we have incorporated all of the relevant local rules for Albany, Bronx, Erie, Kings, Nassau, New York, Onondaga, and Queens Counties into one document for each matter. Now, rather than thumbing through eight separate complaints to find the one that matches your jurisdiction, you will have one complaint that houses all local jurisdictions. The volume enclosed contains all of the information that you are accustomed to finding in KeyRules outlines, but with a different layout.

Highlights

- *Increased portability.* You'll find a more manageable volume without a reduction in content, making it more convenient for you to take your KeyRules book with you.

- *Greater adaptability.* The new design will allow you to easily modify your documents to comply with multiple nearby jurisdictions, as well as compare various local rules without having to sort through multiple documents.

Contact Us

We hope that you will find that this new format allows you to easily tailor your documents to your desired jurisdiction and that it increases the efficiency of your law practice. We encourage your feedback, which can be directed to: editors.us-legal@thomsonreuters.com.

Thank you for subscribing to this product. Should you have any questions regarding this product, please contact Customer Service at 1-800-328-4880 or by fax at 1-800-340-9378. If you would like to inquire about related publications, or to place an order, please contact us at 1-888-728-7677.

ADDITIONAL KEYRULES COVERAGE ON WESTLAW

Documents for additional jurisdictions are available on Thomson Reuters Westlaw.

Table of Contents

NEW YORK SUPREME COURT

Pleadings
Complaint

Document Last Updated August 2020

A. Checklist

(I) ❑ Matters to be considered by party filing the complaint

(a) ❑ Required documents

(1) ❑ Summons and complaint

(2) ❑ Index number

(3) ❑ Filing fees

(4) ❑ Proof of service

(b) ❑ Supplemental documents

(1) ❑ Supporting evidence; Exhibits

(2) ❑ Application to proceed as a poor person

(3) ❑ Working copies

(4) ❑ Statement of authorization in electronic filing cases

(5) ❑ Notice regarding availability of e-filing

(6) ❑ Notice to government of certain claims

(7) ❑ Documents required for specific types of claim

(c) ❑ Timing

(1) ❑ An action, including one brought in the name or for the benefit of the state, must be commenced within the time specified in NY CPLR § 201, et seq. unless a different time is prescribed by law or a shorter time is prescribed by written agreement

(2) ❑ Service of the summons and complaint shall be made within one hundred twenty (120) days after the commencement of the action or proceeding

(II) ❑ Matters to be considered by party filing the answer

(a) ❑ Required documents

(1) ❑ Answer

(2) ❑ Proof of service

(b) ❑ Supplemental documents

(1) ❑ Supporting evidence; Exhibits

(2) ❑ Demand for bill of particulars

(3) ❑ Filing fees

(4) ❑ Application to proceed as a poor person

(5) ❑ Working copies

(6) ❑ Statement of authorization in electronic filing cases

(7) ❑ Notice to government of certain claims

(8) ❑ Initiating documents served to newly added third parties

(9) ❑ ERIE COUNTY: Additional supplemental documents

(i) ❑ Notice of hard copy submission

(10) ❑ KINGS COUNTY: Additional supplemental documents

(i) ❑ Forms when filing in hard copy

(11) ❑ NEW YORK COUNTY: Additional supplemental documents

(i) ❑ Notice of hard copy submission

(12) ❑ ONONDAGA COUNTY: Additional supplemental documents

(i) ❑ Notice of hard copy submission

(13) ❑ QUEENS COUNTY: Additional supplemental documents

(i) ❑ Notice of hard copy submission

(c) ❑ Timing

(1) ❑ Service of an answer or reply shall be made within twenty (20) days after service of the pleading to which it responds

B. Timing

1. *Time to bring complaint.* An action, including one brought in the name or for the benefit of the state, must be commenced within the time specified in NY CPLR § 201, et seq. unless a different time is prescribed by law or a shorter time is prescribed by written agreement. No court shall extend the time limited by law for the commencement of an action. NY CPLR § 201.

   a. *Time when action must be commenced.* The time within which an action must be commenced, except as otherwise expressly prescribed, shall be computed from the time the cause of action accrued to the time the claim is interposed. NY CPLR § 203(a). For information on when a claim is considered to be interposed, refer to NY CPLR § 203.

2. *Time to serve summons and complaint.* Service of the summons and complaint, summons with notice, third-party summons and complaint, or petition with a notice of petition or order to show cause shall be made within one hundred twenty (120) days after the commencement of the action or proceeding, provided that in an action or proceeding, except a proceeding commenced under the election law, where the applicable statute of limitations is four (4) months or less, service shall be made not later than fifteen (15) days after the date on which the applicable statute of limitations expires. If service is not made upon a defendant within the time provided in NY CPLR § 306-b, the court, upon motion, shall dismiss the action without prejudice as to that defendant, or upon good cause shown or in the interest of justice, extend the time for service. NY CPLR § 306-b.

3. *Time to serve complaint after demand from defendant.* If the complaint is not served with the summons, the defendant may serve a written demand for the complaint. Service of the complaint shall be made within twenty (20) days after service of the demand. If no demand is made, the complaint shall be served within twenty (20) days after service of the notice of appearance. The court upon motion may dismiss the action if service of the complaint is not made as provided in NY CPLR § 3012(b). NY CPLR § 3012(b).

4. *Computation of time*

   a. *Units of time*

      i. *Day.* A calendar day includes the time from midnight to midnight. Sunday or any day of the week specifically mentioned means a calendar day. NY GEN CONSTR § 19.

      ii. *Month.* In a statute, contract or public or private instrument, unless otherwise provided in such contract or instrument or by law, the term month means a calendar month and not a lunar month. NY GEN CONSTR § 31.

      iii. *Year.* For information on the definition of a year, including the definitions of a half-year and quarter-year, refer to NY GEN CONSTR § 58 and NY GEN CONSTR § 50. For information on leap years, refer to NY GEN CONSTR § 57.

   b. *Periods of time*

      i. *Number of days.* A number of days specified as a period from a certain day within which or after or before which an act is authorized or required to be done means such number of calendar days exclusive of the calendar day from which the reckoning is made. NY GEN CONSTR § 20.

      - If such period is a period of two (2) days, Saturday, Sunday or a public holiday must be excluded from the reckoning if it is an intervening day between the day from which the reckoning is made and the last day of the period. NY GEN CONSTR § 20.
      - In computing any specified period of time from a specified event, the day upon which the event happens is

deemed the day from which the reckoning is made. The day from which any specified period of time is reckoned shall be excluded in making the reckoning. NY GEN CONSTR § 20.

ii. *Number of months.* A number of months after or before a certain day shall be computed by counting such number of calendar months from such day, exclusive of the calendar month in which such day occurs, and shall include the day of the month in the last month so counted having the same numerical order in days of the month as the day from which the computation is made, unless there be not so many days in the last month so counted, in which case the period computed shall expire with the last day of the month so counted. NY GEN CONSTR § 30.

iii. *Publication of notice; Number of days.* The period of publication of a legal notice shall be computed by excluding the first day of publication and including the day on which the act or event of which notice is given is to take place or which completes the full period of publication. NY CPLR § 2402.

iv. *Periods ending on Saturday, Sunday or public holiday.* When any period of time, computed from a certain day, within which or after which or before which an act is authorized or required to be done, ends on a Saturday, Sunday or a public holiday, such act may be done on the next succeeding business day and if the period ends at a specified hour, such act may be done at or before the same hour of such next succeeding business day, except that where a period of time specified by contract ends on a Saturday, Sunday or a public holiday, the extension of such period is governed by NY GEN CONSTR § 25. NY GEN CONSTR § 25-a(1).

- For a list of public holidays, refer to NY GEN CONSTR § 24.

v. *Additional time after certain kinds of service*

- *Service by mail.* Where a period of time prescribed by law is measured from the service of a paper and service is by mail, five (5) days shall be added to the prescribed period. NY CPLR Rule 2103(b)(2).
- *Service by overnight delivery service.* Where a period of time prescribed by law is measured from the service of a paper and service is by overnight delivery, one (1) business day shall be added to the prescribed period. NY CPLR Rule 2103(b)(6).

vi. *Daylight saving time.* For information on New York's time zone and the effect of daylight saving time, refer to NY GEN CONSTR § 52.

c. *Hours of court.* Notwithstanding any provision of law or rule of court to the contrary, throughout the State of New York the sessions of the Supreme Court for the disposition of business before the court shall commence not later than 9:30 a.m. and conclude not earlier than 5 p.m. Where warranted, the Chief Administrator of the Courts may authorize variances in the opening and closing hours of the courts, but, in such event, daily sessions shall total not less than six (6) hours. NY R CHIEF J § 3.1.

d. *Time limits; Extension of time.* Any act required by or in pursuance of law to be performed at or within a prescribed time, shall be performed according to the standard time. NY GEN CONSTR § 53.

i. Except where otherwise expressly prescribed by law, the court may extend the time fixed by any statute, rule or order for doing any act, upon such terms as may be just and upon good cause shown, whether the application for extension is made before or after the expiration of the time fixed. NY CPLR § 2004. Refer to the New York KeyRules Motion for Continuance/Extension of Time document for more information.

C. General Requirements

1. *Pleading, generally.* Statements in a pleading shall be sufficiently particular to give the court and parties notice of the transactions, occurrences, or series of transactions or occurrences, intended to be proved and the material elements of each cause of action or defense. NY CPLR § 3013.

a. *Pleadings to be liberally construed.* Pleadings shall be liberally construed. Defects shall be ignored if a substantial right of a party is not prejudiced. NY CPLR § 3026.

b. *Pleadings must give notice.* The basic requirement of NY CPLR § 3013 is that the pleading be "sufficiently particular" to give "notice" to the other side of the "transactions" or "occurrences" as seen by the pleader. As long as the pleading may be said to give such "notice," in whatever terminology it chooses, this aspect of the NY CPLR § 3013 requirement is satisfied. NY CPLR § 3013(Practice Commentary, C3013:2). The test is entirely sui generis. The court's inquiry, if a pleading issue is raised, is to ask whether the total verbiage of the pleading at issue may be said to give "notice" to the other side of what the pleader's grievance is. If it is sufficient to put the adversary on "notice," it satisfies this first mandate. NY CPLR § 3013(Practice Commentary, C3013:2).

c. *Pleadings must contain material facts.* The cause of action or defense is the thing the pleading must give notice of. NY CPLR § 3013 elaborates that the "material elements" of the claim or defense must be covered in the pleading.

Where does the practitioner find those elements? They come from the substantive law. The practitioner about to bring suit who turns to the pleadings article must do so with a substantive cause of action in hand. The practitioner must thus gather up the material elements of the claim or defense through analysis and research of the substantive law, if necessary, before even considering pleading. And when now turning to drafting, the practitioner need only see to it that the material elements that are substantive constituents of the claim are somewhere verbalized within the four corners of the complaint. See, e.g., Gershon v. Goldberg, 30 A.D.3d 372, 373, 817 N.Y.S.2d 322, 323 (2006). NY CPLR § 3013(Practice Commentary, C3013:2).

d. *Fulfilling pleading requirements.* The main mission of an affirmative pleading, whether it is the main claim in the complaint, or a counterclaim or cross-claim in the answer, etc., is to give "notice" of the event out of which the grievance arises. If the pleading can be said to give that notice, the first pleading requirement is satisfied. If the allegations also cover the substantive material elements that make up the particular cause of action relied on, the second requirement is met and the pleading satisfies the CPLR. SIEGEL-NYPRAC § 208.

2. *Pleading special matters*

   a. *Conditions precedent.* The performance or occurrence of a condition precedent in a contract need not be pleaded. A denial of performance or occurrence shall be made specifically and with particularity. In case of such denial, the party relying upon the performance or occurrence shall be required to prove on the trial only such performance or occurrence as shall have been so specified. NY CPLR Rule 3015(a).

   b. *Corporate status.* Where any party is a corporation, the complaint shall so state and, where known, it shall specify the state, country or government by or under whose laws the party was created. NY CPLR Rule 3015(b).

   c. *Prior judgment, decision or determination.* A judgment, decision or other determination of a court, judicial or quasi-judicial tribunal, or of a board or officer, may be pleaded without stating matter showing jurisdiction to render it. NY CPLR Rule 3015(c).

   d. *Signatures on negotiable instruments.* Unless specifically denied in the pleadings each signature on a negotiable instrument is admitted. NY CPLR Rule 3015(d).

   e. *Fraud or mistake.* Where a cause of action or defense is based upon misrepresentation, fraud, mistake, wilful default, breach of trust or undue influence, the circumstances constituting the wrong shall be stated in detail. NY CPLR Rule 3016(b).

      i. When relief against a mistake is sought in an action or by way of defense or counterclaim, relief shall not be denied merely because the mistake is one of law rather than one of fact. NY CPLR § 3005.

      ii. The party relying on the mistake should. . .take the initiative of pleading it. The "mistake" listed in NY CPLR Rule 3016(b) does not distinguish between fact or law and should thus be taken as applying to both. NY CPLR § 3005(Practice Commentary, C3005:2).

   f. *Law of a foreign country.* Where a cause of action or defense is based upon the law of a foreign country or its political subdivision, the substance of the foreign law relied upon shall be stated. NY CPLR Rule 3016(e).

   g. *Period of time.* When a time limit for the commencement of an action is a condition precedent to suit instead of a statute of limitations, satisfaction of the time limit must be alleged in the complaint because it is an element of the cause of action. NY CPLR § 201(Practice Commentary, C201:7); SIEGEL-NYPRAC § 34.

   h. *Designation of public body or officer.* When a public officer, body, board, commission or other public agency may sue or be sued in its official capacity, it may be designated by its official title, subject to the power of the court to require names to be added. NY CPLR § 1023.

3. *Complaint.* There shall be a complaint and an answer. NY CPLR § 3011. An action is commenced by filing a summons and complaint or summons with notice in accordance with NY CPLR Rule 2102. A special proceeding is commenced by filing a petition in accordance with NY CPLR Rule 2102. Where a court finds that circumstances prevent immediate filing, the signing of an order requiring the subsequent filing at a specific time and date not later than five (5) days thereafter shall commence the action. NY CPLR § 304(a).

   a. *Actions and special proceedings.* All civil judicial proceedings shall be prosecuted in the form of an action, except where prosecution in the form of a special proceeding is authorized. Except where otherwise prescribed by law, procedure in special proceedings shall be the same as in actions, and the provisions of the civil practice law and rules applicable to actions shall be applicable to special proceedings. NY CPLR § 103(b). The word "action" appearing anywhere in the CPLR includes special proceeding. NY CPLR § 103(Practice Commentary, C103:2).

b. *One form of action.* There is only one form of civil action. The distinctions between actions at law and suits in equity, and the forms of those actions and suits, have been abolished. NY CPLR § 103(a).

i. *Substance of law and equity retained.* Only the forms of action, legal and equitable, have been abolished; but the distinctions between law and equity and the remedies appropriate to each are still very much with us. In the Supreme Court, the court of general legal and equitable jurisdiction, the distinction survives. There are law and equity sides to the court, with jury trial generally a matter of right in the former and a matter of grace, if available at all, in the latter. NY CPLR § 103(Practice Commentary, C103:1).

ii. *Improper form of action.* If a court has obtained jurisdiction over the parties, a civil judicial proceeding shall not be dismissed solely because it is not brought in the proper form, but the court shall make whatever order is required for its proper prosecution. NY CPLR § 103(c).

c. *Jurisdiction.* There is no requirement in New York practice that jurisdiction be pleaded. Even with the lower courts, whose subject matter jurisdiction is limited, there is no statutory requirement, as there is in federal practice, that subject matter jurisdiction be pleaded. Whether there is subject matter jurisdiction is technically an affirmative defense for the defendant to raise by motion or answer, and the plaintiff is allowed, when the defense is raised, to establish the court's subject matter jurisdiction whether the complaint has mentioned it or not. The same is true of personal jurisdiction: the complaint need not say anything about it. If personal jurisdiction is lacking, the defendant must raise the objection by motion or answer, and the plaintiff can, in response, adduce whatever is needed to show that personal jurisdiction exists. SIEGEL-NYPRAC § 215; NY CPLR Rule 3211.

d. *Demand for relief.* Except as otherwise provided in NY CPLR § 3017(c), every complaint, counterclaim, cross-claim, interpleader complaint, and third-party complaint shall contain a demand for the relief to which the pleader deems himself entitled. Relief in the alternative or of several different types may be demanded. Except as provided in NY CPLR § 3215, the court may grant any type of relief within its jurisdiction appropriate to the proof whether or not demanded, imposing such terms as may be just. NY CPLR § 3017(a).

i. *Demand in personal injury or wrongful death action.* In an action to recover damages for personal injuries or wrongful death, the complaint, counterclaim, cross-claim, interpleader complaint, and third-party complaint shall contain a prayer for general relief but shall not state the amount of damages to which the pleader deems himself entitled. If the action is brought in the supreme court, the pleading shall also state whether or not the amount of damages sought exceeds the jurisdictional limits of all lower courts which would otherwise have jurisdiction. Provided, however, that a party against whom an action to recover damages for personal injuries or wrongful death is brought, may at any time request a supplemental demand setting forth the total damages to which the pleader deems himself entitled. A supplemental demand shall be provided by the party bringing the action within fifteen (15) days of the request. In the event the supplemental demand is not served within fifteen (15) days, the court, on motion, may order that it be served. A supplemental demand served pursuant to NY CPLR § 3017(c) shall be treated in all respects as a demand made pursuant to NY CPLR § 3017(a). NY CPLR § 3017(c).

e. *Declaratory judgment.* The supreme court may render a declaratory judgment having the effect of a final judgment as to the rights and other legal relations of the parties to a justiciable controversy whether or not further relief is or could be claimed. If the court declines to render such a judgment it shall state its grounds. A party who has brought a claim for personal injury or wrongful death against another party may maintain a declaratory judgment action directly against the insurer of such other party, as provided in NY INS § 3420(a)(6). NY CPLR § 3001. [Editor's note: NY INS § 3420 was held preempted in Wadsworth v. Allied Professionals Ins. Co., 748 F.3d 100 (2d Cir. 2014)].

i. *Demand for declaratory judgment.* In an action for a declaratory judgment, the demand for relief in the complaint shall specify the rights and other legal relations on which a declaration is requested and state whether further or consequential relief is or could be claimed and the nature and extent of any such relief which is claimed. NY CPLR § 3017(b).

f. *Actions and relief not barred for inconsistency*

i. *Action against several persons; Action against one no bar to action against others.* Where causes of action exist against several persons, the commencement or maintenance of an action against one, or the recovery against one of a judgment which is unsatisfied, shall not be deemed an election of remedies which bars an action against the others. NY CPLR § 3002(a).

ii. *Action against agent and undisclosed principal; Action against one no bar to action against others.* Where causes of action exist against an agent and his undisclosed principal, the commencement or maintenance, after disclosure of the principal, of an action against either, or the recovery of a judgment against either which is unsatisfied, shall not be deemed an election of remedies which bars an action against the other. NY CPLR § 3002(b).

iii. *Action for conversion and on contract.* Where causes of action exist against several persons for the conversion of property and upon express or implied contract, the commencement or maintenance of an action against one, or the recovery against one of a judgment which is unsatisfied, either for the conversion or upon the contract, shall not be deemed an election of remedies which bars an action against the others either for the conversion or upon the contract. NY CPLR § 3002(c).

iv. *Action on contract and to reform.* A judgment denying recovery in an action upon an agreement in writing shall not be deemed to bar an action to reform such agreement and to enforce it as reformed. NY CPLR § 3002(d).

v. *Claim for damages and rescission.* A claim for damages sustained as a result of fraud or misrepresentation in the inducement of a contract or other transaction, shall not be deemed inconsistent with a claim for rescission or based upon rescission. In an action for rescission or based upon rescission the aggrieved party shall be allowed to obtain complete relief in one action, including rescission, restitution of the benefits, if any, conferred by him as a result of the transaction, and damages to which he is entitled because of such fraud or misrepresentation; but such complete relief shall not include duplication of items of recovery. NY CPLR § 3002(e).

vi. *Vendee's lien not to depend upon form of action.* When relief is sought, in an action or by way of defense or counterclaim, by a vendee under an agreement for the sale or exchange of real property, because of the rescission, failure, invalidity or disaffirmance of such agreement, a vendee's lien upon the property shall not be denied merely because the claim is for rescission, or is based upon the rescission, failure, invalidity or disaffirmance of such agreement. NY CPLR § 3002(f).

g. *Special proceedings.* A special proceeding is a civil judicial proceeding in which a right can be established or an obligation enforced in summary fashion. Like an action, it ends in a judgment but the procedure is similar to that on a motion. Statutory authorization must exist for the use of a special proceeding to enforce a particular right. NY CPLR § 401(Practice Commentary, C401:1). For information on when a special proceeding is called for, refer to NY CPLR § 401(Practice Commentary, C401:1).

4. *Particularity in pleadings; Specific actions*

a. *License to do business.* Where the plaintiff's cause of action against a consumer arises from the plaintiff's conduct of a business which is required by state or local law to be licensed by the department of consumer affairs of the city of New York, the Suffolk county department of consumer affairs, the Westchester county department of consumer affairs/weight-measures, the county of Rockland, the county of Putnam or the Nassau county department of consumer affairs, the complaint shall allege, as part of the cause of action, that plaintiff was duly licensed at the time of services rendered and shall contain the name and number, if any, of such license and the governmental agency which issued such license. The failure of the plaintiff to comply with NY CPLR Rule 3015(e) will permit the defendant to move for dismissal pursuant to NY CPLR Rule 3211(a)(7). NY CPLR Rule 3015(e).

b. *Libel or slander.* In an action for libel or slander, the particular words complained of shall be set forth in the complaint, but their application to the plaintiff may be stated generally. NY CPLR Rule 3016(a). In a libel or slander case the defamatory words must be quoted verbatim. This is strictly enforced and any paraphrasing or use of qualifying words makes the complaint defective. The words' applicability to the plaintiff, however, may be stated generally. If extrinsic facts are relied on to give defamatory import to the words, or if the persons to whom the words were uttered had special knowledge that gave the words their defamatory impact, those facts should be pleaded. SIEGEL-NYPRAC § 216.

c. *Separation or divorce.* In an action for separation or divorce, the nature and circumstances of a party's alleged misconduct, if any, and the time and place of each act complained of, if any, shall be specified in the complaint or counterclaim as the case may be. NY CPLR Rule 3016(c).

d. *Prior judgment.* In an action on a judgment, the complaint shall state the extent to which any judgment recovered by the plaintiff against the defendant, or against a person jointly liable with the defendant, on the same cause of action has been satisfied. NY CPLR Rule 3016(d).

e. *Sale and delivery of goods or performing of labor or services.* In an action involving the sale and delivery of goods, or the performing of labor or services, or the furnishing of materials, the plaintiff may set forth and number in his verified complaint the items of his claim and the reasonable value or agreed price of each. Thereupon the defendant by his verified answer shall indicate specifically those items he disputes and whether in respect of delivery or performance, reasonable value or agreed price. NY CPLR Rule 3016(f).

f. *Personal injury resulting from negligent use of motor vehicle.* In an action designated in NY INS § 5104(a), for personal injuries arising out of negligence in the use or operation of a motor vehicle in this state, the complaint shall state that the plaintiff has sustained a serious injury, as defined in NY INS § 5102(d), or economic loss greater than basic economic loss, as defined in NY INS § 5102(a). NY CPLR Rule 3016(g).

g. *Gross negligence or intentional infliction of harm by certain directors, officers or trustees of certain corporations, associations, organizations or trusts.* In an action or proceeding based upon the conduct of a director, officer or trustee described in NY NOT PROF CORP § 720-a or NY ART & CULT AFF § 20.09(6), the complaint shall be verified and shall state whether or not said complaint is based upon gross negligence or intentional infliction of harm. NY CPLR Rule 3016(h).

h. *Legal challenges to college and university disciplinary findings.* In any proceeding brought against a college or university that is chartered by the regents or incorporated by special act of the legislature, which proceeding seeks to vacate or modify a finding that a student was responsible for a violation of college or university rules regarding a violation covered by NY EDUC § 6439, et seq., the name and identifying biographical information of any student shall be presumptively confidential and shall not be included in the pleadings and other papers from such proceeding absent a waiver or cause shown as determined by the court. Such witnesses shall be identified only as numbered witnesses. If such a name or identifying biographical information appears in a pleading or paper filed in such a proceeding, the court, absent such a waiver or cause shown, shall direct the clerk of the court to redact such name and identifying biographical information and so advise the parties. NY CPLR Rule 3016(i).

i. *Review of determinations by administrative officers of the unified court system.* In any action or proceeding brought to review a determination of the chief judge of the court of appeals, of the court of appeals or of the administrative board of the courts, made pursuant to the provisions of article seven-A of the judiciary law (NY JUD § 210, et seq.) or NY CONST Art. 6, § 28, the only proper party to be named therein shall be the chief administrator of the courts, in his representative capacity. No action or proceeding so instituted shall name the chief judge, the court of appeals or any member thereof, or the administrative board or any member thereof as a party. NY CPLR § 1026.

j. *Petition to appoint trustee for property of imprisoned person.* For information on the contents of a petition for appointment of a trustee to care for the property of an imprisoned person, including documents required to be presented with such a petition, refer to NY CORRECT § 350, et seq.

k. *Article 78 proceeding against government body or officer.* For information on proceeding against a government body or officer, refer to NY CPLR § 7801.

5. *Parties named in complaint*

a. *Complaint against partnership or unincorporated association.* Two or more persons conducting a business as a partnership may sue or be sued in the partnership name, and actions may be brought by or against the president or treasurer of an unincorporated association on behalf of the association in accordance with the provisions of the general associations law (NY GEN ASSOC § 1, et seq.). NY CPLR § 1025.

b. *Complaint against unknown party.* A party who is ignorant, in whole or in part, of the name or identity of a person who may properly be made a party, may proceed against such person as an unknown party by designating so much of his name and identity as is known. If the name or remainder of the name becomes known all subsequent proceedings shall be taken under the true name and all prior proceedings shall be deemed amended accordingly. NY CPLR § 1024.

c. *Complaint against jointly liable parties not served; Effect on judgment.* Where less than all of the named defendants in an action based upon a joint obligation, contract or liability are served with the summons, the plaintiff may proceed against the defendants served, unless the court otherwise directs, and if the judgment is for the plaintiff it may be taken against all the defendants. NY CPLR § 1501.

6. *Joinder*

a. *Of claims.* The plaintiff in a complaint or the defendant in an answer setting forth a counterclaim or cross-claim may join as many claims as he may have against an adverse party. There may be like joinder of claims when there are multiple parties. NY CPLR § 601(a).

   i. *Limit on joinder of claims arising from consumer credit transactions.* Two or more plaintiffs may join no more than five claims in any one action or proceeding against the same defendant arising out of separate consumer credit transactions, provided that the plaintiffs are represented by the same attorney. NY CPLR § 601(b).

b. *Of parties; Necessary.* Persons who ought to be parties if complete relief is to be accorded between the persons who are parties to the action or who might be inequitably affected by a judgment in the action shall be made plaintiffs or defendants. When a person who should join as a plaintiff refuses to do so he may be made a defendant. NY CPLR § 1001(a).

   i. When a person who should be joined under NY CPLR § 1001(a) has not been made a party and is subject to the jurisdiction of the court, the court shall order him summoned. If jurisdiction over him can be obtained only by his consent or appearance, the court, when justice requires, may allow the action to proceed without his being made a party. NY CPLR § 1001(b). In determining whether to allow the action to proceed, the court shall consider the factors listed in NY CPLR § 1001(b). NY CPLR § 1001(b).

c. *Of parties; Permissive*

i. *Plaintiffs.* Persons who assert any right to relief jointly, severally, or in the alternative arising out of the same transaction, occurrence, or series of transactions or occurrences, may join in one action as plaintiffs if any common question of law or fact would arise. NY CPLR § 1002(a).

ii. *Defendants.* Persons against whom there is asserted any right to relief jointly, severally, or in the alternative, arising out of the same transaction, occurrence, or series of transactions or occurrences, may be joined in one action as defendants if any common question of law or fact would arise. NY CPLR § 1002(b).

iii. *Separate relief; Separate trials.* It shall not be necessary that each plaintiff be interested in obtaining, or each defendant be interested in defending against, all the relief demanded or as to every claim included in an action; but the court may make such orders as will prevent a party from being embarrassed, delayed, or put to expense by the inclusion of a party against whom he asserts no claim and, who asserts no claim against him, and may order separate trials or make other orders to prevent prejudice. NY CPLR § 1002(c).

d. *When joinder unnecessary.* Except where otherwise prescribed by order of the court, an executor, administrator, guardian of the property of an infant, committee of the property of a judicially declared incompetent, conservator of the property of a conservatee, trustee of an express trust, insured person who has executed to his insurer either a loan or subrogation receipt, trust agreement, or other similar agreement, or person with whom or in whose name a contract has been made for the benefit of another, may sue or be sued without joining with him the person for or against whose interest the action is brought. NY CPLR § 1004.

e. *Class actions.* For information on the requirements for class actions, refer to NY CPLR § 901, et seq. [Editor's note: parts of NY CPLR § 901 were recognized as preempted in Holster v. Gatco, Inc., 618 F.3d 214 (2d Cir. 2010), which was recognized as abrogated by Giovanniello v. ALM Media, LLC, 726 F.3d 106 (2d Cir. 2013)].

f. *Interpleader.* For information on interpleader, refer to NY CPLR § 1006.

g. *Severance of claims and separate trials.* In furtherance of convenience or to avoid prejudice the court may order a severance of claims, or may order a separate trial of any claim, or of any separate issue. The court may order the trial of any claim or issue prior to the trial of the others. NY CPLR § 603.

7. *Simplified procedure for court determination of disputes.* An action may be commenced without the service of a summons, or may be continued after the service of a summons, without pleadings, by the filing of a statement, signed and acknowledged by all the parties or signed by their attorneys, specifying plainly and concisely the claims and defenses between the parties and the relief requested. Signing constitutes a certificate that the issues are genuine, and such filing, together with a note of issue, to be filed at the same time, shall constitute the joinder of issues in the action. The procedure in any action commenced under NY CPLR § 3031 shall constitute "the New York Simplified Procedure for Court Determination of Disputes" and it shall be sufficient so to identify the procedure in any contract or other document referring to it. A submission of a controversy under NY CPLR § 3031 shall constitute a waiver by the parties of the right to trial by jury. NY CPLR § 3031. For more information, refer to NY CPLR § 3031.

8. *Motion for summary judgment in lieu of complaint.* When an action is based upon an instrument for the payment of money only or upon any judgment, the plaintiff may serve with the summons a notice of motion for summary judgment and the supporting papers in lieu of a complaint. NY CPLR § 3213.

9. *Verification of pleadings.* A verification is a statement under oath that the pleading is true to the knowledge of the deponent, except as to matters alleged on information and belief, and that as to those matters he believes it to be true. Unless otherwise specified by law, where a pleading is verified, each subsequent pleading shall also be verified, except the answer of an infant and except as to matter in the pleading concerning which the party would be privileged from testifying as a witness. Where the complaint is not verified, a counterclaim, cross-claim or third-party claim in the answer may be separately verified in the same manner and with the same effect as if it were a separate pleading. NY CPLR § 3020(a).

a. *When verification required.* In only a few instances is verification mandatory. SIEGEL-NYPRAC § 232. Among the CPLR instances of mandatory verification of a complaint are where it contains or has appended the schedule of goods and services available for optional use under NY CPLR Rule 3016(f), or where it seeks to charge an obligor with an amount still unsatisfied after prior suit by the obligee against a co-obligor. The pleadings in an Article 78 (NY CPLR § 7801, et seq.) proceeding also require verification. SIEGEL-NYPRAC § 232.

b. *By whom verification made.* The verification of a pleading shall be made by the affidavit of the party, or, if two or more parties united in interest are pleading together, by at least one of them who is acquainted with the facts, except:

i. If the party is a domestic corporation, the verification shall be made by an officer thereof and shall be deemed a verification by the party;

ii. If the party is the state, a governmental subdivision, board, commission, or agency, or a public officer in behalf of any of them, the verification may be made by any person acquainted with the facts; and

iii. If the party is a foreign corporation, or is not in the county where the attorney has his office, or if there are two or more parties united in interest and pleading together and none of them acquainted with the facts is within that county, or if the action or defense is founded upon a written instrument for the payment of money only which is in the possession of an agent or the attorney, or if all the material allegations of the pleading are within the personal knowledge of an agent or the attorney, the verification may be made by such agent or attorney. NY CPLR § 3020(d).

c. *Form of affidavit of verification.* The affidavit of verification must be to the effect that the pleading is true to the knowledge of the deponent, except as to the matters therein stated to be alleged on information and belief, and that as to those matters he believes it to be true. If it is made by a person other than the party, he must set forth in the affidavit the grounds of his belief as to all matters not stated upon his knowledge and the reason why it is not made by the party. NY CPLR Rule 3021.

d. *Effect of verified pleading.* Unless they are stated to be made upon the information and belief of the party, they must be regarded for all purposes, including a criminal prosecution, as having been made upon the knowledge of the person verifying the pleading. An allegation that the party has not sufficient knowledge or information to form a belief with respect to a matter, must, for the same purposes, be regarded as an allegation that the person verifying the pleading has not such knowledge or information. NY CPLR Rule 3023. A "verified pleading" may be utilized as an affidavit whenever the latter is required. NY CPLR § 105(u).

i. Although pleadings ordinarily need not be verified, a benefit of voluntary verification is that the pleading, pursuant to NY CPLR § 105(u), then qualifies as an affidavit. The Court of Appeals has also held that a verified bill of particulars, which technically is not a pleading, also fell within the scope of NY CPLR § 105(u) and therefore had the effect of an affidavit. NY CPLR § 105(Practice Commentary, C105:7); Sanchez v. Nat'l R.R. Passenger Corp., 21 N.Y.3d 890, 988 N.E.2d 511 (2013). However, a verified pleading will be of no value as an affidavit when the circumstances require evidentiary detail and the pleading is phrased in conclusory terms. NY CPLR § 105(Practice Commentary, C105:7).

e. *Defective verification.* A defectively verified pleading shall be treated as an unverified pleading. Where a pleading is served without a sufficient verification in a case where the adverse party is entitled to a verified pleading, he may treat it as a nullity, provided he gives notice with due diligence to the attorney of the adverse party that he elects so to do. NY CPLR Rule 3022.

10. *Mandatory arbitration.* In each county where an arbitration program is established by order of the Chief Administrator, all civil actions for a sum of money only, except those commenced in small claims parts and not subsequently transferred to a regular part of court, that are noticed for trial or commenced in the Supreme Court, County Court, the Civil Court of the City of New York, a District Court or a City Court, on or after the effective date of the order where recovery sought for each cause of action is six thousand dollars ($6,000) or less, or ten thousand dollars ($10,000) or less in the Civil Court of the City of New York, or such other sum as may be authorized by law, exclusive of costs and interest, shall be heard and decided by a panel of arbitrators. The Chief Administrator may also, at any time, upon the establishment of the program in any particular court or county or thereafter, provide for the submission to arbitration of actions seeking recovery of such sums, that are pending for trial in those courts on the effective date of the order. NY R CHIEF J § 28.2(b). For more information on mandatory arbitration, refer to NY R CHIEF J § 28.1, et seq.

11. *Governing law.* The civil practice law and rules (NY CPLR § 101, et seq.) shall govern the procedure in civil judicial proceedings in all courts of the state and before all judges, except where the procedure is regulated by inconsistent statute. The civil practice law and rules shall succeed the civil practice act and rules of civil practice and shall be deemed substituted therefor throughout the statutes and rules of the state. NY CPLR § 101. The civil practice law and rules shall be liberally construed to secure the just, speedy and inexpensive determination of every civil judicial proceeding. NY CPLR § 104.

a. *Uniform trial court rules.* The uniform civil rules for the Supreme Court and County Court (NY R UNIF TRIAL CTS § 202.1, et seq.) shall be applicable to civil actions and proceedings in the Supreme Court and the County Court. NY R UNIF TRIAL CTS § 202.1(a). The provisions of the uniform rules shall be construed consistent with the Civil

Practice Law and Rules (CPLR), and matters not covered by the uniform rules shall be governed by the CPLR. NY R UNIF TRIAL CTS § 202.1(d).

b. *Local rules.* Local court rules, not inconsistent with law or with uniform civil rules for the Supreme Court and County Court (NY R UNIF TRIAL CTS § 202.1, et seq.), shall comply with Part 9 of the Rules of the Chief Judge (NY R CHIEF J § 9.1). NY R UNIF TRIAL CTS § 202.1(c).

c. *Official forms.* The state administrator shall have the power to adopt, amend and rescind an appendix of forms. Forms adopted pursuant to NY CPLR § 107 shall be sufficient under the civil practice law and rules and shall illustrate the simplicity and brevity of statement which the civil practice law and rules contemplate. NY CPLR § 107.

12. *Rules of the commercial division.* [Editor's note: certain types of civil cases or civil cases meeting certain monetary thresholds that are filed in the state of New York must be filed in the Commercial Division of the New York Supreme Courts. Rules governing practice in the commercial division are found in NY R UNIF TRIAL CTS § 202.70]. Cases which must be filed in the commercial division are listed below. For more information, refer to NY R UNIF TRIAL CTS § 202.70.

a. *Monetary thresholds.* Except as set forth in NY R UNIF TRIAL CTS § 202.70(b), the monetary thresholds of the Commercial Division, exclusive of punitive damages, interests, costs, disbursements and counsel fees claimed, are established as follows: (1) Albany County, fifty thousand dollars ($50,000); (2) Eighth Judicial District, one hundred thousand dollars ($100,000); (3) Kings County, one hundred fifty thousand dollars ($150,000); (4) Nassau County, two hundred thousand dollars ($200,000); (5) New York County, five hundred thousand dollars ($500,000); (6) Onondaga County, fifty thousand dollars ($50,000); (7) Queens County, one hundred thousand dollars ($100,000); (8) Seventh Judicial District, fifty thousand dollars ($50,000); (9) Suffolk County, one hundred thousand dollars ($100,000); and (10) Westchester County, one hundred thousand dollars ($100,000). NY R UNIF TRIAL CTS § 202.70(a).

i. *ALBANY COUNTY.* The Commercial Division of the Albany County Supreme Court exercises jurisdiction over selected business and commercial disputes in which the amount at issue generally involves damage claims in a minimum amount of fifty thousand dollars ($50,000) as well as claims for unspecified amounts where the value of the commercial asset(s) in dispute exceeds fifty thousand dollars ($50,000). A separate publication promulgating the rules and criteria relating to the filing and management of Commercial Court cases in this part may be obtained from the Albany County Supreme Court Clerk's Office. A section of the Uniform Civil Rules for the Supreme Court and County Court sets forth statewide rules. NY R 3 JD SUP Doc. 1(E).

ii. *BRONX COUNTY.* The monetary threshold for commercial cases in Bronx County will be seventy-five thousand dollars ($75,000). All other parameters including the type of matters that will be heard are contained within the Rules of the Commercial Division of the Supreme Court (NY R UNIF TRIAL CTS § 202.70). NY R BRONX FIL R Doc. 12.

iii. *NEW YORK COUNTY.* The monetary threshold in the New York County Commercial Division, which is generally applicable, is an amount in controversy of five hundred thousand dollars ($500,000) or more (exclusive of punitive damages, interest, costs, disbursements, and counsel fees). If the case is designated a commercial one and the Addendum is submitted, the clerk will review the pleadings to determine whether the amount in controversy in the case meets the monetary threshold or whether an exception to the threshold applies. NY R NY CTY Procedure IA(B). For more information on assigning a case to the commercial division in New York County, refer to NY R NY CTY Procedure IA(B).

b. *Commercial cases.* Actions in which the principal claims involve or consist of the following will be heard in the Commercial Division provided that the monetary threshold is met or equitable or declaratory relief is sought:

i. Breach of contract or fiduciary duty, fraud, misrepresentation, business tort (e.g., unfair competition), or statutory and/or common law violation where the breach or violation is alleged to arise out of business dealings (e.g., sales of assets or securities; corporate restructuring; partnership, shareholder, joint venture, and other business agreements; trade secrets; restrictive covenants; and employment agreements not including claims that principally involve alleged discriminatory practices);

ii. Transactions governed by the Uniform Commercial Code (exclusive of those concerning individual cooperative or condominium units);

iii. Transactions involving commercial real property, including Yellowstone injunctions and excluding actions for the payment of rent only;

iv. Shareholder derivative actions—without consideration of the monetary threshold;

v. Commercial class actions—without consideration of the monetary threshold;

vi. Business transactions involving or arising out of dealings with commercial banks and other financial institutions;

vii. Internal affairs of business organizations;

viii. Malpractice by accountants or actuaries, and legal malpractice arising out of representation in commercial matters;

ix. Environmental insurance coverage;

x. Commercial insurance coverage (e.g., directors and officers, errors and omissions, and business interruption coverage);

xi. Dissolution of corporations, partnerships, limited liability companies, limited liability partnerships and joint ventures—without consideration of the monetary threshold; and

xii. Applications to stay or compel arbitration and affirm or disaffirm arbitration awards and related injunctive relief pursuant to Article 75 of the New York Civil Practice Law and Rules (NY CPLR § 7501, et seq.) involving any of the foregoing enumerated commercial issues. Where the applicable arbitration agreement provides for the arbitration to be heard outside the United States, the monetary threshold set forth in NY R UNIF TRIAL CTS § 202.70(a) shall not apply. NY R UNIF TRIAL CTS § 202.70(b).

c. *Non-commercial cases.* The following will not be heard in the Commercial Division even if the monetary threshold is met:

i. Suits to collect professional fees;

ii. Cases seeking a declaratory judgment as to insurance coverage for personal injury or property damage;

iii. Residential real estate disputes, including landlord-tenant matters, and commercial real estate disputes involving the payment of rent only;

iv. Home improvement contracts involving residential properties consisting of one to four residential units or individual units in any residential building, including cooperative or condominium units;

v. Proceedings to enforce a judgment regardless of the nature of the underlying case;

vi. First-party insurance claims and actions by insurers to collect premiums or rescind non-commercial policies; and

vii. Attorney malpractice actions except as otherwise provided in NY R UNIF TRIAL CTS § 202.70(b)(8). NY R UNIF TRIAL CTS § 202.70(c).

d. For more information on the Commercial Division, refer to NY R UNIF TRIAL CTS § 202.70.

D. Documents

1. *Required documents*

a. *Summons and complaint.* Refer to the General Requirements section of this document for information on the summons and complaint.

b. *Index number.* Upon filing the summons and complaint, summons with notice or petition in an action or proceeding commenced in supreme or county court with the clerk of the county, an index number shall be assigned and the fee required by NY CPLR § 8018(a) shall be paid. Upon the filing of a summons and complaint against a person not already a party, as permitted under NY CPLR § 1007 or NY CPLR Rule 1011, the fee required by NY CPLR § 8018(a) shall be paid, but a separate index number shall not be assigned. NY CPLR § 306-a(a). For information on the amount of the index number fee, refer to NY CPLR § 8018(a).

i. No paper in an action in the supreme or a county court, other than an order submitted for signature to a judge out of court, shall be submitted for any purpose to the supreme or county court or to a clerk thereof unless there is endorsed on such paper the index number of the action assigned by the clerk of the county. NY CPLR § 8018(c).

ii. The party causing the first paper to be filed shall communicate in writing the county clerk's index number forthwith to all other parties to the action. NY R UNIF TRIAL CTS § 202.5(a).

c. *Filing fees.* The County Clerk shall require the payment of any applicable statutory fees, or an order of the Court waiving payment of such fees, before accepting a paper for filing. NY R UNIF TRIAL CTS § 202.5(d)(1). For information on filing fees, if any, refer to NY CPLR § 8001, et seq.

i. *ALBANY COUNTY.* A litigant shall first pay for an index number and a request for judicial intervention in the

County Clerk's Office in the county of the venue of the case and then file the request for judicial intervention in the Supreme Court Clerk's Office. NY R 3 JD SUP Doc. 1(A).

ii. *ERIE COUNTY.* Payment for fee-bearing NYSCEF documents must be made online via credit or debit card (American Express, MasterCard or Visa) at the time of submission. NY R ERIE E FIL Doc. 3(III)(E).

iii. *KINGS COUNTY.* Court fees in NYSCEF cases must be paid via NYSCEF by a credit or bank card (MasterCard, Visa, or American Express). Fees are no longer accepted in person in the Kings County Clerk's Office in NYSCEF cases. NY R L KINGS E FIL Doc. 1(B)(6).

iv. *NEW YORK COUNTY.* Filing fees (two hundred and ten dollars ($210) for an index number, except in foreclosure cases) must be paid through NYSCEF by Visa, Mastercard, or American Express credit or bank card. A full list of filing fees appears on Court Fees. NY R NY CTY Procedure I(A); NY R NY CTY E FIL Doc. 2(B)(5).

v. *ONONDAGA COUNTY.* Court fees in e-filed cases must be paid online with the NYSCEF system using a credit card. The document is not considered to have been filed until payment of the fee has been tendered. NY R ONDGA E FIL Protocol(B)(2).

vi. *QUEENS COUNTY.* Court fees (e.g., RJI fee, motion fee) in E-filed cases may be paid for on-line using a credit card. Papers may also be filed with the E-file system and the fee may be paid at the County Clerk's Office. In the latter case, the paper is not considered to have been filed until payment of the fee has been tendered. NY R L QUEENS E-FILE Doc. 1(E)(1).

d. *Proof of service.* In addition to complying with the provisions of NY CPLR Rule 2101, every paper filed in court shall have annexed thereto appropriate proof of service on all parties where required. NY R UNIF TRIAL CTS § 202.5(a). Proof of service shall specify the papers served, the person who was served and the date, time, address, or, in the event there is no address, place and manner of service, and set forth facts showing that the service was made by an authorized person and in an authorized manner. NY CPLR Rule 306(a).

i. *Personal service.* Whenever service is made pursuant to NY CPLR § 301, et seq. by delivery of the summons to an individual, proof of service shall also include, in addition to any other requirement, a description of the person to whom it was so delivered, including, but not limited to, sex, color of skin, hair color, approximate age, approximate weight and height, and other identifying features. NY CPLR Rule 306(b).

ii. *Service other than personal service.* Where service is made pursuant to NY CPLR § 308(4), proof of service shall also specify the dates, addresses and the times of attempted service pursuant to NY CPLR § 308(1), NY CPLR § 308(2) or NY CPLR § 308(3). NY CPLR Rule 306(c).

iii. *Form.* Proof of service shall be in the form of a certificate if the service is made by a sheriff or other authorized public officer, in the form of an affidavit if made by any other person, or in the form of a signed acknowledgement of receipt of a summons and complaint, or summons and notice or notice of petition as provided for in NY CPLR § 312-a. NY CPLR Rule 306(d).

iv. *Writing admitting service.* A writing admitting service by the person to be served is adequate proof of service. NY CPLR Rule 306(e).

2. *Supplemental documents*

a. *Supporting evidence; Exhibits*

i. *Foreign language documents.* Where an affidavit or exhibit annexed to a paper served or filed is in a foreign language, it shall be accompanied by an English translation and an affidavit by the translator stating his qualifications and that the translation is accurate. NY CPLR Rule 2101(b).

ii. *Statement of attorney in lieu of affidavit.* The statement of an attorney admitted to practice in the courts of the state, or of a physician, osteopath or dentist, authorized by law to practice in the state, who is not a party to an action, when subscribed and affirmed by him to be true under the penalties of perjury, may be served or filed in the action in lieu of and with the same force and effect as an affidavit. NY CPLR Rule 2106.

b. *Application to proceed as a poor person.* Upon motion of any person, the court in which an action is triable, or to which an appeal has been or will be taken, may grant permission to proceed as a poor person. The moving party shall file an affidavit setting forth the amount and sources of his or her income and listing his or her property with its value; that he or she is unable to pay the costs, fees and expenses necessary to prosecute or defend the action or to maintain or respond to the appeal; the nature of the action; sufficient facts so that the merit of the contentions can be ascertained; and whether any other person is beneficially interested in any recovery sought and, if so, whether every such person is unable to pay such costs, fees and expenses. An executor, administrator or other representative may move for permission on behalf of a deceased, infant or incompetent poor person. NY CPLR § 1101. For more information on proceeding as a poor person, refer to NY CPLR § 1101, et seq.

i. *Affidavit of inmate's indigence.* As required by NY CPLR § 1101(f), and in addition to such other papers as may be required by law, [a federal, state or local inmate under sentence for conviction of a crime who is seeking to commence a civil action or proceeding, other than a proceeding brought under CPLR Article 78 (NY CPLR § 7801, et seq.) that alleges a failure to correctly award or certify jail time credit due an inmate], shall complete and file with the court the form affidavit referred to in NY CPLR § 1101(d) along with the summons and complaint or petition or notice of petition or order to show cause. Such affidavit shall be in the form set forth in NY R CHIEF ADMIN Pt. 140, App. A-1. NY R CHIEF ADMIN § 140.2; NY R CHIEF ADMIN § 140.1.

c. *Working copies.* The court may require the parties to provide working copies of documents filed electronically. In such event, each working copy shall include, firmly affixed thereto, a copy of a confirmation notice in a form prescribed by the Chief Administrator. NY R UNIF TRIAL CTS § 202.5-b(d)(5).

d. *Statement of authorization in electronic filing cases.* A filing agent (other than one employed by a governmental entity) shall e-file a statement of authorization from counsel of record in an action, in a form approved by the Chief Administrator, prior to or together with the first e-filing in that action by the agent on behalf of that counsel. NY R UNIF TRIAL CTS § 202.5-b(d)(1)(i).

e. *Notice regarding availability of e-filing.* A party who has commenced an action electronically shall serve upon the other parties together with the initiating documents a notice of e-filing in a form approved by the Chief Administrator. Such notice shall provide sufficient information in plain language concerning e-filing. NY R UNIF TRIAL CTS § 202.5-b(b)(2)(ii).

f. *Notice to government of certain claims*

i. When the constitutionality of a statute of the state, or a rule and regulation adopted pursuant thereto is involved in an action to which the state is not a party, the attorney-general, shall be notified and permitted to intervene in support of its constitutionality. NY CPLR § 1012(b)(1).

ii. When the constitutionality of a local law, ordinance, rule or regulation of a city, county, town or village is involved in an action to which the city, county, town or village that enacted the provision is not a party, such city, county, town or village shall be notified and permitted to intervene in support of its constitutionality. NY CPLR § 1012(b)(2).

iii. The court having jurisdiction in an action or proceeding in which the constitutionality of a state statute, local law, ordinance, rule or regulation is challenged shall not consider any challenge to the constitutionality of such state statute, local law, ordinance, rule or regulation unless proof of service of the notice required by NY CPLR § 1012(b) is filed with such court. NY CPLR § 1012(b)(3).

iv. Where public retirement benefits, paid, payable, claimed, or sought to be paid by a state retirement system or any other retirement system established for public employees within this state or any subdivision thereof, or the interpretation of any provisions of law or rules governing any such retirement system or the operation thereof, are involved in an action to which the comptroller of the state of New York is not a party, the court shall notify said comptroller, who shall be permitted, in his discretion, to intervene in such action or to file a brief amicus curiae. NY CPLR § 1012(c).

g. *Documents required for specific types of claim*

i. *Certificate of merit in medical, dental and podiatric malpractice actions.* In any action for medical, dental or podiatric malpractice, the complaint shall be accompanied by a certificate, executed by the attorney for the plaintiff. NY CPLR § 3012-a(a). For information on the required contents of the certificate of merit, refer to NY CPLR § 3012-a.

- *QUEENS COUNTY.* Upon the filing of a Notice of Medical Malpractice in an E-filed case, the Certificate of Merit shall be filed as a separate document. NY R L QUEENS E-FILE Doc. 1(G).

ii. *Notice of dental, medical or podiatric malpractice action.* Not more than sixty (60) days after issue is joined, the plaintiff in an action to recover damages for dental, medical or podiatric malpractice shall file with the clerk of the court in which the action is commenced a notice of dental, medical or podiatric malpractice action, on a form to be specified by the chief administrator of the courts. NY CPLR Rule 3406(a). For more information on the requirements of this notice, refer to NY CPLR Rule 3406(a).

iii. *Certificate of merit in certain residential foreclosure actions.* In any residential foreclosure action involving a home loan, as such term is defined in NY RP ACT & PRO § 1304, in which the defendant is a resident of the property which is subject to foreclosure, the complaint shall be accompanied by a certificate, signed by the attorney for the plaintiff, certifying that the attorney has reviewed the facts of the case and that, based on consultation with representatives of the plaintiff identified in the certificate and the attorney's review of pertinent documents, including the mortgage, security agreement and note or bond underlying the mortgage executed by defendant and all instruments of assignment, if any, and any other instrument of indebtedness including any modification, extension, and consolidation, to the best of such attorney's knowledge, information and belief there is a reasonable basis for the commencement of such action and that the plaintiff is currently the creditor entitled to enforce rights under such documents. NY CPLR § 3012-b(a). For more information on this certificate, refer to NY CPLR § 3012-b.

iv. *Notice of commencement of action for personal injuries.* In the case of an individual who has suffered personal injuries and has received medical assistance pursuant to NY SOC SERV § 363, et seq. on or after the date of such injury, notice of the commencement of an action by or on behalf of such individual for such personal injuries shall be sent to the social services district in the county in which such recipient resides, or to the department of health, by certified mail, return receipt requested, or electronically in accord with regulations promulgated by the commissioner of the department of health, within sixty (60) days of the completion of service upon all parties to such action. Proof of sending such notice shall be filed with the court in accordance with NY CPLR Rule 306. Sending such notice shall not be a jurisdictional requirement to commencing an action. NY CPLR § 306-c.

E. Format

1. *Format of pleadings*

   a. *Numbered paragraphs.* Every pleading shall consist of plain and concise statements in consecutively numbered paragraphs. Each paragraph shall contain, as far as practicable, a single allegation. Reference to and incorporation of allegations may subsequently be by number. NY CPLR Rule 3014.

   b. *Prior statements in pleading.* Prior statements in a pleading shall be deemed repeated or adopted subsequently in the same pleading whenever express repetition or adoption is unnecessary for a clear presentation of the subsequent matters. NY CPLR Rule 3014.

   c. *Causes of action and defenses; Separate statements.* Separate causes of action or defenses shall be separately stated and numbered and may be stated regardless of consistency. NY CPLR Rule 3014.

   d. *Alternative or hypothetical statements.* Causes of action or defenses may be stated alternatively or hypothetically. NY CPLR Rule 3014.

   e. *Papers attached to pleadings.* A copy of any writing which is attached to a pleading is a part thereof for all purposes. NY CPLR Rule 3014.

   f. *Statement in verified pleading.* The allegations or denials in a verified pleading must, in form, be stated to be made by the party pleading. NY CPLR Rule 3023.

2. *Form of documents; Generally*

   a. *Size and form of paper.* Each paper served or filed shall be durable, white and, except for summonses, subpoenas, notices of appearance, notes of issue, orders of protection, temporary orders of protection and exhibits, shall be eleven by eight and one-half (11 x 8-1/2) inches in size. NY CPLR Rule 2101(a).

   b. *Writing and language.* The writing shall be legible and in black ink. NY CPLR Rule 2101(a). Each paper served or filed shall be in the English language which, where practicable, shall be of ordinary usage. NY CPLR Rule 2101(b).

   c. *Caption.* Each paper served or filed shall begin with a caption setting forth the name of the court, the venue, the title of the action, the nature of the paper and the index number of the action if one has been assigned. In a summons, a complaint or a judgment the title shall include the names of all parties. NY CPLR Rule 2101(c). In accordance with NY CPLR Rule 2102(c), a County Clerk and a chief clerk of the Supreme Court or County Court, as appropriate, shall refuse to accept for filing papers filed in actions and proceedings under the following circumstances: the summons, complaint, petition, or judgment sought to be filed with the County Clerk contains an "et al" or otherwise does not contain a full caption. NY R UNIF TRIAL CTS § 202.5(d)(1)(ii).

      i. The party filing the first paper in an action, upon payment of the proper fee, shall obtain from the county clerk an index number, which shall be affixed to the paper. NY R UNIF TRIAL CTS § 202.5(a).

   d. *Line spacing.* Every paper filed in court, if typewritten, shall have at least double space between each line, except for quotations and the names and addresses of attorneys appearing in the action. NY R UNIF TRIAL CTS § 202.5(a).

e. *Font size.* Each. . .paper printed or typed, served or filed, except for summonses. . .and exhibits, shall be in clear type of no less than ten (10) point in size. NY CPLR Rule 2101(a). The letters in the summons shall be in clear type of no less than twelve (12) point in size. NY CPLR Rule 2101(a).

i. Whenever a requirement relating to size of type is stated in point size, the type size requirement shall be deemed met if the x-height of the type is a minimum of forty-five percent (45%) of the specified point size. Each point shall be measured as .351 millimeter. The x-height size shall be measured as it appears on the page. The x-height is the height of the lower case letters, exclusive of ascenders or descenders. NY CPLR § 105(t).

f. *Margins.* Every paper filed in court shall have at least one (1) inch margins. NY R UNIF TRIAL CTS § 202.5(a).

g. *Citations*

i. *Civil practice law and rules.* NY CPLR § 101, et seq. shall be known as the civil practice law and rules, and may be cited as "CPLR". Reference to a provision in the civil practice law and rules may, except when such provision is being enacted or amended, be made without indicating whether it is a rule or section. NY CPLR § 101.

h. *Indorsement by attorney.* Each paper served or filed shall be indorsed with the name, address and telephone number of the attorney for the party serving or filing the paper, or if the party does not appear by attorney, with the name, address and telephone number of the party. NY CPLR Rule 2101(d).

i. *One-sided printing.* In addition, every paper filed in court, other than an exhibit or printed form, shall contain writing on one side only, except that papers that are fastened on the side may contain writing on both sides. NY R UNIF TRIAL CTS § 202.5(a).

j. *Use of copies authorized.* Except where otherwise specifically prescribed, copies, rather than originals, of all papers, including orders, affidavits and exhibits may be served or filed. Where it is required that the original be served or filed and the original is lost or withheld, the court may authorize a copy to be served or filed. NY CPLR Rule 2101(e).

i. Where a certified copy of a paper is required by law, an attorney admitted to practice in the courts of the state may certify that it has been compared by him with the original and found to be a true and complete copy. Such a certificate, when subscribed by such attorney, has the same effect as if made by a clerk. NY CPLR § 2105.

k. *Recycled paper.* It is the policy of the Unified Court System that litigants, where practicable, should file or submit to the courts of the Unified Court System of the State of New York papers printed or reproduced on recycled paper. Paper is considered recycled if it contains a minimum content of thirty percent (30%) waste paper. NY R UNIF TRIAL CTS § 215.2. The signature page of every paper filed or submitted to the court on recycled paper should bear the legend: "Printed [Reproduced] on Recycled Paper." NY R UNIF TRIAL CTS § 215.3.

l. *KINGS COUNTY: Tabs on filings.* Motions, orders and other filed papers shall be indexed with protruding tabs. Clerks are required to reject papers that do not have protruding exhibit tabs, except papers in matrimonial cases and papers filed by pro se litigants. NY R L KINGS Pt. A, Papers.

3. *Form and contents of summons.* A summons shall specify the basis of the venue designated and if based upon the residence of the plaintiff it shall specify the plaintiff's address, and also shall bear the index number assigned and the date of filing with the clerk of the court. NY CPLR Rule 305(a).

a. *Additional requirements if summons not served with complaint.* If the complaint is not served with the summons, the summons shall contain or have attached thereto a notice stating the nature of the action and the relief sought, and, except in an action for medical malpractice, the sum of money for which judgment may be taken in case of default. NY CPLR Rule 305(b).

b. *Third-party summons requirements.* A third-party summons shall also specify the date of filing of the third-party summons with the clerk of the court. NY CPLR Rule 305(a).

c. *Summons in consumer credit action.* The summons in an action arising out of a consumer credit transaction shall prominently display at the top of the summons the words "consumer credit transaction" and, where a purchaser, borrower or debtor is a defendant, shall specify the county of residence of a defendant, if one resides within the state, and the county where the consumer credit transaction took place, if it is within the state. NY CPLR Rule 305(a).

d. *New party joined in action; Supplemental summons.* Where, upon order of the court or by stipulation of all parties or as of right pursuant to NY CPLR § 1003, a new party is joined in the action and the joinder is not made upon the new party's motion, a supplemental summons specifying the pleading which the new party must answer shall be filed with the clerk of the court and served upon such party. NY CPLR Rule 305(a).

e. *Amendment of summons.* At any time, in its discretion and upon such terms as it deems just, the court may allow any summons or proof of service of a summons to be amended, if a substantial right of a party against whom the summons issued is not prejudiced. NY CPLR Rule 305(c).

4. *Form of electronic documents.* Each paper served or filed by electronic means, as defined in NY CPLR Rule 2103(f), shall be capable of being reproduced by the receiver so as to comply with the provisions of NY CPLR Rule 2101(a) through NY CPLR Rule 2101(d). NY CPLR Rule 2101(g).
   a. *File format.* All e-filed documents shall comply with the technical requirements set forth at the NYSCEF site. NY R UNIF TRIAL CTS § 202.5-b(d)(1)(i).
   b. *E-filed documents identification*
      i. *ERIE COUNTY.* E-filed cases must be readily identifiable and marked as such. If counsel presents papers to the Office of the Erie County Clerk or the Office of the Chief Clerk in a NYSCEF matter where authorized, counsel should alert the Clerk that the case is a NYSCEF matter. NY R ERIE E FIL Doc. 3(II).
      ii. *KINGS COUNTY.* The Supreme Court's Civil Case Information System ("CCIS") will further identify e-filed cases by the addition of a suffix to the index number (e.g. 500136/2006E). This suffix should be used on all documents filed with the court in e-filed matters. NY R L KINGS E FIL Doc. 1(A)(1).

5. *Signature blocks.* Every pleading, written motion, and other paper, served on another party or filed or submitted to the court shall be signed by an attorney, or by a party if the party is not represented by an attorney, with the name of the attorney or party clearly printed or typed directly below the signature. NY R CHIEF ADMIN § 130-1.1-a(a); NY R UNIF TRIAL CTS § 202.5(d)(1)(iv).
   a. *Printed name.* Beneath each signature shall be printed the name signed. NY CPLR Rule 2101(a).
   b. *Failure to sign.* Absent good cause shown, the court shall strike any unsigned paper if the omission of the signature is not corrected promptly after being called to the attention of the attorney or party. NY R CHIEF ADMIN § 130-1.1-a(a).
   c. *Signature as certification.* By signing a paper, an attorney or party certifies that, to the best of that person's knowledge, information and belief, formed after an inquiry reasonable under the circumstances the presentation of the paper or the contentions therein are not frivolous as defined in NY R CHIEF ADMIN § 130-1.1(c). NY R CHIEF ADMIN § 130-1.1-a(b)(1).
   d. *Signatures on initiating papers.* By signing a paper, an attorney or party certifies that, to the best of that person's knowledge, information and belief, formed after an inquiry reasonable under the circumstances, where the paper is an initiating pleading,
      i. The matter was not obtained through illegal conduct, or that if it was, the attorney or other persons responsible for the illegal conduct are not participating in the matter or sharing in any fee earned therefrom; and
      ii. The matter was not obtained in violation of NY ST RPC Rule 4.5. NY R CHIEF ADMIN § 130-1.1-a(b)(2).
   e. *Electronic signatures.* A document shall be considered to have been signed by an attorney or party in compliance with NY R CHIEF ADMIN § 130-1.1-a if it has been signed by such attorney or party as provided in NY R UNIF TRIAL CTS § 202.5-b(e)(1) and it bears the signatory's name. NY R UNIF TRIAL CTS § 202.5-b(e)(2). An electronically filed document shall be considered to have been signed by, and shall be binding upon, the person identified as a signatory, if:
      i. It bears the physical signature of such person and is scanned into an electronic format that reproduces such signature; or
      ii. The signatory has electronically affixed the digital image of his or her signature to the document; or
      iii. It is electronically filed under the User ID and password of that person; or
      iv. In a tax certiorari action in which the parties have stipulated to this procedure, it is an initiating document that is electronically filed without the signature of the signatory in a form provided above in NY R UNIF TRIAL CTS § 202.5-b(e)(iv), provided that, prior to filing, the document is signed in full in hard copy (which hard copy must be preserved until the conclusion of all proceedings, including appeals, in the case in which it is filed); or
      v. In a small claims assessment review proceeding, it is a petition recorded by the NYSCEF site upon the filing of a text file as provided in NY R UNIF TRIAL CTS § 202.5-b(b)(1), provided that prior to filing, the document was signed in full in hard copy (which hard copy must be preserved until the conclusion of all proceedings in the matter, including article 78 (NY CPLR § 7801, et seq.) review and any appeals, and must be made available during the proceeding upon request of the respondent or the court); or
      vi. It otherwise bears the electronic signature of the signatory in a format conforming to such standards and requirements as may hereafter be established by the Chief Administrator. NY R UNIF TRIAL CTS § 202.5-b(e).

6. *Confidentiality of personal information.* No person may file any document available for public inspection with any state agency, political subdivision, or in any court of this state that contains a Social Security account number of any other person, unless such other person is a dependent child, or has consented to such filing, except as required by federal or state law or regulation, or by court rule. NY GEN BUS § 399-ddd. Submissions pursuant to e-filing procedures shall have the same confidentiality rights as paper documents. NY R UNIF TRIAL CTS § 202.5-b(k)(1).

   a. *Confidential personal information.* Except in the actions designated in NY R UNIF TRIAL CTS § 202.5(e)(1), or as otherwise provided by rule or law or court order, and whether or not a sealing order is or has been sought, the parties shall omit or redact confidential personal information in papers submitted to the court for filing. For purposes of NY R UNIF TRIAL CTS § 202.5(e), confidential personal information ("CPI") means:

      i. The taxpayer identification number of an individual or an entity, including a Social Security number, an employer identification number, and an individual taxpayer identification number, except the last four (4) digits thereof;

      ii. The date of an individual's birth, except the year thereof;

      iii. The full name of an individual known to be a minor, except the minor's initials;

      iv. A financial account number, including a credit and/or debit card number, a bank account number, an investment account number, and/or an insurance account number, except the last four (4) digits or letters thereof; and

      v. Any of the documents or testimony in a matrimonial action protected by NY DOM REL § 235 or evidence sealed by the court in such an action which are attached as exhibits or referenced in the papers filed in any other civil action. For purposes of NY R UNIF TRIAL CTS § 202.5, a matrimonial action shall mean: an action to annul a marriage or declare the nullity of a void marriage, an action or agreement for a separation, an action for a divorce, or an action or proceeding for custody, visitation, writ of habeus corpus, child support, maintenance or paternity. NY R UNIF TRIAL CTS § 202.5(e)(1).

      vi. *ERIE COUNTY.* An attorney or unrepresented litigant filing a document via the NYSCEF system must comply with the requirements of NY R UNIF TRIAL CTS § 202.5(e) regarding the redaction of Confidential Personal Information and NY GEN BUS § 399-ddd(6) concerning the filing of documents containing Social Security Numbers. It is the sole responsibility of counsel or unrepresented litigant filing to be aware of and to comply with existing laws requiring non-disclosure of personal information contained in any document e-filed in NYSCEF. NY R ERIE E FIL Doc. 3(III)(G); NY R ERIE E FIL Doc. 3(III).

      vii. *KINGS COUNTY.* An attorney or unrepresented litigant filing a document via the NYSCEF system must comply with the requirements of General Business Law § 399-dd(6), which often require redaction of any Social Security number that appear in the original document. The NYSCEF system automatically redacts portions of filed documents which apparently contain Social Security numbers pursuant to NY R UNIF TRIAL CTS § 202.5-b(k). In the event the filing party receives e-mail notice through NYSCEF that a Social Security number in a filed document has been redacted, and the filing party concludes such redaction is erroneous, the filer should click on the link provided in the e-mail to permit the County Clerk to revert the redaction. For Confidential Personal Information, see NY R UNIF TRIAL CTS § 202.5(e) and NY R L KINGS E FIL Doc. 1(B)(11). [Editor's note: the reference to General Business Law § 399-dd(6) is likely a reference to NY GEN BUS § 399-ddd(6)]. NY R L KINGS E FIL Doc. 1(B)(10); NY R L KINGS E FIL Doc. 1(K)(1).

      viii. *NEW YORK COUNTY.* It is the responsibility of counsel and parties to comply with rules restricting disclosure of confidential personal information. Nevertheless, NYSCEF screens filings and endeavors to identify any that contain social security numbers. When such numbers are discovered through this process, NYSCEF will restrict portions of or all of such documents from public view. Where NYSCEF has redacted what it believes to be a social security number, it will transmit to the filer a notice advising of the action taken and requesting that the filer review the matter and provide notification as set forth in the notice if the redaction has been made in error. NY R NY CTY E FIL Doc. 2(K)(1); NY R NY CTY J RUL Rule A-1. Documents filed in the past in "secure status" under a procedure no longer in place will retain that status unless otherwise directed by the court. NY R NY CTY E FIL Doc. 2(K)(2).

   b. *Submission of confidential personal information.* Where a person submitting a paper to a court for filing believes in good faith that the inclusion of the full confidential personal information described in NY R UNIF TRIAL CTS § 202.5(e)(1) is material and necessary to the adjudication of the action or proceeding before the court, he or she may apply to the court for leave to serve and file together with a paper in which such information has been set forth in abbreviated form a confidential affidavit or affirmation setting forth the same information in unabbreviated form, appropriately referenced to the page or pages of the paper at which the abbreviated form appears. NY R UNIF TRIAL CTS § 202.5(e)(3).

c. *Home addresses.* For information on when home addresses and other personal information must be redacted, refer to NY CPLR Rule 2103-a.

7. *Defective papers.* A defect in the form of a paper, if a substantial right of a party is not prejudiced, shall be disregarded by the court, and leave to correct shall be freely given. NY CPLR Rule 2101(f). Papers that are stapled or bound securely shall not be rejected for filing simply because they are not bound with a backer of any kind. NY R UNIF TRIAL CTS § 202.5(a). A paper filed in accordance with the rules of the chief administrator or any local rule or practice established by the court shall be deemed filed. NY CPLR Rule 2102(b).

a. *Objection to defective papers.* The party on whom a paper is served shall be deemed to have waived objection to any defect in form unless, within fifteen (15) days after the receipt thereof, the party on whom the paper is served returns the paper to the party serving it with a statement of particular objections. NY CPLR Rule 2101(f).

F. Filing and Service Requirements

1. *Filing requirements.* Except where otherwise prescribed by law or order of court, papers required to be filed shall be filed with the clerk of the court in which the action is triable. In an action or proceeding in supreme or court, papers required to be filed shall be filed with the clerk of the county in which the proceeding is brought. NY CPLR Rule 2102(a).

a. *Filing of initiating papers.* For purposes of NY CPLR § 304, and for purposes of NY CPLR § 203 and NY CPLR § 306-a, filing shall mean the delivery of the summons with notice, summons and complaint or petition to the clerk of the court in the county in which the action or special proceeding is brought or any other person designated by the clerk of the court for that purpose. Such filing shall not be accepted unless any fee required as specified in NY CPLR § 8018 has been paid. Where filing is by electronic means, any fee required shall be paid in the time and manner authorized by the chief administrator of the court by rule. NY CPLR § 304(c). For purposes of NY CPLR § 304, governing the method of commencing actions and special proceedings, the term "clerk of the court" shall mean the county clerk. NY R UNIF TRIAL CTS § 202.5(c).

i. *Electronic filing of complaint authorized.* Notwithstanding any other provision of law, such filing may be accomplished by facsimile transmission or electronic means, as defined in NY CPLR Rule 2102(f), where and in the manner authorized by the chief administrator of the courts by rule. NY CPLR § 304(b).

- A confirmation record produced by the filing party's facsimile machine or computer and an affidavit of filing by the filing party, shall be prima facie evidence that the filing party transmitted documents consistent with the date, time and place appearing on the confirmation record. NY CPLR § 304(f).
- A party may commence any action in the Supreme Court in any county (provided that e-filing has been authorized in that county and in the class of actions to which that action belongs pursuant to NY R UNIF TRIAL CTS § 202.5-b(a)(1)) by electronically filing the initiating documents with the County Clerk through the NYSCEF site. NY R UNIF TRIAL CTS § 202.5-b(b)(1).

ii. *Electronic filing of complaint mandatory.* Except where otherwise required by statute, all documents filed and served in Supreme Court shall be filed and served by electronic means in such classes of actions and such counties as shall be specified by order of the Chief Administrator of the Courts. NY R UNIF TRIAL CTS § 202.5-bb(a). Except as otherwise provided in NY R UNIF TRIAL CTS § 202.5-bb, every action authorized by NY R UNIF TRIAL CTS § 202.5-bb(a) shall be commenced by electronically filing the initiating documents with the County Clerk through the NYSCEF site. NY R UNIF TRIAL CTS § 202.5-bb(b)(1).

iii. *Emergency exception to mandatory e-filing.* Notwithstanding paragraph NY R UNIF TRIAL CTS § 202.5-bb(b)(1), an action otherwise required to be commenced electronically may or shall be commenced by the filing of initiating documents in hard copy where permitted or required by statute or court order, and may be so commenced provided such documents are accompanied by the affirmation or affidavit of the filing attorney or party stating that: (i) the statute of limitations will expire on the day the documents are being filed or on the following business day; and (ii) the attorney, party or filing agent therefor is unable to electronically file such documents because of technical problems with his or her computer equipment or Internet connection. In the event a filer shall file initiating documents in hard copy pursuant to NY R UNIF TRIAL CTS § 202.5-bb(b), each such document shall include the notice required by NY R UNIF TRIAL CTS § 202.5-b(d)(1), and the filer shall file those documents with the NYSCEF site within three (3) business days thereafter. For purposes of NY R UNIF TRIAL CTS § 202.5-bb(b)(2), such an action shall be deemed to have been commenced electronically. NY R UNIF TRIAL CTS § 202.5-bb(b)(2).

iv. *ERIE COUNTY: Commencing an action electronically.* To commence an action, go to the NYSCEF home page at www.nycourts.gov/efile, choose the link for Supreme Court, log in, choose from the "E-File" menu the option: "Start a New Case" and select the Supreme Court in which you wish to commence your action. Thereafter, follow the system prompts. Please note that the case type chosen may limit the NYSCEF Document Types available. Unless otherwise stated in these Protocols, each document must be uploaded as a separate .pdf file and the correct document type must be selected under the Document Type menu. NY R ERIE E FIL Doc. 3(III)(A).#. KINGS COUNTY: Actions to be commenced electronically. All mandatory e-filed cases must be commenced electronically. Unless otherwise provided by in the E-Filing Rules or NY R L KINGS E FIL Doc. 1, the Kings County Clerk will not accept commencement documents in paper form nor will the court accept subsequent documents in that form in these cases. NY R L KINGS E FIL Doc. 1(B)(1). For information on commencing an e-filed case under seal, refer to NY R L KINGS E FIL Doc. 1(B)(2).#. NEW YORK COUNTY: Commencing an action electronically. All actions (other than Article 78, Mental Hygiene Law, election law, and matrimonial cases and Article 70 habeas corpus proceedings) must be commenced electronically in Supreme Court, Civil Branch, New York County, and all subsequent filings in those cases must be made electronically. NY R NY CTY Procedure I(A). Filings are made through the New York State Courts Electronic Filing System ("NYSCEF") (www.nycourts.gov/efile). If a person seeks to commence in hard-copy format a case that is required to be commenced electronically, the County Clerk will reject the filing, as required by NY R UNIF TRIAL CTS § 202.5(d) (unless the filing falls within one of the exceptions set forth in the rules). NY R NY CTY Procedure I(A); NY R NY CTY Procedure XI(A). To commence an e-filed action or special proceeding, a summons and complaint or summons with notice in an action. . .shall be filed with the County Clerk through NYSCEF by uploading the documents to the NYSCEF site in PDF-A format. NY R NY CTY Procedure I(A).

- To make a filing that commences an authorized hard-copy case, the attorney must deliver the summons and complaint, summons with notice, or petition to the County Clerk in Room 141B in the basement at 60 Centre Street, together with the index number fee. NY R NY CTY Procedure I(A). For more information on filing in hard copy, refer to NY R NY CTY Procedure I(A).
- Important litigation papers must be filed by counsel with the County Clerk. The chief among these are [the] Summons and complaint or summons with notice. NY R NY CTY Procedure XI(A). Except in electronically-filed cases, all of these documents must be submitted by counsel to Room 141B (in the basement at 60 Centre Street). Papers commencing a case are submitted to the Cashier in that room with an index number purchase form and fee. NY R NY CTY Procedure XI(A).

b. *Electronic filing.* On consent, documents may be filed and served by electronic means in Supreme Court in such civil actions and in such counties as shall be authorized by order of the Chief Administrator of the Courts and only to the extent and in the manner provided in NY R UNIF TRIAL CTS § 202.5-b. NY R UNIF TRIAL CTS § 202.5-b(a)(1). For the definitions of terms used in electronic filing, refer to NY R UNIF TRIAL CTS § 202.5-b(a)(2).

i. *E-filing mandatory.* In any action subject to e-filing, all documents required to be filed with the court by an e-filing party shall be filed and served electronically, except as provided in NY R UNIF TRIAL CTS § 202.5-b. NY R UNIF TRIAL CTS § 202.5-b(d)(1)(i).

- *ERIE COUNTY.* Case types currently eligible and accepted for e-filing are listed at the NYSCEF website. Note that some actions or special proceedings, (i.e., name changes) which are otherwise subject to mandatory e-filing, if commenced by unrepresented litigants will NOT be maintained in the NYSCEF system; individual cases may be found either at NYSCEF or in the Erie County Clerk's online records system. NY R ERIE E FIL Doc. 3(I)(E).
- *KINGS COUNTY.* Cases that are commenced by filing of the initiating papers with NYSCEF are identified as e-filed cases by assignment of a special index number (i.e., Index Numbers beginning with 500,000). NY R L KINGS E FIL Doc. 1(A)(1). All cases required to be e-filed are listed in Uniform Rule 202.5-bb (Mandatory E-Filing Rules) and on the NYSCEF website. All such cases must be commenced by filing with the County Clerk electronically through NYSCEF and all subsequent documents in such cases must be e-filed. Any questions regarding mandatory e-filing in Kings County can be e-mailed to kcco-efile@nycourts.gov. NY R L KINGS E FIL Doc. 1(A)(2).
- *NEW YORK COUNTY.* Unless otherwise provided in the Rules or in NY R NY CTY E FIL Doc. 2 or where a special exemption is granted due to physical requirements (e.g., oversized maps; see NY R NY CTY E FIL Doc. 2(B)(10)), all documents to be filed with the court in a NYSCEF case, including all documents on motions and all letters to the court (where permitted), must be filed with the NYSCEF system. Documents that attorneys would not ordinarily file with the court in a hard-copy case need not be e-filed. Unless otherwise provided by the E-Filing Rules or this Protocol, in e-filed cases the County Clerk and the court will not accept documents filed in paper form. NY R NY CTY E FIL Doc. 2(B)(1). E-filing is mandatory in all types of cases (other than election law, matrimonial, Art. 78, and Mental Hygiene Law matters, and Art.

70 habeas corpus proceedings) that are commenced in this court on or after February 19, 2013. All such cases must be commenced by filing with the County Clerk electronically through NYSCEF and all subsequent documents in such cases must be e-filed. NY R NY CTY E FIL Doc. 2(A)(2)(a). For more information, including information on consensual e-filing and filing scanned hard copy documents, refer to NY R NY CTY E FIL Doc. 2(A)(2).

- *QUEENS COUNTY.* All authorized Torts, Commercial and Tax Certiorari cases may be commenced by E-Filing, however all parties must consent for the action to continue as an E-file case. NY R L QUEENS E-FILE Doc. 1(A). All papers to be filed with the court in an E-filed case shall be filed on-line with the E-file system except as directed by the court. Papers that attorneys would not ordinarily file with the court in a hard-copy case need not be filed in an E-filed matter. NY R L QUEENS E-FILE Doc. 1(E)(2).

ii. *Who may file.* Documents may be filed or served electronically only by a person who has registered as an authorized e-filing user or as otherwise provided in NY R UNIF TRIAL CTS § 202.5-b(c)(1). NY R UNIF TRIAL CTS § 202.5-b(c)(1).

iii. *When filing made.* Documents may be transmitted at any time of the day or night to the NYSCEF site. A document other than an order or judgment is filed when its electronic transmission or, in the case of a petition that is e-filed by submission of a text file as provided in NY R UNIF TRIAL CTS § 202.5-b(b)(1), the electronic transmission of the text file is recorded at that site, provided, however, that where payment of a fee is required upon the filing of a document, the document is not filed until transmission of the document and the information or form or information as required in NY R UNIF TRIAL CTS § 202.5-b(d)(2)(i), NY R UNIF TRIAL CTS § 202.5-b(d)(2)(ii) or NY R UNIF TRIAL CTS § 202.5-b(d)(2)(iii) has been recorded at the NYSCEF site; or, if no transmission of that information or form or information is recorded, where permitted by the County Clerk, until payment is presented to the County Clerk. NY R UNIF TRIAL CTS § 202.5-b(d)(3)(i).

iv. *Notification of filing.* No later than the close of business on the business day following the electronic filing of a document, a notification, in a form prescribed by the Chief Administrator, shall be transmitted electronically by the NYSCEF site to the person filing such document and the e-mail service addresses of all other participating parties in such action. NY R UNIF TRIAL CTS § 202.5-b(d)(3)(ii).

v. *Removal of confidential information and other corrections.* If a document filed electronically is subsequently discovered to contain confidential data—including but not limited to trade secrets, information protected by confidentiality agreement, or personal confidential information as defined by statute or court rule—or otherwise to have been filed in error, the filer or another party or affected person may (1) notify the parties and any non-party filers in the action of the confidentiality issue or other error raised by the filing, and of his or her intention to seek judicial relief to correct the filing: (2) following such notification, request that the appropriate County Clerk, exercising his or her administrative discretion, place the document temporarily in "restricted" status on the NYSCEF site, to be made available for viewing by court staff and the parties but not the general public; and (3) file an application to correct the filing by order to show cause within five (5) business days of such notification (or such time as the court may direct), including a request for preliminary injunctive relief limiting interim disclosure of the document at issue. Unless otherwise directed by the court, any document placed in restricted status in response to such a request shall be returned to public view upon expiration of this five (5) day period. The Chief Administrator of the Courts shall promulgate forms to implement this process. NY R UNIF TRIAL CTS § 202.5-b(d)(3)(iii).

- *KINGS COUNTY.* For information on what to do when a document was erroneously filed with confidential information, refer to NY R L KINGS E FIL Doc. 1(B)(11).
- *NEW YORK COUNTY.* For information on what to do when a document was erroneously filed with confidential information, refer to NY R NY CTY E FIL Doc. 2(B)(8).
- *QUEENS COUNTY.* For information on what to do when a document was erroneously filed with confidential information, refer to NY R L QUEENS E-FILE Doc. 1(E)(7).

vi. *Documents requiring judge's signature.* Except where the court directs otherwise, any document that requires a judge's signature shall be transmitted electronically and in hard copy to the court. NY R UNIF TRIAL CTS § 202.5-b(d)(6).

vii. *Documents which would be inconvenient to file electronically; Hard copies.* Notwithstanding any other provision of NY R UNIF TRIAL CTS § 202.5-b, and subject to such guidelines as may be established by the Chief Administrative Judge, the County Clerk or his or her designee may require or permit a party to file in hard copy, in accordance with procedures set by the County Clerk or designee, an exhibit or other document which it is impractical or inconvenient to file electronically. NY R UNIF TRIAL CTS § 202.5-b(d)(7).

- *ERIE COUNTY.* Please contact the Supervisor of Actions & Proceedings, Erie County Clerk's Office by calling (716) 858-6662 or the Deputy County Clerk—Legal at (716) 858-6348 for information. NY R ERIE E FIL Doc. 3(III)(F).
- *KINGS COUNTY.* With limited exceptions, as set forth in the Uniform Rules and herein, all documents to be filed with the court in a NYSCEF case shall be filed online via the NYSCEF system. However, should the size, consistency or context of a hard copy document preclude electronic filing, the user shall electronically file a "Notice of Hard Copy Submission—E-Filed Cases" form EFM-3. Any hard copy submitted pursuant to NY R L KINGS E FIL Doc. 1(B)(9) shall include, as a cover page firmly fastened thereto, a copy of the Confirmation Notice received from the NYSCEF site confirming receipt of the "Notice of Hard Copy Submission—E-Filed Cases". Any party may object to such hard copy filing. The Court, in response to such objection, may, following the hard copy filing, fashion such relief as it deems appropriate pursuant to and in furtherance of the Uniform Rules and NY R L KINGS E FIL Doc. 1, including, but not limited to, an Order directing the filing party to file such documents online via the NYSCEF system. When exhibits are impractical to file pursuant to NY R UNIF TRIAL CTS § 202.5-b(d)(7), an additional "Notice of Hard Copy Exhibit Filing" form EFM-4 is required to be submitted. NY R L KINGS E FIL Doc. 1(B)(9).
- *NEW YORK COUNTY.* If a filer needs to submit unusual exhibits in original form that cannot practically be e-filed, such as oversized maps or electronic recordings, the filer should consult with the County Clerk's E-File Department by telephone at 646-386-3737 (procedural questions only) or by e-mail at ccnyef@nycourts.gov, which will normally require that the filer retain custody of the original subject to possible future directives of the court. NY R NY CTY E FIL Doc. 2(B)(10). In such instances, the filing counsel shall file with NYSCEF a "placeholder" in the form of a Notice of Hard Copy Exhibit Filing (NYSCEF Form EF 21). The Notice should be uploaded to NYSCEF as document type "Exhibit" and the filer should indicate in the "Additional Document Information" field that the filer is retaining custody of the original. Failure to e-file the Notice may result in a gap in the official record of the court. NY R NY CTY E FIL Doc. 2(B)(10).

viii. *Documents containing sensitive or proprietary information.* In an action subject to e-filing, any person may apply for an order prohibiting or restricting the electronic filing in the action of specifically identified materials on the grounds that such materials are subject to copyright or other proprietary rights, or trade secret or other privacy interests, and that electronic filing in the action is likely to result in substantial prejudice to those rights or interests. NY R UNIF TRIAL CTS § 202.5-b(k)(2).

ix. *Refusal to accept paper filings.* In accordance with NY CPLR Rule 2102(c), a County Clerk and a chief clerk of the Supreme Court or County Court, as appropriate, shall refuse to accept for filing papers filed in actions and proceedings when the paper sought to be filed:

- Is in an action subject to electronic filing pursuant to Rules of the Chief Administrator,
- Is not being filed electronically, and
- Does not include the notice required by NY R UNIF TRIAL CTS § 202.5-b(d)(1). NY R UNIF TRIAL CTS § 202.5(d)(1)(v); NY R UNIF TRIAL CTS § 202.5-bb(d).

x. *Emergency filings; Hard copies.* For information on when an emergency filing may be filed and served in hard copy, refer to NY R UNIF TRIAL CTS § 202.5-b(d)(1)(ii), NY R UNIF TRIAL CTS § 202.5-b(d)(1)(iii) and NY R UNIF TRIAL CTS § 202.5-bb(c)(3).

- *KINGS COUNTY.* Under the rules, a participating emergency e-filer must electronically file the documents initially filed in hard copy form within three (3) business days of the emergency filing; the originals will be discarded after the documents have been processed and the failure to e-file as required will therefore lead to an incomplete record. NY R L KINGS E FIL Doc. 1(B)(3).
- *NEW YORK COUNTY.* Occasionally an emergency will arise requiring expedited entry of a document with the County Clerk (e.g., an order issued in the courtroom after a conference or argument of a critical matter), such as for purposes of an immediate appeal. Expedition can be achieved by the Part as follows: the document should be carried by a Court Officer or staff member to the General Clerk's Office to assure immediate and proper recordation in the computer and, as appropriate, the posting of the document to NYSCEF or the Supreme Court Records On-Line Library ("Scroll"). The court will accommodate counsel in emergencies. NY R NY CTY Procedure XI(A).

xi. *Technical failures.* The NYSCEF site shall be considered to be subject to a technical failure on a given day if the site is unable to accept filings or provide access to filed documents continuously or intermittently over the course of any period of time greater than one (1) hour after 12:00 noon of that day. Notice of all such technical failures shall be provided on the site. NY R UNIF TRIAL CTS § 202.5-b(i).

- When e-filing is hindered by a technical failure, a party may file with the appropriate clerk and serve in hard copy. NY R UNIF TRIAL CTS § 202.5-b(i). In the event an attorney or party shall file and serve documents in hard copy pursuant to NY R UNIF TRIAL CTS § 202.5-b(i), each such document shall include the notice required by NY R UNIF TRIAL CTS § 202.5-b(d)(1), and the filer shall file those documents with the NYSCEF site within three (3) business days after restoration of normal operations at that site. NY R UNIF TRIAL CTS § 202.5-b(i).
- With the exception of deadlines that by law cannot be extended, the time for filing of any document that is delayed due to technical failure of the site shall be extended for one (1) day for each day on which such failure occurs, unless otherwise ordered by the court. NY R UNIF TRIAL CTS § 202.5-b(i).
- *ERIE COUNTY.* When filing by electronic means is hindered by a technical failure, please refer to the NY R UNIF TRIAL CTS § 202.5-b(i). NY R ERIE E FIL Doc. 3(III)(K).
- *KINGS COUNTY.* When filing by electronic means is hindered by a NYSCEF technical failure (as set forth in NY R UNIF TRIAL CTS § 202.5-b(i)), a party may file with the appropriate Clerk in hard copy. Except for deadlines that by law cannot be extended (e.g. Statute of limitations, Notice of Appeal), the time for filing of any document that is delayed due to technical failure of the NYSCEF system shall be extended for one day for each day on which such failure occurs, unless otherwise ordered by the court. NY R L KINGS E FIL Doc. 1(B)(13).
- *ONONDAGA COUNTY.* When filing by electronic means is hindered by a technical failure (as set forth in NY R UNIF TRIAL CTS § 202.5-b(h)(3)(i)), a party may file a hard copy with the County Clerk. With the exception of deadlines that by law cannot be extended (e.g., a statute of limitations or the deadline for filing a Notice of Appeal), the time for filing of any document that is delayed due to technical failure of the NYSCEF system will be extended for one day for each day on which such failure occurs, unless otherwise ordered by the court. A "Notice of Hard Copy Filing Submission—E-Filed Case' must accompany any documents not filed via NYSCEF. NY R ONDGA E FIL Protocol(B)(8).

xii. *Filing fees.* For information on what information must be provided to pay filing fees, refer to NY R UNIF TRIAL CTS § 202.5-b(d)(2).

xiii. *Exemption from e-filing.* For information on exemptions from e-filing, refer to NY R UNIF TRIAL CTS § 202.5-bb(e).

xiv. *Filing exhibits*

- *ERIE COUNTY.* In the NYSCEF system, each exhibit must be uploaded as a separate .pdf file. After uploading a primary document, please choose the document type "Exhibit" and enter the appropriate number or letter and a brief description of the exhibit; each exhibit should bear a separate cover sheet clearly marked as "Exhibit A," "Exhibit B," etc. "Exhibit A" or "Exhibit B" is unacceptable as a brief description of the exhibit. Exhibits, where referenced in a signed Order as attached or affixed shall be uploaded with the signed Order as one .pdf document. NY R ERIE E FIL Doc. 3(III)(H).
- *KINGS COUNTY.* In the NYSCEF system, each exhibit should be uploaded as a separate PDF file. After uploading a primary document, please choose the document type "Exhibit", enter the appropriate number or letter, and be sure to place a check mark to the right of "Attach to main document". Each exhibit shall bear a separate cover sheet clearly marked as Exhibit A, Exhibit B, etc. NY R L KINGS E FIL Doc. 1(B)(12).
- *NEW YORK COUNTY.* Attorneys submitting exhibits in NYSCEF cases should make each exhibit a separate attachment to an affidavit/affirmation in the system; i.e., exhibits should not be filed as a single PDF-A together with the affidavit/affirmation or grouped together as a single PDF-A attachment because either of these two formats makes it difficult for the Justice to locate particular exhibits as needed. Counsel must also include appropriate descriptive language in the "Additional Document Information" field in NYSCEF. NY R NY CTY E FIL Doc. 2(D)(6).
- *ONONDAGA COUNTY.* All exhibits in e-filed cases must be e-filed individually as separate attachments. NY R ONDGA E FIL Protocol(B)(9)(b).

xv. *Correcting documents*

- *ERIE COUNTY.* Submission of documents which, upon examination, require correction or addition will result in notification to the filer advising that the document has been returned for correction. The filer shall make the required corrections and/or additions as indicated in the e-mail transmission sent by the County Clerk or Part Clerk through the NYSCEF site. The corrected documents may be resubmitted using the "Re-file this document" link highlighted in the filer's document list for the respective case. Please note that in the case of multiple submissions, all related documents filed at the same time may be removed from the case record and returned until all documents are properly submitted. NY R ERIE E FIL Doc. 3(III)(J).

- *KINGS COUNTY.* Submission of documents which, upon examination, require correction or addition will result in notification to the filer advising that there is a problem with a document. The filer shall make the required corrections and/or additions and resubmit the corrected document using the "Refile this document" link. In the event a document is returned for correction, the original file date will be preserved. For corrections of documents filed with the Kings County Clerk which require a court order, refer to the procedure in NY R UNIF TRIAL CTS § 202.5-b(d)(3)(iii) and NY R L KINGS E FIL Doc. 1(B)(11). NY R L KINGS E FIL Doc. 1(B)(3).
- *ONONDAGA COUNTY.* If there is an error or an additional document is required, the system will notify the filing party, who will make the corrections/additions and resubmit them online. NY R ONDGA E FIL Protocol(B)(6).
- *QUEENS COUNTY.* Generally speaking, documents that have been E-filed will not thereafter be deleted by the County Clerk from NYCEF because the filer asserts that the filing contains an error or a significant omission. When the filer wishes to correct a perceived error or omission in a filed document, he or she should file an amended version of the document, with the original remaining on file, or else obtain a court order providing for deletion of the original. The County Clerk will only delete a document upon request of the filer or on the County Clerk's own initiative when it is obvious from the face of the document alone that the filer made a fundamental error and never intended to file the document that was filed (e.g., a completely unrelated non-litigation document, a different case, or a wrong county). The County Clerk will advise the filer when any such fundamental errors are detected. NY R L QUEENS E-FILE Doc. 1(E)(6).

c. *Facsimile filing.* In the Supreme Court, facsimile filing shall be limited to commercial claims and tax certiorari, conservatorship, and mental hygiene proceedings in Monroe, Westchester, New York and Suffolk Counties. NY R UNIF TRIAL CTS § 202.5-a(a)(1). Refer to NY R UNIF TRIAL CTS § 202.5-a for information on the procedures for facsimile filing.

    i. *NEW YORK COUNTY.* Unless indicated otherwise by the court in a particular case or in NY R NY CTY J RUL Doc. 1, Justices do not accept papers by fax. NY R NY CTY J RUL Rule 4.

2. *Service requirements for commencing an action by service of the summons and complaint*

a. *NY CPLR Rule 2103 inapplicable.* NY CPLR Rule 2103 generally applies to the service of "interlocutory" papers—the myriad litigation documents served and filed after jurisdiction has been obtained, and the action is pending. Initiatory papers, usually the summons and complaint (or an order to show cause or notice of petition and petition), are governed by the rigid service rules under Article 3 of the CPLR (NY CPLR § 301, et seq.) and various other statutes that apply to the acquisition of personal jurisdiction. NY CPLR Rule 2103(Practice Commentary, C:2103:1).

b. *Service of process.* The complaint may be served with the summons. NY CPLR § 3012(a). When the complaint is served together with the summons, the rules of summons service in NY CPLR § 308 ("Personal service upon a natural person") and NY CPLR § 312-a ("Personal service by mail") generally govern. NY CPLR § 3012(Practice Commentaries, C3012:5).

    i. *Sheriff to serve.* Upon written request by the issuer thereof, the sheriff shall serve all civil process regardless of whether it has been issued by the court. NY COUNTY § 650(2).

    ii. *Service on Sunday prohibited.* All service or execution of legal process, of any kind whatever, on the first day of the week is prohibited, except in criminal proceedings or where service or execution is specially authorized by statute. Service or execution of any process upon said day except as herein permitted is absolutely void for any and every purpose whatsoever. NY GEN BUS § 11.

    - *Persons who keep Saturday as holy time.* Whoever maliciously procures any process in a civil action to be served on Saturday, upon any person who keeps Saturday as holy time, and does not labor on that day, or serves upon him any process returnable on that day, or maliciously procures any civil action to which such person is a party to be adjourned to that day for trial, is guilty of a misdemeanor. NY GEN BUS § 13.
    - *Service invalid if maliciously served on Saturday.* Service on a Saturday is a misdemeanor if made

"maliciously" on one who actually celebrates Saturday as the Sabbath, and caselaw permits the service to be invalidated on motion if that showing is made. SIEGEL-NYPRAC § 63; Jewish Ctr. of Baldwin v. Winer, 216 N.Y.S.2d 153, 154 (Sup. Ct. 1961).

iii. *Service of complaint after service of summons.* If the complaint is not served with the summons, the defendant may serve a written demand for the complaint within the time provided in NY CPLR Rule 320(a) for an appearance. NY CPLR § 3012(b). Refer to the Timing section of this document for more information.

c. *Forms of service*

i. *Personal service on an individual.* Personal service upon a natural person shall be made by any of the following methods:

- By delivering the summons within the state to the person to be served. NY CPLR § 308(1).
- By delivering the summons within the state to a person of suitable age and discretion at the actual place of business, dwelling place or usual place of abode of the person to be served and by either mailing the summons to the person to be served at his or her last known residence or by mailing the summons by first class mail to the person to be served at his or her actual place of business in an envelope bearing the legend "personal and confidential" and not indicating on the outside thereof, by return address or otherwise, that the communication is from an attorney or concerns an action against the person to be served, such delivery and mailing to be effected within twenty (20) days of each other; proof of such service shall be filed with the clerk of the court designated in the summons within twenty (20) days of either such delivery or mailing, whichever is effected later; service shall be complete ten (10) days after such filing; proof of service shall identify such person of suitable age and discretion and state the date, time and place of service, except in matrimonial actions where service hereunder may be made pursuant to an order made in accordance with the provisions of NY DOM REL § 232(a). NY CPLR § 308(2).
- By delivering the summons within the state to the agent for service of the person to be served as designated under NY CPLR Rule 318, except in matrimonial actions where service hereunder may be made pursuant to an order made in accordance with the provisions of NY DOM REL § 232(a). NY CPLR § 308(3).
- Where service under NY CPLR § 308(1) and NY CPLR § 308(2) cannot be made with due diligence, by affixing the summons to the door of either the actual place of business, dwelling place or usual place of abode within the state of the person to be served and by either mailing the summons to such person at his or her last known residence or by mailing the summons by first class mail to the person to be served at his or her actual place of business in an envelope bearing the legend "personal and confidential" and not indicating on the outside thereof, by return address or otherwise, that the communication is from an attorney or concerns an action against the person to be served, such affixing and mailing to be effected within twenty (20) days of each other; proof of such service shall be filed with the clerk of the court designated in the summons within twenty (20) days of either such affixing or mailing, whichever is effected later; service shall be complete ten (10) days after such filing, except in matrimonial actions where service hereunder may be made pursuant to an order made in accordance with the provisions of NY DOM REL § 232(a). NY CPLR § 308(4).
- In such manner as the court, upon motion without notice, directs, if service is impracticable under NY CPLR § 308(1), NY CPLR § 308(2) and NY CPLR § 308(4). NY CPLR § 308(5).
- For purposes of NY CPLR § 308, "actual place of business" shall include any location that the defendant, through regular solicitation or advertisement, has held out as its place of business. NY CPLR § 308(6).

ii. *Service on designated agent.* A person may be designated by a natural person, corporation or partnership as an agent for service in a writing, executed and acknowledged in the same manner as a deed, with the consent of the agent endorsed thereon. The writing shall be filed in the office of the clerk of the county in which the principal to be served resides or has its principal office. The designation shall remain in effect for three (3) years from such filing unless it has been revoked by the filing of a revocation, or by the death, judicial declaration of incompetency or legal termination of the agent or principal. NY CPLR Rule 318.

iii. *Service by mail.* As an alternative to the methods of personal service authorized by NY CPLR § 307, NY CPLR § 308, NY CPLR § 310, NY CPLR § 311 or NY CPLR § 312, a summons and complaint, or summons and notice, or notice of petition and petition may be served by the plaintiff or any other person by mailing to the person or entity to be served, by first class mail, postage prepaid, a copy of the summons and complaint, or summons and notice or notice of petition and petition, together with two (2) copies of a statement of service by mail and acknowledgement of receipt in the form set forth in NY CPLR § 312-a(d), with a return envelope, postage prepaid, addressed to the sender. NY CPLR § 312-a(a).

- The defendant, an authorized employee of the defendant, defendant's attorney or an employee of the attorney must complete the acknowledgement of receipt and mail or deliver one (1) copy of it within thirty (30) days from the date of receipt. Service is complete on the date the signed acknowledgement of receipt is mailed or delivered to the sender. The signed acknowledgement of receipt shall constitute proof of service. NY CPLR § 312-a(b)(1).
- Where a duly executed acknowledgement is not returned, upon the subsequent service of process in another manner permitted by law, the summons or notice of petition or paper served with the summons or notice of petition shall indicate that an attempt previously was made to effect service pursuant to NY CPLR § 312-a. NY CPLR § 312-a(e).
- The statement of service by mail and the acknowledgement of receipt of such service shall be in substantially the form found in NY CPLR § 312-a(d). NY CPLR § 312-a(d).

iv. *Electronic service.* Initiating documents may be served in hard copy pursuant to Article 3 of the CPLR (NY CPLR § 301, et seq.) and shall bear full signatures as required thereby, or by electronic means if the party served agrees to accept such service. NY R UNIF TRIAL CTS § 202.5-b(f)(1); NY R UNIF TRIAL CTS § 202.5-bb(b)(3).

- *NEW YORK COUNTY.* Jurisdiction over the defendant/respondent shall be obtained by service of documents in hard-copy format in the usual manner, together with a Notice of Electronic Filing (a form (Form EFM-1) accessible in the "Forms" section of the NYSCEF website at the address www.nycourts.gov/efile). NY R NY CTY Procedure XI(A).

v. *Service by publication.* The court, upon motion without notice, shall order service of a summons by publication in an action described in NY CPLR § 314 if service cannot be made by another prescribed method with due diligence. NY CPLR § 315. For information on the contents of an order for service by publication, refer to NY CPLR Rule 316.

- The first publication of the summons shall be made within thirty (30) days after the order is granted. Service by publication is complete on the twenty-eighth (28th) day after the day of first publication, except that in a matrimonial action it is complete on the twenty-first (21st) day after the day of first publication. NY CPLR Rule 316(c).
- Where because of circumstances beyond the control of a party required to publish, publication required by any statute, rule or court order cannot be made or completed in the specified place or newspaper in the required manner, the court may by order require such other publication as will not unduly prejudice any other party. NY CPLR § 2401(1).
- Notwithstanding the provisions of NY CPLR § 2401(1), if publication required by any statute, rule or court order has been commenced and cannot be completed because of the suspension or termination of publication by a newspaper, publication may be completed in any other newspaper which complies with the statute, rule, or order without further court order. NY CPLR § 2401(2).
- For the definition of a "newspaper" for the purposes of publication, refer to NY GEN CONSTR § 60.

d. *Effect of service outside the state.* A person domiciled in the state or subject to the jurisdiction of the courts of the state under NY CPLR § 301 or NY CPLR § 302, or his executor or administrator, may be served with the summons without the state, in the same manner as service is made within the state, by any person authorized to make service within the state who is a resident of the state or by any person authorized to make service by the laws of the state, territory, possession or country in which service is made or by any duly qualified attorney, solicitor, barrister, or equivalent in such jurisdiction. NY CPLR § 313. For information on cases where service outside the state does not confer personal jurisdiction, refer to NY CPLR § 314.

e. *Service of process; Dependent on entities to be served*

i. *Personal service upon a corporation.* Personal service upon a corporation shall be made by delivering the summons, upon any domestic or foreign corporation, to an officer, director, managing or general agent, or cashier or assistant cashier or to any other agent authorized by appointment or by law to receive service. A business corporation may also be served pursuant to NY BUS CORP § 306 or NY BUS CORP § 307. A not-for-profit corporation may also be served pursuant to NY NOT PROF CORP § 306 or NY NOT PROF CORP § 307. NY CPLR § 311(a)(1).

- If service upon a domestic or foreign corporation within the one hundred twenty (120) days allowed by NY

CPLR § 306-b is impracticable under NY CPLR § 311(a)(1) or any other law, service upon the corporation may be made in such manner, and proof of service may take such form, as the court, upon motion without notice, directs. NY CPLR § 311(b).

ii. *Personal service upon a limited liability company.* Service of process on any domestic or foreign limited liability company shall be made by delivering a copy personally to:

- Any member of the limited liability company in this state, if the management of the limited liability company is vested in its members;
- Any manager of the limited liability company in this state, if the management of the limited liability company is vested in one or more managers;
- To any other agent authorized by appointment to receive process; or
- To any other person designated by the limited liability company to receive process, in the manner provided by law for service of a summons as if such person was a defendant. NY CPLR § 311-a(a).
- Service of process upon a limited liability company may also be made pursuant to article three of the limited liability company law (NY Limit Liab Co § 101, et seq.). NY CPLR § 311-a(a).
- If service is impracticable under NY CPLR § 311-a(a), it may be made in such manner as the court, upon motion without notice, directs. NY CPLR § 311-a(b).

iii. *Personal service upon a partnership.* Personal service upon persons conducting a business as a partnership may be made by personally serving the summons upon any one of them. NY CPLR § 310(a).

- Personal service upon said partnership may also be made within the state by delivering the summons to the managing or general agent of the partnership or the person in charge of the office of the partnership within the state at such office and by either mailing the summons to the partner thereof intended to be served by first class mail to his last known residence or to the place of business of the partnership. Proof of such service shall be filed within twenty (20) days with the clerk of the court designated in the summons; service shall be complete ten (10) days after such filing; proof of service shall identify the person to whom the summons was so delivered and state the date, time of day and place of service. NY CPLR § 310(b).
- Where service under NY CPLR § 310(a) and NY CPLR § 310(b) cannot be made with due diligence, it may be made by affixing a copy of the summons to the door of the actual place of business of the partnership within the state and by either mailing the summons by first class mail to the partner intended to be so served to such person to his last known residence or to said person at the office of said partnership within the state. Proof of such service shall be filed within twenty (20) days thereafter with the clerk of the court designated in the summons; service shall be complete ten (10) days after filing. NY CPLR § 310(c).
- Personal service on such partnership may also be made by delivering the summons to any other agent or employee of the partnership authorized by appointment to receive service; or to any other person designated by the partnership to receive process in writing, filed in the office of the clerk of the county wherein such partnership is located. NY CPLR § 310(d).
- If service is impracticable under NY CPLR § 310(a), NY CPLR § 310(b) and NY CPLR § 310(c), it may be made in such manner as the court, upon motion without notice directs. NY CPLR § 310(e).

iv. *Personal service upon a limited partnership.* Personal service upon any domestic or foreign limited partnership shall be made by delivering a copy personally to any managing or general agent or general partner of the limited partnership in this state, to any other agent or employee of the limited partnership authorized by appointment to receive service or to any other person designated by the limited partnership to receive process, in the manner provided by law for service of summons, as if such person was the defendant. Personal service upon a limited partnership subject to the NY PARTNER § 121-101, et seq. may also be made pursuant to NY PARTNER § 121-109. NY CPLR § 310-a(a).

- If service is impracticable under NY CPLR § 310-a(a), it may be made in such manner as the court, upon motion without notice, directs. NY CPLR § 310-a(b).
- A limited liability partnership may also be served pursuant to NY PARTNER § 121-1505. NY CPLR § 310-a(c).

v. *Personal service upon the state.* Personal service upon the state shall be made by delivering the summons to an assistant attorney-general at an office of the attorney-general or to the attorney-general within the state. NY CPLR § 307(1).

vi. *Personal service upon a state officer.* Personal service on a state officer sued solely in an official capacity or state agency, which shall be required to obtain personal jurisdiction over such an officer or agency, shall be made by (1) delivering the summons to such officer or to the chief executive officer of such agency or to a person designated by such chief executive officer to receive service, or (2) by mailing the summons by certified mail, return receipt requested, to such officer or to the chief executive officer of such agency, and by personal service upon the state in the manner provided by NY CPLR § 307(1). Service by certified mail shall not be complete until the summons is received in a principal office of the agency and until personal service upon the state in the manner provided by NY CPLR § 307(1) is completed. For purposes of NY CPLR § 307(2), the term "principal office of the agency" shall mean the location at which the office of the chief executive officer of the agency is generally located. Service by certified mail shall not be effective unless the front of the envelope bears the legend "URGENT LEGAL MAIL" in capital letters. The chief executive officer of every such agency shall designate at least one person, in addition to himself or herself, to accept personal service on behalf of the agency. For purposes of NY CPLR § 307(2) the term state agency shall be deemed to refer to any agency, board, bureau, commission, division, tribunal or other entity which constitutes the state for purposes of service under NY CPLR § 307(1). NY CPLR § 307(2).

vii. *Personal service upon a governmental subdivision.* Personal service upon a governmental subdivision shall be made by delivering the summons as follows:

- Upon the city of New York, to the corporation counsel or to any person designated to receive process in a writing filed in the office of the clerk of New York county. NY CPLR § 311(a)(2).
- Upon any other city, to the mayor, comptroller, treasurer, counsel or clerk; or, if the city lacks such officers, to an officer performing a corresponding function under another name. NY CPLR § 311(a)(3).
- Upon a county, to the chair or clerk of the board of supervisors, clerk, attorney or treasurer. NY CPLR § 311(a)(4).
- Upon a town, to the supervisor or the clerk. NY CPLR § 311(a)(5).
- Upon a village, to the mayor, clerk, or any trustee. NY CPLR § 311(a)(6).
- Upon a school district, to a school officer, as defined in the education law. NY CPLR § 311(a)(7).
- Upon a park, sewage or other district, to the clerk, any trustee or any member of the board. NY CPLR § 311(a)(8).

viii. *Personal service upon a court, board or commission.* Personal service upon a court consisting of three or more judges may be made by delivering the summons to any one of them. Personal service upon a board or commission having a chairman or other presiding officer, secretary or clerk, by whatever official title he is called, may be made by delivering the summons to him. Personal service upon a board or commission of a town or village may also be made by delivering the summons to the clerk of the town or village. Personal service upon any other board or commission shall be made by delivering the summons to any one of the members. NY CPLR § 312.

ix. *Personal service upon an infant, incompetent, or conservatee*

- *Upon an infant.* Personal service upon an infant shall be made by personally serving the summons within the state upon a parent or any guardian or any person having legal custody or, if the infant is married, upon an adult spouse with whom the infant resides, or, if none are within the state, upon any other person with whom he resides, or by whom he is employed. If the infant is of the age of fourteen (14) years or over, the summons shall also be personally served upon him within the state. NY CPLR § 309(a).
- *Upon a person judicially declared to be incompetent.* Personal service upon a person judicially declared to be incompetent to manage his affairs and for whom a committee has been appointed shall be made by personally serving the summons within the state upon the committee and upon the incompetent, but the court may dispense with service upon the incompetent. NY CPLR § 309(b).
- *Upon a conservatee.* Personal service on a person for whom a conservator has been appointed shall be made by personally serving the summons within the state upon the conservator and upon the conservatee, but the court may dispense with service upon the conservatee. NY CPLR § 309(c).

x. *Other specialized entities.* [Editor's note: New York has numerous rules related to service on specific regulated entities, for example, NY INS § 1212 relates to insurers, NY Limit Liab Co § 304 relates to unauthorized limited liability companies, and NY EXEC § 172-c relates to non-resident charitable organizations. For more information, refer to the chapter of New York law relating to the entity in question].

3. *Service requirements for commencing an action by service of the summons and notice.* When the action is commenced with a summons and notice, which also must be served via one of the methods in NY CPLR § 308, or in accordance with NY CPLR § 312-a, and the complaint is later served after a defendant has served a notice of appearance and/or demand for the complaint pursuant to NY CPLR § 3012(b), the complaint at that stage is not an initiatory paper, but a mere interlocutory one. Therefore, it may be served by the usual intra-action methods of serving papers outlined in NY CPLR Rule 2103. The service of the complaint is to be made not on the defendant, but on the attorney whose name appears on the notice of appearance or demand, NY CPLR Rule 2103(b), and the method used may be any of several authorized by NY CPLR Rule 2103(b), with service by regular mail being the most popular. NY CPLR § 3012(Practice Commentaries, C3012:5).

   a. *Who may serve.* Except where otherwise prescribed by law or order of court, papers may be served by any person not a party of the age of eighteen years or over. NY CPLR Rule 2103(a).

   b. *Service upon attorney.* Except where otherwise prescribed by law or order of court, papers to be served upon a party in a pending action shall be served upon the party's attorney. Where the same attorney appears for two or more parties, only one (1) copy need be served upon the attorney. Such service upon an attorney shall be made:

      i. By delivering the paper to the attorney personally. NY CPLR Rule 2103(b)(1).

      ii. By mailing the paper to the attorney at the address designated by that attorney for that purpose or, if none is designated, at the attorney's last known address; service by mail shall be complete upon mailing. NY CPLR Rule 2103(b)(2).

      iii. If the attorney's office is open, by leaving the paper with a person in charge, or if no person is in charge, by leaving it in a conspicuous place; or if the attorney's office is not open, by depositing the paper, enclosed in a sealed wrapper directed to the attorney, in the attorney's office letter drop or box. NY CPLR Rule 2103(b)(3).

      iv. By leaving it at the attorney's residence within the state with a person of suitable age and discretion. Service upon an attorney shall not be made at the attorney's residence unless service at the attorney's office cannot be made. NY CPLR Rule 2103(b)(4).

      v. By transmitting the paper to the attorney by facsimile transmission, provided that a facsimile telephone number is designated by the attorney for that purpose. Service by facsimile transmission shall be complete upon the receipt by the sender of a signal from the equipment of the attorney served indicating that the transmission was received, and the mailing of a copy of the paper to that attorney. The designation of a facsimile telephone number in the address block subscribed on a paper served or filed in the course of an action or proceeding shall constitute consent to service by facsimile transmission in accordance with NY CPLR Rule 2103(b)(5). An attorney may change or rescind a facsimile telephone number by serving a notice on the other parties. NY CPLR Rule 2103(b)(5).

      vi. By dispatching the paper to the attorney by overnight delivery service at the address designated by the attorney for that purpose or, if none is designated, at the attorney's last known address. Service by overnight delivery service shall be complete upon deposit of the paper enclosed in a properly addressed wrapper into the custody of the overnight delivery service for overnight delivery, prior to the latest time designated by the overnight delivery service for overnight delivery. "Overnight delivery service" means any delivery service which regularly accepts items for overnight delivery to any address in the state. NY CPLR Rule 2103(b)(6).

      vii. By transmitting the paper to the attorney by electronic means where and in the manner authorized by the chief administrator of the courts by rule and, unless such rule shall otherwise provide, such transmission shall be upon the party's written consent. The subject matter heading for each paper sent by electronic means must indicate that the matter being transmitted electronically is related to a court proceeding. NY CPLR Rule 2103(b)(7).

   c. *Electronic service mandatory; Consenting to electronic service; How electronic service may be made.* Except as otherwise provided in NY R UNIF TRIAL CTS § 202.5-bb, filing and service of all documents in an action that has been commenced electronically in accordance with NY R UNIF TRIAL CTS § 202.5-bb shall be by electronic means. NY R UNIF TRIAL CTS § 202.5-bb(c)(1).

      i. *Party's consent required for certain e-filing.* After commencement of an action wherein e-filing is authorized, documents may be electronically filed and served, but only by, and electronic service shall be made only upon, a party or parties who have consented thereto. NY R UNIF TRIAL CTS § 202.5-b(b)(2)(i).

         - A consent to e-filing in an action shall state that the party providing it agrees to the use of e-filing in the action and to be bound by the filing and service provisions in NY R UNIF TRIAL CTS § 202.5-b. NY R UNIF TRIAL CTS § 202.5-b(b)(2)(ii).

      ii. *Address for service; Duty to notify as to changes.* The e-mail service address recorded at the time of registration

is the e-mail address at which service of interlocutory documents on that party may be made through notification transmitted by the NYSCEF site. It is the responsibility of each filing user to monitor that address and promptly notify the Resource Center in the event of a change in his or her e-mail service address. NY R UNIF TRIAL CTS § 202.5-b(f)(2)(i).

iii. *How service made.* An e-filing party causes service of an interlocutory document to be made upon another party participating in e-filing by filing the document electronically. Upon receipt of an interlocutory document, the NYSCEF site shall automatically transmit electronic notification to all e-mail service addresses in such action. NY R UNIF TRIAL CTS § 202.5-b(f)(2)(ii).

- Except as provided otherwise in NY R UNIF TRIAL CTS § 202.5-b(h)(3), the electronic transmission of the notification shall constitute service of the document on the e-mail service addresses identified therein; however, such service will not be effective if the filing party learns that the notification did not reach the address of the person to be served. Proof of such service will be recorded on the NYSCEF site. A party may, however, utilize other service methods permitted by the CPLR provided that, if one of such other methods is used, proof of that service shall be filed electronically. NY R UNIF TRIAL CTS § 202.5-b(f)(2)(ii).

iv. *Signatures on hard copies; Proof of service filed electronically.* When an e-filing party serves a document in hard copy on a non-participating party, the document served shall bear full signatures of all signatories and proof of such service shall be filed electronically. NY R UNIF TRIAL CTS § 202.5-b(b)(2)(i).

v. *Effect of failure to consent.* A party's failure to consent to participation in electronic filing and service shall not bar any other party to the action from filing documents electronically with the County Clerk and the court or serving documents upon any other party who has consented to participation. A party who has not consented to participation shall file documents with the court and the County Clerk, and serve and be served with documents, in hard copy. NY R UNIF TRIAL CTS § 202.5-b(b)(2)(i).

d. *Service upon party.* If a party has not appeared by an attorney or the party's attorney cannot be served, service shall be upon the party by a method specified in NY CPLR Rule 2103(b)(1), NY CPLR Rule 2103(b)(2), NY CPLR Rule 2103(b)(4), NY CPLR Rule 2103(b)(5) or NY CPLR Rule 2103(b)(6). NY CPLR Rule 2103(c).

e. *Service on all parties.* Each paper served on any party shall be served on every other party who has appeared, except as otherwise may be provided by court order or as provided in NY CPLR § 3012 or in NY CPLR § 3215(f). Upon demand by a party, the plaintiff shall supply that party with a list of those who have appeared and the names and addresses of their attorneys. NY CPLR Rule 2103(e).

f. *Service by filing.* If a paper cannot be served by any of the methods specified in NY CPLR Rule 2103(b) and NY CPLR Rule 2103(c), service may be made by filing the paper as if it were a paper required to be filed. NY CPLR Rule 2103(d).

g. *Definitions.* For the purposes of NY CPLR Rule 2103:

i. "Mailing" means the deposit of a paper enclosed in a first class postpaid wrapper, addressed to the address designated by a person for that purpose or, if none is designated, at that person's last known address, in a post office or official depository under the exclusive care and custody of the United States Postal Service within the state;

ii. "Electronic means" means any method of transmission of information between computers or other machines designed for the purpose of sending and receiving such transmissions, and which allows the recipient to reproduce the information transmitted in a tangible medium of expression;

iii. "Facsimile transmission" means any method of transmission of documents to a facsimile machine at a remote location which can automatically produce a tangible copy of such documents. NY CPLR Rule 2103(f).

G. Hearings

1. There is no hearing required or contemplated in the New York rules governing the complaint and service of summons.

H. Forms

1. Official Complaint and Summons Forms for New York

a. Statement of service by mail. NY CPLR § 312-a(d)(A).

b. Acknowledgement of receipt of summons and complaint or summons and notice or notice of petition and petition. NY CPLR § 312-a(d)(B).

c. Affidavit in support of application pursuant to NY CPLR § 1101 (poor person status for an inmate). NY R CHIEF ADMIN Pt. 140, App. A-1.

2. New York Complaint and Summons Forms

a. General form for a complaint. MCF CPLR § 4:3.

b. Summons served with complaint; Official form. MCF CPLR § 2:34.

c. Summons served without complaint with notice of judgment to be taken in case of default; Official form. MCF CPLR § 2:37.

d. Notice of motion for summary judgment in lieu of complaint based on an instrument for payment of money only. MCF CPLR § 5:200.

e. Notice of motion for summary judgment in lieu of complaint based upon judgment secured in foreign state. MCF CPLR § 5:201.

f. Summons and notice of motion for summary judgment under NY CPLR § 3213; Official form. MCF CPLR § 5:202.

I. Applicable Rules

1. *State rules*

a. Short title; Application; Construction; Definitions. NY CPLR § 101; NY CPLR § 103; NY CPLR § 104; NY CPLR § 105.

b. Appendix of official forms. NY CPLR § 107.

c. Timing; Application of article. NY CPLR § 201; NY CPLR § 203.

d. Service of process. NY CPLR § 304; NY CPLR Rule 305; NY CPLR Rule 306; NY CPLR § 306-a; NY CPLR § 306-b; NY CPLR § 306-c; NY CPLR § 307; NY CPLR § 308; NY CPLR § 309; NY CPLR § 310; NY CPLR § 310-a; NY CPLR § 311; NY CPLR § 311-a; NY CPLR § 312; NY CPLR § 312-a; NY CPLR § 313; NY CPLR § 315; NY CPLR Rule 316; NY CPLR Rule 318; NY CPLR § 2401; NY COUNTY § 650; NY GEN BUS § 11; NY GEN BUS § 13.

e. Parties generally. NY CPLR § 401; NY CPLR § 1001; NY CPLR § 1002; NY CPLR § 1004; NY CPLR § 1012; NY CPLR § 1023; NY CPLR § 1024; NY CPLR § 1025; NY CPLR § 1026; NY CPLR § 1501.

f. Joinder. NY CPLR § 601; NY CPLR § 603.

g. Motion for permission to proceed as a poor person; Affidavit; Certificate; Notice; Waiver of fee; When motion not required. NY CPLR § 1101.

h. Extensions of time generally. NY CPLR § 2004.

i. Form of papers. NY CPLR Rule 2101; NY CPLR Rule 2102; NY CPLR Rule 2103; NY CPLR Rule 2103-a; NY CPLR § 2105; NY CPLR Rule 2106; NY GEN BUS § 399-ddd; NY R UNIF TRIAL CTS § 215.2; NY R UNIF TRIAL CTS § 215.3.

j. Service of papers. NY CPLR Rule 2103.

k. Computation of time. NY CPLR § 2402; NY GEN CONSTR § 19; NY GEN CONSTR § 20; NY GEN CONSTR § 25-a; NY GEN CONSTR § 30; NY GEN CONSTR § 31; NY GEN CONSTR § 53.

l. Particularity of statements generally; Particularity as to specific matters or actions. NY CPLR § 3001; NY CPLR § 3002; NY CPLR § 3005; NY CPLR § 3011; NY CPLR § 3012; NY CPLR § 3012-a; NY CPLR § 3012-b; NY CPLR § 3013; NY CPLR Rule 3014; NY CPLR Rule 3015; NY CPLR Rule 3016; NY CPLR § 3017; NY CPLR Rule 3021; NY CPLR Rule 3022; NY CPLR Rule 3023; NY CPLR § 3026; NY CPLR § 3031; NY CPLR Rule 3211; NY CPLR § 3213; NY CPLR Rule 3406.

m. Verification. NY CPLR § 3020.

n. Fees; Index number fees of county clerks. NY CPLR § 8018.

o. Special forms of action. NY R CHIEF ADMIN § 140.1; NY R CHIEF ADMIN § 140.2.

p. Hours of court. NY R CHIEF J § 3.1.

q. Mandatory submission of actions to arbitration. NY R CHIEF J § 28.2.

r. Application of part; Waiver; Additional rules; Application of CPLR; Definitions. NY R UNIF TRIAL CTS § 202.1.

s. Papers filed in court; Electronic filing in supreme court. NY R UNIF TRIAL CTS § 202.5; NY R UNIF TRIAL CTS § 202.5-b; NY R UNIF TRIAL CTS § 202.5-bb.

t. Rules of the commercial division of the Supreme Court. NY R UNIF TRIAL CTS § 202.70.

u. Signing of papers. NY R CHIEF ADMIN § 130-1.1-a.

2. *Local rules*

a. *Albany County*

i. Third judicial district rules. NY R 3 JD SUP Doc. 1.

b. *Bronx County*

i. Commercial division. NY R BRONX FIL R Doc. 12.

c. *Erie County*

i. Joint protocols for New York State Courts E-Filing (NYSCEF) cases filed in Supreme Court, Erie County. NY R ERIE E FIL Doc. 3.

d. *Kings County*

i. Papers. NY R L KINGS Pt. A, Papers.

ii. Protocol on courthouse and county clerk procedures for electronically filed cases. NY R L KINGS E FIL Doc. 1.

e. *New York County*

i. Commencement of cases. NY R NY CTY Procedure I.

ii. RJIs and assignments. NY R NY CTY Procedure IA.

iii. County clerk litigation functions. NY R NY CTY Procedure XI.

iv. Protocol on courthouse and county clerk procedures for electronically filed cases. NY R NY CTY E FIL Doc. 2.

v. Redaction of information in documents filed with the county clerk and the court. NY R NY CTY J RUL Rule A-1.

vi. Papers by fax. NY R NY CTY J RUL Rule 4.

f. *Onondaga County*

i. Onondaga county protocol for case filings New York State Electronic Files (NYSCEF). NY R ONDGA E FIL Protocol.

g. *Queens County*

i. Queens county protocol on courthouse procedures for electronically filed cases. NY R L QUEENS E-FILE Doc. 1.

J. Miscellaneous

NOTE: Individual judges' rules may apply.

ALBANY COUNTY

JUSTICE LISA M. FISHER: NY R 3 JD FISHER Fisher; NY R 3 JD FISHER Fisher, PC Order.

JUSTICE RICHARD MOTT: NY R 3 JD MOTT Mott.

JUSTICE STEPHAN G. SCHICK: NY R 3 JD Schick.

FORECLOSURE SETTLEMENT PART: NY R 3 JD Foreclosure Settlement.

BRONX COUNTY

JUSTICE PAUL L. ALPERT: [NY R BRONX J Part IA-29, as amended by NY ORDER 20-0337].

JUSTICE BEN BARBATO: NY R BRONX J Part IA-21.

JUSTICE MARY ANNE BRIGANTTI: [NY R BRONX J Part IA-15, as amended by NY ORDER 20-0338].

JUSTICE JOSEPH E. CAPELLA: NY R BRONX J Part IA-23.

JUSTICE MITCHELL DANZIGER: NY R BRONX J Part IA-3/33 ; [NY R BRONX J Danziger, Part IA-3/33, as amended by NY ORDER 20-0339].

JUSTICE LAURA G. DOUGLAS: NY R BRONX J Part IA-11.

JUSTICE RUBEN FRANCO: NY R BRONX J Part IA-26.

JUSTICE DORIS M. GONZALEZ: NY R BRONX J Part IA-24.

JUSTICE WILMA GUZMAN: NY R BRONX J Part IA-7; [NY R BRONX J Guzman, Part IA-7 Virtual, as amended by NY ORDER 20-0340].

JUSTICE ROBERT T. JOHNSON: NY R BRONX J Part IA-12.

JUSTICE DONALD A. MILES: NY R BRONX J Part IA-8.

JUSTICE DONNA M. MILLS: NY R BRONX J Part IA-9.

JUSTICE JULIA I. RODRIGUEZ: NY R BRONX J Part IA-18; [NY R BRONX J Part IA-27, as amended by NY ORDER 20-0341].

JUSTICE LLINET M. ROSADO: [NY R BRONX J Part IA-25, as amended by NY ORDER 20-0342].

JUSTICE NORMA RUIZ: NY R BRONX J Part IA-22; [NY R BRONX J Ruiz, Part IA-22 Virtual, as amended by NY ORDER 20-0343].

JUSTICE HOWARD H. SHERMAN: NY R BRONX J Part IA-4.

JUSTICE FERNANDO TAPIA: NY R BRONX J Part IA-13.

JUSTICE ELIZABETH A. TAYLOR: NY R BRONX J Part IA-2.

JUSTICE ALISON Y. TRUITT: NY R BRONX J Part IA-5.

PART IDV: NY R BRONX J Doc. 1.

PRE-TRIAL PART RULES: NY R BRONX J Doc. 2.

PRE TRIAL WORKSHEET: NY R BRONX J Doc. 3.

FORECLOSURE SETTLEMENT PART RULES: NY R BRONX J Doc. 4.

GUARDIANSHIP PART RULES: NY R BRONX J Doc. 5.

LPM PART RULES: NY R BRONX J Doc. 6.

ERIE COUNTY

JUSTICE M. WILLIAM BOLLER: NY R 8 JD J Boller.

JUSTICE RALPH A. BONIELLO: NY R 8 JD J Boniello.

JUSTICE CHRISTOPHER J. BURN: NY R 8 JD J Burns.

JUSTICE RUSSELL P. BUSCAGLIA: NY R 8 JD J Buscaglia.

JUSTICE FRANK CARUSO: NY R 8 JD J Caruso.

JUSTICE STEPHEN W. CASS: NY R 8 JD J Cass.

JUSTICE DEBORAH A. CHIMES: NY R 8 JD J Chimes.

JUSTICE EMILIO COLAIACOVO: [NY R 8 JD J Colaiacovo, as amended by NY ORDER 20-0252].

JUSTICE DIANE Y. DEVLIN: NY R 8 JD J Devlin.

JUSTICE JAMES H. DILLON: NY R 8 JD J Dillon.

JUSTICE PAULA L. FEROLETO: NY R 8 JD J Feroleto.

JUSTICE DANIEL J. FURLONG: [NY R 8 JD J Furlong, as amended by NY ORDER 20-0253].

JUSTICE JOSEPH R. GLOWNIA: NY R 8 JD J Glownia.

JUSTICE MARK J. GRISANTI: NY R 8 JD J Grisanti.

JUSTICE DEBORAH A. HAENDIGES: NY R 8 JD J Haendiges.

JUSTICE LYNN W. KEANE: [NY R 8 JD J Keane, as amended by NY ORDER 20-0254].

JUSTICE RICHARD C. KLOCH, Sr.: NY R 8 JD J Kloch.

JUSTICE FREDERICK J. MARSHALL: [NY R 8 JD J Marshall, as amended by NY ORDER 20-0255.

JUSTICE JOHN L. MICHALSKI: NY R 8 JD J Michalski.

JUSTICE MARK A. MONTOUR: [NY R 8 JD J Montour, as amended by NY ORDER 20-0256].

JUSTICE HENRY NOWAK: NY R 8 JD J Nowak.

JUSTICE JOHN F. O'DONNELL: NY R 8 JD J O'Donnell.

JUSTICE JEANETTE OGDEN: NY R 8 JD J Ogden.
JUSTICE CATHERINE NUGENT-PANEPINTO: NY R 8 JD J Nugent-Panepinto.
JUSTICE FRANK A. SEDITA, III: [NY R 8 JD J Sedita, as amended by NY ORDER 20-0257].
JUSTICE SARA SHELDON: NY R 8 JD J Sheldon.
JUSTICE DONNA M. SIWEK: NY R 8 JD J Siwek.
JUSTICE MARY L. SLISZ: NY R 8 JD J Slisz.
JUSTICE TIMOTHY J. WALKER: [NY R 8 JD J Walker, as amended by NY ORDER 20-0258].
JUSTICE DENNIS E. WARD: NY R 8 JD J Ward.
JUSTICE PAUL B. WOJTASZEK: [NY R 8 JD J Wojtaszek, as amended by NY ORDER 20-0259].
JUSTICE CHARLES N. ZAMBITO: [NY R 8 JD J Zambito, as amended by NY ORDER 20-0260].
SUPREME COURT LEGAL STAFF: NY R 8 JD J Legal Staff.

KINGS COUNTY

JUSTICE RACHEL A. ADAMS: NY R KINGS J Part 5F.
JUSTICE LOREN BAILY-SCHIFFMAN: NY R KINGS J Part 65.
JUSTICE REGINALD A. BODDIE: NY R KINGS J Part 95.
JUSTICE THERESA M. CICCOTTO: NY R KINGS J Part 19; NY R KINGS J Part 5J.
JUSTICE LISSETTE COLON: NY R KINGS J Part Rules.
JUSTICE GENINE EDWARDS: NY R KINGS J Part 80.
JUSTICE PAMELA L. FISHER: [NY R KINGS J Part 94, as amended by NY ORDER 20-0208].
JUSTICE ROBIN GARSON: NY R KINGS J Part 75.
JUSTICE LARA J. GENOVISI: [NY R KINGS J Part 34, as amended by NY ORDER 20-0209].
JUSTICE BERNARD J. GRAHAM: NY R KINGS J Part 36.
JUSTICE DAWN JIMENEZ-SALTA: NY R KINGS J Part 88.
JUSTICE INGRID JOSEPH: [NY R KINGS J Part FRP3 and Part 83, as amended by NY ORDER 20-0210].
JUSTICE KATHY J. KING: NY R KINGS J Part 64, 76K.
JUSTICE LAWRENCE KNIPEL: NY R KINGS J Part 57.
JUSTICE DONALD KURTZ: NY R KINGS J Part 26.
JUSTICE CARL LANDICINO: [NY R KINGS J Part 81, as amended by NY ORDER 20-0211].
JUSTICE KATHERINE LEVINE: [NY R KINGS J Part 20, 25, 92, as amended by NY ORDER 20-0211].
JUSTICE LORNA MCALLISTER: [NY R KINGS J Part 10, as amended by NY ORDER 20-0211].
JUSTICE ROSEMARIE MONTALBANO: [NY R KINGS J Part 19, 71, and 22, as amended by NY ORDER 20-0211].
JUSTICE RICHARD J. MONTELIONE: [NY R KINGS J Part 99 and DJMP, as amended by NY ORDER 20-0215].
JUSTICE LISA S. OTTLEY: NY R KINGS J Part 24.
JUSTICE MARK I. PARTNOW: NY R KINGS J Part 43.
JUSTICE ERIC I. PRUS: NY R KINGS J Part 5A.
JUSTICE FRANCOIS RIVERA: NY R KINGS J Part 52.
JUSTICE KAREN B. ROTHENBERG: NY R KINGS J Part 35.
JUSTICE LEON RUCHELSMAN: NY R KINGS J Part 1.
JUSTICE WAYNE P. SAITTA: NY R KINGS J Part 29.
JUSTICE ROBIN K. SHEARES: NY R KINGS J Part 96.
JUSTICE KENNETH P. SHERMAN: NY R KINGS J Part 67 and 78.
JUSTICE DEBRA SILBER: NY R KINGS J Part 9 and 5K.

JUSTICE ELLEN M. SPODEK: NY R KINGS J Part 63.

JUSTICE MARSHA L. STEINHARDT: NY R KINGS J Part 15.

JUSTICE JEFFREY S. SUNSHINE: NY R KINGS J Part 5G.

JUSTICE PETER P. SWEENEY: [NY R KINGS J Part 35, as amended by NY ORDER 20-0218].

JUSTICE DELORES J. THOMAS: [NY R KINGS J Part 5T, as amended by NY ORDER 20-0221].

JUSTICE WAVNY TOUSSAINT: NY R KINGS J Part 70.

JUSTICE RICHARD VELASQUEZ: NY R KINGS J Part 66.

JUSTICE CAROLYN E. WADE: NY R KINGS J Part 84.

JUSTICE EDWARD G. WALKER: [NY R KINGS J Part 90, as amended by NY ORDER 20-0219].

JUSTICE LILLIAN WAN: [NY R KINGS J Part 17, as amended by NY ORDER 20-0220].

JUSTICE MICHELLE WESTON: NY R KINGS J Part 3.

MENTAL HYGIENE PART: NY R KINGS J Part 77.

MATRIMONIAL PARTS DURING COVID-19 EMERGENCY: JUSTICE KAREN B. ROTHENBERG: NY R KINGS J Doc. 1.

NASSAU COUNTY

JUSTICE ANNA R. ANZALONE: NY R NASSAU S J Anzalone, Part 26.

JUSTICE STACY D. BENNETT: NY R NASSAU S J Bennett; NY R NASSAU S J Bennett, Form 1.

JUSTICE ANTONIO BRANDVEEN: NY R NASSAU S J Brandveen, Part 31.

JUSTICE JEFFREY S. BROWN: [NY R NASSAU S J Brown, as amended by NY ORDER 20-0297].

JUSTICE STEPHEN A. BUCARIA: NY R NASSAU S J Bucaria.

JUSTICE JULIANNE T. CAPETOLA: NY R NASSAU S J Capetola, Part 28.

JUSTICE EDMUND M. DANE: NY R NASSAU S J Dane, Part 33.

JUSTICE VITO M. DESTEFANO: NY R NASSAU S J DeStefano, Part 13; NY R NASSAU S J DeStefano, Form 1.

JUSTICE ARTHUR M. DIAMOND: NY R NASSAU S J Diamond, Part 7.

JUSTICE THOMAS FEINMAN: NY R NASSAU S J Feinman, Part 5.

JUSTICE JOHN M. GALASSO: NY R NASSAU S J Galasso, Part 22.

JUSTICE SHARON M.J. GIANELLI: NY R NASSAU S J Gianelli, Part 22; NY R NASSAU S J Gianelli, Form 1.

JUSTICE JEFFREY A. GOODSTEIN: NY R NASSAU S J Goodstein, Part 33; NY R NASSAU S J Goodstein, Form 1.

JUSTICE DAVID J. GUGERTY: [NY R NASSAU S J Gugerty, Part 31, as amended by NY ORDER 20-0298].

JUSTICE HELENE F. GUGERTY: NY R NASSAU S J Gugerty, Part 47.

JUSTICE STEVEN M. JAEGER: NY R NASSAU S J Jaeger, Part 35; NY R NASSAU S J Jaeger, Form 1.

JUSTICE JACK L. LIBERT: NY R NASSAU S J Libert, Part 23.

JUSTICE JOSEPH H. LORINTZ: NY R NASSAU S J Lorintz, Part 26; NY R NASSAU S J Lorintz, Form 1.

JUSTICE ROY S. MAHON: NY R NASSAU S J Mahon, Part 3.

JUSTICE RANDY SUE MARBER: NY R NASSAU S J Marber, Part 8.

JUSTICE JAMES P. MCCORMACK: [NY R NASSAU S J McCormack, Part 18, as amended by NY ORDER, 20-0299].

JUSTICE DICCIA T. PINEDA-KIRWAN: [NY R NASSAU S J Pineda-Kirwan, as amended by NY ORDER 20-0300].

JUSTICE THOMAS RADEMAKER: [NY R NASSAU S J Rademaker, Part 28, as amended by NY ORDER 20-0301]; [NY R NASSAU S J Rademaker, Form 1, as amended by NY ORDER 20-0301].

JUSTICE DENISE L. SHER: NY R NASSAU S J Rademaker, Part 32.

JUSTICE LEONARD D. STEINMAN: [NY R NASSAU S J Steinman, Part 15, as amended by NY ORDER 20-0303]; NY R NASSAU S J Steinman, Form 1.

JUSTICE HOWARD E. STURIM: NY R NASSAU S J Sturim, Part 50; NY R NASSAU S J Sturim, Form 1.

JUSTICE HELEN VOUTSINAS: [NY R NASSAU S J Voutsinas, Part 25, as amended by NY ORDER 20-0304]; [NY R NASSAU S J Voutsinas, Form 1, as amended by NY ORDER 20-0305].

JUSTICE HOPE SCHWARTZ ZIMMERMAN: NY R NASSAU S J Zimmerman, Part 17.

NEW YORK COUNTY

JUDGE'S RULES; BASIC INFORMATION: [NY R NY CTY J RUL Doc. 1, as amended by NY ORDER 20-0202].

ONONDAGA COUNTY

JUSTICE ROBERT E. ANTONACCI II: [NY R ONDGA E FIL Doc. 1, as amended by 20-0239].

JUSTICE MICHAEL V. COCCOMI: NY R ONDGA E FIL Doc. 2.

JUSTICE GREGORY R. GILBERT: NY R 5 JD JUDGES Gilbert; NY R ONDGA E FIL Doc. 3.

JUSTICE DONALD A. GREENWOOD: NY R ONDGA E FIL Doc. 4.

JUSTICE DEBORAH H. KARALUNAS: NY R ONDGA E FIL Doc. 5.

JUSTICE JAMES MCCLUSKY: NY R 5 JD MCCLUSKY McClusky.

JUSTICE CHARLES C. MERRELL: NY R 5 JD MERRELL Merrell.

JUSTICE PATRICK F. MACRAE: NY R 5 JD MACRAE Doc. 1.

JUSTICE JAMES P. MURPHY: NY R ONDGA E FIL Doc. 7.

JUSTICE GERALD J. NERI: [NY R 5 JD JUDGES Neri, as amended by NY ORDER 20-0236]; [NY R ONDGA E FIL Doc. 8, as amended by NY ORDER 20-0241].

JUSTICE ANTHONY J. PARIS: NY R 5 JD JUDGES Paris; [NY R ONDGA E FIL Doc. 9, as amended by NY ORDER 20-0242].

JUSTICE NORMAN W. SEITER, JR.: NY R 5 JD JUDGES Seiter.

JUSTICE KEVIN G. YOUNG: [NY R ONDGA E FIL Doc. 10, as amended by NY ORDER 20-0243].

QUEENS COUNTY

JUSTICE PAM JACKMAN BROWN: [NY R L QUEENS Brown, Part 19, as amended by NY ORDER 20-0321].

JUSTICE CHEREE A. BUGGS: NY R L QUEENS Buggs, Part 30.

JUSTICE PAM JACKMAN BROWN: [NY R L QUEENS Brown, Part 19, as amended by NY ORDER 20-0321].

JUSTICE DENIS J. BUTLER: NY R L QUEENS Butler, Part 12.

JUSTICE ROBERT I. CALORAS: [NY R L QUEENS Caloras, Part 36, as amended by NY ORDER 20-0322].

JUSTICE ANNA CULLEY: NY R L QUEENS Culley, Part 53.

JUSTICE TIMOTHY DUFFICY: NY R L QUEENS Dufficy, Part 35.

JUSTICE DAVID ELLIOT: NY R L QUEENS Elliot, Part 14.

JUSTICE JOSEPH J. ESPOSITO: NY R L QUEENS Esposito, Part 6.

JUSTICE DARRELL L. GAVRIN: [NY R L QUEENS Gavrin, Part 27, as amended by NY ORDER 20-0323].

JUSTICE WYATT N. GIBBONS: [NY R L QUEENS Gibbons, Part 5, as amended by NY ORDER 20-0330.

JUSTICE DONNA-MARIE E. GOLIA: [NY R L QUEENS Golia, Part 21, as amended by NY ORDER 20-0331].

JUSTICE MARGUERITE A. GRAYS: [NY R L QUEENS Grays, Part 4, as amended by NY ORDER 20-0324].

JUSTICE RUDOLPH E. GRECO: [NY R L QUEENS Greco, Part 32, as amended by NY ORDER 20-0325].

JUSTICE MAUREEN HEALY: NY R L QUEENS Healy, Part 6.

JUSTICE PHILLIP HOM: [NY R L QUEENS Hom, Part 43, as amended by NY ORDER 20-0332].

JUSTICE KEVIN J. KERRIGAN: NY R L QUEENS Kerrigan, Part 10.

JUSTICE MOJGAN C. LANCMAN: NY R L QUEENS Lancman, Part 20.

JUSTICE RICHARD G. LATIN: NY R L QUEENS Latin, Part 40.

JUSTICE ULYSSES B. LEVERETT: [NY R L QUEENS Leverett, Part 6, as amended by NY ORDER 20-0326].

JUSTICE LEONARD LIVOTE: NY R L QUEENS Livote, Part 33.

JUSTICE LEE A. MAYERSOHN: NY R L QUEENS Mayersohn, Part 22; NY R L QUEENS Mayersohn, Part 22G; [NY R L QUEENS Mayersohn, Part 22G COVID, as amended by NY ORDER 20-0327].

JUSTICE ROBERT J. MCDONALD: NY R L QUEENS McDonald, Part 34.

JUSTICE MARGARET MCGOWAN: NY R L QUEENS McGowan, Part 52.

JUSTICE MAURICE E. MUIR: [NY R L QUEENS Muir, Part 42, as amended by NY ORDER 20-0333].

JUSTICE JODI ORLOW: NY R L QUEENS Orlow, Part 51.

JUSTICE LESLIE J. PURIFICCION: NY R L QUEENS Purificcion, Part 39.

JUSTICE JOSEPH RISI: [NY R L QUEENS Risi, Part 3, as amended by NY ORDER 20-0328].

JUSTICE FREDERICK D.R. SAMPSON: [NY R L QUEENS Sampson, Part 31, as amended by NY ORDER 20-0329].

JUSTICE MARTIN J. SCHULMAN: NY R L QUEENS Schulman, Part 29.

JUSTICE BERNICE D. SIEGAL: NY R L QUEENS Siegal, Part 25G.

JUSTICE JANICE A. TAYLOR: NY R L QUEENS Taylor, Part 15.

JUSTICE CARMEN R. VELASQUEZ: NY R L QUEENS Velasquez, Part 38.

JUSTICE LOURDES M VENTURA: [NY R L QUEENS Ventura, Part 37, as amended by NY ORDER 20-0334].

JUSTICE WILLIAM A. VISCOVICH: NY R L QUEENS Viscovich, Part 63.

JUSTICE ALLAN B. WEISS: NY R L QUEENS Weiss, Part 2.

COMPLIANCE, SETTLEMENT AND CONFERENCE PART: NY R L QUEENS Doc 1.

PRELIMINARY CONFERENCE PART: [NY R L QUEENS Doc. 2, as amended by NY ORDER 20-0335].

MEDICAL MALPRACTICE CONFERENCE PART: [NY R L QUEENS Doc. 3, as amended by NY ORDER 20-0336].

TRIAL SCHEDULING PART: NY R L QUEENS Doc. 4.

SUMMARY JURY TRIAL PROGRAM: NY R L QUEENS Doc. 7.

RESIDENTIAL FORECLOSURE PART: NY R L QUEENS Doc. 9.

FORECLOSURE AUCTION RULES: NY R L QUEENS Doc. 10.

MATRIMONIAL PRELIMINARY CONFERENCE PART: NY R L QUEENS Doc. 11.

NON-CUSTODIAL CONTESTED MATRIMONIAL PART: NY R L QUEENS Doc. 12.

Pleadings
Jury Demand

Document Last Updated August 2020

A. Checklist

(I) ❑ Matters to be considered by party demanding jury

- (a) ❑ Required documents
  - (1) ❑ Note of issue containing a jury demand
  - (2) ❑ Certificate of readiness
  - (3) ❑ Filing fees
  - (4) ❑ Proof of service
- (b) ❑ Supplemental documents
  - (1) ❑ Working copies
  - (2) ❑ Statement of authorization in electronic filing cases
  - (3) ❑ ERIE COUNTY: Additional supplemental documents
    - (i) ❑ Notice of hard copy submission in e-filed case

(4) ❑ KINGS COUNTY: Additional supplemental documents

(i) ❑ Forms when filing in hard copy

(5) ❑ NEW YORK COUNTY: Additional supplemental documents

(i) ❑ Notice of hard copy submission

(6) ❑ ONONDAGA COUNTY: Additional supplemental documents

(i) ❑ Notice of hard copy submission

(7) ❑ QUEENS COUNTY: Additional supplemental documents

(i) ❑ Notice of hard copy submission

(c) ❑ Timing

(1) ❑ There are no specific timing requirements for the jury demand

(2) ❑ Any party may demand a trial by jury of any issue of fact triable of right by a jury, by serving upon all other parties and filing a note of issue containing a demand for trial by jury

(i) ❑ Any party served with a note of issue not containing such a demand may demand a trial by jury by serving upon each party a demand for a trial by jury and filing such demand in the office where the note of issue was filed within fifteen (15) days after service of the note of issue

(3) ❑ If a party has demanded trial by jury of only some of the issues, any other party within ten (10) days after service of the demand may serve and file a demand for trial by jury of any other issues in the action so triable

B. Timing

1. *Time for jury demand.* There are no specific timing requirements for the jury demand.

a. *Demand contained in note of issue.* Any party may demand a trial by jury of any issue of fact triable of right by a jury, by serving upon all other parties and filing a note of issue containing a demand for trial by jury. NY CPLR § 4102(a).

i. Any party served with a note of issue not containing such a demand may demand a trial by jury by serving upon each party a demand for a trial by jury and filing such demand in the office where the note of issue was filed within fifteen (15) days after service of the note of issue. NY CPLR § 4102(a).

b. *Demand for remaining issues.* If a party has demanded trial by jury of only some of the issues, any other party within ten (10) days after service of the demand may serve and file a demand for trial by jury of any other issues in the action so triable. NY CPLR § 4102(b).

2. *Computation of time*

a. *Units of time*

i. *Day.* A calendar day includes the time from midnight to midnight. Sunday or any day of the week specifically mentioned means a calendar day. NY GEN CONSTR § 19.

ii. *Month.* In a statute, contract or public or private instrument, unless otherwise provided in such contract or instrument or by law, the term month means a calendar month and not a lunar month. NY GEN CONSTR § 31.

iii. *Year.* For information on the definition of a year, including the definitions of a half-year and quarter-year, refer to NY GEN CONSTR § 58 and NY GEN CONSTR § 50. For information on leap years, refer to NY GEN CONSTR § 57.

b. *Periods of time*

i. *Number of days.* A number of days specified as a period from a certain day within which or after or before which an act is authorized or required to be done means such number of calendar days exclusive of the calendar day from which the reckoning is made. NY GEN CONSTR § 20.

- If such period is a period of two (2) days, Saturday, Sunday or a public holiday must be excluded from the reckoning if it is an intervening day between the day from which the reckoning is made and the last day of the period. NY GEN CONSTR § 20.
- In computing any specified period of time from a specified event, the day upon which the event happens is deemed the day from which the reckoning is made. The day from which any specified period of time is reckoned shall be excluded in making the reckoning. NY GEN CONSTR § 20.

ii. *Number of months.* A number of months after or before a certain day shall be computed by counting such number of calendar months from such day, exclusive of the calendar month in which such day occurs, and shall include the day of the month in the last month so counted having the same numerical order in days of the month as the day from which the computation is made, unless there be not so many days in the last month so counted, in which case the period computed shall expire with the last day of the month so counted. NY GEN CONSTR § 30.

iii. *Publication of notice; Number of days.* The period of publication of a legal notice shall be computed by excluding the first day of publication and including the day on which the act or event of which notice is given is to take place or which completes the full period of publication. NY CPLR § 2402.

iv. *Periods ending on Saturday, Sunday or public holiday.* When any period of time, computed from a certain day, within which or after which or before which an act is authorized or required to be done, ends on a Saturday, Sunday or a public holiday, such act may be done on the next succeeding business day and if the period ends at a specified hour, such act may be done at or before the same hour of such next succeeding business day, except that where a period of time specified by contract ends on a Saturday, Sunday or a public holiday, the extension of such period is governed by NY GEN CONSTR § 25. NY GEN CONSTR § 25-a(1).

- For a list of public holidays, refer to NY GEN CONSTR § 24.

v. *Additional time after certain kinds of service*

- *Service by mail.* Where a period of time prescribed by law is measured from the service of a paper and service is by mail, five (5) days shall be added to the prescribed period. NY CPLR Rule 2103(b)(2).
- *Service by overnight delivery service.* Where a period of time prescribed by law is measured from the service of a paper and service is by overnight delivery, one (1) business day shall be added to the prescribed period. NY CPLR Rule 2103(b)(6).

vi. *Daylight saving time.* For information on New York's time zone and the effect of daylight saving time, refer to NY GEN CONSTR § 52.

c. *Hours of court.* Notwithstanding any provision of law or rule of court to the contrary, throughout the State of New York the sessions of the Supreme Court for the disposition of business before the court shall commence not later than 9:30 a.m. and conclude not earlier than 5 p.m. Where warranted, the Chief Administrator of the Courts may authorize variances in the opening and closing hours of the courts, but, in such event, daily sessions shall total not less than six (6) hours. NY R CHIEF J § 3.1.

d. *Time limits; Extension of time.* Any act required by or in pursuance of law to be performed at or within a prescribed time, shall be performed according to the standard time. NY GEN CONSTR § 53.

i. Except where otherwise expressly prescribed by law, the court may extend the time fixed by any statute, rule or order for doing any act, upon such terms as may be just and upon good cause shown, whether the application for extension is made before or after the expiration of the time fixed. NY CPLR § 2004. Refer to the New York KeyRules Motion for Continuance/Extension of Time document for more information.

C. General Requirements

1. *Trial by jury, generally.* Trial by jury in all cases in which it has heretofore been guaranteed by constitutional provision shall remain inviolate forever; but a jury trial may be waived by the parties in all civil cases in the manner to be prescribed by law. The legislature may provide, however, by law, that a verdict may be rendered by not less than five-sixths of the jury in any civil case. A jury trial may be waived by the defendant in all criminal cases, except those in which the crime charged may be punishable by death, by a written instrument signed by the defendant in person in open court before and with the approval of a judge or justice of a court having jurisdiction to try the offense. The legislature may enact laws, not inconsistent herewith, governing the form, content, manner and time of presentation of the instrument effectuating such waiver. NY CONST Art. 1, § 2. In the following actions, the issues of fact shall be tried by a jury unless a jury trial is waived or a reference is directed under NY CPLR § 4317, except that equitable defenses and equitable counterclaims shall be tried by the court:

a. An action in which a party demands and sets forth facts which would permit a judgment for a sum of money only;

b. An action of ejectment; for dower; for waste; for abatement of and damages for a nuisance; to recover a chattel; or for determination of a claim to real property under article fifteen of the real property actions and proceedings law (NY RP ACT & PRO § 1501, et seq.); and

c. Any other action in which a party is entitled by the constitution or by express provision of law to a trial by jury. NY CPLR § 4101.

2. *Jury demand*

a. *Demand; Filed with note of issue.* A demand shall not be accepted for filing unless a note of issue is filed in the action.

If no party shall demand a trial by jury as provided in NY CPLR § 4102, the right to trial by jury shall be deemed waived by all parties. A party may not withdraw a demand for trial by jury without the consent of the other parties, regardless of whether another party previously filed a note of issue without a demand for trial by jury. NY CPLR § 4102(a).

b. *Specification of issues.* In his demand a party may specify the issues which he wishes tried by jury; otherwise he shall be deemed to have demanded trial by jury of all issues so triable. If he has demanded trial by jury of only some of the issues, any other party within ten (10) days after service of the demand may serve and file a demand for trial by jury of any other issues in the action so triable. NY CPLR § 4102(b).

c. *Waiver.* A party who has demanded the trial of an issue of fact by a jury under NY CPLR § 4102 waives his right by failing to appear at the trial, by filing a written waiver with the clerk or by oral waiver in open court. A waiver does not withdraw a demand for trial by jury without the consent of the other parties. A party shall not be deemed to have waived the right to trial by jury of the issues of fact arising upon a claim, by joining it with another claim with respect to which there is no right to trial by jury and which is based upon a separate transaction; or of the issues of fact arising upon a counterclaim, cross-claim or third party claim, by asserting it in an action in which there is no right to trial by jury. NY CPLR § 4102(c).

   i. Jury waiver can result in other ways than those recited by NY CPLR § 3012(c). It can be waived in a contract between the parties, and as long as no deceit is shown affecting the waiver of jury clause, a mere unawareness of the clause's existence will not necessarily undo the waiver. SIEGEL-NYPRAC § 378; Int'l Roofing Corp. v. Van Der Veer, 43 Misc. 2d 93, 94, 250 N.Y.S.2d 387, 389 (Sup. Ct. 1964); James Talcott, Inc. v. Wilson Hosiery Co., 32 A.D.2d 524, 525, 299 N.Y.S.2d 460, 461 (1969).

   ii. There is some dispute about that, however. SIEGEL-NYPRAC § 378; Colgate Const. Corp. v. Hill, 70 Misc. 2d 646, 647, 334 N.Y.S.2d 1002, 1003—04 (City Ct. 1972). The waiver should in any event be clear and unequivocal, for it will be strictly construed against the party who drafted the instrument containing it. SIEGEL-NYPRAC § 378; Barrow v. Bloomfield, 30 A.D.2d 947, 947, 293 N.Y.S.2d 1007, 1007 (1968).

   iii. Even if the waiver is in an "adhesion" contract, it is apparently valid. SIEGEL-NYPRAC § 378.

   iv. A waiver of trial by jury is itself waivable. If a contract waives trial by jury, for example, but a jury is demanded and no one makes a timely objection to it, trial by jury will proceed. SIEGEL-NYPRAC § 378; Imp. Alley of Mid-Island, Inc. v. Mid-Island Shopping Plaza, Inc., 103 A.D.2d 797, 798, 477 N.Y.S.2d 675, 677 (1984).

d. *Payment of fees.* A trial by jury may be demanded as provided by NY CPLR § 4102. Where a jury trial has been demanded, the action or special proceeding shall be scheduled for jury trial upon payment of the fee prescribed by NY CPLR § 8020 by the party first filing the demand. If no demand for a jury trial is made, it shall constitute a waiver by all parties and the action or special proceeding shall be scheduled for nonjury trial. NY R UNIF TRIAL CTS § 202.21(c).

e. *Local rules.* The chief administrator of the courts may by rule provide that a party shall be deemed to have demanded trial by jury by filing a note of issue not containing an express waiver of trial by jury. NY CPLR § 4102(d).

   i. A note of issue silent as to jury is a waiver of it by the one filing the note. SIEGEL-NYPRAC § 378. The Civil Practice Law and Rules does allow the chief administrator of the courts to provide by rule for the reverse: that a silent note of issue is deemed to demand the jury; but the note of issue filer, if she wants jury trial, does herself no harm by affirmatively making the demand for it in the note of issue even if such a rule is in force. SIEGEL-NYPRAC § 378; NY CPLR § 4102.

   ii. A party who would rely on such a rule, in any event, had best ascertain that it is currently in force. Trial by jury is a substantial right and rule changes are easy to overlook. SIEGEL-NYPRAC § 378.

f. *Relief by court.* The court may relieve a party from the effect of failing to comply with NY CPLR § 4102 if no undue prejudice to the rights of another party would result. NY CPLR § 4102(e).

   i. A waiver resulting from a failure to comply with NY CPLR § 4102, such as by omitting to demand a jury by the methods specified, can be relieved by the court "if no undue prejudice to the rights of another party would result". SIEGEL-NYPRAC § 378; NY CPLR § 4102(e).

   ii. Intentional waivers are not likely to be undone on this authority, but if the waiver was inadvertent, such as where the paper first filed omitted the jury demand but was corrected shortly afterwards by a refiling with a paper containing the demand, it has been forgiven and the late demand accepted. SIEGEL-NYPRAC § 378; Heller v. Hacken, 40 A.D.2d 1012, 1012, 338 N.Y.S.2d 943, 944 (1972); In re Mirsky's Estate, 81 Misc. 2d 9, 11, 365 N.Y.S.2d 122, 124 (Sur. 1975).

iii. Needless to say, the party relying on such an amnesty is tempting fate. Trial by jury is too precious to let pass as a matter of right and then seek as a matter of discretion, which the court possesses in abundance in determining whether to forgive the waiver. SIEGEL-NYPRAC § 378.

g. *Determination of demand.* In gauging whether to allow a jury trial, the courts tend to look at the relief being sought, at least if it's responsive to the facts pleaded. In the event of a conflict, the pleaded facts control the demand for relief. SIEGEL-NYPRAC § 377.

h. *Registration of title to real property; Sales of real estate under court direction*

i. Where an answer is interposed which raises an issue of fact which in an action relating to the title to real property would be triable by a jury, either or any party to the registration proceeding who is entitled to have such issue determined may apply to the appropriate part or judge within twenty (20) days after the issue has been joined to have the issues framed to be tried by a jury, as provided by NY CPLR § 4102(b). NY R UNIF TRIAL CTS § 202.65(c).

ii. The trial of such issues shall be had and the subsequent proceedings in relation thereto shall be such as is prescribed by the Civil Practice Law and Rules. After such issues are disposed of, either or any party to the registration proceeding may apply to the appropriate part or judge, upon eight (8) days' notice to all who have appeared in the registration proceeding, for a final order and judgment of registration, and on such application the court shall try all other issues in the proceeding not disposed of by the jury, or may refer any such issues undisposed of to be tried by an official examiner of title as referee. NY R UNIF TRIAL CTS § 202.65(c).

iii. Where all issues have been disposed of, any party, upon eight (8) days' notice to all who have appeared in the proceeding, may apply for the final order and judgment of registration at the appropriate part or before the appropriate assigned judge. NY R UNIF TRIAL CTS § 202.65(c).

i. *Creditor opposing discharge of insolvency.* In order to entitle a creditor to oppose the discharge of the insolvent, he must, on the day fixed to show cause, or at such other time as the court may direct, file with the clerk a specification of his objections; and he may then, but not afterwards, demand a trial, by a jury, of the questions of fact arising thereupon. If a trial by a jury is not then demanded, the questions of fact must be tried by the court, without a jury. Where one of two or more opposing creditors demands a trial by a jury, all the material questions of fact, arising upon the objections of all the creditors, must be tried in like manner, and at the same time. NY DEBT & CRED § 69.

3. *When the need for jury becomes apparent at trial.* When it appears in the course of a trial by the court that the relief required, although not originally demanded by a party, entitles the adverse party to a trial by jury of certain issues of fact, the court shall give the adverse party an opportunity to demand a jury trial of such issues. Failure to make such demand within the time limited by the court shall be deemed a waiver of the right to trial by jury. Upon such demand, the court shall order a jury trial of any issues of fact which are required to be tried by jury. NY CPLR § 4103.

4. *Governing law.* The civil practice law and rules (NY CPLR § 101, et seq.) shall govern the procedure in civil judicial proceedings in all courts of the state and before all judges, except where the procedure is regulated by inconsistent statute. The civil practice law and rules shall succeed the civil practice act and rules of civil practice and shall be deemed substituted therefor throughout the statutes and rules of the state. NY CPLR § 101. The civil practice law and rules shall be liberally construed to secure the just, speedy and inexpensive determination of every civil judicial proceeding. NY CPLR § 104.

a. *Uniform trial court rules.* The uniform civil rules for the Supreme Court and County Court (NY R UNIF TRIAL CTS § 202.1, et seq.) shall be applicable to civil actions and proceedings in the Supreme Court and the County Court. NY R UNIF TRIAL CTS § 202.1(a). The provisions of the uniform rules shall be construed consistent with the Civil Practice Law and Rules (CPLR), and matters not covered by the uniform rules shall be governed by the CPLR. NY R UNIF TRIAL CTS § 202.1(d).

b. *Local rules.* Local court rules, not inconsistent with law or with uniform civil rules for the Supreme Court and County Court (NY R UNIF TRIAL CTS § 202.1, et seq.), shall comply with Part 9 of the Rules of the Chief Judge (NY R CHIEF J § 9.1). NY R UNIF TRIAL CTS § 202.1(c).

c. *Official forms.* The state administrator shall have the power to adopt, amend and rescind an appendix of forms. Forms adopted pursuant to NY CPLR § 107 shall be sufficient under the civil practice law and rules and shall illustrate the simplicity and brevity of statement which the civil practice law and rules contemplate. NY CPLR § 107.

5. *Rules of the commercial division.* [Editor's note: certain types of civil cases or civil cases meeting certain monetary thresholds that are filed in the state of New York must be filed in the Commercial Division of the New York Supreme

Courts. Rules governing practice in the commercial division are found in NY R UNIF TRIAL CTS § 202.70]. Cases which must be filed in the commercial division are listed below. For more information, refer to NY R UNIF TRIAL CTS § 202.70.

a. *Monetary thresholds.* Except as set forth in NY R UNIF TRIAL CTS § 202.70(b), the monetary thresholds of the Commercial Division, exclusive of punitive damages, interests, costs, disbursements and counsel fees claimed, are established as follows: (1) Albany County, fifty thousand dollars ($50,000); (2) Eighth Judicial District, one hundred thousand dollars ($100,000); (3) Kings County, one hundred fifty thousand dollars ($150,000); (4) Nassau County, two hundred thousand dollars ($200,000); (5) New York County, five hundred thousand dollars ($500,000); (6) Onondaga County, fifty thousand dollars ($50,000); (7) Queens County, one hundred thousand dollars ($100,000); (8) Seventh Judicial District, fifty thousand dollars ($50,000); (9) Suffolk County, one hundred thousand dollars ($100,000); and (10) Westchester County, one hundred thousand dollars ($100,000). NY R UNIF TRIAL CTS § 202.70(a).

   i. *ALBANY COUNTY.* The Commercial Division of the Albany County Supreme Court exercises jurisdiction over selected business and commercial disputes in which the amount at issue generally involves damage claims in a minimum amount of fifty thousand dollars ($50,000) as well as claims for unspecified amounts where the value of the commercial asset(s) in dispute exceeds fifty thousand dollars ($50,000). A separate publication promulgating the rules and criteria relating to the filing and management of Commercial Court cases in this part may be obtained from the Albany County Supreme Court Clerk's Office. A section of the Uniform Civil Rules for the Supreme Court and County Court sets forth statewide rules. NY R 3 JD SUP Doc. 1(E).

   ii. *BRONX COUNTY.* The monetary threshold for commercial cases in Bronx County will be seventy-five thousand dollars ($75,000). All other parameters including the type of matters that will be heard are contained within the Rules of the Commercial Division of the Supreme Court (NY R UNIF TRIAL CTS § 202.70). NY R BRONX FIL R Doc. 12.

   iii. *NEW YORK COUNTY.* The monetary threshold in the New York County Commercial Division, which is generally applicable, is an amount in controversy of five hundred thousand dollars ($500,000) or more (exclusive of punitive damages, interest, costs, disbursements, and counsel fees). If the case is designated a commercial one and the Addendum is submitted, the clerk will review the pleadings to determine whether the amount in controversy in the case meets the monetary threshold or whether an exception to the threshold applies. NY R NY CTY Procedure IA(B). For more information on assigning a case to the commercial division in New York County, refer to NY R NY CTY Procedure IA(B).

b. *Commercial cases.* Actions in which the principal claims involve or consist of the following will be heard in the Commercial Division provided that the monetary threshold is met or equitable or declaratory relief is sought:

   i. Breach of contract or fiduciary duty, fraud, misrepresentation, business tort (e.g., unfair competition), or statutory and/or common law violation where the breach or violation is alleged to arise out of business dealings (e.g., sales of assets or securities; corporate restructuring; partnership, shareholder, joint venture, and other business agreements; trade secrets; restrictive covenants; and employment agreements not including claims that principally involve alleged discriminatory practices);

   ii. Transactions governed by the Uniform Commercial Code (exclusive of those concerning individual cooperative or condominium units);

   iii. Transactions involving commercial real property, including Yellowstone injunctions and excluding actions for the payment of rent only;

   iv. Shareholder derivative actions—without consideration of the monetary threshold;

   v. Commercial class actions—without consideration of the monetary threshold;

   vi. Business transactions involving or arising out of dealings with commercial banks and other financial institutions;

   vii. Internal affairs of business organizations;

   viii. Malpractice by accountants or actuaries, and legal malpractice arising out of representation in commercial matters;

   ix. Environmental insurance coverage;

   x. Commercial insurance coverage (e.g., directors and officers, errors and omissions, and business interruption coverage);

   xi. Dissolution of corporations, partnerships, limited liability companies, limited liability partnerships and joint ventures—without consideration of the monetary threshold; and

xii. Applications to stay or compel arbitration and affirm or disaffirm arbitration awards and related injunctive relief pursuant to Article 75 of the New York Civil Practice Law and Rules (NY CPLR § 7501, et seq.) involving any of the foregoing enumerated commercial issues. Where the applicable arbitration agreement provides for the arbitration to be heard outside the United States, the monetary threshold set forth in NY R UNIF TRIAL CTS § 202.70(a) shall not apply. NY R UNIF TRIAL CTS § 202.70(b).

c. *Non-commercial cases.* The following will not be heard in the Commercial Division even if the monetary threshold is met:

i. Suits to collect professional fees;

ii. Cases seeking a declaratory judgment as to insurance coverage for personal injury or property damage;

iii. Residential real estate disputes, including landlord-tenant matters, and commercial real estate disputes involving the payment of rent only;

iv. Home improvement contracts involving residential properties consisting of one to four residential units or individual units in any residential building, including cooperative or condominium units;

v. Proceedings to enforce a judgment regardless of the nature of the underlying case;

vi. First-party insurance claims and actions by insurers to collect premiums or rescind non-commercial policies; and

vii. Attorney malpractice actions except as otherwise provided in NY R UNIF TRIAL CTS § 202.70(b)(8). NY R UNIF TRIAL CTS § 202.70(c).

d. For more information on the Commercial Division, refer to NY R UNIF TRIAL CTS § 202.70.

D. Documents

1. *Required documents*

a. *Note of issue containing a jury demand.* Any party may demand a trial by jury of any issue of fact triable of right by a jury, by serving upon all other parties and filing a note of issue containing a demand for trial by jury. NY CPLR § 4102(a). For a sample version of the note of issue, refer to NY R UNIF TRIAL CTS § 202.21(b).

b. *Certificate of readiness.* No action or special proceeding shall be deemed ready for trial or inquest unless there is first filed a note of issue accompanied by a certificate of readiness, with proof of service on all parties entitled to notice, in the form prescribed by NY R UNIF TRIAL CTS § 202.21. NY R UNIF TRIAL CTS § 202.21(a).

c. *Filing fees.* The County Clerk shall require the payment of any applicable statutory fees, or an order of the Court waiving payment of such fees, before accepting a paper for filing. NY R UNIF TRIAL CTS § 202.5(d)(1). For information on filing fees, if any, refer to NY CPLR § 8001, et seq.

i. *NEW YORK COUNTY.* The fees for filing a note of issue and jury demand must be paid to the County Clerk through the New York State Courts Electronic Filing System in e-filed cases or, in hard-copy cases, in person in Room 160 at 60 Centre Street (fees are thirty dollars ($30) (where the RJI has previously been paid for) and sixty-five dollars ($65) respectively). The fees must be paid in cash, by Visa, Mastercard, or American Express credit or bank card, by an attorney's check made payable to the New York County Clerk, or in the form of a U.S. postal money order made payable to the New York County Clerk. An attorney's check will be accepted if it is from a New York attorney, provided that words such as "Attorney at Law" or "Esq." appear thereon, together with the attorney's address and phone number. Other checks must be certified. NY R NY CTY Procedure VIII(A).

d. *Proof of service.* In addition to complying with the provisions of NY CPLR Rule 2101, every paper filed in court shall have annexed thereto appropriate proof of service on all parties where required. NY R UNIF TRIAL CTS § 202.5(a).

2. *Supplemental documents*

a. *Working copies.* The court may require the parties to provide working copies of documents filed electronically. In such event, each working copy shall include, firmly affixed thereto, a copy of a confirmation notice in a form prescribed by the Chief Administrator. NY R UNIF TRIAL CTS § 202.5-b(d)(5).

b. *Statement of authorization in electronic filing cases.* A filing agent (other than one employed by a governmental entity) shall e-file a statement of authorization from counsel of record in an action, in a form approved by the Chief Administrator, prior to or together with the first e-filing in that action by the agent on behalf of that counsel. NY R UNIF TRIAL CTS § 202.5-b(d)(1)(i).

c. *ERIE COUNTY: Additional supplemental documents*

i. *Notice of hard copy submission in e-filed case.* In accordance with NY R UNIF TRIAL CTS § 202.5-b(d), the County Clerk shall refuse to accept for filing, hard copy papers filed to an action subject to electronic filing unless hard copy filing is permitted by the Uniform Rules or NY R ERIE E FIL Doc. 3 and the papers bear a completed Notice of Hard Copy Submission—E-Filed Case form. NY R ERIE E FIL Doc. 3(III)(D).

d. *KINGS COUNTY: Additional supplemental documents*

i. *Forms when filing in hard copy.* An attorney who certifies in good faith that he or she lacks the equipment or knowledge needed to e-file and have no staff member or employee under his or her direction who has such knowledge and equipment may opt out of participation in e-filing in a mandatory case by filing a "Notice of Opt-Out from Participation in Action Subject to Mandatory Electronic Filing" form EFM-2 with the Clerk. NY R L KINGS E FIL Doc. 1(A)(2). Where in accordance with the E-Filing Rules a party submits a document in hard copy in an e-filed case (principally, a document submitted by a nonparticipating party (e.g., an attorney) in a consensual case, an emergency filing made in accordance with the Mandatory E-Filing Rules, and any document filed with the court in hard copy by an attorney who has opted out of participation in mandatory e-filing, the document must bear the back page facing out, a "Notice of Hard Copy Submission—E-Filed Cases" form EFM-3. NY R L KINGS E FIL Doc. 1(B)(3).

e. *NEW YORK COUNTY: Additional supplemental documents*

i. *Notice of hard copy submission.* Where in accordance with the E-Filing Rules an attorney or an unrepresented litigant who is participating in e-filing submits a document in hard copy in an e-filed case, the document must bear, as the back page facing out, a Notice of Hard-Copy Submission—E-Filed Case (a form available in the "Forms" section on the NYSCEF website (Form EFM-3) and in the court's back offices). NY R NY CTY E FIL Doc. 2(B)(3). For more information refer to NY R NY CTY E FIL Doc. 2.

f. *ONONDAGA COUNTY: Additional supplemental documents*

i. *Notice of hard copy submission.* Any papers to be filed with the court in an e-filed case must be filed online with the E-filing system except where a special exemption is granted (e.g., oversized maps, photographs). If such an exemption is granted, Form EFM-3, "Notice of Hard Copy Submission—E-Filed Case," must be attached to such documents forms which are not filed on line. Also, Form EFM-4 "Notice of Hard Copy Exhibit Filing" must be completed and uploaded to the action's e-file. Both of these forms may be found on the NYSCEF website. NY R ONDGA E FIL Protocol(B)(4).

g. *QUEENS COUNTY: Additional supplemental documents*

i. *Notice of hard copy submission.* Any party opting out of the e-filing system must have a "Notice of Hard Copy Submission" firmly affixed to the back of the papers. NY R L QUEENS E-FILE Doc. 1(H)(2)(f).

E. Format

1. *Form of documents*

a. *Size and form of paper.* Each paper served or filed shall be durable, white and, except for summonses, subpoenas, notices of appearance, notes of issue, orders of protection, temporary orders of protection and exhibits, shall be eleven by eight and one-half (11 x 8-1/2) inches in size. NY CPLR Rule 2101(a).

b. *Writing and language.* The writing shall be legible and in black ink. NY CPLR Rule 2101(a). Each paper served or filed shall be in the English language which, where practicable, shall be of ordinary usage. NY CPLR Rule 2101(b).

c. *Caption.* Each paper served or filed shall begin with a caption setting forth the name of the court, the venue, the title of the action, the nature of the paper and the index number of the action if one has been assigned. In all papers other than a summons, a complaint or a judgment it shall be sufficient to state the name of the first named party on each side with an appropriate indication of any omissions. NY CPLR Rule 2101(c).

i. *Further contents of first page.* After the first paper has been filed in each case the index number shall appear on the cover and first page to the right of the caption of every paper tendered for filing in the action. Each such cover and first page also shall contain an indication of the county of venue and a brief description of the nature of the paper and, where the case has been assigned to an individual judge, shall contain the name of the assigned judge to the right of the caption. NY R UNIF TRIAL CTS § 202.5(a); NY R UNIF TRIAL CTS § 202.5(b); NY R UNIF TRIAL CTS § 202.5(d)(1)(i).

d. *Index number.* No paper in an action in the supreme or a county court, other than an order submitted for signature to

a judge out of court, shall be submitted for any purpose to the supreme or county court or to a clerk thereof unless there is endorsed on such paper the index number of the action assigned by the clerk of the county. NY CPLR § 8018(c).

i. *ALBANY COUNTY: Index number on all filed documents.* The index number, the request for judicial intervention number and the assigned justice's name shall appear on [all papers filed with the Court subsequent to the complaint]. NY R 3 JD SUP Doc. 1(A).

ii. *ERIE COUNTY: Index number after initial filing.* Cases that are initially commenced by the filing of papers with the NYSCEF system are identified as e-filed cases by assignment of an Index Number that has "800-899" as the first three (3) digits of the index number (i.e. 802391/2012). NY R ERIE E FIL Doc. 3(II). [The] Index Number must be affixed to all document submissions, filings, and communications to the Erie County Clerk and the Court. Cases that are converted from paper to e-filing shall retain the original index number. NY R ERIE E FIL Doc. 3(II).

iii. *KINGS COUNTY: Index number after initial filing.* In cases commenced electronically by the filing of initiating papers with the NYSCEF system and payment of the statutory fees, the Kings County Clerk will issue an NYSCEF designated index number and the filer shall be notified via the NYSCEF system of the index number assigned and filing date. Such index number must be affixed to all document submissions, filings and communications to the Kings County Clerk and Supreme Court. If counsel faces exigent circumstances that require accelerated assignment, counsel may contact Administration of the Kings County Clerk at kcco-efile@nycourts.gov, during normal business hours of the court. NY R L KINGS E FIL Doc. 1(B)(5).

iv. *NEW YORK COUNTY: Index number on hard copy filings.* Papers subsequently presented for filing in hardcopy format will be filed in this jacket. NY R NY CTY Procedure I(B). Index numbers take the form of six digits followed by a slash and the four digits of the year the case began, e.g., 340705/2018. The first or first two integers of the index number identify the type of case. If a case is commenced electronically, the second integer will be a "5", except as indicated otherwise in the list below. There are many tax certiorari matters e-filed annually and the index numbers therefor will normally run over into those with a "6" as the second integer, and the same will occur with general cases if necessary. The principal types of cases and their index number categories are listed in NY R NY CTY Procedure I(B). NY R NY CTY Procedure I(B); NY R NY CTY Procedure XI(A).

v. *ONONDAGA COUNTY: Index number.* The index number must be referenced on all e-filed documents and correspondence. All e-filed case index numbers will contain the letters "EF" between the year and the file number (for example, 2012EF9999). NY R ONDGA E FIL Protocol(B)(1).

vi. *QUEENS COUNTY: Index number on converted cases.* Cases originally commenced in hard-copy form but later converted to an E-file case, either by stipulation or order will bear a regular index number initially. The County Clerk will issue a new E-file index number. NY R L QUEENS E-FILE Doc. 1(B).

e. *Line spacing.* Every paper filed in court, if typewritten, shall have at least double space between each line, except for quotations and the names and addresses of attorneys appearing in the action. NY R UNIF TRIAL CTS § 202.5(a).

f. *Font size.* Each. . .paper printed or typed, served or filed, except for summonses. . .and exhibits, shall be in clear type of no less than ten (10) point in size. NY CPLR Rule 2101(a).

i. Whenever a requirement relating to size of type is stated in point size, the type size requirement shall be deemed met if the x-height of the type is a minimum of forty-five percent (45%) of the specified point size. Each point shall be measured as .351 millimeter. The x-height size shall be measured as it appears on the page. The x-height is the height of the lower case letters, exclusive of ascenders or descenders. NY CPLR § 105(t).

g. *Margins.* Every paper filed in court shall have at least one (1) inch margins. NY R UNIF TRIAL CTS § 202.5(a).

h. *Citations*

i. *Civil practice law and rules.* NY CPLR § 101, et seq. shall be known as the civil practice law and rules, and may be cited as "CPLR". Reference to a provision in the civil practice law and rules may, except when such provision is being enacted or amended, be made without indicating whether it is a rule or section. NY CPLR § 101.

i. *Indorsement by attorney.* Each paper served or filed shall be indorsed with the name, address and telephone number of the attorney for the party serving or filing the paper, or if the party does not appear by attorney, with the name, address and telephone number of the party. NY CPLR Rule 2101(d).

j. *One-sided printing.* In addition, every paper filed in court, other than an exhibit or printed form, shall contain writing on one side only, except that papers that are fastened on the side may contain writing on both sides. NY R UNIF TRIAL CTS § 202.5(a).

k. *Use of copies authorized.* Except where otherwise specifically prescribed, copies, rather than originals, of all papers,

including orders, affidavits and exhibits may be served or filed. Where it is required that the original be served or filed and the original is lost or withheld, the court may authorize a copy to be served or filed. NY CPLR Rule 2101(e).

i. Where a certified copy of a paper is required by law, an attorney admitted to practice in the courts of the state may certify that it has been compared by him with the original and found to be a true and complete copy. Such a certificate, when subscribed by such attorney, has the same effect as if made by a clerk. NY CPLR § 2105.

l. *Recycled paper.* It is the policy of the Unified Court System that litigants, where practicable, should file or submit to the courts of the Unified Court System of the State of New York papers printed or reproduced on recycled paper. Paper is considered recycled if it contains a minimum content of thirty percent (30%) waste paper. NY R UNIF TRIAL CTS § 215.2. The signature page of every paper filed or submitted to the court on recycled paper should bear the legend: "Printed [Reproduced] on Recycled Paper." NY R UNIF TRIAL CTS § 215.3.

m. *KINGS COUNTY: Tabs on filings.* Motions, orders and other filed papers shall be indexed with protruding tabs. Clerks are required to reject papers that do not have protruding exhibit tabs, except papers in matrimonial cases and papers filed by pro se litigants. NY R L KINGS Pt. A, Papers.

2. *Form of electronic documents.* Each paper served or filed by electronic means, as defined in NY CPLR Rule 2103(f), shall be capable of being reproduced by the receiver so as to comply with the provisions of NY CPLR Rule 2101(a) through NY CPLR Rule 2101(d). NY CPLR Rule 2101(g).

a. *File format.* All e-filed documents shall comply with the technical requirements set forth at the NYSCEF site. NY R UNIF TRIAL CTS § 202.5-b(d)(1)(i).

b. *Heading of document.* The subject matter heading for each paper sent by electronic means must indicate that the matter being transmitted electronically is related to a court proceeding. NY CPLR Rule 2103(b)(7).

c. *E-filed documents identification*

i. *ERIE COUNTY.* E-filed cases must be readily identifiable and marked as such. If counsel presents papers to the Office of the Erie County Clerk or the Office of the Chief Clerk in a NYSCEF matter where authorized, counsel should alert the Clerk that the case is a NYSCEF matter. NY R ERIE E FIL Doc. 3(II).

ii. *KINGS COUNTY.* The Supreme Court's Civil Case Information System ("CCIS") will further identify e-filed cases by the addition of a suffix to the index number (e.g. 500136/2006E). This suffix should be used on all documents filed with the court in e-filed matters. NY R L KINGS E FIL Doc. 1(A)(1).

3. *Signature blocks.* Every pleading, written motion, and other paper, served on another party or filed or submitted to the court shall be signed by an attorney, or by a party if the party is not represented by an attorney, with the name of the attorney or party clearly printed or typed directly below the signature. NY R CHIEF ADMIN § 130-1.1-a(a); NY R UNIF TRIAL CTS § 202.5(d)(1)(iv).

a. *Printed name.* Beneath each signature shall be printed the name signed. NY CPLR Rule 2101(a).

b. *Failure to sign.* Absent good cause shown, the court shall strike any unsigned paper if the omission of the signature is not corrected promptly after being called to the attention of the attorney or party. NY R CHIEF ADMIN § 130-1.1-a(a).

c. *Signature as certification.* By signing a paper, an attorney or party certifies that, to the best of that person's knowledge, information and belief, formed after an inquiry reasonable under the circumstances the presentation of the paper or the contentions therein are not frivolous as defined in NY R CHIEF ADMIN § 130-1.1(c). NY R CHIEF ADMIN § 130-1.1-a(b)(1).

d. *Electronic signatures.* A document shall be considered to have been signed by an attorney or party in compliance with NY R CHIEF ADMIN § 130-1.1-a if it has been signed by such attorney or party as provided in NY R UNIF TRIAL CTS § 202.5-b(e)(1) and it bears the signatory's name. NY R UNIF TRIAL CTS § 202.5-b(e)(2). An electronically filed document shall be considered to have been signed by, and shall be binding upon, the person identified as a signatory, if:

i. It bears the physical signature of such person and is scanned into an electronic format that reproduces such signature; or

ii. The signatory has electronically affixed the digital image of his or her signature to the document; or

iii. It is electronically filed under the User ID and password of that person; or

iv. In a tax certiorari action in which the parties have stipulated to this procedure, it is an initiating document that is electronically filed without the signature of the signatory in a form provided above in NY R UNIF TRIAL CTS

§ 202.5-b(e)(iv), provided that, prior to filing, the document is signed in full in hard copy (which hard copy must be preserved until the conclusion of all proceedings, including appeals, in the case in which it is filed); or

v. In a small claims assessment review proceeding, it is a petition recorded by the NYSCEF site upon the filing of a text file as provided in NY R UNIF TRIAL CTS § 202.5-b(b)(1), provided that prior to filing, the document was signed in full in hard copy (which hard copy must be preserved until the conclusion of all proceedings in the matter, including article 78 (NY CPLR § 7801, et seq.) review and any appeals, and must be made available during the proceeding upon request of the respondent or the court); or

vi. It otherwise bears the electronic signature of the signatory in a format conforming to such standards and requirements as may hereafter be established by the Chief Administrator. NY R UNIF TRIAL CTS § 202.5-b(e).

4. *Confidentiality of personal information.* No person may file any document available for public inspection with any state agency, political subdivision, or in any court of this state that contains a Social Security account number of any other person, unless such other person is a dependent child, or has consented to such filing, except as required by federal or state law or regulation, or by court rule. NY GEN BUS § 399-ddd. Submissions pursuant to e-filing procedures shall have the same confidentiality rights as paper documents. NY R UNIF TRIAL CTS § 202.5-b(k)(1).

a. *Confidential personal information.* Except in the actions designated in NY R UNIF TRIAL CTS § 202.5(e)(1), or as otherwise provided by rule or law or court order, and whether or not a sealing order is or has been sought, the parties shall omit or redact confidential personal information in papers submitted to the court for filing. For purposes of NY R UNIF TRIAL CTS § 202.5(e), confidential personal information ("CPI") means:

i. The taxpayer identification number of an individual or an entity, including a Social Security number, an employer identification number, and an individual taxpayer identification number, except the last four (4) digits thereof;

ii. The date of an individual's birth, except the year thereof;

iii. The full name of an individual known to be a minor, except the minor's initials;

iv. A financial account number, including a credit and/or debit card number, a bank account number, an investment account number, and/or an insurance account number, except the last four (4) digits or letters thereof; and

v. Any of the documents or testimony in a matrimonial action protected by NY DOM REL § 235 or evidence sealed by the court in such an action which are attached as exhibits or referenced in the papers filed in any other civil action. For purposes of NY R UNIF TRIAL CTS § 202.5, a matrimonial action shall mean: an action to annul a marriage or declare the nullity of a void marriage, an action or agreement for a separation, an action for a divorce, or an action or proceeding for custody, visitation, writ of habeus corpus, child support, maintenance or paternity. NY R UNIF TRIAL CTS § 202.5(e)(1).

vi. *ERIE COUNTY.* An attorney or unrepresented litigant filing a document via the NYSCEF system must comply with the requirements of NY R UNIF TRIAL CTS § 202.5(e) regarding the redaction of Confidential Personal Information and NY GEN BUS § 399-ddd(6) concerning the filing of documents containing Social Security Numbers. It is the sole responsibility of counsel or unrepresented litigant filing to be aware of and to comply with existing laws requiring non-disclosure of personal information contained in any document e-filed in NYSCEF. NY R ERIE E FIL Doc. 3(III)(G); NY R ERIE E FIL Doc. 3(III).

vii. *KINGS COUNTY.* An attorney or unrepresented litigant filing a document via the NYSCEF system must comply with the requirements of General Business Law § 399-dd(6), which often require redaction of any Social Security number that appear in the original document. The NYSCEF system automatically redacts portions of filed documents which apparently contain Social Security numbers pursuant to NY R UNIF TRIAL CTS § 202.5-b(k). In the event the filing party receives e-mail notice through NYSCEF that a Social Security number in a filed document has been redacted, and the filing party concludes such redaction is erroneous, the filer should click on the link provided in the e-mail to permit the County Clerk to revert the redaction. For Confidential Personal Information, see NY R UNIF TRIAL CTS § 202.5(e) and NY R L KINGS E FIL Doc. 1(B)(11). [Editor's note: the reference to General Business Law § 399-dd(6) is likely a reference to NY GEN BUS § 399-ddd(6)]. NY R L KINGS E FIL Doc. 1(B)(10); NY R L KINGS E FIL Doc. 1(K)(1).

viii. *NEW YORK COUNTY.* It is the responsibility of counsel and parties to comply with rules restricting disclosure of confidential personal information. Nevertheless, NYSCEF screens filings and endeavors to identify any that contain social security numbers. When such numbers are discovered through this process, NYSCEF will restrict portions of or all of such documents from public view. Where NYSCEF has redacted what it believes to be a social security number, it will transmit to the filer a notice advising of the action taken and requesting that the filer review the matter and provide notification as set forth in the notice if the redaction has been made in error. NY R NY CTY E FIL Doc. 2(K)(1); NY R NY CTY J RUL Rule A-1. Documents filed in the past in "secure status" under a procedure no longer in place will retain that status unless otherwise directed by the court. NY R NY CTY E FIL Doc. 2(K)(2).

b. *Submission of confidential personal information.* Where a person submitting a paper to a court for filing believes in good faith that the inclusion of the full confidential personal information described in NY R UNIF TRIAL CTS § 202.5(e)(1) is material and necessary to the adjudication of the action or proceeding before the court, he or she may apply to the court for leave to serve and file together with a paper in which such information has been set forth in abbreviated form a confidential affidavit or affirmation setting forth the same information in unabbreviated form, appropriately referenced to the page or pages of the paper at which the abbreviated form appears. NY R UNIF TRIAL CTS § 202.5(e)(3).

c. *Home addresses.* For information on when home addresses and other personal information must be redacted, refer to NY CPLR Rule 2103-a.

5. *Defective papers.* A defect in the form of a paper, if a substantial right of a party is not prejudiced, shall be disregarded by the court, and leave to correct shall be freely given. NY CPLR Rule 2101(f). Papers that are stapled or bound securely shall not be rejected for filing simply because they are not bound with a backer of any kind. NY R UNIF TRIAL CTS § 202.5(a). A paper filed in accordance with the rules of the chief administrator or any local rule or practice established by the court shall be deemed filed. NY CPLR Rule 2102(b).

a. *Objection to defective papers.* The party on whom a paper is served shall be deemed to have waived objection to any defect in form unless, within fifteen (15) days after the receipt thereof, the party on whom the paper is served returns the paper to the party serving it with a statement of particular objections. NY CPLR Rule 2101(f).

F. Filing and Service Requirements

1. *Filing requirements.* Except where otherwise prescribed by law or order of court, papers required to be filed shall be filed with the clerk of the court in which the action is triable. In an action or proceeding in supreme or court, papers required to be filed shall be filed with the clerk of the county in which the proceeding is brought. NY CPLR Rule 2102(a).

a. *Electronic filing.* On consent, documents may be filed and served by electronic means in Supreme Court in such civil actions and in such counties as shall be authorized by order of the Chief Administrator of the Courts and only to the extent and in the manner provided in NY R UNIF TRIAL CTS § 202.5-b. NY R UNIF TRIAL CTS § 202.5-b(a)(1). For the definitions of terms used in electronic filing, refer to NY R UNIF TRIAL CTS § 202.5-b(a)(2).

i. *E-filing mandatory.* In any action subject to e-filing, all documents required to be filed with the court by an e-filing party shall be filed and served electronically, except as provided in NY R UNIF TRIAL CTS § 202.5-b. NY R UNIF TRIAL CTS § 202.5-b(d)(1)(i).

- *ERIE COUNTY.* Case types currently eligible and accepted for e-filing are listed at the NYSCEF website. Note that some actions or special proceedings, (i.e., name changes) which are otherwise subject to mandatory e-filing, if commenced by unrepresented litigants will NOT be maintained in the NYSCEF system; individual cases may be found either at NYSCEF or in the Erie County Clerk's online records system. NY R ERIE E FIL Doc. 3(I)(E).

- *KINGS COUNTY.* Cases that are commenced by filing of the initiating papers with NYSCEF are identified as e-filed cases by assignment of a special index number (i.e., Index Numbers beginning with 500,000). NY R L KINGS E FIL Doc. 1(A)(1). All cases required to be e-filed are listed in Uniform Rule 202.5-bb (Mandatory E-Filing Rules) and on the NYSCEF website. All such cases must be commenced by filing with the County Clerk electronically through NYSCEF and all subsequent documents in such cases must be e-filed. Any questions regarding mandatory e-filing in Kings County can be e-mailed to kcco-efile@nycourts.gov. NY R L KINGS E FIL Doc. 1(A)(2).

- *NEW YORK COUNTY.* Unless otherwise provided in the Rules or in NY R NY CTY E FIL Doc. 2 or where a special exemption is granted due to physical requirements (e.g., oversized maps; see NY R NY CTY E FIL Doc. 2(B)(10)), all documents to be filed with the court in a NYSCEF case, including all documents on motions and all letters to the court (where permitted), must be filed with the NYSCEF system. Documents that attorneys would not ordinarily file with the court in a hard-copy case need not be e-filed. Unless otherwise provided by the E-Filing Rules or this Protocol, in e-filed cases the County Clerk and the court will not accept documents filed in paper form. NY R NY CTY E FIL Doc. 2(B)(1). E-filing is mandatory in all types of cases (other than election law, matrimonial, Art. 78, and Mental Hygiene Law matters, and Art. 70 habeas corpus proceedings) that are commenced in this court on or after February 19, 2013. All such cases must be commenced by filing with the County Clerk electronically through NYSCEF and all subsequent documents in such cases must be e-filed. NY R NY CTY E FIL Doc. 2(A)(2)(a). For more information, including information on consensual e-filing and filing scanned hard copy documents, refer to NY R NY CTY E FIL Doc. 2(A)(2).

- *QUEENS COUNTY.* All authorized Torts, Commercial and Tax Certiorari cases may be commenced by E-Filing, however all parties must consent for the action to continue as an E-file case. NY R L QUEENS E-FILE Doc. 1(A). All papers to be filed with the court in an E-filed case shall be filed on-line with the E-file system except as directed by the court. Papers that attorneys would not ordinarily file with the court in a hard-copy case need not be filed in an E-filed matter. NY R L QUEENS E-FILE Doc. 1(E)(2).

ii. *Who may file.* Documents may be filed or served electronically only by a person who has registered as an authorized e-filing user or as otherwise provided in NY R UNIF TRIAL CTS § 202.5-b(c). NY R UNIF TRIAL CTS § 202.5-b(c)(1).

iii. *When filing made.* Documents may be transmitted at any time of the day or night to the NYSCEF site. A document other than an order or judgment is filed when its electronic transmission or, in the case of a petition that is e-filed by submission of a text file as provided in NY R UNIF TRIAL CTS § 202.5-b(b)(1), the electronic transmission of the text file is recorded at that site, provided, however, that where payment of a fee is required upon the filing of a document, the document is not filed until transmission of the document and the information or form or information as required in NY R UNIF TRIAL CTS § 202.5-b(d)(2)(i), NY R UNIF TRIAL CTS § 202.5-b(d)(2)(ii) or NY R UNIF TRIAL CTS § 202.5-b(d)(2)(iii) has been recorded at the NYSCEF site; or, if no transmission of that information or form or information is recorded, where permitted by the County Clerk, until payment is presented to the County Clerk. NY R UNIF TRIAL CTS § 202.5-b(d)(3)(i).

iv. *Notification of filing.* No later than the close of business on the business day following the electronic filing of a document, a notification, in a form prescribed by the Chief Administrator, shall be transmitted electronically by the NYSCEF site to the person filing such document and the e-mail service addresses of all other participating parties in such action. NY R UNIF TRIAL CTS § 202.5-b(d)(3)(ii).

v. *Removal of confidential information and other corrections.* If a document filed electronically is subsequently discovered to contain confidential data—including but not limited to trade secrets, information protected by confidentiality agreement, or personal confidential information as defined by statute or court rule—or otherwise to have been filed in error, the filer or another party or affected person may (1) notify the parties and any non-party filers in the action of the confidentiality issue or other error raised by the filing, and of his or her intention to seek judicial relief to correct the filing: (2) following such notification, request that the appropriate County Clerk, exercising his or her administrative discretion, place the document temporarily in "restricted" status on the NYSCEF site, to be made available for viewing by court staff and the parties but not the general public; and (3) file an application to correct the filing by order to show cause within five (5) business days of such notification (or such time as the court may direct), including a request for preliminary injunctive relief limiting interim disclosure of the document at issue. Unless otherwise directed by the court, any document placed in restricted status in response to such a request shall be returned to public view upon expiration of this five (5) day period. The Chief Administrator of the Courts shall promulgate forms to implement this process. NY R UNIF TRIAL CTS § 202.5-b(d)(3)(iii).

- *KINGS COUNTY.* For information on what to do when a document was erroneously filed with confidential information, refer to NY R L KINGS E FIL Doc. 1(B)(11).
- *NEW YORK COUNTY.* For information on what to do when a document was erroneously filed with confidential information, refer to NY R NY CTY E FIL Doc. 2(B)(8).
- *QUEENS COUNTY.* For information on what to do when a document was erroneously filed with confidential information, refer to NY R L QUEENS E-FILE Doc. 1(E)(7).

vi. *Documents requiring judge's signature.* Except where the court directs otherwise, any document that requires a judge's signature shall be transmitted electronically and in hard copy to the court. NY R UNIF TRIAL CTS § 202.5-b(d)(6).

vii. *Documents which would be inconvenient to file electronically; Hard copies.* Notwithstanding any other provision of NY R UNIF TRIAL CTS § 202.5-b, and subject to such guidelines as may be established by the Chief Administrative Judge, the County Clerk or his or her designee may require or permit a party to file in hard copy, in accordance with procedures set by the County Clerk or designee, an exhibit or other document which it is impractical or inconvenient to file electronically. NY R UNIF TRIAL CTS § 202.5-b(d)(7).

- *ERIE COUNTY.* Please contact the Supervisor of Actions & Proceedings, Erie County Clerk's Office by calling (716) 858-6662 or the Deputy County Clerk—Legal at (716) 858-6348 for information. NY R ERIE E FIL Doc. 3(III)(F).

- *KINGS COUNTY.* With limited exceptions, as set forth in the Uniform Rules and herein, all documents to be filed with the court in a NYSCEF case shall be filed online via the NYSCEF system. However, should the size, consistency or context of a hard copy document preclude electronic filing, the user shall electronically file a "Notice of Hard Copy Submission—E-Filed Cases" form EFM-3. Any hard copy submitted pursuant to NY R L KINGS E FIL Doc. 1(B)(9) shall include, as a cover page firmly fastened thereto, a copy of the Confirmation Notice received from the NYSCEF site confirming receipt of the "Notice of Hard Copy Submission—E-Filed Cases". Any party may object to such hard copy filing. The Court, in response to such objection, may, following the hard copy filing, fashion such relief as it deems appropriate pursuant to and in furtherance of the Uniform Rules and NY R L KINGS E FIL Doc. 1, including, but not limited to, an Order directing the filing party to file such documents online via the NYSCEF system. When exhibits are impractical to file pursuant to NY R UNIF TRIAL CTS § 202.5-b(d)(7), an additional "Notice of Hard Copy Exhibit Filing" form EFM-4 is required to be submitted. NY R L KINGS E FIL Doc. 1(B)(9).
- *NEW YORK COUNTY.* If a filer needs to submit unusual exhibits in original form that cannot practically be e-filed, such as oversized maps or electronic recordings, the filer should consult with the County Clerk's E-File Department by telephone at 646-386-3737 (procedural questions only) or by e-mail at ccnyef@nycourts.gov, which will normally require that the filer retain custody of the original subject to possible future directives of the court. NY R NY CTY E FIL Doc. 2(B)(10). In such instances, the filing counsel shall file with NYSCEF a "placeholder" in the form of a Notice of Hard Copy Exhibit Filing (NYSCEF Form EF 21). The Notice should be uploaded to NYSCEF as document type "Exhibit" and the filer should indicate in the "Additional Document Information" field that the filer is retaining custody of the original. Failure to e-file the Notice may result in a gap in the official record of the court. NY R NY CTY E FIL Doc. 2(B)(10).

viii. *Documents containing sensitive or proprietary information.* In an action subject to e-filing, any person may apply for an order prohibiting or restricting the electronic filing in the action of specifically identified materials on the grounds that such materials are subject to copyright or other proprietary rights, or trade secret or other privacy interests, and that electronic filing in the action is likely to result in substantial prejudice to those rights or interests. NY R UNIF TRIAL CTS § 202.5-b(k)(2).

ix. *Refusal to accept paper filings.* In accordance with NY CPLR Rule 2102(c), a County Clerk and a chief clerk of the Supreme Court or County Court, as appropriate, shall refuse to accept for filing papers filed in actions and proceedings when the paper sought to be filed:

- Is in an action subject to electronic filing pursuant to Rules of the Chief Administrator,
- Is not being filed electronically, and
- Does not include the notice required by NY R UNIF TRIAL CTS § 202.5-b(d)(1). NY R UNIF TRIAL CTS § 202.5(d)(1)(v); NY R UNIF TRIAL CTS § 202.5-bb(d).

x. *Emergency filings; Hard copies.* For information on when an emergency filing may be filed and served in hard copy, refer to NY R UNIF TRIAL CTS § 202.5-b(d)(1)(ii), NY R UNIF TRIAL CTS § 202.5-b(d)(1)(iii) and NY R UNIF TRIAL CTS § 202.5-bb(c)(3).

- *KINGS COUNTY.* Under the rules, a participating emergency e-filer must electronically file the documents initially filed in hard copy form within three (3) business days of the emergency filing; the originals will be discarded after the documents have been processed and the failure to e-file as required will therefore lead to an incomplete record. NY R L KINGS E FIL Doc. 1(B)(3).
- *NEW YORK COUNTY.* Occasionally an emergency will arise requiring expedited entry of a document with the County Clerk (e.g., an order issued in the courtroom after a conference or argument of a critical matter), such as for purposes of an immediate appeal. Expedition can be achieved by the Part as follows: the document should be carried by a Court Officer or staff member to the General Clerk's Office to assure immediate and proper recordation in the computer and, as appropriate, the posting of the document to NYSCEF or the Supreme Court Records On-Line Library ("Scroll"). The court will accommodate counsel in emergencies. NY R NY CTY Procedure XI(A).

xi. *Technical failures.* The NYSCEF site shall be considered to be subject to a technical failure on a given day if the site is unable to accept filings or provide access to filed documents continuously or intermittently over the course of any period of time greater than one (1) hour after 12:00 noon of that day. Notice of all such technical failures shall be provided on the site. NY R UNIF TRIAL CTS § 202.5-b(i).

- When e-filing is hindered by a technical failure, a party may file with the appropriate clerk and serve in hard copy. NY R UNIF TRIAL CTS § 202.5-b(i). In the event an attorney or party shall file and serve documents in hard copy pursuant to NY R UNIF TRIAL CTS § 202.5-b(i), each such document shall include the notice required by NY R UNIF TRIAL CTS § 202.5-b(d)(1), and the filer shall file those documents with the NYSCEF site within three (3) business days after restoration of normal operations at that site. NY R UNIF TRIAL CTS § 202.5-b(i).
- With the exception of deadlines that by law cannot be extended, the time for filing of any document that is delayed due to technical failure of the site shall be extended for one (1) day for each day on which such failure occurs, unless otherwise ordered by the court. NY R UNIF TRIAL CTS § 202.5-b(i).
- *ERIE COUNTY.* When filing by electronic means is hindered by a technical failure, please refer to the NY R UNIF TRIAL CTS § 202.5-b(i). NY R ERIE E FIL Doc. 3(III)(K).
- *KINGS COUNTY.* When filing by electronic means is hindered by a NYSCEF technical failure (as set forth in NY R UNIF TRIAL CTS § 202.5-b(i)), a party may file with the appropriate Clerk in hard copy. Except for deadlines that by law cannot be extended (e.g. Statute of limitations, Notice of Appeal), the time for filing of any document that is delayed due to technical failure of the NYSCEF system shall be extended for one day for each day on which such failure occurs, unless otherwise ordered by the court. NY R L KINGS E FIL Doc. 1(B)(13).
- *ONONDAGA COUNTY.* When filing by electronic means is hindered by a technical failure (as set forth in NY R UNIF TRIAL CTS § 202.5-b(h)(3)(i)), a party may file a hard copy with the County Clerk. With the exception of deadlines that by law cannot be extended (e.g., a statute of limitations or the deadline for filing a Notice of Appeal), the time for filing of any document that is delayed due to technical failure of the NYSCEF system will be extended for one day for each day on which such failure occurs, unless otherwise ordered by the court. A "Notice of Hard Copy Filing Submission—E-Filed Case' must accompany any documents not filed via NYSCEF. NY R ONDGA E FIL Protocol(B)(8).

xii. *Filing fees.* For information on what information must be provided to pay filing fees, refer to NY R UNIF TRIAL CTS § 202.5-b(d)(2).

xiii. *Exemption from e-filing.* For information on exemptions from e-filing, refer to NY R UNIF TRIAL CTS § 202.5-bb(e).

xiv. *Filing exhibits*

- *ERIE COUNTY.* In the NYSCEF system, each exhibit must be uploaded as a separate .pdf file. After uploading a primary document, please choose the document type "Exhibit" and enter the appropriate number or letter and a brief description of the exhibit; each exhibit should bear a separate cover sheet clearly marked as "Exhibit A," "Exhibit B," etc. "Exhibit A" or "Exhibit B" is unacceptable as a brief description of the exhibit. Exhibits, where referenced in a signed Order as attached or affixed shall be uploaded with the signed Order as one .pdf document. NY R ERIE E FIL Doc. 3(III)(H).
- *KINGS COUNTY.* In the NYSCEF system, each exhibit should be uploaded as a separate PDF file. After uploading a primary document, please choose the document type "Exhibit", enter the appropriate number or letter, and be sure to place a check mark to the right of "Attach to main document". Each exhibit shall bear a separate cover sheet clearly marked as Exhibit A, Exhibit B, etc. NY R L KINGS E FIL Doc. 1(B)(12).
- *NEW YORK COUNTY.* Attorneys submitting exhibits in NYSCEF cases should make each exhibit a separate attachment to an affidavit/affirmation in the system; i.e., exhibits should not be filed as a single PDF-A together with the affidavit/affirmation or grouped together as a single PDF-A attachment because either of these two formats makes it difficult for the Justice to locate particular exhibits as needed. Counsel must also include appropriate descriptive language in the "Additional Document Information" field in NYSCEF. NY R NY CTY E FIL Doc. 2(D)(6).
- *ONONDAGA COUNTY.* All exhibits in e-filed cases must be e-filed individually as separate attachments. NY R ONDGA E FIL Protocol(B)(9)(b).

xv. *Correcting documents*

- *ERIE COUNTY.* Submission of documents which, upon examination, require correction or addition will result in notification to the filer advising that the document has been returned for correction. The filer shall make the required corrections and/or additions as indicated in the e-mail transmission sent by the County Clerk or Part Clerk through the NYSCEF site. The corrected documents may be resubmitted using the "Re-file this document" link highlighted in the filer's document list for the respective case. Please note that in the case of multiple submissions, all related documents filed at the same time may be removed from the case record and returned until all documents are properly submitted. NY R ERIE E FIL Doc. 3(III)(J).

- *KINGS COUNTY.* Submission of documents which, upon examination, require correction or addition will result in notification to the filer advising that there is a problem with a document. The filer shall make the required corrections and/or additions and resubmit the corrected document using the "Refile this document" link. In the event a document is returned for correction, the original file date will be preserved. For corrections of documents filed with the Kings County Clerk which require a court order, refer to the procedure in NY R UNIF TRIAL CTS § 202.5-b(d)(3)(iii) and NY R L KINGS E FIL Doc. 1(B)(11). NY R L KINGS E FIL Doc. 1(B)(3).
- *ONONDAGA COUNTY.* If there is an error or an additional document is required, the system will notify the filing party, who will make the corrections/additions and resubmit them online. NY R ONDGA E FIL Protocol(B)(6).
- *QUEENS COUNTY.* Generally speaking, documents that have been E-filed will not thereafter be deleted by the County Clerk from NYCEF because the filer asserts that the filing contains an error or a significant omission. When the filer wishes to correct a perceived error or omission in a filed document, he or she should file an amended version of the document, with the original remaining on file, or else obtain a court order providing for deletion of the original. The County Clerk will only delete a document upon request of the filer or on the County Clerk's own initiative when it is obvious from the face of the document alone that the filer made a fundamental error and never intended to file the document that was filed (e.g., a completely unrelated non-litigation document, a different case, or a wrong county). The County Clerk will advise the filer when any such fundamental errors are detected. NY R L QUEENS E-FILE Doc. 1(E)(6).

b. *Facsimile filing.* In the Supreme Court, facsimile filing shall be limited to commercial claims and tax certiorari, conservatorship, and mental hygiene proceedings in Monroe, Westchester, New York and Suffolk Counties. NY R UNIF TRIAL CTS § 202.5-a(a)(1). Refer to NY R UNIF TRIAL CTS § 202.5-a for information on the procedures for facsimile filing.

   i. *NEW YORK COUNTY.* Unless indicated otherwise by the court in a particular case or in NY R NY CTY J RUL Doc. 1, Justices do not accept papers by fax. NY R NY CTY J RUL Rule 4.

2. *Service requirements*

a. *Who may serve.* Except where otherwise prescribed by law or order of court, papers may be served by any person not a party of the age of eighteen years or over. NY CPLR Rule 2103(a).

b. *Service upon attorney.* Except where otherwise prescribed by law or order of court, papers to be served upon a party in a pending action shall be served upon the party's attorney. Where the same attorney appears for two or more parties, only one (1) copy need be served upon the attorney. Such service upon an attorney shall be made:

   i. By delivering the paper to the attorney personally. NY CPLR Rule 2103(b)(1).

   ii. By mailing the paper to the attorney at the address designated by that attorney for that purpose or, if none is designated, at the attorney's last known address; service by mail shall be complete upon mailing. NY CPLR Rule 2103(b)(2).

   iii. If the attorney's office is open, by leaving the paper with a person in charge, or if no person is in charge, by leaving it in a conspicuous place; or if the attorney's office is not open, by depositing the paper, enclosed in a sealed wrapper directed to the attorney, in the attorney's office letter drop or box. NY CPLR Rule 2103(b)(3).

   iv. By leaving it at the attorney's residence within the state with a person of suitable age and discretion. Service upon an attorney shall not be made at the attorney's residence unless service at the attorney's office cannot be made. NY CPLR Rule 2103(b)(4).

   v. By transmitting the paper to the attorney by facsimile transmission, provided that a facsimile telephone number is designated by the attorney for that purpose. Service by facsimile transmission shall be complete upon the receipt by the sender of a signal from the equipment of the attorney served indicating that the transmission was received, and the mailing of a copy of the paper to that attorney. The designation of a facsimile telephone number in the address block subscribed on a paper served or filed in the course of an action or proceeding shall constitute consent to service by facsimile transmission in accordance with NY CPLR Rule 2103(b)(5). An attorney may change or rescind a facsimile telephone number by serving a notice on the other parties. NY CPLR Rule 2103(b)(5).

vi. By dispatching the paper to the attorney by overnight delivery service at the address designated by the attorney for that purpose or, if none is designated, at the attorney's last known address. Service by overnight delivery service shall be complete upon deposit of the paper enclosed in a properly addressed wrapper into the custody of the overnight delivery service for overnight delivery, prior to the latest time designated by the overnight delivery service for overnight delivery. "Overnight delivery service" means any delivery service which regularly accepts items for overnight delivery to any address in the state. NY CPLR Rule 2103(b)(6).

vii. By transmitting the paper to the attorney by electronic means where and in the manner authorized by the chief administrator of the courts by rule and, unless such rule shall otherwise provide, such transmission shall be upon the party's written consent. The subject matter heading for each paper sent by electronic means must indicate that the matter being transmitted electronically is related to a court proceeding. NY CPLR Rule 2103(b)(7).

- *KINGS COUNTY.* Pursuant to the E-Filing Rules, service of interlocutory documents is made by posting a document to the NYSCEF site, which automatically and immediately transmits an email notice of the filing, including a link to the document, to all participating counsel and unrepresented litigants on the case. The Rules also authorize service by other methods permitted by the CPLR. If service by such other method is made, proof of service must be filed with NYSCEF. NY R L KINGS E FIL Doc. 1(I).
- *NEW YORK COUNTY.* Service. . .will be made automatically through NYSCEF upon all participating counsel and unrepresented parties in the case. There are limited exceptions to the requirement for e-filing in the covered kinds of cases. NY R NY CTY Procedure XI(A). Pursuant to the E-Filing Rules, service of interlocutory documents is made by posting a document to the NYSCEF site, which automatically and immediately transmits an e-mail notice of the filing, including a link to the document, to all participating counsel and unrepresented litigants on the case. The Rules also authorize service by other methods permitted by the CPLR. If service by such a method is made, proof of service must be filed with NYSCEF. NY R NY CTY E FIL Doc. 2(I).
- *QUEENS COUNTY.* Filing with the system permits counsel to serve the papers electronically pursuant to NY R UNIF TRIAL CTS § 202.5-b(f) once consent to E-Filing has been filed on-line. Consult NY R UNIF TRIAL CTS § 202.5-bb(c) for service in mandatory e-filing. Any required proof of service should be E-filed as a separate document. NY R L QUEENS E-FILE Doc. 1(E)(4).

c. *Electronic service mandatory; Consenting to electronic service; How electronic service may be made.* Except as otherwise provided in NY R UNIF TRIAL CTS § 202.5-bb, filing and service of all documents in an action that has been commenced electronically in accordance with NY R UNIF TRIAL CTS § 202.5-bb shall be by electronic means. NY R UNIF TRIAL CTS § 202.5-bb(c)(1).

i. *Party's consent required for certain e-filing.* After commencement of an action wherein e-filing is authorized, documents may be electronically filed and served, but only by, and electronic service shall be made only upon, a party or parties who have consented thereto. NY R UNIF TRIAL CTS § 202.5-b(b)(2)(i).

- A consent to e-filing in an action shall state that the party providing it agrees to the use of e-filing in the action and to be bound by the filing and service provisions in NY R UNIF TRIAL CTS § 202.5-b. NY R UNIF TRIAL CTS § 202.5-b(b)(2)(ii).

ii. *Address for service; Duty to notify as to changes.* The e-mail service address recorded at the time of registration is the e-mail address at which service of interlocutory documents on that party may be made through notification transmitted by the NYSCEF site. It is the responsibility of each filing user to monitor that address and promptly notify the Resource Center in the event of a change in his or her e-mail service address. NY R UNIF TRIAL CTS § 202.5-b(f)(2)(i).

iii. *How service made.* An e-filing party causes service of an interlocutory document to be made upon another party participating in e-filing by filing the document electronically. Upon receipt of an interlocutory document, the NYSCEF site shall automatically transmit electronic notification to all e-mail service addresses in such action. NY R UNIF TRIAL CTS § 202.5-b(f)(2)(ii).

- Except as provided otherwise in NY R UNIF TRIAL CTS § 202.5-b(h)(3), the electronic transmission of the notification shall constitute service of the document on the e-mail service addresses identified therein; however, such service will not be effective if the filing party learns that the notification did not reach the address of the person to be served. Proof of such service will be recorded on the NYSCEF site. A party may, however, utilize other service methods permitted by the CPLR provided that, if one of such other methods is used, proof of that service shall be filed electronically. NY R UNIF TRIAL CTS § 202.5-b(f)(2)(ii).

iv. *Signatures on hard copies; Proof of service filed electronically.* When an e-filing party serves a document in hard copy on a non-participating party, the document served shall bear full signatures of all signatories and proof of such service shall be filed electronically. NY R UNIF TRIAL CTS § 202.5-b(b)(2)(i).

- *ERIE COUNTY.* In the NYSCEF system, each Affidavit of Service must be uploaded as a separate .pdf file. After uploading the Affidavit, please choose the document type: "Affirmation/Affidavit of Service" and enter the name of the party served as Additional Document Information. NY R ERIE E FIL Doc. 3(III)(I).

v. *Effect of failure to consent.* A party's failure to consent to participation in electronic filing and service shall not bar any other party to the action from filing documents electronically with the County Clerk and the court or serving documents upon any other party who has consented to participation. A party who has not consented to participation shall file documents with the court and the County Clerk, and serve and be served with documents, in hard copy. NY R UNIF TRIAL CTS § 202.5-b(b)(2)(i).

d. *Service upon party.* If a party has not appeared by an attorney or the party's attorney cannot be served, service shall be upon the party by a method specified in NY CPLR Rule 2103(b)(1), NY CPLR Rule 2103(b)(2), NY CPLR Rule 2103(b)(4), NY CPLR Rule 2103(b)(5) or NY CPLR Rule 2103(b)(6). NY CPLR Rule 2103(c).

e. *Service on all parties.* Each paper served on any party shall be served on every other party who has appeared, except as otherwise may be provided by court order or as provided in NY CPLR § 3012 or in NY CPLR § 3215(f). Upon demand by a party, the plaintiff shall supply that party with a list of those who have appeared and the names and addresses of their attorneys. NY CPLR Rule 2103(e).

f. *Service by filing.* If a paper cannot be served by any of the methods specified in NY CPLR Rule 2103(b) and NY CPLR Rule 2103(c), service may be made by filing the paper as if it were a paper required to be filed. NY CPLR Rule 2103(d).

g. *Definitions.* For the purposes of NY CPLR Rule 2103:

i. "Mailing" means the deposit of a paper enclosed in a first class postpaid wrapper, addressed to the address designated by a person for that purpose or, if none is designated, at that person's last known address, in a post office or official depository under the exclusive care and custody of the United States Postal Service within the state;

ii. "Electronic means" means any method of transmission of information between computers or other machines designed for the purpose of sending and receiving such transmissions, and which allows the recipient to reproduce the information transmitted in a tangible medium of expression;

iii. "Facsimile transmission" means any method of transmission of documents to a facsimile machine at a remote location which can automatically produce a tangible copy of such documents. NY CPLR Rule 2103(f).

G. Hearings

1. There is no hearing required or contemplated in the New York rules governing the jury demand.

H. Forms

1. Official New York Jury Demand Forms

a. Note of issue. NY R UNIF TRIAL CTS § 202.21(b).

b. Certificate of readiness for trial. NY R UNIF TRIAL CTS § 202.21(b).

2. New York Jury Demand Forms

a. Form of note of issue and statement of readiness. SIEGEL-NYPRAC § 371.

b. Complaint and jury demand. NYPRAC-COMM § 7:38.

I. Applicable Rules

1. *State rules*

a. Short title; Application; Construction; Definitions. NY CPLR § 101; NY CPLR § 104; NY CPLR § 105.

b. Appendix of official forms. NY CPLR § 107.

c. Extensions of time generally. NY CPLR § 2004.

d. Form of papers. NY CPLR Rule 2101; NY CPLR Rule 2102; NY CPLR § 2105; NY GEN BUS § 399-ddd; NY R UNIF TRIAL CTS § 215.2; NY R UNIF TRIAL CTS § 215.3.

e. Service of papers. NY CPLR Rule 2103.

f. Computation of time. NY CPLR § 2402; NY GEN CONSTR § 19; NY GEN CONSTR § 20; NY GEN CONSTR § 25-a; NY GEN CONSTR § 30; NY GEN CONSTR § 31; NY GEN CONSTR § 53.

g. Demand and waiver of trial by jury. NY CPLR § 4101; NY CPLR § 4102; NY CPLR § 4103; NY DEBT & CRED § 69; NY R UNIF TRIAL CTS § 202.21; NY R UNIF TRIAL CTS § 202.65.

h. Fees; Index number fees of county clerks. NY CPLR § 8018.

i. Trial by jury; How waived. NY CONST Art. 1, § 2.

j. Hours of court. NY R CHIEF J § 3.1.

k. Application of part; Waiver; Additional rules; Application of CPLR; Definitions. NY R UNIF TRIAL CTS § 202.1.

l. Papers filed in court; Electronic filing in supreme court. NY R UNIF TRIAL CTS § 202.5; NY R UNIF TRIAL CTS § 202.5-a; NY R UNIF TRIAL CTS § 202.5-b; NY R UNIF TRIAL CTS § 202.5-bb.

m. Rules of the commercial division of the Supreme Court. NY R UNIF TRIAL CTS § 202.70.

n. Signing of papers. NY R CHIEF ADMIN § 130-1.1-a.

2. *Local rules*

a. *Albany County*

i. Third judicial district rules. NY R 3 JD SUP Doc. 1.

b. *Bronx County*

i. Commercial division. NY R BRONX FIL R Doc. 12.

c. *Erie County*

i. Joint protocols for New York State Courts E-Filing (NYSCEF) cases filed in Supreme Court, Erie County. NY R ERIE E FIL Doc. 3.

d. *Kings County*

i. Papers. NY R L KINGS Pt. A, Papers.

ii. Protocol on courthouse and county clerk procedures for electronically filed cases. NY R L KINGS E FIL Doc. 1.

e. *New York County*

i. Commencement of cases. NY R NY CTY Procedure I.

ii. RJIs and assignments. NY R NY CTY Procedure IA.

iii. Trials. NY R NY CTY Procedure VIII.

iv. County clerk litigation functions. NY R NY CTY Procedure XI.

v. Protocol on courthouse and county clerk procedures for electronically filed cases. NY R NY CTY E FIL Doc. 2.

vi. Redaction of information in documents filed with the county clerk and the court. NY R NY CTY J RUL Rule A-1.

vii. Papers by fax. NY R NY CTY J RUL Rule 4.

f. *Onondaga County*

i. Onondaga county protocol for case filings New York State Electronic Files (NYSCEF). NY R ONDGA E FIL Protocol.

g. *Queens County*

i. Queens county protocol on courthouse procedures for electronically filed cases. NY R L QUEENS E-FILE Doc. 1.

J. Miscellaneous

NOTE: Individual judges' rules may apply.

ALBANY COUNTY

JUSTICE LISA M. FISHER: NY R 3 JD FISHER Fisher; NY R 3 JD FISHER Fisher, PC Order.

JUSTICE RICHARD MOTT: NY R 3 JD MOTT Mott.

JUSTICE STEPHAN G. SCHICK: NY R 3 JD Schick.

FORECLOSURE SETTLEMENT PART: NY R 3 JD Foreclosure Settlement.

BRONX COUNTY

JUSTICE PAUL L. ALPERT: [NY R BRONX J Part IA-29, as amended by NY ORDER 20-0337].

JUSTICE BEN BARBATO: NY R BRONX J Part IA-21.

JUSTICE MARY ANNE BRIGANTTI: [NY R BRONX J Part IA-15, as amended by NY ORDER 20-0338].

JUSTICE JOSEPH E. CAPELLA: NY R BRONX J Part IA-23.

JUSTICE MITCHELL DANZIGER: NY R BRONX J Part IA-3/33 ; [NY R BRONX J Danziger, Part IA-3/33, as amended by NY ORDER 20-0339].

JUSTICE LAURA G. DOUGLAS: NY R BRONX J Part IA-11.

JUSTICE RUBEN FRANCO: NY R BRONX J Part IA-26.

JUSTICE DORIS M. GONZALEZ: NY R BRONX J Part IA-24.

JUSTICE WILMA GUZMAN: NY R BRONX J Part IA-7; [NY R BRONX J Guzman, Part IA-7 Virtual, as amended by NY ORDER 20-0340].

JUSTICE ROBERT T. JOHNSON: NY R BRONX J Part IA-12.

JUSTICE DONALD A. MILES: NY R BRONX J Part IA-8.

JUSTICE DONNA M. MILLS: NY R BRONX J Part IA-9.

JUSTICE JULIA I. RODRIGUEZ: NY R BRONX J Part IA-18; [NY R BRONX J Part IA-27, as amended by NY ORDER 20-0341].

JUSTICE LLINET M. ROSADO: [NY R BRONX J Part IA-25, as amended by NY ORDER 20-0342].

JUSTICE NORMA RUIZ: NY R BRONX J Part IA-22; [NY R BRONX J Ruiz, Part IA-22 Virtual, as amended by NY ORDER 20-0343].

JUSTICE HOWARD H. SHERMAN: NY R BRONX J Part IA-4.

JUSTICE FERNANDO TAPIA: NY R BRONX J Part IA-13.

JUSTICE ELIZABETH A. TAYLOR: NY R BRONX J Part IA-2.

JUSTICE ALISON Y. TRUITT: NY R BRONX J Part IA-5.

PART IDV: NY R BRONX J Doc. 1.

PRE-TRIAL PART RULES: NY R BRONX J Doc. 2.

PRE TRIAL WORKSHEET: NY R BRONX J Doc. 3.

FORECLOSURE SETTLEMENT PART RULES: NY R BRONX J Doc. 4.

GUARDIANSHIP PART RULES: NY R BRONX J Doc. 5.

LPM PART RULES: NY R BRONX J Doc. 6.

ERIE COUNTY

JUSTICE M. WILLIAM BOLLER: NY R 8 JD J Boller.

JUSTICE RALPH A. BONIELLO: NY R 8 JD J Boniello.

JUSTICE CHRISTOPHER J. BURN: NY R 8 JD J Burns.

JUSTICE RUSSELL P. BUSCAGLIA: NY R 8 JD J Buscaglia.

JUSTICE FRANK CARUSO: NY R 8 JD J Caruso.

JUSTICE STEPHEN W. CASS: NY R 8 JD J Cass.

JUSTICE DEBORAH A. CHIMES: NY R 8 JD J Chimes.

JUSTICE EMILIO COLAIACOVO: [NY R 8 JD J Colaiacovo, as amended by NY ORDER 20-0252].

JUSTICE DIANE Y. DEVLIN: NY R 8 JD J Devlin.

JUSTICE JAMES H. DILLON: NY R 8 JD J Dillon.

JUSTICE PAULA L. FEROLETO: NY R 8 JD J Feroleto.

JUSTICE DANIEL J. FURLONG: [NY R 8 JD J Furlong, as amended by NY ORDER 20-0253].

JUSTICE JOSEPH R. GLOWNIA: NY R 8 JD J Glownia.

JUSTICE MARK J. GRISANTI: NY R 8 JD J Grisanti.

JUSTICE DEBORAH A. HAENDIGES: NY R 8 JD J Haendiges.

JUSTICE LYNN W. KEANE: [NY R 8 JD J Keane, as amended by NY ORDER 20-0254].

JUSTICE RICHARD C. KLOCH, Sr.: NY R 8 JD J Kloch.

JUSTICE FREDERICK J. MARSHALL: [NY R 8 JD J Marshall, as amended by NY ORDER 20-0255.

JUSTICE JOHN L. MICHALSKI: NY R 8 JD J Michalski.

JUSTICE MARK A. MONTOUR: [NY R 8 JD J Montour, as amended by NY ORDER 20-0256].

JUSTICE HENRY NOWAK: NY R 8 JD J Nowak.

JUSTICE JOHN F. O'DONNELL: NY R 8 JD J O'Donnell.

JUSTICE JEANETTE OGDEN: NY R 8 JD J Ogden.

JUSTICE CATHERINE NUGENT-PANEPINTO: NY R 8 JD J Nugent-Panepinto.

JUSTICE FRANK A. SEDITA, III: [NY R 8 JD J Sedita, as amended by NY ORDER 20-0257].

JUSTICE SARA SHELDON: NY R 8 JD J Sheldon.

JUSTICE DONNA M. SIWEK: NY R 8 JD J Siwek.

JUSTICE MARY L. SLISZ: NY R 8 JD J Slisz.

JUSTICE TIMOTHY J. WALKER: [NY R 8 JD J Walker, as amended by NY ORDER 20-0258].

JUSTICE DENNIS E. WARD: NY R 8 JD J Ward.

JUSTICE PAUL B. WOJTASZEK: [NY R 8 JD J Wojtaszek, as amended by NY ORDER 20-0259].

JUSTICE CHARLES N. ZAMBITO: [NY R 8 JD J Zambito, as amended by NY ORDER 20-0260].

SUPREME COURT LEGAL STAFF: NY R 8 JD J Legal Staff.

KINGS COUNTY

JUSTICE RACHEL A. ADAMS: NY R KINGS J Part 5F.

JUSTICE LOREN BAILY-SCHIFFMAN: NY R KINGS J Part 65.

JUSTICE REGINALD A. BODDIE: NY R KINGS J Part 95.

JUSTICE THERESA M. CICCOTTO: NY R KINGS J Part 19; NY R KINGS J Part 5J.

JUSTICE LISSETTE COLON: NY R KINGS J Part Rules.

JUSTICE GENINE EDWARDS: NY R KINGS J Part 80.

JUSTICE PAMELA L. FISHER: [NY R KINGS J Part 94, as amended by NY ORDER 20-0208].

JUSTICE ROBIN GARSON: NY R KINGS J Part 75.

JUSTICE LARA J. GENOVISI: [NY R KINGS J Part 34, as amended by NY ORDER 20-0209].

JUSTICE BERNARD J. GRAHAM: NY R KINGS J Part 36.

JUSTICE DAWN JIMENEZ-SALTA: NY R KINGS J Part 88.

JUSTICE INGRID JOSEPH: [NY R KINGS J Part FRP3 and Part 83, as amended by NY ORDER 20-0210].

JUSTICE KATHY J. KING: NY R KINGS J Part 64, 76K.

JUSTICE LAWRENCE KNIPEL: NY R KINGS J Part 57.

JUSTICE DONALD KURTZ: NY R KINGS J Part 26.

JUSTICE CARL LANDICINO: [NY R KINGS J Part 81, as amended by NY ORDER 20-0211].

JUSTICE KATHERINE LEVINE: [NY R KINGS J Part 20, 25, 92, as amended by NY ORDER 20-0211].

JUSTICE LORNA MCALLISTER: [NY R KINGS J Part 10, as amended by NY ORDER 20-0211].

JUSTICE ROSEMARIE MONTALBANO: [NY R KINGS J Part 19, 71, and 22, as amended by NY ORDER 20-0211].
JUSTICE RICHARD J. MONTELIONE: [NY R KINGS J Part 99 and DJMP, as amended by NY ORDER 20-0215].
JUSTICE LISA S. OTTLEY: NY R KINGS J Part 24.
JUSTICE MARK I. PARTNOW: NY R KINGS J Part 43.
JUSTICE ERIC I. PRUS: NY R KINGS J Part 5A.
JUSTICE FRANCOIS RIVERA: NY R KINGS J Part 52.
JUSTICE KAREN B. ROTHENBERG: NY R KINGS J Part 35.
JUSTICE LEON RUCHELSMAN: NY R KINGS J Part 1.
JUSTICE WAYNE P. SAITTA: NY R KINGS J Part 29.
JUSTICE ROBIN K. SHEARES: NY R KINGS J Part 96.
JUSTICE KENNETH P. SHERMAN: NY R KINGS J Part 67 and 78.
JUSTICE DEBRA SILBER: NY R KINGS J Part 9 and 5K.
JUSTICE ELLEN M. SPODEK: NY R KINGS J Part 63.
JUSTICE MARSHA L. STEINHARDT: NY R KINGS J Part 15.
JUSTICE JEFFREY S. SUNSHINE: NY R KINGS J Part 5G.
JUSTICE PETER P. SWEENEY: [NY R KINGS J Part 35, as amended by NY ORDER 20-0218].
JUSTICE DELORES J. THOMAS: [NY R KINGS J Part 5T, as amended by NY ORDER 20-0221].
JUSTICE WAVNY TOUSSAINT: NY R KINGS J Part 70.
JUSTICE RICHARD VELASQUEZ: NY R KINGS J Part 66.
JUSTICE CAROLYN E. WADE: NY R KINGS J Part 84.
JUSTICE EDWARD G. WALKER: [NY R KINGS J Part 90, as amended by NY ORDER 20-0219].
JUSTICE LILLIAN WAN: [NY R KINGS J Part 17, as amended by NY ORDER 20-0220].
JUSTICE MICHELLE WESTON: NY R KINGS J Part 3.
MENTAL HYGIENE PART: NY R KINGS J Part 77.
MATRIMONIAL PARTS DURING COVID-19 EMERGENCY: JUSTICE KAREN B. ROTHENBERG: NY R KINGS J Doc. 1.

NASSAU COUNTY

JUSTICE ANNA R. ANZALONE: NY R NASSAU S J Anzalone, Part 26.
JUSTICE STACY D. BENNETT: NY R NASSAU S J Bennett; NY R NASSAU S J Bennett, Form 1.
JUSTICE ANTONIO BRANDVEEN: NY R NASSAU S J Brandveen, Part 31.
JUSTICE JEFFREY S. BROWN: [NY R NASSAU S J Brown, as amended by NY ORDER 20-0297].
JUSTICE STEPHEN A. BUCARIA: NY R NASSAU S J Bucaria.
JUSTICE JULIANNE T. CAPETOLA: NY R NASSAU S J Capetola, Part 28.
JUSTICE EDMUND M. DANE: NY R NASSAU S J Dane, Part 33.
JUSTICE VITO M. DESTEFANO: NY R NASSAU S J DeStefano, Part 13; NY R NASSAU S J DeStefano, Form 1.
JUSTICE ARTHUR M. DIAMOND: NY R NASSAU S J Diamond, Part 7.
JUSTICE THOMAS FEINMAN: NY R NASSAU S J Feinman, Part 5.
JUSTICE JOHN M. GALASSO: NY R NASSAU S J Galasso, Part 22.
JUSTICE SHARON M.J. GIANELLI: NY R NASSAU S J Gianelli, Part 22; NY R NASSAU S J Gianelli, Form 1.
JUSTICE JEFFREY A. GOODSTEIN: NY R NASSAU S J Goodstein, Part 33; NY R NASSAU S J Goodstein, Form 1.
JUSTICE DAVID J. GUGERTY: [NY R NASSAU S J Gugerty, Part 31, as amended by NY ORDER 20-0298].
JUSTICE HELENE F. GUGERTY: NY R NASSAU S J Gugerty, Part 47.
JUSTICE STEVEN M. JAEGER: NY R NASSAU S J Jaeger, Part 35; NY R NASSAU S J Jaeger, Form 1.

JUSTICE JACK L. LIBERT: NY R NASSAU S J Libert, Part 23.

JUSTICE JOSEPH H. LORINTZ: NY R NASSAU S J Lorintz, Part 26; NY R NASSAU S J Lorintz, Form 1.

JUSTICE ROY S. MAHON: NY R NASSAU S J Mahon, Part 3.

JUSTICE RANDY SUE MARBER: NY R NASSAU S J Marber, Part 8.

JUSTICE JAMES P. MCCORMACK: [NY R NASSAU S J McCormack, Part 18, as amended by NY ORDER, 20-0299].

JUSTICE DICCIA T. PINEDA-KIRWAN: [NY R NASSAU S J Pineda-Kirwan, as amended by NY ORDER 20-0300].

JUSTICE THOMAS RADEMAKER: [NY R NASSAU S J Rademaker, Part 28, as amended by NY ORDER 20-0301]; [NY R NASSAU S J Rademaker, Form 1, as amended by NY ORDER 20-0301].

JUSTICE DENISE L. SHER: NY R NASSAU S J Rademaker, Part 32.

JUSTICE LEONARD D. STEINMAN: [NY R NASSAU S J Steinman, Part 15, as amended by NY ORDER 20-0303]; NY R NASSAU S J Steinman, Form 1.

JUSTICE HOWARD E. STURIM: NY R NASSAU S J Sturim, Part 50; NY R NASSAU S J Sturim, Form 1.

JUSTICE HELEN VOUTSINAS: [NY R NASSAU S J Voutsinas, Part 25, as amended by NY ORDER 20-0304]; [NY R NASSAU S J Voutsinas, Form 1, as amended by NY ORDER 20-0305].

JUSTICE HOPE SCHWARTZ ZIMMERMAN: NY R NASSAU S J Zimmerman, Part 17.

NEW YORK COUNTY

JUDGE'S RULES; BASIC INFORMATION: [NY R NY CTY J RUL Doc. 1, as amended by NY ORDER 20-0202].

ONONDAGA COUNTY

JUSTICE ROBERT E. ANTONACCI II: [NY R ONDGA E FIL Doc. 1, as amended by 20-0239].

JUSTICE MICHAEL V. COCCOMI: NY R ONDGA E FIL Doc. 2.

JUSTICE GREGORY R. GILBERT: NY R 5 JD JUDGES Gilbert; NY R ONDGA E FIL Doc. 3.

JUSTICE DONALD A. GREENWOOD: NY R ONDGA E FIL Doc. 4.

JUSTICE DEBORAH H. KARALUNAS: NY R ONDGA E FIL Doc. 5.

JUSTICE JAMES MCCLUSKY: NY R 5 JD MCCLUSKY McClusky.

JUSTICE CHARLES C. MERRELL: NY R 5 JD MERRELL Merrell.

JUSTICE PATRICK F. MACRAE: NY R 5 JD MACRAE Doc. 1.

JUSTICE JAMES P. MURPHY: NY R ONDGA E FIL Doc. 7.

JUSTICE GERALD J. NERI: [NY R 5 JD JUDGES Neri, as amended by NY ORDER 20-0236]; [NY R ONDGA E FIL Doc. 8, as amended by NY ORDER 20-0241].

JUSTICE ANTHONY J. PARIS: NY R 5 JD JUDGES Paris; [NY R ONDGA E FIL Doc. 9, as amended by NY ORDER 20-0242].

JUSTICE NORMAN W. SEITER, JR.: NY R 5 JD JUDGES Seiter.

JUSTICE KEVIN G. YOUNG: [NY R ONDGA E FIL Doc. 10, as amended by NY ORDER 20-0243].

QUEENS COUNTY

JUSTICE PAM JACKMAN BROWN: [NY R L QUEENS Brown, Part 19, as amended by NY ORDER 20-0321].

JUSTICE CHEREE A. BUGGS: NY R L QUEENS Buggs, Part 30.

JUSTICE PAM JACKMAN BROWN: [NY R L QUEENS Brown, Part 19, as amended by NY ORDER 20-0321].

JUSTICE DENIS J. BUTLER: NY R L QUEENS Butler, Part 12.

JUSTICE ROBERT I. CALORAS: [NY R L QUEENS Caloras, Part 36, as amended by NY ORDER 20-0322].

JUSTICE ANNA CULLEY: NY R L QUEENS Culley, Part 53.

JUSTICE TIMOTHY DUFFICY: NY R L QUEENS Dufficy, Part 35.

JUSTICE DAVID ELLIOT: NY R L QUEENS Elliot, Part 14.

JUSTICE JOSEPH J. ESPOSITO: NY R L QUEENS Esposito, Part 6.

JUSTICE DARRELL L. GAVRIN: [NY R L QUEENS Gavrin, Part 27, as amended by NY ORDER 20-0323].

JUSTICE WYATT N. GIBBONS: [NY R L QUEENS Gibbons, Part 5, as amended by NY ORDER 20-0330.

JUSTICE DONNA-MARIE E. GOLIA: [NY R L QUEENS Golia, Part 21, as amended by NY ORDER 20-0331].

JUSTICE MARGUERITE A. GRAYS: [NY R L QUEENS Grays, Part 4, as amended by NY ORDER 20-0324].

JUSTICE RUDOLPH E. GRECO: [NY R L QUEENS Greco, Part 32, as amended by NY ORDER 20-0325].

JUSTICE MAUREEN HEALY: NY R L QUEENS Healy, Part 6.

JUSTICE PHILLIP HOM: [NY R L QUEENS Hom, Part 43, as amended by NY ORDER 20-0332].

JUSTICE KEVIN J. KERRIGAN: NY R L QUEENS Kerrigan, Part 10.

JUSTICE MOJGAN C. LANCMAN: NY R L QUEENS Lancman, Part 20.

JUSTICE RICHARD G. LATIN: NY R L QUEENS Latin, Part 40.

JUSTICE ULYSSES B. LEVERETT: [NY R L QUEENS Leverett, Part 6, as amended by NY ORDER 20-0326].

JUSTICE LEONARD LIVOTE: NY R L QUEENS Livote, Part 33.

JUSTICE LEE A. MAYERSOHN: NY R L QUEENS Mayersohn, Part 22; NY R L QUEENS Mayersohn, Part 22G; [NY R L QUEENS Mayersohn, Part 22G COVID, as amended by NY ORDER 20-0327].

JUSTICE ROBERT J. MCDONALD: NY R L QUEENS McDonald, Part 34.

JUSTICE MARGARET MCGOWAN: NY R L QUEENS McGowan, Part 52.

JUSTICE MAURICE E. MUIR: [NY R L QUEENS Muir, Part 42, as amended by NY ORDER 20-0333].

JUSTICE JODI ORLOW: NY R L QUEENS Orlow, Part 51.

JUSTICE LESLIE J. PURIFICCION: NY R L QUEENS Purificcion, Part 39.

JUSTICE JOSEPH RISI: [NY R L QUEENS Risi, Part 3, as amended by NY ORDER 20-0328].

JUSTICE FREDERICK D.R. SAMPSON: [NY R L QUEENS Sampson, Part 31, as amended by NY ORDER 20-0329].

JUSTICE MARTIN J. SCHULMAN: NY R L QUEENS Schulman, Part 29.

JUSTICE BERNICE D. SIEGAL: NY R L QUEENS Siegal, Part 25G.

JUSTICE JANICE A. TAYLOR: NY R L QUEENS Taylor, Part 15.

JUSTICE CARMEN R. VELASQUEZ: NY R L QUEENS Velasquez, Part 38.

JUSTICE LOURDES M VENTURA: [NY R L QUEENS Ventura, Part 37, as amended by NY ORDER 20-0334].

JUSTICE WILLIAM A. VISCOVICH: NY R L QUEENS Viscovich, Part 63.

JUSTICE ALLAN B. WEISS: NY R L QUEENS Weiss, Part 2.

COMPLIANCE, SETTLEMENT AND CONFERENCE PART: NY R L QUEENS Doc 1.

PRELIMINARY CONFERENCE PART: [NY R L QUEENS Doc. 2, as amended by NY ORDER 20-0335].

MEDICAL MALPRACTICE CONFERENCE PART: [NY R L QUEENS Doc. 3, as amended by NY ORDER 20-0336].

TRIAL SCHEDULING PART: NY R L QUEENS Doc. 4.

SUMMARY JURY TRIAL PROGRAM: NY R L QUEENS Doc. 7.

RESIDENTIAL FORECLOSURE PART: NY R L QUEENS Doc. 9.

FORECLOSURE AUCTION RULES: NY R L QUEENS Doc. 10.

MATRIMONIAL PRELIMINARY CONFERENCE PART: NY R L QUEENS Doc. 11.

NON-CUSTODIAL CONTESTED MATRIMONIAL PART: NY R L QUEENS Doc. 12.

Pleadings
Answer

Document Last Updated August 2020

A. Checklist

(I) ❑ Matters to be considered by party filing the complaint

(a) ❑ Required documents

(1) ❑ Summons and complaint

(2) ❑ Index number

(3) ❑ Filing fees

(4) ❑ Proof of service

(b) ❑ Supplemental documents

(1) ❑ Supporting evidence; Exhibits

(2) ❑ Application to proceed as a poor person

(3) ❑ Working copies

(4) ❑ Statement of authorization in electronic filing cases

(5) ❑ Notice regarding availability of e-filing

(6) ❑ Notice to government of certain claims

(7) ❑ Documents required for specific types of claim

(c) ❑ Timing

(1) ❑ An action, including one brought in the name or for the benefit of the state, must be commenced within the time specified in NY CPLR § 201, et seq. unless a different time is prescribed by law or a shorter time is prescribed by written agreement

(2) ❑ Service of the summons and complaint shall be made within one hundred twenty (120) days after the commencement of the action or proceeding

(II) ❑ Matters to be considered by party filing the answer

(a) ❑ Required documents

(1) ❑ Answer

(2) ❑ Proof of service

(b) ❑ Supplemental documents

(1) ❑ Supporting evidence; Exhibits

(2) ❑ Demand for bill of particulars

(3) ❑ Filing fees

(4) ❑ Application to proceed as a poor person

(5) ❑ Working copies

(6) ❑ Statement of authorization in electronic filing cases

(7) ❑ Notice to government of certain claims

(8) ❑ Initiating documents served to newly added third parties

(9) ❑ ERIE COUNTY: Additional supplemental documents

(i) ❑ Notice of hard copy submission

(10) ❑ KINGS COUNTY: Additional supplemental documents

(i) ❑ Forms when filing in hard copy

(11) ❑ NEW YORK COUNTY: Additional supplemental documents

(i) ❑ Notice of hard copy submission

(12) ❑ ONONDAGA COUNTY: Additional supplemental documents

(i) ❑ Notice of hard copy submission

(13) ❑ QUEENS COUNTY: Additional supplemental documents

(i) ❑ Notice of hard copy submission

(c) ❑ Timing

(1) ❑ Service of an answer or reply shall be made within twenty (20) days after service of the pleading to which it responds

B. Timing

1. *Time for answer.* Service of an answer or reply shall be made within twenty (20) days after service of the pleading to which it responds. NY CPLR § 3012(a).

a. *Additional time when complaint served on state official.* If the complaint is served with the summons and the service is made on the defendant by delivering the summons and complaint to an official of the state authorized to receive service in his behalf or if service of the summons and complaint is made pursuant to NY CPLR § 303, NY CPLR § 308(2), NY CPLR § 308(3), NY CPLR § 308(4) or NY CPLR § 308(5), or NY CPLR § 313, NY CPLR § 314 or NY CPLR § 315, service of an answer shall be made within thirty (30) days after service is complete. NY CPLR § 3012(c).

b. *Additional time after motion to dismiss.* Service of a notice of motion under NY CPLR Rule 3211(a) or NY CPLR Rule 3211(b) before service of a pleading responsive to the cause of action or defense sought to be dismissed extends the time to serve the pleading until ten (10) days after service of notice of entry of the order. NY CPLR Rule 3211(f).

c. *Defenses and counterclaims; Statute of limitations.* The time within which an action must be commenced, except as otherwise expressly prescribed, shall be computed from the time the cause of action accrued to the time the claim is interposed. NY CPLR § 203(a).

i. *When defense or counterclaim interposed.* A defense or counterclaim is interposed when a pleading containing it is served. A defense or counterclaim is not barred if it was not barred at the time the claims asserted in the complaint were interposed, except that if the defense or counterclaim arose from the transactions, occurrences, or series of transactions or occurrences, upon which a claim asserted in the complaint depends, it is not barred to the extent of the demand in the complaint notwithstanding that it was barred at the time the claims asserted in the complaint were interposed. NY CPLR § 203(d).

ii. *Recoupment claims.* The defendant may interpose an otherwise time-barred counterclaim if it arose from the "transactions, occurrences, or series of transactions or occurrences, upon which a claim asserted in the complaint depends." NY CPLR § 203(Practice Commentary, C203:9); Delta Funding Corp. v. Murdaugh, 6 A.D.3d 571, 571, 774 N.Y.S.2d 797 (2004). The current doctrine is not limited, as it apparently was under earlier law, to contract actions in which both parties assert breach of the same agreement. A recoupment counterclaim is only viable "to the extent of the demand in the complaint," meaning that such counterclaim can only be used as an offset against plaintiff's damages, if any. No affirmative judgment may be entered for the defendant on a recoupment counterclaim. Recoupment "is really a defense, as it denies the validity of plaintiff's claim in the amount claimed, and does not entitle defendants to any affirmative relief or any amounts in excess of the amount demanded by plaintiff." NY CPLR § 203(Practice Commentary, C203:9); Enrico & Sons Contracting, Inc. v. Bridgemarket Assocs., 252 A.D.2d 429, 430, 675 N.Y.S.2d 351, 353 (1998).

2. *Time for initial appearance.* The defendant appears by serving an answer or a notice of appearance, or by making a motion which has the effect of extending the time to answer. An appearance shall be made within twenty (20) days after service of the summons, except that if the summons was served on the defendant by delivering it to an official of the state authorized to receive service in his behalf or if it was served pursuant to NY CPLR § 303, NY CPLR § 308(2), NY CPLR § 308(3), NY CPLR § 308(4) or NY CPLR § 308(5), or NY CPLR § 313, NY CPLR § 314 or NY CPLR § 315, the appearance shall be made within thirty (30) days after service is complete. NY CPLR Rule 320(a).

a. *Extension of time when complaint not served with summons.* If the complaint is not served with the summons, the time to appear may be extended as provided in NY CPLR § 3012(b). NY CPLR Rule 320(a).

b. *Written demand for complaint; Effect on time to appear.* If the complaint is not served with the summons, the defendant may serve a written demand for the complaint within the time provided in NY CPLR Rule 320(a) for an appearance. Service of the demand shall extend the time to appear until twenty (20) days after service of the complaint. A demand or motion under NY CPLR § 3012(b) does not of itself constitute an appearance in the action. NY CPLR § 3012(b).

3. *Time to acknowledge service of initiating papers*
   a. *Served by electronic means.* A party served by electronic means shall, within twenty-four (24) hours of service, provide the serving party or attorney with an electronic confirmation that the service has been effected. NY R UNIF TRIAL CTS § 202.5-b(f)(1); NY R UNIF TRIAL CTS § 202.5-bb(b)(3).
   b. *Served by mail.* The defendant, an authorized employee of the defendant, defendant's attorney or an employee of the attorney must complete the acknowledgement of receipt and mail or deliver one (1) copy of it within thirty (30) days from the date of receipt. Service is complete on the date the signed acknowledgement of receipt is mailed or delivered to the sender. The signed acknowledgement of receipt shall constitute proof of service. NY CPLR § 312-a(b)(1).
      i. *Acknowledgement to be sworn.* The acknowledgement of receipt of service shall be subscribed and affirmed as true under penalties of perjury and shall have the same force and effect as an affidavit. NY CPLR § 312-a(c).
      ii. *Time for answer after acknowledgement.* Where a complaint or petition is served with the summons or notice of petition, the defendant shall serve an answer within twenty (20) days after the date the signed acknowledgement of receipt is mailed or delivered to the sender. NY CPLR § 312-a(b)(2).
4. *Computation of time*
   a. *Units of time*
      i. *Day.* A calendar day includes the time from midnight to midnight. Sunday or any day of the week specifically mentioned means a calendar day. NY GEN CONSTR § 19.
      ii. *Month.* In a statute, contract or public or private instrument, unless otherwise provided in such contract or instrument or by law, the term month means a calendar month and not a lunar month. NY GEN CONSTR § 31.
      iii. *Year.* For information on the definition of a year, including the definitions of a half-year and quarter-year, refer to NY GEN CONSTR § 58 and NY GEN CONSTR § 50. For information on leap years, refer to NY GEN CONSTR § 57.
   b. *Periods of time*
      i. *Number of days.* A number of days specified as a period from a certain day within which or after or before which an act is authorized or required to be done means such number of calendar days exclusive of the calendar day from which the reckoning is made. NY GEN CONSTR § 20.
         - If such period is a period of two (2) days, Saturday, Sunday or a public holiday must be excluded from the reckoning if it is an intervening day between the day from which the reckoning is made and the last day of the period. NY GEN CONSTR § 20.
         - In computing any specified period of time from a specified event, the day upon which the event happens is deemed the day from which the reckoning is made. The day from which any specified period of time is reckoned shall be excluded in making the reckoning. NY GEN CONSTR § 20.
      ii. *Number of months.* A number of months after or before a certain day shall be computed by counting such number of calendar months from such day, exclusive of the calendar month in which such day occurs, and shall include the day of the month in the last month so counted having the same numerical order in days of the month as the day from which the computation is made, unless there be not so many days in the last month so counted, in which case the period computed shall expire with the last day of the month so counted. NY GEN CONSTR § 30.
      iii. *Publication of notice; Number of days.* The period of publication of a legal notice shall be computed by excluding the first day of publication and including the day on which the act or event of which notice is given is to take place or which completes the full period of publication. NY CPLR § 2402.
      iv. *Periods ending on Saturday, Sunday or public holiday.* When any period of time, computed from a certain day, within which or after which or before which an act is authorized or required to be done, ends on a Saturday, Sunday or a public holiday, such act may be done on the next succeeding business day and if the period ends at a specified hour, such act may be done at or before the same hour of such next succeeding business day, except that where a period of time specified by contract ends on a Saturday, Sunday or a public holiday, the extension of such period is governed by NY GEN CONSTR § 25. NY GEN CONSTR § 25-a(1).
         - For a list of public holidays, refer to NY GEN CONSTR § 24.

v. *Additional time after certain kinds of service*

- *Service by mail.* Where a period of time prescribed by law is measured from the service of a paper and service is by mail, five (5) days shall be added to the prescribed period. NY CPLR Rule 2103(b)(2).
- *Service by overnight delivery service.* Where a period of time prescribed by law is measured from the service of a paper and service is by overnight delivery, one (1) business day shall be added to the prescribed period. NY CPLR Rule 2103(b)(6).

vi. *Daylight saving time.* For information on New York's time zone and the effect of daylight saving time, refer to NY GEN CONSTR § 52.

c. *Hours of court.* Notwithstanding any provision of law or rule of court to the contrary, throughout the State of New York the sessions of the Supreme Court for the disposition of business before the court shall commence not later than 9:30 a.m. and conclude not earlier than 5 p.m. Where warranted, the Chief Administrator of the Courts may authorize variances in the opening and closing hours of the courts, but, in such event, daily sessions shall total not less than six (6) hours. NY R CHIEF J § 3.1.

d. *Time limits; Extension of time.* Any act required by or in pursuance of law to be performed at or within a prescribed time, shall be performed according to the standard time. NY GEN CONSTR § 53.

i. Except where otherwise expressly prescribed by law, the court may extend the time fixed by any statute, rule or order for doing any act, upon such terms as may be just and upon good cause shown, whether the application for extension is made before or after the expiration of the time fixed. NY CPLR § 2004. Refer to the New York KeyRules Motion for Continuance/Extension of Time document for more information.

C. General Requirements

1. *Pleading, generally.* Statements in a pleading shall be sufficiently particular to give the court and parties notice of the transactions, occurrences, or series of transactions or occurrences, intended to be proved and the material elements of each cause of action or defense. NY CPLR § 3013.

a. *Pleadings to be liberally construed.* Pleadings shall be liberally construed. Defects shall be ignored if a substantial right of a party is not prejudiced. NY CPLR § 3026.

b. *Pleadings must give notice.* The basic requirement of NY CPLR § 3013 is that the pleading be "sufficiently particular" to give "notice" to the other side of the "transactions" or "occurrences" as seen by the pleader. As long as the pleading may be said to give such "notice," in whatever terminology it chooses, this aspect of the NY CPLR § 3013 requirement is satisfied. NY CPLR § 3013(Practice Commentary, C3013:2). The test is entirely sui generis. The court's inquiry, if a pleading issue is raised, is to ask whether the total verbiage of the pleading at issue may be said to give "notice" to the other side of what the pleader's grievance is. If it is sufficient to put the adversary on "notice," it satisfies this first mandate. NY CPLR § 3013(Practice Commentary, C3013:2).

c. *Pleadings must contain material facts.* The cause of action or defense is the thing the pleading must give notice of. NY CPLR § 3013 elaborates that the "material elements" of the claim or defense must be covered in the pleading. Where does the practitioner find those elements? They come from the substantive law. The practitioner about to bring suit who turns to the pleadings article must do so with a substantive cause of action in hand. The practitioner must thus gather up the material elements of the claim or defense through analysis and research of the substantive law, if necessary, before even considering pleading. And when now turning to drafting, the practitioner need only see to it that the material elements that are substantive constituents of the claim are somewhere verbalized within the four corners of the complaint. See, e.g., Gershon v. Goldberg, 30 A.D.3d 372, 373, 817 N.Y.S.2d 322, 323 (2006). NY CPLR § 3013(Practice Commentary, C3013:2).

d. *Fulfilling pleading requirements.* The main mission of an affirmative pleading, whether it is the main claim in the complaint, or a counterclaim or cross-claim in the answer, etc., is to give "notice" of the event out of which the grievance arises. If the pleading can be said to give that notice, the first pleading requirement is satisfied. If the allegations also cover the substantive material elements that make up the particular cause of action relied on, the second requirement is met and the pleading satisfies the CPLR. SIEGEL-NYPRAC § 208.

2. *Pleading special matters*

a. *Conditions precedent.* The performance or occurrence of a condition precedent in a contract need not be pleaded. A denial of performance or occurrence shall be made specifically and with particularity. In case of such denial, the party relying upon the performance or occurrence shall be required to prove on the trial only such performance or occurrence as shall have been so specified. NY CPLR Rule 3015(a).

b. *Corporate status.* Where any party is a corporation, the complaint shall so state and, where known, it shall specify the state, country or government by or under whose laws the party was created. NY CPLR Rule 3015(b).

c. *Prior judgment, decision or determination.* A judgment, decision or other determination of a court, judicial or quasi-judicial tribunal, or of a board or officer, may be pleaded without stating matter showing jurisdiction to render it. NY CPLR Rule 3015(c).

d. *Signatures on negotiable instruments.* Unless specifically denied in the pleadings each signature on a negotiable instrument is admitted. NY CPLR Rule 3015(d).

e. *Fraud or mistake.* Where a cause of action or defense is based upon misrepresentation, fraud, mistake, wilful default, breach of trust or undue influence, the circumstances constituting the wrong shall be stated in detail. NY CPLR Rule 3016(b).

i. When relief against a mistake is sought in an action or by way of defense or counterclaim, relief shall not be denied merely because the mistake is one of law rather than one of fact. NY CPLR § 3005.

ii. The party relying on the mistake should. . .take the initiative of pleading it. The "mistake" listed in NY CPLR Rule 3016(b) does not distinguish between fact or law and should thus be taken as applying to both. NY CPLR § 3005(Practice Commentary, C3005:2).

f. *Law of a foreign country.* Where a cause of action or defense is based upon the law of a foreign country or its political subdivision, the substance of the foreign law relied upon shall be stated. NY CPLR Rule 3016(e).

3. *Answer.* There shall be a complaint and an answer. NY CPLR § 3011.

a. *Denials.* A party shall deny those statements known or believed by him to be untrue. He shall specify those statements as to the truth of which he lacks knowledge or information sufficient to form a belief and this shall have the effect of a denial. All other statements of a pleading are deemed admitted, except that where no responsive pleading is permitted they are deemed denied or avoided. NY CPLR § 3018(a).

i. Denials should of course be made in good faith. A denial of knowledge or information sufficient to form a belief of something the defendant must know one way or the other can lead to trouble for the defendant, although the consequences are not clear. If the denials lend an aura of sham to the whole of the defendant's posture in the litigation, they may be deemed to go to the crux of his case and lead to summary judgment. SIEGEL-NYPRAC § 221; Dahlstrom v. Gemunder, 198 N.Y. 449, 453, 92 N.E. 106, 108 (1910).

ii. If the subject of a given allegation of a complaint is only presumptively in the defendant's knowledge, the denial-of-knowledge form is permissible to meet the allegation. If some of the denials in that situation are good while some are bad and some borderline, there is not likely to be enough to support a summary judgment against the responsive pleader. And there is no motion available under the CPLR to strike denials. One risk the bad faith denier runs, however, is that the matter purportedly denied may be deemed admitted. SIEGEL-NYPRAC § 221; Kirschbaum v. Eschmann, 205 N.Y. 127, 132, 98 N.E. 328, 330 (1912); NY CPLR § 3018(Practice Commentaries, C3018:4).

iii. It is not a common result, nor something the other side can assume will happen unless and until the court so holds, but even a denial made upon information and belief may be deemed ineffective and the matter addressed deemed admitted if the court is convinced that the denier had to know the fact at first hand one way or the other. SIEGEL-NYPRAC § 221; City of Rochester v. Diksu Corp., 47 Misc. 2d 407, 408, 262 N.Y.S.2d 690, 692 (Sup. Ct. 1965).

iv. Certain other denial techniques are frowned on and can get the denier in trouble. One of these is the inconsistent-version denial. Here the responsive pleader does not deny a fact directly, but sets forth a different version in the expectation that the reader will imply or infer a denial. This technique should not be used; it has been held inadequate to deny the fact and may therefore result in its admission. SIEGEL-NYPRAC § 221; Smith v. Coe, 170 N.Y. 162, 167, 63 N.E. 57, 59 (1902).

v. Another unacceptable ploy, related to the inconsistent-version denial, is the so-called "negative pregnant"—a negation pregnant with an admission. "The defect known as negative pregnant usually arises where the answer denies immaterial allegations of the complaint, which relate to time and place merely." SIEGEL-NYPRAC § 221; Kellogg v. Freeland, 195 N.Y.S. 912, 913 (Sup. Ct. 1922).

vi. A "general denial", as it is popularly known, is usually a terse but total denial of everything contained in the complaint: "Defendant denies all the allegations of the complaint." If intended in good faith, it is acceptable, and if the complaint is terse it may be appropriate. But the more precise and detailed the complaint is, the less appropriate the general denial becomes. If used against a complaint containing extended allegations, it may create the same aura of frivolity or sham that the wrong kind of specific denial, as previously discussed, can amount to. SIEGEL-NYPRAC § 221.

b. *Affirmative defenses.* A party shall plead all matters which if not pleaded would be likely to take the adverse party by surprise or would raise issues of fact not appearing on the face of a prior pleading such as arbitration and award, collateral estoppel, culpable conduct claimed in diminution of damages as set forth in article fourteen-A of the CPLR (NY CPLR § 1411, et seq.), discharge in bankruptcy, facts showing illegality either by statute or common law, fraud, infancy or other disability of the party defending, payment, release, res judicata, statute of frauds, or statute of limitation. The application of NY CPLR § 3018(b) shall not be confined to the instances enumerated. NY CPLR § 3018(b).

i. *Other affirmative defenses not enumerated in NY CPLR § 3018(b).* Other matters have been held to be affirmative defenses, such as:

- Truth in a defamation action; Fregoe v. Fregoe, 33 A.D.3d 1182, 826 N.Y.S.2d 755 (2006);
- Adverse possession; Falco v. Pollitts, 298 A.D.2d 838, 747 N.Y.S.2d 874 (2002);
- Qualified privilege; Lerwick v. Kelsey, 24 A.D.3d 918, 806 N.Y.S.2d 732 (2005);
- Standing to sue; Fossella v. Dinkins, 66 N.Y.2d 162, 167, 485 N.E.2d 1017, 1019 (1985);
- Article 16 of the New York Civil Practice Law and Rules (NY CPLR § 1600, et seq.) (several-only liability). SIEGEL-NYPRAC § 223.

4. *Counterclaims and cross-claims.* An answer may include a counterclaim against a plaintiff and a cross-claim against a defendant. NY CPLR § 3011.

a. *Counterclaims.* A counterclaim may be any cause of action in favor of one or more defendants or a person whom a defendant represents against one or more plaintiffs, a person whom a plaintiff represents or a plaintiff and other persons alleged to be liable. NY CPLR § 3019(a).

i. *Counterclaims always permissive.* All counterclaims are permissive in New York: defendant can use his claim as a counterclaim or save it and sue on it separately. Defendant may save it for separate suit even when it is a related counterclaim, i.e., when it arises out of the same transaction or occurrence as plaintiff's claim. SIEGEL-NYPRAC § 224; Batavia Kill Watershed Dist. in Greene Cty. v. Charles O. Desch, Inc., 83 A.D.2d 97, 99, 444 N.Y.S.2d 958, 960 (1981), aff'd sub nom. Batavia Kill Watershed Dist. in Cty. of Greene v. Charles O. Desch, Inc., 57 N.Y.2d 796, 441 N.E.2d 1115 (1982).

ii. *Counterclaim against trustee or nominal plaintiff barred.* In an action brought by a trustee or in the name of a plaintiff who has no actual interest in the contract upon which it is founded, a claim against the plaintiff shall not be allowed as a counterclaim, but a claim existing against the person beneficially interested shall be allowed as a counterclaim to the extent of the plaintiff's claim, if it might have been so allowed in an action brought by the person beneficially interested. NY CPLR § 3019(c).

b. *Cross-claims.* A cross-claim may be any cause of action in favor of one or more defendants or a person whom a defendant represents against one or more defendants, a person whom a defendant represents or a defendant and other persons alleged to be liable. A cross-claim may include a claim that the party against whom it is asserted is or may be liable to the cross-claimant for all or part of a claim asserted in the action against the cross-claimant. NY CPLR § 3019(b).

i. A cross-claim is a claim by one defendant against another; in New York it can be for any claim at all, whether or not related to the plaintiff's claim. SIEGEL-NYPRAC § 227; NY CPLR § 3019(b).

ii. This is in contrast to federal practice, where a cross-claim is interposable only if related to some other claim in the case. SIEGEL-NYPRAC § 227.

c. *Cause of action in counterclaim or cross-claim deemed in complaint.* A cause of action contained in a counterclaim or a cross-claim shall be treated, as far as practicable, as if it were contained in a complaint, except that separate process, trial or judgment may not be had unless the court so orders. Where a person not a party is alleged to be liable a summons and answer containing the counterclaim or cross-claim shall be filed, whereupon he or she shall become a defendant. Service upon such a defendant shall be by serving a summons and answer containing the counterclaim or cross-claim. Such defendant shall serve a reply or answer as if he or she were originally a party. NY CPLR § 3019(d).

d. *Pleading in response to counterclaim or cross-claim.* There shall be a reply to a counterclaim denominated as such and an answer to a cross-claim that contains a demand for an answer. If no demand is made, the cross-claim shall be deemed denied or avoided. There shall be no other pleading unless the court orders otherwise. NY CPLR § 3011.

5. *Third-party complaints.* A defendant's pleading against another claimant is an interpleader complaint, or against any other person not already a party is a third-party complaint. NY CPLR § 3011.

   a. *When third-party practice allowed.* After the service of his answer, a defendant may proceed against a person not a party who is or may be liable to that defendant for all or part of the plaintiff's claim against that defendant, by filing pursuant to NY CPLR § 304 a third-party summons and complaint with the clerk of the court in the county in which the main action is pending, for which a separate index number shall not be issued but a separate index number fee shall be collected. The third-party summons and complaint and all prior pleadings served in the action shall be served upon such person within one hundred twenty (120) days of the filing. A defendant serving a third-party complaint shall be styled a third-party plaintiff and the person so served shall be styled a third-party defendant. The defendant shall also serve a copy of such third-party complaint upon the plaintiff's attorney simultaneously upon issuance for service of the third-party complaint on the third-party defendant. NY CPLR § 1007.

   b. *Answer of third-party defendant; Defenses.* The third-party defendant shall answer the claim asserted against him or her by serving copies of his or her answer upon the third-party plaintiff. The third-party defendant may assert against the plaintiff in his or her answer any defenses which the third-party plaintiff has to the plaintiff's claim except an objection or defense that the summons and complaint, summons with notice or notice of petition and petition was not properly served, or that jurisdiction was not obtained over the third-party plaintiff. The third-party defendant shall have the rights of a party adverse to the other parties in the action, including the right to counter-claim, cross-claim and appeal. NY CPLR § 1008.

   c. *Successive third-party proceedings.* A third-party defendant may proceed pursuant to NY CPLR § 1007 against any person who is or may be liable to him for all or part of the third-party claim. When a counterclaim is asserted against a plaintiff, he may proceed pursuant to NY CPLR § 1007 as if he were a defendant. NY CPLR Rule 1011.

      i. NY CPLR Rule 1011 authorizes successive third-party claims by any party who has a claim over against another person. Thus, a plaintiff may implead a third party who may be liable to her on a counterclaim, a third-party defendant may implead a fourth-party defendant, and a fourth-party defendant may implead a fifth-party defendant. NY CPLR Rule 1011(Practice Commentary).

   d. *Dismissal or separate trial of third-party complaint.* The court may dismiss a third-party complaint without prejudice, order a separate trial of the third-party claim or of any separate issue thereof, or make such other order as may be just. In exercising its discretion, the court shall consider whether the controversy between the third-party plaintiff and the third-party defendant will unduly delay the determination of the main action or prejudice the substantial rights of any party. NY CPLR Rule 1010.

   e. *Pleading in response to third-party complaint.* There shall be an answer to an interpleader complaint or third-party complaint. There shall be no other pleading unless the court orders otherwise. NY CPLR § 3011.

6. *Pleading affirmative relief.* Refer to the New York KeyRules Complaint document for information on the pleading requirements of a complaint, include counterclaim, cross-claim, and third-party complaints.

7. *Effect of defendant's appearance.* Subject to the provisions of NY CPLR Rule 320(c), an appearance of the defendant is equivalent to personal service of the summons upon him, unless an objection to jurisdiction under NY CPLR Rule 3211(a)(8) is asserted by motion or in the answer as provided in NY CPLR Rule 3211. NY CPLR Rule 320(b).

   a. *Appearance not conferring jurisdiction; Limited appearance.* When the court's jurisdiction is not based upon personal service on the defendant, an appearance is not equivalent to personal service upon the defendant:

      i. In a case specified in NY CPLR § 314(3), if jurisdiction is based solely upon a levy on defendant's property within the state pursuant to an order of attachment; or

      ii. In any other case specified in NY CPLR § 314, if an objection to jurisdiction under NY CPLR Rule 3211(a)(8) or NY CPLR Rule 3211(a)(9), or both, is asserted by motion or in the answer as provided in NY CPLR Rule 3211, unless the defendant proceeds with the defense after asserting the objection to jurisdiction and the objection is not ultimately sustained. NY CPLR Rule 320(c).

   b. *Effect on publication of summons.* Where the defendant appears during the period of publication of a summons against him, the service by publication shall be deemed completed by the appearance. NY CPLR Rule 320(d).

8. *Joinder*

   a. *Of claims.* The plaintiff in a complaint or the defendant in an answer setting forth a counterclaim or cross-claim may join as many claims as he may have against an adverse party. There may be like joinder of claims when there are multiple parties. NY CPLR § 601(a).

      i. *Limit on joinder of claims arising from consumer credit transactions.* Two or more plaintiffs may join no more than five claims in any one action or proceeding against the same defendant arising out of separate consumer credit transactions, provided that the plaintiffs are represented by the same attorney. NY CPLR § 601(b).

b. *Of parties; Necessary.* Persons who ought to be parties if complete relief is to be accorded between the persons who are parties to the action or who might be inequitably affected by a judgment in the action shall be made plaintiffs or defendants. When a person who should join as a plaintiff refuses to do so he may be made a defendant. NY CPLR § 1001(a).

i. When a person who should be joined under NY CPLR § 1001(a) has not been made a party and is subject to the jurisdiction of the court, the court shall order him summoned. If jurisdiction over him can be obtained only by his consent or appearance, the court, when justice requires, may allow the action to proceed without his being made a party. NY CPLR § 1001(b). In determining whether to allow the action to proceed, the court shall consider the factors listed in NY CPLR § 1001(b). NY CPLR § 1001(b).

c. *Of parties; Permissive*

i. *Plaintiffs.* Persons who assert any right to relief jointly, severally, or in the alternative arising out of the same transaction, occurrence, or series of transactions or occurrences, may join in one action as plaintiffs if any common question of law or fact would arise. NY CPLR § 1002(a).

ii. *Defendants.* Persons against whom there is asserted any right to relief jointly, severally, or in the alternative, arising out of the same transaction, occurrence, or series of transactions or occurrences, may be joined in one action as defendants if any common question of law or fact would arise. NY CPLR § 1002(b).

iii. *Separate relief; Separate trials.* It shall not be necessary that each plaintiff be interested in obtaining, or each defendant be interested in defending against, all the relief demanded or as to every claim included in an action; but the court may make such orders as will prevent a party from being embarrassed, delayed, or put to expense by the inclusion of a party against whom he asserts no claim and, who asserts no claim against him, and may order separate trials or make other orders to prevent prejudice. NY CPLR § 1002(c).

d. *When joinder unnecessary.* Except where otherwise prescribed by order of the court, an executor, administrator, guardian of the property of an infant, committee of the property of a judicially declared incompetent, conservator of the property of a conservatee, trustee of an express trust, insured person who has executed to his insurer either a loan or subrogation receipt, trust agreement, or other similar agreement, or person with whom or in whose name a contract has been made for the benefit of another, may sue or be sued without joining with him the person for or against whose interest the action is brought. NY CPLR § 1004.

e. *Class actions.* For information on the requirements for class actions, refer to NY CPLR § 901, et seq. [Editor's note: parts of NY CPLR § 901 were recognized as preempted in Holster v. Gatco, Inc., 618 F.3d 214 (2d Cir. 2010), which was recognized as abrogated by Giovanniello v. ALM Media, LLC, 726 F.3d 106 (2d Cir. 2013)].

f. *Interpleader.* For information on interpleader, refer to NY CPLR § 1006.

g. *Severance of claims and separate trials.* In furtherance of convenience or to avoid prejudice the court may order a severance of claims, or may order a separate trial of any claim, or of any separate issue. The court may order the trial of any claim or issue prior to the trial of the others. NY CPLR § 603.

9. *Verification of pleadings.* A verification is a statement under oath that the pleading is true to the knowledge of the deponent, except as to matters alleged on information and belief, and that as to those matters he believes it to be true. Unless otherwise specified by law, where a pleading is verified, each subsequent pleading shall also be verified, except the answer of an infant and except as to matter in the pleading concerning which the party would be privileged from testifying as a witness. Where the complaint is not verified, a counterclaim, cross-claim or third-party claim in the answer may be separately verified in the same manner and with the same effect as if it were a separate pleading. NY CPLR § 3020(a).

a. *When verification required.* In only a few instances is verification mandatory. SIEGEL-NYPRAC § 232. Among the CPLR instances of mandatory verification of a complaint are where it contains or has appended the schedule of goods and services available for optional use under NY CPLR Rule 3016(f), or where it seeks to charge an obligor with an amount still unsatisfied after prior suit by the obligee against a co-obligor. The pleadings in an Article 78 (NY CPLR § 7801, et seq.) proceeding also require verification. SIEGEL-NYPRAC § 232. An answer shall be verified:

i. When the complaint charges the defendant with having confessed or suffered a judgment, executed a conveyance, assignment or other instrument, or transferred or delivered money or personal property with intent to hinder, delay or defraud his creditors, or with being a party or privy to such a transaction by another person with like intent towards the creditors of that person, or with any fraud whatever affecting a right or the property of another; or

ii. In an action against a corporation to recover damages for the non-payment of a promissory note or other evidence of debt for the absolute payment of money upon demand or at a particular time. NY CPLR § 3020(b).

iii. Defense not involving the merits. A defense which does not involve the merits of the action shall be verified. NY CPLR § 3020(c).

b. *By whom verification made.* The verification of a pleading shall be made by the affidavit of the party, or, if two or more parties united in interest are pleading together, by at least one of them who is acquainted with the facts, except:

i. If the party is a domestic corporation, the verification shall be made by an officer thereof and shall be deemed a verification by the party;

ii. If the party is the state, a governmental subdivision, board, commission, or agency, or a public officer in behalf of any of them, the verification may be made by any person acquainted with the facts; and

iii. If the party is a foreign corporation, or is not in the county where the attorney has his office, or if there are two or more parties united in interest and pleading together and none of them acquainted with the facts is within that county, or if the action or defense is founded upon a written instrument for the payment of money only which is in the possession of an agent or the attorney, or if all the material allegations of the pleading are within the personal knowledge of an agent or the attorney, the verification may be made by such agent or attorney. NY CPLR § 3020(d).

c. *Form of affidavit of verification.* The affidavit of verification must be to the effect that the pleading is true to the knowledge of the deponent, except as to the matters therein stated to be alleged on information and belief, and that as to those matters he believes it to be true. If it is made by a person other than the party, he must set forth in the affidavit the grounds of his belief as to all matters not stated upon his knowledge and the reason why it is not made by the party. NY CPLR Rule 3021.

d. *Effect of verified pleading.* Unless they are stated to be made upon the information and belief of the party, they must be regarded for all purposes, including a criminal prosecution, as having been made upon the knowledge of the person verifying the pleading. An allegation that the party has not sufficient knowledge or information to form a belief with respect to a matter, must, for the same purposes, be regarded as an allegation that the person verifying the pleading has not such knowledge or information. NY CPLR Rule 3023. A "verified pleading" may be utilized as an affidavit whenever the latter is required. NY CPLR § 105(u).

i. Although pleadings ordinarily need not be verified, a benefit of voluntary verification is that the pleading, pursuant to NY CPLR § 105(u), then qualifies as an affidavit. The Court of Appeals has also held that a verified bill of particulars, which technically is not a pleading, also fell within the scope of NY CPLR § 105(u) and therefore had the effect of an affidavit. NY CPLR § 105(Practice Commentary, C105:7); Sanchez v. Nat'l R.R. Passenger Corp., 21 N.Y.3d 890, 988 N.E.2d 511 (2013). However, a verified pleading will be of no value as an affidavit when the circumstances require evidentiary detail and the pleading is phrased in conclusory terms. NY CPLR § 105(Practice Commentary, C105:7).

e. *Defective verification.* A defectively verified pleading shall be treated as an unverified pleading. Where a pleading is served without a sufficient verification in a case where the adverse party is entitled to a verified pleading, he may treat it as a nullity, provided he gives notice with due diligence to the attorney of the adverse party that he elects so to do. NY CPLR Rule 3022.

10. *Mandatory arbitration.* In each county where an arbitration program is established by order of the Chief Administrator, all civil actions for a sum of money only, except those commenced in small claims parts and not subsequently transferred to a regular part of court, that are noticed for trial or commenced in the Supreme Court, County Court, the Civil Court of the City of New York, a District Court or a City Court, on or after the effective date of the order where recovery sought for each cause of action is six thousand dollars ($6,000) or less, or ten thousand dollars ($10,000) or less in the Civil Court of the City of New York, or such other sum as may be authorized by law, exclusive of costs and interest, shall be heard and decided by a panel of arbitrators. The Chief Administrator may also, at any time, upon the establishment of the program in any particular court or county or thereafter, provide for the submission to arbitration of actions seeking recovery of such sums, that are pending for trial in those courts on the effective date of the order. NY R CHIEF J § 28.2(b). For more information on mandatory arbitration, refer to NY R CHIEF J § 28.1, et seq.

11. *Governing law.* The civil practice law and rules (NY CPLR § 101, et seq.) shall govern the procedure in civil judicial proceedings in all courts of the state and before all judges, except where the procedure is regulated by inconsistent statute. The civil practice law and rules shall succeed the civil practice act and rules of civil practice and shall be deemed substituted therefor throughout the statutes and rules of the state. NY CPLR § 101. The civil practice law and rules shall

be liberally construed to secure the just, speedy and inexpensive determination of every civil judicial proceeding. NY CPLR § 104.

a. *Uniform trial court rules.* The uniform civil rules for the Supreme Court and County Court (NY R UNIF TRIAL CTS § 202.1, et seq.) shall be applicable to civil actions and proceedings in the Supreme Court and the County Court. NY R UNIF TRIAL CTS § 202.1(a). The provisions of the uniform rules shall be construed consistent with the Civil Practice Law and Rules (CPLR), and matters not covered by the uniform rules shall be governed by the CPLR. NY R UNIF TRIAL CTS § 202.1(d).

b. *Local rules.* Local court rules, not inconsistent with law or with uniform civil rules for the Supreme Court and County Court (NY R UNIF TRIAL CTS § 202.1, et seq.), shall comply with Part 9 of the Rules of the Chief Judge (NY R CHIEF J § 9.1). NY R UNIF TRIAL CTS § 202.1(c).

c. *Official forms.* The state administrator shall have the power to adopt, amend and rescind an appendix of forms. Forms adopted pursuant to NY CPLR § 107 shall be sufficient under the civil practice law and rules and shall illustrate the simplicity and brevity of statement which the civil practice law and rules contemplate. NY CPLR § 107.

12. *Rules of the commercial division.* [Editor's note: certain types of civil cases or civil cases meeting certain monetary thresholds that are filed in the state of New York must be filed in the Commercial Division of the New York Supreme Courts. Rules governing practice in the commercial division are found in NY R UNIF TRIAL CTS § 202.70]. Cases which must be filed in the commercial division are listed below. For more information, refer to NY R UNIF TRIAL CTS § 202.70.

a. *Monetary thresholds.* Except as set forth in NY R UNIF TRIAL CTS § 202.70(b), the monetary thresholds of the Commercial Division, exclusive of punitive damages, interests, costs, disbursements and counsel fees claimed, are established as follows: (1) Albany County, fifty thousand dollars ($50,000); (2) Eighth Judicial District, one hundred thousand dollars ($100,000); (3) Kings County, one hundred fifty thousand dollars ($150,000); (4) Nassau County, two hundred thousand dollars ($200,000); (5) New York County, five hundred thousand dollars ($500,000); (6) Onondaga County, fifty thousand dollars ($50,000); (7) Queens County, one hundred thousand dollars ($100,000); (8) Seventh Judicial District, fifty thousand dollars ($50,000); (9) Suffolk County, one hundred thousand dollars ($100,000); and (10) Westchester County, one hundred thousand dollars ($100,000). NY R UNIF TRIAL CTS § 202.70(a).

i. *ALBANY COUNTY.* The Commercial Division of the Albany County Supreme Court exercises jurisdiction over selected business and commercial disputes in which the amount at issue generally involves damage claims in a minimum amount of fifty thousand dollars ($50,000) as well as claims for unspecified amounts where the value of the commercial asset(s) in dispute exceeds fifty thousand dollars ($50,000). A separate publication promulgating the rules and criteria relating to the filing and management of Commercial Court cases in this part may be obtained from the Albany County Supreme Court Clerk's Office. A section of the Uniform Civil Rules for the Supreme Court and County Court sets forth statewide rules. NY R 3 JD SUP Doc. 1(E).

ii. *BRONX COUNTY.* The monetary threshold for commercial cases in Bronx County will be seventy-five thousand dollars ($75,000). All other parameters including the type of matters that will be heard are contained within the Rules of the Commercial Division of the Supreme Court (NY R UNIF TRIAL CTS § 202.70). NY R BRONX FIL R Doc. 12.

iii. *NEW YORK COUNTY.* The monetary threshold in the New York County Commercial Division, which is generally applicable, is an amount in controversy of five hundred thousand dollars ($500,000) or more (exclusive of punitive damages, interest, costs, disbursements, and counsel fees). If the case is designated a commercial one and the Addendum is submitted, the clerk will review the pleadings to determine whether the amount in controversy in the case meets the monetary threshold or whether an exception to the threshold applies. NY R NY CTY Procedure IA(B). For more information on assigning a case to the commercial division in New York County, refer to NY R NY CTY Procedure IA(B).

b. *Commercial cases.* Actions in which the principal claims involve or consist of the following will be heard in the Commercial Division provided that the monetary threshold is met or equitable or declaratory relief is sought:

i. Breach of contract or fiduciary duty, fraud, misrepresentation, business tort (e.g., unfair competition), or statutory and/or common law violation where the breach or violation is alleged to arise out of business dealings (e.g., sales of assets or securities; corporate restructuring; partnership, shareholder, joint venture, and other business agreements; trade secrets; restrictive covenants; and employment agreements not including claims that principally involve alleged discriminatory practices);

ii. Transactions governed by the Uniform Commercial Code (exclusive of those concerning individual cooperative or condominium units);

iii. Transactions involving commercial real property, including Yellowstone injunctions and excluding actions for the payment of rent only;

iv. Shareholder derivative actions—without consideration of the monetary threshold;

v. Commercial class actions—without consideration of the monetary threshold;

vi. Business transactions involving or arising out of dealings with commercial banks and other financial institutions;

vii. Internal affairs of business organizations;

viii. Malpractice by accountants or actuaries, and legal malpractice arising out of representation in commercial matters;

ix. Environmental insurance coverage;

x. Commercial insurance coverage (e.g., directors and officers, errors and omissions, and business interruption coverage);

xi. Dissolution of corporations, partnerships, limited liability companies, limited liability partnerships and joint ventures—without consideration of the monetary threshold; and

xii. Applications to stay or compel arbitration and affirm or disaffirm arbitration awards and related injunctive relief pursuant to Article 75 of the New York Civil Practice Law and Rules (NY CPLR § 7501, et seq.) involving any of the foregoing enumerated commercial issues. Where the applicable arbitration agreement provides for the arbitration to be heard outside the United States, the monetary threshold set forth in NY R UNIF TRIAL CTS § 202.70(a) shall not apply. NY R UNIF TRIAL CTS § 202.70(b).

c. *Non-commercial cases.* The following will not be heard in the Commercial Division even if the monetary threshold is met:

i. Suits to collect professional fees;

ii. Cases seeking a declaratory judgment as to insurance coverage for personal injury or property damage;

iii. Residential real estate disputes, including landlord-tenant matters, and commercial real estate disputes involving the payment of rent only;

iv. Home improvement contracts involving residential properties consisting of one to four residential units or individual units in any residential building, including cooperative or condominium units;

v. Proceedings to enforce a judgment regardless of the nature of the underlying case;

vi. First-party insurance claims and actions by insurers to collect premiums or rescind non-commercial policies; and

vii. Attorney malpractice actions except as otherwise provided in NY R UNIF TRIAL CTS § 202.70(b)(8). NY R UNIF TRIAL CTS § 202.70(c).

d. For more information on the Commercial Division, refer to NY R UNIF TRIAL CTS § 202.70.

D. Documents

1. *Required documents*

a. *Answer.* Refer to the General Requirements section of this document for information on the answer.

b. *Proof of service.* In addition to complying with the provisions of NY CPLR Rule 2101, every paper filed in court shall have annexed thereto appropriate proof of service on all parties where required. NY R UNIF TRIAL CTS § 202.5(a).

2. *Supplemental documents*

a. *Supporting evidence; Exhibits*

i. *Foreign language documents.* Where an affidavit or exhibit annexed to a paper served or filed is in a foreign language, it shall be accompanied by an English translation and an affidavit by the translator stating his qualifications and that the translation is accurate. NY CPLR Rule 2101(b).

ii. *Statement of attorney in lieu of affidavit.* The statement of an attorney admitted to practice in the courts of the state, or of a physician, osteopath or dentist, authorized by law to practice in the state, who is not a party to an action, when subscribed and affirmed by him to be true under the penalties of perjury, may be served or filed in the action in lieu of and with the same force and effect as an affidavit. NY CPLR Rule 2106.

b. *Demand for bill of particulars.* There is no stated time for when the demand may be served, but ordinarily it should not be served before joinder of issue. The common practice for the defendant is to serve the demand with or after the answer. SIEGEL-NYPRAC § 239. Refer to the New York KeyRules Demand for Bill of Particulars document for more information.

c. *Filing fees.* The County Clerk shall require the payment of any applicable statutory fees, or an order of the Court waiving payment of such fees, before accepting a paper for filing. NY R UNIF TRIAL CTS § 202.5(d)(1). For information on filing fees, if any, refer to NY CPLR § 8001, et seq.

d. *Application to proceed as a poor person.* Upon motion of any person, the court in which an action is triable, or to which an appeal has been or will be taken, may grant permission to proceed as a poor person. The moving party shall file an affidavit setting forth the amount and sources of his or her income and listing his or her property with its value; that he or she is unable to pay the costs, fees and expenses necessary to prosecute or defend the action or to maintain or respond to the appeal; the nature of the action; sufficient facts so that the merit of the contentions can be ascertained; and whether any other person is beneficially interested in any recovery sought and, if so, whether every such person is unable to pay such costs, fees and expenses. An executor, administrator or other representative may move for permission on behalf of a deceased, infant or incompetent poor person. NY CPLR § 1101. For more information on proceeding as a poor person, refer to NY CPLR § 1101, et seq.

e. *Working copies.* The court may require the parties to provide working copies of documents filed electronically. In such event, each working copy shall include, firmly affixed thereto, a copy of a confirmation notice in a form prescribed by the Chief Administrator. NY R UNIF TRIAL CTS § 202.5-b(d)(5).

f. *Statement of authorization in electronic filing cases.* A filing agent (other than one employed by a governmental entity) shall e-file a statement of authorization from counsel of record in an action, in a form approved by the Chief Administrator, prior to or together with the first e-filing in that action by the agent on behalf of that counsel. NY R UNIF TRIAL CTS § 202.5-b(d)(1)(i).

g. *Notice to government of certain claims*

    i. When the constitutionality of a statute of the state, or a rule and regulation adopted pursuant thereto is involved in an action to which the state is not a party, the attorney-general, shall be notified and permitted to intervene in support of its constitutionality. NY CPLR § 1012(b)(1).

    ii. When the constitutionality of a local law, ordinance, rule or regulation of a city, county, town or village is involved in an action to which the city, county, town or village that enacted the provision is not a party, such city, county, town or village shall be notified and permitted to intervene in support of its constitutionality. NY CPLR § 1012(b)(2).

    iii. The court having jurisdiction in an action or proceeding in which the constitutionality of a state statute, local law, ordinance, rule or regulation is challenged shall not consider any challenge to the constitutionality of such state statute, local law, ordinance, rule or regulation unless proof of service of the notice required by NY CPLR § 1012(b) is filed with such court. NY CPLR § 1012(b)(3).

    iv. Where public retirement benefits, paid, payable, claimed, or sought to be paid by a state retirement system or any other retirement system established for public employees within this state or any subdivision thereof, or the interpretation of any provisions of law or rules governing any such retirement system or the operation thereof, are involved in an action to which the comptroller of the state of New York is not a party, the court shall notify said comptroller, who shall be permitted, in his discretion, to intervene in such action or to file a brief amicus curiae. NY CPLR § 1012(c).

h. *Initiating documents served to newly added third parties.* A party to be added in an action subject to e-filing shall be served with initiating documents in hard copy together with the notice of e-filing. NY R UNIF TRIAL CTS § 202.5-b(g). A party to be added in an action that has been commenced electronically in accordance with NY R UNIF TRIAL CTS § 202.5-bb shall be served with initiating documents in hard copy together with the notice specified in NY R UNIF TRIAL CTS § 202.5-bb(b)(3). NY R UNIF TRIAL CTS § 202.5-bb(c)(2).

i. *ERIE COUNTY: Additional supplemental documents*

    i. *Notice of hard copy submission in e-filed case.* In accordance with NY R UNIF TRIAL CTS § 202.5-b(d), the County Clerk shall refuse to accept for filing, hard copy papers filed to an action subject to electronic filing unless hard copy filing is permitted by the Uniform Rules or NY R ERIE E FIL Doc. 3 and the papers bear a completed Notice of Hard Copy Submission—E-Filed Case form. NY R ERIE E FIL Doc. 3(III)(D).

j. *KINGS COUNTY: Additional supplemental documents*

    i. *Forms when filing in hard copy.* An attorney who certifies in good faith that he or she lacks the equipment or knowledge needed to e-file and have no staff member or employee under his or her direction who has such knowledge and equipment may opt out of participation in e-filing in a mandatory case by filing a "Notice of Opt-Out from Participation in Action Subject to Mandatory Electronic Filing" form EFM-2 with the Clerk. NY R L KINGS E FIL Doc. 1(A)(2). Where in accordance with the E-Filing Rules a party submits a document in hard copy in an e-filed case (principally, a document submitted by a nonparticipating party (e.g., an attorney) in a consensual case, an emergency filing made in accordance with the Mandatory E-Filing Rules, and any document filed with the court in hard copy by an attorney who has opted out of participation in mandatory e-filing, the document must bear the back page facing out, a "Notice of Hard Copy Submission—E-Filed Cases" form EFM-3. NY R L KINGS E FIL Doc. 1(B)(3).

k. *NEW YORK COUNTY: Additional supplemental documents*

i. *Notice of hard copy submission.* Where in accordance with the E-Filing Rules an attorney or an unrepresented litigant who is participating in e-filing submits a document in hard copy in an e-filed case, the document must bear, as the back page facing out, a Notice of Hard-Copy Submission—E-Filed Case (a form available in the "Forms" section on the NYSCEF website (Form EFM-3) and in the court's back offices). NY R NY CTY E FIL Doc. 2(B)(3). For more information refer to NY R NY CTY E FIL Doc. 2.

l. *ONONDAGA COUNTY: Additional supplemental documents*

i. *Notice of hard copy submission.* Any papers to be filed with the court in an e-filed case must be filed online with the E-filing system except where a special exemption is granted (e.g., oversized maps, photographs). If such an exemption is granted, Form EFM-3, "Notice of Hard Copy Submission—E-Filed Case," must be attached to such documents forms which are not filed on line. Also, Form EFM-4 "Notice of Hard Copy Exhibit Filing" must be completed and uploaded to the action's e-file. Both of these forms may be found on the NYSCEF website. NY R ONDGA E FIL Protocol(B)(4).

m. *QUEENS COUNTY: Additional supplemental documents*

i. *Notice of hard copy submission.* Any party opting out of the e-filing system must have a "Notice of Hard Copy Submission" firmly affixed to the back of the papers. NY R L QUEENS E-FILE Doc. 1(H)(2)(f).

E. Format

1. *Format of pleadings*

a. *Numbered paragraphs.* Every pleading shall consist of plain and concise statements in consecutively numbered paragraphs. Each paragraph shall contain, as far as practicable, a single allegation. Reference to and incorporation of allegations may subsequently be by number. NY CPLR Rule 3014.

b. *Prior statements in pleading.* Prior statements in a pleading shall be deemed repeated or adopted subsequently in the same pleading whenever express repetition or adoption is unnecessary for a clear presentation of the subsequent matters. NY CPLR Rule 3014.

c. *Causes of action and defenses; Separate statements.* Separate causes of action or defenses shall be separately stated and numbered and may be stated regardless of consistency. NY CPLR Rule 3014.

d. *Alternative or hypothetical statements.* Causes of action or defenses may be stated alternatively or hypothetically. NY CPLR Rule 3014.

e. *Papers attached to pleadings.* A copy of any writing which is attached to a pleading is a part thereof for all purposes. NY CPLR Rule 3014.

f. *Statement in verified pleading.* The allegations or denials in a verified pleading must, in form, be stated to be made by the party pleading. NY CPLR Rule 3023.

2. *Form of documents; Generally*

a. *Size and form of paper.* Each paper served or filed shall be durable, white and, except for summonses, subpoenas, notices of appearance, notes of issue, orders of protection, temporary orders of protection and exhibits, shall be eleven by eight and one-half (11 x 8-1/2) inches in size. NY CPLR Rule 2101(a).

b. *Writing and language.* The writing shall be legible and in black ink. NY CPLR Rule 2101(a). Each paper served or filed shall be in the English language which, where practicable, shall be of ordinary usage. NY CPLR Rule 2101(b).

c. *Caption.* Each paper served or filed shall begin with a caption setting forth the name of the court, the venue, the title of the action, the nature of the paper and the index number of the action if one has been assigned. In all papers other

than a summons, a complaint or a judgment it shall be sufficient to state the name of the first named party on each side with an appropriate indication of any omissions. NY CPLR Rule 2101(c).

i. *Further contents of first page.* After the first paper has been filed in each case the index number shall appear on the cover and first page to the right of the caption of every paper tendered for filing in the action. Each such cover and first page also shall contain an indication of the county of venue and a brief description of the nature of the paper and, where the case has been assigned to an individual judge, shall contain the name of the assigned judge to the right of the caption. NY R UNIF TRIAL CTS § 202.5(a); NY R UNIF TRIAL CTS § 202.5(b); NY R UNIF TRIAL CTS § 202.5(d)(1)(i).

d. *Index number.* No paper in an action in the supreme or a county court, other than an order submitted for signature to a judge out of court, shall be submitted for any purpose to the supreme or county court or to a clerk thereof unless there is endorsed on such paper the index number of the action assigned by the clerk of the county. NY CPLR § 8018(c).

i. *ALBANY COUNTY: Index number on all filed documents.* The index number, the request for judicial intervention number and the assigned justice's name shall appear on [all papers filed with the Court subsequent to the complaint]. NY R 3 JD SUP Doc. 1(A).

ii. *ERIE COUNTY: Index number after initial filing.* Cases that are initially commenced by the filing of papers with the NYSCEF system are identified as e-filed cases by assignment of an Index Number that has "800-899" as the first three (3) digits of the index number (i.e. 802391/2012). NY R ERIE E FIL Doc. 3(II). [The] Index Number must be affixed to all document submissions, filings, and communications to the Erie County Clerk and the Court. Cases that are converted from paper to e-filing shall retain the original index number. NY R ERIE E FIL Doc. 3(II).

iii. *KINGS COUNTY: Index number after initial filing.* In cases commenced electronically by the filing of initiating papers with the NYSCEF system and payment of the statutory fees, the Kings County Clerk will issue an NYSCEF designated index number and the filer shall be notified via the NYSCEF system of the index number assigned and filing date. Such index number must be affixed to all document submissions, filings and communications to the Kings County Clerk and Supreme Court. If counsel faces exigent circumstances that require accelerated assignment, counsel may contact Administration of the Kings County Clerk at kcco-efile@nycourts.gov, during normal business hours of the court. NY R L KINGS E FIL Doc. 1(B)(5).

iv. *NEW YORK COUNTY: Index number on hard copy filings.* Papers subsequently presented for filing in hardcopy format will be filed in this jacket. NY R NY CTY Procedure I(B). Index numbers take the form of six digits followed by a slash and the four digits of the year the case began, e.g., 340705/2018. The first or first two integers of the index number identify the type of case. If a case is commenced electronically, the second integer will be a "5", except as indicated otherwise in the list below. There are many tax certiorari matters e-filed annually and the index numbers therefor will normally run over into those with a "6" as the second integer, and the same will occur with general cases if necessary. The principal types of cases and their index number categories are listed in NY R NY CTY Procedure I(B). NY R NY CTY Procedure I(B); NY R NY CTY Procedure XI(A).

v. *ONONDAGA COUNTY: Index number.* The index number must be referenced on all e-filed documents and correspondence. All e-filed case index numbers will contain the letters "EF" between the year and the file number (for example, 2012EF9999). NY R ONDGA E FIL Protocol(B)(1).

vi. *QUEENS COUNTY: Index number on converted cases.* Cases originally commenced in hard-copy form but later converted to an E-file case, either by stipulation or order will bear a regular index number initially. The County Clerk will issue a new E-file index number. NY R L QUEENS E-FILE Doc. 1(B).

e. *Line spacing.* Every paper filed in court, if typewritten, shall have at least double space between each line, except for quotations and the names and addresses of attorneys appearing in the action. NY R UNIF TRIAL CTS § 202.5(a).

f. *Font size.* Each. . .paper printed or typed, served or filed, except for summonses. . .and exhibits, shall be in clear type of no less than ten (10) point in size. NY CPLR Rule 2101(a).

i. Whenever a requirement relating to size of type is stated in point size, the type size requirement shall be deemed met if the x-height of the type is a minimum of forty-five percent (45%) of the specified point size. Each point shall be measured as .351 millimeter. The x-height size shall be measured as it appears on the page. The x-height is the height of the lower case letters, exclusive of ascenders or descenders. NY CPLR § 105(t).

g. *Margins.* Every paper filed in court shall have at least one (1) inch margins. NY R UNIF TRIAL CTS § 202.5(a).

h. *Citations*

i. *Civil practice law and rules.* NY CPLR § 101, et seq. shall be known as the civil practice law and rules, and may be cited as "CPLR". Reference to a provision in the civil practice law and rules may, except when such provision is being enacted or amended, be made without indicating whether it is a rule or section. NY CPLR § 101.

i. *Indorsement by attorney.* Each paper served or filed shall be indorsed with the name, address and telephone number of the attorney for the party serving or filing the paper, or if the party does not appear by attorney, with the name, address and telephone number of the party. NY CPLR Rule 2101(d).

j. *One-sided printing.* In addition, every paper filed in court, other than an exhibit or printed form, shall contain writing on one side only, except that papers that are fastened on the side may contain writing on both sides. NY R UNIF TRIAL CTS § 202.5(a).

k. *Use of copies authorized.* Except where otherwise specifically prescribed, copies, rather than originals, of all papers, including orders, affidavits and exhibits may be served or filed. Where it is required that the original be served or filed and the original is lost or withheld, the court may authorize a copy to be served or filed. NY CPLR Rule 2101(e).

   i. Where a certified copy of a paper is required by law, an attorney admitted to practice in the courts of the state may certify that it has been compared by him with the original and found to be a true and complete copy. Such a certificate, when subscribed by such attorney, has the same effect as if made by a clerk. NY CPLR § 2105.

l. *Recycled paper.* It is the policy of the Unified Court System that litigants, where practicable, should file or submit to the courts of the Unified Court System of the State of New York papers printed or reproduced on recycled paper. Paper is considered recycled if it contains a minimum content of thirty percent (30%) waste paper. NY R UNIF TRIAL CTS § 215.2. The signature page of every paper filed or submitted to the court on recycled paper should bear the legend: "Printed [Reproduced] on Recycled Paper." NY R UNIF TRIAL CTS § 215.3.

m. *KINGS COUNTY: Tabs on filings.* Motions, orders and other filed papers shall be indexed with protruding tabs. Clerks are required to reject papers that do not have protruding exhibit tabs, except papers in matrimonial cases and papers filed by pro se litigants. NY R L KINGS Pt. A, Papers.

3. *Form of electronic documents.* Each paper served or filed by electronic means, as defined in NY CPLR Rule 2103(f), shall be capable of being reproduced by the receiver so as to comply with the provisions of NY CPLR Rule 2101(a) through NY CPLR Rule 2101(d). NY CPLR Rule 2101(g).

   a. *File format.* All e-filed documents shall comply with the technical requirements set forth at the NYSCEF site. NY R UNIF TRIAL CTS § 202.5-b(d)(1)(i).

   b. *Heading of document.* The subject matter heading for each paper sent by electronic means must indicate that the matter being transmitted electronically is related to a court proceeding. NY CPLR Rule 2103(b)(7).

   c. *E-filed documents identification*

      i. *ERIE COUNTY.* E-filed cases must be readily identifiable and marked as such. If counsel presents papers to the Office of the Erie County Clerk or the Office of the Chief Clerk in a NYSCEF matter where authorized, counsel should alert the Clerk that the case is a NYSCEF matter. NY R ERIE E FIL Doc. 3(II).

      ii. *KINGS COUNTY.* The Supreme Court's Civil Case Information System ("CCIS") will further identify e-filed cases by the addition of a suffix to the index number (e.g. 500136/2006E). This suffix should be used on all documents filed with the court in e-filed matters. NY R L KINGS E FIL Doc. 1(A)(1).

4. *Signature blocks.* Every pleading, written motion, and other paper, served on another party or filed or submitted to the court shall be signed by an attorney, or by a party if the party is not represented by an attorney, with the name of the attorney or party clearly printed or typed directly below the signature. NY R CHIEF ADMIN § 130-1.1-a(a); NY R UNIF TRIAL CTS § 202.5(d)(1)(iv).

   a. *Printed name.* Beneath each signature shall be printed the name signed. NY CPLR Rule 2101(a).

   b. *Failure to sign.* Absent good cause shown, the court shall strike any unsigned paper if the omission of the signature is not corrected promptly after being called to the attention of the attorney or party. NY R CHIEF ADMIN § 130-1.1-a(a).

   c. *Signature as certification.* By signing a paper, an attorney or party certifies that, to the best of that person's knowledge, information and belief, formed after an inquiry reasonable under the circumstances the presentation of the paper or the contentions therein are not frivolous as defined in NY R CHIEF ADMIN § 130-1.1(c). NY R CHIEF ADMIN § 130-1.1-a(b)(1).

   d. *Electronic signatures.* A document shall be considered to have been signed by an attorney or party in compliance with NY R CHIEF ADMIN § 130-1.1-a if it has been signed by such attorney or party as provided in NY R UNIF TRIAL

CTS § 202.5-b(e)(1) and it bears the signatory's name. NY R UNIF TRIAL CTS § 202.5-b(e)(2). An electronically filed document shall be considered to have been signed by, and shall be binding upon, the person identified as a signatory, if:

i. It bears the physical signature of such person and is scanned into an electronic format that reproduces such signature; or

ii. The signatory has electronically affixed the digital image of his or her signature to the document; or

iii. It is electronically filed under the User ID and password of that person; or

iv. In a tax certiorari action in which the parties have stipulated to this procedure, it is an initiating document that is electronically filed without the signature of the signatory in a form provided above in NY R UNIF TRIAL CTS § 202.5-b(e)(iv), provided that, prior to filing, the document is signed in full in hard copy (which hard copy must be preserved until the conclusion of all proceedings, including appeals, in the case in which it is filed); or

v. In a small claims assessment review proceeding, it is a petition recorded by the NYSCEF site upon the filing of a text file as provided in NY R UNIF TRIAL CTS § 202.5-b(b)(1), provided that prior to filing, the document was signed in full in hard copy (which hard copy must be preserved until the conclusion of all proceedings in the matter, including article 78 (NY CPLR § 7801, et seq.) review and any appeals, and must be made available during the proceeding upon request of the respondent or the court); or

vi. It otherwise bears the electronic signature of the signatory in a format conforming to such standards and requirements as may hereafter be established by the Chief Administrator. NY R UNIF TRIAL CTS § 202.5-b(e).

5. *Confidentiality of personal information.* No person may file any document available for public inspection with any state agency, political subdivision, or in any court of this state that contains a Social Security account number of any other person, unless such other person is a dependent child, or has consented to such filing, except as required by federal or state law or regulation, or by court rule. NY GEN BUS § 399-ddd. Submissions pursuant to e-filing procedures shall have the same confidentiality rights as paper documents. NY R UNIF TRIAL CTS § 202.5-b(k)(1).

a. *Confidential personal information.* Except in the actions designated in NY R UNIF TRIAL CTS § 202.5(e)(1), or as otherwise provided by rule or law or court order, and whether or not a sealing order is or has been sought, the parties shall omit or redact confidential personal information in papers submitted to the court for filing. For purposes of NY R UNIF TRIAL CTS § 202.5(e), confidential personal information ("CPI") means:

i. The taxpayer identification number of an individual or an entity, including a Social Security number, an employer identification number, and an individual taxpayer identification number, except the last four (4) digits thereof;

ii. The date of an individual's birth, except the year thereof;

iii. The full name of an individual known to be a minor, except the minor's initials;

iv. A financial account number, including a credit and/or debit card number, a bank account number, an investment account number, and/or an insurance account number, except the last four (4) digits or letters thereof; and

v. Any of the documents or testimony in a matrimonial action protected by NY DOM REL § 235 or evidence sealed by the court in such an action which are attached as exhibits or referenced in the papers filed in any other civil action. For purposes of NY R UNIF TRIAL CTS § 202.5, a matrimonial action shall mean: an action to annul a marriage or declare the nullity of a void marriage, an action or agreement for a separation, an action for a divorce, or an action or proceeding for custody, visitation, writ of habeus corpus, child support, maintenance or paternity. NY R UNIF TRIAL CTS § 202.5(e)(1).

vi. *ERIE COUNTY.* An attorney or unrepresented litigant filing a document via the NYSCEF system must comply with the requirements of NY R UNIF TRIAL CTS § 202.5(e) regarding the redaction of Confidential Personal Information and NY GEN BUS § 399-ddd(6) concerning the filing of documents containing Social Security Numbers. It is the sole responsibility of counsel or unrepresented litigant filing to be aware of and to comply with existing laws requiring non-disclosure of personal information contained in any document e-filed in NYSCEF. NY R ERIE E FIL Doc. 3(III)(G); NY R ERIE E FIL Doc. 3(III).

vii. *KINGS COUNTY.* An attorney or unrepresented litigant filing a document via the NYSCEF system must comply with the requirements of General Business Law § 399-dd(6), which often require redaction of any Social Security number that appear in the original document. The NYSCEF system automatically redacts portions of filed documents which apparently contain Social Security numbers pursuant to NY R UNIF TRIAL CTS § 202.5-b(k). In the event the filing party receives e-mail notice through NYSCEF that a Social Security number in a filed document has been redacted, and the filing party concludes such redaction is erroneous, the filer should click on the link provided in the e-mail to permit the County Clerk to revert the redaction. For Confidential Personal Information, see NY R UNIF TRIAL CTS § 202.5(e) and NY R L KINGS E FIL Doc. 1(B)(11). [Editor's note: the reference to General Business Law § 399-dd(6) is likely a reference to NY GEN BUS § 399-ddd(6)]. NY R L KINGS E FIL Doc. 1(B)(10); NY R L KINGS E FIL Doc. 1(K)(1).

viii. *NEW YORK COUNTY.* It is the responsibility of counsel and parties to comply with rules restricting disclosure of confidential personal information. Nevertheless, NYSCEF screens filings and endeavors to identify any that contain social security numbers. When such numbers are discovered through this process, NYSCEF will restrict portions of or all of such documents from public view. Where NYSCEF has redacted what it believes to be a social security number, it will transmit to the filer a notice advising of the action taken and requesting that the filer review the matter and provide notification as set forth in the notice if the redaction has been made in error. NY R NY CTY E FIL Doc. 2(K)(1); NY R NY CTY J RUL Rule A-1. Documents filed in the past in "secure status" under a procedure no longer in place will retain that status unless otherwise directed by the court. NY R NY CTY E FIL Doc. 2(K)(2).

b. *Submission of confidential personal information.* Where a person submitting a paper to a court for filing believes in good faith that the inclusion of the full confidential personal information described in NY R UNIF TRIAL CTS § 202.5(e)(1) is material and necessary to the adjudication of the action or proceeding before the court, he or she may apply to the court for leave to serve and file together with a paper in which such information has been set forth in abbreviated form a confidential affidavit or affirmation setting forth the same information in unabbreviated form, appropriately referenced to the page or pages of the paper at which the abbreviated form appears. NY R UNIF TRIAL CTS § 202.5(e)(3).

c. *Home addresses.* For information on when home addresses and other personal information must be redacted, refer to NY CPLR Rule 2103-a.

6. *Defective papers.* A defect in the form of a paper, if a substantial right of a party is not prejudiced, shall be disregarded by the court, and leave to correct shall be freely given. NY CPLR Rule 2101(f). Papers that are stapled or bound securely shall not be rejected for filing simply because they are not bound with a backer of any kind. NY R UNIF TRIAL CTS § 202.5(a). A paper filed in accordance with the rules of the chief administrator or any local rule or practice established by the court shall be deemed filed. NY CPLR Rule 2102(b).

a. *Objection to defective papers.* The party on whom a paper is served shall be deemed to have waived objection to any defect in form unless, within fifteen (15) days after the receipt thereof, the party on whom the paper is served returns the paper to the party serving it with a statement of particular objections. NY CPLR Rule 2101(f).

F. Filing and Service Requirements

1. *Filing requirements.* Except where otherwise prescribed by law or order of court, papers required to be filed shall be filed with the clerk of the court in which the action is triable. In an action or proceeding in supreme or court, papers required to be filed shall be filed with the clerk of the county in which the proceeding is brought. NY CPLR Rule 2102(a). In any case other than a pleading asserting new or additional claims for relief, a pleading shall be served in the manner provided for service of papers generally. NY CPLR § 3012(a).

a. *Electronic filing.* On consent, documents may be filed and served by electronic means in Supreme Court in such civil actions and in such counties as shall be authorized by order of the Chief Administrator of the Courts and only to the extent and in the manner provided in NY R UNIF TRIAL CTS § 202.5-b. NY R UNIF TRIAL CTS § 202.5-b(a)(1). For the definitions of terms used in electronic filing, refer to NY R UNIF TRIAL CTS § 202.5-b(a)(2).

i. *E-filing mandatory.* In any action subject to e-filing, all documents required to be filed with the court by an e-filing party shall be filed and served electronically, except as provided in NY R UNIF TRIAL CTS § 202.5-b. NY R UNIF TRIAL CTS § 202.5-b(d)(1)(i).

- *ERIE COUNTY.* Case types currently eligible and accepted for e-filing are listed at the NYSCEF website. Note that some actions or special proceedings, (i.e., name changes) which are otherwise subject to mandatory e-filing, if commenced by unrepresented litigants will NOT be maintained in the NYSCEF system; individual cases may be found either at NYSCEF or in the Erie County Clerk's online records system. NY R ERIE E FIL Doc. 3(I)(E).
- *KINGS COUNTY.* Cases that are commenced by filing of the initiating papers with NYSCEF are identified as e-filed cases by assignment of a special index number (i.e., Index Numbers beginning with 500,000). NY R L KINGS E FIL Doc. 1(A)(1). All cases required to be e-filed are listed in Uniform Rule 202.5-bb (Mandatory E-Filing Rules) and on the NYSCEF website. All such cases must be commenced by filing with

the County Clerk electronically through NYSCEF and all subsequent documents in such cases must be e-filed. Any questions regarding mandatory e-filing in Kings County can be e-mailed to kcco-efile@nycourts.gov. NY R L KINGS E FIL Doc. 1(A)(2).

- *NEW YORK COUNTY.* Unless otherwise provided in the Rules or in NY R NY CTY E FIL Doc. 2 or where a special exemption is granted due to physical requirements (e.g., oversized maps; see NY R NY CTY E FIL Doc. 2(B)(10)), all documents to be filed with the court in a NYSCEF case, including all documents on motions and all letters to the court (where permitted), must be filed with the NYSCEF system. Documents that attorneys would not ordinarily file with the court in a hard-copy case need not be e-filed. Unless otherwise provided by the E-Filing Rules or this Protocol, in e-filed cases the County Clerk and the court will not accept documents filed in paper form. NY R NY CTY E FIL Doc. 2(B)(1). E-filing is mandatory in all types of cases (other than election law, matrimonial, Art. 78, and Mental Hygiene Law matters, and Art. 70 habeas corpus proceedings) that are commenced in this court on or after February 19, 2013. All such cases must be commenced by filing with the County Clerk electronically through NYSCEF and all subsequent documents in such cases must be e-filed. NY R NY CTY E FIL Doc. 2(A)(2)(a). For more information, including information on consensual e-filing and filing scanned hard copy documents, refer to NY R NY CTY E FIL Doc. 2(A)(2).
- *QUEENS COUNTY.* All authorized Torts, Commercial and Tax Certiorari cases may be commenced by E-Filing, however all parties must consent for the action to continue as an E-file case. NY R L QUEENS E-FILE Doc. 1(A). All papers to be filed with the court in an E-filed case shall be filed on-line with the E-file system except as directed by the court. Papers that attorneys would not ordinarily file with the court in a hard-copy case need not be filed in an E-filed matter. NY R L QUEENS E-FILE Doc. 1(E)(2).

ii. *Who may file.* Documents may be filed or served electronically only by a person who has registered as an authorized e-filing user or as otherwise provided in NY R UNIF TRIAL CTS § 202.5-b(c). NY R UNIF TRIAL CTS § 202.5-b(c)(1).

iii. *When filing made.* Documents may be transmitted at any time of the day or night to the NYSCEF site. A document other than an order or judgment is filed when its electronic transmission or, in the case of a petition that is e-filed by submission of a text file as provided in NY R UNIF TRIAL CTS § 202.5-b(b)(1), the electronic transmission of the text file is recorded at that site, provided, however, that where payment of a fee is required upon the filing of a document, the document is not filed until transmission of the document and the information or form or information as required in NY R UNIF TRIAL CTS § 202.5-b(d)(2)(i), NY R UNIF TRIAL CTS § 202.5-b(d)(2)(ii) or NY R UNIF TRIAL CTS § 202.5-b(d)(2)(iii) has been recorded at the NYSCEF site; or, if no transmission of that information or form or information is recorded, where permitted by the County Clerk, until payment is presented to the County Clerk. NY R UNIF TRIAL CTS § 202.5-b(d)(3)(i).

iv. *Notification of filing.* No later than the close of business on the business day following the electronic filing of a document, a notification, in a form prescribed by the Chief Administrator, shall be transmitted electronically by the NYSCEF site to the person filing such document and the e-mail service addresses of all other participating parties in such action. NY R UNIF TRIAL CTS § 202.5-b(d)(3)(ii).

v. *Removal of confidential information and other corrections.* If a document filed electronically is subsequently discovered to contain confidential data—including but not limited to trade secrets, information protected by confidentiality agreement, or personal confidential information as defined by statute or court rule—or otherwise to have been filed in error, the filer or another party or affected person may (1) notify the parties and any non-party filers in the action of the confidentiality issue or other error raised by the filing, and of his or her intention to seek judicial relief to correct the filing: (2) following such notification, request that the appropriate County Clerk, exercising his or her administrative discretion, place the document temporarily in "restricted" status on the NYSCEF site, to be made available for viewing by court staff and the parties but not the general public; and (3) file an application to correct the filing by order to show cause within five (5) business days of such notification (or such time as the court may direct), including a request for preliminary injunctive relief limiting interim disclosure of the document at issue. Unless otherwise directed by the court, any document placed in restricted status in response to such a request shall be returned to public view upon expiration of this five (5) day period. The Chief Administrator of the Courts shall promulgate forms to implement this process. NY R UNIF TRIAL CTS § 202.5-b(d)(3)(iii).

- *KINGS COUNTY.* For information on what to do when a document was erroneously filed with confidential information, refer to NY R L KINGS E FIL Doc. 1(B)(11).
- *NEW YORK COUNTY.* For information on what to do when a document was erroneously filed with confidential information, refer to NY R NY CTY E FIL Doc. 2(B)(8).

- *QUEENS COUNTY.* For information on what to do when a document was erroneously filed with confidential information, refer to NY R L QUEENS E-FILE Doc. 1(E)(7).

vi. *Documents requiring judge's signature.* Except where the court directs otherwise, any document that requires a judge's signature shall be transmitted electronically and in hard copy to the court. NY R UNIF TRIAL CTS § 202.5-b(d)(6).

vii. *Documents which would be inconvenient to file electronically; Hard copies.* Notwithstanding any other provision of NY R UNIF TRIAL CTS § 202.5-b, and subject to such guidelines as may be established by the Chief Administrative Judge, the County Clerk or his or her designee may require or permit a party to file in hard copy, in accordance with procedures set by the County Clerk or designee, an exhibit or other document which it is impractical or inconvenient to file electronically. NY R UNIF TRIAL CTS § 202.5-b(d)(7).

- *ERIE COUNTY.* Please contact the Supervisor of Actions & Proceedings, Erie County Clerk's Office by calling (716) 858-6662 or the Deputy County Clerk—Legal at (716) 858-6348 for information. NY R ERIE E FIL Doc. 3(III)(F).
- *KINGS COUNTY.* With limited exceptions, as set forth in the Uniform Rules and herein, all documents to be filed with the court in a NYSCEF case shall be filed online via the NYSCEF system. However, should the size, consistency or context of a hard copy document preclude electronic filing, the user shall electronically file a "Notice of Hard Copy Submission—E-Filed Cases" form EFM-3. Any hard copy submitted pursuant to NY R L KINGS E FIL Doc. 1(B)(9) shall include, as a cover page firmly fastened thereto, a copy of the Confirmation Notice received from the NYSCEF site confirming receipt of the "Notice of Hard Copy Submission—E-Filed Cases". Any party may object to such hard copy filing. The Court, in response to such objection, may, following the hard copy filing, fashion such relief as it deems appropriate pursuant to and in furtherance of the Uniform Rules and NY R L KINGS E FIL Doc. 1, including, but not limited to, an Order directing the filing party to file such documents online via the NYSCEF system. When exhibits are impractical to file pursuant to NY R UNIF TRIAL CTS § 202.5-b(d)(7), an additional "Notice of Hard Copy Exhibit Filing" form EFM-4 is required to be submitted. NY R L KINGS E FIL Doc. 1(B)(9).
- *NEW YORK COUNTY.* If a filer needs to submit unusual exhibits in original form that cannot practically be e-filed, such as oversized maps or electronic recordings, the filer should consult with the County Clerk's E-File Department by telephone at 646-386-3737 (procedural questions only) or by e-mail at ccnyef@nycourts.gov, which will normally require that the filer retain custody of the original subject to possible future directives of the court. NY R NY CTY E FIL Doc. 2(B)(10). In such instances, the filing counsel shall file with NYSCEF a "placeholder" in the form of a Notice of Hard Copy Exhibit Filing (NYSCEF Form EF 21). The Notice should be uploaded to NYSCEF as document type "Exhibit" and the filer should indicate in the "Additional Document Information" field that the filer is retaining custody of the original. Failure to e-file the Notice may result in a gap in the official record of the court. NY R NY CTY E FIL Doc. 2(B)(10).

viii. *Documents containing sensitive or proprietary information.* In an action subject to e-filing, any person may apply for an order prohibiting or restricting the electronic filing in the action of specifically identified materials on the grounds that such materials are subject to copyright or other proprietary rights, or trade secret or other privacy interests, and that electronic filing in the action is likely to result in substantial prejudice to those rights or interests. NY R UNIF TRIAL CTS § 202.5-b(k)(2).

ix. *Refusal to accept paper filings.* In accordance with NY CPLR Rule 2102(c), a County Clerk and a chief clerk of the Supreme Court or County Court, as appropriate, shall refuse to accept for filing papers filed in actions and proceedings when the paper sought to be filed:

- Is in an action subject to electronic filing pursuant to Rules of the Chief Administrator,
- Is not being filed electronically, and
- Does not include the notice required by NY R UNIF TRIAL CTS § 202.5-b(d)(1). NY R UNIF TRIAL CTS § 202.5(d)(1)(v); NY R UNIF TRIAL CTS § 202.5-bb(d).

x. *Emergency filings; Hard copies.* For information on when an emergency filing may be filed and served in hard copy, refer to NY R UNIF TRIAL CTS § 202.5-b(d)(1)(ii), NY R UNIF TRIAL CTS § 202.5-b(d)(1)(iii) and NY R UNIF TRIAL CTS § 202.5-bb(c)(3).

- *KINGS COUNTY.* Under the rules, a participating emergency e-filer must electronically file the documents initially filed in hard copy form within three (3) business days of the emergency filing; the originals will be discarded after the documents have been processed and the failure to e-file as required will therefore lead to an incomplete record. NY R L KINGS E FIL Doc. 1(B)(3).

- *NEW YORK COUNTY.* Occasionally an emergency will arise requiring expedited entry of a document with the County Clerk (e.g., an order issued in the courtroom after a conference or argument of a critical matter), such as for purposes of an immediate appeal. Expedition can be achieved by the Part as follows: the document should be carried by a Court Officer or staff member to the General Clerk's Office to assure immediate and proper recordation in the computer and, as appropriate, the posting of the document to NYSCEF or the Supreme Court Records On-Line Library ("Scroll"). The court will accommodate counsel in emergencies. NY R NY CTY Procedure XI(A).

xi. *Technical failures.* The NYSCEF site shall be considered to be subject to a technical failure on a given day if the site is unable to accept filings or provide access to filed documents continuously or intermittently over the course of any period of time greater than one (1) hour after 12:00 noon of that day. Notice of all such technical failures shall be provided on the site. NY R UNIF TRIAL CTS § 202.5-b(i).

- When e-filing is hindered by a technical failure, a party may file with the appropriate clerk and serve in hard copy. NY R UNIF TRIAL CTS § 202.5-b(i). In the event an attorney or party shall file and serve documents in hard copy pursuant to NY R UNIF TRIAL CTS § 202.5-b(i), each such document shall include the notice required by NY R UNIF TRIAL CTS § 202.5-b(d)(1), and the filer shall file those documents with the NYSCEF site within three (3) business days after restoration of normal operations at that site. NY R UNIF TRIAL CTS § 202.5-b(i).
- With the exception of deadlines that by law cannot be extended, the time for filing of any document that is delayed due to technical failure of the site shall be extended for one (1) day for each day on which such failure occurs, unless otherwise ordered by the court. NY R UNIF TRIAL CTS § 202.5-b(i).
- *ERIE COUNTY.* When filing by electronic means is hindered by a technical failure, please refer to the NY R UNIF TRIAL CTS § 202.5-b(i). NY R ERIE E FIL Doc. 3(III)(K).
- *KINGS COUNTY.* When filing by electronic means is hindered by a NYSCEF technical failure (as set forth in NY R UNIF TRIAL CTS § 202.5-b(i)), a party may file with the appropriate Clerk in hard copy. Except for deadlines that by law cannot be extended (e.g. Statute of limitations, Notice of Appeal), the time for filing of any document that is delayed due to technical failure of the NYSCEF system shall be extended for one day for each day on which such failure occurs, unless otherwise ordered by the court. NY R L KINGS E FIL Doc. 1(B)(13).
- *ONONDAGA COUNTY.* When filing by electronic means is hindered by a technical failure (as set forth in NY R UNIF TRIAL CTS § 202.5-b(h)(3)(i)), a party may file a hard copy with the County Clerk. With the exception of deadlines that by law cannot be extended (e.g., a statute of limitations or the deadline for filing a Notice of Appeal), the time for filing of any document that is delayed due to technical failure of the NYSCEF system will be extended for one day for each day on which such failure occurs, unless otherwise ordered by the court. A "Notice of Hard Copy Filing Submission—E-Filed Case' must accompany any documents not filed via NYSCEF. NY R ONDGA E FIL Protocol(B)(8).

xii. *Filing fees.* For information on what information must be provided to pay filing fees, refer to NY R UNIF TRIAL CTS § 202.5-b(d)(2).

xiii. *Exemption from e-filing.* For information on exemptions from e-filing, refer to NY R UNIF TRIAL CTS § 202.5-bb(e).

xiv. *Filing exhibits*

- *ERIE COUNTY.* In the NYSCEF system, each exhibit must be uploaded as a separate .pdf file. After uploading a primary document, please choose the document type "Exhibit" and enter the appropriate number or letter and a brief description of the exhibit; each exhibit should bear a separate cover sheet clearly marked as "Exhibit A," "Exhibit B," etc. "Exhibit A" or "Exhibit B" is unacceptable as a brief description of the exhibit. Exhibits, where referenced in a signed Order as attached or affixed shall be uploaded with the signed Order as one .pdf document. NY R ERIE E FIL Doc. 3(III)(H).
- *KINGS COUNTY.* In the NYSCEF system, each exhibit should be uploaded as a separate PDF file. After uploading a primary document, please choose the document type "Exhibit", enter the appropriate number or letter, and be sure to place a check mark to the right of "Attach to main document". Each exhibit shall bear a separate cover sheet clearly marked as Exhibit A, Exhibit B, etc. NY R L KINGS E FIL Doc. 1(B)(12).

- *NEW YORK COUNTY.* Attorneys submitting exhibits in NYSCEF cases should make each exhibit a separate attachment to an affidavit/affirmation in the system; i.e., exhibits should not be filed as a single PDF-A together with the affidavit/affirmation or grouped together as a single PDF-A attachment because either of these two formats makes it difficult for the Justice to locate particular exhibits as needed. Counsel must also include appropriate descriptive language in the "Additional Document Information" field in NYSCEF. NY R NY CTY E FIL Doc. 2(D)(6).
- *ONONDAGA COUNTY.* All exhibits in e-filed cases must be e-filed individually as separate attachments. NY R ONDGA E FIL Protocol(B)(9)(b).

xv. *Correcting documents*

- *ERIE COUNTY.* Submission of documents which, upon examination, require correction or addition will result in notification to the filer advising that the document has been returned for correction. The filer shall make the required corrections and/or additions as indicated in the e-mail transmission sent by the County Clerk or Part Clerk through the NYSCEF site. The corrected documents may be resubmitted using the "Re-file this document" link highlighted in the filer's document list for the respective case. Please note that in the case of multiple submissions, all related documents filed at the same time may be removed from the case record and returned until all documents are properly submitted. NY R ERIE E FIL Doc. 3(III)(J).
- *KINGS COUNTY.* Submission of documents which, upon examination, require correction or addition will result in notification to the filer advising that there is a problem with a document. The filer shall make the required corrections and/or additions and resubmit the corrected document using the "Refile this document" link. In the event a document is returned for correction, the original file date will be preserved. For corrections of documents filed with the Kings County Clerk which require a court order, refer to the procedure in NY R UNIF TRIAL CTS § 202.5-b(d)(3)(iii) and NY R L KINGS E FIL Doc. 1(B)(11). NY R L KINGS E FIL Doc. 1(B)(3).
- *ONONDAGA COUNTY.* If there is an error or an additional document is required, the system will notify the filing party, who will make the corrections/additions and resubmit them online. NY R ONDGA E FIL Protocol(B)(6).
- *QUEENS COUNTY.* Generally speaking, documents that have been E-filed will not thereafter be deleted by the County Clerk from NYCEF because the filer asserts that the filing contains an error or a significant omission. When the filer wishes to correct a perceived error or omission in a filed document, he or she should file an amended version of the document, with the original remaining on file, or else obtain a court order providing for deletion of the original. The County Clerk will only delete a document upon request of the filer or on the County Clerk's own initiative when it is obvious from the face of the document alone that the filer made a fundamental error and never intended to file the document that was filed (e.g., a completely unrelated non-litigation document, a different case, or a wrong county). The County Clerk will advise the filer when any such fundamental errors are detected. NY R L QUEENS E-FILE Doc. 1(E)(6).

b. *Facsimile filing.* In the Supreme Court, facsimile filing shall be limited to commercial claims and tax certiorari, conservatorship, and mental hygiene proceedings in Monroe, Westchester, New York and Suffolk Counties. NY R UNIF TRIAL CTS § 202.5-a(a)(1). Refer to NY R UNIF TRIAL CTS § 202.5-a for information on the procedures for facsimile filing.

i. *NEW YORK COUNTY.* Unless indicated otherwise by the court in a particular case or in NY R NY CTY J RUL Doc. 1, Justices do not accept papers by fax. NY R NY CTY J RUL Rule 4.

2. *Service requirements*

a. *Who may serve.* Except where otherwise prescribed by law or order of court, papers may be served by any person not a party of the age of eighteen years or over. NY CPLR Rule 2103(a).

b. *Service upon attorney.* Except where otherwise prescribed by law or order of court, papers to be served upon a party in a pending action shall be served upon the party's attorney. Where the same attorney appears for two or more parties, only one (1) copy need be served upon the attorney. Such service upon an attorney shall be made:

i. By delivering the paper to the attorney personally. NY CPLR Rule 2103(b)(1).

ii. By mailing the paper to the attorney at the address designated by that attorney for that purpose or, if none is designated, at the attorney's last known address; service by mail shall be complete upon mailing. NY CPLR Rule 2103(b)(2).

iii. If the attorney's office is open, by leaving the paper with a person in charge, or if no person is in charge, by leaving it in a conspicuous place; or if the attorney's office is not open, by depositing the paper, enclosed in a sealed wrapper directed to the attorney, in the attorney's office letter drop or box. NY CPLR Rule 2103(b)(3).

iv. By leaving it at the attorney's residence within the state with a person of suitable age and discretion. Service upon an attorney shall not be made at the attorney's residence unless service at the attorney's office cannot be made. NY CPLR Rule 2103(b)(4).

v. By transmitting the paper to the attorney by facsimile transmission, provided that a facsimile telephone number is designated by the attorney for that purpose. Service by facsimile transmission shall be complete upon the receipt by the sender of a signal from the equipment of the attorney served indicating that the transmission was received, and the mailing of a copy of the paper to that attorney. The designation of a facsimile telephone number in the address block subscribed on a paper served or filed in the course of an action or proceeding shall constitute consent to service by facsimile transmission in accordance with NY CPLR Rule 2103(b)(5). An attorney may change or rescind a facsimile telephone number by serving a notice on the other parties. NY CPLR Rule 2103(b)(5).

vi. By dispatching the paper to the attorney by overnight delivery service at the address designated by the attorney for that purpose or, if none is designated, at the attorney's last known address. Service by overnight delivery service shall be complete upon deposit of the paper enclosed in a properly addressed wrapper into the custody of the overnight delivery service for overnight delivery, prior to the latest time designated by the overnight delivery service for overnight delivery. "Overnight delivery service" means any delivery service which regularly accepts items for overnight delivery to any address in the state. NY CPLR Rule 2103(b)(6).

vii. By transmitting the paper to the attorney by electronic means where and in the manner authorized by the chief administrator of the courts by rule and, unless such rule shall otherwise provide, such transmission shall be upon the party's written consent. The subject matter heading for each paper sent by electronic means must indicate that the matter being transmitted electronically is related to a court proceeding. NY CPLR Rule 2103(b)(7).

- *KINGS COUNTY.* Pursuant to the E-Filing Rules, service of interlocutory documents is made by posting a document to the NYSCEF site, which automatically and immediately transmits an email notice of the filing, including a link to the document, to all participating counsel and unrepresented litigants on the case. The Rules also authorize service by other methods permitted by the CPLR. If service by such other method is made, proof of service must be filed with NYSCEF. NY R L KINGS E FIL Doc. 1(I).
- *NEW YORK COUNTY.* Service. . .will be made automatically through NYSCEF upon all participating counsel and unrepresented parties in the case. There are limited exceptions to the requirement for e-filing in the covered kinds of cases. NY R NY CTY Procedure XI(A). Pursuant to the E-Filing Rules, service of interlocutory documents is made by posting a document to the NYSCEF site, which automatically and immediately transmits an e-mail notice of the filing, including a link to the document, to all participating counsel and unrepresented litigants on the case. The Rules also authorize service by other methods permitted by the CPLR. If service by such a method is made, proof of service must be filed with NYSCEF. NY R NY CTY E FIL Doc. 2(I).
- *QUEENS COUNTY.* Filing with the system permits counsel to serve the papers electronically pursuant to NY R UNIF TRIAL CTS § 202.5-b(f) once consent to E-Filing has been filed on-line. Consult NY R UNIF TRIAL CTS § 202.5-bb(c) for service in mandatory e-filing. Any required proof of service should be E-filed as a separate document. NY R L QUEENS E-FILE Doc. 1(E)(4).

c. *Electronic service mandatory; Consenting to electronic service; How electronic service may be made.* Except as otherwise provided in NY R UNIF TRIAL CTS § 202.5-bb, filing and service of all documents in an action that has been commenced electronically in accordance with NY R UNIF TRIAL CTS § 202.5-bb shall be by electronic means. NY R UNIF TRIAL CTS § 202.5-bb(c)(1).

i. *Party's consent required for certain e-filing.* After commencement of an action wherein e-filing is authorized, documents may be electronically filed and served, but only by, and electronic service shall be made only upon, a party or parties who have consented thereto. NY R UNIF TRIAL CTS § 202.5-b(b)(2)(i).

- A consent to e-filing in an action shall state that the party providing it agrees to the use of e-filing in the action and to be bound by the filing and service provisions in NY R UNIF TRIAL CTS § 202.5-b. NY R UNIF TRIAL CTS § 202.5-b(b)(2)(ii).

ii. *Address for service; Duty to notify as to changes.* The e-mail service address recorded at the time of registration is the e-mail address at which service of interlocutory documents on that party may be made through notification transmitted by the NYSCEF site. It is the responsibility of each filing user to monitor that address and promptly notify the Resource Center in the event of a change in his or her e-mail service address. NY R UNIF TRIAL CTS § 202.5-b(f)(2)(i).

iii. *How service made.* An e-filing party causes service of an interlocutory document to be made upon another party participating in e-filing by filing the document electronically. Upon receipt of an interlocutory document, the NYSCEF site shall automatically transmit electronic notification to all e-mail service addresses in such action. NY R UNIF TRIAL CTS § 202.5-b(f)(2)(ii).

- Except as provided otherwise in NY R UNIF TRIAL CTS § 202.5-b(h)(3), the electronic transmission of the notification shall constitute service of the document on the e-mail service addresses identified therein; however, such service will not be effective if the filing party learns that the notification did not reach the address of the person to be served. Proof of such service will be recorded on the NYSCEF site. A party may, however, utilize other service methods permitted by the CPLR provided that, if one of such other methods is used, proof of that service shall be filed electronically. NY R UNIF TRIAL CTS § 202.5-b(f)(2)(ii).

iv. *Signatures on hard copies; Proof of service filed electronically.* When an e-filing party serves a document in hard copy on a non-participating party, the document served shall bear full signatures of all signatories and proof of such service shall be filed electronically. NY R UNIF TRIAL CTS § 202.5-b(b)(2)(i).

- *ERIE COUNTY.* In the NYSCEF system, each Affidavit of Service must be uploaded as a separate .pdf file. After uploading the Affidavit, please choose the document type: "Affirmation/Affidavit of Service" and enter the name of the party served as Additional Document Information. NY R ERIE E FIL Doc. 3(III)(I).

v. *Effect of failure to consent.* A party's failure to consent to participation in electronic filing and service shall not bar any other party to the action from filing documents electronically with the County Clerk and the court or serving documents upon any other party who has consented to participation. A party who has not consented to participation shall file documents with the court and the County Clerk, and serve and be served with documents, in hard copy. NY R UNIF TRIAL CTS § 202.5-b(b)(2)(i).

d. *Service upon party.* If a party has not appeared by an attorney or the party's attorney cannot be served, service shall be upon the party by a method specified in NY CPLR Rule 2103(b)(1), NY CPLR Rule 2103(b)(2), NY CPLR Rule 2103(b)(4), NY CPLR Rule 2103(b)(5) or NY CPLR Rule 2103(b)(6). NY CPLR Rule 2103(c).

e. *Service on all parties.* Each paper served on any party shall be served on every other party who has appeared, except as otherwise may be provided by court order or as provided in NY CPLR § 3012 or in NY CPLR § 3215(f). Upon demand by a party, the plaintiff shall supply that party with a list of those who have appeared and the names and addresses of their attorneys. NY CPLR Rule 2103(e).

f. *Service by filing.* If a paper cannot be served by any of the methods specified in NY CPLR Rule 2103(b) and NY CPLR Rule 2103(c), service may be made by filing the paper as if it were a paper required to be filed. NY CPLR Rule 2103(d).

g. *Definitions.* For the purposes of NY CPLR Rule 2103:

i. "Mailing" means the deposit of a paper enclosed in a first class postpaid wrapper, addressed to the address designated by a person for that purpose or, if none is designated, at that person's last known address, in a post office or official depository under the exclusive care and custody of the United States Postal Service within the state;

ii. "Electronic means" means any method of transmission of information between computers or other machines designed for the purpose of sending and receiving such transmissions, and which allows the recipient to reproduce the information transmitted in a tangible medium of expression;

iii. "Facsimile transmission" means any method of transmission of documents to a facsimile machine at a remote location which can automatically produce a tangible copy of such documents. NY CPLR Rule 2103(f).

3. *Service on third-party defendants.* Refer to the New York KeyRules Complaint document for information on serving process on a newly added party.

G. Hearings

1. There is no hearing required or contemplated in the New York rules governing the answer.

H. Forms

1. New York Answer Forms

a. Form of answer. SIEGEL-NYPRAC § 228.

b. Answer. NYPRAC-COMM § 8:168.
c. Form; Third-party answer. NYPRAC-COMM § 9:34.
d. Sample breach of contract answer. NYPRAC-COMM § 72:45.
e. Answer and cross-claim. NYPRAC-COMM § 85:90.
f. Owner's answer, with affirmative defenses and counterclaims. NYPRAC-COMM § 121:37.
g. Answer with counterclaims. NYPRAC-LT § 14:522.

I. Applicable Rules

1. *State rules*
   a. Short title; Application; Construction; Definitions. NY CPLR § 101; NY CPLR § 104; NY CPLR § 105.
   b. Appendix of official forms. NY CPLR § 107.
   c. Method of computing periods of limitation generally. NY CPLR § 203.
   d. Service of process. NY CPLR § 312-a; NY CPLR Rule 320.
   e. Joinder. NY CPLR § 601; NY CPLR § 603.
   f. Parties generally. NY CPLR § 1001; NY CPLR § 1002; NY CPLR § 1004; NY CPLR § 1007; NY CPLR § 1008; NY CPLR Rule 1010; NY CPLR Rule 1011; NY CPLR § 1012.
   g. Motion for permission to proceed as a poor person; Affidavit; Certificate; Notice; Waiver of fee; When motion not required. NY CPLR § 1101.
   h. Extensions of time generally. NY CPLR § 2004.
   i. Form of papers. NY CPLR Rule 2101; NY CPLR Rule 2102; NY CPLR § 2105; NY CPLR Rule 2106; NY GEN BUS § 399-ddd; NY R UNIF TRIAL CTS § 215.2; NY R UNIF TRIAL CTS § 215.3.
   j. Service of papers. NY CPLR Rule 2103.
   k. Computation of time. NY CPLR § 2402; NY GEN CONSTR § 19; NY GEN CONSTR § 20; NY GEN CONSTR § 25-a; NY GEN CONSTR § 30; NY GEN CONSTR § 31; NY GEN CONSTR § 53.
   l. Particularity of statements generally; Particularity as to specific matters or actions. NY CPLR § 3005; NY CPLR § 3011; NY CPLR § 3012; NY CPLR § 3013; NY CPLR Rule 3014; NY CPLR Rule 3015; NY CPLR Rule 3016; NY CPLR § 3018; NY CPLR § 3019; NY CPLR Rule 3021; NY CPLR Rule 3022; NY CPLR Rule 3023; NY CPLR § 3026.
   m. Verification. NY CPLR § 3020.
   n. Motion to dismiss. NY CPLR Rule 3211.
   o. Fees; Index number fees of county clerks. NY CPLR § 8018.
   p. Hours of court. NY R CHIEF J § 3.1.
   q. Mandatory submission of actions to arbitration. NY R CHIEF J § 28.2.
   r. Application of part; Waiver; Additional rules; Application of CPLR; Definitions. NY R UNIF TRIAL CTS § 202.1.
   s. Papers filed in court; Electronic filing in supreme court. NY R UNIF TRIAL CTS § 202.5; NY R UNIF TRIAL CTS § 202.5-a; NY R UNIF TRIAL CTS § 202.5-b; NY R UNIF TRIAL CTS § 202.5-bb.
   t. Rules of the commercial division of the Supreme Court. NY R UNIF TRIAL CTS § 202.70.
   u. Signing of papers. NY R CHIEF ADMIN § 130-1.1-a.
2. *Local rules*
   a. *Albany County*
      i. Third judicial district rules. NY R 3 JD SUP Doc. 1.
   b. *Bronx County*
      i. Commercial division. NY R BRONX FIL R Doc. 12.
   c. *Erie County*
      i. Joint protocols for New York State Courts E-Filing (NYSCEF) cases filed in Supreme Court, Erie County. NY R ERIE E FIL Doc. 3.

d. *Kings County*
   i. Papers. NY R L KINGS Pt. A, Papers.
   ii. Protocol on courthouse and county clerk procedures for electronically filed cases. NY R L KINGS E FIL Doc. 1.

e. *New York County*
   i. Commencement of cases. NY R NY CTY Procedure I.
   ii. RJIs and assignments. NY R NY CTY Procedure IA.
   iii. County clerk litigation functions. NY R NY CTY Procedure XI.
   iv. Protocol on courthouse and county clerk procedures for electronically filed cases. NY R NY CTY E FIL Doc. 2.
   v. Redaction of information in documents filed with the county clerk and the court. NY R NY CTY J RUL Rule A-1.
   vi. Papers by fax. NY R NY CTY J RUL Rule 4.

f. *Onondaga County*
   i. Onondaga county protocol for case filings New York State Electronic Files (NYSCEF). NY R ONDGA E FIL Protocol.

g. *Queens County*
   i. Queens county protocol on courthouse procedures for electronically filed cases. NY R L QUEENS E-FILE Doc. 1.

J. Miscellaneous

NOTE: Individual judges' rules may apply.

ALBANY COUNTY

JUSTICE LISA M. FISHER: NY R 3 JD FISHER Fisher; NY R 3 JD FISHER Fisher, PC Order.

JUSTICE RICHARD MOTT: NY R 3 JD MOTT Mott.

JUSTICE STEPHAN G. SCHICK: NY R 3 JD Schick.

FORECLOSURE SETTLEMENT PART: NY R 3 JD Foreclosure Settlement.

BRONX COUNTY

JUSTICE PAUL L. ALPERT: [NY R BRONX J Part IA-29, as amended by NY ORDER 20-0337].

JUSTICE BEN BARBATO: NY R BRONX J Part IA-21.

JUSTICE MARY ANNE BRIGANTTI: [NY R BRONX J Part IA-15, as amended by NY ORDER 20-0338].

JUSTICE JOSEPH E. CAPELLA: NY R BRONX J Part IA-23.

JUSTICE MITCHELL DANZIGER: NY R BRONX J Part IA-3/33 ; [NY R BRONX J Danziger, Part IA-3/33, as amended by NY ORDER 20-0339].

JUSTICE LAURA G. DOUGLAS: NY R BRONX J Part IA-11.

JUSTICE RUBEN FRANCO: NY R BRONX J Part IA-26.

JUSTICE DORIS M. GONZALEZ: NY R BRONX J Part IA-24.

JUSTICE WILMA GUZMAN: NY R BRONX J Part IA-7; [NY R BRONX J Guzman, Part IA-7 Virtual, as amended by NY ORDER 20-0340].

JUSTICE ROBERT T. JOHNSON: NY R BRONX J Part IA-12.

JUSTICE DONALD A. MILES: NY R BRONX J Part IA-8.

JUSTICE DONNA M. MILLS: NY R BRONX J Part IA-9.

JUSTICE JULIA I. RODRIGUEZ: NY R BRONX J Part IA-18; [NY R BRONX J Part IA-27, as amended by NY ORDER 20-0341].

JUSTICE LLINET M. ROSADO: [NY R BRONX J Part IA-25, as amended by NY ORDER 20-0342].

JUSTICE NORMA RUIZ: NY R BRONX J Part IA-22; [NY R BRONX J Ruiz, Part IA-22 Virtual, as amended by NY ORDER 20-0343].

JUSTICE HOWARD H. SHERMAN: NY R BRONX J Part IA-4.
JUSTICE FERNANDO TAPIA: NY R BRONX J Part IA-13.
JUSTICE ELIZABETH A. TAYLOR: NY R BRONX J Part IA-2.
JUSTICE ALISON Y. TRUITT: NY R BRONX J Part IA-5.
PART IDV: NY R BRONX J Doc. 1.
PRE-TRIAL PART RULES: NY R BRONX J Doc. 2.
PRE TRIAL WORKSHEET: NY R BRONX J Doc. 3.
FORECLOSURE SETTLEMENT PART RULES: NY R BRONX J Doc. 4.
GUARDIANSHIP PART RULES: NY R BRONX J Doc. 5.
LPM PART RULES: NY R BRONX J Doc. 6.

ERIE COUNTY

JUSTICE M. WILLIAM BOLLER: NY R 8 JD J Boller.
JUSTICE RALPH A. BONIELLO: NY R 8 JD J Boniello.
JUSTICE CHRISTOPHER J. BURN: NY R 8 JD J Burns.
JUSTICE RUSSELL P. BUSCAGLIA: NY R 8 JD J Buscaglia.
JUSTICE FRANK CARUSO: NY R 8 JD J Caruso.
JUSTICE STEPHEN W. CASS: NY R 8 JD J Cass.
JUSTICE DEBORAH A. CHIMES: NY R 8 JD J Chimes.
JUSTICE EMILIO COLAIACOVO: [NY R 8 JD J Colaiacovo, as amended by NY ORDER 20-0252].
JUSTICE DIANE Y. DEVLIN: NY R 8 JD J Devlin.
JUSTICE JAMES H. DILLON: NY R 8 JD J Dillon.
JUSTICE PAULA L. FEROLETO: NY R 8 JD J Feroleto.
JUSTICE DANIEL J. FURLONG: [NY R 8 JD J Furlong, as amended by NY ORDER 20-0253].
JUSTICE JOSEPH R. GLOWNIA: NY R 8 JD J Glownia.
JUSTICE MARK J. GRISANTI: NY R 8 JD J Grisanti.
JUSTICE DEBORAH A. HAENDIGES: NY R 8 JD J Haendiges.
JUSTICE LYNN W. KEANE: [NY R 8 JD J Keane, as amended by NY ORDER 20-0254].
JUSTICE RICHARD C. KLOCH, Sr.: NY R 8 JD J Kloch.
JUSTICE FREDERICK J. MARSHALL: [NY R 8 JD J Marshall, as amended by NY ORDER 20-0255.
JUSTICE JOHN L. MICHALSKI: NY R 8 JD J Michalski.
JUSTICE MARK A. MONTOUR: [NY R 8 JD J Montour, as amended by NY ORDER 20-0256].
JUSTICE HENRY NOWAK: NY R 8 JD J Nowak.
JUSTICE JOHN F. O'DONNELL: NY R 8 JD J O'Donnell.
JUSTICE JEANETTE OGDEN: NY R 8 JD J Ogden.
JUSTICE CATHERINE NUGENT-PANEPINTO: NY R 8 JD J Nugent-Panepinto.
JUSTICE FRANK A. SEDITA, III: [NY R 8 JD J Sedita, as amended by NY ORDER 20-0257].
JUSTICE SARA SHELDON: NY R 8 JD J Sheldon.
JUSTICE DONNA M. SIWEK: NY R 8 JD J Siwek.
JUSTICE MARY L. SLISZ: NY R 8 JD J Slisz.
JUSTICE TIMOTHY J. WALKER: [NY R 8 JD J Walker, as amended by NY ORDER 20-0258].
JUSTICE DENNIS E. WARD: NY R 8 JD J Ward.
JUSTICE PAUL B. WOJTASZEK: [NY R 8 JD J Wojtaszek, as amended by NY ORDER 20-0259].

JUSTICE CHARLES N. ZAMBITO: [NY R 8 JD J Zambito, as amended by NY ORDER 20-0260].

SUPREME COURT LEGAL STAFF: NY R 8 JD J Legal Staff.

KINGS COUNTY

JUSTICE RACHEL A. ADAMS: NY R KINGS J Part 5F.

JUSTICE LOREN BAILY-SCHIFFMAN: NY R KINGS J Part 65.

JUSTICE REGINALD A. BODDIE: NY R KINGS J Part 95.

JUSTICE THERESA M. CICCOTTO: NY R KINGS J Part 19; NY R KINGS J Part 5J.

JUSTICE LISSETTE COLON: NY R KINGS J Part Rules.

JUSTICE GENINE EDWARDS: NY R KINGS J Part 80.

JUSTICE PAMELA L. FISHER: [NY R KINGS J Part 94, as amended by NY ORDER 20-0208].

JUSTICE ROBIN GARSON: NY R KINGS J Part 75.

JUSTICE LARA J. GENOVISI: [NY R KINGS J Part 34, as amended by NY ORDER 20-0209].

JUSTICE BERNARD J. GRAHAM: NY R KINGS J Part 36.

JUSTICE DAWN JIMENEZ-SALTA: NY R KINGS J Part 88.

JUSTICE INGRID JOSEPH: [NY R KINGS J Part FRP3 and Part 83, as amended by NY ORDER 20-0210].

JUSTICE KATHY J. KING: NY R KINGS J Part 64, 76K.

JUSTICE LAWRENCE KNIPEL: NY R KINGS J Part 57.

JUSTICE DONALD KURTZ: NY R KINGS J Part 26.

JUSTICE CARL LANDICINO: [NY R KINGS J Part 81, as amended by NY ORDER 20-0211].

JUSTICE KATHERINE LEVINE: [NY R KINGS J Part 20, 25, 92, as amended by NY ORDER 20-0211].

JUSTICE LORNA MCALLISTER: [NY R KINGS J Part 10, as amended by NY ORDER 20-0211].

JUSTICE ROSEMARIE MONTALBANO: [NY R KINGS J Part 19, 71, and 22, as amended by NY ORDER 20-0211].

JUSTICE RICHARD J. MONTELIONE: [NY R KINGS J Part 99 and DJMP, as amended by NY ORDER 20-0215].

JUSTICE LISA S. OTTLEY: NY R KINGS J Part 24.

JUSTICE MARK I. PARTNOW: NY R KINGS J Part 43.

JUSTICE ERIC I. PRUS: NY R KINGS J Part 5A.

JUSTICE FRANCOIS RIVERA: NY R KINGS J Part 52.

JUSTICE KAREN B. ROTHENBERG: NY R KINGS J Part 35.

JUSTICE LEON RUCHELSMAN: NY R KINGS J Part 1.

JUSTICE WAYNE P. SAITTA: NY R KINGS J Part 29.

JUSTICE ROBIN K. SHEARES: NY R KINGS J Part 96.

JUSTICE KENNETH P. SHERMAN: NY R KINGS J Part 67 and 78.

JUSTICE DEBRA SILBER: NY R KINGS J Part 9 and 5K.

JUSTICE ELLEN M. SPODEK: NY R KINGS J Part 63.

JUSTICE MARSHA L. STEINHARDT: NY R KINGS J Part 15.

JUSTICE JEFFREY S. SUNSHINE: NY R KINGS J Part 5G.

JUSTICE PETER P. SWEENEY: [NY R KINGS J Part 35, as amended by NY ORDER 20-0218].

JUSTICE DELORES J. THOMAS: [NY R KINGS J Part 5T, as amended by NY ORDER 20-0221].

JUSTICE WAVNY TOUSSAINT: NY R KINGS J Part 70.

JUSTICE RICHARD VELASQUEZ: NY R KINGS J Part 66.

JUSTICE CAROLYN E. WADE: NY R KINGS J Part 84.

JUSTICE EDWARD G. WALKER: [NY R KINGS J Part 90, as amended by NY ORDER 20-0219].

JUSTICE LILLIAN WAN: [NY R KINGS J Part 17, as amended by NY ORDER 20-0220].

JUSTICE MICHELLE WESTON: NY R KINGS J Part 3.

MENTAL HYGIENE PART: NY R KINGS J Part 77.

MATRIMONIAL PARTS DURING COVID-19 EMERGENCY: JUSTICE KAREN B. ROTHENBERG: NY R KINGS J Doc. 1.

NASSAU COUNTY

JUSTICE ANNA R. ANZALONE: NY R NASSAU S J Anzalone, Part 26.

JUSTICE STACY D. BENNETT: NY R NASSAU S J Bennett; NY R NASSAU S J Bennett, Form 1.

JUSTICE ANTONIO BRANDVEEN: NY R NASSAU S J Brandveen, Part 31.

JUSTICE JEFFREY S. BROWN: [NY R NASSAU S J Brown, as amended by NY ORDER 20-0297].

JUSTICE STEPHEN A. BUCARIA: NY R NASSAU S J Bucaria.

JUSTICE JULIANNE T. CAPETOLA: NY R NASSAU S J Capetola, Part 28.

JUSTICE EDMUND M. DANE: NY R NASSAU S J Dane, Part 33.

JUSTICE VITO M. DESTEFANO: NY R NASSAU S J DeStefano, Part 13; NY R NASSAU S J DeStefano, Form 1.

JUSTICE ARTHUR M. DIAMOND: NY R NASSAU S J Diamond, Part 7.

JUSTICE THOMAS FEINMAN: NY R NASSAU S J Feinman, Part 5.

JUSTICE JOHN M. GALASSO: NY R NASSAU S J Galasso, Part 22.

JUSTICE SHARON M.J. GIANELLI: NY R NASSAU S J Gianelli, Part 22; NY R NASSAU S J Gianelli, Form 1.

JUSTICE JEFFREY A. GOODSTEIN: NY R NASSAU S J Goodstein, Part 33; NY R NASSAU S J Goodstein, Form 1.

JUSTICE DAVID J. GUGERTY: [NY R NASSAU S J Gugerty, Part 31, as amended by NY ORDER 20-0298].

JUSTICE HELENE F. GUGERTY: NY R NASSAU S J Gugerty, Part 47.

JUSTICE STEVEN M. JAEGER: NY R NASSAU S J Jaeger, Part 35; NY R NASSAU S J Jaeger, Form 1.

JUSTICE JACK L. LIBERT: NY R NASSAU S J Libert, Part 23.

JUSTICE JOSEPH H. LORINTZ: NY R NASSAU S J Lorintz, Part 26; NY R NASSAU S J Lorintz, Form 1.

JUSTICE ROY S. MAHON: NY R NASSAU S J Mahon, Part 3.

JUSTICE RANDY SUE MARBER: NY R NASSAU S J Marber, Part 8.

JUSTICE JAMES P. MCCORMACK: [NY R NASSAU S J McCormack, Part 18, as amended by NY ORDER, 20-0299].

JUSTICE DICCIA T. PINEDA-KIRWAN: [NY R NASSAU S J Pineda-Kirwan, as amended by NY ORDER 20-0300].

JUSTICE THOMAS RADEMAKER: [NY R NASSAU S J Rademaker, Part 28, as amended by NY ORDER 20-0301]; [NY R NASSAU S J Rademaker, Form 1, as amended by NY ORDER 20-0301].

JUSTICE DENISE L. SHER: NY R NASSAU S J Rademaker, Part 32.

JUSTICE LEONARD D. STEINMAN: [NY R NASSAU S J Steinman, Part 15, as amended by NY ORDER 20-0303]; NY R NASSAU S J Steinman, Form 1.

JUSTICE HOWARD E. STURIM: NY R NASSAU S J Sturim, Part 50; NY R NASSAU S J Sturim, Form 1.

JUSTICE HELEN VOUTSINAS: [NY R NASSAU S J Voutsinas, Part 25, as amended by NY ORDER 20-0304]; [NY R NASSAU S J Voutsinas, Form 1, as amended by NY ORDER 20-0305].

JUSTICE HOPE SCHWARTZ ZIMMERMAN: NY R NASSAU S J Zimmerman, Part 17.

NEW YORK COUNTY

JUDGE'S RULES; BASIC INFORMATION: [NY R NY CTY J RUL Doc. 1, as amended by NY ORDER 20-0202].

ONONDAGA COUNTY

JUSTICE ROBERT E. ANTONACCI II: [NY R ONDGA E FIL Doc. 1, as amended by 20-0239].

JUSTICE MICHAEL V. COCCOMI: NY R ONDGA E FIL Doc. 2.

JUSTICE GREGORY R. GILBERT: NY R 5 JD JUDGES Gilbert; NY R ONDGA E FIL Doc. 3.

JUSTICE DONALD A. GREENWOOD: NY R ONDGA E FIL Doc. 4.

JUSTICE DEBORAH H. KARALUNAS: NY R ONDGA E FIL Doc. 5.

JUSTICE JAMES MCCLUSKY: NY R 5 JD MCCLUSKY McClusky.

JUSTICE CHARLES C. MERRELL: NY R 5 JD MERRELL Merrell.

JUSTICE PATRICK F. MACRAE: NY R 5 JD MACRAE Doc. 1.

JUSTICE JAMES P. MURPHY: NY R ONDGA E FIL Doc. 7.

JUSTICE GERALD J. NERI: [NY R 5 JD JUDGES Neri, as amended by NY ORDER 20-0236]; [NY R ONDGA E FIL Doc. 8, as amended by NY ORDER 20-0241].

JUSTICE ANTHONY J. PARIS: NY R 5 JD JUDGES Paris; [NY R ONDGA E FIL Doc. 9, as amended by NY ORDER 20-0242].

JUSTICE NORMAN W. SEITER, JR.: NY R 5 JD JUDGES Seiter.

JUSTICE KEVIN G. YOUNG: [NY R ONDGA E FIL Doc. 10, as amended by NY ORDER 20-0243].

QUEENS COUNTY

JUSTICE PAM JACKMAN BROWN: [NY R L QUEENS Brown, Part 19, as amended by NY ORDER 20-0321].

JUSTICE CHEREE A. BUGGS: NY R L QUEENS Buggs, Part 30.

JUSTICE PAM JACKMAN BROWN: [NY R L QUEENS Brown, Part 19, as amended by NY ORDER 20-0321].

JUSTICE DENIS J. BUTLER: NY R L QUEENS Butler, Part 12.

JUSTICE ROBERT I. CALORAS: [NY R L QUEENS Caloras, Part 36, as amended by NY ORDER 20-0322].

JUSTICE ANNA CULLEY: NY R L QUEENS Culley, Part 53.

JUSTICE TIMOTHY DUFFICY: NY R L QUEENS Dufficy, Part 35.

JUSTICE DAVID ELLIOT: NY R L QUEENS Elliot, Part 14.

JUSTICE JOSEPH J. ESPOSITO: NY R L QUEENS Esposito, Part 6.

JUSTICE DARRELL L. GAVRIN: [NY R L QUEENS Gavrin, Part 27, as amended by NY ORDER 20-0323].

JUSTICE WYATT N. GIBBONS: [NY R L QUEENS Gibbons, Part 5, as amended by NY ORDER 20-0330.

JUSTICE DONNA-MARIE E. GOLIA: [NY R L QUEENS Golia, Part 21, as amended by NY ORDER 20-0331].

JUSTICE MARGUERITE A. GRAYS: [NY R L QUEENS Grays, Part 4, as amended by NY ORDER 20-0324].

JUSTICE RUDOLPH E. GRECO: [NY R L QUEENS Greco, Part 32, as amended by NY ORDER 20-0325].

JUSTICE MAUREEN HEALY: NY R L QUEENS Healy, Part 6.

JUSTICE PHILLIP HOM: [NY R L QUEENS Hom, Part 43, as amended by NY ORDER 20-0332].

JUSTICE KEVIN J. KERRIGAN: NY R L QUEENS Kerrigan, Part 10.

JUSTICE MOJGAN C. LANCMAN: NY R L QUEENS Lancman, Part 20.

JUSTICE RICHARD G. LATIN: NY R L QUEENS Latin, Part 40.

JUSTICE ULYSSES B. LEVERETT: [NY R L QUEENS Leverett, Part 6, as amended by NY ORDER 20-0326].

JUSTICE LEONARD LIVOTE: NY R L QUEENS Livote, Part 33.

JUSTICE LEE A. MAYERSOHN: NY R L QUEENS Mayersohn, Part 22; NY R L QUEENS Mayersohn, Part 22G; [NY R L QUEENS Mayersohn, Part 22G COVID, as amended by NY ORDER 20-0327].

JUSTICE ROBERT J. MCDONALD: NY R L QUEENS McDonald, Part 34.

JUSTICE MARGARET MCGOWAN: NY R L QUEENS McGowan, Part 52.

JUSTICE MAURICE E. MUIR: [NY R L QUEENS Muir, Part 42, as amended by NY ORDER 20-0333].

JUSTICE JODI ORLOW: NY R L QUEENS Orlow, Part 51.

JUSTICE LESLIE J. PURIFICCION: NY R L QUEENS Purificcion, Part 39.

JUSTICE JOSEPH RISI: [NY R L QUEENS Risi, Part 3, as amended by NY ORDER 20-0328].

JUSTICE FREDERICK D.R. SAMPSON: [NY R L QUEENS Sampson, Part 31, as amended by NY ORDER 20-0329].

JUSTICE MARTIN J. SCHULMAN: NY R L QUEENS Schulman, Part 29.

JUSTICE BERNICE D. SIEGAL: NY R L QUEENS Siegal, Part 25G.
JUSTICE JANICE A. TAYLOR: NY R L QUEENS Taylor, Part 15.
JUSTICE CARMEN R. VELASQUEZ: NY R L QUEENS Velasquez, Part 38.
JUSTICE LOURDES M VENTURA: [NY R L QUEENS Ventura, Part 37, as amended by NY ORDER 20-0334].
JUSTICE WILLIAM A. VISCOVICH: NY R L QUEENS Viscovich, Part 63.
JUSTICE ALLAN B. WEISS: NY R L QUEENS Weiss, Part 2.
COMPLIANCE, SETTLEMENT AND CONFERENCE PART: NY R L QUEENS Doc 1.
PRELIMINARY CONFERENCE PART: [NY R L QUEENS Doc. 2, as amended by NY ORDER 20-0335].
MEDICAL MALPRACTICE CONFERENCE PART: [NY R L QUEENS Doc. 3, as amended by NY ORDER 20-0336].
TRIAL SCHEDULING PART: NY R L QUEENS Doc. 4.
SUMMARY JURY TRIAL PROGRAM: NY R L QUEENS Doc. 7.
RESIDENTIAL FORECLOSURE PART: NY R L QUEENS Doc. 9.
FORECLOSURE AUCTION RULES: NY R L QUEENS Doc. 10.
MATRIMONIAL PRELIMINARY CONFERENCE PART: NY R L QUEENS Doc. 11.
NON-CUSTODIAL CONTESTED MATRIMONIAL PART: NY R L QUEENS Doc. 12.

Pleadings
Demand for Bill of Particulars

Document Last Updated August 2020

A. Checklist

(I) ❑ Matters to consider for party demanding bill of particulars
- (a) ❑ Required documents
  - (1) ❑ Demand for bill of particulars
  - (2) ❑ Proof of service
- (b) ❑ Supplemental documents
  - (1) ❑ Filing fees
  - (2) ❑ Working copies
  - (3) ❑ Statement of authorization in electronic filing cases
  - (4) ❑ ERIE COUNTY: Additional supplemental documents
    - (i) ❑ Notice of hard copy submission in e-filed case
  - (5) ❑ KINGS COUNTY: Additional supplemental documents
    - (i) ❑ Forms when filing in hard copy
  - (6) ❑ NEW YORK COUNTY: Additional supplemental documents
    - (i) ❑ Notice of hard copy submission
  - (7) ❑ ONONDAGA COUNTY: Additional supplemental documents
    - (i) ❑ Notice of hard copy submission
  - (8) ❑ QUEENS COUNTY: Additional supplemental documents
    - (i) ❑ Notice of hard copy submission
- (c) ❑ Timing
  - (1) ❑ There is no stated time for when the demand may be served, but ordinarily it should not be served before joinder of issue
  - (2) ❑ The common practice for the defendant is to serve the demand with or after the answer

(3) ❑ If the plaintiff wants a bill regarding affirmative defenses in the answer, the plaintiff can demand it any time after the answer is served; if the answer contains a counterclaim, a demand for a bill of particulars pertaining to the counterclaim may be served with or after the reply

(II) ❑ Matters to consider for party furnishing bill of particulars

(a) ❑ Required documents

(1) ❑ Bill of particulars

(2) ❑ Proof of service

(b) ❑ Supplemental documents

(1) ❑ Supporting evidence; Exhibits

(2) ❑ Filing fees

(3) ❑ Working copies

(4) ❑ ERIE COUNTY: Additional supplemental documents

(i) ❑ Notice of hard copy submission in e-filed case

(5) ❑ KINGS COUNTY: Additional supplemental documents

(i) ❑ Forms when filing in hard copy

(6) ❑ NEW YORK COUNTY: Additional supplemental documents

(i) ❑ Notice of hard copy submission

(7) ❑ ONONDAGA COUNTY: Additional supplemental documents

(i) ❑ Notice of hard copy submission

(8) ❑ QUEENS COUNTY: Additional supplemental documents

(i) ❑ Notice of hard copy submission

(c) ❑ Timing

(1) ❑ Within thirty (30) days of service of a demand for a bill of particulars, the party on whom the demand is made shall serve a bill of particulars complying with each item of the demand, except any item to which the party objects, in which event the reasons for the objection shall be stated with reasonable particularity

B. Timing

1. *Service of demand for bill of particulars.* There is no stated time for when the demand may be served, but ordinarily it should not be served before joinder of issue. The common practice for the defendant is to serve the demand with or after the answer. SIEGEL-NYPRAC § 239.

   a. *Plaintiff's demand.* If the plaintiff wants a bill regarding affirmative defenses in the answer, the plaintiff can demand it any time after the answer is served; if the answer contains a counterclaim, a demand for a bill of particulars pertaining to the counterclaim may be served with or after the reply. SIEGEL-NYPRAC § 239.

2. *Time for initial appearance.* The defendant appears by serving an answer or a notice of appearance, or by making a motion which has the effect of extending the time to answer. An appearance shall be made within twenty (20) days after service of the summons, except that if the summons was served on the defendant by delivering it to an official of the state authorized to receive service in his behalf or if it was served pursuant to NY CPLR § 303, NY CPLR § 308(2), NY CPLR § 308(3), NY CPLR § 308(4) or NY CPLR § 308(5), or NY CPLR § 313, NY CPLR § 314 or NY CPLR § 315, the appearance shall be made within thirty (30) days after service is complete. NY CPLR Rule 320(a).

   a. *Extension of time when complaint not served with summons.* If the complaint is not served with the summons, the time to appear may be extended as provided in NY CPLR § 3012(b). NY CPLR Rule 320(a).

   b. *Written demand for complaint; Effect on time to appear.* If the complaint is not served with the summons, the defendant may serve a written demand for the complaint within the time provided in NY CPLR Rule 320(a) for an appearance. Service of the demand shall extend the time to appear until twenty (20) days after service of the complaint. A demand or motion under NY CPLR § 3012(b) does not of itself constitute an appearance in the action. NY CPLR § 3012(b).

3. *Time to acknowledge service of initiating papers*

   a. *Served by electronic means.* A party served by electronic means shall, within twenty-four (24) hours of service, provide the serving party or attorney with an electronic confirmation that the service has been effected. NY R UNIF TRIAL CTS § 202.5-b(f)(1); NY R UNIF TRIAL CTS § 202.5-bb(b)(3).

b. *Served by mail.* The defendant, an authorized employee of the defendant, defendant's attorney or an employee of the attorney must complete the acknowledgement of receipt and mail or deliver one (1) copy of it within thirty (30) days from the date of receipt. Service is complete on the date the signed acknowledgement of receipt is mailed or delivered to the sender. The signed acknowledgement of receipt shall constitute proof of service. NY CPLR § 312-a(b)(1).

   i. *Acknowledgement to be sworn.* The acknowledgement of receipt of service shall be subscribed and affirmed as true under penalties of perjury and shall have the same force and effect as an affidavit. NY CPLR § 312-a(c).

   ii. *Time for answer after acknowledgement.* Where a complaint or petition is served with the summons or notice of petition, the defendant shall serve an answer within twenty (20) days after the date the signed acknowledgement of receipt is mailed or delivered to the sender. NY CPLR § 312-a(b)(2).

4. *Computation of time*

a. *Units of time*

   i. *Day.* A calendar day includes the time from midnight to midnight. Sunday or any day of the week specifically mentioned means a calendar day. NY GEN CONSTR § 19.

   ii. *Month.* In a statute, contract or public or private instrument, unless otherwise provided in such contract or instrument or by law, the term month means a calendar month and not a lunar month. NY GEN CONSTR § 31.

   iii. *Year.* For information on the definition of a year, including the definitions of a half-year and quarter-year, refer to NY GEN CONSTR § 58 and NY GEN CONSTR § 50. For information on leap years, refer to NY GEN CONSTR § 57.

b. *Periods of time*

   i. *Number of days.* A number of days specified as a period from a certain day within which or after or before which an act is authorized or required to be done means such number of calendar days exclusive of the calendar day from which the reckoning is made. NY GEN CONSTR § 20.

   - If such period is a period of two (2) days, Saturday, Sunday or a public holiday must be excluded from the reckoning if it is an intervening day between the day from which the reckoning is made and the last day of the period. NY GEN CONSTR § 20.
   - In computing any specified period of time from a specified event, the day upon which the event happens is deemed the day from which the reckoning is made. The day from which any specified period of time is reckoned shall be excluded in making the reckoning. NY GEN CONSTR § 20.

   ii. *Number of months.* A number of months after or before a certain day shall be computed by counting such number of calendar months from such day, exclusive of the calendar month in which such day occurs, and shall include the day of the month in the last month so counted having the same numerical order in days of the month as the day from which the computation is made, unless there be not so many days in the last month so counted, in which case the period computed shall expire with the last day of the month so counted. NY GEN CONSTR § 30.

   iii. *Publication of notice; Number of days.* The period of publication of a legal notice shall be computed by excluding the first day of publication and including the day on which the act or event of which notice is given is to take place or which completes the full period of publication. NY CPLR § 2402.

   iv. *Periods ending on Saturday, Sunday or public holiday.* When any period of time, computed from a certain day, within which or after which or before which an act is authorized or required to be done, ends on a Saturday, Sunday or a public holiday, such act may be done on the next succeeding business day and if the period ends at a specified hour, such act may be done at or before the same hour of such next succeeding business day, except that where a period of time specified by contract ends on a Saturday, Sunday or a public holiday, the extension of such period is governed by NY GEN CONSTR § 25. NY GEN CONSTR § 25-a(1).

   - For a list of public holidays, refer to NY GEN CONSTR § 24.

   v. *Additional time after certain kinds of service*

   - *Service by mail.* Where a period of time prescribed by law is measured from the service of a paper and service is by mail, five (5) days shall be added to the prescribed period. NY CPLR Rule 2103(b)(2).
   - *Service by overnight delivery service.* Where a period of time prescribed by law is measured from the service of a paper and service is by overnight delivery, one (1) business day shall be added to the prescribed period. NY CPLR Rule 2103(b)(6).

vi. *Daylight saving time.* For information on New York's time zone and the effect of daylight saving time, refer to NY GEN CONSTR § 52.

c. *Hours of court.* Notwithstanding any provision of law or rule of court to the contrary, throughout the State of New York the sessions of the Supreme Court for the disposition of business before the court shall commence not later than 9:30 a.m. and conclude not earlier than 5 p.m. Where warranted, the Chief Administrator of the Courts may authorize variances in the opening and closing hours of the courts, but, in such event, daily sessions shall total not less than six (6) hours. NY R CHIEF J § 3.1.

d. *Time limits; Extension of time.* Any act required by or in pursuance of law to be performed at or within a prescribed time, shall be performed according to the standard time. NY GEN CONSTR § 53.

i. Except where otherwise expressly prescribed by law, the court may extend the time fixed by any statute, rule or order for doing any act, upon such terms as may be just and upon good cause shown, whether the application for extension is made before or after the expiration of the time fixed. NY CPLR § 2004. Refer to the New York KeyRules Motion for Continuance/Extension of Time document for more information.

C. General Requirements

1. *Demand for bill of particulars.* Any party may require any other party to give a bill of particulars of such party's claim, or a copy of the items of the account alleged in a pleading. As used elsewhere in Article 30 of the CPLR (NY CPLR § 3001, et seq.), the term "bill of particulars" shall include "copy of the items of an account." NY CPLR § 3041. A demand for a bill of particulars shall be made by serving a written demand stating the items concerning which particulars are desired. NY CPLR Rule 3042(a).

a. *Role of bill of particulars.* A "bill of particulars" in civil practice is an amplification of a pleading. It supplies more detail and therefore affords the adverse party a more thorough picture of the claim or defense being particularized. It's designed to limit the proof and prevent surprise at the trial. SIEGEL-NYPRAC § 238; State v. Horsemen's Benev. & Protective Ass'n (New York Div.), 34 A.D.2d 769, 770, 311 N.Y.S.2d 511, 512 (1970).

b. *What must be particularized; Burdens.* Parties are required to particularize only that of which they have the burden of proof, and a bill of particulars is as a rule served only when demanded. Plaintiffs must particularize their claims, and defendants their defenses, counterclaims, cross-claims, and third-party claims. But the defendant need not particularize denials contained in the answer because the matters involved are the plaintiff's burden to prove, not the defendant's. SIEGEL-NYPRAC § 238; NY CPLR § 3041; L. F. Dommerich & Co. v. Diener & Dorskind, Inc., 31 A.D.2d 516, 516, 294 N.Y.S.2d 613, 614 (1968).

c. *Bill of particulars not used to obtain evidence.* It is the general rule that a bill of particulars is not usable to obtain evidence. SIEGEL-NYPRAC § 238; Yardarm Club Hotel, Inc. v. Morgan, 22 A.D.2d 700, 700, 253 N.Y.S.2d 920, 921 (1964).

d. *Demand and bill are specific to case.* What a party may demand in a bill—and the demand, as long as it is reasonable, determines the bill's contents—is necessarily personal to the particular case. Whatever the pleading pleads, the bill must particularize. With the exception of the personal injury action, where the items that may be demanded have been codified into a list, the things that may be demanded and thus must be particularized are a sui generis inquiry. SIEGEL-NYPRAC § 238.

e. *Demand in personal injury case.* In actions to recover for personal injuries the following particulars may be required:

i. The date and approximate time of day of the occurrence;

ii. Its approximate location;

iii. General statement of the acts or omissions constituting the negligence claimed;

iv. Where notice of a condition is a prerequisite, whether actual or constructive notice is claimed;

v. If actual notice is claimed, a statement of when and to whom it was given;

vi. Statement of the injuries and description of those claimed to be permanent, and in an action designated in NY INS § 5104(a), for personal injuries arising out of negligence in the use or operation of a motor vehicle in this state, in what respect plaintiff has sustained a serious injury, as defined in NY INS § 5102(d), or economic loss greater than basic economic loss, as defined in NY INS § 5102(a);

vii. Length of time confined to bed and to house;

viii. Length of time incapacitated from employment; and

ix. Total amounts claimed as special damages for physicians' services and medical supplies; loss of earnings, with name and address of the employer; hospital expenses; nurses' services. NY CPLR Rule 3043(a).

x. A party may serve a supplemental bill of particulars with respect to claims of continuing special damages and disabilities without leave of court at any time, but not less than thirty (30) days prior to trial. Provided however that no new cause of action may be alleged or new injury claimed and that the other party shall upon seven (7) days notice, be entitled to newly exercise any and all rights of discovery but only with respect to such continuing special damages and disabilities. NY CPLR Rule 3043(b).

xi. Nothing contained in the foregoing shall be deemed to limit the court in denying in a proper case, any one or more of the foregoing particulars, or in a proper case, in granting other, further or different particulars. NY CPLR Rule 3043(c). The list is, nonetheless, the standard for personal injury litigation and the court seldom has occasion to stray far from it. SIEGEL-NYPRAC § 238.

f. *Failure to respond or to comply with demand.* If a party fails to respond to a demand in a timely fashion or fails to comply fully with a demand, the party seeking the bill of particulars may move to compel compliance, or, if such failure is willful, for the imposition of penalties pursuant to NY CPLR Rule 3042(d). NY CPLR Rule 3042(c).

i. If a party served with a demand for a bill of particulars willfully fails to provide particulars which the court finds ought to have been provided pursuant to NY CPLR Rule 3042, the court may make such final or conditional order with regard to the failure or refusal as is just, including such relief as is set forth in NY CPLR § 3126. NY CPLR Rule 3042(d).

g. *Improper or unduly burdensome demand.* If the court concludes that the demand for particulars, or a part thereof, is improper or unduly burdensome, in addition to vacating or modifying the demand, the court may make such order with regard to the improper or unduly burdensome demand as is just. NY CPLR Rule 3042(e).

2. *Effect of defendant's appearance.* Subject to the provisions of NY CPLR Rule 320(c), an appearance of the defendant is equivalent to personal service of the summons upon him, unless an objection to jurisdiction under NY CPLR Rule 3211(a)(8) is asserted by motion or in the answer as provided in NY CPLR Rule 3211. NY CPLR Rule 320(b).

a. *Appearance not conferring jurisdiction; Limited appearance.* When the court's jurisdiction is not based upon personal service on the defendant, an appearance is not equivalent to personal service upon the defendant:

i. In a case specified in NY CPLR § 314(3), if jurisdiction is based solely upon a levy on defendant's property within the state pursuant to an order of attachment; or

ii. In any other case specified in NY CPLR § 314, if an objection to jurisdiction under NY CPLR Rule 3211(a)(8) or NY CPLR Rule 3211(a)(9), or both, is asserted by motion or in the answer as provided in NY CPLR Rule 3211, unless the defendant proceeds with the defense after asserting the objection to jurisdiction and the objection is not ultimately sustained. NY CPLR Rule 320(c).

b. *Effect on publication of summons.* Where the defendant appears during the period of publication of a summons against him, the service by publication shall be deemed completed by the appearance. NY CPLR Rule 320(d).

3. *Governing law.* The civil practice law and rules (NY CPLR § 101, et seq.) shall govern the procedure in civil judicial proceedings in all courts of the state and before all judges, except where the procedure is regulated by inconsistent statute. The civil practice law and rules shall succeed the civil practice act and rules of civil practice and shall be deemed substituted therefor throughout the statutes and rules of the state. NY CPLR § 101. The civil practice law and rules shall be liberally construed to secure the just, speedy and inexpensive determination of every civil judicial proceeding. NY CPLR § 104.

a. *Uniform trial court rules.* The uniform civil rules for the Supreme Court and County Court (NY R UNIF TRIAL CTS § 202.1, et seq.) shall be applicable to civil actions and proceedings in the Supreme Court and the County Court. NY R UNIF TRIAL CTS § 202.1(a). The provisions of the uniform rules shall be construed consistent with the Civil Practice Law and Rules (CPLR), and matters not covered by the uniform rules shall be governed by the CPLR. NY R UNIF TRIAL CTS § 202.1(d).

b. *Local rules.* Local court rules, not inconsistent with law or with uniform civil rules for the Supreme Court and County Court (NY R UNIF TRIAL CTS § 202.1, et seq.), shall comply with Part 9 of the Rules of the Chief Judge (NY R CHIEF J § 9.1). NY R UNIF TRIAL CTS § 202.1(c).

c. *Official forms.* The state administrator shall have the power to adopt, amend and rescind an appendix of forms. Forms adopted pursuant to NY CPLR § 107 shall be sufficient under the civil practice law and rules and shall illustrate the simplicity and brevity of statement which the civil practice law and rules contemplate. NY CPLR § 107.

4. *Rules of the commercial division.* [Editor's note: certain types of civil cases or civil cases meeting certain monetary thresholds that are filed in the state of New York must be filed in the Commercial Division of the New York Supreme

Courts. Rules governing practice in the commercial division are found in NY R UNIF TRIAL CTS § 202.70]. Cases which must be filed in the commercial division are listed below. For more information, refer to NY R UNIF TRIAL CTS § 202.70.

a. *Monetary thresholds.* Except as set forth in NY R UNIF TRIAL CTS § 202.70(b), the monetary thresholds of the Commercial Division, exclusive of punitive damages, interests, costs, disbursements and counsel fees claimed, are established as follows: (1) Albany County, fifty thousand dollars ($50,000); (2) Eighth Judicial District, one hundred thousand dollars ($100,000); (3) Kings County, one hundred fifty thousand dollars ($150,000); (4) Nassau County, two hundred thousand dollars ($200,000); (5) New York County, five hundred thousand dollars ($500,000); (6) Onondaga County, fifty thousand dollars ($50,000); (7) Queens County, one hundred thousand dollars ($100,000); (8) Seventh Judicial District, fifty thousand dollars ($50,000); (9) Suffolk County, one hundred thousand dollars ($100,000); and (10) Westchester County, one hundred thousand dollars ($100,000). NY R UNIF TRIAL CTS § 202.70(a).

   i. *ALBANY COUNTY.* The Commercial Division of the Albany County Supreme Court exercises jurisdiction over selected business and commercial disputes in which the amount at issue generally involves damage claims in a minimum amount of fifty thousand dollars ($50,000) as well as claims for unspecified amounts where the value of the commercial asset(s) in dispute exceeds fifty thousand dollars ($50,000). A separate publication promulgating the rules and criteria relating to the filing and management of Commercial Court cases in this part may be obtained from the Albany County Supreme Court Clerk's Office. A section of the Uniform Civil Rules for the Supreme Court and County Court sets forth statewide rules. NY R 3 JD SUP Doc. 1(E).

   ii. *BRONX COUNTY.* The monetary threshold for commercial cases in Bronx County will be seventy-five thousand dollars ($75,000). All other parameters including the type of matters that will be heard are contained within the Rules of the Commercial Division of the Supreme Court (NY R UNIF TRIAL CTS § 202.70). NY R BRONX FIL R Doc. 12.

   iii. *NEW YORK COUNTY.* The monetary threshold in the New York County Commercial Division, which is generally applicable, is an amount in controversy of five hundred thousand dollars ($500,000) or more (exclusive of punitive damages, interest, costs, disbursements, and counsel fees). If the case is designated a commercial one and the Addendum is submitted, the clerk will review the pleadings to determine whether the amount in controversy in the case meets the monetary threshold or whether an exception to the threshold applies. NY R NY CTY Procedure IA(B). For more information on assigning a case to the commercial division in New York County, refer to NY R NY CTY Procedure IA(B).

b. *Commercial cases.* Actions in which the principal claims involve or consist of the following will be heard in the Commercial Division provided that the monetary threshold is met or equitable or declaratory relief is sought:

   i. Breach of contract or fiduciary duty, fraud, misrepresentation, business tort (e.g., unfair competition), or statutory and/or common law violation where the breach or violation is alleged to arise out of business dealings (e.g., sales of assets or securities; corporate restructuring; partnership, shareholder, joint venture, and other business agreements; trade secrets; restrictive covenants; and employment agreements not including claims that principally involve alleged discriminatory practices);

   ii. Transactions governed by the Uniform Commercial Code (exclusive of those concerning individual cooperative or condominium units);

   iii. Transactions involving commercial real property, including Yellowstone injunctions and excluding actions for the payment of rent only;

   iv. Shareholder derivative actions—without consideration of the monetary threshold;

   v. Commercial class actions—without consideration of the monetary threshold;

   vi. Business transactions involving or arising out of dealings with commercial banks and other financial institutions;

   vii. Internal affairs of business organizations;

   viii. Malpractice by accountants or actuaries, and legal malpractice arising out of representation in commercial matters;

   ix. Environmental insurance coverage;

   x. Commercial insurance coverage (e.g., directors and officers, errors and omissions, and business interruption coverage);

   xi. Dissolution of corporations, partnerships, limited liability companies, limited liability partnerships and joint ventures—without consideration of the monetary threshold; and

xii. Applications to stay or compel arbitration and affirm or disaffirm arbitration awards and related injunctive relief pursuant to Article 75 of the New York Civil Practice Law and Rules (NY CPLR § 7501, et seq.) involving any of the foregoing enumerated commercial issues. Where the applicable arbitration agreement provides for the arbitration to be heard outside the United States, the monetary threshold set forth in NY R UNIF TRIAL CTS § 202.70(a) shall not apply. NY R UNIF TRIAL CTS § 202.70(b).

c. *Non-commercial cases.* The following will not be heard in the Commercial Division even if the monetary threshold is met:

i. Suits to collect professional fees;

ii. Cases seeking a declaratory judgment as to insurance coverage for personal injury or property damage;

iii. Residential real estate disputes, including landlord-tenant matters, and commercial real estate disputes involving the payment of rent only;

iv. Home improvement contracts involving residential properties consisting of one to four residential units or individual units in any residential building, including cooperative or condominium units;

v. Proceedings to enforce a judgment regardless of the nature of the underlying case;

vi. First-party insurance claims and actions by insurers to collect premiums or rescind non-commercial policies; and

vii. Attorney malpractice actions except as otherwise provided in NY R UNIF TRIAL CTS § 202.70(b)(8). NY R UNIF TRIAL CTS § 202.70(c).

d. For more information on the Commercial Division, refer to NY R UNIF TRIAL CTS § 202.70.

D. Documents

1. *Required documents*

a. *Demand for bill of particulars.* Refer to the General Requirements section of this document for information on the demand for bill of particulars.

b. *Proof of service.* In addition to complying with the provisions of NY CPLR Rule 2101, every paper filed in court shall have annexed thereto appropriate proof of service on all parties where required. NY R UNIF TRIAL CTS § 202.5(a).

2. *Supplemental documents*

a. *Filing fees.* The County Clerk shall require the payment of any applicable statutory fees, or an order of the Court waiving payment of such fees, before accepting a paper for filing. NY R UNIF TRIAL CTS § 202.5(d)(1). For information on filing fees, if any, refer to NY CPLR § 8001, et seq.

b. *Working copies.* The court may require the parties to provide working copies of documents filed electronically. In such event, each working copy shall include, firmly affixed thereto, a copy of a confirmation notice in a form prescribed by the Chief Administrator. NY R UNIF TRIAL CTS § 202.5-b(d)(5).

c. *Statement of authorization in electronic filing cases.* A filing agent (other than one employed by a governmental entity) shall e-file a statement of authorization from counsel of record in an action, in a form approved by the Chief Administrator, prior to or together with the first e-filing in that action by the agent on behalf of that counsel. NY R UNIF TRIAL CTS § 202.5-b(d)(1)(i).

d. *ERIE COUNTY: Additional supplemental documents*

i. *Notice of hard copy submission in e-filed case.* In accordance with NY R UNIF TRIAL CTS § 202.5-b(d), the County Clerk shall refuse to accept for filing, hard copy papers filed to an action subject to electronic filing unless hard copy filing is permitted by the Uniform Rules or NY R ERIE E FIL Doc. 3 and the papers bear a completed Notice of Hard Copy Submission—E-Filed Case form. NY R ERIE E FIL Doc. 3(III)(D).

e. *KINGS COUNTY: Additional supplemental documents*

i. *Forms when filing in hard copy.* An attorney who certifies in good faith that he or she lacks the equipment or knowledge needed to e-file and have no staff member or employee under his or her direction who has such knowledge and equipment may opt out of participation in e-filing in a mandatory case by filing a "Notice of Opt-Out from Participation in Action Subject to Mandatory Electronic Filing" form EFM-2 with the Clerk. NY R L KINGS E FIL Doc. 1(A)(2). Where in accordance with the E-Filing Rules a party submits a document in hard copy in an e-filed case (principally, a document submitted by a nonparticipating party (e.g., an attorney) in a consensual case, an emergency filing made in accordance with the Mandatory E-Filing Rules, and any document filed with the court in hard copy by an attorney who has opted out of participation in mandatory e-filing, the document must bear the back page facing out, a "Notice of Hard Copy Submission—E-Filed Cases" form EFM-3. NY R L KINGS E FIL Doc. 1(B)(3).

f. *NEW YORK COUNTY: Additional supplemental documents*

i. *Notice of hard copy submission.* Where in accordance with the E-Filing Rules an attorney or an unrepresented litigant who is participating in e-filing submits a document in hard copy in an e-filed case, the document must bear, as the back page facing out, a Notice of Hard-Copy Submission—E-Filed Case (a form available in the "Forms" section on the NYSCEF website (Form EFM-3) and in the court's back offices). NY R NY CTY E FIL Doc. 2(B)(3). For more information refer to NY R NY CTY E FIL Doc. 2.

g. *ONONDAGA COUNTY: Additional supplemental documents*

i. *Notice of hard copy submission.* Any papers to be filed with the court in an e-filed case must be filed online with the E-filing system except where a special exemption is granted (e.g., oversized maps, photographs). If such an exemption is granted, Form EFM-3, "Notice of Hard Copy Submission—E-Filed Case," must be attached to such documents forms which are not filed on line. Also, Form EFM-4 "Notice of Hard Copy Exhibit Filing" must be completed and uploaded to the action's e-file. Both of these forms may be found on the NYSCEF website. NY R ONDGA E FIL Protocol(B)(4).

h. *QUEENS COUNTY: Additional supplemental documents*

i. *Notice of hard copy submission.* Any party opting out of the e-filing system must have a "Notice of Hard Copy Submission" firmly affixed to the back of the papers. NY R L QUEENS E-FILE Doc. 1(H)(2)(f).

E. Format

1. *Form of documents*

a. *Size and form of paper.* Each paper served or filed shall be durable, white and, except for summonses, subpoenas, notices of appearance, notes of issue, orders of protection, temporary orders of protection and exhibits, shall be eleven by eight and one-half (11 x 8-1/2) inches in size. NY CPLR Rule 2101(a).

b. *Writing and language.* The writing shall be legible and in black ink. NY CPLR Rule 2101(a). Each paper served or filed shall be in the English language which, where practicable, shall be of ordinary usage. NY CPLR Rule 2101(b).

c. *Caption.* Each paper served or filed shall begin with a caption setting forth the name of the court, the venue, the title of the action, the nature of the paper and the index number of the action if one has been assigned. In all papers other than a summons, a complaint or a judgment it shall be sufficient to state the name of the first named party on each side with an appropriate indication of any omissions. NY CPLR Rule 2101(c).

i. *Further contents of first page.* After the first paper has been filed in each case the index number shall appear on the cover and first page to the right of the caption of every paper tendered for filing in the action. Each such cover and first page also shall contain an indication of the county of venue and a brief description of the nature of the paper and, where the case has been assigned to an individual judge, shall contain the name of the assigned judge to the right of the caption. NY R UNIF TRIAL CTS § 202.5(a); NY R UNIF TRIAL CTS § 202.5(b); NY R UNIF TRIAL CTS § 202.5(d)(1)(i).

d. *Index number.* No paper in an action in the supreme or a county court, other than an order submitted for signature to a judge out of court, shall be submitted for any purpose to the supreme or county court or to a clerk thereof unless there is endorsed on such paper the index number of the action assigned by the clerk of the county. NY CPLR § 8018(c).

i. *ALBANY COUNTY: Index number on all filed documents.* The index number, the request for judicial intervention number and the assigned justice's name shall appear on [all papers filed with the Court subsequent to the complaint]. NY R 3 JD SUP Doc. 1(A).

ii. *ERIE COUNTY: Index number after initial filing.* Cases that are initially commenced by the filing of papers with the NYSCEF system are identified as e-filed cases by assignment of an Index Number that has "800-899" as the first three (3) digits of the index number (i.e. 802391/2012). NY R ERIE E FIL Doc. 3(II). [The] Index Number must be affixed to all document submissions, filings, and communications to the Erie County Clerk and the Court. Cases that are converted from paper to e-filing shall retain the original index number. NY R ERIE E FIL Doc. 3(II).

iii. *KINGS COUNTY: Index number after initial filing.* In cases commenced electronically by the filing of initiating papers with the NYSCEF system and payment of the statutory fees, the Kings County Clerk will issue an NYSCEF designated index number and the filer shall be notified via the NYSCEF system of the index number assigned and filing date. Such index number must be affixed to all document submissions, filings and communications to the Kings County Clerk and Supreme Court. If counsel faces exigent circumstances that require accelerated assignment, counsel may contact Administration of the Kings County Clerk at kcco-efile@nycourts.gov, during normal business hours of the court. NY R L KINGS E FIL Doc. 1(B)(5).

iv. *NEW YORK COUNTY: Index number on hard copy filings.* Papers subsequently presented for filing in hardcopy format will be filed in this jacket. NY R NY CTY Procedure I(B). Index numbers take the form of six digits followed by a slash and the four digits of the year the case began, e.g., 340705/2018. The first or first two integers of the index number identify the type of case. If a case is commenced electronically, the second integer will be a "5", except as indicated otherwise in the list below. There are many tax certiorari matters e-filed annually and the index numbers therefor will normally run over into those with a "6" as the second integer, and the same will occur with general cases if necessary. The principal types of cases and their index number categories are listed in NY R NY CTY Procedure I(B). NY R NY CTY Procedure I(B); NY R NY CTY Procedure XI(A).

v. *ONONDAGA COUNTY: Index number.* The index number must be referenced on all e-filed documents and correspondence. All e-filed case index numbers will contain the letters "EF" between the year and the file number (for example, 2012EF9999). NY R ONDGA E FIL Protocol(B)(1).

vi. *QUEENS COUNTY: Index number on converted cases.* Cases originally commenced in hard-copy form but later converted to an E-file case, either by stipulation or order will bear a regular index number initially. The County Clerk will issue a new E-file index number. NY R L QUEENS E-FILE Doc. 1(B).

e. *Line spacing.* Every paper filed in court, if typewritten, shall have at least double space between each line, except for quotations and the names and addresses of attorneys appearing in the action. NY R UNIF TRIAL CTS § 202.5(a).

f. *Font size.* Each. . .paper printed or typed, served or filed, except for summonses. . .and exhibits, shall be in clear type of no less than ten (10) point in size. NY CPLR Rule 2101(a).

i. Whenever a requirement relating to size of type is stated in point size, the type size requirement shall be deemed met if the x-height of the type is a minimum of forty-five percent (45%) of the specified point size. Each point shall be measured as .351 millimeter. The x-height size shall be measured as it appears on the page. The x-height is the height of the lower case letters, exclusive of ascenders or descenders. NY CPLR § 105(t).

g. *Margins.* Every paper filed in court shall have at least one (1) inch margins. NY R UNIF TRIAL CTS § 202.5(a).

h. *Citations*

i. *Civil practice law and rules.* NY CPLR § 101, et seq. shall be known as the civil practice law and rules, and may be cited as "CPLR". Reference to a provision in the civil practice law and rules may, except when such provision is being enacted or amended, be made without indicating whether it is a rule or section. NY CPLR § 101.

i. *Indorsement by attorney.* Each paper served or filed shall be indorsed with the name, address and telephone number of the attorney for the party serving or filing the paper, or if the party does not appear by attorney, with the name, address and telephone number of the party. NY CPLR Rule 2101(d).

j. *One-sided printing.* In addition, every paper filed in court, other than an exhibit or printed form, shall contain writing on one side only, except that papers that are fastened on the side may contain writing on both sides. NY R UNIF TRIAL CTS § 202.5(a).

k. *Use of copies authorized.* Except where otherwise specifically prescribed, copies, rather than originals, of all papers, including orders, affidavits and exhibits may be served or filed. Where it is required that the original be served or filed and the original is lost or withheld, the court may authorize a copy to be served or filed. NY CPLR Rule 2101(e).

i. Where a certified copy of a paper is required by law, an attorney admitted to practice in the courts of the state may certify that it has been compared by him with the original and found to be a true and complete copy. Such a certificate, when subscribed by such attorney, has the same effect as if made by a clerk. NY CPLR § 2105.

l. *Recycled paper.* It is the policy of the Unified Court System that litigants, where practicable, should file or submit to the courts of the Unified Court System of the State of New York papers printed or reproduced on recycled paper. Paper is considered recycled if it contains a minimum content of thirty percent (30%) waste paper. NY R UNIF TRIAL CTS § 215.2. The signature page of every paper filed or submitted to the court on recycled paper should bear the legend: "Printed [Reproduced] on Recycled Paper." NY R UNIF TRIAL CTS § 215.3.

m. *KINGS COUNTY: Tabs on filings.* Motions, orders and other filed papers shall be indexed with protruding tabs. Clerks are required to reject papers that do not have protruding exhibit tabs, except papers in matrimonial cases and papers filed by pro se litigants. NY R L KINGS Pt. A, Papers.

2. *Form of electronic documents.* Each paper served or filed by electronic means, as defined in NY CPLR Rule 2103(f), shall be capable of being reproduced by the receiver so as to comply with the provisions of NY CPLR Rule 2101(a) through NY CPLR Rule 2101(d). NY CPLR Rule 2101(g).

    a. *File format.* All e-filed documents shall comply with the technical requirements set forth at the NYSCEF site. NY R UNIF TRIAL CTS § 202.5-b(d)(1)(i).

    b. *Heading of document.* The subject matter heading for each paper sent by electronic means must indicate that the matter being transmitted electronically is related to a court proceeding. NY CPLR Rule 2103(b)(7).

    c. *E-filed documents identification*

        i. *ERIE COUNTY.* E-filed cases must be readily identifiable and marked as such. If counsel presents papers to the Office of the Erie County Clerk or the Office of the Chief Clerk in a NYSCEF matter where authorized, counsel should alert the Clerk that the case is a NYSCEF matter. NY R ERIE E FIL Doc. 3(II).

        ii. *KINGS COUNTY.* The Supreme Court's Civil Case Information System ("CCIS") will further identify e-filed cases by the addition of a suffix to the index number (e.g. 500136/2006E). This suffix should be used on all documents filed with the court in e-filed matters. NY R L KINGS E FIL Doc. 1(A)(1).

3. *Signature blocks.* Every pleading, written motion, and other paper, served on another party or filed or submitted to the court shall be signed by an attorney, or by a party if the party is not represented by an attorney, with the name of the attorney or party clearly printed or typed directly below the signature. NY R CHIEF ADMIN § 130-1.1-a(a); NY R UNIF TRIAL CTS § 202.5(d)(1)(iv).

    a. *Printed name.* Beneath each signature shall be printed the name signed. NY CPLR Rule 2101(a).

    b. *Failure to sign.* Absent good cause shown, the court shall strike any unsigned paper if the omission of the signature is not corrected promptly after being called to the attention of the attorney or party. NY R CHIEF ADMIN § 130-1.1-a(a).

    c. *Signature as certification.* By signing a paper, an attorney or party certifies that, to the best of that person's knowledge, information and belief, formed after an inquiry reasonable under the circumstances the presentation of the paper or the contentions therein are not frivolous as defined in NY R CHIEF ADMIN § 130-1.1(c). NY R CHIEF ADMIN § 130-1.1-a(b)(1).

    d. *Electronic signatures.* A document shall be considered to have been signed by an attorney or party in compliance with NY R CHIEF ADMIN § 130-1.1-a if it has been signed by such attorney or party as provided in NY R UNIF TRIAL CTS § 202.5-b(e)(1) and it bears the signatory's name. NY R UNIF TRIAL CTS § 202.5-b(e)(2). An electronically filed document shall be considered to have been signed by, and shall be binding upon, the person identified as a signatory, if:

        i. It bears the physical signature of such person and is scanned into an electronic format that reproduces such signature; or

        ii. The signatory has electronically affixed the digital image of his or her signature to the document; or

        iii. It is electronically filed under the User ID and password of that person; or

        iv. In a tax certiorari action in which the parties have stipulated to this procedure, it is an initiating document that is electronically filed without the signature of the signatory in a form provided above in NY R UNIF TRIAL CTS § 202.5-b(e)(iv), provided that, prior to filing, the document is signed in full in hard copy (which hard copy must be preserved until the conclusion of all proceedings, including appeals, in the case in which it is filed); or

        v. In a small claims assessment review proceeding, it is a petition recorded by the NYSCEF site upon the filing of a text file as provided in NY R UNIF TRIAL CTS § 202.5-b(b)(1), provided that prior to filing, the document was signed in full in hard copy (which hard copy must be preserved until the conclusion of all proceedings in the matter, including article 78 (NY CPLR § 7801, et seq.) review and any appeals, and must be made available during the proceeding upon request of the respondent or the court); or

        vi. It otherwise bears the electronic signature of the signatory in a format conforming to such standards and requirements as may hereafter be established by the Chief Administrator. NY R UNIF TRIAL CTS § 202.5-b(e).

4. *Confidentiality of personal information.* No person may file any document available for public inspection with any state agency, political subdivision, or in any court of this state that contains a Social Security account number of any other person, unless such other person is a dependent child, or has consented to such filing, except as required by federal or state law or regulation, or by court rule. NY GEN BUS § 399-ddd. Submissions pursuant to e-filing procedures shall have the same confidentiality rights as paper documents. NY R UNIF TRIAL CTS § 202.5-b(k)(1).

    a. *Confidential personal information.* Except in the actions designated in NY R UNIF TRIAL CTS § 202.5(e)(1), or as

otherwise provided by rule or law or court order, and whether or not a sealing order is or has been sought, the parties shall omit or redact confidential personal information in papers submitted to the court for filing. For purposes of NY R UNIF TRIAL CTS § 202.5(e), confidential personal information ("CPI") means:

i. The taxpayer identification number of an individual or an entity, including a Social Security number, an employer identification number, and an individual taxpayer identification number, except the last four (4) digits thereof;

ii. The date of an individual's birth, except the year thereof;

iii. The full name of an individual known to be a minor, except the minor's initials;

iv. A financial account number, including a credit and/or debit card number, a bank account number, an investment account number, and/or an insurance account number, except the last four (4) digits or letters thereof; and

v. Any of the documents or testimony in a matrimonial action protected by NY DOM REL § 235 or evidence sealed by the court in such an action which are attached as exhibits or referenced in the papers filed in any other civil action. For purposes of NY R UNIF TRIAL CTS § 202.5, a matrimonial action shall mean: an action to annul a marriage or declare the nullity of a void marriage, an action or agreement for a separation, an action for a divorce, or an action or proceeding for custody, visitation, writ of habeus corpus, child support, maintenance or paternity. NY R UNIF TRIAL CTS § 202.5(e)(1).

vi. *ERIE COUNTY.* An attorney or unrepresented litigant filing a document via the NYSCEF system must comply with the requirements of NY R UNIF TRIAL CTS § 202.5(e) regarding the redaction of Confidential Personal Information and NY GEN BUS § 399-ddd(6) concerning the filing of documents containing Social Security Numbers. It is the sole responsibility of counsel or unrepresented litigant filing to be aware of and to comply with existing laws requiring non-disclosure of personal information contained in any document e-filed in NYSCEF. NY R ERIE E FIL Doc. 3(III)(G); NY R ERIE E FIL Doc. 3(III).

vii. *KINGS COUNTY.* An attorney or unrepresented litigant filing a document via the NYSCEF system must comply with the requirements of General Business Law § 399-dd(6), which often require redaction of any Social Security number that appear in the original document. The NYSCEF system automatically redacts portions of filed documents which apparently contain Social Security numbers pursuant to NY R UNIF TRIAL CTS § 202.5-b(k). In the event the filing party receives e-mail notice through NYSCEF that a Social Security number in a filed document has been redacted, and the filing party concludes such redaction is erroneous, the filer should click on the link provided in the e-mail to permit the County Clerk to revert the redaction. For Confidential Personal Information, see NY R UNIF TRIAL CTS § 202.5(e) and NY R L KINGS E FIL Doc. 1(B)(11). [Editor's note: the reference to General Business Law § 399-dd(6) is likely a reference to NY GEN BUS § 399-ddd(6)]. NY R L KINGS E FIL Doc. 1(B)(10); NY R L KINGS E FIL Doc. 1(K)(1).

viii. *NEW YORK COUNTY.* It is the responsibility of counsel and parties to comply with rules restricting disclosure of confidential personal information. Nevertheless, NYSCEF screens filings and endeavors to identify any that contain social security numbers. When such numbers are discovered through this process, NYSCEF will restrict portions of or all of such documents from public view. Where NYSCEF has redacted what it believes to be a social security number, it will transmit to the filer a notice advising of the action taken and requesting that the filer review the matter and provide notification as set forth in the notice if the redaction has been made in error. NY R NY CTY E FIL Doc. 2(K)(1); NY R NY CTY J RUL Rule A-1. Documents filed in the past in "secure status" under a procedure no longer in place will retain that status unless otherwise directed by the court. NY R NY CTY E FIL Doc. 2(K)(2).

b. *Submission of confidential personal information.* Where a person submitting a paper to a court for filing believes in good faith that the inclusion of the full confidential personal information described in NY R UNIF TRIAL CTS § 202.5(e)(1) is material and necessary to the adjudication of the action or proceeding before the court, he or she may apply to the court for leave to serve and file together with a paper in which such information has been set forth in abbreviated form a confidential affidavit or affirmation setting forth the same information in unabbreviated form, appropriately referenced to the page or pages of the paper at which the abbreviated form appears. NY R UNIF TRIAL CTS § 202.5(e)(3).

c. *Home addresses.* For information on when home addresses and other personal information must be redacted, refer to NY CPLR Rule 2103-a.

5. *Defective papers.* A defect in the form of a paper, if a substantial right of a party is not prejudiced, shall be disregarded by the court, and leave to correct shall be freely given. NY CPLR Rule 2101(f). Papers that are stapled or bound securely shall not be rejected for filing simply because they are not bound with a backer of any kind. NY R UNIF TRIAL CTS § 202.5(a).

A paper filed in accordance with the rules of the chief administrator or any local rule or practice established by the court shall be deemed filed. NY CPLR Rule 2102(b).

a. *Objection to defective papers.* The party on whom a paper is served shall be deemed to have waived objection to any defect in form unless, within fifteen (15) days after the receipt thereof, the party on whom the paper is served returns the paper to the party serving it with a statement of particular objections. NY CPLR Rule 2101(f).

F. Filing and Service Requirements

1. *Filing requirements.* Except where otherwise prescribed by law or order of court, papers required to be filed shall be filed with the clerk of the court in which the action is triable. In an action or proceeding in supreme or court, papers required to be filed shall be filed with the clerk of the county in which the proceeding is brought. NY CPLR Rule 2102(a).

a. *Electronic filing.* On consent, documents may be filed and served by electronic means in Supreme Court in such civil actions and in such counties as shall be authorized by order of the Chief Administrator of the Courts and only to the extent and in the manner provided in NY R UNIF TRIAL CTS § 202.5-b. NY R UNIF TRIAL CTS § 202.5-b(a)(1). For the definitions of terms used in electronic filing, refer to NY R UNIF TRIAL CTS § 202.5-b(a)(2).

i. *E-filing mandatory.* In any action subject to e-filing, all documents required to be filed with the court by an e-filing party shall be filed and served electronically, except as provided in NY R UNIF TRIAL CTS § 202.5-b. NY R UNIF TRIAL CTS § 202.5-b(d)(1)(i).

- *ERIE COUNTY.* Case types currently eligible and accepted for e-filing are listed at the NYSCEF website. Note that some actions or special proceedings, (i.e., name changes) which are otherwise subject to mandatory e-filing, if commenced by unrepresented litigants will NOT be maintained in the NYSCEF system; individual cases may be found either at NYSCEF or in the Erie County Clerk's online records system. NY R ERIE E FIL Doc. 3(I)(E).
- *KINGS COUNTY.* Cases that are commenced by filing of the initiating papers with NYSCEF are identified as e-filed cases by assignment of a special index number (i.e., Index Numbers beginning with 500,000). NY R L KINGS E FIL Doc. 1(A)(1). All cases required to be e-filed are listed in Uniform Rule 202.5-bb (Mandatory E-Filing Rules) and on the NYSCEF website. All such cases must be commenced by filing with the County Clerk electronically through NYSCEF and all subsequent documents in such cases must be e-filed. Any questions regarding mandatory e-filing in Kings County can be e-mailed to kcco-efile@nycourts.gov. NY R L KINGS E FIL Doc. 1(A)(2).
- *NEW YORK COUNTY.* Unless otherwise provided in the Rules or in NY R NY CTY E FIL Doc. 2 or where a special exemption is granted due to physical requirements (e.g., oversized maps; see NY R NY CTY E FIL Doc. 2(B)(10)), all documents to be filed with the court in a NYSCEF case, including all documents on motions and all letters to the court (where permitted), must be filed with the NYSCEF system. Documents that attorneys would not ordinarily file with the court in a hard-copy case need not be e-filed. Unless otherwise provided by the E-Filing Rules or this Protocol, in e-filed cases the County Clerk and the court will not accept documents filed in paper form. NY R NY CTY E FIL Doc. 2(B)(1). E-filing is mandatory in all types of cases (other than election law, matrimonial, Art. 78, and Mental Hygiene Law matters, and Art. 70 habeas corpus proceedings) that are commenced in this court on or after February 19, 2013. All such cases must be commenced by filing with the County Clerk electronically through NYSCEF and all subsequent documents in such cases must be e-filed. NY R NY CTY E FIL Doc. 2(A)(2)(a). For more information, including information on consensual e-filing and filing scanned hard copy documents, refer to NY R NY CTY E FIL Doc. 2(A)(2).
- *QUEENS COUNTY.* All authorized Torts, Commercial and Tax Certiorari cases may be commenced by E-Filing, however all parties must consent for the action to continue as an E-file case. NY R L QUEENS E-FILE Doc. 1(A). All papers to be filed with the court in an E-filed case shall be filed on-line with the E-file system except as directed by the court. Papers that attorneys would not ordinarily file with the court in a hard-copy case need not be filed in an E-filed matter. NY R L QUEENS E-FILE Doc. 1(E)(2).

ii. *Who may file.* Documents may be filed or served electronically only by a person who has registered as an authorized e-filing user or as otherwise provided in NY R UNIF TRIAL CTS § 202.5-b(c). NY R UNIF TRIAL CTS § 202.5-b(c)(1).

iii. *When filing made.* Documents may be transmitted at any time of the day or night to the NYSCEF site. A document other than an order or judgment is filed when its electronic transmission or, in the case of a petition that is e-filed by submission of a text file as provided in NY R UNIF TRIAL CTS § 202.5-b(b)(1), the electronic transmission of the text file is recorded at that site, provided, however, that where payment of a fee is required upon the filing of a document, the document is not filed until transmission of the document and the information or form or information as required in NY R UNIF TRIAL CTS § 202.5-b(d)(2)(i), NY R UNIF TRIAL CTS § 202.5-b(d)(2)(ii) or NY R UNIF TRIAL CTS § 202.5-b(d)(2)(iii) has been recorded at the NYSCEF site; or, if no transmission of that information or form or information is recorded, where permitted by the County Clerk, until payment is presented to the County Clerk. NY R UNIF TRIAL CTS § 202.5-b(d)(3)(i).

iv. *Notification of filing.* No later than the close of business on the business day following the electronic filing of a document, a notification, in a form prescribed by the Chief Administrator, shall be transmitted electronically by the NYSCEF site to the person filing such document and the e-mail service addresses of all other participating parties in such action. NY R UNIF TRIAL CTS § 202.5-b(d)(3)(ii).

v. *Removal of confidential information and other corrections.* If a document filed electronically is subsequently discovered to contain confidential data—including but not limited to trade secrets, information protected by confidentiality agreement, or personal confidential information as defined by statute or court rule—or otherwise to have been filed in error, the filer or another party or affected person may (1) notify the parties and any non-party filers in the action of the confidentiality issue or other error raised by the filing, and of his or her intention to seek judicial relief to correct the filing: (2) following such notification, request that the appropriate County Clerk, exercising his or her administrative discretion, place the document temporarily in "restricted" status on the NYSCEF site, to be made available for viewing by court staff and the parties but not the general public; and (3) file an application to correct the filing by order to show cause within five (5) business days of such notification (or such time as the court may direct), including a request for preliminary injunctive relief limiting interim disclosure of the document at issue. Unless otherwise directed by the court, any document placed in restricted status in response to such a request shall be returned to public view upon expiration of this five (5) day period. The Chief Administrator of the Courts shall promulgate forms to implement this process. NY R UNIF TRIAL CTS § 202.5-b(d)(3)(iii).

- *KINGS COUNTY.* For information on what to do when a document was erroneously filed with confidential information, refer to NY R L KINGS E FIL Doc. 1(B)(11).
- *NEW YORK COUNTY.* For information on what to do when a document was erroneously filed with confidential information, refer to NY R NY CTY E FIL Doc. 2(B)(8).
- *QUEENS COUNTY.* For information on what to do when a document was erroneously filed with confidential information, refer to NY R L QUEENS E-FILE Doc. 1(E)(7).

vi. *Documents requiring judge's signature.* Except where the court directs otherwise, any document that requires a judge's signature shall be transmitted electronically and in hard copy to the court. NY R UNIF TRIAL CTS § 202.5-b(d)(6).

vii. *Documents which would be inconvenient to file electronically; Hard copies.* Notwithstanding any other provision of NY R UNIF TRIAL CTS § 202.5-b, and subject to such guidelines as may be established by the Chief Administrative Judge, the County Clerk or his or her designee may require or permit a party to file in hard copy, in accordance with procedures set by the County Clerk or designee, an exhibit or other document which it is impractical or inconvenient to file electronically. NY R UNIF TRIAL CTS § 202.5-b(d)(7).

- *ERIE COUNTY.* Please contact the Supervisor of Actions & Proceedings, Erie County Clerk's Office by calling (716) 858-6662 or the Deputy County Clerk—Legal at (716) 858-6348 for information. NY R ERIE E FIL Doc. 3(III)(F).
- *KINGS COUNTY.* With limited exceptions, as set forth in the Uniform Rules and herein, all documents to be filed with the court in a NYSCEF case shall be filed online via the NYSCEF system. However, should the size, consistency or context of a hard copy document preclude electronic filing, the user shall electronically file a "Notice of Hard Copy Submission—E-Filed Cases" form EFM-3. Any hard copy submitted pursuant to NY R L KINGS E FIL Doc. 1(B)(9) shall include, as a cover page firmly fastened thereto, a copy of the Confirmation Notice received from the NYSCEF site confirming receipt of the "Notice of Hard Copy Submission—E-Filed Cases". Any party may object to such hard copy filing. The Court, in response to such objection, may, following the hard copy filing, fashion such relief as it deems appropriate pursuant to and in furtherance of the Uniform Rules and NY R L KINGS E FIL Doc. 1, including, but not limited to, an Order directing the filing party to file such documents online via the NYSCEF system. When exhibits are impractical to file pursuant to NY R UNIF TRIAL CTS § 202.5-b(d)(7), an additional "Notice of Hard Copy Exhibit Filing" form EFM-4 is required to be submitted. NY R L KINGS E FIL Doc. 1(B)(9).

- *NEW YORK COUNTY.* If a filer needs to submit unusual exhibits in original form that cannot practically be e-filed, such as oversized maps or electronic recordings, the filer should consult with the County Clerk's E-File Department by telephone at 646-386-3737 (procedural questions only) or by e-mail at ccnyef@nycourts.gov, which will normally require that the filer retain custody of the original subject to possible future directives of the court. NY R NY CTY E FIL Doc. 2(B)(10). In such instances, the filing counsel shall file with NYSCEF a "placeholder" in the form of a Notice of Hard Copy Exhibit Filing (NYSCEF Form EF 21). The Notice should be uploaded to NYSCEF as document type "Exhibit" and the filer should indicate in the "Additional Document Information" field that the filer is retaining custody of the original. Failure to e-file the Notice may result in a gap in the official record of the court. NY R NY CTY E FIL Doc. 2(B)(10).

viii. *Documents containing sensitive or proprietary information.* In an action subject to e-filing, any person may apply for an order prohibiting or restricting the electronic filing in the action of specifically identified materials on the grounds that such materials are subject to copyright or other proprietary rights, or trade secret or other privacy interests, and that electronic filing in the action is likely to result in substantial prejudice to those rights or interests. NY R UNIF TRIAL CTS § 202.5-b(k)(2).

ix. *Refusal to accept paper filings.* In accordance with NY CPLR Rule 2102(c), a County Clerk and a chief clerk of the Supreme Court or County Court, as appropriate, shall refuse to accept for filing papers filed in actions and proceedings when the paper sought to be filed:

- Is in an action subject to electronic filing pursuant to Rules of the Chief Administrator,
- Is not being filed electronically, and
- Does not include the notice required by NY R UNIF TRIAL CTS § 202.5-b(d)(1). NY R UNIF TRIAL CTS § 202.5(d)(1)(v); NY R UNIF TRIAL CTS § 202.5-bb(d).

x. *Emergency filings; Hard copies.* For information on when an emergency filing may be filed and served in hard copy, refer to NY R UNIF TRIAL CTS § 202.5-b(d)(1)(ii), NY R UNIF TRIAL CTS § 202.5-b(d)(1)(iii) and NY R UNIF TRIAL CTS § 202.5-bb(c)(3).

- *KINGS COUNTY.* Under the rules, a participating emergency e-filer must electronically file the documents initially filed in hard copy form within three (3) business days of the emergency filing; the originals will be discarded after the documents have been processed and the failure to e-file as required will therefore lead to an incomplete record. NY R L KINGS E FIL Doc. 1(B)(3).
- *NEW YORK COUNTY.* Occasionally an emergency will arise requiring expedited entry of a document with the County Clerk (e.g., an order issued in the courtroom after a conference or argument of a critical matter), such as for purposes of an immediate appeal. Expedition can be achieved by the Part as follows: the document should be carried by a Court Officer or staff member to the General Clerk's Office to assure immediate and proper recordation in the computer and, as appropriate, the posting of the document to NYSCEF or the Supreme Court Records On-Line Library ("Scroll"). The court will accommodate counsel in emergencies. NY R NY CTY Procedure XI(A).

xi. *Technical failures.* The NYSCEF site shall be considered to be subject to a technical failure on a given day if the site is unable to accept filings or provide access to filed documents continuously or intermittently over the course of any period of time greater than one (1) hour after 12:00 noon of that day. Notice of all such technical failures shall be provided on the site. NY R UNIF TRIAL CTS § 202.5-b(i).

- When e-filing is hindered by a technical failure, a party may file with the appropriate clerk and serve in hard copy. NY R UNIF TRIAL CTS § 202.5-b(i). In the event an attorney or party shall file and serve documents in hard copy pursuant to NY R UNIF TRIAL CTS § 202.5-b(i), each such document shall include the notice required by NY R UNIF TRIAL CTS § 202.5-b(d)(1), and the filer shall file those documents with the NYSCEF site within three (3) business days after restoration of normal operations at that site. NY R UNIF TRIAL CTS § 202.5-b(i).
- With the exception of deadlines that by law cannot be extended, the time for filing of any document that is delayed due to technical failure of the site shall be extended for one (1) day for each day on which such failure occurs, unless otherwise ordered by the court. NY R UNIF TRIAL CTS § 202.5-b(i).
- *ERIE COUNTY.* When filing by electronic means is hindered by a technical failure, please refer to the NY R UNIF TRIAL CTS § 202.5-b(i). NY R ERIE E FIL Doc. 3(III)(K).
- *KINGS COUNTY.* When filing by electronic means is hindered by a NYSCEF technical failure (as set forth

in NY R UNIF TRIAL CTS § 202.5-b(i)), a party may file with the appropriate Clerk in hard copy. Except for deadlines that by law cannot be extended (e.g. Statute of limitations, Notice of Appeal), the time for filing of any document that is delayed due to technical failure of the NYSCEF system shall be extended for one day for each day on which such failure occurs, unless otherwise ordered by the court. NY R L KINGS E FIL Doc. 1(B)(13).

- *ONONDAGA COUNTY.* When filing by electronic means is hindered by a technical failure (as set forth in NY R UNIF TRIAL CTS § 202.5-b(h)(3)(i)), a party may file a hard copy with the County Clerk. With the exception of deadlines that by law cannot be extended (e.g., a statute of limitations or the deadline for filing a Notice of Appeal), the time for filing of any document that is delayed due to technical failure of the NYSCEF system will be extended for one day for each day on which such failure occurs, unless otherwise ordered by the court. A "Notice of Hard Copy Filing Submission—E-Filed Case' must accompany any documents not filed via NYSCEF. NY R ONDGA E FIL Protocol(B)(8).

xii. *Filing fees.* For information on what information must be provided to pay filing fees, refer to NY R UNIF TRIAL CTS § 202.5-b(d)(2).

xiii. *Exemption from e-filing.* For information on exemptions from e-filing, refer to NY R UNIF TRIAL CTS § 202.5-bb(e).

xiv. *Filing exhibits*

- *ERIE COUNTY.* In the NYSCEF system, each exhibit must be uploaded as a separate .pdf file. After uploading a primary document, please choose the document type "Exhibit" and enter the appropriate number or letter and a brief description of the exhibit; each exhibit should bear a separate cover sheet clearly marked as "Exhibit A," "Exhibit B," etc. "Exhibit A" or "Exhibit B" is unacceptable as a brief description of the exhibit. Exhibits, where referenced in a signed Order as attached or affixed shall be uploaded with the signed Order as one .pdf document. NY R ERIE E FIL Doc. 3(III)(H).
- *KINGS COUNTY.* In the NYSCEF system, each exhibit should be uploaded as a separate PDF file. After uploading a primary document, please choose the document type "Exhibit", enter the appropriate number or letter, and be sure to place a check mark to the right of "Attach to main document". Each exhibit shall bear a separate cover sheet clearly marked as Exhibit A, Exhibit B, etc. NY R L KINGS E FIL Doc. 1(B)(12).
- *NEW YORK COUNTY.* Attorneys submitting exhibits in NYSCEF cases should make each exhibit a separate attachment to an affidavit/affirmation in the system; i.e., exhibits should not be filed as a single PDF-A together with the affidavit/affirmation or grouped together as a single PDF-A attachment because either of these two formats makes it difficult for the Justice to locate particular exhibits as needed. Counsel must also include appropriate descriptive language in the "Additional Document Information" field in NYSCEF. NY R NY CTY E FIL Doc. 2(D)(6).
- *ONONDAGA COUNTY.* All exhibits in e-filed cases must be e-filed individually as separate attachments. NY R ONDGA E FIL Protocol(B)(9)(b).

xv. *Correcting documents*

- *ERIE COUNTY.* Submission of documents which, upon examination, require correction or addition will result in notification to the filer advising that the document has been returned for correction. The filer shall make the required corrections and/or additions as indicated in the e-mail transmission sent by the County Clerk or Part Clerk through the NYSCEF site. The corrected documents may be resubmitted using the "Re-file this document" link highlighted in the filer's document list for the respective case. Please note that in the case of multiple submissions, all related documents filed at the same time may be removed from the case record and returned until all documents are properly submitted. NY R ERIE E FIL Doc. 3(III)(J).
- *KINGS COUNTY.* Submission of documents which, upon examination, require correction or addition will result in notification to the filer advising that there is a problem with a document. The filer shall make the required corrections and/or additions and resubmit the corrected document using the "Refile this document" link. In the event a document is returned for correction, the original file date will be preserved. For corrections of documents filed with the Kings County Clerk which require a court order, refer to the procedure in NY R UNIF TRIAL CTS § 202.5-b(d)(3)(iii) and NY R L KINGS E FIL Doc. 1(B)(11). NY R L KINGS E FIL Doc. 1(B)(3).
- *ONONDAGA COUNTY.* If there is an error or an additional document is required, the system will notify the filing party, who will make the corrections/additions and resubmit them online. NY R ONDGA E FIL Protocol(B)(6).

- *QUEENS COUNTY.* Generally speaking, documents that have been E-filed will not thereafter be deleted by the County Clerk from NYCEF because the filer asserts that the filing contains an error or a significant omission. When the filer wishes to correct a perceived error or omission in a filed document, he or she should file an amended version of the document, with the original remaining on file, or else obtain a court order providing for deletion of the original. The County Clerk will only delete a document upon request of the filer or on the County Clerk's own initiative when it is obvious from the face of the document alone that the filer made a fundamental error and never intended to file the document that was filed (e.g., a completely unrelated non-litigation document, a different case, or a wrong county). The County Clerk will advise the filer when any such fundamental errors are detected. NY R L QUEENS E-FILE Doc. 1(E)(6).

b. *Facsimile filing.* In the Supreme Court, facsimile filing shall be limited to commercial claims and tax certiorari, conservatorship, and mental hygiene proceedings in Monroe, Westchester, New York and Suffolk Counties. NY R UNIF TRIAL CTS § 202.5-a(a)(1). Refer to NY R UNIF TRIAL CTS § 202.5-a for information on the procedures for facsimile filing.

i. *NEW YORK COUNTY.* Unless indicated otherwise by the court in a particular case or in NY R NY CTY J RUL Doc. 1, Justices do not accept papers by fax. NY R NY CTY J RUL Rule 4.

2. *Service requirements*

a. *Who may serve.* Except where otherwise prescribed by law or order of court, papers may be served by any person not a party of the age of eighteen years or over. NY CPLR Rule 2103(a).

b. *Service upon attorney.* Except where otherwise prescribed by law or order of court, papers to be served upon a party in a pending action shall be served upon the party's attorney. Where the same attorney appears for two or more parties, only one (1) copy need be served upon the attorney. Such service upon an attorney shall be made:

i. By delivering the paper to the attorney personally. NY CPLR Rule 2103(b)(1).

ii. By mailing the paper to the attorney at the address designated by that attorney for that purpose or, if none is designated, at the attorney's last known address; service by mail shall be complete upon mailing. NY CPLR Rule 2103(b)(2).

iii. If the attorney's office is open, by leaving the paper with a person in charge, or if no person is in charge, by leaving it in a conspicuous place; or if the attorney's office is not open, by depositing the paper, enclosed in a sealed wrapper directed to the attorney, in the attorney's office letter drop or box. NY CPLR Rule 2103(b)(3).

iv. By leaving it at the attorney's residence within the state with a person of suitable age and discretion. Service upon an attorney shall not be made at the attorney's residence unless service at the attorney's office cannot be made. NY CPLR Rule 2103(b)(4).

v. By transmitting the paper to the attorney by facsimile transmission, provided that a facsimile telephone number is designated by the attorney for that purpose. Service by facsimile transmission shall be complete upon the receipt by the sender of a signal from the equipment of the attorney served indicating that the transmission was received, and the mailing of a copy of the paper to that attorney. The designation of a facsimile telephone number in the address block subscribed on a paper served or filed in the course of an action or proceeding shall constitute consent to service by facsimile transmission in accordance with NY CPLR Rule 2103(b)(5). An attorney may change or rescind a facsimile telephone number by serving a notice on the other parties. NY CPLR Rule 2103(b)(5).

vi. By dispatching the paper to the attorney by overnight delivery service at the address designated by the attorney for that purpose or, if none is designated, at the attorney's last known address. Service by overnight delivery service shall be complete upon deposit of the paper enclosed in a properly addressed wrapper into the custody of the overnight delivery service for overnight delivery, prior to the latest time designated by the overnight delivery service for overnight delivery. "Overnight delivery service" means any delivery service which regularly accepts items for overnight delivery to any address in the state. NY CPLR Rule 2103(b)(6).

vii. By transmitting the paper to the attorney by electronic means where and in the manner authorized by the chief administrator of the courts by rule and, unless such rule shall otherwise provide, such transmission shall be upon the party's written consent. The subject matter heading for each paper sent by electronic means must indicate that the matter being transmitted electronically is related to a court proceeding. NY CPLR Rule 2103(b)(7).

- *KINGS COUNTY.* Pursuant to the E-Filing Rules, service of interlocutory documents is made by posting a document to the NYSCEF site, which automatically and immediately transmits an email notice of the filing, including a link to the document, to all participating counsel and unrepresented litigants on the case.

The Rules also authorize service by other methods permitted by the CPLR. If service by such other method is made, proof of service must be filed with NYSCEF. NY R L KINGS E FIL Doc. 1(I).

- *NEW YORK COUNTY.* Service. . .will be made automatically through NYSCEF upon all participating counsel and unrepresented parties in the case. There are limited exceptions to the requirement for e-filing in the covered kinds of cases. NY R NY CTY Procedure XI(A). Pursuant to the E-Filing Rules, service of interlocutory documents is made by posting a document to the NYSCEF site, which automatically and immediately transmits an e-mail notice of the filing, including a link to the document, to all participating counsel and unrepresented litigants on the case. The Rules also authorize service by other methods permitted by the CPLR. If service by such a method is made, proof of service must be filed with NYSCEF. NY R NY CTY E FIL Doc. 2(I).
- *QUEENS COUNTY.* Filing with the system permits counsel to serve the papers electronically pursuant to NY R UNIF TRIAL CTS § 202.5-b(f) once consent to E-Filing has been filed on-line. Consult NY R UNIF TRIAL CTS § 202.5-bb(c) for service in mandatory e-filing. Any required proof of service should be E-filed as a separate document. NY R L QUEENS E-FILE Doc. 1(E)(4).

c. *Electronic service mandatory; Consenting to electronic service; How electronic service may be made.* Except as otherwise provided in NY R UNIF TRIAL CTS § 202.5-bb, filing and service of all documents in an action that has been commenced electronically in accordance with NY R UNIF TRIAL CTS § 202.5-bb shall be by electronic means. NY R UNIF TRIAL CTS § 202.5-bb(c)(1).

i. *Party's consent required for certain e-filing.* After commencement of an action wherein e-filing is authorized, documents may be electronically filed and served, but only by, and electronic service shall be made only upon, a party or parties who have consented thereto. NY R UNIF TRIAL CTS § 202.5-b(b)(2)(i).

- A consent to e-filing in an action shall state that the party providing it agrees to the use of e-filing in the action and to be bound by the filing and service provisions in NY R UNIF TRIAL CTS § 202.5-b. NY R UNIF TRIAL CTS § 202.5-b(b)(2)(ii).

ii. *Address for service; Duty to notify as to changes.* The e-mail service address recorded at the time of registration is the e-mail address at which service of interlocutory documents on that party may be made through notification transmitted by the NYSCEF site. It is the responsibility of each filing user to monitor that address and promptly notify the Resource Center in the event of a change in his or her e-mail service address. NY R UNIF TRIAL CTS § 202.5-b(f)(2)(i).

iii. *How service made.* An e-filing party causes service of an interlocutory document to be made upon another party participating in e-filing by filing the document electronically. Upon receipt of an interlocutory document, the NYSCEF site shall automatically transmit electronic notification to all e-mail service addresses in such action. NY R UNIF TRIAL CTS § 202.5-b(f)(2)(ii).

- Except as provided otherwise in NY R UNIF TRIAL CTS § 202.5-b(h)(3), the electronic transmission of the notification shall constitute service of the document on the e-mail service addresses identified therein; however, such service will not be effective if the filing party learns that the notification did not reach the address of the person to be served. Proof of such service will be recorded on the NYSCEF site. A party may, however, utilize other service methods permitted by the CPLR provided that, if one of such other methods is used, proof of that service shall be filed electronically. NY R UNIF TRIAL CTS § 202.5-b(f)(2)(ii).

iv. *Signatures on hard copies; Proof of service filed electronically.* When an e-filing party serves a document in hard copy on a non-participating party, the document served shall bear full signatures of all signatories and proof of such service shall be filed electronically. NY R UNIF TRIAL CTS § 202.5-b(b)(2)(i).

- *ERIE COUNTY.* In the NYSCEF system, each Affidavit of Service must be uploaded as a separate .pdf file. After uploading the Affidavit, please choose the document type: "Affirmation/Affidavit of Service" and enter the name of the party served as Additional Document Information. NY R ERIE E FIL Doc. 3(III)(I).

v. *Effect of failure to consent.* A party's failure to consent to participation in electronic filing and service shall not bar any other party to the action from filing documents electronically with the County Clerk and the court or serving documents upon any other party who has consented to participation. A party who has not consented to participation shall file documents with the court and the County Clerk, and serve and be served with documents, in hard copy. NY R UNIF TRIAL CTS § 202.5-b(b)(2)(i).

d. *Service upon party.* If a party has not appeared by an attorney or the party's attorney cannot be served, service shall be upon the party by a method specified in NY CPLR Rule 2103(b)(1), NY CPLR Rule 2103(b)(2), NY CPLR Rule 2103(b)(4), NY CPLR Rule 2103(b)(5) or NY CPLR Rule 2103(b)(6). NY CPLR Rule 2103(c).

e. *Service on all parties.* Each paper served on any party shall be served on every other party who has appeared, except as otherwise may be provided by court order or as provided in NY CPLR § 3012 or in NY CPLR § 3215(f). Upon demand by a party, the plaintiff shall supply that party with a list of those who have appeared and the names and addresses of their attorneys. NY CPLR Rule 2103(e).

f. *Service by filing.* If a paper cannot be served by any of the methods specified in NY CPLR Rule 2103(b) and NY CPLR Rule 2103(c), service may be made by filing the paper as if it were a paper required to be filed. NY CPLR Rule 2103(d).

g. *Definitions.* For the purposes of NY CPLR Rule 2103:

   i. "Mailing" means the deposit of a paper enclosed in a first class postpaid wrapper, addressed to the address designated by a person for that purpose or, if none is designated, at that person's last known address, in a post office or official depository under the exclusive care and custody of the United States Postal Service within the state;

   ii. "Electronic means" means any method of transmission of information between computers or other machines designed for the purpose of sending and receiving such transmissions, and which allows the recipient to reproduce the information transmitted in a tangible medium of expression;

   iii. "Facsimile transmission" means any method of transmission of documents to a facsimile machine at a remote location which can automatically produce a tangible copy of such documents. NY CPLR Rule 2103(f).

G. Hearings

1. There is no hearing required or contemplated in the New York rules governing the demand for bill of particulars.

H. Forms

1. New York Demand for Bill of Particulars Forms

a. Form; The basic form of a defendant's demand for a bill of particulars in an action for breach of a contract for services when the contract is not attached to the complaint. NYPRAC-COMM § 23:25.

b. Form; The basic form of a plaintiff's bill of particulars in an action for breach of a contract for services when the contract was not reduced to writing. NYPRAC-COMM § 23:26.

I. Applicable Rules

1. *State rules*

a. Short title; Application; Construction; Definitions. NY CPLR § 101; NY CPLR § 104; NY CPLR § 105.

b. Appendix of official forms. NY CPLR § 107.

c. Service of process. NY CPLR § 312-a; NY CPLR Rule 320.

d. Extensions of time generally. NY CPLR § 2004.

e. Form of papers. NY CPLR Rule 2101; NY CPLR Rule 2102; NY CPLR § 2105; NY GEN BUS § 399-ddd; NY R UNIF TRIAL CTS § 215.2; NY R UNIF TRIAL CTS § 215.3.

f. Service of papers. NY CPLR Rule 2103.

g. Computation of time. NY CPLR § 2402; NY GEN CONSTR § 19; NY GEN CONSTR § 20; NY GEN CONSTR § 25-a; NY GEN CONSTR § 30; NY GEN CONSTR § 31; NY GEN CONSTR § 53.

h. Service of pleadings and demand for complaint. NY CPLR § 3012.

i. Bill of particulars in any case. NY CPLR § 3041.

j. Procedure for bill of particulars. NY CPLR Rule 3042.

k. Bill of particulars in personal injury actions. NY CPLR Rule 3043.

l. Fees; Index number fees of county clerks. NY CPLR § 8018.

m. Hours of court. NY R CHIEF J § 3.1.

n. Application of part; Waiver; Additional rules; Application of CPLR; Definitions. NY R UNIF TRIAL CTS § 202.1.

o. Papers filed in court; Electronic filing in supreme court. NY R UNIF TRIAL CTS § 202.5; NY R UNIF TRIAL CTS § 202.5-a; NY R UNIF TRIAL CTS § 202.5-b; NY R UNIF TRIAL CTS § 202.5-bb.

p. Rules of the commercial division of the Supreme Court. NY R UNIF TRIAL CTS § 202.70.

q. Signing of papers. NY R CHIEF ADMIN § 130-1.1-a.

2. *Local rules*

a. *Albany County*

i. Third judicial district rules. NY R 3 JD SUP Doc. 1.

b. *Bronx County*

i. Commercial division. NY R BRONX FIL R Doc. 12.

c. *Erie County*

i. Joint protocols for New York State Courts E-Filing (NYSCEF) cases filed in Supreme Court, Erie County. NY R ERIE E FIL Doc. 3.

d. *Kings County*

i. Papers. NY R L KINGS Pt. A, Papers.

ii. Protocol on courthouse and county clerk procedures for electronically filed cases. NY R L KINGS E FIL Doc. 1.

e. *New York County*

i. Commencement of cases. NY R NY CTY Procedure I.

ii. RJIs and assignments. NY R NY CTY Procedure IA.

iii. County clerk litigation functions. NY R NY CTY Procedure XI.

iv. Protocol on courthouse and county clerk procedures for electronically filed cases. NY R NY CTY E FIL Doc. 2.

v. Redaction of information in documents filed with the county clerk and the court. NY R NY CTY J RUL Rule A-1.

vi. Papers by fax. NY R NY CTY J RUL Rule 4.

f. *Onondaga County*

i. Onondaga county protocol for case filings New York State Electronic Files (NYSCEF). NY R ONDGA E FIL Protocol.

g. *Queens County*

i. Queens county protocol on courthouse procedures for electronically filed cases. NY R L QUEENS E-FILE Doc. 1.

J. Miscellaneous

NOTE: Individual judges' rules may apply.

ALBANY COUNTY

JUSTICE LISA M. FISHER: NY R 3 JD FISHER Fisher; NY R 3 JD FISHER Fisher, PC Order.

JUSTICE RICHARD MOTT: NY R 3 JD MOTT Mott.

JUSTICE STEPHAN G. SCHICK: NY R 3 JD Schick.

FORECLOSURE SETTLEMENT PART: NY R 3 JD Foreclosure Settlement.

BRONX COUNTY

JUSTICE PAUL L. ALPERT: [NY R BRONX J Part IA-29, as amended by NY ORDER 20-0337].

JUSTICE BEN BARBATO: NY R BRONX J Part IA-21.

JUSTICE MARY ANNE BRIGANTTI: [NY R BRONX J Part IA-15, as amended by NY ORDER 20-0338].

JUSTICE JOSEPH E. CAPELLA: NY R BRONX J Part IA-23.

JUSTICE MITCHELL DANZIGER: NY R BRONX J Part IA-3/33 ; [NY R BRONX J Danziger, Part IA-3/33, as amended by NY ORDER 20-0339].

JUSTICE LAURA G. DOUGLAS: NY R BRONX J Part IA-11.

JUSTICE RUBEN FRANCO: NY R BRONX J Part IA-26.

JUSTICE DORIS M. GONZALEZ: NY R BRONX J Part IA-24.

JUSTICE WILMA GUZMAN: NY R BRONX J Part IA-7; [NY R BRONX J Guzman, Part IA-7 Virtual, as amended by NY ORDER 20-0340].

JUSTICE ROBERT T. JOHNSON: NY R BRONX J Part IA-12.

JUSTICE DONALD A. MILES: NY R BRONX J Part IA-8.

JUSTICE DONNA M. MILLS: NY R BRONX J Part IA-9.

JUSTICE JULIA I. RODRIGUEZ: NY R BRONX J Part IA-18; [NY R BRONX J Part IA-27, as amended by NY ORDER 20-0341].

JUSTICE LLINET M. ROSADO: [NY R BRONX J Part IA-25, as amended by NY ORDER 20-0342].

JUSTICE NORMA RUIZ: NY R BRONX J Part IA-22; [NY R BRONX J Ruiz, Part IA-22 Virtual, as amended by NY ORDER 20-0343].

JUSTICE HOWARD H. SHERMAN: NY R BRONX J Part IA-4.

JUSTICE FERNANDO TAPIA: NY R BRONX J Part IA-13.

JUSTICE ELIZABETH A. TAYLOR: NY R BRONX J Part IA-2.

JUSTICE ALISON Y. TRUITT: NY R BRONX J Part IA-5.

PART IDV: NY R BRONX J Doc. 1.

PRE-TRIAL PART RULES: NY R BRONX J Doc. 2.

PRE TRIAL WORKSHEET: NY R BRONX J Doc. 3.

FORECLOSURE SETTLEMENT PART RULES: NY R BRONX J Doc. 4.

GUARDIANSHIP PART RULES: NY R BRONX J Doc. 5.

LPM PART RULES: NY R BRONX J Doc. 6.

ERIE COUNTY

JUSTICE M. WILLIAM BOLLER: NY R 8 JD J Boller.

JUSTICE RALPH A. BONIELLO: NY R 8 JD J Boniello.

JUSTICE CHRISTOPHER J. BURN: NY R 8 JD J Burns.

JUSTICE RUSSELL P. BUSCAGLIA: NY R 8 JD J Buscaglia.

JUSTICE FRANK CARUSO: NY R 8 JD J Caruso.

JUSTICE STEPHEN W. CASS: NY R 8 JD J Cass.

JUSTICE DEBORAH A. CHIMES: NY R 8 JD J Chimes.

JUSTICE EMILIO COLAIACOVO: [NY R 8 JD J Colaiacovo, as amended by NY ORDER 20-0252].

JUSTICE DIANE Y. DEVLIN: NY R 8 JD J Devlin.

JUSTICE JAMES H. DILLON: NY R 8 JD J Dillon.

JUSTICE PAULA L. FEROLETO: NY R 8 JD J Feroleto.

JUSTICE DANIEL J. FURLONG: [NY R 8 JD J Furlong, as amended by NY ORDER 20-0253].

JUSTICE JOSEPH R. GLOWNIA: NY R 8 JD J Glownia.

JUSTICE MARK J. GRISANTI: NY R 8 JD J Grisanti.

JUSTICE DEBORAH A. HAENDIGES: NY R 8 JD J Haendiges.

JUSTICE LYNN W. KEANE: [NY R 8 JD J Keane, as amended by NY ORDER 20-0254].

JUSTICE RICHARD C. KLOCH, Sr.: NY R 8 JD J Kloch.

JUSTICE FREDERICK J. MARSHALL: [NY R 8 JD J Marshall, as amended by NY ORDER 20-0255.

JUSTICE JOHN L. MICHALSKI: NY R 8 JD J Michalski.

JUSTICE MARK A. MONTOUR: [NY R 8 JD J Montour, as amended by NY ORDER 20-0256].

JUSTICE HENRY NOWAK: NY R 8 JD J Nowak.

JUSTICE JOHN F. O'DONNELL: NY R 8 JD J O'Donnell.

JUSTICE JEANETTE OGDEN: NY R 8 JD J Ogden.
JUSTICE CATHERINE NUGENT-PANEPINTO: NY R 8 JD J Nugent-Panepinto.
JUSTICE FRANK A. SEDITA, III: [NY R 8 JD J Sedita, as amended by NY ORDER 20-0257].
JUSTICE SARA SHELDON: NY R 8 JD J Sheldon.
JUSTICE DONNA M. SIWEK: NY R 8 JD J Siwek.
JUSTICE MARY L. SLISZ: NY R 8 JD J Slisz.
JUSTICE TIMOTHY J. WALKER: [NY R 8 JD J Walker, as amended by NY ORDER 20-0258].
JUSTICE DENNIS E. WARD: NY R 8 JD J Ward.
JUSTICE PAUL B. WOJTASZEK: [NY R 8 JD J Wojtaszek, as amended by NY ORDER 20-0259].
JUSTICE CHARLES N. ZAMBITO: [NY R 8 JD J Zambito, as amended by NY ORDER 20-0260].
SUPREME COURT LEGAL STAFF: NY R 8 JD J Legal Staff.

KINGS COUNTY

JUSTICE RACHEL A. ADAMS: NY R KINGS J Part 5F.
JUSTICE LOREN BAILY-SCHIFFMAN: NY R KINGS J Part 65.
JUSTICE REGINALD A. BODDIE: NY R KINGS J Part 95.
JUSTICE THERESA M. CICCOTTO: NY R KINGS J Part 19; NY R KINGS J Part 5J.
JUSTICE LISSETTE COLON: NY R KINGS J Part Rules.
JUSTICE GENINE EDWARDS: NY R KINGS J Part 80.
JUSTICE PAMELA L. FISHER: [NY R KINGS J Part 94, as amended by NY ORDER 20-0208].
JUSTICE ROBIN GARSON: NY R KINGS J Part 75.
JUSTICE LARA J. GENOVISI: [NY R KINGS J Part 34, as amended by NY ORDER 20-0209].
JUSTICE BERNARD J. GRAHAM: NY R KINGS J Part 36.
JUSTICE DAWN JIMENEZ-SALTA: NY R KINGS J Part 88.
JUSTICE INGRID JOSEPH: [NY R KINGS J Part FRP3 and Part 83, as amended by NY ORDER 20-0210].
JUSTICE KATHY J. KING: NY R KINGS J Part 64, 76K.
JUSTICE LAWRENCE KNIPEL: NY R KINGS J Part 57.
JUSTICE DONALD KURTZ: NY R KINGS J Part 26.
JUSTICE CARL LANDICINO: [NY R KINGS J Part 81, as amended by NY ORDER 20-0211].
JUSTICE KATHERINE LEVINE: [NY R KINGS J Part 20, 25, 92, as amended by NY ORDER 20-0211].
JUSTICE LORNA MCALLISTER: [NY R KINGS J Part 10, as amended by NY ORDER 20-0211].
JUSTICE ROSEMARIE MONTALBANO: [NY R KINGS J Part 19, 71, and 22, as amended by NY ORDER 20-0211].
JUSTICE RICHARD J. MONTELIONE: [NY R KINGS J Part 99 and DJMP, as amended by NY ORDER 20-0215].
JUSTICE LISA S. OTTLEY: NY R KINGS J Part 24.
JUSTICE MARK I. PARTNOW: NY R KINGS J Part 43.
JUSTICE ERIC I. PRUS: NY R KINGS J Part 5A.
JUSTICE FRANCOIS RIVERA: NY R KINGS J Part 52.
JUSTICE KAREN B. ROTHENBERG: NY R KINGS J Part 35.
JUSTICE LEON RUCHELSMAN: NY R KINGS J Part 1.
JUSTICE WAYNE P. SAITTA: NY R KINGS J Part 29.
JUSTICE ROBIN K. SHEARES: NY R KINGS J Part 96.
JUSTICE KENNETH P. SHERMAN: NY R KINGS J Part 67 and 78.
JUSTICE DEBRA SILBER: NY R KINGS J Part 9 and 5K.

JUSTICE ELLEN M. SPODEK: NY R KINGS J Part 63.

JUSTICE MARSHA L. STEINHARDT: NY R KINGS J Part 15.

JUSTICE JEFFREY S. SUNSHINE: NY R KINGS J Part 5G.

JUSTICE PETER P. SWEENEY: [NY R KINGS J Part 35, as amended by NY ORDER 20-0218].

JUSTICE DELORES J. THOMAS: [NY R KINGS J Part 5T, as amended by NY ORDER 20-0221].

JUSTICE WAVNY TOUSSAINT: NY R KINGS J Part 70.

JUSTICE RICHARD VELASQUEZ: NY R KINGS J Part 66.

JUSTICE CAROLYN E. WADE: NY R KINGS J Part 84.

JUSTICE EDWARD G. WALKER: [NY R KINGS J Part 90, as amended by NY ORDER 20-0219].

JUSTICE LILLIAN WAN: [NY R KINGS J Part 17, as amended by NY ORDER 20-0220].

JUSTICE MICHELLE WESTON: NY R KINGS J Part 3.

MENTAL HYGIENE PART: NY R KINGS J Part 77.

MATRIMONIAL PARTS DURING COVID-19 EMERGENCY: JUSTICE KAREN B. ROTHENBERG: NY R KINGS J Doc. 1.

NASSAU COUNTY

JUSTICE ANNA R. ANZALONE: NY R NASSAU S J Anzalone, Part 26.

JUSTICE STACY D. BENNETT: NY R NASSAU S J Bennett; NY R NASSAU S J Bennett, Form 1.

JUSTICE ANTONIO BRANDVEEN: NY R NASSAU S J Brandveen, Part 31.

JUSTICE JEFFREY S. BROWN: [NY R NASSAU S J Brown, as amended by NY ORDER 20-0297].

JUSTICE STEPHEN A. BUCARIA: NY R NASSAU S J Bucaria.

JUSTICE JULIANNE T. CAPETOLA: NY R NASSAU S J Capetola, Part 28.

JUSTICE EDMUND M. DANE: NY R NASSAU S J Dane, Part 33.

JUSTICE VITO M. DESTEFANO: NY R NASSAU S J DeStefano, Part 13; NY R NASSAU S J DeStefano, Form 1.

JUSTICE ARTHUR M. DIAMOND: NY R NASSAU S J Diamond, Part 7.

JUSTICE THOMAS FEINMAN: NY R NASSAU S J Feinman, Part 5.

JUSTICE JOHN M. GALASSO: NY R NASSAU S J Galasso, Part 22.

JUSTICE SHARON M.J. GIANELLI: NY R NASSAU S J Gianelli, Part 22; NY R NASSAU S J Gianelli, Form 1.

JUSTICE JEFFREY A. GOODSTEIN: NY R NASSAU S J Goodstein, Part 33; NY R NASSAU S J Goodstein, Form 1.

JUSTICE DAVID J. GUGERTY: [NY R NASSAU S J Gugerty, Part 31, as amended by NY ORDER 20-0298].

JUSTICE HELENE F. GUGERTY: NY R NASSAU S J Gugerty, Part 47.

JUSTICE STEVEN M. JAEGER: NY R NASSAU S J Jaeger, Part 35; NY R NASSAU S J Jaeger, Form 1.

JUSTICE JACK L. LIBERT: NY R NASSAU S J Libert, Part 23.

JUSTICE JOSEPH H. LORINTZ: NY R NASSAU S J Lorintz, Part 26; NY R NASSAU S J Lorintz, Form 1.

JUSTICE ROY S. MAHON: NY R NASSAU S J Mahon, Part 3.

JUSTICE RANDY SUE MARBER: NY R NASSAU S J Marber, Part 8.

JUSTICE JAMES P. MCCORMACK: [NY R NASSAU S J McCormack, Part 18, as amended by NY ORDER, 20-0299].

JUSTICE DICCIA T. PINEDA-KIRWAN: [NY R NASSAU S J Pineda-Kirwan, as amended by NY ORDER 20-0300].

JUSTICE THOMAS RADEMAKER: [NY R NASSAU S J Rademaker, Part 28, as amended by NY ORDER 20-0301]; [NY R NASSAU S J Rademaker, Form 1, as amended by NY ORDER 20-0301].

JUSTICE DENISE L. SHER: NY R NASSAU S J Rademaker, Part 32.

JUSTICE LEONARD D. STEINMAN: [NY R NASSAU S J Steinman, Part 15, as amended by NY ORDER 20-0303]; NY R NASSAU S J Steinman, Form 1.

JUSTICE HOWARD E. STURIM: NY R NASSAU S J Sturim, Part 50; NY R NASSAU S J Sturim, Form 1.

JUSTICE HELEN VOUTSINAS: [NY R NASSAU S J Voutsinas, Part 25, as amended by NY ORDER 20-0304]; [NY R NASSAU S J Voutsinas, Form 1, as amended by NY ORDER 20-0305].

JUSTICE HOPE SCHWARTZ ZIMMERMAN: NY R NASSAU S J Zimmerman, Part 17.

NEW YORK COUNTY

JUDGE'S RULES; BASIC INFORMATION: [NY R NY CTY J RUL Doc. 1, as amended by NY ORDER 20-0202].

ONONDAGA COUNTY

JUSTICE ROBERT E. ANTONACCI II: [NY R ONDGA E FIL Doc. 1, as amended by 20-0239].

JUSTICE MICHAEL V. COCCOMI: NY R ONDGA E FIL Doc. 2.

JUSTICE GREGORY R. GILBERT: NY R 5 JD JUDGES Gilbert; NY R ONDGA E FIL Doc. 3.

JUSTICE DONALD A. GREENWOOD: NY R ONDGA E FIL Doc. 4.

JUSTICE DEBORAH H. KARALUNAS: NY R ONDGA E FIL Doc. 5.

JUSTICE JAMES MCCLUSKY: NY R 5 JD MCCLUSKY McClusky.

JUSTICE CHARLES C. MERRELL: NY R 5 JD MERRELL Merrell.

JUSTICE PATRICK F. MACRAE: NY R 5 JD MACRAE Doc. 1.

JUSTICE JAMES P. MURPHY: NY R ONDGA E FIL Doc. 7.

JUSTICE GERALD J. NERI: [NY R 5 JD JUDGES Neri, as amended by NY ORDER 20-0236]; [NY R ONDGA E FIL Doc. 8, as amended by NY ORDER 20-0241].

JUSTICE ANTHONY J. PARIS: NY R 5 JD JUDGES Paris; [NY R ONDGA E FIL Doc. 9, as amended by NY ORDER 20-0242].

JUSTICE NORMAN W. SEITER, JR.: NY R 5 JD JUDGES Seiter.

JUSTICE KEVIN G. YOUNG: [NY R ONDGA E FIL Doc. 10, as amended by NY ORDER 20-0243].

QUEENS COUNTY

JUSTICE PAM JACKMAN BROWN: [NY R L QUEENS Brown, Part 19, as amended by NY ORDER 20-0321].

JUSTICE CHEREE A. BUGGS: NY R L QUEENS Buggs, Part 30.

JUSTICE PAM JACKMAN BROWN: [NY R L QUEENS Brown, Part 19, as amended by NY ORDER 20-0321].

JUSTICE DENIS J. BUTLER: NY R L QUEENS Butler, Part 12.

JUSTICE ROBERT I. CALORAS: [NY R L QUEENS Caloras, Part 36, as amended by NY ORDER 20-0322].

JUSTICE ANNA CULLEY: NY R L QUEENS Culley, Part 53.

JUSTICE TIMOTHY DUFFICY: NY R L QUEENS Dufficy, Part 35.

JUSTICE DAVID ELLIOT: NY R L QUEENS Elliot, Part 14.

JUSTICE JOSEPH J. ESPOSITO: NY R L QUEENS Esposito, Part 6.

JUSTICE DARRELL L. GAVRIN: [NY R L QUEENS Gavrin, Part 27, as amended by NY ORDER 20-0323].

JUSTICE WYATT N. GIBBONS: [NY R L QUEENS Gibbons, Part 5, as amended by NY ORDER 20-0330.

JUSTICE DONNA-MARIE E. GOLIA: [NY R L QUEENS Golia, Part 21, as amended by NY ORDER 20-0331].

JUSTICE MARGUERITE A. GRAYS: [NY R L QUEENS Grays, Part 4, as amended by NY ORDER 20-0324].

JUSTICE RUDOLPH E. GRECO: [NY R L QUEENS Greco, Part 32, as amended by NY ORDER 20-0325].

JUSTICE MAUREEN HEALY: NY R L QUEENS Healy, Part 6.

JUSTICE PHILLIP HOM: [NY R L QUEENS Hom, Part 43, as amended by NY ORDER 20-0332].

JUSTICE KEVIN J. KERRIGAN: NY R L QUEENS Kerrigan, Part 10.

JUSTICE MOJGAN C. LANCMAN: NY R L QUEENS Lancman, Part 20.

JUSTICE RICHARD G. LATIN: NY R L QUEENS Latin, Part 40.

JUSTICE ULYSSES B. LEVERETT: [NY R L QUEENS Leverett, Part 6, as amended by NY ORDER 20-0326].

JUSTICE LEONARD LIVOTE: NY R L QUEENS Livote, Part 33.

JUSTICE LEE A. MAYERSOHN: NY R L QUEENS Mayersohn, Part 22; NY R L QUEENS Mayersohn, Part 22G; [NY R L QUEENS Mayersohn, Part 22G COVID, as amended by NY ORDER 20-0327].

JUSTICE ROBERT J. MCDONALD: NY R L QUEENS McDonald, Part 34.

JUSTICE MARGARET MCGOWAN: NY R L QUEENS McGowan, Part 52.

JUSTICE MAURICE E. MUIR: [NY R L QUEENS Muir, Part 42, as amended by NY ORDER 20-0333].

JUSTICE JODI ORLOW: NY R L QUEENS Orlow, Part 51.

JUSTICE LESLIE J. PURIFICCION: NY R L QUEENS Purificcion, Part 39.

JUSTICE JOSEPH RISI: [NY R L QUEENS Risi, Part 3, as amended by NY ORDER 20-0328].

JUSTICE FREDERICK D.R. SAMPSON: [NY R L QUEENS Sampson, Part 31, as amended by NY ORDER 20-0329].

JUSTICE MARTIN J. SCHULMAN: NY R L QUEENS Schulman, Part 29.

JUSTICE BERNICE D. SIEGAL: NY R L QUEENS Siegal, Part 25G.

JUSTICE JANICE A. TAYLOR: NY R L QUEENS Taylor, Part 15.

JUSTICE CARMEN R. VELASQUEZ: NY R L QUEENS Velasquez, Part 38.

JUSTICE LOURDES M VENTURA: [NY R L QUEENS Ventura, Part 37, as amended by NY ORDER 20-0334].

JUSTICE WILLIAM A. VISCOVICH: NY R L QUEENS Viscovich, Part 63.

JUSTICE ALLAN B. WEISS: NY R L QUEENS Weiss, Part 2.

COMPLIANCE, SETTLEMENT AND CONFERENCE PART: NY R L QUEENS Doc 1.

PRELIMINARY CONFERENCE PART: [NY R L QUEENS Doc. 2, as amended by NY ORDER 20-0335].

MEDICAL MALPRACTICE CONFERENCE PART: [NY R L QUEENS Doc. 3, as amended by NY ORDER 20-0336].

TRIAL SCHEDULING PART: NY R L QUEENS Doc. 4.

SUMMARY JURY TRIAL PROGRAM: NY R L QUEENS Doc. 7.

RESIDENTIAL FORECLOSURE PART: NY R L QUEENS Doc. 9.

FORECLOSURE AUCTION RULES: NY R L QUEENS Doc. 10.

MATRIMONIAL PRELIMINARY CONFERENCE PART: NY R L QUEENS Doc. 11.

NON-CUSTODIAL CONTESTED MATRIMONIAL PART: NY R L QUEENS Doc. 12.

Pleadings
Bill of Particulars

Document Last Updated August 2020

A. Checklist

(I) ❑ Matters to consider for party demanding bill of particulars

- (a) ❑ Required documents
  - (1) ❑ Demand for bill of particulars
  - (2) ❑ Proof of service
- (b) ❑ Supplemental documents
  - (1) ❑ Filing fees
  - (2) ❑ Working copies
  - (3) ❑ Statement of authorization in electronic filing cases
  - (4) ❑ ERIE COUNTY: Additional supplemental documents
    - (i) ❑ Notice of hard copy submission in e-filed case
  - (5) ❑ KINGS COUNTY: Additional supplemental documents
    - (i) ❑ Forms when filing in hard copy

(6) ❑ NEW YORK COUNTY: Additional supplemental documents

(i) ❑ Notice of hard copy submission

(7) ❑ ONONDAGA COUNTY: Additional supplemental documents

(i) ❑ Notice of hard copy submission

(8) ❑ QUEENS COUNTY: Additional supplemental documents

(i) ❑ Notice of hard copy submission

(c) ❑ Timing

(1) ❑ There is no stated time for when the demand may be served, but ordinarily it should not be served before joinder of issue

(2) ❑ The common practice for the defendant is to serve the demand with or after the answer

(3) ❑ If the plaintiff wants a bill regarding affirmative defenses in the answer, the plaintiff can demand it any time after the answer is served; if the answer contains a counterclaim, a demand for a bill of particulars pertaining to the counterclaim may be served with or after the reply

(II) ❑ Matters to consider for party furnishing bill of particulars

(a) ❑ Required documents

(1) ❑ Bill of particulars

(2) ❑ Proof of service

(b) ❑ Supplemental documents

(1) ❑ Supporting evidence; Exhibits

(2) ❑ Filing fees

(3) ❑ Working copies

(4) ❑ ERIE COUNTY: Additional supplemental documents

(i) ❑ Notice of hard copy submission in e-filed case

(5) ❑ KINGS COUNTY: Additional supplemental documents

(i) ❑ Forms when filing in hard copy

(6) ❑ NEW YORK COUNTY: Additional supplemental documents

(i) ❑ Notice of hard copy submission

(7) ❑ ONONDAGA COUNTY: Additional supplemental documents

(i) ❑ Notice of hard copy submission

(8) ❑ QUEENS COUNTY: Additional supplemental documents

(i) ❑ Notice of hard copy submission

(c) ❑ Timing

(1) ❑ Within thirty (30) days of service of a demand for a bill of particulars, the party on whom the demand is made shall serve a bill of particulars complying with each item of the demand, except any item to which the party objects, in which event the reasons for the objection shall be stated with reasonable particularity

B. Timing

1. *Time to serve bill of particulars.* Within thirty (30) days of service of a demand for a bill of particulars, the party on whom the demand is made shall serve a bill of particulars complying with each item of the demand, except any item to which the party objects, in which event the reasons for the objection shall be stated with reasonable particularity. The assertion of an objection to one or more of the items in the demand shall not relieve the party on whom the demand is made from the obligation to respond in full within thirty (30) days of service of the demand to the items of the demand to which no objection has been made. NY CPLR Rule 3042(a).

2. *Computation of time*

a. *Units of time*

i. *Day.* A calendar day includes the time from midnight to midnight. Sunday or any day of the week specifically mentioned means a calendar day. NY GEN CONSTR § 19.

ii. *Month.* In a statute, contract or public or private instrument, unless otherwise provided in such contract or instrument or by law, the term month means a calendar month and not a lunar month. NY GEN CONSTR § 31.

iii. *Year.* For information on the definition of a year, including the definitions of a half-year and quarter-year, refer to NY GEN CONSTR § 58 and NY GEN CONSTR § 50. For information on leap years, refer to NY GEN CONSTR § 57.

b. *Periods of time*

i. *Number of days.* A number of days specified as a period from a certain day within which or after or before which an act is authorized or required to be done means such number of calendar days exclusive of the calendar day from which the reckoning is made. NY GEN CONSTR § 20.

- If such period is a period of two (2) days, Saturday, Sunday or a public holiday must be excluded from the reckoning if it is an intervening day between the day from which the reckoning is made and the last day of the period. NY GEN CONSTR § 20.
- In computing any specified period of time from a specified event, the day upon which the event happens is deemed the day from which the reckoning is made. The day from which any specified period of time is reckoned shall be excluded in making the reckoning. NY GEN CONSTR § 20.

ii. *Number of months.* A number of months after or before a certain day shall be computed by counting such number of calendar months from such day, exclusive of the calendar month in which such day occurs, and shall include the day of the month in the last month so counted having the same numerical order in days of the month as the day from which the computation is made, unless there be not so many days in the last month so counted, in which case the period computed shall expire with the last day of the month so counted. NY GEN CONSTR § 30.

iii. *Publication of notice; Number of days.* The period of publication of a legal notice shall be computed by excluding the first day of publication and including the day on which the act or event of which notice is given is to take place or which completes the full period of publication. NY CPLR § 2402.

iv. *Periods ending on Saturday, Sunday or public holiday.* When any period of time, computed from a certain day, within which or after which or before which an act is authorized or required to be done, ends on a Saturday, Sunday or a public holiday, such act may be done on the next succeeding business day and if the period ends at a specified hour, such act may be done at or before the same hour of such next succeeding business day, except that where a period of time specified by contract ends on a Saturday, Sunday or a public holiday, the extension of such period is governed by NY GEN CONSTR § 25. NY GEN CONSTR § 25-a(1).

- For a list of public holidays, refer to NY GEN CONSTR § 24.

v. *Additional time after certain kinds of service*

- *Service by mail.* Where a period of time prescribed by law is measured from the service of a paper and service is by mail, five (5) days shall be added to the prescribed period. NY CPLR Rule 2103(b)(2).
- *Service by overnight delivery service.* Where a period of time prescribed by law is measured from the service of a paper and service is by overnight delivery, one (1) business day shall be added to the prescribed period. NY CPLR Rule 2103(b)(6).

vi. *Daylight saving time.* For information on New York's time zone and the effect of daylight saving time, refer to NY GEN CONSTR § 52.

c. *Hours of court.* Notwithstanding any provision of law or rule of court to the contrary, throughout the State of New York the sessions of the Supreme Court for the disposition of business before the court shall commence not later than 9:30 a.m. and conclude not earlier than 5 p.m. Where warranted, the Chief Administrator of the Courts may authorize variances in the opening and closing hours of the courts, but, in such event, daily sessions shall total not less than six (6) hours. NY R CHIEF J § 3.1.

d. *Time limits; Extension of time.* Any act required by or in pursuance of law to be performed at or within a prescribed time, shall be performed according to the standard time. NY GEN CONSTR § 53.

i. Except where otherwise expressly prescribed by law, the court may extend the time fixed by any statute, rule or order for doing any act, upon such terms as may be just and upon good cause shown, whether the application for extension is made before or after the expiration of the time fixed. NY CPLR § 2004. Refer to the New York KeyRules Motion for Continuance/Extension of Time document for more information.

C. General Requirements

1. *Bill of particulars.* Any party may require any other party to give a bill of particulars of such party's claim, or a copy of the items of the account alleged in a pleading. As used elsewhere in Article 30 of the CPLR (NY CPLR § 3001, et seq.), the term "bill of particulars" shall include "copy of the items of an account." NY CPLR § 3041. A demand for a bill of particulars shall be made by serving a written demand stating the items concerning which particulars are desired. NY CPLR Rule 3042(a).
   a. *Role of bill of particulars.* A "bill of particulars" in civil practice is an amplification of a pleading. It supplies more detail and therefore affords the adverse party a more thorough picture of the claim or defense being particularized. It's designed to limit the proof and prevent surprise at the trial. SIEGEL-NYPRAC § 238; State v. Horsemen's Benev. & Protective Ass'n (New York Div.), 34 A.D.2d 769, 770, 311 N.Y.S.2d 511, 512 (1970).
   b. *What must be particularized; Burdens.* Parties are required to particularize only that of which they have the burden of proof, and a bill of particulars is as a rule served only when demanded. Plaintiffs must particularize their claims, and defendants their defenses, counterclaims, cross-claims, and third-party claims. But the defendant need not particularize denials contained in the answer because the matters involved are the plaintiff's burden to prove, not the defendant's. SIEGEL-NYPRAC § 238; NY CPLR § 3041; L. F. Dommerich & Co. v. Diener & Dorskind, Inc., 31 A.D.2d 516, 516, 294 N.Y.S.2d 613, 614 (1968).
   c. *Bill of particulars not used to obtain evidence.* It is the general rule that a bill of particulars is not usable to obtain evidence. SIEGEL-NYPRAC § 238; Yardarm Club Hotel, Inc. v. Morgan, 22 A.D.2d 700, 700, 253 N.Y.S.2d 920, 921 (1964).
   d. *Demand and bill are specific to case.* What a party may demand in a bill—and the demand, as long as it is reasonable, determines the bill's contents—is necessarily personal to the particular case. Whatever the pleading pleads, the bill must particularize. With the exception of the personal injury action, where the items that may be demanded have been codified into a list, the things that may be demanded and thus must be particularized are a sui generis inquiry. SIEGEL-NYPRAC § 238.
   e. *Demand in personal injury case.* In actions to recover for personal injuries the following particulars may be required:
      i. The date and approximate time of day of the occurrence;
      ii. Its approximate location;
      iii. General statement of the acts or omissions constituting the negligence claimed;
      iv. Where notice of a condition is a prerequisite, whether actual or constructive notice is claimed;
      v. If actual notice is claimed, a statement of when and to whom it was given;
      vi. Statement of the injuries and description of those claimed to be permanent, and in an action designated in NY INS § 5104(a), for personal injuries arising out of negligence in the use or operation of a motor vehicle in this state, in what respect plaintiff has sustained a serious injury, as defined in NY INS § 5102(d), or economic loss greater than basic economic loss, as defined in NY INS § 5102(a);
      vii. Length of time confined to bed and to house;
      viii. Length of time incapacitated from employment; and
      ix. Total amounts claimed as special damages for physicians' services and medical supplies; loss of earnings, with name and address of the employer; hospital expenses; nurses' services. NY CPLR Rule 3043(a).
      x. A party may serve a supplemental bill of particulars with respect to claims of continuing special damages and disabilities without leave of court at any time, but not less than thirty (30) days prior to trial. Provided however that no new cause of action may be alleged or new injury claimed and that the other party shall upon seven (7) days notice, be entitled to newly exercise any and all rights of discovery but only with respect to such continuing special damages and disabilities. NY CPLR Rule 3043(b).
      xi. Nothing contained in the foregoing shall be deemed to limit the court in denying in a proper case, any one or more of the foregoing particulars, or in a proper case, in granting other, further or different particulars. NY CPLR Rule 3043(c). The list is, nonetheless, the standard for personal injury litigation and the court seldom has occasion to stray far from it. SIEGEL-NYPRAC § 238.

f. *Failure to respond or to comply with demand.* If a party fails to respond to a demand in a timely fashion or fails to comply fully with a demand, the party seeking the bill of particulars may move to compel compliance, or, if such failure is willful, for the imposition of penalties pursuant to NY CPLR Rule 3042(d). NY CPLR Rule 3042(c).

i. If a party served with a demand for a bill of particulars willfully fails to provide particulars which the court finds ought to have been provided pursuant to NY CPLR Rule 3042, the court may make such final or conditional order with regard to the failure or refusal as is just, including such relief as is set forth in NY CPLR § 3126. NY CPLR Rule 3042(d).

g. *Improper or unduly burdensome demand.* If the court concludes that the demand for particulars, or a part thereof, is improper or unduly burdensome, in addition to vacating or modifying the demand, the court may make such order with regard to the improper or unduly burdensome demand as is just. NY CPLR Rule 3042(e).

2. *Amendment of bill of particulars.* In any action or proceeding in a court in which a note of issue is required to be filed, a party may amend the bill of particulars once as of course prior to the filing of a note of issue. NY CPLR Rule 3042(b).

3. *When bill of particulars must be verified.* If a pleading is verified, a subsequent bill of particulars shall also be verified. A bill of particulars of any pleading with respect to a cause of action for negligence shall be verified whether such pleading be verified or not. NY CPLR § 3044.

a. *Verification of pleadings.* A verification is a statement under oath that the pleading is true to the knowledge of the deponent, except as to matters alleged on information and belief, and that as to those matters he believes it to be true. Unless otherwise specified by law, where a pleading is verified, each subsequent pleading shall also be verified, except the answer of an infant and except as to matter in the pleading concerning which the party would be privileged from testifying as a witness. Where the complaint is not verified, a counterclaim, cross-claim or third-party claim in the answer may be separately verified in the same manner and with the same effect as if it were a separate pleading. NY CPLR § 3020(a).

i. *When verification required.* In only a few instances is verification mandatory. SIEGEL-NYPRAC § 232. Among the CPLR instances of mandatory verification of a complaint are where it contains or has appended the schedule of goods and services available for optional use under NY CPLR Rule 3016(f), or where it seeks to charge an obligor with an amount still unsatisfied after prior suit by the obligee against a co-obligor. The pleadings in an Article 78 (NY CPLR § 7801, et seq.) proceeding also require verification. SIEGEL-NYPRAC § 232.

ii. *By whom verification made.* By whom verification made. The verification of a pleading shall be made by the affidavit of the party, or, if two or more parties united in interest are pleading together, by at least one of them who is acquainted with the facts, except:

- If the party is a domestic corporation, the verification shall be made by an officer thereof and shall be deemed a verification by the party;
- If the party is the state, a governmental subdivision, board, commission, or agency, or a public officer in behalf of any of them, the verification may be made by any person acquainted with the facts; and
- If the party is a foreign corporation, or is not in the county where the attorney has his office, or if there are two or more parties united in interest and pleading together and none of them acquainted with the facts is within that county, or if the action or defense is founded upon a written instrument for the payment of money only which is in the possession of an agent or the attorney, or if all the material allegations of the pleading are within the personal knowledge of an agent or the attorney, the verification may be made by such agent or attorney. NY CPLR § 3020(d).

iii. *Form of affidavit of verification.* The affidavit of verification must be to the effect that the pleading is true to the knowledge of the deponent, except as to the matters therein stated to be alleged on information and belief, and that as to those matters he believes it to be true. If it is made by a person other than the party, he must set forth in the affidavit the grounds of his belief as to all matters not stated upon his knowledge and the reason why it is not made by the party. NY CPLR Rule 3021.

iv. *Effect of verified pleading.* Unless they are stated to be made upon the information and belief of the party, they must be regarded for all purposes, including a criminal prosecution, as having been made upon the knowledge of the person verifying the pleading. An allegation that the party has not sufficient knowledge or information to form a belief with respect to a matter, must, for the same purposes, be regarded as an allegation that the person verifying the pleading has not such knowledge or information. NY CPLR Rule 3023. A "verified pleading" may be utilized as an affidavit whenever the latter is required. NY CPLR § 105(u).

- Although pleadings ordinarily need not be verified, a benefit of voluntary verification is that the pleading, pursuant to NY CPLR § 105(u), then qualifies as an affidavit. The Court of Appeals has also held that a verified bill of particulars, which technically is not a pleading, also fell within the scope of NY CPLR § 105(u) and therefore had the effect of an affidavit. NY CPLR § 105(Practice Commentary, C105:7); Sanchez v. Nat'l R.R. Passenger Corp., 21 N.Y.3d 890, 988 N.E.2d 511 (2013). However, a verified pleading will be of no value as an affidavit when the circumstances require evidentiary detail and the pleading is phrased in conclusory terms. NY CPLR § 105(Practice Commentary, C105:7).

v. *Defective verification.* A defectively verified pleading shall be treated as an unverified pleading. Where a pleading is served without a sufficient verification in a case where the adverse party is entitled to a verified pleading, he may treat it as a nullity, provided he gives notice with due diligence to the attorney of the adverse party that he elects so to do. NY CPLR Rule 3022.

4. *Governing law.* The civil practice law and rules (NY CPLR § 101, et seq.) shall govern the procedure in civil judicial proceedings in all courts of the state and before all judges, except where the procedure is regulated by inconsistent statute. The civil practice law and rules shall succeed the civil practice act and rules of civil practice and shall be deemed substituted therefor throughout the statutes and rules of the state. NY CPLR § 101. The civil practice law and rules shall be liberally construed to secure the just, speedy and inexpensive determination of every civil judicial proceeding. NY CPLR § 104.

a. *Uniform trial court rules.* The uniform civil rules for the Supreme Court and County Court (NY R UNIF TRIAL CTS § 202.1, et seq.) shall be applicable to civil actions and proceedings in the Supreme Court and the County Court. NY R UNIF TRIAL CTS § 202.1(a). The provisions of the uniform rules shall be construed consistent with the Civil Practice Law and Rules (CPLR), and matters not covered by the uniform rules shall be governed by the CPLR. NY R UNIF TRIAL CTS § 202.1(d).

b. *Local rules.* Local court rules, not inconsistent with law or with uniform civil rules for the Supreme Court and County Court (NY R UNIF TRIAL CTS § 202.1, et seq.), shall comply with Part 9 of the Rules of the Chief Judge (NY R CHIEF J § 9.1). NY R UNIF TRIAL CTS § 202.1(c).

c. *Official forms.* The state administrator shall have the power to adopt, amend and rescind an appendix of forms. Forms adopted pursuant to NY CPLR § 107 shall be sufficient under the civil practice law and rules and shall illustrate the simplicity and brevity of statement which the civil practice law and rules contemplate. NY CPLR § 107.

5. *Rules of the commercial division.* [Editor's note: certain types of civil cases or civil cases meeting certain monetary thresholds that are filed in the state of New York must be filed in the Commercial Division of the New York Supreme Courts. Rules governing practice in the commercial division are found in NY R UNIF TRIAL CTS § 202.70]. Cases which must be filed in the commercial division are listed below. For more information, refer to NY R UNIF TRIAL CTS § 202.70.

a. *Monetary thresholds.* Except as set forth in NY R UNIF TRIAL CTS § 202.70(b), the monetary thresholds of the Commercial Division, exclusive of punitive damages, interests, costs, disbursements and counsel fees claimed, are established as follows: (1) Albany County, fifty thousand dollars ($50,000); (2) Eighth Judicial District, one hundred thousand dollars ($100,000); (3) Kings County, one hundred fifty thousand dollars ($150,000); (4) Nassau County, two hundred thousand dollars ($200,000); (5) New York County, five hundred thousand dollars ($500,000); (6) Onondaga County, fifty thousand dollars ($50,000); (7) Queens County, one hundred thousand dollars ($100,000); (8) Seventh Judicial District, fifty thousand dollars ($50,000); (9) Suffolk County, one hundred thousand dollars ($100,000); and (10) Westchester County, one hundred thousand dollars ($100,000). NY R UNIF TRIAL CTS § 202.70(a).

i. *ALBANY COUNTY.* The Commercial Division of the Albany County Supreme Court exercises jurisdiction over selected business and commercial disputes in which the amount at issue generally involves damage claims in a minimum amount of fifty thousand dollars ($50,000) as well as claims for unspecified amounts where the value of the commercial asset(s) in dispute exceeds fifty thousand dollars ($50,000). A separate publication promulgating the rules and criteria relating to the filing and management of Commercial Court cases in this part may be obtained from the Albany County Supreme Court Clerk's Office. A section of the Uniform Civil Rules for the Supreme Court and County Court sets forth statewide rules. NY R 3 JD SUP Doc. 1(E).

ii. *BRONX COUNTY.* The monetary threshold for commercial cases in Bronx County will be seventy-five thousand dollars ($75,000). All other parameters including the type of matters that will be heard are contained within the Rules of the Commercial Division of the Supreme Court (NY R UNIF TRIAL CTS § 202.70). NY R BRONX FIL R Doc. 12.

iii. *NEW YORK COUNTY.* The monetary threshold in the New York County Commercial Division, which is generally applicable, is an amount in controversy of five hundred thousand dollars ($500,000) or more (exclusive of punitive damages, interest, costs, disbursements, and counsel fees). If the case is designated a commercial one and the Addendum is submitted, the clerk will review the pleadings to determine whether the amount in controversy in the case meets the monetary threshold or whether an exception to the threshold applies. NY R NY CTY Procedure IA(B). For more information on assigning a case to the commercial division in New York County, refer to NY R NY CTY Procedure IA(B).

b. *Commercial cases.* Actions in which the principal claims involve or consist of the following will be heard in the Commercial Division provided that the monetary threshold is met or equitable or declaratory relief is sought:

   i. Breach of contract or fiduciary duty, fraud, misrepresentation, business tort (e.g., unfair competition), or statutory and/or common law violation where the breach or violation is alleged to arise out of business dealings (e.g., sales of assets or securities; corporate restructuring; partnership, shareholder, joint venture, and other business agreements; trade secrets; restrictive covenants; and employment agreements not including claims that principally involve alleged discriminatory practices);

   ii. Transactions governed by the Uniform Commercial Code (exclusive of those concerning individual cooperative or condominium units);

   iii. Transactions involving commercial real property, including Yellowstone injunctions and excluding actions for the payment of rent only;

   iv. Shareholder derivative actions—without consideration of the monetary threshold;

   v. Commercial class actions—without consideration of the monetary threshold;

   vi. Business transactions involving or arising out of dealings with commercial banks and other financial institutions;

   vii. Internal affairs of business organizations;

   viii. Malpractice by accountants or actuaries, and legal malpractice arising out of representation in commercial matters;

   ix. Environmental insurance coverage;

   x. Commercial insurance coverage (e.g., directors and officers, errors and omissions, and business interruption coverage);

   xi. Dissolution of corporations, partnerships, limited liability companies, limited liability partnerships and joint ventures—without consideration of the monetary threshold; and

   xii. Applications to stay or compel arbitration and affirm or disaffirm arbitration awards and related injunctive relief pursuant to Article 75 of the New York Civil Practice Law and Rules (NY CPLR § 7501, et seq.) involving any of the foregoing enumerated commercial issues. Where the applicable arbitration agreement provides for the arbitration to be heard outside the United States, the monetary threshold set forth in NY R UNIF TRIAL CTS § 202.70(a) shall not apply. NY R UNIF TRIAL CTS § 202.70(b).

c. *Non-commercial cases.* The following will not be heard in the Commercial Division even if the monetary threshold is met:

   i. Suits to collect professional fees;

   ii. Cases seeking a declaratory judgment as to insurance coverage for personal injury or property damage;

   iii. Residential real estate disputes, including landlord-tenant matters, and commercial real estate disputes involving the payment of rent only;

   iv. Home improvement contracts involving residential properties consisting of one to four residential units or individual units in any residential building, including cooperative or condominium units;

   v. Proceedings to enforce a judgment regardless of the nature of the underlying case;

   vi. First-party insurance claims and actions by insurers to collect premiums or rescind non-commercial policies; and

   vii. Attorney malpractice actions except as otherwise provided in NY R UNIF TRIAL CTS § 202.70(b)(8). NY R UNIF TRIAL CTS § 202.70(c).

d. For more information on the Commercial Division, refer to NY R UNIF TRIAL CTS § 202.70.

D. Documents

1. *Required documents*
   a. *Bill of particulars.* Refer to the General Requirements section of this document for information on the bill of particulars.
   b. *Proof of service.* In addition to complying with the provisions of NY CPLR Rule 2101, every paper filed in court shall have annexed thereto appropriate proof of service on all parties where required. NY R UNIF TRIAL CTS § 202.5(a).
2. *Supplemental documents*
   a. *Supporting evidence; Exhibits*
      i. *Foreign language documents.* Where an affidavit or exhibit annexed to a paper served or filed is in a foreign language, it shall be accompanied by an English translation and an affidavit by the translator stating his qualifications and that the translation is accurate. NY CPLR Rule 2101(b).
      ii. *Statement of attorney in lieu of affidavit.* The statement of an attorney admitted to practice in the courts of the state, or of a physician, osteopath or dentist, authorized by law to practice in the state, who is not a party to an action, when subscribed and affirmed by him to be true under the penalties of perjury, may be served or filed in the action in lieu of and with the same force and effect as an affidavit. NY CPLR Rule 2106.
   b. *Filing fees.* The County Clerk shall require the payment of any applicable statutory fees, or an order of the Court waiving payment of such fees, before accepting a paper for filing. NY R UNIF TRIAL CTS § 202.5(d)(1). For information on filing fees, if any, refer to NY CPLR § 8001, et seq.
   c. *Working copies.* The court may require the parties to provide working copies of documents filed electronically. In such event, each working copy shall include, firmly affixed thereto, a copy of a confirmation notice in a form prescribed by the Chief Administrator. NY R UNIF TRIAL CTS § 202.5-b(d)(5).
   d. *ERIE COUNTY: Additional supplemental documents*
      i. *Notice of hard copy submission in e-filed case.* In accordance with NY R UNIF TRIAL CTS § 202.5-b(d), the County Clerk shall refuse to accept for filing, hard copy papers filed to an action subject to electronic filing unless hard copy filing is permitted by the Uniform Rules or NY R ERIE E FIL Doc. 3 and the papers bear a completed Notice of Hard Copy Submission—E-Filed Case form. NY R ERIE E FIL Doc. 3(III)(D).
   e. *KINGS COUNTY: Additional supplemental documents*
      i. *Forms when filing in hard copy.* An attorney who certifies in good faith that he or she lacks the equipment or knowledge needed to e-file and have no staff member or employee under his or her direction who has such knowledge and equipment may opt out of participation in e-filing in a mandatory case by filing a "Notice of Opt-Out from Participation in Action Subject to Mandatory Electronic Filing" form EFM-2 with the Clerk. NY R L KINGS E FIL Doc. 1(A)(2). Where in accordance with the E-Filing Rules a party submits a document in hard copy in an e-filed case (principally, a document submitted by a nonparticipating party (e.g., an attorney) in a consensual case, an emergency filing made in accordance with the Mandatory E-Filing Rules, and any document filed with the court in hard copy by an attorney who has opted out of participation in mandatory e-filing, the document must bear the back page facing out, a "Notice of Hard Copy Submission—E-Filed Cases" form EFM-3. NY R L KINGS E FIL Doc. 1(B)(3).
   f. *NEW YORK COUNTY: Additional supplemental documents*
      i. *Notice of hard copy submission.* Where in accordance with the E-Filing Rules an attorney or an unrepresented litigant who is participating in e-filing submits a document in hard copy in an e-filed case, the document must bear, as the back page facing out, a Notice of Hard-Copy Submission—E-Filed Case (a form available in the "Forms" section on the NYSCEF website (Form EFM-3) and in the court's back offices). NY R NY CTY E FIL Doc. 2(B)(3). For more information refer to NY R NY CTY E FIL Doc. 2.
      ii. *Medical authorizations.* When a defendant in a personal injury action serves a demand for authorizations together with a demand for a bill of particulars, counsel for plaintiff shall serve the authorizations with the bill. NY R NY CTY J RUL Rule 9.
   g. *ONONDAGA COUNTY: Additional supplemental documents*
      i. *Notice of hard copy submission.* Any papers to be filed with the court in an e-filed case must be filed online with the E-filing system except where a special exemption is granted (e.g., oversized maps, photographs). If such an exemption is granted, Form EFM-3, "Notice of Hard Copy Submission—E-Filed Case," must be attached to

such documents forms which are not filed on line. Also, Form EFM-4 "Notice of Hard Copy Exhibit Filing" must be completed and uploaded to the action's e-file. Both of these forms may be found on the NYSCEF website. NY R ONDGA E FIL Protocol(B)(4).

h. *QUEENS COUNTY: Additional supplemental documents*

i. *Notice of hard copy submission.* Any party opting out of the e-filing system must have a "Notice of Hard Copy Submission" firmly affixed to the back of the papers. NY R L QUEENS E-FILE Doc. 1(H)(2)(f).

E. Format

1. *Form of documents*

a. *Size and form of paper.* Each paper served or filed shall be durable, white and, except for summonses, subpoenas, notices of appearance, notes of issue, orders of protection, temporary orders of protection and exhibits, shall be eleven by eight and one-half (11 x 8-1/2) inches in size. NY CPLR Rule 2101(a).

b. *Writing and language.* The writing shall be legible and in black ink. NY CPLR Rule 2101(a). Each paper served or filed shall be in the English language which, where practicable, shall be of ordinary usage. NY CPLR Rule 2101(b).

c. *Caption.* Each paper served or filed shall begin with a caption setting forth the name of the court, the venue, the title of the action, the nature of the paper and the index number of the action if one has been assigned. In all papers other than a summons, a complaint or a judgment it shall be sufficient to state the name of the first named party on each side with an appropriate indication of any omissions. NY CPLR Rule 2101(c).

i. *Further contents of first page.* After the first paper has been filed in each case the index number shall appear on the cover and first page to the right of the caption of every paper tendered for filing in the action. Each such cover and first page also shall contain an indication of the county of venue and a brief description of the nature of the paper and, where the case has been assigned to an individual judge, shall contain the name of the assigned judge to the right of the caption. NY R UNIF TRIAL CTS § 202.5(a); NY R UNIF TRIAL CTS § 202.5(b); NY R UNIF TRIAL CTS § 202.5(d)(1)(i).

d. *Index number.* No paper in an action in the supreme or a county court, other than an order submitted for signature to a judge out of court, shall be submitted for any purpose to the supreme or county court or to a clerk thereof unless there is endorsed on such paper the index number of the action assigned by the clerk of the county. NY CPLR § 8018(c).

i. *ALBANY COUNTY: Index number on all filed documents.* The index number, the request for judicial intervention number and the assigned justice's name shall appear on [all papers filed with the Court subsequent to the complaint]. NY R 3 JD SUP Doc. 1(A).

ii. *ERIE COUNTY: Index number after initial filing.* Cases that are initially commenced by the filing of papers with the NYSCEF system are identified as e-filed cases by assignment of an Index Number that has "800-899" as the first three (3) digits of the index number (i.e. 802391/2012). NY R ERIE E FIL Doc. 3(II). [The] Index Number must be affixed to all document submissions, filings, and communications to the Erie County Clerk and the Court. Cases that are converted from paper to e-filing shall retain the original index number. NY R ERIE E FIL Doc. 3(II).

iii. *KINGS COUNTY: Index number after initial filing.* In cases commenced electronically by the filing of initiating papers with the NYSCEF system and payment of the statutory fees, the Kings County Clerk will issue an NYSCEF designated index number and the filer shall be notified via the NYSCEF system of the index number assigned and filing date. Such index number must be affixed to all document submissions, filings and communications to the Kings County Clerk and Supreme Court. If counsel faces exigent circumstances that require accelerated assignment, counsel may contact Administration of the Kings County Clerk at kcco-efile@nycourts.gov, during normal business hours of the court. NY R L KINGS E FIL Doc. 1(B)(5).

iv. *NEW YORK COUNTY: Index number on hard copy filings.* Papers subsequently presented for filing in hardcopy format will be filed in this jacket. NY R NY CTY Procedure I(B). Index numbers take the form of six digits followed by a slash and the four digits of the year the case began, e.g., 340705/2018. The first or first two integers of the index number identify the type of case. If a case is commenced electronically, the second integer will be a "5", except as indicated otherwise in the list below. There are many tax certiorari matters e-filed annually and the index numbers therefor will normally run over into those with a "6" as the second integer, and the same will occur with general cases if necessary. The principal types of cases and their index number categories are listed in NY R NY CTY Procedure I(B). NY R NY CTY Procedure I(B); NY R NY CTY Procedure XI(A).

v. *ONONDAGA COUNTY: Index number.* The index number must be referenced on all e-filed documents and correspondence. All e-filed case index numbers will contain the letters "EF" between the year and the file number (for example, 2012EF9999). NY R ONDGA E FIL Protocol(B)(1).

vi. *QUEENS COUNTY: Index number on converted cases.* Cases originally commenced in hard-copy form but later converted to an E-file case, either by stipulation or order will bear a regular index number initially. The County Clerk will issue a new E-file index number. NY R L QUEENS E-FILE Doc. 1(B).

e. *Line spacing.* Every paper filed in court, if typewritten, shall have at least double space between each line, except for quotations and the names and addresses of attorneys appearing in the action. NY R UNIF TRIAL CTS § 202.5(a).

f. *Font size.* Each. . .paper printed or typed, served or filed, except for summonses. . .and exhibits, shall be in clear type of no less than ten (10) point in size. NY CPLR Rule 2101(a).

i. Whenever a requirement relating to size of type is stated in point size, the type size requirement shall be deemed met if the x-height of the type is a minimum of forty-five percent (45%) of the specified point size. Each point shall be measured as .351 millimeter. The x-height size shall be measured as it appears on the page. The x-height is the height of the lower case letters, exclusive of ascenders or descenders. NY CPLR § 105(t).

g. *Margins.* Every paper filed in court shall have at least one (1) inch margins. NY R UNIF TRIAL CTS § 202.5(a).

h. *Citations*

i. *Civil practice law and rules.* NY CPLR § 101, et seq. shall be known as the civil practice law and rules, and may be cited as "CPLR". Reference to a provision in the civil practice law and rules may, except when such provision is being enacted or amended, be made without indicating whether it is a rule or section. NY CPLR § 101.

i. *Indorsement by attorney.* Each paper served or filed shall be indorsed with the name, address and telephone number of the attorney for the party serving or filing the paper, or if the party does not appear by attorney, with the name, address and telephone number of the party. NY CPLR Rule 2101(d).

j. *One-sided printing.* In addition, every paper filed in court, other than an exhibit or printed form, shall contain writing on one side only, except that papers that are fastened on the side may contain writing on both sides. NY R UNIF TRIAL CTS § 202.5(a).

k. *Use of copies authorized.* Except where otherwise specifically prescribed, copies, rather than originals, of all papers, including orders, affidavits and exhibits may be served or filed. Where it is required that the original be served or filed and the original is lost or withheld, the court may authorize a copy to be served or filed. NY CPLR Rule 2101(e).

i. Where a certified copy of a paper is required by law, an attorney admitted to practice in the courts of the state may certify that it has been compared by him with the original and found to be a true and complete copy. Such a certificate, when subscribed by such attorney, has the same effect as if made by a clerk. NY CPLR § 2105.

l. *Recycled paper.* It is the policy of the Unified Court System that litigants, where practicable, should file or submit to the courts of the Unified Court System of the State of New York papers printed or reproduced on recycled paper. Paper is considered recycled if it contains a minimum content of thirty percent (30%) waste paper. NY R UNIF TRIAL CTS § 215.2. The signature page of every paper filed or submitted to the court on recycled paper should bear the legend: "Printed [Reproduced] on Recycled Paper." NY R UNIF TRIAL CTS § 215.3.

m. *KINGS COUNTY: Tabs on filings.* Motions, orders and other filed papers shall be indexed with protruding tabs. Clerks are required to reject papers that do not have protruding exhibit tabs, except papers in matrimonial cases and papers filed by pro se litigants. NY R L KINGS Pt. A, Papers.

2. *Form of electronic documents.* Each paper served or filed by electronic means, as defined in NY CPLR Rule 2103(f), shall be capable of being reproduced by the receiver so as to comply with the provisions of NY CPLR Rule 2101(a) through NY CPLR Rule 2101(d). NY CPLR Rule 2101(g).

a. *File format.* All e-filed documents shall comply with the technical requirements set forth at the NYSCEF site. NY R UNIF TRIAL CTS § 202.5-b(d)(1)(i).

b. *Heading of document.* The subject matter heading for each paper sent by electronic means must indicate that the matter being transmitted electronically is related to a court proceeding. NY CPLR Rule 2103(b)(7).

c. *E-filed documents identification*

i. *ERIE COUNTY.* E-filed cases must be readily identifiable and marked as such. If counsel presents papers to the Office of the Erie County Clerk or the Office of the Chief Clerk in a NYSCEF matter where authorized, counsel should alert the Clerk that the case is a NYSCEF matter. NY R ERIE E FIL Doc. 3(II).

ii. *KINGS COUNTY.* The Supreme Court's Civil Case Information System ("CCIS") will further identify e-filed cases by the addition of a suffix to the index number (e.g. 500136/2006E). This suffix should be used on all documents filed with the court in e-filed matters. NY R L KINGS E FIL Doc. 1(A)(1).

3. *Signature blocks.* Every pleading, written motion, and other paper, served on another party or filed or submitted to the court shall be signed by an attorney, or by a party if the party is not represented by an attorney, with the name of the attorney or party clearly printed or typed directly below the signature. NY R CHIEF ADMIN § 130-1.1-a(a); NY R UNIF TRIAL CTS § 202.5(d)(1)(iv).
   a. *Printed name.* Beneath each signature shall be printed the name signed. NY CPLR Rule 2101(a).
   b. *Failure to sign.* Absent good cause shown, the court shall strike any unsigned paper if the omission of the signature is not corrected promptly after being called to the attention of the attorney or party. NY R CHIEF ADMIN § 130-1.1-a(a).
   c. *Signature as certification.* By signing a paper, an attorney or party certifies that, to the best of that person's knowledge, information and belief, formed after an inquiry reasonable under the circumstances the presentation of the paper or the contentions therein are not frivolous as defined in NY R CHIEF ADMIN § 130-1.1(c). NY R CHIEF ADMIN § 130-1.1-a(b)(1).
   d. *Electronic signatures.* A document shall be considered to have been signed by an attorney or party in compliance with NY R CHIEF ADMIN § 130-1.1-a if it has been signed by such attorney or party as provided in NY R UNIF TRIAL CTS § 202.5-b(e)(1) and it bears the signatory's name. NY R UNIF TRIAL CTS § 202.5-b(e)(2). An electronically filed document shall be considered to have been signed by, and shall be binding upon, the person identified as a signatory, if:
      i. It bears the physical signature of such person and is scanned into an electronic format that reproduces such signature; or
      ii. The signatory has electronically affixed the digital image of his or her signature to the document; or
      iii. It is electronically filed under the User ID and password of that person; or
      iv. In a tax certiorari action in which the parties have stipulated to this procedure, it is an initiating document that is electronically filed without the signature of the signatory in a form provided above in NY R UNIF TRIAL CTS § 202.5-b(e)(iv), provided that, prior to filing, the document is signed in full in hard copy (which hard copy must be preserved until the conclusion of all proceedings, including appeals, in the case in which it is filed); or
      v. In a small claims assessment review proceeding, it is a petition recorded by the NYSCEF site upon the filing of a text file as provided in NY R UNIF TRIAL CTS § 202.5-b(b)(1), provided that prior to filing, the document was signed in full in hard copy (which hard copy must be preserved until the conclusion of all proceedings in the matter, including article 78 (NY CPLR § 7801, et seq.) review and any appeals, and must be made available during the proceeding upon request of the respondent or the court); or
      vi. It otherwise bears the electronic signature of the signatory in a format conforming to such standards and requirements as may hereafter be established by the Chief Administrator. NY R UNIF TRIAL CTS § 202.5-b(e).

4. *Confidentiality of personal information.* No person may file any document available for public inspection with any state agency, political subdivision, or in any court of this state that contains a Social Security account number of any other person, unless such other person is a dependent child, or has consented to such filing, except as required by federal or state law or regulation, or by court rule. NY GEN BUS § 399-ddd. Submissions pursuant to e-filing procedures shall have the same confidentiality rights as paper documents. NY R UNIF TRIAL CTS § 202.5-b(k)(1).
   a. *Confidential personal information.* Except in the actions designated in NY R UNIF TRIAL CTS § 202.5(e)(1), or as otherwise provided by rule or law or court order, and whether or not a sealing order is or has been sought, the parties shall omit or redact confidential personal information in papers submitted to the court for filing. For purposes of NY R UNIF TRIAL CTS § 202.5(e), confidential personal information ("CPI") means:
      i. The taxpayer identification number of an individual or an entity, including a Social Security number, an employer identification number, and an individual taxpayer identification number, except the last four (4) digits thereof;
      ii. The date of an individual's birth, except the year thereof;
      iii. The full name of an individual known to be a minor, except the minor's initials;
      iv. A financial account number, including a credit and/or debit card number, a bank account number, an investment account number, and/or an insurance account number, except the last four (4) digits or letters thereof; and
      v. Any of the documents or testimony in a matrimonial action protected by NY DOM REL § 235 or evidence sealed by the court in such an action which are attached as exhibits or referenced in the papers filed in any other civil

action. For purposes of NY R UNIF TRIAL CTS § 202.5, a matrimonial action shall mean: an action to annul a marriage or declare the nullity of a void marriage, an action or agreement for a separation, an action for a divorce, or an action or proceeding for custody, visitation, writ of habeus corpus, child support, maintenance or paternity. NY R UNIF TRIAL CTS § 202.5(e)(1).

vi. *ERIE COUNTY.* An attorney or unrepresented litigant filing a document via the NYSCEF system must comply with the requirements of NY R UNIF TRIAL CTS § 202.5(e) regarding the redaction of Confidential Personal Information and NY GEN BUS § 399-ddd(6) concerning the filing of documents containing Social Security Numbers. It is the sole responsibility of counsel or unrepresented litigant filing to be aware of and to comply with existing laws requiring non-disclosure of personal information contained in any document e-filed in NYSCEF. NY R ERIE E FIL Doc. 3(III)(G); NY R ERIE E FIL Doc. 3(III).

vii. *KINGS COUNTY.* An attorney or unrepresented litigant filing a document via the NYSCEF system must comply with the requirements of General Business Law § 399-dd(6), which often require redaction of any Social Security number that appear in the original document. The NYSCEF system automatically redacts portions of filed documents which apparently contain Social Security numbers pursuant to NY R UNIF TRIAL CTS § 202.5-b(k). In the event the filing party receives e-mail notice through NYSCEF that a Social Security number in a filed document has been redacted, and the filing party concludes such redaction is erroneous, the filer should click on the link provided in the e-mail to permit the County Clerk to revert the redaction. For Confidential Personal Information, see NY R UNIF TRIAL CTS § 202.5(e) and NY R L KINGS E FIL Doc. 1(B)(11). [Editor's note: the reference to General Business Law § 399-dd(6) is likely a reference to NY GEN BUS § 399-ddd(6)]. NY R L KINGS E FIL Doc. 1(B)(10); NY R L KINGS E FIL Doc. 1(K)(1).

viii. *NEW YORK COUNTY.* It is the responsibility of counsel and parties to comply with rules restricting disclosure of confidential personal information. Nevertheless, NYSCEF screens filings and endeavors to identify any that contain social security numbers. When such numbers are discovered through this process, NYSCEF will restrict portions of or all of such documents from public view. Where NYSCEF has redacted what it believes to be a social security number, it will transmit to the filer a notice advising of the action taken and requesting that the filer review the matter and provide notification as set forth in the notice if the redaction has been made in error. NY R NY CTY E FIL Doc. 2(K)(1); NY R NY CTY J RUL Rule A-1. Documents filed in the past in "secure status" under a procedure no longer in place will retain that status unless otherwise directed by the court. NY R NY CTY E FIL Doc. 2(K)(2).

b. *Submission of confidential personal information.* Where a person submitting a paper to a court for filing believes in good faith that the inclusion of the full confidential personal information described in NY R UNIF TRIAL CTS § 202.5(e)(1) is material and necessary to the adjudication of the action or proceeding before the court, he or she may apply to the court for leave to serve and file together with a paper in which such information has been set forth in abbreviated form a confidential affidavit or affirmation setting forth the same information in unabbreviated form, appropriately referenced to the page or pages of the paper at which the abbreviated form appears. NY R UNIF TRIAL CTS § 202.5(e)(3).

c. *Home addresses.* For information on when home addresses and other personal information must be redacted, refer to NY CPLR Rule 2103-a.

5. *Defective papers.* A defect in the form of a paper, if a substantial right of a party is not prejudiced, shall be disregarded by the court, and leave to correct shall be freely given. NY CPLR Rule 2101(f). Papers that are stapled or bound securely shall not be rejected for filing simply because they are not bound with a backer of any kind. NY R UNIF TRIAL CTS § 202.5(a). A paper filed in accordance with the rules of the chief administrator or any local rule or practice established by the court shall be deemed filed. NY CPLR Rule 2102(b).

a. *Objection to defective papers.* The party on whom a paper is served shall be deemed to have waived objection to any defect in form unless, within fifteen (15) days after the receipt thereof, the party on whom the paper is served returns the paper to the party serving it with a statement of particular objections. NY CPLR Rule 2101(f).

F. Filing and Service Requirements

1. *Filing requirements.* Except where otherwise prescribed by law or order of court, papers required to be filed shall be filed with the clerk of the court in which the action is triable. In an action or proceeding in supreme or court, papers required to be filed shall be filed with the clerk of the county in which the proceeding is brought. NY CPLR Rule 2102(a).

a. *Electronic filing.* On consent, documents may be filed and served by electronic means in Supreme Court in such civil actions and in such counties as shall be authorized by order of the Chief Administrator of the Courts and only to the extent and in the manner provided in NY R UNIF TRIAL CTS § 202.5-b. NY R UNIF TRIAL CTS § 202.5-b(a)(1). For the definitions of terms used in electronic filing, refer to NY R UNIF TRIAL CTS § 202.5-b(a)(2).

i. *E-filing mandatory.* In any action subject to e-filing, all documents required to be filed with the court by an e-filing party shall be filed and served electronically, except as provided in NY R UNIF TRIAL CTS § 202.5-b. NY R UNIF TRIAL CTS § 202.5-b(d)(1)(i).

- *ERIE COUNTY.* Case types currently eligible and accepted for e-filing are listed at the NYSCEF website. Note that some actions or special proceedings, (i.e., name changes) which are otherwise subject to mandatory e-filing, if commenced by unrepresented litigants will NOT be maintained in the NYSCEF system; individual cases may be found either at NYSCEF or in the Erie County Clerk's online records system. NY R ERIE E FIL Doc. 3(I)(E).
- *KINGS COUNTY.* Cases that are commenced by filing of the initiating papers with NYSCEF are identified as e-filed cases by assignment of a special index number (i.e., Index Numbers beginning with 500,000). NY R L KINGS E FIL Doc. 1(A)(1). All cases required to be e-filed are listed in Uniform Rule 202.5-bb (Mandatory E-Filing Rules) and on the NYSCEF website. All such cases must be commenced by filing with the County Clerk electronically through NYSCEF and all subsequent documents in such cases must be e-filed. Any questions regarding mandatory e-filing in Kings County can be e-mailed to kcco-efile@nycourts.gov. NY R L KINGS E FIL Doc. 1(A)(2).
- *NEW YORK COUNTY.* Unless otherwise provided in the Rules or in NY R NY CTY E FIL Doc. 2 or where a special exemption is granted due to physical requirements (e.g., oversized maps; see NY R NY CTY E FIL Doc. 2(B)(10)), all documents to be filed with the court in a NYSCEF case, including all documents on motions and all letters to the court (where permitted), must be filed with the NYSCEF system. Documents that attorneys would not ordinarily file with the court in a hard-copy case need not be e-filed. Unless otherwise provided by the E-Filing Rules or this Protocol, in e-filed cases the County Clerk and the court will not accept documents filed in paper form. NY R NY CTY E FIL Doc. 2(B)(1). E-filing is mandatory in all types of cases (other than election law, matrimonial, Art. 78, and Mental Hygiene Law matters, and Art. 70 habeas corpus proceedings) that are commenced in this court on or after February 19, 2013. All such cases must be commenced by filing with the County Clerk electronically through NYSCEF and all subsequent documents in such cases must be e-filed. NY R NY CTY E FIL Doc. 2(A)(2)(a). For more information, including information on consensual e-filing and filing scanned hard copy documents, refer to NY R NY CTY E FIL Doc. 2(A)(2).
- *QUEENS COUNTY.* All authorized Torts, Commercial and Tax Certiorari cases may be commenced by E-Filing, however all parties must consent for the action to continue as an E-file case. NY R L QUEENS E-FILE Doc. 1(A). All papers to be filed with the court in an E-filed case shall be filed on-line with the E-file system except as directed by the court. Papers that attorneys would not ordinarily file with the court in a hard-copy case need not be filed in an E-filed matter. NY R L QUEENS E-FILE Doc. 1(E)(2).

ii. *Who may file.* Documents may be filed or served electronically only by a person who has registered as an authorized e-filing user or as otherwise provided in NY R UNIF TRIAL CTS § 202.5-b(c). NY R UNIF TRIAL CTS § 202.5-b(c)(1).

iii. *When filing made.* Documents may be transmitted at any time of the day or night to the NYSCEF site. A document other than an order or judgment is filed when its electronic transmission or, in the case of a petition that is e-filed by submission of a text file as provided in NY R UNIF TRIAL CTS § 202.5-b(b)(1), the electronic transmission of the text file is recorded at that site, provided, however, that where payment of a fee is required upon the filing of a document, the document is not filed until transmission of the document and the information or form or information as required in NY R UNIF TRIAL CTS § 202.5-b(d)(2)(i), NY R UNIF TRIAL CTS § 202.5-b(d)(2)(ii) or NY R UNIF TRIAL CTS § 202.5-b(d)(2)(iii) has been recorded at the NYSCEF site; or, if no transmission of that information or form or information is recorded, where permitted by the County Clerk, until payment is presented to the County Clerk. NY R UNIF TRIAL CTS § 202.5-b(d)(3)(i).

iv. *Notification of filing.* No later than the close of business on the business day following the electronic filing of a document, a notification, in a form prescribed by the Chief Administrator, shall be transmitted electronically by the NYSCEF site to the person filing such document and the e-mail service addresses of all other participating parties in such action. NY R UNIF TRIAL CTS § 202.5-b(d)(3)(ii).

v. *Removal of confidential information and other corrections.* If a document filed electronically is subsequently discovered to contain confidential data—including but not limited to trade secrets, information protected by confidentiality agreement, or personal confidential information as defined by statute or court rule—or otherwise to have been filed in error, the filer or another party or affected person may (1) notify the parties and any non-party filers in the action of the confidentiality issue or other error raised by the filing, and of his or her intention to seek judicial relief to correct the filing: (2) following such notification, request that the appropriate County Clerk, exercising his or her administrative discretion, place the document temporarily in "restricted" status on the NYSCEF site, to be made available for viewing by court staff and the parties but not the general public; and (3) file an application to correct the filing by order to show cause within five (5) business days of such notification (or such time as the court may direct), including a request for preliminary injunctive relief limiting interim disclosure of the document at issue. Unless otherwise directed by the court, any document placed in restricted status in response to such a request shall be returned to public view upon expiration of this five (5) day period. The Chief Administrator of the Courts shall promulgate forms to implement this process. NY R UNIF TRIAL CTS § 202.5-b(d)(3)(iii).

- *KINGS COUNTY.* For information on what to do when a document was erroneously filed with confidential information, refer to NY R L KINGS E FIL Doc. 1(B)(11).
- *NEW YORK COUNTY.* For information on what to do when a document was erroneously filed with confidential information, refer to NY R NY CTY E FIL Doc. 2(B)(8).
- *QUEENS COUNTY.* For information on what to do when a document was erroneously filed with confidential information, refer to NY R L QUEENS E-FILE Doc. 1(E)(7).

vi. *Documents requiring judge's signature.* Except where the court directs otherwise, any document that requires a judge's signature shall be transmitted electronically and in hard copy to the court. NY R UNIF TRIAL CTS § 202.5-b(d)(6).

vii. *Documents which would be inconvenient to file electronically; Hard copies.* Notwithstanding any other provision of NY R UNIF TRIAL CTS § 202.5-b, and subject to such guidelines as may be established by the Chief Administrative Judge, the County Clerk or his or her designee may require or permit a party to file in hard copy, in accordance with procedures set by the County Clerk or designee, an exhibit or other document which it is impractical or inconvenient to file electronically. NY R UNIF TRIAL CTS § 202.5-b(d)(7).

- *ERIE COUNTY.* Please contact the Supervisor of Actions & Proceedings, Erie County Clerk's Office by calling (716) 858-6662 or the Deputy County Clerk—Legal at (716) 858-6348 for information. NY R ERIE E FIL Doc. 3(III)(F).
- *KINGS COUNTY.* With limited exceptions, as set forth in the Uniform Rules and herein, all documents to be filed with the court in a NYSCEF case shall be filed online via the NYSCEF system. However, should the size, consistency or context of a hard copy document preclude electronic filing, the user shall electronically file a "Notice of Hard Copy Submission—E-Filed Cases" form EFM-3. Any hard copy submitted pursuant to NY R L KINGS E FIL Doc. 1(B)(9) shall include, as a cover page firmly fastened thereto, a copy of the Confirmation Notice received from the NYSCEF site confirming receipt of the "Notice of Hard Copy Submission—E-Filed Cases". Any party may object to such hard copy filing. The Court, in response to such objection, may, following the hard copy filing, fashion such relief as it deems appropriate pursuant to and in furtherance of the Uniform Rules and NY R L KINGS E FIL Doc. 1, including, but not limited to, an Order directing the filing party to file such documents online via the NYSCEF system. When exhibits are impractical to file pursuant to NY R UNIF TRIAL CTS § 202.5-b(d)(7), an additional "Notice of Hard Copy Exhibit Filing" form EFM-4 is required to be submitted. NY R L KINGS E FIL Doc. 1(B)(9).
- *NEW YORK COUNTY.* If a filer needs to submit unusual exhibits in original form that cannot practically be e-filed, such as oversized maps or electronic recordings, the filer should consult with the County Clerk's E-File Department by telephone at 646-386-3737 (procedural questions only) or by e-mail at ccnyef@nycourts.gov, which will normally require that the filer retain custody of the original subject to possible future directives of the court. NY R NY CTY E FIL Doc. 2(B)(10). In such instances, the filing counsel shall file with NYSCEF a "placeholder" in the form of a Notice of Hard Copy Exhibit Filing (NYSCEF Form EF 21). The Notice should be uploaded to NYSCEF as document type "Exhibit" and the filer should indicate in the "Additional Document Information" field that the filer is retaining custody of the original. Failure to e-file the Notice may result in a gap in the official record of the court. NY R NY CTY E FIL Doc. 2(B)(10).

viii. *Documents containing sensitive or proprietary information.* In an action subject to e-filing, any person may apply for an order prohibiting or restricting the electronic filing in the action of specifically identified materials on the grounds that such materials are subject to copyright or other proprietary rights, or trade secret or other privacy interests, and that electronic filing in the action is likely to result in substantial prejudice to those rights or interests. NY R UNIF TRIAL CTS § 202.5-b(k)(2).

ix. *Refusal to accept paper filings.* In accordance with NY CPLR Rule 2102(c), a County Clerk and a chief clerk of the Supreme Court or County Court, as appropriate, shall refuse to accept for filing papers filed in actions and proceedings when the paper sought to be filed:

- Is in an action subject to electronic filing pursuant to Rules of the Chief Administrator,
- Is not being filed electronically, and
- Does not include the notice required by NY R UNIF TRIAL CTS § 202.5-b(d)(1). NY R UNIF TRIAL CTS § 202.5(d)(1)(v); NY R UNIF TRIAL CTS § 202.5-bb(d).

x. *Emergency filings; Hard copies.* For information on when an emergency filing may be filed and served in hard copy, refer to NY R UNIF TRIAL CTS § 202.5-b(d)(1)(ii), NY R UNIF TRIAL CTS § 202.5-b(d)(1)(iii) and NY R UNIF TRIAL CTS § 202.5-bb(c)(3).

- *KINGS COUNTY.* Under the rules, a participating emergency e-filer must electronically file the documents initially filed in hard copy form within three (3) business days of the emergency filing; the originals will be discarded after the documents have been processed and the failure to e-file as required will therefore lead to an incomplete record. NY R L KINGS E FIL Doc. 1(B)(3).
- *NEW YORK COUNTY.* Occasionally an emergency will arise requiring expedited entry of a document with the County Clerk (e.g., an order issued in the courtroom after a conference or argument of a critical matter), such as for purposes of an immediate appeal. Expedition can be achieved by the Part as follows: the document should be carried by a Court Officer or staff member to the General Clerk's Office to assure immediate and proper recordation in the computer and, as appropriate, the posting of the document to NYSCEF or the Supreme Court Records On-Line Library ("Scroll"). The court will accommodate counsel in emergencies. NY R NY CTY Procedure XI(A).

xi. *Technical failures.* The NYSCEF site shall be considered to be subject to a technical failure on a given day if the site is unable to accept filings or provide access to filed documents continuously or intermittently over the course of any period of time greater than one (1) hour after 12:00 noon of that day. Notice of all such technical failures shall be provided on the site. NY R UNIF TRIAL CTS § 202.5-b(i).

- When e-filing is hindered by a technical failure, a party may file with the appropriate clerk and serve in hard copy. NY R UNIF TRIAL CTS § 202.5-b(i). In the event an attorney or party shall file and serve documents in hard copy pursuant to NY R UNIF TRIAL CTS § 202.5-b(i), each such document shall include the notice required by NY R UNIF TRIAL CTS § 202.5-b(d)(1), and the filer shall file those documents with the NYSCEF site within three (3) business days after restoration of normal operations at that site. NY R UNIF TRIAL CTS § 202.5-b(i).
- With the exception of deadlines that by law cannot be extended, the time for filing of any document that is delayed due to technical failure of the site shall be extended for one (1) day for each day on which such failure occurs, unless otherwise ordered by the court. NY R UNIF TRIAL CTS § 202.5-b(i).
- *ERIE COUNTY.* When filing by electronic means is hindered by a technical failure, please refer to the NY R UNIF TRIAL CTS § 202.5-b(i). NY R ERIE E FIL Doc. 3(III)(K).
- *KINGS COUNTY.* When filing by electronic means is hindered by a NYSCEF technical failure (as set forth in NY R UNIF TRIAL CTS § 202.5-b(i)), a party may file with the appropriate Clerk in hard copy. Except for deadlines that by law cannot be extended (e.g. Statute of limitations, Notice of Appeal), the time for filing of any document that is delayed due to technical failure of the NYSCEF system shall be extended for one day for each day on which such failure occurs, unless otherwise ordered by the court. NY R L KINGS E FIL Doc. 1(B)(13).
- *ONONDAGA COUNTY.* When filing by electronic means is hindered by a technical failure (as set forth in NY R UNIF TRIAL CTS § 202.5-b(h)(3)(i)), a party may file a hard copy with the County Clerk. With the exception of deadlines that by law cannot be extended (e.g., a statute of limitations or the deadline for filing a Notice of Appeal), the time for filing of any document that is delayed due to technical failure of the NYSCEF system will be extended for one day for each day on which such failure occurs, unless otherwise ordered by the court. A "Notice of Hard Copy Filing Submission—E-Filed Case' must accompany any documents not filed via NYSCEF. NY R ONDGA E FIL Protocol(B)(8).

xii. *Filing fees.* For information on what information must be provided to pay filing fees, refer to NY R UNIF TRIAL CTS § 202.5-b(d)(2).

xiii. *Exemption from e-filing.* For information on exemptions from e-filing, refer to NY R UNIF TRIAL CTS § 202.5-bb(e).

xiv. *Filing exhibits*

- *ERIE COUNTY.* In the NYSCEF system, each exhibit must be uploaded as a separate .pdf file. After uploading a primary document, please choose the document type "Exhibit" and enter the appropriate number or letter and a brief description of the exhibit; each exhibit should bear a separate cover sheet clearly marked as "Exhibit A," "Exhibit B," etc. "Exhibit A" or "Exhibit B" is unacceptable as a brief description of the exhibit. Exhibits, where referenced in a signed Order as attached or affixed shall be uploaded with the signed Order as one .pdf document. NY R ERIE E FIL Doc. 3(III)(H).
- *KINGS COUNTY.* In the NYSCEF system, each exhibit should be uploaded as a separate PDF file. After uploading a primary document, please choose the document type "Exhibit", enter the appropriate number or letter, and be sure to place a check mark to the right of "Attach to main document". Each exhibit shall bear a separate cover sheet clearly marked as Exhibit A, Exhibit B, etc. NY R L KINGS E FIL Doc. 1(B)(12).
- *NEW YORK COUNTY.* Attorneys submitting exhibits in NYSCEF cases should make each exhibit a separate attachment to an affidavit/affirmation in the system; i.e., exhibits should not be filed as a single PDF-A together with the affidavit/affirmation or grouped together as a single PDF-A attachment because either of these two formats makes it difficult for the Justice to locate particular exhibits as needed. Counsel must also include appropriate descriptive language in the "Additional Document Information" field in NYSCEF. NY R NY CTY E FIL Doc. 2(D)(6).
- *ONONDAGA COUNTY.* All exhibits in e-filed cases must be e-filed individually as separate attachments. NY R ONDGA E FIL Protocol(B)(9)(b).

xv. *Correcting documents*

- *ERIE COUNTY.* Submission of documents which, upon examination, require correction or addition will result in notification to the filer advising that the document has been returned for correction. The filer shall make the required corrections and/or additions as indicated in the e-mail transmission sent by the County Clerk or Part Clerk through the NYSCEF site. The corrected documents may be resubmitted using the "Re-file this document" link highlighted in the filer's document list for the respective case. Please note that in the case of multiple submissions, all related documents filed at the same time may be removed from the case record and returned until all documents are properly submitted. NY R ERIE E FIL Doc. 3(III)(J).
- *KINGS COUNTY.* Submission of documents which, upon examination, require correction or addition will result in notification to the filer advising that there is a problem with a document. The filer shall make the required corrections and/or additions and resubmit the corrected document using the "Refile this document" link. In the event a document is returned for correction, the original file date will be preserved. For corrections of documents filed with the Kings County Clerk which require a court order, refer to the procedure in NY R UNIF TRIAL CTS § 202.5-b(d)(3)(iii) and NY R L KINGS E FIL Doc. 1(B)(11). NY R L KINGS E FIL Doc. 1(B)(3).
- *ONONDAGA COUNTY.* If there is an error or an additional document is required, the system will notify the filing party, who will make the corrections/additions and resubmit them online. NY R ONDGA E FIL Protocol(B)(6).
- *QUEENS COUNTY.* Generally speaking, documents that have been E-filed will not thereafter be deleted by the County Clerk from NYCEF because the filer asserts that the filing contains an error or a significant omission. When the filer wishes to correct a perceived error or omission in a filed document, he or she should file an amended version of the document, with the original remaining on file, or else obtain a court order providing for deletion of the original. The County Clerk will only delete a document upon request of the filer or on the County Clerk's own initiative when it is obvious from the face of the document alone that the filer made a fundamental error and never intended to file the document that was filed (e.g., a completely unrelated non-litigation document, a different case, or a wrong county). The County Clerk will advise the filer when any such fundamental errors are detected. NY R L QUEENS E-FILE Doc. 1(E)(6).

b. *Facsimile filing.* In the Supreme Court, facsimile filing shall be limited to commercial claims and tax certiorari, conservatorship, and mental hygiene proceedings in Monroe, Westchester, New York and Suffolk Counties. NY R

UNIF TRIAL CTS § 202.5-a(a)(1). Refer to NY R UNIF TRIAL CTS § 202.5-a for information on the procedures for facsimile filing.

i. *NEW YORK COUNTY.* Unless indicated otherwise by the court in a particular case or in NY R NY CTY J RUL Doc. 1, Justices do not accept papers by fax. NY R NY CTY J RUL Rule 4.

2. *Service requirements*

a. *Who may serve.* Except where otherwise prescribed by law or order of court, papers may be served by any person not a party of the age of eighteen years or over. NY CPLR Rule 2103(a).

b. *Service upon attorney.* Except where otherwise prescribed by law or order of court, papers to be served upon a party in a pending action shall be served upon the party's attorney. Where the same attorney appears for two or more parties, only one (1) copy need be served upon the attorney. Such service upon an attorney shall be made:

i. By delivering the paper to the attorney personally. NY CPLR Rule 2103(b)(1).

ii. By mailing the paper to the attorney at the address designated by that attorney for that purpose or, if none is designated, at the attorney's last known address; service by mail shall be complete upon mailing. NY CPLR Rule 2103(b)(2).

iii. If the attorney's office is open, by leaving the paper with a person in charge, or if no person is in charge, by leaving it in a conspicuous place; or if the attorney's office is not open, by depositing the paper, enclosed in a sealed wrapper directed to the attorney, in the attorney's office letter drop or box. NY CPLR Rule 2103(b)(3).

iv. By leaving it at the attorney's residence within the state with a person of suitable age and discretion. Service upon an attorney shall not be made at the attorney's residence unless service at the attorney's office cannot be made. NY CPLR Rule 2103(b)(4).

v. By transmitting the paper to the attorney by facsimile transmission, provided that a facsimile telephone number is designated by the attorney for that purpose. Service by facsimile transmission shall be complete upon the receipt by the sender of a signal from the equipment of the attorney served indicating that the transmission was received, and the mailing of a copy of the paper to that attorney. The designation of a facsimile telephone number in the address block subscribed on a paper served or filed in the course of an action or proceeding shall constitute consent to service by facsimile transmission in accordance with NY CPLR Rule 2103(b)(5). An attorney may change or rescind a facsimile telephone number by serving a notice on the other parties. NY CPLR Rule 2103(b)(5).

vi. By dispatching the paper to the attorney by overnight delivery service at the address designated by the attorney for that purpose or, if none is designated, at the attorney's last known address. Service by overnight delivery service shall be complete upon deposit of the paper enclosed in a properly addressed wrapper into the custody of the overnight delivery service for overnight delivery, prior to the latest time designated by the overnight delivery service for overnight delivery. "Overnight delivery service" means any delivery service which regularly accepts items for overnight delivery to any address in the state. NY CPLR Rule 2103(b)(6).

vii. By transmitting the paper to the attorney by electronic means where and in the manner authorized by the chief administrator of the courts by rule and, unless such rule shall otherwise provide, such transmission shall be upon the party's written consent. The subject matter heading for each paper sent by electronic means must indicate that the matter being transmitted electronically is related to a court proceeding. NY CPLR Rule 2103(b)(7).

- *KINGS COUNTY.* Pursuant to the E-Filing Rules, service of interlocutory documents is made by posting a document to the NYSCEF site, which automatically and immediately transmits an email notice of the filing, including a link to the document, to all participating counsel and unrepresented litigants on the case. The Rules also authorize service by other methods permitted by the CPLR. If service by such other method is made, proof of service must be filed with NYSCEF. NY R L KINGS E FIL Doc. 1(I).
- *NEW YORK COUNTY.* Service. . .will be made automatically through NYSCEF upon all participating counsel and unrepresented parties in the case. There are limited exceptions to the requirement for e-filing in the covered kinds of cases. NY R NY CTY Procedure XI(A). Pursuant to the E-Filing Rules, service of interlocutory documents is made by posting a document to the NYSCEF site, which automatically and immediately transmits an e-mail notice of the filing, including a link to the document, to all participating counsel and unrepresented litigants on the case. The Rules also authorize service by other methods permitted by the CPLR. If service by such a method is made, proof of service must be filed with NYSCEF. NY R NY CTY E FIL Doc. 2(I).
- *QUEENS COUNTY.* Filing with the system permits counsel to serve the papers electronically pursuant to

NY R UNIF TRIAL CTS § 202.5-b(f) once consent to E-Filing has been filed on-line. Consult NY R UNIF TRIAL CTS § 202.5-bb(c) for service in mandatory e-filing. Any required proof of service should be E-filed as a separate document. NY R L QUEENS E-FILE Doc. 1(E)(4).

c. *Electronic service mandatory; Consenting to electronic service; How electronic service may be made.* Except as otherwise provided in NY R UNIF TRIAL CTS § 202.5-bb, filing and service of all documents in an action that has been commenced electronically in accordance with NY R UNIF TRIAL CTS § 202.5-bb shall be by electronic means. NY R UNIF TRIAL CTS § 202.5-bb(c)(1).

  i. *Party's consent required for certain e-filing.* After commencement of an action wherein e-filing is authorized, documents may be electronically filed and served, but only by, and electronic service shall be made only upon, a party or parties who have consented thereto. NY R UNIF TRIAL CTS § 202.5-b(b)(2)(i).

    - A consent to e-filing in an action shall state that the party providing it agrees to the use of e-filing in the action and to be bound by the filing and service provisions in NY R UNIF TRIAL CTS § 202.5-b. NY R UNIF TRIAL CTS § 202.5-b(b)(2)(ii).

  ii. *Address for service; Duty to notify as to changes.* The e-mail service address recorded at the time of registration is the e-mail address at which service of interlocutory documents on that party may be made through notification transmitted by the NYSCEF site. It is the responsibility of each filing user to monitor that address and promptly notify the Resource Center in the event of a change in his or her e-mail service address. NY R UNIF TRIAL CTS § 202.5-b(f)(2)(i).

  iii. *How service made.* An e-filing party causes service of an interlocutory document to be made upon another party participating in e-filing by filing the document electronically. Upon receipt of an interlocutory document, the NYSCEF site shall automatically transmit electronic notification to all e-mail service addresses in such action. NY R UNIF TRIAL CTS § 202.5-b(f)(2)(ii).

    - Except as provided otherwise in NY R UNIF TRIAL CTS § 202.5-b(h)(3), the electronic transmission of the notification shall constitute service of the document on the e-mail service addresses identified therein; however, such service will not be effective if the filing party learns that the notification did not reach the address of the person to be served. Proof of such service will be recorded on the NYSCEF site. A party may, however, utilize other service methods permitted by the CPLR provided that, if one of such other methods is used, proof of that service shall be filed electronically. NY R UNIF TRIAL CTS § 202.5-b(f)(2)(ii).

  iv. *Signatures on hard copies; Proof of service filed electronically.* When an e-filing party serves a document in hard copy on a non-participating party, the document served shall bear full signatures of all signatories and proof of such service shall be filed electronically. NY R UNIF TRIAL CTS § 202.5-b(b)(2)(i).

    - *ERIE COUNTY.* In the NYSCEF system, each Affidavit of Service must be uploaded as a separate .pdf file. After uploading the Affidavit, please choose the document type: "Affirmation/Affidavit of Service" and enter the name of the party served as Additional Document Information. NY R ERIE E FIL Doc. 3(III)(I).

  v. *Effect of failure to consent.* A party's failure to consent to participation in electronic filing and service shall not bar any other party to the action from filing documents electronically with the County Clerk and the court or serving documents upon any other party who has consented to participation. A party who has not consented to participation shall file documents with the court and the County Clerk, and serve and be served with documents, in hard copy. NY R UNIF TRIAL CTS § 202.5-b(b)(2)(i).

d. *Service upon party.* If a party has not appeared by an attorney or the party's attorney cannot be served, service shall be upon the party by a method specified in NY CPLR Rule 2103(b)(1), NY CPLR Rule 2103(b)(2), NY CPLR Rule 2103(b)(4), NY CPLR Rule 2103(b)(5) or NY CPLR Rule 2103(b)(6). NY CPLR Rule 2103(c).

e. *Service on all parties.* Each paper served on any party shall be served on every other party who has appeared, except as otherwise may be provided by court order or as provided in NY CPLR § 3012 or in NY CPLR § 3215(f). Upon demand by a party, the plaintiff shall supply that party with a list of those who have appeared and the names and addresses of their attorneys. NY CPLR Rule 2103(e).

f. *Service by filing.* If a paper cannot be served by any of the methods specified in NY CPLR Rule 2103(b) and NY CPLR Rule 2103(c), service may be made by filing the paper as if it were a paper required to be filed. NY CPLR Rule 2103(d).

g. *Definitions.* For the purposes of NY CPLR Rule 2103:

  i. "Mailing" means the deposit of a paper enclosed in a first class postpaid wrapper, addressed to the address designated by a person for that purpose or, if none is designated, at that person's last known address, in a post office or official depository under the exclusive care and custody of the United States Postal Service within the state;

ii. "Electronic means" means any method of transmission of information between computers or other machines designed for the purpose of sending and receiving such transmissions, and which allows the recipient to reproduce the information transmitted in a tangible medium of expression;

iii. "Facsimile transmission" means any method of transmission of documents to a facsimile machine at a remote location which can automatically produce a tangible copy of such documents. NY CPLR Rule 2103(f).

G. Hearings

1. There is no hearing required or contemplated in the New York rules governing the bill of particulars.

H. Forms

1. New York Bill of Particulars Forms

a. Form; The basic form of a defendant's demand for a bill of particulars in an action for breach of a contract for services when the contract is not attached to the complaint. NYPRAC-COMM § 23:25.

b. Form; The basic form of a plaintiff's bill of particulars in an action for breach of a contract for services when the contract was not reduced to writing. NYPRAC-COMM § 23:26.

I. Applicable Rules

1. *State rules*

a. Short title; Application; Construction; Definitions. NY CPLR § 101; NY CPLR § 104; NY CPLR § 105.

b. Appendix of official forms. NY CPLR § 107.

c. Extensions of time generally. NY CPLR § 2004.

d. Form of papers. NY CPLR Rule 2101; NY CPLR Rule 2102; NY CPLR § 2105; NY CPLR Rule 2106; NY GEN BUS § 399-ddd; NY R UNIF TRIAL CTS § 215.2; NY R UNIF TRIAL CTS § 215.3.

e. Service of papers. NY CPLR Rule 2103.

f. Computation of time. NY CPLR § 2402; NY GEN CONSTR § 19; NY GEN CONSTR § 20; NY GEN CONSTR § 25-a; NY GEN CONSTR § 30; NY GEN CONSTR § 31; NY GEN CONSTR § 53.

g. Verification. NY CPLR § 3020; NY CPLR Rule 3021; NY CPLR Rule 3022; NY CPLR Rule 3023.

h. Bill of particulars in any case. NY CPLR § 3041.

i. Procedure for bill of particulars. NY CPLR Rule 3042.

j. Bill of particulars in personal injury actions. NY CPLR Rule 3043.

k. Verification of bill of particulars. NY CPLR § 3044.

l. Fees; Index number fees of county clerks. NY CPLR § 8018.

m. Hours of court. NY R CHIEF J § 3.1.

n. Application of part; Waiver; Additional rules; Application of CPLR; Definitions. NY R UNIF TRIAL CTS § 202.1.

o. Papers filed in court; Electronic filing in supreme court. NY R UNIF TRIAL CTS § 202.5; NY R UNIF TRIAL CTS § 202.5-a; NY R UNIF TRIAL CTS § 202.5-b; NY R UNIF TRIAL CTS § 202.5-bb.

p. Rules of the commercial division of the Supreme Court. NY R UNIF TRIAL CTS § 202.70.

q. Signing of papers. NY R CHIEF ADMIN § 130-1.1-a.

2. *Local rules*

a. *Albany County*

i. Third judicial district rules. NY R 3 JD SUP Doc. 1.

b. *Bronx County*

i. Commercial division. NY R BRONX FIL R Doc. 12.

c. *Erie County*

i. Joint protocols for New York State Courts E-Filing (NYSCEF) cases filed in Supreme Court, Erie County. NY R ERIE E FIL Doc. 3.

d. *Kings County*
   i. Papers. NY R L KINGS Pt. A, Papers.
   ii. Protocol on courthouse and county clerk procedures for electronically filed cases. NY R L KINGS E FIL Doc. 1.
e. *New York County*
   i. Commencement of cases. NY R NY CTY Procedure I.
   ii. RJIs and assignments. NY R NY CTY Procedure IA.
   iii. County clerk litigation functions. NY R NY CTY Procedure XI.
   iv. Protocol on courthouse and county clerk procedures for electronically filed cases. NY R NY CTY E FIL Doc. 2.
   v. Redaction of information in documents filed with the county clerk and the court. NY R NY CTY J RUL Rule A-1.
   vi. Papers by fax. NY R NY CTY J RUL Rule 4.
   vii. Medical authorizations. NY R NY CTY J RUL Rule 9.
f. *Onondaga County*
   i. Onondaga county protocol for case filings New York State Electronic Files (NYSCEF). NY R ONDGA E FIL Protocol.
g. *Queens County*
   i. Queens county protocol on courthouse procedures for electronically filed cases. NY R L QUEENS E-FILE Doc. 1.

J. Miscellaneous

NOTE: Individual judges' rules may apply.

ALBANY COUNTY

JUSTICE LISA M. FISHER: NY R 3 JD FISHER Fisher; NY R 3 JD FISHER Fisher, PC Order.

JUSTICE RICHARD MOTT: NY R 3 JD MOTT Mott.

JUSTICE STEPHAN G. SCHICK: NY R 3 JD Schick.

FORECLOSURE SETTLEMENT PART: NY R 3 JD Foreclosure Settlement.

BRONX COUNTY

JUSTICE PAUL L. ALPERT: [NY R BRONX J Part IA-29, as amended by NY ORDER 20-0337].

JUSTICE BEN BARBATO: NY R BRONX J Part IA-21.

JUSTICE MARY ANNE BRIGANTTI: [NY R BRONX J Part IA-15, as amended by NY ORDER 20-0338].

JUSTICE JOSEPH E. CAPELLA: NY R BRONX J Part IA-23.

JUSTICE MITCHELL DANZIGER: NY R BRONX J Part IA-3/33 ; [NY R BRONX J Danziger, Part IA-3/33, as amended by NY ORDER 20-0339].

JUSTICE LAURA G. DOUGLAS: NY R BRONX J Part IA-11.

JUSTICE RUBEN FRANCO: NY R BRONX J Part IA-26.

JUSTICE DORIS M. GONZALEZ: NY R BRONX J Part IA-24.

JUSTICE WILMA GUZMAN: NY R BRONX J Part IA-7; [NY R BRONX J Guzman, Part IA-7 Virtual, as amended by NY ORDER 20-0340].

JUSTICE ROBERT T. JOHNSON: NY R BRONX J Part IA-12.

JUSTICE DONALD A. MILES: NY R BRONX J Part IA-8.

JUSTICE DONNA M. MILLS: NY R BRONX J Part IA-9.

JUSTICE JULIA I. RODRIGUEZ: NY R BRONX J Part IA-18; [NY R BRONX J Part IA-27, as amended by NY ORDER 20-0341].

JUSTICE LLINET M. ROSADO: [NY R BRONX J Part IA-25, as amended by NY ORDER 20-0342].

JUSTICE NORMA RUIZ: NY R BRONX J Part IA-22; [NY R BRONX J Ruiz, Part IA-22 Virtual, as amended by NY ORDER 20-0343].

JUSTICE HOWARD H. SHERMAN: NY R BRONX J Part IA-4.

JUSTICE FERNANDO TAPIA: NY R BRONX J Part IA-13.

JUSTICE ELIZABETH A. TAYLOR: NY R BRONX J Part IA-2.

JUSTICE ALISON Y. TRUITT: NY R BRONX J Part IA-5.

PART IDV: NY R BRONX J Doc. 1.

PRE-TRIAL PART RULES: NY R BRONX J Doc. 2.

PRE TRIAL WORKSHEET: NY R BRONX J Doc. 3.

FORECLOSURE SETTLEMENT PART RULES: NY R BRONX J Doc. 4.

GUARDIANSHIP PART RULES: NY R BRONX J Doc. 5.

LPM PART RULES: NY R BRONX J Doc. 6.

ERIE COUNTY

JUSTICE M. WILLIAM BOLLER: NY R 8 JD J Boller.

JUSTICE RALPH A. BONIELLO: NY R 8 JD J Boniello.

JUSTICE CHRISTOPHER J. BURN: NY R 8 JD J Burns.

JUSTICE RUSSELL P. BUSCAGLIA: NY R 8 JD J Buscaglia.

JUSTICE FRANK CARUSO: NY R 8 JD J Caruso.

JUSTICE STEPHEN W. CASS: NY R 8 JD J Cass.

JUSTICE DEBORAH A. CHIMES: NY R 8 JD J Chimes.

JUSTICE EMILIO COLAIACOVO: [NY R 8 JD J Colaiacovo, as amended by NY ORDER 20-0252].

JUSTICE DIANE Y. DEVLIN: NY R 8 JD J Devlin.

JUSTICE JAMES H. DILLON: NY R 8 JD J Dillon.

JUSTICE PAULA L. FEROLETO: NY R 8 JD J Feroleto.

JUSTICE DANIEL J. FURLONG: [NY R 8 JD J Furlong, as amended by NY ORDER 20-0253].

JUSTICE JOSEPH R. GLOWNIA: NY R 8 JD J Glownia.

JUSTICE MARK J. GRISANTI: NY R 8 JD J Grisanti.

JUSTICE DEBORAH A. HAENDIGES: NY R 8 JD J Haendiges.

JUSTICE LYNN W. KEANE: [NY R 8 JD J Keane, as amended by NY ORDER 20-0254].

JUSTICE RICHARD C. KLOCH, Sr.: NY R 8 JD J Kloch.

JUSTICE FREDERICK J. MARSHALL: [NY R 8 JD J Marshall, as amended by NY ORDER 20-0255.

JUSTICE JOHN L. MICHALSKI: NY R 8 JD J Michalski.

JUSTICE MARK A. MONTOUR: [NY R 8 JD J Montour, as amended by NY ORDER 20-0256].

JUSTICE HENRY NOWAK: NY R 8 JD J Nowak.

JUSTICE JOHN F. O'DONNELL: NY R 8 JD J O'Donnell.

JUSTICE JEANETTE OGDEN: NY R 8 JD J Ogden.

JUSTICE CATHERINE NUGENT-PANEPINTO: NY R 8 JD J Nugent-Panepinto.

JUSTICE FRANK A. SEDITA, III: [NY R 8 JD J Sedita, as amended by NY ORDER 20-0257].

JUSTICE SARA SHELDON: NY R 8 JD J Sheldon.

JUSTICE DONNA M. SIWEK: NY R 8 JD J Siwek.

JUSTICE MARY L. SLISZ: NY R 8 JD J Slisz.

JUSTICE TIMOTHY J. WALKER: [NY R 8 JD J Walker, as amended by NY ORDER 20-0258].

JUSTICE DENNIS E. WARD: NY R 8 JD J Ward.
JUSTICE PAUL B. WOJTASZEK: [NY R 8 JD J Wojtaszek, as amended by NY ORDER 20-0259].
JUSTICE CHARLES N. ZAMBITO: [NY R 8 JD J Zambito, as amended by NY ORDER 20-0260].
SUPREME COURT LEGAL STAFF: NY R 8 JD J Legal Staff.

KINGS COUNTY

JUSTICE RACHEL A. ADAMS: NY R KINGS J Part 5F.
JUSTICE LOREN BAILY-SCHIFFMAN: NY R KINGS J Part 65.
JUSTICE REGINALD A. BODDIE: NY R KINGS J Part 95.
JUSTICE THERESA M. CICCOTTO: NY R KINGS J Part 19; NY R KINGS J Part 5J.
JUSTICE LISSETTE COLON: NY R KINGS J Part Rules.
JUSTICE GENINE EDWARDS: NY R KINGS J Part 80.
JUSTICE PAMELA L. FISHER: [NY R KINGS J Part 94, as amended by NY ORDER 20-0208].
JUSTICE ROBIN GARSON: NY R KINGS J Part 75.
JUSTICE LARA J. GENOVISI: [NY R KINGS J Part 34, as amended by NY ORDER 20-0209].
JUSTICE BERNARD J. GRAHAM: NY R KINGS J Part 36.
JUSTICE DAWN JIMENEZ-SALTA: NY R KINGS J Part 88.
JUSTICE INGRID JOSEPH: [NY R KINGS J Part FRP3 and Part 83, as amended by NY ORDER 20-0210].
JUSTICE KATHY J. KING: NY R KINGS J Part 64, 76K.
JUSTICE LAWRENCE KNIPEL: NY R KINGS J Part 57.
JUSTICE DONALD KURTZ: NY R KINGS J Part 26.
JUSTICE CARL LANDICINO: [NY R KINGS J Part 81, as amended by NY ORDER 20-0211].
JUSTICE KATHERINE LEVINE: [NY R KINGS J Part 20, 25, 92, as amended by NY ORDER 20-0211].
JUSTICE LORNA MCALLISTER: [NY R KINGS J Part 10, as amended by NY ORDER 20-0211].
JUSTICE ROSEMARIE MONTALBANO: [NY R KINGS J Part 19, 71, and 22, as amended by NY ORDER 20-0211].
JUSTICE RICHARD J. MONTELIONE: [NY R KINGS J Part 99 and DJMP, as amended by NY ORDER 20-0215].
JUSTICE LISA S. OTTLEY: NY R KINGS J Part 24.
JUSTICE MARK I. PARTNOW: NY R KINGS J Part 43.
JUSTICE ERIC I. PRUS: NY R KINGS J Part 5A.
JUSTICE FRANCOIS RIVERA: NY R KINGS J Part 52.
JUSTICE KAREN B. ROTHENBERG: NY R KINGS J Part 35.
JUSTICE LEON RUCHELSMAN: NY R KINGS J Part 1.
JUSTICE WAYNE P. SAITTA: NY R KINGS J Part 29.
JUSTICE ROBIN K. SHEARES: NY R KINGS J Part 96.
JUSTICE KENNETH P. SHERMAN: NY R KINGS J Part 67 and 78.
JUSTICE DEBRA SILBER: NY R KINGS J Part 9 and 5K.
JUSTICE ELLEN M. SPODEK: NY R KINGS J Part 63.
JUSTICE MARSHA L. STEINHARDT: NY R KINGS J Part 15.
JUSTICE JEFFREY S. SUNSHINE: NY R KINGS J Part 5G.
JUSTICE PETER P. SWEENEY: [NY R KINGS J Part 35, as amended by NY ORDER 20-0218].
JUSTICE DELORES J. THOMAS: [NY R KINGS J Part 5T, as amended by NY ORDER 20-0221].
JUSTICE WAVNY TOUSSAINT: NY R KINGS J Part 70.
JUSTICE RICHARD VELASQUEZ: NY R KINGS J Part 66.

JUSTICE CAROLYN E. WADE: NY R KINGS J Part 84.

JUSTICE EDWARD G. WALKER: [NY R KINGS J Part 90, as amended by NY ORDER 20-0219].

JUSTICE LILLIAN WAN: [NY R KINGS J Part 17, as amended by NY ORDER 20-0220].

JUSTICE MICHELLE WESTON: NY R KINGS J Part 3.

MENTAL HYGIENE PART: NY R KINGS J Part 77.

MATRIMONIAL PARTS DURING COVID-19 EMERGENCY: JUSTICE KAREN B. ROTHENBERG: NY R KINGS J Doc. 1.

NASSAU COUNTY

JUSTICE ANNA R. ANZALONE: NY R NASSAU S J Anzalone, Part 26.

JUSTICE STACY D. BENNETT: NY R NASSAU S J Bennett; NY R NASSAU S J Bennett, Form 1.

JUSTICE ANTONIO BRANDVEEN: NY R NASSAU S J Brandveen, Part 31.

JUSTICE JEFFREY S. BROWN: [NY R NASSAU S J Brown, as amended by NY ORDER 20-0297].

JUSTICE STEPHEN A. BUCARIA: NY R NASSAU S J Bucaria.

JUSTICE JULIANNE T. CAPETOLA: NY R NASSAU S J Capetola, Part 28.

JUSTICE EDMUND M. DANE: NY R NASSAU S J Dane, Part 33.

JUSTICE VITO M. DESTEFANO: NY R NASSAU S J DeStefano, Part 13; NY R NASSAU S J DeStefano, Form 1.

JUSTICE ARTHUR M. DIAMOND: NY R NASSAU S J Diamond, Part 7.

JUSTICE THOMAS FEINMAN: NY R NASSAU S J Feinman, Part 5.

JUSTICE JOHN M. GALASSO: NY R NASSAU S J Galasso, Part 22.

JUSTICE SHARON M.J. GIANELLI: NY R NASSAU S J Gianelli, Part 22; NY R NASSAU S J Gianelli, Form 1.

JUSTICE JEFFREY A. GOODSTEIN: NY R NASSAU S J Goodstein, Part 33; NY R NASSAU S J Goodstein, Form 1.

JUSTICE DAVID J. GUGERTY: [NY R NASSAU S J Gugerty, Part 31, as amended by NY ORDER 20-0298].

JUSTICE HELENE F. GUGERTY: NY R NASSAU S J Gugerty, Part 47.

JUSTICE STEVEN M. JAEGER: NY R NASSAU S J Jaeger, Part 35; NY R NASSAU S J Jaeger, Form 1.

JUSTICE JACK L. LIBERT: NY R NASSAU S J Libert, Part 23.

JUSTICE JOSEPH H. LORINTZ: NY R NASSAU S J Lorintz, Part 26; NY R NASSAU S J Lorintz, Form 1.

JUSTICE ROY S. MAHON: NY R NASSAU S J Mahon, Part 3.

JUSTICE RANDY SUE MARBER: NY R NASSAU S J Marber, Part 8.

JUSTICE JAMES P. MCCORMACK: [NY R NASSAU S J McCormack, Part 18, as amended by NY ORDER, 20-0299].

JUSTICE DICCIA T. PINEDA-KIRWAN: [NY R NASSAU S J Pineda-Kirwan, as amended by NY ORDER 20-0300].

JUSTICE THOMAS RADEMAKER: [NY R NASSAU S J Rademaker, Part 28, as amended by NY ORDER 20-0301]; [NY R NASSAU S J Rademaker, Form 1, as amended by NY ORDER 20-0301].

JUSTICE DENISE L. SHER: NY R NASSAU S J Rademaker, Part 32.

JUSTICE LEONARD D. STEINMAN: [NY R NASSAU S J Steinman, Part 15, as amended by NY ORDER 20-0303]; NY R NASSAU S J Steinman, Form 1.

JUSTICE HOWARD E. STURIM: NY R NASSAU S J Sturim, Part 50; NY R NASSAU S J Sturim, Form 1.

JUSTICE HELEN VOUTSINAS: [NY R NASSAU S J Voutsinas, Part 25, as amended by NY ORDER 20-0304]; [NY R NASSAU S J Voutsinas, Form 1, as amended by NY ORDER 20-0305].

JUSTICE HOPE SCHWARTZ ZIMMERMAN: NY R NASSAU S J Zimmerman, Part 17.

NEW YORK COUNTY

JUDGE'S RULES; BASIC INFORMATION: [NY R NY CTY J RUL Doc. 1, as amended by NY ORDER 20-0202].

ONONDAGA COUNTY

JUSTICE ROBERT E. ANTONACCI II: [NY R ONDGA E FIL Doc. 1, as amended by 20-0239].

JUSTICE MICHAEL V. COCCOMI: NY R ONDGA E FIL Doc. 2.

JUSTICE GREGORY R. GILBERT: NY R 5 JD JUDGES Gilbert; NY R ONDGA E FIL Doc. 3.

JUSTICE DONALD A. GREENWOOD: NY R ONDGA E FIL Doc. 4.

JUSTICE DEBORAH H. KARALUNAS: NY R ONDGA E FIL Doc. 5.

JUSTICE JAMES MCCLUSKY: NY R 5 JD MCCLUSKY McClusky.

JUSTICE CHARLES C. MERRELL: NY R 5 JD MERRELL Merrell.

JUSTICE PATRICK F. MACRAE: NY R 5 JD MACRAE Doc. 1.

JUSTICE JAMES P. MURPHY: NY R ONDGA E FIL Doc. 7.

JUSTICE GERALD J. NERI: [NY R 5 JD JUDGES Neri, as amended by NY ORDER 20-0236]; [NY R ONDGA E FIL Doc. 8, as amended by NY ORDER 20-0241].

JUSTICE ANTHONY J. PARIS: NY R 5 JD JUDGES Paris; [NY R ONDGA E FIL Doc. 9, as amended by NY ORDER 20-0242].

JUSTICE NORMAN W. SEITER, JR.: NY R 5 JD JUDGES Seiter.

JUSTICE KEVIN G. YOUNG: [NY R ONDGA E FIL Doc. 10, as amended by NY ORDER 20-0243].

QUEENS COUNTY

JUSTICE PAM JACKMAN BROWN: [NY R L QUEENS Brown, Part 19, as amended by NY ORDER 20-0321].

JUSTICE CHEREE A. BUGGS: NY R L QUEENS Buggs, Part 30.

JUSTICE PAM JACKMAN BROWN: [NY R L QUEENS Brown, Part 19, as amended by NY ORDER 20-0321].

JUSTICE DENIS J. BUTLER: NY R L QUEENS Butler, Part 12.

JUSTICE ROBERT I. CALORAS: [NY R L QUEENS Caloras, Part 36, as amended by NY ORDER 20-0322].

JUSTICE ANNA CULLEY: NY R L QUEENS Culley, Part 53.

JUSTICE TIMOTHY DUFFICY: NY R L QUEENS Dufficy, Part 35.

JUSTICE DAVID ELLIOT: NY R L QUEENS Elliot, Part 14.

JUSTICE JOSEPH J. ESPOSITO: NY R L QUEENS Esposito, Part 6.

JUSTICE DARRELL L. GAVRIN: [NY R L QUEENS Gavrin, Part 27, as amended by NY ORDER 20-0323].

JUSTICE WYATT N. GIBBONS: [NY R L QUEENS Gibbons, Part 5, as amended by NY ORDER 20-0330.

JUSTICE DONNA-MARIE E. GOLIA: [NY R L QUEENS Golia, Part 21, as amended by NY ORDER 20-0331].

JUSTICE MARGUERITE A. GRAYS: [NY R L QUEENS Grays, Part 4, as amended by NY ORDER 20-0324].

JUSTICE RUDOLPH E. GRECO: [NY R L QUEENS Greco, Part 32, as amended by NY ORDER 20-0325].

JUSTICE MAUREEN HEALY: NY R L QUEENS Healy, Part 6.

JUSTICE PHILLIP HOM: [NY R L QUEENS Hom, Part 43, as amended by NY ORDER 20-0332].

JUSTICE KEVIN J. KERRIGAN: NY R L QUEENS Kerrigan, Part 10.

JUSTICE MOJGAN C. LANCMAN: NY R L QUEENS Lancman, Part 20.

JUSTICE RICHARD G. LATIN: NY R L QUEENS Latin, Part 40.

JUSTICE ULYSSES B. LEVERETT: [NY R L QUEENS Leverett, Part 6, as amended by NY ORDER 20-0326].

JUSTICE LEONARD LIVOTE: NY R L QUEENS Livote, Part 33.

JUSTICE LEE A. MAYERSOHN: NY R L QUEENS Mayersohn, Part 22; NY R L QUEENS Mayersohn, Part 22G; [NY R L QUEENS Mayersohn, Part 22G COVID, as amended by NY ORDER 20-0327].

JUSTICE ROBERT J. MCDONALD: NY R L QUEENS McDonald, Part 34.

JUSTICE MARGARET MCGOWAN: NY R L QUEENS McGowan, Part 52.

JUSTICE MAURICE E. MUIR: [NY R L QUEENS Muir, Part 42, as amended by NY ORDER 20-0333].

JUSTICE JODI ORLOW: NY R L QUEENS Orlow, Part 51.

JUSTICE LESLIE J. PURIFICCION: NY R L QUEENS Purificcion, Part 39.

JUSTICE JOSEPH RISI: [NY R L QUEENS Risi, Part 3, as amended by NY ORDER 20-0328].

JUSTICE FREDERICK D.R. SAMPSON: [NY R L QUEENS Sampson, Part 31, as amended by NY ORDER 20-0329].
JUSTICE MARTIN J. SCHULMAN: NY R L QUEENS Schulman, Part 29.
JUSTICE BERNICE D. SIEGAL: NY R L QUEENS Siegal, Part 25G.
JUSTICE JANICE A. TAYLOR: NY R L QUEENS Taylor, Part 15.
JUSTICE CARMEN R. VELASQUEZ: NY R L QUEENS Velasquez, Part 38.
JUSTICE LOURDES M VENTURA: [NY R L QUEENS Ventura, Part 37, as amended by NY ORDER 20-0334].
JUSTICE WILLIAM A. VISCOVICH: NY R L QUEENS Viscovich, Part 63.
JUSTICE ALLAN B. WEISS: NY R L QUEENS Weiss, Part 2.
COMPLIANCE, SETTLEMENT AND CONFERENCE PART: NY R L QUEENS Doc 1.
PRELIMINARY CONFERENCE PART: [NY R L QUEENS Doc. 2, as amended by NY ORDER 20-0335].
MEDICAL MALPRACTICE CONFERENCE PART: [NY R L QUEENS Doc. 3, as amended by NY ORDER 20-0336].
TRIAL SCHEDULING PART: NY R L QUEENS Doc. 4.
SUMMARY JURY TRIAL PROGRAM: NY R L QUEENS Doc. 7.
RESIDENTIAL FORECLOSURE PART: NY R L QUEENS Doc. 9.
FORECLOSURE AUCTION RULES: NY R L QUEENS Doc. 10.
MATRIMONIAL PRELIMINARY CONFERENCE PART: NY R L QUEENS Doc. 11.
NON-CUSTODIAL CONTESTED MATRIMONIAL PART: NY R L QUEENS Doc. 12.

Motions, Oppositions and Replies
Motion for Leave to Amend

Document Last Updated August 2020

A. Checklist

(I) ❑ Matters to consider for moving party
- (a) ❑ Required documents
  - (1) ❑ Notice of motion, order to show cause, or affidavit on ex parte motion
  - (2) ❑ Motion
  - (3) ❑ Request for judicial intervention
  - (4) ❑ Proposed amended pleading
  - (5) ❑ Proof of service
  - (6) ❑ ALBANY COUNTY: Additional required documents
    - (i) ❑ Affirmation of good faith effort
- (b) ❑ Supplemental documents
  - (1) ❑ Supporting evidence; Exhibits
  - (2) ❑ Brief
  - (3) ❑ Notice to produce papers not in possession of the court
  - (4) ❑ Filing fees
  - (5) ❑ Working copies
  - (6) ❑ ERIE COUNTY: Additional supplemental documents
    - (i) ❑ Notice of hard copy submission in e-filed case
  - (7) ❑ KINGS COUNTY: Additional supplemental documents
    - (i) ❑ Forms when filing in hard copy

- (8) ❑ NEW YORK COUNTY: Additional supplemental documents
  - (i) ❑ Notice of hard copy submission
  - (ii) ❑ Unpublished opinions
- (9) ❑ ONONDAGA COUNTY: Additional supplemental documents
  - (i) ❑ Notice of hard copy submission
- (10) ❑ QUEENS COUNTY: Additional supplemental documents
  - (i) ❑ Notice of hard copy submission

(c) ❑ Timing

- (1) ❑ A party may amend his or her pleading at any time by leave of court or by stipulation of all parties
- (2) ❑ The moving party shall serve copies of all affidavits and briefs upon all other parties at the time of service of the notice of motion
- (3) ❑ A notice of motion and supporting affidavits shall be served at least eight (8) days before the time at which the motion is noticed to be heard
- (4) ❑ It is also good practice to make motions returnable at least three (3) weeks away from the planned date of mailing and to always include a demand in the motion that the other side serve answering papers at least seven (7) days before the return day
- (5) ❑ ERIE COUNTY: Additional supplemental documents
  - (i) ❑ Notice of hard copy submission in e-filed case
- (6) ❑ KINGS COUNTY: Additional supplemental documents
  - (i) ❑ Forms when filing in hard copy
- (7) ❑ NEW YORK COUNTY: Additional supplemental documents
  - (i) ❑ Notice of hard copy submission
  - (ii) ❑ Unpublished opinions
- (8) ❑ ONONDAGA COUNTY: Additional supplemental documents
  - (i) ❑ Notice of hard copy submission
- (9) ❑ QUEENS COUNTY: Additional supplemental documents
  - (i) ❑ Notice of hard copy submission

(II) ❑ Matters to consider for opposing party

(a) ❑ Required documents

- (1) ❑ Opposition
- (2) ❑ Proof of service

(b) ❑ Supplemental documents

- (1) ❑ Supporting evidence; Exhibits
- (2) ❑ Brief
- (3) ❑ Filing fees
- (4) ❑ Working copies
- (5) ❑ ERIE COUNTY: Additional supplemental documents
  - (i) ❑ Notice of hard copy submission in e-filed case
- (6) ❑ KINGS COUNTY: Additional supplemental documents
  - (i) ❑ Forms when filing in hard copy
- (7) ❑ NEW YORK COUNTY: Additional supplemental documents
  - (i) ❑ Notice of hard copy submission
  - (ii) ❑ Unpublished opinions

(8) ❑ ONONDAGA COUNTY: Additional supplemental documents

(i) ❑ Notice of hard copy submission

(9) ❑ QUEENS COUNTY: Additional supplemental documents

(i) ❑ Notice of hard copy submission

(c) ❑ Timing

(1) ❑ Answering affidavits shall be served at least two (2) days before the time at which the motion is noticed to be heard

(2) ❑ Answering affidavits and any notice of cross-motion, with supporting papers, if any, shall be served at least seven (7) days before such time if a notice of motion served at least sixteen (16) days before such time so demands

B. Timing

1. *Time to bring motion for leave to amend.* A party may amend his or her pleading, or supplement it by setting forth additional or subsequent transactions or occurrences, at any time by leave of court or by stipulation of all parties. NY CPLR Rule 3025(b).

a. *When leave not required.* A party may amend his pleading once without leave of court within twenty (20) days after its service, or at any time before the period for responding to it expires, or within twenty (20) days after service of a pleading responding to it. NY CPLR Rule 3025(a).

b. *Claim by plaintiff against third-party defendant; Leave not required.* Within twenty (20) days after service of the answer to the third-party complaint upon plaintiff's attorney, the plaintiff may amend his complaint without leave of court to assert against the third-party defendant any claim plaintiff has against the third-party defendant. NY CPLR Rule 1009.

2. *Time to serve.* The moving party shall serve copies of all affidavits and briefs upon all other parties at the time of service of the notice of motion. NY R UNIF TRIAL CTS § 202.8(c). A notice of motion and supporting affidavits shall be served at least eight (8) days before the time at which the motion is noticed to be heard. NY CPLR Rule 2214(b).

a. *Return dates; Best practice.* It is also good practice to make motions returnable at least three (3) weeks away from the planned date of mailing and to always include a demand in the motion that the other side serve answering papers at least seven (7) days before the return day. This enables the motion to be served by mail, gives sufficient notice to support the seven (7) day demand, and leaves a few days for a delayed mailing if some snag prevents posting on the day planned. If speed is needed, the shorter eight (8) day notice period can be used, forfeiting the right to seven (7) day answering papers and a reply. If even eight (8) days notice is too much under the circumstances, the order to show cause is the remedy. SIEGEL-NYPRAC § 247.

i. *ALBANY COUNTY.* All motions, except for certain matters in Albany County as specified in NY R 3 JD SUP Doc. 1(E) and NY R 3 JD SUP Doc. 1(F), brought on by notice of motion or by order to show cause will be made returnable on any day, Monday through Friday, as chosen by the movant in compliance with the CPLR. Parties shall submit all papers in a timely fashion as required by the CPLR by delivering them or mailing them directly to the Supreme Court Clerk's Office[. . .]except that motions and other applications subject to a filing fee shall first be presented to the County Clerk's Office for payment of the requisite fee and then subsequently filed with the Supreme Court Clerk's Office. NY R 3 JD SUP Doc. 1(B).

ii. *BRONX COUNTY.* A Notice of Motion must be served at least eight (8) days, by personal service, nine (9) days by overnight express and thirteen (13) days by mail before the return date. NY R BRONX FIL R Doc. 3. All unassigned motions must be accompanied with a properly filled out RJI and shall be filed in the Motion Support Office, room 217, within five (5) days of service. All motions on actions already assigned to a Justice must be filed at least five (5) business days before the return date. NY R BRONX FIL R Doc. 3. All papers served must strictly comply with the time requirements of NY CPLR Rule 2101, NY CPLR Rule 2103 and NY CPLR Rule 2214(b). NY R BRONX FIL R Doc. 8.

iii. *KINGS COUNTY.* Motion papers, answering affidavits and reply affidavits must be served on adversaries in accordance with NY CPLR Rule 2214. NY R L KINGS Pt. C, Rule 1.

iv. *NEW YORK COUNTY.* In an e-filed case, all of the moving papers shall be e-filed at least eight (8) business days prior to the return date. The clerk will calendar the motion for the Motion Submission Part Courtroom (Room 130) for the return date selected. NY R NY CTY Procedure II(A); NY R NY CTY E FIL Doc. 2(D)(1).

v. *ONONDAGA COUNTY.* Onondaga County local court rules require that any additional papers relating to motions must be e-filed at least two (2) business days prior to the return date, excluding the return date. NY R ONDGA E FIL Protocol(B)(9)(e).

vi. *QUEENS COUNTY.* Motions must be in the possession of the Motion Support Office at least nine (9) days before the noticed return date of the motion. NY R L QUEENS MOT SUP Doc. 1; NY R L QUEENS E-FILE Doc. 1(H)(1).

b. *Order to show cause; Shorter time.* The court in a proper case may grant an order to show cause, to be served in lieu of a notice of motion, at a time and in a manner specified therein. NY CPLR Rule 2214(d). An ordinary notice of motion can't be brought on for hearing earlier than the eighth (8th) day after the motion papers are served. With an order to show cause, the hearing can be brought on at any time the court directs, which can be fewer than eight (8) days or as close as the very day on which it is signed. If the court is convinced there is a real emergency, it can schedule the hearing for a few hours later or, in the direst case, "forthwith" the service of the order to show cause. SIEGEL-NYPRAC § 248.

c. *Time to serve answering affidavits; Other answering papers.* Answering affidavits shall be served at least two (2) days before the time at which the motion is noticed to be heard. Answering affidavits and any notice of cross-motion, with supporting papers, if any, shall be served at least seven (7) days before such time if a notice of motion served at least sixteen (16) days before such time so demands; whereupon any reply or responding affidavits shall be served at least one (1) day before such time. NY CPLR Rule 2214(b); NY R UNIF TRIAL CTS § 202.8(c).

i. *BRONX COUNTY.* All answering papers must be submitted to the Clerk 's Office on the return date of the motion. Answering papers will not be accepted prior to the return date. NY R BRONX FIL R Doc. 8.

ii. *NEW YORK COUNTY.* Cross-motions, papers in opposition, and reply papers on motions/petitions on notice returnable in Room 130 in a hard-copy case shall be submitted to the Motion Submission Part Courtroom (Room 130) on the final return date of the motion/petition and will not be accepted until that date. Subsequent documents on motions/petitions in e-filed cases shall be e-filed in a timely manner. Working copies when required shall be submitted to Room 130 on the final return date. NY R NY CTY Procedure II(A).

d. *Time to serve cross-motion.* At least three (3) days prior to the time at which the motion is noticed to be heard, or seven (7) days prior to such time if demand is properly made pursuant to NY CPLR Rule 2214(b), a party may serve upon the moving party a notice of cross-motion demanding relief, with or without supporting papers; provided, however, that:

i. If such notice and any supporting papers are served by mailing, as provided in NY CPLR Rule 2103(b)(2), they shall be served three (3) days earlier than as prescribed in NY CPLR Rule 2215; and

ii. If served by overnight delivery, as provided in NY CPLR Rule 2103(b)(6), they shall be served one (1) day earlier than as prescribed in NY CPLR Rule 2215. Relief in the alternative or of several different types may be demanded; relief need not be responsive to that demanded by the moving party. NY CPLR Rule 2215(a); NY CPLR Rule 2215(b).

iii. *BRONX COUNTY.* Cross motions may be presented for approval on or before the return date, provided that there is a motion already calendared. NY R BRONX FIL R Doc. 8.

iv. *ERIE COUNTY.* Cross-motions must be filed at least two (2) days before the return date of the motion. NY R L KINGS Pt. A, Papers.

v. *KINGS COUNTY.* Hard copies are required to be filed for any motions, answering papers, stipulations, etc. for E-Filed cases returnable in [the Central Compliance Part] at least [two (2)] days before return date. . .for cross motions. NY R L KINGS Pt. E, Rule 8.

vi. *QUEENS COUNTY.* Motion Support does not process or forward responsive papers, including cross-motions. They must be brought to the calendar call in the judge's part. NY R L QUEENS MOT SUP Doc. 1. E-filed cross motions: across motion must be noticed for the same return date as the main motion and have the confirmation of filing attached in the same manner as a motion. NY R L QUEENS E-FILE Doc. 1(H)(2)(e).

3. *Filing before return date.* All motions shall be returnable before the assigned judge, and all papers shall be filed with the court on or before the return date. NY R UNIF TRIAL CTS § 202.8(a).

a. *BRONX COUNTY: Time for filing*

i. *Unassigned motions.* Unassigned motions must be in the Clerk's Office within five (5) days of the date of service of the motion. NY R BRONX FIL R Doc. 8.

ii. *Assigned motions.* Assigned motions must be filed in the Clerk's Office not less than five (5) business days prior to the return date of the motion. NY R BRONX FIL R Doc. 8.

iii. *Motions returnable in room 217.* The moving documents must be e-filed no later than eight (8) days prior to the return date. NY R BRONX E FIL R Doc. 1(1).

b. *KINGS COUNTY: Time and place of filing.* Motion papers must be filed with the E-file/Motion Support Office located in Room 227. . . at 360 Adams Street at least five (5) business days before the return date of the motion. NY R L KINGS Pt. A, Papers. Hard copies are required to be filed for any motions, answering papers, stipulations, etc. for E-Filed cases returnable in [the Central Compliance Part] at least five (5) days before return date for main motions. NY R L KINGS Pt. E, Rule 8. The moving documents must be e-filed no later than eight (8) days prior to the return date. NY R L KINGS E FIL Doc. 1(D).

4. *NEW YORK COUNTY: Briefing schedule.* Once a motion is made, counsel for all parties are strongly encouraged to agree upon a briefing schedule and submit a stipulation of adjournment reflecting that schedule using service or a clerk. Where a briefing schedule has not been agreed upon, the movant can avoid the need to attend simply to see if anyone will hand up opposing papers by demanding papers as provided by NY CPLR Rule'2214(b). To protect movants against the submission of late opposition papers or cross-motions, the General Clerk's Office will screen motions in which such papers are submitted without a response (reply or opposition respectively) to ensure that proper time to respond has been afforded and it will sua sponte adjourn for one (1) week cases in which such time has not been given. NY R NY CTY Procedure II(C).

5. *QUEENS COUNTY: Time to pay fees.* As motions and petitions are time sensitive, if opting to pay at the County Clerk's Office payment MUST be made, if filed with an RJI, a minimum of nine (9) business days prior to the application's return date and if filed post RJI, a minimum of nine (9) business days prior to the application's return date. NY R L QUEENS E-FILE Doc. 1(H)(1).

6. *Computation of time*

a. *Units of time*

i. *Day.* A calendar day includes the time from midnight to midnight. Sunday or any day of the week specifically mentioned means a calendar day. NY GEN CONSTR § 19.

ii. *Month.* In a statute, contract or public or private instrument, unless otherwise provided in such contract or instrument or by law, the term month means a calendar month and not a lunar month. NY GEN CONSTR § 31.

iii. *Year.* For information on the definition of a year, including the definitions of a half-year and quarter-year, refer to NY GEN CONSTR § 58 and NY GEN CONSTR § 50. For information on leap years, refer to NY GEN CONSTR § 57.

b. *Periods of time*

i. *Number of days.* A number of days specified as a period from a certain day within which or after or before which an act is authorized or required to be done means such number of calendar days exclusive of the calendar day from which the reckoning is made. NY GEN CONSTR § 20.

- If such period is a period of two (2) days, Saturday, Sunday or a public holiday must be excluded from the reckoning if it is an intervening day between the day from which the reckoning is made and the last day of the period. NY GEN CONSTR § 20.
- In computing any specified period of time from a specified event, the day upon which the event happens is deemed the day from which the reckoning is made. The day from which any specified period of time is reckoned shall be excluded in making the reckoning. NY GEN CONSTR § 20.

ii. *Number of months.* A number of months after or before a certain day shall be computed by counting such number of calendar months from such day, exclusive of the calendar month in which such day occurs, and shall include the day of the month in the last month so counted having the same numerical order in days of the month as the day from which the computation is made, unless there be not so many days in the last month so counted, in which case the period computed shall expire with the last day of the month so counted. NY GEN CONSTR § 30.

iii. *Publication of notice; Number of days.* The period of publication of a legal notice shall be computed by excluding the first day of publication and including the day on which the act or event of which notice is given is to take place or which completes the full period of publication. NY CPLR § 2402.

iv. *Periods ending on Saturday, Sunday or public holiday.* When any period of time, computed from a certain day, within which or after which or before which an act is authorized or required to be done, ends on a Saturday, Sunday or a public holiday, such act may be done on the next succeeding business day and if the period ends at a specified hour, such act may be done at or before the same hour of such next succeeding business day, except that where a period of time specified by contract ends on a Saturday, Sunday or a public holiday, the extension of such period is governed by NY GEN CONSTR § 25. NY GEN CONSTR § 25-a(1).

- For a list of public holidays, refer to NY GEN CONSTR § 24.

v. *Additional time after certain kinds of service*

- *Service by mail.* Where a period of time prescribed by law is measured from the service of a paper and service is by mail, five (5) days shall be added to the prescribed period. NY CPLR Rule 2103(b)(2).
- *Service by overnight delivery service.* Where a period of time prescribed by law is measured from the service of a paper and service is by overnight delivery, one (1) business day shall be added to the prescribed period. NY CPLR Rule 2103(b)(6).

vi. *Daylight saving time.* For information on New York's time zone and the effect of daylight saving time, refer to NY GEN CONSTR § 52.

c. *Hours of court.* Notwithstanding any provision of law or rule of court to the contrary, throughout the State of New York the sessions of the Supreme Court for the disposition of business before the court shall commence not later than 9:30 a.m. and conclude not earlier than 5 p.m. Where warranted, the Chief Administrator of the Courts may authorize variances in the opening and closing hours of the courts, but, in such event, daily sessions shall total not less than six (6) hours. NY R CHIEF J § 3.1.

d. *Time limits; Extension of time.* Any act required by or in pursuance of law to be performed at or within a prescribed time, shall be performed according to the standard time. NY GEN CONSTR § 53.

i. Except where otherwise expressly prescribed by law, the court may extend the time fixed by any statute, rule or order for doing any act, upon such terms as may be just and upon good cause shown, whether the application for extension is made before or after the expiration of the time fixed. NY CPLR § 2004. Refer to the New York KeyRules Motion for Continuance/Extension of Time document for more information.

C. General Requirements

1. *Motions, generally.* There shall be compliance with the procedures prescribed in the CPLR for the bringing of motions. NY R UNIF TRIAL CTS § 202.7(a).

a. *Motions on notice.* A notice of motion shall specify the time and place of the hearing on the motion, the supporting papers upon which the motion is based, the relief demanded and the grounds therefor. NY CPLR Rule 2214(a). A motion on notice in an action in the supreme court shall be noticed to be heard in the judicial district where the action is triable or in a county adjoining the county where the action is triable. Unless statute, civil practice rule or local court rule provides otherwise, the motion shall be noticed to be heard before a motion term or, upon order to show cause granted by a justice, before that justice out of court. NY CPLR § 2212(a). Except as provided in NY R UNIF TRIAL CTS § 202.7(d), no motion shall be filed with the court unless there have been served and filed with the motion papers a notice of motion. NY R UNIF TRIAL CTS § 202.7(a)(1).

b. *Ex parte motions.* A motion in an action in the supreme court that may be made without notice may be made at a motion term or to a justice out of court in any county in the state. NY CPLR § 2212(b).

i. *KINGS COUNTY.* For more information on submitting a motion ex parte, refer to NY R L KINGS E FIL Doc. 1(G).

ii. *NEW YORK COUNTY.* For more information on submitting matters ex parte, refer to NY R NY CTY Procedure III and NY R NY CTY E FIL Doc. 2(G).

iii. *QUEENS COUNTY.* For more information on submitting matters ex parte, refer to NY R L QUEENS EX PARTE Doc. 1.

c. *Alternative relief.* Relief in the alternative or of several different types may be demanded. NY CPLR Rule 2214(a). The types of relief need not be related. In one motion, for example, the defendant can seek to dismiss the plaintiff's claim for lack of jurisdiction, to get an extension of time to answer, to require the plaintiff to join X as a party, and to quash a disclosure subpoena served in behalf of the plaintiff on a nonparty witness. So doing, the movant must of course specify all of these items of relief in the notice of motion, and the grounds for them, and the supporting papers must contain the entire proof requisite to the items of relief sought. NY CPLR Rule 2214(Practice Commentary, C2214:4).

d. *General relief.* It is common practice to include at the end of the relief request in the notice of motion a so-called "general relief" clause. This is merely a few words to cover the possibility that the relief appropriate to what the movant proves was not specifically asked for, but is close enough to enable the court to grant it. After stating the specific relief desired, the lawyer will often add something like: and for such other, further, or different relief as this court may deem just and proper. NY CPLR Rule 2214(Practice Commentary, C2214:5).

e. *Motion in improper form.* If the court finds it appropriate in the interests of justice, it may convert a motion into a special proceeding, or vice-versa, upon such terms as may be just, including the payment of fees and costs. NY CPLR § 103(c).

f. *Order to show cause.* An order to show cause is basically only a substitute for a notice of motion. An ordinary notice of motion merely notifies the recipient that a motion is being made for specified relief. The burden of proof is on the movant. Although in most cases it is just as innocent as an ordinary notice of motion, the order to show cause gets its name by directing the recipient to "show cause" why the particular relief being asked for should not be granted. It sounds as if the burden of proof is being shifted to the recipient. It isn't. It specifies the time and place of the hearing on the application but when the hearing comes on, the burden of proof is where it always is on a motion: on the movant. SIEGEL-NYPRAC § 248.

   i. The CPLR says nothing more about an order to show cause than that it may be used "in a proper case", which leaves it entirely to the judge's discretion to determine what a proper case is. Any fact suggesting a problem as to any of the items listed above would be sufficient to invoke judicial discretion and justify the show cause procedure, which is in fact liberally used. SIEGEL-NYPRAC § 248.

   ii. An order to show cause against a state body or officers must be served in addition to service upon the defendant or respondent state body or officers upon the attorney general by delivery to an assistant attorney general at an office of the attorney general in the county in which venue of the action is designated or if there is no office of the attorney general in such county, at the office of the attorney general nearest such county. NY CPLR Rule 2214(d).

   iii. *BRONX COUNTY.* For information on submitting an order to show cause, refer to NY R BRONX E FIL R Doc. 2 and NY R BRONX LEG SUP Doc. 1.

   iv. *ERIE COUNTY.* For information on submitting an order to show cause, refer to NY R ERIE E FIL Doc. 3(VI).

   v. *KINGS COUNTY.* For information on submitting an order to show cause, refer to NY R L KINGS E FIL Doc. 1(F).

   vi. *NEW YORK COUNTY.* For information on submitting an order to show cause, refer to NY R NY CTY E FIL Doc. 2(F).

   vii. *ONONDAGA COUNTY.* For information on submitting an order to show cause, refer to NY R ONDGA E FIL Protocol(B)(10) and NY R ONDGA E FIL Protocol(J).

g. *Motions before preliminary conference.* Motions in actions to which NY R UNIF TRIAL CTS § 202.12 is applicable made after the preliminary conference has been scheduled may be denied unless there is shown good cause why such relief is warranted before the preliminary conference is held. NY R UNIF TRIAL CTS § 202.12(h).

h. *ALBANY COUNTY: Good faith effort to resolve.* Prior to the submission of a notice of motion relating to disclosure or a bill of particulars, the parties must make a good faith effort to resolve the matter in question and submit an affirmation attesting to this good faith effort. NY R 3 JD SUP Doc. 1(B).

i. *NEW YORK COUNTY: Documents with motions.* Counsel must attach to motion papers copies of all pleadings and other documents as required by the CPLR and as necessary for an informed decision on the motion. Documents in a foreign language shall be properly translated. NY R NY CTY J RUL Rule 14(a).

j. *NEW YORK COUNTY: Motions in multiple cases made together.* On occasion, attorneys may wish to make a motion in more than one case on a single set of papers. In such cases, by definition consolidation will not have been directed since consolidation signifies the combination of more than one case into a single one with a single caption and index number and ending in a single judgment. NY R NY CTY Procedure II(B). For more information on motions made with the same papers, refer to NY R NY CTY Procedure II(A).

k. *QUEENS COUNTY: Motion sequence numbers.* A motion sequence number is required for all E-filed motions. After a motion is E-filed, please consult the e-courts website within twenty-four (24) to forty-eight (48) hours to obtain the sequence number. The Confirmation Notice of E-filing MUST indicate the sequence number of any motion submitted at the Centralized Motion Part calendar call. NY R L QUEENS E-FILE Doc. 1(H)(5).

2. *Motion for leave to amend.* A party may amend his or her pleading, or supplement it by setting forth additional or

subsequent transactions or occurrences, at any time by leave of court or by stipulation of all parties. Leave shall be freely given upon such terms as may be just including the granting of costs and continuances. NY CPLR Rule 3025(b).

a. *Court's discretion.* The NY CPLR Rule 3025(b) amendment lies in the discretion of the court and may be denied on such discretionary grounds as prejudice, delay, undue advantage, etc. SIEGEL-NYPRAC § 237; Leutloff v. Leutloff, 47 Misc. 2d 458, 459, 262 N.Y.S.2d 736, 738 (Sup. Ct. 1965).

b. *Changing causes of action.* Causes of action can be added or subtracted by amendment, whether they involve changes of fact or changes of theory. SIEGEL-NYPRAC § 237.

   i. If the theory alone is changed, but the facts remain as originally pleaded, a problem should not often be met because there is little the other party would now have to do by way of new preparation. SIEGEL-NYPRAC § 237; Rife v. Union Coll., 30 A.D.2d 504, 505, 294 N.Y.S.2d 460, 462 (1968). Conceptual rather than factual changes are always easier because the opponent will at least be on notice of the facts. Inadvertent omissions are also curable with the of-leave amendment, as where a denial or even a defense has been left out of an answer through oversight. SIEGEL-NYPRAC § 237; LaBate v. Meyerbank Elec. Co., 23 A.D.2d 503, 256 N.Y.S.2d 420, 421 (1965); Ciunci v. Wella Corp., 23 A.D.2d 754, 755, 258 N.Y.S.2d 994, 995 (1965).

   ii. Objections listed in NY CPLR Rule 3211(a)—NY CPLR Rule 3211(a) objections must be taken either by motion or answer—may be added in an amended answer if omitted from the original one, but while this has been held to be automatically permissible for an amendment as of course under NY CPLR Rule 3025(a), it will be allowed in an amendment by leave under NY CPLR Rule 3025(b) only if there is no prejudice to the plaintiff. It is up to the plaintiff to show prejudice in that situation. SIEGEL-NYPRAC § 237; NY CPLR Rule 3211(e); see NY CPLR Rule 3025(Practice Commentaries, C3025:7); Lermit Plastics Co. v. C. W. Lauman & Co., 40 A.D.2d 680, 680, 336 N.Y.S.2d 187, 188 (1972).

c. *Court less likely to allow amendment for previously known facts.* Courts are more hesitant to grant amendment motions when the facts on which they're based were known to the movant from the beginning and could have been pleaded without trouble earlier. SIEGEL-NYPRAC § 237; L. B. Foster Co. v. Terry Contracting, Inc., 25 A.D.2d 721, 721—22, 268 N.Y.S.2d 618, 619 (1966). As a rule, mere lateness is not a barrier to the amendment, but lateness coupled with significant prejudice is. SIEGEL-NYPRAC § 237.

d. *Merits of proposed new matter.* On a motion to amend, the court will not ordinarily consider the merits of the proposed new matter unless it is so obviously lacking in merit as to have no chance of success whatever, in which case the motion may be denied on that ground. SIEGEL-NYPRAC § 237; B v. B, 78 Misc. 2d 112, 115, 355 N.Y.S.2d 712, 715 (Sup. Ct. 1974). Some courts have even said that a grant of the motion without looking at the merits may needlessly generate a later motion to test the merits. Labeling that procedure wasteful, they hold that at least the prima facie merit of the new matter should be considered on the amendment motion. SIEGEL-NYPRAC § 237; E. Asiatic Co. v. Corash, 34 A.D.2d 432, 434, 312 N.Y.S.2d 311, 313 (1970).

e. *Relation back.* A claim asserted in an amended pleading is deemed to have been interposed at the time the claims in the original pleading were interposed, unless the original pleading does not give notice of the transactions, occurrences, or series of transactions or occurrences, to be proved pursuant to the amended pleading. NY CPLR § 203(f). If such notice is not given by the original pleading, the new claim will be measured for timeliness only by service of the amended pleading that contains it. SIEGEL-NYPRAC § 49.

   i. The key elements of NY CPLR § 203(f)'s relation-back doctrine are the identity of the transaction or occurrence alleged in the original and the amended pleadings and notice of such transaction or occurrence. In some instances, however, courts focus not on the overall transaction but its separate and individual components, and ask whether defendant had notice of the "claim" being asserted in the amended pleading. NY CPLR § 203(Practice Commentary, C203:11).

   ii. A plaintiff can sometimes overcome the statute of limitations defense when joining an additional defendant after the limitations period has expired against such defendant. The united-in-interest rule provides that the assertion of an otherwise time-barred claim against a newly added defendant will relate back to the date of commencement of a timely action against a related party if: (1) the claims arose out of the same conduct, transaction or occurrence; (2) the new defendant and the original party are united in interest and, by reason of their relationship, the defendant can be charged with such notice of the action that he will not be prejudiced in defending the case; and (3) the new defendant reasonably should have known that the plaintiff made a mistake in failing to timely identify the proper parties. NY CPLR § 203(Practice Commentary, C203:3).

f. *Amendment to conform to the evidence.* The court may permit pleadings to be amended before or after judgment to conform them to the evidence, upon such terms as may be just including the granting of costs and continuances. NY CPLR Rule 3025(c).

g. *Opposing party's time to respond to amended or supplemental pleading.* Except where otherwise prescribed by law or order of the court, there shall be an answer or reply to an amended or supplemental pleading if an answer or reply is required to the pleading being amended or supplemented. Service of such an answer or reply shall be made within twenty (20) days after service of the amended or supplemental pleading to which it responds. NY CPLR Rule 3025(d).

3. *Oppositions.* In the absence of statutory provision or court rule, a motion ordinarily does not require a written answer, although an adverse party may be permitted to file an answer in opposition to the showing made in the motion or its supporting affidavits. AMJUR MOTIONS § 26. When a party files a motion and the opposing party fails to respond, the court may construe such failure to respond as non-opposition to the motion or an admission that the motion was meritorious, may take the facts alleged in the motion as true, and may grant the motion if the relief requested appears to be justified. However, the severity of such a result demands that a court impose it only with great caution. AMJUR MOTIONS § 28.

4. *Governing law.* The civil practice law and rules (NY CPLR § 101, et seq.) shall govern the procedure in civil judicial proceedings in all courts of the state and before all judges, except where the procedure is regulated by inconsistent statute. The civil practice law and rules shall succeed the civil practice act and rules of civil practice and shall be deemed substituted therefor throughout the statutes and rules of the state. NY CPLR § 101. The civil practice law and rules shall be liberally construed to secure the just, speedy and inexpensive determination of every civil judicial proceeding. NY CPLR § 104.

   a. *Uniform trial court rules.* The uniform civil rules for the Supreme Court and County Court (NY R UNIF TRIAL CTS § 202.1, et seq.) shall be applicable to civil actions and proceedings in the Supreme Court and the County Court. NY R UNIF TRIAL CTS § 202.1(a). The provisions of the uniform rules shall be construed consistent with the Civil Practice Law and Rules (CPLR), and matters not covered by the uniform rules shall be governed by the CPLR. NY R UNIF TRIAL CTS § 202.1(d).

   b. *Local rules.* Local court rules, not inconsistent with law or with uniform civil rules for the Supreme Court and County Court (NY R UNIF TRIAL CTS § 202.1, et seq.), shall comply with Part 9 of the Rules of the Chief Judge (NY R CHIEF J § 9.1). NY R UNIF TRIAL CTS § 202.1(c).

   c. *Official forms.* The state administrator shall have the power to adopt, amend and rescind an appendix of forms. Forms adopted pursuant to NY CPLR § 107 shall be sufficient under the civil practice law and rules and shall illustrate the simplicity and brevity of statement which the civil practice law and rules contemplate. NY CPLR § 107.

5. *Rules of the commercial division.* [Editor's note: certain types of civil cases or civil cases meeting certain monetary thresholds that are filed in the state of New York must be filed in the Commercial Division of the New York Supreme Courts. Rules governing practice in the commercial division are found in NY R UNIF TRIAL CTS § 202.70]. Cases which must be filed in the commercial division are listed below. For more information, refer to NY R UNIF TRIAL CTS § 202.70.

   a. *Monetary thresholds.* Except as set forth in NY R UNIF TRIAL CTS § 202.70(b), the monetary thresholds of the Commercial Division, exclusive of punitive damages, interests, costs, disbursements and counsel fees claimed, are established as follows: (1) Albany County, fifty thousand dollars ($50,000); (2) Eighth Judicial District, one hundred thousand dollars ($100,000); (3) Kings County, one hundred fifty thousand dollars ($150,000); (4) Nassau County, two hundred thousand dollars ($200,000); (5) New York County, five hundred thousand dollars ($500,000); (6) Onondaga County, fifty thousand dollars ($50,000); (7) Queens County, one hundred thousand dollars ($100,000); (8) Seventh Judicial District, fifty thousand dollars ($50,000); (9) Suffolk County, one hundred thousand dollars ($100,000); and (10) Westchester County, one hundred thousand dollars ($100,000). NY R UNIF TRIAL CTS § 202.70(a).

      i. *ALBANY COUNTY.* The Commercial Division of the Albany County Supreme Court exercises jurisdiction over selected business and commercial disputes in which the amount at issue generally involves damage claims in a minimum amount of fifty thousand dollars ($50,000) as well as claims for unspecified amounts where the value of the commercial asset(s) in dispute exceeds fifty thousand dollars ($50,000). A separate publication promulgating the rules and criteria relating to the filing and management of Commercial Court cases in this part may be obtained from the Albany County Supreme Court Clerk's Office. A section of the Uniform Civil Rules for the Supreme Court and County Court sets forth statewide rules. NY R 3 JD SUP Doc. 1(E).

      ii. *BRONX COUNTY.* The monetary threshold for commercial cases in Bronx County will be seventy-five thousand dollars ($75,000). All other parameters including the type of matters that will be heard are contained within the Rules of the Commercial Division of the Supreme Court (NY R UNIF TRIAL CTS § 202.70). NY R BRONX FIL R Doc. 12.

iii. *NEW YORK COUNTY.* The monetary threshold in the New York County Commercial Division, which is generally applicable, is an amount in controversy of five hundred thousand dollars ($500,000) or more (exclusive of punitive damages, interest, costs, disbursements, and counsel fees). If the case is designated a commercial one and the Addendum is submitted, the clerk will review the pleadings to determine whether the amount in controversy in the case meets the monetary threshold or whether an exception to the threshold applies. NY R NY CTY Procedure IA(B). For more information on assigning a case to the commercial division in New York County, refer to NY R NY CTY Procedure IA(B).

b. *Commercial cases.* Actions in which the principal claims involve or consist of the following will be heard in the Commercial Division provided that the monetary threshold is met or equitable or declaratory relief is sought:

i. Breach of contract or fiduciary duty, fraud, misrepresentation, business tort (e.g., unfair competition), or statutory and/or common law violation where the breach or violation is alleged to arise out of business dealings (e.g., sales of assets or securities; corporate restructuring; partnership, shareholder, joint venture, and other business agreements; trade secrets; restrictive covenants; and employment agreements not including claims that principally involve alleged discriminatory practices);

ii. Transactions governed by the Uniform Commercial Code (exclusive of those concerning individual cooperative or condominium units);

iii. Transactions involving commercial real property, including Yellowstone injunctions and excluding actions for the payment of rent only;

iv. Shareholder derivative actions—without consideration of the monetary threshold;

v. Commercial class actions—without consideration of the monetary threshold;

vi. Business transactions involving or arising out of dealings with commercial banks and other financial institutions;

vii. Internal affairs of business organizations;

viii. Malpractice by accountants or actuaries, and legal malpractice arising out of representation in commercial matters;

ix. Environmental insurance coverage;

x. Commercial insurance coverage (e.g., directors and officers, errors and omissions, and business interruption coverage);

xi. Dissolution of corporations, partnerships, limited liability companies, limited liability partnerships and joint ventures—without consideration of the monetary threshold; and

xii. Applications to stay or compel arbitration and affirm or disaffirm arbitration awards and related injunctive relief pursuant to Article 75 of the New York Civil Practice Law and Rules (NY CPLR § 7501, et seq.) involving any of the foregoing enumerated commercial issues. Where the applicable arbitration agreement provides for the arbitration to be heard outside the United States, the monetary threshold set forth in NY R UNIF TRIAL CTS § 202.70(a) shall not apply. NY R UNIF TRIAL CTS § 202.70(b).

c. *Non-commercial cases.* The following will not be heard in the Commercial Division even if the monetary threshold is met:

i. Suits to collect professional fees;

ii. Cases seeking a declaratory judgment as to insurance coverage for personal injury or property damage;

iii. Residential real estate disputes, including landlord-tenant matters, and commercial real estate disputes involving the payment of rent only;

iv. Home improvement contracts involving residential properties consisting of one to four residential units or individual units in any residential building, including cooperative or condominium units;

v. Proceedings to enforce a judgment regardless of the nature of the underlying case;

vi. First-party insurance claims and actions by insurers to collect premiums or rescind non-commercial policies; and

vii. Attorney malpractice actions except as otherwise provided in NY R UNIF TRIAL CTS § 202.70(b)(8). NY R UNIF TRIAL CTS § 202.70(c).

d. For more information on the Commercial Division, refer to NY R UNIF TRIAL CTS § 202.70.

D. Documents

1. *Documents for moving party*

   a. *Required documents*

      i. *Notice of motion, order to show cause, or affidavit on ex parte motion.* The notice of motion shall be substantially in the form found in NY R UNIF TRIAL CTS § 202.7(b). NY R UNIF TRIAL CTS § 202.7(b). The supporting papers should be referred to in the notice of motion. SIEGEL-NYPRAC § 246. The court in a proper case may grant an order to show cause, to be served in lieu of a notice of motion. NY CPLR Rule 2214(d). An ex parte motion shall be accompanied by an affidavit stating the result of any prior motion for similar relief and specifying the new facts, if any, that were not previously shown. NY CPLR Rule 2217(b).

         - *Request for oral argument.* A party requesting oral argument shall set forth such request in its notice of motion or in its order to show cause or on the first page of the answering papers, as the case may be. Where all parties to a motion request oral argument, oral argument shall be granted unless the court shall determine it to be unnecessary. Where a motion is brought on by order to show cause, the court may set forth in the order that oral argument is required on the return date of the motion. NY R UNIF TRIAL CTS § 202.8(d).

      ii. *Motion.* Refer to the General Requirements section of this document for information on the notice of motion and motion.

      iii. *Request for judicial intervention.* At any time after service of process, a party may file a request for judicial intervention. Except as provided in NY R UNIF TRIAL CTS § 202.6(b), in an action not yet assigned to a judge, the court shall not accept for filing a notice of motion, order to show cause, or application for ex parte order, unless such notice or application is accompanied by a request for judicial intervention. NY R UNIF TRIAL CTS § 202.6(a).

         - *BRONX COUNTY.* Generally, the Request For Judicial Intervention, commonly referred to as an "RJI", is required to be filed in any action where the assignment of a Justice is required. The RJI sets forth the information which is entered into the court system's database. It must be completely and accurately filled out. The full caption, as stated on the Summons, must be set forth. Use of terms "et al." and "etc." are not permitted. Only one (1) RJI may be filed in each action. Either a self represented litigant or an attorney must sign the affirmation at the end of the form. Once completed, the RJI must be filed in duplicate. Except in the case of an ex-parte application, the RJI must also be served together with the accompanying application upon all parties. Proof of accuracy of the index number must accompany the RJI. Check the Fee Schedule[. . .]for any applicable filing fees. NY R BRONX FIL R Doc. 2.
         - *KINGS COUNTY.* An RJI with the relevant required addendum in a NYSCEF case shall be submitted via NYSCEF. Once e-filed, the RJI and any accompanying document will be forwarded to the relevant support office for random assignment of the case and processing of the document. A filer or counsel need not appear (as to Proposed Orders to Show Cause, however, see below). A copy of the pleadings must be submitted only if the document has not previously been e-filed. If the RJI seeks intervention with regard to a document that is intended for review by a Justice, such as a motion, a working copy of the RJI must be submitted with the working copy of the motion and the NYSCEF Confirmation Notice. NY R L KINGS E FIL Doc. 1(C).
         - *NEW YORK COUNTY.* To obtain the assignment of an IAS Justice to a case, a Request for Judicial Intervention (cost ninety-five dollars ($95)) must be filed, with NYSCEF in an e-filed case or in paper in an authorized hard-copy one. A no-fee RJI, which will generally result in the referral of an application to an Ex Parte Justice, is also required with regard to certain kinds of applications for which, prior to 2011, no RJI was required. NY R NY CTY Procedure I(C). A "fillable" form RJI is available on-line. The form must be filed in duplicate in hard-copy cases. NY R NY CTY Procedure IA(A)(1). The filer of an RJI must check off a box identifying the type of case at issue. Where the RJI seeks judicial assignment, this designation will bring about a random assignment of the case by computer to a Justice handling cases of that type. NY R NY CTY Procedure IA(A)(1). The RJI and any addendum can be completed and submitted electronically in an e-filed case. NY R NY CTY Procedure II(A). The RJI shall be marked to reflect the existence of any "related case" as explained on the "Commencement of Cases" page under "Case Processing" on the court's website. NY R NY CTY Procedure II(A); NY R NY CTY E FIL Doc. 2(C).
         - *ONONDAGA COUNTY.* The RJI will be submitted via the NYSCEF system along with any required RJI addendum forms. When the RJI is filed and the fee paid online, the Onondaga County Clerk's Office will electronically forward the RJI and any accompanying documents to the Onondaga Supreme Court Clerk's Office for assignment and processing. Counsel will receive notification of judge assignment via the NYSCEF system. NY R ONDGA E FIL Protocol(B)(3).

- *QUEENS COUNTY.* A Request for Judicial Intervention ("RJI") in an E-filed case shall be submitted via the E-filing System. When the RJI is approved, filed and paid for on-line, it will be forwarded to the relevant back office for random assignment of the case and processing of the document. In the case of RJIs seeking assignment to the Commercial Division, the filer must submit therewith, a Commercial Addendum as required by the standards for assignment of cases to the Commercial Division. NY R L QUEENS E-FILE Doc. 1(F).

iv. *Proposed amended pleading.* Any motion to amend or supplement pleadings shall be accompanied by the proposed amended or supplemental pleading clearly showing the changes or additions to be made to the pleading. NY CPLR Rule 3025(b).

v. *Proof of service.* In addition to complying with the provisions of NY CPLR Rule 2101, every paper filed in court shall have annexed thereto appropriate proof of service on all parties where required. NY R UNIF TRIAL CTS § 202.5(a).

- *QUEENS COUNTY.* With regard to service of a motion/petition on notice in an E-filed action, NY CPLR Rule 2214(b) and NY R UNIF TRIAL CTS § 202.5-b(f) applies. Where required, proof of service shall be filed on-line as a separate document. NY R L QUEENS E-FILE Doc. 1(H)(3).

vi. *ALBANY COUNTY: Additional required documents*

- *Affirmation of good faith effort.* The parties must[. . .]submit an affirmation attesting to [their good faith effort to resolve the matter]. The affirmation of good faith effort to resolve the issues raised by the motion shall indicate the time, place and nature of the consultation and the issues discussed and any resolutions, or shall indicate good cause why no such conferral with counsel for opposing parties was held. An assigned justice or judge may dismiss a motion for failure to demonstrate that such effort was made with leave to renew the motion after such effort has been demonstrated. NY R 3 JD SUP Doc. 1(B).

b. *Supplemental documents*

i. *Supporting evidence; Exhibits.* The main supporting papers on a motion are affidavits, but any relevant exhibits, documents, depositions, etc., are also includible. SIEGEL-NYPRAC § 246.

- *Affidavits accompanying motion.* Affidavits shall be for a statement of the relevant facts. NY R UNIF TRIAL CTS § 202.8(c).
- *Foreign language documents.* Where an affidavit or exhibit annexed to a paper served or filed is in a foreign language, it shall be accompanied by an English translation and an affidavit by the translator stating his qualifications and that the translation is accurate. NY CPLR Rule 2101(b).
- *Statement of attorney in lieu of affidavit.* The statement of an attorney admitted to practice in the courts of the state, or of a physician, osteopath or dentist, authorized by law to practice in the state, who is not a party to an action, when subscribed and affirmed by him to be true under the penalties of perjury, may be served or filed in the action in lieu of and with the same force and effect as an affidavit. NY CPLR Rule 2106.
- *NEW YORK COUNTY: Form of presented exhibits.* Exhibits should be tabbed and be legible; a typed version of any exhibit that is difficult to read should be submitted with the original. Exhibits printed on both sides of the page should be bound and tabbed on the side. NY R NY CTY J RUL Rule 14(a).
- *QUEENS COUNTY.* Attorneys submitting exhibits to the court on E-file cases shall make each exhibit a separate, labeled attachment to an affidavit/affirmation. NY R L QUEENS E-FILE Doc. 1(H)(4).

ii. *Brief.* Briefs shall be for a statement of the relevant law. NY R UNIF TRIAL CTS § 202.8(c).

iii. *Notice to produce papers not in possession of the court.* If a paper relied on by the movant is in the possession of the other side, it may be demanded of that side with a notice to produce it at the hearing. Where such papers are in the possession of an adverse party, they shall be produced by him at the hearing on notice served with the motion papers. NY CPLR Rule 2214(Practice Commentary, C2214:23).

iv. *Filing fees.* The County Clerk shall require the payment of any applicable statutory fees, or an order of the Court waiving payment of such fees, before accepting a paper for filing. NY R UNIF TRIAL CTS § 202.5(d)(1). For information on filing fees, if any, refer to NY CPLR § 8001, et seq.

- *ALBANY COUNTY.* In general, any filing subsequent to the commencement of an action which is designated as a motion or cross-motion requires the payment of a filing fee to the County Clerk's Office prior to submission to the Supreme Court Clerk's Office for referral to the assigned justice. The fee is assessed regardless of whether an application is made by notice of motion, order to show cause or ex parte.

No fee will be charged upon the filing of a motion for poor person status in conjunction with an application which serves to commence an action or special proceeding. In the event a motion is received by the court unaccompanied by proof of payment to the County Clerk, the Supreme Court Clerk's Office will contact the submitting party to advise that the application will be held pending receipt of the filing fee only until the return date of the motion. If proof of payment is not submitted to the Supreme Court Clerk's Office by the return date (ex parte applications will be held ten (10) days), the papers will be returned by mail with a notification that the motion has been removed from the court's calendar and that it must be re-noticed and re-filed with the court along with the requisite filing fee. Inquiries concerning the applicability of the motion fee to a proposed filing may be directed to the Supreme Court Clerk's Office. NY R 3 JD SUP Doc. 1(B).

- *BRONX COUNTY.* In accordance with the new civil fee schedule set forth in Article 80 of the C.P.L.R. (NY CPLR § 8001, et seq.), effective July 14, 2003, all motions, and cross motions must be approved in Room 217 prior to payment of said fees in the County Clerk's Office, Room 118. NY R BRONX FIL R Doc. 8. The motion fee [must be] paid for via NYSCEF by credit/debit card. NY R BRONX E FIL R Doc. 1(1).
- *ERIE COUNTY.* Payment for fee-bearing NYSCEF documents must be made online via credit or debit card (American Express, MasterCard or Visa) at the time of submission. NY R ERIE E FIL Doc. 3(III)(E).
- *KINGS COUNTY.* The motion must be filed with NYSCEF and the motion fee paid. NY R L KINGS E FIL Doc. 1(D). Court fees in NYSCEF cases must be paid via NYSCEF by a credit or bank card (MasterCard, Visa, or American Express). Fees are no longer accepted in person in the Kings County Clerk's Office in NYSCEF cases. NY R L KINGS E FIL Doc. 1(B)(6).
- *NEW YORK COUNTY.* A motion fee must be paid on motions made in writing by notice of motion, order to show cause or ex parte after the commencement of an action. For this purpose, the term "action" shall mean any application to the court that requires the assignment of an index number, regardless of whether a formal pleading is filed. Applications or motions that commence an action and for which an index number fee must be paid require no motion fee. [A]ny motions made after the initial applications in these situations would require payment of the motion fee. A motion that is the initial application in a case commenced by the filing of a summons and complaint would require a motion fee since the filing of the summons and complaint rather than the application itself would require the purchase of an index number. NY R NY CTY Procedure II(A). In e-filed cases the motion fee must be paid when the documents are filed. Payment is made on-line by Visa, Mastercard, or American Express credit or bank card. NY R NY CTY Procedure II(A); NY R NY CTY E FIL Doc. 2(B)(5).
- *ONONDAGA COUNTY.* Court fees in e-filed cases must be paid online with the NYSCEF system using a credit card. The document is not considered to have been filed until payment of the fee has been tendered. NY R ONDGA E FIL Protocol(B)(2). Fees must be paid on all cross motions. NY R ONDGA E FIL Protocol(B)(9)(e).
- *QUEENS COUNTY.* The Motion Support Office does not receive, forward or process any fees or waiver of fees. All applications requiring payment of statutory fees or waiver of fees must be sent directly to the Queens County Clerk's office. NY R L QUEENS MOT SUP Doc. 1. Court fees (e.g., RJI fee, motion fee) in E-filed cases may be paid for on-line using a credit card. Papers may also be filed with the E-file system and the fee may be paid at the County Clerk's Office. In the latter case, the paper is not considered to have been filed until payment of the fee has been tendered. NY R L QUEENS E-FILE Doc. 1(E)(1). The motion/petition shall be filed on-line and the fee paid for either on-line by credit card or by the "Pay at the County Clerk's Office" option. NY R L QUEENS E-FILE Doc. 1(H)(1).

v. *Working copies.* The court may require the parties to provide working copies of documents filed electronically. In such event, each working copy shall include, firmly affixed thereto, a copy of a confirmation notice in a form prescribed by the Chief Administrator. NY R UNIF TRIAL CTS § 202.5-b(d)(5).

- *BRONX COUNTY.* After papers on motions have been e-filed, working copies thereof, with Confirmation Notice firmly attached as the back page facing out, must be submitted. (Each document or group of documents that is separately bound shall bear a Confirmation Notice.) Working copies lacking the Notice will not be accepted. WORKING COPIES OF MOTION PAPERS MUST BE SUBMITTED NO LATER THAN 4:45 P.M. ON THE RETURN DATE IN THE MOTION SUPPORT OFFICE (ROOM 217) AS EXPLAINED in NY R BRONX E FIL R Doc. 1(4). If an attorney has failed to submit required working copies on or before the return date, the motion will be transmitted as is to the Justice for such action as the Justice finds appropriate. Attorneys may submit working copies on motions by mail or overnight delivery.

Any such submission shall be sent in a timely manner to the Motion Support Office (Room 217) and be conspicuously marked on the outside "NYSCEF Matter"; lack of such marking may delay processing. NY R BRONX E FIL R Doc. 1(4)(a).

- *ERIE COUNTY.* Electronically filed documents subject to review and processing by the Part Clerk do not require a working copy unless otherwise directed or provided for in IAS Part Rules. NY R UNIF TRIAL CTS § 202.5-b(d)(4), any working copy submitted shall include, as a cover page firmly fastened thereto, a copy of the Confirmation Notice generated by the NYSCEF site at the time of filing. Please consult the individual Justice's Part Rules and/or consult with the Judge's chambers to determine whether and how working copies are to be provided. Working copies will not be printed or delivered by the Erie County Clerk or the Chief Clerk of the Courts or any of their personnel to chambers. The official record of a document in an electronically filed case is the document filed via the NYSCEF system. Working copies are intended only for use by the Justice. The Court will discard all working copies after the Justice has finished with them. Thus, in the event that counsel fails to file a document via the NYSCEF system, the document will not be part of the court record. NY R ERIE E FIL Doc. 3(III)(O); NY R ERIE E FIL Doc. 3(V)(E).
- *KINGS COUNTY.* No courtesy copies of motion papers are required by the Court, except as may be required for electronic filing or by the Judge's Part Rules. In tort cases against the City of New York, courtesy copies shall be supplied to the Corporation Counsel's office in Brooklyn. NY R L KINGS Pt. C, Rule 5. Unless otherwise directed by the Court or as described herein, and with the exceptions listed below, in all NYSCEF cases in which an RJI has been filed, working copies of e-filed documents that are intended for judicial review must be submitted to the court. Working copies are not required of documents that are only processed by a support office (e.g. preliminary conference request, note of issue). Working copies shall include exhibit tabs and backs; for motion papers, the motion sequence number and the return date and part. The confirmation notice with the motion sequence number on it should be the back page of the motion facing out. In addition, the filer of a working copy must firmly bind thereto, with the back page facing out, a copy of the Confirmation Notice that was generated by NYSCEF when that document was efiled. Working copies that are submitted without the related Confirmation Notice will not be accepted. NY R L KINGS E FIL Doc. 1(B)(7); NY R L KINGS E FIL Doc. 1(D). WORKING COPIES OF MOTION PAPERS MUST BE SUBMITTED IN THE MOTION SUPPORT OFFICE (ROOM 227) AS EXPLAINED HEREIN. THEY MUST NOT BE DELIVERED TO THE PART OR CHAMBERS, EXCEPT WHERE THE INDIVIDUAL JUSTICE'S PART RULES PROVIDE OTHERWISE; DOING SO WILL CAUSE ADMINISTRATIVE CONFUSION AND POSSIBLE MISPLACEMENT OF PAPERS. Any such submission shall be sent in a timely manner (kindly review individual Justice's rules) and be conspicuously marked on the outside "NYSCEF Matter;" lack of such marking may delay processing. NY R L KINGS E FIL Doc. 1(D).
- *NEW YORK COUNTY.* Some Justices require that working copies of e-filed motion papers be submitted. See the E-filing Protocol for information on the many Parts that do not require working copies. Where required, working copies of the moving documents and all other documents on the motion or application shall be submitted to the Motion Submission Part Courtroom (Room 130) on, but not before, the final return date. A Confirmation Notice from the NYSCEF system, which is generated when a document is e-filed, shall be firmly affixed, as the back page facing out, to each separate working copy or group of such copies. NY R NY CTY Procedure II(A) NY R NY CTY E FIL Doc. 2(B)(5)(a); NY R NY CTY J RUL Rule 14(a). For more information on working copies, including which parts don't require them, refer to NY R NY CTY E FIL Doc. 2(B)(6).
- *ONONDAGA COUNTY.* Any courtesy "working" copies, if required (see NY R ONDGA E FIL Protocol(B)(7)), must be provided directly to the assigned justice. NY R ONDGA E FIL Protocol(B)(9)(e). For information as to whether or not an Onondaga Supreme Court Justice requires working (courtesy) copies of e-filed documents, please consult the Onondaga County Individual E-filing Rules. NY R ONDGA E FIL Protocol(B)(7)(a). The Supreme Court Clerk's Office and the Onondaga County Clerk's Office will NOT accept the working copies. Working copies must be sent directly to the assigned justice's chambers. NY R ONDGA E FIL Protocol(B)(7)(b). A copy of the Confirmation Notice, generated by the NYSCEF system at the time a document is e-filed, must be attached to every working copy provided to chambers. If the Confirmation Notice is missing, the copy will not be accepted. NY R ONDGA E FIL Protocol(B)(7)(c). Courtesy copies do not become part of the official court record as maintained by the Onondaga County Clerk's Office and will be destroyed by chambers at the disposition of the case. In the event that counsel fails to file a document via NYSCEF, the document will not be part of the court record. NY R ONDGA E FIL Protocol(B)(7)(d).

- *QUEENS COUNTY.* Working copies of E-Filed notices of motion/notices of petition are NOT to be sent to the Motion Support Office. They must be brought to the calendar call in the judge's part. NY R L QUEENS MOT SUP Doc. 1. Unless otherwise directed or authorized by the court, counsel should file papers with the E-file system first and thereafter deliver a working copy to at the calendar call of the Centralized Motion Part or Assigned Justice in accordance with individual Part Rules. NY R L QUEENS E-FILE Doc. 1(E)(4). On the return date of a motion that has been E-filed, the movant must provide the Centralized Motion Part (CMP) with a working copy of the entire motion including the notice of motion with sequence number and all of the attached exhibits. The motion must have the confirmation of filing firmly affixed to the back of the papers (facing outward). The confirmation of filing is a separate notice from the payment notice and will say confirmation clearly across the top of the page. NY R L QUEENS E-FILE Doc. 1(H)(2)(a). The motion or Order to Show Cause must have clearly written across its face the words "Working Copy," it must also have the assigned Judge's name, motion sequence number and calendar number—which may be obtained from the posted calendar outside courtroom on the return date of the motion. A confirmation of filing must attached thereto. Working copies of e-filed Orders to Show Cause must contain a copy of the signed order and all supporting papers. NY R L QUEENS E-FILE Doc. 1(H)(2)(c). The Confirmation Notice must be an updated version that indicates the sequence number of the motion being submitted at the CMP calendar call. WORKING COPIES WITHOUT A CONFIRMATION NOTICE WILL NOT BE ACCEPTED. NY R L QUEENS E-FILE Doc. 1(H)(7).

vi. *ERIE COUNTY: Additional supplemental documents*

- *Notice of hard copy submission in e-filed case.* In accordance with NY R UNIF TRIAL CTS § 202.5-b(d), the County Clerk shall refuse to accept for filing, hard copy papers filed to an action subject to electronic filing unless hard copy filing is permitted by the Uniform Rules or NY R ERIE E FIL Doc. 3 and the papers bear a completed Notice of Hard Copy Submission—E-Filed Case form. NY R ERIE E FIL Doc. 3(III)(D).

vii. *KINGS COUNTY: Additional supplemental documents*

- *Forms when filing in hard copy.* An attorney who certifies in good faith that he or she lacks the equipment or knowledge needed to e-file and have no staff member or employee under his or her direction who has such knowledge and equipment may opt out of participation in e-filing in a mandatory case by filing a "Notice of Opt-Out from Participation in Action Subject to Mandatory Electronic Filing" form EFM-2 with the Clerk. NY R L KINGS E FIL Doc. 1(A)(2). Where in accordance with the E-Filing Rules a party submits a document in hard copy in an e-filed case (principally, a document submitted by a nonparticipating party (e.g., an attorney) in a consensual case, an emergency filing made in accordance with the Mandatory E-Filing Rules, and any document filed with the court in hard copy by an attorney who has opted out of participation in mandatory e-filing, the document must bear the back page facing out, a "Notice of Hard Copy Submission—E-Filed Cases" form EFM-3. NY R L KINGS E FIL Doc. 1(B)(3).

viii. *NEW YORK COUNTY: Additional supplemental documents*

- *Notice of hard copy submission.* Where in accordance with the E-Filing Rules an attorney or an unrepresented litigant who is participating in e-filing submits a document in hard copy in an e-filed case, the document must bear, as the back page facing out, a Notice of Hard-Copy Submission—E-Filed Case (a form available in the "Forms" section on the NYSCEF website (Form EFM-3) and in the court's back offices). NY R NY CTY E FIL Doc. 2(B)(3). For more information refer to NY R NY CTY E FIL Doc. 2.
- *Unpublished decisions.* Whenever reliance is placed upon a decision or other authority not officially published or readily available to the New York County Supreme Court, a copy of the case or of pertinent portions of the authority shall be submitted with the motion papers. NY R NY CTY J RUL Rule 14(a).

ix. *ONONDAGA COUNTY: Additional supplemental documents*

- *Notice of hard copy submission.* Any papers to be filed with the court in an e-filed case must be filed online with the E-filing system except where a special exemption is granted (e.g., oversized maps, photographs). If such an exemption is granted, Form EFM-3, "Notice of Hard Copy Submission—E-Filed Case," must be attached to such documents forms which are not filed on line. Also, Form EFM-4 "Notice of Hard Copy Exhibit Filing" must be completed and uploaded to the action's e-file. Both of these forms may be found on the NYSCEF website. NY R ONDGA E FIL Protocol(B)(4).

x. *QUEENS COUNTY: Additional supplemental documents*

- *Notice of hard copy submission.* Any party opting out of the e-filing system must have a "Notice of Hard Copy Submission" firmly affixed to the back of the papers. NY R L QUEENS E-FILE Doc. 1(H)(2)(f).

2. *Documents for opposing party*
    a. *Required documents*
        i. *Opposition.* Refer to the General Requirements section of this document for information on the opposition.
            - *Request for oral argument.* A party requesting oral argument shall set forth such request in its notice of motion or in its order to show cause or on the first page of the answering papers, as the case may be. Where all parties to a motion request oral argument, oral argument shall be granted unless the court shall determine it to be unnecessary. Where a motion is brought on by order to show cause, the court may set forth in the order that oral argument is required on the return date of the motion. NY R UNIF TRIAL CTS § 202.8(d).
            - *QUEENS COUNTY: E-filing opposition papers.* E-filed opposition papers and/or reply papers must also be provided to the Centralized Motion Part in the same manner as the moving papers with the confirmation of filing firmly attached to the back of the papers. NY R L QUEENS E-FILE Doc. 1(H)(2)(d).
        ii. *Proof of service.* In addition to complying with the provisions of NY CPLR Rule 2101, every paper filed in court shall have annexed thereto appropriate proof of service on all parties where required. NY R UNIF TRIAL CTS § 202.5(a).
    b. *Supplemental documents*
        i. *Supporting evidence; Exhibits.* The main supporting papers on a motion are affidavits, but any relevant exhibits, documents, depositions, etc., are also includible. SIEGEL-NYPRAC § 246.
            - *Affidavits accompanying opposition.* Affidavits shall be for a statement of the relevant facts. NY R UNIF TRIAL CTS § 202.8(c).
            - *Foreign language documents.* Where an affidavit or exhibit annexed to a paper served or filed is in a foreign language, it shall be accompanied by an English translation and an affidavit by the translator stating his qualifications and that the translation is accurate. NY CPLR Rule 2101(b).
            - *Statement of attorney in lieu of affidavit.* The statement of an attorney admitted to practice in the courts of the state, or of a physician, osteopath or dentist, authorized by law to practice in the state, who is not a party to an action, when subscribed and affirmed by him to be true under the penalties of perjury, may be served or filed in the action in lieu of and with the same force and effect as an affidavit. NY CPLR Rule 2106.
            - *NEW YORK COUNTY: Form of presented exhibits.* Exhibits should be tabbed and be legible; a typed version of any exhibit that is difficult to read should be submitted with the original. Exhibits printed on both sides of the page should be bound and tabbed on the side. NY R NY CTY J RUL Rule 14(a).
            - *QUEENS COUNTY.* Attorneys submitting exhibits to the court on E-file cases shall make each exhibit a separate, labeled attachment to an affidavit/affirmation. NY R L QUEENS E-FILE Doc. 1(H)(4).
        ii. *Brief.* Briefs shall be for a statement of the relevant law. NY R UNIF TRIAL CTS § 202.8(c).
        iii. *Filing fees.* The County Clerk shall require the payment of any applicable statutory fees, or an order of the Court waiving payment of such fees, before accepting a paper for filing. NY R UNIF TRIAL CTS § 202.5(d)(1). For information on filing fees, if any, refer to NY CPLR § 8001, et seq.
            - *ALBANY COUNTY.* In general, any filing subsequent to the commencement of an action which is designated as a motion or cross-motion requires the payment of a filing fee to the County Clerk's Office prior to submission to the Supreme Court Clerk's Office for referral to the assigned justice. The fee is assessed regardless of whether an application is made by notice of motion, order to show cause or ex parte. No fee will be charged upon the filing of a motion for poor person status in conjunction with an application which serves to commence an action or special proceeding. In the event a motion is received by the court unaccompanied by proof of payment to the County Clerk, the Supreme Court Clerk's Office will contact the submitting party to advise that the application will be held pending receipt of the filing fee only until the return date of the motion. If proof of payment is not submitted to the Supreme Court Clerk's Office by the return date (ex parte applications will be held ten (10) days), the papers will be returned by mail with a notification that the motion has been removed from the court's calendar and that it must be re-noticed and re-filed with the court along with the requisite filing fee. Inquiries concerning the applicability of the motion fee to a proposed filing may be directed to the Supreme Court Clerk's Office. NY R 3 JD SUP Doc. 1(B).
            - *BRONX COUNTY.* In accordance with the new civil fee schedule set forth in Article 80 of the C.P.L.R. (NY CPLR § 8001, et seq.), effective July 14, 2003, all motions, and cross motions must be approved in Room

217 prior to payment of said fees in the County Clerk's Office, Room 118. NY R BRONX FIL R Doc. 8. The motion fee [must be] paid for via NYSCEF by credit/debit card. NY R BRONX E FIL R Doc. 1(1).

- *ERIE COUNTY.* Payment for fee-bearing NYSCEF documents must be made online via credit or debit card (American Express, MasterCard or Visa) at the time of submission. NY R ERIE E FIL Doc. 3(III)(E).
- *KINGS COUNTY.* The motion must be filed with NYSCEF and the motion fee paid. NY R L KINGS E FIL Doc. 1(D). Court fees in NYSCEF cases must be paid via NYSCEF by a credit or bank card (MasterCard, Visa, or American Express). Fees are no longer accepted in person in the Kings County Clerk's Office in NYSCEF cases. NY R L KINGS E FIL Doc. 1(B)(6).
- *NEW YORK COUNTY.* A motion fee must be paid on motions made in writing by notice of motion, order to show cause or ex parte after the commencement of an action. For this purpose, the term "action" shall mean any application to the court that requires the assignment of an index number, regardless of whether a formal pleading is filed. Applications or motions that commence an action and for which an index number fee must be paid require no motion fee. [A]ny motions made after the initial applications in these situations would require payment of the motion fee. A motion that is the initial application in a case commenced by the filing of a summons and complaint would require a motion fee since the filing of the summons and complaint rather than the application itself would require the purchase of an index number. NY R NY CTY Procedure II(A). In e-filed cases the motion fee must be paid when the documents are filed. Payment is made on-line by Visa, Mastercard, or American Express credit or bank card. NY R NY CTY Procedure II(A); NY R NY CTY E FIL Doc. 2(B)(5).
- *ONONDAGA COUNTY.* Court fees in e-filed cases must be paid online with the NYSCEF system using a credit card. The document is not considered to have been filed until payment of the fee has been tendered. NY R ONDGA E FIL Protocol(B)(2). Fees must be paid on all cross motions. NY R ONDGA E FIL Protocol(B)(9)(e).
- *QUEENS COUNTY.* The Motion Support Office does not receive, forward or process any fees or waiver of fees. All applications requiring payment of statutory fees or waiver of fees must be sent directly to the Queens County Clerk's office. NY R L QUEENS MOT SUP Doc. 1. Court fees (e.g., RJI fee, motion fee) in E-filed cases may be paid for on-line using a credit card. Papers may also be filed with the E-file system and the fee may be paid at the County Clerk's Office. In the latter case, the paper is not considered to have been filed until payment of the fee has been tendered. NY R L QUEENS E-FILE Doc. 1(E)(1). The motion/petition shall be filed on-line and the fee paid for either on-line by credit card or by the "Pay at the County Clerk's Office" option. NY R L QUEENS E-FILE Doc. 1(H)(1).

iv. *Working copies.* The court may require the parties to provide working copies of documents filed electronically. In such event, each working copy shall include, firmly affixed thereto, a copy of a confirmation notice in a form prescribed by the Chief Administrator. NY R UNIF TRIAL CTS § 202.5-b(d)(5).

- *BRONX COUNTY.* After papers on motions have been e-filed, working copies thereof, with Confirmation Notice firmly attached as the back page facing out, must be submitted. (Each document or group of documents that is separately bound shall bear a Confirmation Notice.) Working copies lacking the Notice will not be accepted. WORKING COPIES OF MOTION PAPERS MUST BE SUBMITTED NO LATER THAN 4:45 P.M. ON THE RETURN DATE IN THE MOTION SUPPORT OFFICE (ROOM 217) AS EXPLAINED in NY R BRONX E FIL R Doc. 1(4). If an attorney has failed to submit required working copies on or before the return date, the motion will be transmitted as is to the Justice for such action as the Justice finds appropriate. Attorneys may submit working copies on motions by mail or overnight delivery. Any such submission shall be sent in a timely manner to the Motion Support Office (Room 217) and be conspicuously marked on the outside "NYSCEF Matter"; lack of such marking may delay processing. NY R BRONX E FIL R Doc. 1(4)(a).
- *ERIE COUNTY.* Electronically filed documents subject to review and processing by the Part Clerk do not require a working copy unless otherwise directed or provided for in IAS Part Rules. NY R UNIF TRIAL CTS § 202.5-b(d)(4), any working copy submitted shall include, as a cover page firmly fastened thereto, a copy of the Confirmation Notice generated by the NYSCEF site at the time of filing. Please consult the individual Justice's Part Rules and/or consult with the Judge's chambers to determine whether and how working copies are to be provided. Working copies will not be printed or delivered by the Erie County Clerk or the Chief Clerk of the Courts or any of their personnel to chambers. The official record of a document in an electronically filed case is the document filed via the NYSCEF system. Working copies are intended only for use by the Justice. The Court will discard all working copies after the Justice has finished with them.

Thus, in the event that counsel fails to file a document via the NYSCEF system, the document will not be part of the court record. NY R ERIE E FIL Doc. 3(III)(O); NY R ERIE E FIL Doc. 3(V)(E).

- *KINGS COUNTY.* No courtesy copies of motion papers are required by the Court, except as may be required for electronic filing or by the Judge's Part Rules. In tort cases against the City of New York, courtesy copies shall be supplied to the Corporation Counsel's office in Brooklyn. NY R L KINGS Pt. C, Rule 5. Unless otherwise directed by the Court or as described herein, and with the exceptions listed below, in all NYSCEF cases in which an RJI has been filed, working copies of e-filed documents that are intended for judicial review must be submitted to the court. Working copies are not required of documents that are only processed by a support office (e.g. preliminary conference request, note of issue). Working copies shall include exhibit tabs and backs; for motion papers, the motion sequence number and the return date and part. The confirmation notice with the motion sequence number on it should be the back page of the motion facing out. In addition, the filer of a working copy must firmly bind thereto, with the back page facing out, a copy of the Confirmation Notice that was generated by NYSCEF when that document was efiled. Working copies that are submitted without the related Confirmation Notice will not be accepted. NY R L KINGS E FIL Doc. 1(B)(7); NY R L KINGS E FIL Doc. 1(D). WORKING COPIES OF MOTION PAPERS MUST BE SUBMITTED IN THE MOTION SUPPORT OFFICE (ROOM 227) AS EXPLAINED HEREIN. THEY MUST NOT BE DELIVERED TO THE PART OR CHAMBERS, EXCEPT WHERE THE INDIVIDUAL JUSTICE'S PART RULES PROVIDE OTHERWISE; DOING SO WILL CAUSE ADMINISTRATIVE CONFUSION AND POSSIBLE MISPLACEMENT OF PAPERS. Any such submission shall be sent in a timely manner (kindly review individual Justice's rules) and be conspicuously marked on the outside "NYSCEF Matter;" lack of such marking may delay processing. NY R L KINGS E FIL Doc. 1(D).
- *NEW YORK COUNTY.* Some Justices require that working copies of e-filed motion papers be submitted. See the E-filing Protocol for information on the many Parts that do not require working copies. Where required, working copies of the moving documents and all other documents on the motion or application shall be submitted to the Motion Submission Part Courtroom (Room 130) on, but not before, the final return date. A Confirmation Notice from the NYSCEF system, which is generated when a document is e-filed, shall be firmly affixed, as the back page facing out, to each separate working copy or group of such copies. NY R NY CTY Procedure II(A) NY R NY CTY E FIL Doc. 2(B)(5)(a); NY R NY CTY J RUL Rule 14(a). For more information on working copies, including which parts don't require them, refer to NY R NY CTY E FIL Doc. 2(B)(6).
- *ONONDAGA COUNTY.* Any courtesy "working" copies, if required (see NY R ONDGA E FIL Protocol(B)(7)), must be provided directly to the assigned justice. NY R ONDGA E FIL Protocol(B)(9)(e). For information as to whether or not an Onondaga Supreme Court Justice requires working (courtesy) copies of e-filed documents, please consult the Onondaga County Individual E-filing Rules. NY R ONDGA E FIL Protocol(B)(7)(a). The Supreme Court Clerk's Office and the Onondaga County Clerk's Office will NOT accept the working copies. Working copies must be sent directly to the assigned justice's chambers. NY R ONDGA E FIL Protocol(B)(7)(b). A copy of the Confirmation Notice, generated by the NYSCEF system at the time a document is e-filed, must be attached to every working copy provided to chambers. If the Confirmation Notice is missing, the copy will not be accepted. NY R ONDGA E FIL Protocol(B)(7)(c). Courtesy copies do not become part of the official court record as maintained by the Onondaga County Clerk's Office and will be destroyed by chambers at the disposition of the case. In the event that counsel fails to file a document via NYSCEF, the document will not be part of the court record. NY R ONDGA E FIL Protocol(B)(7)(d).
- *QUEENS COUNTY.* Working copies of E-Filed notices of motion/notices of petition are NOT to be sent to the Motion Support Office. They must be brought to the calendar call in the judge's part. NY R L QUEENS MOT SUP Doc. 1. Unless otherwise directed or authorized by the court, counsel should file papers with the E-file system first and thereafter deliver a working copy to at the calendar call of the Centralized Motion Part or Assigned Justice in accordance with individual Part Rules. NY R L QUEENS E-FILE Doc. 1(E)(4). On the return date of a motion that has been E-filed, the movant must provide the Centralized Motion Part (CMP) with a working copy of the entire motion including the notice of motion with sequence number and all of the attached exhibits. The motion must have the confirmation of filing firmly affixed to the back of the papers (facing outward). The confirmation of filing is a separate notice from the payment notice and will say confirmation clearly across the top of the page. NY R L QUEENS E-FILE Doc. 1(H)(2)(a). The motion or Order to Show Cause must have clearly written across its face the words "Working Copy," it must also

have the assigned Judge's name, motion sequence number and calendar number—which may be obtained from the posted calendar outside courtroom on the return date of the motion. A confirmation of filing must attached thereto. Working copies of e-filed Orders to Show Cause must contain a copy of the signed order and all supporting papers. NY R L QUEENS E-FILE Doc. 1(H)(2)(c). The Confirmation Notice must be an updated version that indicates the sequence number of the motion being submitted at the CMP calendar call. WORKING COPIES WITHOUT A CONFIRMATION NOTICE WILL NOT BE ACCEPTED. NY R L QUEENS E-FILE Doc. 1(H)(7).

v. *ERIE COUNTY: Additional supplemental documents*

- *Notice of hard copy submission in e-filed case.* In accordance with NY R UNIF TRIAL CTS § 202.5-b(d), the County Clerk shall refuse to accept for filing, hard copy papers filed to an action subject to electronic filing unless hard copy filing is permitted by the Uniform Rules or NY R ERIE E FIL Doc. 3 and the papers bear a completed Notice of Hard Copy Submission—E-Filed Case form. NY R ERIE E FIL Doc. 3(III)(D).

vi. *KINGS COUNTY: Additional supplemental documents*

- *Forms when filing in hard copy.* An attorney who certifies in good faith that he or she lacks the equipment or knowledge needed to e-file and have no staff member or employee under his or her direction who has such knowledge and equipment may opt out of participation in e-filing in a mandatory case by filing a "Notice of Opt-Out from Participation in Action Subject to Mandatory Electronic Filing" form EFM-2 with the Clerk. NY R L KINGS E FIL Doc. 1(A)(2). Where in accordance with the E-Filing Rules a party submits a document in hard copy in an e-filed case (principally, a document submitted by a nonparticipating party (e.g., an attorney) in a consensual case, an emergency filing made in accordance with the Mandatory E-Filing Rules, and any document filed with the court in hard copy by an attorney who has opted out of participation in mandatory e-filing, the document must bear the back page facing out, a "Notice of Hard Copy Submission—E-Filed Cases" form EFM-3. NY R L KINGS E FIL Doc. 1(B)(3).

vii. *NEW YORK COUNTY: Additional supplemental documents*

- *Notice of hard copy submission.* Where in accordance with the E-Filing Rules an attorney or an unrepresented litigant who is participating in e-filing submits a document in hard copy in an e-filed case, the document must bear, as the back page facing out, a Notice of Hard-Copy Submission—E-Filed Case (a form available in the "Forms" section on the NYSCEF website (Form EFM-3) and in the court's back offices). NY R NY CTY E FIL Doc. 2(B)(3). For more information refer to NY R NY CTY E FIL Doc. 2.
- *Unpublished decisions.* Whenever reliance is placed upon a decision or other authority not officially published or readily available to the New York County Supreme Court, a copy of the case or of pertinent portions of the authority shall be submitted with the motion papers. NY R NY CTY J RUL Rule 14(a).

viii. *ONONDAGA COUNTY: Additional supplemental documents*

- *Notice of hard copy submission.* Any papers to be filed with the court in an e-filed case must be filed online with the E-filing system except where a special exemption is granted (e.g., oversized maps, photographs). If such an exemption is granted, Form EFM-3, "Notice of Hard Copy Submission—E-Filed Case," must be attached to such documents forms which are not filed on line. Also, Form EFM-4 "Notice of Hard Copy Exhibit Filing" must be completed and uploaded to the action's e-file. Both of these forms may be found on the NYSCEF website. NY R ONDGA E FIL Protocol(B)(4).

ix. *QUEENS COUNTY: Additional supplemental documents*

- *Notice of hard copy submission.* Any party opting out of the e-filing system must have a "Notice of Hard Copy Submission" firmly affixed to the back of the papers. NY R L QUEENS E-FILE Doc. 1(H)(2)(f).

E. Format

1. *Form of documents*

a. *Size and form of paper.* Each paper served or filed shall be durable, white and, except for summonses, subpoenas, notices of appearance, notes of issue, orders of protection, temporary orders of protection and exhibits, shall be eleven by eight and one-half (11 x 8-1/2) inches in size. NY CPLR Rule 2101(a).

b. *Writing and language.* The writing shall be legible and in black ink. NY CPLR Rule 2101(a). Each paper served or filed shall be in the English language which, where practicable, shall be of ordinary usage. NY CPLR Rule 2101(b).

c. *Caption.* Each paper served or filed shall begin with a caption setting forth the name of the court, the venue, the title of the action, the nature of the paper and the index number of the action if one has been assigned. In all papers other

than a summons, a complaint or a judgment it shall be sufficient to state the name of the first named party on each side with an appropriate indication of any omissions. NY CPLR Rule 2101(c).

i. *Further contents of first page.* After the first paper has been filed in each case the index number shall appear on the cover and first page to the right of the caption of every paper tendered for filing in the action. Each such cover and first page also shall contain an indication of the county of venue and a brief description of the nature of the paper and, where the case has been assigned to an individual judge, shall contain the name of the assigned judge to the right of the caption. NY R UNIF TRIAL CTS § 202.5(a); NY R UNIF TRIAL CTS § 202.5(b); NY R UNIF TRIAL CTS § 202.5(d)(1)(i).

ii. *ALBANY COUNTY: Request for oral argument.* A party may request oral argument on a motion by indicating such request on the first page of the notice of motion, order to show cause, or answering papers in the area across from the caption of the action/proceeding. NY R 3 JD SUP Doc. 1(B).

iii. *NEW YORK COUNTY: Request for oral argument.* Counsel who wish oral argument must so request conspicuously on the front of their papers. NY R NY CTY Procedure II(D).

d. *Index number.* No paper in an action in the supreme or a county court, other than an order submitted for signature to a judge out of court, shall be submitted for any purpose to the supreme or county court or to a clerk thereof unless there is endorsed on such paper the index number of the action assigned by the clerk of the county. NY CPLR § 8018(c).

i. *ALBANY COUNTY: Index number on all filed documents.* The index number, the request for judicial intervention number and the assigned justice's name shall appear on [all papers filed with the Court subsequent to the complaint]. NY R 3 JD SUP Doc. 1(A).

ii. *ERIE COUNTY: Index number after initial filing.* Cases that are initially commenced by the filing of papers with the NYSCEF system are identified as e-filed cases by assignment of an Index Number that has "800-899" as the first three (3) digits of the index number (i.e. 802391/2012). NY R ERIE E FIL Doc. 3(II). [The] Index Number must be affixed to all document submissions, filings, and communications to the Erie County Clerk and the Court. Cases that are converted from paper to e-filing shall retain the original index number. NY R ERIE E FIL Doc. 3(II).

iii. *KINGS COUNTY: Index number after initial filing.* In cases commenced electronically by the filing of initiating papers with the NYSCEF system and payment of the statutory fees, the Kings County Clerk will issue an NYSCEF designated index number and the filer shall be notified via the NYSCEF system of the index number assigned and filing date. Such index number must be affixed to all document submissions, filings and communications to the Kings County Clerk and Supreme Court. If counsel faces exigent circumstances that require accelerated assignment, counsel may contact Administration of the Kings County Clerk at kcco-efile@nycourts.gov, during normal business hours of the court. NY R L KINGS E FIL Doc. 1(B)(5).

iv. *NEW YORK COUNTY: Index number on hard copy filings.* Papers subsequently presented for filing in hardcopy format will be filed in this jacket. NY R NY CTY Procedure I(B). Index numbers take the form of six digits followed by a slash and the four digits of the year the case began, e.g., 340705/2018. The first or first two integers of the index number identify the type of case. If a case is commenced electronically, the second integer will be a "5", except as indicated otherwise in the list below. There are many tax certiorari matters e-filed annually and the index numbers therefor will normally run over into those with a "6" as the second integer, and the same will occur with general cases if necessary. The principal types of cases and their index number categories are listed in NY R NY CTY Procedure I(B). NY R NY CTY Procedure I(B); NY R NY CTY Procedure XI(A).

v. *ONONDAGA COUNTY: Index number.* The index number must be referenced on all e-filed documents and correspondence. All e-filed case index numbers will contain the letters "EF" between the year and the file number (for example, 2012EF9999). NY R ONDGA E FIL Protocol(B)(1).

vi. *QUEENS COUNTY: Index number on converted cases.* Cases originally commenced in hard-copy form but later converted to an E-file case, either by stipulation or order will bear a regular index number initially. The County Clerk will issue a new E-file index number. NY R L QUEENS E-FILE Doc. 1(B).

e. *Line spacing.* Every paper filed in court, if typewritten, shall have at least double space between each line, except for quotations and the names and addresses of attorneys appearing in the action. NY R UNIF TRIAL CTS § 202.5(a).

f. *Font size.* Each. . .paper printed or typed, served or filed, except for summonses. . .and exhibits, shall be in clear type of no less than ten (10) point in size. NY CPLR Rule 2101(a).

i. Whenever a requirement relating to size of type is stated in point size, the type size requirement shall be deemed met if the x-height of the type is a minimum of forty-five percent (45%) of the specified point size. Each point shall be measured as .351 millimeter. The x-height size shall be measured as it appears on the page. The x-height is the height of the lower case letters, exclusive of ascenders or descenders. NY CPLR § 105(t).

g. *Margins.* Every paper filed in court shall have at least one (1) inch margins. NY R UNIF TRIAL CTS § 202.5(a).

h. *Citations*

   i. *Civil practice law and rules.* NY CPLR § 101, et seq. shall be known as the civil practice law and rules, and may be cited as "CPLR". Reference to a provision in the civil practice law and rules may, except when such provision is being enacted or amended, be made without indicating whether it is a rule or section. NY CPLR § 101.

i. *Indorsement by attorney.* Each paper served or filed shall be indorsed with the name, address and telephone number of the attorney for the party serving or filing the paper, or if the party does not appear by attorney, with the name, address and telephone number of the party. NY CPLR Rule 2101(d).

j. *One-sided printing.* In addition, every paper filed in court, other than an exhibit or printed form, shall contain writing on one side only, except that papers that are fastened on the side may contain writing on both sides. NY R UNIF TRIAL CTS § 202.5(a).

k. *Use of copies authorized.* Except where otherwise specifically prescribed, copies, rather than originals, of all papers, including orders, affidavits and exhibits may be served or filed. Where it is required that the original be served or filed and the original is lost or withheld, the court may authorize a copy to be served or filed. NY CPLR Rule 2101(e).

   i. Where a certified copy of a paper is required by law, an attorney admitted to practice in the courts of the state may certify that it has been compared by him with the original and found to be a true and complete copy. Such a certificate, when subscribed by such attorney, has the same effect as if made by a clerk. NY CPLR § 2105.

l. *Recycled paper.* It is the policy of the Unified Court System that litigants, where practicable, should file or submit to the courts of the Unified Court System of the State of New York papers printed or reproduced on recycled paper. Paper is considered recycled if it contains a minimum content of thirty percent (30%) waste paper. NY R UNIF TRIAL CTS § 215.2. The signature page of every paper filed or submitted to the court on recycled paper should bear the legend: "Printed [Reproduced] on Recycled Paper." NY R UNIF TRIAL CTS § 215.3.

m. *Form of request for judicial intervention; Copies.* A request for judicial intervention must be submitted, in duplicate, on a form authorized by the Chief of the Courts, with proof of service on the other parties to the action (but proof of service is not required where the application is ex parte). NY R UNIF TRIAL CTS § 202.6(a).

n. *KINGS COUNTY: Tabs on filings.* Motions, orders and other filed papers shall be indexed with protruding tabs. Clerks are required to reject papers that do not have protruding exhibit tabs, except papers in matrimonial cases and papers filed by pro se litigants. NY R L KINGS Pt. A, Papers.

o. *NEW YORK COUNTY: Length of briefs.* Unless advance permission otherwise is granted by the court for good cause, memoranda of law shall not exceed thirty (30) pages each (exclusive of table of contents and table of authorities) and affidavits/affirmations shall not exceed twenty-five (25) pages each. NY R NY CTY J RUL Rule 14(b).

p. *QUEENS COUNTY: Form and size of motion filings.* All motions filed in Queens Supreme Court-Civil Term, must adhere to the Motion Support rules and the rules of the assigned judge. NY R L QUEENS MOT SUP Doc. 1. Due to space limitations, the Motion Support Office cannot accept notices of motion/notices of petition and accompanying exhibits which measure greater than eight (8) inches. If your documents measure greater than eight (8) inches you are directed to submit only the notice of motion/notice of petition to the Motion Support Office and bring all exhibits to the calendar call on your return date. NY R L QUEENS MOT SUP Doc. 1.

2. *Form of electronic documents.* Each paper served or filed by electronic means, as defined in NY CPLR Rule 2103(f), shall be capable of being reproduced by the receiver so as to comply with the provisions of NY CPLR Rule 2101(a) through NY CPLR Rule 2101(d). NY CPLR Rule 2101(g).

   a. *File format.* All e-filed documents shall comply with the technical requirements set forth at the NYSCEF site. NY R UNIF TRIAL CTS § 202.5-b(d)(1)(i).

   b. *Heading of document.* The subject matter heading for each paper sent by electronic means must indicate that the matter being transmitted electronically is related to a court proceeding. NY CPLR Rule 2103(b)(7).

   c. *E-filed documents identification*

      i. *ERIE COUNTY.* E-filed cases must be readily identifiable and marked as such. If counsel presents papers to the Office of the Erie County Clerk or the Office of the Chief Clerk in a NYSCEF matter where authorized, counsel should alert the Clerk that the case is a NYSCEF matter. NY R ERIE E FIL Doc. 3(II).

ii. *KINGS COUNTY.* The Supreme Court's Civil Case Information System ("CCIS") will further identify e-filed cases by the addition of a suffix to the index number (e.g. 500136/2006E). This suffix should be used on all documents filed with the court in e-filed matters. NY R L KINGS E FIL Doc. 1(A)(1).

3. *Signature blocks.* Every pleading, written motion, and other paper, served on another party or filed or submitted to the court shall be signed by an attorney, or by a party if the party is not represented by an attorney, with the name of the attorney or party clearly printed or typed directly below the signature. NY R CHIEF ADMIN § 130-1.1-a(a); NY R UNIF TRIAL CTS § 202.5(d)(1)(iv).

   a. *Printed name.* Beneath each signature shall be printed the name signed. NY CPLR Rule 2101(a).

   b. *Failure to sign.* Absent good cause shown, the court shall strike any unsigned paper if the omission of the signature is not corrected promptly after being called to the attention of the attorney or party. NY R CHIEF ADMIN § 130-1.1-a(a).

   c. *Signature as certification.* By signing a paper, an attorney or party certifies that, to the best of that person's knowledge, information and belief, formed after an inquiry reasonable under the circumstances the presentation of the paper or the contentions therein are not frivolous as defined in NY R CHIEF ADMIN § 130-1.1(c). NY R CHIEF ADMIN § 130-1.1-a(b)(1).

   d. *Electronic signatures.* A document shall be considered to have been signed by an attorney or party in compliance with NY R CHIEF ADMIN § 130-1.1-a if it has been signed by such attorney or party as provided in NY R UNIF TRIAL CTS § 202.5-b(e)(1) and it bears the signatory's name. NY R UNIF TRIAL CTS § 202.5-b(e)(2). An electronically filed document shall be considered to have been signed by, and shall be binding upon, the person identified as a signatory, if:

      i. It bears the physical signature of such person and is scanned into an electronic format that reproduces such signature; or

      ii. The signatory has electronically affixed the digital image of his or her signature to the document; or

      iii. It is electronically filed under the User ID and password of that person; or

      iv. In a tax certiorari action in which the parties have stipulated to this procedure, it is an initiating document that is electronically filed without the signature of the signatory in a form provided above in NY R UNIF TRIAL CTS § 202.5-b(e)(iv), provided that, prior to filing, the document is signed in full in hard copy (which hard copy must be preserved until the conclusion of all proceedings, including appeals, in the case in which it is filed); or

      v. In a small claims assessment review proceeding, it is a petition recorded by the NYSCEF site upon the filing of a text file as provided in NY R UNIF TRIAL CTS § 202.5-b(b)(1), provided that prior to filing, the document was signed in full in hard copy (which hard copy must be preserved until the conclusion of all proceedings in the matter, including article 78 (NY CPLR § 7801, et seq.) review and any appeals, and must be made available during the proceeding upon request of the respondent or the court); or

      vi. It otherwise bears the electronic signature of the signatory in a format conforming to such standards and requirements as may hereafter be established by the Chief Administrator. NY R UNIF TRIAL CTS § 202.5-b(e).

4. *Confidentiality of personal information.* No person may file any document available for public inspection with any state agency, political subdivision, or in any court of this state that contains a Social Security account number of any other person, unless such other person is a dependent child, or has consented to such filing, except as required by federal or state law or regulation, or by court rule. NY GEN BUS § 399-ddd. Submissions pursuant to e-filing procedures shall have the same confidentiality rights as paper documents. NY R UNIF TRIAL CTS § 202.5-b(k)(1).

   a. *Confidential personal information.* Except in the actions designated in NY R UNIF TRIAL CTS § 202.5(e)(1), or as otherwise provided by rule or law or court order, and whether or not a sealing order is or has been sought, the parties shall omit or redact confidential personal information in papers submitted to the court for filing. For purposes of NY R UNIF TRIAL CTS § 202.5(e), confidential personal information ("CPI") means:

      i. The taxpayer identification number of an individual or an entity, including a Social Security number, an employer identification number, and an individual taxpayer identification number, except the last four (4) digits thereof;

      ii. The date of an individual's birth, except the year thereof;

      iii. The full name of an individual known to be a minor, except the minor's initials;

      iv. A financial account number, including a credit and/or debit card number, a bank account number, an investment account number, and/or an insurance account number, except the last four (4) digits or letters thereof; and

v. Any of the documents or testimony in a matrimonial action protected by NY DOM REL § 235 or evidence sealed by the court in such an action which are attached as exhibits or referenced in the papers filed in any other civil action. For purposes of NY R UNIF TRIAL CTS § 202.5, a matrimonial action shall mean: an action to annul a marriage or declare the nullity of a void marriage, an action or agreement for a separation, an action for a divorce, or an action or proceeding for custody, visitation, writ of habeus corpus, child support, maintenance or paternity. NY R UNIF TRIAL CTS § 202.5(e)(1).

vi. *ERIE COUNTY.* An attorney or unrepresented litigant filing a document via the NYSCEF system must comply with the requirements of NY R UNIF TRIAL CTS § 202.5(e) regarding the redaction of Confidential Personal Information and NY GEN BUS § 399-ddd(6) concerning the filing of documents containing Social Security Numbers. It is the sole responsibility of counsel or unrepresented litigant filing to be aware of and to comply with existing laws requiring non-disclosure of personal information contained in any document e-filed in NYSCEF. NY R ERIE E FIL Doc. 3(III)(G); NY R ERIE E FIL Doc. 3(III).

vii. *KINGS COUNTY.* An attorney or unrepresented litigant filing a document via the NYSCEF system must comply with the requirements of General Business Law § 399-dd(6), which often require redaction of any Social Security number that appear in the original document. The NYSCEF system automatically redacts portions of filed documents which apparently contain Social Security numbers pursuant to NY R UNIF TRIAL CTS § 202.5-b(k). In the event the filing party receives e-mail notice through NYSCEF that a Social Security number in a filed document has been redacted, and the filing party concludes such redaction is erroneous, the filer should click on the link provided in the e-mail to permit the County Clerk to revert the redaction. For Confidential Personal Information, see NY R UNIF TRIAL CTS § 202.5(e) and NY R L KINGS E FIL Doc. 1(B)(11). [Editor's note: the reference to General Business Law § 399-dd(6) is likely a reference to NY GEN BUS § 399-ddd(6)]. NY R L KINGS E FIL Doc. 1(B)(10); NY R L KINGS E FIL Doc. 1(K)(1).

viii. *NEW YORK COUNTY.* It is the responsibility of counsel and parties to comply with rules restricting disclosure of confidential personal information. Nevertheless, NYSCEF screens filings and endeavors to identify any that contain social security numbers. When such numbers are discovered through this process, NYSCEF will restrict portions of or all of such documents from public view. Where NYSCEF has redacted what it believes to be a social security number, it will transmit to the filer a notice advising of the action taken and requesting that the filer review the matter and provide notification as set forth in the notice if the redaction has been made in error. NY R NY CTY E FIL Doc. 2(K)(1); NY R NY CTY J RUL Rule A-1. Documents filed in the past in "secure status" under a procedure no longer in place will retain that status unless otherwise directed by the court. NY R NY CTY E FIL Doc. 2(K)(2).

b. *Submission of confidential personal information.* Where a person submitting a paper to a court for filing believes in good faith that the inclusion of the full confidential personal information described in NY R UNIF TRIAL CTS § 202.5(e)(1) is material and necessary to the adjudication of the action or proceeding before the court, he or she may apply to the court for leave to serve and file together with a paper in which such information has been set forth in abbreviated form a confidential affidavit or affirmation setting forth the same information in unabbreviated form, appropriately referenced to the page or pages of the paper at which the abbreviated form appears. NY R UNIF TRIAL CTS § 202.5(e)(3).

c. *Home addresses.* For information on when home addresses and other personal information must be redacted, refer to NY CPLR Rule 2103-a.

5. *Defective papers.* A defect in the form of a paper, if a substantial right of a party is not prejudiced, shall be disregarded by the court, and leave to correct shall be freely given. NY CPLR Rule 2101(f). Papers that are stapled or bound securely shall not be rejected for filing simply because they are not bound with a backer of any kind. NY R UNIF TRIAL CTS § 202.5(a). A paper filed in accordance with the rules of the chief administrator or any local rule or practice established by the court shall be deemed filed. NY CPLR Rule 2102(b).

a. *Objection to defective papers.* The party on whom a paper is served shall be deemed to have waived objection to any defect in form unless, within fifteen (15) days after the receipt thereof, the party on whom the paper is served returns the paper to the party serving it with a statement of particular objections. NY CPLR Rule 2101(f).

F. Filing and Service Requirements

1. *Filing requirements.* Except where otherwise prescribed by law or order of court, papers required to be filed shall be filed with the clerk of the court in which the action is triable. In an action or proceeding in supreme or court, papers required to be filed shall be filed with the clerk of the county in which the proceeding is brought. NY CPLR Rule 2102(a).

a. *Furnishing papers to the court.* Each party shall furnish to the court all papers served by him. The moving party shall

furnish at the hearing all other papers not already in the possession of the court necessary to the consideration of the questions involved. Where such papers are in the possession of an adverse party, they shall be produced by him at the hearing on notice served with the motion papers. Only papers served in accordance with the provisions of NY CPLR Rule 2214 shall be read in support of, or in opposition to, the motion, unless the court for good cause shall otherwise direct. NY CPLR Rule 2214(c).

i. *Submission to judge.* All papers for signature or consideration of the court shall be presented to the clerk of the trial court in the appropriate courtroom or clerk's office, except that where the clerk is unavailable or the judge so directs, papers may be submitted to the judge and a copy filed with the clerk at the first available opportunity. All papers for any judge that are filed in the clerk's office shall be promptly delivered to the judge by the clerk. The papers shall be clearly addressed to the judge for whom they are intended and prominently show the nature of the papers, the title and index number of the action in which they are filed, the judge's name and the name of the attorney or party submitting them. NY R UNIF TRIAL CTS § 202.5(b).

ii. *BRONX COUNTY: Approval of motions before filing.* All motion papers must be approved by the Motion Support Office, Supreme Court, Civil Term, room 217, before the motion papers are filed and the appropriate fee paid to the County Clerk. NY R BRONX FIL R Doc. 1.

iii. *ERIE COUNTY: Filing motions.* A motion on notice or a notice of petition in a NYSCEF case shall be filed through the NYSCEF system and must be accompanied by a Request for Judicial Intervention if the motion is being filed upon commencement of the action or if the matter has not yet been assigned to an IAS Justice. In addition, cross motions with the appropriate filing fees and opposition and reply papers must be submitted via the NYSCEF system. NY R ERIE E FIL Doc. 3(V)(A).

iv. *NEW YORK COUNTY: Filing hard copies.* Where in the narrow circumstances described by the e-filing rules a motion is made in hard-copy form or opposition papers are submitted in such form in an e-filed case, the hard-copy documents shall be submitted in the same way papers are submitted in non-e-filed cases, except that there shall be firmly affixed to each separate document or group of documents, as the back page facing out, a Notice of Hard Copy Submission—E-Filed Case. NY R NY CTY Procedure II(A). For more information on filing in hard copy cases, refer to NY R NY CTY Procedure II(A).

v. *ONONDAGA COUNTY: Submission of responsive papers and cross-motions.* Cross-motions, opposition and reply papers must be submitted online. NY R ONDGA E FIL Protocol(B)(9)(e). Motions and Orders to Show Cause are assigned a sequence number by the system. Counsel must be sure that cross motions and other filings correspond with the correct sequence number so that a cross motion will not be associated with the wrong original motion. NY R ONDGA E FIL Protocol(B)(9)(f).

b. *Electronic filing.* On consent, documents may be filed and served by electronic means in Supreme Court in such civil actions and in such counties as shall be authorized by order of the Chief Administrator of the Courts and only to the extent and in the manner provided in NY R UNIF TRIAL CTS § 202.5-b. NY R UNIF TRIAL CTS § 202.5-b(a)(1). For the definitions of terms used in electronic filing, refer to NY R UNIF TRIAL CTS § 202.5-b(a)(2).

i. *E-filing mandatory.* In any action subject to e-filing, all documents required to be filed with the court by an e-filing party shall be filed and served electronically, except as provided in NY R UNIF TRIAL CTS § 202.5-b. NY R UNIF TRIAL CTS § 202.5-b(d)(1)(i).

- *ERIE COUNTY.* Case types currently eligible and accepted for e-filing are listed at the NYSCEF website. Note that some actions or special proceedings, (i.e., name changes) which are otherwise subject to mandatory e-filing, if commenced by unrepresented litigants will NOT be maintained in the NYSCEF system; individual cases may be found either at NYSCEF or in the Erie County Clerk's online records system. NY R ERIE E FIL Doc. 3(I)(E).

- *KINGS COUNTY.* Cases that are commenced by filing of the initiating papers with NYSCEF are identified as e-filed cases by assignment of a special index number (i.e., Index Numbers beginning with 500,000). NY R L KINGS E FIL Doc. 1(A)(1). All cases required to be e-filed are listed in Uniform Rule 202.5-bb (Mandatory E-Filing Rules) and on the NYSCEF website. All such cases must be commenced by filing with the County Clerk electronically through NYSCEF and all subsequent documents in such cases must be e-filed. Any questions regarding mandatory e-filing in Kings County can be e-mailed to kcco-efile@nycourts.gov. NY R L KINGS E FIL Doc. 1(A)(2).

- *NEW YORK COUNTY.* Unless otherwise provided in the Rules or in NY R NY CTY E FIL Doc. 2 or where a special exemption is granted due to physical requirements (e.g., oversized maps; see NY R NY CTY E FIL Doc. 2(B)(10)), all documents to be filed with the court in a NYSCEF case, including all documents on

motions and all letters to the court (where permitted), must be filed with the NYSCEF system. Documents that attorneys would not ordinarily file with the court in a hard-copy case need not be e-filed. Unless otherwise provided by the E-Filing Rules or this Protocol, in e-filed cases the County Clerk and the court will not accept documents filed in paper form. NY R NY CTY E FIL Doc. 2(B)(1). E-filing is mandatory in all types of cases (other than election law, matrimonial, Art. 78, and Mental Hygiene Law matters, and Art. 70 habeas corpus proceedings) that are commenced in this court on or after February 19, 2013. All such cases must be commenced by filing with the County Clerk electronically through NYSCEF and all subsequent documents in such cases must be e-filed. NY R NY CTY E FIL Doc. 2(A)(2)(a). For more information, including information on consensual e-filing and filing scanned hard copy documents, refer to NY R NY CTY E FIL Doc. 2(A)(2).

- *QUEENS COUNTY.* All authorized Torts, Commercial and Tax Certiorari cases may be commenced by E-Filing, however all parties must consent for the action to continue as an E-file case. NY R L QUEENS E-FILE Doc. 1(A). All papers to be filed with the court in an E-filed case shall be filed on-line with the E-file system except as directed by the court. Papers that attorneys would not ordinarily file with the court in a hard-copy case need not be filed in an E-filed matter. NY R L QUEENS E-FILE Doc. 1(E)(2).

ii. *Who may file.* Documents may be filed or served electronically only by a person who has registered as an authorized e-filing user or as otherwise provided in NY R UNIF TRIAL CTS § 202.5-b(c). NY R UNIF TRIAL CTS § 202.5-b(c)(1).

iii. *When filing made.* Documents may be transmitted at any time of the day or night to the NYSCEF site. A document other than an order or judgment is filed when its electronic transmission or, in the case of a petition that is e-filed by submission of a text file as provided in NY R UNIF TRIAL CTS § 202.5-b(b)(1), the electronic transmission of the text file is recorded at that site, provided, however, that where payment of a fee is required upon the filing of a document, the document is not filed until transmission of the document and the information or form or information as required in NY R UNIF TRIAL CTS § 202.5-b(d)(2)(i), NY R UNIF TRIAL CTS § 202.5-b(d)(2)(ii) or NY R UNIF TRIAL CTS § 202.5-b(d)(2)(iii) has been recorded at the NYSCEF site; or, if no transmission of that information or form or information is recorded, where permitted by the County Clerk, until payment is presented to the County Clerk. NY R UNIF TRIAL CTS § 202.5-b(d)(3)(i).

iv. *Notification of filing.* No later than the close of business on the business day following the electronic filing of a document, a notification, in a form prescribed by the Chief Administrator, shall be transmitted electronically by the NYSCEF site to the person filing such document and the e-mail service addresses of all other participating parties in such action. NY R UNIF TRIAL CTS § 202.5-b(d)(3)(ii).

v. *Removal of confidential information and other corrections.* If a document filed electronically is subsequently discovered to contain confidential data—including but not limited to trade secrets, information protected by confidentiality agreement, or personal confidential information as defined by statute or court rule—or otherwise to have been filed in error, the filer or another party or affected person may (1) notify the parties and any non-party filers in the action of the confidentiality issue or other error raised by the filing, and of his or her intention to seek judicial relief to correct the filing: (2) following such notification, request that the appropriate County Clerk, exercising his or her administrative discretion, place the document temporarily in "restricted" status on the NYSCEF site, to be made available for viewing by court staff and the parties but not the general public; and (3) file an application to correct the filing by order to show cause within five (5) business days of such notification (or such time as the court may direct), including a request for preliminary injunctive relief limiting interim disclosure of the document at issue. Unless otherwise directed by the court, any document placed in restricted status in response to such a request shall be returned to public view upon expiration of this five (5) day period. The Chief Administrator of the Courts shall promulgate forms to implement this process. NY R UNIF TRIAL CTS § 202.5-b(d)(3)(iii).

- *KINGS COUNTY.* For information on what to do when a document was erroneously filed with confidential information, refer to NY R L KINGS E FIL Doc. 1(B)(11).
- *NEW YORK COUNTY.* For information on what to do when a document was erroneously filed with confidential information, refer to NY R NY CTY E FIL Doc. 2(B)(8).
- *QUEENS COUNTY.* For information on what to do when a document was erroneously filed with confidential information, refer to NY R L QUEENS E-FILE Doc. 1(E)(7).

vi. *Documents requiring judge's signature.* Except where the court directs otherwise, any document that requires a judge's signature shall be transmitted electronically and in hard copy to the court. NY R UNIF TRIAL CTS § 202.5-b(d)(6).

vii. *Documents which would be inconvenient to file electronically; Hard copies.* Notwithstanding any other provision of NY R UNIF TRIAL CTS § 202.5-b, and subject to such guidelines as may be established by the Chief Administrative Judge, the County Clerk or his or her designee may require or permit a party to file in hard copy, in accordance with procedures set by the County Clerk or designee, an exhibit or other document which it is impractical or inconvenient to file electronically. NY R UNIF TRIAL CTS § 202.5-b(d)(7).

- *ERIE COUNTY.* Please contact the Supervisor of Actions & Proceedings, Erie County Clerk's Office by calling (716) 858-6662 or the Deputy County Clerk—Legal at (716) 858-6348 for information. NY R ERIE E FIL Doc. 3(III)(F).
- *KINGS COUNTY.* With limited exceptions, as set forth in the Uniform Rules and herein, all documents to be filed with the court in a NYSCEF case shall be filed online via the NYSCEF system. However, should the size, consistency or context of a hard copy document preclude electronic filing, the user shall electronically file a "Notice of Hard Copy Submission—E-Filed Cases" form EFM-3. Any hard copy submitted pursuant to NY R L KINGS E FIL Doc. 1(B)(9) shall include, as a cover page firmly fastened thereto, a copy of the Confirmation Notice received from the NYSCEF site confirming receipt of the "Notice of Hard Copy Submission—E-Filed Cases". Any party may object to such hard copy filing. The Court, in response to such objection, may, following the hard copy filing, fashion such relief as it deems appropriate pursuant to and in furtherance of the Uniform Rules and NY R L KINGS E FIL Doc. 1, including, but not limited to, an Order directing the filing party to file such documents online via the NYSCEF system. When exhibits are impractical to file pursuant to NY R UNIF TRIAL CTS § 202.5-b(d)(7), an additional "Notice of Hard Copy Exhibit Filing" form EFM-4 is required to be submitted. NY R L KINGS E FIL Doc. 1(B)(9).
- *NEW YORK COUNTY.* If a filer needs to submit unusual exhibits in original form that cannot practically be e-filed, such as oversized maps or electronic recordings, the filer should consult with the County Clerk's E-File Department by telephone at 646-386-3737 (procedural questions only) or by e-mail at ccnyef@nycourts.gov, which will normally require that the filer retain custody of the original subject to possible future directives of the court. NY R NY CTY E FIL Doc. 2(B)(10). In such instances, the filing counsel shall file with NYSCEF a "placeholder" in the form of a Notice of Hard Copy Exhibit Filing (NYSCEF Form EF 21). The Notice should be uploaded to NYSCEF as document type "Exhibit" and the filer should indicate in the "Additional Document Information" field that the filer is retaining custody of the original. Failure to e-file the Notice may result in a gap in the official record of the court. NY R NY CTY E FIL Doc. 2(B)(10).

viii. *Documents containing sensitive or proprietary information.* In an action subject to e-filing, any person may apply for an order prohibiting or restricting the electronic filing in the action of specifically identified materials on the grounds that such materials are subject to copyright or other proprietary rights, or trade secret or other privacy interests, and that electronic filing in the action is likely to result in substantial prejudice to those rights or interests. NY R UNIF TRIAL CTS § 202.5-b(k)(2).

ix. *Refusal to accept paper filings.* In accordance with NY CPLR Rule 2102(c), a County Clerk and a chief clerk of the Supreme Court or County Court, as appropriate, shall refuse to accept for filing papers filed in actions and proceedings when the paper sought to be filed:

- Is in an action subject to electronic filing pursuant to Rules of the Chief Administrator,
- Is not being filed electronically, and
- Does not include the notice required by NY R UNIF TRIAL CTS § 202.5-b(d)(1). NY R UNIF TRIAL CTS § 202.5(d)(1)(v); NY R UNIF TRIAL CTS § 202.5-bb(d).

x. *Emergency filings; Hard copies.* For information on when an emergency filing may be filed and served in hard copy, refer to NY R UNIF TRIAL CTS § 202.5-b(d)(1)(ii), NY R UNIF TRIAL CTS § 202.5-b(d)(1)(iii) and NY R UNIF TRIAL CTS § 202.5-bb(c)(3).

- *KINGS COUNTY.* Under the rules, a participating emergency e-filer must electronically file the documents initially filed in hard copy form within three (3) business days of the emergency filing; the originals will be discarded after the documents have been processed and the failure to e-file as required will therefore lead to an incomplete record. NY R L KINGS E FIL Doc. 1(B)(3).
- *NEW YORK COUNTY.* Occasionally an emergency will arise requiring expedited entry of a document with the County Clerk (e.g., an order issued in the courtroom after a conference or argument of a critical matter), such as for purposes of an immediate appeal. Expedition can be achieved by the Part as follows: the

document should be carried by a Court Officer or staff member to the General Clerk's Office to assure immediate and proper recordation in the computer and, as appropriate, the posting of the document to NYSCEF or the Supreme Court Records On-Line Library ("Scroll"). The court will accommodate counsel in emergencies. NY R NY CTY Procedure XI(A).

- *NEW YORK COUNTY.* For more information on how to bring emergency matters before the court, refer to NY R NY CTY Procedure IV.

xi. *Technical failures.* The NYSCEF site shall be considered to be subject to a technical failure on a given day if the site is unable to accept filings or provide access to filed documents continuously or intermittently over the course of any period of time greater than one (1) hour after 12:00 noon of that day. Notice of all such technical failures shall be provided on the site. NY R UNIF TRIAL CTS § 202.5-b(i).

- When e-filing is hindered by a technical failure, a party may file with the appropriate clerk and serve in hard copy. NY R UNIF TRIAL CTS § 202.5-b(i). In the event an attorney or party shall file and serve documents in hard copy pursuant to NY R UNIF TRIAL CTS § 202.5-b(i), each such document shall include the notice required by NY R UNIF TRIAL CTS § 202.5-b(d)(1), and the filer shall file those documents with the NYSCEF site within three (3) business days after restoration of normal operations at that site. NY R UNIF TRIAL CTS § 202.5-b(i).
- With the exception of deadlines that by law cannot be extended, the time for filing of any document that is delayed due to technical failure of the site shall be extended for one (1) day for each day on which such failure occurs, unless otherwise ordered by the court. NY R UNIF TRIAL CTS § 202.5-b(i).
- *ERIE COUNTY.* When filing by electronic means is hindered by a technical failure, please refer to the NY R UNIF TRIAL CTS § 202.5-b(i). NY R ERIE E FIL Doc. 3(III)(K).
- *KINGS COUNTY.* When filing by electronic means is hindered by a NYSCEF technical failure (as set forth in NY R UNIF TRIAL CTS § 202.5-b(i)), a party may file with the appropriate Clerk in hard copy. Except for deadlines that by law cannot be extended (e.g. Statute of limitations, Notice of Appeal), the time for filing of any document that is delayed due to technical failure of the NYSCEF system shall be extended for one day for each day on which such failure occurs, unless otherwise ordered by the court. NY R L KINGS E FIL Doc. 1(B)(13).
- *ONONDAGA COUNTY.* When filing by electronic means is hindered by a technical failure (as set forth in NY R UNIF TRIAL CTS § 202.5-b(h)(3)(i)), a party may file a hard copy with the County Clerk. With the exception of deadlines that by law cannot be extended (e.g., a statute of limitations or the deadline for filing a Notice of Appeal), the time for filing of any document that is delayed due to technical failure of the NYSCEF system will be extended for one day for each day on which such failure occurs, unless otherwise ordered by the court. A "Notice of Hard Copy Filing Submission—E-Filed Case' must accompany any documents not filed via NYSCEF. NY R ONDGA E FIL Protocol(B)(8).

xii. *Filing fees.* For information on what information must be provided to pay filing fees, refer to NY R UNIF TRIAL CTS § 202.5-b(d)(2).

xiii. *Exemption from e-filing.* For information on exemptions from e-filing, refer to NY R UNIF TRIAL CTS § 202.5-bb(e).

xiv. *Filing exhibits*

- *ERIE COUNTY.* In the NYSCEF system, each exhibit must be uploaded as a separate .pdf file. After uploading a primary document, please choose the document type "Exhibit" and enter the appropriate number or letter and a brief description of the exhibit; each exhibit should bear a separate cover sheet clearly marked as "Exhibit A," "Exhibit B," etc. "Exhibit A" or "Exhibit B" is unacceptable as a brief description of the exhibit. Exhibits, where referenced in a signed Order as attached or affixed shall be uploaded with the signed Order as one .pdf document. NY R ERIE E FIL Doc. 3(III)(H); NY R ERIE E FIL Doc. 3(V)(D).
- *KINGS COUNTY.* In the NYSCEF system, each exhibit should be uploaded as a separate PDF file. After uploading a primary document, please choose the document type "Exhibit", enter the appropriate number or letter, and be sure to place a check mark to the right of "Attach to main document". Each exhibit shall bear a separate cover sheet clearly marked as Exhibit A, Exhibit B, etc. NY R L KINGS E FIL Doc. 1(B)(12). Whenever possible, attorneys submitting exhibits in NYSCEF cases should make each exhibit a separate attachment to an affidavit/affirmation in the system (i.e., multiple exhibits should not be filed as a single PDF). NY R L KINGS E FIL Doc. 1(D)(1).

- *NEW YORK COUNTY.* Attorneys submitting exhibits in NYSCEF cases should make each exhibit a separate attachment to an affidavit/affirmation in the system; i.e., exhibits should not be filed as a single PDF-A together with the affidavit/affirmation or grouped together as a single PDF-A attachment because either of these two formats makes it difficult for the Justice to locate particular exhibits as needed. Counsel must also include appropriate descriptive language in the "Additional Document Information" field in NYSCEF. NY R NY CTY E FIL Doc. 2(D)(6).
- *ONONDAGA COUNTY.* All exhibits in e-filed cases must be e-filed individually as separate attachments. NY R ONDGA E FIL Protocol(B)(9)(b).

xv. *Correcting documents*

- *ERIE COUNTY.* Submission of documents which, upon examination, require correction or addition will result in notification to the filer advising that the document has been returned for correction. The filer shall make the required corrections and/or additions as indicated in the e-mail transmission sent by the County Clerk or Part Clerk through the NYSCEF site. The corrected documents may be resubmitted using the "Re-file this document" link highlighted in the filer's document list for the respective case. Please note that in the case of multiple submissions, all related documents filed at the same time may be removed from the case record and returned until all documents are properly submitted. NY R ERIE E FIL Doc. 3(III)(J).
- *KINGS COUNTY.* Submission of documents which, upon examination, require correction or addition will result in notification to the filer advising that there is a problem with a document. The filer shall make the required corrections and/or additions and resubmit the corrected document using the "Refile this document" link. In the event a document is returned for correction, the original file date will be preserved. For corrections of documents filed with the Kings County Clerk which require a court order, refer to the procedure in NY R UNIF TRIAL CTS § 202.5-b(d)(3)(iii) and NY R L KINGS E FIL Doc. 1(B)(11). NY R L KINGS E FIL Doc. 1(B)(3).
- *ONONDAGA COUNTY.* If there is an error or an additional document is required, the system will notify the filing party, who will make the corrections/additions and resubmit them online. NY R ONDGA E FIL Protocol(B)(6).
- *QUEENS COUNTY.* Generally speaking, documents that have been E-filed will not thereafter be deleted by the County Clerk from NYCEF because the filer asserts that the filing contains an error or a significant omission. When the filer wishes to correct a perceived error or omission in a filed document, he or she should file an amended version of the document, with the original remaining on file, or else obtain a court order providing for deletion of the original. The County Clerk will only delete a document upon request of the filer or on the County Clerk's own initiative when it is obvious from the face of the document alone that the filer made a fundamental error and never intended to file the document that was filed (e.g., a completely unrelated non-litigation document, a different case, or a wrong county). The County Clerk will advise the filer when any such fundamental errors are detected. NY R L QUEENS E-FILE Doc. 1(E)(6).

c. *Facsimile filing.* In the Supreme Court, facsimile filing shall be limited to commercial claims and tax certiorari, conservatorship, and mental hygiene proceedings in Monroe, Westchester, New York and Suffolk Counties. NY R UNIF TRIAL CTS § 202.5-a(a)(1). Refer to NY R UNIF TRIAL CTS § 202.5-a for information on the procedures for facsimile filing.

i. *NEW YORK COUNTY.* Unless indicated otherwise by the court in a particular case or in NY R NY CTY J RUL Doc. 1, Justices do not accept papers by fax. NY R NY CTY J RUL Rule 4.

d. *ERIE COUNTY: Filing request for judicial intervention.* An RJI in a NYSCEF case shall be filed via the NYSCEF system and will be filed after all other documents have been uploaded. The filer may choose between filing a .pdf image of the prepared RJI and any Addendum or having the system prepare the RJI which shall conform to Uniform Rules. Addenda, such as the Commercial Division Addendum, if prepared by the filer must be filed simultaneously with and attached to an RJI and uploaded as one .pdf document with the RJI. If the RJI is prepared by the e-filing system, no separate Addendum is required. Whether or not the filer elects to allow NYSCEF to create the RJI or chooses to upload a prepared RJI, data in addition to the nature of the judicial intervention, including information that appears on any Addenda will be collected through completion of the fields presented. If the filing of the RJI is accomplished through a filing agent, a prepared RJI and Addendum must be filed in lieu of the creation of the RJI by the NYSCEF system, as the RJI must be signed by the attorney. NY R ERIE E FIL Doc. 3(IV). For information on RJIs in specific types of action, refer to NY R ERIE E FIL Doc. 3(IV).

2. *Service requirements*

a. *Who may serve.* Except where otherwise prescribed by law or order of court, papers may be served by any person not a party of the age of eighteen years or over. NY CPLR Rule 2103(a).

b. *Service upon attorney.* Except where otherwise prescribed by law or order of court, papers to be served upon a party in a pending action shall be served upon the party's attorney. Where the same attorney appears for two or more parties, only one (1) copy need be served upon the attorney. Such service upon an attorney shall be made:

i. By delivering the paper to the attorney personally. NY CPLR Rule 2103(b)(1).

ii. By mailing the paper to the attorney at the address designated by that attorney for that purpose or, if none is designated, at the attorney's last known address; service by mail shall be complete upon mailing. NY CPLR Rule 2103(b)(2).

- *BRONX COUNTY.* Service by mail must be within the state. NY R BRONX FIL R Doc. 3.

iii. If the attorney's office is open, by leaving the paper with a person in charge, or if no person is in charge, by leaving it in a conspicuous place; or if the attorney's office is not open, by depositing the paper, enclosed in a sealed wrapper directed to the attorney, in the attorney's office letter drop or box. NY CPLR Rule 2103(b)(3).

iv. By leaving it at the attorney's residence within the state with a person of suitable age and discretion. Service upon an attorney shall not be made at the attorney's residence unless service at the attorney's office cannot be made. NY CPLR Rule 2103(b)(4).

v. By transmitting the paper to the attorney by facsimile transmission, provided that a facsimile telephone number is designated by the attorney for that purpose. Service by facsimile transmission shall be complete upon the receipt by the sender of a signal from the equipment of the attorney served indicating that the transmission was received, and the mailing of a copy of the paper to that attorney. The designation of a facsimile telephone number in the address block subscribed on a paper served or filed in the course of an action or proceeding shall constitute consent to service by facsimile transmission in accordance with NY CPLR Rule 2103(b)(5). An attorney may change or rescind a facsimile telephone number by serving a notice on the other parties. NY CPLR Rule 2103(b)(5).

vi. By dispatching the paper to the attorney by overnight delivery service at the address designated by the attorney for that purpose or, if none is designated, at the attorney's last known address. Service by overnight delivery service shall be complete upon deposit of the paper enclosed in a properly addressed wrapper into the custody of the overnight delivery service for overnight delivery, prior to the latest time designated by the overnight delivery service for overnight delivery. "Overnight delivery service" means any delivery service which regularly accepts items for overnight delivery to any address in the state. NY CPLR Rule 2103(b)(6).

vii. By transmitting the paper to the attorney by electronic means where and in the manner authorized by the chief administrator of the courts by rule and, unless such rule shall otherwise provide, such transmission shall be upon the party's written consent. The subject matter heading for each paper sent by electronic means must indicate that the matter being transmitted electronically is related to a court proceeding. NY CPLR Rule 2103(b)(7).

- *KINGS COUNTY.* Pursuant to the E-Filing Rules, service of interlocutory documents is made by posting a document to the NYSCEF site, which automatically and immediately transmits an email notice of the filing, including a link to the document, to all participating counsel and unrepresented litigants on the case. The Rules also authorize service by other methods permitted by the CPLR. If service by such other method is made, proof of service must be filed with NYSCEF. NY R L KINGS E FIL Doc. 1(I).
- *NEW YORK COUNTY.* Service. . .will be made automatically through NYSCEF upon all participating counsel and unrepresented parties in the case. There are limited exceptions to the requirement for e-filing in the covered kinds of cases. NY R NY CTY Procedure XI(A). Pursuant to the E-Filing Rules, service of interlocutory documents is made by posting a document to the NYSCEF site, which automatically and immediately transmits an e-mail notice of the filing, including a link to the document, to all participating counsel and unrepresented litigants on the case. The Rules also authorize service by other methods permitted by the CPLR. If service by such a method is made, proof of service must be filed with NYSCEF. NY R NY CTY E FIL Doc. 2(I).
- *QUEENS COUNTY.* Filing with the system permits counsel to serve the papers electronically pursuant to NY R UNIF TRIAL CTS § 202.5-b(f) once consent to E-Filing has been filed on-line. Consult NY R UNIF TRIAL CTS § 202.5-bb(c) for service in mandatory e-filing. Any required proof of service should be E-filed as a separate document. NY R L QUEENS E-FILE Doc. 1(E)(4).

c. *Electronic service mandatory; Consenting to electronic service; How electronic service may be made.* Except as otherwise provided in NY R UNIF TRIAL CTS § 202.5-bb, filing and service of all documents in an action that has been commenced electronically in accordance with NY R UNIF TRIAL CTS § 202.5-bb shall be by electronic means. NY R UNIF TRIAL CTS § 202.5-bb(c)(1).

i. *Party's consent required for certain e-filing.* After commencement of an action wherein e-filing is authorized, documents may be electronically filed and served, but only by, and electronic service shall be made only upon, a party or parties who have consented thereto. NY R UNIF TRIAL CTS § 202.5-b(b)(2)(i).

- A consent to e-filing in an action shall state that the party providing it agrees to the use of e-filing in the action and to be bound by the filing and service provisions in NY R UNIF TRIAL CTS § 202.5-b. NY R UNIF TRIAL CTS § 202.5-b(b)(2)(ii).

ii. *Address for service; Duty to notify as to changes.* The e-mail service address recorded at the time of registration is the e-mail address at which service of interlocutory documents on that party may be made through notification transmitted by the NYSCEF site. It is the responsibility of each filing user to monitor that address and promptly notify the Resource Center in the event of a change in his or her e-mail service address. NY R UNIF TRIAL CTS § 202.5-b(f)(2)(i).

iii. *How service made.* An e-filing party causes service of an interlocutory document to be made upon another party participating in e-filing by filing the document electronically. Upon receipt of an interlocutory document, the NYSCEF site shall automatically transmit electronic notification to all e-mail service addresses in such action. NY R UNIF TRIAL CTS § 202.5-b(f)(2)(ii).

- Except as provided otherwise in NY R UNIF TRIAL CTS § 202.5-b(h)(3), the electronic transmission of the notification shall constitute service of the document on the e-mail service addresses identified therein; however, such service will not be effective if the filing party learns that the notification did not reach the address of the person to be served. Proof of such service will be recorded on the NYSCEF site. A party may, however, utilize other service methods permitted by the CPLR provided that, if one of such other methods is used, proof of that service shall be filed electronically. NY R UNIF TRIAL CTS § 202.5-b(f)(2)(ii).

iv. *Signatures on hard copies; Proof of service filed electronically.* When an e-filing party serves a document in hard copy on a non-participating party, the document served shall bear full signatures of all signatories and proof of such service shall be filed electronically. NY R UNIF TRIAL CTS § 202.5-b(b)(2)(i).

- *ERIE COUNTY.* In the NYSCEF system, each Affidavit of Service must be uploaded as a separate .pdf file. After uploading the Affidavit, please choose the document type: "Affirmation/Affidavit of Service" and enter the name of the party served as Additional Document Information. NY R ERIE E FIL Doc. 3(III)(I); NY R ERIE E FIL Doc. 3(V)(F).

v. *Effect of failure to consent.* A party's failure to consent to participation in electronic filing and service shall not bar any other party to the action from filing documents electronically with the County Clerk and the court or serving documents upon any other party who has consented to participation. A party who has not consented to participation shall file documents with the court and the County Clerk, and serve and be served with documents, in hard copy. NY R UNIF TRIAL CTS § 202.5-b(b)(2)(i).

d. *Service upon party.* If a party has not appeared by an attorney or the party's attorney cannot be served, service shall be upon the party by a method specified in NY CPLR Rule 2103(b)(1), NY CPLR Rule 2103(b)(2), NY CPLR Rule 2103(b)(4), NY CPLR Rule 2103(b)(5) or NY CPLR Rule 2103(b)(6). NY CPLR Rule 2103(c).

e. *Service on all parties.* Each paper served on any party shall be served on every other party who has appeared, except as otherwise may be provided by court order or as provided in NY CPLR § 3012 or in NY CPLR § 3215(f). Upon demand by a party, the plaintiff shall supply that party with a list of those who have appeared and the names and addresses of their attorneys. NY CPLR Rule 2103(e).

f. *Service by filing.* If a paper cannot be served by any of the methods specified in NY CPLR Rule 2103(b) and NY CPLR Rule 2103(c), service may be made by filing the paper as if it were a paper required to be filed. NY CPLR Rule 2103(d).

g. *Definitions.* For the purposes of NY CPLR Rule 2103:

i. "Mailing" means the deposit of a paper enclosed in a first class postpaid wrapper, addressed to the address designated by a person for that purpose or, if none is designated, at that person's last known address, in a post office or official depository under the exclusive care and custody of the United States Postal Service within the state;

ii. "Electronic means" means any method of transmission of information between computers or other machines designed for the purpose of sending and receiving such transmissions, and which allows the recipient to reproduce the information transmitted in a tangible medium of expression;

iii. "Facsimile transmission" means any method of transmission of documents to a facsimile machine at a remote location which can automatically produce a tangible copy of such documents. NY CPLR Rule 2103(f).

G. Hearings

1. *Oral argument.* Motion papers received by the clerk of the court on or before the return date shall be deemed submitted as of the return date. The assigned judge, in his or her discretion or at the request of a party, thereafter may determine that any motion be orally argued and may fix a time for oral argument. NY R UNIF TRIAL CTS § 202.8(d).

a. A party requesting oral argument shall set forth such request in its notice of motion or in its order to show cause or on the first page of the answering papers, as the case may be. Where all parties to a motion request oral argument, oral argument shall be granted unless the court shall determine it to be unnecessary. NY R UNIF TRIAL CTS § 202.8(d).

b. Where a motion is brought on by order to show cause, the court may set forth in the order that oral argument is required on the return date of the motion. NY R UNIF TRIAL CTS § 202.8(d).

i. *BRONX COUNTY.* All orders to show cause, with the exception of orders to show cause that are returnable in the City Part, the STP Part, the Matrimonial Part and the Preliminary/Compliance Conference Part (IA-11), submitted on or after August 25, 2003, will be returnable on a Monday in the assigned Justice's part and appear on his or her motion calendar. Appearances will be required on orders to show cause. NY R BRONX FIL R Doc. 8. A motion on notice or a notice of petition in a New York Supreme Court E-File (hereafter known as NYSCEF) case, as in others, shall be made returnable in the Motion Support Office (Room 217). NY R BRONX E FIL R Doc. 1(1).

- After a motion/petition and notice are filed with the NYSCEF system, the Motion Support Office will automatically place the motion/proceeding on the submit calendar in the Motion Support Office (Room 217) for the return date. No appearance or other action by the filing attorney is required in order for the motion to be calendared if the motion fee is paid for via NYSCEF. Motions in e-filed cases (other than tax certiorari cases) appear on the submit calendar in Room 217 on the return date. NY R BRONX E FIL R Doc. 1(2).

c. *KINGS COUNTY.* All motions require appearances and oral argument. NY R L KINGS Pt. C, Rule 3.

2. *Return date; Time for hearing.* A notice of motion shall specify the time and place of the hearing on the motion. NY CPLR Rule 2214(a). The moving party determines when a motion on notice shall be heard, but she has to consult the court's or judge's calendar practice first. The movant picks out a "return day" sufficiently far off to assure that the notice requirements of NY CPLR Rule 2214(b) can be met, and to assure as well that the day picked is a day on which the assigned judge hears motions. SIEGEL-NYPRAC § 247.

a. *Judge assigned to hear motion*

i. *Referral to judge supervising disclosure.* Unless the chief administrator of the courts has, by rule, provided otherwise, if a case has been assigned to a judge to supervise disclosure pursuant to NY CPLR § 3104, all motions preliminary to trial shall be referred to such judge whenever practicable. NY CPLR Rule 3214(a).

ii. *Referral to judge who decided prior motion.* Any motion may be referred to a judge who decided a prior motion in the action. NY CPLR Rule 2217(a).

iii. *Transfer when judge unable to hear motion.* If a motion is made to a judge who is or will be for any reason unable to hear it, it may be transferred by order of such judge or by written stipulation of the parties to any other judge to whom it might originally have been made. NY CPLR Rule 2217(c).

iv. *Procedure for unassigned cases.* If a case has not been assigned to a judge, the motion shall be made returnable before the court, and a copy of the moving papers, together with a request for judicial intervention, shall be filed with the court, with proof of service upon all other parties, where required by NY R UNIF TRIAL CTS § 202.6, within five (5) days of service upon the other parties. The moving party shall give written notice of the index number to all other parties immediately after filing of the papers. NY R UNIF TRIAL CTS § 202.8(b).

- *Responding papers.* Copies of all responding papers shall be submitted to the court, with proof of service and with the index number set forth in the papers, on or before the return date. NY R UNIF TRIAL CTS § 202.8(b).
- *Assignment after request for judicial intervention.* The case shall be assigned to a judge as soon as

practicable after the filing of the request for judicial intervention pursuant to NY R UNIF TRIAL CTS § 202.6, but in no event later than the return date. After assignment to the judge, the court shall provide for appropriate notice to the parties of the name of the assigned judge. NY R UNIF TRIAL CTS § 202.8(b).

- *Motions to be heard in another county.* Motion papers noticed to be heard in a county other than the county where the venue of the action has been placed by the plaintiff shall be assigned to a judge in accordance with procedures established by the Chief Administrator. NY R UNIF TRIAL CTS § 202.8(b).

v. *ALBANY COUNTY: Motions referred to IAS Justice.* All motions made after a case has been assigned a day certain shall be referred to the IAS Justice unless the motion is returnable during the term in which the matter has been assigned a day certain, in that event, the matter will be referred to the Part 1 Justice for that particular term who may entertain the motion or refer such motion to the IAS Justice. Under those circumstances, the Part I Justice shall decide whether or not to strike the note of issue or assign the matter a new day certain. NY R 3 JD SUP Doc. 1(H)(2). All motions shall be returnable before the assigned justice. NY R 3 JD SUP Doc. 1(B).

b. *Trial of issue raised by motion.* The court may order that an issue of fact raised on a motion shall be separately tried by the court or a referee. If the issue is triable of right by jury, the court shall give the parties an opportunity to demand a jury trial of such issue. Failure to make such demand within the time limited by the court, or, if no such time is limited, before trial begins, shall be deemed a waiver of the right to trial by jury. An order under NY CPLR § 2218 shall specify the issue to be tried. NY CPLR § 2218.

c. *Audio-visual coverage of trial court proceeding.* Audio-visual coverage of proceedings in the trial courts shall be permitted only in accordance with the provisions of Part 131 of the Rules of the Chief Administrator (NY R CHIEF ADMIN § 131.1, et seq.). NY R CHIEF J § 29.3.

d. *Adjournment of return date.* Stipulations of adjournment of the return date made by the parties shall be in writing and shall be submitted to the assigned judge. Such stipulation shall be effective unless the court otherwise directs. No more than three (3) stipulated adjournments for an aggregate period of sixty (60) days shall be submitted without prior permission of the court. NY R UNIF TRIAL CTS § 202.8(e)(1).

i. Absent agreement by the parties, a request by any party for an adjournment shall be submitted in writing, upon notice to the other party, to the assigned judge on or before the return date. The court will notify the requesting party whether the adjournment has been granted. NY R UNIF TRIAL CTS § 202.8(e)(2).

ii. *BRONX COUNTY.* Non-disclosure motions for IA5, IA7 and IA22 will be adjourned for oral argument to the Monday of the second week following the week of the return date of the motion. All other non-disclosure motions will be deemed submitted on the return date and forwarded to Chambers unless a stipulation of adjournment complying with the requirements of NY R UNIF TRIAL CTS § 202.8(e) is submitted, in which event, the motion will be adjourned for the requested date and kept in the Clerk's Office. If a non-stipulated request for adjournment or notice is submitted, the motion and request will be forwarded to Chambers for judicial approval or denial of the request. In either event, the attorney requesting the adjournment will be notified, via telephone, of the granting or denial of the request and instructed to notify his adversary. NY R BRONX FIL R Doc. 8.

iii. *BRONX COUNTY.* Motions that have been e-filed may be adjourned in Room 217 if an adjournment complies with the procedures of the Motion Support Office (explained in the "Filing Rules—Motion Procedure" section of the "Courthouse Procedures" link on the website of [the] court). An adjournment that so complies may be obtained by filing a stipulation of all parties with NYSCEF (designated in the filing menu as a "Stipulation to Adjourn Motion"). NY R BRONX E FIL R Doc. 1(3).

iv. *NEW YORK COUNTY.* The Courtroom also maintains a "APB (All Papers By)" Calendar, which is used when a party seeks an adjournment but fails to comply with the Courtroom's procedures or there is a failure to comply with procedures that requires the clerk to adjourn the motion/application (e.g., failure to submit a Confirmation Notice in an e-filed case). The case may be put over for three days to allow compliance with those procedures, as described further below. NY R NY CTY Procedure II(C); NY R NY CTY E FIL Doc. 2(D)(2). E-filed applications may be adjourned in the Part if an adjournment complies with the Part's procedures (see the Uniform Rules of the Justices (Local Rules) on the court's website). An adjournment that so complies may be obtained by filing with NYSCEF a stipulation of all parties (designated in the filing menu as a Stipulation—Adjournment of Motion—Before Judge); the motion number and the current return date of the motion being adjourned shall be set forth in the "Additional Document Information" field in NYSCEF. Absent any problems, the Part will effectuate the adjournment without need for an appearance or any other action by the parties. NY R NY CTY E FIL Doc. 2(D)(4).

v. *QUEENS COUNTY.* The Motion Support Office is NOT authorized to grant adjournments. NY R L QUEENS MOT SUP Doc. 1.

e. *ALBANY COUNTY: Motion terms.* There shall be a. . . Motion Term on each Friday in the Supreme Court, Albany County. The Friday Motion Term shall include all Article 78 Proceedings involving New York State and proceedings commenced pursuant to Article 14 of the Civil Service Law (including applications for injunctive relief made pursuant to section 209-a of the Civil Service Law). NY R 3 JD SUP Doc. 1(F). Generally, parties will be granted only one adjournment for the Friday Motion Term. NY R 3 JD SUP Doc. 1(F).

f. *ALBANY COUNTY: Motion determined without hearing.* All motions are deemed "submitted" on the return date and no appearances are required by the parties. NY R 3 JD SUP Doc. 1(B). In the event oral argument is requested, the parties should not appear on the return date. At the discretion of the assigned Judge and upon the granting of a request for oral argument, the parties will be notified by Chambers of the scheduled time and place at which argument will be heard. Where a motion is brought on by order to show cause, the court may set forth in the order that appearances and/or oral argument are required on the return date of the motion. NY R 3 JD SUP Doc. 1(B).

g. *BRONX COUNTY: Return date.* All assigned and unassigned motions will be returnable five (5) days a week in the Civil Branch Clerk's Office, Room 217, at 9:30 a.m. NY R BRONX FIL R Doc. 8.

   i. If on any submitted non-disclosure motion oral argument is requested and granted, or directed by the Court, the motion shall be adjourned for oral argument before the I.A. Judge on the second Monday following the week of the return date of the motion. Attorneys will be notified via telephone of the adjourned date. NY R BRONX FIL R Doc. 8.

h. *BRONX COUNTY: Oral argument.* Calendars of disclosure motions and other motions adjourned for oral argument will be published for the four (4) business days preceding the rescheduled appearance date and on the rescheduled date of the motion. These repetitive publications will serve as the notification of procedure of adjournment of all motions. In addition, two (2) days before the return date of unassigned motions a list of such motions indicating the assigned Justice and the adjourned date of the motion will be published. NY R BRONX FIL R Doc. 8.

i. *BRONX COUNTY: Resolution before return date.* Counsel/parties must advise the Court in writing on or before the return date of all motions that have been resolved by Counsel/parties themselves and all motions the movant(s) wish to be withdrawn. NY R BRONX FIL R Doc. 8.

j. *ERIE COUNTY: Calendaring of motions.* Refer to individual Justice's Part Rules. NY R ERIE E FIL Doc. 3(V)(B).

k. *KINGS COUNTY: Return date set by court.* Irrespective of the return date indicated in the notice of motion, motions will be rescheduled by the E-file/Motion Support Office to a date designated by the assigned Judge. NY R L KINGS Pt. C, Rule 2.

l. *KINGS COUNTY: Calendar calls.* There shall be two (2) calendar calls on motion days. The first calendar call shall be at 9:30 AM and the second calendar call shall be at 10:45 AM, unless the Judge's Part Rules provide otherwise. Defaults shall only be taken on second call. Attorneys with appearances elsewhere in the courthouse may advise the clerk of their whereabouts to avoid a default. Failure to so advise the clerk or appear at the default calendar call will result in a default order being entered or the motion being marked off the calendar. NY R L KINGS Pt. C, Rule 7.

m. *NEW YORK COUNTY: Return date and assigned courtroom.* Motions made by notice of motion and petitions and notices of petition in special proceedings are processed by the General Clerk's Office (Room 119) and are to be made returnable in the Motion Submission Part Courtroom (Room 130) on any business day of the week at 9:30 AM. There are some differences in electronically-filed cases. NY R NY CTY Procedure II; NY R NY CTY Procedure II(C); NY R NY CTY J RUL Rule 13(a).

   i. For the convenience of counsel, between 9:00 A.M. and 9:30 A.M. each day, in advance of the "call," Room 130 accepts (1) written stipulations; (2) affidavits/affirmations reciting the required details as to an adjournment on consent; (3) stipulations, letters or other writings withdrawing motions; and (4) final papers or complete sets of papers on motions. For motions in which these items are handed in before the "call," no one need remain to answer the "call." Counsel/parties must advise the court, either between 9:00 A.M. and 9:30 A.M. or at the "call," of all motions or cases that have been resolved by counsel/parties themselves and all motions that the movant no longer wishes to pursue. If such resolution occurs subsequent to the "call", the assigned Justice must be advised as soon as possible, by written notice sent to the Part, so that the court does not do unnecessary work. NY R NY CTY Procedure II(C).

   ii. Depending upon the assigned Part, contested motions submitted in the Motion Submission Part Courtroom are submitted without argument, or rescheduled for oral argument if so directed by the assigned Justice. For Justices who schedule argument on a case-by-case basis, notice of the argument date will be transmitted by the court. Counsel may ascertain how a motion submitted in Courtroom 130 was marked by consulting Scroll on the court's website, the e-Track application, or, on the two (2) days immediately following the submission date, the New York Law Journal. NY R NY CTY J RUL Rule 13(a).

n. *NEW YORK COUNTY: Motion call.* Each day in the Motion Submission Part Courtroom, commencing at 9:30 A.M., all motions returnable that day will be "called" for the submission of these papers, which must be handed up at this "call" or, as described below, immediately before. Because hundreds of motions appear on the Room 130 calendars every day, motion papers (other than part of the moving papers as described above) cannot be accepted on any day prior to the return date. Courtesy copies are not required nor accepted, but working copies are required by certain Justices in e-filed cases. NY R NY CTY Procedure II(C). If argument is directed, it will take place on an announced date shortly after the day of submission. NY R NY CTY Procedure II(C).

o. *NEW YORK COUNTY: Oral arguments.* Pursuant to request of some Justices, motions submitted in Room 130 will automatically be scheduled for a set argument date in the Part. Other Justices determine on a case-by-case basis after submission in Room 130 whether to accept a particular substantive motion on submission, to require oral argument, or to hold a conference. NY R NY CTY Procedure II(D). If argument is directed by the Justice automatically, notice of argument and the argument date will be given in Room 130. Any appearing party is expected to give notice to all parties and an announcement to this effect is made in Room 130. If the motion is submitted in Room 130 and the Justice, after examining the file, determines that argument should be directed, notice of the argument and the argument date will not be sent by the court. To obtain notification of the argument date and other developments, counsel should use e-Track. If argument notification is not given or transmitted as just described, counsel should understand that the motion has been taken on submission for decision on the papers. NY R NY CTY Procedure II(D).

   i. Calendars of motions to be argued in the Parts are published on the morning of the argument date and on the day before in the New York Law Journal under each Part. Argument information is available on a case-by-case basis in Scroll, and e-mail notifications are sent by e-Track to participating attorneys whenever a motion is scheduled for argument in the court's computer system. NY R NY CTY J RUL Rule 15(a)

p. *NEW YORK COUNTY: Motion determined without hearing.* Given the purpose of the Room 130 procedure, the substance of motions will not be addressed at the submission "call." No Judge is present. To the extent possible, motions submitted in Room 130 will be decided "on the papers." Indeed, attorneys are encouraged to use service or clerks to deliver papers or working copies, or to agree among themselves to have one of them deliver papers for all parties by service or a clerk. Counsel for the movant need not appear to "take a default" on any motion or for any other reason. Motions will be submitted, not marked off, in the absence of the movant. Opposing counsel similarly need not appear in person in order to avoid suffering a default. Delivery of papers by service or a clerk will suffice. The court's goal is to be able to collect papers on motions in an orderly fashion but without any attorney having to make an appearance in Room 130 at any time. NY R NY CTY Procedure II(C).

q. *ONONDAGA COUNTY: Return date.* If the motion is the first filing in an action, the case will be assigned and counsel will be notified by the Supreme Court Clerk's Office via the NYSCEF system of the assigned justice and return date. NY R ONDGA E FIL Protocol(B)(7)(c). If the motion is on a previously assigned case, counsel may choose a return date from the assigned justice's motion term schedule. If the date in unavailable, the Supreme Court Clerk's Office will assign the motion to the next available motion term date and will notify counsel via e-mail. The change will also appear in the notification generated by the NYSCEF system. NY R ONDGA E FIL Protocol(B)(7)(d).

r. *QUEENS COUNTY: Return date.* Motions must be made returnable on the proper day/time based on the assigned judge. NY R L QUEENS MOT SUP Doc. 1. Failure to make a motion returnable on the proper day/time may result in the motion being administratively rescheduled or marked off. NY R L QUEENS MOT SUP Doc. 1.

s. *QUEENS COUNTY: Unassigned motions.* For RJI/Motions, due to the fact that the movant would not know who the assigned judge will be, the notice of motion may be returnable any day of the week. RJI/Motions shall be made returnable in "Queens Supreme Court" with no address designated. The motion will be administratively rescheduled to the proper day of the week based on the judge (once a judge has been assigned). Within one (1) week of filing, the movant must check online to see who the assigned judge is (and therefore the location/date/time) that their motion is now returnable. Movant must then notify their adversary of this information prior to the return date. NY R L QUEENS MOT SUP Doc. 1.

3. *Entry of order after hearing.* An order determining a motion shall be entered and filed in the office of the clerk of the court where the action is triable, and all papers used on the motion and any opinion or memorandum in writing shall be filed with that clerk unless the order dispenses with such filing. When a statute or civil practice rule requires such filing and entry in a county other than that in which the order was made, the party prevailing on the motion shall file the order and the papers

used on the motion with the proper clerk after receiving them. If a party fails to file any papers required to be filed under NY CPLR Rule 2220(a), the order may be vacated as irregular, with costs. NY CPLR Rule 2220(a). For more information on the entry of an order after a motion, refer to NY CPLR Rule 2219.

a. *BRONX COUNTY: Settled orders.* A Judge's decision will often call for a Settled Order. The purpose of the settled order is to give effect to the decision by directing that some action be done and/or that a court official perform some task. NY R BRONX LEG SUP Doc. 2. A settled order consists of a notice of settlement informing all parties that the proposed order will be presented to the judge who made the decision on a date certain. Next comes the proposed order which will be presented to the judge. This order should conform to the judge's decision and should direct the relief granted in the decision. This should be followed by proof of service upon all parties who were noticed with the decision. It is also helpful if a copy of the judge's decision is included along with the other papers. A settled order should always be noticed before the judge who made the decision. NY R BRONX LEG SUP Doc. 2.

   i. Although an order is usually settled by the party who prevailed on the motion, any party may settle the order. It should be presented to the court within sixty (60) days of the decision. The other parties are entitled to ten (10) days notice where service of the settled order is done by mail, five (5) days if the notice is personally delivered. An attorney who is served with a notice of settlement which he believes does not accurately reflect the decision may settle a counter order. The counter order must be noticed for the same day and must be served not less than seven (7) days if by mail and two (2) days if personally delivered. NY R BRONX LEG SUP Doc. 2.

   ii. Settled orders are usually sent to the judge the day after they noticed for settlement. No appearance is necessary or even contemplated on a settled order. If the decision directs "submit order", then no notice is necessary, and the order will be sent to the judge as soon a practical after it is received. No fees are collected on settled orders. NY R BRONX LEG SUP Doc. 2.

b. *ERIE COUNTY: Proposed orders.* Proposed orders shall be submitted through the NYSCEF system and a working copy provided to the IAS Justice for signature, if Part Rules so require. NY R ERIE E FIL Doc. 3(V)(G).

c. *KINGS COUNTY: Long form orders.* If the Court directs that an order be settled or submitted on a motion in a NYSCEF case, the proposed order, with Notice of Settlement where required, and any proposed counter-order shall be filed with the Court via NYSCEF. The relevant clerk's office will process the documents in the customary manner. NY R L KINGS E FIL Doc. 1(E).

   i. WORKING COPIES OF PROPOSED ORDERS WITH NOTICE OF SETTLEMENT MUST BE SUBMITTED IN THE MOTION SUPPORT OFFICE (ROOM 227) AS EXPLAINED HEREIN. THEY MUST NOT BE DELIVERED TO THE PART OR CHAMBERS, EXCEPT WHERE THE INDIVIDUAL JUSTICE'S PART RULES PROVIDE OTHERWISE; DOING SO WILL CAUSE ADMINISTRATIVE CONFUSION AND POSSIBLE MISPLACEMENT OF PAPERS. Any such submission shall be sent in a timely manner (kindly review individual Justice's rules) and be conspicuously marked on the outside "NYSCEF Matter;" lack of such marking may delay processing. After an order/counter-order has been signed, it will be scanned, and the County Clerk will affix the entry stamp into the NYSCEF system, which will immediately transmit notice of this event via e-mail, including a link to the entered document, to all participating attorneys and unrepresented litigants in the case. Such transmittal does not constitute Notice of Entry. NY R L KINGS E FIL Doc. 1(E).

d. *NEW YORK COUNTY: Long form orders.* Although the court strongly favors the use of short form orders and judgments, there are instances when settlement of an order or judgment is appropriate. When a Justice directs in a decision that a long form order or judgment be settled, that decision is recorded in the court's computer system by the General Clerk's Office and the motion file with decision is held in the Order Section of the Office in Room 119. The settlement process takes place there. NY R NY CTY Procedure II(D); NY R NY CTY E FIL Doc. 2(E).

   i. A proposed long form order or judgment in compliance NY R UNIF TRIAL CTS § 202.48 must be presented to the relevant back office, together with a notice of settlement which bears a settlement date, the date on which the order is to be ready for formal presentation to the Justice. In an e-filed case the submission shall be made electronically. The proposed order or counter-order should be e-filed and it will be transmitted automatically by the NYSCEF system to the appropriate back office. The return date and time of the proposed order must be at 9:30 A.M. no sooner than either five (5) days from personal service of the proposed order or ten (10) days from service by mail. Proof of timely service on the other parties must accompany the proposed order in a hard copy case. If an order or judgment is submitted late (later than sixty (60) days from signing and filing of the decision) and the proponent can show good cause for this tardiness, an affidavit or affirmation justifying the delay should be annexed to the proposed order, together with proof of service thereof. If persuaded, the Justice will consider the proposed order despite its untimeliness. NY R NY CTY Procedure II(D); NY R NY CTY E FIL Doc. 2(E).

   ii. Sometimes a decision will state "Submit Order." The submitting party should prepare a long form order and

make it returnable without notice. Counsel should deliver the proposed order to the Order Section of the appropriate back office, except in an e-filed case, when it shall be submitted electronically. NY R NY CTY Procedure II(D). If the decision of the court directs that a proposed order be settled or submitted in the Part or in Chambers, that direction, should, of course, be followed without presentation of the proposal to the back office. NY R NY CTY Procedure II(D).

iii. For information on proposed counter-orders, refer to NY R NY CTY Procedure II(D) and NY R NY CTY J RUL Rule 16(b).

e. *QUEENS COUNTY: Proposed orders.* If the court directs that an order be settled or submitted on a motion in an E-file case, the proposed order and any proposed counter-order shall be filed with the court on-line with proof of service. (If a decision refers to a proceeding on the record, a copy of the transcript must be submitted.) Working copies of all proposed orders MUST be submitted to the Motion Support Office before an order can be reviewed. NY R L QUEENS E-FILE Doc. 1(I).

i. Counsel are advised to adhere to NY R UNIF TRIAL CTS § 202.48 regarding the submission or settlement of their proposed order or judgment. Persons who are submitting proposed orders/judgments pursuant to a previously issued memorandum decision must submit a copy of the memorandum decision with their proposed order/judgment. Upon E-Filing a proposed order/judgement, a working copy of the proposed order/judgement must be provided to the Motion Support Office. NY R L QUEENS MOT SUP Doc. 1.

4. *NEW YORK COUNTY: Informing clerk after motion for leave to amend granted.* If a motion affecting the caption or the trial status of a case is granted, the prevailing attorney must serve a copy of the court's order on both the County Clerk and the General Clerk's Office in a hard-copy case or via NYSCEF in an e-filed case. NY R NY CTY Procedure VIII(B); NY R NY CTY E FIL Doc. 2(B)(9).

H. Forms

1. Official Motion for Leave to Amend Forms for New York

a. Request for judicial intervention. NY R UNIF TRIAL CTS § 202.6.

b. Notice of motion. NY R UNIF TRIAL CTS § 202.7(b).

2. New York Motion for Leave to Amend Forms

a. Amended complaint or answer; Skeleton form. MCF CPLR § 4:305.

b. Stipulation amending complaint. MCF CPLR § 4:306.

c. Notice of motion for leave to amend complaint; With specific reference to NY CPLR Rule 3025(b). MCF CPLR § 4:307.

d. Notice of motion for leave to amend complaint; Without specific references to NY CPLR Rule 3025(b). MCF CPLR § 4:308.

e. Notice of motion for leave to amend complaint; To add cause of action for exemplary damages. MCF CPLR § 4:309.

f. Notice of motion for leave to amend complaint to add party defendants and claims. MCF CPLR § 4:310.

g. Affidavit in support of motion for leave to serve amended complaint; To increase claim for damages. MCF CPLR § 4:311.

h. Affidavit in support of motion for leave to serve amended complaint; To state cause of action after dismissal. MCF CPLR § 4:312.

i. Affidavit in support of motion for leave to serve amended complaint; Addition of cause of action for exemplary damages. MCF CPLR § 4:313.

j. Affidavit in support of motion for leave to serve amended complaint; Addition of wrongful-death action. MCF CPLR § 4:314.

k. Affidavit in support of motion for leave to amend complaint to add party defendants and claims. MCF CPLR § 4:316.

l. Notice of motion to increase ad damnum clause of complaint. MCF CPLR § 4:325.

m. Affidavit of plaintiff in support of motion to increase ad damnum clause of complaint. MCF CPLR § 4:326.

n. Affidavit of attorney in support of motion to increase ad damnum clause of complaint. MCF CPLR § 4:327.

o. Affidavit of physician in support of motion to increase ad damnum clause of complaint. MCF CPLR § 4:328.

p. Notice of motion for leave to serve amended answer. MCF CPLR § 4:333.

q. Affidavit in support of motion for leave to serve amended answer. MCF CPLR § 4:334.

r. Affidavit in support of motion for leave to serve amended answer; Inclusion of additional affirmative defense. MCF CPLR § 4:335.

s. Notice of motion for leave to serve amended answer to assert cross-claim. MCF CPLR § 4:336.

t. Affidavit in support of motion for leave to serve amended answer to assert cross-claim. MCF CPLR § 4:337.

u. Notice of motion for leave to serve amended reply and for partial summary judgment. MCF CPLR § 4:340.

v. Affidavit in support of motion for leave to serve amended reply and for partial summary judgment. MCF CPLR § 4:341.

w. Supplemental complaint or answer; Skeleton form. MCF CPLR § 4:347.

x. Affidavit in support of motion for leave to serve supplemental complaint. MCF CPLR § 4:350.

y. Affidavit in support of motion for leave to serve supplemental answer. MCF CPLR § 4:352.

z. General form of affidavit of service of motion papers. MCF CPLR § 5:24.

I. Applicable Rules

1. *State rules*

a. Short title; Application; Construction; Definitions. NY CPLR § 101; NY CPLR § 103; NY CPLR § 104; NY CPLR § 105.

b. Appendix of official forms. NY CPLR § 107.

c. Method of computing periods of limitation generally. NY CPLR § 203.

d. Claim by plaintiff against third-party defendant. NY CPLR Rule 1009.

e. Extensions of time generally. NY CPLR § 2004.

f. Form of papers. NY CPLR Rule 2101; NY CPLR Rule 2102; NY CPLR § 2105; NY CPLR Rule 2106; NY GEN BUS § 399-ddd; NY R UNIF TRIAL CTS § 215.2; NY R UNIF TRIAL CTS § 215.3.

g. Service of papers. NY CPLR Rule 2103.

h. Where motion made; In supreme court action. NY CPLR § 2212.

i. Motion papers; Service; Time. NY CPLR Rule 2214.

j. Relief demanded by other than moving party. NY CPLR Rule 2215.

k. Prior motion; Ex parte motion; Transfer of motion; Hearings; Orders. NY CPLR Rule 2217; NY CPLR § 2218; NY CPLR Rule 2220.

l. Computation of time. NY CPLR § 2402; NY GEN CONSTR § 19; NY GEN CONSTR § 20; NY GEN CONSTR § 25-a; NY GEN CONSTR § 30; NY GEN CONSTR § 31; NY GEN CONSTR § 53.

m. Amended and supplemental pleadings. NY CPLR Rule 3025.

n. Motion to dismiss. NY CPLR Rule 3211.

o. Motions heard by judge supervising disclosure; Stay of disclosure. NY CPLR Rule 3214.

p. Fees; Index number fees of county clerks. NY CPLR § 8018.

q. Hours of court; Proceedings in court. NY R CHIEF J § 3.1; NY R CHIEF J § 29.3.

r. Application of part; Waiver; Additional rules; Application of CPLR; Definitions. NY R UNIF TRIAL CTS § 202.1.

s. Papers filed in court; Electronic filing in supreme court. NY R UNIF TRIAL CTS § 202.5; NY R UNIF TRIAL CTS § 202.5-a; NY R UNIF TRIAL CTS § 202.5-b; NY R UNIF TRIAL CTS § 202.5-bb.

t. Request for judicial intervention. NY R UNIF TRIAL CTS § 202.6.

u. Calendaring of motions; Uniform notice of motion form; Affirmation of good faith. NY R UNIF TRIAL CTS § 202.7.

v. Motion procedure; Preliminary conferences. NY R UNIF TRIAL CTS § 202.8; NY R UNIF TRIAL CTS § 202.12.

w. Rules of the commercial division of the Supreme Court. NY R UNIF TRIAL CTS § 202.70.

x. Signing of papers. NY R CHIEF ADMIN § 130-1.1-a.

2. *Local rules*
   a. *Albany County*
      i. Third judicial district rules. NY R 3 JD SUP Doc. 1.
   b. *Bronx County*
      i. Filing of papers in supreme court. NY R BRONX FIL R Doc. 1.
      ii. Request for judicial intervention. NY R BRONX FIL R Doc. 2.
      iii. Motion procedure. NY R BRONX FIL R Doc. 8.
      iv. Commercial division. NY R BRONX FIL R Doc. 12.
      v. Motions on notice. NY R BRONX E FIL R Doc. 1.
      vi. Settled orders. NY R BRONX LEG SUP Doc. 2.
   c. *Erie County*
      i. Joint protocols for New York State Courts E-Filing (NYSCEF) cases filed in Supreme Court, Erie County. NY R ERIE E FIL Doc. 3.
   d. *Kings County*
      i. Papers. NY R L KINGS Pt. A, Papers.
      ii. Service of motion papers. NY R L KINGS Pt. C, Rule 1.
      iii. Scheduling of motions. NY R L KINGS Pt. C, Rule 2.
      iv. Appearance and argument. NY R L KINGS Pt. C, Rule 3.
      v. Courtesy copies. NY R L KINGS Pt. C, Rule 5.
      vi. Motion calendar calls. NY R L KINGS Pt. C, Rule 7.
      vii. Protocol on courthouse and county clerk procedures for electronically filed cases. NY R L KINGS E FIL Doc. 1.
   e. *New York County*
      i. Commencement of cases. NY R NY CTY Procedure I.
      ii. RJIs and assignments. NY R NY CTY Procedure IA.
      iii. Motions and special proceedings by notice of motion/petition. NY R NY CTY Procedure II.
      iv. Trials. NY R NY CTY Procedure VIII.
      v. County clerk litigation functions. NY R NY CTY Procedure XI.
      vi. Protocol on courthouse and county clerk procedures for electronically filed cases. NY R NY CTY E FIL Doc. 2.
      vii. Redaction of information in documents filed with the county clerk and the court. NY R NY CTY J RUL Rule A-1.
      viii. Papers by fax. NY R NY CTY J RUL Rule 4.
      ix. Motions on notice; Orders to show cause. NY R NY CTY J RUL Rule 13.
      x. Motion papers. NY R NY CTY J RUL Rule 14.
      xi. Oral argument; Adjournments. NY R NY CTY J RUL Rule 15.
   f. *Onondaga County*
      i. Onondaga county protocol for case filings New York State Electronic Files (NYSCEF). NY R ONDGA E FIL Protocol.
   g. *Queens County*
      i. Motion support office. NY R L QUEENS MOT SUP Doc. 1.
      ii. Queens county protocol on courthouse procedures for electronically filed cases. NY R L QUEENS E-FILE Doc. 1.

J. Miscellaneous

NOTE: Individual judges' rules may apply.

ALBANY COUNTY

JUSTICE LISA M. FISHER: NY R 3 JD FISHER Fisher; NY R 3 JD FISHER Fisher, PC Order.

JUSTICE RICHARD MOTT: NY R 3 JD MOTT Mott.

JUSTICE STEPHAN G. SCHICK: NY R 3 JD Schick.

FORECLOSURE SETTLEMENT PART: NY R 3 JD Foreclosure Settlement.

BRONX COUNTY

JUSTICE PAUL L. ALPERT: [NY R BRONX J Part IA-29, as amended by NY ORDER 20-0337].

JUSTICE BEN BARBATO: NY R BRONX J Part IA-21.

JUSTICE MARY ANNE BRIGANTTI: [NY R BRONX J Part IA-15, as amended by NY ORDER 20-0338].

JUSTICE JOSEPH E. CAPELLA: NY R BRONX J Part IA-23.

JUSTICE MITCHELL DANZIGER: NY R BRONX J Part IA-3/33 ; [NY R BRONX J Danziger, Part IA-3/33, as amended by NY ORDER 20-0339].

JUSTICE LAURA G. DOUGLAS: NY R BRONX J Part IA-11.

JUSTICE RUBEN FRANCO: NY R BRONX J Part IA-26.

JUSTICE DORIS M. GONZALEZ: NY R BRONX J Part IA-24.

JUSTICE WILMA GUZMAN: NY R BRONX J Part IA-7; [NY R BRONX J Guzman, Part IA-7 Virtual, as amended by NY ORDER 20-0340].

JUSTICE ROBERT T. JOHNSON: NY R BRONX J Part IA-12.

JUSTICE DONALD A. MILES: NY R BRONX J Part IA-8.

JUSTICE DONNA M. MILLS: NY R BRONX J Part IA-9.

JUSTICE JULIA I. RODRIGUEZ: NY R BRONX J Part IA-18; [NY R BRONX J Part IA-27, as amended by NY ORDER 20-0341].

JUSTICE LLINET M. ROSADO: [NY R BRONX J Part IA-25, as amended by NY ORDER 20-0342].

JUSTICE NORMA RUIZ: NY R BRONX J Part IA-22; [NY R BRONX J Ruiz, Part IA-22 Virtual, as amended by NY ORDER 20-0343].

JUSTICE HOWARD H. SHERMAN: NY R BRONX J Part IA-4.

JUSTICE FERNANDO TAPIA: NY R BRONX J Part IA-13.

JUSTICE ELIZABETH A. TAYLOR: NY R BRONX J Part IA-2.

JUSTICE ALISON Y. TRUITT: NY R BRONX J Part IA-5.

PART IDV: NY R BRONX J Doc. 1.

PRE-TRIAL PART RULES: NY R BRONX J Doc. 2.

PRE TRIAL WORKSHEET: NY R BRONX J Doc. 3.

FORECLOSURE SETTLEMENT PART RULES: NY R BRONX J Doc. 4.

GUARDIANSHIP PART RULES: NY R BRONX J Doc. 5.

LPM PART RULES: NY R BRONX J Doc. 6.

ERIE COUNTY

JUSTICE M. WILLIAM BOLLER: NY R 8 JD J Boller.

JUSTICE RALPH A. BONIELLO: NY R 8 JD J Boniello.

JUSTICE CHRISTOPHER J. BURN: NY R 8 JD J Burns.

JUSTICE RUSSELL P. BUSCAGLIA: NY R 8 JD J Buscaglia.

JUSTICE FRANK CARUSO: NY R 8 JD J Caruso.

JUSTICE STEPHEN W. CASS: NY R 8 JD J Cass.
JUSTICE DEBORAH A. CHIMES: NY R 8 JD J Chimes.
JUSTICE EMILIO COLAIACOVO: [NY R 8 JD J Colaiacovo, as amended by NY ORDER 20-0252].
JUSTICE DIANE Y. DEVLIN: NY R 8 JD J Devlin.
JUSTICE JAMES H. DILLON: NY R 8 JD J Dillon.
JUSTICE PAULA L. FEROLETO: NY R 8 JD J Feroleto.
JUSTICE DANIEL J. FURLONG: [NY R 8 JD J Furlong, as amended by NY ORDER 20-0253].
JUSTICE JOSEPH R. GLOWNIA: NY R 8 JD J Glownia.
JUSTICE MARK J. GRISANTI: NY R 8 JD J Grisanti.
JUSTICE DEBORAH A. HAENDIGES: NY R 8 JD J Haendiges.
JUSTICE LYNN W. KEANE: [NY R 8 JD J Keane, as amended by NY ORDER 20-0254].
JUSTICE RICHARD C. KLOCH, Sr.: NY R 8 JD J Kloch.
JUSTICE FREDERICK J. MARSHALL: [NY R 8 JD J Marshall, as amended by NY ORDER 20-0255.
JUSTICE JOHN L. MICHALSKI: NY R 8 JD J Michalski.
JUSTICE MARK A. MONTOUR: [NY R 8 JD J Montour, as amended by NY ORDER 20-0256].
JUSTICE HENRY NOWAK: NY R 8 JD J Nowak.
JUSTICE JOHN F. O'DONNELL: NY R 8 JD J O'Donnell.
JUSTICE JEANETTE OGDEN: NY R 8 JD J Ogden.
JUSTICE CATHERINE NUGENT-PANEPINTO: NY R 8 JD J Nugent-Panepinto.
JUSTICE FRANK A. SEDITA, III: [NY R 8 JD J Sedita, as amended by NY ORDER 20-0257].
JUSTICE SARA SHELDON: NY R 8 JD J Sheldon.
JUSTICE DONNA M. SIWEK: NY R 8 JD J Siwek.
JUSTICE MARY L. SLISZ: NY R 8 JD J Slisz.
JUSTICE TIMOTHY J. WALKER: [NY R 8 JD J Walker, as amended by NY ORDER 20-0258].
JUSTICE DENNIS E. WARD: NY R 8 JD J Ward.
JUSTICE PAUL B. WOJTASZEK: [NY R 8 JD J Wojtaszek, as amended by NY ORDER 20-0259].
JUSTICE CHARLES N. ZAMBITO: [NY R 8 JD J Zambito, as amended by NY ORDER 20-0260].
SUPREME COURT LEGAL STAFF: NY R 8 JD J Legal Staff.

KINGS COUNTY

JUSTICE RACHEL A. ADAMS: NY R KINGS J Part 5F.
JUSTICE LOREN BAILY-SCHIFFMAN: NY R KINGS J Part 65.
JUSTICE REGINALD A. BODDIE: NY R KINGS J Part 95.
JUSTICE THERESA M. CICCOTTO: NY R KINGS J Part 19; NY R KINGS J Part 5J.
JUSTICE LISSETTE COLON: NY R KINGS J Part Rules.
JUSTICE GENINE EDWARDS: NY R KINGS J Part 80.
JUSTICE PAMELA L. FISHER: [NY R KINGS J Part 94, as amended by NY ORDER 20-0208].
JUSTICE ROBIN GARSON: NY R KINGS J Part 75.
JUSTICE LARA J. GENOVISI: [NY R KINGS J Part 34, as amended by NY ORDER 20-0209].
JUSTICE BERNARD J. GRAHAM: NY R KINGS J Part 36.
JUSTICE DAWN JIMENEZ-SALTA: NY R KINGS J Part 88.
JUSTICE INGRID JOSEPH: [NY R KINGS J Part FRP3 and Part 83, as amended by NY ORDER 20-0210].
JUSTICE KATHY J. KING: NY R KINGS J Part 64, 76K.

JUSTICE LAWRENCE KNIPEL: NY R KINGS J Part 57.
JUSTICE DONALD KURTZ: NY R KINGS J Part 26.
JUSTICE CARL LANDICINO: [NY R KINGS J Part 81, as amended by NY ORDER 20-0211].
JUSTICE KATHERINE LEVINE: [NY R KINGS J Part 20, 25, 92, as amended by NY ORDER 20-0211].
JUSTICE LORNA MCALLISTER: [NY R KINGS J Part 10, as amended by NY ORDER 20-0211].
JUSTICE ROSEMARIE MONTALBANO: [NY R KINGS J Part 19, 71, and 22, as amended by NY ORDER 20-0211].
JUSTICE RICHARD J. MONTELIONE: [NY R KINGS J Part 99 and DJMP, as amended by NY ORDER 20-0215].
JUSTICE LISA S. OTTLEY: NY R KINGS J Part 24.
JUSTICE MARK I. PARTNOW: NY R KINGS J Part 43.
JUSTICE ERIC I. PRUS: NY R KINGS J Part 5A.
JUSTICE FRANCOIS RIVERA: NY R KINGS J Part 52.
JUSTICE KAREN B. ROTHENBERG: NY R KINGS J Part 35.
JUSTICE LEON RUCHELSMAN: NY R KINGS J Part 1.
JUSTICE WAYNE P. SAITTA: NY R KINGS J Part 29.
JUSTICE ROBIN K. SHEARES: NY R KINGS J Part 96.
JUSTICE KENNETH P. SHERMAN: NY R KINGS J Part 67 and 78.
JUSTICE DEBRA SILBER: NY R KINGS J Part 9 and 5K.
JUSTICE ELLEN M. SPODEK: NY R KINGS J Part 63.
JUSTICE MARSHA L. STEINHARDT: NY R KINGS J Part 15.
JUSTICE JEFFREY S. SUNSHINE: NY R KINGS J Part 5G.
JUSTICE PETER P. SWEENEY: [NY R KINGS J Part 35, as amended by NY ORDER 20-0218].
JUSTICE DELORES J. THOMAS: [NY R KINGS J Part 5T, as amended by NY ORDER 20-0221].
JUSTICE WAVNY TOUSSAINT: NY R KINGS J Part 70.
JUSTICE RICHARD VELASQUEZ: NY R KINGS J Part 66.
JUSTICE CAROLYN E. WADE: NY R KINGS J Part 84.
JUSTICE EDWARD G. WALKER: [NY R KINGS J Part 90, as amended by NY ORDER 20-0219].
JUSTICE LILLIAN WAN: [NY R KINGS J Part 17, as amended by NY ORDER 20-0220].
JUSTICE MICHELLE WESTON: NY R KINGS J Part 3.
MENTAL HYGIENE PART: NY R KINGS J Part 77.
MATRIMONIAL PARTS DURING COVID-19 EMERGENCY: JUSTICE KAREN B. ROTHENBERG: NY R KINGS J Doc. 1.

NASSAU COUNTY

JUSTICE ANNA R. ANZALONE: NY R NASSAU S J Anzalone, Part 26.
JUSTICE STACY D. BENNETT: NY R NASSAU S J Bennett; NY R NASSAU S J Bennett, Form 1.
JUSTICE ANTONIO BRANDVEEN: NY R NASSAU S J Brandveen, Part 31.
JUSTICE JEFFREY S. BROWN: [NY R NASSAU S J Brown, as amended by NY ORDER 20-0297].
JUSTICE STEPHEN A. BUCARIA: NY R NASSAU S J Bucaria.
JUSTICE JULIANNE T. CAPETOLA: NY R NASSAU S J Capetola, Part 28.
JUSTICE EDMUND M. DANE: NY R NASSAU S J Dane, Part 33.
JUSTICE VITO M. DESTEFANO: NY R NASSAU S J DeStefano, Part 13; NY R NASSAU S J DeStefano, Form 1.
JUSTICE ARTHUR M. DIAMOND: NY R NASSAU S J Diamond, Part 7.
JUSTICE THOMAS FEINMAN: NY R NASSAU S J Feinman, Part 5.
JUSTICE JOHN M. GALASSO: NY R NASSAU S J Galasso, Part 22.

JUSTICE SHARON M.J. GIANELLI: NY R NASSAU S J Gianelli, Part 22; NY R NASSAU S J Gianelli, Form 1.

JUSTICE JEFFREY A. GOODSTEIN: NY R NASSAU S J Goodstein, Part 33; NY R NASSAU S J Goodstein, Form 1.

JUSTICE DAVID J. GUGERTY: [NY R NASSAU S J Gugerty, Part 31, as amended by NY ORDER 20-0298].

JUSTICE HELENE F. GUGERTY: NY R NASSAU S J Gugerty, Part 47.

JUSTICE STEVEN M. JAEGER: NY R NASSAU S J Jaeger, Part 35; NY R NASSAU S J Jaeger, Form 1.

JUSTICE JACK L. LIBERT: NY R NASSAU S J Libert, Part 23.

JUSTICE JOSEPH H. LORINTZ: NY R NASSAU S J Lorintz, Part 26; NY R NASSAU S J Lorintz, Form 1.

JUSTICE ROY S. MAHON: NY R NASSAU S J Mahon, Part 3.

JUSTICE RANDY SUE MARBER: NY R NASSAU S J Marber, Part 8.

JUSTICE JAMES P. MCCORMACK: [NY R NASSAU S J McCormack, Part 18, as amended by NY ORDER, 20-0299].

JUSTICE DICCIA T. PINEDA-KIRWAN: [NY R NASSAU S J Pineda-Kirwan, as amended by NY ORDER 20-0300].

JUSTICE THOMAS RADEMAKER: [NY R NASSAU S J Rademaker, Part 28, as amended by NY ORDER 20-0301]; [NY R NASSAU S J Rademaker, Form 1, as amended by NY ORDER 20-0301].

JUSTICE DENISE L. SHER: NY R NASSAU S J Rademaker, Part 32.

JUSTICE LEONARD D. STEINMAN: [NY R NASSAU S J Steinman, Part 15, as amended by NY ORDER 20-0303]; NY R NASSAU S J Steinman, Form 1.

JUSTICE HOWARD E. STURIM: NY R NASSAU S J Sturim, Part 50; NY R NASSAU S J Sturim, Form 1.

JUSTICE HELEN VOUTSINAS: [NY R NASSAU S J Voutsinas, Part 25, as amended by NY ORDER 20-0304]; [NY R NASSAU S J Voutsinas, Form 1, as amended by NY ORDER 20-0305].

JUSTICE HOPE SCHWARTZ ZIMMERMAN: NY R NASSAU S J Zimmerman, Part 17.

NEW YORK COUNTY

JUDGE'S RULES; BASIC INFORMATION: [NY R NY CTY J RUL Doc. 1, as amended by NY ORDER 20-0202].

ONONDAGA COUNTY

JUSTICE ROBERT E. ANTONACCI II: [NY R ONDGA E FIL Doc. 1, as amended by 20-0239].

JUSTICE MICHAEL V. COCCOMI: NY R ONDGA E FIL Doc. 2.

JUSTICE GREGORY R. GILBERT: NY R 5 JD JUDGES Gilbert; NY R ONDGA E FIL Doc. 3.

JUSTICE DONALD A. GREENWOOD: NY R ONDGA E FIL Doc. 4.

JUSTICE DEBORAH H. KARALUNAS: NY R ONDGA E FIL Doc. 5.

JUSTICE JAMES MCCLUSKY: NY R 5 JD MCCLUSKY McClusky.

JUSTICE CHARLES C. MERRELL: NY R 5 JD MERRELL Merrell.

JUSTICE PATRICK F. MACRAE: NY R 5 JD MACRAE Doc. 1.

JUSTICE JAMES P. MURPHY: NY R ONDGA E FIL Doc. 7.

JUSTICE GERALD J. NERI: [NY R 5 JD JUDGES Neri, as amended by NY ORDER 20-0236]; [NY R ONDGA E FIL Doc. 8, as amended by NY ORDER 20-0241].

JUSTICE ANTHONY J. PARIS: NY R 5 JD JUDGES Paris; [NY R ONDGA E FIL Doc. 9, as amended by NY ORDER 20-0242].

JUSTICE NORMAN W. SEITER, JR.: NY R 5 JD JUDGES Seiter.

JUSTICE KEVIN G. YOUNG: [NY R ONDGA E FIL Doc. 10, as amended by NY ORDER 20-0243].

QUEENS COUNTY

JUSTICE PAM JACKMAN BROWN: [NY R L QUEENS Brown, Part 19, as amended by NY ORDER 20-0321].

JUSTICE CHEREE A. BUGGS: NY R L QUEENS Buggs, Part 30.

JUSTICE PAM JACKMAN BROWN: [NY R L QUEENS Brown, Part 19, as amended by NY ORDER 20-0321].

JUSTICE DENIS J. BUTLER: NY R L QUEENS Butler, Part 12.

JUSTICE ROBERT I. CALORAS: [NY R L QUEENS Caloras, Part 36, as amended by NY ORDER 20-0322].

JUSTICE ANNA CULLEY: NY R L QUEENS Culley, Part 53.

JUSTICE TIMOTHY DUFFICY: NY R L QUEENS Dufficy, Part 35.

JUSTICE DAVID ELLIOT: NY R L QUEENS Elliot, Part 14.

JUSTICE JOSEPH J. ESPOSITO: NY R L QUEENS Esposito, Part 6.

JUSTICE DARRELL L. GAVRIN: [NY R L QUEENS Gavrin, Part 27, as amended by NY ORDER 20-0323].

JUSTICE WYATT N. GIBBONS: [NY R L QUEENS Gibbons, Part 5, as amended by NY ORDER 20-0330.

JUSTICE DONNA-MARIE E. GOLIA: [NY R L QUEENS Golia, Part 21, as amended by NY ORDER 20-0331].

JUSTICE MARGUERITE A. GRAYS: [NY R L QUEENS Grays, Part 4, as amended by NY ORDER 20-0324].

JUSTICE RUDOLPH E. GRECO: [NY R L QUEENS Greco, Part 32, as amended by NY ORDER 20-0325].

JUSTICE MAUREEN HEALY: NY R L QUEENS Healy, Part 6.

JUSTICE PHILLIP HOM: [NY R L QUEENS Hom, Part 43, as amended by NY ORDER 20-0332].

JUSTICE KEVIN J. KERRIGAN: NY R L QUEENS Kerrigan, Part 10.

JUSTICE MOJGAN C. LANCMAN: NY R L QUEENS Lancman, Part 20.

JUSTICE RICHARD G. LATIN: NY R L QUEENS Latin, Part 40.

JUSTICE ULYSSES B. LEVERETT: [NY R L QUEENS Leverett, Part 6, as amended by NY ORDER 20-0326].

JUSTICE LEONARD LIVOTE: NY R L QUEENS Livote, Part 33.

JUSTICE LEE A. MAYERSOHN: NY R L QUEENS Mayersohn, Part 22; NY R L QUEENS Mayersohn, Part 22G; [NY R L QUEENS Mayersohn, Part 22G COVID, as amended by NY ORDER 20-0327].

JUSTICE ROBERT J. MCDONALD: NY R L QUEENS McDonald, Part 34.

JUSTICE MARGARET MCGOWAN: NY R L QUEENS McGowan, Part 52.

JUSTICE MAURICE E. MUIR: [NY R L QUEENS Muir, Part 42, as amended by NY ORDER 20-0333].

JUSTICE JODI ORLOW: NY R L QUEENS Orlow, Part 51.

JUSTICE LESLIE J. PURIFICCION: NY R L QUEENS Purificcion, Part 39.

JUSTICE JOSEPH RISI: [NY R L QUEENS Risi, Part 3, as amended by NY ORDER 20-0328].

JUSTICE FREDERICK D.R. SAMPSON: [NY R L QUEENS Sampson, Part 31, as amended by NY ORDER 20-0329].

JUSTICE MARTIN J. SCHULMAN: NY R L QUEENS Schulman, Part 29.

JUSTICE BERNICE D. SIEGAL: NY R L QUEENS Siegal, Part 25G.

JUSTICE JANICE A. TAYLOR: NY R L QUEENS Taylor, Part 15.

JUSTICE CARMEN R. VELASQUEZ: NY R L QUEENS Velasquez, Part 38.

JUSTICE LOURDES M VENTURA: [NY R L QUEENS Ventura, Part 37, as amended by NY ORDER 20-0334].

JUSTICE WILLIAM A. VISCOVICH: NY R L QUEENS Viscovich, Part 63.

JUSTICE ALLAN B. WEISS: NY R L QUEENS Weiss, Part 2.

COMPLIANCE, SETTLEMENT AND CONFERENCE PART: NY R L QUEENS Doc 1.

PRELIMINARY CONFERENCE PART: [NY R L QUEENS Doc. 2, as amended by NY ORDER 20-0335].

MEDICAL MALPRACTICE CONFERENCE PART: [NY R L QUEENS Doc. 3, as amended by NY ORDER 20-0336].

TRIAL SCHEDULING PART: NY R L QUEENS Doc. 4.

SUMMARY JURY TRIAL PROGRAM: NY R L QUEENS Doc. 7.

RESIDENTIAL FORECLOSURE PART: NY R L QUEENS Doc. 9.

FORECLOSURE AUCTION RULES: NY R L QUEENS Doc. 10.

MATRIMONIAL PRELIMINARY CONFERENCE PART: NY R L QUEENS Doc. 11.

NON-CUSTODIAL CONTESTED MATRIMONIAL PART: NY R L QUEENS Doc. 12.

Motions, Oppositions and Replies
Motion for Continuance/Extension of Time

Document Last Updated August 2020

A. Checklist

(I) ❑ Matters to consider for moving party

(a) ❑ Required documents

(1) ❑ Notice of motion, order to show cause, or affidavit on ex parte motion

(2) ❑ Motion

(3) ❑ Request for judicial intervention

(4) ❑ Proof of service

(5) ❑ ALBANY COUNTY: Additional required documents

(i) ❑ Affirmation of good faith effort

(b) ❑ Supplemental documents

(1) ❑ Supporting evidence; Exhibits

(2) ❑ Brief

(3) ❑ Notice to produce papers not in possession of the court

(4) ❑ Filing fees

(5) ❑ Working copies

(6) ❑ ERIE COUNTY: Additional supplemental documents

(i) ❑ Notice of hard copy submission in e-filed case

(7) ❑ KINGS COUNTY: Additional supplemental documents

(i) ❑ Forms when filing in hard copy

(8) ❑ NEW YORK COUNTY: Additional supplemental documents

(i) ❑ Notice of hard copy submission

(ii) ❑ Unpublished opinions

(9) ❑ ONONDAGA COUNTY: Additional supplemental documents

(i) ❑ Notice of hard copy submission

(10) ❑ QUEENS COUNTY: Additional supplemental documents

(i) ❑ Notice of hard copy submission

(c) ❑ Timing

(1) ❑ The moving party shall serve copies of all affidavits and briefs upon all other parties at the time of service of the notice of motion

(2) ❑ A notice of motion and supporting affidavits shall be served at least eight (8) days before the time at which the motion is noticed to be heard

(3) ❑ It is also good practice to make motions returnable at least three (3) weeks away from the planned date of mailing and to always include a demand in the motion that the other side serve answering papers at least seven (7) days before the return day

(4) ❑ BRONX COUNTY: Additional timing

(i) ❑ A Notice of Motion must be served at least eight (8) days, by personal service, nine (9) days by overnight express and thirteen (13) days by mail before the return date

(5) ❑ NEW YORK COUNTY: Additional timing

(i) ❑ In an e-filed case, all of the moving papers shall be e-filed at least eight (8) business days prior to the return date

(6) ❑ ONONDAGA COUNTY: Additional timing

(i) ❑ Onondaga County local court rules require that any additional papers relating to motions must be e-filed at least two (2) business days prior to the return date, excluding the return date

(7) ❑ QUEENS COUNTY: Additional timing

(i) ❑ Motions must be in the possession of the Motion Support Office at least nine (9) days before the noticed return date of the motion

(II) ❑ Matters to consider for opposing party

(a) ❑ Required documents

(1) ❑ Opposition

(2) ❑ Proof of service

(b) ❑ Supplemental documents

(1) ❑ Supporting evidence; Exhibits

(2) ❑ Brief

(3) ❑ Filing fees

(4) ❑ Working copies

(5) ❑ ERIE COUNTY: Additional supplemental documents

(i) ❑ Notice of hard copy submission in e-filed case

(6) ❑ KINGS COUNTY: Additional supplemental documents

(i) ❑ Forms when filing in hard copy

(7) ❑ NEW YORK COUNTY: Additional supplemental documents

(i) ❑ Notice of hard copy submission

(ii) ❑ Unpublished opinions

(8) ❑ ONONDAGA COUNTY: Additional supplemental documents

(i) ❑ Notice of hard copy submission

(9) ❑ QUEENS COUNTY: Additional supplemental documents

(i) ❑ Notice of hard copy submission

(c) ❑ Timing

(1) ❑ Answering affidavits shall be served at least two (2) days before the time at which the motion is noticed to be heard

(2) ❑ Answering affidavits and any notice of cross-motion, with supporting papers, if any, shall be served at least seven (7) days before such time if a notice of motion served at least sixteen (16) days before such time so demands

B. Timing

1. *Time to bring motion for continuance/extension of time.* There are no specific timing requirements for the motion for continuance/extension of time.

2. *Time to serve.* The moving party shall serve copies of all affidavits and briefs upon all other parties at the time of service of the notice of motion. NY R UNIF TRIAL CTS § 202.8(c). A notice of motion and supporting affidavits shall be served at least eight (8) days before the time at which the motion is noticed to be heard. NY CPLR Rule 2214(b).

   a. *Return dates; Best practice.* It is also good practice to make motions returnable at least three (3) weeks away from the planned date of mailing and to always include a demand in the motion that the other side serve answering papers at least seven (7) days before the return day. This enables the motion to be served by mail, gives sufficient notice to support the seven (7) day demand, and leaves a few days for a delayed mailing if some snag prevents posting on the day planned. If speed is needed, the shorter eight (8) day notice period can be used, forfeiting the right to seven (7) day answering papers and a reply. If even eight (8) days notice is too much under the circumstances, the order to show cause is the remedy. SIEGEL-NYPRAC § 247.

      i. *ALBANY COUNTY.* All motions, except for certain matters in Albany County as specified in NY R 3 JD SUP

Doc. 1(E) and NY R 3 JD SUP Doc. 1(F), brought on by notice of motion or by order to show cause will be made returnable on any day, Monday through Friday, as chosen by the movant in compliance with the CPLR. Parties shall submit all papers in a timely fashion as required by the CPLR by delivering them or mailing them directly to the Supreme Court Clerk's Office[. . .]except that motions and other applications subject to a filing fee shall first be presented to the County Clerk's Office for payment of the requisite fee and then subsequently filed with the Supreme Court Clerk's Office. NY R 3 JD SUP Doc. 1(B).

ii. *BRONX COUNTY.* A Notice of Motion must be served at least eight (8) days, by personal service, nine (9) days by overnight express and thirteen (13) days by mail before the return date. NY R BRONX FIL R Doc. 3. All unassigned motions must be accompanied with a properly filled out RJI and shall be filed in the Motion Support Office, room 217, within five (5) days of service. All motions on actions already assigned to a Justice must be filed at least five (5) business days before the return date. NY R BRONX FIL R Doc. 3. All papers served must strictly comply with the time requirements of NY CPLR Rule 2101, NY CPLR Rule 2103 and NY CPLR Rule 2214(b). NY R BRONX FIL R Doc. 8.

iii. *KINGS COUNTY.* Motion papers, answering affidavits and reply affidavits must be served on adversaries in accordance with NY CPLR Rule 2214. NY R L KINGS Pt. C, Rule 1.

iv. *NEW YORK COUNTY.* In an e-filed case, all of the moving papers shall be e-filed at least eight (8) business days prior to the return date. The clerk will calendar the motion for the Motion Submission Part Courtroom (Room 130) for the return date selected. NY R NY CTY Procedure II(A); NY R NY CTY E FIL Doc. 2(D)(1).

v. *ONONDAGA COUNTY.* Onondaga County local court rules require that any additional papers relating to motions must be e-filed at least two (2) business days prior to the return date, excluding the return date. NY R ONDGA E FIL Protocol(B)(9)(e).

vi. *QUEENS COUNTY.* Motions must be in the possession of the Motion Support Office at least nine (9) days before the noticed return date of the motion. NY R L QUEENS MOT SUP Doc. 1; NY R L QUEENS E-FILE Doc. 1(H)(1).

b. *Order to show cause; Shorter time.* The court in a proper case may grant an order to show cause, to be served in lieu of a notice of motion, at a time and in a manner specified therein. NY CPLR Rule 2214(d). An ordinary notice of motion can't be brought on for hearing earlier than the eighth (8th) day after the motion papers are served. With an order to show cause, the hearing can be brought on at any time the court directs, which can be fewer than eight (8) days or as close as the very day on which it is signed. If the court is convinced there is a real emergency, it can schedule the hearing for a few hours later or, in the direst case, "forthwith" the service of the order to show cause. SIEGEL-NYPRAC § 248.

c. *Time to serve answering affidavits; Other answering papers.* Answering affidavits shall be served at least two (2) days before the time at which the motion is noticed to be heard. Answering affidavits and any notice of cross-motion, with supporting papers, if any, shall be served at least seven (7) days before such time if a notice of motion served at least sixteen (16) days before such time so demands; whereupon any reply or responding affidavits shall be served at least one (1) day before such time. NY CPLR Rule 2214(b); NY R UNIF TRIAL CTS § 202.8(c).

i. *BRONX COUNTY.* All answering papers must be submitted to the Clerk 's Office on the return date of the motion. Answering papers will not be accepted prior to the return date. NY R BRONX FIL R Doc. 8.

ii. *NEW YORK COUNTY.* Cross-motions, papers in opposition, and reply papers on motions/petitions on notice returnable in Room 130 in a hard-copy case shall be submitted to the Motion Submission Part Courtroom (Room 130) on the final return date of the motion/petition and will not be accepted until that date. Subsequent documents on motions/petitions in e-filed cases shall be e-filed in a timely manner. Working copies when required shall be submitted to Room 130 on the final return date. NY R NY CTY Procedure II(A).

d. *Time to serve cross-motion.* At least three (3) days prior to the time at which the motion is noticed to be heard, or seven (7) days prior to such time if demand is properly made pursuant to NY CPLR Rule 2214(b), a party may serve upon the moving party a notice of cross-motion demanding relief, with or without supporting papers; provided, however, that:

i. If such notice and any supporting papers are served by mailing, as provided in NY CPLR Rule 2103(b)(2), they shall be served three (3) days earlier than as prescribed in NY CPLR Rule 2215; and

ii. If served by overnight delivery, as provided in NY CPLR Rule 2103(b)(6), they shall be served one (1) day earlier than as prescribed in NY CPLR Rule 2215. Relief in the alternative or of several different types may be demanded; relief need not be responsive to that demanded by the moving party. NY CPLR Rule 2215(a); NY CPLR Rule 2215(b).

iii. *BRONX COUNTY.* Cross motions may be presented for approval on or before the return date, provided that there is a motion already calendared. NY R BRONX FIL R Doc. 8.

iv. *ERIE COUNTY.* Cross-motions must be filed at least two (2) days before the return date of the motion. NY R L KINGS Pt. A, Papers.

v. *KINGS COUNTY.* Hard copies are required to be filed for any motions, answering papers, stipulations, etc. for E-Filed cases returnable in [the Central Compliance Part] at least [two (2)] days before return date. . . .for cross motions. NY R L KINGS Pt. E, Rule 8.

vi. *QUEENS COUNTY.* Motion Support does not process or forward responsive papers, including cross-motions. They must be brought to the calendar call in the judge's part. NY R L QUEENS MOT SUP Doc. 1. E-filed cross motions: across motion must be noticed for the same return date as the main motion and have the confirmation of filing attached in the same manner as a motion. NY R L QUEENS E-FILE Doc. 1(H)(2)(e).

3. *Filing before return date.* All motions shall be returnable before the assigned judge, and all papers shall be filed with the court on or before the return date. NY R UNIF TRIAL CTS § 202.8(a).

a. *BRONX COUNTY: Time for filing*

i. *Unassigned motions.* Unassigned motions must be in the Clerk's Office within five (5) days of the date of service of the motion. NY R BRONX FIL R Doc. 8.

ii. *Assigned motions.* Assigned motions must be filed in the Clerk's Office not less than five (5) business days prior to the return date of the motion. NY R BRONX FIL R Doc. 8.

iii. *Motions returnable in room 217.* The moving documents must be e-filed no later than eight (8) days prior to the return date. NY R BRONX E FIL R Doc. 1(1).

b. *KINGS COUNTY: Time and place of filing.* Motion papers must be filed with the E-file/Motion Support Office located in Room 227. . . at 360 Adams Street at least five (5) business days before the return date of the motion. NY R L KINGS Pt. A, Papers. Hard copies are required to be filed for any motions, answering papers, stipulations, etc. for E-Filed cases returnable in [the Central Compliance Part] at least five (5) days before return date for main motions. NY R L KINGS Pt. E, Rule 8. The moving documents must be e-filed no later than eight (8) days prior to the return date. NY R L KINGS E FIL Doc. 1(D).

4. *NEW YORK COUNTY: Briefing schedule.* Once a motion is made, counsel for all parties are strongly encouraged to agree upon a briefing schedule and submit a stipulation of adjournment reflecting that schedule using service or a clerk. Where a briefing schedule has not been agreed upon, the movant can avoid the need to attend simply to see if anyone will hand up opposing papers by demanding papers as provided by NY CPLR Rule 2214(b). To protect movants against the submission of late opposition papers or cross-motions, the General Clerk's Office will screen motions in which such papers are submitted without a response (reply or opposition respectively) to ensure that proper time to respond has been afforded and it will sua sponte adjourn for one (1) week cases in which such time has not been given. NY R NY CTY Procedure II(C).

5. *QUEENS COUNTY: Time to pay fees.* As motions and petitions are time sensitive, if opting to pay at the County Clerk's Office payment MUST be made, if filed with an RJI, a minimum of nine (9) business days prior to the application's return date and if filed post RJI, a minimum of nine (9) business days prior to the application's return date. NY R L QUEENS E-FILE Doc. 1(H)(1).

6. *Computation of time*

a. *Units of time*

i. *Day.* A calendar day includes the time from midnight to midnight. Sunday or any day of the week specifically mentioned means a calendar day. NY GEN CONSTR § 19.

ii. *Month.* In a statute, contract or public or private instrument, unless otherwise provided in such contract or instrument or by law, the term month means a calendar month and not a lunar month. NY GEN CONSTR § 31.

iii. *Year.* For information on the definition of a year, including the definitions of a half-year and quarter-year, refer to NY GEN CONSTR § 58 and NY GEN CONSTR § 50. For information on leap years, refer to NY GEN CONSTR § 57.

b. *Periods of time*

i. *Number of days.* A number of days specified as a period from a certain day within which or after or before which

an act is authorized or required to be done means such number of calendar days exclusive of the calendar day from which the reckoning is made. NY GEN CONSTR § 20.

- If such period is a period of two (2) days, Saturday, Sunday or a public holiday must be excluded from the reckoning if it is an intervening day between the day from which the reckoning is made and the last day of the period. NY GEN CONSTR § 20.
- In computing any specified period of time from a specified event, the day upon which the event happens is deemed the day from which the reckoning is made. The day from which any specified period of time is reckoned shall be excluded in making the reckoning. NY GEN CONSTR § 20.

ii. *Number of months.* A number of months after or before a certain day shall be computed by counting such number of calendar months from such day, exclusive of the calendar month in which such day occurs, and shall include the day of the month in the last month so counted having the same numerical order in days of the month as the day from which the computation is made, unless there be not so many days in the last month so counted, in which case the period computed shall expire with the last day of the month so counted. NY GEN CONSTR § 30.

iii. *Publication of notice; Number of days.* The period of publication of a legal notice shall be computed by excluding the first day of publication and including the day on which the act or event of which notice is given is to take place or which completes the full period of publication. NY CPLR § 2402.

iv. *Periods ending on Saturday, Sunday or public holiday.* When any period of time, computed from a certain day, within which or after which or before which an act is authorized or required to be done, ends on a Saturday, Sunday or a public holiday, such act may be done on the next succeeding business day and if the period ends at a specified hour, such act may be done at or before the same hour of such next succeeding business day, except that where a period of time specified by contract ends on a Saturday, Sunday or a public holiday, the extension of such period is governed by NY GEN CONSTR § 25. NY GEN CONSTR § 25-a(1).

- For a list of public holidays, refer to NY GEN CONSTR § 24.

v. *Additional time after certain kinds of service*

- *Service by mail.* Where a period of time prescribed by law is measured from the service of a paper and service is by mail, five (5) days shall be added to the prescribed period. NY CPLR Rule 2103(b)(2).
- *Service by overnight delivery service.* Where a period of time prescribed by law is measured from the service of a paper and service is by overnight delivery, one (1) business day shall be added to the prescribed period. NY CPLR Rule 2103(b)(6).

vi. *Daylight saving time.* For information on New York's time zone and the effect of daylight saving time, refer to NY GEN CONSTR § 52.

c. *Hours of court.* Notwithstanding any provision of law or rule of court to the contrary, throughout the State of New York the sessions of the Supreme Court for the disposition of business before the court shall commence not later than 9:30 a.m. and conclude not earlier than 5 p.m. Where warranted, the Chief Administrator of the Courts may authorize variances in the opening and closing hours of the courts, but, in such event, daily sessions shall total not less than six (6) hours. NY R CHIEF J § 3.1.

d. *Time limits; Extension of time.* Any act required by or in pursuance of law to be performed at or within a prescribed time, shall be performed according to the standard time. NY GEN CONSTR § 53.

i. Refer to the General Requirements section of this document for information on extending.

C. General Requirements

1. *Motions, generally.* There shall be compliance with the procedures prescribed in the CPLR for the bringing of motions. NY R UNIF TRIAL CTS § 202.7(a).

a. *Motions on notice.* A notice of motion shall specify the time and place of the hearing on the motion, the supporting papers upon which the motion is based, the relief demanded and the grounds therefor. NY CPLR Rule 2214(a). A motion on notice in an action in the supreme court shall be noticed to be heard in the judicial district where the action is triable or in a county adjoining the county where the action is triable. Unless statute, civil practice rule or local court rule provides otherwise, the motion shall be noticed to be heard before a motion term or, upon order to show cause granted by a justice, before that justice out of court. NY CPLR § 2212(a). Except as provided in NY R UNIF TRIAL CTS § 202.7(d), no motion shall be filed with the court unless there have been served and filed with the motion papers a notice of motion. NY R UNIF TRIAL CTS § 202.7(a)(1).

b. *Ex parte motions.* A motion in an action in the supreme court that may be made without notice may be made at a motion term or to a justice out of court in any county in the state. NY CPLR § 2212(b).

   i. *KINGS COUNTY.* For more information on submitting a motion ex parte, refer to NY R L KINGS E FIL Doc. 1(G).

   ii. *NEW YORK COUNTY.* For more information on submitting matters ex parte, refer to NY R NY CTY Procedure III and NY R NY CTY E FIL Doc. 2(G).

   iii. *QUEENS COUNTY.* For more information on submitting matters ex parte, refer to NY R L QUEENS EX PARTE Doc. 1.

c. *Alternative relief.* Relief in the alternative or of several different types may be demanded. NY CPLR Rule 2214(a). The types of relief need not be related. In one motion, for example, the defendant can seek to dismiss the plaintiff's claim for lack of jurisdiction, to get an extension of time to answer, to require the plaintiff to join X as a party, and to quash a disclosure subpoena served in behalf of the plaintiff on a nonparty witness. So doing, the movant must of course specify all of these items of relief in the notice of motion, and the grounds for them, and the supporting papers must contain the entire proof requisite to the items of relief sought. NY CPLR Rule 2214(Practice Commentary, C2214:4).

d. *General relief.* It is common practice to include at the end of the relief request in the notice of motion a so-called "general relief" clause. This is merely a few words to cover the possibility that the relief appropriate to what the movant proves was not specifically asked for, but is close enough to enable the court to grant it. After stating the specific relief desired, the lawyer will often add something like: and for such other, further, or different relief as this court may deem just and proper. NY CPLR Rule 2214(Practice Commentary, C2214:5).

e. *Motion in improper form.* If the court finds it appropriate in the interests of justice, it may convert a motion into a special proceeding, or vice-versa, upon such terms as may be just, including the payment of fees and costs. NY CPLR § 103(c).

f. *Order to show cause.* An order to show cause is basically only a substitute for a notice of motion. An ordinary notice of motion merely notifies the recipient that a motion is being made for specified relief. The burden of proof is on the movant. Although in most cases it is just as innocent as an ordinary notice of motion, the order to show cause gets its name by directing the recipient to "show cause" why the particular relief being asked for should not be granted. It sounds as if the burden of proof is being shifted to the recipient. It isn't. It specifies the time and place of the hearing on the application but when the hearing comes on, the burden of proof is where it always is on a motion: on the movant. SIEGEL-NYPRAC § 248.

   i. The CPLR says nothing more about an order to show cause than that it may be used "in a proper case", which leaves it entirely to the judge's discretion to determine what a proper case is. Any fact suggesting a problem as to any of the items listed above would be sufficient to invoke judicial discretion and justify the show cause procedure, which is in fact liberally used. SIEGEL-NYPRAC § 248.

   ii. An order to show cause against a state body or officers must be served in addition to service upon the defendant or respondent state body or officers upon the attorney general by delivery to an assistant attorney general at an office of the attorney general in the county in which venue of the action is designated or if there is no office of the attorney general in such county, at the office of the attorney general nearest such county. NY CPLR Rule 2214(d).

   iii. *BRONX COUNTY.* For information on submitting an order to show cause, refer to NY R BRONX E FIL R Doc. 2 and NY R BRONX LEG SUP Doc. 1.

   iv. *ERIE COUNTY.* For information on submitting an order to show cause, refer to NY R ERIE E FIL Doc. 3(VI).

   v. *KINGS COUNTY.* For information on submitting an order to show cause, refer to NY R L KINGS E FIL Doc. 1(F).

   vi. *NEW YORK COUNTY.* For information on submitting an order to show cause, refer to NY R NY CTY E FIL Doc. 2(F).

   vii. *ONONDAGA COUNTY.* For information on submitting an order to show cause, refer to NY R ONDGA E FIL Protocol(B)(10) and NY R ONDGA E FIL Protocol(J).

g. *Motions before preliminary conference.* Motions in actions to which NY R UNIF TRIAL CTS § 202.12 is applicable made after the preliminary conference has been scheduled may be denied unless there is shown good cause why such relief is warranted before the preliminary conference is held. NY R UNIF TRIAL CTS § 202.12(h).

h. *ALBANY COUNTY: Good faith effort to resolve.* Prior to the submission of a notice of motion relating to disclosure or a bill of particulars, the parties must make a good faith effort to resolve the matter in question and submit an affirmation attesting to this good faith effort. NY R 3 JD SUP Doc. 1(B).

i. *NEW YORK COUNTY: Documents with motions.* Counsel must attach to motion papers copies of all pleadings and other documents as required by the CPLR and as necessary for an informed decision on the motion. Documents in a foreign language shall be properly translated. NY R NY CTY J RUL Rule 14(a).

j. *NEW YORK COUNTY: Motions in multiple cases made together.* On occasion, attorneys may wish to make a motion in more than one case on a single set of papers. In such cases, by definition consolidation will not have been directed since consolidation signifies the combination of more than one case into a single one with a single caption and index number and ending in a single judgment. NY R NY CTY Procedure II(B). For more information on motions made with the same papers, refer to NY R NY CTY Procedure II(A).

k. *QUEENS COUNTY: Motion sequence numbers.* A motion sequence number is required for all E-filed motions. After a motion is E-filed, please consult the e-courts website within twenty-four (24) to forty-eight (48) hours to obtain the sequence number. The Confirmation Notice of E-filing MUST indicate the sequence number of any motion submitted at the Centralized Motion Part calendar call. NY R L QUEENS E-FILE Doc. 1(H)(5).

2. *Motion for continuance/extension of time.* Except where otherwise expressly prescribed by law, the court may extend the time fixed by any statute, rule or order for doing any act, upon such terms as may be just and upon good cause shown, whether the application for extension is made before or after the expiration of the time fixed. NY CPLR § 2004.

   a. *Exceptions.* There are two statutory exceptions to the power of NY CPLR § 2004 to extend time. One is the statute of limitations itself, i.e., the time in which an action has to be commenced. It is not subject to discretionary extensions. The second is the time in which to take an appeal. Occasionally some other time period is treated, perhaps unexpectedly, as a statute of limitations, with the result that it, too, becomes unextendable under NY CPLR § 2004, but the exceptions are few and the uses of NY CPLR § 2004 many. SIEGEL-NYPRAC § 6.

   b. *Extending time for service of summons and complaint.* If service can't be made within the one hundred and twenty (120) days despite the plaintiff's diligent efforts, the plaintiff can move for an extension of time. And there is no arbitrary limit on how long an extension the court can grant. It can grant whatever it believes the facts call for, and can do so in a series of extensions, if need be, when genuine difficulties are being experienced in effecting service. SIEGEL-NYPRAC § 63.

      i. The plaintiff should show "good cause" for the extension, but NY CPLR § 306-b also allows the court to grant it without good cause if the court finds it "in the interest of justice". This poses the anomaly of inviting a court to allow an enlargement of time in its discretion when the plaintiff can show no good cause for invoking that discretion. SIEGEL-NYPRAC § 63.

      ii. The extension can be granted even after the expiration of the one hundred and twenty (120) days. The plaintiff's request for the extension can also take the form of a cross-motion made in opposition to the defendant's motion to dismiss for lack of timely service. But a plaintiff does well to seek the extension within the one hundred and twenty (120) days. Doing so may itself serve as some indication of diligence. SIEGEL-NYPRAC § 63.

      iii. When service is being made by publication, which has to be effected in a series of publishings within a prescribed time period, the availability of a time extension may prove more than helpful; It may prove indispensable. SIEGEL-NYPRAC § 63; SIEGEL-NYPRAC § 107.

      iv. There may be a special need for a time extension when service is being made in a foreign country, especially one with primitive procedures or an indifferent bureaucracy. NY CPLR § 306-b doesn't exempt foreign country service from the one hundred and twenty (120) day requirement, but the situation would be one with a special appeal to the court's discretionary extension powers. SIEGEL-NYPRAC § 63.

      v. If the plaintiff is getting down to the wire and can't make service because (e.g.) she doesn't know where the defendant resides and hence cannot use such substituted service provisions as NY CPLR § 308(2) or NY CPLR § 308(4), she can consider moving for an ex parte order under NY CPLR § 308(5), under which the court can invent a method of service for the plaintiff. SIEGEL-NYPRAC § 63; SIEGEL-NYPRAC § 75.

   c. *Extension of time to appear or plead.* Upon the application of a party, the court may extend the time to appear or plead, or compel the acceptance of a pleading untimely served, upon such terms as may be just and upon a showing of reasonable excuse for delay or default. NY CPLR § 3012(d).

      i. *Law office failure as reasonable excuse.* Upon an application satisfying the requirements of NY CPLR § 3012(d), the court shall not, as a matter of law, be precluded from exercising its discretion in the interests of justice to excuse delay or default resulting from law office failure. NY CPLR § 2005.

d. *Adjournment due to engagement of counsel.* No adjournment shall be granted on the ground of engagement of counsel except in accordance with Part 125 of the Rules of the Chief Administrator of the Courts (NY R CHIEF ADMIN § 125.1, et seq.). NY R UNIF TRIAL CTS § 202.32.

   i. *Engagement of counsel proper ground for adjournment.* Engagement of counsel shall be a ground for adjournment of an action or proceeding in accordance with NY R CHIEF ADMIN § 125.1. NY R CHIEF ADMIN § 125.1(a).

   ii. *Engagement defined.* Engagement of counsel shall mean actual engagement on trial or in argument before any state or federal trial or appellate court, or in a proceeding conducted pursuant to NY CPLR § 3045 and the rules promulgated thereunder. NY R CHIEF ADMIN § 125.1(b).

   iii. For more information on adjournment due to engagement of counsel, refer to NY R CHIEF ADMIN § 125.1.

e. *Adjournment of motion return date*

   i. *By stipulation.* Stipulations of adjournment of the return date made by the parties shall be in writing and shall be submitted to the assigned judge. Such stipulation shall be effective unless the court otherwise directs. No more than three (3) stipulated adjournments for an aggregate period of sixty (60) days shall be submitted without prior permission of the court. NY R UNIF TRIAL CTS § 202.8(e)(1).

   ii. *By request to assigned judge.* Absent agreement by the parties, a request by any party for an adjournment shall be submitted in writing, upon notice to the other party, to the assigned judge on or before the return date. The court will notify the requesting party whether the adjournment has been granted. NY R UNIF TRIAL CTS § 202.8(e)(2).

   iii. *ALBANY COUNTY: Limits on adjournments.* Generally, parties will be granted only one adjournment for the Friday Motion Term. Requests for an adjournment of the proceeding or an extension of time in which to submit papers must be made in writing to the Supreme Court Clerk's Office for referral to the assigned justice or judge for consideration. NY R 3 JD SUP Doc. 1(F).

   iv. *BRONX COUNTY: Stipulated adjournments of non-disclosure motions.* Non-disclosure motions for IA5, IA7 and IA22 will be adjourned for oral argument to the Monday of the second week following the week of the return date of the motion. All other non-disclosure motions will be deemed submitted on the return date and forwarded to Chambers unless a stipulation of adjournment complying with the requirements of NY R UNIF TRIAL CTS § 202.8(e) is submitted, in which event, the motion will be adjourned for the requested date and kept in the Clerk's Office. If a non-stipulated request for adjournment or notice is submitted, the motion and request will be forwarded to Chambers for judicial approval or denial of the request. In either event, the attorney requesting the adjournment will be notified, via telephone, of the granting or denial of the request and instructed to notify his adversary. NY R BRONX FIL R Doc. 8.

      - *BRONX COUNTY.* Motions that have been e-filed may be adjourned in Room 217 if an adjournment complies with the procedures of the Motion Support Office (explained in the "Filing Rules—Motion Procedure" section of the "Courthouse Procedures" link on the website of [the] court). An adjournment that so complies may be obtained by filing a stipulation of all parties with NYSCEF (designated in the filing menu as a "Stipulation to Adjourn Motion"). NY R BRONX E FIL R Doc. 1(3).

   v. *ERIE COUNTY: Adjournment of motion dates.* Refer to individual Justice's Part Rules. NY R ERIE E FIL Doc. 3(V)(C).

   vi. *KINGS COUNTY: Adjournment of motions.* Unless the Judge's Part Rules provide otherwise, motions may be adjourned twice, on consent, without appearance, for a period not to exceed sixty (60) days from the initial return date of the motion. Adjournment of motions without appearance may be done by usage of stipulation or affirmation submitted no later than the previous work day. Any subsequent adjournment shall be by personal application. NY R L KINGS Pt. C, Rule 4.

   vii. *KINGS COUNTY: Adjournment of discovery motions.* Appearances are required on all motions. Motions are heard on the return date, and are only adjourned upon good cause. Applications for adjournment on consent of all parties shall be heard by the court attorneys. NY R L KINGS Pt. E, Rule 12.

      - If all parties are not present, an application may be made by the party(ies) present at the default calendar call at 11:45 a.m. NY R L KINGS Pt. E, Rule 12(a).
      - There shall be no extension of time for filing summary judgment motions after the Note of Issue except upon application to the Court. NY R L KINGS Pt. E, Rule 12(b).

   viii. *NEW YORK COUNTY: Adjournment of oral argument.* Unless provided otherwise in NY R NY CTY J RUL

Doc. 1: argument may be adjourned for good cause; there shall be only one adjournment, for no more than fourteen (14) days, unless otherwise directed by the court. A request for an adjournment shall be made prior to the scheduled date. NY R NY CTY J RUL Rule 15(b).

ix. *NEW YORK COUNTY: Adjournment by stipulation.* [A] party seeking an adjournment must contact all other parties in an effort to obtain consent and demonstrate that that was done. Adjournments are allowed in Room 130 in response to written stipulations. No more than three adjournments for a total of no more than sixty (60) days are allowed except with the permission of the assigned Justice (NY R UNIF TRIAL CTS § 202.8(e)(1)), given by means of a so-ordered stipulation. NY R NY CTY Procedure II(C).

x. *NEW YORK COUNTY: Adjournment by affidavit or affirmation.* If all parties consent to an adjournment as allowed by the Local Rules of New York County but a written stipulation cannot be obtained in time for submission, the applicant for the adjournment on consent may submit an affidavit or affirmation reciting that such consent was obtained. That document must state the reason for the adjournment request, how consent was obtained from all parties, when it was obtained, and the name of each attorney who gave oral consent. The affidavit/affirmation must have been served before the date on which the request for adjournment is made. NY R NY CTY Procedure II(C).

xi. *NEW YORK COUNTY: Adjournment by e-mail.* Parties to a hard-copy case seeking an adjournment on consent in compliance with the procedures outlined here may do so by e-mail. Counsel who wish to avail themselves of this procedure must submit the stipulation or affidavit/affirmation in PDF format as an attachment to an e-mail message sent to the following e-mail address: NYMOTCAL@courts.state.ny.us. Any such message may be sent up to 5 P.M. of the day before the return date of the motion to which it relates. In addition to the caption and the index number, each submission must identify the date on which the motion is then returnable. The party filing the paper must retain the original paper for sixty (60) days in case any issue should later be raised about the PDF copy submitted. NY R NY CTY Procedure II(C); NY R NY CTY E FIL Doc. 2(D)(2). An attorney [in an e-filed case] ho wishes to submit a stipulation for an adjournment, an application for an adjournment, or notice that a motion is being withdrawn must take care to designate correctly the applicable document type from the menu in the NYSCEF e-filing system. A correct designation is necessary to ensure that the clerk takes the proper action on the submission. NY R NY CTY Procedure II(C). For more information on requesting an adjournment by email, refer to NY R NY CTY Procedure II(C).

xii. *NEW YORK COUNTY: Adjournment not on consent.* If consent was not obtained from all parties prior to the return date, any party making an application for adjournment must submit an affidavit or affirmation in support of the application, reciting the reason for the requested adjournment and a description of the efforts made to obtain such consent, including the date when a contact was initiated or attempted, the means used, and the person contacted (if consent was refused) or for whom a message was left (if no contact was made). Furthermore, an applicant must, by phone, fax, e-mail, or mail transmitted with adequate lead time, advise all parties who have not consented that an application will be made, and the affidavit or affirmation must provide specifics on this as well. Applications for adjournments that are not properly supported will not be entertained. Rather, the matter will be adjourned for three (3) days to permit compliance. These matters will then appear on the APB Calendar. If there is no compliance, the Clerk of the General Clerk's Office will mark the case submitted and refer it to the assigned Justice. NY R NY CTY Procedure II(C).

xiii. *ONONDAGA COUNTY: Adjournments on motions in general.* For information regarding requests for adjournments, please see the assigned Justice's individual e-filing rules on the Fifth Judicial District website. NY R ONDGA E FIL Protocol(B)(9)(g).

xiv. *QUEENS COUNTY: Adjournments not available from motion support office.* The Motion Support Office is NOT authorized to grant adjournments. NY R L QUEENS MOT SUP Doc. 1.

f. *Continuance during trial.* At any time during the trial, the court, on motion of any party, may order a continuance in the interest of justice on such terms as may be just. NY CPLR Rule 4402.

g. *Extending time to file motion for summary judgment.* Refer to the New York KeyRules Motion for Summary Judgment document for information on special considerations when extending time to file a motion for summary judgment.

h. *ALBANY COUNTY: Adjournment of trial date.* Applications for adjournment of a scheduled trial date shall be addressed to the IAS Justice until the commencement of the trial term for which the case has been set down for trial. Once a trial term has commenced, applications for adjournment of the trial of a case, scheduled to be tried during that trial term, shall be addressed to the Part I Trial Justice only. NY R 3 JD SUP Doc. 1(H)(1).

i. *BRONX COUNTY: Extending NOI due date.* Stipulations to extend NOI due dates will not be considered by the court. NY R BRONX DCM Doc. 1.

j. *KINGS COUNTY: No adjournment of compliance conference.* There will be no adjournments of a scheduled compliance conference except in special circumstances. NY R L KINGS Pt. E, Rule 3.

k. *KINGS COUNTY: Adjournment of preliminary conference only on good cause.* PC Conference is not to be adjourned, even on consent, unless good cause is shown for the adjournment. Mere failure to serve B/P is insufficient reason to adjourn PC Conference. A PC Order will be entered on default of any non appearing party. NY R L KINGS Rule I(A)(1).

l. *NEW YORK COUNTY: Adjournment of preliminary conference.* Conferences may be adjourned where permitted by the assigned Justice. NY R NY CTY Procedure V. Except as otherwise provided in NY R NY CTY J RUL Doc. 1 or in NY R NY CTY J RUL Rule 26, adjournment of conferences will be allowed only as follows. The parties may adjourn any preliminary conference once for no more than twenty-one (21) days, but only by submission of a written stipulation to the Part Clerk on or before the scheduled date thereof. Appearance by counsel is not required. Further adjournment of preliminary conferences and adjournments of compliance and pretrial conferences will be allowed only with permission of the court for good cause. NY R NY CTY J RUL Rule 6.

m. *NEW YORK COUNTY: Extending NOI due date.* If an attorney wishes to file a note of issue when a deadline for the filing thereof, such as one set forth in a preliminary conference order, has passed, the clerk's office will seek authorization from the assigned Justice to accept it; the court can authorize a late filing by endorsement on the note (a notation of "OK to file by" with a signature by the Justice will suffice); or the parties may seek an extension from the court by presenting a stipulation for "so ordering." In light of Differentiated Case Management deadlines, counsel should not assume that extensions, even by stipulation, can be had without good cause. NY R NY CTY Procedure VIII(A).

n. *NEW YORK COUNTY: Extensions of deadlines in preliminary order.* Unless otherwise provided in NY R NY CTY J RUL Doc. 1 or in the order, no extensions of deadlines set forth in a preliminary conference, compliance conference or other discovery order shall be allowed except with permission of the court for good cause shown. NY R NY CTY J RUL Rule 8.

3. *Oppositions.* In the absence of statutory provision or court rule, a motion ordinarily does not require a written answer, although an adverse party may be permitted to file an answer in opposition to the showing made in the motion or its supporting affidavits. AMJUR MOTIONS § 26. When a party files a motion and the opposing party fails to respond, the court may construe such failure to respond as non-opposition to the motion or an admission that the motion was meritorious, may take the facts alleged in the motion as true, and may grant the motion if the relief requested appears to be justified. However, the severity of such a result demands that a court impose it only with great caution. AMJUR MOTIONS § 28.

4. *Governing law.* The civil practice law and rules (NY CPLR § 101, et seq.) shall govern the procedure in civil judicial proceedings in all courts of the state and before all judges, except where the procedure is regulated by inconsistent statute. The civil practice law and rules shall succeed the civil practice act and rules of civil practice and shall be deemed substituted therefor throughout the statutes and rules of the state. NY CPLR § 101. The civil practice law and rules shall be liberally construed to secure the just, speedy and inexpensive determination of every civil judicial proceeding. NY CPLR § 104.

a. *Uniform trial court rules.* The uniform civil rules for the Supreme Court and County Court (NY R UNIF TRIAL CTS § 202.1, et seq.) shall be applicable to civil actions and proceedings in the Supreme Court and the County Court. NY R UNIF TRIAL CTS § 202.1(a). The provisions of the uniform rules shall be construed consistent with the Civil Practice Law and Rules (CPLR), and matters not covered by the uniform rules shall be governed by the CPLR. NY R UNIF TRIAL CTS § 202.1(d).

b. *Local rules.* Local court rules, not inconsistent with law or with uniform civil rules for the Supreme Court and County Court (NY R UNIF TRIAL CTS § 202.1, et seq.), shall comply with Part 9 of the Rules of the Chief Judge (NY R CHIEF J § 9.1). NY R UNIF TRIAL CTS § 202.1(c).

c. *Official forms.* The state administrator shall have the power to adopt, amend and rescind an appendix of forms. Forms adopted pursuant to NY CPLR § 107 shall be sufficient under the civil practice law and rules and shall illustrate the simplicity and brevity of statement which the civil practice law and rules contemplate. NY CPLR § 107.

5. *Rules of the commercial division.* [Editor's note: certain types of civil cases or civil cases meeting certain monetary thresholds that are filed in the state of New York must be filed in the Commercial Division of the New York Supreme

Courts. Rules governing practice in the commercial division are found in NY R UNIF TRIAL CTS § 202.70]. Cases which must be filed in the commercial division are listed below. For more information, refer to NY R UNIF TRIAL CTS § 202.70.

a. *Monetary thresholds.* Except as set forth in NY R UNIF TRIAL CTS § 202.70(b), the monetary thresholds of the Commercial Division, exclusive of punitive damages, interests, costs, disbursements and counsel fees claimed, are established as follows: (1) Albany County, fifty thousand dollars ($50,000); (2) Eighth Judicial District, one hundred thousand dollars ($100,000); (3) Kings County, one hundred fifty thousand dollars ($150,000); (4) Nassau County, two hundred thousand dollars ($200,000); (5) New York County, five hundred thousand dollars ($500,000); (6) Onondaga County, fifty thousand dollars ($50,000); (7) Queens County, one hundred thousand dollars ($100,000); (8) Seventh Judicial District, fifty thousand dollars ($50,000); (9) Suffolk County, one hundred thousand dollars ($100,000); and (10) Westchester County, one hundred thousand dollars ($100,000). NY R UNIF TRIAL CTS § 202.70(a).

   i. *ALBANY COUNTY.* The Commercial Division of the Albany County Supreme Court exercises jurisdiction over selected business and commercial disputes in which the amount at issue generally involves damage claims in a minimum amount of fifty thousand dollars ($50,000) as well as claims for unspecified amounts where the value of the commercial asset(s) in dispute exceeds fifty thousand dollars ($50,000). A separate publication promulgating the rules and criteria relating to the filing and management of Commercial Court cases in this part may be obtained from the Albany County Supreme Court Clerk's Office. A section of the Uniform Civil Rules for the Supreme Court and County Court sets forth statewide rules. NY R 3 JD SUP Doc. 1(E).

   ii. *BRONX COUNTY.* The monetary threshold for commercial cases in Bronx County will be seventy-five thousand dollars ($75,000). All other parameters including the type of matters that will be heard are contained within the Rules of the Commercial Division of the Supreme Court (NY R UNIF TRIAL CTS § 202.70). NY R BRONX FIL R Doc. 12.

   iii. *NEW YORK COUNTY.* The monetary threshold in the New York County Commercial Division, which is generally applicable, is an amount in controversy of five hundred thousand dollars ($500,000) or more (exclusive of punitive damages, interest, costs, disbursements, and counsel fees). If the case is designated a commercial one and the Addendum is submitted, the clerk will review the pleadings to determine whether the amount in controversy in the case meets the monetary threshold or whether an exception to the threshold applies. NY R NY CTY Procedure IA(B). For more information on assigning a case to the commercial division in New York County, refer to NY R NY CTY Procedure IA(B).

b. *Commercial cases.* Actions in which the principal claims involve or consist of the following will be heard in the Commercial Division provided that the monetary threshold is met or equitable or declaratory relief is sought:

   i. Breach of contract or fiduciary duty, fraud, misrepresentation, business tort (e.g., unfair competition), or statutory and/or common law violation where the breach or violation is alleged to arise out of business dealings (e.g., sales of assets or securities; corporate restructuring; partnership, shareholder, joint venture, and other business agreements; trade secrets; restrictive covenants; and employment agreements not including claims that principally involve alleged discriminatory practices);

   ii. Transactions governed by the Uniform Commercial Code (exclusive of those concerning individual cooperative or condominium units);

   iii. Transactions involving commercial real property, including Yellowstone injunctions and excluding actions for the payment of rent only;

   iv. Shareholder derivative actions—without consideration of the monetary threshold;

   v. Commercial class actions—without consideration of the monetary threshold;

   vi. Business transactions involving or arising out of dealings with commercial banks and other financial institutions;

   vii. Internal affairs of business organizations;

   viii. Malpractice by accountants or actuaries, and legal malpractice arising out of representation in commercial matters;

   ix. Environmental insurance coverage;

   x. Commercial insurance coverage (e.g., directors and officers, errors and omissions, and business interruption coverage);

   xi. Dissolution of corporations, partnerships, limited liability companies, limited liability partnerships and joint ventures—without consideration of the monetary threshold; and

xii. Applications to stay or compel arbitration and affirm or disaffirm arbitration awards and related injunctive relief pursuant to Article 75 of the New York Civil Practice Law and Rules (NY CPLR § 7501, et seq.) involving any of the foregoing enumerated commercial issues. Where the applicable arbitration agreement provides for the arbitration to be heard outside the United States, the monetary threshold set forth in NY R UNIF TRIAL CTS § 202.70(a) shall not apply. NY R UNIF TRIAL CTS § 202.70(b).

c. *Non-commercial cases.* The following will not be heard in the Commercial Division even if the monetary threshold is met:

i. Suits to collect professional fees;

ii. Cases seeking a declaratory judgment as to insurance coverage for personal injury or property damage;

iii. Residential real estate disputes, including landlord-tenant matters, and commercial real estate disputes involving the payment of rent only;

iv. Home improvement contracts involving residential properties consisting of one to four residential units or individual units in any residential building, including cooperative or condominium units;

v. Proceedings to enforce a judgment regardless of the nature of the underlying case;

vi. First-party insurance claims and actions by insurers to collect premiums or rescind non-commercial policies; and

vii. Attorney malpractice actions except as otherwise provided in NY R UNIF TRIAL CTS § 202.70(b)(8). NY R UNIF TRIAL CTS § 202.70(c).

d. For more information on the Commercial Division, refer to NY R UNIF TRIAL CTS § 202.70.

D. Documents

1. *Documents for moving party*

a. *Required documents*

i. *Notice of motion, order to show cause, or affidavit on ex parte motion.* The notice of motion shall be substantially in the form found in NY R UNIF TRIAL CTS § 202.7(b). NY R UNIF TRIAL CTS § 202.7(b). The supporting papers should be referred to in the notice of motion. SIEGEL-NYPRAC § 246. The court in a proper case may grant an order to show cause, to be served in lieu of a notice of motion. NY CPLR Rule 2214(d). An ex parte motion shall be accompanied by an affidavit stating the result of any prior motion for similar relief and specifying the new facts, if any, that were not previously shown. NY CPLR Rule 2217(b).

- *Request for oral argument.* A party requesting oral argument shall set forth such request in its notice of motion or in its order to show cause or on the first page of the answering papers, as the case may be. Where all parties to a motion request oral argument, oral argument shall be granted unless the court shall determine it to be unnecessary. Where a motion is brought on by order to show cause, the court may set forth in the order that oral argument is required on the return date of the motion. NY R UNIF TRIAL CTS § 202.8(d).

ii. *Motion.* Refer to the General Requirements section of this document for information on the notice of motion and motion.

iii. *Request for judicial intervention.* At any time after service of process, a party may file a request for judicial intervention. Except as provided in NY R UNIF TRIAL CTS § 202.6(b), in an action not yet assigned to a judge, the court shall not accept for filing a notice of motion, order to show cause, or application for ex parte order, unless such notice or application is accompanied by a request for judicial intervention. NY R UNIF TRIAL CTS § 202.6(a).

- *BRONX COUNTY.* Generally, the Request For Judicial Intervention, commonly referred to as an "RJI", is required to be filed in any action where the assignment of a Justice is required. The RJI sets forth the information which is entered into the court system's database. It must be completely and accurately filled out. The full caption, as stated on the Summons, must be set forth. Use of terms "et al." and "etc." are not permitted. Only one (1) RJI may be filed in each action. Either a self represented litigant or an attorney must sign the affirmation at the end of the form. Once completed, the RJI must be filed in duplicate. Except in the case of an ex-parte application, the RJI must also be served together with the accompanying application upon all parties. Proof of accuracy of the index number must accompany the RJI. Check the Fee Schedule[. . .]for any applicable filing fees. NY R BRONX FIL R Doc. 2.
- *KINGS COUNTY.* An RJI with the relevant required addendum in a NYSCEF case shall be submitted via

NYSCEF. Once e-filed, the RJI and any accompanying document will be forwarded to the relevant support office for random assignment of the case and processing of the document. A filer or counsel need not appear (as to Proposed Orders to Show Cause, however, see below). A copy of the pleadings must be submitted only if the document has not previously been e-filed. If the RJI seeks intervention with regard to a document that is intended for review by a Justice, such as a motion, a working copy of the RJI must be submitted with the working copy of the motion and the NYSCEF Confirmation Notice. NY R L KINGS E FIL Doc. 1(C).

- *NEW YORK COUNTY.* To obtain the assignment of an IAS Justice to a case, a Request for Judicial Intervention (cost ninety-five dollars ($95)) must be filed, with NYSCEF in an e-filed case or in paper in an authorized hard-copy one. A no-fee RJI, which will generally result in the referral of an application to an Ex Parte Justice, is also required with regard to certain kinds of applications for which, prior to 2011, no RJI was required. NY R NY CTY Procedure I(C). A "fillable" form RJI is available on-line. The form must be filed in duplicate in hard-copy cases. NY R NY CTY Procedure IA(A)(1). The filer of an RJI must check off a box identifying the type of case at issue. Where the RJI seeks judicial assignment, this designation will bring about a random assignment of the case by computer to a Justice handling cases of that type. NY R NY CTY Procedure IA(A)(1). The RJI and any addendum can be completed and submitted electronically in an e-filed case. NY R NY CTY Procedure II(A). The RJI shall be marked to reflect the existence of any "related case" as explained on the "Commencement of Cases" page under "Case Processing" on the court's website. NY R NY CTY Procedure II(A); NY R NY CTY E FIL Doc. 2(C).
- *ONONDAGA COUNTY.* The RJI will be submitted via the NYSCEF system along with any required RJI addendum forms. When the RJI is filed and the fee paid online, the Onondaga County Clerk's Office will electronically forward the RJI and any accompanying documents to the Onondaga Supreme Court Clerk's Office for assignment and processing. Counsel will receive notification of judge assignment via the NYSCEF system. NY R ONDGA E FIL Protocol(B)(3).
- *QUEENS COUNTY.* A Request for Judicial Intervention ("RJI") in an E-filed case shall be submitted via the E-filing System. When the RJI is approved, filed and paid for on-line, it will be forwarded to the relevant back office for random assignment of the case and processing of the document. In the case of RJIs seeking assignment to the Commercial Division, the filer must submit therewith, a Commercial Addendum as required by the standards for assignment of cases to the Commercial Division. NY R L QUEENS E-FILE Doc. 1(F).

iv. *Proof of service.* In addition to complying with the provisions of NY CPLR Rule 2101, every paper filed in court shall have annexed thereto appropriate proof of service on all parties where required. NY R UNIF TRIAL CTS § 202.5(a).

- *QUEENS COUNTY.* With regard to service of a motion/petition on notice in an E-filed action, NY CPLR Rule 2214(b) and NY R UNIF TRIAL CTS § 202.5-b(f) applies. Where required, proof of service shall be filed on-line as a separate document. NY R L QUEENS E-FILE Doc. 1(H)(3).

v. *ALBANY COUNTY: Additional required documents*

- *Affirmation of good faith effort.* The parties must[. . .]submit an affirmation attesting to [their good faith effort to resolve the matter]. The affirmation of good faith effort to resolve the issues raised by the motion shall indicate the time, place and nature of the consultation and the issues discussed and any resolutions, or shall indicate good cause why no such conferral with counsel for opposing parties was held. An assigned justice or judge may dismiss a motion for failure to demonstrate that such effort was made with leave to renew the motion after such effort has been demonstrated. NY R 3 JD SUP Doc. 1(B).

b. *Supplemental documents*

i. *Supporting evidence; Exhibits.* The main supporting papers on a motion are affidavits, but any relevant exhibits, documents, depositions, etc., are also includible. SIEGEL-NYPRAC § 246.

- *Affidavits accompanying motion.* Affidavits shall be for a statement of the relevant facts. NY R UNIF TRIAL CTS § 202.8(c).
- *Foreign language documents.* Where an affidavit or exhibit annexed to a paper served or filed is in a foreign language, it shall be accompanied by an English translation and an affidavit by the translator stating his qualifications and that the translation is accurate. NY CPLR Rule 2101(b).
- *Statement of attorney in lieu of affidavit.* The statement of an attorney admitted to practice in the courts of the state, or of a physician, osteopath or dentist, authorized by law to practice in the state, who is not a party

to an action, when subscribed and affirmed by him to be true under the penalties of perjury, may be served or filed in the action in lieu of and with the same force and effect as an affidavit. NY CPLR Rule 2106.

- *NEW YORK COUNTY: Form of presented exhibits.* Exhibits should be tabbed and be legible; a typed version of any exhibit that is difficult to read should be submitted with the original. Exhibits printed on both sides of the page should be bound and tabbed on the side. NY R NY CTY J RUL Rule 14(a).
- *QUEENS COUNTY.* Attorneys submitting exhibits to the court on E-file cases shall make each exhibit a separate, labeled attachment to an affidavit/affirmation. NY R L QUEENS E-FILE Doc. 1(H)(4).

ii. *Brief.* Briefs shall be for a statement of the relevant law. NY R UNIF TRIAL CTS § 202.8(c).

iii. *Notice to produce papers not in possession of the court.* If a paper relied on by the movant is in the possession of the other side, it may be demanded of that side with a notice to produce it at the hearing. Where such papers are in the possession of an adverse party, they shall be produced by him at the hearing on notice served with the motion papers. NY CPLR Rule 2214(Practice Commentary, C2214:23).

iv. *Filing fees.* The County Clerk shall require the payment of any applicable statutory fees, or an order of the Court waiving payment of such fees, before accepting a paper for filing. NY R UNIF TRIAL CTS § 202.5(d)(1). For information on filing fees, if any, refer to NY CPLR § 8001, et seq.

- *ALBANY COUNTY.* In general, any filing subsequent to the commencement of an action which is designated as a motion or cross-motion requires the payment of a filing fee to the County Clerk's Office prior to submission to the Supreme Court Clerk's Office for referral to the assigned justice. The fee is assessed regardless of whether an application is made by notice of motion, order to show cause or ex parte. No fee will be charged upon the filing of a motion for poor person status in conjunction with an application which serves to commence an action or special proceeding. In the event a motion is received by the court unaccompanied by proof of payment to the County Clerk, the Supreme Court Clerk's Office will contact the submitting party to advise that the application will be held pending receipt of the filing fee only until the return date of the motion. If proof of payment is not submitted to the Supreme Court Clerk's Office by the return date (ex parte applications will be held ten (10) days), the papers will be returned by mail with a notification that the motion has been removed from the court's calendar and that it must be re-noticed and re-filed with the court along with the requisite filing fee. Inquiries concerning the applicability of the motion fee to a proposed filing may be directed to the Supreme Court Clerk's Office. NY R 3 JD SUP Doc. 1(B).
- *BRONX COUNTY.* In accordance with the new civil fee schedule set forth in Article 80 of the C.P.L.R. (NY CPLR § 8001, et seq.), effective July 14, 2003, all motions, and cross motions must be approved in Room 217 prior to payment of said fees in the County Clerk's Office, Room 118. NY R BRONX FIL R Doc. 8. The motion fee [must be] paid for via NYSCEF by credit/debit card. NY R BRONX E FIL R Doc. 1(1).
- *ERIE COUNTY.* Payment for fee-bearing NYSCEF documents must be made online via credit or debit card (American Express, MasterCard or Visa) at the time of submission. NY R ERIE E FIL Doc. 3(III)(E).
- *KINGS COUNTY.* The motion must be filed with NYSCEF and the motion fee paid. NY R L KINGS E FIL Doc. 1(D). Court fees in NYSCEF cases must be paid via NYSCEF by a credit or bank card (MasterCard, Visa, or American Express). Fees are no longer accepted in person in the Kings County Clerk's Office in NYSCEF cases. NY R L KINGS E FIL Doc. 1(B)(6).
- *NEW YORK COUNTY.* A motion fee must be paid on motions made in writing by notice of motion, order to show cause or ex parte after the commencement of an action. For this purpose, the term "action" shall mean any application to the court that requires the assignment of an index number, regardless of whether a formal pleading is filed. Applications or motions that commence an action and for which an index number fee must be paid require no motion fee. [A]ny motions made after the initial applications in these situations would require payment of the motion fee. A motion that is the initial application in a case commenced by the filing of a summons and complaint would require a motion fee since the filing of the summons and complaint rather than the application itself would require the purchase of an index number. NY R NY CTY Procedure II(A). In e-filed cases the motion fee must be paid when the documents are filed. Payment is made on-line by Visa, Mastercard, or American Express credit or bank card. NY R NY CTY Procedure II(A); NY R NY CTY E FIL Doc. 2(B)(5).
- *ONONDAGA COUNTY.* Court fees in e-filed cases must be paid online with the NYSCEF system using a credit card. The document is not considered to have been filed until payment of the fee has been tendered. NY R ONDGA E FIL Protocol(B)(2). Fees must be paid on all cross motions. NY R ONDGA E FIL Protocol(B)(9)(e).

- *QUEENS COUNTY.* The Motion Support Office does not receive, forward or process any fees or waiver of fees. All applications requiring payment of statutory fees or waiver of fees must be sent directly to the Queens County Clerk's office. NY R L QUEENS MOT SUP Doc. 1. Court fees (e.g., RJI fee, motion fee) in E-filed cases may be paid for on-line using a credit card. Papers may also be filed with the E-file system and the fee may be paid at the County Clerk's Office. In the latter case, the paper is not considered to have been filed until payment of the fee has been tendered. NY R L QUEENS E-FILE Doc. 1(E)(1). The motion/petition shall be filed on-line and the fee paid for either on-line by credit card or by the "Pay at the County Clerk's Office" option. NY R L QUEENS E-FILE Doc. 1(H)(1).

v. *Working copies.* The court may require the parties to provide working copies of documents filed electronically. In such event, each working copy shall include, firmly affixed thereto, a copy of a confirmation notice in a form prescribed by the Chief Administrator. NY R UNIF TRIAL CTS § 202.5-b(d)(5).

- *BRONX COUNTY.* After papers on motions have been e-filed, working copies thereof, with Confirmation Notice firmly attached as the back page facing out, must be submitted. (Each document or group of documents that is separately bound shall bear a Confirmation Notice.) Working copies lacking the Notice will not be accepted. WORKING COPIES OF MOTION PAPERS MUST BE SUBMITTED NO LATER THAN 4:45 P.M. ON THE RETURN DATE IN THE MOTION SUPPORT OFFICE (ROOM 217) AS EXPLAINED in NY R BRONX E FIL R Doc. 1(4). If an attorney has failed to submit required working copies on or before the return date, the motion will be transmitted as is to the Justice for such action as the Justice finds appropriate. Attorneys may submit working copies on motions by mail or overnight delivery. Any such submission shall be sent in a timely manner to the Motion Support Office (Room 217) and be conspicuously marked on the outside "NYSCEF Matter"; lack of such marking may delay processing. NY R BRONX E FIL R Doc. 1(4)(a).
- *ERIE COUNTY.* Electronically filed documents subject to review and processing by the Part Clerk do not require a working copy unless otherwise directed or provided for in IAS Part Rules. NY R UNIF TRIAL CTS § 202.5-b(d)(4), any working copy submitted shall include, as a cover page firmly fastened thereto, a copy of the Confirmation Notice generated by the NYSCEF site at the time of filing. Please consult the individual Justice's Part Rules and/or consult with the Judge's chambers to determine whether and how working copies are to be provided. Working copies will not be printed or delivered by the Erie County Clerk or the Chief Clerk of the Courts or any of their personnel to chambers. The official record of a document in an electronically filed case is the document filed via the NYSCEF system. Working copies are intended only for use by the Justice. The Court will discard all working copies after the Justice has finished with them. Thus, in the event that counsel fails to file a document via the NYSCEF system, the document will not be part of the court record. NY R ERIE E FIL Doc. 3(III)(O); NY R ERIE E FIL Doc. 3(V)(E).
- *KINGS COUNTY.* No courtesy copies of motion papers are required by the Court, except as may be required for electronic filing or by the Judge's Part Rules. In tort cases against the City of New York, courtesy copies shall be supplied to the Corporation Counsel's office in Brooklyn. NY R L KINGS Pt. C, Rule 5. Unless otherwise directed by the Court or as described herein, and with the exceptions listed below, in all NYSCEF cases in which an RJI has been filed, working copies of e-filed documents that are intended for judicial review must be submitted to the court. Working copies are not required of documents that are only processed by a support office (e.g. preliminary conference request, note of issue). Working copies shall include exhibit tabs and backs; for motion papers, the motion sequence number and the return date and part. The confirmation notice with the motion sequence number on it should be the back page of the motion facing out. In addition, the filer of a working copy must firmly bind thereto, with the back page facing out, a copy of the Confirmation Notice that was generated by NYSCEF when that document was efiled. Working copies that are submitted without the related Confirmation Notice will not be accepted. NY R L KINGS E FIL Doc. 1(B)(7); NY R L KINGS E FIL Doc. 1(D). WORKING COPIES OF MOTION PAPERS MUST BE SUBMITTED IN THE MOTION SUPPORT OFFICE (ROOM 227) AS EXPLAINED HEREIN. THEY MUST NOT BE DELIVERED TO THE PART OR CHAMBERS, EXCEPT WHERE THE INDIVIDUAL JUSTICE'S PART RULES PROVIDE OTHERWISE; DOING SO WILL CAUSE ADMINISTRATIVE CONFUSION AND POSSIBLE MISPLACEMENT OF PAPERS. Any such submission shall be sent in a timely manner (kindly review individual Justice's rules) and be conspicuously marked on the outside "NYSCEF Matter;" lack of such marking may delay processing. NY R L KINGS E FIL Doc. 1(D).
- *NEW YORK COUNTY.* Some Justices require that working copies of e-filed motion papers be submitted. See the E-filing Protocol for information on the many Parts that do not require working copies. Where

required, working copies of the moving documents and all other documents on the motion or application shall be submitted to the Motion Submission Part Courtroom (Room 130) on, but not before, the final return date. A Confirmation Notice from the NYSCEF system, which is generated when a document is e-filed, shall be firmly affixed, as the back page facing out, to each separate working copy or group of such copies. NY R NY CTY Procedure II(A) NY R NY CTY E FIL Doc. 2(B)(5)(a); NY R NY CTY J RUL Rule 14(a). For more information on working copies, including which parts don't require them, refer to NY R NY CTY E FIL Doc. 2(B)(6).

- *ONONDAGA COUNTY.* Any courtesy "working" copies, if required (see NY R ONDGA E FIL Protocol(B)(7)), must be provided directly to the assigned justice. NY R ONDGA E FIL Protocol(B)(9)(e). For information as to whether or not an Onondaga Supreme Court Justice requires working (courtesy) copies of e-filed documents, please consult the Onondaga County Individual E-filing Rules. NY R ONDGA E FIL Protocol(B)(7)(a). The Supreme Court Clerk's Office and the Onondaga County Clerk's Office will NOT accept the working copies. Working copies must be sent directly to the assigned justice's chambers. NY R ONDGA E FIL Protocol(B)(7)(b). A copy of the Confirmation Notice, generated by the NYSCEF system at the time a document is e-filed, must be attached to every working copy provided to chambers. If the Confirmation Notice is missing, the copy will not be accepted. NY R ONDGA E FIL Protocol(B)(7)(c). Courtesy copies do not become part of the official court record as maintained by the Onondaga County Clerk's Office and will be destroyed by chambers at the disposition of the case. In the event that counsel fails to file a document via NYSCEF, the document will not be part of the court record. NY R ONDGA E FIL Protocol(B)(7)(d).
- *QUEENS COUNTY.* Working copies of E-Filed notices of motion/notices of petition are NOT to be sent to the Motion Support Office. They must be brought to the calendar call in the judge's part. NY R L QUEENS MOT SUP Doc. 1. Unless otherwise directed or authorized by the court, counsel should file papers with the E-file system first and thereafter deliver a working copy to at the calendar call of the Centralized Motion Part or Assigned Justice in accordance with individual Part Rules. NY R L QUEENS E-FILE Doc. 1(E)(4). On the return date of a motion that has been E-filed, the movant must provide the Centralized Motion Part (CMP) with a working copy of the entire motion including the notice of motion with sequence number and all of the attached exhibits. The motion must have the confirmation of filing firmly affixed to the back of the papers (facing outward). The confirmation of filing is a separate notice from the payment notice and will say confirmation clearly across the top of the page. NY R L QUEENS E-FILE Doc. 1(H)(2)(a). The motion or Order to Show Cause must have clearly written across its face the words "Working Copy," it must also have the assigned Judge's name, motion sequence number and calendar number—which may be obtained from the posted calendar outside courtroom on the return date of the motion. A confirmation of filing must attached thereto. Working copies of e-filed Orders to Show Cause must contain a copy of the signed order and all supporting papers. NY R L QUEENS E-FILE Doc. 1(H)(2)(c). The Confirmation Notice must be an updated version that indicates the sequence number of the motion being submitted at the CMP calendar call. WORKING COPIES WITHOUT A CONFIRMATION NOTICE WILL NOT BE ACCEPTED. NY R L QUEENS E-FILE Doc. 1(H)(7).

vi. *ERIE COUNTY: Additional supplemental documents*

- *Notice of hard copy submission in e-filed case.* In accordance with NY R UNIF TRIAL CTS § 202.5-b(d), the County Clerk shall refuse to accept for filing, hard copy papers filed to an action subject to electronic filing unless hard copy filing is permitted by the Uniform Rules or NY R ERIE E FIL Doc. 3 and the papers bear a completed Notice of Hard Copy Submission—E-Filed Case form. NY R ERIE E FIL Doc. 3(III)(D).

vii. *KINGS COUNTY: Additional supplemental documents*

- *Forms when filing in hard copy.* An attorney who certifies in good faith that he or she lacks the equipment or knowledge needed to e-file and have no staff member or employee under his or her direction who has such knowledge and equipment may opt out of participation in e-filing in a mandatory case by filing a "Notice of Opt-Out from Participation in Action Subject to Mandatory Electronic Filing" form EFM-2 with the Clerk. NY R L KINGS E FIL Doc. 1(A)(2). Where in accordance with the E-Filing Rules a party submits a document in hard copy in an e-filed case (principally, a document submitted by a nonparticipating party (e.g., an attorney) in a consensual case, an emergency filing made in accordance with the Mandatory E-Filing Rules, and any document filed with the court in hard copy by an attorney who has opted out of participation in mandatory e-filing, the document must bear the back page facing out, a "Notice of Hard Copy Submission—E-Filed Cases" form EFM-3. NY R L KINGS E FIL Doc. 1(B)(3).

viii. *NEW YORK COUNTY: Additional supplemental documents*

- *Notice of hard copy submission.* Where in accordance with the E-Filing Rules an attorney or an unrepresented litigant who is participating in e-filing submits a document in hard copy in an e-filed case, the document must bear, as the back page facing out, a Notice of Hard-Copy Submission—E-Filed Case (a form available in the "Forms" section on the NYSCEF website (Form EFM-3) and in the court's back offices). NY R NY CTY E FIL Doc. 2(B)(3). For more information refer to NY R NY CTY E FIL Doc. 2.
- *Unpublished decisions.* Whenever reliance is placed upon a decision or other authority not officially published or readily available to the New York County Supreme Court, a copy of the case or of pertinent portions of the authority shall be submitted with the motion papers. NY R NY CTY J RUL Rule 14(a).

ix. *ONONDAGA COUNTY: Additional supplemental documents*

- *Notice of hard copy submission.* Any papers to be filed with the court in an e-filed case must be filed online with the E-filing system except where a special exemption is granted (e.g., oversized maps, photographs). If such an exemption is granted, Form EFM-3, "Notice of Hard Copy Submission—E-Filed Case," must be attached to such documents forms which are not filed on line. Also, Form EFM-4 "Notice of Hard Copy Exhibit Filing" must be completed and uploaded to the action's e-file. Both of these forms may be found on the NYSCEF website. NY R ONDGA E FIL Protocol(B)(4).

x. *QUEENS COUNTY: Additional supplemental documents*

- *Notice of hard copy submission.* Any party opting out of the e-filing system must have a "Notice of Hard Copy Submission" firmly affixed to the back of the papers. NY R L QUEENS E-FILE Doc. 1(H)(2)(f).

2. *Documents for opposing party*

a. *Required documents*

i. *Opposition.* Refer to the General Requirements section of this document for information on the opposition.

- *Request for oral argument.* A party requesting oral argument shall set forth such request in its notice of motion or in its order to show cause or on the first page of the answering papers, as the case may be. Where all parties to a motion request oral argument, oral argument shall be granted unless the court shall determine it to be unnecessary. Where a motion is brought on by order to show cause, the court may set forth in the order that oral argument is required on the return date of the motion. NY R UNIF TRIAL CTS § 202.8(d).
- *QUEENS COUNTY: E-filing opposition papers.* E-filed opposition papers and/or reply papers must also be provided to the Centralized Motion Part in the same manner as the moving papers with the confirmation of filing firmly attached to the back of the papers. NY R L QUEENS E-FILE Doc. 1(H)(2)(d).

ii. *Proof of service.* In addition to complying with the provisions of NY CPLR Rule 2101, every paper filed in court shall have annexed thereto appropriate proof of service on all parties where required. NY R UNIF TRIAL CTS § 202.5(a).

b. *Supplemental documents*

i. *Supporting evidence; Exhibits.* The main supporting papers on a motion are affidavits, but any relevant exhibits, documents, depositions, etc., are also includible. SIEGEL-NYPRAC § 246.

- *Affidavits accompanying opposition.* Affidavits shall be for a statement of the relevant facts. NY R UNIF TRIAL CTS § 202.8(c).
- *Foreign language documents.* Where an affidavit or exhibit annexed to a paper served or filed is in a foreign language, it shall be accompanied by an English translation and an affidavit by the translator stating his qualifications and that the translation is accurate. NY CPLR Rule 2101(b).
- *Statement of attorney in lieu of affidavit.* The statement of an attorney admitted to practice in the courts of the state, or of a physician, osteopath or dentist, authorized by law to practice in the state, who is not a party to an action, when subscribed and affirmed by him to be true under the penalties of perjury, may be served or filed in the action in lieu of and with the same force and effect as an affidavit. NY CPLR Rule 2106.
- *NEW YORK COUNTY: Form of presented exhibits.* Exhibits should be tabbed and be legible; a typed version of any exhibit that is difficult to read should be submitted with the original. Exhibits printed on both sides of the page should be bound and tabbed on the side. NY R NY CTY J RUL Rule 14(a).
- *QUEENS COUNTY.* Attorneys submitting exhibits to the court on E-file cases shall make each exhibit a separate, labeled attachment to an affidavit/affirmation. NY R L QUEENS E-FILE Doc. 1(H)(4).

ii. *Brief.* Briefs shall be for a statement of the relevant law. NY R UNIF TRIAL CTS § 202.8(c).

iii. *Filing fees.* The County Clerk shall require the payment of any applicable statutory fees, or an order of the Court waiving payment of such fees, before accepting a paper for filing. NY R UNIF TRIAL CTS § 202.5(d)(1). For information on filing fees, if any, refer to NY CPLR § 8001, et seq.

- *ALBANY COUNTY.* In general, any filing subsequent to the commencement of an action which is designated as a motion or cross-motion requires the payment of a filing fee to the County Clerk's Office prior to submission to the Supreme Court Clerk's Office for referral to the assigned justice. The fee is assessed regardless of whether an application is made by notice of motion, order to show cause or ex parte. No fee will be charged upon the filing of a motion for poor person status in conjunction with an application which serves to commence an action or special proceeding. In the event a motion is received by the court unaccompanied by proof of payment to the County Clerk, the Supreme Court Clerk's Office will contact the submitting party to advise that the application will be held pending receipt of the filing fee only until the return date of the motion. If proof of payment is not submitted to the Supreme Court Clerk's Office by the return date (ex parte applications will be held ten (10) days), the papers will be returned by mail with a notification that the motion has been removed from the court's calendar and that it must be re-noticed and re-filed with the court along with the requisite filing fee. Inquiries concerning the applicability of the motion fee to a proposed filing may be directed to the Supreme Court Clerk's Office. NY R 3 JD SUP Doc. 1(B).
- *BRONX COUNTY.* In accordance with the new civil fee schedule set forth in Article 80 of the C.P.L.R. (NY CPLR § 8001, et seq.), effective July 14, 2003, all motions, and cross motions must be approved in Room 217 prior to payment of said fees in the County Clerk's Office, Room 118. NY R BRONX FIL R Doc. 8. The motion fee [must be] paid for via NYSCEF by credit/debit card. NY R BRONX E FIL R Doc. 1(1).
- *ERIE COUNTY.* Payment for fee-bearing NYSCEF documents must be made online via credit or debit card (American Express, MasterCard or Visa) at the time of submission. NY R ERIE E FIL Doc. 3(III)(E).
- *KINGS COUNTY.* The motion must be filed with NYSCEF and the motion fee paid. NY R L KINGS E FIL Doc. 1(D). Court fees in NYSCEF cases must be paid via NYSCEF by a credit or bank card (MasterCard, Visa, or American Express). Fees are no longer accepted in person in the Kings County Clerk's Office in NYSCEF cases. NY R L KINGS E FIL Doc. 1(B)(6).
- *NEW YORK COUNTY.* A motion fee must be paid on motions made in writing by notice of motion, order to show cause or ex parte after the commencement of an action. For this purpose, the term "action" shall mean any application to the court that requires the assignment of an index number, regardless of whether a formal pleading is filed. Applications or motions that commence an action and for which an index number fee must be paid require no motion fee. [A]ny motions made after the initial applications in these situations would require payment of the motion fee. A motion that is the initial application in a case commenced by the filing of a summons and complaint would require a motion fee since the filing of the summons and complaint rather than the application itself would require the purchase of an index number. NY R NY CTY Procedure II(A). In e-filed cases the motion fee must be paid when the documents are filed. Payment is made on-line by Visa, Mastercard, or American Express credit or bank card. NY R NY CTY Procedure II(A); NY R NY CTY E FIL Doc. 2(B)(5).
- *ONONDAGA COUNTY.* Court fees in e-filed cases must be paid online with the NYSCEF system using a credit card. The document is not considered to have been filed until payment of the fee has been tendered. NY R ONDGA E FIL Protocol(B)(2). Fees must be paid on all cross motions. NY R ONDGA E FIL Protocol(B)(9)(e).
- *QUEENS COUNTY.* The Motion Support Office does not receive, forward or process any fees or waiver of fees. All applications requiring payment of statutory fees or waiver of fees must be sent directly to the Queens County Clerk's office. NY R L QUEENS MOT SUP Doc. 1. Court fees (e.g., RJI fee, motion fee) in E-filed cases may be paid for on-line using a credit card. Papers may also be filed with the E-file system and the fee may be paid at the County Clerk's Office. In the latter case, the paper is not considered to have been filed until payment of the fee has been tendered. NY R L QUEENS E-FILE Doc. 1(E)(1). The motion/petition shall be filed on-line and the fee paid for either on-line by credit card or by the "Pay at the County Clerk's Office" option. NY R L QUEENS E-FILE Doc. 1(H)(1).

iv. *Working copies.* The court may require the parties to provide working copies of documents filed electronically. In such event, each working copy shall include, firmly affixed thereto, a copy of a confirmation notice in a form prescribed by the Chief Administrator. NY R UNIF TRIAL CTS § 202.5-b(d)(5).

- *BRONX COUNTY.* After papers on motions have been e-filed, working copies thereof, with Confirmation

Notice firmly attached as the back page facing out, must be submitted. (Each document or group of documents that is separately bound shall bear a Confirmation Notice.) Working copies lacking the Notice will not be accepted. WORKING COPIES OF MOTION PAPERS MUST BE SUBMITTED NO LATER THAN 4:45 P.M. ON THE RETURN DATE IN THE MOTION SUPPORT OFFICE (ROOM 217) AS EXPLAINED in NY R BRONX E FIL R Doc. 1(4). If an attorney has failed to submit required working copies on or before the return date, the motion will be transmitted as is to the Justice for such action as the Justice finds appropriate. Attorneys may submit working copies on motions by mail or overnight delivery. Any such submission shall be sent in a timely manner to the Motion Support Office (Room 217) and be conspicuously marked on the outside "NYSCEF Matter"; lack of such marking may delay processing. NY R BRONX E FIL R Doc. 1(4)(a).

- *ERIE COUNTY.* Electronically filed documents subject to review and processing by the Part Clerk do not require a working copy unless otherwise directed or provided for in IAS Part Rules. NY R UNIF TRIAL CTS § 202.5-b(d)(4), any working copy submitted shall include, as a cover page firmly fastened thereto, a copy of the Confirmation Notice generated by the NYSCEF site at the time of filing. Please consult the individual Justice's Part Rules and/or consult with the Judge's chambers to determine whether and how working copies are to be provided. Working copies will not be printed or delivered by the Erie County Clerk or the Chief Clerk of the Courts or any of their personnel to chambers. The official record of a document in an electronically filed case is the document filed via the NYSCEF system. Working copies are intended only for use by the Justice. The Court will discard all working copies after the Justice has finished with them. Thus, in the event that counsel fails to file a document via the NYSCEF system, the document will not be part of the court record. NY R ERIE E FIL Doc. 3(III)(O); NY R ERIE E FIL Doc. 3(V)(E).
- *KINGS COUNTY.* No courtesy copies of motion papers are required by the Court, except as may be required for electronic filing or by the Judge's Part Rules. In tort cases against the City of New York, courtesy copies shall be supplied to the Corporation Counsel's office in Brooklyn. NY R L KINGS Pt. C, Rule 5. Unless otherwise directed by the Court or as described herein, and with the exceptions listed below, in all NYSCEF cases in which an RJI has been filed, working copies of e-filed documents that are intended for judicial review must be submitted to the court. Working copies are not required of documents that are only processed by a support office (e.g. preliminary conference request, note of issue). Working copies shall include exhibit tabs and backs; for motion papers, the motion sequence number and the return date and part. The confirmation notice with the motion sequence number on it should be the back page of the motion facing out. In addition, the filer of a working copy must firmly bind thereto, with the back page facing out, a copy of the Confirmation Notice that was generated by NYSCEF when that document was efiled. Working copies that are submitted without the related Confirmation Notice will not be accepted. NY R L KINGS E FIL Doc. 1(B)(7); NY R L KINGS E FIL Doc. 1(D). WORKING COPIES OF MOTION PAPERS MUST BE SUBMITTED IN THE MOTION SUPPORT OFFICE (ROOM 227) AS EXPLAINED HEREIN. THEY MUST NOT BE DELIVERED TO THE PART OR CHAMBERS, EXCEPT WHERE THE INDIVIDUAL JUSTICE'S PART RULES PROVIDE OTHERWISE; DOING SO WILL CAUSE ADMINISTRATIVE CONFUSION AND POSSIBLE MISPLACEMENT OF PAPERS. Any such submission shall be sent in a timely manner (kindly review individual Justice's rules) and be conspicuously marked on the outside "NYSCEF Matter;" lack of such marking may delay processing. NY R L KINGS E FIL Doc. 1(D).
- *NEW YORK COUNTY.* Some Justices require that working copies of e-filed motion papers be submitted. See the E-filing Protocol for information on the many Parts that do not require working copies. Where required, working copies of the moving documents and all other documents on the motion or application shall be submitted to the Motion Submission Part Courtroom (Room 130) on, but not before, the final return date. A Confirmation Notice from the NYSCEF system, which is generated when a document is e-filed, shall be firmly affixed, as the back page facing out, to each separate working copy or group of such copies. NY R NY CTY Procedure II(A) NY R NY CTY E FIL Doc. 2(B)(5)(a); NY R NY CTY J RUL Rule 14(a). For more information on working copies, including which parts don't require them, refer to NY R NY CTY E FIL Doc. 2(B)(6).
- *ONONDAGA COUNTY.* Any courtesy "working" copies, if required (see NY R ONDGA E FIL Protocol(B)(7)), must be provided directly to the assigned justice. NY R ONDGA E FIL Protocol(B)(9)(e). For information as to whether or not an Onondaga Supreme Court Justice requires working (courtesy) copies of e-filed documents, please consult the Onondaga County Individual E-filing Rules. NY R ONDGA E FIL Protocol(B)(7)(a). The Supreme Court Clerk's Office and the Onondaga County Clerk's Office will

NOT accept the working copies. Working copies must be sent directly to the assigned justice's chambers. NY R ONDGA E FIL Protocol(B)(7)(b). A copy of the Confirmation Notice, generated by the NYSCEF system at the time a document is e-filed, must be attached to every working copy provided to chambers. If the Confirmation Notice is missing, the copy will not be accepted. NY R ONDGA E FIL Protocol(B)(7)(c). Courtesy copies do not become part of the official court record as maintained by the Onondaga County Clerk's Office and will be destroyed by chambers at the disposition of the case. In the event that counsel fails to file a document via NYSCEF, the document will not be part of the court record. NY R ONDGA E FIL Protocol(B)(7)(d).

- *QUEENS COUNTY.* Working copies of E-Filed notices of motion/notices of petition are NOT to be sent to the Motion Support Office. They must be brought to the calendar call in the judge's part. NY R L QUEENS MOT SUP Doc. 1. Unless otherwise directed or authorized by the court, counsel should file papers with the E-file system first and thereafter deliver a working copy to at the calendar call of the Centralized Motion Part or Assigned Justice in accordance with individual Part Rules. NY R L QUEENS E-FILE Doc. 1(E)(4). On the return date of a motion that has been E-filed, the movant must provide the Centralized Motion Part (CMP) with a working copy of the entire motion including the notice of motion with sequence number and all of the attached exhibits. The motion must have the confirmation of filing firmly affixed to the back of the papers (facing outward). The confirmation of filing is a separate notice from the payment notice and will say confirmation clearly across the top of the page. NY R L QUEENS E-FILE Doc. 1(H)(2)(a). The motion or Order to Show Cause must have clearly written across its face the words "Working Copy," it must also have the assigned Judge's name, motion sequence number and calendar number—which may be obtained from the posted calendar outside courtroom on the return date of the motion. A confirmation of filing must attached thereto. Working copies of e-filed Orders to Show Cause must contain a copy of the signed order and all supporting papers. NY R L QUEENS E-FILE Doc. 1(H)(2)(c). The Confirmation Notice must be an updated version that indicates the sequence number of the motion being submitted at the CMP calendar call. WORKING COPIES WITHOUT A CONFIRMATION NOTICE WILL NOT BE ACCEPTED. NY R L QUEENS E-FILE Doc. 1(H)(7).

v. *ERIE COUNTY: Additional supplemental documents*

- *Notice of hard copy submission in e-filed case.* In accordance with NY R UNIF TRIAL CTS § 202.5-b(d), the County Clerk shall refuse to accept for filing, hard copy papers filed to an action subject to electronic filing unless hard copy filing is permitted by the Uniform Rules or NY R ERIE E FIL Doc. 3 and the papers bear a completed Notice of Hard Copy Submission—E-Filed Case form. NY R ERIE E FIL Doc. 3(III)(D).

vi. *KINGS COUNTY: Additional supplemental documents*

- *Forms when filing in hard copy.* An attorney who certifies in good faith that he or she lacks the equipment or knowledge needed to e-file and have no staff member or employee under his or her direction who has such knowledge and equipment may opt out of participation in e-filing in a mandatory case by filing a "Notice of Opt-Out from Participation in Action Subject to Mandatory Electronic Filing" form EFM-2 with the Clerk. NY R L KINGS E FIL Doc. 1(A)(2). Where in accordance with the E-Filing Rules a party submits a document in hard copy in an e-filed case (principally, a document submitted by a nonparticipating party (e.g., an attorney) in a consensual case, an emergency filing made in accordance with the Mandatory E-Filing Rules, and any document filed with the court in hard copy by an attorney who has opted out of participation in mandatory e-filing, the document must bear the back page facing out, a "Notice of Hard Copy Submission—E-Filed Cases" form EFM-3. NY R L KINGS E FIL Doc. 1(B)(3).

vii. *NEW YORK COUNTY: Additional supplemental documents*

- *Notice of hard copy submission.* Where in accordance with the E-Filing Rules an attorney or an unrepresented litigant who is participating in e-filing submits a document in hard copy in an e-filed case, the document must bear, as the back page facing out, a Notice of Hard-Copy Submission—E-Filed Case (a form available in the "Forms" section on the NYSCEF website (Form EFM-3) and in the court's back offices). NY R NY CTY E FIL Doc. 2(B)(3). For more information refer to NY R NY CTY E FIL Doc. 2.
- *Unpublished decisions.* Whenever reliance is placed upon a decision or other authority not officially published or readily available to the New York County Supreme Court, a copy of the case or of pertinent portions of the authority shall be submitted with the motion papers. NY R NY CTY J RUL Rule 14(a).

viii. *ONONDAGA COUNTY: Additional supplemental documents*

- *Notice of hard copy submission.* Any papers to be filed with the court in an e-filed case must be filed online with the E-filing system except where a special exemption is granted (e.g., oversized maps, photographs). If such an exemption is granted, Form EFM-3, "Notice of Hard Copy Submission—E-Filed Case," must be attached to such documents forms which are not filed on line. Also, Form EFM-4 "Notice of Hard Copy Exhibit Filing" must be completed and uploaded to the action's e-file. Both of these forms may be found on the NYSCEF website. NY R ONDGA E FIL Protocol(B)(4).

ix. *QUEENS COUNTY: Additional supplemental documents*

- *Notice of hard copy submission.* Any party opting out of the e-filing system must have a "Notice of Hard Copy Submission" firmly affixed to the back of the papers. NY R L QUEENS E-FILE Doc. 1(H)(2)(f).

E. Format

1. *Form of documents*

a. *Size and form of paper.* Each paper served or filed shall be durable, white and, except for summonses, subpoenas, notices of appearance, notes of issue, orders of protection, temporary orders of protection and exhibits, shall be eleven by eight and one-half (11 x 8-1/2) inches in size. NY CPLR Rule 2101(a).

b. *Writing and language.* The writing shall be legible and in black ink. NY CPLR Rule 2101(a). Each paper served or filed shall be in the English language which, where practicable, shall be of ordinary usage. NY CPLR Rule 2101(b).

c. *Caption.* Each paper served or filed shall begin with a caption setting forth the name of the court, the venue, the title of the action, the nature of the paper and the index number of the action if one has been assigned. In all papers other than a summons, a complaint or a judgment it shall be sufficient to state the name of the first named party on each side with an appropriate indication of any omissions. NY CPLR Rule 2101(c).

i. *Further contents of first page.* After the first paper has been filed in each case the index number shall appear on the cover and first page to the right of the caption of every paper tendered for filing in the action. Each such cover and first page also shall contain an indication of the county of venue and a brief description of the nature of the paper and, where the case has been assigned to an individual judge, shall contain the name of the assigned judge to the right of the caption. NY R UNIF TRIAL CTS § 202.5(a); NY R UNIF TRIAL CTS § 202.5(b); NY R UNIF TRIAL CTS § 202.5(d)(1)(i).

ii. *ALBANY COUNTY: Request for oral argument.* A party may request oral argument on a motion by indicating such request on the first page of the notice of motion, order to show cause, or answering papers in the area across from the caption of the action/proceeding. NY R 3 JD SUP Doc. 1(B).

iii. *NEW YORK COUNTY: Request for oral argument.* Counsel who wish oral argument must so request conspicuously on the front of their papers. NY R NY CTY Procedure II(D).

d. *Index number.* No paper in an action in the supreme or a county court, other than an order submitted for signature to a judge out of court, shall be submitted for any purpose to the supreme or county court or to a clerk thereof unless there is endorsed on such paper the index number of the action assigned by the clerk of the county. NY CPLR § 8018(c).

i. *ALBANY COUNTY: Index number on all filed documents.* The index number, the request for judicial intervention number and the assigned justice's name shall appear on [all papers filed with the Court subsequent to the complaint]. NY R 3 JD SUP Doc. 1(A).

ii. *ERIE COUNTY: Index number after initial filing.* Cases that are initially commenced by the filing of papers with the NYSCEF system are identified as e-filed cases by assignment of an Index Number that has "800-899" as the first three (3) digits of the index number (i.e. 802391/2012). NY R ERIE E FIL Doc. 3(II). [The] Index Number must be affixed to all document submissions, filings, and communications to the Erie County Clerk and the Court. Cases that are converted from paper to e-filing shall retain the original index number. NY R ERIE E FIL Doc. 3(II).

iii. *KINGS COUNTY: Index number after initial filing.* In cases commenced electronically by the filing of initiating papers with the NYSCEF system and payment of the statutory fees, the Kings County Clerk will issue an NYSCEF designated index number and the filer shall be notified via the NYSCEF system of the index number assigned and filing date. Such index number must be affixed to all document submissions, filings and communications to the Kings County Clerk and Supreme Court. If counsel faces exigent circumstances that require accelerated assignment, counsel may contact Administration of the Kings County Clerk at kcco-efile@nycourts.gov, during normal business hours of the court. NY R L KINGS E FIL Doc. 1(B)(5).

iv. *NEW YORK COUNTY: Index number on hard copy filings.* Papers subsequently presented for filing in hardcopy format will be filed in this jacket. NY R NY CTY Procedure I(B). Index numbers take the form of six digits followed by a slash and the four digits of the year the case began, e.g., 340705/2018. The first or first two integers of the index number identify the type of case. If a case is commenced electronically, the second integer will be a "5", except as indicated otherwise in the list below. There are many tax certiorari matters e-filed annually and the index numbers therefor will normally run over into those with a "6" as the second integer, and the same will occur with general cases if necessary. The principal types of cases and their index number categories are listed in NY R NY CTY Procedure I(B). NY R NY CTY Procedure I(B); NY R NY CTY Procedure XI(A).

v. *ONONDAGA COUNTY: Index number.* The index number must be referenced on all e-filed documents and correspondence. All e-filed case index numbers will contain the letters "EF" between the year and the file number (for example, 2012EF9999). NY R ONDGA E FIL Protocol(B)(1).

vi. *QUEENS COUNTY: Index number on converted cases.* Cases originally commenced in hard-copy form but later converted to an E-file case, either by stipulation or order will bear a regular index number initially. The County Clerk will issue a new E-file index number. NY R L QUEENS E-FILE Doc. 1(B).

e. *Line spacing.* Every paper filed in court, if typewritten, shall have at least double space between each line, except for quotations and the names and addresses of attorneys appearing in the action. NY R UNIF TRIAL CTS § 202.5(a).

f. *Font size.* Each. . .paper printed or typed, served or filed, except for summonses. . .and exhibits, shall be in clear type of no less than ten (10) point in size. NY CPLR Rule 2101(a).

i. Whenever a requirement relating to size of type is stated in point size, the type size requirement shall be deemed met if the x-height of the type is a minimum of forty-five percent (45%) of the specified point size. Each point shall be measured as .351 millimeter. The x-height size shall be measured as it appears on the page. The x-height is the height of the lower case letters, exclusive of ascenders or descenders. NY CPLR § 105(t).

g. *Margins.* Every paper filed in court shall have at least one (1) inch margins, NY R UNIF TRIAL CTS § 202.5(a).

h. *Citations*

i. *Civil practice law and rules.* NY CPLR § 101, et seq. shall be known as the civil practice law and rules, and may be cited as "CPLR". Reference to a provision in the civil practice law and rules may, except when such provision is being enacted or amended, be made without indicating whether it is a rule or section. NY CPLR § 101.

i. *Indorsement by attorney.* Each paper served or filed shall be indorsed with the name, address and telephone number of the attorney for the party serving or filing the paper, or if the party does not appear by attorney, with the name, address and telephone number of the party. NY CPLR Rule 2101(d).

j. *One-sided printing.* In addition, every paper filed in court, other than an exhibit or printed form, shall contain writing on one side only, except that papers that are fastened on the side may contain writing on both sides. NY R UNIF TRIAL CTS § 202.5(a).

k. *Use of copies authorized.* Except where otherwise specifically prescribed, copies, rather than originals, of all papers, including orders, affidavits and exhibits may be served or filed. Where it is required that the original be served or filed and the original is lost or withheld, the court may authorize a copy to be served or filed. NY CPLR Rule 2101(e).

i. Where a certified copy of a paper is required by law, an attorney admitted to practice in the courts of the state may certify that it has been compared by him with the original and found to be a true and complete copy. Such a certificate, when subscribed by such attorney, has the same effect as if made by a clerk. NY CPLR § 2105.

l. *Recycled paper.* It is the policy of the Unified Court System that litigants, where practicable, should file or submit to the courts of the Unified Court System of the State of New York papers printed or reproduced on recycled paper. Paper is considered recycled if it contains a minimum content of thirty percent (30%) waste paper. NY R UNIF TRIAL CTS § 215.2. The signature page of every paper filed or submitted to the court on recycled paper should bear the legend: "Printed [Reproduced] on Recycled Paper." NY R UNIF TRIAL CTS § 215.3.

m. *Form of request for judicial intervention; Copies.* A request for judicial intervention must be submitted, in duplicate, on a form authorized by the Chief of the Courts, with proof of service on the other parties to the action (but proof of service is not required where the application is ex parte). NY R UNIF TRIAL CTS § 202.6(a).

n. *KINGS COUNTY: Tabs on filings.* Motions, orders and other filed papers shall be indexed with protruding tabs. Clerks are required to reject papers that do not have protruding exhibit tabs, except papers in matrimonial cases and papers filed by pro se litigants. NY R L KINGS Pt. A, Papers.

o. *NEW YORK COUNTY: Length of briefs.* Unless advance permission otherwise is granted by the court for good cause, memoranda of law shall not exceed thirty (30) pages each (exclusive of table of contents and table of authorities) and affidavits/affirmations shall not exceed twenty-five (25) pages each. NY R NY CTY J RUL Rule 14(b).

p. *QUEENS COUNTY: Form and size of motion filings.* All motions filed in Queens Supreme Court-Civil Term, must adhere to the Motion Support rules and the rules of the assigned judge. NY R L QUEENS MOT SUP Doc. 1. Due to space limitations, the Motion Support Office cannot accept notices of motion/notices of petition and accompanying exhibits which measure greater than eight (8) inches. If your documents measure greater than eight (8) inches you are directed to submit only the notice of motion/notice of petition to the Motion Support Office and bring all exhibits to the calendar call on your return date. NY R L QUEENS MOT SUP Doc. 1.

2. *Form of electronic documents.* Each paper served or filed by electronic means, as defined in NY CPLR Rule 2103(f), shall be capable of being reproduced by the receiver so as to comply with the provisions of NY CPLR Rule 2101(a) through NY CPLR Rule 2101(d). NY CPLR Rule 2101(g).

a. *File format.* All e-filed documents shall comply with the technical requirements set forth at the NYSCEF site. NY R UNIF TRIAL CTS § 202.5-b(d)(1)(i).

b. *Heading of document.* The subject matter heading for each paper sent by electronic means must indicate that the matter being transmitted electronically is related to a court proceeding. NY CPLR Rule 2103(b)(7).

c. *E-filed documents identification*

i. *ERIE COUNTY.* E-filed cases must be readily identifiable and marked as such. If counsel presents papers to the Office of the Erie County Clerk or the Office of the Chief Clerk in a NYSCEF matter where authorized, counsel should alert the Clerk that the case is a NYSCEF matter. NY R ERIE E FIL Doc. 3(II).

ii. *KINGS COUNTY.* The Supreme Court's Civil Case Information System ("CCIS") will further identify e-filed cases by the addition of a suffix to the index number (e.g. 500136/2006E). This suffix should be used on all documents filed with the court in e-filed matters. NY R L KINGS E FIL Doc. 1(A)(1).

3. *Signature blocks.* Every pleading, written motion, and other paper, served on another party or filed or submitted to the court shall be signed by an attorney, or by a party if the party is not represented by an attorney, with the name of the attorney or party clearly printed or typed directly below the signature. NY R CHIEF ADMIN § 130-1.1-a(a); NY R UNIF TRIAL CTS § 202.5(d)(1)(iv).

a. *Printed name.* Beneath each signature shall be printed the name signed. NY CPLR Rule 2101(a).

b. *Failure to sign.* Absent good cause shown, the court shall strike any unsigned paper if the omission of the signature is not corrected promptly after being called to the attention of the attorney or party. NY R CHIEF ADMIN § 130-1.1-a(a).

c. *Signature as certification.* By signing a paper, an attorney or party certifies that, to the best of that person's knowledge, information and belief, formed after an inquiry reasonable under the circumstances the presentation of the paper or the contentions therein are not frivolous as defined in NY R CHIEF ADMIN § 130-1.1(c). NY R CHIEF ADMIN § 130-1.1-a(b)(1).

d. *Electronic signatures.* A document shall be considered to have been signed by an attorney or party in compliance with NY R CHIEF ADMIN § 130-1.1-a if it has been signed by such attorney or party as provided in NY R UNIF TRIAL CTS § 202.5-b(e)(1) and it bears the signatory's name. NY R UNIF TRIAL CTS § 202.5-b(e)(2). An electronically filed document shall be considered to have been signed by, and shall be binding upon, the person identified as a signatory, if:

i. It bears the physical signature of such person and is scanned into an electronic format that reproduces such signature; or

ii. The signatory has electronically affixed the digital image of his or her signature to the document; or

iii. It is electronically filed under the User ID and password of that person; or

iv. In a tax certiorari action in which the parties have stipulated to this procedure, it is an initiating document that is electronically filed without the signature of the signatory in a form provided above in NY R UNIF TRIAL CTS § 202.5-b(e)(iv), provided that, prior to filing, the document is signed in full in hard copy (which hard copy must be preserved until the conclusion of all proceedings, including appeals, in the case in which it is filed); or

v. In a small claims assessment review proceeding, it is a petition recorded by the NYSCEF site upon the filing of a text file as provided in NY R UNIF TRIAL CTS § 202.5-b(b)(1), provided that prior to filing, the document was signed in full in hard copy (which hard copy must be preserved until the conclusion of all proceedings in the matter, including article 78 (NY CPLR § 7801, et seq.) review and any appeals, and must be made available during the proceeding upon request of the respondent or the court); or

vi. It otherwise bears the electronic signature of the signatory in a format conforming to such standards and requirements as may hereafter be established by the Chief Administrator. NY R UNIF TRIAL CTS § 202.5-b(e).

4. *Confidentiality of personal information.* No person may file any document available for public inspection with any state agency, political subdivision, or in any court of this state that contains a Social Security account number of any other person, unless such other person is a dependent child, or has consented to such filing, except as required by federal or state law or regulation, or by court rule. NY GEN BUS § 399-ddd. Submissions pursuant to e-filing procedures shall have the same confidentiality rights as paper documents. NY R UNIF TRIAL CTS § 202.5-b(k)(1).
   a. *Confidential personal information.* Except in the actions designated in NY R UNIF TRIAL CTS § 202.5(e)(1), or as otherwise provided by rule or law or court order, and whether or not a sealing order is or has been sought, the parties shall omit or redact confidential personal information in papers submitted to the court for filing. For purposes of NY R UNIF TRIAL CTS § 202.5(e), confidential personal information ("CPI") means:
      i. The taxpayer identification number of an individual or an entity, including a Social Security number, an employer identification number, and an individual taxpayer identification number, except the last four (4) digits thereof;
      ii. The date of an individual's birth, except the year thereof;
      iii. The full name of an individual known to be a minor, except the minor's initials;
      iv. A financial account number, including a credit and/or debit card number, a bank account number, an investment account number, and/or an insurance account number, except the last four (4) digits or letters thereof; and
      v. Any of the documents or testimony in a matrimonial action protected by NY DOM REL § 235 or evidence sealed by the court in such an action which are attached as exhibits or referenced in the papers filed in any other civil action. For purposes of NY R UNIF TRIAL CTS § 202.5, a matrimonial action shall mean: an action to annul a marriage or declare the nullity of a void marriage, an action or agreement for a separation, an action for a divorce, or an action or proceeding for custody, visitation, writ of habeus corpus, child support, maintenance or paternity. NY R UNIF TRIAL CTS § 202.5(e)(1).
      vi. *ERIE COUNTY.* An attorney or unrepresented litigant filing a document via the NYSCEF system must comply with the requirements of NY R UNIF TRIAL CTS § 202.5(e) regarding the redaction of Confidential Personal Information and NY GEN BUS § 399-ddd(6) concerning the filing of documents containing Social Security Numbers. It is the sole responsibility of counsel or unrepresented litigant filing to be aware of and to comply with existing laws requiring non-disclosure of personal information contained in any document e-filed in NYSCEF. NY R ERIE E FIL Doc. 3(III)(G); NY R ERIE E FIL Doc. 3(III).
      vii. *KINGS COUNTY.* An attorney or unrepresented litigant filing a document via the NYSCEF system must comply with the requirements of General Business Law § 399-dd(6), which often require redaction of any Social Security number that appear in the original document. The NYSCEF system automatically redacts portions of filed documents which apparently contain Social Security numbers pursuant to NY R UNIF TRIAL CTS § 202.5-b(k). In the event the filing party receives e-mail notice through NYSCEF that a Social Security number in a filed document has been redacted, and the filing party concludes such redaction is erroneous, the filer should click on the link provided in the e-mail to permit the County Clerk to revert the redaction. For Confidential Personal Information, see NY R UNIF TRIAL CTS § 202.5(e) and NY R L KINGS E FIL Doc. 1(B)(11). [Editor's note: the reference to General Business Law § 399-dd(6) is likely a reference to NY GEN BUS § 399-ddd(6)]. NY R L KINGS E FIL Doc. 1(B)(10); NY R L KINGS E FIL Doc. 1(K)(1).
      viii. *NEW YORK COUNTY.* It is the responsibility of counsel and parties to comply with rules restricting disclosure of confidential personal information. Nevertheless, NYSCEF screens filings and endeavors to identify any that contain social security numbers. When such numbers are discovered through this process, NYSCEF will restrict portions of or all of such documents from public view. Where NYSCEF has redacted what it believes to be a social security number, it will transmit to the filer a notice advising of the action taken and requesting that the filer review the matter and provide notification as set forth in the notice if the redaction has been made in error. NY R NY CTY E FIL Doc. 2(K)(1); NY R NY CTY J RUL Rule A-1. Documents filed in the past in "secure status" under a procedure no longer in place will retain that status unless otherwise directed by the court. NY R NY CTY E FIL Doc. 2(K)(2).
   b. *Submission of confidential personal information.* Where a person submitting a paper to a court for filing believes in good faith that the inclusion of the full confidential personal information described in NY R UNIF TRIAL CTS § 202.5(e)(1) is material and necessary to the adjudication of the action or proceeding before the court, he or she may apply to the court for leave to serve and file together with a paper in which such information has been set forth in abbreviated form a confidential affidavit or affirmation setting forth the same information in unabbreviated form, appropriately referenced to the page or pages of the paper at which the abbreviated form appears. NY R UNIF TRIAL CTS § 202.5(e)(3).

c. *Home addresses.* For information on when home addresses and other personal information must be redacted, refer to NY CPLR Rule 2103-a.

5. *Defective papers.* A defect in the form of a paper, if a substantial right of a party is not prejudiced, shall be disregarded by the court, and leave to correct shall be freely given. NY CPLR Rule 2101(f). Papers that are stapled or bound securely shall not be rejected for filing simply because they are not bound with a backer of any kind. NY R UNIF TRIAL CTS § 202.5(a). A paper filed in accordance with the rules of the chief administrator or any local rule or practice established by the court shall be deemed filed. NY CPLR Rule 2102(b).

a. *Objection to defective papers.* The party on whom a paper is served shall be deemed to have waived objection to any defect in form unless, within fifteen (15) days after the receipt thereof, the party on whom the paper is served returns the paper to the party serving it with a statement of particular objections. NY CPLR Rule 2101(f).

F. Filing and Service Requirements

1. *Filing requirements.* Except where otherwise prescribed by law or order of court, papers required to be filed shall be filed with the clerk of the court in which the action is triable. In an action or proceeding in supreme or court, papers required to be filed shall be filed with the clerk of the county in which the proceeding is brought. NY CPLR Rule 2102(a).

a. *Furnishing papers to the court.* Each party shall furnish to the court all papers served by him. The moving party shall furnish at the hearing all other papers not already in the possession of the court necessary to the consideration of the questions involved. Where such papers are in the possession of an adverse party, they shall be produced by him at the hearing on notice served with the motion papers. Only papers served in accordance with the provisions of NY CPLR Rule 2214 shall be read in support of, or in opposition to, the motion, unless the court for good cause shall otherwise direct. NY CPLR Rule 2214(c).

i. *Submission to judge.* All papers for signature or consideration of the court shall be presented to the clerk of the trial court in the appropriate courtroom or clerk's office, except that where the clerk is unavailable or the judge so directs, papers may be submitted to the judge and a copy filed with the clerk at the first available opportunity. All papers for any judge that are filed in the clerk's office shall be promptly delivered to the judge by the clerk. The papers shall be clearly addressed to the judge for whom they are intended and prominently show the nature of the papers, the title and index number of the action in which they are filed, the judge's name and the name of the attorney or party submitting them. NY R UNIF TRIAL CTS § 202.5(b).

ii. *BRONX COUNTY: Approval of motions before filing.* All motion papers must be approved by the Motion Support Office, Supreme Court, Civil Term, room 217, before the motion papers are filed and the appropriate fee paid to the County Clerk. NY R BRONX FIL R Doc. 1.

iii. *ERIE COUNTY: Filing motions.* A motion on notice or a notice of petition in a NYSCEF case shall be filed through the NYSCEF system and must be accompanied by a Request for Judicial Intervention if the motion is being filed upon commencement of the action or if the matter has not yet been assigned to an IAS Justice. In addition, cross motions with the appropriate filing fees and opposition and reply papers must be submitted via the NYSCEF system. NY R ERIE E FIL Doc. 3(V)(A).

iv. *NEW YORK COUNTY: Filing hard copies.* Where in the narrow circumstances described by the e-filing rules a motion is made in hard-copy form or opposition papers are submitted in such form in an e-filed case, the hard-copy documents shall be submitted in the same way papers are submitted in non-e-filed cases, except that there shall be firmly affixed to each separate document or group of documents, as the back page facing out, a Notice of Hard Copy Submission—E-Filed Case. NY R NY CTY Procedure II(A). For more information on filing in hard copy cases, refer to NY R NY CTY Procedure II(A).

v. *ONONDAGA COUNTY: Submission of responsive papers and cross-motions.* Cross-motions, opposition and reply papers must be submitted online. NY R ONDGA E FIL Protocol(B)(9)(e). Motions and Orders to Show Cause are assigned a sequence number by the system. Counsel must be sure that cross motions and other filings correspond with the correct sequence number so that a cross motion will not be associated with the wrong original motion. NY R ONDGA E FIL Protocol(B)(9)(f).

b. *Electronic filing.* On consent, documents may be filed and served by electronic means in Supreme Court in such civil actions and in such counties as shall be authorized by order of the Chief Administrator of the Courts and only to the extent and in the manner provided in NY R UNIF TRIAL CTS § 202.5-b. NY R UNIF TRIAL CTS § 202.5-b(a)(1). For the definitions of terms used in electronic filing, refer to NY R UNIF TRIAL CTS § 202.5-b(a)(2).

i. *E-filing mandatory.* In any action subject to e-filing, all documents required to be filed with the court by an e-filing party shall be filed and served electronically, except as provided in NY R UNIF TRIAL CTS § 202.5-b. NY R UNIF TRIAL CTS § 202.5-b(d)(1)(i).

- *ERIE COUNTY.* Case types currently eligible and accepted for e-filing are listed at the NYSCEF website. Note that some actions or special proceedings, (i.e., name changes) which are otherwise subject to mandatory e-filing, if commenced by unrepresented litigants will NOT be maintained in the NYSCEF system; individual cases may be found either at NYSCEF or in the Erie County Clerk's online records system. NY R ERIE E FIL Doc. 3(I)(E).
- *KINGS COUNTY.* Cases that are commenced by filing of the initiating papers with NYSCEF are identified as e-filed cases by assignment of a special index number (i.e., Index Numbers beginning with 500,000). NY R L KINGS E FIL Doc. 1(A)(1). All cases required to be e-filed are listed in Uniform Rule 202.5-bb (Mandatory E-Filing Rules) and on the NYSCEF website. All such cases must be commenced by filing with the County Clerk electronically through NYSCEF and all subsequent documents in such cases must be e-filed. Any questions regarding mandatory e-filing in Kings County can be e-mailed to kcco-efile@nycourts.gov. NY R L KINGS E FIL Doc. 1(A)(2).
- *NEW YORK COUNTY.* Unless otherwise provided in the Rules or in NY R NY CTY E FIL Doc. 2 or where a special exemption is granted due to physical requirements (e.g., oversized maps; see NY R NY CTY E FIL Doc. 2(B)(10)), all documents to be filed with the court in a NYSCEF case, including all documents on motions and all letters to the court (where permitted), must be filed with the NYSCEF system. Documents that attorneys would not ordinarily file with the court in a hard-copy case need not be e-filed. Unless otherwise provided by the E-Filing Rules or this Protocol, in e-filed cases the County Clerk and the court will not accept documents filed in paper form. NY R NY CTY E FIL Doc. 2(B)(1). E-filing is mandatory in all types of cases (other than election law, matrimonial, Art. 78, and Mental Hygiene Law matters, and Art. 70 habeas corpus proceedings) that are commenced in this court on or after February 19, 2013. All such cases must be commenced by filing with the County Clerk electronically through NYSCEF and all subsequent documents in such cases must be e-filed. NY R NY CTY E FIL Doc. 2(A)(2)(a). For more information, including information on consensual e-filing and filing scanned hard copy documents, refer to NY R NY CTY E FIL Doc. 2(A)(2).
- *QUEENS COUNTY.* All authorized Torts, Commercial and Tax Certiorari cases may be commenced by E-Filing, however all parties must consent for the action to continue as an E-file case. NY R L QUEENS E-FILE Doc. 1(A). All papers to be filed with the court in an E-filed case shall be filed on-line with the E-file system except as directed by the court. Papers that attorneys would not ordinarily file with the court in a hard-copy case need not be filed in an E-filed matter. NY R L QUEENS E-FILE Doc. 1(E)(2).

ii. *Who may file.* Documents may be filed or served electronically only by a person who has registered as an authorized e-filing user or as otherwise provided in NY R UNIF TRIAL CTS § 202.5-b(c). NY R UNIF TRIAL CTS § 202.5-b(c)(1).

iii. *When filing made.* Documents may be transmitted at any time of the day or night to the NYSCEF site. A document other than an order or judgment is filed when its electronic transmission or, in the case of a petition that is e-filed by submission of a text file as provided in NY R UNIF TRIAL CTS § 202.5-b(b)(1), the electronic transmission of the text file is recorded at that site, provided, however, that where payment of a fee is required upon the filing of a document, the document is not filed until transmission of the document and the information or form or information as required in NY R UNIF TRIAL CTS § 202.5-b(d)(2)(i), NY R UNIF TRIAL CTS § 202.5-b(d)(2)(ii) or NY R UNIF TRIAL CTS § 202.5-b(d)(2)(iii) has been recorded at the NYSCEF site; or, if no transmission of that information or form or information is recorded, where permitted by the County Clerk, until payment is presented to the County Clerk. NY R UNIF TRIAL CTS § 202.5-b(d)(3)(i).

iv. *Notification of filing.* No later than the close of business on the business day following the electronic filing of a document, a notification, in a form prescribed by the Chief Administrator, shall be transmitted electronically by the NYSCEF site to the person filing such document and the e-mail service addresses of all other participating parties in such action. NY R UNIF TRIAL CTS § 202.5-b(d)(3)(ii).

v. *Removal of confidential information and other corrections.* If a document filed electronically is subsequently discovered to contain confidential data—including but not limited to trade secrets, information protected by confidentiality agreement, or personal confidential information as defined by statute or court rule—or otherwise to have been filed in error, the filer or another party or affected person may (1) notify the parties and any non-party filers in the action of the confidentiality issue or other error raised by the filing, and of his or her intention to seek judicial relief to correct the filing: (2) following such notification, request that the appropriate

County Clerk, exercising his or her administrative discretion, place the document temporarily in "restricted" status on the NYSCEF site, to be made available for viewing by court staff and the parties but not the general public; and (3) file an application to correct the filing by order to show cause within five (5) business days of such notification (or such time as the court may direct), including a request for preliminary injunctive relief limiting interim disclosure of the document at issue. Unless otherwise directed by the court, any document placed in restricted status in response to such a request shall be returned to public view upon expiration of this five (5) day period. The Chief Administrator of the Courts shall promulgate forms to implement this process. NY R UNIF TRIAL CTS § 202.5-b(d)(3)(iii).

- *KINGS COUNTY.* For information on what to do when a document was erroneously filed with confidential information, refer to NY R L KINGS E FIL Doc. 1(B)(11).
- *NEW YORK COUNTY.* For information on what to do when a document was erroneously filed with confidential information, refer to NY R NY CTY E FIL Doc. 2(B)(8).
- *QUEENS COUNTY.* For information on what to do when a document was erroneously filed with confidential information, refer to NY R L QUEENS E-FILE Doc. 1(E)(7).

vi. *Documents requiring judge's signature.* Except where the court directs otherwise, any document that requires a judge's signature shall be transmitted electronically and in hard copy to the court. NY R UNIF TRIAL CTS § 202.5-b(d)(6).

vii. *Documents which would be inconvenient to file electronically; Hard copies.* Notwithstanding any other provision of NY R UNIF TRIAL CTS § 202.5-b, and subject to such guidelines as may be established by the Chief Administrative Judge, the County Clerk or his or her designee may require or permit a party to file in hard copy, in accordance with procedures set by the County Clerk or designee, an exhibit or other document which it is impractical or inconvenient to file electronically. NY R UNIF TRIAL CTS § 202.5-b(d)(7).

- *ERIE COUNTY.* Please contact the Supervisor of Actions & Proceedings, Erie County Clerk's Office by calling (716) 858-6662 or the Deputy County Clerk—Legal at (716) 858-6348 for information. NY R ERIE E FIL Doc. 3(III)(F).
- *KINGS COUNTY.* With limited exceptions, as set forth in the Uniform Rules and herein, all documents to be filed with the court in a NYSCEF case shall be filed online via the NYSCEF system. However, should the size, consistency or context of a hard copy document preclude electronic filing, the user shall electronically file a "Notice of Hard Copy Submission—E-Filed Cases" form EFM-3. Any hard copy submitted pursuant to NY R L KINGS E FIL Doc. 1(B)(9) shall include, as a cover page firmly fastened thereto, a copy of the Confirmation Notice received from the NYSCEF site confirming receipt of the "Notice of Hard Copy Submission—E-Filed Cases". Any party may object to such hard copy filing. The Court, in response to such objection, may, following the hard copy filing, fashion such relief as it deems appropriate pursuant to and in furtherance of the Uniform Rules and NY R L KINGS E FIL Doc. 1, including, but not limited to, an Order directing the filing party to file such documents online via the NYSCEF system. When exhibits are impractical to file pursuant to NY R UNIF TRIAL CTS § 202.5-b(d)(7), an additional "Notice of Hard Copy Exhibit Filing" form EFM-4 is required to be submitted. NY R L KINGS E FIL Doc. 1(B)(9).
- *NEW YORK COUNTY.* If a filer needs to submit unusual exhibits in original form that cannot practically be e-filed, such as oversized maps or electronic recordings, the filer should consult with the County Clerk's E-File Department by telephone at 646-386-3737 (procedural questions only) or by e-mail at ccnyef@nycourts.gov, which will normally require that the filer retain custody of the original subject to possible future directives of the court. NY R NY CTY E FIL Doc. 2(B)(10). In such instances, the filing counsel shall file with NYSCEF a "placeholder" in the form of a Notice of Hard Copy Exhibit Filing (NYSCEF Form EF 21). The Notice should be uploaded to NYSCEF as document type "Exhibit" and the filer should indicate in the "Additional Document Information" field that the filer is retaining custody of the original. Failure to e-file the Notice may result in a gap in the official record of the court. NY R NY CTY E FIL Doc. 2(B)(10).

viii. *Documents containing sensitive or proprietary information.* In an action subject to e-filing, any person may apply for an order prohibiting or restricting the electronic filing in the action of specifically identified materials on the grounds that such materials are subject to copyright or other proprietary rights, or trade secret or other privacy interests, and that electronic filing in the action is likely to result in substantial prejudice to those rights or interests. NY R UNIF TRIAL CTS § 202.5-b(k)(2).

ix. *Refusal to accept paper filings.* In accordance with NY CPLR Rule 2102(c), a County Clerk and a chief clerk of the Supreme Court or County Court, as appropriate, shall refuse to accept for filing papers filed in actions and proceedings when the paper sought to be filed:

- Is in an action subject to electronic filing pursuant to Rules of the Chief Administrator,
- Is not being filed electronically, and
- Does not include the notice required by NY R UNIF TRIAL CTS § 202.5-b(d)(1). NY R UNIF TRIAL CTS § 202.5(d)(1)(v); NY R UNIF TRIAL CTS § 202.5-bb(d).

x. *Emergency filings; Hard copies.* For information on when an emergency filing may be filed and served in hard copy, refer to NY R UNIF TRIAL CTS § 202.5-b(d)(1)(ii), NY R UNIF TRIAL CTS § 202.5-b(d)(1)(iii) and NY R UNIF TRIAL CTS § 202.5-bb(c)(3).

- *KINGS COUNTY.* Under the rules, a participating emergency e-filer must electronically file the documents initially filed in hard copy form within three (3) business days of the emergency filing; the originals will be discarded after the documents have been processed and the failure to e-file as required will therefore lead to an incomplete record. NY R L KINGS E FIL Doc. 1(B)(3).
- *NEW YORK COUNTY.* Occasionally an emergency will arise requiring expedited entry of a document with the County Clerk (e.g., an order issued in the courtroom after a conference or argument of a critical matter), such as for purposes of an immediate appeal. Expedition can be achieved by the Part as follows: the document should be carried by a Court Officer or staff member to the General Clerk's Office to assure immediate and proper recordation in the computer and, as appropriate, the posting of the document to NYSCEF or the Supreme Court Records On-Line Library ("Scroll"). The court will accommodate counsel in emergencies. NY R NY CTY Procedure XI(A).
- *NEW YORK COUNTY.* For more information on how to bring emergency matters before the court, refer to NY R NY CTY Procedure IV.

xi. *Technical failures.* The NYSCEF site shall be considered to be subject to a technical failure on a given day if the site is unable to accept filings or provide access to filed documents continuously or intermittently over the course of any period of time greater than one (1) hour after 12:00 noon of that day. Notice of all such technical failures shall be provided on the site. NY R UNIF TRIAL CTS § 202.5-b(i).

- When e-filing is hindered by a technical failure, a party may file with the appropriate clerk and serve in hard copy. NY R UNIF TRIAL CTS § 202.5-b(i). In the event an attorney or party shall file and serve documents in hard copy pursuant to NY R UNIF TRIAL CTS § 202.5-b(i), each such document shall include the notice required by NY R UNIF TRIAL CTS § 202.5-b(d)(1), and the filer shall file those documents with the NYSCEF site within three (3) business days after restoration of normal operations at that site. NY R UNIF TRIAL CTS § 202.5-b(i).
- With the exception of deadlines that by law cannot be extended, the time for filing of any document that is delayed due to technical failure of the site shall be extended for one (1) day for each day on which such failure occurs, unless otherwise ordered by the court. NY R UNIF TRIAL CTS § 202.5-b(i).
- *ERIE COUNTY.* When filing by electronic means is hindered by a technical failure, please refer to the NY R UNIF TRIAL CTS § 202.5-b(i). NY R ERIE E FIL Doc. 3(III)(K).
- *KINGS COUNTY.* When filing by electronic means is hindered by a NYSCEF technical failure (as set forth in NY R UNIF TRIAL CTS § 202.5-b(i)), a party may file with the appropriate Clerk in hard copy. Except for deadlines that by law cannot be extended (e.g. Statute of limitations, Notice of Appeal), the time for filing of any document that is delayed due to technical failure of the NYSCEF system shall be extended for one day for each day on which such failure occurs, unless otherwise ordered by the court. NY R L KINGS E FIL Doc. 1(B)(13).
- *ONONDAGA COUNTY.* When filing by electronic means is hindered by a technical failure (as set forth in NY R UNIF TRIAL CTS § 202.5-b(h)(3)(i)), a party may file a hard copy with the County Clerk. With the exception of deadlines that by law cannot be extended (e.g., a statute of limitations or the deadline for filing a Notice of Appeal), the time for filing of any document that is delayed due to technical failure of the NYSCEF system will be extended for one day for each day on which such failure occurs, unless otherwise ordered by the court. A "Notice of Hard Copy Filing Submission—E-Filed Case' must accompany any documents not filed via NYSCEF. NY R ONDGA E FIL Protocol(B)(8).

xii. *Filing fees.* For information on what information must be provided to pay filing fees, refer to NY R UNIF TRIAL CTS § 202.5-b(d)(2).

xiii. *Exemption from e-filing.* For information on exemptions from e-filing, refer to NY R UNIF TRIAL CTS § 202.5-bb(e).

xiv. *Filing exhibits*

- *ERIE COUNTY.* In the NYSCEF system, each exhibit must be uploaded as a separate .pdf file. After uploading a primary document, please choose the document type "Exhibit" and enter the appropriate number or letter and a brief description of the exhibit; each exhibit should bear a separate cover sheet clearly marked as "Exhibit A," "Exhibit B," etc. "Exhibit A" or "Exhibit B" is unacceptable as a brief description of the exhibit. Exhibits, where referenced in a signed Order as attached or affixed shall be uploaded with the signed Order as one .pdf document. NY R ERIE E FIL Doc. 3(III)(H); NY R ERIE E FIL Doc. 3(V)(D).
- *KINGS COUNTY.* In the NYSCEF system, each exhibit should be uploaded as a separate PDF file. After uploading a primary document, please choose the document type "Exhibit", enter the appropriate number or letter, and be sure to place a check mark to the right of "Attach to main document". Each exhibit shall bear a separate cover sheet clearly marked as Exhibit A, Exhibit B, etc. NY R L KINGS E FIL Doc. 1(B)(12). Whenever possible, attorneys submitting exhibits in NYSCEF cases should make each exhibit a separate attachment to an affidavit/affirmation in the system (i.e., multiple exhibits should not be filed as a single PDF). NY R L KINGS E FIL Doc. 1(D)(1).
- *NEW YORK COUNTY.* Attorneys submitting exhibits in NYSCEF cases should make each exhibit a separate attachment to an affidavit/affirmation in the system; i.e., exhibits should not be filed as a single PDF-A together with the affidavit/affirmation or grouped together as a single PDF-A attachment because either of these two formats makes it difficult for the Justice to locate particular exhibits as needed. Counsel must also include appropriate descriptive language in the "Additional Document Information" field in NYSCEF. NY R NY CTY E FIL Doc. 2(D)(6).
- *ONONDAGA COUNTY.* All exhibits in e-filed cases must be e-filed individually as separate attachments. NY R ONDGA E FIL Protocol(B)(9)(b).

xv. *Correcting documents*

- *ERIE COUNTY.* Submission of documents which, upon examination, require correction or addition will result in notification to the filer advising that the document has been returned for correction. The filer shall make the required corrections and/or additions as indicated in the e-mail transmission sent by the County Clerk or Part Clerk through the NYSCEF site. The corrected documents may be resubmitted using the "Re-file this document" link highlighted in the filer's document list for the respective case. Please note that in the case of multiple submissions, all related documents filed at the same time may be removed from the case record and returned until all documents are properly submitted. NY R ERIE E FIL Doc. 3(III)(J).
- *KINGS COUNTY.* Submission of documents which, upon examination, require correction or addition will result in notification to the filer advising that there is a problem with a document. The filer shall make the required corrections and/or additions and resubmit the corrected document using the "Refile this document" link. In the event a document is returned for correction, the original file date will be preserved. For corrections of documents filed with the Kings County Clerk which require a court order, refer to the procedure in NY R UNIF TRIAL CTS § 202.5-b(d)(3)(iii) and NY R L KINGS E FIL Doc. 1(B)(11). NY R L KINGS E FIL Doc. 1(B)(3).
- *ONONDAGA COUNTY.* If there is an error or an additional document is required, the system will notify the filing party, who will make the corrections/additions and resubmit them online. NY R ONDGA E FIL Protocol(B)(6).
- *QUEENS COUNTY.* Generally speaking, documents that have been E-filed will not thereafter be deleted by the County Clerk from NYCEF because the filer asserts that the filing contains an error or a significant omission. When the filer wishes to correct a perceived error or omission in a filed document, he or she should file an amended version of the document, with the original remaining on file, or else obtain a court order providing for deletion of the original. The County Clerk will only delete a document upon request of the filer or on the County Clerk's own initiative when it is obvious from the face of the document alone that the filer made a fundamental error and never intended to file the document that was filed (e.g., a completely unrelated non-litigation document, a different case, or a wrong county). The County Clerk will advise the filer when any such fundamental errors are detected. NY R L QUEENS E-FILE Doc. 1(E)(6).

c. *Facsimile filing.* In the Supreme Court, facsimile filing shall be limited to commercial claims and tax certiorari, conservatorship, and mental hygiene proceedings in Monroe, Westchester, New York and Suffolk Counties. NY R UNIF TRIAL CTS § 202.5-a(a)(1). Refer to NY R UNIF TRIAL CTS § 202.5-a for information on the procedures for facsimile filing.

i. *NEW YORK COUNTY.* Unless indicated otherwise by the court in a particular case or in NY R NY CTY J RUL Doc. 1, Justices do not accept papers by fax. NY R NY CTY J RUL Rule 4.

d. *ERIE COUNTY: Filing request for judicial intervention.* An RJI in a NYSCEF case shall be filed via the NYSCEF system and will be filed after all other documents have been uploaded. The filer may choose between filing a .pdf image of the prepared RJI and any Addendum or having the system prepare the RJI which shall conform to Uniform Rules. Addenda, such as the Commercial Division Addendum, if prepared by the filer must be filed simultaneously with and attached to an RJI and uploaded as one .pdf document with the RJI. If the RJI is prepared by the e-filing system, no separate Addendum is required. Whether or not the filer elects to allow NYSCEF to create the RJI or chooses to upload a prepared RJI, data in addition to the nature of the judicial intervention, including information that appears on any Addenda will be collected through completion of the fields presented. If the filing of the RJI is accomplished through a filing agent, a prepared RJI and Addendum must be filed in lieu of the creation of the RJI by the NYSCEF system, as the RJI must be signed by the attorney. NY R ERIE E FIL Doc. 3(IV). For information on RJIs in specific types of action, refer to NY R ERIE E FIL Doc. 3(IV).

2. *Service requirements*

a. *Who may serve.* Except where otherwise prescribed by law or order of court, papers may be served by any person not a party of the age of eighteen years or over. NY CPLR Rule 2103(a).

b. *Service upon attorney.* Except where otherwise prescribed by law or order of court, papers to be served upon a party in a pending action shall be served upon the party's attorney. Where the same attorney appears for two or more parties, only one (1) copy need be served upon the attorney. Such service upon an attorney shall be made:

i. By delivering the paper to the attorney personally. NY CPLR Rule 2103(b)(1).

ii. By mailing the paper to the attorney at the address designated by that attorney for that purpose or, if none is designated, at the attorney's last known address; service by mail shall be complete upon mailing. NY CPLR Rule 2103(b)(2).

- *BRONX COUNTY.* Service by mail must be within the state. NY R BRONX FIL R Doc. 3.

iii. If the attorney's office is open, by leaving the paper with a person in charge, or if no person is in charge, by leaving it in a conspicuous place; or if the attorney's office is not open, by depositing the paper, enclosed in a sealed wrapper directed to the attorney, in the attorney's office letter drop or box. NY CPLR Rule 2103(b)(3).

iv. By leaving it at the attorney's residence within the state with a person of suitable age and discretion. Service upon an attorney shall not be made at the attorney's residence unless service at the attorney's office cannot be made. NY CPLR Rule 2103(b)(4).

v. By transmitting the paper to the attorney by facsimile transmission, provided that a facsimile telephone number is designated by the attorney for that purpose. Service by facsimile transmission shall be complete upon the receipt by the sender of a signal from the equipment of the attorney served indicating that the transmission was received, and the mailing of a copy of the paper to that attorney. The designation of a facsimile telephone number in the address block subscribed on a paper served or filed in the course of an action or proceeding shall constitute consent to service by facsimile transmission in accordance with NY CPLR Rule 2103. An attorney may change or rescind a facsimile telephone number by serving a notice on the other parties. NY CPLR Rule 2103(b)(5).

vi. By dispatching the paper to the attorney by overnight delivery service at the address designated by the attorney for that purpose or, if none is designated, at the attorney's last known address. Service by overnight delivery service shall be complete upon deposit of the paper enclosed in a properly addressed wrapper into the custody of the overnight delivery service for overnight delivery, prior to the latest time designated by the overnight delivery service for overnight delivery. "Overnight delivery service" means any delivery service which regularly accepts items for overnight delivery to any address in the state. NY CPLR Rule 2103(b)(6).

vii. By transmitting the paper to the attorney by electronic means where and in the manner authorized by the chief administrator of the courts by rule and, unless such rule shall otherwise provide, such transmission shall be upon the party's written consent. The subject matter heading for each paper sent by electronic means must indicate that the matter being transmitted electronically is related to a court proceeding. NY CPLR Rule 2103(b)(7).

- *KINGS COUNTY.* Pursuant to the E-Filing Rules, service of interlocutory documents is made by posting a document to the NYSCEF site, which automatically and immediately transmits an email notice of the filing, including a link to the document, to all participating counsel and unrepresented litigants on the case. The Rules also authorize service by other methods permitted by the CPLR. If service by such other method is made, proof of service must be filed with NYSCEF. NY R L KINGS E FIL Doc. 1(I).

- *NEW YORK COUNTY.* Service. . .will be made automatically through NYSCEF upon all participating counsel and unrepresented parties in the case. There are limited exceptions to the requirement for e-filing in the covered kinds of cases. NY R NY CTY Procedure XI(A). Pursuant to the E-Filing Rules, service of interlocutory documents is made by posting a document to the NYSCEF site, which automatically and immediately transmits an e-mail notice of the filing, including a link to the document, to all participating counsel and unrepresented litigants on the case. The Rules also authorize service by other methods permitted by the CPLR. If service by such a method is made, proof of service must be filed with NYSCEF. NY R NY CTY E FIL Doc. 2(I).
- *QUEENS COUNTY.* Filing with the system permits counsel to serve the papers electronically pursuant to NY R UNIF TRIAL CTS § 202.5-b(f) once consent to E-Filing has been filed on-line. Consult NY R UNIF TRIAL CTS § 202.5-bb(c) for service in mandatory e-filing. Any required proof of service should be E-filed as a separate document. NY R L QUEENS E-FILE Doc. 1(E)(4).

c. *Electronic service mandatory; Consenting to electronic service; How electronic service may be made.* Except as otherwise provided in NY R UNIF TRIAL CTS § 202.5-bb, filing and service of all documents in an action that has been commenced electronically in accordance with NY R UNIF TRIAL CTS § 202.5-bb shall be by electronic means. NY R UNIF TRIAL CTS § 202.5-bb(c)(1).

i. *Party's consent required for certain e-filing.* After commencement of an action wherein e-filing is authorized, documents may be electronically filed and served, but only by, and electronic service shall be made only upon, a party or parties who have consented thereto. NY R UNIF TRIAL CTS § 202.5-b(b)(2)(i).

- A consent to e-filing in an action shall state that the party providing it agrees to the use of e-filing in the action and to be bound by the filing and service provisions in NY R UNIF TRIAL CTS § 202.5-b. NY R UNIF TRIAL CTS § 202.5-b(b)(2)(ii).

ii. *Address for service; Duty to notify as to changes.* The e-mail service address recorded at the time of registration is the e-mail address at which service of interlocutory documents on that party may be made through notification transmitted by the NYSCEF site. It is the responsibility of each filing user to monitor that address and promptly notify the Resource Center in the event of a change in his or her e-mail service address. NY R UNIF TRIAL CTS § 202.5-b(f)(2)(i).

iii. *How service made.* An e-filing party causes service of an interlocutory document to be made upon another party participating in e-filing by filing the document electronically. Upon receipt of an interlocutory document, the NYSCEF site shall automatically transmit electronic notification to all e-mail service addresses in such action. NY R UNIF TRIAL CTS § 202.5-b(f)(2)(ii).

- Except as provided otherwise in NY R UNIF TRIAL CTS § 202.5-b(h)(3), the electronic transmission of the notification shall constitute service of the document on the e-mail service addresses identified therein; however, such service will not be effective if the filing party learns that the notification did not reach the address of the person to be served. Proof of such service will be recorded on the NYSCEF site. A party may, however, utilize other service methods permitted by the CPLR provided that, if one of such other methods is used, proof of that service shall be filed electronically. NY R UNIF TRIAL CTS § 202.5-b(f)(2)(ii).

iv. *Signatures on hard copies; Proof of service filed electronically.* When an e-filing party serves a document in hard copy on a non-participating party, the document served shall bear full signatures of all signatories and proof of such service shall be filed electronically. NY R UNIF TRIAL CTS § 202.5-b(b)(2)(i).

- *ERIE COUNTY.* In the NYSCEF system, each Affidavit of Service must be uploaded as a separate .pdf file. After uploading the Affidavit, please choose the document type: "Affirmation/Affidavit of Service" and enter the name of the party served as Additional Document Information. NY R ERIE E FIL Doc. 3(III)(I); NY R ERIE E FIL Doc. 3(V)(F).

v. *Effect of failure to consent.* A party's failure to consent to participation in electronic filing and service shall not bar any other party to the action from filing documents electronically with the County Clerk and the court or serving documents upon any other party who has consented to participation. A party who has not consented to participation shall file documents with the court and the County Clerk, and serve and be served with documents, in hard copy. NY R UNIF TRIAL CTS § 202.5-b(b)(2)(i).

d. *Service upon party.* If a party has not appeared by an attorney or the party's attorney cannot be served, service shall be upon the party by a method specified in NY CPLR Rule 2103(b)(1), NY CPLR Rule 2103(b)(2), NY CPLR Rule 2103(b)(4), NY CPLR Rule 2103(b)(5) or NY CPLR Rule 2103(b)(6). NY CPLR Rule 2103(c).

e. *Service on all parties.* Each paper served on any party shall be served on every other party who has appeared, except as otherwise may be provided by court order or as provided in NY CPLR § 3012 or in NY CPLR § 3215(f). Upon demand by a party, the plaintiff shall supply that party with a list of those who have appeared and the names and addresses of their attorneys. NY CPLR Rule 2103(e).

f. *Service by filing.* If a paper cannot be served by any of the methods specified in NY CPLR Rule 2103(b) and NY CPLR Rule 2103(c), service may be made by filing the paper as if it were a paper required to be filed. NY CPLR Rule 2103(d).

g. *Definitions.* For the purposes of NY CPLR Rule 2103:

i. "Mailing" means the deposit of a paper enclosed in a first class postpaid wrapper, addressed to the address designated by a person for that purpose or, if none is designated, at that person's last known address, in a post office or official depository under the exclusive care and custody of the United States Postal Service within the state;

ii. "Electronic means" means any method of transmission of information between computers or other machines designed for the purpose of sending and receiving such transmissions, and which allows the recipient to reproduce the information transmitted in a tangible medium of expression;

iii. "Facsimile transmission" means any method of transmission of documents to a facsimile machine at a remote location which can automatically produce a tangible copy of such documents. NY CPLR Rule 2103(f).

G. Hearings

1. *Oral argument.* Motion papers received by the clerk of the court on or before the return date shall be deemed submitted as of the return date. The assigned judge, in his or her discretion or at the request of a party, thereafter may determine that any motion be orally argued and may fix a time for oral argument. NY UNIF TRIAL CTS § 202.8(d).

a. A party requesting oral argument shall set forth such request in its notice of motion or in its order to show cause or on the first page of the answering papers, as the case may be. Where all parties to a motion request oral argument, oral argument shall be granted unless the court shall determine it to be unnecessary. NY R UNIF TRIAL CTS § 202.8(d).

b. Where a motion is brought on by order to show cause, the court may set forth in the order that oral argument is required on the return date of the motion. NY R UNIF TRIAL CTS § 202.8(d).

i. *BRONX COUNTY.* All orders to show cause, with the exception of orders to show cause that are returnable in the City Part, the STP Part, the Matrimonial Part and the Preliminary/Compliance Conference Part (IA-11), submitted on or after August 25, 2003, will be returnable on a Monday in the assigned Justice's part and appear on his or her motion calendar. Appearances will be required on orders to show cause. NY R BRONX FIL R Doc. 8. A motion on notice or a notice of petition in a New York Supreme Court E-File (hereafter known as NYSCEF) case, as in others, shall be made returnable in the Motion Support Office (Room 217). NY R BRONX E FIL R Doc. 1(1).

- After a motion/petition and notice are filed with the NYSCEF system, the Motion Support Office will automatically place the motion/proceeding on the submit calendar in the Motion Support Office (Room 217) for the return date. No appearance or other action by the filing attorney is required in order for the motion to be calendared if the motion fee is paid for via NYSCEF. Motions in e-filed cases (other than tax certiorari cases) appear on the submit calendar in Room 217 on the return date. NY R BRONX E FIL R Doc. 1(2).

c. *KINGS COUNTY.* All motions require appearances and oral argument. NY R L KINGS Pt. C, Rule 3.

2. *Return date; Time for hearing.* A notice of motion shall specify the time and place of the hearing on the motion. NY CPLR Rule 2214(a). The moving party determines when a motion on notice shall be heard, but she has to consult the court's or judge's calendar practice first. The movant picks out a "return day" sufficiently far off to assure that the notice requirements of NY CPLR Rule 2214(b) can be met, and to assure as well that the day picked is a day on which the assigned judge hears motions. SIEGEL-NYPRAC § 247.

a. *Judge assigned to hear motion*

i. *Referral to judge supervising disclosure.* Unless the chief administrator of the courts has, by rule, provided otherwise, if a case has been assigned to a judge to supervise disclosure pursuant to NY CPLR § 3104, all motions preliminary to trial shall be referred to such judge whenever practicable. NY CPLR Rule 3214(a).

ii. *Referral to judge who decided prior motion.* Any motion may be referred to a judge who decided a prior motion in the action. NY CPLR Rule 2217(a).

iii. *Transfer when judge unable to hear motion.* If a motion is made to a judge who is or will be for any reason unable to hear it, it may be transferred by order of such judge or by written stipulation of the parties to any other judge to whom it might originally have been made. NY CPLR Rule 2217(c).

iv. *Procedure for unassigned cases.* If a case has not been assigned to a judge, the motion shall be made returnable before the court, and a copy of the moving papers, together with a request for judicial intervention, shall be filed with the court, with proof of service upon all other parties, where required by NY R UNIF TRIAL CTS § 202.6, within five (5) days of service upon the other parties. The moving party shall give written notice of the index number to all other parties immediately after filing of the papers. NY R UNIF TRIAL CTS § 202.8(b).

- *Responding papers.* Copies of all responding papers shall be submitted to the court, with proof of service and with the index number set forth in the papers, on or before the return date. NY R UNIF TRIAL CTS § 202.8(b).
- *Assignment after request for judicial intervention.* The case shall be assigned to a judge as soon as practicable after the filing of the request for judicial intervention pursuant to NY R UNIF TRIAL CTS § 202.6, but in no event later than the return date. After assignment to the judge, the court shall provide for appropriate notice to the parties of the name of the assigned judge. NY R UNIF TRIAL CTS § 202.8(b).
- *Motions to be heard in another county.* Motion papers noticed to be heard in a county other than the county where the venue of the action has been placed by the plaintiff shall be assigned to a judge in accordance with procedures established by the Chief Administrator. NY R UNIF TRIAL CTS § 202.8(b).

v. *ALBANY COUNTY: Motions referred to IAS Justice.* All motions made after a case has been assigned a day certain shall be referred to the IAS Justice unless the motion is returnable during the term in which the matter has been assigned a day certain, in that event, the matter will be referred to the Part 1 Justice for that particular term who may entertain the motion or refer such motion to the IAS Justice. Under those circumstances, the Part I Justice shall decide whether or not to strike the note of issue or assign the matter a new day certain. NY R 3 JD SUP Doc. 1(H)(2). All motions shall be returnable before the assigned justice. NY R 3 JD SUP Doc. 1(B).

b. *Trial of issue raised by motion.* The court may order that an issue of fact raised on a motion shall be separately tried by the court or a referee. If the issue is triable of right by jury, the court shall give the parties an opportunity to demand a jury trial of such issue. Failure to make such demand within the time limited by the court, or, if no such time is limited, before trial begins, shall be deemed a waiver of the right to trial by jury. An order under NY CPLR § 2218 shall specify the issue to be tried. NY CPLR § 2218.

c. *Audio-visual coverage of trial court proceeding.* Audio-visual coverage of proceedings in the trial courts shall be permitted only in accordance with the provisions of Part 131 of the Rules of the Chief Administrator (NY R CHIEF ADMIN § 131.1, et seq.). NY R CHIEF J § 29.3.

d. *Adjournment of return date.* Stipulations of adjournment of the return date made by the parties shall be in writing and shall be submitted to the assigned judge. Such stipulation shall be effective unless the court otherwise directs. No more than three (3) stipulated adjournments for an aggregate period of sixty (60) days shall be submitted without prior permission of the court. NY R UNIF TRIAL CTS § 202.8(e)(1).

i. Absent agreement by the parties, a request by any party for an adjournment shall be submitted in writing, upon notice to the other party, to the assigned judge on or before the return date. The court will notify the requesting party whether the adjournment has been granted. NY R UNIF TRIAL CTS § 202.8(e)(2).

ii. *BRONX COUNTY.* Non-disclosure motions for IA5, IA7 and IA22 will be adjourned for oral argument to the Monday of the second week following the week of the return date of the motion. All other non-disclosure motions will be deemed submitted on the return date and forwarded to Chambers unless a stipulation of adjournment complying with the requirements of NY R UNIF TRIAL CTS § 202.8(e) is submitted, in which event, the motion will be adjourned for the requested date and kept in the Clerk's Office. If a non-stipulated request for adjournment or notice is submitted, the motion and request will be forwarded to Chambers for judicial approval or denial of the request. In either event, the attorney requesting the adjournment will be notified, via telephone, of the granting or denial of the request and instructed to notify his adversary. NY R BRONX FIL R Doc. 8.

iii. *BRONX COUNTY.* Motions that have been e-filed may be adjourned in Room 217 if an adjournment complies with the procedures of the Motion Support Office (explained in the "Filing Rules—Motion Procedure" section of the "Courthouse Procedures" link on the website of [the] court). An adjournment that so complies may be obtained by filing a stipulation of all parties with NYSCEF (designated in the filing menu as a "Stipulation to Adjourn Motion"). NY R BRONX E FIL R Doc. 1(3).

iv. *NEW YORK COUNTY.* The Courtroom also maintains a "APB (All Papers By)" Calendar, which is used when a party seeks an adjournment but fails to comply with the Courtroom's procedures or there is a failure to comply with procedures that requires the clerk to adjourn the motion/application (e.g., failure to submit a Confirmation Notice in an e-filed case). The case may be put over for three days to allow compliance with those procedures, as described further below. NY R NY CTY Procedure II(C); NY R NY CTY E FIL Doc. 2(D)(2). E-filed applications may be adjourned in the Part if an adjournment complies with the Part's procedures (see the Uniform Rules of the Justices (Local Rules) on the court's website). An adjournment that so complies may be obtained by filing with NYSCEF a stipulation of all parties (designated in the filing menu as a Stipulation—Adjournment of Motion—Before Judge); the motion number and the current return date of the motion being adjourned shall be set forth in the "Additional Document Information" field in NYSCEF. Absent any problems, the Part will effectuate the adjournment without need for an appearance or any other action by the parties. NY R NY CTY E FIL Doc. 2(D)(4).

v. *QUEENS COUNTY.* The Motion Support Office is NOT authorized to grant adjournments. NY R L QUEENS MOT SUP Doc. 1.

e. *ALBANY COUNTY: Motion terms.* There shall be a. . . Motion Term on each Friday in the Supreme Court, Albany County. The Friday Motion Term shall include all Article 78 Proceedings involving New York State and proceedings commenced pursuant to Article 14 of the Civil Service Law (including applications for injunctive relief made pursuant to section 209-a of the Civil Service Law). NY R 3 JD SUP Doc. 1(F). Generally, parties will be granted only one adjournment for the Friday Motion Term. NY R 3 JD SUP Doc. 1(F).

f. *ALBANY COUNTY: Motion determined without hearing.* All motions are deemed "submitted" on the return date and no appearances are required by the parties. NY R 3 JD SUP Doc. 1(B). In the event oral argument is requested, the parties should not appear on the return date. At the discretion of the assigned Judge and upon the granting of a request for oral argument, the parties will be notified by Chambers of the scheduled time and place at which argument will be heard. Where a motion is brought on by order to show cause, the court may set forth in the order that appearances and/or oral argument are required on the return date of the motion. NY R 3 JD SUP Doc. 1(B).

g. *BRONX COUNTY: Return date.* All assigned and unassigned motions will be returnable five (5) days a week in the Civil Branch Clerk's Office, Room 217, at 9:30 a.m. NY R BRONX FIL R Doc. 8.

i. If on any submitted non-disclosure motion oral argument is requested and granted, or directed by the Court, the motion shall be adjourned for oral argument before the I.A. Judge on the second Monday following the week of the return date of the motion. Attorneys will be notified via telephone of the adjourned date. NY R BRONX FIL R Doc. 8.

h. *BRONX COUNTY: Oral argument.* Calendars of disclosure motions and other motions adjourned for oral argument will be published for the four (4) business days preceding the rescheduled appearance date and on the rescheduled date of the motion. These repetitive publications will serve as the notification of procedure of adjournment of all motions. In addition, two (2) days before the return date of unassigned motions a list of such motions indicating the assigned Justice and the adjourned date of the motion will be published. NY R BRONX FIL R Doc. 8.

i. *BRONX COUNTY: Resolution before return date.* Counsel/parties must advise the Court in writing on or before the return date of all motions that have been resolved by Counsel/parties themselves and all motions the movant(s) wish to be withdrawn. NY R BRONX FIL R Doc. 8.

j. *ERIE COUNTY: Calendaring of motions.* Refer to individual Justice's Part Rules. NY R ERIE E FIL Doc. 3(V)(B).

k. *KINGS COUNTY: Return date set by court.* Irrespective of the return date indicated in the notice of motion, motions will be rescheduled by the E-file/Motion Support Office to a date designated by the assigned Judge. NY R L KINGS Pt. C, Rule 2.

l. *KINGS COUNTY: Calendar calls.* There shall be two (2) calendar calls on motion days. The first calendar call shall be at 9:30 AM and the second calendar call shall be at 10:45 AM, unless the Judge's Part Rules provide otherwise. Defaults shall only be taken on second call. Attorneys with appearances elsewhere in the courthouse may advise the clerk of their whereabouts to avoid a default. Failure to so advise the clerk or appear at the default calendar call will result in a default order being entered or the motion being marked off the calendar. NY R L KINGS Pt. C, Rule 7.

m. *NEW YORK COUNTY: Return date and assigned courtroom.* Motions made by notice of motion and petitions and notices of petition in special proceedings are processed by the General Clerk's Office (Room 119) and are to be made returnable in the Motion Submission Part Courtroom (Room 130) on any business day of the week at 9:30 AM. There are some differences in electronically-filed cases. NY R NY CTY Procedure II; NY R NY CTY Procedure II(C); NY R NY CTY J RUL Rule 13(a).

i. For the convenience of counsel, between 9:00 A.M. and 9:30 A.M. each day, in advance of the "call," Room 130 accepts (1) written stipulations; (2) affidavits/affirmations reciting the required details as to an adjournment on consent; (3) stipulations, letters or other writings withdrawing motions; and (4) final papers or complete sets of papers on motions. For motions in which these items are handed in before the "call," no one need remain to answer the "call." Counsel/parties must advise the court, either between 9:00 A.M. and 9:30 A.M. or at the "call," of all motions or cases that have been resolved by counsel/parties themselves and all motions that the movant no longer wishes to pursue. If such resolution occurs subsequent to the "call", the assigned Justice must be advised as soon as possible, by written notice sent to the Part, so that the court does not do unnecessary work. NY R NY CTY Procedure II(C).

ii. Depending upon the assigned Part, contested motions submitted in the Motion Submission Part Courtroom are submitted without argument, or rescheduled for oral argument if so directed by the assigned Justice. For Justices who schedule argument on a case-by-case basis, notice of the argument date will be transmitted by the court. Counsel may ascertain how a motion submitted in Courtroom 130 was marked by consulting Scroll on the court's website, the e-Track application, or, on the two (2) days immediately following the submission date, the New York Law Journal. NY R NY CTY J RUL Rule 13(a).

n. *NEW YORK COUNTY: Motion call.* Each day in the Motion Submission Part Courtroom, commencing at 9:30 A.M., all motions returnable that day will be "called" for the submission of these papers, which must be handed up at this "call" or, as described below, immediately before. Because hundreds of motions appear on the Room 130 calendars every day, motion papers (other than part of the moving papers as described above) cannot be accepted on any day prior to the return date. Courtesy copies are not required nor accepted, but working copies are required by certain Justices in e-filed cases. NY R NY CTY Procedure II(C). If argument is directed, it will take place on an announced date shortly after the day of submission. NY R NY CTY Procedure II(C).

o. *NEW YORK COUNTY: Oral arguments.* Pursuant to request of some Justices, motions submitted in Room 130 will automatically be scheduled for a set argument date in the Part. Other Justices determine on a case-by-case basis after submission in Room 130 whether to accept a particular substantive motion on submission, to require oral argument, or to hold a conference. NY R NY CTY Procedure II(D). If argument is directed by the Justice automatically, notice of argument and the argument date will be given in Room 130. Any appearing party is expected to give notice to all parties and an announcement to this effect is made in Room 130. If the motion is submitted in Room 130 and the Justice, after examining the file, determines that argument should be directed, notice of the argument and the argument date will not be sent by the court. To obtain notification of the argument date and other developments, counsel should use e-Track. If argument notification is not given or transmitted as just described, counsel should understand that the motion has been taken on submission for decision on the papers. NY R NY CTY Procedure II(D).

i. Calendars of motions to be argued in the Parts are published on the morning of the argument date and on the day before in the New York Law Journal under each Part. Argument information is available on a case-by-case basis in Scroll, and e-mail notifications are sent by e-Track to participating attorneys whenever a motion is scheduled for argument in the court's computer system. NY R NY CTY J RUL Rule 15(a)

p. *NEW YORK COUNTY: Motion determined without hearing.* Given the purpose of the Room 130 procedure, the substance of motions will not be addressed at the submission "call." No Judge is present. To the extent possible, motions submitted in Room 130 will be decided "on the papers." Indeed, attorneys are encouraged to use service or clerks to deliver papers or working copies, or to agree among themselves to have one of them deliver papers for all parties by service or a clerk. Counsel for the movant need not appear to "take a default" on any motion or for any other reason. Motions will be submitted, not marked off, in the absence of the movant. Opposing counsel similarly need not appear in person in order to avoid suffering a default. Delivery of papers by service or a clerk will suffice. The court's goal is to be able to collect papers on motions in an orderly fashion but without any attorney having to make an appearance in Room 130 at any time. NY R NY CTY Procedure II(C).

q. *ONONDAGA COUNTY: Return date.* If the motion is the first filing in an action, the case will be assigned and counsel will be notified by the Supreme Court Clerk's Office via the NYSCEF system of the assigned justice and return date. NY R ONDGA E FIL Protocol(B)(7)(c). If the motion is on a previously assigned case, counsel may choose a return date from the assigned justice's motion term schedule. If the date in unavailable, the Supreme Court Clerk's Office will assign the motion to the next available motion term date and will notify counsel via e-mail. The change will also appear in the notification generated by the NYSCEF system. NY R ONDGA E FIL Protocol(B)(7)(d).

r. *QUEENS COUNTY: Return date.* Motions must be made returnable on the proper day/time based on the assigned judge. NY R L QUEENS MOT SUP Doc. 1. Failure to make a motion returnable on the proper day/time may result in the motion being administratively rescheduled or marked off. NY R L QUEENS MOT SUP Doc. 1.

s. *QUEENS COUNTY: Unassigned motions.* For RJI/Motions, due to the fact that the movant would not know who the assigned judge will be, the notice of motion may be returnable any day of the week. RJI/Motions shall be made returnable in "Queens Supreme Court" with no address designated. The motion will be administratively rescheduled to the proper day of the week based on the judge (once a judge has been assigned). Within one (1) week of filing, the movant must check online to see who the assigned judge is (and therefore the location/date/time) that their motion is now returnable. Movant must then notify their adversary of this information prior to the return date. NY R L QUEENS MOT SUP Doc. 1.

3. *Entry of order after hearing.* An order determining a motion shall be entered and filed in the office of the clerk of the court where the action is triable, and all papers used on the motion and any opinion or memorandum in writing shall be filed with that clerk unless the order dispenses with such filing. When a statute or civil practice rule requires such filing and entry in a county other than that in which the order was made, the party prevailing on the motion shall file the order and the papers used on the motion with the proper clerk after receiving them. If a party fails to file any papers required to be filed under NY CPLR Rule 2220(a), the order may be vacated as irregular, with costs. NY CPLR Rule 2220(a). For more information on the entry of an order after a motion, refer to NY CPLR Rule 2219.

a. *BRONX COUNTY: Settled orders.* A Judge's decision will often call for a Settled Order. The purpose of the settled order is to give effect to the decision by directing that some action be done and/or that a court official perform some task. NY R BRONX LEG SUP Doc. 2. A settled order consists of a notice of settlement informing all parties that the proposed order will be presented to the judge who made the decision on a date certain. Next comes the proposed order which will be presented to the judge. This order should conform to the judge's decision and should direct the relief granted in the decision. This should be followed by proof of service upon all parties who were noticed with the decision. It is also helpful if a copy of the judge's decision is included along with the other papers. A settled order should always be noticed before the judge who made the decision. NY R BRONX LEG SUP Doc. 2.

i. Although an order is usually settled by the party who prevailed on the motion, any party may settle the order. It should be presented to the court within sixty (60) days of the decision. The other parties are entitled to ten (10) days notice where service of the settled order is done by mail, five (5) days if the notice is personally delivered. An attorney who is served with a notice of settlement which he believes does not accurately reflect the decision may settle a counter order. The counter order must be noticed for the same day and must be served not less than seven (7) days if by mail and two (2) days if personally delivered. NY R BRONX LEG SUP Doc. 2.

ii. Settled orders are usually sent to the judge the day after they noticed for settlement. No appearance is necessary or even contemplated on a settled order. If the decision directs "submit order", then no notice is necessary, and the order will be sent to the judge as soon a practical after it is received. No fees are collected on settled orders. NY R BRONX LEG SUP Doc. 2.

b. *ERIE COUNTY: Proposed orders.* Proposed orders shall be submitted through the NYSCEF system and a working copy provided to the IAS Justice for signature, if Part Rules so require. NY R ERIE E FIL Doc. 3(V)(G).

c. *KINGS COUNTY: Long form orders.* If the Court directs that an order be settled or submitted on a motion in a NYSCEF case, the proposed order, with Notice of Settlement where required, and any proposed counter-order shall be filed with the Court via NYSCEF. The relevant clerk's office will process the documents in the customary manner. NY R L KINGS E FIL Doc. 1(E).

i. WORKING COPIES OF PROPOSED ORDERS WITH NOTICE OF SETTLEMENT MUST BE SUBMITTED IN THE MOTION SUPPORT OFFICE (ROOM 227) AS EXPLAINED HEREIN. THEY MUST NOT BE DELIVERED TO THE PART OR CHAMBERS, EXCEPT WHERE THE INDIVIDUAL JUSTICE'S PART RULES PROVIDE OTHERWISE; DOING SO WILL CAUSE ADMINISTRATIVE CONFUSION AND POSSIBLE MISPLACEMENT OF PAPERS. Any such submission shall be sent in a timely manner (kindly review individual Justice's rules) and be conspicuously marked on the outside "NYSCEF Matter;" lack of such marking may delay processing. After an order/counter-order has been signed, it will be scanned, and the County Clerk will affix the entry stamp into the NYSCEF system, which will immediately transmit notice of this event via e-mail, including a link to the entered document, to all participating attorneys and unrepresented litigants in the case. Such transmittal does not constitute Notice of Entry. NY R L KINGS E FIL Doc. 1(E).

d. *NEW YORK COUNTY: Long form orders.* Although the court strongly favors the use of short form orders and judgments, there are instances when settlement of an order or judgment is appropriate. When a Justice directs in a decision that a long form order or judgment be settled, that decision is recorded in the court's computer system by the General Clerk's Office and the motion file with decision is held in the Order Section of the Office in Room 119. The settlement process takes place there. NY R NY CTY Procedure II(D); NY R NY CTY E FIL Doc. 2(E).

i. A proposed long form order or judgment in compliance NY R UNIF TRIAL CTS § 202.48 must be presented to the relevant back office, together with a notice of settlement which bears a settlement date, the date on which the order is to be ready for formal presentation to the Justice. In an e-filed case the submission shall be made electronically. The proposed order or counter-order should be e-filed and it will be transmitted automatically by the NYSCEF system to the appropriate back office. The return date and time of the proposed order must be at 9:30 A.M. no sooner than either five (5) days from personal service of the proposed order or ten (10) days from service by mail. Proof of timely service on the other parties must accompany the proposed order in a hard copy case. If an order or judgment is submitted late (later than sixty (60) days from signing and filing of the decision) and the proponent can show good cause for this tardiness, an affidavit or affirmation justifying the delay should be annexed to the proposed order, together with proof of service thereof. If persuaded, the Justice will consider the proposed order despite its untimeliness. NY R NY CTY Procedure II(D); NY R NY CTY E FIL Doc. 2(E).

ii. Sometimes a decision will state "Submit Order." The submitting party should prepare a long form order and make it returnable without notice. Counsel should deliver the proposed order to the Order Section of the appropriate back office, except in an e-filed case, when it shall be submitted electronically. NY R NY CTY Procedure II(D). If the decision of the court directs that a proposed order be settled or submitted in the Part or in Chambers, that direction, should, of course, be followed without presentation of the proposal to the back office. NY R NY CTY Procedure II(D).

iii. For information on proposed counter-orders, refer to NY R NY CTY Procedure II(D) and NY R NY CTY J RUL Rule 16(b).

e. *QUEENS COUNTY: Proposed orders.* If the court directs that an order be settled or submitted on a motion in an E-file case, the proposed order and any proposed counter-order shall be filed with the court on-line with proof of service. (If a decision refers to a proceeding on the record, a copy of the transcript must be submitted.) Working copies of all proposed orders MUST be submitted to the Motion Support Office before an order can be reviewed. NY R L QUEENS E-FILE Doc. 1(I).

i. Counsel are advised to adhere to NY R UNIF TRIAL CTS § 202.48 regarding the submission or settlement of their proposed order or judgment. Persons who are submitting proposed orders/judgments pursuant to a previously issued memorandum decision must submit a copy of the memorandum decision with their proposed order/judgment. Upon E-Filing a proposed order/judgement, a working copy of the proposed order/judgement must be provided to the Motion Support Office. NY R L QUEENS MOT SUP Doc. 1.

H. Forms

1. Official Motion for Continuance/Extension of Time Forms for New York

a. Request for judicial intervention. NY R UNIF TRIAL CTS § 202.6.

b. Notice of motion. NY R UNIF TRIAL CTS § 202.7(b).

2. New York Motion for Continuance/Extension of Time Forms

a. Affidavit in support of motion for extension of time to reply to request for admission. MCF CPLR § 6:194.

b. Notice of motion for extension of time to file notice of dental, medical, or podiatric malpractice action. MCF CPLR § 7:9.

c. Affidavit in support of motion for extension of time to file notice of dental, medical, or podiatric malpractice action. MCF CPLR § 7:10.

d. Notice of motion for extension of time to serve complaint. MCF CPLR § 12:54.

e. Affirmation in support of motion for extension of time to serve complaint. MCF CPLR § 12:55.

f. Affidavit in support of motion to extend time to answer or move in relation to complaint. MCF CPLR § 12:59.

g. Affidavit in support of motion to extend time to answer or move in relation to complaint; Attorney's illness. MCF CPLR § 12:60.

h. Affirmation in support of motion for extension of time to serve reply to counterclaim. MCF CPLR § 12:64.

i. General form of affidavit of service of motion papers. MCF CPLR § 5:24.

I. Applicable Rules

1. *State rules*
   a. Short title; Application; Construction; Definitions. NY CPLR § 101; NY CPLR § 103; NY CPLR § 104; NY CPLR § 105.
   b. Appendix of official forms. NY CPLR § 107.
   c. Extensions of time generally. NY CPLR § 2004; NY CPLR § 2005.
   d. Form of papers. NY CPLR Rule 2101; NY CPLR Rule 2102; NY CPLR § 2105; NY CPLR Rule 2106; NY GEN BUS § 399-ddd; NY R UNIF TRIAL CTS § 215.2; NY R UNIF TRIAL CTS § 215.3.
   e. Service of papers. NY CPLR Rule 2103.
   f. Where motion made; In supreme court action. NY CPLR § 2212.
   g. Motion papers; Service; Time. NY CPLR Rule 2214.
   h. Relief demanded by other than moving party. NY CPLR Rule 2215.
   i. Prior motion; Ex parte motion; Transfer of motion; Hearings; Orders. NY CPLR Rule 2217; NY CPLR § 2218; NY CPLR Rule 2220.
   j. Computation of time. NY CPLR § 2402; NY GEN CONSTR § 19; NY GEN CONSTR § 20; NY GEN CONSTR § 25-a; NY GEN CONSTR § 30; NY GEN CONSTR § 31; NY GEN CONSTR § 53.
   k. Service of pleadings and demand for complaint. NY CPLR § 3012.
   l. Motions heard by judge supervising disclosure; Stay of disclosure. NY CPLR Rule 3214.
   m. Continuances. NY CPLR Rule 4402; NY R CHIEF ADMIN § 125.1; NY R UNIF TRIAL CTS § 202.32.
   n. Fees; Index number fees of county clerks. NY CPLR § 8018.
   o. Hours of court; Proceedings in court. NY R CHIEF J § 3.1; NY R CHIEF J § 29.3.
   p. Application of part; Waiver; Additional rules; Application of CPLR; Definitions. NY R UNIF TRIAL CTS § 202.1.
   q. Papers filed in court; Electronic filing in supreme court. NY R UNIF TRIAL CTS § 202.5; NY R UNIF TRIAL CTS § 202.5-a; NY R UNIF TRIAL CTS § 202.5-b; NY R UNIF TRIAL CTS § 202.5-bb.
   r. Request for judicial intervention. NY R UNIF TRIAL CTS § 202.6.
   s. Calendaring of motions; Uniform notice of motion form; Affirmation of good faith. NY R UNIF TRIAL CTS § 202.7.
   t. Motion procedure; Preliminary conferences. NY R UNIF TRIAL CTS § 202.8; NY R UNIF TRIAL CTS § 202.12.
   u. Rules of the commercial division of the Supreme Court. NY R UNIF TRIAL CTS § 202.70.
   v. Signing of papers. NY R CHIEF ADMIN § 130-1.1-a.
2. *Local rules*
   a. *Albany County*
      i. Third judicial district rules. NY R 3 JD SUP Doc. 1.
   b. *Bronx County*
      i. Filing of papers in supreme court. NY R BRONX FIL R Doc. 1.
      ii. Request for judicial intervention. NY R BRONX FIL R Doc. 2.
      iii. Motion procedure. NY R BRONX FIL R Doc. 8.
      iv. Commercial division. NY R BRONX FIL R Doc. 12.
      v. Motions on notice. NY R BRONX E FIL R Doc. 1.
      vi. Settled orders. NY R BRONX LEG SUP Doc. 2.
   c. *Erie County*
      i. Joint protocols for New York State Courts E-Filing (NYSCEF) cases filed in Supreme Court, Erie County. NY R ERIE E FIL Doc. 3.
   d. *Kings County*
      i. Papers. NY R L KINGS Pt. A, Papers.

ii. Service of motion papers. NY R L KINGS Pt. C, Rule 1.

iii. Scheduling of motions. NY R L KINGS Pt. C, Rule 2.

iv. Appearance and argument. NY R L KINGS Pt. C, Rule 3.

v. Adjournment of motions. NY R L KINGS Pt. C, Rule 4.

vi. Courtesy copies. NY R L KINGS Pt. C, Rule 5.

vii. Motion calendar calls. NY R L KINGS Pt. C, Rule 7.

viii. Adjournments. NY R L KINGS Pt. E, Rule 3.

ix. Adjournment of motions. NY R L KINGS Pt. E, Rule 12.

x. Pre calendar procedures. NY R L KINGS Rule I.

xi. Protocol on courthouse and county clerk procedures for electronically filed cases. NY R L KINGS E FIL Doc. 1.

e. *New York County*

i. Commencement of cases. NY R NY CTY Procedure I.

ii. RJIs and assignments. NY R NY CTY Procedure IA.

iii. Motions and special proceedings by notice of motion/petition. NY R NY CTY Procedure II.

iv. Conferences & case management. NY R NY CTY Procedure V.

v. Trials. NY R NY CTY Procedure VIII.

vi. County clerk litigation functions. NY R NY CTY Procedure XI.

vii. Protocol on courthouse and county clerk procedures for electronically filed cases. NY R NY CTY E FIL Doc. 2.

viii. Redaction of information in documents filed with the county clerk and the court. NY R NY CTY J RUL Rule A-1.

ix. Papers by fax. NY R NY CTY J RUL Rule 4.

x. Adjournments of conferences. NY R NY CTY J RUL Rule 6.

xi. Discovery schedule. NY R NY CTY J RUL Rule 8.

xii. Motions on notice; Orders to show cause. NY R NY CTY J RUL Rule 13.

xiii. Motion papers. NY R NY CTY J RUL Rule 14.

xiv. Oral argument; Adjournments. NY R NY CTY J RUL Rule 15.

f. *Onondaga County*

i. Onondaga county protocol for case filings New York State Electronic Files (NYSCEF). NY R ONDGA E FIL Protocol.

g. *Queens County*

i. Motion support office. NY R L QUEENS MOT SUP Doc. 1.

ii. Queens county protocol on courthouse procedures for electronically filed cases. NY R L QUEENS E-FILE Doc. 1.

J. Miscellaneous

NOTE: Individual judges' rules may apply.

ALBANY COUNTY

JUSTICE LISA M. FISHER: NY R 3 JD FISHER Fisher; NY R 3 JD FISHER Fisher, PC Order.

JUSTICE RICHARD MOTT: NY R 3 JD MOTT Mott.

JUSTICE STEPHAN G. SCHICK: NY R 3 JD Schick.

FORECLOSURE SETTLEMENT PART: NY R 3 JD Foreclosure Settlement.

BRONX COUNTY

JUSTICE PAUL L. ALPERT: [NY R BRONX J Part IA-29, as amended by NY ORDER 20-0337].

JUSTICE BEN BARBATO: NY R BRONX J Part IA-21.

JUSTICE MARY ANNE BRIGANTTI: [NY R BRONX J Part IA-15, as amended by NY ORDER 20-0338].

JUSTICE JOSEPH E. CAPELLA: NY R BRONX J Part IA-23.

JUSTICE MITCHELL DANZIGER: NY R BRONX J Part IA-3/33 ; [NY R BRONX J Danziger, Part IA-3/33, as amended by NY ORDER 20-0339].

JUSTICE LAURA G. DOUGLAS: NY R BRONX J Part IA-11.

JUSTICE RUBEN FRANCO: NY R BRONX J Part IA-26.

JUSTICE DORIS M. GONZALEZ: NY R BRONX J Part IA-24.

JUSTICE WILMA GUZMAN: NY R BRONX J Part IA-7; [NY R BRONX J Guzman, Part IA-7 Virtual, as amended by NY ORDER 20-0340].

JUSTICE ROBERT T. JOHNSON: NY R BRONX J Part IA-12.

JUSTICE DONALD A. MILES: NY R BRONX J Part IA-8.

JUSTICE DONNA M. MILLS: NY R BRONX J Part IA-9.

JUSTICE JULIA I. RODRIGUEZ: NY R BRONX J Part IA-18; [NY R BRONX J Part IA-27, as amended by NY ORDER 20-0341].

JUSTICE LLINET M. ROSADO: [NY R BRONX J Part IA-25, as amended by NY ORDER 20-0342].

JUSTICE NORMA RUIZ: NY R BRONX J Part IA-22; [NY R BRONX J Ruiz, Part IA-22 Virtual, as amended by NY ORDER 20-0343].

JUSTICE HOWARD H. SHERMAN: NY R BRONX J Part IA-4.

JUSTICE FERNANDO TAPIA: NY R BRONX J Part IA-13.

JUSTICE ELIZABETH A. TAYLOR: NY R BRONX J Part IA-2.

JUSTICE ALISON Y. TRUITT: NY R BRONX J Part IA-5.

PART IDV: NY R BRONX J Doc. 1.

PRE-TRIAL PART RULES: NY R BRONX J Doc. 2.

PRE TRIAL WORKSHEET: NY R BRONX J Doc. 3.

FORECLOSURE SETTLEMENT PART RULES: NY R BRONX J Doc. 4.

GUARDIANSHIP PART RULES: NY R BRONX J Doc. 5.

LPM PART RULES: NY R BRONX J Doc. 6.

ERIE COUNTY

JUSTICE M. WILLIAM BOLLER: NY R 8 JD J Boller.

JUSTICE RALPH A. BONIELLO: NY R 8 JD J Boniello.

JUSTICE CHRISTOPHER J. BURN: NY R 8 JD J Burns.

JUSTICE RUSSELL P. BUSCAGLIA: NY R 8 JD J Buscaglia.

JUSTICE FRANK CARUSO: NY R 8 JD J Caruso.

JUSTICE STEPHEN W. CASS: NY R 8 JD J Cass.

JUSTICE DEBORAH A. CHIMES: NY R 8 JD J Chimes.

JUSTICE EMILIO COLAIACOVO: [NY R 8 JD J Colaiacovo, as amended by NY ORDER 20-0252].

JUSTICE DIANE Y. DEVLIN: NY R 8 JD J Devlin.

JUSTICE JAMES H. DILLON: NY R 8 JD J Dillon.

JUSTICE PAULA L. FEROLETO: NY R 8 JD J Feroleto.

JUSTICE DANIEL J. FURLONG: [NY R 8 JD J Furlong, as amended by NY ORDER 20-0253].

JUSTICE JOSEPH R. GLOWNIA: NY R 8 JD J Glownia.

JUSTICE MARK J. GRISANTI: NY R 8 JD J Grisanti.

JUSTICE DEBORAH A. HAENDIGES: NY R 8 JD J Haendiges.

JUSTICE LYNN W. KEANE: [NY R 8 JD J Keane, as amended by NY ORDER 20-0254].

JUSTICE RICHARD C. KLOCH, Sr.: NY R 8 JD J Kloch.

JUSTICE FREDERICK J. MARSHALL: [NY R 8 JD J Marshall, as amended by NY ORDER 20-0255.

JUSTICE JOHN L. MICHALSKI: NY R 8 JD J Michalski.

JUSTICE MARK A. MONTOUR: [NY R 8 JD J Montour, as amended by NY ORDER 20-0256].

JUSTICE HENRY NOWAK: NY R 8 JD J Nowak.

JUSTICE JOHN F. O'DONNELL: NY R 8 JD J O'Donnell.

JUSTICE JEANETTE OGDEN: NY R 8 JD J Ogden.

JUSTICE CATHERINE NUGENT-PANEPINTO: NY R 8 JD J Nugent-Panepinto.

JUSTICE FRANK A. SEDITA, III: [NY R 8 JD J Sedita, as amended by NY ORDER 20-0257].

JUSTICE SARA SHELDON: NY R 8 JD J Sheldon.

JUSTICE DONNA M. SIWEK: NY R 8 JD J Siwek.

JUSTICE MARY L. SLISZ: NY R 8 JD J Slisz.

JUSTICE TIMOTHY J. WALKER: [NY R 8 JD J Walker, as amended by NY ORDER 20-0258].

JUSTICE DENNIS E. WARD: NY R 8 JD J Ward.

JUSTICE PAUL B. WOJTASZEK: [NY R 8 JD J Wojtaszek, as amended by NY ORDER 20-0259].

JUSTICE CHARLES N. ZAMBITO: [NY R 8 JD J Zambito, as amended by NY ORDER 20-0260].

SUPREME COURT LEGAL STAFF: NY R 8 JD J Legal Staff.

KINGS COUNTY

JUSTICE RACHEL A. ADAMS: NY R KINGS J Part 5F.

JUSTICE LOREN BAILY-SCHIFFMAN: NY R KINGS J Part 65.

JUSTICE REGINALD A. BODDIE: NY R KINGS J Part 95.

JUSTICE THERESA M. CICCOTTO: NY R KINGS J Part 19; NY R KINGS J Part 5J.

JUSTICE LISSETTE COLON: NY R KINGS J Part Rules.

JUSTICE GENINE EDWARDS: NY R KINGS J Part 80.

JUSTICE PAMELA L. FISHER: [NY R KINGS J Part 94, as amended by NY ORDER 20-0208].

JUSTICE ROBIN GARSON: NY R KINGS J Part 75.

JUSTICE LARA J. GENOVISI: [NY R KINGS J Part 34, as amended by NY ORDER 20-0209].

JUSTICE BERNARD J. GRAHAM: NY R KINGS J Part 36.

JUSTICE DAWN JIMENEZ-SALTA: NY R KINGS J Part 88.

JUSTICE INGRID JOSEPH: [NY R KINGS J Part FRP3 and Part 83, as amended by NY ORDER 20-0210].

JUSTICE KATHY J. KING: NY R KINGS J Part 64, 76K.

JUSTICE LAWRENCE KNIPEL: NY R KINGS J Part 57.

JUSTICE DONALD KURTZ: NY R KINGS J Part 26.

JUSTICE CARL LANDICINO: [NY R KINGS J Part 81, as amended by NY ORDER 20-0211].

JUSTICE KATHERINE LEVINE: [NY R KINGS J Part 20, 25, 92, as amended by NY ORDER 20-0211].

JUSTICE LORNA MCALLISTER: [NY R KINGS J Part 10, as amended by NY ORDER 20-0211].

JUSTICE ROSEMARIE MONTALBANO: [NY R KINGS J Part 19, 71, and 22, as amended by NY ORDER 20-0211].

JUSTICE RICHARD J. MONTELIONE: [NY R KINGS J Part 99 and DJMP, as amended by NY ORDER 20-0215].

JUSTICE LISA S. OTTLEY: NY R KINGS J Part 24.

JUSTICE MARK I. PARTNOW: NY R KINGS J Part 43.

JUSTICE ERIC I. PRUS: NY R KINGS J Part 5A.
JUSTICE FRANCOIS RIVERA: NY R KINGS J Part 52.
JUSTICE KAREN B. ROTHENBERG: NY R KINGS J Part 35.
JUSTICE LEON RUCHELSMAN: NY R KINGS J Part 1.
JUSTICE WAYNE P. SAITTA: NY R KINGS J Part 29.
JUSTICE ROBIN K. SHEARES: NY R KINGS J Part 96.
JUSTICE KENNETH P. SHERMAN: NY R KINGS J Part 67 and 78.
JUSTICE DEBRA SILBER: NY R KINGS J Part 9 and 5K.
JUSTICE ELLEN M. SPODEK: NY R KINGS J Part 63.
JUSTICE MARSHA L. STEINHARDT: NY R KINGS J Part 15.
JUSTICE JEFFREY S. SUNSHINE: NY R KINGS J Part 5G.
JUSTICE PETER P. SWEENEY: [NY R KINGS J Part 35, as amended by NY ORDER 20-0218].
JUSTICE DELORES J. THOMAS: [NY R KINGS J Part 5T, as amended by NY ORDER 20-0221].
JUSTICE WAVNY TOUSSAINT: NY R KINGS J Part 70.
JUSTICE RICHARD VELASQUEZ: NY R KINGS J Part 66.
JUSTICE CAROLYN E. WADE: NY R KINGS J Part 84.
JUSTICE EDWARD G. WALKER: [NY R KINGS J Part 90, as amended by NY ORDER 20-0219].
JUSTICE LILLIAN WAN: [NY R KINGS J Part 17, as amended by NY ORDER 20-0220].
JUSTICE MICHELLE WESTON: NY R KINGS J Part 3.
MENTAL HYGIENE PART: NY R KINGS J Part 77.
MATRIMONIAL PARTS DURING COVID-19 EMERGENCY: JUSTICE KAREN B. ROTHENBERG: NY R KINGS J Doc. 1.

NASSAU COUNTY

JUSTICE ANNA R. ANZALONE: NY R NASSAU S J Anzalone, Part 26.
JUSTICE STACY D. BENNETT: NY R NASSAU S J Bennett; NY R NASSAU S J Bennett, Form 1.
JUSTICE ANTONIO BRANDVEEN: NY R NASSAU S J Brandveen, Part 31.
JUSTICE JEFFREY S. BROWN: [NY R NASSAU S J Brown, as amended by NY ORDER 20-0297].
JUSTICE STEPHEN A. BUCARIA: NY R NASSAU S J Bucaria.
JUSTICE JULIANNE T. CAPETOLA: NY R NASSAU S J Capetola, Part 28.
JUSTICE EDMUND M. DANE: NY R NASSAU S J Dane, Part 33.
JUSTICE VITO M. DESTEFANO: NY R NASSAU S J DeStefano, Part 13; NY R NASSAU S J DeStefano, Form 1.
JUSTICE ARTHUR M. DIAMOND: NY R NASSAU S J Diamond, Part 7.
JUSTICE THOMAS FEINMAN: NY R NASSAU S J Feinman, Part 5.
JUSTICE JOHN M. GALASSO: NY R NASSAU S J Galasso, Part 22.
JUSTICE SHARON M.J. GIANELLI: NY R NASSAU S J Gianelli, Part 22; NY R NASSAU S J Gianelli, Form 1.
JUSTICE JEFFREY A. GOODSTEIN: NY R NASSAU S J Goodstein, Part 33; NY R NASSAU S J Goodstein, Form 1.
JUSTICE DAVID J. GUGERTY: [NY R NASSAU S J Gugerty, Part 31, as amended by NY ORDER 20-0298].
JUSTICE HELENE F. GUGERTY: NY R NASSAU S J Gugerty, Part 47.
JUSTICE STEVEN M. JAEGER: NY R NASSAU S J Jaeger, Part 35; NY R NASSAU S J Jaeger, Form 1.
JUSTICE JACK L. LIBERT: NY R NASSAU S J Libert, Part 23.
JUSTICE JOSEPH H. LORINTZ: NY R NASSAU S J Lorintz, Part 26; NY R NASSAU S J Lorintz, Form 1.
JUSTICE ROY S. MAHON: NY R NASSAU S J Mahon, Part 3.
JUSTICE RANDY SUE MARBER: NY R NASSAU S J Marber, Part 8.

JUSTICE JAMES P. MCCORMACK: [NY R NASSAU S J McCormack, Part 18, as amended by NY ORDER, 20-0299].

JUSTICE DICCIA T. PINEDA-KIRWAN: [NY R NASSAU S J Pineda-Kirwan, as amended by NY ORDER 20-0300].

JUSTICE THOMAS RADEMAKER: [NY R NASSAU S J Rademaker, Part 28, as amended by NY ORDER 20-0301]; [NY R NASSAU S J Rademaker, Form 1, as amended by NY ORDER 20-0301].

JUSTICE DENISE L. SHER: NY R NASSAU S J Rademaker, Part 32.

JUSTICE LEONARD D. STEINMAN: [NY R NASSAU S J Steinman, Part 15, as amended by NY ORDER 20-0303]; NY R NASSAU S J Steinman, Form 1.

JUSTICE HOWARD E. STURIM: NY R NASSAU S J Sturim, Part 50; NY R NASSAU S J Sturim, Form 1.

JUSTICE HELEN VOUTSINAS: [NY R NASSAU S J Voutsinas, Part 25, as amended by NY ORDER 20-0304]; [NY R NASSAU S J Voutsinas, Form 1, as amended by NY ORDER 20-0305].

JUSTICE HOPE SCHWARTZ ZIMMERMAN: NY R NASSAU S J Zimmerman, Part 17.

NEW YORK COUNTY

JUDGE'S RULES; BASIC INFORMATION: [NY R NY CTY J RUL Doc. 1, as amended by NY ORDER 20-0202].

ONONDAGA COUNTY

JUSTICE ROBERT E. ANTONACCI II: [NY R ONDGA E FIL Doc. 1, as amended by 20-0239].

JUSTICE MICHAEL V. COCCOMI: NY R ONDGA E FIL Doc. 2.

JUSTICE GREGORY R. GILBERT: NY R 5 JD JUDGES Gilbert; NY R ONDGA E FIL Doc. 3.

JUSTICE DONALD A. GREENWOOD: NY R ONDGA E FIL Doc. 4.

JUSTICE DEBORAH H. KARALUNAS: NY R ONDGA E FIL Doc. 5.

JUSTICE JAMES MCCLUSKY: NY R 5 JD MCCLUSKY McClusky.

JUSTICE CHARLES C. MERRELL: NY R 5 JD MERRELL Merrell.

JUSTICE PATRICK F. MACRAE: NY R 5 JD MACRAE Doc. 1.

JUSTICE JAMES P. MURPHY: NY R ONDGA E FIL Doc. 7.

JUSTICE GERALD J. NERI: [NY R 5 JD JUDGES Neri, as amended by NY ORDER 20-0236]; [NY R ONDGA E FIL Doc. 8, as amended by NY ORDER 20-0241].

JUSTICE ANTHONY J. PARIS: NY R 5 JD JUDGES Paris; [NY R ONDGA E FIL Doc. 9, as amended by NY ORDER 20-0242].

JUSTICE NORMAN W. SEITER, JR.: NY R 5 JD JUDGES Seiter.

JUSTICE KEVIN G. YOUNG: [NY R ONDGA E FIL Doc. 10, as amended by NY ORDER 20-0243].

QUEENS COUNTY

JUSTICE PAM JACKMAN BROWN: [NY R L QUEENS Brown, Part 19, as amended by NY ORDER 20-0321].

JUSTICE CHEREE A. BUGGS: NY R L QUEENS Buggs, Part 30.

JUSTICE PAM JACKMAN BROWN: [NY R L QUEENS Brown, Part 19, as amended by NY ORDER 20-0321].

JUSTICE DENIS J. BUTLER: NY R L QUEENS Butler, Part 12.

JUSTICE ROBERT I. CALORAS: [NY R L QUEENS Caloras, Part 36, as amended by NY ORDER 20-0322].

JUSTICE ANNA CULLEY: NY R L QUEENS Culley, Part 53.

JUSTICE TIMOTHY DUFFICY: NY R L QUEENS Dufficy, Part 35.

JUSTICE DAVID ELLIOT: NY R L QUEENS Elliot, Part 14.

JUSTICE JOSEPH J. ESPOSITO: NY R L QUEENS Esposito, Part 6.

JUSTICE DARRELL L. GAVRIN: [NY R L QUEENS Gavrin, Part 27, as amended by NY ORDER 20-0323].

JUSTICE WYATT N. GIBBONS: [NY R L QUEENS Gibbons, Part 5, as amended by NY ORDER 20-0330.

JUSTICE DONNA-MARIE E. GOLIA: [NY R L QUEENS Golia, Part 21, as amended by NY ORDER 20-0331].

JUSTICE MARGUERITE A. GRAYS: [NY R L QUEENS Grays, Part 4, as amended by NY ORDER 20-0324].

JUSTICE RUDOLPH E. GRECO: [NY R L QUEENS Greco, Part 32, as amended by NY ORDER 20-0325].

JUSTICE MAUREEN HEALY: NY R L QUEENS Healy, Part 6.
JUSTICE PHILLIP HOM: [NY R L QUEENS Hom, Part 43, as amended by NY ORDER 20-0332].
JUSTICE KEVIN J. KERRIGAN: NY R L QUEENS Kerrigan, Part 10.
JUSTICE MOJGAN C. LANCMAN: NY R L QUEENS Lancman, Part 20.
JUSTICE RICHARD G. LATIN: NY R L QUEENS Latin, Part 40.
JUSTICE ULYSSES B. LEVERETT: [NY R L QUEENS Leverett, Part 6, as amended by NY ORDER 20-0326].
JUSTICE LEONARD LIVOTE: NY R L QUEENS Livote, Part 33.
JUSTICE LEE A. MAYERSOHN: NY R L QUEENS Mayersohn, Part 22; NY R L QUEENS Mayersohn, Part 22G; [NY R L QUEENS Mayersohn, Part 22G COVID, as amended by NY ORDER 20-0327].
JUSTICE ROBERT J. MCDONALD: NY R L QUEENS McDonald, Part 34.
JUSTICE MARGARET MCGOWAN: NY R L QUEENS McGowan, Part 52.
JUSTICE MAURICE E. MUIR: [NY R L QUEENS Muir, Part 42, as amended by NY ORDER 20-0333].
JUSTICE JODI ORLOW: NY R L QUEENS Orlow, Part 51.
JUSTICE LESLIE J. PURIFICCION: NY R L QUEENS Purificcion, Part 39.
JUSTICE JOSEPH RISI: [NY R L QUEENS Risi, Part 3, as amended by NY ORDER 20-0328].
JUSTICE FREDERICK D.R. SAMPSON: [NY R L QUEENS Sampson, Part 31, as amended by NY ORDER 20-0329].
JUSTICE MARTIN J. SCHULMAN: NY R L QUEENS Schulman, Part 29.
JUSTICE BERNICE D. SIEGAL: NY R L QUEENS Siegal, Part 25G.
JUSTICE JANICE A. TAYLOR: NY R L QUEENS Taylor, Part 15.
JUSTICE CARMEN R. VELASQUEZ: NY R L QUEENS Velasquez, Part 38.
JUSTICE LOURDES M VENTURA: [NY R L QUEENS Ventura, Part 37, as amended by NY ORDER 20-0334].
JUSTICE WILLIAM A. VISCOVICH: NY R L QUEENS Viscovich, Part 63.
JUSTICE ALLAN B. WEISS: NY R L QUEENS Weiss, Part 2.
COMPLIANCE, SETTLEMENT AND CONFERENCE PART: NY R L QUEENS Doc 1.
PRELIMINARY CONFERENCE PART: [NY R L QUEENS Doc. 2, as amended by NY ORDER 20-0335].
MEDICAL MALPRACTICE CONFERENCE PART: [NY R L QUEENS Doc. 3, as amended by NY ORDER 20-0336].
TRIAL SCHEDULING PART: NY R L QUEENS Doc. 4.
SUMMARY JURY TRIAL PROGRAM: NY R L QUEENS Doc. 7.
RESIDENTIAL FORECLOSURE PART: NY R L QUEENS Doc. 9.
FORECLOSURE AUCTION RULES: NY R L QUEENS Doc. 10.
MATRIMONIAL PRELIMINARY CONFERENCE PART: NY R L QUEENS Doc. 11.
NON-CUSTODIAL CONTESTED MATRIMONIAL PART: NY R L QUEENS Doc. 12.

Motions, Oppositions and Replies
Motion for Summary Judgment

Document Last Updated August 2020

A. Checklist

(I) ❑ Matters to consider for moving party

(a) ❑ Required documents

(1) ❑ Notice of motion, order to show cause, or affidavit on ex parte motion

(2) ❑ Motion

(3) ❑ Supporting evidence; Exhibits

(4) ❑ Copy of the pleadings

(5) ❑ Request for judicial intervention

(6) ❑ Proof of service

(7) ❑ ALBANY COUNTY: Additional required documents

(i) ❑ Affirmation of good faith effort

(b) ❑ Supplemental documents

(1) ❑ Brief

(2) ❑ Notice to produce papers not in possession of the court

(3) ❑ Filing fees

(4) ❑ Working copies

(5) ❑ Statement of authorization in electronic filing cases

(6) ❑ ERIE COUNTY: Additional supplemental documents

(i) ❑ Notice of hard copy submission in e-filed case

(7) ❑ KINGS COUNTY: Additional supplemental documents

(i) ❑ Forms when filing in hard copy

(8) ❑ NEW YORK COUNTY: Additional supplemental documents

(i) ❑ Notice of hard copy submission

(ii) ❑ Unpublished opinions

(9) ❑ ONONDAGA COUNTY: Additional supplemental documents

(i) ❑ Notice of hard copy submission

(10) ❑ QUEENS COUNTY: Additional supplemental documents

(i) ❑ Notice of hard copy submission

(c) ❑ Timing

(1) ❑ Any party may move for summary judgment in any action, after issue has been joined; provided however, that the court may set a date after which no such motion may be made, such date being no earlier than thirty (30) days after the filing of the note of issue

(2) ❑ If no such date is set by the court, such motion shall be made no later than one hundred twenty (120) days after the filing of the note of issue, except with leave of court on good cause shown

(3) ❑ The moving party shall serve copies of all affidavits and briefs upon all other parties at the time of service of the notice of motion

(4) ❑ A notice of motion and supporting affidavits shall be served at least eight (8) days before the time at which the motion is noticed to be heard

(5) ❑ NEW YORK COUNTY: Additional timing

(i) ❑ Unless otherwise provided in a particular case in the preliminary conference order or other directive of the Justice assigned, a motion for summary judgment shall be made no later than one hundred and twenty (120) days after the filing of the note of issue, except with leave of court for good cause shown

(6) ❑ ONONDAGA COUNTY: Additional timing

(i) ❑ Summary judgment motions are to be made no later than sixty (60) days after the filing of the Note of Issue

(II) ❑ Matters to consider for party moving for summary judgment in lieu of complaint

(a) ❑ Required documents

(1) ❑ Summons

(2) ❑ Notice of motion, order to show cause, or affidavit on ex parte motion

(3) ❑ Motion

(4) ❑ Supporting evidence; Exhibits

(5) ❑ Copy of the pleadings

(6) ❑ Request for judicial intervention

(7) ❑ Proof of service

(8) ❑ ALBANY COUNTY: Additional required documents

(i) ❑ Affirmation of good faith effort

(b) ❑ Supplemental documents

(1) ❑ Brief

(2) ❑ Notice to produce papers not in possession of the court

(3) ❑ Filing fees

(4) ❑ Working copies

(5) ❑ Statement of authorization in electronic filing cases

(6) ❑ ERIE COUNTY: Additional supplemental documents

(i) ❑ Notice of hard copy submission in e-filed case

(7) ❑ KINGS COUNTY: Additional supplemental documents

(i) ❑ Forms when filing in hard copy

(8) ❑ NEW YORK COUNTY: Additional supplemental documents

(i) ❑ Notice of hard copy submission

(ii) ❑ Unpublished opinions

(9) ❑ ONONDAGA COUNTY: Additional supplemental documents

(i) ❑ Notice of hard copy submission

(10) ❑ QUEENS COUNTY: Additional supplemental documents

(i) ❑ Notice of hard copy submission

(c) ❑ Timing

(1) ❑ As an action, the NY CPLR § 3213 application should enjoy the one hundred and twenty (120) day period for service

(2) ❑ However, papers are likely to require service long before the one hundred and twentieth (120th) day

(III) ❑ Matters to consider for opposing party

(a) ❑ Required documents

(1) ❑ Opposition

(2) ❑ Proof of service

(b) ❑ Supplemental documents

(1) ❑ Supporting evidence; Exhibits

(2) ❑ Brief

(3) ❑ Filing fees

(4) ❑ Working copies

(5) ❑ ERIE COUNTY: Additional supplemental documents

(i) ❑ Notice of hard copy submission in e-filed case

(6) ❑ KINGS COUNTY: Additional supplemental documents

(i) ❑ Forms when filing in hard copy

(7) ❑ NEW YORK COUNTY: Additional supplemental documents

(i) ❑ Notice of hard copy submission

(ii) ❑ Unpublished opinions

(8) ❑ ONONDAGA COUNTY: Additional supplemental documents

(i) ❑ Notice of hard copy submission

(9) ❑ QUEENS COUNTY: Additional supplemental documents

(i) ❑ Notice of hard copy submission

(c) ❑ Timing

(1) ❑ Answering affidavits shall be served at least two (2) days before the time at which the motion is noticed to be heard

(2) ❑ Answering affidavits and any notice of cross-motion, with supporting papers, if any, shall be served at least seven (7) days before such time if a notice of motion served at least sixteen (16) days before such time so demands

B. Timing

1. *Time to bring motion for summary judgment.* Any party may move for summary judgment in any action, after issue has been joined; provided however, that the court may set a date after which no such motion may be made, such date being no earlier than thirty (30) days after the filing of the note of issue. If no such date is set by the court, such motion shall be made no later than one hundred twenty (120) days after the filing of the note of issue, except with leave of court on good cause shown. NY CPLR Rule 3212(a).

a. *Good cause.* What will constitute "good cause" permitting a late motion to be considered? A number of lower court decisions had held that a strong showing of the merits of the motion would suffice. The rationale supporting this conclusion was that if the motion, however late, demonstrated that there was no issue of fact and that summary judgment was warranted, it would be idle to force the case to trial. They questioned, irrespective of a late motion, whether a case should have to go to trial when there was nothing to try. SIEGEL-NYPRAC § 279. The Court of Appeals in Brill v. City of New York, 2 N.Y.3d 648, 814 N.E.2d 431 (2004) unambiguously rejected this argument and held that NY CPLR Rule 3212(a) "requires a showing of good cause for the delay in making the motion—a satisfactory explanation for the untimeliness—rather than simply permitting meritorious, nonprejudicial filings, however tardy." Hence it held that even if the merits of the motion are manifest, the delay in its making must be excused by "good cause" and that the consequence of failing to excuse the lateness is that the case will now just have to stay on the calendar until the trial, with the aspiring summary judgment party left to the devices available there. SIEGEL-NYPRAC § 279; Brill v. City of New York, 2 N.Y.3d 648, 814 N.E.2d 431 (2004).

i. *KINGS COUNTY.* Ordinarily to be denied without prejudice to renew at time the motion for Summary Judgment is brought upon showing of Compliance with the criteria set forth by our Court of Appeals in Brill. NY R L KINGS Rule II.

b. *Timeliness of cross-motion for summary judgment.* What about NY CPLR Rule 3212(a)'s time limit as applied to an application for summary judgment made by way of cross-motion? Assume X makes a timely motion for summary judgment and Y then makes a cross-motion for similar relief, affording proper notice under NY CPLR Rule 2215, the cross-motion statute, but just beyond the time limit of NY CPLR Rule 3212(a). May the cross-motion be entertained? The First Department answered yes in Filannino v. Triborough Bridge & Tunnel Auth., 34 A.D.3d 280, 824 N.Y.S.2d 244 (2006), as long as the relief sought in the cross-motion is "nearly identical" to that sought on the main motion, but then concluded that the standard was not satisfied. SIEGEL-NYPRAC § 279; Filannino v. Triborough Bridge & Tunnel Auth., 34 A.D.3d 280, 824 N.Y.S.2d 244 (2006).

c. *KINGS COUNTY: Time limit after note of issue.* In cases where the City of New York is a defendant and is represented by the Tort Division of the Corporation Counsel's office, summary judgment motions may be made no later than one hundred and twenty (120) days after the filing of a Note of Issue. In all other matters, including third party actions, motions for summary judgment may be made no later than sixty (60) days after the filing of a Note of Issue. In both instances the above time limitation may only be extended by the Court upon good cause shown. See NY CPLR Rule 3212(a). NY R L KINGS Pt. C, Rule 6.

d. *NEW YORK COUNTY: Time after note of issue.* Unless otherwise provided in a particular case in the preliminary conference order or other directive of the Justice assigned, a motion for summary judgment shall be made no later than one hundred and twenty (120) days after the filing of the note of issue, except with leave of court for good cause shown. NY R NY CTY J RUL Rule 17.

e. *ONONDAGA COUNTY: Time after note of issue.* Going forward, summary judgment motions are to be made no later than sixty (60) days after the filing of the Note of Issue. NY R ONDGA SUM JUDG Doc. 1.

2. *Motion for summary judgment served in lieu of complaint; Time to serve summons.* The filing system for commencement applies to both actions and special proceedings, but no specific attention was given to how it applies to the NY CPLR § 3213 procedure. Under the rules for commencement by filing, the initiatory papers must be served within one hundred and twenty (120) days after they're filed, but only a fifteen (15) day period for service running from the expiration of the statute of limitations applies in a special proceeding. It is doubtful that this issue will ever be resolved as the plaintiff in a NY CPLR § 3213 action will usually serve the summons and summary judgment papers promptly after they are filed. SIEGEL-NYPRAC § 291.
3. *Time to serve.* The moving party shall serve copies of all affidavits and briefs upon all other parties at the time of service of the notice of motion. NY R UNIF TRIAL CTS § 202.8(c). A notice of motion and supporting affidavits shall be served at least eight (8) days before the time at which the motion is noticed to be heard. NY CPLR Rule 2214(b).
    a. *Return dates; best practice*
        i. *ALBANY COUNTY.* All motions, except for certain matters in Albany County as specified in NY R 3 JD SUP Doc. 1(E) and NY R 3 JD SUP Doc. 1(F), brought on by notice of motion or by order to show cause will be made returnable on any day, Monday through Friday, as chosen by the movant in compliance with the CPLR. Parties shall submit all papers in a timely fashion as required by the CPLR by delivering them or mailing them directly to the Supreme Court Clerk's Office[. . .]except that motions and other applications subject to a filing fee shall first be presented to the County Clerk's Office for payment of the requisite fee and then subsequently filed with the Supreme Court Clerk's Office. NY R 3 JD SUP Doc. 1(B).
        ii. *BRONX COUNTY.* A Notice of Motion must be served at least eight (8) days, by personal service, nine (9) days by overnight express and thirteen (13) days by mail before the return date. NY R BRONX FIL R Doc. 3. All unassigned motions must be accompanied with a properly filled out RJI and shall be filed in the Motion Support Office, room 217, within five (5) days of service. All motions on actions already assigned to a Justice must be filed at least five (5) business days before the return date. NY R BRONX FIL R Doc. 3. All papers served must strictly comply with the time requirements of NY CPLR Rule 2101, NY CPLR Rule 2103 and NY CPLR Rule 2214(b). NY R BRONX FIL R Doc. 8.
        iii. *KINGS COUNTY.* Motion papers, answering affidavits and reply affidavits must be served on adversaries in accordance with NY CPLR Rule 2214. NY R L KINGS Pt. C, Rule 1.
        iv. *NEW YORK COUNTY.* In an e-filed case, all of the moving papers shall be e-filed at least eight (8) business days prior to the return date. The clerk will calendar the motion for the Motion Submission Part Courtroom (Room 130) for the return date selected. NY R NY CTY Procedure II(A); NY R NY CTY E FIL Doc. 2(D)(1).
        v. *ONONDAGA COUNTY.* Onondaga County local court rules require that any additional papers relating to motions must be e-filed at least two (2) business days prior to the return date, excluding the return date. NY R ONDGA E FIL Protocol(B)(9)(e).
        vi. *QUEENS COUNTY.* Motions must be in the possession of the Motion Support Office at least nine (9) days before the noticed return date of the motion. NY R L QUEENS MOT SUP Doc. 1; NY R L QUEENS E-FILE Doc. 1(H)(1).
    b. *Time to serve answering affidavits; Other answering papers.* Answering affidavits shall be served at least two (2) days before the time at which the motion is noticed to be heard. Answering affidavits and any notice of cross-motion, with supporting papers, if any, shall be served at least seven (7) days before such time if a notice of motion served at least sixteen (16) days before such time so demands; whereupon any reply or responding affidavits shall be served at least one (1) day before such time. NY CPLR Rule 2214(b); NY R UNIF TRIAL CTS § 202.8(c).
        i. *BRONX COUNTY.* All answering papers must be submitted to the Clerk 's Office on the return date of the motion. Answering papers will not be accepted prior to the return date. NY R BRONX FIL R Doc. 8.
        ii. *NEW YORK COUNTY.* Cross-motions, papers in opposition, and reply papers on motions/petitions on notice returnable in Room 130 in a hard-copy case shall be submitted to the Motion Submission Part Courtroom (Room 130) on the final return date of the motion/petition and will not be accepted until that date. Subsequent documents on motions/petitions in e-filed cases shall be e-filed in a timely manner. Working copies when required shall be submitted to Room 130 on the final return date. NY R NY CTY Procedure II(A).
    c. *Time to serve cross-motion.* At least three (3) days prior to the time at which the motion is noticed to be heard, or seven (7) days prior to such time if demand is properly made pursuant to NY CPLR Rule 2214(b), a party may serve upon

the moving party a notice of cross-motion demanding relief, with or without supporting papers; provided, however, that:

i. If such notice and any supporting papers are served by mailing, as provided in NY CPLR Rule 2103(b)(2), they shall be served three (3) days earlier than as prescribed in NY CPLR Rule 2215; and

ii. If served by overnight delivery, as provided in NY CPLR Rule 2103(b)(6), they shall be served one (1) day earlier than as prescribed in NY CPLR Rule 2215. Relief in the alternative or of several different types may be demanded; relief need not be responsive to that demanded by the moving party. NY CPLR Rule 2215(a); NY CPLR Rule 2215(b).

iii. *BRONX COUNTY.* Cross motions may be presented for approval on or before the return date, provided that there is a motion already calendared. NY R BRONX FIL R Doc. 8.

iv. *ERIE COUNTY.* Cross-motions must be filed at least two (2) days before the return date of the motion. NY R L KINGS Pt. A, Papers.

v. *KINGS COUNTY.* Hard copies are required to be filed for any motions, answering papers, stipulations, etc. for E-Filed cases returnable in [the Central Compliance Part] at least [two (2)] days before return date. . . .for cross motions. NY R L KINGS Pt. E, Rule 8.

vi. *QUEENS COUNTY.* Motion Support does not process or forward responsive papers, including cross-motions. They must be brought to the calendar call in the judge's part. NY R L QUEENS MOT SUP Doc. 1. E-filed cross motions: across motion must be noticed for the same return date as the main motion and have the confirmation of filing attached in the same manner as a motion. NY R L QUEENS E-FILE Doc. 1(H)(2)(e).

4. *Filing before return date.* All motions shall be returnable before the assigned judge, and all papers shall be filed with the court on or before the return date. NY R UNIF TRIAL CTS § 202.8(a).

a. *BRONX COUNTY: Time for filing*

i. *Unassigned motions.* Unassigned motions must be in the Clerk's Office within five (5) days of the date of service of the motion. NY R BRONX FIL R Doc. 8.

ii. *Assigned motions.* Assigned motions must be filed in the Clerk's Office not less than five (5) business days prior to the return date of the motion. NY R BRONX FIL R Doc. 8.

iii. *Motions returnable in room 217.* The moving documents must be e-filed no later than eight (8) days prior to the return date. NY R BRONX E FIL R Doc. 1(1).

b. *KINGS COUNTY: Time and place of filing.* Motion papers must be filed with the E-file/Motion Support Office located in Room 227. . . at 360 Adams Street at least five (5) business days before the return date of the motion. NY R L KINGS Pt. A, Papers. Hard copies are required to be filed for any motions, answering papers, stipulations, etc. for E-Filed cases returnable in [the Central Compliance Part] at least five (5) days before return date for main motions. NY R L KINGS Pt. E, Rule 8. The moving documents must be e-filed no later than eight (8) days prior to the return date. NY R L KINGS E FIL Doc. 1(D).

5. *NEW YORK COUNTY: Briefing schedule.* Once a motion is made, counsel for all parties are strongly encouraged to agree upon a briefing schedule and submit a stipulation of adjournment reflecting that schedule using service or a clerk. Where a briefing schedule has not been agreed upon, the movant can avoid the need to attend simply to see if anyone will hand up opposing papers by demanding papers as provided by NY CPLR Rule 2214(b). To protect movants against the submission of late opposition papers or cross-motions, the General Clerk's Office will screen motions in which such papers are submitted without a response (reply or opposition respectively) to ensure that proper time to respond has been afforded and it will sua sponte adjourn for one (1) week cases in which such time has not been given. NY R NY CTY Procedure II(C).

6. *QUEENS COUNTY: Time to pay fees.* As motions and petitions are time sensitive, if opting to pay at the County Clerk's Office payment MUST be made, if filed with an RJI, a minimum of nine (9) business days prior to the application's return date and if filed post RJI, a minimum of nine (9) business days prior to the application's return date. NY R L QUEENS E-FILE Doc. 1(H)(1).

7. *Computation of time*

a. *Units of time*

i. *Day.* A calendar day includes the time from midnight to midnight. Sunday or any day of the week specifically mentioned means a calendar day. NY GEN CONSTR § 19.

ii. *Month.* In a statute, contract or public or private instrument, unless otherwise provided in such contract or instrument or by law, the term month means a calendar month and not a lunar month. NY GEN CONSTR § 31.

iii. *Year.* For information on the definition of a year, including the definitions of a half-year and quarter-year, refer to NY GEN CONSTR § 58 and NY GEN CONSTR § 50. For information on leap years, refer to NY GEN CONSTR § 57.

b. *Periods of time*

i. *Number of days.* A number of days specified as a period from a certain day within which or after or before which an act is authorized or required to be done means such number of calendar days exclusive of the calendar day from which the reckoning is made. NY GEN CONSTR § 20.

- If such period is a period of two (2) days, Saturday, Sunday or a public holiday must be excluded from the reckoning if it is an intervening day between the day from which the reckoning is made and the last day of the period. NY GEN CONSTR § 20.
- In computing any specified period of time from a specified event, the day upon which the event happens is deemed the day from which the reckoning is made. The day from which any specified period of time is reckoned shall be excluded in making the reckoning. NY GEN CONSTR § 20.

ii. *Number of months.* A number of months after or before a certain day shall be computed by counting such number of calendar months from such day, exclusive of the calendar month in which such day occurs, and shall include the day of the month in the last month so counted having the same numerical order in days of the month as the day from which the computation is made, unless there be not so many days in the last month so counted, in which case the period computed shall expire with the last day of the month so counted. NY GEN CONSTR § 30.

iii. *Publication of notice; Number of days.* The period of publication of a legal notice shall be computed by excluding the first day of publication and including the day on which the act or event of which notice is given is to take place or which completes the full period of publication. NY CPLR § 2402.

iv. *Periods ending on Saturday, Sunday or public holiday.* When any period of time, computed from a certain day, within which or after which or before which an act is authorized or required to be done, ends on a Saturday, Sunday or a public holiday, such act may be done on the next succeeding business day and if the period ends at a specified hour, such act may be done at or before the same hour of such next succeeding business day, except that where a period of time specified by contract ends on a Saturday, Sunday or a public holiday, the extension of such period is governed by NY GEN CONSTR § 25. NY GEN CONSTR § 25-a(1).

- For a list of public holidays, refer to NY GEN CONSTR § 24.

v. *Additional time after certain kinds of service*

- *Service by mail.* Where a period of time prescribed by law is measured from the service of a paper and service is by mail, five (5) days shall be added to the prescribed period. NY CPLR Rule 2103(b)(2).
- *Service by overnight delivery service.* Where a period of time prescribed by law is measured from the service of a paper and service is by overnight delivery, one (1) business day shall be added to the prescribed period. NY CPLR Rule 2103(b)(6).

vi. *Daylight saving time.* For information on New York's time zone and the effect of daylight saving time, refer to NY GEN CONSTR § 52.

c. *Hours of court.* Notwithstanding any provision of law or rule of court to the contrary, throughout the State of New York the sessions of the Supreme Court for the disposition of business before the court shall commence not later than 9:30 a.m. and conclude not earlier than 5 p.m. Where warranted, the Chief Administrator of the Courts may authorize variances in the opening and closing hours of the courts, but, in such event, daily sessions shall total not less than six (6) hours. NY R CHIEF J § 3.1.

d. *Time limits; Extension of time.* Any act required by or in pursuance of law to be performed at or within a prescribed time, shall be performed according to the standard time. NY GEN CONSTR § 53.

i. Except where otherwise expressly prescribed by law, the court may extend the time fixed by any statute, rule or order for doing any act, upon such terms as may be just and upon good cause shown, whether the application for extension is made before or after the expiration of the time fixed. NY CPLR § 2004. Refer to the New York KeyRules Motion for Continuance/Extension of Time document for more information.

C. General Requirements

1. *Motions, generally.* There shall be compliance with the procedures prescribed in the CPLR for the bringing of motions. NY R UNIF TRIAL CTS § 202.7(a).

   a. *Motions on notice.* A notice of motion shall specify the time and place of the hearing on the motion, the supporting papers upon which the motion is based, the relief demanded and the grounds therefor. NY CPLR Rule 2214(a). A motion on notice in an action in the supreme court shall be noticed to be heard in the judicial district where the action is triable or in a county adjoining the county where the action is triable. Unless statute, civil practice rule or local court rule provides otherwise, the motion shall be noticed to be heard before a motion term or, upon order to show cause granted by a justice, before that justice out of court. NY CPLR § 2212(a). Except as provided in NY R UNIF TRIAL CTS § 202.7(d), no motion shall be filed with the court unless there have been served and filed with the motion papers a notice of motion. NY R UNIF TRIAL CTS § 202.7(a)(1).

   b. *Ex parte motions.* A motion in an action in the supreme court that may be made without notice may be made at a motion term or to a justice out of court in any county in the state. NY CPLR § 2212(b).

      i. *KINGS COUNTY.* For more information on submitting a motion ex parte, refer to NY R L KINGS E FIL Doc. 1(G).

      ii. *NEW YORK COUNTY.* For more information on submitting matters ex parte, refer to NY R NY CTY Procedure III and NY R NY CTY E FIL Doc. 2(G).

      iii. *QUEENS COUNTY.* For more information on submitting matters ex parte, refer to NY R L QUEENS EX PARTE Doc. 1.

   c. *Alternative relief.* Relief in the alternative or of several different types may be demanded. NY CPLR Rule 2214(a). The types of relief need not be related. In one motion, for example, the defendant can seek to dismiss the plaintiff's claim for lack of jurisdiction, to get an extension of time to answer, to require the plaintiff to join X as a party, and to quash a disclosure subpoena served in behalf of the plaintiff on a nonparty witness. So doing, the movant must of course specify all of these items of relief in the notice of motion, and the grounds for them, and the supporting papers must contain the entire proof requisite to the items of relief sought. NY CPLR Rule 2214(Practice Commentary, C2214:4).

   d. *General relief.* It is common practice to include at the end of the relief request in the notice of motion a so-called "general relief" clause. This is merely a few words to cover the possibility that the relief appropriate to what the movant proves was not specifically asked for, but is close enough to enable the court to grant it. After stating the specific relief desired, the lawyer will often add something like: and for such other, further, or different relief as this court may deem just and proper. NY CPLR Rule 2214(Practice Commentary, C2214:5).

   e. *Motion in improper form.* If the court finds it appropriate in the interests of justice, it may convert a motion into a special proceeding, or vice-versa, upon such terms as may be just, including the payment of fees and costs. NY CPLR § 103(c).

   f. *Order to show cause.* An order to show cause is basically only a substitute for a notice of motion. An ordinary notice of motion merely notifies the recipient that a motion is being made for specified relief. The burden of proof is on the movant. Although in most cases it is just as innocent as an ordinary notice of motion, the order to show cause gets its name by directing the recipient to "show cause" why the particular relief being asked for should not be granted. It sounds as if the burden of proof is being shifted to the recipient. It isn't. It specifies the time and place of the hearing on the application but when the hearing comes on, the burden of proof is where it always is on a motion: on the movant. SIEGEL-NYPRAC § 248.

      i. The CPLR says nothing more about an order to show cause than that it may be used "in a proper case", which leaves it entirely to the judge's discretion to determine what a proper case is. Any fact suggesting a problem as to any of the items listed above would be sufficient to invoke judicial discretion and justify the show cause procedure, which is in fact liberally used. SIEGEL-NYPRAC § 248.

      ii. An order to show cause against a state body or officers must be served in addition to service upon the defendant or respondent state body or officers upon the attorney general by delivery to an assistant attorney general at an office of the attorney general in the county in which venue of the action is designated or if there is no office of the attorney general in such county, at the office of the attorney general nearest such county. NY CPLR Rule 2214(d).

      iii. *BRONX COUNTY.* For information on submitting an order to show cause, refer to NY R BRONX E FIL R Doc. 2 and NY R BRONX LEG SUP Doc. 1.

iv. *ERIE COUNTY.* For information on submitting an order to show cause, refer to NY R ERIE E FIL Doc. 3(VI).

v. *KINGS COUNTY.* For information on submitting an order to show cause, refer to NY R L KINGS E FIL Doc. 1(F).

vi. *NEW YORK COUNTY.* For information on submitting an order to show cause, refer to NY R NY CTY E FIL Doc. 2(F).

vii. *ONONDAGA COUNTY.* For information on submitting an order to show cause, refer to NY R ONDGA E FIL Protocol(B)(10) and NY R ONDGA E FIL Protocol(J).

g. *Motions before preliminary conference.* Motions in actions to which NY R UNIF TRIAL CTS § 202.12 is applicable made after the preliminary conference has been scheduled may be denied unless there is shown good cause why such relief is warranted before the preliminary conference is held. NY R UNIF TRIAL CTS § 202.12(h).

h. *ALBANY COUNTY: Good faith effort to resolve.* Prior to the submission of a notice of motion relating to disclosure or a bill of particulars, the parties must make a good faith effort to resolve the matter in question and submit an affirmation attesting to this good faith effort. NY R 3 JD SUP Doc. 1(B).

i. *NEW YORK COUNTY: Documents with motions.* Counsel must attach to motion papers copies of all pleadings and other documents as required by the CPLR and as necessary for an informed decision on the motion. Documents in a foreign language shall be properly translated. NY R NY CTY J RUL Rule 14(a).

j. *NEW YORK COUNTY: Motions in multiple cases made together.* On occasion, attorneys may wish to make a motion in more than one case on a single set of papers. In such cases, by definition consolidation will not have been directed since consolidation signifies the combination of more than one case into a single one with a single caption and index number and ending in a single judgment. NY R NY CTY Procedure II(B). For more information on motions made with the same papers, refer to NY R NY CTY Procedure II(A).

k. *QUEENS COUNTY: Motion sequence numbers.* A motion sequence number is required for all E-filed motions. After a motion is E-filed, please consult the e-courts website within twenty-four (24) to forty-eight (48) hours to obtain the sequence number. The Confirmation Notice of E-filing MUST indicate the sequence number of any motion submitted at the Centralized Motion Part calendar call. NY R L QUEENS E-FILE Doc. 1(H)(5).

2. *Motion for summary judgment.* Any party may move for summary judgment in any action, after issue has been joined. NY CPLR Rule 3212(a).

a. *Stay of disclosure.* Service of a notice of motion under NY CPLR Rule 3211, NY CPLR Rule 3212, or NY CPLR § 3213 stays disclosure until determination of the motion unless the court orders otherwise. If the motion is based solely on the defense that the summons and complaint, summons with notice, or notice of petition and petition was not properly served, disclosure shall not be stayed unless the court orders otherwise. NY CPLR Rule 3214(b).

b. *Immediate trial.* If it appears that the only triable issues of fact arising on a motion for summary judgment relate to the amount or extent of damages, or if the motion is based on any of the grounds enumerated in NY CPLR Rule 3211(a) or NY CPLR Rule 3211(b), the court may, when appropriate for the expeditious disposition of the controversy, order an immediate trial of such issues of fact raised by the motion, before a referee, before the court, or before the court and a jury, whichever may be proper. NY CPLR Rule 3212(c).

i. On a dismissal motion under NY CPLR Rule 3211, the immediate trial of an issue of fact is permissible. SIEGEL-NYPRAC § 284; SIEGEL-NYPRAC § 271; NY CPLR Rule 3211(c). And if the NY CPLR Rule 3211(a) objection is taken by answer instead of by motion, it can be made the basis of a summary judgment motion under NY CPLR Rule 3212. SIEGEL-NYPRAC § 284.

ii. The mode of trial of the damages issue, notably whether it's to be by jury, depends on the nature of the case itself. If the case would have been triable by jury had there been no summary judgment, and either party insists on a jury trial on damages, a jury is required. SIEGEL-NYPRAC § 284; Livingston v. Blumenthal, 248 A.D. 138, 140, 289 N.Y.S. 5, 8 - 9 (N.Y.A.D. 1st Dept. 1936). Under the 1973 amendment authorizing the immediate trial of some liability-related fact issues, the question of whether a jury is required should depend further on whether the ground involved disposes of the case permanently. If it does not, such as where defendant seeks summary judgment dismissing plaintiff's action for the affirmative defense of lack of personal jurisdiction and the statute of limitations has not expired, a trial by jury should not ordinarily be necessary. SIEGEL-NYPRAC § 284; SIEGEL-NYPRAC § 271.

c. *Proof*

i. Drawing the line between what the moving party has to show to earn a summary judgment and what the opposing party has to show to defeat the summary judgment is a perennial battle in the courts, both federal and state. And it is a case-by-case battle, manifesting the relatively limited value of general language about who has what burden. The New York rule governing burdens of proof on a summary judgment motion should be contrasted with the federal rule established in Celotex Corp. v. Catrett, 477 U.S. 317, 106 S. Ct. 2548, 91 L. Ed. 2d 265 (1986). Therein, the Supreme Court held that "the burden on the moving party may be discharged by . . . pointing out to the district court . . . that there is an absence of evidence to support the nonmoving party's case." Such an approach will not satisfy the movant's burden in a New York State court, and parties moving for summary judgment must be alert to this distinction. SIEGEL-NYPRAC § 281; Celotex Corp. v. Catrett, 477 U.S. 317, 106 S. Ct. 2548, 91 L. Ed. 2d 265 (1986).

ii. In New York State courts, the party moving for summary judgment has the burden to establish "a prima facie showing of entitlement to judgment as a matter of law, tendering sufficient evidence to demonstrate the absence of any material issues of fact." If the moving party fails to meet that initial burden, summary judgment should be denied "regardless of the sufficiency of the opposing papers." In these circumstances, the burden does not shift to the party opposing summary judgment to persuade the court against granting it. Stated otherwise, a defendant should not be awarded summary judgment dismissing the action by simply pointing to weaknesses in the plaintiff's case. SIEGEL-NYPRAC § 281.

- If a key fact in issue is within the exclusive knowledge of the moving party, the motion for summary judgment will be denied. SIEGEL-NYPRAC § 281; Krupp v. Aetna Life & Cas. Co., 103 A.D.2d 252, 263, 479 N.Y.S.2d 992, 1000 (1984). Denial of the motion will also result when the fact is one the opposing party cannot know, as where it turns on the scope of the movant's knowledge of his own agent's act. SIEGEL-NYPRAC § 281; Franklin Nat. Bank of Long Island v. DeGiacomo, 20 A.D.2d 797, 797, 248 N.Y.S.2d 586, 587 (1964).
- If a key fact turns on an item of evidence whose admissibility at the trial is arguable, summary judgment must be denied. SIEGEL-NYPRAC § 281; Gallo Painting, Inc. v. Aetna Ins. Co., 49 A.D.2d 746, 746, 372 N.Y.S.2d 699, 701 (1975). Because of the drastic nature of the remedy, a rule has even arisen that occasionally permits the court to consider incompetent evidence, i.e., evidence that would be inadmissible at a trial, but only if it tends to defeat the motion. SIEGEL-NYPRAC § 281.

iii. The failure of the opposing party to respond to a summary judgment motion does not mandate a grant of the motion; that the movant must still make the usual showing needed for summary judgment, which is that there is no issue of fact and that the movant is entitled to judgment as a matter of law. SIEGEL-NYPRAC § 281; Liberty Taxi Mgmt., Inc. v. Gincherman, 32 A.D.3d 276, 820 N.Y.S.2d 49 (2006).

d. *Motion granted.* The motion shall be granted if, upon all the papers and proof submitted, the cause of action or defense shall be established sufficiently to warrant the court as a matter of law in directing judgment in favor of any party. NY CPLR Rule 3212(b).

e. *Motion denied.* Except as provided in NY CPLR Rule 3212(c) the motion shall be denied if any party shall show facts sufficient to require a trial of any issue of fact. NY CPLR Rule 3212(b).

i. *Facts unavailable to opposing party.* Should it appear from affidavits submitted in opposition to the motion that facts essential to justify opposition may exist but cannot then be stated, the court may deny the motion or may order a continuance to permit affidavits to be obtained or disclosure to be had and may make such other order as may be just. NY CPLR Rule 3212(f).

ii. *Judgment for opposing party; Searching the record.* If it shall appear that any party other than the moving party is entitled to a summary judgment, the court may grant such judgment without the necessity of a cross-motion. NY CPLR Rule 3212(b).

- Popularly known to bench and bar as "searching the record," this device is more likely to be remembered as the doctrine of extreme disappointment. It occurs most often when the pleading being attacked by the summary judgment motion is a responsive one, as in the example above where plaintiff's motion is actually an attack on the answer. A motion in that category requires the court to go behind the answer to examine the sufficiency of the complaint. If the complaint is defective, it and not the answer is dismissed and the plaintiff, although the movant, becomes the victim. The theory is that a bad answer is good enough for a bad complaint. SIEGEL-NYPRAC § 282.
- Searching the record is permissible only with respect to the claim on which summary judgment is sought. If plaintiff has several distinct claims and moves for summary judgment only on claim X, it is only with respect to claim X that the court can sua sponte search the record. SIEGEL-NYPRAC § 282; Costello v. Hapco Realty, Inc., 305 A.D.2d 445, 447, 761 N.Y.S.2d 79, 81 (2003).

- In a matrimonial action summary judgment may not be granted in favor of the non-moving party. NY CPLR Rule 3212(e).

f. *Motion for summary judgment on motion to dismiss grounds*

i. The usual summary judgment motion is based on the overall merits of the case rather than on an individual defense like the statute of limitations, lack of jurisdiction, other action pending, etc. But it is permissible to base it on one of those grounds or any of the other grounds listed in NY CPLR Rule 3211(a). SIEGEL-NYPRAC § 283; Houston v. Trans Union Credit Info. Co., 154 A.D.2d 312, 313, 546 N.Y.S.2d 600, 601 (1989). It will be recalled that the long list of NY CPLR Rule 3211(a) objections may, under NY CPLR Rule 3211(e), be taken either by a motion to dismiss or as defenses in the answer. When the latter alternative is used, the objection, duly preserved by inclusion in the answer, may then be made the basis of a NY CPLR Rule 3212(a) summary judgment motion. SIEGEL-NYPRAC § 283. If an affirmative defense was not included in the original answer, but the defendant seeks to include it in an amended answer, the requests to amend to include the defense and for summary judgment based on it may be included in one motion. SIEGEL-NYPRAC § 283; Armstrong v. Peat, Marwick, Mitchell & Co., 150 A.D.2d 189, 191, 540 N.Y.S.2d 799, 802 (1989).

ii. This applies not only to a defense that can constitute an effective disposition on the merits, such as the defense of payment or release, but also to a defense that brings on a mere temporary abatement, i.e., dismisses without precluding a new action, such as lack of jurisdiction or the curable incapacity of the plaintiff. SIEGEL-NYPRAC § 283; NY CPLR Rule 3211(a)(5); NY CPLR Rule 3211(a)(2); NY CPLR Rule 3211(a)(8); NY CPLR Rule 3211(a)(9); NY CPLR Rule 3211(a)(c).

iii. The grant of summary judgment based on one of these "abatement" defenses will not import the full res judicata effect carried by the usual summary judgment aimed at the merits of the case generally. SIEGEL-NYPRAC § 283; SIEGEL-NYPRAC § 287. The lesson to the parties is to see to it that the dispositive order clarifies the particular ground on which the summary judgment is based. If it is based only on the defense of lack of jurisdiction of the defendant, for example, the order should say so. That will clarify that the merits of the claim were not disposed of in this round and that a new action lies if jurisdiction can now be obtained. SIEGEL-NYPRAC § 283.

g. *Cases unsuitable for summary judgment.* If a main element in the case is a highly subjective one, such as fraud (because of the investigation into intent that it entails), the case is likely to be unsuitable for summary judgment, although there is no arbitrary restriction on the categories of action in which summary judgment may be sought. SIEGEL-NYPRAC § 278; SIEGEL-NYPRAC § 280; Falk v. Goodman, 7 N.Y.2d 87, 90, 163 N.E.2d 871, 872 (1959).

h. *Partial summary judgment; Severance.* In any action other than a matrimonial action summary judgment may be granted as to one or more causes of action, or part thereof, in favor of any one or more parties, to the extent warranted, on such terms as may be just. NY CPLR Rule 3212(e).

i. The court may also direct:

- That the cause of action as to which summary judgment is granted shall be severed from any remaining cause of action; or
- That the entry of the summary judgment shall be held in abeyance pending the determination of any remaining cause of action. NY CPLR Rule 3212(e).

ii. Although the provision speaks in terms of partial summary judgment as to one or more "causes of action", it can operate on defenses in the answer as well. Where, for example, one defense is shown to be bad but the other good, the court can grant summary judgment dismissing the bad one. SIEGEL-NYPRAC § 285.

iii. There is a substantial body of law treating the situation in which a plaintiff's claim is summarily established, but where a defendant has interposed a counterclaim that requires trial. Or vice-versa. What effect does the counterclaim have, if any, on a grant of summary judgment for the plaintiff? Despite a quantum of caselaw, it all boils down to a simple conclusion: the court can work out whatever seems fair in the particular case. SIEGEL-NYPRAC § 285.

- It is clear that the mere assertion of the counterclaim does not bar an otherwise warranted summary judgment on the main claim. SIEGEL-NYPRAC § 285; M & S Mercury Air Conditioning Corp. v. Rodolitz, 24 A.D.2d 873, 264 N.Y.S.2d 454, 455 (1965), aff'd, 17 N.Y.2d 909, 218 N.E.2d 898 (1966).
- One alternative is that a plaintiff be given summary judgment for all of the main claim with the entry of it stayed until the counterclaim is tried (to see what effect the counterclaim may have in diminishing a

plaintiff's claim in whole or in part). SIEGEL-NYPRAC § 285; NY CPLR Rule 3212(e)(2); Casten v. Tannenbaum, 42 Misc. 2d 118, 118, 246 N.Y.S.2d 954, 955 (Sup. Ct. 1964).

- If the main claim exceeds the counterclaim, a plaintiff may be given summary judgment for the balance with the right to seek immediate enforcement of it, the rest being held in abeyance for possible offset by whatever the defendant proves on the counterclaim. SIEGEL-NYPRAC § 285; Atlas Arm Co. v. Smith, 25 A.D.2d 669, 670, 268 N.Y.S.2d 385, 387 (1966). If the counterclaim in that situation does not then succeed, a plaintiff can be given summary judgment for the rest of the main claim at that time. SIEGEL-NYPRAC § 285.
- If the defendant's counterclaim exceeds a plaintiff's claim and the plaintiff is given summary judgment on the main claim, the staying of entry or enforcement of the judgment until the counterclaim is adjudicated will protect the defendant. But if there is no prospect of the plaintiff's insolvency, so that the defendant is assured of payment of any judgment that may be warranted on the counterclaim, the stay would not even be required; a plaintiff could go to immediate entry and enforcement of the summary judgment. SIEGEL-NYPRAC § 285; Pease & Elliman, Inc. v. 926 Park Ave. Corp., 23 A.D.2d 361, 362, 260 N.Y.S.2d 693, 696 (1965), aff'd, 17 N.Y.2d 890, 218 N.E.2d 700 (1966).

i. *Limitations of issues of fact for trial.* If a motion for summary judgment is denied or is granted in part, the court, by examining the papers before it and, in the discretion of the court, by interrogating counsel, shall, if practicable, ascertain what facts are not in dispute or are incontrovertible. It shall thereupon make an order specifying such facts and they shall be deemed established for all purposes in the action. The court may make any order as may aid in the disposition of the action. NY CPLR Rule 3212(g).

j. *Summary judgment specific cases.* For information on summary judgment in cases involving public petition and participation, refer to NY CPLR Rule 3212(h). For information on summary judgment in cases involving licensed architects, engineers, land surveyors, or landscape architects, refer to NY CPLR Rule 3212(i).

3. *Motion for summary judgment in lieu of complaint.* When an action is based upon an instrument for the payment of money only or upon any judgment, the plaintiff may serve with the summons a notice of motion for summary judgment and the supporting papers in lieu of a complaint. NY CPLR § 3213.

a. *Instrument for the payment of money only defined*

i. One helpful standard for what qualifies as a proper NY CPLR § 3213 "instrument" case is that offered by Seaman-Andwall Corp. v. Wright Mach. Corp., 31 A.D.2d 136, 295 N.Y.S.2d 752 (1968), aff'd sub nom. Seaman-Andwall Corp v. Wright Mach. Corp, 29 N.Y.2d 617, 273 N.E.2d 138 (1971), which says that a case is made out for NY CPLR § 3213 use if two (2) things are shown:

- The instrument itself, and
- Proof of non-payment. SIEGEL-NYPRAC § 289; Seaman-Andwall Corp. v. Wright Mach. Corp., 31 A.D.2d 136, 295 N.Y.S.2d 752 (1968), aff'd sub nom. Seaman-Andwall Corp v. Wright Mach. Corp, 29 N.Y.2d 617, 273 N.E.2d 138 (1971).

ii. The instrument doesn't qualify "if outside proof is needed." So stating in Weissman v. Sinorm Deli, Inc., 88 N.Y.2d 437, 444, 669 N.E.2d 242, 245 (1996) the Court of Appeals rejected for NY CPLR § 3213 treatment an indemnification commitment included in a stock agreement. SIEGEL-NYPRAC § 289; Weissman v. Sinorm Deli, Inc., 88 N.Y.2d 437, 444, 669 N.E.2d 242, 245 (1996).

iii. Presumably any paper requiring the payment of money only and qualifying as a piece of "commercial paper" under the Uniform Commercial Code would satisfy for NY CPLR § 3213 use. Furthermore, if a given paper, although not formally a money "instrument," contains the requisite (and limited) terms, it will be accepted, as a mere letter was in one case. SIEGEL-NYPRAC § 289; Baker v. Gundermann, 52 Misc. 2d 639, 640, 276 N.Y.S.2d 495, 498 (Sup. Ct. 1966).

b. *Action based on judgment.* Any judgment qualifies to invoke NY CPLR § 3213 and allow the action to be commenced with the motion procedure it supplies, but that is of course no guarantee that the court will grant the motion. That depends entirely on whether the judgment qualifies for recognition and adoption. SIEGEL-NYPRAC § 290.

i. Sister-state judgments and those of the federal and territorial courts and the District of Columbia, since all are entitled to full faith and credit as long as rendered with jurisdiction of subject matter and parties, are of course entitled to recognition and readily qualify for a NY CPLR § 3213 motion. SIEGEL-NYPRAC § 290; U.S.C.A. Const. Art. IV § 1; 28 U.S.C.A. § 1738; SIEGEL-NYPRAC § 471.

ii. The only judgments denied summary registration under Article 54 of the New York Civil Practice Law and Rules

(NY CPLR § 5401, et seq.) are those taken in the earlier forum either by default for non-appearance or by confession. Only those, therefore, normally need to invoke NY CPLR § 3213. SIEGEL-NYPRAC § 290; NY CPLR § 5401.

iii. NY CPLR § 3213 is not restricted to money judgments. It has been held that the statute may be used to convert even a sister-state matrimonial decree into a New York judgment, thus enabling it to be enforced here. But there is still some debate about how far New York will go in "adopting" a sister-state decree, replete with its periodic payment awards. SIEGEL-NYPRAC § 290; Mittenthal v. Mittenthal, 99 Misc. 2d 778, 781, 417 N.Y.S.2d 175, 177 (Sup. Ct. 1979); Blackburn v. Blackburn, 113 Misc. 2d 619, 449 N.Y.S.2d 827 (Sup. Ct. 1982).

iv. It is really the foreign country judgment that can best exploit NY CPLR § 3213—the judgment that is not entitled to full faith and credit under federal law and which therefore depends on New York's willingness to recognize it, an acquiescence loosely known as "comity." Here Article 53 of the Civil Practice Law and Rules (NY CPLR § 5301, et seq.) is relevant, having much to say about which foreign country judgments must be recognized and which need not be. Article 53 applies only to money judgments, however. Other kinds are governed by caselaw, but as it happens New York decisional law is quite generous in recognizing foreign judgments. SIEGEL-NYPRAC § 290; NY CPLR § 5301(b).

c. *Stay of disclosure.* Service of a notice of motion under NY CPLR Rule 3211, NY CPLR Rule 3212, or NY CPLR § 3213 stays disclosure until determination of the motion unless the court orders otherwise. If the motion is based solely on the defense that the summons and complaint, summons with notice, or notice of petition and petition was not properly served, disclosure shall not be stayed unless the court orders otherwise. NY CPLR Rule 3214(b).

d. *Time for response.* The summons served with such motion papers shall require the defendant to submit answering papers on the motion within the time provided in the notice of motion. The minimum time such motion shall be noticed to be heard shall be as provided by NY CPLR Rule 320(a) for making an appearance, depending upon the method of service. If the plaintiff sets the hearing date of the motion later than the minimum time therefor, he may require the defendant to serve a copy of his answering papers upon him within such extended period of time, not exceeding ten (10) days, prior to such hearing date. NY CPLR § 3213.

i. *Time under NY CPLR Rule 320.* An appearance shall be made within twenty (20) days after service of the summons, except that if the summons was served on the defendant by delivering it to an official of the state authorized to receive service in his behalf or if it was served pursuant to NY CPLR § 303, NY CPLR § 308(2), NY CPLR § 308(3), NY CPLR § 308(4), NY CPLR § 308(5), NY CPLR § 313, NY CPLR § 314, or NY CPLR § 315, the appearance shall be made within thirty (30) days after service is complete. NY CPLR Rule 320(a).

ii. *Effect of hearing date.* Since a specific hearing date is set under NY CPLR § 3213 rather than an open-ended requirement to answer within X days as in an ordinary action, it may be difficult to work out the additional requirements of NY CPLR § 308(2) or NY CPLR § 308(4) if the substituted service methods of those provisions are used. They require the filing of proof of service and delay the start of the answering time until ten (10) days after that filing. This suggests that it is wise to use personal delivery under NY CPLR § 308(1) in NY CPLR § 3213 cases. If the other methods must be resorted to, however, it would be reasonable for the court to adjust or even disregard their requirements about filing proof of service and postponing completion of service. Otherwise, it may prove difficult to satisfy both NY CPLR § 3213 and the substituted service provisions of NY CPLR § 308 simultaneously. SIEGEL-NYPRAC § 291; NY CPLR § 2303(Practice Commentaries, C2303:2); NY CPLR § 2303(Practice Commentaries, C2303:4).

e. *No default judgment; Denial of motion.* No default judgment may be entered pursuant to NY CPLR § 3215(a) prior to the hearing date of the motion. If the motion is denied, the moving and answering papers shall be deemed the complaint and answer, respectively, unless the court orders otherwise. NY CPLR § 3213.

i. *Effects of denial.* The defendant may refute the claim, and, if she does, summary judgment may be granted for the defendant instead of the plaintiff. If the refutation is not total, but establishes that genuine issues of fact exist that require trial, the court will deny the motion. In doing so, however, it will not dismiss the action; under NY CPLR § 3213, the court will merely convert the action into an ordinary one, the moving papers becoming the equivalent of a complaint and the answering papers an answer. SIEGEL-NYPRAC § 292; Fine v. Di Stanti, 79 A.D.2d 673, 433 N.Y.S.2d 873, 874 (1980). The case is now the equal of an action brought in conventional form in which a summary judgment motion has just been denied. Whether the issues of fact that resulted in the denial are to be preferred for trial would be governed by the same rules that govern summary judgment motions in general. SIEGEL-NYPRAC § 292; SIEGEL-NYPRAC § 284.

ii. *Conversion to ordinary action; Court's discretion.* This conversion to an ordinary action is the usual remedy, but not the inevitable one. The language of the statute is that the court can order "otherwise." This lays the matter in the court's discretion. SIEGEL-NYPRAC § 292.

f. *Effects of counterclaims.* The question of whether a counterclaim should be entertained in NY CPLR § 3213 context, in view of the statute's intention to get the main claim through to judgment summarily, is an interesting one. The courts are generally reticent about allowing a counterclaim to impede a legitimate NY CPLR § 3213 claim, and while a better case can be made for entertaining a counterclaim if it is related to the plaintiff's claim than if it is not, it has been held that even if a counterclaim arises out of the "same general transaction" as the main claim does, its interposition should not be allowed to impede a plaintiff's ride to summary judgment on the main claim unless the counterclaim also amounts to a "defense" to the main claim. SIEGEL-NYPRAC § 292; Fine v. Di Stanti, 79 A.D.2d 673, 433 N.Y.S.2d 873, 874 (1980); NY CPLR § 3213(Practice Commentaries, C3213:17); NY CPLR § 3213(Practice Commentaries, C3213:18).

g. *Summons; Commencing a case.* Refer to the New York KeyRules Complaint document for further information on commencing a case, including information on the summons.

h. *NEW YORK COUNTY: Filing and bringing case.* In special proceedings and with regard to motions pursuant to NY CPLR § 3213, counsel should file the original petition and a summons and the original motion papers with the County Clerk to commence the case, e-filing them when required. A duplicate original of the petition, the original notice of petition, and an original affidavit of service in a special proceeding, and a duplicate original of the 3213 papers and an original affidavit of service in any such motion-action shall be filed with the General Clerk's Office or e-filed when required. NY R NY CTY Procedure II(A). Important litigation papers must be filed by counsel with the County Clerk. The chief among these are NY CPLR § 3213 motion papers. NY R NY CTY Procedure XI(A). Except in electronically-filed cases, all of these documents must be submitted by counsel to Room 141B (in the basement at 60 Centre Street). Papers commencing a case are submitted to the Cashier in that room with an index number purchase form and fee. NY R NY CTY Procedure XI(A). Except in electronically-filed cases, initiating papers in special proceedings and moving papers in NY CPLR § 3213 motion/actions are filed [according to the procedures in NY R NY CTY Procedure XI(A)]. NY R NY CTY Procedure XI(A).

4. *Oppositions.* In the absence of statutory provision or court rule, a motion ordinarily does not require a written answer, although an adverse party may be permitted to file an answer in opposition to the showing made in the motion or its supporting affidavits. AMJUR MOTIONS § 26. When a party files a motion and the opposing party fails to respond, the court may construe such failure to respond as non-opposition to the motion or an admission that the motion was meritorious, may take the facts alleged in the motion as true, and may grant the motion if the relief requested appears to be justified. However, the severity of such a result demands that a court impose it only with great caution. AMJUR MOTIONS § 28.

a. *Burden of proof.* The opposing party must not overlook his burden if the motion is to be defeated. He must avoid mere conclusory allegations and come forward to lay bare his proof. The consequence of failing to do so will lead the court to infer that there is no genuine fact issue to be tried. SIEGEL-NYPRAC § 281; Hanson v. Ontario Milk Producers Co-op., Inc., 58 Misc. 2d 138, 142, 294 N.Y.S.2d 936, 941 (Sup. Ct. 1968); Banasik v. Reed Prentice Div. of Package Mach. Co., 34 A.D.2d 746, 310 N.Y.S.2d 127, 129 (1970), aff'd, 28 N.Y.2d 770, 269 N.E.2d 918 (1971). Failing to respond to a fact attested to in the moving papers, for example, will be deemed to admit it. SIEGEL-NYPRAC § 281; Kuehne & Nagel, Inc. v. Baiden, 36 N.Y.2d 539, 544, 330 N.E.2d 624, 627, 369 N.Y.S.2d 667, 671 (N.Y. 1975). Nor will pleading ignorance of the fact be a sufficient response, unless it is shown that the ignorance is unavoidable and that with diligent effort the fact could not be ascertained in time for the motion. SIEGEL-NYPRAC § 281; Overseas Reliance Tours & Travel Serv., Inc. v. Sarne Co., 17 A.D.2d 578, 581, 237 N.Y.S.2d 416, 417 (1963).

i. The evidence will be construed in a light most favorable to the one moved against, but this normal rule of summary judgment practice will not be applied if the opposition is evasive, indirect, or coy. SIEGEL-NYPRAC § 281; Weiss v. Garfield, 21 A.D.2d 156, 158, 249 N.Y.S.2d 458, 461 (1964).

ii. Offering only part of one's opposing proof on the assumption that it will suffice to defeat the motion, and for tactical purposes holding back the rest for trial use, can backfire. It can be done safely only when the opposer is sure that what he uses will suffice to beat back the motion. A wrong guess will find the opposer on the wrong side of a summary judgment. Although the courts sometimes grant a motion for summary judgment with leave to move to vacate it, it is rare and should not be anticipated. SIEGEL-NYPRAC § 281; Frutos v. Shapiro, 11 A.D.2d 1005, 1006, 206 N.Y.S.2d 18, 19 (1960).

b. *Disclosure required.* If the opposing party needs further opportunity to secure affidavits or conduct disclosure or otherwise summon forth evidentiary aid in opposing the motion, the court can make any order it deems appropriate, as long as the party attests in an affidavit that such opposing facts may exist. SIEGEL-NYPRAC § 281; NY CPLR

Rule 3212(f). The court can stay the motion and give the party the needed chance to get the additional data or seek the requisite disclosure, or it can deny the motion outright with similar purpose without prejudice to renewal later. SIEGEL-NYPRAC § 281; Kagan v. U.S. Life Ins. Co., 21 A.D.2d 846, 846, 250 N.Y.S.2d 889, 890 (1964).

i. If the motion for summary judgment is made at a late point in the action, however—albeit within the time limits imposed by NY CPLR Rule 3212(a)—and the court finds that the opposing party has already had all the opportunity for disclosure that it now claims the need of, the disclosure may be denied and the opponent left to face the consequences of the summary judgment motion without it. SIEGEL-NYPRAC § 281; SIEGEL-NYPRAC § 279; Dennis v. City of New York, 304 A.D.2d 611, 611, 758 N.Y.S.2d 661, 664 (2003).

c. *Opposing motion for summary judgment in lieu of complaint.* If the case is unsuitable for NY CPLR § 3213 treatment, moreover, but the defendant does not point this out, she may be held to waive objection to the use of NY CPLR § 3213, with the court proceeding right to the merits. SIEGEL-NYPRAC § 292; P. Ballantine & Sons v. Bos. Celtics Basketball Club, 36 A.D.2d 914, 914, 320 N.Y.S.2d 876, 877 (1971).

i. *Failure to timely oppose motion for summary judgment in lieu of complaint.* The defendant's failure to serve answering papers within the required time does not authorize an immediate default, however. The plaintiff who wants a default judgment must ask for it on the return day. And the default may of course be excused by the court for good cause shown. SIEGEL-NYPRAC § 291; NY CPLR § 3213(Practice Commentaries, C3213:14).

5. *Governing law.* The civil practice law and rules (NY CPLR § 101, et seq.) shall govern the procedure in civil judicial proceedings in all courts of the state and before all judges, except where the procedure is regulated by inconsistent statute. The civil practice law and rules shall succeed the civil practice act and rules of civil practice and shall be deemed substituted therefor throughout the statutes and rules of the state. NY CPLR § 101. The civil practice law and rules shall be liberally construed to secure the just, speedy and inexpensive determination of every civil judicial proceeding. NY CPLR § 104.

a. *Uniform trial court rules.* The uniform civil rules for the Supreme Court and County Court (NY R UNIF TRIAL CTS § 202.1, et seq.) shall be applicable to civil actions and proceedings in the Supreme Court and the County Court. NY R UNIF TRIAL CTS § 202.1(a). The provisions of the uniform rules shall be construed consistent with the Civil Practice Law and Rules (CPLR), and matters not covered by the uniform rules shall be governed by the CPLR. NY R UNIF TRIAL CTS § 202.1(d).

b. *Local rules.* Local court rules, not inconsistent with law or with uniform civil rules for the Supreme Court and County Court (NY R UNIF TRIAL CTS § 202.1, et seq.), shall comply with Part 9 of the Rules of the Chief Judge (NY R CHIEF J § 9.1). NY R UNIF TRIAL CTS § 202.1(c).

c. *Official forms.* The state administrator shall have the power to adopt, amend and rescind an appendix of forms. Forms adopted pursuant to NY CPLR § 107 shall be sufficient under the civil practice law and rules and shall illustrate the simplicity and brevity of statement which the civil practice law and rules contemplate. NY CPLR § 107.

6. *Rules of the commercial division.* [Editor's note: certain types of civil cases or civil cases meeting certain monetary thresholds that are filed in the state of New York must be filed in the Commercial Division of the New York Supreme Courts. Rules governing practice in the commercial division are found in NY R UNIF TRIAL CTS § 202.70]. Cases which must be filed in the commercial division are listed below. For more information, refer to NY R UNIF TRIAL CTS § 202.70.

a. *Monetary thresholds.* Except as set forth in NY R UNIF TRIAL CTS § 202.70(b), the monetary thresholds of the Commercial Division, exclusive of punitive damages, interests, costs, disbursements and counsel fees claimed, are established as follows: (1) Albany County, fifty thousand dollars ($50,000); (2) Eighth Judicial District, one hundred thousand dollars ($100,000); (3) Kings County, one hundred fifty thousand dollars ($150,000); (4) Nassau County, two hundred thousand dollars ($200,000); (5) New York County, five hundred thousand dollars ($500,000); (6) Onondaga County, fifty thousand dollars ($50,000); (7) Queens County, one hundred thousand dollars ($100,000); (8) Seventh Judicial District, fifty thousand dollars ($50,000); (9) Suffolk County, one hundred thousand dollars ($100,000); and (10) Westchester County, one hundred thousand dollars ($100,000). NY R UNIF TRIAL CTS § 202.70(a).

i. *ALBANY COUNTY.* The Commercial Division of the Albany County Supreme Court exercises jurisdiction over selected business and commercial disputes in which the amount at issue generally involves damage claims in a minimum amount of fifty thousand dollars ($50,000) as well as claims for unspecified amounts where the value of the commercial asset(s) in dispute exceeds fifty thousand dollars ($50,000). A separate publication promulgating the rules and criteria relating to the filing and management of Commercial Court cases in this part may be obtained from the Albany County Supreme Court Clerk's Office. A section of the Uniform Civil Rules for the Supreme Court and County Court sets forth statewide rules. NY R 3 JD SUP Doc. 1(E).

ii. *BRONX COUNTY.* The monetary threshold for commercial cases in Bronx County will be seventy-five thousand dollars ($75,000). All other parameters including the type of matters that will be heard are contained within the Rules of the Commercial Division of the Supreme Court (NY R UNIF TRIAL CTS § 202.70). NY R BRONX FIL R Doc. 12.

iii. *NEW YORK COUNTY.* The monetary threshold in the New York County Commercial Division, which is generally applicable, is an amount in controversy of five hundred thousand dollars ($500,000) or more (exclusive of punitive damages, interest, costs, disbursements, and counsel fees). If the case is designated a commercial one and the Addendum is submitted, the clerk will review the pleadings to determine whether the amount in controversy in the case meets the monetary threshold or whether an exception to the threshold applies. NY R NY CTY Procedure IA(B). For more information on assigning a case to the commercial division in New York County, refer to NY R NY CTY Procedure IA(B).

b. *Commercial cases.* Actions in which the principal claims involve or consist of the following will be heard in the Commercial Division provided that the monetary threshold is met or equitable or declaratory relief is sought:

i. Breach of contract or fiduciary duty, fraud, misrepresentation, business tort (e.g., unfair competition), or statutory and/or common law violation where the breach or violation is alleged to arise out of business dealings (e.g., sales of assets or securities; corporate restructuring; partnership, shareholder, joint venture, and other business agreements; trade secrets; restrictive covenants; and employment agreements not including claims that principally involve alleged discriminatory practices);

ii. Transactions governed by the Uniform Commercial Code (exclusive of those concerning individual cooperative or condominium units);

iii. Transactions involving commercial real property, including Yellowstone injunctions and excluding actions for the payment of rent only;

iv. Shareholder derivative actions—without consideration of the monetary threshold;

v. Commercial class actions—without consideration of the monetary threshold;

vi. Business transactions involving or arising out of dealings with commercial banks and other financial institutions;

vii. Internal affairs of business organizations;

viii. Malpractice by accountants or actuaries, and legal malpractice arising out of representation in commercial matters;

ix. Environmental insurance coverage;

x. Commercial insurance coverage (e.g., directors and officers, errors and omissions, and business interruption coverage);

xi. Dissolution of corporations, partnerships, limited liability companies, limited liability partnerships and joint ventures—without consideration of the monetary threshold; and

xii. Applications to stay or compel arbitration and affirm or disaffirm arbitration awards and related injunctive relief pursuant to Article 75 of the New York Civil Practice Law and Rules (NY CPLR § 7501, et seq.) involving any of the foregoing enumerated commercial issues. Where the applicable arbitration agreement provides for the arbitration to be heard outside the United States, the monetary threshold set forth in NY R UNIF TRIAL CTS § 202.70(a) shall not apply. NY R UNIF TRIAL CTS § 202.70(b).

c. *Non-commercial cases.* The following will not be heard in the Commercial Division even if the monetary threshold is met:

i. Suits to collect professional fees;

ii. Cases seeking a declaratory judgment as to insurance coverage for personal injury or property damage;

iii. Residential real estate disputes, including landlord-tenant matters, and commercial real estate disputes involving the payment of rent only;

iv. Home improvement contracts involving residential properties consisting of one to four residential units or individual units in any residential building, including cooperative or condominium units;

v. Proceedings to enforce a judgment regardless of the nature of the underlying case;

vi. First-party insurance claims and actions by insurers to collect premiums or rescind non-commercial policies; and

vii. Attorney malpractice actions except as otherwise provided in NY R UNIF TRIAL CTS § 202.70(b)(8). NY R UNIF TRIAL CTS § 202.70(c).

d. For more information on the Commercial Division, refer to NY R UNIF TRIAL CTS § 202.70.

D. Documents

1. *Documents for moving party*

a. *Required documents*

i. *Notice of motion, order to show cause, or affidavit on ex parte motion.* The notice of motion shall be substantially in the form found in NY R UNIF TRIAL CTS § 202.7(b). NY R UNIF TRIAL CTS § 202.7(b). The supporting papers should be referred to in the notice of motion. SIEGEL-NYPRAC § 246. The court in a proper case may grant an order to show cause, to be served in lieu of a notice of motion. NY CPLR Rule 2214(d). An ex parte motion shall be accompanied by an affidavit stating the result of any prior motion for similar relief and specifying the new facts, if any, that were not previously shown. NY CPLR Rule 2217(b).

- *Request for oral argument.* A party requesting oral argument shall set forth such request in its notice of motion or in its order to show cause or on the first page of the answering papers, as the case may be. Where all parties to a motion request oral argument, oral argument shall be granted unless the court shall determine it to be unnecessary. Where a motion is brought on by order to show cause, the court may set forth in the order that oral argument is required on the return date of the motion. NY R UNIF TRIAL CTS § 202.8(d).

ii. *Motion.* Refer to the General Requirements section of this document for information on the notice of motion and motion.

iii. *Supporting evidence; Exhibits.* A motion for summary judgment shall be supported by affidavit, and by other available proof, such as depositions and written admissions. The affidavit shall be by a person having knowledge of the facts; it shall recite all the material facts; and it shall show that there is no defense to the cause of action or that the cause of action or defense has no merit. NY CPLR Rule 3212(b). The main supporting papers on a motion are affidavits, but any relevant exhibits, documents, depositions, etc., are also includible. SIEGEL-NYPRAC § 246.

- *Evidence on summary judgment.* Any form of evidence, documentary or otherwise, may be considered on a motion for summary judgment. SIEGEL-NYPRAC § 281; Wilkinson v. Skinner, 34 N.Y.2d 53, 56, 312 N.E.2d 158, 160 (1974).
- *Affidavits accompanying motion.* Affidavits shall be for a statement of the relevant facts. NY R UNIF TRIAL CTS § 202.8(c).
- *Foreign language documents.* Where an affidavit or exhibit annexed to a paper served or filed is in a foreign language, it shall be accompanied by an English translation and an affidavit by the translator stating his qualifications and that the translation is accurate. NY CPLR Rule 2101(b).
- *Statement of attorney in lieu of affidavit.* The statement of an attorney admitted to practice in the courts of the state, or of a physician, osteopath or dentist, authorized by law to practice in the state, who is not a party to an action, when subscribed and affirmed by him to be true under the penalties of perjury, may be served or filed in the action in lieu of and with the same force and effect as an affidavit. NY CPLR Rule 2106. Affidavits on any motion should be made only by those with knowledge of the facts, and nowhere is this rule more faithfully applied than on the motion for summary judgment. The attorney's affidavit, unless the attorney happens to have first-hand knowledge of the facts—which is the exception rather than the rule—has no probative force. SIEGEL-NYPRAC § 281; S. Bay Ctr., Inc. v. Butler, Herrick & Marshall, 43 Misc. 2d 269, 272, 250 N.Y.S.2d 863, 866 (Sup. Ct. 1964).
- *NEW YORK COUNTY: Form of presented exhibits.* Exhibits should be tabbed and be legible; a typed version of any exhibit that is difficult to read should be submitted with the original. Exhibits printed on both sides of the page should be bound and tabbed on the side. NY R NY CTY J RUL Rule 14(a).
- *QUEENS COUNTY.* Attorneys submitting exhibits to the court on E-file cases shall make each exhibit a separate, labeled attachment to an affidavit/affirmation. NY R L QUEENS E-FILE Doc. 1(H)(4).

iv. *Copy of the pleadings.* A motion for summary judgment shall be supported by a copy of the pleadings. NY CPLR Rule 3212(b).

- A copy of the pleadings should be part of the moving papers on a motion for summary judgment. While their omission could presumably be remediable under NY CPLR § 2001, some courts have held that omitting the pleadings mandates a denial or dismissal of the motion for that reason alone. SIEGEL-NYPRAC § 281; Notaro v. Bison Const. Corp., 32 A.D.3d 1218, 821 N.Y.S.2d 715 (2006).

v. *Request for judicial intervention.* At any time after service of process, a party may file a request for judicial intervention. Except as provided in NY R UNIF TRIAL CTS § 202.6(b), in an action not yet assigned to a judge, the court shall not accept for filing a notice of motion, order to show cause, or application for ex parte order, unless such notice or application is accompanied by a request for judicial intervention. NY R UNIF TRIAL CTS § 202.6(a).

- *BRONX COUNTY.* Generally, the Request For Judicial Intervention, commonly referred to as an "RJI", is required to be filed in any action where the assignment of a Justice is required. The RJI sets forth the information which is entered into the court system's database. It must be completely and accurately filled out. The full caption, as stated on the Summons, must be set forth. Use of terms "et al." and "etc." are not permitted. Only one (1) RJI may be filed in each action. Either a self represented litigant or an attorney must sign the affirmation at the end of the form. Once completed, the RJI must be filed in duplicate. Except in the case of an ex-parte application, the RJI must also be served together with the accompanying application upon all parties. Proof of accuracy of the index number must accompany the RJI. Check the Fee Schedule[. . .]for any applicable filing fees. NY R BRONX FIL R Doc. 2.
- *KINGS COUNTY.* An RJI with the relevant required addendum in a NYSCEF case shall be submitted via NYSCEF. Once e-filed, the RJI and any accompanying document will be forwarded to the relevant support office for random assignment of the case and processing of the document. A filer or counsel need not appear (as to Proposed Orders to Show Cause, however, see below). A copy of the pleadings must be submitted only if the document has not previously been e-filed. If the RJI seeks intervention with regard to a document that is intended for review by a Justice, such as a motion, a working copy of the RJI must be submitted with the working copy of the motion and the NYSCEF Confirmation Notice. NY R L KINGS E FIL Doc. 1(C).
- *NEW YORK COUNTY.* To obtain the assignment of an IAS Justice to a case, a Request for Judicial Intervention (cost ninety-five dollars ($95)) must be filed, with NYSCEF in an e-filed case or in paper in an authorized hard-copy one. A no-fee RJI, which will generally result in the referral of an application to an Ex Parte Justice, is also required with regard to certain kinds of applications for which, prior to 2011, no RJI was required. NY R NY CTY Procedure I(C). A "fillable" form RJI is available on-line. The form must be filed in duplicate in hard-copy cases. NY R NY CTY Procedure IA(A)(1). The filer of an RJI must check off a box identifying the type of case at issue. Where the RJI seeks judicial assignment, this designation will bring about a random assignment of the case by computer to a Justice handling cases of that type. NY R NY CTY Procedure IA(A)(1). The RJI and any addendum can be completed and submitted electronically in an e-filed case. NY R NY CTY Procedure II(A). The RJI shall be marked to reflect the existence of any "related case" as explained on the "Commencement of Cases" page under "Case Processing" on the court's website. NY R NY CTY Procedure II(A); NY R NY CTY E FIL Doc. 2(C).
- *ONONDAGA COUNTY.* The RJI will be submitted via the NYSCEF system along with any required RJI addendum forms. When the RJI is filed and the fee paid online, the Onondaga County Clerk's Office will electronically forward the RJI and any accompanying documents to the Onondaga Supreme Court Clerk's Office for assignment and processing. Counsel will receive notification of judge assignment via the NYSCEF system. NY R ONDGA E FIL Protocol(B)(3).
- *QUEENS COUNTY.* A Request for Judicial Intervention ("RJI") in an E-filed case shall be submitted via the E-filing System. When the RJI is approved, filed and paid for on-line, it will be forwarded to the relevant back office for random assignment of the case and processing of the document. In the case of RJIs seeking assignment to the Commercial Division, the filer must submit therewith, a Commercial Addendum as required by the standards for assignment of cases to the Commercial Division. NY R L QUEENS E-FILE Doc. 1(F).

vi. *Proof of service.* In addition to complying with the provisions of NY CPLR Rule 2101, every paper filed in court shall have annexed thereto appropriate proof of service on all parties where required. NY R UNIF TRIAL CTS § 202.5(a).

- *QUEENS COUNTY.* With regard to service of a motion/petition on notice in an E-filed action, NY CPLR Rule 2214(b) and NY R UNIF TRIAL CTS § 202.5-b(f) applies. Where required, proof of service shall be filed on-line as a separate document. NY R L QUEENS E-FILE Doc. 1(H)(3).

vii. *ALBANY COUNTY: Additional required documents*

- *Affirmation of good faith effort.* The parties must[. . .]submit an affirmation attesting to [their good faith effort to resolve the matter]. The affirmation of good faith effort to resolve the issues raised by the motion shall indicate the time, place and nature of the consultation and the issues discussed and any resolutions, or shall indicate good cause why no such conferral with counsel for opposing parties was held. An assigned justice or judge may dismiss a motion for failure to demonstrate that such effort was made with leave to renew the motion after such effort has been demonstrated. NY R 3 JD SUP Doc. 1(B).

b. *Supplemental documents*

i. *Brief.* Briefs shall be for a statement of the relevant law. NY R UNIF TRIAL CTS § 202.8(c).

ii. *Notice to produce papers not in possession of the court.* If a paper relied on by the movant is in the possession of the other side, it may be demanded of that side with a notice to produce it at the hearing. Where such papers are in the possession of an adverse party, they shall be produced by him at the hearing on notice served with the motion papers. NY CPLR Rule 2214(Practice Commentary, C2214:23).

iii. *Filing fees.* The County Clerk shall require the payment of any applicable statutory fees, or an order of the Court waiving payment of such fees, before accepting a paper for filing. NY R UNIF TRIAL CTS § 202.5(d)(1). For information on filing fees, if any, refer to NY CPLR § 8001, et seq.

- *ALBANY COUNTY.* In general, any filing subsequent to the commencement of an action which is designated as a motion or cross-motion requires the payment of a filing fee to the County Clerk's Office prior to submission to the Supreme Court Clerk's Office for referral to the assigned justice. The fee is assessed regardless of whether an application is made by notice of motion, order to show cause or ex parte. No fee will be charged upon the filing of a motion for poor person status in conjunction with an application which serves to commence an action or special proceeding. In the event a motion is received by the court unaccompanied by proof of payment to the County Clerk, the Supreme Court Clerk's Office will contact the submitting party to advise that the application will be held pending receipt of the filing fee only until the return date of the motion. If proof of payment is not submitted to the Supreme Court Clerk's Office by the return date (ex parte applications will be held ten (10) days), the papers will be returned by mail with a notification that the motion has been removed from the court's calendar and that it must be re-noticed and re-filed with the court along with the requisite filing fee. Inquiries concerning the applicability of the motion fee to a proposed filing may be directed to the Supreme Court Clerk's Office. NY R 3 JD SUP Doc. 1(B).
- *BRONX COUNTY.* In accordance with the new civil fee schedule set forth in Article 80 of the C.P.L.R. (NY CPLR § 8001, et seq.), effective July 14, 2003, all motions, and cross motions must be approved in Room 217 prior to payment of said fees in the County Clerk's Office, Room 118. NY R BRONX FIL R Doc. 8. The motion fee [must be] paid for via NYSCEF by credit/debit card. NY R BRONX E FIL R Doc. 1(1).
- *ERIE COUNTY.* Payment for fee-bearing NYSCEF documents must be made online via credit or debit card (American Express, MasterCard or Visa) at the time of submission. NY R ERIE E FIL Doc. 3(III)(E).
- *KINGS COUNTY.* The motion must be filed with NYSCEF and the motion fee paid. NY R L KINGS E FIL Doc. 1(D). Court fees in NYSCEF cases must be paid via NYSCEF by a credit or bank card (MasterCard, Visa, or American Express). Fees are no longer accepted in person in the Kings County Clerk's Office in NYSCEF cases. NY R L KINGS E FIL Doc. 1(B)(6).
- *NEW YORK COUNTY.* A motion fee must be paid on motions made in writing by notice of motion, order to show cause or ex parte after the commencement of an action. For this purpose, the term "action" shall mean any application to the court that requires the assignment of an index number, regardless of whether a formal pleading is filed. Applications or motions that commence an action and for which an index number fee must be paid require no motion fee. [A]ny motions made after the initial applications in these situations would require payment of the motion fee. A motion that is the initial application in a case commenced by the filing of a summons and complaint would require a motion fee since the filing of the summons and complaint rather than the application itself would require the purchase of an index number. NY R NY CTY Procedure II(A). In e-filed cases the motion fee must be paid when the documents are filed. Payment is made on-line by Visa, Mastercard, or American Express credit or bank card. NY R NY CTY Procedure II(A); NY R NY CTY E FIL Doc. 2(B)(5).
- *ONONDAGA COUNTY.* Court fees in e-filed cases must be paid online with the NYSCEF system using a credit card. The document is not considered to have been filed until payment of the fee has been tendered. NY R ONDGA E FIL Protocol(B)(2). Fees must be paid on all cross motions. NY R ONDGA E FIL Protocol(B)(9)(e).

- *QUEENS COUNTY.* The Motion Support Office does not receive, forward or process any fees or waiver of fees. All applications requiring payment of statutory fees or waiver of fees must be sent directly to the Queens County Clerk's office. NY R L QUEENS MOT SUP Doc. 1. Court fees (e.g., RJI fee, motion fee) in E-filed cases may be paid for on-line using a credit card. Papers may also be filed with the E-file system and the fee may be paid at the County Clerk's Office. In the latter case, the paper is not considered to have been filed until payment of the fee has been tendered. NY R L QUEENS E-FILE Doc. 1(E)(1). The motion/petition shall be filed on-line and the fee paid for either on-line by credit card or by the "Pay at the County Clerk's Office" option. NY R L QUEENS E-FILE Doc. 1(H)(1).

iv. *Working copies.* The court may require the parties to provide working copies of documents filed electronically. In such event, each working copy shall include, firmly affixed thereto, a copy of a confirmation notice in a form prescribed by the Chief Administrator. NY R UNIF TRIAL CTS § 202.5-b(d)(5).

- *BRONX COUNTY.* After papers on motions have been e-filed, working copies thereof, with Confirmation Notice firmly attached as the back page facing out, must be submitted. (Each document or group of documents that is separately bound shall bear a Confirmation Notice.) Working copies lacking the Notice will not be accepted. WORKING COPIES OF MOTION PAPERS MUST BE SUBMITTED NO LATER THAN 4:45 P.M. ON THE RETURN DATE IN THE MOTION SUPPORT OFFICE (ROOM 217) AS EXPLAINED in NY R BRONX E FIL R Doc. 1(4). If an attorney has failed to submit required working copies on or before the return date, the motion will be transmitted as is to the Justice for such action as the Justice finds appropriate. Attorneys may submit working copies on motions by mail or overnight delivery. Any such submission shall be sent in a timely manner to the Motion Support Office (Room 217) and be conspicuously marked on the outside "NYSCEF Matter"; lack of such marking may delay processing. NY R BRONX E FIL R Doc. 1(4)(a).

- *ERIE COUNTY.* Electronically filed documents subject to review and processing by the Part Clerk do not require a working copy unless otherwise directed or provided for in IAS Part Rules. NY R UNIF TRIAL CTS § 202.5-b(d)(4), any working copy submitted shall include, as a cover page firmly fastened thereto, a copy of the Confirmation Notice generated by the NYSCEF site at the time of filing. Please consult the individual Justice's Part Rules and/or consult with the Judge's chambers to determine whether and how working copies are to be provided. Working copies will not be printed or delivered by the Erie County Clerk or the Chief Clerk of the Courts or any of their personnel to chambers. The official record of a document in an electronically filed case is the document filed via the NYSCEF system. Working copies are intended only for use by the Justice. The Court will discard all working copies after the Justice has finished with them. Thus, in the event that counsel fails to file a document via the NYSCEF system, the document will not be part of the court record. NY R ERIE E FIL Doc. 3(III)(O); NY R ERIE E FIL Doc. 3(V)(E).

- *KINGS COUNTY.* No courtesy copies of motion papers are required by the Court, except as may be required for electronic filing or by the Judge's Part Rules. In tort cases against the City of New York, courtesy copies shall be supplied to the Corporation Counsel's office in Brooklyn. NY R L KINGS Pt. C, Rule 5. Unless otherwise directed by the Court or as described herein, and with the exceptions listed below, in all NYSCEF cases in which an RJI has been filed, working copies of e-filed documents that are intended for judicial review must be submitted to the court. Working copies are not required of documents that are only processed by a support office (e.g. preliminary conference request, note of issue). Working copies shall include exhibit tabs and backs; for motion papers, the motion sequence number and the return date and part. The confirmation notice with the motion sequence number on it should be the back page of the motion facing out. In addition, the filer of a working copy must firmly bind thereto, with the back page facing out, a copy of the Confirmation Notice that was generated by NYSCEF when that document was efiled. Working copies that are submitted without the related Confirmation Notice will not be accepted. NY R L KINGS E FIL Doc. 1(B)(7); NY R L KINGS E FIL Doc. 1(D). WORKING COPIES OF MOTION PAPERS MUST BE SUBMITTED IN THE MOTION SUPPORT OFFICE (ROOM 227) AS EXPLAINED HEREIN. THEY MUST NOT BE DELIVERED TO THE PART OR CHAMBERS, EXCEPT WHERE THE INDIVIDUAL JUSTICE'S PART RULES PROVIDE OTHERWISE; DOING SO WILL CAUSE ADMINISTRATIVE CONFUSION AND POSSIBLE MISPLACEMENT OF PAPERS. Any such submission shall be sent in a timely manner (kindly review individual Justice's rules) and be conspicuously marked on the outside "NYSCEF Matter;" lack of such marking may delay processing. NY R L KINGS E FIL Doc. 1(D).

- *NEW YORK COUNTY.* Some Justices require that working copies of e-filed motion papers be submitted. See the E-filing Protocol for information on the many Parts that do not require working copies. Where required, working copies of the moving documents and all other documents on the motion or application shall be submitted to the Motion Submission Part Courtroom (Room 130) on, but not before, the final return date. A Confirmation Notice from the NYSCEF system, which is generated when a document is e-filed, shall be firmly affixed, as the back page facing out, to each separate working copy or group of such copies. NY R NY CTY Procedure II(A) NY R NY CTY E FIL Doc. 2(B)(5)(a); NY R NY CTY J RUL Rule 14(a). For more information on working copies, including which parts don't require them, refer to NY R NY CTY E FIL Doc. 2(B)(6).

- *ONONDAGA COUNTY.* Any courtesy "working" copies, if required (see NY R ONDGA E FIL Protocol(B)(7)), must be provided directly to the assigned justice. NY R ONDGA E FIL Protocol(B)(9)(e). For information as to whether or not an Onondaga Supreme Court Justice requires working (courtesy) copies of e-filed documents, please consult the Onondaga County Individual E-filing Rules. NY R ONDGA E FIL Protocol(B)(7)(a). The Supreme Court Clerk's Office and the Onondaga County Clerk's Office will NOT accept the working copies. Working copies must be sent directly to the assigned justice's chambers. NY R ONDGA E FIL Protocol(B)(7)(b). A copy of the Confirmation Notice, generated by the NYSCEF system at the time a document is e-filed, must be attached to every working copy provided to chambers. If the Confirmation Notice is missing, the copy will not be accepted. NY R ONDGA E FIL Protocol(B)(7)(c). Courtesy copies do not become part of the official court record as maintained by the Onondaga County Clerk's Office and will be destroyed by chambers at the disposition of the case. In the event that counsel fails to file a document via NYSCEF, the document will not be part of the court record. NY R ONDGA E FIL Protocol(B)(7)(d).
- *QUEENS COUNTY.* Working copies of E-Filed notices of motion/notices of petition are NOT to be sent to the Motion Support Office. They must be brought to the calendar call in the judge's part. NY R L QUEENS MOT SUP Doc. 1. Unless otherwise directed or authorized by the court, counsel should file papers with the E-file system first and thereafter deliver a working copy to at the calendar call of the Centralized Motion Part or Assigned Justice in accordance with individual Part Rules. NY R L QUEENS E-FILE Doc. 1(E)(4). On the return date of a motion that has been E-filed, the movant must provide the Centralized Motion Part (CMP) with a working copy of the entire motion including the notice of motion with sequence number and all of the attached exhibits. The motion must have the confirmation of filing firmly affixed to the back of the papers (facing outward). The confirmation of filing is a separate notice from the payment notice and will say confirmation clearly across the top of the page. NY R L QUEENS E-FILE Doc. 1(H)(2)(a). The motion or Order to Show Cause must have clearly written across its face the words "Working Copy," it must also have the assigned Judge's name, motion sequence number and calendar number—which may be obtained from the posted calendar outside courtroom on the return date of the motion. A confirmation of filing must attached thereto. Working copies of e-filed Orders to Show Cause must contain a copy of the signed order and all supporting papers. NY R L QUEENS E-FILE Doc. 1(H)(2)(c). The Confirmation Notice must be an updated version that indicates the sequence number of the motion being submitted at the CMP calendar call. WORKING COPIES WITHOUT A CONFIRMATION NOTICE WILL NOT BE ACCEPTED. NY R L QUEENS E-FILE Doc. 1(H)(7).

v. *Statement of authorization in electronic filing cases.* A filing agent (other than one employed by a governmental entity) shall e-file a statement of authorization from counsel of record in an action, in a form approved by the Chief Administrator, prior to or together with the first e-filing in that action by the agent on behalf of that counsel. NY R UNIF TRIAL CTS § 202.5-b(d)(1)(i).

vi. *ERIE COUNTY: Additional supplemental documents*

- *Notice of hard copy submission in e-filed case.* In accordance with NY R UNIF TRIAL CTS § 202.5-b(d), the County Clerk shall refuse to accept for filing, hard copy papers filed to an action subject to electronic filing unless hard copy filing is permitted by the Uniform Rules or NY R ERIE E FIL Doc. 3 and the papers bear a completed Notice of Hard Copy Submission—E-Filed Case form. NY R ERIE E FIL Doc. 3(III)(D).

vii. *KINGS COUNTY: Additional supplemental documents*

- *Forms when filing in hard copy.* An attorney who certifies in good faith that he or she lacks the equipment or knowledge needed to e-file and have no staff member or employee under his or her direction who has such knowledge and equipment may opt out of participation in e-filing in a mandatory case by filing a "Notice of Opt-Out from Participation in Action Subject to Mandatory Electronic Filing" form EFM-2 with the Clerk. NY R L KINGS E FIL Doc. 1(A)(2). Where in accordance with the E-Filing Rules a party submits a document in hard copy in an e-filed case (principally, a document submitted by a nonparticipating party (e.g., an attorney) in a consensual case, an emergency filing made in accordance with the Mandatory E-Filing Rules, and any document filed with the court in hard copy by an attorney who has opted out of participation in mandatory e-filing, the document must bear the back page facing out, a "Notice of Hard Copy Submission—E-Filed Cases" form EFM-3. NY R L KINGS E FIL Doc. 1(B)(3).

viii. *NEW YORK COUNTY: Additional supplemental documents*

- *Notice of hard copy submission.* Where in accordance with the E-Filing Rules an attorney or an unrepresented litigant who is participating in e-filing submits a document in hard copy in an e-filed case, the document must bear, as the back page facing out, a Notice of Hard-Copy Submission—E-Filed Case (a form available in the "Forms" section on the NYSCEF website (Form EFM-3) and in the court's back offices). NY R NY CTY E FIL Doc. 2(B)(3). For more information refer to NY R NY CTY E FIL Doc. 2.
- *Unpublished decisions.* Whenever reliance is placed upon a decision or other authority not officially published or readily available to the New York County Supreme Court, a copy of the case or of pertinent portions of the authority shall be submitted with the motion papers. NY R NY CTY J RUL Rule 14(a).

ix. *ONONDAGA COUNTY: Additional supplemental documents*

- *Notice of hard copy submission.* Any papers to be filed with the court in an e-filed case must be filed online with the E-filing system except where a special exemption is granted (e.g., oversized maps, photographs). If such an exemption is granted, Form EFM-3, "Notice of Hard Copy Submission—E-Filed Case," must be attached to such documents forms which are not filed on line. Also, Form EFM-4 "Notice of Hard Copy Exhibit Filing" must be completed and uploaded to the action's e-file. Both of these forms may be found on the NYSCEF website. NY R ONDGA E FIL Protocol(B)(4).

x. *QUEENS COUNTY: Additional supplemental documents*

- *Notice of hard copy submission.* Any party opting out of the e-filing system must have a "Notice of Hard Copy Submission" firmly affixed to the back of the papers. NY R L QUEENS E-FILE Doc. 1(H)(2)(f).

2. *Documents for moving party in motion for summary judgment in lieu of complaint*

a. *Required documents*

i. *Summons.* Refer to the New York KeyRules Complaint document for the form and contents of the summons.

- If the complaint is not served with the summons, the summons shall contain or have attached thereto a notice stating the nature of the action and the relief sought, and, except in an action for medical malpractice, the sum of money for which judgment may be taken in case of default. NY CPLR Rule 305(b).

ii. *Notice of motion, order to show cause, or affidavit on ex parte motion.* The notice of motion shall be substantially in the form found in NY R UNIF TRIAL CTS § 202.7(b). NY R UNIF TRIAL CTS § 202.7(b). The supporting papers should be referred to in the notice of motion. SIEGEL-NYPRAC § 246. The court in a proper case may grant an order to show cause, to be served in lieu of a notice of motion. NY CPLR Rule 2214(d). An ex parte motion shall be accompanied by an affidavit stating the result of any prior motion for similar relief and specifying the new facts, if any, that were not previously shown. NY CPLR Rule 2217(b).

- *Request for oral argument.* A party requesting oral argument shall set forth such request in its notice of motion or in its order to show cause or on the first page of the answering papers, as the case may be. Where all parties to a motion request oral argument, oral argument shall be granted unless the court shall determine it to be unnecessary. Where a motion is brought on by order to show cause, the court may set forth in the order that oral argument is required on the return date of the motion. NY R UNIF TRIAL CTS § 202.8(d).

iii. *Motion.* Refer to the General Requirements section of this document for information on the notice of motion and motion.

iv. *Supporting evidence; Exhibits.* A motion for summary judgment shall be supported by affidavit, and by other available proof, such as depositions and written admissions. The affidavit shall be by a person having knowledge of the facts; it shall recite all the material facts; and it shall show that there is no defense to the cause of action or that the cause of action or defense has no merit. NY CPLR Rule 3212(b). The main supporting papers on a motion are affidavits, but any relevant exhibits, documents, depositions, etc., are also includible. SIEGEL-NYPRAC § 246.

- *Evidence on summary judgment.* Any form of evidence, documentary or otherwise, may be considered on a motion for summary judgment. SIEGEL-NYPRAC § 281; Wilkinson v. Skinner, 34 N.Y.2d 53, 56, 312 N.E.2d 158, 160 (1974).

- *Affidavits accompanying motion.* Affidavits shall be for a statement of the relevant facts. NY R UNIF TRIAL CTS § 202.8(c).
- *Foreign language documents.* Where an affidavit or exhibit annexed to a paper served or filed is in a foreign language, it shall be accompanied by an English translation and an affidavit by the translator stating his qualifications and that the translation is accurate. NY CPLR Rule 2101(b).
- *Statement of attorney in lieu of affidavit.* The statement of an attorney admitted to practice in the courts of the state, or of a physician, osteopath or dentist, authorized by law to practice in the state, who is not a party to an action, when subscribed and affirmed by him to be true under the penalties of perjury, may be served or filed in the action in lieu of and with the same force and effect as an affidavit. NY CPLR Rule 2106. Affidavits on any motion should be made only by those with knowledge of the facts, and nowhere is this rule more faithfully applied than on the motion for summary judgment. The attorney's affidavit, unless the attorney happens to have first-hand knowledge of the facts—which is the exception rather than the rule—has no probative force. SIEGEL-NYPRAC § 281; S. Bay Ctr., Inc. v. Butler, Herrick & Marshall, 43 Misc. 2d 269, 272, 250 N.Y.S.2d 863, 866 (Sup. Ct. 1964).
- *NEW YORK COUNTY: Form of presented exhibits.* Exhibits should be tabbed and be legible; a typed version of any exhibit that is difficult to read should be submitted with the original. Exhibits printed on both sides of the page should be bound and tabbed on the side. NY R NY CTY J RUL Rule 14(a).
- *QUEENS COUNTY.* Attorneys submitting exhibits to the court on E-file cases shall make each exhibit a separate, labeled attachment to an affidavit/affirmation. NY R L QUEENS E-FILE Doc. 1(H)(4).

v. *Copy of the pleadings.* A motion for summary judgment shall be supported by a copy of the pleadings. NY CPLR Rule 3212(b).

- A copy of the pleadings should be part of the moving papers on a motion for summary judgment. While their omission could presumably be remediable under NY CPLR § 2001, some courts have held that omitting the pleadings mandates a denial or dismissal of the motion for that reason alone. SIEGEL-NYPRAC § 281; Notaro v. Bison Const. Corp., 32 A.D.3d 1218, 821 N.Y.S.2d 715 (2006).

vi. *Request for judicial intervention.* At any time after service of process, a party may file a request for judicial intervention. Except as provided in NY R UNIF TRIAL CTS § 202.6(b), in an action not yet assigned to a judge, the court shall not accept for filing a notice of motion, order to show cause, or application for ex parte order, unless such notice or application is accompanied by a request for judicial intervention. NY R UNIF TRIAL CTS § 202.6(a).

- *BRONX COUNTY.* Generally, the Request For Judicial Intervention, commonly referred to as an "RJI", is required to be filed in any action where the assignment of a Justice is required. The RJI sets forth the information which is entered into the court system's database. It must be completely and accurately filled out. The full caption, as stated on the Summons, must be set forth. Use of terms "et al." and "etc." are not permitted. Only one (1) RJI may be filed in each action. Either a self represented litigant or an attorney must sign the affirmation at the end of the form. Once completed, the RJI must be filed in duplicate. Except in the case of an ex-parte application, the RJI must also be served together with the accompanying application upon all parties. Proof of accuracy of the index number must accompany the RJI. Check the Fee Schedule[. . .]for any applicable filing fees. NY R BRONX FIL R Doc. 2.
- *KINGS COUNTY.* An RJI with the relevant required addendum in a NYSCEF case shall be submitted via NYSCEF. Once e-filed, the RJI and any accompanying document will be forwarded to the relevant support office for random assignment of the case and processing of the document. A filer or counsel need not appear (as to Proposed Orders to Show Cause, however, see below). A copy of the pleadings must be submitted only if the document has not previously been e-filed. If the RJI seeks intervention with regard to a document that is intended for review by a Justice, such as a motion, a working copy of the RJI must be submitted with the working copy of the motion and the NYSCEF Confirmation Notice. NY R L KINGS E FIL Doc. 1(C).
- *NEW YORK COUNTY.* To obtain the assignment of an IAS Justice to a case, a Request for Judicial Intervention (cost ninety-five dollars ($95)) must be filed, with NYSCEF in an e-filed case or in paper in an authorized hard-copy one. A no-fee RJI, which will generally result in the referral of an application to an Ex Parte Justice, is also required with regard to certain kinds of applications for which, prior to 2011, no RJI was required. NY R NY CTY Procedure I(C). A "fillable" form RJI is available on-line. The form must be filed in duplicate in hard-copy cases. NY R NY CTY Procedure IA(A)(1). The filer of an RJI must check off a box identifying the type of case at issue. Where the RJI seeks judicial assignment, this designation will

bring about a random assignment of the case by computer to a Justice handling cases of that type. NY R NY CTY Procedure IA(A)(1). The RJI and any addendum can be completed and submitted electronically in an e-filed case. NY R NY CTY Procedure II(A). The RJI shall be marked to reflect the existence of any "related case" as explained on the "Commencement of Cases" page under "Case Processing" on the court's website. NY R NY CTY Procedure II(A); NY R NY CTY E FIL Doc. 2(C).

- *ONONDAGA COUNTY.* The RJI will be submitted via the NYSCEF system along with any required RJI addendum forms. When the RJI is filed and the fee paid online, the Onondaga County Clerk's Office will electronically forward the RJI and any accompanying documents to the Onondaga Supreme Court Clerk's Office for assignment and processing. Counsel will receive notification of judge assignment via the NYSCEF system. NY R ONDGA E FIL Protocol(B)(3).
- *QUEENS COUNTY.* A Request for Judicial Intervention ("RJI") in an E-filed case shall be submitted via the E-filing System. When the RJI is approved, filed and paid for on-line, it will be forwarded to the relevant back office for random assignment of the case and processing of the document. In the case of RJIs seeking assignment to the Commercial Division, the filer must submit therewith, a Commercial Addendum as required by the standards for assignment of cases to the Commercial Division. NY R L QUEENS E-FILE Doc. 1(F).

vii. *Proof of service.* In addition to complying with the provisions of NY CPLR Rule 2101, every paper filed in court shall have annexed thereto appropriate proof of service on all parties where required. NY R UNIF TRIAL CTS § 202.5(a).

- *QUEENS COUNTY.* With regard to service of a motion/petition on notice in an E-filed action, NY CPLR Rule 2214(b) and NY R UNIF TRIAL CTS § 202.5-b(f) applies. Where required, proof of service shall be filed on-line as a separate document. NY R L QUEENS E-FILE Doc. 1(H)(3).

viii. *ALBANY COUNTY: Additional required documents*

- *Affirmation of good faith effort.* The parties must[. . .]submit an affirmation attesting to [their good faith effort to resolve the matter]. The affirmation of good faith effort to resolve the issues raised by the motion shall indicate the time, place and nature of the consultation and the issues discussed and any resolutions, or shall indicate good cause why no such conferral with counsel for opposing parties was held. An assigned justice or judge may dismiss a motion for failure to demonstrate that such effort was made with leave to renew the motion after such effort has been demonstrated. NY R 3 JD SUP Doc. 1(B).

b. *Supplemental documents*

i. *Brief.* Briefs shall be for a statement of the relevant law. NY R UNIF TRIAL CTS § 202.8(c).

ii. *Notice to produce papers not in possession of the court.* If a paper relied on by the movant is in the possession of the other side, it may be demanded of that side with a notice to produce it at the hearing. Where such papers are in the possession of an adverse party, they shall be produced by him at the hearing on notice served with the motion papers. NY CPLR Rule 2214(Practice Commentary, C2214:23).

iii. *Filing fees.* The County Clerk shall require the payment of any applicable statutory fees, or an order of the Court waiving payment of such fees, before accepting a paper for filing. NY R UNIF TRIAL CTS § 202.5(d)(1). For information on filing fees, if any, refer to NY CPLR § 8001, et seq.

- *ALBANY COUNTY.* In general, any filing subsequent to the commencement of an action which is designated as a motion or cross-motion requires the payment of a filing fee to the County Clerk's Office prior to submission to the Supreme Court Clerk's Office for referral to the assigned justice. The fee is assessed regardless of whether an application is made by notice of motion, order to show cause or ex parte. No fee will be charged upon the filing of a motion for poor person status in conjunction with an application which serves to commence an action or special proceeding. In the event a motion is received by the court unaccompanied by proof of payment to the County Clerk, the Supreme Court Clerk's Office will contact the submitting party to advise that the application will be held pending receipt of the filing fee only until the return date of the motion. If proof of payment is not submitted to the Supreme Court Clerk's Office by the return date (ex parte applications will be held ten (10) days), the papers will be returned by mail with a notification that the motion has been removed from the court's calendar and that it must be re-noticed and re-filed with the court along with the requisite filing fee. Inquiries concerning the applicability of the motion fee to a proposed filing may be directed to the Supreme Court Clerk's Office. NY R 3 JD SUP Doc. 1(B).
- *BRONX COUNTY.* In accordance with the new civil fee schedule set forth in Article 80 of the C.P.L.R. (NY

CPLR § 8001, et seq.), effective July 14, 2003, all motions, and cross motions must be approved in Room 217 prior to payment of said fees in the County Clerk's Office, Room 118. NY R BRONX FIL R Doc. 8. The motion fee [must be] paid for via NYSCEF by credit/debit card. NY R BRONX E FIL R Doc. 1(1).

- *ERIE COUNTY.* Payment for fee-bearing NYSCEF documents must be made online via credit or debit card (American Express, MasterCard or Visa) at the time of submission. NY R ERIE E FIL Doc. 3(III)(E).
- *KINGS COUNTY.* The motion must be filed with NYSCEF and the motion fee paid. NY R L KINGS E FIL Doc. 1(D). Court fees in NYSCEF cases must be paid via NYSCEF by a credit or bank card (MasterCard, Visa, or American Express). Fees are no longer accepted in person in the Kings County Clerk's Office in NYSCEF cases. NY R L KINGS E FIL Doc. 1(B)(6).
- *NEW YORK COUNTY.* A motion fee must be paid on motions made in writing by notice of motion, order to show cause or ex parte after the commencement of an action. For this purpose, the term "action" shall mean any application to the court that requires the assignment of an index number, regardless of whether a formal pleading is filed. Applications or motions that commence an action and for which an index number fee must be paid require no motion fee. [A]ny motions made after the initial applications in these situations would require payment of the motion fee. A motion that is the initial application in a case commenced by the filing of a summons and complaint would require a motion fee since the filing of the summons and complaint rather than the application itself would require the purchase of an index number. NY R NY CTY Procedure II(A). In e-filed cases the motion fee must be paid when the documents are filed. Payment is made on-line by Visa, Mastercard, or American Express credit or bank card. NY R NY CTY Procedure II(A); NY R NY CTY E FIL Doc. 2(B)(5).
- *ONONDAGA COUNTY.* Court fees in e-filed cases must be paid online with the NYSCEF system using a credit card. The document is not considered to have been filed until payment of the fee has been tendered. NY R ONDGA E FIL Protocol(B)(2). Fees must be paid on all cross motions. NY R ONDGA E FIL Protocol(B)(9)(e).
- *QUEENS COUNTY.* The Motion Support Office does not receive, forward or process any fees or waiver of fees. All applications requiring payment of statutory fees or waiver of fees must be sent directly to the Queens County Clerk's office. NY R L QUEENS MOT SUP Doc. 1. Court fees (e.g., RJI fee, motion fee) in E-filed cases may be paid for on-line using a credit card. Papers may also be filed with the E-file system and the fee may be paid at the County Clerk's Office. In the latter case, the paper is not considered to have been filed until payment of the fee has been tendered. NY R L QUEENS E-FILE Doc. 1(E)(1). The motion/petition shall be filed on-line and the fee paid for either on-line by credit card or by the "Pay at the County Clerk's Office" option. NY R L QUEENS E-FILE Doc. 1(H)(1).

iv. *Working copies.* The court may require the parties to provide working copies of documents filed electronically. In such event, each working copy shall include, firmly affixed thereto, a copy of a confirmation notice in a form prescribed by the Chief Administrator. NY R UNIF TRIAL CTS § 202.5-b(d)(5).

- *BRONX COUNTY.* After papers on motions have been e-filed, working copies thereof, with Confirmation Notice firmly attached as the back page facing out, must be submitted. (Each document or group of documents that is separately bound shall bear a Confirmation Notice.) Working copies lacking the Notice will not be accepted. WORKING COPIES OF MOTION PAPERS MUST BE SUBMITTED NO LATER THAN 4:45 P.M. ON THE RETURN DATE IN THE MOTION SUPPORT OFFICE (ROOM 217) AS EXPLAINED in NY R BRONX E FIL R Doc. 1(4). If an attorney has failed to submit required working copies on or before the return date, the motion will be transmitted as is to the Justice for such action as the Justice finds appropriate. Attorneys may submit working copies on motions by mail or overnight delivery. Any such submission shall be sent in a timely manner to the Motion Support Office (Room 217) and be conspicuously marked on the outside "NYSCEF Matter"; lack of such marking may delay processing. NY R BRONX E FIL R Doc. 1(4)(a).
- *ERIE COUNTY.* Electronically filed documents subject to review and processing by the Part Clerk do not require a working copy unless otherwise directed or provided for in IAS Part Rules. NY R UNIF TRIAL CTS § 202.5-b(d)(4), any working copy submitted shall include, as a cover page firmly fastened thereto, a copy of the Confirmation Notice generated by the NYSCEF site at the time of filing. Please consult the individual Justice's Part Rules and/or consult with the Judge's chambers to determine whether and how working copies are to be provided. Working copies will not be printed or delivered by the Erie County Clerk or the Chief Clerk of the Courts or any of their personnel to chambers. The official record of a document in an electronically filed case is the document filed via the NYSCEF system. Working copies are intended only

for use by the Justice. The Court will discard all working copies after the Justice has finished with them. Thus, in the event that counsel fails to file a document via the NYSCEF system, the document will not be part of the court record. NY R ERIE E FIL Doc. 3(III)(O); NY R ERIE E FIL Doc. 3(V)(E).

- *KINGS COUNTY.* No courtesy copies of motion papers are required by the Court, except as may be required for electronic filing or by the Judge's Part Rules. In tort cases against the City of New York, courtesy copies shall be supplied to the Corporation Counsel's office in Brooklyn. NY R L KINGS Pt. C, Rule 5. Unless otherwise directed by the Court or as described herein, and with the exceptions listed below, in all NYSCEF cases in which an RJI has been filed, working copies of e-filed documents that are intended for judicial review must be submitted to the court. Working copies are not required of documents that are only processed by a support office (e.g. preliminary conference request, note of issue). Working copies shall include exhibit tabs and backs; for motion papers, the motion sequence number and the return date and part. The confirmation notice with the motion sequence number on it should be the back page of the motion facing out. In addition, the filer of a working copy must firmly bind thereto, with the back page facing out, a copy of the Confirmation Notice that was generated by NYSCEF when that document was efiled. Working copies that are submitted without the related Confirmation Notice will not be accepted. NY R L KINGS E FIL Doc. 1(B)(7); NY R L KINGS E FIL Doc. 1(D). WORKING COPIES OF MOTION PAPERS MUST BE SUBMITTED IN THE MOTION SUPPORT OFFICE (ROOM 227) AS EXPLAINED HEREIN. THEY MUST NOT BE DELIVERED TO THE PART OR CHAMBERS, EXCEPT WHERE THE INDIVIDUAL JUSTICE'S PART RULES PROVIDE OTHERWISE; DOING SO WILL CAUSE ADMINISTRATIVE CONFUSION AND POSSIBLE MISPLACEMENT OF PAPERS. Any such submission shall be sent in a timely manner (kindly review individual Justice's rules) and be conspicuously marked on the outside "NYSCEF Matter;" lack of such marking may delay processing. NY R L KINGS E FIL Doc. 1(D).
- *NEW YORK COUNTY.* Some Justices require that working copies of e-filed motion papers be submitted. See the E-filing Protocol for information on the many Parts that do not require working copies. Where required, working copies of the moving documents and all other documents on the motion or application shall be submitted to the Motion Submission Part Courtroom (Room 130) on, but not before, the final return date. A Confirmation Notice from the NYSCEF system, which is generated when a document is e-filed, shall be firmly affixed, as the back page facing out, to each separate working copy or group of such copies. NY R NY CTY Procedure II(A) NY R NY CTY E FIL Doc. 2(B)(5)(a); NY R NY CTY J RUL Rule 14(a). For more information on working copies, including which parts don't require them, refer to NY R NY CTY E FIL Doc. 2(B)(6).
- *ONONDAGA COUNTY.* Any courtesy "working" copies, if required (see NY R ONDGA E FIL Protocol(B)(7)), must be provided directly to the assigned justice. NY R ONDGA E FIL Protocol(B)(9)(e). For information as to whether or not an Onondaga Supreme Court Justice requires working (courtesy) copies of e-filed documents, please consult the Onondaga County Individual E-filing Rules. NY R ONDGA E FIL Protocol(B)(7)(a). The Supreme Court Clerk's Office and the Onondaga County Clerk's Office will NOT accept the working copies. Working copies must be sent directly to the assigned justice's chambers. NY R ONDGA E FIL Protocol(B)(7)(b). A copy of the Confirmation Notice, generated by the NYSCEF system at the time a document is e-filed, must be attached to every working copy provided to chambers. If the Confirmation Notice is missing, the copy will not be accepted. NY R ONDGA E FIL Protocol(B)(7)(c). Courtesy copies do not become part of the official court record as maintained by the Onondaga County Clerk's Office and will be destroyed by chambers at the disposition of the case. In the event that counsel fails to file a document via NYSCEF, the document will not be part of the court record. NY R ONDGA E FIL Protocol(B)(7)(d).
- *QUEENS COUNTY.* Working copies of E-Filed notices of motion/notices of petition are NOT to be sent to the Motion Support Office. They must be brought to the calendar call in the judge's part. NY R L QUEENS MOT SUP Doc. 1. Unless otherwise directed or authorized by the court, counsel should file papers with the E-file system first and thereafter deliver a working copy to at the calendar call of the Centralized Motion Part or Assigned Justice in accordance with individual Part Rules. NY R L QUEENS E-FILE Doc. 1(E)(4). On the return date of a motion that has been E-filed, the movant must provide the Centralized Motion Part (CMP) with a working copy of the entire motion including the notice of motion with sequence number and all of the attached exhibits. The motion must have the confirmation of filing firmly affixed to the back of the papers (facing outward). The confirmation of filing is a separate notice from the payment notice and will say confirmation clearly across the top of the page. NY R L QUEENS E-FILE Doc. 1(H)(2)(a). The motion

or Order to Show Cause must have clearly written across its face the words "Working Copy," it must also have the assigned Judge's name, motion sequence number and calendar number—which may be obtained from the posted calendar outside courtroom on the return date of the motion. A confirmation of filing must attached thereto. Working copies of e-filed Orders to Show Cause must contain a copy of the signed order and all supporting papers. NY R L QUEENS E-FILE Doc. 1(H)(2)(c). The Confirmation Notice must be an updated version that indicates the sequence number of the motion being submitted at the CMP calendar call. WORKING COPIES WITHOUT A CONFIRMATION NOTICE WILL NOT BE ACCEPTED. NY R L QUEENS E-FILE Doc. 1(H)(7).

v. *Statement of authorization in electronic filing cases.* A filing agent (other than one employed by a governmental entity) shall e-file a statement of authorization from counsel of record in an action, in a form approved by the Chief Administrator, prior to or together with the first e-filing in that action by the agent on behalf of that counsel. NY R UNIF TRIAL CTS § 202.5-b(d)(1)(i).

vi. *ERIE COUNTY: Additional supplemental documents*

- *Notice of hard copy submission in e-filed case.* In accordance with NY R UNIF TRIAL CTS § 202.5-b(d), the County Clerk shall refuse to accept for filing, hard copy papers filed to an action subject to electronic filing unless hard copy filing is permitted by the Uniform Rules or NY R ERIE E FIL Doc. 3 and the papers bear a completed Notice of Hard Copy Submission—E-Filed Case form. NY R ERIE E FIL Doc. 3(III)(D).

vii. *KINGS COUNTY: Additional supplemental documents*

- *Forms when filing in hard copy.* An attorney who certifies in good faith that he or she lacks the equipment or knowledge needed to e-file and have no staff member or employee under his or her direction who has such knowledge and equipment may opt out of participation in e-filing in a mandatory case by filing a "Notice of Opt-Out from Participation in Action Subject to Mandatory Electronic Filing" form EFM-2 with the Clerk. NY R L KINGS E FIL Doc. 1(A)(2). Where in accordance with the E-Filing Rules a party submits a document in hard copy in an e-filed case (principally, a document submitted by a nonparticipating party (e.g., an attorney) in a consensual case, an emergency filing made in accordance with the Mandatory E-Filing Rules, and any document filed with the court in hard copy by an attorney who has opted out of participation in mandatory e-filing, the document must bear the back page facing out, a "Notice of Hard Copy Submission—E-Filed Cases" form EFM-3. NY R L KINGS E FIL Doc. 1(B)(3).

viii. *NEW YORK COUNTY: Additional supplemental documents*

- *Notice of hard copy submission.* Where in accordance with the E-Filing Rules an attorney or an unrepresented litigant who is participating in e-filing submits a document in hard copy in an e-filed case, the document must bear, as the back page facing out, a Notice of Hard-Copy Submission—E-Filed Case (a form available in the "Forms" section on the NYSCEF website (Form EFM-3) and in the court's back offices). NY R NY CTY E FIL Doc. 2(B)(3). For more information refer to NY R NY CTY E FIL Doc. 2.
- *Unpublished decisions.* Whenever reliance is placed upon a decision or other authority not officially published or readily available to the New York County Supreme Court, a copy of the case or of pertinent portions of the authority shall be submitted with the motion papers. NY R NY CTY J RUL Rule 14(a).

ix. *ONONDAGA COUNTY: Additional supplemental documents*

- *Notice of hard copy submission.* Any papers to be filed with the court in an e-filed case must be filed online with the E-filing system except where a special exemption is granted (e.g., oversized maps, photographs). If such an exemption is granted, Form EFM-3, "Notice of Hard Copy Submission—E-Filed Case," must be attached to such documents forms which are not filed on line. Also, Form EFM-4 "Notice of Hard Copy Exhibit Filing" must be completed and uploaded to the action's e-file. Both of these forms may be found on the NYSCEF website. NY R ONDGA E FIL Protocol(B)(4).

x. *QUEENS COUNTY: Additional supplemental documents*

- *Notice of hard copy submission.* Any party opting out of the e-filing system must have a "Notice of Hard Copy Submission" firmly affixed to the back of the papers. NY R L QUEENS E-FILE Doc. 1(H)(2)(f).

3. *Documents for opposing party*

a. *Required documents*

i. *Opposition.* Refer to the General Requirements section of this document for information on the opposition.

- *Request for oral argument.* A party requesting oral argument shall set forth such request in its notice of motion or in its order to show cause or on the first page of the answering papers, as the case may be. Where all parties to a motion request oral argument, oral argument shall be granted unless the court shall determine it to be unnecessary. Where a motion is brought on by order to show cause, the court may set forth in the order that oral argument is required on the return date of the motion. NY R UNIF TRIAL CTS § 202.8(d).

- *QUEENS COUNTY: E-filing opposition papers.* E-filed opposition papers and/or reply papers must also be provided to the Centralized Motion Part in the same manner as the moving papers with the confirmation of filing firmly attached to the back of the papers. NY R L QUEENS E-FILE Doc. 1(H)(2)(d).

ii. *Proof of service.* In addition to complying with the provisions of NY CPLR Rule 2101, every paper filed in court shall have annexed thereto appropriate proof of service on all parties where required. NY R UNIF TRIAL CTS § 202.5(a).

b. *Supplemental documents*

i. *Supporting evidence; Exhibits.* The main supporting papers on a motion are affidavits, but any relevant exhibits, documents, depositions, etc., are also includible. SIEGEL-NYPRAC § 246.

- *Evidence on summary judgment.* Any form of evidence, documentary or otherwise, may be considered on a motion for summary judgment. SIEGEL-NYPRAC § 281; Wilkinson v. Skinner, 34 N.Y.2d 53, 56, 312 N.E.2d 158, 160 (1974).
- *Affidavits accompanying motion.* Affidavits shall be for a statement of the relevant facts. NY R UNIF TRIAL CTS § 202.8(c).
- *Foreign language documents.* Where an affidavit or exhibit annexed to a paper served or filed is in a foreign language, it shall be accompanied by an English translation and an affidavit by the translator stating his qualifications and that the translation is accurate. NY CPLR Rule 2101(b).
- *Statement of attorney in lieu of affidavit.* The statement of an attorney admitted to practice in the courts of the state, or of a physician, osteopath or dentist, authorized by law to practice in the state, who is not a party to an action, when subscribed and affirmed by him to be true under the penalties of perjury, may be served or filed in the action in lieu of and with the same force and effect as an affidavit. NY CPLR Rule 2106. Affidavits on any motion should be made only by those with knowledge of the facts, and nowhere is this rule more faithfully applied than on the motion for summary judgment. The attorney's affidavit, unless the attorney happens to have first-hand knowledge of the facts—which is the exception rather than the rule—has no probative force. SIEGEL-NYPRAC § 281; S. Bay Ctr., Inc. v. Butler, Herrick & Marshall, 43 Misc. 2d 269, 272, 250 N.Y.S.2d 863, 866 (Sup. Ct. 1964).
- *NEW YORK COUNTY: Form of presented exhibits.* Exhibits should be tabbed and be legible; a typed version of any exhibit that is difficult to read should be submitted with the original. Exhibits printed on both sides of the page should be bound and tabbed on the side. NY R NY CTY J RUL Rule 14(a).
- *QUEENS COUNTY.* Attorneys submitting exhibits to the court on E-file cases shall make each exhibit a separate, labeled attachment to an affidavit/affirmation. NY R L QUEENS E-FILE Doc. 1(H)(4).

ii. *Brief.* Briefs shall be for a statement of the relevant law. NY R UNIF TRIAL CTS § 202.8(c).

iii. *Filing fees.* The County Clerk shall require the payment of any applicable statutory fees, or an order of the Court waiving payment of such fees, before accepting a paper for filing. NY R UNIF TRIAL CTS § 202.5(d)(1). For information on filing fees, if any, refer to NY CPLR § 8020.

- *ALBANY COUNTY.* In general, any filing subsequent to the commencement of an action which is designated as a motion or cross-motion requires the payment of a filing fee to the County Clerk's Office prior to submission to the Supreme Court Clerk's Office for referral to the assigned justice. The fee is assessed regardless of whether an application is made by notice of motion, order to show cause or ex parte. No fee will be charged upon the filing of a motion for poor person status in conjunction with an application which serves to commence an action or special proceeding. In the event a motion is received by the court unaccompanied by proof of payment to the County Clerk, the Supreme Court Clerk's Office will contact the submitting party to advise that the application will be held pending receipt of the filing fee only until the return date of the motion. If proof of payment is not submitted to the Supreme Court Clerk's Office by the return date (ex parte applications will be held ten (10) days), the papers will be returned by mail with a notification that the motion has been removed from the court's calendar and that it must be re-noticed and re-filed with the court along with the requisite filing fee. Inquiries concerning the applicability of the motion fee to a proposed filing may be directed to the Supreme Court Clerk's Office. NY R 3 JD SUP Doc. 1(B).

- *BRONX COUNTY.* In accordance with the new civil fee schedule set forth in Article 80 of the C.P.L.R. (NY CPLR § 8001, et seq.), effective July 14, 2003, all motions, and cross motions must be approved in Room 217 prior to payment of said fees in the County Clerk's Office, Room 118. NY R BRONX FIL R Doc. 8. The motion fee [must be] paid for via NYSCEF by credit/debit card. NY R BRONX E FIL R Doc. 1(1).
- *ERIE COUNTY.* Payment for fee-bearing NYSCEF documents must be made online via credit or debit card (American Express, MasterCard or Visa) at the time of submission. NY R ERIE E FIL Doc. 3(III)(E).
- *KINGS COUNTY.* The motion must be filed with NYSCEF and the motion fee paid. NY R L KINGS E FIL Doc. 1(D). Court fees in NYSCEF cases must be paid via NYSCEF by a credit or bank card (MasterCard, Visa, or American Express). Fees are no longer accepted in person in the Kings County Clerk's Office in NYSCEF cases. NY R L KINGS E FIL Doc. 1(B)(6).
- *NEW YORK COUNTY.* A motion fee must be paid on motions made in writing by notice of motion, order to show cause or ex parte after the commencement of an action. For this purpose, the term "action" shall mean any application to the court that requires the assignment of an index number, regardless of whether a formal pleading is filed. Applications or motions that commence an action and for which an index number fee must be paid require no motion fee. [A]ny motions made after the initial applications in these situations would require payment of the motion fee. A motion that is the initial application in a case commenced by the filing of a summons and complaint would require a motion fee since the filing of the summons and complaint rather than the application itself would require the purchase of an index number. NY R NY CTY Procedure II(A). In e-filed cases the motion fee must be paid when the documents are filed. Payment is made on-line by Visa, Mastercard, or American Express credit or bank card. NY R NY CTY Procedure II(A); NY R NY CTY E FIL Doc. 2(B)(5).
- *ONONDAGA COUNTY.* Court fees in e-filed cases must be paid online with the NYSCEF system using a credit card. The document is not considered to have been filed until payment of the fee has been tendered. NY R ONDGA E FIL Protocol(B)(2). Fees must be paid on all cross motions. NY R ONDGA E FIL Protocol(B)(9)(e).
- *QUEENS COUNTY.* The Motion Support Office does not receive, forward or process any fees or waiver of fees. All applications requiring payment of statutory fees or waiver of fees must be sent directly to the Queens County Clerk's office. NY R L QUEENS MOT SUP Doc. 1. Court fees (e.g., RJI fee, motion fee) in E-filed cases may be paid for on-line using a credit card. Papers may also be filed with the E-file system and the fee may be paid at the County Clerk's Office. In the latter case, the paper is not considered to have been filed until payment of the fee has been tendered. NY R L QUEENS E-FILE Doc. 1(E)(1). The motion/petition shall be filed on-line and the fee paid for either on-line by credit card or by the "Pay at the County Clerk's Office" option. NY R L QUEENS E-FILE Doc. 1(H)(1).

iv. *Working copies.* The court may require the parties to provide working copies of documents filed electronically. In such event, each working copy shall include, firmly affixed thereto, a copy of a confirmation notice in a form prescribed by the Chief Administrator. NY R UNIF TRIAL CTS § 202.5-b(d)(5).

- *BRONX COUNTY.* After papers on motions have been e-filed, working copies thereof, with Confirmation Notice firmly attached as the back page facing out, must be submitted. (Each document or group of documents that is separately bound shall bear a Confirmation Notice.) Working copies lacking the Notice will not be accepted. WORKING COPIES OF MOTION PAPERS MUST BE SUBMITTED NO LATER THAN 4:45 P.M. ON THE RETURN DATE IN THE MOTION SUPPORT OFFICE (ROOM 217) AS EXPLAINED in NY R BRONX E FIL R Doc. 1(4). If an attorney has failed to submit required working copies on or before the return date, the motion will be transmitted as is to the Justice for such action as the Justice finds appropriate. Attorneys may submit working copies on motions by mail or overnight delivery. Any such submission shall be sent in a timely manner to the Motion Support Office (Room 217) and be conspicuously marked on the outside "NYSCEF Matter"; lack of such marking may delay processing. NY R BRONX E FIL R Doc. 1(4)(a).
- *ERIE COUNTY.* Electronically filed documents subject to review and processing by the Part Clerk do not require a working copy unless otherwise directed or provided for in IAS Part Rules. NY R UNIF TRIAL CTS § 202.5-b(d)(4), any working copy submitted shall include, as a cover page firmly fastened thereto, a copy of the Confirmation Notice generated by the NYSCEF site at the time of filing. Please consult the individual Justice's Part Rules and/or consult with the Judge's chambers to determine whether and how working copies are to be provided. Working copies will not be printed or delivered by the Erie County Clerk or the Chief Clerk of the Courts or any of their personnel to chambers. The official record of a document in

an electronically filed case is the document filed via the NYSCEF system. Working copies are intended only for use by the Justice. The Court will discard all working copies after the Justice has finished with them. Thus, in the event that counsel fails to file a document via the NYSCEF system, the document will not be part of the court record. NY R ERIE E FIL Doc. 3(III)(O); NY R ERIE E FIL Doc. 3(V)(E).

- *KINGS COUNTY.* No courtesy copies of motion papers are required by the Court, except as may be required for electronic filing or by the Judge's Part Rules. In tort cases against the City of New York, courtesy copies shall be supplied to the Corporation Counsel's office in Brooklyn. NY R L KINGS Pt. C, Rule 5. Unless otherwise directed by the Court or as described herein, and with the exceptions listed below, in all NYSCEF cases in which an RJI has been filed, working copies of e-filed documents that are intended for judicial review must be submitted to the court. Working copies are not required of documents that are only processed by a support office (e.g. preliminary conference request, note of issue). Working copies shall include exhibit tabs and backs; for motion papers, the motion sequence number and the return date and part. The confirmation notice with the motion sequence number on it should be the back page of the motion facing out. In addition, the filer of a working copy must firmly bind thereto, with the back page facing out, a copy of the Confirmation Notice that was generated by NYSCEF when that document was efiled. Working copies that are submitted without the related Confirmation Notice will not be accepted. NY R L KINGS E FIL Doc. 1(B)(7); NY R L KINGS E FIL Doc. 1(D). WORKING COPIES OF MOTION PAPERS MUST BE SUBMITTED IN THE MOTION SUPPORT OFFICE (ROOM 227) AS EXPLAINED HEREIN. THEY MUST NOT BE DELIVERED TO THE PART OR CHAMBERS, EXCEPT WHERE THE INDIVIDUAL JUSTICE'S PART RULES PROVIDE OTHERWISE; DOING SO WILL CAUSE ADMINISTRATIVE CONFUSION AND POSSIBLE MISPLACEMENT OF PAPERS. Any such submission shall be sent in a timely manner (kindly review individual Justice's rules) and be conspicuously marked on the outside "NYSCEF Matter;" lack of such marking may delay processing. NY R L KINGS E FIL Doc. 1(D).
- *NEW YORK COUNTY.* Some Justices require that working copies of e-filed motion papers be submitted. See the E-filing Protocol for information on the many Parts that do not require working copies. Where required, working copies of the moving documents and all other documents on the motion or application shall be submitted to the Motion Submission Part Courtroom (Room 130) on, but not before, the final return date. A Confirmation Notice from the NYSCEF system, which is generated when a document is e-filed, shall be firmly affixed, as the back page facing out, to each separate working copy or group of such copies. NY R NY CTY Procedure II(A) NY R NY CTY E FIL Doc. 2(B)(5)(a); NY R NY CTY J RUL Rule 14(a). For more information on working copies, including which parts don't require them, refer to NY R NY CTY E FIL Doc. 2(B)(6).
- *ONONDAGA COUNTY.* Any courtesy "working" copies, if required (see NY R ONDGA E FIL Protocol(B)(7)), must be provided directly to the assigned justice. NY R ONDGA E FIL Protocol(B)(9)(e). For information as to whether or not an Onondaga Supreme Court Justice requires working (courtesy) copies of e-filed documents, please consult the Onondaga County Individual E-filing Rules. NY R ONDGA E FIL Protocol(B)(7)(a). The Supreme Court Clerk's Office and the Onondaga County Clerk's Office will NOT accept the working copies. Working copies must be sent directly to the assigned justice's chambers. NY R ONDGA E FIL Protocol(B)(7)(b). A copy of the Confirmation Notice, generated by the NYSCEF system at the time a document is e-filed, must be attached to every working copy provided to chambers. If the Confirmation Notice is missing, the copy will not be accepted. NY R ONDGA E FIL Protocol(B)(7)(c). Courtesy copies do not become part of the official court record as maintained by the Onondaga County Clerk's Office and will be destroyed by chambers at the disposition of the case. In the event that counsel fails to file a document via NYSCEF, the document will not be part of the court record. NY R ONDGA E FIL Protocol(B)(7)(d).
- *QUEENS COUNTY.* Working copies of E-Filed notices of motion/notices of petition are NOT to be sent to the Motion Support Office. They must be brought to the calendar call in the judge's part. NY R L QUEENS MOT SUP Doc. 1. Unless otherwise directed or authorized by the court, counsel should file papers with the E-file system first and thereafter deliver a working copy to at the calendar call of the Centralized Motion Part or Assigned Justice in accordance with individual Part Rules. NY R L QUEENS E-FILE Doc. 1(E)(4). On the return date of a motion that has been E-filed, the movant must provide the Centralized Motion Part (CMP) with a working copy of the entire motion including the notice of motion with sequence number and all of the attached exhibits. The motion must have the confirmation of filing firmly affixed to the back of the papers (facing outward). The confirmation of filing is a separate notice from the payment notice and will

say confirmation clearly across the top of the page. NY R L QUEENS E-FILE Doc. 1(H)(2)(a). The motion or Order to Show Cause must have clearly written across its face the words "Working Copy," it must also have the assigned Judge's name, motion sequence number and calendar number—which may be obtained from the posted calendar outside courtroom on the return date of the motion. A confirmation of filing must attached thereto. Working copies of e-filed Orders to Show Cause must contain a copy of the signed order and all supporting papers. NY R L QUEENS E-FILE Doc. 1(H)(2)(c). The Confirmation Notice must be an updated version that indicates the sequence number of the motion being submitted at the CMP calendar call. WORKING COPIES WITHOUT A CONFIRMATION NOTICE WILL NOT BE ACCEPTED. NY R L QUEENS E-FILE Doc. 1(H)(7).

v. *ERIE COUNTY: Additional supplemental documents*

- *Notice of hard copy submission in e-filed case.* In accordance with NY R UNIF TRIAL CTS § 202.5-b(d), the County Clerk shall refuse to accept for filing, hard copy papers filed to an action subject to electronic filing unless hard copy filing is permitted by the Uniform Rules or NY R ERIE E FIL Doc. 3 and the papers bear a completed Notice of Hard Copy Submission—E-Filed Case form. NY R ERIE E FIL Doc. 3(III)(D).

vi. *KINGS COUNTY: Additional supplemental documents*

- *Forms when filing in hard copy.* An attorney who certifies in good faith that he or she lacks the equipment or knowledge needed to e-file and have no staff member or employee under his or her direction who has such knowledge and equipment may opt out of participation in e-filing in a mandatory case by filing a "Notice of Opt-Out from Participation in Action Subject to Mandatory Electronic Filing" form EFM-2 with the Clerk. NY R L KINGS E FIL Doc. 1(A)(2). Where in accordance with the E-Filing Rules a party submits a document in hard copy in an e-filed case (principally, a document submitted by a nonparticipating party (e.g., an attorney) in a consensual case, an emergency filing made in accordance with the Mandatory E-Filing Rules, and any document filed with the court in hard copy by an attorney who has opted out of participation in mandatory e-filing, the document must bear the back page facing out, a "Notice of Hard Copy Submission—E-Filed Cases" form EFM-3. NY R L KINGS E FIL Doc. 1(B)(3).

vii. *NEW YORK COUNTY: Additional supplemental documents*

- *Notice of hard copy submission.* Where in accordance with the E-Filing Rules an attorney or an unrepresented litigant who is participating in e-filing submits a document in hard copy in an e-filed case, the document must bear, as the back page facing out, a Notice of Hard-Copy Submission—E-Filed Case (a form available in the "Forms" section on the NYSCEF website (Form EFM-3) and in the court's back offices). NY R NY CTY E FIL Doc. 2(B)(3). For more information refer to NY R NY CTY E FIL Doc. 2.
- *Unpublished decisions.* Whenever reliance is placed upon a decision or other authority not officially published or readily available to the New York County Supreme Court, a copy of the case or of pertinent portions of the authority shall be submitted with the motion papers. NY R NY CTY J RUL Rule 14(a).

viii. *ONONDAGA COUNTY: Additional supplemental documents*

- *Notice of hard copy submission.* Any papers to be filed with the court in an e-filed case must be filed online with the E-filing system except where a special exemption is granted (e.g., oversized maps, photographs). If such an exemption is granted, Form EFM-3, "Notice of Hard Copy Submission—E-Filed Case," must be attached to such documents forms which are not filed on line. Also, Form EFM-4 "Notice of Hard Copy Exhibit Filing" must be completed and uploaded to the action's e-file. Both of these forms may be found on the NYSCEF website. NY R ONDGA E FIL Protocol(B)(4).

ix. *QUEENS COUNTY: Additional supplemental documents*

- *Notice of hard copy submission.* Any party opting out of the e-filing system must have a "Notice of Hard Copy Submission" firmly affixed to the back of the papers. NY R L QUEENS E-FILE Doc. 1(H)(2)(f).

E. Format

1. *Form of documents*

a. *Size and form of paper.* Each paper served or filed shall be durable, white and, except for summonses, subpoenas, notices of appearance, notes of issue, orders of protection, temporary orders of protection and exhibits, shall be eleven by eight and one-half (11 x 8-1/2) inches in size. NY CPLR Rule 2101(a).

b. *Writing and language.* The writing shall be legible and in black ink. NY CPLR Rule 2101(a). Each paper served or filed shall be in the English language which, where practicable, shall be of ordinary usage. NY CPLR Rule 2101(b).

c. *Caption.* Each paper served or filed shall begin with a caption setting forth the name of the court, the venue, the title of the action, the nature of the paper and the index number of the action if one has been assigned. In all papers other than a summons, a complaint or a judgment it shall be sufficient to state the name of the first named party on each side with an appropriate indication of any omissions. NY CPLR Rule 2101(c).

   i. *Further contents of first page.* After the first paper has been filed in each case the index number shall appear on the cover and first page to the right of the caption of every paper tendered for filing in the action. Each such cover and first page also shall contain an indication of the county of venue and a brief description of the nature of the paper and, where the case has been assigned to an individual judge, shall contain the name of the assigned judge to the right of the caption. NY R UNIF TRIAL CTS § 202.5(a); NY R UNIF TRIAL CTS § 202.5(b); NY R UNIF TRIAL CTS § 202.5(d)(1)(i).

   ii. *ALBANY COUNTY: Request for oral argument.* A party may request oral argument on a motion by indicating such request on the first page of the notice of motion, order to show cause, or answering papers in the area across from the caption of the action/proceeding. NY R 3 JD SUP Doc. 1(B).

   iii. *NEW YORK COUNTY: Request for oral argument.* Counsel who wish oral argument must so request conspicuously on the front of their papers. NY R NY CTY Procedure II(D).

d. *Index number.* No paper in an action in the supreme or a county court, other than an order submitted for signature to a judge out of court, shall be submitted for any purpose to the supreme or county court or to a clerk thereof unless there is endorsed on such paper the index number of the action assigned by the clerk of the county. NY CPLR § 8018(c).

   i. *ALBANY COUNTY: Index number on all filed documents.* The index number, the request for judicial intervention number and the assigned justice's name shall appear on [all papers filed with the Court subsequent to the complaint]. NY R 3 JD SUP Doc. 1(A).

   ii. *ERIE COUNTY: Index number after initial filing.* Cases that are initially commenced by the filing of papers with the NYSCEF system are identified as e-filed cases by assignment of an Index Number that has "800-899" as the first three (3) digits of the index number (i.e. 802391/2012). NY R ERIE E FIL Doc. 3(II). [The] Index Number must be affixed to all document submissions, filings, and communications to the Erie County Clerk and the Court. Cases that are converted from paper to e-filing shall retain the original index number. NY R ERIE E FIL Doc. 3(II).

   iii. *KINGS COUNTY: Index number after initial filing.* In cases commenced electronically by the filing of initiating papers with the NYSCEF system and payment of the statutory fees, the Kings County Clerk will issue an NYSCEF designated index number and the filer shall be notified via the NYSCEF system of the index number assigned and filing date. Such index number must be affixed to all document submissions, filings and communications to the Kings County Clerk and Supreme Court. If counsel faces exigent circumstances that require accelerated assignment, counsel may contact Administration of the Kings County Clerk at kcco-efile@nycourts.gov, during normal business hours of the court. NY R L KINGS E FIL Doc. 1(B)(5).

   iv. *NEW YORK COUNTY: Index number on hard copy filings.* Papers subsequently presented for filing in hardcopy format will be filed in this jacket. NY R NY CTY Procedure I(B). Index numbers take the form of six digits followed by a slash and the four digits of the year the case began, e.g., 340705/2018. The first or first two integers of the index number identify the type of case. If a case is commenced electronically, the second integer will be a "5", except as indicated otherwise in the list below. There are many tax certiorari matters e-filed annually and the index numbers therefor will normally run over into those with a "6" as the second integer, and the same will occur with general cases if necessary. The principal types of cases and their index number categories are listed in NY R NY CTY Procedure I(B). NY R NY CTY Procedure I(B); NY R NY CTY Procedure XI(A).

   v. *ONONDAGA COUNTY: Index number.* The index number must be referenced on all e-filed documents and correspondence. All e-filed case index numbers will contain the letters "EF" between the year and the file number (for example, 2012EF9999). NY R ONDGA E FIL Protocol(B)(1).

   vi. *QUEENS COUNTY: Index number on converted cases.* Cases originally commenced in hard-copy form but later converted to an E-file case, either by stipulation or order will bear a regular index number initially. The County Clerk will issue a new E-file index number. NY R L QUEENS E-FILE Doc. 1(B).

e. *Line spacing.* Every paper filed in court, if typewritten, shall have at least double space between each line, except for quotations and the names and addresses of attorneys appearing in the action. NY R UNIF TRIAL CTS § 202.5(a).

f. *Font size.* Each. . .paper printed or typed, served or filed, except for summonses. . .and exhibits, shall be in clear type of no less than ten (10) point in size. NY CPLR Rule 2101(a).

   i. Whenever a requirement relating to size of type is stated in point size, the type size requirement shall be deemed met if the x-height of the type is a minimum of forty-five percent (45%) of the specified point size. Each point shall be measured as .351 millimeter. The x-height size shall be measured as it appears on the page. The x-height is the height of the lower case letters, exclusive of ascenders or descenders. NY CPLR § 105(t).

g. *Margins.* Every paper filed in court shall have at least one (1) inch margins. NY R UNIF TRIAL CTS § 202.5(a).

h. *Citations*

   i. *Civil practice law and rules.* NY CPLR § 101, et seq. shall be known as the civil practice law and rules, and may be cited as "CPLR". Reference to a provision in the civil practice law and rules may, except when such provision is being enacted or amended, be made without indicating whether it is a rule or section. NY CPLR § 101.

i. *Indorsement by attorney.* Each paper served or filed shall be indorsed with the name, address and telephone number of the attorney for the party serving or filing the paper, or if the party does not appear by attorney, with the name, address and telephone number of the party. NY CPLR Rule 2101(d).

j. *One-sided printing.* In addition, every paper filed in court, other than an exhibit or printed form, shall contain writing on one side only, except that papers that are fastened on the side may contain writing on both sides. NY R UNIF TRIAL CTS § 202.5(a).

k. *Use of copies authorized.* Except where otherwise specifically prescribed, copies, rather than originals, of all papers, including orders, affidavits and exhibits may be served or filed. Where it is required that the original be served or filed and the original is lost or withheld, the court may authorize a copy to be served or filed. NY CPLR Rule 2101(e).

   i. Where a certified copy of a paper is required by law, an attorney admitted to practice in the courts of the state may certify that it has been compared by him with the original and found to be a true and complete copy. Such a certificate, when subscribed by such attorney, has the same effect as if made by a clerk. NY CPLR § 2105.

l. *Recycled paper.* It is the policy of the Unified Court System that litigants, where practicable, should file or submit to the courts of the Unified Court System of the State of New York papers printed or reproduced on recycled paper. Paper is considered recycled if it contains a minimum content of thirty percent (30%) waste paper. NY R UNIF TRIAL CTS § 215.2. The signature page of every paper filed or submitted to the court on recycled paper should bear the legend: "Printed [Reproduced] on Recycled Paper." NY R UNIF TRIAL CTS § 215.3.

m. *Form of request for judicial intervention; Copies.* A request for judicial intervention must be submitted, in duplicate, on a form authorized by the Chief of the Courts, with proof of service on the other parties to the action (but proof of service is not required where the application is ex parte). NY R UNIF TRIAL CTS § 202.6(a).

n. *KINGS COUNTY: Tabs on filings.* Motions, orders and other filed papers shall be indexed with protruding tabs. Clerks are required to reject papers that do not have protruding exhibit tabs, except papers in matrimonial cases and papers filed by pro se litigants. NY R L KINGS Pt. A, Papers.

o. *NEW YORK COUNTY: Length of briefs.* Unless advance permission otherwise is granted by the court for good cause, memoranda of law shall not exceed thirty (30) pages each (exclusive of table of contents and table of authorities) and affidavits/affirmations shall not exceed twenty-five (25) pages each. NY R NY CTY J RUL Rule 14(b).

p. *QUEENS COUNTY: Form and size of motion filings.* All motions filed in Queens Supreme Court-Civil Term, must adhere to the Motion Support rules and the rules of the assigned judge. NY R L QUEENS MOT SUP Doc. 1. Due to space limitations, the Motion Support Office cannot accept notices of motion/notices of petition and accompanying exhibits which measure greater than eight (8) inches. If your documents measure greater than eight (8) inches you are directed to submit only the notice of motion/notice of petition to the Motion Support Office and bring all exhibits to the calendar call on your return date. NY R L QUEENS MOT SUP Doc. 1.

2. *Form of electronic documents.* Each paper served or filed by electronic means, as defined in NY CPLR Rule 2103(f), shall be capable of being reproduced by the receiver so as to comply with the provisions of NY CPLR Rule 2101(a) through NY CPLR Rule 2101(d). NY CPLR Rule 2101(g).

a. *File format.* All e-filed documents shall comply with the technical requirements set forth at the NYSCEF site. NY R UNIF TRIAL CTS § 202.5-b(d)(1)(i).

b. *Heading of document.* The subject matter heading for each paper sent by electronic means must indicate that the matter being transmitted electronically is related to a court proceeding. NY CPLR Rule 2103(b)(7).

c. *E-filed documents identification*

   i. *ERIE COUNTY.* E-filed cases must be readily identifiable and marked as such. If counsel presents papers to the Office of the Erie County Clerk or the Office of the Chief Clerk in a NYSCEF matter where authorized, counsel should alert the Clerk that the case is a NYSCEF matter. NY R ERIE E FIL Doc. 3(II).

ii. *KINGS COUNTY.* The Supreme Court's Civil Case Information System ("CCIS") will further identify e-filed cases by the addition of a suffix to the index number (e.g. 500136/2006E). This suffix should be used on all documents filed with the court in e-filed matters. NY R L KINGS E FIL Doc. 1(A)(1).

3. *Signature blocks.* Every pleading, written motion, and other paper, served on another party or filed or submitted to the court shall be signed by an attorney, or by a party if the party is not represented by an attorney, with the name of the attorney or party clearly printed or typed directly below the signature. NY R CHIEF ADMIN § 130-1.1-a(a); NY R UNIF TRIAL CTS § 202.5(d)(1)(iv).

a. *Printed name.* Beneath each signature shall be printed the name signed. NY CPLR Rule 2101(a).

b. *Failure to sign.* Absent good cause shown, the court shall strike any unsigned paper if the omission of the signature is not corrected promptly after being called to the attention of the attorney or party. NY R CHIEF ADMIN § 130-1.1-a(a).

c. *Signature as certification.* By signing a paper, an attorney or party certifies that, to the best of that person's knowledge, information and belief, formed after an inquiry reasonable under the circumstances the presentation of the paper or the contentions therein are not frivolous as defined in NY R CHIEF ADMIN § 130-1.1(c). NY R CHIEF ADMIN § 130-1.1-a(b)(1).

d. *Electronic signatures.* A document shall be considered to have been signed by an attorney or party in compliance with NY R CHIEF ADMIN § 130-1.1-a if it has been signed by such attorney or party as provided in NY R UNIF TRIAL CTS § 202.5-b(e)(1) and it bears the signatory's name. NY R UNIF TRIAL CTS § 202.5-b(e)(2). An electronically filed document shall be considered to have been signed by, and shall be binding upon, the person identified as a signatory, if:

i. It bears the physical signature of such person and is scanned into an electronic format that reproduces such signature; or

ii. The signatory has electronically affixed the digital image of his or her signature to the document; or

iii. It is electronically filed under the User ID and password of that person; or

iv. In a tax certiorari action in which the parties have stipulated to this procedure, it is an initiating document that is electronically filed without the signature of the signatory in a form provided above in NY R UNIF TRIAL CTS § 202.5-b(e)(iv), provided that, prior to filing, the document is signed in full in hard copy (which hard copy must be preserved until the conclusion of all proceedings, including appeals, in the case in which it is filed); or

v. In a small claims assessment review proceeding, it is a petition recorded by the NYSCEF site upon the filing of a text file as provided in NY R UNIF TRIAL CTS § 202.5-b(b)(1), provided that prior to filing, the document was signed in full in hard copy (which hard copy must be preserved until the conclusion of all proceedings in the matter, including article 78 (NY CPLR § 7801, et seq.) review and any appeals, and must be made available during the proceeding upon request of the respondent or the court); or

vi. It otherwise bears the electronic signature of the signatory in a format conforming to such standards and requirements as may hereafter be established by the Chief Administrator. NY R UNIF TRIAL CTS § 202.5-b(e).

4. *Confidentiality of personal information.* No person may file any document available for public inspection with any state agency, political subdivision, or in any court of this state that contains a Social Security account number of any other person, unless such other person is a dependent child, or has consented to such filing, except as required by federal or state law or regulation, or by court rule. NY GEN BUS § 399-ddd. Submissions pursuant to e-filing procedures shall have the same confidentiality rights as paper documents. NY R UNIF TRIAL CTS § 202.5-b(k)(1).

a. *Confidential personal information.* Except in the actions designated in NY R UNIF TRIAL CTS § 202.5(e)(1), or as otherwise provided by rule or law or court order, and whether or not a sealing order is or has been sought, the parties shall omit or redact confidential personal information in papers submitted to the court for filing. For purposes of NY R UNIF TRIAL CTS § 202.5(e), confidential personal information ("CPI") means:

i. The taxpayer identification number of an individual or an entity, including a Social Security number, an employer identification number, and an individual taxpayer identification number, except the last four (4) digits thereof;

ii. The date of an individual's birth, except the year thereof;

iii. The full name of an individual known to be a minor, except the minor's initials;

iv. A financial account number, including a credit and/or debit card number, a bank account number, an investment account number, and/or an insurance account number, except the last four (4) digits or letters thereof; and

v. Any of the documents or testimony in a matrimonial action protected by NY DOM REL § 235 or evidence sealed by the court in such an action which are attached as exhibits or referenced in the papers filed in any other civil action. For purposes of NY R UNIF TRIAL CTS § 202.5, a matrimonial action shall mean: an action to annul a marriage or declare the nullity of a void marriage, an action or agreement for a separation, an action for a divorce, or an action or proceeding for custody, visitation, writ of habeus corpus, child support, maintenance or paternity. NY R UNIF TRIAL CTS § 202.5(e)(1).

vi. *ERIE COUNTY.* An attorney or unrepresented litigant filing a document via the NYSCEF system must comply with the requirements of NY R UNIF TRIAL CTS § 202.5(e) regarding the redaction of Confidential Personal Information and NY GEN BUS § 399-ddd(6) concerning the filing of documents containing Social Security Numbers. It is the sole responsibility of counsel or unrepresented litigant filing to be aware of and to comply with existing laws requiring non-disclosure of personal information contained in any document e-filed in NYSCEF. NY R ERIE E FIL Doc. 3(III)(G); NY R ERIE E FIL Doc. 3(III).

vii. *KINGS COUNTY.* An attorney or unrepresented litigant filing a document via the NYSCEF system must comply with the requirements of General Business Law § 399-dd(6), which often require redaction of any Social Security number that appear in the original document. The NYSCEF system automatically redacts portions of filed documents which apparently contain Social Security numbers pursuant to NY R UNIF TRIAL CTS § 202.5-b(k). In the event the filing party receives e-mail notice through NYSCEF that a Social Security number in a filed document has been redacted, and the filing party concludes such redaction is erroneous, the filer should click on the link provided in the e-mail to permit the County Clerk to revert the redaction. For Confidential Personal Information, see NY R UNIF TRIAL CTS § 202.5(e) and NY R L KINGS E FIL Doc. 1(B)(11). [Editor's note: the reference to General Business Law § 399-dd(6) is likely a reference to NY GEN BUS § 399-ddd(6)]. NY R L KINGS E FIL Doc. 1(B)(10); NY R L KINGS E FIL Doc. 1(K)(1).

viii. *NEW YORK COUNTY.* It is the responsibility of counsel and parties to comply with rules restricting disclosure of confidential personal information. Nevertheless, NYSCEF screens filings and endeavors to identify any that contain social security numbers. When such numbers are discovered through this process, NYSCEF will restrict portions of or all of such documents from public view. Where NYSCEF has redacted what it believes to be a social security number, it will transmit to the filer a notice advising of the action taken and requesting that the filer review the matter and provide notification as set forth in the notice if the redaction has been made in error. NY R NY CTY E FIL Doc. 2(K)(1); NY R NY CTY J RUL Rule A-1. Documents filed in the past in "secure status" under a procedure no longer in place will retain that status unless otherwise directed by the court. NY R NY CTY E FIL Doc. 2(K)(2).

b. *Submission of confidential personal information.* Where a person submitting a paper to a court for filing believes in good faith that the inclusion of the full confidential personal information described in NY R UNIF TRIAL CTS § 202.5(e)(1) is material and necessary to the adjudication of the action or proceeding before the court, he or she may apply to the court for leave to serve and file together with a paper in which such information has been set forth in abbreviated form a confidential affidavit or affirmation setting forth the same information in unabbreviated form, appropriately referenced to the page or pages of the paper at which the abbreviated form appears. NY R UNIF TRIAL CTS § 202.5(e)(3).

c. *Home addresses.* For information on when home addresses and other personal information must be redacted, refer to NY CPLR Rule 2103-a.

5. *Defective papers.* A defect in the form of a paper, if a substantial right of a party is not prejudiced, shall be disregarded by the court, and leave to correct shall be freely given. NY CPLR Rule 2101(f). Papers that are stapled or bound securely shall not be rejected for filing simply because they are not bound with a backer of any kind. NY R UNIF TRIAL CTS § 202.5(a). A paper filed in accordance with the rules of the chief administrator or any local rule or practice established by the court shall be deemed filed. NY CPLR Rule 2102(b).

a. *Objection to defective papers.* The party on whom a paper is served shall be deemed to have waived objection to any defect in form unless, within fifteen (15) days after the receipt thereof, the party on whom the paper is served returns the paper to the party serving it with a statement of particular objections. NY CPLR Rule 2101(f).

F. Filing and Service Requirements

1. *Filing requirements.* Except where otherwise prescribed by law or order of court, papers required to be filed shall be filed with the clerk of the court in which the action is triable. In an action or proceeding in supreme or court, papers required to be filed shall be filed with the clerk of the county in which the proceeding is brought. NY CPLR Rule 2102(a).

a. *Furnishing papers to the court.* Each party shall furnish to the court all papers served by him. The moving party shall

furnish at the hearing all other papers not already in the possession of the court necessary to the consideration of the questions involved. Where such papers are in the possession of an adverse party, they shall be produced by him at the hearing on notice served with the motion papers. Only papers served in accordance with the provisions of NY CPLR Rule 2214 shall be read in support of, or in opposition to, the motion, unless the court for good cause shall otherwise direct. NY CPLR Rule 2214(c).

i. *Submission to judge.* All papers for signature or consideration of the court shall be presented to the clerk of the trial court in the appropriate courtroom or clerk's office, except that where the clerk is unavailable or the judge so directs, papers may be submitted to the judge and a copy filed with the clerk at the first available opportunity. All papers for any judge that are filed in the clerk's office shall be promptly delivered to the judge by the clerk. The papers shall be clearly addressed to the judge for whom they are intended and prominently show the nature of the papers, the title and index number of the action in which they are filed, the judge's name and the name of the attorney or party submitting them. NY R UNIF TRIAL CTS § 202.5(b).

ii. *BRONX COUNTY: Approval of motions before filing.* All motion papers must be approved by the Motion Support Office, Supreme Court, Civil Term, room 217, before the motion papers are filed and the appropriate fee paid to the County Clerk. NY R BRONX FIL R Doc. 1.

iii. *ERIE COUNTY: Filing motions.* A motion on notice or a notice of petition in a NYSCEF case shall be filed through the NYSCEF system and must be accompanied by a Request for Judicial Intervention if the motion is being filed upon commencement of the action or if the matter has not yet been assigned to an IAS Justice. In addition, cross motions with the appropriate filing fees and opposition and reply papers must be submitted via the NYSCEF system. NY R ERIE E FIL Doc. 3(V)(A).

iv. *NEW YORK COUNTY: Filing hard copies.* Where in the narrow circumstances described by the e-filing rules a motion is made in hard-copy form or opposition papers are submitted in such form in an e-filed case, the hard-copy documents shall be submitted in the same way papers are submitted in non-e-filed cases, except that there shall be firmly affixed to each separate document or group of documents, as the back page facing out, a Notice of Hard Copy Submission—E-Filed Case. NY R NY CTY Procedure II(A). For more information on filing in hard copy cases, refer to NY R NY CTY Procedure II(A).

v. *ONONDAGA COUNTY: Submission of responsive papers and cross-motions.* Cross-motions, opposition and reply papers must be submitted online. NY R ONDGA E FIL Protocol(B)(9)(e). Motions and Orders to Show Cause are assigned a sequence number by the system. Counsel must be sure that cross motions and other filings correspond with the correct sequence number so that a cross motion will not be associated with the wrong original motion. NY R ONDGA E FIL Protocol(B)(9)(f).

b. *Electronic filing.* On consent, documents may be filed and served by electronic means in Supreme Court in such civil actions and in such counties as shall be authorized by order of the Chief Administrator of the Courts and only to the extent and in the manner provided in NY R UNIF TRIAL CTS § 202.5-b. NY R UNIF TRIAL CTS § 202.5-b(a)(1). For the definitions of terms used in electronic filing, refer to NY R UNIF TRIAL CTS § 202.5-b(a)(2).

i. *E-filing mandatory.* In any action subject to e-filing, all documents required to be filed with the court by an e-filing party shall be filed and served electronically, except as provided in NY R UNIF TRIAL CTS § 202.5-b. NY R UNIF TRIAL CTS § 202.5-b(d)(1)(i).

- *ERIE COUNTY.* Case types currently eligible and accepted for e-filing are listed at the NYSCEF website. Note that some actions or special proceedings, (i.e., name changes) which are otherwise subject to mandatory e-filing, if commenced by unrepresented litigants will NOT be maintained in the NYSCEF system; individual cases may be found either at NYSCEF or in the Erie County Clerk's online records system. NY R ERIE E FIL Doc. 3(I)(E).
- *KINGS COUNTY.* Cases that are commenced by filing of the initiating papers with NYSCEF are identified as e-filed cases by assignment of a special index number (i.e., Index Numbers beginning with 500,000). NY R L KINGS E FIL Doc. 1(A)(1). All cases required to be e-filed are listed in Uniform Rule 202.5-bb (Mandatory E-Filing Rules) and on the NYSCEF website. All such cases must be commenced by filing with the County Clerk electronically through NYSCEF and all subsequent documents in such cases must be e-filed. Any questions regarding mandatory e-filing in Kings County can be e-mailed to kcco-efile@nycourts.gov. NY R L KINGS E FIL Doc. 1(A)(2).
- *NEW YORK COUNTY.* Unless otherwise provided in the Rules or in NY R NY CTY E FIL Doc. 2 or where a special exemption is granted due to physical requirements (e.g., oversized maps; see NY R NY CTY E FIL Doc. 2(B)(10)), all documents to be filed with the court in a NYSCEF case, including all documents on

motions and all letters to the court (where permitted), must be filed with the NYSCEF system. Documents that attorneys would not ordinarily file with the court in a hard-copy case need not be e-filed. Unless otherwise provided by the E-Filing Rules or this Protocol, in e-filed cases the County Clerk and the court will not accept documents filed in paper form. NY R NY CTY E FIL Doc. 2(B)(1). E-filing is mandatory in all types of cases (other than election law, matrimonial, Art. 78, and Mental Hygiene Law matters, and Art. 70 habeas corpus proceedings) that are commenced in this court on or after February 19, 2013. All such cases must be commenced by filing with the County Clerk electronically through NYSCEF and all subsequent documents in such cases must be e-filed. NY R NY CTY E FIL Doc. 2(A)(2)(a). For more information, including information on consensual e-filing and filing scanned hard copy documents, refer to NY R NY CTY E FIL Doc. 2(A)(2).

- *QUEENS COUNTY.* All authorized Torts, Commercial and Tax Certiorari cases may be commenced by E-Filing, however all parties must consent for the action to continue as an E-file case. NY R L QUEENS E-FILE Doc. 1(A). All papers to be filed with the court in an E-filed case shall be filed on-line with the E-file system except as directed by the court. Papers that attorneys would not ordinarily file with the court in a hard-copy case need not be filed in an E-filed matter. NY R L QUEENS E-FILE Doc. 1(E)(2).

ii. *Who may file.* Documents may be filed or served electronically only by a person who has registered as an authorized e-filing user or as otherwise provided in NY R UNIF TRIAL CTS § 202.5-b(c). NY R UNIF TRIAL CTS § 202.5-b(c)(1).

iii. *When filing made.* Documents may be transmitted at any time of the day or night to the NYSCEF site. A document other than an order or judgment is filed when its electronic transmission or, in the case of a petition that is e-filed by submission of a text file as provided in NY R UNIF TRIAL CTS § 202.5-b(b)(1), the electronic transmission of the text file is recorded at that site, provided, however, that where payment of a fee is required upon the filing of a document, the document is not filed until transmission of the document and the information or form or information as required in NY R UNIF TRIAL CTS § 202.5-b(d)(2)(i), NY R UNIF TRIAL CTS § 202.5-b(d)(2)(ii) or NY R UNIF TRIAL CTS § 202.5-b(d)(2)(iii) has been recorded at the NYSCEF site; or, if no transmission of that information or form or information is recorded, where permitted by the County Clerk, until payment is presented to the County Clerk. NY R UNIF TRIAL CTS § 202.5-b(d)(3)(i).

iv. *Notification of filing.* No later than the close of business on the business day following the electronic filing of a document, a notification, in a form prescribed by the Chief Administrator, shall be transmitted electronically by the NYSCEF site to the person filing such document and the e-mail service addresses of all other participating parties in such action. NY R UNIF TRIAL CTS § 202.5-b(d)(3)(ii).

v. *Removal of confidential information and other corrections.* If a document filed electronically is subsequently discovered to contain confidential data—including but not limited to trade secrets, information protected by confidentiality agreement, or personal confidential information as defined by statute or court rule—or otherwise to have been filed in error, the filer or another party or affected person may (1) notify the parties and any non-party filers in the action of the confidentiality issue or other error raised by the filing, and of his or her intention to seek judicial relief to correct the filing: (2) following such notification, request that the appropriate County Clerk, exercising his or her administrative discretion, place the document temporarily in "restricted" status on the NYSCEF site, to be made available for viewing by court staff and the parties but not the general public; and (3) file an application to correct the filing by order to show cause within five (5) business days of such notification (or such time as the court may direct), including a request for preliminary injunctive relief limiting interim disclosure of the document at issue. Unless otherwise directed by the court, any document placed in restricted status in response to such a request shall be returned to public view upon expiration of this five (5) day period. The Chief Administrator of the Courts shall promulgate forms to implement this process. NY R UNIF TRIAL CTS § 202.5-b(d)(3)(iii).

- *KINGS COUNTY.* For information on what to do when a document was erroneously filed with confidential information, refer to NY R L KINGS E FIL Doc. 1(B)(11).
- *NEW YORK COUNTY.* For information on what to do when a document was erroneously filed with confidential information, refer to NY R NY CTY E FIL Doc. 2(B)(8).
- *QUEENS COUNTY.* For information on what to do when a document was erroneously filed with confidential information, refer to NY R L QUEENS E-FILE Doc. 1(E)(7).

vi. *Documents requiring judge's signature.* Except where the court directs otherwise, any document that requires a judge's signature shall be transmitted electronically and in hard copy to the court. NY R UNIF TRIAL CTS § 202.5-b(d)(6).

vii. *Documents which would be inconvenient to file electronically; Hard copies.* Notwithstanding any other provision of NY R UNIF TRIAL CTS § 202.5-b, and subject to such guidelines as may be established by the Chief Administrative Judge, the County Clerk or his or her designee may require or permit a party to file in hard copy, in accordance with procedures set by the County Clerk or designee, an exhibit or other document which it is impractical or inconvenient to file electronically. NY R UNIF TRIAL CTS § 202.5-b(d)(7).

- *ERIE COUNTY.* Please contact the Supervisor of Actions & Proceedings, Erie County Clerk's Office by calling (716) 858-6662 or the Deputy County Clerk—Legal at (716) 858-6348 for information. NY R ERIE E FIL Doc. 3(III)(F).
- *KINGS COUNTY.* With limited exceptions, as set forth in the Uniform Rules and herein, all documents to be filed with the court in a NYSCEF case shall be filed online via the NYSCEF system. However, should the size, consistency or context of a hard copy document preclude electronic filing, the user shall electronically file a "Notice of Hard Copy Submission—E-Filed Cases" form EFM-3. Any hard copy submitted pursuant to NY R L KINGS E FIL Doc. 1(B)(9) shall include, as a cover page firmly fastened thereto, a copy of the Confirmation Notice received from the NYSCEF site confirming receipt of the "Notice of Hard Copy Submission—E-Filed Cases". Any party may object to such hard copy filing. The Court, in response to such objection, may, following the hard copy filing, fashion such relief as it deems appropriate pursuant to and in furtherance of the Uniform Rules and NY R L KINGS E FIL Doc. 1, including, but not limited to, an Order directing the filing party to file such documents online via the NYSCEF system. When exhibits are impractical to file pursuant to NY R UNIF TRIAL CTS § 202.5-b(d)(7), an additional "Notice of Hard Copy Exhibit Filing" form EFM-4 is required to be submitted. NY R L KINGS E FIL Doc. 1(B)(9).
- *NEW YORK COUNTY.* If a filer needs to submit unusual exhibits in original form that cannot practically be e-filed, such as oversized maps or electronic recordings, the filer should consult with the County Clerk's E-File Department by telephone at 646-386-3737 (procedural questions only) or by e-mail at ccnyef@nycourts.gov, which will normally require that the filer retain custody of the original subject to possible future directives of the court. NY R NY CTY E FIL Doc. 2(B)(10). In such instances, the filing counsel shall file with NYSCEF a "placeholder" in the form of a Notice of Hard Copy Exhibit Filing (NYSCEF Form EF 21). The Notice should be uploaded to NYSCEF as document type "Exhibit" and the filer should indicate in the "Additional Document Information" field that the filer is retaining custody of the original. Failure to e-file the Notice may result in a gap in the official record of the court. NY R NY CTY E FIL Doc. 2(B)(10).

viii. *Documents containing sensitive or proprietary information.* In an action subject to e-filing, any person may apply for an order prohibiting or restricting the electronic filing in the action of specifically identified materials on the grounds that such materials are subject to copyright or other proprietary rights, or trade secret or other privacy interests, and that electronic filing in the action is likely to result in substantial prejudice to those rights or interests. NY R UNIF TRIAL CTS § 202.5-b(k)(2).

ix. *Refusal to accept paper filings.* In accordance with NY CPLR Rule 2102(c), a County Clerk and a chief clerk of the Supreme Court or County Court, as appropriate, shall refuse to accept for filing papers filed in actions and proceedings when the paper sought to be filed:

- Is in an action subject to electronic filing pursuant to Rules of the Chief Administrator,
- Is not being filed electronically, and
- Does not include the notice required by NY R UNIF TRIAL CTS § 202.5-b(d)(1). NY R UNIF TRIAL CTS § 202.5(d)(1)(v); NY R UNIF TRIAL CTS § 202.5-bb(d).

x. *Emergency filings; Hard copies.* For information on when an emergency filing may be filed and served in hard copy, refer to NY R UNIF TRIAL CTS § 202.5-b(d)(1)(ii), NY R UNIF TRIAL CTS § 202.5-b(d)(1)(iii) and NY R UNIF TRIAL CTS § 202.5-bb(c)(3).

- *KINGS COUNTY.* Under the rules, a participating emergency e-filer must electronically file the documents initially filed in hard copy form within three (3) business days of the emergency filing; the originals will be discarded after the documents have been processed and the failure to e-file as required will therefore lead to an incomplete record. NY R L KINGS E FIL Doc. 1(B)(3).
- *NEW YORK COUNTY.* Occasionally an emergency will arise requiring expedited entry of a document with the County Clerk (e.g., an order issued in the courtroom after a conference or argument of a critical matter), such as for purposes of an immediate appeal. Expedition can be achieved by the Part as follows: the

document should be carried by a Court Officer or staff member to the General Clerk's Office to assure immediate and proper recordation in the computer and, as appropriate, the posting of the document to NYSCEF or the Supreme Court Records On-Line Library ("Scroll"). The court will accommodate counsel in emergencies. NY R NY CTY Procedure XI(A).

- *NEW YORK COUNTY.* For more information on how to bring emergency matters before the court, refer to NY R NY CTY Procedure IV.

xi. *Technical failures.* The NYSCEF site shall be considered to be subject to a technical failure on a given day if the site is unable to accept filings or provide access to filed documents continuously or intermittently over the course of any period of time greater than one (1) hour after 12:00 noon of that day. Notice of all such technical failures shall be provided on the site. NY R UNIF TRIAL CTS § 202.5-b(i).

- When e-filing is hindered by a technical failure, a party may file with the appropriate clerk and serve in hard copy. NY R UNIF TRIAL CTS § 202.5-b(i). In the event an attorney or party shall file and serve documents in hard copy pursuant to NY R UNIF TRIAL CTS § 202.5-b(i), each such document shall include the notice required by NY R UNIF TRIAL CTS § 202.5-b(d)(1), and the filer shall file those documents with the NYSCEF site within three (3) business days after restoration of normal operations at that site. NY R UNIF TRIAL CTS § 202.5-b(i).
- With the exception of deadlines that by law cannot be extended, the time for filing of any document that is delayed due to technical failure of the site shall be extended for one (1) day for each day on which such failure occurs, unless otherwise ordered by the court. NY R UNIF TRIAL CTS § 202.5-b(i).
- *ERIE COUNTY.* When filing by electronic means is hindered by a technical failure, please refer to the NY R UNIF TRIAL CTS § 202.5-b(i). NY R ERIE E FIL Doc. 3(III)(K).
- *KINGS COUNTY.* When filing by electronic means is hindered by a NYSCEF technical failure (as set forth in NY R UNIF TRIAL CTS § 202.5-b(i)), a party may file with the appropriate Clerk in hard copy. Except for deadlines that by law cannot be extended (e.g. Statute of limitations, Notice of Appeal), the time for filing of any document that is delayed due to technical failure of the NYSCEF system shall be extended for one day for each day on which such failure occurs, unless otherwise ordered by the court. NY R L KINGS E FIL Doc. 1(B)(13).
- *ONONDAGA COUNTY.* When filing by electronic means is hindered by a technical failure (as set forth in NY R UNIF TRIAL CTS § 202.5-b(h)(3)(i)), a party may file a hard copy with the County Clerk. With the exception of deadlines that by law cannot be extended (e.g., a statute of limitations or the deadline for filing a Notice of Appeal), the time for filing of any document that is delayed due to technical failure of the NYSCEF system will be extended for one day for each day on which such failure occurs, unless otherwise ordered by the court. A "Notice of Hard Copy Filing Submission—E-Filed Case' must accompany any documents not filed via NYSCEF. NY R ONDGA E FIL Protocol(B)(8).

xii. *Filing fees.* For information on what information must be provided to pay filing fees, refer to NY R UNIF TRIAL CTS § 202.5-b(d)(2).

xiii. *Exemption from e-filing.* For information on exemptions from e-filing, refer to NY R UNIF TRIAL CTS § 202.5-bb(e).

xiv. *Filing exhibits*

- *ERIE COUNTY.* In the NYSCEF system, each exhibit must be uploaded as a separate .pdf file. After uploading a primary document, please choose the document type "Exhibit" and enter the appropriate number or letter and a brief description of the exhibit; each exhibit should bear a separate cover sheet clearly marked as "Exhibit A," "Exhibit B," etc. "Exhibit A" or "Exhibit B" is unacceptable as a brief description of the exhibit. Exhibits, where referenced in a signed Order as attached or affixed shall be uploaded with the signed Order as one .pdf document. NY R ERIE E FIL Doc. 3(III)(H); NY R ERIE E FIL Doc. 3(V)(D).
- *KINGS COUNTY.* In the NYSCEF system, each exhibit should be uploaded as a separate PDF file. After uploading a primary document, please choose the document type "Exhibit", enter the appropriate number or letter, and be sure to place a check mark to the right of "Attach to main document". Each exhibit shall bear a separate cover sheet clearly marked as Exhibit A, Exhibit B, etc. NY R L KINGS E FIL Doc. 1(B)(12). Whenever possible, attorneys submitting exhibits in NYSCEF cases should make each exhibit a separate attachment to an affidavit/affirmation in the system (i.e., multiple exhibits should not be filed as a single PDF). NY R L KINGS E FIL Doc. 1(D)(1).

- *NEW YORK COUNTY.* Attorneys submitting exhibits in NYSCEF cases should make each exhibit a separate attachment to an affidavit/affirmation in the system; i.e., exhibits should not be filed as a single PDF-A together with the affidavit/affirmation or grouped together as a single PDF-A attachment because either of these two formats makes it difficult for the Justice to locate particular exhibits as needed. Counsel must also include appropriate descriptive language in the "Additional Document Information" field in NYSCEF. NY R NY CTY E FIL Doc. 2(D)(6).
- *ONONDAGA COUNTY.* All exhibits in e-filed cases must be e-filed individually as separate attachments. NY R ONDGA E FIL Protocol(B)(9)(b).

xv. *Correcting documents*

- *ERIE COUNTY.* Submission of documents which, upon examination, require correction or addition will result in notification to the filer advising that the document has been returned for correction. The filer shall make the required corrections and/or additions as indicated in the e-mail transmission sent by the County Clerk or Part Clerk through the NYSCEF site. The corrected documents may be resubmitted using the "Re-file this document" link highlighted in the filer's document list for the respective case. Please note that in the case of multiple submissions, all related documents filed at the same time may be removed from the case record and returned until all documents are properly submitted. NY R ERIE E FIL Doc. 3(III)(J).
- *KINGS COUNTY.* Submission of documents which, upon examination, require correction or addition will result in notification to the filer advising that there is a problem with a document. The filer shall make the required corrections and/or additions and resubmit the corrected document using the "Refile this document" link. In the event a document is returned for correction, the original file date will be preserved. For corrections of documents filed with the Kings County Clerk which require a court order, refer to the procedure in NY R UNIF TRIAL CTS § 202.5-b(d)(3)(iii) and NY R L KINGS E FIL Doc. 1(B)(11). NY R L KINGS E FIL Doc. 1(B)(3).
- *ONONDAGA COUNTY.* If there is an error or an additional document is required, the system will notify the filing party, who will make the corrections/additions and resubmit them online. NY R ONDGA E FIL Protocol(B)(6).
- *QUEENS COUNTY.* Generally speaking, documents that have been E-filed will not thereafter be deleted by the County Clerk from NYCEF because the filer asserts that the filing contains an error or a significant omission. When the filer wishes to correct a perceived error or omission in a filed document, he or she should file an amended version of the document, with the original remaining on file, or else obtain a court order providing for deletion of the original. The County Clerk will only delete a document upon request of the filer or on the County Clerk's own initiative when it is obvious from the face of the document alone that the filer made a fundamental error and never intended to file the document that was filed (e.g., a completely unrelated non-litigation document, a different case, or a wrong county). The County Clerk will advise the filer when any such fundamental errors are detected. NY R L QUEENS E-FILE Doc. 1(E)(6).

c. *Facsimile filing.* In the Supreme Court, facsimile filing shall be limited to commercial claims and tax certiorari, conservatorship, and mental hygiene proceedings in Monroe, Westchester, New York and Suffolk Counties. NY R UNIF TRIAL CTS § 202.5-a(a)(1). Refer to NY R UNIF TRIAL CTS § 202.5-a for information on the procedures for facsimile filing.

   i. *NEW YORK COUNTY.* Unless indicated otherwise by the court in a particular case or in NY R NY CTY J RUL Doc. 1, Justices do not accept papers by fax. NY R NY CTY J RUL Rule 4.

d. *ERIE COUNTY: Filing request for judicial intervention.* An RJI in a NYSCEF case shall be filed via the NYSCEF system and will be filed after all other documents have been uploaded. The filer may choose between filing a .pdf image of the prepared RJI and any Addendum or having the system prepare the RJI which shall conform to Uniform Rules. Addenda, such as the Commercial Division Addendum, if prepared by the filer must be filed simultaneously with and attached to an RJI and uploaded as one .pdf document with the RJI. If the RJI is prepared by the e-filing system, no separate Addendum is required. Whether or not the filer elects to allow NYSCEF to create the RJI or chooses to upload a prepared RJI, data in addition to the nature of the judicial intervention, including information that appears on any Addenda will be collected through completion of the fields presented. If the filing of the RJI is accomplished through a filing agent, a prepared RJI and Addendum must be filed in lieu of the creation of the RJI by the NYSCEF system, as the RJI must be signed by the attorney. NY R ERIE E FIL Doc. 3(IV). For information on RJIs in specific types of action, refer to NY R ERIE E FIL Doc. 3(IV).

2. *Service requirements*

a. *Who may serve.* Except where otherwise prescribed by law or order of court, papers may be served by any person not a party of the age of eighteen years or over. NY CPLR Rule 2103(a).

b. *Service upon attorney.* Except where otherwise prescribed by law or order of court, papers to be served upon a party in a pending action shall be served upon the party's attorney. Where the same attorney appears for two or more parties, only one (1) copy need be served upon the attorney. Such service upon an attorney shall be made:

i. By delivering the paper to the attorney personally. NY CPLR Rule 2103(b)(1).

ii. By mailing the paper to the attorney at the address designated by that attorney for that purpose or, if none is designated, at the attorney's last known address; service by mail shall be complete upon mailing. NY CPLR Rule 2103(b)(2).

- *BRONX COUNTY.* Service by mail must be within the state. NY R BRONX FIL R Doc. 3.

iii. If the attorney's office is open, by leaving the paper with a person in charge, or if no person is in charge, by leaving it in a conspicuous place; or if the attorney's office is not open, by depositing the paper, enclosed in a sealed wrapper directed to the attorney, in the attorney's office letter drop or box. NY CPLR Rule 2103(b)(3).

iv. By leaving it at the attorney's residence within the state with a person of suitable age and discretion. Service upon an attorney shall not be made at the attorney's residence unless service at the attorney's office cannot be made. NY CPLR Rule 2103(b)(4).

v. By transmitting the paper to the attorney by facsimile transmission, provided that a facsimile telephone number is designated by the attorney for that purpose. Service by facsimile transmission shall be complete upon the receipt by the sender of a signal from the equipment of the attorney served indicating that the transmission was received, and the mailing of a copy of the paper to that attorney. The designation of a facsimile telephone number in the address block subscribed on a paper served or filed in the course of an action or proceeding shall constitute consent to service by facsimile transmission in accordance with NY CPLR Rule 2103(b)(5). An attorney may change or rescind a facsimile telephone number by serving a notice on the other parties. NY CPLR Rule 2103(b)(5).

vi. By dispatching the paper to the attorney by overnight delivery service at the address designated by the attorney for that purpose or, if none is designated, at the attorney's last known address. Service by overnight delivery service shall be complete upon deposit of the paper enclosed in a properly addressed wrapper into the custody of the overnight delivery service for overnight delivery, prior to the latest time designated by the overnight delivery service for overnight delivery. "Overnight delivery service" means any delivery service which regularly accepts items for overnight delivery to any address in the state. NY CPLR Rule 2103(b)(6).

vii. By transmitting the paper to the attorney by electronic means where and in the manner authorized by the chief administrator of the courts by rule and, unless such rule shall otherwise provide, such transmission shall be upon the party's written consent. The subject matter heading for each paper sent by electronic means must indicate that the matter being transmitted electronically is related to a court proceeding. NY CPLR Rule 2103(b)(7).

- *KINGS COUNTY.* Pursuant to the E-Filing Rules, service of interlocutory documents is made by posting a document to the NYSCEF site, which automatically and immediately transmits an email notice of the filing, including a link to the document, to all participating counsel and unrepresented litigants on the case. The Rules also authorize service by other methods permitted by the CPLR. If service by such other method is made, proof of service must be filed with NYSCEF. NY R L KINGS E FIL Doc. 1(I).

- *NEW YORK COUNTY.* Service. . .will be made automatically through NYSCEF upon all participating counsel and unrepresented parties in the case. There are limited exceptions to the requirement for e-filing in the covered kinds of cases. NY R NY CTY Procedure XI(A). Pursuant to the E-Filing Rules, service of interlocutory documents is made by posting a document to the NYSCEF site, which automatically and immediately transmits an e-mail notice of the filing, including a link to the document, to all participating counsel and unrepresented litigants on the case. The Rules also authorize service by other methods permitted by the CPLR. If service by such a method is made, proof of service must be filed with NYSCEF. NY R NY CTY E FIL Doc. 2(I).

- *QUEENS COUNTY.* Filing with the system permits counsel to serve the papers electronically pursuant to NY R UNIF TRIAL CTS § 202.5-b(f) once consent to E-Filing has been filed on-line. Consult NY R UNIF TRIAL CTS § 202.5-bb(c) for service in mandatory e-filing. Any required proof of service should be E-filed as a separate document. NY R L QUEENS E-FILE Doc. 1(E)(4).

c. *Electronic service mandatory; Consenting to electronic service; How electronic service may be made.* Except as otherwise provided in NY R UNIF TRIAL CTS § 202.5-bb, filing and service of all documents in an action that has been commenced electronically in accordance with NY R UNIF TRIAL CTS § 202.5-bb shall be by electronic means. NY R UNIF TRIAL CTS § 202.5-bb(c)(1).

i. *Party's consent required for certain e-filing.* After commencement of an action wherein e-filing is authorized, documents may be electronically filed and served, but only by, and electronic service shall be made only upon, a party or parties who have consented thereto. NY R UNIF TRIAL CTS § 202.5-b(b)(2)(i).

- A consent to e-filing in an action shall state that the party providing it agrees to the use of e-filing in the action and to be bound by the filing and service provisions in NY R UNIF TRIAL CTS § 202.5-b. NY R UNIF TRIAL CTS § 202.5-b(b)(2)(ii).

ii. *Address for service; Duty to notify as to changes.* The e-mail service address recorded at the time of registration is the e-mail address at which service of interlocutory documents on that party may be made through notification transmitted by the NYSCEF site. It is the responsibility of each filing user to monitor that address and promptly notify the Resource Center in the event of a change in his or her e-mail service address. NY R UNIF TRIAL CTS § 202.5-b(f)(2)(i).

iii. *How service made.* An e-filing party causes service of an interlocutory document to be made upon another party participating in e-filing by filing the document electronically. Upon receipt of an interlocutory document, the NYSCEF site shall automatically transmit electronic notification to all e-mail service addresses in such action. NY R UNIF TRIAL CTS § 202.5-b(f)(2)(ii).

- Except as provided otherwise in NY R UNIF TRIAL CTS § 202.5-b(h)(3), the electronic transmission of the notification shall constitute service of the document on the e-mail service addresses identified therein; however, such service will not be effective if the filing party learns that the notification did not reach the address of the person to be served. Proof of such service will be recorded on the NYSCEF site. A party may, however, utilize other service methods permitted by the CPLR provided that, if one of such other methods is used, proof of that service shall be filed electronically. NY R UNIF TRIAL CTS § 202.5-b(f)(2)(ii).

iv. *Signatures on hard copies; Proof of service filed electronically.* When an e-filing party serves a document in hard copy on a non-participating party, the document served shall bear full signatures of all signatories and proof of such service shall be filed electronically. NY R UNIF TRIAL CTS § 202.5-b(b)(2)(i).

- *ERIE COUNTY.* In the NYSCEF system, each Affidavit of Service must be uploaded as a separate .pdf file. After uploading the Affidavit, please choose the document type: "Affirmation/Affidavit of Service" and enter the name of the party served as Additional Document Information. NY R ERIE E FIL Doc. 3(III)(I); NY R ERIE E FIL Doc. 3(V)(F).

v. *Effect of failure to consent.* A party's failure to consent to participation in electronic filing and service shall not bar any other party to the action from filing documents electronically with the County Clerk and the court or serving documents upon any other party who has consented to participation. A party who has not consented to participation shall file documents with the court and the County Clerk, and serve and be served with documents, in hard copy. NY R UNIF TRIAL CTS § 202.5-b(b)(2)(i).

d. *Service upon party.* If a party has not appeared by an attorney or the party's attorney cannot be served, service shall be upon the party by a method specified in NY CPLR Rule 2103(b)(1), NY CPLR Rule 2103(b)(2), NY CPLR Rule 2103(b)(4), NY CPLR Rule 2103(b)(5) or NY CPLR Rule 2103(b)(6). NY CPLR Rule 2103(c).

e. *Service on all parties.* Each paper served on any party shall be served on every other party who has appeared, except as otherwise may be provided by court order or as provided in NY CPLR § 3012 or in NY CPLR § 3215(f). Upon demand by a party, the plaintiff shall supply that party with a list of those who have appeared and the names and addresses of their attorneys. NY CPLR Rule 2103(e).

f. *Service by filing.* If a paper cannot be served by any of the methods specified in NY CPLR Rule 2103(b) and NY CPLR Rule 2103(c), service may be made by filing the paper as if it were a paper required to be filed. NY CPLR Rule 2103(d).

g. *Definitions.* For the purposes of NY CPLR Rule 2103:

i. "Mailing" means the deposit of a paper enclosed in a first class postpaid wrapper, addressed to the address designated by a person for that purpose or, if none is designated, at that person's last known address, in a post office or official depository under the exclusive care and custody of the United States Postal Service within the state;

ii. "Electronic means" means any method of transmission of information between computers or other machines designed for the purpose of sending and receiving such transmissions, and which allows the recipient to reproduce the information transmitted in a tangible medium of expression;

iii. "Facsimile transmission" means any method of transmission of documents to a facsimile machine at a remote location which can automatically produce a tangible copy of such documents. NY CPLR Rule 2103(f).

G. Hearings

1. *Oral argument.* Motion papers received by the clerk of the court on or before the return date shall be deemed submitted as of the return date. The assigned judge, in his or her discretion or at the request of a party, thereafter may determine that any motion be orally argued and may fix a time for oral argument. NY R UNIF TRIAL CTS § 202.8(d).

a. A party requesting oral argument shall set forth such request in its notice of motion or in its order to show cause or on the first page of the answering papers, as the case may be. Where all parties to a motion request oral argument, oral argument shall be granted unless the court shall determine it to be unnecessary. NY R UNIF TRIAL CTS § 202.8(d).

b. Where a motion is brought on by order to show cause, the court may set forth in the order that oral argument is required on the return date of the motion. NY R UNIF TRIAL CTS § 202.8(d).

i. *BRONX COUNTY.* All orders to show cause, with the exception of orders to show cause that are returnable in the City Part, the STP Part, the Matrimonial Part and the Preliminary/Compliance Conference Part (IA-11), submitted on or after August 25, 2003, will be returnable on a Monday in the assigned Justice's part and appear on his or her motion calendar. Appearances will be required on orders to show cause. NY R BRONX FIL R Doc. 8. A motion on notice or a notice of petition in a New York Supreme Court E-File (hereafter known as NYSCEF) case, as in others, shall be made returnable in the Motion Support Office (Room 217). NY R BRONX E FIL R Doc. 1(1).

- After a motion/petition and notice are filed with the NYSCEF system, the Motion Support Office will automatically place the motion/proceeding on the submit calendar in the Motion Support Office (Room 217) for the return date. No appearance or other action by the filing attorney is required in order for the motion to be calendared if the motion fee is paid for via NYSCEF. Motions in e-filed cases (other than tax certiorari cases) appear on the submit calendar in Room 217 on the return date. NY R BRONX E FIL R Doc. 1(2).

c. *KINGS COUNTY.* All motions require appearances and oral argument. NY R L KINGS Pt. C, Rule 3.

2. *Return date; Time for hearing.* A notice of motion shall specify the time and place of the hearing on the motion. NY CPLR Rule 2214(a). The moving party determines when a motion on notice shall be heard, but she has to consult the court's or judge's calendar practice first. The movant picks out a "return day" sufficiently far off to assure that the notice requirements of NY CPLR Rule 2214(b) can be met, and to assure as well that the day picked is a day on which the assigned judge hears motions. SIEGEL-NYPRAC § 247.

a. *Judge assigned to hear motion*

i. *Referral to judge supervising disclosure.* Unless the chief administrator of the courts has, by rule, provided otherwise, if a case has been assigned to a judge to supervise disclosure pursuant to NY CPLR § 3104, all motions preliminary to trial shall be referred to such judge whenever practicable. NY CPLR Rule 3214(a).

ii. *Referral to judge who decided prior motion.* Any motion may be referred to a judge who decided a prior motion in the action. NY CPLR Rule 2217(a).

iii. *Transfer when judge unable to hear motion.* If a motion is made to a judge who is or will be for any reason unable to hear it, it may be transferred by order of such judge or by written stipulation of the parties to any other judge to whom it might originally have been made. NY CPLR Rule 2217(c).

iv. *Procedure for unassigned cases.* If a case has not been assigned to a judge, the motion shall be made returnable before the court, and a copy of the moving papers, together with a request for judicial intervention, shall be filed with the court, with proof of service upon all other parties, where required by NY R UNIF TRIAL CTS § 202.6, within five (5) days of service upon the other parties. The moving party shall give written notice of the index number to all other parties immediately after filing of the papers. NY R UNIF TRIAL CTS § 202.8(b).

- *Responding papers.* Copies of all responding papers shall be submitted to the court, with proof of service and with the index number set forth in the papers, on or before the return date. NY R UNIF TRIAL CTS § 202.8(b).
- *Assignment after request for judicial intervention.* The case shall be assigned to a judge as soon as

practicable after the filing of the request for judicial intervention pursuant to NY R UNIF TRIAL CTS § 202.6, but in no event later than the return date. After assignment to the judge, the court shall provide for appropriate notice to the parties of the name of the assigned judge. NY R UNIF TRIAL CTS § 202.8(b).

- *Motions to be heard in another county.* Motion papers noticed to be heard in a county other than the county where the venue of the action has been placed by the plaintiff shall be assigned to a judge in accordance with procedures established by the Chief Administrator. NY R UNIF TRIAL CTS § 202.8(b).

v. *ALBANY COUNTY: Motions referred to IAS Justice.* All motions made after a case has been assigned a day certain shall be referred to the IAS Justice unless the motion is returnable during the term in which the matter has been assigned a day certain, in that event, the matter will be referred to the Part 1 Justice for that particular term who may entertain the motion or refer such motion to the IAS Justice. Under those circumstances, the Part I Justice shall decide whether or not to strike the note of issue or assign the matter a new day certain. NY R 3 JD SUP Doc. 1(H)(2). All motions shall be returnable before the assigned justice. NY R 3 JD SUP Doc. 1(B).

b. *Trial of issue raised by motion.* The court may order that an issue of fact raised on a motion shall be separately tried by the court or a referee. If the issue is triable of right by jury, the court shall give the parties an opportunity to demand a jury trial of such issue. Failure to make such demand within the time limited by the court, or, if no such time is limited, before trial begins, shall be deemed a waiver of the right to trial by jury. An order under NY CPLR § 2218 shall specify the issue to be tried. NY CPLR § 2218.

c. *Audio-visual coverage of trial court proceeding.* Audio-visual coverage of proceedings in the trial courts shall be permitted only in accordance with the provisions of Part 131 of the Rules of the Chief Administrator (NY R CHIEF ADMIN § 131.1, et seq.). NY R CHIEF J § 29.3.

d. *Adjournment of return date.* Stipulations of adjournment of the return date made by the parties shall be in writing and shall be submitted to the assigned judge. Such stipulation shall be effective unless the court otherwise directs. No more than three (3) stipulated adjournments for an aggregate period of sixty (60) days shall be submitted without prior permission of the court. NY R UNIF TRIAL CTS § 202.8(e)(1).

i. Absent agreement by the parties, a request by any party for an adjournment shall be submitted in writing, upon notice to the other party, to the assigned judge on or before the return date. The court will notify the requesting party whether the adjournment has been granted. NY R UNIF TRIAL CTS § 202.8(e)(2).

ii. *BRONX COUNTY.* Non-disclosure motions for IA5, IA7 and IA22 will be adjourned for oral argument to the Monday of the second week following the week of the return date of the motion. All other non-disclosure motions will be deemed submitted on the return date and forwarded to Chambers unless a stipulation of adjournment complying with the requirements of NY R UNIF TRIAL CTS § 202.8(e) is submitted, in which event, the motion will be adjourned for the requested date and kept in the Clerk's Office. If a non-stipulated request for adjournment or notice is submitted, the motion and request will be forwarded to Chambers for judicial approval or denial of the request. In either event, the attorney requesting the adjournment will be notified, via telephone, of the granting or denial of the request and instructed to notify his adversary. NY R BRONX FIL R Doc. 8.

iii. *BRONX COUNTY.* Motions that have been e-filed may be adjourned in Room 217 if an adjournment complies with the procedures of the Motion Support Office (explained in the "Filing Rules—Motion Procedure" section of the "Courthouse Procedures" link on the website of [the] court). An adjournment that so complies may be obtained by filing a stipulation of all parties with NYSCEF (designated in the filing menu as a "Stipulation to Adjourn Motion"). NY R BRONX E FIL R Doc. 1(3).

iv. *NEW YORK COUNTY.* The Courtroom also maintains a "APB (All Papers By)" Calendar, which is used when a party seeks an adjournment but fails to comply with the Courtroom's procedures or there is a failure to comply with procedures that requires the clerk to adjourn the motion/application (e.g., failure to submit a Confirmation Notice in an e-filed case). The case may be put over for three days to allow compliance with those procedures, as described further below. NY R NY CTY Procedure II(C); NY R NY CTY E FIL Doc. 2(D)(2). E-filed applications may be adjourned in the Part if an adjournment complies with the Part's procedures (see the Uniform Rules of the Justices (Local Rules) on the court's website). An adjournment that so complies may be obtained by filing with NYSCEF a stipulation of all parties (designated in the filing menu as a Stipulation—Adjournment of Motion—Before Judge); the motion number and the current return date of the motion being adjourned shall be set forth in the "Additional Document Information" field in NYSCEF. Absent any problems, the Part will effectuate the adjournment without need for an appearance or any other action by the parties. NY R NY CTY E FIL Doc. 2(D)(4).

v. *QUEENS COUNTY.* The Motion Support Office is NOT authorized to grant adjournments. NY R L QUEENS MOT SUP Doc. 1.

e. *ALBANY COUNTY: Motion terms.* There shall be a. . . Motion Term on each Friday in the Supreme Court, Albany County. The Friday Motion Term shall include all Article 78 Proceedings involving New York State and proceedings commenced pursuant to Article 14 of the Civil Service Law (including applications for injunctive relief made pursuant to section 209-a of the Civil Service Law). NY R 3 JD SUP Doc. 1(F). Generally, parties will be granted only one adjournment for the Friday Motion Term. NY R 3 JD SUP Doc. 1(F).

f. *ALBANY COUNTY: Motion determined without hearing.* All motions are deemed "submitted" on the return date and no appearances are required by the parties. NY R 3 JD SUP Doc. 1(B). In the event oral argument is requested, the parties should not appear on the return date. At the discretion of the assigned Judge and upon the granting of a request for oral argument, the parties will be notified by Chambers of the scheduled time and place at which argument will be heard. Where a motion is brought on by order to show cause, the court may set forth in the order that appearances and/or oral argument are required on the return date of the motion. NY R 3 JD SUP Doc. 1(B).

g. *BRONX COUNTY: Return date.* All assigned and unassigned motions will be returnable five (5) days a week in the Civil Branch Clerk's Office, Room 217, at 9:30 a.m. NY R BRONX FIL R Doc. 8.

i. If on any submitted non-disclosure motion oral argument is requested and granted, or directed by the Court, the motion shall be adjourned for oral argument before the I.A. Judge on the second Monday following the week of the return date of the motion. Attorneys will be notified via telephone of the adjourned date. NY R BRONX FIL R Doc. 8.

h. *BRONX COUNTY: Oral argument.* Calendars of disclosure motions and other motions adjourned for oral argument will be published for the four (4) business days preceding the rescheduled appearance date and on the rescheduled date of the motion. These repetitive publications will serve as the notification of procedure of adjournment of all motions. In addition, two (2) days before the return date of unassigned motions a list of such motions indicating the assigned Justice and the adjourned date of the motion will be published. NY R BRONX FIL R Doc. 8.

i. *BRONX COUNTY: Resolution before return date.* Counsel/parties must advise the Court in writing on or before the return date of all motions that have been resolved by Counsel/parties themselves and all motions the movant(s) wish to be withdrawn. NY R BRONX FIL R Doc. 8.

j. *ERIE COUNTY: Calendaring of motions.* Refer to individual Justice's Part Rules. NY R ERIE E FIL Doc. 3(V)(B).

k. *KINGS COUNTY: Return date set by court.* Irrespective of the return date indicated in the notice of motion, motions will be rescheduled by the E-file/Motion Support Office to a date designated by the assigned Judge. NY R L KINGS Pt. C, Rule 2.

l. *KINGS COUNTY: Calendar calls.* There shall be two (2) calendar calls on motion days. The first calendar call shall be at 9:30 AM and the second calendar call shall be at 10:45 AM, unless the Judge's Part Rules provide otherwise. Defaults shall only be taken on second call. Attorneys with appearances elsewhere in the courthouse may advise the clerk of their whereabouts to avoid a default. Failure to so advise the clerk or appear at the default calendar call will result in a default order being entered or the motion being marked off the calendar. NY R L KINGS Pt. C, Rule 7.

m. *NEW YORK COUNTY: Return date and assigned courtroom.* Motions made by notice of motion and petitions and notices of petition in special proceedings are processed by the General Clerk's Office (Room 119) and are to be made returnable in the Motion Submission Part Courtroom (Room 130) on any business day of the week at 9:30 AM. There are some differences in electronically-filed cases. NY R NY CTY Procedure II; NY R NY CTY Procedure II(C); NY R NY CTY J RUL Rule 13(a).

i. For the convenience of counsel, between 9:00 A.M. and 9:30 A.M. each day, in advance of the "call," Room 130 accepts (1) written stipulations; (2) affidavits/affirmations reciting the required details as to an adjournment on consent; (3) stipulations, letters or other writings withdrawing motions; and (4) final papers or complete sets of papers on motions. For motions in which these items are handed in before the "call," no one need remain to answer the "call." Counsel/parties must advise the court, either between 9:00 A.M. and 9:30 A.M. or at the "call," of all motions or cases that have been resolved by counsel/parties themselves and all motions that the movant no longer wishes to pursue. If such resolution occurs subsequent to the "call", the assigned Justice must be advised as soon as possible, by written notice sent to the Part, so that the court does not do unnecessary work. NY R NY CTY Procedure II(C).

ii. Depending upon the assigned Part, contested motions submitted in the Motion Submission Part Courtroom are submitted without argument, or rescheduled for oral argument if so directed by the assigned Justice. For Justices who schedule argument on a case-by-case basis, notice of the argument date will be transmitted by the court. Counsel may ascertain how a motion submitted in Courtroom 130 was marked by consulting Scroll on the court's website, the e-Track application, or, on the two (2) days immediately following the submission date, the New York Law Journal. NY R NY CTY J RUL Rule 13(a).

n. *NEW YORK COUNTY: Motion call.* Each day in the Motion Submission Part Courtroom, commencing at 9:30 A.M., all motions returnable that day will be "called" for the submission of these papers, which must be handed up at this "call" or, as described below, immediately before. Because hundreds of motions appear on the Room 130 calendars every day, motion papers (other than part of the moving papers as described above) cannot be accepted on any day prior to the return date. Courtesy copies are not required nor accepted, but working copies are required by certain Justices in e-filed cases. NY R NY CTY Procedure II(C). If argument is directed, it will take place on an announced date shortly after the day of submission. NY R NY CTY Procedure II(C).

o. *NEW YORK COUNTY: Oral arguments.* Pursuant to request of some Justices, motions submitted in Room 130 will automatically be scheduled for a set argument date in the Part. Other Justices determine on a case-by-case basis after submission in Room 130 whether to accept a particular substantive motion on submission, to require oral argument, or to hold a conference. NY R NY CTY Procedure II(D). If argument is directed by the Justice automatically, notice of argument and the argument date will be given in Room 130. Any appearing party is expected to give notice to all parties and an announcement to this effect is made in Room 130. If the motion is submitted in Room 130 and the Justice, after examining the file, determines that argument should be directed, notice of the argument and the argument date will not be sent by the court. To obtain notification of the argument date and other developments, counsel should use e-Track. If argument notification is not given or transmitted as just described, counsel should understand that the motion has been taken on submission for decision on the papers. NY R NY CTY Procedure II(D).

   i. Calendars of motions to be argued in the Parts are published on the morning of the argument date and on the day before in the New York Law Journal under each Part. Argument information is available on a case-by-case basis in Scroll, and e-mail notifications are sent by e-Track to participating attorneys whenever a motion is scheduled for argument in the court's computer system. NY R NY CTY J RUL Rule 15(a)

p. *NEW YORK COUNTY: Motion determined without hearing.* Given the purpose of the Room 130 procedure, the substance of motions will not be addressed at the submission "call." No Judge is present. To the extent possible, motions submitted in Room 130 will be decided "on the papers." Indeed, attorneys are encouraged to use service or clerks to deliver papers or working copies, or to agree among themselves to have one of them deliver papers for all parties by service or a clerk. Counsel for the movant need not appear to "take a default" on any motion or for any other reason. Motions will be submitted, not marked off, in the absence of the movant. Opposing counsel similarly need not appear in person in order to avoid suffering a default. Delivery of papers by service or a clerk will suffice. The court's goal is to be able to collect papers on motions in an orderly fashion but without any attorney having to make an appearance in Room 130 at any time. NY R NY CTY Procedure II(C).

q. *ONONDAGA COUNTY: Return date.* If the motion is the first filing in an action, the case will be assigned and counsel will be notified by the Supreme Court Clerk's Office via the NYSCEF system of the assigned justice and return date. NY R ONDGA E FIL Protocol(B)(7)(c). If the motion is on a previously assigned case, counsel may choose a return date from the assigned justice's motion term schedule. If the date in unavailable, the Supreme Court Clerk's Office will assign the motion to the next available motion term date and will notify counsel via e-mail. The change will also appear in the notification generated by the NYSCEF system. NY R ONDGA E FIL Protocol(B)(7)(d).

r. *QUEENS COUNTY: Return date.* Motions must be made returnable on the proper day/time based on the assigned judge. NY R L QUEENS MOT SUP Doc. 1. Failure to make a motion returnable on the proper day/time may result in the motion being administratively rescheduled or marked off. NY R L QUEENS MOT SUP Doc. 1.

s. *QUEENS COUNTY: Unassigned motions.* For RJI/Motions, due to the fact that the movant would not know who the assigned judge will be, the notice of motion may be returnable any day of the week. RJI/Motions shall be made returnable in "Queens Supreme Court" with no address designated. The motion will be administratively rescheduled to the proper day of the week based on the judge (once a judge has been assigned). Within one (1) week of filing, the movant must check online to see who the assigned judge is (and therefore the location/date/time) that their motion is now returnable. Movant must then notify their adversary of this information prior to the return date. NY R L QUEENS MOT SUP Doc. 1.

3. *Entry of order after hearing.* An order determining a motion shall be entered and filed in the office of the clerk of the court where the action is triable, and all papers used on the motion and any opinion or memorandum in writing shall be filed with that clerk unless the order dispenses with such filing. When a statute or civil practice rule requires such filing and entry in a county other than that in which the order was made, the party prevailing on the motion shall file the order and the papers

used on the motion with the proper clerk after receiving them. If a party fails to file any papers required to be filed under NY CPLR Rule 2220(a), the order may be vacated as irregular, with costs. NY CPLR Rule 2220(a). For more information on the entry of an order after a motion, refer to NY CPLR Rule 2219.

a. *BRONX COUNTY: Settled orders.* A Judge's decision will often call for a Settled Order. The purpose of the settled order is to give effect to the decision by directing that some action be done and/or that a court official perform some task. NY R BRONX LEG SUP Doc. 2. A settled order consists of a notice of settlement informing all parties that the proposed order will be presented to the judge who made the decision on a date certain. Next comes the proposed order which will be presented to the judge. This order should conform to the judge's decision and should direct the relief granted in the decision. This should be followed by proof of service upon all parties who were noticed with the decision. It is also helpful if a copy of the judge's decision is included along with the other papers. A settled order should always be noticed before the judge who made the decision. NY R BRONX LEG SUP Doc. 2.

   i. Although an order is usually settled by the party who prevailed on the motion, any party may settle the order. It should be presented to the court within sixty (60) days of the decision. The other parties are entitled to ten (10) days notice where service of the settled order is done by mail, five (5) days if the notice is personally delivered. An attorney who is served with a notice of settlement which he believes does not accurately reflect the decision may settle a counter order. The counter order must be noticed for the same day and must be served not less than seven (7) days if by mail and two (2) days if personally delivered. NY R BRONX LEG SUP Doc. 2.

   ii. Settled orders are usually sent to the judge the day after they noticed for settlement. No appearance is necessary or even contemplated on a settled order. If the decision directs "submit order", then no notice is necessary, and the order will be sent to the judge as soon a practical after it is received. No fees are collected on settled orders. NY R BRONX LEG SUP Doc. 2.

b. *ERIE COUNTY: Proposed orders.* Proposed orders shall be submitted through the NYSCEF system and a working copy provided to the IAS Justice for signature, if Part Rules so require. NY R ERIE E FIL Doc. 3(V)(G).

c. *KINGS COUNTY: Long form orders.* If the Court directs that an order be settled or submitted on a motion in a NYSCEF case, the proposed order, with Notice of Settlement where required, and any proposed counter-order shall be filed with the Court via NYSCEF. The relevant clerk's office will process the documents in the customary manner. NY R L KINGS E FIL Doc. 1(E).

   i. WORKING COPIES OF PROPOSED ORDERS WITH NOTICE OF SETTLEMENT MUST BE SUBMITTED IN THE MOTION SUPPORT OFFICE (ROOM 227) AS EXPLAINED HEREIN. THEY MUST NOT BE DELIVERED TO THE PART OR CHAMBERS, EXCEPT WHERE THE INDIVIDUAL JUSTICE'S PART RULES PROVIDE OTHERWISE; DOING SO WILL CAUSE ADMINISTRATIVE CONFUSION AND POSSIBLE MISPLACEMENT OF PAPERS. Any such submission shall be sent in a timely manner (kindly review individual Justice's rules) and be conspicuously marked on the outside "NYSCEF Matter;" lack of such marking may delay processing. After an order/counter-order has been signed, it will be scanned, and the County Clerk will affix the entry stamp into the NYSCEF system, which will immediately transmit notice of this event via e-mail, including a link to the entered document, to all participating attorneys and unrepresented litigants in the case. Such transmittal does not constitute Notice of Entry. NY R L KINGS E FIL Doc. 1(E).

d. *NEW YORK COUNTY: Long form orders.* Although the court strongly favors the use of short form orders and judgments, there are instances when settlement of an order or judgment is appropriate. When a Justice directs in a decision that a long form order or judgment be settled, that decision is recorded in the court's computer system by the General Clerk's Office and the motion file with decision is held in the Order Section of the Office in Room 119. The settlement process takes place there. NY R NY CTY Procedure II(D); NY R NY CTY E FIL Doc. 2(E).

   i. A proposed long form order or judgment in compliance NY R UNIF TRIAL CTS § 202.48 must be presented to the relevant back office, together with a notice of settlement which bears a settlement date, the date on which the order is to be ready for formal presentation to the Justice. In an e-filed case the submission shall be made electronically. The proposed order or counter-order should be e-filed and it will be transmitted automatically by the NYSCEF system to the appropriate back office. The return date and time of the proposed order must be at 9:30 A.M. no sooner than either five (5) days from personal service of the proposed order or ten (10) days from service by mail. Proof of timely service on the other parties must accompany the proposed order in a hard copy case. If an order or judgment is submitted late (later than sixty (60) days from signing and filing of the decision) and the proponent can show good cause for this tardiness, an affidavit or affirmation justifying the delay should be annexed to the proposed order, together with proof of service thereof. If persuaded, the Justice will consider the proposed order despite its untimeliness. NY R NY CTY Procedure II(D); NY R NY CTY E FIL Doc. 2(E).

   ii. Sometimes a decision will state "Submit Order." The submitting party should prepare a long form order and

make it returnable without notice. Counsel should deliver the proposed order to the Order Section of the appropriate back office, except in an e-filed case, when it shall be submitted electronically. NY R NY CTY Procedure II(D). If the decision of the court directs that a proposed order be settled or submitted in the Part or in Chambers, that direction, should, of course, be followed without presentation of the proposal to the back office. NY R NY CTY Procedure II(D).

iii. For information on proposed counter-orders, refer to NY R NY CTY Procedure II(D) and NY R NY CTY J RUL Rule 16(b).

e. *QUEENS COUNTY: Proposed orders.* If the court directs that an order be settled or submitted on a motion in an E-file case, the proposed order and any proposed counter-order shall be filed with the court on-line with proof of service. (If a decision refers to a proceeding on the record, a copy of the transcript must be submitted.) Working copies of all proposed orders MUST be submitted to the Motion Support Office before an order can be reviewed. NY R L QUEENS E-FILE Doc. 1(I).

i. Counsel are advised to adhere to NY R UNIF TRIAL CTS § 202.48 regarding the submission or settlement of their proposed order or judgment. Persons who are submitting proposed orders/judgments pursuant to a previously issued memorandum decision must submit a copy of the memorandum decision with their proposed order/judgment. Upon E-Filing a proposed order/judgement, a working copy of the proposed order/judgement must be provided to the Motion Support Office. NY R L QUEENS MOT SUP Doc. 1.

4. *NEW YORK COUNTY: Judgment after motion.* A decision on a motion will usually be a decision and order. In some instances, the order will direct the Clerk to enter judgment in favor of the plaintiff for a particular sum (again, where that can be determined on papers alone) or in favor of defendant usually dismissing the case. The Clerk will then sign and enter a judgment in accordance with the order of the Court. This will happen when counsel submits to the Judgment Clerk, in hard copy form or, in an e-filed case, via NYSCEF, a judgment in proper form that substantively complies with the order of the court. NY R NY CTY Procedure XI(B)(2).

H. Forms

1. Official Motion for Summary Judgment Forms for New York

a. Request for judicial intervention. NY R UNIF TRIAL CTS § 202.6.

b. Notice of motion. NY R UNIF TRIAL CTS § 202.7(b).

2. New York Motion for Summary Judgment Forms

a. Notice of motion for summary judgment by plaintiff. MCF CPLR § 5:167.

b. Affidavit in support of motion for summary judgment by plaintiff. MCF CPLR § 5:168.

c. Notice of motion for summary judgment by defendant; Example 1. MCF CPLR § 5:173.

d. Notice of motion for summary judgment by defendant; Example 2. MCF CPLR § 5:174.

e. Affidavit in support of motion for summary judgment by defendant; Example 1. MCF CPLR § 5:175.

f. Affidavit in support of motion for summary judgment by defendant; Example 2. MCF CPLR § 5:176.

g. Notice of motion by defendant for summary judgment dismissing personal injury complaint on ground of Fireman's Rule. MCF CPLR § 5:180.

h. Affidavit of attorney in support of motion by defendant for summary judgment dismissing personal injury complaint on ground of Fireman's Rule. MCF CPLR § 5:181.

i. Affidavit of defendant in support of motion by defendant for summary judgment dismissing personal injury complaint on ground of Fireman's Rule. MCF CPLR § 5:182.

j. Notice of cross-motion by defendant for summary judgment; Escrow funds. MCF CPLR § 5:183.

k. Affidavit of attorney in support of cross-motion by defendant for summary judgment; Escrow funds. MCF CPLR § 5:184.

l. Notice of motion by defendant for summary judgment; Negligence. MCF CPLR § 5:186.

m. Affirmation of attorney in support of motion by defendant for summary judgment; Negligence. MCF CPLR § 5:187.

n. Affidavit in support of motion by defendant for summary judgment; Negligence. MCF CPLR § 5:188.

o. Notice of motion for partial summary judgment; Example 1. MCF CPLR § 5:191.

p. Affidavit in support of motion for partial summary judgment; Example 1. MCF CPLR § 5:193.

q. Notice of motion for summary judgment in lieu of complaint based on an instrument for payment of money only. MCF CPLR § 5:200.

r. Notice of motion for summary judgment in lieu of complaint based upon judgment secured in foreign state. MCF CPLR § 5:201.

s. Affidavit in support of motion for summary judgment under NY CPLR § 3213; Example 1. MCF CPLR § 5:205.

t. Affidavit in support of motion for summary judgment under NY CPLR § 3213; Example 2. MCF CPLR § 5:206.

u. Affidavit in support of motion for summary judgment under NY CPLR § 3213; Example 3. MCF CPLR § 5:207.

v. Affidavit in support of motion for summary judgment under NY CPLR § 3213; Example 4. MCF CPLR § 5:208.

w. Affidavit in support of motion for summary judgment in lieu of complaint based upon judgment secured in foreign state. MCF CPLR § 5:209.

x. Notice of motion for summary judgment in lieu of complaint. NYPRAC-COLL § 9:105.

y. Affidavit in support of plaintiff's motion for summary judgment in lieu of complaint. NYPRAC-COLL § 9:106.

z. General form of affidavit of service of motion papers. MCF CPLR § 5:24.

I. Applicable Rules

1. *State rules*

a. Short title; Application; Construction; Definitions. NY CPLR § 101; NY CPLR § 103; NY CPLR § 104; NY CPLR § 105.

b. Appendix of official forms. NY CPLR § 107.

c. Service of process. NY CPLR Rule 305; NY CPLR § 306-b; NY CPLR Rule 320.

d. Extensions of time generally. NY CPLR § 2004.

e. Form of papers. NY CPLR Rule 2101; NY CPLR Rule 2102; NY CPLR § 2105; NY CPLR Rule 2106; NY GEN BUS § 399-ddd; NY R UNIF TRIAL CTS § 215.2; NY R UNIF TRIAL CTS § 215.3.

f. Service of papers. NY CPLR Rule 2103.

g. Where motion made; In supreme court action. NY CPLR § 2212.

h. Motion papers; Service; Time. NY CPLR Rule 2214.

i. Relief demanded by other than moving party. NY CPLR Rule 2215.

j. Prior motion; Ex parte motion; Transfer of motion; Hearings; Orders. NY CPLR Rule 2217; NY CPLR § 2218; NY CPLR Rule 2220.

k. Computation of time. NY CPLR § 2402; NY GEN CONSTR § 19; NY GEN CONSTR § 20; NY GEN CONSTR § 25-a; NY GEN CONSTR § 30; NY GEN CONSTR § 31; NY GEN CONSTR § 53.

l. Motion to dismiss. NY CPLR Rule 3211.

m. Motion for summary judgment; Summary judgment in lieu of complaint. NY CPLR § 2303; NY CPLR Rule 3212; NY CPLR § 3213; NY CPLR § 5301; NY CPLR § 5401; U.S.C.A. Const. Art. IV § 1; 28 U.S.C.A. § 1738.

n. Motions heard by judge supervising disclosure; Stay of disclosure. NY CPLR Rule 3214.

o. Fees; Index number fees of county clerks. NY CPLR § 8018.

p. Hours of court; Proceedings in court. NY R CHIEF J § 3.1; NY R CHIEF J § 29.3.

q. Application of part; Waiver; Additional rules; Application of CPLR; Definitions. NY R UNIF TRIAL CTS § 202.1.

r. Papers filed in court; Electronic filing in supreme court. NY R UNIF TRIAL CTS § 202.5; NY R UNIF TRIAL CTS § 202.5-a; NY R UNIF TRIAL CTS § 202.5-b; NY R UNIF TRIAL CTS § 202.5-bb.

s. Request for judicial intervention. NY R UNIF TRIAL CTS § 202.6.

t. Calendaring of motions; Uniform notice of motion form; Affirmation of good faith. NY R UNIF TRIAL CTS § 202.7.

u. Motion procedure; Preliminary conferences. NY R UNIF TRIAL CTS § 202.8; NY R UNIF TRIAL CTS § 202.12.

v. Rules of the commercial division of the Supreme Court. NY R UNIF TRIAL CTS § 202.70.

w. Signing of papers. NY R CHIEF ADMIN § 130-1.1-a.

2. *Local rules*
    a. *Albany County*
        i. Third judicial district rules. NY R 3 JD SUP Doc. 1.
    b. *Bronx County*
        i. Filing of papers in supreme court. NY R BRONX FIL R Doc. 1.
        ii. Request for judicial intervention. NY R BRONX FIL R Doc. 2.
        iii. Motion procedure. NY R BRONX FIL R Doc. 8.
        iv. Commercial division. NY R BRONX FIL R Doc. 12.
        v. Motions on notice. NY R BRONX E FIL R Doc. 1.
        vi. Settled orders. NY R BRONX LEG SUP Doc. 2.
    c. *Erie County*
        i. Joint protocols for New York State Courts E-Filing (NYSCEF) cases filed in Supreme Court, Erie County. NY R ERIE E FIL Doc. 3.
    d. *Kings County*
        i. Papers. NY R L KINGS Pt. A, Papers.
        ii. Service of motion papers. NY R L KINGS Pt. C, Rule 1.
        iii. Scheduling of motions. NY R L KINGS Pt. C, Rule 2.
        iv. Appearance and argument. NY R L KINGS Pt. C, Rule 3.
        v. Courtesy copies. NY R L KINGS Pt. C, Rule 5.
        vi. Summary judgment motions. NY R L KINGS Pt. C, Rule 6.
        vii. Motion calendar calls. NY R L KINGS Pt. C, Rule 7.
        viii. Motions to extend time within which to move for summary judgment. NY R L KINGS Rule II.
        ix. Protocol on courthouse and county clerk procedures for electronically filed cases. NY R L KINGS E FIL Doc. 1.
    e. *New York County*
        i. Commencement of cases. NY R NY CTY Procedure I.
        ii. RJIs and assignments. NY R NY CTY Procedure IA.
        iii. Motions and special proceedings by notice of motion/petition. NY R NY CTY Procedure II.
        iv. County clerk litigation functions. NY R NY CTY Procedure XI.
        v. Protocol on courthouse and county clerk procedures for electronically filed cases. NY R NY CTY E FIL Doc. 2.
        vi. Redaction of information in documents filed with the county clerk and the court. NY R NY CTY J RUL Rule A-1.
        vii. Papers by fax. NY R NY CTY J RUL Rule 4.
        viii. Motions on notice; Orders to show cause. NY R NY CTY J RUL Rule 13.
        ix. Motion papers. NY R NY CTY J RUL Rule 14.
        x. Oral argument; Adjournments. NY R NY CTY J RUL Rule 15.
        xi. Motions for summary judgment. NY R NY CTY J RUL Rule 17.
    f. *Onondaga County*
        i. Summary judgment motion uniform time period. NY R ONDGA SUM JUDG Doc. 1.
        ii. Onondaga county protocol for case filings New York State Electronic Files (NYSCEF). NY R ONDGA E FIL Protocol.
    g. *Queens County*
        i. Motion support office. NY R L QUEENS MOT SUP Doc. 1.

ii. Queens county protocol on courthouse procedures for electronically filed cases. NY R L QUEENS E-FILE Doc. 1.

J. Miscellaneous

NOTE: Individual judges' rules may apply.

ALBANY COUNTY

JUSTICE LISA M. FISHER: NY R 3 JD FISHER Fisher; NY R 3 JD FISHER Fisher, PC Order.

JUSTICE RICHARD MOTT: NY R 3 JD MOTT Mott.

JUSTICE STEPHAN G. SCHICK: NY R 3 JD Schick.

FORECLOSURE SETTLEMENT PART: NY R 3 JD Foreclosure Settlement.

BRONX COUNTY

JUSTICE PAUL L. ALPERT: [NY R BRONX J Part IA-29, as amended by NY ORDER 20-0337].

JUSTICE BEN BARBATO: NY R BRONX J Part IA-21.

JUSTICE MARY ANNE BRIGANTTI: [NY R BRONX J Part IA-15, as amended by NY ORDER 20-0338].

JUSTICE JOSEPH E. CAPELLA: NY R BRONX J Part IA-23.

JUSTICE MITCHELL DANZIGER: NY R BRONX J Part IA-3/33 ; [NY R BRONX J Danziger, Part IA-3/33, as amended by NY ORDER 20-0339].

JUSTICE LAURA G. DOUGLAS: NY R BRONX J Part IA-11.

JUSTICE RUBEN FRANCO: NY R BRONX J Part IA-26.

JUSTICE DORIS M. GONZALEZ: NY R BRONX J Part IA-24.

JUSTICE WILMA GUZMAN: NY R BRONX J Part IA-7; [NY R BRONX J Guzman, Part IA-7 Virtual, as amended by NY ORDER 20-0340].

JUSTICE ROBERT T. JOHNSON: NY R BRONX J Part IA-12.

JUSTICE DONALD A. MILES: NY R BRONX J Part IA-8.

JUSTICE DONNA M. MILLS: NY R BRONX J Part IA-9.

JUSTICE JULIA I. RODRIGUEZ: NY R BRONX J Part IA-18; [NY R BRONX J Part IA-27, as amended by NY ORDER 20-0341].

JUSTICE LLINET M. ROSADO: [NY R BRONX J Part IA-25, as amended by NY ORDER 20-0342].

JUSTICE NORMA RUIZ: NY R BRONX J Part IA-22; [NY R BRONX J Ruiz, Part IA-22 Virtual, as amended by NY ORDER 20-0343].

JUSTICE HOWARD H. SHERMAN: NY R BRONX J Part IA-4.

JUSTICE FERNANDO TAPIA: NY R BRONX J Part IA-13.

JUSTICE ELIZABETH A. TAYLOR: NY R BRONX J Part IA-2.

JUSTICE ALISON Y. TRUITT: NY R BRONX J Part IA-5.

PART IDV: NY R BRONX J Doc. 1.

PRE-TRIAL PART RULES: NY R BRONX J Doc. 2.

PRE TRIAL WORKSHEET: NY R BRONX J Doc. 3.

FORECLOSURE SETTLEMENT PART RULES: NY R BRONX J Doc. 4.

GUARDIANSHIP PART RULES: NY R BRONX J Doc. 5.

LPM PART RULES: NY R BRONX J Doc. 6.

ERIE COUNTY

JUSTICE M. WILLIAM BOLLER: NY R 8 JD J Boller.

JUSTICE RALPH A. BONIELLO: NY R 8 JD J Boniello.

JUSTICE CHRISTOPHER J. BURN: NY R 8 JD J Burns.

JUSTICE RUSSELL P. BUSCAGLIA: NY R 8 JD J Buscaglia.
JUSTICE FRANK CARUSO: NY R 8 JD J Caruso.
JUSTICE STEPHEN W. CASS: NY R 8 JD J Cass.
JUSTICE DEBORAH A. CHIMES: NY R 8 JD J Chimes.
JUSTICE EMILIO COLAIACOVO: [NY R 8 JD J Colaiacovo, as amended by NY ORDER 20-0252].
JUSTICE DIANE Y. DEVLIN: NY R 8 JD J Devlin.
JUSTICE JAMES H. DILLON: NY R 8 JD J Dillon.
JUSTICE PAULA L. FEROLETO: NY R 8 JD J Feroleto.
JUSTICE DANIEL J. FURLONG: [NY R 8 JD J Furlong, as amended by NY ORDER 20-0253].
JUSTICE JOSEPH R. GLOWNIA: NY R 8 JD J Glownia.
JUSTICE MARK J. GRISANTI: NY R 8 JD J Grisanti.
JUSTICE DEBORAH A. HAENDIGES: NY R 8 JD J Haendiges.
JUSTICE LYNN W. KEANE: [NY R 8 JD J Keane, as amended by NY ORDER 20-0254].
JUSTICE RICHARD C. KLOCH, Sr.: NY R 8 JD J Kloch.
JUSTICE FREDERICK J. MARSHALL: [NY R 8 JD J Marshall, as amended by NY ORDER 20-0255.
JUSTICE JOHN L. MICHALSKI: NY R 8 JD J Michalski.
JUSTICE MARK A. MONTOUR: [NY R 8 JD J Montour, as amended by NY ORDER 20-0256].
JUSTICE HENRY NOWAK: NY R 8 JD J Nowak.
JUSTICE JOHN F. O'DONNELL: NY R 8 JD J O'Donnell.
JUSTICE JEANETTE OGDEN: NY R 8 JD J Ogden.
JUSTICE CATHERINE NUGENT-PANEPINTO: NY R 8 JD J Nugent-Panepinto.
JUSTICE FRANK A. SEDITA, III: [NY R 8 JD J Sedita, as amended by NY ORDER 20-0257].
JUSTICE SARA SHELDON: NY R 8 JD J Sheldon.
JUSTICE DONNA M. SIWEK: NY R 8 JD J Siwek.
JUSTICE MARY L. SLISZ: NY R 8 JD J Slisz.
JUSTICE TIMOTHY J. WALKER: [NY R 8 JD J Walker, as amended by NY ORDER 20-0258].
JUSTICE DENNIS E. WARD: NY R 8 JD J Ward.
JUSTICE PAUL B. WOJTASZEK: [NY R 8 JD J Wojtaszek, as amended by NY ORDER 20-0259].
JUSTICE CHARLES N. ZAMBITO: [NY R 8 JD J Zambito, as amended by NY ORDER 20-0260].
SUPREME COURT LEGAL STAFF: NY R 8 JD J Legal Staff.

KINGS COUNTY

JUSTICE RACHEL A. ADAMS: NY R KINGS J Part 5F.
JUSTICE LOREN BAILY-SCHIFFMAN: NY R KINGS J Part 65.
JUSTICE REGINALD A. BODDIE: NY R KINGS J Part 95.
JUSTICE THERESA M. CICCOTTO: NY R KINGS J Part 19; NY R KINGS J Part 5J.
JUSTICE LISSETTE COLON: NY R KINGS J Part Rules.
JUSTICE GENINE EDWARDS: NY R KINGS J Part 80.
JUSTICE PAMELA L. FISHER: [NY R KINGS J Part 94, as amended by NY ORDER 20-0208].
JUSTICE ROBIN GARSON: NY R KINGS J Part 75.
JUSTICE LARA J. GENOVISI: [NY R KINGS J Part 34, as amended by NY ORDER 20-0209].
JUSTICE BERNARD J. GRAHAM: NY R KINGS J Part 36.
JUSTICE DAWN JIMENEZ-SALTA: NY R KINGS J Part 88.

JUSTICE INGRID JOSEPH: [NY R KINGS J Part FRP3 and Part 83, as amended by NY ORDER 20-0210].
JUSTICE KATHY J. KING: NY R KINGS J Part 64, 76K.
JUSTICE LAWRENCE KNIPEL: NY R KINGS J Part 57.
JUSTICE DONALD KURTZ: NY R KINGS J Part 26.
JUSTICE CARL LANDICINO: [NY R KINGS J Part 81, as amended by NY ORDER 20-0211].
JUSTICE KATHERINE LEVINE: [NY R KINGS J Part 20, 25, 92, as amended by NY ORDER 20-0211].
JUSTICE LORNA MCALLISTER: [NY R KINGS J Part 10, as amended by NY ORDER 20-0211].
JUSTICE ROSEMARIE MONTALBANO: [NY R KINGS J Part 19, 71, and 22, as amended by NY ORDER 20-0211].
JUSTICE RICHARD J. MONTELIONE: [NY R KINGS J Part 99 and DJMP, as amended by NY ORDER 20-0215].
JUSTICE LISA S. OTTLEY: NY R KINGS J Part 24.
JUSTICE MARK I. PARTNOW: NY R KINGS J Part 43.
JUSTICE ERIC I. PRUS: NY R KINGS J Part 5A.
JUSTICE FRANCOIS RIVERA: NY R KINGS J Part 52.
JUSTICE KAREN B. ROTHENBERG: NY R KINGS J Part 35.
JUSTICE LEON RUCHELSMAN: NY R KINGS J Part 1.
JUSTICE WAYNE P. SAITTA: NY R KINGS J Part 29.
JUSTICE ROBIN K. SHEARES: NY R KINGS J Part 96.
JUSTICE KENNETH P. SHERMAN: NY R KINGS J Part 67 and 78.
JUSTICE DEBRA SILBER: NY R KINGS J Part 9 and 5K.
JUSTICE ELLEN M. SPODEK: NY R KINGS J Part 63.
JUSTICE MARSHA L. STEINHARDT: NY R KINGS J Part 15.
JUSTICE JEFFREY S. SUNSHINE: NY R KINGS J Part 5G.
JUSTICE PETER P. SWEENEY: [NY R KINGS J Part 35, as amended by NY ORDER 20-0218].
JUSTICE DELORES J. THOMAS: [NY R KINGS J Part 5T, as amended by NY ORDER 20-0221].
JUSTICE WAVNY TOUSSAINT: NY R KINGS J Part 70.
JUSTICE RICHARD VELASQUEZ: NY R KINGS J Part 66.
JUSTICE CAROLYN E. WADE: NY R KINGS J Part 84.
JUSTICE EDWARD G. WALKER: [NY R KINGS J Part 90, as amended by NY ORDER 20-0219].
JUSTICE LILLIAN WAN: [NY R KINGS J Part 17, as amended by NY ORDER 20-0220].
JUSTICE MICHELLE WESTON: NY R KINGS J Part 3.
MENTAL HYGIENE PART: NY R KINGS J Part 77.
MATRIMONIAL PARTS DURING COVID-19 EMERGENCY: JUSTICE KAREN B. ROTHENBERG: NY R KINGS J Doc. 1.

NASSAU COUNTY

JUSTICE ANNA R. ANZALONE: NY R NASSAU S J Anzalone, Part 26.
JUSTICE STACY D. BENNETT: NY R NASSAU S J Bennett; NY R NASSAU S J Bennett, Form 1.
JUSTICE ANTONIO BRANDVEEN: NY R NASSAU S J Brandveen, Part 31.
JUSTICE JEFFREY S. BROWN: [NY R NASSAU S J Brown, as amended by NY ORDER 20-0297].
JUSTICE STEPHEN A. BUCARIA: NY R NASSAU S J Bucaria.
JUSTICE JULIANNE T. CAPETOLA: NY R NASSAU S J Capetola, Part 28.
JUSTICE EDMUND M. DANE: NY R NASSAU S J Dane, Part 33.
JUSTICE VITO M. DESTEFANO: NY R NASSAU S J DeStefano, Part 13; NY R NASSAU S J DeStefano, Form 1.
JUSTICE ARTHUR M. DIAMOND: NY R NASSAU S J Diamond, Part 7.

JUSTICE THOMAS FEINMAN: NY R NASSAU S J Feinman, Part 5.

JUSTICE JOHN M. GALASSO: NY R NASSAU S J Galasso, Part 22.

JUSTICE SHARON M.J. GIANELLI: NY R NASSAU S J Gianelli, Part 22; NY R NASSAU S J Gianelli, Form 1.

JUSTICE JEFFREY A. GOODSTEIN: NY R NASSAU S J Goodstein, Part 33; NY R NASSAU S J Goodstein, Form 1.

JUSTICE DAVID J. GUGERTY: [NY R NASSAU S J Gugerty, Part 31, as amended by NY ORDER 20-0298].

JUSTICE HELENE F. GUGERTY: NY R NASSAU S J Gugerty, Part 47.

JUSTICE STEVEN M. JAEGER: NY R NASSAU S J Jaeger, Part 35; NY R NASSAU S J Jaeger, Form 1.

JUSTICE JACK L. LIBERT: NY R NASSAU S J Libert, Part 23.

JUSTICE JOSEPH H. LORINTZ: NY R NASSAU S J Lorintz, Part 26; NY R NASSAU S J Lorintz, Form 1.

JUSTICE ROY S. MAHON: NY R NASSAU S J Mahon, Part 3.

JUSTICE RANDY SUE MARBER: NY R NASSAU S J Marber, Part 8.

JUSTICE JAMES P. MCCORMACK: [NY R NASSAU S J McCormack, Part 18, as amended by NY ORDER, 20-0299].

JUSTICE DICCIA T. PINEDA-KIRWAN: [NY R NASSAU S J Pineda-Kirwan, as amended by NY ORDER 20-0300].

JUSTICE THOMAS RADEMAKER: [NY R NASSAU S J Rademaker, Part 28, as amended by NY ORDER 20-0301]; [NY R NASSAU S J Rademaker, Form 1, as amended by NY ORDER 20-0301].

JUSTICE DENISE L. SHER: NY R NASSAU S J Rademaker, Part 32.

JUSTICE LEONARD D. STEINMAN: [NY R NASSAU S J Steinman, Part 15, as amended by NY ORDER 20-0303]; NY R NASSAU S J Steinman, Form 1.

JUSTICE HOWARD E. STURIM: NY R NASSAU S J Sturim, Part 50; NY R NASSAU S J Sturim, Form 1.

JUSTICE HELEN VOUTSINAS: [NY R NASSAU S J Voutsinas, Part 25, as amended by NY ORDER 20-0304]; [NY R NASSAU S J Voutsinas, Form 1, as amended by NY ORDER 20-0305].

JUSTICE HOPE SCHWARTZ ZIMMERMAN: NY R NASSAU S J Zimmerman, Part 17.

NEW YORK COUNTY

JUDGE'S RULES; BASIC INFORMATION: [NY R NY CTY J RUL Doc. 1, as amended by NY ORDER 20-0202].

ONONDAGA COUNTY

JUSTICE ROBERT E. ANTONACCI II: [NY R ONDGA E FIL Doc. 1, as amended by 20-0239].

JUSTICE MICHAEL V. COCCOMI: NY R ONDGA E FIL Doc. 2.

JUSTICE GREGORY R. GILBERT: NY R 5 JD JUDGES Gilbert; NY R ONDGA E FIL Doc. 3.

JUSTICE DONALD A. GREENWOOD: NY R ONDGA E FIL Doc. 4.

JUSTICE DEBORAH H. KARALUNAS: NY R ONDGA E FIL Doc. 5.

JUSTICE JAMES MCCLUSKY: NY R 5 JD MCCLUSKY McClusky.

JUSTICE CHARLES C. MERRELL: NY R 5 JD MERRELL Merrell.

JUSTICE PATRICK F. MACRAE: NY R 5 JD MACRAE Doc. 1.

JUSTICE JAMES P. MURPHY: NY R ONDGA E FIL Doc. 7.

JUSTICE GERALD J. NERI: [NY R 5 JD JUDGES Neri, as amended by NY ORDER 20-0236]; [NY R ONDGA E FIL Doc. 8, as amended by NY ORDER 20-0241].

JUSTICE ANTHONY J. PARIS: NY R 5 JD JUDGES Paris; [NY R ONDGA E FIL Doc. 9, as amended by NY ORDER 20-0242].

JUSTICE NORMAN W. SEITER, JR.: NY R 5 JD JUDGES Seiter.

JUSTICE KEVIN G. YOUNG: [NY R ONDGA E FIL Doc. 10, as amended by NY ORDER 20-0243].

QUEENS COUNTY

JUSTICE PAM JACKMAN BROWN: [NY R L QUEENS Brown, Part 19, as amended by NY ORDER 20-0321].

JUSTICE CHEREE A. BUGGS: NY R L QUEENS Buggs, Part 30.

JUSTICE PAM JACKMAN BROWN: [NY R L QUEENS Brown, Part 19, as amended by NY ORDER 20-0321].

JUSTICE DENIS J. BUTLER: NY R L QUEENS Butler, Part 12.
JUSTICE ROBERT I. CALORAS: [NY R L QUEENS Caloras, Part 36, as amended by NY ORDER 20-0322].
JUSTICE ANNA CULLEY: NY R L QUEENS Culley, Part 53.
JUSTICE TIMOTHY DUFFICY: NY R L QUEENS Dufficy, Part 35.
JUSTICE DAVID ELLIOT: NY R L QUEENS Elliot, Part 14.
JUSTICE JOSEPH J. ESPOSITO: NY R L QUEENS Esposito, Part 6.
JUSTICE DARRELL L. GAVRIN: [NY R L QUEENS Gavrin, Part 27, as amended by NY ORDER 20-0323].
JUSTICE WYATT N. GIBBONS: [NY R L QUEENS Gibbons, Part 5, as amended by NY ORDER 20-0330.
JUSTICE DONNA-MARIE E. GOLIA: [NY R L QUEENS Golia, Part 21, as amended by NY ORDER 20-0331].
JUSTICE MARGUERITE A. GRAYS: [NY R L QUEENS Grays, Part 4, as amended by NY ORDER 20-0324].
JUSTICE RUDOLPH E. GRECO: [NY R L QUEENS Greco, Part 32, as amended by NY ORDER 20-0325].
JUSTICE MAUREEN HEALY: NY R L QUEENS Healy, Part 6.
JUSTICE PHILLIP HOM: [NY R L QUEENS Hom, Part 43, as amended by NY ORDER 20-0332].
JUSTICE KEVIN J. KERRIGAN: NY R L QUEENS Kerrigan, Part 10.
JUSTICE MOJGAN C. LANCMAN: NY R L QUEENS Lancman, Part 20.
JUSTICE RICHARD G. LATIN: NY R L QUEENS Latin, Part 40.
JUSTICE ULYSSES B. LEVERETT: [NY R L QUEENS Leverett, Part 6, as amended by NY ORDER 20-0326].
JUSTICE LEONARD LIVOTE: NY R L QUEENS Livote, Part 33.
JUSTICE LEE A. MAYERSOHN: NY R L QUEENS Mayersohn, Part 22; NY R L QUEENS Mayersohn, Part 22G; [NY R L QUEENS Mayersohn, Part 22G COVID, as amended by NY ORDER 20-0327].
JUSTICE ROBERT J. MCDONALD: NY R L QUEENS McDonald, Part 34.
JUSTICE MARGARET MCGOWAN: NY R L QUEENS McGowan, Part 52.
JUSTICE MAURICE E. MUIR: [NY R L QUEENS Muir, Part 42, as amended by NY ORDER 20-0333].
JUSTICE JODI ORLOW: NY R L QUEENS Orlow, Part 51.
JUSTICE LESLIE J. PURIFICCION: NY R L QUEENS Purificcion, Part 39.
JUSTICE JOSEPH RISI: [NY R L QUEENS Risi, Part 3, as amended by NY ORDER 20-0328].
JUSTICE FREDERICK D.R. SAMPSON: [NY R L QUEENS Sampson, Part 31, as amended by NY ORDER 20-0329].
JUSTICE MARTIN J. SCHULMAN: NY R L QUEENS Schulman, Part 29.
JUSTICE BERNICE D. SIEGAL: NY R L QUEENS Siegal, Part 25G.
JUSTICE JANICE A. TAYLOR: NY R L QUEENS Taylor, Part 15.
JUSTICE CARMEN R. VELASQUEZ: NY R L QUEENS Velasquez, Part 38.
JUSTICE LOURDES M VENTURA: [NY R L QUEENS Ventura, Part 37, as amended by NY ORDER 20-0334].
JUSTICE WILLIAM A. VISCOVICH: NY R L QUEENS Viscovich, Part 63.
JUSTICE ALLAN B. WEISS: NY R L QUEENS Weiss, Part 2.
COMPLIANCE, SETTLEMENT AND CONFERENCE PART: NY R L QUEENS Doc 1.
PRELIMINARY CONFERENCE PART: [NY R L QUEENS Doc. 2, as amended by NY ORDER 20-0335].
MEDICAL MALPRACTICE CONFERENCE PART: [NY R L QUEENS Doc. 3, as amended by NY ORDER 20-0336].
TRIAL SCHEDULING PART: NY R L QUEENS Doc. 4.
SUMMARY JURY TRIAL PROGRAM: NY R L QUEENS Doc. 7.
RESIDENTIAL FORECLOSURE PART: NY R L QUEENS Doc. 9.
FORECLOSURE AUCTION RULES: NY R L QUEENS Doc. 10.
MATRIMONIAL PRELIMINARY CONFERENCE PART: NY R L QUEENS Doc. 11.

NON-CUSTODIAL CONTESTED MATRIMONIAL PART: NY R L QUEENS Doc. 12.

Motions, Oppositions and Replies
Motion for Sanctions

Document Last Updated August 2020

A. Checklist

(I) ❑ Matters to consider for moving party
- (a) ❑ Required documents
  - (1) ❑ Notice of motion, order to show cause, or affidavit on ex parte motion
  - (2) ❑ Motion
  - (3) ❑ Request for judicial intervention
  - (4) ❑ Proof of service
  - (5) ❑ ALBANY COUNTY: Additional required documents
    - (i) ❑ Affirmation of good faith effort
- (b) ❑ Supplemental documents
  - (1) ❑ Supporting evidence; Exhibits
  - (2) ❑ Brief
  - (3) ❑ Notice to produce papers not in possession of the court
  - (4) ❑ Filing fees
  - (5) ❑ Working copies
  - (6) ❑ ERIE COUNTY: Additional supplemental documents
    - (i) ❑ Notice of hard copy submission in e-filed case
  - (7) ❑ KINGS COUNTY: Additional supplemental documents
    - (i) ❑ Forms when filing in hard copy
  - (8) ❑ NEW YORK COUNTY: Additional supplemental documents
    - (i) ❑ Notice of hard copy submission
    - (ii) ❑ Unpublished opinions
  - (9) ❑ ONONDAGA COUNTY: Additional supplemental documents
    - (i) ❑ Notice of hard copy submission
  - (10) ❑ QUEENS COUNTY: Additional supplemental documents
    - (i) ❑ Notice of hard copy submission
- (c) ❑ Timing
  - (1) ❑ There are no specific timing requirements for the motion for sanctions
  - (2) ❑ The moving party shall serve copies of all affidavits and briefs upon all other parties at the time of service of the notice of motion
  - (3) ❑ A notice of motion and supporting affidavits shall be served at least eight (8) days before the time at which the motion is noticed to be heard
  - (4) ❑ It is also good practice to make motions returnable at least three (3) weeks away from the planned date of mailing and to always include a demand in the motion that the other side serve answering papers at least seven (7) days before the return day
  - (5) ❑ BRONX COUNTY: Additional timing
    - (i) ❑ A Notice of Motion must be served at least eight (8) days, by personal service, nine (9) days by overnight express and thirteen (13) days by mail before the return date

(6) ❑ NEW YORK COUNTY: Additional timing

(i) ❑ In an e-filed case, all of the moving papers shall be e-filed at least eight (8) business days prior to the return date

(7) ❑ ONONDAGA COUNTY: Additional timing

(i) ❑ Onondaga County local court rules require that any additional papers relating to motions must be e-filed at least two (2) business days prior to the return date, excluding the return date

(8) ❑ QUEENS COUNTY: Additional timing

(i) ❑ Motions must be in the possession of the Motion Support Office at least nine (9) days before the noticed return date of the motion

(II) ❑ Matters to consider for opposing party

(a) ❑ Required documents

(1) ❑ Opposition

(2) ❑ Proof of service

(b) ❑ Supplemental documents

(1) ❑ Supporting evidence; Exhibits

(2) ❑ Brief

(3) ❑ Filing fees

(4) ❑ Working copies

(5) ❑ ERIE COUNTY: Additional supplemental documents

(i) ❑ Notice of hard copy submission in e-filed case

(6) ❑ KINGS COUNTY: Additional supplemental documents

(i) ❑ Forms when filing in hard copy

(7) ❑ NEW YORK COUNTY: Additional supplemental documents

(i) ❑ Notice of hard copy submission

(ii) ❑ Unpublished opinions

(8) ❑ ONONDAGA COUNTY: Additional supplemental documents

(i) ❑ Notice of hard copy submission

(9) ❑ QUEENS COUNTY: Additional supplemental documents

(i) ❑ Notice of hard copy submission

(c) ❑ Timing

(1) ❑ Answering affidavits shall be served at least two (2) days before the time at which the motion is noticed to be heard

(2) ❑ Answering affidavits and any notice of cross-motion, with supporting papers, if any, shall be served at least seven (7) days before such time if a notice of motion served at least sixteen (16) days before such time so demands

B. Timing

1. *Time to bring motion for sanctions.* There are no specific timing requirements for the motion for sanctions.
2. *Time to serve.* The moving party shall serve copies of all affidavits and briefs upon all other parties at the time of service of the notice of motion. NY R UNIF TRIAL CTS § 202.8(c). A notice of motion and supporting affidavits shall be served at least eight (8) days before the time at which the motion is noticed to be heard. NY CPLR Rule 2214(b).
   a. *Return dates; Best practice.* It is also good practice to make motions returnable at least three (3) weeks away from the planned date of mailing and to always include a demand in the motion that the other side serve answering papers at least seven (7) days before the return day. This enables the motion to be served by mail, gives sufficient notice to support the seven (7) day demand, and leaves a few days for a delayed mailing if some snag prevents posting on the day planned. If speed is needed, the shorter eight (8) day notice period can be used, forfeiting the right to seven (7)

day answering papers and a reply. If even eight (8) days notice is too much under the circumstances, the order to show cause is the remedy. SIEGEL-NYPRAC § 247.

i. *ALBANY COUNTY.* All motions, except for certain matters in Albany County as specified in NY R 3 JD SUP Doc. 1(E) and NY R 3 JD SUP Doc. 1(F), brought on by notice of motion or by order to show cause will be made returnable on any day, Monday through Friday, as chosen by the movant in compliance with the CPLR. Parties shall submit all papers in a timely fashion as required by the CPLR by delivering them or mailing them directly to the Supreme Court Clerk's Office[. . .]except that motions and other applications subject to a filing fee shall first be presented to the County Clerk's Office for payment of the requisite fee and then subsequently filed with the Supreme Court Clerk's Office. NY R 3 JD SUP Doc. 1(B).

ii. *BRONX COUNTY.* A Notice of Motion must be served at least eight (8) days, by personal service, nine (9) days by overnight express and thirteen (13) days by mail before the return date. NY R BRONX FIL R Doc. 3. All unassigned motions must be accompanied with a properly filled out RJI and shall be filed in the Motion Support Office, room 217, within five (5) days of service. All motions on actions already assigned to a Justice must be filed at least five (5) business days before the return date. NY R BRONX FIL R Doc. 3. All papers served must strictly comply with the time requirements of NY CPLR Rule 2101, NY CPLR Rule 2103 and NY CPLR Rule 2214(b). NY R BRONX FIL R Doc. 8.

iii. *KINGS COUNTY.* Motion papers, answering affidavits and reply affidavits must be served on adversaries in accordance with NY CPLR Rule 2214. NY R L KINGS Pt. C, Rule 1.

iv. *NEW YORK COUNTY.* In an e-filed case, all of the moving papers shall be e-filed at least eight (8) business days prior to the return date. The clerk will calendar the motion for the Motion Submission Part Courtroom (Room 130) for the return date selected. NY R NY CTY Procedure II(A); NY R NY CTY E FIL Doc. 2(D)(1).

v. *ONONDAGA COUNTY.* Onondaga County local court rules require that any additional papers relating to motions must be e-filed at least two (2) business days prior to the return date, excluding the return date. NY R ONDGA E FIL Protocol(B)(9)(e).

vi. *QUEENS COUNTY.* Motions must be in the possession of the Motion Support Office at least nine (9) days before the noticed return date of the motion. NY R L QUEENS MOT SUP Doc. 1; NY R L QUEENS E-FILE Doc. 1(H)(1).

b. *Order to show cause; Shorter time.* The court in a proper case may grant an order to show cause, to be served in lieu of a notice of motion, at a time and in a manner specified therein. NY CPLR Rule 2214(d). An ordinary notice of motion can't be brought on for hearing earlier than the eighth (8th) day after the motion papers are served. With an order to show cause, the hearing can be brought on at any time the court directs, which can be fewer than eight (8) days or as close as the very day on which it is signed. If the court is convinced there is a real emergency, it can schedule the hearing for a few hours later or, in the direst case, "forthwith" the service of the order to show cause. SIEGEL-NYPRAC § 248.

c. *Time to serve answering affidavits; Other answering papers.* Answering affidavits shall be served at least two (2) days before the time at which the motion is noticed to be heard. Answering affidavits and any notice of cross-motion, with supporting papers, if any, shall be served at least seven (7) days before such time if a notice of motion served at least sixteen (16) days before such time so demands; whereupon any reply or responding affidavits shall be served at least one (1) day before such time. NY CPLR Rule 2214(b); NY R UNIF TRIAL CTS § 202.8(c).

i. *BRONX COUNTY.* All answering papers must be submitted to the Clerk 's Office on the return date of the motion. Answering papers will not be accepted prior to the return date. NY R BRONX FIL R Doc. 8.

ii. *NEW YORK COUNTY.* Cross-motions, papers in opposition, and reply papers on motions/petitions on notice returnable in Room 130 in a hard-copy case shall be submitted to the Motion Submission Part Courtroom (Room 130) on the final return date of the motion/petition and will not be accepted until that date. Subsequent documents on motions/petitions in e-filed cases shall be e-filed in a timely manner. Working copies when required shall be submitted to Room 130 on the final return date. NY R NY CTY Procedure II(A).

d. *Time to serve cross-motion.* At least three (3) days prior to the time at which the motion is noticed to be heard, or seven (7) days prior to such time if demand is properly made pursuant to NY CPLR Rule 2214(b), a party may serve upon the moving party a notice of cross-motion demanding relief, with or without supporting papers; provided, however, that:

i. If such notice and any supporting papers are served by mailing, as provided in NY CPLR Rule 2103(b)(2), they shall be served three (3) days earlier than as prescribed in NY CPLR Rule 2215; and

ii. If served by overnight delivery, as provided in NY CPLR Rule 2103(b)(6), they shall be served one (1) day earlier than as prescribed in NY CPLR Rule 2215. Relief in the alternative or of several different types may be demanded; relief need not be responsive to that demanded by the moving party. NY CPLR Rule 2215(a); NY CPLR Rule 2215(b).

iii. *BRONX COUNTY.* Cross motions may be presented for approval on or before the return date, provided that there is a motion already calendared. NY R BRONX FIL R Doc. 8.

iv. *ERIE COUNTY.* Cross-motions must be filed at least two (2) days before the return date of the motion. NY R L KINGS Pt. A, Papers.

v. *KINGS COUNTY.* Hard copies are required to be filed for any motions, answering papers, stipulations, etc. for E-Filed cases returnable in [the Central Compliance Part] at least [two (2)] days before return date. . . .for cross motions. NY R L KINGS Pt. E, Rule 8.

vi. *QUEENS COUNTY.* Motion Support does not process or forward responsive papers, including cross-motions. They must be brought to the calendar call in the judge's part. NY R L QUEENS MOT SUP Doc. 1. E-filed cross motions: across motion must be noticed for the same return date as the main motion and have the confirmation of filing attached in the same manner as a motion. NY R L QUEENS E-FILE Doc. 1(H)(2)(e).

3. *Filing before return date.* All motions shall be returnable before the assigned judge, and all papers shall be filed with the court on or before the return date. NY R UNIF TRIAL CTS § 202.8(a).

a. *BRONX COUNTY: Time for filing*

i. *Unassigned motions.* Unassigned motions must be in the Clerk's Office within five (5) days of the date of service of the motion. NY R BRONX FIL R Doc. 8.

ii. *Assigned motions.* Assigned motions must be filed in the Clerk's Office not less than five (5) business days prior to the return date of the motion. NY R BRONX FIL R Doc. 8.

iii. *Motions returnable in room 217.* The moving documents must be e-filed no later than eight (8) days prior to the return date. NY R BRONX E FIL R Doc. 1(1).

b. *KINGS COUNTY: Time and place of filing.* Motion papers must be filed with the E-file/Motion Support Office located in Room 227. . . at 360 Adams Street at least five (5) business days before the return date of the motion. NY R L KINGS Pt. A, Papers. Hard copies are required to be filed for any motions, answering papers, stipulations, etc. for E-Filed cases returnable in [the Central Compliance Part] at least five (5) days before return date for main motions. NY R L KINGS Pt. E, Rule 8. The moving documents must be e-filed no later than eight (8) days prior to the return date. NY R L KINGS E FIL Doc. 1(D).

4. *NEW YORK COUNTY: Briefing schedule.* Once a motion is made, counsel for all parties are strongly encouraged to agree upon a briefing schedule and submit a stipulation of adjournment reflecting that schedule using service or a clerk. Where a briefing schedule has not been agreed upon, the movant can avoid the need to attend simply to see if anyone will hand up opposing papers by demanding papers as provided by NY CPLR Rule 2214(b). To protect movants against the submission of late opposition papers or cross-motions, the General Clerk's Office will screen motions in which such papers are submitted without a response (reply or opposition respectively) to ensure that proper time to respond has been afforded and it will sua sponte adjourn for one (1) week cases in which such time has not been given. NY R NY CTY Procedure II(C).

5. *QUEENS COUNTY: Time to pay fees.* As motions and petitions are time sensitive, if opting to pay at the County Clerk's Office payment MUST be made, if filed with an RJI, a minimum of nine (9) business days prior to the application's return date and if filed post RJI, a minimum of nine (9) business days prior to the application's return date. NY R L QUEENS E-FILE Doc. 1(H)(1).

6. *Computation of time*

a. *Units of time*

i. *Day.* A calendar day includes the time from midnight to midnight. Sunday or any day of the week specifically mentioned means a calendar day. NY GEN CONSTR § 19.

ii. *Month.* In a statute, contract or public or private instrument, unless otherwise provided in such contract or instrument or by law, the term month means a calendar month and not a lunar month. NY GEN CONSTR § 31.

iii. *Year.* For information on the definition of a year, including the definitions of a half-year and quarter-year, refer to NY GEN CONSTR § 58 and NY GEN CONSTR § 50. For information on leap years, refer to NY GEN CONSTR § 57.

b. *Periods of time*

i. *Number of days.* A number of days specified as a period from a certain day within which or after or before which an act is authorized or required to be done means such number of calendar days exclusive of the calendar day from which the reckoning is made. NY GEN CONSTR § 20.

- If such period is a period of two (2) days, Saturday, Sunday or a public holiday must be excluded from the reckoning if it is an intervening day between the day from which the reckoning is made and the last day of the period. NY GEN CONSTR § 20.
- In computing any specified period of time from a specified event, the day upon which the event happens is deemed the day from which the reckoning is made. The day from which any specified period of time is reckoned shall be excluded in making the reckoning. NY GEN CONSTR § 20.

ii. *Number of months.* A number of months after or before a certain day shall be computed by counting such number of calendar months from such day, exclusive of the calendar month in which such day occurs, and shall include the day of the month in the last month so counted having the same numerical order in days of the month as the day from which the computation is made, unless there be not so many days in the last month so counted, in which case the period computed shall expire with the last day of the month so counted. NY GEN CONSTR § 30.

iii. *Publication of notice; Number of days.* The period of publication of a legal notice shall be computed by excluding the first day of publication and including the day on which the act or event of which notice is given is to take place or which completes the full period of publication. NY CPLR § 2402.

iv. *Periods ending on Saturday, Sunday or public holiday.* When any period of time, computed from a certain day, within which or after which or before which an act is authorized or required to be done, ends on a Saturday, Sunday or a public holiday, such act may be done on the next succeeding business day and if the period ends at a specified hour, such act may be done at or before the same hour of such next succeeding business day, except that where a period of time specified by contract ends on a Saturday, Sunday or a public holiday, the extension of such period is governed by NY GEN CONSTR § 25. NY GEN CONSTR § 25-a(1).

- For a list of public holidays, refer to NY GEN CONSTR § 24.

v. *Additional time after certain kinds of service*

- *Service by mail.* Where a period of time prescribed by law is measured from the service of a paper and service is by mail, five (5) days shall be added to the prescribed period. NY CPLR Rule 2103(b)(2).
- *Service by overnight delivery service.* Where a period of time prescribed by law is measured from the service of a paper and service is by overnight delivery, one (1) business day shall be added to the prescribed period. NY CPLR Rule 2103(b)(6).

vi. *Daylight saving time.* For information on New York's time zone and the effect of daylight saving time, refer to NY GEN CONSTR § 52.

c. *Hours of court.* Notwithstanding any provision of law or rule of court to the contrary, throughout the State of New York the sessions of the Supreme Court for the disposition of business before the court shall commence not later than 9:30 a.m. and conclude not earlier than 5 p.m. Where warranted, the Chief Administrator of the Courts may authorize variances in the opening and closing hours of the courts, but, in such event, daily sessions shall total not less than six (6) hours. NY R CHIEF J § 3.1.

d. *Time limits; Extension of time.* Any act required by or in pursuance of law to be performed at or within a prescribed time, shall be performed according to the standard time. NY GEN CONSTR § 53.

i. Except where otherwise expressly prescribed by law, the court may extend the time fixed by any statute, rule or order for doing any act, upon such terms as may be just and upon good cause shown, whether the application for extension is made before or after the expiration of the time fixed. NY CPLR § 2004. Refer to the New York KeyRules Motion for Continuance/Extension of Time document for more information.

C. General Requirements

1. *Motions, generally.* There shall be compliance with the procedures prescribed in the CPLR for the bringing of motions. NY R UNIF TRIAL CTS § 202.7(a).

a. *Motions on notice.* A notice of motion shall specify the time and place of the hearing on the motion, the supporting papers upon which the motion is based, the relief demanded and the grounds therefor. NY CPLR Rule 2214(a). A motion on notice in an action in the supreme court shall be noticed to be heard in the judicial district where the action is triable or in a county adjoining the county where the action is triable. Unless statute, civil practice rule or local court rule provides otherwise, the motion shall be noticed to be heard before a motion term or, upon order to show cause granted by a justice, before that justice out of court. NY CPLR § 2212(a). Except as provided in NY R UNIF TRIAL CTS § 202.7(d), no motion shall be filed with the court unless there have been served and filed with the motion papers a notice of motion. NY R UNIF TRIAL CTS § 202.7(a)(1).

b. *Ex parte motions.* A motion in an action in the supreme court that may be made without notice may be made at a motion term or to a justice out of court in any county in the state. NY CPLR § 2212(b).
   i. *KINGS COUNTY.* For more information on submitting a motion ex parte, refer to NY R L KINGS E FIL Doc. 1(G).
   ii. *NEW YORK COUNTY.* For more information on submitting matters ex parte, refer to NY R NY CTY Procedure III and NY R NY CTY E FIL Doc. 2(G).
   iii. *QUEENS COUNTY.* For more information on submitting matters ex parte, refer to NY R L QUEENS EX PARTE Doc. 1.

c. *Alternative relief.* Relief in the alternative or of several different types may be demanded. NY CPLR Rule 2214(a). The types of relief need not be related. In one motion, for example, the defendant can seek to dismiss the plaintiff's claim for lack of jurisdiction, to get an extension of time to answer, to require the plaintiff to join X as a party, and to quash a disclosure subpoena served in behalf of the plaintiff on a nonparty witness. So doing, the movant must of course specify all of these items of relief in the notice of motion, and the grounds for them, and the supporting papers must contain the entire proof requisite to the items of relief sought. NY CPLR Rule 2214(Practice Commentary, C2214:4).

d. *General relief.* It is common practice to include at the end of the relief request in the notice of motion a so-called "general relief" clause. This is merely a few words to cover the possibility that the relief appropriate to what the movant proves was not specifically asked for, but is close enough to enable the court to grant it. After stating the specific relief desired, the lawyer will often add something like: and for such other, further, or different relief as this court may deem just and proper. NY CPLR Rule 2214(Practice Commentary, C2214:5).

e. *Motion in improper form.* If the court finds it appropriate in the interests of justice, it may convert a motion into a special proceeding, or vice-versa, upon such terms as may be just, including the payment of fees and costs. NY CPLR § 103(c).

f. *Order to show cause.* An order to show cause is basically only a substitute for a notice of motion. An ordinary notice of motion merely notifies the recipient that a motion is being made for specified relief. The burden of proof is on the movant. Although in most cases it is just as innocent as an ordinary notice of motion, the order to show cause gets its name by directing the recipient to "show cause" why the particular relief being asked for should not be granted. It sounds as if the burden of proof is being shifted to the recipient. It isn't. It specifies the time and place of the hearing on the application but when the hearing comes on, the burden of proof is where it always is on a motion: on the movant. SIEGEL-NYPRAC § 248.
   i. The CPLR says nothing more about an order to show cause than that it may be used "in a proper case", which leaves it entirely to the judge's discretion to determine what a proper case is. Any fact suggesting a problem as to any of the items listed above would be sufficient to invoke judicial discretion and justify the show cause procedure, which is in fact liberally used. SIEGEL-NYPRAC § 248.
   ii. An order to show cause against a state body or officers must be served in addition to service upon the defendant or respondent state body or officers upon the attorney general by delivery to an assistant attorney general at an office of the attorney general in the county in which venue of the action is designated or if there is no office of the attorney general in such county, at the office of the attorney general nearest such county. NY CPLR Rule 2214(d).
   iii. *BRONX COUNTY.* For information on submitting an order to show cause, refer to NY R BRONX E FIL R Doc. 2 and NY R BRONX LEG SUP Doc. 1.
   iv. *ERIE COUNTY.* For information on submitting an order to show cause, refer to NY R ERIE E FIL Doc. 3(VI).
   v. *KINGS COUNTY.* For information on submitting an order to show cause, refer to NY R L KINGS E FIL Doc. 1(F).
   vi. *NEW YORK COUNTY.* For information on submitting an order to show cause, refer to NY R NY CTY E FIL Doc. 2(F).
   vii. *ONONDAGA COUNTY.* For information on submitting an order to show cause, refer to NY R ONDGA E FIL Protocol(B)(10) and NY R ONDGA E FIL Protocol(J).

g. *Motions before preliminary conference.* Motions in actions to which NY R UNIF TRIAL CTS § 202.12 is applicable made after the preliminary conference has been scheduled may be denied unless there is shown good cause why such relief is warranted before the preliminary conference is held. NY R UNIF TRIAL CTS § 202.12(h).

h. *ALBANY COUNTY: Good faith effort to resolve.* Prior to the submission of a notice of motion relating to disclosure or a bill of particulars, the parties must make a good faith effort to resolve the matter in question and submit an affirmation attesting to this good faith effort. NY R 3 JD SUP Doc. 1(B).

i. *NEW YORK COUNTY: Documents with motions.* Counsel must attach to motion papers copies of all pleadings and other documents as required by the CPLR and as necessary for an informed decision on the motion. Documents in a foreign language shall be properly translated. NY R NY CTY J RUL Rule 14(a).

j. *NEW YORK COUNTY: Motions in multiple cases made together.* On occasion, attorneys may wish to make a motion in more than one case on a single set of papers. In such cases, by definition consolidation will not have been directed since consolidation signifies the combination of more than one case into a single one with a single caption and index number and ending in a single judgment. NY R NY CTY Procedure II(B). For more information on motions made with the same papers, refer to NY R NY CTY Procedure II(A).

k. *QUEENS COUNTY: Motion sequence numbers.* A motion sequence number is required for all E-filed motions. After a motion is E-filed, please consult the e-courts website within twenty-four (24) to forty-eight (48) hours to obtain the sequence number. The Confirmation Notice of E-filing MUST indicate the sequence number of any motion submitted at the Centralized Motion Part calendar call. NY R L QUEENS E-FILE Doc. 1(H)(5).

2. *Sanctions, generally.* The court may award costs or impose sanctions or both only upon a written decision setting forth the conduct on which the award or imposition is based, the reasons why the court found the conduct to be frivolous, and the reasons why the court found the amount awarded or imposed to be appropriate. An award of costs or the imposition of sanctions or both shall be entered as a judgment of the court. In no event shall the amount of sanctions imposed exceed ten thousand dollars ($10,000) for any single occurrence of frivolous conduct. NY R CHIEF ADMIN § 130-1.2; NY R CHIEF ADMIN § 130-2.2.

3. *Sanctions for frivolous conduct in civil litigation.* The court, in its discretion, may award to any party or attorney in any civil action or proceeding before the court, except where prohibited by law, costs in the form of reimbursement for actual expenses reasonably incurred and reasonable attorney's fees, resulting from frivolous conduct as defined in Part 130 of the Rules of the Chief Administrator of the Courts (NY R CHIEF ADMIN § 130-1.1, et seq.). NY R CHIEF ADMIN § 130-1.1(a).

a. *Nature of sanctions; Sanctions against attorney.* The court, as appropriate, may make such award of costs or impose such financial sanctions against either an attorney or a party to the litigation or against both. Where the award or sanction is against an attorney, it may be against the attorney personally or upon a partnership, firm, corporation, government agency, prosecutor's office, legal aid society or public defender's office with which the attorney is associated and that has appeared as attorney of record. The award or sanctions may be imposed upon any attorney appearing in the action or upon a partnership, firm or corporation with which the attorney is associated. NY R CHIEF ADMIN § 130-1.1(b).

b. *Sanctions above and beyond costs.* In addition to or in lieu of awarding costs, the court, in its discretion may impose financial sanctions upon any party or attorney in a civil action or proceeding who engages in frivolous conduct as defined in NY R CHIEF ADMIN § 130-1.1, et seq., which shall be payable as provided in NY R CHIEF ADMIN § 130-1.3. NY R CHIEF ADMIN § 130-1.1(a).

c. *Frivolous conduct defined.* For purposes of NY R CHIEF ADMIN § 130-1.1, et seq., conduct is frivolous if:

i. It is completely without merit in law and cannot be supported by a reasonable argument for an extension, modification or reversal of existing law;

ii. It is undertaken primarily to delay or prolong the resolution of the litigation, or to harass or maliciously injure another; or

iii. It asserts material factual statements that are false. NY R CHIEF ADMIN § 130-1.1(c).

iv. Frivolous conduct shall include the making of a frivolous motion for costs or sanctions under NY R CHIEF ADMIN § 130-1.1. In determining whether the conduct undertaken was frivolous, the court shall consider, among other issues,

- The circumstances under which the conduct took place, including the time available for investigating the legal or factual basis of the conduct; and
- Whether or not the conduct was continued when its lack of legal or factual basis was apparent, should have been apparent, or was brought to the attention of counsel or the party. NY R CHIEF ADMIN § 130-1.1(c).

v. It has been held frivolous, and made the subject of a sanction, to take evasive steps to try to avoid the judge who has been assigned to the case. SIEGEL-NYPRAC § 414A; Int'l 800 Telecom Corp. v. Kramer, Levin, Nessen, Kamin & Frankel, 155 Misc. 2d 975, 979, 591 N.Y.S.2d 313, 317 (Sup. Ct. 1992).

d. *Malicious claims.* If the motive for interposing a claim is found to be malicious, the claimant has been held subject to the sanction of NY R CHIEF ADMIN § 130-1.1 even if the claim is found to have some colorable basis. SIEGEL-NYPRAC § 414A; Gordon v. Marrone, 202 A.D.2d 104, 109, 616 N.Y.S.2d 98, 101 (1994).

e. *Hearing required for imposition of sanctions.* An award of costs or the imposition of sanctions may be made either upon motion in compliance with NY CPLR Rule 2214 or NY CPLR Rule 2215 or upon the court's own initiative, after a reasonable opportunity to be heard. The form of the hearing shall depend upon the nature of the conduct and the circumstances of the case. NY R CHIEF ADMIN § 130-1.1(d).

i. It has been held that a request for sanctions may not be asserted as a separate claim. SIEGEL-NYPRAC § 414A.

ii. Presumably the court can order an immediate hearing on a costs or sanctions application, suspending further attention to the merits of the case while the hearing goes forward, or postpone it to some later point, perhaps depending on what the allegedly frivolous conduct affected (the whole case? just a defense? some incidental step like a motion? etc.). SIEGEL-NYPRAC § 414A.

iii. A discussion of what kind of hearing is required appears in Bruckner v. Jaitor Apartments Co., 147 Misc. 2d 796, 555 N.Y.S.2d 563 (Civ. Ct. 1990), where the court said that if a motion is made for sanctions, the return day of the motion is the hearing. SIEGEL-NYPRAC § 414A; Bruckner v. Jaitor Apartments Co., 147 Misc. 2d 796, 798, 555 N.Y.S.2d 563, 564 (Civ. Ct. 1990). Reviewing earlier cases, the court also noted that when the offense occurs right in front of the judge, no further hearing is necessary. SIEGEL-NYPRAC § 414A.

iv. Refer to the Hearings section of this document for more information on the hearing.

f. *Inapplicable to requests under NY CPLR § 8303-a.* NY R CHIEF ADMIN § 130-1.1 shall not apply to requests for costs or attorneys' fees subject to the provisions of NY CPLR § 8303-a. NY R CHIEF ADMIN § 130-1.5.

g. *Award of sanctions.* The court may award costs or impose sanctions or both only upon a written decision setting forth the conduct on which the award or imposition is based, the reasons why the court found the conduct to be frivolous, and the reasons why the court found the amount awarded or imposed to be appropriate. An award of costs or the imposition of sanctions or both shall be entered as a judgment of the court. In no event shall the amount of sanctions imposed exceed ten thousand dollars ($10,000) for any single occurrence of frivolous conduct. NY R CHIEF ADMIN § 130-1.2.

4. *Costs upon frivolous claims and counterclaims in actions to recover damages for personal injury, injury to property or wrongful death*

a. *Frivolous claim against victim of crime.* If in an action to recover damages for personal injury, injury to property or wrongful death, or an action brought by the individual who committed a crime against the victim of the crime, and such action or claim is commenced or continued by a plaintiff or a counterclaim, defense or cross claim is commenced or continued by a defendant and is found, at any time during the proceedings or upon judgment, to be frivolous by the court, the court shall award to the successful party costs and reasonable attorney's fees not exceeding ten thousand dollars ($10,000). NY CPLR § 8303-a(a).

b. *Nature of sanctions.* The costs and fees awarded under NY CPLR § 8303-a(a) shall be assessed either against the party bringing the action, claim, cross claim, defense or counterclaim or against the attorney for such party, or against both, as may be determined by the court, based upon the circumstances of the case. Such costs and fees shall be in addition to any other judgment awarded to the successful party. NY CPLR § 8303-a(b).

c. *Finding of frivolousness.* In order to find the action, claim, counterclaim, defense or cross claim to be frivolous under NY CPLR § 8303-a(a), the court must find one or more of the following:

i. The action, claim, counterclaim, defense or cross claim was commenced, used or continued in bad faith, solely to delay or prolong the resolution of the litigation or to harass or maliciously injure another;

ii. The action, claim, counterclaim, defense or cross claim was commenced or continued in bad faith without any reasonable basis in law or fact and could not be supported by a good faith argument for an extension, modification or reversal of existing law. If the action, claim, counterclaim, defense or cross claim was promptly discontinued when the party or the attorney learned or should have learned that the action, claim, counterclaim, defense or cross claim lacked such a reasonable basis, the court may find that the party or the attorney did not act in bad faith. NY CPLR § 8303-a(c).

5. *Sanctions for failure to appear.* Notwithstanding and in addition to the provisions of NY R CHIEF ADMIN § 130-1.1-a,

et seq., the court, in its discretion, may impose financial sanctions or, in addition to or in lieu of imposing sanctions, may award costs in the form of reimbursement for actual expenses reasonably incurred and reasonable attorney's fees, upon any attorney who, without good cause, fails to appear at a time and place scheduled for an action or proceeding to be heard before a designated court. NY R CHIEF ADMIN § 130-2.1, et seq. shall not apply to town or village courts or to proceedings in a small claims part of any court. NY R CHIEF ADMIN § 130-2.1(a).

a. *Determination of good cause for failure to appear or attend.* In determining whether an attorney's failure to appear at a scheduled court appearance was without good cause and in determining the measure of sanctions or costs to be imposed, the court shall consider all of the attendant circumstances, including but not limited to:
   i. The explanation, if any, offered by the attorney for his or her nonappearance;
   ii. The adequacy of the notice to the attorney of the time and date of the scheduled appearance;
   iii. Whether the attorney notified the court and opposing counsel in advance that he or she would be unable to appear;
   iv. Whether substitute counsel appeared in court at the time previously scheduled to proffer an explanation of the attorney's nonappearance and whether such substitute counsel was prepared to go forward with the case;
   v. Whether an affidavit or affirmation of actual engagement was filed in the manner prescribed in NY R CHIEF ADMIN § 125.1;
   vi. Whether the attorney on prior occasions in the same action or proceeding failed to appear at a scheduled court action or proceeding;
   vii. Whether financial sanctions or costs have been imposed upon the attorney pursuant to NY R CHIEF ADMIN § 130-2.1 in some other action or proceeding; and
   viii. The extent and nature of the harm caused by the attorney's failure to appear. NY R CHIEF ADMIN § 130-2.1(b).

b. *Nature of sanctions.* The court, as appropriate, may impose any such financial sanctions or award costs upon an attorney personally or upon a partnership, firm, corporation, government agency, prosecutor's office, legal aid society or public defender's office with which the attorney is associated and that has appeared as attorney of record. NY R CHIEF ADMIN § 130-2.1(c).

c. *Nature of hearing on sanctions.* The imposition of sanctions or award of costs may be made either upon motion or upon the court's own initiative, after a reasonable opportunity to be heard. The form of the hearing shall depend upon the nature of the attorney's failure to appear and the totality of the circumstances of the case. NY R CHIEF ADMIN § 130-2.1(d).

6. *Sanctions in connection with default.* Before NY R CHIEF ADMIN § 130-1.1 and NY CPLR § 8303-a, the most common and most visible source of an award of attorney's fees seen in New York practice was the penalty imposed against a party as a condition for getting out from under a default. SIEGEL-NYPRAC § 414A; SIEGEL-NYPRAC § 414.

   a. The situation there is that a party has been guilty of so serious a default that the court, on motion of the other side, has clear power to make the default stick. Doing so, however, exacts a forfeiture of the party's claim or defense and is often viewed by the judges as too severe, a draconian requisition that penalizes the client for what is most often the fault of the lawyer. The judicial predilection in this category has therefore been to excuse the default, but only on the condition that the defaulter's lawyer pay the other side (or some worthy outside source like the Lawyers' Fund for Client Protection) a sum of money commensurate with the defaulter's delay and his proffered excuse. SIEGEL-NYPRAC § 414A; McLoughlin v. Henke, 130 Misc. 2d 1091, 1094, 499 N.Y.S.2d 332, 334 (Sup. Ct. 1986). The court may require the lawyer to pay this out of pocket, not to be reimbursed by the client, or may allot it between client and lawyer. SIEGEL-NYPRAC § 414A.

   b. Pleading defaults have been the most common illustration of this, but they are not the only ones. Defaults in connection with a bill of particulars, disclosure, a failure to prosecute, and calendar calls are other examples. SIEGEL-NYPRAC § 414A; SIEGEL-NYPRAC § 231; SIEGEL-NYPRAC § 241; SIEGEL-NYPRAC § 367; SIEGEL-NYPRAC § 375; SIEGEL-NYPRAC § 376.

7. *Oppositions.* In the absence of statutory provision or court rule, a motion ordinarily does not require a written answer, although an adverse party may be permitted to file an answer in opposition to the showing made in the motion or its supporting affidavits. AMJUR MOTIONS § 26. When a party files a motion and the opposing party fails to respond, the court may construe such failure to respond as non-opposition to the motion or an admission that the motion was meritorious, may take the facts alleged in the motion as true, and may grant the motion if the relief requested appears to be justified. However, the severity of such a result demands that a court impose it only with great caution. AMJUR MOTIONS § 28.

8. *Governing law.* The civil practice law and rules (NY CPLR § 101, et seq.) shall govern the procedure in civil judicial proceedings in all courts of the state and before all judges, except where the procedure is regulated by inconsistent statute. The civil practice law and rules shall succeed the civil practice act and rules of civil practice and shall be deemed substituted therefor throughout the statutes and rules of the state. NY CPLR § 101. The civil practice law and rules shall be liberally construed to secure the just, speedy and inexpensive determination of every civil judicial proceeding. NY CPLR § 104.
   a. *Uniform trial court rules.* The uniform civil rules for the Supreme Court and County Court (NY R UNIF TRIAL CTS § 202.1, et seq.) shall be applicable to civil actions and proceedings in the Supreme Court and the County Court. NY R UNIF TRIAL CTS § 202.1(a). The provisions of the uniform rules shall be construed consistent with the Civil Practice Law and Rules (CPLR), and matters not covered by the uniform rules shall be governed by the CPLR. NY R UNIF TRIAL CTS § 202.1(d).
   b. *Local rules.* Local court rules, not inconsistent with law or with uniform civil rules for the Supreme Court and County Court (NY R UNIF TRIAL CTS § 202.1, et seq.), shall comply with Part 9 of the Rules of the Chief Judge (NY R CHIEF J § 9.1). NY R UNIF TRIAL CTS § 202.1(c).
   c. *Official forms.* The state administrator shall have the power to adopt, amend and rescind an appendix of forms. Forms adopted pursuant to NY CPLR § 107 shall be sufficient under the civil practice law and rules and shall illustrate the simplicity and brevity of statement which the civil practice law and rules contemplate. NY CPLR § 107.
9. *Rules of the commercial division.* [Editor's note: certain types of civil cases or civil cases meeting certain monetary thresholds that are filed in the state of New York must be filed in the Commercial Division of the New York Supreme Courts. Rules governing practice in the commercial division are found in NY R UNIF TRIAL CTS § 202.70]. Cases which must be filed in the commercial division are listed below. For more information, refer to NY R UNIF TRIAL CTS § 202.70.
   a. *Monetary thresholds.* Except as set forth in NY R UNIF TRIAL CTS § 202.70(b), the monetary thresholds of the Commercial Division, exclusive of punitive damages, interests, costs, disbursements and counsel fees claimed, are established as follows: (1) Albany County, fifty thousand dollars ($50,000); (2) Eighth Judicial District, one hundred thousand dollars ($100,000); (3) Kings County, one hundred fifty thousand dollars ($150,000); (4) Nassau County, two hundred thousand dollars ($200,000); (5) New York County, five hundred thousand dollars ($500,000); (6) Onondaga County, fifty thousand dollars ($50,000); (7) Queens County, one hundred thousand dollars ($100,000); (8) Seventh Judicial District, fifty thousand dollars ($50,000); (9) Suffolk County, one hundred thousand dollars ($100,000); and (10) Westchester County, one hundred thousand dollars ($100,000). NY R UNIF TRIAL CTS § 202.70(a).
      i. *ALBANY COUNTY.* The Commercial Division of the Albany County Supreme Court exercises jurisdiction over selected business and commercial disputes in which the amount at issue generally involves damage claims in a minimum amount of fifty thousand dollars ($50,000) as well as claims for unspecified amounts where the value of the commercial asset(s) in dispute exceeds fifty thousand dollars ($50,000). A separate publication promulgating the rules and criteria relating to the filing and management of Commercial Court cases in this part may be obtained from the Albany County Supreme Court Clerk's Office. A section of the Uniform Civil Rules for the Supreme Court and County Court sets forth statewide rules. NY R 3 JD SUP Doc. 1(E).
      ii. *BRONX COUNTY.* The monetary threshold for commercial cases in Bronx County will be seventy-five thousand dollars ($75,000). All other parameters including the type of matters that will be heard are contained within the Rules of the Commercial Division of the Supreme Court (NY R UNIF TRIAL CTS § 202.70). NY R BRONX FIL R Doc. 12.
      iii. *NEW YORK COUNTY.* The monetary threshold in the New York County Commercial Division, which is generally applicable, is an amount in controversy of five hundred thousand dollars ($500,000) or more (exclusive of punitive damages, interest, costs, disbursements, and counsel fees). If the case is designated a commercial one and the Addendum is submitted, the clerk will review the pleadings to determine whether the amount in controversy in the case meets the monetary threshold or whether an exception to the threshold applies. NY R NY CTY Procedure IA(B). For more information on assigning a case to the commercial division in New York County, refer to NY R NY CTY Procedure IA(B).
   b. *Commercial cases.* Actions in which the principal claims involve or consist of the following will be heard in the Commercial Division provided that the monetary threshold is met or equitable or declaratory relief is sought:
      i. Breach of contract or fiduciary duty, fraud, misrepresentation, business tort (e.g., unfair competition), or statutory and/or common law violation where the breach or violation is alleged to arise out of business dealings (e.g., sales of assets or securities; corporate restructuring; partnership, shareholder, joint venture, and other

business agreements; trade secrets; restrictive covenants; and employment agreements not including claims that principally involve alleged discriminatory practices);

ii. Transactions governed by the Uniform Commercial Code (exclusive of those concerning individual cooperative or condominium units);

iii. Transactions involving commercial real property, including Yellowstone injunctions and excluding actions for the payment of rent only;

iv. Shareholder derivative actions—without consideration of the monetary threshold;

v. Commercial class actions—without consideration of the monetary threshold;

vi. Business transactions involving or arising out of dealings with commercial banks and other financial institutions;

vii. Internal affairs of business organizations;

viii. Malpractice by accountants or actuaries, and legal malpractice arising out of representation in commercial matters;

ix. Environmental insurance coverage;

x. Commercial insurance coverage (e.g., directors and officers, errors and omissions, and business interruption coverage);

xi. Dissolution of corporations, partnerships, limited liability companies, limited liability partnerships and joint ventures—without consideration of the monetary threshold; and

xii. Applications to stay or compel arbitration and affirm or disaffirm arbitration awards and related injunctive relief pursuant to Article 75 of the New York Civil Practice Law and Rules (NY CPLR § 7501, et seq.) involving any of the foregoing enumerated commercial issues. Where the applicable arbitration agreement provides for the arbitration to be heard outside the United States, the monetary threshold set forth in NY R UNIF TRIAL CTS § 202.70(a) shall not apply. NY R UNIF TRIAL CTS § 202.70(b).

c. *Non-commercial cases.* The following will not be heard in the Commercial Division even if the monetary threshold is met:

i. Suits to collect professional fees;

ii. Cases seeking a declaratory judgment as to insurance coverage for personal injury or property damage;

iii. Residential real estate disputes, including landlord-tenant matters, and commercial real estate disputes involving the payment of rent only;

iv. Home improvement contracts involving residential properties consisting of one to four residential units or individual units in any residential building, including cooperative or condominium units;

v. Proceedings to enforce a judgment regardless of the nature of the underlying case;

vi. First-party insurance claims and actions by insurers to collect premiums or rescind non-commercial policies; and

vii. Attorney malpractice actions except as otherwise provided in NY R UNIF TRIAL CTS § 202.70(b)(8). NY R UNIF TRIAL CTS § 202.70(c).

d. For more information on the Commercial Division, refer to NY R UNIF TRIAL CTS § 202.70.

D. Documents

1. *Documents for moving party*

a. ***Required documents***

i. *Notice of motion, order to show cause, or affidavit on ex parte motion.* The notice of motion shall be substantially in the form found in NY R UNIF TRIAL CTS § 202.7(b). NY R UNIF TRIAL CTS § 202.7(b). The supporting papers should be referred to in the notice of motion. SIEGEL-NYPRAC § 246. The court in a proper case may grant an order to show cause, to be served in lieu of a notice of motion. NY CPLR Rule 2214(d). An ex parte motion shall be accompanied by an affidavit stating the result of any prior motion for similar relief and specifying the new facts, if any, that were not previously shown. NY CPLR Rule 2217(b).

- *Request for oral argument.* A party requesting oral argument shall set forth such request in its notice of motion or in its order to show cause or on the first page of the answering papers, as the case may be. Where all parties to a motion request oral argument, oral argument shall be granted unless the court shall determine it to be unnecessary. Where a motion is brought on by order to show cause, the court may set forth in the order that oral argument is required on the return date of the motion. NY R UNIF TRIAL CTS § 202.8(d).

ii. *Motion.* Refer to the General Requirements section of this document for information on the notice of motion and motion.

iii. *Request for judicial intervention.* At any time after service of process, a party may file a request for judicial intervention. Except as provided in NY R UNIF TRIAL CTS § 202.6(b), in an action not yet assigned to a judge, the court shall not accept for filing a notice of motion, order to show cause, or application for ex parte order, unless such notice or application is accompanied by a request for judicial intervention. NY R UNIF TRIAL CTS § 202.6(a).

- *BRONX COUNTY.* Generally, the Request For Judicial Intervention, commonly referred to as an "RJI", is required to be filed in any action where the assignment of a Justice is required. The RJI sets forth the information which is entered into the court system's database. It must be completely and accurately filled out. The full caption, as stated on the Summons, must be set forth. Use of terms "et al." and "etc." are not permitted. Only one (1) RJI may be filed in each action. Either a self represented litigant or an attorney must sign the affirmation at the end of the form. Once completed, the RJI must be filed in duplicate. Except in the case of an ex-parte application, the RJI must also be served together with the accompanying application upon all parties. Proof of accuracy of the index number must accompany the RJI. Check the Fee Schedule[. . .]for any applicable filing fees. NY R BRONX FIL R Doc. 2.
- *KINGS COUNTY.* An RJI with the relevant required addendum in a NYSCEF case shall be submitted via NYSCEF. Once e-filed, the RJI and any accompanying document will be forwarded to the relevant support office for random assignment of the case and processing of the document. A filer or counsel need not appear (as to Proposed Orders to Show Cause, however, see below). A copy of the pleadings must be submitted only if the document has not previously been e-filed. If the RJI seeks intervention with regard to a document that is intended for review by a Justice, such as a motion, a working copy of the RJI must be submitted with the working copy of the motion and the NYSCEF Confirmation Notice. NY R L KINGS E FIL Doc. 1(C).
- *NEW YORK COUNTY.* To obtain the assignment of an IAS Justice to a case, a Request for Judicial Intervention (cost ninety-five dollars ($95)) must be filed, with NYSCEF in an e-filed case or in paper in an authorized hard-copy one. A no-fee RJI, which will generally result in the referral of an application to an Ex Parte Justice, is also required with regard to certain kinds of applications for which, prior to 2011, no RJI was required. NY R NY CTY Procedure I(C). A "fillable" form RJI is available on-line. The form must be filed in duplicate in hard-copy cases. NY R NY CTY Procedure IA(A)(1). The filer of an RJI must check off a box identifying the type of case at issue. Where the RJI seeks judicial assignment, this designation will bring about a random assignment of the case by computer to a Justice handling cases of that type. NY R NY CTY Procedure IA(A)(1). The RJI and any addendum can be completed and submitted electronically in an e-filed case. NY R NY CTY Procedure II(A). The RJI shall be marked to reflect the existence of any "related case" as explained on the "Commencement of Cases" page under "Case Processing" on the court's website. NY R NY CTY Procedure II(A); NY R NY CTY E FIL Doc. 2(C).
- *ONONDAGA COUNTY.* The RJI will be submitted via the NYSCEF system along with any required RJI addendum forms. When the RJI is filed and the fee paid online, the Onondaga County Clerk's Office will electronically forward the RJI and any accompanying documents to the Onondaga Supreme Court Clerk's Office for assignment and processing. Counsel will receive notification of judge assignment via the NYSCEF system. NY R ONDGA E FIL Protocol(B)(3).
- *QUEENS COUNTY.* A Request for Judicial Intervention ("RJI") in an E-filed case shall be submitted via the E-filing System. When the RJI is approved, filed and paid for on-line, it will be forwarded to the relevant back office for random assignment of the case and processing of the document. In the case of RJIs seeking assignment to the Commercial Division, the filer must submit therewith, a Commercial Addendum as required by the standards for assignment of cases to the Commercial Division. NY R L QUEENS E-FILE Doc. 1(F).

iv. *Proof of service.* In addition to complying with the provisions of NY CPLR Rule 2101, every paper filed in court shall have annexed thereto appropriate proof of service on all parties where required. NY R UNIF TRIAL CTS § 202.5(a).

- *QUEENS COUNTY.* With regard to service of a motion/petition on notice in an E-filed action, NY CPLR

Rule 2214(b) and NY R UNIF TRIAL CTS § 202.5-b(f) applies. Where required, proof of service shall be filed on-line as a separate document. NY R L QUEENS E-FILE Doc. 1(H)(3).

v. *ALBANY COUNTY: Additional required documents*

- *Affirmation of good faith effort.* The parties must[. . .]submit an affirmation attesting to [their good faith effort to resolve the matter]. The affirmation of good faith effort to resolve the issues raised by the motion shall indicate the time, place and nature of the consultation and the issues discussed and any resolutions, or shall indicate good cause why no such conferral with counsel for opposing parties was held. An assigned justice or judge may dismiss a motion for failure to demonstrate that such effort was made with leave to renew the motion after such effort has been demonstrated. NY R 3 JD SUP Doc. 1(B).

b. *Supplemental documents*

i. *Supporting evidence; Exhibits.* The main supporting papers on a motion are affidavits, but any relevant exhibits, documents, depositions, etc., are also includible. SIEGEL-NYPRAC § 246.

- *Affidavits accompanying motion.* Affidavits shall be for a statement of the relevant facts. NY R UNIF TRIAL CTS § 202.8(c).
- *Foreign language documents.* Where an affidavit or exhibit annexed to a paper served or filed is in a foreign language, it shall be accompanied by an English translation and an affidavit by the translator stating his qualifications and that the translation is accurate. NY CPLR Rule 2101(b).
- *Statement of attorney in lieu of affidavit.* The statement of an attorney admitted to practice in the courts of the state, or of a physician, osteopath or dentist, authorized by law to practice in the state, who is not a party to an action, when subscribed and affirmed by him to be true under the penalties of perjury, may be served or filed in the action in lieu of and with the same force and effect as an affidavit. NY CPLR Rule 2106.
- *NEW YORK COUNTY: Form of presented exhibits.* Exhibits should be tabbed and be legible; a typed version of any exhibit that is difficult to read should be submitted with the original. Exhibits printed on both sides of the page should be bound and tabbed on the side. NY R NY CTY J RUL Rule 14(a).
- *QUEENS COUNTY.* Attorneys submitting exhibits to the court on E-file cases shall make each exhibit a separate, labeled attachment to an affidavit/affirmation. NY R L QUEENS E-FILE Doc. 1(H)(4).

ii. *Brief.* Briefs shall be for a statement of the relevant law. NY R UNIF TRIAL CTS § 202.8(c).

iii. *Notice to produce papers not in possession of the court.* If a paper relied on by the movant is in the possession of the other side, it may be demanded of that side with a notice to produce it at the hearing. Where such papers are in the possession of an adverse party, they shall be produced by him at the hearing on notice served with the motion papers. NY CPLR Rule 2214(Practice Commentary, C2214:23).

iv. *Filing fees.* The County Clerk shall require the payment of any applicable statutory fees, or an order of the Court waiving payment of such fees, before accepting a paper for filing. NY R UNIF TRIAL CTS § 202.5(d)(1). For information on filing fees, if any, refer to NY CPLR § 8001, et seq.

- *ALBANY COUNTY.* In general, any filing subsequent to the commencement of an action which is designated as a motion or cross-motion requires the payment of a filing fee to the County Clerk's Office prior to submission to the Supreme Court Clerk's Office for referral to the assigned justice. The fee is assessed regardless of whether an application is made by notice of motion, order to show cause or ex parte. No fee will be charged upon the filing of a motion for poor person status in conjunction with an application which serves to commence an action or special proceeding. In the event a motion is received by the court unaccompanied by proof of payment to the County Clerk, the Supreme Court Clerk's Office will contact the submitting party to advise that the application will be held pending receipt of the filing fee only until the return date of the motion. If proof of payment is not submitted to the Supreme Court Clerk's Office by the return date (ex parte applications will be held ten (10) days), the papers will be returned by mail with a notification that the motion has been removed from the court's calendar and that it must be re-noticed and re-filed with the court along with the requisite filing fee. Inquiries concerning the applicability of the motion fee to a proposed filing may be directed to the Supreme Court Clerk's Office. NY R 3 JD SUP Doc. 1(B).
- *BRONX COUNTY.* In accordance with the new civil fee schedule set forth in Article 80 of the C.P.L.R. (NY CPLR § 8001, et seq.), effective July 14, 2003, all motions, and cross motions must be approved in Room 217 prior to payment of said fees in the County Clerk's Office, Room 118. NY R BRONX FIL R Doc. 8. The motion fee [must be] paid for via NYSCEF by credit/debit card. NY R BRONX E FIL R Doc. 1(1).

- *ERIE COUNTY.* Payment for fee-bearing NYSCEF documents must be made online via credit or debit card (American Express, MasterCard or Visa) at the time of submission. NY R ERIE E FIL Doc. 3(III)(E).
- *KINGS COUNTY.* The motion must be filed with NYSCEF and the motion fee paid. NY R L KINGS E FIL Doc. 1(D). Court fees in NYSCEF cases must be paid via NYSCEF by a credit or bank card (MasterCard, Visa, or American Express). Fees are no longer accepted in person in the Kings County Clerk's Office in NYSCEF cases. NY R L KINGS E FIL Doc. 1(B)(6).
- *NEW YORK COUNTY.* A motion fee must be paid on motions made in writing by notice of motion, order to show cause or ex parte after the commencement of an action. For this purpose, the term "action" shall mean any application to the court that requires the assignment of an index number, regardless of whether a formal pleading is filed. Applications or motions that commence an action and for which an index number fee must be paid require no motion fee. [A]ny motions made after the initial applications in these situations would require payment of the motion fee. A motion that is the initial application in a case commenced by the filing of a summons and complaint would require a motion fee since the filing of the summons and complaint rather than the application itself would require the purchase of an index number. NY R NY CTY Procedure II(A). In e-filed cases the motion fee must be paid when the documents are filed. Payment is made on-line by Visa, Mastercard, or American Express credit or bank card. NY R NY CTY Procedure II(A); NY R NY CTY E FIL Doc. 2(B)(5).
- *ONONDAGA COUNTY.* Court fees in e-filed cases must be paid online with the NYSCEF system using a credit card. The document is not considered to have been filed until payment of the fee has been tendered. NY R ONDGA E FIL Protocol(B)(2). Fees must be paid on all cross motions. NY R ONDGA E FIL Protocol(B)(9)(e).
- *QUEENS COUNTY.* The Motion Support Office does not receive, forward or process any fees or waiver of fees. All applications requiring payment of statutory fees or waiver of fees must be sent directly to the Queens County Clerk's office. NY R L QUEENS MOT SUP Doc. 1. Court fees (e.g., RJI fee, motion fee) in E-filed cases may be paid for on-line using a credit card. Papers may also be filed with the E-file system and the fee may be paid at the County Clerk's Office. In the latter case, the paper is not considered to have been filed until payment of the fee has been tendered. NY R L QUEENS E-FILE Doc. 1(E)(1). The motion/petition shall be filed on-line and the fee paid for either on-line by credit card or by the "Pay at the County Clerk's Office" option. NY R L QUEENS E-FILE Doc. 1(H)(1).

v. *Working copies.* The court may require the parties to provide working copies of documents filed electronically. In such event, each working copy shall include, firmly affixed thereto, a copy of a confirmation notice in a form prescribed by the Chief Administrator. NY R UNIF TRIAL CTS § 202.5-b(d)(5).

- *BRONX COUNTY.* After papers on motions have been e-filed, working copies thereof, with Confirmation Notice firmly attached as the back page facing out, must be submitted. (Each document or group of documents that is separately bound shall bear a Confirmation Notice.) Working copies lacking the Notice will not be accepted. WORKING COPIES OF MOTION PAPERS MUST BE SUBMITTED NO LATER THAN 4:45 P.M. ON THE RETURN DATE IN THE MOTION SUPPORT OFFICE (ROOM 217) AS EXPLAINED in NY R BRONX E FIL R Doc. 1(4). If an attorney has failed to submit required working copies on or before the return date, the motion will be transmitted as is to the Justice for such action as the Justice finds appropriate. Attorneys may submit working copies on motions by mail or overnight delivery. Any such submission shall be sent in a timely manner to the Motion Support Office (Room 217) and be conspicuously marked on the outside "NYSCEF Matter"; lack of such marking may delay processing. NY R BRONX E FIL R Doc. 1(4)(a).
- *ERIE COUNTY.* Electronically filed documents subject to review and processing by the Part Clerk do not require a working copy unless otherwise directed or provided for in IAS Part Rules. NY R UNIF TRIAL CTS § 202.5-b(d)(4), any working copy submitted shall include, as a cover page firmly fastened thereto, a copy of the Confirmation Notice generated by the NYSCEF site at the time of filing. Please consult the individual Justice's Part Rules and/or consult with the Judge's chambers to determine whether and how working copies are to be provided. Working copies will not be printed or delivered by the Erie County Clerk or the Chief Clerk of the Courts or any of their personnel to chambers. The official record of a document in an electronically filed case is the document filed via the NYSCEF system. Working copies are intended only for use by the Justice. The Court will discard all working copies after the Justice has finished with them. Thus, in the event that counsel fails to file a document via the NYSCEF system, the document will not be part of the court record. NY R ERIE E FIL Doc. 3(III)(O); NY R ERIE E FIL Doc. 3(V)(E).

- *KINGS COUNTY.* No courtesy copies of motion papers are required by the Court, except as may be required for electronic filing or by the Judge's Part Rules. In tort cases against the City of New York, courtesy copies shall be supplied to the Corporation Counsel's office in Brooklyn. NY R L KINGS Pt. C, Rule 5. Unless otherwise directed by the Court or as described herein, and with the exceptions listed below, in all NYSCEF cases in which an RJI has been filed, working copies of e-filed documents that are intended for judicial review must be submitted to the court. Working copies are not required of documents that are only processed by a support office (e.g. preliminary conference request, note of issue). Working copies shall include exhibit tabs and backs; for motion papers, the motion sequence number and the return date and part. The confirmation notice with the motion sequence number on it should be the back page of the motion facing out. In addition, the filer of a working copy must firmly bind thereto, with the back page facing out, a copy of the Confirmation Notice that was generated by NYSCEF when that document was efiled. Working copies that are submitted without the related Confirmation Notice will not be accepted. NY R L KINGS E FIL Doc. 1(B)(7); NY R L KINGS E FIL Doc. 1(D). WORKING COPIES OF MOTION PAPERS MUST BE SUBMITTED IN THE MOTION SUPPORT OFFICE (ROOM 227) AS EXPLAINED HEREIN. THEY MUST NOT BE DELIVERED TO THE PART OR CHAMBERS, EXCEPT WHERE THE INDIVIDUAL JUSTICE'S PART RULES PROVIDE OTHERWISE; DOING SO WILL CAUSE ADMINISTRATIVE CONFUSION AND POSSIBLE MISPLACEMENT OF PAPERS. Any such submission shall be sent in a timely manner (kindly review individual Justice's rules) and be conspicuously marked on the outside "NYSCEF Matter;" lack of such marking may delay processing. NY R L KINGS E FIL Doc. 1(D).
- *NEW YORK COUNTY.* Some Justices require that working copies of e-filed motion papers be submitted. See the E-filing Protocol for information on the many Parts that do not require working copies. Where required, working copies of the moving documents and all other documents on the motion or application shall be submitted to the Motion Submission Part Courtroom (Room 130) on, but not before, the final return date. A Confirmation Notice from the NYSCEF system, which is generated when a document is e-filed, shall be firmly affixed, as the back page facing out, to each separate working copy or group of such copies. NY R NY CTY Procedure II(A) NY R NY CTY E FIL Doc. 2(B)(5)(a); NY R NY CTY J RUL Rule 14(a). For more information on working copies, including which parts don't require them, refer to NY R NY CTY E FIL Doc. 2(B)(6).
- *ONONDAGA COUNTY.* Any courtesy "working" copies, if required (see NY R ONDGA E FIL Protocol(B)(7)), must be provided directly to the assigned justice. NY R ONDGA E FIL Protocol(B)(9)(e). For information as to whether or not an Onondaga Supreme Court Justice requires working (courtesy) copies of e-filed documents, please consult the Onondaga County Individual E-filing Rules. NY R ONDGA E FIL Protocol(B)(7)(a). The Supreme Court Clerk's Office and the Onondaga County Clerk's Office will NOT accept the working copies. Working copies must be sent directly to the assigned justice's chambers. NY R ONDGA E FIL Protocol(B)(7)(b). A copy of the Confirmation Notice, generated by the NYSCEF system at the time a document is e-filed, must be attached to every working copy provided to chambers. If the Confirmation Notice is missing, the copy will not be accepted. NY R ONDGA E FIL Protocol(B)(7)(c). Courtesy copies do not become part of the official court record as maintained by the Onondaga County Clerk's Office and will be destroyed by chambers at the disposition of the case. In the event that counsel fails to file a document via NYSCEF, the document will not be part of the court record. NY R ONDGA E FIL Protocol(B)(7)(d).
- *QUEENS COUNTY.* Working copies of E-Filed notices of motion/notices of petition are NOT to be sent to the Motion Support Office. They must be brought to the calendar call in the judge's part. NY R L QUEENS MOT SUP Doc. 1. Unless otherwise directed or authorized by the court, counsel should file papers with the E-file system first and thereafter deliver a working copy to at the calendar call of the Centralized Motion Part or Assigned Justice in accordance with individual Part Rules. NY R L QUEENS E-FILE Doc. 1(E)(4). On the return date of a motion that has been E-filed, the movant must provide the Centralized Motion Part (CMP) with a working copy of the entire motion including the notice of motion with sequence number and all of the attached exhibits. The motion must have the confirmation of filing firmly affixed to the back of the papers (facing outward). The confirmation of filing is a separate notice from the payment notice and will say confirmation clearly across the top of the page. NY R L QUEENS E-FILE Doc. 1(H)(2)(a). The motion or Order to Show Cause must have clearly written across its face the words "Working Copy," it must also have the assigned Judge's name, motion sequence number and calendar number—which may be obtained from the posted calendar outside courtroom on the return date of the motion. A confirmation of filing must attached thereto. Working copies of e-filed Orders to Show Cause must contain a copy of the signed order

and all supporting papers. NY R L QUEENS E-FILE Doc. 1(H)(2)(c). The Confirmation Notice must be an updated version that indicates the sequence number of the motion being submitted at the CMP calendar call. WORKING COPIES WITHOUT A CONFIRMATION NOTICE WILL NOT BE ACCEPTED. NY R L QUEENS E-FILE Doc. 1(H)(7).

vi. *ERIE COUNTY: Additional supplemental documents*

- *Notice of hard copy submission in e-filed case.* In accordance with NY R UNIF TRIAL CTS § 202.5-b(d), the County Clerk shall refuse to accept for filing, hard copy papers filed to an action subject to electronic filing unless hard copy filing is permitted by the Uniform Rules or NY R ERIE E FIL Doc. 3 and the papers bear a completed Notice of Hard Copy Submission—E-Filed Case form. NY R ERIE E FIL Doc. 3(III)(D).

vii. *KINGS COUNTY: Additional supplemental documents*

- *Forms when filing in hard copy.* An attorney who certifies in good faith that he or she lacks the equipment or knowledge needed to e-file and have no staff member or employee under his or her direction who has such knowledge and equipment may opt out of participation in e-filing in a mandatory case by filing a "Notice of Opt-Out from Participation in Action Subject to Mandatory Electronic Filing" form EFM-2 with the Clerk. NY R L KINGS E FIL Doc. 1(A)(2). Where in accordance with the E-Filing Rules a party submits a document in hard copy in an e-filed case (principally, a document submitted by a nonparticipating party (e.g., an attorney) in a consensual case, an emergency filing made in accordance with the Mandatory E-Filing Rules, and any document filed with the court in hard copy by an attorney who has opted out of participation in mandatory e-filing, the document must bear the back page facing out, a "Notice of Hard Copy Submission—E-Filed Cases" form EFM-3. NY R L KINGS E FIL Doc. 1(B)(3).

viii. *NEW YORK COUNTY: Additional supplemental documents*

- *Notice of hard copy submission.* Where in accordance with the E-Filing Rules an attorney or an unrepresented litigant who is participating in e-filing submits a document in hard copy in an e-filed case, the document must bear, as the back page facing out, a Notice of Hard-Copy Submission—E-Filed Case (a form available in the "Forms" section on the NYSCEF website (Form EFM-3) and in the court's back offices). NY R NY CTY E FIL Doc. 2(B)(3). For more information refer to NY R NY CTY E FIL Doc. 2.
- *Unpublished decisions.* Whenever reliance is placed upon a decision or other authority not officially published or readily available to the New York County Supreme Court, a copy of the case or of pertinent portions of the authority shall be submitted with the motion papers. NY R NY CTY J RUL Rule 14(a).

ix. *ONONDAGA COUNTY: Additional supplemental documents*

- *Notice of hard copy submission.* Any papers to be filed with the court in an e-filed case must be filed online with the E-filing system except where a special exemption is granted (e.g., oversized maps, photographs). If such an exemption is granted, Form EFM-3, "Notice of Hard Copy Submission—E-Filed Case," must be attached to such documents forms which are not filed on line. Also, Form EFM-4 "Notice of Hard Copy Exhibit Filing" must be completed and uploaded to the action's e-file. Both of these forms may be found on the NYSCEF website. NY R ONDGA E FIL Protocol(B)(4).

x. *QUEENS COUNTY: Additional supplemental documents*

- *Notice of hard copy submission.* Any party opting out of the e-filing system must have a "Notice of Hard Copy Submission" firmly affixed to the back of the papers. NY R L QUEENS E-FILE Doc. 1(H)(2)(f).

2. *Documents for opposing party*

a. *Required documents*

i. *Opposition.* Refer to the General Requirements section of this document for information on the opposition.

- *Request for oral argument.* A party requesting oral argument shall set forth such request in its notice of motion or in its order to show cause or on the first page of the answering papers, as the case may be. Where all parties to a motion request oral argument, oral argument shall be granted unless the court shall determine it to be unnecessary. Where a motion is brought on by order to show cause, the court may set forth in the order that oral argument is required on the return date of the motion. NY R UNIF TRIAL CTS § 202.8(d).
- *QUEENS COUNTY: E-filing opposition papers.* E-filed opposition papers and/or reply papers must also be provided to the Centralized Motion Part in the same manner as the moving papers with the confirmation of filing firmly attached to the back of the papers. NY R L QUEENS E-FILE Doc. 1(H)(2)(d).

ii. *Proof of service.* In addition to complying with the provisions of NY CPLR Rule 2101, every paper filed in court shall have annexed thereto appropriate proof of service on all parties where required. NY R UNIF TRIAL CTS § 202.5(a).

b. *Supplemental documents*

i. *Supporting evidence; Exhibits.* The main supporting papers on a motion are affidavits, but any relevant exhibits, documents, depositions, etc., are also includible. SIEGEL-NYPRAC § 246.

- *Affidavits accompanying opposition.* Affidavits shall be for a statement of the relevant facts. NY R UNIF TRIAL CTS § 202.8(c).
- *Foreign language documents.* Where an affidavit or exhibit annexed to a paper served or filed is in a foreign language, it shall be accompanied by an English translation and an affidavit by the translator stating his qualifications and that the translation is accurate. NY CPLR Rule 2101(b).
- *Statement of attorney in lieu of affidavit.* The statement of an attorney admitted to practice in the courts of the state, or of a physician, osteopath or dentist, authorized by law to practice in the state, who is not a party to an action, when subscribed and affirmed by him to be true under the penalties of perjury, may be served or filed in the action in lieu of and with the same force and effect as an affidavit. NY CPLR Rule 2106.
- *NEW YORK COUNTY: Form of presented exhibits.* Exhibits should be tabbed and be legible; a typed version of any exhibit that is difficult to read should be submitted with the original. Exhibits printed on both sides of the page should be bound and tabbed on the side. NY R NY CTY J RUL Rule 14(a).
- *QUEENS COUNTY.* Attorneys submitting exhibits to the court on E-file cases shall make each exhibit a separate, labeled attachment to an affidavit/affirmation. NY R L QUEENS E-FILE Doc. 1(H)(4).

ii. *Brief.* Briefs shall be for a statement of the relevant law. NY R UNIF TRIAL CTS § 202.8(c).

iii. *Filing fees.* The County Clerk shall require the payment of any applicable statutory fees, or an order of the Court waiving payment of such fees, before accepting a paper for filing. NY R UNIF TRIAL CTS § 202.5(d)(1). For information on filing fees, if any, refer to NY CPLR § 8001, et seq.

- *ALBANY COUNTY.* In general, any filing subsequent to the commencement of an action which is designated as a motion or cross-motion requires the payment of a filing fee to the County Clerk's Office prior to submission to the Supreme Court Clerk's Office for referral to the assigned justice. The fee is assessed regardless of whether an application is made by notice of motion, order to show cause or ex parte. No fee will be charged upon the filing of a motion for poor person status in conjunction with an application which serves to commence an action or special proceeding. In the event a motion is received by the court unaccompanied by proof of payment to the County Clerk, the Supreme Court Clerk's Office will contact the submitting party to advise that the application will be held pending receipt of the filing fee only until the return date of the motion. If proof of payment is not submitted to the Supreme Court Clerk's Office by the return date (ex parte applications will be held ten (10) days), the papers will be returned by mail with a notification that the motion has been removed from the court's calendar and that it must be re-noticed and re-filed with the court along with the requisite filing fee. Inquiries concerning the applicability of the motion fee to a proposed filing may be directed to the Supreme Court Clerk's Office. NY R 3 JD SUP Doc. 1(B).
- *BRONX COUNTY.* In accordance with the new civil fee schedule set forth in Article 80 of the C.P.L.R. (NY CPLR § 8001, et seq.), effective July 14, 2003, all motions, and cross motions must be approved in Room 217 prior to payment of said fees in the County Clerk's Office, Room 118. NY R BRONX FIL R Doc. 8. The motion fee [must be] paid for via NYSCEF by credit/debit card. NY R BRONX E FIL R Doc. 1(1).
- *ERIE COUNTY.* Payment for fee-bearing NYSCEF documents must be made online via credit or debit card (American Express, MasterCard or Visa) at the time of submission. NY R ERIE E FIL Doc. 3(III)(E).
- *KINGS COUNTY.* The motion must be filed with NYSCEF and the motion fee paid. NY R L KINGS E FIL Doc. 1(D). Court fees in NYSCEF cases must be paid via NYSCEF by a credit or bank card (MasterCard, Visa, or American Express). Fees are no longer accepted in person in the Kings County Clerk's Office in NYSCEF cases. NY R L KINGS E FIL Doc. 1(B)(6).
- *NEW YORK COUNTY.* A motion fee must be paid on motions made in writing by notice of motion, order to show cause or ex parte after the commencement of an action. For this purpose, the term "action" shall mean any application to the court that requires the assignment of an index number, regardless of whether a formal pleading is filed. Applications or motions that commence an action and for which an index number fee must be paid require no motion fee. [A]ny motions made after the initial applications in these situations

would require payment of the motion fee. A motion that is the initial application in a case commenced by the filing of a summons and complaint would require a motion fee since the filing of the summons and complaint rather than the application itself would require the purchase of an index number. NY R NY CTY Procedure II(A). In e-filed cases the motion fee must be paid when the documents are filed. Payment is made on-line by Visa, Mastercard, or American Express credit or bank card. NY R NY CTY Procedure II(A); NY R NY CTY E FIL Doc. 2(B)(5).

- *ONONDAGA COUNTY.* Court fees in e-filed cases must be paid online with the NYSCEF system using a credit card. The document is not considered to have been filed until payment of the fee has been tendered. NY R ONDGA E FIL Protocol(B)(2). Fees must be paid on all cross motions. NY R ONDGA E FIL Protocol(B)(9)(e).
- *QUEENS COUNTY.* The Motion Support Office does not receive, forward or process any fees or waiver of fees. All applications requiring payment of statutory fees or waiver of fees must be sent directly to the Queens County Clerk's office. NY R L QUEENS MOT SUP Doc. 1. Court fees (e.g., RJI fee, motion fee) in E-filed cases may be paid for on-line using a credit card. Papers may also be filed with the E-file system and the fee may be paid at the County Clerk's Office. In the latter case, the paper is not considered to have been filed until payment of the fee has been tendered. NY R L QUEENS E-FILE Doc. 1(E)(1). The motion/petition shall be filed on-line and the fee paid for either on-line by credit card or by the "Pay at the County Clerk's Office" option. NY R L QUEENS E-FILE Doc. 1(H)(1).

iv. *Working copies.* The court may require the parties to provide working copies of documents filed electronically. In such event, each working copy shall include, firmly affixed thereto, a copy of a confirmation notice in a form prescribed by the Chief Administrator. NY R UNIF TRIAL CTS § 202.5-b(d)(5).

- *BRONX COUNTY.* After papers on motions have been e-filed, working copies thereof, with Confirmation Notice firmly attached as the back page facing out, must be submitted. (Each document or group of documents that is separately bound shall bear a Confirmation Notice.) Working copies lacking the Notice will not be accepted. WORKING COPIES OF MOTION PAPERS MUST BE SUBMITTED NO LATER THAN 4:45 P.M. ON THE RETURN DATE IN THE MOTION SUPPORT OFFICE (ROOM 217) AS EXPLAINED in NY R BRONX E FIL R Doc. 1(4). If an attorney has failed to submit required working copies on or before the return date, the motion will be transmitted as is to the Justice for such action as the Justice finds appropriate. Attorneys may submit working copies on motions by mail or overnight delivery. Any such submission shall be sent in a timely manner to the Motion Support Office (Room 217) and be conspicuously marked on the outside "NYSCEF Matter"; lack of such marking may delay processing. NY R BRONX E FIL R Doc. 1(4)(a).
- *ERIE COUNTY.* Electronically filed documents subject to review and processing by the Part Clerk do not require a working copy unless otherwise directed or provided for in IAS Part Rules. NY R UNIF TRIAL CTS § 202.5-b(d)(4), any working copy submitted shall include, as a cover page firmly fastened thereto, a copy of the Confirmation Notice generated by the NYSCEF site at the time of filing. Please consult the individual Justice's Part Rules and/or consult with the Judge's chambers to determine whether and how working copies are to be provided. Working copies will not be printed or delivered by the Erie County Clerk or the Chief Clerk of the Courts or any of their personnel to chambers. The official record of a document in an electronically filed case is the document filed via the NYSCEF system. Working copies are intended only for use by the Justice. The Court will discard all working copies after the Justice has finished with them. Thus, in the event that counsel fails to file a document via the NYSCEF system, the document will not be part of the court record. NY R ERIE E FIL Doc. 3(III)(O); NY R ERIE E FIL Doc. 3(V)(E).
- *KINGS COUNTY.* No courtesy copies of motion papers are required by the Court, except as may be required for electronic filing or by the Judge's Part Rules. In tort cases against the City of New York, courtesy copies shall be supplied to the Corporation Counsel's office in Brooklyn. NY R L KINGS Pt. C, Rule 5. Unless otherwise directed by the Court or as described herein, and with the exceptions listed below, in all NYSCEF cases in which an RJI has been filed, working copies of e-filed documents that are intended for judicial review must be submitted to the court. Working copies are not required of documents that are only processed by a support office (e.g. preliminary conference request, note of issue). Working copies shall include exhibit tabs and backs; for motion papers, the motion sequence number and the return date and part. The confirmation notice with the motion sequence number on it should be the back page of the motion facing out. In addition, the filer of a working copy must firmly bind thereto, with the back page facing out, a copy of the Confirmation Notice that was generated by NYSCEF when that document was efiled.

Working copies that are submitted without the related Confirmation Notice will not be accepted. NY R L KINGS E FIL Doc. 1(B)(7); NY R L KINGS E FIL Doc. 1(D). WORKING COPIES OF MOTION PAPERS MUST BE SUBMITTED IN THE MOTION SUPPORT OFFICE (ROOM 227) AS EXPLAINED HEREIN. THEY MUST NOT BE DELIVERED TO THE PART OR CHAMBERS, EXCEPT WHERE THE INDIVIDUAL JUSTICE'S PART RULES PROVIDE OTHERWISE; DOING SO WILL CAUSE ADMINISTRATIVE CONFUSION AND POSSIBLE MISPLACEMENT OF PAPERS. Any such submission shall be sent in a timely manner (kindly review individual Justice's rules) and be conspicuously marked on the outside "NYSCEF Matter;" lack of such marking may delay processing. NY R L KINGS E FIL Doc. 1(D).

- *NEW YORK COUNTY.* Some Justices require that working copies of e-filed motion papers be submitted. See the E-filing Protocol for information on the many Parts that do not require working copies. Where required, working copies of the moving documents and all other documents on the motion or application shall be submitted to the Motion Submission Part Courtroom (Room 130) on, but not before, the final return date. A Confirmation Notice from the NYSCEF system, which is generated when a document is e-filed, shall be firmly affixed, as the back page facing out, to each separate working copy or group of such copies. NY R NY CTY Procedure II(A) NY R NY CTY E FIL Doc. 2(B)(5)(a); NY R NY CTY J RUL Rule 14(a). For more information on working copies, including which parts don't require them, refer to NY R NY CTY E FIL Doc. 2(B)(6).
- *ONONDAGA COUNTY.* Any courtesy "working" copies, if required (see NY R ONDGA E FIL Protocol(B)(7)), must be provided directly to the assigned justice. NY R ONDGA E FIL Protocol(B)(9)(e). For information as to whether or not an Onondaga Supreme Court Justice requires working (courtesy) copies of e-filed documents, please consult the Onondaga County Individual E-filing Rules. NY R ONDGA E FIL Protocol(B)(7)(a). The Supreme Court Clerk's Office and the Onondaga County Clerk's Office will NOT accept the working copies. Working copies must be sent directly to the assigned justice's chambers. NY R ONDGA E FIL Protocol(B)(7)(b). A copy of the Confirmation Notice, generated by the NYSCEF system at the time a document is e-filed, must be attached to every working copy provided to chambers. If the Confirmation Notice is missing, the copy will not be accepted. NY R ONDGA E FIL Protocol(B)(7)(c). Courtesy copies do not become part of the official court record as maintained by the Onondaga County Clerk's Office and will be destroyed by chambers at the disposition of the case. In the event that counsel fails to file a document via NYSCEF, the document will not be part of the court record. NY R ONDGA E FIL Protocol(B)(7)(d).
- *QUEENS COUNTY.* Working copies of E-Filed notices of motion/notices of petition are NOT to be sent to the Motion Support Office. They must be brought to the calendar call in the judge's part. NY R L QUEENS MOT SUP Doc. 1. Unless otherwise directed or authorized by the court, counsel should file papers with the E-file system first and thereafter deliver a working copy to at the calendar call of the Centralized Motion Part or Assigned Justice in accordance with individual Part Rules. NY R L QUEENS E-FILE Doc. 1(E)(4). On the return date of a motion that has been E-filed, the movant must provide the Centralized Motion Part (CMP) with a working copy of the entire motion including the notice of motion with sequence number and all of the attached exhibits. The motion must have the confirmation of filing firmly affixed to the back of the papers (facing outward). The confirmation of filing is a separate notice from the payment notice and will say confirmation clearly across the top of the page. NY R L QUEENS E-FILE Doc. 1(H)(2)(a). The motion or Order to Show Cause must have clearly written across its face the words "Working Copy," it must also have the assigned Judge's name, motion sequence number and calendar number—which may be obtained from the posted calendar outside courtroom on the return date of the motion. A confirmation of filing must attached thereto. Working copies of e-filed Orders to Show Cause must contain a copy of the signed order and all supporting papers. NY R L QUEENS E-FILE Doc. 1(H)(2)(c). The Confirmation Notice must be an updated version that indicates the sequence number of the motion being submitted at the CMP calendar call. WORKING COPIES WITHOUT A CONFIRMATION NOTICE WILL NOT BE ACCEPTED. NY R L QUEENS E-FILE Doc. 1(H)(7).

v. *ERIE COUNTY: Additional supplemental documents*

- *Notice of hard copy submission in e-filed case.* In accordance with NY R UNIF TRIAL CTS § 202.5-b(d), the County Clerk shall refuse to accept for filing, hard copy papers filed to an action subject to electronic filing unless hard copy filing is permitted by the Uniform Rules or NY R ERIE E FIL Doc. 3 and the papers bear a completed Notice of Hard Copy Submission—E-Filed Case form. NY R ERIE E FIL Doc. 3(III)(D).

vi. *KINGS COUNTY: Additional supplemental documents*

- *Forms when filing in hard copy.* An attorney who certifies in good faith that he or she lacks the equipment or knowledge needed to e-file and have no staff member or employee under his or her direction who has such knowledge and equipment may opt out of participation in e-filing in a mandatory case by filing a "Notice of Opt-Out from Participation in Action Subject to Mandatory Electronic Filing" form EFM-2 with the Clerk. NY R L KINGS E FIL Doc. 1(A)(2). Where in accordance with the E-Filing Rules a party submits a document in hard copy in an e-filed case (principally, a document submitted by a nonparticipating party (e.g., an attorney) in a consensual case, an emergency filing made in accordance with the Mandatory E-Filing Rules, and any document filed with the court in hard copy by an attorney who has opted out of participation in mandatory e-filing, the document must bear the back page facing out, a "Notice of Hard Copy Submission—E-Filed Cases" form EFM-3. NY R L KINGS E FIL Doc. 1(B)(3).

vii. *NEW YORK COUNTY: Additional supplemental documents*

- *Notice of hard copy submission.* Where in accordance with the E-Filing Rules an attorney or an unrepresented litigant who is participating in e-filing submits a document in hard copy in an e-filed case, the document must bear, as the back page facing out, a Notice of Hard-Copy Submission—E-Filed Case (a form available in the "Forms" section on the NYSCEF website (Form EFM-3) and in the court's back offices). NY R NY CTY E FIL Doc. 2(B)(3). For more information refer to NY R NY CTY E FIL Doc. 2.
- *Unpublished decisions.* Whenever reliance is placed upon a decision or other authority not officially published or readily available to the New York County Supreme Court, a copy of the case or of pertinent portions of the authority shall be submitted with the motion papers. NY R NY CTY J RUL Rule 14(a).

viii. *ONONDAGA COUNTY: Additional supplemental documents*

- *Notice of hard copy submission.* Any papers to be filed with the court in an e-filed case must be filed online with the E-filing system except where a special exemption is granted (e.g., oversized maps, photographs). If such an exemption is granted, Form EFM-3, "Notice of Hard Copy Submission—E-Filed Case," must be attached to such documents forms which are not filed on line. Also, Form EFM-4 "Notice of Hard Copy Exhibit Filing" must be completed and uploaded to the action's e-file. Both of these forms may be found on the NYSCEF website. NY R ONDGA E FIL Protocol(B)(4).

ix. *QUEENS COUNTY: Additional supplemental documents*

- *Notice of hard copy submission.* Any party opting out of the e-filing system must have a "Notice of Hard Copy Submission" firmly affixed to the back of the papers. NY R L QUEENS E-FILE Doc. 1(H)(2)(f).

E. Format

1. *Form of documents*

a. *Size and form of paper.* Each paper served or filed shall be durable, white and, except for summonses, subpoenas, notices of appearance, notes of issue, orders of protection, temporary orders of protection and exhibits, shall be eleven by eight and one-half (11 x 8-1/2) inches in size. NY CPLR Rule 2101(a).

b. *Writing and language.* The writing shall be legible and in black ink. NY CPLR Rule 2101(a). Each paper served or filed shall be in the English language which, where practicable, shall be of ordinary usage. NY CPLR Rule 2101(b).

c. *Caption.* Each paper served or filed shall begin with a caption setting forth the name of the court, the venue, the title of the action, the nature of the paper and the index number of the action if one has been assigned. In all papers other than a summons, a complaint or a judgment it shall be sufficient to state the name of the first named party on each side with an appropriate indication of any omissions. NY CPLR Rule 2101(c).

i. *Further contents of first page.* After the first paper has been filed in each case the index number shall appear on the cover and first page to the right of the caption of every paper tendered for filing in the action. Each such cover and first page also shall contain an indication of the county of venue and a brief description of the nature of the paper and, where the case has been assigned to an individual judge, shall contain the name of the assigned judge to the right of the caption. NY R UNIF TRIAL CTS § 202.5(a); NY R UNIF TRIAL CTS § 202.5(b); NY R UNIF TRIAL CTS § 202.5(d)(1)(i).

ii. *ALBANY COUNTY: Request for oral argument.* A party may request oral argument on a motion by indicating such request on the first page of the notice of motion, order to show cause, or answering papers in the area across from the caption of the action/proceeding. NY R 3 JD SUP Doc. 1(B).

iii. *NEW YORK COUNTY: Request for oral argument.* Counsel who wish oral argument must so request conspicuously on the front of their papers. NY R NY CTY Procedure II(D).

d. *Index number.* No paper in an action in the supreme or a county court, other than an order submitted for signature to

a judge out of court, shall be submitted for any purpose to the supreme or county court or to a clerk thereof unless there is endorsed on such paper the index number of the action assigned by the clerk of the county. NY CPLR § 8018(c).

i. *ALBANY COUNTY: Index number on all filed documents.* The index number, the request for judicial intervention number and the assigned justice's name shall appear on [all papers filed with the Court subsequent to the complaint]. NY R 3 JD SUP Doc. 1(A).

ii. *ERIE COUNTY: Index number after initial filing.* Cases that are initially commenced by the filing of papers with the NYSCEF system are identified as e-filed cases by assignment of an Index Number that has "800-899" as the first three (3) digits of the index number (i.e. 802391/2012). NY R ERIE E FIL Doc. 3(II). [The] Index Number must be affixed to all document submissions, filings, and communications to the Erie County Clerk and the Court. Cases that are converted from paper to e-filing shall retain the original index number. NY R ERIE E FIL Doc. 3(II).

iii. *KINGS COUNTY: Index number after initial filing.* In cases commenced electronically by the filing of initiating papers with the NYSCEF system and payment of the statutory fees, the Kings County Clerk will issue an NYSCEF designated index number and the filer shall be notified via the NYSCEF system of the index number assigned and filing date. Such index number must be affixed to all document submissions, filings and communications to the Kings County Clerk and Supreme Court. If counsel faces exigent circumstances that require accelerated assignment, counsel may contact Administration of the Kings County Clerk at kcco-efile@nycourts.gov, during normal business hours of the court. NY R L KINGS E FIL Doc. 1(B)(5).

iv. *NEW YORK COUNTY: Index number on hard copy filings.* Papers subsequently presented for filing in hardcopy format will be filed in this jacket. NY R NY CTY Procedure I(B). Index numbers take the form of six digits followed by a slash and the four digits of the year the case began, e.g., 340705/2018. The first or first two integers of the index number identify the type of case. If a case is commenced electronically, the second integer will be a "5", except as indicated otherwise in the list below. There are many tax certiorari matters e-filed annually and the index numbers therefor will normally run over into those with a "6" as the second integer, and the same will occur with general cases if necessary. The principal types of cases and their index number categories are listed in NY R NY CTY Procedure I(B). NY R NY CTY Procedure I(B); NY R NY CTY Procedure XI(A).

v. *ONONDAGA COUNTY: Index number.* The index number must be referenced on all e-filed documents and correspondence. All e-filed case index numbers will contain the letters "EF" between the year and the file number (for example, 2012EF9999). NY R ONDGA E FIL Protocol(B)(1).

vi. *QUEENS COUNTY: Index number on converted cases.* Cases originally commenced in hard-copy form but later converted to an E-file case, either by stipulation or order will bear a regular index number initially. The County Clerk will issue a new E-file index number. NY R L QUEENS E-FILE Doc. 1(B).

e. *Line spacing.* Every paper filed in court, if typewritten, shall have at least double space between each line, except for quotations and the names and addresses of attorneys appearing in the action. NY R UNIF TRIAL CTS § 202.5(a).

f. *Font size.* Each. . .paper printed or typed, served or filed, except for summonses. . .and exhibits, shall be in clear type of no less than ten (10) point in size. NY CPLR Rule 2101(a).

i. Whenever a requirement relating to size of type is stated in point size, the type size requirement shall be deemed met if the x-height of the type is a minimum of forty-five percent (45%) of the specified point size. Each point shall be measured as .351 millimeter. The x-height size shall be measured as it appears on the page. The x-height is the height of the lower case letters, exclusive of ascenders or descenders. NY CPLR § 105(t).

g. *Margins.* Every paper filed in court shall have at least one (1) inch margins. NY R UNIF TRIAL CTS § 202.5(a).

h. *Citations*

i. *Civil practice law and rules.* NY CPLR § 101, et seq. shall be known as the civil practice law and rules, and may be cited as "CPLR". Reference to a provision in the civil practice law and rules may, except when such provision is being enacted or amended, be made without indicating whether it is a rule or section. NY CPLR § 101.

i. *Indorsement by attorney.* Each paper served or filed shall be indorsed with the name, address and telephone number of the attorney for the party serving or filing the paper, or if the party does not appear by attorney, with the name, address and telephone number of the party. NY CPLR Rule 2101(d).

j. *One-sided printing.* In addition, every paper filed in court, other than an exhibit or printed form, shall contain writing on one side only, except that papers that are fastened on the side may contain writing on both sides. NY R UNIF TRIAL CTS § 202.5(a).

k. *Use of copies authorized.* Except where otherwise specifically prescribed, copies, rather than originals, of all papers,

including orders, affidavits and exhibits may be served or filed. Where it is required that the original be served or filed and the original is lost or withheld, the court may authorize a copy to be served or filed. NY CPLR Rule 2101(e).

i. Where a certified copy of a paper is required by law, an attorney admitted to practice in the courts of the state may certify that it has been compared by him with the original and found to be a true and complete copy. Such a certificate, when subscribed by such attorney, has the same effect as if made by a clerk. NY CPLR § 2105.

l. *Recycled paper.* It is the policy of the Unified Court System that litigants, where practicable, should file or submit to the courts of the Unified Court System of the State of New York papers printed or reproduced on recycled paper. Paper is considered recycled if it contains a minimum content of thirty percent (30%) waste paper. NY R UNIF TRIAL CTS § 215.2. The signature page of every paper filed or submitted to the court on recycled paper should bear the legend: "Printed [Reproduced] on Recycled Paper." NY R UNIF TRIAL CTS § 215.3.

m. *Form of request for judicial intervention; Copies.* A request for judicial intervention must be submitted, in duplicate, on a form authorized by the Chief of the Courts, with proof of service on the other parties to the action (but proof of service is not required where the application is ex parte). NY R UNIF TRIAL CTS § 202.6(a).

n. *KINGS COUNTY: Tabs on filings.* Motions, orders and other filed papers shall be indexed with protruding tabs. Clerks are required to reject papers that do not have protruding exhibit tabs, except papers in matrimonial cases and papers filed by pro se litigants. NY R L KINGS Pt. A, Papers.

o. *NEW YORK COUNTY: Length of briefs.* Unless advance permission otherwise is granted by the court for good cause, memoranda of law shall not exceed thirty (30) pages each (exclusive of table of contents and table of authorities) and affidavits/affirmations shall not exceed twenty-five (25) pages each. NY R NY CTY J RUL Rule 14(b).

p. *QUEENS COUNTY: Form and size of motion filings.* All motions filed in Queens Supreme Court-Civil Term, must adhere to the Motion Support rules and the rules of the assigned judge. NY R L QUEENS MOT SUP Doc. 1. Due to space limitations, the Motion Support Office cannot accept notices of motion/notices of petition and accompanying exhibits which measure greater than eight (8) inches. If your documents measure greater than eight (8) inches you are directed to submit only the notice of motion/notice of petition to the Motion Support Office and bring all exhibits to the calendar call on your return date. NY R L QUEENS MOT SUP Doc. 1.

2. *Form of electronic documents.* Each paper served or filed by electronic means, as defined in NY CPLR Rule 2103(f), shall be capable of being reproduced by the receiver so as to comply with the provisions of NY CPLR Rule 2101(a) through NY CPLR Rule 2101(d). NY CPLR Rule 2101(g).

a. *File format.* All e-filed documents shall comply with the technical requirements set forth at the NYSCEF site. NY R UNIF TRIAL CTS § 202.5-b(d)(1)(i).

b. *Heading of document.* The subject matter heading for each paper sent by electronic means must indicate that the matter being transmitted electronically is related to a court proceeding. NY CPLR Rule 2103(b)(7).

c. *E-filed documents identification*

i. *ERIE COUNTY.* E-filed cases must be readily identifiable and marked as such. If counsel presents papers to the Office of the Erie County Clerk or the Office of the Chief Clerk in a NYSCEF matter where authorized, counsel should alert the Clerk that the case is a NYSCEF matter. NY R ERIE E FIL Doc. 3(II).

ii. *KINGS COUNTY.* The Supreme Court's Civil Case Information System ("CCIS") will further identify e-filed cases by the addition of a suffix to the index number (e.g. 500136/2006E). This suffix should be used on all documents filed with the court in e-filed matters. NY R L KINGS E FIL Doc. 1(A)(1).

3. *Signature blocks.* Every pleading, written motion, and other paper, served on another party or filed or submitted to the court shall be signed by an attorney, or by a party if the party is not represented by an attorney, with the name of the attorney or party clearly printed or typed directly below the signature. NY R CHIEF ADMIN § 130-1.1-a(a); NY R UNIF TRIAL CTS § 202.5(d)(1)(iv).

a. *Printed name.* Beneath each signature shall be printed the name signed. NY CPLR Rule 2101(a).

b. *Failure to sign.* Absent good cause shown, the court shall strike any unsigned paper if the omission of the signature is not corrected promptly after being called to the attention of the attorney or party. NY R CHIEF ADMIN § 130-1.1-a(a).

c. *Signature as certification.* By signing a paper, an attorney or party certifies that, to the best of that person's knowledge, information and belief, formed after an inquiry reasonable under the circumstances the presentation of the paper or the contentions therein are not frivolous as defined in NY R CHIEF ADMIN § 130-1.1(c). NY R CHIEF ADMIN § 130-1.1-a(b)(1).

d. *Electronic signatures.* A document shall be considered to have been signed by an attorney or party in compliance with NY R CHIEF ADMIN § 130-1.1-a if it has been signed by such attorney or party as provided in NY R UNIF TRIAL CTS § 202.5-b(e)(1) and it bears the signatory's name. NY R UNIF TRIAL CTS § 202.5-b(e)(2). An electronically filed document shall be considered to have been signed by, and shall be binding upon, the person identified as a signatory, if:

i. It bears the physical signature of such person and is scanned into an electronic format that reproduces such signature; or

ii. The signatory has electronically affixed the digital image of his or her signature to the document; or

iii. It is electronically filed under the User ID and password of that person; or

iv. In a tax certiorari action in which the parties have stipulated to this procedure, it is an initiating document that is electronically filed without the signature of the signatory in a form provided above in NY R UNIF TRIAL CTS § 202.5-b(e)(iv), provided that, prior to filing, the document is signed in full in hard copy (which hard copy must be preserved until the conclusion of all proceedings, including appeals, in the case in which it is filed); or

v. In a small claims assessment review proceeding, it is a petition recorded by the NYSCEF site upon the filing of a text file as provided in NY R UNIF TRIAL CTS § 202.5-b(b)(1), provided that prior to filing, the document was signed in full in hard copy (which hard copy must be preserved until the conclusion of all proceedings in the matter, including article 78 (NY CPLR § 7801, et seq.) review and any appeals, and must be made available during the proceeding upon request of the respondent or the court); or

vi. It otherwise bears the electronic signature of the signatory in a format conforming to such standards and requirements as may hereafter be established by the Chief Administrator. NY R UNIF TRIAL CTS § 202.5-b(e).

4. *Confidentiality of personal information.* No person may file any document available for public inspection with any state agency, political subdivision, or in any court of this state that contains a Social Security account number of any other person, unless such other person is a dependent child, or has consented to such filing, except as required by federal or state law or regulation, or by court rule. NY GEN BUS § 399-ddd. Submissions pursuant to e-filing procedures shall have the same confidentiality rights as paper documents. NY R UNIF TRIAL CTS § 202.5-b(k)(1).

a. *Confidential personal information.* Except in the actions designated in NY R UNIF TRIAL CTS § 202.5(e)(1), or as otherwise provided by rule or law or court order, and whether or not a sealing order is or has been sought, the parties shall omit or redact confidential personal information in papers submitted to the court for filing. For purposes of NY R UNIF TRIAL CTS § 202.5(e), confidential personal information ("CPI") means:

i. The taxpayer identification number of an individual or an entity, including a Social Security number, an employer identification number, and an individual taxpayer identification number, except the last four (4) digits thereof;

ii. The date of an individual's birth, except the year thereof;

iii. The full name of an individual known to be a minor, except the minor's initials;

iv. A financial account number, including a credit and/or debit card number, a bank account number, an investment account number, and/or an insurance account number, except the last four (4) digits or letters thereof; and

v. Any of the documents or testimony in a matrimonial action protected by NY DOM REL § 235 or evidence sealed by the court in such an action which are attached as exhibits or referenced in the papers filed in any other civil action. For purposes of NY R UNIF TRIAL CTS § 202.5, a matrimonial action shall mean: an action to annul a marriage or declare the nullity of a void marriage, an action or agreement for a separation, an action for a divorce, or an action or proceeding for custody, visitation, writ of habeus corpus, child support, maintenance or paternity. NY R UNIF TRIAL CTS § 202.5(e)(1).

vi. *ERIE COUNTY.* An attorney or unrepresented litigant filing a document via the NYSCEF system must comply with the requirements of NY R UNIF TRIAL CTS § 202.5(e) regarding the redaction of Confidential Personal Information and NY GEN BUS § 399-ddd(6) concerning the filing of documents containing Social Security Numbers. It is the sole responsibility of counsel or unrepresented litigant filing to be aware of and to comply with existing laws requiring non-disclosure of personal information contained in any document e-filed in NYSCEF. NY R ERIE E FIL Doc. 3(III)(G); NY R ERIE E FIL Doc. 3(III).

vii. *KINGS COUNTY.* An attorney or unrepresented litigant filing a document via the NYSCEF system must comply with the requirements of General Business Law § 399-dd(6), which often require redaction of any Social Security number that appear in the original document. The NYSCEF system automatically redacts portions of filed documents which apparently contain Social Security numbers pursuant to NY R UNIF TRIAL CTS § 202.5-b(k). In the event the filing party receives e-mail notice through NYSCEF that a Social Security number in a filed document has been redacted, and the filing party concludes such redaction is erroneous, the filer should click on the link provided in the e-mail to permit the County Clerk to revert the redaction. For Confidential Personal Information, see NY R UNIF TRIAL CTS § 202.5(e) and NY R L KINGS E FIL Doc. 1(B)(11). [Editor's note: the reference to General Business Law § 399-dd(6) is likely a reference to NY GEN BUS § 399-ddd(6)]. NY R L KINGS E FIL Doc. 1(B)(10); NY R L KINGS E FIL Doc. 1(K)(1).

viii. *NEW YORK COUNTY.* It is the responsibility of counsel and parties to comply with rules restricting disclosure of confidential personal information. Nevertheless, NYSCEF screens filings and endeavors to identify any that contain social security numbers. When such numbers are discovered through this process, NYSCEF will restrict portions of or all of such documents from public view. Where NYSCEF has redacted what it believes to be a social security number, it will transmit to the filer a notice advising of the action taken and requesting that the filer review the matter and provide notification as set forth in the notice if the redaction has been made in error. NY R NY CTY E FIL Doc. 2(K)(1); NY R NY CTY J RUL Rule A-1. Documents filed in the past in "secure status" under a procedure no longer in place will retain that status unless otherwise directed by the court. NY R NY CTY E FIL Doc. 2(K)(2).

b. *Submission of confidential personal information.* Where a person submitting a paper to a court for filing believes in good faith that the inclusion of the full confidential personal information described in NY R UNIF TRIAL CTS § 202.5(e)(1) is material and necessary to the adjudication of the action or proceeding before the court, he or she may apply to the court for leave to serve and file together with a paper in which such information has been set forth in abbreviated form a confidential affidavit or affirmation setting forth the same information in unabbreviated form, appropriately referenced to the page or pages of the paper at which the abbreviated form appears. NY R UNIF TRIAL CTS § 202.5(e)(3).

c. *Home addresses.* For information on when home addresses and other personal information must be redacted, refer to NY CPLR Rule 2103-a.

5. *Defective papers.* A defect in the form of a paper, if a substantial right of a party is not prejudiced, shall be disregarded by the court, and leave to correct shall be freely given. NY CPLR Rule 2101(f). Papers that are stapled or bound securely shall not be rejected for filing simply because they are not bound with a backer of any kind. NY R UNIF TRIAL CTS § 202.5(a). A paper filed in accordance with the rules of the chief administrator or any local rule or practice established by the court shall be deemed filed. NY CPLR Rule 2102(b).

a. *Objection to defective papers.* The party on whom a paper is served shall be deemed to have waived objection to any defect in form unless, within fifteen (15) days after the receipt thereof, the party on whom the paper is served returns the paper to the party serving it with a statement of particular objections. NY CPLR Rule 2101(f).

F. Filing and Service Requirements

1. *Filing requirements.* Except where otherwise prescribed by law or order of court, papers required to be filed shall be filed with the clerk of the court in which the action is triable. In an action or proceeding in supreme or court, papers required to be filed shall be filed with the clerk of the county in which the proceeding is brought. NY CPLR Rule 2102(a).

a. *Furnishing papers to the court.* Each party shall furnish to the court all papers served by him. The moving party shall furnish at the hearing all other papers not already in the possession of the court necessary to the consideration of the questions involved. Where such papers are in the possession of an adverse party, they shall be produced by him at the hearing on notice served with the motion papers. Only papers served in accordance with the provisions of NY CPLR Rule 2214 shall be read in support of, or in opposition to, the motion, unless the court for good cause shall otherwise direct. NY CPLR Rule 2214(c).

i. *Submission to judge.* All papers for signature or consideration of the court shall be presented to the clerk of the trial court in the appropriate courtroom or clerk's office, except that where the clerk is unavailable or the judge so directs, papers may be submitted to the judge and a copy filed with the clerk at the first available opportunity. All papers for any judge that are filed in the clerk's office shall be promptly delivered to the judge by the clerk. The papers shall be clearly addressed to the judge for whom they are intended and prominently show the nature of the papers, the title and index number of the action in which they are filed, the judge's name and the name of the attorney or party submitting them. NY R UNIF TRIAL CTS § 202.5(b).

ii. *BRONX COUNTY: Approval of motions before filing.* All motion papers must be approved by the Motion Support Office, Supreme Court, Civil Term, room 217, before the motion papers are filed and the appropriate fee paid to the County Clerk. NY R BRONX FIL R Doc. 1.

iii. *ERIE COUNTY: Filing motions.* A motion on notice or a notice of petition in a NYSCEF case shall be filed through the NYSCEF system and must be accompanied by a Request for Judicial Intervention if the motion is being filed upon commencement of the action or if the matter has not yet been assigned to an IAS Justice. In addition, cross motions with the appropriate filing fees and opposition and reply papers must be submitted via the NYSCEF system. NY R ERIE E FIL Doc. 3(V)(A).

iv. *NEW YORK COUNTY: Filing hard copies.* Where in the narrow circumstances described by the e-filing rules a motion is made in hard-copy form or opposition papers are submitted in such form in an e-filed case, the hard-copy documents shall be submitted in the same way papers are submitted in non-e-filed cases, except that there shall be firmly affixed to each separate document or group of documents, as the back page facing out, a Notice of Hard Copy Submission—E-Filed Case. NY R NY CTY Procedure II(A). For more information on filing in hard copy cases, refer to NY R NY CTY Procedure II(A).

v. *ONONDAGA COUNTY: Submission of responsive papers and cross-motions.* Cross-motions, opposition and reply papers must be submitted online. NY R ONDGA E FIL Protocol(B)(9)(e). Motions and Orders to Show Cause are assigned a sequence number by the system. Counsel must be sure that cross motions and other filings correspond with the correct sequence number so that a cross motion will not be associated with the wrong original motion. NY R ONDGA E FIL Protocol(B)(9)(f).

b. *Electronic filing.* On consent, documents may be filed and served by electronic means in Supreme Court in such civil actions and in such counties as shall be authorized by order of the Chief Administrator of the Courts and only to the extent and in the manner provided in NY R UNIF TRIAL CTS § 202.5-b. NY R UNIF TRIAL CTS § 202.5-b(a)(1). For the definitions of terms used in electronic filing, refer to NY R UNIF TRIAL CTS § 202.5-b(a)(2).

i. *E-filing mandatory.* In any action subject to e-filing, all documents required to be filed with the court by an e-filing party shall be filed and served electronically, except as provided in NY R UNIF TRIAL CTS § 202.5-b. NY R UNIF TRIAL CTS § 202.5-b(d)(1)(i).

- *ERIE COUNTY.* Case types currently eligible and accepted for e-filing are listed at the NYSCEF website. Note that some actions or special proceedings, (i.e., name changes) which are otherwise subject to mandatory e-filing, if commenced by unrepresented litigants will NOT be maintained in the NYSCEF system; individual cases may be found either at NYSCEF or in the Erie County Clerk's online records system. NY R ERIE E FIL Doc. 3(I)(E).
- *KINGS COUNTY.* Cases that are commenced by filing of the initiating papers with NYSCEF are identified as e-filed cases by assignment of a special index number (i.e., Index Numbers beginning with 500,000). NY R L KINGS E FIL Doc. 1(A)(1). All cases required to be e-filed are listed in Uniform Rule 202.5-bb (Mandatory E-Filing Rules) and on the NYSCEF website. All such cases must be commenced by filing with the County Clerk electronically through NYSCEF and all subsequent documents in such cases must be e-filed. Any questions regarding mandatory e-filing in Kings County can be e-mailed to kcco-efile@nycourts.gov. NY R L KINGS E FIL Doc. 1(A)(2).
- *NEW YORK COUNTY.* Unless otherwise provided in the Rules or in NY R NY CTY E FIL Doc. 2 or where a special exemption is granted due to physical requirements (e.g., oversized maps; see NY R NY CTY E FIL Doc. 2(B)(10)), all documents to be filed with the court in a NYSCEF case, including all documents on motions and all letters to the court (where permitted), must be filed with the NYSCEF system. Documents that attorneys would not ordinarily file with the court in a hard-copy case need not be e-filed. Unless otherwise provided by the E-Filing Rules or this Protocol, in e-filed cases the County Clerk and the court will not accept documents filed in paper form. NY R NY CTY E FIL Doc. 2(B)(1). E-filing is mandatory in all types of cases (other than election law, matrimonial, Art. 78, and Mental Hygiene Law matters, and Art. 70 habeas corpus proceedings) that are commenced in this court on or after February 19, 2013. All such cases must be commenced by filing with the County Clerk electronically through NYSCEF and all subsequent documents in such cases must be e-filed. NY R NY CTY E FIL Doc. 2(A)(2)(a). For more information, including information on consensual e-filing and filing scanned hard copy documents, refer to NY R NY CTY E FIL Doc. 2(A)(2).
- *QUEENS COUNTY.* All authorized Torts, Commercial and Tax Certiorari cases may be commenced by E-Filing, however all parties must consent for the action to continue as an E-file case. NY R L QUEENS E-FILE Doc. 1(A). All papers to be filed with the court in an E-filed case shall be filed on-line with the E-file system except as directed by the court. Papers that attorneys would not ordinarily file with the court in a hard-copy case need not be filed in an E-filed matter. NY R L QUEENS E-FILE Doc. 1(E)(2).

ii. *Who may file.* Documents may be filed or served electronically only by a person who has registered as an authorized e-filing user or as otherwise provided in NY R UNIF TRIAL CTS § 202.5-b(c). NY R UNIF TRIAL CTS § 202.5-b(c)(1).

iii. *When filing made.* Documents may be transmitted at any time of the day or night to the NYSCEF site. A document other than an order or judgment is filed when its electronic transmission or, in the case of a petition that is e-filed by submission of a text file as provided in NY R UNIF TRIAL CTS § 202.5-b(b)(1), the electronic transmission of the text file is recorded at that site, provided, however, that where payment of a fee is required upon the filing of a document, the document is not filed until transmission of the document and the information or form or information as required in NY R UNIF TRIAL CTS § 202.5-b(d)(2)(i), NY R UNIF TRIAL CTS § 202.5-b(d)(2)(ii) or NY R UNIF TRIAL CTS § 202.5-b(d)(2)(iii) has been recorded at the NYSCEF site; or, if no transmission of that information or form or information is recorded, where permitted by the County Clerk, until payment is presented to the County Clerk. NY R UNIF TRIAL CTS § 202.5-b(d)(3)(i).

iv. *Notification of filing.* No later than the close of business on the business day following the electronic filing of a document, a notification, in a form prescribed by the Chief Administrator, shall be transmitted electronically by the NYSCEF site to the person filing such document and the e-mail service addresses of all other participating parties in such action. NY R UNIF TRIAL CTS § 202.5-b(d)(3)(ii).

v. *Removal of confidential information and other corrections.* If a document filed electronically is subsequently discovered to contain confidential data—including but not limited to trade secrets, information protected by confidentiality agreement, or personal confidential information as defined by statute or court rule—or otherwise to have been filed in error, the filer or another party or affected person may (1) notify the parties and any non-party filers in the action of the confidentiality issue or other error raised by the filing, and of his or her intention to seek judicial relief to correct the filing: (2) following such notification, request that the appropriate County Clerk, exercising his or her administrative discretion, place the document temporarily in "restricted" status on the NYSCEF site, to be made available for viewing by court staff and the parties but not the general public; and (3) file an application to correct the filing by order to show cause within five (5) business days of such notification (or such time as the court may direct), including a request for preliminary injunctive relief limiting interim disclosure of the document at issue. Unless otherwise directed by the court, any document placed in restricted status in response to such a request shall be returned to public view upon expiration of this five (5) day period. The Chief Administrator of the Courts shall promulgate forms to implement this process. NY R UNIF TRIAL CTS § 202.5-b(d)(3)(iii).

- *KINGS COUNTY.* For information on what to do when a document was erroneously filed with confidential information, refer to NY R L KINGS E FIL Doc. 1(B)(11).
- *NEW YORK COUNTY.* For information on what to do when a document was erroneously filed with confidential information, refer to NY R NY CTY E FIL Doc. 2(B)(8).
- *QUEENS COUNTY.* For information on what to do when a document was erroneously filed with confidential information, refer to NY R L QUEENS E-FILE Doc. 1(E)(7).

vi. *Documents requiring judge's signature.* Except where the court directs otherwise, any document that requires a judge's signature shall be transmitted electronically and in hard copy to the court. NY R UNIF TRIAL CTS § 202.5-b(d)(6).

vii. *Documents which would be inconvenient to file electronically; Hard copies.* Notwithstanding any other provision of NY R UNIF TRIAL CTS § 202.5-b, and subject to such guidelines as may be established by the Chief Administrative Judge, the County Clerk or his or her designee may require or permit a party to file in hard copy, in accordance with procedures set by the County Clerk or designee, an exhibit or other document which it is impractical or inconvenient to file electronically. NY R UNIF TRIAL CTS § 202.5-b(d)(7).

- *ERIE COUNTY.* Please contact the Supervisor of Actions & Proceedings, Erie County Clerk's Office by calling (716) 858-6662 or the Deputy County Clerk—Legal at (716) 858-6348 for information. NY R ERIE E FIL Doc. 3(III)(F).
- *KINGS COUNTY.* With limited exceptions, as set forth in the Uniform Rules and herein, all documents to be filed with the court in a NYSCEF case shall be filed online via the NYSCEF system. However, should the size, consistency or context of a hard copy document preclude electronic filing, the user shall electronically file a "Notice of Hard Copy Submission—E-Filed Cases" form EFM-3. Any hard copy submitted pursuant to NY R L KINGS E FIL Doc. 1(B)(9) shall include, as a cover page firmly fastened thereto, a copy of the Confirmation Notice received from the NYSCEF site confirming receipt of the "Notice of Hard Copy Submission—E-Filed Cases". Any party may object to such hard copy filing. The

Court, in response to such objection, may, following the hard copy filing, fashion such relief as it deems appropriate pursuant to and in furtherance of the Uniform Rules and NY R L KINGS E FIL Doc. 1, including, but not limited to, an Order directing the filing party to file such documents online via the NYSCEF system. When exhibits are impractical to file pursuant to NY R UNIF TRIAL CTS § 202.5-b(d)(7), an additional "Notice of Hard Copy Exhibit Filing" form EFM-4 is required to be submitted. NY R L KINGS E FIL Doc. 1(B)(9).

- *NEW YORK COUNTY.* If a filer needs to submit unusual exhibits in original form that cannot practically be e-filed, such as oversized maps or electronic recordings, the filer should consult with the County Clerk's E-File Department by telephone at 646-386-3737 (procedural questions only) or by e-mail at ccnyef@nycourts.gov, which will normally require that the filer retain custody of the original subject to possible future directives of the court. NY R NY CTY E FIL Doc. 2(B)(10). In such instances, the filing counsel shall file with NYSCEF a "placeholder" in the form of a Notice of Hard Copy Exhibit Filing (NYSCEF Form EF 21). The Notice should be uploaded to NYSCEF as document type "Exhibit" and the filer should indicate in the "Additional Document Information" field that the filer is retaining custody of the original. Failure to e-file the Notice may result in a gap in the official record of the court. NY R NY CTY E FIL Doc. 2(B)(10).

viii. *Documents containing sensitive or proprietary information.* In an action subject to e-filing, any person may apply for an order prohibiting or restricting the electronic filing in the action of specifically identified materials on the grounds that such materials are subject to copyright or other proprietary rights, or trade secret or other privacy interests, and that electronic filing in the action is likely to result in substantial prejudice to those rights or interests. NY R UNIF TRIAL CTS § 202.5-b(k)(2).

ix. *Refusal to accept paper filings.* In accordance with NY CPLR Rule 2102(c), a County Clerk and a chief clerk of the Supreme Court or County Court, as appropriate, shall refuse to accept for filing papers filed in actions and proceedings when the paper sought to be filed:

- Is in an action subject to electronic filing pursuant to Rules of the Chief Administrator,
- Is not being filed electronically, and
- Does not include the notice required by NY R UNIF TRIAL CTS § 202.5-b(d)(1). NY R UNIF TRIAL CTS § 202.5(d)(1)(v); NY R UNIF TRIAL CTS § 202.5-bb(d).

x. *Emergency filings; Hard copies.* For information on when an emergency filing may be filed and served in hard copy, refer to NY R UNIF TRIAL CTS § 202.5-b(d)(1)(ii), NY R UNIF TRIAL CTS § 202.5-b(d)(1)(iii) and NY R UNIF TRIAL CTS § 202.5-bb(c)(3).

- *KINGS COUNTY.* Under the rules, a participating emergency e-filer must electronically file the documents initially filed in hard copy form within three (3) business days of the emergency filing; the originals will be discarded after the documents have been processed and the failure to e-file as required will therefore lead to an incomplete record. NY R L KINGS E FIL Doc. 1(B)(3).
- *NEW YORK COUNTY.* Occasionally an emergency will arise requiring expedited entry of a document with the County Clerk (e.g., an order issued in the courtroom after a conference or argument of a critical matter), such as for purposes of an immediate appeal. Expedition can be achieved by the Part as follows: the document should be carried by a Court Officer or staff member to the General Clerk's Office to assure immediate and proper recordation in the computer and, as appropriate, the posting of the document to NYSCEF or the Supreme Court Records On-Line Library ("Scroll"). The court will accommodate counsel in emergencies. NY R NY CTY Procedure XI(A).
- *NEW YORK COUNTY.* For more information on how to bring emergency matters before the court, refer to NY R NY CTY Procedure IV.

xi. *Technical failures.* The NYSCEF site shall be considered to be subject to a technical failure on a given day if the site is unable to accept filings or provide access to filed documents continuously or intermittently over the course of any period of time greater than one (1) hour after 12:00 noon of that day. Notice of all such technical failures shall be provided on the site. NY R UNIF TRIAL CTS § 202.5-b(i).

- When e-filing is hindered by a technical failure, a party may file with the appropriate clerk and serve in hard copy. NY R UNIF TRIAL CTS § 202.5-b(i). In the event an attorney or party shall file and serve documents in hard copy pursuant to NY R UNIF TRIAL CTS § 202.5-b(i), each such document shall include the notice required by NY R UNIF TRIAL CTS § 202.5-b(d)(1), and the filer shall file those documents with the

NYSCEF site within three (3) business days after restoration of normal operations at that site. NY R UNIF TRIAL CTS § 202.5-b(i).

- With the exception of deadlines that by law cannot be extended, the time for filing of any document that is delayed due to technical failure of the site shall be extended for one (1) day for each day on which such failure occurs, unless otherwise ordered by the court. NY R UNIF TRIAL CTS § 202.5-b(i).
- *ERIE COUNTY.* When filing by electronic means is hindered by a technical failure, please refer to the NY R UNIF TRIAL CTS § 202.5-b(i). NY R ERIE E FIL Doc. 3(III)(K).
- *KINGS COUNTY.* When filing by electronic means is hindered by a NYSCEF technical failure (as set forth in NY R UNIF TRIAL CTS § 202.5-b(i)), a party may file with the appropriate Clerk in hard copy. Except for deadlines that by law cannot be extended (e.g. Statute of limitations, Notice of Appeal), the time for filing of any document that is delayed due to technical failure of the NYSCEF system shall be extended for one day for each day on which such failure occurs, unless otherwise ordered by the court. NY R L KINGS E FIL Doc. 1(B)(13).
- *ONONDAGA COUNTY.* When filing by electronic means is hindered by a technical failure (as set forth in NY R UNIF TRIAL CTS § 202.5-b(h)(3)(i)), a party may file a hard copy with the County Clerk. With the exception of deadlines that by law cannot be extended (e.g., a statute of limitations or the deadline for filing a Notice of Appeal), the time for filing of any document that is delayed due to technical failure of the NYSCEF system will be extended for one day for each day on which such failure occurs, unless otherwise ordered by the court. A "Notice of Hard Copy Filing Submission—E-Filed Case' must accompany any documents not filed via NYSCEF. NY R ONDGA E FIL Protocol(B)(8).

xii. *Filing fees.* For information on what information must be provided to pay filing fees, refer to NY R UNIF TRIAL CTS § 202.5-b(d)(2).

xiii. *Exemption from e-filing.* For information on exemptions from e-filing, refer to NY R UNIF TRIAL CTS § 202.5-bb(e).

xiv. *Filing exhibits*

- *ERIE COUNTY.* In the NYSCEF system, each exhibit must be uploaded as a separate .pdf file. After uploading a primary document, please choose the document type "Exhibit" and enter the appropriate number or letter and a brief description of the exhibit; each exhibit should bear a separate cover sheet clearly marked as "Exhibit A," "Exhibit B," etc. "Exhibit A" or "Exhibit B" is unacceptable as a brief description of the exhibit. Exhibits, where referenced in a signed Order as attached or affixed shall be uploaded with the signed Order as one .pdf document. NY R ERIE E FIL Doc. 3(III)(H); NY R ERIE E FIL Doc. 3(V)(D).
- *KINGS COUNTY.* In the NYSCEF system, each exhibit should be uploaded as a separate PDF file. After uploading a primary document, please choose the document type "Exhibit", enter the appropriate number or letter, and be sure to place a check mark to the right of "Attach to main document". Each exhibit shall bear a separate cover sheet clearly marked as Exhibit A, Exhibit B, etc. NY R L KINGS E FIL Doc. 1(B)(12). Whenever possible, attorneys submitting exhibits in NYSCEF cases should make each exhibit a separate attachment to an affidavit/affirmation in the system (i.e., multiple exhibits should not be filed as a single PDF). NY R L KINGS E FIL Doc. 1(D)(1).
- *NEW YORK COUNTY.* Attorneys submitting exhibits in NYSCEF cases should make each exhibit a separate attachment to an affidavit/affirmation in the system; i.e., exhibits should not be filed as a single PDF-A together with the affidavit/affirmation or grouped together as a single PDF-A attachment because either of these two formats makes it difficult for the Justice to locate particular exhibits as needed. Counsel must also include appropriate descriptive language in the "Additional Document Information" field in NYSCEF. NY R NY CTY E FIL Doc. 2(D)(6).
- *ONONDAGA COUNTY.* All exhibits in e-filed cases must be e-filed individually as separate attachments. NY R ONDGA E FIL Protocol(B)(9)(b).

xv. *Correcting documents*

- *ERIE COUNTY.* Submission of documents which, upon examination, require correction or addition will result in notification to the filer advising that the document has been returned for correction. The filer shall make the required corrections and/or additions as indicated in the e-mail transmission sent by the County Clerk or Part Clerk through the NYSCEF site. The corrected documents may be resubmitted using the

"Re-file this document" link highlighted in the filer's document list for the respective case. Please note that in the case of multiple submissions, all related documents filed at the same time may be removed from the case record and returned until all documents are properly submitted. NY R ERIE E FIL Doc. 3(III)(J).

- *KINGS COUNTY.* Submission of documents which, upon examination, require correction or addition will result in notification to the filer advising that there is a problem with a document. The filer shall make the required corrections and/or additions and resubmit the corrected document using the "Refile this document" link. In the event a document is returned for correction, the original file date will be preserved. For corrections of documents filed with the Kings County Clerk which require a court order, refer to the procedure in NY R UNIF TRIAL CTS § 202.5-b(d)(3)(iii) and NY R L KINGS E FIL Doc. 1(B)(11). NY R L KINGS E FIL Doc. 1(B)(3).
- *ONONDAGA COUNTY.* If there is an error or an additional document is required, the system will notify the filing party, who will make the corrections/additions and resubmit them online. NY R ONDGA E FIL Protocol(B)(6).
- *QUEENS COUNTY.* Generally speaking, documents that have been E-filed will not thereafter be deleted by the County Clerk from NYCEF because the filer asserts that the filing contains an error or a significant omission. When the filer wishes to correct a perceived error or omission in a filed document, he or she should file an amended version of the document, with the original remaining on file, or else obtain a court order providing for deletion of the original. The County Clerk will only delete a document upon request of the filer or on the County Clerk's own initiative when it is obvious from the face of the document alone that the filer made a fundamental error and never intended to file the document that was filed (e.g., a completely unrelated non-litigation document, a different case, or a wrong county). The County Clerk will advise the filer when any such fundamental errors are detected. NY R L QUEENS E-FILE Doc. 1(E)(6).

c. *Facsimile filing.* In the Supreme Court, facsimile filing shall be limited to commercial claims and tax certiorari, conservatorship, and mental hygiene proceedings in Monroe, Westchester, New York and Suffolk Counties. NY R UNIF TRIAL CTS § 202.5-a(a)(1). Refer to NY R UNIF TRIAL CTS § 202.5-a for information on the procedures for facsimile filing.

   i. *NEW YORK COUNTY.* Unless indicated otherwise by the court in a particular case or in NY R NY CTY J RUL Doc. 1, Justices do not accept papers by fax. NY R NY CTY J RUL Rule 4.

d. *ERIE COUNTY: Filing request for judicial intervention.* An RJI in a NYSCEF case shall be filed via the NYSCEF system and will be filed after all other documents have been uploaded. The filer may choose between filing a .pdf image of the prepared RJI and any Addendum or having the system prepare the RJI which shall conform to Uniform Rules. Addenda, such as the Commercial Division Addendum, if prepared by the filer must be filed simultaneously with and attached to an RJI and uploaded as one .pdf document with the RJI. If the RJI is prepared by the e-filing system, no separate Addendum is required. Whether or not the filer elects to allow NYSCEF to create the RJI or chooses to upload a prepared RJI, data in addition to the nature of the judicial intervention, including information that appears on any Addenda will be collected through completion of the fields presented. If the filing of the RJI is accomplished through a filing agent, a prepared RJI and Addendum must be filed in lieu of the creation of the RJI by the NYSCEF system, as the RJI must be signed by the attorney. NY R ERIE E FIL Doc. 3(IV). For information on RJIs in specific types of action, refer to NY R ERIE E FIL Doc. 3(IV).

2. *Service requirements*

a. *Who may serve.* Except where otherwise prescribed by law or order of court, papers may be served by any person not a party of the age of eighteen years or over. NY CPLR Rule 2103(a).

b. *Service upon attorney.* Except where otherwise prescribed by law or order of court, papers to be served upon a party in a pending action shall be served upon the party's attorney. Where the same attorney appears for two or more parties, only one (1) copy need be served upon the attorney. Such service upon an attorney shall be made:

   i. By delivering the paper to the attorney personally. NY CPLR Rule 2103(b)(1).

   ii. By mailing the paper to the attorney at the address designated by that attorney for that purpose or, if none is designated, at the attorney's last known address; service by mail shall be complete upon mailing. NY CPLR Rule 2103(b)(2).

   - *BRONX COUNTY.* Service by mail must be within the state. NY R BRONX FIL R Doc. 3.

   iii. If the attorney's office is open, by leaving the paper with a person in charge, or if no person is in charge, by leaving it in a conspicuous place; or if the attorney's office is not open, by depositing the paper, enclosed in a sealed wrapper directed to the attorney, in the attorney's office letter drop or box. NY CPLR Rule 2103(b)(3).

iv. By leaving it at the attorney's residence within the state with a person of suitable age and discretion. Service upon an attorney shall not be made at the attorney's residence unless service at the attorney's office cannot be made. NY CPLR Rule 2103(b)(4).

v. By transmitting the paper to the attorney by facsimile transmission, provided that a facsimile telephone number is designated by the attorney for that purpose. Service by facsimile transmission shall be complete upon the receipt by the sender of a signal from the equipment of the attorney served indicating that the transmission was received, and the mailing of a copy of the paper to that attorney. The designation of a facsimile telephone number in the address block subscribed on a paper served or filed in the course of an action or proceeding shall constitute consent to service by facsimile transmission in accordance with NY CPLR Rule 2103(b)(5). An attorney may change or rescind a facsimile telephone number by serving a notice on the other parties. NY CPLR Rule 2103(b)(5).

vi. By dispatching the paper to the attorney by overnight delivery service at the address designated by the attorney for that purpose or, if none is designated, at the attorney's last known address. Service by overnight delivery service shall be complete upon deposit of the paper enclosed in a properly addressed wrapper into the custody of the overnight delivery service for overnight delivery, prior to the latest time designated by the overnight delivery service for overnight delivery. "Overnight delivery service" means any delivery service which regularly accepts items for overnight delivery to any address in the state. NY CPLR Rule 2103(b)(6).

vii. By transmitting the paper to the attorney by electronic means where and in the manner authorized by the chief administrator of the courts by rule and, unless such rule shall otherwise provide, such transmission shall be upon the party's written consent. The subject matter heading for each paper sent by electronic means must indicate that the matter being transmitted electronically is related to a court proceeding. NY CPLR Rule 2103(b)(7).

- *KINGS COUNTY.* Pursuant to the E-Filing Rules, service of interlocutory documents is made by posting a document to the NYSCEF site, which automatically and immediately transmits an email notice of the filing, including a link to the document, to all participating counsel and unrepresented litigants on the case. The Rules also authorize service by other methods permitted by the CPLR. If service by such other method is made, proof of service must be filed with NYSCEF. NY R L KINGS E FIL Doc. 1(I).
- *NEW YORK COUNTY.* Service. . .will be made automatically through NYSCEF upon all participating counsel and unrepresented parties in the case. There are limited exceptions to the requirement for e-filing in the covered kinds of cases. NY R NY CTY Procedure XI(A). Pursuant to the E-Filing Rules, service of interlocutory documents is made by posting a document to the NYSCEF site, which automatically and immediately transmits an e-mail notice of the filing, including a link to the document, to all participating counsel and unrepresented litigants on the case. The Rules also authorize service by other methods permitted by the CPLR. If service by such a method is made, proof of service must be filed with NYSCEF. NY R NY CTY E FIL Doc. 2(I).
- *QUEENS COUNTY.* Filing with the system permits counsel to serve the papers electronically pursuant to NY R UNIF TRIAL CTS § 202.5-b(f) once consent to E-Filing has been filed on-line. Consult NY R UNIF TRIAL CTS § 202.5-bb(c) for service in mandatory e-filing. Any required proof of service should be E-filed as a separate document. NY R L QUEENS E-FILE Doc. 1(E)(4).

c. *Electronic service mandatory; Consenting to electronic service; How electronic service may be made.* Except as otherwise provided in NY R UNIF TRIAL CTS § 202.5-bb, filing and service of all documents in an action that has been commenced electronically in accordance with NY R UNIF TRIAL CTS § 202.5-bb shall be by electronic means. NY R UNIF TRIAL CTS § 202.5-bb(c)(1).

i. *Party's consent required for certain e-filing.* After commencement of an action wherein e-filing is authorized, documents may be electronically filed and served, but only by, and electronic service shall be made only upon, a party or parties who have consented thereto. NY R UNIF TRIAL CTS § 202.5-b(b)(2)(i).

- A consent to e-filing in an action shall state that the party providing it agrees to the use of e-filing in the action and to be bound by the filing and service provisions in NY R UNIF TRIAL CTS § 202.5-b. NY R UNIF TRIAL CTS § 202.5-b(b)(2)(ii).

ii. *Address for service; Duty to notify as to changes.* The e-mail service address recorded at the time of registration is the e-mail address at which service of interlocutory documents on that party may be made through notification transmitted by the NYSCEF site. It is the responsibility of each filing user to monitor that address and promptly notify the Resource Center in the event of a change in his or her e-mail service address. NY R UNIF TRIAL CTS § 202.5-b(f)(2)(i).

iii. *How service made.* An e-filing party causes service of an interlocutory document to be made upon another party participating in e-filing by filing the document electronically. Upon receipt of an interlocutory document, the NYSCEF site shall automatically transmit electronic notification to all e-mail service addresses in such action. NY R UNIF TRIAL CTS § 202.5-b(f)(2)(ii).

- Except as provided otherwise in NY R UNIF TRIAL CTS § 202.5-b(h)(3), the electronic transmission of the notification shall constitute service of the document on the e-mail service addresses identified therein; however, such service will not be effective if the filing party learns that the notification did not reach the address of the person to be served. Proof of such service will be recorded on the NYSCEF site. A party may, however, utilize other service methods permitted by the CPLR provided that, if one of such other methods is used, proof of that service shall be filed electronically. NY R UNIF TRIAL CTS § 202.5-b(f)(2)(ii).

iv. *Signatures on hard copies; Proof of service filed electronically.* When an e-filing party serves a document in hard copy on a non-participating party, the document served shall bear full signatures of all signatories and proof of such service shall be filed electronically. NY R UNIF TRIAL CTS § 202.5-b(b)(2)(i).

- *ERIE COUNTY.* In the NYSCEF system, each Affidavit of Service must be uploaded as a separate .pdf file. After uploading the Affidavit, please choose the document type: "Affirmation/Affidavit of Service" and enter the name of the party served as Additional Document Information. NY R ERIE E FIL Doc. 3(III)(I); NY R ERIE E FIL Doc. 3(V)(F).

v. *Effect of failure to consent.* A party's failure to consent to participation in electronic filing and service shall not bar any other party to the action from filing documents electronically with the County Clerk and the court or serving documents upon any other party who has consented to participation. A party who has not consented to participation shall file documents with the court and the County Clerk, and serve and be served with documents, in hard copy. NY R UNIF TRIAL CTS § 202.5-b(b)(2)(i).

d. *Service upon party.* If a party has not appeared by an attorney or the party's attorney cannot be served, service shall be upon the party by a method specified in NY CPLR Rule 2103(b)(1), NY CPLR Rule 2103(b)(2), NY CPLR Rule 2103(b)(4), NY CPLR Rule 2103(b)(5) or NY CPLR Rule 2103(b)(6). NY CPLR Rule 2103(c).

e. *Service on all parties.* Each paper served on any party shall be served on every other party who has appeared, except as otherwise may be provided by court order or as provided in NY CPLR § 3012 or in NY CPLR § 3215(f). Upon demand by a party, the plaintiff shall supply that party with a list of those who have appeared and the names and addresses of their attorneys. NY CPLR Rule 2103(e).

f. *Service by filing.* If a paper cannot be served by any of the methods specified in NY CPLR Rule 2103(b) and NY CPLR Rule 2103(c), service may be made by filing the paper as if it were a paper required to be filed. NY CPLR Rule 2103(d).

g. *Definitions.* For the purposes of NY CPLR Rule 2103:

i. "Mailing" means the deposit of a paper enclosed in a first class postpaid wrapper, addressed to the address designated by a person for that purpose or, if none is designated, at that person's last known address, in a post office or official depository under the exclusive care and custody of the United States Postal Service within the state;

ii. "Electronic means" means any method of transmission of information between computers or other machines designed for the purpose of sending and receiving such transmissions, and which allows the recipient to reproduce the information transmitted in a tangible medium of expression;

iii. "Facsimile transmission" means any method of transmission of documents to a facsimile machine at a remote location which can automatically produce a tangible copy of such documents. NY CPLR Rule 2103(f).

G. Hearings

1. *Oral argument.* Motion papers received by the clerk of the court on or before the return date shall be deemed submitted as of the return date. The assigned judge, in his or her discretion or at the request of a party, thereafter may determine that any motion be orally argued and may fix a time for oral argument. NY R UNIF TRIAL CTS § 202.8(d).

a. A party requesting oral argument shall set forth such request in its notice of motion or in its order to show cause or on the first page of the answering papers, as the case may be. Where all parties to a motion request oral argument, oral argument shall be granted unless the court shall determine it to be unnecessary. NY R UNIF TRIAL CTS § 202.8(d).

b. Where a motion is brought on by order to show cause, the court may set forth in the order that oral argument is required on the return date of the motion. NY R UNIF TRIAL CTS § 202.8(d).

i. *BRONX COUNTY.* All orders to show cause, with the exception of orders to show cause that are returnable in the

City Part, the STP Part, the Matrimonial Part and the Preliminary/Compliance Conference Part (IA-11), submitted on or after August 25, 2003, will be returnable on a Monday in the assigned Justice's part and appear on his or her motion calendar. Appearances will be required on orders to show cause. NY R BRONX FIL R Doc. 8. A motion on notice or a notice of petition in a New York Supreme Court E-File (hereafter known as NYSCEF) case, as in others, shall be made returnable in the Motion Support Office (Room 217). NY R BRONX E FIL R Doc. 1(1).

- After a motion/petition and notice are filed with the NYSCEF system, the Motion Support Office will automatically place the motion/proceeding on the submit calendar in the Motion Support Office (Room 217) for the return date. No appearance or other action by the filing attorney is required in order for the motion to be calendared if the motion fee is paid for via NYSCEF. Motions in e-filed cases (other than tax certiorari cases) appear on the submit calendar in Room 217 on the return date. NY R BRONX E FIL R Doc. 1(2).

c. *KINGS COUNTY.* All motions require appearances and oral argument. NY R L KINGS Pt. C, Rule 3.

2. *Return date; Time for hearing.* A notice of motion shall specify the time and place of the hearing on the motion. NY CPLR Rule 2214(a). The moving party determines when a motion on notice shall be heard, but she has to consult the court's or judge's calendar practice first. The movant picks out a "return day" sufficiently far off to assure that the notice requirements of NY CPLR Rule 2214(b) can be met, and to assure as well that the day picked is a day on which the assigned judge hears motions. SIEGEL-NYPRAC § 247.

a. *Judge assigned to hear motion*

i. *Referral to judge supervising disclosure.* Unless the chief administrator of the courts has, by rule, provided otherwise, if a case has been assigned to a judge to supervise disclosure pursuant to NY CPLR § 3104, all motions preliminary to trial shall be referred to such judge whenever practicable. NY CPLR Rule 3214(a).

ii. *Referral to judge who decided prior motion.* Any motion may be referred to a judge who decided a prior motion in the action. NY CPLR Rule 2217(a).

iii. *Transfer when judge unable to hear motion.* If a motion is made to a judge who is or will be for any reason unable to hear it, it may be transferred by order of such judge or by written stipulation of the parties to any other judge to whom it might originally have been made. NY CPLR Rule 2217(c).

iv. *Procedure for unassigned cases.* If a case has not been assigned to a judge, the motion shall be made returnable before the court, and a copy of the moving papers, together with a request for judicial intervention, shall be filed with the court, with proof of service upon all other parties, where required by NY R UNIF TRIAL CTS § 202.6, within five (5) days of service upon the other parties. The moving party shall give written notice of the index number to all other parties immediately after filing of the papers. NY R UNIF TRIAL CTS § 202.8(b).

- *Responding papers.* Copies of all responding papers shall be submitted to the court, with proof of service and with the index number set forth in the papers, on or before the return date. NY R UNIF TRIAL CTS § 202.8(b).
- *Assignment after request for judicial intervention.* The case shall be assigned to a judge as soon as practicable after the filing of the request for judicial intervention pursuant to NY R UNIF TRIAL CTS § 202.6, but in no event later than the return date. After assignment to the judge, the court shall provide for appropriate notice to the parties of the name of the assigned judge. NY R UNIF TRIAL CTS § 202.8(b).
- *Motions to be heard in another county.* Motion papers noticed to be heard in a county other than the county where the venue of the action has been placed by the plaintiff shall be assigned to a judge in accordance with procedures established by the Chief Administrator. NY R UNIF TRIAL CTS § 202.8(b).

v. *ALBANY COUNTY: Motions referred to IAS Justice.* All motions made after a case has been assigned a day certain shall be referred to the IAS Justice unless the motion is returnable during the term in which the matter has been assigned a day certain, in that event, the matter will be referred to the Part 1 Justice for that particular term who may entertain the motion or refer such motion to the IAS Justice. Under those circumstances, the Part I Justice shall decide whether or not to strike the note of issue or assign the matter a new day certain. NY R 3 JD SUP Doc. 1(H)(2). All motions shall be returnable before the assigned justice. NY R 3 JD SUP Doc. 1(B).

b. *Trial of issue raised by motion.* The court may order that an issue of fact raised on a motion shall be separately tried by the court or a referee. If the issue is triable of right by jury, the court shall give the parties an opportunity to demand a jury trial of such issue. Failure to make such demand within the time limited by the court, or, if no such time is limited, before trial begins, shall be deemed a waiver of the right to trial by jury. An order under NY CPLR § 2218 shall specify the issue to be tried. NY CPLR § 2218.

c. *Audio-visual coverage of trial court proceeding.* Audio-visual coverage of proceedings in the trial courts shall be permitted only in accordance with the provisions of Part 131 of the Rules of the Chief Administrator (NY R CHIEF ADMIN § 131.1, et seq.). NY R CHIEF J § 29.3.

d. *Adjournment of return date.* Stipulations of adjournment of the return date made by the parties shall be in writing and shall be submitted to the assigned judge. Such stipulation shall be effective unless the court otherwise directs. No more than three (3) stipulated adjournments for an aggregate period of sixty (60) days shall be submitted without prior permission of the court. NY R UNIF TRIAL CTS § 202.8(e)(1).

i. Absent agreement by the parties, a request by any party for an adjournment shall be submitted in writing, upon notice to the other party, to the assigned judge on or before the return date. The court will notify the requesting party whether the adjournment has been granted. NY R UNIF TRIAL CTS § 202.8(e)(2).

ii. *BRONX COUNTY.* Non-disclosure motions for IA5, IA7 and IA22 will be adjourned for oral argument to the Monday of the second week following the week of the return date of the motion. All other non-disclosure motions will be deemed submitted on the return date and forwarded to Chambers unless a stipulation of adjournment complying with the requirements of NY R UNIF TRIAL CTS § 202.8(e) is submitted, in which event, the motion will be adjourned for the requested date and kept in the Clerk's Office. If a non-stipulated request for adjournment or notice is submitted, the motion and request will be forwarded to Chambers for judicial approval or denial of the request. In either event, the attorney requesting the adjournment will be notified, via telephone, of the granting or denial of the request and instructed to notify his adversary. NY R BRONX FIL R Doc. 8.

iii. *BRONX COUNTY.* Motions that have been e-filed may be adjourned in Room 217 if an adjournment complies with the procedures of the Motion Support Office (explained in the "Filing Rules—Motion Procedure" section of the "Courthouse Procedures" link on the website of [the] court). An adjournment that so complies may be obtained by filing a stipulation of all parties with NYSCEF (designated in the filing menu as a "Stipulation to Adjourn Motion"). NY R BRONX E FIL R Doc. 1(3).

iv. *NEW YORK COUNTY.* The Courtroom also maintains a "APB (All Papers By)" Calendar, which is used when a party seeks an adjournment but fails to comply with the Courtroom's procedures or there is a failure to comply with procedures that requires the clerk to adjourn the motion/application (e.g., failure to submit a Confirmation Notice in an e-filed case). The case may be put over for three days to allow compliance with those procedures, as described further below. NY R NY CTY Procedure II(C); NY R NY CTY E FIL Doc. 2(D)(2). E-filed applications may be adjourned in the Part if an adjournment complies with the Part's procedures (see the Uniform Rules of the Justices (Local Rules) on the court's website). An adjournment that so complies may be obtained by filing with NYSCEF a stipulation of all parties (designated in the filing menu as a Stipulation—Adjournment of Motion—Before Judge); the motion number and the current return date of the motion being adjourned shall be set forth in the "Additional Document Information" field in NYSCEF. Absent any problems, the Part will effectuate the adjournment without need for an appearance or any other action by the parties. NY R NY CTY E FIL Doc. 2(D)(4).

v. *QUEENS COUNTY.* The Motion Support Office is NOT authorized to grant adjournments. NY R L QUEENS MOT SUP Doc. 1.

e. *ALBANY COUNTY: Motion terms.* There shall be a. . . Motion Term on each Friday in the Supreme Court, Albany County. The Friday Motion Term shall include all Article 78 Proceedings involving New York State and proceedings commenced pursuant to Article 14 of the Civil Service Law (including applications for injunctive relief made pursuant to section 209-a of the Civil Service Law). NY R 3 JD SUP Doc. 1(F). Generally, parties will be granted only one adjournment for the Friday Motion Term. NY R 3 JD SUP Doc. 1(F).

f. *ALBANY COUNTY: Motion determined without hearing.* All motions are deemed "submitted" on the return date and no appearances are required by the parties. NY R 3 JD SUP Doc. 1(B). In the event oral argument is requested, the parties should not appear on the return date. At the discretion of the assigned Judge and upon the granting of a request for oral argument, the parties will be notified by Chambers of the scheduled time and place at which argument will be heard. Where a motion is brought on by order to show cause, the court may set forth in the order that appearances and/or oral argument are required on the return date of the motion. NY R 3 JD SUP Doc. 1(B).

g. *BRONX COUNTY: Return date.* All assigned and unassigned motions will be returnable five (5) days a week in the Civil Branch Clerk's Office, Room 217, at 9:30 a.m. NY R BRONX FIL R Doc. 8.

i. If on any submitted non-disclosure motion oral argument is requested and granted, or directed by the Court, the motion shall be adjourned for oral argument before the I.A. Judge on the second Monday following the week of the return date of the motion. Attorneys will be notified via telephone of the adjourned date. NY R BRONX FIL R Doc. 8.

h. *BRONX COUNTY: Oral argument.* Calendars of disclosure motions and other motions adjourned for oral argument will be published for the four (4) business days preceding the rescheduled appearance date and on the rescheduled date of the motion. These repetitive publications will serve as the notification of procedure of adjournment of all motions. In addition, two (2) days before the return date of unassigned motions a list of such motions indicating the assigned Justice and the adjourned date of the motion will be published. NY R BRONX FIL R Doc. 8.

i. *BRONX COUNTY: Resolution before return date.* Counsel/parties must advise the Court in writing on or before the return date of all motions that have been resolved by Counsel/parties themselves and all motions the movant(s) wish to be withdrawn. NY R BRONX FIL R Doc. 8.

j. *ERIE COUNTY: Calendaring of motions.* Refer to individual Justice's Part Rules. NY R ERIE E FIL Doc. 3(V)(B).

k. *KINGS COUNTY: Return date set by court.* Irrespective of the return date indicated in the notice of motion, motions will be rescheduled by the E-file/Motion Support Office to a date designated by the assigned Judge. NY R L KINGS Pt. C, Rule 2.

l. *KINGS COUNTY: Calendar calls.* There shall be two (2) calendar calls on motion days. The first calendar call shall be at 9:30 AM and the second calendar call shall be at 10:45 AM, unless the Judge's Part Rules provide otherwise. Defaults shall only be taken on second call. Attorneys with appearances elsewhere in the courthouse may advise the clerk of their whereabouts to avoid a default. Failure to so advise the clerk or appear at the default calendar call will result in a default order being entered or the motion being marked off the calendar. NY R L KINGS Pt. C, Rule 7.

m. *NEW YORK COUNTY: Return date and assigned courtroom.* Motions made by notice of motion and petitions and notices of petition in special proceedings are processed by the General Clerk's Office (Room 119) and are to be made returnable in the Motion Submission Part Courtroom (Room 130) on any business day of the week at 9:30 AM. There are some differences in electronically-filed cases. NY R NY CTY Procedure II; NY R NY CTY Procedure II(C); NY R NY CTY J RUL Rule 13(a).

   i. For the convenience of counsel, between 9:00 A.M. and 9:30 A.M. each day, in advance of the "call," Room 130 accepts (1) written stipulations; (2) affidavits/affirmations reciting the required details as to an adjournment on consent; (3) stipulations, letters or other writings withdrawing motions; and (4) final papers or complete sets of papers on motions. For motions in which these items are handed in before the "call," no one need remain to answer the "call." Counsel/parties must advise the court, either between 9:00 A.M. and 9:30 A.M. or at the "call," of all motions or cases that have been resolved by counsel/parties themselves and all motions that the movant no longer wishes to pursue. If such resolution occurs subsequent to the "call", the assigned Justice must be advised as soon as possible, by written notice sent to the Part, so that the court does not do unnecessary work. NY R NY CTY Procedure II(C).

   ii. Depending upon the assigned Part, contested motions submitted in the Motion Submission Part Courtroom are submitted without argument, or rescheduled for oral argument if so directed by the assigned Justice. For Justices who schedule argument on a case-by-case basis, notice of the argument date will be transmitted by the court. Counsel may ascertain how a motion submitted in Courtroom 130 was marked by consulting Scroll on the court's website, the e-Track application, or, on the two (2) days immediately following the submission date, the New York Law Journal. NY R NY CTY J RUL Rule 13(a).

n. *NEW YORK COUNTY: Motion call.* Each day in the Motion Submission Part Courtroom, commencing at 9:30 A.M., all motions returnable that day will be "called" for the submission of these papers, which must be handed up at this "call" or, as described below, immediately before. Because hundreds of motions appear on the Room 130 calendars every day, motion papers (other than part of the moving papers as described above) cannot be accepted on any day prior to the return date. Courtesy copies are not required nor accepted, but working copies are required by certain Justices in e-filed cases. NY R NY CTY Procedure II(C). If argument is directed, it will take place on an announced date shortly after the day of submission. NY R NY CTY Procedure II(C).

o. *NEW YORK COUNTY: Oral arguments.* Pursuant to request of some Justices, motions submitted in Room 130 will automatically be scheduled for a set argument date in the Part. Other Justices determine on a case-by-case basis after submission in Room 130 whether to accept a particular substantive motion on submission, to require oral argument, or to hold a conference. NY R NY CTY Procedure II(D). If argument is directed by the Justice automatically, notice of argument and the argument date will be given in Room 130. Any appearing party is expected to give notice to all parties and an announcement to this effect is made in Room 130. If the motion is submitted in Room 130 and the Justice, after examining the file, determines that argument should be directed, notice of the argument and the argument date will not be sent by the court. To obtain notification of the argument date and other developments, counsel should use e-Track. If argument notification is not given or transmitted as just described, counsel should understand that the motion has been taken on submission for decision on the papers. NY R NY CTY Procedure II(D).

i. Calendars of motions to be argued in the Parts are published on the morning of the argument date and on the day before in the New York Law Journal under each Part. Argument information is available on a case-by-case basis in Scroll, and e-mail notifications are sent by e-Track to participating attorneys whenever a motion is scheduled for argument in the court's computer system. NY R NY CTY J RUL Rule 15(a)

p. *NEW YORK COUNTY: Motion determined without hearing.* Given the purpose of the Room 130 procedure, the substance of motions will not be addressed at the submission "call." No Judge is present. To the extent possible, motions submitted in Room 130 will be decided "on the papers." Indeed, attorneys are encouraged to use service or clerks to deliver papers or working copies, or to agree among themselves to have one of them deliver papers for all parties by service or a clerk. Counsel for the movant need not appear to "take a default" on any motion or for any other reason. Motions will be submitted, not marked off, in the absence of the movant. Opposing counsel similarly need not appear in person in order to avoid suffering a default. Delivery of papers by service or a clerk will suffice. The court's goal is to be able to collect papers on motions in an orderly fashion but without any attorney having to make an appearance in Room 130 at any time. NY R NY CTY Procedure II(C).

q. *ONONDAGA COUNTY: Return date.* If the motion is the first filing in an action, the case will be assigned and counsel will be notified by the Supreme Court Clerk's Office via the NYSCEF system of the assigned justice and return date. NY R ONDGA E FIL Protocol(B)(7)(c). If the motion is on a previously assigned case, counsel may choose a return date from the assigned justice's motion term schedule. If the date in unavailable, the Supreme Court Clerk's Office will assign the motion to the next available motion term date and will notify counsel via e-mail. The change will also appear in the notification generated by the NYSCEF system. NY R ONDGA E FIL Protocol(B)(7)(d).

r. *QUEENS COUNTY: Return date.* Motions must be made returnable on the proper day/time based on the assigned judge. NY R L QUEENS MOT SUP Doc. 1. Failure to make a motion returnable on the proper day/time may result in the motion being administratively rescheduled or marked off. NY R L QUEENS MOT SUP Doc. 1.

s. *QUEENS COUNTY: Unassigned motions.* For RJI/Motions, due to the fact that the movant would not know who the assigned judge will be, the notice of motion may be returnable any day of the week. RJI/Motions shall be made returnable in "Queens Supreme Court" with no address designated. The motion will be administratively rescheduled to the proper day of the week based on the judge (once a judge has been assigned). Within one (1) week of filing, the movant must check online to see who the assigned judge is (and therefore the location/date/time) that their motion is now returnable. Movant must then notify their adversary of this information prior to the return date. NY R L QUEENS MOT SUP Doc. 1.

3. *Entry of order after hearing.* An order determining a motion shall be entered and filed in the office of the clerk of the court where the action is triable, and all papers used on the motion and any opinion or memorandum in writing shall be filed with that clerk unless the order dispenses with such filing. When a statute or civil practice rule requires such filing and entry in a county other than that in which the order was made, the party prevailing on the motion shall file the order and the papers used on the motion with the proper clerk after receiving them. If a party fails to file any papers required to be filed under NY CPLR Rule 2220(a), the order may be vacated as irregular, with costs. NY CPLR Rule 2220(a). For more information on the entry of an order after a motion, refer to NY CPLR Rule 2219.

a. *BRONX COUNTY: Settled orders.* A Judge's decision will often call for a Settled Order. The purpose of the settled order is to give effect to the decision by directing that some action be done and/or that a court official perform some task. NY R BRONX LEG SUP Doc. 2. A settled order consists of a notice of settlement informing all parties that the proposed order will be presented to the judge who made the decision on a date certain. Next comes the proposed order which will be presented to the judge. This order should conform to the judge's decision and should direct the relief granted in the decision. This should be followed by proof of service upon all parties who were noticed with the decision. It is also helpful if a copy of the judge's decision is included along with the other papers. A settled order should always be noticed before the judge who made the decision. NY R BRONX LEG SUP Doc. 2.

i. Although an order is usually settled by the party who prevailed on the motion, any party may settle the order. It should be presented to the court within sixty (60) days of the decision. The other parties are entitled to ten (10) days notice where service of the settled order is done by mail, five (5) days if the notice is personally delivered. An attorney who is served with a notice of settlement which he believes does not accurately reflect the decision may settle a counter order. The counter order must be noticed for the same day and must be served not less than seven (7) days if by mail and two (2) days if personally delivered. NY R BRONX LEG SUP Doc. 2.

ii. Settled orders are usually sent to the judge the day after they noticed for settlement. No appearance is necessary or even contemplated on a settled order. If the decision directs "submit order", then no notice is necessary, and the order will be sent to the judge as soon a practical after it is received. No fees are collected on settled orders. NY R BRONX LEG SUP Doc. 2.

b. *ERIE COUNTY: Proposed orders.* Proposed orders shall be submitted through the NYSCEF system and a working copy provided to the IAS Justice for signature, if Part Rules so require. NY R ERIE E FIL Doc. 3(V)(G).

c. *KINGS COUNTY: Long form orders.* If the Court directs that an order be settled or submitted on a motion in a NYSCEF case, the proposed order, with Notice of Settlement where required, and any proposed counter-order shall be filed with the Court via NYSCEF. The relevant clerk's office will process the documents in the customary manner. NY R L KINGS E FIL Doc. 1(E).

   i. WORKING COPIES OF PROPOSED ORDERS WITH NOTICE OF SETTLEMENT MUST BE SUBMITTED IN THE MOTION SUPPORT OFFICE (ROOM 227) AS EXPLAINED HEREIN. THEY MUST NOT BE DELIVERED TO THE PART OR CHAMBERS, EXCEPT WHERE THE INDIVIDUAL JUSTICE'S PART RULES PROVIDE OTHERWISE; DOING SO WILL CAUSE ADMINISTRATIVE CONFUSION AND POSSIBLE MISPLACEMENT OF PAPERS. Any such submission shall be sent in a timely manner (kindly review individual Justice's rules) and be conspicuously marked on the outside "NYSCEF Matter;" lack of such marking may delay processing. After an order/counter-order has been signed, it will be scanned, and the County Clerk will affix the entry stamp into the NYSCEF system, which will immediately transmit notice of this event via e-mail, including a link to the entered document, to all participating attorneys and unrepresented litigants in the case. Such transmittal does not constitute Notice of Entry. NY R L KINGS E FIL Doc. 1(E).

d. *NEW YORK COUNTY: Long form orders.* Although the court strongly favors the use of short form orders and judgments, there are instances when settlement of an order or judgment is appropriate. When a Justice directs in a decision that a long form order or judgment be settled, that decision is recorded in the court's computer system by the General Clerk's Office and the motion file with decision is held in the Order Section of the Office in Room 119. The settlement process takes place there. NY R NY CTY Procedure II(D); NY R NY CTY E FIL Doc. 2(E).

   i. A proposed long form order or judgment in compliance NY R UNIF TRIAL CTS § 202.48 must be presented to the relevant back office, together with a notice of settlement which bears a settlement date, the date on which the order is to be ready for formal presentation to the Justice. In an e-filed case the submission shall be made electronically. The proposed order or counter-order should be e-filed and it will be transmitted automatically by the NYSCEF system to the appropriate back office. The return date and time of the proposed order must be at 9:30 A.M. no sooner than either five (5) days from personal service of the proposed order or ten (10) days from service by mail. Proof of timely service on the other parties must accompany the proposed order in a hard copy case. If an order or judgment is submitted late (later than sixty (60) days from signing and filing of the decision) and the proponent can show good cause for this tardiness, an affidavit or affirmation justifying the delay should be annexed to the proposed order, together with proof of service thereof. If persuaded, the Justice will consider the proposed order despite its untimeliness. NY R NY CTY Procedure II(D); NY R NY CTY E FIL Doc. 2(E).

   ii. Sometimes a decision will state "Submit Order." The submitting party should prepare a long form order and make it returnable without notice. Counsel should deliver the proposed order to the Order Section of the appropriate back office, except in an e-filed case, when it shall be submitted electronically. NY R NY CTY Procedure II(D). If the decision of the court directs that a proposed order be settled or submitted in the Part or in Chambers, that direction, should, of course, be followed without presentation of the proposal to the back office. NY R NY CTY Procedure II(D).

   iii. For information on proposed counter-orders, refer to NY R NY CTY Procedure II(D) and NY R NY CTY J RUL Rule 16(b).

e. *QUEENS COUNTY: Proposed orders.* If the court directs that an order be settled or submitted on a motion in an E-file case, the proposed order and any proposed counter-order shall be filed with the court on-line with proof of service. (If a decision refers to a proceeding on the record, a copy of the transcript must be submitted.) Working copies of all proposed orders MUST be submitted to the Motion Support Office before an order can be reviewed. NY R L QUEENS E-FILE Doc. 1(I).

   i. Counsel are advised to adhere to NY R UNIF TRIAL CTS § 202.48 regarding the submission or settlement of their proposed order or judgment. Persons who are submitting proposed orders/judgments pursuant to a previously issued memorandum decision must submit a copy of the memorandum decision with their proposed order/judgment. Upon E-Filing a proposed order/judgement, a working copy of the proposed order/judgement must be provided to the Motion Support Office. NY R L QUEENS MOT SUP Doc. 1.

H. Forms

1. Official Motion for Sanctions Forms for New York

a. Request for judicial intervention. NY R UNIF TRIAL CTS § 202.6.

b. Notice of motion. NY R UNIF TRIAL CTS § 202.7(b).

2. New York Motion for Sanctions Forms

a. Notice of motion by defendant in libel action for summary judgment and the imposition of sanctions for frivolous actions; Short form. MCF CPLR § 12:326.

b. Affirmation in support of motion by defendant in libel action for summary judgment and the imposition of sanctions for frivolous action. MCF CPLR § 12:327.

c. Affidavit in support of motion by defendant in libel action for summary judgment and the imposition of sanctions for frivolous action. MCF CPLR § 12:328.

d. General form of affidavit of service of motion papers. MCF CPLR § 5:24.

I. Applicable Rules

1. *State rules*

a. Short title; Application; Construction; Definitions. NY CPLR § 101; NY CPLR § 103; NY CPLR § 104; NY CPLR § 105.

b. Appendix of official forms. NY CPLR § 107.

c. Extensions of time generally. NY CPLR § 2004.

d. Form of papers. NY CPLR Rule 2101; NY CPLR Rule 2102; NY CPLR § 2105; NY CPLR Rule 2106; NY GEN BUS § 399-ddd; NY R UNIF TRIAL CTS § 215.2; NY R UNIF TRIAL CTS § 215.3.

e. Service of papers. NY CPLR Rule 2103.

f. Where motion made; In supreme court action. NY CPLR § 2212.

g. Motion papers; Service; Time. NY CPLR Rule 2214.

h. Relief demanded by other than moving party. NY CPLR Rule 2215.

i. Prior motion; Ex parte motion; Transfer of motion; Hearings; Orders. NY CPLR Rule 2217; NY CPLR § 2218; NY CPLR Rule 2220.

j. Computation of time. NY CPLR § 2402; NY GEN CONSTR § 19; NY GEN CONSTR § 20; NY GEN CONSTR § 25-a; NY GEN CONSTR § 30; NY GEN CONSTR § 31; NY GEN CONSTR § 53.

k. Motions heard by judge supervising disclosure; Stay of disclosure. NY CPLR Rule 3214.

l. Fees; Index number fees of county clerks. NY CPLR § 8018.

m. Costs upon frivolous claims and counterclaims in actions to recover damages for personal injury, injury to property or wrongful death. NY CPLR § 8303-a.

n. Hours of court; Proceedings in court. NY R CHIEF J § 3.1; NY R CHIEF J § 29.3.

o. Application of part; Waiver; Additional rules; Application of CPLR; Definitions. NY R UNIF TRIAL CTS § 202.1.

p. Papers filed in court; Electronic filing in supreme court. NY R UNIF TRIAL CTS § 202.5; NY R UNIF TRIAL CTS § 202.5-a; NY R UNIF TRIAL CTS § 202.5-b; NY R UNIF TRIAL CTS § 202.5-bb.

q. Request for judicial intervention. NY R UNIF TRIAL CTS § 202.6.

r. Calendaring of motions; Uniform notice of motion form; Affirmation of good faith. NY R UNIF TRIAL CTS § 202.7.

s. Motion procedure; Preliminary conferences. NY R UNIF TRIAL CTS § 202.8; NY R UNIF TRIAL CTS § 202.12.

t. Rules of the commercial division of the Supreme Court. NY R UNIF TRIAL CTS § 202.70.

u. Costs; Sanctions. NY R CHIEF ADMIN § 130-1.1; NY R CHIEF ADMIN § 130-1.1-a; NY R CHIEF ADMIN § 130-1.2; NY R CHIEF ADMIN § 130-1.5; NY R CHIEF ADMIN § 130-2.1; NY R CHIEF ADMIN § 130-2.2.

2. *Local rules*

a. *Albany County*

i. Third judicial district rules. NY R 3 JD SUP Doc. 1.

b. *Bronx County*

  i. Filing of papers in supreme court. NY R BRONX FIL R Doc. 1.
  ii. Request for judicial intervention. NY R BRONX FIL R Doc. 2.
  iii. Motion procedure. NY R BRONX FIL R Doc. 8.
  iv. Commercial division. NY R BRONX FIL R Doc. 12.
  v. Motions on notice. NY R BRONX E FIL R Doc. 1.
  vi. Settled orders. NY R BRONX LEG SUP Doc. 2.

c. *Erie County*

  i. Joint protocols for New York State Courts E-Filing (NYSCEF) cases filed in Supreme Court, Erie County. NY R ERIE E FIL Doc. 3.

d. *Kings County*

  i. Papers. NY R L KINGS Pt. A, Papers.
  ii. Service of motion papers. NY R L KINGS Pt. C, Rule 1.
  iii. Scheduling of motions. NY R L KINGS Pt. C, Rule 2.
  iv. Appearance and argument. NY R L KINGS Pt. C, Rule 3.
  v. Courtesy copies. NY R L KINGS Pt. C, Rule 5.
  vi. Motion calendar calls. NY R L KINGS Pt. C, Rule 7.
  vii. Protocol on courthouse and county clerk procedures for electronically filed cases. NY R L KINGS E FIL Doc. 1.

e. *New York County*

  i. Commencement of cases. NY R NY CTY Procedure I.
  ii. RJIs and assignments. NY R NY CTY Procedure IA.
  iii. Motions and special proceedings by notice of motion/petition. NY R NY CTY Procedure II.
  iv. County clerk litigation functions. NY R NY CTY Procedure XI.
  v. Protocol on courthouse and county clerk procedures for electronically filed cases. NY R NY CTY E FIL Doc. 2.
  vi. Redaction of information in documents filed with the county clerk and the court. NY R NY CTY J RUL Rule A-1.
  vii. Papers by fax. NY R NY CTY J RUL Rule 4.
  viii. Motions on notice; Orders to show cause. NY R NY CTY J RUL Rule 13.
  ix. Motion papers. NY R NY CTY J RUL Rule 14.
  x. Oral argument; Adjournments. NY R NY CTY J RUL Rule 15.

f. *Onondaga County*

  i. Onondaga county protocol for case filings New York State Electronic Files (NYSCEF). NY R ONDGA E FIL Protocol.

g. *Queens County*

  i. Motion support office. NY R L QUEENS MOT SUP Doc. 1.
  ii. Queens county protocol on courthouse procedures for electronically filed cases. NY R L QUEENS E-FILE Doc. 1.

J. Miscellaneous

NOTE: Individual judges' rules may apply.

ALBANY COUNTY

JUSTICE LISA M. FISHER: NY R 3 JD FISHER Fisher; NY R 3 JD FISHER Fisher, PC Order.

JUSTICE RICHARD MOTT: NY R 3 JD MOTT Mott.

JUSTICE STEPHAN G. SCHICK: NY R 3 JD Schick.

FORECLOSURE SETTLEMENT PART: NY R 3 JD Foreclosure Settlement.

BRONX COUNTY

JUSTICE PAUL L. ALPERT: [NY R BRONX J Part IA-29, as amended by NY ORDER 20-0337].

JUSTICE BEN BARBATO: NY R BRONX J Part IA-21.

JUSTICE MARY ANNE BRIGANTTI: [NY R BRONX J Part IA-15, as amended by NY ORDER 20-0338].

JUSTICE JOSEPH E. CAPELLA: NY R BRONX J Part IA-23.

JUSTICE MITCHELL DANZIGER: NY R BRONX J Part IA-3/33 ; [NY R BRONX J Danziger, Part IA-3/33, as amended by NY ORDER 20-0339].

JUSTICE LAURA G. DOUGLAS: NY R BRONX J Part IA-11.

JUSTICE RUBEN FRANCO: NY R BRONX J Part IA-26.

JUSTICE DORIS M. GONZALEZ: NY R BRONX J Part IA-24.

JUSTICE WILMA GUZMAN: NY R BRONX J Part IA-7; [NY R BRONX J Guzman, Part IA-7 Virtual, as amended by NY ORDER 20-0340].

JUSTICE ROBERT T. JOHNSON: NY R BRONX J Part IA-12.

JUSTICE DONALD A. MILES: NY R BRONX J Part IA-8.

JUSTICE DONNA M. MILLS: NY R BRONX J Part IA-9.

JUSTICE JULIA I. RODRIGUEZ: NY R BRONX J Part IA-18; [NY R BRONX J Part IA-27, as amended by NY ORDER 20-0341].

JUSTICE LLINET M. ROSADO: [NY R BRONX J Part IA-25, as amended by NY ORDER 20-0342].

JUSTICE NORMA RUIZ: NY R BRONX J Part IA-22; [NY R BRONX J Ruiz, Part IA-22 Virtual, as amended by NY ORDER 20-0343].

JUSTICE HOWARD H. SHERMAN: NY R BRONX J Part IA-4.

JUSTICE FERNANDO TAPIA: NY R BRONX J Part IA-13.

JUSTICE ELIZABETH A. TAYLOR: NY R BRONX J Part IA-2.

JUSTICE ALISON Y. TRUITT: NY R BRONX J Part IA-5.

PART IDV: NY R BRONX J Doc. 1.

PRE-TRIAL PART RULES: NY R BRONX J Doc. 2.

PRE TRIAL WORKSHEET: NY R BRONX J Doc. 3.

FORECLOSURE SETTLEMENT PART RULES: NY R BRONX J Doc. 4.

GUARDIANSHIP PART RULES: NY R BRONX J Doc. 5.

LPM PART RULES: NY R BRONX J Doc. 6.

ERIE COUNTY

JUSTICE M. WILLIAM BOLLER: NY R 8 JD J Boller.

JUSTICE RALPH A. BONIELLO: NY R 8 JD J Boniello.

JUSTICE CHRISTOPHER J. BURN: NY R 8 JD J Burns.

JUSTICE RUSSELL P. BUSCAGLIA: NY R 8 JD J Buscaglia.

JUSTICE FRANK CARUSO: NY R 8 JD J Caruso.

JUSTICE STEPHEN W. CASS: NY R 8 JD J Cass.

JUSTICE DEBORAH A. CHIMES: NY R 8 JD J Chimes.

JUSTICE EMILIO COLAIACOVO: [NY R 8 JD J Colaiacovo, as amended by NY ORDER 20-0252].

JUSTICE DIANE Y. DEVLIN: NY R 8 JD J Devlin.

JUSTICE JAMES H. DILLON: NY R 8 JD J Dillon.

JUSTICE PAULA L. FEROLETO: NY R 8 JD J Feroleto.

JUSTICE DANIEL J. FURLONG: [NY R 8 JD J Furlong, as amended by NY ORDER 20-0253].

JUSTICE JOSEPH R. GLOWNIA: NY R 8 JD J Glownia.

JUSTICE MARK J. GRISANTI: NY R 8 JD J Grisanti.

JUSTICE DEBORAH A. HAENDIGES: NY R 8 JD J Haendiges.

JUSTICE LYNN W. KEANE: [NY R 8 JD J Keane, as amended by NY ORDER 20-0254].

JUSTICE RICHARD C. KLOCH, Sr.: NY R 8 JD J Kloch.

JUSTICE FREDERICK J. MARSHALL: [NY R 8 JD J Marshall, as amended by NY ORDER 20-0255.

JUSTICE JOHN L. MICHALSKI: NY R 8 JD J Michalski.

JUSTICE MARK A. MONTOUR: [NY R 8 JD J Montour, as amended by NY ORDER 20-0256].

JUSTICE HENRY NOWAK: NY R 8 JD J Nowak.

JUSTICE JOHN F. O'DONNELL: NY R 8 JD J O'Donnell.

JUSTICE JEANETTE OGDEN: NY R 8 JD J Ogden.

JUSTICE CATHERINE NUGENT-PANEPINTO: NY R 8 JD J Nugent-Panepinto.

JUSTICE FRANK A. SEDITA, III: [NY R 8 JD J Sedita, as amended by NY ORDER 20-0257].

JUSTICE SARA SHELDON: NY R 8 JD J Sheldon.

JUSTICE DONNA M. SIWEK: NY R 8 JD J Siwek.

JUSTICE MARY L. SLISZ: NY R 8 JD J Slisz.

JUSTICE TIMOTHY J. WALKER: [NY R 8 JD J Walker, as amended by NY ORDER 20-0258].

JUSTICE DENNIS E. WARD: NY R 8 JD J Ward.

JUSTICE PAUL B. WOJTASZEK: [NY R 8 JD J Wojtaszek, as amended by NY ORDER 20-0259].

JUSTICE CHARLES N. ZAMBITO: [NY R 8 JD J Zambito, as amended by NY ORDER 20-0260].

SUPREME COURT LEGAL STAFF: NY R 8 JD J Legal Staff.

KINGS COUNTY

JUSTICE RACHEL A. ADAMS: NY R KINGS J Part 5F.

JUSTICE LOREN BAILY-SCHIFFMAN: NY R KINGS J Part 65.

JUSTICE REGINALD A. BODDIE: NY R KINGS J Part 95.

JUSTICE THERESA M. CICCOTTO: NY R KINGS J Part 19; NY R KINGS J Part 5J.

JUSTICE LISSETTE COLON: NY R KINGS J Part Rules.

JUSTICE GENINE EDWARDS: NY R KINGS J Part 80.

JUSTICE PAMELA L. FISHER: [NY R KINGS J Part 94, as amended by NY ORDER 20-0208].

JUSTICE ROBIN GARSON: NY R KINGS J Part 75.

JUSTICE LARA J. GENOVISI: [NY R KINGS J Part 34, as amended by NY ORDER 20-0209].

JUSTICE BERNARD J. GRAHAM: NY R KINGS J Part 36.

JUSTICE DAWN JIMENEZ-SALTA: NY R KINGS J Part 88.

JUSTICE INGRID JOSEPH: [NY R KINGS J Part FRP3 and Part 83, as amended by NY ORDER 20-0210].

JUSTICE KATHY J. KING: NY R KINGS J Part 64, 76K.

JUSTICE LAWRENCE KNIPEL: NY R KINGS J Part 57.

JUSTICE DONALD KURTZ: NY R KINGS J Part 26.

JUSTICE CARL LANDICINO: [NY R KINGS J Part 81, as amended by NY ORDER 20-0211].

JUSTICE KATHERINE LEVINE: [NY R KINGS J Part 20, 25, 92, as amended by NY ORDER 20-0211].

JUSTICE LORNA MCALLISTER: [NY R KINGS J Part 10, as amended by NY ORDER 20-0211].

JUSTICE ROSEMARIE MONTALBANO: [NY R KINGS J Part 19, 71, and 22, as amended by NY ORDER 20-0211].
JUSTICE RICHARD J. MONTELIONE: [NY R KINGS J Part 99 and DJMP, as amended by NY ORDER 20-0215].
JUSTICE LISA S. OTTLEY: NY R KINGS J Part 24.
JUSTICE MARK I. PARTNOW: NY R KINGS J Part 43.
JUSTICE ERIC I. PRUS: NY R KINGS J Part 5A.
JUSTICE FRANCOIS RIVERA: NY R KINGS J Part 52.
JUSTICE KAREN B. ROTHENBERG: NY R KINGS J Part 35.
JUSTICE LEON RUCHELSMAN: NY R KINGS J Part 1.
JUSTICE WAYNE P. SAITTA: NY R KINGS J Part 29.
JUSTICE ROBIN K. SHEARES: NY R KINGS J Part 96.
JUSTICE KENNETH P. SHERMAN: NY R KINGS J Part 67 and 78.
JUSTICE DEBRA SILBER: NY R KINGS J Part 9 and 5K.
JUSTICE ELLEN M. SPODEK: NY R KINGS J Part 63.
JUSTICE MARSHA L. STEINHARDT: NY R KINGS J Part 15.
JUSTICE JEFFREY S. SUNSHINE: NY R KINGS J Part 5G.
JUSTICE PETER P. SWEENEY: [NY R KINGS J Part 35, as amended by NY ORDER 20-0218].
JUSTICE DELORES J. THOMAS: [NY R KINGS J Part 5T, as amended by NY ORDER 20-0221].
JUSTICE WAVNY TOUSSAINT: NY R KINGS J Part 70.
JUSTICE RICHARD VELASQUEZ: NY R KINGS J Part 66.
JUSTICE CAROLYN E. WADE: NY R KINGS J Part 84.
JUSTICE EDWARD G. WALKER: [NY R KINGS J Part 90, as amended by NY ORDER 20-0219].
JUSTICE LILLIAN WAN: [NY R KINGS J Part 17, as amended by NY ORDER 20-0220].
JUSTICE MICHELLE WESTON: NY R KINGS J Part 3.
MENTAL HYGIENE PART: NY R KINGS J Part 77.
MATRIMONIAL PARTS DURING COVID-19 EMERGENCY: JUSTICE KAREN B. ROTHENBERG: NY R KINGS J Doc. 1.

NASSAU COUNTY

JUSTICE ANNA R. ANZALONE: NY R NASSAU S J Anzalone, Part 26.
JUSTICE STACY D. BENNETT: NY R NASSAU S J Bennett; NY R NASSAU S J Bennett, Form 1.
JUSTICE ANTONIO BRANDVEEN: NY R NASSAU S J Brandveen, Part 31.
JUSTICE JEFFREY S. BROWN: [NY R NASSAU S J Brown, as amended by NY ORDER 20-0297].
JUSTICE STEPHEN A. BUCARIA: NY R NASSAU S J Bucaria.
JUSTICE JULIANNE T. CAPETOLA: NY R NASSAU S J Capetola, Part 28.
JUSTICE EDMUND M. DANE: NY R NASSAU S J Dane, Part 33.
JUSTICE VITO M. DESTEFANO: NY R NASSAU S J DeStefano, Part 13; NY R NASSAU S J DeStefano, Form 1.
JUSTICE ARTHUR M. DIAMOND: NY R NASSAU S J Diamond, Part 7.
JUSTICE THOMAS FEINMAN: NY R NASSAU S J Feinman, Part 5.
JUSTICE JOHN M. GALASSO: NY R NASSAU S J Galasso, Part 22.
JUSTICE SHARON M.J. GIANELLI: NY R NASSAU S J Gianelli, Part 22; NY R NASSAU S J Gianelli, Form 1.
JUSTICE JEFFREY A. GOODSTEIN: NY R NASSAU S J Goodstein, Part 33; NY R NASSAU S J Goodstein, Form 1.
JUSTICE DAVID J. GUGERTY: [NY R NASSAU S J Gugerty, Part 31, as amended by NY ORDER 20-0298].
JUSTICE HELENE F. GUGERTY: NY R NASSAU S J Gugerty, Part 47.
JUSTICE STEVEN M. JAEGER: NY R NASSAU S J Jaeger, Part 35; NY R NASSAU S J Jaeger, Form 1.

JUSTICE JACK L. LIBERT: NY R NASSAU S J Libert, Part 23.

JUSTICE JOSEPH H. LORINTZ: NY R NASSAU S J Lorintz, Part 26; NY R NASSAU S J Lorintz, Form 1.

JUSTICE ROY S. MAHON: NY R NASSAU S J Mahon, Part 3.

JUSTICE RANDY SUE MARBER: NY R NASSAU S J Marber, Part 8.

JUSTICE JAMES P. MCCORMACK: [NY R NASSAU S J McCormack, Part 18, as amended by NY ORDER, 20-0299].

JUSTICE DICCIA T. PINEDA-KIRWAN: [NY R NASSAU S J Pineda-Kirwan, as amended by NY ORDER 20-0300].

JUSTICE THOMAS RADEMAKER: [NY R NASSAU S J Rademaker, Part 28, as amended by NY ORDER 20-0301]; [NY R NASSAU S J Rademaker, Form 1, as amended by NY ORDER 20-0301].

JUSTICE DENISE L. SHER: NY R NASSAU S J Rademaker, Part 32.

JUSTICE LEONARD D. STEINMAN: [NY R NASSAU S J Steinman, Part 15, as amended by NY ORDER 20-0303]; NY R NASSAU S J Steinman, Form 1.

JUSTICE HOWARD E. STURIM: NY R NASSAU S J Sturim, Part 50; NY R NASSAU S J Sturim, Form 1.

JUSTICE HELEN VOUTSINAS: [NY R NASSAU S J Voutsinas, Part 25, as amended by NY ORDER 20-0304]; [NY R NASSAU S J Voutsinas, Form 1, as amended by NY ORDER 20-0305].

JUSTICE HOPE SCHWARTZ ZIMMERMAN: NY R NASSAU S J Zimmerman, Part 17.

NEW YORK COUNTY

JUDGE'S RULES; BASIC INFORMATION: [NY R NY CTY J RUL Doc. 1, as amended by NY ORDER 20-0202].

ONONDAGA COUNTY

JUSTICE ROBERT E. ANTONACCI II: [NY R ONDGA E FIL Doc. 1, as amended by 20-0239].

JUSTICE MICHAEL V. COCCOMI: NY R ONDGA E FIL Doc. 2.

JUSTICE GREGORY R. GILBERT: NY R 5 JD JUDGES Gilbert; NY R ONDGA E FIL Doc. 3.

JUSTICE DONALD A. GREENWOOD: NY R ONDGA E FIL Doc. 4.

JUSTICE DEBORAH H. KARALUNAS: NY R ONDGA E FIL Doc. 5.

JUSTICE JAMES MCCLUSKY: NY R 5 JD MCCLUSKY McClusky.

JUSTICE CHARLES C. MERRELL: NY R 5 JD MERRELL Merrell.

JUSTICE PATRICK F. MACRAE: NY R 5 JD MACRAE Doc. 1.

JUSTICE JAMES P. MURPHY: NY R ONDGA E FIL Doc. 7.

JUSTICE GERALD J. NERI: [NY R 5 JD JUDGES Neri, as amended by NY ORDER 20-0236]; [NY R ONDGA E FIL Doc. 8, as amended by NY ORDER 20-0241].

JUSTICE ANTHONY J. PARIS: NY R 5 JD JUDGES Paris; [NY R ONDGA E FIL Doc. 9, as amended by NY ORDER 20-0242].

JUSTICE NORMAN W. SEITER, JR.: NY R 5 JD JUDGES Seiter.

JUSTICE KEVIN G. YOUNG: [NY R ONDGA E FIL Doc. 10, as amended by NY ORDER 20-0243].

QUEENS COUNTY

JUSTICE PAM JACKMAN BROWN: [NY R L QUEENS Brown, Part 19, as amended by NY ORDER 20-0321].

JUSTICE CHEREE A. BUGGS: NY R L QUEENS Buggs, Part 30.

JUSTICE PAM JACKMAN BROWN: [NY R L QUEENS Brown, Part 19, as amended by NY ORDER 20-0321].

JUSTICE DENIS J. BUTLER: NY R L QUEENS Butler, Part 12.

JUSTICE ROBERT I. CALORAS: [NY R L QUEENS Caloras, Part 36, as amended by NY ORDER 20-0322].

JUSTICE ANNA CULLEY: NY R L QUEENS Culley, Part 53.

JUSTICE TIMOTHY DUFFICY: NY R L QUEENS Dufficy, Part 35.

JUSTICE DAVID ELLIOT: NY R L QUEENS Elliot, Part 14.

JUSTICE JOSEPH J. ESPOSITO: NY R L QUEENS Esposito, Part 6.

JUSTICE DARRELL L. GAVRIN: [NY R L QUEENS Gavrin, Part 27, as amended by NY ORDER 20-0323].

JUSTICE WYATT N. GIBBONS: [NY R L QUEENS Gibbons, Part 5, as amended by NY ORDER 20-0330.
JUSTICE DONNA-MARIE E. GOLIA: [NY R L QUEENS Golia, Part 21, as amended by NY ORDER 20-0331].
JUSTICE MARGUERITE A. GRAYS: [NY R L QUEENS Grays, Part 4, as amended by NY ORDER 20-0324].
JUSTICE RUDOLPH E. GRECO: [NY R L QUEENS Greco, Part 32, as amended by NY ORDER 20-0325].
JUSTICE MAUREEN HEALY: NY R L QUEENS Healy, Part 6.
JUSTICE PHILLIP HOM: [NY R L QUEENS Hom, Part 43, as amended by NY ORDER 20-0332].
JUSTICE KEVIN J. KERRIGAN: NY R L QUEENS Kerrigan, Part 10.
JUSTICE MOJGAN C. LANCMAN: NY R L QUEENS Lancman, Part 20.
JUSTICE RICHARD G. LATIN: NY R L QUEENS Latin, Part 40.
JUSTICE ULYSSES B. LEVERETT: [NY R L QUEENS Leverett, Part 6, as amended by NY ORDER 20-0326].
JUSTICE LEONARD LIVOTE: NY R L QUEENS Livote, Part 33.
JUSTICE LEE A. MAYERSOHN: NY R L QUEENS Mayersohn, Part 22; NY R L QUEENS Mayersohn, Part 22G; [NY R L QUEENS Mayersohn, Part 22G COVID, as amended by NY ORDER 20-0327].
JUSTICE ROBERT J. MCDONALD: NY R L QUEENS McDonald, Part 34.
JUSTICE MARGARET MCGOWAN: NY R L QUEENS McGowan, Part 52.
JUSTICE MAURICE E. MUIR: [NY R L QUEENS Muir, Part 42, as amended by NY ORDER 20-0333].
JUSTICE JODI ORLOW: NY R L QUEENS Orlow, Part 51.
JUSTICE LESLIE J. PURIFICCION: NY R L QUEENS Purificcion, Part 39.
JUSTICE JOSEPH RISI: [NY R L QUEENS Risi, Part 3, as amended by NY ORDER 20-0328].
JUSTICE FREDERICK D.R. SAMPSON: [NY R L QUEENS Sampson, Part 31, as amended by NY ORDER 20-0329].
JUSTICE MARTIN J. SCHULMAN: NY R L QUEENS Schulman, Part 29.
JUSTICE BERNICE D. SIEGAL: NY R L QUEENS Siegal, Part 25G.
JUSTICE JANICE A. TAYLOR: NY R L QUEENS Taylor, Part 15.
JUSTICE CARMEN R. VELASQUEZ: NY R L QUEENS Velasquez, Part 38.
JUSTICE LOURDES M VENTURA: [NY R L QUEENS Ventura, Part 37, as amended by NY ORDER 20-0334].
JUSTICE WILLIAM A. VISCOVICH: NY R L QUEENS Viscovich, Part 63.
JUSTICE ALLAN B. WEISS: NY R L QUEENS Weiss, Part 2.
COMPLIANCE, SETTLEMENT AND CONFERENCE PART: NY R L QUEENS Doc 1.
PRELIMINARY CONFERENCE PART: [NY R L QUEENS Doc. 2, as amended by NY ORDER 20-0335].
MEDICAL MALPRACTICE CONFERENCE PART: [NY R L QUEENS Doc. 3, as amended by NY ORDER 20-0336].
TRIAL SCHEDULING PART: NY R L QUEENS Doc. 4.
SUMMARY JURY TRIAL PROGRAM: NY R L QUEENS Doc. 7.
RESIDENTIAL FORECLOSURE PART: NY R L QUEENS Doc. 9.
FORECLOSURE AUCTION RULES: NY R L QUEENS Doc. 10.
MATRIMONIAL PRELIMINARY CONFERENCE PART: NY R L QUEENS Doc. 11.
NON-CUSTODIAL CONTESTED MATRIMONIAL PART: NY R L QUEENS Doc. 12.

Motions, Oppositions and Replies
Motion in Limine

Document Last Updated August 2020

A. Checklist

(I) ❑ Matters to consider for moving party

(a) ❑ Required documents

(1) ❑ Notice of motion, order to show cause, or affidavit on ex parte motion

(2) ❑ Motion

(3) ❑ Request for judicial intervention

(4) ❑ Proof of service

(5) ❑ ALBANY COUNTY: Additional required documents

(i) ❑ Affirmation of good faith effort

(b) ❑ Supplemental documents

(1) ❑ Supporting evidence; Exhibits

(2) ❑ Brief

(3) ❑ Notice to produce papers not in possession of the court

(4) ❑ Filing fees

(5) ❑ Working copies

(6) ❑ ERIE COUNTY: Additional supplemental documents

(i) ❑ Notice of hard copy submission in e-filed case

(7) ❑ KINGS COUNTY: Additional supplemental documents

(i) ❑ Forms when filing in hard copy

(8) ❑ NEW YORK COUNTY: Additional supplemental documents

(i) ❑ Notice of hard copy submission

(ii) ❑ Unpublished opinions

(9) ❑ ONONDAGA COUNTY: Additional supplemental documents

(i) ❑ Notice of hard copy submission

(10) ❑ QUEENS COUNTY: Additional supplemental documents

(i) ❑ Notice of hard copy submission

(c) ❑ Timing

(1) ❑ The timing of motions in limine may be specified by the court

(2) ❑ The moving party shall serve copies of all affidavits and briefs upon all other parties at the time of service of the notice of motion

(3) ❑ A notice of motion and supporting affidavits shall be served at least eight (8) days before the time at which the motion is noticed to be heard

(4) ❑ It is also good practice to make motions returnable at least three (3) weeks away from the planned date of mailing and to always include a demand in the motion that the other side serve answering papers at least seven (7) days before the return day

(5) ❑ ALBANY COUNTY: Additional timing

(i) ❑ All motions in limine should be in writing and should be prepared and filed at the earliest possible time to the extent that the basis for these motions are known by a party and will arise during the trial of the action

(6) ❑ BRONX COUNTY: Additional timing

(i) ❑ A Notice of Motion must be served at least eight (8) days, by personal service, nine (9) days by overnight express and thirteen (13) days by mail before the return date

(7) ❑ NEW YORK COUNTY: Additional timing

(i) ❑ In an e-filed case, all of the moving papers shall be e-filed at least eight (8) business days prior to the return date

(8) ❑ ONONDAGA COUNTY: Additional timing

(i) ❑ Onondaga County local court rules require that any additional papers relating to motions must be e-filed at least two (2) business days prior to the return date, excluding the return date

(ii) ❑ Motions in limine must be filed with the Onondaga County Clerk's Office and served on opposing counsel at least one(1) week prior to the trial date

(9) ❑ QUEENS COUNTY: Additional timing

(i) ❑ Motions must be in the possession of the Motion Support Office at least nine (9) days before the noticed return date of the motion

(II) ❑ Matters to consider for opposing party

(a) ❑ Required documents

(1) ❑ Opposition

(2) ❑ Proof of service

(b) ❑ Supplemental documents

(1) ❑ Supporting evidence; Exhibits

(2) ❑ Brief

(3) ❑ Filing fees

(4) ❑ Working copies

(5) ❑ ERIE COUNTY: Additional supplemental documents

(i) ❑ Notice of hard copy submission in e-filed case

(6) ❑ KINGS COUNTY: Additional supplemental documents

(i) ❑ Forms when filing in hard copy

(7) ❑ NEW YORK COUNTY: Additional supplemental documents

(i) ❑ Notice of hard copy submission

(ii) ❑ Unpublished opinions

(8) ❑ ONONDAGA COUNTY: Additional supplemental documents

(i) ❑ Notice of hard copy submission

(9) ❑ QUEENS COUNTY: Additional supplemental documents

(i) ❑ Notice of hard copy submission

(c) ❑ Timing

(1) ❑ Answering affidavits shall be served at least two (2) days before the time at which the motion is noticed to be heard

(2) ❑ Answering affidavits and any notice of cross-motion, with supporting papers, if any, shall be served at least seven (7) days before such time if a notice of motion served at least sixteen (16) days before such time so demands

(3) ❑ ONONDAGA COUNTY: Additional timing

(i) ❑ Opposing papers, if any, must be filed and served no later than two (2) business days prior to the trial date

B. Timing

1. *Motion in limine.* Since in limine motions are typically made shortly before trial to obtain rulings on evidentiary concerns,

whether actual items of evidence or testimony, counsel should be sensitive to reading the Individual Rules of the assigned trial judge to learn the court's specific requirements for the timing and briefing of such a motion. NYPRAC-COMM § 65:61.

a. *ALBANY COUNTY: Filed as soon as possible.* All motions in limine should be in writing and should be prepared and filed at the earliest possible time to the extent that the basis for these motions are known by a party and will arise during the trial of the action. NY R 3 JD SUP Doc. 1(H)(4)(e).

b. *ONONDAGA COUNTY: Filing in advance of jury trial.* Motions in limine must be filed with the Onondaga County Clerk's Office and served on opposing counsel at least one (1) week prior to the trial date. Opposing papers, if any, must be filed and served, no later than two (2) business days prior to the trial date. Motions in limine are to be made returnable in chambers at 9:30 a.m. on the trial date. NY R ONDGA JURY TRIAL Rule 3.

c. *ONONDAGA COUNTY: Filing in advance of non-jury trial.* Motions in limine must be filed with the Onondaga County Clerk's Office and served on opposing counsel at least one(1) week prior to the trial date. Opposing papers, if any, must be filed and served no later than two (2) business days prior to the trial date. Motions in limine are to be made returnable in chambers at 9:30 A.M. on the trial date. NY R ONDGA NON JURY TRIAL Rule 3.

2. *Time to serve.* The moving party shall serve copies of all affidavits and briefs upon all other parties at the time of service of the notice of motion. NY R UNIF TRIAL CTS § 202.8(c). A notice of motion and supporting affidavits shall be served at least eight (8) days before the time at which the motion is noticed to be heard. NY CPLR Rule 2214(b).

a. *Return dates; Best practice.* It is also good practice to make motions returnable at least three (3) weeks away from the planned date of mailing and to always include a demand in the motion that the other side serve answering papers at least seven (7) days before the return day. This enables the motion to be served by mail, gives sufficient notice to support the seven (7) day demand, and leaves a few days for a delayed mailing if some snag prevents posting on the day planned. If speed is needed, the shorter eight (8) day notice period can be used, forfeiting the right to seven (7) day answering papers and a reply. If even eight (8) days notice is too much under the circumstances, the order to show cause is the remedy. SIEGEL-NYPRAC § 247.

i. *ALBANY COUNTY.* All motions, except for certain matters in Albany County as specified in NY R 3 JD SUP Doc. 1(E) and NY R 3 JD SUP Doc. 1(F), brought on by notice of motion or by order to show cause will be made returnable on any day, Monday through Friday, as chosen by the movant in compliance with the CPLR. Parties shall submit all papers in a timely fashion as required by the CPLR by delivering them or mailing them directly to the Supreme Court Clerk's Office[. . .]except that motions and other applications subject to a filing fee shall first be presented to the County Clerk's Office for payment of the requisite fee and then subsequently filed with the Supreme Court Clerk's Office. NY R 3 JD SUP Doc. 1(B).

ii. *BRONX COUNTY.* A Notice of Motion must be served at least eight (8) days, by personal service, nine (9) days by overnight express and thirteen (13) days by mail before the return date. NY R BRONX FIL R Doc. 3. All unassigned motions must be accompanied with a properly filled out RJI and shall be filed in the Motion Support Office, room 217, within five (5) days of service. All motions on actions already assigned to a Justice must be filed at least five (5) business days before the return date. NY R BRONX FIL R Doc. 3. All papers served must strictly comply with the time requirements of NY CPLR Rule 2101, NY CPLR Rule 2103 and NY CPLR Rule 2214(b). NY R BRONX FIL R Doc. 8.

iii. *KINGS COUNTY.* Motion papers, answering affidavits and reply affidavits must be served on adversaries in accordance with NY CPLR Rule 2214. NY R L KINGS Pt. C, Rule 1.

iv. *NEW YORK COUNTY.* In an e-filed case, all of the moving papers shall be e-filed at least eight (8) business days prior to the return date. The clerk will calendar the motion for the Motion Submission Part Courtroom (Room 130) for the return date selected. NY R NY CTY Procedure II(A); NY R NY CTY E FIL Doc. 2(D)(1).

v. *ONONDAGA COUNTY.* Onondaga County local court rules require that any additional papers relating to motions must be e-filed at least two (2) business days prior to the return date, excluding the return date. NY R ONDGA E FIL Protocol(B)(9)(e).

vi. *QUEENS COUNTY.* Motions must be in the possession of the Motion Support Office at least nine (9) days before the noticed return date of the motion. NY R L QUEENS MOT SUP Doc. 1; NY R L QUEENS E-FILE Doc. 1(H)(1).

b. *Order to show cause; Shorter time.* The court in a proper case may grant an order to show cause, to be served in lieu of a notice of motion, at a time and in a manner specified therein. NY CPLR Rule 2214(d). An ordinary notice of motion can't be brought on for hearing earlier than the eighth (8th) day after the motion papers are served. With an order to show cause, the hearing can be brought on at any time the court directs, which can be fewer than eight (8) days or as close as the very day on which it is signed. If the court is convinced there is a real emergency, it can schedule the hearing for a few hours later or, in the direst case, "forthwith" the service of the order to show cause. SIEGEL-NYPRAC § 248.

c. *Time to serve answering affidavits; Other answering papers.* Answering affidavits shall be served at least two (2) days before the time at which the motion is noticed to be heard. Answering affidavits and any notice of cross-motion, with supporting papers, if any, shall be served at least seven (7) days before such time if a notice of motion served at least sixteen (16) days before such time so demands; whereupon any reply or responding affidavits shall be served at least one (1) day before such time. NY CPLR Rule 2214(b); NY R UNIF TRIAL CTS § 202.8(c).

   i. *BRONX COUNTY.* All answering papers must be submitted to the Clerk 's Office on the return date of the motion. Answering papers will not be accepted prior to the return date. NY R BRONX FIL R Doc. 8.

   ii. *NEW YORK COUNTY.* Cross-motions, papers in opposition, and reply papers on motions/petitions on notice returnable in Room 130 in a hard-copy case shall be submitted to the Motion Submission Part Courtroom (Room 130) on the final return date of the motion/petition and will not be accepted until that date. Subsequent documents on motions/petitions in e-filed cases shall be e-filed in a timely manner. Working copies when required shall be submitted to Room 130 on the final return date. NY R NY CTY Procedure II(A).

d. *Time to serve cross-motion.* At least three (3) days prior to the time at which the motion is noticed to be heard, or seven (7) days prior to such time if demand is properly made pursuant to NY CPLR Rule 2214(b), a party may serve upon the moving party a notice of cross-motion demanding relief, with or without supporting papers; provided, however, that:

   i. If such notice and any supporting papers are served by mailing, as provided in NY CPLR Rule 2103(b)(2), they shall be served three (3) days earlier than as prescribed in NY CPLR Rule 2215; and

   ii. If served by overnight delivery, as provided in NY CPLR Rule 2103(b)(6), they shall be served one (1) day earlier than as prescribed in NY CPLR Rule 2215. Relief in the alternative or of several different types may be demanded; relief need not be responsive to that demanded by the moving party. NY CPLR Rule 2215(a); NY CPLR Rule 2215(b).

   iii. *BRONX COUNTY.* Cross motions may be presented for approval on or before the return date, provided that there is a motion already calendared. NY R BRONX FIL R Doc. 8.

   iv. *ERIE COUNTY.* Cross-motions must be filed at least two (2) days before the return date of the motion. NY R L KINGS Pt. A, Papers.

   v. *KINGS COUNTY.* Hard copies are required to be filed for any motions, answering papers, stipulations, etc. for E-Filed cases returnable in [the Central Compliance Part] at least [two (2)] days before return date. . . .for cross motions. NY R L KINGS Pt. E, Rule 8.

   vi. *QUEENS COUNTY.* Motion Support does not process or forward responsive papers, including cross-motions. They must be brought to the calendar call in the judge's part. NY R L QUEENS MOT SUP Doc. 1. E-filed cross motions: across motion must be noticed for the same return date as the main motion and have the confirmation of filing attached in the same manner as a motion. NY R L QUEENS E-FILE Doc. 1(H)(2)(e).

3. *Filing before return date.* All motions shall be returnable before the assigned judge, and all papers shall be filed with the court on or before the return date. NY R UNIF TRIAL CTS § 202.8(a).

   a. *BRONX COUNTY: Time for filing*

      i. *Unassigned motions.* Unassigned motions must be in the Clerk's Office within five (5) days of the date of service of the motion. NY R BRONX FIL R Doc. 8.

      ii. *Assigned motions.* Assigned motions must be filed in the Clerk's Office not less than five (5) business days prior to the return date of the motion. NY R BRONX FIL R Doc. 8.

      iii. *Motions returnable in room 217.* The moving documents must be e-filed no later than eight (8) days prior to the return date. NY R BRONX E FIL R Doc. 1(1).

   b. *KINGS COUNTY: Time and place of filing.* Motion papers must be filed with the E-file/Motion Support Office located in Room 227. . . at 360 Adams Street at least five (5) business days before the return date of the motion. NY R L KINGS Pt. A, Papers. Hard copies are required to be filed for any motions, answering papers, stipulations, etc. for E-Filed cases returnable in [the Central Compliance Part] at least five (5) days before return date for main motions. NY R L KINGS Pt. E, Rule 8. The moving documents must be e-filed no later than eight (8) days prior to the return date. NY R L KINGS E FIL Doc. 1(D).

4. *NEW YORK COUNTY: Briefing schedule.* Once a motion is made, counsel for all parties are strongly encouraged to agree upon a briefing schedule and submit a stipulation of adjournment reflecting that schedule using service or a clerk. Where a briefing schedule has not been agreed upon, the movant can avoid the need to attend simply to see if anyone will hand up opposing papers by demanding papers as provided by NY CPLR Rule 2214(b). To protect movants against the submission of late opposition papers or cross-motions, the General Clerk's Office will screen motions in which such papers are submitted without a response (reply or opposition respectively) to ensure that proper time to respond has been afforded and it will sua sponte adjourn for one (1) week cases in which such time has not been given. NY R NY CTY Procedure II(C).
5. *QUEENS COUNTY: Time to pay fees.* As motions and petitions are time sensitive, if opting to pay at the County Clerk's Office payment MUST be made, if filed with an RJI, a minimum of nine (9) business days prior to the application's return date and if filed post RJI, a minimum of nine (9) business days prior to the application's return date. NY R L QUEENS E-FILE Doc. 1(H)(1).
6. *Computation of time*
   a. *Units of time*
      i. *Day.* A calendar day includes the time from midnight to midnight. Sunday or any day of the week specifically mentioned means a calendar day. NY GEN CONSTR § 19.
      ii. *Month.* In a statute, contract or public or private instrument, unless otherwise provided in such contract or instrument or by law, the term month means a calendar month and not a lunar month. NY GEN CONSTR § 31.
      iii. *Year.* For information on the definition of a year, including the definitions of a half-year and quarter-year, refer to NY GEN CONSTR § 58 and NY GEN CONSTR § 50. For information on leap years, refer to NY GEN CONSTR § 57.
   b. *Periods of time*
      i. *Number of days.* A number of days specified as a period from a certain day within which or after or before which an act is authorized or required to be done means such number of calendar days exclusive of the calendar day from which the reckoning is made. NY GEN CONSTR § 20.
         - If such period is a period of two (2) days, Saturday, Sunday or a public holiday must be excluded from the reckoning if it is an intervening day between the day from which the reckoning is made and the last day of the period. NY GEN CONSTR § 20.
         - In computing any specified period of time from a specified event, the day upon which the event happens is deemed the day from which the reckoning is made. The day from which any specified period of time is reckoned shall be excluded in making the reckoning. NY GEN CONSTR § 20.
      ii. *Number of months.* A number of months after or before a certain day shall be computed by counting such number of calendar months from such day, exclusive of the calendar month in which such day occurs, and shall include the day of the month in the last month so counted having the same numerical order in days of the month as the day from which the computation is made, unless there be not so many days in the last month so counted, in which case the period computed shall expire with the last day of the month so counted. NY GEN CONSTR § 30.
      iii. *Publication of notice; Number of days.* The period of publication of a legal notice shall be computed by excluding the first day of publication and including the day on which the act or event of which notice is given is to take place or which completes the full period of publication. NY CPLR § 2402.
      iv. *Periods ending on Saturday, Sunday or public holiday.* When any period of time, computed from a certain day, within which or after which or before which an act is authorized or required to be done, ends on a Saturday, Sunday or a public holiday, such act may be done on the next succeeding business day and if the period ends at a specified hour, such act may be done at or before the same hour of such next succeeding business day, except that where a period of time specified by contract ends on a Saturday, Sunday or a public holiday, the extension of such period is governed by NY GEN CONSTR § 25. NY GEN CONSTR § 25-a(1).
         - For a list of public holidays, refer to NY GEN CONSTR § 24.
      v. *Additional time after certain kinds of service*
         - *Service by mail.* Where a period of time prescribed by law is measured from the service of a paper and service is by mail, five (5) days shall be added to the prescribed period. NY CPLR Rule 2103(b)(2).
         - *Service by overnight delivery service.* Where a period of time prescribed by law is measured from the

service of a paper and service is by overnight delivery, one (1) business day shall be added to the prescribed period. NY CPLR Rule 2103(b)(6).

vi. *Daylight saving time.* For information on New York's time zone and the effect of daylight saving time, refer to NY GEN CONSTR § 52.

c. *Hours of court.* Notwithstanding any provision of law or rule of court to the contrary, throughout the State of New York the sessions of the Supreme Court for the disposition of business before the court shall commence not later than 9:30 a.m. and conclude not earlier than 5 p.m. Where warranted, the Chief Administrator of the Courts may authorize variances in the opening and closing hours of the courts, but, in such event, daily sessions shall total not less than six (6) hours. NY R CHIEF J § 3.1.

d. *Time limits; Extension of time.* Any act required by or in pursuance of law to be performed at or within a prescribed time, shall be performed according to the standard time. NY GEN CONSTR § 53.

i. Except where otherwise expressly prescribed by law, the court may extend the time fixed by any statute, rule or order for doing any act, upon such terms as may be just and upon good cause shown, whether the application for extension is made before or after the expiration of the time fixed. NY CPLR § 2004. Refer to the New York KeyRules Motion for Continuance/Extension of Time document for more information.

C. General Requirements

1. *Motions, generally.* There shall be compliance with the procedures prescribed in the CPLR for the bringing of motions. NY R UNIF TRIAL CTS § 202.7(a).

a. *Motions on notice.* A notice of motion shall specify the time and place of the hearing on the motion, the supporting papers upon which the motion is based, the relief demanded and the grounds therefor. NY CPLR Rule 2214(a). A motion on notice in an action in the supreme court shall be noticed to be heard in the judicial district where the action is triable or in a county adjoining the county where the action is triable. Unless statute, civil practice rule or local court rule provides otherwise, the motion shall be noticed to be heard before a motion term or, upon order to show cause granted by a justice, before that justice out of court. NY CPLR § 2212(a). Except as provided in NY R UNIF TRIAL CTS § 202.7(d), no motion shall be filed with the court unless there have been served and filed with the motion papers a notice of motion. NY R UNIF TRIAL CTS § 202.7(a)(1).

b. *Ex parte motions.* A motion in an action in the supreme court that may be made without notice may be made at a motion term or to a justice out of court in any county in the state. NY CPLR § 2212(b).

i. *KINGS COUNTY.* For more information on submitting a motion ex parte, refer to NY R L KINGS E FIL Doc. 1(G).

ii. *NEW YORK COUNTY.* For more information on submitting matters ex parte, refer to NY R NY CTY Procedure III and NY R NY CTY E FIL Doc. 2(G).

iii. *QUEENS COUNTY.* For more information on submitting matters ex parte, refer to NY R L QUEENS EX PARTE Doc. 1.

c. *Alternative relief.* Relief in the alternative or of several different types may be demanded. NY CPLR Rule 2214(a). The types of relief need not be related. In one motion, for example, the defendant can seek to dismiss the plaintiff's claim for lack of jurisdiction, to get an extension of time to answer, to require the plaintiff to join X as a party, and to quash a disclosure subpoena served in behalf of the plaintiff on a nonparty witness. So doing, the movant must of course specify all of these items of relief in the notice of motion, and the grounds for them, and the supporting papers must contain the entire proof requisite to the items of relief sought. NY CPLR Rule 2214(Practice Commentary, C2214:4).

d. *General relief.* It is common practice to include at the end of the relief request in the notice of motion a so-called "general relief" clause. This is merely a few words to cover the possibility that the relief appropriate to what the movant proves was not specifically asked for, but is close enough to enable the court to grant it. After stating the specific relief desired, the lawyer will often add something like: and for such other, further, or different relief as this court may deem just and proper. NY CPLR Rule 2214(Practice Commentary, C2214:5).

e. *Motion in improper form.* If the court finds it appropriate in the interests of justice, it may convert a motion into a special proceeding, or vice-versa, upon such terms as may be just, including the payment of fees and costs. NY CPLR § 103(c).

f. *Order to show cause.* An order to show cause is basically only a substitute for a notice of motion. An ordinary notice of motion merely notifies the recipient that a motion is being made for specified relief. The burden of proof is on the movant. Although in most cases it is just as innocent as an ordinary notice of motion, the order to show cause gets its name by directing the recipient to "show cause" why the particular relief being asked for should not be granted. It sounds as if the burden of proof is being shifted to the recipient. It isn't. It specifies the time and place of the hearing on the application but when the hearing comes on, the burden of proof is where it always is on a motion: on the movant. SIEGEL-NYPRAC § 248.

i. The CPLR says nothing more about an order to show cause than that it may be used "in a proper case", which leaves it entirely to the judge's discretion to determine what a proper case is. Any fact suggesting a problem as to any of the items listed above would be sufficient to invoke judicial discretion and justify the show cause procedure, which is in fact liberally used. SIEGEL-NYPRAC § 248.

ii. An order to show cause against a state body or officers must be served in addition to service upon the defendant or respondent state body or officers upon the attorney general by delivery to an assistant attorney general at an office of the attorney general in the county in which venue of the action is designated or if there is no office of the attorney general in such county, at the office of the attorney general nearest such county. NY CPLR Rule 2214(d).

iii. *BRONX COUNTY.* For information on submitting an order to show cause, refer to NY R BRONX E FIL R Doc. 2 and NY R BRONX LEG SUP Doc. 1.

iv. *ERIE COUNTY.* For information on submitting an order to show cause, refer to NY R ERIE E FIL Doc. 3(VI).

v. *KINGS COUNTY.* For information on submitting an order to show cause, refer to NY R L KINGS E FIL Doc. 1(F).

vi. *NEW YORK COUNTY.* For information on submitting an order to show cause, refer to NY R NY CTY E FIL Doc. 2(F).

vii. *ONONDAGA COUNTY.* For information on submitting an order to show cause, refer to NY R ONDGA E FIL Protocol(B)(10) and NY R ONDGA E FIL Protocol(J).

g. *Motions before preliminary conference.* Motions in actions to which NY R UNIF TRIAL CTS § 202.12 is applicable made after the preliminary conference has been scheduled may be denied unless there is shown good cause why such relief is warranted before the preliminary conference is held. NY R UNIF TRIAL CTS § 202.12(h).

h. *ALBANY COUNTY: Good faith effort to resolve.* Prior to the submission of a notice of motion relating to disclosure or a bill of particulars, the parties must make a good faith effort to resolve the matter in question and submit an affirmation attesting to this good faith effort. NY R 3 JD SUP Doc. 1(B).

i. *NEW YORK COUNTY: Documents with motions.* Counsel must attach to motion papers copies of all pleadings and other documents as required by the CPLR and as necessary for an informed decision on the motion. Documents in a foreign language shall be properly translated. NY R NY CTY J RUL Rule 14(a).

j. *NEW YORK COUNTY: Motions in multiple cases made together.* On occasion, attorneys may wish to make a motion in more than one case on a single set of papers. In such cases, by definition consolidation will not have been directed since consolidation signifies the combination of more than one case into a single one with a single caption and index number and ending in a single judgment. NY R NY CTY Procedure II(B). For more information on motions made with the same papers, refer to NY R NY CTY Procedure II(A).

k. *QUEENS COUNTY: Motion sequence numbers.* A motion sequence number is required for all E-filed motions. After a motion is E-filed, please consult the e-courts website within twenty-four (24) to forty-eight (48) hours to obtain the sequence number. The Confirmation Notice of E-filing MUST indicate the sequence number of any motion submitted at the Centralized Motion Part calendar call. NY R L QUEENS E-FILE Doc. 1(H)(5).

2. *Motion in limine*

a. *Generally*

i. *Purpose.* The motion in limine is an application by either party for a pretrial ruling precluding the use of prejudicial evidence at trial, whether in an opening statement or during the evidentiary process. NYPRAC-COMM § 40:6; Wilkinson v. British Airways, 292 A.D.2d 263, 264, 740 N.Y.S.2d 294, 296 (2002). The motion in limine is a valuable strategic tool that should be used to limit or exclude extraneous, collateral, or otherwise damaging evidence. The United States Supreme Court has indicated that judicial authority for the motion in limine stems from the court's "inherent authority to manage the course of trials," and the motion is used extensively in commercial and other civil cases. NYPRAC-COMM § 40:6; Luce v. United States, 469 U.S. 38, 40, 105 S. Ct. 460, 463, 83 L. Ed. 2d 443 (1984).

- The primary purpose of the motion in limine is to reduce the likelihood that the jury will be prejudiced by hearing inadmissible, irrelevant, or inflammatory evidence. This function is obviously applicable primarily to jury trials, as judges in bench trials are often prone to admit evidence liberally, reasoning that they can ignore evidence that should not technically be considered and will base their determination on only properly admitted evidence. NYPRAC-COMM § 40:6.

- In a bench trial, however, the motion in limine may still be valuable for purposes of streamlining the case or focusing attention on an important issue before the trial begins. Thus its use should not be overlooked in appropriate situations in bench trials. NYPRAC-COMM § 40:6.

ii. *Shortening or streamlining trial.* The motion in limine can also be used to shorten the trial and simplify or bifurcate issues. For example, the motion in limine has been used in New York courts to preclude evidence on an issue not in dispute and to limit proof to one issue. NYPRAC-COMM § 40:6; Loughran v. Orange & Rockland Utilities Inc., 209 A.D.2d 917, 918, 619 N.Y.S.2d 200, 201 (1994) (holding that a motion in limine to preclude the plaintiff from challenging the easement was properly granted); Siewert v. Loudonville Elementary Sch., 210 A.D.2d 568, 620 N.Y.S.2d 149 (1994) (involving a motion in limine to limit the plaintiff's proof to a negligent supervision theory). Motions in limine streamline trials by obviating the need for piecemeal legal arguments in the middle of trial that slow down the proceedings. NYPRAC-COMM § 65:61. Successful motions in limine can also shorten trials by reducing the volume of evidence. NYPRAC-COMM § 65:61.

iii. *Promoting certainty and settlement.* Motions in limine can also promote settlement by confirming whether or not certain crucial evidence will be admissible, leading to reconsideration of the risks and rewards of trial. NYPRAC-COMM § 65:61.

iv. *Reducing reversible error and mistrial.* Motions in limine also reduce the likelihood of reversible error on evidentiary rulings because they are made before trial, and therefore the court will not be asked to strike evidence or testimony that the jury has already seen. NYPRAC-COMM § 65:61. By obtaining an in limine ruling from the court on the admissibility of evidence, litigants can also avoid the risk of a mistrial through the mere mention of inadmissible or unduly prejudicial evidence that could otherwise taint the trial. NYPRAC-COMM § 38:2.

v. *Pretrial preparation.* Finally, before a party incurs significant costs in constructing sophisticated technological trial presentations, motions in limine may determine whether the evidence behind such presentations is even admissible. NYPRAC-COMM § 65:61.

vi. *Immediate appeal.* Rulings of in limine motions typically are not immediately appealable. Narrow exceptions exist for an immediate appeal of an in limine ruling under NY CPLR § 5701. One word of caution, under such narrow circumstances, invoking an immediate appeal, a motion in limine may delay the ultimate dispostion of the case. A motion in limine may also be subject to appellate review on the grounds that the motion was actually a motion for partial summary judgment on a legal issue in the case or otherwise dispositive. NYPRAC-COMM § 65:61.

b. *Authority*

i. In civil cases there are no statutory provisions or Court of Appeals decisions explicitly authorizing pretrial rulings on evidentiary issues. The lower courts, however, appear to have assumed the existence of an inherent authority to entertain in limine motions to decide such questions as:

- Whether a witness was incompetent to testify under the "Dead Man's Statute";
- Whether certain portions of medical records qualified for admission under the hearsay exception for business records;
- Whether a witness who had been hypnotized could testify to her post-hypnotic recollections;
- Whether certain expert testimony satisfied the required standard of reliability; and
- Whether certain videotaped deposition testimony should be precluded due to procedural irregularities. NYPRAC-EVID § 1:7; Endervelt v. Slade, 214 A.D.2d 456, 625 N.Y.S.2d 210, 211 (1995); Passino v. DeRosa, 199 A.D.2d 1017, 1017, 606 N.Y.S.2d 107, 108 (1993); Bennett v. Saeger Hotels, Inc., 209 A.D.2d 946, 946, 619 N.Y.S.2d 424, 425 (1994); Drago v. Tishman Const. Corp. of New York, 4 Misc. 3d 354, 358, 777 N.Y.S.2d 889, 893 (Sup. Ct. 2004); Wilkinson v. British Airways, 292 A.D.2d 263, 740 N.Y.S.2d 294 (2002).

ii. One basis for this inherent power is reflected in NY CPLR Rule 4011, which provides that "[t]he court may determine the sequence in which the issues shall be tried and otherwise regulate the conduct of the trial in order to achieve a speedy and unprejudiced disposition of the matters at issue . . ." Objections to evidence are governed by NY CPLR § 4017, which provides that "[a]t the time a ruling or order of the court is requested or made a party shall make known* * * his objection to the action of the court." Although NY CPLR § 4017 is silent as to when such an objection or ruling is to be made, the provision is broad enough to apply to motions in limine. In addition, NY R UNIF TRIAL CTS § 202.26(c) permits courts to consider at the pretrial conference "simplification and limitation of the issues" and "any other matters deemed relevant." NYPRAC-COMM § 38:3.

iii. In a case involving the applicability of the best evidence rule, the Court of Appeals itself noted, without criticism of the procedure, that the issue had been addressed by the trial court in an in limine motion. NYPRAC-EVID § 1:7; Schozer v. William Penn Life Ins. Co. of New York, 84 N.Y.2d 639, 643, 644 N.E.2d 1353, 1355 (1994).

c. *Types of motions in limine.* There are two basic types of motions in limine. "Prohibitive" motions seek an order prohibiting counsel or any witness from referring to the evidence in question in the jury's presence and are made by the party seeking to exclude the evidence. "Permissive" motions seek a determination that the evidence in question is admissible and are made by the party seeking to offer the evidence. NYPRAC-COMM § 38:3; 20 AMJUR TRIALS 441.

d. *Form.* The motion for an in limine ruling need not be in writing if the issue is relatively simple. NYPRAC-EVID § 1:7; Wilkinson v. British Airways, 292 A.D.2d 263, 264, 740 N.Y.S.2d 294, 296 (2002). On the other hand, if the matter is complex, as, for example, the admissibility of scientific evidence, the movant will need to submit appropriate documentary support. NYPRAC-EVID § 1:7; Drago v. Tishman Const. Corp. of New York, 4 Misc. 3d 354, 360, 777 N.Y.S.2d 889, 894 (Sup. Ct. 2004).

e. *Procedure for in limine motions*

i. A motion in limine is typically brought by notice of motion accompanied by a memorandum of law and affidavits setting forth the factual basis of the motion in accordance with NY CPLR Rule 2214. NYPRAC-COMM § 38:4. While there is no requirement that the motion be made in writing, strategic considerations weigh in favor of submitting a written motion. NYPRAC-COMM § 38:4.

ii. The timing of motions in limine may be specified by the court. Before bringing the motion in limine, it is important to check the applicable rules of the trial court to ensure compliance with any applicable local rules. NYPRAC-COMM § 38:4.

iii. The determination of a motion in limine may require an evidentiary hearing pursuant to NY CPLR § 2218. NYPRAC-COMM § 38:4; DeMeyer v. Advantage Auto, 9 Misc. 3d 306, 316, 797 N.Y.S.2d 743, 752 (Sup. Ct. 2005). Evidentiary hearings are often necessary on motions to exclude or include certain kinds of scientific or technical expert opinion testimony that require a determination of the expert's qualifications and the reliability of the underlying methodology employed by the expert. NYPRAC-COMM § 38:4.

f. *Objections to motions in limine.* Objections to the results of in limine motions should be renewed at trial to ensure preservation of the issue for appellate review. See, e.g., People v. Zayas, 202 A.D.2d 324, 324, 609 N.Y.S.2d 9, 10 (1994) ("Defendant's in limine application to the trial court did not outline any specific proposed questioning of the complainant based upon the witness' employment records, and thus defendant did not preserve by appropriate record his current claim that the trial court improperly restricted his cross-examination of the complainant."). NYPRAC-EVID § 1:7.

i. It should be noted that a court's ruling on a motion in limine as to the admissibility of evidence prior to trial is inherently without prejudice as it is subject to reconsideration by the court based on evidence proffered at trial. NYPRAC-COMM § 38:2; Britvan v. Plaza At Latham L.L.C., 266 A.D.2d 799, 800, 698 N.Y.S.2d 759, 761 (1999).

3. *Oppositions.* In the absence of statutory provision or court rule, a motion ordinarily does not require a written answer, although an adverse party may be permitted to file an answer in opposition to the showing made in the motion or its supporting affidavits. AMJUR MOTIONS § 26. When a party files a motion and the opposing party fails to respond, the court may construe such failure to respond as non-opposition to the motion or an admission that the motion was meritorious, may take the facts alleged in the motion as true, and may grant the motion if the relief requested appears to be justified. However, the severity of such a result demands that a court impose it only with great caution. AMJUR MOTIONS § 28.

4. *Governing law.* The civil practice law and rules (NY CPLR § 101, et seq.) shall govern the procedure in civil judicial proceedings in all courts of the state and before all judges, except where the procedure is regulated by inconsistent statute. The civil practice law and rules shall succeed the civil practice act and rules of civil practice and shall be deemed substituted therefor throughout the statutes and rules of the state. NY CPLR § 101. The civil practice law and rules shall be liberally construed to secure the just, speedy and inexpensive determination of every civil judicial proceeding. NY CPLR § 104.

a. *Uniform trial court rules.* The uniform civil rules for the Supreme Court and County Court (NY R UNIF TRIAL CTS

§ 202.1, et seq.) shall be applicable to civil actions and proceedings in the Supreme Court and the County Court. NY R UNIF TRIAL CTS § 202.1(a). The provisions of the uniform rules shall be construed consistent with the Civil Practice Law and Rules (CPLR), and matters not covered by the uniform rules shall be governed by the CPLR. NY R UNIF TRIAL CTS § 202.1(d).

b. *Local rules.* Local court rules, not inconsistent with law or with uniform civil rules for the Supreme Court and County Court (NY R UNIF TRIAL CTS § 202.1, et seq.), shall comply with Part 9 of the Rules of the Chief Judge (NY R CHIEF J § 9.1). NY R UNIF TRIAL CTS § 202.1(c).

c. *Official forms.* The state administrator shall have the power to adopt, amend and rescind an appendix of forms. Forms adopted pursuant to NY CPLR § 107 shall be sufficient under the civil practice law and rules and shall illustrate the simplicity and brevity of statement which the civil practice law and rules contemplate. NY CPLR § 107.

5. *Rules of the commercial division.* [Editor's note: certain types of civil cases or civil cases meeting certain monetary thresholds that are filed in the state of New York must be filed in the Commercial Division of the New York Supreme Courts. Rules governing practice in the commercial division are found in NY R UNIF TRIAL CTS § 202.70]. Cases which must be filed in the commercial division are listed below. For more information, refer to NY R UNIF TRIAL CTS § 202.70.

a. *Monetary thresholds.* Except as set forth in NY R UNIF TRIAL CTS § 202.70(b), the monetary thresholds of the Commercial Division, exclusive of punitive damages, interests, costs, disbursements and counsel fees claimed, are established as follows: (1) Albany County, fifty thousand dollars ($50,000); (2) Eighth Judicial District, one hundred thousand dollars ($100,000); (3) Kings County, one hundred fifty thousand dollars ($150,000); (4) Nassau County, two hundred thousand dollars ($200,000); (5) New York County, five hundred thousand dollars ($500,000); (6) Onondaga County, fifty thousand dollars ($50,000); (7) Queens County, one hundred thousand dollars ($100,000); (8) Seventh Judicial District, fifty thousand dollars ($50,000); (9) Suffolk County, one hundred thousand dollars ($100,000); and (10) Westchester County, one hundred thousand dollars ($100,000). NY R UNIF TRIAL CTS § 202.70(a).

i. *ALBANY COUNTY.* The Commercial Division of the Albany County Supreme Court exercises jurisdiction over selected business and commercial disputes in which the amount at issue generally involves damage claims in a minimum amount of fifty thousand dollars ($50,000) as well as claims for unspecified amounts where the value of the commercial asset(s) in dispute exceeds fifty thousand dollars ($50,000). A separate publication promulgating the rules and criteria relating to the filing and management of Commercial Court cases in this part may be obtained from the Albany County Supreme Court Clerk's Office. A section of the Uniform Civil Rules for the Supreme Court and County Court sets forth statewide rules. NY R 3 JD SUP Doc. 1(E).

ii. *BRONX COUNTY.* The monetary threshold for commercial cases in Bronx County will be seventy-five thousand dollars ($75,000). All other parameters including the type of matters that will be heard are contained within the Rules of the Commercial Division of the Supreme Court (NY R UNIF TRIAL CTS § 202.70). NY R BRONX FIL R Doc. 12.

iii. *NEW YORK COUNTY.* The monetary threshold in the New York County Commercial Division, which is generally applicable, is an amount in controversy of five hundred thousand dollars ($500,000) or more (exclusive of punitive damages, interest, costs, disbursements, and counsel fees). If the case is designated a commercial one and the Addendum is submitted, the clerk will review the pleadings to determine whether the amount in controversy in the case meets the monetary threshold or whether an exception to the threshold applies. NY R NY CTY Procedure IA(B). For more information on assigning a case to the commercial division in New York County, refer to NY R NY CTY Procedure IA(B).

b. *Commercial cases.* Actions in which the principal claims involve or consist of the following will be heard in the Commercial Division provided that the monetary threshold is met or equitable or declaratory relief is sought:

i. Breach of contract or fiduciary duty, fraud, misrepresentation, business tort (e.g., unfair competition), or statutory and/or common law violation where the breach or violation is alleged to arise out of business dealings (e.g., sales of assets or securities; corporate restructuring; partnership, shareholder, joint venture, and other business agreements; trade secrets; restrictive covenants; and employment agreements not including claims that principally involve alleged discriminatory practices);

ii. Transactions governed by the Uniform Commercial Code (exclusive of those concerning individual cooperative or condominium units);

iii. Transactions involving commercial real property, including Yellowstone injunctions and excluding actions for the payment of rent only;

iv. Shareholder derivative actions—without consideration of the monetary threshold;

v. Commercial class actions—without consideration of the monetary threshold;

vi. Business transactions involving or arising out of dealings with commercial banks and other financial institutions;

vii. Internal affairs of business organizations;

viii. Malpractice by accountants or actuaries, and legal malpractice arising out of representation in commercial matters;

ix. Environmental insurance coverage;

x. Commercial insurance coverage (e.g., directors and officers, errors and omissions, and business interruption coverage);

xi. Dissolution of corporations, partnerships, limited liability companies, limited liability partnerships and joint ventures—without consideration of the monetary threshold; and

xii. Applications to stay or compel arbitration and affirm or disaffirm arbitration awards and related injunctive relief pursuant to Article 75 of the New York Civil Practice Law and Rules (NY CPLR § 7501, et seq.) involving any of the foregoing enumerated commercial issues. Where the applicable arbitration agreement provides for the arbitration to be heard outside the United States, the monetary threshold set forth in NY R UNIF TRIAL CTS § 202.70(a) shall not apply. NY R UNIF TRIAL CTS § 202.70(b).

c. *Non-commercial cases.* The following will not be heard in the Commercial Division even if the monetary threshold is met:

i. Suits to collect professional fees;

ii. Cases seeking a declaratory judgment as to insurance coverage for personal injury or property damage;

iii. Residential real estate disputes, including landlord-tenant matters, and commercial real estate disputes involving the payment of rent only;

iv. Home improvement contracts involving residential properties consisting of one to four residential units or individual units in any residential building, including cooperative or condominium units;

v. Proceedings to enforce a judgment regardless of the nature of the underlying case;

vi. First-party insurance claims and actions by insurers to collect premiums or rescind non-commercial policies; and

vii. Attorney malpractice actions except as otherwise provided in NY R UNIF TRIAL CTS § 202.70(b)(8). NY R UNIF TRIAL CTS § 202.70(c).

d. For more information on the Commercial Division, refer to NY R UNIF TRIAL CTS § 202.70.

D. Documents

1. *Documents for moving party*

a. *Required documents*

i. *Notice of motion, order to show cause, or affidavit on ex parte motion.* The notice of motion shall be substantially in the form found in NY R UNIF TRIAL CTS § 202.7(b). NY R UNIF TRIAL CTS § 202.7(b). The supporting papers should be referred to in the notice of motion. SIEGEL-NYPRAC § 246. The court in a proper case may grant an order to show cause, to be served in lieu of a notice of motion. NY CPLR Rule 2214(d). An ex parte motion shall be accompanied by an affidavit stating the result of any prior motion for similar relief and specifying the new facts, if any, that were not previously shown. NY CPLR Rule 2217(b).

- *Request for oral argument.* A party requesting oral argument shall set forth such request in its notice of motion or in its order to show cause or on the first page of the answering papers, as the case may be. Where all parties to a motion request oral argument, oral argument shall be granted unless the court shall determine it to be unnecessary. Where a motion is brought on by order to show cause, the court may set forth in the order that oral argument is required on the return date of the motion. NY R UNIF TRIAL CTS § 202.8(d).

ii. *Motion.* Refer to the General Requirements section of this document for information on the notice of motion and motion.

iii. *Request for judicial intervention.* At any time after service of process, a party may file a request for judicial intervention. Except as provided in NY R UNIF TRIAL CTS § 202.6(b), in an action not yet assigned to a judge, the court shall not accept for filing a notice of motion, order to show cause, or application for ex parte order, unless such notice or application is accompanied by a request for judicial intervention. NY R UNIF TRIAL CTS § 202.6(a).

- *BRONX COUNTY.* Generally, the Request For Judicial Intervention, commonly referred to as an "RJI", is required to be filed in any action where the assignment of a Justice is required. The RJI sets forth the information which is entered into the court system's database. It must be completely and accurately filled out. The full caption, as stated on the Summons, must be set forth. Use of terms "et al." and "etc." are not permitted. Only one (1) RJI may be filed in each action. Either a self represented litigant or an attorney must sign the affirmation at the end of the form. Once completed, the RJI must be filed in duplicate. Except in the case of an ex-parte application, the RJI must also be served together with the accompanying application upon all parties. Proof of accuracy of the index number must accompany the RJI. Check the Fee Schedule[. . .]for any applicable filing fees. NY R BRONX FIL R Doc. 2.
- *KINGS COUNTY.* An RJI with the relevant required addendum in a NYSCEF case shall be submitted via NYSCEF. Once e-filed, the RJI and any accompanying document will be forwarded to the relevant support office for random assignment of the case and processing of the document. A filer or counsel need not appear (as to Proposed Orders to Show Cause, however, see below). A copy of the pleadings must be submitted only if the document has not previously been e-filed. If the RJI seeks intervention with regard to a document that is intended for review by a Justice, such as a motion, a working copy of the RJI must be submitted with the working copy of the motion and the NYSCEF Confirmation Notice. NY R L KINGS E FIL Doc. 1(C).
- *NEW YORK COUNTY.* To obtain the assignment of an IAS Justice to a case, a Request for Judicial Intervention (cost ninety-five dollars ($95)) must be filed, with NYSCEF in an e-filed case or in paper in an authorized hard-copy one. A no-fee RJI, which will generally result in the referral of an application to an Ex Parte Justice, is also required with regard to certain kinds of applications for which, prior to 2011, no RJI was required. NY R NY CTY Procedure I(C). A "fillable" form RJI is available on-line. The form must be filed in duplicate in hard-copy cases. NY R NY CTY Procedure IA(A)(1). The filer of an RJI must check off a box identifying the type of case at issue. Where the RJI seeks judicial assignment, this designation will bring about a random assignment of the case by computer to a Justice handling cases of that type. NY R NY CTY Procedure IA(A)(1). The RJI and any addendum can be completed and submitted electronically in an e-filed case. NY R NY CTY Procedure II(A). The RJI shall be marked to reflect the existence of any "related case" as explained on the "Commencement of Cases" page under "Case Processing" on the court's website. NY R NY CTY Procedure II(A); NY R NY CTY E FIL Doc. 2(C).
- *ONONDAGA COUNTY.* The RJI will be submitted via the NYSCEF system along with any required RJI addendum forms. When the RJI is filed and the fee paid online, the Onondaga County Clerk's Office will electronically forward the RJI and any accompanying documents to the Onondaga Supreme Court Clerk's Office for assignment and processing. Counsel will receive notification of judge assignment via the NYSCEF system. NY R ONDGA E FIL Protocol(B)(3).
- *QUEENS COUNTY.* A Request for Judicial Intervention ("RJI") in an E-filed case shall be submitted via the E-filing System. When the RJI is approved, filed and paid for on-line, it will be forwarded to the relevant back office for random assignment of the case and processing of the document. In the case of RJIs seeking assignment to the Commercial Division, the filer must submit therewith, a Commercial Addendum as required by the standards for assignment of cases to the Commercial Division. NY R L QUEENS E-FILE Doc. 1(F).

iv. *Proof of service.* In addition to complying with the provisions of NY CPLR Rule 2101, every paper filed in court shall have annexed thereto appropriate proof of service on all parties where required. NY R UNIF TRIAL CTS § 202.5(a).

- *QUEENS COUNTY.* With regard to service of a motion/petition on notice in an E-filed action, NY CPLR Rule 2214(b) and NY R UNIF TRIAL CTS § 202.5-b(f) applies. Where required, proof of service shall be filed on-line as a separate document. NY R L QUEENS E-FILE Doc. 1(H)(3).

v. *ALBANY COUNTY: Additional required documents*

- *Affirmation of good faith effort.* The parties must[. . .]submit an affirmation attesting to [their good faith effort to resolve the matter]. The affirmation of good faith effort to resolve the issues raised by the motion shall indicate the time, place and nature of the consultation and the issues discussed and any resolutions, or shall indicate good cause why no such conferral with counsel for opposing parties was held. An assigned justice or judge may dismiss a motion for failure to demonstrate that such effort was made with leave to renew the motion after such effort has been demonstrated. NY R 3 JD SUP Doc. 1(B).

b. *Supplemental documents*

i. *Supporting evidence; Exhibits.* The main supporting papers on a motion are affidavits, but any relevant exhibits, documents, depositions, etc., are also includible. SIEGEL-NYPRAC § 246.

- *Affidavits accompanying motion.* Affidavits shall be for a statement of the relevant facts. NY R UNIF TRIAL CTS § 202.8(c).
- *Foreign language documents.* Where an affidavit or exhibit annexed to a paper served or filed is in a foreign language, it shall be accompanied by an English translation and an affidavit by the translator stating his qualifications and that the translation is accurate. NY CPLR Rule 2101(b).
- *Statement of attorney in lieu of affidavit.* The statement of an attorney admitted to practice in the courts of the state, or of a physician, osteopath or dentist, authorized by law to practice in the state, who is not a party to an action, when subscribed and affirmed by him to be true under the penalties of perjury, may be served or filed in the action in lieu of and with the same force and effect as an affidavit. NY CPLR Rule 2106.
- *NEW YORK COUNTY: Form of presented exhibits.* Exhibits should be tabbed and be legible; a typed version of any exhibit that is difficult to read should be submitted with the original. Exhibits printed on both sides of the page should be bound and tabbed on the side. NY R NY CTY J RUL Rule 14(a).
- *QUEENS COUNTY.* Attorneys submitting exhibits to the court on E-file cases shall make each exhibit a separate, labeled attachment to an affidavit/affirmation. NY R L QUEENS E-FILE Doc. 1(H)(4).

ii. *Brief.* Briefs shall be for a statement of the relevant law. NY R UNIF TRIAL CTS § 202.8(c).

iii. *Notice to produce papers not in possession of the court.* If a paper relied on by the movant is in the possession of the other side, it may be demanded of that side with a notice to produce it at the hearing. Where such papers are in the possession of an adverse party, they shall be produced by him at the hearing on notice served with the motion papers. NY CPLR Rule 2214(Practice Commentary, C2214:23).

iv. *Filing fees.* The County Clerk shall require the payment of any applicable statutory fees, or an order of the Court waiving payment of such fees, before accepting a paper for filing. NY R UNIF TRIAL CTS § 202.5(d)(1). For information on filing fees, if any, refer to NY CPLR § 8001, et seq.

- *ALBANY COUNTY.* In general, any filing subsequent to the commencement of an action which is designated as a motion or cross-motion requires the payment of a filing fee to the County Clerk's Office prior to submission to the Supreme Court Clerk's Office for referral to the assigned justice. The fee is assessed regardless of whether an application is made by notice of motion, order to show cause or ex parte. No fee will be charged upon the filing of a motion for poor person status in conjunction with an application which serves to commence an action or special proceeding. In the event a motion is received by the court unaccompanied by proof of payment to the County Clerk, the Supreme Court Clerk's Office will contact the submitting party to advise that the application will be held pending receipt of the filing fee only until the return date of the motion. If proof of payment is not submitted to the Supreme Court Clerk's Office by the return date (ex parte applications will be held ten (10) days), the papers will be returned by mail with a notification that the motion has been removed from the court's calendar and that it must be re-noticed and re-filed with the court along with the requisite filing fee. Inquiries concerning the applicability of the motion fee to a proposed filing may be directed to the Supreme Court Clerk's Office. NY R 3 JD SUP Doc. 1(B).
- *BRONX COUNTY.* In accordance with the new civil fee schedule set forth in Article 80 of the C.P.L.R. (NY CPLR § 8001, et seq.), effective July 14, 2003, all motions, and cross motions must be approved in Room 217 prior to payment of said fees in the County Clerk's Office, Room 118. NY R BRONX FIL R Doc. 8. The motion fee [must be] paid for via NYSCEF by credit/debit card. NY R BRONX E FIL R Doc. 1(1).
- *ERIE COUNTY.* Payment for fee-bearing NYSCEF documents must be made online via credit or debit card (American Express, MasterCard or Visa) at the time of submission. NY R ERIE E FIL Doc. 3(III)(E).
- *KINGS COUNTY.* The motion must be filed with NYSCEF and the motion fee paid. NY R L KINGS E FIL Doc. 1(D). Court fees in NYSCEF cases must be paid via NYSCEF by a credit or bank card (MasterCard, Visa, or American Express). Fees are no longer accepted in person in the Kings County Clerk's Office in NYSCEF cases. NY R L KINGS E FIL Doc. 1(B)(6).
- *NEW YORK COUNTY.* A motion fee must be paid on motions made in writing by notice of motion, order

to show cause or ex parte after the commencement of an action. For this purpose, the term "action" shall mean any application to the court that requires the assignment of an index number, regardless of whether a formal pleading is filed. Applications or motions that commence an action and for which an index number fee must be paid require no motion fee. [A]ny motions made after the initial applications in these situations would require payment of the motion fee. A motion that is the initial application in a case commenced by the filing of a summons and complaint would require a motion fee since the filing of the summons and complaint rather than the application itself would require the purchase of an index number. NY R NY CTY Procedure II(A). In e-filed cases the motion fee must be paid when the documents are filed. Payment is made on-line by Visa, Mastercard, or American Express credit or bank card. NY R NY CTY Procedure II(A); NY R NY CTY E FIL Doc. 2(B)(5).

- *ONONDAGA COUNTY.* Court fees in e-filed cases must be paid online with the NYSCEF system using a credit card. The document is not considered to have been filed until payment of the fee has been tendered. NY R ONDGA E FIL Protocol(B)(2). Fees must be paid on all cross motions. NY R ONDGA E FIL Protocol(B)(9)(e).
- *QUEENS COUNTY.* The Motion Support Office does not receive, forward or process any fees or waiver of fees. All applications requiring payment of statutory fees or waiver of fees must be sent directly to the Queens County Clerk's office. NY R L QUEENS MOT SUP Doc. 1. Court fees (e.g., RJI fee, motion fee) in E-filed cases may be paid for on-line using a credit card. Papers may also be filed with the E-file system and the fee may be paid at the County Clerk's Office. In the latter case, the paper is not considered to have been filed until payment of the fee has been tendered. NY R L QUEENS E-FILE Doc. 1(E)(1). The motion/petition shall be filed on-line and the fee paid for either on-line by credit card or by the "Pay at the County Clerk's Office" option. NY R L QUEENS E-FILE Doc. 1(H)(1).

v. *Working copies.* The court may require the parties to provide working copies of documents filed electronically. In such event, each working copy shall include, firmly affixed thereto, a copy of a confirmation notice in a form prescribed by the Chief Administrator. NY R UNIF TRIAL CTS § 202.5-b(d)(5).

- *BRONX COUNTY.* After papers on motions have been e-filed, working copies thereof, with Confirmation Notice firmly attached as the back page facing out, must be submitted. (Each document or group of documents that is separately bound shall bear a Confirmation Notice.) Working copies lacking the Notice will not be accepted. WORKING COPIES OF MOTION PAPERS MUST BE SUBMITTED NO LATER THAN 4:45 P.M. ON THE RETURN DATE IN THE MOTION SUPPORT OFFICE (ROOM 217) AS EXPLAINED in NY R BRONX E FIL R Doc. 1(4). If an attorney has failed to submit required working copies on or before the return date, the motion will be transmitted as is to the Justice for such action as the Justice finds appropriate. Attorneys may submit working copies on motions by mail or overnight delivery. Any such submission shall be sent in a timely manner to the Motion Support Office (Room 217) and be conspicuously marked on the outside "NYSCEF Matter"; lack of such marking may delay processing. NY R BRONX E FIL R Doc. 1(4)(a).
- *ERIE COUNTY.* Electronically filed documents subject to review and processing by the Part Clerk do not require a working copy unless otherwise directed or provided for in IAS Part Rules. NY R UNIF TRIAL CTS § 202.5-b(d)(4), any working copy submitted shall include, as a cover page firmly fastened thereto, a copy of the Confirmation Notice generated by the NYSCEF site at the time of filing. Please consult the individual Justice's Part Rules and/or consult with the Judge's chambers to determine whether and how working copies are to be provided. Working copies will not be printed or delivered by the Erie County Clerk or the Chief Clerk of the Courts or any of their personnel to chambers. The official record of a document in an electronically filed case is the document filed via the NYSCEF system. Working copies are intended only for use by the Justice. The Court will discard all working copies after the Justice has finished with them. Thus, in the event that counsel fails to file a document via the NYSCEF system, the document will not be part of the court record. NY R ERIE E FIL Doc. 3(III)(O); NY R ERIE E FIL Doc. 3(V)(E).
- *KINGS COUNTY.* No courtesy copies of motion papers are required by the Court, except as may be required for electronic filing or by the Judge's Part Rules. In tort cases against the City of New York, courtesy copies shall be supplied to the Corporation Counsel's office in Brooklyn. NY R L KINGS Pt. C, Rule 5. Unless otherwise directed by the Court or as described herein, and with the exceptions listed below, in all NYSCEF cases in which an RJI has been filed, working copies of e-filed documents that are intended for judicial review must be submitted to the court. Working copies are not required of documents that are only processed by a support office (e.g. preliminary conference request, note of issue). Working copies

shall include exhibit tabs and backs; for motion papers, the motion sequence number and the return date and part. The confirmation notice with the motion sequence number on it should be the back page of the motion facing out. In addition, the filer of a working copy must firmly bind thereto, with the back page facing out, a copy of the Confirmation Notice that was generated by NYSCEF when that document was efiled. Working copies that are submitted without the related Confirmation Notice will not be accepted. NY R L KINGS E FIL Doc. 1(B)(7); NY R L KINGS E FIL Doc. 1(D). WORKING COPIES OF MOTION PAPERS MUST BE SUBMITTED IN THE MOTION SUPPORT OFFICE (ROOM 227) AS EXPLAINED HEREIN. THEY MUST NOT BE DELIVERED TO THE PART OR CHAMBERS, EXCEPT WHERE THE INDIVIDUAL JUSTICE'S PART RULES PROVIDE OTHERWISE; DOING SO WILL CAUSE ADMINISTRATIVE CONFUSION AND POSSIBLE MISPLACEMENT OF PAPERS. Any such submission shall be sent in a timely manner (kindly review individual Justice's rules) and be conspicuously marked on the outside "NYSCEF Matter;" lack of such marking may delay processing. NY R L KINGS E FIL Doc. 1(D).

- *NEW YORK COUNTY.* Some Justices require that working copies of e-filed motion papers be submitted. See the E-filing Protocol for information on the many Parts that do not require working copies. Where required, working copies of the moving documents and all other documents on the motion or application shall be submitted to the Motion Submission Part Courtroom (Room 130) on, but not before, the final return date. A Confirmation Notice from the NYSCEF system, which is generated when a document is e-filed, shall be firmly affixed, as the back page facing out, to each separate working copy or group of such copies. NY R NY CTY Procedure II(A) NY R NY CTY E FIL Doc. 2(B)(5)(a); NY R NY CTY J RUL Rule 14(a). For more information on working copies, including which parts don't require them, refer to NY R NY CTY E FIL Doc. 2(B)(6).
- *ONONDAGA COUNTY.* Any courtesy "working" copies, if required (see NY R ONDGA E FIL Protocol(B)(7)), must be provided directly to the assigned justice. NY R ONDGA E FIL Protocol(B)(9)(e). For information as to whether or not an Onondaga Supreme Court Justice requires working (courtesy) copies of e-filed documents, please consult the Onondaga County Individual E-filing Rules. NY R ONDGA E FIL Protocol(B)(7)(a). The Supreme Court Clerk's Office and the Onondaga County Clerk's Office will NOT accept the working copies. Working copies must be sent directly to the assigned justice's chambers. NY R ONDGA E FIL Protocol(B)(7)(b). A copy of the Confirmation Notice, generated by the NYSCEF system at the time a document is e-filed, must be attached to every working copy provided to chambers. If the Confirmation Notice is missing, the copy will not be accepted. NY R ONDGA E FIL Protocol(B)(7)(c). Courtesy copies do not become part of the official court record as maintained by the Onondaga County Clerk's Office and will be destroyed by chambers at the disposition of the case. In the event that counsel fails to file a document via NYSCEF, the document will not be part of the court record. NY R ONDGA E FIL Protocol(B)(7)(d).
- *QUEENS COUNTY.* Working copies of E-Filed notices of motion/notices of petition are NOT to be sent to the Motion Support Office. They must be brought to the calendar call in the judge's part. NY R L QUEENS MOT SUP Doc. 1. Unless otherwise directed or authorized by the court, counsel should file papers with the E-file system first and thereafter deliver a working copy to at the calendar call of the Centralized Motion Part or Assigned Justice in accordance with individual Part Rules. NY R L QUEENS E-FILE Doc. 1(E)(4). On the return date of a motion that has been E-filed, the movant must provide the Centralized Motion Part (CMP) with a working copy of the entire motion including the notice of motion with sequence number and all of the attached exhibits. The motion must have the confirmation of filing firmly affixed to the back of the papers (facing outward). The confirmation of filing is a separate notice from the payment notice and will say confirmation clearly across the top of the page. NY R L QUEENS E-FILE Doc. 1(H)(2)(a). The motion or Order to Show Cause must have clearly written across its face the words "Working Copy," it must also have the assigned Judge's name, motion sequence number and calendar number—which may be obtained from the posted calendar outside courtroom on the return date of the motion. A confirmation of filing must attached thereto. Working copies of e-filed Orders to Show Cause must contain a copy of the signed order and all supporting papers. NY R L QUEENS E-FILE Doc. 1(H)(2)(c). The Confirmation Notice must be an updated version that indicates the sequence number of the motion being submitted at the CMP calendar call. WORKING COPIES WITHOUT A CONFIRMATION NOTICE WILL NOT BE ACCEPTED. NY R L QUEENS E-FILE Doc. 1(H)(7).

vi. *ERIE COUNTY: Additional supplemental documents*

- *Notice of hard copy submission in e-filed case.* In accordance with NY R UNIF TRIAL CTS § 202.5-b(d),

the County Clerk shall refuse to accept for filing, hard copy papers filed to an action subject to electronic filing unless hard copy filing is permitted by the Uniform Rules or NY R ERIE E FIL Doc. 3 and the papers bear a completed Notice of Hard Copy Submission—E-Filed Case form. NY R ERIE E FIL Doc. 3(III)(D).

vii. *KINGS COUNTY: Additional supplemental documents*

- *Forms when filing in hard copy.* An attorney who certifies in good faith that he or she lacks the equipment or knowledge needed to e-file and have no staff member or employee under his or her direction who has such knowledge and equipment may opt out of participation in e-filing in a mandatory case by filing a "Notice of Opt-Out from Participation in Action Subject to Mandatory Electronic Filing" form EFM-2 with the Clerk. NY R L KINGS E FIL Doc. 1(A)(2). Where in accordance with the E-Filing Rules a party submits a document in hard copy in an e-filed case (principally, a document submitted by a nonparticipating party (e.g., an attorney) in a consensual case, an emergency filing made in accordance with the Mandatory E-Filing Rules, and any document filed with the court in hard copy by an attorney who has opted out of participation in mandatory e-filing, the document must bear the back page facing out, a "Notice of Hard Copy Submission—E-Filed Cases" form EFM-3. NY R L KINGS E FIL Doc. 1(B)(3).

viii. *NEW YORK COUNTY: Additional supplemental documents*

- *Notice of hard copy submission.* Where in accordance with the E-Filing Rules an attorney or an unrepresented litigant who is participating in e-filing submits a document in hard copy in an e-filed case, the document must bear, as the back page facing out, a Notice of Hard-Copy Submission—E-Filed Case (a form available in the "Forms" section on the NYSCEF website (Form EFM-3) and in the court's back offices). NY R NY CTY E FIL Doc. 2(B)(3). For more information refer to NY R NY CTY E FIL Doc. 2.
- *Unpublished decisions.* Whenever reliance is placed upon a decision or other authority not officially published or readily available to the New York County Supreme Court, a copy of the case or of pertinent portions of the authority shall be submitted with the motion papers. NY R NY CTY J RUL Rule 14(a).

ix. *ONONDAGA COUNTY: Additional supplemental documents*

- *Notice of hard copy submission.* Any papers to be filed with the court in an e-filed case must be filed online with the E-filing system except where a special exemption is granted (e.g., oversized maps, photographs). If such an exemption is granted, Form EFM-3, "Notice of Hard Copy Submission—E-Filed Case," must be attached to such documents forms which are not filed on line. Also, Form EFM-4 "Notice of Hard Copy Exhibit Filing" must be completed and uploaded to the action's e-file. Both of these forms may be found on the NYSCEF website. NY R ONDGA E FIL Protocol(B)(4).

x. *QUEENS COUNTY: Additional supplemental documents*

- *Notice of hard copy submission.* Any party opting out of the e-filing system must have a "Notice of Hard Copy Submission" firmly affixed to the back of the papers. NY R L QUEENS E-FILE Doc. 1(H)(2)(f).

2. *Documents for opposing party*

a. *Required documents*

i. *Opposition.* Refer to the General Requirements section of this document for information on the opposition.

- *Request for oral argument.* A party requesting oral argument shall set forth such request in its notice of motion or in its order to show cause or on the first page of the answering papers, as the case may be. Where all parties to a motion request oral argument, oral argument shall be granted unless the court shall determine it to be unnecessary. Where a motion is brought on by order to show cause, the court may set forth in the order that oral argument is required on the return date of the motion. NY R UNIF TRIAL CTS § 202.8(d).
- *QUEENS COUNTY: E-filing opposition papers.* E-filed opposition papers and/or reply papers must also be provided to the Centralized Motion Part in the same manner as the moving papers with the confirmation of filing firmly attached to the back of the papers. NY R L QUEENS E-FILE Doc. 1(H)(2)(d).

ii. *Proof of service.* In addition to complying with the provisions of NY CPLR Rule 2101, every paper filed in court shall have annexed thereto appropriate proof of service on all parties where required. NY R UNIF TRIAL CTS § 202.5(a).

b. *Supplemental documents*

i. *Supporting evidence; Exhibits.* The main supporting papers on a motion are affidavits, but any relevant exhibits, documents, depositions, etc., are also includible. SIEGEL-NYPRAC § 246.

- *Affidavits accompanying opposition.* Affidavits shall be for a statement of the relevant facts. NY R UNIF TRIAL CTS § 202.8(c).

- *Foreign language documents.* Where an affidavit or exhibit annexed to a paper served or filed is in a foreign language, it shall be accompanied by an English translation and an affidavit by the translator stating his qualifications and that the translation is accurate. NY CPLR Rule 2101(b).
- *Statement of attorney in lieu of affidavit.* The statement of an attorney admitted to practice in the courts of the state, or of a physician, osteopath or dentist, authorized by law to practice in the state, who is not a party to an action, when subscribed and affirmed by him to be true under the penalties of perjury, may be served or filed in the action in lieu of and with the same force and effect as an affidavit. NY CPLR Rule 2106.
- *NEW YORK COUNTY: Form of presented exhibits.* Exhibits should be tabbed and be legible; a typed version of any exhibit that is difficult to read should be submitted with the original. Exhibits printed on both sides of the page should be bound and tabbed on the side. NY R NY CTY J RUL Rule 14(a).
- *QUEENS COUNTY.* Attorneys submitting exhibits to the court on E-file cases shall make each exhibit a separate, labeled attachment to an affidavit/affirmation. NY R L QUEENS E-FILE Doc. 1(H)(4).

ii. *Brief.* Briefs shall be for a statement of the relevant law. NY R UNIF TRIAL CTS § 202.8(c).

iii. *Filing fees.* The County Clerk shall require the payment of any applicable statutory fees, or an order of the Court waiving payment of such fees, before accepting a paper for filing. NY R UNIF TRIAL CTS § 202.5(d)(1). For information on filing fees, if any, refer to NY CPLR § 8001, et seq.

- *ALBANY COUNTY.* In general, any filing subsequent to the commencement of an action which is designated as a motion or cross-motion requires the payment of a filing fee to the County Clerk's Office prior to submission to the Supreme Court Clerk's Office for referral to the assigned justice. The fee is assessed regardless of whether an application is made by notice of motion, order to show cause or ex parte. No fee will be charged upon the filing of a motion for poor person status in conjunction with an application which serves to commence an action or special proceeding. In the event a motion is received by the court unaccompanied by proof of payment to the County Clerk, the Supreme Court Clerk's Office will contact the submitting party to advise that the application will be held pending receipt of the filing fee only until the return date of the motion. If proof of payment is not submitted to the Supreme Court Clerk's Office by the return date (ex parte applications will be held ten (10) days), the papers will be returned by mail with a notification that the motion has been removed from the court's calendar and that it must be re-noticed and re-filed with the court along with the requisite filing fee. Inquiries concerning the applicability of the motion fee to a proposed filing may be directed to the Supreme Court Clerk's Office. NY R 3 JD SUP Doc. 1(B).
- *BRONX COUNTY.* In accordance with the new civil fee schedule set forth in Article 80 of the C.P.L.R. (NY CPLR § 8001, et seq.), effective July 14, 2003, all motions, and cross motions must be approved in Room 217 prior to payment of said fees in the County Clerk's Office, Room 118. NY R BRONX FIL R Doc. 8. The motion fee [must be] paid for via NYSCEF by credit/debit card. NY R BRONX E FIL R Doc. 1(1).
- *ERIE COUNTY.* Payment for fee-bearing NYSCEF documents must be made online via credit or debit card (American Express, MasterCard or Visa) at the time of submission. NY R ERIE E FIL Doc. 3(III)(E).
- *KINGS COUNTY.* The motion must be filed with NYSCEF and the motion fee paid. NY R L KINGS E FIL Doc. 1(D). Court fees in NYSCEF cases must be paid via NYSCEF by a credit or bank card (MasterCard, Visa, or American Express). Fees are no longer accepted in person in the Kings County Clerk's Office in NYSCEF cases. NY R L KINGS E FIL Doc. 1(B)(6).
- *NEW YORK COUNTY.* A motion fee must be paid on motions made in writing by notice of motion, order to show cause or ex parte after the commencement of an action. For this purpose, the term "action" shall mean any application to the court that requires the assignment of an index number, regardless of whether a formal pleading is filed. Applications or motions that commence an action and for which an index number fee must be paid require no motion fee. [A]ny motions made after the initial applications in these situations would require payment of the motion fee. A motion that is the initial application in a case commenced by the filing of a summons and complaint would require a motion fee since the filing of the summons and complaint rather than the application itself would require the purchase of an index number. NY R NY CTY Procedure II(A). In e-filed cases the motion fee must be paid when the documents are filed. Payment is made on-line by Visa, Mastercard, or American Express credit or bank card. NY R NY CTY Procedure II(A); NY R NY CTY E FIL Doc. 2(B)(5).
- *ONONDAGA COUNTY.* Court fees in e-filed cases must be paid online with the NYSCEF system using a credit card. The document is not considered to have been filed until payment of the fee has been tendered.

NY R ONDGA E FIL Protocol(B)(2). Fees must be paid on all cross motions. NY R ONDGA E FIL Protocol(B)(9)(e).

- *QUEENS COUNTY.* The Motion Support Office does not receive, forward or process any fees or waiver of fees. All applications requiring payment of statutory fees or waiver of fees must be sent directly to the Queens County Clerk's office. NY R L QUEENS MOT SUP Doc. 1. Court fees (e.g., RJI fee, motion fee) in E-filed cases may be paid for on-line using a credit card. Papers may also be filed with the E-file system and the fee may be paid at the County Clerk's Office. In the latter case, the paper is not considered to have been filed until payment of the fee has been tendered. NY R L QUEENS E-FILE Doc. 1(E)(1). The motion/petition shall be filed on-line and the fee paid for either on-line by credit card or by the "Pay at the County Clerk's Office" option. NY R L QUEENS E-FILE Doc. 1(H)(1).

iv. *Working copies.* The court may require the parties to provide working copies of documents filed electronically. In such event, each working copy shall include, firmly affixed thereto, a copy of a confirmation notice in a form prescribed by the Chief Administrator. NY R UNIF TRIAL CTS § 202.5-b(d)(5).

- *BRONX COUNTY.* After papers on motions have been e-filed, working copies thereof, with Confirmation Notice firmly attached as the back page facing out, must be submitted. (Each document or group of documents that is separately bound shall bear a Confirmation Notice.) Working copies lacking the Notice will not be accepted. WORKING COPIES OF MOTION PAPERS MUST BE SUBMITTED NO LATER THAN 4:45 P.M. ON THE RETURN DATE IN THE MOTION SUPPORT OFFICE (ROOM 217) AS EXPLAINED in NY R BRONX E FIL R Doc. 1(4). If an attorney has failed to submit required working copies on or before the return date, the motion will be transmitted as is to the Justice for such action as the Justice finds appropriate. Attorneys may submit working copies on motions by mail or overnight delivery. Any such submission shall be sent in a timely manner to the Motion Support Office (Room 217) and be conspicuously marked on the outside "NYSCEF Matter"; lack of such marking may delay processing. NY R BRONX E FIL R Doc. 1(4)(a).
- *ERIE COUNTY.* Electronically filed documents subject to review and processing by the Part Clerk do not require a working copy unless otherwise directed or provided for in IAS Part Rules. NY R UNIF TRIAL CTS § 202.5-b(d)(4), any working copy submitted shall include, as a cover page firmly fastened thereto, a copy of the Confirmation Notice generated by the NYSCEF site at the time of filing. Please consult the individual Justice's Part Rules and/or consult with the Judge's chambers to determine whether and how working copies are to be provided. Working copies will not be printed or delivered by the Erie County Clerk or the Chief Clerk of the Courts or any of their personnel to chambers. The official record of a document in an electronically filed case is the document filed via the NYSCEF system. Working copies are intended only for use by the Justice. The Court will discard all working copies after the Justice has finished with them. Thus, in the event that counsel fails to file a document via the NYSCEF system, the document will not be part of the court record. NY R ERIE E FIL Doc. 3(III)(O); NY R ERIE E FIL Doc. 3(V)(E).
- *KINGS COUNTY.* No courtesy copies of motion papers are required by the Court, except as may be required for electronic filing or by the Judge's Part Rules. In tort cases against the City of New York, courtesy copies shall be supplied to the Corporation Counsel's office in Brooklyn. NY R L KINGS Pt. C, Rule 5. Unless otherwise directed by the Court or as described herein, and with the exceptions listed below, in all NYSCEF cases in which an RJI has been filed, working copies of e-filed documents that are intended for judicial review must be submitted to the court. Working copies are not required of documents that are only processed by a support office (e.g. preliminary conference request, note of issue). Working copies shall include exhibit tabs and backs; for motion papers, the motion sequence number and the return date and part. The confirmation notice with the motion sequence number on it should be the back page of the motion facing out. In addition, the filer of a working copy must firmly bind thereto, with the back page facing out, a copy of the Confirmation Notice that was generated by NYSCEF when that document was efiled. Working copies that are submitted without the related Confirmation Notice will not be accepted. NY R L KINGS E FIL Doc. 1(B)(7); NY R L KINGS E FIL Doc. 1(D). WORKING COPIES OF MOTION PAPERS MUST BE SUBMITTED IN THE MOTION SUPPORT OFFICE (ROOM 227) AS EXPLAINED HEREIN. THEY MUST NOT BE DELIVERED TO THE PART OR CHAMBERS, EXCEPT WHERE THE INDIVIDUAL JUSTICE'S PART RULES PROVIDE OTHERWISE; DOING SO WILL CAUSE ADMINISTRATIVE CONFUSION AND POSSIBLE MISPLACEMENT OF PAPERS. Any such submission shall be sent in a timely manner (kindly review individual Justice's rules) and be conspicuously marked on the outside "NYSCEF Matter;" lack of such marking may delay processing. NY R L KINGS E FIL Doc. 1(D).

- *NEW YORK COUNTY.* Some Justices require that working copies of e-filed motion papers be submitted. See the E-filing Protocol for information on the many Parts that do not require working copies. Where required, working copies of the moving documents and all other documents on the motion or application shall be submitted to the Motion Submission Part Courtroom (Room 130) on, but not before, the final return date. A Confirmation Notice from the NYSCEF system, which is generated when a document is e-filed, shall be firmly affixed, as the back page facing out, to each separate working copy or group of such copies. NY R NY CTY Procedure II(A) NY R NY CTY E FIL Doc. 2(B)(5)(a); NY R NY CTY J RUL Rule 14(a). For more information on working copies, including which parts don't require them, refer to NY R NY CTY E FIL Doc. 2(B)(6).
- *ONONDAGA COUNTY.* Any courtesy "working" copies, if required (see NY R ONDGA E FIL Protocol(B)(7)), must be provided directly to the assigned justice. NY R ONDGA E FIL Protocol(B)(9)(e). For information as to whether or not an Onondaga Supreme Court Justice requires working (courtesy) copies of e-filed documents, please consult the Onondaga County Individual E-filing Rules. NY R ONDGA E FIL Protocol(B)(7)(a). The Supreme Court Clerk's Office and the Onondaga County Clerk's Office will NOT accept the working copies. Working copies must be sent directly to the assigned justice's chambers. NY R ONDGA E FIL Protocol(B)(7)(b). A copy of the Confirmation Notice, generated by the NYSCEF system at the time a document is e-filed, must be attached to every working copy provided to chambers. If the Confirmation Notice is missing, the copy will not be accepted. NY R ONDGA E FIL Protocol(B)(7)(c). Courtesy copies do not become part of the official court record as maintained by the Onondaga County Clerk's Office and will be destroyed by chambers at the disposition of the case. In the event that counsel fails to file a document via NYSCEF, the document will not be part of the court record. NY R ONDGA E FIL Protocol(B)(7)(d).
- *QUEENS COUNTY.* Working copies of E-Filed notices of motion/notices of petition are NOT to be sent to the Motion Support Office. They must be brought to the calendar call in the judge's part. NY R L QUEENS MOT SUP Doc. 1. Unless otherwise directed or authorized by the court, counsel should file papers with the E-file system first and thereafter deliver a working copy to at the calendar call of the Centralized Motion Part or Assigned Justice in accordance with individual Part Rules. NY R L QUEENS E-FILE Doc. 1(E)(4). On the return date of a motion that has been E-filed, the movant must provide the Centralized Motion Part (CMP) with a working copy of the entire motion including the notice of motion with sequence number and all of the attached exhibits. The motion must have the confirmation of filing firmly affixed to the back of the papers (facing outward). The confirmation of filing is a separate notice from the payment notice and will say confirmation clearly across the top of the page. NY R L QUEENS E-FILE Doc. 1(H)(2)(a). The motion or Order to Show Cause must have clearly written across its face the words "Working Copy," it must also have the assigned Judge's name, motion sequence number and calendar number—which may be obtained from the posted calendar outside courtroom on the return date of the motion. A confirmation of filing must attached thereto. Working copies of e-filed Orders to Show Cause must contain a copy of the signed order and all supporting papers. NY R L QUEENS E-FILE Doc. 1(H)(2)(c). The Confirmation Notice must be an updated version that indicates the sequence number of the motion being submitted at the CMP calendar call. WORKING COPIES WITHOUT A CONFIRMATION NOTICE WILL NOT BE ACCEPTED. NY R L QUEENS E-FILE Doc. 1(H)(7).

v. *ERIE COUNTY: Additional supplemental documents*

- *Notice of hard copy submission in e-filed case.* In accordance with NY R UNIF TRIAL CTS § 202.5-b(d), the County Clerk shall refuse to accept for filing, hard copy papers filed to an action subject to electronic filing unless hard copy filing is permitted by the Uniform Rules or NY R ERIE E FIL Doc. 3 and the papers bear a completed Notice of Hard Copy Submission—E-Filed Case form. NY R ERIE E FIL Doc. 3(III)(D).

vi. *KINGS COUNTY: Additional supplemental documents*

- *Forms when filing in hard copy.* An attorney who certifies in good faith that he or she lacks the equipment or knowledge needed to e-file and have no staff member or employee under his or her direction who has such knowledge and equipment may opt out of participation in e-filing in a mandatory case by filing a "Notice of Opt-Out from Participation in Action Subject to Mandatory Electronic Filing" form EFM-2 with the Clerk. NY R L KINGS E FIL Doc. 1(A)(2). Where in accordance with the E-Filing Rules a party submits a document in hard copy in an e-filed case (principally, a document submitted by a nonparticipating party (e.g., an attorney) in a consensual case, an emergency filing made in accordance with the Mandatory E-Filing Rules, and any document filed with the court in hard copy by an attorney who has opted out of

participation in mandatory e-filing, the document must bear the back page facing out, a "Notice of Hard Copy Submission—E-Filed Cases" form EFM-3. NY R L KINGS E FIL Doc. 1(B)(3).

vii. *NEW YORK COUNTY: Additional supplemental documents*

- *Notice of hard copy submission.* Where in accordance with the E-Filing Rules an attorney or an unrepresented litigant who is participating in e-filing submits a document in hard copy in an e-filed case, the document must bear, as the back page facing out, a Notice of Hard-Copy Submission—E-Filed Case (a form available in the "Forms" section on the NYSCEF website (Form EFM-3) and in the court's back offices). NY R NY CTY E FIL Doc. 2(B)(3). For more information refer to NY R NY CTY E FIL Doc. 2.
- *Unpublished decisions.* Whenever reliance is placed upon a decision or other authority not officially published or readily available to the New York County Supreme Court, a copy of the case or of pertinent portions of the authority shall be submitted with the motion papers. NY R NY CTY J RUL Rule 14(a).

viii. *ONONDAGA COUNTY: Additional supplemental documents*

- *Notice of hard copy submission.* Any papers to be filed with the court in an e-filed case must be filed online with the E-filing system except where a special exemption is granted (e.g., oversized maps, photographs). If such an exemption is granted, Form EFM-3, "Notice of Hard Copy Submission—E-Filed Case," must be attached to such documents forms which are not filed on line. Also, Form EFM-4 "Notice of Hard Copy Exhibit Filing" must be completed and uploaded to the action's e-file. Both of these forms may be found on the NYSCEF website. NY R ONDGA E FIL Protocol(B)(4).

ix. *QUEENS COUNTY: Additional supplemental documents*

- *Notice of hard copy submission.* Any party opting out of the e-filing system must have a "Notice of Hard Copy Submission" firmly affixed to the back of the papers. NY R L QUEENS E-FILE Doc. 1(H)(2)(f).

E. Format

1. *Form of documents*

a. *Size and form of paper.* Each paper served or filed shall be durable, white and, except for summonses, subpoenas, notices of appearance, notes of issue, orders of protection, temporary orders of protection and exhibits, shall be eleven by eight and one-half (11 x 8-1/2) inches in size. NY CPLR Rule 2101(a).

b. *Writing and language.* The writing shall be legible and in black ink. NY CPLR Rule 2101(a). Each paper served or filed shall be in the English language which, where practicable, shall be of ordinary usage. NY CPLR Rule 2101(b).

c. *Caption.* Each paper served or filed shall begin with a caption setting forth the name of the court, the venue, the title of the action, the nature of the paper and the index number of the action if one has been assigned. In all papers other than a summons, a complaint or a judgment it shall be sufficient to state the name of the first named party on each side with an appropriate indication of any omissions. NY CPLR Rule 2101(c).

i. *Further contents of first page.* After the first paper has been filed in each case the index number shall appear on the cover and first page to the right of the caption of every paper tendered for filing in the action. Each such cover and first page also shall contain an indication of the county of venue and a brief description of the nature of the paper and, where the case has been assigned to an individual judge, shall contain the name of the assigned judge to the right of the caption. NY R UNIF TRIAL CTS § 202.5(a); NY R UNIF TRIAL CTS § 202.5(b); NY R UNIF TRIAL CTS § 202.5(d)(1)(i).

ii. *ALBANY COUNTY: Request for oral argument.* A party may request oral argument on a motion by indicating such request on the first page of the notice of motion, order to show cause, or answering papers in the area across from the caption of the action/proceeding. NY R 3 JD SUP Doc. 1(B).

iii. *NEW YORK COUNTY: Request for oral argument.* Counsel who wish oral argument must so request conspicuously on the front of their papers. NY R NY CTY Procedure II(D).

d. *Index number.* No paper in an action in the supreme or a county court, other than an order submitted for signature to a judge out of court, shall be submitted for any purpose to the supreme or county court or to a clerk thereof unless there is endorsed on such paper the index number of the action assigned by the clerk of the county. NY CPLR § 8018(c).

i. *ALBANY COUNTY: Index number on all filed documents.* The index number, the request for judicial intervention number and the assigned justice's name shall appear on [all papers filed with the Court subsequent to the complaint]. NY R 3 JD SUP Doc. 1(A).

ii. *ERIE COUNTY: Index number after initial filing.* Cases that are initially commenced by the filing of papers with

the NYSCEF system are identified as e-filed cases by assignment of an Index Number that has "800-899" as the first three (3) digits of the index number (i.e. 802391/2012). NY R ERIE E FIL Doc. 3(II). [The] Index Number must be affixed to all document submissions, filings, and communications to the Erie County Clerk and the Court. Cases that are converted from paper to e-filing shall retain the original index number. NY R ERIE E FIL Doc. 3(II).

iii. *KINGS COUNTY: Index number after initial filing.* In cases commenced electronically by the filing of initiating papers with the NYSCEF system and payment of the statutory fees, the Kings County Clerk will issue an NYSCEF designated index number and the filer shall be notified via the NYSCEF system of the index number assigned and filing date. Such index number must be affixed to all document submissions, filings and communications to the Kings County Clerk and Supreme Court. If counsel faces exigent circumstances that require accelerated assignment, counsel may contact Administration of the Kings County Clerk at kcco-efile@nycourts.gov, during normal business hours of the court. NY R L KINGS E FIL Doc. 1(B)(5).

iv. *NEW YORK COUNTY: Index number on hard copy filings.* Papers subsequently presented for filing in hardcopy format will be filed in this jacket. NY R NY CTY Procedure I(B). Index numbers take the form of six digits followed by a slash and the four digits of the year the case began, e.g., 340705/2018. The first or first two integers of the index number identify the type of case. If a case is commenced electronically, the second integer will be a "5", except as indicated otherwise in the list below. There are many tax certiorari matters e-filed annually and the index numbers therefor will normally run over into those with a "6" as the second integer, and the same will occur with general cases if necessary. The principal types of cases and their index number categories are listed in NY R NY CTY Procedure I(B). NY R NY CTY Procedure I(B); NY R NY CTY Procedure XI(A).

v. *ONONDAGA COUNTY: Index number.* The index number must be referenced on all e-filed documents and correspondence. All e-filed case index numbers will contain the letters "EF" between the year and the file number (for example, 2012EF9999). NY R ONDGA E FIL Protocol(B)(1).

vi. *QUEENS COUNTY: Index number on converted cases.* Cases originally commenced in hard-copy form but later converted to an E-file case, either by stipulation or order will bear a regular index number initially. The County Clerk will issue a new E-file index number. NY R L QUEENS E-FILE Doc. 1(B).

e. *Line spacing.* Every paper filed in court, if typewritten, shall have at least double space between each line, except for quotations and the names and addresses of attorneys appearing in the action. NY R UNIF TRIAL CTS § 202.5(a).

f. *Font size.* Each. . .paper printed or typed, served or filed, except for summonses. . .and exhibits, shall be in clear type of no less than ten (10) point in size. NY CPLR Rule 2101(a).

i. Whenever a requirement relating to size of type is stated in point size, the type size requirement shall be deemed met if the x-height of the type is a minimum of forty-five percent (45%) of the specified point size. Each point shall be measured as .351 millimeter. The x-height size shall be measured as it appears on the page. The x-height is the height of the lower case letters, exclusive of ascenders or descenders. NY CPLR § 105(t).

g. *Margins.* Every paper filed in court shall have at least one (1) inch margins. NY R UNIF TRIAL CTS § 202.5(a).

h. *Citations*

i. *Civil practice law and rules.* NY CPLR § 101, et seq. shall be known as the civil practice law and rules, and may be cited as "CPLR". Reference to a provision in the civil practice law and rules may, except when such provision is being enacted or amended, be made without indicating whether it is a rule or section. NY CPLR § 101.

i. *Indorsement by attorney.* Each paper served or filed shall be indorsed with the name, address and telephone number of the attorney for the party serving or filing the paper, or if the party does not appear by attorney, with the name, address and telephone number of the party. NY CPLR Rule 2101(d).

j. *One-sided printing.* In addition, every paper filed in court, other than an exhibit or printed form, shall contain writing on one side only, except that papers that are fastened on the side may contain writing on both sides. NY R UNIF TRIAL CTS § 202.5(a).

k. *Use of copies authorized.* Except where otherwise specifically prescribed, copies, rather than originals, of all papers, including orders, affidavits and exhibits may be served or filed. Where it is required that the original be served or filed and the original is lost or withheld, the court may authorize a copy to be served or filed. NY CPLR Rule 2101(e).

i. Where a certified copy of a paper is required by law, an attorney admitted to practice in the courts of the state may certify that it has been compared by him with the original and found to be a true and complete copy. Such a certificate, when subscribed by such attorney, has the same effect as if made by a clerk. NY CPLR § 2105.

l. *Recycled paper.* It is the policy of the Unified Court System that litigants, where practicable, should file or submit to

the courts of the Unified Court System of the State of New York papers printed or reproduced on recycled paper. Paper is considered recycled if it contains a minimum content of thirty percent (30%) waste paper. NY R UNIF TRIAL CTS § 215.2. The signature page of every paper filed or submitted to the court on recycled paper should bear the legend: "Printed [Reproduced] on Recycled Paper." NY R UNIF TRIAL CTS § 215.3.

m. *Form of request for judicial intervention; Copies.* A request for judicial intervention must be submitted, in duplicate, on a form authorized by the Chief of the Courts, with proof of service on the other parties to the action (but proof of service is not required where the application is ex parte). NY R UNIF TRIAL CTS § 202.6(a).

n. *KINGS COUNTY: Tabs on filings.* Motions, orders and other filed papers shall be indexed with protruding tabs. Clerks are required to reject papers that do not have protruding exhibit tabs, except papers in matrimonial cases and papers filed by pro se litigants. NY R L KINGS Pt. A, Papers.

o. *NEW YORK COUNTY: Length of briefs.* Unless advance permission otherwise is granted by the court for good cause, memoranda of law shall not exceed thirty (30) pages each (exclusive of table of contents and table of authorities) and affidavits/affirmations shall not exceed twenty-five (25) pages each. NY R NY CTY J RUL Rule 14(b).

p. *QUEENS COUNTY: Form and size of motion filings.* All motions filed in Queens Supreme Court-Civil Term, must adhere to the Motion Support rules and the rules of the assigned judge. NY R L QUEENS MOT SUP Doc. 1. Due to space limitations, the Motion Support Office cannot accept notices of motion/notices of petition and accompanying exhibits which measure greater than eight (8) inches. If your documents measure greater than eight (8) inches you are directed to submit only the notice of motion/notice of petition to the Motion Support Office and bring all exhibits to the calendar call on your return date. NY R L QUEENS MOT SUP Doc. 1.

2. *Form of electronic documents.* Each paper served or filed by electronic means, as defined in NY CPLR Rule 2103(f), shall be capable of being reproduced by the receiver so as to comply with the provisions of NY CPLR Rule 2101(a) through NY CPLR Rule 2101(d). NY CPLR Rule 2101(g).

   a. *File format.* All e-filed documents shall comply with the technical requirements set forth at the NYSCEF site. NY R UNIF TRIAL CTS § 202.5-b(d)(1)(i).

   b. *Heading of document.* The subject matter heading for each paper sent by electronic means must indicate that the matter being transmitted electronically is related to a court proceeding. NY CPLR Rule 2103(b)(7).

   c. *E-filed documents identification*

      i. *ERIE COUNTY.* E-filed cases must be readily identifiable and marked as such. If counsel presents papers to the Office of the Erie County Clerk or the Office of the Chief Clerk in a NYSCEF matter where authorized, counsel should alert the Clerk that the case is a NYSCEF matter. NY R ERIE E FIL Doc. 3(II).

      ii. *KINGS COUNTY.* The Supreme Court's Civil Case Information System ("CCIS") will further identify e-filed cases by the addition of a suffix to the index number (e.g. 500136/2006E). This suffix should be used on all documents filed with the court in e-filed matters. NY R L KINGS E FIL Doc. 1(A)(1).

3. *Signature blocks.* Every pleading, written motion, and other paper, served on another party or filed or submitted to the court shall be signed by an attorney, or by a party if the party is not represented by an attorney, with the name of the attorney or party clearly printed or typed directly below the signature. NY R CHIEF ADMIN § 130-1.1-a(a); NY R UNIF TRIAL CTS § 202.5(d)(1)(iv).

   a. *Printed name.* Beneath each signature shall be printed the name signed. NY CPLR Rule 2101(a).

   b. *Failure to sign.* Absent good cause shown, the court shall strike any unsigned paper if the omission of the signature is not corrected promptly after being called to the attention of the attorney or party. NY R CHIEF ADMIN § 130-1.1-a(a).

   c. *Signature as certification.* By signing a paper, an attorney or party certifies that, to the best of that person's knowledge, information and belief, formed after an inquiry reasonable under the circumstances the presentation of the paper or the contentions therein are not frivolous as defined in NY R CHIEF ADMIN § 130-1.1(c). NY R CHIEF ADMIN § 130-1.1-a(b)(1).

   d. *Electronic signatures.* A document shall be considered to have been signed by an attorney or party in compliance with NY R CHIEF ADMIN § 130-1.1-a if it has been signed by such attorney or party as provided in NY R UNIF TRIAL CTS § 202.5-b(e)(1) and it bears the signatory's name. NY R UNIF TRIAL CTS § 202.5-b(e)(2). An electronically filed document shall be considered to have been signed by, and shall be binding upon, the person identified as a signatory, if:

      i. It bears the physical signature of such person and is scanned into an electronic format that reproduces such signature; or

ii. The signatory has electronically affixed the digital image of his or her signature to the document; or

iii. It is electronically filed under the User ID and password of that person; or

iv. In a tax certiorari action in which the parties have stipulated to this procedure, it is an initiating document that is electronically filed without the signature of the signatory in a form provided above in NY R UNIF TRIAL CTS § 202.5-b(e)(iv), provided that, prior to filing, the document is signed in full in hard copy (which hard copy must be preserved until the conclusion of all proceedings, including appeals, in the case in which it is filed); or

v. In a small claims assessment review proceeding, it is a petition recorded by the NYSCEF site upon the filing of a text file as provided in NY R UNIF TRIAL CTS § 202.5-b(b)(1), provided that prior to filing, the document was signed in full in hard copy (which hard copy must be preserved until the conclusion of all proceedings in the matter, including article 78 (NY CPLR § 7801, et seq.) review and any appeals, and must be made available during the proceeding upon request of the respondent or the court); or

vi. It otherwise bears the electronic signature of the signatory in a format conforming to such standards and requirements as may hereafter be established by the Chief Administrator. NY R UNIF TRIAL CTS § 202.5-b(e).

4. *Confidentiality of personal information.* No person may file any document available for public inspection with any state agency, political subdivision, or in any court of this state that contains a Social Security account number of any other person, unless such other person is a dependent child, or has consented to such filing, except as required by federal or state law or regulation, or by court rule. NY GEN BUS § 399-ddd. Submissions pursuant to e-filing procedures shall have the same confidentiality rights as paper documents. NY R UNIF TRIAL CTS § 202.5-b(k)(1).

a. *Confidential personal information.* Except in the actions designated in NY R UNIF TRIAL CTS § 202.5(e)(1), or as otherwise provided by rule or law or court order, and whether or not a sealing order is or has been sought, the parties shall omit or redact confidential personal information in papers submitted to the court for filing. For purposes of NY R UNIF TRIAL CTS § 202.5(e), confidential personal information ("CPI") means:

i. The taxpayer identification number of an individual or an entity, including a Social Security number, an employer identification number, and an individual taxpayer identification number, except the last four (4) digits thereof;

ii. The date of an individual's birth, except the year thereof;

iii. The full name of an individual known to be a minor, except the minor's initials;

iv. A financial account number, including a credit and/or debit card number, a bank account number, an investment account number, and/or an insurance account number, except the last four (4) digits or letters thereof; and

v. Any of the documents or testimony in a matrimonial action protected by NY DOM REL § 235 or evidence sealed by the court in such an action which are attached as exhibits or referenced in the papers filed in any other civil action. For purposes of NY R UNIF TRIAL CTS § 202.5, a matrimonial action shall mean: an action to annul a marriage or declare the nullity of a void marriage, an action or agreement for a separation, an action for a divorce, or an action or proceeding for custody, visitation, writ of habeus corpus, child support, maintenance or paternity. NY R UNIF TRIAL CTS § 202.5(e)(1).

vi. *ERIE COUNTY.* An attorney or unrepresented litigant filing a document via the NYSCEF system must comply with the requirements of NY R UNIF TRIAL CTS § 202.5(e) regarding the redaction of Confidential Personal Information and NY GEN BUS § 399-ddd(6) concerning the filing of documents containing Social Security Numbers. It is the sole responsibility of counsel or unrepresented litigant filing to be aware of and to comply with existing laws requiring non-disclosure of personal information contained in any document e-filed in NYSCEF. NY R ERIE E FIL Doc. 3(III)(G); NY R ERIE E FIL Doc. 3(III).

vii. *KINGS COUNTY.* An attorney or unrepresented litigant filing a document via the NYSCEF system must comply with the requirements of General Business Law § 399-dd(6), which often require redaction of any Social Security number that appear in the original document. The NYSCEF system automatically redacts portions of filed documents which apparently contain Social Security numbers pursuant to NY R UNIF TRIAL CTS § 202.5-b(k). In the event the filing party receives e-mail notice through NYSCEF that a Social Security number in a filed document has been redacted, and the filing party concludes such redaction is erroneous, the filer should click on the link provided in the e-mail to permit the County Clerk to revert the redaction. For Confidential Personal Information, see NY R UNIF TRIAL CTS § 202.5(e) and NY R L KINGS E FIL Doc. 1(B)(11). [Editor's note: the reference to General Business Law § 399-dd(6) is likely a reference to NY GEN BUS § 399-ddd(6)]. NY R L KINGS E FIL Doc. 1(B)(10); NY R L KINGS E FIL Doc. 1(K)(1).

viii. *NEW YORK COUNTY.* It is the responsibility of counsel and parties to comply with rules restricting disclosure

of confidential personal information. Nevertheless, NYSCEF screens filings and endeavors to identify any that contain social security numbers. When such numbers are discovered through this process, NYSCEF will restrict portions of or all of such documents from public view. Where NYSCEF has redacted what it believes to be a social security number, it will transmit to the filer a notice advising of the action taken and requesting that the filer review the matter and provide notification as set forth in the notice if the redaction has been made in error. NY R NY CTY E FIL Doc. 2(K)(1); NY R NY CTY J RUL Rule A-1. Documents filed in the past in "secure status" under a procedure no longer in place will retain that status unless otherwise directed by the court. NY R NY CTY E FIL Doc. 2(K)(2).

b. *Submission of confidential personal information.* Where a person submitting a paper to a court for filing believes in good faith that the inclusion of the full confidential personal information described in NY R UNIF TRIAL CTS § 202.5(e)(1) is material and necessary to the adjudication of the action or proceeding before the court, he or she may apply to the court for leave to serve and file together with a paper in which such information has been set forth in abbreviated form a confidential affidavit or affirmation setting forth the same information in unabbreviated form, appropriately referenced to the page or pages of the paper at which the abbreviated form appears. NY R UNIF TRIAL CTS § 202.5(e)(3).

c. *Home addresses.* For information on when home addresses and other personal information must be redacted, refer to NY CPLR Rule 2103-a.

5. *Defective papers.* A defect in the form of a paper, if a substantial right of a party is not prejudiced, shall be disregarded by the court, and leave to correct shall be freely given. NY CPLR Rule 2101(f). Papers that are stapled or bound securely shall not be rejected for filing simply because they are not bound with a backer of any kind. NY R UNIF TRIAL CTS § 202.5(a). A paper filed in accordance with the rules of the chief administrator or any local rule or practice established by the court shall be deemed filed. NY CPLR Rule 2102(b).

a. *Objection to defective papers.* The party on whom a paper is served shall be deemed to have waived objection to any defect in form unless, within fifteen (15) days after the receipt thereof, the party on whom the paper is served returns the paper to the party serving it with a statement of particular objections. NY CPLR Rule 2101(f).

F. Filing and Service Requirements

1. *Filing requirements.* Except where otherwise prescribed by law or order of court, papers required to be filed shall be filed with the clerk of the court in which the action is triable. In an action or proceeding in supreme or court, papers required to be filed shall be filed with the clerk of the county in which the proceeding is brought. NY CPLR Rule 2102(a).

a. *Furnishing papers to the court.* Each party shall furnish to the court all papers served by him. The moving party shall furnish at the hearing all other papers not already in the possession of the court necessary to the consideration of the questions involved. Where such papers are in the possession of an adverse party, they shall be produced by him at the hearing on notice served with the motion papers. Only papers served in accordance with the provisions of NY CPLR Rule 2214 shall be read in support of, or in opposition to, the motion, unless the court for good cause shall otherwise direct. NY CPLR Rule 2214(c).

i. *Submission to judge.* All papers for signature or consideration of the court shall be presented to the clerk of the trial court in the appropriate courtroom or clerk's office, except that where the clerk is unavailable or the judge so directs, papers may be submitted to the judge and a copy filed with the clerk at the first available opportunity. All papers for any judge that are filed in the clerk's office shall be promptly delivered to the judge by the clerk. The papers shall be clearly addressed to the judge for whom they are intended and prominently show the nature of the papers, the title and index number of the action in which they are filed, the judge's name and the name of the attorney or party submitting them. NY R UNIF TRIAL CTS § 202.5(b).

ii. *BRONX COUNTY: Approval of motions before filing.* All motion papers must be approved by the Motion Support Office, Supreme Court, Civil Term, room 217, before the motion papers are filed and the appropriate fee paid to the County Clerk. NY R BRONX FIL R Doc. 1.

iii. *ERIE COUNTY: Filing motions.* A motion on notice or a notice of petition in a NYSCEF case shall be filed through the NYSCEF system and must be accompanied by a Request for Judicial Intervention if the motion is being filed upon commencement of the action or if the matter has not yet been assigned to an IAS Justice. In addition, cross motions with the appropriate filing fees and opposition and reply papers must be submitted via the NYSCEF system. NY R ERIE E FIL Doc. 3(V)(A).

iv. *NEW YORK COUNTY: Filing hard copies.* Where in the narrow circumstances described by the e-filing rules a motion is made in hard-copy form or opposition papers are submitted in such form in an e-filed case, the hard-copy documents shall be submitted in the same way papers are submitted in non-e-filed cases, except that

there shall be firmly affixed to each separate document or group of documents, as the back page facing out, a Notice of Hard Copy Submission—E-Filed Case. NY R NY CTY Procedure II(A). For more information on filing in hard copy cases, refer to NY R NY CTY Procedure II(A).

v. *ONONDAGA COUNTY: Submission of responsive papers and cross-motions.* Cross-motions, opposition and reply papers must be submitted online. NY R ONDGA E FIL Protocol(B)(9)(e). Motions and Orders to Show Cause are assigned a sequence number by the system. Counsel must be sure that cross motions and other filings correspond with the correct sequence number so that a cross motion will not be associated with the wrong original motion. NY R ONDGA E FIL Protocol(B)(9)(f).

b. *Electronic filing.* On consent, documents may be filed and served by electronic means in Supreme Court in such civil actions and in such counties as shall be authorized by order of the Chief Administrator of the Courts and only to the extent and in the manner provided in NY R UNIF TRIAL CTS § 202.5-b. NY R UNIF TRIAL CTS § 202.5-b(a)(1). For the definitions of terms used in electronic filing, refer to NY R UNIF TRIAL CTS § 202.5-b(a)(2).

i. *E-filing mandatory.* In any action subject to e-filing, all documents required to be filed with the court by an e-filing party shall be filed and served electronically, except as provided in NY R UNIF TRIAL CTS § 202.5-b. NY R UNIF TRIAL CTS § 202.5-b(d)(1)(i).

- *ERIE COUNTY.* Case types currently eligible and accepted for e-filing are listed at the NYSCEF website. Note that some actions or special proceedings, (i.e., name changes) which are otherwise subject to mandatory e-filing, if commenced by unrepresented litigants will NOT be maintained in the NYSCEF system; individual cases may be found either at NYSCEF or in the Erie County Clerk's online records system. NY R ERIE E FIL Doc. 3(I)(E).
- *KINGS COUNTY.* Cases that are commenced by filing of the initiating papers with NYSCEF are identified as e-filed cases by assignment of a special index number (i.e., Index Numbers beginning with 500,000). NY R L KINGS E FIL Doc. 1(A)(1). All cases required to be e-filed are listed in Uniform Rule 202.5-bb (Mandatory E-Filing Rules) and on the NYSCEF website. All such cases must be commenced by filing with the County Clerk electronically through NYSCEF and all subsequent documents in such cases must be e-filed. Any questions regarding mandatory e-filing in Kings County can be e-mailed to kcco-efile@nycourts.gov. NY R L KINGS E FIL Doc. 1(A)(2).
- *NEW YORK COUNTY.* Unless otherwise provided in the Rules or in NY R NY CTY E FIL Doc. 2 or where a special exemption is granted due to physical requirements (e.g., oversized maps; see NY R NY CTY E FIL Doc. 2(B)(10)), all documents to be filed with the court in a NYSCEF case, including all documents on motions and all letters to the court (where permitted), must be filed with the NYSCEF system. Documents that attorneys would not ordinarily file with the court in a hard-copy case need not be e-filed. Unless otherwise provided by the E-Filing Rules or this Protocol, in e-filed cases the County Clerk and the court will not accept documents filed in paper form. NY R NY CTY E FIL Doc. 2(B)(1). E-filing is mandatory in all types of cases (other than election law, matrimonial, Art. 78, and Mental Hygiene Law matters, and Art. 70 habeas corpus proceedings) that are commenced in this court on or after February 19, 2013. All such cases must be commenced by filing with the County Clerk electronically through NYSCEF and all subsequent documents in such cases must be e-filed. NY R NY CTY E FIL Doc. 2(A)(2)(a). For more information, including information on consensual e-filing and filing scanned hard copy documents, refer to NY R NY CTY E FIL Doc. 2(A)(2).
- *QUEENS COUNTY.* All authorized Torts, Commercial and Tax Certiorari cases may be commenced by E-Filing, however all parties must consent for the action to continue as an E-file case. NY R L QUEENS E-FILE Doc. 1(A). All papers to be filed with the court in an E-filed case shall be filed on-line with the E-file system except as directed by the court. Papers that attorneys would not ordinarily file with the court in a hard-copy case need not be filed in an E-filed matter. NY R L QUEENS E-FILE Doc. 1(E)(2).

ii. *Who may file.* Documents may be filed or served electronically only by a person who has registered as an authorized e-filing user or as otherwise provided in NY R UNIF TRIAL CTS § 202.5-b(c). NY R UNIF TRIAL CTS § 202.5-b(c)(1).

iii. *When filing made.* Documents may be transmitted at any time of the day or night to the NYSCEF site. A document other than an order or judgment is filed when its electronic transmission or, in the case of a petition that is e-filed by submission of a text file as provided in NY R UNIF TRIAL CTS § 202.5-b(b)(1), the electronic transmission of the text file is recorded at that site, provided, however, that where payment of a fee is required upon the filing of a document, the document is not filed until transmission of the document and the information

or form or information as required in NY R UNIF TRIAL CTS § 202.5-b(d)(2)(i), NY R UNIF TRIAL CTS § 202.5-b(d)(2)(ii) or NY R UNIF TRIAL CTS § 202.5-b(d)(2)(iii) has been recorded at the NYSCEF site; or, if no transmission of that information or form or information is recorded, where permitted by the County Clerk, until payment is presented to the County Clerk. NY R UNIF TRIAL CTS § 202.5-b(d)(3)(i).

iv. *Notification of filing.* No later than the close of business on the business day following the electronic filing of a document, a notification, in a form prescribed by the Chief Administrator, shall be transmitted electronically by the NYSCEF site to the person filing such document and the e-mail service addresses of all other participating parties in such action. NY R UNIF TRIAL CTS § 202.5-b(d)(3)(ii).

v. *Removal of confidential information and other corrections.* If a document filed electronically is subsequently discovered to contain confidential data—including but not limited to trade secrets, information protected by confidentiality agreement, or personal confidential information as defined by statute or court rule—or otherwise to have been filed in error, the filer or another party or affected person may (1) notify the parties and any non-party filers in the action of the confidentiality issue or other error raised by the filing, and of his or her intention to seek judicial relief to correct the filing: (2) following such notification, request that the appropriate County Clerk, exercising his or her administrative discretion, place the document temporarily in "restricted" status on the NYSCEF site, to be made available for viewing by court staff and the parties but not the general public; and (3) file an application to correct the filing by order to show cause within five (5) business days of such notification (or such time as the court may direct), including a request for preliminary injunctive relief limiting interim disclosure of the document at issue. Unless otherwise directed by the court, any document placed in restricted status in response to such a request shall be returned to public view upon expiration of this five (5) day period. The Chief Administrator of the Courts shall promulgate forms to implement this process. NY R UNIF TRIAL CTS § 202.5-b(d)(3)(iii).

- *KINGS COUNTY.* For information on what to do when a document was erroneously filed with confidential information, refer to NY R L KINGS E FIL Doc. 1(B)(11).
- *NEW YORK COUNTY.* For information on what to do when a document was erroneously filed with confidential information, refer to NY R NY CTY E FIL Doc. 2(B)(8).
- *QUEENS COUNTY.* For information on what to do when a document was erroneously filed with confidential information, refer to NY R L QUEENS E-FILE Doc. 1(E)(7).

vi. *Documents requiring judge's signature.* Except where the court directs otherwise, any document that requires a judge's signature shall be transmitted electronically and in hard copy to the court. NY R UNIF TRIAL CTS § 202.5-b(d)(6).

vii. *Documents which would be inconvenient to file electronically; Hard copies.* Notwithstanding any other provision of NY R UNIF TRIAL CTS § 202.5-b, and subject to such guidelines as may be established by the Chief Administrative Judge, the County Clerk or his or her designee may require or permit a party to file in hard copy, in accordance with procedures set by the County Clerk or designee, an exhibit or other document which it is impractical or inconvenient to file electronically. NY R UNIF TRIAL CTS § 202.5-b(d)(7).

- *ERIE COUNTY.* Please contact the Supervisor of Actions & Proceedings, Erie County Clerk's Office by calling (716) 858-6662 or the Deputy County Clerk—Legal at (716) 858-6348 for information. NY R ERIE E FIL Doc. 3(III)(F).
- *KINGS COUNTY.* With limited exceptions, as set forth in the Uniform Rules and herein, all documents to be filed with the court in a NYSCEF case shall be filed online via the NYSCEF system. However, should the size, consistency or context of a hard copy document preclude electronic filing, the user shall electronically file a "Notice of Hard Copy Submission—E-Filed Cases" form EFM-3. Any hard copy submitted pursuant to NY R L KINGS E FIL Doc. 1(B)(9) shall include, as a cover page firmly fastened thereto, a copy of the Confirmation Notice received from the NYSCEF site confirming receipt of the "Notice of Hard Copy Submission—E-Filed Cases". Any party may object to such hard copy filing. The Court, in response to such objection, may, following the hard copy filing, fashion such relief as it deems appropriate pursuant to and in furtherance of the Uniform Rules and NY R L KINGS E FIL Doc. 1, including, but not limited to, an Order directing the filing party to file such documents online via the NYSCEF system. When exhibits are impractical to file pursuant to NY R UNIF TRIAL CTS § 202.5-b(d)(7), an additional "Notice of Hard Copy Exhibit Filing" form EFM-4 is required to be submitted. NY R L KINGS E FIL Doc. 1(B)(9).
- *NEW YORK COUNTY.* If a filer needs to submit unusual exhibits in original form that cannot practically be

e-filed, such as oversized maps or electronic recordings, the filer should consult with the County Clerk's E-File Department by telephone at 646-386-3737 (procedural questions only) or by e-mail at ccnyef@nycourts.gov, which will normally require that the filer retain custody of the original subject to possible future directives of the court. NY R NY CTY E FIL Doc. 2(B)(10). In such instances, the filing counsel shall file with NYSCEF a "placeholder" in the form of a Notice of Hard Copy Exhibit Filing (NYSCEF Form EF 21). The Notice should be uploaded to NYSCEF as document type "Exhibit" and the filer should indicate in the "Additional Document Information" field that the filer is retaining custody of the original. Failure to e-file the Notice may result in a gap in the official record of the court. NY R NY CTY E FIL Doc. 2(B)(10).

viii. *Documents containing sensitive or proprietary information.* In an action subject to e-filing, any person may apply for an order prohibiting or restricting the electronic filing in the action of specifically identified materials on the grounds that such materials are subject to copyright or other proprietary rights, or trade secret or other privacy interests, and that electronic filing in the action is likely to result in substantial prejudice to those rights or interests. NY R UNIF TRIAL CTS § 202.5-b(k)(2).

ix. *Refusal to accept paper filings.* In accordance with NY CPLR Rule 2102(c), a County Clerk and a chief clerk of the Supreme Court or County Court, as appropriate, shall refuse to accept for filing papers filed in actions and proceedings when the paper sought to be filed:

- Is in an action subject to electronic filing pursuant to Rules of the Chief Administrator,
- Is not being filed electronically, and
- Does not include the notice required by NY R UNIF TRIAL CTS § 202.5-b(d)(1). NY R UNIF TRIAL CTS § 202.5(d)(1)(v); NY R UNIF TRIAL CTS § 202.5-bb(d).

x. *Emergency filings; Hard copies.* For information on when an emergency filing may be filed and served in hard copy, refer to NY R UNIF TRIAL CTS § 202.5-b(d)(1)(ii), NY R UNIF TRIAL CTS § 202.5-b(d)(1)(iii) and NY R UNIF TRIAL CTS § 202.5-bb(c)(3).

- *KINGS COUNTY.* Under the rules, a participating emergency e-filer must electronically file the documents initially filed in hard copy form within three (3) business days of the emergency filing; the originals will be discarded after the documents have been processed and the failure to e-file as required will therefore lead to an incomplete record. NY R L KINGS E FIL Doc. 1(B)(3).
- *NEW YORK COUNTY.* Occasionally an emergency will arise requiring expedited entry of a document with the County Clerk (e.g., an order issued in the courtroom after a conference or argument of a critical matter), such as for purposes of an immediate appeal. Expedition can be achieved by the Part as follows: the document should be carried by a Court Officer or staff member to the General Clerk's Office to assure immediate and proper recordation in the computer and, as appropriate, the posting of the document to NYSCEF or the Supreme Court Records On-Line Library ("Scroll"). The court will accommodate counsel in emergencies. NY R NY CTY Procedure XI(A).
- *NEW YORK COUNTY.* For more information on how to bring emergency matters before the court, refer to NY R NY CTY Procedure IV.

xi. *Technical failures.* The NYSCEF site shall be considered to be subject to a technical failure on a given day if the site is unable to accept filings or provide access to filed documents continuously or intermittently over the course of any period of time greater than one (1) hour after 12:00 noon of that day. Notice of all such technical failures shall be provided on the site. NY R UNIF TRIAL CTS § 202.5-b(i).

- When e-filing is hindered by a technical failure, a party may file with the appropriate clerk and serve in hard copy. NY R UNIF TRIAL CTS § 202.5-b(i). In the event an attorney or party shall file and serve documents in hard copy pursuant to NY R UNIF TRIAL CTS § 202.5-b(i), each such document shall include the notice required by NY R UNIF TRIAL CTS § 202.5-b(d)(1), and the filer shall file those documents with the NYSCEF site within three (3) business days after restoration of normal operations at that site. NY R UNIF TRIAL CTS § 202.5-b(i).
- With the exception of deadlines that by law cannot be extended, the time for filing of any document that is delayed due to technical failure of the site shall be extended for one (1) day for each day on which such failure occurs, unless otherwise ordered by the court. NY R UNIF TRIAL CTS § 202.5-b(i).
- *ERIE COUNTY.* When filing by electronic means is hindered by a technical failure, please refer to the NY R UNIF TRIAL CTS § 202.5-b(i). NY R ERIE E FIL Doc. 3(III)(K).

- *KINGS COUNTY.* When filing by electronic means is hindered by a NYSCEF technical failure (as set forth in NY R UNIF TRIAL CTS § 202.5-b(i)), a party may file with the appropriate Clerk in hard copy. Except for deadlines that by law cannot be extended (e.g. Statute of limitations, Notice of Appeal), the time for filing of any document that is delayed due to technical failure of the NYSCEF system shall be extended for one day for each day on which such failure occurs, unless otherwise ordered by the court. NY R L KINGS E FIL Doc. 1(B)(13).
- *ONONDAGA COUNTY.* When filing by electronic means is hindered by a technical failure (as set forth in NY R UNIF TRIAL CTS § 202.5-b(h)(3)(i)), a party may file a hard copy with the County Clerk. With the exception of deadlines that by law cannot be extended (e.g., a statute of limitations or the deadline for filing a Notice of Appeal), the time for filing of any document that is delayed due to technical failure of the NYSCEF system will be extended for one day for each day on which such failure occurs, unless otherwise ordered by the court. A "Notice of Hard Copy Filing Submission—E-Filed Case' must accompany any documents not filed via NYSCEF. NY R ONDGA E FIL Protocol(B)(8).

xii. *Filing fees.* For information on what information must be provided to pay filing fees, refer to NY R UNIF TRIAL CTS § 202.5-b(d)(2).

xiii. *Exemption from e-filing.* For information on exemptions from e-filing, refer to NY R UNIF TRIAL CTS § 202.5-bb(e).

xiv. *Filing exhibits*

- *ERIE COUNTY.* In the NYSCEF system, each exhibit must be uploaded as a separate .pdf file. After uploading a primary document, please choose the document type "Exhibit" and enter the appropriate number or letter and a brief description of the exhibit; each exhibit should bear a separate cover sheet clearly marked as "Exhibit A," "Exhibit B," etc. "Exhibit A" or "Exhibit B" is unacceptable as a brief description of the exhibit. Exhibits, where referenced in a signed Order as attached or affixed shall be uploaded with the signed Order as one .pdf document. NY R ERIE E FIL Doc. 3(III)(H); NY R ERIE E FIL Doc. 3(V)(D).
- *KINGS COUNTY.* In the NYSCEF system, each exhibit should be uploaded as a separate PDF file. After uploading a primary document, please choose the document type "Exhibit", enter the appropriate number or letter, and be sure to place a check mark to the right of "Attach to main document". Each exhibit shall bear a separate cover sheet clearly marked as Exhibit A, Exhibit B, etc. NY R L KINGS E FIL Doc. 1(B)(12). Whenever possible, attorneys submitting exhibits in NYSCEF cases should make each exhibit a separate attachment to an affidavit/affirmation in the system (i.e., multiple exhibits should not be filed as a single PDF). NY R L KINGS E FIL Doc. 1(D)(1).
- *NEW YORK COUNTY.* Attorneys submitting exhibits in NYSCEF cases should make each exhibit a separate attachment to an affidavit/affirmation in the system; i.e., exhibits should not be filed as a single PDF-A together with the affidavit/affirmation or grouped together as a single PDF-A attachment because either of these two formats makes it difficult for the Justice to locate particular exhibits as needed. Counsel must also include appropriate descriptive language in the "Additional Document Information" field in NYSCEF. NY R NY CTY E FIL Doc. 2(D)(6).
- *ONONDAGA COUNTY.* All exhibits in e-filed cases must be e-filed individually as separate attachments. NY R ONDGA E FIL Protocol(B)(9)(b).

xv. *Correcting documents*

- *ERIE COUNTY.* Submission of documents which, upon examination, require correction or addition will result in notification to the filer advising that the document has been returned for correction. The filer shall make the required corrections and/or additions as indicated in the e-mail transmission sent by the County Clerk or Part Clerk through the NYSCEF site. The corrected documents may be resubmitted using the "Re-file this document" link highlighted in the filer's document list for the respective case. Please note that in the case of multiple submissions, all related documents filed at the same time may be removed from the case record and returned until all documents are properly submitted. NY R ERIE E FIL Doc. 3(III)(J).
- *KINGS COUNTY.* Submission of documents which, upon examination, require correction or addition will result in notification to the filer advising that there is a problem with a document. The filer shall make the required corrections and/or additions and resubmit the corrected document using the "Refile this document" link. In the event a document is returned for correction, the original file date will be preserved. For corrections of documents filed with the Kings County Clerk which require a court order, refer to the

procedure in NY R UNIF TRIAL CTS § 202.5-b(d)(3)(iii) and NY R L KINGS E FIL Doc. 1(B)(11). NY R L KINGS E FIL Doc. 1(B)(3).

- *ONONDAGA COUNTY.* If there is an error or an additional document is required, the system will notify the filing party, who will make the corrections/additions and resubmit them online. NY R ONDGA E FIL Protocol(B)(6).
- *QUEENS COUNTY.* Generally speaking, documents that have been E-filed will not thereafter be deleted by the County Clerk from NYCEF because the filer asserts that the filing contains an error or a significant omission. When the filer wishes to correct a perceived error or omission in a filed document, he or she should file an amended version of the document, with the original remaining on file, or else obtain a court order providing for deletion of the original. The County Clerk will only delete a document upon request of the filer or on the County Clerk's own initiative when it is obvious from the face of the document alone that the filer made a fundamental error and never intended to file the document that was filed (e.g., a completely unrelated non-litigation document, a different case, or a wrong county). The County Clerk will advise the filer when any such fundamental errors are detected. NY R L QUEENS E-FILE Doc. 1(E)(6).

c. *Facsimile filing.* In the Supreme Court, facsimile filing shall be limited to commercial claims and tax certiorari, conservatorship, and mental hygiene proceedings in Monroe, Westchester, New York and Suffolk Counties. NY R UNIF TRIAL CTS § 202.5-a(a)(1). Refer to NY R UNIF TRIAL CTS § 202.5-a for information on the procedures for facsimile filing.

   i. *NEW YORK COUNTY.* Unless indicated otherwise by the court in a particular case or in NY R NY CTY J RUL Doc. 1, Justices do not accept papers by fax. NY R NY CTY J RUL Rule 4.

d. *ERIE COUNTY: Filing request for judicial intervention.* An RJI in a NYSCEF case shall be filed via the NYSCEF system and will be filed after all other documents have been uploaded. The filer may choose between filing a .pdf image of the prepared RJI and any Addendum or having the system prepare the RJI which shall conform to Uniform Rules. Addenda, such as the Commercial Division Addendum, if prepared by the filer must be filed simultaneously with and attached to an RJI and uploaded as one .pdf document with the RJI. If the RJI is prepared by the e-filing system, no separate Addendum is required. Whether or not the filer elects to allow NYSCEF to create the RJI or chooses to upload a prepared RJI, data in addition to the nature of the judicial intervention, including information that appears on any Addenda will be collected through completion of the fields presented. If the filing of the RJI is accomplished through a filing agent, a prepared RJI and Addendum must be filed in lieu of the creation of the RJI by the NYSCEF system, as the RJI must be signed by the attorney. NY R ERIE E FIL Doc. 3(IV). For information on RJIs in specific types of action, refer to NY R ERIE E FIL Doc. 3(IV).

2. *Service requirements*

a. *Who may serve.* Except where otherwise prescribed by law or order of court, papers may be served by any person not a party of the age of eighteen years or over. NY CPLR Rule 2103(a).

b. *Service upon attorney.* Except where otherwise prescribed by law or order of court, papers to be served upon a party in a pending action shall be served upon the party's attorney. Where the same attorney appears for two or more parties, only one (1) copy need be served upon the attorney. Such service upon an attorney shall be made:

   i. By delivering the paper to the attorney personally. NY CPLR Rule 2103(b)(1).

   ii. By mailing the paper to the attorney at the address designated by that attorney for that purpose or, if none is designated, at the attorney's last known address; service by mail shall be complete upon mailing. NY CPLR Rule 2103(b)(2).

   - *BRONX COUNTY.* Service by mail must be within the state. NY R BRONX FIL R Doc. 3.

   iii. If the attorney's office is open, by leaving the paper with a person in charge, or if no person is in charge, by leaving it in a conspicuous place; or if the attorney's office is not open, by depositing the paper, enclosed in a sealed wrapper directed to the attorney, in the attorney's office letter drop or box. NY CPLR Rule 2103(b)(3).

   iv. By leaving it at the attorney's residence within the state with a person of suitable age and discretion. Service upon an attorney shall not be made at the attorney's residence unless service at the attorney's office cannot be made. NY CPLR Rule 2103(b)(4).

   v. By transmitting the paper to the attorney by facsimile transmission, provided that a facsimile telephone number is designated by the attorney for that purpose. Service by facsimile transmission shall be complete upon the receipt by the sender of a signal from the equipment of the attorney served indicating that the transmission was received, and the mailing of a copy of the paper to that attorney. The designation of a facsimile telephone number

in the address block subscribed on a paper served or filed in the course of an action or proceeding shall constitute consent to service by facsimile transmission in accordance with NY CPLR Rule 2103(b)(5). An attorney may change or rescind a facsimile telephone number by serving a notice on the other parties. NY CPLR Rule 2103(b)(5).

vi. By dispatching the paper to the attorney by overnight delivery service at the address designated by the attorney for that purpose or, if none is designated, at the attorney's last known address. Service by overnight delivery service shall be complete upon deposit of the paper enclosed in a properly addressed wrapper into the custody of the overnight delivery service for overnight delivery, prior to the latest time designated by the overnight delivery service for overnight delivery. "Overnight delivery service" means any delivery service which regularly accepts items for overnight delivery to any address in the state. NY CPLR Rule 2103(b)(6).

vii. By transmitting the paper to the attorney by electronic means where and in the manner authorized by the chief administrator of the courts by rule and, unless such rule shall otherwise provide, such transmission shall be upon the party's written consent. The subject matter heading for each paper sent by electronic means must indicate that the matter being transmitted electronically is related to a court proceeding. NY CPLR Rule 2103(b)(7).

- *KINGS COUNTY.* Pursuant to the E-Filing Rules, service of interlocutory documents is made by posting a document to the NYSCEF site, which automatically and immediately transmits an email notice of the filing, including a link to the document, to all participating counsel and unrepresented litigants on the case. The Rules also authorize service by other methods permitted by the CPLR. If service by such other method is made, proof of service must be filed with NYSCEF. NY R L KINGS E FIL Doc. 1(I).
- *NEW YORK COUNTY.* Service. . .will be made automatically through NYSCEF upon all participating counsel and unrepresented parties in the case. There are limited exceptions to the requirement for e-filing in the covered kinds of cases. NY R NY CTY Procedure XI(A). Pursuant to the E-Filing Rules, service of interlocutory documents is made by posting a document to the NYSCEF site, which automatically and immediately transmits an e-mail notice of the filing, including a link to the document, to all participating counsel and unrepresented litigants on the case. The Rules also authorize service by other methods permitted by the CPLR. If service by such a method is made, proof of service must be filed with NYSCEF. NY R NY CTY E FIL Doc. 2(I).
- *QUEENS COUNTY.* Filing with the system permits counsel to serve the papers electronically pursuant to NY R UNIF TRIAL CTS § 202.5-b(f) once consent to E-Filing has been filed on-line. Consult NY R UNIF TRIAL CTS § 202.5-bb(c) for service in mandatory e-filing. Any required proof of service should be E-filed as a separate document. NY R L QUEENS E-FILE Doc. 1(E)(4).

c. *Electronic service mandatory; Consenting to electronic service; How electronic service may be made.* Except as otherwise provided in NY R UNIF TRIAL CTS § 202.5-bb, filing and service of all documents in an action that has been commenced electronically in accordance with NY R UNIF TRIAL CTS § 202.5-bb shall be by electronic means. NY R UNIF TRIAL CTS § 202.5-bb(c)(1).

i. *Party's consent required for certain e-filing.* After commencement of an action wherein e-filing is authorized, documents may be electronically filed and served, but only by, and electronic service shall be made only upon, a party or parties who have consented thereto. NY R UNIF TRIAL CTS § 202.5-b(b)(2)(i).

- A consent to e-filing in an action shall state that the party providing it agrees to the use of e-filing in the action and to be bound by the filing and service provisions in NY R UNIF TRIAL CTS § 202.5-b. NY R UNIF TRIAL CTS § 202.5-b(b)(2)(ii).

ii. *Address for service; Duty to notify as to changes.* The e-mail service address recorded at the time of registration is the e-mail address at which service of interlocutory documents on that party may be made through notification transmitted by the NYSCEF site. It is the responsibility of each filing user to monitor that address and promptly notify the Resource Center in the event of a change in his or her e-mail service address. NY R UNIF TRIAL CTS § 202.5-b(f)(2)(i).

iii. *How service made.* An e-filing party causes service of an interlocutory document to be made upon another party participating in e-filing by filing the document electronically. Upon receipt of an interlocutory document, the NYSCEF site shall automatically transmit electronic notification to all e-mail service addresses in such action. NY R UNIF TRIAL CTS § 202.5-b(f)(2)(ii).

- Except as provided otherwise in NY R UNIF TRIAL CTS § 202.5-b(h)(3), the electronic transmission of the notification shall constitute service of the document on the e-mail service addresses identified therein; however, such service will not be effective if the filing party learns that the notification did not reach the

address of the person to be served. Proof of such service will be recorded on the NYSCEF site. A party may, however, utilize other service methods permitted by the CPLR provided that, if one of such other methods is used, proof of that service shall be filed electronically. NY R UNIF TRIAL CTS § 202.5-b(f)(2)(ii).

iv. *Signatures on hard copies; Proof of service filed electronically.* When an e-filing party serves a document in hard copy on a non-participating party, the document served shall bear full signatures of all signatories and proof of such service shall be filed electronically. NY R UNIF TRIAL CTS § 202.5-b(b)(2)(i).

- *ERIE COUNTY.* In the NYSCEF system, each Affidavit of Service must be uploaded as a separate .pdf file. After uploading the Affidavit, please choose the document type: "Affirmation/Affidavit of Service" and enter the name of the party served as Additional Document Information. NY R ERIE E FIL Doc. 3(III)(I); NY R ERIE E FIL Doc. 3(V)(F).

v. *Effect of failure to consent.* A party's failure to consent to participation in electronic filing and service shall not bar any other party to the action from filing documents electronically with the County Clerk and the court or serving documents upon any other party who has consented to participation. A party who has not consented to participation shall file documents with the court and the County Clerk, and serve and be served with documents, in hard copy. NY R UNIF TRIAL CTS § 202.5-b(b)(2)(i).

d. *Service upon party.* If a party has not appeared by an attorney or the party's attorney cannot be served, service shall be upon the party by a method specified in NY CPLR Rule 2103(b)(1), NY CPLR Rule 2103(b)(2), NY CPLR Rule 2103(b)(4), NY CPLR Rule 2103(b)(5) or NY CPLR Rule 2103(b)(6). NY CPLR Rule 2103(c).

e. *Service on all parties.* Each paper served on any party shall be served on every other party who has appeared, except as otherwise may be provided by court order or as provided in NY CPLR § 3012 or in NY CPLR § 3215(f). Upon demand by a party, the plaintiff shall supply that party with a list of those who have appeared and the names and addresses of their attorneys. NY CPLR Rule 2103(e).

f. *Service by filing.* If a paper cannot be served by any of the methods specified in NY CPLR Rule 2103(b) and NY CPLR Rule 2103(c), service may be made by filing the paper as if it were a paper required to be filed. NY CPLR Rule 2103(d).

g. *Definitions.* For the purposes of NY CPLR Rule 2103:

i. "Mailing" means the deposit of a paper enclosed in a first class postpaid wrapper, addressed to the address designated by a person for that purpose or, if none is designated, at that person's last known address, in a post office or official depository under the exclusive care and custody of the United States Postal Service within the state;

ii. "Electronic means" means any method of transmission of information between computers or other machines designed for the purpose of sending and receiving such transmissions, and which allows the recipient to reproduce the information transmitted in a tangible medium of expression;

iii. "Facsimile transmission" means any method of transmission of documents to a facsimile machine at a remote location which can automatically produce a tangible copy of such documents. NY CPLR Rule 2103(f).

G. Hearings

1. *Oral argument.* Motion papers received by the clerk of the court on or before the return date shall be deemed submitted as of the return date. The assigned judge, in his or her discretion or at the request of a party, thereafter may determine that any motion be orally argued and may fix a time for oral argument. NY R UNIF TRIAL CTS § 202.8(d).

a. A party requesting oral argument shall set forth such request in its notice of motion or in its order to show cause or on the first page of the answering papers, as the case may be. Where all parties to a motion request oral argument, oral argument shall be granted unless the court shall determine it to be unnecessary. NY R UNIF TRIAL CTS § 202.8(d).

b. Where a motion is brought on by order to show cause, the court may set forth in the order that oral argument is required on the return date of the motion. NY R UNIF TRIAL CTS § 202.8(d).

i. *BRONX COUNTY.* All orders to show cause, with the exception of orders to show cause that are returnable in the City Part, the STP Part, the Matrimonial Part and the Preliminary/Compliance Conference Part (IA-11), submitted on or after August 25, 2003, will be returnable on a Monday in the assigned Justice's part and appear on his or her motion calendar. Appearances will be required on orders to show cause. NY R BRONX FIL R Doc. 8. A motion on notice or a notice of petition in a New York Supreme Court E-File (hereafter known as NYSCEF) case, as in others, shall be made returnable in the Motion Support Office (Room 217). NY R BRONX E FIL R Doc. 1(1).

- After a motion/petition and notice are filed with the NYSCEF system, the Motion Support Office will automatically place the motion/proceeding on the submit calendar in the Motion Support Office (Room 217) for the return date. No appearance or other action by the filing attorney is required in order for the motion to be calendared if the motion fee is paid for via NYSCEF. Motions in e-filed cases (other than tax certiorari cases) appear on the submit calendar in Room 217 on the return date. NY R BRONX E FIL R Doc. 1(2).

c. *KINGS COUNTY.* All motions require appearances and oral argument. NY R L KINGS Pt. C, Rule 3.

2. *Return date; Time for hearing.* A notice of motion shall specify the time and place of the hearing on the motion. NY CPLR Rule 2214(a). The moving party determines when a motion on notice shall be heard, but she has to consult the court's or judge's calendar practice first. The movant picks out a "return day" sufficiently far off to assure that the notice requirements of NY CPLR Rule 2214(b) can be met, and to assure as well that the day picked is a day on which the assigned judge hears motions. SIEGEL-NYPRAC § 247.

a. *Judge assigned to hear motion*

i. *Referral to judge supervising disclosure.* Unless the chief administrator of the courts has, by rule, provided otherwise, if a case has been assigned to a judge to supervise disclosure pursuant to NY CPLR § 3104, all motions preliminary to trial shall be referred to such judge whenever practicable. NY CPLR Rule 3214(a).

ii. *Referral to judge who decided prior motion.* Any motion may be referred to a judge who decided a prior motion in the action. NY CPLR Rule 2217(a).

iii. *Transfer when judge unable to hear motion.* If a motion is made to a judge who is or will be for any reason unable to hear it, it may be transferred by order of such judge or by written stipulation of the parties to any other judge to whom it might originally have been made. NY CPLR Rule 2217(c).

iv. *Procedure for unassigned cases.* If a case has not been assigned to a judge, the motion shall be made returnable before the court, and a copy of the moving papers, together with a request for judicial intervention, shall be filed with the court, with proof of service upon all other parties, where required by NY R UNIF TRIAL CTS § 202.6, within five (5) days of service upon the other parties. The moving party shall give written notice of the index number to all other parties immediately after filing of the papers. NY R UNIF TRIAL CTS § 202.8(b).

- *Responding papers.* Copies of all responding papers shall be submitted to the court, with proof of service and with the index number set forth in the papers, on or before the return date. NY R UNIF TRIAL CTS § 202.8(b).
- *Assignment after request for judicial intervention.* The case shall be assigned to a judge as soon as practicable after the filing of the request for judicial intervention pursuant to NY R UNIF TRIAL CTS § 202.6, but in no event later than the return date. After assignment to the judge, the court shall provide for appropriate notice to the parties of the name of the assigned judge. NY R UNIF TRIAL CTS § 202.8(b).
- *Motions to be heard in another county.* Motion papers noticed to be heard in a county other than the county where the venue of the action has been placed by the plaintiff shall be assigned to a judge in accordance with procedures established by the Chief Administrator. NY R UNIF TRIAL CTS § 202.8(b).

v. *ALBANY COUNTY: Motions referred to IAS Justice.* All motions made after a case has been assigned a day certain shall be referred to the IAS Justice unless the motion is returnable during the term in which the matter has been assigned a day certain, in that event, the matter will be referred to the Part 1 Justice for that particular term who may entertain the motion or refer such motion to the IAS Justice. Under those circumstances, the Part I Justice shall decide whether or not to strike the note of issue or assign the matter a new day certain. NY R 3 JD SUP Doc. 1(H)(2). All motions shall be returnable before the assigned justice. NY R 3 JD SUP Doc. 1(B).

b. *Trial of issue raised by motion.* The court may order that an issue of fact raised on a motion shall be separately tried by the court or a referee. If the issue is triable of right by jury, the court shall give the parties an opportunity to demand a jury trial of such issue. Failure to make such demand within the time limited by the court, or, if no such time is limited, before trial begins, shall be deemed a waiver of the right to trial by jury. An order under NY CPLR § 2218 shall specify the issue to be tried. NY CPLR § 2218.

c. *Audio-visual coverage of trial court proceeding.* Audio-visual coverage of proceedings in the trial courts shall be permitted only in accordance with the provisions of Part 131 of the Rules of the Chief Administrator (NY R CHIEF ADMIN § 131.1, et seq.). NY R CHIEF J § 29.3.

d. *Adjournment of return date.* Stipulations of adjournment of the return date made by the parties shall be in writing and shall be submitted to the assigned judge. Such stipulation shall be effective unless the court otherwise directs. No more than three (3) stipulated adjournments for an aggregate period of sixty (60) days shall be submitted without prior permission of the court. NY R UNIF TRIAL CTS § 202.8(e)(1).

i. Absent agreement by the parties, a request by any party for an adjournment shall be submitted in writing, upon notice to the other party, to the assigned judge on or before the return date. The court will notify the requesting party whether the adjournment has been granted. NY R UNIF TRIAL CTS § 202.8(e)(2).

ii. *BRONX COUNTY.* Non-disclosure motions for IA5, IA7 and IA22 will be adjourned for oral argument to the Monday of the second week following the week of the return date of the motion. All other non-disclosure motions will be deemed submitted on the return date and forwarded to Chambers unless a stipulation of adjournment complying with the requirements of NY R UNIF TRIAL CTS § 202.8(e) is submitted, in which event, the motion will be adjourned for the requested date and kept in the Clerk's Office. If a non-stipulated request for adjournment or notice is submitted, the motion and request will be forwarded to Chambers for judicial approval or denial of the request. In either event, the attorney requesting the adjournment will be notified, via telephone, of the granting or denial of the request and instructed to notify his adversary. NY R BRONX FIL R Doc. 8.

iii. *BRONX COUNTY.* Motions that have been e-filed may be adjourned in Room 217 if an adjournment complies with the procedures of the Motion Support Office (explained in the "Filing Rules—Motion Procedure" section of the "Courthouse Procedures" link on the website of [the] court). An adjournment that so complies may be obtained by filing a stipulation of all parties with NYSCEF (designated in the filing menu as a "Stipulation to Adjourn Motion"). NY R BRONX E FIL R Doc. 1(3).

iv. *NEW YORK COUNTY.* The Courtroom also maintains a "APB (All Papers By)" Calendar, which is used when a party seeks an adjournment but fails to comply with the Courtroom's procedures or there is a failure to comply with procedures that requires the clerk to adjourn the motion/application (e.g., failure to submit a Confirmation Notice in an e-filed case). The case may be put over for three days to allow compliance with those procedures, as described further below. NY R NY CTY Procedure II(C); NY R NY CTY E FIL Doc. 2(D)(2). E-filed applications may be adjourned in the Part if an adjournment complies with the Part's procedures (see the Uniform Rules of the Justices (Local Rules) on the court's website). An adjournment that so complies may be obtained by filing with NYSCEF a stipulation of all parties (designated in the filing menu as a Stipulation—Adjournment of Motion—Before Judge); the motion number and the current return date of the motion being adjourned shall be set forth in the "Additional Document Information" field in NYSCEF. Absent any problems, the Part will effectuate the adjournment without need for an appearance or any other action by the parties. NY R NY CTY E FIL Doc. 2(D)(4).

v. *QUEENS COUNTY.* The Motion Support Office is NOT authorized to grant adjournments. NY R L QUEENS MOT SUP Doc. 1.

e. *ALBANY COUNTY: Motion terms.* There shall be a. . . Motion Term on each Friday in the Supreme Court, Albany County. The Friday Motion Term shall include all Article 78 Proceedings involving New York State and proceedings commenced pursuant to Article 14 of the Civil Service Law (including applications for injunctive relief made pursuant to section 209-a of the Civil Service Law). NY R 3 JD SUP Doc. 1(F). Generally, parties will be granted only one adjournment for the Friday Motion Term. NY R 3 JD SUP Doc. 1(F).

f. *ALBANY COUNTY: Motion determined without hearing.* All motions are deemed "submitted" on the return date and no appearances are required by the parties. NY R 3 JD SUP Doc. 1(B). In the event oral argument is requested, the parties should not appear on the return date. At the discretion of the assigned Judge and upon the granting of a request for oral argument, the parties will be notified by Chambers of the scheduled time and place at which argument will be heard. Where a motion is brought on by order to show cause, the court may set forth in the order that appearances and/or oral argument are required on the return date of the motion. NY R 3 JD SUP Doc. 1(B).

g. *BRONX COUNTY: Return date.* All assigned and unassigned motions will be returnable five (5) days a week in the Civil Branch Clerk's Office, Room 217, at 9:30 a.m. NY R BRONX FIL R Doc. 8.

i. If on any submitted non-disclosure motion oral argument is requested and granted, or directed by the Court, the motion shall be adjourned for oral argument before the I.A. Judge on the second Monday following the week of the return date of the motion. Attorneys will be notified via telephone of the adjourned date. NY R BRONX FIL R Doc. 8.

h. *BRONX COUNTY: Oral argument.* Calendars of disclosure motions and other motions adjourned for oral argument will be published for the four (4) business days preceding the rescheduled appearance date and on the rescheduled date of the motion. These repetitive publications will serve as the notification of procedure of adjournment of all motions. In addition, two (2) days before the return date of unassigned motions a list of such motions indicating the assigned Justice and the adjourned date of the motion will be published. NY R BRONX FIL R Doc. 8.

i. *BRONX COUNTY: Resolution before return date.* Counsel/parties must advise the Court in writing on or before the return date of all motions that have been resolved by Counsel/parties themselves and all motions the movant(s) wish to be withdrawn. NY R BRONX FIL R Doc. 8.

j. *ERIE COUNTY: Calendaring of motions.* Refer to individual Justice's Part Rules. NY R ERIE E FIL Doc. 3(V)(B).

k. *KINGS COUNTY: Return date set by court.* Irrespective of the return date indicated in the notice of motion, motions will be rescheduled by the E-file/Motion Support Office to a date designated by the assigned Judge. NY R L KINGS Pt. C, Rule 2.

l. *KINGS COUNTY: Calendar calls.* There shall be two (2) calendar calls on motion days. The first calendar call shall be at 9:30 AM and the second calendar call shall be at 10:45 AM, unless the Judge's Part Rules provide otherwise. Defaults shall only be taken on second call. Attorneys with appearances elsewhere in the courthouse may advise the clerk of their whereabouts to avoid a default. Failure to so advise the clerk or appear at the default calendar call will result in a default order being entered or the motion being marked off the calendar. NY R L KINGS Pt. C, Rule 7.

m. *NEW YORK COUNTY: Return date and assigned courtroom.* Motions made by notice of motion and petitions and notices of petition in special proceedings are processed by the General Clerk's Office (Room 119) and are to be made returnable in the Motion Submission Part Courtroom (Room 130) on any business day of the week at 9:30 AM. There are some differences in electronically-filed cases. NY R NY CTY Procedure II; NY R NY CTY Procedure II(C); NY R NY CTY J RUL Rule 13(a).

   i. For the convenience of counsel, between 9:00 A.M. and 9:30 A.M. each day, in advance of the "call," Room 130 accepts (1) written stipulations; (2) affidavits/affirmations reciting the required details as to an adjournment on consent; (3) stipulations, letters or other writings withdrawing motions; and (4) final papers or complete sets of papers on motions. For motions in which these items are handed in before the "call," no one need remain to answer the "call." Counsel/parties must advise the court, either between 9:00 A.M. and 9:30 A.M. or at the "call," of all motions or cases that have been resolved by counsel/parties themselves and all motions that the movant no longer wishes to pursue. If such resolution occurs subsequent to the "call", the assigned Justice must be advised as soon as possible, by written notice sent to the Part, so that the court does not do unnecessary work. NY R NY CTY Procedure II(C).

   ii. Depending upon the assigned Part, contested motions submitted in the Motion Submission Part Courtroom are submitted without argument, or rescheduled for oral argument if so directed by the assigned Justice. For Justices who schedule argument on a case-by-case basis, notice of the argument date will be transmitted by the court. Counsel may ascertain how a motion submitted in Courtroom 130 was marked by consulting Scroll on the court's website, the e-Track application, or, on the two (2) days immediately following the submission date, the New York Law Journal. NY R NY CTY J RUL Rule 13(a).

n. *NEW YORK COUNTY: Motion call.* Each day in the Motion Submission Part Courtroom, commencing at 9:30 A.M., all motions returnable that day will be "called" for the submission of these papers, which must be handed up at this "call" or, as described below, immediately before. Because hundreds of motions appear on the Room 130 calendars every day, motion papers (other than part of the moving papers as described above) cannot be accepted on any day prior to the return date. Courtesy copies are not required nor accepted, but working copies are required by certain Justices in e-filed cases. NY R NY CTY Procedure II(C). If argument is directed, it will take place on an announced date shortly after the day of submission. NY R NY CTY Procedure II(C).

o. *NEW YORK COUNTY: Oral arguments.* Pursuant to request of some Justices, motions submitted in Room 130 will automatically be scheduled for a set argument date in the Part. Other Justices determine on a case-by-case basis after submission in Room 130 whether to accept a particular substantive motion on submission, to require oral argument, or to hold a conference. NY R NY CTY Procedure II(D). If argument is directed by the Justice automatically, notice of argument and the argument date will be given in Room 130. Any appearing party is expected to give notice to all parties and an announcement to this effect is made in Room 130. If the motion is submitted in Room 130 and the Justice, after examining the file, determines that argument should be directed, notice of the argument and the argument date will not be sent by the court. To obtain notification of the argument date and other developments, counsel should use e-Track. If argument notification is not given or transmitted as just described, counsel should understand that the motion has been taken on submission for decision on the papers. NY R NY CTY Procedure II(D).

   i. Calendars of motions to be argued in the Parts are published on the morning of the argument date and on the day before in the New York Law Journal under each Part. Argument information is available on a case-by-case basis in Scroll, and e-mail notifications are sent by e-Track to participating attorneys whenever a motion is scheduled for argument in the court's computer system. NY R NY CTY J RUL Rule 15(a)

p. *NEW YORK COUNTY: Motion determined without hearing.* Given the purpose of the Room 130 procedure, the substance of motions will not be addressed at the submission "call." No Judge is present. To the extent possible, motions submitted in Room 130 will be decided "on the papers." Indeed, attorneys are encouraged to use service or clerks to deliver papers or working copies, or to agree among themselves to have one of them deliver papers for all parties by service or a clerk. Counsel for the movant need not appear to "take a default" on any motion or for any other reason. Motions will be submitted, not marked off, in the absence of the movant. Opposing counsel similarly need not appear in person in order to avoid suffering a default. Delivery of papers by service or a clerk will suffice. The court's goal is to be able to collect papers on motions in an orderly fashion but without any attorney having to make an appearance in Room 130 at any time. NY R NY CTY Procedure II(C).

q. *ONONDAGA COUNTY: Return date.* If the motion is the first filing in an action, the case will be assigned and counsel will be notified by the Supreme Court Clerk's Office via the NYSCEF system of the assigned justice and return date. NY R ONDGA E FIL Protocol(B)(7)(c). If the motion is on a previously assigned case, counsel may choose a return date from the assigned justice's motion term schedule. If the date in unavailable, the Supreme Court Clerk's Office will assign the motion to the next available motion term date and will notify counsel via e-mail. The change will also appear in the notification generated by the NYSCEF system. NY R ONDGA E FIL Protocol(B)(7)(d).

r. *QUEENS COUNTY: Return date.* Motions must be made returnable on the proper day/time based on the assigned judge. NY R L QUEENS MOT SUP Doc. 1. Failure to make a motion returnable on the proper day/time may result in the motion being administratively rescheduled or marked off. NY R L QUEENS MOT SUP Doc. 1.

s. *QUEENS COUNTY: Unassigned motions.* For RJI/Motions, due to the fact that the movant would not know who the assigned judge will be, the notice of motion may be returnable any day of the week. RJI/Motions shall be made returnable in "Queens Supreme Court" with no address designated. The motion will be administratively rescheduled to the proper day of the week based on the judge (once a judge has been assigned). Within one (1) week of filing, the movant must check online to see who the assigned judge is (and therefore the location/date/time) that their motion is now returnable. Movant must then notify their adversary of this information prior to the return date. NY R L QUEENS MOT SUP Doc. 1.

3. *Entry of order after hearing.* An order determining a motion shall be entered and filed in the office of the clerk of the court where the action is triable, and all papers used on the motion and any opinion or memorandum in writing shall be filed with that clerk unless the order dispenses with such filing. When a statute or civil practice rule requires such filing and entry in a county other than that in which the order was made, the party prevailing on the motion shall file the order and the papers used on the motion with the proper clerk after receiving them. If a party fails to file any papers required to be filed under NY CPLR Rule 2220(a), the order may be vacated as irregular, with costs. NY CPLR Rule 2220(a). For more information on the entry of an order after a motion, refer to NY CPLR Rule 2219.

a. *BRONX COUNTY: Settled orders.* A Judge's decision will often call for a Settled Order. The purpose of the settled order is to give effect to the decision by directing that some action be done and/or that a court official perform some task. NY R BRONX LEG SUP Doc. 2. A settled order consists of a notice of settlement informing all parties that the proposed order will be presented to the judge who made the decision on a date certain. Next comes the proposed order which will be presented to the judge. This order should conform to the judge's decision and should direct the relief granted in the decision. This should be followed by proof of service upon all parties who were noticed with the decision. It is also helpful if a copy of the judge's decision is included along with the other papers. A settled order should always be noticed before the judge who made the decision. NY R BRONX LEG SUP Doc. 2.

i. Although an order is usually settled by the party who prevailed on the motion, any party may settle the order. It should be presented to the court within sixty (60) days of the decision. The other parties are entitled to ten (10) days notice where service of the settled order is done by mail, five (5) days if the notice is personally delivered. An attorney who is served with a notice of settlement which he believes does not accurately reflect the decision may settle a counter order. The counter order must be noticed for the same day and must be served not less than seven (7) days if by mail and two (2) days if personally delivered. NY R BRONX LEG SUP Doc. 2.

ii. Settled orders are usually sent to the judge the day after they noticed for settlement. No appearance is necessary or even contemplated on a settled order. If the decision directs "submit order", then no notice is necessary, and the order will be sent to the judge as soon a practical after it is received. No fees are collected on settled orders. NY R BRONX LEG SUP Doc. 2.

b. *ERIE COUNTY: Proposed orders.* Proposed orders shall be submitted through the NYSCEF system and a working copy provided to the IAS Justice for signature, if Part Rules so require. NY R ERIE E FIL Doc. 3(V)(G).

c. *KINGS COUNTY: Long form orders.* If the Court directs that an order be settled or submitted on a motion in a NYSCEF case, the proposed order, with Notice of Settlement where required, and any proposed counter-order shall be filed with the Court via NYSCEF. The relevant clerk's office will process the documents in the customary manner. NY R L KINGS E FIL Doc. 1(E).

i. WORKING COPIES OF PROPOSED ORDERS WITH NOTICE OF SETTLEMENT MUST BE SUBMITTED IN THE MOTION SUPPORT OFFICE (ROOM 227) AS EXPLAINED HEREIN. THEY MUST NOT BE DELIVERED TO THE PART OR CHAMBERS, EXCEPT WHERE THE INDIVIDUAL JUSTICE'S PART RULES PROVIDE OTHERWISE; DOING SO WILL CAUSE ADMINISTRATIVE CONFUSION AND POSSIBLE MISPLACEMENT OF PAPERS. Any such submission shall be sent in a timely manner (kindly review individual Justice's rules) and be conspicuously marked on the outside "NYSCEF Matter;" lack of such marking may delay processing. After an order/counter-order has been signed, it will be scanned, and the County Clerk will affix the entry stamp into the NYSCEF system, which will immediately transmit notice of this event via e-mail, including a link to the entered document, to all participating attorneys and unrepresented litigants in the case. Such transmittal does not constitute Notice of Entry. NY R L KINGS E FIL Doc. 1(E).

d. *NEW YORK COUNTY: Long form orders.* Although the court strongly favors the use of short form orders and judgments, there are instances when settlement of an order or judgment is appropriate. When a Justice directs in a decision that a long form order or judgment be settled, that decision is recorded in the court's computer system by the General Clerk's Office and the motion file with decision is held in the Order Section of the Office in Room 119. The settlement process takes place there. NY R NY CTY Procedure II(D); NY R NY CTY E FIL Doc. 2(E).

i. A proposed long form order or judgment in compliance NY R UNIF TRIAL CTS § 202.48 must be presented to the relevant back office, together with a notice of settlement which bears a settlement date, the date on which the order is to be ready for formal presentation to the Justice. In an e-filed case the submission shall be made electronically. The proposed order or counter-order should be e-filed and it will be transmitted automatically by the NYSCEF system to the appropriate back office. The return date and time of the proposed order must be at 9:30 A.M. no sooner than either five (5) days from personal service of the proposed order or ten (10) days from service by mail. Proof of timely service on the other parties must accompany the proposed order in a hard copy case. If an order or judgment is submitted late (later than sixty (60) days from signing and filing of the decision) and the proponent can show good cause for this tardiness, an affidavit or affirmation justifying the delay should be annexed to the proposed order, together with proof of service thereof. If persuaded, the Justice will consider the proposed order despite its untimeliness. NY R NY CTY Procedure II(D); NY R NY CTY E FIL Doc. 2(E).

ii. Sometimes a decision will state "Submit Order." The submitting party should prepare a long form order and make it returnable without notice. Counsel should deliver the proposed order to the Order Section of the appropriate back office, except in an e-filed case, when it shall be submitted electronically. NY R NY CTY Procedure II(D). If the decision of the court directs that a proposed order be settled or submitted in the Part or in Chambers, that direction, should, of course, be followed without presentation of the proposal to the back office. NY R NY CTY Procedure II(D).

iii. For information on proposed counter-orders, refer to NY R NY CTY Procedure II(D) and NY R NY CTY J RUL Rule 16(b).

e. *QUEENS COUNTY: Proposed orders.* If the court directs that an order be settled or submitted on a motion in an E-file case, the proposed order and any proposed counter-order shall be filed with the court on-line with proof of service. (If a decision refers to a proceeding on the record, a copy of the transcript must be submitted.) Working copies of all proposed orders MUST be submitted to the Motion Support Office before an order can be reviewed. NY R L QUEENS E-FILE Doc. 1(I).

i. Counsel are advised to adhere to NY R UNIF TRIAL CTS § 202.48 regarding the submission or settlement of their proposed order or judgment. Persons who are submitting proposed orders/judgments pursuant to a previously issued memorandum decision must submit a copy of the memorandum decision with their proposed order/judgment. Upon E-Filing a proposed order/judgement, a working copy of the proposed order/judgement must be provided to the Motion Support Office. NY R L QUEENS MOT SUP Doc. 1.

H. Forms

1. Official Motion in Limine Forms for New York

a. Request for judicial intervention. NY R UNIF TRIAL CTS § 202.6.

b. Notice of motion. NY R UNIF TRIAL CTS § 202.7(b).

2. **New York Motion in Limine Forms**
    a. Forms. NYPRAC-COMM § 38:8.
    b. General form of affidavit of service of motion papers. MCF CPLR § 5:24.

I. Applicable Rules

1. *State rules*
    a. Short title; Application; Construction; Definitions. NY CPLR § 101; NY CPLR § 103; NY CPLR § 104; NY CPLR § 105.
    b. Appendix of official forms. NY CPLR § 107.
    c. Extensions of time generally. NY CPLR § 2004.
    d. Form of papers. NY CPLR Rule 2101; NY CPLR Rule 2102; NY CPLR § 2105; NY CPLR Rule 2106; NY GEN BUS § 399-ddd; NY R UNIF TRIAL CTS § 215.2; NY R UNIF TRIAL CTS § 215.3.
    e. Service of papers. NY CPLR Rule 2103.
    f. Where motion made; In supreme court action. NY CPLR § 2212.
    g. Motion papers; Service; Time. NY CPLR Rule 2214.
    h. Relief demanded by other than moving party. NY CPLR Rule 2215.
    i. Prior motion; Ex parte motion; Transfer of motion; Hearings; Orders. NY CPLR Rule 2217; NY CPLR § 2218; NY CPLR Rule 2220.
    j. Computation of time. NY CPLR § 2402; NY GEN CONSTR § 19; NY GEN CONSTR § 20; NY GEN CONSTR § 25-a; NY GEN CONSTR § 30; NY GEN CONSTR § 31; NY GEN CONSTR § 53.
    k. Motions heard by judge supervising disclosure; Stay of disclosure. NY CPLR Rule 3214.
    l. Fees; Index number fees of county clerks. NY CPLR § 8018.
    m. Hours of court; Proceedings in court. NY R CHIEF J § 3.1; NY R CHIEF J § 29.3.
    n. Application of part; Waiver; Additional rules; Application of CPLR; Definitions. NY R UNIF TRIAL CTS § 202.1.
    o. Papers filed in court; Electronic filing in supreme court. NY R UNIF TRIAL CTS § 202.5; NY R UNIF TRIAL CTS § 202.5-a; NY R UNIF TRIAL CTS § 202.5-b; NY R UNIF TRIAL CTS § 202.5-bb.
    p. Request for judicial intervention. NY R UNIF TRIAL CTS § 202.6.
    q. Calendaring of motions; Uniform notice of motion form; Affirmation of good faith. NY R UNIF TRIAL CTS § 202.7.
    r. Motion procedure; Preliminary conferences. NY R UNIF TRIAL CTS § 202.8; NY R UNIF TRIAL CTS § 202.12.
    s. Rules of the commercial division of the Supreme Court. NY R UNIF TRIAL CTS § 202.70.
    t. Signing of papers. NY R CHIEF ADMIN § 130-1.1-a.
2. *Local rules*
    a. *Albany County*
        i. Third judicial district rules. NY R 3 JD SUP Doc. 1.
    b. *Bronx County*
        i. Filing of papers in supreme court. NY R BRONX FIL R Doc. 1.
        ii. Request for judicial intervention. NY R BRONX FIL R Doc. 2.
        iii. Motion procedure. NY R BRONX FIL R Doc. 8.
        iv. Commercial division. NY R BRONX FIL R Doc. 12.
        v. Motions on notice. NY R BRONX E FIL R Doc. 1.
        vi. Settled orders. NY R BRONX LEG SUP Doc. 2.
    c. *Erie County*
        i. Joint protocols for New York State Courts E-Filing (NYSCEF) cases filed in Supreme Court, Erie County. NY R ERIE E FIL Doc. 3.

d. *Kings County*

i. Papers. NY R L KINGS Pt. A, Papers.

ii. Service of motion papers. NY R L KINGS Pt. C, Rule 1.

iii. Scheduling of motions. NY R L KINGS Pt. C, Rule 2.

iv. Appearance and argument. NY R L KINGS Pt. C, Rule 3.

v. Courtesy copies. NY R L KINGS Pt. C, Rule 5.

vi. Motion calendar calls. NY R L KINGS Pt. C, Rule 7.

vii. Protocol on courthouse and county clerk procedures for electronically filed cases. NY R L KINGS E FIL Doc. 1.

e. *New York County*

i. Commencement of cases. NY R NY CTY Procedure I.

ii. RJIs and assignments. NY R NY CTY Procedure IA.

iii. Motions and special proceedings by notice of motion/petition. NY R NY CTY Procedure II.

iv. County clerk litigation functions. NY R NY CTY Procedure XI.

v. Protocol on courthouse and county clerk procedures for electronically filed cases. NY R NY CTY E FIL Doc. 2.

vi. Redaction of information in documents filed with the county clerk and the court. NY R NY CTY J RUL Rule A-1.

vii. Papers by fax. NY R NY CTY J RUL Rule 4.

viii. Motions on notice; Orders to show cause. NY R NY CTY J RUL Rule 13.

ix. Motion papers. NY R NY CTY J RUL Rule 14.

x. Oral argument; Adjournments. NY R NY CTY J RUL Rule 15.

f. *Onondaga County*

i. Onondaga county protocol for case filings New York State Electronic Files (NYSCEF). NY R ONDGA E FIL Protocol.

ii. Motions in limine. NY R ONDGA JURY TRIAL Rule 3.

iii. Motions in limine. NY R ONDGA NON JURY TRIAL Rule 3.

g. *Queens County*

i. Motion support office. NY R L QUEENS MOT SUP Doc. 1.

ii. Queens county protocol on courthouse procedures for electronically filed cases. NY R L QUEENS E-FILE Doc. 1.

J. Miscellaneous

NOTE: Individual judges' rules may apply.

ALBANY COUNTY

JUSTICE LISA M. FISHER: NY R 3 JD FISHER Fisher; NY R 3 JD FISHER Fisher, PC Order.

JUSTICE RICHARD MOTT: NY R 3 JD MOTT Mott.

JUSTICE STEPHAN G. SCHICK: NY R 3 JD Schick.

FORECLOSURE SETTLEMENT PART: NY R 3 JD Foreclosure Settlement.

BRONX COUNTY

JUSTICE PAUL L. ALPERT: [NY R BRONX J Part IA-29, as amended by NY ORDER 20-0337].

JUSTICE BEN BARBATO: NY R BRONX J Part IA-21.

JUSTICE MARY ANNE BRIGANTTI: [NY R BRONX J Part IA-15, as amended by NY ORDER 20-0338].

JUSTICE JOSEPH E. CAPELLA: NY R BRONX J Part IA-23.

JUSTICE MITCHELL DANZIGER: NY R BRONX J Part IA-3/33 ; [NY R BRONX J Danziger, Part IA-3/33, as amended by NY ORDER 20-0339].

JUSTICE LAURA G. DOUGLAS: NY R BRONX J Part IA-11.

JUSTICE RUBEN FRANCO: NY R BRONX J Part IA-26.

JUSTICE DORIS M. GONZALEZ: NY R BRONX J Part IA-24.

JUSTICE WILMA GUZMAN: NY R BRONX J Part IA-7; [NY R BRONX J Guzman, Part IA-7 Virtual, as amended by NY ORDER 20-0340].

JUSTICE ROBERT T. JOHNSON: NY R BRONX J Part IA-12.

JUSTICE DONALD A. MILES: NY R BRONX J Part IA-8.

JUSTICE DONNA M. MILLS: NY R BRONX J Part IA-9.

JUSTICE JULIA I. RODRIGUEZ: NY R BRONX J Part IA-18; [NY R BRONX J Part IA-27, as amended by NY ORDER 20-0341].

JUSTICE LLINET M. ROSADO: [NY R BRONX J Part IA-25, as amended by NY ORDER 20-0342].

JUSTICE NORMA RUIZ: NY R BRONX J Part IA-22; [NY R BRONX J Ruiz, Part IA-22 Virtual, as amended by NY ORDER 20-0343].

JUSTICE HOWARD H. SHERMAN: NY R BRONX J Part IA-4.

JUSTICE FERNANDO TAPIA: NY R BRONX J Part IA-13.

JUSTICE ELIZABETH A. TAYLOR: NY R BRONX J Part IA-2.

JUSTICE ALISON Y. TRUITT: NY R BRONX J Part IA-5.

PART IDV: NY R BRONX J Doc. 1.

PRE-TRIAL PART RULES: NY R BRONX J Doc. 2.

PRE TRIAL WORKSHEET: NY R BRONX J Doc. 3.

FORECLOSURE SETTLEMENT PART RULES: NY R BRONX J Doc. 4.

GUARDIANSHIP PART RULES: NY R BRONX J Doc. 5.

LPM PART RULES: NY R BRONX J Doc. 6.

ERIE COUNTY

JUSTICE M. WILLIAM BOLLER: NY R 8 JD J Boller.

JUSTICE RALPH A. BONIELLO: NY R 8 JD J Boniello.

JUSTICE CHRISTOPHER J. BURN: NY R 8 JD J Burns.

JUSTICE RUSSELL P. BUSCAGLIA: NY R 8 JD J Buscaglia.

JUSTICE FRANK CARUSO: NY R 8 JD J Caruso.

JUSTICE STEPHEN W. CASS: NY R 8 JD J Cass.

JUSTICE DEBORAH A. CHIMES: NY R 8 JD J Chimes.

JUSTICE EMILIO COLAIACOVO: [NY R 8 JD J Colaiacovo, as amended by NY ORDER 20-0252].

JUSTICE DIANE Y. DEVLIN: NY R 8 JD J Devlin.

JUSTICE JAMES H. DILLON: NY R 8 JD J Dillon.

JUSTICE PAULA L. FEROLETO: NY R 8 JD J Feroleto.

JUSTICE DANIEL J. FURLONG: [NY R 8 JD J Furlong, as amended by NY ORDER 20-0253].

JUSTICE JOSEPH R. GLOWNIA: NY R 8 JD J Glownia.

JUSTICE MARK J. GRISANTI: NY R 8 JD J Grisanti.

JUSTICE DEBORAH A. HAENDIGES: NY R 8 JD J Haendiges.

JUSTICE LYNN W. KEANE: [NY R 8 JD J Keane, as amended by NY ORDER 20-0254].

JUSTICE RICHARD C. KLOCH, Sr.: NY R 8 JD J Kloch.

JUSTICE FREDERICK J. MARSHALL: [NY R 8 JD J Marshall, as amended by NY ORDER 20-0255.

JUSTICE JOHN L. MICHALSKI: NY R 8 JD J Michalski.

JUSTICE MARK A. MONTOUR: [NY R 8 JD J Montour, as amended by NY ORDER 20-0256].
JUSTICE HENRY NOWAK: NY R 8 JD J Nowak.
JUSTICE JOHN F. O'DONNELL: NY R 8 JD J O'Donnell.
JUSTICE JEANETTE OGDEN: NY R 8 JD J Ogden.
JUSTICE CATHERINE NUGENT-PANEPINTO: NY R 8 JD J Nugent-Panepinto.
JUSTICE FRANK A. SEDITA, III: [NY R 8 JD J Sedita, as amended by NY ORDER 20-0257].
JUSTICE SARA SHELDON: NY R 8 JD J Sheldon.
JUSTICE DONNA M. SIWEK: NY R 8 JD J Siwek.
JUSTICE MARY L. SLISZ: NY R 8 JD J Slisz.
JUSTICE TIMOTHY J. WALKER: [NY R 8 JD J Walker, as amended by NY ORDER 20-0258].
JUSTICE DENNIS E. WARD: NY R 8 JD J Ward.
JUSTICE PAUL B. WOJTASZEK: [NY R 8 JD J Wojtaszek, as amended by NY ORDER 20-0259].
JUSTICE CHARLES N. ZAMBITO: [NY R 8 JD J Zambito, as amended by NY ORDER 20-0260].
SUPREME COURT LEGAL STAFF: NY R 8 JD J Legal Staff.

KINGS COUNTY

JUSTICE RACHEL A. ADAMS: NY R KINGS J Part 5F.
JUSTICE LOREN BAILY-SCHIFFMAN: NY R KINGS J Part 65.
JUSTICE REGINALD A. BODDIE: NY R KINGS J Part 95.
JUSTICE THERESA M. CICCOTTO: NY R KINGS J Part 19; NY R KINGS J Part 5J.
JUSTICE LISSETTE COLON: NY R KINGS J Part Rules.
JUSTICE GENINE EDWARDS: NY R KINGS J Part 80.
JUSTICE PAMELA L. FISHER: [NY R KINGS J Part 94, as amended by NY ORDER 20-0208].
JUSTICE ROBIN GARSON: NY R KINGS J Part 75.
JUSTICE LARA J. GENOVISI: [NY R KINGS J Part 34, as amended by NY ORDER 20-0209].
JUSTICE BERNARD J. GRAHAM: NY R KINGS J Part 36.
JUSTICE DAWN JIMENEZ-SALTA: NY R KINGS J Part 88.
JUSTICE INGRID JOSEPH: [NY R KINGS J Part FRP3 and Part 83, as amended by NY ORDER 20-0210].
JUSTICE KATHY J. KING: NY R KINGS J Part 64, 76K.
JUSTICE LAWRENCE KNIPEL: NY R KINGS J Part 57.
JUSTICE DONALD KURTZ: NY R KINGS J Part 26.
JUSTICE CARL LANDICINO: [NY R KINGS J Part 81, as amended by NY ORDER 20-0211].
JUSTICE KATHERINE LEVINE: [NY R KINGS J Part 20, 25, 92, as amended by NY ORDER 20-0211].
JUSTICE LORNA MCALLISTER: [NY R KINGS J Part 10, as amended by NY ORDER 20-0211].
JUSTICE ROSEMARIE MONTALBANO: [NY R KINGS J Part 19, 71, and 22, as amended by NY ORDER 20-0211].
JUSTICE RICHARD J. MONTELIONE: [NY R KINGS J Part 99 and DJMP, as amended by NY ORDER 20-0215].
JUSTICE LISA S. OTTLEY: NY R KINGS J Part 24.
JUSTICE MARK I. PARTNOW: NY R KINGS J Part 43.
JUSTICE ERIC I. PRUS: NY R KINGS J Part 5A.
JUSTICE FRANCOIS RIVERA: NY R KINGS J Part 52.
JUSTICE KAREN B. ROTHENBERG: NY R KINGS J Part 35.
JUSTICE LEON RUCHELSMAN: NY R KINGS J Part 1.
JUSTICE WAYNE P. SAITTA: NY R KINGS J Part 29.

JUSTICE ROBIN K. SHEARES: NY R KINGS J Part 96.

JUSTICE KENNETH P. SHERMAN: NY R KINGS J Part 67 and 78.

JUSTICE DEBRA SILBER: NY R KINGS J Part 9 and 5K.

JUSTICE ELLEN M. SPODEK: NY R KINGS J Part 63.

JUSTICE MARSHA L. STEINHARDT: NY R KINGS J Part 15.

JUSTICE JEFFREY S. SUNSHINE: NY R KINGS J Part 5G.

JUSTICE PETER P. SWEENEY: [NY R KINGS J Part 35, as amended by NY ORDER 20-0218].

JUSTICE DELORES J. THOMAS: [NY R KINGS J Part 5T, as amended by NY ORDER 20-0221].

JUSTICE WAVNY TOUSSAINT: NY R KINGS J Part 70.

JUSTICE RICHARD VELASQUEZ: NY R KINGS J Part 66.

JUSTICE CAROLYN E. WADE: NY R KINGS J Part 84.

JUSTICE EDWARD G. WALKER: [NY R KINGS J Part 90, as amended by NY ORDER 20-0219].

JUSTICE LILLIAN WAN: [NY R KINGS J Part 17, as amended by NY ORDER 20-0220].

JUSTICE MICHELLE WESTON: NY R KINGS J Part 3.

MENTAL HYGIENE PART: NY R KINGS J Part 77.

MATRIMONIAL PARTS DURING COVID-19 EMERGENCY: JUSTICE KAREN B. ROTHENBERG: NY R KINGS J Doc. 1.

NASSAU COUNTY

JUSTICE ANNA R. ANZALONE: NY R NASSAU S J Anzalone, Part 26.

JUSTICE STACY D. BENNETT: NY R NASSAU S J Bennett; NY R NASSAU S J Bennett, Form 1.

JUSTICE ANTONIO BRANDVEEN: NY R NASSAU S J Brandveen, Part 31.

JUSTICE JEFFREY S. BROWN: [NY R NASSAU S J Brown, as amended by NY ORDER 20-0297].

JUSTICE STEPHEN A. BUCARIA: NY R NASSAU S J Bucaria.

JUSTICE JULIANNE T. CAPETOLA: NY R NASSAU S J Capetola, Part 28.

JUSTICE EDMUND M. DANE: NY R NASSAU S J Dane, Part 33.

JUSTICE VITO M. DESTEFANO: NY R NASSAU S J DeStefano, Part 13; NY R NASSAU S J DeStefano, Form 1.

JUSTICE ARTHUR M. DIAMOND: NY R NASSAU S J Diamond, Part 7.

JUSTICE THOMAS FEINMAN: NY R NASSAU S J Feinman, Part 5.

JUSTICE JOHN M. GALASSO: NY R NASSAU S J Galasso, Part 22.

JUSTICE SHARON M.J. GIANELLI: NY R NASSAU S J Gianelli, Part 22; NY R NASSAU S J Gianelli, Form 1.

JUSTICE JEFFREY A. GOODSTEIN: NY R NASSAU S J Goodstein, Part 33; NY R NASSAU S J Goodstein, Form 1.

JUSTICE DAVID J. GUGERTY: [NY R NASSAU S J Gugerty, Part 31, as amended by NY ORDER 20-0298].

JUSTICE HELENE F. GUGERTY: NY R NASSAU S J Gugerty, Part 47.

JUSTICE STEVEN M. JAEGER: NY R NASSAU S J Jaeger, Part 35; NY R NASSAU S J Jaeger, Form 1.

JUSTICE JACK L. LIBERT: NY R NASSAU S J Libert, Part 23.

JUSTICE JOSEPH H. LORINTZ: NY R NASSAU S J Lorintz, Part 26; NY R NASSAU S J Lorintz, Form 1.

JUSTICE ROY S. MAHON: NY R NASSAU S J Mahon, Part 3.

JUSTICE RANDY SUE MARBER: NY R NASSAU S J Marber, Part 8.

JUSTICE JAMES P. MCCORMACK: [NY R NASSAU S J McCormack, Part 18, as amended by NY ORDER, 20-0299].

JUSTICE DICCIA T. PINEDA-KIRWAN: [NY R NASSAU S J Pineda-Kirwan, as amended by NY ORDER 20-0300].

JUSTICE THOMAS RADEMAKER: [NY R NASSAU S J Rademaker, Part 28, as amended by NY ORDER 20-0301]; [NY R NASSAU S J Rademaker, Form 1, as amended by NY ORDER 20-0301].

JUSTICE DENISE L. SHER: NY R NASSAU S J Rademaker, Part 32.

JUSTICE LEONARD D. STEINMAN: [NY R NASSAU S J Steinman, Part 15, as amended by NY ORDER 20-0303]; NY R NASSAU S J Steinman, Form 1.

JUSTICE HOWARD E. STURIM: NY R NASSAU S J Sturim, Part 50; NY R NASSAU S J Sturim, Form 1.

JUSTICE HELEN VOUTSINAS: [NY R NASSAU S J Voutsinas, Part 25, as amended by NY ORDER 20-0304]; [NY R NASSAU S J Voutsinas, Form 1, as amended by NY ORDER 20-0305].

JUSTICE HOPE SCHWARTZ ZIMMERMAN: NY R NASSAU S J Zimmerman, Part 17.

NEW YORK COUNTY

JUDGE'S RULES; BASIC INFORMATION: [NY R NY CTY J RUL Doc. 1, as amended by NY ORDER 20-0202].

ONONDAGA COUNTY

JUSTICE ROBERT E. ANTONACCI II: [NY R ONDGA E FIL Doc. 1, as amended by 20-0239].

JUSTICE MICHAEL V. COCCOMI: NY R ONDGA E FIL Doc. 2.

JUSTICE GREGORY R. GILBERT: NY R 5 JD JUDGES Gilbert; NY R ONDGA E FIL Doc. 3.

JUSTICE DONALD A. GREENWOOD: NY R ONDGA E FIL Doc. 4.

JUSTICE DEBORAH H. KARALUNAS: NY R ONDGA E FIL Doc. 5.

JUSTICE JAMES MCCLUSKY: NY R 5 JD MCCLUSKY McClusky.

JUSTICE CHARLES C. MERRELL: NY R 5 JD MERRELL Merrell.

JUSTICE PATRICK F. MACRAE: NY R 5 JD MACRAE Doc. 1.

JUSTICE JAMES P. MURPHY: NY R ONDGA E FIL Doc. 7.

JUSTICE GERALD J. NERI: [NY R 5 JD JUDGES Neri, as amended by NY ORDER 20-0236]; [NY R ONDGA E FIL Doc. 8, as amended by NY ORDER 20-0241].

JUSTICE ANTHONY J. PARIS: NY R 5 JD JUDGES Paris; [NY R ONDGA E FIL Doc. 9, as amended by NY ORDER 20-0242].

JUSTICE NORMAN W. SEITER, JR.: NY R 5 JD JUDGES Seiter.

JUSTICE KEVIN G. YOUNG: [NY R ONDGA E FIL Doc. 10, as amended by NY ORDER 20-0243].

QUEENS COUNTY

JUSTICE PAM JACKMAN BROWN: [NY R L QUEENS Brown, Part 19, as amended by NY ORDER 20-0321].

JUSTICE CHEREE A. BUGGS: NY R L QUEENS Buggs, Part 30.

JUSTICE PAM JACKMAN BROWN: [NY R L QUEENS Brown, Part 19, as amended by NY ORDER 20-0321].

JUSTICE DENIS J. BUTLER: NY R L QUEENS Butler, Part 12.

JUSTICE ROBERT I. CALORAS: [NY R L QUEENS Caloras, Part 36, as amended by NY ORDER 20-0322].

JUSTICE ANNA CULLEY: NY R L QUEENS Culley, Part 53.

JUSTICE TIMOTHY DUFFICY: NY R L QUEENS Dufficy, Part 35.

JUSTICE DAVID ELLIOT: NY R L QUEENS Elliot, Part 14.

JUSTICE JOSEPH J. ESPOSITO: NY R L QUEENS Esposito, Part 6.

JUSTICE DARRELL L. GAVRIN: [NY R L QUEENS Gavrin, Part 27, as amended by NY ORDER 20-0323].

JUSTICE WYATT N. GIBBONS: [NY R L QUEENS Gibbons, Part 5, as amended by NY ORDER 20-0330.

JUSTICE DONNA-MARIE E. GOLIA: [NY R L QUEENS Golia, Part 21, as amended by NY ORDER 20-0331].

JUSTICE MARGUERITE A. GRAYS: [NY R L QUEENS Grays, Part 4, as amended by NY ORDER 20-0324].

JUSTICE RUDOLPH E. GRECO: [NY R L QUEENS Greco, Part 32, as amended by NY ORDER 20-0325].

JUSTICE MAUREEN HEALY: NY R L QUEENS Healy, Part 6.

JUSTICE PHILLIP HOM: [NY R L QUEENS Hom, Part 43, as amended by NY ORDER 20-0332].

JUSTICE KEVIN J. KERRIGAN: NY R L QUEENS Kerrigan, Part 10.

JUSTICE MOJGAN C. LANCMAN: NY R L QUEENS Lancman, Part 20.

JUSTICE RICHARD G. LATIN: NY R L QUEENS Latin, Part 40.

JUSTICE ULYSSES B. LEVERETT: [NY R L QUEENS Leverett, Part 6, as amended by NY ORDER 20-0326].

JUSTICE LEONARD LIVOTE: NY R L QUEENS Livote, Part 33.

JUSTICE LEE A. MAYERSOHN: NY R L QUEENS Mayersohn, Part 22; NY R L QUEENS Mayersohn, Part 22G; [NY R L QUEENS Mayersohn, Part 22G COVID, as amended by NY ORDER 20-0327].

JUSTICE ROBERT J. MCDONALD: NY R L QUEENS McDonald, Part 34.

JUSTICE MARGARET MCGOWAN: NY R L QUEENS McGowan, Part 52.

JUSTICE MAURICE E. MUIR: [NY R L QUEENS Muir, Part 42, as amended by NY ORDER 20-0333].

JUSTICE JODI ORLOW: NY R L QUEENS Orlow, Part 51.

JUSTICE LESLIE J. PURIFICCION: NY R L QUEENS Purificcion, Part 39.

JUSTICE JOSEPH RISI: [NY R L QUEENS Risi, Part 3, as amended by NY ORDER 20-0328].

JUSTICE FREDERICK D.R. SAMPSON: [NY R L QUEENS Sampson, Part 31, as amended by NY ORDER 20-0329].

JUSTICE MARTIN J. SCHULMAN: NY R L QUEENS Schulman, Part 29.

JUSTICE BERNICE D. SIEGAL: NY R L QUEENS Siegal, Part 25G.

JUSTICE JANICE A. TAYLOR: NY R L QUEENS Taylor, Part 15.

JUSTICE CARMEN R. VELASQUEZ: NY R L QUEENS Velasquez, Part 38.

JUSTICE LOURDES M VENTURA: [NY R L QUEENS Ventura, Part 37, as amended by NY ORDER 20-0334].

JUSTICE WILLIAM A. VISCOVICH: NY R L QUEENS Viscovich, Part 63.

JUSTICE ALLAN B. WEISS: NY R L QUEENS Weiss, Part 2.

COMPLIANCE, SETTLEMENT AND CONFERENCE PART: NY R L QUEENS Doc 1.

PRELIMINARY CONFERENCE PART: [NY R L QUEENS Doc. 2, as amended by NY ORDER 20-0335].

MEDICAL MALPRACTICE CONFERENCE PART: [NY R L QUEENS Doc. 3, as amended by NY ORDER 20-0336].

TRIAL SCHEDULING PART: NY R L QUEENS Doc. 4.

SUMMARY JURY TRIAL PROGRAM: NY R L QUEENS Doc. 7.

RESIDENTIAL FORECLOSURE PART: NY R L QUEENS Doc. 9.

FORECLOSURE AUCTION RULES: NY R L QUEENS Doc. 10.

MATRIMONIAL PRELIMINARY CONFERENCE PART: NY R L QUEENS Doc. 11.

NON-CUSTODIAL CONTESTED MATRIMONIAL PART: NY R L QUEENS Doc. 12.

Motions, Oppositions and Replies
Motion to Compel Disclosure

Document Last Updated August 2020

A. Checklist

(I) ❑ Matters to consider for moving party

(a) ❑ Required documents

(1) ❑ Notice of motion, order to show cause, or affidavit on ex parte motion

(2) ❑ Motion

(3) ❑ Affirmation of counsel

(4) ❑ Request for judicial intervention

(5) ❑ Proof of service

(6) ❑ ALBANY COUNTY: Additional required documents

(i) ❑ Affirmation of good faith effort

(b) ❑ Supplemental documents

(1) ❑ Supporting evidence; Exhibits

(2) ❑ Brief

(3) ❑ Notice to produce papers not in possession of the court

(4) ❑ Filing fees

(5) ❑ Working copies

(6) ❑ ERIE COUNTY: Additional supplemental documents

(i) ❑ Notice of hard copy submission in e-filed case

(7) ❑ KINGS COUNTY: Additional supplemental documents

(i) ❑ Forms when filing in hard copy

(8) ❑ NEW YORK COUNTY: Additional supplemental documents

(i) ❑ Notice of hard copy submission

(ii) ❑ Unpublished opinions

(9) ❑ ONONDAGA COUNTY: Additional supplemental documents

(i) ❑ Notice of hard copy submission

(10) ❑ QUEENS COUNTY: Additional supplemental documents

(i) ❑ Notice of hard copy submission

(c) ❑ Timing

(1) ❑ There are no specific timing requirements for the motion to compel disclosure

(2) ❑ The moving party shall serve copies of all affidavits and briefs upon all other parties at the time of service of the notice of motion

(3) ❑ A notice of motion and supporting affidavits shall be served at least eight (8) days before the time at which the motion is noticed to be heard

(4) ❑ It is also good practice to make motions returnable at least three (3) weeks away from the planned date of mailing and to always include a demand in the motion that the other side serve answering papers at least seven (7) days before the return day

(5) ❑ BRONX COUNTY: Additional timing

(i) ❑ A Notice of Motion must be served at least eight (8) days, by personal service, nine (9) days by overnight express and thirteen (13) days by mail before the return date

(6) ❑ NEW YORK COUNTY: Additional timing

(i) ❑ In an e-filed case, all of the moving papers shall be e-filed at least eight (8) business days prior to the return date

(7) ❑ ONONDAGA COUNTY: Additional timing

(i) ❑ Onondaga County local court rules require that any additional papers relating to motions must be e-filed at least two (2) business days prior to the return date, excluding the return date

(8) ❑ QUEENS COUNTY: Additional timing

(i) ❑ Motions must be in the possession of the Motion Support Office at least nine (9) days before the noticed return date of the motion

(II) ❑ Matters to consider for opposing party

(a) ❑ Required documents

(1) ❑ Opposition

(2) ❑ Proof of service

(b) ❑ Supplemental documents

(1) ❑ Supporting evidence; Exhibits

(2) ❑ Brief

(3) ❑ Filing fees

(4) ❑ Working copies

(5) ❑ ERIE COUNTY: Additional supplemental documents

(i) ❑ Notice of hard copy submission in e-filed case

(6) ❑ KINGS COUNTY: Additional supplemental documents

(i) ❑ Forms when filing in hard copy

(7) ❑ NEW YORK COUNTY: Additional supplemental documents

(i) ❑ Notice of hard copy submission

(ii) ❑ Unpublished opinions

(8) ❑ ONONDAGA COUNTY: Additional supplemental documents

(i) ❑ Notice of hard copy submission

(9) ❑ QUEENS COUNTY: Additional supplemental documents

(i) ❑ Notice of hard copy submission

(c) ❑ Timing

(1) ❑ Answering affidavits shall be served at least two (2) days before the time at which the motion is noticed to be heard

(2) ❑ Answering affidavits and any notice of cross-motion, with supporting papers, if any, shall be served at least seven (7) days before such time if a notice of motion served at least sixteen (16) days before such time so demands

B. Timing

1. *Motion to compel disclosure.* There are no specific timing requirements for the motion to compel disclosure.
2. *Time to serve.* The moving party shall serve copies of all affidavits and briefs upon all other parties at the time of service of the notice of motion. NY R UNIF TRIAL CTS § 202.8(c). A notice of motion and supporting affidavits shall be served at least eight (8) days before the time at which the motion is noticed to be heard. NY CPLR Rule 2214(b).

a. *Return dates; Best practice.* It is also good practice to make motions returnable at least three (3) weeks away from the planned date of mailing and to always include a demand in the motion that the other side serve answering papers at least seven (7) days before the return day. This enables the motion to be served by mail, gives sufficient notice to support the seven (7) day demand, and leaves a few days for a delayed mailing if some snag prevents posting on the day planned. If speed is needed, the shorter eight (8) day notice period can be used, forfeiting the right to seven (7) day answering papers and a reply. If even eight (8) days notice is too much under the circumstances, the order to show cause is the remedy. SIEGEL-NYPRAC § 247.

i. *ALBANY COUNTY.* All motions, except for certain matters in Albany County as specified in NY R 3 JD SUP Doc. 1(E) and NY R 3 JD SUP Doc. 1(F), brought on by notice of motion or by order to show cause will be made returnable on any day, Monday through Friday, as chosen by the movant in compliance with the CPLR. Parties shall submit all papers in a timely fashion as required by the CPLR by delivering them or mailing them directly to the Supreme Court Clerk's Office[. . .]except that motions and other applications subject to a filing fee shall first be presented to the County Clerk's Office for payment of the requisite fee and then subsequently filed with the Supreme Court Clerk's Office. NY R 3 JD SUP Doc. 1(B).

ii. *BRONX COUNTY.* A Notice of Motion must be served at least eight (8) days, by personal service, nine (9) days by overnight express and thirteen (13) days by mail before the return date. NY R BRONX FIL R Doc. 3. All unassigned motions must be accompanied with a properly filled out RJI and shall be filed in the Motion Support Office, room 217, within five (5) days of service. All motions on actions already assigned to a Justice must be filed at least five (5) business days before the return date. NY R BRONX FIL R Doc. 3. All papers served must strictly comply with the time requirements of NY CPLR Rule 2101, NY CPLR Rule 2103 and NY CPLR Rule 2214(b). NY R BRONX FIL R Doc. 8.

iii. *KINGS COUNTY.* Motion papers, answering affidavits and reply affidavits must be served on adversaries in accordance with NY CPLR Rule 2214. NY R L KINGS Pt. C, Rule 1.

iv. *NEW YORK COUNTY.* In an e-filed case, all of the moving papers shall be e-filed at least eight (8) business days prior to the return date. The clerk will calendar the motion for the Motion Submission Part Courtroom (Room 130) for the return date selected. NY R NY CTY Procedure II(A); NY R NY CTY E FIL Doc. 2(D)(1).

v. *ONONDAGA COUNTY.* Onondaga County local court rules require that any additional papers relating to motions must be e-filed at least two (2) business days prior to the return date, excluding the return date. NY R ONDGA E FIL Protocol(B)(9)(e).

vi. *QUEENS COUNTY.* Motions must be in the possession of the Motion Support Office at least nine (9) days before the noticed return date of the motion. NY R L QUEENS MOT SUP Doc. 1; NY R L QUEENS E-FILE Doc. 1(H)(1).

b. *Order to show cause; Shorter time.* The court in a proper case may grant an order to show cause, to be served in lieu of a notice of motion, at a time and in a manner specified therein. NY CPLR Rule 2214(d). An ordinary notice of motion can't be brought on for hearing earlier than the eighth (8th) day after the motion papers are served. With an order to show cause, the hearing can be brought on at any time the court directs, which can be fewer than eight (8) days or as close as the very day on which it is signed. If the court is convinced there is a real emergency, it can schedule the hearing for a few hours later or, in the direst case, "forthwith" the service of the order to show cause. SIEGEL-NYPRAC § 248.

c. *Time to serve answering affidavits; Other answering papers.* Answering affidavits shall be served at least two (2) days before the time at which the motion is noticed to be heard. Answering affidavits and any notice of cross-motion, with supporting papers, if any, shall be served at least seven (7) days before such time if a notice of motion served at least sixteen (16) days before such time so demands; whereupon any reply or responding affidavits shall be served at least one (1) day before such time. NY CPLR Rule 2214(b); NY R UNIF TRIAL CTS § 202.8(c).

i. *BRONX COUNTY.* All answering papers must be submitted to the Clerk 's Office on the return date of the motion. Answering papers will not be accepted prior to the return date. NY R BRONX FIL R Doc. 8.

ii. *NEW YORK COUNTY.* Cross-motions, papers in opposition, and reply papers on motions/petitions on notice returnable in Room 130 in a hard-copy case shall be submitted to the Motion Submission Part Courtroom (Room 130) on the final return date of the motion/petition and will not be accepted until that date. Subsequent documents on motions/petitions in e-filed cases shall be e-filed in a timely manner. Working copies when required shall be submitted to Room 130 on the final return date. NY R NY CTY Procedure II(A).

d. *Time to serve cross-motion.* At least three (3) days prior to the time at which the motion is noticed to be heard, or seven (7) days prior to such time if demand is properly made pursuant to NY CPLR Rule 2214(b), a party may serve upon the moving party a notice of cross-motion demanding relief, with or without supporting papers; provided, however, that:

i. If such notice and any supporting papers are served by mailing, as provided in NY CPLR Rule 2103(b)(2), they shall be served three (3) days earlier than as prescribed in NY CPLR Rule 2215; and

ii. If served by overnight delivery, as provided in NY CPLR Rule 2103(b)(6), they shall be served one (1) day earlier than as prescribed in NY CPLR Rule 2215. Relief in the alternative or of several different types may be demanded; relief need not be responsive to that demanded by the moving party. NY CPLR Rule 2215(a); NY CPLR Rule 2215(b).

iii. *BRONX COUNTY.* Cross motions may be presented for approval on or before the return date, provided that there is a motion already calendared. NY R BRONX FIL R Doc. 8.

iv. *ERIE COUNTY.* Cross-motions must be filed at least two (2) days before the return date of the motion. NY R L KINGS Pt. A, Papers.

v. *KINGS COUNTY.* Hard copies are required to be filed for any motions, answering papers, stipulations, etc. for E-Filed cases returnable in [the Central Compliance Part] at least [two (2)] days before return date. . .for cross motions. NY R L KINGS Pt. E, Rule 8.

vi. *QUEENS COUNTY.* Motion Support does not process or forward responsive papers, including cross-motions. They must be brought to the calendar call in the judge's part. NY R L QUEENS MOT SUP Doc. 1. E-filed cross motions: across motion must be noticed for the same return date as the main motion and have the confirmation of filing attached in the same manner as a motion. NY R L QUEENS E-FILE Doc. 1(H)(2)(e).

3. *Filing before return date.* All motions shall be returnable before the assigned judge, and all papers shall be filed with the court on or before the return date. NY R UNIF TRIAL CTS § 202.8(a).
   a. *BRONX COUNTY: Time for filing*
      i. *Unassigned motions.* Unassigned motions must be in the Clerk's Office within five (5) days of the date of service of the motion. NY R BRONX FIL R Doc. 8.
      ii. *Assigned motions.* Assigned motions must be filed in the Clerk's Office not less than five (5) business days prior to the return date of the motion. NY R BRONX FIL R Doc. 8.
      iii. *Motions returnable in room 217.* The moving documents must be e-filed no later than eight (8) days prior to the return date. NY R BRONX E FIL R Doc. 1(1).
   b. *KINGS COUNTY: Time and place of filing.* Motion papers must be filed with the E-file/Motion Support Office located in Room 227. . . at 360 Adams Street at least five (5) business days before the return date of the motion. NY R L KINGS Pt. A, Papers. Hard copies are required to be filed for any motions, answering papers, stipulations, etc. for E-Filed cases returnable in [the Central Compliance Part] at least five (5) days before return date for main motions. NY R L KINGS Pt. E, Rule 8. The moving documents must be e-filed no later than eight (8) days prior to the return date. NY R L KINGS E FIL Doc. 1(D).
4. *NEW YORK COUNTY: Briefing schedule.* Once a motion is made, counsel for all parties are strongly encouraged to agree upon a briefing schedule and submit a stipulation of adjournment reflecting that schedule using service or a clerk. Where a briefing schedule has not been agreed upon, the movant can avoid the need to attend simply to see if anyone will hand up opposing papers by demanding papers as provided by NY CPLR Rule 2214(b). To protect movants against the submission of late opposition papers or cross-motions, the General Clerk's Office will screen motions in which such papers are submitted without a response (reply or opposition respectively) to ensure that proper time to respond has been afforded and it will sua sponte adjourn for one (1) week cases in which such time has not been given. NY R NY CTY Procedure II(C).
5. *QUEENS COUNTY: Time to pay fees.* As motions and petitions are time sensitive, if opting to pay at the County Clerk's Office payment MUST be made, if filed with an RJI, a minimum of nine (9) business days prior to the application's return date and if filed post RJI, a minimum of nine (9) business days prior to the application's return date. NY R L QUEENS E-FILE Doc. 1(H)(1).
6. *Computation of time*
   a. *Units of time*
      i. *Day.* A calendar day includes the time from midnight to midnight. Sunday or any day of the week specifically mentioned means a calendar day. NY GEN CONSTR § 19.
      ii. *Month.* In a statute, contract or public or private instrument, unless otherwise provided in such contract or instrument or by law, the term month means a calendar month and not a lunar month. NY GEN CONSTR § 31.
      iii. *Year.* For information on the definition of a year, including the definitions of a half-year and quarter-year, refer to NY GEN CONSTR § 58 and NY GEN CONSTR § 50. For information on leap years, refer to NY GEN CONSTR § 57.
   b. *Periods of time*
      i. *Number of days.* A number of days specified as a period from a certain day within which or after or before which an act is authorized or required to be done means such number of calendar days exclusive of the calendar day from which the reckoning is made. NY GEN CONSTR § 20.
         - If such period is a period of two (2) days, Saturday, Sunday or a public holiday must be excluded from the reckoning if it is an intervening day between the day from which the reckoning is made and the last day of the period. NY GEN CONSTR § 20.
         - In computing any specified period of time from a specified event, the day upon which the event happens is deemed the day from which the reckoning is made. The day from which any specified period of time is reckoned shall be excluded in making the reckoning. NY GEN CONSTR § 20.
      ii. *Number of months.* A number of months after or before a certain day shall be computed by counting such number of calendar months from such day, exclusive of the calendar month in which such day occurs, and shall include the day of the month in the last month so counted having the same numerical order in days of the month as the day from which the computation is made, unless there be not so many days in the last month so counted, in which case the period computed shall expire with the last day of the month so counted. NY GEN CONSTR § 30.

iii. *Publication of notice; Number of days.* The period of publication of a legal notice shall be computed by excluding the first day of publication and including the day on which the act or event of which notice is given is to take place or which completes the full period of publication. NY CPLR § 2402.

iv. *Periods ending on Saturday, Sunday or public holiday.* When any period of time, computed from a certain day, within which or after which or before which an act is authorized or required to be done, ends on a Saturday, Sunday or a public holiday, such act may be done on the next succeeding business day and if the period ends at a specified hour, such act may be done at or before the same hour of such next succeeding business day, except that where a period of time specified by contract ends on a Saturday, Sunday or a public holiday, the extension of such period is governed by NY GEN CONSTR § 25. NY GEN CONSTR § 25-a(1).

- For a list of public holidays, refer to NY GEN CONSTR § 24.

v. *Additional time after certain kinds of service*

- *Service by mail.* Where a period of time prescribed by law is measured from the service of a paper and service is by mail, five (5) days shall be added to the prescribed period. NY CPLR Rule 2103(b)(2).
- *Service by overnight delivery service.* Where a period of time prescribed by law is measured from the service of a paper and service is by overnight delivery, one (1) business day shall be added to the prescribed period. NY CPLR Rule 2103(b)(6).

vi. *Daylight saving time.* For information on New York's time zone and the effect of daylight saving time, refer to NY GEN CONSTR § 52.

c. *Hours of court.* Notwithstanding any provision of law or rule of court to the contrary, throughout the State of New York the sessions of the Supreme Court for the disposition of business before the court shall commence not later than 9:30 a.m. and conclude not earlier than 5 p.m. Where warranted, the Chief Administrator of the Courts may authorize variances in the opening and closing hours of the courts, but, in such event, daily sessions shall total not less than six (6) hours. NY R CHIEF J § 3.1.

d. *Time limits; Extension of time.* Any act required by or in pursuance of law to be performed at or within a prescribed time, shall be performed according to the standard time. NY GEN CONSTR § 53.

i. Except where otherwise expressly prescribed by law, the court may extend the time fixed by any statute, rule or order for doing any act, upon such terms as may be just and upon good cause shown, whether the application for extension is made before or after the expiration of the time fixed. NY CPLR § 2004. Refer to the New York KeyRules Motion for Continuance/Extension of Time document for more information.

C. General Requirements

1. *Motions, generally.* There shall be compliance with the procedures prescribed in the CPLR for the bringing of motions. NY R UNIF TRIAL CTS § 202.7(a).

a. *Motions on notice.* A notice of motion shall specify the time and place of the hearing on the motion, the supporting papers upon which the motion is based, the relief demanded and the grounds therefor. NY CPLR Rule 2214(a). A motion on notice in an action in the supreme court shall be noticed to be heard in the judicial district where the action is triable or in a county adjoining the county where the action is triable. Unless statute, civil practice rule or local court rule provides otherwise, the motion shall be noticed to be heard before a motion term or, upon order to show cause granted by a justice, before that justice out of court. NY CPLR § 2212(a). Except as provided in NY R UNIF TRIAL CTS § 202.7(d), no motion shall be filed with the court unless there have been served and filed with the motion papers a notice of motion. NY R UNIF TRIAL CTS § 202.7(a)(1).

b. *Ex parte motions.* A motion in an action in the supreme court that may be made without notice may be made at a motion term or to a justice out of court in any county in the state. NY CPLR § 2212(b).

i. *KINGS COUNTY.* For more information on submitting a motion ex parte, refer to NY R L KINGS E FIL Doc. 1(G).

ii. *NEW YORK COUNTY.* For more information on submitting matters ex parte, refer to NY R NY CTY Procedure III and NY R NY CTY E FIL Doc. 2(G).

iii. *QUEENS COUNTY.* For more information on submitting matters ex parte, refer to NY R L QUEENS EX PARTE Doc. 1.

c. *Alternative relief.* Relief in the alternative or of several different types may be demanded. NY CPLR Rule 2214(a). The types of relief need not be related. In one motion, for example, the defendant can seek to dismiss the plaintiff's claim for lack of jurisdiction, to get an extension of time to answer, to require the plaintiff to join X as a party, and to quash a disclosure subpoena served in behalf of the plaintiff on a nonparty witness. So doing, the movant must of course specify all of these items of relief in the notice of motion, and the grounds for them, and the supporting papers must contain the entire proof requisite to the items of relief sought. NY CPLR Rule 2214(Practice Commentary, C2214:4).

d. *General relief.* It is common practice to include at the end of the relief request in the notice of motion a so-called "general relief" clause. This is merely a few words to cover the possibility that the relief appropriate to what the movant proves was not specifically asked for, but is close enough to enable the court to grant it. After stating the specific relief desired, the lawyer will often add something like: and for such other, further, or different relief as this court may deem just and proper. NY CPLR Rule 2214(Practice Commentary, C2214:5).

e. *Motion in improper form.* If the court finds it appropriate in the interests of justice, it may convert a motion into a special proceeding, or vice-versa, upon such terms as may be just, including the payment of fees and costs. NY CPLR § 103(c).

f. *Order to show cause.* An order to show cause is basically only a substitute for a notice of motion. An ordinary notice of motion merely notifies the recipient that a motion is being made for specified relief. The burden of proof is on the movant. Although in most cases it is just as innocent as an ordinary notice of motion, the order to show cause gets its name by directing the recipient to "show cause" why the particular relief being asked for should not be granted. It sounds as if the burden of proof is being shifted to the recipient. It isn't. It specifies the time and place of the hearing on the application but when the hearing comes on, the burden of proof is where it always is on a motion: on the movant. SIEGEL-NYPRAC § 248.

   i. The CPLR says nothing more about an order to show cause than that it may be used "in a proper case", which leaves it entirely to the judge's discretion to determine what a proper case is. Any fact suggesting a problem as to any of the items listed above would be sufficient to invoke judicial discretion and justify the show cause procedure, which is in fact liberally used. SIEGEL-NYPRAC § 248.

   ii. An order to show cause against a state body or officers must be served in addition to service upon the defendant or respondent state body or officers upon the attorney general by delivery to an assistant attorney general at an office of the attorney general in the county in which venue of the action is designated or if there is no office of the attorney general in such county, at the office of the attorney general nearest such county. NY CPLR Rule 2214(d).

   iii. *BRONX COUNTY.* For information on submitting an order to show cause, refer to NY R BRONX E FIL R Doc. 2 and NY R BRONX LEG SUP Doc. 1.

   iv. *ERIE COUNTY.* For information on submitting an order to show cause, refer to NY R ERIE E FIL Doc. 3(VI).

   v. *KINGS COUNTY.* For information on submitting an order to show cause, refer to NY R L KINGS E FIL Doc. 1(F).

   vi. *NEW YORK COUNTY.* For information on submitting an order to show cause, refer to NY R NY CTY E FIL Doc. 2(F).

   vii. *ONONDAGA COUNTY.* For information on submitting an order to show cause, refer to NY R ONDGA E FIL Protocol(B)(10) and NY R ONDGA E FIL Protocol(J).

g. *Motions before preliminary conference.* Motions in actions to which NY R UNIF TRIAL CTS § 202.12 is applicable made after the preliminary conference has been scheduled may be denied unless there is shown good cause why such relief is warranted before the preliminary conference is held. NY R UNIF TRIAL CTS § 202.12(h).

h. *ALBANY COUNTY: Good faith effort to resolve.* Prior to the submission of a notice of motion relating to disclosure or a bill of particulars, the parties must make a good faith effort to resolve the matter in question and submit an affirmation attesting to this good faith effort. NY R 3 JD SUP Doc. 1(B).

i. *NEW YORK COUNTY: Documents with motions.* Counsel must attach to motion papers copies of all pleadings and other documents as required by the CPLR and as necessary for an informed decision on the motion. Documents in a foreign language shall be properly translated. NY R NY CTY J RUL Rule 14(a).

j. *NEW YORK COUNTY: Motions in multiple cases made together.* On occasion, attorneys may wish to make a motion in more than one case on a single set of papers. In such cases, by definition consolidation will not have been directed since consolidation signifies the combination of more than one case into a single one with a single caption and index number and ending in a single judgment. NY R NY CTY Procedure II(B). For more information on motions made with the same papers, refer to NY R NY CTY Procedure II(A).

k. *QUEENS COUNTY: Motion sequence numbers.* A motion sequence number is required for all E-filed motions. After a motion is E-filed, please consult the e-courts website within twenty-four (24) to forty-eight (48) hours to obtain the sequence number. The Confirmation Notice of E-filing MUST indicate the sequence number of any motion submitted at the Centralized Motion Part calendar call. NY R L QUEENS E-FILE Doc. 1(H)(5).

2. *Rules governing disclosure*

a. *Generally.* There shall be full disclosure of all matter material and necessary in the prosecution or defense of an action, regardless of the burden of proof, by:

i. A party, or the officer, director, member, agent or employee of a party;

ii. A person who possessed a cause of action or defense asserted in the action;

iii. A person about to depart from the state, or without the state, or residing at a greater distance from the place of trial than one hundred miles, or so sick or infirm as to afford reasonable grounds of belief that he or she will not be able to attend the trial, or a person authorized to practice medicine, dentistry or podiatry who has provided medical, dental or podiatric care or diagnosis to the party demanding disclosure, or who has been retained by such party as an expert witness; and

iv. Any other person, upon notice stating the circumstances or reasons such disclosure is sought or required. NY CPLR § 3101(a).

v. The statutory phrase "material and necessary", said the Court of Appeals, must be interpreted liberally to require disclosure upon request, of any facts bearing on the controversy which will assist preparation for trial by sharpening the issues and reducing delay and prolixity. The test is one of usefulness and reason. SIEGEL-NYPRAC § 344; Allen v. Crowell-Collier Pub. Co., 21 N.Y.2d 403, 235 N.E.2d 430 (1968).

vi. Another potential problem that the original NY CPLR § 3101(a) posed was that it spoke of "evidence" that is material and necessary, which might have been construed to permit disclosure to elicit only that which would itself qualify as "evidence" admissible at trial. It was, however, construed more broadly than that. Well-considered caselaw specifically rejected this "evidence in chief" doctrine, stating that disclosure extends as well "to all relevant information calculated to lead to relevant evidence," a standard similar to that applicable in federal court. With an amendment that took effect on January 1, 1994, changing "evidence" to "matter" in NY CPLR § 3101(a), these generous interpretations of the statute were in effect approved by the legislature. SIEGEL-NYPRAC § 344.

vii. If a party is a corporation, each of its officers, directors, members, agents, and employees is also deemed a "party" for disclosure purposes. A party who needs relevant data or material from a nonparty corporation can seek it through NY CPLR § 3101(a)(2), NY CPLR § 3101(a)(3) or NY CPLR § 3101(a)(4), under which the corporate entity is treated as a "person." These subdivisions should also apply to any entity, corporate or otherwise, from whom disclosure is sought through its agents. A corporate employee who has the requisite knowledge and information may respond to a disclosure request on behalf of the corporation. A party who can't single out the particular person in the corporation's employ to whom a disclosure request should be properly directed can direct it to the corporation as such and leave it to the corporation to designate the appropriate person to respond. Whenever disclosure is sought from a corporation through a deposition, whether as a party or as a nonparty witness, the choice in the first instance of who will be produced in the corporate behalf is with the corporation rather than the examining party. SIEGEL-NYPRAC § 345.

viii. NY CPLR § 3101(a)(4) permits a party to obtain disclosure from a nonparty by merely serving a subpoena on the nonparty providing notice of "the circumstances or reasons such disclosure is sought or required." SIEGEL-NYPRAC § 345.

b. *Privileged matter.* Upon objection by a person entitled to assert the privilege, privileged matter shall not be obtainable. NY CPLR § 3101(b).

i. A determination of whether information is privileged is governed by the rules of evidence, which apply as they would at a trial. Whatever is privileged at the trial is privileged as well on pretrial disclosure. SIEGEL-NYPRAC § 346.

c. *Attorney's work product.* The work product of an attorney shall not be obtainable. NY CPLR § 3101(c).

i. NY CPLR § 3101(c) makes unobtainable the "work product of an attorney"—an ill-defined category whose potential for mischief has been avoided only because the judiciary has accorded it a very narrow scope. It is a category wholly distinct from the "materials . . . prepared in anticipation of litigation" of NY CPLR § 3101(d)(2). The fact that immunity is absolute under NY CPLR § 3101(c), while that of NY CPLR § 3101(d)(2) is only conditional, is the factor that requires as sharp a line as possible between the two categories. SIEGEL-NYPRAC § 347.

ii. The judiciary has cast precious little under the "work product" category of NY CPLR § 3101(c), preferring instead to fit doubtful items under the "materials . . . prepared in anticipation of litigation" banner of NY CPLR § 3101(d)(2), where the conditional immunity can be overcome and the matters ordered disclosed when stated conditions are met. SIEGEL-NYPRAC § 347.

d. *Trial preparation*

i. *Experts.* Upon request, each party shall identify each person whom the party expects to call as an expert witness at trial and shall disclose in reasonable detail the subject matter on which each expert is expected to testify, the substance of the facts and opinions on which each expert is expected to testify, the qualifications of each expert witness and a summary of the grounds for each expert's opinion. NY CPLR § 3101(d)(1)(i).

- However, where a party for good cause shown retains an expert an insufficient period of time before the commencement of trial to give appropriate notice thereof, the party shall not thereupon be precluded from introducing the expert's testimony at the trial solely on grounds of noncompliance with NY CPLR § 3101(d)(1). In that instance, upon motion of any party, made before or at trial, or on its own initiative, the court may make whatever order may be just. In an action for medical, dental or podiatric malpractice, a party, in responding to a request, may omit the names of medical, dental or podiatric experts but shall be required to disclose all other information concerning such experts otherwise required by NY CPLR § 3101(d)(1). NY CPLR § 3101(d)(1)(i).

- In an action for medical, dental or podiatric malpractice, any party may, by written offer made to and served upon all other parties and filed with the court, offer to disclose the name of, and to make available for examination upon oral deposition, any person the party making the offer expects to call as an expert witness at trial. Within twenty (20) days of service of the offer, a party shall accept or reject the offer by serving a written reply upon all parties and filing a copy thereof with the court. Failure to serve a reply within twenty (20) days of service of the offer shall be deemed a rejection of the offer. If all parties accept the offer, each party shall be required to produce his or her expert witness for examination upon oral deposition upon receipt of a notice to take oral deposition in accordance with NY CPLR Rule 3107. If any party, having made or accepted the offer, fails to make that party's expert available for oral deposition, that party shall be precluded from offering expert testimony at the trial of the action. NY CPLR § 3101(d)(1)(ii).

- Further disclosure concerning the expected testimony of any expert may be obtained only by court order upon a showing of special circumstances and subject to restrictions as to scope and provisions concerning fees and expenses as the court may deem appropriate. However, a party, without court order, may take the testimony of a person authorized to practice medicine, dentistry or podiatry who is the party's treating or retained expert, as described in NY CPLR § 3101(a)(3), in which event any other party shall be entitled to the full disclosure authorized by Article 31 of Chapter 8 of the Civil Practice Law and Rules (NY CPLR § 3101, et seq.) with respect to that expert without court order. NY CPLR § 3101(d)(1)(iii).

ii. *Materials.* Subject to the provisions of NY CPLR § 3101(d)(1), materials otherwise discoverable under NY CPLR § 3101(a) and prepared in anticipation of litigation or for trial by or for another party, or by or for that other party's representative (including an attorney, consultant, surety, indemnitor, insurer or agent), may be obtained only upon a showing that the party seeking discovery has substantial need of the materials in the preparation of the case and is unable without undue hardship to obtain the substantial equivalent of the materials by other means. In ordering discovery of the materials when the required showing has been made, the court shall protect against disclosure of the mental impressions, conclusions, opinions or legal theories of an attorney or other representative of a party concerning the litigation. NY CPLR § 3101(d)(2).

- In order to qualify as "litigation" material the item must have been prepared exclusively for litigation. Incidental potential use in litigation, the courts have observed, may also be a function of such reports, but they have at least an equal if not greater mission "to prevent future accidents, discipline careless employees, or, generally, to increase the economy and efficiency of the operation." SIEGEL-NYPRAC § 348.

e. *Party's statement.* A party may obtain a copy of his own statement. NY CPLR § 3101(e).

i. Moreover, NY CPLR § 3101(e) has been broadly interpreted to include photographs. Items such as photographs and videotapes are now independently subject to disclosure under NY CPLR § 3101(i). SIEGEL-NYPRAC § 348.

f. *Contents of insurance agreement.* A party may obtain discovery of the existence and contents of any insurance agreement under which any person carrying on an insurance business may be liable to satisfy part or all of a judgment which may be entered in the action or to indemnify or reimburse for payments made to satisfy the judgment. Information concerning the insurance agreement is not by reason of disclosure admissible in evidence at trial. For purpose of NY CPLR § 3101(f), an application for insurance shall not be treated as part of an insurance agreement. NY CPLR § 3101(f).

g. *Accident reports.* Except as is otherwise provided by law, in addition to any other matter which may be subject to disclosure, there shall be full disclosure of any written report of an accident prepared in the regular course of business operations or practices of any person, firm, corporation, association or other public or private entity, unless prepared by a police or peace officer for a criminal investigation or prosecution and disclosure would interfere with a criminal investigation or prosecution. NY CPLR § 3101(g).

h. *Amendment or supplementation of responses.* A party shall amend or supplement a response previously given to a request for disclosure promptly upon the party's thereafter obtaining information that the response was incorrect or incomplete when made, or that the response, though correct and complete when made, no longer is correct and complete, and the circumstances are such that a failure to amend or supplement the response would be materially misleading. NY CPLR § 3101(h).

    i. Where a party obtains such information an insufficient period of time before the commencement of trial appropriately to amend or supplement the response, the party shall not thereupon be precluded from introducing evidence at the trial solely on grounds of noncompliance with NY CPLR § 3101(h). In that instance, upon motion of any party, made before or at trial, or on its own initiative, the court may make whatever order may be just. Further amendment or supplementation may be obtained by court order. NY CPLR § 3101(h).

i. *Other disclosures.* In addition to any other matter which may be subject to disclosure, there shall be full disclosure of any films, photographs, video tapes or audio tapes, including transcripts or memoranda thereof, involving a person referred to in NY CPLR § 3101(a)(1). There shall be disclosure of all portions of such material, including out-takes, rather than only those portions a party intends to use. The provisions of NY CPLR § 3101(i) shall not apply to materials compiled for law enforcement purposes which are exempt from disclosure under NY PUB OFF § 87. NY CPLR § 3101(i).

    i. While NY CPLR § 3101(i) was enacted with the defendant's surreptitious tapes of the plaintiff in mind, its language is broad enough to embrace any films, photographs, and audio or video tapes of a party, even those made by the party from whom disclosure is sought. SIEGEL-NYPRAC § 348.

j. *Protective orders.* The court may at any time on its own initiative, or on motion of any party or of any person from whom discovery is sought, make a protective order denying, limiting, conditioning or regulating the use of any disclosure device. NY CPLR § 3103(a). Refer to the New York KeyRules Motion for Protective Order document for more information.

k. *Supervision of disclosure.* Upon the motion of any party or witness on notice to all parties or on its own initiative without notice, the court in which an action is pending may by one of its judges or a referee supervise all or part of any disclosure procedure. NY CPLR § 3104(a).

    i. *Selection of referee.* A judicial hearing officer may be designated as a referee under NY CPLR § 3104, or the court may permit all of the parties in an action to stipulate that a named attorney may act as referee. In such latter event, the stipulation shall provide for payment of his fees which shall, unless otherwise agreed, be taxed as disbursements. NY CPLR § 3104(b).

    ii. *Powers of referee; Motions referred to person supervising disclosure.* A referee under NY CPLR § 3104 shall have all the powers of the court under NY CPLR § 3101, et seq. except the power to relieve himself of his duties, to appoint a successor, or to adjudge any person guilty of contempt. All motions or applications made under Article 31 of Chapter 8 of the Civil Practice Law and Rules (NY CPLR § 3101, et seq.) shall be returnable before the judge or referee, designated under NY CPLR § 3104 and after disposition, if requested by any party, his order shall be filed in the office of the clerk. NY CPLR § 3104(c).

    iii. *Review of order of referee.* Any party or witness may apply for review of an order made under NY CPLR § 3104 by a referee. The application shall be by motion made in the court in which the action is pending within five (5) days after the order is made. Service of a notice of motion for review shall suspend disclosure of the particular matter in dispute. If the question raised by the motion may affect the rights of a witness, notice shall be served on him personally or by mail at his last known address. It shall set forth succinctly the order complained of, the reason it is objectionable and the relief demanded. NY CPLR § 3104(d).

    iv. *Payment of expenses of referee.* Except where a judicial hearing officer has been designated a referee hereunder, the court may make an appropriate order for the payment of the reasonable expenses of the referee. NY CPLR § 3104(e).

3. *Resolution of disclosure disputes*
   a. *BRONX COUNTY: Written application for conference in place of formal motion.* In lieu of a formal motion, parties may make written application to schedule a Discovery Status or Compliance Conference. Such application shall be forwarded to Bronx Supreme Civil, 851 Grand Concourse, Bronx, New York 10451 Room 217 DCM Department, Email BXDCM@NYCOURTS.GOV, FAX: 212 884 8955, PHONE: 212 884 8955. NY R BRONX FIL R Doc. 5. Such application shall set forth:
      i. The case caption and index number;
      ii. E Mail address for notification;
      iii. Must specify all discovery issues and any other relief being requested;
      iv. The request must state the courts intervention is necessary to resolve these issues. NY R BRONX FIL R Doc. 5.
      v. Identify all prior orders addressing discovery issues. NY R BRONX FIL R Doc. 5(5).
      vi. The request must be CCed to all appearing parties. NY R BRONX FIL R Doc. 5(6).
   b. *KINGS COUNTY: Attempt to reach agreement.* The attorneys shall, in the first instance, attempt to reach an agreement on all relevant discovery. Disputed matters will be adjudicated by the Court. NY R L KINGS Pt. B, Rule 2.
   c. *NEW YORK COUNTY: Good faith effort to resolve.* Prior to making a discovery motion, counsel shall consult one another in a good faith effort to resolve any discovery disputes. If a dispute is not thus resolved, the party seeking disclosure, unless otherwise directed in the Background Information section above, is advised to contact the Part Clerk promptly, and within any applicable deadline, for the purpose of arranging a conference, in court or by telephone. NY R NY CTY J RUL Rule 10.
4. *Motion to compel disclosure.* If a person fails to respond to or comply with any request, notice, interrogatory, demand, question or order under Article 31 (NY CPLR § 3101, et seq.), except a notice to admit under NY CPLR § 3123, the party seeking disclosure may move to compel compliance or a response. NY CPLR Rule 3124.
   a. *Place where motion made.* Unless otherwise provided by rule of the chief administrator of the courts, the county in which a deposition is being taken or an examination or inspection is being sought may be treated by the moving party as the county in which the action is pending for purposes of NY CPLR Rule 3124. NY CPLR Rule 3125.
   b. *Discovery sanctions not included*
      i. NY CPLR Rule 3124 contemplates a disclosure order without a penalty. If a sanction of some kind is sought for the disobedience of either a notice or an order, the application is made under NY CPLR § 3126. SIEGEL-NYPRAC § 366.
      ii. Caselaw under the original statute held that a NY CPLR § 3126 sanction motion need not necessarily be preceded by a disclosure order under NY CPLR Rule 3124, which of course made the motion under NY CPLR § 3126 the preferred one. SIEGEL-NYPRAC § 366; Wolfson v. Nassau Cty. Med. Ctr., 141 A.D.2d 815, 815, 530 N.Y.S.2d 27, 28 (1988). The design was to avoid the two-motion procedure generated by making a party go to NY CPLR Rule 3124 first and allowing access to NY CPLR § 3126 only as a follow-up. SIEGEL-NYPRAC § 366.
      iii. Under the 1993 amendments, however, there are at least two instances in which it appears that a bypass of NY CPLR Rule 3124 in favor of a direct motion under NY CPLR § 3126 may be barred. When the devices involved are the discovery of NY CPLR Rule 3120 or the physical or mental examination of NY CPLR § 3121, the also-amended NY CPLR Rule 3122 appears to require that a preliminary NY CPLR Rule 3124 application be made—for a court order directing disclosure without a sanction—before a sanction can be invoked with a NY CPLR § 3126 motion. SIEGEL-NYPRAC § 366. Refer to the New York KeyRules Motion for Discovery Sanctions document for more information on discovery sanctions under NY CPLR § 3126.
      iv. The court might also have authority to impose sanctions independent of NY CPLR § 3126. If the party resisting disclosure has engaged in frivolous conduct, the court has the power to impose sanctions under Part 130 (NY R CHIEF ADMIN § 130-1.1, et seq.). NY CPLR Rule 3124(Practice Commentary, C3124:6). Refer to the New York KeyRules Motion for Sanctions document for more information.
   c. *Relationship with preliminary conference; Disclosure timetable.* Where the motion relates to disclosure or to a bill of particulars, and a preliminary conference has not been held, the court shall notify all parties of a scheduled date to

appear for a preliminary conference, which shall be not more than forty-five (45) days from the return date of the motion unless the court orders otherwise, and a form of a stipulation and order, prescribed by the Chief Administrator of the Courts, shall be made available which the parties may sign, agreeing to a timetable which shall provide for completion of disclosure within twelve (12) months, and for a resolution of any other issues raised by the motion. If all parties sign the form and return it to the court before the return date of the motion, such form shall be "so ordered" by the court, and the motion shall be deemed withdrawn. If such stipulation is not returned by all parties, the conference shall be held on the assigned date. Issues raised by the motion and not resolved at the conference shall be determined by the court. NY R UNIF TRIAL CTS § 202.8(f).

5. *Oppositions.* In the absence of statutory provision or court rule, a motion ordinarily does not require a written answer, although an adverse party may be permitted to file an answer in opposition to the showing made in the motion or its supporting affidavits. AMJUR MOTIONS § 26. When a party files a motion and the opposing party fails to respond, the court may construe such failure to respond as non-opposition to the motion or an admission that the motion was meritorious, may take the facts alleged in the motion as true, and may grant the motion if the relief requested appears to be justified. However, the severity of such a result demands that a court impose it only with great caution. AMJUR MOTIONS § 28.
6. *Governing law.* The civil practice law and rules (NY CPLR § 101, et seq.) shall govern the procedure in civil judicial proceedings in all courts of the state and before all judges, except where the procedure is regulated by inconsistent statute. The civil practice law and rules shall succeed the civil practice act and rules of civil practice and shall be deemed substituted therefor throughout the statutes and rules of the state. NY CPLR § 101. The civil practice law and rules shall be liberally construed to secure the just, speedy and inexpensive determination of every civil judicial proceeding. NY CPLR § 104.
   a. *Uniform trial court rules.* The uniform civil rules for the Supreme Court and County Court (NY R UNIF TRIAL CTS § 202.1, et seq.) shall be applicable to civil actions and proceedings in the Supreme Court and the County Court. NY R UNIF TRIAL CTS § 202.1(a). The provisions of the uniform rules shall be construed consistent with the Civil Practice Law and Rules (CPLR), and matters not covered by the uniform rules shall be governed by the CPLR. NY R UNIF TRIAL CTS § 202.1(d).
   b. *Local rules.* Local court rules, not inconsistent with law or with uniform civil rules for the Supreme Court and County Court (NY R UNIF TRIAL CTS § 202.1, et seq.), shall comply with Part 9 of the Rules of the Chief Judge (NY R CHIEF J § 9.1). NY R UNIF TRIAL CTS § 202.1(c).
   c. *Official forms.* The state administrator shall have the power to adopt, amend and rescind an appendix of forms. Forms adopted pursuant to NY CPLR § 107 shall be sufficient under the civil practice law and rules and shall illustrate the simplicity and brevity of statement which the civil practice law and rules contemplate. NY CPLR § 107.
7. *Rules of the commercial division.* [Editor's note: certain types of civil cases or civil cases meeting certain monetary thresholds that are filed in the state of New York must be filed in the Commercial Division of the New York Supreme Courts. Rules governing practice in the commercial division are found in NY R UNIF TRIAL CTS § 202.70]. Cases which must be filed in the commercial division are listed below. For more information, refer to NY R UNIF TRIAL CTS § 202.70.
   a. *Monetary thresholds.* Except as set forth in NY R UNIF TRIAL CTS § 202.70(b), the monetary thresholds of the Commercial Division, exclusive of punitive damages, interests, costs, disbursements and counsel fees claimed, are established as follows: (1) Albany County, fifty thousand dollars ($50,000); (2) Eighth Judicial District, one hundred thousand dollars ($100,000); (3) Kings County, one hundred fifty thousand dollars ($150,000); (4) Nassau County, two hundred thousand dollars ($200,000); (5) New York County, five hundred thousand dollars ($500,000); (6) Onondaga County, fifty thousand dollars ($50,000); (7) Queens County, one hundred thousand dollars ($100,000); (8) Seventh Judicial District, fifty thousand dollars ($50,000); (9) Suffolk County, one hundred thousand dollars ($100,000); and (10) Westchester County, one hundred thousand dollars ($100,000). NY R UNIF TRIAL CTS § 202.70(a).
      i. *ALBANY COUNTY.* The Commercial Division of the Albany County Supreme Court exercises jurisdiction over selected business and commercial disputes in which the amount at issue generally involves damage claims in a minimum amount of fifty thousand dollars ($50,000) as well as claims for unspecified amounts where the value of the commercial asset(s) in dispute exceeds fifty thousand dollars ($50,000). A separate publication promulgating the rules and criteria relating to the filing and management of Commercial Court cases in this part may be obtained from the Albany County Supreme Court Clerk's Office. A section of the Uniform Civil Rules for the Supreme Court and County Court sets forth statewide rules. NY R 3 JD SUP Doc. 1(E).
      ii. *BRONX COUNTY.* The monetary threshold for commercial cases in Bronx County will be seventy-five thousand

dollars ($75,000). All other parameters including the type of matters that will be heard are contained within the Rules of the Commercial Division of the Supreme Court (NY R UNIF TRIAL CTS § 202.70). NY R BRONX FIL R Doc. 12.

iii. *NEW YORK COUNTY.* The monetary threshold in the New York County Commercial Division, which is generally applicable, is an amount in controversy of five hundred thousand dollars ($500,000) or more (exclusive of punitive damages, interest, costs, disbursements, and counsel fees). If the case is designated a commercial one and the Addendum is submitted, the clerk will review the pleadings to determine whether the amount in controversy in the case meets the monetary threshold or whether an exception to the threshold applies. NY R NY CTY Procedure IA(B). For more information on assigning a case to the commercial division in New York County, refer to NY R NY CTY Procedure IA(B).

b. *Commercial cases.* Actions in which the principal claims involve or consist of the following will be heard in the Commercial Division provided that the monetary threshold is met or equitable or declaratory relief is sought:

i. Breach of contract or fiduciary duty, fraud, misrepresentation, business tort (e.g., unfair competition), or statutory and/or common law violation where the breach or violation is alleged to arise out of business dealings (e.g., sales of assets or securities; corporate restructuring; partnership, shareholder, joint venture, and other business agreements; trade secrets; restrictive covenants; and employment agreements not including claims that principally involve alleged discriminatory practices);

ii. Transactions governed by the Uniform Commercial Code (exclusive of those concerning individual cooperative or condominium units);

iii. Transactions involving commercial real property, including Yellowstone injunctions and excluding actions for the payment of rent only;

iv. Shareholder derivative actions—without consideration of the monetary threshold;

v. Commercial class actions—without consideration of the monetary threshold;

vi. Business transactions involving or arising out of dealings with commercial banks and other financial institutions;

vii. Internal affairs of business organizations;

viii. Malpractice by accountants or actuaries, and legal malpractice arising out of representation in commercial matters;

ix. Environmental insurance coverage;

x. Commercial insurance coverage (e.g., directors and officers, errors and omissions, and business interruption coverage);

xi. Dissolution of corporations, partnerships, limited liability companies, limited liability partnerships and joint ventures—without consideration of the monetary threshold; and

xii. Applications to stay or compel arbitration and affirm or disaffirm arbitration awards and related injunctive relief pursuant to Article 75 of the New York Civil Practice Law and Rules (NY CPLR § 7501, et seq.) involving any of the foregoing enumerated commercial issues. Where the applicable arbitration agreement provides for the arbitration to be heard outside the United States, the monetary threshold set forth in NY R UNIF TRIAL CTS § 202.70(a) shall not apply. NY R UNIF TRIAL CTS § 202.70(b).

c. *Non-commercial cases.* The following will not be heard in the Commercial Division even if the monetary threshold is met:

i. Suits to collect professional fees;

ii. Cases seeking a declaratory judgment as to insurance coverage for personal injury or property damage;

iii. Residential real estate disputes, including landlord-tenant matters, and commercial real estate disputes involving the payment of rent only;

iv. Home improvement contracts involving residential properties consisting of one to four residential units or individual units in any residential building, including cooperative or condominium units;

v. Proceedings to enforce a judgment regardless of the nature of the underlying case;

vi. First-party insurance claims and actions by insurers to collect premiums or rescind non-commercial policies; and

vii. Attorney malpractice actions except as otherwise provided in NY R UNIF TRIAL CTS § 202.70(b)(8). NY R UNIF TRIAL CTS § 202.70(c).

d. For more information on the Commercial Division, refer to NY R UNIF TRIAL CTS § 202.70.

D. Documents

1. *Documents for moving party*

a. *Required documents*

i. *Notice of motion, order to show cause, or affidavit on ex parte motion.* The notice of motion shall be substantially in the form found in NY R UNIF TRIAL CTS § 202.7(b). NY R UNIF TRIAL CTS § 202.7(b). The supporting papers should be referred to in the notice of motion. SIEGEL-NYPRAC § 246. The court in a proper case may grant an order to show cause, to be served in lieu of a notice of motion. NY CPLR Rule 2214(d). An ex parte motion shall be accompanied by an affidavit stating the result of any prior motion for similar relief and specifying the new facts, if any, that were not previously shown. NY CPLR Rule 2217(b).

- *Request for oral argument.* A party requesting oral argument shall set forth such request in its notice of motion or in its order to show cause or on the first page of the answering papers, as the case may be. Where all parties to a motion request oral argument, oral argument shall be granted unless the court shall determine it to be unnecessary. Where a motion is brought on by order to show cause, the court may set forth in the order that oral argument is required on the return date of the motion. NY R UNIF TRIAL CTS § 202.8(d).

ii. *Motion.* Refer to the General Requirements section of this document for information on the notice of motion and motion.

iii. *Affirmation of counsel.* No motion shall be filed with the court unless there have been served and filed with the motion papers with respect to a motion relating to disclosure or to a bill of particulars, an affirmation that counsel has conferred with counsel for the opposing party in a good faith effort to resolve the issues raised by the motion. NY R UNIF TRIAL CTS § 202.7(a)(2).

- The affirmation of the good faith effort to resolve the issues raised by the motion shall indicate the time, place and nature of the consultation and the issues discussed and any resolutions, or shall indicate good cause why no such conferral with counsel for opposing parties was held. NY R UNIF TRIAL CTS § 202.7(c).
- *KINGS COUNTY.* Motions must be accompanied by an affirmation of good faith pursuant to NY R UNIF TRIAL CTS § 202.7(a), indicating what efforts have been made to resolve the motion. NY R L KINGS Pt. E, Rule 9.

iv. *Request for judicial intervention.* At any time after service of process, a party may file a request for judicial intervention. Except as provided in NY R UNIF TRIAL CTS § 202.6(b), in an action not yet assigned to a judge, the court shall not accept for filing a notice of motion, order to show cause, or application for ex parte order, unless such notice or application is accompanied by a request for judicial intervention. NY R UNIF TRIAL CTS § 202.6(a).

- *BRONX COUNTY.* Generally, the Request For Judicial Intervention, commonly referred to as an "RJI", is required to be filed in any action where the assignment of a Justice is required. The RJI sets forth the information which is entered into the court system's database. It must be completely and accurately filled out. The full caption, as stated on the Summons, must be set forth. Use of terms "et al." and "etc." are not permitted. Only one (1) RJI may be filed in each action. Either a self represented litigant or an attorney must sign the affirmation at the end of the form. Once completed, the RJI must be filed in duplicate. Except in the case of an ex-parte application, the RJI must also be served together with the accompanying application upon all parties. Proof of accuracy of the index number must accompany the RJI. Check the Fee Schedule[. . .]for any applicable filing fees. NY R BRONX FIL R Doc. 2.
- *KINGS COUNTY.* An RJI with the relevant required addendum in a NYSCEF case shall be submitted via NYSCEF. Once e-filed, the RJI and any accompanying document will be forwarded to the relevant support office for random assignment of the case and processing of the document. A filer or counsel need not appear (as to Proposed Orders to Show Cause, however, see below). A copy of the pleadings must be submitted only if the document has not previously been e-filed. If the RJI seeks intervention with regard to a document that is intended for review by a Justice, such as a motion, a working copy of the RJI must be submitted with the working copy of the motion and the NYSCEF Confirmation Notice. NY R L KINGS E FIL Doc. 1(C).
- *NEW YORK COUNTY.* To obtain the assignment of an IAS Justice to a case, a Request for Judicial

Intervention (cost ninety-five dollars ($95)) must be filed, with NYSCEF in an e-filed case or in paper in an authorized hard-copy one. A no-fee RJI, which will generally result in the referral of an application to an Ex Parte Justice, is also required with regard to certain kinds of applications for which, prior to 2011, no RJI was required. NY R NY CTY Procedure I(C). A "fillable" form RJI is available on-line. The form must be filed in duplicate in hard-copy cases. NY R NY CTY Procedure IA(A)(1). The filer of an RJI must check off a box identifying the type of case at issue. Where the RJI seeks judicial assignment, this designation will bring about a random assignment of the case by computer to a Justice handling cases of that type. NY R NY CTY Procedure IA(A)(1). The RJI and any addendum can be completed and submitted electronically in an e-filed case. NY R NY CTY Procedure II(A). The RJI shall be marked to reflect the existence of any "related case" as explained on the "Commencement of Cases" page under "Case Processing" on the court's website. NY R NY CTY Procedure II(A); NY R NY CTY E FIL Doc. 2(C).

- *ONONDAGA COUNTY.* The RJI will be submitted via the NYSCEF system along with any required RJI addendum forms. When the RJI is filed and the fee paid online, the Onondaga County Clerk's Office will electronically forward the RJI and any accompanying documents to the Onondaga Supreme Court Clerk's Office for assignment and processing. Counsel will receive notification of judge assignment via the NYSCEF system. NY R ONDGA E FIL Protocol(B)(3).
- *QUEENS COUNTY.* A Request for Judicial Intervention ("RJI") in an E-filed case shall be submitted via the E-filing System. When the RJI is approved, filed and paid for on-line, it will be forwarded to the relevant back office for random assignment of the case and processing of the document. In the case of RJIs seeking assignment to the Commercial Division, the filer must submit therewith, a Commercial Addendum as required by the standards for assignment of cases to the Commercial Division. NY R L QUEENS E-FILE Doc. 1(F).

v. *Proof of service.* In addition to complying with the provisions of NY CPLR Rule 2101, every paper filed in court shall have annexed thereto appropriate proof of service on all parties where required. NY R UNIF TRIAL CTS § 202.5(a).

- *QUEENS COUNTY.* With regard to service of a motion/petition on notice in an E-filed action, NY CPLR Rule 2214(b) and NY R UNIF TRIAL CTS § 202.5-b(f) applies. Where required, proof of service shall be filed on-line as a separate document. NY R L QUEENS E-FILE Doc. 1(H)(3).

vi. *ALBANY COUNTY: Additional required documents*

- *Affirmation of good faith effort.* The parties must[. . .]submit an affirmation attesting to [their good faith effort to resolve the matter]. The affirmation of good faith effort to resolve the issues raised by the motion shall indicate the time, place and nature of the consultation and the issues discussed and any resolutions, or shall indicate good cause why no such conferral with counsel for opposing parties was held. An assigned justice or judge may dismiss a motion for failure to demonstrate that such effort was made with leave to renew the motion after such effort has been demonstrated. NY R 3 JD SUP Doc. 1(B).

b. *Supplemental documents*

i. *Supporting evidence; Exhibits.* The main supporting papers on a motion are affidavits, but any relevant exhibits, documents, depositions, etc., are also includible. SIEGEL-NYPRAC § 246.

- *Affidavits accompanying motion.* Affidavits shall be for a statement of the relevant facts. NY R UNIF TRIAL CTS § 202.8(c).
- *Foreign language documents.* Where an affidavit or exhibit annexed to a paper served or filed is in a foreign language, it shall be accompanied by an English translation and an affidavit by the translator stating his qualifications and that the translation is accurate. NY CPLR Rule 2101(b).
- *Statement of attorney in lieu of affidavit.* The statement of an attorney admitted to practice in the courts of the state, or of a physician, osteopath or dentist, authorized by law to practice in the state, who is not a party to an action, when subscribed and affirmed by him to be true under the penalties of perjury, may be served or filed in the action in lieu of and with the same force and effect as an affidavit. NY CPLR Rule 2106.
- *NEW YORK COUNTY: Form of presented exhibits.* Exhibits should be tabbed and be legible; a typed version of any exhibit that is difficult to read should be submitted with the original. Exhibits printed on both sides of the page should be bound and tabbed on the side. NY R NY CTY J RUL Rule 14(a).
- *QUEENS COUNTY.* Attorneys submitting exhibits to the court on E-file cases shall make each exhibit a separate, labeled attachment to an affidavit/affirmation. NY R L QUEENS E-FILE Doc. 1(H)(4).

ii. *Brief.* Briefs shall be for a statement of the relevant law. NY R UNIF TRIAL CTS § 202.8(c).

iii. *Notice to produce papers not in possession of the court.* If a paper relied on by the movant is in the possession of the other side, it may be demanded of that side with a notice to produce it at the hearing. Where such papers are in the possession of an adverse party, they shall be produced by him at the hearing on notice served with the motion papers. NY CPLR Rule 2214(Practice Commentary, C2214:23).

iv. *Filing fees.* The County Clerk shall require the payment of any applicable statutory fees, or an order of the Court waiving payment of such fees, before accepting a paper for filing. NY R UNIF TRIAL CTS § 202.5(d)(1). For information on filing fees, if any, refer to NY CPLR § 8001, et seq.

- *ALBANY COUNTY.* In general, any filing subsequent to the commencement of an action which is designated as a motion or cross-motion requires the payment of a filing fee to the County Clerk's Office prior to submission to the Supreme Court Clerk's Office for referral to the assigned justice. The fee is assessed regardless of whether an application is made by notice of motion, order to show cause or ex parte. No fee will be charged upon the filing of a motion for poor person status in conjunction with an application which serves to commence an action or special proceeding. In the event a motion is received by the court unaccompanied by proof of payment to the County Clerk, the Supreme Court Clerk's Office will contact the submitting party to advise that the application will be held pending receipt of the filing fee only until the return date of the motion. If proof of payment is not submitted to the Supreme Court Clerk's Office by the return date (ex parte applications will be held ten (10) days), the papers will be returned by mail with a notification that the motion has been removed from the court's calendar and that it must be re-noticed and re-filed with the court along with the requisite filing fee. Inquiries concerning the applicability of the motion fee to a proposed filing may be directed to the Supreme Court Clerk's Office. NY R 3 JD SUP Doc. 1(B).
- *BRONX COUNTY.* In accordance with the new civil fee schedule set forth in Article 80 of the C.P.L.R. (NY CPLR § 8001, et seq.), effective July 14, 2003, all motions, and cross motions must be approved in Room 217 prior to payment of said fees in the County Clerk's Office, Room 118. NY R BRONX FIL R Doc. 8. The motion fee [must be] paid for via NYSCEF by credit/debit card. NY R BRONX E FIL R Doc. 1(1).
- *ERIE COUNTY.* Payment for fee-bearing NYSCEF documents must be made online via credit or debit card (American Express, MasterCard or Visa) at the time of submission. NY R ERIE E FIL Doc. 3(III)(E).
- *KINGS COUNTY.* The motion must be filed with NYSCEF and the motion fee paid. NY R L KINGS E FIL Doc. 1(D). Court fees in NYSCEF cases must be paid via NYSCEF by a credit or bank card (MasterCard, Visa, or American Express). Fees are no longer accepted in person in the Kings County Clerk's Office in NYSCEF cases. NY R L KINGS E FIL Doc. 1(B)(6).
- *NEW YORK COUNTY.* A motion fee must be paid on motions made in writing by notice of motion, order to show cause or ex parte after the commencement of an action. For this purpose, the term "action" shall mean any application to the court that requires the assignment of an index number, regardless of whether a formal pleading is filed. Applications or motions that commence an action and for which an index number fee must be paid require no motion fee. [A]ny motions made after the initial applications in these situations would require payment of the motion fee. A motion that is the initial application in a case commenced by the filing of a summons and complaint would require a motion fee since the filing of the summons and complaint rather than the application itself would require the purchase of an index number. NY R NY CTY Procedure II(A). In e-filed cases the motion fee must be paid when the documents are filed. Payment is made on-line by Visa, Mastercard, or American Express credit or bank card. NY R NY CTY Procedure II(A); NY R NY CTY E FIL Doc. 2(B)(5).
- *ONONDAGA COUNTY.* Court fees in e-filed cases must be paid online with the NYSCEF system using a credit card. The document is not considered to have been filed until payment of the fee has been tendered. NY R ONDGA E FIL Protocol(B)(2). Fees must be paid on all cross motions. NY R ONDGA E FIL Protocol(B)(9)(e).
- *QUEENS COUNTY.* The Motion Support Office does not receive, forward or process any fees or waiver of fees. All applications requiring payment of statutory fees or waiver of fees must be sent directly to the Queens County Clerk's office. NY R L QUEENS MOT SUP Doc. 1. Court fees (e.g., RJI fee, motion fee) in E-filed cases may be paid for on-line using a credit card. Papers may also be filed with the E-file system and the fee may be paid at the County Clerk's Office. In the latter case, the paper is not considered to have been filed until payment of the fee has been tendered. NY R L QUEENS E-FILE Doc. 1(E)(1). The

motion/petition shall be filed on-line and the fee paid for either on-line by credit card or by the "Pay at the County Clerk's Office" option. NY R L QUEENS E-FILE Doc. 1(H)(1).

v. *Working copies.* The court may require the parties to provide working copies of documents filed electronically. In such event, each working copy shall include, firmly affixed thereto, a copy of a confirmation notice in a form prescribed by the Chief Administrator. NY R UNIF TRIAL CTS § 202.5-b(d)(5).

- *BRONX COUNTY.* After papers on motions have been e-filed, working copies thereof, with Confirmation Notice firmly attached as the back page facing out, must be submitted. (Each document or group of documents that is separately bound shall bear a Confirmation Notice.) Working copies lacking the Notice will not be accepted. WORKING COPIES OF MOTION PAPERS MUST BE SUBMITTED NO LATER THAN 4:45 P.M. ON THE RETURN DATE IN THE MOTION SUPPORT OFFICE (ROOM 217) AS EXPLAINED in NY R BRONX E FIL R Doc. 1(4). If an attorney has failed to submit required working copies on or before the return date, the motion will be transmitted as is to the Justice for such action as the Justice finds appropriate. Attorneys may submit working copies on motions by mail or overnight delivery. Any such submission shall be sent in a timely manner to the Motion Support Office (Room 217) and be conspicuously marked on the outside "NYSCEF Matter"; lack of such marking may delay processing. NY R BRONX E FIL R Doc. 1(4)(a).
- *ERIE COUNTY.* Electronically filed documents subject to review and processing by the Part Clerk do not require a working copy unless otherwise directed or provided for in IAS Part Rules. NY R UNIF TRIAL CTS § 202.5-b(d)(4), any working copy submitted shall include, as a cover page firmly fastened thereto, a copy of the Confirmation Notice generated by the NYSCEF site at the time of filing. Please consult the individual Justice's Part Rules and/or consult with the Judge's chambers to determine whether and how working copies are to be provided. Working copies will not be printed or delivered by the Erie County Clerk or the Chief Clerk of the Courts or any of their personnel to chambers. The official record of a document in an electronically filed case is the document filed via the NYSCEF system. Working copies are intended only for use by the Justice. The Court will discard all working copies after the Justice has finished with them. Thus, in the event that counsel fails to file a document via the NYSCEF system, the document will not be part of the court record. NY R ERIE E FIL Doc. 3(III)(O); NY R ERIE E FIL Doc. 3(V)(E).
- *KINGS COUNTY.* No courtesy copies of motion papers are required by the Court, except as may be required for electronic filing or by the Judge's Part Rules. In tort cases against the City of New York, courtesy copies shall be supplied to the Corporation Counsel's office in Brooklyn. NY R L KINGS Pt. C, Rule 5. Unless otherwise directed by the Court or as described herein, and with the exceptions listed below, in all NYSCEF cases in which an RJI has been filed, working copies of e-filed documents that are intended for judicial review must be submitted to the court. Working copies are not required of documents that are only processed by a support office (e.g. preliminary conference request, note of issue). Working copies shall include exhibit tabs and backs; for motion papers, the motion sequence number and the return date and part. The confirmation notice with the motion sequence number on it should be the back page of the motion facing out. In addition, the filer of a working copy must firmly bind thereto, with the back page facing out, a copy of the Confirmation Notice that was generated by NYSCEF when that document was efiled. Working copies that are submitted without the related Confirmation Notice will not be accepted. NY R L KINGS E FIL Doc. 1(B)(7); NY R L KINGS E FIL Doc. 1(D). WORKING COPIES OF MOTION PAPERS MUST BE SUBMITTED IN THE MOTION SUPPORT OFFICE (ROOM 227) AS EXPLAINED HEREIN. THEY MUST NOT BE DELIVERED TO THE PART OR CHAMBERS, EXCEPT WHERE THE INDIVIDUAL JUSTICE'S PART RULES PROVIDE OTHERWISE; DOING SO WILL CAUSE ADMINISTRATIVE CONFUSION AND POSSIBLE MISPLACEMENT OF PAPERS. Any such submission shall be sent in a timely manner (kindly review individual Justice's rules) and be conspicuously marked on the outside "NYSCEF Matter;" lack of such marking may delay processing. NY R L KINGS E FIL Doc. 1(D).
- *NEW YORK COUNTY.* Some Justices require that working copies of e-filed motion papers be submitted. See the E-filing Protocol for information on the many Parts that do not require working copies. Where required, working copies of the moving documents and all other documents on the motion or application shall be submitted to the Motion Submission Part Courtroom (Room 130) on, but not before, the final return date. A Confirmation Notice from the NYSCEF system, which is generated when a document is e-filed, shall be firmly affixed, as the back page facing out, to each separate working copy or group of such copies. NY R NY CTY Procedure II(A) NY R NY CTY E FIL Doc. 2(B)(5)(a); NY R NY CTY J RUL Rule 14(a). For more information on working copies, including which parts don't require them, refer to NY R NY CTY E FIL Doc. 2(B)(6).

- *ONONDAGA COUNTY.* Any courtesy "working" copies, if required (see NY R ONDGA E FIL Protocol(B)(7)), must be provided directly to the assigned justice. NY R ONDGA E FIL Protocol(B)(9)(e). For information as to whether or not an Onondaga Supreme Court Justice requires working (courtesy) copies of e-filed documents, please consult the Onondaga County Individual E-filing Rules. NY R ONDGA E FIL Protocol(B)(7)(a). The Supreme Court Clerk's Office and the Onondaga County Clerk's Office will NOT accept the working copies. Working copies must be sent directly to the assigned justice's chambers. NY R ONDGA E FIL Protocol(B)(7)(b). A copy of the Confirmation Notice, generated by the NYSCEF system at the time a document is e-filed, must be attached to every working copy provided to chambers. If the Confirmation Notice is missing, the copy will not be accepted. NY R ONDGA E FIL Protocol(B)(7)(c). Courtesy copies do not become part of the official court record as maintained by the Onondaga County Clerk's Office and will be destroyed by chambers at the disposition of the case. In the event that counsel fails to file a document via NYSCEF, the document will not be part of the court record. NY R ONDGA E FIL Protocol(B)(7)(d).
- *QUEENS COUNTY.* Working copies of E-Filed notices of motion/notices of petition are NOT to be sent to the Motion Support Office. They must be brought to the calendar call in the judge's part. NY R L QUEENS MOT SUP Doc. 1. Unless otherwise directed or authorized by the court, counsel should file papers with the E-file system first and thereafter deliver a working copy to at the calendar call of the Centralized Motion Part or Assigned Justice in accordance with individual Part Rules. NY R L QUEENS E-FILE Doc. 1(E)(4). On the return date of a motion that has been E-filed, the movant must provide the Centralized Motion Part (CMP) with a working copy of the entire motion including the notice of motion with sequence number and all of the attached exhibits. The motion must have the confirmation of filing firmly affixed to the back of the papers (facing outward). The confirmation of filing is a separate notice from the payment notice and will say confirmation clearly across the top of the page. NY R L QUEENS E-FILE Doc. 1(H)(2)(a). The motion or Order to Show Cause must have clearly written across its face the words "Working Copy," it must also have the assigned Judge's name, motion sequence number and calendar number—which may be obtained from the posted calendar outside courtroom on the return date of the motion. A confirmation of filing must attached thereto. Working copies of e-filed Orders to Show Cause must contain a copy of the signed order and all supporting papers. NY R L QUEENS E-FILE Doc. 1(H)(2)(c). The Confirmation Notice must be an updated version that indicates the sequence number of the motion being submitted at the CMP calendar call. WORKING COPIES WITHOUT A CONFIRMATION NOTICE WILL NOT BE ACCEPTED. NY R L QUEENS E-FILE Doc. 1(H)(7).

vi. *ERIE COUNTY: Additional supplemental documents*

- *Notice of hard copy submission in e-filed case.* In accordance with NY R UNIF TRIAL CTS § 202.5-b(d), the County Clerk shall refuse to accept for filing, hard copy papers filed to an action subject to electronic filing unless hard copy filing is permitted by the Uniform Rules or NY R ERIE E FIL Doc. 3 and the papers bear a completed Notice of Hard Copy Submission—E-Filed Case form. NY R ERIE E FIL Doc. 3(III)(D).

vii. *KINGS COUNTY: Additional supplemental documents*

- *Forms when filing in hard copy.* An attorney who certifies in good faith that he or she lacks the equipment or knowledge needed to e-file and have no staff member or employee under his or her direction who has such knowledge and equipment may opt out of participation in e-filing in a mandatory case by filing a "Notice of Opt-Out from Participation in Action Subject to Mandatory Electronic Filing" form EFM-2 with the Clerk. NY R L KINGS E FIL Doc. 1(A)(2). Where in accordance with the E-Filing Rules a party submits a document in hard copy in an e-filed case (principally, a document submitted by a nonparticipating party (e.g., an attorney) in a consensual case, an emergency filing made in accordance with the Mandatory E-Filing Rules, and any document filed with the court in hard copy by an attorney who has opted out of participation in mandatory e-filing, the document must bear the back page facing out, a "Notice of Hard Copy Submission—E-Filed Cases" form EFM-3. NY R L KINGS E FIL Doc. 1(B)(3).

viii. *NEW YORK COUNTY: Additional supplemental documents*

- *Notice of hard copy submission.* Where in accordance with the E-Filing Rules an attorney or an unrepresented litigant who is participating in e-filing submits a document in hard copy in an e-filed case, the document must bear, as the back page facing out, a Notice of Hard-Copy Submission—E-Filed Case (a form available in the "Forms" section on the NYSCEF website (Form EFM-3) and in the court's back offices). NY R NY CTY E FIL Doc. 2(B)(3). For more information refer to NY R NY CTY E FIL Doc. 2.
- *Unpublished decisions.* Whenever reliance is placed upon a decision or other authority not officially

published or readily available to the New York County Supreme Court, a copy of the case or of pertinent portions of the authority shall be submitted with the motion papers. NY R NY CTY J RUL Rule 14(a).

ix. *ONONDAGA COUNTY: Additional supplemental documents*

- *Notice of hard copy submission.* Any papers to be filed with the court in an e-filed case must be filed online with the E-filing system except where a special exemption is granted (e.g., oversized maps, photographs). If such an exemption is granted, Form EFM-3, "Notice of Hard Copy Submission—E-Filed Case," must be attached to such documents forms which are not filed on line. Also, Form EFM-4 "Notice of Hard Copy Exhibit Filing" must be completed and uploaded to the action's e-file. Both of these forms may be found on the NYSCEF website. NY R ONDGA E FIL Protocol(B)(4).

x. *QUEENS COUNTY: Additional supplemental documents*

- *Notice of hard copy submission.* Any party opting out of the e-filing system must have a "Notice of Hard Copy Submission" firmly affixed to the back of the papers. NY R L QUEENS E-FILE Doc. 1(H)(2)(f).

2. *Documents for opposing party*

a. *Required documents*

i. *Opposition.* Refer to the General Requirements section of this document for information on the opposition.

- *Request for oral argument.* A party requesting oral argument shall set forth such request in its notice of motion or in its order to show cause or on the first page of the answering papers, as the case may be. Where all parties to a motion request oral argument, oral argument shall be granted unless the court shall determine it to be unnecessary. Where a motion is brought on by order to show cause, the court may set forth in the order that oral argument is required on the return date of the motion. NY R UNIF TRIAL CTS § 202.8(d).
- *QUEENS COUNTY: E-filing opposition papers.* E-filed opposition papers and/or reply papers must also be provided to the Centralized Motion Part in the same manner as the moving papers with the confirmation of filing firmly attached to the back of the papers. NY R L QUEENS E-FILE Doc. 1(H)(2)(d).

ii. *Proof of service.* In addition to complying with the provisions of NY CPLR Rule 2101, every paper filed in court shall have annexed thereto appropriate proof of service on all parties where required. NY R UNIF TRIAL CTS § 202.5(a).

b. *Supplemental documents*

i. *Supporting evidence; Exhibits.* The main supporting papers on a motion are affidavits, but any relevant exhibits, documents, depositions, etc., are also includible. SIEGEL-NYPRAC § 246.

- *Affidavits accompanying opposition.* Affidavits shall be for a statement of the relevant facts. NY R UNIF TRIAL CTS § 202.8(c).
- *Foreign language documents.* Where an affidavit or exhibit annexed to a paper served or filed is in a foreign language, it shall be accompanied by an English translation and an affidavit by the translator stating his qualifications and that the translation is accurate. NY CPLR Rule 2101(b).
- *Statement of attorney in lieu of affidavit.* The statement of an attorney admitted to practice in the courts of the state, or of a physician, osteopath or dentist, authorized by law to practice in the state, who is not a party to an action, when subscribed and affirmed by him to be true under the penalties of perjury, may be served or filed in the action in lieu of and with the same force and effect as an affidavit. NY CPLR Rule 2106.
- *NEW YORK COUNTY: Form of presented exhibits.* Exhibits should be tabbed and be legible; a typed version of any exhibit that is difficult to read should be submitted with the original. Exhibits printed on both sides of the page should be bound and tabbed on the side. NY R NY CTY J RUL Rule 14(a).
- *QUEENS COUNTY.* Attorneys submitting exhibits to the court on E-file cases shall make each exhibit a separate, labeled attachment to an affidavit/affirmation. NY R L QUEENS E-FILE Doc. 1(H)(4).

ii. *Brief.* Briefs shall be for a statement of the relevant law. NY R UNIF TRIAL CTS § 202.8(c).

iii. *Filing fees.* The County Clerk shall require the payment of any applicable statutory fees, or an order of the Court waiving payment of such fees, before accepting a paper for filing. NY R UNIF TRIAL CTS § 202.5(d)(1). For information on filing fees, if any, refer to NY CPLR § 8001, et seq.

- *ALBANY COUNTY.* In general, any filing subsequent to the commencement of an action which is designated as a motion or cross-motion requires the payment of a filing fee to the County Clerk's Office

prior to submission to the Supreme Court Clerk's Office for referral to the assigned justice. The fee is assessed regardless of whether an application is made by notice of motion, order to show cause or ex parte. No fee will be charged upon the filing of a motion for poor person status in conjunction with an application which serves to commence an action or special proceeding. In the event a motion is received by the court unaccompanied by proof of payment to the County Clerk, the Supreme Court Clerk's Office will contact the submitting party to advise that the application will be held pending receipt of the filing fee only until the return date of the motion. If proof of payment is not submitted to the Supreme Court Clerk's Office by the return date (ex parte applications will be held ten (10) days), the papers will be returned by mail with a notification that the motion has been removed from the court's calendar and that it must be re-noticed and re-filed with the court along with the requisite filing fee. Inquiries concerning the applicability of the motion fee to a proposed filing may be directed to the Supreme Court Clerk's Office. NY R 3 JD SUP Doc. 1(B).

- *BRONX COUNTY.* In accordance with the new civil fee schedule set forth in Article 80 of the C.P.L.R. (NY CPLR § 8001, et seq.), effective July 14, 2003, all motions, and cross motions must be approved in Room 217 prior to payment of said fees in the County Clerk's Office, Room 118. NY R BRONX FIL R Doc. 8. The motion fee [must be] paid for via NYSCEF by credit/debit card. NY R BRONX E FIL R Doc. 1(1).
- *ERIE COUNTY.* Payment for fee-bearing NYSCEF documents must be made online via credit or debit card (American Express, MasterCard or Visa) at the time of submission. NY R ERIE E FIL Doc. 3(III)(E).
- *KINGS COUNTY.* The motion must be filed with NYSCEF and the motion fee paid. NY R L KINGS E FIL Doc. 1(D). Court fees in NYSCEF cases must be paid via NYSCEF by a credit or bank card (MasterCard, Visa, or American Express). Fees are no longer accepted in person in the Kings County Clerk's Office in NYSCEF cases. NY R L KINGS E FIL Doc. 1(B)(6).
- *NEW YORK COUNTY.* A motion fee must be paid on motions made in writing by notice of motion, order to show cause or ex parte after the commencement of an action. For this purpose, the term "action" shall mean any application to the court that requires the assignment of an index number, regardless of whether a formal pleading is filed. Applications or motions that commence an action and for which an index number fee must be paid require no motion fee. [A]ny motions made after the initial applications in these situations would require payment of the motion fee. A motion that is the initial application in a case commenced by the filing of a summons and complaint would require a motion fee since the filing of the summons and complaint rather than the application itself would require the purchase of an index number. NY R NY CTY Procedure II(A). In e-filed cases the motion fee must be paid when the documents are filed. Payment is made on-line by Visa, Mastercard, or American Express credit or bank card. NY R NY CTY Procedure II(A); NY R NY CTY E FIL Doc. 2(B)(5).
- *ONONDAGA COUNTY.* Court fees in e-filed cases must be paid online with the NYSCEF system using a credit card. The document is not considered to have been filed until payment of the fee has been tendered. NY R ONDGA E FIL Protocol(B)(2). Fees must be paid on all cross motions. NY R ONDGA E FIL Protocol(B)(9)(e).
- *QUEENS COUNTY.* The Motion Support Office does not receive, forward or process any fees or waiver of fees. All applications requiring payment of statutory fees or waiver of fees must be sent directly to the Queens County Clerk's office. NY R L QUEENS MOT SUP Doc. 1. Court fees (e.g., RJI fee, motion fee) in E-filed cases may be paid for on-line using a credit card. Papers may also be filed with the E-file system and the fee may be paid at the County Clerk's Office. In the latter case, the paper is not considered to have been filed until payment of the fee has been tendered. NY R L QUEENS E-FILE Doc. 1(E)(1). The motion/petition shall be filed on-line and the fee paid for either on-line by credit card or by the "Pay at the County Clerk's Office" option. NY R L QUEENS E-FILE Doc. 1(H)(1).

iv. *Working copies.* The court may require the parties to provide working copies of documents filed electronically. In such event, each working copy shall include, firmly affixed thereto, a copy of a confirmation notice in a form prescribed by the Chief Administrator. NY R UNIF TRIAL CTS § 202.5-b(d)(5).

- *BRONX COUNTY.* After papers on motions have been e-filed, working copies thereof, with Confirmation Notice firmly attached as the back page facing out, must be submitted. (Each document or group of documents that is separately bound shall bear a Confirmation Notice.) Working copies lacking the Notice will not be accepted. WORKING COPIES OF MOTION PAPERS MUST BE SUBMITTED NO LATER THAN 4:45 P.M. ON THE RETURN DATE IN THE MOTION SUPPORT OFFICE (ROOM 217) AS EXPLAINED in NY R BRONX E FIL R Doc. 1(4). If an attorney has failed to submit required working

copies on or before the return date, the motion will be transmitted as is to the Justice for such action as the Justice finds appropriate. Attorneys may submit working copies on motions by mail or overnight delivery. Any such submission shall be sent in a timely manner to the Motion Support Office (Room 217) and be conspicuously marked on the outside "NYSCEF Matter"; lack of such marking may delay processing. NY R BRONX E FIL R Doc. 1(4)(a).

- *ERIE COUNTY.* Electronically filed documents subject to review and processing by the Part Clerk do not require a working copy unless otherwise directed or provided for in IAS Part Rules. NY R UNIF TRIAL CTS § 202.5-b(d)(4), any working copy submitted shall include, as a cover page firmly fastened thereto, a copy of the Confirmation Notice generated by the NYSCEF site at the time of filing. Please consult the individual Justice's Part Rules and/or consult with the Judge's chambers to determine whether and how working copies are to be provided. Working copies will not be printed or delivered by the Erie County Clerk or the Chief Clerk of the Courts or any of their personnel to chambers. The official record of a document in an electronically filed case is the document filed via the NYSCEF system. Working copies are intended only for use by the Justice. The Court will discard all working copies after the Justice has finished with them. Thus, in the event that counsel fails to file a document via the NYSCEF system, the document will not be part of the court record. NY R ERIE E FIL Doc. 3(III)(O); NY R ERIE E FIL Doc. 3(V)(E).
- *KINGS COUNTY.* No courtesy copies of motion papers are required by the Court, except as may be required for electronic filing or by the Judge's Part Rules. In tort cases against the City of New York, courtesy copies shall be supplied to the Corporation Counsel's office in Brooklyn. NY R L KINGS Pt. C, Rule 5. Unless otherwise directed by the Court or as described herein, and with the exceptions listed below, in all NYSCEF cases in which an RJI has been filed, working copies of e-filed documents that are intended for judicial review must be submitted to the court. Working copies are not required of documents that are only processed by a support office (e.g. preliminary conference request, note of issue). Working copies shall include exhibit tabs and backs; for motion papers, the motion sequence number and the return date and part. The confirmation notice with the motion sequence number on it should be the back page of the motion facing out. In addition, the filer of a working copy must firmly bind thereto, with the back page facing out, a copy of the Confirmation Notice that was generated by NYSCEF when that document was efiled. Working copies that are submitted without the related Confirmation Notice will not be accepted. NY R L KINGS E FIL Doc. 1(B)(7); NY R L KINGS E FIL Doc. 1(D). WORKING COPIES OF MOTION PAPERS MUST BE SUBMITTED IN THE MOTION SUPPORT OFFICE (ROOM 227) AS EXPLAINED HEREIN. THEY MUST NOT BE DELIVERED TO THE PART OR CHAMBERS, EXCEPT WHERE THE INDIVIDUAL JUSTICE'S PART RULES PROVIDE OTHERWISE; DOING SO WILL CAUSE ADMINISTRATIVE CONFUSION AND POSSIBLE MISPLACEMENT OF PAPERS. Any such submission shall be sent in a timely manner (kindly review individual Justice's rules) and be conspicuously marked on the outside "NYSCEF Matter;" lack of such marking may delay processing. NY R L KINGS E FIL Doc. 1(D).
- *NEW YORK COUNTY.* Some Justices require that working copies of e-filed motion papers be submitted. See the E-filing Protocol for information on the many Parts that do not require working copies. Where required, working copies of the moving documents and all other documents on the motion or application shall be submitted to the Motion Submission Part Courtroom (Room 130) on, but not before, the final return date. A Confirmation Notice from the NYSCEF system, which is generated when a document is e-filed, shall be firmly affixed, as the back page facing out, to each separate working copy or group of such copies. NY R NY CTY Procedure II(A) NY R NY CTY E FIL Doc. 2(B)(5)(a); NY R NY CTY J RUL Rule 14(a). For more information on working copies, including which parts don't require them, refer to NY R NY CTY E FIL Doc. 2(B)(6).
- *ONONDAGA COUNTY.* Any courtesy "working" copies, if required (see NY R ONDGA E FIL Protocol(B)(7)), must be provided directly to the assigned justice. NY R ONDGA E FIL Protocol(B)(9)(e). For information as to whether or not an Onondaga Supreme Court Justice requires working (courtesy) copies of e-filed documents, please consult the Onondaga County Individual E-filing Rules. NY R ONDGA E FIL Protocol(B)(7)(a). The Supreme Court Clerk's Office and the Onondaga County Clerk's Office will NOT accept the working copies. Working copies must be sent directly to the assigned justice's chambers. NY R ONDGA E FIL Protocol(B)(7)(b). A copy of the Confirmation Notice, generated by the NYSCEF system at the time a document is e-filed, must be attached to every working copy provided to chambers. If the Confirmation Notice is missing, the copy will not be accepted. NY R ONDGA E FIL Protocol(B)(7)(c). Courtesy copies do not become part of the official court record as maintained by the Onondaga County

Clerk's Office and will be destroyed by chambers at the disposition of the case. In the event that counsel fails to file a document via NYSCEF, the document will not be part of the court record. NY R ONDGA E FIL Protocol(B)(7)(d).

- *QUEENS COUNTY.* Working copies of E-Filed notices of motion/notices of petition are NOT to be sent to the Motion Support Office. They must be brought to the calendar call in the judge's part. NY R L QUEENS MOT SUP Doc. 1. Unless otherwise directed or authorized by the court, counsel should file papers with the E-file system first and thereafter deliver a working copy to at the calendar call of the Centralized Motion Part or Assigned Justice in accordance with individual Part Rules. NY R L QUEENS E-FILE Doc. 1(E)(4). On the return date of a motion that has been E-filed, the movant must provide the Centralized Motion Part (CMP) with a working copy of the entire motion including the notice of motion with sequence number and all of the attached exhibits. The motion must have the confirmation of filing firmly affixed to the back of the papers (facing outward). The confirmation of filing is a separate notice from the payment notice and will say confirmation clearly across the top of the page. NY R L QUEENS E-FILE Doc. 1(H)(2)(a). The motion or Order to Show Cause must have clearly written across its face the words "Working Copy," it must also have the assigned Judge's name, motion sequence number and calendar number—which may be obtained from the posted calendar outside courtroom on the return date of the motion. A confirmation of filing must attached thereto. Working copies of e-filed Orders to Show Cause must contain a copy of the signed order and all supporting papers. NY R L QUEENS E-FILE Doc. 1(H)(2)(c). The Confirmation Notice must be an updated version that indicates the sequence number of the motion being submitted at the CMP calendar call. WORKING COPIES WITHOUT A CONFIRMATION NOTICE WILL NOT BE ACCEPTED. NY R L QUEENS E-FILE Doc. 1(H)(7).

v. *ERIE COUNTY: Additional supplemental documents*

- *Notice of hard copy submission in e-filed case.* In accordance with NY R UNIF TRIAL CTS § 202.5-b(d), the County Clerk shall refuse to accept for filing, hard copy papers filed to an action subject to electronic filing unless hard copy filing is permitted by the Uniform Rules or NY R ERIE E FIL Doc. 3 and the papers bear a completed Notice of Hard Copy Submission—E-Filed Case form. NY R ERIE E FIL Doc. 3(III)(D).

vi. *KINGS COUNTY: Additional supplemental documents*

- *Forms when filing in hard copy.* An attorney who certifies in good faith that he or she lacks the equipment or knowledge needed to e-file and have no staff member or employee under his or her direction who has such knowledge and equipment may opt out of participation in e-filing in a mandatory case by filing a "Notice of Opt-Out from Participation in Action Subject to Mandatory Electronic Filing" form EFM-2 with the Clerk. NY R L KINGS E FIL Doc. 1(A)(2). Where in accordance with the E-Filing Rules a party submits a document in hard copy in an e-filed case (principally, a document submitted by a nonparticipating party (e.g., an attorney) in a consensual case, an emergency filing made in accordance with the Mandatory E-Filing Rules, and any document filed with the court in hard copy by an attorney who has opted out of participation in mandatory e-filing, the document must bear the back page facing out, a "Notice of Hard Copy Submission—E-Filed Cases" form EFM-3. NY R L KINGS E FIL Doc. 1(B)(3).

vii. *NEW YORK COUNTY: Additional supplemental documents*

- *Notice of hard copy submission.* Where in accordance with the E-Filing Rules an attorney or an unrepresented litigant who is participating in e-filing submits a document in hard copy in an e-filed case, the document must bear, as the back page facing out, a Notice of Hard-Copy Submission—E-Filed Case (a form available in the "Forms" section on the NYSCEF website (Form EFM-3) and in the court's back offices). NY R NY CTY E FIL Doc. 2(B)(3). For more information refer to NY R NY CTY E FIL Doc. 2.
- *Unpublished decisions.* Whenever reliance is placed upon a decision or other authority not officially published or readily available to the New York County Supreme Court, a copy of the case or of pertinent portions of the authority shall be submitted with the motion papers. NY R NY CTY J RUL Rule 14(a).

viii. *ONONDAGA COUNTY: Additional supplemental documents*

- *Notice of hard copy submission.* Any papers to be filed with the court in an e-filed case must be filed online with the E-filing system except where a special exemption is granted (e.g., oversized maps, photographs). If such an exemption is granted, Form EFM-3, "Notice of Hard Copy Submission—E-Filed Case," must be attached to such documents forms which are not filed on line. Also, Form EFM-4 "Notice of Hard Copy Exhibit Filing" must be completed and uploaded to the action's e-file. Both of these forms may be found on the NYSCEF website. NY R ONDGA E FIL Protocol(B)(4).

ix. *QUEENS COUNTY: Additional supplemental documents*

- *Notice of hard copy submission.* Any party opting out of the e-filing system must have a "Notice of Hard Copy Submission" firmly affixed to the back of the papers. NY R L QUEENS E-FILE Doc. 1(H)(2)(f).

E. Format

1. *Form of documents*

a. *Size and form of paper.* Each paper served or filed shall be durable, white and, except for summonses, subpoenas, notices of appearance, notes of issue, orders of protection, temporary orders of protection and exhibits, shall be eleven by eight and one-half (11 x 8-1/2) inches in size. NY CPLR Rule 2101(a).

b. *Writing and language.* The writing shall be legible and in black ink. NY CPLR Rule 2101(a). Each paper served or filed shall be in the English language which, where practicable, shall be of ordinary usage. NY CPLR Rule 2101(b).

c. *Caption.* Each paper served or filed shall begin with a caption setting forth the name of the court, the venue, the title of the action, the nature of the paper and the index number of the action if one has been assigned. In all papers other than a summons, a complaint or a judgment it shall be sufficient to state the name of the first named party on each side with an appropriate indication of any omissions. NY CPLR Rule 2101(c).

i. *Further contents of first page.* After the first paper has been filed in each case the index number shall appear on the cover and first page to the right of the caption of every paper tendered for filing in the action. Each such cover and first page also shall contain an indication of the county of venue and a brief description of the nature of the paper and, where the case has been assigned to an individual judge, shall contain the name of the assigned judge to the right of the caption. NY R UNIF TRIAL CTS § 202.5(a); NY R UNIF TRIAL CTS § 202.5(b); NY R UNIF TRIAL CTS § 202.5(d)(1)(i).

ii. *ALBANY COUNTY: Request for oral argument.* A party may request oral argument on a motion by indicating such request on the first page of the notice of motion, order to show cause, or answering papers in the area across from the caption of the action/proceeding. NY R 3 JD SUP Doc. 1(B).

iii. *NEW YORK COUNTY: Request for oral argument.* Counsel who wish oral argument must so request conspicuously on the front of their papers. NY R NY CTY Procedure II(D).

d. *Index number.* No paper in an action in the supreme or a county court, other than an order submitted for signature to a judge out of court, shall be submitted for any purpose to the supreme or county court or to a clerk thereof unless there is endorsed on such paper the index number of the action assigned by the clerk of the county. NY CPLR § 8018(c).

i. *ALBANY COUNTY: Index number on all filed documents.* The index number, the request for judicial intervention number and the assigned justice's name shall appear on [all papers filed with the Court subsequent to the complaint]. NY R 3 JD SUP Doc. 1(A).

ii. *ERIE COUNTY: Index number after initial filing.* Cases that are initially commenced by the filing of papers with the NYSCEF system are identified as e-filed cases by assignment of an Index Number that has "800-899" as the first three (3) digits of the index number (i.e. 802391/2012). NY R ERIE E FIL Doc. 3(II). [The] Index Number must be affixed to all document submissions, filings, and communications to the Erie County Clerk and the Court. Cases that are converted from paper to e-filing shall retain the original index number. NY R ERIE E FIL Doc. 3(II).

iii. *KINGS COUNTY: Index number after initial filing.* In cases commenced electronically by the filing of initiating papers with the NYSCEF system and payment of the statutory fees, the Kings County Clerk will issue an NYSCEF designated index number and the filer shall be notified via the NYSCEF system of the index number assigned and filing date. Such index number must be affixed to all document submissions, filings and communications to the Kings County Clerk and Supreme Court. If counsel faces exigent circumstances that require accelerated assignment, counsel may contact Administration of the Kings County Clerk at kcco-efile@nycourts.gov, during normal business hours of the court. NY R L KINGS E FIL Doc. 1(B)(5).

iv. *NEW YORK COUNTY: Index number on hard copy filings.* Papers subsequently presented for filing in hardcopy format will be filed in this jacket. NY R NY CTY Procedure I(B). Index numbers take the form of six digits followed by a slash and the four digits of the year the case began, e.g., 340705/2018. The first or first two integers of the index number identify the type of case. If a case is commenced electronically, the second integer will be a "5", except as indicated otherwise in the list below. There are many tax certiorari matters e-filed annually and the index numbers therefor will normally run over into those with a "6" as the second integer, and the same will occur with general cases if necessary. The principal types of cases and their index number categories are listed in NY R NY CTY Procedure I(B). NY R NY CTY Procedure I(B); NY R NY CTY Procedure XI(A).

v. *ONONDAGA COUNTY: Index number.* The index number must be referenced on all e-filed documents and correspondence. All e-filed case index numbers will contain the letters "EF" between the year and the file number (for example, 2012EF9999). NY R ONDGA E FIL Protocol(B)(1).

vi. *QUEENS COUNTY: Index number on converted cases.* Cases originally commenced in hard-copy form but later converted to an E-file case, either by stipulation or order will bear a regular index number initially. The County Clerk will issue a new E-file index number. NY R L QUEENS E-FILE Doc. 1(B).

e. *Line spacing.* Every paper filed in court, if typewritten, shall have at least double space between each line, except for quotations and the names and addresses of attorneys appearing in the action. NY R UNIF TRIAL CTS § 202.5(a).

f. *Font size.* Each. . .paper printed or typed, served or filed, except an exhibit or a summons, shall be in clear type of no less than ten (10) point in size. NY CPLR Rule 2101(a).

i. Whenever a requirement relating to size of type is stated in point size, the type size requirement shall be deemed met if the x-height of the type is a minimum of forty-five percent (45%) of the specified point size. Each point shall be measured as .351 millimeter. The x-height size shall be measured as it appears on the page. The x-height is the height of the lower case letters, exclusive of ascenders or descenders. NY CPLR § 105(t).

g. *Margins.* Every paper filed in court shall have at least one (1) inch margins. NY R UNIF TRIAL CTS § 202.5(a).

h. *Citations*

i. *Civil practice law and rules.* NY CPLR § 101, et seq. shall be known as the civil practice law and rules, and may be cited as "CPLR". Reference to a provision in the civil practice law and rules may, except when such provision is being enacted or amended, be made without indicating whether it is a rule or section. NY CPLR § 101.

i. *Indorsement by attorney.* Each paper served or filed shall be indorsed with the name, address and telephone number of the attorney for the party serving or filing the paper, or if the party does not appear by attorney, with the name, address and telephone number of the party. NY CPLR Rule 2101(d).

j. *One-sided printing.* In addition, every paper filed in court, other than an exhibit or printed form, shall contain writing on one side only, except that papers that are fastened on the side may contain writing on both sides. NY R UNIF TRIAL CTS § 202.5(a).

k. *Use of copies authorized.* Except where otherwise specifically prescribed, copies, rather than originals, of all papers, including orders, affidavits and exhibits may be served or filed. Where it is required that the original be served or filed and the original is lost or withheld, the court may authorize a copy to be served or filed. NY CPLR Rule 2101(e).

i. Where a certified copy of a paper is required by law, an attorney admitted to practice in the courts of the state may certify that it has been compared by him with the original and found to be a true and complete copy. Such a certificate, when subscribed by such attorney, has the same effect as if made by a clerk. NY CPLR § 2105.

l. *Recycled paper.* It is the policy of the Unified Court System that litigants, where practicable, should file or submit to the courts of the Unified Court System of the State of New York papers printed or reproduced on recycled paper. Paper is considered recycled if it contains a minimum content of thirty percent (30%) waste paper. NY R UNIF TRIAL CTS § 215.2. The signature page of every paper filed or submitted to the court on recycled paper should bear the legend: "Printed [Reproduced] on Recycled Paper." NY R UNIF TRIAL CTS § 215.3.

m. *Form of request for judicial intervention; Copies.* A request for judicial intervention must be submitted, in duplicate, on a form authorized by the Chief of the Courts, with proof of service on the other parties to the action (but proof of service is not required where the application is ex parte). NY R UNIF TRIAL CTS § 202.6(a).

n. *KINGS COUNTY: Tabs on filings.* Motions, orders and other filed papers shall be indexed with protruding tabs. Clerks are required to reject papers that do not have protruding exhibit tabs, except papers in matrimonial cases and papers filed by pro se litigants. NY R L KINGS Pt. A, Papers.

o. *NEW YORK COUNTY: Length of briefs.* Unless advance permission otherwise is granted by the court for good cause, memoranda of law shall not exceed thirty (30) pages each (exclusive of table of contents and table of authorities) and affidavits/affirmations shall not exceed twenty-five (25) pages each. NY R NY CTY J RUL Rule 14(b).

p. *QUEENS COUNTY: Form and size of motion filings.* All motions filed in Queens Supreme Court-Civil Term, must adhere to the Motion Support rules and the rules of the assigned judge. NY R L QUEENS MOT SUP Doc. 1. Due to space limitations, the Motion Support Office cannot accept notices of motion/notices of petition and accompanying exhibits which measure greater than eight (8) inches. If your documents measure greater than eight (8) inches you are directed to submit only the notice of motion/notice of petition to the Motion Support Office and bring all exhibits to the calendar call on your return date. NY R L QUEENS MOT SUP Doc. 1.

2. *Form of electronic documents.* Each paper served or filed by electronic means, as defined in NY CPLR Rule 2103(f), shall be capable of being reproduced by the receiver so as to comply with the provisions of NY CPLR Rule 2101(a) through NY CPLR Rule 2101(d). NY CPLR Rule 2101(g).
   a. *File format.* All e-filed documents shall comply with the technical requirements set forth at the NYSCEF site. NY R UNIF TRIAL CTS § 202.5-b(d)(1)(i).
   b. *Heading of document.* The subject matter heading for each paper sent by electronic means must indicate that the matter being transmitted electronically is related to a court proceeding. NY CPLR Rule 2103(b)(7).
   c. *E-filed documents identification*
      i. *ERIE COUNTY.* E-filed cases must be readily identifiable and marked as such. If counsel presents papers to the Office of the Erie County Clerk or the Office of the Chief Clerk in a NYSCEF matter where authorized, counsel should alert the Clerk that the case is a NYSCEF matter. NY R ERIE E FIL Doc. 3(II).
      ii. *KINGS COUNTY.* The Supreme Court's Civil Case Information System ("CCIS") will further identify e-filed cases by the addition of a suffix to the index number (e.g. 500136/2006E). This suffix should be used on all documents filed with the court in e-filed matters. NY R L KINGS E FIL Doc. 1(A)(1).
3. *Signature blocks.* Every pleading, written motion, and other paper, served on another party or filed or submitted to the court shall be signed by an attorney, or by a party if the party is not represented by an attorney, with the name of the attorney or party clearly printed or typed directly below the signature. NY R CHIEF ADMIN § 130-1.1-a(a); NY R UNIF TRIAL CTS § 202.5(d)(1)(iv).
   a. *Printed name.* Beneath each signature shall be printed the name signed. NY CPLR Rule 2101(a).
   b. *Failure to sign.* Absent good cause shown, the court shall strike any unsigned paper if the omission of the signature is not corrected promptly after being called to the attention of the attorney or party. NY R CHIEF ADMIN § 130-1.1-a(a).
   c. *Signature as certification.* By signing a paper, an attorney or party certifies that, to the best of that person's knowledge, information and belief, formed after an inquiry reasonable under the circumstances the presentation of the paper or the contentions therein are not frivolous as defined in NY R CHIEF ADMIN § 130-1.1(c). NY R CHIEF ADMIN § 130-1.1-a(b)(1).
   d. *Electronic signatures.* A document shall be considered to have been signed by an attorney or party in compliance with NY R CHIEF ADMIN § 130-1.1-a if it has been signed by such attorney or party as provided in NY R UNIF TRIAL CTS § 202.5-b(e)(1) and it bears the signatory's name. NY R UNIF TRIAL CTS § 202.5-b(e)(2). An electronically filed document shall be considered to have been signed by, and shall be binding upon, the person identified as a signatory, if:
      i. It bears the physical signature of such person and is scanned into an electronic format that reproduces such signature; or
      ii. The signatory has electronically affixed the digital image of his or her signature to the document; or
      iii. It is electronically filed under the User ID and password of that person; or
      iv. In a tax certiorari action in which the parties have stipulated to this procedure, it is an initiating document that is electronically filed without the signature of the signatory in a form provided above in NY R UNIF TRIAL CTS § 202.5-b(e)(iv), provided that, prior to filing, the document is signed in full in hard copy (which hard copy must be preserved until the conclusion of all proceedings, including appeals, in the case in which it is filed); or
      v. In a small claims assessment review proceeding, it is a petition recorded by the NYSCEF site upon the filing of a text file as provided in NY R UNIF TRIAL CTS § 202.5-b(b)(1), provided that prior to filing, the document was signed in full in hard copy (which hard copy must be preserved until the conclusion of all proceedings in the matter, including article 78 (NY CPLR § 7801, et seq.) review and any appeals, and must be made available during the proceeding upon request of the respondent or the court); or
      vi. It otherwise bears the electronic signature of the signatory in a format conforming to such standards and requirements as may hereafter be established by the Chief Administrator. NY R UNIF TRIAL CTS § 202.5-b(e).
4. *Confidentiality of personal information.* No person may file any document available for public inspection with any state agency, political subdivision, or in any court of this state that contains a Social Security account number of any other person, unless such other person is a dependent child, or has consented to such filing, except as required by federal or state law or regulation, or by court rule. NY GEN BUS § 399-ddd. Submissions pursuant to e-filing procedures shall have the same confidentiality rights as paper documents. NY R UNIF TRIAL CTS § 202.5-b(k)(1).
   a. *Confidential personal information.* Except in the actions designated in NY R UNIF TRIAL CTS § 202.5(e)(1), or as

otherwise provided by rule or law or court order, and whether or not a sealing order is or has been sought, the parties shall omit or redact confidential personal information in papers submitted to the court for filing. For purposes of NY R UNIF TRIAL CTS § 202.5(e), confidential personal information ("CPI") means:

i. The taxpayer identification number of an individual or an entity, including a Social Security number, an employer identification number, and an individual taxpayer identification number, except the last four (4) digits thereof;

ii. The date of an individual's birth, except the year thereof;

iii. The full name of an individual known to be a minor, except the minor's initials;

iv. A financial account number, including a credit and/or debit card number, a bank account number, an investment account number, and/or an insurance account number, except the last four (4) digits or letters thereof; and

v. Any of the documents or testimony in a matrimonial action protected by NY DOM REL § 235 or evidence sealed by the court in such an action which are attached as exhibits or referenced in the papers filed in any other civil action. For purposes of NY R UNIF TRIAL CTS § 202.5, a matrimonial action shall mean: an action to annul a marriage or declare the nullity of a void marriage, an action or agreement for a separation, an action for a divorce, or an action or proceeding for custody, visitation, writ of habeus corpus, child support, maintenance or paternity. NY R UNIF TRIAL CTS § 202.5(e)(1).

vi. *ERIE COUNTY.* An attorney or unrepresented litigant filing a document via the NYSCEF system must comply with the requirements of NY R UNIF TRIAL CTS § 202.5(e) regarding the redaction of Confidential Personal Information and NY GEN BUS § 399-ddd(6) concerning the filing of documents containing Social Security Numbers. It is the sole responsibility of counsel or unrepresented litigant filing to be aware of and to comply with existing laws requiring non-disclosure of personal information contained in any document e-filed in NYSCEF. NY R ERIE E FIL Doc. 3(III)(G); NY R ERIE E FIL Doc. 3(III).

vii. *KINGS COUNTY.* An attorney or unrepresented litigant filing a document via the NYSCEF system must comply with the requirements of General Business Law § 399-dd(6), which often require redaction of any Social Security number that appear in the original document. The NYSCEF system automatically redacts portions of filed documents which apparently contain Social Security numbers pursuant to NY R UNIF TRIAL CTS § 202.5-b(k). In the event the filing party receives e-mail notice through NYSCEF that a Social Security number in a filed document has been redacted, and the filing party concludes such redaction is erroneous, the filer should click on the link provided in the e-mail to permit the County Clerk to revert the redaction. For Confidential Personal Information, see NY R UNIF TRIAL CTS § 202.5(e) and NY R L KINGS E FIL Doc. 1(B)(11). [Editor's note: the reference to General Business Law § 399-dd(6) is likely a reference to NY GEN BUS § 399-ddd(6)]. NY R L KINGS E FIL Doc. 1(B)(10); NY R L KINGS E FIL Doc. 1(K)(1).

viii. *NEW YORK COUNTY.* It is the responsibility of counsel and parties to comply with rules restricting disclosure of confidential personal information. Nevertheless, NYSCEF screens filings and endeavors to identify any that contain social security numbers. When such numbers are discovered through this process, NYSCEF will restrict portions of or all of such documents from public view. Where NYSCEF has redacted what it believes to be a social security number, it will transmit to the filer a notice advising of the action taken and requesting that the filer review the matter and provide notification as set forth in the notice if the redaction has been made in error. NY R NY CTY E FIL Doc. 2(K)(1); NY R NY CTY J RUL Rule A-1. Documents filed in the past in "secure status" under a procedure no longer in place will retain that status unless otherwise directed by the court. NY R NY CTY E FIL Doc. 2(K)(2).

b. *Submission of confidential personal information.* Where a person submitting a paper to a court for filing believes in good faith that the inclusion of the full confidential personal information described in NY R UNIF TRIAL CTS § 202.5(e)(1) is material and necessary to the adjudication of the action or proceeding before the court, he or she may apply to the court for leave to serve and file together with a paper in which such information has been set forth in abbreviated form a confidential affidavit or affirmation setting forth the same information in unabbreviated form, appropriately referenced to the page or pages of the paper at which the abbreviated form appears. NY R UNIF TRIAL CTS § 202.5(e)(3).

c. *Home addresses.* For information on when home addresses and other personal information must be redacted, refer to NY CPLR Rule 2103-a.

5. *Defective papers.* A defect in the form of a paper, if a substantial right of a party is not prejudiced, shall be disregarded by the court, and leave to correct shall be freely given. NY CPLR Rule 2101(f). Papers that are stapled or bound securely shall not be rejected for filing simply because they are not bound with a backer of any kind. NY R UNIF TRIAL CTS § 202.5(a).

A paper filed in accordance with the rules of the chief administrator or any local rule or practice established by the court shall be deemed filed. NY CPLR Rule 2102(b).

a. *Objection to defective papers.* The party on whom a paper is served shall be deemed to have waived objection to any defect in form unless, within fifteen (15) days after the receipt thereof, the party on whom the paper is served returns the paper to the party serving it with a statement of particular objections. NY CPLR Rule 2101(f).

F. Filing and Service Requirements

1. *Filing requirements.* Except where otherwise prescribed by law or order of court, papers required to be filed shall be filed with the clerk of the court in which the action is triable. In an action or proceeding in supreme or court, papers required to be filed shall be filed with the clerk of the county in which the proceeding is brought. NY CPLR Rule 2102(a).

a. *Furnishing papers to the court.* Each party shall furnish to the court all papers served by him. The moving party shall furnish at the hearing all other papers not already in the possession of the court necessary to the consideration of the questions involved. Where such papers are in the possession of an adverse party, they shall be produced by him at the hearing on notice served with the motion papers. Only papers served in accordance with the provisions of NY CPLR Rule 2214 shall be read in support of, or in opposition to, the motion, unless the court for good cause shall otherwise direct. NY CPLR Rule 2214(c).

i. *Submission to judge.* All papers for signature or consideration of the court shall be presented to the clerk of the trial court in the appropriate courtroom or clerk's office, except that where the clerk is unavailable or the judge so directs, papers may be submitted to the judge and a copy filed with the clerk at the first available opportunity. All papers for any judge that are filed in the clerk's office shall be promptly delivered to the judge by the clerk. The papers shall be clearly addressed to the judge for whom they are intended and prominently show the nature of the papers, the title and index number of the action in which they are filed, the judge's name and the name of the attorney or party submitting them. NY R UNIF TRIAL CTS § 202.5(b).

ii. *BRONX COUNTY: Approval of motions before filing.* All motion papers must be approved by the Motion Support Office, Supreme Court, Civil Term, room 217, before the motion papers are filed and the appropriate fee paid to the County Clerk. NY R BRONX FIL R Doc. 1.

iii. *ERIE COUNTY: Filing motions.* A motion on notice or a notice of petition in a NYSCEF case shall be filed through the NYSCEF system and must be accompanied by a Request for Judicial Intervention if the motion is being filed upon commencement of the action or if the matter has not yet been assigned to an IAS Justice. In addition, cross motions with the appropriate filing fees and opposition and reply papers must be submitted via the NYSCEF system. NY R ERIE E FIL Doc. 3(V)(A).

iv. *NEW YORK COUNTY: Filing hard copies.* Where in the narrow circumstances described by the e-filing rules a motion is made in hard-copy form or opposition papers are submitted in such form in an e-filed case, the hard-copy documents shall be submitted in the same way papers are submitted in non-e-filed cases, except that there shall be firmly affixed to each separate document or group of documents, as the back page facing out, a Notice of Hard Copy Submission—E-Filed Case. NY R NY CTY Procedure II(A). For more information on filing in hard copy cases, refer to NY R NY CTY Procedure II(A).

v. *ONONDAGA COUNTY: Submission of responsive papers and cross-motions.* Cross-motions, opposition and reply papers must be submitted online. NY R ONDGA E FIL Protocol(B)(9)(e). Motions and Orders to Show Cause are assigned a sequence number by the system. Counsel must be sure that cross motions and other filings correspond with the correct sequence number so that a cross motion will not be associated with the wrong original motion. NY R ONDGA E FIL Protocol(B)(9)(f).

b. *Electronic filing.* On consent, documents may be filed and served by electronic means in Supreme Court in such civil actions and in such counties as shall be authorized by order of the Chief Administrator of the Courts and only to the extent and in the manner provided in NY R UNIF TRIAL CTS § 202.5-b. NY R UNIF TRIAL CTS § 202.5-b(a)(1). For the definitions of terms used in electronic filing, refer to NY R UNIF TRIAL CTS § 202.5-b(a)(2).

i. *E-filing mandatory.* In any action subject to e-filing, all documents required to be filed with the court by an e-filing party shall be filed and served electronically, except as provided in NY R UNIF TRIAL CTS § 202.5-b. NY R UNIF TRIAL CTS § 202.5-b(d)(1)(i).

- *ERIE COUNTY.* Case types currently eligible and accepted for e-filing are listed at the NYSCEF website. Note that some actions or special proceedings, (i.e., name changes) which are otherwise subject to mandatory e-filing, if commenced by unrepresented litigants will NOT be maintained in the NYSCEF system; individual cases may be found either at NYSCEF or in the Erie County Clerk's online records system. NY R ERIE E FIL Doc. 3(I)(E).

- *KINGS COUNTY.* Cases that are commenced by filing of the initiating papers with NYSCEF are identified as e-filed cases by assignment of a special index number (i.e., Index Numbers beginning with 500,000). NY R L KINGS E FIL Doc. 1(A)(1). All cases required to be e-filed are listed in Uniform Rule 202.5-bb (Mandatory E-Filing Rules) and on the NYSCEF website. All such cases must be commenced by filing with the County Clerk electronically through NYSCEF and all subsequent documents in such cases must be e-filed. Any questions regarding mandatory e-filing in Kings County can be e-mailed to kcco-efile@nycourts.gov. NY R L KINGS E FIL Doc. 1(A)(2).
- *NEW YORK COUNTY.* Unless otherwise provided in the Rules or in NY R NY CTY E FIL Doc. 2 or where a special exemption is granted due to physical requirements (e.g., oversized maps; see NY R NY CTY E FIL Doc. 2(B)(10)), all documents to be filed with the court in a NYSCEF case, including all documents on motions and all letters to the court (where permitted), must be filed with the NYSCEF system. Documents that attorneys would not ordinarily file with the court in a hard-copy case need not be e-filed. Unless otherwise provided by the E-Filing Rules or this Protocol, in e-filed cases the County Clerk and the court will not accept documents filed in paper form. NY R NY CTY E FIL Doc. 2(B)(1). E-filing is mandatory in all types of cases (other than election law, matrimonial, Art. 78, and Mental Hygiene Law matters, and Art. 70 habeas corpus proceedings) that are commenced in this court on or after February 19, 2013. All such cases must be commenced by filing with the County Clerk electronically through NYSCEF and all subsequent documents in such cases must be e-filed. NY R NY CTY E FIL Doc. 2(A)(2)(a). For more information, including information on consensual e-filing and filing scanned hard copy documents, refer to NY R NY CTY E FIL Doc. 2(A)(2).
- *QUEENS COUNTY.* All authorized Torts, Commercial and Tax Certiorari cases may be commenced by E-Filing, however all parties must consent for the action to continue as an E-file case. NY R L QUEENS E-FILE Doc. 1(A). All papers to be filed with the court in an E-filed case shall be filed on-line with the E-file system except as directed by the court. Papers that attorneys would not ordinarily file with the court in a hard-copy case need not be filed in an E-filed matter. NY R L QUEENS E-FILE Doc. 1(E)(2).

ii. *Who may file.* Documents may be filed or served electronically only by a person who has registered as an authorized e-filing user or as otherwise provided in NY R UNIF TRIAL CTS § 202.5-b(c). NY R UNIF TRIAL CTS § 202.5-b(c)(1).

iii. *When filing made.* Documents may be transmitted at any time of the day or night to the NYSCEF site. A document other than an order or judgment is filed when its electronic transmission or, in the case of a petition that is e-filed by submission of a text file as provided in NY R UNIF TRIAL CTS § 202.5-b(b)(1), the electronic transmission of the text file is recorded at that site, provided, however, that where payment of a fee is required upon the filing of a document, the document is not filed until transmission of the document and the information or form or information as required in NY R UNIF TRIAL CTS § 202.5-b(d)(2)(i), NY R UNIF TRIAL CTS § 202.5-b(d)(2)(ii) or NY R UNIF TRIAL CTS § 202.5-b(d)(2)(iii) has been recorded at the NYSCEF site; or, if no transmission of that information or form or information is recorded, where permitted by the County Clerk, until payment is presented to the County Clerk. NY R UNIF TRIAL CTS § 202.5-b(d)(3)(i).

iv. *Notification of filing.* No later than the close of business on the business day following the electronic filing of a document, a notification, in a form prescribed by the Chief Administrator, shall be transmitted electronically by the NYSCEF site to the person filing such document and the e-mail service addresses of all other participating parties in such action. NY R UNIF TRIAL CTS § 202.5-b(d)(3)(ii).

v. *Removal of confidential information and other corrections.* If a document filed electronically is subsequently discovered to contain confidential data—including but not limited to trade secrets, information protected by confidentiality agreement, or personal confidential information as defined by statute or court rule—or otherwise to have been filed in error, the filer or another party or affected person may (1) notify the parties and any non-party filers in the action of the confidentiality issue or other error raised by the filing, and of his or her intention to seek judicial relief to correct the filing: (2) following such notification, request that the appropriate County Clerk, exercising his or her administrative discretion, place the document temporarily in "restricted" status on the NYSCEF site, to be made available for viewing by court staff and the parties but not the general public; and (3) file an application to correct the filing by order to show cause within five (5) business days of such notification (or such time as the court may direct), including a request for preliminary injunctive relief limiting interim disclosure of the document at issue. Unless otherwise directed by the court, any document placed in restricted status in response to such a request shall be returned to public view upon expiration of this five (5) day

period. The Chief Administrator of the Courts shall promulgate forms to implement this process. NY R UNIF TRIAL CTS § 202.5-b(d)(3)(iii).

- *KINGS COUNTY.* For information on what to do when a document was erroneously filed with confidential information, refer to NY R L KINGS E FIL Doc. 1(B)(11).
- *NEW YORK COUNTY.* For information on what to do when a document was erroneously filed with confidential information, refer to NY R NY CTY E FIL Doc. 2(B)(8).
- *QUEENS COUNTY.* For information on what to do when a document was erroneously filed with confidential information, refer to NY R L QUEENS E-FILE Doc. 1(E)(7).

vi. *Documents requiring judge's signature.* Except where the court directs otherwise, any document that requires a judge's signature shall be transmitted electronically and in hard copy to the court. NY R UNIF TRIAL CTS § 202.5-b(d)(6).

vii. *Documents which would be inconvenient to file electronically; Hard copies.* Notwithstanding any other provision of NY R UNIF TRIAL CTS § 202.5-b, and subject to such guidelines as may be established by the Chief Administrative Judge, the County Clerk or his or her designee may require or permit a party to file in hard copy, in accordance with procedures set by the County Clerk or designee, an exhibit or other document which it is impractical or inconvenient to file electronically. NY R UNIF TRIAL CTS § 202.5-b(d)(7).

- *ERIE COUNTY.* Please contact the Supervisor of Actions & Proceedings, Erie County Clerk's Office by calling (716) 858-6662 or the Deputy County Clerk—Legal at (716) 858-6348 for information. NY R ERIE E FIL Doc. 3(III)(F).
- *KINGS COUNTY.* With limited exceptions, as set forth in the Uniform Rules and herein, all documents to be filed with the court in a NYSCEF case shall be filed online via the NYSCEF system. However, should the size, consistency or context of a hard copy document preclude electronic filing, the user shall electronically file a "Notice of Hard Copy Submission—E-Filed Cases" form EFM-3. Any hard copy submitted pursuant to NY R L KINGS E FIL Doc. 1(B)(9) shall include, as a cover page firmly fastened thereto, a copy of the Confirmation Notice received from the NYSCEF site confirming receipt of the "Notice of Hard Copy Submission—E-Filed Cases". Any party may object to such hard copy filing. The Court, in response to such objection, may, following the hard copy filing, fashion such relief as it deems appropriate pursuant to and in furtherance of the Uniform Rules and NY R L KINGS E FIL Doc. 1, including, but not limited to, an Order directing the filing party to file such documents online via the NYSCEF system. When exhibits are impractical to file pursuant to NY R UNIF TRIAL CTS § 202.5-b(d)(7), an additional "Notice of Hard Copy Exhibit Filing" form EFM-4 is required to be submitted. NY R L KINGS E FIL Doc. 1(B)(9).
- *NEW YORK COUNTY.* If a filer needs to submit unusual exhibits in original form that cannot practically be e-filed, such as oversized maps or electronic recordings, the filer should consult with the County Clerk's E-File Department by telephone at 646-386-3737 (procedural questions only) or by e-mail at ccnyef@nycourts.gov, which will normally require that the filer retain custody of the original subject to possible future directives of the court. NY R NY CTY E FIL Doc. 2(B)(10). In such instances, the filing counsel shall file with NYSCEF a "placeholder" in the form of a Notice of Hard Copy Exhibit Filing (NYSCEF Form EF 21). The Notice should be uploaded to NYSCEF as document type "Exhibit" and the filer should indicate in the "Additional Document Information" field that the filer is retaining custody of the original. Failure to e-file the Notice may result in a gap in the official record of the court. NY R NY CTY E FIL Doc. 2(B)(10).

viii. *Documents containing sensitive or proprietary information.* In an action subject to e-filing, any person may apply for an order prohibiting or restricting the electronic filing in the action of specifically identified materials on the grounds that such materials are subject to copyright or other proprietary rights, or trade secret or other privacy interests, and that electronic filing in the action is likely to result in substantial prejudice to those rights or interests. NY R UNIF TRIAL CTS § 202.5-b(k)(2).

ix. *Refusal to accept paper filings.* In accordance with NY CPLR Rule 2102(c), a County Clerk and a chief clerk of the Supreme Court or County Court, as appropriate, shall refuse to accept for filing papers filed in actions and proceedings when the paper sought to be filed:

- Is in an action subject to electronic filing pursuant to Rules of the Chief Administrator,
- Is not being filed electronically, and

- Does not include the notice required by NY R UNIF TRIAL CTS § 202.5-b(d)(1). NY R UNIF TRIAL CTS § 202.5(d)(1)(v); NY R UNIF TRIAL CTS § 202.5-bb(d).

x. *Emergency filings; Hard copies.* For information on when an emergency filing may be filed and served in hard copy, refer to NY R UNIF TRIAL CTS § 202.5-b(d)(1)(ii), NY R UNIF TRIAL CTS § 202.5-b(d)(1)(iii) and NY R UNIF TRIAL CTS § 202.5-bb(c)(3).

- *KINGS COUNTY.* Under the rules, a participating emergency e-filer must electronically file the documents initially filed in hard copy form within three (3) business days of the emergency filing; the originals will be discarded after the documents have been processed and the failure to e-file as required will therefore lead to an incomplete record. NY R L KINGS E FIL Doc. 1(B)(3).
- *NEW YORK COUNTY.* Occasionally an emergency will arise requiring expedited entry of a document with the County Clerk (e.g., an order issued in the courtroom after a conference or argument of a critical matter), such as for purposes of an immediate appeal. Expedition can be achieved by the Part as follows: the document should be carried by a Court Officer or staff member to the General Clerk's Office to assure immediate and proper recordation in the computer and, as appropriate, the posting of the document to NYSCEF or the Supreme Court Records On-Line Library ("Scroll"). The court will accommodate counsel in emergencies. NY R NY CTY Procedure XI(A).
- *NEW YORK COUNTY.* For more information on how to bring emergency matters before the court, refer to NY R NY CTY Procedure IV.

xi. *Technical failures.* The NYSCEF site shall be considered to be subject to a technical failure on a given day if the site is unable to accept filings or provide access to filed documents continuously or intermittently over the course of any period of time greater than one (1) hour after 12:00 noon of that day. Notice of all such technical failures shall be provided on the site. NY R UNIF TRIAL CTS § 202.5-b(i).

- When e-filing is hindered by a technical failure, a party may file with the appropriate clerk and serve in hard copy. NY R UNIF TRIAL CTS § 202.5-b(i). In the event an attorney or party shall file and serve documents in hard copy pursuant to NY R UNIF TRIAL CTS § 202.5-b(i), each such document shall include the notice required by NY R UNIF TRIAL CTS § 202.5-b(d)(1), and the filer shall file those documents with the NYSCEF site within three (3) business days after restoration of normal operations at that site. NY R UNIF TRIAL CTS § 202.5-b(i).
- With the exception of deadlines that by law cannot be extended, the time for filing of any document that is delayed due to technical failure of the site shall be extended for one (1) day for each day on which such failure occurs, unless otherwise ordered by the court. NY R UNIF TRIAL CTS § 202.5-b(i).
- *ERIE COUNTY.* When filing by electronic means is hindered by a technical failure, please refer to the NY R UNIF TRIAL CTS § 202.5-b(i). NY R ERIE E FIL Doc. 3(III)(K).
- *KINGS COUNTY.* When filing by electronic means is hindered by a NYSCEF technical failure (as set forth in NY R UNIF TRIAL CTS § 202.5-b(i)), a party may file with the appropriate Clerk in hard copy. Except for deadlines that by law cannot be extended (e.g. Statute of limitations, Notice of Appeal), the time for filing of any document that is delayed due to technical failure of the NYSCEF system shall be extended for one day for each day on which such failure occurs, unless otherwise ordered by the court. NY R L KINGS E FIL Doc. 1(B)(13).
- *ONONDAGA COUNTY.* When filing by electronic means is hindered by a technical failure (as set forth in NY R UNIF TRIAL CTS § 202.5-b(h)(3)(i)), a party may file a hard copy with the County Clerk. With the exception of deadlines that by law cannot be extended (e.g., a statute of limitations or the deadline for filing a Notice of Appeal), the time for filing of any document that is delayed due to technical failure of the NYSCEF system will be extended for one day for each day on which such failure occurs, unless otherwise ordered by the court. A "Notice of Hard Copy Filing Submission—E-Filed Case' must accompany any documents not filed via NYSCEF. NY R ONDGA E FIL Protocol(B)(8).

xii. *Filing fees.* For information on what information must be provided to pay filing fees, refer to NY R UNIF TRIAL CTS § 202.5-b(d)(2).

xiii. *Exemption from e-filing.* For information on exemptions from e-filing, refer to NY R UNIF TRIAL CTS § 202.5-bb(e).

xiv. *Filing exhibits*

- *ERIE COUNTY.* In the NYSCEF system, each exhibit must be uploaded as a separate .pdf file. After

uploading a primary document, please choose the document type "Exhibit" and enter the appropriate number or letter and a brief description of the exhibit; each exhibit should bear a separate cover sheet clearly marked as "Exhibit A," "Exhibit B," etc. "Exhibit A" or "Exhibit B" is unacceptable as a brief description of the exhibit. Exhibits, where referenced in a signed Order as attached or affixed shall be uploaded with the signed Order as one .pdf document. NY R ERIE E FIL Doc. 3(III)(H); NY R ERIE E FIL Doc. 3(V)(D).

- *KINGS COUNTY.* In the NYSCEF system, each exhibit should be uploaded as a separate PDF file. After uploading a primary document, please choose the document type "Exhibit", enter the appropriate number or letter, and be sure to place a check mark to the right of "Attach to main document". Each exhibit shall bear a separate cover sheet clearly marked as Exhibit A, Exhibit B, etc. NY R L KINGS E FIL Doc. 1(B)(12). Whenever possible, attorneys submitting exhibits in NYSCEF cases should make each exhibit a separate attachment to an affidavit/affirmation in the system (i.e., multiple exhibits should not be filed as a single PDF). NY R L KINGS E FIL Doc. 1(D)(1).
- *NEW YORK COUNTY.* Attorneys submitting exhibits in NYSCEF cases should make each exhibit a separate attachment to an affidavit/affirmation in the system; i.e., exhibits should not be filed as a single PDF-A together with the affidavit/affirmation or grouped together as a single PDF-A attachment because either of these two formats makes it difficult for the Justice to locate particular exhibits as needed. Counsel must also include appropriate descriptive language in the "Additional Document Information" field in NYSCEF. NY R NY CTY E FIL Doc. 2(D)(6).
- *ONONDAGA COUNTY.* All exhibits in e-filed cases must be e-filed individually as separate attachments. NY R ONDGA E FIL Protocol(B)(9)(b).

xv. *Correcting documents*

- *ERIE COUNTY.* Submission of documents which, upon examination, require correction or addition will result in notification to the filer advising that the document has been returned for correction. The filer shall make the required corrections and/or additions as indicated in the e-mail transmission sent by the County Clerk or Part Clerk through the NYSCEF site. The corrected documents may be resubmitted using the "Re-file this document" link highlighted in the filer's document list for the respective case. Please note that in the case of multiple submissions, all related documents filed at the same time may be removed from the case record and returned until all documents are properly submitted. NY R ERIE E FIL Doc. 3(III)(J).
- *KINGS COUNTY.* Submission of documents which, upon examination, require correction or addition will result in notification to the filer advising that there is a problem with a document. The filer shall make the required corrections and/or additions and resubmit the corrected document using the "Refile this document" link. In the event a document is returned for correction, the original file date will be preserved. For corrections of documents filed with the Kings County Clerk which require a court order, refer to the procedure in NY R UNIF TRIAL CTS § 202.5-b(d)(3)(iii) and NY R L KINGS E FIL Doc. 1(B)(11). NY R L KINGS E FIL Doc. 1(B)(3).
- *ONONDAGA COUNTY.* If there is an error or an additional document is required, the system will notify the filing party, who will make the corrections/additions and resubmit them online. NY R ONDGA E FIL Protocol(B)(6).
- *QUEENS COUNTY.* Generally speaking, documents that have been E-filed will not thereafter be deleted by the County Clerk from NYCEF because the filer asserts that the filing contains an error or a significant omission. When the filer wishes to correct a perceived error or omission in a filed document, he or she should file an amended version of the document, with the original remaining on file, or else obtain a court order providing for deletion of the original. The County Clerk will only delete a document upon request of the filer or on the County Clerk's own initiative when it is obvious from the face of the document alone that the filer made a fundamental error and never intended to file the document that was filed (e.g., a completely unrelated non-litigation document, a different case, or a wrong county). The County Clerk will advise the filer when any such fundamental errors are detected. NY R L QUEENS E-FILE Doc. 1(E)(6).

c. *Facsimile filing.* In the Supreme Court, facsimile filing shall be limited to commercial claims and tax certiorari, conservatorship, and mental hygiene proceedings in Monroe, Westchester, New York and Suffolk Counties. NY R UNIF TRIAL CTS § 202.5-a(a)(1). Refer to NY R UNIF TRIAL CTS § 202.5-a for information on the procedures for facsimile filing.

i. *NEW YORK COUNTY.* Unless indicated otherwise by the court in a particular case or in NY R NY CTY J RUL Doc. 1, Justices do not accept papers by fax. NY R NY CTY J RUL Rule 4.

d. *ERIE COUNTY: Filing request for judicial intervention.* An RJI in a NYSCEF case shall be filed via the NYSCEF system and will be filed after all other documents have been uploaded. The filer may choose between filing a .pdf image of the prepared RJI and any Addendum or having the system prepare the RJI which shall conform to Uniform Rules. Addenda, such as the Commercial Division Addendum, if prepared by the filer must be filed simultaneously with and attached to an RJI and uploaded as one .pdf document with the RJI. If the RJI is prepared by the e-filing system, no separate Addendum is required. Whether or not the filer elects to allow NYSCEF to create the RJI or chooses to upload a prepared RJI, data in addition to the nature of the judicial intervention, including information that appears on any Addenda will be collected through completion of the fields presented. If the filing of the RJI is accomplished through a filing agent, a prepared RJI and Addendum must be filed in lieu of the creation of the RJI by the NYSCEF system, as the RJI must be signed by the attorney. NY R ERIE E FIL Doc. 3(IV). For information on RJIs in specific types of action, refer to NY R ERIE E FIL Doc. 3(IV).

2. *Service requirements*

a. *Who may serve.* Except where otherwise prescribed by law or order of court, papers may be served by any person not a party of the age of eighteen years or over. NY CPLR Rule 2103(a).

b. *Service upon attorney.* Except where otherwise prescribed by law or order of court, papers to be served upon a party in a pending action shall be served upon the party's attorney. Where the same attorney appears for two or more parties, only one (1) copy need be served upon the attorney. Such service upon an attorney shall be made:

i. By delivering the paper to the attorney personally. NY CPLR Rule 2103(b)(1).

ii. By mailing the paper to the attorney at the address designated by that attorney for that purpose or, if none is designated, at the attorney's last known address; service by mail shall be complete upon mailing. NY CPLR Rule 2103(b)(2).

- *BRONX COUNTY.* Service by mail must be within the state. NY R BRONX FIL R Doc. 3.

iii. If the attorney's office is open, by leaving the paper with a person in charge, or if no person is in charge, by leaving it in a conspicuous place; or if the attorney's office is not open, by depositing the paper, enclosed in a sealed wrapper directed to the attorney, in the attorney's office letter drop or box. NY CPLR Rule 2103(b)(3).

iv. By leaving it at the attorney's residence within the state with a person of suitable age and discretion. Service upon an attorney shall not be made at the attorney's residence unless service at the attorney's office cannot be made. NY CPLR Rule 2103(b)(4).

v. By transmitting the paper to the attorney by facsimile transmission, provided that a facsimile telephone number is designated by the attorney for that purpose. Service by facsimile transmission shall be complete upon the receipt by the sender of a signal from the equipment of the attorney served indicating that the transmission was received, and the mailing of a copy of the paper to that attorney. The designation of a facsimile telephone number in the address block subscribed on a paper served or filed in the course of an action or proceeding shall constitute consent to service by facsimile transmission in accordance with NY CPLR Rule 2103(b)(5). An attorney may change or rescind a facsimile telephone number by serving a notice on the other parties. NY CPLR Rule 2103(b)(5).

vi. By dispatching the paper to the attorney by overnight delivery service at the address designated by the attorney for that purpose or, if none is designated, at the attorney's last known address. Service by overnight delivery service shall be complete upon deposit of the paper enclosed in a properly addressed wrapper into the custody of the overnight delivery service for overnight delivery, prior to the latest time designated by the overnight delivery service for overnight delivery. "Overnight delivery service" means any delivery service which regularly accepts items for overnight delivery to any address in the state. NY CPLR Rule 2103(b)(6).

vii. By transmitting the paper to the attorney by electronic means where and in the manner authorized by the chief administrator of the courts by rule and, unless such rule shall otherwise provide, such transmission shall be upon the party's written consent. The subject matter heading for each paper sent by electronic means must indicate that the matter being transmitted electronically is related to a court proceeding. NY CPLR Rule 2103(b)(7).

- *KINGS COUNTY.* Pursuant to the E-Filing Rules, service of interlocutory documents is made by posting a document to the NYSCEF site, which automatically and immediately transmits an email notice of the filing, including a link to the document, to all participating counsel and unrepresented litigants on the case. The Rules also authorize service by other methods permitted by the CPLR. If service by such other method is made, proof of service must be filed with NYSCEF. NY R L KINGS E FIL Doc. 1(I).
- *NEW YORK COUNTY.* Service. . .will be made automatically through NYSCEF upon all participating

counsel and unrepresented parties in the case. There are limited exceptions to the requirement for e-filing in the covered kinds of cases. NY R NY CTY Procedure XI(A). Pursuant to the E-Filing Rules, service of interlocutory documents is made by posting a document to the NYSCEF site, which automatically and immediately transmits an e-mail notice of the filing, including a link to the document, to all participating counsel and unrepresented litigants on the case. The Rules also authorize service by other methods permitted by the CPLR. If service by such a method is made, proof of service must be filed with NYSCEF. NY R NY CTY E FIL Doc. 2(I).

- *QUEENS COUNTY.* Filing with the system permits counsel to serve the papers electronically pursuant to NY R UNIF TRIAL CTS § 202.5-b(f) once consent to E-Filing has been filed on-line. Consult NY R UNIF TRIAL CTS § 202.5-bb(c) for service in mandatory e-filing. Any required proof of service should be E-filed as a separate document. NY R L QUEENS E-FILE Doc. 1(E)(4).

c. *Electronic service mandatory; Consenting to electronic service; How electronic service may be made.* Except as otherwise provided in NY R UNIF TRIAL CTS § 202.5-bb, filing and service of all documents in an action that has been commenced electronically in accordance with NY R UNIF TRIAL CTS § 202.5-bb shall be by electronic means. NY R UNIF TRIAL CTS § 202.5-bb(c)(1).

i. *Party's consent required for certain e-filing.* After commencement of an action wherein e-filing is authorized, documents may be electronically filed and served, but only by, and electronic service shall be made only upon, a party or parties who have consented thereto. NY R UNIF TRIAL CTS § 202.5-b(b)(2)(i).

- A consent to e-filing in an action shall state that the party providing it agrees to the use of e-filing in the action and to be bound by the filing and service provisions in NY R UNIF TRIAL CTS § 202.5-b. NY R UNIF TRIAL CTS § 202.5-b(b)(2)(ii).

ii. *Address for service; Duty to notify as to changes.* The e-mail service address recorded at the time of registration is the e-mail address at which service of interlocutory documents on that party may be made through notification transmitted by the NYSCEF site. It is the responsibility of each filing user to monitor that address and promptly notify the Resource Center in the event of a change in his or her e-mail service address. NY R UNIF TRIAL CTS § 202.5-b(f)(2)(i).

iii. *How service made.* An e-filing party causes service of an interlocutory document to be made upon another party participating in e-filing by filing the document electronically. Upon receipt of an interlocutory document, the NYSCEF site shall automatically transmit electronic notification to all e-mail service addresses in such action. NY R UNIF TRIAL CTS § 202.5-b(f)(2)(ii).

- Except as provided otherwise in NY R UNIF TRIAL CTS § 202.5-b(h)(3), the electronic transmission of the notification shall constitute service of the document on the e-mail service addresses identified therein; however, such service will not be effective if the filing party learns that the notification did not reach the address of the person to be served. Proof of such service will be recorded on the NYSCEF site. A party may, however, utilize other service methods permitted by the CPLR provided that, if one of such other methods is used, proof of that service shall be filed electronically. NY R UNIF TRIAL CTS § 202.5-b(f)(2)(ii).

iv. *Signatures on hard copies; Proof of service filed electronically.* When an e-filing party serves a document in hard copy on a non-participating party, the document served shall bear full signatures of all signatories and proof of such service shall be filed electronically. NY R UNIF TRIAL CTS § 202.5-b(b)(2)(i).

- *ERIE COUNTY.* In the NYSCEF system, each Affidavit of Service must be uploaded as a separate .pdf file. After uploading the Affidavit, please choose the document type: "Affirmation/Affidavit of Service" and enter the name of the party served as Additional Document Information. NY R ERIE E FIL Doc. 3(III)(I); NY R ERIE E FIL Doc. 3(V)(F).

v. *Effect of failure to consent.* A party's failure to consent to participation in electronic filing and service shall not bar any other party to the action from filing documents electronically with the County Clerk and the court or serving documents upon any other party who has consented to participation. A party who has not consented to participation shall file documents with the court and the County Clerk, and serve and be served with documents, in hard copy. NY R UNIF TRIAL CTS § 202.5-b(b)(2)(i).

d. *Service upon party.* If a party has not appeared by an attorney or the party's attorney cannot be served, service shall be upon the party by a method specified in NY CPLR Rule 2103(b)(1), NY CPLR Rule 2103(b)(2), NY CPLR Rule 2103(b)(4), NY CPLR Rule 2103(b)(5) or NY CPLR Rule 2103(b)(6). NY CPLR Rule 2103(c).

e. *Service on all parties.* Each paper served on any party shall be served on every other party who has appeared, except

as otherwise may be provided by court order or as provided in NY CPLR § 3012 or in NY CPLR § 3215(f). Upon demand by a party, the plaintiff shall supply that party with a list of those who have appeared and the names and addresses of their attorneys. NY CPLR Rule 2103(e).

f. *Service by filing.* If a paper cannot be served by any of the methods specified in NY CPLR Rule 2103(b) and NY CPLR Rule 2103(c), service may be made by filing the paper as if it were a paper required to be filed. NY CPLR Rule 2103(d).

g. *Definitions.* For the purposes of NY CPLR Rule 2103:

i. "Mailing" means the deposit of a paper enclosed in a first class postpaid wrapper, addressed to the address designated by a person for that purpose or, if none is designated, at that person's last known address, in a post office or official depository under the exclusive care and custody of the United States Postal Service within the state;

ii. "Electronic means" means any method of transmission of information between computers or other machines designed for the purpose of sending and receiving such transmissions, and which allows the recipient to reproduce the information transmitted in a tangible medium of expression;

iii. "Facsimile transmission" means any method of transmission of documents to a facsimile machine at a remote location which can automatically produce a tangible copy of such documents. NY CPLR Rule 2103(f).

h. *No service on parties in default.* When a party is in default for failure to appear, he shall not be entitled to notice or service of any copy required under NY CPLR § 3101, et seq. NY CPLR Rule 3105.

G. Hearings

1. *Oral argument.* Motion papers received by the clerk of the court on or before the return date shall be deemed submitted as of the return date. The assigned judge, in his or her discretion or at the request of a party, thereafter may determine that any motion be orally argued and may fix a time for oral argument. NY R UNIF TRIAL CTS § 202.8(d).

a. A party requesting oral argument shall set forth such request in its notice of motion or in its order to show cause or on the first page of the answering papers, as the case may be. Where all parties to a motion request oral argument, oral argument shall be granted unless the court shall determine it to be unnecessary. NY R UNIF TRIAL CTS § 202.8(d).

b. Where a motion is brought on by order to show cause, the court may set forth in the order that oral argument is required on the return date of the motion. NY R UNIF TRIAL CTS § 202.8(d).

i. *BRONX COUNTY.* All orders to show cause, with the exception of orders to show cause that are returnable in the City Part, the STP Part, the Matrimonial Part and the Preliminary/Compliance Conference Part (IA-11), submitted on or after August 25, 2003, will be returnable on a Monday in the assigned Justice's part and appear on his or her motion calendar. Appearances will be required on orders to show cause. NY R BRONX FIL R Doc. 8. A motion on notice or a notice of petition in a New York Supreme Court E-File (hereafter known as NYSCEF) case, as in others, shall be made returnable in the Motion Support Office (Room 217). NY R BRONX E FIL R Doc. 1(1).

- After a motion/petition and notice are filed with the NYSCEF system, the Motion Support Office will automatically place the motion/proceeding on the submit calendar in the Motion Support Office (Room 217) for the return date. No appearance or other action by the filing attorney is required in order for the motion to be calendared if the motion fee is paid for via NYSCEF. Motions in e-filed cases (other than tax certiorari cases) appear on the submit calendar in Room 217 on the return date. NY R BRONX E FIL R Doc. 1(2).

c. *KINGS COUNTY.* All motions require appearances and oral argument. NY R L KINGS Pt. C, Rule 3.

2. *Return date; Time for hearing.* A notice of motion shall specify the time and place of the hearing on the motion. NY CPLR Rule 2214(a). The moving party determines when a motion on notice shall be heard, but she has to consult the court's or judge's calendar practice first. The movant picks out a "return day" sufficiently far off to assure that the notice requirements of NY CPLR Rule 2214(b) can be met, and to assure as well that the day picked is a day on which the assigned judge hears motions. SIEGEL-NYPRAC § 247.

a. *Judge assigned to hear motion*

i. *Referral to judge supervising disclosure.* Unless the chief administrator of the courts has, by rule, provided otherwise, if a case has been assigned to a judge to supervise disclosure pursuant to NY CPLR § 3104, all motions preliminary to trial shall be referred to such judge whenever practicable. NY CPLR Rule 3214(a).

ii. *Referral to judge who decided prior motion.* Any motion may be referred to a judge who decided a prior motion in the action. NY CPLR Rule 2217(a).

iii. *Transfer when judge unable to hear motion.* If a motion is made to a judge who is or will be for any reason unable to hear it, it may be transferred by order of such judge or by written stipulation of the parties to any other judge to whom it might originally have been made. NY CPLR Rule 2217(c).

iv. *Procedure for unassigned cases.* If a case has not been assigned to a judge, the motion shall be made returnable before the court, and a copy of the moving papers, together with a request for judicial intervention, shall be filed with the court, with proof of service upon all other parties, where required by NY R UNIF TRIAL CTS § 202.6, within five (5) days of service upon the other parties. The moving party shall give written notice of the index number to all other parties immediately after filing of the papers. NY R UNIF TRIAL CTS § 202.8(b).

- *Responding papers.* Copies of all responding papers shall be submitted to the court, with proof of service and with the index number set forth in the papers, on or before the return date. NY R UNIF TRIAL CTS § 202.8(b).
- *Assignment after request for judicial intervention.* The case shall be assigned to a judge as soon as practicable after the filing of the request for judicial intervention pursuant to NY R UNIF TRIAL CTS § 202.6, but in no event later than the return date. After assignment to the judge, the court shall provide for appropriate notice to the parties of the name of the assigned judge. NY R UNIF TRIAL CTS § 202.8(b).
- *Motions to be heard in another county.* Motion papers noticed to be heard in a county other than the county where the venue of the action has been placed by the plaintiff shall be assigned to a judge in accordance with procedures established by the Chief Administrator. NY R UNIF TRIAL CTS § 202.8(b).

v. *ALBANY COUNTY: Motions referred to IAS Justice.* All motions made after a case has been assigned a day certain shall be referred to the IAS Justice unless the motion is returnable during the term in which the matter has been assigned a day certain, in that event, the matter will be referred to the Part 1 Justice for that particular term who may entertain the motion or refer such motion to the IAS Justice. Under those circumstances, the Part I Justice shall decide whether or not to strike the note of issue or assign the matter a new day certain. NY R 3 JD SUP Doc. 1(H)(2). All motions shall be returnable before the assigned justice. NY R 3 JD SUP Doc. 1(B).

b. *Trial of issue raised by motion.* The court may order that an issue of fact raised on a motion shall be separately tried by the court or a referee. If the issue is triable of right by jury, the court shall give the parties an opportunity to demand a jury trial of such issue. Failure to make such demand within the time limited by the court, or, if no such time is limited, before trial begins, shall be deemed a waiver of the right to trial by jury. An order under NY CPLR § 2218 shall specify the issue to be tried. NY CPLR § 2218.

c. *Audio-visual coverage of trial court proceeding.* Audio-visual coverage of proceedings in the trial courts shall be permitted only in accordance with the provisions of Part 131 of the Rules of the Chief Administrator (NY R CHIEF ADMIN § 131.1, et seq.). NY R CHIEF J § 29.3.

d. *Adjournment of return date.* Stipulations of adjournment of the return date made by the parties shall be in writing and shall be submitted to the assigned judge. Such stipulation shall be effective unless the court otherwise directs. No more than three (3) stipulated adjournments for an aggregate period of sixty (60) days shall be submitted without prior permission of the court. NY R UNIF TRIAL CTS § 202.8(e)(1).

i. Absent agreement by the parties, a request by any party for an adjournment shall be submitted in writing, upon notice to the other party, to the assigned judge on or before the return date. The court will notify the requesting party whether the adjournment has been granted. NY R UNIF TRIAL CTS § 202.8(e)(2).

ii. *BRONX COUNTY.* Motions that have been e-filed may be adjourned in Room 217 if an adjournment complies with the procedures of the Motion Support Office (explained in the "Filing Rules—Motion Procedure" section of the "Courthouse Procedures" link on the website of [the] court). An adjournment that so complies may be obtained by filing a stipulation of all parties with NYSCEF (designated in the filing menu as a "Stipulation to Adjourn Motion"). NY R BRONX E FIL R Doc. 1(3).

iii. *NEW YORK COUNTY.* The Courtroom also maintains a "APB (All Papers By)" Calendar, which is used when a party seeks an adjournment but fails to comply with the Courtroom's procedures or there is a failure to comply with procedures that requires the clerk to adjourn the motion/application (e.g., failure to submit a Confirmation Notice in an e-filed case). The case may be put over for three days to allow compliance with those procedures, as described further below. NY R NY CTY Procedure II(C); NY R NY CTY E FIL Doc. 2(D)(2). E-filed applications may be adjourned in the Part if an adjournment complies with the Part's procedures (see the Uniform Rules of the Justices (Local Rules) on the court's website). An adjournment that so complies may be obtained by filing with NYSCEF a stipulation of all parties (designated in the filing menu as a Stipulation—Adjournment of Motion—Before Judge); the motion number and the current return date of the motion being adjourned shall be set forth in the "Additional Document Information" field in NYSCEF. Absent any problems, the Part will effectuate the adjournment without need for an appearance or any other action by the parties. NY R NY CTY E FIL Doc. 2(D)(4).

iv. *QUEENS COUNTY.* The Motion Support Office is NOT authorized to grant adjournments. NY R L QUEENS MOT SUP Doc. 1.

e. *ALBANY COUNTY: Motion terms.* There shall be a. . . Motion Term on each Friday in the Supreme Court, Albany County. The Friday Motion Term shall include all Article 78 Proceedings involving New York State and proceedings commenced pursuant to Article 14 of the Civil Service Law (including applications for injunctive relief made pursuant to section 209-a of the Civil Service Law). NY R 3 JD SUP Doc. 1(F). Generally, parties will be granted only one adjournment for the Friday Motion Term. NY R 3 JD SUP Doc. 1(F).

f. *ALBANY COUNTY: Motion determined without hearing.* All motions are deemed "submitted" on the return date and no appearances are required by the parties. NY R 3 JD SUP Doc. 1(B). In the event oral argument is requested, the parties should not appear on the return date. At the discretion of the assigned Judge and upon the granting of a request for oral argument, the parties will be notified by Chambers of the scheduled time and place at which argument will be heard. Where a motion is brought on by order to show cause, the court may set forth in the order that appearances and/or oral argument are required on the return date of the motion. NY R 3 JD SUP Doc. 1(B).

g. *BRONX COUNTY: Return date.* All assigned and unassigned motions will be returnable five (5) days a week in the Civil Branch Clerk's Office, Room 217, at 9:30 a.m. NY R BRONX FIL R Doc. 8.

h. *BRONX COUNTY: Oral argument.* Calendars of disclosure motions and other motions adjourned for oral argument will be published for the four (4) business days preceding the rescheduled appearance date and on the rescheduled date of the motion. These repetitive publications will serve as the notification of procedure of adjournment of all motions. In addition, two (2) days before the return date of unassigned motions a list of such motions indicating the assigned Justice and the adjourned date of the motion will be published. NY R BRONX FIL R Doc. 8.

i. *BRONX COUNTY: Resolution before return date.* Counsel/parties must advise the Court in writing on or before the return date of all motions that have been resolved by Counsel/parties themselves and all motions the movant(s) wish to be withdrawn. NY R BRONX FIL R Doc. 8.

j. *ERIE COUNTY: Calendaring of motions.* Refer to individual Justice's Part Rules. NY R ERIE E FIL Doc. 3(V)(B).

k. *KINGS COUNTY: Return date set by court.* Irrespective of the return date indicated in the notice of motion, motions will be rescheduled by the E-file/Motion Support Office to a date designated by the assigned Judge. NY R L KINGS Pt. C, Rule 2.

l. *KINGS COUNTY: Calendar calls.* There shall be two (2) calendar calls on motion days. The first calendar call shall be at 9:30 AM and the second calendar call shall be at 10:45 AM, unless the Judge's Part Rules provide otherwise. Defaults shall only be taken on second call. Attorneys with appearances elsewhere in the courthouse may advise the clerk of their whereabouts to avoid a default. Failure to so advise the clerk or appear at the default calendar call will result in a default order being entered or the motion being marked off the calendar. NY R L KINGS Pt. C, Rule 7.

m. *NEW YORK COUNTY: Return date and assigned courtroom.* Motions made by notice of motion and petitions and notices of petition in special proceedings are processed by the General Clerk's Office (Room 119) and are to be made returnable in the Motion Submission Part Courtroom (Room 130) on any business day of the week at 9:30 AM. There are some differences in electronically-filed cases. NY R NY CTY Procedure II; NY R NY CTY Procedure II(C); NY R NY CTY J RUL Rule 13(a).

i. For the convenience of counsel, between 9:00 A.M. and 9:30 A.M. each day, in advance of the "call," Room 130 accepts (1) written stipulations; (2) affidavits/affirmations reciting the required details as to an adjournment on consent; (3) stipulations, letters or other writings withdrawing motions; and (4) final papers or complete sets of papers on motions. For motions in which these items are handed in before the "call," no one need remain to answer the "call." Counsel/parties must advise the court, either between 9:00 A.M. and 9:30 A.M. or at the "call," of all motions or cases that have been resolved by counsel/parties themselves and all motions that the movant no longer wishes to pursue. If such resolution occurs subsequent to the "call", the assigned Justice must be advised as soon as possible, by written notice sent to the Part, so that the court does not do unnecessary work. NY R NY CTY Procedure II(C).

ii. Depending upon the assigned Part, contested motions submitted in the Motion Submission Part Courtroom are submitted without argument, or rescheduled for oral argument if so directed by the assigned Justice. For Justices who schedule argument on a case-by-case basis, notice of the argument date will be transmitted by the court.

Counsel may ascertain how a motion submitted in Courtroom 130 was marked by consulting Scroll on the court's website, the e-Track application, or, on the two (2) days immediately following the submission date, the New York Law Journal. NY R NY CTY J RUL Rule 13(a).

n. *NEW YORK COUNTY: Motion call.* Each day in the Motion Submission Part Courtroom, commencing at 9:30 A.M., all motions returnable that day will be "called" for the submission of these papers, which must be handed up at this "call" or, as described below, immediately before. Because hundreds of motions appear on the Room 130 calendars every day, motion papers (other than part of the moving papers as described above) cannot be accepted on any day prior to the return date. Courtesy copies are not required nor accepted, but working copies are required by certain Justices in e-filed cases. NY R NY CTY Procedure II(C). If argument is directed, it will take place on an announced date shortly after the day of submission. NY R NY CTY Procedure II(C).

o. *NEW YORK COUNTY: Oral arguments.* Pursuant to request of some Justices, motions submitted in Room 130 will automatically be scheduled for a set argument date in the Part. Other Justices determine on a case-by-case basis after submission in Room 130 whether to accept a particular substantive motion on submission, to require oral argument, or to hold a conference. NY R NY CTY Procedure II(D). If argument is directed by the Justice automatically, notice of argument and the argument date will be given in Room 130. Any appearing party is expected to give notice to all parties and an announcement to this effect is made in Room 130. If the motion is submitted in Room 130 and the Justice, after examining the file, determines that argument should be directed, notice of the argument and the argument date will not be sent by the court. To obtain notification of the argument date and other developments, counsel should use e-Track. If argument notification is not given or transmitted as just described, counsel should understand that the motion has been taken on submission for decision on the papers. NY R NY CTY Procedure II(D).

i. Calendars of motions to be argued in the Parts are published on the morning of the argument date and on the day before in the New York Law Journal under each Part. Argument information is available on a case-by-case basis in Scroll, and e-mail notifications are sent by e-Track to participating attorneys whenever a motion is scheduled for argument in the court's computer system. NY R NY CTY J RUL Rule 15(a)

p. *NEW YORK COUNTY: Motion determined without hearing.* Given the purpose of the Room 130 procedure, the substance of motions will not be addressed at the submission "call." No Judge is present. To the extent possible, motions submitted in Room 130 will be decided "on the papers." Indeed, attorneys are encouraged to use service or clerks to deliver papers or working copies, or to agree among themselves to have one of them deliver papers for all parties by service or a clerk. Counsel for the movant need not appear to "take a default" on any motion or for any other reason. Motions will be submitted, not marked off, in the absence of the movant. Opposing counsel similarly need not appear in person in order to avoid suffering a default. Delivery of papers by service or a clerk will suffice. The court's goal is to be able to collect papers on motions in an orderly fashion but without any attorney having to make an appearance in Room 130 at any time. NY R NY CTY Procedure II(C).

q. *ONONDAGA COUNTY: Return date.* If the motion is the first filing in an action, the case will be assigned and counsel will be notified by the Supreme Court Clerk's Office via the NYSCEF system of the assigned justice and return date. NY R ONDGA E FIL Protocol(B)(7)(c). If the motion is on a previously assigned case, counsel may choose a return date from the assigned justice's motion term schedule. If the date in unavailable, the Supreme Court Clerk's Office will assign the motion to the next available motion term date and will notify counsel via e-mail. The change will also appear in the notification generated by the NYSCEF system. NY R ONDGA E FIL Protocol(B)(7)(d).

r. *QUEENS COUNTY: Return date.* Motions must be made returnable on the proper day/time based on the assigned judge. NY R L QUEENS MOT SUP Doc. 1. Failure to make a motion returnable on the proper day/time may result in the motion being administratively rescheduled or marked off. NY R L QUEENS MOT SUP Doc. 1.

s. *QUEENS COUNTY: Unassigned motions.* For RJI/Motions, due to the fact that the movant would not know who the assigned judge will be, the notice of motion may be returnable any day of the week. RJI/Motions shall be made returnable in "Queens Supreme Court" with no address designated. The motion will be administratively rescheduled to the proper day of the week based on the judge (once a judge has been assigned). Within one (1) week of filing, the movant must check online to see who the assigned judge is (and therefore the location/date/time) that their motion is now returnable. Movant must then notify their adversary of this information prior to the return date. NY R L QUEENS MOT SUP Doc. 1.

3. *Entry of order after hearing.* An order determining a motion shall be entered and filed in the office of the clerk of the court where the action is triable, and all papers used on the motion and any opinion or memorandum in writing shall be filed with that clerk unless the order dispenses with such filing. When a statute or civil practice rule requires such filing and entry in a county other than that in which the order was made, the party prevailing on the motion shall file the order and the papers used on the motion with the proper clerk after receiving them. If a party fails to file any papers required to be filed under

NY CPLR Rule 2220(a), the order may be vacated as irregular, with costs. NY CPLR Rule 2220(a). For more information on the entry of an order after a motion, refer to NY CPLR Rule 2219.

a. *BRONX COUNTY: Settled orders.* A Judge's decision will often call for a Settled Order. The purpose of the settled order is to give effect to the decision by directing that some action be done and/or that a court official perform some task. NY R BRONX LEG SUP Doc. 2. A settled order consists of a notice of settlement informing all parties that the proposed order will be presented to the judge who made the decision on a date certain. Next comes the proposed order which will be presented to the judge. This order should conform to the judge's decision and should direct the relief granted in the decision. This should be followed by proof of service upon all parties who were noticed with the decision. It is also helpful if a copy of the judge's decision is included along with the other papers. A settled order should always be noticed before the judge who made the decision. NY R BRONX LEG SUP Doc. 2.

   i. Although an order is usually settled by the party who prevailed on the motion, any party may settle the order. It should be presented to the court within sixty (60) days of the decision. The other parties are entitled to ten (10) days notice where service of the settled order is done by mail, five (5) days if the notice is personally delivered. An attorney who is served with a notice of settlement which he believes does not accurately reflect the decision may settle a counter order. The counter order must be noticed for the same day and must be served not less than seven (7) days if by mail and two (2) days if personally delivered. NY R BRONX LEG SUP Doc. 2.

   ii. Settled orders are usually sent to the judge the day after they noticed for settlement. No appearance is necessary or even contemplated on a settled order. If the decision directs "submit order", then no notice is necessary, and the order will be sent to the judge as soon a practical after it is received. No fees are collected on settled orders. NY R BRONX LEG SUP Doc. 2.

b. *ERIE COUNTY: Proposed orders.* Proposed orders shall be submitted through the NYSCEF system and a working copy provided to the IAS Justice for signature, if Part Rules so require. NY R ERIE E FIL Doc. 3(V)(G).

c. *KINGS COUNTY: Long form orders.* If the Court directs that an order be settled or submitted on a motion in a NYSCEF case, the proposed order, with Notice of Settlement where required, and any proposed counter-order shall be filed with the Court via NYSCEF. The relevant clerk's office will process the documents in the customary manner. NY R L KINGS E FIL Doc. 1(E).

   i. WORKING COPIES OF PROPOSED ORDERS WITH NOTICE OF SETTLEMENT MUST BE SUBMITTED IN THE MOTION SUPPORT OFFICE (ROOM 227) AS EXPLAINED HEREIN. THEY MUST NOT BE DELIVERED TO THE PART OR CHAMBERS, EXCEPT WHERE THE INDIVIDUAL JUSTICE'S PART RULES PROVIDE OTHERWISE; DOING SO WILL CAUSE ADMINISTRATIVE CONFUSION AND POSSIBLE MISPLACEMENT OF PAPERS. Any such submission shall be sent in a timely manner (kindly review individual Justice's rules) and be conspicuously marked on the outside "NYSCEF Matter;" lack of such marking may delay processing. After an order/counter-order has been signed, it will be scanned, and the County Clerk will affix the entry stamp into the NYSCEF system, which will immediately transmit notice of this event via e-mail, including a link to the entered document, to all participating attorneys and unrepresented litigants in the case. Such transmittal does not constitute Notice of Entry. NY R L KINGS E FIL Doc. 1(E).

d. *NEW YORK COUNTY: Long form orders.* Although the court strongly favors the use of short form orders and judgments, there are instances when settlement of an order or judgment is appropriate. When a Justice directs in a decision that a long form order or judgment be settled, that decision is recorded in the court's computer system by the General Clerk's Office and the motion file with decision is held in the Order Section of the Office in Room 119. The settlement process takes place there. NY R NY CTY Procedure II(D); NY R NY CTY E FIL Doc. 2(E).

   i. A proposed long form order or judgment in compliance NY R UNIF TRIAL CTS § 202.48 must be presented to the relevant back office, together with a notice of settlement which bears a settlement date, the date on which the order is to be ready for formal presentation to the Justice. In an e-filed case the submission shall be made electronically. The proposed order or counter-order should be e-filed and it will be transmitted automatically by the NYSCEF system to the appropriate back office. The return date and time of the proposed order must be at 9:30 A.M. no sooner than either five (5) days from personal service of the proposed order or ten (10) days from service by mail. Proof of timely service on the other parties must accompany the proposed order in a hard copy case. If an order or judgment is submitted late (later than sixty (60) days from signing and filing of the decision) and the proponent can show good cause for this tardiness, an affidavit or affirmation justifying the delay should be annexed to the proposed order, together with proof of service thereof. If persuaded, the Justice will consider the proposed order despite its untimeliness. NY R NY CTY Procedure II(D); NY R NY CTY E FIL Doc. 2(E).

   ii. Sometimes a decision will state "Submit Order." The submitting party should prepare a long form order and

make it returnable without notice. Counsel should deliver the proposed order to the Order Section of the appropriate back office, except in an e-filed case, when it shall be submitted electronically. NY R NY CTY Procedure II(D). If the decision of the court directs that a proposed order be settled or submitted in the Part or in Chambers, that direction, should, of course, be followed without presentation of the proposal to the back office. NY R NY CTY Procedure II(D).

iii. For information on proposed counter-orders, refer to NY R NY CTY Procedure II(D) and NY R NY CTY J RUL Rule 16(b).

e. *QUEENS COUNTY: Proposed orders.* If the court directs that an order be settled or submitted on a motion in an E-file case, the proposed order and any proposed counter-order shall be filed with the court on-line with proof of service. (If a decision refers to a proceeding on the record, a copy of the transcript must be submitted.) Working copies of all proposed orders MUST be submitted to the Motion Support Office before an order can be reviewed. NY R L QUEENS E-FILE Doc. 1(I).

i. Counsel are advised to adhere to NY R UNIF TRIAL CTS § 202.48 regarding the submission or settlement of their proposed order or judgment. Persons who are submitting proposed orders/judgments pursuant to a previously issued memorandum decision must submit a copy of the memorandum decision with their proposed order/judgment. Upon E-Filing a proposed order/judgement, a working copy of the proposed order/judgement must be provided to the Motion Support Office. NY R L QUEENS MOT SUP Doc. 1.

4. *Hearing in disclosure matters*

a. *BRONX COUNTY.* On the return date of the motion all non-City and non-Matrimonial disclosure motions, assigned and unassigned, will be scheduled for appearance in the Preliminary and Compliance Conference Part, IA-11, Room 707. The appearance date shall be no earlier than two (2) weeks from the initial return date of the motion. NY R BRONX FIL R Doc. 8.

b. *KINGS COUNTY.* Motions which only seek discovery related relief are scheduled in the Centralized Compliance Part by the E-file/Motion Support Office, on the date the motion is scheduled to be heard, regardless of judicial assignment. Attorneys are advised to consult, inter alia, the New York Law Journal or the Unified Court System's Future Court Appearance Website for the return dates. NY R L KINGS Pt. E, Rule 7. Any motion seeking discovery related relief filed prior to the PC shall be scheduled concurrently with the PC in the Intake Part. NY R L KINGS Pt. B, Rule 6.

i. If all parties served with the motion are present, they may enter into a consent order. If a new Note of Issue date is required, the order should be filled out and signed by all parties leaving a space for the Note of Issue filing date to be entered by a court attorney. Order should include all outstanding discovery, or indicate that discovery is complete. Consent orders are not effective, or allowed to be copied until they have been reviewed by a court attorney and signed by Judge or JHO. NY R L KINGS Pt. E, Rule 11.

H. Forms

1. Official Motion to Compel Disclosure Forms for New York

a. Request for judicial intervention. NY R UNIF TRIAL CTS § 202.6.

b. Notice of motion. NY R UNIF TRIAL CTS § 202.7(b).

2. New York Motion to Compel Disclosure Forms

a. Notice of motion to compel disclosure and for preclusion. NYDISC § 46:11.

b. Notice of motion to compel disclosure and for preclusion; Affirmation. NYDISC § 46:12.

c. Notice of motion to compel disclosure and for preclusion; Affidavit in support. NYDISC § 46:13.

d. Notice of motion to compel disclosure and for preclusion; 30-day notice. NYDISC § 46:14.

e. Notice of motion to compel compliance with combined discovery demands. NYDISC § 46:15.

f. Notice of motion to compel compliance with combined discovery demands; Affirmation of good faith. NYDISC § 46:16.

g. Notice of motion to compel compliance with combined discovery demands; Affirmation in support. NYDISC § 46:17.

h. Notice of motion to compel discovery and inspection. NYPRAC-COMM § 27:72.

i. Notice of motion to compel response to demand for address. MCF CPLR § 6:222.

j. Affidavit in support of motion to compel response to demand for address. MCF CPLR § 6:223.
k. Notice of motion to compel submission to physical examination. MCF CPLR § 6:225.
l. Affidavit in support of motion to compel submission to physical examination. MCF CPLR § 6:226.
m. Notice of motion to compel discovery and inspection. MCF CPLR § 6:228.
n. Affidavit in support of motion to compel discovery and inspection. MCF CPLR § 6:230.
o. Notice of motion to compel further and complete responses to interrogatories. MCF CPLR § 6:239.
p. Affirmation in support of motion to compel further and complete responses to interrogatories. MCF CPLR § 6:240.
q. General form of affidavit of service of motion papers. MCF CPLR § 5:24.

I. Applicable Rules

1. *State rules*
   a. Short title; Application; Construction; Definitions. NY CPLR § 101; NY CPLR § 103; NY CPLR § 104; NY CPLR § 105.
   b. Appendix of official forms. NY CPLR § 107.
   c. Extensions of time generally. NY CPLR § 2004.
   d. Form of papers. NY CPLR Rule 2101; NY CPLR Rule 2102; NY CPLR § 2105; NY CPLR Rule 2106; NY GEN BUS § 399-ddd; NY R UNIF TRIAL CTS § 215.2; NY R UNIF TRIAL CTS § 215.3.
   e. Service of papers. NY CPLR Rule 2103.
   f. Where motion made; In supreme court action. NY CPLR § 2212.
   g. Motion papers; Service; Time. NY CPLR Rule 2214.
   h. Relief demanded by other than moving party. NY CPLR Rule 2215.
   i. Prior motion; Ex parte motion; Transfer of motion; Hearings; Orders. NY CPLR Rule 2217; NY CPLR § 2218; NY CPLR Rule 2220.
   j. Computation of time. NY CPLR § 2402; NY GEN CONSTR § 19; NY GEN CONSTR § 20; NY GEN CONSTR § 25-a; NY GEN CONSTR § 30; NY GEN CONSTR § 31; NY GEN CONSTR § 53.
   k. Disclosure. NY CPLR § 3101; NY CPLR § 3103; NY CPLR § 3104; NY CPLR Rule 3105; NY CPLR Rule 3125.
   l. Failure to disclose; Motion to compel disclosure. NY CPLR Rule 3124.
   m. Motions heard by judge supervising disclosure; Stay of disclosure. NY CPLR Rule 3214.
   n. Fees; Index number fees of county clerks. NY CPLR § 8018.
   o. Hours of court; Proceedings in court. NY R CHIEF J § 3.1; NY R CHIEF J § 29.3.
   p. Application of part; Waiver; Additional rules; Application of CPLR; Definitions. NY R UNIF TRIAL CTS § 202.1.
   q. Papers filed in court; Electronic filing in supreme court. NY R UNIF TRIAL CTS § 202.5; NY R UNIF TRIAL CTS § 202.5-a; NY R UNIF TRIAL CTS § 202.5-b; NY R UNIF TRIAL CTS § 202.5-bb.
   r. Request for judicial intervention. NY R UNIF TRIAL CTS § 202.6.
   s. Calendaring of motions; Uniform notice of motion form; Affirmation of good faith. NY R UNIF TRIAL CTS § 202.7.
   t. Motion procedure; Preliminary conferences. NY R UNIF TRIAL CTS § 202.8; NY R UNIF TRIAL CTS § 202.12.
   u. Rules of the commercial division of the Supreme Court. NY R UNIF TRIAL CTS § 202.70.
   v. Sanctions; Signing of papers. NY R CHIEF ADMIN § 130-1.1-a.
2. *Local rules*
   a. *Albany County*
      i. Third judicial district rules. NY R 3 JD SUP Doc. 1.
   b. *Bronx County*
      i. Filing of papers in supreme court. NY R BRONX FIL R Doc. 1.
      ii. Request for judicial intervention. NY R BRONX FIL R Doc. 2.

iii. Discovery part conference requests. NY R BRONX FIL R Doc. 5.

iv. Motion procedure. NY R BRONX FIL R Doc. 8.

v. Commercial division. NY R BRONX FIL R Doc. 12.

vi. Motions on notice. NY R BRONX E FIL R Doc. 1.

vii. Settled orders. NY R BRONX LEG SUP Doc. 2.

c. *Erie County*

i. Joint protocols for New York State Courts E-Filing (NYSCEF) cases filed in Supreme Court, Erie County. NY R ERIE E FIL Doc. 3.

d. *Kings County*

i. Papers. NY R L KINGS Pt. A, Papers.

ii. Discovery agreements. NY R L KINGS Pt. B, Rule 2.

iii. Motion scheduling. NY R L KINGS Pt. B, Rule 6.

iv. Service of motion papers. NY R L KINGS Pt. C, Rule 1.

v. Scheduling of motions. NY R L KINGS Pt. C, Rule 2.

vi. Appearance and argument. NY R L KINGS Pt. C, Rule 3.

vii. Courtesy copies. NY R L KINGS Pt. C, Rule 5.

viii. Motion calendar calls. NY R L KINGS Pt. C, Rule 7.

ix. Scheduling of motions. NY R L KINGS Pt. E, Rule 7.

x. Affirmation of good faith. NY R L KINGS Pt. E, Rule 9.

xi. Consent orders. NY R L KINGS Pt. E, Rule 11.

xii. Disclosure disputes. NY R NY CTY J RUL Rule 10.

xiii. Protocol on courthouse and county clerk procedures for electronically filed cases. NY R L KINGS E FIL Doc. 1.

e. *New York County*

i. Commencement of cases. NY R NY CTY Procedure I.

ii. RJIs and assignments. NY R NY CTY Procedure IA.

iii. Motions and special proceedings by notice of motion/petition. NY R NY CTY Procedure II.

iv. County clerk litigation functions. NY R NY CTY Procedure XI.

v. Protocol on courthouse and county clerk procedures for electronically filed cases. NY R NY CTY E FIL Doc. 2.

vi. Redaction of information in documents filed with the county clerk and the court. NY R NY CTY J RUL Rule A-1.

vii. Papers by fax. NY R NY CTY J RUL Rule 4.

viii. Motions on notice; Orders to show cause. NY R NY CTY J RUL Rule 13.

ix. Motion papers. NY R NY CTY J RUL Rule 14.

x. Oral argument; Adjournments. NY R NY CTY J RUL Rule 15.

f. *Onondaga County*

i. Onondaga county protocol for case filings New York State Electronic Files (NYSCEF). NY R ONDGA E FIL Protocol.

g. *Queens County*

i. Motion support office. NY R L QUEENS MOT SUP Doc. 1.

ii. Queens county protocol on courthouse procedures for electronically filed cases. NY R L QUEENS E-FILE Doc. 1.

J. Miscellaneous

NOTE: Individual judges' rules may apply.

ALBANY COUNTY

JUSTICE LISA M. FISHER: NY R 3 JD FISHER Fisher; NY R 3 JD FISHER Fisher, PC Order.

JUSTICE RICHARD MOTT: NY R 3 JD MOTT Mott.

JUSTICE STEPHAN G. SCHICK: NY R 3 JD Schick.

FORECLOSURE SETTLEMENT PART: NY R 3 JD Foreclosure Settlement.

BRONX COUNTY

JUSTICE PAUL L. ALPERT: [NY R BRONX J Part IA-29, as amended by NY ORDER 20-0337].

JUSTICE BEN BARBATO: NY R BRONX J Part IA-21.

JUSTICE MARY ANNE BRIGANTTI: [NY R BRONX J Part IA-15, as amended by NY ORDER 20-0338].

JUSTICE JOSEPH E. CAPELLA: NY R BRONX J Part IA-23.

JUSTICE MITCHELL DANZIGER: NY R BRONX J Part IA-3/33 ; [NY R BRONX J Danziger, Part IA-3/33, as amended by NY ORDER 20-0339].

JUSTICE LAURA G. DOUGLAS: NY R BRONX J Part IA-11.

JUSTICE RUBEN FRANCO: NY R BRONX J Part IA-26.

JUSTICE DORIS M. GONZALEZ: NY R BRONX J Part IA-24.

JUSTICE WILMA GUZMAN: NY R BRONX J Part IA-7; [NY R BRONX J Guzman, Part IA-7 Virtual, as amended by NY ORDER 20-0340].

JUSTICE ROBERT T. JOHNSON: NY R BRONX J Part IA-12.

JUSTICE DONALD A. MILES: NY R BRONX J Part IA-8.

JUSTICE DONNA M. MILLS: NY R BRONX J Part IA-9.

JUSTICE JULIA I. RODRIGUEZ: NY R BRONX J Part IA-18; [NY R BRONX J Part IA-27, as amended by NY ORDER 20-0341].

JUSTICE LLINET M. ROSADO: [NY R BRONX J Part IA-25, as amended by NY ORDER 20-0342].

JUSTICE NORMA RUIZ: NY R BRONX J Part IA-22; [NY R BRONX J Ruiz, Part IA-22 Virtual, as amended by NY ORDER 20-0343].

JUSTICE HOWARD H. SHERMAN: NY R BRONX J Part IA-4.

JUSTICE FERNANDO TAPIA: NY R BRONX J Part IA-13.

JUSTICE ELIZABETH A. TAYLOR: NY R BRONX J Part IA-2.

JUSTICE ALISON Y. TRUITT: NY R BRONX J Part IA-5.

PART IDV: NY R BRONX J Doc. 1.

PRE-TRIAL PART RULES: NY R BRONX J Doc. 2.

PRE TRIAL WORKSHEET: NY R BRONX J Doc. 3.

FORECLOSURE SETTLEMENT PART RULES: NY R BRONX J Doc. 4.

GUARDIANSHIP PART RULES: NY R BRONX J Doc. 5.

LPM PART RULES: NY R BRONX J Doc. 6.

ERIE COUNTY

JUSTICE M. WILLIAM BOLLER: NY R 8 JD J Boller.

JUSTICE RALPH A. BONIELLO: NY R 8 JD J Boniello.

JUSTICE CHRISTOPHER J. BURN: NY R 8 JD J Burns.

JUSTICE RUSSELL P. BUSCAGLIA: NY R 8 JD J Buscaglia.

JUSTICE FRANK CARUSO: NY R 8 JD J Caruso.

JUSTICE STEPHEN W. CASS: NY R 8 JD J Cass.
JUSTICE DEBORAH A. CHIMES: NY R 8 JD J Chimes.
JUSTICE EMILIO COLAIACOVO: [NY R 8 JD J Colaiacovo, as amended by NY ORDER 20-0252].
JUSTICE DIANE Y. DEVLIN: NY R 8 JD J Devlin.
JUSTICE JAMES H. DILLON: NY R 8 JD J Dillon.
JUSTICE PAULA L. FEROLETO: NY R 8 JD J Feroleto.
JUSTICE DANIEL J. FURLONG: [NY R 8 JD J Furlong, as amended by NY ORDER 20-0253].
JUSTICE JOSEPH R. GLOWNIA: NY R 8 JD J Glownia.
JUSTICE MARK J. GRISANTI: NY R 8 JD J Grisanti.
JUSTICE DEBORAH A. HAENDIGES: NY R 8 JD J Haendiges.
JUSTICE LYNN W. KEANE: [NY R 8 JD J Keane, as amended by NY ORDER 20-0254].
JUSTICE RICHARD C. KLOCH, Sr.: NY R 8 JD J Kloch.
JUSTICE FREDERICK J. MARSHALL: [NY R 8 JD J Marshall, as amended by NY ORDER 20-0255.
JUSTICE JOHN L. MICHALSKI: NY R 8 JD J Michalski.
JUSTICE MARK A. MONTOUR: [NY R 8 JD J Montour, as amended by NY ORDER 20-0256].
JUSTICE HENRY NOWAK: NY R 8 JD J Nowak.
JUSTICE JOHN F. O'DONNELL: NY R 8 JD J O'Donnell.
JUSTICE JEANETTE OGDEN: NY R 8 JD J Ogden.
JUSTICE CATHERINE NUGENT-PANEPINTO: NY R 8 JD J Nugent-Panepinto.
JUSTICE FRANK A. SEDITA, III: [NY R 8 JD J Sedita, as amended by NY ORDER 20-0257].
JUSTICE SARA SHELDON: NY R 8 JD J Sheldon.
JUSTICE DONNA M. SIWEK: NY R 8 JD J Siwek.
JUSTICE MARY L. SLISZ: NY R 8 JD J Slisz.
JUSTICE TIMOTHY J. WALKER: [NY R 8 JD J Walker, as amended by NY ORDER 20-0258].
JUSTICE DENNIS E. WARD: NY R 8 JD J Ward.
JUSTICE PAUL B. WOJTASZEK: [NY R 8 JD J Wojtaszek, as amended by NY ORDER 20-0259].
JUSTICE CHARLES N. ZAMBITO: [NY R 8 JD J Zambito, as amended by NY ORDER 20-0260].
SUPREME COURT LEGAL STAFF: NY R 8 JD J Legal Staff.

KINGS COUNTY

JUSTICE RACHEL A. ADAMS: NY R KINGS J Part 5F.
JUSTICE LOREN BAILY-SCHIFFMAN: NY R KINGS J Part 65.
JUSTICE REGINALD A. BODDIE: NY R KINGS J Part 95.
JUSTICE THERESA M. CICCOTTO: NY R KINGS J Part 19; NY R KINGS J Part 5J.
JUSTICE LISSETTE COLON: NY R KINGS J Part Rules.
JUSTICE GENINE EDWARDS: NY R KINGS J Part 80.
JUSTICE PAMELA L. FISHER: [NY R KINGS J Part 94, as amended by NY ORDER 20-0208].
JUSTICE ROBIN GARSON: NY R KINGS J Part 75.
JUSTICE LARA J. GENOVISI: [NY R KINGS J Part 34, as amended by NY ORDER 20-0209].
JUSTICE BERNARD J. GRAHAM: NY R KINGS J Part 36.
JUSTICE DAWN JIMENEZ-SALTA: NY R KINGS J Part 88.
JUSTICE INGRID JOSEPH: [NY R KINGS J Part FRP3 and Part 83, as amended by NY ORDER 20-0210].
JUSTICE KATHY J. KING: NY R KINGS J Part 64, 76K.

JUSTICE LAWRENCE KNIPEL: NY R KINGS J Part 57.
JUSTICE DONALD KURTZ: NY R KINGS J Part 26.
JUSTICE CARL LANDICINO: [NY R KINGS J Part 81, as amended by NY ORDER 20-0211].
JUSTICE KATHERINE LEVINE: [NY R KINGS J Part 20, 25, 92, as amended by NY ORDER 20-0211].
JUSTICE LORNA MCALLISTER: [NY R KINGS J Part 10, as amended by NY ORDER 20-0211].
JUSTICE ROSEMARIE MONTALBANO: [NY R KINGS J Part 19, 71, and 22, as amended by NY ORDER 20-0211].
JUSTICE RICHARD J. MONTELIONE: [NY R KINGS J Part 99 and DJMP, as amended by NY ORDER 20-0215].
JUSTICE LISA S. OTTLEY: NY R KINGS J Part 24.
JUSTICE MARK I. PARTNOW: NY R KINGS J Part 43.
JUSTICE ERIC I. PRUS: NY R KINGS J Part 5A.
JUSTICE FRANCOIS RIVERA: NY R KINGS J Part 52.
JUSTICE KAREN B. ROTHENBERG: NY R KINGS J Part 35.
JUSTICE LEON RUCHELSMAN: NY R KINGS J Part 1.
JUSTICE WAYNE P. SAITTA: NY R KINGS J Part 29.
JUSTICE ROBIN K. SHEARES: NY R KINGS J Part 96.
JUSTICE KENNETH P. SHERMAN: NY R KINGS J Part 67 and 78.
JUSTICE DEBRA SILBER: NY R KINGS J Part 9 and 5K.
JUSTICE ELLEN M. SPODEK: NY R KINGS J Part 63.
JUSTICE MARSHA L. STEINHARDT: NY R KINGS J Part 15.
JUSTICE JEFFREY S. SUNSHINE: NY R KINGS J Part 5G.
JUSTICE PETER P. SWEENEY: [NY R KINGS J Part 35, as amended by NY ORDER 20-0218].
JUSTICE DELORES J. THOMAS: [NY R KINGS J Part 5T, as amended by NY ORDER 20-0221].
JUSTICE WAVNY TOUSSAINT: NY R KINGS J Part 70.
JUSTICE RICHARD VELASQUEZ: NY R KINGS J Part 66.
JUSTICE CAROLYN E. WADE: NY R KINGS J Part 84.
JUSTICE EDWARD G. WALKER: [NY R KINGS J Part 90, as amended by NY ORDER 20-0219].
JUSTICE LILLIAN WAN: [NY R KINGS J Part 17, as amended by NY ORDER 20-0220].
JUSTICE MICHELLE WESTON: NY R KINGS J Part 3.
MENTAL HYGIENE PART: NY R KINGS J Part 77.
MATRIMONIAL PARTS DURING COVID-19 EMERGENCY: JUSTICE KAREN B. ROTHENBERG: NY R KINGS J Doc. 1.

NASSAU COUNTY

JUSTICE ANNA R. ANZALONE: NY R NASSAU S J Anzalone, Part 26.
JUSTICE STACY D. BENNETT: NY R NASSAU S J Bennett; NY R NASSAU S J Bennett, Form 1.
JUSTICE ANTONIO BRANDVEEN: NY R NASSAU S J Brandveen, Part 31.
JUSTICE JEFFREY S. BROWN: [NY R NASSAU S J Brown, as amended by NY ORDER 20-0297].
JUSTICE STEPHEN A. BUCARIA: NY R NASSAU S J Bucaria.
JUSTICE JULIANNE T. CAPETOLA: NY R NASSAU S J Capetola, Part 28.
JUSTICE EDMUND M. DANE: NY R NASSAU S J Dane, Part 33.
JUSTICE VITO M. DESTEFANO: NY R NASSAU S J DeStefano, Part 13; NY R NASSAU S J DeStefano, Form 1.
JUSTICE ARTHUR M. DIAMOND: NY R NASSAU S J Diamond, Part 7.
JUSTICE THOMAS FEINMAN: NY R NASSAU S J Feinman, Part 5.
JUSTICE JOHN M. GALASSO: NY R NASSAU S J Galasso, Part 22.

JUSTICE SHARON M.J. GIANELLI: NY R NASSAU S J Gianelli, Part 22; NY R NASSAU S J Gianelli, Form 1.

JUSTICE JEFFREY A. GOODSTEIN: NY R NASSAU S J Goodstein, Part 33; NY R NASSAU S J Goodstein, Form 1.

JUSTICE DAVID J. GUGERTY: [NY R NASSAU S J Gugerty, Part 31, as amended by NY ORDER 20-0298].

JUSTICE HELENE F. GUGERTY: NY R NASSAU S J Gugerty, Part 47.

JUSTICE STEVEN M. JAEGER: NY R NASSAU S J Jaeger, Part 35; NY R NASSAU S J Jaeger, Form 1.

JUSTICE JACK L. LIBERT: NY R NASSAU S J Libert, Part 23.

JUSTICE JOSEPH H. LORINTZ: NY R NASSAU S J Lorintz, Part 26; NY R NASSAU S J Lorintz, Form 1.

JUSTICE ROY S. MAHON: NY R NASSAU S J Mahon, Part 3.

JUSTICE RANDY SUE MARBER: NY R NASSAU S J Marber, Part 8.

JUSTICE JAMES P. MCCORMACK: [NY R NASSAU S J McCormack, Part 18, as amended by NY ORDER, 20-0299].

JUSTICE DICCIA T. PINEDA-KIRWAN: [NY R NASSAU S J Pineda-Kirwan, as amended by NY ORDER 20-0300].

JUSTICE THOMAS RADEMAKER: [NY R NASSAU S J Rademaker, Part 28, as amended by NY ORDER 20-0301]; [NY R NASSAU S J Rademaker, Form 1, as amended by NY ORDER 20-0301].

JUSTICE DENISE L. SHER: NY R NASSAU S J Rademaker, Part 32.

JUSTICE LEONARD D. STEINMAN: [NY R NASSAU S J Steinman, Part 15, as amended by NY ORDER 20-0303]; NY R NASSAU S J Steinman, Form 1.

JUSTICE HOWARD E. STURIM: NY R NASSAU S J Sturim, Part 50; NY R NASSAU S J Sturim, Form 1.

JUSTICE HELEN VOUTSINAS: [NY R NASSAU S J Voutsinas, Part 25, as amended by NY ORDER 20-0304]; [NY R NASSAU S J Voutsinas, Form 1, as amended by NY ORDER 20-0305].

JUSTICE HOPE SCHWARTZ ZIMMERMAN: NY R NASSAU S J Zimmerman, Part 17.

NEW YORK COUNTY

JUDGE'S RULES; BASIC INFORMATION: [NY R NY CTY J RUL Doc. 1, as amended by NY ORDER 20-0202].

ONONDAGA COUNTY

JUSTICE ROBERT E. ANTONACCI II: [NY R ONDGA E FIL Doc. 1, as amended by 20-0239].

JUSTICE MICHAEL V. COCCOMI: NY R ONDGA E FIL Doc. 2.

JUSTICE GREGORY R. GILBERT: NY R 5 JD JUDGES Gilbert; NY R ONDGA E FIL Doc. 3.

JUSTICE DONALD A. GREENWOOD: NY R ONDGA E FIL Doc. 4.

JUSTICE DEBORAH H. KARALUNAS: NY R ONDGA E FIL Doc. 5.

JUSTICE JAMES MCCLUSKY: NY R 5 JD MCCLUSKY McClusky.

JUSTICE CHARLES C. MERRELL: NY R 5 JD MERRELL Merrell.

JUSTICE PATRICK F. MACRAE: NY R 5 JD MACRAE Doc. 1.

JUSTICE JAMES P. MURPHY: NY R ONDGA E FIL Doc. 7.

JUSTICE GERALD J. NERI: [NY R 5 JD JUDGES Neri, as amended by NY ORDER 20-0236]; [NY R ONDGA E FIL Doc. 8, as amended by NY ORDER 20-0241].

JUSTICE ANTHONY J. PARIS: NY R 5 JD JUDGES Paris; [NY R ONDGA E FIL Doc. 9, as amended by NY ORDER 20-0242].

JUSTICE NORMAN W. SEITER, JR.: NY R 5 JD JUDGES Seiter.

JUSTICE KEVIN G. YOUNG: [NY R ONDGA E FIL Doc. 10, as amended by NY ORDER 20-0243].

QUEENS COUNTY

JUSTICE PAM JACKMAN BROWN: [NY R L QUEENS Brown, Part 19, as amended by NY ORDER 20-0321].

JUSTICE CHEREE A. BUGGS: NY R L QUEENS Buggs, Part 30.

JUSTICE PAM JACKMAN BROWN: [NY R L QUEENS Brown, Part 19, as amended by NY ORDER 20-0321].

JUSTICE DENIS J. BUTLER: NY R L QUEENS Butler, Part 12.

JUSTICE ROBERT I. CALORAS: [NY R L QUEENS Caloras, Part 36, as amended by NY ORDER 20-0322].

JUSTICE ANNA CULLEY: NY R L QUEENS Culley, Part 53.

JUSTICE TIMOTHY DUFFICY: NY R L QUEENS Dufficy, Part 35.

JUSTICE DAVID ELLIOT: NY R L QUEENS Elliot, Part 14.

JUSTICE JOSEPH J. ESPOSITO: NY R L QUEENS Esposito, Part 6.

JUSTICE DARRELL L. GAVRIN: [NY R L QUEENS Gavrin, Part 27, as amended by NY ORDER 20-0323].

JUSTICE WYATT N. GIBBONS: [NY R L QUEENS Gibbons, Part 5, as amended by NY ORDER 20-0330.

JUSTICE DONNA-MARIE E. GOLIA: [NY R L QUEENS Golia, Part 21, as amended by NY ORDER 20-0331].

JUSTICE MARGUERITE A. GRAYS: [NY R L QUEENS Grays, Part 4, as amended by NY ORDER 20-0324].

JUSTICE RUDOLPH E. GRECO: [NY R L QUEENS Greco, Part 32, as amended by NY ORDER 20-0325].

JUSTICE MAUREEN HEALY: NY R L QUEENS Healy, Part 6.

JUSTICE PHILLIP HOM: [NY R L QUEENS Hom, Part 43, as amended by NY ORDER 20-0332].

JUSTICE KEVIN J. KERRIGAN: NY R L QUEENS Kerrigan, Part 10.

JUSTICE MOJGAN C. LANCMAN: NY R L QUEENS Lancman, Part 20.

JUSTICE RICHARD G. LATIN: NY R L QUEENS Latin, Part 40.

JUSTICE ULYSSES B. LEVERETT: [NY R L QUEENS Leverett, Part 6, as amended by NY ORDER 20-0326].

JUSTICE LEONARD LIVOTE: NY R L QUEENS Livote, Part 33.

JUSTICE LEE A. MAYERSOHN: NY R L QUEENS Mayersohn, Part 22; NY R L QUEENS Mayersohn, Part 22G; [NY R L QUEENS Mayersohn, Part 22G COVID, as amended by NY ORDER 20-0327].

JUSTICE ROBERT J. MCDONALD: NY R L QUEENS McDonald, Part 34.

JUSTICE MARGARET MCGOWAN: NY R L QUEENS McGowan, Part 52.

JUSTICE MAURICE E. MUIR: [NY R L QUEENS Muir, Part 42, as amended by NY ORDER 20-0333].

JUSTICE JODI ORLOW: NY R L QUEENS Orlow, Part 51.

JUSTICE LESLIE J. PURIFICCION: NY R L QUEENS Purificcion, Part 39.

JUSTICE JOSEPH RISI: [NY R L QUEENS Risi, Part 3, as amended by NY ORDER 20-0328].

JUSTICE FREDERICK D.R. SAMPSON: [NY R L QUEENS Sampson, Part 31, as amended by NY ORDER 20-0329].

JUSTICE MARTIN J. SCHULMAN: NY R L QUEENS Schulman, Part 29.

JUSTICE BERNICE D. SIEGAL: NY R L QUEENS Siegal, Part 25G.

JUSTICE JANICE A. TAYLOR: NY R L QUEENS Taylor, Part 15.

JUSTICE CARMEN R. VELASQUEZ: NY R L QUEENS Velasquez, Part 38.

JUSTICE LOURDES M VENTURA: [NY R L QUEENS Ventura, Part 37, as amended by NY ORDER 20-0334].

JUSTICE WILLIAM A. VISCOVICH: NY R L QUEENS Viscovich, Part 63.

JUSTICE ALLAN B. WEISS: NY R L QUEENS Weiss, Part 2.

COMPLIANCE, SETTLEMENT AND CONFERENCE PART: NY R L QUEENS Doc 1.

PRELIMINARY CONFERENCE PART: [NY R L QUEENS Doc. 2, as amended by NY ORDER 20-0335].

MEDICAL MALPRACTICE CONFERENCE PART: [NY R L QUEENS Doc. 3, as amended by NY ORDER 20-0336].

TRIAL SCHEDULING PART: NY R L QUEENS Doc. 4.

SUMMARY JURY TRIAL PROGRAM: NY R L QUEENS Doc. 7.

RESIDENTIAL FORECLOSURE PART: NY R L QUEENS Doc. 9.

FORECLOSURE AUCTION RULES: NY R L QUEENS Doc. 10.

MATRIMONIAL PRELIMINARY CONFERENCE PART: NY R L QUEENS Doc. 11.

NON-CUSTODIAL CONTESTED MATRIMONIAL PART: NY R L QUEENS Doc. 12.

Motions, Oppositions and Replies
Motion for Protective Order

Document Last Updated August 2020

A. Checklist

(I) ❑ Matters to consider for moving party

(a) ❑ Required documents

(1) ❑ Notice of motion, order to show cause, or affidavit on ex parte motion

(2) ❑ Motion

(3) ❑ Affirmation of counsel

(4) ❑ Request for judicial intervention

(5) ❑ Proof of service

(6) ❑ ALBANY COUNTY: Additional required documents

(i) ❑ Affirmation of good faith effort

(b) ❑ Supplemental documents

(1) ❑ Supporting evidence; Exhibits

(2) ❑ Brief

(3) ❑ Notice to produce papers not in possession of the court

(4) ❑ Filing fees

(5) ❑ Working copies

(6) ❑ ERIE COUNTY: Additional supplemental documents

(i) ❑ Notice of hard copy submission in e-filed case

(7) ❑ KINGS COUNTY: Additional supplemental documents

(i) ❑ Forms when filing in hard copy

(8) ❑ NEW YORK COUNTY: Additional supplemental documents

(i) ❑ Notice of hard copy submission

(ii) ❑ Unpublished opinions

(9) ❑ ONONDAGA COUNTY: Additional supplemental documents

(i) ❑ Notice of hard copy submission

(10) ❑ QUEENS COUNTY: Additional supplemental documents

(i) ❑ Notice of hard copy submission

(c) ❑ Timing

(1) ❑ There are no specific timing requirements for the motion for protective order

(2) ❑ The moving party shall serve copies of all affidavits and briefs upon all other parties at the time of service of the notice of motion

(3) ❑ A notice of motion and supporting affidavits shall be served at least eight (8) days before the time at which the motion is noticed to be heard

(4) ❑ It is also good practice to make motions returnable at least three (3) weeks away from the planned date of mailing and to always include a demand in the motion that the other side serve answering papers at least seven (7) days before the return day

(5) ❑ BRONX COUNTY: Additional timing

(i) ❑ A Notice of Motion must be served at least eight (8) days, by personal service, nine (9) days by overnight express and thirteen (13) days by mail before the return date

(6) ❑ NEW YORK COUNTY: Additional timing

(i) ❑ In an e-filed case, all of the moving papers shall be e-filed at least eight (8) business days prior to the return date

(7) ❑ ONONDAGA COUNTY: Additional timing

(i) ❑ Onondaga County local court rules require that any additional papers relating to motions must be e-filed at least two (2) business days prior to the return date, excluding the return date

(8) ❑ QUEENS COUNTY: Additional timing

(i) ❑ Motions must be in the possession of the Motion Support Office at least nine (9) days before the noticed return date of the motion

(II) ❑ Matters to consider for opposing party

(a) ❑ Required documents

(1) ❑ Opposition

(2) ❑ Proof of service

(b) ❑ Supplemental documents

(1) ❑ Supporting evidence; Exhibits

(2) ❑ Brief

(3) ❑ Filing fees

(4) ❑ Working copies

(5) ❑ ERIE COUNTY: Additional supplemental documents

(i) ❑ Notice of hard copy submission in e-filed case

(6) ❑ KINGS COUNTY: Additional supplemental documents

(i) ❑ Forms when filing in hard copy

(7) ❑ NEW YORK COUNTY: Additional supplemental documents

(i) ❑ Notice of hard copy submission

(ii) ❑ Unpublished opinions

(8) ❑ ONONDAGA COUNTY: Additional supplemental documents

(i) ❑ Notice of hard copy submission

(9) ❑ QUEENS COUNTY: Additional supplemental documents

(i) ❑ Notice of hard copy submission

(c) ❑ Timing

(1) ❑ Answering affidavits shall be served at least two (2) days before the time at which the motion is noticed to be heard

(2) ❑ Answering affidavits and any notice of cross-motion, with supporting papers, if any, shall be served at least seven (7) days before such time if a notice of motion served at least sixteen (16) days before such time so demands

B. Timing

1. *Time to bring motion for protective order.* There are no specific timing requirements for the motion for protective order.

   a. As a general rule, the time is always open to move for a protective order. The best time to move is obviously before the disclosure has been had because, as noted above, the motion's mere making stays the disclosure until the court decides whether it is to proceed. But if the disclosure has already gone forward and the testimony or item has already been provided, a protective order may still prove useful. Any information "improperly or irregularly obtained" may be ordered suppressed under NY CPLR § 3103(c), i.e., barred from any use at the trial. SIEGEL-NYPRAC § 353; NY CPLR § 3103(c); Juskowitz v. Hahn, 56 Misc. 2d 647, 648, 289 N.Y.S.2d 870, 872 (Sup. Ct. 1968).

2. *Time to serve.* The moving party shall serve copies of all affidavits and briefs upon all other parties at the time of service

of the notice of motion. NY R UNIF TRIAL CTS § 202.8(c). A notice of motion and supporting affidavits shall be served at least eight (8) days before the time at which the motion is noticed to be heard. NY CPLR Rule 2214(b).

a. *Return dates; Best practice.* It is also good practice to make motions returnable at least three (3) weeks away from the planned date of mailing and to always include a demand in the motion that the other side serve answering papers at least seven (7) days before the return day. This enables the motion to be served by mail, gives sufficient notice to support the seven (7) day demand, and leaves a few days for a delayed mailing if some snag prevents posting on the day planned. If speed is needed, the shorter eight (8) day notice period can be used, forfeiting the right to seven (7) day answering papers and a reply. If even eight (8) days notice is too much under the circumstances, the order to show cause is the remedy. SIEGEL-NYPRAC § 247.

   i. *ALBANY COUNTY.* All motions, except for certain matters in Albany County as specified in NY R 3 JD SUP Doc. 1(E) and NY R 3 JD SUP Doc. 1(F), brought on by notice of motion or by order to show cause will be made returnable on any day, Monday through Friday, as chosen by the movant in compliance with the CPLR. Parties shall submit all papers in a timely fashion as required by the CPLR by delivering them or mailing them directly to the Supreme Court Clerk's Office[. . .]except that motions and other applications subject to a filing fee shall first be presented to the County Clerk's Office for payment of the requisite fee and then subsequently filed with the Supreme Court Clerk's Office. NY R 3 JD SUP Doc. 1(B).

   ii. *BRONX COUNTY.* A Notice of Motion must be served at least eight (8) days, by personal service, nine (9) days by overnight express and thirteen (13) days by mail before the return date. NY R BRONX FIL R Doc. 3. All unassigned motions must be accompanied with a properly filled out RJI and shall be filed in the Motion Support Office, room 217, within five (5) days of service. All motions on actions already assigned to a Justice must be filed at least five (5) business days before the return date. NY R BRONX FIL R Doc. 3. All papers served must strictly comply with the time requirements of NY CPLR Rule 2101, NY CPLR Rule 2103 and NY CPLR Rule 2214(b). NY R BRONX FIL R Doc. 8.

   iii. *KINGS COUNTY.* Motion papers, answering affidavits and reply affidavits must be served on adversaries in accordance with NY CPLR Rule 2214. NY R L KINGS Pt. C, Rule 1.

   iv. *NEW YORK COUNTY.* In an e-filed case, all of the moving papers shall be e-filed at least eight (8) business days prior to the return date. The clerk will calendar the motion for the Motion Submission Part Courtroom (Room 130) for the return date selected. NY R NY CTY Procedure II(A); NY R NY CTY E FIL Doc. 2(D)(1).

   v. *ONONDAGA COUNTY.* Onondaga County local court rules require that any additional papers relating to motions must be e-filed at least two (2) business days prior to the return date, excluding the return date. NY R ONDGA E FIL Protocol(B)(9)(e).

   vi. *QUEENS COUNTY.* Motions must be in the possession of the Motion Support Office at least nine (9) days before the noticed return date of the motion. NY R L QUEENS MOT SUP Doc. 1; NY R L QUEENS E-FILE Doc. 1(H)(1).

b. *Order to show cause; Shorter time.* The court in a proper case may grant an order to show cause, to be served in lieu of a notice of motion, at a time and in a manner specified therein. NY CPLR Rule 2214(d). An ordinary notice of motion can't be brought on for hearing earlier than the eighth (8th) day after the motion papers are served. With an order to show cause, the hearing can be brought on at any time the court directs, which can be fewer than eight (8) days or as close as the very day on which it is signed. If the court is convinced there is a real emergency, it can schedule the hearing for a few hours later or, in the direst case, "forthwith" the service of the order to show cause. SIEGEL-NYPRAC § 248.

c. *Time to serve answering affidavits; Other answering papers.* Answering affidavits shall be served at least two (2) days before the time at which the motion is noticed to be heard. Answering affidavits and any notice of cross-motion, with supporting papers, if any, shall be served at least seven (7) days before such time if a notice of motion served at least sixteen (16) days before such time so demands; whereupon any reply or responding affidavits shall be served at least one (1) day before such time. NY CPLR Rule 2214(b); NY R UNIF TRIAL CTS § 202.8(c).

   i. *BRONX COUNTY.* All answering papers must be submitted to the Clerk 's Office on the return date of the motion. Answering papers will not be accepted prior to the return date. NY R BRONX FIL R Doc. 8.

   ii. *NEW YORK COUNTY.* Cross-motions, papers in opposition, and reply papers on motions/petitions on notice returnable in Room 130 in a hard-copy case shall be submitted to the Motion Submission Part Courtroom (Room 130) on the final return date of the motion/petition and will not be accepted until that date. Subsequent documents on motions/petitions in e-filed cases shall be e-filed in a timely manner. Working copies when required shall be submitted to Room 130 on the final return date. NY R NY CTY Procedure II(A).

d. *Time to serve cross-motion.* At least three (3) days prior to the time at which the motion is noticed to be heard, or seven (7) days prior to such time if demand is properly made pursuant to NY CPLR Rule 2214(b), a party may serve upon the moving party a notice of cross-motion demanding relief, with or without supporting papers; provided, however, that:

   i. If such notice and any supporting papers are served by mailing, as provided in NY CPLR Rule 2103(b)(2), they shall be served three (3) days earlier than as prescribed in NY CPLR Rule 2215; and

   ii. If served by overnight delivery, as provided in NY CPLR Rule 2103(b)(6), they shall be served one (1) day earlier than as prescribed in NY CPLR Rule 2215. Relief in the alternative or of several different types may be demanded; relief need not be responsive to that demanded by the moving party. NY CPLR Rule 2215(a); NY CPLR Rule 2215(b).

   iii. *BRONX COUNTY.* Cross motions may be presented for approval on or before the return date, provided that there is a motion already calendared. NY R BRONX FIL R Doc. 8.

   iv. *ERIE COUNTY.* Cross-motions must be filed at least two (2) days before the return date of the motion. NY R L KINGS Pt. A, Papers.

   v. *KINGS COUNTY.* Hard copies are required to be filed for any motions, answering papers, stipulations, etc. for E-Filed cases returnable in [the Central Compliance Part] at least [two (2)] days before return date. . . .for cross motions. NY R L KINGS Pt. E, Rule 8.

   vi. *QUEENS COUNTY.* Motion Support does not process or forward responsive papers, including cross-motions. They must be brought to the calendar call in the judge's part. NY R L QUEENS MOT SUP Doc. 1. E-filed cross motions: across motion must be noticed for the same return date as the main motion and have the confirmation of filing attached in the same manner as a motion. NY R L QUEENS E-FILE Doc. 1(H)(2)(e).

3. *Filing before return date.* All motions shall be returnable before the assigned judge, and all papers shall be filed with the court on or before the return date. NY R UNIF TRIAL CTS § 202.8(a).

   a. *BRONX COUNTY: Time for filing*

      i. *Unassigned motions.* Unassigned motions must be in the Clerk's Office within five (5) days of the date of service of the motion. NY R BRONX FIL R Doc. 8.

      ii. *Assigned motions.* Assigned motions must be filed in the Clerk's Office not less than five (5) business days prior to the return date of the motion. NY R BRONX FIL R Doc. 8.

      iii. *Motions returnable in room 217.* The moving documents must be e-filed no later than eight (8) days prior to the return date. NY R BRONX E FIL R Doc. 1(1).

   b. *KINGS COUNTY: Time and place of filing.* Motion papers must be filed with the E-file/Motion Support Office located in Room 227. . . at 360 Adams Street at least five (5) business days before the return date of the motion. NY R L KINGS Pt. A, Papers. Hard copies are required to be filed for any motions, answering papers, stipulations, etc. for E-Filed cases returnable in [the Central Compliance Part] at least five (5) days before return date for main motions. NY R L KINGS Pt. E, Rule 8. The moving documents must be e-filed no later than eight (8) days prior to the return date. NY R L KINGS E FIL Doc. 1(D).

4. *NEW YORK COUNTY: Briefing schedule.* Once a motion is made, counsel for all parties are strongly encouraged to agree upon a briefing schedule and submit a stipulation of adjournment reflecting that schedule using service or a clerk. Where a briefing schedule has not been agreed upon, the movant can avoid the need to attend simply to see if anyone will hand up opposing papers by demanding papers as provided by NY CPLR Rule 2214(b). To protect movants against the submission of late opposition papers or cross-motions, the General Clerk's Office will screen motions in which such papers are submitted without a response (reply or opposition respectively) to ensure that proper time to respond has been afforded and it will sua sponte adjourn for one (1) week cases in which such time has not been given. NY R NY CTY Procedure II(C).

5. *QUEENS COUNTY: Time to pay fees.* As motions and petitions are time sensitive, if opting to pay at the County Clerk's Office payment MUST be made, if filed with an RJI, a minimum of nine (9) business days prior to the application's return date and if filed post RJI, a minimum of nine (9) business days prior to the application's return date. NY R L QUEENS E-FILE Doc. 1(H)(1).

6. *Computation of time*

   a. *Units of time*

      i. *Day.* A calendar day includes the time from midnight to midnight. Sunday or any day of the week specifically mentioned means a calendar day. NY GEN CONSTR § 19.

ii. *Month.* In a statute, contract or public or private instrument, unless otherwise provided in such contract or instrument or by law, the term month means a calendar month and not a lunar month. NY GEN CONSTR § 31.

iii. *Year.* For information on the definition of a year, including the definitions of a half-year and quarter-year, refer to NY GEN CONSTR § 58 and NY GEN CONSTR § 50. For information on leap years, refer to NY GEN CONSTR § 57.

b. *Periods of time*

i. *Number of days.* A number of days specified as a period from a certain day within which or after or before which an act is authorized or required to be done means such number of calendar days exclusive of the calendar day from which the reckoning is made. NY GEN CONSTR § 20.

- If such period is a period of two (2) days, Saturday, Sunday or a public holiday must be excluded from the reckoning if it is an intervening day between the day from which the reckoning is made and the last day of the period. NY GEN CONSTR § 20.
- In computing any specified period of time from a specified event, the day upon which the event happens is deemed the day from which the reckoning is made. The day from which any specified period of time is reckoned shall be excluded in making the reckoning. NY GEN CONSTR § 20.

ii. *Number of months.* A number of months after or before a certain day shall be computed by counting such number of calendar months from such day, exclusive of the calendar month in which such day occurs, and shall include the day of the month in the last month so counted having the same numerical order in days of the month as the day from which the computation is made, unless there be not so many days in the last month so counted, in which case the period computed shall expire with the last day of the month so counted. NY GEN CONSTR § 30.

iii. *Publication of notice; Number of days.* The period of publication of a legal notice shall be computed by excluding the first day of publication and including the day on which the act or event of which notice is given is to take place or which completes the full period of publication. NY CPLR § 2402.

iv. *Periods ending on Saturday, Sunday or public holiday.* When any period of time, computed from a certain day, within which or after which or before which an act is authorized or required to be done, ends on a Saturday, Sunday or a public holiday, such act may be done on the next succeeding business day and if the period ends at a specified hour, such act may be done at or before the same hour of such next succeeding business day, except that where a period of time specified by contract ends on a Saturday, Sunday or a public holiday, the extension of such period is governed by NY GEN CONSTR § 25. NY GEN CONSTR § 25-a(1).

- For a list of public holidays, refer to NY GEN CONSTR § 24.

v. *Additional time after certain kinds of service*

- *Service by mail.* Where a period of time prescribed by law is measured from the service of a paper and service is by mail, five (5) days shall be added to the prescribed period. NY CPLR Rule 2103(b)(2).
- *Service by overnight delivery service.* Where a period of time prescribed by law is measured from the service of a paper and service is by overnight delivery, one (1) business day shall be added to the prescribed period. NY CPLR Rule 2103(b)(6).

vi. *Daylight saving time.* For information on New York's time zone and the effect of daylight saving time, refer to NY GEN CONSTR § 52.

c. *Hours of court.* Notwithstanding any provision of law or rule of court to the contrary, throughout the State of New York the sessions of the Supreme Court for the disposition of business before the court shall commence not later than 9:30 a.m. and conclude not earlier than 5 p.m. Where warranted, the Chief Administrator of the Courts may authorize variances in the opening and closing hours of the courts, but, in such event, daily sessions shall total not less than six (6) hours. NY R CHIEF J § 3.1.

d. *Time limits; Extension of time.* Any act required by or in pursuance of law to be performed at or within a prescribed time, shall be performed according to the standard time. NY GEN CONSTR § 53.

i. Except where otherwise expressly prescribed by law, the court may extend the time fixed by any statute, rule or order for doing any act, upon such terms as may be just and upon good cause shown, whether the application for extension is made before or after the expiration of the time fixed. NY CPLR § 2004. Refer to the New York KeyRules Motion for Continuance/Extension of Time document for more information.

C. General Requirements

1. *Motions, generally.* There shall be compliance with the procedures prescribed in the CPLR for the bringing of motions. NY R UNIF TRIAL CTS § 202.7(a).
   a. *Motions on notice.* A notice of motion shall specify the time and place of the hearing on the motion, the supporting papers upon which the motion is based, the relief demanded and the grounds therefor. NY CPLR Rule 2214(a). A motion on notice in an action in the supreme court shall be noticed to be heard in the judicial district where the action is triable or in a county adjoining the county where the action is triable. Unless statute, civil practice rule or local court rule provides otherwise, the motion shall be noticed to be heard before a motion term or, upon order to show cause granted by a justice, before that justice out of court. NY CPLR § 2212(a). Except as provided in NY R UNIF TRIAL CTS § 202.7(d), no motion shall be filed with the court unless there have been served and filed with the motion papers a notice of motion. NY R UNIF TRIAL CTS § 202.7(a)(1).
   b. *Ex parte motions.* A motion in an action in the supreme court that may be made without notice may be made at a motion term or to a justice out of court in any county in the state. NY CPLR § 2212(b).
      i. *KINGS COUNTY.* For more information on submitting a motion ex parte, refer to NY R L KINGS E FIL Doc. 1(G).
      ii. *NEW YORK COUNTY.* For more information on submitting matters ex parte, refer to NY R NY CTY Procedure III and NY R NY CTY E FIL Doc. 2(G).
      iii. *QUEENS COUNTY.* For more information on submitting matters ex parte, refer to NY R L QUEENS EX PARTE Doc. 1.
   c. *Alternative relief.* Relief in the alternative or of several different types may be demanded. NY CPLR Rule 2214(a). The types of relief need not be related. In one motion, for example, the defendant can seek to dismiss the plaintiff's claim for lack of jurisdiction, to get an extension of time to answer, to require the plaintiff to join X as a party, and to quash a disclosure subpoena served in behalf of the plaintiff on a nonparty witness. So doing, the movant must of course specify all of these items of relief in the notice of motion, and the grounds for them, and the supporting papers must contain the entire proof requisite to the items of relief sought. NY CPLR Rule 2214(Practice Commentary, C2214:4).
   d. *General relief.* It is common practice to include at the end of the relief request in the notice of motion a so-called "general relief" clause. This is merely a few words to cover the possibility that the relief appropriate to what the movant proves was not specifically asked for, but is close enough to enable the court to grant it. After stating the specific relief desired, the lawyer will often add something like: and for such other, further, or different relief as this court may deem just and proper. NY CPLR Rule 2214(Practice Commentary, C2214:5).
   e. *Motion in improper form.* If the court finds it appropriate in the interests of justice, it may convert a motion into a special proceeding, or vice-versa, upon such terms as may be just, including the payment of fees and costs. NY CPLR § 103(c).
   f. *Order to show cause.* An order to show cause is basically only a substitute for a notice of motion. An ordinary notice of motion merely notifies the recipient that a motion is being made for specified relief. The burden of proof is on the movant. Although in most cases it is just as innocent as an ordinary notice of motion, the order to show cause gets its name by directing the recipient to "show cause" why the particular relief being asked for should not be granted. It sounds as if the burden of proof is being shifted to the recipient. It isn't. It specifies the time and place of the hearing on the application but when the hearing comes on, the burden of proof is where it always is on a motion: on the movant. SIEGEL-NYPRAC § 248.
      i. The CPLR says nothing more about an order to show cause than that it may be used "in a proper case", which leaves it entirely to the judge's discretion to determine what a proper case is. Any fact suggesting a problem as to any of the items listed above would be sufficient to invoke judicial discretion and justify the show cause procedure, which is in fact liberally used. SIEGEL-NYPRAC § 248.
      ii. An order to show cause against a state body or officers must be served in addition to service upon the defendant or respondent state body or officers upon the attorney general by delivery to an assistant attorney general at an office of the attorney general in the county in which venue of the action is designated or if there is no office of the attorney general in such county, at the office of the attorney general nearest such county. NY CPLR Rule 2214(d).
      iii. *BRONX COUNTY.* For information on submitting an order to show cause, refer to NY R BRONX E FIL R Doc. 2 and NY R BRONX LEG SUP Doc. 1.

iv. *ERIE COUNTY.* For information on submitting an order to show cause, refer to NY R ERIE E FIL Doc. 3(VI).

v. *KINGS COUNTY.* For information on submitting an order to show cause, refer to NY R L KINGS E FIL Doc. 1(F).

vi. *NEW YORK COUNTY.* For information on submitting an order to show cause, refer to NY R NY CTY E FIL Doc. 2(F).

vii. *ONONDAGA COUNTY.* For information on submitting an order to show cause, refer to NY R ONDGA E FIL Protocol(B)(10) and NY R ONDGA E FIL Protocol(J).

g. *Motions before preliminary conference.* Motions in actions to which NY R UNIF TRIAL CTS § 202.12 is applicable made after the preliminary conference has been scheduled may be denied unless there is shown good cause why such relief is warranted before the preliminary conference is held. NY R UNIF TRIAL CTS § 202.12(h).

h. *ALBANY COUNTY: Good faith effort to resolve.* Prior to the submission of a notice of motion relating to disclosure or a bill of particulars, the parties must make a good faith effort to resolve the matter in question and submit an affirmation attesting to this good faith effort. NY R 3 JD SUP Doc. 1(B).

i. *NEW YORK COUNTY: Documents with motions.* Counsel must attach to motion papers copies of all pleadings and other documents as required by the CPLR and as necessary for an informed decision on the motion. Documents in a foreign language shall be properly translated. NY R NY CTY J RUL Rule 14(a).

j. *NEW YORK COUNTY: Motions in multiple cases made together.* On occasion, attorneys may wish to make a motion in more than one case on a single set of papers. In such cases, by definition consolidation will not have been directed since consolidation signifies the combination of more than one case into a single one with a single caption and index number and ending in a single judgment. NY R NY CTY Procedure II(B). For more information on motions made with the same papers, refer to NY R NY CTY Procedure II(A).

k. *QUEENS COUNTY: Motion sequence numbers.* A motion sequence number is required for all E-filed motions. After a motion is E-filed, please consult the e-courts website within twenty-four (24) to forty-eight (48) hours to obtain the sequence number. The Confirmation Notice of E-filing MUST indicate the sequence number of any motion submitted at the Centralized Motion Part calendar call. NY R L QUEENS E-FILE Doc. 1(H)(5).

2. *Rules governing disclosure*

a. *Generally.* There shall be full disclosure of all matter material and necessary in the prosecution or defense of an action, regardless of the burden of proof, by:

i. A party, or the officer, director, member, agent or employee of a party;

ii. A person who possessed a cause of action or defense asserted in the action;

iii. A person about to depart from the state, or without the state, or residing at a greater distance from the place of trial than one hundred miles, or so sick or infirm as to afford reasonable grounds of belief that he or she will not be able to attend the trial, or a person authorized to practice medicine, dentistry or podiatry who has provided medical, dental or podiatric care or diagnosis to the party demanding disclosure, or who has been retained by such party as an expert witness; and

iv. Any other person, upon notice stating the circumstances or reasons such disclosure is sought or required. NY CPLR § 3101(a).

v. The statutory phrase "material and necessary", said the Court of Appeals, must be interpreted liberally to require disclosure upon request, of any facts bearing on the controversy which will assist preparation for trial by sharpening the issues and reducing delay and prolixity. The test is one of usefulness and reason. SIEGEL-NYPRAC § 344; Allen v. Crowell-Collier Pub. Co., 21 N.Y.2d 403, 235 N.E.2d 430 (1968).

vi. Another potential problem that the original NY CPLR § 3101(a) posed was that it spoke of "evidence" that is material and necessary, which might have been construed to permit disclosure to elicit only that which would itself qualify as "evidence" admissible at trial. It was, however, construed more broadly than that. Well-considered caselaw specifically rejected this "evidence in chief" doctrine, stating that disclosure extends as well "to all relevant information calculated to lead to relevant evidence," a standard similar to that applicable in federal court. With an amendment that took effect on January 1, 1994, changing "evidence" to "matter" in NY CPLR § 3101(a), these generous interpretations of the statute were in effect approved by the legislature. SIEGEL-NYPRAC § 344.

vii. If a party is a corporation, each of its officers, directors, members, agents, and employees is also deemed a "party" for disclosure purposes. A party who needs relevant data or material from a nonparty corporation can seek it through NY CPLR § 3101(a)(2), NY CPLR § 3101(a)(3) or NY CPLR § 3101(a)(4), under which the corporate entity is treated as a "person." These subdivisions should also apply to any entity, corporate or otherwise, from whom disclosure is sought through its agents. A corporate employee who has the requisite knowledge and information may respond to a disclosure request on behalf of the corporation. A party who can't single out the particular person in the corporation's employ to whom a disclosure request should be properly directed can direct it to the corporation as such and leave it to the corporation to designate the appropriate person to respond. Whenever disclosure is sought from a corporation through a deposition, whether as a party or as a nonparty witness, the choice in the first instance of who will be produced in the corporate behalf is with the corporation rather than the examining party. SIEGEL-NYPRAC § 345.

viii. NY CPLR § 3101(a)(4) permits a party to obtain disclosure from a nonparty by merely serving a subpoena on the nonparty providing notice of "the circumstances or reasons such disclosure is sought or required." SIEGEL-NYPRAC § 345.

b. *Privileged matter.* Upon objection by a person entitled to assert the privilege, privileged matter shall not be obtainable. NY CPLR § 3101(b).

i. A determination of whether information is privileged is governed by the rules of evidence, which apply as they would at a trial. Whatever is privileged at the trial is privileged as well on pretrial disclosure. SIEGEL-NYPRAC § 346.

c. *Attorney's work product.* The work product of an attorney shall not be obtainable. NY CPLR § 3101(c).

i. NY CPLR § 3101(c) makes unobtainable the "work product of an attorney"—an ill-defined category whose potential for mischief has been avoided only because the judiciary has accorded it a very narrow scope. It is a category wholly distinct from the "materials . . . prepared in anticipation of litigation" of NY CPLR § 3101(d)(2). The fact that immunity is absolute under NY CPLR § 3101(c), while that of NY CPLR § 3101(d)(2) is only conditional, is the factor that requires as sharp a line as possible between the two categories. SIEGEL-NYPRAC § 347.

ii. The judiciary has cast precious little under the "work product" category of NY CPLR § 3101(c), preferring instead to fit doubtful items under the "materials . . . prepared in anticipation of litigation" banner of NY CPLR § 3101(d)(2), where the conditional immunity can be overcome and the matters ordered disclosed when stated conditions are met. SIEGEL-NYPRAC § 347.

d. *Trial preparation*

i. *Experts.* Upon request, each party shall identify each person whom the party expects to call as an expert witness at trial and shall disclose in reasonable detail the subject matter on which each expert is expected to testify, the substance of the facts and opinions on which each expert is expected to testify, the qualifications of each expert witness and a summary of the grounds for each expert's opinion. NY CPLR § 3101(d)(1)(i).

- However, where a party for good cause shown retains an expert an insufficient period of time before the commencement of trial to give appropriate notice thereof, the party shall not thereupon be precluded from introducing the expert's testimony at the trial solely on grounds of noncompliance with NY CPLR § 3101(d)(1). In that instance, upon motion of any party, made before or at trial, or on its own initiative, the court may make whatever order may be just. In an action for medical, dental or podiatric malpractice, a party, in responding to a request, may omit the names of medical, dental or podiatric experts but shall be required to disclose all other information concerning such experts otherwise required by NY CPLR § 3101(d)(1). NY CPLR § 3101(d)(1)(i).
- In an action for medical, dental or podiatric malpractice, any party may, by written offer made to and served upon all other parties and filed with the court, offer to disclose the name of, and to make available for examination upon oral deposition, any person the party making the offer expects to call as an expert witness at trial. Within twenty (20) days of service of the offer, a party shall accept or reject the offer by serving a written reply upon all parties and filing a copy thereof with the court. Failure to serve a reply within twenty (20) days of service of the offer shall be deemed a rejection of the offer. If all parties accept the offer, each party shall be required to produce his or her expert witness for examination upon oral deposition upon receipt of a notice to take oral deposition in accordance with NY CPLR Rule 3107. If any party, having made or accepted the offer, fails to make that party's expert available for oral deposition, that party shall be precluded from offering expert testimony at the trial of the action. NY CPLR § 3101(d)(1)(ii).
- Further disclosure concerning the expected testimony of any expert may be obtained only by court order

upon a showing of special circumstances and subject to restrictions as to scope and provisions concerning fees and expenses as the court may deem appropriate. However, a party, without court order, may take the testimony of a person authorized to practice medicine, dentistry or podiatry who is the party's treating or retained expert, as described in NY CPLR § 3101(a)(3), in which event any other party shall be entitled to the full disclosure authorized by Article 31 of Chapter 8 of the Civil Practice Law and Rules (NY CPLR § 3101, et seq.) with respect to that expert without court order. NY CPLR § 3101(d)(1)(iii).

ii. *Materials.* Subject to the provisions of NY CPLR § 3101(d)(1), materials otherwise discoverable under NY CPLR § 3101(a) and prepared in anticipation of litigation or for trial by or for another party, or by or for that other party's representative (including an attorney, consultant, surety, indemnitor, insurer or agent), may be obtained only upon a showing that the party seeking discovery has substantial need of the materials in the preparation of the case and is unable without undue hardship to obtain the substantial equivalent of the materials by other means. In ordering discovery of the materials when the required showing has been made, the court shall protect against disclosure of the mental impressions, conclusions, opinions or legal theories of an attorney or other representative of a party concerning the litigation. NY CPLR § 3101(d)(2).

- In order to qualify as "litigation" material the item must have been prepared exclusively for litigation. Incidental potential use in litigation, the courts have observed, may also be a function of such reports, but they have at least an equal if not greater mission "to prevent future accidents, discipline careless employees, or, generally, to increase the economy and efficiency of the operation." SIEGEL-NYPRAC § 348.

e. *Party's statement.* A party may obtain a copy of his own statement. NY CPLR § 3101(e).

i. Moreover, NY CPLR § 3101(e) has been broadly interpreted to include photographs. Items such as photographs and videotapes are now independently subject to disclosure under NY CPLR § 3101(i). SIEGEL-NYPRAC § 348.

f. *Contents of insurance agreement.* A party may obtain discovery of the existence and contents of any insurance agreement under which any person carrying on an insurance business may be liable to satisfy part or all of a judgment which may be entered in the action or to indemnify or reimburse for payments made to satisfy the judgment. Information concerning the insurance agreement is not by reason of disclosure admissible in evidence at trial. For purpose of NY CPLR § 3101(f), an application for insurance shall not be treated as part of an insurance agreement. NY CPLR § 3101(f).

g. *Accident reports.* Except as is otherwise provided by law, in addition to any other matter which may be subject to disclosure, there shall be full disclosure of any written report of an accident prepared in the regular course of business operations or practices of any person, firm, corporation, association or other public or private entity, unless prepared by a police or peace officer for a criminal investigation or prosecution and disclosure would interfere with a criminal investigation or prosecution. NY CPLR § 3101(g).

h. *Amendment or supplementation of responses.* A party shall amend or supplement a response previously given to a request for disclosure promptly upon the party's thereafter obtaining information that the response was incorrect or incomplete when made, or that the response, though correct and complete when made, no longer is correct and complete, and the circumstances are such that a failure to amend or supplement the response would be materially misleading. NY CPLR § 3101(h).

i. Where a party obtains such information an insufficient period of time before the commencement of trial appropriately to amend or supplement the response, the party shall not thereupon be precluded from introducing evidence at the trial solely on grounds of noncompliance with NY CPLR § 3101(h). In that instance, upon motion of any party, made before or at trial, or on its own initiative, the court may make whatever order may be just. Further amendment or supplementation may be obtained by court order. NY CPLR § 3101(h).

i. *Other disclosures.* In addition to any other matter which may be subject to disclosure, there shall be full disclosure of any films, photographs, video tapes or audio tapes, including transcripts or memoranda thereof, involving a person referred to in NY CPLR § 3101(a)(1). There shall be disclosure of all portions of such material, including out-takes, rather than only those portions a party intends to use. The provisions of NY CPLR § 3101(i) shall not apply to materials compiled for law enforcement purposes which are exempt from disclosure under NY PUB OFF § 87. NY CPLR § 3101(i).

i. While NY CPLR § 3101(i) was enacted with the defendant's surreptitious tapes of the plaintiff in mind, its language is broad enough to embrace any films, photographs, and audio or video tapes of a party, even those made by the party from whom disclosure is sought. SIEGEL-NYPRAC § 348.

j. *Protective orders.* The court may at any time on its own initiative, or on motion of any party or of any person from whom discovery is sought, make a protective order denying, limiting, conditioning or regulating the use of any disclosure device. NY CPLR § 3103(a).

k. *Supervision of disclosure.* Upon the motion of any party or witness on notice to all parties or on its own initiative without notice, the court in which an action is pending may by one of its judges or a referee supervise all or part of any disclosure procedure. NY CPLR § 3104(a).

i. *Selection of referee.* A judicial hearing officer may be designated as a referee under NY CPLR § 3104, or the court may permit all of the parties in an action to stipulate that a named attorney may act as referee. In such latter event, the stipulation shall provide for payment of his fees which shall, unless otherwise agreed, be taxed as disbursements. NY CPLR § 3104(b).

ii. *Powers of referee; Motions referred to person supervising disclosure.* A referee under NY CPLR § 3104 shall have all the powers of the court under NY CPLR § 3101, et seq. except the power to relieve himself of his duties, to appoint a successor, or to adjudge any person guilty of contempt. All motions or applications made under Article 31 of Chapter 8 of the Civil Practice Law and Rules (NY CPLR § 3101, et seq.) shall be returnable before the judge or referee, designated under NY CPLR § 3104 and after disposition, if requested by any party, his order shall be filed in the office of the clerk. NY CPLR § 3104(c).

iii. *Review of order of referee.* Any party or witness may apply for review of an order made under NY CPLR § 3104 by a referee. The application shall be by motion made in the court in which the action is pending within five (5) days after the order is made. Service of a notice of motion for review shall suspend disclosure of the particular matter in dispute. If the question raised by the motion may affect the rights of a witness, notice shall be served on him personally or by mail at his last known address. It shall set forth succinctly the order complained of, the reason it is objectionable and the relief demanded. NY CPLR § 3104(d).

iv. *Payment of expenses of referee.* Except where a judicial hearing officer has been designated a referee hereunder, the court may make an appropriate order for the payment of the reasonable expenses of the referee. NY CPLR § 3104(e).

3. *Resolution of disclosure disputes*

a. *BRONX COUNTY: Written application for conference in place of formal motion.* In lieu of a formal motion, parties may make written application to schedule a Discovery Status or Compliance Conference. Such application shall be forwarded to Bronx Supreme Civil, 851 Grand Concourse, Bronx, New York 10451 Room 217 DCM Department, Email BXDCM@NYCOURTS.GOV, FAX: 212 884 8955, PHONE: 212 884 8955. NY R BRONX FIL R Doc. 5. Such application shall set forth:

i. The case caption and index number;

ii. E Mail address for notification;

iii. Must specify all discovery issues and any other relief being requested;

iv. The request must state the courts intervention is necessary to resolve these issues. NY R BRONX FIL R Doc. 5.

v. Identify all prior orders addressing discovery issues. NY R BRONX FIL R Doc. 5(5).

vi. The request must be CCed to all appearing parties. NY R BRONX FIL R Doc. 5(6).

b. *KINGS COUNTY: Attempt to reach agreement.* The attorneys shall, in the first instance, attempt to reach an agreement on all relevant discovery. Disputed matters will be adjudicated by the Court. NY R L KINGS Pt. B, Rule 2.

c. *NEW YORK COUNTY: Good faith effort to resolve.* Prior to making a discovery motion, counsel shall consult one another in a good faith effort to resolve any discovery disputes. If a dispute is not thus resolved, the party seeking disclosure, unless otherwise directed in the Background Information section above, is advised to contact the Part Clerk promptly, and within any applicable deadline, for the purpose of arranging a conference, in court or by telephone. NY R NY CTY J RUL Rule 10.

4. *Motion for protective order*

a. *Prevention of abuse.* The court may at any time on its own initiative, or on motion of any party or of any person from whom or about whom discovery is sought, make a protective order denying, limiting, conditioning or regulating the use of any disclosure device. Such order shall be designed to prevent unreasonable annoyance, expense, embarrassment, disadvantage, or other prejudice to any person or the courts. NY CPLR § 3103(a).

i. The protective order is available no matter what disclosure device is implicated. Early conflict about whether the protective order can be used to test the validity of a request to admit under NY CPLR § 3123 has been resolved.

It can be. SIEGEL-NYPRAC § 353; Epstein v. Consol. Edison Co. of New York, 31 A.D.2d 746, 746, 297 N.Y.S.2d 260, 261 (1969). In the lower courts, the protective order is available against a bill of particulars if the bill is being used for harassment. SIEGEL-NYPRAC § 353.

b. *Suspension of disclosure pending application for protective order.* Service of a notice of motion for a protective order shall suspend disclosure of the particular matter in dispute. NY CPLR § 3103(b).

   i. Where a motion for a protective order against an examination of a witness is made, the witness shall be notified by the moving party that the examination is stayed. NY CPLR Rule 3106(b).

c. *Suppression of information improperly obtained.* If any disclosure under Article 31 of Chapter 8 of the Civil Practice Law and Rules (NY CPLR § 3101, et seq.) has been improperly or irregularly obtained so that a substantial right of a party is prejudiced, the court, on motion, may make an appropriate order, including an order that the information be suppressed. NY CPLR § 3103(c).

d. *Motion by witness.* NY CPLR § 3103(a) permits the witness to seek the protective order, but by contacting an opposing party, the witness may be able to get that party to make the motion in the witness's behalf. SIEGEL-NYPRAC § 353; NY CPLR § 3103(a).

e. *Reach of a protective order.* The court can regulate on a motion for a protective order:

   i. The time, order, and place of taking depositions;

   ii. The number and names of persons to be questioned;

   iii. The time within which the information must be obtained;

   iv. The number, kinds of questions, or specific questions that may be asked;

   v. The disclosure device or combination of devices that may be used; and

   vi. The matters that may or may not be inquired into. SIEGEL-NYPRAC § 353.

f. *Additional uses for a protective order*

   i. The protective order can step in to balance the situation in which a disparity in the economic resources of the parties is disabling one from participating in the disclosure process, or empowering another to take undue advantage of it. The court can order one party to defray initially the costs of another's participation in disclosure, but this is not a favored step. SIEGEL-NYPRAC § 353; Buffone v. Aronson, 45 Misc. 2d 454, 455, 257 N.Y.S.2d 47, 49 (Sup. Ct. 1965). The later winner on the merits can recover these expenses, or at least a segment of them, from the loser as post-judgment disbursements. SIEGEL-NYPRAC § 353; Fairchild Camera & Instrument Corp. v. Barletta, 21 A.D.2d 768, 250 N.Y.S.2d 679 (1964).

   ii. With a protective order, the court can limit the number of disclosure devices that may be used. SIEGEL-NYPRAC § 353; Estates Roofing Co. v. Savo, 85 Misc. 2d 1028, 1028—29, 381 N.Y.S.2d 198, 199 (Dist. Ct. 1976).

g. *Relationship with preliminary conference; Disclosure timetable.* Where the motion relates to disclosure or to a bill of particulars, and a preliminary conference has not been held, the court shall notify all parties of a scheduled date to appear for a preliminary conference, which shall be not more than forty-five (45) days from the return date of the motion unless the court orders otherwise, and a form of a stipulation and order, prescribed by the Chief Administrator of the Courts, shall be made available which the parties may sign, agreeing to a timetable which shall provide for completion of disclosure within twelve (12) months, and for a resolution of any other issues raised by the motion. If all parties sign the form and return it to the court before the return date of the motion, such form shall be "so ordered" by the court, and the motion shall be deemed withdrawn. If such stipulation is not returned by all parties, the conference shall be held on the assigned date. Issues raised by the motion and not resolved at the conference shall be determined by the court. NY R UNIF TRIAL CTS § 202.8(f).

5. *Oppositions.* In the absence of statutory provision or court rule, a motion ordinarily does not require a written answer, although an adverse party may be permitted to file an answer in opposition to the showing made in the motion or its supporting affidavits. AMJUR MOTIONS § 26. When a party files a motion and the opposing party fails to respond, the court may construe such failure to respond as non-opposition to the motion or an admission that the motion was meritorious, may take the facts alleged in the motion as true, and may grant the motion if the relief requested appears to be justified. However, the severity of such a result demands that a court impose it only with great caution. AMJUR MOTIONS § 28.

6. *Governing law.* The civil practice law and rules (NY CPLR § 101, et seq.) shall govern the procedure in civil judicial

proceedings in all courts of the state and before all judges, except where the procedure is regulated by inconsistent statute. The civil practice law and rules shall succeed the civil practice act and rules of civil practice and shall be deemed substituted therefor throughout the statutes and rules of the state. NY CPLR § 101. The civil practice law and rules shall be liberally construed to secure the just, speedy and inexpensive determination of every civil judicial proceeding. NY CPLR § 104.

a. *Uniform trial court rules.* The uniform civil rules for the Supreme Court and County Court (NY R UNIF TRIAL CTS § 202.1, et seq.) shall be applicable to civil actions and proceedings in the Supreme Court and the County Court. NY R UNIF TRIAL CTS § 202.1(a). The provisions of the uniform rules shall be construed consistent with the Civil Practice Law and Rules (CPLR), and matters not covered by the uniform rules shall be governed by the CPLR. NY R UNIF TRIAL CTS § 202.1(d).

b. *Local rules.* Local court rules, not inconsistent with law or with uniform civil rules for the Supreme Court and County Court (NY R UNIF TRIAL CTS § 202.1, et seq.), shall comply with Part 9 of the Rules of the Chief Judge (NY R CHIEF J § 9.1). NY R UNIF TRIAL CTS § 202.1(c).

c. *Official forms.* The state administrator shall have the power to adopt, amend and rescind an appendix of forms. Forms adopted pursuant to NY CPLR § 107 shall be sufficient under the civil practice law and rules and shall illustrate the simplicity and brevity of statement which the civil practice law and rules contemplate. NY CPLR § 107.

7. *Rules of the commercial division.* [Editor's note: certain types of civil cases or civil cases meeting certain monetary thresholds that are filed in the state of New York must be filed in the Commercial Division of the New York Supreme Courts. Rules governing practice in the commercial division are found in NY R UNIF TRIAL CTS § 202.70]. Cases which must be filed in the commercial division are listed below. For more information, refer to NY R UNIF TRIAL CTS § 202.70.

a. *Monetary thresholds.* Except as set forth in NY R UNIF TRIAL CTS § 202.70(b), the monetary thresholds of the Commercial Division, exclusive of punitive damages, interests, costs, disbursements and counsel fees claimed, are established as follows: (1) Albany County, fifty thousand dollars ($50,000); (2) Eighth Judicial District, one hundred thousand dollars ($100,000); (3) Kings County, one hundred fifty thousand dollars ($150,000); (4) Nassau County, two hundred thousand dollars ($200,000); (5) New York County, five hundred thousand dollars ($500,000); (6) Onondaga County, fifty thousand dollars ($50,000); (7) Queens County, one hundred thousand dollars ($100,000); (8) Seventh Judicial District, fifty thousand dollars ($50,000); (9) Suffolk County, one hundred thousand dollars ($100,000); and (10) Westchester County, one hundred thousand dollars ($100,000). NY R UNIF TRIAL CTS § 202.70(a).

i. *ALBANY COUNTY.* The Commercial Division of the Albany County Supreme Court exercises jurisdiction over selected business and commercial disputes in which the amount at issue generally involves damage claims in a minimum amount of fifty thousand dollars ($50,000) as well as claims for unspecified amounts where the value of the commercial asset(s) in dispute exceeds fifty thousand dollars ($50,000). A separate publication promulgating the rules and criteria relating to the filing and management of Commercial Court cases in this part may be obtained from the Albany County Supreme Court Clerk's Office. A section of the Uniform Civil Rules for the Supreme Court and County Court sets forth statewide rules. NY R 3 JD SUP Doc. 1(E).

ii. *BRONX COUNTY.* The monetary threshold for commercial cases in Bronx County will be seventy-five thousand dollars ($75,000). All other parameters including the type of matters that will be heard are contained within the Rules of the Commercial Division of the Supreme Court (NY R UNIF TRIAL CTS § 202.70). NY R BRONX FIL R Doc. 12.

iii. *NEW YORK COUNTY.* The monetary threshold in the New York County Commercial Division, which is generally applicable, is an amount in controversy of five hundred thousand dollars ($500,000) or more (exclusive of punitive damages, interest, costs, disbursements, and counsel fees). If the case is designated a commercial one and the Addendum is submitted, the clerk will review the pleadings to determine whether the amount in controversy in the case meets the monetary threshold or whether an exception to the threshold applies. NY R NY CTY Procedure IA(B). For more information on assigning a case to the commercial division in New York County, refer to NY R NY CTY Procedure IA(B).

b. *Commercial cases.* Actions in which the principal claims involve or consist of the following will be heard in the Commercial Division provided that the monetary threshold is met or equitable or declaratory relief is sought:

i. Breach of contract or fiduciary duty, fraud, misrepresentation, business tort (e.g., unfair competition), or statutory and/or common law violation where the breach or violation is alleged to arise out of business dealings (e.g., sales of assets or securities; corporate restructuring; partnership, shareholder, joint venture, and other business agreements; trade secrets; restrictive covenants; and employment agreements not including claims that principally involve alleged discriminatory practices);

ii. Transactions governed by the Uniform Commercial Code (exclusive of those concerning individual cooperative or condominium units);

iii. Transactions involving commercial real property, including Yellowstone injunctions and excluding actions for the payment of rent only;

iv. Shareholder derivative actions—without consideration of the monetary threshold;

v. Commercial class actions—without consideration of the monetary threshold;

vi. Business transactions involving or arising out of dealings with commercial banks and other financial institutions;

vii. Internal affairs of business organizations;

viii. Malpractice by accountants or actuaries, and legal malpractice arising out of representation in commercial matters;

ix. Environmental insurance coverage;

x. Commercial insurance coverage (e.g., directors and officers, errors and omissions, and business interruption coverage);

xi. Dissolution of corporations, partnerships, limited liability companies, limited liability partnerships and joint ventures—without consideration of the monetary threshold; and

xii. Applications to stay or compel arbitration and affirm or disaffirm arbitration awards and related injunctive relief pursuant to Article 75 of the New York Civil Practice Law and Rules (NY CPLR § 7501, et seq.) involving any of the foregoing enumerated commercial issues. Where the applicable arbitration agreement provides for the arbitration to be heard outside the United States, the monetary threshold set forth in NY R UNIF TRIAL CTS § 202.70(a) shall not apply. NY R UNIF TRIAL CTS § 202.70(b).

c. *Non-commercial cases.* The following will not be heard in the Commercial Division even if the monetary threshold is met:

i. Suits to collect professional fees;

ii. Cases seeking a declaratory judgment as to insurance coverage for personal injury or property damage;

iii. Residential real estate disputes, including landlord-tenant matters, and commercial real estate disputes involving the payment of rent only;

iv. Home improvement contracts involving residential properties consisting of one to four residential units or individual units in any residential building, including cooperative or condominium units;

v. Proceedings to enforce a judgment regardless of the nature of the underlying case;

vi. First-party insurance claims and actions by insurers to collect premiums or rescind non-commercial policies; and

vii. Attorney malpractice actions except as otherwise provided in NY R UNIF TRIAL CTS § 202.70(b)(8). NY R UNIF TRIAL CTS § 202.70(c).

d. For more information on the Commercial Division, refer to NY R UNIF TRIAL CTS § 202.70.

D. Documents

1. *Documents for moving party*

a. *Required documents*

i. *Notice of motion, order to show cause, or affidavit on ex parte motion.* The notice of motion shall be substantially in the form found in NY R UNIF TRIAL CTS § 202.7(b). NY R UNIF TRIAL CTS § 202.7(b). The supporting papers should be referred to in the notice of motion. SIEGEL-NYPRAC § 246. The court in a proper case may grant an order to show cause, to be served in lieu of a notice of motion. NY CPLR Rule 2214(d). An ex parte motion shall be accompanied by an affidavit stating the result of any prior motion for similar relief and specifying the new facts, if any, that were not previously shown. NY CPLR Rule 2217(b).

- *Request for oral argument.* A party requesting oral argument shall set forth such request in its notice of motion or in its order to show cause or on the first page of the answering papers, as the case may be. Where all parties to a motion request oral argument, oral argument shall be granted unless the court shall determine it to be unnecessary. Where a motion is brought on by order to show cause, the court may set forth in the order that oral argument is required on the return date of the motion. NY R UNIF TRIAL CTS § 202.8(d).

ii. *Motion.* Refer to the General Requirements section of this document for information on the notice of motion and motion.

iii. *Affirmation of counsel.* No motion shall be filed with the court unless there have been served and filed with the motion papers with respect to a motion relating to disclosure or to a bill of particulars, an affirmation that counsel has conferred with counsel for the opposing party in a good faith effort to resolve the issues raised by the motion. NY R UNIF TRIAL CTS § 202.7(a)(2).

- The affirmation of the good faith effort to resolve the issues raised by the motion shall indicate the time, place and nature of the consultation and the issues discussed and any resolutions, or shall indicate good cause why no such conferral with counsel for opposing parties was held. NY R UNIF TRIAL CTS § 202.7(c).
- *KINGS COUNTY.* Motions must be accompanied by an affirmation of good faith pursuant to NY R UNIF TRIAL CTS § 202.7(a), indicating what efforts have been made to resolve the motion. NY R L KINGS Pt. E, Rule 9.

iv. *Request for judicial intervention.* At any time after service of process, a party may file a request for judicial intervention. Except as provided in NY R UNIF TRIAL CTS § 202.6(b), in an action not yet assigned to a judge, the court shall not accept for filing a notice of motion, order to show cause, or application for ex parte order, unless such notice or application is accompanied by a request for judicial intervention. NY R UNIF TRIAL CTS § 202.6(a).

- *BRONX COUNTY.* Generally, the Request For Judicial Intervention, commonly referred to as an "RJI", is required to be filed in any action where the assignment of a Justice is required. The RJI sets forth the information which is entered into the court system's database. It must be completely and accurately filled out. The full caption, as stated on the Summons, must be set forth. Use of terms "et al." and "etc." are not permitted. Only one (1) RJI may be filed in each action. Either a self represented litigant or an attorney must sign the affirmation at the end of the form. Once completed, the RJI must be filed in duplicate. Except in the case of an ex-parte application, the RJI must also be served together with the accompanying application upon all parties. Proof of accuracy of the index number must accompany the RJI. Check the Fee Schedule[. . .]for any applicable filing fees. NY R BRONX FIL R Doc. 2.
- *KINGS COUNTY.* An RJI with the relevant required addendum in a NYSCEF case shall be submitted via NYSCEF. Once e-filed, the RJI and any accompanying document will be forwarded to the relevant support office for random assignment of the case and processing of the document. A filer or counsel need not appear (as to Proposed Orders to Show Cause, however, see below). A copy of the pleadings must be submitted only if the document has not previously been e-filed. If the RJI seeks intervention with regard to a document that is intended for review by a Justice, such as a motion, a working copy of the RJI must be submitted with the working copy of the motion and the NYSCEF Confirmation Notice. NY R L KINGS E FIL Doc. 1(C).
- *NEW YORK COUNTY.* To obtain the assignment of an IAS Justice to a case, a Request for Judicial Intervention (cost ninety-five dollars ($95)) must be filed, with NYSCEF in an e-filed case or in paper in an authorized hard-copy one. A no-fee RJI, which will generally result in the referral of an application to an Ex Parte Justice, is also required with regard to certain kinds of applications for which, prior to 2011, no RJI was required. NY R NY CTY Procedure I(C). A "fillable" form RJI is available on-line. The form must be filed in duplicate in hard-copy cases. NY R NY CTY Procedure IA(A)(1). The filer of an RJI must check off a box identifying the type of case at issue. Where the RJI seeks judicial assignment, this designation will bring about a random assignment of the case by computer to a Justice handling cases of that type. NY R NY CTY Procedure IA(A)(1). The RJI and any addendum can be completed and submitted electronically in an e-filed case. NY R NY CTY Procedure II(A). The RJI shall be marked to reflect the existence of any "related case" as explained on the "Commencement of Cases" page under "Case Processing" on the court's website. NY R NY CTY Procedure II(A); NY R NY CTY E FIL Doc. 2(C).
- *ONONDAGA COUNTY.* The RJI will be submitted via the NYSCEF system along with any required RJI addendum forms. When the RJI is filed and the fee paid online, the Onondaga County Clerk's Office will electronically forward the RJI and any accompanying documents to the Onondaga Supreme Court Clerk's Office for assignment and processing. Counsel will receive notification of judge assignment via the NYSCEF system. NY R ONDGA E FIL Protocol(B)(3).
- *QUEENS COUNTY.* A Request for Judicial Intervention ("RJI") in an E-filed case shall be submitted via the E-filing System. When the RJI is approved, filed and paid for on-line, it will be forwarded to the relevant

back office for random assignment of the case and processing of the document. In the case of RJIs seeking assignment to the Commercial Division, the filer must submit therewith, a Commercial Addendum as required by the standards for assignment of cases to the Commercial Division. NY R L QUEENS E-FILE Doc. 1(F).

v. *Proof of service.* In addition to complying with the provisions of NY CPLR Rule 2101, every paper filed in court shall have annexed thereto appropriate proof of service on all parties where required. NY R UNIF TRIAL CTS § 202.5(a).

- *QUEENS COUNTY.* With regard to service of a motion/petition on notice in an E-filed action, NY CPLR Rule 2214(b) and NY R UNIF TRIAL CTS § 202.5-b(f) applies. Where required, proof of service shall be filed on-line as a separate document. NY R L QUEENS E-FILE Doc. 1(H)(3).

vi. *ALBANY COUNTY: Additional required documents*

- *Affirmation of good faith effort.* The parties must[. . .]submit an affirmation attesting to [their good faith effort to resolve the matter]. The affirmation of good faith effort to resolve the issues raised by the motion shall indicate the time, place and nature of the consultation and the issues discussed and any resolutions, or shall indicate good cause why no such conferral with counsel for opposing parties was held. An assigned justice or judge may dismiss a motion for failure to demonstrate that such effort was made with leave to renew the motion after such effort has been demonstrated. NY R 3 JD SUP Doc. 1(B).

b. *Supplemental documents*

i. *Supporting evidence; Exhibits.* The main supporting papers on a motion are affidavits, but any relevant exhibits, documents, depositions, etc., are also includible. SIEGEL-NYPRAC § 246.

- *Affidavits accompanying motion.* Affidavits shall be for a statement of the relevant facts. NY R UNIF TRIAL CTS § 202.8(c).
- *Foreign language documents.* Where an affidavit or exhibit annexed to a paper served or filed is in a foreign language, it shall be accompanied by an English translation and an affidavit by the translator stating his qualifications and that the translation is accurate. NY CPLR Rule 2101(b).
- *Statement of attorney in lieu of affidavit.* The statement of an attorney admitted to practice in the courts of the state, or of a physician, osteopath or dentist, authorized by law to practice in the state, who is not a party to an action, when subscribed and affirmed by him to be true under the penalties of perjury, may be served or filed in the action in lieu of and with the same force and effect as an affidavit. NY CPLR Rule 2106.
- *NEW YORK COUNTY: Form of presented exhibits.* Exhibits should be tabbed and be legible; a typed version of any exhibit that is difficult to read should be submitted with the original. Exhibits printed on both sides of the page should be bound and tabbed on the side. NY R NY CTY J RUL Rule 14(a).
- *QUEENS COUNTY.* Attorneys submitting exhibits to the court on E-file cases shall make each exhibit a separate, labeled attachment to an affidavit/affirmation. NY R L QUEENS E-FILE Doc. 1(H)(4).

ii. *Brief.* Briefs shall be for a statement of the relevant law. NY R UNIF TRIAL CTS § 202.8(c).

iii. *Notice to produce papers not in possession of the court.* If a paper relied on by the movant is in the possession of the other side, it may be demanded of that side with a notice to produce it at the hearing. Where such papers are in the possession of an adverse party, they shall be produced by him at the hearing on notice served with the motion papers. NY CPLR Rule 2214(Practice Commentary, C2214:23).

iv. *Filing fees.* The County Clerk shall require the payment of any applicable statutory fees, or an order of the Court waiving payment of such fees, before accepting a paper for filing. NY R UNIF TRIAL CTS § 202.5(d)(1). For information on filing fees, if any, refer to NY CPLR § 8001, et seq.

- *ALBANY COUNTY.* In general, any filing subsequent to the commencement of an action which is designated as a motion or cross-motion requires the payment of a filing fee to the County Clerk's Office prior to submission to the Supreme Court Clerk's Office for referral to the assigned justice. The fee is assessed regardless of whether an application is made by notice of motion, order to show cause or ex parte. No fee will be charged upon the filing of a motion for poor person status in conjunction with an application which serves to commence an action or special proceeding. In the event a motion is received by the court unaccompanied by proof of payment to the County Clerk, the Supreme Court Clerk's Office will contact the submitting party to advise that the application will be held pending receipt of the filing fee only until the return date of the motion. If proof of payment is not submitted to the Supreme Court Clerk's Office by the return date (ex parte applications will be held ten (10) days), the papers will be returned by mail with a notification that the motion has been removed from the court's calendar and that it must be re-noticed and re-filed with the court along with the requisite filing fee. Inquiries concerning the applicability of the motion fee to a proposed filing may be directed to the Supreme Court Clerk's Office. NY R 3 JD SUP Doc. 1(B).

- *BRONX COUNTY.* In accordance with the new civil fee schedule set forth in Article 80 of the C.P.L.R. (NY CPLR § 8001, et seq.), effective July 14, 2003, all motions, and cross motions must be approved in Room 217 prior to payment of said fees in the County Clerk's Office, Room 118. NY R BRONX FIL R Doc. 8. The motion fee [must be] paid for via NYSCEF by credit/debit card. NY R BRONX E FIL R Doc. 1(1).
- *ERIE COUNTY.* Payment for fee-bearing NYSCEF documents must be made online via credit or debit card (American Express, MasterCard or Visa) at the time of submission. NY R ERIE E FIL Doc. 3(III)(E).
- *KINGS COUNTY.* The motion must be filed with NYSCEF and the motion fee paid. NY R L KINGS E FIL Doc. 1(D). Court fees in NYSCEF cases must be paid via NYSCEF by a credit or bank card (MasterCard, Visa, or American Express). Fees are no longer accepted in person in the Kings County Clerk's Office in NYSCEF cases. NY R L KINGS E FIL Doc. 1(B)(6).
- *NEW YORK COUNTY.* A motion fee must be paid on motions made in writing by notice of motion, order to show cause or ex parte after the commencement of an action. For this purpose, the term "action" shall mean any application to the court that requires the assignment of an index number, regardless of whether a formal pleading is filed. Applications or motions that commence an action and for which an index number fee must be paid require no motion fee. [A]ny motions made after the initial applications in these situations would require payment of the motion fee. A motion that is the initial application in a case commenced by the filing of a summons and complaint would require a motion fee since the filing of the summons and complaint rather than the application itself would require the purchase of an index number. NY R NY CTY Procedure II(A). In e-filed cases the motion fee must be paid when the documents are filed. Payment is made on-line by Visa, Mastercard, or American Express credit or bank card. NY R NY CTY Procedure II(A); NY R NY CTY E FIL Doc. 2(B)(5).
- *ONONDAGA COUNTY.* Court fees in e-filed cases must be paid online with the NYSCEF system using a credit card. The document is not considered to have been filed until payment of the fee has been tendered. NY R ONDGA E FIL Protocol(B)(2). Fees must be paid on all cross motions. NY R ONDGA E FIL Protocol(B)(9)(e).
- *QUEENS COUNTY.* The Motion Support Office does not receive, forward or process any fees or waiver of fees. All applications requiring payment of statutory fees or waiver of fees must be sent directly to the Queens County Clerk's office. NY R L QUEENS MOT SUP Doc. 1. Court fees (e.g., RJI fee, motion fee) in E-filed cases may be paid for on-line using a credit card. Papers may also be filed with the E-file system and the fee may be paid at the County Clerk's Office. In the latter case, the paper is not considered to have been filed until payment of the fee has been tendered. NY R L QUEENS E-FILE Doc. 1(E)(1). The motion/petition shall be filed on-line and the fee paid for either on-line by credit card or by the "Pay at the County Clerk's Office" option. NY R L QUEENS E-FILE Doc. 1(H)(1).

v. *Working copies.* The court may require the parties to provide working copies of documents filed electronically. In such event, each working copy shall include, firmly affixed thereto, a copy of a confirmation notice in a form prescribed by the Chief Administrator. NY R UNIF TRIAL CTS § 202.5-b(d)(5).

- *BRONX COUNTY.* After papers on motions have been e-filed, working copies thereof, with Confirmation Notice firmly attached as the back page facing out, must be submitted. (Each document or group of documents that is separately bound shall bear a Confirmation Notice.) Working copies lacking the Notice will not be accepted. WORKING COPIES OF MOTION PAPERS MUST BE SUBMITTED NO LATER THAN 4:45 P.M. ON THE RETURN DATE IN THE MOTION SUPPORT OFFICE (ROOM 217) AS EXPLAINED in NY R BRONX E FIL R Doc. 1(4). If an attorney has failed to submit required working copies on or before the return date, the motion will be transmitted as is to the Justice for such action as the Justice finds appropriate. Attorneys may submit working copies on motions by mail or overnight delivery. Any such submission shall be sent in a timely manner to the Motion Support Office (Room 217) and be conspicuously marked on the outside "NYSCEF Matter"; lack of such marking may delay processing. NY R BRONX E FIL R Doc. 1(4)(a).
- *ERIE COUNTY.* Electronically filed documents subject to review and processing by the Part Clerk do not

require a working copy unless otherwise directed or provided for in IAS Part Rules. NY R UNIF TRIAL CTS § 202.5-b(d)(4), any working copy submitted shall include, as a cover page firmly fastened thereto, a copy of the Confirmation Notice generated by the NYSCEF site at the time of filing. Please consult the individual Justice's Part Rules and/or consult with the Judge's chambers to determine whether and how working copies are to be provided. Working copies will not be printed or delivered by the Erie County Clerk or the Chief Clerk of the Courts or any of their personnel to chambers. The official record of a document in an electronically filed case is the document filed via the NYSCEF system. Working copies are intended only for use by the Justice. The Court will discard all working copies after the Justice has finished with them. Thus, in the event that counsel fails to file a document via the NYSCEF system, the document will not be part of the court record. NY R ERIE E FIL Doc. 3(III)(O); NY R ERIE E FIL Doc. 3(V)(E).

- *KINGS COUNTY.* No courtesy copies of motion papers are required by the Court, except as may be required for electronic filing or by the Judge's Part Rules. In tort cases against the City of New York, courtesy copies shall be supplied to the Corporation Counsel's office in Brooklyn. NY R L KINGS Pt. C, Rule 5. Unless otherwise directed by the Court or as described herein, and with the exceptions listed below, in all NYSCEF cases in which an RJI has been filed, working copies of e-filed documents that are intended for judicial review must be submitted to the court. Working copies are not required of documents that are only processed by a support office (e.g. preliminary conference request, note of issue). Working copies shall include exhibit tabs and backs; for motion papers, the motion sequence number and the return date and part. The confirmation notice with the motion sequence number on it should be the back page of the motion facing out. In addition, the filer of a working copy must firmly bind thereto, with the back page facing out, a copy of the Confirmation Notice that was generated by NYSCEF when that document was efiled. Working copies that are submitted without the related Confirmation Notice will not be accepted. NY R L KINGS E FIL Doc. 1(B)(7); NY R L KINGS E FIL Doc. 1(D). WORKING COPIES OF MOTION PAPERS MUST BE SUBMITTED IN THE MOTION SUPPORT OFFICE (ROOM 227) AS EXPLAINED HEREIN. THEY MUST NOT BE DELIVERED TO THE PART OR CHAMBERS, EXCEPT WHERE THE INDIVIDUAL JUSTICE'S PART RULES PROVIDE OTHERWISE; DOING SO WILL CAUSE ADMINISTRATIVE CONFUSION AND POSSIBLE MISPLACEMENT OF PAPERS. Any such submission shall be sent in a timely manner (kindly review individual Justice's rules) and be conspicuously marked on the outside "NYSCEF Matter;" lack of such marking may delay processing. NY R L KINGS E FIL Doc. 1(D).
- *NEW YORK COUNTY.* Some Justices require that working copies of e-filed motion papers be submitted. See the E-filing Protocol for information on the many Parts that do not require working copies. Where required, working copies of the moving documents and all other documents on the motion or application shall be submitted to the Motion Submission Part Courtroom (Room 130) on, but not before, the final return date. A Confirmation Notice from the NYSCEF system, which is generated when a document is e-filed, shall be firmly affixed, as the back page facing out, to each separate working copy or group of such copies. NY R NY CTY Procedure II(A) NY R NY CTY E FIL Doc. 2(B)(5)(a); NY R NY CTY J RUL Rule 14(a). For more information on working copies, including which parts don't require them, refer to NY R NY CTY E FIL Doc. 2(B)(6).
- *ONONDAGA COUNTY.* Any courtesy "working" copies, if required (see NY R ONDGA E FIL Protocol(B)(7)), must be provided directly to the assigned justice. NY R ONDGA E FIL Protocol(B)(9)(e). For information as to whether or not an Onondaga Supreme Court Justice requires working (courtesy) copies of e-filed documents, please consult the Onondaga County Individual E-filing Rules. NY R ONDGA E FIL Protocol(B)(7)(a). The Supreme Court Clerk's Office and the Onondaga County Clerk's Office will NOT accept the working copies. Working copies must be sent directly to the assigned justice's chambers. NY R ONDGA E FIL Protocol(B)(7)(b). A copy of the Confirmation Notice, generated by the NYSCEF system at the time a document is e-filed, must be attached to every working copy provided to chambers. If the Confirmation Notice is missing, the copy will not be accepted. NY R ONDGA E FIL Protocol(B)(7)(c). Courtesy copies do not become part of the official court record as maintained by the Onondaga County Clerk's Office and will be destroyed by chambers at the disposition of the case. In the event that counsel fails to file a document via NYSCEF, the document will not be part of the court record. NY R ONDGA E FIL Protocol(B)(7)(d).
- *QUEENS COUNTY.* Working copies of E-Filed notices of motion/notices of petition are NOT to be sent to the Motion Support Office. They must be brought to the calendar call in the judge's part. NY R L QUEENS MOT SUP Doc. 1. Unless otherwise directed or authorized by the court, counsel should file papers with the

E-file system first and thereafter deliver a working copy to at the calendar call of the Centralized Motion Part or Assigned Justice in accordance with individual Part Rules. NY R L QUEENS E-FILE Doc. 1(E)(4). On the return date of a motion that has been E-filed, the movant must provide the Centralized Motion Part (CMP) with a working copy of the entire motion including the notice of motion with sequence number and all of the attached exhibits. The motion must have the confirmation of filing firmly affixed to the back of the papers (facing outward). The confirmation of filing is a separate notice from the payment notice and will say confirmation clearly across the top of the page. NY R L QUEENS E-FILE Doc. 1(H)(2)(a). The motion or Order to Show Cause must have clearly written across its face the words "Working Copy," it must also have the assigned Judge's name, motion sequence number and calendar number—which may be obtained from the posted calendar outside courtroom on the return date of the motion. A confirmation of filing must attached thereto. Working copies of e-filed Orders to Show Cause must contain a copy of the signed order and all supporting papers. NY R L QUEENS E-FILE Doc. 1(H)(2)(c). The Confirmation Notice must be an updated version that indicates the sequence number of the motion being submitted at the CMP calendar call. WORKING COPIES WITHOUT A CONFIRMATION NOTICE WILL NOT BE ACCEPTED. NY R L QUEENS E-FILE Doc. 1(H)(7).

vi. *ERIE COUNTY: Additional supplemental documents*

- *Notice of hard copy submission in e-filed case.* In accordance with NY R UNIF TRIAL CTS § 202.5-b(d), the County Clerk shall refuse to accept for filing, hard copy papers filed to an action subject to electronic filing unless hard copy filing is permitted by the Uniform Rules or NY R ERIE E FIL Doc. 3 and the papers bear a completed Notice of Hard Copy Submission—E-Filed Case form. NY R ERIE E FIL Doc. 3(III)(D).

vii. *KINGS COUNTY: Additional supplemental documents*

- *Forms when filing in hard copy.* An attorney who certifies in good faith that he or she lacks the equipment or knowledge needed to e-file and have no staff member or employee under his or her direction who has such knowledge and equipment may opt out of participation in e-filing in a mandatory case by filing a "Notice of Opt-Out from Participation in Action Subject to Mandatory Electronic Filing" form EFM-2 with the Clerk. NY R L KINGS E FIL Doc. 1(A)(2). Where in accordance with the E-Filing Rules a party submits a document in hard copy in an e-filed case (principally, a document submitted by a nonparticipating party (e.g., an attorney) in a consensual case, an emergency filing made in accordance with the Mandatory E-Filing Rules, and any document filed with the court in hard copy by an attorney who has opted out of participation in mandatory e-filing, the document must bear the back page facing out, a "Notice of Hard Copy Submission—E-Filed Cases" form EFM-3. NY R L KINGS E FIL Doc. 1(B)(3).

viii. *NEW YORK COUNTY: Additional supplemental documents*

- *Notice of hard copy submission.* Where in accordance with the E-Filing Rules an attorney or an unrepresented litigant who is participating in e-filing submits a document in hard copy in an e-filed case, the document must bear, as the back page facing out, a Notice of Hard-Copy Submission—E-Filed Case (a form available in the "Forms" section on the NYSCEF website (Form EFM-3) and in the court's back offices). NY R NY CTY E FIL Doc. 2(B)(3). For more information refer to NY R NY CTY E FIL Doc. 2.
- *Unpublished decisions.* Whenever reliance is placed upon a decision or other authority not officially published or readily available to the New York County Supreme Court, a copy of the case or of pertinent portions of the authority shall be submitted with the motion papers. NY R NY CTY J RUL Rule 14(a).

ix. *ONONDAGA COUNTY: Additional supplemental documents*

- *Notice of hard copy submission.* Any papers to be filed with the court in an e-filed case must be filed online with the E-filing system except where a special exemption is granted (e.g., oversized maps, photographs). If such an exemption is granted, Form EFM-3, "Notice of Hard Copy Submission—E-Filed Case," must be attached to such documents forms which are not filed on line. Also, Form EFM-4 "Notice of Hard Copy Exhibit Filing" must be completed and uploaded to the action's e-file. Both of these forms may be found on the NYSCEF website. NY R ONDGA E FIL Protocol(B)(4).

x. *QUEENS COUNTY: Additional supplemental documents*

- *Notice of hard copy submission.* Any party opting out of the e-filing system must have a "Notice of Hard Copy Submission" firmly affixed to the back of the papers. NY R L QUEENS E-FILE Doc. 1(H)(2)(f).

2. *Documents for opposing party*
   a. *Required documents*
      i. *Opposition.* Refer to the General Requirements section of this document for information on the opposition.
         - *Request for oral argument.* A party requesting oral argument shall set forth such request in its notice of motion or in its order to show cause or on the first page of the answering papers, as the case may be. Where all parties to a motion request oral argument, oral argument shall be granted unless the court shall determine it to be unnecessary. Where a motion is brought on by order to show cause, the court may set forth in the order that oral argument is required on the return date of the motion. NY R UNIF TRIAL CTS § 202.8(d).
         - *QUEENS COUNTY: E-filing opposition papers.* E-filed opposition papers and/or reply papers must also be provided to the Centralized Motion Part in the same manner as the moving papers with the confirmation of filing firmly attached to the back of the papers. NY R L QUEENS E-FILE Doc. 1(H)(2)(d).
      ii. *Proof of service.* In addition to complying with the provisions of NY CPLR Rule 2101, every paper filed in court shall have annexed thereto appropriate proof of service on all parties where required. NY R UNIF TRIAL CTS § 202.5(a).
   b. *Supplemental documents*
      i. *Supporting evidence; Exhibits.* The main supporting papers on a motion are affidavits, but any relevant exhibits, documents, depositions, etc., are also includible. SIEGEL-NYPRAC § 246.
         - *Affidavits accompanying opposition.* Affidavits shall be for a statement of the relevant facts. NY R UNIF TRIAL CTS § 202.8(c).
         - *Foreign language documents.* Where an affidavit or exhibit annexed to a paper served or filed is in a foreign language, it shall be accompanied by an English translation and an affidavit by the translator stating his qualifications and that the translation is accurate. NY CPLR Rule 2101(b).
         - *Statement of attorney in lieu of affidavit.* The statement of an attorney admitted to practice in the courts of the state, or of a physician, osteopath or dentist, authorized by law to practice in the state, who is not a party to an action, when subscribed and affirmed by him to be true under the penalties of perjury, may be served or filed in the action in lieu of and with the same force and effect as an affidavit. NY CPLR Rule 2106.
         - *NEW YORK COUNTY: Form of presented exhibits.* Exhibits should be tabbed and be legible; a typed version of any exhibit that is difficult to read should be submitted with the original. Exhibits printed on both sides of the page should be bound and tabbed on the side. NY R NY CTY J RUL Rule 14(a).
         - *QUEENS COUNTY.* Attorneys submitting exhibits to the court on E-file cases shall make each exhibit a separate, labeled attachment to an affidavit/affirmation. NY R L QUEENS E-FILE Doc. 1(H)(4).
      ii. *Brief.* Briefs shall be for a statement of the relevant law. NY R UNIF TRIAL CTS § 202.8(c).
      iii. *Filing fees.* The County Clerk shall require the payment of any applicable statutory fees, or an order of the Court waiving payment of such fees, before accepting a paper for filing. NY R UNIF TRIAL CTS § 202.5(d)(1). For information on filing fees, if any, refer to NY CPLR § 8001, et seq.
         - *ALBANY COUNTY.* In general, any filing subsequent to the commencement of an action which is designated as a motion or cross-motion requires the payment of a filing fee to the County Clerk's Office prior to submission to the Supreme Court Clerk's Office for referral to the assigned justice. The fee is assessed regardless of whether an application is made by notice of motion, order to show cause or ex parte. No fee will be charged upon the filing of a motion for poor person status in conjunction with an application which serves to commence an action or special proceeding. In the event a motion is received by the court unaccompanied by proof of payment to the County Clerk, the Supreme Court Clerk's Office will contact the submitting party to advise that the application will be held pending receipt of the filing fee only until the return date of the motion. If proof of payment is not submitted to the Supreme Court Clerk's Office by the return date (ex parte applications will be held ten (10) days), the papers will be returned by mail with a notification that the motion has been removed from the court's calendar and that it must be re-noticed and re-filed with the court along with the requisite filing fee. Inquiries concerning the applicability of the motion fee to a proposed filing may be directed to the Supreme Court Clerk's Office. NY R 3 JD SUP Doc. 1(B).
         - *BRONX COUNTY.* In accordance with the new civil fee schedule set forth in Article 80 of the C.P.L.R. (NY CPLR § 8001, et seq.), effective July 14, 2003, all motions, and cross motions must be approved in Room

217 prior to payment of said fees in the County Clerk's Office, Room 118. NY R BRONX FIL R Doc. 8. The motion fee [must be] paid for via NYSCEF by credit/debit card. NY R BRONX E FIL R Doc. 1(1).

- *ERIE COUNTY.* Payment for fee-bearing NYSCEF documents must be made online via credit or debit card (American Express, MasterCard or Visa) at the time of submission. NY R ERIE E FIL Doc. 3(III)(E).
- *KINGS COUNTY.* The motion must be filed with NYSCEF and the motion fee paid. NY R L KINGS E FIL Doc. 1(D). Court fees in NYSCEF cases must be paid via NYSCEF by a credit or bank card (MasterCard, Visa, or American Express). Fees are no longer accepted in person in the Kings County Clerk's Office in NYSCEF cases. NY R L KINGS E FIL Doc. 1(B)(6).
- *NEW YORK COUNTY.* A motion fee must be paid on motions made in writing by notice of motion, order to show cause or ex parte after the commencement of an action. For this purpose, the term "action" shall mean any application to the court that requires the assignment of an index number, regardless of whether a formal pleading is filed. Applications or motions that commence an action and for which an index number fee must be paid require no motion fee. [A]ny motions made after the initial applications in these situations would require payment of the motion fee. A motion that is the initial application in a case commenced by the filing of a summons and complaint would require a motion fee since the filing of the summons and complaint rather than the application itself would require the purchase of an index number. NY R NY CTY Procedure II(A). In e-filed cases the motion fee must be paid when the documents are filed. Payment is made on-line by Visa, Mastercard, or American Express credit or bank card. NY R NY CTY Procedure II(A); NY R NY CTY E FIL Doc. 2(B)(5).
- *ONONDAGA COUNTY.* Court fees in e-filed cases must be paid online with the NYSCEF system using a credit card. The document is not considered to have been filed until payment of the fee has been tendered. NY R ONDGA E FIL Protocol(B)(2). Fees must be paid on all cross motions. NY R ONDGA E FIL Protocol(B)(9)(e).
- *QUEENS COUNTY.* The Motion Support Office does not receive, forward or process any fees or waiver of fees. All applications requiring payment of statutory fees or waiver of fees must be sent directly to the Queens County Clerk's office. NY R L QUEENS MOT SUP Doc. 1. Court fees (e.g., RJI fee, motion fee) in E-filed cases may be paid for on-line using a credit card. Papers may also be filed with the E-file system and the fee may be paid at the County Clerk's Office. In the latter case, the paper is not considered to have been filed until payment of the fee has been tendered. NY R L QUEENS E-FILE Doc. 1(E)(1). The motion/petition shall be filed on-line and the fee paid for either on-line by credit card or by the "Pay at the County Clerk's Office" option. NY R L QUEENS E-FILE Doc. 1(H)(1).

iv. *Working copies.* The court may require the parties to provide working copies of documents filed electronically. In such event, each working copy shall include, firmly affixed thereto, a copy of a confirmation notice in a form prescribed by the Chief Administrator. NY R UNIF TRIAL CTS § 202.5-b(d)(5).

- *BRONX COUNTY.* After papers on motions have been e-filed, working copies thereof, with Confirmation Notice firmly attached as the back page facing out, must be submitted. (Each document or group of documents that is separately bound shall bear a Confirmation Notice.) Working copies lacking the Notice will not be accepted. WORKING COPIES OF MOTION PAPERS MUST BE SUBMITTED NO LATER THAN 4:45 P.M. ON THE RETURN DATE IN THE MOTION SUPPORT OFFICE (ROOM 217) AS EXPLAINED in NY R BRONX E FIL R Doc. 1(4). If an attorney has failed to submit required working copies on or before the return date, the motion will be transmitted as is to the Justice for such action as the Justice finds appropriate. Attorneys may submit working copies on motions by mail or overnight delivery. Any such submission shall be sent in a timely manner to the Motion Support Office (Room 217) and be conspicuously marked on the outside "NYSCEF Matter"; lack of such marking may delay processing. NY R BRONX E FIL R Doc. 1(4)(a).
- *ERIE COUNTY.* Electronically filed documents subject to review and processing by the Part Clerk do not require a working copy unless otherwise directed or provided for in IAS Part Rules. NY R UNIF TRIAL CTS § 202.5-b(d)(4), any working copy submitted shall include, as a cover page firmly fastened thereto, a copy of the Confirmation Notice generated by the NYSCEF site at the time of filing. Please consult the individual Justice's Part Rules and/or consult with the Judge's chambers to determine whether and how working copies are to be provided. Working copies will not be printed or delivered by the Erie County Clerk or the Chief Clerk of the Courts or any of their personnel to chambers. The official record of a document in an electronically filed case is the document filed via the NYSCEF system. Working copies are intended only for use by the Justice. The Court will discard all working copies after the Justice has finished with them.

Thus, in the event that counsel fails to file a document via the NYSCEF system, the document will not be part of the court record. NY R ERIE E FIL Doc. 3(III)(O); NY R ERIE E FIL Doc. 3(V)(E).

- *KINGS COUNTY.* No courtesy copies of motion papers are required by the Court, except as may be required for electronic filing or by the Judge's Part Rules. In tort cases against the City of New York, courtesy copies shall be supplied to the Corporation Counsel's office in Brooklyn. NY R L KINGS Pt. C, Rule 5. Unless otherwise directed by the Court or as described herein, and with the exceptions listed below, in all NYSCEF cases in which an RJI has been filed, working copies of e-filed documents that are intended for judicial review must be submitted to the court. Working copies are not required of documents that are only processed by a support office (e.g. preliminary conference request, note of issue). Working copies shall include exhibit tabs and backs; for motion papers, the motion sequence number and the return date and part. The confirmation notice with the motion sequence number on it should be the back page of the motion facing out. In addition, the filer of a working copy must firmly bind thereto, with the back page facing out, a copy of the Confirmation Notice that was generated by NYSCEF when that document was efiled. Working copies that are submitted without the related Confirmation Notice will not be accepted. NY R L KINGS E FIL Doc. 1(B)(7); NY R L KINGS E FIL Doc. 1(D). WORKING COPIES OF MOTION PAPERS MUST BE SUBMITTED IN THE MOTION SUPPORT OFFICE (ROOM 227) AS EXPLAINED HEREIN. THEY MUST NOT BE DELIVERED TO THE PART OR CHAMBERS, EXCEPT WHERE THE INDIVIDUAL JUSTICE'S PART RULES PROVIDE OTHERWISE; DOING SO WILL CAUSE ADMINISTRATIVE CONFUSION AND POSSIBLE MISPLACEMENT OF PAPERS. Any such submission shall be sent in a timely manner (kindly review individual Justice's rules) and be conspicuously marked on the outside "NYSCEF Matter;" lack of such marking may delay processing. NY R L KINGS E FIL Doc. 1(D).
- *NEW YORK COUNTY.* Some Justices require that working copies of e-filed motion papers be submitted. See the E-filing Protocol for information on the many Parts that do not require working copies. Where required, working copies of the moving documents and all other documents on the motion or application shall be submitted to the Motion Submission Part Courtroom (Room 130) on, but not before, the final return date. A Confirmation Notice from the NYSCEF system, which is generated when a document is e-filed, shall be firmly affixed, as the back page facing out, to each separate working copy or group of such copies. NY R NY CTY Procedure II(A) NY R NY CTY E FIL Doc. 2(B)(5)(a); NY R NY CTY J RUL Rule 14(a). For more information on working copies, including which parts don't require them, refer to NY R NY CTY E FIL Doc. 2(B)(6).
- *ONONDAGA COUNTY.* Any courtesy "working" copies, if required (see NY R ONDGA E FIL Protocol(B)(7)), must be provided directly to the assigned justice. NY R ONDGA E FIL Protocol(B)(9)(e). For information as to whether or not an Onondaga Supreme Court Justice requires working (courtesy) copies of e-filed documents, please consult the Onondaga County Individual E-filing Rules. NY R ONDGA E FIL Protocol(B)(7)(a). The Supreme Court Clerk's Office and the Onondaga County Clerk's Office will NOT accept the working copies. Working copies must be sent directly to the assigned justice's chambers. NY R ONDGA E FIL Protocol(B)(7)(b). A copy of the Confirmation Notice, generated by the NYSCEF system at the time a document is e-filed, must be attached to every working copy provided to chambers. If the Confirmation Notice is missing, the copy will not be accepted. NY R ONDGA E FIL Protocol(B)(7)(c). Courtesy copies do not become part of the official court record as maintained by the Onondaga County Clerk's Office and will be destroyed by chambers at the disposition of the case. In the event that counsel fails to file a document via NYSCEF, the document will not be part of the court record. NY R ONDGA E FIL Protocol(B)(7)(d).
- *QUEENS COUNTY.* Working copies of E-Filed notices of motion/notices of petition are NOT to be sent to the Motion Support Office. They must be brought to the calendar call in the judge's part. NY R L QUEENS MOT SUP Doc. 1. Unless otherwise directed or authorized by the court, counsel should file papers with the E-file system first and thereafter deliver a working copy to at the calendar call of the Centralized Motion Part or Assigned Justice in accordance with individual Part Rules. NY R L QUEENS E-FILE Doc. 1(E)(4). On the return date of a motion that has been E-filed, the movant must provide the Centralized Motion Part (CMP) with a working copy of the entire motion including the notice of motion with sequence number and all of the attached exhibits. The motion must have the confirmation of filing firmly affixed to the back of the papers (facing outward). The confirmation of filing is a separate notice from the payment notice and will say confirmation clearly across the top of the page. NY R L QUEENS E-FILE Doc. 1(H)(2)(a). The motion or Order to Show Cause must have clearly written across its face the words "Working Copy," it must also

have the assigned Judge's name, motion sequence number and calendar number—which may be obtained from the posted calendar outside courtroom on the return date of the motion. A confirmation of filing must attached thereto. Working copies of e-filed Orders to Show Cause must contain a copy of the signed order and all supporting papers. NY R L QUEENS E-FILE Doc. 1(H)(2)(c). The Confirmation Notice must be an updated version that indicates the sequence number of the motion being submitted at the CMP calendar call. WORKING COPIES WITHOUT A CONFIRMATION NOTICE WILL NOT BE ACCEPTED. NY R L QUEENS E-FILE Doc. 1(H)(7).

v. *ERIE COUNTY: Additional supplemental documents*

- *Notice of hard copy submission in e-filed case.* In accordance with NY R UNIF TRIAL CTS § 202.5-b(d), the County Clerk shall refuse to accept for filing, hard copy papers filed to an action subject to electronic filing unless hard copy filing is permitted by the Uniform Rules or NY R ERIE E FIL Doc. 3 and the papers bear a completed Notice of Hard Copy Submission—E-Filed Case form. NY R ERIE E FIL Doc. 3(III)(D).

vi. *KINGS COUNTY: Additional supplemental documents*

- *Forms when filing in hard copy.* An attorney who certifies in good faith that he or she lacks the equipment or knowledge needed to e-file and have no staff member or employee under his or her direction who has such knowledge and equipment may opt out of participation in e-filing in a mandatory case by filing a "Notice of Opt-Out from Participation in Action Subject to Mandatory Electronic Filing" form EFM-2 with the Clerk. NY R L KINGS E FIL Doc. 1(A)(2). Where in accordance with the E-Filing Rules a party submits a document in hard copy in an e-filed case (principally, a document submitted by a nonparticipating party (e.g., an attorney) in a consensual case, an emergency filing made in accordance with the Mandatory E-Filing Rules, and any document filed with the court in hard copy by an attorney who has opted out of participation in mandatory e-filing, the document must bear the back page facing out, a "Notice of Hard Copy Submission—E-Filed Cases" form EFM-3. NY R L KINGS E FIL Doc. 1(B)(3).

vii. *NEW YORK COUNTY: Additional supplemental documents*

- *Notice of hard copy submission.* Where in accordance with the E-Filing Rules an attorney or an unrepresented litigant who is participating in e-filing submits a document in hard copy in an e-filed case, the document must bear, as the back page facing out, a Notice of Hard-Copy Submission—E-Filed Case (a form available in the "Forms" section on the NYSCEF website (Form EFM-3) and in the court's back offices). NY R NY CTY E FIL Doc. 2(B)(3). For more information refer to NY R NY CTY E FIL Doc. 2.
- *Unpublished decisions.* Whenever reliance is placed upon a decision or other authority not officially published or readily available to the New York County Supreme Court, a copy of the case or of pertinent portions of the authority shall be submitted with the motion papers. NY R NY CTY J RUL Rule 14(a).

viii. *ONONDAGA COUNTY: Additional supplemental documents*

- *Notice of hard copy submission.* Any papers to be filed with the court in an e-filed case must be filed online with the E-filing system except where a special exemption is granted (e.g., oversized maps, photographs). If such an exemption is granted, Form EFM-3, "Notice of Hard Copy Submission—E-Filed Case," must be attached to such documents forms which are not filed on line. Also, Form EFM-4 "Notice of Hard Copy Exhibit Filing" must be completed and uploaded to the action's e-file. Both of these forms may be found on the NYSCEF website. NY R ONDGA E FIL Protocol(B)(4).

ix. *QUEENS COUNTY: Additional supplemental documents*

- *Notice of hard copy submission.* Any party opting out of the e-filing system must have a "Notice of Hard Copy Submission" firmly affixed to the back of the papers. NY R L QUEENS E-FILE Doc. 1(H)(2)(f).

E. Format

1. *Form of documents*

a. *Size and form of paper.* Each paper served or filed shall be durable, white and, except for summonses, subpoenas, notices of appearance, notes of issue, orders of protection, temporary orders of protection and exhibits, shall be eleven by eight and one-half (11 x 8-1/2) inches in size. NY CPLR Rule 2101(a).

b. *Writing and language.* The writing shall be legible and in black ink. NY CPLR Rule 2101(a). Each paper served or filed shall be in the English language which, where practicable, shall be of ordinary usage. NY CPLR Rule 2101(b).

c. *Caption.* Each paper served or filed shall begin with a caption setting forth the name of the court, the venue, the title of the action, the nature of the paper and the index number of the action if one has been assigned. In all papers other

than a summons, a complaint or a judgment it shall be sufficient to state the name of the first named party on each side with an appropriate indication of any omissions. NY CPLR Rule 2101(c).

i. *Further contents of first page.* After the first paper has been filed in each case the index number shall appear on the cover and first page to the right of the caption of every paper tendered for filing in the action. Each such cover and first page also shall contain an indication of the county of venue and a brief description of the nature of the paper and, where the case has been assigned to an individual judge, shall contain the name of the assigned judge to the right of the caption. NY R UNIF TRIAL CTS § 202.5(a); NY R UNIF TRIAL CTS § 202.5(b); NY R UNIF TRIAL CTS § 202.5(d)(1)(i).

ii. *ALBANY COUNTY: Request for oral argument.* A party may request oral argument on a motion by indicating such request on the first page of the notice of motion, order to show cause, or answering papers in the area across from the caption of the action/proceeding. NY R 3 JD SUP Doc. 1(B).

iii. *NEW YORK COUNTY: Request for oral argument.* Counsel who wish oral argument must so request conspicuously on the front of their papers. NY R NY CTY Procedure II(D).

d. *Index number.* No paper in an action in the supreme or a county court, other than an order submitted for signature to a judge out of court, shall be submitted for any purpose to the supreme or county court or to a clerk thereof unless there is endorsed on such paper the index number of the action assigned by the clerk of the county. NY CPLR § 8018(c).

i. *ALBANY COUNTY: Index number on all filed documents.* The index number, the request for judicial intervention number and the assigned justice's name shall appear on [all papers filed with the Court subsequent to the complaint]. NY R 3 JD SUP Doc. 1(A).

ii. *ERIE COUNTY: Index number after initial filing.* Cases that are initially commenced by the filing of papers with the NYSCEF system are identified as e-filed cases by assignment of an Index Number that has "800-899" as the first three (3) digits of the index number (i.e. 802391/2012). NY R ERIE E FIL Doc. 3(II). [The] Index Number must be affixed to all document submissions, filings, and communications to the Erie County Clerk and the Court. Cases that are converted from paper to e-filing shall retain the original index number. NY R ERIE E FIL Doc. 3(II).

iii. *KINGS COUNTY: Index number after initial filing.* In cases commenced electronically by the filing of initiating papers with the NYSCEF system and payment of the statutory fees, the Kings County Clerk will issue an NYSCEF designated index number and the filer shall be notified via the NYSCEF system of the index number assigned and filing date. Such index number must be affixed to all document submissions, filings and communications to the Kings County Clerk and Supreme Court. If counsel faces exigent circumstances that require accelerated assignment, counsel may contact Administration of the Kings County Clerk at kcco-efile@nycourts.gov, during normal business hours of the court. NY R L KINGS E FIL Doc. 1(B)(5).

iv. *NEW YORK COUNTY: Index number on hard copy filings.* Papers subsequently presented for filing in hardcopy format will be filed in this jacket. NY R NY CTY Procedure I(B). Index numbers take the form of six digits followed by a slash and the four digits of the year the case began, e.g., 340705/2018. The first or first two integers of the index number identify the type of case. If a case is commenced electronically, the second integer will be a "5", except as indicated otherwise in the list below. There are many tax certiorari matters e-filed annually and the index numbers therefor will normally run over into those with a "6" as the second integer, and the same will occur with general cases if necessary. The principal types of cases and their index number categories are listed in NY R NY CTY Procedure I(B). NY R NY CTY Procedure I(B); NY R NY CTY Procedure XI(A).

v. *ONONDAGA COUNTY: Index number.* The index number must be referenced on all e-filed documents and correspondence. All e-filed case index numbers will contain the letters "EF" between the year and the file number (for example, 2012EF9999). NY R ONDGA E FIL Protocol(B)(1).

vi. *QUEENS COUNTY: Index number on converted cases.* Cases originally commenced in hard-copy form but later converted to an E-file case, either by stipulation or order will bear a regular index number initially. The County Clerk will issue a new E-file index number. NY R L QUEENS E-FILE Doc. 1(B).

e. *Line spacing.* Every paper filed in court, if typewritten, shall have at least double space between each line, except for quotations and the names and addresses of attorneys appearing in the action. NY R UNIF TRIAL CTS § 202.5(a).

f. *Font size.* Each. . .paper printed or typed, served or filed, except an exhibit or a summons, shall be in clear type of no less than ten (10) point in size. NY CPLR Rule 2101(a).

i. Whenever a requirement relating to size of type is stated in point size, the type size requirement shall be deemed met if the x-height of the type is a minimum of forty-five percent (45%) of the specified point size. Each point shall be measured as .351 millimeter. The x-height size shall be measured as it appears on the page. The x-height is the height of the lower case letters, exclusive of ascenders or descenders. NY CPLR § 105(t).

g. *Margins.* Every paper filed in court shall have at least one (1) inch margins. NY R UNIF TRIAL CTS § 202.5(a).

h. *Citations*

   i. *Civil practice law and rules.* NY CPLR § 101, et seq. shall be known as the civil practice law and rules, and may be cited as "CPLR". Reference to a provision in the civil practice law and rules may, except when such provision is being enacted or amended, be made without indicating whether it is a rule or section. NY CPLR § 101.

i. *Indorsement by attorney.* Each paper served or filed shall be indorsed with the name, address and telephone number of the attorney for the party serving or filing the paper, or if the party does not appear by attorney, with the name, address and telephone number of the party. NY CPLR Rule 2101(d).

j. *One-sided printing.* In addition, every paper filed in court, other than an exhibit or printed form, shall contain writing on one side only, except that papers that are fastened on the side may contain writing on both sides. NY R UNIF TRIAL CTS § 202.5(a).

k. *Use of copies authorized.* Except where otherwise specifically prescribed, copies, rather than originals, of all papers, including orders, affidavits and exhibits may be served or filed. Where it is required that the original be served or filed and the original is lost or withheld, the court may authorize a copy to be served or filed. NY CPLR Rule 2101(e).

   i. Where a certified copy of a paper is required by law, an attorney admitted to practice in the courts of the state may certify that it has been compared by him with the original and found to be a true and complete copy. Such a certificate, when subscribed by such attorney, has the same effect as if made by a clerk. NY CPLR § 2105.

l. *Recycled paper.* It is the policy of the Unified Court System that litigants, where practicable, should file or submit to the courts of the Unified Court System of the State of New York papers printed or reproduced on recycled paper. Paper is considered recycled if it contains a minimum content of thirty percent (30%) waste paper. NY R UNIF TRIAL CTS § 215.2. The signature page of every paper filed or submitted to the court on recycled paper should bear the legend: "Printed [Reproduced] on Recycled Paper." NY R UNIF TRIAL CTS § 215.3.

m. *Form of request for judicial intervention; Copies.* A request for judicial intervention must be submitted, in duplicate, on a form authorized by the Chief of the Courts, with proof of service on the other parties to the action (but proof of service is not required where the application is ex parte). NY R UNIF TRIAL CTS § 202.6(a).

n. *KINGS COUNTY: Tabs on filings.* Motions, orders and other filed papers shall be indexed with protruding tabs. Clerks are required to reject papers that do not have protruding exhibit tabs, except papers in matrimonial cases and papers filed by pro se litigants. NY R L KINGS Pt. A, Papers.

o. *NEW YORK COUNTY: Length of briefs.* Unless advance permission otherwise is granted by the court for good cause, memoranda of law shall not exceed thirty (30) pages each (exclusive of table of contents and table of authorities) and affidavits/affirmations shall not exceed twenty-five (25) pages each. NY R NY CTY J RUL Rule 14(b).

p. *QUEENS COUNTY: Form and size of motion filings.* All motions filed in Queens Supreme Court-Civil Term, must adhere to the Motion Support rules and the rules of the assigned judge. NY R L QUEENS MOT SUP Doc. 1. Due to space limitations, the Motion Support Office cannot accept notices of motion/notices of petition and accompanying exhibits which measure greater than eight (8) inches. If your documents measure greater than eight (8) inches you are directed to submit only the notice of motion/notice of petition to the Motion Support Office and bring all exhibits to the calendar call on your return date. NY R L QUEENS MOT SUP Doc. 1.

2. *Form of electronic documents.* Each paper served or filed by electronic means, as defined in NY CPLR Rule 2103(f), shall be capable of being reproduced by the receiver so as to comply with the provisions of NY CPLR Rule 2101(a) through NY CPLR Rule 2101(d). NY CPLR Rule 2101(g).

   a. *File format.* All e-filed documents shall comply with the technical requirements set forth at the NYSCEF site. NY R UNIF TRIAL CTS § 202.5-b(d)(1)(i).

   b. *Heading of document.* The subject matter heading for each paper sent by electronic means must indicate that the matter being transmitted electronically is related to a court proceeding. NY CPLR Rule 2103(b)(7).

   c. *E-filed documents identification*

      i. *ERIE COUNTY.* E-filed cases must be readily identifiable and marked as such. If counsel presents papers to the Office of the Erie County Clerk or the Office of the Chief Clerk in a NYSCEF matter where authorized, counsel should alert the Clerk that the case is a NYSCEF matter. NY R ERIE E FIL Doc. 3(II).

ii. *KINGS COUNTY.* The Supreme Court's Civil Case Information System ("CCIS") will further identify e-filed cases by the addition of a suffix to the index number (e.g. 500136/2006E). This suffix should be used on all documents filed with the court in e-filed matters. NY R L KINGS E FIL Doc. 1(A)(1).

3. *Signature blocks.* Every pleading, written motion, and other paper, served on another party or filed or submitted to the court shall be signed by an attorney, or by a party if the party is not represented by an attorney, with the name of the attorney or party clearly printed or typed directly below the signature. NY R CHIEF ADMIN § 130-1.1-a(a); NY R UNIF TRIAL CTS § 202.5(d)(1)(iv).

a. *Printed name.* Beneath each signature shall be printed the name signed. NY CPLR Rule 2101(a).

b. *Failure to sign.* Absent good cause shown, the court shall strike any unsigned paper if the omission of the signature is not corrected promptly after being called to the attention of the attorney or party. NY R CHIEF ADMIN § 130-1.1-a(a).

c. *Signature as certification.* By signing a paper, an attorney or party certifies that, to the best of that person's knowledge, information and belief, formed after an inquiry reasonable under the circumstances the presentation of the paper or the contentions therein are not frivolous as defined in NY R CHIEF ADMIN § 130-1.1(c). NY R CHIEF ADMIN § 130-1.1-a(b)(1).

d. *Electronic signatures.* A document shall be considered to have been signed by an attorney or party in compliance with NY R CHIEF ADMIN § 130-1.1-a if it has been signed by such attorney or party as provided in NY R UNIF TRIAL CTS § 202.5-b(e)(1) and it bears the signatory's name. NY R UNIF TRIAL CTS § 202.5-b(e)(2). An electronically filed document shall be considered to have been signed by, and shall be binding upon, the person identified as a signatory, if:

i. It bears the physical signature of such person and is scanned into an electronic format that reproduces such signature; or

ii. The signatory has electronically affixed the digital image of his or her signature to the document; or

iii. It is electronically filed under the User ID and password of that person; or

iv. In a tax certiorari action in which the parties have stipulated to this procedure, it is an initiating document that is electronically filed without the signature of the signatory in a form provided above in NY R UNIF TRIAL CTS § 202.5-b(e)(iv), provided that, prior to filing, the document is signed in full in hard copy (which hard copy must be preserved until the conclusion of all proceedings, including appeals, in the case in which it is filed); or

v. In a small claims assessment review proceeding, it is a petition recorded by the NYSCEF site upon the filing of a text file as provided in NY R UNIF TRIAL CTS § 202.5-b(b)(1), provided that prior to filing, the document was signed in full in hard copy (which hard copy must be preserved until the conclusion of all proceedings in the matter, including article 78 (NY CPLR § 7801, et seq.) review and any appeals, and must be made available during the proceeding upon request of the respondent or the court); or

vi. It otherwise bears the electronic signature of the signatory in a format conforming to such standards and requirements as may hereafter be established by the Chief Administrator. NY R UNIF TRIAL CTS § 202.5-b(e).

4. *Confidentiality of personal information.* No person may file any document available for public inspection with any state agency, political subdivision, or in any court of this state that contains a Social Security account number of any other person, unless such other person is a dependent child, or has consented to such filing, except as required by federal or state law or regulation, or by court rule. NY GEN BUS § 399-ddd. Submissions pursuant to e-filing procedures shall have the same confidentiality rights as paper documents. NY R UNIF TRIAL CTS § 202.5-b(k)(1).

a. *Confidential personal information.* Except in the actions designated in NY R UNIF TRIAL CTS § 202.5(e)(1), or as otherwise provided by rule or law or court order, and whether or not a sealing order is or has been sought, the parties shall omit or redact confidential personal information in papers submitted to the court for filing. For purposes of NY R UNIF TRIAL CTS § 202.5(e), confidential personal information ("CPI") means:

i. The taxpayer identification number of an individual or an entity, including a Social Security number, an employer identification number, and an individual taxpayer identification number, except the last four (4) digits thereof;

ii. The date of an individual's birth, except the year thereof;

iii. The full name of an individual known to be a minor, except the minor's initials;

iv. A financial account number, including a credit and/or debit card number, a bank account number, an investment account number, and/or an insurance account number, except the last four (4) digits or letters thereof; and

v. Any of the documents or testimony in a matrimonial action protected by NY DOM REL § 235 or evidence sealed by the court in such an action which are attached as exhibits or referenced in the papers filed in any other civil action. For purposes of NY R UNIF TRIAL CTS § 202.5, a matrimonial action shall mean: an action to annul a marriage or declare the nullity of a void marriage, an action or agreement for a separation, an action for a divorce, or an action or proceeding for custody, visitation, writ of habeus corpus, child support, maintenance or paternity. NY R UNIF TRIAL CTS § 202.5(e)(1).

vi. *ERIE COUNTY.* An attorney or unrepresented litigant filing a document via the NYSCEF system must comply with the requirements of NY R UNIF TRIAL CTS § 202.5(e) regarding the redaction of Confidential Personal Information and NY GEN BUS § 399-ddd(6) concerning the filing of documents containing Social Security Numbers. It is the sole responsibility of counsel or unrepresented litigant filing to be aware of and to comply with existing laws requiring non-disclosure of personal information contained in any document e-filed in NYSCEF. NY R ERIE E FIL Doc. 3(III)(G); NY R ERIE E FIL Doc. 3(III).

vii. *KINGS COUNTY.* An attorney or unrepresented litigant filing a document via the NYSCEF system must comply with the requirements of General Business Law § 399-dd(6), which often require redaction of any Social Security number that appear in the original document. The NYSCEF system automatically redacts portions of filed documents which apparently contain Social Security numbers pursuant to NY R UNIF TRIAL CTS § 202.5-b(k). In the event the filing party receives e-mail notice through NYSCEF that a Social Security number in a filed document has been redacted, and the filing party concludes such redaction is erroneous, the filer should click on the link provided in the e-mail to permit the County Clerk to revert the redaction. For Confidential Personal Information, see NY R UNIF TRIAL CTS § 202.5(e) and NY R L KINGS E FIL Doc. 1(B)(11). [Editor's note: the reference to General Business Law § 399-dd(6) is likely a reference to NY GEN BUS § 399-ddd(6)]. NY R L KINGS E FIL Doc. 1(B)(10); NY R L KINGS E FIL Doc. 1(K)(1).

viii. *NEW YORK COUNTY.* It is the responsibility of counsel and parties to comply with rules restricting disclosure of confidential personal information. Nevertheless, NYSCEF screens filings and endeavors to identify any that contain social security numbers. When such numbers are discovered through this process, NYSCEF will restrict portions of or all of such documents from public view. Where NYSCEF has redacted what it believes to be a social security number, it will transmit to the filer a notice advising of the action taken and requesting that the filer review the matter and provide notification as set forth in the notice if the redaction has been made in error. NY R NY CTY E FIL Doc. 2(K)(1); NY R NY CTY J RUL Rule A-1. Documents filed in the past in "secure status" under a procedure no longer in place will retain that status unless otherwise directed by the court. NY R NY CTY E FIL Doc. 2(K)(2).

b. *Submission of confidential personal information.* Where a person submitting a paper to a court for filing believes in good faith that the inclusion of the full confidential personal information described in NY R UNIF TRIAL CTS § 202.5(e)(1) is material and necessary to the adjudication of the action or proceeding before the court, he or she may apply to the court for leave to serve and file together with a paper in which such information has been set forth in abbreviated form a confidential affidavit or affirmation setting forth the same information in unabbreviated form, appropriately referenced to the page or pages of the paper at which the abbreviated form appears. NY R UNIF TRIAL CTS § 202.5(e)(3).

c. *Home addresses.* For information on when home addresses and other personal information must be redacted, refer to NY CPLR Rule 2103-a.

5. *Defective papers.* A defect in the form of a paper, if a substantial right of a party is not prejudiced, shall be disregarded by the court, and leave to correct shall be freely given. NY CPLR Rule 2101(f). Papers that are stapled or bound securely shall not be rejected for filing simply because they are not bound with a backer of any kind. NY R UNIF TRIAL CTS § 202.5(a). A paper filed in accordance with the rules of the chief administrator or any local rule or practice established by the court shall be deemed filed. NY CPLR Rule 2102(b).

a. *Objection to defective papers.* The party on whom a paper is served shall be deemed to have waived objection to any defect in form unless, within fifteen (15) days after the receipt thereof, the party on whom the paper is served returns the paper to the party serving it with a statement of particular objections. NY CPLR Rule 2101(f).

F. Filing and Service Requirements

1. *Filing requirements.* Except where otherwise prescribed by law or order of court, papers required to be filed shall be filed with the clerk of the court in which the action is triable. In an action or proceeding in supreme or court, papers required to be filed shall be filed with the clerk of the county in which the proceeding is brought. NY CPLR Rule 2102(a).

a. *Furnishing papers to the court.* Each party shall furnish to the court all papers served by him. The moving party shall

furnish at the hearing all other papers not already in the possession of the court necessary to the consideration of the questions involved. Where such papers are in the possession of an adverse party, they shall be produced by him at the hearing on notice served with the motion papers. Only papers served in accordance with the provisions of NY CPLR Rule 2214 shall be read in support of, or in opposition to, the motion, unless the court for good cause shall otherwise direct. NY CPLR Rule 2214(c).

i. *Submission to judge.* All papers for signature or consideration of the court shall be presented to the clerk of the trial court in the appropriate courtroom or clerk's office, except that where the clerk is unavailable or the judge so directs, papers may be submitted to the judge and a copy filed with the clerk at the first available opportunity. All papers for any judge that are filed in the clerk's office shall be promptly delivered to the judge by the clerk. The papers shall be clearly addressed to the judge for whom they are intended and prominently show the nature of the papers, the title and index number of the action in which they are filed, the judge's name and the name of the attorney or party submitting them. NY R UNIF TRIAL CTS § 202.5(b).

ii. *BRONX COUNTY: Approval of motions before filing.* All motion papers must be approved by the Motion Support Office, Supreme Court, Civil Term, room 217, before the motion papers are filed and the appropriate fee paid to the County Clerk. NY R BRONX FIL R Doc. 1.

iii. *ERIE COUNTY: Filing motions.* A motion on notice or a notice of petition in a NYSCEF case shall be filed through the NYSCEF system and must be accompanied by a Request for Judicial Intervention if the motion is being filed upon commencement of the action or if the matter has not yet been assigned to an IAS Justice. In addition, cross motions with the appropriate filing fees and opposition and reply papers must be submitted via the NYSCEF system. NY R ERIE E FIL Doc. 3(V)(A).

iv. *NEW YORK COUNTY: Filing hard copies.* Where in the narrow circumstances described by the e-filing rules a motion is made in hard-copy form or opposition papers are submitted in such form in an e-filed case, the hard-copy documents shall be submitted in the same way papers are submitted in non-e-filed cases, except that there shall be firmly affixed to each separate document or group of documents, as the back page facing out, a Notice of Hard Copy Submission—E-Filed Case. NY R NY CTY Procedure II(A). For more information on filing in hard copy cases, refer to NY R NY CTY Procedure II(A).

v. *ONONDAGA COUNTY: Submission of responsive papers and cross-motions.* Cross-motions, opposition and reply papers must be submitted online. NY R ONDGA E FIL Protocol(B)(9)(e). Motions and Orders to Show Cause are assigned a sequence number by the system. Counsel must be sure that cross motions and other filings correspond with the correct sequence number so that a cross motion will not be associated with the wrong original motion. NY R ONDGA E FIL Protocol(B)(9)(f).

b. *Electronic filing.* On consent, documents may be filed and served by electronic means in Supreme Court in such civil actions and in such counties as shall be authorized by order of the Chief Administrator of the Courts and only to the extent and in the manner provided in NY R UNIF TRIAL CTS § 202.5-b. NY R UNIF TRIAL CTS § 202.5-b(a)(1). For the definitions of terms used in electronic filing, refer to NY R UNIF TRIAL CTS § 202.5-b(a)(2).

i. *E-filing mandatory.* In any action subject to e-filing, all documents required to be filed with the court by an e-filing party shall be filed and served electronically, except as provided in NY R UNIF TRIAL CTS § 202.5-b. NY R UNIF TRIAL CTS § 202.5-b(d)(1)(i).

- *ERIE COUNTY.* Case types currently eligible and accepted for e-filing are listed at the NYSCEF website. Note that some actions or special proceedings, (i.e., name changes) which are otherwise subject to mandatory e-filing, if commenced by unrepresented litigants will NOT be maintained in the NYSCEF system; individual cases may be found either at NYSCEF or in the Erie County Clerk's online records system. NY R ERIE E FIL Doc. 3(I)(E).
- *KINGS COUNTY.* Cases that are commenced by filing of the initiating papers with NYSCEF are identified as e-filed cases by assignment of a special index number (i.e., Index Numbers beginning with 500,000). NY R L KINGS E FIL Doc. 1(A)(1). All cases required to be e-filed are listed in Uniform Rule 202.5-bb (Mandatory E-Filing Rules) and on the NYSCEF website. All such cases must be commenced by filing with the County Clerk electronically through NYSCEF and all subsequent documents in such cases must be e-filed. Any questions regarding mandatory e-filing in Kings County can be e-mailed to kcco-efile@nycourts.gov. NY R L KINGS E FIL Doc. 1(A)(2).
- *NEW YORK COUNTY.* Unless otherwise provided in the Rules or in NY R NY CTY E FIL Doc. 2 or where a special exemption is granted due to physical requirements (e.g., oversized maps; see NY R NY CTY E FIL Doc. 2(B)(10)), all documents to be filed with the court in a NYSCEF case, including all documents on

motions and all letters to the court (where permitted), must be filed with the NYSCEF system. Documents that attorneys would not ordinarily file with the court in a hard-copy case need not be e-filed. Unless otherwise provided by the E-Filing Rules or this Protocol, in e-filed cases the County Clerk and the court will not accept documents filed in paper form. NY R NY CTY E FIL Doc. 2(B)(1). E-filing is mandatory in all types of cases (other than election law, matrimonial, Art. 78, and Mental Hygiene Law matters, and Art. 70 habeas corpus proceedings) that are commenced in this court on or after February 19, 2013. All such cases must be commenced by filing with the County Clerk electronically through NYSCEF and all subsequent documents in such cases must be e-filed. NY R NY CTY E FIL Doc. 2(A)(2)(a). For more information, including information on consensual e-filing and filing scanned hard copy documents, refer to NY R NY CTY E FIL Doc. 2(A)(2).

- *QUEENS COUNTY.* All authorized Torts, Commercial and Tax Certiorari cases may be commenced by E-Filing, however all parties must consent for the action to continue as an E-file case. NY R L QUEENS E-FILE Doc. 1(A). All papers to be filed with the court in an E-filed case shall be filed on-line with the E-file system except as directed by the court. Papers that attorneys would not ordinarily file with the court in a hard-copy case need not be filed in an E-filed matter. NY R L QUEENS E-FILE Doc. 1(E)(2).

ii. *Who may file.* Documents may be filed or served electronically only by a person who has registered as an authorized e-filing user or as otherwise provided in NY R UNIF TRIAL CTS § 202.5-b(c). NY R UNIF TRIAL CTS § 202.5-b(c)(1).

iii. *When filing made.* Documents may be transmitted at any time of the day or night to the NYSCEF site. A document other than an order or judgment is filed when its electronic transmission or, in the case of a petition that is e-filed by submission of a text file as provided in NY R UNIF TRIAL CTS § 202.5-b(b)(1), the electronic transmission of the text file is recorded at that site, provided, however, that where payment of a fee is required upon the filing of a document, the document is not filed until transmission of the document and the information or form or information as required in NY R UNIF TRIAL CTS § 202.5-b(d)(2)(i), NY R UNIF TRIAL CTS § 202.5-b(d)(2)(ii) or NY R UNIF TRIAL CTS § 202.5-b(d)(2)(iii) has been recorded at the NYSCEF site; or, if no transmission of that information or form or information is recorded, where permitted by the County Clerk, until payment is presented to the County Clerk. NY R UNIF TRIAL CTS § 202.5-b(d)(3)(i).

iv. *Notification of filing.* No later than the close of business on the business day following the electronic filing of a document, a notification, in a form prescribed by the Chief Administrator, shall be transmitted electronically by the NYSCEF site to the person filing such document and the e-mail service addresses of all other participating parties in such action. NY R UNIF TRIAL CTS § 202.5-b(d)(3)(ii).

v. *Removal of confidential information and other corrections.* If a document filed electronically is subsequently discovered to contain confidential data—including but not limited to trade secrets, information protected by confidentiality agreement, or personal confidential information as defined by statute or court rule—or otherwise to have been filed in error, the filer or another party or affected person may (1) notify the parties and any non-party filers in the action of the confidentiality issue or other error raised by the filing, and of his or her intention to seek judicial relief to correct the filing: (2) following such notification, request that the appropriate County Clerk, exercising his or her administrative discretion, place the document temporarily in "restricted" status on the NYSCEF site, to be made available for viewing by court staff and the parties but not the general public; and (3) file an application to correct the filing by order to show cause within five (5) business days of such notification (or such time as the court may direct), including a request for preliminary injunctive relief limiting interim disclosure of the document at issue. Unless otherwise directed by the court, any document placed in restricted status in response to such a request shall be returned to public view upon expiration of this five (5) day period. The Chief Administrator of the Courts shall promulgate forms to implement this process. NY R UNIF TRIAL CTS § 202.5-b(d)(3)(iii).

- *KINGS COUNTY.* For information on what to do when a document was erroneously filed with confidential information, refer to NY R L KINGS E FIL Doc. 1(B)(11).
- *NEW YORK COUNTY.* For information on what to do when a document was erroneously filed with confidential information, refer to NY R NY CTY E FIL Doc. 2(B)(8).
- *QUEENS COUNTY.* For information on what to do when a document was erroneously filed with confidential information, refer to NY R L QUEENS E-FILE Doc. 1(E)(7).

vi. *Documents requiring judge's signature.* Except where the court directs otherwise, any document that requires a judge's signature shall be transmitted electronically and in hard copy to the court. NY R UNIF TRIAL CTS § 202.5-b(d)(6).

vii. *Documents which would be inconvenient to file electronically; Hard copies.* Notwithstanding any other provision of NY R UNIF TRIAL CTS § 202.5-b, and subject to such guidelines as may be established by the Chief Administrative Judge, the County Clerk or his or her designee may require or permit a party to file in hard copy, in accordance with procedures set by the County Clerk or designee, an exhibit or other document which it is impractical or inconvenient to file electronically. NY R UNIF TRIAL CTS § 202.5-b(d)(7).

- *ERIE COUNTY.* Please contact the Supervisor of Actions & Proceedings, Erie County Clerk's Office by calling (716) 858-6662 or the Deputy County Clerk—Legal at (716) 858-6348 for information. NY R ERIE E FIL Doc. 3(III)(F).
- *KINGS COUNTY.* With limited exceptions, as set forth in the Uniform Rules and herein, all documents to be filed with the court in a NYSCEF case shall be filed online via the NYSCEF system. However, should the size, consistency or context of a hard copy document preclude electronic filing, the user shall electronically file a "Notice of Hard Copy Submission—E-Filed Cases" form EFM-3. Any hard copy submitted pursuant to NY R L KINGS E FIL Doc. 1(B)(9) shall include, as a cover page firmly fastened thereto, a copy of the Confirmation Notice received from the NYSCEF site confirming receipt of the "Notice of Hard Copy Submission—E-Filed Cases". Any party may object to such hard copy filing. The Court, in response to such objection, may, following the hard copy filing, fashion such relief as it deems appropriate pursuant to and in furtherance of the Uniform Rules and NY R L KINGS E FIL Doc. 1, including, but not limited to, an Order directing the filing party to file such documents online via the NYSCEF system. When exhibits are impractical to file pursuant to NY R UNIF TRIAL CTS § 202.5-b(d)(7), an additional "Notice of Hard Copy Exhibit Filing" form EFM-4 is required to be submitted. NY R L KINGS E FIL Doc. 1(B)(9).
- *NEW YORK COUNTY.* If a filer needs to submit unusual exhibits in original form that cannot practically be e-filed, such as oversized maps or electronic recordings, the filer should consult with the County Clerk's E-File Department by telephone at 646-386-3737 (procedural questions only) or by e-mail at ccnyef@nycourts.gov, which will normally require that the filer retain custody of the original subject to possible future directives of the court. NY R NY CTY E FIL Doc. 2(B)(10). In such instances, the filing counsel shall file with NYSCEF a "placeholder" in the form of a Notice of Hard Copy Exhibit Filing (NYSCEF Form EF 21). The Notice should be uploaded to NYSCEF as document type "Exhibit" and the filer should indicate in the "Additional Document Information" field that the filer is retaining custody of the original. Failure to e-file the Notice may result in a gap in the official record of the court. NY R NY CTY E FIL Doc. 2(B)(10).

viii. *Documents containing sensitive or proprietary information.* In an action subject to e-filing, any person may apply for an order prohibiting or restricting the electronic filing in the action of specifically identified materials on the grounds that such materials are subject to copyright or other proprietary rights, or trade secret or other privacy interests, and that electronic filing in the action is likely to result in substantial prejudice to those rights or interests. NY R UNIF TRIAL CTS § 202.5-b(k)(2).

ix. *Refusal to accept paper filings.* In accordance with NY CPLR Rule 2102(c), a County Clerk and a chief clerk of the Supreme Court or County Court, as appropriate, shall refuse to accept for filing papers filed in actions and proceedings when the paper sought to be filed:

- Is in an action subject to electronic filing pursuant to Rules of the Chief Administrator,
- Is not being filed electronically, and
- Does not include the notice required by NY R UNIF TRIAL CTS § 202.5-b(d)(1). NY R UNIF TRIAL CTS § 202.5(d)(1)(v); NY R UNIF TRIAL CTS § 202.5-bb(d).

x. *Emergency filings; Hard copies.* For information on when an emergency filing may be filed and served in hard copy, refer to NY R UNIF TRIAL CTS § 202.5-b(d)(1)(ii), NY R UNIF TRIAL CTS § 202.5-b(d)(1)(iii) and NY R UNIF TRIAL CTS § 202.5-bb(c)(3).

- *KINGS COUNTY.* Under the rules, a participating emergency e-filer must electronically file the documents initially filed in hard copy form within three (3) business days of the emergency filing; the originals will be discarded after the documents have been processed and the failure to e-file as required will therefore lead to an incomplete record. NY R L KINGS E FIL Doc. 1(B)(3).
- *NEW YORK COUNTY.* Occasionally an emergency will arise requiring expedited entry of a document with the County Clerk (e.g., an order issued in the courtroom after a conference or argument of a critical matter), such as for purposes of an immediate appeal. Expedition can be achieved by the Part as follows: the

document should be carried by a Court Officer or staff member to the General Clerk's Office to assure immediate and proper recordation in the computer and, as appropriate, the posting of the document to NYSCEF or the Supreme Court Records On-Line Library ("Scroll"). The court will accommodate counsel in emergencies. NY R NY CTY Procedure XI(A).

- *NEW YORK COUNTY.* For more information on how to bring emergency matters before the court, refer to NY R NY CTY Procedure IV.

xi. *Technical failures.* The NYSCEF site shall be considered to be subject to a technical failure on a given day if the site is unable to accept filings or provide access to filed documents continuously or intermittently over the course of any period of time greater than one (1) hour after 12:00 noon of that day. Notice of all such technical failures shall be provided on the site. NY R UNIF TRIAL CTS § 202.5-b(i).

- When e-filing is hindered by a technical failure, a party may file with the appropriate clerk and serve in hard copy. NY R UNIF TRIAL CTS § 202.5-b(i). In the event an attorney or party shall file and serve documents in hard copy pursuant to NY R UNIF TRIAL CTS § 202.5-b(i), each such document shall include the notice required by NY R UNIF TRIAL CTS § 202.5-b(d)(1), and the filer shall file those documents with the NYSCEF site within three (3) business days after restoration of normal operations at that site. NY R UNIF TRIAL CTS § 202.5-b(i).
- With the exception of deadlines that by law cannot be extended, the time for filing of any document that is delayed due to technical failure of the site shall be extended for one (1) day for each day on which such failure occurs, unless otherwise ordered by the court. NY R UNIF TRIAL CTS § 202.5-b(i).
- *ERIE COUNTY.* When filing by electronic means is hindered by a technical failure, please refer to the NY R UNIF TRIAL CTS § 202.5-b(i). NY R ERIE E FIL Doc. 3(III)(K).
- *KINGS COUNTY.* When filing by electronic means is hindered by a NYSCEF technical failure (as set forth in NY R UNIF TRIAL CTS § 202.5-b(i)), a party may file with the appropriate Clerk in hard copy. Except for deadlines that by law cannot be extended (e.g. Statute of limitations, Notice of Appeal), the time for filing of any document that is delayed due to technical failure of the NYSCEF system shall be extended for one day for each day on which such failure occurs, unless otherwise ordered by the court. NY R L KINGS E FIL Doc. 1(B)(13).
- *ONONDAGA COUNTY.* When filing by electronic means is hindered by a technical failure (as set forth in NY R UNIF TRIAL CTS § 202.5-b(h)(3)(i)), a party may file a hard copy with the County Clerk. With the exception of deadlines that by law cannot be extended (e.g., a statute of limitations or the deadline for filing a Notice of Appeal), the time for filing of any document that is delayed due to technical failure of the NYSCEF system will be extended for one day for each day on which such failure occurs, unless otherwise ordered by the court. A "Notice of Hard Copy Filing Submission—E-Filed Case' must accompany any documents not filed via NYSCEF. NY R ONDGA E FIL Protocol(B)(8).

xii. *Filing fees.* For information on what information must be provided to pay filing fees, refer to NY R UNIF TRIAL CTS § 202.5-b(d)(2).

xiii. *Exemption from e-filing.* For information on exemptions from e-filing, refer to NY R UNIF TRIAL CTS § 202.5-bb(e).

xiv. *Filing exhibits*

- *ERIE COUNTY.* In the NYSCEF system, each exhibit must be uploaded as a separate .pdf file. After uploading a primary document, please choose the document type "Exhibit" and enter the appropriate number or letter and a brief description of the exhibit; each exhibit should bear a separate cover sheet clearly marked as "Exhibit A," "Exhibit B," etc. "Exhibit A" or "Exhibit B" is unacceptable as a brief description of the exhibit. Exhibits, where referenced in a signed Order as attached or affixed shall be uploaded with the signed Order as one .pdf document. NY R ERIE E FIL Doc. 3(III)(H); NY R ERIE E FIL Doc. 3(V)(D).
- *KINGS COUNTY.* In the NYSCEF system, each exhibit should be uploaded as a separate PDF file. After uploading a primary document, please choose the document type "Exhibit", enter the appropriate number or letter, and be sure to place a check mark to the right of "Attach to main document". Each exhibit shall bear a separate cover sheet clearly marked as Exhibit A, Exhibit B, etc. NY R L KINGS E FIL Doc. 1(B)(12). Whenever possible, attorneys submitting exhibits in NYSCEF cases should make each exhibit a separate attachment to an affidavit/affirmation in the system (i.e., multiple exhibits should not be filed as a single PDF). NY R L KINGS E FIL Doc. 1(D)(1).

- *NEW YORK COUNTY.* Attorneys submitting exhibits in NYSCEF cases should make each exhibit a separate attachment to an affidavit/affirmation in the system; i.e., exhibits should not be filed as a single PDF-A together with the affidavit/affirmation or grouped together as a single PDF-A attachment because either of these two formats makes it difficult for the Justice to locate particular exhibits as needed. Counsel must also include appropriate descriptive language in the "Additional Document Information" field in NYSCEF. NY R NY CTY E FIL Doc. 2(D)(6).
- *ONONDAGA COUNTY.* All exhibits in e-filed cases must be e-filed individually as separate attachments. NY R ONDGA E FIL Protocol(B)(9)(b).

xv. *Correcting documents*

- *ERIE COUNTY.* Submission of documents which, upon examination, require correction or addition will result in notification to the filer advising that the document has been returned for correction. The filer shall make the required corrections and/or additions as indicated in the e-mail transmission sent by the County Clerk or Part Clerk through the NYSCEF site. The corrected documents may be resubmitted using the "Re-file this document" link highlighted in the filer's document list for the respective case. Please note that in the case of multiple submissions, all related documents filed at the same time may be removed from the case record and returned until all documents are properly submitted. NY R ERIE E FIL Doc. 3(III)(J).
- *KINGS COUNTY.* Submission of documents which, upon examination, require correction or addition will result in notification to the filer advising that there is a problem with a document. The filer shall make the required corrections and/or additions and resubmit the corrected document using the "Refile this document" link. In the event a document is returned for correction, the original file date will be preserved. For corrections of documents filed with the Kings County Clerk which require a court order, refer to the procedure in NY R UNIF TRIAL CTS § 202.5-b(d)(3)(iii) and NY R L KINGS E FIL Doc. 1(B)(11). NY R L KINGS E FIL Doc. 1(B)(3).
- *ONONDAGA COUNTY.* If there is an error or an additional document is required, the system will notify the filing party, who will make the corrections/additions and resubmit them online. NY R ONDGA E FIL Protocol(B)(6).
- *QUEENS COUNTY.* Generally speaking, documents that have been E-filed will not thereafter be deleted by the County Clerk from NYCEF because the filer asserts that the filing contains an error or a significant omission. When the filer wishes to correct a perceived error or omission in a filed document, he or she should file an amended version of the document, with the original remaining on file, or else obtain a court order providing for deletion of the original. The County Clerk will only delete a document upon request of the filer or on the County Clerk's own initiative when it is obvious from the face of the document alone that the filer made a fundamental error and never intended to file the document that was filed (e.g., a completely unrelated non-litigation document, a different case, or a wrong county). The County Clerk will advise the filer when any such fundamental errors are detected. NY R L QUEENS E-FILE Doc. 1(E)(6).

c. *Facsimile filing.* In the Supreme Court, facsimile filing shall be limited to commercial claims and tax certiorari, conservatorship, and mental hygiene proceedings in Monroe, Westchester, New York and Suffolk Counties. NY R UNIF TRIAL CTS § 202.5-a(a)(1). Refer to NY R UNIF TRIAL CTS § 202.5-a for information on the procedures for facsimile filing.

   i. *NEW YORK COUNTY.* Unless indicated otherwise by the court in a particular case or in NY R NY CTY J RUL Doc. 1, Justices do not accept papers by fax. NY R NY CTY J RUL Rule 4.

d. *ERIE COUNTY: Filing request for judicial intervention.* An RJI in a NYSCEF case shall be filed via the NYSCEF system and will be filed after all other documents have been uploaded. The filer may choose between filing a .pdf image of the prepared RJI and any Addendum or having the system prepare the RJI which shall conform to Uniform Rules. Addenda, such as the Commercial Division Addendum, if prepared by the filer must be filed simultaneously with and attached to an RJI and uploaded as one .pdf document with the RJI. If the RJI is prepared by the e-filing system, no separate Addendum is required. Whether or not the filer elects to allow NYSCEF to create the RJI or chooses to upload a prepared RJI, data in addition to the nature of the judicial intervention, including information that appears on any Addenda will be collected through completion of the fields presented. If the filing of the RJI is accomplished through a filing agent, a prepared RJI and Addendum must be filed in lieu of the creation of the RJI by the NYSCEF system, as the RJI must be signed by the attorney. NY R ERIE E FIL Doc. 3(IV). For information on RJIs in specific types of action, refer to NY R ERIE E FIL Doc. 3(IV).

2. *Service requirements*

   a. *Who may serve.* Except where otherwise prescribed by law or order of court, papers may be served by any person not a party of the age of eighteen years or over. NY CPLR Rule 2103(a).

   b. *Service upon attorney.* Except where otherwise prescribed by law or order of court, papers to be served upon a party in a pending action shall be served upon the party's attorney. Where the same attorney appears for two or more parties, only one (1) copy need be served upon the attorney. Such service upon an attorney shall be made:

      i. By delivering the paper to the attorney personally. NY CPLR Rule 2103(b)(1).

      ii. By mailing the paper to the attorney at the address designated by that attorney for that purpose or, if none is designated, at the attorney's last known address; service by mail shall be complete upon mailing. NY CPLR Rule 2103(b)(2).

         - *BRONX COUNTY.* Service by mail must be within the state. NY R BRONX FIL R Doc. 3.

      iii. If the attorney's office is open, by leaving the paper with a person in charge, or if no person is in charge, by leaving it in a conspicuous place; or if the attorney's office is not open, by depositing the paper, enclosed in a sealed wrapper directed to the attorney, in the attorney's office letter drop or box. NY CPLR Rule 2103(b)(3).

      iv. By leaving it at the attorney's residence within the state with a person of suitable age and discretion. Service upon an attorney shall not be made at the attorney's residence unless service at the attorney's office cannot be made. NY CPLR Rule 2103(b)(4).

      v. By transmitting the paper to the attorney by facsimile transmission, provided that a facsimile telephone number is designated by the attorney for that purpose. Service by facsimile transmission shall be complete upon the receipt by the sender of a signal from the equipment of the attorney served indicating that the transmission was received, and the mailing of a copy of the paper to that attorney. The designation of a facsimile telephone number in the address block subscribed on a paper served or filed in the course of an action or proceeding shall constitute consent to service by facsimile transmission in accordance with NY CPLR Rule 2103(b)(5). An attorney may change or rescind a facsimile telephone number by serving a notice on the other parties. NY CPLR Rule 2103(b)(5).

      vi. By dispatching the paper to the attorney by overnight delivery service at the address designated by the attorney for that purpose or, if none is designated, at the attorney's last known address. Service by overnight delivery service shall be complete upon deposit of the paper enclosed in a properly addressed wrapper into the custody of the overnight delivery service for overnight delivery, prior to the latest time designated by the overnight delivery service for overnight delivery. "Overnight delivery service" means any delivery service which regularly accepts items for overnight delivery to any address in the state. NY CPLR Rule 2103(b)(6).

      vii. By transmitting the paper to the attorney by electronic means where and in the manner authorized by the chief administrator of the courts by rule and, unless such rule shall otherwise provide, such transmission shall be upon the party's written consent. The subject matter heading for each paper sent by electronic means must indicate that the matter being transmitted electronically is related to a court proceeding. NY CPLR Rule 2103(b)(7).

         - *KINGS COUNTY.* Pursuant to the E-Filing Rules, service of interlocutory documents is made by posting a document to the NYSCEF site, which automatically and immediately transmits an email notice of the filing, including a link to the document, to all participating counsel and unrepresented litigants on the case. The Rules also authorize service by other methods permitted by the CPLR. If service by such other method is made, proof of service must be filed with NYSCEF. NY R L KINGS E FIL Doc. 1(I).
         - *NEW YORK COUNTY.* Service. . .will be made automatically through NYSCEF upon all participating counsel and unrepresented parties in the case. There are limited exceptions to the requirement for e-filing in the covered kinds of cases. NY R NY CTY Procedure XI(A). Pursuant to the E-Filing Rules, service of interlocutory documents is made by posting a document to the NYSCEF site, which automatically and immediately transmits an e-mail notice of the filing, including a link to the document, to all participating counsel and unrepresented litigants on the case. The Rules also authorize service by other methods permitted by the CPLR. If service by such a method is made, proof of service must be filed with NYSCEF. NY R NY CTY E FIL Doc. 2(I).
         - *QUEENS COUNTY.* Filing with the system permits counsel to serve the papers electronically pursuant to NY R UNIF TRIAL CTS § 202.5-b(f) once consent to E-Filing has been filed on-line. Consult NY R UNIF TRIAL CTS § 202.5-bb(c) for service in mandatory e-filing. Any required proof of service should be E-filed as a separate document. NY R L QUEENS E-FILE Doc. 1(E)(4).

c. *Electronic service mandatory; Consenting to electronic service; How electronic service may be made.* Except as otherwise provided in NY R UNIF TRIAL CTS § 202.5-bb, filing and service of all documents in an action that has been commenced electronically in accordance with NY R UNIF TRIAL CTS § 202.5-bb shall be by electronic means. NY R UNIF TRIAL CTS § 202.5-bb(c)(1).

   i. *Party's consent required for certain e-filing.* After commencement of an action wherein e-filing is authorized, documents may be electronically filed and served, but only by, and electronic service shall be made only upon, a party or parties who have consented thereto. NY R UNIF TRIAL CTS § 202.5-b(b)(2)(i).

      - A consent to e-filing in an action shall state that the party providing it agrees to the use of e-filing in the action and to be bound by the filing and service provisions in NY R UNIF TRIAL CTS § 202.5-b. NY R UNIF TRIAL CTS § 202.5-b(b)(2)(ii).

   ii. *Address for service; Duty to notify as to changes.* The e-mail service address recorded at the time of registration is the e-mail address at which service of interlocutory documents on that party may be made through notification transmitted by the NYSCEF site. It is the responsibility of each filing user to monitor that address and promptly notify the Resource Center in the event of a change in his or her e-mail service address. NY R UNIF TRIAL CTS § 202.5-b(f)(2)(i).

   iii. *How service made.* An e-filing party causes service of an interlocutory document to be made upon another party participating in e-filing by filing the document electronically. Upon receipt of an interlocutory document, the NYSCEF site shall automatically transmit electronic notification to all e-mail service addresses in such action. NY R UNIF TRIAL CTS § 202.5-b(f)(2)(ii).

      - Except as provided otherwise in NY R UNIF TRIAL CTS § 202.5-b(h)(3), the electronic transmission of the notification shall constitute service of the document on the e-mail service addresses identified therein; however, such service will not be effective if the filing party learns that the notification did not reach the address of the person to be served. Proof of such service will be recorded on the NYSCEF site. A party may, however, utilize other service methods permitted by the CPLR provided that, if one of such other methods is used, proof of that service shall be filed electronically. NY R UNIF TRIAL CTS § 202.5-b(f)(2)(ii).

   iv. *Signatures on hard copies; Proof of service filed electronically.* When an e-filing party serves a document in hard copy on a non-participating party, the document served shall bear full signatures of all signatories and proof of such service shall be filed electronically. NY R UNIF TRIAL CTS § 202.5-b(b)(2)(i).

      - *ERIE COUNTY.* In the NYSCEF system, each Affidavit of Service must be uploaded as a separate .pdf file. After uploading the Affidavit, please choose the document type: "Affirmation/Affidavit of Service" and enter the name of the party served as Additional Document Information. NY R ERIE E FIL Doc. 3(III)(I); NY R ERIE E FIL Doc. 3(V)(F).

   v. *Effect of failure to consent.* A party's failure to consent to participation in electronic filing and service shall not bar any other party to the action from filing documents electronically with the County Clerk and the court or serving documents upon any other party who has consented to participation. A party who has not consented to participation shall file documents with the court and the County Clerk, and serve and be served with documents, in hard copy. NY R UNIF TRIAL CTS § 202.5-b(b)(2)(i).

d. *Service upon party.* If a party has not appeared by an attorney or the party's attorney cannot be served, service shall be upon the party by a method specified in NY CPLR Rule 2103(b)(1), NY CPLR Rule 2103(b)(2), NY CPLR Rule 2103(b)(4), NY CPLR Rule 2103(b)(5) or NY CPLR Rule 2103(b)(6). NY CPLR Rule 2103(c).

e. *Service on all parties.* Each paper served on any party shall be served on every other party who has appeared, except as otherwise may be provided by court order or as provided in NY CPLR § 3012 or in NY CPLR § 3215(f). Upon demand by a party, the plaintiff shall supply that party with a list of those who have appeared and the names and addresses of their attorneys. NY CPLR Rule 2103(e).

f. *Service by filing.* If a paper cannot be served by any of the methods specified in NY CPLR Rule 2103(b) and NY CPLR Rule 2103(c), service may be made by filing the paper as if it were a paper required to be filed. NY CPLR Rule 2103(d).

g. *Definitions.* For the purposes of NY CPLR Rule 2103:

   i. "Mailing" means the deposit of a paper enclosed in a first class postpaid wrapper, addressed to the address designated by a person for that purpose or, if none is designated, at that person's last known address, in a post office or official depository under the exclusive care and custody of the United States Postal Service within the state;

ii. "Electronic means" means any method of transmission of information between computers or other machines designed for the purpose of sending and receiving such transmissions, and which allows the recipient to reproduce the information transmitted in a tangible medium of expression;

iii. "Facsimile transmission" means any method of transmission of documents to a facsimile machine at a remote location which can automatically produce a tangible copy of such documents. NY CPLR Rule 2103(f).

h. *No service on parties in default.* When a party is in default for failure to appear, he shall not be entitled to notice or service of any copy required under NY CPLR § 3101, et seq. NY CPLR Rule 3105.

G. Hearings

1. *Oral argument.* Motion papers received by the clerk of the court on or before the return date shall be deemed submitted as of the return date. The assigned judge, in his or her discretion or at the request of a party, thereafter may determine that any motion be orally argued and may fix a time for oral argument. NY R UNIF TRIAL CTS § 202.8(d).

a. A party requesting oral argument shall set forth such request in its notice of motion or in its order to show cause or on the first page of the answering papers, as the case may be. Where all parties to a motion request oral argument, oral argument shall be granted unless the court shall determine it to be unnecessary. NY R UNIF TRIAL CTS § 202.8(d).

b. Where a motion is brought on by order to show cause, the court may set forth in the order that oral argument is required on the return date of the motion. NY R UNIF TRIAL CTS § 202.8(d).

i. *BRONX COUNTY.* All orders to show cause, with the exception of orders to show cause that are returnable in the City Part, the STP Part, the Matrimonial Part and the Preliminary/Compliance Conference Part (IA-11), submitted on or after August 25, 2003, will be returnable on a Monday in the assigned Justice's part and appear on his or her motion calendar. Appearances will be required on orders to show cause. NY R BRONX FIL R Doc. 8. A motion on notice or a notice of petition in a New York Supreme Court E-File (hereafter known as NYSCEF) case, as in others, shall be made returnable in the Motion Support Office (Room 217). NY R BRONX E FIL R Doc. 1(1).

- After a motion/petition and notice are filed with the NYSCEF system, the Motion Support Office will automatically place the motion/proceeding on the submit calendar in the Motion Support Office (Room 217) for the return date. No appearance or other action by the filing attorney is required in order for the motion to be calendared if the motion fee is paid for via NYSCEF. Motions in e-filed cases (other than tax certiorari cases) appear on the submit calendar in Room 217 on the return date. NY R BRONX E FIL R Doc. 1(2).

c. *KINGS COUNTY.* All motions require appearances and oral argument. NY R L KINGS Pt. C, Rule 3.

2. *Return date; Time for hearing.* A notice of motion shall specify the time and place of the hearing on the motion. NY CPLR Rule 2214(a). The moving party determines when a motion on notice shall be heard, but she has to consult the court's or judge's calendar practice first. The movant picks out a "return day" sufficiently far off to assure that the notice requirements of NY CPLR Rule 2214(b) can be met, and to assure as well that the day picked is a day on which the assigned judge hears motions. SIEGEL-NYPRAC § 247.

a. *Judge assigned to hear motion*

i. *Referral to judge supervising disclosure.* Unless the chief administrator of the courts has, by rule, provided otherwise, if a case has been assigned to a judge to supervise disclosure pursuant to NY CPLR § 3104, all motions preliminary to trial shall be referred to such judge whenever practicable. NY CPLR Rule 3214(a).

ii. *Referral to judge who decided prior motion.* Any motion may be referred to a judge who decided a prior motion in the action. NY CPLR Rule 2217(a).

iii. *Transfer when judge unable to hear motion.* If a motion is made to a judge who is or will be for any reason unable to hear it, it may be transferred by order of such judge or by written stipulation of the parties to any other judge to whom it might originally have been made. NY CPLR Rule 2217(c).

iv. *Procedure for unassigned cases.* If a case has not been assigned to a judge, the motion shall be made returnable before the court, and a copy of the moving papers, together with a request for judicial intervention, shall be filed with the court, with proof of service upon all other parties, where required by NY R UNIF TRIAL CTS § 202.6, within five (5) days of service upon the other parties. The moving party shall give written notice of the index number to all other parties immediately after filing of the papers. NY R UNIF TRIAL CTS § 202.8(b).

- *Responding papers.* Copies of all responding papers shall be submitted to the court, with proof of service and with the index number set forth in the papers, on or before the return date. NY R UNIF TRIAL CTS § 202.8(b).

- *Assignment after request for judicial intervention.* The case shall be assigned to a judge as soon as practicable after the filing of the request for judicial intervention pursuant to NY R UNIF TRIAL CTS § 202.6, but in no event later than the return date. After assignment to the judge, the court shall provide for appropriate notice to the parties of the name of the assigned judge. NY R UNIF TRIAL CTS § 202.8(b).
- *Motions to be heard in another county.* Motion papers noticed to be heard in a county other than the county where the venue of the action has been placed by the plaintiff shall be assigned to a judge in accordance with procedures established by the Chief Administrator. NY R UNIF TRIAL CTS § 202.8(b).

v. *ALBANY COUNTY: Motions referred to IAS Justice.* All motions made after a case has been assigned a day certain shall be referred to the IAS Justice unless the motion is returnable during the term in which the matter has been assigned a day certain, in that event, the matter will be referred to the Part 1 Justice for that particular term who may entertain the motion or refer such motion to the IAS Justice. Under those circumstances, the Part I Justice shall decide whether or not to strike the note of issue or assign the matter a new day certain. NY R 3 JD SUP Doc. 1(H)(2). All motions shall be returnable before the assigned justice. NY R 3 JD SUP Doc. 1(B).

b. *Trial of issue raised by motion.* The court may order that an issue of fact raised on a motion shall be separately tried by the court or a referee. If the issue is triable of right by jury, the court shall give the parties an opportunity to demand a jury trial of such issue. Failure to make such demand within the time limited by the court, or, if no such time is limited, before trial begins, shall be deemed a waiver of the right to trial by jury. An order under NY CPLR § 2218 shall specify the issue to be tried. NY CPLR § 2218.

c. *Audio-visual coverage of trial court proceeding.* Audio-visual coverage of proceedings in the trial courts shall be permitted only in accordance with the provisions of Part 131 of the Rules of the Chief Administrator (NY R CHIEF ADMIN § 131.1, et seq.). NY R CHIEF J § 29.3.

d. *Adjournment of return date.* Stipulations of adjournment of the return date made by the parties shall be in writing and shall be submitted to the assigned judge. Such stipulation shall be effective unless the court otherwise directs. No more than three (3) stipulated adjournments for an aggregate period of sixty (60) days shall be submitted without prior permission of the court. NY R UNIF TRIAL CTS § 202.8(e)(1).

i. Absent agreement by the parties, a request by any party for an adjournment shall be submitted in writing, upon notice to the other party, to the assigned judge on or before the return date. The court will notify the requesting party whether the adjournment has been granted. NY R UNIF TRIAL CTS § 202.8(e)(2).

ii. *BRONX COUNTY.* Motions that have been e-filed may be adjourned in Room 217 if an adjournment complies with the procedures of the Motion Support Office (explained in the "Filing Rules—Motion Procedure" section of the "Courthouse Procedures" link on the website of [the] court). An adjournment that so complies may be obtained by filing a stipulation of all parties with NYSCEF (designated in the filing menu as a "Stipulation to Adjourn Motion"). NY R BRONX E FIL R Doc. 1(3).

iii. *NEW YORK COUNTY.* The Courtroom also maintains a "APB (All Papers By)" Calendar, which is used when a party seeks an adjournment but fails to comply with the Courtroom's procedures or there is a failure to comply with procedures that requires the clerk to adjourn the motion/application (e.g., failure to submit a Confirmation Notice in an e-filed case). The case may be put over for three days to allow compliance with those procedures, as described further below. NY R NY CTY Procedure II(C); NY R NY CTY E FIL Doc. 2(D)(2). E-filed applications may be adjourned in the Part if an adjournment complies with the Part's procedures (see the Uniform Rules of the Justices (Local Rules) on the court's website). An adjournment that so complies may be obtained by filing with NYSCEF a stipulation of all parties (designated in the filing menu as a Stipulation—Adjournment of Motion—Before Judge); the motion number and the current return date of the motion being adjourned shall be set forth in the "Additional Document Information" field in NYSCEF. Absent any problems, the Part will effectuate the adjournment without need for an appearance or any other action by the parties. NY R NY CTY E FIL Doc. 2(D)(4).

iv. *QUEENS COUNTY.* The Motion Support Office is NOT authorized to grant adjournments. NY R L QUEENS MOT SUP Doc. 1.

e. *ALBANY COUNTY: Motion terms.* There shall be a. . . Motion Term on each Friday in the Supreme Court, Albany County. The Friday Motion Term shall include all Article 78 Proceedings involving New York State and proceedings commenced pursuant to Article 14 of the Civil Service Law (including applications for injunctive relief made pursuant to section 209-a of the Civil Service Law). NY R 3 JD SUP Doc. 1(F). Generally, parties will be granted only one adjournment for the Friday Motion Term. NY R 3 JD SUP Doc. 1(F).

f. *ALBANY COUNTY: Motion determined without hearing.* All motions are deemed "submitted" on the return date and no appearances are required by the parties. NY R 3 JD SUP Doc. 1(B). In the event oral argument is requested, the parties should not appear on the return date. At the discretion of the assigned Judge and upon the granting of a request for oral argument, the parties will be notified by Chambers of the scheduled time and place at which argument will be heard. Where a motion is brought on by order to show cause, the court may set forth in the order that appearances and/or oral argument are required on the return date of the motion. NY R 3 JD SUP Doc. 1(B).

g. *BRONX COUNTY: Return date.* All assigned and unassigned motions will be returnable five (5) days a week in the Civil Branch Clerk's Office, Room 217, at 9:30 a.m. NY R BRONX FIL R Doc. 8.

h. *BRONX COUNTY: Oral argument.* Calendars of disclosure motions and other motions adjourned for oral argument will be published for the four (4) business days preceding the rescheduled appearance date and on the rescheduled date of the motion. These repetitive publications will serve as the notification of procedure of adjournment of all motions. In addition, two (2) days before the return date of unassigned motions a list of such motions indicating the assigned Justice and the adjourned date of the motion will be published. NY R BRONX FIL R Doc. 8.

i. *BRONX COUNTY: Resolution before return date.* Counsel/parties must advise the Court in writing on or before the return date of all motions that have been resolved by Counsel/parties themselves and all motions the movant(s) wish to be withdrawn. NY R BRONX FIL R Doc. 8.

j. *ERIE COUNTY: Calendaring of motions.* Refer to individual Justice's Part Rules. NY R ERIE E FIL Doc. 3(V)(B).

k. *KINGS COUNTY: Return date set by court.* Irrespective of the return date indicated in the notice of motion, motions will be rescheduled by the E-file/Motion Support Office to a date designated by the assigned Judge. NY R L KINGS Pt. C, Rule 2.

l. *KINGS COUNTY: Calendar calls.* There shall be two (2) calendar calls on motion days. The first calendar call shall be at 9:30 AM and the second calendar call shall be at 10:45 AM, unless the Judge's Part Rules provide otherwise. Defaults shall only be taken on second call. Attorneys with appearances elsewhere in the courthouse may advise the clerk of their whereabouts to avoid a default. Failure to so advise the clerk or appear at the default calendar call will result in a default order being entered or the motion being marked off the calendar. NY R L KINGS Pt. C, Rule 7.

m. *NEW YORK COUNTY: Return date and assigned courtroom.* Motions made by notice of motion and petitions and notices of petition in special proceedings are processed by the General Clerk's Office (Room 119) and are to be made returnable in the Motion Submission Part Courtroom (Room 130) on any business day of the week at 9:30 AM. There are some differences in electronically-filed cases. NY R NY CTY Procedure II; NY R NY CTY Procedure II(C); NY R NY CTY J RUL Rule 13(a).

   i. For the convenience of counsel, between 9:00 A.M. and 9:30 A.M. each day, in advance of the "call," Room 130 accepts (1) written stipulations; (2) affidavits/affirmations reciting the required details as to an adjournment on consent; (3) stipulations, letters or other writings withdrawing motions; and (4) final papers or complete sets of papers on motions. For motions in which these items are handed in before the "call," no one need remain to answer the "call." Counsel/parties must advise the court, either between 9:00 A.M. and 9:30 A.M. or at the "call," of all motions or cases that have been resolved by counsel/parties themselves and all motions that the movant no longer wishes to pursue. If such resolution occurs subsequent to the "call", the assigned Justice must be advised as soon as possible, by written notice sent to the Part, so that the court does not do unnecessary work. NY R NY CTY Procedure II(C).

   ii. Depending upon the assigned Part, contested motions submitted in the Motion Submission Part Courtroom are submitted without argument, or rescheduled for oral argument if so directed by the assigned Justice. For Justices who schedule argument on a case-by-case basis, notice of the argument date will be transmitted by the court. Counsel may ascertain how a motion submitted in Courtroom 130 was marked by consulting Scroll on the court's website, the e-Track application, or, on the two (2) days immediately following the submission date, the New York Law Journal. NY R NY CTY J RUL Rule 13(a).

n. *NEW YORK COUNTY: Motion call.* Each day in the Motion Submission Part Courtroom, commencing at 9:30 A.M., all motions returnable that day will be "called" for the submission of these papers, which must be handed up at this "call" or, as described below, immediately before. Because hundreds of motions appear on the Room 130 calendars every day, motion papers (other than part of the moving papers as described above) cannot be accepted on any day prior to the return date. Courtesy copies are not required nor accepted, but working copies are required by certain Justices in e-filed cases. NY R NY CTY Procedure II(C). If argument is directed, it will take place on an announced date shortly after the day of submission. NY R NY CTY Procedure II(C).

o. *NEW YORK COUNTY: Oral arguments.* Pursuant to request of some Justices, motions submitted in Room 130 will automatically be scheduled for a set argument date in the Part. Other Justices determine on a case-by-case basis after submission in Room 130 whether to accept a particular substantive motion on submission, to require oral argument, or to hold a conference. NY R NY CTY Procedure II(D). If argument is directed by the Justice automatically, notice of argument and the argument date will be given in Room 130. Any appearing party is expected to give notice to all parties and an announcement to this effect is made in Room 130. If the motion is submitted in Room 130 and the Justice, after examining the file, determines that argument should be directed, notice of the argument and the argument date will not be sent by the court. To obtain notification of the argument date and other developments, counsel should use e-Track. If argument notification is not given or transmitted as just described, counsel should understand that the motion has been taken on submission for decision on the papers. NY R NY CTY Procedure II(D).

i. Calendars of motions to be argued in the Parts are published on the morning of the argument date and on the day before in the New York Law Journal under each Part. Argument information is available on a case-by-case basis in Scroll, and e-mail notifications are sent by e-Track to participating attorneys whenever a motion is scheduled for argument in the court's computer system. NY R NY CTY J RUL Rule 15(a)

p. *NEW YORK COUNTY: Motion determined without hearing.* Given the purpose of the Room 130 procedure, the substance of motions will not be addressed at the submission "call." No Judge is present. To the extent possible, motions submitted in Room 130 will be decided "on the papers." Indeed, attorneys are encouraged to use service or clerks to deliver papers or working copies, or to agree among themselves to have one of them deliver papers for all parties by service or a clerk. Counsel for the movant need not appear to "take a default" on any motion or for any other reason. Motions will be submitted, not marked off, in the absence of the movant. Opposing counsel similarly need not appear in person in order to avoid suffering a default. Delivery of papers by service or a clerk will suffice. The court's goal is to be able to collect papers on motions in an orderly fashion but without any attorney having to make an appearance in Room 130 at any time. NY R NY CTY Procedure II(C).

q. *ONONDAGA COUNTY: Return date.* If the motion is the first filing in an action, the case will be assigned and counsel will be notified by the Supreme Court Clerk's Office via the NYSCEF system of the assigned justice and return date. NY R ONDGA E FIL Protocol(B)(7)(c). If the motion is on a previously assigned case, counsel may choose a return date from the assigned justice's motion term schedule. If the date in unavailable, the Supreme Court Clerk's Office will assign the motion to the next available motion term date and will notify counsel via e-mail. The change will also appear in the notification generated by the NYSCEF system. NY R ONDGA E FIL Protocol(B)(7)(d).

r. *QUEENS COUNTY: Return date.* Motions must be made returnable on the proper day/time based on the assigned judge. NY R L QUEENS MOT SUP Doc. 1. Failure to make a motion returnable on the proper day/time may result in the motion being administratively rescheduled or marked off. NY R L QUEENS MOT SUP Doc. 1.

s. *QUEENS COUNTY: Unassigned motions.* For RJI/Motions, due to the fact that the movant would not know who the assigned judge will be, the notice of motion may be returnable any day of the week. RJI/Motions shall be made returnable in "Queens Supreme Court" with no address designated. The motion will be administratively rescheduled to the proper day of the week based on the judge (once a judge has been assigned). Within one (1) week of filing, the movant must check online to see who the assigned judge is (and therefore the location/date/time) that their motion is now returnable. Movant must then notify their adversary of this information prior to the return date. NY R L QUEENS MOT SUP Doc. 1.

3. *Entry of order after hearing.* An order determining a motion shall be entered and filed in the office of the clerk of the court where the action is triable, and all papers used on the motion and any opinion or memorandum in writing shall be filed with that clerk unless the order dispenses with such filing. When a statute or civil practice rule requires such filing and entry in a county other than that in which the order was made, the party prevailing on the motion shall file the order and the papers used on the motion with the proper clerk after receiving them. If a party fails to file any papers required to be filed under NY CPLR Rule 2220(a), the order may be vacated as irregular, with costs. NY CPLR Rule 2220(a). For more information on the entry of an order after a motion, refer to NY CPLR Rule 2219.

a. *BRONX COUNTY: Settled orders.* A Judge's decision will often call for a Settled Order. The purpose of the settled order is to give effect to the decision by directing that some action be done and/or that a court official perform some task. NY R BRONX LEG SUP Doc. 2. A settled order consists of a notice of settlement informing all parties that the proposed order will be presented to the judge who made the decision on a date certain. Next comes the proposed order which will be presented to the judge. This order should conform to the judge's decision and should direct the relief granted in the decision. This should be followed by proof of service upon all parties who were noticed with the decision. It is also helpful if a copy of the judge's decision is included along with the other papers. A settled order should always be noticed before the judge who made the decision. NY R BRONX LEG SUP Doc. 2.

i. Although an order is usually settled by the party who prevailed on the motion, any party may settle the order. It should be presented to the court within sixty (60) days of the decision. The other parties are entitled to ten (10) days notice where service of the settled order is done by mail, five (5) days if the notice is personally delivered. An attorney who is served with a notice of settlement which he believes does not accurately reflect the decision may settle a counter order. The counter order must be noticed for the same day and must be served not less than seven (7) days if by mail and two (2) days if personally delivered. NY R BRONX LEG SUP Doc. 2.

ii. Settled orders are usually sent to the judge the day after they noticed for settlement. No appearance is necessary or even contemplated on a settled order. If the decision directs "submit order", then no notice is necessary, and the order will be sent to the judge as soon a practical after it is received. No fees are collected on settled orders. NY R BRONX LEG SUP Doc. 2.

b. *ERIE COUNTY: Proposed orders.* Proposed orders shall be submitted through the NYSCEF system and a working copy provided to the IAS Justice for signature, if Part Rules so require. NY R ERIE E FIL Doc. 3(V)(G).

c. *KINGS COUNTY: Long form orders.* If the Court directs that an order be settled or submitted on a motion in a NYSCEF case, the proposed order, with Notice of Settlement where required, and any proposed counter-order shall be filed with the Court via NYSCEF. The relevant clerk's office will process the documents in the customary manner. NY R L KINGS E FIL Doc. 1(E).

i. WORKING COPIES OF PROPOSED ORDERS WITH NOTICE OF SETTLEMENT MUST BE SUBMITTED IN THE MOTION SUPPORT OFFICE (ROOM 227) AS EXPLAINED HEREIN. THEY MUST NOT BE DELIVERED TO THE PART OR CHAMBERS, EXCEPT WHERE THE INDIVIDUAL JUSTICE'S PART RULES PROVIDE OTHERWISE; DOING SO WILL CAUSE ADMINISTRATIVE CONFUSION AND POSSIBLE MISPLACEMENT OF PAPERS. Any such submission shall be sent in a timely manner (kindly review individual Justice's rules) and be conspicuously marked on the outside "NYSCEF Matter;" lack of such marking may delay processing. After an order/counter-order has been signed, it will be scanned, and the County Clerk will affix the entry stamp into the NYSCEF system, which will immediately transmit notice of this event via e-mail, including a link to the entered document, to all participating attorneys and unrepresented litigants in the case. Such transmittal does not constitute Notice of Entry. NY R L KINGS E FIL Doc. 1(E).

d. *NEW YORK COUNTY: Long form orders.* Although the court strongly favors the use of short form orders and judgments, there are instances when settlement of an order or judgment is appropriate. When a Justice directs in a decision that a long form order or judgment be settled, that decision is recorded in the court's computer system by the General Clerk's Office and the motion file with decision is held in the Order Section of the Office in Room 119. The settlement process takes place there. NY R NY CTY Procedure II(D); NY R NY CTY E FIL Doc. 2(E).

i. A proposed long form order or judgment in compliance NY R UNIF TRIAL CTS § 202.48 must be presented to the relevant back office, together with a notice of settlement which bears a settlement date, the date on which the order is to be ready for formal presentation to the Justice. In an e-filed case the submission shall be made electronically. The proposed order or counter-order should be e-filed and it will be transmitted automatically by the NYSCEF system to the appropriate back office. The return date and time of the proposed order must be at 9:30 A.M. no sooner than either five (5) days from personal service of the proposed order or ten (10) days from service by mail. Proof of timely service on the other parties must accompany the proposed order in a hard copy case. If an order or judgment is submitted late (later than sixty (60) days from signing and filing of the decision) and the proponent can show good cause for this tardiness, an affidavit or affirmation justifying the delay should be annexed to the proposed order, together with proof of service thereof. If persuaded, the Justice will consider the proposed order despite its untimeliness. NY R NY CTY Procedure II(D); NY R NY CTY E FIL Doc. 2(E).

ii. Sometimes a decision will state "Submit Order." The submitting party should prepare a long form order and make it returnable without notice. Counsel should deliver the proposed order to the Order Section of the appropriate back office, except in an e-filed case, when it shall be submitted electronically. NY R NY CTY Procedure II(D). If the decision of the court directs that a proposed order be settled or submitted in the Part or in Chambers, that direction, should, of course, be followed without presentation of the proposal to the back office. NY R NY CTY Procedure II(D).

iii. For information on proposed counter-orders, refer to NY R NY CTY Procedure II(D) and NY R NY CTY J RUL Rule 16(b).

e. *QUEENS COUNTY: Proposed orders.* If the court directs that an order be settled or submitted on a motion in an E-file case, the proposed order and any proposed counter-order shall be filed with the court on-line with proof of service. (If a decision refers to a proceeding on the record, a copy of the transcript must be submitted.) Working copies of all proposed orders MUST be submitted to the Motion Support Office before an order can be reviewed. NY R L QUEENS E-FILE Doc. 1(I).

i. Counsel are advised to adhere to NY R UNIF TRIAL CTS § 202.48 regarding the submission or settlement of their proposed order or judgment. Persons who are submitting proposed orders/judgments pursuant to a previously issued memorandum decision must submit a copy of the memorandum decision with their proposed order/judgment. Upon E-Filing a proposed order/judgement, a working copy of the proposed order/judgement must be provided to the Motion Support Office. NY R L QUEENS MOT SUP Doc. 1.

4. *Hearing in disclosure matters*

a. *BRONX COUNTY.* On the return date of the motion all non-City and non-Matrimonial disclosure motions, assigned and unassigned, will be scheduled for appearance in the Preliminary and Compliance Conference Part, IA-11, Room 707. The appearance date shall be no earlier than two (2) weeks from the initial return date of the motion. NY R BRONX FIL R Doc. 8.

b. *KINGS COUNTY.* Motions which only seek discovery related relief are scheduled in the Centralized Compliance Part by the E-file/Motion Support Office, on the date the motion is scheduled to be heard, regardless of judicial assignment. Attorneys are advised to consult, inter alia, the New York Law Journal or the Unified Court System's Future Court Appearance Website for the return dates. NY R L KINGS Pt. E, Rule 7. Any motion seeking discovery related relief filed prior to the PC shall be scheduled concurrently with the PC in the Intake Part. NY R L KINGS Pt. B, Rule 6.

i. If all parties served with the motion are present, they may enter into a consent order. If a new Note of Issue date is required, the order should be filled out and signed by all parties leaving a space for the Note of Issue filing date to be entered by a court attorney. Order should include all outstanding discovery, or indicate that discovery is complete. Consent orders are not effective, or allowed to be copied until they have been reviewed by a court attorney and signed by Judge or JHO. NY R L KINGS Pt. E, Rule 11.

H. Forms

1. Official Motion for Protective Order Forms for New York

a. Request for judicial intervention. NY R UNIF TRIAL CTS § 202.6.

b. Notice of motion. NY R UNIF TRIAL CTS § 202.7(b).

2. New York Motion for Protective Order Forms

a. Notice of motion for protective order. NYDISC § 46:6.

b. Notice of motion for protective order; Affirmation in support. NYDISC § 46:7.

c. Notice of motion to compel disclosure and for preclusion; Affidavit in support. NYDISC § 46:13.

d. To stay proceedings pending compliance; Supporting affidavit. NYDISC § 46:21.

e. Notice of motion for protective order denying use of disclosure device. MCF CPLR § 6:53.

f. Notice of motion for protective order vacating notice of deposition. MCF CPLR § 6:54.

g. Notice of motion for protective order denying use of oral deposition. MCF CPLR § 6:55.

h. Notice of motion for protective order striking notice of discovery and inspection. MCF CPLR § 6:56.

i. Notice of motion for protective order striking interrogatories. MCF CPLR § 6:57.

j. Affidavit in support of motion for protective order denying use of disclosure device. MCF CPLR § 6:58.

k. Affirmation in support of motion for protective order vacating notice of deposition. MCF CPLR § 6:59.

l. Affirmation in support of motion for protective order denying use of oral deposition. MCF CPLR § 6:60.

m. Affidavit in support of motion for protective order striking notice of discovery and inspection. MCF CPLR § 6:61.

n. Affirmation in support of motion for protective order striking interrogatories. MCF CPLR § 6:62.

o. Affidavit in support of motion for protective order denying disclosure of documents which could harm the public interest. MCF CPLR § 6:63.

p. Notice of motion for protective order limiting use of disclosure device. MCF CPLR § 6:66.

q. Affidavit in support of motion for protective order limiting use of disclosure device. MCF CPLR § 6:67.

r. Notice of motion for protective order of confidentiality. MCF CPLR § 6:69.

s. Affirmation of attorney in support of motion for protective order of confidentiality. MCF CPLR § 6:70.

t. Affidavit of client in support of motion for protective order of confidentiality. MCF CPLR § 6:71.

u. Notice of motion to suppress information improperly or irregularly obtained. MCF CPLR § 6:74.
v. Affidavit in support of motion to suppress information improperly or irregularly obtained. MCF CPLR § 6:75.
w. Notice of motion for protective order suspending disclosure, or for a stay of disclosure, pending appeal. MCF CPLR § 6:77.
x. Affirmation in support of motion for protective order suspending disclosure, or for a stay of disclosure, pending appeal. MCF CPLR § 6:78.
y. Affirmation of good faith in support of motion for protective order suspending disclosure, or for a stay of disclosure, pending appeal. MCF CPLR § 6:79.
z. General form of affidavit of service of motion papers. MCF CPLR § 5:24.

I. Applicable Rules

1. *State rules*
   a. Short title; Application; Construction; Definitions. NY CPLR § 101; NY CPLR § 103; NY CPLR § 104; NY CPLR § 105.
   b. Appendix of official forms. NY CPLR § 107.
   c. Extensions of time generally. NY CPLR § 2004.
   d. Form of papers. NY CPLR Rule 2101; NY CPLR Rule 2102; NY CPLR § 2105; NY CPLR Rule 2106; NY GEN BUS § 399-ddd; NY R UNIF TRIAL CTS § 215.2; NY R UNIF TRIAL CTS § 215.3.
   e. Service of papers. NY CPLR Rule 2103.
   f. Where motion made; In supreme court action. NY CPLR § 2212.
   g. Motion papers; Service; Time. NY CPLR Rule 2214.
   h. Relief demanded by other than moving party. NY CPLR Rule 2215.
   i. Prior motion; Ex parte motion; Transfer of motion; Hearings; Orders. NY CPLR Rule 2217; NY CPLR § 2218; NY CPLR Rule 2220.
   j. Computation of time. NY CPLR § 2402; NY GEN CONSTR § 19; NY GEN CONSTR § 20; NY GEN CONSTR § 25-a; NY GEN CONSTR § 30; NY GEN CONSTR § 31; NY GEN CONSTR § 53.
   k. Scope of disclosure. NY CPLR § 3101; NY CPLR § 3104; NY CPLR Rule 3105; NY CPLR Rule 3106.
   l. Protective orders. NY CPLR § 3103.
   m. Motions heard by judge supervising disclosure; Stay of disclosure. NY CPLR Rule 3214.
   n. Fees; Index number fees of county clerks. NY CPLR § 8018.
   o. Hours of court; Proceedings in court. NY R CHIEF J § 3.1; NY R CHIEF J § 29.3.
   p. Application of part; Waiver; Additional rules; Application of CPLR; Definitions. NY R UNIF TRIAL CTS § 202.1.
   q. Papers filed in court; Electronic filing in supreme court. NY R UNIF TRIAL CTS § 202.5; NY R UNIF TRIAL CTS § 202.5-a; NY R UNIF TRIAL CTS § 202.5-b; NY R UNIF TRIAL CTS § 202.5-bb.
   r. Request for judicial intervention. NY R UNIF TRIAL CTS § 202.6.
   s. Calendaring of motions; Uniform notice of motion form; Affirmation of good faith. NY R UNIF TRIAL CTS § 202.7.
   t. Motion procedure; Preliminary conferences. NY R UNIF TRIAL CTS § 202.8; NY R UNIF TRIAL CTS § 202.12.
   u. Rules of the commercial division of the Supreme Court. NY R UNIF TRIAL CTS § 202.70.
   v. Signing of papers. NY R CHIEF ADMIN § 130-1.1-a.
2. *Local rules*
   a. *Albany County*
      i. Third judicial district rules. NY R 3 JD SUP Doc. 1.
   b. *Bronx County*
      i. Filing of papers in supreme court. NY R BRONX FIL R Doc. 1.
      ii. Request for judicial intervention. NY R BRONX FIL R Doc. 2.

iii. Discovery part conference requests. NY R BRONX FIL R Doc. 5.

iv. Motion procedure. NY R BRONX FIL R Doc. 8.

v. Commercial division. NY R BRONX FIL R Doc. 12.

vi. Motions on notice. NY R BRONX E FIL R Doc. 1.

vii. Settled orders. NY R BRONX LEG SUP Doc. 2.

c. *Erie County*

i. Joint protocols for New York State Courts E-Filing (NYSCEF) cases filed in Supreme Court, Erie County. NY R ERIE E FIL Doc. 3.

d. *Kings County*

i. Papers. NY R L KINGS Pt. A, Papers.

ii. Discovery agreements. NY R L KINGS Pt. B, Rule 2.

iii. Motion scheduling. NY R L KINGS Pt. B, Rule 6.

iv. Service of motion papers. NY R L KINGS Pt. C, Rule 1.

v. Scheduling of motions. NY R L KINGS Pt. C, Rule 2.

vi. Appearance and argument. NY R L KINGS Pt. C, Rule 3.

vii. Courtesy copies. NY R L KINGS Pt. C, Rule 5.

viii. Motion calendar calls. NY R L KINGS Pt. C, Rule 7.

ix. Scheduling of motions. NY R L KINGS Pt. E, Rule 7.

x. Affirmation of good faith. NY R L KINGS Pt. E, Rule 9.

xi. Consent orders. NY R L KINGS Pt. E, Rule 11.

xii. Disclosure disputes. NY R NY CTY J RUL Rule 10.

xiii. Protocol on courthouse and county clerk procedures for electronically filed cases. NY R L KINGS E FIL Doc. 1.

e. *New York County*

i. Commencement of cases. NY R NY CTY Procedure I.

ii. RJIs and assignments. NY R NY CTY Procedure IA.

iii. Motions and special proceedings by notice of motion/petition. NY R NY CTY Procedure II.

iv. County clerk litigation functions. NY R NY CTY Procedure XI.

v. Protocol on courthouse and county clerk procedures for electronically filed cases. NY R NY CTY E FIL Doc. 2.

vi. Redaction of information in documents filed with the county clerk and the court. NY R NY CTY J RUL Rule A-1.

vii. Papers by fax. NY R NY CTY J RUL Rule 4.

viii. Motions on notice; Orders to show cause. NY R NY CTY J RUL Rule 13.

ix. Motion papers. NY R NY CTY J RUL Rule 14.

x. Oral argument; Adjournments. NY R NY CTY J RUL Rule 15.

f. *Onondaga County*

i. Onondaga county protocol for case filings New York State Electronic Files (NYSCEF). NY R ONDGA E FIL Protocol.

g. *Queens County*

i. Motion support office. NY R L QUEENS MOT SUP Doc. 1.

ii. Queens county protocol on courthouse procedures for electronically filed cases. NY R L QUEENS E-FILE Doc. 1.

J. Miscellaneous

NOTE: Individual judges' rules may apply.

ALBANY COUNTY

JUSTICE LISA M. FISHER: NY R 3 JD FISHER Fisher; NY R 3 JD FISHER Fisher, PC Order.

JUSTICE RICHARD MOTT: NY R 3 JD MOTT Mott.

JUSTICE STEPHAN G. SCHICK: NY R 3 JD Schick.

FORECLOSURE SETTLEMENT PART: NY R 3 JD Foreclosure Settlement.

BRONX COUNTY

JUSTICE PAUL L. ALPERT: [NY R BRONX J Part IA-29, as amended by NY ORDER 20-0337].

JUSTICE BEN BARBATO: NY R BRONX J Part IA-21.

JUSTICE MARY ANNE BRIGANTTI: [NY R BRONX J Part IA-15, as amended by NY ORDER 20-0338].

JUSTICE JOSEPH E. CAPELLA: NY R BRONX J Part IA-23.

JUSTICE MITCHELL DANZIGER: NY R BRONX J Part IA-3/33 ; [NY R BRONX J Danziger, Part IA-3/33, as amended by NY ORDER 20-0339].

JUSTICE LAURA G. DOUGLAS: NY R BRONX J Part IA-11.

JUSTICE RUBEN FRANCO: NY R BRONX J Part IA-26.

JUSTICE DORIS M. GONZALEZ: NY R BRONX J Part IA-24.

JUSTICE WILMA GUZMAN: NY R BRONX J Part IA-7; [NY R BRONX J Guzman, Part IA-7 Virtual, as amended by NY ORDER 20-0340].

JUSTICE ROBERT T. JOHNSON: NY R BRONX J Part IA-12.

JUSTICE DONALD A. MILES: NY R BRONX J Part IA-8.

JUSTICE DONNA M. MILLS: NY R BRONX J Part IA-9.

JUSTICE JULIA I. RODRIGUEZ: NY R BRONX J Part IA-18; [NY R BRONX J Part IA-27, as amended by NY ORDER 20-0341].

JUSTICE LLINET M. ROSADO: [NY R BRONX J Part IA-25, as amended by NY ORDER 20-0342].

JUSTICE NORMA RUIZ: NY R BRONX J Part IA-22; [NY R BRONX J Ruiz, Part IA-22 Virtual, as amended by NY ORDER 20-0343].

JUSTICE HOWARD H. SHERMAN: NY R BRONX J Part IA-4.

JUSTICE FERNANDO TAPIA: NY R BRONX J Part IA-13.

JUSTICE ELIZABETH A. TAYLOR: NY R BRONX J Part IA-2.

JUSTICE ALISON Y. TRUITT: NY R BRONX J Part IA-5.

PART IDV: NY R BRONX J Doc. 1.

PRE-TRIAL PART RULES: NY R BRONX J Doc. 2.

PRE TRIAL WORKSHEET: NY R BRONX J Doc. 3.

FORECLOSURE SETTLEMENT PART RULES: NY R BRONX J Doc. 4.

GUARDIANSHIP PART RULES: NY R BRONX J Doc. 5.

LPM PART RULES: NY R BRONX J Doc. 6.

ERIE COUNTY

JUSTICE M. WILLIAM BOLLER: NY R 8 JD J Boller.

JUSTICE RALPH A. BONIELLO: NY R 8 JD J Boniello.

JUSTICE CHRISTOPHER J. BURN: NY R 8 JD J Burns.

JUSTICE RUSSELL P. BUSCAGLIA: NY R 8 JD J Buscaglia.

JUSTICE FRANK CARUSO: NY R 8 JD J Caruso.

JUSTICE STEPHEN W. CASS: NY R 8 JD J Cass.

JUSTICE DEBORAH A. CHIMES: NY R 8 JD J Chimes.

JUSTICE EMILIO COLAIACOVO: [NY R 8 JD J Colaiacovo, as amended by NY ORDER 20-0252].

JUSTICE DIANE Y. DEVLIN: NY R 8 JD J Devlin.

JUSTICE JAMES H. DILLON: NY R 8 JD J Dillon.

JUSTICE PAULA L. FEROLETO: NY R 8 JD J Feroleto.

JUSTICE DANIEL J. FURLONG: [NY R 8 JD J Furlong, as amended by NY ORDER 20-0253].

JUSTICE JOSEPH R. GLOWNIA: NY R 8 JD J Glownia.

JUSTICE MARK J. GRISANTI: NY R 8 JD J Grisanti.

JUSTICE DEBORAH A. HAENDIGES: NY R 8 JD J Haendiges.

JUSTICE LYNN W. KEANE: [NY R 8 JD J Keane, as amended by NY ORDER 20-0254].

JUSTICE RICHARD C. KLOCH, Sr.: NY R 8 JD J Kloch.

JUSTICE FREDERICK J. MARSHALL: [NY R 8 JD J Marshall, as amended by NY ORDER 20-0255.

JUSTICE JOHN L. MICHALSKI: NY R 8 JD J Michalski.

JUSTICE MARK A. MONTOUR: [NY R 8 JD J Montour, as amended by NY ORDER 20-0256].

JUSTICE HENRY NOWAK: NY R 8 JD J Nowak.

JUSTICE JOHN F. O'DONNELL: NY R 8 JD J O'Donnell.

JUSTICE JEANETTE OGDEN: NY R 8 JD J Ogden.

JUSTICE CATHERINE NUGENT-PANEPINTO: NY R 8 JD J Nugent-Panepinto.

JUSTICE FRANK A. SEDITA, III: [NY R 8 JD J Sedita, as amended by NY ORDER 20-0257].

JUSTICE SARA SHELDON: NY R 8 JD J Sheldon.

JUSTICE DONNA M. SIWEK: NY R 8 JD J Siwek.

JUSTICE MARY L. SLISZ: NY R 8 JD J Slisz.

JUSTICE TIMOTHY J. WALKER: [NY R 8 JD J Walker, as amended by NY ORDER 20-0258].

JUSTICE DENNIS E. WARD: NY R 8 JD J Ward.

JUSTICE PAUL B. WOJTASZEK: [NY R 8 JD J Wojtaszek, as amended by NY ORDER 20-0259].

JUSTICE CHARLES N. ZAMBITO: [NY R 8 JD J Zambito, as amended by NY ORDER 20-0260].

SUPREME COURT LEGAL STAFF: NY R 8 JD J Legal Staff.

KINGS COUNTY

JUSTICE RACHEL A. ADAMS: NY R KINGS J Part 5F.

JUSTICE LOREN BAILY-SCHIFFMAN: NY R KINGS J Part 65.

JUSTICE REGINALD A. BODDIE: NY R KINGS J Part 95.

JUSTICE THERESA M. CICCOTTO: NY R KINGS J Part 19; NY R KINGS J Part 5J.

JUSTICE LISSETTE COLON: NY R KINGS J Part Rules.

JUSTICE GENINE EDWARDS: NY R KINGS J Part 80.

JUSTICE PAMELA L. FISHER: [NY R KINGS J Part 94, as amended by NY ORDER 20-0208].

JUSTICE ROBIN GARSON: NY R KINGS J Part 75.

JUSTICE LARA J. GENOVISI: [NY R KINGS J Part 34, as amended by NY ORDER 20-0209].

JUSTICE BERNARD J. GRAHAM: NY R KINGS J Part 36.

JUSTICE DAWN JIMENEZ-SALTA: NY R KINGS J Part 88.

JUSTICE INGRID JOSEPH: [NY R KINGS J Part FRP3 and Part 83, as amended by NY ORDER 20-0210].

JUSTICE KATHY J. KING: NY R KINGS J Part 64, 76K.

JUSTICE LAWRENCE KNIPEL: NY R KINGS J Part 57.
JUSTICE DONALD KURTZ: NY R KINGS J Part 26.
JUSTICE CARL LANDICINO: [NY R KINGS J Part 81, as amended by NY ORDER 20-0211].
JUSTICE KATHERINE LEVINE: [NY R KINGS J Part 20, 25, 92, as amended by NY ORDER 20-0211].
JUSTICE LORNA MCALLISTER: [NY R KINGS J Part 10, as amended by NY ORDER 20-0211].
JUSTICE ROSEMARIE MONTALBANO: [NY R KINGS J Part 19, 71, and 22, as amended by NY ORDER 20-0211].
JUSTICE RICHARD J. MONTELIONE: [NY R KINGS J Part 99 and DJMP, as amended by NY ORDER 20-0215].
JUSTICE LISA S. OTTLEY: NY R KINGS J Part 24.
JUSTICE MARK I. PARTNOW: NY R KINGS J Part 43.
JUSTICE ERIC I. PRUS: NY R KINGS J Part 5A.
JUSTICE FRANCOIS RIVERA: NY R KINGS J Part 52.
JUSTICE KAREN B. ROTHENBERG: NY R KINGS J Part 35.
JUSTICE LEON RUCHELSMAN: NY R KINGS J Part 1.
JUSTICE WAYNE P. SAITTA: NY R KINGS J Part 29.
JUSTICE ROBIN K. SHEARES: NY R KINGS J Part 96.
JUSTICE KENNETH P. SHERMAN: NY R KINGS J Part 67 and 78.
JUSTICE DEBRA SILBER: NY R KINGS J Part 9 and 5K.
JUSTICE ELLEN M. SPODEK: NY R KINGS J Part 63.
JUSTICE MARSHA L. STEINHARDT: NY R KINGS J Part 15.
JUSTICE JEFFREY S. SUNSHINE: NY R KINGS J Part 5G.
JUSTICE PETER P. SWEENEY: [NY R KINGS J Part 35, as amended by NY ORDER 20-0218].
JUSTICE DELORES J. THOMAS: [NY R KINGS J Part 5T, as amended by NY ORDER 20-0221].
JUSTICE WAVNY TOUSSAINT: NY R KINGS J Part 70.
JUSTICE RICHARD VELASQUEZ: NY R KINGS J Part 66.
JUSTICE CAROLYN E. WADE: NY R KINGS J Part 84.
JUSTICE EDWARD G. WALKER: [NY R KINGS J Part 90, as amended by NY ORDER 20-0219].
JUSTICE LILLIAN WAN: [NY R KINGS J Part 17, as amended by NY ORDER 20-0220].
JUSTICE MICHELLE WESTON: NY R KINGS J Part 3.
MENTAL HYGIENE PART: NY R KINGS J Part 77.
MATRIMONIAL PARTS DURING COVID-19 EMERGENCY: JUSTICE KAREN B. ROTHENBERG: NY R KINGS J Doc. 1.

NASSAU COUNTY

JUSTICE ANNA R. ANZALONE: NY R NASSAU S J Anzalone, Part 26.
JUSTICE STACY D. BENNETT: NY R NASSAU S J Bennett; NY R NASSAU S J Bennett, Form 1.
JUSTICE ANTONIO BRANDVEEN: NY R NASSAU S J Brandveen, Part 31.
JUSTICE JEFFREY S. BROWN: [NY R NASSAU S J Brown, as amended by NY ORDER 20-0297].
JUSTICE STEPHEN A. BUCARIA: NY R NASSAU S J Bucaria.
JUSTICE JULIANNE T. CAPETOLA: NY R NASSAU S J Capetola, Part 28.
JUSTICE EDMUND M. DANE: NY R NASSAU S J Dane, Part 33.
JUSTICE VITO M. DESTEFANO: NY R NASSAU S J DeStefano, Part 13; NY R NASSAU S J DeStefano, Form 1.
JUSTICE ARTHUR M. DIAMOND: NY R NASSAU S J Diamond, Part 7.
JUSTICE THOMAS FEINMAN: NY R NASSAU S J Feinman, Part 5.
JUSTICE JOHN M. GALASSO: NY R NASSAU S J Galasso, Part 22.

JUSTICE SHARON M.J. GIANELLI: NY R NASSAU S J Gianelli, Part 22; NY R NASSAU S J Gianelli, Form 1.

JUSTICE JEFFREY A. GOODSTEIN: NY R NASSAU S J Goodstein, Part 33; NY R NASSAU S J Goodstein, Form 1.

JUSTICE DAVID J. GUGERTY: [NY R NASSAU S J Gugerty, Part 31, as amended by NY ORDER 20-0298].

JUSTICE HELENE F. GUGERTY: NY R NASSAU S J Gugerty, Part 47.

JUSTICE STEVEN M. JAEGER: NY R NASSAU S J Jaeger, Part 35; NY R NASSAU S J Jaeger, Form 1.

JUSTICE JACK L. LIBERT: NY R NASSAU S J Libert, Part 23.

JUSTICE JOSEPH H. LORINTZ: NY R NASSAU S J Lorintz, Part 26; NY R NASSAU S J Lorintz, Form 1.

JUSTICE ROY S. MAHON: NY R NASSAU S J Mahon, Part 3.

JUSTICE RANDY SUE MARBER: NY R NASSAU S J Marber, Part 8.

JUSTICE JAMES P. MCCORMACK: [NY R NASSAU S J McCormack, Part 18, as amended by NY ORDER, 20-0299].

JUSTICE DICCIA T. PINEDA-KIRWAN: [NY R NASSAU S J Pineda-Kirwan, as amended by NY ORDER 20-0300].

JUSTICE THOMAS RADEMAKER: [NY R NASSAU S J Rademaker, Part 28, as amended by NY ORDER 20-0301]; [NY R NASSAU S J Rademaker, Form 1, as amended by NY ORDER 20-0301].

JUSTICE DENISE L. SHER: NY R NASSAU S J Rademaker, Part 32.

JUSTICE LEONARD D. STEINMAN: [NY R NASSAU S J Steinman, Part 15, as amended by NY ORDER 20-0303]; NY R NASSAU S J Steinman, Form 1.

JUSTICE HOWARD E. STURIM: NY R NASSAU S J Sturim, Part 50; NY R NASSAU S J Sturim, Form 1.

JUSTICE HELEN VOUTSINAS: [NY R NASSAU S J Voutsinas, Part 25, as amended by NY ORDER 20-0304]; [NY R NASSAU S J Voutsinas, Form 1, as amended by NY ORDER 20-0305].

JUSTICE HOPE SCHWARTZ ZIMMERMAN: NY R NASSAU S J Zimmerman, Part 17.

NEW YORK COUNTY

JUDGE'S RULES; BASIC INFORMATION: [NY R NY CTY J RUL Doc. 1, as amended by NY ORDER 20-0202].

ONONDAGA COUNTY

JUSTICE ROBERT E. ANTONACCI II: [NY R ONDGA E FIL Doc. 1, as amended by 20-0239].

JUSTICE MICHAEL V. COCCOMI: NY R ONDGA E FIL Doc. 2.

JUSTICE GREGORY R. GILBERT: NY R 5 JD JUDGES Gilbert; NY R ONDGA E FIL Doc. 3.

JUSTICE DONALD A. GREENWOOD: NY R ONDGA E FIL Doc. 4.

JUSTICE DEBORAH H. KARALUNAS: NY R ONDGA E FIL Doc. 5.

JUSTICE JAMES MCCLUSKY: NY R 5 JD MCCLUSKY McClusky.

JUSTICE CHARLES C. MERRELL: NY R 5 JD MERRELL Merrell.

JUSTICE PATRICK F. MACRAE: NY R 5 JD MACRAE Doc. 1.

JUSTICE JAMES P. MURPHY: NY R ONDGA E FIL Doc. 7.

JUSTICE GERALD J. NERI: [NY R 5 JD JUDGES Neri, as amended by NY ORDER 20-0236]; [NY R ONDGA E FIL Doc. 8, as amended by NY ORDER 20-0241].

JUSTICE ANTHONY J. PARIS: NY R 5 JD JUDGES Paris; [NY R ONDGA E FIL Doc. 9, as amended by NY ORDER 20-0242].

JUSTICE NORMAN W. SEITER, JR.: NY R 5 JD JUDGES Seiter.

JUSTICE KEVIN G. YOUNG: [NY R ONDGA E FIL Doc. 10, as amended by NY ORDER 20-0243].

QUEENS COUNTY

JUSTICE PAM JACKMAN BROWN: [NY R L QUEENS Brown, Part 19, as amended by NY ORDER 20-0321].

JUSTICE CHEREE A. BUGGS: NY R L QUEENS Buggs, Part 30.

JUSTICE PAM JACKMAN BROWN: [NY R L QUEENS Brown, Part 19, as amended by NY ORDER 20-0321].

JUSTICE DENIS J. BUTLER: NY R L QUEENS Butler, Part 12.

JUSTICE ROBERT I. CALORAS: [NY R L QUEENS Caloras, Part 36, as amended by NY ORDER 20-0322].

JUSTICE ANNA CULLEY: NY R L QUEENS Culley, Part 53.

JUSTICE TIMOTHY DUFFICY: NY R L QUEENS Dufficy, Part 35.

JUSTICE DAVID ELLIOT: NY R L QUEENS Elliot, Part 14.

JUSTICE JOSEPH J. ESPOSITO: NY R L QUEENS Esposito, Part 6.

JUSTICE DARRELL L. GAVRIN: [NY R L QUEENS Gavrin, Part 27, as amended by NY ORDER 20-0323].

JUSTICE WYATT N. GIBBONS: [NY R L QUEENS Gibbons, Part 5, as amended by NY ORDER 20-0330.

JUSTICE DONNA-MARIE E. GOLIA: [NY R L QUEENS Golia, Part 21, as amended by NY ORDER 20-0331].

JUSTICE MARGUERITE A. GRAYS: [NY R L QUEENS Grays, Part 4, as amended by NY ORDER 20-0324].

JUSTICE RUDOLPH E. GRECO: [NY R L QUEENS Greco, Part 32, as amended by NY ORDER 20-0325].

JUSTICE MAUREEN HEALY: NY R L QUEENS Healy, Part 6.

JUSTICE PHILLIP HOM: [NY R L QUEENS Hom, Part 43, as amended by NY ORDER 20-0332].

JUSTICE KEVIN J. KERRIGAN: NY R L QUEENS Kerrigan, Part 10.

JUSTICE MOJGAN C. LANCMAN: NY R L QUEENS Lancman, Part 20.

JUSTICE RICHARD G. LATIN: NY R L QUEENS Latin, Part 40.

JUSTICE ULYSSES B. LEVERETT: [NY R L QUEENS Leverett, Part 6, as amended by NY ORDER 20-0326].

JUSTICE LEONARD LIVOTE: NY R L QUEENS Livote, Part 33.

JUSTICE LEE A. MAYERSOHN: NY R L QUEENS Mayersohn, Part 22; NY R L QUEENS Mayersohn, Part 22G; [NY R L QUEENS Mayersohn, Part 22G COVID, as amended by NY ORDER 20-0327].

JUSTICE ROBERT J. MCDONALD: NY R L QUEENS McDonald, Part 34.

JUSTICE MARGARET MCGOWAN: NY R L QUEENS McGowan, Part 52.

JUSTICE MAURICE E. MUIR: [NY R L QUEENS Muir, Part 42, as amended by NY ORDER 20-0333].

JUSTICE JODI ORLOW: NY R L QUEENS Orlow, Part 51.

JUSTICE LESLIE J. PURIFICCION: NY R L QUEENS Purificcion, Part 39.

JUSTICE JOSEPH RISI: [NY R L QUEENS Risi, Part 3, as amended by NY ORDER 20-0328].

JUSTICE FREDERICK D.R. SAMPSON: [NY R L QUEENS Sampson, Part 31, as amended by NY ORDER 20-0329].

JUSTICE MARTIN J. SCHULMAN: NY R L QUEENS Schulman, Part 29.

JUSTICE BERNICE D. SIEGAL: NY R L QUEENS Siegal, Part 25G.

JUSTICE JANICE A. TAYLOR: NY R L QUEENS Taylor, Part 15.

JUSTICE CARMEN R. VELASQUEZ: NY R L QUEENS Velasquez, Part 38.

JUSTICE LOURDES M VENTURA: [NY R L QUEENS Ventura, Part 37, as amended by NY ORDER 20-0334].

JUSTICE WILLIAM A. VISCOVICH: NY R L QUEENS Viscovich, Part 63.

JUSTICE ALLAN B. WEISS: NY R L QUEENS Weiss, Part 2.

COMPLIANCE, SETTLEMENT AND CONFERENCE PART: NY R L QUEENS Doc 1.

PRELIMINARY CONFERENCE PART: [NY R L QUEENS Doc. 2, as amended by NY ORDER 20-0335].

MEDICAL MALPRACTICE CONFERENCE PART: [NY R L QUEENS Doc. 3, as amended by NY ORDER 20-0336].

TRIAL SCHEDULING PART: NY R L QUEENS Doc. 4.

SUMMARY JURY TRIAL PROGRAM: NY R L QUEENS Doc. 7.

RESIDENTIAL FORECLOSURE PART: NY R L QUEENS Doc. 9.

FORECLOSURE AUCTION RULES: NY R L QUEENS Doc. 10.

MATRIMONIAL PRELIMINARY CONFERENCE PART: NY R L QUEENS Doc. 11.

NON-CUSTODIAL CONTESTED MATRIMONIAL PART: NY R L QUEENS Doc. 12.

Motions, Oppositions and Replies
Motion for Discovery Sanctions

Document Last Updated August 2020

A. Checklist

(I) ❑ Matters to consider for moving party

(a) ❑ Required documents

(1) ❑ Notice of motion, order to show cause, or affidavit on ex parte motion

(2) ❑ Motion

(3) ❑ Affirmation of counsel

(4) ❑ Request for judicial intervention

(5) ❑ Proof of service

(6) ❑ ALBANY COUNTY: Additional required documents

(i) ❑ Affirmation of good faith effort

(b) ❑ Supplemental documents

(1) ❑ Supporting evidence; Exhibits

(2) ❑ Brief

(3) ❑ Notice to produce papers not in possession of the court

(4) ❑ Filing fees

(5) ❑ Working copies

(6) ❑ ERIE COUNTY: Additional supplemental documents

(i) ❑ Notice of hard copy submission in e-filed case

(7) ❑ KINGS COUNTY: Additional supplemental documents

(i) ❑ Forms when filing in hard copy

(8) ❑ NEW YORK COUNTY: Additional supplemental documents

(i) ❑ Notice of hard copy submission

(ii) ❑ Unpublished opinions

(9) ❑ ONONDAGA COUNTY: Additional supplemental documents

(i) ❑ Notice of hard copy submission

(10) ❑ QUEENS COUNTY: Additional supplemental documents

(i) ❑ Notice of hard copy submission

(c) ❑ Timing

(1) ❑ There are no specific timing requirements for the motion for discovery sanctions

(2) ❑ The moving party shall serve copies of all affidavits and briefs upon all other parties at the time of service of the notice of motion

(3) ❑ A notice of motion and supporting affidavits shall be served at least eight (8) days before the time at which the motion is noticed to be heard

(4) ❑ It is also good practice to make motions returnable at least three (3) weeks away from the planned date of mailing and to always include a demand in the motion that the other side serve answering papers at least seven (7) days before the return day

(5) ❑ BRONX COUNTY: Additional timing

(i) ❑ A Notice of Motion must be served at least eight (8) days, by personal service, nine (9) days by overnight express and thirteen (13) days by mail before the return date

(6) ❑ NEW YORK COUNTY: Additional timing

(i) ❑ In an e-filed case, all of the moving papers shall be e-filed at least eight (8) business days prior to the return date

(7) ❑ ONONDAGA COUNTY: Additional timing

(i) ❑ Onondaga County local court rules require that any additional papers relating to motions must be e-filed at least two (2) business days prior to the return date, excluding the return date

(8) ❑ QUEENS COUNTY: Additional timing

(i) ❑ Motions must be in the possession of the Motion Support Office at least nine (9) days before the noticed return date of the motion

(II) ❑ Matters to consider for opposing party

(a) ❑ Required documents

(1) ❑ Opposition

(2) ❑ Proof of service

(b) ❑ Supplemental documents

(1) ❑ Supporting evidence; Exhibits

(2) ❑ Brief

(3) ❑ Filing fees

(4) ❑ Working copies

(5) ❑ ERIE COUNTY: Additional supplemental documents

(i) ❑ Notice of hard copy submission in e-filed case

(6) ❑ KINGS COUNTY: Additional supplemental documents

(i) ❑ Forms when filing in hard copy

(7) ❑ NEW YORK COUNTY: Additional supplemental documents

(i) ❑ Notice of hard copy submission

(ii) ❑ Unpublished opinions

(8) ❑ ONONDAGA COUNTY: Additional supplemental documents

(i) ❑ Notice of hard copy submission

(9) ❑ QUEENS COUNTY: Additional supplemental documents

(i) ❑ Notice of hard copy submission

(c) ❑ Timing

(1) ❑ Answering affidavits shall be served at least two (2) days before the time at which the motion is noticed to be heard

(2) ❑ Answering affidavits and any notice of cross-motion, with supporting papers, if any, shall be served at least seven (7) days before such time if a notice of motion served at least sixteen (16) days before such time so demands

B. Timing

1. *Time to bring motion for discovery sanctions.* There are no specific timing requirements for the motion for discovery sanctions.

2. *Time to serve.* The moving party shall serve copies of all affidavits and briefs upon all other parties at the time of service of the notice of motion. NY R UNIF TRIAL CTS § 202.8(c). A notice of motion and supporting affidavits shall be served at least eight (8) days before the time at which the motion is noticed to be heard. NY CPLR Rule 2214(b).

a. *Return dates; Best practice.* It is also good practice to make motions returnable at least three (3) weeks away from the planned date of mailing and to always include a demand in the motion that the other side serve answering papers at least seven (7) days before the return day. This enables the motion to be served by mail, gives sufficient notice to support the seven (7) day demand, and leaves a few days for a delayed mailing if some snag prevents posting on the day planned. If speed is needed, the shorter eight (8) day notice period can be used, forfeiting the right to seven (7) day answering papers and a reply. If even eight (8) days notice is too much under the circumstances, the order to show cause is the remedy. SIEGEL-NYPRAC § 247.

i. *ALBANY COUNTY.* All motions, except for certain matters in Albany County as specified in NY R 3 JD SUP Doc. 1(E) and NY R 3 JD SUP Doc. 1(F), brought on by notice of motion or by order to show cause will be made returnable on any day, Monday through Friday, as chosen by the movant in compliance with the CPLR. Parties shall submit all papers in a timely fashion as required by the CPLR by delivering them or mailing them directly to the Supreme Court Clerk's Office[. . .]except that motions and other applications subject to a filing fee shall first be presented to the County Clerk's Office for payment of the requisite fee and then subsequently filed with the Supreme Court Clerk's Office. NY R 3 JD SUP Doc. 1(B).

ii. *BRONX COUNTY.* A Notice of Motion must be served at least eight (8) days, by personal service, nine (9) days by overnight express and thirteen (13) days by mail before the return date. NY R BRONX FIL R Doc. 3. All unassigned motions must be accompanied with a properly filled out RJI and shall be filed in the Motion Support Office, room 217, within five (5) days of service. All motions on actions already assigned to a Justice must be filed at least five (5) business days before the return date. NY R BRONX FIL R Doc. 3. All papers served must strictly comply with the time requirements of NY CPLR Rule 2101, NY CPLR Rule 2103 and NY CPLR Rule 2214(b). NY R BRONX FIL R Doc. 8.

iii. *KINGS COUNTY.* Motion papers, answering affidavits and reply affidavits must be served on adversaries in accordance with NY CPLR Rule 2214. NY R L KINGS Pt. C, Rule 1.

iv. *NEW YORK COUNTY.* In an e-filed case, all of the moving papers shall be e-filed at least eight (8) business days prior to the return date. The clerk will calendar the motion for the Motion Submission Part Courtroom (Room 130) for the return date selected. NY R NY CTY Procedure II(A); NY R NY CTY E FIL Doc. 2(D)(1).

v. *ONONDAGA COUNTY.* Onondaga County local court rules require that any additional papers relating to motions must be e-filed at least two (2) business days prior to the return date, excluding the return date. NY R ONDGA E FIL Protocol(B)(9)(e).

vi. *QUEENS COUNTY.* Motions must be in the possession of the Motion Support Office at least nine (9) days before the noticed return date of the motion. NY R L QUEENS MOT SUP Doc. 1; NY R L QUEENS E-FILE Doc. 1(H)(1).

b. *Order to show cause; Shorter time.* The court in a proper case may grant an order to show cause, to be served in lieu of a notice of motion, at a time and in a manner specified therein. NY CPLR Rule 2214(d). An ordinary notice of motion can't be brought on for hearing earlier than the eighth (8th) day after the motion papers are served. With an order to show cause, the hearing can be brought on at any time the court directs, which can be fewer than eight (8) days or as close as the very day on which it is signed. If the court is convinced there is a real emergency, it can schedule the hearing for a few hours later or, in the direst case, "forthwith" the service of the order to show cause. SIEGEL-NYPRAC § 248.

c. *Time to serve answering affidavits; Other answering papers.* Answering affidavits shall be served at least two (2) days before the time at which the motion is noticed to be heard. Answering affidavits and any notice of cross-motion, with supporting papers, if any, shall be served at least seven (7) days before such time if a notice of motion served at least sixteen (16) days before such time so demands; whereupon any reply or responding affidavits shall be served at least one (1) day before such time. NY CPLR Rule 2214(b); NY R UNIF TRIAL CTS § 202.8(c).

i. *BRONX COUNTY.* All answering papers must be submitted to the Clerk 's Office on the return date of the motion. Answering papers will not be accepted prior to the return date. NY R BRONX FIL R Doc. 8.

ii. *NEW YORK COUNTY.* Cross-motions, papers in opposition, and reply papers on motions/petitions on notice returnable in Room 130 in a hard-copy case shall be submitted to the Motion Submission Part Courtroom (Room 130) on the final return date of the motion/petition and will not be accepted until that date. Subsequent documents on motions/petitions in e-filed cases shall be e-filed in a timely manner. Working copies when required shall be submitted to Room 130 on the final return date. NY R NY CTY Procedure II(A).

d. *Time to serve cross-motion.* At least three (3) days prior to the time at which the motion is noticed to be heard, or seven (7) days prior to such time if demand is properly made pursuant to NY CPLR Rule 2214(b), a party may serve upon the moving party a notice of cross-motion demanding relief, with or without supporting papers; provided, however, that:

i. If such notice and any supporting papers are served by mailing, as provided in NY CPLR Rule 2103(b)(2), they shall be served three (3) days earlier than as prescribed in NY CPLR Rule 2215; and

ii. If served by overnight delivery, as provided in NY CPLR Rule 2103(b)(6), they shall be served one (1) day earlier than as prescribed in NY CPLR Rule 2215. Relief in the alternative or of several different types may be demanded; relief need not be responsive to that demanded by the moving party. NY CPLR Rule 2215(a); NY CPLR Rule 2215(b).

iii. *BRONX COUNTY.* Cross motions may be presented for approval on or before the return date, provided that there is a motion already calendared. NY R BRONX FIL R Doc. 8.

iv. *ERIE COUNTY.* Cross-motions must be filed at least two (2) days before the return date of the motion. NY R L KINGS Pt. A, Papers.

v. *KINGS COUNTY.* Hard copies are required to be filed for any motions, answering papers, stipulations, etc. for E-Filed cases returnable in [the Central Compliance Part] at least [two (2)] days before return date. . . .for cross motions. NY R L KINGS Pt. E, Rule 8.

vi. *QUEENS COUNTY.* Motion Support does not process or forward responsive papers, including cross-motions. They must be brought to the calendar call in the judge's part. NY R L QUEENS MOT SUP Doc. 1. E-filed cross motions: across motion must be noticed for the same return date as the main motion and have the confirmation of filing attached in the same manner as a motion. NY R L QUEENS E-FILE Doc. 1(H)(2)(e).

3. *Filing before return date.* All motions shall be returnable before the assigned judge, and all papers shall be filed with the court on or before the return date. NY R UNIF TRIAL CTS § 202.8(a).

a. *BRONX COUNTY: Time for filing*

i. *Unassigned motions.* Unassigned motions must be in the Clerk's Office within five (5) days of the date of service of the motion. NY R BRONX FIL R Doc. 8.

ii. *Assigned motions.* Assigned motions must be filed in the Clerk's Office not less than five (5) business days prior to the return date of the motion. NY R BRONX FIL R Doc. 8.

iii. *Motions returnable in room 217.* The moving documents must be e-filed no later than eight (8) days prior to the return date. NY R BRONX E FIL R Doc. 1(1).

b. *KINGS COUNTY: Time and place of filing.* Motion papers must be filed with the E-file/Motion Support Office located in Room 227. . . at 360 Adams Street at least five (5) business days before the return date of the motion. NY R L KINGS Pt. A, Papers. Hard copies are required to be filed for any motions, answering papers, stipulations, etc. for E-Filed cases returnable in [the Central Compliance Part] at least five (5) days before return date for main motions. NY R L KINGS Pt. E, Rule 8. The moving documents must be e-filed no later than eight (8) days prior to the return date. NY R L KINGS E FIL Doc. 1(D).

4. *NEW YORK COUNTY: Briefing schedule.* Once a motion is made, counsel for all parties are strongly encouraged to agree upon a briefing schedule and submit a stipulation of adjournment reflecting that schedule using service or a clerk. Where a briefing schedule has not been agreed upon, the movant can avoid the need to attend simply to see if anyone will hand up opposing papers by demanding papers as provided by NY CPLR Rule 2214(b). To protect movants against the submission of late opposition papers or cross-motions, the General Clerk's Office will screen motions in which such papers are submitted without a response (reply or opposition respectively) to ensure that proper time to respond has been afforded and it will sua sponte adjourn for one (1) week cases in which such time has not been given. NY R NY CTY Procedure II(C).

5. *QUEENS COUNTY: Time to pay fees.* As motions and petitions are time sensitive, if opting to pay at the County Clerk's Office payment MUST be made, if filed with an RJI, a minimum of nine (9) business days prior to the application's return date and if filed post RJI, a minimum of nine (9) business days prior to the application's return date. NY R L QUEENS E-FILE Doc. 1(H)(1).

6. *Computation of time*

a. *Units of time*

i. *Day.* A calendar day includes the time from midnight to midnight. Sunday or any day of the week specifically mentioned means a calendar day. NY GEN CONSTR § 19.

ii. *Month.* In a statute, contract or public or private instrument, unless otherwise provided in such contract or instrument or by law, the term month means a calendar month and not a lunar month. NY GEN CONSTR § 31.

iii. *Year.* For information on the definition of a year, including the definitions of a half-year and quarter-year, refer to NY GEN CONSTR § 58 and NY GEN CONSTR § 50. For information on leap years, refer to NY GEN CONSTR § 57.

b. *Periods of time*

i. *Number of days.* A number of days specified as a period from a certain day within which or after or before which an act is authorized or required to be done means such number of calendar days exclusive of the calendar day from which the reckoning is made. NY GEN CONSTR § 20.

- If such period is a period of two (2) days, Saturday, Sunday or a public holiday must be excluded from the reckoning if it is an intervening day between the day from which the reckoning is made and the last day of the period. NY GEN CONSTR § 20.
- In computing any specified period of time from a specified event, the day upon which the event happens is deemed the day from which the reckoning is made. The day from which any specified period of time is reckoned shall be excluded in making the reckoning. NY GEN CONSTR § 20.

ii. *Number of months.* A number of months after or before a certain day shall be computed by counting such number of calendar months from such day, exclusive of the calendar month in which such day occurs, and shall include the day of the month in the last month so counted having the same numerical order in days of the month as the day from which the computation is made, unless there be not so many days in the last month so counted, in which case the period computed shall expire with the last day of the month so counted. NY GEN CONSTR § 30.

iii. *Publication of notice; Number of days.* The period of publication of a legal notice shall be computed by excluding the first day of publication and including the day on which the act or event of which notice is given is to take place or which completes the full period of publication. NY CPLR § 2402.

iv. *Periods ending on Saturday, Sunday or public holiday.* When any period of time, computed from a certain day, within which or after which or before which an act is authorized or required to be done, ends on a Saturday, Sunday or a public holiday, such act may be done on the next succeeding business day and if the period ends at a specified hour, such act may be done at or before the same hour of such next succeeding business day, except that where a period of time specified by contract ends on a Saturday, Sunday or a public holiday, the extension of such period is governed by NY GEN CONSTR § 25. NY GEN CONSTR § 25-a(1).

- For a list of public holidays, refer to NY GEN CONSTR § 24.

v. *Additional time after certain kinds of service*

- *Service by mail.* Where a period of time prescribed by law is measured from the service of a paper and service is by mail, five (5) days shall be added to the prescribed period. NY CPLR Rule 2103(b)(2).
- *Service by overnight delivery service.* Where a period of time prescribed by law is measured from the service of a paper and service is by overnight delivery, one (1) business day shall be added to the prescribed period. NY CPLR Rule 2103(b)(6).

vi. *Daylight saving time.* For information on New York's time zone and the effect of daylight saving time, refer to NY GEN CONSTR § 52.

c. *Hours of court.* Notwithstanding any provision of law or rule of court to the contrary, throughout the State of New York the sessions of the Supreme Court for the disposition of business before the court shall commence not later than 9:30 a.m. and conclude not earlier than 5 p.m. Where warranted, the Chief Administrator of the Courts may authorize variances in the opening and closing hours of the courts, but, in such event, daily sessions shall total not less than six (6) hours. NY R CHIEF J § 3.1.

d. *Time limits; Extension of time.* Any act required by or in pursuance of law to be performed at or within a prescribed time, shall be performed according to the standard time. NY GEN CONSTR § 53.

i. Except where otherwise expressly prescribed by law, the court may extend the time fixed by any statute, rule or order for doing any act, upon such terms as may be just and upon good cause shown, whether the application for extension is made before or after the expiration of the time fixed. NY CPLR § 2004. Refer to the New York KeyRules Motion for Continuance/Extension of Time document for more information.

C. General Requirements

1. *Motions, generally.* There shall be compliance with the procedures prescribed in the CPLR for the bringing of motions. NY R UNIF TRIAL CTS § 202.7(a).

a. *Motions on notice.* A notice of motion shall specify the time and place of the hearing on the motion, the supporting papers upon which the motion is based, the relief demanded and the grounds therefor. NY CPLR Rule 2214(a). A motion on notice in an action in the supreme court shall be noticed to be heard in the judicial district where the action is triable or in a county adjoining the county where the action is triable. Unless statute, civil practice rule or local court rule provides otherwise, the motion shall be noticed to be heard before a motion term or, upon order to show cause granted by a justice, before that justice out of court. NY CPLR § 2212(a). Except as provided in NY R UNIF TRIAL CTS § 202.7(d), no motion shall be filed with the court unless there have been served and filed with the motion papers a notice of motion. NY R UNIF TRIAL CTS § 202.7(a)(1).

b. *Ex parte motions.* A motion in an action in the supreme court that may be made without notice may be made at a motion term or to a justice out of court in any county in the state. NY CPLR § 2212(b).

  i. *KINGS COUNTY.* For more information on submitting a motion ex parte, refer to NY R L KINGS E FIL Doc. 1(G).

  ii. *NEW YORK COUNTY.* For more information on submitting matters ex parte, refer to NY R NY CTY Procedure III and NY R NY CTY E FIL Doc. 2(G).

  iii. *QUEENS COUNTY.* For more information on submitting matters ex parte, refer to NY R L QUEENS EX PARTE Doc. 1.

c. *Alternative relief.* Relief in the alternative or of several different types may be demanded. NY CPLR Rule 2214(a). The types of relief need not be related. In one motion, for example, the defendant can seek to dismiss the plaintiff's claim for lack of jurisdiction, to get an extension of time to answer, to require the plaintiff to join X as a party, and to quash a disclosure subpoena served in behalf of the plaintiff on a nonparty witness. So doing, the movant must of course specify all of these items of relief in the notice of motion, and the grounds for them, and the supporting papers must contain the entire proof requisite to the items of relief sought. NY CPLR Rule 2214(Practice Commentary, C2214:4).

d. *General relief.* It is common practice to include at the end of the relief request in the notice of motion a so-called "general relief" clause. This is merely a few words to cover the possibility that the relief appropriate to what the movant proves was not specifically asked for, but is close enough to enable the court to grant it. After stating the specific relief desired, the lawyer will often add something like: and for such other, further, or different relief as this court may deem just and proper. NY CPLR Rule 2214(Practice Commentary, C2214:5).

e. *Motion in improper form.* If the court finds it appropriate in the interests of justice, it may convert a motion into a special proceeding, or vice-versa, upon such terms as may be just, including the payment of fees and costs. NY CPLR § 103(c).

f. *Order to show cause.* An order to show cause is basically only a substitute for a notice of motion. An ordinary notice of motion merely notifies the recipient that a motion is being made for specified relief. The burden of proof is on the movant. Although in most cases it is just as innocent as an ordinary notice of motion, the order to show cause gets its name by directing the recipient to "show cause" why the particular relief being asked for should not be granted. It sounds as if the burden of proof is being shifted to the recipient. It isn't. It specifies the time and place of the hearing on the application but when the hearing comes on, the burden of proof is where it always is on a motion: on the movant. SIEGEL-NYPRAC § 248.

  i. The CPLR says nothing more about an order to show cause than that it may be used "in a proper case", which leaves it entirely to the judge's discretion to determine what a proper case is. Any fact suggesting a problem as to any of the items listed above would be sufficient to invoke judicial discretion and justify the show cause procedure, which is in fact liberally used. SIEGEL-NYPRAC § 248.

  ii. An order to show cause against a state body or officers must be served in addition to service upon the defendant or respondent state body or officers upon the attorney general by delivery to an assistant attorney general at an office of the attorney general in the county in which venue of the action is designated or if there is no office of the attorney general in such county, at the office of the attorney general nearest such county. NY CPLR Rule 2214(d).

  iii. *BRONX COUNTY.* For information on submitting an order to show cause, refer to NY R BRONX E FIL R Doc. 2 and NY R BRONX LEG SUP Doc. 1.

  iv. *ERIE COUNTY.* For information on submitting an order to show cause, refer to NY R ERIE E FIL Doc. 3(VI).

  v. *KINGS COUNTY.* For information on submitting an order to show cause, refer to NY R L KINGS E FIL Doc. 1(F).

  vi. *NEW YORK COUNTY.* For information on submitting an order to show cause, refer to NY R NY CTY E FIL Doc. 2(F).

  vii. *ONONDAGA COUNTY.* For information on submitting an order to show cause, refer to NY R ONDGA E FIL Protocol(B)(10) and NY R ONDGA E FIL Protocol(J).

g. *Motions before preliminary conference.* Motions in actions to which NY R UNIF TRIAL CTS § 202.12 is applicable made after the preliminary conference has been scheduled may be denied unless there is shown good cause why such relief is warranted before the preliminary conference is held. NY R UNIF TRIAL CTS § 202.12(h).

h. *ALBANY COUNTY: Good faith effort to resolve.* Prior to the submission of a notice of motion relating to disclosure or a bill of particulars, the parties must make a good faith effort to resolve the matter in question and submit an affirmation attesting to this good faith effort. NY R 3 JD SUP Doc. 1(B).

i. *NEW YORK COUNTY: Documents with motions.* Counsel must attach to motion papers copies of all pleadings and other documents as required by the CPLR and as necessary for an informed decision on the motion. Documents in a foreign language shall be properly translated. NY R NY CTY J RUL Rule 14(a).

j. *NEW YORK COUNTY: Motions in multiple cases made together.* On occasion, attorneys may wish to make a motion in more than one case on a single set of papers. In such cases, by definition consolidation will not have been directed since consolidation signifies the combination of more than one case into a single one with a single caption and index number and ending in a single judgment. NY R NY CTY Procedure II(B). For more information on motions made with the same papers, refer to NY R NY CTY Procedure II(A).

k. *QUEENS COUNTY: Motion sequence numbers.* A motion sequence number is required for all E-filed motions. After a motion is E-filed, please consult the e-courts website within twenty-four (24) to forty-eight (48) hours to obtain the sequence number. The Confirmation Notice of E-filing MUST indicate the sequence number of any motion submitted at the Centralized Motion Part calendar call. NY R L QUEENS E-FILE Doc. 1(H)(5).

2. *Rules governing disclosure*

a. *Generally.* There shall be full disclosure of all matter material and necessary in the prosecution or defense of an action, regardless of the burden of proof, by:

i. A party, or the officer, director, member, agent or employee of a party;

ii. A person who possessed a cause of action or defense asserted in the action;

iii. A person about to depart from the state, or without the state, or residing at a greater distance from the place of trial than one hundred miles, or so sick or infirm as to afford reasonable grounds of belief that he or she will not be able to attend the trial, or a person authorized to practice medicine, dentistry or podiatry who has provided medical, dental or podiatric care or diagnosis to the party demanding disclosure, or who has been retained by such party as an expert witness; and

iv. Any other person, upon notice stating the circumstances or reasons such disclosure is sought or required. NY CPLR § 3101(a).

v. The statutory phrase "material and necessary", said the Court of Appeals, must be interpreted liberally to require disclosure upon request, of any facts bearing on the controversy which will assist preparation for trial by sharpening the issues and reducing delay and prolixity. The test is one of usefulness and reason. SIEGEL-NYPRAC § 344; Allen v. Crowell-Collier Pub. Co., 21 N.Y.2d 403, 235 N.E.2d 430 (1968).

vi. Another potential problem that the original NY CPLR § 3101(a) posed was that it spoke of "evidence" that is material and necessary, which might have been construed to permit disclosure to elicit only that which would itself qualify as "evidence" admissible at trial. It was, however, construed more broadly than that. Well-considered caselaw specifically rejected this "evidence in chief" doctrine, stating that disclosure extends as well "to all relevant information calculated to lead to relevant evidence," a standard similar to that applicable in federal court. With an amendment that took effect on January 1, 1994, changing "evidence" to "matter" in NY CPLR § 3101(a), these generous interpretations of the statute were in effect approved by the legislature. SIEGEL-NYPRAC § 344.

vii. If a party is a corporation, each of its officers, directors, members, agents, and employees is also deemed a "party" for disclosure purposes. A party who needs relevant data or material from a nonparty corporation can seek it through NY CPLR § 3101(a)(2), NY CPLR § 3101(a)(3) or NY CPLR § 3101(a)(4), under which the corporate entity is treated as a "person." These subdivisions should also apply to any entity, corporate or otherwise, from whom disclosure is sought through its agents. A corporate employee who has the requisite knowledge and information may respond to a disclosure request on behalf of the corporation. A party who can't single out the particular person in the corporation's employ to whom a disclosure request should be properly directed can direct it to the corporation as such and leave it to the corporation to designate the appropriate person to respond. Whenever disclosure is sought from a corporation through a deposition, whether as a party or as a nonparty witness, the choice in the first instance of who will be produced in the corporate behalf is with the corporation rather than the examining party. SIEGEL-NYPRAC § 345.

viii. NY CPLR § 3101(a)(4) permits a party to obtain disclosure from a nonparty by merely serving a subpoena on the nonparty providing notice of "the circumstances or reasons such disclosure is sought or required." SIEGEL-NYPRAC § 345.

b. *Privileged matter.* Upon objection by a person entitled to assert the privilege, privileged matter shall not be obtainable. NY CPLR § 3101(b).

i. A determination of whether information is privileged is governed by the rules of evidence, which apply as they would at a trial. Whatever is privileged at the trial is privileged as well on pretrial disclosure. SIEGEL-NYPRAC § 346.

c. *Attorney's work product.* The work product of an attorney shall not be obtainable. NY CPLR § 3101(c).

i. NY CPLR § 3101(c) makes unobtainable the "work product of an attorney"—an ill-defined category whose potential for mischief has been avoided only because the judiciary has accorded it a very narrow scope. It is a category wholly distinct from the "materials . . . prepared in anticipation of litigation" of NY CPLR § 3101(d)(2). The fact that immunity is absolute under NY CPLR § 3101(c), while that of NY CPLR § 3101(d)(2) is only conditional, is the factor that requires as sharp a line as possible between the two categories. SIEGEL-NYPRAC § 347.

ii. The judiciary has cast precious little under the "work product" category of NY CPLR § 3101(c), preferring instead to fit doubtful items under the "materials . . . prepared in anticipation of litigation" banner of NY CPLR § 3101(d)(2), where the conditional immunity can be overcome and the matters ordered disclosed when stated conditions are met. SIEGEL-NYPRAC § 347.

d. *Trial preparation* .

i. *Experts.* Upon request, each party shall identify each person whom the party expects to call as an expert witness at trial and shall disclose in reasonable detail the subject matter on which each expert is expected to testify, the substance of the facts and opinions on which each expert is expected to testify, the qualifications of each expert witness and a summary of the grounds for each expert's opinion. NY CPLR § 3101(d)(1)(i).

- However, where a party for good cause shown retains an expert an insufficient period of time before the commencement of trial to give appropriate notice thereof, the party shall not thereupon be precluded from introducing the expert's testimony at the trial solely on grounds of noncompliance with NY CPLR § 3101(d)(1). In that instance, upon motion of any party, made before or at trial, or on its own initiative, the court may make whatever order may be just. In an action for medical, dental or podiatric malpractice, a party, in responding to a request, may omit the names of medical, dental or podiatric experts but shall be required to disclose all other information concerning such experts otherwise required by NY CPLR § 3101(d)(1). NY CPLR § 3101(d)(1)(i).
- In an action for medical, dental or podiatric malpractice, any party may, by written offer made to and served upon all other parties and filed with the court, offer to disclose the name of, and to make available for examination upon oral deposition, any person the party making the offer expects to call as an expert witness at trial. Within twenty (20) days of service of the offer, a party shall accept or reject the offer by serving a written reply upon all parties and filing a copy thereof with the court. Failure to serve a reply within twenty (20) days of service of the offer shall be deemed a rejection of the offer. If all parties accept the offer, each party shall be required to produce his or her expert witness for examination upon oral deposition upon receipt of a notice to take oral deposition in accordance with NY CPLR Rule 3107. If any party, having made or accepted the offer, fails to make that party's expert available for oral deposition, that party shall be precluded from offering expert testimony at the trial of the action. NY CPLR § 3101(d)(1)(ii).
- Further disclosure concerning the expected testimony of any expert may be obtained only by court order upon a showing of special circumstances and subject to restrictions as to scope and provisions concerning fees and expenses as the court may deem appropriate. However, a party, without court order, may take the testimony of a person authorized to practice medicine, dentistry or podiatry who is the party's treating or retained expert, as described in NY CPLR § 3101(a)(3), in which event any other party shall be entitled to the full disclosure authorized by Article 31 of Chapter 8 of the Civil Practice Law and Rules (NY CPLR § 3101, et seq.) with respect to that expert without court order. NY CPLR § 3101(d)(1)(iii).

ii. *Materials.* Subject to the provisions of NY CPLR § 3101(d)(1), materials otherwise discoverable under NY CPLR § 3101(a) and prepared in anticipation of litigation or for trial by or for another party, or by or for that other party's representative (including an attorney, consultant, surety, indemnitor, insurer or agent), may be obtained only upon a showing that the party seeking discovery has substantial need of the materials in the preparation of the case and is unable without undue hardship to obtain the substantial equivalent of the materials by other means. In ordering discovery of the materials when the required showing has been made, the court shall protect against disclosure of the mental impressions, conclusions, opinions or legal theories of an attorney or other representative of a party concerning the litigation. NY CPLR § 3101(d)(2).

- In order to qualify as "litigation" material the item must have been prepared exclusively for litigation. Incidental potential use in litigation, the courts have observed, may also be a function of such reports, but they have at least an equal if not greater mission "to prevent future accidents, discipline careless employees, or, generally, to increase the economy and efficiency of the operation." SIEGEL-NYPRAC § 348.

e. *Party's statement.* A party may obtain a copy of his own statement. NY CPLR § 3101(e).

i. Moreover, NY CPLR § 3101(e) has been broadly interpreted to include photographs. Items such as photographs and videotapes are now independently subject to disclosure under NY CPLR § 3101(i). SIEGEL-NYPRAC § 348.

f. *Contents of insurance agreement.* A party may obtain discovery of the existence and contents of any insurance agreement under which any person carrying on an insurance business may be liable to satisfy part or all of a judgment which may be entered in the action or to indemnify or reimburse for payments made to satisfy the judgment. Information concerning the insurance agreement is not by reason of disclosure admissible in evidence at trial. For purpose of NY CPLR § 3101(f), an application for insurance shall not be treated as part of an insurance agreement. NY CPLR § 3101(f).

g. *Accident reports.* Except as is otherwise provided by law, in addition to any other matter which may be subject to disclosure, there shall be full disclosure of any written report of an accident prepared in the regular course of business operations or practices of any person, firm, corporation, association or other public or private entity, unless prepared by a police or peace officer for a criminal investigation or prosecution and disclosure would interfere with a criminal investigation or prosecution. NY CPLR § 3101(g).

h. *Amendment or supplementation of responses.* A party shall amend or supplement a response previously given to a request for disclosure promptly upon the party's thereafter obtaining information that the response was incorrect or incomplete when made, or that the response, though correct and complete when made, no longer is correct and complete, and the circumstances are such that a failure to amend or supplement the response would be materially misleading. NY CPLR § 3101(h).

i. Where a party obtains such information an insufficient period of time before the commencement of trial appropriately to amend or supplement the response, the party shall not thereupon be precluded from introducing evidence at the trial solely on grounds of noncompliance with NY CPLR § 3101(h). In that instance, upon motion of any party, made before or at trial, or on its own initiative, the court may make whatever order may be just. Further amendment or supplementation may be obtained by court order. NY CPLR § 3101(h).

i. *Other disclosures.* In addition to any other matter which may be subject to disclosure, there shall be full disclosure of any films, photographs, video tapes or audio tapes, including transcripts or memoranda thereof, involving a person referred to in NY CPLR § 3101(a)(1). There shall be disclosure of all portions of such material, including out-takes, rather than only those portions a party intends to use. The provisions of NY CPLR § 3101(i) shall not apply to materials compiled for law enforcement purposes which are exempt from disclosure under NY PUB OFF § 87. NY CPLR § 3101(i).

i. While NY CPLR § 3101(i) was enacted with the defendant's surreptitious tapes of the plaintiff in mind, its language is broad enough to embrace any films, photographs, and audio or video tapes of a party, even those made by the party from whom disclosure is sought. SIEGEL-NYPRAC § 348.

j. *Protective orders.* The court may at any time on its own initiative, or on motion of any party or of any person from whom discovery is sought, make a protective order denying, limiting, conditioning or regulating the use of any disclosure device. NY CPLR § 3103(a). Refer to the New York KeyRules Motion for Protective Order document for more information.

k. *Supervision of disclosure.* Upon the motion of any party or witness on notice to all parties or on its own initiative without notice, the court in which an action is pending may by one of its judges or a referee supervise all or part of any disclosure procedure. NY CPLR § 3104(a).

i. *Selection of referee.* A judicial hearing officer may be designated as a referee under NY CPLR § 3104, or the court may permit all of the parties in an action to stipulate that a named attorney may act as referee. In such latter event, the stipulation shall provide for payment of his fees which shall, unless otherwise agreed, be taxed as disbursements. NY CPLR § 3104(b).

ii. *Powers of referee; Motions referred to person supervising disclosure.* A referee under NY CPLR § 3104 shall have all the powers of the court under NY CPLR § 3101, et seq. except the power to relieve himself of his duties, to appoint a successor, or to adjudge any person guilty of contempt. All motions or applications made under Article 31 of Chapter 8 of the Civil Practice Law and Rules (NY CPLR § 3101, et seq.) shall be returnable before the judge or referee, designated under NY CPLR § 3104 and after disposition, if requested by any party, his order shall be filed in the office of the clerk. NY CPLR § 3104(c).

iii. *Review of order of referee.* Any party or witness may apply for review of an order made under NY CPLR § 3104 by a referee. The application shall be by motion made in the court in which the action is pending within five (5) days after the order is made. Service of a notice of motion for review shall suspend disclosure of the particular matter in dispute. If the question raised by the motion may affect the rights of a witness, notice shall be served on him personally or by mail at his last known address. It shall set forth succinctly the order complained of, the reason it is objectionable and the relief demanded. NY CPLR § 3104(d).

iv. *Payment of expenses of referee.* Except where a judicial hearing officer has been designated a referee hereunder, the court may make an appropriate order for the payment of the reasonable expenses of the referee. NY CPLR § 3104(e).

3. *Resolution of disclosure disputes*

a. *BRONX COUNTY: Written application for conference in place of formal motion.* In lieu of a formal motion, parties may make written application to schedule a Discovery Status or Compliance Conference. Such application shall be forwarded to Bronx Supreme Civil, 851 Grand Concourse, Bronx, New York 10451 Room 217 DCM Department, Email BXDCM@NYCOURTS.GOV, FAX: 212 884 8955, PHONE: 212 884 8955. NY R BRONX FIL R Doc. 5. Such application shall set forth:

i. The case caption and index number;

ii. E Mail address for notification;

iii. Must specify all discovery issues and any other relief being requested;

iv. The request must state the courts intervention is necessary to resolve these issues. NY R BRONX FIL R Doc. 5.

v. Identify all prior orders addressing discovery issues. NY R BRONX FIL R Doc. 5(5).

vi. The request must be CCed to all appearing parties. NY R BRONX FIL R Doc. 5(6).

b. *KINGS COUNTY: Attempt to reach agreement.* The attorneys shall, in the first instance, attempt to reach an agreement on all relevant discovery. Disputed matters will be adjudicated by the Court. NY R L KINGS Pt. B, Rule 2.

c. *NEW YORK COUNTY: Good faith effort to resolve.* Prior to making a discovery motion, counsel shall consult one another in a good faith effort to resolve any discovery disputes. If a dispute is not thus resolved, the party seeking disclosure, unless otherwise directed in the Background Information section above, is advised to contact the Part Clerk promptly, and within any applicable deadline, for the purpose of arranging a conference, in court or by telephone. NY R NY CTY J RUL Rule 10.

4. *Motion for discovery sanctions*

a. *Generally.* All of the disclosure devices are backed by the sanctions of NY CPLR § 3126, with the exception of the request to admit, which carries its own set of consequences. SIEGEL-NYPRAC § 367. If any party, or a person who at the time a deposition is taken or an examination or inspection is made is an officer, director, member, employee or agent of a party or otherwise under a party's control, refuses to obey an order for disclosure or willfully fails to disclose information which the court finds ought to have been disclosed pursuant to Article 31 of the New York Civil Practice Law and Rules (NY CPLR § 3101, et seq.), the court may make such orders with regard to the failure or refusal as are just, among them:

i. An order that the issues to which the information is relevant shall be deemed resolved for purposes of the action in accordance with the claims of the party obtaining the order; or

ii. An order prohibiting the disobedient party from supporting or opposing designated claims or defenses, from producing in evidence designated things or items of testimony, or from introducing any evidence of the physical, mental or blood condition sought to be determined, or from using certain witnesses; or

iii. An order striking out pleadings or parts thereof, or staying further proceedings until the order is obeyed, or dismissing the action or any part thereof, or rendering a judgment by default against the disobedient party. NY CPLR § 3126.

- This ultimate penalty for nondisclosure is not favored by the courts. They save it for cases of aggravated resistance, where "[l]ess drastic action would only serve to encourage dilatory conduct and reward an obstructionist approach to discovery proceedings." SIEGEL-NYPRAC § 367; Sawh v. Bridges, 120 A.D.2d 74, 78, 507 N.Y.S.2d 632, 635 (1986).

b. *Sanctions for nondisclosure, generally.* The NY CPLR § 3126 sanctions are available not only when an order for disclosure has been disobeyed, but also when there is wilful disobedience of a mere notice. A court order, such as one under NY CPLR Rule 3124 directing disclosure, is not a condition precedent to the invocation of NY CPLR § 3126. SIEGEL-NYPRAC § 367; Wolfson v. Nassau Cty. Med. Ctr., 141 A.D.2d 815, 530 N.Y.S.2d 27 (1988). The statute so provides explicitly in that it applies when the party either disobeys an order, "or" wilfilly fails to disclose information which the court finds ought to have been disclosed. SIEGEL-NYPRAC § 367; Coffey v. Orbachs, Inc., 22 A.D.2d 317, 320, 254 N.Y.S.2d 596, 599 (1964); Goldner v. Lendor Structures, Inc., 29 A.D.2d 978, 979, 289 N.Y.S.2d 687, 689 (1968). This may account, at least in part, for some diminished use NY CPLR Rule 3124 today, which prescribes an order directing disclosure without a sanction. SIEGEL-NYPRAC § 367.

   i. Caselaw under the original statute held that a NY CPLR § 3126 sanction motion need not necessarily be preceded by a disclosure order under NY CPLR Rule 3124, which of course made the motion under NY CPLR § 3126 the preferred one. SIEGEL-NYPRAC § 366; Wolfson v. Nassau Cty. Med. Ctr., 141 A.D.2d 815, 815-16, 530 N.Y.S.2d 27, 28 (1988). The design was to avoid the two-motion procedure generated by making a party go to NY CPLR Rule 3124 first and allowing access to NY CPLR § 3126 only as a follow-up. SIEGEL-NYPRAC § 366.

   ii. Under the 1993 amendments, however, there are at least two instances in which it appears that a bypass of NY CPLR Rule 3124 in favor of a direct motion under NY CPLR § 3126 may be barred. When the devices involved are the discovery of NY CPLR Rule 3120 or the physical or mental examination of NY CPLR § 3121, the also-amended NY CPLR Rule 3122 appears to require that a preliminary NY CPLR Rule 3124 application be made—for a court order directing disclosure without a sanction—before a sanction can be invoked with a NY CPLR § 3126 motion. SIEGEL-NYPRAC § 366.

   iii. Another reason some courts will not require resort to a NY CPLR Rule 3124 order before entertaining a motion under NY CPLR § 3126 is that an order under NY CPLR § 3126 can be made conditionally, with the court directing the disclosure accompanied by a sanction if the direction should be disobeyed. This is a very popular step among judges today. SIEGEL-NYPRAC § 367.

   iv. Refer to the New York KeyRules Motion to Compel Disclosure document for more information regarding to motions to compel discovery under NY CPLR Rule 3124.

c. *Failure of a party to supplement prior disclosure responses.* The sanctions of NY CPLR § 3126 are in fact available not just for the disobedience of an order or the disregard of a notice. Under NY CPLR § 3101(h), a party is required to supplement prior responses in certain circumstances, and to do so voluntarily, i.e., without the other side having to serve a new notice, demand, request, interrogatory, or anything else. SIEGEL-NYPRAC § 367; SIEGEL-NYPRAC § 352A. The NY CPLR § 3126 sanctions are available for a failure to honor the NY CPLR § 3101(h) supplementation requirement even though no order or notice has specifically requested supplementation. SIEGEL-NYPRAC § 367.

d. *Motion addressed to notice to disclose*

   i. If a NY CPLR § 3126 sanction motion is addressed to a mere notice to disclose, as opposed to an order, it must be shown that the disobedience was "wilful." One might guess that the cases would be filled with discussion of what is and what is not "wilful" in this sense, but the law is not altogether clear in this realm. In any event, the courts usually prefer to determine whether the disclosure is required and, if it is, to issue a conditional order directing the party to make the disclosure whether the prior refusal was wilful or not. SIEGEL-NYPRAC § 367.

   ii. The order will normally impose a sanction "unless" the disclosure is made within a stated time. With this conditioning, the court relieves itself of the unrewarding inquiry into whether a party's resistance was wilful. The court usually reserves the "willful" finding for cases where it is convinced not only that the party refused disclosure in the past, but apparently will not, without judicial prodding, make it in the future either. In one case, the court considered a party's failure to comply with disclosure in related actions outside New York State as part of a "programmed response to discovery." Any unnecessary trouble the seeking party has been caused in this process is usually remedied, as will be seen, by a conditional order requiring the resisting party to make the disclosure now and pay the seeking party an attorney's fee. SIEGEL-NYPRAC § 367.

e. *Refusal to disclose based on privilege.* When the refusal to disclose is based on privilege, such as that against self-incrimination, the availability of a sanction may depend on who is invoking the privilege. If the defendant does, and legitimately, no sanction may be invoked because the privilege is a shield and that's the way the defendant is using it. But when the plaintiff invokes it—the very person who brought the case to court—the invocation amounts to an attempt to use the privilege as a sword. Although the plaintiff can't be precluded from using the privilege, he will face a civil sanction under NY CPLR § 3126 if he does, up to and including the ultimate sanction of a dismissal or default. SIEGEL-NYPRAC § 367; Levine v. Bornstein, 13 Misc. 2d 161, 163, 174 N.Y.S.2d 574, 576 (Sup. Ct. 1958), aff'd, 7 A.D.2d 995, 183 N.Y.S.2d 868 (1959), aff'd, 6 N.Y.2d 892, 160 N.E.2d 921 (1959).

f. *Relationship with preliminary conference; Disclosure timetable.* Where the motion relates to disclosure or to a bill of particulars, and a preliminary conference has not been held, the court shall notify all parties of a scheduled date to appear for a preliminary conference, which shall be not more than forty-five (45) days from the return date of the motion unless the court orders otherwise, and a form of a stipulation and order, prescribed by the Chief Administrator of the Courts, shall be made available which the parties may sign, agreeing to a timetable which shall provide for completion of disclosure within twelve (12) months, and for a resolution of any other issues raised by the motion. If all parties sign the form and return it to the court before the return date of the motion, such form shall be "so ordered" by the court, and the motion shall be deemed withdrawn. If such stipulation is not returned by all parties, the conference shall be held on the assigned date. Issues raised by the motion and not resolved at the conference shall be determined by the court. NY R UNIF TRIAL CTS § 202.8(f).

5. *Penalty for unreasonable denial of a matter of fact, papers, documents and photographs*
   a. If a party, after being served with a request under NY CPLR § 3123(a) does not admit and if the party requesting the admission thereafter proves the genuineness of any such paper or document, or the correctness or fairness of representation of any such photograph, or the truth of any such matter of fact, he may move at or immediately following the trial for an order requiring the other party to pay him the reasonable expenses incurred in making such proof, including reasonable attorney's fees. NY CPLR § 3123(c).
   b. Unless the court finds that there were good reasons for the denial or the refusal otherwise to admit or that the admissions sought were of no substantial importance, the order shall be made irrespective of the result of the action. Upon a trial by jury, the motion for such an order shall be determined by the court outside the presence of the jury. NY CPLR § 3123(c).
6. *Availability of other penalties.* The court might also have authority to impose sanctions independent of NY CPLR § 3126. If the party resisting disclosure has engaged in frivolous conduct, the court has the power to impose sanctions under Part 130 (NY R CHIEF ADMIN § 130-1.1, et seq.). NY CPLR Rule 3124(Practice Commentary, C3124:6). Refer to the New York KeyRules Motion for Sanctions document for more information.
7. *Oppositions.* In the absence of statutory provision or court rule, a motion ordinarily does not require a written answer, although an adverse party may be permitted to file an answer in opposition to the showing made in the motion or its supporting affidavits. AMJUR MOTIONS § 26. When a party files a motion and the opposing party fails to respond, the court may construe such failure to respond as non-opposition to the motion or an admission that the motion was meritorious, may take the facts alleged in the motion as true, and may grant the motion if the relief requested appears to be justified. However, the severity of such a result demands that a court impose it only with great caution. AMJUR MOTIONS § 28.
8. *Governing law.* The civil practice law and rules (NY CPLR § 101, et seq.) shall govern the procedure in civil judicial proceedings in all courts of the state and before all judges, except where the procedure is regulated by inconsistent statute. The civil practice law and rules shall succeed the civil practice act and rules of civil practice and shall be deemed substituted therefor throughout the statutes and rules of the state. NY CPLR § 101. The civil practice law and rules shall be liberally construed to secure the just, speedy and inexpensive determination of every civil judicial proceeding. NY CPLR § 104.
   a. *Uniform trial court rules.* The uniform civil rules for the Supreme Court and County Court (NY R UNIF TRIAL CTS § 202.1, et seq.) shall be applicable to civil actions and proceedings in the Supreme Court and the County Court. NY R UNIF TRIAL CTS § 202.1(a). The provisions of the uniform rules shall be construed consistent with the Civil Practice Law and Rules (CPLR), and matters not covered by the uniform rules shall be governed by the CPLR. NY R UNIF TRIAL CTS § 202.1(d).
   b. *Local rules.* Local court rules, not inconsistent with law or with uniform civil rules for the Supreme Court and County Court (NY R UNIF TRIAL CTS § 202.1, et seq.), shall comply with Part 9 of the Rules of the Chief Judge (NY R CHIEF J § 9.1). NY R UNIF TRIAL CTS § 202.1(c).
   c. *Official forms.* The state administrator shall have the power to adopt, amend and rescind an appendix of forms. Forms adopted pursuant to NY CPLR § 107 shall be sufficient under the civil practice law and rules and shall illustrate the simplicity and brevity of statement which the civil practice law and rules contemplate. NY CPLR § 107.

9. *Rules of the commercial division.* [Editor's note: certain types of civil cases or civil cases meeting certain monetary thresholds that are filed in the state of New York must be filed in the Commercial Division of the New York Supreme Courts. Rules governing practice in the commercial division are found in NY R UNIF TRIAL CTS § 202.70]. Cases which must be filed in the commercial division are listed below. For more information, refer to NY R UNIF TRIAL CTS § 202.70.

   a. *Monetary thresholds.* Except as set forth in NY R UNIF TRIAL CTS § 202.70(b), the monetary thresholds of the Commercial Division, exclusive of punitive damages, interests, costs, disbursements and counsel fees claimed, are established as follows: (1) Albany County, fifty thousand dollars ($50,000); (2) Eighth Judicial District, one hundred thousand dollars ($100,000); (3) Kings County, one hundred fifty thousand dollars ($150,000); (4) Nassau County, two hundred thousand dollars ($200,000); (5) New York County, five hundred thousand dollars ($500,000); (6) Onondaga County, fifty thousand dollars ($50,000); (7) Queens County, one hundred thousand dollars ($100,000); (8) Seventh Judicial District, fifty thousand dollars ($50,000); (9) Suffolk County, one hundred thousand dollars ($100,000); and (10) Westchester County, one hundred thousand dollars ($100,000). NY R UNIF TRIAL CTS § 202.70(a).

      i. *ALBANY COUNTY.* The Commercial Division of the Albany County Supreme Court exercises jurisdiction over selected business and commercial disputes in which the amount at issue generally involves damage claims in a minimum amount of fifty thousand dollars ($50,000) as well as claims for unspecified amounts where the value of the commercial asset(s) in dispute exceeds fifty thousand dollars ($50,000). A separate publication promulgating the rules and criteria relating to the filing and management of Commercial Court cases in this part may be obtained from the Albany County Supreme Court Clerk's Office. A section of the Uniform Civil Rules for the Supreme Court and County Court sets forth statewide rules. NY R 3 JD SUP Doc. 1(E).

      ii. *BRONX COUNTY.* The monetary threshold for commercial cases in Bronx County will be seventy-five thousand dollars ($75,000). All other parameters including the type of matters that will be heard are contained within the Rules of the Commercial Division of the Supreme Court (NY R UNIF TRIAL CTS § 202.70). NY R BRONX FIL R Doc. 12.

      iii. *NEW YORK COUNTY.* The monetary threshold in the New York County Commercial Division, which is generally applicable, is an amount in controversy of five hundred thousand dollars ($500,000) or more (exclusive of punitive damages, interest, costs, disbursements, and counsel fees). If the case is designated a commercial one and the Addendum is submitted, the clerk will review the pleadings to determine whether the amount in controversy in the case meets the monetary threshold or whether an exception to the threshold applies. NY R NY CTY Procedure IA(B). For more information on assigning a case to the commercial division in New York County, refer to NY R NY CTY Procedure IA(B).

   b. *Commercial cases.* Actions in which the principal claims involve or consist of the following will be heard in the Commercial Division provided that the monetary threshold is met or equitable or declaratory relief is sought:

      i. Breach of contract or fiduciary duty, fraud, misrepresentation, business tort (e.g., unfair competition), or statutory and/or common law violation where the breach or violation is alleged to arise out of business dealings (e.g., sales of assets or securities; corporate restructuring; partnership, shareholder, joint venture, and other business agreements; trade secrets; restrictive covenants; and employment agreements not including claims that principally involve alleged discriminatory practices);

      ii. Transactions governed by the Uniform Commercial Code (exclusive of those concerning individual cooperative or condominium units);

      iii. Transactions involving commercial real property, including Yellowstone injunctions and excluding actions for the payment of rent only;

      iv. Shareholder derivative actions—without consideration of the monetary threshold;

      v. Commercial class actions—without consideration of the monetary threshold;

      vi. Business transactions involving or arising out of dealings with commercial banks and other financial institutions;

      vii. Internal affairs of business organizations;

      viii. Malpractice by accountants or actuaries, and legal malpractice arising out of representation in commercial matters;

      ix. Environmental insurance coverage;

      x. Commercial insurance coverage (e.g., directors and officers, errors and omissions, and business interruption coverage);

xi. Dissolution of corporations, partnerships, limited liability companies, limited liability partnerships and joint ventures—without consideration of the monetary threshold; and

xii. Applications to stay or compel arbitration and affirm or disaffirm arbitration awards and related injunctive relief pursuant to Article 75 of the New York Civil Practice Law and Rules (NY CPLR § 7501, et seq.) involving any of the foregoing enumerated commercial issues. Where the applicable arbitration agreement provides for the arbitration to be heard outside the United States, the monetary threshold set forth in NY R UNIF TRIAL CTS § 202.70(a) shall not apply. NY R UNIF TRIAL CTS § 202.70(b).

c. *Non-commercial cases.* The following will not be heard in the Commercial Division even if the monetary threshold is met:

i. Suits to collect professional fees;

ii. Cases seeking a declaratory judgment as to insurance coverage for personal injury or property damage;

iii. Residential real estate disputes, including landlord-tenant matters, and commercial real estate disputes involving the payment of rent only;

iv. Home improvement contracts involving residential properties consisting of one to four residential units or individual units in any residential building, including cooperative or condominium units;

v. Proceedings to enforce a judgment regardless of the nature of the underlying case;

vi. First-party insurance claims and actions by insurers to collect premiums or rescind non-commercial policies; and

vii. Attorney malpractice actions except as otherwise provided in NY R UNIF TRIAL CTS § 202.70(b)(8). NY R UNIF TRIAL CTS § 202.70(c).

d. For more information on the Commercial Division, refer to NY R UNIF TRIAL CTS § 202.70.

D. Documents

1. *Documents for moving party*

a. *Required documents*

i. *Notice of motion, order to show cause, or affidavit on ex parte motion.* The notice of motion shall be substantially in the form found in NY R UNIF TRIAL CTS § 202.7(b). NY R UNIF TRIAL CTS § 202.7(b). The supporting papers should be referred to in the notice of motion. SIEGEL-NYPRAC § 246. The court in a proper case may grant an order to show cause, to be served in lieu of a notice of motion. NY CPLR Rule 2214(d). An ex parte motion shall be accompanied by an affidavit stating the result of any prior motion for similar relief and specifying the new facts, if any, that were not previously shown. NY CPLR Rule 2217(b).

- *Request for oral argument.* A party requesting oral argument shall set forth such request in its notice of motion or in its order to show cause or on the first page of the answering papers, as the case may be. Where all parties to a motion request oral argument, oral argument shall be granted unless the court shall determine it to be unnecessary. Where a motion is brought on by order to show cause, the court may set forth in the order that oral argument is required on the return date of the motion. NY R UNIF TRIAL CTS § 202.8(d).

ii. *Motion.* Refer to the General Requirements section of this document for information on the notice of motion and motion.

iii. *Affirmation of counsel.* No motion shall be filed with the court unless there have been served and filed with the motion papers with respect to a motion relating to disclosure or to a bill of particulars, an affirmation that counsel has conferred with counsel for the opposing party in a good faith effort to resolve the issues raised by the motion. NY R UNIF TRIAL CTS § 202.7(a)(2).

- The affirmation of the good faith effort to resolve the issues raised by the motion shall indicate the time, place and nature of the consultation and the issues discussed and any resolutions, or shall indicate good cause why no such conferral with counsel for opposing parties was held. NY R UNIF TRIAL CTS § 202.7(c).
- *KINGS COUNTY.* Motions must be accompanied by an affirmation of good faith pursuant to NY R UNIF TRIAL CTS § 202.7(a), indicating what efforts have been made to resolve the motion. NY R L KINGS Pt. E, Rule 9.

iv. *Request for judicial intervention.* At any time after service of process, a party may file a request for judicial intervention. Except as provided in NY R UNIF TRIAL CTS § 202.6(b), in an action not yet assigned to a judge, the court shall not accept for filing a notice of motion, order to show cause, or application for ex parte order, unless such notice or application is accompanied by a request for judicial intervention. NY R UNIF TRIAL CTS § 202.6(a).

- *BRONX COUNTY.* Generally, the Request For Judicial Intervention, commonly referred to as an "RJI", is required to be filed in any action where the assignment of a Justice is required. The RJI sets forth the information which is entered into the court system's database. It must be completely and accurately filled out. The full caption, as stated on the Summons, must be set forth. Use of terms "et al." and "etc." are not permitted. Only one (1) RJI may be filed in each action. Either a self represented litigant or an attorney must sign the affirmation at the end of the form. Once completed, the RJI must be filed in duplicate. Except in the case of an ex-parte application, the RJI must also be served together with the accompanying application upon all parties. Proof of accuracy of the index number must accompany the RJI. Check the Fee Schedule[. . .]for any applicable filing fees. NY R BRONX FIL R Doc. 2.
- *KINGS COUNTY.* An RJI with the relevant required addendum in a NYSCEF case shall be submitted via NYSCEF. Once e-filed, the RJI and any accompanying document will be forwarded to the relevant support office for random assignment of the case and processing of the document. A filer or counsel need not appear (as to Proposed Orders to Show Cause, however, see below). A copy of the pleadings must be submitted only if the document has not previously been e-filed. If the RJI seeks intervention with regard to a document that is intended for review by a Justice, such as a motion, a working copy of the RJI must be submitted with the working copy of the motion and the NYSCEF Confirmation Notice. NY R L KINGS E FIL Doc. 1(C).
- *NEW YORK COUNTY.* To obtain the assignment of an IAS Justice to a case, a Request for Judicial Intervention (cost ninety-five dollars ($95)) must be filed, with NYSCEF in an e-filed case or in paper in an authorized hard-copy one. A no-fee RJI, which will generally result in the referral of an application to an Ex Parte Justice, is also required with regard to certain kinds of applications for which, prior to 2011, no RJI was required. NY R NY CTY Procedure I(C). A "fillable" form RJI is available on-line. The form must be filed in duplicate in hard-copy cases. NY R NY CTY Procedure IA(A)(1). The filer of an RJI must check off a box identifying the type of case at issue. Where the RJI seeks judicial assignment, this designation will bring about a random assignment of the case by computer to a Justice handling cases of that type. NY R NY CTY Procedure IA(A)(1). The RJI and any addendum can be completed and submitted electronically in an e-filed case. NY R NY CTY Procedure II(A). The RJI shall be marked to reflect the existence of any "related case" as explained on the "Commencement of Cases" page under "Case Processing" on the court's website. NY R NY CTY Procedure II(A); NY R NY CTY E FIL Doc. 2(C).
- *ONONDAGA COUNTY.* The RJI will be submitted via the NYSCEF system along with any required RJI addendum forms. When the RJI is filed and the fee paid online, the Onondaga County Clerk's Office will electronically forward the RJI and any accompanying documents to the Onondaga Supreme Court Clerk's Office for assignment and processing. Counsel will receive notification of judge assignment via the NYSCEF system. NY R ONDGA E FIL Protocol(B)(3).
- *QUEENS COUNTY.* A Request for Judicial Intervention ("RJI") in an E-filed case shall be submitted via the E-filing System. When the RJI is approved, filed and paid for on-line, it will be forwarded to the relevant back office for random assignment of the case and processing of the document. In the case of RJIs seeking assignment to the Commercial Division, the filer must submit therewith, a Commercial Addendum as required by the standards for assignment of cases to the Commercial Division. NY R L QUEENS E-FILE Doc. 1(F).

v. *Proof of service.* In addition to complying with the provisions of NY CPLR Rule 2101, every paper filed in court shall have annexed thereto appropriate proof of service on all parties where required. NY R UNIF TRIAL CTS § 202.5(a).

- *QUEENS COUNTY.* With regard to service of a motion/petition on notice in an E-filed action, NY CPLR Rule 2214(b) and NY R UNIF TRIAL CTS § 202.5-b(f) applies. Where required, proof of service shall be filed on-line as a separate document. NY R L QUEENS E-FILE Doc. 1(H)(3).

vi. *ALBANY COUNTY: Additional required documents*

- *Affirmation of good faith effort.* The parties must[. . .]submit an affirmation attesting to [their good faith effort to resolve the matter]. The affirmation of good faith effort to resolve the issues raised by the motion shall indicate the time, place and nature of the consultation and the issues discussed and any resolutions, or shall indicate good cause why no such conferral with counsel for opposing parties was held. An assigned justice or judge may dismiss a motion for failure to demonstrate that such effort was made with leave to renew the motion after such effort has been demonstrated. NY R 3 JD SUP Doc. 1(B).

b. *Supplemental documents*

i. *Supporting evidence; Exhibits.* The main supporting papers on a motion are affidavits, but any relevant exhibits, documents, depositions, etc., are also includible. SIEGEL-NYPRAC § 246.

- *Affidavits accompanying motion.* Affidavits shall be for a statement of the relevant facts. NY R UNIF TRIAL CTS § 202.8(c).
- *Foreign language documents.* Where an affidavit or exhibit annexed to a paper served or filed is in a foreign language, it shall be accompanied by an English translation and an affidavit by the translator stating his qualifications and that the translation is accurate. NY CPLR Rule 2101(b).
- *Statement of attorney in lieu of affidavit.* The statement of an attorney admitted to practice in the courts of the state, or of a physician, osteopath or dentist, authorized by law to practice in the state, who is not a party to an action, when subscribed and affirmed by him to be true under the penalties of perjury, may be served or filed in the action in lieu of and with the same force and effect as an affidavit. NY CPLR Rule 2106.
- *NEW YORK COUNTY: Form of presented exhibits.* Exhibits should be tabbed and be legible; a typed version of any exhibit that is difficult to read should be submitted with the original. Exhibits printed on both sides of the page should be bound and tabbed on the side. NY R NY CTY J RUL Rule 14(a).
- *QUEENS COUNTY.* Attorneys submitting exhibits to the court on E-file cases shall make each exhibit a separate, labeled attachment to an affidavit/affirmation. NY R L QUEENS E-FILE Doc. 1(H)(4).

ii. *Brief.* Briefs shall be for a statement of the relevant law. NY R UNIF TRIAL CTS § 202.8(c).

iii. *Notice to produce papers not in possession of the court.* If a paper relied on by the movant is in the possession of the other side, it may be demanded of that side with a notice to produce it at the hearing. Where such papers are in the possession of an adverse party, they shall be produced by him at the hearing on notice served with the motion papers. NY CPLR Rule 2214(Practice Commentary, C2214:23).

iv. *Filing fees.* The County Clerk shall require the payment of any applicable statutory fees, or an order of the Court waiving payment of such fees, before accepting a paper for filing. NY R UNIF TRIAL CTS § 202.5(d)(1). For information on filing fees, if any, refer to NY CPLR § 8001, et seq.

- *ALBANY COUNTY.* In general, any filing subsequent to the commencement of an action which is designated as a motion or cross-motion requires the payment of a filing fee to the County Clerk's Office prior to submission to the Supreme Court Clerk's Office for referral to the assigned justice. The fee is assessed regardless of whether an application is made by notice of motion, order to show cause or ex parte. No fee will be charged upon the filing of a motion for poor person status in conjunction with an application which serves to commence an action or special proceeding. In the event a motion is received by the court unaccompanied by proof of payment to the County Clerk, the Supreme Court Clerk's Office will contact the submitting party to advise that the application will be held pending receipt of the filing fee only until the return date of the motion. If proof of payment is not submitted to the Supreme Court Clerk's Office by the return date (ex parte applications will be held ten (10) days), the papers will be returned by mail with a notification that the motion has been removed from the court's calendar and that it must be re-noticed and re-filed with the court along with the requisite filing fee. Inquiries concerning the applicability of the motion fee to a proposed filing may be directed to the Supreme Court Clerk's Office. NY R 3 JD SUP Doc. 1(B).
- *BRONX COUNTY.* In accordance with the new civil fee schedule set forth in Article 80 of the C.P.L.R. (NY CPLR § 8001, et seq.), effective July 14, 2003, all motions, and cross motions must be approved in Room 217 prior to payment of said fees in the County Clerk's Office, Room 118. NY R BRONX FIL R Doc. 8. The motion fee [must be] paid for via NYSCEF by credit/debit card. NY R BRONX E FIL R Doc. 1(1).
- *ERIE COUNTY.* Payment for fee-bearing NYSCEF documents must be made online via credit or debit card (American Express, MasterCard or Visa) at the time of submission. NY R ERIE E FIL Doc. 3(III)(E).
- *KINGS COUNTY.* The motion must be filed with NYSCEF and the motion fee paid. NY R L KINGS E FIL Doc. 1(D). Court fees in NYSCEF cases must be paid via NYSCEF by a credit or bank card (MasterCard, Visa, or American Express). Fees are no longer accepted in person in the Kings County Clerk's Office in NYSCEF cases. NY R L KINGS E FIL Doc. 1(B)(6).

- *NEW YORK COUNTY.* A motion fee must be paid on motions made in writing by notice of motion, order to show cause or ex parte after the commencement of an action. For this purpose, the term "action" shall mean any application to the court that requires the assignment of an index number, regardless of whether a formal pleading is filed. Applications or motions that commence an action and for which an index number fee must be paid require no motion fee. [A]ny motions made after the initial applications in these situations would require payment of the motion fee. A motion that is the initial application in a case commenced by the filing of a summons and complaint would require a motion fee since the filing of the summons and complaint rather than the application itself would require the purchase of an index number. NY R NY CTY Procedure II(A). In e-filed cases the motion fee must be paid when the documents are filed. Payment is made on-line by Visa, Mastercard, or American Express credit or bank card. NY R NY CTY Procedure II(A); NY R NY CTY E FIL Doc. 2(B)(5).
- *ONONDAGA COUNTY.* Court fees in e-filed cases must be paid online with the NYSCEF system using a credit card. The document is not considered to have been filed until payment of the fee has been tendered. NY R ONDGA E FIL Protocol(B)(2). Fees must be paid on all cross motions. NY R ONDGA E FIL Protocol(B)(9)(e).
- *QUEENS COUNTY.* The Motion Support Office does not receive, forward or process any fees or waiver of fees. All applications requiring payment of statutory fees or waiver of fees must be sent directly to the Queens County Clerk's office. NY R L QUEENS MOT SUP Doc. 1. Court fees (e.g., RJI fee, motion fee) in E-filed cases may be paid for on-line using a credit card. Papers may also be filed with the E-file system and the fee may be paid at the County Clerk's Office. In the latter case, the paper is not considered to have been filed until payment of the fee has been tendered. NY R L QUEENS E-FILE Doc. 1(E)(1). The motion/petition shall be filed on-line and the fee paid for either on-line by credit card or by the "Pay at the County Clerk's Office" option. NY R L QUEENS E-FILE Doc. 1(H)(1).

v. *Working copies.* The court may require the parties to provide working copies of documents filed electronically. In such event, each working copy shall include, firmly affixed thereto, a copy of a confirmation notice in a form prescribed by the Chief Administrator. NY R UNIF TRIAL CTS § 202.5-b(d)(5).

- *BRONX COUNTY.* After papers on motions have been e-filed, working copies thereof, with Confirmation Notice firmly attached as the back page facing out, must be submitted. (Each document or group of documents that is separately bound shall bear a Confirmation Notice.) Working copies lacking the Notice will not be accepted. WORKING COPIES OF MOTION PAPERS MUST BE SUBMITTED NO LATER THAN 4:45 P.M. ON THE RETURN DATE IN THE MOTION SUPPORT OFFICE (ROOM 217) AS EXPLAINED in NY R BRONX E FIL R Doc. 1(4). If an attorney has failed to submit required working copies on or before the return date, the motion will be transmitted as is to the Justice for such action as the Justice finds appropriate. Attorneys may submit working copies on motions by mail or overnight delivery. Any such submission shall be sent in a timely manner to the Motion Support Office (Room 217) and be conspicuously marked on the outside "NYSCEF Matter"; lack of such marking may delay processing. NY R BRONX E FIL R Doc. 1(4)(a).
- *ERIE COUNTY.* Electronically filed documents subject to review and processing by the Part Clerk do not require a working copy unless otherwise directed or provided for in IAS Part Rules. NY R UNIF TRIAL CTS § 202.5-b(d)(4), any working copy submitted shall include, as a cover page firmly fastened thereto, a copy of the Confirmation Notice generated by the NYSCEF site at the time of filing. Please consult the individual Justice's Part Rules and/or consult with the Judge's chambers to determine whether and how working copies are to be provided. Working copies will not be printed or delivered by the Erie County Clerk or the Chief Clerk of the Courts or any of their personnel to chambers. The official record of a document in an electronically filed case is the document filed via the NYSCEF system. Working copies are intended only for use by the Justice. The Court will discard all working copies after the Justice has finished with them. Thus, in the event that counsel fails to file a document via the NYSCEF system, the document will not be part of the court record. NY R ERIE E FIL Doc. 3(III)(O); NY R ERIE E FIL Doc. 3(V)(E).
- *KINGS COUNTY.* No courtesy copies of motion papers are required by the Court, except as may be required for electronic filing or by the Judge's Part Rules. In tort cases against the City of New York, courtesy copies shall be supplied to the Corporation Counsel's office in Brooklyn. NY R L KINGS Pt. C, Rule 5. Unless otherwise directed by the Court or as described herein, and with the exceptions listed below, in all NYSCEF cases in which an RJI has been filed, working copies of e-filed documents that are intended for judicial review must be submitted to the court. Working copies are not required of documents that are

only processed by a support office (e.g. preliminary conference request, note of issue). Working copies shall include exhibit tabs and backs; for motion papers, the motion sequence number and the return date and part. The confirmation notice with the motion sequence number on it should be the back page of the motion facing out. In addition, the filer of a working copy must firmly bind thereto, with the back page facing out, a copy of the Confirmation Notice that was generated by NYSCEF when that document was efiled. Working copies that are submitted without the related Confirmation Notice will not be accepted. NY R L KINGS E FIL Doc. 1(B)(7); NY R L KINGS E FIL Doc. 1(D). WORKING COPIES OF MOTION PAPERS MUST BE SUBMITTED IN THE MOTION SUPPORT OFFICE (ROOM 227) AS EXPLAINED HEREIN. THEY MUST NOT BE DELIVERED TO THE PART OR CHAMBERS, EXCEPT WHERE THE INDIVIDUAL JUSTICE'S PART RULES PROVIDE OTHERWISE; DOING SO WILL CAUSE ADMINISTRATIVE CONFUSION AND POSSIBLE MISPLACEMENT OF PAPERS. Any such submission shall be sent in a timely manner (kindly review individual Justice's rules) and be conspicuously marked on the outside "NYSCEF Matter;" lack of such marking may delay processing. NY R L KINGS E FIL Doc. 1(D).

- *NEW YORK COUNTY.* Some Justices require that working copies of e-filed motion papers be submitted. See the E-filing Protocol for information on the many Parts that do not require working copies. Where required, working copies of the moving documents and all other documents on the motion or application shall be submitted to the Motion Submission Part Courtroom (Room 130) on, but not before, the final return date. A Confirmation Notice from the NYSCEF system, which is generated when a document is e-filed, shall be firmly affixed, as the back page facing out, to each separate working copy or group of such copies. NY R NY CTY Procedure II(A) NY R NY CTY E FIL Doc. 2(B)(5)(a); NY R NY CTY J RUL Rule 14(a). For more information on working copies, including which parts don't require them, refer to NY R NY CTY E FIL Doc. 2(B)(6).
- *ONONDAGA COUNTY.* Any courtesy "working" copies, if required (see NY R ONDGA E FIL Protocol(B)(7)), must be provided directly to the assigned justice. NY R ONDGA E FIL Protocol(B)(9)(e). For information as to whether or not an Onondaga Supreme Court Justice requires working (courtesy) copies of e-filed documents, please consult the Onondaga County Individual E-filing Rules. NY R ONDGA E FIL Protocol(B)(7)(a). The Supreme Court Clerk's Office and the Onondaga County Clerk's Office will NOT accept the working copies. Working copies must be sent directly to the assigned justice's chambers. NY R ONDGA E FIL Protocol(B)(7)(b). A copy of the Confirmation Notice, generated by the NYSCEF system at the time a document is e-filed, must be attached to every working copy provided to chambers. If the Confirmation Notice is missing, the copy will not be accepted. NY R ONDGA E FIL Protocol(B)(7)(c). Courtesy copies do not become part of the official court record as maintained by the Onondaga County Clerk's Office and will be destroyed by chambers at the disposition of the case. In the event that counsel fails to file a document via NYSCEF, the document will not be part of the court record. NY R ONDGA E FIL Protocol(B)(7)(d).
- *QUEENS COUNTY.* Working copies of E-Filed notices of motion/notices of petition are NOT to be sent to the Motion Support Office. They must be brought to the calendar call in the judge's part. NY R L QUEENS MOT SUP Doc. 1. Unless otherwise directed or authorized by the court, counsel should file papers with the E-file system first and thereafter deliver a working copy to at the calendar call of the Centralized Motion Part or Assigned Justice in accordance with individual Part Rules. NY R L QUEENS E-FILE Doc. 1(E)(4). On the return date of a motion that has been E-filed, the movant must provide the Centralized Motion Part (CMP) with a working copy of the entire motion including the notice of motion with sequence number and all of the attached exhibits. The motion must have the confirmation of filing firmly affixed to the back of the papers (facing outward). The confirmation of filing is a separate notice from the payment notice and will say confirmation clearly across the top of the page. NY R L QUEENS E-FILE Doc. 1(H)(2)(a). The motion or Order to Show Cause must have clearly written across its face the words "Working Copy," it must also have the assigned Judge's name, motion sequence number and calendar number—which may be obtained from the posted calendar outside courtroom on the return date of the motion. A confirmation of filing must attached thereto. Working copies of e-filed Orders to Show Cause must contain a copy of the signed order and all supporting papers. NY R L QUEENS E-FILE Doc. 1(H)(2)(c). The Confirmation Notice must be an updated version that indicates the sequence number of the motion being submitted at the CMP calendar call. WORKING COPIES WITHOUT A CONFIRMATION NOTICE WILL NOT BE ACCEPTED. NY R L QUEENS E-FILE Doc. 1(H)(7).

vi. *ERIE COUNTY: Additional supplemental documents*

- *Notice of hard copy submission in e-filed case.* In accordance with NY R UNIF TRIAL CTS § 202.5-b(d),

the County Clerk shall refuse to accept for filing, hard copy papers filed to an action subject to electronic filing unless hard copy filing is permitted by the Uniform Rules or NY R ERIE E FIL Doc. 3 and the papers bear a completed Notice of Hard Copy Submission—E-Filed Case form. NY R ERIE E FIL Doc. 3(III)(D).

vii. *KINGS COUNTY: Additional supplemental documents*

- *Forms when filing in hard copy.* An attorney who certifies in good faith that he or she lacks the equipment or knowledge needed to e-file and have no staff member or employee under his or her direction who has such knowledge and equipment may opt out of participation in e-filing in a mandatory case by filing a "Notice of Opt-Out from Participation in Action Subject to Mandatory Electronic Filing" form EFM-2 with the Clerk. NY R L KINGS E FIL Doc. 1(A)(2). Where in accordance with the E-Filing Rules a party submits a document in hard copy in an e-filed case (principally, a document submitted by a nonparticipating party (e.g., an attorney) in a consensual case, an emergency filing made in accordance with the Mandatory E-Filing Rules, and any document filed with the court in hard copy by an attorney who has opted out of participation in mandatory e-filing, the document must bear the back page facing out, a "Notice of Hard Copy Submission—E-Filed Cases" form EFM-3. NY R L KINGS E FIL Doc. 1(B)(3).

viii. *NEW YORK COUNTY: Additional supplemental documents*

- *Notice of hard copy submission.* Where in accordance with the E-Filing Rules an attorney or an unrepresented litigant who is participating in e-filing submits a document in hard copy in an e-filed case, the document must bear, as the back page facing out, a Notice of Hard-Copy Submission—E-Filed Case (a form available in the "Forms" section on the NYSCEF website (Form EFM-3) and in the court's back offices). NY R NY CTY E FIL Doc. 2(B)(3). For more information refer to NY R NY CTY E FIL Doc. 2.
- *Unpublished decisions.* Whenever reliance is placed upon a decision or other authority not officially published or readily available to the New York County Supreme Court, a copy of the case or of pertinent portions of the authority shall be submitted with the motion papers. NY R NY CTY J RUL Rule 14(a).

ix. *ONONDAGA COUNTY: Additional supplemental documents*

- *Notice of hard copy submission.* Any papers to be filed with the court in an e-filed case must be filed online with the E-filing system except where a special exemption is granted (e.g., oversized maps, photographs). If such an exemption is granted, Form EFM-3, "Notice of Hard Copy Submission—E-Filed Case," must be attached to such documents forms which are not filed on line. Also, Form EFM-4 "Notice of Hard Copy Exhibit Filing" must be completed and uploaded to the action's e-file. Both of these forms may be found on the NYSCEF website. NY R ONDGA E FIL Protocol(B)(4).

x. *QUEENS COUNTY: Additional supplemental documents*

- *Notice of hard copy submission.* Any party opting out of the e-filing system must have a "Notice of Hard Copy Submission" firmly affixed to the back of the papers. NY R L QUEENS E-FILE Doc. 1(H)(2)(f).

2. *Documents for opposing party*

a. *Required documents*

i. *Opposition.* Refer to the General Requirements section of this document for information on the opposition.

- *Request for oral argument.* A party requesting oral argument shall set forth such request in its notice of motion or in its order to show cause or on the first page of the answering papers, as the case may be. Where all parties to a motion request oral argument, oral argument shall be granted unless the court shall determine it to be unnecessary. Where a motion is brought on by order to show cause, the court may set forth in the order that oral argument is required on the return date of the motion. NY R UNIF TRIAL CTS § 202.8(d).
- *QUEENS COUNTY: E-filing opposition papers.* E-filed opposition papers and/or reply papers must also be provided to the Centralized Motion Part in the same manner as the moving papers with the confirmation of filing firmly attached to the back of the papers. NY R L QUEENS E-FILE Doc. 1(H)(2)(d).

ii. *Proof of service.* In addition to complying with the provisions of NY CPLR Rule 2101, every paper filed in court shall have annexed thereto appropriate proof of service on all parties where required. NY R UNIF TRIAL CTS § 202.5(a).

b. *Supplemental documents*

i. *Supporting evidence; Exhibits.* The main supporting papers on a motion are affidavits, but any relevant exhibits, documents, depositions, etc., are also includible. SIEGEL-NYPRAC § 246.

- *Affidavits accompanying opposition.* Affidavits shall be for a statement of the relevant facts. NY R UNIF TRIAL CTS § 202.8(c).

- *Foreign language documents.* Where an affidavit or exhibit annexed to a paper served or filed is in a foreign language, it shall be accompanied by an English translation and an affidavit by the translator stating his qualifications and that the translation is accurate. NY CPLR Rule 2101(b).
- *Statement of attorney in lieu of affidavit.* The statement of an attorney admitted to practice in the courts of the state, or of a physician, osteopath or dentist, authorized by law to practice in the state, who is not a party to an action, when subscribed and affirmed by him to be true under the penalties of perjury, may be served or filed in the action in lieu of and with the same force and effect as an affidavit. NY CPLR Rule 2106.
- *NEW YORK COUNTY: Form of presented exhibits.* Exhibits should be tabbed and be legible; a typed version of any exhibit that is difficult to read should be submitted with the original. Exhibits printed on both sides of the page should be bound and tabbed on the side. NY R NY CTY J RUL Rule 14(a).
- *QUEENS COUNTY.* Attorneys submitting exhibits to the court on E-file cases shall make each exhibit a separate, labeled attachment to an affidavit/affirmation. NY R L QUEENS E-FILE Doc. 1(H)(4).

ii. *Brief.* Briefs shall be for a statement of the relevant law. NY R UNIF TRIAL CTS § 202.8(c).

iii. *Filing fees.* The County Clerk shall require the payment of any applicable statutory fees, or an order of the Court waiving payment of such fees, before accepting a paper for filing. NY R UNIF TRIAL CTS § 202.5(d)(1). For information on filing fees, if any, refer to NY CPLR § 8001, et seq.

- *ALBANY COUNTY.* In general, any filing subsequent to the commencement of an action which is designated as a motion or cross-motion requires the payment of a filing fee to the County Clerk's Office prior to submission to the Supreme Court Clerk's Office for referral to the assigned justice. The fee is assessed regardless of whether an application is made by notice of motion, order to show cause or ex parte. No fee will be charged upon the filing of a motion for poor person status in conjunction with an application which serves to commence an action or special proceeding. In the event a motion is received by the court unaccompanied by proof of payment to the County Clerk, the Supreme Court Clerk's Office will contact the submitting party to advise that the application will be held pending receipt of the filing fee only until the return date of the motion. If proof of payment is not submitted to the Supreme Court Clerk's Office by the return date (ex parte applications will be held ten (10) days), the papers will be returned by mail with a notification that the motion has been removed from the court's calendar and that it must be re-noticed and re-filed with the court along with the requisite filing fee. Inquiries concerning the applicability of the motion fee to a proposed filing may be directed to the Supreme Court Clerk's Office. NY R 3 JD SUP Doc. 1(B).
- *BRONX COUNTY.* In accordance with the new civil fee schedule set forth in Article 80 of the C.P.L.R. (NY CPLR § 8001, et seq.), effective July 14, 2003, all motions, and cross motions must be approved in Room 217 prior to payment of said fees in the County Clerk's Office, Room 118. NY R BRONX FIL R Doc. 8. The motion fee [must be] paid for via NYSCEF by credit/debit card. NY R BRONX E FIL R Doc. 1(1).
- *ERIE COUNTY.* Payment for fee-bearing NYSCEF documents must be made online via credit or debit card (American Express, MasterCard or Visa) at the time of submission. NY R ERIE E FIL Doc. 3(III)(E).
- *KINGS COUNTY.* The motion must be filed with NYSCEF and the motion fee paid. NY R L KINGS E FIL Doc. 1(D). Court fees in NYSCEF cases must be paid via NYSCEF by a credit or bank card (MasterCard, Visa, or American Express). Fees are no longer accepted in person in the Kings County Clerk's Office in NYSCEF cases. NY R L KINGS E FIL Doc. 1(B)(6).
- *NEW YORK COUNTY.* A motion fee must be paid on motions made in writing by notice of motion, order to show cause or ex parte after the commencement of an action. For this purpose, the term "action" shall mean any application to the court that requires the assignment of an index number, regardless of whether a formal pleading is filed. Applications or motions that commence an action and for which an index number fee must be paid require no motion fee. [A]ny motions made after the initial applications in these situations would require payment of the motion fee. A motion that is the initial application in a case commenced by the filing of a summons and complaint would require a motion fee since the filing of the summons and complaint rather than the application itself would require the purchase of an index number. NY R NY CTY Procedure II(A). In e-filed cases the motion fee must be paid when the documents are filed. Payment is made on-line by Visa, Mastercard, or American Express credit or bank card. NY R NY CTY Procedure II(A); NY R NY CTY E FIL Doc. 2(B)(5).
- *ONONDAGA COUNTY.* Court fees in e-filed cases must be paid online with the NYSCEF system using a credit card. The document is not considered to have been filed until payment of the fee has been tendered.

NY R ONDGA E FIL Protocol(B)(2). Fees must be paid on all cross motions. NY R ONDGA E FIL Protocol(B)(9)(e).

- *QUEENS COUNTY.* The Motion Support Office does not receive, forward or process any fees or waiver of fees. All applications requiring payment of statutory fees or waiver of fees must be sent directly to the Queens County Clerk's office. NY R L QUEENS MOT SUP Doc. 1. Court fees (e.g., RJI fee, motion fee) in E-filed cases may be paid for on-line using a credit card. Papers may also be filed with the E-file system and the fee may be paid at the County Clerk's Office. In the latter case, the paper is not considered to have been filed until payment of the fee has been tendered. NY R L QUEENS E-FILE Doc. 1(E)(1). The motion/petition shall be filed on-line and the fee paid for either on-line by credit card or by the "Pay at the County Clerk's Office" option. NY R L QUEENS E-FILE Doc. 1(H)(1).

iv. *Working copies.* The court may require the parties to provide working copies of documents filed electronically. In such event, each working copy shall include, firmly affixed thereto, a copy of a confirmation notice in a form prescribed by the Chief Administrator. NY R UNIF TRIAL CTS § 202.5-b(d)(5).

- *BRONX COUNTY.* After papers on motions have been e-filed, working copies thereof, with Confirmation Notice firmly attached as the back page facing out, must be submitted. (Each document or group of documents that is separately bound shall bear a Confirmation Notice.) Working copies lacking the Notice will not be accepted. WORKING COPIES OF MOTION PAPERS MUST BE SUBMITTED NO LATER THAN 4:45 P.M. ON THE RETURN DATE IN THE MOTION SUPPORT OFFICE (ROOM 217) AS EXPLAINED in NY R BRONX E FIL R Doc. 1(4). If an attorney has failed to submit required working copies on or before the return date, the motion will be transmitted as is to the Justice for such action as the Justice finds appropriate. Attorneys may submit working copies on motions by mail or overnight delivery. Any such submission shall be sent in a timely manner to the Motion Support Office (Room 217) and be conspicuously marked on the outside "NYSCEF Matter"; lack of such marking may delay processing. NY R BRONX E FIL R Doc. 1(4)(a).
- *ERIE COUNTY.* Electronically filed documents subject to review and processing by the Part Clerk do not require a working copy unless otherwise directed or provided for in IAS Part Rules. NY R UNIF TRIAL CTS § 202.5-b(d)(4), any working copy submitted shall include, as a cover page firmly fastened thereto, a copy of the Confirmation Notice generated by the NYSCEF site at the time of filing. Please consult the individual Justice's Part Rules and/or consult with the Judge's chambers to determine whether and how working copies are to be provided. Working copies will not be printed or delivered by the Erie County Clerk or the Chief Clerk of the Courts or any of their personnel to chambers. The official record of a document in an electronically filed case is the document filed via the NYSCEF system. Working copies are intended only for use by the Justice. The Court will discard all working copies after the Justice has finished with them. Thus, in the event that counsel fails to file a document via the NYSCEF system, the document will not be part of the court record. NY R ERIE E FIL Doc. 3(III)(O); NY R ERIE E FIL Doc. 3(V)(E).
- *KINGS COUNTY.* No courtesy copies of motion papers are required by the Court, except as may be required for electronic filing or by the Judge's Part Rules. In tort cases against the City of New York, courtesy copies shall be supplied to the Corporation Counsel's office in Brooklyn. NY R L KINGS Pt. C, Rule 5. Unless otherwise directed by the Court or as described herein, and with the exceptions listed below, in all NYSCEF cases in which an RJI has been filed, working copies of e-filed documents that are intended for judicial review must be submitted to the court. Working copies are not required of documents that are only processed by a support office (e.g. preliminary conference request, note of issue). Working copies shall include exhibit tabs and backs; for motion papers, the motion sequence number and the return date and part. The confirmation notice with the motion sequence number on it should be the back page of the motion facing out. In addition, the filer of a working copy must firmly bind thereto, with the back page facing out, a copy of the Confirmation Notice that was generated by NYSCEF when that document was efiled. Working copies that are submitted without the related Confirmation Notice will not be accepted. NY R L KINGS E FIL Doc. 1(B)(7); NY R L KINGS E FIL Doc. 1(D). WORKING COPIES OF MOTION PAPERS MUST BE SUBMITTED IN THE MOTION SUPPORT OFFICE (ROOM 227) AS EXPLAINED HEREIN. THEY MUST NOT BE DELIVERED TO THE PART OR CHAMBERS, EXCEPT WHERE THE INDIVIDUAL JUSTICE'S PART RULES PROVIDE OTHERWISE; DOING SO WILL CAUSE ADMINISTRATIVE CONFUSION AND POSSIBLE MISPLACEMENT OF PAPERS. Any such submission shall be sent in a timely manner (kindly review individual Justice's rules) and be conspicuously marked on the outside "NYSCEF Matter;" lack of such marking may delay processing. NY R L KINGS E FIL Doc. 1(D).

- *NEW YORK COUNTY.* Some Justices require that working copies of e-filed motion papers be submitted. See the E-filing Protocol for information on the many Parts that do not require working copies. Where required, working copies of the moving documents and all other documents on the motion or application shall be submitted to the Motion Submission Part Courtroom (Room 130) on, but not before, the final return date. A Confirmation Notice from the NYSCEF system, which is generated when a document is e-filed, shall be firmly affixed, as the back page facing out, to each separate working copy or group of such copies. NY R NY CTY Procedure II(A) NY R NY CTY E FIL Doc. 2(B)(5)(a); NY R NY CTY J RUL Rule 14(a). For more information on working copies, including which parts don't require them, refer to NY R NY CTY E FIL Doc. 2(B)(6).
- *ONONDAGA COUNTY.* Any courtesy "working" copies, if required (see NY R ONDGA E FIL Protocol(B)(7)), must be provided directly to the assigned justice. NY R ONDGA E FIL Protocol(B)(9)(e). For information as to whether or not an Onondaga Supreme Court Justice requires working (courtesy) copies of e-filed documents, please consult the Onondaga County Individual E-filing Rules. NY R ONDGA E FIL Protocol(B)(7)(a). The Supreme Court Clerk's Office and the Onondaga County Clerk's Office will NOT accept the working copies. Working copies must be sent directly to the assigned justice's chambers. NY R ONDGA E FIL Protocol(B)(7)(b). A copy of the Confirmation Notice, generated by the NYSCEF system at the time a document is e-filed, must be attached to every working copy provided to chambers. If the Confirmation Notice is missing, the copy will not be accepted. NY R ONDGA E FIL Protocol(B)(7)(c). Courtesy copies do not become part of the official court record as maintained by the Onondaga County Clerk's Office and will be destroyed by chambers at the disposition of the case. In the event that counsel fails to file a document via NYSCEF, the document will not be part of the court record. NY R ONDGA E FIL Protocol(B)(7)(d).
- *QUEENS COUNTY.* Working copies of E-Filed notices of motion/notices of petition are NOT to be sent to the Motion Support Office. They must be brought to the calendar call in the judge's part. NY R L QUEENS MOT SUP Doc. 1. Unless otherwise directed or authorized by the court, counsel should file papers with the E-file system first and thereafter deliver a working copy to at the calendar call of the Centralized Motion Part or Assigned Justice in accordance with individual Part Rules. NY R L QUEENS E-FILE Doc. 1(E)(4). On the return date of a motion that has been E-filed, the movant must provide the Centralized Motion Part (CMP) with a working copy of the entire motion including the notice of motion with sequence number and all of the attached exhibits. The motion must have the confirmation of filing firmly affixed to the back of the papers (facing outward). The confirmation of filing is a separate notice from the payment notice and will say confirmation clearly across the top of the page. NY R L QUEENS E-FILE Doc. 1(H)(2)(a). The motion or Order to Show Cause must have clearly written across its face the words "Working Copy," it must also have the assigned Judge's name, motion sequence number and calendar number—which may be obtained from the posted calendar outside courtroom on the return date of the motion. A confirmation of filing must attached thereto. Working copies of e-filed Orders to Show Cause must contain a copy of the signed order and all supporting papers. NY R L QUEENS E-FILE Doc. 1(H)(2)(c). The Confirmation Notice must be an updated version that indicates the sequence number of the motion being submitted at the CMP calendar call. WORKING COPIES WITHOUT A CONFIRMATION NOTICE WILL NOT BE ACCEPTED. NY R L QUEENS E-FILE Doc. 1(H)(7).

v. *ERIE COUNTY: Additional supplemental documents*

- *Notice of hard copy submission in e-filed case.* In accordance with NY R UNIF TRIAL CTS § 202.5-b(d), the County Clerk shall refuse to accept for filing, hard copy papers filed to an action subject to electronic filing unless hard copy filing is permitted by the Uniform Rules or NY R ERIE E FIL Doc. 3 and the papers bear a completed Notice of Hard Copy Submission—E-Filed Case form. NY R ERIE E FIL Doc. 3(III)(D).

vi. *KINGS COUNTY: Additional supplemental documents*

- *Forms when filing in hard copy.* An attorney who certifies in good faith that he or she lacks the equipment or knowledge needed to e-file and have no staff member or employee under his or her direction who has such knowledge and equipment may opt out of participation in e-filing in a mandatory case by filing a "Notice of Opt-Out from Participation in Action Subject to Mandatory Electronic Filing" form EFM-2 with the Clerk. NY R L KINGS E FIL Doc. 1(A)(2). Where in accordance with the E-Filing Rules a party submits a document in hard copy in an e-filed case (principally, a document submitted by a nonparticipating party (e.g., an attorney) in a consensual case, an emergency filing made in accordance with the Mandatory E-Filing Rules, and any document filed with the court in hard copy by an attorney who has opted out of

participation in mandatory e-filing, the document must bear the back page facing out, a "Notice of Hard Copy Submission—E-Filed Cases" form EFM-3. NY R L KINGS E FIL Doc. 1(B)(3).

vii. *NEW YORK COUNTY: Additional supplemental documents*

- *Notice of hard copy submission.* Where in accordance with the E-Filing Rules an attorney or an unrepresented litigant who is participating in e-filing submits a document in hard copy in an e-filed case, the document must bear, as the back page facing out, a Notice of Hard-Copy Submission—E-Filed Case (a form available in the "Forms" section on the NYSCEF website (Form EFM-3) and in the court's back offices). NY R NY CTY E FIL Doc. 2(B)(3). For more information refer to NY R NY CTY E FIL Doc. 2.

- *Unpublished decisions.* Whenever reliance is placed upon a decision or other authority not officially published or readily available to the New York County Supreme Court, a copy of the case or of pertinent portions of the authority shall be submitted with the motion papers. NY R NY CTY J RUL Rule 14(a).

viii. *ONONDAGA COUNTY: Additional supplemental documents*

- *Notice of hard copy submission.* Any papers to be filed with the court in an e-filed case must be filed online with the E-filing system except where a special exemption is granted (e.g., oversized maps, photographs). If such an exemption is granted, Form EFM-3, "Notice of Hard Copy Submission—E-Filed Case," must be attached to such documents forms which are not filed on line. Also, Form EFM-4 "Notice of Hard Copy Exhibit Filing" must be completed and uploaded to the action's e-file. Both of these forms may be found on the NYSCEF website. NY R ONDGA E FIL Protocol(B)(4).

ix. *QUEENS COUNTY: Additional supplemental documents*

- *Notice of hard copy submission.* Any party opting out of the e-filing system must have a "Notice of Hard Copy Submission" firmly affixed to the back of the papers. NY R L QUEENS E-FILE Doc. 1(H)(2)(f).

E. Format

1. *Form of documents*

a. *Size and form of paper.* Each paper served or filed shall be durable, white and, except for summonses, subpoenas, notices of appearance, notes of issue, orders of protection, temporary orders of protection and exhibits, shall be eleven by eight and one-half (11 x 8-1/2) inches in size. NY CPLR Rule 2101(a).

b. *Writing and language.* The writing shall be legible and in black ink. NY CPLR Rule 2101(a). Each paper served or filed shall be in the English language which, where practicable, shall be of ordinary usage. NY CPLR Rule 2101(b).

c. *Caption.* Each paper served or filed shall begin with a caption setting forth the name of the court, the venue, the title of the action, the nature of the paper and the index number of the action if one has been assigned. In all papers other than a summons, a complaint or a judgment it shall be sufficient to state the name of the first named party on each side with an appropriate indication of any omissions. NY CPLR Rule 2101(c).

i. *Further contents of first page.* After the first paper has been filed in each case the index number shall appear on the cover and first page to the right of the caption of every paper tendered for filing in the action. Each such cover and first page also shall contain an indication of the county of venue and a brief description of the nature of the paper and, where the case has been assigned to an individual judge, shall contain the name of the assigned judge to the right of the caption. NY R UNIF TRIAL CTS § 202.5(a); NY R UNIF TRIAL CTS § 202.5(b); NY R UNIF TRIAL CTS § 202.5(d)(1)(i).

ii. *ALBANY COUNTY: Request for oral argument.* A party may request oral argument on a motion by indicating such request on the first page of the notice of motion, order to show cause, or answering papers in the area across from the caption of the action/proceeding. NY R 3 JD SUP Doc. 1(B).

iii. *NEW YORK COUNTY: Request for oral argument.* Counsel who wish oral argument must so request conspicuously on the front of their papers. NY R NY CTY Procedure II(D).

d. *Index number.* No paper in an action in the supreme or a county court, other than an order submitted for signature to a judge out of court, shall be submitted for any purpose to the supreme or county court or to a clerk thereof unless there is endorsed on such paper the index number of the action assigned by the clerk of the county. NY CPLR § 8018(c).

i. *ALBANY COUNTY: Index number on all filed documents.* The index number, the request for judicial intervention number and the assigned justice's name shall appear on [all papers filed with the Court subsequent to the complaint]. NY R 3 JD SUP Doc. 1(A).

ii. *ERIE COUNTY: Index number after initial filing.* Cases that are initially commenced by the filing of papers with

the NYSCEF system are identified as e-filed cases by assignment of an Index Number that has "800-899" as the first three (3) digits of the index number (i.e. 802391/2012). NY R ERIE E FIL Doc. 3(II). [The] Index Number must be affixed to all document submissions, filings, and communications to the Erie County Clerk and the Court. Cases that are converted from paper to e-filing shall retain the original index number. NY R ERIE E FIL Doc. 3(II).

iii. *KINGS COUNTY: Index number after initial filing.* In cases commenced electronically by the filing of initiating papers with the NYSCEF system and payment of the statutory fees, the Kings County Clerk will issue an NYSCEF designated index number and the filer shall be notified via the NYSCEF system of the index number assigned and filing date. Such index number must be affixed to all document submissions, filings and communications to the Kings County Clerk and Supreme Court. If counsel faces exigent circumstances that require accelerated assignment, counsel may contact Administration of the Kings County Clerk at kcco-efile@nycourts.gov, during normal business hours of the court. NY R L KINGS E FIL Doc. 1(B)(5).

iv. *NEW YORK COUNTY: Index number on hard copy filings.* Papers subsequently presented for filing in hardcopy format will be filed in this jacket. NY R NY CTY Procedure I(B). Index numbers take the form of six digits followed by a slash and the four digits of the year the case began, e.g., 340705/2018. The first or first two integers of the index number identify the type of case. If a case is commenced electronically, the second integer will be a "5", except as indicated otherwise in the list below. There are many tax certiorari matters e-filed annually and the index numbers therefor will normally run over into those with a "6" as the second integer, and the same will occur with general cases if necessary. The principal types of cases and their index number categories are listed in NY R NY CTY Procedure I(B). NY R NY CTY Procedure I(B); NY R NY CTY Procedure XI(A).

v. *ONONDAGA COUNTY: Index number.* The index number must be referenced on all e-filed documents and correspondence. All e-filed case index numbers will contain the letters "EF" between the year and the file number (for example, 2012EF9999). NY R ONDGA E FIL Protocol(B)(1).

vi. *QUEENS COUNTY: Index number on converted cases.* Cases originally commenced in hard-copy form but later converted to an E-file case, either by stipulation or order will bear a regular index number initially. The County Clerk will issue a new E-file index number. NY R L QUEENS E-FILE Doc. 1(B).

e. *Line spacing.* Every paper filed in court, if typewritten, shall have at least double space between each line, except for quotations and the names and addresses of attorneys appearing in the action. NY R UNIF TRIAL CTS § 202.5(a).

f. *Font size.* Each. . .paper printed or typed, served or filed, except an exhibit or a summons, shall be in clear type of no less than ten (10) point in size. NY CPLR Rule 2101(a).

i. Whenever a requirement relating to size of type is stated in point size, the type size requirement shall be deemed met if the x-height of the type is a minimum of forty-five percent (45%) of the specified point size. Each point shall be measured as .351 millimeter. The x-height size shall be measured as it appears on the page. The x-height is the height of the lower case letters, exclusive of ascenders or descenders. NY CPLR § 105(t).

g. *Margins.* Every paper filed in court shall have at least one (1) inch margins. NY R UNIF TRIAL CTS § 202.5(a).

h. *Citations*

i. *Civil practice law and rules.* NY CPLR § 101, et seq. shall be known as the civil practice law and rules, and may be cited as "CPLR". Reference to a provision in the civil practice law and rules may, except when such provision is being enacted or amended, be made without indicating whether it is a rule or section. NY CPLR § 101.

i. *Indorsement by attorney.* Each paper served or filed shall be indorsed with the name, address and telephone number of the attorney for the party serving or filing the paper, or if the party does not appear by attorney, with the name, address and telephone number of the party. NY CPLR Rule 2101(d).

j. *One-sided printing.* In addition, every paper filed in court, other than an exhibit or printed form, shall contain writing on one side only, except that papers that are fastened on the side may contain writing on both sides. NY R UNIF TRIAL CTS § 202.5(a).

k. *Use of copies authorized.* Except where otherwise specifically prescribed, copies, rather than originals, of all papers, including orders, affidavits and exhibits may be served or filed. Where it is required that the original be served or filed and the original is lost or withheld, the court may authorize a copy to be served or filed. NY CPLR Rule 2101(e).

i. Where a certified copy of a paper is required by law, an attorney admitted to practice in the courts of the state may certify that it has been compared by him with the original and found to be a true and complete copy. Such a certificate, when subscribed by such attorney, has the same effect as if made by a clerk. NY CPLR § 2105.

l. *Recycled paper.* It is the policy of the Unified Court System that litigants, where practicable, should file or submit to

the courts of the Unified Court System of the State of New York papers printed or reproduced on recycled paper. Paper is considered recycled if it contains a minimum content of thirty percent (30%) waste paper. NY R UNIF TRIAL CTS § 215.2. The signature page of every paper filed or submitted to the court on recycled paper should bear the legend: "Printed [Reproduced] on Recycled Paper." NY R UNIF TRIAL CTS § 215.3.

m. *Form of request for judicial intervention; Copies.* A request for judicial intervention must be submitted, in duplicate, on a form authorized by the Chief of the Courts, with proof of service on the other parties to the action (but proof of service is not required where the application is ex parte). NY R UNIF TRIAL CTS § 202.6(a).

n. *KINGS COUNTY: Tabs on filings.* Motions, orders and other filed papers shall be indexed with protruding tabs. Clerks are required to reject papers that do not have protruding exhibit tabs, except papers in matrimonial cases and papers filed by pro se litigants. NY R L KINGS Pt. A, Papers.

o. *NEW YORK COUNTY: Length of briefs.* Unless advance permission otherwise is granted by the court for good cause, memoranda of law shall not exceed thirty (30) pages each (exclusive of table of contents and table of authorities) and affidavits/affirmations shall not exceed twenty-five (25) pages each. NY R NY CTY J RUL Rule 14(b).

p. *QUEENS COUNTY: Form and size of motion filings.* All motions filed in Queens Supreme Court-Civil Term, must adhere to the Motion Support rules and the rules of the assigned judge. NY R L QUEENS MOT SUP Doc. 1. Due to space limitations, the Motion Support Office cannot accept notices of motion/notices of petition and accompanying exhibits which measure greater than eight (8) inches. If your documents measure greater than eight (8) inches you are directed to submit only the notice of motion/notice of petition to the Motion Support Office and bring all exhibits to the calendar call on your return date. NY R L QUEENS MOT SUP Doc. 1.

2. *Form of electronic documents.* Each paper served or filed by electronic means, as defined in NY CPLR Rule 2103(f), shall be capable of being reproduced by the receiver so as to comply with the provisions of NY CPLR Rule 2101(a) through NY CPLR Rule 2101(d). NY CPLR Rule 2101(g).

   a. *File format.* All e-filed documents shall comply with the technical requirements set forth at the NYSCEF site. NY R UNIF TRIAL CTS § 202.5-b(d)(1)(i).

   b. *Heading of document.* The subject matter heading for each paper sent by electronic means must indicate that the matter being transmitted electronically is related to a court proceeding. NY CPLR Rule 2103(b)(7).

   c. *E-filed documents identification*

      i. *ERIE COUNTY.* E-filed cases must be readily identifiable and marked as such. If counsel presents papers to the Office of the Erie County Clerk or the Office of the Chief Clerk in a NYSCEF matter where authorized, counsel should alert the Clerk that the case is a NYSCEF matter. NY R ERIE E FIL Doc. 3(II).

      ii. *KINGS COUNTY.* The Supreme Court's Civil Case Information System ("CCIS") will further identify e-filed cases by the addition of a suffix to the index number (e.g. 500136/2006E). This suffix should be used on all documents filed with the court in e-filed matters. NY R L KINGS E FIL Doc. 1(A)(1).

3. *Signature blocks.* Every pleading, written motion, and other paper, served on another party or filed or submitted to the court shall be signed by an attorney, or by a party if the party is not represented by an attorney, with the name of the attorney or party clearly printed or typed directly below the signature. NY R CHIEF ADMIN § 130-1.1-a(a); NY R UNIF TRIAL CTS § 202.5(d)(1)(iv).

   a. *Printed name.* Beneath each signature shall be printed the name signed. NY CPLR Rule 2101(a).

   b. *Failure to sign.* Absent good cause shown, the court shall strike any unsigned paper if the omission of the signature is not corrected promptly after being called to the attention of the attorney or party. NY R CHIEF ADMIN § 130-1.1-a(a).

   c. *Signature as certification.* By signing a paper, an attorney or party certifies that, to the best of that person's knowledge, information and belief, formed after an inquiry reasonable under the circumstances the presentation of the paper or the contentions therein are not frivolous as defined in NY R CHIEF ADMIN § 130-1.1(c). NY R CHIEF ADMIN § 130-1.1-a(b)(1).

   d. *Electronic signatures.* A document shall be considered to have been signed by an attorney or party in compliance with NY R CHIEF ADMIN § 130-1.1-a if it has been signed by such attorney or party as provided in NY R UNIF TRIAL CTS § 202.5-b(e)(1) and it bears the signatory's name. NY R UNIF TRIAL CTS § 202.5-b(e)(2). An electronically filed document shall be considered to have been signed by, and shall be binding upon, the person identified as a signatory, if:

      i. It bears the physical signature of such person and is scanned into an electronic format that reproduces such signature; or

ii. The signatory has electronically affixed the digital image of his or her signature to the document; or

iii. It is electronically filed under the User ID and password of that person; or

iv. In a tax certiorari action in which the parties have stipulated to this procedure, it is an initiating document that is electronically filed without the signature of the signatory in a form provided above in NY R UNIF TRIAL CTS § 202.5-b(e)(iv), provided that, prior to filing, the document is signed in full in hard copy (which hard copy must be preserved until the conclusion of all proceedings, including appeals, in the case in which it is filed); or

v. In a small claims assessment review proceeding, it is a petition recorded by the NYSCEF site upon the filing of a text file as provided in NY R UNIF TRIAL CTS § 202.5-b(b)(1), provided that prior to filing, the document was signed in full in hard copy (which hard copy must be preserved until the conclusion of all proceedings in the matter, including article 78 (NY CPLR § 7801, et seq.) review and any appeals, and must be made available during the proceeding upon request of the respondent or the court); or

vi. It otherwise bears the electronic signature of the signatory in a format conforming to such standards and requirements as may hereafter be established by the Chief Administrator. NY R UNIF TRIAL CTS § 202.5-b(e).

4. *Confidentiality of personal information.* No person may file any document available for public inspection with any state agency, political subdivision, or in any court of this state that contains a Social Security account number of any other person, unless such other person is a dependent child, or has consented to such filing, except as required by federal or state law or regulation, or by court rule. NY GEN BUS § 399-ddd. Submissions pursuant to e-filing procedures shall have the same confidentiality rights as paper documents. NY R UNIF TRIAL CTS § 202.5-b(k)(1).

a. *Confidential personal information.* Except in the actions designated in NY R UNIF TRIAL CTS § 202.5(e)(1), or as otherwise provided by rule or law or court order, and whether or not a sealing order is or has been sought, the parties shall omit or redact confidential personal information in papers submitted to the court for filing. For purposes of NY R UNIF TRIAL CTS § 202.5(e), confidential personal information ("CPI") means:

i. The taxpayer identification number of an individual or an entity, including a Social Security number, an employer identification number, and an individual taxpayer identification number, except the last four (4) digits thereof;

ii. The date of an individual's birth, except the year thereof;

iii. The full name of an individual known to be a minor, except the minor's initials;

iv. A financial account number, including a credit and/or debit card number, a bank account number, an investment account number, and/or an insurance account number, except the last four (4) digits or letters thereof; and

v. Any of the documents or testimony in a matrimonial action protected by NY DOM REL § 235 or evidence sealed by the court in such an action which are attached as exhibits or referenced in the papers filed in any other civil action. For purposes of NY R UNIF TRIAL CTS § 202.5, a matrimonial action shall mean: an action to annul a marriage or declare the nullity of a void marriage, an action or agreement for a separation, an action for a divorce, or an action or proceeding for custody, visitation, writ of habeus corpus, child support, maintenance or paternity. NY R UNIF TRIAL CTS § 202.5(e)(1).

vi. *ERIE COUNTY.* An attorney or unrepresented litigant filing a document via the NYSCEF system must comply with the requirements of NY R UNIF TRIAL CTS § 202.5(e) regarding the redaction of Confidential Personal Information and NY GEN BUS § 399-ddd(6) concerning the filing of documents containing Social Security Numbers. It is the sole responsibility of counsel or unrepresented litigant filing to be aware of and to comply with existing laws requiring non-disclosure of personal information contained in any document e-filed in NYSCEF. NY R ERIE E FIL Doc. 3(III)(G); NY R ERIE E FIL Doc. 3(III).

vii. *KINGS COUNTY.* An attorney or unrepresented litigant filing a document via the NYSCEF system must comply with the requirements of General Business Law § 399-dd(6), which often require redaction of any Social Security number that appear in the original document. The NYSCEF system automatically redacts portions of filed documents which apparently contain Social Security numbers pursuant to NY R UNIF TRIAL CTS § 202.5-b(k). In the event the filing party receives e-mail notice through NYSCEF that a Social Security number in a filed document has been redacted, and the filing party concludes such redaction is erroneous, the filer should click on the link provided in the e-mail to permit the County Clerk to revert the redaction. For Confidential Personal Information, see NY R UNIF TRIAL CTS § 202.5(e) and NY R L KINGS E FIL Doc. 1(B)(11). [Editor's note: the reference to General Business Law § 399-dd(6) is likely a reference to NY GEN BUS § 399-ddd(6)]. NY R L KINGS E FIL Doc. 1(B)(10); NY R L KINGS E FIL Doc. 1(K)(1).

viii. *NEW YORK COUNTY.* It is the responsibility of counsel and parties to comply with rules restricting disclosure

of confidential personal information. Nevertheless, NYSCEF screens filings and endeavors to identify any that contain social security numbers. When such numbers are discovered through this process, NYSCEF will restrict portions of or all of such documents from public view. Where NYSCEF has redacted what it believes to be a social security number, it will transmit to the filer a notice advising of the action taken and requesting that the filer review the matter and provide notification as set forth in the notice if the redaction has been made in error. NY R NY CTY E FIL Doc. 2(K)(1); NY R NY CTY J RUL Rule A-1. Documents filed in the past in "secure status" under a procedure no longer in place will retain that status unless otherwise directed by the court. NY R NY CTY E FIL Doc. 2(K)(2).

b. *Submission of confidential personal information.* Where a person submitting a paper to a court for filing believes in good faith that the inclusion of the full confidential personal information described in NY R UNIF TRIAL CTS § 202.5(e)(1) is material and necessary to the adjudication of the action or proceeding before the court, he or she may apply to the court for leave to serve and file together with a paper in which such information has been set forth in abbreviated form a confidential affidavit or affirmation setting forth the same information in unabbreviated form, appropriately referenced to the page or pages of the paper at which the abbreviated form appears. NY R UNIF TRIAL CTS § 202.5(e)(3).

c. *Home addresses.* For information on when home addresses and other personal information must be redacted, refer to NY CPLR Rule 2103-a.

5. *Defective papers.* A defect in the form of a paper, if a substantial right of a party is not prejudiced, shall be disregarded by the court, and leave to correct shall be freely given. NY CPLR Rule 2101(f). Papers that are stapled or bound securely shall not be rejected for filing simply because they are not bound with a backer of any kind. NY R UNIF TRIAL CTS § 202.5(a). A paper filed in accordance with the rules of the chief administrator or any local rule or practice established by the court shall be deemed filed. NY CPLR Rule 2102(b).

   a. *Objection to defective papers.* The party on whom a paper is served shall be deemed to have waived objection to any defect in form unless, within fifteen (15) days after the receipt thereof, the party on whom the paper is served returns the paper to the party serving it with a statement of particular objections. NY CPLR Rule 2101(f).

F. Filing and Service Requirements

1. *Filing requirements.* Except where otherwise prescribed by law or order of court, papers required to be filed shall be filed with the clerk of the court in which the action is triable. In an action or proceeding in supreme or court, papers required to be filed shall be filed with the clerk of the county in which the proceeding is brought. NY CPLR Rule 2102(a).

   a. *Furnishing papers to the court.* Each party shall furnish to the court all papers served by him. The moving party shall furnish at the hearing all other papers not already in the possession of the court necessary to the consideration of the questions involved. Where such papers are in the possession of an adverse party, they shall be produced by him at the hearing on notice served with the motion papers. Only papers served in accordance with the provisions of NY CPLR Rule 2214 shall be read in support of, or in opposition to, the motion, unless the court for good cause shall otherwise direct. NY CPLR Rule 2214(c).

      i. *Submission to judge.* All papers for signature or consideration of the court shall be presented to the clerk of the trial court in the appropriate courtroom or clerk's office, except that where the clerk is unavailable or the judge so directs, papers may be submitted to the judge and a copy filed with the clerk at the first available opportunity. All papers for any judge that are filed in the clerk's office shall be promptly delivered to the judge by the clerk. The papers shall be clearly addressed to the judge for whom they are intended and prominently show the nature of the papers, the title and index number of the action in which they are filed, the judge's name and the name of the attorney or party submitting them. NY R UNIF TRIAL CTS § 202.5(b).

      ii. *BRONX COUNTY: Approval of motions before filing.* All motion papers must be approved by the Motion Support Office, Supreme Court, Civil Term, room 217, before the motion papers are filed and the appropriate fee paid to the County Clerk. NY R BRONX FIL R Doc. 1.

      iii. *ERIE COUNTY: Filing motions.* A motion on notice or a notice of petition in a NYSCEF case shall be filed through the NYSCEF system and must be accompanied by a Request for Judicial Intervention if the motion is being filed upon commencement of the action or if the matter has not yet been assigned to an IAS Justice. In addition, cross motions with the appropriate filing fees and opposition and reply papers must be submitted via the NYSCEF system. NY R ERIE E FIL Doc. 3(V)(A).

      iv. *NEW YORK COUNTY: Filing hard copies.* Where in the narrow circumstances described by the e-filing rules a motion is made in hard-copy form or opposition papers are submitted in such form in an e-filed case, the hard-copy documents shall be submitted in the same way papers are submitted in non-e-filed cases, except that

there shall be firmly affixed to each separate document or group of documents, as the back page facing out, a Notice of Hard Copy Submission—E-Filed Case. NY R NY CTY Procedure II(A). For more information on filing in hard copy cases, refer to NY R NY CTY Procedure II(A).

v. *ONONDAGA COUNTY: Submission of responsive papers and cross-motions.* Cross-motions, opposition and reply papers must be submitted online. NY R ONDGA E FIL Protocol(B)(9)(e). Motions and Orders to Show Cause are assigned a sequence number by the system. Counsel must be sure that cross motions and other filings correspond with the correct sequence number so that a cross motion will not be associated with the wrong original motion. NY R ONDGA E FIL Protocol(B)(9)(f).

b. *Electronic filing.* On consent, documents may be filed and served by electronic means in Supreme Court in such civil actions and in such counties as shall be authorized by order of the Chief Administrator of the Courts and only to the extent and in the manner provided in NY R UNIF TRIAL CTS § 202.5-b. NY R UNIF TRIAL CTS § 202.5-b(a)(1). For the definitions of terms used in electronic filing, refer to NY R UNIF TRIAL CTS § 202.5-b(a)(2).

i. *E-filing mandatory.* In any action subject to e-filing, all documents required to be filed with the court by an e-filing party shall be filed and served electronically, except as provided in NY R UNIF TRIAL CTS § 202.5-b. NY R UNIF TRIAL CTS § 202.5-b(d)(1)(i).

- *ERIE COUNTY.* Case types currently eligible and accepted for e-filing are listed at the NYSCEF website. Note that some actions or special proceedings, (i.e., name changes) which are otherwise subject to mandatory e-filing, if commenced by unrepresented litigants will NOT be maintained in the NYSCEF system; individual cases may be found either at NYSCEF or in the Erie County Clerk's online records system. NY R ERIE E FIL Doc. 3(I)(E).
- *KINGS COUNTY.* Cases that are commenced by filing of the initiating papers with NYSCEF are identified as e-filed cases by assignment of a special index number (i.e., Index Numbers beginning with 500,000). NY R L KINGS E FIL Doc. 1(A)(1). All cases required to be e-filed are listed in Uniform Rule 202.5-bb (Mandatory E-Filing Rules) and on the NYSCEF website. All such cases must be commenced by filing with the County Clerk electronically through NYSCEF and all subsequent documents in such cases must be e-filed. Any questions regarding mandatory e-filing in Kings County can be e-mailed to kcco-efile@nycourts.gov. NY R L KINGS E FIL Doc. 1(A)(2).
- *NEW YORK COUNTY.* Unless otherwise provided in the Rules or in NY R NY CTY E FIL Doc. 2 or where a special exemption is granted due to physical requirements (e.g., oversized maps; see NY R NY CTY E FIL Doc. 2(B)(10)), all documents to be filed with the court in a NYSCEF case, including all documents on motions and all letters to the court (where permitted), must be filed with the NYSCEF system. Documents that attorneys would not ordinarily file with the court in a hard-copy case need not be e-filed. Unless otherwise provided by the E-Filing Rules or this Protocol, in e-filed cases the County Clerk and the court will not accept documents filed in paper form. NY R NY CTY E FIL Doc. 2(B)(1). E-filing is mandatory in all types of cases (other than election law, matrimonial, Art. 78, and Mental Hygiene Law matters, and Art. 70 habeas corpus proceedings) that are commenced in this court on or after February 19, 2013. All such cases must be commenced by filing with the County Clerk electronically through NYSCEF and all subsequent documents in such cases must be e-filed. NY R NY CTY E FIL Doc. 2(A)(2)(a). For more information, including information on consensual e-filing and filing scanned hard copy documents, refer to NY R NY CTY E FIL Doc. 2(A)(2).
- *QUEENS COUNTY.* All authorized Torts, Commercial and Tax Certiorari cases may be commenced by E-Filing, however all parties must consent for the action to continue as an E-file case. NY R L QUEENS E-FILE Doc. 1(A). All papers to be filed with the court in an E-filed case shall be filed on-line with the E-file system except as directed by the court. Papers that attorneys would not ordinarily file with the court in a hard-copy case need not be filed in an E-filed matter. NY R L QUEENS E-FILE Doc. 1(E)(2).

ii. *Who may file.* Documents may be filed or served electronically only by a person who has registered as an authorized e-filing user or as otherwise provided in NY R UNIF TRIAL CTS § 202.5-b(c). NY R UNIF TRIAL CTS § 202.5-b(c)(1).

iii. *When filing made.* Documents may be transmitted at any time of the day or night to the NYSCEF site. A document other than an order or judgment is filed when its electronic transmission or, in the case of a petition that is e-filed by submission of a text file as provided in NY R UNIF TRIAL CTS § 202.5-b(b)(1), the electronic transmission of the text file is recorded at that site, provided, however, that where payment of a fee is required upon the filing of a document, the document is not filed until transmission of the document and the information

or form or information as required in NY R UNIF TRIAL CTS § 202.5-b(d)(2)(i), NY R UNIF TRIAL CTS § 202.5-b(d)(2)(ii) or NY R UNIF TRIAL CTS § 202.5-b(d)(2)(iii) has been recorded at the NYSCEF site; or, if no transmission of that information or form or information is recorded, where permitted by the County Clerk, until payment is presented to the County Clerk. NY R UNIF TRIAL CTS § 202.5-b(d)(3)(i).

iv. *Notification of filing.* No later than the close of business on the business day following the electronic filing of a document, a notification, in a form prescribed by the Chief Administrator, shall be transmitted electronically by the NYSCEF site to the person filing such document and the e-mail service addresses of all other participating parties in such action. NY R UNIF TRIAL CTS § 202.5-b(d)(3)(ii).

v. *Removal of confidential information and other corrections.* If a document filed electronically is subsequently discovered to contain confidential data—including but not limited to trade secrets, information protected by confidentiality agreement, or personal confidential information as defined by statute or court rule—or otherwise to have been filed in error, the filer or another party or affected person may (1) notify the parties and any non-party filers in the action of the confidentiality issue or other error raised by the filing, and of his or her intention to seek judicial relief to correct the filing: (2) following such notification, request that the appropriate County Clerk, exercising his or her administrative discretion, place the document temporarily in "restricted" status on the NYSCEF site, to be made available for viewing by court staff and the parties but not the general public; and (3) file an application to correct the filing by order to show cause within five (5) business days of such notification (or such time as the court may direct), including a request for preliminary injunctive relief limiting interim disclosure of the document at issue. Unless otherwise directed by the court, any document placed in restricted status in response to such a request shall be returned to public view upon expiration of this five (5) day period. The Chief Administrator of the Courts shall promulgate forms to implement this process. NY R UNIF TRIAL CTS § 202.5-b(d)(3)(iii).

- *KINGS COUNTY.* For information on what to do when a document was erroneously filed with confidential information, refer to NY R L KINGS E FIL Doc. 1(B)(11).
- *NEW YORK COUNTY.* For information on what to do when a document was erroneously filed with confidential information, refer to NY R NY CTY E FIL Doc. 2(B)(8).
- *QUEENS COUNTY.* For information on what to do when a document was erroneously filed with confidential information, refer to NY R L QUEENS E-FILE Doc. 1(E)(7).

vi. *Documents requiring judge's signature.* Except where the court directs otherwise, any document that requires a judge's signature shall be transmitted electronically and in hard copy to the court. NY R UNIF TRIAL CTS § 202.5-b(d)(6).

vii. *Documents which would be inconvenient to file electronically; Hard copies.* Notwithstanding any other provision of NY R UNIF TRIAL CTS § 202.5-b, and subject to such guidelines as may be established by the Chief Administrative Judge, the County Clerk or his or her designee may require or permit a party to file in hard copy, in accordance with procedures set by the County Clerk or designee, an exhibit or other document which it is impractical or inconvenient to file electronically. NY R UNIF TRIAL CTS § 202.5-b(d)(7).

- *ERIE COUNTY.* Please contact the Supervisor of Actions & Proceedings, Erie County Clerk's Office by calling (716) 858-6662 or the Deputy County Clerk—Legal at (716) 858-6348 for information. NY R ERIE E FIL Doc. 3(III)(F).
- *KINGS COUNTY.* With limited exceptions, as set forth in the Uniform Rules and herein, all documents to be filed with the court in a NYSCEF case shall be filed online via the NYSCEF system. However, should the size, consistency or context of a hard copy document preclude electronic filing, the user shall electronically file a "Notice of Hard Copy Submission—E-Filed Cases" form EFM-3. Any hard copy submitted pursuant to NY R L KINGS E FIL Doc. 1(B)(9) shall include, as a cover page firmly fastened thereto, a copy of the Confirmation Notice received from the NYSCEF site confirming receipt of the "Notice of Hard Copy Submission—E-Filed Cases". Any party may object to such hard copy filing. The Court, in response to such objection, may, following the hard copy filing, fashion such relief as it deems appropriate pursuant to and in furtherance of the Uniform Rules and NY R L KINGS E FIL Doc. 1, including, but not limited to, an Order directing the filing party to file such documents online via the NYSCEF system. When exhibits are impractical to file pursuant to NY R UNIF TRIAL CTS § 202.5-b(d)(7), an additional "Notice of Hard Copy Exhibit Filing" form EFM-4 is required to be submitted. NY R L KINGS E FIL Doc. 1(B)(9).
- *NEW YORK COUNTY.* If a filer needs to submit unusual exhibits in original form that cannot practically be

e-filed, such as oversized maps or electronic recordings, the filer should consult with the County Clerk's E-File Department by telephone at 646-386-3737 (procedural questions only) or by e-mail at ccnyef@nycourts.gov, which will normally require that the filer retain custody of the original subject to possible future directives of the court. NY R NY CTY E FIL Doc. 2(B)(10). In such instances, the filing counsel shall file with NYSCEF a "placeholder" in the form of a Notice of Hard Copy Exhibit Filing (NYSCEF Form EF 21). The Notice should be uploaded to NYSCEF as document type "Exhibit" and the filer should indicate in the "Additional Document Information" field that the filer is retaining custody of the original. Failure to e-file the Notice may result in a gap in the official record of the court. NY R NY CTY E FIL Doc. 2(B)(10).

viii. *Documents containing sensitive or proprietary information.* In an action subject to e-filing, any person may apply for an order prohibiting or restricting the electronic filing in the action of specifically identified materials on the grounds that such materials are subject to copyright or other proprietary rights, or trade secret or other privacy interests, and that electronic filing in the action is likely to result in substantial prejudice to those rights or interests. NY R UNIF TRIAL CTS § 202.5-b(k)(2).

ix. *Refusal to accept paper filings.* In accordance with NY CPLR Rule 2102(c), a County Clerk and a chief clerk of the Supreme Court or County Court, as appropriate, shall refuse to accept for filing papers filed in actions and proceedings when the paper sought to be filed:

- Is in an action subject to electronic filing pursuant to Rules of the Chief Administrator,
- Is not being filed electronically, and
- Does not include the notice required by NY R UNIF TRIAL CTS § 202.5-b(d)(1). NY R UNIF TRIAL CTS § 202.5(d)(1)(v); NY R UNIF TRIAL CTS § 202.5-bb(d).

x. *Emergency filings; Hard copies.* For information on when an emergency filing may be filed and served in hard copy, refer to NY R UNIF TRIAL CTS § 202.5-b(d)(1)(ii), NY R UNIF TRIAL CTS § 202.5-b(d)(1)(iii) and NY R UNIF TRIAL CTS § 202.5-bb(c)(3).

- *KINGS COUNTY.* Under the rules, a participating emergency e-filer must electronically file the documents initially filed in hard copy form within three (3) business days of the emergency filing; the originals will be discarded after the documents have been processed and the failure to e-file as required will therefore lead to an incomplete record. NY R L KINGS E FIL Doc. 1(B)(3).
- *NEW YORK COUNTY.* Occasionally an emergency will arise requiring expedited entry of a document with the County Clerk (e.g., an order issued in the courtroom after a conference or argument of a critical matter), such as for purposes of an immediate appeal. Expedition can be achieved by the Part as follows: the document should be carried by a Court Officer or staff member to the General Clerk's Office to assure immediate and proper recordation in the computer and, as appropriate, the posting of the document to NYSCEF or the Supreme Court Records On-Line Library ("Scroll"). The court will accommodate counsel in emergencies. NY R NY CTY Procedure XI(A).
- *NEW YORK COUNTY.* For more information on how to bring emergency matters before the court, refer to NY R NY CTY Procedure IV.

xi. *Technical failures.* The NYSCEF site shall be considered to be subject to a technical failure on a given day if the site is unable to accept filings or provide access to filed documents continuously or intermittently over the course of any period of time greater than one (1) hour after 12:00 noon of that day. Notice of all such technical failures shall be provided on the site. NY R UNIF TRIAL CTS § 202.5-b(i).

- When e-filing is hindered by a technical failure, a party may file with the appropriate clerk and serve in hard copy. NY R UNIF TRIAL CTS § 202.5-b(i). In the event an attorney or party shall file and serve documents in hard copy pursuant to NY R UNIF TRIAL CTS § 202.5-b(i), each such document shall include the notice required by NY R UNIF TRIAL CTS § 202.5-b(d)(1), and the filer shall file those documents with the NYSCEF site within three (3) business days after restoration of normal operations at that site. NY R UNIF TRIAL CTS § 202.5-b(i).
- With the exception of deadlines that by law cannot be extended, the time for filing of any document that is delayed due to technical failure of the site shall be extended for one (1) day for each day on which such failure occurs, unless otherwise ordered by the court. NY R UNIF TRIAL CTS § 202.5-b(i).
- *ERIE COUNTY.* When filing by electronic means is hindered by a technical failure, please refer to the NY R UNIF TRIAL CTS § 202.5-b(i). NY R ERIE E FIL Doc. 3(III)(K).

- *KINGS COUNTY.* When filing by electronic means is hindered by a NYSCEF technical failure (as set forth in NY R UNIF TRIAL CTS § 202.5-b(i)), a party may file with the appropriate Clerk in hard copy. Except for deadlines that by law cannot be extended (e.g. Statute of limitations, Notice of Appeal), the time for filing of any document that is delayed due to technical failure of the NYSCEF system shall be extended for one day for each day on which such failure occurs, unless otherwise ordered by the court. NY R L KINGS E FIL Doc. 1(B)(13).
- *ONONDAGA COUNTY.* When filing by electronic means is hindered by a technical failure (as set forth in NY R UNIF TRIAL CTS § 202.5-b(h)(3)(i)), a party may file a hard copy with the County Clerk. With the exception of deadlines that by law cannot be extended (e.g., a statute of limitations or the deadline for filing a Notice of Appeal), the time for filing of any document that is delayed due to technical failure of the NYSCEF system will be extended for one day for each day on which such failure occurs, unless otherwise ordered by the court. A "Notice of Hard Copy Filing Submission—E-Filed Case' must accompany any documents not filed via NYSCEF. NY R ONDGA E FIL Protocol(B)(8).

xii. *Filing fees.* For information on what information must be provided to pay filing fees, refer to NY R UNIF TRIAL CTS § 202.5-b(d)(2).

xiii. *Exemption from e-filing.* For information on exemptions from e-filing, refer to NY R UNIF TRIAL CTS § 202.5-bb(e).

xiv. *Filing exhibits*

- *ERIE COUNTY.* In the NYSCEF system, each exhibit must be uploaded as a separate .pdf file. After uploading a primary document, please choose the document type "Exhibit" and enter the appropriate number or letter and a brief description of the exhibit; each exhibit should bear a separate cover sheet clearly marked as "Exhibit A," "Exhibit B," etc. "Exhibit A" or "Exhibit B" is unacceptable as a brief description of the exhibit. Exhibits, where referenced in a signed Order as attached or affixed shall be uploaded with the signed Order as one .pdf document. NY R ERIE E FIL Doc. 3(III)(H); NY R ERIE E FIL Doc. 3(V)(D).
- *KINGS COUNTY.* In the NYSCEF system, each exhibit should be uploaded as a separate PDF file. After uploading a primary document, please choose the document type "Exhibit", enter the appropriate number or letter, and be sure to place a check mark to the right of "Attach to main document". Each exhibit shall bear a separate cover sheet clearly marked as Exhibit A, Exhibit B, etc. NY R L KINGS E FIL Doc. 1(B)(12). Whenever possible, attorneys submitting exhibits in NYSCEF cases should make each exhibit a separate attachment to an affidavit/affirmation in the system (i.e., multiple exhibits should not be filed as a single PDF). NY R L KINGS E FIL Doc. 1(D)(1).
- *NEW YORK COUNTY.* Attorneys submitting exhibits in NYSCEF cases should make each exhibit a separate attachment to an affidavit/affirmation in the system; i.e., exhibits should not be filed as a single PDF-A together with the affidavit/affirmation or grouped together as a single PDF-A attachment because either of these two formats makes it difficult for the Justice to locate particular exhibits as needed. Counsel must also include appropriate descriptive language in the "Additional Document Information" field in NYSCEF. NY R NY CTY E FIL Doc. 2(D)(6).
- *ONONDAGA COUNTY.* All exhibits in e-filed cases must be e-filed individually as separate attachments. NY R ONDGA E FIL Protocol(B)(9)(b).

xv. *Correcting documents*

- *ERIE COUNTY.* Submission of documents which, upon examination, require correction or addition will result in notification to the filer advising that the document has been returned for correction. The filer shall make the required corrections and/or additions as indicated in the e-mail transmission sent by the County Clerk or Part Clerk through the NYSCEF site. The corrected documents may be resubmitted using the "Re-file this document" link highlighted in the filer's document list for the respective case. Please note that in the case of multiple submissions, all related documents filed at the same time may be removed from the case record and returned until all documents are properly submitted. NY R ERIE E FIL Doc. 3(III)(J).
- *KINGS COUNTY.* Submission of documents which, upon examination, require correction or addition will result in notification to the filer advising that there is a problem with a document. The filer shall make the required corrections and/or additions and resubmit the corrected document using the "Refile this document" link. In the event a document is returned for correction, the original file date will be preserved. For corrections of documents filed with the Kings County Clerk which require a court order, refer to the

procedure in NY R UNIF TRIAL CTS § 202.5-b(d)(3)(iii) and NY R L KINGS E FIL Doc. 1(B)(11). NY R L KINGS E FIL Doc. 1(B)(3).

- *ONONDAGA COUNTY.* If there is an error or an additional document is required, the system will notify the filing party, who will make the corrections/additions and resubmit them online. NY R ONDGA E FIL Protocol(B)(6).
- *QUEENS COUNTY.* Generally speaking, documents that have been E-filed will not thereafter be deleted by the County Clerk from NYCEF because the filer asserts that the filing contains an error or a significant omission. When the filer wishes to correct a perceived error or omission in a filed document, he or she should file an amended version of the document, with the original remaining on file, or else obtain a court order providing for deletion of the original. The County Clerk will only delete a document upon request of the filer or on the County Clerk's own initiative when it is obvious from the face of the document alone that the filer made a fundamental error and never intended to file the document that was filed (e.g., a completely unrelated non-litigation document, a different case, or a wrong county). The County Clerk will advise the filer when any such fundamental errors are detected. NY R L QUEENS E-FILE Doc. 1(E)(6).

c. *Facsimile filing.* In the Supreme Court, facsimile filing shall be limited to commercial claims and tax certiorari, conservatorship, and mental hygiene proceedings in Monroe, Westchester, New York and Suffolk Counties. NY R UNIF TRIAL CTS § 202.5-a(a)(1). Refer to NY R UNIF TRIAL CTS § 202.5-a for information on the procedures for facsimile filing.

i. *NEW YORK COUNTY.* Unless indicated otherwise by the court in a particular case or in NY R NY CTY J RUL Doc. 1, Justices do not accept papers by fax. NY R NY CTY J RUL Rule 4.

d. *ERIE COUNTY: Filing request for judicial intervention.* An RJI in a NYSCEF case shall be filed via the NYSCEF system and will be filed after all other documents have been uploaded. The filer may choose between filing a .pdf image of the prepared RJI and any Addendum or having the system prepare the RJI which shall conform to Uniform Rules. Addenda, such as the Commercial Division Addendum, if prepared by the filer must be filed simultaneously with and attached to an RJI and uploaded as one .pdf document with the RJI. If the RJI is prepared by the e-filing system, no separate Addendum is required. Whether or not the filer elects to allow NYSCEF to create the RJI or chooses to upload a prepared RJI, data in addition to the nature of the judicial intervention, including information that appears on any Addenda will be collected through completion of the fields presented. If the filing of the RJI is accomplished through a filing agent, a prepared RJI and Addendum must be filed in lieu of the creation of the RJI by the NYSCEF system, as the RJI must be signed by the attorney. NY R ERIE E FIL Doc. 3(IV). For information on RJIs in specific types of action, refer to NY R ERIE E FIL Doc. 3(IV).

2. *Service requirements*

a. *Who may serve.* Except where otherwise prescribed by law or order of court, papers may be served by any person not a party of the age of eighteen years or over. NY CPLR Rule 2103(a).

b. *Service upon attorney.* Except where otherwise prescribed by law or order of court, papers to be served upon a party in a pending action shall be served upon the party's attorney. Where the same attorney appears for two or more parties, only one (1) copy need be served upon the attorney. Such service upon an attorney shall be made:

i. By delivering the paper to the attorney personally. NY CPLR Rule 2103(b)(1).

ii. By mailing the paper to the attorney at the address designated by that attorney for that purpose or, if none is designated, at the attorney's last known address; service by mail shall be complete upon mailing. NY CPLR Rule 2103(b)(2).

- *BRONX COUNTY.* Service by mail must be within the state. NY R BRONX FIL R Doc. 3.

iii. If the attorney's office is open, by leaving the paper with a person in charge, or if no person is in charge, by leaving it in a conspicuous place; or if the attorney's office is not open, by depositing the paper, enclosed in a sealed wrapper directed to the attorney, in the attorney's office letter drop or box. NY CPLR Rule 2103(b)(3).

iv. By leaving it at the attorney's residence within the state with a person of suitable age and discretion. Service upon an attorney shall not be made at the attorney's residence unless service at the attorney's office cannot be made. NY CPLR Rule 2103(b)(4).

v. By transmitting the paper to the attorney by facsimile transmission, provided that a facsimile telephone number is designated by the attorney for that purpose. Service by facsimile transmission shall be complete upon the receipt by the sender of a signal from the equipment of the attorney served indicating that the transmission was received, and the mailing of a copy of the paper to that attorney. The designation of a facsimile telephone number

in the address block subscribed on a paper served or filed in the course of an action or proceeding shall constitute consent to service by facsimile transmission in accordance with NY CPLR Rule 2103(b)(5). An attorney may change or rescind a facsimile telephone number by serving a notice on the other parties. NY CPLR Rule 2103(b)(5).

vi. By dispatching the paper to the attorney by overnight delivery service at the address designated by the attorney for that purpose or, if none is designated, at the attorney's last known address. Service by overnight delivery service shall be complete upon deposit of the paper enclosed in a properly addressed wrapper into the custody of the overnight delivery service for overnight delivery, prior to the latest time designated by the overnight delivery service for overnight delivery. "Overnight delivery service" means any delivery service which regularly accepts items for overnight delivery to any address in the state. NY CPLR Rule 2103(b)(6).

vii. By transmitting the paper to the attorney by electronic means where and in the manner authorized by the chief administrator of the courts by rule and, unless such rule shall otherwise provide, such transmission shall be upon the party's written consent. The subject matter heading for each paper sent by electronic means must indicate that the matter being transmitted electronically is related to a court proceeding. NY CPLR Rule 2103(b)(7).

- *KINGS COUNTY.* Pursuant to the E-Filing Rules, service of interlocutory documents is made by posting a document to the NYSCEF site, which automatically and immediately transmits an email notice of the filing, including a link to the document, to all participating counsel and unrepresented litigants on the case. The Rules also authorize service by other methods permitted by the CPLR. If service by such other method is made, proof of service must be filed with NYSCEF. NY R L KINGS E FIL Doc. 1(I).
- *NEW YORK COUNTY.* Service. . .will be made automatically through NYSCEF upon all participating counsel and unrepresented parties in the case. There are limited exceptions to the requirement for e-filing in the covered kinds of cases. NY R NY CTY Procedure XI(A). Pursuant to the E-Filing Rules, service of interlocutory documents is made by posting a document to the NYSCEF site, which automatically and immediately transmits an e-mail notice of the filing, including a link to the document, to all participating counsel and unrepresented litigants on the case. The Rules also authorize service by other methods permitted by the CPLR. If service by such a method is made, proof of service must be filed with NYSCEF. NY R NY CTY E FIL Doc. 2(I).
- *QUEENS COUNTY.* Filing with the system permits counsel to serve the papers electronically pursuant to NY R UNIF TRIAL CTS § 202.5-b(f) once consent to E-Filing has been filed on-line. Consult NY R UNIF TRIAL CTS § 202.5-bb(c) for service in mandatory e-filing. Any required proof of service should be E-filed as a separate document. NY R L QUEENS E-FILE Doc. 1(E)(4).

c. *Electronic service mandatory; Consenting to electronic service; How electronic service may be made.* Except as otherwise provided in NY R UNIF TRIAL CTS § 202.5-bb, filing and service of all documents in an action that has been commenced electronically in accordance with NY R UNIF TRIAL CTS § 202.5-bb shall be by electronic means. NY R UNIF TRIAL CTS § 202.5-bb(c)(1).

i. *Party's consent required for certain e-filing.* After commencement of an action wherein e-filing is authorized, documents may be electronically filed and served, but only by, and electronic service shall be made only upon, a party or parties who have consented thereto. NY R UNIF TRIAL CTS § 202.5-b(b)(2)(i).

- A consent to e-filing in an action shall state that the party providing it agrees to the use of e-filing in the action and to be bound by the filing and service provisions in NY R UNIF TRIAL CTS § 202.5-b. NY R UNIF TRIAL CTS § 202.5-b(b)(2)(ii).

ii. *Address for service; Duty to notify as to changes.* The e-mail service address recorded at the time of registration is the e-mail address at which service of interlocutory documents on that party may be made through notification transmitted by the NYSCEF site. It is the responsibility of each filing user to monitor that address and promptly notify the Resource Center in the event of a change in his or her e-mail service address. NY R UNIF TRIAL CTS § 202.5-b(f)(2)(i).

iii. *How service made.* An e-filing party causes service of an interlocutory document to be made upon another party participating in e-filing by filing the document electronically. Upon receipt of an interlocutory document, the NYSCEF site shall automatically transmit electronic notification to all e-mail service addresses in such action. NY R UNIF TRIAL CTS § 202.5-b(f)(2)(ii).

- Except as provided otherwise in NY R UNIF TRIAL CTS § 202.5-b(h)(3), the electronic transmission of the notification shall constitute service of the document on the e-mail service addresses identified therein; however, such service will not be effective if the filing party learns that the notification did not reach the

address of the person to be served. Proof of such service will be recorded on the NYSCEF site. A party may, however, utilize other service methods permitted by the CPLR provided that, if one of such other methods is used, proof of that service shall be filed electronically. NY R UNIF TRIAL CTS § 202.5-b(f)(2)(ii).

iv. *Signatures on hard copies; Proof of service filed electronically.* When an e-filing party serves a document in hard copy on a non-participating party, the document served shall bear full signatures of all signatories and proof of such service shall be filed electronically. NY R UNIF TRIAL CTS § 202.5-b(b)(2)(i).

- *ERIE COUNTY.* In the NYSCEF system, each Affidavit of Service must be uploaded as a separate .pdf file. After uploading the Affidavit, please choose the document type: "Affirmation/Affidavit of Service" and enter the name of the party served as Additional Document Information. NY R ERIE E FIL Doc. 3(III)(I); NY R ERIE E FIL Doc. 3(V)(F).

v. *Effect of failure to consent.* A party's failure to consent to participation in electronic filing and service shall not bar any other party to the action from filing documents electronically with the County Clerk and the court or serving documents upon any other party who has consented to participation. A party who has not consented to participation shall file documents with the court and the County Clerk, and serve and be served with documents, in hard copy. NY R UNIF TRIAL CTS § 202.5-b(b)(2)(i).

d. *Service upon party.* If a party has not appeared by an attorney or the party's attorney cannot be served, service shall be upon the party by a method specified in NY CPLR Rule 2103(b)(1), NY CPLR Rule 2103(b)(2), NY CPLR Rule 2103(b)(4), NY CPLR Rule 2103(b)(5) or NY CPLR Rule 2103(b)(6). NY CPLR Rule 2103(c).

e. *Service on all parties.* Each paper served on any party shall be served on every other party who has appeared, except as otherwise may be provided by court order or as provided in NY CPLR § 3012 or in NY CPLR § 3215(f). Upon demand by a party, the plaintiff shall supply that party with a list of those who have appeared and the names and addresses of their attorneys. NY CPLR Rule 2103(e).

f. *Service by filing.* If a paper cannot be served by any of the methods specified in NY CPLR Rule 2103(b) and NY CPLR Rule 2103(c), service may be made by filing the paper as if it were a paper required to be filed. NY CPLR Rule 2103(d).

g. *Definitions.* For the purposes of NY CPLR Rule 2103:

i. "Mailing" means the deposit of a paper enclosed in a first class postpaid wrapper, addressed to the address designated by a person for that purpose or, if none is designated, at that person's last known address, in a post office or official depository under the exclusive care and custody of the United States Postal Service within the state;

ii. "Electronic means" means any method of transmission of information between computers or other machines designed for the purpose of sending and receiving such transmissions, and which allows the recipient to reproduce the information transmitted in a tangible medium of expression;

iii. "Facsimile transmission" means any method of transmission of documents to a facsimile machine at a remote location which can automatically produce a tangible copy of such documents. NY CPLR Rule 2103(f).

h. *No service on parties in default.* When a party is in default for failure to appear, he shall not be entitled to notice or service of any copy required under NY CPLR § 3101, et seq. NY CPLR Rule 3105.

G. Hearings

1. *Oral argument.* Motion papers received by the clerk of the court on or before the return date shall be deemed submitted as of the return date. The assigned judge, in his or her discretion or at the request of a party, thereafter may determine that any motion be orally argued and may fix a time for oral argument. NY R UNIF TRIAL CTS § 202.8(d).

a. A party requesting oral argument shall set forth such request in its notice of motion or in its order to show cause or on the first page of the answering papers, as the case may be. Where all parties to a motion request oral argument, oral argument shall be granted unless the court shall determine it to be unnecessary. NY R UNIF TRIAL CTS § 202.8(d).

b. Where a motion is brought on by order to show cause, the court may set forth in the order that oral argument is required on the return date of the motion. NY R UNIF TRIAL CTS § 202.8(d).

i. *BRONX COUNTY.* All orders to show cause, with the exception of orders to show cause that are returnable in the City Part, the STP Part, the Matrimonial Part and the Preliminary/Compliance Conference Part (IA-11), submitted on or after August 25, 2003, will be returnable on a Monday in the assigned Justice's part and appear on his or her motion calendar. Appearances will be required on orders to show cause. NY R BRONX FIL R Doc. 8. A motion on notice or a notice of petition in a New York Supreme Court E-File (hereafter known as NYSCEF) case, as in others, shall be made returnable in the Motion Support Office (Room 217). NY R BRONX E FIL R Doc. 1(1).

- After a motion/petition and notice are filed with the NYSCEF system, the Motion Support Office will automatically place the motion/proceeding on the submit calendar in the Motion Support Office (Room 217) for the return date. No appearance or other action by the filing attorney is required in order for the motion to be calendared if the motion fee is paid for via NYSCEF. Motions in e-filed cases (other than tax certiorari cases) appear on the submit calendar in Room 217 on the return date. NY R BRONX E FIL R Doc. 1(2).

c. *KINGS COUNTY.* All motions require appearances and oral argument. NY R L KINGS Pt. C, Rule 3.

2. *Return date; Time for hearing.* A notice of motion shall specify the time and place of the hearing on the motion. NY CPLR Rule 2214(a). The moving party determines when a motion on notice shall be heard, but she has to consult the court's or judge's calendar practice first. The movant picks out a "return day" sufficiently far off to assure that the notice requirements of NY CPLR Rule 2214(b) can be met, and to assure as well that the day picked is a day on which the assigned judge hears motions. SIEGEL-NYPRAC § 247.

a. *Judge assigned to hear motion*

i. *Referral to judge supervising disclosure.* Unless the chief administrator of the courts has, by rule, provided otherwise, if a case has been assigned to a judge to supervise disclosure pursuant to NY CPLR § 3104, all motions preliminary to trial shall be referred to such judge whenever practicable. NY CPLR Rule 3214(a).

ii. *Referral to judge who decided prior motion.* Any motion may be referred to a judge who decided a prior motion in the action. NY CPLR Rule 2217(a).

iii. *Transfer when judge unable to hear motion.* If a motion is made to a judge who is or will be for any reason unable to hear it, it may be transferred by order of such judge or by written stipulation of the parties to any other judge to whom it might originally have been made. NY CPLR Rule 2217(c).

iv. *Procedure for unassigned cases.* If a case has not been assigned to a judge, the motion shall be made returnable before the court, and a copy of the moving papers, together with a request for judicial intervention, shall be filed with the court, with proof of service upon all other parties, where required by NY R UNIF TRIAL CTS § 202.6, within five (5) days of service upon the other parties. The moving party shall give written notice of the index number to all other parties immediately after filing of the papers. NY R UNIF TRIAL CTS § 202.8(b).

- *Responding papers.* Copies of all responding papers shall be submitted to the court, with proof of service and with the index number set forth in the papers, on or before the return date. NY R UNIF TRIAL CTS § 202.8(b).
- *Assignment after request for judicial intervention.* The case shall be assigned to a judge as soon as practicable after the filing of the request for judicial intervention pursuant to NY R UNIF TRIAL CTS § 202.6, but in no event later than the return date. After assignment to the judge, the court shall provide for appropriate notice to the parties of the name of the assigned judge. NY R UNIF TRIAL CTS § 202.8(b).
- *Motions to be heard in another county.* Motion papers noticed to be heard in a county other than the county where the venue of the action has been placed by the plaintiff shall be assigned to a judge in accordance with procedures established by the Chief Administrator. NY R UNIF TRIAL CTS § 202.8(b).

v. *ALBANY COUNTY: Motions referred to IAS Justice.* All motions made after a case has been assigned a day certain shall be referred to the IAS Justice unless the motion is returnable during the term in which the matter has been assigned a day certain, in that event, the matter will be referred to the Part 1 Justice for that particular term who may entertain the motion or refer such motion to the IAS Justice. Under those circumstances, the Part I Justice shall decide whether or not to strike the note of issue or assign the matter a new day certain. NY R 3 JD SUP Doc. 1(H)(2). All motions shall be returnable before the assigned justice. NY R 3 JD SUP Doc. 1(B).

b. *Trial of issue raised by motion.* The court may order that an issue of fact raised on a motion shall be separately tried by the court or a referee. If the issue is triable of right by jury, the court shall give the parties an opportunity to demand a jury trial of such issue. Failure to make such demand within the time limited by the court, or, if no such time is limited, before trial begins, shall be deemed a waiver of the right to trial by jury. An order under NY CPLR § 2218 shall specify the issue to be tried. NY CPLR § 2218.

c. *Audio-visual coverage of trial court proceeding.* Audio-visual coverage of proceedings in the trial courts shall be permitted only in accordance with the provisions of Part 131 of the Rules of the Chief Administrator (NY R CHIEF ADMIN § 131.1, et seq.). NY R CHIEF J § 29.3.

d. *Adjournment of return date.* Stipulations of adjournment of the return date made by the parties shall be in writing and shall be submitted to the assigned judge. Such stipulation shall be effective unless the court otherwise directs. No more than three (3) stipulated adjournments for an aggregate period of sixty (60) days shall be submitted without prior permission of the court. NY R UNIF TRIAL CTS § 202.8(e)(1).

   i. Absent agreement by the parties, a request by any party for an adjournment shall be submitted in writing, upon notice to the other party, to the assigned judge on or before the return date. The court will notify the requesting party whether the adjournment has been granted. NY R UNIF TRIAL CTS § 202.8(e)(2).

   ii. *BRONX COUNTY.* Motions that have been e-filed may be adjourned in Room 217 if an adjournment complies with the procedures of the Motion Support Office (explained in the "Filing Rules—Motion Procedure" section of the "Courthouse Procedures" link on the website of [the] court). An adjournment that so complies may be obtained by filing a stipulation of all parties with NYSCEF (designated in the filing menu as a "Stipulation to Adjourn Motion"). NY R BRONX E FIL R Doc. 1(3).

   iii. *NEW YORK COUNTY.* The Courtroom also maintains a "APB (All Papers By)" Calendar, which is used when a party seeks an adjournment but fails to comply with the Courtroom's procedures or there is a failure to comply with procedures that requires the clerk to adjourn the motion/application (e.g., failure to submit a Confirmation Notice in an e-filed case). The case may be put over for three days to allow compliance with those procedures, as described further below. NY R NY CTY Procedure II(C); NY R NY CTY E FIL Doc. 2(D)(2). E-filed applications may be adjourned in the Part if an adjournment complies with the Part's procedures (see the Uniform Rules of the Justices (Local Rules) on the court's website). An adjournment that so complies may be obtained by filing with NYSCEF a stipulation of all parties (designated in the filing menu as a Stipulation—Adjournment of Motion—Before Judge); the motion number and the current return date of the motion being adjourned shall be set forth in the "Additional Document Information" field in NYSCEF. Absent any problems, the Part will effectuate the adjournment without need for an appearance or any other action by the parties. NY R NY CTY E FIL Doc. 2(D)(4).

   iv. *QUEENS COUNTY.* The Motion Support Office is NOT authorized to grant adjournments. NY R L QUEENS MOT SUP Doc. 1.

e. *ALBANY COUNTY: Motion terms.* There shall be a. . . Motion Term on each Friday in the Supreme Court, Albany County. The Friday Motion Term shall include all Article 78 Proceedings involving New York State and proceedings commenced pursuant to Article 14 of the Civil Service Law (including applications for injunctive relief made pursuant to section 209-a of the Civil Service Law). NY R 3 JD SUP Doc. 1(F). Generally, parties will be granted only one adjournment for the Friday Motion Term. NY R 3 JD SUP Doc. 1(F).

f. *ALBANY COUNTY: Motion determined without hearing.* All motions are deemed "submitted" on the return date and no appearances are required by the parties. NY R 3 JD SUP Doc. 1(B). In the event oral argument is requested, the parties should not appear on the return date. At the discretion of the assigned Judge and upon the granting of a request for oral argument, the parties will be notified by Chambers of the scheduled time and place at which argument will be heard. Where a motion is brought on by order to show cause, the court may set forth in the order that appearances and/or oral argument are required on the return date of the motion. NY R 3 JD SUP Doc. 1(B).

g. *BRONX COUNTY: Return date.* All assigned and unassigned motions will be returnable five (5) days a week in the Civil Branch Clerk's Office, Room 217, at 9:30 a.m. NY R BRONX FIL R Doc. 8.

h. *BRONX COUNTY: Oral argument.* Calendars of disclosure motions and other motions adjourned for oral argument will be published for the four (4) business days preceding the rescheduled appearance date and on the rescheduled date of the motion. These repetitive publications will serve as the notification of procedure of adjournment of all motions. In addition, two (2) days before the return date of unassigned motions a list of such motions indicating the assigned Justice and the adjourned date of the motion will be published. NY R BRONX FIL R Doc. 8.

i. *BRONX COUNTY: Resolution before return date.* Counsel/parties must advise the Court in writing on or before the return date of all motions that have been resolved by Counsel/parties themselves and all motions the movant(s) wish to be withdrawn. NY R BRONX FIL R Doc. 8.

j. *ERIE COUNTY: Calendaring of motions.* Refer to individual Justice's Part Rules. NY R ERIE E FIL Doc. 3(V)(B).

k. *KINGS COUNTY: Return date set by court.* Irrespective of the return date indicated in the notice of motion, motions will be rescheduled by the E-file/Motion Support Office to a date designated by the assigned Judge. NY R L KINGS Pt. C, Rule 2.

l. *KINGS COUNTY: Calendar calls.* There shall be two (2) calendar calls on motion days. The first calendar call shall be at 9:30 AM and the second calendar call shall be at 10:45 AM, unless the Judge's Part Rules provide otherwise. Defaults shall only be taken on second call. Attorneys with appearances elsewhere in the courthouse may advise the clerk of their whereabouts to avoid a default. Failure to so advise the clerk or appear at the default calendar call will result in a default order being entered or the motion being marked off the calendar. NY R L KINGS Pt. C, Rule 7.

m. *NEW YORK COUNTY: Return date and assigned courtroom.* Motions made by notice of motion and petitions and notices of petition in special proceedings are processed by the General Clerk's Office (Room 119) and are to be made returnable in the Motion Submission Part Courtroom (Room 130) on any business day of the week at 9:30 AM. There are some differences in electronically-filed cases. NY R NY CTY Procedure II; NY R NY CTY Procedure II(C); NY R NY CTY J RUL Rule 13(a).

   i. For the convenience of counsel, between 9:00 A.M. and 9:30 A.M. each day, in advance of the "call," Room 130 accepts (1) written stipulations; (2) affidavits/affirmations reciting the required details as to an adjournment on consent; (3) stipulations, letters or other writings withdrawing motions; and (4) final papers or complete sets of papers on motions. For motions in which these items are handed in before the "call," no one need remain to answer the "call." Counsel/parties must advise the court, either between 9:00 A.M. and 9:30 A.M. or at the "call," of all motions or cases that have been resolved by counsel/parties themselves and all motions that the movant no longer wishes to pursue. If such resolution occurs subsequent to the "call", the assigned Justice must be advised as soon as possible, by written notice sent to the Part, so that the court does not do unnecessary work. NY R NY CTY Procedure II(C).

   ii. Depending upon the assigned Part, contested motions submitted in the Motion Submission Part Courtroom are submitted without argument, or rescheduled for oral argument if so directed by the assigned Justice. For Justices who schedule argument on a case-by-case basis, notice of the argument date will be transmitted by the court. Counsel may ascertain how a motion submitted in Courtroom 130 was marked by consulting Scroll on the court's website, the e-Track application, or, on the two (2) days immediately following the submission date, the New York Law Journal. NY R NY CTY J RUL Rule 13(a).

n. *NEW YORK COUNTY: Motion call.* Each day in the Motion Submission Part Courtroom, commencing at 9:30 A.M., all motions returnable that day will be "called" for the submission of these papers, which must be handed up at this "call" or, as described below, immediately before. Because hundreds of motions appear on the Room 130 calendars every day, motion papers (other than part of the moving papers as described above) cannot be accepted on any day prior to the return date. Courtesy copies are not required nor accepted, but working copies are required by certain Justices in e-filed cases. NY R NY CTY Procedure II(C). If argument is directed, it will take place on an announced date shortly after the day of submission. NY R NY CTY Procedure II(C).

o. *NEW YORK COUNTY: Oral arguments.* Pursuant to request of some Justices, motions submitted in Room 130 will automatically be scheduled for a set argument date in the Part. Other Justices determine on a case-by-case basis after submission in Room 130 whether to accept a particular substantive motion on submission, to require oral argument, or to hold a conference. NY R NY CTY Procedure II(D). If argument is directed by the Justice automatically, notice of argument and the argument date will be given in Room 130. Any appearing party is expected to give notice to all parties and an announcement to this effect is made in Room 130. If the motion is submitted in Room 130 and the Justice, after examining the file, determines that argument should be directed, notice of the argument and the argument date will not be sent by the court. To obtain notification of the argument date and other developments, counsel should use e-Track. If argument notification is not given or transmitted as just described, counsel should understand that the motion has been taken on submission for decision on the papers. NY R NY CTY Procedure II(D).

   i. Calendars of motions to be argued in the Parts are published on the morning of the argument date and on the day before in the New York Law Journal under each Part. Argument information is available on a case-by-case basis in Scroll, and e-mail notifications are sent by e-Track to participating attorneys whenever a motion is scheduled for argument in the court's computer system. NY R NY CTY J RUL Rule 15(a)

p. *NEW YORK COUNTY: Motion determined without hearing.* Given the purpose of the Room 130 procedure, the substance of motions will not be addressed at the submission "call." No Judge is present. To the extent possible, motions submitted in Room 130 will be decided "on the papers." Indeed, attorneys are encouraged to use service or clerks to deliver papers or working copies, or to agree among themselves to have one of them deliver papers for all parties by service or a clerk. Counsel for the movant need not appear to "take a default" on any motion or for any other reason. Motions will be submitted, not marked off, in the absence of the movant. Opposing counsel similarly need not appear in person in order to avoid suffering a default. Delivery of papers by service or a clerk will suffice. The court's goal is to be able to collect papers on motions in an orderly fashion but without any attorney having to make an appearance in Room 130 at any time. NY R NY CTY Procedure II(C).

q. *ONONDAGA COUNTY: Return date.* If the motion is the first filing in an action, the case will be assigned and counsel will be notified by the Supreme Court Clerk's Office via the NYSCEF system of the assigned justice and return date. NY R ONDGA E FIL Protocol(B)(7)(c). If the motion is on a previously assigned case, counsel may choose a return date from the assigned justice's motion term schedule. If the date in unavailable, the Supreme Court Clerk's Office will assign the motion to the next available motion term date and will notify counsel via e-mail. The change will also appear in the notification generated by the NYSCEF system. NY R ONDGA E FIL Protocol(B)(7)(d).

r. *QUEENS COUNTY: Return date.* Motions must be made returnable on the proper day/time based on the assigned judge. NY R L QUEENS MOT SUP Doc. 1. Failure to make a motion returnable on the proper day/time may result in the motion being administratively rescheduled or marked off. NY R L QUEENS MOT SUP Doc. 1.

s. *QUEENS COUNTY: Unassigned motions.* For RJI/Motions, due to the fact that the movant would not know who the assigned judge will be, the notice of motion may be returnable any day of the week. RJI/Motions shall be made returnable in "Queens Supreme Court" with no address designated. The motion will be administratively rescheduled to the proper day of the week based on the judge (once a judge has been assigned). Within one (1) week of filing, the movant must check online to see who the assigned judge is (and therefore the location/date/time) that their motion is now returnable. Movant must then notify their adversary of this information prior to the return date. NY R L QUEENS MOT SUP Doc. 1.

3. *Entry of order after hearing.* An order determining a motion shall be entered and filed in the office of the clerk of the court where the action is triable, and all papers used on the motion and any opinion or memorandum in writing shall be filed with that clerk unless the order dispenses with such filing. When a statute or civil practice rule requires such filing and entry in a county other than that in which the order was made, the party prevailing on the motion shall file the order and the papers used on the motion with the proper clerk after receiving them. If a party fails to file any papers required to be filed under NY CPLR Rule 2220(a), the order may be vacated as irregular, with costs. NY CPLR Rule 2220(a). For more information on the entry of an order after a motion, refer to NY CPLR Rule 2219.

a. *BRONX COUNTY: Settled orders.* A Judge's decision will often call for a Settled Order. The purpose of the settled order is to give effect to the decision by directing that some action be done and/or that a court official perform some task. NY R BRONX LEG SUP Doc. 2. A settled order consists of a notice of settlement informing all parties that the proposed order will be presented to the judge who made the decision on a date certain. Next comes the proposed order which will be presented to the judge. This order should conform to the judge's decision and should direct the relief granted in the decision. This should be followed by proof of service upon all parties who were noticed with the decision. It is also helpful if a copy of the judge's decision is included along with the other papers. A settled order should always be noticed before the judge who made the decision. NY R BRONX LEG SUP Doc. 2.

i. Although an order is usually settled by the party who prevailed on the motion, any party may settle the order. It should be presented to the court within sixty (60) days of the decision. The other parties are entitled to ten (10) days notice where service of the settled order is done by mail, five (5) days if the notice is personally delivered. An attorney who is served with a notice of settlement which he believes does not accurately reflect the decision may settle a counter order. The counter order must be noticed for the same day and must be served not less than seven (7) days if by mail and two (2) days if personally delivered. NY R BRONX LEG SUP Doc. 2.

ii. Settled orders are usually sent to the judge the day after they noticed for settlement. No appearance is necessary or even contemplated on a settled order. If the decision directs "submit order", then no notice is necessary, and the order will be sent to the judge as soon a practical after it is received. No fees are collected on settled orders. NY R BRONX LEG SUP Doc. 2.

b. *ERIE COUNTY: Proposed orders.* Proposed orders shall be submitted through the NYSCEF system and a working copy provided to the IAS Justice for signature, if Part Rules so require. NY R ERIE E FIL Doc. 3(V)(G).

c. *KINGS COUNTY: Long form orders.* If the Court directs that an order be settled or submitted on a motion in a NYSCEF case, the proposed order, with Notice of Settlement where required, and any proposed counter-order shall be filed with the Court via NYSCEF. The relevant clerk's office will process the documents in the customary manner. NY R L KINGS E FIL Doc. 1(E).

i. WORKING COPIES OF PROPOSED ORDERS WITH NOTICE OF SETTLEMENT MUST BE SUBMITTED IN THE MOTION SUPPORT OFFICE (ROOM 227) AS EXPLAINED HEREIN. THEY MUST NOT BE DELIVERED TO THE PART OR CHAMBERS, EXCEPT WHERE THE INDIVIDUAL JUSTICE'S PART RULES PROVIDE OTHERWISE; DOING SO WILL CAUSE ADMINISTRATIVE CONFUSION AND POSSIBLE MISPLACEMENT OF PAPERS. Any such submission shall be sent in a timely manner (kindly review individual Justice's rules) and be conspicuously marked on the outside "NYSCEF Matter;" lack of such marking may delay processing. After an order/counter-order has been signed, it will be scanned, and the County Clerk will affix the entry stamp into the NYSCEF system, which will immediately transmit notice of this event via e-mail, including a link to the entered document, to all participating attorneys and unrepresented litigants in the case. Such transmittal does not constitute Notice of Entry. NY R L KINGS E FIL Doc. 1(E).

d. *NEW YORK COUNTY: Long form orders.* Although the court strongly favors the use of short form orders and judgments, there are instances when settlement of an order or judgment is appropriate. When a Justice directs in a decision that a long form order or judgment be settled, that decision is recorded in the court's computer system by the General Clerk's Office and the motion file with decision is held in the Order Section of the Office in Room 119. The settlement process takes place there. NY R NY CTY Procedure II(D); NY R NY CTY E FIL Doc. 2(E).

i. A proposed long form order or judgment in compliance NY R UNIF TRIAL CTS § 202.48 must be presented to the relevant back office, together with a notice of settlement which bears a settlement date, the date on which the order is to be ready for formal presentation to the Justice. In an e-filed case the submission shall be made electronically. The proposed order or counter-order should be e-filed and it will be transmitted automatically by the NYSCEF system to the appropriate back office. The return date and time of the proposed order must be at 9:30 A.M. no sooner than either five (5) days from personal service of the proposed order or ten (10) days from service by mail. Proof of timely service on the other parties must accompany the proposed order in a hard copy case. If an order or judgment is submitted late (later than sixty (60) days from signing and filing of the decision) and the proponent can show good cause for this tardiness, an affidavit or affirmation justifying the delay should be annexed to the proposed order, together with proof of service thereof. If persuaded, the Justice will consider the proposed order despite its untimeliness. NY R NY CTY Procedure II(D); NY R NY CTY E FIL Doc. 2(E).

ii. Sometimes a decision will state "Submit Order." The submitting party should prepare a long form order and make it returnable without notice. Counsel should deliver the proposed order to the Order Section of the appropriate back office, except in an e-filed case, when it shall be submitted electronically. NY R NY CTY Procedure II(D). If the decision of the court directs that a proposed order be settled or submitted in the Part or in Chambers, that direction, should, of course, be followed without presentation of the proposal to the back office. NY R NY CTY Procedure II(D).

iii. For information on proposed counter-orders, refer to NY R NY CTY Procedure II(D) and NY R NY CTY J RUL Rule 16(b).

e. *QUEENS COUNTY: Proposed orders.* If the court directs that an order be settled or submitted on a motion in an E-file case, the proposed order and any proposed counter-order shall be filed with the court on-line with proof of service. (If a decision refers to a proceeding on the record, a copy of the transcript must be submitted.) Working copies of all proposed orders MUST be submitted to the Motion Support Office before an order can be reviewed. NY R L QUEENS E-FILE Doc. 1(I).

i. Counsel are advised to adhere to NY R UNIF TRIAL CTS § 202.48 regarding the submission or settlement of their proposed order or judgment. Persons who are submitting proposed orders/judgments pursuant to a previously issued memorandum decision must submit a copy of the memorandum decision with their proposed order/judgment. Upon E-Filing a proposed order/judgement, a working copy of the proposed order/judgement must be provided to the Motion Support Office. NY R L QUEENS MOT SUP Doc. 1.

4. *Hearing in disclosure matters*

a. *BRONX COUNTY.* On the return date of the motion all non-City and non-Matrimonial disclosure motions, assigned and unassigned, will be scheduled for appearance in the Preliminary and Compliance Conference Part, IA-11, Room 707. The appearance date shall be no earlier than two (2) weeks from the initial return date of the motion. NY R BRONX FIL R Doc. 8.

b. *KINGS COUNTY.* Motions which only seek discovery related relief are scheduled in the Centralized Compliance Part by the E-file/Motion Support Office, on the date the motion is scheduled to be heard, regardless of judicial assignment. Attorneys are advised to consult, inter alia, the New York Law Journal or the Unified Court System's Future Court Appearance Website for the return dates. NY R L KINGS Pt. E, Rule 7. Any motion seeking discovery related relief filed prior to the PC shall be scheduled concurrently with the PC in the Intake Part. NY R L KINGS Pt. B, Rule 6.

i. If all parties served with the motion are present, they may enter into a consent order. If a new Note of Issue date is required, the order should be filled out and signed by all parties leaving a space for the Note of Issue filing date to be entered by a court attorney. Order should include all outstanding discovery, or indicate that discovery is complete. Consent orders are not effective, or allowed to be copied until they have been reviewed by a court attorney and signed by Judge or JHO. NY R L KINGS Pt. E, Rule 11.

H. Forms

1. Official Motion for Discovery Sanctions Forms for New York

a. Request for judicial intervention. NY R UNIF TRIAL CTS § 202.6.

b. Notice of motion. NY R UNIF TRIAL CTS § 202.7(b).

2. New York Motion for Discovery Sanctions Forms

a. To prohibit introduction of evidence at trial; Notice of motion. NYDISC § 46:18.

b. To prohibit introduction of evidence at trial; Supporting affidavit. NYDISC § 46:19.

c. To strike pleadings; Notice of motion. NYDISC § 46:23.

d. To strike pleadings; Supporting affidavit. NYDISC § 46:24.

e. To preclude expert testimony; Notice of motion. NYDISC § 46:26.

f. To preclude expert testimony; Supporting affidavit. NYDISC § 46:27.

g. Notice of motion to deem issues resolved. MCF CPLR § 6:242.

h. Notice of motion to deem issues resolved; Specific relief sought. MCF CPLR § 6:243.

i. Affidavit in support of motion to deem issues resolved. MCF CPLR § 6:244.

j. Affidavit in support of motion to deem issues resolved; In property damage negligence action. MCF CPLR § 6:245.

k. Notice of motion to prohibit disobedient party from supporting claim. MCF CPLR § 6:249.

l. Affidavit in support of motion to prohibit disobedient party from supporting claim. MCF CPLR § 6:250.

m. Notice of motion to prohibit introduction of evidence at trial or, alternatively, to compel additional disclosure. MCF CPLR § 6:252.

n. Affidavit in support of motion to prohibit introduction of evidence at trial or, alternatively, to compel additional disclosure. MCF CPLR § 6:253.

o. Affidavit in support of motion to stay further proceedings until disclosure order is obeyed. MCF CPLR § 6:255.

p. Affirmation in support of cross-motion to strike case from calendar until plaintiff submits to examination before trial. MCF CPLR § 6:256.

q. Notice of motion to strike out pleadings. MCF CPLR § 6:258.

r. Affidavit in support of motion to strike out pleadings. MCF CPLR § 6:259.

s. Notice of motion to preclude party in medical, dental, or podiatric malpractice action from offering expert testimony at trial for failure to make party's expert witness available for oral deposition after accepting offer to do so. MCF CPLR § 6:261.

t. Affidavit in support of motion to preclude party in medical, dental, or podiatric malpractice action from offering expert testimony at trial for failure to make party's expert witness available for oral deposition after accepting offer to do so. MCF CPLR § 6:262.

u. Affidavit in support of motion to dismiss complaints. MCF CPLR § 6:265.

v. Notice of motion to dismiss complaint with prejudice for delay in responding to interrogatories. MCF CPLR § 6:269.

w. Affirmation in support of motion to dismiss complaint with prejudice for delay in responding to interrogatories. MCF CPLR § 6:270.

x. Notice of motion to strike answer for failure to obey order for discovery and inspection. MCF CPLR § 6:271.

y. Affidavit in support of motion to strike answer for failure to obey order for discovery and inspection. MCF CPLR § 6:272.

z. General form of affidavit of service of motion papers. MCF CPLR § 5:24.

I. Applicable Rules

1. *State rules*

a. Short title; Application; Construction; Definitions. NY CPLR § 101; NY CPLR § 103; NY CPLR § 104; NY CPLR § 105.

b. Appendix of official forms. NY CPLR § 107.

c. Extensions of time generally. NY CPLR § 2004.

d. Form of papers. NY CPLR Rule 2101; NY CPLR Rule 2102; NY CPLR § 2105; NY CPLR Rule 2106; NY GEN BUS § 399-ddd; NY R UNIF TRIAL CTS § 215.2; NY R UNIF TRIAL CTS § 215.3.

e. Service of papers. NY CPLR Rule 2103.

f. Where motion made; In supreme court action. NY CPLR § 2212.

g. Motion papers; Service; Time. NY CPLR Rule 2214.

h. Relief demanded by other than moving party. NY CPLR Rule 2215.

i. Prior motion; Ex parte motion; Transfer of motion; Hearings; Orders. NY CPLR Rule 2217; NY CPLR § 2218; NY CPLR Rule 2220.

j. Computation of time. NY CPLR § 2402; NY GEN CONSTR § 19; NY GEN CONSTR § 20; NY GEN CONSTR § 25-a; NY GEN CONSTR § 30; NY GEN CONSTR § 31; NY GEN CONSTR § 53.

k. Scope of disclosure. NY CPLR § 3101; NY CPLR § 3103; NY CPLR § 3104; NY CPLR § 3123; NY CPLR Rule 3124.

l. Penalties for refusal to comply with order or to disclose. NY CPLR § 3126.

m. Motions heard by judge supervising disclosure; Stay of disclosure. NY CPLR Rule 3214.

n. Fees; Index number fees of county clerks. NY CPLR § 8018.

o. Hours of court; Proceedings in court. NY R CHIEF J § 3.1; NY R CHIEF J § 29.3.

p. Application of part; Waiver; Additional rules; Application of CPLR; Definitions. NY R UNIF TRIAL CTS § 202.1.

q. Papers filed in court; Electronic filing in supreme court. NY R UNIF TRIAL CTS § 202.5; NY R UNIF TRIAL CTS § 202.5-a; NY R UNIF TRIAL CTS § 202.5-b; NY R UNIF TRIAL CTS § 202.5-bb.

r. Request for judicial intervention. NY R UNIF TRIAL CTS § 202.6.

s. Calendaring of motions; Uniform notice of motion form; Affirmation of good faith. NY R UNIF TRIAL CTS § 202.7.

t. Motion procedure; Preliminary conferences. NY R UNIF TRIAL CTS § 202.8; NY R UNIF TRIAL CTS § 202.12.

u. Rules of the commercial division of the Supreme Court. NY R UNIF TRIAL CTS § 202.70.

v. Sanctions; Signing of papers. NY R CHIEF ADMIN § 130-1.1-a.

2. *Local rules*

a. *Albany County*

i. Third judicial district rules. NY R 3 JD SUP Doc. 1.

b. *Bronx County*

i. Filing of papers in supreme court. NY R BRONX FIL R Doc. 1.

ii. Request for judicial intervention. NY R BRONX FIL R Doc. 2.

iii. Discovery part conference requests. NY R BRONX FIL R Doc. 5.

iv. Motion procedure. NY R BRONX FIL R Doc. 8.

v. Commercial division. NY R BRONX FIL R Doc. 12.

vi. Motions on notice. NY R BRONX E FIL R Doc. 1.

vii. Settled orders. NY R BRONX LEG SUP Doc. 2.

c. *Erie County*

i. Joint protocols for New York State Courts E-Filing (NYSCEF) cases filed in Supreme Court, Erie County. NY R ERIE E FIL Doc. 3.

d. *Kings County*

i. Papers. NY R L KINGS Pt. A, Papers.

ii. Discovery agreements. NY R L KINGS Pt. B, Rule 2.

iii. Motion scheduling. NY R L KINGS Pt. B, Rule 6.

iv. Service of motion papers. NY R L KINGS Pt. C, Rule 1.

v. Scheduling of motions. NY R L KINGS Pt. C, Rule 2.
vi. Appearance and argument. NY R L KINGS Pt. C, Rule 3.
vii. Courtesy copies. NY R L KINGS Pt. C, Rule 5.
viii. Motion calendar calls. NY R L KINGS Pt. C, Rule 7.
ix. Scheduling of motions. NY R L KINGS Pt. E, Rule 7.
x. Affirmation of good faith. NY R L KINGS Pt. E, Rule 9.
xi. Consent orders. NY R L KINGS Pt. E, Rule 11.
xii. Disclosure disputes. NY R NY CTY J RUL Rule 10.
xiii. Protocol on courthouse and county clerk procedures for electronically filed cases. NY R L KINGS E FIL Doc. 1.

e. *New York County*

i. Commencement of cases. NY R NY CTY Procedure I.
ii. RJIs and assignments. NY R NY CTY Procedure IA.
iii. Motions and special proceedings by notice of motion/petition. NY R NY CTY Procedure II.
iv. County clerk litigation functions. NY R NY CTY Procedure XI.
v. Protocol on courthouse and county clerk procedures for electronically filed cases. NY R NY CTY E FIL Doc. 2.
vi. Redaction of information in documents filed with the county clerk and the court. NY R NY CTY J RUL Rule A-1.
vii. Papers by fax. NY R NY CTY J RUL Rule 4.
viii. Motions on notice; Orders to show cause. NY R NY CTY J RUL Rule 13.
ix. Motion papers. NY R NY CTY J RUL Rule 14.
x. Oral argument; Adjournments. NY R NY CTY J RUL Rule 15.

f. *Onondaga County*

i. Onondaga county protocol for case filings New York State Electronic Files (NYSCEF). NY R ONDGA E FIL Protocol.

g. *Queens County*

i. Motion support office. NY R L QUEENS MOT SUP Doc. 1.
ii. Queens county protocol on courthouse procedures for electronically filed cases. NY R L QUEENS E-FILE Doc. 1.

J. Miscellaneous

NOTE: Individual judges' rules may apply.

ALBANY COUNTY

JUSTICE LISA M. FISHER: NY R 3 JD FISHER Fisher; NY R 3 JD FISHER Fisher, PC Order.

JUSTICE RICHARD MOTT: NY R 3 JD MOTT Mott.

JUSTICE STEPHAN G. SCHICK: NY R 3 JD Schick.

FORECLOSURE SETTLEMENT PART: NY R 3 JD Foreclosure Settlement.

BRONX COUNTY

JUSTICE PAUL L. ALPERT: [NY R BRONX J Part IA-29, as amended by NY ORDER 20-0337].

JUSTICE BEN BARBATO: NY R BRONX J Part IA-21.

JUSTICE MARY ANNE BRIGANTTI: [NY R BRONX J Part IA-15, as amended by NY ORDER 20-0338].

JUSTICE JOSEPH E. CAPELLA: NY R BRONX J Part IA-23.

JUSTICE MITCHELL DANZIGER: NY R BRONX J Part IA-3/33 ; [NY R BRONX J Danziger, Part IA-3/33, as amended by NY ORDER 20-0339].

JUSTICE LAURA G. DOUGLAS: NY R BRONX J Part IA-11.

JUSTICE RUBEN FRANCO: NY R BRONX J Part IA-26.

JUSTICE DORIS M. GONZALEZ: NY R BRONX J Part IA-24.

JUSTICE WILMA GUZMAN: NY R BRONX J Part IA-7; [NY R BRONX J Guzman, Part IA-7 Virtual, as amended by NY ORDER 20-0340].

JUSTICE ROBERT T. JOHNSON: NY R BRONX J Part IA-12.

JUSTICE DONALD A. MILES: NY R BRONX J Part IA-8.

JUSTICE DONNA M. MILLS: NY R BRONX J Part IA-9.

JUSTICE JULIA I. RODRIGUEZ: NY R BRONX J Part IA-18; [NY R BRONX J Part IA-27, as amended by NY ORDER 20-0341].

JUSTICE LLINET M. ROSADO: [NY R BRONX J Part IA-25, as amended by NY ORDER 20-0342].

JUSTICE NORMA RUIZ: NY R BRONX J Part IA-22; [NY R BRONX J Ruiz, Part IA-22 Virtual, as amended by NY ORDER 20-0343].

JUSTICE HOWARD H. SHERMAN: NY R BRONX J Part IA-4.

JUSTICE FERNANDO TAPIA: NY R BRONX J Part IA-13.

JUSTICE ELIZABETH A. TAYLOR: NY R BRONX J Part IA-2.

JUSTICE ALISON Y. TRUITT: NY R BRONX J Part IA-5.

PART IDV: NY R BRONX J Doc. 1.

PRE-TRIAL PART RULES: NY R BRONX J Doc. 2.

PRE TRIAL WORKSHEET: NY R BRONX J Doc. 3.

FORECLOSURE SETTLEMENT PART RULES: NY R BRONX J Doc. 4.

GUARDIANSHIP PART RULES: NY R BRONX J Doc. 5.

LPM PART RULES: NY R BRONX J Doc. 6.

ERIE COUNTY

JUSTICE M. WILLIAM BOLLER: NY R 8 JD J Boller.

JUSTICE RALPH A. BONIELLO: NY R 8 JD J Boniello.

JUSTICE CHRISTOPHER J. BURN: NY R 8 JD J Burns.

JUSTICE RUSSELL P. BUSCAGLIA: NY R 8 JD J Buscaglia.

JUSTICE FRANK CARUSO: NY R 8 JD J Caruso.

JUSTICE STEPHEN W. CASS: NY R 8 JD J Cass.

JUSTICE DEBORAH A. CHIMES: NY R 8 JD J Chimes.

JUSTICE EMILIO COLAIACOVO: [NY R 8 JD J Colaiacovo, as amended by NY ORDER 20-0252].

JUSTICE DIANE Y. DEVLIN: NY R 8 JD J Devlin.

JUSTICE JAMES H. DILLON: NY R 8 JD J Dillon.

JUSTICE PAULA L. FEROLETO: NY R 8 JD J Feroleto.

JUSTICE DANIEL J. FURLONG: [NY R 8 JD J Furlong, as amended by NY ORDER 20-0253].

JUSTICE JOSEPH R. GLOWNIA: NY R 8 JD J Glownia.

JUSTICE MARK J. GRISANTI: NY R 8 JD J Grisanti.

JUSTICE DEBORAH A. HAENDIGES: NY R 8 JD J Haendiges.

JUSTICE LYNN W. KEANE: [NY R 8 JD J Keane, as amended by NY ORDER 20-0254].

JUSTICE RICHARD C. KLOCH, Sr.: NY R 8 JD J Kloch.

JUSTICE FREDERICK J. MARSHALL: [NY R 8 JD J Marshall, as amended by NY ORDER 20-0255.

JUSTICE JOHN L. MICHALSKI: NY R 8 JD J Michalski.

JUSTICE MARK A. MONTOUR: [NY R 8 JD J Montour, as amended by NY ORDER 20-0256].
JUSTICE HENRY NOWAK: NY R 8 JD J Nowak.
JUSTICE JOHN F. O'DONNELL: NY R 8 JD J O'Donnell.
JUSTICE JEANETTE OGDEN: NY R 8 JD J Ogden.
JUSTICE CATHERINE NUGENT-PANEPINTO: NY R 8 JD J Nugent-Panepinto.
JUSTICE FRANK A. SEDITA, III: [NY R 8 JD J Sedita, as amended by NY ORDER 20-0257].
JUSTICE SARA SHELDON: NY R 8 JD J Sheldon.
JUSTICE DONNA M. SIWEK: NY R 8 JD J Siwek.
JUSTICE MARY L. SLISZ: NY R 8 JD J Slisz.
JUSTICE TIMOTHY J. WALKER: [NY R 8 JD J Walker, as amended by NY ORDER 20-0258].
JUSTICE DENNIS E. WARD: NY R 8 JD J Ward.
JUSTICE PAUL B. WOJTASZEK: [NY R 8 JD J Wojtaszek, as amended by NY ORDER 20-0259].
JUSTICE CHARLES N. ZAMBITO: [NY R 8 JD J Zambito, as amended by NY ORDER 20-0260].
SUPREME COURT LEGAL STAFF: NY R 8 JD J Legal Staff.

KINGS COUNTY

JUSTICE RACHEL A. ADAMS: NY R KINGS J Part 5F.
JUSTICE LOREN BAILY-SCHIFFMAN: NY R KINGS J Part 65.
JUSTICE REGINALD A. BODDIE: NY R KINGS J Part 95.
JUSTICE THERESA M. CICCOTTO: NY R KINGS J Part 19; NY R KINGS J Part 5J.
JUSTICE LISSETTE COLON: NY R KINGS J Part Rules.
JUSTICE GENINE EDWARDS: NY R KINGS J Part 80.
JUSTICE PAMELA L. FISHER: [NY R KINGS J Part 94, as amended by NY ORDER 20-0208].
JUSTICE ROBIN GARSON: NY R KINGS J Part 75.
JUSTICE LARA J. GENOVISI: [NY R KINGS J Part 34, as amended by NY ORDER 20-0209].
JUSTICE BERNARD J. GRAHAM: NY R KINGS J Part 36.
JUSTICE DAWN JIMENEZ-SALTA: NY R KINGS J Part 88.
JUSTICE INGRID JOSEPH: [NY R KINGS J Part FRP3 and Part 83, as amended by NY ORDER 20-0210].
JUSTICE KATHY J. KING: NY R KINGS J Part 64, 76K.
JUSTICE LAWRENCE KNIPEL: NY R KINGS J Part 57.
JUSTICE DONALD KURTZ: NY R KINGS J Part 26.
JUSTICE CARL LANDICINO: [NY R KINGS J Part 81, as amended by NY ORDER 20-0211].
JUSTICE KATHERINE LEVINE: [NY R KINGS J Part 20, 25, 92, as amended by NY ORDER 20-0211].
JUSTICE LORNA MCALLISTER: [NY R KINGS J Part 10, as amended by NY ORDER 20-0211].
JUSTICE ROSEMARIE MONTALBANO: [NY R KINGS J Part 19, 71, and 22, as amended by NY ORDER 20-0211].
JUSTICE RICHARD J. MONTELIONE: [NY R KINGS J Part 99 and DJMP, as amended by NY ORDER 20-0215].
JUSTICE LISA S. OTTLEY: NY R KINGS J Part 24.
JUSTICE MARK I. PARTNOW: NY R KINGS J Part 43.
JUSTICE ERIC I. PRUS: NY R KINGS J Part 5A.
JUSTICE FRANCOIS RIVERA: NY R KINGS J Part 52.
JUSTICE KAREN B. ROTHENBERG: NY R KINGS J Part 35.
JUSTICE LEON RUCHELSMAN: NY R KINGS J Part 1.
JUSTICE WAYNE P. SAITTA: NY R KINGS J Part 29.

JUSTICE ROBIN K. SHEARES: NY R KINGS J Part 96.

JUSTICE KENNETH P. SHERMAN: NY R KINGS J Part 67 and 78.

JUSTICE DEBRA SILBER: NY R KINGS J Part 9 and 5K.

JUSTICE ELLEN M. SPODEK: NY R KINGS J Part 63.

JUSTICE MARSHA L. STEINHARDT: NY R KINGS J Part 15.

JUSTICE JEFFREY S. SUNSHINE: NY R KINGS J Part 5G.

JUSTICE PETER P. SWEENEY: [NY R KINGS J Part 35, as amended by NY ORDER 20-0218].

JUSTICE DELORES J. THOMAS: [NY R KINGS J Part 5T, as amended by NY ORDER 20-0221].

JUSTICE WAVNY TOUSSAINT: NY R KINGS J Part 70.

JUSTICE RICHARD VELASQUEZ: NY R KINGS J Part 66.

JUSTICE CAROLYN E. WADE: NY R KINGS J Part 84.

JUSTICE EDWARD G. WALKER: [NY R KINGS J Part 90, as amended by NY ORDER 20-0219].

JUSTICE LILLIAN WAN: [NY R KINGS J Part 17, as amended by NY ORDER 20-0220].

JUSTICE MICHELLE WESTON: NY R KINGS J Part 3.

MENTAL HYGIENE PART: NY R KINGS J Part 77.

MATRIMONIAL PARTS DURING COVID-19 EMERGENCY: JUSTICE KAREN B. ROTHENBERG: NY R KINGS J Doc. 1.

NASSAU COUNTY

JUSTICE ANNA R. ANZALONE: NY R NASSAU S J Anzalone, Part 26.

JUSTICE STACY D. BENNETT: NY R NASSAU S J Bennett; NY R NASSAU S J Bennett, Form 1.

JUSTICE ANTONIO BRANDVEEN: NY R NASSAU S J Brandveen, Part 31.

JUSTICE JEFFREY S. BROWN: [NY R NASSAU S J Brown, as amended by NY ORDER 20-0297].

JUSTICE STEPHEN A. BUCARIA: NY R NASSAU S J Bucaria.

JUSTICE JULIANNE T. CAPETOLA: NY R NASSAU S J Capetola, Part 28.

JUSTICE EDMUND M. DANE: NY R NASSAU S J Dane, Part 33.

JUSTICE VITO M. DESTEFANO: NY R NASSAU S J DeStefano, Part 13; NY R NASSAU S J DeStefano, Form 1.

JUSTICE ARTHUR M. DIAMOND: NY R NASSAU S J Diamond, Part 7.

JUSTICE THOMAS FEINMAN: NY R NASSAU S J Feinman, Part 5.

JUSTICE JOHN M. GALASSO: NY R NASSAU S J Galasso, Part 22.

JUSTICE SHARON M.J. GIANELLI: NY R NASSAU S J Gianelli, Part 22; NY R NASSAU S J Gianelli, Form 1.

JUSTICE JEFFREY A. GOODSTEIN: NY R NASSAU S J Goodstein, Part 33; NY R NASSAU S J Goodstein, Form 1.

JUSTICE DAVID J. GUGERTY: [NY R NASSAU S J Gugerty, Part 31, as amended by NY ORDER 20-0298].

JUSTICE HELENE F. GUGERTY: NY R NASSAU S J Gugerty, Part 47.

JUSTICE STEVEN M. JAEGER: NY R NASSAU S J Jaeger, Part 35; NY R NASSAU S J Jaeger, Form 1.

JUSTICE JACK L. LIBERT: NY R NASSAU S J Libert, Part 23.

JUSTICE JOSEPH H. LORINTZ: NY R NASSAU S J Lorintz, Part 26; NY R NASSAU S J Lorintz, Form 1.

JUSTICE ROY S. MAHON: NY R NASSAU S J Mahon, Part 3.

JUSTICE RANDY SUE MARBER: NY R NASSAU S J Marber, Part 8.

JUSTICE JAMES P. MCCORMACK: [NY R NASSAU S J McCormack, Part 18, as amended by NY ORDER, 20-0299].

JUSTICE DICCIA T. PINEDA-KIRWAN: [NY R NASSAU S J Pineda-Kirwan, as amended by NY ORDER 20-0300].

JUSTICE THOMAS RADEMAKER: [NY R NASSAU S J Rademaker, Part 28, as amended by NY ORDER 20-0301]; [NY R NASSAU S J Rademaker, Form 1, as amended by NY ORDER 20-0301].

JUSTICE DENISE L. SHER: NY R NASSAU S J Rademaker, Part 32.

JUSTICE LEONARD D. STEINMAN: [NY R NASSAU S J Steinman, Part 15, as amended by NY ORDER 20-0303]; NY R NASSAU S J Steinman, Form 1.

JUSTICE HOWARD E. STURIM: NY R NASSAU S J Sturim, Part 50; NY R NASSAU S J Sturim, Form 1.

JUSTICE HELEN VOUTSINAS: [NY R NASSAU S J Voutsinas, Part 25, as amended by NY ORDER 20-0304]; [NY R NASSAU S J Voutsinas, Form 1, as amended by NY ORDER 20-0305].

JUSTICE HOPE SCHWARTZ ZIMMERMAN: NY R NASSAU S J Zimmerman, Part 17.

NEW YORK COUNTY

JUDGE'S RULES; BASIC INFORMATION: [NY R NY CTY J RUL Doc. 1, as amended by NY ORDER 20-0202].

ONONDAGA COUNTY

JUSTICE ROBERT E. ANTONACCI II: [NY R ONDGA E FIL Doc. 1, as amended by 20-0239].

JUSTICE MICHAEL V. COCCOMI: NY R ONDGA E FIL Doc. 2.

JUSTICE GREGORY R. GILBERT: NY R 5 JD JUDGES Gilbert; NY R ONDGA E FIL Doc. 3.

JUSTICE DONALD A. GREENWOOD: NY R ONDGA E FIL Doc. 4.

JUSTICE DEBORAH H. KARALUNAS: NY R ONDGA E FIL Doc. 5.

JUSTICE JAMES MCCLUSKY: NY R 5 JD MCCLUSKY McClusky.

JUSTICE CHARLES C. MERRELL: NY R 5 JD MERRELL Merrell.

JUSTICE PATRICK F. MACRAE: NY R 5 JD MACRAE Doc. 1.

JUSTICE JAMES P. MURPHY: NY R ONDGA E FIL Doc. 7.

JUSTICE GERALD J. NERI: [NY R 5 JD JUDGES Neri, as amended by NY ORDER 20-0236]; [NY R ONDGA E FIL Doc. 8, as amended by NY ORDER 20-0241].

JUSTICE ANTHONY J. PARIS: NY R 5 JD JUDGES Paris; [NY R ONDGA E FIL Doc. 9, as amended by NY ORDER 20-0242].

JUSTICE NORMAN W. SEITER, JR.: NY R 5 JD JUDGES Seiter.

JUSTICE KEVIN G. YOUNG: [NY R ONDGA E FIL Doc. 10, as amended by NY ORDER 20-0243].

QUEENS COUNTY

JUSTICE PAM JACKMAN BROWN: [NY R L QUEENS Brown, Part 19, as amended by NY ORDER 20-0321].

JUSTICE CHEREE A. BUGGS: NY R L QUEENS Buggs, Part 30.

JUSTICE PAM JACKMAN BROWN: [NY R L QUEENS Brown, Part 19, as amended by NY ORDER 20-0321].

JUSTICE DENIS J. BUTLER: NY R L QUEENS Butler, Part 12.

JUSTICE ROBERT I. CALORAS: [NY R L QUEENS Caloras, Part 36, as amended by NY ORDER 20-0322].

JUSTICE ANNA CULLEY: NY R L QUEENS Culley, Part 53.

JUSTICE TIMOTHY DUFFICY: NY R L QUEENS Dufficy, Part 35.

JUSTICE DAVID ELLIOT: NY R L QUEENS Elliot, Part 14.

JUSTICE JOSEPH J. ESPOSITO: NY R L QUEENS Esposito, Part 6.

JUSTICE DARRELL L. GAVRIN: [NY R L QUEENS Gavrin, Part 27, as amended by NY ORDER 20-0323].

JUSTICE WYATT N. GIBBONS: [NY R L QUEENS Gibbons, Part 5, as amended by NY ORDER 20-0330.

JUSTICE DONNA-MARIE E. GOLIA: [NY R L QUEENS Golia, Part 21, as amended by NY ORDER 20-0331].

JUSTICE MARGUERITE A. GRAYS: [NY R L QUEENS Grays, Part 4, as amended by NY ORDER 20-0324].

JUSTICE RUDOLPH E. GRECO: [NY R L QUEENS Greco, Part 32, as amended by NY ORDER 20-0325].

JUSTICE MAUREEN HEALY: NY R L QUEENS Healy, Part 6.

JUSTICE PHILLIP HOM: [NY R L QUEENS Hom, Part 43, as amended by NY ORDER 20-0332].

JUSTICE KEVIN J. KERRIGAN: NY R L QUEENS Kerrigan, Part 10.

JUSTICE MOJGAN C. LANCMAN: NY R L QUEENS Lancman, Part 20.

JUSTICE RICHARD G. LATIN: NY R L QUEENS Latin, Part 40.

JUSTICE ULYSSES B. LEVERETT: [NY R L QUEENS Leverett, Part 6, as amended by NY ORDER 20-0326].

JUSTICE LEONARD LIVOTE: NY R L QUEENS Livote, Part 33.

JUSTICE LEE A. MAYERSOHN: NY R L QUEENS Mayersohn, Part 22; NY R L QUEENS Mayersohn, Part 22G; [NY R L QUEENS Mayersohn, Part 22G COVID, as amended by NY ORDER 20-0327].

JUSTICE ROBERT J. MCDONALD: NY R L QUEENS McDonald, Part 34.

JUSTICE MARGARET MCGOWAN: NY R L QUEENS McGowan, Part 52.

JUSTICE MAURICE E. MUIR: [NY R L QUEENS Muir, Part 42, as amended by NY ORDER 20-0333].

JUSTICE JODI ORLOW: NY R L QUEENS Orlow, Part 51.

JUSTICE LESLIE J. PURIFICCION: NY R L QUEENS Purificcion, Part 39.

JUSTICE JOSEPH RISI: [NY R L QUEENS Risi, Part 3, as amended by NY ORDER 20-0328].

JUSTICE FREDERICK D.R. SAMPSON: [NY R L QUEENS Sampson, Part 31, as amended by NY ORDER 20-0329].

JUSTICE MARTIN J. SCHULMAN: NY R L QUEENS Schulman, Part 29.

JUSTICE BERNICE D. SIEGAL: NY R L QUEENS Siegal, Part 25G.

JUSTICE JANICE A. TAYLOR: NY R L QUEENS Taylor, Part 15.

JUSTICE CARMEN R. VELASQUEZ: NY R L QUEENS Velasquez, Part 38.

JUSTICE LOURDES M VENTURA: [NY R L QUEENS Ventura, Part 37, as amended by NY ORDER 20-0334].

JUSTICE WILLIAM A. VISCOVICH: NY R L QUEENS Viscovich, Part 63.

JUSTICE ALLAN B. WEISS: NY R L QUEENS Weiss, Part 2.

COMPLIANCE, SETTLEMENT AND CONFERENCE PART: NY R L QUEENS Doc 1.

PRELIMINARY CONFERENCE PART: [NY R L QUEENS Doc. 2, as amended by NY ORDER 20-0335].

MEDICAL MALPRACTICE CONFERENCE PART; [NY R L QUEENS Doc. 3, as amended by NY ORDER 20-0336].

TRIAL SCHEDULING PART: NY R L QUEENS Doc. 4.

SUMMARY JURY TRIAL PROGRAM: NY R L QUEENS Doc. 7.

RESIDENTIAL FORECLOSURE PART: NY R L QUEENS Doc. 9.

FORECLOSURE AUCTION RULES: NY R L QUEENS Doc. 10.

MATRIMONIAL PRELIMINARY CONFERENCE PART: NY R L QUEENS Doc. 11.

NON-CUSTODIAL CONTESTED MATRIMONIAL PART: NY R L QUEENS Doc. 12.

Motions, Oppositions and Replies
Motion for Preliminary Injunction

Document Last Updated August 2020

A. Checklist

(I) ❑ Matters to consider for moving party

- (a) ❑ Required documents
  - (1) ❑ Notice of motion, order to show cause, or affidavit on ex parte motion
  - (2) ❑ Motion
  - (3) ❑ Undertaking
  - (4) ❑ Request for judicial intervention
  - (5) ❑ Proof of service
  - (6) ❑ ALBANY COUNTY: Additional required documents
    - (i) ❑ Affirmation of good faith effort

(b) ❑ Supplemental documents
- (1) ❑ Supporting evidence; Exhibits
- (2) ❑ Brief
- (3) ❑ Application for temporary restraining order
- (4) ❑ Notice to produce papers not in possession of the court
- (5) ❑ Filing fees
- (6) ❑ Working copies
- (7) ❑ Statement of authorization in electronic filing cases
- (8) ❑ ERIE COUNTY: Additional supplemental documents
  - (i) ❑ Notice of hard copy submission in e-filed case
- (9) ❑ KINGS COUNTY: Additional supplemental documents
  - (i) ❑ Forms when filing in hard copy
- (10) ❑ NEW YORK COUNTY: Additional supplemental documents
  - (i) ❑ Notice of hard copy submission
  - (ii) ❑ Unpublished opinions
- (11) ❑ ONONDAGA COUNTY: Additional supplemental documents
  - (i) ❑ Notice of hard copy submission
- (12) ❑ QUEENS COUNTY: Additional supplemental documents
  - (i) ❑ Notice of hard copy submission

(c) ❑ Timing
- (1) ❑ Notice of the motion may be served with the summons or at any time thereafter and prior to judgment
- (2) ❑ The moving party shall serve copies of all affidavits and briefs upon all other parties at the time of service of the notice of motion
- (3) ❑ A notice of motion and supporting affidavits shall be served at least eight (8) days before the time at which the motion is noticed to be heard
- (4) ❑ It is also good practice to make motions returnable at least three (3) weeks away from the planned date of mailing and to always include a demand in the motion that the other side serve answering papers at least seven (7) days before the return day

(II) ❑ Matters to consider for opposing party

(a) ❑ Required documents
- (1) ❑ Opposition
- (2) ❑ Proof of service

(b) ❑ Supplemental documents
- (1) ❑ Supporting evidence; Exhibits
- (2) ❑ Brief
- (3) ❑ Filing fees
- (4) ❑ Working copies
- (5) ❑ ERIE COUNTY: Additional supplemental documents
  - (i) ❑ Notice of hard copy submission in e-filed case
- (6) ❑ KINGS COUNTY: Additional supplemental documents
  - (i) ❑ Forms when filing in hard copy
- (7) ❑ NEW YORK COUNTY: Additional supplemental documents
  - (i) ❑ Notice of hard copy submission

(ii) ❑ Unpublished opinions

(8) ❑ ONONDAGA COUNTY: Additional supplemental documents

(i) ❑ Notice of hard copy submission

(9) ❑ QUEENS COUNTY: Additional supplemental documents

(i) ❑ Notice of hard copy submission

(c) ❑ Timing

(1) ❑ Answering affidavits shall be served at least two (2) days before the time at which the motion is noticed to be heard

(2) ❑ Answering affidavits and any notice of cross-motion, with supporting papers, if any, shall be served at least seven (7) days before such time if a notice of motion served at least sixteen (16) days before such time so demands

B. Timing

1. *Time to bring motion for preliminary injunction.* Notice of the motion may be served with the summons or at any time thereafter and prior to judgment. NY CPLR § 6311(1). A preliminary injunction is available only in a pending action or proceeding. SIEGEL-NYPRAC § 329.

2. *Time to serve.* The moving party shall serve copies of all affidavits and briefs upon all other parties at the time of service of the notice of motion. NY R UNIF TRIAL CTS § 202.8(c). A notice of motion and supporting affidavits shall be served at least eight (8) days before the time at which the motion is noticed to be heard. NY CPLR Rule 2214(b).

a. *Return dates; Best practice.* It is also good practice to make motions returnable at least three (3) weeks away from the planned date of mailing and to always include a demand in the motion that the other side serve answering papers at least seven (7) days before the return day. This enables the motion to be served by mail, gives sufficient notice to support the seven (7) day demand, and leaves a few days for a delayed mailing if some snag prevents posting on the day planned. If speed is needed, the shorter eight (8) day notice period can be used, forfeiting the right to seven (7) day answering papers and a reply. If even eight (8) days notice is too much under the circumstances, the order to show cause is the remedy. SIEGEL-NYPRAC § 247.

i. *ALBANY COUNTY.* All motions, except for certain matters in Albany County as specified in NY R 3 JD SUP Doc. 1(E) and NY R 3 JD SUP Doc. 1(F), brought on by notice of motion or by order to show cause will be made returnable on any day, Monday through Friday, as chosen by the movant in compliance with the CPLR. Parties shall submit all papers in a timely fashion as required by the CPLR by delivering them or mailing them directly to the Supreme Court Clerk's Office[. . .]except that motions and other applications subject to a filing fee shall first be presented to the County Clerk's Office for payment of the requisite fee and then subsequently filed with the Supreme Court Clerk's Office. NY R 3 JD SUP Doc. 1(B).

ii. *BRONX COUNTY.* A Notice of Motion must be served at least eight (8) days, by personal service, nine (9) days by overnight express and thirteen (13) days by mail before the return date. NY R BRONX FIL R Doc. 3. All unassigned motions must be accompanied with a properly filled out RJI and shall be filed in the Motion Support Office, room 217, within five (5) days of service. All motions on actions already assigned to a Justice must be filed at least five (5) business days before the return date. NY R BRONX FIL R Doc. 3. All papers served must strictly comply with the time requirements of NY CPLR Rule 2101, NY CPLR Rule 2103 and NY CPLR Rule 2214(b). NY R BRONX FIL R Doc. 8.

iii. *KINGS COUNTY.* Motion papers, answering affidavits and reply affidavits must be served on adversaries in accordance with NY CPLR Rule 2214. NY R L KINGS Pt. C, Rule 1.

iv. *NEW YORK COUNTY.* In an e-filed case, all of the moving papers shall be e-filed at least eight (8) business days prior to the return date. The clerk will calendar the motion for the Motion Submission Part Courtroom (Room 130) for the return date selected. NY R NY CTY Procedure II(A); NY R NY CTY E FIL Doc. 2(D)(1).

v. *ONONDAGA COUNTY.* Onondaga County local court rules require that any additional papers relating to motions must be e-filed at least two (2) business days prior to the return date, excluding the return date. NY R ONDGA E FIL Protocol(B)(9)(e).

vi. *QUEENS COUNTY.* Motions must be in the possession of the Motion Support Office at least nine (9) days before the noticed return date of the motion. NY R L QUEENS MOT SUP Doc. 1; NY R L QUEENS E-FILE Doc. 1(H)(1).

b. *Order to show cause; Shorter time.* The court in a proper case may grant an order to show cause, to be served in lieu of a notice of motion, at a time and in a manner specified therein. NY CPLR Rule 2214(d). An ordinary notice of motion can't be brought on for hearing earlier than the eighth (8th) day after the motion papers are served. With an order to show cause, the hearing can be brought on at any time the court directs, which can be fewer than eight (8) days or as close as the very day on which it is signed. If the court is convinced there is a real emergency, it can schedule the hearing for a few hours later or, in the direst case, "forthwith" the service of the order to show cause. SIEGEL-NYPRAC § 248.

c. *Time to serve answering affidavits; Other answering papers.* Answering affidavits shall be served at least two (2) days before the time at which the motion is noticed to be heard. Answering affidavits and any notice of cross-motion, with supporting papers, if any, shall be served at least seven (7) days before such time if a notice of motion served at least sixteen (16) days before such time so demands; whereupon any reply or responding affidavits shall be served at least one (1) day before such time. NY CPLR Rule 2214(b); NY R UNIF TRIAL CTS § 202.8(c).

   i. *BRONX COUNTY.* All answering papers must be submitted to the Clerk 's Office on the return date of the motion. Answering papers will not be accepted prior to the return date. NY R BRONX FIL R Doc. 8.

   ii. *NEW YORK COUNTY.* Cross-motions, papers in opposition, and reply papers on motions/petitions on notice returnable in Room 130 in a hard-copy case shall be submitted to the Motion Submission Part Courtroom (Room 130) on the final return date of the motion/petition and will not be accepted until that date. Subsequent documents on motions/petitions in e-filed cases shall be e-filed in a timely manner. Working copies when required shall be submitted to Room 130 on the final return date. NY R NY CTY Procedure II(A).

d. *Time to serve cross-motion.* At least three (3) days prior to the time at which the motion is noticed to be heard, or seven (7) days prior to such time if demand is properly made pursuant to NY CPLR Rule 2214(b), a party may serve upon the moving party a notice of cross-motion demanding relief, with or without supporting papers; provided, however, that:

   i. If such notice and any supporting papers are served by mailing, as provided in NY CPLR Rule 2103(b)(2), they shall be served three (3) days earlier than as prescribed in NY CPLR Rule 2215; and

   ii. If served by overnight delivery, as provided in NY CPLR Rule 2103(b)(6), they shall be served one (1) day earlier than as prescribed in NY CPLR Rule 2215. Relief in the alternative or of several different types may be demanded; relief need not be responsive to that demanded by the moving party. NY CPLR Rule 2215(a); NY CPLR Rule 2215(b).

   iii. *BRONX COUNTY.* Cross motions may be presented for approval on or before the return date, provided that there is a motion already calendared. NY R BRONX FIL R Doc. 8.

   iv. *ERIE COUNTY.* Cross-motions must be filed at least two (2) days before the return date of the motion. NY R L KINGS Pt. A, Papers.

   v. *KINGS COUNTY.* Hard copies are required to be filed for any motions, answering papers, stipulations, etc. for E-Filed cases returnable in [the Central Compliance Part] at least [two (2)] days before return date. . .for cross motions. NY R L KINGS Pt. E, Rule 8.

   vi. *QUEENS COUNTY.* Motion Support does not process or forward responsive papers, including cross-motions. They must be brought to the calendar call in the judge's part. NY R L QUEENS MOT SUP Doc. 1. E-filed cross motions: across motion must be noticed for the same return date as the main motion and have the confirmation of filing attached in the same manner as a motion. NY R L QUEENS E-FILE Doc. 1(H)(2)(e).

3. *Filing before return date.* All motions shall be returnable before the assigned judge, and all papers shall be filed with the court on or before the return date. NY R UNIF TRIAL CTS § 202.8(a).

   a. *BRONX COUNTY: Time for filing*

      i. *Unassigned motions.* Unassigned motions must be in the Clerk's Office within five (5) days of the date of service of the motion. NY R BRONX FIL R Doc. 8.

      ii. *Assigned motions.* Assigned motions must be filed in the Clerk's Office not less than five (5) business days prior to the return date of the motion. NY R BRONX FIL R Doc. 8.

      iii. *Motions returnable in room 217.* The moving documents must be e-filed no later than eight (8) days prior to the return date. NY R BRONX E FIL R Doc. 1(1).

   b. *KINGS COUNTY: Time and place of filing.* Motion papers must be filed with the E-file/Motion Support Office located in Room 227. . . at 360 Adams Street at least five (5) business days before the return date of the motion. NY R L

KINGS Pt. A, Papers. Hard copies are required to be filed for any motions, answering papers, stipulations, etc. for E-Filed cases returnable in [the Central Compliance Part] at least five (5) days before return date for main motions. NY R L KINGS Pt. E, Rule 8. The moving documents must be e-filed no later than eight (8) days prior to the return date. NY R L KINGS E FIL Doc. 1(D).

4. *NEW YORK COUNTY: Briefing schedule.* Once a motion is made, counsel for all parties are strongly encouraged to agree upon a briefing schedule and submit a stipulation of adjournment reflecting that schedule using service or a clerk. Where a briefing schedule has not been agreed upon, the movant can avoid the need to attend simply to see if anyone will hand up opposing papers by demanding papers as provided by NY CPLR Rule 2214(b). To protect movants against the submission of late opposition papers or cross-motions, the General Clerk's Office will screen motions in which such papers are submitted without a response (reply or opposition respectively) to ensure that proper time to respond has been afforded and it will sua sponte adjourn for one (1) week cases in which such time has not been given. NY R NY CTY Procedure II(C).
5. *QUEENS COUNTY: Time to pay fees.* As motions and petitions are time sensitive, if opting to pay at the County Clerk's Office payment MUST be made, if filed with an RJI, a minimum of nine (9) business days prior to the application's return date and if filed post RJI, a minimum of nine (9) business days prior to the application's return date. NY R L QUEENS E-FILE Doc. 1(H)(1).
6. *Computation of time*
   a. *Units of time*
      i. *Day.* A calendar day includes the time from midnight to midnight. Sunday or any day of the week specifically mentioned means a calendar day. NY GEN CONSTR § 19.
      ii. *Month.* In a statute, contract or public or private instrument, unless otherwise provided in such contract or instrument or by law, the term month means a calendar month and not a lunar month. NY GEN CONSTR § 31.
      iii. *Year.* For information on the definition of a year, including the definitions of a half-year and quarter-year, refer to NY GEN CONSTR § 58 and NY GEN CONSTR § 50. For information on leap years, refer to NY GEN CONSTR § 57.
   b. *Periods of time*
      i. *Number of days.* A number of days specified as a period from a certain day within which or after or before which an act is authorized or required to be done means such number of calendar days exclusive of the calendar day from which the reckoning is made. NY GEN CONSTR § 20.
         - If such period is a period of two (2) days, Saturday, Sunday or a public holiday must be excluded from the reckoning if it is an intervening day between the day from which the reckoning is made and the last day of the period. NY GEN CONSTR § 20.
         - In computing any specified period of time from a specified event, the day upon which the event happens is deemed the day from which the reckoning is made. The day from which any specified period of time is reckoned shall be excluded in making the reckoning. NY GEN CONSTR § 20.
      ii. *Number of months.* A number of months after or before a certain day shall be computed by counting such number of calendar months from such day, exclusive of the calendar month in which such day occurs, and shall include the day of the month in the last month so counted having the same numerical order in days of the month as the day from which the computation is made, unless there be not so many days in the last month so counted, in which case the period computed shall expire with the last day of the month so counted. NY GEN CONSTR § 30.
      iii. *Publication of notice; Number of days.* The period of publication of a legal notice shall be computed by excluding the first day of publication and including the day on which the act or event of which notice is given is to take place or which completes the full period of publication. NY CPLR § 2402.
      iv. *Periods ending on Saturday, Sunday or public holiday.* When any period of time, computed from a certain day, within which or after which or before which an act is authorized or required to be done, ends on a Saturday, Sunday or a public holiday, such act may be done on the next succeeding business day and if the period ends at a specified hour, such act may be done at or before the same hour of such next succeeding business day, except that where a period of time specified by contract ends on a Saturday, Sunday or a public holiday, the extension of such period is governed by NY GEN CONSTR § 25. NY GEN CONSTR § 25-a(1).
         - For a list of public holidays, refer to NY GEN CONSTR § 24.

v. *Additional time after certain kinds of service*

- *Service by mail.* Where a period of time prescribed by law is measured from the service of a paper and service is by mail, five (5) days shall be added to the prescribed period. NY CPLR Rule 2103(b)(2).
- *Service by overnight delivery service.* Where a period of time prescribed by law is measured from the service of a paper and service is by overnight delivery, one (1) business day shall be added to the prescribed period. NY CPLR Rule 2103(b)(6).

vi. *Daylight saving time.* For information on New York's time zone and the effect of daylight saving time, refer to NY GEN CONSTR § 52.

c. *Hours of court.* Notwithstanding any provision of law or rule of court to the contrary, throughout the State of New York the sessions of the Supreme Court for the disposition of business before the court shall commence not later than 9:30 a.m. and conclude not earlier than 5 p.m. Where warranted, the Chief Administrator of the Courts may authorize variances in the opening and closing hours of the courts, but, in such event, daily sessions shall total not less than six (6) hours. NY R CHIEF J § 3.1.

d. *Time limits; Extension of time.* Any act required by or in pursuance of law to be performed at or within a prescribed time, shall be performed according to the standard time. NY GEN CONSTR § 53.

i. Except where otherwise expressly prescribed by law, the court may extend the time fixed by any statute, rule or order for doing any act, upon such terms as may be just and upon good cause shown, whether the application for extension is made before or after the expiration of the time fixed. NY CPLR § 2004. Refer to the New York KeyRules Motion for Continuance/Extension of Time document for more information.

C. General Requirements

1. *Motions, generally.* There shall be compliance with the procedures prescribed in the CPLR for the bringing of motions. NY R UNIF TRIAL CTS § 202.7(a).

a. *Motions on notice.* A notice of motion shall specify the time and place of the hearing on the motion, the supporting papers upon which the motion is based, the relief demanded and the grounds therefor. NY CPLR Rule 2214(a). A motion on notice in an action in the supreme court shall be noticed to be heard in the judicial district where the action is triable or in a county adjoining the county where the action is triable. Unless statute, civil practice rule or local court rule provides otherwise, the motion shall be noticed to be heard before a motion term or, upon order to show cause granted by a justice, before that justice out of court. NY CPLR § 2212(a). Except as provided in NY R UNIF TRIAL CTS § 202.7(d), no motion shall be filed with the court unless there have been served and filed with the motion papers a notice of motion. NY R UNIF TRIAL CTS § 202.7(a)(1).

b. *Ex parte motions.* A motion in an action in the supreme court that may be made without notice may be made at a motion term or to a justice out of court in any county in the state. NY CPLR § 2212(b).

i. *KINGS COUNTY.* For more information on submitting a motion ex parte, refer to NY R L KINGS E FIL Doc. 1(G).

ii. *NEW YORK COUNTY.* For more information on submitting matters ex parte, refer to NY R NY CTY Procedure III and NY R NY CTY E FIL Doc. 2(G).

iii. *QUEENS COUNTY.* For more information on submitting matters ex parte, refer to NY R L QUEENS EX PARTE Doc. 1.

c. *Alternative relief.* Relief in the alternative or of several different types may be demanded. NY CPLR Rule 2214(a). The types of relief need not be related. In one motion, for example, the defendant can seek to dismiss the plaintiff's claim for lack of jurisdiction, to get an extension of time to answer, to require the plaintiff to join X as a party, and to quash a disclosure subpoena served in behalf of the plaintiff on a nonparty witness. So doing, the movant must of course specify all of these items of relief in the notice of motion, and the grounds for them, and the supporting papers must contain the entire proof requisite to the items of relief sought. NY CPLR Rule 2214(Practice Commentary, C2214:4).

d. *General relief.* It is common practice to include at the end of the relief request in the notice of motion a so-called "general relief" clause. This is merely a few words to cover the possibility that the relief appropriate to what the movant proves was not specifically asked for, but is close enough to enable the court to grant it. After stating the specific relief desired, the lawyer will often add something like: and for such other, further, or different relief as this court may deem just and proper. NY CPLR Rule 2214(Practice Commentary, C2214:5).

e. *Motion in improper form.* If the court finds it appropriate in the interests of justice, it may convert a motion into a

special proceeding, or vice-versa, upon such terms as may be just, including the payment of fees and costs. NY CPLR § 103(c).

f. *Order to show cause.* An order to show cause is basically only a substitute for a notice of motion. An ordinary notice of motion merely notifies the recipient that a motion is being made for specified relief. The burden of proof is on the movant. Although in most cases it is just as innocent as an ordinary notice of motion, the order to show cause gets its name by directing the recipient to "show cause" why the particular relief being asked for should not be granted. It sounds as if the burden of proof is being shifted to the recipient. It isn't. It specifies the time and place of the hearing on the application but when the hearing comes on, the burden of proof is where it always is on a motion: on the movant. SIEGEL-NYPRAC § 248.

i. The CPLR says nothing more about an order to show cause than that it may be used "in a proper case", which leaves it entirely to the judge's discretion to determine what a proper case is. Any fact suggesting a problem as to any of the items listed above would be sufficient to invoke judicial discretion and justify the show cause procedure, which is in fact liberally used. SIEGEL-NYPRAC § 248.

ii. An order to show cause against a state body or officers must be served in addition to service upon the defendant or respondent state body or officers upon the attorney general by delivery to an assistant attorney general at an office of the attorney general in the county in which venue of the action is designated or if there is no office of the attorney general in such county, at the office of the attorney general nearest such county. NY CPLR Rule 2214(d).

iii. *BRONX COUNTY.* For information on submitting an order to show cause, refer to NY R BRONX E FIL R Doc. 2 and NY R BRONX LEG SUP Doc. 1.

iv. *ERIE COUNTY.* For information on submitting an order to show cause, refer to NY R ERIE E FIL Doc. 3(VI).

v. *KINGS COUNTY.* For information on submitting an order to show cause, refer to NY R L KINGS E FIL Doc. 1(F).

vi. *NEW YORK COUNTY.* For information on submitting an order to show cause, refer to NY R NY CTY E FIL Doc. 2(F).

vii. *ONONDAGA COUNTY.* For information on submitting an order to show cause, refer to NY R ONDGA E FIL Protocol(B)(10) and NY R ONDGA E FIL Protocol(J).

g. *Motions before preliminary conference.* Motions in actions to which NY R UNIF TRIAL CTS § 202.12 is applicable made after the preliminary conference has been scheduled may be denied unless there is shown good cause why such relief is warranted before the preliminary conference is held. NY R UNIF TRIAL CTS § 202.12(h).

h. *ALBANY COUNTY: Good faith effort to resolve.* Prior to the submission of a notice of motion relating to disclosure or a bill of particulars, the parties must make a good faith effort to resolve the matter in question and submit an affirmation attesting to this good faith effort. NY R 3 JD SUP Doc. 1(B).

i. *NEW YORK COUNTY: Documents with motions.* Counsel must attach to motion papers copies of all pleadings and other documents as required by the CPLR and as necessary for an informed decision on the motion. Documents in a foreign language shall be properly translated. NY R NY CTY J RUL Rule 14(a).

j. *NEW YORK COUNTY: Motions in multiple cases made together.* On occasion, attorneys may wish to make a motion in more than one case on a single set of papers. In such cases, by definition consolidation will not have been directed since consolidation signifies the combination of more than one case into a single one with a single caption and index number and ending in a single judgment. NY R NY CTY Procedure II(B). For more information on motions made with the same papers, refer to NY R NY CTY Procedure II(A).

k. *QUEENS COUNTY: Motion sequence numbers.* A motion sequence number is required for all E-filed motions. After a motion is E-filed, please consult the e-courts website within twenty-four (24) to forty-eight (48) hours to obtain the sequence number. The Confirmation Notice of E-filing MUST indicate the sequence number of any motion submitted at the Centralized Motion Part calendar call. NY R L QUEENS E-FILE Doc. 1(H)(5).

2. *Motion for preliminary injunction*

a. *Provisional remedies generally.* The provisional remedies are attachment, injunction, receivership and notice of pendency. On a motion for a provisional remedy, the plaintiff shall state whether any other provisional remedy has been secured or sought in the same action against the same defendant, and the court may require the plaintiff to elect between those remedies to which he would otherwise be entitled; for this purpose, seizure of a chattel in an action to recover a chattel is a provisional remedy. A cause of action contained in a counterclaim or a cross-claim, and a judgment demanded thereon, shall entitle the defendant to the same provisional remedies to which he would be entitled if he were the plaintiff, the party against whom the judgment is demanded were the defendant and the cause of action were contained in a complaint. NY CPLR § 6001.

b. *Grounds for preliminary injunction*

i. A preliminary injunction may be granted in any action where it appears that the defendant threatens or is about to do, or is doing or procuring or suffering to be done, an act in violation of the plaintiff's rights respecting the subject of the action, and tending to render the judgment ineffectual. NY CPLR § 6301.

- Since the first part of NY CPLR § 6301 requires a specific "subject matter," an action for money only does not qualify, and of course a money action does not qualify under the second part of the statute, in which the object of the action itself is a permanent injunction. The provisional remedy of injunction is therefore unavailable in that most numerous of all actions, the money action. SIEGEL-NYPRAC § 327.
- A plaintiff seeking to prevent the defendant from transferring assets during the pendency of a money action and unable to secure the help of a preliminary injunction might look to the remedy of attachment under NY CPLR § 6201(3) instead. SIEGEL-NYPRAC § 327.
- Although the inclusion of a money demand will not necessarily preclude an injunction if other relief, which would satisfy this provision of NY CPLR § 6301, is also sought, the court will refuse the injunction if convinced that a money judgment is the true object of the action and that all else is incidental. SIEGEL-NYPRAC § 327.

ii. A preliminary injunction may be granted in any action where the plaintiff has demanded and would be entitled to a judgment restraining the defendant from the commission or continuance of an act, which, if committed or continued during the pendency of the action, would produce injury to the plaintiff. NY CPLR § 6301.

c. *Notice*

i. A preliminary injunction may be granted only upon notice to the defendant. Notice of the motion may be served with the summons or at any time thereafter and prior to judgment. A preliminary injunction to restrain a public officer, board or municipal corporation of the state from performing a statutory duty may be granted only by the supreme court at a term in the department in which the officer or board is located or in which the duty is required to be performed. NY CPLR § 6311(1).

ii. Notice of motion for a preliminary injunction to restrain state officers or boards of state officers under the provisions of NY CPLR § 6311 must be upon notice served upon the defendant or respondent, state officers or board of state officers and must be served upon the attorney general by delivery of such notice to an assistant attorney general at an office of the attorney general in the county in which venue of the action is designated or if there is no office of the attorney general in such county, at the office of the attorney general nearest such county. NY CPLR § 6311(2).

d. *Proof*

i. On a motion for a preliminary injunction the plaintiff shall show, by affidavit and such other evidence as may be submitted, that there is a cause of action, and either that the defendant threatens or is about to do, or is doing or procuring or suffering to be done, an act in violation of the plaintiff's rights respecting the subject of the action and tending to render the judgment ineffectual; or that the plaintiff has demanded and would be entitled to a judgment restraining the defendant from the commission or continuance of an act, which, if committed or continued during the pendency of the action, would produce injury to the plaintiff. NY CPLR Rule 6312(a). The plaintiff's showing on an application for a preliminary injunction must be convincing. SIEGEL-NYPRAC § 328; Etter v. Littwitz, 47 Misc. 2d 473, 477, 262 N.Y.S.2d 924, 928 (Sup. Ct. 1965).

- It will not suffice for the plaintiff merely to make out a prima facie possibility of success on the merits of the claim. The plaintiff has the burden of proof and must demonstrate a likelihood of success on the merits, which means a strong showing in affidavits and other proof supplying evidentiary detail. SIEGEL-NYPRAC § 328; Metz v. People, 73 Misc. 2d 219, 220, 341 N.Y.S.2d 940, 942 (Sup. Ct. 1973). The plaintiff should then show "that he would be irreparably damaged if an injunction were not granted before trial," and should demonstrate this factually and convincingly. SIEGEL-NYPRAC § 328; De Candido v. Young Stars, Inc., 10 A.D.2d 922, 922, 200 N.Y.S.2d 695, 696 (1960).
- If the defendant, opposing the application, offers substantial proof of defenses tending to negate the plaintiff's claim on the merits, such as laches and unclean hands, the injunction is likely to be denied. SIEGEL-NYPRAC § 328; De Candido v. Young Stars, Inc., 10 A.D.2d 922, 922, 200 N.Y.S.2d 695, 696 (1960).

e. *Statement of prejudice.* Any application for temporary injunctive relief, including but not limited to a motion for a stay or a temporary restraining order, shall contain, in addition to the other information required by NY R UNIF TRIAL CTS § 202.7, an affirmation demonstrating there will be significant prejudice to the party seeking the restraining order by giving of notice. In the absence of a showing of significant prejudice, the affirmation must demonstrate that a good faith effort has been made to notify the party against whom the temporary restraining order is sought of the time, date and place that the application will be made in a manner sufficient to permit the party an opportunity to appear in response to the application. NY R UNIF TRIAL CTS § 202.7(f).

  i. *ALBANY COUNTY.* Prior to submitting an order to show cause which contains an application for temporary injunctive relief, an applicant must comply with NY R UNIF TRIAL CTS § 202.7(f). NY R 3 JD SUP Doc. 1(B).

f. *Undertaking required.* Except as provided in NY CPLR § 2512, prior to the granting of a preliminary injunction, the plaintiff shall give an undertaking in an amount to be fixed by the court, that the plaintiff, if it is finally determined that he or she was not entitled to an injunction, will pay to the defendant all damages and costs which may be sustained by reason of the injunction, including:

  i. If the injunction is to stay proceedings in another action, on any ground other than that a report, verdict or decision was obtained by actual fraud, all damages and costs which may be, or which have been, awarded in the other action to the defendant as well as all damages and costs which may be awarded him or her in the action in which the injunction was granted; or,

  ii. If the injunction is to stay proceedings in an action to recover real property, or for dower, on any ground other than that a verdict, report or decision was obtained by actual fraud, all damages and costs which may be, or which have been, awarded to the defendant in the action in which the injunction was granted, including the reasonable rents and profits of, and any wastes committed upon, the real property which is sought to be recovered or which is the subject of the action for dower, after the granting of the injunction; or,

  iii. If the injunction is to stay proceedings upon a judgment for a sum of money on any ground other than that the judgment was obtained by actual fraud, the full amount of the judgment as well as all damages and costs which may be awarded to the defendant in the action in which the injunction was granted. NY CPLR Rule 6312(b).

  iv. For information on undertakings, refer to NY CPLR § 2501, et seq.

g. *Issues of fact.* Provided that the elements required for the issuance of a preliminary injunction are demonstrated in the plaintiff's papers, the presentation by the defendant of evidence sufficient to raise an issue of fact as to any of such elements shall not in itself be grounds for denial of the motion. In such event the court shall make a determination by hearing or otherwise whether each of the elements required for issuance of a preliminary injunction exists. NY CPLR Rule 6312(c).

  i. An evidentiary hearing is permissible, but not mandatory. The court may, as it usually does in these situations, determine the application on the papers alone. SIEGEL-NYPRAC § 328; Indep. Health Ass'n, Inc. v. Murray, 233 A.D.2d 883, 883, 649 N.Y.S.2d 616, 618 (1996).

h. *Discretion of court.* Perhaps the most instructive point about the preliminary injunction is that its granting is discretionary with the court. This is so even though the plaintiff has made out the minimum showing under NY CPLR § 6301. SIEGEL-NYPRAC § 328; Sartwell v. Field, 68 N.Y. 341, 341 (1877).

  i. Perhaps the highest role discretion plays is in determining whether the plaintiff would be "irreparably" injured if the injunction were withheld. The adverb is often seen in opinions treating injunctions, and yet if it were literally applied, few injunctions would issue. Whether the plaintiff's harm would be "irreparable" turns on many things, all of which can be weighed and balanced by an astute judicial exercise of discretion. If all past cases granting provisional injunctions were collated and analyzed, many if not most would not pass a rigid "irreparable injury" test. The test must be applied common sensically to give appropriate consideration to all factors. With a banner of discretion waving over the field of injunctions, pragmatism is the theme. This tends to prevent any single factor, no matter what its individual dictate might be, from rejecting the injunction out of hand in the face of countervailing considerations. SIEGEL-NYPRAC § 328.

i. *Temporary restraining order.* A temporary restraining order may be granted pending a hearing for a preliminary injunction where it appears that immediate and irreparable injury, loss or damage will result unless the defendant is restrained before the hearing can be had. NY CPLR § 6301.

  i. *Generally.* If, on a motion for a preliminary injunction, the plaintiff shall show that immediate and irreparable injury, loss or damages will result unless the defendant is restrained before a hearing can be had, a temporary restraining order may be granted without notice. Upon granting a temporary restraining order, the court shall set the hearing for the preliminary injunction at the earliest possible time. No temporary restraining order may be granted in an action arising out of a labor dispute as defined in NY LABOR § 807, nor against a public officer, board or municipal corporation of the state to restrain the performance of statutory duties. NY CPLR § 6313(a).

ii. *Purpose.* Since a motion for a preliminary injunction may be made only on notice under NY CPLR § 6311, there is a risk that between the time the motion papers are served and the day set for the hearing, the return day, the defendant will consummate the act the plaintiff wants restrained and make all further proceedings futile. The sole mission of the temporary restraining order (TRO) is to effect a restraint against the defendant during that brief interim and keep the status quo until the judge can hear both sides. SIEGEL-NYPRAC § 330.

iii. *Contents.* A plaintiff who wants a temporary restraining order does not use the ordinary motion on notice procedure to bring on the application for a preliminary injunction, but rather an order to show cause, and it's the order to show cause that includes the temporary restraining order. SIEGEL-NYPRAC § 330.

- *Order to show cause.* The plaintiff who wants a TRO frequently applies for it ex parte by presenting an order to show cause to the court. Since an order to show cause is, in this instance, a species of ex parte application, the plaintiff must inform the court in an affidavit whether this or like relief was previously applied for and what the result was of any such prior application, and must establish the requirements in NY R UNIF TRIAL CTS § 202.7(f). SIEGEL-NYPRAC § 330; NY CPLR Rule 2217(b).
- *Contents of order.* If the judge signs the order to show cause, the judge will determine in the order itself (1) the time and place of the hearing for the preliminary injunction, (2) who shall be served with the order, (3) how and when the service shall be made, and (4) the terms of the temporary restraining order. SIEGEL-NYPRAC § 330; SIEGEL-NYPRAC § 248. After signing by the judge, the order is returned to the plaintiff's attorney, who then effects service of it on the defendant pursuant to its terms. SIEGEL-NYPRAC § 330. If the court grants a temporary restraining order, it must set the hearing for the preliminary injunction for "the earliest possible time," which merely recognizes that an ex parte restraint against a defendant should be as brief as possible. SIEGEL-NYPRAC § 330; NY CPLR § 6313(a). If an order to show cause containing a temporary restraining order does not contain directions as to the method of service, then service is to be made in the same manner as a summons. The papers served must include the papers on which the temporary restraining order is based. SIEGEL-NYPRAC § 330; NY CPLR § 6313(b).

iv. *Service.* Unless the court orders otherwise, a temporary restraining order together with the papers upon which it was based, and a notice of hearing for the preliminary injunction, shall be personally served in the same manner as a summons. NY CPLR § 6313(b). If the summons has not yet been served, the summons should accompany the order to show cause and be served on the defendant at the same time. Since the order to show cause serves as the notice of application for the preliminary injunction, this procedure will satisfy the requirement of NY CPLR § 6311(1) that notice of the application be served with or after the summons. SIEGEL-NYPRAC § 330. Refer to the New York KeyRules Complaint document for information on service of the summons.

- The usual practice is for the plaintiff to file the summons and complaint when applying for the temporary restraining order, so that an action will immediately be pending and give its context to the application. It will also enable the plaintiff to secure an index number and include it on the summons and complaint, as well as on the order to show cause. SIEGEL-NYPRAC § 330.

v. *Undertaking.* Prior to the granting of a temporary restraining order the court may, in its discretion, require the plaintiff to give an undertaking in an amount to be fixed by the court, containing terms similar to those set forth in NY CPLR Rule 6312(b), and subject to the exception set forth therein. NY CPLR § 6313(c).

j. *Violation of order.* The violation of either a preliminary injunction or a temporary restraining order is of course a contempt of court and may be punished as such. SIEGEL-NYPRAC § 331.

k. *Vacating or modifying injunction.* A defendant enjoined by a preliminary injunction may move at any time, on notice to the plaintiff, to vacate or modify it. On motion, without notice, made by a defendant enjoined by a temporary restraining order, the judge who granted it, or in his absence or disability, another judge, may vacate or modify the order. An order granted without notice and vacating or modifying a temporary restraining order shall be effective when, together with the papers upon which it is based, it is filed with the clerk and served upon the plaintiff. As a condition to granting an order vacating or modifying a preliminary injunction or a temporary restraining order, a court may require the defendant, except where the defendant is a public body or officer, to give an undertaking, in an amount to be fixed by the court, that the defendant shall pay to the plaintiff any loss sustained by reason of the vacating or modifying order. NY CPLR § 6314.

i. *Ascertaining damages.* The damages sustained by reason of a preliminary injunction or temporary restraining order may be ascertained upon motion on such notice to all interested persons as the court shall direct. Where the defendant enjoined was an officer of a corporation or joint-stock association or a representative of another person, and the amount of the undertaking exceeds the damages sustained by the defendant by reason of the preliminary injunction or temporary restraining order, the damages sustained by such corporation, association or person represented, to the amount of such excess, may also be ascertained. The amount of damages so ascertained is conclusive upon all persons who were served with notice of the motion and such amount may be recovered by the person entitled thereto in a separate action. NY CPLR § 6315.

- This is designed to facilitate things by enabling the defendant, with a mere motion procedure, to have the amount of her damages ascertained within the framework of the plaintiff's action before bringing a separate action on the undertaking to recover judgment for those damages. SIEGEL-NYPRAC § 329; Gross v. Shields, 130 Misc. 2d 641, 645, 496 N.Y.S.2d 894, 897 (Sup. Ct. 1985).
- This procedure is optional; the damages can be ascertained in the separate action. It has also been held that if the damages are ascertained by motion in the plaintiff's action, a judgment for them can be awarded without even requiring a separate action. SIEGEL-NYPRAC § 329; Carroll v. Kenin, 25 A.D.2d 743, 269 N.Y.S.2d 226, 227 (1966).

l. *Labor injunctions.* For information on special requirements for injunctions sought in labor disputes, refer to NY LABOR § 807.

3. *Oppositions.* In the absence of statutory provision or court rule, a motion ordinarily does not require a written answer, although an adverse party may be permitted to file an answer in opposition to the showing made in the motion or its supporting affidavits. AMJUR MOTIONS § 26. When a party files a motion and the opposing party fails to respond, the court may construe such failure to respond as non-opposition to the motion or an admission that the motion was meritorious, may take the facts alleged in the motion as true, and may grant the motion if the relief requested appears to be justified. However, the severity of such a result demands that a court impose it only with great caution. AMJUR MOTIONS § 28.

4. *Governing law.* The civil practice law and rules (NY CPLR § 101, et seq.) shall govern the procedure in civil judicial proceedings in all courts of the state and before all judges, except where the procedure is regulated by inconsistent statute. The civil practice law and rules shall succeed the civil practice act and rules of civil practice and shall be deemed substituted therefor throughout the statutes and rules of the state. NY CPLR § 101. The civil practice law and rules shall be liberally construed to secure the just, speedy and inexpensive determination of every civil judicial proceeding. NY CPLR § 104.

   a. *Uniform trial court rules.* The uniform civil rules for the Supreme Court and County Court (NY R UNIF TRIAL CTS § 202.1, et seq.) shall be applicable to civil actions and proceedings in the Supreme Court and the County Court. NY R UNIF TRIAL CTS § 202.1(a). The provisions of the uniform rules shall be construed consistent with the Civil Practice Law and Rules (CPLR), and matters not covered by the uniform rules shall be governed by the CPLR. NY R UNIF TRIAL CTS § 202.1(d).

   b. *Local rules.* Local court rules, not inconsistent with law or with uniform civil rules for the Supreme Court and County Court (NY R UNIF TRIAL CTS § 202.1, et seq.), shall comply with Part 9 of the Rules of the Chief Judge (NY R CHIEF J § 9.1). NY R UNIF TRIAL CTS § 202.1(c).

   c. *Official forms.* The state administrator shall have the power to adopt, amend and rescind an appendix of forms. Forms adopted pursuant to NY CPLR § 107 shall be sufficient under the civil practice law and rules and shall illustrate the simplicity and brevity of statement which the civil practice law and rules contemplate. NY CPLR § 107.

5. *Rules of the commercial division.* [Editor's note: certain types of civil cases or civil cases meeting certain monetary thresholds that are filed in the state of New York must be filed in the Commercial Division of the New York Supreme Courts. Rules governing practice in the commercial division are found in NY R UNIF TRIAL CTS § 202.70]. Cases which must be filed in the commercial division are listed below. For more information, refer to NY R UNIF TRIAL CTS § 202.70.

   a. *Monetary thresholds.* Except as set forth in NY R UNIF TRIAL CTS § 202.70(b), the monetary thresholds of the Commercial Division, exclusive of punitive damages, interests, costs, disbursements and counsel fees claimed, are established as follows: (1) Albany County, fifty thousand dollars ($50,000); (2) Eighth Judicial District, one hundred thousand dollars ($100,000); (3) Kings County, one hundred fifty thousand dollars ($150,000); (4) Nassau County, two hundred thousand dollars ($200,000); (5) New York County, five hundred thousand dollars ($500,000); (6) Onondaga County, fifty thousand dollars ($50,000); (7) Queens County, one hundred thousand dollars ($100,000); (8) Seventh Judicial District, fifty thousand dollars ($50,000); (9) Suffolk County, one hundred thousand dollars

($100,000); and (10) Westchester County, one hundred thousand dollars ($100,000). NY R UNIF TRIAL CTS § 202.70(a).

i. *ALBANY COUNTY.* The Commercial Division of the Albany County Supreme Court exercises jurisdiction over selected business and commercial disputes in which the amount at issue generally involves damage claims in a minimum amount of fifty thousand dollars ($50,000) as well as claims for unspecified amounts where the value of the commercial asset(s) in dispute exceeds fifty thousand dollars ($50,000). A separate publication promulgating the rules and criteria relating to the filing and management of Commercial Court cases in this part may be obtained from the Albany County Supreme Court Clerk's Office. A section of the Uniform Civil Rules for the Supreme Court and County Court sets forth statewide rules. NY R 3 JD SUP Doc. 1(E).

ii. *BRONX COUNTY.* The monetary threshold for commercial cases in Bronx County will be seventy-five thousand dollars ($75,000). All other parameters including the type of matters that will be heard are contained within the Rules of the Commercial Division of the Supreme Court (NY R UNIF TRIAL CTS § 202.70). NY R BRONX FIL R Doc. 12.

iii. *NEW YORK COUNTY.* The monetary threshold in the New York County Commercial Division, which is generally applicable, is an amount in controversy of five hundred thousand dollars ($500,000) or more (exclusive of punitive damages, interest, costs, disbursements, and counsel fees). If the case is designated a commercial one and the Addendum is submitted, the clerk will review the pleadings to determine whether the amount in controversy in the case meets the monetary threshold or whether an exception to the threshold applies. NY R NY CTY Procedure IA(B). For more information on assigning a case to the commercial division in New York County, refer to NY R NY CTY Procedure IA(B).

b. *Commercial cases.* Actions in which the principal claims involve or consist of the following will be heard in the Commercial Division provided that the monetary threshold is met or equitable or declaratory relief is sought:

i. Breach of contract or fiduciary duty, fraud, misrepresentation, business tort (e.g., unfair competition), or statutory and/or common law violation where the breach or violation is alleged to arise out of business dealings (e.g., sales of assets or securities; corporate restructuring; partnership, shareholder, joint venture, and other business agreements; trade secrets; restrictive covenants; and employment agreements not including claims that principally involve alleged discriminatory practices);

ii. Transactions governed by the Uniform Commercial Code (exclusive of those concerning individual cooperative or condominium units);

iii. Transactions involving commercial real property, including Yellowstone injunctions and excluding actions for the payment of rent only;

iv. Shareholder derivative actions—without consideration of the monetary threshold;

v. Commercial class actions—without consideration of the monetary threshold;

vi. Business transactions involving or arising out of dealings with commercial banks and other financial institutions;

vii. Internal affairs of business organizations;

viii. Malpractice by accountants or actuaries, and legal malpractice arising out of representation in commercial matters;

ix. Environmental insurance coverage;

x. Commercial insurance coverage (e.g., directors and officers, errors and omissions, and business interruption coverage);

xi. Dissolution of corporations, partnerships, limited liability companies, limited liability partnerships and joint ventures—without consideration of the monetary threshold; and

xii. Applications to stay or compel arbitration and affirm or disaffirm arbitration awards and related injunctive relief pursuant to Article 75 of the New York Civil Practice Law and Rules (NY CPLR § 7501, et seq.) involving any of the foregoing enumerated commercial issues. Where the applicable arbitration agreement provides for the arbitration to be heard outside the United States, the monetary threshold set forth in NY R UNIF TRIAL CTS § 202.70(a) shall not apply. NY R UNIF TRIAL CTS § 202.70(b).

c. *Non-commercial cases.* The following will not be heard in the Commercial Division even if the monetary threshold is met:

i. Suits to collect professional fees;

ii. Cases seeking a declaratory judgment as to insurance coverage for personal injury or property damage;

iii. Residential real estate disputes, including landlord-tenant matters, and commercial real estate disputes involving the payment of rent only;

iv. Home improvement contracts involving residential properties consisting of one to four residential units or individual units in any residential building, including cooperative or condominium units;

v. Proceedings to enforce a judgment regardless of the nature of the underlying case;

vi. First-party insurance claims and actions by insurers to collect premiums or rescind non-commercial policies; and

vii. Attorney malpractice actions except as otherwise provided in NY R UNIF TRIAL CTS § 202.70(b)(8). NY R UNIF TRIAL CTS § 202.70(c).

d. For more information on the Commercial Division, refer to NY R UNIF TRIAL CTS § 202.70.

D. Documents

1. *Documents for moving party*

a. *Required documents*

i. *Notice of motion, order to show cause, or affidavit on ex parte motion.* The notice of motion shall be substantially in the form found in NY R UNIF TRIAL CTS § 202.7(b). NY R UNIF TRIAL CTS § 202.7(b). The supporting papers should be referred to in the notice of motion. SIEGEL-NYPRAC § 246. The court in a proper case may grant an order to show cause, to be served in lieu of a notice of motion. NY CPLR Rule 2214(d). An ex parte motion shall be accompanied by an affidavit stating the result of any prior motion for similar relief and specifying the new facts, if any, that were not previously shown. NY CPLR Rule 2217(b).

- *Request for oral argument.* A party requesting oral argument shall set forth such request in its notice of motion or in its order to show cause or on the first page of the answering papers, as the case may be. Where all parties to a motion request oral argument, oral argument shall be granted unless the court shall determine it to be unnecessary. Where a motion is brought on by order to show cause, the court may set forth in the order that oral argument is required on the return date of the motion. NY R UNIF TRIAL CTS § 202.8(d).

ii. *Motion.* Refer to the General Requirements section of this document for information on the notice of motion and motion.

iii. *Undertaking.* Refer to the General Requirements section of this document for information on the undertaking.

iv. *Request for judicial intervention.* At any time after service of process, a party may file a request for judicial intervention. Except as provided in NY R UNIF TRIAL CTS § 202.6(b), in an action not yet assigned to a judge, the court shall not accept for filing a notice of motion, order to show cause, or application for ex parte order, unless such notice or application is accompanied by a request for judicial intervention. NY R UNIF TRIAL CTS § 202.6(a).

- *BRONX COUNTY.* Generally, the Request For Judicial Intervention, commonly referred to as an "RJI", is required to be filed in any action where the assignment of a Justice is required. The RJI sets forth the information which is entered into the court system's database. It must be completely and accurately filled out. The full caption, as stated on the Summons, must be set forth. Use of terms "et al." and "etc." are not permitted. Only one (1) RJI may be filed in each action. Either a self represented litigant or an attorney must sign the affirmation at the end of the form. Once completed, the RJI must be filed in duplicate. Except in the case of an ex-parte application, the RJI must also be served together with the accompanying application upon all parties. Proof of accuracy of the index number must accompany the RJI. Check the Fee Schedule[. . .]for any applicable filing fees. NY R BRONX FIL R Doc. 2.
- *KINGS COUNTY.* An RJI with the relevant required addendum in a NYSCEF case shall be submitted via NYSCEF. Once e-filed, the RJI and any accompanying document will be forwarded to the relevant support office for random assignment of the case and processing of the document. A filer or counsel need not appear (as to Proposed Orders to Show Cause, however, see below). A copy of the pleadings must be submitted only if the document has not previously been e-filed. If the RJI seeks intervention with regard to a document that is intended for review by a Justice, such as a motion, a working copy of the RJI must be submitted with the working copy of the motion and the NYSCEF Confirmation Notice. NY R L KINGS E FIL Doc. 1(C).
- *NEW YORK COUNTY.* To obtain the assignment of an IAS Justice to a case, a Request for Judicial

Intervention (cost ninety-five dollars ($95)) must be filed, with NYSCEF in an e-filed case or in paper in an authorized hard-copy one. A no-fee RJI, which will generally result in the referral of an application to an Ex Parte Justice, is also required with regard to certain kinds of applications for which, prior to 2011, no RJI was required. NY R NY CTY Procedure I(C). A "fillable" form RJI is available on-line. The form must be filed in duplicate in hard-copy cases. NY R NY CTY Procedure IA(A)(1). The filer of an RJI must check off a box identifying the type of case at issue. Where the RJI seeks judicial assignment, this designation will bring about a random assignment of the case by computer to a Justice handling cases of that type. NY R NY CTY Procedure IA(A)(1). The RJI and any addendum can be completed and submitted electronically in an e-filed case. NY R NY CTY Procedure II(A). The RJI shall be marked to reflect the existence of any "related case" as explained on the "Commencement of Cases" page under "Case Processing" on the court's website. NY R NY CTY Procedure II(A); NY R NY CTY E FIL Doc. 2(C).

- *ONONDAGA COUNTY.* The RJI will be submitted via the NYSCEF system along with any required RJI addendum forms. When the RJI is filed and the fee paid online, the Onondaga County Clerk's Office will electronically forward the RJI and any accompanying documents to the Onondaga Supreme Court Clerk's Office for assignment and processing. Counsel will receive notification of judge assignment via the NYSCEF system. NY R ONDGA E FIL Protocol(B)(3).
- *QUEENS COUNTY.* A Request for Judicial Intervention ("RJI") in an E-filed case shall be submitted via the E-filing System. When the RJI is approved, filed and paid for on-line, it will be forwarded to the relevant back office for random assignment of the case and processing of the document. In the case of RJIs seeking assignment to the Commercial Division, the filer must submit therewith, a Commercial Addendum as required by the standards for assignment of cases to the Commercial Division. NY R L QUEENS E-FILE Doc. 1(F).

v. *Proof of service.* In addition to complying with the provisions of NY CPLR Rule 2101, every paper filed in court shall have annexed thereto appropriate proof of service on all parties where required. NY R UNIF TRIAL CTS § 202.5(a).

- *QUEENS COUNTY.* With regard to service of a motion/petition on notice in an E-filed action, NY CPLR Rule 2214(b) and NY R UNIF TRIAL CTS § 202.5-b(f) applies. Where required, proof of service shall be filed on-line as a separate document. NY R L QUEENS E-FILE Doc. 1(H)(3).

vi. *ALBANY COUNTY: Additional required documents*

- *Affirmation of good faith effort.* The parties must[. . .]submit an affirmation attesting to [their good faith effort to resolve the matter]. The affirmation of good faith effort to resolve the issues raised by the motion shall indicate the time, place and nature of the consultation and the issues discussed and any resolutions, or shall indicate good cause why no such conferral with counsel for opposing parties was held. An assigned justice or judge may dismiss a motion for failure to demonstrate that such effort was made with leave to renew the motion after such effort has been demonstrated. NY R 3 JD SUP Doc. 1(B).

b. *Supplemental documents*

i. *Supporting evidence; Exhibits.* The main supporting papers on a motion are affidavits, but any relevant exhibits, documents, depositions, etc., are also includible. SIEGEL-NYPRAC § 246.

- *Affidavits accompanying motion.* Affidavits shall be for a statement of the relevant facts. NY R UNIF TRIAL CTS § 202.8(c).
- *Foreign language documents.* Where an affidavit or exhibit annexed to a paper served or filed is in a foreign language, it shall be accompanied by an English translation and an affidavit by the translator stating his qualifications and that the translation is accurate. NY CPLR Rule 2101(b).
- *Statement of attorney in lieu of affidavit.* The statement of an attorney admitted to practice in the courts of the state, or of a physician, osteopath or dentist, authorized by law to practice in the state, who is not a party to an action, when subscribed and affirmed by him to be true under the penalties of perjury, may be served or filed in the action in lieu of and with the same force and effect as an affidavit. NY CPLR Rule 2106.
- *NEW YORK COUNTY: Form of presented exhibits.* Exhibits should be tabbed and be legible; a typed version of any exhibit that is difficult to read should be submitted with the original. Exhibits printed on both sides of the page should be bound and tabbed on the side. NY R NY CTY J RUL Rule 14(a).
- *QUEENS COUNTY.* Attorneys submitting exhibits to the court on E-file cases shall make each exhibit a separate, labeled attachment to an affidavit/affirmation. NY R L QUEENS E-FILE Doc. 1(H)(4).

ii. *Brief.* Briefs shall be for a statement of the relevant law. NY R UNIF TRIAL CTS § 202.8(c).

iii. *Application for temporary restraining order.* Refer to the General Requirements section of this document for more information on the application for temporary restraining order.

iv. *Notice to produce papers not in possession of the court.* If a paper relied on by the movant is in the possession of the other side, it may be demanded of that side with a notice to produce it at the hearing. Where such papers are in the possession of an adverse party, they shall be produced by him at the hearing on notice served with the motion papers. NY CPLR Rule 2214(Practice Commentary, C2214:23).

v. *Filing fees.* The County Clerk shall require the payment of any applicable statutory fees, or an order of the Court waiving payment of such fees, before accepting a paper for filing. NY R UNIF TRIAL CTS § 202.5(d)(1). For information on filing fees, if any, refer to NY CPLR § 8001, et seq.

- *ALBANY COUNTY.* In general, any filing subsequent to the commencement of an action which is designated as a motion or cross-motion requires the payment of a filing fee to the County Clerk's Office prior to submission to the Supreme Court Clerk's Office for referral to the assigned justice. The fee is assessed regardless of whether an application is made by notice of motion, order to show cause or ex parte. No fee will be charged upon the filing of a motion for poor person status in conjunction with an application which serves to commence an action or special proceeding. In the event a motion is received by the court unaccompanied by proof of payment to the County Clerk, the Supreme Court Clerk's Office will contact the submitting party to advise that the application will be held pending receipt of the filing fee only until the return date of the motion. If proof of payment is not submitted to the Supreme Court Clerk's Office by the return date (ex parte applications will be held ten (10) days), the papers will be returned by mail with a notification that the motion has been removed from the court's calendar and that it must be re-noticed and re-filed with the court along with the requisite filing fee. Inquiries concerning the applicability of the motion fee to a proposed filing may be directed to the Supreme Court Clerk's Office. NY R 3 JD SUP Doc. 1(B).

- *BRONX COUNTY.* In accordance with the new civil fee schedule set forth in Article 80 of the C.P.L.R. (NY CPLR § 8001, et seq.), effective July 14, 2003, all motions, and cross motions must be approved in Room 217 prior to payment of said fees in the County Clerk's Office, Room 118. NY R BRONX FIL R Doc. 8. The motion fee [must be] paid for via NYSCEF by credit/debit card. NY R BRONX E FIL R Doc. 1(1).

- *ERIE COUNTY.* Payment for fee-bearing NYSCEF documents must be made online via credit or debit card (American Express, MasterCard or Visa) at the time of submission. NY R ERIE E FIL Doc. 3(III)(E).

- *KINGS COUNTY.* The motion must be filed with NYSCEF and the motion fee paid. NY R L KINGS E FIL Doc. 1(D). Court fees in NYSCEF cases must be paid via NYSCEF by a credit or bank card (MasterCard, Visa, or American Express). Fees are no longer accepted in person in the Kings County Clerk's Office in NYSCEF cases. NY R L KINGS E FIL Doc. 1(B)(6).

- *NEW YORK COUNTY.* A motion fee must be paid on motions made in writing by notice of motion, order to show cause or ex parte after the commencement of an action. For this purpose, the term "action" shall mean any application to the court that requires the assignment of an index number, regardless of whether a formal pleading is filed. Applications or motions that commence an action and for which an index number fee must be paid require no motion fee. [A]ny motions made after the initial applications in these situations would require payment of the motion fee. A motion that is the initial application in a case commenced by the filing of a summons and complaint would require a motion fee since the filing of the summons and complaint rather than the application itself would require the purchase of an index number. NY R NY CTY Procedure II(A). In e-filed cases the motion fee must be paid when the documents are filed. Payment is made on-line by Visa, Mastercard, or American Express credit or bank card. NY R NY CTY Procedure II(A); NY R NY CTY E FIL Doc. 2(B)(5).

- *ONONDAGA COUNTY.* Court fees in e-filed cases must be paid online with the NYSCEF system using a credit card. The document is not considered to have been filed until payment of the fee has been tendered. NY R ONDGA E FIL Protocol(B)(2). Fees must be paid on all cross motions. NY R ONDGA E FIL Protocol(B)(9)(e).

- *QUEENS COUNTY.* The Motion Support Office does not receive, forward or process any fees or waiver of fees. All applications requiring payment of statutory fees or waiver of fees must be sent directly to the Queens County Clerk's office. NY R L QUEENS MOT SUP Doc. 1. Court fees (e.g., RJI fee, motion fee) in E-filed cases may be paid for on-line using a credit card. Papers may also be filed with the E-file system and the fee may be paid at the County Clerk's Office. In the latter case, the paper is not considered to have been filed until payment of the fee has been tendered. NY R L QUEENS E-FILE Doc. 1(E)(1). The motion/petition shall be filed on-line and the fee paid for either on-line by credit card or by the "Pay at the County Clerk's Office" option. NY R L QUEENS E-FILE Doc. 1(H)(1).

vi. *Working copies.* The court may require the parties to provide working copies of documents filed electronically. In such event, each working copy shall include, firmly affixed thereto, a copy of a confirmation notice in a form prescribed by the Chief Administrator. NY R UNIF TRIAL CTS § 202.5-b(d)(5).

- *BRONX COUNTY.* After papers on motions have been e-filed, working copies thereof, with Confirmation Notice firmly attached as the back page facing out, must be submitted. (Each document or group of documents that is separately bound shall bear a Confirmation Notice.) Working copies lacking the Notice will not be accepted. WORKING COPIES OF MOTION PAPERS MUST BE SUBMITTED NO LATER THAN 4:45 P.M. ON THE RETURN DATE IN THE MOTION SUPPORT OFFICE (ROOM 217) AS EXPLAINED in NY R BRONX E FIL R Doc. 1(4). If an attorney has failed to submit required working copies on or before the return date, the motion will be transmitted as is to the Justice for such action as the Justice finds appropriate. Attorneys may submit working copies on motions by mail or overnight delivery. Any such submission shall be sent in a timely manner to the Motion Support Office (Room 217) and be conspicuously marked on the outside "NYSCEF Matter"; lack of such marking may delay processing. NY R BRONX E FIL R Doc. 1(4)(a).
- *ERIE COUNTY.* Electronically filed documents subject to review and processing by the Part Clerk do not require a working copy unless otherwise directed or provided for in IAS Part Rules. NY R UNIF TRIAL CTS § 202.5-b(d)(4), any working copy submitted shall include, as a cover page firmly fastened thereto, a copy of the Confirmation Notice generated by the NYSCEF site at the time of filing. Please consult the individual Justice's Part Rules and/or consult with the Judge's chambers to determine whether and how working copies are to be provided. Working copies will not be printed or delivered by the Erie County Clerk or the Chief Clerk of the Courts or any of their personnel to chambers. The official record of a document in an electronically filed case is the document filed via the NYSCEF system. Working copies are intended only for use by the Justice. The Court will discard all working copies after the Justice has finished with them. Thus, in the event that counsel fails to file a document via the NYSCEF system, the document will not be part of the court record. NY R ERIE E FIL Doc. 3(III)(O); NY R ERIE E FIL Doc. 3(V)(E).
- *KINGS COUNTY.* No courtesy copies of motion papers are required by the Court, except as may be required for electronic filing or by the Judge's Part Rules. In tort cases against the City of New York, courtesy copies shall be supplied to the Corporation Counsel's office in Brooklyn. NY R L KINGS Pt. C, Rule 5. Unless otherwise directed by the Court or as described herein, and with the exceptions listed below, in all NYSCEF cases in which an RJI has been filed, working copies of e-filed documents that are intended for judicial review must be submitted to the court. Working copies are not required of documents that are only processed by a support office (e.g. preliminary conference request, note of issue). Working copies shall include exhibit tabs and backs; for motion papers, the motion sequence number and the return date and part. The confirmation notice with the motion sequence number on it should be the back page of the motion facing out. In addition, the filer of a working copy must firmly bind thereto, with the back page facing out, a copy of the Confirmation Notice that was generated by NYSCEF when that document was efiled. Working copies that are submitted without the related Confirmation Notice will not be accepted. NY R L KINGS E FIL Doc. 1(B)(7); NY R L KINGS E FIL Doc. 1(D). WORKING COPIES OF MOTION PAPERS MUST BE SUBMITTED IN THE MOTION SUPPORT OFFICE (ROOM 227) AS EXPLAINED HEREIN. THEY MUST NOT BE DELIVERED TO THE PART OR CHAMBERS, EXCEPT WHERE THE INDIVIDUAL JUSTICE'S PART RULES PROVIDE OTHERWISE; DOING SO WILL CAUSE ADMINISTRATIVE CONFUSION AND POSSIBLE MISPLACEMENT OF PAPERS. Any such submission shall be sent in a timely manner (kindly review individual Justice's rules) and be conspicuously marked on the outside "NYSCEF Matter;" lack of such marking may delay processing. NY R L KINGS E FIL Doc. 1(D).
- *NEW YORK COUNTY.* Some Justices require that working copies of e-filed motion papers be submitted. See the E-filing Protocol for information on the many Parts that do not require working copies. Where required, working copies of the moving documents and all other documents on the motion or application shall be submitted to the Motion Submission Part Courtroom (Room 130) on, but not before, the final return date. A Confirmation Notice from the NYSCEF system, which is generated when a document is e-filed, shall be firmly affixed, as the back page facing out, to each separate working copy or group of such copies.

NY R NY CTY Procedure II(A) NY R NY CTY E FIL Doc. 2(B)(5)(a); NY R NY CTY J RUL Rule 14(a). For more information on working copies, including which parts don't require them, refer to NY R NY CTY E FIL Doc. 2(B)(6).

- *ONONDAGA COUNTY.* Any courtesy "working" copies, if required (see NY R ONDGA E FIL Protocol(B)(7)), must be provided directly to the assigned justice. NY R ONDGA E FIL Protocol(B)(9)(e). For information as to whether or not an Onondaga Supreme Court Justice requires working (courtesy) copies of e-filed documents, please consult the Onondaga County Individual E-filing Rules. NY R ONDGA E FIL Protocol(B)(7)(a). The Supreme Court Clerk's Office and the Onondaga County Clerk's Office will NOT accept the working copies. Working copies must be sent directly to the assigned justice's chambers. NY R ONDGA E FIL Protocol(B)(7)(b). A copy of the Confirmation Notice, generated by the NYSCEF system at the time a document is e-filed, must be attached to every working copy provided to chambers. If the Confirmation Notice is missing, the copy will not be accepted. NY R ONDGA E FIL Protocol(B)(7)(c). Courtesy copies do not become part of the official court record as maintained by the Onondaga County Clerk's Office and will be destroyed by chambers at the disposition of the case. In the event that counsel fails to file a document via NYSCEF, the document will not be part of the court record. NY R ONDGA E FIL Protocol(B)(7)(d).
- *QUEENS COUNTY.* Working copies of E-Filed notices of motion/notices of petition are NOT to be sent to the Motion Support Office. They must be brought to the calendar call in the judge's part. NY R L QUEENS MOT SUP Doc. 1. Unless otherwise directed or authorized by the court, counsel should file papers with the E-file system first and thereafter deliver a working copy to at the calendar call of the Centralized Motion Part or Assigned Justice in accordance with individual Part Rules. NY R L QUEENS E-FILE Doc. 1(E)(4). On the return date of a motion that has been E-filed, the movant must provide the Centralized Motion Part (CMP) with a working copy of the entire motion including the notice of motion with sequence number and all of the attached exhibits. The motion must have the confirmation of filing firmly affixed to the back of the papers (facing outward). The confirmation of filing is a separate notice from the payment notice and will say confirmation clearly across the top of the page. NY R L QUEENS E-FILE Doc. 1(H)(2)(a). The motion or Order to Show Cause must have clearly written across its face the words "Working Copy," it must also have the assigned Judge's name, motion sequence number and calendar number—which may be obtained from the posted calendar outside courtroom on the return date of the motion. A confirmation of filing must attached thereto. Working copies of e-filed Orders to Show Cause must contain a copy of the signed order and all supporting papers. NY R L QUEENS E-FILE Doc. 1(H)(2)(c). The Confirmation Notice must be an updated version that indicates the sequence number of the motion being submitted at the CMP calendar call. WORKING COPIES WITHOUT A CONFIRMATION NOTICE WILL NOT BE ACCEPTED. NY R L QUEENS E-FILE Doc. 1(H)(7).

vii. *Statement of authorization in electronic filing cases.* A filing agent (other than one employed by a governmental entity) shall e-file a statement of authorization from counsel of record in an action, in a form approved by the Chief Administrator, prior to or together with the first e-filing in that action by the agent on behalf of that counsel. NY R UNIF TRIAL CTS § 202.5-b(d)(1)(i).

viii. *ERIE COUNTY: Additional supplemental documents*

- *Notice of hard copy submission in e-filed case.* In accordance with NY R UNIF TRIAL CTS § 202.5-b(d), the County Clerk shall refuse to accept for filing, hard copy papers filed to an action subject to electronic filing unless hard copy filing is permitted by the Uniform Rules or NY R ERIE E FIL Doc. 3 and the papers bear a completed Notice of Hard Copy Submission—E-Filed Case form. NY R ERIE E FIL Doc. 3(III)(D).

ix. *KINGS COUNTY: Additional supplemental documents*

- *Forms when filing in hard copy.* An attorney who certifies in good faith that he or she lacks the equipment or knowledge needed to e-file and have no staff member or employee under his or her direction who has such knowledge and equipment may opt out of participation in e-filing in a mandatory case by filing a "Notice of Opt-Out from Participation in Action Subject to Mandatory Electronic Filing" form EFM-2 with the Clerk. NY R L KINGS E FIL Doc. 1(A)(2). Where in accordance with the E-Filing Rules a party submits a document in hard copy in an e-filed case (principally, a document submitted by a nonparticipating party (e.g., an attorney) in a consensual case, an emergency filing made in accordance with the Mandatory E-Filing Rules, and any document filed with the court in hard copy by an attorney who has opted out of participation in mandatory e-filing, the document must bear the back page facing out, a "Notice of Hard Copy Submission—E-Filed Cases" form EFM-3. NY R L KINGS E FIL Doc. 1(B)(3).

x. *NEW YORK COUNTY: Additional supplemental documents*

- *Notice of hard copy submission.* Where in accordance with the E-Filing Rules an attorney or an unrepresented litigant who is participating in e-filing submits a document in hard copy in an e-filed case, the document must bear, as the back page facing out, a Notice of Hard-Copy Submission—E-Filed Case (a form available in the "Forms" section on the NYSCEF website (Form EFM-3) and in the court's back offices). NY R NY CTY E FIL Doc. 2(B)(3). For more information refer to NY R NY CTY E FIL Doc. 2.
- *Unpublished decisions.* Whenever reliance is placed upon a decision or other authority not officially published or readily available to the New York County Supreme Court, a copy of the case or of pertinent portions of the authority shall be submitted with the motion papers. NY R NY CTY J RUL Rule 14(a).

xi. *ONONDAGA COUNTY: Additional supplemental documents*

- *Notice of hard copy submission.* Any papers to be filed with the court in an e-filed case must be filed online with the E-filing system except where a special exemption is granted (e.g., oversized maps, photographs). If such an exemption is granted, Form EFM-3, "Notice of Hard Copy Submission—E-Filed Case," must be attached to such documents forms which are not filed on line. Also, Form EFM-4 "Notice of Hard Copy Exhibit Filing" must be completed and uploaded to the action's e-file. Both of these forms may be found on the NYSCEF website. NY R ONDGA E FIL Protocol(B)(4).

xii. *QUEENS COUNTY: Additional supplemental documents*

- *Notice of hard copy submission.* Any party opting out of the e-filing system must have a "Notice of Hard Copy Submission" firmly affixed to the back of the papers. NY R L QUEENS E-FILE Doc. 1(H)(2)(f).

2. *Documents for opposing party*

a. *Required documents*

i. *Opposition.* Refer to the General Requirements section of this document for information on the opposition.

- *Request for oral argument.* A party requesting oral argument shall set forth such request in its notice of motion or in its order to show cause or on the first page of the answering papers, as the case may be. Where all parties to a motion request oral argument, oral argument shall be granted unless the court shall determine it to be unnecessary. Where a motion is brought on by order to show cause, the court may set forth in the order that oral argument is required on the return date of the motion. NY R UNIF TRIAL CTS § 202.8(d).
- *QUEENS COUNTY: E-filing opposition papers.* E-filed opposition papers and/or reply papers must also be provided to the Centralized Motion Part in the same manner as the moving papers with the confirmation of filing firmly attached to the back of the papers. NY R L QUEENS E-FILE Doc. 1(H)(2)(d).

ii. *Proof of service.* In addition to complying with the provisions of NY CPLR Rule 2101, every paper filed in court shall have annexed thereto appropriate proof of service on all parties where required. NY R UNIF TRIAL CTS § 202.5(a).

b. *Supplemental documents*

i. *Supporting evidence; Exhibits.* The main supporting papers on a motion are affidavits, but any relevant exhibits, documents, depositions, etc., are also includible. SIEGEL-NYPRAC § 246.

- *Affidavits accompanying opposition.* Affidavits shall be for a statement of the relevant facts. NY R UNIF TRIAL CTS § 202.8(c).
- *Foreign language documents.* Where an affidavit or exhibit annexed to a paper served or filed is in a foreign language, it shall be accompanied by an English translation and an affidavit by the translator stating his qualifications and that the translation is accurate. NY CPLR Rule 2101(b).
- *Statement of attorney in lieu of affidavit.* The statement of an attorney admitted to practice in the courts of the state, or of a physician, osteopath or dentist, authorized by law to practice in the state, who is not a party to an action, when subscribed and affirmed by him to be true under the penalties of perjury, may be served or filed in the action in lieu of and with the same force and effect as an affidavit. NY CPLR Rule 2106.
- *NEW YORK COUNTY: Form of presented exhibits.* Exhibits should be tabbed and be legible; a typed version of any exhibit that is difficult to read should be submitted with the original. Exhibits printed on both sides of the page should be bound and tabbed on the side. NY R NY CTY J RUL Rule 14(a).
- *QUEENS COUNTY.* Attorneys submitting exhibits to the court on E-file cases shall make each exhibit a separate, labeled attachment to an affidavit/affirmation. NY R L QUEENS E-FILE Doc. 1(H)(4).

ii. *Brief.* Briefs shall be for a statement of the relevant law. NY R UNIF TRIAL CTS § 202.8(c).

iii. *Filing fees.* The County Clerk shall require the payment of any applicable statutory fees, or an order of the Court waiving payment of such fees, before accepting a paper for filing. NY R UNIF TRIAL CTS § 202.5(d)(1). For information on filing fees, if any, refer to NY CPLR § 8001, et seq.

- *ALBANY COUNTY.* In general, any filing subsequent to the commencement of an action which is designated as a motion or cross-motion requires the payment of a filing fee to the County Clerk's Office prior to submission to the Supreme Court Clerk's Office for referral to the assigned justice. The fee is assessed regardless of whether an application is made by notice of motion, order to show cause or ex parte. No fee will be charged upon the filing of a motion for poor person status in conjunction with an application which serves to commence an action or special proceeding. In the event a motion is received by the court unaccompanied by proof of payment to the County Clerk, the Supreme Court Clerk's Office will contact the submitting party to advise that the application will be held pending receipt of the filing fee only until the return date of the motion. If proof of payment is not submitted to the Supreme Court Clerk's Office by the return date (ex parte applications will be held ten (10) days), the papers will be returned by mail with a notification that the motion has been removed from the court's calendar and that it must be re-noticed and re-filed with the court along with the requisite filing fee. Inquiries concerning the applicability of the motion fee to a proposed filing may be directed to the Supreme Court Clerk's Office. NY R 3 JD SUP Doc. 1(B).
- *BRONX COUNTY.* In accordance with the new civil fee schedule set forth in Article 80 of the C.P.L.R. (NY CPLR § 8001, et seq.), effective July 14, 2003, all motions, and cross motions must be approved in Room 217 prior to payment of said fees in the County Clerk's Office, Room 118. NY R BRONX FIL R Doc. 8. The motion fee [must be] paid for via NYSCEF by credit/debit card. NY R BRONX E FIL R Doc. 1(1).
- *ERIE COUNTY.* Payment for fee-bearing NYSCEF documents must be made online via credit or debit card (American Express, MasterCard or Visa) at the time of submission. NY R ERIE E FIL Doc. 3(III)(E).
- *KINGS COUNTY.* The motion must be filed with NYSCEF and the motion fee paid. NY R L KINGS E FIL Doc. 1(D). Court fees in NYSCEF cases must be paid via NYSCEF by a credit or bank card (MasterCard, Visa, or American Express). Fees are no longer accepted in person in the Kings County Clerk's Office in NYSCEF cases. NY R L KINGS E FIL Doc. 1(B)(6).
- *NEW YORK COUNTY.* A motion fee must be paid on motions made in writing by notice of motion, order to show cause or ex parte after the commencement of an action. For this purpose, the term "action" shall mean any application to the court that requires the assignment of an index number, regardless of whether a formal pleading is filed. Applications or motions that commence an action and for which an index number fee must be paid require no motion fee. [A]ny motions made after the initial applications in these situations would require payment of the motion fee. A motion that is the initial application in a case commenced by the filing of a summons and complaint would require a motion fee since the filing of the summons and complaint rather than the application itself would require the purchase of an index number. NY R NY CTY Procedure II(A). In e-filed cases the motion fee must be paid when the documents are filed. Payment is made on-line by Visa, Mastercard, or American Express credit or bank card. NY R NY CTY Procedure II(A); NY R NY CTY E FIL Doc. 2(B)(5).
- *ONONDAGA COUNTY.* Court fees in e-filed cases must be paid online with the NYSCEF system using a credit card. The document is not considered to have been filed until payment of the fee has been tendered. NY R ONDGA E FIL Protocol(B)(2). Fees must be paid on all cross motions. NY R ONDGA E FIL Protocol(B)(9)(e).
- *QUEENS COUNTY.* The Motion Support Office does not receive, forward or process any fees or waiver of fees. All applications requiring payment of statutory fees or waiver of fees must be sent directly to the Queens County Clerk's office. NY R L QUEENS MOT SUP Doc. 1. Court fees (e.g., RJI fee, motion fee) in E-filed cases may be paid for on-line using a credit card. Papers may also be filed with the E-file system and the fee may be paid at the County Clerk's Office. In the latter case, the paper is not considered to have been filed until payment of the fee has been tendered. NY R L QUEENS E-FILE Doc. 1(E)(1). The motion/petition shall be filed on-line and the fee paid for either on-line by credit card or by the "Pay at the County Clerk's Office" option. NY R L QUEENS E-FILE Doc. 1(H)(1).

iv. *Working copies.* The court may require the parties to provide working copies of documents filed electronically. In such event, each working copy shall include, firmly affixed thereto, a copy of a confirmation notice in a form prescribed by the Chief Administrator. NY R UNIF TRIAL CTS § 202.5-b(d)(5).

- *BRONX COUNTY.* After papers on motions have been e-filed, working copies thereof, with Confirmation

Notice firmly attached as the back page facing out, must be submitted. (Each document or group of documents that is separately bound shall bear a Confirmation Notice.) Working copies lacking the Notice will not be accepted. WORKING COPIES OF MOTION PAPERS MUST BE SUBMITTED NO LATER THAN 4:45 P.M. ON THE RETURN DATE IN THE MOTION SUPPORT OFFICE (ROOM 217) AS EXPLAINED in NY R BRONX E FIL R Doc. 1(4). If an attorney has failed to submit required working copies on or before the return date, the motion will be transmitted as is to the Justice for such action as the Justice finds appropriate. Attorneys may submit working copies on motions by mail or overnight delivery. Any such submission shall be sent in a timely manner to the Motion Support Office (Room 217) and be conspicuously marked on the outside "NYSCEF Matter"; lack of such marking may delay processing. NY R BRONX E FIL R Doc. 1(4)(a).

- *ERIE COUNTY.* Electronically filed documents subject to review and processing by the Part Clerk do not require a working copy unless otherwise directed or provided for in IAS Part Rules. NY R UNIF TRIAL CTS § 202.5-b(d)(4), any working copy submitted shall include, as a cover page firmly fastened thereto, a copy of the Confirmation Notice generated by the NYSCEF site at the time of filing. Please consult the individual Justice's Part Rules and/or consult with the Judge's chambers to determine whether and how working copies are to be provided. Working copies will not be printed or delivered by the Erie County Clerk or the Chief Clerk of the Courts or any of their personnel to chambers. The official record of a document in an electronically filed case is the document filed via the NYSCEF system. Working copies are intended only for use by the Justice. The Court will discard all working copies after the Justice has finished with them. Thus, in the event that counsel fails to file a document via the NYSCEF system, the document will not be part of the court record. NY R ERIE E FIL Doc. 3(III)(O); NY R ERIE E FIL Doc. 3(V)(E).

- *KINGS COUNTY.* No courtesy copies of motion papers are required by the Court, except as may be required for electronic filing or by the Judge's Part Rules. In tort cases against the City of New York, courtesy copies shall be supplied to the Corporation Counsel's office in Brooklyn. NY R L KINGS Pt. C, Rule 5. Unless otherwise directed by the Court or as described herein, and with the exceptions listed below, in all NYSCEF cases in which an RJI has been filed, working copies of e-filed documents that are intended for judicial review must be submitted to the court. Working copies are not required of documents that are only processed by a support office (e.g. preliminary conference request, note of issue). Working copies shall include exhibit tabs and backs; for motion papers, the motion sequence number and the return date and part. The confirmation notice with the motion sequence number on it should be the back page of the motion facing out. In addition, the filer of a working copy must firmly bind thereto, with the back page facing out, a copy of the Confirmation Notice that was generated by NYSCEF when that document was efiled. Working copies that are submitted without the related Confirmation Notice will not be accepted. NY R L KINGS E FIL Doc. 1(B)(7); NY R L KINGS E FIL Doc. 1(D). WORKING COPIES OF MOTION PAPERS MUST BE SUBMITTED IN THE MOTION SUPPORT OFFICE (ROOM 227) AS EXPLAINED HEREIN. THEY MUST NOT BE DELIVERED TO THE PART OR CHAMBERS, EXCEPT WHERE THE INDIVIDUAL JUSTICE'S PART RULES PROVIDE OTHERWISE; DOING SO WILL CAUSE ADMINISTRATIVE CONFUSION AND POSSIBLE MISPLACEMENT OF PAPERS. Any such submission shall be sent in a timely manner (kindly review individual Justice's rules) and be conspicuously marked on the outside "NYSCEF Matter;" lack of such marking may delay processing. NY R L KINGS E FIL Doc. 1(D).

- *NEW YORK COUNTY.* Some Justices require that working copies of e-filed motion papers be submitted. See the E-filing Protocol for information on the many Parts that do not require working copies. Where required, working copies of the moving documents and all other documents on the motion or application shall be submitted to the Motion Submission Part Courtroom (Room 130) on, but not before, the final return date. A Confirmation Notice from the NYSCEF system, which is generated when a document is e-filed, shall be firmly affixed, as the back page facing out, to each separate working copy or group of such copies. NY R NY CTY Procedure II(A) NY R NY CTY E FIL Doc. 2(B)(5)(a); NY R NY CTY J RUL Rule 14(a). For more information on working copies, including which parts don't require them, refer to NY R NY CTY E FIL Doc. 2(B)(6).

- *ONONDAGA COUNTY.* Any courtesy "working" copies, if required (see NY R ONDGA E FIL Protocol(B)(7)), must be provided directly to the assigned justice. NY R ONDGA E FIL Protocol(B)(9)(e). For information as to whether or not an Onondaga Supreme Court Justice requires working (courtesy) copies of e-filed documents, please consult the Onondaga County Individual E-filing Rules. NY R ONDGA E FIL Protocol(B)(7)(a). The Supreme Court Clerk's Office and the Onondaga County Clerk's Office will

NOT accept the working copies. Working copies must be sent directly to the assigned justice's chambers. NY R ONDGA E FIL Protocol(B)(7)(b). A copy of the Confirmation Notice, generated by the NYSCEF system at the time a document is e-filed, must be attached to every working copy provided to chambers. If the Confirmation Notice is missing, the copy will not be accepted. NY R ONDGA E FIL Protocol(B)(7)(c). Courtesy copies do not become part of the official court record as maintained by the Onondaga County Clerk's Office and will be destroyed by chambers at the disposition of the case. In the event that counsel fails to file a document via NYSCEF, the document will not be part of the court record. NY R ONDGA E FIL Protocol(B)(7)(d).

- *QUEENS COUNTY.* Working copies of E-Filed notices of motion/notices of petition are NOT to be sent to the Motion Support Office. They must be brought to the calendar call in the judge's part. NY R L QUEENS MOT SUP Doc. 1. Unless otherwise directed or authorized by the court, counsel should file papers with the E-file system first and thereafter deliver a working copy to at the calendar call of the Centralized Motion Part or Assigned Justice in accordance with individual Part Rules. NY R L QUEENS E-FILE Doc. 1(E)(4). On the return date of a motion that has been E-filed, the movant must provide the Centralized Motion Part (CMP) with a working copy of the entire motion including the notice of motion with sequence number and all of the attached exhibits. The motion must have the confirmation of filing firmly affixed to the back of the papers (facing outward). The confirmation of filing is a separate notice from the payment notice and will say confirmation clearly across the top of the page. NY R L QUEENS E-FILE Doc. 1(H)(2)(a). The motion or Order to Show Cause must have clearly written across its face the words "Working Copy," it must also have the assigned Judge's name, motion sequence number and calendar number—which may be obtained from the posted calendar outside courtroom on the return date of the motion. A confirmation of filing must attached thereto. Working copies of e-filed Orders to Show Cause must contain a copy of the signed order and all supporting papers. NY R L QUEENS E-FILE Doc. 1(H)(2)(c). The Confirmation Notice must be an updated version that indicates the sequence number of the motion being submitted at the CMP calendar call. WORKING COPIES WITHOUT A CONFIRMATION NOTICE WILL NOT BE ACCEPTED. NY R L QUEENS E-FILE Doc. 1(H)(7).

v. *ERIE COUNTY: Additional supplemental documents*

- *Notice of hard copy submission in e-filed case.* In accordance with NY R UNIF TRIAL CTS § 202.5-b(d), the County Clerk shall refuse to accept for filing, hard copy papers filed to an action subject to electronic filing unless hard copy filing is permitted by the Uniform Rules or NY R ERIE E FIL Doc. 3 and the papers bear a completed Notice of Hard Copy Submission—E-Filed Case form. NY R ERIE E FIL Doc. 3(III)(D).

vi. *KINGS COUNTY: Additional supplemental documents*

- *Forms when filing in hard copy.* An attorney who certifies in good faith that he or she lacks the equipment or knowledge needed to e-file and have no staff member or employee under his or her direction who has such knowledge and equipment may opt out of participation in e-filing in a mandatory case by filing a "Notice of Opt-Out from Participation in Action Subject to Mandatory Electronic Filing" form EFM-2 with the Clerk. NY R L KINGS E FIL Doc. 1(A)(2). Where in accordance with the E-Filing Rules a party submits a document in hard copy in an e-filed case (principally, a document submitted by a nonparticipating party (e.g., an attorney) in a consensual case, an emergency filing made in accordance with the Mandatory E-Filing Rules, and any document filed with the court in hard copy by an attorney who has opted out of participation in mandatory e-filing, the document must bear the back page facing out, a "Notice of Hard Copy Submission—E-Filed Cases" form EFM-3. NY R L KINGS E FIL Doc. 1(B)(3).

vii. *NEW YORK COUNTY: Additional supplemental documents*

- *Notice of hard copy submission.* Where in accordance with the E-Filing Rules an attorney or an unrepresented litigant who is participating in e-filing submits a document in hard copy in an e-filed case, the document must bear, as the back page facing out, a Notice of Hard-Copy Submission—E-Filed Case (a form available in the "Forms" section on the NYSCEF website (Form EFM-3) and in the court's back offices). NY R NY CTY E FIL Doc. 2(B)(3). For more information refer to NY R NY CTY E FIL Doc. 2.

- *Unpublished decisions.* Whenever reliance is placed upon a decision or other authority not officially published or readily available to the New York County Supreme Court, a copy of the case or of pertinent portions of the authority shall be submitted with the motion papers. NY R NY CTY J RUL Rule 14(a).

viii. *ONONDAGA COUNTY: Additional supplemental documents*

- *Notice of hard copy submission.* Any papers to be filed with the court in an e-filed case must be filed online with the E-filing system except where a special exemption is granted (e.g., oversized maps, photographs). If such an exemption is granted, Form EFM-3, "Notice of Hard Copy Submission—E-Filed Case," must be attached to such documents forms which are not filed on line. Also, Form EFM-4 "Notice of Hard Copy Exhibit Filing" must be completed and uploaded to the action's e-file. Both of these forms may be found on the NYSCEF website. NY R ONDGA E FIL Protocol(B)(4).

ix. *QUEENS COUNTY: Additional supplemental documents*

- *Notice of hard copy submission.* Any party opting out of the e-filing system must have a "Notice of Hard Copy Submission" firmly affixed to the back of the papers. NY R L QUEENS E-FILE Doc. 1(H)(2)(f).

E. Format

1. *Form of documents*

a. *Size and form of paper.* Each paper served or filed shall be durable, white and, except for summonses, subpoenas, notices of appearance, notes of issue, orders of protection, temporary orders of protection and exhibits, shall be eleven by eight and one-half (11 x 8-1/2) inches in size. NY CPLR Rule 2101(a).

b. *Writing and language.* The writing shall be legible and in black ink. NY CPLR Rule 2101(a). Each paper served or filed shall be in the English language which, where practicable, shall be of ordinary usage. NY CPLR Rule 2101(b).

c. *Caption.* Each paper served or filed shall begin with a caption setting forth the name of the court, the venue, the title of the action, the nature of the paper and the index number of the action if one has been assigned. In all papers other than a summons, a complaint or a judgment it shall be sufficient to state the name of the first named party on each side with an appropriate indication of any omissions. NY CPLR Rule 2101(c).

i. *Further contents of first page.* After the first paper has been filed in each case the index number shall appear on the cover and first page to the right of the caption of every paper tendered for filing in the action. Each such cover and first page also shall contain an indication of the county of venue and a brief description of the nature of the paper and, where the case has been assigned to an individual judge, shall contain the name of the assigned judge to the right of the caption. NY R UNIF TRIAL CTS § 202.5(a); NY R UNIF TRIAL CTS § 202.5(b); NY R UNIF TRIAL CTS § 202.5(d)(1)(i).

ii. *ALBANY COUNTY: Request for oral argument.* A party may request oral argument on a motion by indicating such request on the first page of the notice of motion, order to show cause, or answering papers in the area across from the caption of the action/proceeding. NY R 3 JD SUP Doc. 1(B).

iii. *NEW YORK COUNTY: Request for oral argument.* Counsel who wish oral argument must so request conspicuously on the front of their papers. NY R NY CTY Procedure II(D).

d. *Index number.* No paper in an action in the supreme or a county court, other than an order submitted for signature to a judge out of court, shall be submitted for any purpose to the supreme or county court or to a clerk thereof unless there is endorsed on such paper the index number of the action assigned by the clerk of the county. NY CPLR § 8018(c).

i. *ALBANY COUNTY: Index number on all filed documents.* The index number, the request for judicial intervention number and the assigned justice's name shall appear on [all papers filed with the Court subsequent to the complaint]. NY R 3 JD SUP Doc. 1(A).

ii. *ERIE COUNTY: Index number after initial filing.* Cases that are initially commenced by the filing of papers with the NYSCEF system are identified as e-filed cases by assignment of an Index Number that has "800-899" as the first three (3) digits of the index number (i.e. 802391/2012). NY R ERIE E FIL Doc. 3(II). [The] Index Number must be affixed to all document submissions, filings, and communications to the Erie County Clerk and the Court. Cases that are converted from paper to e-filing shall retain the original index number. NY R ERIE E FIL Doc. 3(II).

iii. *KINGS COUNTY: Index number after initial filing.* In cases commenced electronically by the filing of initiating papers with the NYSCEF system and payment of the statutory fees, the Kings County Clerk will issue an NYSCEF designated index number and the filer shall be notified via the NYSCEF system of the index number assigned and filing date. Such index number must be affixed to all document submissions, filings and communications to the Kings County Clerk and Supreme Court. If counsel faces exigent circumstances that require accelerated assignment, counsel may contact Administration of the Kings County Clerk at kcco-efile@nycourts.gov, during normal business hours of the court. NY R L KINGS E FIL Doc. 1(B)(5).

iv. *NEW YORK COUNTY: Index number on hard copy filings.* Papers subsequently presented for filing in hardcopy format will be filed in this jacket. NY R NY CTY Procedure I(B). Index numbers take the form of six digits followed by a slash and the four digits of the year the case began, e.g., 340705/2018. The first or first two integers of the index number identify the type of case. If a case is commenced electronically, the second integer will be a "5", except as indicated otherwise in the list below. There are many tax certiorari matters e-filed annually and the index numbers therefor will normally run over into those with a "6" as the second integer, and the same will occur with general cases if necessary. The principal types of cases and their index number categories are listed in NY R NY CTY Procedure I(B). NY R NY CTY Procedure I(B); NY R NY CTY Procedure XI(A).

v. *ONONDAGA COUNTY: Index number.* The index number must be referenced on all e-filed documents and correspondence. All e-filed case index numbers will contain the letters "EF" between the year and the file number (for example, 2012EF9999). NY R ONDGA E FIL Protocol(B)(1).

vi. *QUEENS COUNTY: Index number on converted cases.* Cases originally commenced in hard-copy form but later converted to an E-file case, either by stipulation or order will bear a regular index number initially. The County Clerk will issue a new E-file index number. NY R L QUEENS E-FILE Doc. 1(B).

e. *Line spacing.* Every paper filed in court, if typewritten, shall have at least double space between each line, except for quotations and the names and addresses of attorneys appearing in the action. NY R UNIF TRIAL CTS § 202.5(a).

f. *Font size.* Each. . .paper printed or typed, served or filed, except an exhibit or a summons, shall be in clear type of no less than ten (10) point in size. NY CPLR Rule 2101(a).

i. Whenever a requirement relating to size of type is stated in point size, the type size requirement shall be deemed met if the x-height of the type is a minimum of forty-five percent (45%) of the specified point size. Each point shall be measured as .351 millimeter. The x-height size shall be measured as it appears on the page. The x-height is the height of the lower case letters, exclusive of ascenders or descenders. NY CPLR § 105(t).

g. *Margins.* Every paper filed in court shall have at least one (1) inch margins. NY R UNIF TRIAL CTS § 202.5(a).

h. *Citations*

i. *Civil practice law and rules.* NY CPLR § 101, et seq. shall be known as the civil practice law and rules, and may be cited as "CPLR". Reference to a provision in the civil practice law and rules may, except when such provision is being enacted or amended, be made without indicating whether it is a rule or section. NY CPLR § 101.

i. *Indorsement by attorney.* Each paper served or filed shall be indorsed with the name, address and telephone number of the attorney for the party serving or filing the paper, or if the party does not appear by attorney, with the name, address and telephone number of the party. NY CPLR Rule 2101(d).

j. *One-sided printing.* In addition, every paper filed in court, other than an exhibit or printed form, shall contain writing on one side only, except that papers that are fastened on the side may contain writing on both sides. NY R UNIF TRIAL CTS § 202.5(a).

k. *Use of copies authorized.* Except where otherwise specifically prescribed, copies, rather than originals, of all papers, including orders, affidavits and exhibits may be served or filed. Where it is required that the original be served or filed and the original is lost or withheld, the court may authorize a copy to be served or filed. NY CPLR Rule 2101(e).

i. Where a certified copy of a paper is required by law, an attorney admitted to practice in the courts of the state may certify that it has been compared by him with the original and found to be a true and complete copy. Such a certificate, when subscribed by such attorney, has the same effect as if made by a clerk. NY CPLR § 2105.

l. *Recycled paper.* It is the policy of the Unified Court System that litigants, where practicable, should file or submit to the courts of the Unified Court System of the State of New York papers printed or reproduced on recycled paper. Paper is considered recycled if it contains a minimum content of thirty percent (30%) waste paper. NY R UNIF TRIAL CTS § 215.2. The signature page of every paper filed or submitted to the court on recycled paper should bear the legend: "Printed [Reproduced] on Recycled Paper." NY R UNIF TRIAL CTS § 215.3.

m. *Form of request for judicial intervention; Copies.* A request for judicial intervention must be submitted, in duplicate, on a form authorized by the Chief of the Courts, with proof of service on the other parties to the action (but proof of service is not required where the application is ex parte). NY R UNIF TRIAL CTS § 202.6(a).

n. *KINGS COUNTY: Tabs on filings.* Motions, orders and other filed papers shall be indexed with protruding tabs. Clerks are required to reject papers that do not have protruding exhibit tabs, except papers in matrimonial cases and papers filed by pro se litigants. NY R L KINGS Pt. A, Papers.

o. *NEW YORK COUNTY: Length of briefs.* Unless advance permission otherwise is granted by the court for good cause, memoranda of law shall not exceed thirty (30) pages each (exclusive of table of contents and table of authorities) and affidavits/affirmations shall not exceed twenty-five (25) pages each. NY R NY CTY J RUL Rule 14(b).

p. *QUEENS COUNTY: Form and size of motion filings.* All motions filed in Queens Supreme Court-Civil Term, must adhere to the Motion Support rules and the rules of the assigned judge. NY R L QUEENS MOT SUP Doc. 1. Due to space limitations, the Motion Support Office cannot accept notices of motion/notices of petition and accompanying exhibits which measure greater than eight (8) inches. If your documents measure greater than eight (8) inches you are directed to submit only the notice of motion/notice of petition to the Motion Support Office and bring all exhibits to the calendar call on your return date. NY R L QUEENS MOT SUP Doc. 1.

2. *Form of electronic documents.* Each paper served or filed by electronic means, as defined in NY CPLR Rule 2103(f), shall be capable of being reproduced by the receiver so as to comply with the provisions of NY CPLR Rule 2101(a) through NY CPLR Rule 2101(d). NY CPLR Rule 2101(g).
   a. *File format.* All e-filed documents shall comply with the technical requirements set forth at the NYSCEF site. NY R UNIF TRIAL CTS § 202.5-b(d)(1)(i).
   b. *Heading of document.* The subject matter heading for each paper sent by electronic means must indicate that the matter being transmitted electronically is related to a court proceeding. NY CPLR Rule 2103(b)(7).
   c. *E-filed documents identification*
      i. *ERIE COUNTY.* E-filed cases must be readily identifiable and marked as such. If counsel presents papers to the Office of the Erie County Clerk or the Office of the Chief Clerk in a NYSCEF matter where authorized, counsel should alert the Clerk that the case is a NYSCEF matter. NY R ERIE E FIL Doc. 3(II).
      ii. *KINGS COUNTY.* The Supreme Court's Civil Case Information System ("CCIS") will further identify e-filed cases by the addition of a suffix to the index number (e.g. 500136/2006E). This suffix should be used on all documents filed with the court in e-filed matters. NY R L KINGS E FIL Doc. 1(A)(1).

3. *Signature blocks.* Every pleading, written motion, and other paper, served on another party or filed or submitted to the court shall be signed by an attorney, or by a party if the party is not represented by an attorney, with the name of the attorney or party clearly printed or typed directly below the signature. NY R CHIEF ADMIN § 130-1.1-a(a); NY R UNIF TRIAL CTS § 202.5(d)(1)(iv).
   a. *Printed name.* Beneath each signature shall be printed the name signed. NY CPLR Rule 2101(a).
   b. *Failure to sign.* Absent good cause shown, the court shall strike any unsigned paper if the omission of the signature is not corrected promptly after being called to the attention of the attorney or party. NY R CHIEF ADMIN § 130-1.1-a(a).
   c. *Signature as certification.* By signing a paper, an attorney or party certifies that, to the best of that person's knowledge, information and belief, formed after an inquiry reasonable under the circumstances the presentation of the paper or the contentions therein are not frivolous as defined in NY R CHIEF ADMIN § 130-1.1(c). NY R CHIEF ADMIN § 130-1.1-a(b)(1).
   d. *Electronic signatures.* A document shall be considered to have been signed by an attorney or party in compliance with NY R CHIEF ADMIN § 130-1.1-a if it has been signed by such attorney or party as provided in NY R UNIF TRIAL CTS § 202.5-b(e)(1) and it bears the signatory's name. NY R UNIF TRIAL CTS § 202.5-b(e)(2). An electronically filed document shall be considered to have been signed by, and shall be binding upon, the person identified as a signatory, if:
      i. It bears the physical signature of such person and is scanned into an electronic format that reproduces such signature; or
      ii. The signatory has electronically affixed the digital image of his or her signature to the document; or
      iii. It is electronically filed under the User ID and password of that person; or
      iv. In a tax certiorari action in which the parties have stipulated to this procedure, it is an initiating document that is electronically filed without the signature of the signatory in a form provided above in NY R UNIF TRIAL CTS § 202.5-b(e)(iv), provided that, prior to filing, the document is signed in full in hard copy (which hard copy must be preserved until the conclusion of all proceedings, including appeals, in the case in which it is filed); or
      v. In a small claims assessment review proceeding, it is a petition recorded by the NYSCEF site upon the filing of a text file as provided in NY R UNIF TRIAL CTS § 202.5-b(b)(1), provided that prior to filing, the document was signed in full in hard copy (which hard copy must be preserved until the conclusion of all proceedings in the matter, including article 78 (NY CPLR § 7801, et seq.) review and any appeals, and must be made available during the proceeding upon request of the respondent or the court); or
      vi. It otherwise bears the electronic signature of the signatory in a format conforming to such standards and requirements as may hereafter be established by the Chief Administrator. NY R UNIF TRIAL CTS § 202.5-b(e).

4. *Confidentiality of personal information.* No person may file any document available for public inspection with any state agency, political subdivision, or in any court of this state that contains a Social Security account number of any other person, unless such other person is a dependent child, or has consented to such filing, except as required by federal or state law or regulation, or by court rule. NY GEN BUS § 399-ddd. Submissions pursuant to e-filing procedures shall have the same confidentiality rights as paper documents. NY R UNIF TRIAL CTS § 202.5-b(k)(1).

   a. *Confidential personal information.* Except in the actions designated in NY R UNIF TRIAL CTS § 202.5(e)(1), or as otherwise provided by rule or law or court order, and whether or not a sealing order is or has been sought, the parties shall omit or redact confidential personal information in papers submitted to the court for filing. For purposes of NY R UNIF TRIAL CTS § 202.5(e), confidential personal information ("CPI") means:

      i. The taxpayer identification number of an individual or an entity, including a Social Security number, an employer identification number, and an individual taxpayer identification number, except the last four (4) digits thereof;

      ii. The date of an individual's birth, except the year thereof;

      iii. The full name of an individual known to be a minor, except the minor's initials;

      iv. A financial account number, including a credit and/or debit card number, a bank account number, an investment account number, and/or an insurance account number, except the last four (4) digits or letters thereof; and

      v. Any of the documents or testimony in a matrimonial action protected by NY DOM REL § 235 or evidence sealed by the court in such an action which are attached as exhibits or referenced in the papers filed in any other civil action. For purposes of NY R UNIF TRIAL CTS § 202.5, a matrimonial action shall mean: an action to annul a marriage or declare the nullity of a void marriage, an action or agreement for a separation, an action for a divorce, or an action or proceeding for custody, visitation, writ of habeus corpus, child support, maintenance or paternity. NY R UNIF TRIAL CTS § 202.5(e)(1).

      vi. *ERIE COUNTY.* An attorney or unrepresented litigant filing a document via the NYSCEF system must comply with the requirements of NY R UNIF TRIAL CTS § 202.5(e) regarding the redaction of Confidential Personal Information and NY GEN BUS § 399-ddd(6) concerning the filing of documents containing Social Security Numbers. It is the sole responsibility of counsel or unrepresented litigant filing to be aware of and to comply with existing laws requiring non-disclosure of personal information contained in any document e-filed in NYSCEF. NY R ERIE E FIL Doc. 3(III)(G); NY R ERIE E FIL Doc. 3(III).

      vii. *KINGS COUNTY.* An attorney or unrepresented litigant filing a document via the NYSCEF system must comply with the requirements of General Business Law § 399-dd(6), which often require redaction of any Social Security number that appear in the original document. The NYSCEF system automatically redacts portions of filed documents which apparently contain Social Security numbers pursuant to NY R UNIF TRIAL CTS § 202.5-b(k). In the event the filing party receives e-mail notice through NYSCEF that a Social Security number in a filed document has been redacted, and the filing party concludes such redaction is erroneous, the filer should click on the link provided in the e-mail to permit the County Clerk to revert the redaction. For Confidential Personal Information, see NY R UNIF TRIAL CTS § 202.5(e) and NY R L KINGS E FIL Doc. 1(B)(11). [Editor's note: the reference to General Business Law § 399-dd(6) is likely a reference to NY GEN BUS § 399-ddd(6)]. NY R L KINGS E FIL Doc. 1(B)(10); NY R L KINGS E FIL Doc. 1(K)(1).

      viii. *NEW YORK COUNTY.* It is the responsibility of counsel and parties to comply with rules restricting disclosure of confidential personal information. Nevertheless, NYSCEF screens filings and endeavors to identify any that contain social security numbers. When such numbers are discovered through this process, NYSCEF will restrict portions of or all of such documents from public view. Where NYSCEF has redacted what it believes to be a social security number, it will transmit to the filer a notice advising of the action taken and requesting that the filer review the matter and provide notification as set forth in the notice if the redaction has been made in error. NY R NY CTY E FIL Doc. 2(K)(1); NY R NY CTY J RUL Rule A-1. Documents filed in the past in "secure status" under a procedure no longer in place will retain that status unless otherwise directed by the court. NY R NY CTY E FIL Doc. 2(K)(2).

   b. *Submission of confidential personal information.* Where a person submitting a paper to a court for filing believes in good faith that the inclusion of the full confidential personal information described in NY R UNIF TRIAL CTS § 202.5(e)(1) is material and necessary to the adjudication of the action or proceeding before the court, he or she may apply to the court for leave to serve and file together with a paper in which such information has been set forth in abbreviated form a confidential affidavit or affirmation setting forth the same information in unabbreviated form, appropriately referenced to the page or pages of the paper at which the abbreviated form appears. NY R UNIF TRIAL CTS § 202.5(e)(3).

c. *Home addresses.* For information on when home addresses and other personal information must be redacted, refer to NY CPLR Rule 2103-a.

5. *Defective papers.* A defect in the form of a paper, if a substantial right of a party is not prejudiced, shall be disregarded by the court, and leave to correct shall be freely given. NY CPLR Rule 2101(f). Papers that are stapled or bound securely shall not be rejected for filing simply because they are not bound with a backer of any kind. NY R UNIF TRIAL CTS § 202.5(a). A paper filed in accordance with the rules of the chief administrator or any local rule or practice established by the court shall be deemed filed. NY CPLR Rule 2102(b).

a. *Objection to defective papers.* The party on whom a paper is served shall be deemed to have waived objection to any defect in form unless, within fifteen (15) days after the receipt thereof, the party on whom the paper is served returns the paper to the party serving it with a statement of particular objections. NY CPLR Rule 2101(f).

F. Filing and Service Requirements

1. *Filing requirements.* Except where otherwise prescribed by law or order of court, papers required to be filed shall be filed with the clerk of the court in which the action is triable. In an action or proceeding in supreme or court, papers required to be filed shall be filed with the clerk of the county in which the proceeding is brought. NY CPLR Rule 2102(a).

a. *Furnishing papers to the court.* Each party shall furnish to the court all papers served by him. The moving party shall furnish at the hearing all other papers not already in the possession of the court necessary to the consideration of the questions involved. Where such papers are in the possession of an adverse party, they shall be produced by him at the hearing on notice served with the motion papers. Only papers served in accordance with the provisions of NY CPLR Rule 2214 shall be read in support of, or in opposition to, the motion, unless the court for good cause shall otherwise direct. NY CPLR Rule 2214(c).

i. *Submission to judge.* All papers for signature or consideration of the court shall be presented to the clerk of the trial court in the appropriate courtroom or clerk's office, except that where the clerk is unavailable or the judge so directs, papers may be submitted to the judge and a copy filed with the clerk at the first available opportunity. All papers for any judge that are filed in the clerk's office shall be promptly delivered to the judge by the clerk. The papers shall be clearly addressed to the judge for whom they are intended and prominently show the nature of the papers, the title and index number of the action in which they are filed, the judge's name and the name of the attorney or party submitting them. NY R UNIF TRIAL CTS § 202.5(b).

ii. *BRONX COUNTY: Approval of motions before filing.* All motion papers must be approved by the Motion Support Office, Supreme Court, Civil Term, room 217, before the motion papers are filed and the appropriate fee paid to the County Clerk. NY R BRONX FIL R Doc. 1.

iii. *ERIE COUNTY: Filing motions.* A motion on notice or a notice of petition in a NYSCEF case shall be filed through the NYSCEF system and must be accompanied by a Request for Judicial Intervention if the motion is being filed upon commencement of the action or if the matter has not yet been assigned to an IAS Justice. In addition, cross motions with the appropriate filing fees and opposition and reply papers must be submitted via the NYSCEF system. NY R ERIE E FIL Doc. 3(V)(A).

iv. *NEW YORK COUNTY: Filing hard copies.* Where in the narrow circumstances described by the e-filing rules a motion is made in hard-copy form or opposition papers are submitted in such form in an e-filed case, the hard-copy documents shall be submitted in the same way papers are submitted in non-e-filed cases, except that there shall be firmly affixed to each separate document or group of documents, as the back page facing out, a Notice of Hard Copy Submission—E-Filed Case. NY R NY CTY Procedure II(A). For more information on filing in hard copy cases, refer to NY R NY CTY Procedure II(A).

v. *ONONDAGA COUNTY: Submission of responsive papers and cross-motions.* Cross-motions, opposition and reply papers must be submitted online. NY R ONDGA E FIL Protocol(B)(9)(e). Motions and Orders to Show Cause are assigned a sequence number by the system. Counsel must be sure that cross motions and other filings correspond with the correct sequence number so that a cross motion will not be associated with the wrong original motion. NY R ONDGA E FIL Protocol(B)(9)(f).

b. *Electronic filing.* On consent, documents may be filed and served by electronic means in Supreme Court in such civil actions and in such counties as shall be authorized by order of the Chief Administrator of the Courts and only to the extent and in the manner provided in NY R UNIF TRIAL CTS § 202.5-b. NY R UNIF TRIAL CTS § 202.5-b(a)(1). For the definitions of terms used in electronic filing, refer to NY R UNIF TRIAL CTS § 202.5-b(a)(2).

i. *E-filing mandatory.* In any action subject to e-filing, all documents required to be filed with the court by an e-filing party shall be filed and served electronically, except as provided in NY R UNIF TRIAL CTS § 202.5-b. NY R UNIF TRIAL CTS § 202.5-b(d)(1)(i).

- *ERIE COUNTY.* Case types currently eligible and accepted for e-filing are listed at the NYSCEF website. Note that some actions or special proceedings, (i.e., name changes) which are otherwise subject to mandatory e-filing, if commenced by unrepresented litigants will NOT be maintained in the NYSCEF system; individual cases may be found either at NYSCEF or in the Erie County Clerk's online records system. NY R ERIE E FIL Doc. 3(I)(E).
- *KINGS COUNTY.* Cases that are commenced by filing of the initiating papers with NYSCEF are identified as e-filed cases by assignment of a special index number (i.e., Index Numbers beginning with 500,000). NY R L KINGS E FIL Doc. 1(A)(1). All cases required to be e-filed are listed in Uniform Rule 202.5-bb (Mandatory E-Filing Rules) and on the NYSCEF website. All such cases must be commenced by filing with the County Clerk electronically through NYSCEF and all subsequent documents in such cases must be e-filed. Any questions regarding mandatory e-filing in Kings County can be e-mailed to kcco-efile@nycourts.gov. NY R L KINGS E FIL Doc. 1(A)(2).
- *NEW YORK COUNTY.* Unless otherwise provided in the Rules or in NY R NY CTY E FIL Doc. 2 or where a special exemption is granted due to physical requirements (e.g., oversized maps; see NY R NY CTY E FIL Doc. 2(B)(10)), all documents to be filed with the court in a NYSCEF case, including all documents on motions and all letters to the court (where permitted), must be filed with the NYSCEF system. Documents that attorneys would not ordinarily file with the court in a hard-copy case need not be e-filed. Unless otherwise provided by the E-Filing Rules or this Protocol, in e-filed cases the County Clerk and the court will not accept documents filed in paper form. NY R NY CTY E FIL Doc. 2(B)(1). E-filing is mandatory in all types of cases (other than election law, matrimonial, Art. 78, and Mental Hygiene Law matters, and Art. 70 habeas corpus proceedings) that are commenced in this court on or after February 19, 2013. All such cases must be commenced by filing with the County Clerk electronically through NYSCEF and all subsequent documents in such cases must be e-filed. NY R NY CTY E FIL Doc. 2(A)(2)(a). For more information, including information on consensual e-filing and filing scanned hard copy documents, refer to NY R NY CTY E FIL Doc. 2(A)(2).
- *QUEENS COUNTY.* All authorized Torts, Commercial and Tax Certiorari cases may be commenced by E-Filing, however all parties must consent for the action to continue as an E-file case. NY R L QUEENS E-FILE Doc. 1(A). All papers to be filed with the court in an E-filed case shall be filed on-line with the E-file system except as directed by the court. Papers that attorneys would not ordinarily file with the court in a hard-copy case need not be filed in an E-filed matter. NY R L QUEENS E-FILE Doc. 1(E)(2).

ii. *Who may file.* Documents may be filed or served electronically only by a person who has registered as an authorized e-filing user or as otherwise provided in NY R UNIF TRIAL CTS § 202.5-b(c). NY R UNIF TRIAL CTS § 202.5-b(c)(1).

iii. *When filing made.* Documents may be transmitted at any time of the day or night to the NYSCEF site. A document other than an order or judgment is filed when its electronic transmission or, in the case of a petition that is e-filed by submission of a text file as provided in NY R UNIF TRIAL CTS § 202.5-b(b)(1), the electronic transmission of the text file is recorded at that site, provided, however, that where payment of a fee is required upon the filing of a document, the document is not filed until transmission of the document and the information or form or information as required in NY R UNIF TRIAL CTS § 202.5-b(d)(2)(i), NY R UNIF TRIAL CTS § 202.5-b(d)(2)(ii) or NY R UNIF TRIAL CTS § 202.5-b(d)(2)(iii) has been recorded at the NYSCEF site; or, if no transmission of that information or form or information is recorded, where permitted by the County Clerk, until payment is presented to the County Clerk. NY R UNIF TRIAL CTS § 202.5-b(d)(3)(i).

iv. *Notification of filing.* No later than the close of business on the business day following the electronic filing of a document, a notification, in a form prescribed by the Chief Administrator, shall be transmitted electronically by the NYSCEF site to the person filing such document and the e-mail service addresses of all other participating parties in such action. NY R UNIF TRIAL CTS § 202.5-b(d)(3)(ii).

v. *Removal of confidential information and other corrections.* If a document filed electronically is subsequently discovered to contain confidential data—including but not limited to trade secrets, information protected by confidentiality agreement, or personal confidential information as defined by statute or court rule—or otherwise to have been filed in error, the filer or another party or affected person may (1) notify the parties and any non-party filers in the action of the confidentiality issue or other error raised by the filing, and of his or her intention to seek judicial relief to correct the filing: (2) following such notification, request that the appropriate

County Clerk, exercising his or her administrative discretion, place the document temporarily in "restricted" status on the NYSCEF site, to be made available for viewing by court staff and the parties but not the general public; and (3) file an application to correct the filing by order to show cause within five (5) business days of such notification (or such time as the court may direct), including a request for preliminary injunctive relief limiting interim disclosure of the document at issue. Unless otherwise directed by the court, any document placed in restricted status in response to such a request shall be returned to public view upon expiration of this five (5) day period. The Chief Administrator of the Courts shall promulgate forms to implement this process. NY R UNIF TRIAL CTS § 202.5-b(d)(3)(iii).

- *KINGS COUNTY.* For information on what to do when a document was erroneously filed with confidential information, refer to NY R L KINGS E FIL Doc. 1(B)(11).
- *NEW YORK COUNTY.* For information on what to do when a document was erroneously filed with confidential information, refer to NY R NY CTY E FIL Doc. 2(B)(8).
- *QUEENS COUNTY.* For information on what to do when a document was erroneously filed with confidential information, refer to NY R L QUEENS E-FILE Doc. 1(E)(7).

vi. *Documents requiring judge's signature.* Except where the court directs otherwise, any document that requires a judge's signature shall be transmitted electronically and in hard copy to the court. NY R UNIF TRIAL CTS § 202.5-b(d)(6).

vii. *Documents which would be inconvenient to file electronically; Hard copies.* Notwithstanding any other provision of NY R UNIF TRIAL CTS § 202.5-b, and subject to such guidelines as may be established by the Chief Administrative Judge, the County Clerk or his or her designee may require or permit a party to file in hard copy, in accordance with procedures set by the County Clerk or designee, an exhibit or other document which it is impractical or inconvenient to file electronically. NY R UNIF TRIAL CTS § 202.5-b(d)(7).

- *ERIE COUNTY.* Please contact the Supervisor of Actions & Proceedings, Erie County Clerk's Office by calling (716) 858-6662 or the Deputy County Clerk—Legal at (716) 858-6348 for information. NY R ERIE E FIL Doc. 3(III)(F).
- *KINGS COUNTY.* With limited exceptions, as set forth in the Uniform Rules and herein, all documents to be filed with the court in a NYSCEF case shall be filed online via the NYSCEF system. However, should the size, consistency or context of a hard copy document preclude electronic filing, the user shall electronically file a "Notice of Hard Copy Submission—E-Filed Cases" form EFM-3. Any hard copy submitted pursuant to NY R L KINGS E FIL Doc. 1(B)(9) shall include, as a cover page firmly fastened thereto, a copy of the Confirmation Notice received from the NYSCEF site confirming receipt of the "Notice of Hard Copy Submission—E-Filed Cases". Any party may object to such hard copy filing. The Court, in response to such objection, may, following the hard copy filing, fashion such relief as it deems appropriate pursuant to and in furtherance of the Uniform Rules and NY R L KINGS E FIL Doc. 1, including, but not limited to, an Order directing the filing party to file such documents online via the NYSCEF system. When exhibits are impractical to file pursuant to NY R UNIF TRIAL CTS § 202.5-b(d)(7), an additional "Notice of Hard Copy Exhibit Filing" form EFM-4 is required to be submitted. NY R L KINGS E FIL Doc. 1(B)(9).
- *NEW YORK COUNTY.* If a filer needs to submit unusual exhibits in original form that cannot practically be e-filed, such as oversized maps or electronic recordings, the filer should consult with the County Clerk's E-File Department by telephone at 646-386-3737 (procedural questions only) or by e-mail at ccnyef@nycourts.gov, which will normally require that the filer retain custody of the original subject to possible future directives of the court. NY R NY CTY E FIL Doc. 2(B)(10). In such instances, the filing counsel shall file with NYSCEF a "placeholder" in the form of a Notice of Hard Copy Exhibit Filing (NYSCEF Form EF 21). The Notice should be uploaded to NYSCEF as document type "Exhibit" and the filer should indicate in the "Additional Document Information" field that the filer is retaining custody of the original. Failure to e-file the Notice may result in a gap in the official record of the court. NY R NY CTY E FIL Doc. 2(B)(10).

viii. *Documents containing sensitive or proprietary information.* In an action subject to e-filing, any person may apply for an order prohibiting or restricting the electronic filing in the action of specifically identified materials on the grounds that such materials are subject to copyright or other proprietary rights, or trade secret or other privacy interests, and that electronic filing in the action is likely to result in substantial prejudice to those rights or interests. NY R UNIF TRIAL CTS § 202.5-b(k)(2).

ix. *Refusal to accept paper filings.* In accordance with NY CPLR Rule 2102(c), a County Clerk and a chief clerk of the Supreme Court or County Court, as appropriate, shall refuse to accept for filing papers filed in actions and proceedings when the paper sought to be filed:

- Is in an action subject to electronic filing pursuant to Rules of the Chief Administrator,
- Is not being filed electronically, and
- Does not include the notice required by NY R UNIF TRIAL CTS § 202.5-b(d)(1). NY R UNIF TRIAL CTS § 202.5(d)(1)(v); NY R UNIF TRIAL CTS § 202.5-bb(d).

x. *Emergency filings; Hard copies.* For information on when an emergency filing may be filed and served in hard copy, refer to NY R UNIF TRIAL CTS § 202.5-b(d)(1)(ii), NY R UNIF TRIAL CTS § 202.5-b(d)(1)(iii) and NY R UNIF TRIAL CTS § 202.5-bb(c)(3).

- *KINGS COUNTY.* Under the rules, a participating emergency e-filer must electronically file the documents initially filed in hard copy form within three (3) business days of the emergency filing; the originals will be discarded after the documents have been processed and the failure to e-file as required will therefore lead to an incomplete record. NY R L KINGS E FIL Doc. 1(B)(3).
- *NEW YORK COUNTY.* Occasionally an emergency will arise requiring expedited entry of a document with the County Clerk (e.g., an order issued in the courtroom after a conference or argument of a critical matter), such as for purposes of an immediate appeal. Expedition can be achieved by the Part as follows: the document should be carried by a Court Officer or staff member to the General Clerk's Office to assure immediate and proper recordation in the computer and, as appropriate, the posting of the document to NYSCEF or the Supreme Court Records On-Line Library ("Scroll"). The court will accommodate counsel in emergencies. NY R NY CTY Procedure XI(A).
- *NEW YORK COUNTY.* For more information on how to bring emergency matters before the court, refer to NY R NY CTY Procedure IV.

xi. *Technical failures.* The NYSCEF site shall be considered to be subject to a technical failure on a given day if the site is unable to accept filings or provide access to filed documents continuously or intermittently over the course of any period of time greater than one (1) hour after 12:00 noon of that day. Notice of all such technical failures shall be provided on the site. NY R UNIF TRIAL CTS § 202.5-b(i).

- When e-filing is hindered by a technical failure, a party may file with the appropriate clerk and serve in hard copy. NY R UNIF TRIAL CTS § 202.5-b(i). In the event an attorney or party shall file and serve documents in hard copy pursuant to NY R UNIF TRIAL CTS § 202.5-b(i), each such document shall include the notice required by NY R UNIF TRIAL CTS § 202.5-b(d)(1), and the filer shall file those documents with the NYSCEF site within three (3) business days after restoration of normal operations at that site. NY R UNIF TRIAL CTS § 202.5-b(i).
- With the exception of deadlines that by law cannot be extended, the time for filing of any document that is delayed due to technical failure of the site shall be extended for one (1) day for each day on which such failure occurs, unless otherwise ordered by the court. NY R UNIF TRIAL CTS § 202.5-b(i).
- *ERIE COUNTY.* When filing by electronic means is hindered by a technical failure, please refer to the NY R UNIF TRIAL CTS § 202.5-b(i). NY R ERIE E FIL Doc. 3(III)(K).
- *KINGS COUNTY.* When filing by electronic means is hindered by a NYSCEF technical failure (as set forth in NY R UNIF TRIAL CTS § 202.5-b(i)), a party may file with the appropriate Clerk in hard copy. Except for deadlines that by law cannot be extended (e.g. Statute of limitations, Notice of Appeal), the time for filing of any document that is delayed due to technical failure of the NYSCEF system shall be extended for one day for each day on which such failure occurs, unless otherwise ordered by the court. NY R L KINGS E FIL Doc. 1(B)(13).
- *ONONDAGA COUNTY.* When filing by electronic means is hindered by a technical failure (as set forth in NY R UNIF TRIAL CTS § 202.5-b(h)(3)(i)), a party may file a hard copy with the County Clerk. With the exception of deadlines that by law cannot be extended (e.g., a statute of limitations or the deadline for filing a Notice of Appeal), the time for filing of any document that is delayed due to technical failure of the NYSCEF system will be extended for one day for each day on which such failure occurs, unless otherwise ordered by the court. A "Notice of Hard Copy Filing Submission—E-Filed Case' must accompany any documents not filed via NYSCEF. NY R ONDGA E FIL Protocol(B)(8).

xii. *Filing fees.* For information on what information must be provided to pay filing fees, refer to NY R UNIF TRIAL CTS § 202.5-b(d)(2).

xiii. *Exemption from e-filing.* For information on exemptions from e-filing, refer to NY R UNIF TRIAL CTS § 202.5-bb(e).

xiv. *Filing exhibits*

- *ERIE COUNTY.* In the NYSCEF system, each exhibit must be uploaded as a separate .pdf file. After uploading a primary document, please choose the document type "Exhibit" and enter the appropriate number or letter and a brief description of the exhibit; each exhibit should bear a separate cover sheet clearly marked as "Exhibit A," "Exhibit B," etc. "Exhibit A" or "Exhibit B" is unacceptable as a brief description of the exhibit. Exhibits, where referenced in a signed Order as attached or affixed shall be uploaded with the signed Order as one .pdf document. NY R ERIE E FIL Doc. 3(III)(H); NY R ERIE E FIL Doc. 3(V)(D).
- *KINGS COUNTY.* In the NYSCEF system, each exhibit should be uploaded as a separate PDF file. After uploading a primary document, please choose the document type "Exhibit", enter the appropriate number or letter, and be sure to place a check mark to the right of "Attach to main document". Each exhibit shall bear a separate cover sheet clearly marked as Exhibit A, Exhibit B, etc. NY R L KINGS E FIL Doc. 1(B)(12). Whenever possible, attorneys submitting exhibits in NYSCEF cases should make each exhibit a separate attachment to an affidavit/affirmation in the system (i.e., multiple exhibits should not be filed as a single PDF). NY R L KINGS E FIL Doc. 1(D)(1).
- *NEW YORK COUNTY.* Attorneys submitting exhibits in NYSCEF cases should make each exhibit a separate attachment to an affidavit/affirmation in the system; i.e., exhibits should not be filed as a single PDF-A together with the affidavit/affirmation or grouped together as a single PDF-A attachment because either of these two formats makes it difficult for the Justice to locate particular exhibits as needed. Counsel must also include appropriate descriptive language in the "Additional Document Information" field in NYSCEF. NY R NY CTY E FIL Doc. 2(D)(6).
- *ONONDAGA COUNTY.* All exhibits in e-filed cases must be e-filed individually as separate attachments. NY R ONDGA E FIL Protocol(B)(9)(b).

xv. *Correcting documents*

- *ERIE COUNTY.* Submission of documents which, upon examination, require correction or addition will result in notification to the filer advising that the document has been returned for correction. The filer shall make the required corrections and/or additions as indicated in the e-mail transmission sent by the County Clerk or Part Clerk through the NYSCEF site. The corrected documents may be resubmitted using the "Re-file this document" link highlighted in the filer's document list for the respective case. Please note that in the case of multiple submissions, all related documents filed at the same time may be removed from the case record and returned until all documents are properly submitted. NY R ERIE E FIL Doc. 3(III)(J).
- *KINGS COUNTY.* Submission of documents which, upon examination, require correction or addition will result in notification to the filer advising that there is a problem with a document. The filer shall make the required corrections and/or additions and resubmit the corrected document using the "Refile this document" link. In the event a document is returned for correction, the original file date will be preserved. For corrections of documents filed with the Kings County Clerk which require a court order, refer to the procedure in NY R UNIF TRIAL CTS § 202.5-b(d)(3)(iii) and NY R L KINGS E FIL Doc. 1(B)(11). NY R L KINGS E FIL Doc. 1(B)(3).
- *ONONDAGA COUNTY.* If there is an error or an additional document is required, the system will notify the filing party, who will make the corrections/additions and resubmit them online. NY R ONDGA E FIL Protocol(B)(6).
- *QUEENS COUNTY.* Generally speaking, documents that have been E-filed will not thereafter be deleted by the County Clerk from NYCEF because the filer asserts that the filing contains an error or a significant omission. When the filer wishes to correct a perceived error or omission in a filed document, he or she should file an amended version of the document, with the original remaining on file, or else obtain a court order providing for deletion of the original. The County Clerk will only delete a document upon request of the filer or on the County Clerk's own initiative when it is obvious from the face of the document alone that the filer made a fundamental error and never intended to file the document that was filed (e.g., a completely unrelated non-litigation document, a different case, or a wrong county). The County Clerk will advise the filer when any such fundamental errors are detected. NY R L QUEENS E-FILE Doc. 1(E)(6).

c. *Facsimile filing.* In the Supreme Court, facsimile filing shall be limited to commercial claims and tax certiorari, conservatorship, and mental hygiene proceedings in Monroe, Westchester, New York and Suffolk Counties. NY R UNIF TRIAL CTS § 202.5-a(a)(1). Refer to NY R UNIF TRIAL CTS § 202.5-a for information on the procedures for facsimile filing.

i. *NEW YORK COUNTY.* Unless indicated otherwise by the court in a particular case or in NY R NY CTY J RUL Doc. 1, Justices do not accept papers by fax. NY R NY CTY J RUL Rule 4.

d. *ERIE COUNTY: Filing request for judicial intervention.* An RJI in a NYSCEF case shall be filed via the NYSCEF system and will be filed after all other documents have been uploaded. The filer may choose between filing a .pdf image of the prepared RJI and any Addendum or having the system prepare the RJI which shall conform to Uniform Rules. Addenda, such as the Commercial Division Addendum, if prepared by the filer must be filed simultaneously with and attached to an RJI and uploaded as one .pdf document with the RJI. If the RJI is prepared by the e-filing system, no separate Addendum is required. Whether or not the filer elects to allow NYSCEF to create the RJI or chooses to upload a prepared RJI, data in addition to the nature of the judicial intervention, including information that appears on any Addenda will be collected through completion of the fields presented. If the filing of the RJI is accomplished through a filing agent, a prepared RJI and Addendum must be filed in lieu of the creation of the RJI by the NYSCEF system, as the RJI must be signed by the attorney. NY R ERIE E FIL Doc. 3(IV). For information on RJIs in specific types of action, refer to NY R ERIE E FIL Doc. 3(IV).

2. *Service requirements*

a. *Who may serve.* Except where otherwise prescribed by law or order of court, papers may be served by any person not a party of the age of eighteen years or over. NY CPLR Rule 2103(a).

b. *Service upon attorney.* Except where otherwise prescribed by law or order of court, papers to be served upon a party in a pending action shall be served upon the party's attorney. Where the same attorney appears for two or more parties, only one (1) copy need be served upon the attorney. Such service upon an attorney shall be made:

i. By delivering the paper to the attorney personally. NY CPLR Rule 2103(b)(1).

ii. By mailing the paper to the attorney at the address designated by that attorney for that purpose or, if none is designated, at the attorney's last known address; service by mail shall be complete upon mailing. NY CPLR Rule 2103(b)(2).

- *BRONX COUNTY.* Service by mail must be within the state. NY R BRONX FIL R Doc. 3.

iii. If the attorney's office is open, by leaving the paper with a person in charge, or if no person is in charge, by leaving it in a conspicuous place; or if the attorney's office is not open, by depositing the paper, enclosed in a sealed wrapper directed to the attorney, in the attorney's office letter drop or box. NY CPLR Rule 2103(b)(3).

iv. By leaving it at the attorney's residence within the state with a person of suitable age and discretion. Service upon an attorney shall not be made at the attorney's residence unless service at the attorney's office cannot be made. NY CPLR Rule 2103(b)(4).

v. By transmitting the paper to the attorney by facsimile transmission, provided that a facsimile telephone number is designated by the attorney for that purpose. Service by facsimile transmission shall be complete upon the receipt by the sender of a signal from the equipment of the attorney served indicating that the transmission was received, and the mailing of a copy of the paper to that attorney. The designation of a facsimile telephone number in the address block subscribed on a paper served or filed in the course of an action or proceeding shall constitute consent to service by facsimile transmission in accordance with NY CPLR Rule 2103(b)(5). An attorney may change or rescind a facsimile telephone number by serving a notice on the other parties. NY CPLR Rule 2103(b)(5).

vi. By dispatching the paper to the attorney by overnight delivery service at the address designated by the attorney for that purpose or, if none is designated, at the attorney's last known address. Service by overnight delivery service shall be complete upon deposit of the paper enclosed in a properly addressed wrapper into the custody of the overnight delivery service for overnight delivery, prior to the latest time designated by the overnight delivery service for overnight delivery. "Overnight delivery service" means any delivery service which regularly accepts items for overnight delivery to any address in the state. NY CPLR Rule 2103(b)(6).

vii. By transmitting the paper to the attorney by electronic means where and in the manner authorized by the chief administrator of the courts by rule and, unless such rule shall otherwise provide, such transmission shall be upon the party's written consent. The subject matter heading for each paper sent by electronic means must indicate that the matter being transmitted electronically is related to a court proceeding. NY CPLR Rule 2103(b)(7).

- *KINGS COUNTY.* Pursuant to the E-Filing Rules, service of interlocutory documents is made by posting a document to the NYSCEF site, which automatically and immediately transmits an email notice of the filing, including a link to the document, to all participating counsel and unrepresented litigants on the case. The Rules also authorize service by other methods permitted by the CPLR. If service by such other method is made, proof of service must be filed with NYSCEF. NY R L KINGS E FIL Doc. 1(I).

- *NEW YORK COUNTY.* Service. . .will be made automatically through NYSCEF upon all participating counsel and unrepresented parties in the case. There are limited exceptions to the requirement for e-filing in the covered kinds of cases. NY R NY CTY Procedure XI(A). Pursuant to the E-Filing Rules, service of interlocutory documents is made by posting a document to the NYSCEF site, which automatically and immediately transmits an e-mail notice of the filing, including a link to the document, to all participating counsel and unrepresented litigants on the case. The Rules also authorize service by other methods permitted by the CPLR. If service by such a method is made, proof of service must be filed with NYSCEF. NY R NY CTY E FIL Doc. 2(I).
- *QUEENS COUNTY.* Filing with the system permits counsel to serve the papers electronically pursuant to NY R UNIF TRIAL CTS § 202.5-b(f) once consent to E-Filing has been filed on-line. Consult NY R UNIF TRIAL CTS § 202.5-bb(c) for service in mandatory e-filing. Any required proof of service should be E-filed as a separate document. NY R L QUEENS E-FILE Doc. 1(E)(4).

c. *Electronic service mandatory; Consenting to electronic service; How electronic service may be made.* Except as otherwise provided in NY R UNIF TRIAL CTS § 202.5-bb, filing and service of all documents in an action that has been commenced electronically in accordance with NY R UNIF TRIAL CTS § 202.5-bb shall be by electronic means. NY R UNIF TRIAL CTS § 202.5-bb(c)(1).

i. *Party's consent required for certain e-filing.* After commencement of an action wherein e-filing is authorized, documents may be electronically filed and served, but only by, and electronic service shall be made only upon, a party or parties who have consented thereto. NY R UNIF TRIAL CTS § 202.5-b(b)(2)(i).

- A consent to e-filing in an action shall state that the party providing it agrees to the use of e-filing in the action and to be bound by the filing and service provisions in NY R UNIF TRIAL CTS § 202.5-b. NY R UNIF TRIAL CTS § 202.5-b(b)(2)(ii).

ii. *Address for service; Duty to notify as to changes.* The e-mail service address recorded at the time of registration is the e-mail address at which service of interlocutory documents on that party may be made through notification transmitted by the NYSCEF site. It is the responsibility of each filing user to monitor that address and promptly notify the Resource Center in the event of a change in his or her e-mail service address. NY R UNIF TRIAL CTS § 202.5-b(f)(2)(i).

iii. *How service made.* An e-filing party causes service of an interlocutory document to be made upon another party participating in e-filing by filing the document electronically. Upon receipt of an interlocutory document, the NYSCEF site shall automatically transmit electronic notification to all e-mail service addresses in such action. NY R UNIF TRIAL CTS § 202.5-b(f)(2)(ii).

- Except as provided otherwise in NY R UNIF TRIAL CTS § 202.5-b(h)(3), the electronic transmission of the notification shall constitute service of the document on the e-mail service addresses identified therein; however, such service will not be effective if the filing party learns that the notification did not reach the address of the person to be served. Proof of such service will be recorded on the NYSCEF site. A party may, however, utilize other service methods permitted by the CPLR provided that, if one of such other methods is used, proof of that service shall be filed electronically. NY R UNIF TRIAL CTS § 202.5-b(f)(2)(ii).

iv. *Signatures on hard copies; Proof of service filed electronically.* When an e-filing party serves a document in hard copy on a non-participating party, the document served shall bear full signatures of all signatories and proof of such service shall be filed electronically. NY R UNIF TRIAL CTS § 202.5-b(b)(2)(i).

- *ERIE COUNTY.* In the NYSCEF system, each Affidavit of Service must be uploaded as a separate .pdf file. After uploading the Affidavit, please choose the document type: "Affirmation/Affidavit of Service" and enter the name of the party served as Additional Document Information. NY R ERIE E FIL Doc. 3(III)(I); NY R ERIE E FIL Doc. 3(V)(F).

v. *Effect of failure to consent.* A party's failure to consent to participation in electronic filing and service shall not bar any other party to the action from filing documents electronically with the County Clerk and the court or serving documents upon any other party who has consented to participation. A party who has not consented to participation shall file documents with the court and the County Clerk, and serve and be served with documents, in hard copy. NY R UNIF TRIAL CTS § 202.5-b(b)(2)(i).

d. *Service upon party.* If a party has not appeared by an attorney or the party's attorney cannot be served, service shall be upon the party by a method specified in NY CPLR Rule 2103(b)(1), NY CPLR Rule 2103(b)(2), NY CPLR Rule 2103(b)(4), NY CPLR Rule 2103(b)(5) or NY CPLR Rule 2103(b)(6). NY CPLR Rule 2103(c).

e. *Service on all parties.* Each paper served on any party shall be served on every other party who has appeared, except as otherwise may be provided by court order or as provided in NY CPLR § 3012 or in NY CPLR § 3215(f). Upon demand by a party, the plaintiff shall supply that party with a list of those who have appeared and the names and addresses of their attorneys. NY CPLR Rule 2103(e).

f. *Service by filing.* If a paper cannot be served by any of the methods specified in NY CPLR Rule 2103(b) and NY CPLR Rule 2103(c), service may be made by filing the paper as if it were a paper required to be filed. NY CPLR Rule 2103(d).

g. *Definitions.* For the purposes of NY CPLR Rule 2103:

i. "Mailing" means the deposit of a paper enclosed in a first class postpaid wrapper, addressed to the address designated by a person for that purpose or, if none is designated, at that person's last known address, in a post office or official depository under the exclusive care and custody of the United States Postal Service within the state;

ii. "Electronic means" means any method of transmission of information between computers or other machines designed for the purpose of sending and receiving such transmissions, and which allows the recipient to reproduce the information transmitted in a tangible medium of expression;

iii. "Facsimile transmission" means any method of transmission of documents to a facsimile machine at a remote location which can automatically produce a tangible copy of such documents. NY CPLR Rule 2103(f).

G. Hearings

1. *Oral argument.* Motion papers received by the clerk of the court on or before the return date shall be deemed submitted as of the return date. The assigned judge, in his or her discretion or at the request of a party, thereafter may determine that any motion be orally argued and may fix a time for oral argument. NY R UNIF TRIAL CTS § 202.8(d).

a. A party requesting oral argument shall set forth such request in its notice of motion or in its order to show cause or on the first page of the answering papers, as the case may be. Where all parties to a motion request oral argument, oral argument shall be granted unless the court shall determine it to be unnecessary. NY R UNIF TRIAL CTS § 202.8(d).

b. Where a motion is brought on by order to show cause, the court may set forth in the order that oral argument is required on the return date of the motion. NY R UNIF TRIAL CTS § 202.8(d).

i. *BRONX COUNTY.* All orders to show cause, with the exception of orders to show cause that are returnable in the City Part, the STP Part, the Matrimonial Part and the Preliminary/Compliance Conference Part (IA-11), submitted on or after August 25, 2003, will be returnable on a Monday in the assigned Justice's part and appear on his or her motion calendar. Appearances will be required on orders to show cause. NY R BRONX FIL R Doc. 8. A motion on notice or a notice of petition in a New York Supreme Court E-File (hereafter known as NYSCEF) case, as in others, shall be made returnable in the Motion Support Office (Room 217). NY R BRONX E FIL R Doc. 1(1).

- After a motion/petition and notice are filed with the NYSCEF system, the Motion Support Office will automatically place the motion/proceeding on the submit calendar in the Motion Support Office (Room 217) for the return date. No appearance or other action by the filing attorney is required in order for the motion to be calendared if the motion fee is paid for via NYSCEF. Motions in e-filed cases (other than tax certiorari cases) appear on the submit calendar in Room 217 on the return date. NY R BRONX E FIL R Doc. 1(2).

c. *KINGS COUNTY.* All motions require appearances and oral argument. NY R L KINGS Pt. C, Rule 3.

2. *Return date; Time for hearing.* A notice of motion shall specify the time and place of the hearing on the motion. NY CPLR Rule 2214(a). The moving party determines when a motion on notice shall be heard, but she has to consult the court's or judge's calendar practice first. The movant picks out a "return day" sufficiently far off to assure that the notice requirements of NY CPLR Rule 2214(b) can be met, and to assure as well that the day picked is a day on which the assigned judge hears motions. SIEGEL-NYPRAC § 247.

a. *Judge assigned to hear motion*

i. *Referral to judge supervising disclosure.* Unless the chief administrator of the courts has, by rule, provided otherwise, if a case has been assigned to a judge to supervise disclosure pursuant to NY CPLR § 3104, all motions preliminary to trial shall be referred to such judge whenever practicable. NY CPLR Rule 3214(a).

ii. *Referral to judge who decided prior motion.* Any motion may be referred to a judge who decided a prior motion in the action. NY CPLR Rule 2217(a).

iii. *Transfer when judge unable to hear motion.* If a motion is made to a judge who is or will be for any reason unable to hear it, it may be transferred by order of such judge or by written stipulation of the parties to any other judge to whom it might originally have been made. NY CPLR Rule 2217(c).

iv. *Procedure for unassigned cases.* If a case has not been assigned to a judge, the motion shall be made returnable before the court, and a copy of the moving papers, together with a request for judicial intervention, shall be filed with the court, with proof of service upon all other parties, where required by NY R UNIF TRIAL CTS § 202.6, within five (5) days of service upon the other parties. The moving party shall give written notice of the index number to all other parties immediately after filing of the papers. NY R UNIF TRIAL CTS § 202.8(b).

- *Responding papers.* Copies of all responding papers shall be submitted to the court, with proof of service and with the index number set forth in the papers, on or before the return date. NY R UNIF TRIAL CTS § 202.8(b).
- *Assignment after request for judicial intervention.* The case shall be assigned to a judge as soon as practicable after the filing of the request for judicial intervention pursuant to NY R UNIF TRIAL CTS § 202.6, but in no event later than the return date. After assignment to the judge, the court shall provide for appropriate notice to the parties of the name of the assigned judge. NY R UNIF TRIAL CTS § 202.8(b).
- *Motions to be heard in another county.* Motion papers noticed to be heard in a county other than the county where the venue of the action has been placed by the plaintiff shall be assigned to a judge in accordance with procedures established by the Chief Administrator. NY R UNIF TRIAL CTS § 202.8(b).

v. *ALBANY COUNTY: Motions referred to IAS Justice.* All motions made after a case has been assigned a day certain shall be referred to the IAS Justice unless the motion is returnable during the term in which the matter has been assigned a day certain, in that event, the matter will be referred to the Part 1 Justice for that particular term who may entertain the motion or refer such motion to the IAS Justice. Under those circumstances, the Part I Justice shall decide whether or not to strike the note of issue or assign the matter a new day certain. NY R 3 JD SUP Doc. 1(H)(2). All motions shall be returnable before the assigned justice. NY R 3 JD SUP Doc. 1(B).

b. *Trial of issue raised by motion.* The court may order that an issue of fact raised on a motion shall be separately tried by the court or a referee. If the issue is triable of right by jury, the court shall give the parties an opportunity to demand a jury trial of such issue. Failure to make such demand within the time limited by the court, or, if no such time is limited, before trial begins, shall be deemed a waiver of the right to trial by jury. An order under NY CPLR § 2218 shall specify the issue to be tried. NY CPLR § 2218.

c. *Audio-visual coverage of trial court proceeding.* Audio-visual coverage of proceedings in the trial courts shall be permitted only in accordance with the provisions of Part 131 of the Rules of the Chief Administrator (NY R CHIEF ADMIN § 131.1, et seq.). NY R CHIEF J § 29.3.

d. *Adjournment of return date.* Stipulations of adjournment of the return date made by the parties shall be in writing and shall be submitted to the assigned judge. Such stipulation shall be effective unless the court otherwise directs. No more than three (3) stipulated adjournments for an aggregate period of sixty (60) days shall be submitted without prior permission of the court. NY R UNIF TRIAL CTS § 202.8(e)(1).

i. Absent agreement by the parties, a request by any party for an adjournment shall be submitted in writing, upon notice to the other party, to the assigned judge on or before the return date. The court will notify the requesting party whether the adjournment has been granted. NY R UNIF TRIAL CTS § 202.8(e)(2).

ii. *BRONX COUNTY.* Non-disclosure motions for IA5, IA7 and IA22 will be adjourned for oral argument to the Monday of the second week following the week of the return date of the motion. All other non-disclosure motions will be deemed submitted on the return date and forwarded to Chambers unless a stipulation of adjournment complying with the requirements of NY R UNIF TRIAL CTS § 202.8(e) is submitted, in which event, the motion will be adjourned for the requested date and kept in the Clerk's Office. If a non-stipulated request for adjournment or notice is submitted, the motion and request will be forwarded to Chambers for judicial approval or denial of the request. In either event, the attorney requesting the adjournment will be notified, via telephone, of the granting or denial of the request and instructed to notify his adversary. NY R BRONX FIL R Doc. 8.

iii. *BRONX COUNTY.* Motions that have been e-filed may be adjourned in Room 217 if an adjournment complies with the procedures of the Motion Support Office (explained in the "Filing Rules—Motion Procedure" section of the "Courthouse Procedures" link on the website of [the] court). An adjournment that so complies may be obtained by filing a stipulation of all parties with NYSCEF (designated in the filing menu as a "Stipulation to Adjourn Motion"). NY R BRONX E FIL R Doc. 1(3).

iv. *NEW YORK COUNTY.* The Courtroom also maintains a "APB (All Papers By)" Calendar, which is used when a party seeks an adjournment but fails to comply with the Courtroom's procedures or there is a failure to comply with procedures that requires the clerk to adjourn the motion/application (e.g., failure to submit a Confirmation Notice in an e-filed case). The case may be put over for three days to allow compliance with those procedures, as described further below. NY R NY CTY Procedure II(C); NY R NY CTY E FIL Doc. 2(D)(2). E-filed applications may be adjourned in the Part if an adjournment complies with the Part's procedures (see the Uniform Rules of the Justices (Local Rules) on the court's website). An adjournment that so complies may be obtained by filing with NYSCEF a stipulation of all parties (designated in the filing menu as a Stipulation—Adjournment of Motion—Before Judge); the motion number and the current return date of the motion being adjourned shall be set forth in the "Additional Document Information" field in NYSCEF. Absent any problems, the Part will effectuate the adjournment without need for an appearance or any other action by the parties. NY R NY CTY E FIL Doc. 2(D)(4).

v. *QUEENS COUNTY.* The Motion Support Office is NOT authorized to grant adjournments. NY R L QUEENS MOT SUP Doc. 1.

e. *ALBANY COUNTY: Motion terms.* There shall be a. . . Motion Term on each Friday in the Supreme Court, Albany County. The Friday Motion Term shall include all Article 78 Proceedings involving New York State and proceedings commenced pursuant to Article 14 of the Civil Service Law (including applications for injunctive relief made pursuant to section 209-a of the Civil Service Law). NY R 3 JD SUP Doc. 1(F). Generally, parties will be granted only one adjournment for the Friday Motion Term. NY R 3 JD SUP Doc. 1(F).

f. *ALBANY COUNTY: Motion determined without hearing.* All motions are deemed "submitted" on the return date and no appearances are required by the parties. NY R 3 JD SUP Doc. 1(B). In the event oral argument is requested, the parties should not appear on the return date. At the discretion of the assigned Judge and upon the granting of a request for oral argument, the parties will be notified by Chambers of the scheduled time and place at which argument will be heard. Where a motion is brought on by order to show cause, the court may set forth in the order that appearances and/or oral argument are required on the return date of the motion. NY R 3 JD SUP Doc. 1(B).

g. *BRONX COUNTY: Return date.* All assigned and unassigned motions will be returnable five (5) days a week in the Civil Branch Clerk's Office, Room 217, at 9:30 a.m. NY R BRONX FIL R Doc. 8.

i. If on any submitted non-disclosure motion oral argument is requested and granted, or directed by the Court, the motion shall be adjourned for oral argument before the I.A. Judge on the second Monday following the week of the return date of the motion. Attorneys will be notified via telephone of the adjourned date. NY R BRONX FIL R Doc. 8.

h. *BRONX COUNTY: Oral argument.* Calendars of disclosure motions and other motions adjourned for oral argument will be published for the four (4) business days preceding the rescheduled appearance date and on the rescheduled date of the motion. These repetitive publications will serve as the notification of procedure of adjournment of all motions. In addition, two (2) days before the return date of unassigned motions a list of such motions indicating the assigned Justice and the adjourned date of the motion will be published. NY R BRONX FIL R Doc. 8.

i. *BRONX COUNTY: Resolution before return date.* Counsel/parties must advise the Court in writing on or before the return date of all motions that have been resolved by Counsel/parties themselves and all motions the movant(s) wish to be withdrawn. NY R BRONX FIL R Doc. 8.

j. *ERIE COUNTY: Calendaring of motions.* Refer to individual Justice's Part Rules. NY R ERIE E FIL Doc. 3(V)(B).

k. *KINGS COUNTY: Return date set by court.* Irrespective of the return date indicated in the notice of motion, motions will be rescheduled by the E-file/Motion Support Office to a date designated by the assigned Judge. NY R L KINGS Pt. C, Rule 2.

l. *KINGS COUNTY: Calendar calls.* There shall be two (2) calendar calls on motion days. The first calendar call shall be at 9:30 AM and the second calendar call shall be at 10:45 AM, unless the Judge's Part Rules provide otherwise. Defaults shall only be taken on second call. Attorneys with appearances elsewhere in the courthouse may advise the clerk of their whereabouts to avoid a default. Failure to so advise the clerk or appear at the default calendar call will result in a default order being entered or the motion being marked off the calendar. NY R L KINGS Pt. C, Rule 7.

m. *NEW YORK COUNTY: Return date and assigned courtroom.* Motions made by notice of motion and petitions and notices of petition in special proceedings are processed by the General Clerk's Office (Room 119) and are to be made returnable in the Motion Submission Part Courtroom (Room 130) on any business day of the week at 9:30 AM. There are some differences in electronically-filed cases. NY R NY CTY Procedure II; NY R NY CTY Procedure II(C); NY R NY CTY J RUL Rule 13(a).

i. For the convenience of counsel, between 9:00 A.M. and 9:30 A.M. each day, in advance of the "call," Room 130 accepts (1) written stipulations; (2) affidavits/affirmations reciting the required details as to an adjournment on consent; (3) stipulations, letters or other writings withdrawing motions; and (4) final papers or complete sets of papers on motions. For motions in which these items are handed in before the "call," no one need remain to answer the "call." Counsel/parties must advise the court, either between 9:00 A.M. and 9:30 A.M. or at the "call," of all motions or cases that have been resolved by counsel/parties themselves and all motions that the movant no longer wishes to pursue. If such resolution occurs subsequent to the "call", the assigned Justice must be advised as soon as possible, by written notice sent to the Part, so that the court does not do unnecessary work. NY R NY CTY Procedure II(C).

ii. Depending upon the assigned Part, contested motions submitted in the Motion Submission Part Courtroom are submitted without argument, or rescheduled for oral argument if so directed by the assigned Justice. For Justices who schedule argument on a case-by-case basis, notice of the argument date will be transmitted by the court. Counsel may ascertain how a motion submitted in Courtroom 130 was marked by consulting Scroll on the court's website, the e-Track application, or, on the two (2) days immediately following the submission date, the New York Law Journal. NY R NY CTY J RUL Rule 13(a).

n. *NEW YORK COUNTY: Motion call.* Each day in the Motion Submission Part Courtroom, commencing at 9:30 A.M., all motions returnable that day will be "called" for the submission of these papers, which must be handed up at this "call" or, as described below, immediately before. Because hundreds of motions appear on the Room 130 calendars every day, motion papers (other than part of the moving papers as described above) cannot be accepted on any day prior to the return date. Courtesy copies are not required nor accepted, but working copies are required by certain Justices in e-filed cases. NY R NY CTY Procedure II(C). If argument is directed, it will take place on an announced date shortly after the day of submission. NY R NY CTY Procedure II(C).

o. *NEW YORK COUNTY: Oral arguments.* Pursuant to request of some Justices, motions submitted in Room 130 will automatically be scheduled for a set argument date in the Part. Other Justices determine on a case-by-case basis after submission in Room 130 whether to accept a particular substantive motion on submission, to require oral argument, or to hold a conference. NY R NY CTY Procedure II(D). If argument is directed by the Justice automatically, notice of argument and the argument date will be given in Room 130. Any appearing party is expected to give notice to all parties and an announcement to this effect is made in Room 130. If the motion is submitted in Room 130 and the Justice, after examining the file, determines that argument should be directed, notice of the argument and the argument date will not be sent by the court. To obtain notification of the argument date and other developments, counsel should use e-Track. If argument notification is not given or transmitted as just described, counsel should understand that the motion has been taken on submission for decision on the papers. NY R NY CTY Procedure II(D).

i. Calendars of motions to be argued in the Parts are published on the morning of the argument date and on the day before in the New York Law Journal under each Part. Argument information is available on a case-by-case basis in Scroll, and e-mail notifications are sent by e-Track to participating attorneys whenever a motion is scheduled for argument in the court's computer system. NY R NY CTY J RUL Rule 15(a)

p. *NEW YORK COUNTY: Motion determined without hearing.* Given the purpose of the Room 130 procedure, the substance of motions will not be addressed at the submission "call." No Judge is present. To the extent possible, motions submitted in Room 130 will be decided "on the papers." Indeed, attorneys are encouraged to use service or clerks to deliver papers or working copies, or to agree among themselves to have one of them deliver papers for all parties by service or a clerk. Counsel for the movant need not appear to "take a default" on any motion or for any other reason. Motions will be submitted, not marked off, in the absence of the movant. Opposing counsel similarly need not appear in person in order to avoid suffering a default. Delivery of papers by service or a clerk will suffice. The court's goal is to be able to collect papers on motions in an orderly fashion but without any attorney having to make an appearance in Room 130 at any time. NY R NY CTY Procedure II(C).

q. *ONONDAGA COUNTY: Return date.* If the motion is the first filing in an action, the case will be assigned and counsel will be notified by the Supreme Court Clerk's Office via the NYSCEF system of the assigned justice and return date. NY R ONDGA E FIL Protocol(B)(7)(c). If the motion is on a previously assigned case, counsel may choose a return date from the assigned justice's motion term schedule. If the date in unavailable, the Supreme Court Clerk's Office will assign the motion to the next available motion term date and will notify counsel via e-mail. The change will also appear in the notification generated by the NYSCEF system. NY R ONDGA E FIL Protocol(B)(7)(d).

r. *QUEENS COUNTY: Return date.* Motions must be made returnable on the proper day/time based on the assigned judge. NY R L QUEENS MOT SUP Doc. 1. Failure to make a motion returnable on the proper day/time may result in the motion being administratively rescheduled or marked off. NY R L QUEENS MOT SUP Doc. 1.

s. *QUEENS COUNTY: Unassigned motions.* For RJI/Motions, due to the fact that the movant would not know who the assigned judge will be, the notice of motion may be returnable any day of the week. RJI/Motions shall be made returnable in "Queens Supreme Court" with no address designated. The motion will be administratively rescheduled to the proper day of the week based on the judge (once a judge has been assigned). Within one (1) week of filing, the movant must check online to see who the assigned judge is (and therefore the location/date/time) that their motion is now returnable. Movant must then notify their adversary of this information prior to the return date. NY R L QUEENS MOT SUP Doc. 1.

3. *Entry of order after hearing.* An order determining a motion shall be entered and filed in the office of the clerk of the court where the action is triable, and all papers used on the motion and any opinion or memorandum in writing shall be filed with that clerk unless the order dispenses with such filing. When a statute or civil practice rule requires such filing and entry in a county other than that in which the order was made, the party prevailing on the motion shall file the order and the papers used on the motion with the proper clerk after receiving them. If a party fails to file any papers required to be filed under NY CPLR Rule 2220(a), the order may be vacated as irregular, with costs. NY CPLR Rule 2220(a). For more information on the entry of an order after a motion, refer to NY CPLR Rule 2219.

a. *BRONX COUNTY: Settled orders.* A Judge's decision will often call for a Settled Order. The purpose of the settled order is to give effect to the decision by directing that some action be done and/or that a court official perform some task. NY R BRONX LEG SUP Doc. 2. A settled order consists of a notice of settlement informing all parties that the proposed order will be presented to the judge who made the decision on a date certain. Next comes the proposed order which will be presented to the judge. This order should conform to the judge's decision and should direct the relief granted in the decision. This should be followed by proof of service upon all parties who were noticed with the decision. It is also helpful if a copy of the judge's decision is included along with the other papers. A settled order should always be noticed before the judge who made the decision. NY R BRONX LEG SUP Doc. 2.

i. Although an order is usually settled by the party who prevailed on the motion, any party may settle the order. It should be presented to the court within sixty (60) days of the decision. The other parties are entitled to ten (10) days notice where service of the settled order is done by mail, five (5) days if the notice is personally delivered. An attorney who is served with a notice of settlement which he believes does not accurately reflect the decision may settle a counter order. The counter order must be noticed for the same day and must be served not less than seven (7) days if by mail and two (2) days if personally delivered. NY R BRONX LEG SUP Doc. 2.

ii. Settled orders are usually sent to the judge the day after they noticed for settlement. No appearance is necessary or even contemplated on a settled order. If the decision directs "submit order", then no notice is necessary, and the order will be sent to the judge as soon a practical after it is received. No fees are collected on settled orders. NY R BRONX LEG SUP Doc. 2.

b. *ERIE COUNTY: Proposed orders.* Proposed orders shall be submitted through the NYSCEF system and a working copy provided to the IAS Justice for signature, if Part Rules so require. NY R ERIE E FIL Doc. 3(V)(G).

c. *KINGS COUNTY: Long form orders.* If the Court directs that an order be settled or submitted on a motion in a NYSCEF case, the proposed order, with Notice of Settlement where required, and any proposed counter-order shall be filed with the Court via NYSCEF. The relevant clerk's office will process the documents in the customary manner. NY R L KINGS E FIL Doc. 1(E).

i. WORKING COPIES OF PROPOSED ORDERS WITH NOTICE OF SETTLEMENT MUST BE SUBMITTED IN THE MOTION SUPPORT OFFICE (ROOM 227) AS EXPLAINED HEREIN. THEY MUST NOT BE DELIVERED TO THE PART OR CHAMBERS, EXCEPT WHERE THE INDIVIDUAL JUSTICE'S PART RULES PROVIDE OTHERWISE; DOING SO WILL CAUSE ADMINISTRATIVE CONFUSION AND POSSIBLE MISPLACEMENT OF PAPERS. Any such submission shall be sent in a timely manner (kindly review individual Justice's rules) and be conspicuously marked on the outside "NYSCEF Matter;" lack of such marking may delay processing. After an order/counter-order has been signed, it will be scanned, and the County Clerk will affix the entry stamp into the NYSCEF system, which will immediately transmit notice of this event via e-mail, including a link to the entered document, to all participating attorneys and unrepresented litigants in the case. Such transmittal does not constitute Notice of Entry. NY R L KINGS E FIL Doc. 1(E).

d. *NEW YORK COUNTY: Long form orders.* Although the court strongly favors the use of short form orders and judgments, there are instances when settlement of an order or judgment is appropriate. When a Justice directs in a decision that a long form order or judgment be settled, that decision is recorded in the court's computer system by the General Clerk's Office and the motion file with decision is held in the Order Section of the Office in Room 119. The settlement process takes place there. NY R NY CTY Procedure II(D); NY R NY CTY E FIL Doc. 2(E).

i. A proposed long form order or judgment in compliance NY R UNIF TRIAL CTS § 202.48 must be presented to the relevant back office, together with a notice of settlement which bears a settlement date, the date on which the order is to be ready for formal presentation to the Justice. In an e-filed case the submission shall be made electronically. The proposed order or counter-order should be e-filed and it will be transmitted automatically by the NYSCEF system to the appropriate back office. The return date and time of the proposed order must be at 9:30 A.M. no sooner than either five (5) days from personal service of the proposed order or ten (10) days from service by mail. Proof of timely service on the other parties must accompany the proposed order in a hard copy case. If an order or judgment is submitted late (later than sixty (60) days from signing and filing of the decision) and the proponent can show good cause for this tardiness, an affidavit or affirmation justifying the delay should be annexed to the proposed order, together with proof of service thereof. If persuaded, the Justice will consider the proposed order despite its untimeliness. NY R NY CTY Procedure II(D); NY R NY CTY E FIL Doc. 2(E).

ii. Sometimes a decision will state "Submit Order." The submitting party should prepare a long form order and make it returnable without notice. Counsel should deliver the proposed order to the Order Section of the appropriate back office, except in an e-filed case, when it shall be submitted electronically. NY R NY CTY Procedure II(D). If the decision of the court directs that a proposed order be settled or submitted in the Part or in Chambers, that direction, should, of course, be followed without presentation of the proposal to the back office. NY R NY CTY Procedure II(D).

iii. For information on proposed counter-orders, refer to NY R NY CTY Procedure II(D) and NY R NY CTY J RUL Rule 16(b).

e. *QUEENS COUNTY: Proposed orders.* If the court directs that an order be settled or submitted on a motion in an E-file case, the proposed order and any proposed counter-order shall be filed with the court on-line with proof of service. (If a decision refers to a proceeding on the record, a copy of the transcript must be submitted.) Working copies of all proposed orders MUST be submitted to the Motion Support Office before an order can be reviewed. NY R L QUEENS E-FILE Doc. 1(I).

i. Counsel are advised to adhere to NY R UNIF TRIAL CTS § 202.48 regarding the submission or settlement of their proposed order or judgment. Persons who are submitting proposed orders/judgments pursuant to a previously issued memorandum decision must submit a copy of the memorandum decision with their proposed order/judgment. Upon E-Filing a proposed order/judgement, a working copy of the proposed order/judgement must be provided to the Motion Support Office. NY R L QUEENS MOT SUP Doc. 1.

4. *ALBANY COUNTY: Additional hearing on temporary restraining order.* A justice or judge who signs an order to show cause which contains a stay or temporary restraining order may, if appropriate, require a hearing on short notice to determine if the stay or TRO should be continued until the return date before the assigned justice or judge. NY R 3 JD SUP Doc. 1(B).

H. Forms

1. Official Motion for Preliminary Injunction Forms for New York

a. Request for judicial intervention. NY R UNIF TRIAL CTS § 202.6.

b. Notice of motion. NY R UNIF TRIAL CTS § 202.7(b).

2. New York Motion for Preliminary Injunction Forms

a. Notice of motion for preliminary injunction. NYPRAC-COLL § 4:302.

b. Affidavit in support of motion for preliminary injunction. NYPRAC-COLL § 4:303.

c. Undertaking upon motion for preliminary injunction. NYPRAC-COLL § 4:305.

d. Notice of motion to vacate or modify preliminary injunction. NYPRAC-COLL § 4:308.

e. Affidavit in support of motion to vacate preliminary injunction. NYPRAC-COLL § 4:309.

f. Affidavit in support of order to show cause (containing temporary restraining order) for preliminary injunction in relation to unique chattel. NYPRAC-COLL § 4:357.

g. Notice of motion for preliminary injunction. MCF CPLR § 11:97.

h. Notice of motion for preliminary injunction; Copyright trademark. MCF CPLR § 11:98.

i. Affidavit in support of motion for preliminary injunction. MCF CPLR § 11:99.
j. Affirmation in support of order to show cause why preliminary injunction should not issue. MCF CPLR § 11:105.
k. Affidavit in support of order to show cause why preliminary injunction should not issue. MCF CPLR § 11:106.
l. Notice of motion for reargument and renewal of motion for preliminary injunction. MCF CPLR § 11:108.
m. Affidavit in support of motion for reargument and renewal of motion for preliminary injunction. MCF CPLR § 11:109.
n. Affidavit in support of motion for preliminary injunction and stay of action. MCF CPLR § 11:111.
o. Attorney's affidavit in support of motion for preliminary injunction and stay of action. MCF CPLR § 11:112.
p. Notice of motion to vacate or modify preliminary injunction. MCF CPLR § 11:113.
q. Affidavit in support of motion to vacate preliminary injunction. MCF CPLR § 11:114.
r. Affidavit in support of motion to vacate temporary restraining order. MCF CPLR § 11:117.
s. General form of affidavit of service of motion papers. MCF CPLR § 5:24.

I. Applicable Rules

1. *State rules*
   a. Short title; Application; Construction; Definitions. NY CPLR § 101; NY CPLR § 103; NY CPLR § 104; NY CPLR § 105.
   b. Appendix of official forms. NY CPLR § 107.
   c. Extensions of time generally. NY CPLR § 2004.
   d. Form of papers. NY CPLR Rule 2101; NY CPLR Rule 2102; NY CPLR § 2105; NY CPLR Rule 2106; NY GEN BUS § 399-ddd; NY R UNIF TRIAL CTS § 215.2; NY R UNIF TRIAL CTS § 215.3.
   e. Service of papers. NY CPLR Rule 2103.
   f. Where motion made; In supreme court action. NY CPLR § 2212.
   g. Motion papers; Service; Time. NY CPLR Rule 2214.
   h. Relief demanded by other than moving party. NY CPLR Rule 2215.
   i. Prior motion; Ex parte motion; Transfer of motion; Hearings; Orders. NY CPLR Rule 2217; NY CPLR § 2218; NY CPLR Rule 2220.
   j. Computation of time. NY CPLR § 2402; NY GEN CONSTR § 19; NY GEN CONSTR § 20; NY GEN CONSTR § 25-a; NY GEN CONSTR § 30; NY GEN CONSTR § 31; NY GEN CONSTR § 53.
   k. Motions heard by judge supervising disclosure; Stay of disclosure. NY CPLR Rule 3214.
   l. Provisional remedies; Preliminary injunction. NY CPLR § 6001; NY CPLR § 6301; NY CPLR § 6311; NY CPLR Rule 6312; NY CPLR § 6313; NY CPLR § 6314; NY CPLR § 6315.
   m. Fees; Index number fees of county clerks. NY CPLR § 8018.
   n. Hours of court; Proceedings in court. NY R CHIEF J § 3.1; NY R CHIEF J § 29.3.
   o. Application of part; Waiver; Additional rules; Application of CPLR; Definitions. NY R UNIF TRIAL CTS § 202.1.
   p. Papers filed in court; Electronic filing in supreme court. NY R UNIF TRIAL CTS § 202.5; NY R UNIF TRIAL CTS § 202.5-a; NY R UNIF TRIAL CTS § 202.5-b; NY R UNIF TRIAL CTS § 202.5-bb.
   q. Request for judicial intervention. NY R UNIF TRIAL CTS § 202.6.
   r. Calendaring of motions; Uniform notice of motion form; Affirmation of good faith. NY R UNIF TRIAL CTS § 202.7.
   s. Motion procedure; Preliminary conferences. NY R UNIF TRIAL CTS § 202.8; NY R UNIF TRIAL CTS § 202.12.
   t. Rules of the commercial division of the Supreme Court. NY R UNIF TRIAL CTS § 202.70.
   u. Signing of papers. NY R CHIEF ADMIN § 130-1.1-a.
2. *Local rules*
   a. *Albany County*
      i. Third judicial district rules. NY R 3 JD SUP Doc. 1.

b. *Bronx County*
   i. Filing of papers in supreme court. NY R BRONX FIL R Doc. 1.
   ii. Request for judicial intervention. NY R BRONX FIL R Doc. 2.
   iii. Motion procedure. NY R BRONX FIL R Doc. 8.
   iv. Commercial division. NY R BRONX FIL R Doc. 12.
   v. Motions on notice. NY R BRONX E FIL R Doc. 1.
   vi. Settled orders. NY R BRONX LEG SUP Doc. 2.
c. *Erie County*
   i. Joint protocols for New York State Courts E-Filing (NYSCEF) cases filed in Supreme Court, Erie County. NY R ERIE E FIL Doc. 3.
d. *Kings County*
   i. Papers. NY R L KINGS Pt. A, Papers.
   ii. Service of motion papers. NY R L KINGS Pt. C, Rule 1.
   iii. Scheduling of motions. NY R L KINGS Pt. C, Rule 2.
   iv. Appearance and argument. NY R L KINGS Pt. C, Rule 3.
   v. Courtesy copies. NY R L KINGS Pt. C, Rule 5.
   vi. Motion calendar calls. NY R L KINGS Pt. C, Rule 7.
   vii. Protocol on courthouse and county clerk procedures for electronically filed cases. NY R L KINGS E FIL Doc. 1.
e. *New York County*
   i. Commencement of cases. NY R NY CTY Procedure I.
   ii. RJIs and assignments. NY R NY CTY Procedure IA.
   iii. Motions and special proceedings by notice of motion/petition. NY R NY CTY Procedure II.
   iv. County clerk litigation functions. NY R NY CTY Procedure XI.
   v. Protocol on courthouse and county clerk procedures for electronically filed cases. NY R NY CTY E FIL Doc. 2.
   vi. Redaction of information in documents filed with the county clerk and the court. NY R NY CTY J RUL Rule A-1.
   vii. Papers by fax. NY R NY CTY J RUL Rule 4.
   viii. Motions on notice; Orders to show cause. NY R NY CTY J RUL Rule 13.
   ix. Motion papers. NY R NY CTY J RUL Rule 14.
   x. Oral argument; Adjournments. NY R NY CTY J RUL Rule 15.
f. *Onondaga County*
   i. Onondaga county protocol for case filings New York State Electronic Files (NYSCEF). NY R ONDGA E FIL Protocol.
g. *Queens County*
   i. Motion support office. NY R L QUEENS MOT SUP Doc. 1.
   ii. Queens county protocol on courthouse procedures for electronically filed cases. NY R L QUEENS E-FILE Doc. 1.

J. Miscellaneous

NOTE: Individual judges' rules may apply.

ALBANY COUNTY

JUSTICE LISA M. FISHER: NY R 3 JD FISHER Fisher; NY R 3 JD FISHER Fisher, PC Order.

JUSTICE RICHARD MOTT: NY R 3 JD MOTT Mott.

JUSTICE STEPHAN G. SCHICK: NY R 3 JD Schick.

FORECLOSURE SETTLEMENT PART: NY R 3 JD Foreclosure Settlement.

BRONX COUNTY

JUSTICE PAUL L. ALPERT: [NY R BRONX J Part IA-29, as amended by NY ORDER 20-0337].

JUSTICE BEN BARBATO: NY R BRONX J Part IA-21.

JUSTICE MARY ANNE BRIGANTTI: [NY R BRONX J Part IA-15, as amended by NY ORDER 20-0338].

JUSTICE JOSEPH E. CAPELLA: NY R BRONX J Part IA-23.

JUSTICE MITCHELL DANZIGER: NY R BRONX J Part IA-3/33 ; [NY R BRONX J Danziger, Part IA-3/33, as amended by NY ORDER 20-0339].

JUSTICE LAURA G. DOUGLAS: NY R BRONX J Part IA-11.

JUSTICE RUBEN FRANCO: NY R BRONX J Part IA-26.

JUSTICE DORIS M. GONZALEZ: NY R BRONX J Part IA-24.

JUSTICE WILMA GUZMAN: NY R BRONX J Part IA-7; [NY R BRONX J Guzman, Part IA-7 Virtual, as amended by NY ORDER 20-0340].

JUSTICE ROBERT T. JOHNSON: NY R BRONX J Part IA-12.

JUSTICE DONALD A. MILES: NY R BRONX J Part IA-8.

JUSTICE DONNA M. MILLS: NY R BRONX J Part IA-9.

JUSTICE JULIA I. RODRIGUEZ: NY R BRONX J Part IA-18; [NY R BRONX J Part IA-27, as amended by NY ORDER 20-0341].

JUSTICE LLINET M. ROSADO: [NY R BRONX J Part IA-25, as amended by NY ORDER 20-0342].

JUSTICE NORMA RUIZ: NY R BRONX J Part IA-22; [NY R BRONX J Ruiz, Part IA-22 Virtual, as amended by NY ORDER 20-0343].

JUSTICE HOWARD H. SHERMAN: NY R BRONX J Part IA-4.

JUSTICE FERNANDO TAPIA: NY R BRONX J Part IA-13.

JUSTICE ELIZABETH A. TAYLOR: NY R BRONX J Part IA-2.

JUSTICE ALISON Y. TRUITT: NY R BRONX J Part IA-5.

PART IDV: NY R BRONX J Doc. 1.

PRE-TRIAL PART RULES: NY R BRONX J Doc. 2.

PRE TRIAL WORKSHEET: NY R BRONX J Doc. 3.

FORECLOSURE SETTLEMENT PART RULES: NY R BRONX J Doc. 4.

GUARDIANSHIP PART RULES: NY R BRONX J Doc. 5.

LPM PART RULES: NY R BRONX J Doc. 6.

ERIE COUNTY

JUSTICE M. WILLIAM BOLLER: NY R 8 JD J Boller.

JUSTICE RALPH A. BONIELLO: NY R 8 JD J Boniello.

JUSTICE CHRISTOPHER J. BURN: NY R 8 JD J Burns.

JUSTICE RUSSELL P. BUSCAGLIA: NY R 8 JD J Buscaglia.

JUSTICE FRANK CARUSO: NY R 8 JD J Caruso.

JUSTICE STEPHEN W. CASS: NY R 8 JD J Cass.

JUSTICE DEBORAH A. CHIMES: NY R 8 JD J Chimes.

JUSTICE EMILIO COLAIACOVO: [NY R 8 JD J Colaiacovo, as amended by NY ORDER 20-0252].

JUSTICE DIANE Y. DEVLIN: NY R 8 JD J Devlin.

JUSTICE JAMES H. DILLON: NY R 8 JD J Dillon.

JUSTICE PAULA L. FEROLETO: NY R 8 JD J Feroleto.
JUSTICE DANIEL J. FURLONG: [NY R 8 JD J Furlong, as amended by NY ORDER 20-0253].
JUSTICE JOSEPH R. GLOWNIA: NY R 8 JD J Glownia.
JUSTICE MARK J. GRISANTI: NY R 8 JD J Grisanti.
JUSTICE DEBORAH A. HAENDIGES: NY R 8 JD J Haendiges.
JUSTICE LYNN W. KEANE: [NY R 8 JD J Keane, as amended by NY ORDER 20-0254].
JUSTICE RICHARD C. KLOCH, Sr.: NY R 8 JD J Kloch.
JUSTICE FREDERICK J. MARSHALL: [NY R 8 JD J Marshall, as amended by NY ORDER 20-0255.
JUSTICE JOHN L. MICHALSKI: NY R 8 JD J Michalski.
JUSTICE MARK A. MONTOUR: [NY R 8 JD J Montour, as amended by NY ORDER 20-0256].
JUSTICE HENRY NOWAK: NY R 8 JD J Nowak.
JUSTICE JOHN F. O'DONNELL: NY R 8 JD J O'Donnell.
JUSTICE JEANETTE OGDEN: NY R 8 JD J Ogden.
JUSTICE CATHERINE NUGENT-PANEPINTO: NY R 8 JD J Nugent-Panepinto.
JUSTICE FRANK A. SEDITA, III: [NY R 8 JD J Sedita, as amended by NY ORDER 20-0257].
JUSTICE SARA SHELDON: NY R 8 JD J Sheldon.
JUSTICE DONNA M. SIWEK: NY R 8 JD J Siwek.
JUSTICE MARY L. SLISZ: NY R 8 JD J Slisz.
JUSTICE TIMOTHY J. WALKER: [NY R 8 JD J Walker, as amended by NY ORDER 20-0258].
JUSTICE DENNIS E. WARD: NY R 8 JD J Ward.
JUSTICE PAUL B. WOJTASZEK: [NY R 8 JD J Wojtaszek, as amended by NY ORDER 20-0259].
JUSTICE CHARLES N. ZAMBITO: [NY R 8 JD J Zambito, as amended by NY ORDER 20-0260].
SUPREME COURT LEGAL STAFF: NY R 8 JD J Legal Staff.

KINGS COUNTY

JUSTICE RACHEL A. ADAMS: NY R KINGS J Part 5F.
JUSTICE LOREN BAILY-SCHIFFMAN: NY R KINGS J Part 65.
JUSTICE REGINALD A. BODDIE: NY R KINGS J Part 95.
JUSTICE THERESA M. CICCOTTO: NY R KINGS J Part 19; NY R KINGS J Part 5J.
JUSTICE LISSETTE COLON: NY R KINGS J Part Rules.
JUSTICE GENINE EDWARDS: NY R KINGS J Part 80.
JUSTICE PAMELA L. FISHER: [NY R KINGS J Part 94, as amended by NY ORDER 20-0208].
JUSTICE ROBIN GARSON: NY R KINGS J Part 75.
JUSTICE LARA J. GENOVISI: [NY R KINGS J Part 34, as amended by NY ORDER 20-0209].
JUSTICE BERNARD J. GRAHAM: NY R KINGS J Part 36.
JUSTICE DAWN JIMENEZ-SALTA: NY R KINGS J Part 88.
JUSTICE INGRID JOSEPH: [NY R KINGS J Part FRP3 and Part 83, as amended by NY ORDER 20-0210].
JUSTICE KATHY J. KING: NY R KINGS J Part 64, 76K.
JUSTICE LAWRENCE KNIPEL: NY R KINGS J Part 57.
JUSTICE DONALD KURTZ: NY R KINGS J Part 26.
JUSTICE CARL LANDICINO: [NY R KINGS J Part 81, as amended by NY ORDER 20-0211].
JUSTICE KATHERINE LEVINE: [NY R KINGS J Part 20, 25, 92, as amended by NY ORDER 20-0211].
JUSTICE LORNA MCALLISTER: [NY R KINGS J Part 10, as amended by NY ORDER 20-0211].

JUSTICE ROSEMARIE MONTALBANO: [NY R KINGS J Part 19, 71, and 22, as amended by NY ORDER 20-0211].
JUSTICE RICHARD J. MONTELIONE: [NY R KINGS J Part 99 and DJMP, as amended by NY ORDER 20-0215].
JUSTICE LISA S. OTTLEY: NY R KINGS J Part 24.
JUSTICE MARK I. PARTNOW: NY R KINGS J Part 43.
JUSTICE ERIC I. PRUS: NY R KINGS J Part 5A.
JUSTICE FRANCOIS RIVERA: NY R KINGS J Part 52.
JUSTICE KAREN B. ROTHENBERG: NY R KINGS J Part 35.
JUSTICE LEON RUCHELSMAN: NY R KINGS J Part 1.
JUSTICE WAYNE P. SAITTA: NY R KINGS J Part 29.
JUSTICE ROBIN K. SHEARES: NY R KINGS J Part 96.
JUSTICE KENNETH P. SHERMAN: NY R KINGS J Part 67 and 78.
JUSTICE DEBRA SILBER: NY R KINGS J Part 9 and 5K.
JUSTICE ELLEN M. SPODEK: NY R KINGS J Part 63.
JUSTICE MARSHA L. STEINHARDT: NY R KINGS J Part 15.
JUSTICE JEFFREY S. SUNSHINE: NY R KINGS J Part 5G.
JUSTICE PETER P. SWEENEY: [NY R KINGS J Part 35, as amended by NY ORDER 20-0218].
JUSTICE DELORES J. THOMAS: [NY R KINGS J Part 5T, as amended by NY ORDER 20-0221].
JUSTICE WAVNY TOUSSAINT: NY R KINGS J Part 70.
JUSTICE RICHARD VELASQUEZ: NY R KINGS J Part 66.
JUSTICE CAROLYN E. WADE: NY R KINGS J Part 84.
JUSTICE EDWARD G. WALKER: [NY R KINGS J Part 90, as amended by NY ORDER 20-0219].
JUSTICE LILLIAN WAN: [NY R KINGS J Part 17, as amended by NY ORDER 20-0220].
JUSTICE MICHELLE WESTON: NY R KINGS J Part 3.
MENTAL HYGIENE PART: NY R KINGS J Part 77.
MATRIMONIAL PARTS DURING COVID-19 EMERGENCY: JUSTICE KAREN B. ROTHENBERG: NY R KINGS J Doc. 1.

NASSAU COUNTY

JUSTICE ANNA R. ANZALONE: NY R NASSAU S J Anzalone, Part 26.
JUSTICE STACY D. BENNETT: NY R NASSAU S J Bennett; NY R NASSAU S J Bennett, Form 1.
JUSTICE ANTONIO BRANDVEEN: NY R NASSAU S J Brandveen, Part 31.
JUSTICE JEFFREY S. BROWN: [NY R NASSAU S J Brown, as amended by NY ORDER 20-0297].
JUSTICE STEPHEN A. BUCARIA: NY R NASSAU S J Bucaria.
JUSTICE JULIANNE T. CAPETOLA: NY R NASSAU S J Capetola, Part 28.
JUSTICE EDMUND M. DANE: NY R NASSAU S J Dane, Part 33.
JUSTICE VITO M. DESTEFANO: NY R NASSAU S J DeStefano, Part 13; NY R NASSAU S J DeStefano, Form 1.
JUSTICE ARTHUR M. DIAMOND: NY R NASSAU S J Diamond, Part 7.
JUSTICE THOMAS FEINMAN: NY R NASSAU S J Feinman, Part 5.
JUSTICE JOHN M. GALASSO: NY R NASSAU S J Galasso, Part 22.
JUSTICE SHARON M.J. GIANELLI: NY R NASSAU S J Gianelli, Part 22; NY R NASSAU S J Gianelli, Form 1.
JUSTICE JEFFREY A. GOODSTEIN: NY R NASSAU S J Goodstein, Part 33; NY R NASSAU S J Goodstein, Form 1.
JUSTICE DAVID J. GUGERTY: [NY R NASSAU S J Gugerty, Part 31, as amended by NY ORDER 20-0298].
JUSTICE HELENE F. GUGERTY: NY R NASSAU S J Gugerty, Part 47.
JUSTICE STEVEN M. JAEGER: NY R NASSAU S J Jaeger, Part 35; NY R NASSAU S J Jaeger, Form 1.

JUSTICE JACK L. LIBERT: NY R NASSAU S J Libert, Part 23.

JUSTICE JOSEPH H. LORINTZ: NY R NASSAU S J Lorintz, Part 26; NY R NASSAU S J Lorintz, Form 1.

JUSTICE ROY S. MAHON: NY R NASSAU S J Mahon, Part 3.

JUSTICE RANDY SUE MARBER: NY R NASSAU S J Marber, Part 8.

JUSTICE JAMES P. MCCORMACK: [NY R NASSAU S J McCormack, Part 18, as amended by NY ORDER, 20-0299].

JUSTICE DICCIA T. PINEDA-KIRWAN: [NY R NASSAU S J Pineda-Kirwan, as amended by NY ORDER 20-0300].

JUSTICE THOMAS RADEMAKER: [NY R NASSAU S J Rademaker, Part 28, as amended by NY ORDER 20-0301]; [NY R NASSAU S J Rademaker, Form 1, as amended by NY ORDER 20-0301].

JUSTICE DENISE L. SHER: NY R NASSAU S J Rademaker, Part 32.

JUSTICE LEONARD D. STEINMAN: [NY R NASSAU S J Steinman, Part 15, as amended by NY ORDER 20-0303]; NY R NASSAU S J Steinman, Form 1.

JUSTICE HOWARD E. STURIM: NY R NASSAU S J Sturim, Part 50; NY R NASSAU S J Sturim, Form 1.

JUSTICE HELEN VOUTSINAS: [NY R NASSAU S J Voutsinas, Part 25, as amended by NY ORDER 20-0304]; [NY R NASSAU S J Voutsinas, Form 1, as amended by NY ORDER 20-0305].

JUSTICE HOPE SCHWARTZ ZIMMERMAN: NY R NASSAU S J Zimmerman, Part 17.

NEW YORK COUNTY

JUDGE'S RULES; BASIC INFORMATION: [NY R NY CTY J RUL Doc. 1, as amended by NY ORDER 20-0202].

ONONDAGA COUNTY

JUSTICE ROBERT E. ANTONACCI II: [NY R ONDGA E FIL Doc. 1, as amended by 20-0239].

JUSTICE MICHAEL V. COCCOMI: NY R ONDGA E FIL Doc. 2.

JUSTICE GREGORY R. GILBERT: NY R 5 JD JUDGES Gilbert; NY R ONDGA E FIL Doc. 3.

JUSTICE DONALD A. GREENWOOD: NY R ONDGA E FIL Doc. 4.

JUSTICE DEBORAH H. KARALUNAS: NY R ONDGA E FIL Doc. 5.

JUSTICE JAMES MCCLUSKY: NY R 5 JD MCCLUSKY McClusky.

JUSTICE CHARLES C. MERRELL: NY R 5 JD MERRELL Merrell.

JUSTICE PATRICK F. MACRAE: NY R 5 JD MACRAE Doc. 1.

JUSTICE JAMES P. MURPHY: NY R ONDGA E FIL Doc. 7.

JUSTICE GERALD J. NERI: [NY R 5 JD JUDGES Neri, as amended by NY ORDER 20-0236]; [NY R ONDGA E FIL Doc. 8, as amended by NY ORDER 20-0241].

JUSTICE ANTHONY J. PARIS: NY R 5 JD JUDGES Paris; [NY R ONDGA E FIL Doc. 9, as amended by NY ORDER 20-0242].

JUSTICE NORMAN W. SEITER, JR.: NY R 5 JD JUDGES Seiter.

JUSTICE KEVIN G. YOUNG: [NY R ONDGA E FIL Doc. 10, as amended by NY ORDER 20-0243].

QUEENS COUNTY

JUSTICE PAM JACKMAN BROWN: [NY R L QUEENS Brown, Part 19, as amended by NY ORDER 20-0321].

JUSTICE CHEREE A. BUGGS: NY R L QUEENS Buggs, Part 30.

JUSTICE PAM JACKMAN BROWN: [NY R L QUEENS Brown, Part 19, as amended by NY ORDER 20-0321].

JUSTICE DENIS J. BUTLER: NY R L QUEENS Butler, Part 12.

JUSTICE ROBERT I. CALORAS: [NY R L QUEENS Caloras, Part 36, as amended by NY ORDER 20-0322].

JUSTICE ANNA CULLEY: NY R L QUEENS Culley, Part 53.

JUSTICE TIMOTHY DUFFICY: NY R L QUEENS Dufficy, Part 35.

JUSTICE DAVID ELLIOT: NY R L QUEENS Elliot, Part 14.

JUSTICE JOSEPH J. ESPOSITO: NY R L QUEENS Esposito, Part 6.

JUSTICE DARRELL L. GAVRIN: [NY R L QUEENS Gavrin, Part 27, as amended by NY ORDER 20-0323].

JUSTICE WYATT N. GIBBONS: [NY R L QUEENS Gibbons, Part 5, as amended by NY ORDER 20-0330.

JUSTICE DONNA-MARIE E. GOLIA: [NY R L QUEENS Golia, Part 21, as amended by NY ORDER 20-0331].

JUSTICE MARGUERITE A. GRAYS: [NY R L QUEENS Grays, Part 4, as amended by NY ORDER 20-0324].

JUSTICE RUDOLPH E. GRECO: [NY R L QUEENS Greco, Part 32, as amended by NY ORDER 20-0325].

JUSTICE MAUREEN HEALY: NY R L QUEENS Healy, Part 6.

JUSTICE PHILLIP HOM: [NY R L QUEENS Hom, Part 43, as amended by NY ORDER 20-0332].

JUSTICE KEVIN J. KERRIGAN: NY R L QUEENS Kerrigan, Part 10.

JUSTICE MOJGAN C. LANCMAN: NY R L QUEENS Lancman, Part 20.

JUSTICE RICHARD G. LATIN: NY R L QUEENS Latin, Part 40.

JUSTICE ULYSSES B. LEVERETT: [NY R L QUEENS Leverett, Part 6, as amended by NY ORDER 20-0326].

JUSTICE LEONARD LIVOTE: NY R L QUEENS Livote, Part 33.

JUSTICE LEE A. MAYERSOHN: NY R L QUEENS Mayersohn, Part 22; NY R L QUEENS Mayersohn, Part 22G; [NY R L QUEENS Mayersohn, Part 22G COVID, as amended by NY ORDER 20-0327].

JUSTICE ROBERT J. MCDONALD: NY R L QUEENS McDonald, Part 34.

JUSTICE MARGARET MCGOWAN: NY R L QUEENS McGowan, Part 52.

JUSTICE MAURICE E. MUIR: [NY R L QUEENS Muir, Part 42, as amended by NY ORDER 20-0333].

JUSTICE JODI ORLOW: NY R L QUEENS Orlow, Part 51.

JUSTICE LESLIE J. PURIFICCION: NY R L QUEENS Purificcion, Part 39.

JUSTICE JOSEPH RISI: [NY R L QUEENS Risi, Part 3, as amended by NY ORDER 20-0328].

JUSTICE FREDERICK D.R. SAMPSON: [NY R L QUEENS Sampson, Part 31, as amended by NY ORDER 20-0329].

JUSTICE MARTIN J. SCHULMAN: NY R L QUEENS Schulman, Part 29.

JUSTICE BERNICE D. SIEGAL: NY R L QUEENS Siegal, Part 25G.

JUSTICE JANICE A. TAYLOR: NY R L QUEENS Taylor, Part 15.

JUSTICE CARMEN R. VELASQUEZ: NY R L QUEENS Velasquez, Part 38.

JUSTICE LOURDES M VENTURA: [NY R L QUEENS Ventura, Part 37, as amended by NY ORDER 20-0334].

JUSTICE WILLIAM A. VISCOVICH: NY R L QUEENS Viscovich, Part 63.

JUSTICE ALLAN B. WEISS: NY R L QUEENS Weiss, Part 2.

COMPLIANCE, SETTLEMENT AND CONFERENCE PART: NY R L QUEENS Doc 1.

PRELIMINARY CONFERENCE PART: [NY R L QUEENS Doc. 2, as amended by NY ORDER 20-0335].

MEDICAL MALPRACTICE CONFERENCE PART: [NY R L QUEENS Doc. 3, as amended by NY ORDER 20-0336].

TRIAL SCHEDULING PART: NY R L QUEENS Doc. 4.

SUMMARY JURY TRIAL PROGRAM: NY R L QUEENS Doc. 7.

RESIDENTIAL FORECLOSURE PART: NY R L QUEENS Doc. 9.

FORECLOSURE AUCTION RULES: NY R L QUEENS Doc. 10.

MATRIMONIAL PRELIMINARY CONFERENCE PART: NY R L QUEENS Doc. 11.

NON-CUSTODIAL CONTESTED MATRIMONIAL PART: NY R L QUEENS Doc. 12.

Motions, Oppositions and Replies
Motion for Relief from Judgment

Document Last Updated August 2020

A. Checklist

(I) ❑ Matters to consider for moving party

(a) ❑ Required documents

(1) ❑ Notice of motion, order to show cause, or affidavit on ex parte motion

(2) ❑ Motion

(3) ❑ Request for judicial intervention

(4) ❑ Proof of service

(5) ❑ ALBANY COUNTY: Additional required documents

(i) ❑ Affirmation of good faith effort

(b) ❑ Supplemental documents

(1) ❑ Supporting evidence; Exhibits

(2) ❑ Brief

(3) ❑ Affidavit of merits

(4) ❑ Notice to produce papers not in possession of the court

(5) ❑ Filing fees

(6) ❑ Working copies

(7) ❑ Statement of authorization in electronic filing cases

(8) ❑ ERIE COUNTY: Additional supplemental documents

(i) ❑ Notice of hard copy submission in e-filed case

(9) ❑ KINGS COUNTY: Additional supplemental documents

(i) ❑ Forms when filing in hard copy

(10) ❑ NEW YORK COUNTY: Additional supplemental documents

(i) ❑ Notice of hard copy submission

(ii) ❑ Unpublished opinions

(11) ❑ ONONDAGA COUNTY: Additional supplemental documents

(i) ❑ Notice of hard copy submission

(12) ❑ QUEENS COUNTY: Additional supplemental documents

(i) ❑ Notice of hard copy submission

(c) ❑ Timing

(1) ❑ Motion for relief from judgment based on excusable default: the court which rendered a judgment or order may relieve a party from it upon such terms as may be just, on motion of any interested person with such notice as the court may direct, upon the ground of excusable default, if such motion is made within one (1) year after service of a copy of the judgment or order with written notice of its entry upon the moving party, or, if the moving party has entered the judgment or order, within one (1) year after such entry

(2) ❑ No stated time limit for motion based on other NY CPLR Rule 5015(a) grounds; the standard is within a reasonable time

(3) ❑ The moving party shall serve copies of all affidavits and briefs upon all other parties at the time of service of the notice of motion

(4) ❑ A notice of motion and supporting affidavits shall be served at least eight (8) days before the time at which the motion is noticed to be heard

(5) ❑ It is also good practice to make motions returnable at least three (3) weeks away from the planned date of mailing and to always include a demand in the motion that the other side serve answering papers at least seven (7) days before the return day

(6) ❑ BRONX COUNTY: Additional timing

(i) ❑ A Notice of Motion must be served at least eight (8) days, by personal service, nine (9) days by overnight express and thirteen (13) days by mail before the return date

(7) ❑ NEW YORK COUNTY: Additional timing

(i) ❑ In an e-filed case, all of the moving papers shall be e-filed at least eight (8) business days prior to the return date

(8) ❑ ONONDAGA COUNTY: Additional timing

(i) ❑ Onondaga County local court rules require that any additional papers relating to motions must be e-filed at least two (2) business days prior to the return date, excluding the return date

(9) ❑ QUEENS COUNTY: Additional timing

(i) ❑ Motions must be in the possession of the Motion Support Office at least nine (9) days before the noticed return date of the motion

(II) ❑ Matters to consider for opposing party

(a) ❑ Required documents

(1) ❑ Opposition

(2) ❑ Proof of service

(b) ❑ Supplemental documents

(1) ❑ Supporting evidence; Exhibits

(2) ❑ Brief

(3) ❑ Filing fees

(4) ❑ Working copies

(5) ❑ ERIE COUNTY: Additional supplemental documents

(i) ❑ Notice of hard copy submission in e-filed case

(6) ❑ KINGS COUNTY: Additional supplemental documents

(i) ❑ Forms when filing in hard copy

(7) ❑ NEW YORK COUNTY: Additional supplemental documents

(i) ❑ Notice of hard copy submission

(ii) ❑ Unpublished opinions

(8) ❑ ONONDAGA COUNTY: Additional supplemental documents

(i) ❑ Notice of hard copy submission

(9) ❑ QUEENS COUNTY: Additional supplemental documents

(i) ❑ Notice of hard copy submission

(c) ❑ Timing

(1) ❑ Answering affidavits shall be served at least two (2) days before the time at which the motion is noticed to be heard

(2) ❑ Answering affidavits and any notice of cross-motion, with supporting papers, if any, shall be served at least seven (7) days before such time if a notice of motion served at least sixteen (16) days before such time so demands

B. Timing

1. *Time to move for relief from judgment*

a. *Based on excusable default.* The court which rendered a judgment or order may relieve a party from it upon such terms as may be just, on motion of any interested person with such notice as the court may direct, upon the ground of excusable default, if such motion is made within one (1) year after service of a copy of the judgment or order with written notice of its entry upon the moving party, or, if the moving party has entered the judgment or order, within one (1) year after such entry. NY CPLR Rule 5015(a)(1).

b. *No time limit for motion based on other grounds*

i. *Newly discovered evidence.* There is no stated time limit for a motion to vacate based on newly discovered evidence. The law implies a reasonable time, and what is reasonable is determined sui generis. SIEGEL-NYPRAC § 428; NY CPLR Rule 5015(a)(2).

ii. *Fraud or misconduct.* There being no stated time, a reasonable time will govern the motion to vacate on the ground of fraud or misconduct, with the court determining reasonableness on a sui generis basis. SIEGEL-NYPRAC § 429; NY CPLR Rule 5015(a)(3).

iii. *Jurisdictional defect.* For the same reason, the jurisdictional defect permits the vacatur motion without a time limit. SIEGEL-NYPRAC § 430; NY CPLR Rule 5015(a)(4).

iv. *Reversal of underlying judgment.* There is no stated time limit on a vacatur motion under NY CPLR Rule 5015(a)(5). A reasonable time is therefore the standard, with the court to gauge reasonableness on the facts of the particular case. SIEGEL-NYPRAC § 431; NY CPLR Rule 5015(a)(5).

2. *Time to serve.* The moving party shall serve copies of all affidavits and briefs upon all other parties at the time of service of the notice of motion. NY R UNIF TRIAL CTS § 202.8(c). A notice of motion and supporting affidavits shall be served at least eight (8) days before the time at which the motion is noticed to be heard. NY CPLR Rule 2214(b).

a. *Return dates; Best practice.* It is also good practice to make motions returnable at least three (3) weeks away from the planned date of mailing and to always include a demand in the motion that the other side serve answering papers at least seven (7) days before the return day. This enables the motion to be served by mail, gives sufficient notice to support the seven (7) day demand, and leaves a few days for a delayed mailing if some snag prevents posting on the day planned. If speed is needed, the shorter eight (8) day notice period can be used, forfeiting the right to seven (7) day answering papers and a reply. If even eight (8) days notice is too much under the circumstances, the order to show cause is the remedy. SIEGEL-NYPRAC § 247.

i. *ALBANY COUNTY.* All motions, except for certain matters in Albany County as specified in NY R 3 JD SUP Doc. 1(E) and NY R 3 JD SUP Doc. 1(F), brought on by notice of motion or by order to show cause will be made returnable on any day, Monday through Friday, as chosen by the movant in compliance with the CPLR. Parties shall submit all papers in a timely fashion as required by the CPLR by delivering them or mailing them directly to the Supreme Court Clerk's Office[. . .]except that motions and other applications subject to a filing fee shall first be presented to the County Clerk's Office for payment of the requisite fee and then subsequently filed with the Supreme Court Clerk's Office. NY R 3 JD SUP Doc. 1(B).

ii. *BRONX COUNTY.* A Notice of Motion must be served at least eight (8) days, by personal service, nine (9) days by overnight express and thirteen (13) days by mail before the return date. NY R BRONX FIL R Doc. 3. All unassigned motions must be accompanied with a properly filled out RJI and shall be filed in the Motion Support Office, room 217, within five (5) days of service. All motions on actions already assigned to a Justice must be filed at least five (5) business days before the return date. NY R BRONX FIL R Doc. 3. All papers served must strictly comply with the time requirements of NY CPLR Rule 2101, NY CPLR Rule 2103 and NY CPLR Rule 2214(b). NY R BRONX FIL R Doc. 8.

iii. *KINGS COUNTY.* Motion papers, answering affidavits and reply affidavits must be served on adversaries in accordance with NY CPLR Rule 2214. NY R L KINGS Pt. C, Rule 1.

iv. *NEW YORK COUNTY.* In an e-filed case, all of the moving papers shall be e-filed at least eight (8) business days prior to the return date. The clerk will calendar the motion for the Motion Submission Part Courtroom (Room 130) for the return date selected. NY R NY CTY Procedure II(A); NY R NY CTY E FIL Doc. 2(D)(1).

v. *ONONDAGA COUNTY.* Onondaga County local court rules require that any additional papers relating to motions must be e-filed at least two (2) business days prior to the return date, excluding the return date. NY R ONDGA E FIL Protocol(B)(9)(e).

vi. *QUEENS COUNTY.* Motions must be in the possession of the Motion Support Office at least nine (9) days before the noticed return date of the motion. NY R L QUEENS MOT SUP Doc. 1; NY R L QUEENS E-FILE Doc. 1(H)(1).

b. *Order to show cause; Shorter time.* The court in a proper case may grant an order to show cause, to be served in lieu of a notice of motion, at a time and in a manner specified therein. NY CPLR Rule 2214(d). An ordinary notice of motion can't be brought on for hearing earlier than the eighth (8th) day after the motion papers are served. With an order to show cause, the hearing can be brought on at any time the court directs, which can be fewer than eight (8) days or as close as the very day on which it is signed. If the court is convinced there is a real emergency, it can schedule the hearing for a few hours later or, in the direst case, "forthwith" the service of the order to show cause. SIEGEL-NYPRAC § 248.

c. *Time to serve answering affidavits; Other answering papers.* Answering affidavits shall be served at least two (2) days before the time at which the motion is noticed to be heard. Answering affidavits and any notice of cross-motion, with supporting papers, if any, shall be served at least seven (7) days before such time if a notice of motion served at least sixteen (16) days before such time so demands; whereupon any reply or responding affidavits shall be served at least one (1) day before such time. NY CPLR Rule 2214(b); NY R UNIF TRIAL CTS § 202.8(c).

   i. *BRONX COUNTY.* All answering papers must be submitted to the Clerk 's Office on the return date of the motion. Answering papers will not be accepted prior to the return date. NY R BRONX FIL R Doc. 8.

   ii. *NEW YORK COUNTY.* Cross-motions, papers in opposition, and reply papers on motions/petitions on notice returnable in Room 130 in a hard-copy case shall be submitted to the Motion Submission Part Courtroom (Room 130) on the final return date of the motion/petition and will not be accepted until that date. Subsequent documents on motions/petitions in e-filed cases shall be e-filed in a timely manner. Working copies when required shall be submitted to Room 130 on the final return date. NY R NY CTY Procedure II(A).

d. *Time to serve cross-motion.* At least three (3) days prior to the time at which the motion is noticed to be heard, or seven (7) days prior to such time if demand is properly made pursuant to NY CPLR Rule 2214(b), a party may serve upon the moving party a notice of cross-motion demanding relief, with or without supporting papers; provided, however, that:

   i. If such notice and any supporting papers are served by mailing, as provided in NY CPLR Rule 2103(b)(2), they shall be served three (3) days earlier than as prescribed in NY CPLR Rule 2215; and

   ii. If served by overnight delivery, as provided in NY CPLR Rule 2103(b)(6), they shall be served one (1) day earlier than as prescribed in NY CPLR Rule 2215. Relief in the alternative or of several different types may be demanded; relief need not be responsive to that demanded by the moving party. NY CPLR Rule 2215(a); NY CPLR Rule 2215(b).

   iii. *BRONX COUNTY.* Cross motions may be presented for approval on or before the return date, provided that there is a motion already calendared. NY R BRONX FIL R Doc. 8.

   iv. *ERIE COUNTY.* Cross-motions must be filed at least two (2) days before the return date of the motion. NY R L KINGS Pt. A, Papers.

   v. *KINGS COUNTY.* Hard copies are required to be filed for any motions, answering papers, stipulations, etc. for E-Filed cases returnable in [the Central Compliance Part] at least [two (2)] days before return date. . . .for cross motions. NY R L KINGS Pt. E, Rule 8.

   vi. *QUEENS COUNTY.* Motion Support does not process or forward responsive papers, including cross-motions. They must be brought to the calendar call in the judge's part. NY R L QUEENS MOT SUP Doc. 1. E-filed cross motions: across motion must be noticed for the same return date as the main motion and have the confirmation of filing attached in the same manner as a motion. NY R L QUEENS E-FILE Doc. 1(H)(2)(e).

3. *Filing before return date.* All motions shall be returnable before the assigned judge, and all papers shall be filed with the court on or before the return date. NY R UNIF TRIAL CTS § 202.8(a).

   a. *BRONX COUNTY: Time for filing*

      i. *Unassigned motions.* Unassigned motions must be in the Clerk's Office within five (5) days of the date of service of the motion. NY R BRONX FIL R Doc. 8.

      ii. *Assigned motions.* Assigned motions must be filed in the Clerk's Office not less than five (5) business days prior to the return date of the motion. NY R BRONX FIL R Doc. 8.

      iii. *Motions returnable in room 217.* The moving documents must be e-filed no later than eight (8) days prior to the return date. NY R BRONX E FIL R Doc. 1(1).

   b. *KINGS COUNTY: Time and place of filing.* Motion papers must be filed with the E-file/Motion Support Office located in Room 227. . . at 360 Adams Street at least five (5) business days before the return date of the motion. NY R L KINGS Pt. A, Papers. Hard copies are required to be filed for any motions, answering papers, stipulations, etc. for

E-Filed cases returnable in [the Central Compliance Part] at least five (5) days before return date for main motions. NY R L KINGS Pt. E, Rule 8. The moving documents must be e-filed no later than eight (8) days prior to the return date. NY R L KINGS E FIL Doc. 1(D).

4. *NEW YORK COUNTY: Briefing schedule.* Once a motion is made, counsel for all parties are strongly encouraged to agree upon a briefing schedule and submit a stipulation of adjournment reflecting that schedule using service or a clerk. Where a briefing schedule has not been agreed upon, the movant can avoid the need to attend simply to see if anyone will hand up opposing papers by demanding papers as provided by NY CPLR Rule 2214(b). To protect movants against the submission of late opposition papers or cross-motions, the General Clerk's Office will screen motions in which such papers are submitted without a response (reply or opposition respectively) to ensure that proper time to respond has been afforded and it will sua sponte adjourn for one (1) week cases in which such time has not been given. NY R NY CTY Procedure II(C).

5. *QUEENS COUNTY: Time to pay fees.* As motions and petitions are time sensitive, if opting to pay at the County Clerk's Office payment MUST be made, if filed with an RJI, a minimum of nine (9) business days prior to the application's return date and if filed post RJI, a minimum of nine (9) business days prior to the application's return date. NY R L QUEENS E-FILE Doc. 1(H)(1).

6. *Computation of time*

   a. *Units of time*

      i. *Day.* A calendar day includes the time from midnight to midnight. Sunday or any day of the week specifically mentioned means a calendar day. NY GEN CONSTR § 19.

      ii. *Month.* In a statute, contract or public or private instrument, unless otherwise provided in such contract or instrument or by law, the term month means a calendar month and not a lunar month. NY GEN CONSTR § 31.

      iii. *Year.* For information on the definition of a year, including the definitions of a half-year and quarter-year, refer to NY GEN CONSTR § 58 and NY GEN CONSTR § 50. For information on leap years, refer to NY GEN CONSTR § 57.

   b. *Periods of time*

      i. *Number of days.* A number of days specified as a period from a certain day within which or after or before which an act is authorized or required to be done means such number of calendar days exclusive of the calendar day from which the reckoning is made. NY GEN CONSTR § 20.

         - If such period is a period of two (2) days, Saturday, Sunday or a public holiday must be excluded from the reckoning if it is an intervening day between the day from which the reckoning is made and the last day of the period. NY GEN CONSTR § 20.
         - In computing any specified period of time from a specified event, the day upon which the event happens is deemed the day from which the reckoning is made. The day from which any specified period of time is reckoned shall be excluded in making the reckoning. NY GEN CONSTR § 20.

      ii. *Number of months.* A number of months after or before a certain day shall be computed by counting such number of calendar months from such day, exclusive of the calendar month in which such day occurs, and shall include the day of the month in the last month so counted having the same numerical order in days of the month as the day from which the computation is made, unless there be not so many days in the last month so counted, in which case the period computed shall expire with the last day of the month so counted. NY GEN CONSTR § 30.

      iii. *Publication of notice; Number of days.* The period of publication of a legal notice shall be computed by excluding the first day of publication and including the day on which the act or event of which notice is given is to take place or which completes the full period of publication. NY CPLR § 2402.

      iv. *Periods ending on Saturday, Sunday or public holiday.* When any period of time, computed from a certain day, within which or after which or before which an act is authorized or required to be done, ends on a Saturday, Sunday or a public holiday, such act may be done on the next succeeding business day and if the period ends at a specified hour, such act may be done at or before the same hour of such next succeeding business day, except that where a period of time specified by contract ends on a Saturday, Sunday or a public holiday, the extension of such period is governed by NY GEN CONSTR § 25. NY GEN CONSTR § 25-a(1).

         - For a list of public holidays, refer to NY GEN CONSTR § 24.

      v. *Additional time after certain kinds of service*

         - *Service by mail.* Where a period of time prescribed by law is measured from the service of a paper and service is by mail, five (5) days shall be added to the prescribed period. NY CPLR Rule 2103(b)(2).

- *Service by overnight delivery service.* Where a period of time prescribed by law is measured from the service of a paper and service is by overnight delivery, one (1) business day shall be added to the prescribed period. NY CPLR Rule 2103(b)(6).

vi. *Daylight saving time.* For information on New York's time zone and the effect of daylight saving time, refer to NY GEN CONSTR § 52.

c. *Hours of court.* Notwithstanding any provision of law or rule of court to the contrary, throughout the State of New York the sessions of the Supreme Court for the disposition of business before the court shall commence not later than 9:30 a.m. and conclude not earlier than 5 p.m. Where warranted, the Chief Administrator of the Courts may authorize variances in the opening and closing hours of the courts, but, in such event, daily sessions shall total not less than six (6) hours. NY R CHIEF J § 3.1.

d. *Time limits; Extension of time.* Any act required by or in pursuance of law to be performed at or within a prescribed time, shall be performed according to the standard time. NY GEN CONSTR § 53.

i. Except where otherwise expressly prescribed by law, the court may extend the time fixed by any statute, rule or order for doing any act, upon such terms as may be just and upon good cause shown, whether the application for extension is made before or after the expiration of the time fixed. NY CPLR § 2004. Refer to the New York KeyRules Motion for Continuance/Extension of Time document for more information.

C. General Requirements

1. *Motions, generally.* There shall be compliance with the procedures prescribed in the CPLR for the bringing of motions. NY R UNIF TRIAL CTS § 202.7(a).

a. *Motions on notice.* A notice of motion shall specify the time and place of the hearing on the motion, the supporting papers upon which the motion is based, the relief demanded and the grounds therefor. NY CPLR Rule 2214(a). A motion on notice in an action in the supreme court shall be noticed to be heard in the judicial district where the action is triable or in a county adjoining the county where the action is triable. Unless statute, civil practice rule or local court rule provides otherwise, the motion shall be noticed to be heard before a motion term or, upon order to show cause granted by a justice, before that justice out of court. NY CPLR § 2212(a). Except as provided in NY R UNIF TRIAL CTS § 202.7(d), no motion shall be filed with the court unless there have been served and filed with the motion papers a notice of motion. NY R UNIF TRIAL CTS § 202.7(a)(1).

b. *Ex parte motions.* A motion in an action in the supreme court that may be made without notice may be made at a motion term or to a justice out of court in any county in the state. NY CPLR § 2212(b).

i. *KINGS COUNTY.* For more information on submitting a motion ex parte, refer to NY R L KINGS E FIL Doc. 1(G).

ii. *NEW YORK COUNTY.* For more information on submitting matters ex parte, refer to NY R NY CTY Procedure III and NY R NY CTY E FIL Doc. 2(G).

iii. *QUEENS COUNTY.* For more information on submitting matters ex parte, refer to NY R L QUEENS EX PARTE Doc. 1.

c. *Alternative relief.* Relief in the alternative or of several different types may be demanded. NY CPLR Rule 2214(a). The types of relief need not be related. In one motion, for example, the defendant can seek to dismiss the plaintiff's claim for lack of jurisdiction, to get an extension of time to answer, to require the plaintiff to join X as a party, and to quash a disclosure subpoena served in behalf of the plaintiff on a nonparty witness. So doing, the movant must of course specify all of these items of relief in the notice of motion, and the grounds for them, and the supporting papers must contain the entire proof requisite to the items of relief sought. NY CPLR Rule 2214(Practice Commentary, C2214:4).

d. *General relief.* It is common practice to include at the end of the relief request in the notice of motion a so-called "general relief" clause. This is merely a few words to cover the possibility that the relief appropriate to what the movant proves was not specifically asked for, but is close enough to enable the court to grant it. After stating the specific relief desired, the lawyer will often add something like: and for such other, further, or different relief as this court may deem just and proper. NY CPLR Rule 2214(Practice Commentary, C2214:5).

e. *Motion in improper form.* If the court finds it appropriate in the interests of justice, it may convert a motion into a special proceeding, or vice-versa, upon such terms as may be just, including the payment of fees and costs. NY CPLR § 103(c).

f. *Order to show cause.* An order to show cause is basically only a substitute for a notice of motion. An ordinary notice of motion merely notifies the recipient that a motion is being made for specified relief. The burden of proof is on the movant. Although in most cases it is just as innocent as an ordinary notice of motion, the order to show cause gets its name by directing the recipient to "show cause" why the particular relief being asked for should not be granted. It sounds as if the burden of proof is being shifted to the recipient. It isn't. It specifies the time and place of the hearing on the application but when the hearing comes on, the burden of proof is where it always is on a motion: on the movant. SIEGEL-NYPRAC § 248.

i. The CPLR says nothing more about an order to show cause than that it may be used "in a proper case", which leaves it entirely to the judge's discretion to determine what a proper case is. Any fact suggesting a problem as to any of the items listed above would be sufficient to invoke judicial discretion and justify the show cause procedure, which is in fact liberally used. SIEGEL-NYPRAC § 248.

ii. An order to show cause against a state body or officers must be served in addition to service upon the defendant or respondent state body or officers upon the attorney general by delivery to an assistant attorney general at an office of the attorney general in the county in which venue of the action is designated or if there is no office of the attorney general in such county, at the office of the attorney general nearest such county. NY CPLR Rule 2214(d).

iii. *BRONX COUNTY.* For information on submitting an order to show cause, refer to NY R BRONX E FIL R Doc. 2 and NY R BRONX LEG SUP Doc. 1.

iv. *ERIE COUNTY.* For information on submitting an order to show cause, refer to NY R ERIE E FIL Doc. 3(VI).

v. *KINGS COUNTY.* For information on submitting an order to show cause, refer to NY R L KINGS E FIL Doc. 1(F).

vi. *NEW YORK COUNTY.* For information on submitting an order to show cause, refer to NY R NY CTY E FIL Doc. 2(F).

vii. *ONONDAGA COUNTY.* For information on submitting an order to show cause, refer to NY R ONDGA E FIL Protocol(B)(10) and NY R ONDGA E FIL Protocol(J).

g. *Motions before preliminary conference.* Motions in actions to which NY R UNIF TRIAL CTS § 202.12 is applicable made after the preliminary conference has been scheduled may be denied unless there is shown good cause why such relief is warranted before the preliminary conference is held. NY R UNIF TRIAL CTS § 202.12(h).

h. *ALBANY COUNTY: Good faith effort to resolve.* Prior to the submission of a notice of motion relating to disclosure or a bill of particulars, the parties must make a good faith effort to resolve the matter in question and submit an affirmation attesting to this good faith effort. NY R 3 JD SUP Doc. 1(B).

i. *NEW YORK COUNTY: Documents with motions.* Counsel must attach to motion papers copies of all pleadings and other documents as required by the CPLR and as necessary for an informed decision on the motion. Documents in a foreign language shall be properly translated. NY R NY CTY J RUL Rule 14(a).

j. *NEW YORK COUNTY: Motions in multiple cases made together.* On occasion, attorneys may wish to make a motion in more than one case on a single set of papers. In such cases, by definition consolidation will not have been directed since consolidation signifies the combination of more than one case into a single one with a single caption and index number and ending in a single judgment. NY R NY CTY Procedure II(B). For more information on motions made with the same papers, refer to NY R NY CTY Procedure II(A).

k. *QUEENS COUNTY: Motion sequence numbers.* A motion sequence number is required for all E-filed motions. After a motion is E-filed, please consult the e-courts website within twenty-four (24) to forty-eight (48) hours to obtain the sequence number. The Confirmation Notice of E-filing MUST indicate the sequence number of any motion submitted at the Centralized Motion Part calendar call. NY R L QUEENS E-FILE Doc. 1(H)(5).

2. *Motion for relief from judgment*

a. *Grounds.* The court which rendered a judgment or order may relieve a party from it upon such terms as may be just, on motion of any interested person with such notice as the court may direct, upon the ground of:

i. *Excusable default.* Excusable default, if such motion is made within one (1) year after service of a copy of the judgment or order with written notice of its entry upon the moving party, or, if the moving party has entered the judgment or order, within one (1) year after such entry. NY CPLR Rule 5015(a)(1).

ii. *Newly discovered evidence.* Newly-discovered evidence which, if introduced at the trial, would probably have produced a different result and which could not have been discovered in time to move for a new trial under NY CPLR Rule 4404. NY CPLR Rule 5015(a)(2).

iii. *Fraud, misrepresentation, or other misconduct.* Fraud, misrepresentation, or other misconduct of an adverse party. NY CPLR Rule 5015(a)(3).

iv. *Lack of jurisdiction.* Lack of jurisdiction to render the judgment or order. NY CPLR Rule 5015(a)(4).

v. *Reversal, modification or vacatur of a prior judgment or order.* Reversal, modification or vacatur of a prior judgment or order upon which it is based. NY CPLR Rule 5015(a)(5).

b. *Relief based on excusable default.* The courts are liberal in vacating default judgments. They want disputes resolved on the merits and are therefore inclined, practically speaking, to accept a generous range of excuses, sometimes even vacating deliberate defaults, but there is a limit to their patience and from time to time a warning is issued to potential defaulters. SIEGEL-NYPRAC § 427; Hensey Properties, Inc. v. Lamagna, 23 A.D.2d 742, 742-43, 258 N.Y.S.2d 495, 496 (1965).

i. The New York rule of thumb is that a motion to vacate a default requires two showings: (1) an excuse for the default and (2) an "affidavit of merits", as it is commonly called, in which the defendant is required to satisfy the court that she has a meritorious defense. SIEGEL-NYPRAC § 108; Benadon v. Antonio, 10 A.D.2d 40, 41, 197 N.Y.S.2d 1, 3, modified, 10 A.D.2d 929, 205 N.Y.S.2d 800 (1960). This offers assurance that vacating the default will not be a wasted effort; that the defendant does have a reasonable position on the merits and is not just wasting time. (If the defendant has no defense on the merits, the rule's theory is that a default judgment is just as good as any other to close out the case.) SIEGEL-NYPRAC § 108.

ii. The affidavit of merits should be made by the defendant herself, or by someone else with first-hand knowledge of the facts. An affidavit of merits made by one without such knowledge will be ignored as having no probative force, which means that the motion papers will be deficient and that the motion to vacate will likely be denied. SIEGEL-NYPRAC § 108.

c. *Relief based on newly discovered evidence.* Newly discovered evidence will not suffice to open the judgment and permit retrial of the merits unless the court is convinced that the new evidence would "probably" change the result. Perhaps the best known illustration of this motion, while by no means the only one, is the post-judgment appearance of a key witness to the event, unknown-of or unlocatable earlier in spite of diligent effort. SIEGEL-NYPRAC § 428; Cizler v. Cizler, 19 A.D.2d 819, 820, 243 N.Y.S.2d 614, 615-16 (1963).

i. Newly discovered matter such as would reopen the judgment must as a rule be competent evidence, although occasionally even incompetent evidence may be allowed to do it if it tends "dramatically" to undermine the original judgment. SIEGEL-NYPRAC § 428; Delagi v. Delagi, 34 A.D.2d 1005, 1007, 313 N.Y.S.2d 265, 269 (1970).

ii. A further requirement for a motion under NY CPLR Rule 5015(a)(2) is that the newly discovered evidence could not have been discovered in time to move for a new trial under NY CPLR Rule 4404. Since a motion under NY CPLR Rule 4404 must be made within fifteen (15) days after the decision or verdict, the discovery of the new evidence before the expiration of that fifteen (15) day period would presumably fit that motion and therefore preclude this one. SIEGEL-NYPRAC § 428; NY CPLR Rule 4404.

d. *Relief based on fraud or other misconduct.* The power of the court to relieve a party from a judgment taken through mistake, inadvertence, surprise, or excusable neglect "does not depend on any statute, but is inherent." SIEGEL-NYPRAC § 429; Ladd v. Stevenson, 112 N.Y. 325, 331, 19 N.E. 842, 844 (1889).

i. The fraud involved can qualify as either "intrinsic" or "extrinsic." Airtight distinctions are probably impossible, but perhaps a reasonably accurate general statement is that conduct which in effect denies a hearing is extrinsic while conduct that injects fraud into the hearing is intrinsic. If the fraud does get stamped "extrinsic," it technically dispenses with an affidavit of merits as part of the moving papers because it is deemed to go to jurisdiction. SIEGEL-NYPRAC § 429; Shaw v. Shaw, 97 A.D.2d 403, 403, 467 N.Y.S.2d 231, 233 (1983). But here the movant may be too easily misled. Since it is often difficult if not impossible to predict in advance which "trinsic" describes the case, the inclusion of a strong affidavit of merits can do no harm. SIEGEL-NYPRAC § 429.

e. *Relief based on lack of jurisdiction.* The jurisdictional defect permits the vacatur motion without a time limit: the judgment in this instance is theoretically void and the order sought under NY CPLR Rule 5015(a)(4) is not what makes it so; the order merely declares it to be so, cancelling of record a judgment that has had the presumption to stand on the books without a jurisdictional invitation. SIEGEL-NYPRAC § 430.

i. The motion can rest on a lack of subject matter jurisdiction. More frequently it's based on a lack of personal jurisdiction, but seldom is NY CPLR Rule 5015(a)(4) cited. The reason is that lack of jurisdiction is so deep a defect, and so obviously a basis for vacatur, that a statute authorizing the vacatur on this ground is like the proverbial fifth wheel. SIEGEL-NYPRAC § 430.

ii. It is generally a good idea for the defendant to hedge his bets and make the motion in the alternative—to vacate the judgment and (1) dismiss for want of jurisdiction or, if the court finds jurisdiction present, (2) to open the default and let the defendant defend on the merits. Since the second alternative requires the affidavit of merits even if the first does not, the affidavit of merits should be included not as an adjunct of the first part of the motion, but of the second. The bottom line is that it should be included. To omit it because the first part—the jurisdictional ground—doesn't require it is to forfeit the second part—the discretionary vacatur—altogether: the defendant would have to prevail on the jurisdictional point or lose everything, including the very substantial right to a hearing on the merits. SIEGEL-NYPRAC § 430.

f. *Relief based on reversal, vacatur, or modification of prior judgment or order.* If the judgment or order is based on some other judgment or order, and the latter is in some way undermined, as by reversal, modification, or vacatur, the dependent judgment can similarly be cancelled or adjusted. SIEGEL-NYPRAC § 431. The most likely context for this happening is where a sister-state or foreign country judgment has been converted into a New York one, only to be afterwards undone in some way at home. SIEGEL-NYPRAC § 431.

i. The provision also applies to original New York judgments. For example, plaintiff sued defendant, who impleaded X—an ordinary indemnity situation—but defendant won against plaintiff, which naturally gave X judgment against defendant on the third-party claim because there was nothing to indemnify. Only plaintiff appealed, but he succeeded, and the judgment for defendant was reversed. On motion by defendant under CPLR 5015(a)(5) after remand from the appellate court, X's judgment dismissing defendant's indemnity claim was also vacated. The court held that the revival of plaintiff's claim against defendant automatically reinstated defendant's indemnity claim against X. SIEGEL-NYPRAC § 431; Frank L. Ciminelli Const. Co. v. City of Buffalo, 110 A.D.2d 1075, 1076, 488 N.Y.S.2d 932, 934 (1985).

g. *Conditional relief*

i. There is express authority in NY CPLR Rule 5015(a) for the court to allow the vacatur "upon such terms as may be just." The conditions can include the granting of costs and disbursements for the trial or appellate levels or both, an attorney's fee, and such other sums as would defray actual expenses to which the other side has been put. SIEGEL-NYPRAC § 432; Hensey Properties, Inc. v. Lamagna, 23 A.D.2d 742, 258 N.Y.S.2d 495, 496 (1965).

ii. If the vacating of the judgment contemplates further proceedings, as where a default is opened and a trial on the merits is directed, or where a retrial results from newly discovered evidence, the judgment can be made to stand as security for the plaintiff pending the trial's outcome, or the defendant can be required to post a bond in the amount of all or part of the judgment. SIEGEL-NYPRAC § 432; Treitel v. Arnold Chait, Ltd., 20 A.D.2d 711, 711, 247 N.Y.S.2d 373, 374 (1964); E. Tetz & Sons, Inc. v. Carriage Hill Apartment Co., 48 A.D.2d 875, 875, 369 N.Y.S.2d 192, 193 (1975).

iii. There are no arbitrary limits on the court's discretion in fixing terms under NY CPLR Rule 5015(a), as long as the ground relied on can be disposed of as a matter of discretion. SIEGEL-NYPRAC § 432.

h. *Discretion of court.* Should a ground arise not expressly listed, however, and not susceptible of being lodged under a ground listed in NY CPLR Rule 5015(a) the lawyer can take note that thorough as the list may seem, it is not exhaustive. The court has inherent discretionary power to vacate its judgments and orders for good cause shown, not limited by the NY CPLR Rule 5015(a) list. SIEGEL-NYPRAC § 426; McMahon v. City of New York, 105 A.D.2d 101, 103, 483 N.Y.S.2d 228, 230 (1984).

i. *Order to show cause.* The requirement that the vacatur motion be made "with such notice as the court may direct" means that it should be brought on by order to show cause. This recognizes that applications of this kind can take place long after the judgment was rendered and that uncertainties can arise concerning, for example, the continued authority of the other side's lawyer. The court in the order to show cause can take cognizance of the applicable facts, including lapse of time, and direct accordingly about whom and how to serve. SIEGEL-NYPRAC § 426.

j. *On stipulation.* The clerk of the court may vacate a default judgment entered pursuant to NY CPLR § 3215 upon the filing with him of a stipulation of consent to such vacatur by the parties personally or by their attorneys. NY CPLR Rule 5015(b).

k. *On application of an administrative judge.* An administrative judge, upon a showing that default judgments were obtained by fraud, misrepresentation, illegality, unconscionability, lack of due service, violations of law, or other illegalities or where such default judgments were obtained in cases in which those defendants would be uniformly entitled to interpose a defense predicated upon but not limited to the foregoing defenses, and where such default judgments have been obtained in a number deemed sufficient by him to justify such action as set forth herein, and upon appropriate notice to counsel for the respective parties, or to the parties themselves, may bring a proceeding to relieve a party or parties from them upon such terms as may be just. The disposition of any proceeding so instituted shall be determined by a judge other than the administrative judge. NY CPLR Rule 5015(c).

l. *Restitution.* Where a judgment or order is set aside or vacated, the court may direct and enforce restitution in like manner and subject to the same conditions as where a judgment is reversed or modified on appeal. NY CPLR Rule 5015(d).

   i. An order directing restitution is the equivalent of an ordinary money judgment and may be docketed and enforced as such, which makes the usual enforcement devices of Article 52 of the New York Civil Practice Law & Rules (NY CPLR § 5201, et seq.) available. But despite its being an "order" to pay the money back, it is not ordinarily enforceable through the contempt punishment. SIEGEL-NYPRAC § 433; NY CPLR Rule 2222; Marlee, Inc., v. Bittar, 257 N.Y. 240, 243, 177 N.E. 434, 435 (1931).

3. *Oppositions.* In the absence of statutory provision or court rule, a motion ordinarily does not require a written answer, although an adverse party may be permitted to file an answer in opposition to the showing made in the motion or its supporting affidavits. AMJUR MOTIONS § 26. When a party files a motion and the opposing party fails to respond, the court may construe such failure to respond as non-opposition to the motion or an admission that the motion was meritorious, may take the facts alleged in the motion as true, and may grant the motion if the relief requested appears to be justified. However, the severity of such a result demands that a court impose it only with great caution. AMJUR MOTIONS § 28.

4. *Governing law.* The civil practice law and rules (NY CPLR § 101, et seq.) shall govern the procedure in civil judicial proceedings in all courts of the state and before all judges, except where the procedure is regulated by inconsistent statute. The civil practice law and rules shall succeed the civil practice act and rules of civil practice and shall be deemed substituted therefor throughout the statutes and rules of the state. NY CPLR § 101. The civil practice law and rules shall be liberally construed to secure the just, speedy and inexpensive determination of every civil judicial proceeding. NY CPLR § 104.

   a. *Uniform trial court rules.* The uniform civil rules for the Supreme Court and County Court (NY R UNIF TRIAL CTS § 202.1, et seq.) shall be applicable to civil actions and proceedings in the Supreme Court and the County Court. NY R UNIF TRIAL CTS § 202.1(a). The provisions of the uniform rules shall be construed consistent with the Civil Practice Law and Rules (CPLR), and matters not covered by the uniform rules shall be governed by the CPLR. NY R UNIF TRIAL CTS § 202.1(d).

   b. *Local rules.* Local court rules, not inconsistent with law or with uniform civil rules for the Supreme Court and County Court (NY R UNIF TRIAL CTS § 202.1, et seq.), shall comply with Part 9 of the Rules of the Chief Judge (NY R CHIEF J § 9.1). NY R UNIF TRIAL CTS § 202.1(c).

   c. *Official forms.* The state administrator shall have the power to adopt, amend and rescind an appendix of forms. Forms adopted pursuant to NY CPLR § 107 shall be sufficient under the civil practice law and rules and shall illustrate the simplicity and brevity of statement which the civil practice law and rules contemplate. NY CPLR § 107.

5. *Rules of the commercial division.* [Editor's note: certain types of civil cases or civil cases meeting certain monetary thresholds that are filed in the state of New York must be filed in the Commercial Division of the New York Supreme Courts. Rules governing practice in the commercial division are found in NY R UNIF TRIAL CTS § 202.70]. Cases which must be filed in the commercial division are listed below. For more information, refer to NY R UNIF TRIAL CTS § 202.70.

   a. *Monetary thresholds.* Except as set forth in NY R UNIF TRIAL CTS § 202.70(b), the monetary thresholds of the Commercial Division, exclusive of punitive damages, interests, costs, disbursements and counsel fees claimed, are established as follows: (1) Albany County, fifty thousand dollars ($50,000); (2) Eighth Judicial District, one hundred thousand dollars ($100,000); (3) Kings County, one hundred fifty thousand dollars ($150,000); (4) Nassau County, two hundred thousand dollars ($200,000); (5) New York County, five hundred thousand dollars ($500,000); (6) Onondaga County, fifty thousand dollars ($50,000); (7) Queens County, one hundred thousand dollars ($100,000); (8) Seventh Judicial District, fifty thousand dollars ($50,000); (9) Suffolk County, one hundred thousand dollars ($100,000); and (10) Westchester County, one hundred thousand dollars ($100,000). NY R UNIF TRIAL CTS § 202.70(a).

      i. *ALBANY COUNTY.* The Commercial Division of the Albany County Supreme Court exercises jurisdiction over selected business and commercial disputes in which the amount at issue generally involves damage claims in a minimum amount of fifty thousand dollars ($50,000) as well as claims for unspecified amounts where the value of the commercial asset(s) in dispute exceeds fifty thousand dollars ($50,000). A separate publication promulgating the rules and criteria relating to the filing and management of Commercial Court cases in this part may be obtained from the Albany County Supreme Court Clerk's Office. A section of the Uniform Civil Rules for the Supreme Court and County Court sets forth statewide rules. NY R 3 JD SUP Doc. 1(E).

ii. *BRONX COUNTY.* The monetary threshold for commercial cases in Bronx County will be seventy-five thousand dollars ($75,000). All other parameters including the type of matters that will be heard are contained within the Rules of the Commercial Division of the Supreme Court (NY R UNIF TRIAL CTS § 202.70). NY R BRONX FIL R Doc. 12.

iii. *NEW YORK COUNTY.* The monetary threshold in the New York County Commercial Division, which is generally applicable, is an amount in controversy of five hundred thousand dollars ($500,000) or more (exclusive of punitive damages, interest, costs, disbursements, and counsel fees). If the case is designated a commercial one and the Addendum is submitted, the clerk will review the pleadings to determine whether the amount in controversy in the case meets the monetary threshold or whether an exception to the threshold applies. NY R NY CTY Procedure IA(B). For more information on assigning a case to the commercial division in New York County, refer to NY R NY CTY Procedure IA(B).

b. *Commercial cases.* Actions in which the principal claims involve or consist of the following will be heard in the Commercial Division provided that the monetary threshold is met or equitable or declaratory relief is sought:

i. Breach of contract or fiduciary duty, fraud, misrepresentation, business tort (e.g., unfair competition), or statutory and/or common law violation where the breach or violation is alleged to arise out of business dealings (e.g., sales of assets or securities; corporate restructuring; partnership, shareholder, joint venture, and other business agreements; trade secrets; restrictive covenants; and employment agreements not including claims that principally involve alleged discriminatory practices);

ii. Transactions governed by the Uniform Commercial Code (exclusive of those concerning individual cooperative or condominium units);

iii. Transactions involving commercial real property, including Yellowstone injunctions and excluding actions for the payment of rent only;

iv. Shareholder derivative actions—without consideration of the monetary threshold;

v. Commercial class actions—without consideration of the monetary threshold;

vi. Business transactions involving or arising out of dealings with commercial banks and other financial institutions;

vii. Internal affairs of business organizations;

viii. Malpractice by accountants or actuaries, and legal malpractice arising out of representation in commercial matters;

ix. Environmental insurance coverage;

x. Commercial insurance coverage (e.g., directors and officers, errors and omissions, and business interruption coverage);

xi. Dissolution of corporations, partnerships, limited liability companies, limited liability partnerships and joint ventures—without consideration of the monetary threshold; and

xii. Applications to stay or compel arbitration and affirm or disaffirm arbitration awards and related injunctive relief pursuant to Article 75 of the New York Civil Practice Law and Rules (NY CPLR § 7501, et seq.) involving any of the foregoing enumerated commercial issues. Where the applicable arbitration agreement provides for the arbitration to be heard outside the United States, the monetary threshold set forth in NY R UNIF TRIAL CTS § 202.70(a) shall not apply. NY R UNIF TRIAL CTS § 202.70(b).

c. *Non-commercial cases.* The following will not be heard in the Commercial Division even if the monetary threshold is met:

i. Suits to collect professional fees;

ii. Cases seeking a declaratory judgment as to insurance coverage for personal injury or property damage;

iii. Residential real estate disputes, including landlord-tenant matters, and commercial real estate disputes involving the payment of rent only;

iv. Home improvement contracts involving residential properties consisting of one to four residential units or individual units in any residential building, including cooperative or condominium units;

v. Proceedings to enforce a judgment regardless of the nature of the underlying case;

vi. First-party insurance claims and actions by insurers to collect premiums or rescind non-commercial policies; and

vii. Attorney malpractice actions except as otherwise provided in NY R UNIF TRIAL CTS § 202.70(b)(8). NY R UNIF TRIAL CTS § 202.70(c).

d. For more information on the Commercial Division, refer to NY R UNIF TRIAL CTS § 202.70.

D. Documents

1. *Documents for moving party*

a. *Required documents*

i. *Notice of motion, order to show cause, or affidavit on ex parte motion.* The notice of motion shall be substantially in the form found in NY R UNIF TRIAL CTS § 202.7(b). NY R UNIF TRIAL CTS § 202.7(b). The supporting papers should be referred to in the notice of motion. SIEGEL-NYPRAC § 246. The court in a proper case may grant an order to show cause, to be served in lieu of a notice of motion. NY CPLR Rule 2214(d). An ex parte motion shall be accompanied by an affidavit stating the result of any prior motion for similar relief and specifying the new facts, if any, that were not previously shown. NY CPLR Rule 2217(b).

- *Request for oral argument.* A party requesting oral argument shall set forth such request in its notice of motion or in its order to show cause or on the first page of the answering papers, as the case may be. Where all parties to a motion request oral argument, oral argument shall be granted unless the court shall determine it to be unnecessary. Where a motion is brought on by order to show cause, the court may set forth in the order that oral argument is required on the return date of the motion. NY R UNIF TRIAL CTS § 202.8(d).

ii. *Motion.* Refer to the General Requirements section of this document for information on the notice of motion and motion.

iii. *Request for judicial intervention.* At any time after service of process, a party may file a request for judicial intervention. Except as provided in NY R UNIF TRIAL CTS § 202.6(b), in an action not yet assigned to a judge, the court shall not accept for filing a notice of motion, order to show cause, or application for ex parte order, unless such notice or application is accompanied by a request for judicial intervention. NY R UNIF TRIAL CTS § 202.6(a).

- *BRONX COUNTY.* Generally, the Request For Judicial Intervention, commonly referred to as an "RJI", is required to be filed in any action where the assignment of a Justice is required. The RJI sets forth the information which is entered into the court system's database. It must be completely and accurately filled out. The full caption, as stated on the Summons, must be set forth. Use of terms "et al." and "etc." are not permitted. Only one (1) RJI may be filed in each action. Either a self represented litigant or an attorney must sign the affirmation at the end of the form. Once completed, the RJI must be filed in duplicate. Except in the case of an ex-parte application, the RJI must also be served together with the accompanying application upon all parties. Proof of accuracy of the index number must accompany the RJI. Check the Fee Schedule[. . .]for any applicable filing fees. NY R BRONX FIL R Doc. 2.
- *KINGS COUNTY.* An RJI with the relevant required addendum in a NYSCEF case shall be submitted via NYSCEF. Once e-filed, the RJI and any accompanying document will be forwarded to the relevant support office for random assignment of the case and processing of the document. A filer or counsel need not appear (as to Proposed Orders to Show Cause, however, see below). A copy of the pleadings must be submitted only if the document has not previously been e-filed. If the RJI seeks intervention with regard to a document that is intended for review by a Justice, such as a motion, a working copy of the RJI must be submitted with the working copy of the motion and the NYSCEF Confirmation Notice. NY R L KINGS E FIL Doc. 1(C).
- *NEW YORK COUNTY.* To obtain the assignment of an IAS Justice to a case, a Request for Judicial Intervention (cost ninety-five dollars ($95)) must be filed, with NYSCEF in an e-filed case or in paper in an authorized hard-copy one. A no-fee RJI, which will generally result in the referral of an application to an Ex Parte Justice, is also required with regard to certain kinds of applications for which, prior to 2011, no RJI was required. NY R NY CTY Procedure I(C). A "fillable" form RJI is available on-line. The form must be filed in duplicate in hard-copy cases. NY R NY CTY Procedure IA(A)(1). The filer of an RJI must check off a box identifying the type of case at issue. Where the RJI seeks judicial assignment, this designation will bring about a random assignment of the case by computer to a Justice handling cases of that type. NY R NY CTY Procedure IA(A)(1). The RJI and any addendum can be completed and submitted electronically in an

e-filed case. NY R NY CTY Procedure II(A). The RJI shall be marked to reflect the existence of any "related case" as explained on the "Commencement of Cases" page under "Case Processing" on the court's website. NY R NY CTY Procedure II(A); NY R NY CTY E FIL Doc. 2(C).

- *ONONDAGA COUNTY.* The RJI will be submitted via the NYSCEF system along with any required RJI addendum forms. When the RJI is filed and the fee paid online, the Onondaga County Clerk's Office will electronically forward the RJI and any accompanying documents to the Onondaga Supreme Court Clerk's Office for assignment and processing. Counsel will receive notification of judge assignment via the NYSCEF system. NY R ONDGA E FIL Protocol(B)(3).
- *QUEENS COUNTY.* A Request for Judicial Intervention ("RJI") in an E-filed case shall be submitted via the E-filing System. When the RJI is approved, filed and paid for on-line, it will be forwarded to the relevant back office for random assignment of the case and processing of the document. In the case of RJIs seeking assignment to the Commercial Division, the filer must submit therewith, a Commercial Addendum as required by the standards for assignment of cases to the Commercial Division. NY R L QUEENS E-FILE Doc. 1(F).

iv. *Proof of service.* In addition to complying with the provisions of NY CPLR Rule 2101, every paper filed in court shall have annexed thereto appropriate proof of service on all parties where required. NY R UNIF TRIAL CTS § 202.5(a).

- *QUEENS COUNTY.* With regard to service of a motion/petition on notice in an E-filed action, NY CPLR Rule 2214(b) and NY R UNIF TRIAL CTS § 202.5-b(f) applies. Where required, proof of service shall be filed on-line as a separate document. NY R L QUEENS E-FILE Doc. 1(H)(3).

v. *ALBANY COUNTY: Additional required documents*

- *Affirmation of good faith effort.* The parties must[. . .]submit an affirmation attesting to [their good faith effort to resolve the matter]. The affirmation of good faith effort to resolve the issues raised by the motion shall indicate the time, place and nature of the consultation and the issues discussed and any resolutions, or shall indicate good cause why no such conferral with counsel for opposing parties was held. An assigned justice or judge may dismiss a motion for failure to demonstrate that such effort was made with leave to renew the motion after such effort has been demonstrated. NY R 3 JD SUP Doc. 1(B).

b. *Supplemental documents*

i. *Supporting evidence; Exhibits.* The main supporting papers on a motion are affidavits, but any relevant exhibits, documents, depositions, etc., are also includible. SIEGEL-NYPRAC § 246.

- *Affidavits accompanying motion.* Affidavits shall be for a statement of the relevant facts. NY R UNIF TRIAL CTS § 202.8(c).
- *Foreign language documents.* Where an affidavit or exhibit annexed to a paper served or filed is in a foreign language, it shall be accompanied by an English translation and an affidavit by the translator stating his qualifications and that the translation is accurate. NY CPLR Rule 2101(b).
- *Statement of attorney in lieu of affidavit.* The statement of an attorney admitted to practice in the courts of the state, or of a physician, osteopath or dentist, authorized by law to practice in the state, who is not a party to an action, when subscribed and affirmed by him to be true under the penalties of perjury, may be served or filed in the action in lieu of and with the same force and effect as an affidavit. NY CPLR Rule 2106.
- *NEW YORK COUNTY: Form of presented exhibits.* Exhibits should be tabbed and be legible; a typed version of any exhibit that is difficult to read should be submitted with the original. Exhibits printed on both sides of the page should be bound and tabbed on the side. NY R NY CTY J RUL Rule 14(a).
- *QUEENS COUNTY.* Attorneys submitting exhibits to the court on E-file cases shall make each exhibit a separate, labeled attachment to an affidavit/affirmation. NY R L QUEENS E-FILE Doc. 1(H)(4).

ii. *Brief.* Briefs shall be for a statement of the relevant law. NY R UNIF TRIAL CTS § 202.8(c).

iii. *Affidavit of merits.* Refer to the General Requirements section of this document for information on when an affidavit of merits is required.

iv. *Notice to produce papers not in possession of the court.* If a paper relied on by the movant is in the possession of the other side, it may be demanded of that side with a notice to produce it at the hearing. Where such papers are in the possession of an adverse party, they shall be produced by him at the hearing on notice served with the motion papers. NY CPLR Rule 2214(Practice Commentary, C2214:23).

v. *Filing fees.* The County Clerk shall require the payment of any applicable statutory fees, or an order of the Court waiving payment of such fees, before accepting a paper for filing. NY R UNIF TRIAL CTS § 202.5(d)(1). For information on filing fees, if any, refer to NY CPLR § 8001, et seq.

- *ALBANY COUNTY.* In general, any filing subsequent to the commencement of an action which is designated as a motion or cross-motion requires the payment of a filing fee to the County Clerk's Office prior to submission to the Supreme Court Clerk's Office for referral to the assigned justice. The fee is assessed regardless of whether an application is made by notice of motion, order to show cause or ex parte. No fee will be charged upon the filing of a motion for poor person status in conjunction with an application which serves to commence an action or special proceeding. In the event a motion is received by the court unaccompanied by proof of payment to the County Clerk, the Supreme Court Clerk's Office will contact the submitting party to advise that the application will be held pending receipt of the filing fee only until the return date of the motion. If proof of payment is not submitted to the Supreme Court Clerk's Office by the return date (ex parte applications will be held ten (10) days), the papers will be returned by mail with a notification that the motion has been removed from the court's calendar and that it must be re-noticed and re-filed with the court along with the requisite filing fee. Inquiries concerning the applicability of the motion fee to a proposed filing may be directed to the Supreme Court Clerk's Office. NY R 3 JD SUP Doc. 1(B).
- *BRONX COUNTY.* In accordance with the new civil fee schedule set forth in Article 80 of the C.P.L.R. (NY CPLR § 8001, et seq.), effective July 14, 2003, all motions, and cross motions must be approved in Room 217 prior to payment of said fees in the County Clerk's Office, Room 118. NY R BRONX FIL R Doc. 8. The motion fee [must be] paid for via NYSCEF by credit/debit card. NY R BRONX E FIL R Doc. 1(1).
- *ERIE COUNTY.* Payment for fee-bearing NYSCEF documents must be made online via credit or debit card (American Express, MasterCard or Visa) at the time of submission. NY R ERIE E FIL Doc. 3(III)(E).
- *KINGS COUNTY.* The motion must be filed with NYSCEF and the motion fee paid. NY R L KINGS E FIL Doc. 1(D). Court fees in NYSCEF cases must be paid via NYSCEF by a credit or bank card (MasterCard, Visa, or American Express). Fees are no longer accepted in person in the Kings County Clerk's Office in NYSCEF cases. NY R L KINGS E FIL Doc. 1(B)(6).
- *NEW YORK COUNTY.* A motion fee must be paid on motions made in writing by notice of motion, order to show cause or ex parte after the commencement of an action. For this purpose, the term "action" shall mean any application to the court that requires the assignment of an index number, regardless of whether a formal pleading is filed. Applications or motions that commence an action and for which an index number fee must be paid require no motion fee. [A]ny motions made after the initial applications in these situations would require payment of the motion fee. A motion that is the initial application in a case commenced by the filing of a summons and complaint would require a motion fee since the filing of the summons and complaint rather than the application itself would require the purchase of an index number. NY R NY CTY Procedure II(A). In e-filed cases the motion fee must be paid when the documents are filed. Payment is made on-line by Visa, Mastercard, or American Express credit or bank card. NY R NY CTY Procedure II(A); NY R NY CTY E FIL Doc. 2(B)(5).
- *ONONDAGA COUNTY.* Court fees in e-filed cases must be paid online with the NYSCEF system using a credit card. The document is not considered to have been filed until payment of the fee has been tendered. NY R ONDGA E FIL Protocol(B)(2). Fees must be paid on all cross motions. NY R ONDGA E FIL Protocol(B)(9)(e).
- *QUEENS COUNTY.* The Motion Support Office does not receive, forward or process any fees or waiver of fees. All applications requiring payment of statutory fees or waiver of fees must be sent directly to the Queens County Clerk's office. NY R L QUEENS MOT SUP Doc. 1. Court fees (e.g., RJI fee, motion fee) in E-filed cases may be paid for on-line using a credit card. Papers may also be filed with the E-file system and the fee may be paid at the County Clerk's Office. In the latter case, the paper is not considered to have been filed until payment of the fee has been tendered. NY R L QUEENS E-FILE Doc. 1(E)(1). The motion/petition shall be filed on-line and the fee paid for either on-line by credit card or by the "Pay at the County Clerk's Office" option. NY R L QUEENS E-FILE Doc. 1(H)(1).

vi. *Working copies.* The court may require the parties to provide working copies of documents filed electronically. In such event, each working copy shall include, firmly affixed thereto, a copy of a confirmation notice in a form prescribed by the Chief Administrator. NY R UNIF TRIAL CTS § 202.5-b(d)(5).

- *BRONX COUNTY.* After papers on motions have been e-filed, working copies thereof, with Confirmation

Notice firmly attached as the back page facing out, must be submitted. (Each document or group of documents that is separately bound shall bear a Confirmation Notice.) Working copies lacking the Notice will not be accepted. WORKING COPIES OF MOTION PAPERS MUST BE SUBMITTED NO LATER THAN 4:45 P.M. ON THE RETURN DATE IN THE MOTION SUPPORT OFFICE (ROOM 217) AS EXPLAINED in NY R BRONX E FIL R Doc. 1(4). If an attorney has failed to submit required working copies on or before the return date, the motion will be transmitted as is to the Justice for such action as the Justice finds appropriate. Attorneys may submit working copies on motions by mail or overnight delivery. Any such submission shall be sent in a timely manner to the Motion Support Office (Room 217) and be conspicuously marked on the outside "NYSCEF Matter"; lack of such marking may delay processing. NY R BRONX E FIL R Doc. 1(4)(a).

- *ERIE COUNTY.* Electronically filed documents subject to review and processing by the Part Clerk do not require a working copy unless otherwise directed or provided for in IAS Part Rules. NY R UNIF TRIAL CTS § 202.5-b(d)(4), any working copy submitted shall include, as a cover page firmly fastened thereto, a copy of the Confirmation Notice generated by the NYSCEF site at the time of filing. Please consult the individual Justice's Part Rules and/or consult with the Judge's chambers to determine whether and how working copies are to be provided. Working copies will not be printed or delivered by the Erie County Clerk or the Chief Clerk of the Courts or any of their personnel to chambers. The official record of a document in an electronically filed case is the document filed via the NYSCEF system. Working copies are intended only for use by the Justice. The Court will discard all working copies after the Justice has finished with them. Thus, in the event that counsel fails to file a document via the NYSCEF system, the document will not be part of the court record. NY R ERIE E FIL Doc. 3(III)(O); NY R ERIE E FIL Doc. 3(V)(E).
- *KINGS COUNTY.* No courtesy copies of motion papers are required by the Court, except as may be required for electronic filing or by the Judge's Part Rules. In tort cases against the City of New York, courtesy copies shall be supplied to the Corporation Counsel's office in Brooklyn. NY R L KINGS Pt. C, Rule 5. Unless otherwise directed by the Court or as described herein, and with the exceptions listed below, in all NYSCEF cases in which an RJI has been filed, working copies of e-filed documents that are intended for judicial review must be submitted to the court. Working copies are not required of documents that are only processed by a support office (e.g. preliminary conference request, note of issue). Working copies shall include exhibit tabs and backs; for motion papers, the motion sequence number and the return date and part. The confirmation notice with the motion sequence number on it should be the back page of the motion facing out. In addition, the filer of a working copy must firmly bind thereto, with the back page facing out, a copy of the Confirmation Notice that was generated by NYSCEF when that document was efiled. Working copies that are submitted without the related Confirmation Notice will not be accepted. NY R L KINGS E FIL Doc. 1(B)(7); NY R L KINGS E FIL Doc. 1(D). WORKING COPIES OF MOTION PAPERS MUST BE SUBMITTED IN THE MOTION SUPPORT OFFICE (ROOM 227) AS EXPLAINED HEREIN. THEY MUST NOT BE DELIVERED TO THE PART OR CHAMBERS, EXCEPT WHERE THE INDIVIDUAL JUSTICE'S PART RULES PROVIDE OTHERWISE; DOING SO WILL CAUSE ADMINISTRATIVE CONFUSION AND POSSIBLE MISPLACEMENT OF PAPERS. Any such submission shall be sent in a timely manner (kindly review individual Justice's rules) and be conspicuously marked on the outside "NYSCEF Matter;" lack of such marking may delay processing. NY R L KINGS E FIL Doc. 1(D).
- *NEW YORK COUNTY.* Some Justices require that working copies of e-filed motion papers be submitted. See the E-filing Protocol for information on the many Parts that do not require working copies. Where required, working copies of the moving documents and all other documents on the motion or application shall be submitted to the Motion Submission Part Courtroom (Room 130) on, but not before, the final return date. A Confirmation Notice from the NYSCEF system, which is generated when a document is e-filed, shall be firmly affixed, as the back page facing out, to each separate working copy or group of such copies. NY R NY CTY Procedure II(A) NY R NY CTY E FIL Doc. 2(B)(5)(a); NY R NY CTY J RUL Rule 14(a). For more information on working copies, including which parts don't require them, refer to NY R NY CTY E FIL Doc. 2(B)(6).
- *ONONDAGA COUNTY.* Any courtesy "working" copies, if required (see NY R ONDGA E FIL Protocol(B)(7)), must be provided directly to the assigned justice. NY R ONDGA E FIL Protocol(B)(9)(e). For information as to whether or not an Onondaga Supreme Court Justice requires working (courtesy) copies of e-filed documents, please consult the Onondaga County Individual E-filing Rules. NY R ONDGA E FIL Protocol(B)(7)(a). The Supreme Court Clerk's Office and the Onondaga County Clerk's Office will

NOT accept the working copies. Working copies must be sent directly to the assigned justice's chambers. NY R ONDGA E FIL Protocol(B)(7)(b). A copy of the Confirmation Notice, generated by the NYSCEF system at the time a document is e-filed, must be attached to every working copy provided to chambers. If the Confirmation Notice is missing, the copy will not be accepted. NY R ONDGA E FIL Protocol(B)(7)(c). Courtesy copies do not become part of the official court record as maintained by the Onondaga County Clerk's Office and will be destroyed by chambers at the disposition of the case. In the event that counsel fails to file a document via NYSCEF, the document will not be part of the court record. NY R ONDGA E FIL Protocol(B)(7)(d).

- *QUEENS COUNTY.* Working copies of E-Filed notices of motion/notices of petition are NOT to be sent to the Motion Support Office. They must be brought to the calendar call in the judge's part. NY R L QUEENS MOT SUP Doc. 1. Unless otherwise directed or authorized by the court, counsel should file papers with the E-file system first and thereafter deliver a working copy to at the calendar call of the Centralized Motion Part or Assigned Justice in accordance with individual Part Rules. NY R L QUEENS E-FILE Doc. 1(E)(4). On the return date of a motion that has been E-filed, the movant must provide the Centralized Motion Part (CMP) with a working copy of the entire motion including the notice of motion with sequence number and all of the attached exhibits. The motion must have the confirmation of filing firmly affixed to the back of the papers (facing outward). The confirmation of filing is a separate notice from the payment notice and will say confirmation clearly across the top of the page. NY R L QUEENS E-FILE Doc. 1(H)(2)(a). The motion or Order to Show Cause must have clearly written across its face the words "Working Copy," it must also have the assigned Judge's name, motion sequence number and calendar number—which may be obtained from the posted calendar outside courtroom on the return date of the motion. A confirmation of filing must attached thereto. Working copies of e-filed Orders to Show Cause must contain a copy of the signed order and all supporting papers. NY R L QUEENS E-FILE Doc. 1(H)(2)(c). The Confirmation Notice must be an updated version that indicates the sequence number of the motion being submitted at the CMP calendar call. WORKING COPIES WITHOUT A CONFIRMATION NOTICE WILL NOT BE ACCEPTED. NY R L QUEENS E-FILE Doc. 1(H)(7).

vii. *Statement of authorization in electronic filing cases.* A filing agent (other than one employed by a governmental entity) shall e-file a statement of authorization from counsel of record in an action, in a form approved by the Chief Administrator, prior to or together with the first e-filing in that action by the agent on behalf of that counsel. NY R UNIF TRIAL CTS § 202.5-b(d)(1)(i).

viii. *ERIE COUNTY: Additional supplemental documents*

- *Notice of hard copy submission in e-filed case.* In accordance with NY R UNIF TRIAL CTS § 202.5-b(d), the County Clerk shall refuse to accept for filing, hard copy papers filed to an action subject to electronic filing unless hard copy filing is permitted by the Uniform Rules or NY R ERIE E FIL Doc. 3 and the papers bear a completed Notice of Hard Copy Submission—E-Filed Case form. NY R ERIE E FIL Doc. 3(III)(D).

ix. *KINGS COUNTY: Additional supplemental documents*

- *Forms when filing in hard copy.* An attorney who certifies in good faith that he or she lacks the equipment or knowledge needed to e-file and have no staff member or employee under his or her direction who has such knowledge and equipment may opt out of participation in e-filing in a mandatory case by filing a "Notice of Opt-Out from Participation in Action Subject to Mandatory Electronic Filing" form EFM-2 with the Clerk. NY R L KINGS E FIL Doc. 1(A)(2). Where in accordance with the E-Filing Rules a party submits a document in hard copy in an e-filed case (principally, a document submitted by a nonparticipating party (e.g., an attorney) in a consensual case, an emergency filing made in accordance with the Mandatory E-Filing Rules, and any document filed with the court in hard copy by an attorney who has opted out of participation in mandatory e-filing, the document must bear the back page facing out, a "Notice of Hard Copy Submission—E-Filed Cases" form EFM-3. NY R L KINGS E FIL Doc. 1(B)(3).

x. *NEW YORK COUNTY: Additional supplemental documents*

- *Notice of hard copy submission.* Where in accordance with the E-Filing Rules an attorney or an unrepresented litigant who is participating in e-filing submits a document in hard copy in an e-filed case, the document must bear, as the back page facing out, a Notice of Hard-Copy Submission—E-Filed Case (a form available in the "Forms" section on the NYSCEF website (Form EFM-3) and in the court's back offices). NY R NY CTY E FIL Doc. 2(B)(3). For more information refer to NY R NY CTY E FIL Doc. 2.
- *Unpublished decisions.* Whenever reliance is placed upon a decision or other authority not officially

published or readily available to the New York County Supreme Court, a copy of the case or of pertinent portions of the authority shall be submitted with the motion papers. NY R NY CTY J RUL Rule 14(a).

xi. *ONONDAGA COUNTY: Additional supplemental documents*

- *Notice of hard copy submission.* Any papers to be filed with the court in an e-filed case must be filed online with the E-filing system except where a special exemption is granted (e.g., oversized maps, photographs). If such an exemption is granted, Form EFM-3, "Notice of Hard Copy Submission—E-Filed Case," must be attached to such documents forms which are not filed on line. Also, Form EFM-4 "Notice of Hard Copy Exhibit Filing" must be completed and uploaded to the action's e-file. Both of these forms may be found on the NYSCEF website. NY R ONDGA E FIL Protocol(B)(4).

xii. *QUEENS COUNTY: Additional supplemental documents*

- *Notice of hard copy submission.* Any party opting out of the e-filing system must have a "Notice of Hard Copy Submission" firmly affixed to the back of the papers. NY R L QUEENS E-FILE Doc. 1(H)(2)(f).

2. *Documents for opposing party*

a. *Required documents*

i. *Opposition.* Refer to the General Requirements section of this document for information on the opposition.

- *Request for oral argument.* A party requesting oral argument shall set forth such request in its notice of motion or in its order to show cause or on the first page of the answering papers, as the case may be. Where all parties to a motion request oral argument, oral argument shall be granted unless the court shall determine it to be unnecessary. Where a motion is brought on by order to show cause, the court may set forth in the order that oral argument is required on the return date of the motion. NY R UNIF TRIAL CTS § 202.8(d).
- *QUEENS COUNTY: E-filing opposition papers.* E-filed opposition papers and/or reply papers must also be provided to the Centralized Motion Part in the same manner as the moving papers with the confirmation of filing firmly attached to the back of the papers. NY R L QUEENS E-FILE Doc. 1(H)(2)(d).

ii. *Proof of service.* In addition to complying with the provisions of NY CPLR Rule 2101, every paper filed in court shall have annexed thereto appropriate proof of service on all parties where required. NY R UNIF TRIAL CTS § 202.5(a).

b. *Supplemental documents*

i. *Supporting evidence; Exhibits.* The main supporting papers on a motion are affidavits, but any relevant exhibits, documents, depositions, etc., are also includible. SIEGEL-NYPRAC § 246.

- *Affidavits accompanying opposition.* Affidavits shall be for a statement of the relevant facts. NY R UNIF TRIAL CTS § 202.8(c).
- *Foreign language documents.* Where an affidavit or exhibit annexed to a paper served or filed is in a foreign language, it shall be accompanied by an English translation and an affidavit by the translator stating his qualifications and that the translation is accurate. NY CPLR Rule 2101(b).
- *Statement of attorney in lieu of affidavit.* The statement of an attorney admitted to practice in the courts of the state, or of a physician, osteopath or dentist, authorized by law to practice in the state, who is not a party to an action, when subscribed and affirmed by him to be true under the penalties of perjury, may be served or filed in the action in lieu of and with the same force and effect as an affidavit. NY CPLR Rule 2106.
- *NEW YORK COUNTY: Form of presented exhibits.* Exhibits should be tabbed and be legible; a typed version of any exhibit that is difficult to read should be submitted with the original. Exhibits printed on both sides of the page should be bound and tabbed on the side. NY R NY CTY J RUL Rule 14(a).
- *QUEENS COUNTY.* Attorneys submitting exhibits to the court on E-file cases shall make each exhibit a separate, labeled attachment to an affidavit/affirmation. NY R L QUEENS E-FILE Doc. 1(H)(4).

ii. *Brief.* Briefs shall be for a statement of the relevant law. NY R UNIF TRIAL CTS § 202.8(c).

iii. *Filing fees.* The County Clerk shall require the payment of any applicable statutory fees, or an order of the Court waiving payment of such fees, before accepting a paper for filing. NY R UNIF TRIAL CTS § 202.5(d)(1). For information on filing fees, if any, refer to NY CPLR § 8001, et seq.

- *ALBANY COUNTY.* In general, any filing subsequent to the commencement of an action which is designated as a motion or cross-motion requires the payment of a filing fee to the County Clerk's Office

prior to submission to the Supreme Court Clerk's Office for referral to the assigned justice. The fee is assessed regardless of whether an application is made by notice of motion, order to show cause or ex parte. No fee will be charged upon the filing of a motion for poor person status in conjunction with an application which serves to commence an action or special proceeding. In the event a motion is received by the court unaccompanied by proof of payment to the County Clerk, the Supreme Court Clerk's Office will contact the submitting party to advise that the application will be held pending receipt of the filing fee only until the return date of the motion. If proof of payment is not submitted to the Supreme Court Clerk's Office by the return date (ex parte applications will be held ten (10) days), the papers will be returned by mail with a notification that the motion has been removed from the court's calendar and that it must be re-noticed and re-filed with the court along with the requisite filing fee. Inquiries concerning the applicability of the motion fee to a proposed filing may be directed to the Supreme Court Clerk's Office. NY R 3 JD SUP Doc. 1(B).

- *BRONX COUNTY.* In accordance with the new civil fee schedule set forth in Article 80 of the C.P.L.R. (NY CPLR § 8001, et seq.), effective July 14, 2003, all motions, and cross motions must be approved in Room 217 prior to payment of said fees in the County Clerk's Office, Room 118. NY R BRONX FIL R Doc. 8. The motion fee [must be] paid for via NYSCEF by credit/debit card. NY R BRONX E FIL R Doc. 1(1).
- *ERIE COUNTY.* Payment for fee-bearing NYSCEF documents must be made online via credit or debit card (American Express, MasterCard or Visa) at the time of submission. NY R ERIE E FIL Doc. 3(III)(E).
- *KINGS COUNTY.* The motion must be filed with NYSCEF and the motion fee paid. NY R L KINGS E FIL Doc. 1(D). Court fees in NYSCEF cases must be paid via NYSCEF by a credit or bank card (MasterCard, Visa, or American Express). Fees are no longer accepted in person in the Kings County Clerk's Office in NYSCEF cases. NY R L KINGS E FIL Doc. 1(B)(6).
- *NEW YORK COUNTY.* A motion fee must be paid on motions made in writing by notice of motion, order to show cause or ex parte after the commencement of an action. For this purpose, the term "action" shall mean any application to the court that requires the assignment of an index number, regardless of whether a formal pleading is filed. Applications or motions that commence an action and for which an index number fee must be paid require no motion fee. [A]ny motions made after the initial applications in these situations would require payment of the motion fee. A motion that is the initial application in a case commenced by the filing of a summons and complaint would require a motion fee since the filing of the summons and complaint rather than the application itself would require the purchase of an index number. NY R NY CTY Procedure II(A). In e-filed cases the motion fee must be paid when the documents are filed. Payment is made on-line by Visa, Mastercard, or American Express credit or bank card. NY R NY CTY Procedure II(A); NY R NY CTY E FIL Doc. 2(B)(5).
- *ONONDAGA COUNTY.* Court fees in e-filed cases must be paid online with the NYSCEF system using a credit card. The document is not considered to have been filed until payment of the fee has been tendered. NY R ONDGA E FIL Protocol(B)(2). Fees must be paid on all cross motions. NY R ONDGA E FIL Protocol(B)(9)(e).
- *QUEENS COUNTY.* The Motion Support Office does not receive, forward or process any fees or waiver of fees. All applications requiring payment of statutory fees or waiver of fees must be sent directly to the Queens County Clerk's office. NY R L QUEENS MOT SUP Doc. 1. Court fees (e.g., RJI fee, motion fee) in E-filed cases may be paid for on-line using a credit card. Papers may also be filed with the E-file system and the fee may be paid at the County Clerk's Office. In the latter case, the paper is not considered to have been filed until payment of the fee has been tendered. NY R L QUEENS E-FILE Doc. 1(E)(1). The motion/petition shall be filed on-line and the fee paid for either on-line by credit card or by the "Pay at the County Clerk's Office" option. NY R L QUEENS E-FILE Doc. 1(H)(1).

iv. *Working copies.* The court may require the parties to provide working copies of documents filed electronically. In such event, each working copy shall include, firmly affixed thereto, a copy of a confirmation notice in a form prescribed by the Chief Administrator. NY R UNIF TRIAL CTS § 202.5-b(d)(5).

- *BRONX COUNTY.* After papers on motions have been e-filed, working copies thereof, with Confirmation Notice firmly attached as the back page facing out, must be submitted. (Each document or group of documents that is separately bound shall bear a Confirmation Notice.) Working copies lacking the Notice will not be accepted. WORKING COPIES OF MOTION PAPERS MUST BE SUBMITTED NO LATER THAN 4:45 P.M. ON THE RETURN DATE IN THE MOTION SUPPORT OFFICE (ROOM 217) AS EXPLAINED in NY R BRONX E FIL R Doc. 1(4). If an attorney has failed to submit required working

copies on or before the return date, the motion will be transmitted as is to the Justice for such action as the Justice finds appropriate. Attorneys may submit working copies on motions by mail or overnight delivery. Any such submission shall be sent in a timely manner to the Motion Support Office (Room 217) and be conspicuously marked on the outside "NYSCEF Matter"; lack of such marking may delay processing. NY R BRONX E FIL R Doc. 1(4)(a).

- *ERIE COUNTY.* Electronically filed documents subject to review and processing by the Part Clerk do not require a working copy unless otherwise directed or provided for in IAS Part Rules. NY R UNIF TRIAL CTS § 202.5-b(d)(4), any working copy submitted shall include, as a cover page firmly fastened thereto, a copy of the Confirmation Notice generated by the NYSCEF site at the time of filing. Please consult the individual Justice's Part Rules and/or consult with the Judge's chambers to determine whether and how working copies are to be provided. Working copies will not be printed or delivered by the Erie County Clerk or the Chief Clerk of the Courts or any of their personnel to chambers. The official record of a document in an electronically filed case is the document filed via the NYSCEF system. Working copies are intended only for use by the Justice. The Court will discard all working copies after the Justice has finished with them. Thus, in the event that counsel fails to file a document via the NYSCEF system, the document will not be part of the court record. NY R ERIE E FIL Doc. 3(III)(O); NY R ERIE E FIL Doc. 3(V)(E).
- *KINGS COUNTY.* No courtesy copies of motion papers are required by the Court, except as may be required for electronic filing or by the Judge's Part Rules. In tort cases against the City of New York, courtesy copies shall be supplied to the Corporation Counsel's office in Brooklyn. NY R L KINGS Pt. C, Rule 5. Unless otherwise directed by the Court or as described herein, and with the exceptions listed below, in all NYSCEF cases in which an RJI has been filed, working copies of e-filed documents that are intended for judicial review must be submitted to the court. Working copies are not required of documents that are only processed by a support office (e.g. preliminary conference request, note of issue). Working copies shall include exhibit tabs and backs; for motion papers, the motion sequence number and the return date and part. The confirmation notice with the motion sequence number on it should be the back page of the motion facing out. In addition, the filer of a working copy must firmly bind thereto, with the back page facing out, a copy of the Confirmation Notice that was generated by NYSCEF when that document was efiled. Working copies that are submitted without the related Confirmation Notice will not be accepted. NY R L KINGS E FIL Doc. 1(B)(7); NY R L KINGS E FIL Doc. 1(D). WORKING COPIES OF MOTION PAPERS MUST BE SUBMITTED IN THE MOTION SUPPORT OFFICE (ROOM 227) AS EXPLAINED HEREIN. THEY MUST NOT BE DELIVERED TO THE PART OR CHAMBERS, EXCEPT WHERE THE INDIVIDUAL JUSTICE'S PART RULES PROVIDE OTHERWISE; DOING SO WILL CAUSE ADMINISTRATIVE CONFUSION AND POSSIBLE MISPLACEMENT OF PAPERS. Any such submission shall be sent in a timely manner (kindly review individual Justice's rules) and be conspicuously marked on the outside "NYSCEF Matter;" lack of such marking may delay processing. NY R L KINGS E FIL Doc. 1(D).
- *NEW YORK COUNTY.* Some Justices require that working copies of e-filed motion papers be submitted. See the E-filing Protocol for information on the many Parts that do not require working copies. Where required, working copies of the moving documents and all other documents on the motion or application shall be submitted to the Motion Submission Part Courtroom (Room 130) on, but not before, the final return date. A Confirmation Notice from the NYSCEF system, which is generated when a document is e-filed, shall be firmly affixed, as the back page facing out, to each separate working copy or group of such copies. NY R NY CTY Procedure II(A) NY R NY CTY E FIL Doc. 2(B)(5)(a); NY R NY CTY J RUL Rule 14(a). For more information on working copies, including which parts don't require them, refer to NY R NY CTY E FIL Doc. 2(B)(6).
- *ONONDAGA COUNTY.* Any courtesy "working" copies, if required (see NY R ONDGA E FIL Protocol(B)(7)), must be provided directly to the assigned justice. NY R ONDGA E FIL Protocol(B)(9)(e). For information as to whether or not an Onondaga Supreme Court Justice requires working (courtesy) copies of e-filed documents, please consult the Onondaga County Individual E-filing Rules. NY R ONDGA E FIL Protocol(B)(7)(a). The Supreme Court Clerk's Office and the Onondaga County Clerk's Office will NOT accept the working copies. Working copies must be sent directly to the assigned justice's chambers. NY R ONDGA E FIL Protocol(B)(7)(b). A copy of the Confirmation Notice, generated by the NYSCEF system at the time a document is e-filed, must be attached to every working copy provided to chambers. If the Confirmation Notice is missing, the copy will not be accepted. NY R ONDGA E FIL Protocol(B)(7)(c). Courtesy copies do not become part of the official court record as maintained by the Onondaga County

Clerk's Office and will be destroyed by chambers at the disposition of the case. In the event that counsel fails to file a document via NYSCEF, the document will not be part of the court record. NY R ONDGA E FIL Protocol(B)(7)(d).

- *QUEENS COUNTY.* Working copies of E-Filed notices of motion/notices of petition are NOT to be sent to the Motion Support Office. They must be brought to the calendar call in the judge's part. NY R L QUEENS MOT SUP Doc. 1. Unless otherwise directed or authorized by the court, counsel should file papers with the E-file system first and thereafter deliver a working copy to at the calendar call of the Centralized Motion Part or Assigned Justice in accordance with individual Part Rules. NY R L QUEENS E-FILE Doc. 1(E)(4). On the return date of a motion that has been E-filed, the movant must provide the Centralized Motion Part (CMP) with a working copy of the entire motion including the notice of motion with sequence number and all of the attached exhibits. The motion must have the confirmation of filing firmly affixed to the back of the papers (facing outward). The confirmation of filing is a separate notice from the payment notice and will say confirmation clearly across the top of the page. NY R L QUEENS E-FILE Doc. 1(H)(2)(a). The motion or Order to Show Cause must have clearly written across its face the words "Working Copy," it must also have the assigned Judge's name, motion sequence number and calendar number—which may be obtained from the posted calendar outside courtroom on the return date of the motion. A confirmation of filing must attached thereto. Working copies of e-filed Orders to Show Cause must contain a copy of the signed order and all supporting papers. NY R L QUEENS E-FILE Doc. 1(H)(2)(c). The Confirmation Notice must be an updated version that indicates the sequence number of the motion being submitted at the CMP calendar call. WORKING COPIES WITHOUT A CONFIRMATION NOTICE WILL NOT BE ACCEPTED. NY R L QUEENS E-FILE Doc. 1(H)(7).

v. *ERIE COUNTY: Additional supplemental documents*

- *Notice of hard copy submission in e-filed case.* In accordance with NY R UNIF TRIAL CTS § 202.5-b(d), the County Clerk shall refuse to accept for filing, hard copy papers filed to an action subject to electronic filing unless hard copy filing is permitted by the Uniform Rules or NY R ERIE E FIL Doc. 3 and the papers bear a completed Notice of Hard Copy Submission—E-Filed Case form. NY R ERIE E FIL Doc. 3(III)(D).

vi. *KINGS COUNTY: Additional supplemental documents*

- *Forms when filing in hard copy.* An attorney who certifies in good faith that he or she lacks the equipment or knowledge needed to e-file and have no staff member or employee under his or her direction who has such knowledge and equipment may opt out of participation in e-filing in a mandatory case by filing a "Notice of Opt-Out from Participation in Action Subject to Mandatory Electronic Filing" form EFM-2 with the Clerk. NY R L KINGS E FIL Doc. 1(A)(2). Where in accordance with the E-Filing Rules a party submits a document in hard copy in an e-filed case (principally, a document submitted by a nonparticipating party (e.g., an attorney) in a consensual case, an emergency filing made in accordance with the Mandatory E-Filing Rules, and any document filed with the court in hard copy by an attorney who has opted out of participation in mandatory e-filing, the document must bear the back page facing out, a "Notice of Hard Copy Submission—E-Filed Cases" form EFM-3. NY R L KINGS E FIL Doc. 1(B)(3).

vii. *NEW YORK COUNTY: Additional supplemental documents*

- *Notice of hard copy submission.* Where in accordance with the E-Filing Rules an attorney or an unrepresented litigant who is participating in e-filing submits a document in hard copy in an e-filed case, the document must bear, as the back page facing out, a Notice of Hard-Copy Submission—E-Filed Case (a form available in the "Forms" section on the NYSCEF website (Form EFM-3) and in the court's back offices). NY R NY CTY E FIL Doc. 2(B)(3). For more information refer to NY R NY CTY E FIL Doc. 2.
- *Unpublished decisions.* Whenever reliance is placed upon a decision or other authority not officially published or readily available to the New York County Supreme Court, a copy of the case or of pertinent portions of the authority shall be submitted with the motion papers. NY R NY CTY J RUL Rule 14(a).

viii. *ONONDAGA COUNTY: Additional supplemental documents*

- *Notice of hard copy submission.* Any papers to be filed with the court in an e-filed case must be filed online with the E-filing system except where a special exemption is granted (e.g., oversized maps, photographs). If such an exemption is granted, Form EFM-3, "Notice of Hard Copy Submission—E-Filed Case," must be attached to such documents forms which are not filed on line. Also, Form EFM-4 "Notice of Hard Copy Exhibit Filing" must be completed and uploaded to the action's e-file. Both of these forms may be found on the NYSCEF website. NY R ONDGA E FIL Protocol(B)(4).

ix. *QUEENS COUNTY: Additional supplemental documents*

- *Notice of hard copy submission.* Any party opting out of the e-filing system must have a "Notice of Hard Copy Submission" firmly affixed to the back of the papers. NY R L QUEENS E-FILE Doc. 1(H)(2)(f).

E. Format

1. *Form of documents*

a. *Size and form of paper.* Each paper served or filed shall be durable, white and, except for summonses, subpoenas, notices of appearance, notes of issue, orders of protection, temporary orders of protection and exhibits, shall be eleven by eight and one-half (11 x 8-1/2) inches in size. NY CPLR Rule 2101(a).

b. *Writing and language.* The writing shall be legible and in black ink. NY CPLR Rule 2101(a). Each paper served or filed shall be in the English language which, where practicable, shall be of ordinary usage. NY CPLR Rule 2101(b).

c. *Caption.* Each paper served or filed shall begin with a caption setting forth the name of the court, the venue, the title of the action, the nature of the paper and the index number of the action if one has been assigned. In all papers other than a summons, a complaint or a judgment it shall be sufficient to state the name of the first named party on each side with an appropriate indication of any omissions. NY CPLR Rule 2101(c).

i. *Further contents of first page.* After the first paper has been filed in each case the index number shall appear on the cover and first page to the right of the caption of every paper tendered for filing in the action. Each such cover and first page also shall contain an indication of the county of venue and a brief description of the nature of the paper and, where the case has been assigned to an individual judge, shall contain the name of the assigned judge to the right of the caption. NY R UNIF TRIAL CTS § 202.5(a); NY R UNIF TRIAL CTS § 202.5(b); NY R UNIF TRIAL CTS § 202.5(d)(1)(i).

ii. *ALBANY COUNTY: Request for oral argument.* A party may request oral argument on a motion by indicating such request on the first page of the notice of motion, order to show cause, or answering papers in the area across from the caption of the action/proceeding. NY R 3 JD SUP Doc. 1(B).

iii. *NEW YORK COUNTY: Request for oral argument.* Counsel who wish oral argument must so request conspicuously on the front of their papers. NY R NY CTY Procedure II(D).

d. *Index number.* No paper in an action in the supreme or a county court, other than an order submitted for signature to a judge out of court, shall be submitted for any purpose to the supreme or county court or to a clerk thereof unless there is endorsed on such paper the index number of the action assigned by the clerk of the county. NY CPLR § 8018(c).

i. *ALBANY COUNTY: Index number on all filed documents.* The index number, the request for judicial intervention number and the assigned justice's name shall appear on [all papers filed with the Court subsequent to the complaint]. NY R 3 JD SUP Doc. 1(A).

ii. *ERIE COUNTY: Index number after initial filing.* Cases that are initially commenced by the filing of papers with the NYSCEF system are identified as e-filed cases by assignment of an Index Number that has "800-899" as the first three (3) digits of the index number (i.e. 802391/2012). NY R ERIE E FIL Doc. 3(II). [The] Index Number must be affixed to all document submissions, filings, and communications to the Erie County Clerk and the Court. Cases that are converted from paper to e-filing shall retain the original index number. NY R ERIE E FIL Doc. 3(II).

iii. *KINGS COUNTY: Index number after initial filing.* In cases commenced electronically by the filing of initiating papers with the NYSCEF system and payment of the statutory fees, the Kings County Clerk will issue an NYSCEF designated index number and the filer shall be notified via the NYSCEF system of the index number assigned and filing date. Such index number must be affixed to all document submissions, filings and communications to the Kings County Clerk and Supreme Court. If counsel faces exigent circumstances that require accelerated assignment, counsel may contact Administration of the Kings County Clerk at kcco-efile@nycourts.gov, during normal business hours of the court. NY R L KINGS E FIL Doc. 1(B)(5).

iv. *NEW YORK COUNTY: Index number on hard copy filings.* Papers subsequently presented for filing in hardcopy format will be filed in this jacket. NY R NY CTY Procedure I(B). Index numbers take the form of six digits followed by a slash and the four digits of the year the case began, e.g., 340705/2018. The first or first two integers of the index number identify the type of case. If a case is commenced electronically, the second integer will be a "5", except as indicated otherwise in the list below. There are many tax certiorari matters e-filed annually and the index numbers therefor will normally run over into those with a "6" as the second integer, and the same will occur with general cases if necessary. The principal types of cases and their index number categories are listed in NY R NY CTY Procedure I(B). NY R NY CTY Procedure I(B); NY R NY CTY Procedure XI(A).

v. *ONONDAGA COUNTY: Index number.* The index number must be referenced on all e-filed documents and correspondence. All e-filed case index numbers will contain the letters "EF" between the year and the file number (for example, 2012EF9999). NY R ONDGA E FIL Protocol(B)(1).

vi. *QUEENS COUNTY: Index number on converted cases.* Cases originally commenced in hard-copy form but later converted to an E-file case, either by stipulation or order will bear a regular index number initially. The County Clerk will issue a new E-file index number. NY R L QUEENS E-FILE Doc. 1(B).

e. *Line spacing.* Every paper filed in court, if typewritten, shall have at least double space between each line, except for quotations and the names and addresses of attorneys appearing in the action. NY R UNIF TRIAL CTS § 202.5(a).

f. *Font size.* Each. . .paper printed or typed, served or filed, except an exhibit or a summons, shall be in clear type of no less than ten (10) point in size. NY CPLR Rule 2101(a).

i. Whenever a requirement relating to size of type is stated in point size, the type size requirement shall be deemed met if the x-height of the type is a minimum of forty-five percent (45%) of the specified point size. Each point shall be measured as .351 millimeter. The x-height size shall be measured as it appears on the page. The x-height is the height of the lower case letters, exclusive of ascenders or descenders. NY CPLR § 105(t).

g. *Margins.* Every paper filed in court shall have at least one (1) inch margins. NY R UNIF TRIAL CTS § 202.5(a).

h. *Citations*

i. *Civil practice law and rules.* NY CPLR § 101, et seq. shall be known as the civil practice law and rules, and may be cited as "CPLR". Reference to a provision in the civil practice law and rules may, except when such provision is being enacted or amended, be made without indicating whether it is a rule or section. NY CPLR § 101.

i. *Indorsement by attorney.* Each paper served or filed shall be indorsed with the name, address and telephone number of the attorney for the party serving or filing the paper, or if the party does not appear by attorney, with the name, address and telephone number of the party. NY CPLR Rule 2101(d).

j. *One-sided printing.* In addition, every paper filed in court, other than an exhibit or printed form, shall contain writing on one side only, except that papers that are fastened on the side may contain writing on both sides. NY R UNIF TRIAL CTS § 202.5(a).

k. *Use of copies authorized.* Except where otherwise specifically prescribed, copies, rather than originals, of all papers, including orders, affidavits and exhibits may be served or filed. Where it is required that the original be served or filed and the original is lost or withheld, the court may authorize a copy to be served or filed. NY CPLR Rule 2101(e).

i. Where a certified copy of a paper is required by law, an attorney admitted to practice in the courts of the state may certify that it has been compared by him with the original and found to be a true and complete copy. Such a certificate, when subscribed by such attorney, has the same effect as if made by a clerk. NY CPLR § 2105.

l. *Recycled paper.* It is the policy of the Unified Court System that litigants, where practicable, should file or submit to the courts of the Unified Court System of the State of New York papers printed or reproduced on recycled paper. Paper is considered recycled if it contains a minimum content of thirty percent (30%) waste paper. NY R UNIF TRIAL CTS § 215.2. The signature page of every paper filed or submitted to the court on recycled paper should bear the legend: "Printed [Reproduced] on Recycled Paper." NY R UNIF TRIAL CTS § 215.3.

m. *Form of request for judicial intervention; Copies.* A request for judicial intervention must be submitted, in duplicate, on a form authorized by the Chief of the Courts, with proof of service on the other parties to the action (but proof of service is not required where the application is ex parte). NY R UNIF TRIAL CTS § 202.6(a).

n. *KINGS COUNTY: Tabs on filings.* Motions, orders and other filed papers shall be indexed with protruding tabs. Clerks are required to reject papers that do not have protruding exhibit tabs, except papers in matrimonial cases and papers filed by pro se litigants. NY R L KINGS Pt. A, Papers.

o. *NEW YORK COUNTY: Length of briefs.* Unless advance permission otherwise is granted by the court for good cause, memoranda of law shall not exceed thirty (30) pages each (exclusive of table of contents and table of authorities) and affidavits/affirmations shall not exceed twenty-five (25) pages each. NY R NY CTY J RUL Rule 14(b).

p. *QUEENS COUNTY: Form and size of motion filings.* All motions filed in Queens Supreme Court-Civil Term, must adhere to the Motion Support rules and the rules of the assigned judge. NY R L QUEENS MOT SUP Doc. 1. Due to space limitations, the Motion Support Office cannot accept notices of motion/notices of petition and accompanying exhibits which measure greater than eight (8) inches. If your documents measure greater than eight (8) inches you are directed to submit only the notice of motion/notice of petition to the Motion Support Office and bring all exhibits to the calendar call on your return date. NY R L QUEENS MOT SUP Doc. 1.

2. *Form of electronic documents.* Each paper served or filed by electronic means, as defined in NY CPLR Rule 2103(f), shall be capable of being reproduced by the receiver so as to comply with the provisions of NY CPLR Rule 2101(a) through NY CPLR Rule 2101(d). NY CPLR Rule 2101(g).
   a. *File format.* All e-filed documents shall comply with the technical requirements set forth at the NYSCEF site. NY R UNIF TRIAL CTS § 202.5-b(d)(1)(i).
   b. *Heading of document.* The subject matter heading for each paper sent by electronic means must indicate that the matter being transmitted electronically is related to a court proceeding. NY CPLR Rule 2103(b)(7).
   c. *E-filed documents identification*
      i. *ERIE COUNTY.* E-filed cases must be readily identifiable and marked as such. If counsel presents papers to the Office of the Erie County Clerk or the Office of the Chief Clerk in a NYSCEF matter where authorized, counsel should alert the Clerk that the case is a NYSCEF matter. NY R ERIE E FIL Doc. 3(II).
      ii. *KINGS COUNTY.* The Supreme Court's Civil Case Information System ("CCIS") will further identify e-filed cases by the addition of a suffix to the index number (e.g. 500136/2006E). This suffix should be used on all documents filed with the court in e-filed matters. NY R L KINGS E FIL Doc. 1(A)(1).
3. *Signature blocks.* Every pleading, written motion, and other paper, served on another party or filed or submitted to the court shall be signed by an attorney, or by a party if the party is not represented by an attorney, with the name of the attorney or party clearly printed or typed directly below the signature. NY R CHIEF ADMIN § 130-1.1-a(a); NY R UNIF TRIAL CTS § 202.5(d)(1)(iv).
   a. *Printed name.* Beneath each signature shall be printed the name signed. NY CPLR Rule 2101(a).
   b. *Failure to sign.* Absent good cause shown, the court shall strike any unsigned paper if the omission of the signature is not corrected promptly after being called to the attention of the attorney or party. NY R CHIEF ADMIN § 130-1.1-a(a).
   c. *Signature as certification.* By signing a paper, an attorney or party certifies that, to the best of that person's knowledge, information and belief, formed after an inquiry reasonable under the circumstances the presentation of the paper or the contentions therein are not frivolous as defined in NY R CHIEF ADMIN § 130-1.1(c). NY R CHIEF ADMIN § 130-1.1-a(b)(1).
   d. *Electronic signatures.* A document shall be considered to have been signed by an attorney or party in compliance with NY R CHIEF ADMIN § 130-1.1-a if it has been signed by such attorney or party as provided in NY R UNIF TRIAL CTS § 202.5-b(e)(1) and it bears the signatory's name. NY R UNIF TRIAL CTS § 202.5-b(e)(2). An electronically filed document shall be considered to have been signed by, and shall be binding upon, the person identified as a signatory, if:
      i. It bears the physical signature of such person and is scanned into an electronic format that reproduces such signature; or
      ii. The signatory has electronically affixed the digital image of his or her signature to the document; or
      iii. It is electronically filed under the User ID and password of that person; or
      iv. In a tax certiorari action in which the parties have stipulated to this procedure, it is an initiating document that is electronically filed without the signature of the signatory in a form provided above in NY R UNIF TRIAL CTS § 202.5-b(e)(iv), provided that, prior to filing, the document is signed in full in hard copy (which hard copy must be preserved until the conclusion of all proceedings, including appeals, in the case in which it is filed); or
      v. In a small claims assessment review proceeding, it is a petition recorded by the NYSCEF site upon the filing of a text file as provided in NY R UNIF TRIAL CTS § 202.5-b(b)(1), provided that prior to filing, the document was signed in full in hard copy (which hard copy must be preserved until the conclusion of all proceedings in the matter, including article 78 (NY CPLR § 7801, et seq.) review and any appeals, and must be made available during the proceeding upon request of the respondent or the court); or
      vi. It otherwise bears the electronic signature of the signatory in a format conforming to such standards and requirements as may hereafter be established by the Chief Administrator. NY R UNIF TRIAL CTS § 202.5-b(e).
4. *Confidentiality of personal information.* No person may file any document available for public inspection with any state agency, political subdivision, or in any court of this state that contains a Social Security account number of any other person, unless such other person is a dependent child, or has consented to such filing, except as required by federal or state law or regulation, or by court rule. NY GEN BUS § 399-ddd. Submissions pursuant to e-filing procedures shall have the same confidentiality rights as paper documents. NY R UNIF TRIAL CTS § 202.5-b(k)(1).
   a. *Confidential personal information.* Except in the actions designated in NY R UNIF TRIAL CTS § 202.5(e)(1), or as

otherwise provided by rule or law or court order, and whether or not a sealing order is or has been sought, the parties shall omit or redact confidential personal information in papers submitted to the court for filing. For purposes of NY R UNIF TRIAL CTS § 202.5(e), confidential personal information ("CPI") means:

i. The taxpayer identification number of an individual or an entity, including a Social Security number, an employer identification number, and an individual taxpayer identification number, except the last four (4) digits thereof;

ii. The date of an individual's birth, except the year thereof;

iii. The full name of an individual known to be a minor, except the minor's initials;

iv. A financial account number, including a credit and/or debit card number, a bank account number, an investment account number, and/or an insurance account number, except the last four (4) digits or letters thereof; and

v. Any of the documents or testimony in a matrimonial action protected by NY DOM REL § 235 or evidence sealed by the court in such an action which are attached as exhibits or referenced in the papers filed in any other civil action. For purposes of NY R UNIF TRIAL CTS § 202.5, a matrimonial action shall mean: an action to annul a marriage or declare the nullity of a void marriage, an action or agreement for a separation, an action for a divorce, or an action or proceeding for custody, visitation, writ of habeus corpus, child support, maintenance or paternity. NY R UNIF TRIAL CTS § 202.5(e)(1).

vi. *ERIE COUNTY.* An attorney or unrepresented litigant filing a document via the NYSCEF system must comply with the requirements of NY R UNIF TRIAL CTS § 202.5(e) regarding the redaction of Confidential Personal Information and NY GEN BUS § 399-ddd(6) concerning the filing of documents containing Social Security Numbers. It is the sole responsibility of counsel or unrepresented litigant filing to be aware of and to comply with existing laws requiring non-disclosure of personal information contained in any document e-filed in NYSCEF. NY R ERIE E FIL Doc. 3(III)(G); NY R ERIE E FIL Doc. 3(III).

vii. *KINGS COUNTY.* An attorney or unrepresented litigant filing a document via the NYSCEF system must comply with the requirements of General Business Law § 399-dd(6), which often require redaction of any Social Security number that appear in the original document. The NYSCEF system automatically redacts portions of filed documents which apparently contain Social Security numbers pursuant to NY R UNIF TRIAL CTS § 202.5-b(k). In the event the filing party receives e-mail notice through NYSCEF that a Social Security number in a filed document has been redacted, and the filing party concludes such redaction is erroneous, the filer should click on the link provided in the e-mail to permit the County Clerk to revert the redaction. For Confidential Personal Information, see NY R UNIF TRIAL CTS § 202.5(e) and NY R L KINGS E FIL Doc. 1(B)(11). [Editor's note: the reference to General Business Law § 399-dd(6) is likely a reference to NY GEN BUS § 399-ddd(6)]. NY R L KINGS E FIL Doc. 1(B)(10); NY R L KINGS E FIL Doc. 1(K)(1).

viii. *NEW YORK COUNTY.* It is the responsibility of counsel and parties to comply with rules restricting disclosure of confidential personal information. Nevertheless, NYSCEF screens filings and endeavors to identify any that contain social security numbers. When such numbers are discovered through this process, NYSCEF will restrict portions of or all of such documents from public view. Where NYSCEF has redacted what it believes to be a social security number, it will transmit to the filer a notice advising of the action taken and requesting that the filer review the matter and provide notification as set forth in the notice if the redaction has been made in error. NY R NY CTY E FIL Doc. 2(K)(1); NY R NY CTY J RUL Rule A-1. Documents filed in the past in "secure status" under a procedure no longer in place will retain that status unless otherwise directed by the court. NY R NY CTY E FIL Doc. 2(K)(2).

b. *Submission of confidential personal information.* Where a person submitting a paper to a court for filing believes in good faith that the inclusion of the full confidential personal information described in NY R UNIF TRIAL CTS § 202.5(e)(1) is material and necessary to the adjudication of the action or proceeding before the court, he or she may apply to the court for leave to serve and file together with a paper in which such information has been set forth in abbreviated form a confidential affidavit or affirmation setting forth the same information in unabbreviated form, appropriately referenced to the page or pages of the paper at which the abbreviated form appears. NY R UNIF TRIAL CTS § 202.5(e)(3).

c. *Home addresses.* For information on when home addresses and other personal information must be redacted, refer to NY CPLR Rule 2103-a.

5. *Defective papers.* A defect in the form of a paper, if a substantial right of a party is not prejudiced, shall be disregarded by the court, and leave to correct shall be freely given. NY CPLR Rule 2101(f). Papers that are stapled or bound securely shall not be rejected for filing simply because they are not bound with a backer of any kind. NY R UNIF TRIAL CTS § 202.5(a).

A paper filed in accordance with the rules of the chief administrator or any local rule or practice established by the court shall be deemed filed. NY CPLR Rule 2102(b).

a. *Objection to defective papers.* The party on whom a paper is served shall be deemed to have waived objection to any defect in form unless, within fifteen (15) days after the receipt thereof, the party on whom the paper is served returns the paper to the party serving it with a statement of particular objections. NY CPLR Rule 2101(f).

F. Filing and Service Requirements

1. *Filing requirements.* Except where otherwise prescribed by law or order of court, papers required to be filed shall be filed with the clerk of the court in which the action is triable. In an action or proceeding in supreme or court, papers required to be filed shall be filed with the clerk of the county in which the proceeding is brought. NY CPLR Rule 2102(a).

a. *Furnishing papers to the court.* Each party shall furnish to the court all papers served by him. The moving party shall furnish at the hearing all other papers not already in the possession of the court necessary to the consideration of the questions involved. Where such papers are in the possession of an adverse party, they shall be produced by him at the hearing on notice served with the motion papers. Only papers served in accordance with the provisions of NY CPLR Rule 2214 shall be read in support of, or in opposition to, the motion, unless the court for good cause shall otherwise direct. NY CPLR Rule 2214(c).

i. *Submission to judge.* All papers for signature or consideration of the court shall be presented to the clerk of the trial court in the appropriate courtroom or clerk's office, except that where the clerk is unavailable or the judge so directs, papers may be submitted to the judge and a copy filed with the clerk at the first available opportunity. All papers for any judge that are filed in the clerk's office shall be promptly delivered to the judge by the clerk. The papers shall be clearly addressed to the judge for whom they are intended and prominently show the nature of the papers, the title and index number of the action in which they are filed, the judge's name and the name of the attorney or party submitting them. NY R UNIF TRIAL CTS § 202.5(b).

ii. *BRONX COUNTY: Approval of motions before filing.* All motion papers must be approved by the Motion Support Office, Supreme Court, Civil Term, room 217, before the motion papers are filed and the appropriate fee paid to the County Clerk. NY R BRONX FIL R Doc. 1.

iii. *ERIE COUNTY: Filing motions.* A motion on notice or a notice of petition in a NYSCEF case shall be filed through the NYSCEF system and must be accompanied by a Request for Judicial Intervention if the motion is being filed upon commencement of the action or if the matter has not yet been assigned to an IAS Justice. In addition, cross motions with the appropriate filing fees and opposition and reply papers must be submitted via the NYSCEF system. NY R ERIE E FIL Doc. 3(V)(A).

iv. *NEW YORK COUNTY: Filing hard copies.* Where in the narrow circumstances described by the e-filing rules a motion is made in hard-copy form or opposition papers are submitted in such form in an e-filed case, the hard-copy documents shall be submitted in the same way papers are submitted in non-e-filed cases, except that there shall be firmly affixed to each separate document or group of documents, as the back page facing out, a Notice of Hard Copy Submission—E-Filed Case. NY R NY CTY Procedure II(A). For more information on filing in hard copy cases, refer to NY R NY CTY Procedure II(A).

v. *ONONDAGA COUNTY: Submission of responsive papers and cross-motions.* Cross-motions, opposition and reply papers must be submitted online. NY R ONDGA E FIL Protocol(B)(9)(e). Motions and Orders to Show Cause are assigned a sequence number by the system. Counsel must be sure that cross motions and other filings correspond with the correct sequence number so that a cross motion will not be associated with the wrong original motion. NY R ONDGA E FIL Protocol(B)(9)(f).

b. *Electronic filing.* On consent, documents may be filed and served by electronic means in Supreme Court in such civil actions and in such counties as shall be authorized by order of the Chief Administrator of the Courts and only to the extent and in the manner provided in NY R UNIF TRIAL CTS § 202.5-b. NY R UNIF TRIAL CTS § 202.5-b(a)(1). For the definitions of terms used in electronic filing, refer to NY R UNIF TRIAL CTS § 202.5-b(a)(2).

i. *E-filing mandatory.* In any action subject to e-filing, all documents required to be filed with the court by an e-filing party shall be filed and served electronically, except as provided in NY R UNIF TRIAL CTS § 202.5-b. NY R UNIF TRIAL CTS § 202.5-b(d)(1)(i).

- *ERIE COUNTY.* Case types currently eligible and accepted for e-filing are listed at the NYSCEF website. Note that some actions or special proceedings, (i.e., name changes) which are otherwise subject to mandatory e-filing, if commenced by unrepresented litigants will NOT be maintained in the NYSCEF system; individual cases may be found either at NYSCEF or in the Erie County Clerk's online records system. NY R ERIE E FIL Doc. 3(I)(E).

- *KINGS COUNTY.* Cases that are commenced by filing of the initiating papers with NYSCEF are identified as e-filed cases by assignment of a special index number (i.e., Index Numbers beginning with 500,000). NY R L KINGS E FIL Doc. 1(A)(1). All cases required to be e-filed are listed in Uniform Rule 202.5-bb (Mandatory E-Filing Rules) and on the NYSCEF website. All such cases must be commenced by filing with the County Clerk electronically through NYSCEF and all subsequent documents in such cases must be e-filed. Any questions regarding mandatory e-filing in Kings County can be e-mailed to kcco-efile@nycourts.gov. NY R L KINGS E FIL Doc. 1(A)(2).
- *NEW YORK COUNTY.* Unless otherwise provided in the Rules or in NY R NY CTY E FIL Doc. 2 or where a special exemption is granted due to physical requirements (e.g., oversized maps; see NY R NY CTY E FIL Doc. 2(B)(10)), all documents to be filed with the court in a NYSCEF case, including all documents on motions and all letters to the court (where permitted), must be filed with the NYSCEF system. Documents that attorneys would not ordinarily file with the court in a hard-copy case need not be e-filed. Unless otherwise provided by the E-Filing Rules or this Protocol, in e-filed cases the County Clerk and the court will not accept documents filed in paper form. NY R NY CTY E FIL Doc. 2(B)(1). E-filing is mandatory in all types of cases (other than election law, matrimonial, Art. 78, and Mental Hygiene Law matters, and Art. 70 habeas corpus proceedings) that are commenced in this court on or after February 19, 2013. All such cases must be commenced by filing with the County Clerk electronically through NYSCEF and all subsequent documents in such cases must be e-filed. NY R NY CTY E FIL Doc. 2(A)(2)(a). For more information, including information on consensual e-filing and filing scanned hard copy documents, refer to NY R NY CTY E FIL Doc. 2(A)(2).
- *QUEENS COUNTY.* All authorized Torts, Commercial and Tax Certiorari cases may be commenced by E-Filing, however all parties must consent for the action to continue as an E-file case. NY R L QUEENS E-FILE Doc. 1(A). All papers to be filed with the court in an E-filed case shall be filed on-line with the E-file system except as directed by the court. Papers that attorneys would not ordinarily file with the court in a hard-copy case need not be filed in an E-filed matter. NY R L QUEENS E-FILE Doc. 1(E)(2).

ii. *Who may file.* Documents may be filed or served electronically only by a person who has registered as an authorized e-filing user or as otherwise provided in NY R UNIF TRIAL CTS § 202.5-b(c). NY R UNIF TRIAL CTS § 202.5-b(c)(1).

iii. *When filing made.* Documents may be transmitted at any time of the day or night to the NYSCEF site. A document other than an order or judgment is filed when its electronic transmission or, in the case of a petition that is e-filed by submission of a text file as provided in NY R UNIF TRIAL CTS § 202.5-b(b)(1), the electronic transmission of the text file is recorded at that site, provided, however, that where payment of a fee is required upon the filing of a document, the document is not filed until transmission of the document and the information or form or information as required in NY R UNIF TRIAL CTS § 202.5-b(d)(2)(i), NY R UNIF TRIAL CTS § 202.5-b(d)(2)(ii) or NY R UNIF TRIAL CTS § 202.5-b(d)(2)(iii) has been recorded at the NYSCEF site; or, if no transmission of that information or form or information is recorded, where permitted by the County Clerk, until payment is presented to the County Clerk. NY R UNIF TRIAL CTS § 202.5-b(d)(3)(i).

iv. *Notification of filing.* No later than the close of business on the business day following the electronic filing of a document, a notification, in a form prescribed by the Chief Administrator, shall be transmitted electronically by the NYSCEF site to the person filing such document and the e-mail service addresses of all other participating parties in such action. NY R UNIF TRIAL CTS § 202.5-b(d)(3)(ii).

v. *Removal of confidential information and other corrections.* If a document filed electronically is subsequently discovered to contain confidential data—including but not limited to trade secrets, information protected by confidentiality agreement, or personal confidential information as defined by statute or court rule—or otherwise to have been filed in error, the filer or another party or affected person may (1) notify the parties and any non-party filers in the action of the confidentiality issue or other error raised by the filing, and of his or her intention to seek judicial relief to correct the filing: (2) following such notification, request that the appropriate County Clerk, exercising his or her administrative discretion, place the document temporarily in "restricted" status on the NYSCEF site, to be made available for viewing by court staff and the parties but not the general public; and (3) file an application to correct the filing by order to show cause within five (5) business days of such notification (or such time as the court may direct), including a request for preliminary injunctive relief limiting interim disclosure of the document at issue. Unless otherwise directed by the court, any document placed in restricted status in response to such a request shall be returned to public view upon expiration of this five (5) day

period. The Chief Administrator of the Courts shall promulgate forms to implement this process. NY R UNIF TRIAL CTS § 202.5-b(d)(3)(iii).

- *KINGS COUNTY.* For information on what to do when a document was erroneously filed with confidential information, refer to NY R L KINGS E FIL Doc. 1(B)(11).
- *NEW YORK COUNTY.* For information on what to do when a document was erroneously filed with confidential information, refer to NY R NY CTY E FIL Doc. 2(B)(8).
- *QUEENS COUNTY.* For information on what to do when a document was erroneously filed with confidential information, refer to NY R L QUEENS E-FILE Doc. 1(E)(7).

vi. *Documents requiring judge's signature.* Except where the court directs otherwise, any document that requires a judge's signature shall be transmitted electronically and in hard copy to the court. NY R UNIF TRIAL CTS § 202.5-b(d)(6).

vii. *Documents which would be inconvenient to file electronically; Hard copies.* Notwithstanding any other provision of NY R UNIF TRIAL CTS § 202.5-b, and subject to such guidelines as may be established by the Chief Administrative Judge, the County Clerk or his or her designee may require or permit a party to file in hard copy, in accordance with procedures set by the County Clerk or designee, an exhibit or other document which it is impractical or inconvenient to file electronically. NY R UNIF TRIAL CTS § 202.5-b(d)(7).

- *ERIE COUNTY.* Please contact the Supervisor of Actions & Proceedings, Erie County Clerk's Office by calling (716) 858-6662 or the Deputy County Clerk—Legal at (716) 858-6348 for information. NY R ERIE E FIL Doc. 3(III)(F).
- *KINGS COUNTY.* With limited exceptions, as set forth in the Uniform Rules and herein, all documents to be filed with the court in a NYSCEF case shall be filed online via the NYSCEF system. However, should the size, consistency or context of a hard copy document preclude electronic filing, the user shall electronically file a "Notice of Hard Copy Submission—E-Filed Cases" form EFM-3. Any hard copy submitted pursuant to NY R L KINGS E FIL Doc. 1(B)(9) shall include, as a cover page firmly fastened thereto, a copy of the Confirmation Notice received from the NYSCEF site confirming receipt of the "Notice of Hard Copy Submission—E-Filed Cases". Any party may object to such hard copy filing. The Court, in response to such objection, may, following the hard copy filing, fashion such relief as it deems appropriate pursuant to and in furtherance of the Uniform Rules and NY R L KINGS E FIL Doc. 1, including, but not limited to, an Order directing the filing party to file such documents online via the NYSCEF system. When exhibits are impractical to file pursuant to NY R UNIF TRIAL CTS § 202.5-b(d)(7), an additional "Notice of Hard Copy Exhibit Filing" form EFM-4 is required to be submitted. NY R L KINGS E FIL Doc. 1(B)(9).
- *NEW YORK COUNTY.* If a filer needs to submit unusual exhibits in original form that cannot practically be e-filed, such as oversized maps or electronic recordings, the filer should consult with the County Clerk's E-File Department by telephone at 646-386-3737 (procedural questions only) or by e-mail at ccnyef@nycourts.gov, which will normally require that the filer retain custody of the original subject to possible future directives of the court. NY R NY CTY E FIL Doc. 2(B)(10). In such instances, the filing counsel shall file with NYSCEF a "placeholder" in the form of a Notice of Hard Copy Exhibit Filing (NYSCEF Form EF 21). The Notice should be uploaded to NYSCEF as document type "Exhibit" and the filer should indicate in the "Additional Document Information" field that the filer is retaining custody of the original. Failure to e-file the Notice may result in a gap in the official record of the court. NY R NY CTY E FIL Doc. 2(B)(10).

viii. *Documents containing sensitive or proprietary information.* In an action subject to e-filing, any person may apply for an order prohibiting or restricting the electronic filing in the action of specifically identified materials on the grounds that such materials are subject to copyright or other proprietary rights, or trade secret or other privacy interests, and that electronic filing in the action is likely to result in substantial prejudice to those rights or interests. NY R UNIF TRIAL CTS § 202.5-b(k)(2).

ix. *Refusal to accept paper filings.* In accordance with NY CPLR Rule 2102(c), a County Clerk and a chief clerk of the Supreme Court or County Court, as appropriate, shall refuse to accept for filing papers filed in actions and proceedings when the paper sought to be filed:

- Is in an action subject to electronic filing pursuant to Rules of the Chief Administrator,
- Is not being filed electronically, and

- Does not include the notice required by NY R UNIF TRIAL CTS § 202.5-b(d)(1). NY R UNIF TRIAL CTS § 202.5(d)(1)(v); NY R UNIF TRIAL CTS § 202.5-bb(d).

x. *Emergency filings; Hard copies.* For information on when an emergency filing may be filed and served in hard copy, refer to NY R UNIF TRIAL CTS § 202.5-b(d)(1)(ii), NY R UNIF TRIAL CTS § 202.5-b(d)(1)(iii) and NY R UNIF TRIAL CTS § 202.5-bb(c)(3).

- *KINGS COUNTY.* Under the rules, a participating emergency e-filer must electronically file the documents initially filed in hard copy form within three (3) business days of the emergency filing; the originals will be discarded after the documents have been processed and the failure to e-file as required will therefore lead to an incomplete record. NY R L KINGS E FIL Doc. 1(B)(3).
- *NEW YORK COUNTY.* Occasionally an emergency will arise requiring expedited entry of a document with the County Clerk (e.g., an order issued in the courtroom after a conference or argument of a critical matter), such as for purposes of an immediate appeal. Expedition can be achieved by the Part as follows: the document should be carried by a Court Officer or staff member to the General Clerk's Office to assure immediate and proper recordation in the computer and, as appropriate, the posting of the document to NYSCEF or the Supreme Court Records On-Line Library ("Scroll"). The court will accommodate counsel in emergencies. NY R NY CTY Procedure XI(A).
- *NEW YORK COUNTY.* For more information on how to bring emergency matters before the court, refer to NY R NY CTY Procedure IV.

xi. *Technical failures.* The NYSCEF site shall be considered to be subject to a technical failure on a given day if the site is unable to accept filings or provide access to filed documents continuously or intermittently over the course of any period of time greater than one (1) hour after 12:00 noon of that day. Notice of all such technical failures shall be provided on the site. NY R UNIF TRIAL CTS § 202.5-b(i).

- When e-filing is hindered by a technical failure, a party may file with the appropriate clerk and serve in hard copy. NY R UNIF TRIAL CTS § 202.5-b(i). In the event an attorney or party shall file and serve documents in hard copy pursuant to NY R UNIF TRIAL CTS § 202.5-b(i), each such document shall include the notice required by NY R UNIF TRIAL CTS § 202.5-b(d)(1), and the filer shall file those documents with the NYSCEF site within three (3) business days after restoration of normal operations at that site. NY R UNIF TRIAL CTS § 202.5-b(i).
- With the exception of deadlines that by law cannot be extended, the time for filing of any document that is delayed due to technical failure of the site shall be extended for one (1) day for each day on which such failure occurs, unless otherwise ordered by the court. NY R UNIF TRIAL CTS § 202.5-b(i).
- *ERIE COUNTY.* When filing by electronic means is hindered by a technical failure, please refer to the NY R UNIF TRIAL CTS § 202.5-b(i). NY R ERIE E FIL Doc. 3(III)(K).
- *KINGS COUNTY.* When filing by electronic means is hindered by a NYSCEF technical failure (as set forth in NY R UNIF TRIAL CTS § 202.5-b(i)), a party may file with the appropriate Clerk in hard copy. Except for deadlines that by law cannot be extended (e.g. Statute of limitations, Notice of Appeal), the time for filing of any document that is delayed due to technical failure of the NYSCEF system shall be extended for one day for each day on which such failure occurs, unless otherwise ordered by the court. NY R L KINGS E FIL Doc. 1(B)(13).
- *ONONDAGA COUNTY.* When filing by electronic means is hindered by a technical failure (as set forth in NY R UNIF TRIAL CTS § 202.5-b(h)(3)(i)), a party may file a hard copy with the County Clerk. With the exception of deadlines that by law cannot be extended (e.g., a statute of limitations or the deadline for filing a Notice of Appeal), the time for filing of any document that is delayed due to technical failure of the NYSCEF system will be extended for one day for each day on which such failure occurs, unless otherwise ordered by the court. A "Notice of Hard Copy Filing Submission—E-Filed Case' must accompany any documents not filed via NYSCEF. NY R ONDGA E FIL Protocol(B)(8).

xii. *Filing fees.* For information on what information must be provided to pay filing fees, refer to NY R UNIF TRIAL CTS § 202.5-b(d)(2).

xiii. *Exemption from e-filing.* For information on exemptions from e-filing, refer to NY R UNIF TRIAL CTS § 202.5-bb(e).

xiv. *Filing exhibits*

- *ERIE COUNTY.* In the NYSCEF system, each exhibit must be uploaded as a separate .pdf file. After

uploading a primary document, please choose the document type "Exhibit" and enter the appropriate number or letter and a brief description of the exhibit; each exhibit should bear a separate cover sheet clearly marked as "Exhibit A," "Exhibit B," etc. "Exhibit A" or "Exhibit B" is unacceptable as a brief description of the exhibit. Exhibits, where referenced in a signed Order as attached or affixed shall be uploaded with the signed Order as one .pdf document. NY R ERIE E FIL Doc. 3(III)(H); NY R ERIE E FIL Doc. 3(V)(D).

- *KINGS COUNTY.* In the NYSCEF system, each exhibit should be uploaded as a separate PDF file. After uploading a primary document, please choose the document type "Exhibit", enter the appropriate number or letter, and be sure to place a check mark to the right of "Attach to main document". Each exhibit shall bear a separate cover sheet clearly marked as Exhibit A, Exhibit B, etc. NY R L KINGS E FIL Doc. 1(B)(12). Whenever possible, attorneys submitting exhibits in NYSCEF cases should make each exhibit a separate attachment to an affidavit/affirmation in the system (i.e., multiple exhibits should not be filed as a single PDF). NY R L KINGS E FIL Doc. 1(D)(1).
- *NEW YORK COUNTY.* Attorneys submitting exhibits in NYSCEF cases should make each exhibit a separate attachment to an affidavit/affirmation in the system; i.e., exhibits should not be filed as a single PDF-A together with the affidavit/affirmation or grouped together as a single PDF-A attachment because either of these two formats makes it difficult for the Justice to locate particular exhibits as needed. Counsel must also include appropriate descriptive language in the "Additional Document Information" field in NYSCEF. NY R NY CTY E FIL Doc. 2(D)(6).
- *ONONDAGA COUNTY.* All exhibits in e-filed cases must be e-filed individually as separate attachments. NY R ONDGA E FIL Protocol(B)(9)(b).

xv. *Correcting documents*

- *ERIE COUNTY.* Submission of documents which, upon examination, require correction or addition will result in notification to the filer advising that the document has been returned for correction. The filer shall make the required corrections and/or additions as indicated in the e-mail transmission sent by the County Clerk or Part Clerk through the NYSCEF site. The corrected documents may be resubmitted using the "Re-file this document" link highlighted in the filer's document list for the respective case. Please note that in the case of multiple submissions, all related documents filed at the same time may be removed from the case record and returned until all documents are properly submitted. NY R ERIE E FIL Doc. 3(III)(J).
- *KINGS COUNTY.* Submission of documents which, upon examination, require correction or addition will result in notification to the filer advising that there is a problem with a document. The filer shall make the required corrections and/or additions and resubmit the corrected document using the "Refile this document" link. In the event a document is returned for correction, the original file date will be preserved. For corrections of documents filed with the Kings County Clerk which require a court order, refer to the procedure in NY R UNIF TRIAL CTS § 202.5-b(d)(3)(iii) and NY R L KINGS E FIL Doc. 1(B)(11). NY R L KINGS E FIL Doc. 1(B)(3).
- *ONONDAGA COUNTY.* If there is an error or an additional document is required, the system will notify the filing party, who will make the corrections/additions and resubmit them online. NY R ONDGA E FIL Protocol(B)(6).
- *QUEENS COUNTY.* Generally speaking, documents that have been E-filed will not thereafter be deleted by the County Clerk from NYCEF because the filer asserts that the filing contains an error or a significant omission. When the filer wishes to correct a perceived error or omission in a filed document, he or she should file an amended version of the document, with the original remaining on file, or else obtain a court order providing for deletion of the original. The County Clerk will only delete a document upon request of the filer or on the County Clerk's own initiative when it is obvious from the face of the document alone that the filer made a fundamental error and never intended to file the document that was filed (e.g., a completely unrelated non-litigation document, a different case, or a wrong county). The County Clerk will advise the filer when any such fundamental errors are detected. NY R L QUEENS E-FILE Doc. 1(E)(6).

c. *Facsimile filing.* In the Supreme Court, facsimile filing shall be limited to commercial claims and tax certiorari, conservatorship, and mental hygiene proceedings in Monroe, Westchester, New York and Suffolk Counties. NY R UNIF TRIAL CTS § 202.5-a(a)(1). Refer to NY R UNIF TRIAL CTS § 202.5-a for information on the procedures for facsimile filing.

i. *NEW YORK COUNTY.* Unless indicated otherwise by the court in a particular case or in NY R NY CTY J RUL Doc. 1, Justices do not accept papers by fax. NY R NY CTY J RUL Rule 4.

d. *ERIE COUNTY: Filing request for judicial intervention.* An RJI in a NYSCEF case shall be filed via the NYSCEF system and will be filed after all other documents have been uploaded. The filer may choose between filing a .pdf image of the prepared RJI and any Addendum or having the system prepare the RJI which shall conform to Uniform Rules. Addenda, such as the Commercial Division Addendum, if prepared by the filer must be filed simultaneously with and attached to an RJI and uploaded as one .pdf document with the RJI. If the RJI is prepared by the e-filing system, no separate Addendum is required. Whether or not the filer elects to allow NYSCEF to create the RJI or chooses to upload a prepared RJI, data in addition to the nature of the judicial intervention, including information that appears on any Addenda will be collected through completion of the fields presented. If the filing of the RJI is accomplished through a filing agent, a prepared RJI and Addendum must be filed in lieu of the creation of the RJI by the NYSCEF system, as the RJI must be signed by the attorney. NY R ERIE E FIL Doc. 3(IV). For information on RJIs in specific types of action, refer to NY R ERIE E FIL Doc. 3(IV).

2. *Service requirements*

a. *Who may serve.* Except where otherwise prescribed by law or order of court, papers may be served by any person not a party of the age of eighteen years or over. NY CPLR Rule 2103(a).

b. *Service upon attorney.* Except where otherwise prescribed by law or order of court, papers to be served upon a party in a pending action shall be served upon the party's attorney. Where the same attorney appears for two or more parties, only one (1) copy need be served upon the attorney. Such service upon an attorney shall be made:

i. By delivering the paper to the attorney personally. NY CPLR Rule 2103(b)(1).

ii. By mailing the paper to the attorney at the address designated by that attorney for that purpose or, if none is designated, at the attorney's last known address; service by mail shall be complete upon mailing. NY CPLR Rule 2103(b)(2).

- *BRONX COUNTY.* Service by mail must be within the state. NY R BRONX FIL R Doc. 3.

iii. If the attorney's office is open, by leaving the paper with a person in charge, or if no person is in charge, by leaving it in a conspicuous place; or if the attorney's office is not open, by depositing the paper, enclosed in a sealed wrapper directed to the attorney, in the attorney's office letter drop or box. NY CPLR Rule 2103(b)(3).

iv. By leaving it at the attorney's residence within the state with a person of suitable age and discretion. Service upon an attorney shall not be made at the attorney's residence unless service at the attorney's office cannot be made. NY CPLR Rule 2103(b)(4).

v. By transmitting the paper to the attorney by facsimile transmission, provided that a facsimile telephone number is designated by the attorney for that purpose. Service by facsimile transmission shall be complete upon the receipt by the sender of a signal from the equipment of the attorney served indicating that the transmission was received, and the mailing of a copy of the paper to that attorney. The designation of a facsimile telephone number in the address block subscribed on a paper served or filed in the course of an action or proceeding shall constitute consent to service by facsimile transmission in accordance with NY CPLR Rule 2103(b)(5). An attorney may change or rescind a facsimile telephone number by serving a notice on the other parties. NY CPLR Rule 2103(b)(5).

vi. By dispatching the paper to the attorney by overnight delivery service at the address designated by the attorney for that purpose or, if none is designated, at the attorney's last known address. Service by overnight delivery service shall be complete upon deposit of the paper enclosed in a properly addressed wrapper into the custody of the overnight delivery service for overnight delivery, prior to the latest time designated by the overnight delivery service for overnight delivery. "Overnight delivery service" means any delivery service which regularly accepts items for overnight delivery to any address in the state. NY CPLR Rule 2103(b)(6).

vii. By transmitting the paper to the attorney by electronic means where and in the manner authorized by the chief administrator of the courts by rule and, unless such rule shall otherwise provide, such transmission shall be upon the party's written consent. The subject matter heading for each paper sent by electronic means must indicate that the matter being transmitted electronically is related to a court proceeding. NY CPLR Rule 2103(b)(7).

- *KINGS COUNTY.* Pursuant to the E-Filing Rules, service of interlocutory documents is made by posting a document to the NYSCEF site, which automatically and immediately transmits an email notice of the filing, including a link to the document, to all participating counsel and unrepresented litigants on the case. The Rules also authorize service by other methods permitted by the CPLR. If service by such other method is made, proof of service must be filed with NYSCEF. NY R L KINGS E FIL Doc. 1(I).
- *NEW YORK COUNTY.* Service. . .will be made automatically through NYSCEF upon all participating

counsel and unrepresented parties in the case. There are limited exceptions to the requirement for e-filing in the covered kinds of cases. NY R NY CTY Procedure XI(A). Pursuant to the E-Filing Rules, service of interlocutory documents is made by posting a document to the NYSCEF site, which automatically and immediately transmits an e-mail notice of the filing, including a link to the document, to all participating counsel and unrepresented litigants on the case. The Rules also authorize service by other methods permitted by the CPLR. If service by such a method is made, proof of service must be filed with NYSCEF. NY R NY CTY E FIL Doc. 2(I).

- *QUEENS COUNTY.* Filing with the system permits counsel to serve the papers electronically pursuant to NY R UNIF TRIAL CTS § 202.5-b(f) once consent to E-Filing has been filed on-line. Consult NY R UNIF TRIAL CTS § 202.5-bb(c) for service in mandatory e-filing. Any required proof of service should be E-filed as a separate document. NY R L QUEENS E-FILE Doc. 1(E)(4).

c. *Electronic service mandatory; Consenting to electronic service; How electronic service may be made.* Except as otherwise provided in NY R UNIF TRIAL CTS § 202.5-bb, filing and service of all documents in an action that has been commenced electronically in accordance with NY R UNIF TRIAL CTS § 202.5-bb shall be by electronic means. NY R UNIF TRIAL CTS § 202.5-bb(c)(1).

i. *Party's consent required for certain e-filing.* After commencement of an action wherein e-filing is authorized, documents may be electronically filed and served, but only by, and electronic service shall be made only upon, a party or parties who have consented thereto. NY R UNIF TRIAL CTS § 202.5-b(b)(2)(i).

- A consent to e-filing in an action shall state that the party providing it agrees to the use of e-filing in the action and to be bound by the filing and service provisions in NY R UNIF TRIAL CTS § 202.5-b. NY R UNIF TRIAL CTS § 202.5-b(b)(2)(ii).

ii. *Address for service; Duty to notify as to changes.* The e-mail service address recorded at the time of registration is the e-mail address at which service of interlocutory documents on that party may be made through notification transmitted by the NYSCEF site. It is the responsibility of each filing user to monitor that address and promptly notify the Resource Center in the event of a change in his or her e-mail service address. NY R UNIF TRIAL CTS § 202.5-b(f)(2)(i).

iii. *How service made.* An e-filing party causes service of an interlocutory document to be made upon another party participating in e-filing by filing the document electronically. Upon receipt of an interlocutory document, the NYSCEF site shall automatically transmit electronic notification to all e-mail service addresses in such action. NY R UNIF TRIAL CTS § 202.5-b(f)(2)(ii).

- Except as provided otherwise in NY R UNIF TRIAL CTS § 202.5-b(h)(3), the electronic transmission of the notification shall constitute service of the document on the e-mail service addresses identified therein; however, such service will not be effective if the filing party learns that the notification did not reach the address of the person to be served. Proof of such service will be recorded on the NYSCEF site. A party may, however, utilize other service methods permitted by the CPLR provided that, if one of such other methods is used, proof of that service shall be filed electronically. NY R UNIF TRIAL CTS § 202.5-b(f)(2)(ii).

iv. *Signatures on hard copies; Proof of service filed electronically.* When an e-filing party serves a document in hard copy on a non-participating party, the document served shall bear full signatures of all signatories and proof of such service shall be filed electronically. NY R UNIF TRIAL CTS § 202.5-b(b)(2)(i).

- *ERIE COUNTY.* In the NYSCEF system, each Affidavit of Service must be uploaded as a separate .pdf file. After uploading the Affidavit, please choose the document type: "Affirmation/Affidavit of Service" and enter the name of the party served as Additional Document Information. NY R ERIE E FIL Doc. 3(III)(I); NY R ERIE E FIL Doc. 3(V)(F).

v. *Effect of failure to consent.* A party's failure to consent to participation in electronic filing and service shall not bar any other party to the action from filing documents electronically with the County Clerk and the court or serving documents upon any other party who has consented to participation. A party who has not consented to participation shall file documents with the court and the County Clerk, and serve and be served with documents, in hard copy. NY R UNIF TRIAL CTS § 202.5-b(b)(2)(i).

d. *Service upon party.* If a party has not appeared by an attorney or the party's attorney cannot be served, service shall be upon the party by a method specified in NY CPLR Rule 2103(b)(1), NY CPLR Rule 2103(b)(2), NY CPLR Rule 2103(b)(4), NY CPLR Rule 2103(b)(5) or NY CPLR Rule 2103(b)(6). NY CPLR Rule 2103(c).

e. *Service on all parties.* Each paper served on any party shall be served on every other party who has appeared, except

as otherwise may be provided by court order or as provided in NY CPLR § 3012 or in NY CPLR § 3215(f). Upon demand by a party, the plaintiff shall supply that party with a list of those who have appeared and the names and addresses of their attorneys. NY CPLR Rule 2103(e).

f. *Service by filing.* If a paper cannot be served by any of the methods specified in NY CPLR Rule 2103(b) and NY CPLR Rule 2103(c), service may be made by filing the paper as if it were a paper required to be filed. NY CPLR Rule 2103(d).

g. *Definitions.* For the purposes of NY CPLR Rule 2103:

i. "Mailing" means the deposit of a paper enclosed in a first class postpaid wrapper, addressed to the address designated by a person for that purpose or, if none is designated, at that person's last known address, in a post office or official depository under the exclusive care and custody of the United States Postal Service within the state;

ii. "Electronic means" means any method of transmission of information between computers or other machines designed for the purpose of sending and receiving such transmissions, and which allows the recipient to reproduce the information transmitted in a tangible medium of expression;

iii. "Facsimile transmission" means any method of transmission of documents to a facsimile machine at a remote location which can automatically produce a tangible copy of such documents. NY CPLR Rule 2103(f).

G. Hearings

1. *Oral argument.* Motion papers received by the clerk of the court on or before the return date shall be deemed submitted as of the return date. The assigned judge, in his or her discretion or at the request of a party, thereafter may determine that any motion be orally argued and may fix a time for oral argument. NY R UNIF TRIAL CTS § 202.8(d).

a. A party requesting oral argument shall set forth such request in its notice of motion or in its order to show cause or on the first page of the answering papers, as the case may be. Where all parties to a motion request oral argument, oral argument shall be granted unless the court shall determine it to be unnecessary. NY R UNIF TRIAL CTS § 202.8(d).

b. Where a motion is brought on by order to show cause, the court may set forth in the order that oral argument is required on the return date of the motion. NY R UNIF TRIAL CTS § 202.8(d).

i. *BRONX COUNTY.* All orders to show cause, with the exception of orders to show cause that are returnable in the City Part, the STP Part, the Matrimonial Part and the Preliminary/Compliance Conference Part (IA-11), submitted on or after August 25, 2003, will be returnable on a Monday in the assigned Justice's part and appear on his or her motion calendar. Appearances will be required on orders to show cause. NY R BRONX FIL R Doc. 8. A motion on notice or a notice of petition in a New York Supreme Court E-File (hereafter known as NYSCEF) case, as in others, shall be made returnable in the Motion Support Office (Room 217). NY R BRONX E FIL R Doc. 1(1).

- After a motion/petition and notice are filed with the NYSCEF system, the Motion Support Office will automatically place the motion/proceeding on the submit calendar in the Motion Support Office (Room 217) for the return date. No appearance or other action by the filing attorney is required in order for the motion to be calendared if the motion fee is paid for via NYSCEF. Motions in e-filed cases (other than tax certiorari cases) appear on the submit calendar in Room 217 on the return date. NY R BRONX E FIL R Doc. 1(2).

c. *KINGS COUNTY.* All motions require appearances and oral argument. NY R L KINGS Pt. C, Rule 3.

2. *Return date; Time for hearing.* A notice of motion shall specify the time and place of the hearing on the motion. NY CPLR Rule 2214(a). The moving party determines when a motion on notice shall be heard, but she has to consult the court's or judge's calendar practice first. The movant picks out a "return day" sufficiently far off to assure that the notice requirements of NY CPLR Rule 2214(b) can be met, and to assure as well that the day picked is a day on which the assigned judge hears motions. SIEGEL-NYPRAC § 247.

a. *Judge assigned to hear motion*

i. *Referral to judge supervising disclosure.* Unless the chief administrator of the courts has, by rule, provided otherwise, if a case has been assigned to a judge to supervise disclosure pursuant to NY CPLR § 3104, all motions preliminary to trial shall be referred to such judge whenever practicable. NY CPLR Rule 3214(a).

ii. *Referral to judge who decided prior motion.* Any motion may be referred to a judge who decided a prior motion in the action. NY CPLR Rule 2217(a).

iii. *Transfer when judge unable to hear motion.* If a motion is made to a judge who is or will be for any reason unable

to hear it, it may be transferred by order of such judge or by written stipulation of the parties to any other judge to whom it might originally have been made. NY CPLR Rule 2217(c).

iv. *Procedure for unassigned cases.* If a case has not been assigned to a judge, the motion shall be made returnable before the court, and a copy of the moving papers, together with a request for judicial intervention, shall be filed with the court, with proof of service upon all other parties, where required by NY R UNIF TRIAL CTS § 202.6, within five (5) days of service upon the other parties. The moving party shall give written notice of the index number to all other parties immediately after filing of the papers. NY R UNIF TRIAL CTS § 202.8(b).

- *Responding papers.* Copies of all responding papers shall be submitted to the court, with proof of service and with the index number set forth in the papers, on or before the return date. NY R UNIF TRIAL CTS § 202.8(b).
- *Assignment after request for judicial intervention.* The case shall be assigned to a judge as soon as practicable after the filing of the request for judicial intervention pursuant to NY R UNIF TRIAL CTS § 202.6, but in no event later than the return date. After assignment to the judge, the court shall provide for appropriate notice to the parties of the name of the assigned judge. NY R UNIF TRIAL CTS § 202.8(b).
- *Motions to be heard in another county.* Motion papers noticed to be heard in a county other than the county where the venue of the action has been placed by the plaintiff shall be assigned to a judge in accordance with procedures established by the Chief Administrator. NY R UNIF TRIAL CTS § 202.8(b).

v. *ALBANY COUNTY: Motions referred to IAS Justice.* All motions made after a case has been assigned a day certain shall be referred to the IAS Justice unless the motion is returnable during the term in which the matter has been assigned a day certain, in that event, the matter will be referred to the Part 1 Justice for that particular term who may entertain the motion or refer such motion to the IAS Justice. Under those circumstances, the Part I Justice shall decide whether or not to strike the note of issue or assign the matter a new day certain. NY R 3 JD SUP Doc. 1(H)(2). All motions shall be returnable before the assigned justice. NY R 3 JD SUP Doc. 1(B).

b. *Trial of issue raised by motion.* The court may order that an issue of fact raised on a motion shall be separately tried by the court or a referee. If the issue is triable of right by jury, the court shall give the parties an opportunity to demand a jury trial of such issue. Failure to make such demand within the time limited by the court, or, if no such time is limited, before trial begins, shall be deemed a waiver of the right to trial by jury. An order under NY CPLR § 2218 shall specify the issue to be tried. NY CPLR § 2218.

c. *Audio-visual coverage of trial court proceeding.* Audio-visual coverage of proceedings in the trial courts shall be permitted only in accordance with the provisions of Part 131 of the Rules of the Chief Administrator (NY R CHIEF ADMIN § 131.1, et seq.). NY R CHIEF J § 29.3.

d. *Adjournment of return date.* Stipulations of adjournment of the return date made by the parties shall be in writing and shall be submitted to the assigned judge. Such stipulation shall be effective unless the court otherwise directs. No more than three (3) stipulated adjournments for an aggregate period of sixty (60) days shall be submitted without prior permission of the court. NY R UNIF TRIAL CTS § 202.8(e)(1).

i. Absent agreement by the parties, a request by any party for an adjournment shall be submitted in writing, upon notice to the other party, to the assigned judge on or before the return date. The court will notify the requesting party whether the adjournment has been granted. NY R UNIF TRIAL CTS § 202.8(e)(2).

ii. *BRONX COUNTY.* Non-disclosure motions for IA5, IA7 and IA22 will be adjourned for oral argument to the Monday of the second week following the week of the return date of the motion. All other non-disclosure motions will be deemed submitted on the return date and forwarded to Chambers unless a stipulation of adjournment complying with the requirements of NY R UNIF TRIAL CTS § 202.8(e) is submitted, in which event, the motion will be adjourned for the requested date and kept in the Clerk's Office. If a non-stipulated request for adjournment or notice is submitted, the motion and request will be forwarded to Chambers for judicial approval or denial of the request. In either event, the attorney requesting the adjournment will be notified, via telephone, of the granting or denial of the request and instructed to notify his adversary. NY R BRONX FIL R Doc. 8.

iii. *BRONX COUNTY.* Motions that have been e-filed may be adjourned in Room 217 if an adjournment complies with the procedures of the Motion Support Office (explained in the "Filing Rules—Motion Procedure" section of the "Courthouse Procedures" link on the website of [the] court). An adjournment that so complies may be obtained by filing a stipulation of all parties with NYSCEF (designated in the filing menu as a "Stipulation to Adjourn Motion"). NY R BRONX E FIL R Doc. 1(3).

iv. *NEW YORK COUNTY.* The Courtroom also maintains a "APB (All Papers By)" Calendar, which is used when

a party seeks an adjournment but fails to comply with the Courtroom's procedures or there is a failure to comply with procedures that requires the clerk to adjourn the motion/application (e.g., failure to submit a Confirmation Notice in an e-filed case). The case may be put over for three days to allow compliance with those procedures, as described further below. NY R NY CTY Procedure II(C); NY R NY CTY E FIL Doc. 2(D)(2). E-filed applications may be adjourned in the Part if an adjournment complies with the Part's procedures (see the Uniform Rules of the Justices (Local Rules) on the court's website). An adjournment that so complies may be obtained by filing with NYSCEF a stipulation of all parties (designated in the filing menu as a Stipulation—Adjournment of Motion—Before Judge); the motion number and the current return date of the motion being adjourned shall be set forth in the "Additional Document Information" field in NYSCEF. Absent any problems, the Part will effectuate the adjournment without need for an appearance or any other action by the parties. NY R NY CTY E FIL Doc. 2(D)(4).

v. *QUEENS COUNTY.* The Motion Support Office is NOT authorized to grant adjournments. NY R L QUEENS MOT SUP Doc. 1.

e. *ALBANY COUNTY: Motion terms.* There shall be a. . . Motion Term on each Friday in the Supreme Court, Albany County. The Friday Motion Term shall include all Article 78 Proceedings involving New York State and proceedings commenced pursuant to Article 14 of the Civil Service Law (including applications for injunctive relief made pursuant to section 209-a of the Civil Service Law). NY R 3 JD SUP Doc. 1(F). Generally, parties will be granted only one adjournment for the Friday Motion Term. NY R 3 JD SUP Doc. 1(F).

f. *ALBANY COUNTY: Motion determined without hearing.* All motions are deemed "submitted" on the return date and no appearances are required by the parties. NY R 3 JD SUP Doc. 1(B). In the event oral argument is requested, the parties should not appear on the return date. At the discretion of the assigned Judge and upon the granting of a request for oral argument, the parties will be notified by Chambers of the scheduled time and place at which argument will be heard. Where a motion is brought on by order to show cause, the court may set forth in the order that appearances and/or oral argument are required on the return date of the motion. NY R 3 JD SUP Doc. 1(B).

g. *BRONX COUNTY: Return date.* All assigned and unassigned motions will be returnable five (5) days a week in the Civil Branch Clerk's Office, Room 217, at 9:30 a.m. NY R BRONX FIL R Doc. 8.

i. If on any submitted non-disclosure motion oral argument is requested and granted, or directed by the Court, the motion shall be adjourned for oral argument before the I.A. Judge on the second Monday following the week of the return date of the motion. Attorneys will be notified via telephone of the adjourned date. NY R BRONX FIL R Doc. 8.

h. *BRONX COUNTY: Oral argument.* Calendars of disclosure motions and other motions adjourned for oral argument will be published for the four (4) business days preceding the rescheduled appearance date and on the rescheduled date of the motion. These repetitive publications will serve as the notification of procedure of adjournment of all motions. In addition, two (2) days before the return date of unassigned motions a list of such motions indicating the assigned Justice and the adjourned date of the motion will be published. NY R BRONX FIL R Doc. 8.

i. *BRONX COUNTY: Resolution before return date.* Counsel/parties must advise the Court in writing on or before the return date of all motions that have been resolved by Counsel/parties themselves and all motions the movant(s) wish to be withdrawn. NY R BRONX FIL R Doc. 8.

j. *ERIE COUNTY: Calendaring of motions.* Refer to individual Justice's Part Rules. NY R ERIE E FIL Doc. 3(V)(B).

k. *KINGS COUNTY: Return date set by court.* Irrespective of the return date indicated in the notice of motion, motions will be rescheduled by the E-file/Motion Support Office to a date designated by the assigned Judge. NY R L KINGS Pt. C, Rule 2.

l. *KINGS COUNTY: Calendar calls.* There shall be two (2) calendar calls on motion days. The first calendar call shall be at 9:30 AM and the second calendar call shall be at 10:45 AM, unless the Judge's Part Rules provide otherwise. Defaults shall only be taken on second call. Attorneys with appearances elsewhere in the courthouse may advise the clerk of their whereabouts to avoid a default. Failure to so advise the clerk or appear at the default calendar call will result in a default order being entered or the motion being marked off the calendar. NY R L KINGS Pt. C, Rule 7.

m. *NEW YORK COUNTY: Return date and assigned courtroom.* Motions made by notice of motion and petitions and notices of petition in special proceedings are processed by the General Clerk's Office (Room 119) and are to be made returnable in the Motion Submission Part Courtroom (Room 130) on any business day of the week at 9:30 AM. There are some differences in electronically-filed cases. NY R NY CTY Procedure II; NY R NY CTY Procedure II(C); NY R NY CTY J RUL Rule 13(a).

i. For the convenience of counsel, between 9:00 A.M. and 9:30 A.M. each day, in advance of the "call," Room 130

accepts (1) written stipulations; (2) affidavits/affirmations reciting the required details as to an adjournment on consent; (3) stipulations, letters or other writings withdrawing motions; and (4) final papers or complete sets of papers on motions. For motions in which these items are handed in before the "call," no one need remain to answer the "call." Counsel/parties must advise the court, either between 9:00 A.M. and 9:30 A.M. or at the "call," of all motions or cases that have been resolved by counsel/parties themselves and all motions that the movant no longer wishes to pursue. If such resolution occurs subsequent to the "call", the assigned Justice must be advised as soon as possible, by written notice sent to the Part, so that the court does not do unnecessary work. NY R NY CTY Procedure II(C).

ii. Depending upon the assigned Part, contested motions submitted in the Motion Submission Part Courtroom are submitted without argument, or rescheduled for oral argument if so directed by the assigned Justice. For Justices who schedule argument on a case-by-case basis, notice of the argument date will be transmitted by the court. Counsel may ascertain how a motion submitted in Courtroom 130 was marked by consulting Scroll on the court's website, the e-Track application, or, on the two (2) days immediately following the submission date, the New York Law Journal. NY R NY CTY J RUL Rule 13(a).

n. *NEW YORK COUNTY: Motion call.* Each day in the Motion Submission Part Courtroom, commencing at 9:30 A.M., all motions returnable that day will be "called" for the submission of these papers, which must be handed up at this "call" or, as described below, immediately before. Because hundreds of motions appear on the Room 130 calendars every day, motion papers (other than part of the moving papers as described above) cannot be accepted on any day prior to the return date. Courtesy copies are not required nor accepted, but working copies are required by certain Justices in e-filed cases. NY R NY CTY Procedure II(C). If argument is directed, it will take place on an announced date shortly after the day of submission. NY R NY CTY Procedure II(C).

o. *NEW YORK COUNTY: Oral arguments.* Pursuant to request of some Justices, motions submitted in Room 130 will automatically be scheduled for a set argument date in the Part. Other Justices determine on a case-by-case basis after submission in Room 130 whether to accept a particular substantive motion on submission, to require oral argument, or to hold a conference. NY R NY CTY Procedure II(D). If argument is directed by the Justice automatically, notice of argument and the argument date will be given in Room 130. Any appearing party is expected to give notice to all parties and an announcement to this effect is made in Room 130. If the motion is submitted in Room 130 and the Justice, after examining the file, determines that argument should be directed, notice of the argument and the argument date will not be sent by the court. To obtain notification of the argument date and other developments, counsel should use e-Track. If argument notification is not given or transmitted as just described, counsel should understand that the motion has been taken on submission for decision on the papers. NY R NY CTY Procedure II(D).

i. Calendars of motions to be argued in the Parts are published on the morning of the argument date and on the day before in the New York Law Journal under each Part. Argument information is available on a case-by-case basis in Scroll, and e-mail notifications are sent by e-Track to participating attorneys whenever a motion is scheduled for argument in the court's computer system. NY R NY CTY J RUL Rule 15(a)

p. *NEW YORK COUNTY: Motion determined without hearing.* Given the purpose of the Room 130 procedure, the substance of motions will not be addressed at the submission "call." No Judge is present. To the extent possible, motions submitted in Room 130 will be decided "on the papers." Indeed, attorneys are encouraged to use service or clerks to deliver papers or working copies, or to agree among themselves to have one of them deliver papers for all parties by service or a clerk. Counsel for the movant need not appear to "take a default" on any motion or for any other reason. Motions will be submitted, not marked off, in the absence of the movant. Opposing counsel similarly need not appear in person in order to avoid suffering a default. Delivery of papers by service or a clerk will suffice. The court's goal is to be able to collect papers on motions in an orderly fashion but without any attorney having to make an appearance in Room 130 at any time. NY R NY CTY Procedure II(C).

q. *ONONDAGA COUNTY: Return date.* If the motion is the first filing in an action, the case will be assigned and counsel will be notified by the Supreme Court Clerk's Office via the NYSCEF system of the assigned justice and return date. NY R ONDGA E FIL Protocol(B)(7)(c). If the motion is on a previously assigned case, counsel may choose a return date from the assigned justice's motion term schedule. If the date in unavailable, the Supreme Court Clerk's Office will assign the motion to the next available motion term date and will notify counsel via e-mail. The change will also appear in the notification generated by the NYSCEF system. NY R ONDGA E FIL Protocol(B)(7)(d).

r. *QUEENS COUNTY: Return date.* Motions must be made returnable on the proper day/time based on the assigned judge. NY R L QUEENS MOT SUP Doc. 1. Failure to make a motion returnable on the proper day/time may result in the motion being administratively rescheduled or marked off. NY R L QUEENS MOT SUP Doc. 1.

s. *QUEENS COUNTY: Unassigned motions.* For RJI/Motions, due to the fact that the movant would not know who the

assigned judge will be, the notice of motion may be returnable any day of the week. RJI/Motions shall be made returnable in "Queens Supreme Court" with no address designated. The motion will be administratively rescheduled to the proper day of the week based on the judge (once a judge has been assigned). Within one (1) week of filing, the movant must check online to see who the assigned judge is (and therefore the location/date/time) that their motion is now returnable. Movant must then notify their adversary of this information prior to the return date. NY R L QUEENS MOT SUP Doc. 1.

3. *Entry of order after hearing.* An order determining a motion shall be entered and filed in the office of the clerk of the court where the action is triable, and all papers used on the motion and any opinion or memorandum in writing shall be filed with that clerk unless the order dispenses with such filing. When a statute or civil practice rule requires such filing and entry in a county other than that in which the order was made, the party prevailing on the motion shall file the order and the papers used on the motion with the proper clerk after receiving them. If a party fails to file any papers required to be filed under NY CPLR Rule 2220(a), the order may be vacated as irregular, with costs. NY CPLR Rule 2220(a). For more information on the entry of an order after a motion, refer to NY CPLR Rule 2219.

   a. *BRONX COUNTY: Settled orders.* A Judge's decision will often call for a Settled Order. The purpose of the settled order is to give effect to the decision by directing that some action be done and/or that a court official perform some task. NY R BRONX LEG SUP Doc. 2. A settled order consists of a notice of settlement informing all parties that the proposed order will be presented to the judge who made the decision on a date certain. Next comes the proposed order which will be presented to the judge. This order should conform to the judge's decision and should direct the relief granted in the decision. This should be followed by proof of service upon all parties who were noticed with the decision. It is also helpful if a copy of the judge's decision is included along with the other papers. A settled order should always be noticed before the judge who made the decision. NY R BRONX LEG SUP Doc. 2.

      i. Although an order is usually settled by the party who prevailed on the motion, any party may settle the order. It should be presented to the court within sixty (60) days of the decision. The other parties are entitled to ten (10) days notice where service of the settled order is done by mail, five (5) days if the notice is personally delivered. An attorney who is served with a notice of settlement which he believes does not accurately reflect the decision may settle a counter order. The counter order must be noticed for the same day and must be served not less than seven (7) days if by mail and two (2) days if personally delivered. NY R BRONX LEG SUP Doc. 2.

      ii. Settled orders are usually sent to the judge the day after they noticed for settlement. No appearance is necessary or even contemplated on a settled order. If the decision directs "submit order", then no notice is necessary, and the order will be sent to the judge as soon a practical after it is received. No fees are collected on settled orders. NY R BRONX LEG SUP Doc. 2.

   b. *ERIE COUNTY: Proposed orders.* Proposed orders shall be submitted through the NYSCEF system and a working copy provided to the IAS Justice for signature, if Part Rules so require. NY R ERIE E FIL Doc. 3(V)(G).

   c. *KINGS COUNTY: Long form orders.* If the Court directs that an order be settled or submitted on a motion in a NYSCEF case, the proposed order, with Notice of Settlement where required, and any proposed counter-order shall be filed with the Court via NYSCEF. The relevant clerk's office will process the documents in the customary manner. NY R L KINGS E FIL Doc. 1(E).

      i. WORKING COPIES OF PROPOSED ORDERS WITH NOTICE OF SETTLEMENT MUST BE SUBMITTED IN THE MOTION SUPPORT OFFICE (ROOM 227) AS EXPLAINED HEREIN. THEY MUST NOT BE DELIVERED TO THE PART OR CHAMBERS, EXCEPT WHERE THE INDIVIDUAL JUSTICE'S PART RULES PROVIDE OTHERWISE; DOING SO WILL CAUSE ADMINISTRATIVE CONFUSION AND POSSIBLE MISPLACEMENT OF PAPERS. Any such submission shall be sent in a timely manner (kindly review individual Justice's rules) and be conspicuously marked on the outside "NYSCEF Matter;" lack of such marking may delay processing. After an order/counter-order has been signed, it will be scanned, and the County Clerk will affix the entry stamp into the NYSCEF system, which will immediately transmit notice of this event via e-mail, including a link to the entered document, to all participating attorneys and unrepresented litigants in the case. Such transmittal does not constitute Notice of Entry. NY R L KINGS E FIL Doc. 1(E).

   d. *NEW YORK COUNTY: Long form orders.* Although the court strongly favors the use of short form orders and judgments, there are instances when settlement of an order or judgment is appropriate. When a Justice directs in a decision that a long form order or judgment be settled, that decision is recorded in the court's computer system by the General Clerk's Office and the motion file with decision is held in the Order Section of the Office in Room 119. The settlement process takes place there. NY R NY CTY Procedure II(D); NY R NY CTY E FIL Doc. 2(E).

      i. A proposed long form order or judgment in compliance NY R UNIF TRIAL CTS § 202.48 must be presented to

the relevant back office, together with a notice of settlement which bears a settlement date, the date on which the order is to be ready for formal presentation to the Justice. In an e-filed case the submission shall be made electronically. The proposed order or counter-order should be e-filed and it will be transmitted automatically by the NYSCEF system to the appropriate back office. The return date and time of the proposed order must be at 9:30 A.M. no sooner than either five (5) days from personal service of the proposed order or ten (10) days from service by mail. Proof of timely service on the other parties must accompany the proposed order in a hard copy case. If an order or judgment is submitted late (later than sixty (60) days from signing and filing of the decision) and the proponent can show good cause for this tardiness, an affidavit or affirmation justifying the delay should be annexed to the proposed order, together with proof of service thereof. If persuaded, the Justice will consider the proposed order despite its untimeliness. NY R NY CTY Procedure II(D); NY R NY CTY E FIL Doc. 2(E).

ii. Sometimes a decision will state "Submit Order." The submitting party should prepare a long form order and make it returnable without notice. Counsel should deliver the proposed order to the Order Section of the appropriate back office, except in an e-filed case, when it shall be submitted electronically. NY R NY CTY Procedure II(D). If the decision of the court directs that a proposed order be settled or submitted in the Part or in Chambers, that direction, should, of course, be followed without presentation of the proposal to the back office. NY R NY CTY Procedure II(D).

iii. For information on proposed counter-orders, refer to NY R NY CTY Procedure II(D) and NY R NY CTY J RUL Rule 16(b).

e. *QUEENS COUNTY: Proposed orders.* If the court directs that an order be settled or submitted on a motion in an E-file case, the proposed order and any proposed counter-order shall be filed with the court on-line with proof of service. (If a decision refers to a proceeding on the record, a copy of the transcript must be submitted.) Working copies of all proposed orders MUST be submitted to the Motion Support Office before an order can be reviewed. NY R L QUEENS E-FILE Doc. 1(I).

i. Counsel are advised to adhere to NY R UNIF TRIAL CTS § 202.48 regarding the submission or settlement of their proposed order or judgment. Persons who are submitting proposed orders/judgments pursuant to a previously issued memorandum decision must submit a copy of the memorandum decision with their proposed order/judgment. Upon E-Filing a proposed order/judgement, a working copy of the proposed order/judgement must be provided to the Motion Support Office. NY R L QUEENS MOT SUP Doc. 1.

H. Forms

1. Official Motion for Relief from Judgment Forms for New York

a. Request for judicial intervention. NY R UNIF TRIAL CTS § 202.6.

b. Notice of motion. NY R UNIF TRIAL CTS § 202.7(b).

2. New York Motion for Relief from Judgment Forms

a. Affidavit in support of motion for relief from judgment upon ground of excusable default. MCF CPLR § 8:91.

b. Affidavit in support of motion for relief from judgment upon ground of excusable default; Long form. MCF CPLR § 8:92.

c. Affidavit in support of motion for relief from judgment upon ground of excusable default and fraud. MCF CPLR § 8:94.

d. Affirmation in support of motion for relief from judgment upon ground of excusable default; Law office failure. MCF CPLR § 8:95.

e. Affidavit of officer of plaintiff in support of motion for relief from dismissal of complaint and from judgment entered on counterclaim upon ground of excusable default (containing allegations as to meritorious cause of action). MCF CPLR § 8:96.

f. Affidavit of merits of defendant in support of motion for relief from judgment upon ground of excusable default. MCF CPLR § 8:97.

g. Notice of motion for relief from judgment upon ground that court lacked jurisdiction to render judgment or, alternatively, upon ground of excusable default. MCF CPLR § 8:98.

h. Affidavit of attorney in support of motion for relief from judgment upon ground that court lacked jurisdiction to render judgment or, alternatively, upon ground of excusable default. MCF CPLR § 8:99.

i. Affidavit of defendant in support of motion for relief from judgment upon ground that court lacked jurisdiction to render judgment or, alternatively, upon ground of excusable default. MCF CPLR § 8:100.

j. Notice of motion for relief from judgment upon ground of newly discovered evidence and for new trial. MCF CPLR § 8:105.

k. Affidavit in support of motion for relief from judgment upon ground of newly discovered evidence. MCF CPLR § 8:106.

l. Affidavit in support of motion for relief from judgment upon ground of newly discovered evidence; Long form. MCF CPLR § 8:107.

m. Affidavit of new witness in support of motion for relief from judgment upon ground of newly discovered evidence. MCF CPLR § 8:108.

n. Affirmation in support of motion for relief from judgment upon ground of newly discovered evidence and for a new trial. MCF CPLR § 8:109.

o. Affirmation in support of motion for relief from judgment upon ground of newly discovered evidence and for new trial; Long form. MCF CPLR § 8:110.

p. Affidavit of plaintiff in support of motion for relief from judgment upon ground of newly discovered evidence and for new trial. MCF CPLR § 8:111.

q. Affirmation of physician in support of motion for relief from judgment upon ground of newly discovered evidence and for new trial. MCF CPLR § 8:112.

r. Affidavit in support of motion for relief from judgment upon ground of fraud, misrepresentation, or other misconduct of adverse party. MCF CPLR § 8:117.

s. Affidavit of attorney in support of motion for relief from judgment upon ground of fraud, misrepresentation, or other misconduct of adverse party. MCF CPLR § 8:118.

t. Affidavit of officer of defendant in support of motion for relief from judgment upon ground of fraud, misrepresentation, or other misconduct of adverse party. MCF CPLR § 8:119.

u. Affidavit in support of motion for relief from judgment upon ground that court lacked jurisdiction to render judgment. MCF CPLR § 8:122.

v. Stipulation of consent to vacatur of default judgment. MCF CPLR § 8:125.

w. Notice of motion for restitution after judgment set aside. MCF CPLR § 8:127.

x. Affidavit in support of motion for restitution after judgment set aside. MCF CPLR § 8:128.

y. General form of affidavit of service of motion papers. MCF CPLR § 5:24.

I. Applicable Rules

1. *State rules*

a. Short title; Application; Construction; Definitions. NY CPLR § 101; NY CPLR § 103; NY CPLR § 104; NY CPLR § 105.

b. Appendix of official forms. NY CPLR § 107.

c. Extensions of time generally. NY CPLR § 2004.

d. Form of papers. NY CPLR Rule 2101; NY CPLR Rule 2102; NY CPLR § 2105; NY CPLR Rule 2106; NY GEN BUS § 399-ddd; NY R UNIF TRIAL CTS § 215.2; NY R UNIF TRIAL CTS § 215.3.

e. Service of papers. NY CPLR Rule 2103.

f. Where motion made; In supreme court action. NY CPLR § 2212.

g. Motion papers; Service; Time. NY CPLR Rule 2214.

h. Relief demanded by other than moving party. NY CPLR Rule 2215.

i. Prior motion; Ex parte motion; Transfer of motion; Hearings; Orders. NY CPLR Rule 2217; NY CPLR § 2218; NY CPLR Rule 2220; NY CPLR Rule 2222.

j. Computation of time. NY CPLR § 2402; NY GEN CONSTR § 19; NY GEN CONSTR § 20; NY GEN CONSTR § 25-a; NY GEN CONSTR § 30; NY GEN CONSTR § 31; NY GEN CONSTR § 53.

k. Motions heard by judge supervising disclosure; Stay of disclosure. NY CPLR Rule 3214.

l. Post-trial motion for judgment and new trial. NY CPLR Rule 4404.

m. Relief from judgment or order. NY CPLR Rule 5015.
n. Debt or property subject to enforcement; Proper garnishee. NY CPLR § 5201.
o. Fees; Index number fees of county clerks. NY CPLR § 8018.
p. Hours of court; Proceedings in court. NY R CHIEF J § 3.1; NY R CHIEF J § 29.3.
q. Application of part; Waiver; Additional rules; Application of CPLR; Definitions. NY R UNIF TRIAL CTS § 202.1.
r. Papers filed in court; Electronic filing in supreme court. NY R UNIF TRIAL CTS § 202.5; NY R UNIF TRIAL CTS § 202.5-a; NY R UNIF TRIAL CTS § 202.5-b; NY R UNIF TRIAL CTS § 202.5-bb.
s. Request for judicial intervention. NY R UNIF TRIAL CTS § 202.6.
t. Calendaring of motions; Uniform notice of motion form; Affirmation of good faith. NY R UNIF TRIAL CTS § 202.7.
u. Motion procedure; Preliminary conferences. NY R UNIF TRIAL CTS § 202.8; NY R UNIF TRIAL CTS § 202.12.
v. Rules of the commercial division of the Supreme Court. NY R UNIF TRIAL CTS § 202.70.
w. Signing of papers. NY R CHIEF ADMIN § 130-1.1-a.

2. *Local rules*
   a. *Albany County*
      i. Third judicial district rules. NY R 3 JD SUP Doc. 1.
   b. *Bronx County*
      i. Filing of papers in supreme court. NY R BRONX FIL R Doc. 1.
      ii. Request for judicial intervention. NY R BRONX FIL R Doc. 2.
      iii. Motion procedure. NY R BRONX FIL R Doc. 8.
      iv. Commercial division. NY R BRONX FIL R Doc. 12.
      v. Motions on notice. NY R BRONX E FIL R Doc. 1.
      vi. Settled orders. NY R BRONX LEG SUP Doc. 2.
   c. *Erie County*
      i. Joint protocols for New York State Courts E-Filing (NYSCEF) cases filed in Supreme Court, Erie County. NY R ERIE E FIL Doc. 3.
   d. *Kings County*
      i. Papers. NY R L KINGS Pt. A, Papers.
      ii. Service of motion papers. NY R L KINGS Pt. C, Rule 1.
      iii. Scheduling of motions. NY R L KINGS Pt. C, Rule 2.
      iv. Appearance and argument. NY R L KINGS Pt. C, Rule 3.
      v. Courtesy copies. NY R L KINGS Pt. C, Rule 5.
      vi. Motion calendar calls. NY R L KINGS Pt. C, Rule 7.
      vii. Protocol on courthouse and county clerk procedures for electronically filed cases. NY R L KINGS E FIL Doc. 1.
   e. *New York County*
      i. Commencement of cases. NY R NY CTY Procedure I.
      ii. RJIs and assignments. NY R NY CTY Procedure IA.
      iii. Motions and special proceedings by notice of motion/petition. NY R NY CTY Procedure II.
      iv. County clerk litigation functions. NY R NY CTY Procedure XI.
      v. Protocol on courthouse and county clerk procedures for electronically filed cases. NY R NY CTY E FIL Doc. 2.
      vi. Redaction of information in documents filed with the county clerk and the court. NY R NY CTY J RUL Rule A-1.
      vii. Papers by fax. NY R NY CTY J RUL Rule 4.

viii. Motions on notice; Orders to show cause. NY R NY CTY J RUL Rule 13.

ix. Motion papers. NY R NY CTY J RUL Rule 14.

x. Oral argument; Adjournments. NY R NY CTY J RUL Rule 15.

f. *Onondaga County*

i. Onondaga county protocol for case filings New York State Electronic Files (NYSCEF). NY R ONDGA E FIL Protocol.

g. *Queens County*

i. Motion support office. NY R L QUEENS MOT SUP Doc. 1.

ii. Queens county protocol on courthouse procedures for electronically filed cases. NY R L QUEENS E-FILE Doc. 1.

J. Miscellaneous

NOTE: Individual judges' rules may apply.

ALBANY COUNTY

JUSTICE LISA M. FISHER: NY R 3 JD FISHER Fisher; NY R 3 JD FISHER Fisher, PC Order.

JUSTICE RICHARD MOTT: NY R 3 JD MOTT Mott.

JUSTICE STEPHAN G. SCHICK: NY R 3 JD Schick.

FORECLOSURE SETTLEMENT PART: NY R 3 JD Foreclosure Settlement.

BRONX COUNTY

JUSTICE PAUL L. ALPERT: [NY R BRONX J Part IA-29, as amended by NY ORDER 20-0337].

JUSTICE BEN BARBATO: NY R BRONX J Part IA-21.

JUSTICE MARY ANNE BRIGANTTI: [NY R BRONX J Part IA-15, as amended by NY ORDER 20-0338].

JUSTICE JOSEPH E. CAPELLA: NY R BRONX J Part IA-23.

JUSTICE MITCHELL DANZIGER: NY R BRONX J Part IA-3/33 ; [NY R BRONX J Danziger, Part IA-3/33, as amended by NY ORDER 20-0339].

JUSTICE LAURA G. DOUGLAS: NY R BRONX J Part IA-11.

JUSTICE RUBEN FRANCO: NY R BRONX J Part IA-26.

JUSTICE DORIS M. GONZALEZ: NY R BRONX J Part IA-24.

JUSTICE WILMA GUZMAN: NY R BRONX J Part IA-7; [NY R BRONX J Guzman, Part IA-7 Virtual, as amended by NY ORDER 20-0340].

JUSTICE ROBERT T. JOHNSON: NY R BRONX J Part IA-12.

JUSTICE DONALD A. MILES: NY R BRONX J Part IA-8.

JUSTICE DONNA M. MILLS: NY R BRONX J Part IA-9.

JUSTICE JULIA I. RODRIGUEZ: NY R BRONX J Part IA-18; [NY R BRONX J Part IA-27, as amended by NY ORDER 20-0341].

JUSTICE LLINET M. ROSADO: [NY R BRONX J Part IA-25, as amended by NY ORDER 20-0342].

JUSTICE NORMA RUIZ: NY R BRONX J Part IA-22; [NY R BRONX J Ruiz, Part IA-22 Virtual, as amended by NY ORDER 20-0343].

JUSTICE HOWARD H. SHERMAN: NY R BRONX J Part IA-4.

JUSTICE FERNANDO TAPIA: NY R BRONX J Part IA-13.

JUSTICE ELIZABETH A. TAYLOR: NY R BRONX J Part IA-2.

JUSTICE ALISON Y. TRUITT: NY R BRONX J Part IA-5.

PART IDV: NY R BRONX J Doc. 1.

PRE-TRIAL PART RULES: NY R BRONX J Doc. 2.

PRE TRIAL WORKSHEET: NY R BRONX J Doc. 3.

FORECLOSURE SETTLEMENT PART RULES: NY R BRONX J Doc. 4.
GUARDIANSHIP PART RULES: NY R BRONX J Doc. 5.
LPM PART RULES: NY R BRONX J Doc. 6.

ERIE COUNTY

JUSTICE M. WILLIAM BOLLER: NY R 8 JD J Boller.
JUSTICE RALPH A. BONIELLO: NY R 8 JD J Boniello.
JUSTICE CHRISTOPHER J. BURN: NY R 8 JD J Burns.
JUSTICE RUSSELL P. BUSCAGLIA: NY R 8 JD J Buscaglia.
JUSTICE FRANK CARUSO: NY R 8 JD J Caruso.
JUSTICE STEPHEN W. CASS: NY R 8 JD J Cass.
JUSTICE DEBORAH A. CHIMES: NY R 8 JD J Chimes.
JUSTICE EMILIO COLAIACOVO: [NY R 8 JD J Colaiacovo, as amended by NY ORDER 20-0252].
JUSTICE DIANE Y. DEVLIN: NY R 8 JD J Devlin.
JUSTICE JAMES H. DILLON: NY R 8 JD J Dillon.
JUSTICE PAULA L. FEROLETO: NY R 8 JD J Feroleto.
JUSTICE DANIEL J. FURLONG: [NY R 8 JD J Furlong, as amended by NY ORDER 20-0253].
JUSTICE JOSEPH R. GLOWNIA: NY R 8 JD J Glownia.
JUSTICE MARK J. GRISANTI: NY R 8 JD J Grisanti.
JUSTICE DEBORAH A. HAENDIGES: NY R 8 JD J Haendiges.
JUSTICE LYNN W. KEANE: [NY R 8 JD J Keane, as amended by NY ORDER 20-0254].
JUSTICE RICHARD C. KLOCH, Sr.: NY R 8 JD J Kloch.
JUSTICE FREDERICK J. MARSHALL: [NY R 8 JD J Marshall, as amended by NY ORDER 20-0255.
JUSTICE JOHN L. MICHALSKI: NY R 8 JD J Michalski.
JUSTICE MARK A. MONTOUR: [NY R 8 JD J Montour, as amended by NY ORDER 20-0256].
JUSTICE HENRY NOWAK: NY R 8 JD J Nowak.
JUSTICE JOHN F. O'DONNELL: NY R 8 JD J O'Donnell.
JUSTICE JEANETTE OGDEN: NY R 8 JD J Ogden.
JUSTICE CATHERINE NUGENT-PANEPINTO: NY R 8 JD J Nugent-Panepinto.
JUSTICE FRANK A. SEDITA, III: [NY R 8 JD J Sedita, as amended by NY ORDER 20-0257].
JUSTICE SARA SHELDON: NY R 8 JD J Sheldon.
JUSTICE DONNA M. SIWEK: NY R 8 JD J Siwek.
JUSTICE MARY L. SLISZ: NY R 8 JD J Slisz.
JUSTICE TIMOTHY J. WALKER: [NY R 8 JD J Walker, as amended by NY ORDER 20-0258].
JUSTICE DENNIS E. WARD: NY R 8 JD J Ward.
JUSTICE PAUL B. WOJTASZEK: [NY R 8 JD J Wojtaszek, as amended by NY ORDER 20-0259].
JUSTICE CHARLES N. ZAMBITO: [NY R 8 JD J Zambito, as amended by NY ORDER 20-0260].
SUPREME COURT LEGAL STAFF: NY R 8 JD J Legal Staff.

KINGS COUNTY

JUSTICE RACHEL A. ADAMS: NY R KINGS J Part 5F.
JUSTICE LOREN BAILY-SCHIFFMAN: NY R KINGS J Part 65.
JUSTICE REGINALD A. BODDIE: NY R KINGS J Part 95.
JUSTICE THERESA M. CICCOTTO: NY R KINGS J Part 19; NY R KINGS J Part 5J.

JUSTICE LISSETTE COLON: NY R KINGS J Part Rules.
JUSTICE GENINE EDWARDS: NY R KINGS J Part 80.
JUSTICE PAMELA L. FISHER: [NY R KINGS J Part 94, as amended by NY ORDER 20-0208].
JUSTICE ROBIN GARSON: NY R KINGS J Part 75.
JUSTICE LARA J. GENOVISI: [NY R KINGS J Part 34, as amended by NY ORDER 20-0209].
JUSTICE BERNARD J. GRAHAM: NY R KINGS J Part 36.
JUSTICE DAWN JIMENEZ-SALTA: NY R KINGS J Part 88.
JUSTICE INGRID JOSEPH: [NY R KINGS J Part FRP3 and Part 83, as amended by NY ORDER 20-0210].
JUSTICE KATHY J. KING: NY R KINGS J Part 64, 76K.
JUSTICE LAWRENCE KNIPEL: NY R KINGS J Part 57.
JUSTICE DONALD KURTZ: NY R KINGS J Part 26.
JUSTICE CARL LANDICINO: [NY R KINGS J Part 81, as amended by NY ORDER 20-0211].
JUSTICE KATHERINE LEVINE: [NY R KINGS J Part 20, 25, 92, as amended by NY ORDER 20-0211].
JUSTICE LORNA MCALLISTER: [NY R KINGS J Part 10, as amended by NY ORDER 20-0211].
JUSTICE ROSEMARIE MONTALBANO: [NY R KINGS J Part 19, 71, and 22, as amended by NY ORDER 20-0211].
JUSTICE RICHARD J. MONTELIONE: [NY R KINGS J Part 99 and DJMP, as amended by NY ORDER 20-0215].
JUSTICE LISA S. OTTLEY: NY R KINGS J Part 24.
JUSTICE MARK I. PARTNOW: NY R KINGS J Part 43.
JUSTICE ERIC I. PRUS: NY R KINGS J Part 5A.
JUSTICE FRANCOIS RIVERA: NY R KINGS J Part 52.
JUSTICE KAREN B. ROTHENBERG: NY R KINGS J Part 35.
JUSTICE LEON RUCHELSMAN: NY R KINGS J Part 1.
JUSTICE WAYNE P. SAITTA: NY R KINGS J Part 29.
JUSTICE ROBIN K. SHEARES: NY R KINGS J Part 96.
JUSTICE KENNETH P. SHERMAN: NY R KINGS J Part 67 and 78.
JUSTICE DEBRA SILBER: NY R KINGS J Part 9 and 5K.
JUSTICE ELLEN M. SPODEK: NY R KINGS J Part 63.
JUSTICE MARSHA L. STEINHARDT: NY R KINGS J Part 15.
JUSTICE JEFFREY S. SUNSHINE: NY R KINGS J Part 5G.
JUSTICE PETER P. SWEENEY: [NY R KINGS J Part 35, as amended by NY ORDER 20-0218].
JUSTICE DELORES J. THOMAS: [NY R KINGS J Part 5T, as amended by NY ORDER 20-0221].
JUSTICE WAVNY TOUSSAINT: NY R KINGS J Part 70.
JUSTICE RICHARD VELASQUEZ: NY R KINGS J Part 66.
JUSTICE CAROLYN E. WADE: NY R KINGS J Part 84.
JUSTICE EDWARD G. WALKER: [NY R KINGS J Part 90, as amended by NY ORDER 20-0219].
JUSTICE LILLIAN WAN: [NY R KINGS J Part 17, as amended by NY ORDER 20-0220].
JUSTICE MICHELLE WESTON: NY R KINGS J Part 3.
MENTAL HYGIENE PART: NY R KINGS J Part 77.
MATRIMONIAL PARTS DURING COVID-19 EMERGENCY: JUSTICE KAREN B. ROTHENBERG: NY R KINGS J Doc. 1.

NASSAU COUNTY

JUSTICE ANNA R. ANZALONE: NY R NASSAU S J Anzalone, Part 26.
JUSTICE STACY D. BENNETT: NY R NASSAU S J Bennett; NY R NASSAU S J Bennett, Form 1.

JUSTICE ANTONIO BRANDVEEN: NY R NASSAU S J Brandveen, Part 31.

JUSTICE JEFFREY S. BROWN: [NY R NASSAU S J Brown, as amended by NY ORDER 20-0297].

JUSTICE STEPHEN A. BUCARIA: NY R NASSAU S J Bucaria.

JUSTICE JULIANNE T. CAPETOLA: NY R NASSAU S J Capetola, Part 28.

JUSTICE EDMUND M. DANE: NY R NASSAU S J Dane, Part 33.

JUSTICE VITO M. DESTEFANO: NY R NASSAU S J DeStefano, Part 13; NY R NASSAU S J DeStefano, Form 1.

JUSTICE ARTHUR M. DIAMOND: NY R NASSAU S J Diamond, Part 7.

JUSTICE THOMAS FEINMAN: NY R NASSAU S J Feinman, Part 5.

JUSTICE JOHN M. GALASSO: NY R NASSAU S J Galasso, Part 22.

JUSTICE SHARON M.J. GIANELLI: NY R NASSAU S J Gianelli, Part 22; NY R NASSAU S J Gianelli, Form 1.

JUSTICE JEFFREY A. GOODSTEIN: NY R NASSAU S J Goodstein, Part 33; NY R NASSAU S J Goodstein, Form 1.

JUSTICE DAVID J. GUGERTY: [NY R NASSAU S J Gugerty, Part 31, as amended by NY ORDER 20-0298].

JUSTICE HELENE F. GUGERTY: NY R NASSAU S J Gugerty, Part 47.

JUSTICE STEVEN M. JAEGER: NY R NASSAU S J Jaeger, Part 35; NY R NASSAU S J Jaeger, Form 1.

JUSTICE JACK L. LIBERT: NY R NASSAU S J Libert, Part 23.

JUSTICE JOSEPH H. LORINTZ: NY R NASSAU S J Lorintz, Part 26; NY R NASSAU S J Lorintz, Form 1.

JUSTICE ROY S. MAHON: NY R NASSAU S J Mahon, Part 3.

JUSTICE RANDY SUE MARBER: NY R NASSAU S J Marber, Part 8.

JUSTICE JAMES P. MCCORMACK: [NY R NASSAU S J McCormack, Part 18, as amended by NY ORDER, 20-0299].

JUSTICE DICCIA T. PINEDA-KIRWAN: [NY R NASSAU S J Pineda-Kirwan, as amended by NY ORDER 20-0300].

JUSTICE THOMAS RADEMAKER: [NY R NASSAU S J Rademaker, Part 28, as amended by NY ORDER 20-0301]; [NY R NASSAU S J Rademaker, Form 1, as amended by NY ORDER 20-0301].

JUSTICE DENISE L. SHER: NY R NASSAU S J Rademaker, Part 32.

JUSTICE LEONARD D. STEINMAN: [NY R NASSAU S J Steinman, Part 15, as amended by NY ORDER 20-0303]; NY R NASSAU S J Steinman, Form 1.

JUSTICE HOWARD E. STURIM: NY R NASSAU S J Sturim, Part 50; NY R NASSAU S J Sturim, Form 1.

JUSTICE HELEN VOUTSINAS: [NY R NASSAU S J Voutsinas, Part 25, as amended by NY ORDER 20-0304]; [NY R NASSAU S J Voutsinas, Form 1, as amended by NY ORDER 20-0305].

JUSTICE HOPE SCHWARTZ ZIMMERMAN: NY R NASSAU S J Zimmerman, Part 17.

NEW YORK COUNTY

JUDGE'S RULES; BASIC INFORMATION: [NY R NY CTY J RUL Doc. 1, as amended by NY ORDER 20-0202].

ONONDAGA COUNTY

JUSTICE ROBERT E. ANTONACCI II: [NY R ONDGA E FIL Doc. 1, as amended by 20-0239].

JUSTICE MICHAEL V. COCCOMI: NY R ONDGA E FIL Doc. 2.

JUSTICE GREGORY R. GILBERT: NY R 5 JD JUDGES Gilbert; NY R ONDGA E FIL Doc. 3.

JUSTICE DONALD A. GREENWOOD: NY R ONDGA E FIL Doc. 4.

JUSTICE DEBORAH H. KARALUNAS: NY R ONDGA E FIL Doc. 5.

JUSTICE JAMES MCCLUSKY: NY R 5 JD MCCLUSKY McClusky.

JUSTICE CHARLES C. MERRELL: NY R 5 JD MERRELL Merrell.

JUSTICE PATRICK F. MACRAE: NY R 5 JD MACRAE Doc. 1.

JUSTICE JAMES P. MURPHY: NY R ONDGA E FIL Doc. 7.

JUSTICE GERALD J. NERI: [NY R 5 JD JUDGES Neri, as amended by NY ORDER 20-0236]; [NY R ONDGA E FIL Doc. 8, as amended by NY ORDER 20-0241].

JUSTICE ANTHONY J. PARIS: NY R 5 JD JUDGES Paris; [NY R ONDGA E FIL Doc. 9, as amended by NY ORDER 20-0242].

JUSTICE NORMAN W. SEITER, JR.: NY R 5 JD JUDGES Seiter.

JUSTICE KEVIN G. YOUNG: [NY R ONDGA E FIL Doc. 10, as amended by NY ORDER 20-0243].

QUEENS COUNTY

JUSTICE PAM JACKMAN BROWN: [NY R L QUEENS Brown, Part 19, as amended by NY ORDER 20-0321].

JUSTICE CHEREE A. BUGGS: NY R L QUEENS Buggs, Part 30.

JUSTICE PAM JACKMAN BROWN: [NY R L QUEENS Brown, Part 19, as amended by NY ORDER 20-0321].

JUSTICE DENIS J. BUTLER: NY R L QUEENS Butler, Part 12.

JUSTICE ROBERT I. CALORAS: [NY R L QUEENS Caloras, Part 36, as amended by NY ORDER 20-0322].

JUSTICE ANNA CULLEY: NY R L QUEENS Culley, Part 53.

JUSTICE TIMOTHY DUFFICY: NY R L QUEENS Dufficy, Part 35.

JUSTICE DAVID ELLIOT: NY R L QUEENS Elliot, Part 14.

JUSTICE JOSEPH J. ESPOSITO: NY R L QUEENS Esposito, Part 6.

JUSTICE DARRELL L. GAVRIN: [NY R L QUEENS Gavrin, Part 27, as amended by NY ORDER 20-0323].

JUSTICE WYATT N. GIBBONS: [NY R L QUEENS Gibbons, Part 5, as amended by NY ORDER 20-0330.

JUSTICE DONNA-MARIE E. GOLIA: [NY R L QUEENS Golia, Part 21, as amended by NY ORDER 20-0331].

JUSTICE MARGUERITE A. GRAYS: [NY R L QUEENS Grays, Part 4, as amended by NY ORDER 20-0324].

JUSTICE RUDOLPH E. GRECO: [NY R L QUEENS Greco, Part 32, as amended by NY ORDER 20-0325].

JUSTICE MAUREEN HEALY: NY R L QUEENS Healy, Part 6.

JUSTICE PHILLIP HOM: [NY R L QUEENS Hom, Part 43, as amended by NY ORDER 20-0332].

JUSTICE KEVIN J. KERRIGAN: NY R L QUEENS Kerrigan, Part 10.

JUSTICE MOJGAN C. LANCMAN: NY R L QUEENS Lancman, Part 20.

JUSTICE RICHARD G. LATIN: NY R L QUEENS Latin, Part 40.

JUSTICE ULYSSES B. LEVERETT: [NY R L QUEENS Leverett, Part 6, as amended by NY ORDER 20-0326].

JUSTICE LEONARD LIVOTE: NY R L QUEENS Livote, Part 33.

JUSTICE LEE A. MAYERSOHN: NY R L QUEENS Mayersohn, Part 22; NY R L QUEENS Mayersohn, Part 22G; [NY R L QUEENS Mayersohn, Part 22G COVID, as amended by NY ORDER 20-0327].

JUSTICE ROBERT J. MCDONALD: NY R L QUEENS McDonald, Part 34.

JUSTICE MARGARET MCGOWAN: NY R L QUEENS McGowan, Part 52.

JUSTICE MAURICE E. MUIR: [NY R L QUEENS Muir, Part 42, as amended by NY ORDER 20-0333].

JUSTICE JODI ORLOW: NY R L QUEENS Orlow, Part 51.

JUSTICE LESLIE J. PURIFICCION: NY R L QUEENS Purificcion, Part 39.

JUSTICE JOSEPH RISI: [NY R L QUEENS Risi, Part 3, as amended by NY ORDER 20-0328].

JUSTICE FREDERICK D.R. SAMPSON: [NY R L QUEENS Sampson, Part 31, as amended by NY ORDER 20-0329].

JUSTICE MARTIN J. SCHULMAN: NY R L QUEENS Schulman, Part 29.

JUSTICE BERNICE D. SIEGAL: NY R L QUEENS Siegal, Part 25G.

JUSTICE JANICE A. TAYLOR: NY R L QUEENS Taylor, Part 15.

JUSTICE CARMEN R. VELASQUEZ: NY R L QUEENS Velasquez, Part 38.

JUSTICE LOURDES M VENTURA: [NY R L QUEENS Ventura, Part 37, as amended by NY ORDER 20-0334].

JUSTICE WILLIAM A. VISCOVICH: NY R L QUEENS Viscovich, Part 63.

JUSTICE ALLAN B. WEISS: NY R L QUEENS Weiss, Part 2.

COMPLIANCE, SETTLEMENT AND CONFERENCE PART: NY R L QUEENS Doc 1.

PRELIMINARY CONFERENCE PART: [NY R L QUEENS Doc. 2, as amended by NY ORDER 20-0335].
MEDICAL MALPRACTICE CONFERENCE PART: [NY R L QUEENS Doc. 3, as amended by NY ORDER 20-0336].
TRIAL SCHEDULING PART: NY R L QUEENS Doc. 4.
SUMMARY JURY TRIAL PROGRAM: NY R L QUEENS Doc. 7.
RESIDENTIAL FORECLOSURE PART: NY R L QUEENS Doc. 9.
FORECLOSURE AUCTION RULES: NY R L QUEENS Doc. 10.
MATRIMONIAL PRELIMINARY CONFERENCE PART: NY R L QUEENS Doc. 11.
NON-CUSTODIAL CONTESTED MATRIMONIAL PART: NY R L QUEENS Doc. 12.

Motions, Oppositions and Replies
Motion for Judgment as a Matter of Law or New Trial

Document Last Updated August 2020

A. Checklist

(I) ❑ Matters to consider for moving party
- (a) ❑ Required documents
  - (1) ❑ Notice of motion, order to show cause, or affidavit on ex parte motion
  - (2) ❑ Motion
  - (3) ❑ Request for judicial intervention
  - (4) ❑ Proof of service
- (b) ❑ Supplemental documents
  - (1) ❑ Supporting evidence; Exhibits
  - (2) ❑ Brief
  - (3) ❑ Notice to produce papers not in possession of the court
  - (4) ❑ Filing fees
  - (5) ❑ Working copies
  - (6) ❑ ERIE COUNTY: Additional supplemental documents
    - (i) ❑ Notice of hard copy submission in e-filed case
  - (7) ❑ KINGS COUNTY: Additional supplemental documents
    - (i) ❑ Forms when filing in hard copy
  - (8) ❑ NEW YORK COUNTY: Additional supplemental documents
    - (i) ❑ Notice of hard copy submission
    - (ii) ❑ Unpublished opinions
  - (9) ❑ ONONDAGA COUNTY: Additional supplemental documents
    - (i) ❑ Notice of hard copy submission
  - (10) ❑ QUEENS COUNTY: Additional supplemental documents
    - (i) ❑ Notice of hard copy submission
- (c) ❑ Timing
  - (1) ❑ Any party may move for judgment with respect to a cause of action or issue upon the ground that the moving party is entitled to judgment as a matter of law, after the close of the evidence presented by an opposing party with respect to such cause of action or issue, or at any time on the basis of admissions
  - (2) ❑ A motion under Article 44 of the CPLR (NY CPLR Rule 4401, et seq.) shall be made within fifteen (15) days after decision, verdict or discharge of the jury

(3) ❑ The moving party shall serve copies of all affidavits and briefs upon all other parties at the time of service of the notice of motion

(4) ❑ A notice of motion and supporting affidavits shall be served at least eight (8) days before the time at which the motion is noticed to be heard

(5) ❑ It is also good practice to make motions returnable at least three (3) weeks away from the planned date of mailing and to always include a demand in the motion that the other side serve answering papers at least seven (7) days before the return day

(6) ❑ BRONX COUNTY: Additional timing

(i) ❑ A Notice of Motion must be served at least eight (8) days, by personal service, nine (9) days by overnight express and thirteen (13) days by mail before the return date

(7) ❑ NEW YORK COUNTY: Additional timing

(i) ❑ In an e-filed case, all of the moving papers shall be e-filed at least eight (8) business days prior to the return date

(8) ❑ ONONDAGA COUNTY: Additional timing

(i) ❑ Onondaga County local court rules require that any additional papers relating to motions must be e-filed at least two (2) business days prior to the return date, excluding the return date

(9) ❑ QUEENS COUNTY: Additional timing

(i) ❑ Motions must be in the possession of the Motion Support Office at least nine (9) days before the noticed return date of the motion

(II) ❑ Matters to consider for opposing party

(a) ❑ Required documents

(1) ❑ Opposition

(2) ❑ Proof of service

(b) ❑ Supplemental documents

(1) ❑ Supporting evidence; Exhibits

(2) ❑ Brief

(3) ❑ Filing fees

(4) ❑ Working copies

(5) ❑ ERIE COUNTY: Additional supplemental documents

(i) ❑ Notice of hard copy submission in e-filed case

(6) ❑ KINGS COUNTY: Additional supplemental documents

(i) ❑ Forms when filing in hard copy

(7) ❑ NEW YORK COUNTY: Additional supplemental documents

(i) ❑ Notice of hard copy submission

(ii) ❑ Unpublished opinions

(8) ❑ ONONDAGA COUNTY: Additional supplemental documents

(i) ❑ Notice of hard copy submission

(9) ❑ QUEENS COUNTY: Additional supplemental documents

(i) ❑ Notice of hard copy submission

(c) ❑ Timing

(1) ❑ Answering affidavits shall be served at least two (2) days before the time at which the motion is noticed to be heard

(2) ❑ Answering affidavits and any notice of cross-motion, with supporting papers, if any, shall be served at least seven (7) days before such time if a notice of motion served at least sixteen (16) days before such time so demands

B. Timing

1. *Time to bring motion for judgment as a matter of law or new trial.* Any party may move for judgment with respect to a cause of action or issue upon the ground that the moving party is entitled to judgment as a matter of law, after the close of the evidence presented by an opposing party with respect to such cause of action or issue, or at any time on the basis of admissions. NY CPLR Rule 4401.

   a. *Time to bring motion after trial.* A motion under Article 44 of the CPLR (NY CPLR Rule 4401, et seq.) shall be made within fifteen (15) days after decision, verdict or discharge of the jury. The court shall have no power to grant relief after argument or submission of an appeal from the final judgment. NY CPLR Rule 4405.

   b. *Motion for new trial after report of advisory jury.* Upon the motion of any party or on his own initiative, the judge required to decide the issue may confirm or reject, in whole or in part, the verdict of an advisory jury or the report of a referee to report; may make new findings with or without taking additional testimony; and may order a new trial or hearing. The motion shall be made within fifteen (15) days after the verdict or the filing of the report and prior to further trial in the action. Where no issues remain to be tried the court shall render decision directing judgment in the action. NY CPLR Rule 4403.

2. *Time to serve.* The moving party shall serve copies of all affidavits and briefs upon all other parties at the time of service of the notice of motion. NY R UNIF TRIAL CTS § 202.8(c). A notice of motion and supporting affidavits shall be served at least eight (8) days before the time at which the motion is noticed to be heard. NY CPLR Rule 2214(b).

   a. *Return dates; Best practice.* It is also good practice to make motions returnable at least three (3) weeks away from the planned date of mailing and to always include a demand in the motion that the other side serve answering papers at least seven (7) days before the return day. This enables the motion to be served by mail, gives sufficient notice to support the seven (7) day demand, and leaves a few days for a delayed mailing if some snag prevents posting on the day planned. If speed is needed, the shorter eight (8) day notice period can be used, forfeiting the right to seven (7) day answering papers and a reply. If even eight (8) days notice is too much under the circumstances, the order to show cause is the remedy. SIEGEL-NYPRAC § 247.

      i. *ALBANY COUNTY.* All motions, except for certain matters in Albany County as specified in NY R 3 JD SUP Doc. 1(E) and NY R 3 JD SUP Doc. 1(F), brought on by notice of motion or by order to show cause will be made returnable on any day, Monday through Friday, as chosen by the movant in compliance with the CPLR. Parties shall submit all papers in a timely fashion as required by the CPLR by delivering them or mailing them directly to the Supreme Court Clerk's Office[. . .]except that motions and other applications subject to a filing fee shall first be presented to the County Clerk's Office for payment of the requisite fee and then subsequently filed with the Supreme Court Clerk's Office. NY R 3 JD SUP Doc. 1(B).

      ii. *BRONX COUNTY.* A Notice of Motion must be served at least eight (8) days, by personal service, nine (9) days by overnight express and thirteen (13) days by mail before the return date. NY R BRONX FIL R Doc. 3. All unassigned motions must be accompanied with a properly filled out RJI and shall be filed in the Motion Support Office, room 217, within five (5) days of service. All motions on actions already assigned to a Justice must be filed at least five (5) business days before the return date. NY R BRONX FIL R Doc. 3. All papers served must strictly comply with the time requirements of NY CPLR Rule 2101, NY CPLR Rule 2103 and NY CPLR Rule 2214(b). NY R BRONX FIL R Doc. 8.

      iii. *KINGS COUNTY.* Motion papers, answering affidavits and reply affidavits must be served on adversaries in accordance with NY CPLR Rule 2214. NY R L KINGS Pt. C, Rule 1.

      iv. *NEW YORK COUNTY.* In an e-filed case, all of the moving papers shall be e-filed at least eight (8) business days prior to the return date. The clerk will calendar the motion for the Motion Submission Part Courtroom (Room 130) for the return date selected. NY R NY CTY Procedure II(A); NY R NY CTY E FIL Doc. 2(D)(1).

      v. *ONONDAGA COUNTY.* Onondaga County local court rules require that any additional papers relating to motions must be e-filed at least two (2) business days prior to the return date, excluding the return date. NY R ONDGA E FIL Protocol(B)(9)(e).

      vi. *QUEENS COUNTY.* Motions must be in the possession of the Motion Support Office at least nine (9) days before the noticed return date of the motion. NY R L QUEENS MOT SUP Doc. 1; NY R L QUEENS E-FILE Doc. 1(H)(1).

   b. *Order to show cause; Shorter time.* The court in a proper case may grant an order to show cause, to be served in lieu of a notice of motion, at a time and in a manner specified therein. NY CPLR Rule 2214(d). An ordinary notice of motion can't be brought on for hearing earlier than the eighth (8th) day after the motion papers are served. With an order to show cause, the hearing can be brought on at any time the court directs, which can be fewer than eight (8) days or as close as the very day on which it is signed. If the court is convinced there is a real emergency, it can schedule the hearing for a few hours later or, in the direst case, "forthwith" the service of the order to show cause. SIEGEL-NYPRAC § 248.

c. *Time to serve answering affidavits; Other answering papers.* Answering affidavits shall be served at least two (2) days before the time at which the motion is noticed to be heard. Answering affidavits and any notice of cross-motion, with supporting papers, if any, shall be served at least seven (7) days before such time if a notice of motion served at least sixteen (16) days before such time so demands; whereupon any reply or responding affidavits shall be served at least one (1) day before such time. NY CPLR Rule 2214(b); NY R UNIF TRIAL CTS § 202.8(c).

   i. *BRONX COUNTY.* All answering papers must be submitted to the Clerk 's Office on the return date of the motion. Answering papers will not be accepted prior to the return date. NY R BRONX FIL R Doc. 8.

   ii. *NEW YORK COUNTY.* Cross-motions, papers in opposition, and reply papers on motions/petitions on notice returnable in Room 130 in a hard-copy case shall be submitted to the Motion Submission Part Courtroom (Room 130) on the final return date of the motion/petition and will not be accepted until that date. Subsequent documents on motions/petitions in e-filed cases shall be e-filed in a timely manner. Working copies when required shall be submitted to Room 130 on the final return date. NY R NY CTY Procedure II(A).

d. *Time to serve cross-motion.* At least three (3) days prior to the time at which the motion is noticed to be heard, or seven (7) days prior to such time if demand is properly made pursuant to NY CPLR Rule 2214(b), a party may serve upon the moving party a notice of cross-motion demanding relief, with or without supporting papers; provided, however, that:

   i. If such notice and any supporting papers are served by mailing, as provided in NY CPLR Rule 2103(b)(2), they shall be served three (3) days earlier than as prescribed in NY CPLR Rule 2215; and

   ii. If served by overnight delivery, as provided in NY CPLR Rule 2103(b)(6), they shall be served one (1) day earlier than as prescribed in NY CPLR Rule 2215. Relief in the alternative or of several different types may be demanded; relief need not be responsive to that demanded by the moving party. NY CPLR Rule 2215(a); NY CPLR Rule 2215(b).

   iii. *BRONX COUNTY.* Cross motions may be presented for approval on or before the return date, provided that there is a motion already calendared. NY R BRONX FIL R Doc. 8.

   iv. *ERIE COUNTY.* Cross-motions must be filed at least two (2) days before the return date of the motion. NY R L KINGS Pt. A, Papers.

   v. *KINGS COUNTY.* Hard copies are required to be filed for any motions, answering papers, stipulations, etc. for E-Filed cases returnable in [the Central Compliance Part] at least [two (2)] days before return date. . . .for cross motions. NY R L KINGS Pt. E, Rule 8.

   vi. *QUEENS COUNTY.* Motion Support does not process or forward responsive papers, including cross-motions. They must be brought to the calendar call in the judge's part. NY R L QUEENS MOT SUP Doc. 1. E-filed cross motions: across motion must be noticed for the same return date as the main motion and have the confirmation of filing attached in the same manner as a motion. NY R L QUEENS E-FILE Doc. 1(H)(2)(e).

3. *Filing before return date.* All motions shall be returnable before the assigned judge, and all papers shall be filed with the court on or before the return date. NY R UNIF TRIAL CTS § 202.8(a).

   a. *BRONX COUNTY: Time for filing*

      i. *Unassigned motions.* Unassigned motions must be in the Clerk's Office within five (5) days of the date of service of the motion. NY R BRONX FIL R Doc. 8.

      ii. *Assigned motions.* Assigned motions must be filed in the Clerk's Office not less than five (5) business days prior to the return date of the motion. NY R BRONX FIL R Doc. 8.

      iii. *Motions returnable in room 217.* The moving documents must be e-filed no later than eight (8) days prior to the return date. NY R BRONX E FIL R Doc. 1(1).

   b. *KINGS COUNTY: Time and place of filing.* Motion papers must be filed with the E-file/Motion Support Office located in Room 227. . . at 360 Adams Street at least five (5) business days before the return date of the motion. NY R L KINGS Pt. A, Papers. Hard copies are required to be filed for any motions, answering papers, stipulations, etc. for E-Filed cases returnable in [the Central Compliance Part] at least five (5) days before return date for main motions. NY R L KINGS Pt. E, Rule 8. The moving documents must be e-filed no later than eight (8) days prior to the return date. NY R L KINGS E FIL Doc. 1(D).

4. *NEW YORK COUNTY: Briefing schedule.* Once a motion is made, counsel for all parties are strongly encouraged to agree upon a briefing schedule and submit a stipulation of adjournment reflecting that schedule using service or a clerk. Where a briefing schedule has not been agreed upon, the movant can avoid the need to attend simply to see if anyone will hand up opposing papers by demanding papers as provided by NY CPLR Rule 2214(b). To protect movants against the submission of late opposition papers or cross-motions, the General Clerk's Office will screen motions in which such papers are submitted without a response (reply or opposition respectively) to ensure that proper time to respond has been afforded and it will sua sponte adjourn for one (1) week cases in which such time has not been given. NY R NY CTY Procedure II(C).
5. *QUEENS COUNTY: Time to pay fees.* As motions and petitions are time sensitive, if opting to pay at the County Clerk's Office payment MUST be made, if filed with an RJI, a minimum of nine (9) business days prior to the application's return date and if filed post RJI, a minimum of nine (9) business days prior to the application's return date. NY R L QUEENS E-FILE Doc. 1(H)(1).
6. *Computation of time*
    a. *Units of time*
        i. *Day.* A calendar day includes the time from midnight to midnight. Sunday or any day of the week specifically mentioned means a calendar day. NY GEN CONSTR § 19.
        ii. *Month.* In a statute, contract or public or private instrument, unless otherwise provided in such contract or instrument or by law, the term month means a calendar month and not a lunar month. NY GEN CONSTR § 31.
        iii. *Year.* For information on the definition of a year, including the definitions of a half-year and quarter-year, refer to NY GEN CONSTR § 58 and NY GEN CONSTR § 50. For information on leap years, refer to NY GEN CONSTR § 57.
    b. *Periods of time*
        i. *Number of days.* A number of days specified as a period from a certain day within which or after or before which an act is authorized or required to be done means such number of calendar days exclusive of the calendar day from which the reckoning is made. NY GEN CONSTR § 20.
            - If such period is a period of two (2) days, Saturday, Sunday or a public holiday must be excluded from the reckoning if it is an intervening day between the day from which the reckoning is made and the last day of the period. NY GEN CONSTR § 20.
            - In computing any specified period of time from a specified event, the day upon which the event happens is deemed the day from which the reckoning is made. The day from which any specified period of time is reckoned shall be excluded in making the reckoning. NY GEN CONSTR § 20.
        ii. *Number of months.* A number of months after or before a certain day shall be computed by counting such number of calendar months from such day, exclusive of the calendar month in which such day occurs, and shall include the day of the month in the last month so counted having the same numerical order in days of the month as the day from which the computation is made, unless there be not so many days in the last month so counted, in which case the period computed shall expire with the last day of the month so counted. NY GEN CONSTR § 30.
        iii. *Publication of notice; Number of days.* The period of publication of a legal notice shall be computed by excluding the first day of publication and including the day on which the act or event of which notice is given is to take place or which completes the full period of publication. NY CPLR § 2402.
        iv. *Periods ending on Saturday, Sunday or public holiday.* When any period of time, computed from a certain day, within which or after which or before which an act is authorized or required to be done, ends on a Saturday, Sunday or a public holiday, such act may be done on the next succeeding business day and if the period ends at a specified hour, such act may be done at or before the same hour of such next succeeding business day, except that where a period of time specified by contract ends on a Saturday, Sunday or a public holiday, the extension of such period is governed by NY GEN CONSTR § 25. NY GEN CONSTR § 25-a(1).
            - For a list of public holidays, refer to NY GEN CONSTR § 24.
        v. *Additional time after certain kinds of service*
            - *Service by mail.* Where a period of time prescribed by law is measured from the service of a paper and service is by mail, five (5) days shall be added to the prescribed period. NY CPLR Rule 2103(b)(2).
            - *Service by overnight delivery service.* Where a period of time prescribed by law is measured from the

service of a paper and service is by overnight delivery, one (1) business day shall be added to the prescribed period. NY CPLR Rule 2103(b)(6).

vi. *Daylight saving time.* For information on New York's time zone and the effect of daylight saving time, refer to NY GEN CONSTR § 52.

c. *Hours of court.* Notwithstanding any provision of law or rule of court to the contrary, throughout the State of New York the sessions of the Supreme Court for the disposition of business before the court shall commence not later than 9:30 a.m. and conclude not earlier than 5 p.m. Where warranted, the Chief Administrator of the Courts may authorize variances in the opening and closing hours of the courts, but, in such event, daily sessions shall total not less than six (6) hours. NY R CHIEF J § 3.1.

d. *Time limits; Extension of time.* Any act required by or in pursuance of law to be performed at or within a prescribed time, shall be performed according to the standard time. NY GEN CONSTR § 53.

i. Except where otherwise expressly prescribed by law, the court may extend the time fixed by any statute, rule or order for doing any act, upon such terms as may be just and upon good cause shown, whether the application for extension is made before or after the expiration of the time fixed. NY CPLR § 2004. Refer to the New York KeyRules Motion for Continuance/Extension of Time document for more information.

C. General Requirements

1. *Motions, generally.* There shall be compliance with the procedures prescribed in the CPLR for the bringing of motions. NY R UNIF TRIAL CTS § 202.7(a).

a. *Motions on notice.* A notice of motion shall specify the time and place of the hearing on the motion, the supporting papers upon which the motion is based, the relief demanded and the grounds therefor. NY CPLR Rule 2214(a). A motion on notice in an action in the supreme court shall be noticed to be heard in the judicial district where the action is triable or in a county adjoining the county where the action is triable. Unless statute, civil practice rule or local court rule provides otherwise, the motion shall be noticed to be heard before a motion term or, upon order to show cause granted by a justice, before that justice out of court. NY CPLR § 2212(a). Except as provided in NY R UNIF TRIAL CTS § 202.7(d), no motion shall be filed with the court unless there have been served and filed with the motion papers a notice of motion. NY R UNIF TRIAL CTS § 202.7(a)(1).

b. *Ex parte motions.* A motion in an action in the supreme court that may be made without notice may be made at a motion term or to a justice out of court in any county in the state. NY CPLR § 2212(b).

i. *KINGS COUNTY.* For more information on submitting a motion ex parte, refer to NY R L KINGS E FIL Doc. 1(G).

ii. *NEW YORK COUNTY.* For more information on submitting matters ex parte, refer to NY R NY CTY Procedure III and NY R NY CTY E FIL Doc. 2(G).

iii. *QUEENS COUNTY.* For more information on submitting matters ex parte, refer to NY R L QUEENS EX PARTE Doc. 1.

c. *Alternative relief.* Relief in the alternative or of several different types may be demanded. NY CPLR Rule 2214(a). The types of relief need not be related. In one motion, for example, the defendant can seek to dismiss the plaintiff's claim for lack of jurisdiction, to get an extension of time to answer, to require the plaintiff to join X as a party, and to quash a disclosure subpoena served in behalf of the plaintiff on a nonparty witness. So doing, the movant must of course specify all of these items of relief in the notice of motion, and the grounds for them, and the supporting papers must contain the entire proof requisite to the items of relief sought. NY CPLR Rule 2214(Practice Commentary, C2214:4).

d. *General relief.* It is common practice to include at the end of the relief request in the notice of motion a so-called "general relief" clause. This is merely a few words to cover the possibility that the relief appropriate to what the movant proves was not specifically asked for, but is close enough to enable the court to grant it. After stating the specific relief desired, the lawyer will often add something like: and for such other, further, or different relief as this court may deem just and proper. NY CPLR Rule 2214(Practice Commentary, C2214:5).

e. *Motion in improper form.* If the court finds it appropriate in the interests of justice, it may convert a motion into a special proceeding, or vice-versa, upon such terms as may be just, including the payment of fees and costs. NY CPLR § 103(c).

f. *Order to show cause.* An order to show cause is basically only a substitute for a notice of motion. An ordinary notice of motion merely notifies the recipient that a motion is being made for specified relief. The burden of proof is on the movant. Although in most cases it is just as innocent as an ordinary notice of motion, the order to show cause gets its name by directing the recipient to "show cause" why the particular relief being asked for should not be granted. It sounds as if the burden of proof is being shifted to the recipient. It isn't. It specifies the time and place of the hearing on the application but when the hearing comes on, the burden of proof is where it always is on a motion: on the movant. SIEGEL-NYPRAC § 248.

i. The CPLR says nothing more about an order to show cause than that it may be used "in a proper case", which leaves it entirely to the judge's discretion to determine what a proper case is. Any fact suggesting a problem as to any of the items listed above would be sufficient to invoke judicial discretion and justify the show cause procedure, which is in fact liberally used. SIEGEL-NYPRAC § 248.

ii. An order to show cause against a state body or officers must be served in addition to service upon the defendant or respondent state body or officers upon the attorney general by delivery to an assistant attorney general at an office of the attorney general in the county in which venue of the action is designated or if there is no office of the attorney general in such county, at the office of the attorney general nearest such county. NY CPLR Rule 2214(d).

iii. *BRONX COUNTY.* For information on submitting an order to show cause, refer to NY R BRONX E FIL R Doc. 2 and NY R BRONX LEG SUP Doc. 1.

iv. *ERIE COUNTY.* For information on submitting an order to show cause, refer to NY R ERIE E FIL Doc. 3(VI).

v. *KINGS COUNTY.* For information on submitting an order to show cause, refer to NY R L KINGS E FIL Doc. 1(F).

vi. *NEW YORK COUNTY.* For information on submitting an order to show cause, refer to NY R NY CTY E FIL Doc. 2(F).

vii. *ONONDAGA COUNTY.* For information on submitting an order to show cause, refer to NY R ONDGA E FIL Protocol(B)(10) and NY R ONDGA E FIL Protocol(J).

g. *Motions before preliminary conference.* Motions in actions to which NY R UNIF TRIAL CTS § 202.12 is applicable made after the preliminary conference has been scheduled may be denied unless there is shown good cause why such relief is warranted before the preliminary conference is held. NY R UNIF TRIAL CTS § 202.12(h).

h. *ALBANY COUNTY: Good faith effort to resolve.* Prior to the submission of a notice of motion relating to disclosure or a bill of particulars, the parties must make a good faith effort to resolve the matter in question and submit an affirmation attesting to this good faith effort. NY R 3 JD SUP Doc. 1(B).

i. *NEW YORK COUNTY: Documents with motions.* Counsel must attach to motion papers copies of all pleadings and other documents as required by the CPLR and as necessary for an informed decision on the motion. Documents in a foreign language shall be properly translated. NY R NY CTY J RUL Rule 14(a).

j. *NEW YORK COUNTY: Motions in multiple cases made together.* On occasion, attorneys may wish to make a motion in more than one case on a single set of papers. In such cases, by definition consolidation will not have been directed since consolidation signifies the combination of more than one case into a single one with a single caption and index number and ending in a single judgment. NY R NY CTY Procedure II(B). For more information on motions made with the same papers, refer to NY R NY CTY Procedure II(A).

k. *QUEENS COUNTY: Motion sequence numbers.* A motion sequence number is required for all E-filed motions. After a motion is E-filed, please consult the e-courts website within twenty-four (24) to forty-eight (48) hours to obtain the sequence number. The Confirmation Notice of E-filing MUST indicate the sequence number of any motion submitted at the Centralized Motion Part calendar call. NY R L QUEENS E-FILE Doc. 1(H)(5).

2. *Motion for judgment as a matter of law or new trial*

a. *Single post-trial motion.* In addition to motions made orally immediately after decision, verdict or discharge of the jury, there shall be only one motion under Article 44 of the CPLR (NY CPLR Rule 4401, et seq.) with respect to any decision by a court, or to a verdict on issues triable of right by a jury; and each party shall raise by the motion or by demand under NY CPLR Rule 2215 every ground for post-trial relief then available to him. NY CPLR Rule 4406.

b. *Judge to whom motion made.* A motion under Article 44 of the CPLR (NY CPLR Rule 4401, et seq.) shall be made before the judge who presided at the trial. NY CPLR Rule 4405.

c. *Judgment as a matter of law generally.* Any party may move for judgment with respect to a cause of action or issue upon the ground that the moving party is entitled to judgment as a matter of law. Grounds for the motion shall be specified. The motion does not waive the right to trial by jury or to present further evidence even where it is made by all parties. NY CPLR Rule 4401. The main motion authorized by this provision is better known to the bar as the motion for a "directed verdict." That terminology is still used, but in official CPLR parlance today, it is simply a motion for "judgment as a matter of law" under NY CPLR Rule 4401. SIEGEL-NYPRAC § 402.

i. *Judgment sought during trial.* As a general and salutary rule, the courts prefer to deny NY CPLR Rule 4401 motions during the trial in deference to the NY CPLR Rule 4404 motion after it. SIEGEL-NYPRAC § 402.

- *Standard for granting motion.* The judge may grant the motion, which of course takes the case out of the jury's hands, only when convinced that the jury could not find for the other party by any rational process; when, in support of the party against whom it proposes to order judgment, the court can find "no evidence and no substantial inferences"; when reasonable minds reacting to the evidence could not differ and would have to conclude just one way. SIEGEL-NYPRAC § 402; Prince v. City of New York, 21 A.D.2d 668, 668, 250 N.Y.S.2d 107, 108 (1964); African Metals Corp. v. Bullowa, 288 N.Y. 78, 81, 41 N.E.2d 466, 468 (1942); Cesario v. Chiapparine, 21 A.D.2d 272, 275, 250 N.Y.S.2d 584, 588 (1964).
- *Procedure on motion; Evidence.* The court must accept as true all of the evidence offered by the party against whom the motion for judgment aims, and must even resolve in that party's favor all questions relating to the credibility of witnesses. SIEGEL-NYPRAC § 402; Hurder v. Samuel Kosoff & Sons, Inc., 23 A.D.2d 804, 804, 258 N.Y.S.2d 1, 2 (1965).
- *Medical malpractice; Failure to prove insufficiency of consent.* A motion for judgment at the end of the plaintiff's case must be granted as to any cause of action for medical malpractice based solely on lack of informed consent if the plaintiff has failed to adduce expert medical testimony in support of the alleged qualitative insufficiency of the consent. NY CPLR § 4401-a.
- *Granting of motion; Res judicata.* There is a tie-in between NY CPLR Rule 4401 and NY CPLR Rule 5013. The latter provides that a dismissal against a plaintiff before the close of the plaintiff's evidence is not on the merits (which means that a dismissal made at that point will not bar a fresh suit), while a dismissal after the close of the plaintiff's evidence does qualify as a merits determination (which would subject a new action to the defense of res judicata). SIEGEL-NYPRAC § 402; NY CPLR Rule 5013. The juncture at which NY CPLR Rule 4401 authorizes its main motion for judgment is therefore a juncture at which, if the motion is granted, the movant will ordinarily draw the added advantage of the res judicata doctrine. SIEGEL-NYPRAC § 402.
- *Court's discretion to give res judicata effect to early motion.* The court does have power to provide otherwise, however, i.e., to give res judicata effect to a dismissal made before the close of the plaintiff's evidence or to deprive of res judicata effect a dismissal made after it. SIEGEL-NYPRAC § 402; NY CPLR Rule 5013. Whether the court will exercise this discretionary power depends on the state of the evidence. SIEGEL-NYPRAC § 402. If the dismissal is based, for example, on a failure of proof that the plaintiff may yet be able to come up with, the dismissal after the close of plaintiff's case should be without prejudice, i.e., not on the merits. SIEGEL-NYPRAC § 402; Harsco Corp. v. Rodolitz Realty Corp., 61 Misc. 2d 644, 652, 307 N.Y.S.2d 531, 539 (Sup. Ct. 1969). But if there is no indication that curative proof exists, the dismissal at that stage should not be qualified and should thus be left to stand as a judgment on the merits. SIEGEL-NYPRAC § 402; Hansen v. City of New York, 274 A.D. 196, 200, 80 N.Y.S.2d 249, 253 (App. Div. 1948), aff'd, 299 N.Y. 136, 85 N.E.2d 905 (1949).

ii. *Motion based on admissions*

- While a motion for judgment based on admissions is authorized "at any time", one must today be circumspect about what will satisfy as an admission for this purpose. The courts are justifiably reticent about putting an abrupt end to a case—after it has survived all the pretrial stages and at last arrived at trial—before the parties have put in their evidence. The motion for judgment based on admissions will therefore be granted only when counsel "deliberately and intentionally states or admits some fact that in any view of the case is fatal to the action," and counsel obviously does not make a habit of that. SIEGEL-NYPRAC § 402; Hoffman House v. Foote, 172 N.Y. 348, 351, 65 N.E. 169, 169 (1902).
- The admissions should be of a kind intended as the virtual equivalent of a pleading rather than some mere evidentiary statement that the party is not precluded from contradicting with other evidence. SIEGEL-NYPRAC § 402; Martin Fireproofing Corp. v. Maryland Cas. Co., 45 Misc. 2d 354, 358—59, 257 N.Y.S.2d 100, 105 (Sup. Ct. 1965), aff'd, 26 A.D.2d 910, 275 N.Y.S.2d 375 (1966). A formal admission made under NY CPLR § 3123, if sufficient to warrant judgment against the admitter as a matter of law, should suffice, but it is tactically unlikely that the opposing party—who would presumably have initiated and secured the

admission during the pretrial stage—would have saved the admission to use on a dispositive motion at the trial when she could have used it to ground a summary judgment motion under NY CPLR Rule 3212 long before. SIEGEL-NYPRAC § 402.

- Much of the caselaw on this phase of NY CPLR Rule 4401 involves the plaintiff's opening to the jury and whether counsel made some fatal admission during it. The complaint will not be dismissed on the opening statement, however, unless it plainly appears that there is really no issue of fact holding the case up; that taking as true every fact the plaintiff alleges and resolving in the plaintiff's favor every fact the defendant disputes, the plaintiff has no case. SIEGEL-NYPRAC § 402; Runkel v. City of New York, 282 A.D. 173, 175, 123 N.Y.S.2d 485, 487 (App. Div. 1953). An admission in the opening that amounts to nothing more than an immaterial variance from the complaint or bill of particulars, or even from a deposition, will not ground a dismissal. SIEGEL-NYPRAC § 402. An authoritative case on this matter said that a dismissal based on the plaintiff's opening to the jury has to be reserved for a most unique case; that a strong general rule exists against so narrowly based a dismissal. SIEGEL-NYPRAC § 402; De Vito v. Katsch, 157 A.D.2d 413, 416, 556 N.Y.S.2d 649, 652 (1990).

iii. *Judgment sought after trial.* A party may move for judgment n.o.v. after the verdict without having moved for judgment before it. One is not a condition precedent to the other. Still, a party who loses the verdict and wants judgment n.o.v. is in a more consistent position if she can show that she moved for judgment as a matter of law before the jury retired. SIEGEL-NYPRAC § 405.

- A party may make an NY CPLR Rule 4404 motion after the trial even though he made no NY CPLR Rule 4401 motion during it. One is not a condition precedent to the other. SIEGEL-NYPRAC § 405.
- If the court finds the verdict to be against the "weight of the evidence", it orders a new trial rather than directing judgment for the opposing party. This is a long recognized alternative for the court when it sets aside a verdict on a post-trial motion under NY CPLR Rule 4404(a). SIEGEL-NYPRAC § 405.

d. *New trial generally*

i. *Motion made during trial.* At any time during the trial, the court, on motion of any party, may order a new trial in the interest of justice on such terms as may be just. NY CPLR Rule 4402. If the defect is something that does not induce jury bias and is curable by a mere adjournment, a new trial is not necessary under NY CPLR Rule 4402 and a mere continuance will be ordered. SIEGEL-NYPRAC § 403.

- Which if any step to take depends on the defect to be remedied and perhaps even on whether it was inadvertent or contrived. Inadvertent and unobtrusive mentions of the existence of insurance in a personal injury case, for example, have been held curable by a mere instruction, while a deliberate attempt by the plaintiff to show that insurance exists or by the defendant to show that it does not will necessitate a new trial before a new jury. SIEGEL-NYPRAC § 403; Ismail v. City of New York, 18 Misc. 2d 818, 825, 181 N.Y.S.2d 848, 855 (Sup. Ct. 1959); Rendo v. Schermerhorn, 24 A.D.2d 773, 773, 263 N.Y.S.2d 743, 744 (1965).
- Misconduct that may necessitate a new trial is not restricted to that of a party or lawyer. The intemperate comments or conduct of a judge, for example, suggesting the judge's prejudice against a party or cause, will require a new trial and may even occasion an appellate reprimand. SIEGEL-NYPRAC § 403; Habenicht v. R.K.O. Theatres, Inc., 23 A.D.2d 378, 381, 260 N.Y.S.2d 890, 891 (1965). The misconduct of a juror will do the same, as where a juror walks the plaintiff home during the trial and assures her that everything will be okay. SIEGEL-NYPRAC § 403; Campbell v. Towber, 46 Misc. 2d 891, 893, 261 N.Y.S.2d 458, 460 (Sup. Ct. 1965).
- There are no arbitrary limits on the trial judge's power to declare a mistrial. Whatever the source of the prejudicial conduct, if it deprives an innocent party of a fair trial, the court can make it the basis of a mistrial. SIEGEL-NYPRAC § 403.
- The use of the words "on motion of any party" in NY CPLR Rule 4402 indicates that a mistrial may not be granted by the court sua sponte. Instances exist, however, in which the court has done that, and as a practical matter there is no cure for it if it is done before the verdict is rendered: there is no verdict to reinstate and a new trial is necessary anyway. SIEGEL-NYPRAC § 403; Jaworski v. New Cassel Fuel Corp., 21 A.D.2d 753, 251 N.Y.S.2d 929, 930 (1964). A judge bent on granting a mistrial because of something prejudicial occurring during the trial, whether through his own conduct or another person's, should advise the presumably prejudiced party of the court's willingness to entertain a mistrial motion. A party failing to respond to that invitation may be held to have waived a mistrial. If a mistrial is declared, the case should be

rescheduled for trial. A specific rule may even require it. SIEGEL-NYPRAC § 403; NY R UNIF TRIAL CTS § 202.45.

ii. *Motion made after trial; Jury required.* After a trial of a cause of action or issue triable of right by a jury, upon the motion of any party or on its own initiative, the court may set aside a verdict or any judgment entered thereon and direct that judgment be entered in favor of a party entitled to judgment as a matter of law or it may order a new trial of a cause of action or separable issue where the verdict is contrary to the weight of the evidence, in the interest of justice or where the jury cannot agree after being kept together for as long as is deemed reasonable by the court. NY CPLR Rule 4404(a).

iii. *Motion made after trial; Jury not required.* After a trial not triable of right by a jury, upon the motion of any party or on its own initiative, the court may set aside its decision or any judgment entered thereon. It may make new findings of fact or conclusions of law, with or without taking additional testimony, render a new decision and direct entry of judgment, or it may order a new trial of a cause of action or separable issue. NY CPLR Rule 4404(b).

e. *Special rules when motion made after trial and verdict.* The technical rules, such as the time for the making of the motion—measured now from "decision" instead of "verdict"—are the same as govern the trial by jury, but the court's powers are of course more extensive. In a court-tried case, the judge on the post-trial motion can make new findings and conclusions, take additional testimony if need be, and render a new and entirely different decision; while in a trial by jury, the judge's powers are necessarily more restricted. SIEGEL-NYPRAC § 405.

i. The post-trial motion is usually made promptly upon the delivery of the verdict, and made orally in the courtroom. In addition to such an oral application, however, each party aggrieved by the verdict is entitled to make one formal, written motion under NY CPLR Rule 4404. For the written motion, the several requirements of NY CPLR Rule 4405 and NY CPLR Rule 4406 must be met. The motion may be made only to the judge who presided at the trial and must be made within fifteen (15) days after the verdict. SIEGEL-NYPRAC § 405; NY CPLR Rule 4405. If a judgment has been entered in the interim, the granting of the motion can incidentally vacate the judgment. SIEGEL-NYPRAC § 405; NY CPLR Rule 4404(a).

ii. When the court sets aside a verdict on a post-trial motion under NY CPLR Rule 4404(a), it has the alternative of granting a new trial instead of awarding outright judgment to the other side. The new trial is the route the court takes when, while not confident that any party is entitled to judgment as a matter of law, it nonetheless finds the verdict contrary to the "weight of the evidence." Here NY CPLR Rule 4404(a) allows a new trial "in the interest of justice," but neither of the quoted phrases is very informative. Precision about what is meant is elusive if not impossible: the "weight" of the evidence involves the judge's viscera as much as her intellect. SIEGEL-NYPRAC § 406.

iii. The key is the judge's common sense reaction to the evidence, because there can of course be no precise standard by which to "weigh" it. SIEGEL-NYPRAC § 406; Micallef v. Miehle Co., Div. of Miehle-Goss Dexter, 39 N.Y.2d 376, 381, 348 N.E.2d 571, 574 (1976). The scale is in the court's exclusive keeping and not every judge will read it the same way. A lawyer inexperienced in trial practice may even be surprised to learn that the weighing of the evidence is left entirely to the court's discretion and that this discretion may be exercised to set aside the verdict even where the evidence may be technically sufficient to sustain it. SIEGEL-NYPRAC § 406; Cohen v. Hallmark Cards, Inc., 45 N.Y.2d 493, 499, 382 N.E.2d 1145, 1147-48 (1978).

f. *Motion fails; Alternative relief.* The losing party who finds the NY CPLR Rule 4404 door closed may find relief under NY CPLR Rule 5015(a). SIEGEL-NYPRAC § 405; SIEGEL-NYPRAC § 428. Refer to the New York KeyRules Motion for Relief from Judgment document for more information.

3. *Oppositions.* In the absence of statutory provision or court rule, a motion ordinarily does not require a written answer, although an adverse party may be permitted to file an answer in opposition to the showing made in the motion or its supporting affidavits. AMJUR MOTIONS § 26. When a party files a motion and the opposing party fails to respond, the court may construe such failure to respond as non-opposition to the motion or an admission that the motion was meritorious, may take the facts alleged in the motion as true, and may grant the motion if the relief requested appears to be justified. However, the severity of such a result demands that a court impose it only with great caution. AMJUR MOTIONS § 28.

4. *Governing law.* The civil practice law and rules (NY CPLR § 101, et seq.) shall govern the procedure in civil judicial proceedings in all courts of the state and before all judges, except where the procedure is regulated by inconsistent statute. The civil practice law and rules shall succeed the civil practice act and rules of civil practice and shall be deemed substituted therefor throughout the statutes and rules of the state. NY CPLR § 101. The civil practice law and rules shall

be liberally construed to secure the just, speedy and inexpensive determination of every civil judicial proceeding. NY CPLR § 104.

a. *Uniform trial court rules.* The uniform civil rules for the Supreme Court and County Court (NY R UNIF TRIAL CTS § 202.1, et seq.) shall be applicable to civil actions and proceedings in the Supreme Court and the County Court. NY R UNIF TRIAL CTS § 202.1(a). The provisions of the uniform rules shall be construed consistent with the Civil Practice Law and Rules (CPLR), and matters not covered by the uniform rules shall be governed by the CPLR. NY R UNIF TRIAL CTS § 202.1(d).

b. *Local rules.* Local court rules, not inconsistent with law or with uniform civil rules for the Supreme Court and County Court (NY R UNIF TRIAL CTS § 202.1, et seq.), shall comply with Part 9 of the Rules of the Chief Judge (NY R CHIEF J § 9.1). NY R UNIF TRIAL CTS § 202.1(c).

c. *Official forms.* The state administrator shall have the power to adopt, amend and rescind an appendix of forms. Forms adopted pursuant to NY CPLR § 107 shall be sufficient under the civil practice law and rules and shall illustrate the simplicity and brevity of statement which the civil practice law and rules contemplate. NY CPLR § 107.

5. *Rules of the commercial division.* [Editor's note: certain types of civil cases or civil cases meeting certain monetary thresholds that are filed in the state of New York must be filed in the Commercial Division of the New York Supreme Courts. Rules governing practice in the commercial division are found in NY R UNIF TRIAL CTS § 202.70]. Cases which must be filed in the commercial division are listed below. For more information, refer to NY R UNIF TRIAL CTS § 202.70.

a. *Monetary thresholds.* Except as set forth in NY R UNIF TRIAL CTS § 202.70(b), the monetary thresholds of the Commercial Division, exclusive of punitive damages, interests, costs, disbursements and counsel fees claimed, are established as follows: (1) Albany County, fifty thousand dollars ($50,000); (2) Eighth Judicial District, one hundred thousand dollars ($100,000); (3) Kings County, one hundred fifty thousand dollars ($150,000); (4) Nassau County, two hundred thousand dollars ($200,000); (5) New York County, five hundred thousand dollars ($500,000); (6) Onondaga County, fifty thousand dollars ($50,000); (7) Queens County, one hundred thousand dollars ($100,000); (8) Seventh Judicial District, fifty thousand dollars ($50,000); (9) Suffolk County, one hundred thousand dollars ($100,000); and (10) Westchester County, one hundred thousand dollars ($100,000). NY R UNIF TRIAL CTS § 202.70(a).

i. *ALBANY COUNTY.* The Commercial Division of the Albany County Supreme Court exercises jurisdiction over selected business and commercial disputes in which the amount at issue generally involves damage claims in a minimum amount of fifty thousand dollars ($50,000) as well as claims for unspecified amounts where the value of the commercial asset(s) in dispute exceeds fifty thousand dollars ($50,000). A separate publication promulgating the rules and criteria relating to the filing and management of Commercial Court cases in this part may be obtained from the Albany County Supreme Court Clerk's Office. A section of the Uniform Civil Rules for the Supreme Court and County Court sets forth statewide rules. NY R 3 JD SUP Doc. 1(E).

ii. *BRONX COUNTY.* The monetary threshold for commercial cases in Bronx County will be seventy-five thousand dollars ($75,000). All other parameters including the type of matters that will be heard are contained within the Rules of the Commercial Division of the Supreme Court (NY R UNIF TRIAL CTS § 202.70). NY R BRONX FIL R Doc. 12.

iii. *NEW YORK COUNTY.* The monetary threshold in the New York County Commercial Division, which is generally applicable, is an amount in controversy of five hundred thousand dollars ($500,000) or more (exclusive of punitive damages, interest, costs, disbursements, and counsel fees). If the case is designated a commercial one and the Addendum is submitted, the clerk will review the pleadings to determine whether the amount in controversy in the case meets the monetary threshold or whether an exception to the threshold applies. NY R NY CTY Procedure IA(B). For more information on assigning a case to the commercial division in New York County, refer to NY R NY CTY Procedure IA(B).

b. *Commercial cases.* Actions in which the principal claims involve or consist of the following will be heard in the Commercial Division provided that the monetary threshold is met or equitable or declaratory relief is sought:

i. Breach of contract or fiduciary duty, fraud, misrepresentation, business tort (e.g., unfair competition), or statutory and/or common law violation where the breach or violation is alleged to arise out of business dealings (e.g., sales of assets or securities; corporate restructuring; partnership, shareholder, joint venture, and other business agreements; trade secrets; restrictive covenants; and employment agreements not including claims that principally involve alleged discriminatory practices);

ii. Transactions governed by the Uniform Commercial Code (exclusive of those concerning individual cooperative or condominium units);

iii. Transactions involving commercial real property, including Yellowstone injunctions and excluding actions for the payment of rent only;

iv. Shareholder derivative actions—without consideration of the monetary threshold;

v. Commercial class actions—without consideration of the monetary threshold;

vi. Business transactions involving or arising out of dealings with commercial banks and other financial institutions;

vii. Internal affairs of business organizations;

viii. Malpractice by accountants or actuaries, and legal malpractice arising out of representation in commercial matters;

ix. Environmental insurance coverage;

x. Commercial insurance coverage (e.g., directors and officers, errors and omissions, and business interruption coverage);

xi. Dissolution of corporations, partnerships, limited liability companies, limited liability partnerships and joint ventures—without consideration of the monetary threshold; and

xii. Applications to stay or compel arbitration and affirm or disaffirm arbitration awards and related injunctive relief pursuant to Article 75 of the New York Civil Practice Law and Rules (NY CPLR § 7501, et seq.) involving any of the foregoing enumerated commercial issues. Where the applicable arbitration agreement provides for the arbitration to be heard outside the United States, the monetary threshold set forth in NY R UNIF TRIAL CTS § 202.70(a) shall not apply. NY R UNIF TRIAL CTS § 202.70(b).

c. *Non-commercial cases.* The following will not be heard in the Commercial Division even if the monetary threshold is met:

i. Suits to collect professional fees;

ii. Cases seeking a declaratory judgment as to insurance coverage for personal injury or property damage;

iii. Residential real estate disputes, including landlord-tenant matters, and commercial real estate disputes involving the payment of rent only;

iv. Home improvement contracts involving residential properties consisting of one to four residential units or individual units in any residential building, including cooperative or condominium units;

v. Proceedings to enforce a judgment regardless of the nature of the underlying case;

vi. First-party insurance claims and actions by insurers to collect premiums or rescind non-commercial policies; and

vii. Attorney malpractice actions except as otherwise provided in NY R UNIF TRIAL CTS § 202.70(b)(8). NY R UNIF TRIAL CTS § 202.70(c).

d. For more information on the Commercial Division, refer to NY R UNIF TRIAL CTS § 202.70.

D. Documents

1. *Documents for moving party*

a. *Required documents*

i. *Notice of motion, order to show cause, or affidavit on ex parte motion.* The notice of motion shall be substantially in the form found in NY R UNIF TRIAL CTS § 202.7(b). NY R UNIF TRIAL CTS § 202.7(b). The supporting papers should be referred to in the notice of motion. SIEGEL-NYPRAC § 246. The court in a proper case may grant an order to show cause, to be served in lieu of a notice of motion. NY CPLR Rule 2214(d). An ex parte motion shall be accompanied by an affidavit stating the result of any prior motion for similar relief and specifying the new facts, if any, that were not previously shown. NY CPLR Rule 2217(b).

- *Request for oral argument.* A party requesting oral argument shall set forth such request in its notice of motion or in its order to show cause or on the first page of the answering papers, as the case may be. Where all parties to a motion request oral argument, oral argument shall be granted unless the court shall determine it to be unnecessary. Where a motion is brought on by order to show cause, the court may set forth in the order that oral argument is required on the return date of the motion. NY R UNIF TRIAL CTS § 202.8(d).

ii. *Motion.* Refer to the General Requirements section of this document for information on the notice of motion and motion.

iii. *Request for judicial intervention.* At any time after service of process, a party may file a request for judicial intervention. Except as provided in NY R UNIF TRIAL CTS § 202.6(b), in an action not yet assigned to a judge, the court shall not accept for filing a notice of motion, order to show cause, or application for ex parte order, unless such notice or application is accompanied by a request for judicial intervention. NY R UNIF TRIAL CTS § 202.6(a).

- *BRONX COUNTY.* Generally, the Request For Judicial Intervention, commonly referred to as an "RJI", is required to be filed in any action where the assignment of a Justice is required. The RJI sets forth the information which is entered into the court system's database. It must be completely and accurately filled out. The full caption, as stated on the Summons, must be set forth. Use of terms "et al." and "etc." are not permitted. Only one (1) RJI may be filed in each action. Either a self represented litigant or an attorney must sign the affirmation at the end of the form. Once completed, the RJI must be filed in duplicate. Except in the case of an ex-parte application, the RJI must also be served together with the accompanying application upon all parties. Proof of accuracy of the index number must accompany the RJI. Check the Fee Schedule[. . .]for any applicable filing fees. NY R BRONX FIL R Doc. 2.
- *KINGS COUNTY.* An RJI with the relevant required addendum in a NYSCEF case shall be submitted via NYSCEF. Once e-filed, the RJI and any accompanying document will be forwarded to the relevant support office for random assignment of the case and processing of the document. A filer or counsel need not appear (as to Proposed Orders to Show Cause, however, see below). A copy of the pleadings must be submitted only if the document has not previously been e-filed. If the RJI seeks intervention with regard to a document that is intended for review by a Justice, such as a motion, a working copy of the RJI must be submitted with the working copy of the motion and the NYSCEF Confirmation Notice. NY R L KINGS E FIL Doc. 1(C).
- *NEW YORK COUNTY.* To obtain the assignment of an IAS Justice to a case, a Request for Judicial Intervention (cost ninety-five dollars ($95)) must be filed, with NYSCEF in an e-filed case or in paper in an authorized hard-copy one. A no-fee RJI, which will generally result in the referral of an application to an Ex Parte Justice, is also required with regard to certain kinds of applications for which, prior to 2011, no RJI was required. NY R NY CTY Procedure I(C). A "fillable" form RJI is available on-line. The form must be filed in duplicate in hard-copy cases. NY R NY CTY Procedure IA(A)(1). The filer of an RJI must check off a box identifying the type of case at issue. Where the RJI seeks judicial assignment, this designation will bring about a random assignment of the case by computer to a Justice handling cases of that type. NY R NY CTY Procedure IA(A)(1). The RJI and any addendum can be completed and submitted electronically in an e-filed case. NY R NY CTY Procedure II(A). The RJI shall be marked to reflect the existence of any "related case" as explained on the "Commencement of Cases" page under "Case Processing" on the court's website. NY R NY CTY Procedure II(A); NY R NY CTY E FIL Doc. 2(C).
- *ONONDAGA COUNTY.* The RJI will be submitted via the NYSCEF system along with any required RJI addendum forms. When the RJI is filed and the fee paid online, the Onondaga County Clerk's Office will electronically forward the RJI and any accompanying documents to the Onondaga Supreme Court Clerk's Office for assignment and processing. Counsel will receive notification of judge assignment via the NYSCEF system. NY R ONDGA E FIL Protocol(B)(3).
- *QUEENS COUNTY.* A Request for Judicial Intervention ("RJI") in an E-filed case shall be submitted via the E-filing System. When the RJI is approved, filed and paid for on-line, it will be forwarded to the relevant back office for random assignment of the case and processing of the document. In the case of RJIs seeking assignment to the Commercial Division, the filer must submit therewith, a Commercial Addendum as required by the standards for assignment of cases to the Commercial Division. NY R L QUEENS E-FILE Doc. 1(F).

iv. *Proof of service.* In addition to complying with the provisions of NY CPLR Rule 2101, every paper filed in court shall have annexed thereto appropriate proof of service on all parties where required. NY R UNIF TRIAL CTS § 202.5(a).

- *QUEENS COUNTY.* With regard to service of a motion/petition on notice in an E-filed action, NY CPLR Rule 2214(b) and NY R UNIF TRIAL CTS § 202.5-b(f) applies. Where required, proof of service shall be filed on-line as a separate document. NY R L QUEENS E-FILE Doc. 1(H)(3).

v. *ALBANY COUNTY: Additional required documents*

- *Affirmation of good faith effort.* The parties must[. . .]submit an affirmation attesting to [their good faith effort to resolve the matter]. The affirmation of good faith effort to resolve the issues raised by the motion shall indicate the time, place and nature of the consultation and the issues discussed and any resolutions, or shall indicate good cause why no such conferral with counsel for opposing parties was held. An assigned justice or judge may dismiss a motion for failure to demonstrate that such effort was made with leave to renew the motion after such effort has been demonstrated. NY R 3 JD SUP Doc. 1(B).

b. *Supplemental documents*

i. *Supporting evidence; Exhibits.* The main supporting papers on a motion are affidavits, but any relevant exhibits, documents, depositions, etc., are also includible. SIEGEL-NYPRAC § 246.

- *Affidavits accompanying motion.* Affidavits shall be for a statement of the relevant facts. NY R UNIF TRIAL CTS § 202.8(c).
- *Foreign language documents.* Where an affidavit or exhibit annexed to a paper served or filed is in a foreign language, it shall be accompanied by an English translation and an affidavit by the translator stating his qualifications and that the translation is accurate. NY CPLR Rule 2101(b).
- *Statement of attorney in lieu of affidavit.* The statement of an attorney admitted to practice in the courts of the state, or of a physician, osteopath or dentist, authorized by law to practice in the state, who is not a party to an action, when subscribed and affirmed by him to be true under the penalties of perjury, may be served or filed in the action in lieu of and with the same force and effect as an affidavit. NY CPLR Rule 2106.
- *NEW YORK COUNTY: Form of presented exhibits.* Exhibits should be tabbed and be legible; a typed version of any exhibit that is difficult to read should be submitted with the original. Exhibits printed on both sides of the page should be bound and tabbed on the side. NY R NY CTY J RUL Rule 14(a).
- *QUEENS COUNTY.* Attorneys submitting exhibits to the court on E-file cases shall make each exhibit a separate, labeled attachment to an affidavit/affirmation. NY R L QUEENS E-FILE Doc. 1(H)(4).

ii. *Brief.* Briefs shall be for a statement of the relevant law. NY R UNIF TRIAL CTS § 202.8(c).

iii. *Notice to produce papers not in possession of the court.* If a paper relied on by the movant is in the possession of the other side, it may be demanded of that side with a notice to produce it at the hearing. Where such papers are in the possession of an adverse party, they shall be produced by him at the hearing on notice served with the motion papers. NY CPLR Rule 2214(Practice Commentary, C2214:23).

iv. *Filing fees.* The County Clerk shall require the payment of any applicable statutory fees, or an order of the Court waiving payment of such fees, before accepting a paper for filing. NY R UNIF TRIAL CTS § 202.5(d)(1). For information on filing fees, if any, refer to NY CPLR § 8001, et seq.

- *ALBANY COUNTY.* In general, any filing subsequent to the commencement of an action which is designated as a motion or cross-motion requires the payment of a filing fee to the County Clerk's Office prior to submission to the Supreme Court Clerk's Office for referral to the assigned justice. The fee is assessed regardless of whether an application is made by notice of motion, order to show cause or ex parte. No fee will be charged upon the filing of a motion for poor person status in conjunction with an application which serves to commence an action or special proceeding. In the event a motion is received by the court unaccompanied by proof of payment to the County Clerk, the Supreme Court Clerk's Office will contact the submitting party to advise that the application will be held pending receipt of the filing fee only until the return date of the motion. If proof of payment is not submitted to the Supreme Court Clerk's Office by the return date (ex parte applications will be held ten (10) days), the papers will be returned by mail with a notification that the motion has been removed from the court's calendar and that it must be re-noticed and re-filed with the court along with the requisite filing fee. Inquiries concerning the applicability of the motion fee to a proposed filing may be directed to the Supreme Court Clerk's Office. NY R 3 JD SUP Doc. 1(B).
- *BRONX COUNTY.* In accordance with the new civil fee schedule set forth in Article 80 of the C.P.L.R. (NY CPLR § 8001, et seq.), effective July 14, 2003, all motions, and cross motions must be approved in Room 217 prior to payment of said fees in the County Clerk's Office, Room 118. NY R BRONX FIL R Doc. 8. The motion fee [must be] paid for via NYSCEF by credit/debit card. NY R BRONX E FIL R Doc. 1(1).
- *ERIE COUNTY.* Payment for fee-bearing NYSCEF documents must be made online via credit or debit card (American Express, MasterCard or Visa) at the time of submission. NY R ERIE E FIL Doc. 3(III)(E).
- *KINGS COUNTY.* The motion must be filed with NYSCEF and the motion fee paid. NY R L KINGS E FIL Doc. 1(D). Court fees in NYSCEF cases must be paid via NYSCEF by a credit or bank card (MasterCard, Visa, or American Express). Fees are no longer accepted in person in the Kings County Clerk's Office in NYSCEF cases. NY R L KINGS E FIL Doc. 1(B)(6).

- *NEW YORK COUNTY.* A motion fee must be paid on motions made in writing by notice of motion, order to show cause or ex parte after the commencement of an action. For this purpose, the term "action" shall mean any application to the court that requires the assignment of an index number, regardless of whether a formal pleading is filed. Applications or motions that commence an action and for which an index number fee must be paid require no motion fee. [A]ny motions made after the initial applications in these situations would require payment of the motion fee. A motion that is the initial application in a case commenced by the filing of a summons and complaint would require a motion fee since the filing of the summons and complaint rather than the application itself would require the purchase of an index number. NY R NY CTY Procedure II(A). In e-filed cases the motion fee must be paid when the documents are filed. Payment is made on-line by Visa, Mastercard, or American Express credit or bank card. NY R NY CTY Procedure II(A); NY R NY CTY E FIL Doc. 2(B)(5).
- *ONONDAGA COUNTY.* Court fees in e-filed cases must be paid online with the NYSCEF system using a credit card. The document is not considered to have been filed until payment of the fee has been tendered. NY R ONDGA E FIL Protocol(B)(2). Fees must be paid on all cross motions. NY R ONDGA E FIL Protocol(B)(9)(e).
- *QUEENS COUNTY.* The Motion Support Office does not receive, forward or process any fees or waiver of fees. All applications requiring payment of statutory fees or waiver of fees must be sent directly to the Queens County Clerk's office. NY R L QUEENS MOT SUP Doc. 1. Court fees (e.g., RJI fee, motion fee) in E-filed cases may be paid for on-line using a credit card. Papers may also be filed with the E-file system and the fee may be paid at the County Clerk's Office. In the latter case, the paper is not considered to have been filed until payment of the fee has been tendered. NY R L QUEENS E-FILE Doc. 1(E)(1). The motion/petition shall be filed on-line and the fee paid for either on-line by credit card or by the "Pay at the County Clerk's Office" option. NY R L QUEENS E-FILE Doc. 1(H)(1).

v. *Working copies.* The court may require the parties to provide working copies of documents filed electronically. In such event, each working copy shall include, firmly affixed thereto, a copy of a confirmation notice in a form prescribed by the Chief Administrator. NY R UNIF TRIAL CTS § 202.5-b(d)(5).

- *BRONX COUNTY.* After papers on motions have been e-filed, working copies thereof, with Confirmation Notice firmly attached as the back page facing out, must be submitted. (Each document or group of documents that is separately bound shall bear a Confirmation Notice.) Working copies lacking the Notice will not be accepted. WORKING COPIES OF MOTION PAPERS MUST BE SUBMITTED NO LATER THAN 4:45 P.M. ON THE RETURN DATE IN THE MOTION SUPPORT OFFICE (ROOM 217) AS EXPLAINED in NY R BRONX E FIL R Doc. 1(4). If an attorney has failed to submit required working copies on or before the return date, the motion will be transmitted as is to the Justice for such action as the Justice finds appropriate. Attorneys may submit working copies on motions by mail or overnight delivery. Any such submission shall be sent in a timely manner to the Motion Support Office (Room 217) and be conspicuously marked on the outside "NYSCEF Matter"; lack of such marking may delay processing. NY R BRONX E FIL R Doc. 1(4)(a).
- *ERIE COUNTY.* Electronically filed documents subject to review and processing by the Part Clerk do not require a working copy unless otherwise directed or provided for in IAS Part Rules. NY R UNIF TRIAL CTS § 202.5-b(d)(4), any working copy submitted shall include, as a cover page firmly fastened thereto, a copy of the Confirmation Notice generated by the NYSCEF site at the time of filing. Please consult the individual Justice's Part Rules and/or consult with the Judge's chambers to determine whether and how working copies are to be provided. Working copies will not be printed or delivered by the Erie County Clerk or the Chief Clerk of the Courts or any of their personnel to chambers. The official record of a document in an electronically filed case is the document filed via the NYSCEF system. Working copies are intended only for use by the Justice. The Court will discard all working copies after the Justice has finished with them. Thus, in the event that counsel fails to file a document via the NYSCEF system, the document will not be part of the court record. NY R ERIE E FIL Doc. 3(III)(O); NY R ERIE E FIL Doc. 3(V)(E).
- *KINGS COUNTY.* No courtesy copies of motion papers are required by the Court, except as may be required for electronic filing or by the Judge's Part Rules. In tort cases against the City of New York, courtesy copies shall be supplied to the Corporation Counsel's office in Brooklyn. NY R L KINGS Pt. C, Rule 5. Unless otherwise directed by the Court or as described herein, and with the exceptions listed below, in all NYSCEF cases in which an RJI has been filed, working copies of e-filed documents that are intended for judicial review must be submitted to the court. Working copies are not required of documents that are

only processed by a support office (e.g. preliminary conference request, note of issue). Working copies shall include exhibit tabs and backs; for motion papers, the motion sequence number and the return date and part. The confirmation notice with the motion sequence number on it should be the back page of the motion facing out. In addition, the filer of a working copy must firmly bind thereto, with the back page facing out, a copy of the Confirmation Notice that was generated by NYSCEF when that document was efiled. Working copies that are submitted without the related Confirmation Notice will not be accepted. NY R L KINGS E FIL Doc. 1(B)(7); NY R L KINGS E FIL Doc. 1(D). WORKING COPIES OF MOTION PAPERS MUST BE SUBMITTED IN THE MOTION SUPPORT OFFICE (ROOM 227) AS EXPLAINED HEREIN. THEY MUST NOT BE DELIVERED TO THE PART OR CHAMBERS, EXCEPT WHERE THE INDIVIDUAL JUSTICE'S PART RULES PROVIDE OTHERWISE; DOING SO WILL CAUSE ADMINISTRATIVE CONFUSION AND POSSIBLE MISPLACEMENT OF PAPERS. Any such submission shall be sent in a timely manner (kindly review individual Justice's rules) and be conspicuously marked on the outside "NYSCEF Matter;" lack of such marking may delay processing. NY R L KINGS E FIL Doc. 1(D).

- *NEW YORK COUNTY.* Some Justices require that working copies of e-filed motion papers be submitted. See the E-filing Protocol for information on the many Parts that do not require working copies. Where required, working copies of the moving documents and all other documents on the motion or application shall be submitted to the Motion Submission Part Courtroom (Room 130) on, but not before, the final return date. A Confirmation Notice from the NYSCEF system, which is generated when a document is e-filed, shall be firmly affixed, as the back page facing out, to each separate working copy or group of such copies. NY R NY CTY Procedure II(A) NY R NY CTY E FIL Doc. 2(B)(5)(a); NY R NY CTY J RUL Rule 14(a). For more information on working copies, including which parts don't require them, refer to NY R NY CTY E FIL Doc. 2(B)(6).
- *ONONDAGA COUNTY.* Any courtesy "working" copies, if required (see NY R ONDGA E FIL Protocol(B)(7)), must be provided directly to the assigned justice. NY R ONDGA E FIL Protocol(B)(9)(e). For information as to whether or not an Onondaga Supreme Court Justice requires working (courtesy) copies of e-filed documents, please consult the Onondaga County Individual E-filing Rules. NY R ONDGA E FIL Protocol(B)(7)(a). The Supreme Court Clerk's Office and the Onondaga County Clerk's Office will NOT accept the working copies. Working copies must be sent directly to the assigned justice's chambers. NY R ONDGA E FIL Protocol(B)(7)(b). A copy of the Confirmation Notice, generated by the NYSCEF system at the time a document is e-filed, must be attached to every working copy provided to chambers. If the Confirmation Notice is missing, the copy will not be accepted. NY R ONDGA E FIL Protocol(B)(7)(c). Courtesy copies do not become part of the official court record as maintained by the Onondaga County Clerk's Office and will be destroyed by chambers at the disposition of the case. In the event that counsel fails to file a document via NYSCEF, the document will not be part of the court record. NY R ONDGA E FIL Protocol(B)(7)(d).
- *QUEENS COUNTY.* Working copies of E-Filed notices of motion/notices of petition are NOT to be sent to the Motion Support Office. They must be brought to the calendar call in the judge's part. NY R L QUEENS MOT SUP Doc. 1. Unless otherwise directed or authorized by the court, counsel should file papers with the E-file system first and thereafter deliver a working copy to at the calendar call of the Centralized Motion Part or Assigned Justice in accordance with individual Part Rules. NY R L QUEENS E-FILE Doc. 1(E)(4). On the return date of a motion that has been E-filed, the movant must provide the Centralized Motion Part (CMP) with a working copy of the entire motion including the notice of motion with sequence number and all of the attached exhibits. The motion must have the confirmation of filing firmly affixed to the back of the papers (facing outward). The confirmation of filing is a separate notice from the payment notice and will say confirmation clearly across the top of the page. NY R L QUEENS E-FILE Doc. 1(H)(2)(a). The motion or Order to Show Cause must have clearly written across its face the words "Working Copy," it must also have the assigned Judge's name, motion sequence number and calendar number—which may be obtained from the posted calendar outside courtroom on the return date of the motion. A confirmation of filing must attached thereto. Working copies of e-filed Orders to Show Cause must contain a copy of the signed order and all supporting papers. NY R L QUEENS E-FILE Doc. 1(H)(2)(c). The Confirmation Notice must be an updated version that indicates the sequence number of the motion being submitted at the CMP calendar call. WORKING COPIES WITHOUT A CONFIRMATION NOTICE WILL NOT BE ACCEPTED. NY R L QUEENS E-FILE Doc. 1(H)(7).

vi. *ERIE COUNTY: Additional supplemental documents*

- *Notice of hard copy submission in e-filed case.* In accordance with NY R UNIF TRIAL CTS § 202.5-b(d),

the County Clerk shall refuse to accept for filing, hard copy papers filed to an action subject to electronic filing unless hard copy filing is permitted by the Uniform Rules or NY R ERIE E FIL Doc. 3 and the papers bear a completed Notice of Hard Copy Submission—E-Filed Case form. NY R ERIE E FIL Doc. 3(III)(D).

vii. *KINGS COUNTY: Additional supplemental documents*

- *Forms when filing in hard copy.* An attorney who certifies in good faith that he or she lacks the equipment or knowledge needed to e-file and have no staff member or employee under his or her direction who has such knowledge and equipment may opt out of participation in e-filing in a mandatory case by filing a "Notice of Opt-Out from Participation in Action Subject to Mandatory Electronic Filing" form EFM-2 with the Clerk. NY R L KINGS E FIL Doc. 1(A)(2). Where in accordance with the E-Filing Rules a party submits a document in hard copy in an e-filed case (principally, a document submitted by a nonparticipating party (e.g., an attorney) in a consensual case, an emergency filing made in accordance with the Mandatory E-Filing Rules, and any document filed with the court in hard copy by an attorney who has opted out of participation in mandatory e-filing, the document must bear the back page facing out, a "Notice of Hard Copy Submission—E-Filed Cases" form EFM-3. NY R L KINGS E FIL Doc. 1(B)(3).

viii. *NEW YORK COUNTY: Additional supplemental documents*

- *Notice of hard copy submission.* Where in accordance with the E-Filing Rules an attorney or an unrepresented litigant who is participating in e-filing submits a document in hard copy in an e-filed case, the document must bear, as the back page facing out, a Notice of Hard-Copy Submission—E-Filed Case (a form available in the "Forms" section on the NYSCEF website (Form EFM-3) and in the court's back offices). NY R NY CTY E FIL Doc. 2(B)(3). For more information refer to NY R NY CTY E FIL Doc. 2.
- *Unpublished decisions.* Whenever reliance is placed upon a decision or other authority not officially published or readily available to the New York County Supreme Court, a copy of the case or of pertinent portions of the authority shall be submitted with the motion papers. NY R NY CTY J RUL Rule 14(a).

ix. *ONONDAGA COUNTY: Additional supplemental documents*

- *Notice of hard copy submission.* Any papers to be filed with the court in an e-filed case must be filed online with the E-filing system except where a special exemption is granted (e.g., oversized maps, photographs). If such an exemption is granted, Form EFM-3, "Notice of Hard Copy Submission—E-Filed Case," must be attached to such documents forms which are not filed on line. Also, Form EFM-4 "Notice of Hard Copy Exhibit Filing" must be completed and uploaded to the action's e-file. Both of these forms may be found on the NYSCEF website. NY R ONDGA E FIL Protocol(B)(4).

x. *QUEENS COUNTY: Additional supplemental documents*

- *Notice of hard copy submission.* Any party opting out of the e-filing system must have a "Notice of Hard Copy Submission" firmly affixed to the back of the papers. NY R L QUEENS E-FILE Doc. 1(H)(2)(f).

2. *Documents for opposing party*

a. *Required documents*

i. *Opposition.* Refer to the General Requirements section of this document for information on the opposition.

- *Request for oral argument.* A party requesting oral argument shall set forth such request in its notice of motion or in its order to show cause or on the first page of the answering papers, as the case may be. Where all parties to a motion request oral argument, oral argument shall be granted unless the court shall determine it to be unnecessary. Where a motion is brought on by order to show cause, the court may set forth in the order that oral argument is required on the return date of the motion. NY R UNIF TRIAL CTS § 202.8(d).
- *QUEENS COUNTY: E-filing opposition papers.* E-filed opposition papers and/or reply papers must also be provided to the Centralized Motion Part in the same manner as the moving papers with the confirmation of filing firmly attached to the back of the papers. NY R L QUEENS E-FILE Doc. 1(H)(2)(d).

ii. *Proof of service.* In addition to complying with the provisions of NY CPLR Rule 2101, every paper filed in court shall have annexed thereto appropriate proof of service on all parties where required. NY R UNIF TRIAL CTS § 202.5(a).

b. *Supplemental documents*

i. *Supporting evidence; Exhibits.* The main supporting papers on a motion are affidavits, but any relevant exhibits, documents, depositions, etc., are also includible. SIEGEL-NYPRAC § 246.

- *Affidavits accompanying opposition.* Affidavits shall be for a statement of the relevant facts. NY R UNIF TRIAL CTS § 202.8(c).

- *Foreign language documents.* Where an affidavit or exhibit annexed to a paper served or filed is in a foreign language, it shall be accompanied by an English translation and an affidavit by the translator stating his qualifications and that the translation is accurate. NY CPLR Rule 2101(b).
- *Statement of attorney in lieu of affidavit.* The statement of an attorney admitted to practice in the courts of the state, or of a physician, osteopath or dentist, authorized by law to practice in the state, who is not a party to an action, when subscribed and affirmed by him to be true under the penalties of perjury, may be served or filed in the action in lieu of and with the same force and effect as an affidavit. NY CPLR Rule 2106.
- *NEW YORK COUNTY: Form of presented exhibits.* Exhibits should be tabbed and be legible; a typed version of any exhibit that is difficult to read should be submitted with the original. Exhibits printed on both sides of the page should be bound and tabbed on the side. NY R NY CTY J RUL Rule 14(a).
- *QUEENS COUNTY.* Attorneys submitting exhibits to the court on E-file cases shall make each exhibit a separate, labeled attachment to an affidavit/affirmation. NY R L QUEENS E-FILE Doc. 1(H)(4).

ii. *Brief.* Briefs shall be for a statement of the relevant law. NY R UNIF TRIAL CTS § 202.8(c).

iii. *Filing fees.* The County Clerk shall require the payment of any applicable statutory fees, or an order of the Court waiving payment of such fees, before accepting a paper for filing. NY R UNIF TRIAL CTS § 202.5(d)(1). For information on filing fees, if any, refer to NY CPLR § 8001, et seq.

- *ALBANY COUNTY.* In general, any filing subsequent to the commencement of an action which is designated as a motion or cross-motion requires the payment of a filing fee to the County Clerk's Office prior to submission to the Supreme Court Clerk's Office for referral to the assigned justice. The fee is assessed regardless of whether an application is made by notice of motion, order to show cause or ex parte. No fee will be charged upon the filing of a motion for poor person status in conjunction with an application which serves to commence an action or special proceeding. In the event a motion is received by the court unaccompanied by proof of payment to the County Clerk, the Supreme Court Clerk's Office will contact the submitting party to advise that the application will be held pending receipt of the filing fee only until the return date of the motion. If proof of payment is not submitted to the Supreme Court Clerk's Office by the return date (ex parte applications will be held ten (10) days), the papers will be returned by mail with a notification that the motion has been removed from the court's calendar and that it must be re-noticed and re-filed with the court along with the requisite filing fee. Inquiries concerning the applicability of the motion fee to a proposed filing may be directed to the Supreme Court Clerk's Office. NY R 3 JD SUP Doc. 1(B).
- *BRONX COUNTY.* In accordance with the new civil fee schedule set forth in Article 80 of the C.P.L.R. (NY CPLR § 8001, et seq.), effective July 14, 2003, all motions, and cross motions must be approved in Room 217 prior to payment of said fees in the County Clerk's Office, Room 118. NY R BRONX FIL R Doc. 8. The motion fee [must be] paid for via NYSCEF by credit/debit card. NY R BRONX E FIL R Doc. 1(1).
- *ERIE COUNTY.* Payment for fee-bearing NYSCEF documents must be made online via credit or debit card (American Express, MasterCard or Visa) at the time of submission. NY R ERIE E FIL Doc. 3(III)(E).
- *KINGS COUNTY.* The motion must be filed with NYSCEF and the motion fee paid. NY R L KINGS E FIL Doc. 1(D). Court fees in NYSCEF cases must be paid via NYSCEF by a credit or bank card (MasterCard, Visa, or American Express). Fees are no longer accepted in person in the Kings County Clerk's Office in NYSCEF cases. NY R L KINGS E FIL Doc. 1(B)(6).
- *NEW YORK COUNTY.* A motion fee must be paid on motions made in writing by notice of motion, order to show cause or ex parte after the commencement of an action. For this purpose, the term "action" shall mean any application to the court that requires the assignment of an index number, regardless of whether a formal pleading is filed. Applications or motions that commence an action and for which an index number fee must be paid require no motion fee. [A]ny motions made after the initial applications in these situations would require payment of the motion fee. A motion that is the initial application in a case commenced by the filing of a summons and complaint would require a motion fee since the filing of the summons and complaint rather than the application itself would require the purchase of an index number. NY R NY CTY Procedure II(A). In e-filed cases the motion fee must be paid when the documents are filed. Payment is made on-line by Visa, Mastercard, or American Express credit or bank card. NY R NY CTY Procedure II(A); NY R NY CTY E FIL Doc. 2(B)(5).
- *ONONDAGA COUNTY.* Court fees in e-filed cases must be paid online with the NYSCEF system using a credit card. The document is not considered to have been filed until payment of the fee has been tendered.

NY R ONDGA E FIL Protocol(B)(2). Fees must be paid on all cross motions. NY R ONDGA E FIL Protocol(B)(9)(e).

- *QUEENS COUNTY.* The Motion Support Office does not receive, forward or process any fees or waiver of fees. All applications requiring payment of statutory fees or waiver of fees must be sent directly to the Queens County Clerk's office. NY R L QUEENS MOT SUP Doc. 1. Court fees (e.g., RJI fee, motion fee) in E-filed cases may be paid for on-line using a credit card. Papers may also be filed with the E-file system and the fee may be paid at the County Clerk's Office. In the latter case, the paper is not considered to have been filed until payment of the fee has been tendered. NY R L QUEENS E-FILE Doc. 1(E)(1). The motion/petition shall be filed on-line and the fee paid for either on-line by credit card or by the "Pay at the County Clerk's Office" option. NY R L QUEENS E-FILE Doc. 1(H)(1).

iv. *Working copies.* The court may require the parties to provide working copies of documents filed electronically. In such event, each working copy shall include, firmly affixed thereto, a copy of a confirmation notice in a form prescribed by the Chief Administrator. NY R UNIF TRIAL CTS § 202.5-b(d)(5).

- *BRONX COUNTY.* After papers on motions have been e-filed, working copies thereof, with Confirmation Notice firmly attached as the back page facing out, must be submitted. (Each document or group of documents that is separately bound shall bear a Confirmation Notice.) Working copies lacking the Notice will not be accepted. WORKING COPIES OF MOTION PAPERS MUST BE SUBMITTED NO LATER THAN 4:45 P.M. ON THE RETURN DATE IN THE MOTION SUPPORT OFFICE (ROOM 217) AS EXPLAINED in NY R BRONX E FIL R Doc. 1(4). If an attorney has failed to submit required working copies on or before the return date, the motion will be transmitted as is to the Justice for such action as the Justice finds appropriate. Attorneys may submit working copies on motions by mail or overnight delivery. Any such submission shall be sent in a timely manner to the Motion Support Office (Room 217) and be conspicuously marked on the outside "NYSCEF Matter"; lack of such marking may delay processing. NY R BRONX E FIL R Doc. 1(4)(a).
- *ERIE COUNTY.* Electronically filed documents subject to review and processing by the Part Clerk do not require a working copy unless otherwise directed or provided for in IAS Part Rules. NY R UNIF TRIAL CTS § 202.5-b(d)(4), any working copy submitted shall include, as a cover page firmly fastened thereto, a copy of the Confirmation Notice generated by the NYSCEF site at the time of filing. Please consult the individual Justice's Part Rules and/or consult with the Judge's chambers to determine whether and how working copies are to be provided. Working copies will not be printed or delivered by the Erie County Clerk or the Chief Clerk of the Courts or any of their personnel to chambers. The official record of a document in an electronically filed case is the document filed via the NYSCEF system. Working copies are intended only for use by the Justice. The Court will discard all working copies after the Justice has finished with them. Thus, in the event that counsel fails to file a document via the NYSCEF system, the document will not be part of the court record. NY R ERIE E FIL Doc. 3(III)(O); NY R ERIE E FIL Doc. 3(V)(E).
- *KINGS COUNTY.* No courtesy copies of motion papers are required by the Court, except as may be required for electronic filing or by the Judge's Part Rules. In tort cases against the City of New York, courtesy copies shall be supplied to the Corporation Counsel's office in Brooklyn. NY R L KINGS Pt. C, Rule 5. Unless otherwise directed by the Court or as described herein, and with the exceptions listed below, in all NYSCEF cases in which an RJI has been filed, working copies of e-filed documents that are intended for judicial review must be submitted to the court. Working copies are not required of documents that are only processed by a support office (e.g. preliminary conference request, note of issue). Working copies shall include exhibit tabs and backs; for motion papers, the motion sequence number and the return date and part. The confirmation notice with the motion sequence number on it should be the back page of the motion facing out. In addition, the filer of a working copy must firmly bind thereto, with the back page facing out, a copy of the Confirmation Notice that was generated by NYSCEF when that document was efiled. Working copies that are submitted without the related Confirmation Notice will not be accepted. NY R L KINGS E FIL Doc. 1(B)(7); NY R L KINGS E FIL Doc. 1(D). WORKING COPIES OF MOTION PAPERS MUST BE SUBMITTED IN THE MOTION SUPPORT OFFICE (ROOM 227) AS EXPLAINED HEREIN. THEY MUST NOT BE DELIVERED TO THE PART OR CHAMBERS, EXCEPT WHERE THE INDIVIDUAL JUSTICE'S PART RULES PROVIDE OTHERWISE; DOING SO WILL CAUSE ADMINISTRATIVE CONFUSION AND POSSIBLE MISPLACEMENT OF PAPERS. Any such submission shall be sent in a timely manner (kindly review individual Justice's rules) and be conspicuously marked on the outside "NYSCEF Matter;" lack of such marking may delay processing. NY R L KINGS E FIL Doc. 1(D).

- *NEW YORK COUNTY.* Some Justices require that working copies of e-filed motion papers be submitted. See the E-filing Protocol for information on the many Parts that do not require working copies. Where required, working copies of the moving documents and all other documents on the motion or application shall be submitted to the Motion Submission Part Courtroom (Room 130) on, but not before, the final return date. A Confirmation Notice from the NYSCEF system, which is generated when a document is e-filed, shall be firmly affixed, as the back page facing out, to each separate working copy or group of such copies. NY R NY CTY Procedure II(A) NY R NY CTY E FIL Doc. 2(B)(5)(a); NY R NY CTY J RUL Rule 14(a). For more information on working copies, including which parts don't require them, refer to NY R NY CTY E FIL Doc. 2(B)(6).
- *ONONDAGA COUNTY.* Any courtesy "working" copies, if required (see NY R ONDGA E FIL Protocol(B)(7)), must be provided directly to the assigned justice. NY R ONDGA E FIL Protocol(B)(9)(e). For information as to whether or not an Onondaga Supreme Court Justice requires working (courtesy) copies of e-filed documents, please consult the Onondaga County Individual E-filing Rules. NY R ONDGA E FIL Protocol(B)(7)(a). The Supreme Court Clerk's Office and the Onondaga County Clerk's Office will NOT accept the working copies. Working copies must be sent directly to the assigned justice's chambers. NY R ONDGA E FIL Protocol(B)(7)(b). A copy of the Confirmation Notice, generated by the NYSCEF system at the time a document is e-filed, must be attached to every working copy provided to chambers. If the Confirmation Notice is missing, the copy will not be accepted. NY R ONDGA E FIL Protocol(B)(7)(c). Courtesy copies do not become part of the official court record as maintained by the Onondaga County Clerk's Office and will be destroyed by chambers at the disposition of the case. In the event that counsel fails to file a document via NYSCEF, the document will not be part of the court record. NY R ONDGA E FIL Protocol(B)(7)(d).
- *QUEENS COUNTY.* Working copies of E-Filed notices of motion/notices of petition are NOT to be sent to the Motion Support Office. They must be brought to the calendar call in the judge's part. NY R L QUEENS MOT SUP Doc. 1. Unless otherwise directed or authorized by the court, counsel should file papers with the E-file system first and thereafter deliver a working copy to at the calendar call of the Centralized Motion Part or Assigned Justice in accordance with individual Part Rules. NY R L QUEENS E-FILE Doc. 1(E)(4). On the return date of a motion that has been E-filed, the movant must provide the Centralized Motion Part (CMP) with a working copy of the entire motion including the notice of motion with sequence number and all of the attached exhibits. The motion must have the confirmation of filing firmly affixed to the back of the papers (facing outward). The confirmation of filing is a separate notice from the payment notice and will say confirmation clearly across the top of the page. NY R L QUEENS E-FILE Doc. 1(H)(2)(a). The motion or Order to Show Cause must have clearly written across its face the words "Working Copy," it must also have the assigned Judge's name, motion sequence number and calendar number—which may be obtained from the posted calendar outside courtroom on the return date of the motion. A confirmation of filing must attached thereto. Working copies of e-filed Orders to Show Cause must contain a copy of the signed order and all supporting papers. NY R L QUEENS E-FILE Doc. 1(H)(2)(c). The Confirmation Notice must be an updated version that indicates the sequence number of the motion being submitted at the CMP calendar call. WORKING COPIES WITHOUT A CONFIRMATION NOTICE WILL NOT BE ACCEPTED. NY R L QUEENS E-FILE Doc. 1(H)(7).

v. *ERIE COUNTY: Additional supplemental documents*

- *Notice of hard copy submission in e-filed case.* In accordance with NY R UNIF TRIAL CTS § 202.5-b(d), the County Clerk shall refuse to accept for filing, hard copy papers filed to an action subject to electronic filing unless hard copy filing is permitted by the Uniform Rules or NY R ERIE E FIL Doc. 3 and the papers bear a completed Notice of Hard Copy Submission—E-Filed Case form. NY R ERIE E FIL Doc. 3(III)(D).

vi. *KINGS COUNTY: Additional supplemental documents*

- *Forms when filing in hard copy.* An attorney who certifies in good faith that he or she lacks the equipment or knowledge needed to e-file and have no staff member or employee under his or her direction who has such knowledge and equipment may opt out of participation in e-filing in a mandatory case by filing a "Notice of Opt-Out from Participation in Action Subject to Mandatory Electronic Filing" form EFM-2 with the Clerk. NY R L KINGS E FIL Doc. 1(A)(2). Where in accordance with the E-Filing Rules a party submits a document in hard copy in an e-filed case (principally, a document submitted by a nonparticipating party (e.g., an attorney) in a consensual case, an emergency filing made in accordance with the Mandatory E-Filing Rules, and any document filed with the court in hard copy by an attorney who has opted out of

participation in mandatory e-filing, the document must bear the back page facing out, a "Notice of Hard Copy Submission—E-Filed Cases" form EFM-3. NY R L KINGS E FIL Doc. 1(B)(3).

vii. *NEW YORK COUNTY: Additional supplemental documents*

- *Notice of hard copy submission.* Where in accordance with the E-Filing Rules an attorney or an unrepresented litigant who is participating in e-filing submits a document in hard copy in an e-filed case, the document must bear, as the back page facing out, a Notice of Hard-Copy Submission—E-Filed Case (a form available in the "Forms" section on the NYSCEF website (Form EFM-3) and in the court's back offices). NY R NY CTY E FIL Doc. 2(B)(3). For more information refer to NY R NY CTY E FIL Doc. 2.
- *Unpublished decisions.* Whenever reliance is placed upon a decision or other authority not officially published or readily available to the New York County Supreme Court, a copy of the case or of pertinent portions of the authority shall be submitted with the motion papers. NY R NY CTY J RUL Rule 14(a).

viii. *ONONDAGA COUNTY: Additional supplemental documents*

- *Notice of hard copy submission.* Any papers to be filed with the court in an e-filed case must be filed online with the E-filing system except where a special exemption is granted (e.g., oversized maps, photographs). If such an exemption is granted, Form EFM-3, "Notice of Hard Copy Submission—E-Filed Case," must be attached to such documents forms which are not filed on line. Also, Form EFM-4 "Notice of Hard Copy Exhibit Filing" must be completed and uploaded to the action's e-file. Both of these forms may be found on the NYSCEF website. NY R ONDGA E FIL Protocol(B)(4).

ix. *QUEENS COUNTY: Additional supplemental documents*

- *Notice of hard copy submission.* Any party opting out of the e-filing system must have a "Notice of Hard Copy Submission" firmly affixed to the back of the papers. NY R L QUEENS E-FILE Doc. 1(H)(2)(f).

E. Format

1. *Form of documents*

a. *Size and form of paper.* Each paper served or filed shall be durable, white and, except for summonses, subpoenas, notices of appearance, notes of issue, orders of protection, temporary orders of protection and exhibits, shall be eleven by eight and one-half (11 x 8-1/2) inches in size. NY CPLR Rule 2101(a).

b. *Writing and language.* The writing shall be legible and in black ink. NY CPLR Rule 2101(a). Each paper served or filed shall be in the English language which, where practicable, shall be of ordinary usage. NY CPLR Rule 2101(b).

c. *Caption.* Each paper served or filed shall begin with a caption setting forth the name of the court, the venue, the title of the action, the nature of the paper and the index number of the action if one has been assigned. In all papers other than a summons, a complaint or a judgment it shall be sufficient to state the name of the first named party on each side with an appropriate indication of any omissions. NY CPLR Rule 2101(c).

i. *Further contents of first page.* After the first paper has been filed in each case the index number shall appear on the cover and first page to the right of the caption of every paper tendered for filing in the action. Each such cover and first page also shall contain an indication of the county of venue and a brief description of the nature of the paper and, where the case has been assigned to an individual judge, shall contain the name of the assigned judge to the right of the caption. NY R UNIF TRIAL CTS § 202.5(a); NY R UNIF TRIAL CTS § 202.5(b); NY R UNIF TRIAL CTS § 202.5(d)(1)(i).

ii. *ALBANY COUNTY: Request for oral argument.* A party may request oral argument on a motion by indicating such request on the first page of the notice of motion, order to show cause, or answering papers in the area across from the caption of the action/proceeding. NY R 3 JD SUP Doc. 1(B).

iii. *NEW YORK COUNTY: Request for oral argument.* Counsel who wish oral argument must so request conspicuously on the front of their papers. NY R NY CTY Procedure II(D).

d. *Index number.* No paper in an action in the supreme or a county court, other than an order submitted for signature to a judge out of court, shall be submitted for any purpose to the supreme or county court or to a clerk thereof unless there is endorsed on such paper the index number of the action assigned by the clerk of the county. NY CPLR § 8018(c).

i. *ALBANY COUNTY: Index number on all filed documents.* The index number, the request for judicial intervention number and the assigned justice's name shall appear on [all papers filed with the Court subsequent to the complaint]. NY R 3 JD SUP Doc. 1(A).

ii. *ERIE COUNTY: Index number after initial filing.* Cases that are initially commenced by the filing of papers with

the NYSCEF system are identified as e-filed cases by assignment of an Index Number that has "800-899" as the first three (3) digits of the index number (i.e. 802391/2012). NY R ERIE E FIL Doc. 3(II). [The] Index Number must be affixed to all document submissions, filings, and communications to the Erie County Clerk and the Court. Cases that are converted from paper to e-filing shall retain the original index number. NY R ERIE E FIL Doc. 3(II).

iii. *KINGS COUNTY: Index number after initial filing.* In cases commenced electronically by the filing of initiating papers with the NYSCEF system and payment of the statutory fees, the Kings County Clerk will issue an NYSCEF designated index number and the filer shall be notified via the NYSCEF system of the index number assigned and filing date. Such index number must be affixed to all document submissions, filings and communications to the Kings County Clerk and Supreme Court. If counsel faces exigent circumstances that require accelerated assignment, counsel may contact Administration of the Kings County Clerk at kcco-efile@nycourts.gov, during normal business hours of the court. NY R L KINGS E FIL Doc. 1(B)(5).

iv. *NEW YORK COUNTY: Index number on hard copy filings.* Papers subsequently presented for filing in hardcopy format will be filed in this jacket. NY R NY CTY Procedure I(B). Index numbers take the form of six digits followed by a slash and the four digits of the year the case began, e.g., 340705/2018. The first or first two integers of the index number identify the type of case. If a case is commenced electronically, the second integer will be a "5", except as indicated otherwise in the list below. There are many tax certiorari matters e-filed annually and the index numbers therefor will normally run over into those with a "6" as the second integer, and the same will occur with general cases if necessary. The principal types of cases and their index number categories are listed in NY R NY CTY Procedure I(B). NY R NY CTY Procedure I(B); NY R NY CTY Procedure XI(A).

v. *ONONDAGA COUNTY: Index number.* The index number must be referenced on all e-filed documents and correspondence. All e-filed case index numbers will contain the letters "EF" between the year and the file number (for example, 2012EF9999). NY R ONDGA E FIL Protocol(B)(1).

vi. *QUEENS COUNTY: Index number on converted cases.* Cases originally commenced in hard-copy form but later converted to an E-file case, either by stipulation or order will bear a regular index number initially. The County Clerk will issue a new E-file index number. NY R L QUEENS E-FILE Doc. 1(B).

e. *Line spacing.* Every paper filed in court, if typewritten, shall have at least double space between each line, except for quotations and the names and addresses of attorneys appearing in the action. NY R UNIF TRIAL CTS § 202.5(a).

f. *Font size.* Each. . .paper printed or typed, served or filed, except an exhibit or a summons, shall be in clear type of no less than ten (10) point in size. NY CPLR Rule 2101(a).

i. Whenever a requirement relating to size of type is stated in point size, the type size requirement shall be deemed met if the x-height of the type is a minimum of forty-five percent (45%) of the specified point size. Each point shall be measured as .351 millimeter. The x-height size shall be measured as it appears on the page. The x-height is the height of the lower case letters, exclusive of ascenders or descenders. NY CPLR § 105(t).

g. *Margins.* Every paper filed in court shall have at least one (1) inch margins. NY R UNIF TRIAL CTS § 202.5(a).

h. *Citations*

i. *Civil practice law and rules.* NY CPLR § 101, et seq. shall be known as the civil practice law and rules, and may be cited as "CPLR". Reference to a provision in the civil practice law and rules may, except when such provision is being enacted or amended, be made without indicating whether it is a rule or section. NY CPLR § 101.

i. *Indorsement by attorney.* Each paper served or filed shall be indorsed with the name, address and telephone number of the attorney for the party serving or filing the paper, or if the party does not appear by attorney, with the name, address and telephone number of the party. NY CPLR Rule 2101(d).

j. *One-sided printing.* In addition, every paper filed in court, other than an exhibit or printed form, shall contain writing on one side only, except that papers that are fastened on the side may contain writing on both sides. NY R UNIF TRIAL CTS § 202.5(a).

k. *Use of copies authorized.* Except where otherwise specifically prescribed, copies, rather than originals, of all papers, including orders, affidavits and exhibits may be served or filed. Where it is required that the original be served or filed and the original is lost or withheld, the court may authorize a copy to be served or filed. NY CPLR Rule 2101(e).

i. Where a certified copy of a paper is required by law, an attorney admitted to practice in the courts of the state may certify that it has been compared by him with the original and found to be a true and complete copy. Such a certificate, when subscribed by such attorney, has the same effect as if made by a clerk. NY CPLR § 2105.

l. *Recycled paper.* It is the policy of the Unified Court System that litigants, where practicable, should file or submit to

the courts of the Unified Court System of the State of New York papers printed or reproduced on recycled paper. Paper is considered recycled if it contains a minimum content of thirty percent (30%) waste paper. NY R UNIF TRIAL CTS § 215.2. The signature page of every paper filed or submitted to the court on recycled paper should bear the legend: "Printed [Reproduced] on Recycled Paper." NY R UNIF TRIAL CTS § 215.3.

m. *Form of request for judicial intervention; Copies.* A request for judicial intervention must be submitted, in duplicate, on a form authorized by the Chief of the Courts, with proof of service on the other parties to the action (but proof of service is not required where the application is ex parte). NY R UNIF TRIAL CTS § 202.6(a).

n. *KINGS COUNTY: Tabs on filings.* Motions, orders and other filed papers shall be indexed with protruding tabs. Clerks are required to reject papers that do not have protruding exhibit tabs, except papers in matrimonial cases and papers filed by pro se litigants. NY R L KINGS Pt. A, Papers.

o. *NEW YORK COUNTY: Length of briefs.* Unless advance permission otherwise is granted by the court for good cause, memoranda of law shall not exceed thirty (30) pages each (exclusive of table of contents and table of authorities) and affidavits/affirmations shall not exceed twenty-five (25) pages each. NY R NY CTY J RUL Rule 14(b).

p. *QUEENS COUNTY: Form and size of motion filings.* All motions filed in Queens Supreme Court-Civil Term, must adhere to the Motion Support rules and the rules of the assigned judge. NY R L QUEENS MOT SUP Doc. 1. Due to space limitations, the Motion Support Office cannot accept notices of motion/notices of petition and accompanying exhibits which measure greater than eight (8) inches. If your documents measure greater than eight (8) inches you are directed to submit only the notice of motion/notice of petition to the Motion Support Office and bring all exhibits to the calendar call on your return date. NY R L QUEENS MOT SUP Doc. 1.

2. *Form of electronic documents.* Each paper served or filed by electronic means, as defined in NY CPLR Rule 2103(f), shall be capable of being reproduced by the receiver so as to comply with the provisions of NY CPLR Rule 2101(a) through NY CPLR Rule 2101(d). NY CPLR Rule 2101(g).

   a. *File format.* All e-filed documents shall comply with the technical requirements set forth at the NYSCEF site. NY R UNIF TRIAL CTS § 202.5-b(d)(1)(i).

   b. *Heading of document.* The subject matter heading for each paper sent by electronic means must indicate that the matter being transmitted electronically is related to a court proceeding. NY CPLR Rule 2103(b)(7).

   c. *E-filed documents identification*

      i. *ERIE COUNTY.* E-filed cases must be readily identifiable and marked as such. If counsel presents papers to the Office of the Erie County Clerk or the Office of the Chief Clerk in a NYSCEF matter where authorized, counsel should alert the Clerk that the case is a NYSCEF matter. NY R ERIE E FIL Doc. 3(II).

      ii. *KINGS COUNTY.* The Supreme Court's Civil Case Information System ("CCIS") will further identify e-filed cases by the addition of a suffix to the index number (e.g. 500136/2006E). This suffix should be used on all documents filed with the court in e-filed matters. NY R L KINGS E FIL Doc. 1(A)(1).

3. *Signature blocks.* Every pleading, written motion, and other paper, served on another party or filed or submitted to the court shall be signed by an attorney, or by a party if the party is not represented by an attorney, with the name of the attorney or party clearly printed or typed directly below the signature. NY R CHIEF ADMIN § 130-1.1-a(a); NY R UNIF TRIAL CTS § 202.5(d)(1)(iv).

   a. *Printed name.* Beneath each signature shall be printed the name signed. NY CPLR Rule 2101(a).

   b. *Failure to sign.* Absent good cause shown, the court shall strike any unsigned paper if the omission of the signature is not corrected promptly after being called to the attention of the attorney or party. NY R CHIEF ADMIN § 130-1.1-a(a).

   c. *Signature as certification.* By signing a paper, an attorney or party certifies that, to the best of that person's knowledge, information and belief, formed after an inquiry reasonable under the circumstances the presentation of the paper or the contentions therein are not frivolous as defined in NY R CHIEF ADMIN § 130-1.1(c). NY R CHIEF ADMIN § 130-1.1-a(b)(1).

   d. *Electronic signatures.* A document shall be considered to have been signed by an attorney or party in compliance with NY R CHIEF ADMIN § 130-1.1-a if it has been signed by such attorney or party as provided in NY R UNIF TRIAL CTS § 202.5-b(e)(1) and it bears the signatory's name. NY R UNIF TRIAL CTS § 202.5-b(e)(2). An electronically filed document shall be considered to have been signed by, and shall be binding upon, the person identified as a signatory, if:

      i. It bears the physical signature of such person and is scanned into an electronic format that reproduces such signature; or

ii. The signatory has electronically affixed the digital image of his or her signature to the document; or

iii. It is electronically filed under the User ID and password of that person; or

iv. In a tax certiorari action in which the parties have stipulated to this procedure, it is an initiating document that is electronically filed without the signature of the signatory in a form provided above in NY R UNIF TRIAL CTS § 202.5-b(e)(iv), provided that, prior to filing, the document is signed in full in hard copy (which hard copy must be preserved until the conclusion of all proceedings, including appeals, in the case in which it is filed); or

v. In a small claims assessment review proceeding, it is a petition recorded by the NYSCEF site upon the filing of a text file as provided in NY R UNIF TRIAL CTS § 202.5-b(b)(1), provided that prior to filing, the document was signed in full in hard copy (which hard copy must be preserved until the conclusion of all proceedings in the matter, including article 78 (NY CPLR § 7801, et seq.) review and any appeals, and must be made available during the proceeding upon request of the respondent or the court); or

vi. It otherwise bears the electronic signature of the signatory in a format conforming to such standards and requirements as may hereafter be established by the Chief Administrator. NY R UNIF TRIAL CTS § 202.5-b(e).

4. *Confidentiality of personal information.* No person may file any document available for public inspection with any state agency, political subdivision, or in any court of this state that contains a Social Security account number of any other person, unless such other person is a dependent child, or has consented to such filing, except as required by federal or state law or regulation, or by court rule. NY GEN BUS § 399-ddd. Submissions pursuant to e-filing procedures shall have the same confidentiality rights as paper documents. NY R UNIF TRIAL CTS § 202.5-b(k)(1).

a. *Confidential personal information.* Except in the actions designated in NY R UNIF TRIAL CTS § 202.5(e)(1), or as otherwise provided by rule or law or court order, and whether or not a sealing order is or has been sought, the parties shall omit or redact confidential personal information in papers submitted to the court for filing. For purposes of NY R UNIF TRIAL CTS § 202.5(e), confidential personal information ("CPI") means:

i. The taxpayer identification number of an individual or an entity, including a Social Security number, an employer identification number, and an individual taxpayer identification number, except the last four (4) digits thereof;

ii. The date of an individual's birth, except the year thereof;

iii. The full name of an individual known to be a minor, except the minor's initials;

iv. A financial account number, including a credit and/or debit card number, a bank account number, an investment account number, and/or an insurance account number, except the last four (4) digits or letters thereof; and

v. Any of the documents or testimony in a matrimonial action protected by NY DOM REL § 235 or evidence sealed by the court in such an action which are attached as exhibits or referenced in the papers filed in any other civil action. For purposes of NY R UNIF TRIAL CTS § 202.5, a matrimonial action shall mean: an action to annul a marriage or declare the nullity of a void marriage, an action or agreement for a separation, an action for a divorce, or an action or proceeding for custody, visitation, writ of habeus corpus, child support, maintenance or paternity. NY R UNIF TRIAL CTS § 202.5(e)(1).

vi. *ERIE COUNTY.* An attorney or unrepresented litigant filing a document via the NYSCEF system must comply with the requirements of NY R UNIF TRIAL CTS § 202.5(e) regarding the redaction of Confidential Personal Information and NY GEN BUS § 399-ddd(6) concerning the filing of documents containing Social Security Numbers. It is the sole responsibility of counsel or unrepresented litigant filing to be aware of and to comply with existing laws requiring non-disclosure of personal information contained in any document e-filed in NYSCEF. NY R ERIE E FIL Doc. 3(III)(G); NY R ERIE E FIL Doc. 3(III).

vii. *KINGS COUNTY.* An attorney or unrepresented litigant filing a document via the NYSCEF system must comply with the requirements of General Business Law § 399-dd(6), which often require redaction of any Social Security number that appear in the original document. The NYSCEF system automatically redacts portions of filed documents which apparently contain Social Security numbers pursuant to NY R UNIF TRIAL CTS § 202.5-b(k). In the event the filing party receives e-mail notice through NYSCEF that a Social Security number in a filed document has been redacted, and the filing party concludes such redaction is erroneous, the filer should click on the link provided in the e-mail to permit the County Clerk to revert the redaction. For Confidential Personal Information, see NY R UNIF TRIAL CTS § 202.5(e) and NY R L KINGS E FIL Doc. 1(B)(11). [Editor's note: the reference to General Business Law § 399-dd(6) is likely a reference to NY GEN BUS § 399-ddd(6)]. NY R L KINGS E FIL Doc. 1(B)(10); NY R L KINGS E FIL Doc. 1(K)(1).

viii. *NEW YORK COUNTY.* It is the responsibility of counsel and parties to comply with rules restricting disclosure

of confidential personal information. Nevertheless, NYSCEF screens filings and endeavors to identify any that contain social security numbers. When such numbers are discovered through this process, NYSCEF will restrict portions of or all of such documents from public view. Where NYSCEF has redacted what it believes to be a social security number, it will transmit to the filer a notice advising of the action taken and requesting that the filer review the matter and provide notification as set forth in the notice if the redaction has been made in error. NY R NY CTY E FIL Doc. 2(K)(1); NY R NY CTY J RUL Rule A-1. Documents filed in the past in "secure status" under a procedure no longer in place will retain that status unless otherwise directed by the court. NY R NY CTY E FIL Doc. 2(K)(2).

b. *Submission of confidential personal information.* Where a person submitting a paper to a court for filing believes in good faith that the inclusion of the full confidential personal information described in NY R UNIF TRIAL CTS § 202.5(e)(1) is material and necessary to the adjudication of the action or proceeding before the court, he or she may apply to the court for leave to serve and file together with a paper in which such information has been set forth in abbreviated form a confidential affidavit or affirmation setting forth the same information in unabbreviated form, appropriately referenced to the page or pages of the paper at which the abbreviated form appears. NY R UNIF TRIAL CTS § 202.5(e)(3).

c. *Home addresses.* For information on when home addresses and other personal information must be redacted, refer to NY CPLR Rule 2103-a.

5. *Defective papers.* A defect in the form of a paper, if a substantial right of a party is not prejudiced, shall be disregarded by the court, and leave to correct shall be freely given. NY CPLR Rule 2101(f). Papers that are stapled or bound securely shall not be rejected for filing simply because they are not bound with a backer of any kind. NY R UNIF TRIAL CTS § 202.5(a). A paper filed in accordance with the rules of the chief administrator or any local rule or practice established by the court shall be deemed filed. NY CPLR Rule 2102(b).

a. *Objection to defective papers.* The party on whom a paper is served shall be deemed to have waived objection to any defect in form unless, within fifteen (15) days after the receipt thereof, the party on whom the paper is served returns the paper to the party serving it with a statement of particular objections. NY CPLR Rule 2101(f).

F. Filing and Service Requirements

1. *Filing requirements.* Except where otherwise prescribed by law or order of court, papers required to be filed shall be filed with the clerk of the court in which the action is triable. In an action or proceeding in supreme or court, papers required to be filed shall be filed with the clerk of the county in which the proceeding is brought. NY CPLR Rule 2102(a).

a. *Furnishing papers to the court.* Each party shall furnish to the court all papers served by him. The moving party shall furnish at the hearing all other papers not already in the possession of the court necessary to the consideration of the questions involved. Where such papers are in the possession of an adverse party, they shall be produced by him at the hearing on notice served with the motion papers. Only papers served in accordance with the provisions of NY CPLR Rule 2214 shall be read in support of, or in opposition to, the motion, unless the court for good cause shall otherwise direct. NY CPLR Rule 2214(c).

i. *Submission to judge.* All papers for signature or consideration of the court shall be presented to the clerk of the trial court in the appropriate courtroom or clerk's office, except that where the clerk is unavailable or the judge so directs, papers may be submitted to the judge and a copy filed with the clerk at the first available opportunity. All papers for any judge that are filed in the clerk's office shall be promptly delivered to the judge by the clerk. The papers shall be clearly addressed to the judge for whom they are intended and prominently show the nature of the papers, the title and index number of the action in which they are filed, the judge's name and the name of the attorney or party submitting them. NY R UNIF TRIAL CTS § 202.5(b).

ii. *BRONX COUNTY: Approval of motions before filing.* All motion papers must be approved by the Motion Support Office, Supreme Court, Civil Term, room 217, before the motion papers are filed and the appropriate fee paid to the County Clerk. NY R BRONX FIL R Doc. 1.

iii. *ERIE COUNTY: Filing motions.* A motion on notice or a notice of petition in a NYSCEF case shall be filed through the NYSCEF system and must be accompanied by a Request for Judicial Intervention if the motion is being filed upon commencement of the action or if the matter has not yet been assigned to an IAS Justice. In addition, cross motions with the appropriate filing fees and opposition and reply papers must be submitted via the NYSCEF system. NY R ERIE E FIL Doc. 3(V)(A).

iv. *NEW YORK COUNTY: Filing hard copies.* Where in the narrow circumstances described by the e-filing rules a motion is made in hard-copy form or opposition papers are submitted in such form in an e-filed case, the hard-copy documents shall be submitted in the same way papers are submitted in non-e-filed cases, except that

there shall be firmly affixed to each separate document or group of documents, as the back page facing out, a Notice of Hard Copy Submission—E-Filed Case. NY R NY CTY Procedure II(A). For more information on filing in hard copy cases, refer to NY R NY CTY Procedure II(A).

v. *ONONDAGA COUNTY: Submission of responsive papers and cross-motions.* Cross-motions, opposition and reply papers must be submitted online. NY R ONDGA E FIL Protocol(B)(9)(e). Motions and Orders to Show Cause are assigned a sequence number by the system. Counsel must be sure that cross motions and other filings correspond with the correct sequence number so that a cross motion will not be associated with the wrong original motion. NY R ONDGA E FIL Protocol(B)(9)(f).

b. *Electronic filing.* On consent, documents may be filed and served by electronic means in Supreme Court in such civil actions and in such counties as shall be authorized by order of the Chief Administrator of the Courts and only to the extent and in the manner provided in NY R UNIF TRIAL CTS § 202.5-b. NY R UNIF TRIAL CTS § 202.5-b(a)(1). For the definitions of terms used in electronic filing, refer to NY R UNIF TRIAL CTS § 202.5-b(a)(2).

i. *E-filing mandatory.* In any action subject to e-filing, all documents required to be filed with the court by an e-filing party shall be filed and served electronically, except as provided in NY R UNIF TRIAL CTS § 202.5-b. NY R UNIF TRIAL CTS § 202.5-b(d)(1)(i).

- *ERIE COUNTY.* Case types currently eligible and accepted for e-filing are listed at the NYSCEF website. Note that some actions or special proceedings, (i.e., name changes) which are otherwise subject to mandatory e-filing, if commenced by unrepresented litigants will NOT be maintained in the NYSCEF system; individual cases may be found either at NYSCEF or in the Erie County Clerk's online records system. NY R ERIE E FIL Doc. 3(I)(E).
- *KINGS COUNTY.* Cases that are commenced by filing of the initiating papers with NYSCEF are identified as e-filed cases by assignment of a special index number (i.e., Index Numbers beginning with 500,000). NY R L KINGS E FIL Doc. 1(A)(1). All cases required to be e-filed are listed in Uniform Rule 202.5-bb (Mandatory E-Filing Rules) and on the NYSCEF website. All such cases must be commenced by filing with the County Clerk electronically through NYSCEF and all subsequent documents in such cases must be e-filed. Any questions regarding mandatory e-filing in Kings County can be e-mailed to kcco-efile@nycourts.gov. NY R L KINGS E FIL Doc. 1(A)(2).
- *NEW YORK COUNTY.* Unless otherwise provided in the Rules or in NY R NY CTY E FIL Doc. 2 or where a special exemption is granted due to physical requirements (e.g., oversized maps; see NY R NY CTY E FIL Doc. 2(B)(10)), all documents to be filed with the court in a NYSCEF case, including all documents on motions and all letters to the court (where permitted), must be filed with the NYSCEF system. Documents that attorneys would not ordinarily file with the court in a hard-copy case need not be e-filed. Unless otherwise provided by the E-Filing Rules or this Protocol, in e-filed cases the County Clerk and the court will not accept documents filed in paper form. NY R NY CTY E FIL Doc. 2(B)(1). E-filing is mandatory in all types of cases (other than election law, matrimonial, Art. 78, and Mental Hygiene Law matters, and Art. 70 habeas corpus proceedings) that are commenced in this court on or after February 19, 2013. All such cases must be commenced by filing with the County Clerk electronically through NYSCEF and all subsequent documents in such cases must be e-filed. NY R NY CTY E FIL Doc. 2(A)(2)(a). For more information, including information on consensual e-filing and filing scanned hard copy documents, refer to NY R NY CTY E FIL Doc. 2(A)(2).
- *QUEENS COUNTY.* All authorized Torts, Commercial and Tax Certiorari cases may be commenced by E-Filing, however all parties must consent for the action to continue as an E-file case. NY R L QUEENS E-FILE Doc. 1(A). All papers to be filed with the court in an E-filed case shall be filed on-line with the E-file system except as directed by the court. Papers that attorneys would not ordinarily file with the court in a hard-copy case need not be filed in an E-filed matter. NY R L QUEENS E-FILE Doc. 1(E)(2).

ii. *Who may file.* Documents may be filed or served electronically only by a person who has registered as an authorized e-filing user or as otherwise provided in NY R UNIF TRIAL CTS § 202.5-b(c). NY R UNIF TRIAL CTS § 202.5-b(c)(1).

iii. *When filing made.* Documents may be transmitted at any time of the day or night to the NYSCEF site. A document other than an order or judgment is filed when its electronic transmission or, in the case of a petition that is e-filed by submission of a text file as provided in NY R UNIF TRIAL CTS § 202.5-b(b)(1), the electronic transmission of the text file is recorded at that site, provided, however, that where payment of a fee is required upon the filing of a document, the document is not filed until transmission of the document and the information

or form or information as required in NY R UNIF TRIAL CTS § 202.5-b(d)(2)(i), NY R UNIF TRIAL CTS § 202.5-b(d)(2)(ii) or NY R UNIF TRIAL CTS § 202.5-b(d)(2)(iii) has been recorded at the NYSCEF site; or, if no transmission of that information or form or information is recorded, where permitted by the County Clerk, until payment is presented to the County Clerk. NY R UNIF TRIAL CTS § 202.5-b(d)(3)(i).

iv. *Notification of filing.* No later than the close of business on the business day following the electronic filing of a document, a notification, in a form prescribed by the Chief Administrator, shall be transmitted electronically by the NYSCEF site to the person filing such document and the e-mail service addresses of all other participating parties in such action. NY R UNIF TRIAL CTS § 202.5-b(d)(3)(ii).

v. *Removal of confidential information and other corrections.* If a document filed electronically is subsequently discovered to contain confidential data—including but not limited to trade secrets, information protected by confidentiality agreement, or personal confidential information as defined by statute or court rule—or otherwise to have been filed in error, the filer or another party or affected person may (1) notify the parties and any non-party filers in the action of the confidentiality issue or other error raised by the filing, and of his or her intention to seek judicial relief to correct the filing: (2) following such notification, request that the appropriate County Clerk, exercising his or her administrative discretion, place the document temporarily in "restricted" status on the NYSCEF site, to be made available for viewing by court staff and the parties but not the general public; and (3) file an application to correct the filing by order to show cause within five (5) business days of such notification (or such time as the court may direct), including a request for preliminary injunctive relief limiting interim disclosure of the document at issue. Unless otherwise directed by the court, any document placed in restricted status in response to such a request shall be returned to public view upon expiration of this five (5) day period. The Chief Administrator of the Courts shall promulgate forms to implement this process. NY R UNIF TRIAL CTS § 202.5-b(d)(3)(iii).

- *KINGS COUNTY.* For information on what to do when a document was erroneously filed with confidential information, refer to NY R L KINGS E FIL Doc. 1(B)(11).
- *NEW YORK COUNTY.* For information on what to do when a document was erroneously filed with confidential information, refer to NY R NY CTY E FIL Doc. 2(B)(8).
- *QUEENS COUNTY.* For information on what to do when a document was erroneously filed with confidential information, refer to NY R L QUEENS E-FILE Doc. 1(E)(7).

vi. *Documents requiring judge's signature.* Except where the court directs otherwise, any document that requires a judge's signature shall be transmitted electronically and in hard copy to the court. NY R UNIF TRIAL CTS § 202.5-b(d)(6).

vii. *Documents which would be inconvenient to file electronically; Hard copies.* Notwithstanding any other provision of NY R UNIF TRIAL CTS § 202.5-b, and subject to such guidelines as may be established by the Chief Administrative Judge, the County Clerk or his or her designee may require or permit a party to file in hard copy, in accordance with procedures set by the County Clerk or designee, an exhibit or other document which it is impractical or inconvenient to file electronically. NY R UNIF TRIAL CTS § 202.5-b(d)(7).

- *ERIE COUNTY.* Please contact the Supervisor of Actions & Proceedings, Erie County Clerk's Office by calling (716) 858-6662 or the Deputy County Clerk—Legal at (716) 858-6348 for information. NY R ERIE E FIL Doc. 3(III)(F).
- *KINGS COUNTY.* With limited exceptions, as set forth in the Uniform Rules and herein, all documents to be filed with the court in a NYSCEF case shall be filed online via the NYSCEF system. However, should the size, consistency or context of a hard copy document preclude electronic filing, the user shall electronically file a "Notice of Hard Copy Submission—E-Filed Cases" form EFM-3. Any hard copy submitted pursuant to NY R L KINGS E FIL Doc. 1(B)(9) shall include, as a cover page firmly fastened thereto, a copy of the Confirmation Notice received from the NYSCEF site confirming receipt of the "Notice of Hard Copy Submission—E-Filed Cases". Any party may object to such hard copy filing. The Court, in response to such objection, may, following the hard copy filing, fashion such relief as it deems appropriate pursuant to and in furtherance of the Uniform Rules and NY R L KINGS E FIL Doc. 1, including, but not limited to, an Order directing the filing party to file such documents online via the NYSCEF system. When exhibits are impractical to file pursuant to NY R UNIF TRIAL CTS § 202.5-b(d)(7), an additional "Notice of Hard Copy Exhibit Filing" form EFM-4 is required to be submitted. NY R L KINGS E FIL Doc. 1(B)(9).
- *NEW YORK COUNTY.* If a filer needs to submit unusual exhibits in original form that cannot practically be

e-filed, such as oversized maps or electronic recordings, the filer should consult with the County Clerk's E-File Department by telephone at 646-386-3737 (procedural questions only) or by e-mail at ccnyef@nycourts.gov, which will normally require that the filer retain custody of the original subject to possible future directives of the court. NY R NY CTY E FIL Doc. 2(B)(10). In such instances, the filing counsel shall file with NYSCEF a "placeholder" in the form of a Notice of Hard Copy Exhibit Filing (NYSCEF Form EF 21). The Notice should be uploaded to NYSCEF as document type "Exhibit" and the filer should indicate in the "Additional Document Information" field that the filer is retaining custody of the original. Failure to e-file the Notice may result in a gap in the official record of the court. NY R NY CTY E FIL Doc. 2(B)(10).

viii. *Documents containing sensitive or proprietary information.* In an action subject to e-filing, any person may apply for an order prohibiting or restricting the electronic filing in the action of specifically identified materials on the grounds that such materials are subject to copyright or other proprietary rights, or trade secret or other privacy interests, and that electronic filing in the action is likely to result in substantial prejudice to those rights or interests. NY R UNIF TRIAL CTS § 202.5-b(k)(2).

ix. *Refusal to accept paper filings.* In accordance with NY CPLR Rule 2102(c), a County Clerk and a chief clerk of the Supreme Court or County Court, as appropriate, shall refuse to accept for filing papers filed in actions and proceedings when the paper sought to be filed:

- Is in an action subject to electronic filing pursuant to Rules of the Chief Administrator,
- Is not being filed electronically, and
- Does not include the notice required by NY R UNIF TRIAL CTS § 202.5-b(d)(1). NY R UNIF TRIAL CTS § 202.5(d)(1)(v); NY R UNIF TRIAL CTS § 202.5-bb(d).

x. *Emergency filings; Hard copies.* For information on when an emergency filing may be filed and served in hard copy, refer to NY R UNIF TRIAL CTS § 202.5-b(d)(1)(ii), NY R UNIF TRIAL CTS § 202.5-b(d)(1)(iii) and NY R UNIF TRIAL CTS § 202.5-bb(c)(3).

- *KINGS COUNTY.* Under the rules, a participating emergency e-filer must electronically file the documents initially filed in hard copy form within three (3) business days of the emergency filing; the originals will be discarded after the documents have been processed and the failure to e-file as required will therefore lead to an incomplete record. NY R L KINGS E FIL Doc. 1(B)(3).
- *NEW YORK COUNTY.* Occasionally an emergency will arise requiring expedited entry of a document with the County Clerk (e.g., an order issued in the courtroom after a conference or argument of a critical matter), such as for purposes of an immediate appeal. Expedition can be achieved by the Part as follows: the document should be carried by a Court Officer or staff member to the General Clerk's Office to assure immediate and proper recordation in the computer and, as appropriate, the posting of the document to NYSCEF or the Supreme Court Records On-Line Library ("Scroll"). The court will accommodate counsel in emergencies. NY R NY CTY Procedure XI(A).
- *NEW YORK COUNTY.* For more information on how to bring emergency matters before the court, refer to NY R NY CTY Procedure IV.

xi. *Technical failures.* The NYSCEF site shall be considered to be subject to a technical failure on a given day if the site is unable to accept filings or provide access to filed documents continuously or intermittently over the course of any period of time greater than one (1) hour after 12:00 noon of that day. Notice of all such technical failures shall be provided on the site. NY R UNIF TRIAL CTS § 202.5-b(i).

- When e-filing is hindered by a technical failure, a party may file with the appropriate clerk and serve in hard copy. NY R UNIF TRIAL CTS § 202.5-b(i). In the event an attorney or party shall file and serve documents in hard copy pursuant to NY R UNIF TRIAL CTS § 202.5-b(i), each such document shall include the notice required by NY R UNIF TRIAL CTS § 202.5-b(d)(1), and the filer shall file those documents with the NYSCEF site within three (3) business days after restoration of normal operations at that site. NY R UNIF TRIAL CTS § 202.5-b(i).
- With the exception of deadlines that by law cannot be extended, the time for filing of any document that is delayed due to technical failure of the site shall be extended for one (1) day for each day on which such failure occurs, unless otherwise ordered by the court. NY R UNIF TRIAL CTS § 202.5-b(i).
- *ERIE COUNTY.* When filing by electronic means is hindered by a technical failure, please refer to the NY R UNIF TRIAL CTS § 202.5-b(i). NY R ERIE E FIL Doc. 3(III)(K).

- *KINGS COUNTY.* When filing by electronic means is hindered by a NYSCEF technical failure (as set forth in NY R UNIF TRIAL CTS § 202.5-b(i)), a party may file with the appropriate Clerk in hard copy. Except for deadlines that by law cannot be extended (e.g. Statute of limitations, Notice of Appeal), the time for filing of any document that is delayed due to technical failure of the NYSCEF system shall be extended for one day for each day on which such failure occurs, unless otherwise ordered by the court. NY R L KINGS E FIL Doc. 1(B)(13).
- *ONONDAGA COUNTY.* When filing by electronic means is hindered by a technical failure (as set forth in NY R UNIF TRIAL CTS § 202.5-b(h)(3)(i)), a party may file a hard copy with the County Clerk. With the exception of deadlines that by law cannot be extended (e.g., a statute of limitations or the deadline for filing a Notice of Appeal), the time for filing of any document that is delayed due to technical failure of the NYSCEF system will be extended for one day for each day on which such failure occurs, unless otherwise ordered by the court. A "Notice of Hard Copy Filing Submission—E-Filed Case' must accompany any documents not filed via NYSCEF. NY R ONDGA E FIL Protocol(B)(8).

xii. *Filing fees.* For information on what information must be provided to pay filing fees, refer to NY R UNIF TRIAL CTS § 202.5-b(d)(2).

xiii. *Exemption from e-filing.* For information on exemptions from e-filing, refer to NY R UNIF TRIAL CTS § 202.5-bb(e).

xiv. *Filing exhibits*

- *ERIE COUNTY.* In the NYSCEF system, each exhibit must be uploaded as a separate .pdf file. After uploading a primary document, please choose the document type "Exhibit" and enter the appropriate number or letter and a brief description of the exhibit; each exhibit should bear a separate cover sheet clearly marked as "Exhibit A," "Exhibit B," etc. "Exhibit A" or "Exhibit B" is unacceptable as a brief description of the exhibit. Exhibits, where referenced in a signed Order as attached or affixed shall be uploaded with the signed Order as one .pdf document. NY R ERIE E FIL Doc. 3(III)(H); NY R ERIE E FIL Doc. 3(V)(D).
- *KINGS COUNTY.* In the NYSCEF system, each exhibit should be uploaded as a separate PDF file. After uploading a primary document, please choose the document type "Exhibit", enter the appropriate number or letter, and be sure to place a check mark to the right of "Attach to main document". Each exhibit shall bear a separate cover sheet clearly marked as Exhibit A, Exhibit B, etc. NY R L KINGS E FIL Doc. 1(B)(12). Whenever possible, attorneys submitting exhibits in NYSCEF cases should make each exhibit a separate attachment to an affidavit/affirmation in the system (i.e., multiple exhibits should not be filed as a single PDF). NY R L KINGS E FIL Doc. 1(D)(1).
- *NEW YORK COUNTY.* Attorneys submitting exhibits in NYSCEF cases should make each exhibit a separate attachment to an affidavit/affirmation in the system; i.e., exhibits should not be filed as a single PDF-A together with the affidavit/affirmation or grouped together as a single PDF-A attachment because either of these two formats makes it difficult for the Justice to locate particular exhibits as needed. Counsel must also include appropriate descriptive language in the "Additional Document Information" field in NYSCEF. NY R NY CTY E FIL Doc. 2(D)(6).
- *ONONDAGA COUNTY.* All exhibits in e-filed cases must be e-filed individually as separate attachments. NY R ONDGA E FIL Protocol(B)(9)(b).

xv. *Correcting documents*

- *ERIE COUNTY.* Submission of documents which, upon examination, require correction or addition will result in notification to the filer advising that the document has been returned for correction. The filer shall make the required corrections and/or additions as indicated in the e-mail transmission sent by the County Clerk or Part Clerk through the NYSCEF site. The corrected documents may be resubmitted using the "Re-file this document" link highlighted in the filer's document list for the respective case. Please note that in the case of multiple submissions, all related documents filed at the same time may be removed from the case record and returned until all documents are properly submitted. NY R ERIE E FIL Doc. 3(III)(J).
- *KINGS COUNTY.* Submission of documents which, upon examination, require correction or addition will result in notification to the filer advising that there is a problem with a document. The filer shall make the required corrections and/or additions and resubmit the corrected document using the "Refile this document" link. In the event a document is returned for correction, the original file date will be preserved. For corrections of documents filed with the Kings County Clerk which require a court order, refer to the

procedure in NY R UNIF TRIAL CTS § 202.5-b(d)(3)(iii) and NY R L KINGS E FIL Doc. 1(B)(11). NY R L KINGS E FIL Doc. 1(B)(3).

- *ONONDAGA COUNTY.* If there is an error or an additional document is required, the system will notify the filing party, who will make the corrections/additions and resubmit them online. NY R ONDGA E FIL Protocol(B)(6).
- *QUEENS COUNTY.* Generally speaking, documents that have been E-filed will not thereafter be deleted by the County Clerk from NYCEF because the filer asserts that the filing contains an error or a significant omission. When the filer wishes to correct a perceived error or omission in a filed document, he or she should file an amended version of the document, with the original remaining on file, or else obtain a court order providing for deletion of the original. The County Clerk will only delete a document upon request of the filer or on the County Clerk's own initiative when it is obvious from the face of the document alone that the filer made a fundamental error and never intended to file the document that was filed (e.g., a completely unrelated non-litigation document, a different case, or a wrong county). The County Clerk will advise the filer when any such fundamental errors are detected. NY R L QUEENS E-FILE Doc. 1(E)(6).

c. *Facsimile filing.* In the Supreme Court, facsimile filing shall be limited to commercial claims and tax certiorari, conservatorship, and mental hygiene proceedings in Monroe, Westchester, New York and Suffolk Counties. NY R UNIF TRIAL CTS § 202.5-a(a)(1). Refer to NY R UNIF TRIAL CTS § 202.5-a for information on the procedures for facsimile filing.

i. *NEW YORK COUNTY.* Unless indicated otherwise by the court in a particular case or in NY R NY CTY J RUL Doc. 1, Justices do not accept papers by fax. NY R NY CTY J RUL Rule 4.

d. *ERIE COUNTY: Filing request for judicial intervention.* An RJI in a NYSCEF case shall be filed via the NYSCEF system and will be filed after all other documents have been uploaded. The filer may choose between filing a .pdf image of the prepared RJI and any Addendum or having the system prepare the RJI which shall conform to Uniform Rules. Addenda, such as the Commercial Division Addendum, if prepared by the filer must be filed simultaneously with and attached to an RJI and uploaded as one .pdf document with the RJI. If the RJI is prepared by the e-filing system, no separate Addendum is required. Whether or not the filer elects to allow NYSCEF to create the RJI or chooses to upload a prepared RJI, data in addition to the nature of the judicial intervention, including information that appears on any Addenda will be collected through completion of the fields presented. If the filing of the RJI is accomplished through a filing agent, a prepared RJI and Addendum must be filed in lieu of the creation of the RJI by the NYSCEF system, as the RJI must be signed by the attorney. NY R ERIE E FIL Doc. 3(IV). For information on RJIs in specific types of action, refer to NY R ERIE E FIL Doc. 3(IV).

2. *Service requirements*

a. *Who may serve.* Except where otherwise prescribed by law or order of court, papers may be served by any person not a party of the age of eighteen years or over. NY CPLR Rule 2103(a).

b. *Service upon attorney.* Except where otherwise prescribed by law or order of court, papers to be served upon a party in a pending action shall be served upon the party's attorney. Where the same attorney appears for two or more parties, only one (1) copy need be served upon the attorney. Such service upon an attorney shall be made:

i. By delivering the paper to the attorney personally. NY CPLR Rule 2103(b)(1).

ii. By mailing the paper to the attorney at the address designated by that attorney for that purpose or, if none is designated, at the attorney's last known address; service by mail shall be complete upon mailing. NY CPLR Rule 2103(b)(2).

- *BRONX COUNTY.* Service by mail must be within the state. NY R BRONX FIL R Doc. 3.

iii. If the attorney's office is open, by leaving the paper with a person in charge, or if no person is in charge, by leaving it in a conspicuous place; or if the attorney's office is not open, by depositing the paper, enclosed in a sealed wrapper directed to the attorney, in the attorney's office letter drop or box. NY CPLR Rule 2103(b)(3).

iv. By leaving it at the attorney's residence within the state with a person of suitable age and discretion. Service upon an attorney shall not be made at the attorney's residence unless service at the attorney's office cannot be made. NY CPLR Rule 2103(b)(4).

v. By transmitting the paper to the attorney by facsimile transmission, provided that a facsimile telephone number is designated by the attorney for that purpose. Service by facsimile transmission shall be complete upon the receipt by the sender of a signal from the equipment of the attorney served indicating that the transmission was received, and the mailing of a copy of the paper to that attorney. The designation of a facsimile telephone number

in the address block subscribed on a paper served or filed in the course of an action or proceeding shall constitute consent to service by facsimile transmission in accordance with NY CPLR Rule 2103(b)(5). An attorney may change or rescind a facsimile telephone number by serving a notice on the other parties. NY CPLR Rule 2103(b)(5).

vi. By dispatching the paper to the attorney by overnight delivery service at the address designated by the attorney for that purpose or, if none is designated, at the attorney's last known address. Service by overnight delivery service shall be complete upon deposit of the paper enclosed in a properly addressed wrapper into the custody of the overnight delivery service for overnight delivery, prior to the latest time designated by the overnight delivery service for overnight delivery. "Overnight delivery service" means any delivery service which regularly accepts items for overnight delivery to any address in the state. NY CPLR Rule 2103(b)(6).

vii. By transmitting the paper to the attorney by electronic means where and in the manner authorized by the chief administrator of the courts by rule and, unless such rule shall otherwise provide, such transmission shall be upon the party's written consent. The subject matter heading for each paper sent by electronic means must indicate that the matter being transmitted electronically is related to a court proceeding. NY CPLR Rule 2103(b)(7).

- *KINGS COUNTY.* Pursuant to the E-Filing Rules, service of interlocutory documents is made by posting a document to the NYSCEF site, which automatically and immediately transmits an email notice of the filing, including a link to the document, to all participating counsel and unrepresented litigants on the case. The Rules also authorize service by other methods permitted by the CPLR. If service by such other method is made, proof of service must be filed with NYSCEF. NY R L KINGS E FIL Doc. 1(I).
- *NEW YORK COUNTY.* Service. . .will be made automatically through NYSCEF upon all participating counsel and unrepresented parties in the case. There are limited exceptions to the requirement for e-filing in the covered kinds of cases. NY R NY CTY Procedure XI(A). Pursuant to the E-Filing Rules, service of interlocutory documents is made by posting a document to the NYSCEF site, which automatically and immediately transmits an e-mail notice of the filing, including a link to the document, to all participating counsel and unrepresented litigants on the case. The Rules also authorize service by other methods permitted by the CPLR. If service by such a method is made, proof of service must be filed with NYSCEF. NY R NY CTY E FIL Doc. 2(I).
- *QUEENS COUNTY.* Filing with the system permits counsel to serve the papers electronically pursuant to NY R UNIF TRIAL CTS § 202.5-b(f) once consent to E-Filing has been filed on-line. Consult NY R UNIF TRIAL CTS § 202.5-bb(c) for service in mandatory e-filing. Any required proof of service should be E-filed as a separate document. NY R L QUEENS E-FILE Doc. 1(E)(4).

c. *Electronic service mandatory; Consenting to electronic service; How electronic service may be made.* Except as otherwise provided in NY R UNIF TRIAL CTS § 202.5-bb, filing and service of all documents in an action that has been commenced electronically in accordance with NY R UNIF TRIAL CTS § 202.5-bb shall be by electronic means. NY R UNIF TRIAL CTS § 202.5-bb(c)(1).

i. *Party's consent required for certain e-filing.* After commencement of an action wherein e-filing is authorized, documents may be electronically filed and served, but only by, and electronic service shall be made only upon, a party or parties who have consented thereto. NY R UNIF TRIAL CTS § 202.5-b(b)(2)(i).

- A consent to e-filing in an action shall state that the party providing it agrees to the use of e-filing in the action and to be bound by the filing and service provisions in NY R UNIF TRIAL CTS § 202.5-b. NY R UNIF TRIAL CTS § 202.5-b(b)(2)(ii).

ii. *Address for service; Duty to notify as to changes.* The e-mail service address recorded at the time of registration is the e-mail address at which service of interlocutory documents on that party may be made through notification transmitted by the NYSCEF site. It is the responsibility of each filing user to monitor that address and promptly notify the Resource Center in the event of a change in his or her e-mail service address. NY R UNIF TRIAL CTS § 202.5-b(f)(2)(i).

iii. *How service made.* An e-filing party causes service of an interlocutory document to be made upon another party participating in e-filing by filing the document electronically. Upon receipt of an interlocutory document, the NYSCEF site shall automatically transmit electronic notification to all e-mail service addresses in such action. NY R UNIF TRIAL CTS § 202.5-b(f)(2)(ii).

- Except as provided otherwise in NY R UNIF TRIAL CTS § 202.5-b(h)(3), the electronic transmission of the notification shall constitute service of the document on the e-mail service addresses identified therein; however, such service will not be effective if the filing party learns that the notification did not reach the

address of the person to be served. Proof of such service will be recorded on the NYSCEF site. A party may, however, utilize other service methods permitted by the CPLR provided that, if one of such other methods is used, proof of that service shall be filed electronically. NY R UNIF TRIAL CTS § 202.5-b(f)(2)(ii).

iv. *Signatures on hard copies; Proof of service filed electronically.* When an e-filing party serves a document in hard copy on a non-participating party, the document served shall bear full signatures of all signatories and proof of such service shall be filed electronically. NY R UNIF TRIAL CTS § 202.5-b(b)(2)(i).

- *ERIE COUNTY.* In the NYSCEF system, each Affidavit of Service must be uploaded as a separate .pdf file. After uploading the Affidavit, please choose the document type: "Affirmation/Affidavit of Service" and enter the name of the party served as Additional Document Information. NY R ERIE E FIL Doc. 3(III)(I); NY R ERIE E FIL Doc. 3(V)(F).

v. *Effect of failure to consent.* A party's failure to consent to participation in electronic filing and service shall not bar any other party to the action from filing documents electronically with the County Clerk and the court or serving documents upon any other party who has consented to participation. A party who has not consented to participation shall file documents with the court and the County Clerk, and serve and be served with documents, in hard copy. NY R UNIF TRIAL CTS § 202.5-b(b)(2)(i).

d. *Service upon party.* If a party has not appeared by an attorney or the party's attorney cannot be served, service shall be upon the party by a method specified in NY CPLR Rule 2103(b)(1), NY CPLR Rule 2103(b)(2), NY CPLR Rule 2103(b)(4), NY CPLR Rule 2103(b)(5) or NY CPLR Rule 2103(b)(6). NY CPLR Rule 2103(c).

e. *Service on all parties.* Each paper served on any party shall be served on every other party who has appeared, except as otherwise may be provided by court order or as provided in NY CPLR § 3012 or in NY CPLR § 3215(f). Upon demand by a party, the plaintiff shall supply that party with a list of those who have appeared and the names and addresses of their attorneys. NY CPLR Rule 2103(e).

f. *Service by filing.* If a paper cannot be served by any of the methods specified in NY CPLR Rule 2103(b) and NY CPLR Rule 2103(c), service may be made by filing the paper as if it were a paper required to be filed. NY CPLR Rule 2103(d).

g. *Definitions.* For the purposes of NY CPLR Rule 2103:

i. "Mailing" means the deposit of a paper enclosed in a first class postpaid wrapper, addressed to the address designated by a person for that purpose or, if none is designated, at that person's last known address, in a post office or official depository under the exclusive care and custody of the United States Postal Service within the state;

ii. "Electronic means" means any method of transmission of information between computers or other machines designed for the purpose of sending and receiving such transmissions, and which allows the recipient to reproduce the information transmitted in a tangible medium of expression;

iii. "Facsimile transmission" means any method of transmission of documents to a facsimile machine at a remote location which can automatically produce a tangible copy of such documents. NY CPLR Rule 2103(f).

G. Hearings

1. *Oral argument.* Motion papers received by the clerk of the court on or before the return date shall be deemed submitted as of the return date. The assigned judge, in his or her discretion or at the request of a party, thereafter may determine that any motion be orally argued and may fix a time for oral argument. NY R UNIF TRIAL CTS § 202.8(d).

a. A party requesting oral argument shall set forth such request in its notice of motion or in its order to show cause or on the first page of the answering papers, as the case may be. Where all parties to a motion request oral argument, oral argument shall be granted unless the court shall determine it to be unnecessary. NY R UNIF TRIAL CTS § 202.8(d).

b. Where a motion is brought on by order to show cause, the court may set forth in the order that oral argument is required on the return date of the motion. NY R UNIF TRIAL CTS § 202.8(d).

i. *BRONX COUNTY.* All orders to show cause, with the exception of orders to show cause that are returnable in the City Part, the STP Part, the Matrimonial Part and the Preliminary/Compliance Conference Part (IA-11), submitted on or after August 25, 2003, will be returnable on a Monday in the assigned Justice's part and appear on his or her motion calendar. Appearances will be required on orders to show cause. NY R BRONX FIL R Doc. 8. A motion on notice or a notice of petition in a New York Supreme Court E-File (hereafter known as NYSCEF) case, as in others, shall be made returnable in the Motion Support Office (Room 217). NY R BRONX E FIL R Doc. 1(1).

- After a motion/petition and notice are filed with the NYSCEF system, the Motion Support Office will automatically place the motion/proceeding on the submit calendar in the Motion Support Office (Room 217) for the return date. No appearance or other action by the filing attorney is required in order for the motion to be calendared if the motion fee is paid for via NYSCEF. Motions in e-filed cases (other than tax certiorari cases) appear on the submit calendar in Room 217 on the return date. NY R BRONX E FIL R Doc. 1(2).

c. *KINGS COUNTY.* All motions require appearances and oral argument. NY R L KINGS Pt. C, Rule 3.

2. *Return date; Time for hearing.* A notice of motion shall specify the time and place of the hearing on the motion. NY CPLR Rule 2214(a). The moving party determines when a motion on notice shall be heard, but she has to consult the court's or judge's calendar practice first. The movant picks out a "return day" sufficiently far off to assure that the notice requirements of NY CPLR Rule 2214(b) can be met, and to assure as well that the day picked is a day on which the assigned judge hears motions. SIEGEL-NYPRAC § 247.

a. *Judge assigned to hear motion*

i. *Referral to judge supervising disclosure.* Unless the chief administrator of the courts has, by rule, provided otherwise, if a case has been assigned to a judge to supervise disclosure pursuant to NY CPLR § 3104, all motions preliminary to trial shall be referred to such judge whenever practicable. NY CPLR Rule 3214(a).

ii. *Referral to judge who decided prior motion.* Any motion may be referred to a judge who decided a prior motion in the action. NY CPLR Rule 2217(a).

iii. *Transfer when judge unable to hear motion.* If a motion is made to a judge who is or will be for any reason unable to hear it, it may be transferred by order of such judge or by written stipulation of the parties to any other judge to whom it might originally have been made. NY CPLR Rule 2217(c).

iv. *Procedure for unassigned cases.* If a case has not been assigned to a judge, the motion shall be made returnable before the court, and a copy of the moving papers, together with a request for judicial intervention, shall be filed with the court, with proof of service upon all other parties, where required by NY R UNIF TRIAL CTS § 202.6, within five (5) days of service upon the other parties. The moving party shall give written notice of the index number to all other parties immediately after filing of the papers. NY R UNIF TRIAL CTS § 202.8(b).

- *Responding papers.* Copies of all responding papers shall be submitted to the court, with proof of service and with the index number set forth in the papers, on or before the return date. NY R UNIF TRIAL CTS § 202.8(b).
- *Assignment after request for judicial intervention.* The case shall be assigned to a judge as soon as practicable after the filing of the request for judicial intervention pursuant to NY R UNIF TRIAL CTS § 202.6, but in no event later than the return date. After assignment to the judge, the court shall provide for appropriate notice to the parties of the name of the assigned judge. NY R UNIF TRIAL CTS § 202.8(b).
- *Motions to be heard in another county.* Motion papers noticed to be heard in a county other than the county where the venue of the action has been placed by the plaintiff shall be assigned to a judge in accordance with procedures established by the Chief Administrator. NY R UNIF TRIAL CTS § 202.8(b).

v. *ALBANY COUNTY: Motions referred to IAS Justice.* All motions made after a case has been assigned a day certain shall be referred to the IAS Justice unless the motion is returnable during the term in which the matter has been assigned a day certain, in that event, the matter will be referred to the Part 1 Justice for that particular term who may entertain the motion or refer such motion to the IAS Justice. Under those circumstances, the Part I Justice shall decide whether or not to strike the note of issue or assign the matter a new day certain. NY R 3 JD SUP Doc. 1(H)(2). All motions shall be returnable before the assigned justice. NY R 3 JD SUP Doc. 1(B).

b. *Trial of issue raised by motion.* The court may order that an issue of fact raised on a motion shall be separately tried by the court or a referee. If the issue is triable of right by jury, the court shall give the parties an opportunity to demand a jury trial of such issue. Failure to make such demand within the time limited by the court, or, if no such time is limited, before trial begins, shall be deemed a waiver of the right to trial by jury. An order under NY CPLR § 2218 shall specify the issue to be tried. NY CPLR § 2218.

c. *Audio-visual coverage of trial court proceeding.* Audio-visual coverage of proceedings in the trial courts shall be permitted only in accordance with the provisions of Part 131 of the Rules of the Chief Administrator (NY R CHIEF ADMIN § 131.1, et seq.). NY R CHIEF J § 29.3.

d. *Adjournment of return date.* Stipulations of adjournment of the return date made by the parties shall be in writing and shall be submitted to the assigned judge. Such stipulation shall be effective unless the court otherwise directs. No more than three (3) stipulated adjournments for an aggregate period of sixty (60) days shall be submitted without prior permission of the court. NY R UNIF TRIAL CTS § 202.8(e)(1).

i. Absent agreement by the parties, a request by any party for an adjournment shall be submitted in writing, upon notice to the other party, to the assigned judge on or before the return date. The court will notify the requesting party whether the adjournment has been granted. NY R UNIF TRIAL CTS § 202.8(e)(2).

ii. *BRONX COUNTY.* Non-disclosure motions for IA5, IA7 and IA22 will be adjourned for oral argument to the Monday of the second week following the week of the return date of the motion. All other non-disclosure motions will be deemed submitted on the return date and forwarded to Chambers unless a stipulation of adjournment complying with the requirements of NY R UNIF TRIAL CTS § 202.8(e) is submitted, in which event, the motion will be adjourned for the requested date and kept in the Clerk's Office. If a non-stipulated request for adjournment or notice is submitted, the motion and request will be forwarded to Chambers for judicial approval or denial of the request. In either event, the attorney requesting the adjournment will be notified, via telephone, of the granting or denial of the request and instructed to notify his adversary. NY R BRONX FIL R Doc. 8.

iii. *BRONX COUNTY.* Motions that have been e-filed may be adjourned in Room 217 if an adjournment complies with the procedures of the Motion Support Office (explained in the "Filing Rules—Motion Procedure" section of the "Courthouse Procedures" link on the website of [the] court). An adjournment that so complies may be obtained by filing a stipulation of all parties with NYSCEF (designated in the filing menu as a "Stipulation to Adjourn Motion"). NY R BRONX E FIL R Doc. 1(3).

iv. *NEW YORK COUNTY.* The Courtroom also maintains a "APB (All Papers By)" Calendar, which is used when a party seeks an adjournment but fails to comply with the Courtroom's procedures or there is a failure to comply with procedures that requires the clerk to adjourn the motion/application (e.g., failure to submit a Confirmation Notice in an e-filed case). The case may be put over for three days to allow compliance with those procedures, as described further below. NY R NY CTY Procedure II(C); NY R NY CTY E FIL Doc. 2(D)(2). E-filed applications may be adjourned in the Part if an adjournment complies with the Part's procedures (see the Uniform Rules of the Justices (Local Rules) on the court's website). An adjournment that so complies may be obtained by filing with NYSCEF a stipulation of all parties (designated in the filing menu as a Stipulation—Adjournment of Motion—Before Judge); the motion number and the current return date of the motion being adjourned shall be set forth in the "Additional Document Information" field in NYSCEF. Absent any problems, the Part will effectuate the adjournment without need for an appearance or any other action by the parties. NY R NY CTY E FIL Doc. 2(D)(4).

v. *QUEENS COUNTY.* The Motion Support Office is NOT authorized to grant adjournments. NY R L QUEENS MOT SUP Doc. 1.

e. *ALBANY COUNTY: Motion terms.* There shall be a. . . Motion Term on each Friday in the Supreme Court, Albany County. The Friday Motion Term shall include all Article 78 Proceedings involving New York State and proceedings commenced pursuant to Article 14 of the Civil Service Law (including applications for injunctive relief made pursuant to section 209-a of the Civil Service Law). NY R 3 JD SUP Doc. 1(F). Generally, parties will be granted only one adjournment for the Friday Motion Term. NY R 3 JD SUP Doc. 1(F).

f. *ALBANY COUNTY: Motion determined without hearing.* All motions are deemed "submitted" on the return date and no appearances are required by the parties. NY R 3 JD SUP Doc. 1(B). In the event oral argument is requested, the parties should not appear on the return date. At the discretion of the assigned Judge and upon the granting of a request for oral argument, the parties will be notified by Chambers of the scheduled time and place at which argument will be heard. Where a motion is brought on by order to show cause, the court may set forth in the order that appearances and/or oral argument are required on the return date of the motion. NY R 3 JD SUP Doc. 1(B).

g. *BRONX COUNTY: Return date.* All assigned and unassigned motions will be returnable five (5) days a week in the Civil Branch Clerk's Office, Room 217, at 9:30 a.m. NY R BRONX FIL R Doc. 8.

i. If on any submitted non-disclosure motion oral argument is requested and granted, or directed by the Court, the motion shall be adjourned for oral argument before the I.A. Judge on the second Monday following the week of the return date of the motion. Attorneys will be notified via telephone of the adjourned date. NY R BRONX FIL R Doc. 8.

h. *BRONX COUNTY: Oral argument.* Calendars of disclosure motions and other motions adjourned for oral argument will be published for the four (4) business days preceding the rescheduled appearance date and on the rescheduled date of the motion. These repetitive publications will serve as the notification of procedure of adjournment of all motions. In addition, two (2) days before the return date of unassigned motions a list of such motions indicating the assigned Justice and the adjourned date of the motion will be published. NY R BRONX FIL R Doc. 8.

i. *BRONX COUNTY: Resolution before return date.* Counsel/parties must advise the Court in writing on or before the return date of all motions that have been resolved by Counsel/parties themselves and all motions the movant(s) wish to be withdrawn. NY R BRONX FIL R Doc. 8.

j. *ERIE COUNTY: Calendaring of motions.* Refer to individual Justice's Part Rules. NY R ERIE E FIL Doc. 3(V)(B).

k. *KINGS COUNTY: Return date set by court.* Irrespective of the return date indicated in the notice of motion, motions will be rescheduled by the E-file/Motion Support Office to a date designated by the assigned Judge. NY R L KINGS Pt. C, Rule 2.

l. *KINGS COUNTY: Calendar calls.* There shall be two (2) calendar calls on motion days. The first calendar call shall be at 9:30 AM and the second calendar call shall be at 10:45 AM, unless the Judge's Part Rules provide otherwise. Defaults shall only be taken on second call. Attorneys with appearances elsewhere in the courthouse may advise the clerk of their whereabouts to avoid a default. Failure to so advise the clerk or appear at the default calendar call will result in a default order being entered or the motion being marked off the calendar. NY R L KINGS Pt. C, Rule 7.

m. *NEW YORK COUNTY: Return date and assigned courtroom.* Motions made by notice of motion and petitions and notices of petition in special proceedings are processed by the General Clerk's Office (Room 119) and are to be made returnable in the Motion Submission Part Courtroom (Room 130) on any business day of the week at 9:30 AM. There are some differences in electronically-filed cases. NY R NY CTY Procedure II; NY R NY CTY Procedure II(C); NY R NY CTY J RUL Rule 13(a).

   i. For the convenience of counsel, between 9:00 A.M. and 9:30 A.M. each day, in advance of the "call," Room 130 accepts (1) written stipulations; (2) affidavits/affirmations reciting the required details as to an adjournment on consent; (3) stipulations, letters or other writings withdrawing motions; and (4) final papers or complete sets of papers on motions. For motions in which these items are handed in before the "call," no one need remain to answer the "call." Counsel/parties must advise the court, either between 9:00 A.M. and 9:30 A.M. or at the "call," of all motions or cases that have been resolved by counsel/parties themselves and all motions that the movant no longer wishes to pursue. If such resolution occurs subsequent to the "call", the assigned Justice must be advised as soon as possible, by written notice sent to the Part, so that the court does not do unnecessary work. NY R NY CTY Procedure II(C).

   ii. Depending upon the assigned Part, contested motions submitted in the Motion Submission Part Courtroom are submitted without argument, or rescheduled for oral argument if so directed by the assigned Justice. For Justices who schedule argument on a case-by-case basis, notice of the argument date will be transmitted by the court. Counsel may ascertain how a motion submitted in Courtroom 130 was marked by consulting Scroll on the court's website, the e-Track application, or, on the two (2) days immediately following the submission date, the New York Law Journal. NY R NY CTY J RUL Rule 13(a).

n. *NEW YORK COUNTY: Motion call.* Each day in the Motion Submission Part Courtroom, commencing at 9:30 A.M., all motions returnable that day will be "called" for the submission of these papers, which must be handed up at this "call" or, as described below, immediately before. Because hundreds of motions appear on the Room 130 calendars every day, motion papers (other than part of the moving papers as described above) cannot be accepted on any day prior to the return date. Courtesy copies are not required nor accepted, but working copies are required by certain Justices in e-filed cases. NY R NY CTY Procedure II(C). If argument is directed, it will take place on an announced date shortly after the day of submission. NY R NY CTY Procedure II(C).

o. *NEW YORK COUNTY: Oral arguments.* Pursuant to request of some Justices, motions submitted in Room 130 will automatically be scheduled for a set argument date in the Part. Other Justices determine on a case-by-case basis after submission in Room 130 whether to accept a particular substantive motion on submission, to require oral argument, or to hold a conference. NY R NY CTY Procedure II(D). If argument is directed by the Justice automatically, notice of argument and the argument date will be given in Room 130. Any appearing party is expected to give notice to all parties and an announcement to this effect is made in Room 130. If the motion is submitted in Room 130 and the Justice, after examining the file, determines that argument should be directed, notice of the argument and the argument date will not be sent by the court. To obtain notification of the argument date and other developments, counsel should use e-Track. If argument notification is not given or transmitted as just described, counsel should understand that the motion has been taken on submission for decision on the papers. NY R NY CTY Procedure II(D).

   i. Calendars of motions to be argued in the Parts are published on the morning of the argument date and on the day before in the New York Law Journal under each Part. Argument information is available on a case-by-case basis in Scroll, and e-mail notifications are sent by e-Track to participating attorneys whenever a motion is scheduled for argument in the court's computer system. NY R NY CTY J RUL Rule 15(a)

p. *NEW YORK COUNTY: Motion determined without hearing.* Given the purpose of the Room 130 procedure, the substance of motions will not be addressed at the submission "call." No Judge is present. To the extent possible, motions submitted in Room 130 will be decided "on the papers." Indeed, attorneys are encouraged to use service or clerks to deliver papers or working copies, or to agree among themselves to have one of them deliver papers for all parties by service or a clerk. Counsel for the movant need not appear to "take a default" on any motion or for any other reason. Motions will be submitted, not marked off, in the absence of the movant. Opposing counsel similarly need not appear in person in order to avoid suffering a default. Delivery of papers by service or a clerk will suffice. The court's goal is to be able to collect papers on motions in an orderly fashion but without any attorney having to make an appearance in Room 130 at any time. NY R NY CTY Procedure II(C).

q. *ONONDAGA COUNTY: Return date.* If the motion is the first filing in an action, the case will be assigned and counsel will be notified by the Supreme Court Clerk's Office via the NYSCEF system of the assigned justice and return date. NY R ONDGA E FIL Protocol(B)(7)(c). If the motion is on a previously assigned case, counsel may choose a return date from the assigned justice's motion term schedule. If the date in unavailable, the Supreme Court Clerk's Office will assign the motion to the next available motion term date and will notify counsel via e-mail. The change will also appear in the notification generated by the NYSCEF system. NY R ONDGA E FIL Protocol(B)(7)(d).

r. *QUEENS COUNTY: Return date.* Motions must be made returnable on the proper day/time based on the assigned judge. NY R L QUEENS MOT SUP Doc. 1. Failure to make a motion returnable on the proper day/time may result in the motion being administratively rescheduled or marked off. NY R L QUEENS MOT SUP Doc. 1.

s. *QUEENS COUNTY: Unassigned motions.* For RJI/Motions, due to the fact that the movant would not know who the assigned judge will be, the notice of motion may be returnable any day of the week. RJI/Motions shall be made returnable in "Queens Supreme Court" with no address designated. The motion will be administratively rescheduled to the proper day of the week based on the judge (once a judge has been assigned). Within one (1) week of filing, the movant must check online to see who the assigned judge is (and therefore the location/date/time) that their motion is now returnable. Movant must then notify their adversary of this information prior to the return date. NY R L QUEENS MOT SUP Doc. 1.

3. *Entry of order after hearing.* An order determining a motion shall be entered and filed in the office of the clerk of the court where the action is triable, and all papers used on the motion and any opinion or memorandum in writing shall be filed with that clerk unless the order dispenses with such filing. When a statute or civil practice rule requires such filing and entry in a county other than that in which the order was made, the party prevailing on the motion shall file the order and the papers used on the motion with the proper clerk after receiving them. If a party fails to file any papers required to be filed under NY CPLR Rule 2220(a), the order may be vacated as irregular, with costs. NY CPLR Rule 2220(a). For more information on the entry of an order after a motion, refer to NY CPLR Rule 2219.

a. *BRONX COUNTY: Settled orders.* A Judge's decision will often call for a Settled Order. The purpose of the settled order is to give effect to the decision by directing that some action be done and/or that a court official perform some task. NY R BRONX LEG SUP Doc. 2. A settled order consists of a notice of settlement informing all parties that the proposed order will be presented to the judge who made the decision on a date certain. Next comes the proposed order which will be presented to the judge. This order should conform to the judge's decision and should direct the relief granted in the decision. This should be followed by proof of service upon all parties who were noticed with the decision. It is also helpful if a copy of the judge's decision is included along with the other papers. A settled order should always be noticed before the judge who made the decision. NY R BRONX LEG SUP Doc. 2.

i. Although an order is usually settled by the party who prevailed on the motion, any party may settle the order. It should be presented to the court within sixty (60) days of the decision. The other parties are entitled to ten (10) days notice where service of the settled order is done by mail, five (5) days if the notice is personally delivered. An attorney who is served with a notice of settlement which he believes does not accurately reflect the decision may settle a counter order. The counter order must be noticed for the same day and must be served not less than seven (7) days if by mail and two (2) days if personally delivered. NY R BRONX LEG SUP Doc. 2.

ii. Settled orders are usually sent to the judge the day after they noticed for settlement. No appearance is necessary or even contemplated on a settled order. If the decision directs "submit order", then no notice is necessary, and the order will be sent to the judge as soon a practical after it is received. No fees are collected on settled orders. NY R BRONX LEG SUP Doc. 2.

b. *ERIE COUNTY: Proposed orders.* Proposed orders shall be submitted through the NYSCEF system and a working copy provided to the IAS Justice for signature, if Part Rules so require. NY R ERIE E FIL Doc. 3(V)(G).

c. *KINGS COUNTY: Long form orders.* If the Court directs that an order be settled or submitted on a motion in a NYSCEF case, the proposed order, with Notice of Settlement where required, and any proposed counter-order shall be filed with the Court via NYSCEF. The relevant clerk's office will process the documents in the customary manner. NY R L KINGS E FIL Doc. 1(E).

   i. WORKING COPIES OF PROPOSED ORDERS WITH NOTICE OF SETTLEMENT MUST BE SUBMITTED IN THE MOTION SUPPORT OFFICE (ROOM 227) AS EXPLAINED HEREIN. THEY MUST NOT BE DELIVERED TO THE PART OR CHAMBERS, EXCEPT WHERE THE INDIVIDUAL JUSTICE'S PART RULES PROVIDE OTHERWISE; DOING SO WILL CAUSE ADMINISTRATIVE CONFUSION AND POSSIBLE MISPLACEMENT OF PAPERS. Any such submission shall be sent in a timely manner (kindly review individual Justice's rules) and be conspicuously marked on the outside "NYSCEF Matter;" lack of such marking may delay processing. After an order/counter-order has been signed, it will be scanned, and the County Clerk will affix the entry stamp into the NYSCEF system, which will immediately transmit notice of this event via e-mail, including a link to the entered document, to all participating attorneys and unrepresented litigants in the case. Such transmittal does not constitute Notice of Entry. NY R L KINGS E FIL Doc. 1(E).

d. *NEW YORK COUNTY: Long form orders.* Although the court strongly favors the use of short form orders and judgments, there are instances when settlement of an order or judgment is appropriate. When a Justice directs in a decision that a long form order or judgment be settled, that decision is recorded in the court's computer system by the General Clerk's Office and the motion file with decision is held in the Order Section of the Office in Room 119. The settlement process takes place there. NY R NY CTY Procedure II(D); NY R NY CTY E FIL Doc. 2(E).

   i. A proposed long form order or judgment in compliance NY R UNIF TRIAL CTS § 202.48 must be presented to the relevant back office, together with a notice of settlement which bears a settlement date, the date on which the order is to be ready for formal presentation to the Justice. In an e-filed case the submission shall be made electronically. The proposed order or counter-order should be e-filed and it will be transmitted automatically by the NYSCEF system to the appropriate back office. The return date and time of the proposed order must be at 9:30 A.M. no sooner than either five (5) days from personal service of the proposed order or ten (10) days from service by mail. Proof of timely service on the other parties must accompany the proposed order in a hard copy case. If an order or judgment is submitted late (later than sixty (60) days from signing and filing of the decision) and the proponent can show good cause for this tardiness, an affidavit or affirmation justifying the delay should be annexed to the proposed order, together with proof of service thereof. If persuaded, the Justice will consider the proposed order despite its untimeliness. NY R NY CTY Procedure II(D); NY R NY CTY E FIL Doc. 2(E).

   ii. Sometimes a decision will state "Submit Order." The submitting party should prepare a long form order and make it returnable without notice. Counsel should deliver the proposed order to the Order Section of the appropriate back office, except in an e-filed case, when it shall be submitted electronically. NY R NY CTY Procedure II(D). If the decision of the court directs that a proposed order be settled or submitted in the Part or in Chambers, that direction, should, of course, be followed without presentation of the proposal to the back office. NY R NY CTY Procedure II(D).

   iii. For information on proposed counter-orders, refer to NY R NY CTY Procedure II(D) and NY R NY CTY J RUL Rule 16(b).

e. *QUEENS COUNTY: Proposed orders.* If the court directs that an order be settled or submitted on a motion in an E-file case, the proposed order and any proposed counter-order shall be filed with the court on-line with proof of service. (If a decision refers to a proceeding on the record, a copy of the transcript must be submitted.) Working copies of all proposed orders MUST be submitted to the Motion Support Office before an order can be reviewed. NY R L QUEENS E-FILE Doc. 1(I).

   i. Counsel are advised to adhere to NY R UNIF TRIAL CTS § 202.48 regarding the submission or settlement of their proposed order or judgment. Persons who are submitting proposed orders/judgments pursuant to a previously issued memorandum decision must submit a copy of the memorandum decision with their proposed order/judgment. Upon E-Filing a proposed order/judgement, a working copy of the proposed order/judgement must be provided to the Motion Support Office. NY R L QUEENS MOT SUP Doc. 1.

H. Forms

1. Official Motion for Judgment as a Matter of Law or New Trial Forms for New York

a. Request for judicial intervention. NY R UNIF TRIAL CTS § 202.6.

b. Notice of motion. NY R UNIF TRIAL CTS § 202.7(b).

2. New York Motion for Judgment as a Matter of Law or New Trial Forms

a. Notice of motion to set aside verdict of jury and grant judgment or new trial. MCF CPLR § 7:213.

b. Notice of motion to set aside verdict of jury as contrary to weight of evidence and grant new trial. MCF CPLR § 7:214.

c. Notice of motion to set aside verdict of jury for reversible error in admitting evidence and to grant new trial. MCF CPLR § 7:215.

d. Affidavit in support of motion to set aside verdict of jury as contrary to weight of evidence and grant judgment or new trial. MCF CPLR § 7:216.

e. Affirmation in support of motion to set aside verdict of jury as contrary to weight of evidence and grant new trial. MCF CPLR § 7:217.

f. Affidavit in support of motion to set aside verdict of jury for reversible error in admitting evidence and to grant new trial. MCF CPLR § 7:218.

g. Notice of motion to set aside verdict as contrary to weight of evidence and to enter judgment or, in alternative, for new trial. MCF CPLR § 7:221.

h. Affidavit in support of motion to set aside verdict as contrary to weight of evidence and to enter judgment or, in alternative, for new trial. MCF CPLR § 7:222.

i. Notice of motion to set aside decision of court and grant judgment or new trial. MCF CPLR § 7:224.

j. Affidavit in support of motion to set aside decision of court. MCF CPLR § 7:225.

k. General form of affidavit of service of motion papers. MCF CPLR § 5:24.

I. Applicable Rules

1. *State rules*

a. Short title; Application; Construction; Definitions. NY CPLR § 101; NY CPLR § 103; NY CPLR § 104; NY CPLR § 105.

b. Appendix of official forms. NY CPLR § 107.

c. Extensions of time generally. NY CPLR § 2004.

d. Form of papers. NY CPLR Rule 2101; NY CPLR Rule 2102; NY CPLR § 2105; NY CPLR Rule 2106; NY GEN BUS § 399-ddd; NY R UNIF TRIAL CTS § 215.2; NY R UNIF TRIAL CTS § 215.3.

e. Service of papers. NY CPLR Rule 2103.

f. Where motion made; In supreme court action. NY CPLR § 2212.

g. Motion papers; Service; Time. NY CPLR Rule 2214.

h. Relief demanded by other than moving party. NY CPLR Rule 2215.

i. Prior motion; Ex parte motion; Transfer of motion; Hearings; Orders. NY CPLR Rule 2217; NY CPLR § 2218; NY CPLR Rule 2220.

j. Computation of time. NY CPLR § 2402; NY GEN CONSTR § 19; NY GEN CONSTR § 20; NY GEN CONSTR § 25-a; NY GEN CONSTR § 30; NY GEN CONSTR § 31; NY GEN CONSTR § 53.

k. Motions heard by judge supervising disclosure; Stay of disclosure. NY CPLR Rule 3214.

l. Motion for judgment during trial. NY CPLR Rule 4401; NY CPLR § 4401-a; NY CPLR Rule 4402.

m. Post-trial motions. NY CPLR Rule 4403; NY CPLR Rule 4404; NY CPLR Rule 4405; NY CPLR Rule 4406.

n. Effect of judgment dismissing claim. NY CPLR Rule 5013.

o. Fees; Index number fees of county clerks. NY CPLR § 8018.

p. Hours of court; Proceedings in court. NY R CHIEF J § 3.1; NY R CHIEF J § 29.3.

q. Application of part; Waiver; Additional rules; Application of CPLR; Definitions. NY R UNIF TRIAL CTS § 202.1.

r. Papers filed in court; Electronic filing in supreme court. NY R UNIF TRIAL CTS § 202.5; NY R UNIF TRIAL CTS § 202.5-a; NY R UNIF TRIAL CTS § 202.5-b; NY R UNIF TRIAL CTS § 202.5-bb.

s. Request for judicial intervention. NY R UNIF TRIAL CTS § 202.6.

t. Calendaring of motions; Uniform notice of motion form; Affirmation of good faith. NY R UNIF TRIAL CTS § 202.7.

u. Motion procedure; Preliminary conferences. NY R UNIF TRIAL CTS § 202.8; NY R UNIF TRIAL CTS § 202.12.
v. Rescheduling after jury disagreement, mistrial or order for new trial. NY R UNIF TRIAL CTS § 202.45.
w. Rules of the commercial division of the Supreme Court. NY R UNIF TRIAL CTS § 202.70.
x. Signing of papers. NY R CHIEF ADMIN § 130-1.1-a.

2. *Local rules*
   a. *Albany County*
      i. Third judicial district rules. NY R 3 JD SUP Doc. 1.
   b. *Bronx County*
      i. Filing of papers in supreme court. NY R BRONX FIL R Doc. 1.
      ii. Request for judicial intervention. NY R BRONX FIL R Doc. 2.
      iii. Motion procedure. NY R BRONX FIL R Doc. 8.
      iv. Commercial division. NY R BRONX FIL R Doc. 12.
      v. Motions on notice. NY R BRONX E FIL R Doc. 1.
      vi. Settled orders. NY R BRONX LEG SUP Doc. 2.
   c. *Erie County*
      i. Joint protocols for New York State Courts E-Filing (NYSCEF) cases filed in Supreme Court, Erie County. NY R ERIE E FIL Doc. 3.
   d. *Kings County*
      i. Papers. NY R L KINGS Pt. A, Papers.
      ii. Service of motion papers. NY R L KINGS Pt. C, Rule 1.
      iii. Scheduling of motions. NY R L KINGS Pt. C, Rule 2.
      iv. Appearance and argument. NY R L KINGS Pt. C, Rule 3.
      v. Courtesy copies. NY R L KINGS Pt. C, Rule 5.
      vi. Motion calendar calls. NY R L KINGS Pt. C, Rule 7.
      vii. Protocol on courthouse and county clerk procedures for electronically filed cases. NY R L KINGS E FIL Doc. 1.
   e. *New York County*
      i. Commencement of cases. NY R NY CTY Procedure I.
      ii. RJIs and assignments. NY R NY CTY Procedure IA.
      iii. Motions and special proceedings by notice of motion/petition. NY R NY CTY Procedure II.
      iv. County clerk litigation functions. NY R NY CTY Procedure XI.
      v. Protocol on courthouse and county clerk procedures for electronically filed cases. NY R NY CTY E FIL Doc. 2.
      vi. Redaction of information in documents filed with the county clerk and the court. NY R NY CTY J RUL Rule A-1.
      vii. Papers by fax. NY R NY CTY J RUL Rule 4.
      viii. Motions on notice; Orders to show cause. NY R NY CTY J RUL Rule 13.
      ix. Motion papers. NY R NY CTY J RUL Rule 14.
      x. Oral argument; Adjournments. NY R NY CTY J RUL Rule 15.
   f. *Onondaga County*
      i. Onondaga county protocol for case filings New York State Electronic Files (NYSCEF). NY R ONDGA E FIL Protocol.
   g. *Queens County*
      i. Motion support office. NY R L QUEENS MOT SUP Doc. 1.

ii. Queens county protocol on courthouse procedures for electronically filed cases. NY R L QUEENS E-FILE Doc. 1.

J. Miscellaneous

NOTE: Individual judges' rules may apply.

ALBANY COUNTY

JUSTICE LISA M. FISHER: NY R 3 JD FISHER Fisher; NY R 3 JD FISHER Fisher, PC Order.

JUSTICE RICHARD MOTT: NY R 3 JD MOTT Mott.

JUSTICE STEPHAN G. SCHICK: NY R 3 JD Schick.

FORECLOSURE SETTLEMENT PART: NY R 3 JD Foreclosure Settlement.

BRONX COUNTY

JUSTICE PAUL L. ALPERT: [NY R BRONX J Part IA-29, as amended by NY ORDER 20-0337].

JUSTICE BEN BARBATO: NY R BRONX J Part IA-21.

JUSTICE MARY ANNE BRIGANTTI: [NY R BRONX J Part IA-15, as amended by NY ORDER 20-0338].

JUSTICE JOSEPH E. CAPELLA: NY R BRONX J Part IA-23.

JUSTICE MITCHELL DANZIGER: NY R BRONX J Part IA-3/33 ; [NY R BRONX J Danziger, Part IA-3/33, as amended by NY ORDER 20-0339].

JUSTICE LAURA G. DOUGLAS: NY R BRONX J Part IA-11.

JUSTICE RUBEN FRANCO: NY R BRONX J Part IA-26.

JUSTICE DORIS M. GONZALEZ: NY R BRONX J Part IA-24.

JUSTICE WILMA GUZMAN: NY R BRONX J Part IA-7; [NY R BRONX J Guzman, Part IA-7 Virtual, as amended by NY ORDER 20-0340].

JUSTICE ROBERT T. JOHNSON: NY R BRONX J Part IA-12.

JUSTICE DONALD A. MILES: NY R BRONX J Part IA-8.

JUSTICE DONNA M. MILLS: NY R BRONX J Part IA-9.

JUSTICE JULIA I. RODRIGUEZ: NY R BRONX J Part IA-18; [NY R BRONX J Part IA-27, as amended by NY ORDER 20-0341].

JUSTICE LLINET M. ROSADO: [NY R BRONX J Part IA-25, as amended by NY ORDER 20-0342].

JUSTICE NORMA RUIZ: NY R BRONX J Part IA-22; [NY R BRONX J Ruiz, Part IA-22 Virtual, as amended by NY ORDER 20-0343].

JUSTICE HOWARD H. SHERMAN: NY R BRONX J Part IA-4.

JUSTICE FERNANDO TAPIA: NY R BRONX J Part IA-13.

JUSTICE ELIZABETH A. TAYLOR: NY R BRONX J Part IA-2.

JUSTICE ALISON Y. TRUITT: NY R BRONX J Part IA-5.

PART IDV: NY R BRONX J Doc. 1.

PRE-TRIAL PART RULES: NY R BRONX J Doc. 2.

PRE TRIAL WORKSHEET: NY R BRONX J Doc. 3.

FORECLOSURE SETTLEMENT PART RULES: NY R BRONX J Doc. 4.

GUARDIANSHIP PART RULES: NY R BRONX J Doc. 5.

LPM PART RULES: NY R BRONX J Doc. 6.

ERIE COUNTY

JUSTICE M. WILLIAM BOLLER: NY R 8 JD J Boller.

JUSTICE RALPH A. BONIELLO: NY R 8 JD J Boniello.

JUSTICE CHRISTOPHER J. BURN: NY R 8 JD J Burns.

JUSTICE RUSSELL P. BUSCAGLIA: NY R 8 JD J Buscaglia.
JUSTICE FRANK CARUSO: NY R 8 JD J Caruso.
JUSTICE STEPHEN W. CASS: NY R 8 JD J Cass.
JUSTICE DEBORAH A. CHIMES: NY R 8 JD J Chimes.
JUSTICE EMILIO COLAIACOVO: [NY R 8 JD J Colaiacovo, as amended by NY ORDER 20-0252].
JUSTICE DIANE Y. DEVLIN: NY R 8 JD J Devlin.
JUSTICE JAMES H. DILLON: NY R 8 JD J Dillon.
JUSTICE PAULA L. FEROLETO: NY R 8 JD J Feroleto.
JUSTICE DANIEL J. FURLONG: [NY R 8 JD J Furlong, as amended by NY ORDER 20-0253].
JUSTICE JOSEPH R. GLOWNIA: NY R 8 JD J Glownia.
JUSTICE MARK J. GRISANTI: NY R 8 JD J Grisanti.
JUSTICE DEBORAH A. HAENDIGES: NY R 8 JD J Haendiges.
JUSTICE LYNN W. KEANE: [NY R 8 JD J Keane, as amended by NY ORDER 20-0254].
JUSTICE RICHARD C. KLOCH, Sr.: NY R 8 JD J Kloch.
JUSTICE FREDERICK J. MARSHALL: [NY R 8 JD J Marshall, as amended by NY ORDER 20-0255.
JUSTICE JOHN L. MICHALSKI: NY R 8 JD J Michalski.
JUSTICE MARK A. MONTOUR: [NY R 8 JD J Montour, as amended by NY ORDER 20-0256].
JUSTICE HENRY NOWAK: NY R 8 JD J Nowak.
JUSTICE JOHN F. O'DONNELL: NY R 8 JD J O'Donnell.
JUSTICE JEANETTE OGDEN: NY R 8 JD J Ogden.
JUSTICE CATHERINE NUGENT-PANEPINTO: NY R 8 JD J Nugent-Panepinto.
JUSTICE FRANK A. SEDITA, III: [NY R 8 JD J Sedita, as amended by NY ORDER 20-0257].
JUSTICE SARA SHELDON: NY R 8 JD J Sheldon.
JUSTICE DONNA M. SIWEK: NY R 8 JD J Siwek.
JUSTICE MARY L. SLISZ: NY R 8 JD J Slisz.
JUSTICE TIMOTHY J. WALKER: [NY R 8 JD J Walker, as amended by NY ORDER 20-0258].
JUSTICE DENNIS E. WARD: NY R 8 JD J Ward.
JUSTICE PAUL B. WOJTASZEK: [NY R 8 JD J Wojtaszek, as amended by NY ORDER 20-0259].
JUSTICE CHARLES N. ZAMBITO: [NY R 8 JD J Zambito, as amended by NY ORDER 20-0260].
SUPREME COURT LEGAL STAFF: NY R 8 JD J Legal Staff.

KINGS COUNTY

JUSTICE RACHEL A. ADAMS: NY R KINGS J Part 5F.
JUSTICE LOREN BAILY-SCHIFFMAN: NY R KINGS J Part 65.
JUSTICE REGINALD A. BODDIE: NY R KINGS J Part 95.
JUSTICE THERESA M. CICCOTTO: NY R KINGS J Part 19; NY R KINGS J Part 5J.
JUSTICE LISSETTE COLON: NY R KINGS J Part Rules.
JUSTICE GENINE EDWARDS: NY R KINGS J Part 80.
JUSTICE PAMELA L. FISHER: [NY R KINGS J Part 94, as amended by NY ORDER 20-0208].
JUSTICE ROBIN GARSON: NY R KINGS J Part 75.
JUSTICE LARA J. GENOVISI: [NY R KINGS J Part 34, as amended by NY ORDER 20-0209].
JUSTICE BERNARD J. GRAHAM: NY R KINGS J Part 36.
JUSTICE DAWN JIMENEZ-SALTA: NY R KINGS J Part 88.

JUSTICE INGRID JOSEPH: [NY R KINGS J Part FRP3 and Part 83, as amended by NY ORDER 20-0210].
JUSTICE KATHY J. KING: NY R KINGS J Part 64, 76K.
JUSTICE LAWRENCE KNIPEL: NY R KINGS J Part 57.
JUSTICE DONALD KURTZ: NY R KINGS J Part 26.
JUSTICE CARL LANDICINO: [NY R KINGS J Part 81, as amended by NY ORDER 20-0211].
JUSTICE KATHERINE LEVINE: [NY R KINGS J Part 20, 25, 92, as amended by NY ORDER 20-0211].
JUSTICE LORNA MCALLISTER: [NY R KINGS J Part 10, as amended by NY ORDER 20-0211].
JUSTICE ROSEMARIE MONTALBANO: [NY R KINGS J Part 19, 71, and 22, as amended by NY ORDER 20-0211].
JUSTICE RICHARD J. MONTELIONE: [NY R KINGS J Part 99 and DJMP, as amended by NY ORDER 20-0215].
JUSTICE LISA S. OTTLEY: NY R KINGS J Part 24.
JUSTICE MARK I. PARTNOW: NY R KINGS J Part 43.
JUSTICE ERIC I. PRUS: NY R KINGS J Part 5A.
JUSTICE FRANCOIS RIVERA: NY R KINGS J Part 52.
JUSTICE KAREN B. ROTHENBERG: NY R KINGS J Part 35.
JUSTICE LEON RUCHELSMAN: NY R KINGS J Part 1.
JUSTICE WAYNE P. SAITTA: NY R KINGS J Part 29.
JUSTICE ROBIN K. SHEARES: NY R KINGS J Part 96.
JUSTICE KENNETH P. SHERMAN: NY R KINGS J Part 67 and 78.
JUSTICE DEBRA SILBER: NY R KINGS J Part 9 and 5K.
JUSTICE ELLEN M. SPODEK: NY R KINGS J Part 63.
JUSTICE MARSHA L. STEINHARDT: NY R KINGS J Part 15.
JUSTICE JEFFREY S. SUNSHINE: NY R KINGS J Part 5G.
JUSTICE PETER P. SWEENEY: [NY R KINGS J Part 35, as amended by NY ORDER 20-0218].
JUSTICE DELORES J. THOMAS: [NY R KINGS J Part 5T, as amended by NY ORDER 20-0221].
JUSTICE WAVNY TOUSSAINT: NY R KINGS J Part 70.
JUSTICE RICHARD VELASQUEZ: NY R KINGS J Part 66.
JUSTICE CAROLYN E. WADE: NY R KINGS J Part 84.
JUSTICE EDWARD G. WALKER: [NY R KINGS J Part 90, as amended by NY ORDER 20-0219].
JUSTICE LILLIAN WAN: [NY R KINGS J Part 17, as amended by NY ORDER 20-0220].
JUSTICE MICHELLE WESTON: NY R KINGS J Part 3.
MENTAL HYGIENE PART: NY R KINGS J Part 77.
MATRIMONIAL PARTS DURING COVID-19 EMERGENCY: JUSTICE KAREN B. ROTHENBERG: NY R KINGS J Doc. 1.

NASSAU COUNTY

JUSTICE ANNA R. ANZALONE: NY R NASSAU S J Anzalone, Part 26.
JUSTICE STACY D. BENNETT: NY R NASSAU S J Bennett; NY R NASSAU S J Bennett, Form 1.
JUSTICE ANTONIO BRANDVEEN: NY R NASSAU S J Brandveen, Part 31.
JUSTICE JEFFREY S. BROWN: [NY R NASSAU S J Brown, as amended by NY ORDER 20-0297].
JUSTICE STEPHEN A. BUCARIA: NY R NASSAU S J Bucaria.
JUSTICE JULIANNE T. CAPETOLA: NY R NASSAU S J Capetola, Part 28.
JUSTICE EDMUND M. DANE: NY R NASSAU S J Dane, Part 33.
JUSTICE VITO M. DESTEFANO: NY R NASSAU S J DeStefano, Part 13; NY R NASSAU S J DeStefano, Form 1.
JUSTICE ARTHUR M. DIAMOND: NY R NASSAU S J Diamond, Part 7.

JUSTICE THOMAS FEINMAN: NY R NASSAU S J Feinman, Part 5.

JUSTICE JOHN M. GALASSO: NY R NASSAU S J Galasso, Part 22.

JUSTICE SHARON M.J. GIANELLI: NY R NASSAU S J Gianelli, Part 22; NY R NASSAU S J Gianelli, Form 1.

JUSTICE JEFFREY A. GOODSTEIN: NY R NASSAU S J Goodstein, Part 33; NY R NASSAU S J Goodstein, Form 1.

JUSTICE DAVID J. GUGERTY: [NY R NASSAU S J Gugerty, Part 31, as amended by NY ORDER 20-0298].

JUSTICE HELENE F. GUGERTY: NY R NASSAU S J Gugerty, Part 47.

JUSTICE STEVEN M. JAEGER: NY R NASSAU S J Jaeger, Part 35; NY R NASSAU S J Jaeger, Form 1.

JUSTICE JACK L. LIBERT: NY R NASSAU S J Libert, Part 23.

JUSTICE JOSEPH H. LORINTZ: NY R NASSAU S J Lorintz, Part 26; NY R NASSAU S J Lorintz, Form 1.

JUSTICE ROY S. MAHON: NY R NASSAU S J Mahon, Part 3.

JUSTICE RANDY SUE MARBER: NY R NASSAU S J Marber, Part 8.

JUSTICE JAMES P. MCCORMACK: [NY R NASSAU S J McCormack, Part 18, as amended by NY ORDER, 20-0299].

JUSTICE DICCIA T. PINEDA-KIRWAN: [NY R NASSAU S J Pineda-Kirwan, as amended by NY ORDER 20-0300].

JUSTICE THOMAS RADEMAKER: [NY R NASSAU S J Rademaker, Part 28, as amended by NY ORDER 20-0301]; [NY R NASSAU S J Rademaker, Form 1, as amended by NY ORDER 20-0301].

JUSTICE DENISE L. SHER: NY R NASSAU S J Rademaker, Part 32.

JUSTICE LEONARD D. STEINMAN: [NY R NASSAU S J Steinman, Part 15, as amended by NY ORDER 20-0303]; NY R NASSAU S J Steinman, Form 1.

JUSTICE HOWARD E. STURIM: NY R NASSAU S J Sturim, Part 50; NY R NASSAU S J Sturim, Form 1.

JUSTICE HELEN VOUTSINAS: [NY R NASSAU S J Voutsinas, Part 25, as amended by NY ORDER 20-0304]; [NY R NASSAU S J Voutsinas, Form 1, as amended by NY ORDER 20-0305].

JUSTICE HOPE SCHWARTZ ZIMMERMAN: NY R NASSAU S J Zimmerman, Part 17.

NEW YORK COUNTY

JUDGE'S RULES; BASIC INFORMATION: [NY R NY CTY J RUL Doc. 1, as amended by NY ORDER 20-0202].

ONONDAGA COUNTY

JUSTICE ROBERT E. ANTONACCI II: [NY R ONDGA E FIL Doc. 1, as amended by 20-0239].

JUSTICE MICHAEL V. COCCOMI: NY R ONDGA E FIL Doc. 2.

JUSTICE GREGORY R. GILBERT: NY R 5 JD JUDGES Gilbert; NY R ONDGA E FIL Doc. 3.

JUSTICE DONALD A. GREENWOOD: NY R ONDGA E FIL Doc. 4.

JUSTICE DEBORAH H. KARALUNAS: NY R ONDGA E FIL Doc. 5.

JUSTICE JAMES MCCLUSKY: NY R 5 JD MCCLUSKY McClusky.

JUSTICE CHARLES C. MERRELL: NY R 5 JD MERRELL Merrell.

JUSTICE PATRICK F. MACRAE: NY R 5 JD MACRAE Doc. 1.

JUSTICE JAMES P. MURPHY: NY R ONDGA E FIL Doc. 7.

JUSTICE GERALD J. NERI: [NY R 5 JD JUDGES Neri, as amended by NY ORDER 20-0236]; [NY R ONDGA E FIL Doc. 8, as amended by NY ORDER 20-0241].

JUSTICE ANTHONY J. PARIS: NY R 5 JD JUDGES Paris; [NY R ONDGA E FIL Doc. 9, as amended by NY ORDER 20-0242].

JUSTICE NORMAN W. SEITER, JR.: NY R 5 JD JUDGES Seiter.

JUSTICE KEVIN G. YOUNG: [NY R ONDGA E FIL Doc. 10, as amended by NY ORDER 20-0243].

QUEENS COUNTY

JUSTICE PAM JACKMAN BROWN: [NY R L QUEENS Brown, Part 19, as amended by NY ORDER 20-0321].

JUSTICE CHEREE A. BUGGS: NY R L QUEENS Buggs, Part 30.

JUSTICE PAM JACKMAN BROWN: [NY R L QUEENS Brown, Part 19, as amended by NY ORDER 20-0321].

JUSTICE DENIS J. BUTLER: NY R L QUEENS Butler, Part 12.

JUSTICE ROBERT I. CALORAS: [NY R L QUEENS Caloras, Part 36, as amended by NY ORDER 20-0322].

JUSTICE ANNA CULLEY: NY R L QUEENS Culley, Part 53.

JUSTICE TIMOTHY DUFFICY: NY R L QUEENS Dufficy, Part 35.

JUSTICE DAVID ELLIOT: NY R L QUEENS Elliot, Part 14.

JUSTICE JOSEPH J. ESPOSITO: NY R L QUEENS Esposito, Part 6.

JUSTICE DARRELL L. GAVRIN: [NY R L QUEENS Gavrin, Part 27, as amended by NY ORDER 20-0323].

JUSTICE WYATT N. GIBBONS: [NY R L QUEENS Gibbons, Part 5, as amended by NY ORDER 20-0330.

JUSTICE DONNA-MARIE E. GOLIA: [NY R L QUEENS Golia, Part 21, as amended by NY ORDER 20-0331].

JUSTICE MARGUERITE A. GRAYS: [NY R L QUEENS Grays, Part 4, as amended by NY ORDER 20-0324].

JUSTICE RUDOLPH E. GRECO: [NY R L QUEENS Greco, Part 32, as amended by NY ORDER 20-0325].

JUSTICE MAUREEN HEALY: NY R L QUEENS Healy, Part 6.

JUSTICE PHILLIP HOM: [NY R L QUEENS Hom, Part 43, as amended by NY ORDER 20-0332].

JUSTICE KEVIN J. KERRIGAN: NY R L QUEENS Kerrigan, Part 10.

JUSTICE MOJGAN C. LANCMAN: NY R L QUEENS Lancman, Part 20.

JUSTICE RICHARD G. LATIN: NY R L QUEENS Latin, Part 40.

JUSTICE ULYSSES B. LEVERETT: [NY R L QUEENS Leverett, Part 6, as amended by NY ORDER 20-0326].

JUSTICE LEONARD LIVOTE: NY R L QUEENS Livote, Part 33.

JUSTICE LEE A. MAYERSOHN: NY R L QUEENS Mayersohn, Part 22; NY R L QUEENS Mayersohn, Part 22G; [NY R L QUEENS Mayersohn, Part 22G COVID, as amended by NY ORDER 20-0327].

JUSTICE ROBERT J. MCDONALD: NY R L QUEENS McDonald, Part 34.

JUSTICE MARGARET MCGOWAN: NY R L QUEENS McGowan, Part 52.

JUSTICE MAURICE E. MUIR: [NY R L QUEENS Muir, Part 42, as amended by NY ORDER 20-0333].

JUSTICE JODI ORLOW: NY R L QUEENS Orlow, Part 51.

JUSTICE LESLIE J. PURIFICCION: NY R L QUEENS Purificcion, Part 39.

JUSTICE JOSEPH RISI: [NY R L QUEENS Risi, Part 3, as amended by NY ORDER 20-0328].

JUSTICE FREDERICK D.R. SAMPSON: [NY R L QUEENS Sampson, Part 31, as amended by NY ORDER 20-0329].

JUSTICE MARTIN J. SCHULMAN: NY R L QUEENS Schulman, Part 29.

JUSTICE BERNICE D. SIEGAL: NY R L QUEENS Siegal, Part 25G.

JUSTICE JANICE A. TAYLOR: NY R L QUEENS Taylor, Part 15.

JUSTICE CARMEN R. VELASQUEZ: NY R L QUEENS Velasquez, Part 38.

JUSTICE LOURDES M VENTURA: [NY R L QUEENS Ventura, Part 37, as amended by NY ORDER 20-0334].

JUSTICE WILLIAM A. VISCOVICH: NY R L QUEENS Viscovich, Part 63.

JUSTICE ALLAN B. WEISS: NY R L QUEENS Weiss, Part 2.

COMPLIANCE, SETTLEMENT AND CONFERENCE PART: NY R L QUEENS Doc 1.

PRELIMINARY CONFERENCE PART: [NY R L QUEENS Doc. 2, as amended by NY ORDER 20-0335].

MEDICAL MALPRACTICE CONFERENCE PART: [NY R L QUEENS Doc. 3, as amended by NY ORDER 20-0336].

TRIAL SCHEDULING PART: NY R L QUEENS Doc. 4.

SUMMARY JURY TRIAL PROGRAM: NY R L QUEENS Doc. 7.

RESIDENTIAL FORECLOSURE PART: NY R L QUEENS Doc. 9.

FORECLOSURE AUCTION RULES: NY R L QUEENS Doc. 10.

MATRIMONIAL PRELIMINARY CONFERENCE PART: NY R L QUEENS Doc. 11.

NON-CUSTODIAL CONTESTED MATRIMONIAL PART: NY R L QUEENS Doc. 12.

Motions, Oppositions and Replies
Motion to Intervene

Document Last Updated August 2020

A. Checklist

(I) ❑ Matters to consider for moving party
- (a) ❑ Required documents
  - (1) ❑ Notice of motion, order to show cause, or affidavit on ex parte motion
  - (2) ❑ Motion
  - (3) ❑ Proposed intervention pleading
  - (4) ❑ Request for judicial intervention
  - (5) ❑ Proof of service
  - (6) ❑ ALBANY COUNTY: Additional required documents
    - (i) ❑ Affirmation of good faith effort
- (b) ❑ Supplemental documents
  - (1) ❑ Supporting evidence; Exhibits
  - (2) ❑ Brief
  - (3) ❑ Notice to produce papers not in possession of the court
  - (4) ❑ Filing fees
  - (5) ❑ Working copies
  - (6) ❑ Statement of authorization in electronic filing cases
  - (7) ❑ ERIE COUNTY: Additional supplemental documents
    - (i) ❑ Notice of hard copy submission in e-filed case
  - (8) ❑ KINGS COUNTY: Additional supplemental documents
    - (i) ❑ Forms when filing in hard copy
  - (9) ❑ NEW YORK COUNTY: Additional supplemental documents
    - (i) ❑ Notice of hard copy submission
    - (ii) ❑ Unpublished opinions
  - (10) ❑ ONONDAGA COUNTY: Additional supplemental documents
    - (i) ❑ Notice of hard copy submission
  - (11) ❑ QUEENS COUNTY: Additional supplemental documents
    - (i) ❑ Notice of hard copy submission
- (c) ❑ Timing
  - (1) ❑ The movant should of course apply as early as possible, but intervention has been allowed in appropriate circumstances even at the appellate stage, for the purpose of permitting the intervenor to take the appeal
  - (2) ❑ The moving party shall serve copies of all affidavits and briefs upon all other parties at the time of service of the notice of motion
  - (3) ❑ A notice of motion and supporting affidavits shall be served at least eight (8) days before the time at which the motion is noticed to be heard
  - (4) ❑ It is also good practice to make motions returnable at least three (3) weeks away from the planned date of mailing and to always include a demand in the motion that the other side serve answering papers at least seven (7) days before the return day

(5) ❑ BRONX COUNTY: Additional timing

(i) ❑ A Notice of Motion must be served at least eight (8) days, by personal service, nine (9) days by overnight express and thirteen (13) days by mail before the return date

(6) ❑ NEW YORK COUNTY: Additional timing

(i) ❑ In an e-filed case, all of the moving papers shall be e-filed at least eight (8) business days prior to the return date

(7) ❑ ONONDAGA COUNTY: Additional timing

(i) ❑ Onondaga County local court rules require that any additional papers relating to motions must be e-filed at least two (2) business days prior to the return date, excluding the return date

(8) ❑ QUEENS COUNTY: Additional timing

(i) ❑ Motions must be in the possession of the Motion Support Office at least nine (9) days before the noticed return date of the motion

(II) ❑ Matters to consider for opposing party

(a) ❑ Required documents

(1) ❑ Opposition

(2) ❑ Proof of service

(b) ❑ Supplemental documents

(1) ❑ Supporting evidence; Exhibits

(2) ❑ Brief

(3) ❑ Filing fees

(4) ❑ Working copies

(5) ❑ ERIE COUNTY: Additional supplemental documents

(i) ❑ Notice of hard copy submission in e-filed case

(6) ❑ KINGS COUNTY: Additional supplemental documents

(i) ❑ Forms when filing in hard copy

(7) ❑ NEW YORK COUNTY: Additional supplemental documents

(i) ❑ Notice of hard copy submission

(ii) ❑ Unpublished opinions

(8) ❑ ONONDAGA COUNTY: Additional supplemental documents

(i) ❑ Notice of hard copy submission

(9) ❑ QUEENS COUNTY: Additional supplemental documents

(i) ❑ Notice of hard copy submission

(c) ❑ Timing

(1) ❑ Answering affidavits shall be served at least two (2) days before the time at which the motion is noticed to be heard

(2) ❑ Answering affidavits and any notice of cross-motion, with supporting papers, if any, shall be served at least seven (7) days before such time if a notice of motion served at least sixteen (16) days before such time so demands

B. Timing

1. *Time to bring motion to intervene.* Whether made under NY CPLR § 1012 or NY CPLR § 1013, the application for intervention must be "timely." That question is always sui generis. The movant should of course apply as early as possible, but intervention has been allowed in appropriate circumstances even at the appellate stage, for the purpose of permitting the intervenor to take the appeal. SIEGEL-NYPRAC § 183.

2. *Time to serve.* The moving party shall serve copies of all affidavits and briefs upon all other parties at the time of service

of the notice of motion. NY R UNIF TRIAL CTS § 202.8(c). A notice of motion and supporting affidavits shall be served at least eight (8) days before the time at which the motion is noticed to be heard. NY CPLR Rule 2214(b).

a. *Return dates; Best practice.* It is also good practice to make motions returnable at least three (3) weeks away from the planned date of mailing and to always include a demand in the motion that the other side serve answering papers at least seven (7) days before the return day. This enables the motion to be served by mail, gives sufficient notice to support the seven (7) day demand, and leaves a few days for a delayed mailing if some snag prevents posting on the day planned. If speed is needed, the shorter eight (8) day notice period can be used, forfeiting the right to seven (7) day answering papers and a reply. If even eight (8) days notice is too much under the circumstances, the order to show cause is the remedy. SIEGEL-NYPRAC § 247.

   i. *ALBANY COUNTY.* All motions, except for certain matters in Albany County as specified in NY R 3 JD SUP Doc. 1(E) and NY R 3 JD SUP Doc. 1(F), brought on by notice of motion or by order to show cause will be made returnable on any day, Monday through Friday, as chosen by the movant in compliance with the CPLR. Parties shall submit all papers in a timely fashion as required by the CPLR by delivering them or mailing them directly to the Supreme Court Clerk's Office[. . .]except that motions and other applications subject to a filing fee shall first be presented to the County Clerk's Office for payment of the requisite fee and then subsequently filed with the Supreme Court Clerk's Office. NY R 3 JD SUP Doc. 1(B).

   ii. *BRONX COUNTY.* A Notice of Motion must be served at least eight (8) days, by personal service, nine (9) days by overnight express and thirteen (13) days by mail before the return date. NY R BRONX FIL R Doc. 3. All unassigned motions must be accompanied with a properly filled out RJI and shall be filed in the Motion Support Office, room 217, within five (5) days of service. All motions on actions already assigned to a Justice must be filed at least five (5) business days before the return date. NY R BRONX FIL R Doc. 3. All papers served must strictly comply with the time requirements of NY CPLR Rule 2101, NY CPLR Rule 2103 and NY CPLR Rule 2214(b). NY R BRONX FIL R Doc. 8.

   iii. *KINGS COUNTY.* Motion papers, answering affidavits and reply affidavits must be served on adversaries in accordance with NY CPLR Rule 2214. NY R L KINGS Pt. C, Rule 1.

   iv. *NEW YORK COUNTY.* In an e-filed case, all of the moving papers shall be e-filed at least eight (8) business days prior to the return date. The clerk will calendar the motion for the Motion Submission Part Courtroom (Room 130) for the return date selected. NY R NY CTY Procedure II(A); NY R NY CTY E FIL Doc. 2(D)(1).

   v. *ONONDAGA COUNTY.* Onondaga County local court rules require that any additional papers relating to motions must be e-filed at least two (2) business days prior to the return date, excluding the return date. NY R ONDGA E FIL Protocol(B)(9)(e).

   vi. *QUEENS COUNTY.* Motions must be in the possession of the Motion Support Office at least nine (9) days before the noticed return date of the motion. NY R L QUEENS MOT SUP Doc. 1; NY R L QUEENS E-FILE Doc. 1(H)(1).

b. *Order to show cause; Shorter time.* The court in a proper case may grant an order to show cause, to be served in lieu of a notice of motion, at a time and in a manner specified therein. NY CPLR Rule 2214(d). An ordinary notice of motion can't be brought on for hearing earlier than the eighth (8th) day after the motion papers are served. With an order to show cause, the hearing can be brought on at any time the court directs, which can be fewer than eight (8) days or as close as the very day on which it is signed. If the court is convinced there is a real emergency, it can schedule the hearing for a few hours later or, in the direst case, "forthwith" the service of the order to show cause. SIEGEL-NYPRAC § 248.

c. *Time to serve answering affidavits; Other answering papers.* Answering affidavits shall be served at least two (2) days before the time at which the motion is noticed to be heard. Answering affidavits and any notice of cross-motion, with supporting papers, if any, shall be served at least seven (7) days before such time if a notice of motion served at least sixteen (16) days before such time so demands; whereupon any reply or responding affidavits shall be served at least one (1) day before such time. NY CPLR Rule 2214(b); NY R UNIF TRIAL CTS § 202.8(c).

   i. *BRONX COUNTY.* All answering papers must be submitted to the Clerk 's Office on the return date of the motion. Answering papers will not be accepted prior to the return date. NY R BRONX FIL R Doc. 8.

   ii. *NEW YORK COUNTY.* Cross-motions, papers in opposition, and reply papers on motions/petitions on notice returnable in Room 130 in a hard-copy case shall be submitted to the Motion Submission Part Courtroom (Room 130) on the final return date of the motion/petition and will not be accepted until that date. Subsequent documents on motions/petitions in e-filed cases shall be e-filed in a timely manner. Working copies when required shall be submitted to Room 130 on the final return date. NY R NY CTY Procedure II(A).

d. *Time to serve cross-motion.* At least three (3) days prior to the time at which the motion is noticed to be heard, or seven (7) days prior to such time if demand is properly made pursuant to NY CPLR Rule 2214(b), a party may serve upon the moving party a notice of cross-motion demanding relief, with or without supporting papers; provided, however, that:

   i. If such notice and any supporting papers are served by mailing, as provided in NY CPLR Rule 2103(b)(2), they shall be served three (3) days earlier than as prescribed in NY CPLR Rule 2215; and

   ii. If served by overnight delivery, as provided in NY CPLR Rule 2103(b)(6), they shall be served one (1) day earlier than as prescribed in NY CPLR Rule 2215. Relief in the alternative or of several different types may be demanded; relief need not be responsive to that demanded by the moving party. NY CPLR Rule 2215(a); NY CPLR Rule 2215(b).

   iii. *BRONX COUNTY.* Cross motions may be presented for approval on or before the return date, provided that there is a motion already calendared. NY R BRONX FIL R Doc. 8.

   iv. *ERIE COUNTY.* Cross-motions must be filed at least two (2) days before the return date of the motion. NY R L KINGS Pt. A, Papers.

   v. *KINGS COUNTY.* Hard copies are required to be filed for any motions, answering papers, stipulations, etc. for E-Filed cases returnable in [the Central Compliance Part] at least [two (2)] days before return date. . .for cross motions. NY R L KINGS Pt. E, Rule 8.

   vi. *QUEENS COUNTY.* Motion Support does not process or forward responsive papers, including cross-motions. They must be brought to the calendar call in the judge's part. NY R L QUEENS MOT SUP Doc. 1. E-filed cross motions: across motion must be noticed for the same return date as the main motion and have the confirmation of filing attached in the same manner as a motion. NY R L QUEENS E-FILE Doc. 1(H)(2)(e).

3. *Filing before return date.* All motions shall be returnable before the assigned judge, and all papers shall be filed with the court on or before the return date. NY R UNIF TRIAL CTS § 202.8(a).

   a. *BRONX COUNTY: Time for filing*

      i. *Unassigned motions.* Unassigned motions must be in the Clerk's Office within five (5) days of the date of service of the motion. NY R BRONX FIL R Doc. 8.

      ii. *Assigned motions.* Assigned motions must be filed in the Clerk's Office not less than five (5) business days prior to the return date of the motion. NY R BRONX FIL R Doc. 8.

      iii. *Motions returnable in room 217.* The moving documents must be e-filed no later than eight (8) days prior to the return date. NY R BRONX E FIL R Doc. 1(1).

   b. *KINGS COUNTY: Time and place of filing.* Motion papers must be filed with the E-file/Motion Support Office located in Room 227. . . at 360 Adams Street at least five (5) business days before the return date of the motion. NY R L KINGS Pt. A, Papers. Hard copies are required to be filed for any motions, answering papers, stipulations, etc. for E-Filed cases returnable in [the Central Compliance Part] at least five (5) days before return date for main motions. NY R L KINGS Pt. E, Rule 8. The moving documents must be e-filed no later than eight (8) days prior to the return date. NY R L KINGS E FIL Doc. 1(D).

4. *NEW YORK COUNTY: Briefing schedule.* Once a motion is made, counsel for all parties are strongly encouraged to agree upon a briefing schedule and submit a stipulation of adjournment reflecting that schedule using service or a clerk. Where a briefing schedule has not been agreed upon, the movant can avoid the need to attend simply to see if anyone will hand up opposing papers by demanding papers as provided by NY CPLR Rule 2214(b). To protect movants against the submission of late opposition papers or cross-motions, the General Clerk's Office will screen motions in which such papers are submitted without a response (reply or opposition respectively) to ensure that proper time to respond has been afforded and it will sua sponte adjourn for one (1) week cases in which such time has not been given. NY R NY CTY Procedure II(C).

5. *QUEENS COUNTY: Time to pay fees.* As motions and petitions are time sensitive, if opting to pay at the County Clerk's Office payment MUST be made, if filed with an RJI, a minimum of nine (9) business days prior to the application's return date and if filed post RJI, a minimum of nine (9) business days prior to the application's return date. NY R L QUEENS E-FILE Doc. 1(H)(1).

6. *Computation of time*

   a. *Units of time*

      i. *Day.* A calendar day includes the time from midnight to midnight. Sunday or any day of the week specifically mentioned means a calendar day. NY GEN CONSTR § 19.

ii. *Month.* In a statute, contract or public or private instrument, unless otherwise provided in such contract or instrument or by law, the term month means a calendar month and not a lunar month. NY GEN CONSTR § 31.

iii. *Year.* For information on the definition of a year, including the definitions of a half-year and quarter-year, refer to NY GEN CONSTR § 58 and NY GEN CONSTR § 50. For information on leap years, refer to NY GEN CONSTR § 57.

b. *Periods of time*

i. *Number of days.* A number of days specified as a period from a certain day within which or after or before which an act is authorized or required to be done means such number of calendar days exclusive of the calendar day from which the reckoning is made. NY GEN CONSTR § 20.

- If such period is a period of two (2) days, Saturday, Sunday or a public holiday must be excluded from the reckoning if it is an intervening day between the day from which the reckoning is made and the last day of the period. NY GEN CONSTR § 20.
- In computing any specified period of time from a specified event, the day upon which the event happens is deemed the day from which the reckoning is made. The day from which any specified period of time is reckoned shall be excluded in making the reckoning. NY GEN CONSTR § 20.

ii. *Number of months.* A number of months after or before a certain day shall be computed by counting such number of calendar months from such day, exclusive of the calendar month in which such day occurs, and shall include the day of the month in the last month so counted having the same numerical order in days of the month as the day from which the computation is made, unless there be not so many days in the last month so counted, in which case the period computed shall expire with the last day of the month so counted. NY GEN CONSTR § 30.

iii. *Publication of notice; Number of days.* The period of publication of a legal notice shall be computed by excluding the first day of publication and including the day on which the act or event of which notice is given is to take place or which completes the full period of publication. NY CPLR § 2402.

iv. *Periods ending on Saturday, Sunday or public holiday.* When any period of time, computed from a certain day, within which or after which or before which an act is authorized or required to be done, ends on a Saturday, Sunday or a public holiday, such act may be done on the next succeeding business day and if the period ends at a specified hour, such act may be done at or before the same hour of such next succeeding business day, except that where a period of time specified by contract ends on a Saturday, Sunday or a public holiday, the extension of such period is governed by NY GEN CONSTR § 25. NY GEN CONSTR § 25-a(1).

- For a list of public holidays, refer to NY GEN CONSTR § 24.

v. *Additional time after certain kinds of service*

- *Service by mail.* Where a period of time prescribed by law is measured from the service of a paper and service is by mail, five (5) days shall be added to the prescribed period. NY CPLR Rule 2103(b)(2).
- *Service by overnight delivery service.* Where a period of time prescribed by law is measured from the service of a paper and service is by overnight delivery, one (1) business day shall be added to the prescribed period. NY CPLR Rule 2103(b)(6).

vi. *Daylight saving time.* For information on New York's time zone and the effect of daylight saving time, refer to NY GEN CONSTR § 52.

c. *Hours of court.* Notwithstanding any provision of law or rule of court to the contrary, throughout the State of New York the sessions of the Supreme Court for the disposition of business before the court shall commence not later than 9:30 a.m. and conclude not earlier than 5 p.m. Where warranted, the Chief Administrator of the Courts may authorize variances in the opening and closing hours of the courts, but, in such event, daily sessions shall total not less than six (6) hours. NY R CHIEF J § 3.1.

d. *Time limits; Extension of time.* Any act required by or in pursuance of law to be performed at or within a prescribed time, shall be performed according to the standard time. NY GEN CONSTR § 53.

i. Except where otherwise expressly prescribed by law, the court may extend the time fixed by any statute, rule or order for doing any act, upon such terms as may be just and upon good cause shown, whether the application for extension is made before or after the expiration of the time fixed. NY CPLR § 2004. Refer to the New York KeyRules Motion for Continuance/Extension of Time document for more information.

C. General Requirements

1. *Motions, generally.* There shall be compliance with the procedures prescribed in the CPLR for the bringing of motions. NY R UNIF TRIAL CTS § 202.7(a).

   a. *Motions on notice.* A notice of motion shall specify the time and place of the hearing on the motion, the supporting papers upon which the motion is based, the relief demanded and the grounds therefor. NY CPLR Rule 2214(a). A motion on notice in an action in the supreme court shall be noticed to be heard in the judicial district where the action is triable or in a county adjoining the county where the action is triable. Unless statute, civil practice rule or local court rule provides otherwise, the motion shall be noticed to be heard before a motion term or, upon order to show cause granted by a justice, before that justice out of court. NY CPLR § 2212(a). Except as provided in NY R UNIF TRIAL CTS § 202.7(d), no motion shall be filed with the court unless there have been served and filed with the motion papers a notice of motion. NY R UNIF TRIAL CTS § 202.7(a)(1).

   b. *Ex parte motions.* A motion in an action in the supreme court that may be made without notice may be made at a motion term or to a justice out of court in any county in the state. NY CPLR § 2212(b).

      i. *KINGS COUNTY.* For more information on submitting a motion ex parte, refer to NY R L KINGS E FIL Doc. 1(G).

      ii. *NEW YORK COUNTY.* For more information on submitting matters ex parte, refer to NY R NY CTY Procedure III and NY R NY CTY E FIL Doc. 2(G).

      iii. *QUEENS COUNTY.* For more information on submitting matters ex parte, refer to NY R L QUEENS EX PARTE Doc. 1.

   c. *Alternative relief.* Relief in the alternative or of several different types may be demanded. NY CPLR Rule 2214(a). The types of relief need not be related. In one motion, for example, the defendant can seek to dismiss the plaintiff's claim for lack of jurisdiction, to get an extension of time to answer, to require the plaintiff to join X as a party, and to quash a disclosure subpoena served in behalf of the plaintiff on a nonparty witness. So doing, the movant must of course specify all of these items of relief in the notice of motion, and the grounds for them, and the supporting papers must contain the entire proof requisite to the items of relief sought. NY CPLR Rule 2214(Practice Commentary, C2214:4).

   d. *General relief.* It is common practice to include at the end of the relief request in the notice of motion a so-called "general relief" clause. This is merely a few words to cover the possibility that the relief appropriate to what the movant proves was not specifically asked for, but is close enough to enable the court to grant it. After stating the specific relief desired, the lawyer will often add something like: and for such other, further, or different relief as this court may deem just and proper. NY CPLR Rule 2214(Practice Commentary, C2214:5).

   e. *Motion in improper form.* If the court finds it appropriate in the interests of justice, it may convert a motion into a special proceeding, or vice-versa, upon such terms as may be just, including the payment of fees and costs. NY CPLR § 103(c).

   f. *Order to show cause.* An order to show cause is basically only a substitute for a notice of motion. An ordinary notice of motion merely notifies the recipient that a motion is being made for specified relief. The burden of proof is on the movant. Although in most cases it is just as innocent as an ordinary notice of motion, the order to show cause gets its name by directing the recipient to "show cause" why the particular relief being asked for should not be granted. It sounds as if the burden of proof is being shifted to the recipient. It isn't. It specifies the time and place of the hearing on the application but when the hearing comes on, the burden of proof is where it always is on a motion: on the movant. SIEGEL-NYPRAC § 248.

      i. The CPLR says nothing more about an order to show cause than that it may be used "in a proper case", which leaves it entirely to the judge's discretion to determine what a proper case is. Any fact suggesting a problem as to any of the items listed above would be sufficient to invoke judicial discretion and justify the show cause procedure, which is in fact liberally used. SIEGEL-NYPRAC § 248.

      ii. An order to show cause against a state body or officers must be served in addition to service upon the defendant or respondent state body or officers upon the attorney general by delivery to an assistant attorney general at an office of the attorney general in the county in which venue of the action is designated or if there is no office of the attorney general in such county, at the office of the attorney general nearest such county. NY CPLR Rule 2214(d).

      iii. *BRONX COUNTY.* For information on submitting an order to show cause, refer to NY R BRONX E FIL R Doc. 2 and NY R BRONX LEG SUP Doc. 1.

iv. *ERIE COUNTY.* For information on submitting an order to show cause, refer to NY R ERIE E FIL Doc. 3(VI).

v. *KINGS COUNTY.* For information on submitting an order to show cause, refer to NY R L KINGS E FIL Doc. 1(F).

vi. *NEW YORK COUNTY.* For information on submitting an order to show cause, refer to NY R NY CTY E FIL Doc. 2(F).

vii. *ONONDAGA COUNTY.* For information on submitting an order to show cause, refer to NY R ONDGA E FIL Protocol(B)(10) and NY R ONDGA E FIL Protocol(J).

g. *Motions before preliminary conference.* Motions in actions to which NY R UNIF TRIAL CTS § 202.12 is applicable made after the preliminary conference has been scheduled may be denied unless there is shown good cause why such relief is warranted before the preliminary conference is held. NY R UNIF TRIAL CTS § 202.12(h).

h. *ALBANY COUNTY: Good faith effort to resolve.* Prior to the submission of a notice of motion relating to disclosure or a bill of particulars, the parties must make a good faith effort to resolve the matter in question and submit an affirmation attesting to this good faith effort. NY R 3 JD SUP Doc. 1(B).

i. *NEW YORK COUNTY: Documents with motions.* Counsel must attach to motion papers copies of all pleadings and other documents as required by the CPLR and as necessary for an informed decision on the motion. Documents in a foreign language shall be properly translated. NY R NY CTY J RUL Rule 14(a).

j. *NEW YORK COUNTY: Motions in multiple cases made together.* On occasion, attorneys may wish to make a motion in more than one case on a single set of papers. In such cases, by definition consolidation will not have been directed since consolidation signifies the combination of more than one case into a single one with a single caption and index number and ending in a single judgment. NY R NY CTY Procedure II(B). For more information on motions made with the same papers, refer to NY R NY CTY Procedure II(A).

k. *QUEENS COUNTY: Motion sequence numbers.* A motion sequence number is required for all E-filed motions. After a motion is E-filed, please consult the e-courts website within twenty-four (24) to forty-eight (48) hours to obtain the sequence number. The Confirmation Notice of E-filing MUST indicate the sequence number of any motion submitted at the Centralized Motion Part calendar call. NY R L QUEENS E-FILE Doc. 1(H)(5).

2. *Intervention, generally.* Intervention is a procedure whereby an outsider can become a party to a pending action on her own initiative. It is sometimes available as of right, sometimes only in the court's discretion, but it must be sought by motion in all instances. SIEGEL-NYPRAC § 178; NY CPLR § 1012; NY CPLR § 1013; SIEGEL-NYPRAC § 183. The courts are liberal in its allowance today—a relatively recent development—and distinctions between intervention of right and discretionary intervention are not sharply drawn. SIEGEL-NYPRAC § 178; Raymond v. Honeywell, 58 Misc. 2d 903, 904, 297 N.Y.S.2d 66, 67 (Sup. Ct. 1968). The applicant can seek to intervene on either side of the case, plaintiff's or defendant's. Once let in, the intervenor becomes a party for all purposes. SIEGEL-NYPRAC § 178; Inc. Vill. of Island Park v. Island Park-Long Beach, Inc., 81 N.Y.S.2d 407, 409 (Sup. Ct.), aff'd sub nom. Inc. Vill. of Island Park v. Island Park-Long Beach, 274 A.D. 930, 83 N.Y.S.2d 542 (App. Div. 1948).

3. *Intervention as of right*

a. *When intervention shall be permitted.* Upon timely motion, any person shall be permitted to intervene in any action:

i. When a statute of the state confers an absolute right to intervene; or

ii. When the representation of the person's interest by the parties is or may be inadequate and the person is or may be bound by the judgment; or

iii. When the action involves the disposition or distribution of, or the title or a claim for damages for injury to, property and the person may be affected adversely by the judgment. NY CPLR § 1012(a).

iv. For information on when certain government entities may intervene as of right, refer to NY CPLR § 1012(b) and NY CPLR § 1012(c).

b. *Intervention by statutory right.* The first basis recognized for intervention as of right under NY CPLR § 1012 is when a statute confers "an absolute right to intervene". This is of course superfluous in that if some special statute confers the right, it doesn't need additional permission from the CPLR. The provision can be taken as a simple reminder of the existence of such statutes. SIEGEL-NYPRAC § 179. For more information on intervention based on statutory right, refer to SIEGEL-NYPRAC § 179.

c. *Intervention based on inadequate representation.* The showing required under NY CPLR § 1012(a)(2) is that the representation "may" be inadequate and that the proposed intervenor "may" be bound by the judgment. It is the possibility rather than the certainty that governs. Well-reasoned caselaw holds that the movant should be given the benefit of the doubt. SIEGEL-NYPRAC § 180. The potentially binding nature of the judgment on the proposed intervenor is the factor that invokes NY CPLR § 1012(a)(2), even if the law that purports to do the binding is foreign rather than New York law. SIEGEL-NYPRAC § 180; Nardone v. Morris A. Fierberg Co., 40 A.D.2d 60, 62, 337 N.Y.S.2d 884, 886 (1972).

i. Whether the movant will be "bound" by the judgment has reference to the res judicata family of doctrines. SIEGEL-NYPRAC § 180; SIEGEL-NYPRAC § 443. "The stare decisis effect of the judgment is not enough," although it may be relevant for permissive intervention, which can be sought under NY CPLR § 1013 when the intervenor's claim or defense has a question of law in common with the pending action. SIEGEL-NYPRAC § 180; SIEGEL-NYPRAC § 182.

d. *Intervention based on property rights.* The courts are especially prone to authorize intervention when it appears needed to assure an adversary proceeding. SIEGEL-NYPRAC § 181.

i. In New York at present, the notion prevails that when plaintiffs injured in a single accident bring separate suits against the tortfeasor in separate courts, the race to the coverage offered by the tortfeasor's liability insurance policy is to the swift; that whoever gets judgment first is entitled to first crack at the insurance proceeds even if the judgment would exhaust the proceeds and leave nothing for the other injured persons whose suits are still pending. One set of plaintiffs in such a position sought in one case to intervene in the other set's lawsuit when it appeared that judgment in the latter was imminent. They were denied leave to intervene. The main objection was untimeliness, the court said, citing its obligation under NY CPLR § 1013 (permissive intervention) to consider whether the parties to the pending action would be prejudiced by the application. SIEGEL-NYPRAC § 181; NY CPLR § 1013.

e. *Discretion of the court.* It has been held that even with regard to the of-right provisions, the courts have some discretion. SIEGEL-NYPRAC § 180; Reurs v. Carlson, 66 Misc. 2d 968, 968, 323 N.Y.S.2d 370, 371 (Sup. Ct. 1971). This appears to contradict the seemingly mandatory nature of NY CPLR § 1012, but the statute does say that the intervention must be "timely." Timeliness itself is a factor that varies from case to case and the court of course has some discretion in measuring it. SIEGEL-NYPRAC § 180.

4. *Intervention by permission.* Upon timely motion, any person may be permitted to intervene in any action when a statute of the state confers a right to intervene in the discretion of the court, or when the person's claim or defense and the main action have a common question of law or fact. In exercising its discretion, the court shall consider whether the intervention will unduly delay the determination of the action or prejudice the substantial rights of any party. NY CPLR § 1013.

a. When the common question relied on is one of law, the endeavor to intervene is analogous to an application to an appellate court for leave to file a brief amicus curiae, and the disposition is governed by similar factors. Are both sides of the legal issue already well represented in the action? If they are, adding parties may merely make the case more cumbersome. If they are not, the intervention motion of course enables the court to strengthen the existing representation. SIEGEL-NYPRAC § 182.

b. Since intervention under NY CPLR § 1013 is permissive, the court can of course impose conditions on its allowance. SIEGEL-NYPRAC § 182; City of Buffalo v. State Bd. of Equalization & Assessment, 44 Misc. 2d 716, 719, 254 N.Y.S.2d 699, 701 (Sup. Ct. 1964).

c. On an NY CPLR § 1013 application, the court must consider whether the intervention (1) "will unduly delay the determination of the action" or (2) "prejudice the substantial rights of any party." The two factors listed are not exclusive, however. Another that the court can consider is whether, if intervention is refused, the applicant is likely to bring a separate action and then move for consolidation, and how that motion would likely be decided. If consolidation is perceived as inevitable, the court may as well permit intervention. SIEGEL-NYPRAC § 182.

5. *Substitution of parties.* For information on substitution of parties, refer to NY CPLR § 1015, et seq.

6. *Oppositions.* In the absence of statutory provision or court rule, a motion ordinarily does not require a written answer, although an adverse party may be permitted to file an answer in opposition to the showing made in the motion or its supporting affidavits. AMJUR MOTIONS § 26. When a party files a motion and the opposing party fails to respond, the court may construe such failure to respond as non-opposition to the motion or an admission that the motion was meritorious, may take the facts alleged in the motion as true, and may grant the motion if the relief requested appears to be justified. However, the severity of such a result demands that a court impose it only with great caution. AMJUR MOTIONS § 28.

7. *Governing law.* The civil practice law and rules (NY CPLR § 101, et seq.) shall govern the procedure in civil judicial proceedings in all courts of the state and before all judges, except where the procedure is regulated by inconsistent statute.

The civil practice law and rules shall succeed the civil practice act and rules of civil practice and shall be deemed substituted therefor throughout the statutes and rules of the state. NY CPLR § 101. The civil practice law and rules shall be liberally construed to secure the just, speedy and inexpensive determination of every civil judicial proceeding. NY CPLR § 104.

a. *Uniform trial court rules.* The uniform civil rules for the Supreme Court and County Court (NY R UNIF TRIAL CTS § 202.1, et seq.) shall be applicable to civil actions and proceedings in the Supreme Court and the County Court. NY R UNIF TRIAL CTS § 202.1(a). The provisions of the uniform rules shall be construed consistent with the Civil Practice Law and Rules (CPLR), and matters not covered by the uniform rules shall be governed by the CPLR. NY R UNIF TRIAL CTS § 202.1(d).

b. *Local rules.* Local court rules, not inconsistent with law or with uniform civil rules for the Supreme Court and County Court (NY R UNIF TRIAL CTS § 202.1, et seq.), shall comply with Part 9 of the Rules of the Chief Judge (NY R CHIEF J § 9.1). NY R UNIF TRIAL CTS § 202.1(c).

c. *Official forms.* The state administrator shall have the power to adopt, amend and rescind an appendix of forms. Forms adopted pursuant to NY CPLR § 107 shall be sufficient under the civil practice law and rules and shall illustrate the simplicity and brevity of statement which the civil practice law and rules contemplate. NY CPLR § 107.

8. *Rules of the commercial division.* [Editor's note: certain types of civil cases or civil cases meeting certain monetary thresholds that are filed in the state of New York must be filed in the Commercial Division of the New York Supreme Courts. Rules governing practice in the commercial division are found in NY R UNIF TRIAL CTS § 202.70]. Cases which must be filed in the commercial division are listed below. For more information, refer to NY R UNIF TRIAL CTS § 202.70.

a. *Monetary thresholds.* Except as set forth in NY R UNIF TRIAL CTS § 202.70(b), the monetary thresholds of the Commercial Division, exclusive of punitive damages, interests, costs, disbursements and counsel fees claimed, are established as follows: (1) Albany County, fifty thousand dollars ($50,000); (2) Eighth Judicial District, one hundred thousand dollars ($100,000); (3) Kings County, one hundred fifty thousand dollars ($150,000); (4) Nassau County, two hundred thousand dollars ($200,000); (5) New York County, five hundred thousand dollars ($500,000); (6) Onondaga County, fifty thousand dollars ($50,000); (7) Queens County, one hundred thousand dollars ($100,000); (8) Seventh Judicial District, fifty thousand dollars ($50,000); (9) Suffolk County, one hundred thousand dollars ($100,000); and (10) Westchester County, one hundred thousand dollars ($100,000). NY R UNIF TRIAL CTS § 202.70(a).

i. *ALBANY COUNTY.* The Commercial Division of the Albany County Supreme Court exercises jurisdiction over selected business and commercial disputes in which the amount at issue generally involves damage claims in a minimum amount of fifty thousand dollars ($50,000) as well as claims for unspecified amounts where the value of the commercial asset(s) in dispute exceeds fifty thousand dollars ($50,000). A separate publication promulgating the rules and criteria relating to the filing and management of Commercial Court cases in this part may be obtained from the Albany County Supreme Court Clerk's Office. A section of the Uniform Civil Rules for the Supreme Court and County Court sets forth statewide rules. NY R 3 JD SUP Doc. 1(E).

ii. *BRONX COUNTY.* The monetary threshold for commercial cases in Bronx County will be seventy-five thousand dollars ($75,000). All other parameters including the type of matters that will be heard are contained within the Rules of the Commercial Division of the Supreme Court (NY R UNIF TRIAL CTS § 202.70). NY R BRONX FIL R Doc. 12.

iii. *NEW YORK COUNTY.* The monetary threshold in the New York County Commercial Division, which is generally applicable, is an amount in controversy of five hundred thousand dollars ($500,000) or more (exclusive of punitive damages, interest, costs, disbursements, and counsel fees). If the case is designated a commercial one and the Addendum is submitted, the clerk will review the pleadings to determine whether the amount in controversy in the case meets the monetary threshold or whether an exception to the threshold applies. NY R NY CTY Procedure IA(B). For more information on assigning a case to the commercial division in New York County, refer to NY R NY CTY Procedure IA(B).

b. *Commercial cases.* Actions in which the principal claims involve or consist of the following will be heard in the Commercial Division provided that the monetary threshold is met or equitable or declaratory relief is sought:

i. Breach of contract or fiduciary duty, fraud, misrepresentation, business tort (e.g., unfair competition), or statutory and/or common law violation where the breach or violation is alleged to arise out of business dealings (e.g., sales of assets or securities; corporate restructuring; partnership, shareholder, joint venture, and other business agreements; trade secrets; restrictive covenants; and employment agreements not including claims that principally involve alleged discriminatory practices);

ii. Transactions governed by the Uniform Commercial Code (exclusive of those concerning individual cooperative or condominium units);

iii. Transactions involving commercial real property, including Yellowstone injunctions and excluding actions for the payment of rent only;

iv. Shareholder derivative actions—without consideration of the monetary threshold;

v. Commercial class actions—without consideration of the monetary threshold;

vi. Business transactions involving or arising out of dealings with commercial banks and other financial institutions;

vii. Internal affairs of business organizations;

viii. Malpractice by accountants or actuaries, and legal malpractice arising out of representation in commercial matters;

ix. Environmental insurance coverage;

x. Commercial insurance coverage (e.g., directors and officers, errors and omissions, and business interruption coverage);

xi. Dissolution of corporations, partnerships, limited liability companies, limited liability partnerships and joint ventures—without consideration of the monetary threshold; and

xii. Applications to stay or compel arbitration and affirm or disaffirm arbitration awards and related injunctive relief pursuant to Article 75 of the New York Civil Practice Law and Rules (NY CPLR § 7501, et seq.) involving any of the foregoing enumerated commercial issues. Where the applicable arbitration agreement provides for the arbitration to be heard outside the United States, the monetary threshold set forth in NY R UNIF TRIAL CTS § 202.70(a) shall not apply. NY R UNIF TRIAL CTS § 202.70(b).

c. *Non-commercial cases.* The following will not be heard in the Commercial Division even if the monetary threshold is met:

i. Suits to collect professional fees;

ii. Cases seeking a declaratory judgment as to insurance coverage for personal injury or property damage;

iii. Residential real estate disputes, including landlord-tenant matters, and commercial real estate disputes involving the payment of rent only;

iv. Home improvement contracts involving residential properties consisting of one to four residential units or individual units in any residential building, including cooperative or condominium units;

v. Proceedings to enforce a judgment regardless of the nature of the underlying case;

vi. First-party insurance claims and actions by insurers to collect premiums or rescind non-commercial policies; and

vii. Attorney malpractice actions except as otherwise provided in NY R UNIF TRIAL CTS § 202.70(b)(8). NY R UNIF TRIAL CTS § 202.70(c).

d. For more information on the Commercial Division, refer to NY R UNIF TRIAL CTS § 202.70.

D. Documents

1. *Documents for moving party*

a. *Required documents*

i. *Notice of motion, order to show cause, or affidavit on ex parte motion.* The notice of motion shall be substantially in the form found in NY R UNIF TRIAL CTS § 202.7(b). NY R UNIF TRIAL CTS § 202.7(b). The supporting papers should be referred to in the notice of motion. SIEGEL-NYPRAC § 246. The court in a proper case may grant an order to show cause, to be served in lieu of a notice of motion. NY CPLR Rule 2214(d). An ex parte motion shall be accompanied by an affidavit stating the result of any prior motion for similar relief and specifying the new facts, if any, that were not previously shown. NY CPLR Rule 2217(b).

- *Request for oral argument.* A party requesting oral argument shall set forth such request in its notice of motion or in its order to show cause or on the first page of the answering papers, as the case may be. Where all parties to a motion request oral argument, oral argument shall be granted unless the court shall determine it to be unnecessary. Where a motion is brought on by order to show cause, the court may set forth in the order that oral argument is required on the return date of the motion. NY R UNIF TRIAL CTS § 202.8(d).

ii. *Motion.* Refer to the General Requirements section of this document for information on the notice of motion and motion.

iii. *Proposed intervention pleading.* A motion to intervene shall be accompanied by a proposed pleading setting forth the claim or defense for which intervention is sought. NY CPLR § 1014.

iv. *Request for judicial intervention.* At any time after service of process, a party may file a request for judicial intervention. Except as provided in NY R UNIF TRIAL CTS § 202.6(b), in an action not yet assigned to a judge, the court shall not accept for filing a notice of motion, order to show cause, or application for ex parte order, unless such notice or application is accompanied by a request for judicial intervention. NY R UNIF TRIAL CTS § 202.6(a).

- *BRONX COUNTY.* Generally, the Request For Judicial Intervention, commonly referred to as an "RJI", is required to be filed in any action where the assignment of a Justice is required. The RJI sets forth the information which is entered into the court system's database. It must be completely and accurately filled out. The full caption, as stated on the Summons, must be set forth. Use of terms "et al." and "etc." are not permitted. Only one (1) RJI may be filed in each action. Either a self represented litigant or an attorney must sign the affirmation at the end of the form. Once completed, the RJI must be filed in duplicate. Except in the case of an ex-parte application, the RJI must also be served together with the accompanying application upon all parties. Proof of accuracy of the index number must accompany the RJI. Check the Fee Schedule[. . .]for any applicable filing fees. NY R BRONX FIL R Doc. 2.
- *KINGS COUNTY.* An RJI with the relevant required addendum in a NYSCEF case shall be submitted via NYSCEF. Once e-filed, the RJI and any accompanying document will be forwarded to the relevant support office for random assignment of the case and processing of the document. A filer or counsel need not appear (as to Proposed Orders to Show Cause, however, see below). A copy of the pleadings must be submitted only if the document has not previously been e-filed. If the RJI seeks intervention with regard to a document that is intended for review by a Justice, such as a motion, a working copy of the RJI must be submitted with the working copy of the motion and the NYSCEF Confirmation Notice. NY R L KINGS E FIL Doc. 1(C).
- *NEW YORK COUNTY.* To obtain the assignment of an IAS Justice to a case, a Request for Judicial Intervention (cost ninety-five dollars ($95)) must be filed, with NYSCEF in an e-filed case or in paper in an authorized hard-copy one. A no-fee RJI, which will generally result in the referral of an application to an Ex Parte Justice, is also required with regard to certain kinds of applications for which, prior to 2011, no RJI was required. NY R NY CTY Procedure I(C). A "fillable" form RJI is available on-line. The form must be filed in duplicate in hard-copy cases. NY R NY CTY Procedure IA(A)(1). The filer of an RJI must check off a box identifying the type of case at issue. Where the RJI seeks judicial assignment, this designation will bring about a random assignment of the case by computer to a Justice handling cases of that type. NY R NY CTY Procedure IA(A)(1). The RJI and any addendum can be completed and submitted electronically in an e-filed case. NY R NY CTY Procedure II(A). The RJI shall be marked to reflect the existence of any "related case" as explained on the "Commencement of Cases" page under "Case Processing" on the court's website. NY R NY CTY Procedure II(A); NY R NY CTY E FIL Doc. 2(C).
- *ONONDAGA COUNTY.* The RJI will be submitted via the NYSCEF system along with any required RJI addendum forms. When the RJI is filed and the fee paid online, the Onondaga County Clerk's Office will electronically forward the RJI and any accompanying documents to the Onondaga Supreme Court Clerk's Office for assignment and processing. Counsel will receive notification of judge assignment via the NYSCEF system. NY R ONDGA E FIL Protocol(B)(3).
- *QUEENS COUNTY.* A Request for Judicial Intervention ("RJI") in an E-filed case shall be submitted via the E-filing System. When the RJI is approved, filed and paid for on-line, it will be forwarded to the relevant back office for random assignment of the case and processing of the document. In the case of RJIs seeking assignment to the Commercial Division, the filer must submit therewith, a Commercial Addendum as required by the standards for assignment of cases to the Commercial Division. NY R L QUEENS E-FILE Doc. 1(F).

v. *Proof of service.* In addition to complying with the provisions of NY CPLR Rule 2101, every paper filed in court shall have annexed thereto appropriate proof of service on all parties where required. NY R UNIF TRIAL CTS § 202.5(a).

- *QUEENS COUNTY.* With regard to service of a motion/petition on notice in an E-filed action, NY CPLR Rule 2214(b) and NY R UNIF TRIAL CTS § 202.5-b(f) applies. Where required, proof of service shall be filed on-line as a separate document. NY R L QUEENS E-FILE Doc. 1(H)(3).

vi. *ALBANY COUNTY: Additional required documents*

- *Affirmation of good faith effort.* The parties must[. . .]submit an affirmation attesting to [their good faith effort to resolve the matter]. The affirmation of good faith effort to resolve the issues raised by the motion shall indicate the time, place and nature of the consultation and the issues discussed and any resolutions, or shall indicate good cause why no such conferral with counsel for opposing parties was held. An assigned justice or judge may dismiss a motion for failure to demonstrate that such effort was made with leave to renew the motion after such effort has been demonstrated. NY R 3 JD SUP Doc. 1(B).

b. *Supplemental documents*

i. *Supporting evidence; Exhibits.* The main supporting papers on a motion are affidavits, but any relevant exhibits, documents, depositions, etc., are also includible. SIEGEL-NYPRAC § 246.

- *Affidavits accompanying motion.* Affidavits shall be for a statement of the relevant facts. NY R UNIF TRIAL CTS § 202.8(c).
- *Foreign language documents.* Where an affidavit or exhibit annexed to a paper served or filed is in a foreign language, it shall be accompanied by an English translation and an affidavit by the translator stating his qualifications and that the translation is accurate. NY CPLR Rule 2101(b).
- *Statement of attorney in lieu of affidavit.* The statement of an attorney admitted to practice in the courts of the state, or of a physician, osteopath or dentist, authorized by law to practice in the state, who is not a party to an action, when subscribed and affirmed by him to be true under the penalties of perjury, may be served or filed in the action in lieu of and with the same force and effect as an affidavit. NY CPLR Rule 2106.
- *NEW YORK COUNTY: Form of presented exhibits.* Exhibits should be tabbed and be legible; a typed version of any exhibit that is difficult to read should be submitted with the original. Exhibits printed on both sides of the page should be bound and tabbed on the side. NY R NY CTY J RUL Rule 14(a).
- *QUEENS COUNTY.* Attorneys submitting exhibits to the court on E-file cases shall make each exhibit a separate, labeled attachment to an affidavit/affirmation. NY R L QUEENS E-FILE Doc. 1(H)(4).

ii. *Brief.* Briefs shall be for a statement of the relevant law. NY R UNIF TRIAL CTS § 202.8(c).

iii. *Notice to produce papers not in possession of the court.* If a paper relied on by the movant is in the possession of the other side, it may be demanded of that side with a notice to produce it at the hearing. Where such papers are in the possession of an adverse party, they shall be produced by him at the hearing on notice served with the motion papers. NY CPLR Rule 2214(Practice Commentary, C2214:23).

iv. *Filing fees.* The County Clerk shall require the payment of any applicable statutory fees, or an order of the Court waiving payment of such fees, before accepting a paper for filing. NY R UNIF TRIAL CTS § 202.5(d)(1). For information on filing fees, if any, refer to NY CPLR § 8001, et seq.

- *ALBANY COUNTY.* In general, any filing subsequent to the commencement of an action which is designated as a motion or cross-motion requires the payment of a filing fee to the County Clerk's Office prior to submission to the Supreme Court Clerk's Office for referral to the assigned justice. The fee is assessed regardless of whether an application is made by notice of motion, order to show cause or ex parte. No fee will be charged upon the filing of a motion for poor person status in conjunction with an application which serves to commence an action or special proceeding. In the event a motion is received by the court unaccompanied by proof of payment to the County Clerk, the Supreme Court Clerk's Office will contact the submitting party to advise that the application will be held pending receipt of the filing fee only until the return date of the motion. If proof of payment is not submitted to the Supreme Court Clerk's Office by the return date (ex parte applications will be held ten (10) days), the papers will be returned by mail with a notification that the motion has been removed from the court's calendar and that it must be re-noticed and re-filed with the court along with the requisite filing fee. Inquiries concerning the applicability of the motion fee to a proposed filing may be directed to the Supreme Court Clerk's Office. NY R 3 JD SUP Doc. 1(B).
- *BRONX COUNTY.* In accordance with the new civil fee schedule set forth in Article 80 of the C.P.L.R. (NY CPLR § 8001, et seq.), effective July 14, 2003, all motions, and cross motions must be approved in Room 217 prior to payment of said fees in the County Clerk's Office, Room 118. NY R BRONX FIL R Doc. 8. The motion fee [must be] paid for via NYSCEF by credit/debit card. NY R BRONX E FIL R Doc. 1(1).
- *ERIE COUNTY.* Payment for fee-bearing NYSCEF documents must be made online via credit or debit card (American Express, MasterCard or Visa) at the time of submission. NY R ERIE E FIL Doc. 3(III)(E).

- *KINGS COUNTY.* The motion must be filed with NYSCEF and the motion fee paid. NY R L KINGS E FIL Doc. 1(D). Court fees in NYSCEF cases must be paid via NYSCEF by a credit or bank card (MasterCard, Visa, or American Express). Fees are no longer accepted in person in the Kings County Clerk's Office in NYSCEF cases. NY R L KINGS E FIL Doc. 1(B)(6).
- *NEW YORK COUNTY.* A motion fee must be paid on motions made in writing by notice of motion, order to show cause or ex parte after the commencement of an action. For this purpose, the term "action" shall mean any application to the court that requires the assignment of an index number, regardless of whether a formal pleading is filed. Applications or motions that commence an action and for which an index number fee must be paid require no motion fee. [A]ny motions made after the initial applications in these situations would require payment of the motion fee. A motion that is the initial application in a case commenced by the filing of a summons and complaint would require a motion fee since the filing of the summons and complaint rather than the application itself would require the purchase of an index number. NY R NY CTY Procedure II(A). In e-filed cases the motion fee must be paid when the documents are filed. Payment is made on-line by Visa, Mastercard, or American Express credit or bank card. NY R NY CTY Procedure II(A); NY R NY CTY E FIL Doc. 2(B)(5).
- *ONONDAGA COUNTY.* Court fees in e-filed cases must be paid online with the NYSCEF system using a credit card. The document is not considered to have been filed until payment of the fee has been tendered. NY R ONDGA E FIL Protocol(B)(2). Fees must be paid on all cross motions. NY R ONDGA E FIL Protocol(B)(9)(e).
- *QUEENS COUNTY.* The Motion Support Office does not receive, forward or process any fees or waiver of fees. All applications requiring payment of statutory fees or waiver of fees must be sent directly to the Queens County Clerk's office. NY R L QUEENS MOT SUP Doc. 1. Court fees (e.g., RJI fee, motion fee) in E-filed cases may be paid for on-line using a credit card. Papers may also be filed with the E-file system and the fee may be paid at the County Clerk's Office. In the latter case, the paper is not considered to have been filed until payment of the fee has been tendered. NY R L QUEENS E-FILE Doc. 1(E)(1). The motion/petition shall be filed on-line and the fee paid for either on-line by credit card or by the "Pay at the County Clerk's Office" option. NY R L QUEENS E-FILE Doc. 1(H)(1).

v. *Working copies.* The court may require the parties to provide working copies of documents filed electronically. In such event, each working copy shall include, firmly affixed thereto, a copy of a confirmation notice in a form prescribed by the Chief Administrator. NY R UNIF TRIAL CTS § 202.5-b(d)(5).

- *BRONX COUNTY.* After papers on motions have been e-filed, working copies thereof, with Confirmation Notice firmly attached as the back page facing out, must be submitted. (Each document or group of documents that is separately bound shall bear a Confirmation Notice.) Working copies lacking the Notice will not be accepted. WORKING COPIES OF MOTION PAPERS MUST BE SUBMITTED NO LATER THAN 4:45 P.M. ON THE RETURN DATE IN THE MOTION SUPPORT OFFICE (ROOM 217) AS EXPLAINED in NY R BRONX E FIL R Doc. 1(4). If an attorney has failed to submit required working copies on or before the return date, the motion will be transmitted as is to the Justice for such action as the Justice finds appropriate. Attorneys may submit working copies on motions by mail or overnight delivery. Any such submission shall be sent in a timely manner to the Motion Support Office (Room 217) and be conspicuously marked on the outside "NYSCEF Matter"; lack of such marking may delay processing. NY R BRONX E FIL R Doc. 1(4)(a).
- *ERIE COUNTY.* Electronically filed documents subject to review and processing by the Part Clerk do not require a working copy unless otherwise directed or provided for in IAS Part Rules. NY R UNIF TRIAL CTS § 202.5-b(d)(4), any working copy submitted shall include, as a cover page firmly fastened thereto, a copy of the Confirmation Notice generated by the NYSCEF site at the time of filing. Please consult the individual Justice's Part Rules and/or consult with the Judge's chambers to determine whether and how working copies are to be provided. Working copies will not be printed or delivered by the Erie County Clerk or the Chief Clerk of the Courts or any of their personnel to chambers. The official record of a document in an electronically filed case is the document filed via the NYSCEF system. Working copies are intended only for use by the Justice. The Court will discard all working copies after the Justice has finished with them. Thus, in the event that counsel fails to file a document via the NYSCEF system, the document will not be part of the court record. NY R ERIE E FIL Doc. 3(III)(O); NY R ERIE E FIL Doc. 3(V)(E).
- *KINGS COUNTY.* No courtesy copies of motion papers are required by the Court, except as may be required for electronic filing or by the Judge's Part Rules. In tort cases against the City of New York,

courtesy copies shall be supplied to the Corporation Counsel's office in Brooklyn. NY R L KINGS Pt. C, Rule 5. Unless otherwise directed by the Court or as described herein, and with the exceptions listed below, in all NYSCEF cases in which an RJI has been filed, working copies of e-filed documents that are intended for judicial review must be submitted to the court. Working copies are not required of documents that are only processed by a support office (e.g. preliminary conference request, note of issue). Working copies shall include exhibit tabs and backs; for motion papers, the motion sequence number and the return date and part. The confirmation notice with the motion sequence number on it should be the back page of the motion facing out. In addition, the filer of a working copy must firmly bind thereto, with the back page facing out, a copy of the Confirmation Notice that was generated by NYSCEF when that document was efiled. Working copies that are submitted without the related Confirmation Notice will not be accepted. NY R L KINGS E FIL Doc. 1(B)(7); NY R L KINGS E FIL Doc. 1(D). WORKING COPIES OF MOTION PAPERS MUST BE SUBMITTED IN THE MOTION SUPPORT OFFICE (ROOM 227) AS EXPLAINED HEREIN. THEY MUST NOT BE DELIVERED TO THE PART OR CHAMBERS, EXCEPT WHERE THE INDIVIDUAL JUSTICE'S PART RULES PROVIDE OTHERWISE; DOING SO WILL CAUSE ADMINISTRATIVE CONFUSION AND POSSIBLE MISPLACEMENT OF PAPERS. Any such submission shall be sent in a timely manner (kindly review individual Justice's rules) and be conspicuously marked on the outside "NYSCEF Matter;" lack of such marking may delay processing. NY R L KINGS E FIL Doc. 1(D).

- *NEW YORK COUNTY.* Some Justices require that working copies of e-filed motion papers be submitted. See the E-filing Protocol for information on the many Parts that do not require working copies. Where required, working copies of the moving documents and all other documents on the motion or application shall be submitted to the Motion Submission Part Courtroom (Room 130) on, but not before, the final return date. A Confirmation Notice from the NYSCEF system, which is generated when a document is e-filed, shall be firmly affixed, as the back page facing out, to each separate working copy or group of such copies. NY R NY CTY Procedure II(A) NY R NY CTY E FIL Doc. 2(B)(5)(a); NY R NY CTY J RUL Rule 14(a). For more information on working copies, including which parts don't require them, refer to NY R NY CTY E FIL Doc. 2(B)(6).
- *ONONDAGA COUNTY.* Any courtesy "working" copies, if required (see NY R ONDGA E FIL Protocol(B)(7)), must be provided directly to the assigned justice. NY R ONDGA E FIL Protocol(B)(9)(e). For information as to whether or not an Onondaga Supreme Court Justice requires working (courtesy) copies of e-filed documents, please consult the Onondaga County Individual E-filing Rules. NY R ONDGA E FIL Protocol(B)(7)(a). The Supreme Court Clerk's Office and the Onondaga County Clerk's Office will NOT accept the working copies. Working copies must be sent directly to the assigned justice's chambers. NY R ONDGA E FIL Protocol(B)(7)(b). A copy of the Confirmation Notice, generated by the NYSCEF system at the time a document is e-filed, must be attached to every working copy provided to chambers. If the Confirmation Notice is missing, the copy will not be accepted. NY R ONDGA E FIL Protocol(B)(7)(c). Courtesy copies do not become part of the official court record as maintained by the Onondaga County Clerk's Office and will be destroyed by chambers at the disposition of the case. In the event that counsel fails to file a document via NYSCEF, the document will not be part of the court record. NY R ONDGA E FIL Protocol(B)(7)(d).
- *QUEENS COUNTY.* Working copies of E-Filed notices of motion/notices of petition are NOT to be sent to the Motion Support Office. They must be brought to the calendar call in the judge's part. NY R L QUEENS MOT SUP Doc. 1. Unless otherwise directed or authorized by the court, counsel should file papers with the E-file system first and thereafter deliver a working copy to at the calendar call of the Centralized Motion Part or Assigned Justice in accordance with individual Part Rules. NY R L QUEENS E-FILE Doc. 1(E)(4). On the return date of a motion that has been E-filed, the movant must provide the Centralized Motion Part (CMP) with a working copy of the entire motion including the notice of motion with sequence number and all of the attached exhibits. The motion must have the confirmation of filing firmly affixed to the back of the papers (facing outward). The confirmation of filing is a separate notice from the payment notice and will say confirmation clearly across the top of the page. NY R L QUEENS E-FILE Doc. 1(H)(2)(a). The motion or Order to Show Cause must have clearly written across its face the words "Working Copy," it must also have the assigned Judge's name, motion sequence number and calendar number—which may be obtained from the posted calendar outside courtroom on the return date of the motion. A confirmation of filing must attached thereto. Working copies of e-filed Orders to Show Cause must contain a copy of the signed order and all supporting papers. NY R L QUEENS E-FILE Doc. 1(H)(2)(c). The Confirmation Notice must be an updated version that indicates the sequence number of the motion being submitted at the CMP calendar call.

WORKING COPIES WITHOUT A CONFIRMATION NOTICE WILL NOT BE ACCEPTED. NY R L QUEENS E-FILE Doc. 1(H)(7).

vi. *Statement of authorization in electronic filing cases.* A filing agent (other than one employed by a governmental entity) shall e-file a statement of authorization from counsel of record in an action, in a form approved by the Chief Administrator, prior to or together with the first e-filing in that action by the agent on behalf of that counsel. NY R UNIF TRIAL CTS § 202.5-b(d)(1)(i).

vii. *ERIE COUNTY: Additional supplemental documents*

- *Notice of hard copy submission in e-filed case.* In accordance with NY R UNIF TRIAL CTS § 202.5-b(d), the County Clerk shall refuse to accept for filing, hard copy papers filed to an action subject to electronic filing unless hard copy filing is permitted by the Uniform Rules or NY R ERIE E FIL Doc. 3 and the papers bear a completed Notice of Hard Copy Submission—E-Filed Case form. NY R ERIE E FIL Doc. 3(III)(D).

viii. *KINGS COUNTY: Additional supplemental documents*

- *Forms when filing in hard copy.* An attorney who certifies in good faith that he or she lacks the equipment or knowledge needed to e-file and have no staff member or employee under his or her direction who has such knowledge and equipment may opt out of participation in e-filing in a mandatory case by filing a "Notice of Opt-Out from Participation in Action Subject to Mandatory Electronic Filing" form EFM-2 with the Clerk. NY R L KINGS E FIL Doc. 1(A)(2). Where in accordance with the E-Filing Rules a party submits a document in hard copy in an e-filed case (principally, a document submitted by a nonparticipating party (e.g., an attorney) in a consensual case, an emergency filing made in accordance with the Mandatory E-Filing Rules, and any document filed with the court in hard copy by an attorney who has opted out of participation in mandatory e-filing, the document must bear the back page facing out, a "Notice of Hard Copy Submission—E-Filed Cases" form EFM-3. NY R L KINGS E FIL Doc. 1(B)(3).

ix. *NEW YORK COUNTY: Additional supplemental documents*

- *Notice of hard copy submission.* Where in accordance with the E-Filing Rules an attorney or an unrepresented litigant who is participating in e-filing submits a document in hard copy in an e-filed case, the document must bear, as the back page facing out, a Notice of Hard-Copy Submission—E-Filed Case (a form available in the "Forms" section on the NYSCEF website (Form EFM-3) and in the court's back offices). NY R NY CTY E FIL Doc. 2(B)(3). For more information refer to NY R NY CTY E FIL Doc. 2.
- *Unpublished decisions.* Whenever reliance is placed upon a decision or other authority not officially published or readily available to the New York County Supreme Court, a copy of the case or of pertinent portions of the authority shall be submitted with the motion papers. NY R NY CTY J RUL Rule 14(a).

x. *ONONDAGA COUNTY: Additional supplemental documents*

- *Notice of hard copy submission.* Any papers to be filed with the court in an e-filed case must be filed online with the E-filing system except where a special exemption is granted (e.g., oversized maps, photographs). If such an exemption is granted, Form EFM-3, "Notice of Hard Copy Submission—E-Filed Case," must be attached to such documents forms which are not filed on line. Also, Form EFM-4 "Notice of Hard Copy Exhibit Filing" must be completed and uploaded to the action's e-file. Both of these forms may be found on the NYSCEF website. NY R ONDGA E FIL Protocol(B)(4).

xi. *QUEENS COUNTY: Additional supplemental documents*

- *Notice of hard copy submission.* Any party opting out of the e-filing system must have a "Notice of Hard Copy Submission" firmly affixed to the back of the papers. NY R L QUEENS E-FILE Doc. 1(H)(2)(f).

2. *Documents for opposing party*

a. *Required documents*

i. *Opposition.* Refer to the General Requirements section of this document for information on the opposition.

- *Request for oral argument.* A party requesting oral argument shall set forth such request in its notice of motion or in its order to show cause or on the first page of the answering papers, as the case may be. Where all parties to a motion request oral argument, oral argument shall be granted unless the court shall determine it to be unnecessary. Where a motion is brought on by order to show cause, the court may set forth in the order that oral argument is required on the return date of the motion. NY R UNIF TRIAL CTS § 202.8(d).
- *QUEENS COUNTY: E-filing opposition papers.* E-filed opposition papers and/or reply papers must also be

provided to the Centralized Motion Part in the same manner as the moving papers with the confirmation of filing firmly attached to the back of the papers. NY R L QUEENS E-FILE Doc. 1(H)(2)(d).

ii. *Proof of service.* In addition to complying with the provisions of NY CPLR Rule 2101, every paper filed in court shall have annexed thereto appropriate proof of service on all parties where required. NY R UNIF TRIAL CTS § 202.5(a).

b. *Supplemental documents*

i. *Supporting evidence; Exhibits.* The main supporting papers on a motion are affidavits, but any relevant exhibits, documents, depositions, etc., are also includible. SIEGEL-NYPRAC § 246.

- *Affidavits accompanying opposition.* Affidavits shall be for a statement of the relevant facts. NY R UNIF TRIAL CTS § 202.8(c).
- *Foreign language documents.* Where an affidavit or exhibit annexed to a paper served or filed is in a foreign language, it shall be accompanied by an English translation and an affidavit by the translator stating his qualifications and that the translation is accurate. NY CPLR Rule 2101(b).
- *Statement of attorney in lieu of affidavit.* The statement of an attorney admitted to practice in the courts of the state, or of a physician, osteopath or dentist, authorized by law to practice in the state, who is not a party to an action, when subscribed and affirmed by him to be true under the penalties of perjury, may be served or filed in the action in lieu of and with the same force and effect as an affidavit. NY CPLR Rule 2106.
- *NEW YORK COUNTY: Form of presented exhibits.* Exhibits should be tabbed and be legible; a typed version of any exhibit that is difficult to read should be submitted with the original. Exhibits printed on both sides of the page should be bound and tabbed on the side. NY R NY CTY J RUL Rule 14(a).
- *QUEENS COUNTY.* Attorneys submitting exhibits to the court on E-file cases shall make each exhibit a separate, labeled attachment to an affidavit/affirmation. NY R L QUEENS E-FILE Doc. 1(H)(4).

ii. *Brief.* Briefs shall be for a statement of the relevant law. NY R UNIF TRIAL CTS § 202.8(c).

iii. *Filing fees.* The County Clerk shall require the payment of any applicable statutory fees, or an order of the Court waiving payment of such fees, before accepting a paper for filing. NY R UNIF TRIAL CTS § 202.5(d)(1). For information on filing fees, if any, refer to NY CPLR § 8001, et seq.

- *ALBANY COUNTY.* In general, any filing subsequent to the commencement of an action which is designated as a motion or cross-motion requires the payment of a filing fee to the County Clerk's Office prior to submission to the Supreme Court Clerk's Office for referral to the assigned justice. The fee is assessed regardless of whether an application is made by notice of motion, order to show cause or ex parte. No fee will be charged upon the filing of a motion for poor person status in conjunction with an application which serves to commence an action or special proceeding. In the event a motion is received by the court unaccompanied by proof of payment to the County Clerk, the Supreme Court Clerk's Office will contact the submitting party to advise that the application will be held pending receipt of the filing fee only until the return date of the motion. If proof of payment is not submitted to the Supreme Court Clerk's Office by the return date (ex parte applications will be held ten (10) days), the papers will be returned by mail with a notification that the motion has been removed from the court's calendar and that it must be re-noticed and re-filed with the court along with the requisite filing fee. Inquiries concerning the applicability of the motion fee to a proposed filing may be directed to the Supreme Court Clerk's Office. NY R 3 JD SUP Doc. 1(B).
- *BRONX COUNTY.* In accordance with the new civil fee schedule set forth in Article 80 of the C.P.L.R. (NY CPLR § 8001, et seq.), effective July 14, 2003, all motions, and cross motions must be approved in Room 217 prior to payment of said fees in the County Clerk's Office, Room 118. NY R BRONX FIL R Doc. 8. The motion fee [must be] paid for via NYSCEF by credit/debit card. NY R BRONX E FIL R Doc. 1(1).
- *ERIE COUNTY.* Payment for fee-bearing NYSCEF documents must be made online via credit or debit card (American Express, MasterCard or Visa) at the time of submission. NY R ERIE E FIL Doc. 3(III)(E).
- *KINGS COUNTY.* The motion must be filed with NYSCEF and the motion fee paid. NY R L KINGS E FIL Doc. 1(D). Court fees in NYSCEF cases must be paid via NYSCEF by a credit or bank card (MasterCard, Visa, or American Express). Fees are no longer accepted in person in the Kings County Clerk's Office in NYSCEF cases. NY R L KINGS E FIL Doc. 1(B)(6).
- *NEW YORK COUNTY.* A motion fee must be paid on motions made in writing by notice of motion, order

to show cause or ex parte after the commencement of an action. For this purpose, the term "action" shall mean any application to the court that requires the assignment of an index number, regardless of whether a formal pleading is filed. Applications or motions that commence an action and for which an index number fee must be paid require no motion fee. [A]ny motions made after the initial applications in these situations would require payment of the motion fee. A motion that is the initial application in a case commenced by the filing of a summons and complaint would require a motion fee since the filing of the summons and complaint rather than the application itself would require the purchase of an index number. NY R NY CTY Procedure II(A). In e-filed cases the motion fee must be paid when the documents are filed. Payment is made on-line by Visa, Mastercard, or American Express credit or bank card. NY R NY CTY Procedure II(A); NY R NY CTY E FIL Doc. 2(B)(5).

- *ONONDAGA COUNTY.* Court fees in e-filed cases must be paid online with the NYSCEF system using a credit card. The document is not considered to have been filed until payment of the fee has been tendered. NY R ONDGA E FIL Protocol(B)(2). Fees must be paid on all cross motions. NY R ONDGA E FIL Protocol(B)(9)(e).
- *QUEENS COUNTY.* The Motion Support Office does not receive, forward or process any fees or waiver of fees. All applications requiring payment of statutory fees or waiver of fees must be sent directly to the Queens County Clerk's office. NY R L QUEENS MOT SUP Doc. 1. Court fees (e.g., RJI fee, motion fee) in E-filed cases may be paid for on-line using a credit card. Papers may also be filed with the E-file system and the fee may be paid at the County Clerk's Office. In the latter case, the paper is not considered to have been filed until payment of the fee has been tendered. NY R L QUEENS E-FILE Doc. 1(E)(1). The motion/petition shall be filed on-line and the fee paid for either on-line by credit card or by the "Pay at the County Clerk's Office" option. NY R L QUEENS E-FILE Doc. 1(H)(1).

iv. *Working copies.* The court may require the parties to provide working copies of documents filed electronically. In such event, each working copy shall include, firmly affixed thereto, a copy of a confirmation notice in a form prescribed by the Chief Administrator. NY R UNIF TRIAL CTS § 202.5-b(d)(5).

- *BRONX COUNTY.* After papers on motions have been e-filed, working copies thereof, with Confirmation Notice firmly attached as the back page facing out, must be submitted. (Each document or group of documents that is separately bound shall bear a Confirmation Notice.) Working copies lacking the Notice will not be accepted. WORKING COPIES OF MOTION PAPERS MUST BE SUBMITTED NO LATER THAN 4:45 P.M. ON THE RETURN DATE IN THE MOTION SUPPORT OFFICE (ROOM 217) AS EXPLAINED in NY R BRONX E FIL R Doc. 1(4). If an attorney has failed to submit required working copies on or before the return date, the motion will be transmitted as is to the Justice for such action as the Justice finds appropriate. Attorneys may submit working copies on motions by mail or overnight delivery. Any such submission shall be sent in a timely manner to the Motion Support Office (Room 217) and be conspicuously marked on the outside "NYSCEF Matter"; lack of such marking may delay processing. NY R BRONX E FIL R Doc. 1(4)(a).
- *ERIE COUNTY.* Electronically filed documents subject to review and processing by the Part Clerk do not require a working copy unless otherwise directed or provided for in IAS Part Rules. NY R UNIF TRIAL CTS § 202.5-b(d)(4), any working copy submitted shall include, as a cover page firmly fastened thereto, a copy of the Confirmation Notice generated by the NYSCEF site at the time of filing. Please consult the individual Justice's Part Rules and/or consult with the Judge's chambers to determine whether and how working copies are to be provided. Working copies will not be printed or delivered by the Erie County Clerk or the Chief Clerk of the Courts or any of their personnel to chambers. The official record of a document in an electronically filed case is the document filed via the NYSCEF system. Working copies are intended only for use by the Justice. The Court will discard all working copies after the Justice has finished with them. Thus, in the event that counsel fails to file a document via the NYSCEF system, the document will not be part of the court record. NY R ERIE E FIL Doc. 3(III)(O); NY R ERIE E FIL Doc. 3(V)(E).
- *KINGS COUNTY.* No courtesy copies of motion papers are required by the Court, except as may be required for electronic filing or by the Judge's Part Rules. In tort cases against the City of New York, courtesy copies shall be supplied to the Corporation Counsel's office in Brooklyn. NY R L KINGS Pt. C, Rule 5. Unless otherwise directed by the Court or as described herein, and with the exceptions listed below, in all NYSCEF cases in which an RJI has been filed, working copies of e-filed documents that are intended for judicial review must be submitted to the court. Working copies are not required of documents that are only processed by a support office (e.g. preliminary conference request, note of issue). Working copies

shall include exhibit tabs and backs; for motion papers, the motion sequence number and the return date and part. The confirmation notice with the motion sequence number on it should be the back page of the motion facing out. In addition, the filer of a working copy must firmly bind thereto, with the back page facing out, a copy of the Confirmation Notice that was generated by NYSCEF when that document was efiled. Working copies that are submitted without the related Confirmation Notice will not be accepted. NY R L KINGS E FIL Doc. 1(B)(7); NY R L KINGS E FIL Doc. 1(D). WORKING COPIES OF MOTION PAPERS MUST BE SUBMITTED IN THE MOTION SUPPORT OFFICE (ROOM 227) AS EXPLAINED HEREIN. THEY MUST NOT BE DELIVERED TO THE PART OR CHAMBERS, EXCEPT WHERE THE INDIVIDUAL JUSTICE'S PART RULES PROVIDE OTHERWISE; DOING SO WILL CAUSE ADMINISTRATIVE CONFUSION AND POSSIBLE MISPLACEMENT OF PAPERS. Any such submission shall be sent in a timely manner (kindly review individual Justice's rules) and be conspicuously marked on the outside "NYSCEF Matter;" lack of such marking may delay processing. NY R L KINGS E FIL Doc. 1(D).

- *NEW YORK COUNTY.* Some Justices require that working copies of e-filed motion papers be submitted. See the E-filing Protocol for information on the many Parts that do not require working copies. Where required, working copies of the moving documents and all other documents on the motion or application shall be submitted to the Motion Submission Part Courtroom (Room 130) on, but not before, the final return date. A Confirmation Notice from the NYSCEF system, which is generated when a document is e-filed, shall be firmly affixed, as the back page facing out, to each separate working copy or group of such copies. NY R NY CTY Procedure II(A) NY R NY CTY E FIL Doc. 2(B)(5)(a); NY R NY CTY J RUL Rule 14(a). For more information on working copies, including which parts don't require them, refer to NY R NY CTY E FIL Doc. 2(B)(6).
- *ONONDAGA COUNTY.* Any courtesy "working" copies, if required (see NY R ONDGA E FIL Protocol(B)(7)), must be provided directly to the assigned justice. NY R ONDGA E FIL Protocol(B)(9)(e). For information as to whether or not an Onondaga Supreme Court Justice requires working (courtesy) copies of e-filed documents, please consult the Onondaga County Individual E-filing Rules. NY R ONDGA E FIL Protocol(B)(7)(a). The Supreme Court Clerk's Office and the Onondaga County Clerk's Office will NOT accept the working copies. Working copies must be sent directly to the assigned justice's chambers. NY R ONDGA E FIL Protocol(B)(7)(b). A copy of the Confirmation Notice, generated by the NYSCEF system at the time a document is e-filed, must be attached to every working copy provided to chambers. If the Confirmation Notice is missing, the copy will not be accepted. NY R ONDGA E FIL Protocol(B)(7)(c). Courtesy copies do not become part of the official court record as maintained by the Onondaga County Clerk's Office and will be destroyed by chambers at the disposition of the case. In the event that counsel fails to file a document via NYSCEF, the document will not be part of the court record. NY R ONDGA E FIL Protocol(B)(7)(d).
- *QUEENS COUNTY.* Working copies of E-Filed notices of motion/notices of petition are NOT to be sent to the Motion Support Office. They must be brought to the calendar call in the judge's part. NY R L QUEENS MOT SUP Doc. 1. Unless otherwise directed or authorized by the court, counsel should file papers with the E-file system first and thereafter deliver a working copy to at the calendar call of the Centralized Motion Part or Assigned Justice in accordance with individual Part Rules. NY R L QUEENS E-FILE Doc. 1(E)(4). On the return date of a motion that has been E-filed, the movant must provide the Centralized Motion Part (CMP) with a working copy of the entire motion including the notice of motion with sequence number and all of the attached exhibits. The motion must have the confirmation of filing firmly affixed to the back of the papers (facing outward). The confirmation of filing is a separate notice from the payment notice and will say confirmation clearly across the top of the page. NY R L QUEENS E-FILE Doc. 1(H)(2)(a). The motion or Order to Show Cause must have clearly written across its face the words "Working Copy," it must also have the assigned Judge's name, motion sequence number and calendar number—which may be obtained from the posted calendar outside courtroom on the return date of the motion. A confirmation of filing must attached thereto. Working copies of e-filed Orders to Show Cause must contain a copy of the signed order and all supporting papers. NY R L QUEENS E-FILE Doc. 1(H)(2)(c). The Confirmation Notice must be an updated version that indicates the sequence number of the motion being submitted at the CMP calendar call. WORKING COPIES WITHOUT A CONFIRMATION NOTICE WILL NOT BE ACCEPTED. NY R L QUEENS E-FILE Doc. 1(H)(7).

v. *ERIE COUNTY: Additional supplemental documents*

- *Notice of hard copy submission in e-filed case.* In accordance with NY R UNIF TRIAL CTS § 202.5-b(d),

the County Clerk shall refuse to accept for filing, hard copy papers filed to an action subject to electronic filing unless hard copy filing is permitted by the Uniform Rules or NY R ERIE E FIL Doc. 3 and the papers bear a completed Notice of Hard Copy Submission—E-Filed Case form. NY R ERIE E FIL Doc. 3(III)(D).

vi. *KINGS COUNTY: Additional supplemental documents*

- *Forms when filing in hard copy.* An attorney who certifies in good faith that he or she lacks the equipment or knowledge needed to e-file and have no staff member or employee under his or her direction who has such knowledge and equipment may opt out of participation in e-filing in a mandatory case by filing a "Notice of Opt-Out from Participation in Action Subject to Mandatory Electronic Filing" form EFM-2 with the Clerk. NY R L KINGS E FIL Doc. 1(A)(2). Where in accordance with the E-Filing Rules a party submits a document in hard copy in an e-filed case (principally, a document submitted by a nonparticipating party (e.g., an attorney) in a consensual case, an emergency filing made in accordance with the Mandatory E-Filing Rules, and any document filed with the court in hard copy by an attorney who has opted out of participation in mandatory e-filing, the document must bear the back page facing out, a "Notice of Hard Copy Submission—E-Filed Cases" form EFM-3. NY R L KINGS E FIL Doc. 1(B)(3).

vii. *NEW YORK COUNTY: Additional supplemental documents*

- *Notice of hard copy submission.* Where in accordance with the E-Filing Rules an attorney or an unrepresented litigant who is participating in e-filing submits a document in hard copy in an e-filed case, the document must bear, as the back page facing out, a Notice of Hard-Copy Submission—E-Filed Case (a form available in the "Forms" section on the NYSCEF website (Form EFM-3) and in the court's back offices). NY R NY CTY E FIL Doc. 2(B)(3). For more information refer to NY R NY CTY E FIL Doc. 2.
- *Unpublished decisions.* Whenever reliance is placed upon a decision or other authority not officially published or readily available to the New York County Supreme Court, a copy of the case or of pertinent portions of the authority shall be submitted with the motion papers. NY R NY CTY J RUL Rule 14(a).

viii. *ONONDAGA COUNTY: Additional supplemental documents*

- *Notice of hard copy submission.* Any papers to be filed with the court in an e-filed case must be filed online with the E-filing system except where a special exemption is granted (e.g., oversized maps, photographs). If such an exemption is granted, Form EFM-3, "Notice of Hard Copy Submission—E-Filed Case," must be attached to such documents forms which are not filed on line. Also, Form EFM-4 "Notice of Hard Copy Exhibit Filing" must be completed and uploaded to the action's e-file. Both of these forms may be found on the NYSCEF website. NY R ONDGA E FIL Protocol(B)(4).

ix. *QUEENS COUNTY: Additional supplemental documents*

- *Notice of hard copy submission.* Any party opting out of the e-filing system must have a "Notice of Hard Copy Submission" firmly affixed to the back of the papers. NY R L QUEENS E-FILE Doc. 1(H)(2)(f).

E. Format

1. *Form of documents*

a. *Size and form of paper.* Each paper served or filed shall be durable, white and, except for summonses, subpoenas, notices of appearance, notes of issue, orders of protection, temporary orders of protection and exhibits, shall be eleven by eight and one-half (11 x 8-1/2) inches in size. NY CPLR Rule 2101(a).

b. *Writing and language.* The writing shall be legible and in black ink. NY CPLR Rule 2101(a). Each paper served or filed shall be in the English language which, where practicable, shall be of ordinary usage. NY CPLR Rule 2101(b).

c. *Caption.* Each paper served or filed shall begin with a caption setting forth the name of the court, the venue, the title of the action, the nature of the paper and the index number of the action if one has been assigned. In all papers other than a summons, a complaint or a judgment it shall be sufficient to state the name of the first named party on each side with an appropriate indication of any omissions. NY CPLR Rule 2101(c).

i. *Further contents of first page.* After the first paper has been filed in each case the index number shall appear on the cover and first page to the right of the caption of every paper tendered for filing in the action. Each such cover and first page also shall contain an indication of the county of venue and a brief description of the nature of the paper and, where the case has been assigned to an individual judge, shall contain the name of the assigned judge to the right of the caption. NY R UNIF TRIAL CTS § 202.5(a); NY R UNIF TRIAL CTS § 202.5(b); NY R UNIF TRIAL CTS § 202.5(d)(1)(i).

ii. *ALBANY COUNTY: Request for oral argument.* A party may request oral argument on a motion by indicating such request on the first page of the notice of motion, order to show cause, or answering papers in the area across from the caption of the action/proceeding. NY R 3 JD SUP Doc. 1(B).

iii. *NEW YORK COUNTY: Request for oral argument.* Counsel who wish oral argument must so request conspicuously on the front of their papers. NY R NY CTY Procedure II(D).

d. *Index number.* No paper in an action in the supreme or a county court, other than an order submitted for signature to a judge out of court, shall be submitted for any purpose to the supreme or county court or to a clerk thereof unless there is endorsed on such paper the index number of the action assigned by the clerk of the county. NY CPLR § 8018(c).

i. *ALBANY COUNTY: Index number on all filed documents.* The index number, the request for judicial intervention number and the assigned justice's name shall appear on [all papers filed with the Court subsequent to the complaint]. NY R 3 JD SUP Doc. 1(A).

ii. *ERIE COUNTY: Index number after initial filing.* Cases that are initially commenced by the filing of papers with the NYSCEF system are identified as e-filed cases by assignment of an Index Number that has "800-899" as the first three (3) digits of the index number (i.e. 802391/2012). NY R ERIE E FIL Doc. 3(II). [The] Index Number must be affixed to all document submissions, filings, and communications to the Erie County Clerk and the Court. Cases that are converted from paper to e-filing shall retain the original index number. NY R ERIE E FIL Doc. 3(II).

iii. *KINGS COUNTY: Index number after initial filing.* In cases commenced electronically by the filing of initiating papers with the NYSCEF system and payment of the statutory fees, the Kings County Clerk will issue an NYSCEF designated index number and the filer shall be notified via the NYSCEF system of the index number assigned and filing date. Such index number must be affixed to all document submissions, filings and communications to the Kings County Clerk and Supreme Court. If counsel faces exigent circumstances that require accelerated assignment, counsel may contact Administration of the Kings County Clerk at kcco-efile@nycourts.gov, during normal business hours of the court. NY R L KINGS E FIL Doc. 1(B)(5).

iv. *NEW YORK COUNTY: Index number on hard copy filings.* Papers subsequently presented for filing in hardcopy format will be filed in this jacket. NY R NY CTY Procedure I(B). Index numbers take the form of six digits followed by a slash and the four digits of the year the case began, e.g., 340705/2018. The first or first two integers of the index number identify the type of case. If a case is commenced electronically, the second integer will be a "5", except as indicated otherwise in the list below. There are many tax certiorari matters e-filed annually and the index numbers therefor will normally run over into those with a "6" as the second integer, and the same will occur with general cases if necessary. The principal types of cases and their index number categories are listed in NY R NY CTY Procedure I(B). NY R NY CTY Procedure I(B); NY R NY CTY Procedure XI(A).

v. *ONONDAGA COUNTY: Index number.* The index number must be referenced on all e-filed documents and correspondence. All e-filed case index numbers will contain the letters "EF" between the year and the file number (for example, 2012EF9999). NY R ONDGA E FIL Protocol(B)(1).

vi. *QUEENS COUNTY: Index number on converted cases.* Cases originally commenced in hard-copy form but later converted to an E-file case, either by stipulation or order will bear a regular index number initially. The County Clerk will issue a new E-file index number. NY R L QUEENS E-FILE Doc. 1(B).

e. *Line spacing.* Every paper filed in court, if typewritten, shall have at least double space between each line, except for quotations and the names and addresses of attorneys appearing in the action. NY R UNIF TRIAL CTS § 202.5(a).

f. *Font size.* Each. . .paper printed or typed, served or filed, except an exhibit or a summons, shall be in clear type of no less than ten (10) point in size. NY CPLR Rule 2101(a).

i. Whenever a requirement relating to size of type is stated in point size, the type size requirement shall be deemed met if the x-height of the type is a minimum of forty-five percent (45%) of the specified point size. Each point shall be measured as .351 millimeter. The x-height size shall be measured as it appears on the page. The x-height is the height of the lower case letters, exclusive of ascenders or descenders. NY CPLR § 105(t).

g. *Margins.* Every paper filed in court shall have at least one (1) inch margins. NY R UNIF TRIAL CTS § 202.5(a).

h. *Citations*

i. *Civil practice law and rules.* NY CPLR § 101, et seq. shall be known as the civil practice law and rules, and may be cited as "CPLR". Reference to a provision in the civil practice law and rules may, except when such provision is being enacted or amended, be made without indicating whether it is a rule or section. NY CPLR § 101.

i. *Indorsement by attorney.* Each paper served or filed shall be indorsed with the name, address and telephone number of the attorney for the party serving or filing the paper, or if the party does not appear by attorney, with the name, address and telephone number of the party. NY CPLR Rule 2101(d).

j. *One-sided printing.* In addition, every paper filed in court, other than an exhibit or printed form, shall contain writing on one side only, except that papers that are fastened on the side may contain writing on both sides. NY R UNIF TRIAL CTS § 202.5(a).

k. *Use of copies authorized.* Except where otherwise specifically prescribed, copies, rather than originals, of all papers, including orders, affidavits and exhibits may be served or filed. Where it is required that the original be served or filed and the original is lost or withheld, the court may authorize a copy to be served or filed. NY CPLR Rule 2101(e).

   i. Where a certified copy of a paper is required by law, an attorney admitted to practice in the courts of the state may certify that it has been compared by him with the original and found to be a true and complete copy. Such a certificate, when subscribed by such attorney, has the same effect as if made by a clerk. NY CPLR § 2105.

l. *Recycled paper.* It is the policy of the Unified Court System that litigants, where practicable, should file or submit to the courts of the Unified Court System of the State of New York papers printed or reproduced on recycled paper. Paper is considered recycled if it contains a minimum content of thirty percent (30%) waste paper. NY R UNIF TRIAL CTS § 215.2. The signature page of every paper filed or submitted to the court on recycled paper should bear the legend: "Printed [Reproduced] on Recycled Paper." NY R UNIF TRIAL CTS § 215.3.

m. *Form of request for judicial intervention; Copies.* A request for judicial intervention must be submitted, in duplicate, on a form authorized by the Chief of the Courts, with proof of service on the other parties to the action (but proof of service is not required where the application is ex parte). NY R UNIF TRIAL CTS § 202.6(a).

n. *KINGS COUNTY: Tabs on filings.* Motions, orders and other filed papers shall be indexed with protruding tabs. Clerks are required to reject papers that do not have protruding exhibit tabs, except papers in matrimonial cases and papers filed by pro se litigants. NY R L KINGS Pt. A, Papers.

o. *NEW YORK COUNTY: Length of briefs.* Unless advance permission otherwise is granted by the court for good cause, memoranda of law shall not exceed thirty (30) pages each (exclusive of table of contents and table of authorities) and affidavits/affirmations shall not exceed twenty-five (25) pages each. NY R NY CTY J RUL Rule 14(b).

p. *QUEENS COUNTY: Form and size of motion filings.* All motions filed in Queens Supreme Court-Civil Term, must adhere to the Motion Support rules and the rules of the assigned judge. NY R L QUEENS MOT SUP Doc. 1. Due to space limitations, the Motion Support Office cannot accept notices of motion/notices of petition and accompanying exhibits which measure greater than eight (8) inches. If your documents measure greater than eight (8) inches you are directed to submit only the notice of motion/notice of petition to the Motion Support Office and bring all exhibits to the calendar call on your return date. NY R L QUEENS MOT SUP Doc. 1.

2. *Form of electronic documents.* Each paper served or filed by electronic means, as defined in NY CPLR Rule 2103(f), shall be capable of being reproduced by the receiver so as to comply with the provisions of NY CPLR Rule 2101(a) through NY CPLR Rule 2101(d). NY CPLR Rule 2101(g).

   a. *File format.* All e-filed documents shall comply with the technical requirements set forth at the NYSCEF site. NY R UNIF TRIAL CTS § 202.5-b(d)(1)(i).

   b. *Heading of document.* The subject matter heading for each paper sent by electronic means must indicate that the matter being transmitted electronically is related to a court proceeding. NY CPLR Rule 2103(b)(7).

   c. *E-filed documents identification*

      i. *ERIE COUNTY.* E-filed cases must be readily identifiable and marked as such. If counsel presents papers to the Office of the Erie County Clerk or the Office of the Chief Clerk in a NYSCEF matter where authorized, counsel should alert the Clerk that the case is a NYSCEF matter. NY R ERIE E FIL Doc. 3(II).

      ii. *KINGS COUNTY.* The Supreme Court's Civil Case Information System ("CCIS") will further identify e-filed cases by the addition of a suffix to the index number (e.g. 500136/2006E). This suffix should be used on all documents filed with the court in e-filed matters. NY R L KINGS E FIL Doc. 1(A)(1).

3. *Signature blocks.* Every pleading, written motion, and other paper, served on another party or filed or submitted to the court shall be signed by an attorney, or by a party if the party is not represented by an attorney, with the name of the attorney or party clearly printed or typed directly below the signature. NY R CHIEF ADMIN § 130-1.1-a(a); NY R UNIF TRIAL CTS § 202.5(d)(1)(iv).

   a. *Printed name.* Beneath each signature shall be printed the name signed. NY CPLR Rule 2101(a).

   b. *Failure to sign.* Absent good cause shown, the court shall strike any unsigned paper if the omission of the signature is not corrected promptly after being called to the attention of the attorney or party. NY R CHIEF ADMIN § 130-1.1-a(a).

c. *Signature as certification.* By signing a paper, an attorney or party certifies that, to the best of that person's knowledge, information and belief, formed after an inquiry reasonable under the circumstances the presentation of the paper or the contentions therein are not frivolous as defined in NY R CHIEF ADMIN § 130-1.1(c). NY R CHIEF ADMIN § 130-1.1-a(b)(1).

d. *Electronic signatures.* A document shall be considered to have been signed by an attorney or party in compliance with NY R CHIEF ADMIN § 130-1.1-a if it has been signed by such attorney or party as provided in NY R UNIF TRIAL CTS § 202.5-b(e)(1) and it bears the signatory's name. NY R UNIF TRIAL CTS § 202.5-b(e)(2). An electronically filed document shall be considered to have been signed by, and shall be binding upon, the person identified as a signatory, if:

i. It bears the physical signature of such person and is scanned into an electronic format that reproduces such signature; or

ii. The signatory has electronically affixed the digital image of his or her signature to the document; or

iii. It is electronically filed under the User ID and password of that person; or

iv. In a tax certiorari action in which the parties have stipulated to this procedure, it is an initiating document that is electronically filed without the signature of the signatory in a form provided above in NY R UNIF TRIAL CTS § 202.5-b(e), provided that, prior to filing, the document is signed in full in hard copy (which hard copy must be preserved until the conclusion of all proceedings, including appeals, in the case in which it is filed); or

v. In a small claims assessment review proceeding, it is a petition recorded by the NYSCEF site upon the filing of a text file as provided in NY R UNIF TRIAL CTS § 202.5-b(b)(1), provided that prior to filing, the document was signed in full in hard copy (which hard copy must be preserved until the conclusion of all proceedings in the matter, including article 78 (NY CPLR § 7801, et seq.) review and any appeals, and must be made available during the proceeding upon request of the respondent or the court); or

vi. It otherwise bears the electronic signature of the signatory in a format conforming to such standards and requirements as may hereafter be established by the Chief Administrator. NY R UNIF TRIAL CTS § 202.5-b(e).

4. *Confidentiality of personal information.* No person may file any document available for public inspection with any state agency, political subdivision, or in any court of this state that contains a Social Security account number of any other person, unless such other person is a dependent child, or has consented to such filing, except as required by federal or state law or regulation, or by court rule. NY GEN BUS § 399-ddd. Submissions pursuant to e-filing procedures shall have the same confidentiality rights as paper documents. NY R UNIF TRIAL CTS § 202.5-b(k)(1).

a. *Confidential personal information.* Except in the actions designated in NY R UNIF TRIAL CTS § 202.5(e)(1), or as otherwise provided by rule or law or court order, and whether or not a sealing order is or has been sought, the parties shall omit or redact confidential personal information in papers submitted to the court for filing. For purposes of NY R UNIF TRIAL CTS § 202.5(e), confidential personal information ("CPI") means:

i. The taxpayer identification number of an individual or an entity, including a Social Security number, an employer identification number, and an individual taxpayer identification number, except the last four (4) digits thereof;

ii. The date of an individual's birth, except the year thereof;

iii. The full name of an individual known to be a minor, except the minor's initials;

iv. A financial account number, including a credit and/or debit card number, a bank account number, an investment account number, and/or an insurance account number, except the last four (4) digits or letters thereof; and

v. Any of the documents or testimony in a matrimonial action protected by NY DOM REL § 235 or evidence sealed by the court in such an action which are attached as exhibits or referenced in the papers filed in any other civil action. For purposes of NY R UNIF TRIAL CTS § 202.5, a matrimonial action shall mean: an action to annul a marriage or declare the nullity of a void marriage, an action or agreement for a separation, an action for a divorce, or an action or proceeding for custody, visitation, writ of habeus corpus, child support, maintenance or paternity. NY R UNIF TRIAL CTS § 202.5(e)(1).

vi. *ERIE COUNTY.* An attorney or unrepresented litigant filing a document via the NYSCEF system must comply with the requirements of NY R UNIF TRIAL CTS § 202.5(e) regarding the redaction of Confidential Personal Information and NY GEN BUS § 399-ddd(6) concerning the filing of documents containing Social Security

Numbers. It is the sole responsibility of counsel or unrepresented litigant filing to be aware of and to comply with existing laws requiring non-disclosure of personal information contained in any document e-filed in NYSCEF. NY R ERIE E FIL Doc. 3(III)(G); NY R ERIE E FIL Doc. 3(III).

vii. *KINGS COUNTY.* An attorney or unrepresented litigant filing a document via the NYSCEF system must comply with the requirements of General Business Law § 399-dd(6), which often require redaction of any Social Security number that appear in the original document. The NYSCEF system automatically redacts portions of filed documents which apparently contain Social Security numbers pursuant to NY R UNIF TRIAL CTS § 202.5-b(k). In the event the filing party receives e-mail notice through NYSCEF that a Social Security number in a filed document has been redacted, and the filing party concludes such redaction is erroneous, the filer should click on the link provided in the e-mail to permit the County Clerk to revert the redaction. For Confidential Personal Information, see NY R UNIF TRIAL CTS § 202.5(e) and NY R L KINGS E FIL Doc. 1(B)(11). [Editor's note: the reference to General Business Law § 399-dd(6) is likely a reference to NY GEN BUS § 399-ddd(6)]. NY R L KINGS E FIL Doc. 1(B)(10); NY R L KINGS E FIL Doc. 1(K)(1).

viii. *NEW YORK COUNTY.* It is the responsibility of counsel and parties to comply with rules restricting disclosure of confidential personal information. Nevertheless, NYSCEF screens filings and endeavors to identify any that contain social security numbers. When such numbers are discovered through this process, NYSCEF will restrict portions of or all of such documents from public view. Where NYSCEF has redacted what it believes to be a social security number, it will transmit to the filer a notice advising of the action taken and requesting that the filer review the matter and provide notification as set forth in the notice if the redaction has been made in error. NY R NY CTY E FIL Doc. 2(K)(1); NY R NY CTY J RUL Rule A-1. Documents filed in the past in "secure status" under a procedure no longer in place will retain that status unless otherwise directed by the court. NY R NY CTY E FIL Doc. 2(K)(2).

b. *Submission of confidential personal information.* Where a person submitting a paper to a court for filing believes in good faith that the inclusion of the full confidential personal information described in NY R UNIF TRIAL CTS § 202.5(e)(1) is material and necessary to the adjudication of the action or proceeding before the court, he or she may apply to the court for leave to serve and file together with a paper in which such information has been set forth in abbreviated form a confidential affidavit or affirmation setting forth the same information in unabbreviated form, appropriately referenced to the page or pages of the paper at which the abbreviated form appears. NY R UNIF TRIAL CTS § 202.5(e)(3).

c. *Home addresses.* For information on when home addresses and other personal information must be redacted, refer to NY CPLR Rule 2103-a.

5. *Defective papers.* A defect in the form of a paper, if a substantial right of a party is not prejudiced, shall be disregarded by the court, and leave to correct shall be freely given. NY CPLR Rule 2101(f). Papers that are stapled or bound securely shall not be rejected for filing simply because they are not bound with a backer of any kind. NY R UNIF TRIAL CTS § 202.5(a). A paper filed in accordance with the rules of the chief administrator or any local rule or practice established by the court shall be deemed filed. NY CPLR Rule 2102(b).

a. *Objection to defective papers.* The party on whom a paper is served shall be deemed to have waived objection to any defect in form unless, within fifteen (15) days after the receipt thereof, the party on whom the paper is served returns the paper to the party serving it with a statement of particular objections. NY CPLR Rule 2101(f).

F. Filing and Service Requirements

1. *Filing requirements.* Except where otherwise prescribed by law or order of court, papers required to be filed shall be filed with the clerk of the court in which the action is triable. In an action or proceeding in supreme or court, papers required to be filed shall be filed with the clerk of the county in which the proceeding is brought. NY CPLR Rule 2102(a).

a. *Furnishing papers to the court.* Each party shall furnish to the court all papers served by him. The moving party shall furnish at the hearing all other papers not already in the possession of the court necessary to the consideration of the questions involved. Where such papers are in the possession of an adverse party, they shall be produced by him at the hearing on notice served with the motion papers. Only papers served in accordance with the provisions of NY CPLR Rule 2214 shall be read in support of, or in opposition to, the motion, unless the court for good cause shall otherwise direct. NY CPLR Rule 2214(c).

i. *Submission to judge.* All papers for signature or consideration of the court shall be presented to the clerk of the trial court in the appropriate courtroom or clerk's office, except that where the clerk is unavailable or the judge so directs, papers may be submitted to the judge and a copy filed with the clerk at the first available opportunity. All papers for any judge that are filed in the clerk's office shall be promptly delivered to the judge by the clerk.

The papers shall be clearly addressed to the judge for whom they are intended and prominently show the nature of the papers, the title and index number of the action in which they are filed, the judge's name and the name of the attorney or party submitting them. NY R UNIF TRIAL CTS § 202.5(b).

ii. *BRONX COUNTY: Approval of motions before filing.* All motion papers must be approved by the Motion Support Office, Supreme Court, Civil Term, room 217, before the motion papers are filed and the appropriate fee paid to the County Clerk. NY R BRONX FIL R Doc. 1.

iii. *ERIE COUNTY: Filing motions.* A motion on notice or a notice of petition in a NYSCEF case shall be filed through the NYSCEF system and must be accompanied by a Request for Judicial Intervention if the motion is being filed upon commencement of the action or if the matter has not yet been assigned to an IAS Justice. In addition, cross motions with the appropriate filing fees and opposition and reply papers must be submitted via the NYSCEF system. NY R ERIE E FIL Doc. 3(V)(A).

iv. *NEW YORK COUNTY: Filing hard copies.* Where in the narrow circumstances described by the e-filing rules a motion is made in hard-copy form or opposition papers are submitted in such form in an e-filed case, the hard-copy documents shall be submitted in the same way papers are submitted in non-e-filed cases, except that there shall be firmly affixed to each separate document or group of documents, as the back page facing out, a Notice of Hard Copy Submission—E-Filed Case. NY R NY CTY Procedure II(A). For more information on filing in hard copy cases, refer to NY R NY CTY Procedure II(A).

v. *ONONDAGA COUNTY: Submission of responsive papers and cross-motions.* Cross-motions, opposition and reply papers must be submitted online. NY R ONDGA E FIL Protocol(B)(9)(e). Motions and Orders to Show Cause are assigned a sequence number by the system. Counsel must be sure that cross motions and other filings correspond with the correct sequence number so that a cross motion will not be associated with the wrong original motion. NY R ONDGA E FIL Protocol(B)(9)(f).

b. *Electronic filing.* On consent, documents may be filed and served by electronic means in Supreme Court in such civil actions and in such counties as shall be authorized by order of the Chief Administrator of the Courts and only to the extent and in the manner provided in NY R UNIF TRIAL CTS § 202.5-b. NY R UNIF TRIAL CTS § 202.5-b(a)(1). For the definitions of terms used in electronic filing, refer to NY R UNIF TRIAL CTS § 202.5-b(a)(2).

i. *E-filing mandatory.* In any action subject to e-filing, all documents required to be filed with the court by an e-filing party shall be filed and served electronically, except as provided in NY R UNIF TRIAL CTS § 202.5-b. NY R UNIF TRIAL CTS § 202.5-b(d)(1)(i).

- *ERIE COUNTY.* Case types currently eligible and accepted for e-filing are listed at the NYSCEF website. Note that some actions or special proceedings, (i.e., name changes) which are otherwise subject to mandatory e-filing, if commenced by unrepresented litigants will NOT be maintained in the NYSCEF system; individual cases may be found either at NYSCEF or in the Erie County Clerk's online records system. NY R ERIE E FIL Doc. 3(I)(E).
- *KINGS COUNTY.* Cases that are commenced by filing of the initiating papers with NYSCEF are identified as e-filed cases by assignment of a special index number (i.e., Index Numbers beginning with 500,000). NY R L KINGS E FIL Doc. 1(A)(1). All cases required to be e-filed are listed in Uniform Rule 202.5-bb (Mandatory E-Filing Rules) and on the NYSCEF website. All such cases must be commenced by filing with the County Clerk electronically through NYSCEF and all subsequent documents in such cases must be e-filed. Any questions regarding mandatory e-filing in Kings County can be e-mailed to kcco-efile@nycourts.gov. NY R L KINGS E FIL Doc. 1(A)(2).
- *NEW YORK COUNTY.* Unless otherwise provided in the Rules or in NY R NY CTY E FIL Doc. 2 or where a special exemption is granted due to physical requirements (e.g., oversized maps; see NY R NY CTY E FIL Doc. 2(B)(10)), all documents to be filed with the court in a NYSCEF case, including all documents on motions and all letters to the court (where permitted), must be filed with the NYSCEF system. Documents that attorneys would not ordinarily file with the court in a hard-copy case need not be e-filed. Unless otherwise provided by the E-Filing Rules or this Protocol, in e-filed cases the County Clerk and the court will not accept documents filed in paper form. NY R NY CTY E FIL Doc. 2(B)(1). E-filing is mandatory in all types of cases (other than election law, matrimonial, Art. 78, and Mental Hygiene Law matters, and Art. 70 habeas corpus proceedings) that are commenced in this court on or after February 19, 2013. All such cases must be commenced by filing with the County Clerk electronically through NYSCEF and all subsequent documents in such cases must be e-filed. NY R NY CTY E FIL Doc. 2(A)(2)(a). For more information, including information on consensual e-filing and filing scanned hard copy documents, refer to NY R NY CTY E FIL Doc. 2(A)(2).

- *QUEENS COUNTY.* All authorized Torts, Commercial and Tax Certiorari cases may be commenced by E-Filing, however all parties must consent for the action to continue as an E-file case. NY R L QUEENS E-FILE Doc. 1(A). All papers to be filed with the court in an E-filed case shall be filed on-line with the E-file system except as directed by the court. Papers that attorneys would not ordinarily file with the court in a hard-copy case need not be filed in an E-filed matter. NY R L QUEENS E-FILE Doc. 1(E)(2).

ii. *Who may file.* Documents may be filed or served electronically only by a person who has registered as an authorized e-filing user or as otherwise provided in NY R UNIF TRIAL CTS § 202.5-b(c). NY R UNIF TRIAL CTS § 202.5-b(c)(1).

iii. *When filing made.* Documents may be transmitted at any time of the day or night to the NYSCEF site. A document other than an order or judgment is filed when its electronic transmission or, in the case of a petition that is e-filed by submission of a text file as provided in NY R UNIF TRIAL CTS § 202.5-b(b)(1), the electronic transmission of the text file is recorded at that site, provided, however, that where payment of a fee is required upon the filing of a document, the document is not filed until transmission of the document and the information or form or information as required in NY R UNIF TRIAL CTS § 202.5-b(d)(2)(i), NY R UNIF TRIAL CTS § 202.5-b(d)(2)(ii) or NY R UNIF TRIAL CTS § 202.5-b(d)(2)(iii) has been recorded at the NYSCEF site; or, if no transmission of that information or form or information is recorded, where permitted by the County Clerk, until payment is presented to the County Clerk. NY R UNIF TRIAL CTS § 202.5-b(d)(3)(i).

iv. *Notification of filing.* No later than the close of business on the business day following the electronic filing of a document, a notification, in a form prescribed by the Chief Administrator, shall be transmitted electronically by the NYSCEF site to the person filing such document and the e-mail service addresses of all other participating parties in such action. NY R UNIF TRIAL CTS § 202.5-b(d)(3)(ii).

v. *Removal of confidential information and other corrections.* If a document filed electronically is subsequently discovered to contain confidential data—including but not limited to trade secrets, information protected by confidentiality agreement, or personal confidential information as defined by statute or court rule—or otherwise to have been filed in error, the filer or another party or affected person may (1) notify the parties and any non-party filers in the action of the confidentiality issue or other error raised by the filing, and of his or her intention to seek judicial relief to correct the filing: (2) following such notification, request that the appropriate County Clerk, exercising his or her administrative discretion, place the document temporarily in "restricted" status on the NYSCEF site, to be made available for viewing by court staff and the parties but not the general public; and (3) file an application to correct the filing by order to show cause within five (5) business days of such notification (or such time as the court may direct), including a request for preliminary injunctive relief limiting interim disclosure of the document at issue. Unless otherwise directed by the court, any document placed in restricted status in response to such a request shall be returned to public view upon expiration of this five (5) day period. The Chief Administrator of the Courts shall promulgate forms to implement this process. NY R UNIF TRIAL CTS § 202.5-b(d)(3)(iii).

- *KINGS COUNTY.* For information on what to do when a document was erroneously filed with confidential information, refer to NY R L KINGS E FIL Doc. 1(B)(11).
- *NEW YORK COUNTY.* For information on what to do when a document was erroneously filed with confidential information, refer to NY R NY CTY E FIL Doc. 2(B)(8).
- *QUEENS COUNTY.* For information on what to do when a document was erroneously filed with confidential information, refer to NY R L QUEENS E-FILE Doc. 1(E)(7).

vi. *Documents requiring judge's signature.* Except where the court directs otherwise, any document that requires a judge's signature shall be transmitted electronically and in hard copy to the court. NY R UNIF TRIAL CTS § 202.5-b(d)(6).

vii. *Documents which would be inconvenient to file electronically; Hard copies.* Notwithstanding any other provision of NY R UNIF TRIAL CTS § 202.5-b, and subject to such guidelines as may be established by the Chief Administrative Judge, the County Clerk or his or her designee may require or permit a party to file in hard copy, in accordance with procedures set by the County Clerk or designee, an exhibit or other document which it is impractical or inconvenient to file electronically. NY R UNIF TRIAL CTS § 202.5-b(d)(7).

- *ERIE COUNTY.* Please contact the Supervisor of Actions & Proceedings, Erie County Clerk's Office by calling (716) 858-6662 or the Deputy County Clerk—Legal at (716) 858-6348 for information. NY R ERIE E FIL Doc. 3(III)(F).
- *KINGS COUNTY.* With limited exceptions, as set forth in the Uniform Rules and herein, all documents to

be filed with the court in a NYSCEF case shall be filed online via the NYSCEF system. However, should the size, consistency or context of a hard copy document preclude electronic filing, the user shall electronically file a "Notice of Hard Copy Submission—E-Filed Cases" form EFM-3. Any hard copy submitted pursuant to NY R L KINGS E FIL Doc. 1(B)(9) shall include, as a cover page firmly fastened thereto, a copy of the Confirmation Notice received from the NYSCEF site confirming receipt of the "Notice of Hard Copy Submission—E-Filed Cases". Any party may object to such hard copy filing. The Court, in response to such objection, may, following the hard copy filing, fashion such relief as it deems appropriate pursuant to and in furtherance of the Uniform Rules and NY R L KINGS E FIL Doc. 1, including, but not limited to, an Order directing the filing party to file such documents online via the NYSCEF system. When exhibits are impractical to file pursuant to NY R UNIF TRIAL CTS § 202.5-b(d)(7), an additional "Notice of Hard Copy Exhibit Filing" form EFM-4 is required to be submitted. NY R L KINGS E FIL Doc. 1(B)(9).

- *NEW YORK COUNTY.* If a filer needs to submit unusual exhibits in original form that cannot practically be e-filed, such as oversized maps or electronic recordings, the filer should consult with the County Clerk's E-File Department by telephone at 646-386-3737 (procedural questions only) or by e-mail at ccnyef@nycourts.gov, which will normally require that the filer retain custody of the original subject to possible future directives of the court. NY R NY CTY E FIL Doc. 2(B)(10). In such instances, the filing counsel shall file with NYSCEF a "placeholder" in the form of a Notice of Hard Copy Exhibit Filing (NYSCEF Form EF 21). The Notice should be uploaded to NYSCEF as document type "Exhibit" and the filer should indicate in the "Additional Document Information" field that the filer is retaining custody of the original. Failure to e-file the Notice may result in a gap in the official record of the court. NY R NY CTY E FIL Doc. 2(B)(10).

viii. *Documents containing sensitive or proprietary information.* In an action subject to e-filing, any person may apply for an order prohibiting or restricting the electronic filing in the action of specifically identified materials on the grounds that such materials are subject to copyright or other proprietary rights, or trade secret or other privacy interests, and that electronic filing in the action is likely to result in substantial prejudice to those rights or interests. NY R UNIF TRIAL CTS § 202.5-b(k)(2).

ix. *Refusal to accept paper filings.* In accordance with NY CPLR Rule 2102(c), a County Clerk and a chief clerk of the Supreme Court or County Court, as appropriate, shall refuse to accept for filing papers filed in actions and proceedings when the paper sought to be filed:

- Is in an action subject to electronic filing pursuant to Rules of the Chief Administrator,
- Is not being filed electronically, and
- Does not include the notice required by NY R UNIF TRIAL CTS § 202.5-b(d)(1). NY R UNIF TRIAL CTS § 202.5(d)(1)(v); NY R UNIF TRIAL CTS § 202.5-bb(d).

x. *Emergency filings; Hard copies.* For information on when an emergency filing may be filed and served in hard copy, refer to NY R UNIF TRIAL CTS § 202.5-b(d)(1)(ii), NY R UNIF TRIAL CTS § 202.5-b(d)(1)(iii) and NY R UNIF TRIAL CTS § 202.5-bb(c)(3).

- *KINGS COUNTY.* Under the rules, a participating emergency e-filer must electronically file the documents initially filed in hard copy form within three (3) business days of the emergency filing; the originals will be discarded after the documents have been processed and the failure to e-file as required will therefore lead to an incomplete record. NY R L KINGS E FIL Doc. 1(B)(3).
- *NEW YORK COUNTY.* Occasionally an emergency will arise requiring expedited entry of a document with the County Clerk (e.g., an order issued in the courtroom after a conference or argument of a critical matter), such as for purposes of an immediate appeal. Expedition can be achieved by the Part as follows: the document should be carried by a Court Officer or staff member to the General Clerk's Office to assure immediate and proper recordation in the computer and, as appropriate, the posting of the document to NYSCEF or the Supreme Court Records On-Line Library ("Scroll"). The court will accommodate counsel in emergencies. NY R NY CTY Procedure XI(A).
- *NEW YORK COUNTY.* For more information on how to bring emergency matters before the court, refer to NY R NY CTY Procedure IV.

xi. *Technical failures.* The NYSCEF site shall be considered to be subject to a technical failure on a given day if the site is unable to accept filings or provide access to filed documents continuously or intermittently over the course of any period of time greater than one (1) hour after 12:00 noon of that day. Notice of all such technical failures shall be provided on the site. NY R UNIF TRIAL CTS § 202.5-b(i).

- When e-filing is hindered by a technical failure, a party may file with the appropriate clerk and serve in hard copy. NY R UNIF TRIAL CTS § 202.5-b(i). In the event an attorney or party shall file and serve documents in hard copy pursuant to NY R UNIF TRIAL CTS § 202.5-b(i), each such document shall include the notice required by NY R UNIF TRIAL CTS § 202.5-b(d)(1), and the filer shall file those documents with the NYSCEF site within three (3) business days after restoration of normal operations at that site. NY R UNIF TRIAL CTS § 202.5-b(i).
- With the exception of deadlines that by law cannot be extended, the time for filing of any document that is delayed due to technical failure of the site shall be extended for one (1) day for each day on which such failure occurs, unless otherwise ordered by the court. NY R UNIF TRIAL CTS § 202.5-b(i).
- *ERIE COUNTY.* When filing by electronic means is hindered by a technical failure, please refer to the NY R UNIF TRIAL CTS § 202.5-b(i). NY R ERIE E FIL Doc. 3(III)(K).
- *KINGS COUNTY.* When filing by electronic means is hindered by a NYSCEF technical failure (as set forth in NY R UNIF TRIAL CTS § 202.5-b(i)), a party may file with the appropriate Clerk in hard copy. Except for deadlines that by law cannot be extended (e.g. Statute of limitations, Notice of Appeal), the time for filing of any document that is delayed due to technical failure of the NYSCEF system shall be extended for one day for each day on which such failure occurs, unless otherwise ordered by the court. NY R L KINGS E FIL Doc. 1(B)(13).
- *ONONDAGA COUNTY.* When filing by electronic means is hindered by a technical failure (as set forth in NY R UNIF TRIAL CTS § 202.5-b(h)(3)(i)), a party may file a hard copy with the County Clerk. With the exception of deadlines that by law cannot be extended (e.g., a statute of limitations or the deadline for filing a Notice of Appeal), the time for filing of any document that is delayed due to technical failure of the NYSCEF system will be extended for one day for each day on which such failure occurs, unless otherwise ordered by the court. A "Notice of Hard Copy Filing Submission—E-Filed Case' must accompany any documents not filed via NYSCEF. NY R ONDGA E FIL Protocol(B)(8).

xii. *Filing fees.* For information on what information must be provided to pay filing fees, refer to NY R UNIF TRIAL CTS § 202.5-b(d)(2).

xiii. *Exemption from e-filing.* For information on exemptions from e-filing, refer to NY R UNIF TRIAL CTS § 202.5-bb(e).

xiv. *Filing exhibits*

- *ERIE COUNTY.* In the NYSCEF system, each exhibit must be uploaded as a separate .pdf file. After uploading a primary document, please choose the document type "Exhibit" and enter the appropriate number or letter and a brief description of the exhibit; each exhibit should bear a separate cover sheet clearly marked as "Exhibit A," "Exhibit B," etc. "Exhibit A" or "Exhibit B" is unacceptable as a brief description of the exhibit. Exhibits, where referenced in a signed Order as attached or affixed shall be uploaded with the signed Order as one .pdf document. NY R ERIE E FIL Doc. 3(III)(H); NY R ERIE E FIL Doc. 3(V)(D).
- *KINGS COUNTY.* In the NYSCEF system, each exhibit should be uploaded as a separate PDF file. After uploading a primary document, please choose the document type "Exhibit", enter the appropriate number or letter, and be sure to place a check mark to the right of "Attach to main document". Each exhibit shall bear a separate cover sheet clearly marked as Exhibit A, Exhibit B, etc. NY R L KINGS E FIL Doc. 1(B)(12). Whenever possible, attorneys submitting exhibits in NYSCEF cases should make each exhibit a separate attachment to an affidavit/affirmation in the system (i.e., multiple exhibits should not be filed as a single PDF). NY R L KINGS E FIL Doc. 1(D)(1).
- *NEW YORK COUNTY.* Attorneys submitting exhibits in NYSCEF cases should make each exhibit a separate attachment to an affidavit/affirmation in the system; i.e., exhibits should not be filed as a single PDF-A together with the affidavit/affirmation or grouped together as a single PDF-A attachment because either of these two formats makes it difficult for the Justice to locate particular exhibits as needed. Counsel must also include appropriate descriptive language in the "Additional Document Information" field in NYSCEF. NY R NY CTY E FIL Doc. 2(D)(6).
- *ONONDAGA COUNTY.* All exhibits in e-filed cases must be e-filed individually as separate attachments. NY R ONDGA E FIL Protocol(B)(9)(b).

xv. *Correcting documents*

- *ERIE COUNTY.* Submission of documents which, upon examination, require correction or addition will result in notification to the filer advising that the document has been returned for correction. The filer shall make the required corrections and/or additions as indicated in the e-mail transmission sent by the County Clerk or Part Clerk through the NYSCEF site. The corrected documents may be resubmitted using the "Re-file this document" link highlighted in the filer's document list for the respective case. Please note that in the case of multiple submissions, all related documents filed at the same time may be removed from the case record and returned until all documents are properly submitted. NY R ERIE E FIL Doc. 3(III)(J).
- *KINGS COUNTY.* Submission of documents which, upon examination, require correction or addition will result in notification to the filer advising that there is a problem with a document. The filer shall make the required corrections and/or additions and resubmit the corrected document using the "Refile this document" link. In the event a document is returned for correction, the original file date will be preserved. For corrections of documents filed with the Kings County Clerk which require a court order, refer to the procedure in NY R UNIF TRIAL CTS § 202.5-b(d)(3)(iii) and NY R L KINGS E FIL Doc. 1(B)(11). NY R L KINGS E FIL Doc. 1(B)(3).
- *ONONDAGA COUNTY.* If there is an error or an additional document is required, the system will notify the filing party, who will make the corrections/additions and resubmit them online. NY R ONDGA E FIL Protocol(B)(6).
- *QUEENS COUNTY.* Generally speaking, documents that have been E-filed will not thereafter be deleted by the County Clerk from NYCEF because the filer asserts that the filing contains an error or a significant omission. When the filer wishes to correct a perceived error or omission in a filed document, he or she should file an amended version of the document, with the original remaining on file, or else obtain a court order providing for deletion of the original. The County Clerk will only delete a document upon request of the filer or on the County Clerk's own initiative when it is obvious from the face of the document alone that the filer made a fundamental error and never intended to file the document that was filed (e.g., a completely unrelated non-litigation document, a different case, or a wrong county). The County Clerk will advise the filer when any such fundamental errors are detected. NY R L QUEENS E-FILE Doc. 1(E)(6).

c. *Facsimile filing.* In the Supreme Court, facsimile filing shall be limited to commercial claims and tax certiorari, conservatorship, and mental hygiene proceedings in Monroe, Westchester, New York and Suffolk Counties. NY R UNIF TRIAL CTS § 202.5-a(a)(1). Refer to NY R UNIF TRIAL CTS § 202.5-a for information on the procedures for facsimile filing.

i. *NEW YORK COUNTY.* Unless indicated otherwise by the court in a particular case or in NY R NY CTY J RUL Doc. 1, Justices do not accept papers by fax. NY R NY CTY J RUL Rule 4.

d. *ERIE COUNTY: Filing request for judicial intervention.* An RJI in a NYSCEF case shall be filed via the NYSCEF system and will be filed after all other documents have been uploaded. The filer may choose between filing a .pdf image of the prepared RJI and any Addendum or having the system prepare the RJI which shall conform to Uniform Rules. Addenda, such as the Commercial Division Addendum, if prepared by the filer must be filed simultaneously with and attached to an RJI and uploaded as one .pdf document with the RJI. If the RJI is prepared by the e-filing system, no separate Addendum is required. Whether or not the filer elects to allow NYSCEF to create the RJI or chooses to upload a prepared RJI, data in addition to the nature of the judicial intervention, including information that appears on any Addenda will be collected through completion of the fields presented. If the filing of the RJI is accomplished through a filing agent, a prepared RJI and Addendum must be filed in lieu of the creation of the RJI by the NYSCEF system, as the RJI must be signed by the attorney. NY R ERIE E FIL Doc. 3(IV). For information on RJIs in specific types of action, refer to NY R ERIE E FIL Doc. 3(IV).

2. *Service requirements*

a. *Who may serve.* Except where otherwise prescribed by law or order of court, papers may be served by any person not a party of the age of eighteen years or over. NY CPLR Rule 2103(a).

b. *Service upon attorney.* Except where otherwise prescribed by law or order of court, papers to be served upon a party in a pending action shall be served upon the party's attorney. Where the same attorney appears for two or more parties, only one (1) copy need be served upon the attorney. Such service upon an attorney shall be made:

i. By delivering the paper to the attorney personally. NY CPLR Rule 2103(b)(1).

ii. By mailing the paper to the attorney at the address designated by that attorney for that purpose or, if none is designated, at the attorney's last known address; service by mail shall be complete upon mailing. NY CPLR Rule 2103(b)(2).

- *BRONX COUNTY.* Service by mail must be within the state. NY R BRONX FIL R Doc. 3.

iii. If the attorney's office is open, by leaving the paper with a person in charge, or if no person is in charge, by leaving it in a conspicuous place; or if the attorney's office is not open, by depositing the paper, enclosed in a sealed wrapper directed to the attorney, in the attorney's office letter drop or box. NY CPLR Rule 2103(b)(3).

iv. By leaving it at the attorney's residence within the state with a person of suitable age and discretion. Service upon an attorney shall not be made at the attorney's residence unless service at the attorney's office cannot be made. NY CPLR Rule 2103(b)(4).

v. By transmitting the paper to the attorney by facsimile transmission, provided that a facsimile telephone number is designated by the attorney for that purpose. Service by facsimile transmission shall be complete upon the receipt by the sender of a signal from the equipment of the attorney served indicating that the transmission was received, and the mailing of a copy of the paper to that attorney. The designation of a facsimile telephone number in the address block subscribed on a paper served or filed in the course of an action or proceeding shall constitute consent to service by facsimile transmission in accordance with NY CPLR Rule 2103(b)(5). An attorney may change or rescind a facsimile telephone number by serving a notice on the other parties. NY CPLR Rule 2103(b)(5).

vi. By dispatching the paper to the attorney by overnight delivery service at the address designated by the attorney for that purpose or, if none is designated, at the attorney's last known address. Service by overnight delivery service shall be complete upon deposit of the paper enclosed in a properly addressed wrapper into the custody of the overnight delivery service for overnight delivery, prior to the latest time designated by the overnight delivery service for overnight delivery. "Overnight delivery service" means any delivery service which regularly accepts items for overnight delivery to any address in the state. NY CPLR Rule 2103(b)(6).

vii. By transmitting the paper to the attorney by electronic means where and in the manner authorized by the chief administrator of the courts by rule and, unless such rule shall otherwise provide, such transmission shall be upon the party's written consent. The subject matter heading for each paper sent by electronic means must indicate that the matter being transmitted electronically is related to a court proceeding. NY CPLR Rule 2103(b)(7).

- *KINGS COUNTY.* Pursuant to the E-Filing Rules, service of interlocutory documents is made by posting a document to the NYSCEF site, which automatically and immediately transmits an email notice of the filing, including a link to the document, to all participating counsel and unrepresented litigants on the case. The Rules also authorize service by other methods permitted by the CPLR. If service by such other method is made, proof of service must be filed with NYSCEF. NY R L KINGS E FIL Doc. 1(I).
- *NEW YORK COUNTY.* Service. . .will be made automatically through NYSCEF upon all participating counsel and unrepresented parties in the case. There are limited exceptions to the requirement for e-filing in the covered kinds of cases. NY R NY CTY Procedure XI(A). Pursuant to the E-Filing Rules, service of interlocutory documents is made by posting a document to the NYSCEF site, which automatically and immediately transmits an e-mail notice of the filing, including a link to the document, to all participating counsel and unrepresented litigants on the case. The Rules also authorize service by other methods permitted by the CPLR. If service by such a method is made, proof of service must be filed with NYSCEF. NY R NY CTY E FIL Doc. 2(I).
- *QUEENS COUNTY.* Filing with the system permits counsel to serve the papers electronically pursuant to NY R UNIF TRIAL CTS § 202.5-b(f) once consent to E-Filing has been filed on-line. Consult NY R UNIF TRIAL CTS § 202.5-bb(c) for service in mandatory e-filing. Any required proof of service should be E-filed as a separate document. NY R L QUEENS E-FILE Doc. 1(E)(4).

c. *Electronic service mandatory; Consenting to electronic service; How electronic service may be made.* Except as otherwise provided in NY R UNIF TRIAL CTS § 202.5-bb, filing and service of all documents in an action that has been commenced electronically in accordance with NY R UNIF TRIAL CTS § 202.5-bb shall be by electronic means. NY R UNIF TRIAL CTS § 202.5-bb(c)(1).

i. *Party's consent required for certain e-filing.* After commencement of an action wherein e-filing is authorized, documents may be electronically filed and served, but only by, and electronic service shall be made only upon, a party or parties who have consented thereto. NY R UNIF TRIAL CTS § 202.5-b(b)(2)(i).

- A consent to e-filing in an action shall state that the party providing it agrees to the use of e-filing in the action and to be bound by the filing and service provisions in NY R UNIF TRIAL CTS § 202.5-b. NY R UNIF TRIAL CTS § 202.5-b(b)(2)(ii).

ii. *Address for service; Duty to notify as to changes.* The e-mail service address recorded at the time of registration is the e-mail address at which service of interlocutory documents on that party may be made through notification transmitted by the NYSCEF site. It is the responsibility of each filing user to monitor that address and promptly notify the Resource Center in the event of a change in his or her e-mail service address. NY R UNIF TRIAL CTS § 202.5-b(f)(2)(i).

iii. *How service made.* An e-filing party causes service of an interlocutory document to be made upon another party participating in e-filing by filing the document electronically. Upon receipt of an interlocutory document, the NYSCEF site shall automatically transmit electronic notification to all e-mail service addresses in such action. NY R UNIF TRIAL CTS § 202.5-b(f)(2)(ii).

- Except as provided otherwise in NY R UNIF TRIAL CTS § 202.5-b(h)(3), the electronic transmission of the notification shall constitute service of the document on the e-mail service addresses identified therein; however, such service will not be effective if the filing party learns that the notification did not reach the address of the person to be served. Proof of such service will be recorded on the NYSCEF site. A party may, however, utilize other service methods permitted by the CPLR provided that, if one of such other methods is used, proof of that service shall be filed electronically. NY R UNIF TRIAL CTS § 202.5-b(f)(2)(ii).

iv. *Signatures on hard copies; Proof of service filed electronically.* When an e-filing party serves a document in hard copy on a non-participating party, the document served shall bear full signatures of all signatories and proof of such service shall be filed electronically. NY R UNIF TRIAL CTS § 202.5-b(b)(2)(i).

- *ERIE COUNTY.* In the NYSCEF system, each Affidavit of Service must be uploaded as a separate .pdf file. After uploading the Affidavit, please choose the document type: "Affirmation/Affidavit of Service" and enter the name of the party served as Additional Document Information. NY R ERIE E FIL Doc. 3(III)(I); NY R ERIE E FIL Doc. 3(V)(F).

v. *Effect of failure to consent.* A party's failure to consent to participation in electronic filing and service shall not bar any other party to the action from filing documents electronically with the County Clerk and the court or serving documents upon any other party who has consented to participation. A party who has not consented to participation shall file documents with the court and the County Clerk, and serve and be served with documents, in hard copy. NY R UNIF TRIAL CTS § 202.5-b(b)(2)(i).

d. *Service upon party.* If a party has not appeared by an attorney or the party's attorney cannot be served, service shall be upon the party by a method specified in NY CPLR Rule 2103(b)(1), NY CPLR Rule 2103(b)(2), NY CPLR Rule 2103(b)(4), NY CPLR Rule 2103(b)(5) or NY CPLR Rule 2103(b)(6). NY CPLR Rule 2103(c).

e. *Service on all parties.* Each paper served on any party shall be served on every other party who has appeared, except as otherwise may be provided by court order or as provided in NY CPLR § 3012 or in NY CPLR § 3215(f). Upon demand by a party, the plaintiff shall supply that party with a list of those who have appeared and the names and addresses of their attorneys. NY CPLR Rule 2103(e).

f. *Service by filing.* If a paper cannot be served by any of the methods specified in NY CPLR Rule 2103(b) and NY CPLR Rule 2103(c), service may be made by filing the paper as if it were a paper required to be filed. NY CPLR Rule 2103(d).

g. *Definitions.* For the purposes of NY CPLR Rule 2103:

i. "Mailing" means the deposit of a paper enclosed in a first class postpaid wrapper, addressed to the address designated by a person for that purpose or, if none is designated, at that person's last known address, in a post office or official depository under the exclusive care and custody of the United States Postal Service within the state;

ii. "Electronic means" means any method of transmission of information between computers or other machines designed for the purpose of sending and receiving such transmissions, and which allows the recipient to reproduce the information transmitted in a tangible medium of expression;

iii. "Facsimile transmission" means any method of transmission of documents to a facsimile machine at a remote location which can automatically produce a tangible copy of such documents. NY CPLR Rule 2103(f).

G. Hearings

1. *Oral argument.* Motion papers received by the clerk of the court on or before the return date shall be deemed submitted as

of the return date. The assigned judge, in his or her discretion or at the request of a party, thereafter may determine that any motion be orally argued and may fix a time for oral argument. NY R UNIF TRIAL CTS § 202.8(d).

a. A party requesting oral argument shall set forth such request in its notice of motion or in its order to show cause or on the first page of the answering papers, as the case may be. Where all parties to a motion request oral argument, oral argument shall be granted unless the court shall determine it to be unnecessary. NY R UNIF TRIAL CTS § 202.8(d).

b. Where a motion is brought on by order to show cause, the court may set forth in the order that oral argument is required on the return date of the motion. NY R UNIF TRIAL CTS § 202.8(d).

i. *BRONX COUNTY.* All orders to show cause, with the exception of orders to show cause that are returnable in the City Part, the STP Part, the Matrimonial Part and the Preliminary/Compliance Conference Part (IA-11), submitted on or after August 25, 2003, will be returnable on a Monday in the assigned Justice's part and appear on his or her motion calendar. Appearances will be required on orders to show cause. NY R BRONX FIL R Doc. 8. A motion on notice or a notice of petition in a New York Supreme Court E-File (hereafter known as NYSCEF) case, as in others, shall be made returnable in the Motion Support Office (Room 217). NY R BRONX E FIL R Doc. 1(1).

- After a motion/petition and notice are filed with the NYSCEF system, the Motion Support Office will automatically place the motion/proceeding on the submit calendar in the Motion Support Office (Room 217) for the return date. No appearance or other action by the filing attorney is required in order for the motion to be calendared if the motion fee is paid for via NYSCEF. Motions in e-filed cases (other than tax certiorari cases) appear on the submit calendar in Room 217 on the return date. NY R BRONX E FIL R Doc. 1(2).

c. *KINGS COUNTY.* All motions require appearances and oral argument. NY R L KINGS Pt. C, Rule 3.

2. *Return date; Time for hearing.* A notice of motion shall specify the time and place of the hearing on the motion. NY CPLR Rule 2214(a). The moving party determines when a motion on notice shall be heard, but she has to consult the court's or judge's calendar practice first. The movant picks out a "return day" sufficiently far off to assure that the notice requirements of NY CPLR Rule 2214(b) can be met, and to assure as well that the day picked is a day on which the assigned judge hears motions. SIEGEL-NYPRAC § 247.

a. *Judge assigned to hear motion*

i. *Referral to judge supervising disclosure.* Unless the chief administrator of the courts has, by rule, provided otherwise, if a case has been assigned to a judge to supervise disclosure pursuant to NY CPLR § 3104, all motions preliminary to trial shall be referred to such judge whenever practicable. NY CPLR Rule 3214(a).

ii. *Referral to judge who decided prior motion.* Any motion may be referred to a judge who decided a prior motion in the action. NY CPLR Rule 2217(a).

iii. *Transfer when judge unable to hear motion.* If a motion is made to a judge who is or will be for any reason unable to hear it, it may be transferred by order of such judge or by written stipulation of the parties to any other judge to whom it might originally have been made. NY CPLR Rule 2217(c).

iv. *Procedure for unassigned cases.* If a case has not been assigned to a judge, the motion shall be made returnable before the court, and a copy of the moving papers, together with a request for judicial intervention, shall be filed with the court, with proof of service upon all other parties, where required by NY R UNIF TRIAL CTS § 202.6, within five (5) days of service upon the other parties. The moving party shall give written notice of the index number to all other parties immediately after filing of the papers. NY R UNIF TRIAL CTS § 202.8(b).

- *Responding papers.* Copies of all responding papers shall be submitted to the court, with proof of service and with the index number set forth in the papers, on or before the return date. NY R UNIF TRIAL CTS § 202.8(b).
- *Assignment after request for judicial intervention.* The case shall be assigned to a judge as soon as practicable after the filing of the request for judicial intervention pursuant to NY R UNIF TRIAL CTS § 202.6, but in no event later than the return date. After assignment to the judge, the court shall provide for appropriate notice to the parties of the name of the assigned judge. NY R UNIF TRIAL CTS § 202.8(b).
- *Motions to be heard in another county.* Motion papers noticed to be heard in a county other than the county where the venue of the action has been placed by the plaintiff shall be assigned to a judge in accordance with procedures established by the Chief Administrator. NY R UNIF TRIAL CTS § 202.8(b).

v. *ALBANY COUNTY: Motions referred to IAS Justice.* All motions made after a case has been assigned a day certain shall be referred to the IAS Justice unless the motion is returnable during the term in which the matter has been assigned a day certain, in that event, the matter will be referred to the Part 1 Justice for that particular term who may entertain the motion or refer such motion to the IAS Justice. Under those circumstances, the Part I Justice shall decide whether or not to strike the note of issue or assign the matter a new day certain. NY R 3 JD SUP Doc. 1(H)(2). All motions shall be returnable before the assigned justice. NY R 3 JD SUP Doc. 1(B).

b. *Trial of issue raised by motion.* The court may order that an issue of fact raised on a motion shall be separately tried by the court or a referee. If the issue is triable of right by jury, the court shall give the parties an opportunity to demand a jury trial of such issue. Failure to make such demand within the time limited by the court, or, if no such time is limited, before trial begins, shall be deemed a waiver of the right to trial by jury. An order under NY CPLR § 2218 shall specify the issue to be tried. NY CPLR § 2218.

c. *Audio-visual coverage of trial court proceeding.* Audio-visual coverage of proceedings in the trial courts shall be permitted only in accordance with the provisions of Part 131 of the Rules of the Chief Administrator (NY R CHIEF ADMIN § 131.1, et seq.). NY R CHIEF J § 29.3.

d. *Adjournment of return date.* Stipulations of adjournment of the return date made by the parties shall be in writing and shall be submitted to the assigned judge. Such stipulation shall be effective unless the court otherwise directs. No more than three (3) stipulated adjournments for an aggregate period of sixty (60) days shall be submitted without prior permission of the court. NY R UNIF TRIAL CTS § 202.8(e)(1).

i. Absent agreement by the parties, a request by any party for an adjournment shall be submitted in writing, upon notice to the other party, to the assigned judge on or before the return date. The court will notify the requesting party whether the adjournment has been granted. NY R UNIF TRIAL CTS § 202.8(e)(2).

ii. *BRONX COUNTY.* Non-disclosure motions for IA5, IA7 and IA22 will be adjourned for oral argument to the Monday of the second week following the week of the return date of the motion. All other non-disclosure motions will be deemed submitted on the return date and forwarded to Chambers unless a stipulation of adjournment complying with the requirements of NY R UNIF TRIAL CTS § 202.8(e) is submitted, in which event, the motion will be adjourned for the requested date and kept in the Clerk's Office. If a non-stipulated request for adjournment or notice is submitted, the motion and request will be forwarded to Chambers for judicial approval or denial of the request. In either event, the attorney requesting the adjournment will be notified, via telephone, of the granting or denial of the request and instructed to notify his adversary. NY R BRONX FIL R Doc. 8.

iii. *BRONX COUNTY.* Motions that have been e-filed may be adjourned in Room 217 if an adjournment complies with the procedures of the Motion Support Office (explained in the "Filing Rules—Motion Procedure" section of the "Courthouse Procedures" link on the website of [the] court). An adjournment that so complies may be obtained by filing a stipulation of all parties with NYSCEF (designated in the filing menu as a "Stipulation to Adjourn Motion"). NY R BRONX E FIL R Doc. 1(3).

iv. *NEW YORK COUNTY.* The Courtroom also maintains a "APB (All Papers By)" Calendar, which is used when a party seeks an adjournment but fails to comply with the Courtroom's procedures or there is a failure to comply with procedures that requires the clerk to adjourn the motion/application (e.g., failure to submit a Confirmation Notice in an e-filed case). The case may be put over for three days to allow compliance with those procedures, as described further below. NY R NY CTY Procedure II(C); NY R NY CTY E FIL Doc. 2(D)(2). E-filed applications may be adjourned in the Part if an adjournment complies with the Part's procedures (see the Uniform Rules of the Justices (Local Rules) on the court's website). An adjournment that so complies may be obtained by filing with NYSCEF a stipulation of all parties (designated in the filing menu as a Stipulation—Adjournment of Motion—Before Judge); the motion number and the current return date of the motion being adjourned shall be set forth in the "Additional Document Information" field in NYSCEF. Absent any problems, the Part will effectuate the adjournment without need for an appearance or any other action by the parties. NY R NY CTY E FIL Doc. 2(D)(4).

v. *QUEENS COUNTY.* The Motion Support Office is NOT authorized to grant adjournments. NY R L QUEENS MOT SUP Doc. 1.

e. *ALBANY COUNTY: Motion terms.* There shall be a. . . Motion Term on each Friday in the Supreme Court, Albany County. The Friday Motion Term shall include all Article 78 Proceedings involving New York State and proceedings commenced pursuant to Article 14 of the Civil Service Law (including applications for injunctive relief made pursuant to section 209-a of the Civil Service Law). NY R 3 JD SUP Doc. 1(F). Generally, parties will be granted only one adjournment for the Friday Motion Term. NY R 3 JD SUP Doc. 1(F).

f. *ALBANY COUNTY: Motion determined without hearing.* All motions are deemed "submitted" on the return date and no appearances are required by the parties. NY R 3 JD SUP Doc. 1(B). In the event oral argument is requested, the parties should not appear on the return date. At the discretion of the assigned Judge and upon the granting of a request for oral argument, the parties will be notified by Chambers of the scheduled time and place at which argument will be heard. Where a motion is brought on by order to show cause, the court may set forth in the order that appearances and/or oral argument are required on the return date of the motion. NY R 3 JD SUP Doc. 1(B).

g. *BRONX COUNTY: Return date.* All assigned and unassigned motions will be returnable five (5) days a week in the Civil Branch Clerk's Office, Room 217, at 9:30 a.m. NY R BRONX FIL R Doc. 8.

  i. If on any submitted non-disclosure motion oral argument is requested and granted, or directed by the Court, the motion shall be adjourned for oral argument before the I.A. Judge on the second Monday following the week of the return date of the motion. Attorneys will be notified via telephone of the adjourned date. NY R BRONX FIL R Doc. 8.

h. *BRONX COUNTY: Oral argument.* Calendars of disclosure motions and other motions adjourned for oral argument will be published for the four (4) business days preceding the rescheduled appearance date and on the rescheduled date of the motion. These repetitive publications will serve as the notification of procedure of adjournment of all motions. In addition, two (2) days before the return date of unassigned motions a list of such motions indicating the assigned Justice and the adjourned date of the motion will be published. NY R BRONX FIL R Doc. 8.

i. *BRONX COUNTY: Resolution before return date.* Counsel/parties must advise the Court in writing on or before the return date of all motions that have been resolved by Counsel/parties themselves and all motions the movant(s) wish to be withdrawn. NY R BRONX FIL R Doc. 8.

j. *ERIE COUNTY: Calendaring of motions.* Refer to individual Justice's Part Rules. NY R ERIE E FIL Doc. 3(V)(B).

k. *KINGS COUNTY: Return date set by court.* Irrespective of the return date indicated in the notice of motion, motions will be rescheduled by the E-file/Motion Support Office to a date designated by the assigned Judge. NY R L KINGS Pt. C, Rule 2.

l. *KINGS COUNTY: Calendar calls.* There shall be two (2) calendar calls on motion days. The first calendar call shall be at 9:30 AM and the second calendar call shall be at 10:45 AM, unless the Judge's Part Rules provide otherwise. Defaults shall only be taken on second call. Attorneys with appearances elsewhere in the courthouse may advise the clerk of their whereabouts to avoid a default. Failure to so advise the clerk or appear at the default calendar call will result in a default order being entered or the motion being marked off the calendar. NY R L KINGS Pt. C, Rule 7.

m. *NEW YORK COUNTY: Return date and assigned courtroom.* Motions made by notice of motion and petitions and notices of petition in special proceedings are processed by the General Clerk's Office (Room 119) and are to be made returnable in the Motion Submission Part Courtroom (Room 130) on any business day of the week at 9:30 AM. There are some differences in electronically-filed cases. NY R NY CTY Procedure II; NY R NY CTY Procedure II(C); NY R NY CTY J RUL Rule 13(a).

  i. For the convenience of counsel, between 9:00 A.M. and 9:30 A.M. each day, in advance of the "call," Room 130 accepts (1) written stipulations; (2) affidavits/affirmations reciting the required details as to an adjournment on consent; (3) stipulations, letters or other writings withdrawing motions; and (4) final papers or complete sets of papers on motions. For motions in which these items are handed in before the "call," no one need remain to answer the "call." Counsel/parties must advise the court, either between 9:00 A.M. and 9:30 A.M. or at the "call," of all motions or cases that have been resolved by counsel/parties themselves and all motions that the movant no longer wishes to pursue. If such resolution occurs subsequent to the "call", the assigned Justice must be advised as soon as possible, by written notice sent to the Part, so that the court does not do unnecessary work. NY R NY CTY Procedure II(C).

  ii. Depending upon the assigned Part, contested motions submitted in the Motion Submission Part Courtroom are submitted without argument, or rescheduled for oral argument if so directed by the assigned Justice. For Justices who schedule argument on a case-by-case basis, notice of the argument date will be transmitted by the court. Counsel may ascertain how a motion submitted in Courtroom 130 was marked by consulting Scroll on the court's website, the e-Track application, or, on the two (2) days immediately following the submission date, the New York Law Journal. NY R NY CTY J RUL Rule 13(a).

n. *NEW YORK COUNTY: Motion call.* Each day in the Motion Submission Part Courtroom, commencing at 9:30 A.M., all motions returnable that day will be "called" for the submission of these papers, which must be handed up at this "call" or, as described below, immediately before. Because hundreds of motions appear on the Room 130 calendars every day, motion papers (other than part of the moving papers as described above) cannot be accepted on any day prior to the return date. Courtesy copies are not required nor accepted, but working copies are required by certain Justices in e-filed cases. NY R NY CTY Procedure II(C). If argument is directed, it will take place on an announced date shortly after the day of submission. NY R NY CTY Procedure II(C).

o. *NEW YORK COUNTY: Oral arguments.* Pursuant to request of some Justices, motions submitted in Room 130 will automatically be scheduled for a set argument date in the Part. Other Justices determine on a case-by-case basis after submission in Room 130 whether to accept a particular substantive motion on submission, to require oral argument, or to hold a conference. NY R NY CTY Procedure II(D). If argument is directed by the Justice automatically, notice of argument and the argument date will be given in Room 130. Any appearing party is expected to give notice to all parties and an announcement to this effect is made in Room 130. If the motion is submitted in Room 130 and the Justice, after examining the file, determines that argument should be directed, notice of the argument and the argument date will not be sent by the court. To obtain notification of the argument date and other developments, counsel should use e-Track. If argument notification is not given or transmitted as just described, counsel should understand that the motion has been taken on submission for decision on the papers. NY R NY CTY Procedure II(D).

   i. Calendars of motions to be argued in the Parts are published on the morning of the argument date and on the day before in the New York Law Journal under each Part. Argument information is available on a case-by-case basis in Scroll, and e-mail notifications are sent by e-Track to participating attorneys whenever a motion is scheduled for argument in the court's computer system. NY R NY CTY J RUL Rule 15(a)

p. *NEW YORK COUNTY: Motion determined without hearing.* Given the purpose of the Room 130 procedure, the substance of motions will not be addressed at the submission "call." No Judge is present. To the extent possible, motions submitted in Room 130 will be decided "on the papers." Indeed, attorneys are encouraged to use service or clerks to deliver papers or working copies, or to agree among themselves to have one of them deliver papers for all parties by service or a clerk. Counsel for the movant need not appear to "take a default" on any motion or for any other reason. Motions will be submitted, not marked off, in the absence of the movant. Opposing counsel similarly need not appear in person in order to avoid suffering a default. Delivery of papers by service or a clerk will suffice. The court's goal is to be able to collect papers on motions in an orderly fashion but without any attorney having to make an appearance in Room 130 at any time. NY R NY CTY Procedure II(C).

q. *ONONDAGA COUNTY: Return date.* If the motion is the first filing in an action, the case will be assigned and counsel will be notified by the Supreme Court Clerk's Office via the NYSCEF system of the assigned justice and return date. NY R ONDGA E FIL Protocol(B)(7)(c). If the motion is on a previously assigned case, counsel may choose a return date from the assigned justice's motion term schedule. If the date in unavailable, the Supreme Court Clerk's Office will assign the motion to the next available motion term date and will notify counsel via e-mail. The change will also appear in the notification generated by the NYSCEF system. NY R ONDGA E FIL Protocol(B)(7)(d).

r. *QUEENS COUNTY: Return date.* Motions must be made returnable on the proper day/time based on the assigned judge. NY R L QUEENS MOT SUP Doc. 1. Failure to make a motion returnable on the proper day/time may result in the motion being administratively rescheduled or marked off. NY R L QUEENS MOT SUP Doc. 1.

s. *QUEENS COUNTY: Unassigned motions.* For RJI/Motions, due to the fact that the movant would not know who the assigned judge will be, the notice of motion may be returnable any day of the week. RJI/Motions shall be made returnable in "Queens Supreme Court" with no address designated. The motion will be administratively rescheduled to the proper day of the week based on the judge (once a judge has been assigned). Within one (1) week of filing, the movant must check online to see who the assigned judge is (and therefore the location/date/time) that their motion is now returnable. Movant must then notify their adversary of this information prior to the return date. NY R L QUEENS MOT SUP Doc. 1.

3. *Entry of order after hearing.* An order determining a motion shall be entered and filed in the office of the clerk of the court where the action is triable, and all papers used on the motion and any opinion or memorandum in writing shall be filed with that clerk unless the order dispenses with such filing. When a statute or civil practice rule requires such filing and entry in a county other than that in which the order was made, the party prevailing on the motion shall file the order and the papers used on the motion with the proper clerk after receiving them. If a party fails to file any papers required to be filed under NY CPLR Rule 2220(a), the order may be vacated as irregular, with costs. NY CPLR Rule 2220(a). For more information on the entry of an order after a motion, refer to NY CPLR Rule 2219.

   a. *BRONX COUNTY: Settled orders.* A Judge's decision will often call for a Settled Order. The purpose of the settled order is to give effect to the decision by directing that some action be done and/or that a court official perform some task. NY R BRONX LEG SUP Doc. 2. A settled order consists of a notice of settlement informing all parties that the proposed order will be presented to the judge who made the decision on a date certain. Next comes the proposed order which will be presented to the judge. This order should conform to the judge's decision and should direct the relief granted in the decision. This should be followed by proof of service upon all parties who were noticed with the decision. It is also helpful if a copy of the judge's decision is included along with the other papers. A settled order should always be noticed before the judge who made the decision. NY R BRONX LEG SUP Doc. 2.

i. Although an order is usually settled by the party who prevailed on the motion, any party may settle the order. It should be presented to the court within sixty (60) days of the decision. The other parties are entitled to ten (10) days notice where service of the settled order is done by mail, five (5) days if the notice is personally delivered. An attorney who is served with a notice of settlement which he believes does not accurately reflect the decision may settle a counter order. The counter order must be noticed for the same day and must be served not less than seven (7) days if by mail and two (2) days if personally delivered. NY R BRONX LEG SUP Doc. 2.

ii. Settled orders are usually sent to the judge the day after they noticed for settlement. No appearance is necessary or even contemplated on a settled order. If the decision directs "submit order", then no notice is necessary, and the order will be sent to the judge as soon a practical after it is received. No fees are collected on settled orders. NY R BRONX LEG SUP Doc. 2.

b. *ERIE COUNTY: Proposed orders.* Proposed orders shall be submitted through the NYSCEF system and a working copy provided to the IAS Justice for signature, if Part Rules so require. NY R ERIE E FIL Doc. 3(V)(G).

c. *KINGS COUNTY: Long form orders.* If the Court directs that an order be settled or submitted on a motion in a NYSCEF case, the proposed order, with Notice of Settlement where required, and any proposed counter-order shall be filed with the Court via NYSCEF. The relevant clerk's office will process the documents in the customary manner. NY R L KINGS E FIL Doc. 1(E).

i. WORKING COPIES OF PROPOSED ORDERS WITH NOTICE OF SETTLEMENT MUST BE SUBMITTED IN THE MOTION SUPPORT OFFICE (ROOM 227) AS EXPLAINED HEREIN. THEY MUST NOT BE DELIVERED TO THE PART OR CHAMBERS, EXCEPT WHERE THE INDIVIDUAL JUSTICE'S PART RULES PROVIDE OTHERWISE; DOING SO WILL CAUSE ADMINISTRATIVE CONFUSION AND POSSIBLE MISPLACEMENT OF PAPERS. Any such submission shall be sent in a timely manner (kindly review individual Justice's rules) and be conspicuously marked on the outside "NYSCEF Matter;" lack of such marking may delay processing. After an order/counter-order has been signed, it will be scanned, and the County Clerk will affix the entry stamp into the NYSCEF system, which will immediately transmit notice of this event via e-mail, including a link to the entered document, to all participating attorneys and unrepresented litigants in the case. Such transmittal does not constitute Notice of Entry. NY R L KINGS E FIL Doc. 1(E).

d. *NEW YORK COUNTY: Long form orders.* Although the court strongly favors the use of short form orders and judgments, there are instances when settlement of an order or judgment is appropriate. When a Justice directs in a decision that a long form order or judgment be settled, that decision is recorded in the court's computer system by the General Clerk's Office and the motion file with decision is held in the Order Section of the Office in Room 119. The settlement process takes place there. NY R NY CTY Procedure II(D); NY R NY CTY E FIL Doc. 2(E).

i. A proposed long form order or judgment in compliance NY R UNIF TRIAL CTS § 202.48 must be presented to the relevant back office, together with a notice of settlement which bears a settlement date, the date on which the order is to be ready for formal presentation to the Justice. In an e-filed case the submission shall be made electronically. The proposed order or counter-order should be e-filed and it will be transmitted automatically by the NYSCEF system to the appropriate back office. The return date and time of the proposed order must be at 9:30 A.M. no sooner than either five (5) days from personal service of the proposed order or ten (10) days from service by mail. Proof of timely service on the other parties must accompany the proposed order in a hard copy case. If an order or judgment is submitted late (later than sixty (60) days from signing and filing of the decision) and the proponent can show good cause for this tardiness, an affidavit or affirmation justifying the delay should be annexed to the proposed order, together with proof of service thereof. If persuaded, the Justice will consider the proposed order despite its untimeliness. NY R NY CTY Procedure II(D); NY R NY CTY E FIL Doc. 2(E).

ii. Sometimes a decision will state "Submit Order." The submitting party should prepare a long form order and make it returnable without notice. Counsel should deliver the proposed order to the Order Section of the appropriate back office, except in an e-filed case, when it shall be submitted electronically. NY R NY CTY Procedure II(D). If the decision of the court directs that a proposed order be settled or submitted in the Part or in Chambers, that direction, should, of course, be followed without presentation of the proposal to the back office. NY R NY CTY Procedure II(D).

iii. For information on proposed counter-orders, refer to NY R NY CTY Procedure II(D) and NY R NY CTY J RUL Rule 16(b).

e. *QUEENS COUNTY: Proposed orders.* If the court directs that an order be settled or submitted on a motion in an E-file case, the proposed order and any proposed counter-order shall be filed with the court on-line with proof of service. (If a decision refers to a proceeding on the record, a copy of the transcript must be submitted.) Working copies of all proposed orders MUST be submitted to the Motion Support Office before an order can be reviewed. NY R L QUEENS E-FILE Doc. 1(I).

   i. Counsel are advised to adhere to NY R UNIF TRIAL CTS § 202.48 regarding the submission or settlement of their proposed order or judgment. Persons who are submitting proposed orders/judgments pursuant to a previously issued memorandum decision must submit a copy of the memorandum decision with their proposed order/judgment. Upon E-Filing a proposed order/judgement, a working copy of the proposed order/judgement must be provided to the Motion Support Office. NY R L QUEENS MOT SUP Doc. 1.

H. Forms

1. Official Motion to Intervene Forms for New York

a. Request for judicial intervention. NY R UNIF TRIAL CTS § 202.6.

b. Notice of motion. NY R UNIF TRIAL CTS § 202.7(b).

2. New York Motion to Intervene Forms

a. Form; Notice of motion to intervene. NYPRAC-CIVAPP § 8:10.

b. Form; Affidavit in support of motion to intervene. NYPRAC-CIVAPP § 8:11.

c. Notice of motion to intervene when state statute confers absolute right to intervene. MCF CPLR § 3:162.

d. Affidavit in support of motion to intervene when state statute confers absolute right to intervene. MCF CPLR § 3:163.

e. Notice of motion to intervene as of right when representation of person's interest by parties is or may be inadequate. MCF CPLR § 3:165.

f. Affidavit in support of motion to intervene as of right when representation of person's interest by parties is or may be inadequate. MCF CPLR § 3:166.

g. Notice of motion to intervene as of right when action involves disposition or distribution of, or title or claim for damages for injury to, property. MCF CPLR § 3:168.

h. Affidavit in support of motion to intervene as of right when action involves disposition or distribution of, or title or claim for damages for injury to, property. MCF CPLR § 3:169.

i. Affidavit in support of motion to intervene as of right when action involves disposition or distribution of, or title or claim for damages for injury to, property; Intervenors initially named as defendants. MCF CPLR § 3:170.

j. Affidavit in support of motion to intervene as of right (with stay of proceedings to discharge mortgage) when action involves disposition or distribution of, or title or claim for damages for injury to, property. MCF CPLR § 3:175.

k. Reply affidavit in support of motion to intervene as of right (with stay of proceedings to discharge mortgage) when action involves disposition or distribution of, or title or claim for damages for injury to, property. MCF CPLR § 3:176.

l. Notice of motion to intervene when state statute confers right to intervene in discretion of court. MCF CPLR § 3:179.

m. Affidavit in support of motion to intervene when state statute confers right to intervene in discretion of court. MCF CPLR § 3:180.

n. Notice of motion to intervene in discretion of court when person's claim or defense and main action have common question of law and fact. MCF CPLR § 3:182.

o. Affidavit in support of motion to intervene in discretion of court when person's claim or defense and main action have common question of law and fact. MCF CPLR § 3:183.

p. Affirmation in support of motion to intervene when representation of person's interest by parties is or may be inadequate and when person's defense and main action have common question of law and fact, and to vacate default judgment. MCF CPLR § 3:186.

q. Affidavit in support of motion to intervene when representation of person's interest by parties is or may be inadequate and when person's defense and main action have common question of law and fact, and to vacate default judgment. MCF CPLR § 3:187.

r. General form of affidavit of service of motion papers. MCF CPLR § 5:24.

I. Applicable Rules

1. *State rules*
   - a. Short title; Application; Construction; Definitions. NY CPLR § 101; NY CPLR § 103; NY CPLR § 104; NY CPLR § 105.
   - b. Appendix of official forms. NY CPLR § 107.
   - c. Intervention as of right; Notice to attorney-general, city, county, town or village where constitutionality in issue. NY CPLR § 1012.
   - d. Intervention by permission. NY CPLR § 1013.
   - e. Proposed intervention pleading. NY CPLR § 1014.
   - f. Extensions of time generally. NY CPLR § 2004.
   - g. Form of papers. NY CPLR Rule 2101; NY CPLR Rule 2102; NY CPLR § 2105; NY CPLR Rule 2106; NY GEN BUS § 399-ddd; NY R UNIF TRIAL CTS § 215.2; NY R UNIF TRIAL CTS § 215.3.
   - h. Service of papers. NY CPLR Rule 2103.
   - i. Where motion made; In supreme court action. NY CPLR § 2212.
   - j. Motion papers; Service; Time. NY CPLR Rule 2214.
   - k. Relief demanded by other than moving party. NY CPLR Rule 2215.
   - l. Prior motion; Ex parte motion; Transfer of motion; Hearings; Orders. NY CPLR Rule 2217; NY CPLR § 2218; NY CPLR Rule 2220.
   - m. Computation of time. NY CPLR § 2402; NY GEN CONSTR § 19; NY GEN CONSTR § 20; NY GEN CONSTR § 25-a; NY GEN CONSTR § 30; NY GEN CONSTR § 31; NY GEN CONSTR § 53.
   - n. Motions heard by judge supervising disclosure; Stay of disclosure. NY CPLR Rule 3214.
   - o. Fees; Index number fees of county clerks. NY CPLR § 8018.
   - p. Hours of court; Proceedings in court. NY R CHIEF J § 3.1; NY R CHIEF J § 29.3.
   - q. Application of part; Waiver; Additional rules; Application of CPLR; Definitions. NY R UNIF TRIAL CTS § 202.1.
   - r. Papers filed in court; Electronic filing in supreme court. NY R UNIF TRIAL CTS § 202.5; NY R UNIF TRIAL CTS § 202.5-a, NY R UNIF TRIAL CTS § 202.5-b; NY R UNIF TRIAL CTS § 202.5-bb.
   - s. Request for judicial intervention. NY R UNIF TRIAL CTS § 202.6.
   - t. Calendaring of motions; Uniform notice of motion form; Affirmation of good faith. NY R UNIF TRIAL CTS § 202.7.
   - u. Motion procedure; Preliminary conferences. NY R UNIF TRIAL CTS § 202.8; NY R UNIF TRIAL CTS § 202.12.
   - v. Rules of the commercial division of the Supreme Court. NY R UNIF TRIAL CTS § 202.70.
   - w. Signing of papers. NY R CHIEF ADMIN § 130-1.1-a.
2. *Local rules*
   - a. *Albany County*
     - i. Third judicial district rules. NY R 3 JD SUP Doc. 1.
   - b. *Bronx County*
     - i. Filing of papers in supreme court. NY R BRONX FIL R Doc. 1.
     - ii. Request for judicial intervention. NY R BRONX FIL R Doc. 2.
     - iii. Motion procedure. NY R BRONX FIL R Doc. 8.
     - iv. Commercial division. NY R BRONX FIL R Doc. 12.
     - v. Motions on notice. NY R BRONX E FIL R Doc. 1.
     - vi. Settled orders. NY R BRONX LEG SUP Doc. 2.
   - c. *Erie County*
     - i. Joint protocols for New York State Courts E-Filing (NYSCEF) cases filed in Supreme Court, Erie County. NY R ERIE E FIL Doc. 3.

d. *Kings County*

i. Papers. NY R L KINGS Pt. A, Papers.
ii. Service of motion papers. NY R L KINGS Pt. C, Rule 1.
iii. Scheduling of motions. NY R L KINGS Pt. C, Rule 2.
iv. Appearance and argument. NY R L KINGS Pt. C, Rule 3.
v. Courtesy copies. NY R L KINGS Pt. C, Rule 5.
vi. Motion calendar calls. NY R L KINGS Pt. C, Rule 7.
vii. Protocol on courthouse and county clerk procedures for electronically filed cases. NY R L KINGS E FIL Doc. 1.

e. *New York County*

i. Commencement of cases. NY R NY CTY Procedure I.
ii. RJIs and assignments. NY R NY CTY Procedure IA.
iii. Motions and special proceedings by notice of motion/petition. NY R NY CTY Procedure II.
iv. County clerk litigation functions. NY R NY CTY Procedure XI.
v. Protocol on courthouse and county clerk procedures for electronically filed cases. NY R NY CTY E FIL Doc. 2.
vi. Redaction of information in documents filed with the county clerk and the court. NY R NY CTY J RUL Rule A-1.
vii. Papers by fax. NY R NY CTY J RUL Rule 4.
viii. Motions on notice; Orders to show cause. NY R NY CTY J RUL Rule 13.
ix. Motion papers. NY R NY CTY J RUL Rule 14.
x. Oral argument; Adjournments. NY R NY CTY J RUL Rule 15.

f. *Onondaga County*

i. Onondaga county protocol for case filings New York State Electronic Files (NYSCEF). NY R ONDGA E FIL Protocol.

g. *Queens County*

i. Motion support office. NY R L QUEENS MOT SUP Doc. 1.
ii. Queens county protocol on courthouse procedures for electronically filed cases. NY R L QUEENS E-FILE Doc. 1.

J. Miscellaneous

NOTE: Individual judges' rules may apply.

ALBANY COUNTY

JUSTICE LISA M. FISHER: NY R 3 JD FISHER Fisher; NY R 3 JD FISHER Fisher, PC Order.

JUSTICE RICHARD MOTT: NY R 3 JD MOTT Mott.

JUSTICE STEPHAN G. SCHICK: NY R 3 JD Schick.

FORECLOSURE SETTLEMENT PART: NY R 3 JD Foreclosure Settlement.

BRONX COUNTY

JUSTICE PAUL L. ALPERT: [NY R BRONX J Part IA-29, as amended by NY ORDER 20-0337].

JUSTICE BEN BARBATO: NY R BRONX J Part IA-21.

JUSTICE MARY ANNE BRIGANTTI: [NY R BRONX J Part IA-15, as amended by NY ORDER 20-0338].

JUSTICE JOSEPH E. CAPELLA: NY R BRONX J Part IA-23.

JUSTICE MITCHELL DANZIGER: NY R BRONX J Part IA-3/33 ; [NY R BRONX J Danziger, Part IA-3/33, as amended by NY ORDER 20-0339].

JUSTICE LAURA G. DOUGLAS: NY R BRONX J Part IA-11.

JUSTICE RUBEN FRANCO: NY R BRONX J Part IA-26.

JUSTICE DORIS M. GONZALEZ: NY R BRONX J Part IA-24.

JUSTICE WILMA GUZMAN: NY R BRONX J Part IA-7; [NY R BRONX J Guzman, Part IA-7 Virtual, as amended by NY ORDER 20-0340].

JUSTICE ROBERT T. JOHNSON: NY R BRONX J Part IA-12.

JUSTICE DONALD A. MILES: NY R BRONX J Part IA-8.

JUSTICE DONNA M. MILLS: NY R BRONX J Part IA-9.

JUSTICE JULIA I. RODRIGUEZ: NY R BRONX J Part IA-18; [NY R BRONX J Part IA-27, as amended by NY ORDER 20-0341].

JUSTICE LLINET M. ROSADO: [NY R BRONX J Part IA-25, as amended by NY ORDER 20-0342].

JUSTICE NORMA RUIZ: NY R BRONX J Part IA-22; [NY R BRONX J Ruiz, Part IA-22 Virtual, as amended by NY ORDER 20-0343].

JUSTICE HOWARD H. SHERMAN: NY R BRONX J Part IA-4.

JUSTICE FERNANDO TAPIA: NY R BRONX J Part IA-13.

JUSTICE ELIZABETH A. TAYLOR: NY R BRONX J Part IA-2.

JUSTICE ALISON Y. TRUITT: NY R BRONX J Part IA-5.

PART IDV: NY R BRONX J Doc. 1.

PRE-TRIAL PART RULES: NY R BRONX J Doc. 2.

PRE TRIAL WORKSHEET: NY R BRONX J Doc. 3.

FORECLOSURE SETTLEMENT PART RULES: NY R BRONX J Doc. 4.

GUARDIANSHIP PART RULES: NY R BRONX J Doc. 5.

LPM PART RULES: NY R BRONX J Doc. 6.

ERIE COUNTY

JUSTICE M. WILLIAM BOLLER: NY R 8 JD J Boller.

JUSTICE RALPH A. BONIELLO: NY R 8 JD J Boniello.

JUSTICE CHRISTOPHER J. BURN: NY R 8 JD J Burns.

JUSTICE RUSSELL P. BUSCAGLIA: NY R 8 JD J Buscaglia.

JUSTICE FRANK CARUSO: NY R 8 JD J Caruso.

JUSTICE STEPHEN W. CASS: NY R 8 JD J Cass.

JUSTICE DEBORAH A. CHIMES: NY R 8 JD J Chimes.

JUSTICE EMILIO COLAIACOVO: [NY R 8 JD J Colaiacovo, as amended by NY ORDER 20-0252].

JUSTICE DIANE Y. DEVLIN: NY R 8 JD J Devlin.

JUSTICE JAMES H. DILLON: NY R 8 JD J Dillon.

JUSTICE PAULA L. FEROLETO: NY R 8 JD J Feroleto.

JUSTICE DANIEL J. FURLONG: [NY R 8 JD J Furlong, as amended by NY ORDER 20-0253].

JUSTICE JOSEPH R. GLOWNIA: NY R 8 JD J Glownia.

JUSTICE MARK J. GRISANTI: NY R 8 JD J Grisanti.

JUSTICE DEBORAH A. HAENDIGES: NY R 8 JD J Haendiges.

JUSTICE LYNN W. KEANE: [NY R 8 JD J Keane, as amended by NY ORDER 20-0254].

JUSTICE RICHARD C. KLOCH, Sr.: NY R 8 JD J Kloch.

JUSTICE FREDERICK J. MARSHALL: [NY R 8 JD J Marshall, as amended by NY ORDER 20-0255.

JUSTICE JOHN L. MICHALSKI: NY R 8 JD J Michalski.

JUSTICE MARK A. MONTOUR: [NY R 8 JD J Montour, as amended by NY ORDER 20-0256].

JUSTICE HENRY NOWAK: NY R 8 JD J Nowak.

JUSTICE JOHN F. O'DONNELL: NY R 8 JD J O'Donnell.

JUSTICE JEANETTE OGDEN: NY R 8 JD J Ogden.

JUSTICE CATHERINE NUGENT-PANEPINTO: NY R 8 JD J Nugent-Panepinto.

JUSTICE FRANK A. SEDITA, III: [NY R 8 JD J Sedita, as amended by NY ORDER 20-0257].

JUSTICE SARA SHELDON: NY R 8 JD J Sheldon.

JUSTICE DONNA M. SIWEK: NY R 8 JD J Siwek.

JUSTICE MARY L. SLISZ: NY R 8 JD J Slisz.

JUSTICE TIMOTHY J. WALKER: [NY R 8 JD J Walker, as amended by NY ORDER 20-0258].

JUSTICE DENNIS E. WARD: NY R 8 JD J Ward.

JUSTICE PAUL B. WOJTASZEK: [NY R 8 JD J Wojtaszek, as amended by NY ORDER 20-0259].

JUSTICE CHARLES N. ZAMBITO: [NY R 8 JD J Zambito, as amended by NY ORDER 20-0260].

SUPREME COURT LEGAL STAFF: NY R 8 JD J Legal Staff.

KINGS COUNTY

JUSTICE RACHEL A. ADAMS: NY R KINGS J Part 5F.

JUSTICE LOREN BAILY-SCHIFFMAN: NY R KINGS J Part 65.

JUSTICE REGINALD A. BODDIE: NY R KINGS J Part 95.

JUSTICE THERESA M. CICCOTTO: NY R KINGS J Part 19; NY R KINGS J Part 5J.

JUSTICE LISSETTE COLON: NY R KINGS J Part Rules.

JUSTICE GENINE EDWARDS: NY R KINGS J Part 80.

JUSTICE PAMELA L. FISHER: [NY R KINGS J Part 94, as amended by NY ORDER 20-0208].

JUSTICE ROBIN GARSON: NY R KINGS J Part 75.

JUSTICE LARA J. GENOVISI: [NY R KINGS J Part 34, as amended by NY ORDER 20-0209].

JUSTICE BERNARD J. GRAHAM: NY R KINGS J Part 36.

JUSTICE DAWN JIMENEZ-SALTA: NY R KINGS J Part 88.

JUSTICE INGRID JOSEPH: [NY R KINGS J Part FRP3 and Part 83, as amended by NY ORDER 20-0210].

JUSTICE KATHY J. KING: NY R KINGS J Part 64, 76K.

JUSTICE LAWRENCE KNIPEL: NY R KINGS J Part 57.

JUSTICE DONALD KURTZ: NY R KINGS J Part 26.

JUSTICE CARL LANDICINO: [NY R KINGS J Part 81, as amended by NY ORDER 20-0211].

JUSTICE KATHERINE LEVINE: [NY R KINGS J Part 20, 25, 92, as amended by NY ORDER 20-0211].

JUSTICE LORNA MCALLISTER: [NY R KINGS J Part 10, as amended by NY ORDER 20-0211].

JUSTICE ROSEMARIE MONTALBANO: [NY R KINGS J Part 19, 71, and 22, as amended by NY ORDER 20-0211].

JUSTICE RICHARD J. MONTELIONE: [NY R KINGS J Part 99 and DJMP, as amended by NY ORDER 20-0215].

JUSTICE LISA S. OTTLEY: NY R KINGS J Part 24.

JUSTICE MARK I. PARTNOW: NY R KINGS J Part 43.

JUSTICE ERIC I. PRUS: NY R KINGS J Part 5A.

JUSTICE FRANCOIS RIVERA: NY R KINGS J Part 52.

JUSTICE KAREN B. ROTHENBERG: NY R KINGS J Part 35.

JUSTICE LEON RUCHELSMAN: NY R KINGS J Part 1.

JUSTICE WAYNE P. SAITTA: NY R KINGS J Part 29.

JUSTICE ROBIN K. SHEARES: NY R KINGS J Part 96.

JUSTICE KENNETH P. SHERMAN: NY R KINGS J Part 67 and 78.

JUSTICE DEBRA SILBER: NY R KINGS J Part 9 and 5K.

JUSTICE ELLEN M. SPODEK: NY R KINGS J Part 63.

JUSTICE MARSHA L. STEINHARDT: NY R KINGS J Part 15.

JUSTICE JEFFREY S. SUNSHINE: NY R KINGS J Part 5G.

JUSTICE PETER P. SWEENEY: [NY R KINGS J Part 35, as amended by NY ORDER 20-0218].

JUSTICE DELORES J. THOMAS: [NY R KINGS J Part 5T, as amended by NY ORDER 20-0221].

JUSTICE WAVNY TOUSSAINT: NY R KINGS J Part 70.

JUSTICE RICHARD VELASQUEZ: NY R KINGS J Part 66.

JUSTICE CAROLYN E. WADE: NY R KINGS J Part 84.

JUSTICE EDWARD G. WALKER: [NY R KINGS J Part 90, as amended by NY ORDER 20-0219].

JUSTICE LILLIAN WAN: [NY R KINGS J Part 17, as amended by NY ORDER 20-0220].

JUSTICE MICHELLE WESTON: NY R KINGS J Part 3.

MENTAL HYGIENE PART: NY R KINGS J Part 77.

MATRIMONIAL PARTS DURING COVID-19 EMERGENCY: JUSTICE KAREN B. ROTHENBERG: NY R KINGS J Doc. 1.

NASSAU COUNTY

JUSTICE ANNA R. ANZALONE: NY R NASSAU S J Anzalone, Part 26.

JUSTICE STACY D. BENNETT: NY R NASSAU S J Bennett; NY R NASSAU S J Bennett, Form 1.

JUSTICE ANTONIO BRANDVEEN: NY R NASSAU S J Brandveen, Part 31.

JUSTICE JEFFREY S. BROWN: [NY R NASSAU S J Brown, as amended by NY ORDER 20-0297].

JUSTICE STEPHEN A. BUCARIA: NY R NASSAU S J Bucaria.

JUSTICE JULIANNE T. CAPETOLA: NY R NASSAU S J Capetola, Part 28.

JUSTICE EDMUND M. DANE: NY R NASSAU S J Dane, Part 33.

JUSTICE VITO M. DESTEFANO: NY R NASSAU S J DeStefano, Part 13; NY R NASSAU S J DeStefano, Form 1.

JUSTICE ARTHUR M. DIAMOND: NY R NASSAU S J Diamond, Part 7.

JUSTICE THOMAS FEINMAN: NY R NASSAU S J Feinman, Part 5.

JUSTICE JOHN M. GALASSO: NY R NASSAU S J Galasso, Part 22.

JUSTICE SHARON M.J. GIANELLI: NY R NASSAU S J Gianelli, Part 22; NY R NASSAU S J Gianelli, Form 1.

JUSTICE JEFFREY A. GOODSTEIN: NY R NASSAU S J Goodstein, Part 33; NY R NASSAU S J Goodstein, Form 1.

JUSTICE DAVID J. GUGERTY: [NY R NASSAU S J Gugerty, Part 31, as amended by NY ORDER 20-0298].

JUSTICE HELENE F. GUGERTY: NY R NASSAU S J Gugerty, Part 47.

JUSTICE STEVEN M. JAEGER: NY R NASSAU S J Jaeger, Part 35; NY R NASSAU S J Jaeger, Form 1.

JUSTICE JACK L. LIBERT: NY R NASSAU S J Libert, Part 23.

JUSTICE JOSEPH H. LORINTZ: NY R NASSAU S J Lorintz, Part 26; NY R NASSAU S J Lorintz, Form 1.

JUSTICE ROY S. MAHON: NY R NASSAU S J Mahon, Part 3.

JUSTICE RANDY SUE MARBER: NY R NASSAU S J Marber, Part 8.

JUSTICE JAMES P. MCCORMACK: [NY R NASSAU S J McCormack, Part 18, as amended by NY ORDER, 20-0299].

JUSTICE DICCIA T. PINEDA-KIRWAN: [NY R NASSAU S J Pineda-Kirwan, as amended by NY ORDER 20-0300].

JUSTICE THOMAS RADEMAKER: [NY R NASSAU S J Rademaker, Part 28, as amended by NY ORDER 20-0301]; [NY R NASSAU S J Rademaker, Form 1, as amended by NY ORDER 20-0301].

JUSTICE DENISE L. SHER: NY R NASSAU S J Rademaker, Part 32.

JUSTICE LEONARD D. STEINMAN: [NY R NASSAU S J Steinman, Part 15, as amended by NY ORDER 20-0303]; NY R NASSAU S J Steinman, Form 1.

JUSTICE HOWARD E. STURIM: NY R NASSAU S J Sturim, Part 50; NY R NASSAU S J Sturim, Form 1.

JUSTICE HELEN VOUTSINAS: [NY R NASSAU S J Voutsinas, Part 25, as amended by NY ORDER 20-0304]; [NY R NASSAU S J Voutsinas, Form 1, as amended by NY ORDER 20-0305].

JUSTICE HOPE SCHWARTZ ZIMMERMAN: NY R NASSAU S J Zimmerman, Part 17.

NEW YORK COUNTY

JUDGE'S RULES; BASIC INFORMATION: [NY R NY CTY J RUL Doc. 1, as amended by NY ORDER 20-0202].

ONONDAGA COUNTY

JUSTICE ROBERT E. ANTONACCI II: [NY R ONDGA E FIL Doc. 1, as amended by 20-0239].

JUSTICE MICHAEL V. COCCOMI: NY R ONDGA E FIL Doc. 2.

JUSTICE GREGORY R. GILBERT: NY R 5 JD JUDGES Gilbert; NY R ONDGA E FIL Doc. 3.

JUSTICE DONALD A. GREENWOOD: NY R ONDGA E FIL Doc. 4.

JUSTICE DEBORAH H. KARALUNAS: NY R ONDGA E FIL Doc. 5.

JUSTICE JAMES MCCLUSKY: NY R 5 JD MCCLUSKY McClusky.

JUSTICE CHARLES C. MERRELL: NY R 5 JD MERRELL Merrell.

JUSTICE PATRICK F. MACRAE: NY R 5 JD MACRAE Doc. 1.

JUSTICE JAMES P. MURPHY: NY R ONDGA E FIL Doc. 7.

JUSTICE GERALD J. NERI: [NY R 5 JD JUDGES Neri, as amended by NY ORDER 20-0236]; [NY R ONDGA E FIL Doc. 8, as amended by NY ORDER 20-0241].

JUSTICE ANTHONY J. PARIS: NY R 5 JD JUDGES Paris; [NY R ONDGA E FIL Doc. 9, as amended by NY ORDER 20-0242].

JUSTICE NORMAN W. SEITER, JR.: NY R 5 JD JUDGES Seiter.

JUSTICE KEVIN G. YOUNG: [NY R ONDGA E FIL Doc. 10, as amended by NY ORDER 20-0243].

QUEENS COUNTY

JUSTICE PAM JACKMAN BROWN: [NY R L QUEENS Brown, Part 19, as amended by NY ORDER 20-0321].

JUSTICE CHEREE A. BUGGS: NY R L QUEENS Buggs, Part 30.

JUSTICE PAM JACKMAN BROWN: [NY R L QUEENS Brown, Part 19, as amended by NY ORDER 20-0321].

JUSTICE DENIS J. BUTLER: NY R L QUEENS Butler, Part 12.

JUSTICE ROBERT I. CALORAS: [NY R L QUEENS Caloras, Part 36, as amended by NY ORDER 20-0322].

JUSTICE ANNA CULLEY: NY R L QUEENS Culley, Part 53.

JUSTICE TIMOTHY DUFFICY: NY R L QUEENS Dufficy, Part 35.

JUSTICE DAVID ELLIOT: NY R L QUEENS Elliot, Part 14.

JUSTICE JOSEPH J. ESPOSITO: NY R L QUEENS Esposito, Part 6.

JUSTICE DARRELL L. GAVRIN: [NY R L QUEENS Gavrin, Part 27, as amended by NY ORDER 20-0323].

JUSTICE WYATT N. GIBBONS: [NY R L QUEENS Gibbons, Part 5, as amended by NY ORDER 20-0330.

JUSTICE DONNA-MARIE E. GOLIA: [NY R L QUEENS Golia, Part 21, as amended by NY ORDER 20-0331].

JUSTICE MARGUERITE A. GRAYS: [NY R L QUEENS Grays, Part 4, as amended by NY ORDER 20-0324].

JUSTICE RUDOLPH E. GRECO: [NY R L QUEENS Greco, Part 32, as amended by NY ORDER 20-0325].

JUSTICE MAUREEN HEALY: NY R L QUEENS Healy, Part 6.

JUSTICE PHILLIP HOM: [NY R L QUEENS Hom, Part 43, as amended by NY ORDER 20-0332].

JUSTICE KEVIN J. KERRIGAN: NY R L QUEENS Kerrigan, Part 10.

JUSTICE MOJGAN C. LANCMAN: NY R L QUEENS Lancman, Part 20.

JUSTICE RICHARD G. LATIN: NY R L QUEENS Latin, Part 40.

JUSTICE ULYSSES B. LEVERETT: [NY R L QUEENS Leverett, Part 6, as amended by NY ORDER 20-0326].

JUSTICE LEONARD LIVOTE: NY R L QUEENS Livote, Part 33.

JUSTICE LEE A. MAYERSOHN: NY R L QUEENS Mayersohn, Part 22; NY R L QUEENS Mayersohn, Part 22G; [NY R L QUEENS Mayersohn, Part 22G COVID, as amended by NY ORDER 20-0327].

JUSTICE ROBERT J. MCDONALD: NY R L QUEENS McDonald, Part 34.

JUSTICE MARGARET MCGOWAN: NY R L QUEENS McGowan, Part 52.

JUSTICE MAURICE E. MUIR: [NY R L QUEENS Muir, Part 42, as amended by NY ORDER 20-0333].

JUSTICE JODI ORLOW: NY R L QUEENS Orlow, Part 51.

JUSTICE LESLIE J. PURIFICCION: NY R L QUEENS Purificcion, Part 39.

JUSTICE JOSEPH RISI: [NY R L QUEENS Risi, Part 3, as amended by NY ORDER 20-0328].

JUSTICE FREDERICK D.R. SAMPSON: [NY R L QUEENS Sampson, Part 31, as amended by NY ORDER 20-0329].

JUSTICE MARTIN J. SCHULMAN: NY R L QUEENS Schulman, Part 29.

JUSTICE BERNICE D. SIEGAL: NY R L QUEENS Siegal, Part 25G.

JUSTICE JANICE A. TAYLOR: NY R L QUEENS Taylor, Part 15.

JUSTICE CARMEN R. VELASQUEZ: NY R L QUEENS Velasquez, Part 38.

JUSTICE LOURDES M VENTURA: [NY R L QUEENS Ventura, Part 37, as amended by NY ORDER 20-0334].

JUSTICE WILLIAM A. VISCOVICH: NY R L QUEENS Viscovich, Part 63.

JUSTICE ALLAN B. WEISS: NY R L QUEENS Weiss, Part 2.

COMPLIANCE, SETTLEMENT AND CONFERENCE PART: NY R L QUEENS Doc 1.

PRELIMINARY CONFERENCE PART: [NY R L QUEENS Doc. 2, as amended by NY ORDER 20-0335].

MEDICAL MALPRACTICE CONFERENCE PART: [NY R L QUEENS Doc. 3, as amended by NY ORDER 20-0336].

TRIAL SCHEDULING PART: NY R L QUEENS Doc. 4.

SUMMARY JURY TRIAL PROGRAM: NY R L QUEENS Doc. 7.

RESIDENTIAL FORECLOSURE PART: NY R L QUEENS Doc. 9.

FORECLOSURE AUCTION RULES: NY R L QUEENS Doc. 10.

MATRIMONIAL PRELIMINARY CONFERENCE PART: NY R L QUEENS Doc. 11.

NON-CUSTODIAL CONTESTED MATRIMONIAL PART: NY R L QUEENS Doc. 12.

Motions, Oppositions and Replies
Motion to Correct Pleadings

Document Last Updated August 2020

A. Checklist

(I) ❑ Matters to consider for moving party

- (a) ❑ Required documents
  - (1) ❑ Notice of motion, order to show cause, or affidavit on ex parte motion
  - (2) ❑ Motion
  - (3) ❑ Request for judicial intervention
  - (4) ❑ Proof of service
  - (5) ❑ ALBANY COUNTY: Additional required documents
    - (i) ❑ Affirmation of good faith effort
- (b) ❑ Supplemental documents
  - (1) ❑ Supporting evidence; Exhibits
  - (2) ❑ Brief

(3) ❑ Notice to produce papers not in possession of the court

(4) ❑ Filing fees

(5) ❑ Working copies

(6) ❑ Statement of authorization in electronic filing cases

(7) ❑ ERIE COUNTY: Additional supplemental documents

(i) ❑ Notice of hard copy submission in e-filed case

(8) ❑ KINGS COUNTY: Additional supplemental documents

(i) ❑ Forms when filing in hard copy

(9) ❑ NEW YORK COUNTY: Additional supplemental documents

(i) ❑ Notice of hard copy submission

(ii) ❑ Unpublished opinions

(10) ❑ ONONDAGA COUNTY: Additional supplemental documents

(i) ❑ Notice of hard copy submission

(11) ❑ QUEENS COUNTY: Additional supplemental documents

(i) ❑ Notice of hard copy submission

(c) ❑ Timing

(1) ❑ A notice of motion under NY CPLR Rule 3024 shall be served within twenty (20) days after service of the challenged pleading

(2) ❑ The moving party shall serve copies of all affidavits and briefs upon all other parties at the time of service of the notice of motion

(3) ❑ A notice of motion and supporting affidavits shall be served at least eight (8) days before the time at which the motion is noticed to be heard

(4) ❑ It is also good practice to make motions returnable at least three (3) weeks away from the planned date of mailing and to always include a demand in the motion that the other side serve answering papers at least seven (7) days before the return day

(5) ❑ BRONX COUNTY: Additional timing

(i) ❑ A Notice of Motion must be served at least eight (8) days, by personal service, nine (9) days by overnight express and thirteen (13) days by mail before the return date

(6) ❑ NEW YORK COUNTY: Additional timing

(i) ❑ In an e-filed case, all of the moving papers shall be e-filed at least eight (8) business days prior to the return date

(7) ❑ ONONDAGA COUNTY: Additional timing

(i) ❑ Onondaga County local court rules require that any additional papers relating to motions must be e-filed at least two (2) business days prior to the return date, excluding the return date

(8) ❑ QUEENS COUNTY: Additional timing

(i) ❑ Motions must be in the possession of the Motion Support Office at least nine (9) days before the noticed return date of the motion

(II) ❑ Matters to consider for opposing party

(a) ❑ Required documents

(1) ❑ Opposition

(2) ❑ Proof of service

(b) ❑ Supplemental documents

(1) ❑ Supporting evidence; Exhibits

(2) ❑ Brief

(3) ❑ Filing fees

(4) ❑ Working copies

(5) ❑ ERIE COUNTY: Additional supplemental documents

(i) ❑ Notice of hard copy submission in e-filed case

(6) ❑ KINGS COUNTY: Additional supplemental documents

(i) ❑ Forms when filing in hard copy

(7) ❑ NEW YORK COUNTY: Additional supplemental documents

(i) ❑ Notice of hard copy submission

(ii) ❑ Unpublished opinions

(8) ❑ ONONDAGA COUNTY: Additional supplemental documents

(i) ❑ Notice of hard copy submission

(9) ❑ QUEENS COUNTY: Additional supplemental documents

(i) ❑ Notice of hard copy submission

(c) ❑ Timing

(1) ❑ Answering affidavits shall be served at least two (2) days before the time at which the motion is noticed to be heard

(2) ❑ Answering affidavits and any notice of cross-motion, with supporting papers, if any, shall be served at least seven (7) days before such time if a notice of motion served at least sixteen (16) days before such time so demands

B. Timing

1. *Time to bring motion to correct pleadings.* A notice of motion under NY CPLR Rule 3024 shall be served within twenty (20) days after service of the challenged pleading. If the motion is denied, the responsive pleading shall be served within ten (10) days after service of notice of entry of the order and, if it is granted, an amended pleading complying with the order shall be served within that time. NY CPLR Rule 3024(c).

2. *Time to serve.* The moving party shall serve copies of all affidavits and briefs upon all other parties at the time of service of the notice of motion. NY R UNIF TRIAL CTS § 202.8(c). A notice of motion and supporting affidavits shall be served at least eight (8) days before the time at which the motion is noticed to be heard. NY CPLR Rule 2214(b).

a. *Return dates; Best practice.* It is also good practice to make motions returnable at least three (3) weeks away from the planned date of mailing and to always include a demand in the motion that the other side serve answering papers at least seven (7) days before the return day. This enables the motion to be served by mail, gives sufficient notice to support the seven (7) day demand, and leaves a few days for a delayed mailing if some snag prevents posting on the day planned. If speed is needed, the shorter eight (8) day notice period can be used, forfeiting the right to seven (7) day answering papers and a reply. If even eight (8) days notice is too much under the circumstances, the order to show cause is the remedy. SIEGEL-NYPRAC § 247.

i. *ALBANY COUNTY.* All motions, except for certain matters in Albany County as specified in NY R 3 JD SUP Doc. 1(E) and NY R 3 JD SUP Doc. 1(F), brought on by notice of motion or by order to show cause will be made returnable on any day, Monday through Friday, as chosen by the movant in compliance with the CPLR. Parties shall submit all papers in a timely fashion as required by the CPLR by delivering them or mailing them directly to the Supreme Court Clerk's Office[. . .]except that motions and other applications subject to a filing fee shall first be presented to the County Clerk's Office for payment of the requisite fee and then subsequently filed with the Supreme Court Clerk's Office. NY R 3 JD SUP Doc. 1(B).

ii. *BRONX COUNTY.* A Notice of Motion must be served at least eight (8) days, by personal service, nine (9) days by overnight express and thirteen (13) days by mail before the return date. NY R BRONX FIL R Doc. 3. All unassigned motions must be accompanied with a properly filled out RJI and shall be filed in the Motion Support Office, room 217, within five (5) days of service. All motions on actions already assigned to a Justice must be filed at least five (5) business days before the return date. NY R BRONX FIL R Doc. 3. All papers served must strictly comply with the time requirements of NY CPLR Rule 2101, NY CPLR Rule 2103 and NY CPLR Rule 2214(b). NY R BRONX FIL R Doc. 8.

iii. *KINGS COUNTY.* Motion papers, answering affidavits and reply affidavits must be served on adversaries in accordance with NY CPLR Rule 2214. NY R L KINGS Pt. C, Rule 1.

iv. *NEW YORK COUNTY.* In an e-filed case, all of the moving papers shall be e-filed at least eight (8) business days prior to the return date. The clerk will calendar the motion for the Motion Submission Part Courtroom (Room 130) for the return date selected. NY R NY CTY Procedure II(A); NY R NY CTY E FIL Doc. 2(D)(1).

v. *ONONDAGA COUNTY.* Onondaga County local court rules require that any additional papers relating to motions must be e-filed at least two (2) business days prior to the return date, excluding the return date. NY R ONDGA E FIL Protocol(B)(9)(e).

vi. *QUEENS COUNTY.* Motions must be in the possession of the Motion Support Office at least nine (9) days before the noticed return date of the motion. NY R L QUEENS MOT SUP Doc. 1; NY R L QUEENS E-FILE Doc. 1(H)(1).

b. *Order to show cause; Shorter time.* The court in a proper case may grant an order to show cause, to be served in lieu of a notice of motion, at a time and in a manner specified therein. NY CPLR Rule 2214(d). An ordinary notice of motion can't be brought on for hearing earlier than the eighth (8th) day after the motion papers are served. With an order to show cause, the hearing can be brought on at any time the court directs, which can be fewer than eight (8) days or as close as the very day on which it is signed. If the court is convinced there is a real emergency, it can schedule the hearing for a few hours later or, in the direst case, "forthwith" the service of the order to show cause. SIEGEL-NYPRAC § 248.

c. *Time to serve answering affidavits; Other answering papers.* Answering affidavits shall be served at least two (2) days before the time at which the motion is noticed to be heard. Answering affidavits and any notice of cross-motion, with supporting papers, if any, shall be served at least seven (7) days before such time if a notice of motion served at least sixteen (16) days before such time so demands; whereupon any reply or responding affidavits shall be served at least one (1) day before such time. NY CPLR Rule 2214(b); NY R UNIF TRIAL CTS § 202.8(c).

i. *BRONX COUNTY.* All answering papers must be submitted to the Clerk 's Office on the return date of the motion. Answering papers will not be accepted prior to the return date. NY R BRONX FIL R Doc. 8.

ii. *NEW YORK COUNTY.* Cross-motions, papers in opposition, and reply papers on motions/petitions on notice returnable in Room 130 in a hard-copy case shall be submitted to the Motion Submission Part Courtroom (Room 130) on the final return date of the motion/petition and will not be accepted until that date. Subsequent documents on motions/petitions in e-filed cases shall be e-filed in a timely manner. Working copies when required shall be submitted to Room 130 on the final return date. NY R NY CTY Procedure II(A).

d. *Time to serve cross-motion.* At least three (3) days prior to the time at which the motion is noticed to be heard, or seven (7) days prior to such time if demand is properly made pursuant to NY CPLR Rule 2214(b), a party may serve upon the moving party a notice of cross-motion demanding relief, with or without supporting papers; provided, however, that:

i. If such notice and any supporting papers are served by mailing, as provided in NY CPLR Rule 2103(b)(2), they shall be served three (3) days earlier than as prescribed in NY CPLR Rule 2215; and

ii. If served by overnight delivery, as provided in NY CPLR Rule 2103(b)(6), they shall be served one (1) day earlier than as prescribed in NY CPLR Rule 2215. Relief in the alternative or of several different types may be demanded; relief need not be responsive to that demanded by the moving party. NY CPLR Rule 2215(a); NY CPLR Rule 2215(b).

iii. *BRONX COUNTY.* Cross motions may be presented for approval on or before the return date, provided that there is a motion already calendared. NY R BRONX FIL R Doc. 8.

iv. *ERIE COUNTY.* Cross-motions must be filed at least two (2) days before the return date of the motion. NY R L KINGS Pt. A, Papers.

v. *KINGS COUNTY.* Hard copies are required to be filed for any motions, answering papers, stipulations, etc. for E-Filed cases returnable in [the Central Compliance Part] at least [two (2)] days before return date. . .for cross motions. NY R L KINGS Pt. E, Rule 8.

vi. *QUEENS COUNTY.* Motion Support does not process or forward responsive papers, including cross-motions. They must be brought to the calendar call in the judge's part. NY R L QUEENS MOT SUP Doc. 1. E-filed cross motions: across motion must be noticed for the same return date as the main motion and have the confirmation of filing attached in the same manner as a motion. NY R L QUEENS E-FILE Doc. 1(H)(2)(e).

3. *Time for initial appearance.* The defendant appears by serving an answer or a notice of appearance, or by making a motion which has the effect of extending the time to answer. An appearance shall be made within twenty (20) days after service of the summons, except that if the summons was served on the defendant by delivering it to an official of the state

authorized to receive service in his behalf or if it was served pursuant to NY CPLR § 303, NY CPLR § 308(2), NY CPLR § 308(3), NY CPLR § 308(4) or NY CPLR § 308(5), or NY CPLR § 313, NY CPLR § 314 or NY CPLR § 315, the appearance shall be made within thirty (30) days after service is complete. NY CPLR Rule 320(a).

a. *Extension of time when complaint not served with summons.* If the complaint is not served with the summons, the time to appear may be extended as provided in NY CPLR § 3012(b). NY CPLR Rule 320(a).

b. *Written demand for complaint; Effect on time to appear.* If the complaint is not served with the summons, the defendant may serve a written demand for the complaint within the time provided in NY CPLR Rule 320(a) for an appearance. Service of the demand shall extend the time to appear until twenty (20) days after service of the complaint. A demand or motion under NY CPLR § 3012(b) does not of itself constitute an appearance in the action. NY CPLR § 3012(b).

4. *Time to acknowledge service of initiating papers*

a. *Served by electronic means.* A party served by electronic means shall, within twenty-four (24) hours of service, provide the serving party or attorney with an electronic confirmation that the service has been effected. NY R UNIF TRIAL CTS § 202.5-b(f)(1); NY R UNIF TRIAL CTS § 202.5-bb(b)(3).

b. *Served by mail.* The defendant, an authorized employee of the defendant, defendant's attorney or an employee of the attorney must complete the acknowledgement of receipt and mail or deliver one (1) copy of it within thirty (30) days from the date of receipt. Service is complete on the date the signed acknowledgement of receipt is mailed or delivered to the sender. The signed acknowledgement of receipt shall constitute proof of service. NY CPLR § 312-a(b)(1).

i. *Acknowledgement to be sworn.* The acknowledgement of receipt of service shall be subscribed and affirmed as true under penalties of perjury and shall have the same force and effect as an affidavit. NY CPLR § 312-a(c).

ii. *Time for answer after acknowledgement.* Where a complaint or petition is served with the summons or notice of petition, the defendant shall serve an answer within twenty (20) days after the date the signed acknowledgement of receipt is mailed or delivered to the sender. NY CPLR § 312-a(b)(2).

5. *Filing before return date.* All motions shall be returnable before the assigned judge, and all papers shall be filed with the court on or before the return date. NY R UNIF TRIAL CTS § 202.8(a).

a. *BRONX COUNTY: Time for filing*

i. *Unassigned motions.* Unassigned motions must be in the Clerk's Office within five (5) days of the date of service of the motion. NY R BRONX FIL R Doc. 8.

ii. *Assigned motions.* Assigned motions must be filed in the Clerk's Office not less than five (5) business days prior to the return date of the motion. NY R BRONX FIL R Doc. 8.

iii. *Motions returnable in room 217.* The moving documents must be e-filed no later than eight (8) days prior to the return date. NY R BRONX E FIL R Doc. 1(1).

b. *KINGS COUNTY: Time and place of filing.* Motion papers must be filed with the E-file/Motion Support Office located in Room 227. . . at 360 Adams Street at least five (5) business days before the return date of the motion. NY R L KINGS Pt. A, Papers. Hard copies are required to be filed for any motions, answering papers, stipulations, etc. for E-Filed cases returnable in [the Central Compliance Part] at least five (5) days before return date for main motions. NY R L KINGS Pt. E, Rule 8. The moving documents must be e-filed no later than eight (8) days prior to the return date. NY R L KINGS E FIL Doc. 1(D).

6. *NEW YORK COUNTY: Briefing schedule.* Once a motion is made, counsel for all parties are strongly encouraged to agree upon a briefing schedule and submit a stipulation of adjournment reflecting that schedule using service or a clerk. Where a briefing schedule has not been agreed upon, the movant can avoid the need to attend simply to see if anyone will hand up opposing papers by demanding papers as provided by NY CPLR Rule 2214(b). To protect movants against the submission of late opposition papers or cross-motions, the General Clerk's Office will screen motions in which such papers are submitted without a response (reply or opposition respectively) to ensure that proper time to respond has been afforded and it will sua sponte adjourn for one (1) week cases in which such time has not been given. NY R NY CTY Procedure II(C).

7. *QUEENS COUNTY: Time to pay fees.* As motions and petitions are time sensitive, if opting to pay at the County Clerk's Office payment MUST be made, if filed with an RJI, a minimum of nine (9) business days prior to the application's return date and if filed post RJI, a minimum of nine (9) business days prior to the application's return date. NY R L QUEENS E-FILE Doc. 1(H)(1).

8. *Computation of time*
   a. *Units of time*
      i. *Day.* A calendar day includes the time from midnight to midnight. Sunday or any day of the week specifically mentioned means a calendar day. NY GEN CONSTR § 19.
      ii. *Month.* In a statute, contract or public or private instrument, unless otherwise provided in such contract or instrument or by law, the term month means a calendar month and not a lunar month. NY GEN CONSTR § 31.
      iii. *Year.* For information on the definition of a year, including the definitions of a half-year and quarter-year, refer to NY GEN CONSTR § 58 and NY GEN CONSTR § 50. For information on leap years, refer to NY GEN CONSTR § 57.
   b. *Periods of time*
      i. *Number of days.* A number of days specified as a period from a certain day within which or after or before which an act is authorized or required to be done means such number of calendar days exclusive of the calendar day from which the reckoning is made. NY GEN CONSTR § 20.
         - If such period is a period of two (2) days, Saturday, Sunday or a public holiday must be excluded from the reckoning if it is an intervening day between the day from which the reckoning is made and the last day of the period. NY GEN CONSTR § 20.
         - In computing any specified period of time from a specified event, the day upon which the event happens is deemed the day from which the reckoning is made. The day from which any specified period of time is reckoned shall be excluded in making the reckoning. NY GEN CONSTR § 20.
      ii. *Number of months.* A number of months after or before a certain day shall be computed by counting such number of calendar months from such day, exclusive of the calendar month in which such day occurs, and shall include the day of the month in the last month so counted having the same numerical order in days of the month as the day from which the computation is made, unless there be not so many days in the last month so counted, in which case the period computed shall expire with the last day of the month so counted. NY GEN CONSTR § 30.
      iii. *Publication of notice; Number of days.* The period of publication of a legal notice shall be computed by excluding the first day of publication and including the day on which the act or event of which notice is given is to take place or which completes the full period of publication. NY CPLR § 2402.
      iv. *Periods ending on Saturday, Sunday or public holiday.* When any period of time, computed from a certain day, within which or after which or before which an act is authorized or required to be done, ends on a Saturday, Sunday or a public holiday, such act may be done on the next succeeding business day and if the period ends at a specified hour, such act may be done at or before the same hour of such next succeeding business day, except that where a period of time specified by contract ends on a Saturday, Sunday or a public holiday, the extension of such period is governed by NY GEN CONSTR § 25. NY GEN CONSTR § 25-a(1).
         - For a list of public holidays, refer to NY GEN CONSTR § 24.
      v. *Additional time after certain kinds of service*
         - *Service by mail.* Where a period of time prescribed by law is measured from the service of a paper and service is by mail, five (5) days shall be added to the prescribed period. NY CPLR Rule 2103(b)(2).
         - *Service by overnight delivery service.* Where a period of time prescribed by law is measured from the service of a paper and service is by overnight delivery, one (1) business day shall be added to the prescribed period. NY CPLR Rule 2103(b)(6).
      vi. *Daylight saving time.* For information on New York's time zone and the effect of daylight saving time, refer to NY GEN CONSTR § 52.
   c. *Hours of court.* Notwithstanding any provision of law or rule of court to the contrary, throughout the State of New York the sessions of the Supreme Court for the disposition of business before the court shall commence not later than 9:30 a.m. and conclude not earlier than 5 p.m. Where warranted, the Chief Administrator of the Courts may authorize variances in the opening and closing hours of the courts, but, in such event, daily sessions shall total not less than six (6) hours. NY R CHIEF J § 3.1.
   d. *Time limits; Extension of time.* Any act required by or in pursuance of law to be performed at or within a prescribed time, shall be performed according to the standard time. NY GEN CONSTR § 53.
      i. Except where otherwise expressly prescribed by law, the court may extend the time fixed by any statute, rule or

order for doing any act, upon such terms as may be just and upon good cause shown, whether the application for extension is made before or after the expiration of the time fixed. NY CPLR § 2004. Refer to the New York KeyRules Motion for Continuance/Extension of Time document for more information.

C. General Requirements

1. *Motions, generally.* There shall be compliance with the procedures prescribed in the CPLR for the bringing of motions. NY R UNIF TRIAL CTS § 202.7(a).
   a. *Motions on notice.* A notice of motion shall specify the time and place of the hearing on the motion, the supporting papers upon which the motion is based, the relief demanded and the grounds therefor. NY CPLR Rule 2214(a). A motion on notice in an action in the supreme court shall be noticed to be heard in the judicial district where the action is triable or in a county adjoining the county where the action is triable. Unless statute, civil practice rule or local court rule provides otherwise, the motion shall be noticed to be heard before a motion term or, upon order to show cause granted by a justice, before that justice out of court. NY CPLR § 2212(a). Except as provided in NY R UNIF TRIAL CTS § 202.7(d), no motion shall be filed with the court unless there have been served and filed with the motion papers a notice of motion. NY R UNIF TRIAL CTS § 202.7(a)(1).
   b. *Ex parte motions.* A motion in an action in the supreme court that may be made without notice may be made at a motion term or to a justice out of court in any county in the state. NY CPLR § 2212(b).
      i. *KINGS COUNTY.* For more information on submitting a motion ex parte, refer to NY R L KINGS E FIL Doc. 1(G).
      ii. *NEW YORK COUNTY.* For more information on submitting matters ex parte, refer to NY R NY CTY Procedure III and NY R NY CTY E FIL Doc. 2(G).
      iii. *QUEENS COUNTY.* For more information on submitting matters ex parte, refer to NY R L QUEENS EX PARTE Doc. 1.
   c. *Alternative relief.* Relief in the alternative or of several different types may be demanded. NY CPLR Rule 2214(a). The types of relief need not be related. In one motion, for example, the defendant can seek to dismiss the plaintiff's claim for lack of jurisdiction, to get an extension of time to answer, to require the plaintiff to join X as a party, and to quash a disclosure subpoena served in behalf of the plaintiff on a nonparty witness. So doing, the movant must of course specify all of these items of relief in the notice of motion, and the grounds for them, and the supporting papers must contain the entire proof requisite to the items of relief sought. NY CPLR Rule 2214(Practice Commentary, C2214:4).
   d. *General relief.* It is common practice to include at the end of the relief request in the notice of motion a so-called "general relief" clause. This is merely a few words to cover the possibility that the relief appropriate to what the movant proves was not specifically asked for, but is close enough to enable the court to grant it. After stating the specific relief desired, the lawyer will often add something like: and for such other, further, or different relief as this court may deem just and proper. NY CPLR Rule 2214(Practice Commentary, C2214:5).
   e. *Motion in improper form.* If the court finds it appropriate in the interests of justice, it may convert a motion into a special proceeding, or vice-versa, upon such terms as may be just, including the payment of fees and costs. NY CPLR § 103(c).
   f. *Order to show cause.* An order to show cause is basically only a substitute for a notice of motion. An ordinary notice of motion merely notifies the recipient that a motion is being made for specified relief. The burden of proof is on the movant. Although in most cases it is just as innocent as an ordinary notice of motion, the order to show cause gets its name by directing the recipient to "show cause" why the particular relief being asked for should not be granted. It sounds as if the burden of proof is being shifted to the recipient. It isn't. It specifies the time and place of the hearing on the application but when the hearing comes on, the burden of proof is where it always is on a motion: on the movant. SIEGEL-NYPRAC § 248.
      i. The CPLR says nothing more about an order to show cause than that it may be used "in a proper case", which leaves it entirely to the judge's discretion to determine what a proper case is. Any fact suggesting a problem as to any of the items listed above would be sufficient to invoke judicial discretion and justify the show cause procedure, which is in fact liberally used. SIEGEL-NYPRAC § 248.
      ii. An order to show cause against a state body or officers must be served in addition to service upon the defendant or respondent state body or officers upon the attorney general by delivery to an assistant attorney general at an office of the attorney general in the county in which venue of the action is designated or if there is no office of the attorney general in such county, at the office of the attorney general nearest such county. NY CPLR Rule 2214(d).

iii. *BRONX COUNTY.* For information on submitting an order to show cause, refer to NY R BRONX E FIL R Doc. 2 and NY R BRONX LEG SUP Doc. 1.

iv. *ERIE COUNTY.* For information on submitting an order to show cause, refer to NY R ERIE E FIL Doc. 3(VI).

v. *KINGS COUNTY.* For information on submitting an order to show cause, refer to NY R L KINGS E FIL Doc. 1(F).

vi. *NEW YORK COUNTY.* For information on submitting an order to show cause, refer to NY R NY CTY E FIL Doc. 2(F).

vii. *ONONDAGA COUNTY.* For information on submitting an order to show cause, refer to NY R ONDGA E FIL Protocol(B)(10) and NY R ONDGA E FIL Protocol(J).

g. *Motions before preliminary conference.* Motions in actions to which NY R UNIF TRIAL CTS § 202.12 is applicable made after the preliminary conference has been scheduled may be denied unless there is shown good cause why such relief is warranted before the preliminary conference is held. NY R UNIF TRIAL CTS § 202.12(h).

h. *ALBANY COUNTY: Good faith effort to resolve.* Prior to the submission of a notice of motion relating to disclosure or a bill of particulars, the parties must make a good faith effort to resolve the matter in question and submit an affirmation attesting to this good faith effort. NY R 3 JD SUP Doc. 1(B).

i. *NEW YORK COUNTY: Documents with motions.* Counsel must attach to motion papers copies of all pleadings and other documents as required by the CPLR and as necessary for an informed decision on the motion. Documents in a foreign language shall be properly translated. NY R NY CTY J RUL Rule 14(a).

j. *NEW YORK COUNTY: Motions in multiple cases made together.* On occasion, attorneys may wish to make a motion in more than one case on a single set of papers. In such cases, by definition consolidation will not have been directed since consolidation signifies the combination of more than one case into a single one with a single caption and index number and ending in a single judgment. NY R NY CTY Procedure II(B). For more information on motions made with the same papers, refer to NY R NY CTY Procedure II(A).

k. *QUEENS COUNTY: Motion sequence numbers.* A motion sequence number is required for all E-filed motions. After a motion is E-filed, please consult the e-courts website within twenty-four (24) to forty-eight (48) hours to obtain the sequence number. The Confirmation Notice of E-filing MUST indicate the sequence number of any motion submitted at the Centralized Motion Part calendar call. NY R L QUEENS E-FILE Doc. 1(H)(5).

2. *Motion to correct pleadings*

a. *Motion for more definite statement.* If a pleading is so vague or ambiguous that a party cannot reasonably be required to frame a response he may move for a more definite statement. NY CPLR Rule 3024(a).

i. *Generally.* A motion for a more definite statement may be used by the defendant against the complaint and by the plaintiff against a counterclaim, for example, but it's not available to the plaintiff if the answer contains no counterclaim because in that case the plaintiff doesn't have to respond to the answer. SIEGEL-NYPRAC § 230.

ii. *Burden.* The movant's burden is to show that the pleading, whether it states a claim or not, is so jumbled or disorderly that she "cannot reasonably be required to frame a response." If the pleading is answerable and what the movant is really seeking is an amplification of it, the motion for a more definite statement will be denied and the movant remitted to seek a bill of particulars. SIEGEL-NYPRAC § 230; State v. New York Movers Tariff Bureau, Inc., 48 Misc. 2d 225, 254, 264 N.Y.S.2d 931, 963 (Sup. Ct. 1965).

iii. *Waiver.* The service of an answer waives the right to move for a more definite statement, since answering establishes answerability. SIEGEL-NYPRAC § 230; Albemarle Theatre, Inc. v. Bayberry Realty Corp., 27 A.D.2d 172, 177-78, 277 N.Y.S.2d 505, 512 (1967).

b. *Motion to strike scandalous or prejudicial matter.* A party may move to strike any scandalous or prejudicial matter unnecessarily inserted in a pleading. NY CPLR Rule 3024(b). The motion under NY CPLR Rule 3024(b) is the sole surviving motion to "strike" under the CPLR. The various others of prior law are gone. NY CPLR Rule 3024(Practice Commentaries, C3024:4).

i. "Prejudice" by itself has little meaning here because most of what a party pleads is intended to prejudice the other side. The key words are "unnecessarily inserted", which makes relevancy the measuring rod. SIEGEL-NYPRAC § 230. Matter directly relevant to the claim stays in. If something is prejudicial or scandalous, while only indirectly relevant at best, it has been held that it may be stricken out even if it can later be made to appear sufficiently relevant at the trial to be admitted into evidence. SIEGEL-NYPRAC § 230; Schachter v. Massachusetts Protective Ass'n, 30 A.D.2d 540, 540, 291 N.Y.S.2d 128, 129-30 (1968).

3. *Oppositions.* In the absence of statutory provision or court rule, a motion ordinarily does not require a written answer, although an adverse party may be permitted to file an answer in opposition to the showing made in the motion or its supporting affidavits. AMJUR MOTIONS § 26. When a party files a motion and the opposing party fails to respond, the court may construe such failure to respond as non-opposition to the motion or an admission that the motion was meritorious, may take the facts alleged in the motion as true, and may grant the motion if the relief requested appears to be justified. However, the severity of such a result demands that a court impose it only with great caution. AMJUR MOTIONS § 28.

4. *Effect of defendant's appearance.* Subject to the provisions of NY CPLR Rule 320(c), an appearance of the defendant is equivalent to personal service of the summons upon him, unless an objection to jurisdiction under NY CPLR Rule 3211(a)(8) is asserted by motion or in the answer as provided in NY CPLR Rule 3211. NY CPLR Rule 320(b).
   a. *Appearance not conferring jurisdiction; Limited appearance.* When the court's jurisdiction is not based upon personal service on the defendant, an appearance is not equivalent to personal service upon the defendant:
      i. In a case specified in NY CPLR § 314(3), if jurisdiction is based solely upon a levy on defendant's property within the state pursuant to an order of attachment; or
      ii. In any other case specified in NY CPLR § 314, if an objection to jurisdiction under NY CPLR Rule 3211(a)(8) or NY CPLR Rule 3211(a)(9), or both, is asserted by motion or in the answer as provided in NY CPLR Rule 3211, unless the defendant proceeds with the defense after asserting the objection to jurisdiction and the objection is not ultimately sustained. NY CPLR Rule 320(c).
   b. *Effect on publication of summons.* Where the defendant appears during the period of publication of a summons against him, the service by publication shall be deemed completed by the appearance. NY CPLR Rule 320(d).

5. *Governing law.* The civil practice law and rules (NY CPLR § 101, et seq.) shall govern the procedure in civil judicial proceedings in all courts of the state and before all judges, except where the procedure is regulated by inconsistent statute. The civil practice law and rules shall succeed the civil practice act and rules of civil practice and shall be deemed substituted therefor throughout the statutes and rules of the state. NY CPLR § 101. The civil practice law and rules shall be liberally construed to secure the just, speedy and inexpensive determination of every civil judicial proceeding. NY CPLR § 104.
   a. *Uniform trial court rules.* The uniform civil rules for the Supreme Court and County Court (NY R UNIF TRIAL CTS § 202.1, et seq.) shall be applicable to civil actions and proceedings in the Supreme Court and the County Court. NY R UNIF TRIAL CTS § 202.1(a). The provisions of the uniform rules shall be construed consistent with the Civil Practice Law and Rules (CPLR), and matters not covered by the uniform rules shall be governed by the CPLR. NY R UNIF TRIAL CTS § 202.1(d).
   b. *Local rules.* Local court rules, not inconsistent with law or with uniform civil rules for the Supreme Court and County Court (NY R UNIF TRIAL CTS § 202.1, et seq.), shall comply with Part 9 of the Rules of the Chief Judge (NY R CHIEF J § 9.1). NY R UNIF TRIAL CTS § 202.1(c).
   c. *Official forms.* The state administrator shall have the power to adopt, amend and rescind an appendix of forms. Forms adopted pursuant to NY CPLR § 107 shall be sufficient under the civil practice law and rules and shall illustrate the simplicity and brevity of statement which the civil practice law and rules contemplate. NY CPLR § 107.

6. *Rules of the commercial division.* [Editor's note: certain types of civil cases or civil cases meeting certain monetary thresholds that are filed in the state of New York must be filed in the Commercial Division of the New York Supreme Courts. Rules governing practice in the commercial division are found in NY R UNIF TRIAL CTS § 202.70]. Cases which must be filed in the commercial division are listed below. For more information, refer to NY R UNIF TRIAL CTS § 202.70.
   a. *Monetary thresholds.* Except as set forth in NY R UNIF TRIAL CTS § 202.70(b), the monetary thresholds of the Commercial Division, exclusive of punitive damages, interests, costs, disbursements and counsel fees claimed, are established as follows: (1) Albany County, fifty thousand dollars ($50,000); (2) Eighth Judicial District, one hundred thousand dollars ($100,000); (3) Kings County, one hundred fifty thousand dollars ($150,000); (4) Nassau County, two hundred thousand dollars ($200,000); (5) New York County, five hundred thousand dollars ($500,000); (6) Onondaga County, fifty thousand dollars ($50,000); (7) Queens County, one hundred thousand dollars ($100,000); (8) Seventh Judicial District, fifty thousand dollars ($50,000); (9) Suffolk County, one hundred thousand dollars ($100,000); and (10) Westchester County, one hundred thousand dollars ($100,000). NY R UNIF TRIAL CTS § 202.70(a).
      i. *ALBANY COUNTY.* The Commercial Division of the Albany County Supreme Court exercises jurisdiction over selected business and commercial disputes in which the amount at issue generally involves damage claims in a

minimum amount of fifty thousand dollars ($50,000) as well as claims for unspecified amounts where the value of the commercial asset(s) in dispute exceeds fifty thousand dollars ($50,000). A separate publication promulgating the rules and criteria relating to the filing and management of Commercial Court cases in this part may be obtained from the Albany County Supreme Court Clerk's Office. A section of the Uniform Civil Rules for the Supreme Court and County Court sets forth statewide rules. NY R 3 JD SUP Doc. 1(E).

ii. *BRONX COUNTY.* The monetary threshold for commercial cases in Bronx County will be seventy-five thousand dollars ($75,000). All other parameters including the type of matters that will be heard are contained within the Rules of the Commercial Division of the Supreme Court (NY R UNIF TRIAL CTS § 202.70). NY R BRONX FIL R Doc. 12.

iii. *NEW YORK COUNTY.* The monetary threshold in the New York County Commercial Division, which is generally applicable, is an amount in controversy of five hundred thousand dollars ($500,000) or more (exclusive of punitive damages, interest, costs, disbursements, and counsel fees). If the case is designated a commercial one and the Addendum is submitted, the clerk will review the pleadings to determine whether the amount in controversy in the case meets the monetary threshold or whether an exception to the threshold applies. NY R NY CTY Procedure IA(B). For more information on assigning a case to the commercial division in New York County, refer to NY R NY CTY Procedure IA(B).

b. *Commercial cases.* Actions in which the principal claims involve or consist of the following will be heard in the Commercial Division provided that the monetary threshold is met or equitable or declaratory relief is sought:

i. Breach of contract or fiduciary duty, fraud, misrepresentation, business tort (e.g., unfair competition), or statutory and/or common law violation where the breach or violation is alleged to arise out of business dealings (e.g., sales of assets or securities; corporate restructuring; partnership, shareholder, joint venture, and other business agreements; trade secrets; restrictive covenants; and employment agreements not including claims that principally involve alleged discriminatory practices);

ii. Transactions governed by the Uniform Commercial Code (exclusive of those concerning individual cooperative or condominium units);

iii. Transactions involving commercial real property, including Yellowstone injunctions and excluding actions for the payment of rent only;

iv. Shareholder derivative actions—without consideration of the monetary threshold;

v. Commercial class actions—without consideration of the monetary threshold;

vi. Business transactions involving or arising out of dealings with commercial banks and other financial institutions;

vii. Internal affairs of business organizations;

viii. Malpractice by accountants or actuaries, and legal malpractice arising out of representation in commercial matters;

ix. Environmental insurance coverage;

x. Commercial insurance coverage (e.g., directors and officers, errors and omissions, and business interruption coverage);

xi. Dissolution of corporations, partnerships, limited liability companies, limited liability partnerships and joint ventures—without consideration of the monetary threshold; and

xii. Applications to stay or compel arbitration and affirm or disaffirm arbitration awards and related injunctive relief pursuant to Article 75 of the New York Civil Practice Law and Rules (NY CPLR § 7501, et seq.) involving any of the foregoing enumerated commercial issues. Where the applicable arbitration agreement provides for the arbitration to be heard outside the United States, the monetary threshold set forth in NY R UNIF TRIAL CTS § 202.70(a) shall not apply. NY R UNIF TRIAL CTS § 202.70(b).

c. *Non-commercial cases.* The following will not be heard in the Commercial Division even if the monetary threshold is met:

i. Suits to collect professional fees;

ii. Cases seeking a declaratory judgment as to insurance coverage for personal injury or property damage;

iii. Residential real estate disputes, including landlord-tenant matters, and commercial real estate disputes involving the payment of rent only;

iv. Home improvement contracts involving residential properties consisting of one to four residential units or individual units in any residential building, including cooperative or condominium units;

v. Proceedings to enforce a judgment regardless of the nature of the underlying case;

vi. First-party insurance claims and actions by insurers to collect premiums or rescind non-commercial policies; and

vii. Attorney malpractice actions except as otherwise provided in NY R UNIF TRIAL CTS § 202.70(b)(8). NY R UNIF TRIAL CTS § 202.70(c).

d. For more information on the Commercial Division, refer to NY R UNIF TRIAL CTS § 202.70.

D. Documents

1. *Documents for moving party*

a. *Required documents*

i. *Notice of motion, order to show cause, or affidavit on ex parte motion.* The notice of motion shall be substantially in the form found in NY R UNIF TRIAL CTS § 202.7(b). NY R UNIF TRIAL CTS § 202.7(b). The supporting papers should be referred to in the notice of motion. SIEGEL-NYPRAC § 246. The court in a proper case may grant an order to show cause, to be served in lieu of a notice of motion. NY CPLR Rule 2214(d). An ex parte motion shall be accompanied by an affidavit stating the result of any prior motion for similar relief and specifying the new facts, if any, that were not previously shown. NY CPLR Rule 2217(b).

- *Request for oral argument.* A party requesting oral argument shall set forth such request in its notice of motion or in its order to show cause or on the first page of the answering papers, as the case may be. Where all parties to a motion request oral argument, oral argument shall be granted unless the court shall determine it to be unnecessary. Where a motion is brought on by order to show cause, the court may set forth in the order that oral argument is required on the return date of the motion. NY R UNIF TRIAL CTS § 202.8(d).

ii. *Motion.* Refer to the General Requirements section of this document for information on the notice of motion and motion.

iii. *Request for judicial intervention.* At any time after service of process, a party may file a request for judicial intervention. Except as provided in NY R UNIF TRIAL CTS § 202.6(b), in an action not yet assigned to a judge, the court shall not accept for filing a notice of motion, order to show cause, or application for ex parte order, unless such notice or application is accompanied by a request for judicial intervention. NY R UNIF TRIAL CTS § 202.6(a).

- *BRONX COUNTY.* Generally, the Request For Judicial Intervention, commonly referred to as an "RJI", is required to be filed in any action where the assignment of a Justice is required. The RJI sets forth the information which is entered into the court system's database. It must be completely and accurately filled out. The full caption, as stated on the Summons, must be set forth. Use of terms "et al." and "etc." are not permitted. Only one (1) RJI may be filed in each action. Either a self represented litigant or an attorney must sign the affirmation at the end of the form. Once completed, the RJI must be filed in duplicate. Except in the case of an ex-parte application, the RJI must also be served together with the accompanying application upon all parties. Proof of accuracy of the index number must accompany the RJI. Check the Fee Schedule[. . .]for any applicable filing fees. NY R BRONX FIL R Doc. 2.
- *KINGS COUNTY.* An RJI with the relevant required addendum in a NYSCEF case shall be submitted via NYSCEF. Once e-filed, the RJI and any accompanying document will be forwarded to the relevant support office for random assignment of the case and processing of the document. A filer or counsel need not appear (as to Proposed Orders to Show Cause, however, see below). A copy of the pleadings must be submitted only if the document has not previously been e-filed. If the RJI seeks intervention with regard to a document that is intended for review by a Justice, such as a motion, a working copy of the RJI must be submitted with the working copy of the motion and the NYSCEF Confirmation Notice. NY R L KINGS E FIL Doc. 1(C).
- *NEW YORK COUNTY.* To obtain the assignment of an IAS Justice to a case, a Request for Judicial Intervention (cost ninety-five dollars ($95)) must be filed, with NYSCEF in an e-filed case or in paper in an authorized hard-copy one. A no-fee RJI, which will generally result in the referral of an application to an Ex Parte Justice, is also required with regard to certain kinds of applications for which, prior to 2011, no RJI was required. NY R NY CTY Procedure I(C). A "fillable" form RJI is available on-line. The form must be filed in duplicate in hard-copy cases. NY R NY CTY Procedure IA(A)(1). The filer of an RJI must check off a box identifying the type of case at issue. Where the RJI seeks judicial assignment, this designation will

bring about a random assignment of the case by computer to a Justice handling cases of that type. NY R NY CTY Procedure IA(A)(1). The RJI and any addendum can be completed and submitted electronically in an e-filed case. NY R NY CTY Procedure II(A). The RJI shall be marked to reflect the existence of any "related case" as explained on the "Commencement of Cases" page under "Case Processing" on the court's website. NY R NY CTY Procedure II(A); NY R NY CTY E FIL Doc. 2(C).

- *ONONDAGA COUNTY.* The RJI will be submitted via the NYSCEF system along with any required RJI addendum forms. When the RJI is filed and the fee paid online, the Onondaga County Clerk's Office will electronically forward the RJI and any accompanying documents to the Onondaga Supreme Court Clerk's Office for assignment and processing. Counsel will receive notification of judge assignment via the NYSCEF system. NY R ONDGA E FIL Protocol(B)(3).
- *QUEENS COUNTY.* A Request for Judicial Intervention ("RJI") in an E-filed case shall be submitted via the E-filing System. When the RJI is approved, filed and paid for on-line, it will be forwarded to the relevant back office for random assignment of the case and processing of the document. In the case of RJIs seeking assignment to the Commercial Division, the filer must submit therewith, a Commercial Addendum as required by the standards for assignment of cases to the Commercial Division. NY R L QUEENS E-FILE Doc. 1(F).

iv. *Proof of service.* In addition to complying with the provisions of NY CPLR Rule 2101, every paper filed in court shall have annexed thereto appropriate proof of service on all parties where required. NY R UNIF TRIAL CTS § 202.5(a).

- *QUEENS COUNTY.* With regard to service of a motion/petition on notice in an E-filed action, NY CPLR Rule 2214(b) and NY R UNIF TRIAL CTS § 202.5-b(f) applies. Where required, proof of service shall be filed on-line as a separate document. NY R L QUEENS E-FILE Doc. 1(H)(3).

v. *ALBANY COUNTY: Additional required documents*

- *Affirmation of good faith effort.* The parties must[. . .]submit an affirmation attesting to [their good faith effort to resolve the matter]. The affirmation of good faith effort to resolve the issues raised by the motion shall indicate the time, place and nature of the consultation and the issues discussed and any resolutions, or shall indicate good cause why no such conferral with counsel for opposing parties was held. An assigned justice or judge may dismiss a motion for failure to demonstrate that such effort was made with leave to renew the motion after such effort has been demonstrated. NY R 3 JD SUP Doc. 1(B).

b. *Supplemental documents*

i. *Supporting evidence; Exhibits.* The main supporting papers on a motion are affidavits, but any relevant exhibits, documents, depositions, etc., are also includible. SIEGEL-NYPRAC § 246.

- *Affidavits accompanying motion.* Affidavits shall be for a statement of the relevant facts. NY R UNIF TRIAL CTS § 202.8(c).
- *Foreign language documents.* Where an affidavit or exhibit annexed to a paper served or filed is in a foreign language, it shall be accompanied by an English translation and an affidavit by the translator stating his qualifications and that the translation is accurate. NY CPLR Rule 2101(b).
- *Statement of attorney in lieu of affidavit.* The statement of an attorney admitted to practice in the courts of the state, or of a physician, osteopath or dentist, authorized by law to practice in the state, who is not a party to an action, when subscribed and affirmed by him to be true under the penalties of perjury, may be served or filed in the action in lieu of and with the same force and effect as an affidavit. NY CPLR Rule 2106.
- *NEW YORK COUNTY: Form of presented exhibits.* Exhibits should be tabbed and be legible; a typed version of any exhibit that is difficult to read should be submitted with the original. Exhibits printed on both sides of the page should be bound and tabbed on the side. NY R NY CTY J RUL Rule 14(a).
- *QUEENS COUNTY.* Attorneys submitting exhibits to the court on E-file cases shall make each exhibit a separate, labeled attachment to an affidavit/affirmation. NY R L QUEENS E-FILE Doc. 1(H)(4).

ii. *Brief.* Briefs shall be for a statement of the relevant law. NY R UNIF TRIAL CTS § 202.8(c).

iii. *Notice to produce papers not in possession of the court.* If a paper relied on by the movant is in the possession of the other side, it may be demanded of that side with a notice to produce it at the hearing. Where such papers are in the possession of an adverse party, they shall be produced by him at the hearing on notice served with the motion papers. NY CPLR Rule 2214(Practice Commentary, C2214:23).

iv. *Filing fees.* The County Clerk shall require the payment of any applicable statutory fees, or an order of the Court waiving payment of such fees, before accepting a paper for filing. NY R UNIF TRIAL CTS § 202.5(d)(1). For information on filing fees, if any, refer to NY CPLR § 8001, et seq.

- *ALBANY COUNTY.* In general, any filing subsequent to the commencement of an action which is designated as a motion or cross-motion requires the payment of a filing fee to the County Clerk's Office prior to submission to the Supreme Court Clerk's Office for referral to the assigned justice. The fee is assessed regardless of whether an application is made by notice of motion, order to show cause or ex parte. No fee will be charged upon the filing of a motion for poor person status in conjunction with an application which serves to commence an action or special proceeding. In the event a motion is received by the court unaccompanied by proof of payment to the County Clerk, the Supreme Court Clerk's Office will contact the submitting party to advise that the application will be held pending receipt of the filing fee only until the return date of the motion. If proof of payment is not submitted to the Supreme Court Clerk's Office by the return date (ex parte applications will be held ten (10) days), the papers will be returned by mail with a notification that the motion has been removed from the court's calendar and that it must be re-noticed and re-filed with the court along with the requisite filing fee. Inquiries concerning the applicability of the motion fee to a proposed filing may be directed to the Supreme Court Clerk's Office. NY R 3 JD SUP Doc. 1(B).
- *BRONX COUNTY.* In accordance with the new civil fee schedule set forth in Article 80 of the C.P.L.R. (NY CPLR § 8001, et seq.), effective July 14, 2003, all motions, and cross motions must be approved in Room 217 prior to payment of said fees in the County Clerk's Office, Room 118. NY R BRONX FIL R Doc. 8. The motion fee [must be] paid for via NYSCEF by credit/debit card. NY R BRONX E FIL R Doc. 1(1).
- *ERIE COUNTY.* Payment for fee-bearing NYSCEF documents must be made online via credit or debit card (American Express, MasterCard or Visa) at the time of submission. NY R ERIE E FIL Doc. 3(III)(E).
- *KINGS COUNTY.* The motion must be filed with NYSCEF and the motion fee paid. NY R L KINGS E FIL Doc. 1(D). Court fees in NYSCEF cases must be paid via NYSCEF by a credit or bank card (MasterCard, Visa, or American Express). Fees are no longer accepted in person in the Kings County Clerk's Office in NYSCEF cases. NY R L KINGS E FIL Doc. 1(B)(6).
- *NEW YORK COUNTY.* A motion fee must be paid on motions made in writing by notice of motion, order to show cause or ex parte after the commencement of an action. For this purpose, the term "action" shall mean any application to the court that requires the assignment of an index number, regardless of whether a formal pleading is filed. Applications or motions that commence an action and for which an index number fee must be paid require no motion fee. [A]ny motions made after the initial applications in these situations would require payment of the motion fee. A motion that is the initial application in a case commenced by the filing of a summons and complaint would require a motion fee since the filing of the summons and complaint rather than the application itself would require the purchase of an index number. NY R NY CTY Procedure II(A). In e-filed cases the motion fee must be paid when the documents are filed. Payment is made on-line by Visa, Mastercard, or American Express credit or bank card. NY R NY CTY Procedure II(A); NY R NY CTY E FIL Doc. 2(B)(5).
- *ONONDAGA COUNTY.* Court fees in e-filed cases must be paid online with the NYSCEF system using a credit card. The document is not considered to have been filed until payment of the fee has been tendered. NY R ONDGA E FIL Protocol(B)(2). Fees must be paid on all cross motions. NY R ONDGA E FIL Protocol(B)(9)(e).
- *QUEENS COUNTY.* The Motion Support Office does not receive, forward or process any fees or waiver of fees. All applications requiring payment of statutory fees or waiver of fees must be sent directly to the Queens County Clerk's office. NY R L QUEENS MOT SUP Doc. 1. Court fees (e.g., RJI fee, motion fee) in E-filed cases may be paid for on-line using a credit card. Papers may also be filed with the E-file system and the fee may be paid at the County Clerk's Office. In the latter case, the paper is not considered to have been filed until payment of the fee has been tendered. NY R L QUEENS E-FILE Doc. 1(E)(1). The motion/petition shall be filed on-line and the fee paid for either on-line by credit card or by the "Pay at the County Clerk's Office" option. NY R L QUEENS E-FILE Doc. 1(H)(1).

v. *Working copies.* The court may require the parties to provide working copies of documents filed electronically. In such event, each working copy shall include, firmly affixed thereto, a copy of a confirmation notice in a form prescribed by the Chief Administrator. NY R UNIF TRIAL CTS § 202.5-b(d)(5).

- *BRONX COUNTY.* After papers on motions have been e-filed, working copies thereof, with Confirmation

Notice firmly attached as the back page facing out, must be submitted. (Each document or group of documents that is separately bound shall bear a Confirmation Notice.) Working copies lacking the Notice will not be accepted. WORKING COPIES OF MOTION PAPERS MUST BE SUBMITTED NO LATER THAN 4:45 P.M. ON THE RETURN DATE IN THE MOTION SUPPORT OFFICE (ROOM 217) AS EXPLAINED in NY R BRONX E FIL R Doc. 1(4). If an attorney has failed to submit required working copies on or before the return date, the motion will be transmitted as is to the Justice for such action as the Justice finds appropriate. Attorneys may submit working copies on motions by mail or overnight delivery. Any such submission shall be sent in a timely manner to the Motion Support Office (Room 217) and be conspicuously marked on the outside "NYSCEF Matter"; lack of such marking may delay processing. NY R BRONX E FIL R Doc. 1(4)(a).

- *ERIE COUNTY.* Electronically filed documents subject to review and processing by the Part Clerk do not require a working copy unless otherwise directed or provided for in IAS Part Rules. NY R UNIF TRIAL CTS § 202.5-b(d)(4), any working copy submitted shall include, as a cover page firmly fastened thereto, a copy of the Confirmation Notice generated by the NYSCEF site at the time of filing. Please consult the individual Justice's Part Rules and/or consult with the Judge's chambers to determine whether and how working copies are to be provided. Working copies will not be printed or delivered by the Erie County Clerk or the Chief Clerk of the Courts or any of their personnel to chambers. The official record of a document in an electronically filed case is the document filed via the NYSCEF system. Working copies are intended only for use by the Justice. The Court will discard all working copies after the Justice has finished with them. Thus, in the event that counsel fails to file a document via the NYSCEF system, the document will not be part of the court record. NY R ERIE E FIL Doc. 3(III)(O); NY R ERIE E FIL Doc. 3(V)(E).
- *KINGS COUNTY.* No courtesy copies of motion papers are required by the Court, except as may be required for electronic filing or by the Judge's Part Rules. In tort cases against the City of New York, courtesy copies shall be supplied to the Corporation Counsel's office in Brooklyn. NY R L KINGS Pt. C, Rule 5. Unless otherwise directed by the Court or as described herein, and with the exceptions listed below, in all NYSCEF cases in which an RJI has been filed, working copies of e-filed documents that are intended for judicial review must be submitted to the court. Working copies are not required of documents that are only processed by a support office (e.g. preliminary conference request, note of issue). Working copies shall include exhibit tabs and backs; for motion papers, the motion sequence number and the return date and part. The confirmation notice with the motion sequence number on it should be the back page of the motion facing out. In addition, the filer of a working copy must firmly bind thereto, with the back page facing out, a copy of the Confirmation Notice that was generated by NYSCEF when that document was efiled. Working copies that are submitted without the related Confirmation Notice will not be accepted. NY R L KINGS E FIL Doc. 1(B)(7); NY R L KINGS E FIL Doc. 1(D). WORKING COPIES OF MOTION PAPERS MUST BE SUBMITTED IN THE MOTION SUPPORT OFFICE (ROOM 227) AS EXPLAINED HEREIN. THEY MUST NOT BE DELIVERED TO THE PART OR CHAMBERS, EXCEPT WHERE THE INDIVIDUAL JUSTICE'S PART RULES PROVIDE OTHERWISE; DOING SO WILL CAUSE ADMINISTRATIVE CONFUSION AND POSSIBLE MISPLACEMENT OF PAPERS. Any such submission shall be sent in a timely manner (kindly review individual Justice's rules) and be conspicuously marked on the outside "NYSCEF Matter;" lack of such marking may delay processing. NY R L KINGS E FIL Doc. 1(D).
- *NEW YORK COUNTY.* Some Justices require that working copies of e-filed motion papers be submitted. See the E-filing Protocol for information on the many Parts that do not require working copies. Where required, working copies of the moving documents and all other documents on the motion or application shall be submitted to the Motion Submission Part Courtroom (Room 130) on, but not before, the final return date. A Confirmation Notice from the NYSCEF system, which is generated when a document is e-filed, shall be firmly affixed, as the back page facing out, to each separate working copy or group of such copies. NY R NY CTY Procedure II(A) NY R NY CTY E FIL Doc. 2(B)(5)(a); NY R NY CTY J RUL Rule 14(a). For more information on working copies, including which parts don't require them, refer to NY R NY CTY E FIL Doc. 2(B)(6).
- *ONONDAGA COUNTY.* Any courtesy "working" copies, if required (see NY R ONDGA E FIL Protocol(B)(7)), must be provided directly to the assigned justice. NY R ONDGA E FIL Protocol(B)(9)(e). For information as to whether or not an Onondaga Supreme Court Justice requires working (courtesy) copies of e-filed documents, please consult the Onondaga County Individual E-filing Rules. NY R ONDGA E FIL Protocol(B)(7)(a). The Supreme Court Clerk's Office and the Onondaga County Clerk's Office will

NOT accept the working copies. Working copies must be sent directly to the assigned justice's chambers. NY R ONDGA E FIL Protocol(B)(7)(b). A copy of the Confirmation Notice, generated by the NYSCEF system at the time a document is e-filed, must be attached to every working copy provided to chambers. If the Confirmation Notice is missing, the copy will not be accepted. NY R ONDGA E FIL Protocol(B)(7)(c). Courtesy copies do not become part of the official court record as maintained by the Onondaga County Clerk's Office and will be destroyed by chambers at the disposition of the case. In the event that counsel fails to file a document via NYSCEF, the document will not be part of the court record. NY R ONDGA E FIL Protocol(B)(7)(d).

- *QUEENS COUNTY.* Working copies of E-Filed notices of motion/notices of petition are NOT to be sent to the Motion Support Office. They must be brought to the calendar call in the judge's part. NY R L QUEENS MOT SUP Doc. 1. Unless otherwise directed or authorized by the court, counsel should file papers with the E-file system first and thereafter deliver a working copy to at the calendar call of the Centralized Motion Part or Assigned Justice in accordance with individual Part Rules. NY R L QUEENS E-FILE Doc. 1(E)(4). On the return date of a motion that has been E-filed, the movant must provide the Centralized Motion Part (CMP) with a working copy of the entire motion including the notice of motion with sequence number and all of the attached exhibits. The motion must have the confirmation of filing firmly affixed to the back of the papers (facing outward). The confirmation of filing is a separate notice from the payment notice and will say confirmation clearly across the top of the page. NY R L QUEENS E-FILE Doc. 1(H)(2)(a). The motion or Order to Show Cause must have clearly written across its face the words "Working Copy," it must also have the assigned Judge's name, motion sequence number and calendar number—which may be obtained from the posted calendar outside courtroom on the return date of the motion. A confirmation of filing must attached thereto. Working copies of e-filed Orders to Show Cause must contain a copy of the signed order and all supporting papers. NY R L QUEENS E-FILE Doc. 1(H)(2)(c). The Confirmation Notice must be an updated version that indicates the sequence number of the motion being submitted at the CMP calendar call. WORKING COPIES WITHOUT A CONFIRMATION NOTICE WILL NOT BE ACCEPTED. NY R L QUEENS E-FILE Doc. 1(H)(7).

vi. *Statement of authorization in electronic filing cases.* A filing agent (other than one employed by a governmental entity) shall e-file a statement of authorization from counsel of record in an action, in a form approved by the Chief Administrator, prior to or together with the first e-filing in that action by the agent on behalf of that counsel. NY R UNIF TRIAL CTS § 202.5-b(d)(1)(i).

vii. *ERIE COUNTY: Additional supplemental documents*

- *Notice of hard copy submission in e-filed case.* In accordance with NY R UNIF TRIAL CTS § 202.5-b(d), the County Clerk shall refuse to accept for filing, hard copy papers filed to an action subject to electronic filing unless hard copy filing is permitted by the Uniform Rules or NY R ERIE E FIL Doc. 3 and the papers bear a completed Notice of Hard Copy Submission—E-Filed Case form. NY R ERIE E FIL Doc. 3(III)(D).

viii. *KINGS COUNTY: Additional supplemental documents*

- *Forms when filing in hard copy.* An attorney who certifies in good faith that he or she lacks the equipment or knowledge needed to e-file and have no staff member or employee under his or her direction who has such knowledge and equipment may opt out of participation in e-filing in a mandatory case by filing a "Notice of Opt-Out from Participation in Action Subject to Mandatory Electronic Filing" form EFM-2 with the Clerk. NY R L KINGS E FIL Doc. 1(A)(2). Where in accordance with the E-Filing Rules a party submits a document in hard copy in an e-filed case (principally, a document submitted by a nonparticipating party (e.g., an attorney) in a consensual case, an emergency filing made in accordance with the Mandatory E-Filing Rules, and any document filed with the court in hard copy by an attorney who has opted out of participation in mandatory e-filing, the document must bear the back page facing out, a "Notice of Hard Copy Submission—E-Filed Cases" form EFM-3. NY R L KINGS E FIL Doc. 1(B)(3).

ix. *NEW YORK COUNTY: Additional supplemental documents*

- *Notice of hard copy submission.* Where in accordance with the E-Filing Rules an attorney or an unrepresented litigant who is participating in e-filing submits a document in hard copy in an e-filed case, the document must bear, as the back page facing out, a Notice of Hard-Copy Submission—E-Filed Case (a form available in the "Forms" section on the NYSCEF website (Form EFM-3) and in the court's back offices). NY R NY CTY E FIL Doc. 2(B)(3). For more information refer to NY R NY CTY E FIL Doc. 2.
- *Unpublished decisions.* Whenever reliance is placed upon a decision or other authority not officially

published or readily available to the New York County Supreme Court, a copy of the case or of pertinent portions of the authority shall be submitted with the motion papers. NY R NY CTY J RUL Rule 14(a).

x. *ONONDAGA COUNTY: Additional supplemental documents*

- *Notice of hard copy submission.* Any papers to be filed with the court in an e-filed case must be filed online with the E-filing system except where a special exemption is granted (e.g., oversized maps, photographs). If such an exemption is granted, Form EFM-3, "Notice of Hard Copy Submission—E-Filed Case," must be attached to such documents forms which are not filed on line. Also, Form EFM-4 "Notice of Hard Copy Exhibit Filing" must be completed and uploaded to the action's e-file. Both of these forms may be found on the NYSCEF website. NY R ONDGA E FIL Protocol(B)(4).

xi. *QUEENS COUNTY: Additional supplemental documents*

- *Notice of hard copy submission.* Any party opting out of the e-filing system must have a "Notice of Hard Copy Submission" firmly affixed to the back of the papers. NY R L QUEENS E-FILE Doc. 1(H)(2)(f).

2. *Documents for opposing party*

a. *Required documents*

i. *Opposition.* Refer to the General Requirements section of this document for information on the opposition.

- *Request for oral argument.* A party requesting oral argument shall set forth such request in its notice of motion or in its order to show cause or on the first page of the answering papers, as the case may be. Where all parties to a motion request oral argument, oral argument shall be granted unless the court shall determine it to be unnecessary. Where a motion is brought on by order to show cause, the court may set forth in the order that oral argument is required on the return date of the motion. NY R UNIF TRIAL CTS § 202.8(d).
- *QUEENS COUNTY: E-filing opposition papers.* E-filed opposition papers and/or reply papers must also be provided to the Centralized Motion Part in the same manner as the moving papers with the confirmation of filing firmly attached to the back of the papers. NY R L QUEENS E-FILE Doc. 1(H)(2)(d).

ii. *Proof of service.* In addition to complying with the provisions of NY CPLR Rule 2101, every paper filed in court shall have annexed thereto appropriate proof of service on all parties where required. NY R UNIF TRIAL CTS § 202.5(a).

b. *Supplemental documents*

i. *Supporting evidence; Exhibits.* The main supporting papers on a motion are affidavits, but any relevant exhibits, documents, depositions, etc., are also includible. SIEGEL-NYPRAC § 246.

- *Affidavits accompanying opposition.* Affidavits shall be for a statement of the relevant facts. NY R UNIF TRIAL CTS § 202.8(c).
- *Foreign language documents.* Where an affidavit or exhibit annexed to a paper served or filed is in a foreign language, it shall be accompanied by an English translation and an affidavit by the translator stating his qualifications and that the translation is accurate. NY CPLR Rule 2101(b).
- *Statement of attorney in lieu of affidavit.* The statement of an attorney admitted to practice in the courts of the state, or of a physician, osteopath or dentist, authorized by law to practice in the state, who is not a party to an action, when subscribed and affirmed by him to be true under the penalties of perjury, may be served or filed in the action in lieu of and with the same force and effect as an affidavit. NY CPLR Rule 2106.
- *NEW YORK COUNTY: Form of presented exhibits.* Exhibits should be tabbed and be legible; a typed version of any exhibit that is difficult to read should be submitted with the original. Exhibits printed on both sides of the page should be bound and tabbed on the side. NY R NY CTY J RUL Rule 14(a).
- *QUEENS COUNTY.* Attorneys submitting exhibits to the court on E-file cases shall make each exhibit a separate, labeled attachment to an affidavit/affirmation. NY R L QUEENS E-FILE Doc. 1(H)(4).

ii. *Brief.* Briefs shall be for a statement of the relevant law. NY R UNIF TRIAL CTS § 202.8(c).

iii. *Filing fees.* The County Clerk shall require the payment of any applicable statutory fees, or an order of the Court waiving payment of such fees, before accepting a paper for filing. NY R UNIF TRIAL CTS § 202.5(d)(1). For information on filing fees, if any, refer to NY CPLR § 8001, et seq.

- *ALBANY COUNTY.* In general, any filing subsequent to the commencement of an action which is designated as a motion or cross-motion requires the payment of a filing fee to the County Clerk's Office

prior to submission to the Supreme Court Clerk's Office for referral to the assigned justice. The fee is assessed regardless of whether an application is made by notice of motion, order to show cause or ex parte. No fee will be charged upon the filing of a motion for poor person status in conjunction with an application which serves to commence an action or special proceeding. In the event a motion is received by the court unaccompanied by proof of payment to the County Clerk, the Supreme Court Clerk's Office will contact the submitting party to advise that the application will be held pending receipt of the filing fee only until the return date of the motion. If proof of payment is not submitted to the Supreme Court Clerk's Office by the return date (ex parte applications will be held ten (10) days), the papers will be returned by mail with a notification that the motion has been removed from the court's calendar and that it must be re-noticed and re-filed with the court along with the requisite filing fee. Inquiries concerning the applicability of the motion fee to a proposed filing may be directed to the Supreme Court Clerk's Office. NY R 3 JD SUP Doc. 1(B).

- *BRONX COUNTY.* In accordance with the new civil fee schedule set forth in Article 80 of the C.P.L.R. (NY CPLR § 8001, et seq.), effective July 14, 2003, all motions, and cross motions must be approved in Room 217 prior to payment of said fees in the County Clerk's Office, Room 118. NY R BRONX FIL R Doc. 8. The motion fee [must be] paid for via NYSCEF by credit/debit card. NY R BRONX E FIL R Doc. 1(1).
- *ERIE COUNTY.* Payment for fee-bearing NYSCEF documents must be made online via credit or debit card (American Express, MasterCard or Visa) at the time of submission. NY R ERIE E FIL Doc. 3(III)(E).
- *KINGS COUNTY.* The motion must be filed with NYSCEF and the motion fee paid. NY R L KINGS E FIL Doc. 1(D). Court fees in NYSCEF cases must be paid via NYSCEF by a credit or bank card (MasterCard, Visa, or American Express). Fees are no longer accepted in person in the Kings County Clerk's Office in NYSCEF cases. NY R L KINGS E FIL Doc. 1(B)(6).
- *NEW YORK COUNTY.* A motion fee must be paid on motions made in writing by notice of motion, order to show cause or ex parte after the commencement of an action. For this purpose, the term "action" shall mean any application to the court that requires the assignment of an index number, regardless of whether a formal pleading is filed. Applications or motions that commence an action and for which an index number fee must be paid require no motion fee. [A]ny motions made after the initial applications in these situations would require payment of the motion fee. A motion that is the initial application in a case commenced by the filing of a summons and complaint would require a motion fee since the filing of the summons and complaint rather than the application itself would require the purchase of an index number. NY R NY CTY Procedure II(A). In e-filed cases the motion fee must be paid when the documents are filed. Payment is made on-line by Visa, Mastercard, or American Express credit or bank card. NY R NY CTY Procedure II(A); NY R NY CTY E FIL Doc. 2(B)(5).
- *ONONDAGA COUNTY.* Court fees in e-filed cases must be paid online with the NYSCEF system using a credit card. The document is not considered to have been filed until payment of the fee has been tendered. NY R ONDGA E FIL Protocol(B)(2). Fees must be paid on all cross motions. NY R ONDGA E FIL Protocol(B)(9)(e).
- *QUEENS COUNTY.* The Motion Support Office does not receive, forward or process any fees or waiver of fees. All applications requiring payment of statutory fees or waiver of fees must be sent directly to the Queens County Clerk's office. NY R L QUEENS MOT SUP Doc. 1. Court fees (e.g., RJI fee, motion fee) in E-filed cases may be paid for on-line using a credit card. Papers may also be filed with the E-file system and the fee may be paid at the County Clerk's Office. In the latter case, the paper is not considered to have been filed until payment of the fee has been tendered. NY R L QUEENS E-FILE Doc. 1(E)(1). The motion/petition shall be filed on-line and the fee paid for either on-line by credit card or by the "Pay at the County Clerk's Office" option. NY R L QUEENS E-FILE Doc. 1(H)(1).

iv. *Working copies.* The court may require the parties to provide working copies of documents filed electronically. In such event, each working copy shall include, firmly affixed thereto, a copy of a confirmation notice in a form prescribed by the Chief Administrator. NY R UNIF TRIAL CTS § 202.5-b(d)(5).

- *BRONX COUNTY.* After papers on motions have been e-filed, working copies thereof, with Confirmation Notice firmly attached as the back page facing out, must be submitted. (Each document or group of documents that is separately bound shall bear a Confirmation Notice.) Working copies lacking the Notice will not be accepted. WORKING COPIES OF MOTION PAPERS MUST BE SUBMITTED NO LATER THAN 4:45 P.M. ON THE RETURN DATE IN THE MOTION SUPPORT OFFICE (ROOM 217) AS EXPLAINED in NY R BRONX E FIL R Doc. 1(4). If an attorney has failed to submit required working

copies on or before the return date, the motion will be transmitted as is to the Justice for such action as the Justice finds appropriate. Attorneys may submit working copies on motions by mail or overnight delivery. Any such submission shall be sent in a timely manner to the Motion Support Office (Room 217) and be conspicuously marked on the outside "NYSCEF Matter"; lack of such marking may delay processing. NY R BRONX E FIL R Doc. 1(4)(a).

- *ERIE COUNTY.* Electronically filed documents subject to review and processing by the Part Clerk do not require a working copy unless otherwise directed or provided for in IAS Part Rules. NY R UNIF TRIAL CTS § 202.5-b(d)(4), any working copy submitted shall include, as a cover page firmly fastened thereto, a copy of the Confirmation Notice generated by the NYSCEF site at the time of filing. Please consult the individual Justice's Part Rules and/or consult with the Judge's chambers to determine whether and how working copies are to be provided. Working copies will not be printed or delivered by the Erie County Clerk or the Chief Clerk of the Courts or any of their personnel to chambers. The official record of a document in an electronically filed case is the document filed via the NYSCEF system. Working copies are intended only for use by the Justice. The Court will discard all working copies after the Justice has finished with them. Thus, in the event that counsel fails to file a document via the NYSCEF system, the document will not be part of the court record. NY R ERIE E FIL Doc. 3(III)(O); NY R ERIE E FIL Doc. 3(V)(E).
- *KINGS COUNTY.* No courtesy copies of motion papers are required by the Court, except as may be required for electronic filing or by the Judge's Part Rules. In tort cases against the City of New York, courtesy copies shall be supplied to the Corporation Counsel's office in Brooklyn. NY R L KINGS Pt. C, Rule 5. Unless otherwise directed by the Court or as described herein, and with the exceptions listed below, in all NYSCEF cases in which an RJI has been filed, working copies of e-filed documents that are intended for judicial review must be submitted to the court. Working copies are not required of documents that are only processed by a support office (e.g. preliminary conference request, note of issue). Working copies shall include exhibit tabs and backs; for motion papers, the motion sequence number and the return date and part. The confirmation notice with the motion sequence number on it should be the back page of the motion facing out. In addition, the filer of a working copy must firmly bind thereto, with the back page facing out, a copy of the Confirmation Notice that was generated by NYSCEF when that document was efiled. Working copies that are submitted without the related Confirmation Notice will not be accepted. NY R L KINGS E FIL Doc. 1(B)(7); NY R L KINGS E FIL Doc. 1(D). WORKING COPIES OF MOTION PAPERS MUST BE SUBMITTED IN THE MOTION SUPPORT OFFICE (ROOM 227) AS EXPLAINED HEREIN. THEY MUST NOT BE DELIVERED TO THE PART OR CHAMBERS, EXCEPT WHERE THE INDIVIDUAL JUSTICE'S PART RULES PROVIDE OTHERWISE; DOING SO WILL CAUSE ADMINISTRATIVE CONFUSION AND POSSIBLE MISPLACEMENT OF PAPERS. Any such submission shall be sent in a timely manner (kindly review individual Justice's rules) and be conspicuously marked on the outside "NYSCEF Matter;" lack of such marking may delay processing. NY R L KINGS E FIL Doc. 1(D).
- *NEW YORK COUNTY.* Some Justices require that working copies of e-filed motion papers be submitted. See the E-filing Protocol for information on the many Parts that do not require working copies. Where required, working copies of the moving documents and all other documents on the motion or application shall be submitted to the Motion Submission Part Courtroom (Room 130) on, but not before, the final return date. A Confirmation Notice from the NYSCEF system, which is generated when a document is e-filed, shall be firmly affixed, as the back page facing out, to each separate working copy or group of such copies. NY R NY CTY Procedure II(A) NY R NY CTY E FIL Doc. 2(B)(5)(a); NY R NY CTY J RUL Rule 14(a). For more information on working copies, including which parts don't require them, refer to NY R NY CTY E FIL Doc. 2(B)(6).
- *ONONDAGA COUNTY.* Any courtesy "working" copies, if required (see NY R ONDGA E FIL Protocol(B)(7)), must be provided directly to the assigned justice. NY R ONDGA E FIL Protocol(B)(9)(e). For information as to whether or not an Onondaga Supreme Court Justice requires working (courtesy) copies of e-filed documents, please consult the Onondaga County Individual E-filing Rules. NY R ONDGA E FIL Protocol(B)(7)(a). The Supreme Court Clerk's Office and the Onondaga County Clerk's Office will NOT accept the working copies. Working copies must be sent directly to the assigned justice's chambers. NY R ONDGA E FIL Protocol(B)(7)(b). A copy of the Confirmation Notice, generated by the NYSCEF system at the time a document is e-filed, must be attached to every working copy provided to chambers. If the Confirmation Notice is missing, the copy will not be accepted. NY R ONDGA E FIL Protocol(B)(7)(c). Courtesy copies do not become part of the official court record as maintained by the Onondaga County

Clerk's Office and will be destroyed by chambers at the disposition of the case. In the event that counsel fails to file a document via NYSCEF, the document will not be part of the court record. NY R ONDGA E FIL Protocol(B)(7)(d).

- *QUEENS COUNTY.* Working copies of E-Filed notices of motion/notices of petition are NOT to be sent to the Motion Support Office. They must be brought to the calendar call in the judge's part. NY R L QUEENS MOT SUP Doc. 1. Unless otherwise directed or authorized by the court, counsel should file papers with the E-file system first and thereafter deliver a working copy to at the calendar call of the Centralized Motion Part or Assigned Justice in accordance with individual Part Rules. NY R L QUEENS E-FILE Doc. 1(E)(4). On the return date of a motion that has been E-filed, the movant must provide the Centralized Motion Part (CMP) with a working copy of the entire motion including the notice of motion with sequence number and all of the attached exhibits. The motion must have the confirmation of filing firmly affixed to the back of the papers (facing outward). The confirmation of filing is a separate notice from the payment notice and will say confirmation clearly across the top of the page. NY R L QUEENS E-FILE Doc. 1(H)(2)(a). The motion or Order to Show Cause must have clearly written across its face the words "Working Copy," it must also have the assigned Judge's name, motion sequence number and calendar number—which may be obtained from the posted calendar outside courtroom on the return date of the motion. A confirmation of filing must attached thereto. Working copies of e-filed Orders to Show Cause must contain a copy of the signed order and all supporting papers. NY R L QUEENS E-FILE Doc. 1(H)(2)(c). The Confirmation Notice must be an updated version that indicates the sequence number of the motion being submitted at the CMP calendar call. WORKING COPIES WITHOUT A CONFIRMATION NOTICE WILL NOT BE ACCEPTED. NY R L QUEENS E-FILE Doc. 1(H)(7).

v. *ERIE COUNTY: Additional supplemental documents*

- *Notice of hard copy submission in e-filed case.* In accordance with NY R UNIF TRIAL CTS § 202.5-b(d), the County Clerk shall refuse to accept for filing, hard copy papers filed to an action subject to electronic filing unless hard copy filing is permitted by the Uniform Rules or NY R ERIE E FIL Doc. 3 and the papers bear a completed Notice of Hard Copy Submission—E-Filed Case form. NY R ERIE E FIL Doc. 3(III)(D).

vi. *KINGS COUNTY: Additional supplemental documents*

- *Forms when filing in hard copy.* An attorney who certifies in good faith that he or she lacks the equipment or knowledge needed to e-file and have no staff member or employee under his or her direction who has such knowledge and equipment may opt out of participation in e-filing in a mandatory case by filing a "Notice of Opt-Out from Participation in Action Subject to Mandatory Electronic Filing" form EFM-2 with the Clerk. NY R L KINGS E FIL Doc. 1(A)(2). Where in accordance with the E-Filing Rules a party submits a document in hard copy in an e-filed case (principally, a document submitted by a nonparticipating party (e.g., an attorney) in a consensual case, an emergency filing made in accordance with the Mandatory E-Filing Rules, and any document filed with the court in hard copy by an attorney who has opted out of participation in mandatory e-filing, the document must bear the back page facing out, a "Notice of Hard Copy Submission—E-Filed Cases" form EFM-3. NY R L KINGS E FIL Doc. 1(B)(3).

vii. *NEW YORK COUNTY: Additional supplemental documents*

- *Notice of hard copy submission.* Where in accordance with the E-Filing Rules an attorney or an unrepresented litigant who is participating in e-filing submits a document in hard copy in an e-filed case, the document must bear, as the back page facing out, a Notice of Hard-Copy Submission—E-Filed Case (a form available in the "Forms" section on the NYSCEF website (Form EFM-3) and in the court's back offices). NY R NY CTY E FIL Doc. 2(B)(3). For more information refer to NY R NY CTY E FIL Doc. 2.
- *Unpublished decisions.* Whenever reliance is placed upon a decision or other authority not officially published or readily available to the New York County Supreme Court, a copy of the case or of pertinent portions of the authority shall be submitted with the motion papers. NY R NY CTY J RUL Rule 14(a).

viii. *ONONDAGA COUNTY: Additional supplemental documents*

- *Notice of hard copy submission.* Any papers to be filed with the court in an e-filed case must be filed online with the E-filing system except where a special exemption is granted (e.g., oversized maps, photographs). If such an exemption is granted, Form EFM-3, "Notice of Hard Copy Submission—E-Filed Case," must be attached to such documents forms which are not filed on line. Also, Form EFM-4 "Notice of Hard Copy Exhibit Filing" must be completed and uploaded to the action's e-file. Both of these forms may be found on the NYSCEF website. NY R ONDGA E FIL Protocol(B)(4).

ix. *QUEENS COUNTY: Additional supplemental documents*

- *Notice of hard copy submission.* Any party opting out of the e-filing system must have a "Notice of Hard Copy Submission" firmly affixed to the back of the papers. NY R L QUEENS E-FILE Doc. 1(H)(2)(f).

E. Format

1. *Form of documents*

a. *Size and form of paper.* Each paper served or filed shall be durable, white and, except for summonses, subpoenas, notices of appearance, notes of issue, orders of protection, temporary orders of protection and exhibits, shall be eleven by eight and one-half (11 x 8-1/2) inches in size. NY CPLR Rule 2101(a).

b. *Writing and language.* The writing shall be legible and in black ink. NY CPLR Rule 2101(a). Each paper served or filed shall be in the English language which, where practicable, shall be of ordinary usage. NY CPLR Rule 2101(b).

c. *Caption.* Each paper served or filed shall begin with a caption setting forth the name of the court, the venue, the title of the action, the nature of the paper and the index number of the action if one has been assigned. In all papers other than a summons, a complaint or a judgment it shall be sufficient to state the name of the first named party on each side with an appropriate indication of any omissions. NY CPLR Rule 2101(c).

i. *Further contents of first page.* After the first paper has been filed in each case the index number shall appear on the cover and first page to the right of the caption of every paper tendered for filing in the action. Each such cover and first page also shall contain an indication of the county of venue and a brief description of the nature of the paper and, where the case has been assigned to an individual judge, shall contain the name of the assigned judge to the right of the caption. NY R UNIF TRIAL CTS § 202.5(a); NY R UNIF TRIAL CTS § 202.5(b); NY R UNIF TRIAL CTS § 202.5(d)(1)(i).

ii. *ALBANY COUNTY: Request for oral argument.* A party may request oral argument on a motion by indicating such request on the first page of the notice of motion, order to show cause, or answering papers in the area across from the caption of the action/proceeding. NY R 3 JD SUP Doc. 1(B).

iii. *NEW YORK COUNTY: Request for oral argument.* Counsel who wish oral argument must so request conspicuously on the front of their papers. NY R NY CTY Procedure II(D).

d. *Index number.* No paper in an action in the supreme or a county court, other than an order submitted for signature to a judge out of court, shall be submitted for any purpose to the supreme or county court or to a clerk thereof unless there is endorsed on such paper the index number of the action assigned by the clerk of the county. NY CPLR § 8018(c).

i. *ALBANY COUNTY: Index number on all filed documents.* The index number, the request for judicial intervention number and the assigned justice's name shall appear on [all papers filed with the Court subsequent to the complaint]. NY R 3 JD SUP Doc. 1(A).

ii. *ERIE COUNTY: Index number after initial filing.* Cases that are initially commenced by the filing of papers with the NYSCEF system are identified as e-filed cases by assignment of an Index Number that has "800-899" as the first three (3) digits of the index number (i.e. 802391/2012). NY R ERIE E FIL Doc. 3(II). [The] Index Number must be affixed to all document submissions, filings, and communications to the Erie County Clerk and the Court. Cases that are converted from paper to e-filing shall retain the original index number. NY R ERIE E FIL Doc. 3(II).

iii. *KINGS COUNTY: Index number after initial filing.* In cases commenced electronically by the filing of initiating papers with the NYSCEF system and payment of the statutory fees, the Kings County Clerk will issue an NYSCEF designated index number and the filer shall be notified via the NYSCEF system of the index number assigned and filing date. Such index number must be affixed to all document submissions, filings and communications to the Kings County Clerk and Supreme Court. If counsel faces exigent circumstances that require accelerated assignment, counsel may contact Administration of the Kings County Clerk at kcco-efile@nycourts.gov, during normal business hours of the court. NY R L KINGS E FIL Doc. 1(B)(5).

iv. *NEW YORK COUNTY: Index number on hard copy filings.* Papers subsequently presented for filing in hardcopy format will be filed in this jacket. NY R NY CTY Procedure I(B). Index numbers take the form of six digits followed by a slash and the four digits of the year the case began, e.g., 340705/2018. The first or first two integers of the index number identify the type of case. If a case is commenced electronically, the second integer will be a "5", except as indicated otherwise in the list below. There are many tax certiorari matters e-filed annually and the index numbers therefor will normally run over into those with a "6" as the second integer, and the same will occur with general cases if necessary. The principal types of cases and their index number categories are listed in NY R NY CTY Procedure I(B). NY R NY CTY Procedure I(B); NY R NY CTY Procedure XI(A).

v. *ONONDAGA COUNTY: Index number.* The index number must be referenced on all e-filed documents and correspondence. All e-filed case index numbers will contain the letters "EF" between the year and the file number (for example, 2012EF9999). NY R ONDGA E FIL Protocol(B)(1).

vi. *QUEENS COUNTY: Index number on converted cases.* Cases originally commenced in hard-copy form but later converted to an E-file case, either by stipulation or order will bear a regular index number initially. The County Clerk will issue a new E-file index number. NY R L QUEENS E-FILE Doc. 1(B).

e. *Line spacing.* Every paper filed in court, if typewritten, shall have at least double space between each line, except for quotations and the names and addresses of attorneys appearing in the action. NY R UNIF TRIAL CTS § 202.5(a).

f. *Font size.* Each. . .paper printed or typed, served or filed, except for summonses. . .and exhibits, shall be in clear type of no less than ten (10) point in size. NY CPLR Rule 2101(a).

i. Whenever a requirement relating to size of type is stated in point size, the type size requirement shall be deemed met if the x-height of the type is a minimum of forty-five percent (45%) of the specified point size. Each point shall be measured as .351 millimeter. The x-height size shall be measured as it appears on the page. The x-height is the height of the lower case letters, exclusive of ascenders or descenders. NY CPLR § 105(t).

g. *Margins.* Every paper filed in court shall have at least one (1) inch margins. NY R UNIF TRIAL CTS § 202.5(a).

h. *Citations*

i. *Civil practice law and rules.* NY CPLR § 101, et seq. shall be known as the civil practice law and rules, and may be cited as "CPLR". Reference to a provision in the civil practice law and rules may, except when such provision is being enacted or amended, be made without indicating whether it is a rule or section. NY CPLR § 101.

i. *Indorsement by attorney.* Each paper served or filed shall be indorsed with the name, address and telephone number of the attorney for the party serving or filing the paper, or if the party does not appear by attorney, with the name, address and telephone number of the party. NY CPLR Rule 2101(d).

j. *One-sided printing.* In addition, every paper filed in court, other than an exhibit or printed form, shall contain writing on one side only, except that papers that are fastened on the side may contain writing on both sides. NY R UNIF TRIAL CTS § 202.5(a).

k. *Use of copies authorized.* Except where otherwise specifically prescribed, copies, rather than originals, of all papers, including orders, affidavits and exhibits may be served or filed. Where it is required that the original be served or filed and the original is lost or withheld, the court may authorize a copy to be served or filed. NY CPLR Rule 2101(e).

i. Where a certified copy of a paper is required by law, an attorney admitted to practice in the courts of the state may certify that it has been compared by him with the original and found to be a true and complete copy. Such a certificate, when subscribed by such attorney, has the same effect as if made by a clerk. NY CPLR § 2105.

l. *Recycled paper.* It is the policy of the Unified Court System that litigants, where practicable, should file or submit to the courts of the Unified Court System of the State of New York papers printed or reproduced on recycled paper. Paper is considered recycled if it contains a minimum content of thirty percent (30%) waste paper. NY R UNIF TRIAL CTS § 215.2. The signature page of every paper filed or submitted to the court on recycled paper should bear the legend: "Printed [Reproduced] on Recycled Paper." NY R UNIF TRIAL CTS § 215.3.

m. *Form of request for judicial intervention; Copies.* A request for judicial intervention must be submitted, in duplicate, on a form authorized by the Chief of the Courts, with proof of service on the other parties to the action (but proof of service is not required where the application is ex parte). NY R UNIF TRIAL CTS § 202.6(a).

n. *KINGS COUNTY: Tabs on filings.* Motions, orders and other filed papers shall be indexed with protruding tabs. Clerks are required to reject papers that do not have protruding exhibit tabs, except papers in matrimonial cases and papers filed by pro se litigants. NY R L KINGS Pt. A, Papers.

o. *NEW YORK COUNTY: Length of briefs.* Unless advance permission otherwise is granted by the court for good cause, memoranda of law shall not exceed thirty (30) pages each (exclusive of table of contents and table of authorities) and affidavits/affirmations shall not exceed twenty-five (25) pages each. NY R NY CTY J RUL Rule 14(b).

p. *QUEENS COUNTY: Form and size of motion filings.* All motions filed in Queens Supreme Court-Civil Term, must adhere to the Motion Support rules and the rules of the assigned judge. NY R L QUEENS MOT SUP Doc. 1. Due to space limitations, the Motion Support Office cannot accept notices of motion/notices of petition and accompanying exhibits which measure greater than eight (8) inches. If your documents measure greater than eight (8) inches you are directed to submit only the notice of motion/notice of petition to the Motion Support Office and bring all exhibits to the calendar call on your return date. NY R L QUEENS MOT SUP Doc. 1.

2. *Form of electronic documents.* Each paper served or filed by electronic means, as defined in NY CPLR Rule 2103(f), shall be capable of being reproduced by the receiver so as to comply with the provisions of NY CPLR Rule 2101(a) through NY CPLR Rule 2101(d). NY CPLR Rule 2101(g).
   a. *File format.* All e-filed documents shall comply with the technical requirements set forth at the NYSCEF site. NY R UNIF TRIAL CTS § 202.5-b(d)(1)(i).
   b. *Heading of document.* The subject matter heading for each paper sent by electronic means must indicate that the matter being transmitted electronically is related to a court proceeding. NY CPLR Rule 2103(b)(7).
   c. *E-filed documents identification*
      i. *ERIE COUNTY.* E-filed cases must be readily identifiable and marked as such. If counsel presents papers to the Office of the Erie County Clerk or the Office of the Chief Clerk in a NYSCEF matter where authorized, counsel should alert the Clerk that the case is a NYSCEF matter. NY R ERIE E FIL Doc. 3(II).
      ii. *KINGS COUNTY.* The Supreme Court's Civil Case Information System ("CCIS") will further identify e-filed cases by the addition of a suffix to the index number (e.g. 500136/2006E). This suffix should be used on all documents filed with the court in e-filed matters. NY R L KINGS E FIL Doc. 1(A)(1).
3. *Signature blocks.* Every pleading, written motion, and other paper, served on another party or filed or submitted to the court shall be signed by an attorney, or by a party if the party is not represented by an attorney, with the name of the attorney or party clearly printed or typed directly below the signature. NY R CHIEF ADMIN § 130-1.1-a(a); NY R UNIF TRIAL CTS § 202.5(d)(1)(iv).
   a. *Printed name.* Beneath each signature shall be printed the name signed. NY CPLR Rule 2101(a).
   b. *Failure to sign.* Absent good cause shown, the court shall strike any unsigned paper if the omission of the signature is not corrected promptly after being called to the attention of the attorney or party. NY R CHIEF ADMIN § 130-1.1-a(a).
   c. *Signature as certification.* By signing a paper, an attorney or party certifies that, to the best of that person's knowledge, information and belief, formed after an inquiry reasonable under the circumstances the presentation of the paper or the contentions therein are not frivolous as defined in NY R CHIEF ADMIN § 130-1.1(c). NY R CHIEF ADMIN § 130-1.1-a(b)(1).
   d. *Electronic signatures.* A document shall be considered to have been signed by an attorney or party in compliance with NY R CHIEF ADMIN § 130-1.1-a if it has been signed by such attorney or party as provided in NY R UNIF TRIAL CTS § 202.5-b(e)(1) and it bears the signatory's name. NY R UNIF TRIAL CTS § 202.5-b(e)(2). An electronically filed document shall be considered to have been signed by, and shall be binding upon, the person identified as a signatory, if:
      i. It bears the physical signature of such person and is scanned into an electronic format that reproduces such signature; or
      ii. The signatory has electronically affixed the digital image of his or her signature to the document; or
      iii. It is electronically filed under the User ID and password of that person; or
      iv. In a tax certiorari action in which the parties have stipulated to this procedure, it is an initiating document that is electronically filed without the signature of the signatory in a form provided above in NY R UNIF TRIAL CTS § 202.5-b(e)(iv), provided that, prior to filing, the document is signed in full in hard copy (which hard copy must be preserved until the conclusion of all proceedings, including appeals, in the case in which it is filed); or
      v. In a small claims assessment review proceeding, it is a petition recorded by the NYSCEF site upon the filing of a text file as provided in NY R UNIF TRIAL CTS § 202.5-b(b)(1), provided that prior to filing, the document was signed in full in hard copy (which hard copy must be preserved until the conclusion of all proceedings in the matter, including article 78 (NY CPLR § 7801, et seq.) review and any appeals, and must be made available during the proceeding upon request of the respondent or the court); or
      vi. It otherwise bears the electronic signature of the signatory in a format conforming to such standards and requirements as may hereafter be established by the Chief Administrator. NY R UNIF TRIAL CTS § 202.5-b(e).
4. *Confidentiality of personal information.* No person may file any document available for public inspection with any state agency, political subdivision, or in any court of this state that contains a Social Security account number of any other person, unless such other person is a dependent child, or has consented to such filing, except as required by federal or state law or regulation, or by court rule. NY GEN BUS § 399-ddd. Submissions pursuant to e-filing procedures shall have the same confidentiality rights as paper documents. NY R UNIF TRIAL CTS § 202.5-b(k)(1).
   a. *Confidential personal information.* Except in the actions designated in NY R UNIF TRIAL CTS § 202.5(e)(1), or as

otherwise provided by rule or law or court order, and whether or not a sealing order is or has been sought, the parties shall omit or redact confidential personal information in papers submitted to the court for filing. For purposes of NY R UNIF TRIAL CTS § 202.5(e), confidential personal information ("CPI") means:

i. The taxpayer identification number of an individual or an entity, including a Social Security number, an employer identification number, and an individual taxpayer identification number, except the last four (4) digits thereof;

ii. The date of an individual's birth, except the year thereof;

iii. The full name of an individual known to be a minor, except the minor's initials;

iv. A financial account number, including a credit and/or debit card number, a bank account number, an investment account number, and/or an insurance account number, except the last four (4) digits or letters thereof; and

v. Any of the documents or testimony in a matrimonial action protected by NY DOM REL § 235 or evidence sealed by the court in such an action which are attached as exhibits or referenced in the papers filed in any other civil action. For purposes of NY R UNIF TRIAL CTS § 202.5, a matrimonial action shall mean: an action to annul a marriage or declare the nullity of a void marriage, an action or agreement for a separation, an action for a divorce, or an action or proceeding for custody, visitation, writ of habeus corpus, child support, maintenance or paternity. NY R UNIF TRIAL CTS § 202.5(e)(1).

vi. *ERIE COUNTY.* An attorney or unrepresented litigant filing a document via the NYSCEF system must comply with the requirements of NY R UNIF TRIAL CTS § 202.5(e) regarding the redaction of Confidential Personal Information and NY GEN BUS § 399-ddd(6) concerning the filing of documents containing Social Security Numbers. It is the sole responsibility of counsel or unrepresented litigant filing to be aware of and to comply with existing laws requiring non-disclosure of personal information contained in any document e-filed in NYSCEF. NY R ERIE E FIL Doc. 3(III)(G); NY R ERIE E FIL Doc. 3(III).

vii. *KINGS COUNTY.* An attorney or unrepresented litigant filing a document via the NYSCEF system must comply with the requirements of General Business Law § 399-dd(6), which often require redaction of any Social Security number that appear in the original document. The NYSCEF system automatically redacts portions of filed documents which apparently contain Social Security numbers pursuant to NY R UNIF TRIAL CTS § 202.5-b(k). In the event the filing party receives e-mail notice through NYSCEF that a Social Security number in a filed document has been redacted, and the filing party concludes such redaction is erroneous, the filer should click on the link provided in the e-mail to permit the County Clerk to revert the redaction. For Confidential Personal Information, see NY R UNIF TRIAL CTS § 202.5(e) and NY R L KINGS E FIL Doc. 1(B)(11). [Editor's note: the reference to General Business Law § 399-dd(6) is likely a reference to NY GEN BUS § 399-ddd(6)]. NY R L KINGS E FIL Doc. 1(B)(10); NY R L KINGS E FIL Doc. 1(K)(1).

viii. *NEW YORK COUNTY.* It is the responsibility of counsel and parties to comply with rules restricting disclosure of confidential personal information. Nevertheless, NYSCEF screens filings and endeavors to identify any that contain social security numbers. When such numbers are discovered through this process, NYSCEF will restrict portions of or all of such documents from public view. Where NYSCEF has redacted what it believes to be a social security number, it will transmit to the filer a notice advising of the action taken and requesting that the filer review the matter and provide notification as set forth in the notice if the redaction has been made in error. NY R NY CTY E FIL Doc. 2(K)(1); NY R NY CTY J RUL Rule A-1. Documents filed in the past in "secure status" under a procedure no longer in place will retain that status unless otherwise directed by the court. NY R NY CTY E FIL Doc. 2(K)(2).

b. *Submission of confidential personal information.* Where a person submitting a paper to a court for filing believes in good faith that the inclusion of the full confidential personal information described in NY R UNIF TRIAL CTS § 202.5(e)(1) is material and necessary to the adjudication of the action or proceeding before the court, he or she may apply to the court for leave to serve and file together with a paper in which such information has been set forth in abbreviated form a confidential affidavit or affirmation setting forth the same information in unabbreviated form, appropriately referenced to the page or pages of the paper at which the abbreviated form appears. NY R UNIF TRIAL CTS § 202.5(e)(3).

c. *Home addresses.* For information on when home addresses and other personal information must be redacted, refer to NY CPLR Rule 2103-a.

5. *Defective papers.* A defect in the form of a paper, if a substantial right of a party is not prejudiced, shall be disregarded by the court, and leave to correct shall be freely given. NY CPLR Rule 2101(f). Papers that are stapled or bound securely shall not be rejected for filing simply because they are not bound with a backer of any kind. NY R UNIF TRIAL CTS § 202.5(a).

A paper filed in accordance with the rules of the chief administrator or any local rule or practice established by the court shall be deemed filed. NY CPLR Rule 2102(b).

a. *Objection to defective papers.* The party on whom a paper is served shall be deemed to have waived objection to any defect in form unless, within fifteen (15) days after the receipt thereof, the party on whom the paper is served returns the paper to the party serving it with a statement of particular objections. NY CPLR Rule 2101(f).

F. Filing and Service Requirements

1. *Filing requirements.* Except where otherwise prescribed by law or order of court, papers required to be filed shall be filed with the clerk of the court in which the action is triable. In an action or proceeding in supreme or court, papers required to be filed shall be filed with the clerk of the county in which the proceeding is brought. NY CPLR Rule 2102(a).

a. *Furnishing papers to the court.* Each party shall furnish to the court all papers served by him. The moving party shall furnish at the hearing all other papers not already in the possession of the court necessary to the consideration of the questions involved. Where such papers are in the possession of an adverse party, they shall be produced by him at the hearing on notice served with the motion papers. Only papers served in accordance with the provisions of NY CPLR Rule 2214 shall be read in support of, or in opposition to, the motion, unless the court for good cause shall otherwise direct. NY CPLR Rule 2214(c).

i. *Submission to judge.* All papers for signature or consideration of the court shall be presented to the clerk of the trial court in the appropriate courtroom or clerk's office, except that where the clerk is unavailable or the judge so directs, papers may be submitted to the judge and a copy filed with the clerk at the first available opportunity. All papers for any judge that are filed in the clerk's office shall be promptly delivered to the judge by the clerk. The papers shall be clearly addressed to the judge for whom they are intended and prominently show the nature of the papers, the title and index number of the action in which they are filed, the judge's name and the name of the attorney or party submitting them. NY R UNIF TRIAL CTS § 202.5(b).

ii. *BRONX COUNTY: Approval of motions before filing.* All motion papers must be approved by the Motion Support Office, Supreme Court, Civil Term, room 217, before the motion papers are filed and the appropriate fee paid to the County Clerk. NY R BRONX FIL R Doc. 1.

iii. *ERIE COUNTY: Filing motions.* A motion on notice or a notice of petition in a NYSCEF case shall be filed through the NYSCEF system and must be accompanied by a Request for Judicial Intervention if the motion is being filed upon commencement of the action or if the matter has not yet been assigned to an IAS Justice. In addition, cross motions with the appropriate filing fees and opposition and reply papers must be submitted via the NYSCEF system. NY R ERIE E FIL Doc. 3(V)(A).

iv. *NEW YORK COUNTY: Filing hard copies.* Where in the narrow circumstances described by the e-filing rules a motion is made in hard-copy form or opposition papers are submitted in such form in an e-filed case, the hard-copy documents shall be submitted in the same way papers are submitted in non-e-filed cases, except that there shall be firmly affixed to each separate document or group of documents, as the back page facing out, a Notice of Hard Copy Submission—E-Filed Case. NY R NY CTY Procedure II(A). For more information on filing in hard copy cases, refer to NY R NY CTY Procedure II(A).

v. *ONONDAGA COUNTY: Submission of responsive papers and cross-motions.* Cross-motions, opposition and reply papers must be submitted online. NY R ONDGA E FIL Protocol(B)(9)(e). Motions and Orders to Show Cause are assigned a sequence number by the system. Counsel must be sure that cross motions and other filings correspond with the correct sequence number so that a cross motion will not be associated with the wrong original motion. NY R ONDGA E FIL Protocol(B)(9)(f).

b. *Electronic filing.* On consent, documents may be filed and served by electronic means in Supreme Court in such civil actions and in such counties as shall be authorized by order of the Chief Administrator of the Courts and only to the extent and in the manner provided in NY R UNIF TRIAL CTS § 202.5-b. NY R UNIF TRIAL CTS § 202.5-b(a)(1). For the definitions of terms used in electronic filing, refer to NY R UNIF TRIAL CTS § 202.5-b(a)(2).

i. *E-filing mandatory.* In any action subject to e-filing, all documents required to be filed with the court by an e-filing party shall be filed and served electronically, except as provided in NY R UNIF TRIAL CTS § 202.5-b. NY R UNIF TRIAL CTS § 202.5-b(d)(1)(i).

- *ERIE COUNTY.* Case types currently eligible and accepted for e-filing are listed at the NYSCEF website. Note that some actions or special proceedings, (i.e., name changes) which are otherwise subject to mandatory e-filing, if commenced by unrepresented litigants will NOT be maintained in the NYSCEF system; individual cases may be found either at NYSCEF or in the Erie County Clerk's online records system. NY R ERIE E FIL Doc. 3(I)(E).

- *KINGS COUNTY.* Cases that are commenced by filing of the initiating papers with NYSCEF are identified as e-filed cases by assignment of a special index number (i.e., Index Numbers beginning with 500,000). NY R L KINGS E FIL Doc. 1(A)(1). All cases required to be e-filed are listed in Uniform Rule 202.5-bb (Mandatory E-Filing Rules) and on the NYSCEF website. All such cases must be commenced by filing with the County Clerk electronically through NYSCEF and all subsequent documents in such cases must be e-filed. Any questions regarding mandatory e-filing in Kings County can be e-mailed to kcco-efile@nycourts.gov. NY R L KINGS E FIL Doc. 1(A)(2).
- *NEW YORK COUNTY.* Unless otherwise provided in the Rules or in NY R NY CTY E FIL Doc. 2 or where a special exemption is granted due to physical requirements (e.g., oversized maps; see NY R NY CTY E FIL Doc. 2(B)(10)), all documents to be filed with the court in a NYSCEF case, including all documents on motions and all letters to the court (where permitted), must be filed with the NYSCEF system. Documents that attorneys would not ordinarily file with the court in a hard-copy case need not be e-filed. Unless otherwise provided by the E-Filing Rules or this Protocol, in e-filed cases the County Clerk and the court will not accept documents filed in paper form. NY R NY CTY E FIL Doc. 2(B)(1). E-filing is mandatory in all types of cases (other than election law, matrimonial, Art. 78, and Mental Hygiene Law matters, and Art. 70 habeas corpus proceedings) that are commenced in this court on or after February 19, 2013. All such cases must be commenced by filing with the County Clerk electronically through NYSCEF and all subsequent documents in such cases must be e-filed. NY R NY CTY E FIL Doc. 2(A)(2)(a). For more information, including information on consensual e-filing and filing scanned hard copy documents, refer to NY R NY CTY E FIL Doc. 2(A)(2).
- *QUEENS COUNTY.* All authorized Torts, Commercial and Tax Certiorari cases may be commenced by E-Filing, however all parties must consent for the action to continue as an E-file case. NY R L QUEENS E-FILE Doc. 1(A). All papers to be filed with the court in an E-filed case shall be filed on-line with the E-file system except as directed by the court. Papers that attorneys would not ordinarily file with the court in a hard-copy case need not be filed in an E-filed matter. NY R L QUEENS E-FILE Doc. 1(E)(2).

ii. *Who may file.* Documents may be filed or served electronically only by a person who has registered as an authorized e-filing user or as otherwise provided in NY R UNIF TRIAL CTS § 202.5-b(c). NY R UNIF TRIAL CTS § 202.5-b(c)(1).

iii. *When filing made.* Documents may be transmitted at any time of the day or night to the NYSCEF site. A document other than an order or judgment is filed when its electronic transmission or, in the case of a petition that is e-filed by submission of a text file as provided in NY R UNIF TRIAL CTS § 202.5-b(b)(1), the electronic transmission of the text file is recorded at that site, provided, however, that where payment of a fee is required upon the filing of a document, the document is not filed until transmission of the document and the information or form or information as required in NY R UNIF TRIAL CTS § 202.5-b(d)(2)(i), NY R UNIF TRIAL CTS § 202.5-b(d)(2)(ii) or NY R UNIF TRIAL CTS § 202.5-b(d)(2)(iii) has been recorded at the NYSCEF site; or, if no transmission of that information or form or information is recorded, where permitted by the County Clerk, until payment is presented to the County Clerk. NY R UNIF TRIAL CTS § 202.5-b(d)(3)(i).

iv. *Notification of filing.* No later than the close of business on the business day following the electronic filing of a document, a notification, in a form prescribed by the Chief Administrator, shall be transmitted electronically by the NYSCEF site to the person filing such document and the e-mail service addresses of all other participating parties in such action. NY R UNIF TRIAL CTS § 202.5-b(d)(3)(ii).

v. *Removal of confidential information and other corrections.* If a document filed electronically is subsequently discovered to contain confidential data—including but not limited to trade secrets, information protected by confidentiality agreement, or personal confidential information as defined by statute or court rule—or otherwise to have been filed in error, the filer or another party or affected person may (1) notify the parties and any non-party filers in the action of the confidentiality issue or other error raised by the filing, and of his or her intention to seek judicial relief to correct the filing: (2) following such notification, request that the appropriate County Clerk, exercising his or her administrative discretion, place the document temporarily in "restricted" status on the NYSCEF site, to be made available for viewing by court staff and the parties but not the general public; and (3) file an application to correct the filing by order to show cause within five (5) business days of such notification (or such time as the court may direct), including a request for preliminary injunctive relief limiting interim disclosure of the document at issue. Unless otherwise directed by the court, any document placed in restricted status in response to such a request shall be returned to public view upon expiration of this five (5) day

period. The Chief Administrator of the Courts shall promulgate forms to implement this process. NY R UNIF TRIAL CTS § 202.5-b(d)(3)(iii).

- *KINGS COUNTY.* For information on what to do when a document was erroneously filed with confidential information, refer to NY R L KINGS E FIL Doc. 1(B)(11).
- *NEW YORK COUNTY.* For information on what to do when a document was erroneously filed with confidential information, refer to NY R NY CTY E FIL Doc. 2(B)(8).
- *QUEENS COUNTY.* For information on what to do when a document was erroneously filed with confidential information, refer to NY R L QUEENS E-FILE Doc. 1(E)(7).

vi. *Documents requiring judge's signature.* Except where the court directs otherwise, any document that requires a judge's signature shall be transmitted electronically and in hard copy to the court. NY R UNIF TRIAL CTS § 202.5-b(d)(6).

vii. *Documents which would be inconvenient to file electronically; Hard copies.* Notwithstanding any other provision of NY R UNIF TRIAL CTS § 202.5-b, and subject to such guidelines as may be established by the Chief Administrative Judge, the County Clerk or his or her designee may require or permit a party to file in hard copy, in accordance with procedures set by the County Clerk or designee, an exhibit or other document which it is impractical or inconvenient to file electronically. NY R UNIF TRIAL CTS § 202.5-b(d)(7).

- *ERIE COUNTY.* Please contact the Supervisor of Actions & Proceedings, Erie County Clerk's Office by calling (716) 858-6662 or the Deputy County Clerk—Legal at (716) 858-6348 for information. NY R ERIE E FIL Doc. 3(III)(F).
- *KINGS COUNTY.* With limited exceptions, as set forth in the Uniform Rules and herein, all documents to be filed with the court in a NYSCEF case shall be filed online via the NYSCEF system. However, should the size, consistency or context of a hard copy document preclude electronic filing, the user shall electronically file a "Notice of Hard Copy Submission—E-Filed Cases" form EFM-3. Any hard copy submitted pursuant to NY R L KINGS E FIL Doc. 1(B)(9) shall include, as a cover page firmly fastened thereto, a copy of the Confirmation Notice received from the NYSCEF site confirming receipt of the "Notice of Hard Copy Submission—E-Filed Cases". Any party may object to such hard copy filing. The Court, in response to such objection, may, following the hard copy filing, fashion such relief as it deems appropriate pursuant to and in furtherance of the Uniform Rules and NY R L KINGS E FIL Doc. 1, including, but not limited to, an Order directing the filing party to file such documents online via the NYSCEF system. When exhibits are impractical to file pursuant to NY R UNIF TRIAL CTS § 202.5-b(d)(7), an additional "Notice of Hard Copy Exhibit Filing" form EFM-4 is required to be submitted. NY R L KINGS E FIL Doc. 1(B)(9).
- *NEW YORK COUNTY.* If a filer needs to submit unusual exhibits in original form that cannot practically be e-filed, such as oversized maps or electronic recordings, the filer should consult with the County Clerk's E-File Department by telephone at 646-386-3737 (procedural questions only) or by e-mail at ccnyef@nycourts.gov, which will normally require that the filer retain custody of the original subject to possible future directives of the court. NY R NY CTY E FIL Doc. 2(B)(10). In such instances, the filing counsel shall file with NYSCEF a "placeholder" in the form of a Notice of Hard Copy Exhibit Filing (NYSCEF Form EF 21). The Notice should be uploaded to NYSCEF as document type "Exhibit" and the filer should indicate in the "Additional Document Information" field that the filer is retaining custody of the original. Failure to e-file the Notice may result in a gap in the official record of the court. NY R NY CTY E FIL Doc. 2(B)(10).

viii. *Documents containing sensitive or proprietary information.* In an action subject to e-filing, any person may apply for an order prohibiting or restricting the electronic filing in the action of specifically identified materials on the grounds that such materials are subject to copyright or other proprietary rights, or trade secret or other privacy interests, and that electronic filing in the action is likely to result in substantial prejudice to those rights or interests. NY R UNIF TRIAL CTS § 202.5-b(k)(2).

ix. *Refusal to accept paper filings.* In accordance with NY CPLR Rule 2102(c), a County Clerk and a chief clerk of the Supreme Court or County Court, as appropriate, shall refuse to accept for filing papers filed in actions and proceedings when the paper sought to be filed:

- Is in an action subject to electronic filing pursuant to Rules of the Chief Administrator,
- Is not being filed electronically, and

- Does not include the notice required by NY R UNIF TRIAL CTS § 202.5-b(d)(1). NY R UNIF TRIAL CTS § 202.5(d)(1)(v); NY R UNIF TRIAL CTS § 202.5-bb(d).

x. *Emergency filings; Hard copies.* For information on when an emergency filing may be filed and served in hard copy, refer to NY R UNIF TRIAL CTS § 202.5-b(d)(1)(ii), NY R UNIF TRIAL CTS § 202.5-b(d)(1)(iii) and NY R UNIF TRIAL CTS § 202.5-bb(c)(3).

- *KINGS COUNTY.* Under the rules, a participating emergency e-filer must electronically file the documents initially filed in hard copy form within three (3) business days of the emergency filing; the originals will be discarded after the documents have been processed and the failure to e-file as required will therefore lead to an incomplete record. NY R L KINGS E FIL Doc. 1(B)(3).
- *NEW YORK COUNTY.* Occasionally an emergency will arise requiring expedited entry of a document with the County Clerk (e.g., an order issued in the courtroom after a conference or argument of a critical matter), such as for purposes of an immediate appeal. Expedition can be achieved by the Part as follows: the document should be carried by a Court Officer or staff member to the General Clerk's Office to assure immediate and proper recordation in the computer and, as appropriate, the posting of the document to NYSCEF or the Supreme Court Records On-Line Library ("Scroll"). The court will accommodate counsel in emergencies. NY R NY CTY Procedure XI(A).
- *NEW YORK COUNTY.* For more information on how to bring emergency matters before the court, refer to NY R NY CTY Procedure IV.

xi. *Technical failures.* The NYSCEF site shall be considered to be subject to a technical failure on a given day if the site is unable to accept filings or provide access to filed documents continuously or intermittently over the course of any period of time greater than one (1) hour after 12:00 noon of that day. Notice of all such technical failures shall be provided on the site. NY R UNIF TRIAL CTS § 202.5-b(i).

- When e-filing is hindered by a technical failure, a party may file with the appropriate clerk and serve in hard copy. NY R UNIF TRIAL CTS § 202.5-b(i). In the event an attorney or party shall file and serve documents in hard copy pursuant to NY R UNIF TRIAL CTS § 202.5-b(i), each such document shall include the notice required by NY R UNIF TRIAL CTS § 202.5-b(d)(1), and the filer shall file those documents with the NYSCEF site within three (3) business days after restoration of normal operations at that site. NY R UNIF TRIAL CTS § 202.5-b(i).
- With the exception of deadlines that by law cannot be extended, the time for filing of any document that is delayed due to technical failure of the site shall be extended for one (1) day for each day on which such failure occurs, unless otherwise ordered by the court. NY R UNIF TRIAL CTS § 202.5-b(i).
- *ERIE COUNTY.* When filing by electronic means is hindered by a technical failure, please refer to the NY R UNIF TRIAL CTS § 202.5-b(i). NY R ERIE E FIL Doc. 3(III)(K).
- *KINGS COUNTY.* When filing by electronic means is hindered by a NYSCEF technical failure (as set forth in NY R UNIF TRIAL CTS § 202.5-b(i)), a party may file with the appropriate Clerk in hard copy. Except for deadlines that by law cannot be extended (e.g. Statute of limitations, Notice of Appeal), the time for filing of any document that is delayed due to technical failure of the NYSCEF system shall be extended for one day for each day on which such failure occurs, unless otherwise ordered by the court. NY R L KINGS E FIL Doc. 1(B)(13).
- *ONONDAGA COUNTY.* When filing by electronic means is hindered by a technical failure (as set forth in NY R UNIF TRIAL CTS § 202.5-b(h)(3)(i)), a party may file a hard copy with the County Clerk. With the exception of deadlines that by law cannot be extended (e.g., a statute of limitations or the deadline for filing a Notice of Appeal), the time for filing of any document that is delayed due to technical failure of the NYSCEF system will be extended for one day for each day on which such failure occurs, unless otherwise ordered by the court. A "Notice of Hard Copy Filing Submission—E-Filed Case' must accompany any documents not filed via NYSCEF. NY R ONDGA E FIL Protocol(B)(8).

xii. *Filing fees.* For information on what information must be provided to pay filing fees, refer to NY R UNIF TRIAL CTS § 202.5-b(d)(2).

xiii. *Exemption from e-filing.* For information on exemptions from e-filing, refer to NY R UNIF TRIAL CTS § 202.5-bb(e).

xiv. *Filing exhibits*

- *ERIE COUNTY.* In the NYSCEF system, each exhibit must be uploaded as a separate .pdf file. After

uploading a primary document, please choose the document type "Exhibit" and enter the appropriate number or letter and a brief description of the exhibit; each exhibit should bear a separate cover sheet clearly marked as "Exhibit A," "Exhibit B," etc. "Exhibit A" or "Exhibit B" is unacceptable as a brief description of the exhibit. Exhibits, where referenced in a signed Order as attached or affixed shall be uploaded with the signed Order as one .pdf document. NY R ERIE E FIL Doc. 3(III)(H); NY R ERIE E FIL Doc. 3(V)(D).

- *KINGS COUNTY.* In the NYSCEF system, each exhibit should be uploaded as a separate PDF file. After uploading a primary document, please choose the document type "Exhibit", enter the appropriate number or letter, and be sure to place a check mark to the right of "Attach to main document". Each exhibit shall bear a separate cover sheet clearly marked as Exhibit A, Exhibit B, etc. NY R L KINGS E FIL Doc. 1(B)(12). Whenever possible, attorneys submitting exhibits in NYSCEF cases should make each exhibit a separate attachment to an affidavit/affirmation in the system (i.e., multiple exhibits should not be filed as a single PDF). NY R L KINGS E FIL Doc. 1(D)(1).
- *NEW YORK COUNTY.* Attorneys submitting exhibits in NYSCEF cases should make each exhibit a separate attachment to an affidavit/affirmation in the system; i.e., exhibits should not be filed as a single PDF-A together with the affidavit/affirmation or grouped together as a single PDF-A attachment because either of these two formats makes it difficult for the Justice to locate particular exhibits as needed. Counsel must also include appropriate descriptive language in the "Additional Document Information" field in NYSCEF. NY R NY CTY E FIL Doc. 2(D)(6).
- *ONONDAGA COUNTY.* All exhibits in e-filed cases must be e-filed individually as separate attachments. NY R ONDGA E FIL Protocol(B)(9)(b).

xv. *Correcting documents*

- *ERIE COUNTY.* Submission of documents which, upon examination, require correction or addition will result in notification to the filer advising that the document has been returned for correction. The filer shall make the required corrections and/or additions as indicated in the e-mail transmission sent by the County Clerk or Part Clerk through the NYSCEF site. The corrected documents may be resubmitted using the "Re-file this document" link highlighted in the filer's document list for the respective case. Please note that in the case of multiple submissions, all related documents filed at the same time may be removed from the case record and returned until all documents are properly submitted. NY R ERIE E FIL Doc. 3(III)(J).
- *KINGS COUNTY.* Submission of documents which, upon examination, require correction or addition will result in notification to the filer advising that there is a problem with a document. The filer shall make the required corrections and/or additions and resubmit the corrected document using the "Refile this document" link. In the event a document is returned for correction, the original file date will be preserved. For corrections of documents filed with the Kings County Clerk which require a court order, refer to the procedure in NY R UNIF TRIAL CTS § 202.5-b(d)(3)(iii) and NY R L KINGS E FIL Doc. 1(B)(11). NY R L KINGS E FIL Doc. 1(B)(3).
- *ONONDAGA COUNTY.* If there is an error or an additional document is required, the system will notify the filing party, who will make the corrections/additions and resubmit them online. NY R ONDGA E FIL Protocol(B)(6).
- *QUEENS COUNTY.* Generally speaking, documents that have been E-filed will not thereafter be deleted by the County Clerk from NYCEF because the filer asserts that the filing contains an error or a significant omission. When the filer wishes to correct a perceived error or omission in a filed document, he or she should file an amended version of the document, with the original remaining on file, or else obtain a court order providing for deletion of the original. The County Clerk will only delete a document upon request of the filer or on the County Clerk's own initiative when it is obvious from the face of the document alone that the filer made a fundamental error and never intended to file the document that was filed (e.g., a completely unrelated non-litigation document, a different case, or a wrong county). The County Clerk will advise the filer when any such fundamental errors are detected. NY R L QUEENS E-FILE Doc. 1(E)(6).

c. *Facsimile filing.* In the Supreme Court, facsimile filing shall be limited to commercial claims and tax certiorari, conservatorship, and mental hygiene proceedings in Monroe, Westchester, New York and Suffolk Counties. NY R UNIF TRIAL CTS § 202.5-a(a)(1). Refer to NY R UNIF TRIAL CTS § 202.5-a for information on the procedures for facsimile filing.

i. *NEW YORK COUNTY.* Unless indicated otherwise by the court in a particular case or in NY R NY CTY J RUL Doc. 1, Justices do not accept papers by fax. NY R NY CTY J RUL Rule 4.

d. *ERIE COUNTY: Filing request for judicial intervention.* An RJI in a NYSCEF case shall be filed via the NYSCEF system and will be filed after all other documents have been uploaded. The filer may choose between filing a .pdf image of the prepared RJI and any Addendum or having the system prepare the RJI which shall conform to Uniform Rules. Addenda, such as the Commercial Division Addendum, if prepared by the filer must be filed simultaneously with and attached to an RJI and uploaded as one .pdf document with the RJI. If the RJI is prepared by the e-filing system, no separate Addendum is required. Whether or not the filer elects to allow NYSCEF to create the RJI or chooses to upload a prepared RJI, data in addition to the nature of the judicial intervention, including information that appears on any Addenda will be collected through completion of the fields presented. If the filing of the RJI is accomplished through a filing agent, a prepared RJI and Addendum must be filed in lieu of the creation of the RJI by the NYSCEF system, as the RJI must be signed by the attorney. NY R ERIE E FIL Doc. 3(IV). For information on RJIs in specific types of action, refer to NY R ERIE E FIL Doc. 3(IV).

2. *Service requirements*

a. *Who may serve.* Except where otherwise prescribed by law or order of court, papers may be served by any person not a party of the age of eighteen years or over. NY CPLR Rule 2103(a).

b. *Service upon attorney.* Except where otherwise prescribed by law or order of court, papers to be served upon a party in a pending action shall be served upon the party's attorney. Where the same attorney appears for two or more parties, only one (1) copy need be served upon the attorney. Such service upon an attorney shall be made:

i. By delivering the paper to the attorney personally. NY CPLR Rule 2103(b)(1).

ii. By mailing the paper to the attorney at the address designated by that attorney for that purpose or, if none is designated, at the attorney's last known address; service by mail shall be complete upon mailing. NY CPLR Rule 2103(b)(2).

- *BRONX COUNTY.* Service by mail must be within the state. NY R BRONX FIL R Doc. 3.

iii. If the attorney's office is open, by leaving the paper with a person in charge, or if no person is in charge, by leaving it in a conspicuous place; or if the attorney's office is not open, by depositing the paper, enclosed in a sealed wrapper directed to the attorney, in the attorney's office letter drop or box. NY CPLR Rule 2103(b)(3).

iv. By leaving it at the attorney's residence within the state with a person of suitable age and discretion. Service upon an attorney shall not be made at the attorney's residence unless service at the attorney's office cannot be made. NY CPLR Rule 2103(b)(4).

v. By transmitting the paper to the attorney by facsimile transmission, provided that a facsimile telephone number is designated by the attorney for that purpose. Service by facsimile transmission shall be complete upon the receipt by the sender of a signal from the equipment of the attorney served indicating that the transmission was received, and the mailing of a copy of the paper to that attorney. The designation of a facsimile telephone number in the address block subscribed on a paper served or filed in the course of an action or proceeding shall constitute consent to service by facsimile transmission in accordance with NY CPLR Rule 2103(b)(5). An attorney may change or rescind a facsimile telephone number by serving a notice on the other parties. NY CPLR Rule 2103(b)(5).

vi. By dispatching the paper to the attorney by overnight delivery service at the address designated by the attorney for that purpose or, if none is designated, at the attorney's last known address. Service by overnight delivery service shall be complete upon deposit of the paper enclosed in a properly addressed wrapper into the custody of the overnight delivery service for overnight delivery, prior to the latest time designated by the overnight delivery service for overnight delivery. "Overnight delivery service" means any delivery service which regularly accepts items for overnight delivery to any address in the state. NY CPLR Rule 2103(b)(6).

vii. By transmitting the paper to the attorney by electronic means where and in the manner authorized by the chief administrator of the courts by rule and, unless such rule shall otherwise provide, such transmission shall be upon the party's written consent. The subject matter heading for each paper sent by electronic means must indicate that the matter being transmitted electronically is related to a court proceeding. NY CPLR Rule 2103(b)(7).

- *KINGS COUNTY.* Pursuant to the E-Filing Rules, service of interlocutory documents is made by posting a document to the NYSCEF site, which automatically and immediately transmits an email notice of the filing, including a link to the document, to all participating counsel and unrepresented litigants on the case. The Rules also authorize service by other methods permitted by the CPLR. If service by such other method is made, proof of service must be filed with NYSCEF. NY R L KINGS E FIL Doc. 1(I).
- *NEW YORK COUNTY.* Service. . .will be made automatically through NYSCEF upon all participating

counsel and unrepresented parties in the case. There are limited exceptions to the requirement for e-filing in the covered kinds of cases. NY R NY CTY Procedure XI(A). Pursuant to the E-Filing Rules, service of interlocutory documents is made by posting a document to the NYSCEF site, which automatically and immediately transmits an e-mail notice of the filing, including a link to the document, to all participating counsel and unrepresented litigants on the case. The Rules also authorize service by other methods permitted by the CPLR. If service by such a method is made, proof of service must be filed with NYSCEF. NY R NY CTY E FIL Doc. 2(I).

- *QUEENS COUNTY.* Filing with the system permits counsel to serve the papers electronically pursuant to NY R UNIF TRIAL CTS § 202.5-b(f) once consent to E-Filing has been filed on-line. Consult NY R UNIF TRIAL CTS § 202.5-bb(c) for service in mandatory e-filing. Any required proof of service should be E-filed as a separate document. NY R L QUEENS E-FILE Doc. 1(E)(4).

c. *Electronic service mandatory; Consenting to electronic service; How electronic service may be made.* Except as otherwise provided in NY R UNIF TRIAL CTS § 202.5-bb, filing and service of all documents in an action that has been commenced electronically in accordance with NY R UNIF TRIAL CTS § 202.5-bb shall be by electronic means. NY R UNIF TRIAL CTS § 202.5-bb(c)(1).

i. *Party's consent required for certain e-filing.* After commencement of an action wherein e-filing is authorized, documents may be electronically filed and served, but only by, and electronic service shall be made only upon, a party or parties who have consented thereto. NY R UNIF TRIAL CTS § 202.5-b(b)(2)(i).

- A consent to e-filing in an action shall state that the party providing it agrees to the use of e-filing in the action and to be bound by the filing and service provisions in NY R UNIF TRIAL CTS § 202.5-b. NY R UNIF TRIAL CTS § 202.5-b(b)(2)(ii).

ii. *Address for service; Duty to notify as to changes.* The e-mail service address recorded at the time of registration is the e-mail address at which service of interlocutory documents on that party may be made through notification transmitted by the NYSCEF site. It is the responsibility of each filing user to monitor that address and promptly notify the Resource Center in the event of a change in his or her e-mail service address. NY R UNIF TRIAL CTS § 202.5-b(f)(2)(i).

iii. *How service made.* An e-filing party causes service of an interlocutory document to be made upon another party participating in e-filing by filing the document electronically. Upon receipt of an interlocutory document, the NYSCEF site shall automatically transmit electronic notification to all e-mail service addresses in such action. NY R UNIF TRIAL CTS § 202.5-b(f)(2)(ii).

- Except as provided otherwise in NY R UNIF TRIAL CTS § 202.5-b(h)(3), the electronic transmission of the notification shall constitute service of the document on the e-mail service addresses identified therein; however, such service will not be effective if the filing party learns that the notification did not reach the address of the person to be served. Proof of such service will be recorded on the NYSCEF site. A party may, however, utilize other service methods permitted by the CPLR provided that, if one of such other methods is used, proof of that service shall be filed electronically. NY R UNIF TRIAL CTS § 202.5-b(f)(2)(ii).

iv. *Signatures on hard copies; Proof of service filed electronically.* When an e-filing party serves a document in hard copy on a non-participating party, the document served shall bear full signatures of all signatories and proof of such service shall be filed electronically. NY R UNIF TRIAL CTS § 202.5-b(b)(2)(i).

- *ERIE COUNTY.* In the NYSCEF system, each Affidavit of Service must be uploaded as a separate .pdf file. After uploading the Affidavit, please choose the document type: "Affirmation/Affidavit of Service" and enter the name of the party served as Additional Document Information. NY R ERIE E FIL Doc. 3(III)(I); NY R ERIE E FIL Doc. 3(V)(F).

v. *Effect of failure to consent.* A party's failure to consent to participation in electronic filing and service shall not bar any other party to the action from filing documents electronically with the County Clerk and the court or serving documents upon any other party who has consented to participation. A party who has not consented to participation shall file documents with the court and the County Clerk, and serve and be served with documents, in hard copy. NY R UNIF TRIAL CTS § 202.5-b(b)(2)(i).

d. *Service upon party.* If a party has not appeared by an attorney or the party's attorney cannot be served, service shall be upon the party by a method specified in NY CPLR Rule 2103(b)(1), NY CPLR Rule 2103(b)(2), NY CPLR Rule 2103(b)(4), NY CPLR Rule 2103(b)(5) or NY CPLR Rule 2103(b)(6). NY CPLR Rule 2103(c).

e. *Service on all parties.* Each paper served on any party shall be served on every other party who has appeared, except

as otherwise may be provided by court order or as provided in NY CPLR § 3012 or in NY CPLR § 3215(f). Upon demand by a party, the plaintiff shall supply that party with a list of those who have appeared and the names and addresses of their attorneys. NY CPLR Rule 2103(e).

f. *Service by filing.* If a paper cannot be served by any of the methods specified in NY CPLR Rule 2103(b) and NY CPLR Rule 2103(c), service may be made by filing the paper as if it were a paper required to be filed. NY CPLR Rule 2103(d).

g. *Definitions.* For the purposes of NY CPLR Rule 2103:

i. "Mailing" means the deposit of a paper enclosed in a first class postpaid wrapper, addressed to the address designated by a person for that purpose or, if none is designated, at that person's last known address, in a post office or official depository under the exclusive care and custody of the United States Postal Service within the state;

ii. "Electronic means" means any method of transmission of information between computers or other machines designed for the purpose of sending and receiving such transmissions, and which allows the recipient to reproduce the information transmitted in a tangible medium of expression;

iii. "Facsimile transmission" means any method of transmission of documents to a facsimile machine at a remote location which can automatically produce a tangible copy of such documents. NY CPLR Rule 2103(f).

G. Hearings

1. *Oral argument.* Motion papers received by the clerk of the court on or before the return date shall be deemed submitted as of the return date. The assigned judge, in his or her discretion or at the request of a party, thereafter may determine that any motion be orally argued and may fix a time for oral argument. NY R UNIF TRIAL CTS § 202.8(d).

a. A party requesting oral argument shall set forth such request in its notice of motion or in its order to show cause or on the first page of the answering papers, as the case may be. Where all parties to a motion request oral argument, oral argument shall be granted unless the court shall determine it to be unnecessary. NY R UNIF TRIAL CTS § 202.8(d).

b. Where a motion is brought on by order to show cause, the court may set forth in the order that oral argument is required on the return date of the motion. NY R UNIF TRIAL CTS § 202.8(d).

i. *BRONX COUNTY.* All orders to show cause, with the exception of orders to show cause that are returnable in the City Part, the STP Part, the Matrimonial Part and the Preliminary/Compliance Conference Part (IA-11), submitted on or after August 25, 2003, will be returnable on a Monday in the assigned Justice's part and appear on his or her motion calendar. Appearances will be required on orders to show cause. NY R BRONX FIL R Doc. 8. A motion on notice or a notice of petition in a New York Supreme Court E-File (hereafter known as NYSCEF) case, as in others, shall be made returnable in the Motion Support Office (Room 217). NY R BRONX E FIL R Doc. 1(1).

- After a motion/petition and notice are filed with the NYSCEF system, the Motion Support Office will automatically place the motion/proceeding on the submit calendar in the Motion Support Office (Room 217) for the return date. No appearance or other action by the filing attorney is required in order for the motion to be calendared if the motion fee is paid for via NYSCEF. Motions in e-filed cases (other than tax certiorari cases) appear on the submit calendar in Room 217 on the return date. NY R BRONX E FIL R Doc. 1(2).

c. *KINGS COUNTY.* All motions require appearances and oral argument. NY R L KINGS Pt. C, Rule 3.

2. *Return date; Time for hearing.* A notice of motion shall specify the time and place of the hearing on the motion. NY CPLR Rule 2214(a). The moving party determines when a motion on notice shall be heard, but she has to consult the court's or judge's calendar practice first. The movant picks out a "return day" sufficiently far off to assure that the notice requirements of NY CPLR Rule 2214(b) can be met, and to assure as well that the day picked is a day on which the assigned judge hears motions. SIEGEL-NYPRAC § 247.

a. *Judge assigned to hear motion*

i. *Referral to judge supervising disclosure.* Unless the chief administrator of the courts has, by rule, provided otherwise, if a case has been assigned to a judge to supervise disclosure pursuant to NY CPLR § 3104, all motions preliminary to trial shall be referred to such judge whenever practicable. NY CPLR Rule 3214(a).

ii. *Referral to judge who decided prior motion.* Any motion may be referred to a judge who decided a prior motion in the action. NY CPLR Rule 2217(a).

iii. *Transfer when judge unable to hear motion.* If a motion is made to a judge who is or will be for any reason unable

to hear it, it may be transferred by order of such judge or by written stipulation of the parties to any other judge to whom it might originally have been made. NY CPLR Rule 2217(c).

iv. *Procedure for unassigned cases.* If a case has not been assigned to a judge, the motion shall be made returnable before the court, and a copy of the moving papers, together with a request for judicial intervention, shall be filed with the court, with proof of service upon all other parties, where required by NY R UNIF TRIAL CTS § 202.6, within five (5) days of service upon the other parties. The moving party shall give written notice of the index number to all other parties immediately after filing of the papers. NY R UNIF TRIAL CTS § 202.8(b).

- *Responding papers.* Copies of all responding papers shall be submitted to the court, with proof of service and with the index number set forth in the papers, on or before the return date. NY R UNIF TRIAL CTS § 202.8(b).
- *Assignment after request for judicial intervention.* The case shall be assigned to a judge as soon as practicable after the filing of the request for judicial intervention pursuant to NY R UNIF TRIAL CTS § 202.6, but in no event later than the return date. After assignment to the judge, the court shall provide for appropriate notice to the parties of the name of the assigned judge. NY R UNIF TRIAL CTS § 202.8(b).
- *Motions to be heard in another county.* Motion papers noticed to be heard in a county other than the county where the venue of the action has been placed by the plaintiff shall be assigned to a judge in accordance with procedures established by the Chief Administrator. NY R UNIF TRIAL CTS § 202.8(b).

v. *ALBANY COUNTY: Motions referred to IAS Justice.* All motions made after a case has been assigned a day certain shall be referred to the IAS Justice unless the motion is returnable during the term in which the matter has been assigned a day certain, in that event, the matter will be referred to the Part 1 Justice for that particular term who may entertain the motion or refer such motion to the IAS Justice. Under those circumstances, the Part I Justice shall decide whether or not to strike the note of issue or assign the matter a new day certain. NY R 3 JD SUP Doc. 1(H)(2). All motions shall be returnable before the assigned justice. NY R 3 JD SUP Doc. 1(B).

b. *Trial of issue raised by motion.* The court may order that an issue of fact raised on a motion shall be separately tried by the court or a referee. If the issue is triable of right by jury, the court shall give the parties an opportunity to demand a jury trial of such issue. Failure to make such demand within the time limited by the court, or, if no such time is limited, before trial begins, shall be deemed a waiver of the right to trial by jury. An order under NY CPLR § 2218 shall specify the issue to be tried. NY CPLR § 2218.

c. *Audio-visual coverage of trial court proceeding.* Audio-visual coverage of proceedings in the trial courts shall be permitted only in accordance with the provisions of Part 131 of the Rules of the Chief Administrator (NY R CHIEF ADMIN § 131.1, et seq.). NY R CHIEF J § 29.3.

d. *Adjournment of return date.* Stipulations of adjournment of the return date made by the parties shall be in writing and shall be submitted to the assigned judge. Such stipulation shall be effective unless the court otherwise directs. No more than three (3) stipulated adjournments for an aggregate period of sixty (60) days shall be submitted without prior permission of the court. NY R UNIF TRIAL CTS § 202.8(e)(1).

i. Absent agreement by the parties, a request by any party for an adjournment shall be submitted in writing, upon notice to the other party, to the assigned judge on or before the return date. The court will notify the requesting party whether the adjournment has been granted. NY R UNIF TRIAL CTS § 202.8(e)(2).

ii. *BRONX COUNTY.* Non-disclosure motions for IA5, IA7 and IA22 will be adjourned for oral argument to the Monday of the second week following the week of the return date of the motion. All other non-disclosure motions will be deemed submitted on the return date and forwarded to Chambers unless a stipulation of adjournment complying with the requirements of NY R UNIF TRIAL CTS § 202.8(e) is submitted, in which event, the motion will be adjourned for the requested date and kept in the Clerk's Office. If a non-stipulated request for adjournment or notice is submitted, the motion and request will be forwarded to Chambers for judicial approval or denial of the request. In either event, the attorney requesting the adjournment will be notified, via telephone, of the granting or denial of the request and instructed to notify his adversary. NY R BRONX FIL R Doc. 8.

iii. *BRONX COUNTY.* Motions that have been e-filed may be adjourned in Room 217 if an adjournment complies with the procedures of the Motion Support Office (explained in the "Filing Rules—Motion Procedure" section of the "Courthouse Procedures" link on the website of [the] court). An adjournment that so complies may be obtained by filing a stipulation of all parties with NYSCEF (designated in the filing menu as a "Stipulation to Adjourn Motion"). NY R BRONX E FIL R Doc. 1(3).

iv. *NEW YORK COUNTY.* The Courtroom also maintains a "APB (All Papers By)" Calendar, which is used when

a party seeks an adjournment but fails to comply with the Courtroom's procedures or there is a failure to comply with procedures that requires the clerk to adjourn the motion/application (e.g., failure to submit a Confirmation Notice in an e-filed case). The case may be put over for three days to allow compliance with those procedures, as described further below. NY R NY CTY Procedure II(C); NY R NY CTY E FIL Doc. 2(D)(2). E-filed applications may be adjourned in the Part if an adjournment complies with the Part's procedures (see the Uniform Rules of the Justices (Local Rules) on the court's website). An adjournment that so complies may be obtained by filing with NYSCEF a stipulation of all parties (designated in the filing menu as a Stipulation—Adjournment of Motion—Before Judge); the motion number and the current return date of the motion being adjourned shall be set forth in the "Additional Document Information" field in NYSCEF. Absent any problems, the Part will effectuate the adjournment without need for an appearance or any other action by the parties. NY R NY CTY E FIL Doc. 2(D)(4).

v. *QUEENS COUNTY.* The Motion Support Office is NOT authorized to grant adjournments. NY R L QUEENS MOT SUP Doc. 1.

e. *ALBANY COUNTY: Motion terms.* There shall be a. . . Motion Term on each Friday in the Supreme Court, Albany County. The Friday Motion Term shall include all Article 78 Proceedings involving New York State and proceedings commenced pursuant to Article 14 of the Civil Service Law (including applications for injunctive relief made pursuant to section 209-a of the Civil Service Law). NY R 3 JD SUP Doc. 1(F). Generally, parties will be granted only one adjournment for the Friday Motion Term. NY R 3 JD SUP Doc. 1(F).

f. *ALBANY COUNTY: Motion determined without hearing.* All motions are deemed "submitted" on the return date and no appearances are required by the parties. NY R 3 JD SUP Doc. 1(B). In the event oral argument is requested, the parties should not appear on the return date. At the discretion of the assigned Judge and upon the granting of a request for oral argument, the parties will be notified by Chambers of the scheduled time and place at which argument will be heard. Where a motion is brought on by order to show cause, the court may set forth in the order that appearances and/or oral argument are required on the return date of the motion. NY R 3 JD SUP Doc. 1(B).

g. *BRONX COUNTY: Return date.* All assigned and unassigned motions will be returnable five (5) days a week in the Civil Branch Clerk's Office, Room 217, at 9:30 a.m. NY R BRONX FIL R Doc. 8.

i. If on any submitted non-disclosure motion oral argument is requested and granted, or directed by the Court, the motion shall be adjourned for oral argument before the I.A. Judge on the second Monday following the week of the return date of the motion. Attorneys will be notified via telephone of the adjourned date. NY R BRONX FIL R Doc. 8.

h. *BRONX COUNTY: Oral argument.* Calendars of disclosure motions and other motions adjourned for oral argument will be published for the four (4) business days preceding the rescheduled appearance date and on the rescheduled date of the motion. These repetitive publications will serve as the notification of procedure of adjournment of all motions. In addition, two (2) days before the return date of unassigned motions a list of such motions indicating the assigned Justice and the adjourned date of the motion will be published. NY R BRONX FIL R Doc. 8.

i. *BRONX COUNTY: Resolution before return date.* Counsel/parties must advise the Court in writing on or before the return date of all motions that have been resolved by Counsel/parties themselves and all motions the movant(s) wish to be withdrawn. NY R BRONX FIL R Doc. 8.

j. *ERIE COUNTY: Calendaring of motions.* Refer to individual Justice's Part Rules. NY R ERIE E FIL Doc. 3(V)(B).

k. *KINGS COUNTY: Return date set by court.* Irrespective of the return date indicated in the notice of motion, motions will be rescheduled by the E-file/Motion Support Office to a date designated by the assigned Judge. NY R L KINGS Pt. C, Rule 2.

l. *KINGS COUNTY: Calendar calls.* There shall be two (2) calendar calls on motion days. The first calendar call shall be at 9:30 AM and the second calendar call shall be at 10:45 AM, unless the Judge's Part Rules provide otherwise. Defaults shall only be taken on second call. Attorneys with appearances elsewhere in the courthouse may advise the clerk of their whereabouts to avoid a default. Failure to so advise the clerk or appear at the default calendar call will result in a default order being entered or the motion being marked off the calendar. NY R L KINGS Pt. C, Rule 7.

m. *NEW YORK COUNTY: Return date and assigned courtroom.* Motions made by notice of motion and petitions and notices of petition in special proceedings are processed by the General Clerk's Office (Room 119) and are to be made returnable in the Motion Submission Part Courtroom (Room 130) on any business day of the week at 9:30 AM. There are some differences in electronically-filed cases. NY R NY CTY Procedure II; NY R NY CTY Procedure II(C); NY R NY CTY J RUL Rule 13(a).

i. For the convenience of counsel, between 9:00 A.M. and 9:30 A.M. each day, in advance of the "call," Room 130

accepts (1) written stipulations; (2) affidavits/affirmations reciting the required details as to an adjournment on consent; (3) stipulations, letters or other writings withdrawing motions; and (4) final papers or complete sets of papers on motions. For motions in which these items are handed in before the "call," no one need remain to answer the "call." Counsel/parties must advise the court, either between 9:00 A.M. and 9:30 A.M. or at the "call," of all motions or cases that have been resolved by counsel/parties themselves and all motions that the movant no longer wishes to pursue. If such resolution occurs subsequent to the "call", the assigned Justice must be advised as soon as possible, by written notice sent to the Part, so that the court does not do unnecessary work. NY R NY CTY Procedure II(C).

ii. Depending upon the assigned Part, contested motions submitted in the Motion Submission Part Courtroom are submitted without argument, or rescheduled for oral argument if so directed by the assigned Justice. For Justices who schedule argument on a case-by-case basis, notice of the argument date will be transmitted by the court. Counsel may ascertain how a motion submitted in Courtroom 130 was marked by consulting Scroll on the court's website, the e-Track application, or, on the two (2) days immediately following the submission date, the New York Law Journal. NY R NY CTY J RUL Rule 13(a).

n. *NEW YORK COUNTY: Motion call.* Each day in the Motion Submission Part Courtroom, commencing at 9:30 A.M., all motions returnable that day will be "called" for the submission of these papers, which must be handed up at this "call" or, as described below, immediately before. Because hundreds of motions appear on the Room 130 calendars every day, motion papers (other than part of the moving papers as described above) cannot be accepted on any day prior to the return date. Courtesy copies are not required nor accepted, but working copies are required by certain Justices in e-filed cases. NY R NY CTY Procedure II(C). If argument is directed, it will take place on an announced date shortly after the day of submission. NY R NY CTY Procedure II(C).

o. *NEW YORK COUNTY: Oral arguments.* Pursuant to request of some Justices, motions submitted in Room 130 will automatically be scheduled for a set argument date in the Part. Other Justices determine on a case-by-case basis after submission in Room 130 whether to accept a particular substantive motion on submission, to require oral argument, or to hold a conference. NY R NY CTY Procedure II(D). If argument is directed by the Justice automatically, notice of argument and the argument date will be given in Room 130. Any appearing party is expected to give notice to all parties and an announcement to this effect is made in Room 130. If the motion is submitted in Room 130 and the Justice, after examining the file, determines that argument should be directed, notice of the argument and the argument date will not be sent by the court. To obtain notification of the argument date and other developments, counsel should use e-Track. If argument notification is not given or transmitted as just described, counsel should understand that the motion has been taken on submission for decision on the papers. NY R NY CTY Procedure II(D).

i. Calendars of motions to be argued in the Parts are published on the morning of the argument date and on the day before in the New York Law Journal under each Part. Argument information is available on a case-by-case basis in Scroll, and e-mail notifications are sent by e-Track to participating attorneys whenever a motion is scheduled for argument in the court's computer system. NY R NY CTY J RUL Rule 15(a)

p. *NEW YORK COUNTY: Motion determined without hearing.* Given the purpose of the Room 130 procedure, the substance of motions will not be addressed at the submission "call." No Judge is present. To the extent possible, motions submitted in Room 130 will be decided "on the papers." Indeed, attorneys are encouraged to use service or clerks to deliver papers or working copies, or to agree among themselves to have one of them deliver papers for all parties by service or a clerk. Counsel for the movant need not appear to "take a default" on any motion or for any other reason. Motions will be submitted, not marked off, in the absence of the movant. Opposing counsel similarly need not appear in person in order to avoid suffering a default. Delivery of papers by service or a clerk will suffice. The court's goal is to be able to collect papers on motions in an orderly fashion but without any attorney having to make an appearance in Room 130 at any time. NY R NY CTY Procedure II(C).

q. *ONONDAGA COUNTY: Return date.* If the motion is the first filing in an action, the case will be assigned and counsel will be notified by the Supreme Court Clerk's Office via the NYSCEF system of the assigned justice and return date. NY R ONDGA E FIL Protocol(B)(7)(c). If the motion is on a previously assigned case, counsel may choose a return date from the assigned justice's motion term schedule. If the date in unavailable, the Supreme Court Clerk's Office will assign the motion to the next available motion term date and will notify counsel via e-mail. The change will also appear in the notification generated by the NYSCEF system. NY R ONDGA E FIL Protocol(B)(7)(d).

r. *QUEENS COUNTY: Return date.* Motions must be made returnable on the proper day/time based on the assigned judge. NY R L QUEENS MOT SUP Doc. 1. Failure to make a motion returnable on the proper day/time may result in the motion being administratively rescheduled or marked off. NY R L QUEENS MOT SUP Doc. 1.

s. *QUEENS COUNTY: Unassigned motions.* For RJI/Motions, due to the fact that the movant would not know who the

assigned judge will be, the notice of motion may be returnable any day of the week. RJI/Motions shall be made returnable in "Queens Supreme Court" with no address designated. The motion will be administratively rescheduled to the proper day of the week based on the judge (once a judge has been assigned). Within one (1) week of filing, the movant must check online to see who the assigned judge is (and therefore the location/date/time) that their motion is now returnable. Movant must then notify their adversary of this information prior to the return date. NY R L QUEENS MOT SUP Doc. 1.

3. *Entry of order after hearing.* An order determining a motion shall be entered and filed in the office of the clerk of the court where the action is triable, and all papers used on the motion and any opinion or memorandum in writing shall be filed with that clerk unless the order dispenses with such filing. When a statute or civil practice rule requires such filing and entry in a county other than that in which the order was made, the party prevailing on the motion shall file the order and the papers used on the motion with the proper clerk after receiving them. If a party fails to file any papers required to be filed under NY CPLR Rule 2220(a), the order may be vacated as irregular, with costs. NY CPLR Rule 2220(a). For more information on the entry of an order after a motion, refer to NY CPLR Rule 2219.

    a. *BRONX COUNTY: Settled orders.* A Judge's decision will often call for a Settled Order. The purpose of the settled order is to give effect to the decision by directing that some action be done and/or that a court official perform some task. NY R BRONX LEG SUP Doc. 2. A settled order consists of a notice of settlement informing all parties that the proposed order will be presented to the judge who made the decision on a date certain. Next comes the proposed order which will be presented to the judge. This order should conform to the judge's decision and should direct the relief granted in the decision. This should be followed by proof of service upon all parties who were noticed with the decision. It is also helpful if a copy of the judge's decision is included along with the other papers. A settled order should always be noticed before the judge who made the decision. NY R BRONX LEG SUP Doc. 2.

        i. Although an order is usually settled by the party who prevailed on the motion, any party may settle the order. It should be presented to the court within sixty (60) days of the decision. The other parties are entitled to ten (10) days notice where service of the settled order is done by mail, five (5) days if the notice is personally delivered. An attorney who is served with a notice of settlement which he believes does not accurately reflect the decision may settle a counter order. The counter order must be noticed for the same day and must be served not less than seven (7) days if by mail and two (2) days if personally delivered. NY R BRONX LEG SUP Doc. 2.

        ii. Settled orders are usually sent to the judge the day after they noticed for settlement. No appearance is necessary or even contemplated on a settled order. If the decision directs "submit order", then no notice is necessary, and the order will be sent to the judge as soon a practical after it is received. No fees are collected on settled orders. NY R BRONX LEG SUP Doc. 2.

    b. *ERIE COUNTY: Proposed orders.* Proposed orders shall be submitted through the NYSCEF system and a working copy provided to the IAS Justice for signature, if Part Rules so require. NY R ERIE E FIL Doc. 3(V)(G).

    c. *KINGS COUNTY: Long form orders.* If the Court directs that an order be settled or submitted on a motion in a NYSCEF case, the proposed order, with Notice of Settlement where required, and any proposed counter-order shall be filed with the Court via NYSCEF. The relevant clerk's office will process the documents in the customary manner. NY R L KINGS E FIL Doc. 1(E).

        i. WORKING COPIES OF PROPOSED ORDERS WITH NOTICE OF SETTLEMENT MUST BE SUBMITTED IN THE MOTION SUPPORT OFFICE (ROOM 227) AS EXPLAINED HEREIN. THEY MUST NOT BE DELIVERED TO THE PART OR CHAMBERS, EXCEPT WHERE THE INDIVIDUAL JUSTICE'S PART RULES PROVIDE OTHERWISE; DOING SO WILL CAUSE ADMINISTRATIVE CONFUSION AND POSSIBLE MISPLACEMENT OF PAPERS. Any such submission shall be sent in a timely manner (kindly review individual Justice's rules) and be conspicuously marked on the outside "NYSCEF Matter;" lack of such marking may delay processing. After an order/counter-order has been signed, it will be scanned, and the County Clerk will affix the entry stamp into the NYSCEF system, which will immediately transmit notice of this event via e-mail, including a link to the entered document, to all participating attorneys and unrepresented litigants in the case. Such transmittal does not constitute Notice of Entry. NY R L KINGS E FIL Doc. 1(E).

    d. *NEW YORK COUNTY: Long form orders.* Although the court strongly favors the use of short form orders and judgments, there are instances when settlement of an order or judgment is appropriate. When a Justice directs in a decision that a long form order or judgment be settled, that decision is recorded in the court's computer system by the General Clerk's Office and the motion file with decision is held in the Order Section of the Office in Room 119. The settlement process takes place there. NY R NY CTY Procedure II(D); NY R NY CTY E FIL Doc. 2(E).

        i. A proposed long form order or judgment in compliance NY R UNIF TRIAL CTS § 202.48 must be presented to

the relevant back office, together with a notice of settlement which bears a settlement date, the date on which the order is to be ready for formal presentation to the Justice. In an e-filed case the submission shall be made electronically. The proposed order or counter-order should be e-filed and it will be transmitted automatically by the NYSCEF system to the appropriate back office. The return date and time of the proposed order must be at 9:30 A.M. no sooner than either five (5) days from personal service of the proposed order or ten (10) days from service by mail. Proof of timely service on the other parties must accompany the proposed order in a hard copy case. If an order or judgment is submitted late (later than sixty (60) days from signing and filing of the decision) and the proponent can show good cause for this tardiness, an affidavit or affirmation justifying the delay should be annexed to the proposed order, together with proof of service thereof. If persuaded, the Justice will consider the proposed order despite its untimeliness. NY R NY CTY Procedure II(D); NY R NY CTY E FIL Doc. 2(E).

ii. Sometimes a decision will state "Submit Order." The submitting party should prepare a long form order and make it returnable without notice. Counsel should deliver the proposed order to the Order Section of the appropriate back office, except in an e-filed case, when it shall be submitted electronically. NY R NY CTY Procedure II(D). If the decision of the court directs that a proposed order be settled or submitted in the Part or in Chambers, that direction, should, of course, be followed without presentation of the proposal to the back office. NY R NY CTY Procedure II(D).

iii. For information on proposed counter-orders, refer to NY R NY CTY Procedure II(D) and NY R NY CTY J RUL Rule 16(b).

e. *QUEENS COUNTY: Proposed orders.* If the court directs that an order be settled or submitted on a motion in an E-file case, the proposed order and any proposed counter-order shall be filed with the court on-line with proof of service. (If a decision refers to a proceeding on the record, a copy of the transcript must be submitted.) Working copies of all proposed orders MUST be submitted to the Motion Support Office before an order can be reviewed. NY R L QUEENS E-FILE Doc. 1(I).

i. Counsel are advised to adhere to NY R UNIF TRIAL CTS § 202.48 regarding the submission or settlement of their proposed order or judgment. Persons who are submitting proposed orders/judgments pursuant to a previously issued memorandum decision must submit a copy of the memorandum decision with their proposed order/judgment. Upon E-Filing a proposed order/judgement, a working copy of the proposed order/judgement must be provided to the Motion Support Office. NY R L QUEENS MOT SUP Doc. 1.

H. Forms

1. Official Motion to Correct Pleadings Forms for New York

a. Request for judicial intervention. NY R UNIF TRIAL CTS § 202.6.

b. Notice of motion. NY R UNIF TRIAL CTS § 202.7(b).

2. New York Motion to Correct Pleadings Forms

a. Forms; Notice of motion to strike out pleadings. NYPRAC-COMM § 65:79.

b. Notice of motion to correct complaint; Official form 24. MCF CPLR § 4:295.

c. Notice of motion to correct complaint; Proposed official form 28. MCF CPLR § 4:296.

d. General form of attorney's affirmation upon notice of motion. MCF CPLR § 5:19.

e. General form of affidavit upon notice of motion. MCF CPLR § 5:20.

f. General form of affidavit of service of motion papers. MCF CPLR § 5:24.

I. Applicable Rules

1. *State rules*

a. Short title; Application; Construction; Definitions. NY CPLR § 101; NY CPLR § 103; NY CPLR § 104; NY CPLR § 105.

b. Appendix of official forms. NY CPLR § 107.

c. Service of process. NY CPLR § 312-a; NY CPLR Rule 320.

d. Extensions of time generally. NY CPLR § 2004.

e. Form of papers. NY CPLR Rule 2101; NY CPLR Rule 2102; NY CPLR § 2105; NY CPLR Rule 2106; NY GEN BUS § 399-ddd; NY R UNIF TRIAL CTS § 215.2; NY R UNIF TRIAL CTS § 215.3.

f. Service of papers. NY CPLR Rule 2103.

g. Where motion made; In supreme court action. NY CPLR § 2212.
h. Motion papers; Service; Time. NY CPLR Rule 2214.
i. Relief demanded by other than moving party. NY CPLR Rule 2215.
j. Prior motion; Ex parte motion; Transfer of motion; Hearings; Orders. NY CPLR Rule 2217; NY CPLR § 2218; NY CPLR Rule 2220.
k. Computation of time. NY CPLR § 2402; NY GEN CONSTR § 19; NY GEN CONSTR § 20; NY GEN CONSTR § 25-a; NY GEN CONSTR § 30; NY GEN CONSTR § 31; NY GEN CONSTR § 53.
l. Service of pleadings and demand for complaint. NY CPLR § 3012.
m. Motion to correct pleadings. NY CPLR Rule 3024.
n. Motions heard by judge supervising disclosure; Stay of disclosure. NY CPLR Rule 3214.
o. Fees; Index number fees of county clerks. NY CPLR § 8018.
p. Hours of court; Proceedings in court. NY R CHIEF J § 3.1; NY R CHIEF J § 29.3.
q. Application of part; Waiver; Additional rules; Application of CPLR; Definitions. NY R UNIF TRIAL CTS § 202.1.
r. Papers filed in court; Electronic filing in supreme court. NY R UNIF TRIAL CTS § 202.5; NY R UNIF TRIAL CTS § 202.5-a; NY R UNIF TRIAL CTS § 202.5-b; NY R UNIF TRIAL CTS § 202.5-bb.
s. Request for judicial intervention. NY R UNIF TRIAL CTS § 202.6.
t. Calendaring of motions; Uniform notice of motion form; Affirmation of good faith. NY R UNIF TRIAL CTS § 202.7.
u. Motion procedure; Preliminary conferences. NY R UNIF TRIAL CTS § 202.8; NY R UNIF TRIAL CTS § 202.12.
v. Rules of the commercial division of the Supreme Court. NY R UNIF TRIAL CTS § 202.70.
w. Signing of papers. NY R CHIEF ADMIN § 130-1.1-a.

2. *Local rules*
    a. *Albany County*
        i. Third judicial district rules. NY R 3 JD SUP Doc. 1.
    b. *Bronx County*
        i. Filing of papers in supreme court. NY R BRONX FIL R Doc. 1.
        ii. Request for judicial intervention. NY R BRONX FIL R Doc. 2.
        iii. Motion procedure. NY R BRONX FIL R Doc. 8.
        iv. Commercial division. NY R BRONX FIL R Doc. 12.
        v. Motions on notice. NY R BRONX E FIL R Doc. 1.
        vi. Settled orders. NY R BRONX LEG SUP Doc. 2.
    c. *Erie County*
        i. Joint protocols for New York State Courts E-Filing (NYSCEF) cases filed in Supreme Court, Erie County. NY R ERIE E FIL Doc. 3.
    d. *Kings County*
        i. Papers. NY R L KINGS Pt. A, Papers.
        ii. Service of motion papers. NY R L KINGS Pt. C, Rule 1.
        iii. Scheduling of motions. NY R L KINGS Pt. C, Rule 2.
        iv. Appearance and argument. NY R L KINGS Pt. C, Rule 3.
        v. Courtesy copies. NY R L KINGS Pt. C, Rule 5.
        vi. Motion calendar calls. NY R L KINGS Pt. C, Rule 7.
        vii. Protocol on courthouse and county clerk procedures for electronically filed cases. NY R L KINGS E FIL Doc. 1.
    e. *New York County*
        i. Commencement of cases. NY R NY CTY Procedure I.

ii. RJIs and assignments. NY R NY CTY Procedure IA.

iii. Motions and special proceedings by notice of motion/petition. NY R NY CTY Procedure II.

iv. County clerk litigation functions. NY R NY CTY Procedure XI.

v. Protocol on courthouse and county clerk procedures for electronically filed cases. NY R NY CTY E FIL Doc. 2.

vi. Redaction of information in documents filed with the county clerk and the court. NY R NY CTY J RUL Rule A-1.

vii. Papers by fax. NY R NY CTY J RUL Rule 4.

viii. Motions on notice; Orders to show cause. NY R NY CTY J RUL Rule 13.

ix. Motion papers. NY R NY CTY J RUL Rule 14.

x. Oral argument; Adjournments. NY R NY CTY J RUL Rule 15.

f. *Onondaga County*

i. Onondaga county protocol for case filings New York State Electronic Files (NYSCEF). NY R ONDGA E FIL Protocol.

g. *Queens County*

i. Motion support office. NY R L QUEENS MOT SUP Doc. 1.

ii. Queens county protocol on courthouse procedures for electronically filed cases. NY R L QUEENS E-FILE Doc. 1.

J. Miscellaneous

NOTE: Individual judges' rules may apply.

ALBANY COUNTY

JUSTICE LISA M. FISHER: NY R 3 JD FISHER Fisher; NY R 3 JD FISHER Fisher, PC Order.

JUSTICE RICHARD MOTT: NY R 3 JD MOTT Mott.

JUSTICE STEPHAN G. SCHICK: NY R 3 JD Schick.

FORECLOSURE SETTLEMENT PART: NY R 3 JD Foreclosure Settlement.

BRONX COUNTY

JUSTICE PAUL L. ALPERT: [NY R BRONX J Part IA-29, as amended by NY ORDER 20-0337].

JUSTICE BEN BARBATO: NY R BRONX J Part IA-21.

JUSTICE MARY ANNE BRIGANTTI: [NY R BRONX J Part IA-15, as amended by NY ORDER 20-0338].

JUSTICE JOSEPH E. CAPELLA: NY R BRONX J Part IA-23.

JUSTICE MITCHELL DANZIGER: NY R BRONX J Part IA-3/33 ; [NY R BRONX J Danziger, Part IA-3/33, as amended by NY ORDER 20-0339].

JUSTICE LAURA G. DOUGLAS: NY R BRONX J Part IA-11.

JUSTICE RUBEN FRANCO: NY R BRONX J Part IA-26.

JUSTICE DORIS M. GONZALEZ: NY R BRONX J Part IA-24.

JUSTICE WILMA GUZMAN: NY R BRONX J Part IA-7; [NY R BRONX J Guzman, Part IA-7 Virtual, as amended by NY ORDER 20-0340].

JUSTICE ROBERT T. JOHNSON: NY R BRONX J Part IA-12.

JUSTICE DONALD A. MILES: NY R BRONX J Part IA-8.

JUSTICE DONNA M. MILLS: NY R BRONX J Part IA-9.

JUSTICE JULIA I. RODRIGUEZ: NY R BRONX J Part IA-18; [NY R BRONX J Part IA-27, as amended by NY ORDER 20-0341].

JUSTICE LLINET M. ROSADO: [NY R BRONX J Part IA-25, as amended by NY ORDER 20-0342].

JUSTICE NORMA RUIZ: NY R BRONX J Part IA-22; [NY R BRONX J Ruiz, Part IA-22 Virtual, as amended by NY ORDER 20-0343].

JUSTICE HOWARD H. SHERMAN: NY R BRONX J Part IA-4.
JUSTICE FERNANDO TAPIA: NY R BRONX J Part IA-13.
JUSTICE ELIZABETH A. TAYLOR: NY R BRONX J Part IA-2.
JUSTICE ALISON Y. TRUITT: NY R BRONX J Part IA-5.
PART IDV: NY R BRONX J Doc. 1.
PRE-TRIAL PART RULES: NY R BRONX J Doc. 2.
PRE TRIAL WORKSHEET: NY R BRONX J Doc. 3.
FORECLOSURE SETTLEMENT PART RULES: NY R BRONX J Doc. 4.
GUARDIANSHIP PART RULES: NY R BRONX J Doc. 5.
LPM PART RULES: NY R BRONX J Doc. 6.

ERIE COUNTY

JUSTICE M. WILLIAM BOLLER: NY R 8 JD J Boller.
JUSTICE RALPH A. BONIELLO: NY R 8 JD J Boniello.
JUSTICE CHRISTOPHER J. BURN: NY R 8 JD J Burns.
JUSTICE RUSSELL P. BUSCAGLIA: NY R 8 JD J Buscaglia.
JUSTICE FRANK CARUSO: NY R 8 JD J Caruso.
JUSTICE STEPHEN W. CASS: NY R 8 JD J Cass.
JUSTICE DEBORAH A. CHIMES: NY R 8 JD J Chimes.
JUSTICE EMILIO COLAIACOVO: [NY R 8 JD J Colaiacovo, as amended by NY ORDER 20-0252].
JUSTICE DIANE Y. DEVLIN: NY R 8 JD J Devlin.
JUSTICE JAMES H. DILLON: NY R 8 JD J Dillon.
JUSTICE PAULA L. FEROLETO: NY R 8 JD J Feroleto.
JUSTICE DANIEL J. FURLONG: [NY R 8 JD J Furlong, as amended by NY ORDER 20-0253].
JUSTICE JOSEPH R. GLOWNIA: NY R 8 JD J Glownia.
JUSTICE MARK J. GRISANTI: NY R 8 JD J Grisanti.
JUSTICE DEBORAH A. HAENDIGES: NY R 8 JD J Haendiges.
JUSTICE LYNN W. KEANE: [NY R 8 JD J Keane, as amended by NY ORDER 20-0254].
JUSTICE RICHARD C. KLOCH, Sr.: NY R 8 JD J Kloch.
JUSTICE FREDERICK J. MARSHALL: [NY R 8 JD J Marshall, as amended by NY ORDER 20-0255.
JUSTICE JOHN L. MICHALSKI: NY R 8 JD J Michalski.
JUSTICE MARK A. MONTOUR: [NY R 8 JD J Montour, as amended by NY ORDER 20-0256].
JUSTICE HENRY NOWAK: NY R 8 JD J Nowak.
JUSTICE JOHN F. O'DONNELL: NY R 8 JD J O'Donnell.
JUSTICE JEANETTE OGDEN: NY R 8 JD J Ogden.
JUSTICE CATHERINE NUGENT-PANEPINTO: NY R 8 JD J Nugent-Panepinto.
JUSTICE FRANK A. SEDITA, III: [NY R 8 JD J Sedita, as amended by NY ORDER 20-0257].
JUSTICE SARA SHELDON: NY R 8 JD J Sheldon.
JUSTICE DONNA M. SIWEK: NY R 8 JD J Siwek.
JUSTICE MARY L. SLISZ: NY R 8 JD J Slisz.
JUSTICE TIMOTHY J. WALKER: [NY R 8 JD J Walker, as amended by NY ORDER 20-0258].
JUSTICE DENNIS E. WARD: NY R 8 JD J Ward.
JUSTICE PAUL B. WOJTASZEK: [NY R 8 JD J Wojtaszek, as amended by NY ORDER 20-0259].

JUSTICE CHARLES N. ZAMBITO: [NY R 8 JD J Zambito, as amended by NY ORDER 20-0260].

SUPREME COURT LEGAL STAFF: NY R 8 JD J Legal Staff.

KINGS COUNTY

JUSTICE RACHEL A. ADAMS: NY R KINGS J Part 5F.

JUSTICE LOREN BAILY-SCHIFFMAN: NY R KINGS J Part 65.

JUSTICE REGINALD A. BODDIE: NY R KINGS J Part 95.

JUSTICE THERESA M. CICCOTTO: NY R KINGS J Part 19; NY R KINGS J Part 5J.

JUSTICE LISSETTE COLON: NY R KINGS J Part Rules.

JUSTICE GENINE EDWARDS: NY R KINGS J Part 80.

JUSTICE PAMELA L. FISHER: [NY R KINGS J Part 94, as amended by NY ORDER 20-0208].

JUSTICE ROBIN GARSON: NY R KINGS J Part 75.

JUSTICE LARA J. GENOVISI: [NY R KINGS J Part 34, as amended by NY ORDER 20-0209].

JUSTICE BERNARD J. GRAHAM: NY R KINGS J Part 36.

JUSTICE DAWN JIMENEZ-SALTA: NY R KINGS J Part 88.

JUSTICE INGRID JOSEPH: [NY R KINGS J Part FRP3 and Part 83, as amended by NY ORDER 20-0210].

JUSTICE KATHY J. KING: NY R KINGS J Part 64, 76K.

JUSTICE LAWRENCE KNIPEL: NY R KINGS J Part 57.

JUSTICE DONALD KURTZ: NY R KINGS J Part 26.

JUSTICE CARL LANDICINO: [NY R KINGS J Part 81, as amended by NY ORDER 20-0211].

JUSTICE KATHERINE LEVINE: [NY R KINGS J Part 20, 25, 92, as amended by NY ORDER 20-0211].

JUSTICE LORNA MCALLISTER: [NY R KINGS J Part 10, as amended by NY ORDER 20-0211].

JUSTICE ROSEMARIE MONTALBANO: [NY R KINGS J Part 19, 71, and 22, as amended by NY ORDER 20-0211].

JUSTICE RICHARD J. MONTELIONE: [NY R KINGS J Part 99 and DJMP, as amended by NY ORDER 20-0215].

JUSTICE LISA S. OTTLEY: NY R KINGS J Part 24.

JUSTICE MARK I. PARTNOW: NY R KINGS J Part 43.

JUSTICE ERIC I. PRUS: NY R KINGS J Part 5A.

JUSTICE FRANCOIS RIVERA: NY R KINGS J Part 52.

JUSTICE KAREN B. ROTHENBERG: NY R KINGS J Part 35.

JUSTICE LEON RUCHELSMAN: NY R KINGS J Part 1.

JUSTICE WAYNE P. SAITTA: NY R KINGS J Part 29.

JUSTICE ROBIN K. SHEARES: NY R KINGS J Part 96.

JUSTICE KENNETH P. SHERMAN: NY R KINGS J Part 67 and 78.

JUSTICE DEBRA SILBER: NY R KINGS J Part 9 and 5K.

JUSTICE ELLEN M. SPODEK: NY R KINGS J Part 63.

JUSTICE MARSHA L. STEINHARDT: NY R KINGS J Part 15.

JUSTICE JEFFREY S. SUNSHINE: NY R KINGS J Part 5G.

JUSTICE PETER P. SWEENEY: [NY R KINGS J Part 35, as amended by NY ORDER 20-0218].

JUSTICE DELORES J. THOMAS: [NY R KINGS J Part 5T, as amended by NY ORDER 20-0221].

JUSTICE WAVNY TOUSSAINT: NY R KINGS J Part 70.

JUSTICE RICHARD VELASQUEZ: NY R KINGS J Part 66.

JUSTICE CAROLYN E. WADE: NY R KINGS J Part 84.

JUSTICE EDWARD G. WALKER: [NY R KINGS J Part 90, as amended by NY ORDER 20-0219].

JUSTICE LILLIAN WAN: [NY R KINGS J Part 17, as amended by NY ORDER 20-0220].

JUSTICE MICHELLE WESTON: NY R KINGS J Part 3.

MENTAL HYGIENE PART: NY R KINGS J Part 77.

MATRIMONIAL PARTS DURING COVID-19 EMERGENCY: JUSTICE KAREN B. ROTHENBERG: NY R KINGS J Doc. 1.

NASSAU COUNTY

JUSTICE ANNA R. ANZALONE: NY R NASSAU S J Anzalone, Part 26.

JUSTICE STACY D. BENNETT: NY R NASSAU S J Bennett; NY R NASSAU S J Bennett, Form 1.

JUSTICE ANTONIO BRANDVEEN: NY R NASSAU S J Brandveen, Part 31.

JUSTICE JEFFREY S. BROWN: [NY R NASSAU S J Brown, as amended by NY ORDER 20-0297].

JUSTICE STEPHEN A. BUCARIA: NY R NASSAU S J Bucaria.

JUSTICE JULIANNE T. CAPETOLA: NY R NASSAU S J Capetola, Part 28.

JUSTICE EDMUND M. DANE: NY R NASSAU S J Dane, Part 33.

JUSTICE VITO M. DESTEFANO: NY R NASSAU S J DeStefano, Part 13; NY R NASSAU S J DeStefano, Form 1.

JUSTICE ARTHUR M. DIAMOND: NY R NASSAU S J Diamond, Part 7.

JUSTICE THOMAS FEINMAN: NY R NASSAU S J Feinman, Part 5.

JUSTICE JOHN M. GALASSO: NY R NASSAU S J Galasso, Part 22.

JUSTICE SHARON M.J. GIANELLI: NY R NASSAU S J Gianelli, Part 22; NY R NASSAU S J Gianelli, Form 1.

JUSTICE JEFFREY A. GOODSTEIN: NY R NASSAU S J Goodstein, Part 33; NY R NASSAU S J Goodstein, Form 1.

JUSTICE DAVID J. GUGERTY: [NY R NASSAU S J Gugerty, Part 31, as amended by NY ORDER 20-0298].

JUSTICE HELENE F. GUGERTY: NY R NASSAU S J Gugerty, Part 47.

JUSTICE STEVEN M. JAEGER: NY R NASSAU S J Jaeger, Part 35; NY R NASSAU S J Jaeger, Form 1.

JUSTICE JACK L. LIBERT: NY R NASSAU S J Libert, Part 23.

JUSTICE JOSEPH H. LORINTZ: NY R NASSAU S J Lorintz, Part 26; NY R NASSAU S J Lorintz, Form 1.

JUSTICE ROY S. MAHON: NY R NASSAU S J Mahon, Part 3.

JUSTICE RANDY SUE MARBER: NY R NASSAU S J Marber, Part 8.

JUSTICE JAMES P. MCCORMACK: [NY R NASSAU S J McCormack, Part 18, as amended by NY ORDER, 20-0299].

JUSTICE DICCIA T. PINEDA-KIRWAN: [NY R NASSAU S J Pineda-Kirwan, as amended by NY ORDER 20-0300].

JUSTICE THOMAS RADEMAKER: [NY R NASSAU S J Rademaker, Part 28, as amended by NY ORDER 20-0301]; [NY R NASSAU S J Rademaker, Form 1, as amended by NY ORDER 20-0301].

JUSTICE DENISE L. SHER: NY R NASSAU S J Rademaker, Part 32.

JUSTICE LEONARD D. STEINMAN: [NY R NASSAU S J Steinman, Part 15, as amended by NY ORDER 20-0303]; NY R NASSAU S J Steinman, Form 1.

JUSTICE HOWARD E. STURIM: NY R NASSAU S J Sturim, Part 50; NY R NASSAU S J Sturim, Form 1.

JUSTICE HELEN VOUTSINAS: [NY R NASSAU S J Voutsinas, Part 25, as amended by NY ORDER 20-0304]; [NY R NASSAU S J Voutsinas, Form 1, as amended by NY ORDER 20-0305].

JUSTICE HOPE SCHWARTZ ZIMMERMAN: NY R NASSAU S J Zimmerman, Part 17.

NEW YORK COUNTY

JUDGE'S RULES; BASIC INFORMATION: [NY R NY CTY J RUL Doc. 1, as amended by NY ORDER 20-0202].

ONONDAGA COUNTY

JUSTICE ROBERT E. ANTONACCI II: [NY R ONDGA E FIL Doc. 1, as amended by 20-0239].

JUSTICE MICHAEL V. COCCOMI: NY R ONDGA E FIL Doc. 2.

JUSTICE GREGORY R. GILBERT: NY R 5 JD JUDGES Gilbert; NY R ONDGA E FIL Doc. 3.

JUSTICE DONALD A. GREENWOOD: NY R ONDGA E FIL Doc. 4.

JUSTICE DEBORAH H. KARALUNAS: NY R ONDGA E FIL Doc. 5.

JUSTICE JAMES MCCLUSKY: NY R 5 JD MCCLUSKY McClusky.

JUSTICE CHARLES C. MERRELL: NY R 5 JD MERRELL Merrell.

JUSTICE PATRICK F. MACRAE: NY R 5 JD MACRAE Doc. 1.

JUSTICE JAMES P. MURPHY: NY R ONDGA E FIL Doc. 7.

JUSTICE GERALD J. NERI: [NY R 5 JD JUDGES Neri, as amended by NY ORDER 20-0236]; [NY R ONDGA E FIL Doc. 8, as amended by NY ORDER 20-0241].

JUSTICE ANTHONY J. PARIS: NY R 5 JD JUDGES Paris; [NY R ONDGA E FIL Doc. 9, as amended by NY ORDER 20-0242].

JUSTICE NORMAN W. SEITER, JR.: NY R 5 JD JUDGES Seiter.

JUSTICE KEVIN G. YOUNG: [NY R ONDGA E FIL Doc. 10, as amended by NY ORDER 20-0243].

QUEENS COUNTY

JUSTICE PAM JACKMAN BROWN: [NY R L QUEENS Brown, Part 19, as amended by NY ORDER 20-0321].

JUSTICE CHEREE A. BUGGS: NY R L QUEENS Buggs, Part 30.

JUSTICE PAM JACKMAN BROWN: [NY R L QUEENS Brown, Part 19, as amended by NY ORDER 20-0321].

JUSTICE DENIS J. BUTLER: NY R L QUEENS Butler, Part 12.

JUSTICE ROBERT I. CALORAS: [NY R L QUEENS Caloras, Part 36, as amended by NY ORDER 20-0322].

JUSTICE ANNA CULLEY: NY R L QUEENS Culley, Part 53.

JUSTICE TIMOTHY DUFFICY: NY R L QUEENS Dufficy, Part 35.

JUSTICE DAVID ELLIOT: NY R L QUEENS Elliot, Part 14.

JUSTICE JOSEPH J. ESPOSITO: NY R L QUEENS Esposito, Part 6.

JUSTICE DARRELL L. GAVRIN: [NY R L QUEENS Gavrin, Part 27, as amended by NY ORDER 20-0323].

JUSTICE WYATT N. GIBBONS: [NY R L QUEENS Gibbons, Part 5, as amended by NY ORDER 20-0330.

JUSTICE DONNA-MARIE E. GOLIA: [NY R L QUEENS Golia, Part 21, as amended by NY ORDER 20-0331].

JUSTICE MARGUERITE A. GRAYS: [NY R L QUEENS Grays, Part 4, as amended by NY ORDER 20-0324].

JUSTICE RUDOLPH E. GRECO: [NY R L QUEENS Greco, Part 32, as amended by NY ORDER 20-0325].

JUSTICE MAUREEN HEALY: NY R L QUEENS Healy, Part 6.

JUSTICE PHILLIP HOM: [NY R L QUEENS Hom, Part 43, as amended by NY ORDER 20-0332].

JUSTICE KEVIN J. KERRIGAN: NY R L QUEENS Kerrigan, Part 10.

JUSTICE MOJGAN C. LANCMAN: NY R L QUEENS Lancman, Part 20.

JUSTICE RICHARD G. LATIN: NY R L QUEENS Latin, Part 40.

JUSTICE ULYSSES B. LEVERETT: [NY R L QUEENS Leverett, Part 6, as amended by NY ORDER 20-0326].

JUSTICE LEONARD LIVOTE: NY R L QUEENS Livote, Part 33.

JUSTICE LEE A. MAYERSOHN: NY R L QUEENS Mayersohn, Part 22; NY R L QUEENS Mayersohn, Part 22G; [NY R L QUEENS Mayersohn, Part 22G COVID, as amended by NY ORDER 20-0327].

JUSTICE ROBERT J. MCDONALD: NY R L QUEENS McDonald, Part 34.

JUSTICE MARGARET MCGOWAN: NY R L QUEENS McGowan, Part 52.

JUSTICE MAURICE E. MUIR: [NY R L QUEENS Muir, Part 42, as amended by NY ORDER 20-0333].

JUSTICE JODI ORLOW: NY R L QUEENS Orlow, Part 51.

JUSTICE LESLIE J. PURIFICCION: NY R L QUEENS Purificcion, Part 39.

JUSTICE JOSEPH RISI: [NY R L QUEENS Risi, Part 3, as amended by NY ORDER 20-0328].

JUSTICE FREDERICK D.R. SAMPSON: [NY R L QUEENS Sampson, Part 31, as amended by NY ORDER 20-0329].

JUSTICE MARTIN J. SCHULMAN: NY R L QUEENS Schulman, Part 29.

JUSTICE BERNICE D. SIEGAL: NY R L QUEENS Siegal, Part 25G.

JUSTICE JANICE A. TAYLOR: NY R L QUEENS Taylor, Part 15.

JUSTICE CARMEN R. VELASQUEZ: NY R L QUEENS Velasquez, Part 38.

JUSTICE LOURDES M VENTURA: [NY R L QUEENS Ventura, Part 37, as amended by NY ORDER 20-0334].

JUSTICE WILLIAM A. VISCOVICH: NY R L QUEENS Viscovich, Part 63.

JUSTICE ALLAN B. WEISS: NY R L QUEENS Weiss, Part 2.

COMPLIANCE, SETTLEMENT AND CONFERENCE PART: NY R L QUEENS Doc 1.

PRELIMINARY CONFERENCE PART: [NY R L QUEENS Doc. 2, as amended by NY ORDER 20-0335].

MEDICAL MALPRACTICE CONFERENCE PART: [NY R L QUEENS Doc. 3, as amended by NY ORDER 20-0336].

TRIAL SCHEDULING PART: NY R L QUEENS Doc. 4.

SUMMARY JURY TRIAL PROGRAM: NY R L QUEENS Doc. 7.

RESIDENTIAL FORECLOSURE PART: NY R L QUEENS Doc. 9.

FORECLOSURE AUCTION RULES: NY R L QUEENS Doc. 10.

MATRIMONIAL PRELIMINARY CONFERENCE PART: NY R L QUEENS Doc. 11.

NON-CUSTODIAL CONTESTED MATRIMONIAL PART: NY R L QUEENS Doc. 12.

Motions, Oppositions and Replies
Motion to Quash or Modify Subpoena

Document Last Updated August 2020

A. Checklist

(I) ❑ Matters to consider for moving party
- (a) ❑ Required documents
  - (1) ❑ Notice of motion, order to show cause, or affidavit on ex parte motion
  - (2) ❑ Motion
  - (3) ❑ Request for judicial intervention
  - (4) ❑ Proof of service
  - (5) ❑ ALBANY COUNTY: Additional required documents
    - (i) ❑ Affirmation of good faith effort
- (b) ❑ Supplemental documents
  - (1) ❑ Supporting evidence; Exhibits
  - (2) ❑ Brief
  - (3) ❑ Notice to produce papers not in possession of the court
  - (4) ❑ Filing fees
  - (5) ❑ Working copies
  - (6) ❑ ERIE COUNTY: Additional supplemental documents
    - (i) ❑ Notice of hard copy submission in e-filed case
  - (7) ❑ KINGS COUNTY: Additional supplemental documents
    - (i) ❑ Forms when filing in hard copy
  - (8) ❑ NEW YORK COUNTY: Additional supplemental documents
    - (i) ❑ Notice of hard copy submission
    - (ii) ❑ Unpublished opinions

(9) ❑ ONONDAGA COUNTY: Additional supplemental documents

(i) ❑ Notice of hard copy submission

(10) ❑ QUEENS COUNTY: Additional supplemental documents

(i) ❑ Notice of hard copy submission

(c) ❑ Timing

(1) ❑ A motion to quash, fix conditions or modify a subpoena shall be made promptly in the court in which the subpoena is returnable

(2) ❑ The moving party shall serve copies of all affidavits and briefs upon all other parties at the time of service of the notice of motion

(3) ❑ A notice of motion and supporting affidavits shall be served at least eight (8) days before the time at which the motion is noticed to be heard

(4) ❑ It is also good practice to make motions returnable at least three (3) weeks away from the planned date of mailing and to always include a demand in the motion that the other side serve answering papers at least seven (7) days before the return day

(5) ❑ BRONX COUNTY: Additional timing

(i) ❑ A Notice of Motion must be served at least eight (8) days, by personal service, nine (9) days by overnight express and thirteen (13) days by mail before the return date

(6) ❑ NEW YORK COUNTY: Additional timing

(i) ❑ In an e-filed case, all of the moving papers shall be e-filed at least eight (8) business days prior to the return date

(7) ❑ ONONDAGA COUNTY: Additional timing

(i) ❑ Onondaga County local court rules require that any additional papers relating to motions must be e-filed at least two (2) business days prior to the return date, excluding the return date

(8) ❑ QUEENS COUNTY: Additional timing

(i) ❑ Motions must be in the possession of the Motion Support Office at least nine (9) days before the noticed return date of the motion

(II) ❑ Matters to consider for opposing party

(a) ❑ Required documents

(1) ❑ Opposition

(2) ❑ Proof of service

(b) ❑ Supplemental documents

(1) ❑ Supporting evidence; Exhibits

(2) ❑ Brief

(3) ❑ Filing fees

(4) ❑ Working copies

(5) ❑ ERIE COUNTY: Additional supplemental documents

(i) ❑ Notice of hard copy submission in e-filed case

(6) ❑ KINGS COUNTY: Additional supplemental documents

(i) ❑ Forms when filing in hard copy

(7) ❑ NEW YORK COUNTY: Additional supplemental documents

(i) ❑ Notice of hard copy submission

(ii) ❑ Unpublished opinions

(8) ❑ ONONDAGA COUNTY: Additional supplemental documents

(i) ❑ Notice of hard copy submission

(9) ❑ QUEENS COUNTY: Additional supplemental documents

(i) ❑ Notice of hard copy submission

(c) ❑ Timing

(1) ❑ Answering affidavits shall be served at least two (2) days before the time at which the motion is noticed to be heard

(2) ❑ Answering affidavits and any notice of cross-motion, with supporting papers, if any, shall be served at least seven (7) days before such time if a notice of motion served at least sixteen (16) days before such time so demands

B. Timing

1. *Time to bring motion to quash or modify subpoena.* A motion to quash, fix conditions or modify a subpoena shall be made promptly in the court in which the subpoena is returnable. NY CPLR § 2304.

a. NY CPLR § 2304 does not specify the time within which a motion to quash, condition, or modify has to be made. It only states that the motion should be made "promptly," which automatically makes the question of timeliness sui generis. It will all depend on the circumstances of the case. Certainly it would be a futility to make the motion returnable after the return date prescribed by the subpoena itself. NY CPLR § 2304(Practice Commentary: C2304:3).

b. Since there is usually no minimum notice period that must be given when serving a subpoena, it may be returnable in very short order—much too short to move to quash or modify by ordinary motion on ordinary notice. The answer to that problem, of course, is to bring the application on by order to show cause, NY CPLR Rule 2214(d), asking the judge to whom it is presented to make it returnable before, or at, the subpoena's return time. NY CPLR § 2304(Practice Commentary: C2304:3).

2. *Time to serve.* The moving party shall serve copies of all affidavits and briefs upon all other parties at the time of service of the notice of motion. NY R UNIF TRIAL CTS § 202.8(c). A notice of motion and supporting affidavits shall be served at least eight (8) days before the time at which the motion is noticed to be heard. NY CPLR Rule 2214(b).

a. *Return dates; Best practice.* It is also good practice to make motions returnable at least three (3) weeks away from the planned date of mailing and to always include a demand in the motion that the other side serve answering papers at least seven (7) days before the return day. This enables the motion to be served by mail, gives sufficient notice to support the seven (7) day demand, and leaves a few days for a delayed mailing if some snag prevents posting on the day planned. If speed is needed, the shorter eight (8) day notice period can be used, forfeiting the right to seven (7) day answering papers and a reply. If even eight (8) days notice is too much under the circumstances, the order to show cause is the remedy. SIEGEL-NYPRAC § 247.

i. *ALBANY COUNTY.* All motions, except for certain matters in Albany County as specified in NY R 3 JD SUP Doc. 1(E) and NY R 3 JD SUP Doc. 1(F), brought on by notice of motion or by order to show cause will be made returnable on any day, Monday through Friday, as chosen by the movant in compliance with the CPLR. Parties shall submit all papers in a timely fashion as required by the CPLR by delivering them or mailing them directly to the Supreme Court Clerk's Office[. . .]except that motions and other applications subject to a filing fee shall first be presented to the County Clerk's Office for payment of the requisite fee and then subsequently filed with the Supreme Court Clerk's Office. NY R 3 JD SUP Doc. 1(B).

ii. *BRONX COUNTY.* A Notice of Motion must be served at least eight (8) days, by personal service, nine (9) days by overnight express and thirteen (13) days by mail before the return date. NY R BRONX FIL R Doc. 3. All unassigned motions must be accompanied with a properly filled out RJI and shall be filed in the Motion Support Office, room 217, within five (5) days of service. All motions on actions already assigned to a Justice must be filed at least five (5) business days before the return date. NY R BRONX FIL R Doc. 3. All papers served must strictly comply with the time requirements of NY CPLR Rule 2101, NY CPLR Rule 2103 and NY CPLR Rule 2214(b). NY R BRONX FIL R Doc. 8.

iii. *KINGS COUNTY.* Motion papers, answering affidavits and reply affidavits must be served on adversaries in accordance with NY CPLR Rule 2214. NY R L KINGS Pt. C, Rule 1.

iv. *NEW YORK COUNTY.* In an e-filed case, all of the moving papers shall be e-filed at least eight (8) business days prior to the return date. The clerk will calendar the motion for the Motion Submission Part Courtroom (Room 130) for the return date selected. NY R NY CTY Procedure II(A); NY R NY CTY E FIL Doc. 2(D)(1).

v. *ONONDAGA COUNTY.* Onondaga County local court rules require that any additional papers relating to motions must be e-filed at least two (2) business days prior to the return date, excluding the return date. NY R ONDGA E FIL Protocol(B)(9)(e).

vi. *QUEENS COUNTY.* Motions must be in the possession of the Motion Support Office at least nine (9) days before the noticed return date of the motion. NY R L QUEENS MOT SUP Doc. 1; NY R L QUEENS E-FILE Doc. 1(H)(1).

b. *Order to show cause; Shorter time.* The court in a proper case may grant an order to show cause, to be served in lieu of a notice of motion, at a time and in a manner specified therein. NY CPLR Rule 2214(d). An ordinary notice of motion can't be brought on for hearing earlier than the eighth (8th) day after the motion papers are served. With an order to show cause, the hearing can be brought on at any time the court directs, which can be fewer than eight (8) days or as close as the very day on which it is signed. If the court is convinced there is a real emergency, it can schedule the hearing for a few hours later or, in the direst case, "forthwith" the service of the order to show cause. SIEGEL-NYPRAC § 248.

c. *Time to serve answering affidavits; Other answering papers.* Answering affidavits shall be served at least two (2) days before the time at which the motion is noticed to be heard. Answering affidavits and any notice of cross-motion, with supporting papers, if any, shall be served at least seven (7) days before such time if a notice of motion served at least sixteen (16) days before such time so demands; whereupon any reply or responding affidavits shall be served at least one (1) day before such time. NY CPLR Rule 2214(b); NY R UNIF TRIAL CTS § 202.8(c).

i. *BRONX COUNTY.* All answering papers must be submitted to the Clerk 's Office on the return date of the motion. Answering papers will not be accepted prior to the return date. NY R BRONX FIL R Doc. 8.

ii. *NEW YORK COUNTY.* Cross-motions, papers in opposition, and reply papers on motions/petitions on notice returnable in Room 130 in a hard-copy case shall be submitted to the Motion Submission Part Courtroom (Room 130) on the final return date of the motion/petition and will not be accepted until that date. Subsequent documents on motions/petitions in e-filed cases shall be e-filed in a timely manner. Working copies when required shall be submitted to Room 130 on the final return date. NY R NY CTY Procedure II(A).

d. *Time to serve cross-motion.* At least three (3) days prior to the time at which the motion is noticed to be heard, or seven (7) days prior to such time if demand is properly made pursuant to NY CPLR Rule 2214(b), a party may serve upon the moving party a notice of cross-motion demanding relief, with or without supporting papers; provided, however, that:

i. If such notice and any supporting papers are served by mailing, as provided in NY CPLR Rule 2103(b)(2), they shall be served three (3) days earlier than as prescribed in NY CPLR Rule 2215; and

ii. If served by overnight delivery, as provided in NY CPLR Rule 2103(b)(6), they shall be served one (1) day earlier than as prescribed in NY CPLR Rule 2215. Relief in the alternative or of several different types may be demanded; relief need not be responsive to that demanded by the moving party. NY CPLR Rule 2215(a); NY CPLR Rule 2215(b).

iii. *BRONX COUNTY.* Cross motions may be presented for approval on or before the return date, provided that there is a motion already calendared. NY R BRONX FIL R Doc. 8.

iv. *ERIE COUNTY.* Cross-motions must be filed at least two (2) days before the return date of the motion. NY R L KINGS Pt. A, Papers.

v. *KINGS COUNTY.* Hard copies are required to be filed for any motions, answering papers, stipulations, etc. for E-Filed cases returnable in [the Central Compliance Part] at least [two (2)] days before return date. . .for cross motions. NY R L KINGS Pt. E, Rule 8.

vi. *QUEENS COUNTY.* Motion Support does not process or forward responsive papers, including cross-motions. They must be brought to the calendar call in the judge's part. NY R L QUEENS MOT SUP Doc. 1. E-filed cross motions: across motion must be noticed for the same return date as the main motion and have the confirmation of filing attached in the same manner as a motion. NY R L QUEENS E-FILE Doc. 1(H)(2)(e).

3. *Filing before return date.* All motions shall be returnable before the assigned judge, and all papers shall be filed with the court on or before the return date. NY R UNIF TRIAL CTS § 202.8(a).

a. *BRONX COUNTY: Time for filing*

i. *Unassigned motions.* Unassigned motions must be in the Clerk's Office within five (5) days of the date of service of the motion. NY R BRONX FIL R Doc. 8.

ii. *Assigned motions.* Assigned motions must be filed in the Clerk's Office not less than five (5) business days prior to the return date of the motion. NY R BRONX FIL R Doc. 8.

iii. *Motions returnable in room 217.* The moving documents must be e-filed no later than eight (8) days prior to the return date. NY R BRONX E FIL R Doc. 1(1).

b. *KINGS COUNTY: Time and place of filing.* Motion papers must be filed with the E-file/Motion Support Office located in Room 227. . . at 360 Adams Street at least five (5) business days before the return date of the motion. NY R L KINGS Pt. A, Papers. Hard copies are required to be filed for any motions, answering papers, stipulations, etc. for E-Filed cases returnable in [the Central Compliance Part] at least five (5) days before return date for main motions. NY R L KINGS Pt. E, Rule 8. The moving documents must be e-filed no later than eight (8) days prior to the return date. NY R L KINGS E FIL Doc. 1(D).

4. *NEW YORK COUNTY: Briefing schedule.* Once a motion is made, counsel for all parties are strongly encouraged to agree upon a briefing schedule and submit a stipulation of adjournment reflecting that schedule using service or a clerk. Where a briefing schedule has not been agreed upon, the movant can avoid the need to attend simply to see if anyone will hand up opposing papers by demanding papers as provided by NY CPLR Rule 2214(b). To protect movants against the submission of late opposition papers or cross-motions, the General Clerk's Office will screen motions in which such papers are submitted without a response (reply or opposition respectively) to ensure that proper time to respond has been afforded and it will sua sponte adjourn for one (1) week cases in which such time has not been given. NY R NY CTY Procedure II(C).

5. *QUEENS COUNTY: Time to pay fees.* As motions and petitions are time sensitive, if opting to pay at the County Clerk's Office payment MUST be made, if filed with an RJI, a minimum of nine (9) business days prior to the application's return date and if filed post RJI, a minimum of nine (9) business days prior to the application's return date. NY R L QUEENS E-FILE Doc. 1(H)(1).

6. *Computation of time*

   a. *Units of time*

      i. *Day.* A calendar day includes the time from midnight to midnight. Sunday or any day of the week specifically mentioned means a calendar day. NY GEN CONSTR § 19.

      ii. *Month.* In a statute, contract or public or private instrument, unless otherwise provided in such contract or instrument or by law, the term month means a calendar month and not a lunar month. NY GEN CONSTR § 31.

      iii. *Year.* For information on the definition of a year, including the definitions of a half-year and quarter-year, refer to NY GEN CONSTR § 58 and NY GEN CONSTR § 50. For information on leap years, refer to NY GEN CONSTR § 57.

   b. *Periods of time*

      i. *Number of days.* A number of days specified as a period from a certain day within which or after or before which an act is authorized or required to be done means such number of calendar days exclusive of the calendar day from which the reckoning is made. NY GEN CONSTR § 20.

         - If such period is a period of two (2) days, Saturday, Sunday or a public holiday must be excluded from the reckoning if it is an intervening day between the day from which the reckoning is made and the last day of the period. NY GEN CONSTR § 20.
         - In computing any specified period of time from a specified event, the day upon which the event happens is deemed the day from which the reckoning is made. The day from which any specified period of time is reckoned shall be excluded in making the reckoning. NY GEN CONSTR § 20.

      ii. *Number of months.* A number of months after or before a certain day shall be computed by counting such number of calendar months from such day, exclusive of the calendar month in which such day occurs, and shall include the day of the month in the last month so counted having the same numerical order in days of the month as the day from which the computation is made, unless there be not so many days in the last month so counted, in which case the period computed shall expire with the last day of the month so counted. NY GEN CONSTR § 30.

      iii. *Publication of notice; Number of days.* The period of publication of a legal notice shall be computed by excluding the first day of publication and including the day on which the act or event of which notice is given is to take place or which completes the full period of publication. NY CPLR § 2402.

      iv. *Periods ending on Saturday, Sunday or public holiday.* When any period of time, computed from a certain day, within which or after which or before which an act is authorized or required to be done, ends on a Saturday, Sunday or a public holiday, such act may be done on the next succeeding business day and if the period ends at a specified hour, such act may be done at or before the same hour of such next succeeding business day, except that where a period of time specified by contract ends on a Saturday, Sunday or a public holiday, the extension of such period is governed by NY GEN CONSTR § 25. NY GEN CONSTR § 25-a(1).

         - For a list of public holidays, refer to NY GEN CONSTR § 24.

v. *Additional time after certain kinds of service*

- *Service by mail.* Where a period of time prescribed by law is measured from the service of a paper and service is by mail, five (5) days shall be added to the prescribed period. NY CPLR Rule 2103(b)(2).
- *Service by overnight delivery service.* Where a period of time prescribed by law is measured from the service of a paper and service is by overnight delivery, one (1) business day shall be added to the prescribed period. NY CPLR Rule 2103(b)(6).

vi. *Daylight saving time.* For information on New York's time zone and the effect of daylight saving time, refer to NY GEN CONSTR § 52.

c. *Hours of court.* Notwithstanding any provision of law or rule of court to the contrary, throughout the State of New York the sessions of the Supreme Court for the disposition of business before the court shall commence not later than 9:30 a.m. and conclude not earlier than 5 p.m. Where warranted, the Chief Administrator of the Courts may authorize variances in the opening and closing hours of the courts, but, in such event, daily sessions shall total not less than six (6) hours. NY R CHIEF J § 3.1.

d. *Time limits; Extension of time.* Any act required by or in pursuance of law to be performed at or within a prescribed time, shall be performed according to the standard time. NY GEN CONSTR § 53.

i. Except where otherwise expressly prescribed by law, the court may extend the time fixed by any statute, rule or order for doing any act, upon such terms as may be just and upon good cause shown, whether the application for extension is made before or after the expiration of the time fixed. NY CPLR § 2004. Refer to the New York KeyRules Motion for Continuance/Extension of Time document for more information.

C. General Requirements

1. *Motions, generally.* There shall be compliance with the procedures prescribed in the CPLR for the bringing of motions. NY R UNIF TRIAL CTS § 202.7(a).

a. *Motions on notice.* A notice of motion shall specify the time and place of the hearing on the motion, the supporting papers upon which the motion is based, the relief demanded and the grounds therefor. NY CPLR Rule 2214(a). A motion on notice in an action in the supreme court shall be noticed to be heard in the judicial district where the action is triable or in a county adjoining the county where the action is triable. Unless statute, civil practice rule or local court rule provides otherwise, the motion shall be noticed to be heard before a motion term or, upon order to show cause granted by a justice, before that justice out of court. NY CPLR § 2212(a). Except as provided in NY R UNIF TRIAL CTS § 202.7(d), no motion shall be filed with the court unless there have been served and filed with the motion papers a notice of motion. NY R UNIF TRIAL CTS § 202.7(a)(1).

b. *Ex parte motions.* A motion in an action in the supreme court that may be made without notice may be made at a motion term or to a justice out of court in any county in the state. NY CPLR § 2212(b).

i. *KINGS COUNTY.* For more information on submitting a motion ex parte, refer to NY R L KINGS E FIL Doc. 1(G).

ii. *NEW YORK COUNTY.* For more information on submitting matters ex parte, refer to NY R NY CTY Procedure III and NY R NY CTY E FIL Doc. 2(G).

iii. *QUEENS COUNTY.* For more information on submitting matters ex parte, refer to NY R L QUEENS EX PARTE Doc. 1.

c. *Alternative relief.* Relief in the alternative or of several different types may be demanded. NY CPLR Rule 2214(a). The types of relief need not be related. In one motion, for example, the defendant can seek to dismiss the plaintiff's claim for lack of jurisdiction, to get an extension of time to answer, to require the plaintiff to join X as a party, and to quash a disclosure subpoena served in behalf of the plaintiff on a nonparty witness. So doing, the movant must of course specify all of these items of relief in the notice of motion, and the grounds for them, and the supporting papers must contain the entire proof requisite to the items of relief sought. NY CPLR Rule 2214(Practice Commentary, C2214:4).

d. *General relief.* It is common practice to include at the end of the relief request in the notice of motion a so-called "general relief" clause. This is merely a few words to cover the possibility that the relief appropriate to what the movant proves was not specifically asked for, but is close enough to enable the court to grant it. After stating the specific relief desired, the lawyer will often add something like: and for such other, further, or different relief as this court may deem just and proper. NY CPLR Rule 2214(Practice Commentary, C2214:5).

e. *Motion in improper form.* If the court finds it appropriate in the interests of justice, it may convert a motion into a

special proceeding, or vice-versa, upon such terms as may be just, including the payment of fees and costs. NY CPLR § 103(c).

f. *Order to show cause.* An order to show cause is basically only a substitute for a notice of motion. An ordinary notice of motion merely notifies the recipient that a motion is being made for specified relief. The burden of proof is on the movant. Although in most cases it is just as innocent as an ordinary notice of motion, the order to show cause gets its name by directing the recipient to "show cause" why the particular relief being asked for should not be granted. It sounds as if the burden of proof is being shifted to the recipient. It isn't. It specifies the time and place of the hearing on the application but when the hearing comes on, the burden of proof is where it always is on a motion: on the movant. SIEGEL-NYPRAC § 248.

i. The CPLR says nothing more about an order to show cause than that it may be used "in a proper case", which leaves it entirely to the judge's discretion to determine what a proper case is. Any fact suggesting a problem as to any of the items listed above would be sufficient to invoke judicial discretion and justify the show cause procedure, which is in fact liberally used. SIEGEL-NYPRAC § 248.

ii. An order to show cause against a state body or officers must be served in addition to service upon the defendant or respondent state body or officers upon the attorney general by delivery to an assistant attorney general at an office of the attorney general in the county in which venue of the action is designated or if there is no office of the attorney general in such county, at the office of the attorney general nearest such county. NY CPLR Rule 2214(d).

iii. *BRONX COUNTY.* For information on submitting an order to show cause, refer to NY R BRONX E FIL R Doc. 2 and NY R BRONX LEG SUP Doc. 1.

iv. *ERIE COUNTY.* For information on submitting an order to show cause, refer to NY R ERIE E FIL Doc. 3(VI).

v. *KINGS COUNTY.* For information on submitting an order to show cause, refer to NY R L KINGS E FIL Doc. 1(F).

vi. *NEW YORK COUNTY.* For information on submitting an order to show cause, refer to NY R NY CTY E FIL Doc. 2(F).

vii. *ONONDAGA COUNTY.* For information on submitting an order to show cause, refer to NY R ONDGA E FIL Protocol(B)(10) and NY R ONDGA E FIL Protocol(J).

g. *Motions before preliminary conference.* Motions in actions to which NY R UNIF TRIAL CTS § 202.12 is applicable made after the preliminary conference has been scheduled may be denied unless there is shown good cause why such relief is warranted before the preliminary conference is held. NY R UNIF TRIAL CTS § 202.12(h).

h. *ALBANY COUNTY: Good faith effort to resolve.* Prior to the submission of a notice of motion relating to disclosure or a bill of particulars, the parties must make a good faith effort to resolve the matter in question and submit an affirmation attesting to this good faith effort. NY R 3 JD SUP Doc. 1(B).

i. *NEW YORK COUNTY: Documents with motions.* Counsel must attach to motion papers copies of all pleadings and other documents as required by the CPLR and as necessary for an informed decision on the motion. Documents in a foreign language shall be properly translated. NY R NY CTY J RUL Rule 14(a).

j. *NEW YORK COUNTY: Motions in multiple cases made together.* On occasion, attorneys may wish to make a motion in more than one case on a single set of papers. In such cases, by definition consolidation will not have been directed since consolidation signifies the combination of more than one case into a single one with a single caption and index number and ending in a single judgment. NY R NY CTY Procedure II(B). For more information on motions made with the same papers, refer to NY R NY CTY Procedure II(A).

k. *QUEENS COUNTY: Motion sequence numbers.* A motion sequence number is required for all E-filed motions. After a motion is E-filed, please consult the e-courts website within twenty-four (24) to forty-eight (48) hours to obtain the sequence number. The Confirmation Notice of E-filing MUST indicate the sequence number of any motion submitted at the Centralized Motion Part calendar call. NY R L QUEENS E-FILE Doc. 1(H)(5).

2. *Motion to quash or modify subpoena.* If the person served with a subpoena has some objection to it or wishes to test its validity, the remedy is a motion to quash, condition, or modify the subpoena. SIEGEL-NYPRAC § 384.

a. *Generally.* A motion to quash, fix conditions or modify a subpoena shall be made promptly in the court in which the subpoena is returnable. If the subpoena is not returnable in a court, a request to withdraw or modify the subpoena shall first be made to the person who issued it and a motion to quash, fix conditions or modify may thereafter be made in the supreme court; except that such motion with respect to a child support subpoena issued pursuant to NY SOC

SERV § 111-p shall be made to a judge of the family court or the supreme court. Reasonable conditions may be imposed upon the granting or denial of a motion to quash or modify. NY CPLR § 2304.

b. *Nature of motion.* A motion to quash challenges the validity of the subpoena or the jurisdiction of the issuing authority. SIEGEL-NYPRAC § 384; Santangello v. People, 38 N.Y.2d 536, 539, 344 N.E.2d 404, 406 (1976). These categories can embrace a myriad of defects, however, ranging from the most substantive, such as where the subpoena seeks matter irrelevant to the proceeding, to the most procedural, such as where there was some formal defect in its service. SIEGEL-NYPRAC § 384; Temp. State Comm'n on Living Costs & Econ. v. Bergman, 80 Misc. 2d 448, 453, 363 N.Y.S.2d 977, 985 (Sup. Ct. 1975). Other grounds, perhaps not technically sufficient to affect "validity" or "jurisdiction", may also be raised. Perhaps the demands of the subpoena are such that the witness can't afford to meet them on the meager fees tendered. SIEGEL-NYPRAC § 384; NY CPLR § 8001.

c. *Who may bring motion.* The motion to quash may be made on behalf of the witness by the witness's own lawyer, if the witness has one, or by one of the parties' lawyers. On its merits, of course, the subpoena will be quashed only when jurisdictionally defective or groundless. NY CPLR § 2304(Practice Commentary: C2304:1).

d. *Remedy; Conditions imposed by court.* The court is empowered, on a motion to quash or modify, to impose any condition the court finds just. SIEGEL-NYPRAC § 384; NY CPLR § 2304. One condition the court may resort to is that the issuing party advance to the subpoenaed person, in addition to the nominal statutory fees, the reasonable actual cost of honoring the subpoena, especially when it is a subpoena duces tecum requiring the witness to go to expense to produce the papers or things sought. Conditionings of this kind are not frequent, probably because a party in need of a witness's testimony or materials will ordinarily advance such expenses voluntarily, thereby propitiating the witness and obviating the motion to condition and possibly even the subpoena itself. SIEGEL-NYPRAC § 384.

3. *Oppositions.* In the absence of statutory provision or court rule, a motion ordinarily does not require a written answer, although an adverse party may be permitted to file an answer in opposition to the showing made in the motion or its supporting affidavits. AMJUR MOTIONS § 26. When a party files a motion and the opposing party fails to respond, the court may construe such failure to respond as non-opposition to the motion or an admission that the motion was meritorious, may take the facts alleged in the motion as true, and may grant the motion if the relief requested appears to be justified. However, the severity of such a result demands that a court impose it only with great caution. AMJUR MOTIONS § 28.

4. *Governing law.* The civil practice law and rules (NY CPLR § 101, et seq.) shall govern the procedure in civil judicial proceedings in all courts of the state and before all judges, except where the procedure is regulated by inconsistent statute. The civil practice law and rules shall succeed the civil practice act and rules of civil practice and shall be deemed substituted therefor throughout the statutes and rules of the state. NY CPLR § 101. The civil practice law and rules shall be liberally construed to secure the just, speedy and inexpensive determination of every civil judicial proceeding. NY CPLR § 104.

a. *Uniform trial court rules.* The uniform civil rules for the Supreme Court and County Court (NY R UNIF TRIAL CTS § 202.1, et seq.) shall be applicable to civil actions and proceedings in the Supreme Court and the County Court. NY R UNIF TRIAL CTS § 202.1(a). The provisions of the uniform rules shall be construed consistent with the Civil Practice Law and Rules (CPLR), and matters not covered by the uniform rules shall be governed by the CPLR. NY R UNIF TRIAL CTS § 202.1(d).

b. *Local rules.* Local court rules, not inconsistent with law or with uniform civil rules for the Supreme Court and County Court (NY R UNIF TRIAL CTS § 202.1, et seq.), shall comply with Part 9 of the Rules of the Chief Judge (NY R CHIEF J § 9.1). NY R UNIF TRIAL CTS § 202.1(c).

c. *Official forms.* The state administrator shall have the power to adopt, amend and rescind an appendix of forms. Forms adopted pursuant to NY CPLR § 107 shall be sufficient under the civil practice law and rules and shall illustrate the simplicity and brevity of statement which the civil practice law and rules contemplate. NY CPLR § 107.

5. *Rules of the commercial division.* [Editor's note: certain types of civil cases or civil cases meeting certain monetary thresholds that are filed in the state of New York must be filed in the Commercial Division of the New York Supreme Courts. Rules governing practice in the commercial division are found in NY R UNIF TRIAL CTS § 202.70]. Cases which must be filed in the commercial division are listed below. For more information, refer to NY R UNIF TRIAL CTS § 202.70.

a. *Monetary thresholds.* Except as set forth in NY R UNIF TRIAL CTS § 202.70(b), the monetary thresholds of the Commercial Division, exclusive of punitive damages, interests, costs, disbursements and counsel fees claimed, are established as follows: (1) Albany County, fifty thousand dollars ($50,000); (2) Eighth Judicial District, one hundred thousand dollars ($100,000); (3) Kings County, one hundred fifty thousand dollars ($150,000); (4) Nassau County, two hundred thousand dollars ($200,000); (5) New York County, five hundred thousand dollars ($500,000); (6)

Onondaga County, fifty thousand dollars ($50,000); (7) Queens County, one hundred thousand dollars ($100,000); (8) Seventh Judicial District, fifty thousand dollars ($50,000); (9) Suffolk County, one hundred thousand dollars ($100,000); and (10) Westchester County, one hundred thousand dollars ($100,000). NY R UNIF TRIAL CTS § 202.70(a).

i. *ALBANY COUNTY.* The Commercial Division of the Albany County Supreme Court exercises jurisdiction over selected business and commercial disputes in which the amount at issue generally involves damage claims in a minimum amount of fifty thousand dollars ($50,000) as well as claims for unspecified amounts where the value of the commercial asset(s) in dispute exceeds fifty thousand dollars ($50,000). A separate publication promulgating the rules and criteria relating to the filing and management of Commercial Court cases in this part may be obtained from the Albany County Supreme Court Clerk's Office. A section of the Uniform Civil Rules for the Supreme Court and County Court sets forth statewide rules. NY R 3 JD SUP Doc. 1(E).

ii. *BRONX COUNTY.* The monetary threshold for commercial cases in Bronx County will be seventy-five thousand dollars ($75,000). All other parameters including the type of matters that will be heard are contained within the Rules of the Commercial Division of the Supreme Court (NY R UNIF TRIAL CTS § 202.70). NY R BRONX FIL R Doc. 12.

iii. *NEW YORK COUNTY.* The monetary threshold in the New York County Commercial Division, which is generally applicable, is an amount in controversy of five hundred thousand dollars ($500,000) or more (exclusive of punitive damages, interest, costs, disbursements, and counsel fees). If the case is designated a commercial one and the Addendum is submitted, the clerk will review the pleadings to determine whether the amount in controversy in the case meets the monetary threshold or whether an exception to the threshold applies. NY R NY CTY Procedure IA(B). For more information on assigning a case to the commercial division in New York County, refer to NY R NY CTY Procedure IA(B).

b. *Commercial cases.* Actions in which the principal claims involve or consist of the following will be heard in the Commercial Division provided that the monetary threshold is met or equitable or declaratory relief is sought:

i. Breach of contract or fiduciary duty, fraud, misrepresentation, business tort (e.g., unfair competition), or statutory and/or common law violation where the breach or violation is alleged to arise out of business dealings (e.g., sales of assets or securities; corporate restructuring; partnership, shareholder, joint venture, and other business agreements; trade secrets; restrictive covenants; and employment agreements not including claims that principally involve alleged discriminatory practices);

ii. Transactions governed by the Uniform Commercial Code (exclusive of those concerning individual cooperative or condominium units);

iii. Transactions involving commercial real property, including Yellowstone injunctions and excluding actions for the payment of rent only;

iv. Shareholder derivative actions—without consideration of the monetary threshold;

v. Commercial class actions—without consideration of the monetary threshold;

vi. Business transactions involving or arising out of dealings with commercial banks and other financial institutions;

vii. Internal affairs of business organizations;

viii. Malpractice by accountants or actuaries, and legal malpractice arising out of representation in commercial matters;

ix. Environmental insurance coverage;

x. Commercial insurance coverage (e.g., directors and officers, errors and omissions, and business interruption coverage);

xi. Dissolution of corporations, partnerships, limited liability companies, limited liability partnerships and joint ventures—without consideration of the monetary threshold; and

xii. Applications to stay or compel arbitration and affirm or disaffirm arbitration awards and related injunctive relief pursuant to Article 75 of the New York Civil Practice Law and Rules (NY CPLR § 7501, et seq.) involving any of the foregoing enumerated commercial issues. Where the applicable arbitration agreement provides for the arbitration to be heard outside the United States, the monetary threshold set forth in NY R UNIF TRIAL CTS § 202.70(a) shall not apply. NY R UNIF TRIAL CTS § 202.70(b).

c. *Non-commercial cases.* The following will not be heard in the Commercial Division even if the monetary threshold is met:

i. Suits to collect professional fees;

ii. Cases seeking a declaratory judgment as to insurance coverage for personal injury or property damage;

iii. Residential real estate disputes, including landlord-tenant matters, and commercial real estate disputes involving the payment of rent only;

iv. Home improvement contracts involving residential properties consisting of one to four residential units or individual units in any residential building, including cooperative or condominium units;

v. Proceedings to enforce a judgment regardless of the nature of the underlying case;

vi. First-party insurance claims and actions by insurers to collect premiums or rescind non-commercial policies; and

vii. Attorney malpractice actions except as otherwise provided in NY R UNIF TRIAL CTS § 202.70(b)(8). NY R UNIF TRIAL CTS § 202.70(c).

d. For more information on the Commercial Division, refer to NY R UNIF TRIAL CTS § 202.70.

D. Documents

1. *Documents for moving party*

a. *Required documents*

i. *Notice of motion, order to show cause, or affidavit on ex parte motion.* The notice of motion shall be substantially in the form found in NY R UNIF TRIAL CTS § 202.7(b). NY R UNIF TRIAL CTS § 202.7(b). The supporting papers should be referred to in the notice of motion. SIEGEL-NYPRAC § 246. The court in a proper case may grant an order to show cause, to be served in lieu of a notice of motion. NY CPLR Rule 2214(d). An ex parte motion shall be accompanied by an affidavit stating the result of any prior motion for similar relief and specifying the new facts, if any, that were not previously shown. NY CPLR Rule 2217(b).

- *Request for oral argument.* A party requesting oral argument shall set forth such request in its notice of motion or in its order to show cause or on the first page of the answering papers, as the case may be. Where all parties to a motion request oral argument, oral argument shall be granted unless the court shall determine it to be unnecessary. Where a motion is brought on by order to show cause, the court may set forth in the order that oral argument is required on the return date of the motion. NY R UNIF TRIAL CTS § 202.8(d).

ii. *Motion.* Refer to the General Requirements section of this document for information on the notice of motion and motion.

iii. *Request for judicial intervention.* At any time after service of process, a party may file a request for judicial intervention. Except as provided in NY R UNIF TRIAL CTS § 202.6(b), in an action not yet assigned to a judge, the court shall not accept for filing a notice of motion, order to show cause, or application for ex parte order, unless such notice or application is accompanied by a request for judicial intervention. NY R UNIF TRIAL CTS § 202.6(a).

- *BRONX COUNTY.* Generally, the Request For Judicial Intervention, commonly referred to as an "RJI", is required to be filed in any action where the assignment of a Justice is required. The RJI sets forth the information which is entered into the court system's database. It must be completely and accurately filled out. The full caption, as stated on the Summons, must be set forth. Use of terms "et al." and "etc." are not permitted. Only one (1) RJI may be filed in each action. Either a self represented litigant or an attorney must sign the affirmation at the end of the form. Once completed, the RJI must be filed in duplicate. Except in the case of an ex-parte application, the RJI must also be served together with the accompanying application upon all parties. Proof of accuracy of the index number must accompany the RJI. Check the Fee Schedule[. . .]for any applicable filing fees. NY R BRONX FIL R Doc. 2.

- *KINGS COUNTY.* An RJI with the relevant required addendum in a NYSCEF case shall be submitted via NYSCEF. Once e-filed, the RJI and any accompanying document will be forwarded to the relevant support office for random assignment of the case and processing of the document. A filer or counsel need not appear (as to Proposed Orders to Show Cause, however, see below). A copy of the pleadings must be submitted only if the document has not previously been e-filed. If the RJI seeks intervention with regard to a document that is intended for review by a Justice, such as a motion, a working copy of the RJI must be submitted with the working copy of the motion and the NYSCEF Confirmation Notice. NY R L KINGS E FIL Doc. 1(C).

- *NEW YORK COUNTY.* To obtain the assignment of an IAS Justice to a case, a Request for Judicial Intervention (cost ninety-five dollars ($95)) must be filed, with NYSCEF in an e-filed case or in paper in an authorized hard-copy one. A no-fee RJI, which will generally result in the referral of an application to an Ex Parte Justice, is also required with regard to certain kinds of applications for which, prior to 2011, no RJI was required. NY R NY CTY Procedure I(C). A "fillable" form RJI is available on-line. The form must be filed in duplicate in hard-copy cases. NY R NY CTY Procedure IA(A)(1). The filer of an RJI must check off a box identifying the type of case at issue. Where the RJI seeks judicial assignment, this designation will bring about a random assignment of the case by computer to a Justice handling cases of that type. NY R NY CTY Procedure IA(A)(1). The RJI and any addendum can be completed and submitted electronically in an e-filed case. NY R NY CTY Procedure II(A). The RJI shall be marked to reflect the existence of any "related case" as explained on the "Commencement of Cases" page under "Case Processing" on the court's website. NY R NY CTY Procedure II(A); NY R NY CTY E FIL Doc. 2(C).
- *ONONDAGA COUNTY.* The RJI will be submitted via the NYSCEF system along with any required RJI addendum forms. When the RJI is filed and the fee paid online, the Onondaga County Clerk's Office will electronically forward the RJI and any accompanying documents to the Onondaga Supreme Court Clerk's Office for assignment and processing. Counsel will receive notification of judge assignment via the NYSCEF system. NY R ONDGA E FIL Protocol(B)(3).
- *QUEENS COUNTY.* A Request for Judicial Intervention ("RJI") in an E-filed case shall be submitted via the E-filing System. When the RJI is approved, filed and paid for on-line, it will be forwarded to the relevant back office for random assignment of the case and processing of the document. In the case of RJIs seeking assignment to the Commercial Division, the filer must submit therewith, a Commercial Addendum as required by the standards for assignment of cases to the Commercial Division. NY R L QUEENS E-FILE Doc. 1(F).

iv. *Proof of service.* In addition to complying with the provisions of NY CPLR Rule 2101, every paper filed in court shall have annexed thereto appropriate proof of service on all parties where required. NY R UNIF TRIAL CTS § 202.5(a).

v. *ALBANY COUNTY: Additional required documents*

- *Affirmation of good faith effort.* The parties must[. . .]submit an affirmation attesting to [their good faith effort to resolve the matter]. The affirmation of good faith effort to resolve the issues raised by the motion shall indicate the time, place and nature of the consultation and the issues discussed and any resolutions, or shall indicate good cause why no such conferral with counsel for opposing parties was held. An assigned justice or judge may dismiss a motion for failure to demonstrate that such effort was made with leave to renew the motion after such effort has been demonstrated. NY R 3 JD SUP Doc. 1(B).

b. *Supplemental documents*

i. *Supporting evidence; Exhibits.* The main supporting papers on a motion are affidavits, but any relevant exhibits, documents, depositions, etc., are also includible. SIEGEL-NYPRAC § 246.

- *Affidavits accompanying motion.* Affidavits shall be for a statement of the relevant facts. NY R UNIF TRIAL CTS § 202.8(c).
- *Foreign language documents.* Where an affidavit or exhibit annexed to a paper served or filed is in a foreign language, it shall be accompanied by an English translation and an affidavit by the translator stating his qualifications and that the translation is accurate. NY CPLR Rule 2101(b).
- *Statement of attorney in lieu of affidavit.* The statement of an attorney admitted to practice in the courts of the state, or of a physician, osteopath or dentist, authorized by law to practice in the state, who is not a party to an action, when subscribed and affirmed by him to be true under the penalties of perjury, may be served or filed in the action in lieu of and with the same force and effect as an affidavit. NY CPLR Rule 2106.
- *NEW YORK COUNTY: Form of presented exhibits.* Exhibits should be tabbed and be legible; a typed version of any exhibit that is difficult to read should be submitted with the original. Exhibits printed on both sides of the page should be bound and tabbed on the side. NY R NY CTY J RUL Rule 14(a).
- *QUEENS COUNTY.* Attorneys submitting exhibits to the court on E-file cases shall make each exhibit a separate, labeled attachment to an affidavit/affirmation. NY R L QUEENS E-FILE Doc. 1(H)(4).

ii. *Brief.* Briefs shall be for a statement of the relevant law. NY R UNIF TRIAL CTS § 202.8(c).

iii. *Notice to produce papers not in possession of the court.* If a paper relied on by the movant is in the possession of the other side, it may be demanded of that side with a notice to produce it at the hearing. Where such papers are in the possession of an adverse party, they shall be produced by him at the hearing on notice served with the motion papers. NY CPLR Rule 2214(Practice Commentary, C2214:23).

iv. *Filing fees.* The County Clerk shall require the payment of any applicable statutory fees, or an order of the Court waiving payment of such fees, before accepting a paper for filing. NY R UNIF TRIAL CTS § 202.5(d)(1). For information on filing fees, if any, refer to NY CPLR § 8001, et seq.

- *ALBANY COUNTY.* In general, any filing subsequent to the commencement of an action which is designated as a motion or cross-motion requires the payment of a filing fee to the County Clerk's Office prior to submission to the Supreme Court Clerk's Office for referral to the assigned justice. The fee is assessed regardless of whether an application is made by notice of motion, order to show cause or ex parte. No fee will be charged upon the filing of a motion for poor person status in conjunction with an application which serves to commence an action or special proceeding. In the event a motion is received by the court unaccompanied by proof of payment to the County Clerk, the Supreme Court Clerk's Office will contact the submitting party to advise that the application will be held pending receipt of the filing fee only until the return date of the motion. If proof of payment is not submitted to the Supreme Court Clerk's Office by the return date (ex parte applications will be held ten (10) days), the papers will be returned by mail with a notification that the motion has been removed from the court's calendar and that it must be re-noticed and re-filed with the court along with the requisite filing fee. Inquiries concerning the applicability of the motion fee to a proposed filing may be directed to the Supreme Court Clerk's Office. NY R 3 JD SUP Doc. 1(B).
- *BRONX COUNTY.* In accordance with the new civil fee schedule set forth in Article 80 of the C.P.L.R. (NY CPLR § 8001, et seq.), effective July 14, 2003, all motions, and cross motions must be approved in Room 217 prior to payment of said fees in the County Clerk's Office, Room 118. NY R BRONX FIL R Doc. 8. The motion fee [must be] paid for via NYSCEF by credit/debit card. NY R BRONX E FIL R Doc. 1(1).
- *ERIE COUNTY.* Payment for fee-bearing NYSCEF documents must be made online via credit or debit card (American Express, MasterCard or Visa) at the time of submission. NY R ERIE E FIL Doc. 3(III)(E).
- *KINGS COUNTY.* The motion must be filed with NYSCEF and the motion fee paid. NY R L KINGS E FIL Doc. 1(D). Court fees in NYSCEF cases must be paid via NYSCEF by a credit or bank card (MasterCard, Visa, or American Express). Fees are no longer accepted in person in the Kings County Clerk's Office in NYSCEF cases. NY R L KINGS E FIL Doc. 1(B)(6).
- *NEW YORK COUNTY.* A motion fee must be paid on motions made in writing by notice of motion, order to show cause or ex parte after the commencement of an action. For this purpose, the term "action" shall mean any application to the court that requires the assignment of an index number, regardless of whether a formal pleading is filed. Applications or motions that commence an action and for which an index number fee must be paid require no motion fee. [A]ny motions made after the initial applications in these situations would require payment of the motion fee. A motion that is the initial application in a case commenced by the filing of a summons and complaint would require a motion fee since the filing of the summons and complaint rather than the application itself would require the purchase of an index number. NY R NY CTY Procedure II(A). In e-filed cases the motion fee must be paid when the documents are filed. Payment is made on-line by Visa, Mastercard, or American Express credit or bank card. NY R NY CTY Procedure II(A); NY R NY CTY E FIL Doc. 2(B)(5).
- *ONONDAGA COUNTY.* Court fees in e-filed cases must be paid online with the NYSCEF system using a credit card. The document is not considered to have been filed until payment of the fee has been tendered. NY R ONDGA E FIL Protocol(B)(2). Fees must be paid on all cross motions. NY R ONDGA E FIL Protocol(B)(9)(e).
- *QUEENS COUNTY.* The Motion Support Office does not receive, forward or process any fees or waiver of fees. All applications requiring payment of statutory fees or waiver of fees must be sent directly to the Queens County Clerk's office. NY R L QUEENS MOT SUP Doc. 1. Court fees (e.g., RJI fee, motion fee) in E-filed cases may be paid for on-line using a credit card. Papers may also be filed with the E-file system and the fee may be paid at the County Clerk's Office. In the latter case, the paper is not considered to have been filed until payment of the fee has been tendered. NY R L QUEENS E-FILE Doc. 1(E)(1). The motion/petition shall be filed on-line and the fee paid for either on-line by credit card or by the "Pay at the County Clerk's Office" option. NY R L QUEENS E-FILE Doc. 1(H)(1).

v. *Working copies.* The court may require the parties to provide working copies of documents filed electronically.

In such event, each working copy shall include, firmly affixed thereto, a copy of a confirmation notice in a form prescribed by the Chief Administrator. NY R UNIF TRIAL CTS § 202.5-b(d)(5).

- *BRONX COUNTY.* After papers on motions have been e-filed, working copies thereof, with Confirmation Notice firmly attached as the back page facing out, must be submitted. (Each document or group of documents that is separately bound shall bear a Confirmation Notice.) Working copies lacking the Notice will not be accepted. WORKING COPIES OF MOTION PAPERS MUST BE SUBMITTED NO LATER THAN 4:45 P.M. ON THE RETURN DATE IN THE MOTION SUPPORT OFFICE (ROOM 217) AS EXPLAINED in NY R BRONX E FIL R Doc. 1(4). If an attorney has failed to submit required working copies on or before the return date, the motion will be transmitted as is to the Justice for such action as the Justice finds appropriate. Attorneys may submit working copies on motions by mail or overnight delivery. Any such submission shall be sent in a timely manner to the Motion Support Office (Room 217) and be conspicuously marked on the outside "NYSCEF Matter"; lack of such marking may delay processing. NY R BRONX E FIL R Doc. 1(4)(a).
- *ERIE COUNTY.* Electronically filed documents subject to review and processing by the Part Clerk do not require a working copy unless otherwise directed or provided for in IAS Part Rules. NY R UNIF TRIAL CTS § 202.5-b(d)(4), any working copy submitted shall include, as a cover page firmly fastened thereto, a copy of the Confirmation Notice generated by the NYSCEF site at the time of filing. Please consult the individual Justice's Part Rules and/or consult with the Judge's chambers to determine whether and how working copies are to be provided. Working copies will not be printed or delivered by the Erie County Clerk or the Chief Clerk of the Courts or any of their personnel to chambers. The official record of a document in an electronically filed case is the document filed via the NYSCEF system. Working copies are intended only for use by the Justice. The Court will discard all working copies after the Justice has finished with them. Thus, in the event that counsel fails to file a document via the NYSCEF system, the document will not be part of the court record. NY R ERIE E FIL Doc. 3(III)(O); NY R ERIE E FIL Doc. 3(V)(E).
- *KINGS COUNTY.* No courtesy copies of motion papers are required by the Court, except as may be required for electronic filing or by the Judge's Part Rules. In tort cases against the City of New York, courtesy copies shall be supplied to the Corporation Counsel's office in Brooklyn. NY R L KINGS Pt. C, Rule 5. Unless otherwise directed by the Court or as described herein, and with the exceptions listed below, in all NYSCEF cases in which an RJI has been filed, working copies of e-filed documents that are intended for judicial review must be submitted to the court. Working copies are not required of documents that are only processed by a support office (e.g. preliminary conference request, note of issue). Working copies shall include exhibit tabs and backs; for motion papers, the motion sequence number and the return date and part. The confirmation notice with the motion sequence number on it should be the back page of the motion facing out. In addition, the filer of a working copy must firmly bind thereto, with the back page facing out, a copy of the Confirmation Notice that was generated by NYSCEF when that document was efiled. Working copies that are submitted without the related Confirmation Notice will not be accepted. NY R L KINGS E FIL Doc. 1(B)(7); NY R L KINGS E FIL Doc. 1(D). WORKING COPIES OF MOTION PAPERS MUST BE SUBMITTED IN THE MOTION SUPPORT OFFICE (ROOM 227) AS EXPLAINED HEREIN. THEY MUST NOT BE DELIVERED TO THE PART OR CHAMBERS, EXCEPT WHERE THE INDIVIDUAL JUSTICE'S PART RULES PROVIDE OTHERWISE; DOING SO WILL CAUSE ADMINISTRATIVE CONFUSION AND POSSIBLE MISPLACEMENT OF PAPERS. Any such submission shall be sent in a timely manner (kindly review individual Justice's rules) and be conspicuously marked on the outside "NYSCEF Matter;" lack of such marking may delay processing. NY R L KINGS E FIL Doc. 1(D).
- *NEW YORK COUNTY.* Some Justices require that working copies of e-filed motion papers be submitted. See the E-filing Protocol for information on the many Parts that do not require working copies. Where required, working copies of the moving documents and all other documents on the motion or application shall be submitted to the Motion Submission Part Courtroom (Room 130) on, but not before, the final return date. A Confirmation Notice from the NYSCEF system, which is generated when a document is e-filed, shall be firmly affixed, as the back page facing out, to each separate working copy or group of such copies. NY R NY CTY Procedure II(A) NY R NY CTY E FIL Doc. 2(B)(5)(a); NY R NY CTY J RUL Rule 14(a). For more information on working copies, including which parts don't require them, refer to NY R NY CTY E FIL Doc. 2(B)(6).
- *ONONDAGA COUNTY.* Any courtesy "working" copies, if required (see NY R ONDGA E FIL Protocol(B)(7)), must be provided directly to the assigned justice. NY R ONDGA E FIL Protocol(B)(9)(e).

For information as to whether or not an Onondaga Supreme Court Justice requires working (courtesy) copies of e-filed documents, please consult the Onondaga County Individual E-filing Rules. NY R ONDGA E FIL Protocol(B)(7)(a). The Supreme Court Clerk's Office and the Onondaga County Clerk's Office will NOT accept the working copies. Working copies must be sent directly to the assigned justice's chambers. NY R ONDGA E FIL Protocol(B)(7)(b). A copy of the Confirmation Notice, generated by the NYSCEF system at the time a document is e-filed, must be attached to every working copy provided to chambers. If the Confirmation Notice is missing, the copy will not be accepted. NY R ONDGA E FIL Protocol(B)(7)(c). Courtesy copies do not become part of the official court record as maintained by the Onondaga County Clerk's Office and will be destroyed by chambers at the disposition of the case. In the event that counsel fails to file a document via NYSCEF, the document will not be part of the court record. NY R ONDGA E FIL Protocol(B)(7)(d).

- *QUEENS COUNTY.* Working copies of E-Filed notices of motion/notices of petition are NOT to be sent to the Motion Support Office. They must be brought to the calendar call in the judge's part. NY R L QUEENS MOT SUP Doc. 1. Unless otherwise directed or authorized by the court, counsel should file papers with the E-file system first and thereafter deliver a working copy to at the calendar call of the Centralized Motion Part or Assigned Justice in accordance with individual Part Rules. NY R L QUEENS E-FILE Doc. 1(E)(4). On the return date of a motion that has been E-filed, the movant must provide the Centralized Motion Part (CMP) with a working copy of the entire motion including the notice of motion with sequence number and all of the attached exhibits. The motion must have the confirmation of filing firmly affixed to the back of the papers (facing outward). The confirmation of filing is a separate notice from the payment notice and will say confirmation clearly across the top of the page. NY R L QUEENS E-FILE Doc. 1(H)(2)(a). The motion or Order to Show Cause must have clearly written across its face the words "Working Copy," it must also have the assigned Judge's name, motion sequence number and calendar number—which may be obtained from the posted calendar outside courtroom on the return date of the motion. A confirmation of filing must attached thereto. Working copies of e-filed Orders to Show Cause must contain a copy of the signed order and all supporting papers. NY R L QUEENS E-FILE Doc. 1(H)(2)(c). The Confirmation Notice must be an updated version that indicates the sequence number of the motion being submitted at the CMP calendar call. WORKING COPIES WITHOUT A CONFIRMATION NOTICE WILL NOT BE ACCEPTED. NY R L QUEENS E-FILE Doc. 1(H)(7).

vi. *ERIE COUNTY: Additional supplemental documents*

- *Notice of hard copy submission in e-filed case.* In accordance with NY R UNIF TRIAL CTS § 202.5-b(d), the County Clerk shall refuse to accept for filing, hard copy papers filed to an action subject to electronic filing unless hard copy filing is permitted by the Uniform Rules or NY R ERIE E FIL Doc. 3 and the papers bear a completed Notice of Hard Copy Submission—E-Filed Case form. NY R ERIE E FIL Doc. 3(III)(D).

vii. *KINGS COUNTY: Additional supplemental documents*

- *Forms when filing in hard copy.* An attorney who certifies in good faith that he or she lacks the equipment or knowledge needed to e-file and have no staff member or employee under his or her direction who has such knowledge and equipment may opt out of participation in e-filing in a mandatory case by filing a "Notice of Opt-Out from Participation in Action Subject to Mandatory Electronic Filing" form EFM-2 with the Clerk. NY R L KINGS E FIL Doc. 1(A)(2). Where in accordance with the E-Filing Rules a party submits a document in hard copy in an e-filed case (principally, a document submitted by a nonparticipating party (e.g., an attorney) in a consensual case, an emergency filing made in accordance with the Mandatory E-Filing Rules, and any document filed with the court in hard copy by an attorney who has opted out of participation in mandatory e-filing, the document must bear the back page facing out, a "Notice of Hard Copy Submission—E-Filed Cases" form EFM-3. NY R L KINGS E FIL Doc. 1(B)(3).

viii. *NEW YORK COUNTY: Additional supplemental documents*

- *Notice of hard copy submission.* Where in accordance with the E-Filing Rules an attorney or an unrepresented litigant who is participating in e-filing submits a document in hard copy in an e-filed case, the document must bear, as the back page facing out, a Notice of Hard-Copy Submission—E-Filed Case (a form available in the "Forms" section on the NYSCEF website (Form EFM-3) and in the court's back offices). NY R NY CTY E FIL Doc. 2(B)(3). For more information refer to NY R NY CTY E FIL Doc. 2.

- *Unpublished decisions.* Whenever reliance is placed upon a decision or other authority not officially published or readily available to the New York County Supreme Court, a copy of the case or of pertinent portions of the authority shall be submitted with the motion papers. NY R NY CTY J RUL Rule 14(a).

ix. *ONONDAGA COUNTY: Additional supplemental documents*

- *Notice of hard copy submission.* Any papers to be filed with the court in an e-filed case must be filed online with the E-filing system except where a special exemption is granted (e.g., oversized maps, photographs). If such an exemption is granted, Form EFM-3, "Notice of Hard Copy Submission—E-Filed Case," must be attached to such documents forms which are not filed on line. Also, Form EFM-4 "Notice of Hard Copy Exhibit Filing" must be completed and uploaded to the action's e-file. Both of these forms may be found on the NYSCEF website. NY R ONDGA E FIL Protocol(B)(4).

x. *QUEENS COUNTY: Additional supplemental documents*

- *Notice of hard copy submission.* Any party opting out of the e-filing system must have a "Notice of Hard Copy Submission" firmly affixed to the back of the papers. NY R L QUEENS E-FILE Doc. 1(H)(2)(f).

2. *Documents for opposing party*

a. *Required documents*

i. *Opposition.* Refer to the General Requirements section of this document for information on the opposition.

- *Request for oral argument.* A party requesting oral argument shall set forth such request in its notice of motion or in its order to show cause or on the first page of the answering papers, as the case may be. Where all parties to a motion request oral argument, oral argument shall be granted unless the court shall determine it to be unnecessary. Where a motion is brought on by order to show cause, the court may set forth in the order that oral argument is required on the return date of the motion. NY R UNIF TRIAL CTS § 202.8(d).
- *QUEENS COUNTY: E-filing opposition papers.* E-filed opposition papers and/or reply papers must also be provided to the Centralized Motion Part in the same manner as the moving papers with the confirmation of filing firmly attached to the back of the papers. NY R L QUEENS E-FILE Doc. 1(H)(2)(d).

ii. *Proof of service.* In addition to complying with the provisions of NY CPLR Rule 2101, every paper filed in court shall have annexed thereto appropriate proof of service on all parties where required. NY R UNIF TRIAL CTS § 202.5(a).

- *QUEENS COUNTY.* With regard to service of a motion/petition on notice in an E-filed action, NY CPLR Rule 2214(b) and NY R UNIF TRIAL CTS § 202.5-b(f) applies. Where required, proof of service shall be filed on-line as a separate document. NY R L QUEENS E-FILE Doc. 1(H)(3).

b. *Supplemental documents*

i. *Supporting evidence; Exhibits.* The main supporting papers on a motion are affidavits, but any relevant exhibits, documents, depositions, etc., are also includible. SIEGEL-NYPRAC § 246.

- *Affidavits accompanying opposition.* Affidavits shall be for a statement of the relevant facts. NY R UNIF TRIAL CTS § 202.8(c).
- *Foreign language documents.* Where an affidavit or exhibit annexed to a paper served or filed is in a foreign language, it shall be accompanied by an English translation and an affidavit by the translator stating his qualifications and that the translation is accurate. NY CPLR Rule 2101(b).
- *Statement of attorney in lieu of affidavit.* The statement of an attorney admitted to practice in the courts of the state, or of a physician, osteopath or dentist, authorized by law to practice in the state, who is not a party to an action, when subscribed and affirmed by him to be true under the penalties of perjury, may be served or filed in the action in lieu of and with the same force and effect as an affidavit. NY CPLR Rule 2106.
- *NEW YORK COUNTY: Form of presented exhibits.* Exhibits should be tabbed and be legible; a typed version of any exhibit that is difficult to read should be submitted with the original. Exhibits printed on both sides of the page should be bound and tabbed on the side. NY R NY CTY J RUL Rule 14(a).
- *QUEENS COUNTY.* Attorneys submitting exhibits to the court on E-file cases shall make each exhibit a separate, labeled attachment to an affidavit/affirmation. NY R L QUEENS E-FILE Doc. 1(H)(4).

ii. *Brief.* Briefs shall be for a statement of the relevant law. NY R UNIF TRIAL CTS § 202.8(c).

iii. *Filing fees.* The County Clerk shall require the payment of any applicable statutory fees, or an order of the Court waiving payment of such fees, before accepting a paper for filing. NY R UNIF TRIAL CTS § 202.5(d)(1). For information on filing fees, if any, refer to NY CPLR § 8001, et seq.

- *ALBANY COUNTY.* In general, any filing subsequent to the commencement of an action which is designated as a motion or cross-motion requires the payment of a filing fee to the County Clerk's Office prior to submission to the Supreme Court Clerk's Office for referral to the assigned justice. The fee is assessed regardless of whether an application is made by notice of motion, order to show cause or ex parte. No fee will be charged upon the filing of a motion for poor person status in conjunction with an application which serves to commence an action or special proceeding. In the event a motion is received by the court unaccompanied by proof of payment to the County Clerk, the Supreme Court Clerk's Office will contact the submitting party to advise that the application will be held pending receipt of the filing fee only until the return date of the motion. If proof of payment is not submitted to the Supreme Court Clerk's Office by the return date (ex parte applications will be held ten (10) days), the papers will be returned by mail with a notification that the motion has been removed from the court's calendar and that it must be re-noticed and re-filed with the court along with the requisite filing fee. Inquiries concerning the applicability of the motion fee to a proposed filing may be directed to the Supreme Court Clerk's Office. NY R 3 JD SUP Doc. 1(B).

- *BRONX COUNTY.* In accordance with the new civil fee schedule set forth in Article 80 of the C.P.L.R. (NY CPLR § 8001, et seq.), effective July 14, 2003, all motions, and cross motions must be approved in Room 217 prior to payment of said fees in the County Clerk's Office, Room 118. NY R BRONX FIL R Doc. 8. The motion fee [must be] paid for via NYSCEF by credit/debit card. NY R BRONX E FIL R Doc. 1(1).
- *ERIE COUNTY.* Payment for fee-bearing NYSCEF documents must be made online via credit or debit card (American Express, MasterCard or Visa) at the time of submission. NY R ERIE E FIL Doc. 3(III)(E).
- *KINGS COUNTY.* The motion must be filed with NYSCEF and the motion fee paid. NY R L KINGS E FIL Doc. 1(D). Court fees in NYSCEF cases must be paid via NYSCEF by a credit or bank card (MasterCard, Visa, or American Express). Fees are no longer accepted in person in the Kings County Clerk's Office in NYSCEF cases. NY R L KINGS E FIL Doc. 1(B)(6).
- *NEW YORK COUNTY.* A motion fee must be paid on motions made in writing by notice of motion, order to show cause or ex parte after the commencement of an action. For this purpose, the term "action" shall mean any application to the court that requires the assignment of an index number, regardless of whether a formal pleading is filed. Applications or motions that commence an action and for which an index number fee must be paid require no motion fee. [A]ny motions made after the initial applications in these situations would require payment of the motion fee. A motion that is the initial application in a case commenced by the filing of a summons and complaint would require a motion fee since the filing of the summons and complaint rather than the application itself would require the purchase of an index number. NY R NY CTY Procedure II(A). In e-filed cases the motion fee must be paid when the documents are filed. Payment is made on-line by Visa, Mastercard, or American Express credit or bank card. NY R NY CTY Procedure II(A); NY R NY CTY E FIL Doc. 2(B)(5).
- *ONONDAGA COUNTY.* Court fees in e-filed cases must be paid online with the NYSCEF system using a credit card. The document is not considered to have been filed until payment of the fee has been tendered. NY R ONDGA E FIL Protocol(B)(2). Fees must be paid on all cross motions. NY R ONDGA E FIL Protocol(B)(9)(e).
- *QUEENS COUNTY.* The Motion Support Office does not receive, forward or process any fees or waiver of fees. All applications requiring payment of statutory fees or waiver of fees must be sent directly to the Queens County Clerk's office. NY R L QUEENS MOT SUP Doc. 1. Court fees (e.g., RJI fee, motion fee) in E-filed cases may be paid for on-line using a credit card. Papers may also be filed with the E-file system and the fee may be paid at the County Clerk's Office. In the latter case, the paper is not considered to have been filed until payment of the fee has been tendered. NY R L QUEENS E-FILE Doc. 1(E)(1). The motion/petition shall be filed on-line and the fee paid for either on-line by credit card or by the "Pay at the County Clerk's Office" option. NY R L QUEENS E-FILE Doc. 1(H)(1).

iv. *Working copies.* The court may require the parties to provide working copies of documents filed electronically. In such event, each working copy shall include, firmly affixed thereto, a copy of a confirmation notice in a form prescribed by the Chief Administrator. NY R UNIF TRIAL CTS § 202.5-b(d)(5).

- *BRONX COUNTY.* After papers on motions have been e-filed, working copies thereof, with Confirmation Notice firmly attached as the back page facing out, must be submitted. (Each document or group of documents that is separately bound shall bear a Confirmation Notice.) Working copies lacking the Notice will not be accepted. WORKING COPIES OF MOTION PAPERS MUST BE SUBMITTED NO LATER THAN 4:45 P.M. ON THE RETURN DATE IN THE MOTION SUPPORT OFFICE (ROOM 217) AS

EXPLAINED in NY R BRONX E FIL R Doc. 1(4). If an attorney has failed to submit required working copies on or before the return date, the motion will be transmitted as is to the Justice for such action as the Justice finds appropriate. Attorneys may submit working copies on motions by mail or overnight delivery. Any such submission shall be sent in a timely manner to the Motion Support Office (Room 217) and be conspicuously marked on the outside "NYSCEF Matter"; lack of such marking may delay processing. NY R BRONX E FIL R Doc. 1(4)(a).

- *ERIE COUNTY.* Electronically filed documents subject to review and processing by the Part Clerk do not require a working copy unless otherwise directed or provided for in IAS Part Rules. NY R UNIF TRIAL CTS § 202.5-b(d)(4), any working copy submitted shall include, as a cover page firmly fastened thereto, a copy of the Confirmation Notice generated by the NYSCEF site at the time of filing. Please consult the individual Justice's Part Rules and/or consult with the Judge's chambers to determine whether and how working copies are to be provided. Working copies will not be printed or delivered by the Erie County Clerk or the Chief Clerk of the Courts or any of their personnel to chambers. The official record of a document in an electronically filed case is the document filed via the NYSCEF system. Working copies are intended only for use by the Justice. The Court will discard all working copies after the Justice has finished with them. Thus, in the event that counsel fails to file a document via the NYSCEF system, the document will not be part of the court record. NY R ERIE E FIL Doc. 3(III)(O); NY R ERIE E FIL Doc. 3(V)(E).
- *KINGS COUNTY.* No courtesy copies of motion papers are required by the Court, except as may be required for electronic filing or by the Judge's Part Rules. In tort cases against the City of New York, courtesy copies shall be supplied to the Corporation Counsel's office in Brooklyn. NY R L KINGS Pt. C, Rule 5. Unless otherwise directed by the Court or as described herein, and with the exceptions listed below, in all NYSCEF cases in which an RJI has been filed, working copies of e-filed documents that are intended for judicial review must be submitted to the court. Working copies are not required of documents that are only processed by a support office (e.g. preliminary conference request, note of issue). Working copies shall include exhibit tabs and backs; for motion papers, the motion sequence number and the return date and part. The confirmation notice with the motion sequence number on it should be the back page of the motion facing out. In addition, the filer of a working copy must firmly bind thereto, with the back page facing out, a copy of the Confirmation Notice that was generated by NYSCEF when that document was efiled. Working copies that are submitted without the related Confirmation Notice will not be accepted. NY R L KINGS E FIL Doc. 1(B)(7); NY R L KINGS E FIL Doc. 1(D). WORKING COPIES OF MOTION PAPERS MUST BE SUBMITTED IN THE MOTION SUPPORT OFFICE (ROOM 227) AS EXPLAINED HEREIN. THEY MUST NOT BE DELIVERED TO THE PART OR CHAMBERS, EXCEPT WHERE THE INDIVIDUAL JUSTICE'S PART RULES PROVIDE OTHERWISE; DOING SO WILL CAUSE ADMINISTRATIVE CONFUSION AND POSSIBLE MISPLACEMENT OF PAPERS. Any such submission shall be sent in a timely manner (kindly review individual Justice's rules) and be conspicuously marked on the outside "NYSCEF Matter;" lack of such marking may delay processing. NY R L KINGS E FIL Doc. 1(D).
- *NEW YORK COUNTY.* Some Justices require that working copies of e-filed motion papers be submitted. See the E-filing Protocol for information on the many Parts that do not require working copies. Where required, working copies of the moving documents and all other documents on the motion or application shall be submitted to the Motion Submission Part Courtroom (Room 130) on, but not before, the final return date. A Confirmation Notice from the NYSCEF system, which is generated when a document is e-filed, shall be firmly affixed, as the back page facing out, to each separate working copy or group of such copies. NY R NY CTY Procedure II(A) NY R NY CTY E FIL Doc. 2(B)(5)(a); NY R NY CTY J RUL Rule 14(a). For more information on working copies, including which parts don't require them, refer to NY R NY CTY E FIL Doc. 2(B)(6).
- *ONONDAGA COUNTY.* Any courtesy "working" copies, if required (see NY R ONDGA E FIL Protocol(B)(7)), must be provided directly to the assigned justice. NY R ONDGA E FIL Protocol(B)(9)(e). For information as to whether or not an Onondaga Supreme Court Justice requires working (courtesy) copies of e-filed documents, please consult the Onondaga County Individual E-filing Rules. NY R ONDGA E FIL Protocol(B)(7)(a). The Supreme Court Clerk's Office and the Onondaga County Clerk's Office will NOT accept the working copies. Working copies must be sent directly to the assigned justice's chambers. NY R ONDGA E FIL Protocol(B)(7)(b). A copy of the Confirmation Notice, generated by the NYSCEF system at the time a document is e-filed, must be attached to every working copy provided to chambers. If the Confirmation Notice is missing, the copy will not be accepted. NY R ONDGA E FIL Protocol(B)(7)(c).

Courtesy copies do not become part of the official court record as maintained by the Onondaga County Clerk's Office and will be destroyed by chambers at the disposition of the case. In the event that counsel fails to file a document via NYSCEF, the document will not be part of the court record. NY R ONDGA E FIL Protocol(B)(7)(d).

- *QUEENS COUNTY.* Working copies of E-Filed notices of motion/notices of petition are NOT to be sent to the Motion Support Office. They must be brought to the calendar call in the judge's part. NY R L QUEENS MOT SUP Doc. 1. Unless otherwise directed or authorized by the court, counsel should file papers with the E-file system first and thereafter deliver a working copy to at the calendar call of the Centralized Motion Part or Assigned Justice in accordance with individual Part Rules. NY R L QUEENS E-FILE Doc. 1(E)(4). On the return date of a motion that has been E-filed, the movant must provide the Centralized Motion Part (CMP) with a working copy of the entire motion including the notice of motion with sequence number and all of the attached exhibits. The motion must have the confirmation of filing firmly affixed to the back of the papers (facing outward). The confirmation of filing is a separate notice from the payment notice and will say confirmation clearly across the top of the page. NY R L QUEENS E-FILE Doc. 1(H)(2)(a). The motion or Order to Show Cause must have clearly written across its face the words "Working Copy," it must also have the assigned Judge's name, motion sequence number and calendar number—which may be obtained from the posted calendar outside courtroom on the return date of the motion. A confirmation of filing must attached thereto. Working copies of e-filed Orders to Show Cause must contain a copy of the signed order and all supporting papers. NY R L QUEENS E-FILE Doc. 1(H)(2)(c). The Confirmation Notice must be an updated version that indicates the sequence number of the motion being submitted at the CMP calendar call. WORKING COPIES WITHOUT A CONFIRMATION NOTICE WILL NOT BE ÁCCEPTED. NY R L QUEENS E-FILE Doc. 1(H)(7).

v. *ERIE COUNTY: Additional supplemental documents*

- *Notice of hard copy submission in e-filed case.* In accordance with NY R UNIF TRIAL CTS § 202.5-b(d), the County Clerk shall refuse to accept for filing, hard copy papers filed to an action subject to electronic filing unless hard copy filing is permitted by the Uniform Rules or NY R ERIE E FIL Doc. 3 and the papers bear a completed Notice of Hard Copy Submission—E-Filed Case form. NY R ERIE E FIL Doc. 3(III)(D).

vi. *KINGS COUNTY: Additional supplemental documents*

- *Forms when filing in hard copy.* An attorney who certifies in good faith that he or she lacks the equipment or knowledge needed to e-file and have no staff member or employee under his or her direction who has such knowledge and equipment may opt out of participation in e-filing in a mandatory case by filing a "Notice of Opt-Out from Participation in Action Subject to Mandatory Electronic Filing" form EFM-2 with the Clerk. NY R L KINGS E FIL Doc. 1(A)(2). Where in accordance with the E-Filing Rules a party submits a document in hard copy in an e-filed case (principally, a document submitted by a nonparticipating party (e.g., an attorney) in a consensual case, an emergency filing made in accordance with the Mandatory E-Filing Rules, and any document filed with the court in hard copy by an attorney who has opted out of participation in mandatory e-filing, the document must bear the back page facing out, a "Notice of Hard Copy Submission—E-Filed Cases" form EFM-3. NY R L KINGS E FIL Doc. 1(B)(3).

vii. *NEW YORK COUNTY: Additional supplemental documents*

- *Notice of hard copy submission.* Where in accordance with the E-Filing Rules an attorney or an unrepresented litigant who is participating in e-filing submits a document in hard copy in an e-filed case, the document must bear, as the back page facing out, a Notice of Hard-Copy Submission—E-Filed Case (a form available in the "Forms" section on the NYSCEF website (Form EFM-3) and in the court's back offices). NY R NY CTY E FIL Doc. 2(B)(3). For more information refer to NY R NY CTY E FIL Doc. 2.
- *Unpublished decisions.* Whenever reliance is placed upon a decision or other authority not officially published or readily available to the New York County Supreme Court, a copy of the case or of pertinent portions of the authority shall be submitted with the motion papers. NY R NY CTY J RUL Rule 14(a).

viii. *ONONDAGA COUNTY: Additional supplemental documents*

- *Notice of hard copy submission.* Any papers to be filed with the court in an e-filed case must be filed online with the E-filing system except where a special exemption is granted (e.g., oversized maps, photographs). If such an exemption is granted, Form EFM-3, "Notice of Hard Copy Submission—E-Filed Case," must be attached to such documents forms which are not filed on line. Also, Form EFM-4 "Notice of Hard Copy Exhibit Filing" must be completed and uploaded to the action's e-file. Both of these forms may be found on the NYSCEF website. NY R ONDGA E FIL Protocol(B)(4).

ix. *QUEENS COUNTY: Additional supplemental documents*

- *Notice of hard copy submission.* Any party opting out of the e-filing system must have a "Notice of Hard Copy Submission" firmly affixed to the back of the papers. NY R L QUEENS E-FILE Doc. 1(H)(2)(f).

E. Format

1. *Form of documents*

a. *Size and form of paper.* Each paper served or filed shall be durable, white and, except for summonses, subpoenas, notices of appearance, notes of issue, orders of protection, temporary orders of protection and exhibits, shall be eleven by eight and one-half (11 x 8-1/2) inches in size. NY CPLR Rule 2101(a).

b. *Writing and language.* The writing shall be legible and in black ink. NY CPLR Rule 2101(a). Each paper served or filed shall be in the English language which, where practicable, shall be of ordinary usage. NY CPLR Rule 2101(b).

c. *Caption.* Each paper served or filed shall begin with a caption setting forth the name of the court, the venue, the title of the action, the nature of the paper and the index number of the action if one has been assigned. In all papers other than a summons, a complaint or a judgment it shall be sufficient to state the name of the first named party on each side with an appropriate indication of any omissions. NY CPLR Rule 2101(c).

i. *Further contents of first page.* After the first paper has been filed in each case the index number shall appear on the cover and first page to the right of the caption of every paper tendered for filing in the action. Each such cover and first page also shall contain an indication of the county of venue and a brief description of the nature of the paper and, where the case has been assigned to an individual judge, shall contain the name of the assigned judge to the right of the caption. NY R UNIF TRIAL CTS § 202.5(a); NY R UNIF TRIAL CTS § 202.5(b); NY R UNIF TRIAL CTS § 202.5(d)(1)(i).

ii. *ALBANY COUNTY: Request for oral argument.* A party may request oral argument on a motion by indicating such request on the first page of the notice of motion, order to show cause, or answering papers in the area across from the caption of the action/proceeding. NY R 3 JD SUP Doc. 1(B).

iii. *NEW YORK COUNTY: Request for oral argument.* Counsel who wish oral argument must so request conspicuously on the front of their papers. NY R NY CTY Procedure II(D).

d. *Index number.* No paper in an action in the supreme or a county court, other than an order submitted for signature to a judge out of court, shall be submitted for any purpose to the supreme or county court or to a clerk thereof unless there is endorsed on such paper the index number of the action assigned by the clerk of the county. NY CPLR § 8018(c).

i. *ALBANY COUNTY: Index number on all filed documents.* The index number, the request for judicial intervention number and the assigned justice's name shall appear on [all papers filed with the Court subsequent to the complaint]. NY R 3 JD SUP Doc. 1(A).

ii. *ERIE COUNTY: Index number after initial filing.* Cases that are initially commenced by the filing of papers with the NYSCEF system are identified as e-filed cases by assignment of an Index Number that has "800-899" as the first three (3) digits of the index number (i.e. 802391/2012). NY R ERIE E FIL Doc. 3(II). [The] Index Number must be affixed to all document submissions, filings, and communications to the Erie County Clerk and the Court. Cases that are converted from paper to e-filing shall retain the original index number. NY R ERIE E FIL Doc. 3(II).

iii. *KINGS COUNTY: Index number after initial filing.* In cases commenced electronically by the filing of initiating papers with the NYSCEF system and payment of the statutory fees, the Kings County Clerk will issue an NYSCEF designated index number and the filer shall be notified via the NYSCEF system of the index number assigned and filing date. Such index number must be affixed to all document submissions, filings and communications to the Kings County Clerk and Supreme Court. If counsel faces exigent circumstances that require accelerated assignment, counsel may contact Administration of the Kings County Clerk at kcco-efile@nycourts.gov, during normal business hours of the court. NY R L KINGS E FIL Doc. 1(B)(5).

iv. *NEW YORK COUNTY: Index number on hard copy filings.* Papers subsequently presented for filing in hardcopy format will be filed in this jacket. NY R NY CTY Procedure I(B). Index numbers take the form of six digits followed by a slash and the four digits of the year the case began, e.g., 340705/2018. The first or first two integers of the index number identify the type of case. If a case is commenced electronically, the second integer will be a "5", except as indicated otherwise in the list below. There are many tax certiorari matters e-filed annually and the index numbers therefor will normally run over into those with a "6" as the second integer, and the same will occur with general cases if necessary. The principal types of cases and their index number categories are listed in NY R NY CTY Procedure I(B). NY R NY CTY Procedure I(B); NY R NY CTY Procedure XI(A).

v. *ONONDAGA COUNTY: Index number.* The index number must be referenced on all e-filed documents and correspondence. All e-filed case index numbers will contain the letters "EF" between the year and the file number (for example, 2012EF9999). NY R ONDGA E FIL Protocol(B)(1).

vi. *QUEENS COUNTY: Index number on converted cases.* Cases originally commenced in hard-copy form but later converted to an E-file case, either by stipulation or order will bear a regular index number initially. The County Clerk will issue a new E-file index number. NY R L QUEENS E-FILE Doc. 1(B).

e. *Line spacing.* Every paper filed in court, if typewritten, shall have at least double space between each line, except for quotations and the names and addresses of attorneys appearing in the action. NY R UNIF TRIAL CTS § 202.5(a).

f. *Font size.* Each. . .paper printed or typed, served or filed, except for summonses. . .and exhibits, shall be in clear type of no less than ten (10) point in size. NY CPLR Rule 2101(a).

i. Whenever a requirement relating to size of type is stated in point size, the type size requirement shall be deemed met if the x-height of the type is a minimum of forty-five percent (45%) of the specified point size. Each point shall be measured as .351 millimeter. The x-height size shall be measured as it appears on the page. The x-height is the height of the lower case letters, exclusive of ascenders or descenders. NY CPLR § 105(t).

g. *Margins.* Every paper filed in court shall have at least one (1) inch margins. NY R UNIF TRIAL CTS § 202.5(a).

h. *Citations*

i. *Civil practice law and rules.* NY CPLR § 101, et seq. shall be known as the civil practice law and rules, and may be cited as "CPLR". Reference to a provision in the civil practice law and rules may, except when such provision is being enacted or amended, be made without indicating whether it is a rule or section. NY CPLR § 101.

i. *Indorsement by attorney.* Each paper served or filed shall be indorsed with the name, address and telephone number of the attorney for the party serving or filing the paper, or if the party does not appear by attorney, with the name, address and telephone number of the party. NY CPLR Rule 2101(d).

j. *One-sided printing.* In addition, every paper filed in court, other than an exhibit or printed form, shall contain writing on one side only, except that papers that are fastened on the side may contain writing on both sides. NY R UNIF TRIAL CTS § 202.5(a).

k. *Use of copies authorized.* Except where otherwise specifically prescribed, copies, rather than originals, of all papers, including orders, affidavits and exhibits may be served or filed. Where it is required that the original be served or filed and the original is lost or withheld, the court may authorize a copy to be served or filed. NY CPLR Rule 2101(e).

i. Where a certified copy of a paper is required by law, an attorney admitted to practice in the courts of the state may certify that it has been compared by him with the original and found to be a true and complete copy. Such a certificate, when subscribed by such attorney, has the same effect as if made by a clerk. NY CPLR § 2105.

l. *Recycled paper.* It is the policy of the Unified Court System that litigants, where practicable, should file or submit to the courts of the Unified Court System of the State of New York papers printed or reproduced on recycled paper. Paper is considered recycled if it contains a minimum content of thirty percent (30%) waste paper. NY R UNIF TRIAL CTS § 215.2. The signature page of every paper filed or submitted to the court on recycled paper should bear the legend: "Printed [Reproduced] on Recycled Paper." NY R UNIF TRIAL CTS § 215.3.

m. *Form of request for judicial intervention; Copies.* A request for judicial intervention must be submitted, in duplicate, on a form authorized by the Chief of the Courts, with proof of service on the other parties to the action (but proof of service is not required where the application is ex parte). NY R UNIF TRIAL CTS § 202.6(a).

n. *KINGS COUNTY: Tabs on filings.* Motions, orders and other filed papers shall be indexed with protruding tabs. Clerks are required to reject papers that do not have protruding exhibit tabs, except papers in matrimonial cases and papers filed by pro se litigants. NY R L KINGS Pt. A, Papers.

o. *NEW YORK COUNTY: Length of briefs.* Unless advance permission otherwise is granted by the court for good cause, memoranda of law shall not exceed thirty (30) pages each (exclusive of table of contents and table of authorities) and affidavits/affirmations shall not exceed twenty-five (25) pages each. NY R NY CTY J RUL Rule 14(b).

p. *QUEENS COUNTY: Form and size of motion filings.* All motions filed in Queens Supreme Court-Civil Term, must adhere to the Motion Support rules and the rules of the assigned judge. NY R L QUEENS MOT SUP Doc. 1. Due to space limitations, the Motion Support Office cannot accept notices of motion/notices of petition and accompanying exhibits which measure greater than eight (8) inches. If your documents measure greater than eight (8) inches you are directed to submit only the notice of motion/notice of petition to the Motion Support Office and bring all exhibits to the calendar call on your return date. NY R L QUEENS MOT SUP Doc. 1.

2. *Form of electronic documents.* Each paper served or filed by electronic means, as defined in NY CPLR Rule 2103(f), shall be capable of being reproduced by the receiver so as to comply with the provisions of NY CPLR Rule 2101(a) through NY CPLR Rule 2101(d). NY CPLR Rule 2101(g).
    a. *File format.* All e-filed documents shall comply with the technical requirements set forth at the NYSCEF site. NY R UNIF TRIAL CTS § 202.5-b(d)(1)(i).
    b. *Heading of document.* The subject matter heading for each paper sent by electronic means must indicate that the matter being transmitted electronically is related to a court proceeding. NY CPLR Rule 2103(b)(7).
    c. *E-filed documents identification*
        i. *ERIE COUNTY.* E-filed cases must be readily identifiable and marked as such. If counsel presents papers to the Office of the Erie County Clerk or the Office of the Chief Clerk in a NYSCEF matter where authorized, counsel should alert the Clerk that the case is a NYSCEF matter. NY R ERIE E FIL Doc. 3(II).
        ii. *KINGS COUNTY.* The Supreme Court's Civil Case Information System ("CCIS") will further identify e-filed cases by the addition of a suffix to the index number (e.g. 500136/2006E). This suffix should be used on all documents filed with the court in e-filed matters. NY R L KINGS E FIL Doc. 1(A)(1).
3. *Signature blocks.* Every pleading, written motion, and other paper, served on another party or filed or submitted to the court shall be signed by an attorney, or by a party if the party is not represented by an attorney, with the name of the attorney or party clearly printed or typed directly below the signature. NY R CHIEF ADMIN § 130-1.1-a(a); NY R UNIF TRIAL CTS § 202.5(d)(1)(iv).
    a. *Printed name.* Beneath each signature shall be printed the name signed. NY CPLR Rule 2101(a).
    b. *Failure to sign.* Absent good cause shown, the court shall strike any unsigned paper if the omission of the signature is not corrected promptly after being called to the attention of the attorney or party. NY R CHIEF ADMIN § 130-1.1-a(a).
    c. *Signature as certification.* By signing a paper, an attorney or party certifies that, to the best of that person's knowledge, information and belief, formed after an inquiry reasonable under the circumstances the presentation of the paper or the contentions therein are not frivolous as defined in NY R CHIEF ADMIN § 130-1.1(c). NY R CHIEF ADMIN § 130-1.1-a(b)(1).
    d. *Electronic signatures.* A document shall be considered to have been signed by an attorney or party in compliance with NY R CHIEF ADMIN § 130-1.1-a if it has been signed by such attorney or party as provided in NY R UNIF TRIAL CTS § 202.5-b(e)(1) and it bears the signatory's name. NY R UNIF TRIAL CTS § 202.5-b(e)(2). An electronically filed document shall be considered to have been signed by, and shall be binding upon, the person identified as a signatory, if:
        i. It bears the physical signature of such person and is scanned into an electronic format that reproduces such signature; or
        ii. The signatory has electronically affixed the digital image of his or her signature to the document; or
        iii. It is electronically filed under the User ID and password of that person; or
        iv. In a tax certiorari action in which the parties have stipulated to this procedure, it is an initiating document that is electronically filed without the signature of the signatory in a form provided above in NY R UNIF TRIAL CTS § 202.5-b(e)(iv), provided that, prior to filing, the document is signed in full in hard copy (which hard copy must be preserved until the conclusion of all proceedings, including appeals, in the case in which it is filed); or
        v. In a small claims assessment review proceeding, it is a petition recorded by the NYSCEF site upon the filing of a text file as provided in NY R UNIF TRIAL CTS § 202.5-b(b)(1), provided that prior to filing, the document was signed in full in hard copy (which hard copy must be preserved until the conclusion of all proceedings in the matter, including article 78 (NY CPLR § 7801, et seq.) review and any appeals, and must be made available during the proceeding upon request of the respondent or the court); or
        vi. It otherwise bears the electronic signature of the signatory in a format conforming to such standards and requirements as may hereafter be established by the Chief Administrator. NY R UNIF TRIAL CTS § 202.5-b(e).
4. *Confidentiality of personal information.* No person may file any document available for public inspection with any state agency, political subdivision, or in any court of this state that contains a Social Security account number of any other person, unless such other person is a dependent child, or has consented to such filing, except as required by federal or state law or regulation, or by court rule. NY GEN BUS § 399-ddd. Submissions pursuant to e-filing procedures shall have the same confidentiality rights as paper documents. NY R UNIF TRIAL CTS § 202.5-b(k)(1).
    a. *Confidential personal information.* Except in the actions designated in NY R UNIF TRIAL CTS § 202.5(e)(1), or as

otherwise provided by rule or law or court order, and whether or not a sealing order is or has been sought, the parties shall omit or redact confidential personal information in papers submitted to the court for filing. For purposes of NY R UNIF TRIAL CTS § 202.5(e), confidential personal information ("CPI") means:

i. The taxpayer identification number of an individual or an entity, including a Social Security number, an employer identification number, and an individual taxpayer identification number, except the last four (4) digits thereof;

ii. The date of an individual's birth, except the year thereof;

iii. The full name of an individual known to be a minor, except the minor's initials;

iv. A financial account number, including a credit and/or debit card number, a bank account number, an investment account number, and/or an insurance account number, except the last four (4) digits or letters thereof; and

v. Any of the documents or testimony in a matrimonial action protected by NY DOM REL § 235 or evidence sealed by the court in such an action which are attached as exhibits or referenced in the papers filed in any other civil action. For purposes of NY R UNIF TRIAL CTS § 202.5, a matrimonial action shall mean: an action to annul a marriage or declare the nullity of a void marriage, an action or agreement for a separation, an action for a divorce, or an action or proceeding for custody, visitation, writ of habeus corpus, child support, maintenance or paternity. NY R UNIF TRIAL CTS § 202.5(e)(1).

vi. *ERIE COUNTY.* An attorney or unrepresented litigant filing a document via the NYSCEF system must comply with the requirements of NY R UNIF TRIAL CTS § 202.5(e) regarding the redaction of Confidential Personal Information and NY GEN BUS § 399-ddd(6) concerning the filing of documents containing Social Security Numbers. It is the sole responsibility of counsel or unrepresented litigant filing to be aware of and to comply with existing laws requiring non-disclosure of personal information contained in any document e-filed in NYSCEF. NY R ERIE E FIL Doc. 3(III)(G); NY R ERIE E FIL Doc. 3(III).

vii. *KINGS COUNTY.* An attorney or unrepresented litigant filing a document via the NYSCEF system must comply with the requirements of General Business Law § 399-dd(6), which often require redaction of any Social Security number that appear in the original document. The NYSCEF system automatically redacts portions of filed documents which apparently contain Social Security numbers pursuant to NY R UNIF TRIAL CTS § 202.5-b(k). In the event the filing party receives e-mail notice through NYSCEF that a Social Security number in a filed document has been redacted, and the filing party concludes such redaction is erroneous, the filer should click on the link provided in the e-mail to permit the County Clerk to revert the redaction. For Confidential Personal Information, see NY R UNIF TRIAL CTS § 202.5(e) and NY R L KINGS E FIL Doc. 1(B)(11). [Editor's note: the reference to General Business Law § 399-dd(6) is likely a reference to NY GEN BUS § 399-ddd(6)]. NY R L KINGS E FIL Doc. 1(B)(10); NY R L KINGS E FIL Doc. 1(K)(1).

viii. *NEW YORK COUNTY.* It is the responsibility of counsel and parties to comply with rules restricting disclosure of confidential personal information. Nevertheless, NYSCEF screens filings and endeavors to identify any that contain social security numbers. When such numbers are discovered through this process, NYSCEF will restrict portions of or all of such documents from public view. Where NYSCEF has redacted what it believes to be a social security number, it will transmit to the filer a notice advising of the action taken and requesting that the filer review the matter and provide notification as set forth in the notice if the redaction has been made in error. NY R NY CTY E FIL Doc. 2(K)(1); NY R NY CTY J RUL Rule A-1. Documents filed in the past in "secure status" under a procedure no longer in place will retain that status unless otherwise directed by the court. NY R NY CTY E FIL Doc. 2(K)(2).

b. *Submission of confidential personal information.* Where a person submitting a paper to a court for filing believes in good faith that the inclusion of the full confidential personal information described in NY R UNIF TRIAL CTS § 202.5(e)(1) is material and necessary to the adjudication of the action or proceeding before the court, he or she may apply to the court for leave to serve and file together with a paper in which such information has been set forth in abbreviated form a confidential affidavit or affirmation setting forth the same information in unabbreviated form, appropriately referenced to the page or pages of the paper at which the abbreviated form appears. NY R UNIF TRIAL CTS § 202.5(e)(3).

c. *Home addresses.* For information on when home addresses and other personal information must be redacted, refer to NY CPLR Rule 2103-a.

5. *Defective papers.* A defect in the form of a paper, if a substantial right of a party is not prejudiced, shall be disregarded by the court, and leave to correct shall be freely given. NY CPLR Rule 2101(f). Papers that are stapled or bound securely shall not be rejected for filing simply because they are not bound with a backer of any kind. NY R UNIF TRIAL CTS § 202.5(a).

A paper filed in accordance with the rules of the chief administrator or any local rule or practice established by the court shall be deemed filed. NY CPLR Rule 2102(b).

a. *Objection to defective papers.* The party on whom a paper is served shall be deemed to have waived objection to any defect in form unless, within fifteen (15) days after the receipt thereof, the party on whom the paper is served returns the paper to the party serving it with a statement of particular objections. NY CPLR Rule 2101(f).

F. Filing and Service Requirements

1. *Filing requirements.* Except where otherwise prescribed by law or order of court, papers required to be filed shall be filed with the clerk of the court in which the action is triable. In an action or proceeding in supreme or court, papers required to be filed shall be filed with the clerk of the county in which the proceeding is brought. NY CPLR Rule 2102(a).

a. *Furnishing papers to the court.* Each party shall furnish to the court all papers served by him. The moving party shall furnish at the hearing all other papers not already in the possession of the court necessary to the consideration of the questions involved. Where such papers are in the possession of an adverse party, they shall be produced by him at the hearing on notice served with the motion papers. Only papers served in accordance with the provisions of NY CPLR Rule 2214 shall be read in support of, or in opposition to, the motion, unless the court for good cause shall otherwise direct. NY CPLR Rule 2214(c).

i. *Submission to judge.* All papers for signature or consideration of the court shall be presented to the clerk of the trial court in the appropriate courtroom or clerk's office, except that where the clerk is unavailable or the judge so directs, papers may be submitted to the judge and a copy filed with the clerk at the first available opportunity. All papers for any judge that are filed in the clerk's office shall be promptly delivered to the judge by the clerk. The papers shall be clearly addressed to the judge for whom they are intended and prominently show the nature of the papers, the title and index number of the action in which they are filed, the judge's name and the name of the attorney or party submitting them. NY R UNIF TRIAL CTS § 202.5(b).

ii. *BRONX COUNTY: Approval of motions before filing.* All motion papers must be approved by the Motion Support Office, Supreme Court, Civil Term, room 217, before the motion papers are filed and the appropriate fee paid to the County Clerk. NY R BRONX FIL R Doc. 1.

iii. *ERIE COUNTY: Filing motions.* A motion on notice or a notice of petition in a NYSCEF case shall be filed through the NYSCEF system and must be accompanied by a Request for Judicial Intervention if the motion is being filed upon commencement of the action or if the matter has not yet been assigned to an IAS Justice. In addition, cross motions with the appropriate filing fees and opposition and reply papers must be submitted via the NYSCEF system. NY R ERIE E FIL Doc. 3(V)(A).

iv. *NEW YORK COUNTY: Filing hard copies.* Where in the narrow circumstances described by the e-filing rules a motion is made in hard-copy form or opposition papers are submitted in such form in an e-filed case, the hard-copy documents shall be submitted in the same way papers are submitted in non-e-filed cases, except that there shall be firmly affixed to each separate document or group of documents, as the back page facing out, a Notice of Hard Copy Submission—E-Filed Case. NY R NY CTY Procedure II(A). For more information on filing in hard copy cases, refer to NY R NY CTY Procedure II(A).

v. *ONONDAGA COUNTY: Submission of responsive papers and cross-motions.* Cross-motions, opposition and reply papers must be submitted online. NY R ONDGA E FIL Protocol(B)(9)(e). Motions and Orders to Show Cause are assigned a sequence number by the system. Counsel must be sure that cross motions and other filings correspond with the correct sequence number so that a cross motion will not be associated with the wrong original motion. NY R ONDGA E FIL Protocol(B)(9)(f).

b. *Electronic filing.* On consent, documents may be filed and served by electronic means in Supreme Court in such civil actions and in such counties as shall be authorized by order of the Chief Administrator of the Courts and only to the extent and in the manner provided in NY R UNIF TRIAL CTS § 202.5-b. NY R UNIF TRIAL CTS § 202.5-b(a)(1). For the definitions of terms used in electronic filing, refer to NY R UNIF TRIAL CTS § 202.5-b(a)(2).

i. *E-filing mandatory.* In any action subject to e-filing, all documents required to be filed with the court by an e-filing party shall be filed and served electronically, except as provided in NY R UNIF TRIAL CTS § 202.5-b. NY R UNIF TRIAL CTS § 202.5-b(d)(1)(i).

- *ERIE COUNTY.* Case types currently eligible and accepted for e-filing are listed at the NYSCEF website. Note that some actions or special proceedings, (i.e., name changes) which are otherwise subject to mandatory e-filing, if commenced by unrepresented litigants will NOT be maintained in the NYSCEF system; individual cases may be found either at NYSCEF or in the Erie County Clerk's online records system. NY R ERIE E FIL Doc. 3(I)(E).

- *KINGS COUNTY.* Cases that are commenced by filing of the initiating papers with NYSCEF are identified as e-filed cases by assignment of a special index number (i.e., Index Numbers beginning with 500,000). NY R L KINGS E FIL Doc. 1(A)(1). All cases required to be e-filed are listed in Uniform Rule 202.5-bb (Mandatory E-Filing Rules) and on the NYSCEF website. All such cases must be commenced by filing with the County Clerk electronically through NYSCEF and all subsequent documents in such cases must be e-filed. Any questions regarding mandatory e-filing in Kings County can be e-mailed to kcco-efile@nycourts.gov. NY R L KINGS E FIL Doc. 1(A)(2).
- *NEW YORK COUNTY.* Unless otherwise provided in the Rules or in NY R NY CTY E FIL Doc. 2 or where a special exemption is granted due to physical requirements (e.g., oversized maps; see NY R NY CTY E FIL Doc. 2(B)(10)), all documents to be filed with the court in a NYSCEF case, including all documents on motions and all letters to the court (where permitted), must be filed with the NYSCEF system. Documents that attorneys would not ordinarily file with the court in a hard-copy case need not be e-filed. Unless otherwise provided by the E-Filing Rules or this Protocol, in e-filed cases the County Clerk and the court will not accept documents filed in paper form. NY R NY CTY E FIL Doc. 2(B)(1). E-filing is mandatory in all types of cases (other than election law, matrimonial, Art. 78, and Mental Hygiene Law matters, and Art. 70 habeas corpus proceedings) that are commenced in this court on or after February 19, 2013. All such cases must be commenced by filing with the County Clerk electronically through NYSCEF and all subsequent documents in such cases must be e-filed. NY R NY CTY E FIL Doc. 2(A)(2)(a). For more information, including information on consensual e-filing and filing scanned hard copy documents, refer to NY R NY CTY E FIL Doc. 2(A)(2).
- *QUEENS COUNTY.* All authorized Torts, Commercial and Tax Certiorari cases may be commenced by E-Filing, however all parties must consent for the action to continue as an E-file case. NY R L QUEENS E-FILE Doc. 1(A). All papers to be filed with the court in an E-filed case shall be filed on-line with the E-file system except as directed by the court. Papers that attorneys would not ordinarily file with the court in a hard-copy case need not be filed in an E-filed matter. NY R L QUEENS E-FILE Doc. 1(E)(2).

ii. *Who may file.* Documents may be filed or served electronically only by a person who has registered as an authorized e-filing user or as otherwise provided in NY R UNIF TRIAL CTS § 202.5-b(c). NY R UNIF TRIAL CTS § 202.5-b(c)(1).

iii. *When filing made.* Documents may be transmitted at any time of the day or night to the NYSCEF site. A document other than an order or judgment is filed when its electronic transmission or, in the case of a petition that is e-filed by submission of a text file as provided in NY R UNIF TRIAL CTS § 202.5-b(b)(1), the electronic transmission of the text file is recorded at that site, provided, however, that where payment of a fee is required upon the filing of a document, the document is not filed until transmission of the document and the information or form or information as required in NY R UNIF TRIAL CTS § 202.5-b(d)(2)(i), NY R UNIF TRIAL CTS § 202.5-b(d)(2)(ii) or NY R UNIF TRIAL CTS § 202.5-b(d)(2)(iii) has been recorded at the NYSCEF site; or, if no transmission of that information or form or information is recorded, where permitted by the County Clerk, until payment is presented to the County Clerk. NY R UNIF TRIAL CTS § 202.5-b(d)(3)(i).

iv. *Notification of filing.* No later than the close of business on the business day following the electronic filing of a document, a notification, in a form prescribed by the Chief Administrator, shall be transmitted electronically by the NYSCEF site to the person filing such document and the e-mail service addresses of all other participating parties in such action. NY R UNIF TRIAL CTS § 202.5-b(d)(3)(ii).

v. *Removal of confidential information and other corrections.* If a document filed electronically is subsequently discovered to contain confidential data—including but not limited to trade secrets, information protected by confidentiality agreement, or personal confidential information as defined by statute or court rule—or otherwise to have been filed in error, the filer or another party or affected person may (1) notify the parties and any non-party filers in the action of the confidentiality issue or other error raised by the filing, and of his or her intention to seek judicial relief to correct the filing: (2) following such notification, request that the appropriate County Clerk, exercising his or her administrative discretion, place the document temporarily in "restricted" status on the NYSCEF site, to be made available for viewing by court staff and the parties but not the general public; and (3) file an application to correct the filing by order to show cause within five (5) business days of such notification (or such time as the court may direct), including a request for preliminary injunctive relief limiting interim disclosure of the document at issue. Unless otherwise directed by the court, any document placed in restricted status in response to such a request shall be returned to public view upon expiration of this five (5) day

period. The Chief Administrator of the Courts shall promulgate forms to implement this process. NY R UNIF TRIAL CTS § 202.5-b(d)(3)(iii).

- *KINGS COUNTY.* For information on what to do when a document was erroneously filed with confidential information, refer to NY R L KINGS E FIL Doc. 1(B)(11).
- *NEW YORK COUNTY.* For information on what to do when a document was erroneously filed with confidential information, refer to NY R NY CTY E FIL Doc. 2(B)(8).
- *QUEENS COUNTY.* For information on what to do when a document was erroneously filed with confidential information, refer to NY R L QUEENS E-FILE Doc. 1(E)(7).

vi. *Documents requiring judge's signature.* Except where the court directs otherwise, any document that requires a judge's signature shall be transmitted electronically and in hard copy to the court. NY R UNIF TRIAL CTS § 202.5-b(d)(6).

vii. *Documents which would be inconvenient to file electronically; Hard copies.* Notwithstanding any other provision of NY R UNIF TRIAL CTS § 202.5-b, and subject to such guidelines as may be established by the Chief Administrative Judge, the County Clerk or his or her designee may require or permit a party to file in hard copy, in accordance with procedures set by the County Clerk or designee, an exhibit or other document which it is impractical or inconvenient to file electronically. NY R UNIF TRIAL CTS § 202.5-b(d)(7).

- *ERIE COUNTY.* Please contact the Supervisor of Actions & Proceedings, Erie County Clerk's Office by calling (716) 858-6662 or the Deputy County Clerk—Legal at (716) 858-6348 for information. NY R ERIE E FIL Doc. 3(III)(F).
- *KINGS COUNTY.* With limited exceptions, as set forth in the Uniform Rules and herein, all documents to be filed with the court in a NYSCEF case shall be filed online via the NYSCEF system. However, should the size, consistency or context of a hard copy document preclude electronic filing, the user shall electronically file a "Notice of Hard Copy Submission—E-Filed Cases" form EFM-3. Any hard copy submitted pursuant to NY R L KINGS E FIL Doc. 1(B)(9) shall include, as a cover page firmly fastened thereto, a copy of the Confirmation Notice received from the NYSCEF site confirming receipt of the "Notice of Hard Copy Submission—E-Filed Cases". Any party may object to such hard copy filing. The Court, in response to such objection, may, following the hard copy filing, fashion such relief as it deems appropriate pursuant to and in furtherance of the Uniform Rules and NY R L KINGS E FIL Doc. 1, including, but not limited to, an Order directing the filing party to file such documents online via the NYSCEF system. When exhibits are impractical to file pursuant to NY R UNIF TRIAL CTS § 202.5-b(d)(7), an additional "Notice of Hard Copy Exhibit Filing" form EFM-4 is required to be submitted. NY R L KINGS E FIL Doc. 1(B)(9).
- *NEW YORK COUNTY.* If a filer needs to submit unusual exhibits in original form that cannot practically be e-filed, such as oversized maps or electronic recordings, the filer should consult with the County Clerk's E-File Department by telephone at 646-386-3737 (procedural questions only) or by e-mail at ccnyef@nycourts.gov, which will normally require that the filer retain custody of the original subject to possible future directives of the court. NY R NY CTY E FIL Doc. 2(B)(10). In such instances, the filing counsel shall file with NYSCEF a "placeholder" in the form of a Notice of Hard Copy Exhibit Filing (NYSCEF Form EF 21). The Notice should be uploaded to NYSCEF as document type "Exhibit" and the filer should indicate in the "Additional Document Information" field that the filer is retaining custody of the original. Failure to e-file the Notice may result in a gap in the official record of the court. NY R NY CTY E FIL Doc. 2(B)(10).

viii. *Documents containing sensitive or proprietary information.* In an action subject to e-filing, any person may apply for an order prohibiting or restricting the electronic filing in the action of specifically identified materials on the grounds that such materials are subject to copyright or other proprietary rights, or trade secret or other privacy interests, and that electronic filing in the action is likely to result in substantial prejudice to those rights or interests. NY R UNIF TRIAL CTS § 202.5-b(k)(2).

ix. *Refusal to accept paper filings.* In accordance with NY CPLR Rule 2102(c), a County Clerk and a chief clerk of the Supreme Court or County Court, as appropriate, shall refuse to accept for filing papers filed in actions and proceedings when the paper sought to be filed:

- Is in an action subject to electronic filing pursuant to Rules of the Chief Administrator,
- Is not being filed electronically, and

- Does not include the notice required by NY R UNIF TRIAL CTS § 202.5-b(d)(1). NY R UNIF TRIAL CTS § 202.5(d)(1)(v); NY R UNIF TRIAL CTS § 202.5-bb(d).

x. *Emergency filings; Hard copies.* For information on when an emergency filing may be filed and served in hard copy, refer to NY R UNIF TRIAL CTS § 202.5-b(d)(1)(ii), NY R UNIF TRIAL CTS § 202.5-b(d)(1)(iii) and NY R UNIF TRIAL CTS § 202.5-bb(c)(3).

- *KINGS COUNTY.* Under the rules, a participating emergency e-filer must electronically file the documents initially filed in hard copy form within three (3) business days of the emergency filing; the originals will be discarded after the documents have been processed and the failure to e-file as required will therefore lead to an incomplete record. NY R L KINGS E FIL Doc. 1(B)(3).
- *NEW YORK COUNTY.* Occasionally an emergency will arise requiring expedited entry of a document with the County Clerk (e.g., an order issued in the courtroom after a conference or argument of a critical matter), such as for purposes of an immediate appeal. Expedition can be achieved by the Part as follows: the document should be carried by a Court Officer or staff member to the General Clerk's Office to assure immediate and proper recordation in the computer and, as appropriate, the posting of the document to NYSCEF or the Supreme Court Records On-Line Library ("Scroll"). The court will accommodate counsel in emergencies. NY R NY CTY Procedure XI(A).
- *NEW YORK COUNTY.* For more information on how to bring emergency matters before the court, refer to NY R NY CTY Procedure IV.

xi. *Technical failures.* The NYSCEF site shall be considered to be subject to a technical failure on a given day if the site is unable to accept filings or provide access to filed documents continuously or intermittently over the course of any period of time greater than one (1) hour after 12:00 noon of that day. Notice of all such technical failures shall be provided on the site. NY R UNIF TRIAL CTS § 202.5-b(i).

- When e-filing is hindered by a technical failure, a party may file with the appropriate clerk and serve in hard copy. NY R UNIF TRIAL CTS § 202.5-b(i). In the event an attorney or party shall file and serve documents in hard copy pursuant to NY R UNIF TRIAL CTS § 202.5-b(i), each such document shall include the notice required by NY R UNIF TRIAL CTS § 202.5-b(d)(1), and the filer shall file those documents with the NYSCEF site within three (3) business days after restoration of normal operations at that site. NY R UNIF TRIAL CTS § 202.5-b(i).
- With the exception of deadlines that by law cannot be extended, the time for filing of any document that is delayed due to technical failure of the site shall be extended for one (1) day for each day on which such failure occurs, unless otherwise ordered by the court. NY R UNIF TRIAL CTS § 202.5-b(i).
- *ERIE COUNTY.* When filing by electronic means is hindered by a technical failure, please refer to the NY R UNIF TRIAL CTS § 202.5-b(i). NY R ERIE E FIL Doc. 3(III)(K).
- *KINGS COUNTY.* When filing by electronic means is hindered by a NYSCEF technical failure (as set forth in NY R UNIF TRIAL CTS § 202.5-b(i)), a party may file with the appropriate Clerk in hard copy. Except for deadlines that by law cannot be extended (e.g. Statute of limitations, Notice of Appeal), the time for filing of any document that is delayed due to technical failure of the NYSCEF system shall be extended for one day for each day on which such failure occurs, unless otherwise ordered by the court. NY R L KINGS E FIL Doc. 1(B)(13).
- *ONONDAGA COUNTY.* When filing by electronic means is hindered by a technical failure (as set forth in NY R UNIF TRIAL CTS § 202.5-b(h)(3)(i)), a party may file a hard copy with the County Clerk. With the exception of deadlines that by law cannot be extended (e.g., a statute of limitations or the deadline for filing a Notice of Appeal), the time for filing of any document that is delayed due to technical failure of the NYSCEF system will be extended for one day for each day on which such failure occurs, unless otherwise ordered by the court. A "Notice of Hard Copy Filing Submission—E-Filed Case' must accompany any documents not filed via NYSCEF. NY R ONDGA E FIL Protocol(B)(8).

xii. *Filing fees.* For information on what information must be provided to pay filing fees, refer to NY R UNIF TRIAL CTS § 202.5-b(d)(2).

xiii. *Exemption from e-filing.* For information on exemptions from e-filing, refer to NY R UNIF TRIAL CTS § 202.5-bb(e).

xiv. *Filing exhibits*

- *ERIE COUNTY.* In the NYSCEF system, each exhibit must be uploaded as a separate .pdf file. After

uploading a primary document, please choose the document type "Exhibit" and enter the appropriate number or letter and a brief description of the exhibit; each exhibit should bear a separate cover sheet clearly marked as "Exhibit A," "Exhibit B," etc. "Exhibit A" or "Exhibit B" is unacceptable as a brief description of the exhibit. Exhibits, where referenced in a signed Order as attached or affixed shall be uploaded with the signed Order as one .pdf document. NY R ERIE E FIL Doc. 3(III)(H); NY R ERIE E FIL Doc. 3(V)(D).

- *KINGS COUNTY.* In the NYSCEF system, each exhibit should be uploaded as a separate PDF file. After uploading a primary document, please choose the document type "Exhibit", enter the appropriate number or letter, and be sure to place a check mark to the right of "Attach to main document". Each exhibit shall bear a separate cover sheet clearly marked as Exhibit A, Exhibit B, etc. NY R L KINGS E FIL Doc. 1(B)(12). Whenever possible, attorneys submitting exhibits in NYSCEF cases should make each exhibit a separate attachment to an affidavit/affirmation in the system (i.e., multiple exhibits should not be filed as a single PDF). NY R L KINGS E FIL Doc. 1(D)(1).
- *NEW YORK COUNTY.* Attorneys submitting exhibits in NYSCEF cases should make each exhibit a separate attachment to an affidavit/affirmation in the system; i.e., exhibits should not be filed as a single PDF-A together with the affidavit/affirmation or grouped together as a single PDF-A attachment because either of these two formats makes it difficult for the Justice to locate particular exhibits as needed. Counsel must also include appropriate descriptive language in the "Additional Document Information" field in NYSCEF. NY R NY CTY E FIL Doc. 2(D)(6).
- *ONONDAGA COUNTY.* All exhibits in e-filed cases must be e-filed individually as separate attachments. NY R ONDGA E FIL Protocol(B)(9)(b).

xv. *Correcting documents*

- *ERIE COUNTY.* Submission of documents which, upon examination, require correction or addition will result in notification to the filer advising that the document has been returned for correction. The filer shall make the required corrections and/or additions as indicated in the e-mail transmission sent by the County Clerk or Part Clerk through the NYSCEF site. The corrected documents may be resubmitted using the "Re-file this document" link highlighted in the filer's document list for the respective case. Please note that in the case of multiple submissions, all related documents filed at the same time may be removed from the case record and returned until all documents are properly submitted. NY R ERIE E FIL Doc. 3(III)(J).
- *KINGS COUNTY.* Submission of documents which, upon examination, require correction or addition will result in notification to the filer advising that there is a problem with a document. The filer shall make the required corrections and/or additions and resubmit the corrected document using the "Refile this document" link. In the event a document is returned for correction, the original file date will be preserved. For corrections of documents filed with the Kings County Clerk which require a court order, refer to the procedure in NY R UNIF TRIAL CTS § 202.5-b(d)(3)(iii) and NY R L KINGS E FIL Doc. 1(B)(11). NY R L KINGS E FIL Doc. 1(B)(3).
- *ONONDAGA COUNTY.* If there is an error or an additional document is required, the system will notify the filing party, who will make the corrections/additions and resubmit them online. NY R ONDGA E FIL Protocol(B)(6).
- *QUEENS COUNTY.* Generally speaking, documents that have been E-filed will not thereafter be deleted by the County Clerk from NYCEF because the filer asserts that the filing contains an error or a significant omission. When the filer wishes to correct a perceived error or omission in a filed document, he or she should file an amended version of the document, with the original remaining on file, or else obtain a court order providing for deletion of the original. The County Clerk will only delete a document upon request of the filer or on the County Clerk's own initiative when it is obvious from the face of the document alone that the filer made a fundamental error and never intended to file the document that was filed (e.g., a completely unrelated non-litigation document, a different case, or a wrong county). The County Clerk will advise the filer when any such fundamental errors are detected. NY R L QUEENS E-FILE Doc. 1(E)(6).

c. *Facsimile filing.* In the Supreme Court, facsimile filing shall be limited to commercial claims and tax certiorari, conservatorship, and mental hygiene proceedings in Monroe, Westchester, New York and Suffolk Counties. NY R UNIF TRIAL CTS § 202.5-a(a)(1). Refer to NY R UNIF TRIAL CTS § 202.5-a for information on the procedures for facsimile filing.

i. *NEW YORK COUNTY.* Unless indicated otherwise by the court in a particular case or in NY R NY CTY J RUL Doc. 1, Justices do not accept papers by fax. NY R NY CTY J RUL Rule 4.

d. *ERIE COUNTY: Filing request for judicial intervention.* An RJI in a NYSCEF case shall be filed via the NYSCEF system and will be filed after all other documents have been uploaded. The filer may choose between filing a .pdf image of the prepared RJI and any Addendum or having the system prepare the RJI which shall conform to Uniform Rules. Addenda, such as the Commercial Division Addendum, if prepared by the filer must be filed simultaneously with and attached to an RJI and uploaded as one .pdf document with the RJI. If the RJI is prepared by the e-filing system, no separate Addendum is required. Whether or not the filer elects to allow NYSCEF to create the RJI or chooses to upload a prepared RJI, data in addition to the nature of the judicial intervention, including information that appears on any Addenda will be collected through completion of the fields presented. If the filing of the RJI is accomplished through a filing agent, a prepared RJI and Addendum must be filed in lieu of the creation of the RJI by the NYSCEF system, as the RJI must be signed by the attorney. NY R ERIE E FIL Doc. 3(IV). For information on RJIs in specific types of action, refer to NY R ERIE E FIL Doc. 3(IV).

2. *Service requirements*

a. *Who may serve.* Except where otherwise prescribed by law or order of court, papers may be served by any person not a party of the age of eighteen years or over. NY CPLR Rule 2103(a).

b. *Service upon attorney.* Except where otherwise prescribed by law or order of court, papers to be served upon a party in a pending action shall be served upon the party's attorney. Where the same attorney appears for two or more parties, only one (1) copy need be served upon the attorney. Such service upon an attorney shall be made:

i. By delivering the paper to the attorney personally. NY CPLR Rule 2103(b)(1).

ii. By mailing the paper to the attorney at the address designated by that attorney for that purpose or, if none is designated, at the attorney's last known address; service by mail shall be complete upon mailing. NY CPLR Rule 2103(b)(2).

- *BRONX COUNTY.* Service by mail must be within the state. NY R BRONX FIL R Doc. 3.

iii. If the attorney's office is open, by leaving the paper with a person in charge, or if no person is in charge, by leaving it in a conspicuous place; or if the attorney's office is not open, by depositing the paper, enclosed in a sealed wrapper directed to the attorney, in the attorney's office letter drop or box. NY CPLR Rule 2103(b)(3).

iv. By leaving it at the attorney's residence within the state with a person of suitable age and discretion. Service upon an attorney shall not be made at the attorney's residence unless service at the attorney's office cannot be made. NY CPLR Rule 2103(b)(4).

v. By transmitting the paper to the attorney by facsimile transmission, provided that a facsimile telephone number is designated by the attorney for that purpose. Service by facsimile transmission shall be complete upon the receipt by the sender of a signal from the equipment of the attorney served indicating that the transmission was received, and the mailing of a copy of the paper to that attorney. The designation of a facsimile telephone number in the address block subscribed on a paper served or filed in the course of an action or proceeding shall constitute consent to service by facsimile transmission in accordance with NY CPLR Rule 2103(b)(5). An attorney may change or rescind a facsimile telephone number by serving a notice on the other parties. NY CPLR Rule 2103(b)(5).

vi. By dispatching the paper to the attorney by overnight delivery service at the address designated by the attorney for that purpose or, if none is designated, at the attorney's last known address. Service by overnight delivery service shall be complete upon deposit of the paper enclosed in a properly addressed wrapper into the custody of the overnight delivery service for overnight delivery, prior to the latest time designated by the overnight delivery service for overnight delivery. "Overnight delivery service" means any delivery service which regularly accepts items for overnight delivery to any address in the state. NY CPLR Rule 2103(b)(6).

vii. By transmitting the paper to the attorney by electronic means where and in the manner authorized by the chief administrator of the courts by rule and, unless such rule shall otherwise provide, such transmission shall be upon the party's written consent. The subject matter heading for each paper sent by electronic means must indicate that the matter being transmitted electronically is related to a court proceeding. NY CPLR Rule 2103(b)(7).

- *KINGS COUNTY.* Pursuant to the E-Filing Rules, service of interlocutory documents is made by posting a document to the NYSCEF site, which automatically and immediately transmits an email notice of the filing, including a link to the document, to all participating counsel and unrepresented litigants on the case. The Rules also authorize service by other methods permitted by the CPLR. If service by such other method is made, proof of service must be filed with NYSCEF. NY R L KINGS E FIL Doc. 1(I).
- *NEW YORK COUNTY.* Service. . .will be made automatically through NYSCEF upon all participating

counsel and unrepresented parties in the case. There are limited exceptions to the requirement for e-filing in the covered kinds of cases. NY R NY CTY Procedure XI(A). Pursuant to the E-Filing Rules, service of interlocutory documents is made by posting a document to the NYSCEF site, which automatically and immediately transmits an e-mail notice of the filing, including a link to the document, to all participating counsel and unrepresented litigants on the case. The Rules also authorize service by other methods permitted by the CPLR. If service by such a method is made, proof of service must be filed with NYSCEF. NY R NY CTY E FIL Doc. 2(I).

- *QUEENS COUNTY.* Filing with the system permits counsel to serve the papers electronically pursuant to NY R UNIF TRIAL CTS § 202.5-b(f) once consent to E-Filing has been filed on-line. Consult NY R UNIF TRIAL CTS § 202.5-bb(c) for service in mandatory e-filing. Any required proof of service should be E-filed as a separate document. NY R L QUEENS E-FILE Doc. 1(E)(4).

c. *Electronic service mandatory; Consenting to electronic service; How electronic service may be made.* Except as otherwise provided in NY R UNIF TRIAL CTS § 202.5-bb, filing and service of all documents in an action that has been commenced electronically in accordance with NY R UNIF TRIAL CTS § 202.5-bb shall be by electronic means. NY R UNIF TRIAL CTS § 202.5-bb(c)(1).

i. *Party's consent required for certain e-filing.* After commencement of an action wherein e-filing is authorized, documents may be electronically filed and served, but only by, and electronic service shall be made only upon, a party or parties who have consented thereto. NY R UNIF TRIAL CTS § 202.5-b(b)(2)(i).

- A consent to e-filing in an action shall state that the party providing it agrees to the use of e-filing in the action and to be bound by the filing and service provisions in NY R UNIF TRIAL CTS § 202.5-b. NY R UNIF TRIAL CTS § 202.5-b(b)(2)(ii).

ii. *Address for service; Duty to notify as to changes.* The e-mail service address recorded at the time of registration is the e-mail address at which service of interlocutory documents on that party may be made through notification transmitted by the NYSCEF site. It is the responsibility of each filing user to monitor that address and promptly notify the Resource Center in the event of a change in his or her e-mail service address. NY R UNIF TRIAL CTS § 202.5-b(f)(2)(i).

iii. *How service made.* An e-filing party causes service of an interlocutory document to be made upon another party participating in e-filing by filing the document electronically. Upon receipt of an interlocutory document, the NYSCEF site shall automatically transmit electronic notification to all e-mail service addresses in such action. NY R UNIF TRIAL CTS § 202.5-b(f)(2)(ii).

- Except as provided otherwise in NY R UNIF TRIAL CTS § 202.5-b(h)(3), the electronic transmission of the notification shall constitute service of the document on the e-mail service addresses identified therein; however, such service will not be effective if the filing party learns that the notification did not reach the address of the person to be served. Proof of such service will be recorded on the NYSCEF site. A party may, however, utilize other service methods permitted by the CPLR provided that, if one of such other methods is used, proof of that service shall be filed electronically. NY R UNIF TRIAL CTS § 202.5-b(f)(2)(ii).

iv. *Signatures on hard copies; Proof of service filed electronically.* When an e-filing party serves a document in hard copy on a non-participating party, the document served shall bear full signatures of all signatories and proof of such service shall be filed electronically. NY R UNIF TRIAL CTS § 202.5-b(b)(2)(i).

- *ERIE COUNTY.* In the NYSCEF system, each Affidavit of Service must be uploaded as a separate .pdf file. After uploading the Affidavit, please choose the document type: "Affirmation/Affidavit of Service" and enter the name of the party served as Additional Document Information. NY R ERIE E FIL Doc. 3(III)(I); NY R ERIE E FIL Doc. 3(V)(F).

v. *Effect of failure to consent.* A party's failure to consent to participation in electronic filing and service shall not bar any other party to the action from filing documents electronically with the County Clerk and the court or serving documents upon any other party who has consented to participation. A party who has not consented to participation shall file documents with the court and the County Clerk, and serve and be served with documents, in hard copy. NY R UNIF TRIAL CTS § 202.5-b(b)(2)(i).

d. *Service upon party.* If a party has not appeared by an attorney or the party's attorney cannot be served, service shall be upon the party by a method specified in NY CPLR Rule 2103(b)(1), NY CPLR Rule 2103(b)(2), NY CPLR Rule 2103(b)(4), NY CPLR Rule 2103(b)(5) or NY CPLR Rule 2103(b)(6). NY CPLR Rule 2103(c).

e. *Service on all parties.* Each paper served on any party shall be served on every other party who has appeared, except

as otherwise may be provided by court order or as provided in NY CPLR § 3012 or in NY CPLR § 3215(f). Upon demand by a party, the plaintiff shall supply that party with a list of those who have appeared and the names and addresses of their attorneys. NY CPLR Rule 2103(e).

f. *Service by filing.* If a paper cannot be served by any of the methods specified in NY CPLR Rule 2103(b) and NY CPLR Rule 2103(c), service may be made by filing the paper as if it were a paper required to be filed. NY CPLR Rule 2103(d).

g. *Definitions.* For the purposes of NY CPLR Rule 2103:

i. "Mailing" means the deposit of a paper enclosed in a first class postpaid wrapper, addressed to the address designated by a person for that purpose or, if none is designated, at that person's last known address, in a post office or official depository under the exclusive care and custody of the United States Postal Service within the state;

ii. "Electronic means" means any method of transmission of information between computers or other machines designed for the purpose of sending and receiving such transmissions, and which allows the recipient to reproduce the information transmitted in a tangible medium of expression;

iii. "Facsimile transmission" means any method of transmission of documents to a facsimile machine at a remote location which can automatically produce a tangible copy of such documents. NY CPLR Rule 2103(f).

G. Hearings

1. *Oral argument.* Motion papers received by the clerk of the court on or before the return date shall be deemed submitted as of the return date. The assigned judge, in his or her discretion or at the request of a party, thereafter may determine that any motion be orally argued and may fix a time for oral argument. NY R UNIF TRIAL CTS § 202.8(d).

a. A party requesting oral argument shall set forth such request in its notice of motion or in its order to show cause or on the first page of the answering papers, as the case may be. Where all parties to a motion request oral argument, oral argument shall be granted unless the court shall determine it to be unnecessary. NY R UNIF TRIAL CTS § 202.8(d).

b. Where a motion is brought on by order to show cause, the court may set forth in the order that oral argument is required on the return date of the motion. NY R UNIF TRIAL CTS § 202.8(d).

i. *BRONX COUNTY.* All orders to show cause, with the exception of orders to show cause that are returnable in the City Part, the STP Part, the Matrimonial Part and the Preliminary/Compliance Conference Part (IA-11), submitted on or after August 25, 2003, will be returnable on a Monday in the assigned Justice's part and appear on his or her motion calendar. Appearances will be required on orders to show cause. NY R BRONX FIL R Doc. 8. A motion on notice or a notice of petition in a New York Supreme Court E-File (hereafter known as NYSCEF) case, as in others, shall be made returnable in the Motion Support Office (Room 217). NY R BRONX E FIL R Doc. 1(1).

- After a motion/petition and notice are filed with the NYSCEF system, the Motion Support Office will automatically place the motion/proceeding on the submit calendar in the Motion Support Office (Room 217) for the return date. No appearance or other action by the filing attorney is required in order for the motion to be calendared if the motion fee is paid for via NYSCEF. Motions in e-filed cases (other than tax certiorari cases) appear on the submit calendar in Room 217 on the return date. NY R BRONX E FIL R Doc. 1(2).

c. *KINGS COUNTY.* All motions require appearances and oral argument. NY R L KINGS Pt. C, Rule 3.

2. *Return date; Time for hearing.* A notice of motion shall specify the time and place of the hearing on the motion. NY CPLR Rule 2214(a). The moving party determines when a motion on notice shall be heard, but she has to consult the court's or judge's calendar practice first. The movant picks out a "return day" sufficiently far off to assure that the notice requirements of NY CPLR Rule 2214(b) can be met, and to assure as well that the day picked is a day on which the assigned judge hears motions. SIEGEL-NYPRAC § 247.

a. *Judge assigned to hear motion*

i. *Referral to judge supervising disclosure.* Unless the chief administrator of the courts has, by rule, provided otherwise, if a case has been assigned to a judge to supervise disclosure pursuant to NY CPLR § 3104, all motions preliminary to trial shall be referred to such judge whenever practicable. NY CPLR Rule 3214(a).

ii. *Referral to judge who decided prior motion.* Any motion may be referred to a judge who decided a prior motion in the action. NY CPLR Rule 2217(a).

iii. *Transfer when judge unable to hear motion.* If a motion is made to a judge who is or will be for any reason unable

to hear it, it may be transferred by order of such judge or by written stipulation of the parties to any other judge to whom it might originally have been made. NY CPLR Rule 2217(c).

iv. *Procedure for unassigned cases.* If a case has not been assigned to a judge, the motion shall be made returnable before the court, and a copy of the moving papers, together with a request for judicial intervention, shall be filed with the court, with proof of service upon all other parties, where required by NY R UNIF TRIAL CTS § 202.6, within five (5) days of service upon the other parties. The moving party shall give written notice of the index number to all other parties immediately after filing of the papers. NY R UNIF TRIAL CTS § 202.8(b).

- *Responding papers.* Copies of all responding papers shall be submitted to the court, with proof of service and with the index number set forth in the papers, on or before the return date. NY R UNIF TRIAL CTS § 202.8(b).
- *Assignment after request for judicial intervention.* The case shall be assigned to a judge as soon as practicable after the filing of the request for judicial intervention pursuant to NY R UNIF TRIAL CTS § 202.6, but in no event later than the return date. After assignment to the judge, the court shall provide for appropriate notice to the parties of the name of the assigned judge. NY R UNIF TRIAL CTS § 202.8(b).
- *Motions to be heard in another county.* Motion papers noticed to be heard in a county other than the county where the venue of the action has been placed by the plaintiff shall be assigned to a judge in accordance with procedures established by the Chief Administrator. NY R UNIF TRIAL CTS § 202.8(b).

v. *ALBANY COUNTY: Motions referred to IAS Justice.* All motions made after a case has been assigned a day certain shall be referred to the IAS Justice unless the motion is returnable during the term in which the matter has been assigned a day certain, in that event, the matter will be referred to the Part 1 Justice for that particular term who may entertain the motion or refer such motion to the IAS Justice. Under those circumstances, the Part I Justice shall decide whether or not to strike the note of issue or assign the matter a new day certain. NY R 3 JD SUP Doc. 1(H)(2). All motions shall be returnable before the assigned justice. NY R 3 JD SUP Doc. 1(B).

b. *Trial of issue raised by motion.* The court may order that an issue of fact raised on a motion shall be separately tried by the court or a referee. If the issue is triable of right by jury, the court shall give the parties an opportunity to demand a jury trial of such issue. Failure to make such demand within the time limited by the court, or, if no such time is limited, before trial begins, shall be deemed a waiver of the right to trial by jury. An order under NY CPLR § 2218 shall specify the issue to be tried. NY CPLR § 2218.

c. *Audio-visual coverage of trial court proceeding.* Audio-visual coverage of proceedings in the trial courts shall be permitted only in accordance with the provisions of Part 131 of the Rules of the Chief Administrator (NY R CHIEF ADMIN § 131.1, et seq.). NY R CHIEF J § 29.3.

d. *Adjournment of return date.* Stipulations of adjournment of the return date made by the parties shall be in writing and shall be submitted to the assigned judge. Such stipulation shall be effective unless the court otherwise directs. No more than three (3) stipulated adjournments for an aggregate period of sixty (60) days shall be submitted without prior permission of the court. NY R UNIF TRIAL CTS § 202.8(e)(1).

i. Absent agreement by the parties, a request by any party for an adjournment shall be submitted in writing, upon notice to the other party, to the assigned judge on or before the return date. The court will notify the requesting party whether the adjournment has been granted. NY R UNIF TRIAL CTS § 202.8(e)(2).

ii. *BRONX COUNTY.* Non-disclosure motions for IA5, IA7 and IA22 will be adjourned for oral argument to the Monday of the second week following the week of the return date of the motion. All other non-disclosure motions will be deemed submitted on the return date and forwarded to Chambers unless a stipulation of adjournment complying with the requirements of NY R UNIF TRIAL CTS § 202.8(e) is submitted, in which event, the motion will be adjourned for the requested date and kept in the Clerk's Office. If a non-stipulated request for adjournment or notice is submitted, the motion and request will be forwarded to Chambers for judicial approval or denial of the request. In either event, the attorney requesting the adjournment will be notified, via telephone, of the granting or denial of the request and instructed to notify his adversary. NY R BRONX FIL R Doc. 8.

iii. *BRONX COUNTY.* Motions that have been e-filed may be adjourned in Room 217 if an adjournment complies with the procedures of the Motion Support Office (explained in the "Filing Rules—Motion Procedure" section of the "Courthouse Procedures" link on the website of [the] court). An adjournment that so complies may be obtained by filing a stipulation of all parties with NYSCEF (designated in the filing menu as a "Stipulation to Adjourn Motion"). NY R BRONX E FIL R Doc. 1(3).

iv. *NEW YORK COUNTY.* The Courtroom also maintains a "APB (All Papers By)" Calendar, which is used when

a party seeks an adjournment but fails to comply with the Courtroom's procedures or there is a failure to comply with procedures that requires the clerk to adjourn the motion/application (e.g., failure to submit a Confirmation Notice in an e-filed case). The case may be put over for three days to allow compliance with those procedures, as described further below. NY R NY CTY Procedure II(C); NY R NY CTY E FIL Doc. 2(D)(2). E-filed applications may be adjourned in the Part if an adjournment complies with the Part's procedures (see the Uniform Rules of the Justices (Local Rules) on the court's website). An adjournment that so complies may be obtained by filing with NYSCEF a stipulation of all parties (designated in the filing menu as a Stipulation—Adjournment of Motion—Before Judge); the motion number and the current return date of the motion being adjourned shall be set forth in the "Additional Document Information" field in NYSCEF. Absent any problems, the Part will effectuate the adjournment without need for an appearance or any other action by the parties. NY R NY CTY E FIL Doc. 2(D)(4).

v. *QUEENS COUNTY.* The Motion Support Office is NOT authorized to grant adjournments. NY R L QUEENS MOT SUP Doc. 1.

e. *ALBANY COUNTY: Motion terms.* There shall be a. . . Motion Term on each Friday in the Supreme Court, Albany County. The Friday Motion Term shall include all Article 78 Proceedings involving New York State and proceedings commenced pursuant to Article 14 of the Civil Service Law (including applications for injunctive relief made pursuant to section 209-a of the Civil Service Law). NY R 3 JD SUP Doc. 1(F). Generally, parties will be granted only one adjournment for the Friday Motion Term. NY R 3 JD SUP Doc. 1(F).

f. *ALBANY COUNTY: Motion determined without hearing.* All motions are deemed "submitted" on the return date and no appearances are required by the parties. NY R 3 JD SUP Doc. 1(B). In the event oral argument is requested, the parties should not appear on the return date. At the discretion of the assigned Judge and upon the granting of a request for oral argument, the parties will be notified by Chambers of the scheduled time and place at which argument will be heard. Where a motion is brought on by order to show cause, the court may set forth in the order that appearances and/or oral argument are required on the return date of the motion. NY R 3 JD SUP Doc. 1(B).

g. *BRONX COUNTY: Return date.* All assigned and unassigned motions will be returnable five (5) days a week in the Civil Branch Clerk's Office, Room 217, at 9:30 a.m. NY R BRONX FIL R Doc. 8.

i. If on any submitted non-disclosure motion oral argument is requested and granted, or directed by the Court, the motion shall be adjourned for oral argument before the I.A. Judge on the second Monday following the week of the return date of the motion. Attorneys will be notified via telephone of the adjourned date. NY R BRONX FIL R Doc. 8.

h. *BRONX COUNTY: Oral argument.* Calendars of disclosure motions and other motions adjourned for oral argument will be published for the four (4) business days preceding the rescheduled appearance date and on the rescheduled date of the motion. These repetitive publications will serve as the notification of procedure of adjournment of all motions. In addition, two (2) days before the return date of unassigned motions a list of such motions indicating the assigned Justice and the adjourned date of the motion will be published. NY R BRONX FIL R Doc. 8.

i. *BRONX COUNTY: Resolution before return date.* Counsel/parties must advise the Court in writing on or before the return date of all motions that have been resolved by Counsel/parties themselves and all motions the movant(s) wish to be withdrawn. NY R BRONX FIL R Doc. 8.

j. *ERIE COUNTY: Calendaring of motions.* Refer to individual Justice's Part Rules. NY R ERIE E FIL Doc. 3(V)(B).

k. *KINGS COUNTY: Return date set by court.* Irrespective of the return date indicated in the notice of motion, motions will be rescheduled by the E-file/Motion Support Office to a date designated by the assigned Judge. NY R L KINGS Pt. C, Rule 2.

l. *KINGS COUNTY: Calendar calls.* There shall be two (2) calendar calls on motion days. The first calendar call shall be at 9:30 AM and the second calendar call shall be at 10:45 AM, unless the Judge's Part Rules provide otherwise. Defaults shall only be taken on second call. Attorneys with appearances elsewhere in the courthouse may advise the clerk of their whereabouts to avoid a default. Failure to so advise the clerk or appear at the default calendar call will result in a default order being entered or the motion being marked off the calendar. NY R L KINGS Pt. C, Rule 7.

m. *NEW YORK COUNTY: Return date and assigned courtroom.* Motions made by notice of motion and petitions and notices of petition in special proceedings are processed by the General Clerk's Office (Room 119) and are to be made returnable in the Motion Submission Part Courtroom (Room 130) on any business day of the week at 9:30 AM. There are some differences in electronically-filed cases. NY R NY CTY Procedure II; NY R NY CTY Procedure II(C); NY R NY CTY J RUL Rule 13(a).

i. For the convenience of counsel, between 9:00 A.M. and 9:30 A.M. each day, in advance of the "call," Room 130

accepts (1) written stipulations; (2) affidavits/affirmations reciting the required details as to an adjournment on consent; (3) stipulations, letters or other writings withdrawing motions; and (4) final papers or complete sets of papers on motions. For motions in which these items are handed in before the "call," no one need remain to answer the "call." Counsel/parties must advise the court, either between 9:00 A.M. and 9:30 A.M. or at the "call," of all motions or cases that have been resolved by counsel/parties themselves and all motions that the movant no longer wishes to pursue. If such resolution occurs subsequent to the "call", the assigned Justice must be advised as soon as possible, by written notice sent to the Part, so that the court does not do unnecessary work. NY R NY CTY Procedure II(C).

ii. Depending upon the assigned Part, contested motions submitted in the Motion Submission Part Courtroom are submitted without argument, or rescheduled for oral argument if so directed by the assigned Justice. For Justices who schedule argument on a case-by-case basis, notice of the argument date will be transmitted by the court. Counsel may ascertain how a motion submitted in Courtroom 130 was marked by consulting Scroll on the court's website, the e-Track application, or, on the two (2) days immediately following the submission date, the New York Law Journal. NY R NY CTY J RUL Rule 13(a).

n. *NEW YORK COUNTY: Motion call.* Each day in the Motion Submission Part Courtroom, commencing at 9:30 A.M., all motions returnable that day will be "called" for the submission of these papers, which must be handed up at this "call" or, as described below, immediately before. Because hundreds of motions appear on the Room 130 calendars every day, motion papers (other than part of the moving papers as described above) cannot be accepted on any day prior to the return date. Courtesy copies are not required nor accepted, but working copies are required by certain Justices in e-filed cases. NY R NY CTY Procedure II(C). If argument is directed, it will take place on an announced date shortly after the day of submission. NY R NY CTY Procedure II(C).

o. *NEW YORK COUNTY: Oral arguments.* Pursuant to request of some Justices, motions submitted in Room 130 will automatically be scheduled for a set argument date in the Part. Other Justices determine on a case-by-case basis after submission in Room 130 whether to accept a particular substantive motion on submission, to require oral argument, or to hold a conference. NY R NY CTY Procedure II(D). If argument is directed by the Justice automatically, notice of argument and the argument date will be given in Room 130. Any appearing party is expected to give notice to all parties and an announcement to this effect is made in Room 130. If the motion is submitted in Room 130 and the Justice, after examining the file, determines that argument should be directed, notice of the argument and the argument date will not be sent by the court. To obtain notification of the argument date and other developments, counsel should use e-Track. If argument notification is not given or transmitted as just described, counsel should understand that the motion has been taken on submission for decision on the papers. NY R NY CTY Procedure II(D).

i. Calendars of motions to be argued in the Parts are published on the morning of the argument date and on the day before in the New York Law Journal under each Part. Argument information is available on a case-by-case basis in Scroll, and e-mail notifications are sent by e-Track to participating attorneys whenever a motion is scheduled for argument in the court's computer system. NY R NY CTY J RUL Rule 15(a)

p. *NEW YORK COUNTY: Motion determined without hearing.* Given the purpose of the Room 130 procedure, the substance of motions will not be addressed at the submission "call." No Judge is present. To the extent possible, motions submitted in Room 130 will be decided "on the papers." Indeed, attorneys are encouraged to use service or clerks to deliver papers or working copies, or to agree among themselves to have one of them deliver papers for all parties by service or a clerk. Counsel for the movant need not appear to "take a default" on any motion or for any other reason. Motions will be submitted, not marked off, in the absence of the movant. Opposing counsel similarly need not appear in person in order to avoid suffering a default. Delivery of papers by service or a clerk will suffice. The court's goal is to be able to collect papers on motions in an orderly fashion but without any attorney having to make an appearance in Room 130 at any time. NY R NY CTY Procedure II(C).

q. *ONONDAGA COUNTY: Return date.* If the motion is the first filing in an action, the case will be assigned and counsel will be notified by the Supreme Court Clerk's Office via the NYSCEF system of the assigned justice and return date. NY R ONDGA E FIL Protocol(B)(7)(c). If the motion is on a previously assigned case, counsel may choose a return date from the assigned justice's motion term schedule. If the date in unavailable, the Supreme Court Clerk's Office will assign the motion to the next available motion term date and will notify counsel via e-mail. The change will also appear in the notification generated by the NYSCEF system. NY R ONDGA E FIL Protocol(B)(7)(d).

r. *QUEENS COUNTY: Return date.* Motions must be made returnable on the proper day/time based on the assigned judge. NY R L QUEENS MOT SUP Doc. 1. Failure to make a motion returnable on the proper day/time may result in the motion being administratively rescheduled or marked off. NY R L QUEENS MOT SUP Doc. 1.

s. *QUEENS COUNTY: Unassigned motions.* For RJI/Motions, due to the fact that the movant would not know who the

assigned judge will be, the notice of motion may be returnable any day of the week. RJI/Motions shall be made returnable in "Queens Supreme Court" with no address designated. The motion will be administratively rescheduled to the proper day of the week based on the judge (once a judge has been assigned). Within one (1) week of filing, the movant must check online to see who the assigned judge is (and therefore the location/date/time) that their motion is now returnable. Movant must then notify their adversary of this information prior to the return date. NY R L QUEENS MOT SUP Doc. 1.

3. *Entry of order after hearing.* An order determining a motion shall be entered and filed in the office of the clerk of the court where the action is triable, and all papers used on the motion and any opinion or memorandum in writing shall be filed with that clerk unless the order dispenses with such filing. When a statute or civil practice rule requires such filing and entry in a county other than that in which the order was made, the party prevailing on the motion shall file the order and the papers used on the motion with the proper clerk after receiving them. If a party fails to file any papers required to be filed under NY CPLR Rule 2220(a), the order may be vacated as irregular, with costs. NY CPLR Rule 2220(a). For more information on the entry of an order after a motion, refer to NY CPLR Rule 2219.

   a. *BRONX COUNTY: Settled orders.* A Judge's decision will often call for a Settled Order. The purpose of the settled order is to give effect to the decision by directing that some action be done and/or that a court official perform some task. NY R BRONX LEG SUP Doc. 2. A settled order consists of a notice of settlement informing all parties that the proposed order will be presented to the judge who made the decision on a date certain. Next comes the proposed order which will be presented to the judge. This order should conform to the judge's decision and should direct the relief granted in the decision. This should be followed by proof of service upon all parties who were noticed with the decision. It is also helpful if a copy of the judge's decision is included along with the other papers. A settled order should always be noticed before the judge who made the decision. NY R BRONX LEG SUP Doc. 2.

      i. Although an order is usually settled by the party who prevailed on the motion, any party may settle the order. It should be presented to the court within sixty (60) days of the decision. The other parties are entitled to ten (10) days notice where service of the settled order is done by mail, five (5) days if the notice is personally delivered. An attorney who is served with a notice of settlement which he believes does not accurately reflect the decision may settle a counter order. The counter order must be noticed for the same day and must be served not less than seven (7) days if by mail and two (2) days if personally delivered. NY R BRONX LEG SUP Doc. 2.

      ii. Settled orders are usually sent to the judge the day after they noticed for settlement. No appearance is necessary or even contemplated on a settled order. If the decision directs "submit order", then no notice is necessary, and the order will be sent to the judge as soon a practical after it is received. No fees are collected on settled orders. NY R BRONX LEG SUP Doc. 2.

   b. *ERIE COUNTY: Proposed orders.* Proposed orders shall be submitted through the NYSCEF system and a working copy provided to the IAS Justice for signature, if Part Rules so require. NY R ERIE E FIL Doc. 3(V)(G).

   c. *KINGS COUNTY: Long form orders.* If the Court directs that an order be settled or submitted on a motion in a NYSCEF case, the proposed order, with Notice of Settlement where required, and any proposed counter-order shall be filed with the Court via NYSCEF. The relevant clerk's office will process the documents in the customary manner. NY R L KINGS E FIL Doc. 1(E).

      i. WORKING COPIES OF PROPOSED ORDERS WITH NOTICE OF SETTLEMENT MUST BE SUBMITTED IN THE MOTION SUPPORT OFFICE (ROOM 227) AS EXPLAINED HEREIN. THEY MUST NOT BE DELIVERED TO THE PART OR CHAMBERS, EXCEPT WHERE THE INDIVIDUAL JUSTICE'S PART RULES PROVIDE OTHERWISE; DOING SO WILL CAUSE ADMINISTRATIVE CONFUSION AND POSSIBLE MISPLACEMENT OF PAPERS. Any such submission shall be sent in a timely manner (kindly review individual Justice's rules) and be conspicuously marked on the outside "NYSCEF Matter;" lack of such marking may delay processing. After an order/counter-order has been signed, it will be scanned, and the County Clerk will affix the entry stamp into the NYSCEF system, which will immediately transmit notice of this event via e-mail, including a link to the entered document, to all participating attorneys and unrepresented litigants in the case. Such transmittal does not constitute Notice of Entry. NY R L KINGS E FIL Doc. 1(E).

   d. *NEW YORK COUNTY: Long form orders.* Although the court strongly favors the use of short form orders and judgments, there are instances when settlement of an order or judgment is appropriate. When a Justice directs in a decision that a long form order or judgment be settled, that decision is recorded in the court's computer system by the General Clerk's Office and the motion file with decision is held in the Order Section of the Office in Room 119. The settlement process takes place there. NY R NY CTY Procedure II(D); NY R NY CTY E FIL Doc. 2(E).

      i. A proposed long form order or judgment in compliance NY R UNIF TRIAL CTS § 202.48 must be presented to

the relevant back office, together with a notice of settlement which bears a settlement date, the date on which the order is to be ready for formal presentation to the Justice. In an e-filed case the submission shall be made electronically. The proposed order or counter-order should be e-filed and it will be transmitted automatically by the NYSCEF system to the appropriate back office. The return date and time of the proposed order must be at 9:30 A.M. no sooner than either five (5) days from personal service of the proposed order or ten (10) days from service by mail. Proof of timely service on the other parties must accompany the proposed order in a hard copy case. If an order or judgment is submitted late (later than sixty (60) days from signing and filing of the decision) and the proponent can show good cause for this tardiness, an affidavit or affirmation justifying the delay should be annexed to the proposed order, together with proof of service thereof. If persuaded, the Justice will consider the proposed order despite its untimeliness. NY R NY CTY Procedure II(D); NY R NY CTY E FIL Doc. 2(E).

ii. Sometimes a decision will state "Submit Order." The submitting party should prepare a long form order and make it returnable without notice. Counsel should deliver the proposed order to the Order Section of the appropriate back office, except in an e-filed case, when it shall be submitted electronically. NY R NY CTY Procedure II(D). If the decision of the court directs that a proposed order be settled or submitted in the Part or in Chambers, that direction, should, of course, be followed without presentation of the proposal to the back office. NY R NY CTY Procedure II(D).

iii. For information on proposed counter-orders, refer to NY R NY CTY Procedure II(D) and NY R NY CTY J RUL Rule 16(b).

e. *QUEENS COUNTY: Proposed orders.* If the court directs that an order be settled or submitted on a motion in an E-file case, the proposed order and any proposed counter-order shall be filed with the court on-line with proof of service. (If a decision refers to a proceeding on the record, a copy of the transcript must be submitted.) Working copies of all proposed orders MUST be submitted to the Motion Support Office before an order can be reviewed. NY R L QUEENS E-FILE Doc. 1(I).

i. Counsel are advised to adhere to NY R UNIF TRIAL CTS § 202.48 regarding the submission or settlement of their proposed order or judgment. Persons who are submitting proposed orders/judgments pursuant to a previously issued memorandum decision must submit a copy of the memorandum decision with their proposed order/judgment. Upon E-Filing a proposed order/judgement, a working copy of the proposed order/judgement must be provided to the Motion Support Office. NY R L QUEENS MOT SUP Doc. 1.

H. Forms

1. Official Motion to Quash Subpoena Forms for New York

a. Request for judicial intervention. NY R UNIF TRIAL CTS § 202.6.

b. Notice of motion. NY R UNIF TRIAL CTS § 202.7(b).

2. New York Motion to Quash Subpoena Forms

a. Notice of motion to quash subpoena. MCF CPLR § 12:97.

b. Affidavit in support of motion to quash subpoena. MCF CPLR § 12:100.

c. Affidavit in support of motion to quash subpoena; President of corporation. MCF CPLR § 12:101.

d. Affidavit in support of motion to quash subpoena; From Attorney General. MCF CPLR § 12:102.

e. Affirmation in support of motion to quash subpoena. MCF CPLR § 12:103.

f. Affirmation in support of motion to quash subpoena and in opposition to motion to enforce subpoena. MCF CPLR § 12:104.

g. General form of affidavit of service of motion papers. MCF CPLR § 5:24.

I. Applicable Rules

1. *State rules*

a. Short title; Application; Construction; Definitions. NY CPLR § 101; NY CPLR § 103; NY CPLR § 104; NY CPLR § 105.

b. Appendix of official forms. NY CPLR § 107.

c. Extensions of time generally. NY CPLR § 2004.

d. Form of papers. NY CPLR Rule 2101; NY CPLR Rule 2102; NY CPLR § 2105; NY CPLR Rule 2106; NY GEN BUS § 399-ddd; NY R UNIF TRIAL CTS § 215.2; NY R UNIF TRIAL CTS § 215.3.

e. Service of papers. NY CPLR Rule 2103.
f. Where motion made; In supreme court action. NY CPLR § 2212.
g. Motion papers; Service; Time. NY CPLR Rule 2214.
h. Relief demanded by other than moving party. NY CPLR Rule 2215.
i. Prior motion; Ex parte motion; Transfer of motion; Hearings; Orders. NY CPLR Rule 2217; NY CPLR § 2218; NY CPLR Rule 2220.
j. Computation of time. NY CPLR § 2402; NY GEN CONSTR § 19; NY GEN CONSTR § 20; NY GEN CONSTR § 25-a; NY GEN CONSTR § 30; NY GEN CONSTR § 31; NY GEN CONSTR § 53.
k. Motion to quash, fix conditions or modify. NY CPLR § 2304.
l. Motions heard by judge supervising disclosure; Stay of disclosure. NY CPLR Rule 3214.
m. Proceeding against body or officer; Nature of proceeding. NY CPLR § 7801.
n. Fees; Index number fees of county clerks. NY CPLR § 8001; NY CPLR § 8018.
o. Hours of court; Proceedings in court. NY R CHIEF J § 3.1; NY R CHIEF J § 29.3.
p. Application of part; Waiver; Additional rules; Application of CPLR; Definitions. NY R UNIF TRIAL CTS § 202.1.
q. Papers filed in court; Electronic filing in supreme court. NY R UNIF TRIAL CTS § 202.5; NY R UNIF TRIAL CTS § 202.5-a; NY R UNIF TRIAL CTS § 202.5-b; NY R UNIF TRIAL CTS § 202.5-bb.
r. Request for judicial intervention. NY R UNIF TRIAL CTS § 202.6.
s. Calendaring of motions; Uniform notice of motion form; Affirmation of good faith. NY R UNIF TRIAL CTS § 202.7.
t. Motion procedure; Preliminary conferences. NY R UNIF TRIAL CTS § 202.8; NY R UNIF TRIAL CTS § 202.12.
u. Rules of the commercial division of the Supreme Court. NY R UNIF TRIAL CTS § 202.70.
v. Signing of papers. NY R CHIEF ADMIN § 130-1.1-a.

2. *Local rules*
   a. *Albany County*
      i. Third judicial district rules. NY R 3 JD SUP Doc. 1.
   b. *Bronx County*
      i. Filing of papers in supreme court. NY R BRONX FIL R Doc. 1.
      ii. Request for judicial intervention. NY R BRONX FIL R Doc. 2.
      iii. Motion procedure. NY R BRONX FIL R Doc. 8.
      iv. Commercial division. NY R BRONX FIL R Doc. 12.
      v. Motions on notice. NY R BRONX E FIL R Doc. 1.
      vi. Settled orders. NY R BRONX LEG SUP Doc. 2.
   c. *Erie County*
      i. Joint protocols for New York State Courts E-Filing (NYSCEF) cases filed in Supreme Court, Erie County. NY R ERIE E FIL Doc. 3.
   d. *Kings County*
      i. Papers. NY R L KINGS Pt. A, Papers.
      ii. Service of motion papers. NY R L KINGS Pt. C, Rule 1.
      iii. Scheduling of motions. NY R L KINGS Pt. C, Rule 2.
      iv. Appearance and argument. NY R L KINGS Pt. C, Rule 3.
      v. Courtesy copies. NY R L KINGS Pt. C, Rule 5.
      vi. Motion calendar calls. NY R L KINGS Pt. C, Rule 7.
      vii. Protocol on courthouse and county clerk procedures for electronically filed cases. NY R L KINGS E FIL Doc. 1.

e. *New York County*

   i. Commencement of cases. NY R NY CTY Procedure I.

   ii. RJIs and assignments. NY R NY CTY Procedure IA.

   iii. Motions and special proceedings by notice of motion/petition. NY R NY CTY Procedure II.

   iv. County clerk litigation functions. NY R NY CTY Procedure XI.

   v. Protocol on courthouse and county clerk procedures for electronically filed cases. NY R NY CTY E FIL Doc. 2.

   vi. Redaction of information in documents filed with the county clerk and the court. NY R NY CTY J RUL Rule A-1.

   vii. Papers by fax. NY R NY CTY J RUL Rule 4.

   viii. Motions on notice; Orders to show cause. NY R NY CTY J RUL Rule 13.

   ix. Motion papers. NY R NY CTY J RUL Rule 14.

   x. Oral argument; Adjournments. NY R NY CTY J RUL Rule 15.

f. *Onondaga County*

   i. Onondaga county protocol for case filings New York State Electronic Files (NYSCEF). NY R ONDGA E FIL Protocol.

g. *Queens County*

   i. Motion support office. NY R L QUEENS MOT SUP Doc. 1.

   ii. Queens county protocol on courthouse procedures for electronically filed cases. NY R L QUEENS E-FILE Doc. 1.

J. Miscellaneous

NOTE: Individual judges' rules may apply.

ALBANY COUNTY

JUSTICE LISA M. FISHER: NY R 3 JD FISHER Fisher; NY R 3 JD FISHER Fisher, PC Order.

JUSTICE RICHARD MOTT: NY R 3 JD MOTT Mott.

JUSTICE STEPHAN G. SCHICK: NY R 3 JD Schick.

FORECLOSURE SETTLEMENT PART: NY R 3 JD Foreclosure Settlement.

BRONX COUNTY

JUSTICE PAUL L. ALPERT: [NY R BRONX J Part IA-29, as amended by NY ORDER 20-0337].

JUSTICE BEN BARBATO: NY R BRONX J Part IA-21.

JUSTICE MARY ANNE BRIGANTTI: [NY R BRONX J Part IA-15, as amended by NY ORDER 20-0338].

JUSTICE JOSEPH E. CAPELLA: NY R BRONX J Part IA-23.

JUSTICE MITCHELL DANZIGER: NY R BRONX J Part IA-3/33 ; [NY R BRONX J Danziger, Part IA-3/33, as amended by NY ORDER 20-0339].

JUSTICE LAURA G. DOUGLAS: NY R BRONX J Part IA-11.

JUSTICE RUBEN FRANCO: NY R BRONX J Part IA-26.

JUSTICE DORIS M. GONZALEZ: NY R BRONX J Part IA-24.

JUSTICE WILMA GUZMAN: NY R BRONX J Part IA-7; [NY R BRONX J Guzman, Part IA-7 Virtual, as amended by NY ORDER 20-0340].

JUSTICE ROBERT T. JOHNSON: NY R BRONX J Part IA-12.

JUSTICE DONALD A. MILES: NY R BRONX J Part IA-8.

JUSTICE DONNA M. MILLS: NY R BRONX J Part IA-9.

JUSTICE JULIA I. RODRIGUEZ: NY R BRONX J Part IA-18; [NY R BRONX J Part IA-27, as amended by NY ORDER 20-0341].

JUSTICE LLINET M. ROSADO: [NY R BRONX J Part IA-25, as amended by NY ORDER 20-0342].

JUSTICE NORMA RUIZ: NY R BRONX J Part IA-22; [NY R BRONX J Ruiz, Part IA-22 Virtual, as amended by NY ORDER 20-0343].

JUSTICE HOWARD H. SHERMAN: NY R BRONX J Part IA-4.

JUSTICE FERNANDO TAPIA: NY R BRONX J Part IA-13.

JUSTICE ELIZABETH A. TAYLOR: NY R BRONX J Part IA-2.

JUSTICE ALISON Y. TRUITT: NY R BRONX J Part IA-5.

PART IDV: NY R BRONX J Doc. 1.

PRE-TRIAL PART RULES: NY R BRONX J Doc. 2.

PRE TRIAL WORKSHEET: NY R BRONX J Doc. 3.

FORECLOSURE SETTLEMENT PART RULES: NY R BRONX J Doc. 4.

GUARDIANSHIP PART RULES: NY R BRONX J Doc. 5.

LPM PART RULES: NY R BRONX J Doc. 6.

ERIE COUNTY

JUSTICE M. WILLIAM BOLLER: NY R 8 JD J Boller.

JUSTICE RALPH A. BONIELLO: NY R 8 JD J Boniello.

JUSTICE CHRISTOPHER J. BURN: NY R 8 JD J Burns.

JUSTICE RUSSELL P. BUSCAGLIA: NY R 8 JD J Buscaglia.

JUSTICE FRANK CARUSO: NY R 8 JD J Caruso.

JUSTICE STEPHEN W. CASS: NY R 8 JD J Cass.

JUSTICE DEBORAH A. CHIMES: NY R 8 JD J Chimes.

JUSTICE EMILIO COLAIACOVO: [NY R 8 JD J Colaiacovo, as amended by NY ORDER 20-0252].

JUSTICE DIANE Y. DEVLIN: NY R 8 JD J Devlin.

JUSTICE JAMES H. DILLON: NY R 8 JD J Dillon.

JUSTICE PAULA L. FEROLETO: NY R 8 JD J Feroleto.

JUSTICE DANIEL J. FURLONG: [NY R 8 JD J Furlong, as amended by NY ORDER 20-0253].

JUSTICE JOSEPH R. GLOWNIA: NY R 8 JD J Glownia.

JUSTICE MARK J. GRISANTI: NY R 8 JD J Grisanti.

JUSTICE DEBORAH A. HAENDIGES: NY R 8 JD J Haendiges.

JUSTICE LYNN W. KEANE: [NY R 8 JD J Keane, as amended by NY ORDER 20-0254].

JUSTICE RICHARD C. KLOCH, Sr.: NY R 8 JD J Kloch.

JUSTICE FREDERICK J. MARSHALL: [NY R 8 JD J Marshall, as amended by NY ORDER 20-0255.

JUSTICE JOHN L. MICHALSKI: NY R 8 JD J Michalski.

JUSTICE MARK A. MONTOUR: [NY R 8 JD J Montour, as amended by NY ORDER 20-0256].

JUSTICE HENRY NOWAK: NY R 8 JD J Nowak.

JUSTICE JOHN F. O'DONNELL: NY R 8 JD J O'Donnell.

JUSTICE JEANETTE OGDEN: NY R 8 JD J Ogden.

JUSTICE CATHERINE NUGENT-PANEPINTO: NY R 8 JD J Nugent-Panepinto.

JUSTICE FRANK A. SEDITA, III: [NY R 8 JD J Sedita, as amended by NY ORDER 20-0257].

JUSTICE SARA SHELDON: NY R 8 JD J Sheldon.

JUSTICE DONNA M. SIWEK: NY R 8 JD J Siwek.

JUSTICE MARY L. SLISZ: NY R 8 JD J Slisz.

JUSTICE TIMOTHY J. WALKER: [NY R 8 JD J Walker, as amended by NY ORDER 20-0258].

JUSTICE DENNIS E. WARD: NY R 8 JD J Ward.

JUSTICE PAUL B. WOJTASZEK: [NY R 8 JD J Wojtaszek, as amended by NY ORDER 20-0259].

JUSTICE CHARLES N. ZAMBITO: [NY R 8 JD J Zambito, as amended by NY ORDER 20-0260].

SUPREME COURT LEGAL STAFF: NY R 8 JD J Legal Staff.

KINGS COUNTY

JUSTICE RACHEL A. ADAMS: NY R KINGS J Part 5F.

JUSTICE LOREN BAILY-SCHIFFMAN: NY R KINGS J Part 65.

JUSTICE REGINALD A. BODDIE: NY R KINGS J Part 95.

JUSTICE THERESA M. CICCOTTO: NY R KINGS J Part 19; NY R KINGS J Part 5J.

JUSTICE LISSETTE COLON: NY R KINGS J Part Rules.

JUSTICE GENINE EDWARDS: NY R KINGS J Part 80.

JUSTICE PAMELA L. FISHER: [NY R KINGS J Part 94, as amended by NY ORDER 20-0208].

JUSTICE ROBIN GARSON: NY R KINGS J Part 75.

JUSTICE LARA J. GENOVISI: [NY R KINGS J Part 34, as amended by NY ORDER 20-0209].

JUSTICE BERNARD J. GRAHAM: NY R KINGS J Part 36.

JUSTICE DAWN JIMENEZ-SALTA: NY R KINGS J Part 88.

JUSTICE INGRID JOSEPH: [NY R KINGS J Part FRP3 and Part 83, as amended by NY ORDER 20-0210].

JUSTICE KATHY J. KING: NY R KINGS J Part 64, 76K.

JUSTICE LAWRENCE KNIPEL: NY R KINGS J Part 57.

JUSTICE DONALD KURTZ: NY R KINGS J Part 26.

JUSTICE CARL LANDICINO: [NY R KINGS J Part 81, as amended by NY ORDER 20-0211].

JUSTICE KATHERINE LEVINE: [NY R KINGS J Part 20, 25, 92, as amended by NY ORDER 20-0211].

JUSTICE LORNA MCALLISTER: [NY R KINGS J Part 10, as amended by NY ORDER 20-0211].

JUSTICE ROSEMARIE MONTALBANO: [NY R KINGS J Part 19, 71, and 22, as amended by NY ORDER 20-0211].

JUSTICE RICHARD J. MONTELIONE: [NY R KINGS J Part 99 and DJMP, as amended by NY ORDER 20-0215].

JUSTICE LISA S. OTTLEY: NY R KINGS J Part 24.

JUSTICE MARK I. PARTNOW: NY R KINGS J Part 43.

JUSTICE ERIC I. PRUS: NY R KINGS J Part 5A.

JUSTICE FRANCOIS RIVERA: NY R KINGS J Part 52.

JUSTICE KAREN B. ROTHENBERG: NY R KINGS J Part 35.

JUSTICE LEON RUCHELSMAN: NY R KINGS J Part 1.

JUSTICE WAYNE P. SAITTA: NY R KINGS J Part 29.

JUSTICE ROBIN K. SHEARES: NY R KINGS J Part 96.

JUSTICE KENNETH P. SHERMAN: NY R KINGS J Part 67 and 78.

JUSTICE DEBRA SILBER: NY R KINGS J Part 9 and 5K.

JUSTICE ELLEN M. SPODEK: NY R KINGS J Part 63.

JUSTICE MARSHA L. STEINHARDT: NY R KINGS J Part 15.

JUSTICE JEFFREY S. SUNSHINE: NY R KINGS J Part 5G.

JUSTICE PETER P. SWEENEY: [NY R KINGS J Part 35, as amended by NY ORDER 20-0218].

JUSTICE DELORES J. THOMAS: [NY R KINGS J Part 5T, as amended by NY ORDER 20-0221].

JUSTICE WAVNY TOUSSAINT: NY R KINGS J Part 70.

JUSTICE RICHARD VELASQUEZ: NY R KINGS J Part 66.

JUSTICE CAROLYN E. WADE: NY R KINGS J Part 84.

JUSTICE EDWARD G. WALKER: [NY R KINGS J Part 90, as amended by NY ORDER 20-0219].

JUSTICE LILLIAN WAN: [NY R KINGS J Part 17, as amended by NY ORDER 20-0220].

JUSTICE MICHELLE WESTON: NY R KINGS J Part 3.

MENTAL HYGIENE PART: NY R KINGS J Part 77.

MATRIMONIAL PARTS DURING COVID-19 EMERGENCY: JUSTICE KAREN B. ROTHENBERG: NY R KINGS J Doc. 1.

NASSAU COUNTY

JUSTICE ANNA R. ANZALONE: NY R NASSAU S J Anzalone, Part 26.

JUSTICE STACY D. BENNETT: NY R NASSAU S J Bennett; NY R NASSAU S J Bennett, Form 1.

JUSTICE ANTONIO BRANDVEEN: NY R NASSAU S J Brandveen, Part 31.

JUSTICE JEFFREY S. BROWN: [NY R NASSAU S J Brown, as amended by NY ORDER 20-0297].

JUSTICE STEPHEN A. BUCARIA: NY R NASSAU S J Bucaria.

JUSTICE JULIANNE T. CAPETOLA: NY R NASSAU S J Capetola, Part 28.

JUSTICE EDMUND M. DANE: NY R NASSAU S J Dane, Part 33.

JUSTICE VITO M. DESTEFANO: NY R NASSAU S J DeStefano, Part 13; NY R NASSAU S J DeStefano, Form 1.

JUSTICE ARTHUR M. DIAMOND: NY R NASSAU S J Diamond, Part 7.

JUSTICE THOMAS FEINMAN: NY R NASSAU S J Feinman, Part 5.

JUSTICE JOHN M. GALASSO: NY R NASSAU S J Galasso, Part 22.

JUSTICE SHARON M.J. GIANELLI: NY R NASSAU S J Gianelli, Part 22; NY R NASSAU S J Gianelli, Form 1.

JUSTICE JEFFREY A. GOODSTEIN: NY R NASSAU S J Goodstein, Part 33; NY R NASSAU S J Goodstein, Form 1.

JUSTICE DAVID J. GUGERTY: [NY R NASSAU S J Gugerty, Part 31, as amended by NY ORDER 20-0298].

JUSTICE HELENE F. GUGERTY: NY R NASSAU S J Gugerty, Part 47.

JUSTICE STEVEN M. JAEGER: NY R NASSAU S J Jaeger, Part 35; NY R NASSAU S J Jaeger, Form 1.

JUSTICE JACK L. LIBERT: NY R NASSAU S J Libert, Part 23.

JUSTICE JOSEPH H. LORINTZ: NY R NASSAU S J Lorintz, Part 26; NY R NASSAU S J Lorintz, Form 1.

JUSTICE ROY S. MAHON: NY R NASSAU S J Mahon, Part 3.

JUSTICE RANDY SUE MARBER: NY R NASSAU S J Marber, Part 8.

JUSTICE JAMES P. MCCORMACK: [NY R NASSAU S J McCormack, Part 18, as amended by NY ORDER, 20-0299].

JUSTICE DICCIA T. PINEDA-KIRWAN: [NY R NASSAU S J Pineda-Kirwan, as amended by NY ORDER 20-0300].

JUSTICE THOMAS RADEMAKER: [NY R NASSAU S J Rademaker, Part 28, as amended by NY ORDER 20-0301]; [NY R NASSAU S J Rademaker, Form 1, as amended by NY ORDER 20-0301].

JUSTICE DENISE L. SHER: NY R NASSAU S J Rademaker, Part 32.

JUSTICE LEONARD D. STEINMAN: [NY R NASSAU S J Steinman, Part 15, as amended by NY ORDER 20-0303]; NY R NASSAU S J Steinman, Form 1.

JUSTICE HOWARD E. STURIM: NY R NASSAU S J Sturim, Part 50; NY R NASSAU S J Sturim, Form 1.

JUSTICE HELEN VOUTSINAS: [NY R NASSAU S J Voutsinas, Part 25, as amended by NY ORDER 20-0304]; [NY R NASSAU S J Voutsinas, Form 1, as amended by NY ORDER 20-0305].

JUSTICE HOPE SCHWARTZ ZIMMERMAN: NY R NASSAU S J Zimmerman, Part 17.

NEW YORK COUNTY

JUDGE'S RULES; BASIC INFORMATION: [NY R NY CTY J RUL Doc. 1, as amended by NY ORDER 20-0202].

ONONDAGA COUNTY

JUSTICE ROBERT E. ANTONACCI II: [NY R ONDGA E FIL Doc. 1, as amended by 20-0239].

JUSTICE MICHAEL V. COCCOMI: NY R ONDGA E FIL Doc. 2.

JUSTICE GREGORY R. GILBERT: NY R 5 JD JUDGES Gilbert; NY R ONDGA E FIL Doc. 3.

JUSTICE DONALD A. GREENWOOD: NY R ONDGA E FIL Doc. 4.

JUSTICE DEBORAH H. KARALUNAS: NY R ONDGA E FIL Doc. 5.

JUSTICE JAMES MCCLUSKY: NY R 5 JD MCCLUSKY McClusky.

JUSTICE CHARLES C. MERRELL: NY R 5 JD MERRELL Merrell.

JUSTICE PATRICK F. MACRAE: NY R 5 JD MACRAE Doc. 1.

JUSTICE JAMES P. MURPHY: NY R ONDGA E FIL Doc. 7.

JUSTICE GERALD J. NERI: [NY R 5 JD JUDGES Neri, as amended by NY ORDER 20-0236]; [NY R ONDGA E FIL Doc. 8, as amended by NY ORDER 20-0241].

JUSTICE ANTHONY J. PARIS: NY R 5 JD JUDGES Paris; [NY R ONDGA E FIL Doc. 9, as amended by NY ORDER 20-0242].

JUSTICE NORMAN W. SEITER, JR.: NY R 5 JD JUDGES Seiter.

JUSTICE KEVIN G. YOUNG: [NY R ONDGA E FIL Doc. 10, as amended by NY ORDER 20-0243].

QUEENS COUNTY

JUSTICE PAM JACKMAN BROWN: [NY R L QUEENS Brown, Part 19, as amended by NY ORDER 20-0321].

JUSTICE CHEREE A. BUGGS: NY R L QUEENS Buggs, Part 30.

JUSTICE PAM JACKMAN BROWN: [NY R L QUEENS Brown, Part 19, as amended by NY ORDER 20-0321].

JUSTICE DENIS J. BUTLER: NY R L QUEENS Butler, Part 12.

JUSTICE ROBERT I. CALORAS: [NY R L QUEENS Caloras, Part 36, as amended by NY ORDER 20-0322].

JUSTICE ANNA CULLEY: NY R L QUEENS Culley, Part 53.

JUSTICE TIMOTHY DUFFICY: NY R L QUEENS Dufficy, Part 35.

JUSTICE DAVID ELLIOT: NY R L QUEENS Elliot, Part 14.

JUSTICE JOSEPH J. ESPOSITO: NY R L QUEENS Esposito, Part 6.

JUSTICE DARRELL L. GAVRIN: [NY R L QUEENS Gavrin, Part 27, as amended by NY ORDER 20-0323].

JUSTICE WYATT N. GIBBONS: [NY R L QUEENS Gibbons, Part 5, as amended by NY ORDER 20-0330.

JUSTICE DONNA-MARIE E. GOLIA: [NY R L QUEENS Golia, Part 21, as amended by NY ORDER 20-0331].

JUSTICE MARGUERITE A. GRAYS: [NY R L QUEENS Grays, Part 4, as amended by NY ORDER 20-0324].

JUSTICE RUDOLPH E. GRECO: [NY R L QUEENS Greco, Part 32, as amended by NY ORDER 20-0325].

JUSTICE MAUREEN HEALY: NY R L QUEENS Healy, Part 6.

JUSTICE PHILLIP HOM: [NY R L QUEENS Hom, Part 43, as amended by NY ORDER 20-0332].

JUSTICE KEVIN J. KERRIGAN: NY R L QUEENS Kerrigan, Part 10.

JUSTICE MOJGAN C. LANCMAN: NY R L QUEENS Lancman, Part 20.

JUSTICE RICHARD G. LATIN: NY R L QUEENS Latin, Part 40.

JUSTICE ULYSSES B. LEVERETT: [NY R L QUEENS Leverett, Part 6, as amended by NY ORDER 20-0326].

JUSTICE LEONARD LIVOTE: NY R L QUEENS Livote, Part 33.

JUSTICE LEE A. MAYERSOHN: NY R L QUEENS Mayersohn, Part 22; NY R L QUEENS Mayersohn, Part 22G; [NY R L QUEENS Mayersohn, Part 22G COVID, as amended by NY ORDER 20-0327].

JUSTICE ROBERT J. MCDONALD: NY R L QUEENS McDonald, Part 34.

JUSTICE MARGARET MCGOWAN: NY R L QUEENS McGowan, Part 52.

JUSTICE MAURICE E. MUIR: [NY R L QUEENS Muir, Part 42, as amended by NY ORDER 20-0333].

JUSTICE JODI ORLOW: NY R L QUEENS Orlow, Part 51.

JUSTICE LESLIE J. PURIFICCION: NY R L QUEENS Purificcion, Part 39.

JUSTICE JOSEPH RISI: [NY R L QUEENS Risi, Part 3, as amended by NY ORDER 20-0328].

JUSTICE FREDERICK D.R. SAMPSON: [NY R L QUEENS Sampson, Part 31, as amended by NY ORDER 20-0329].
JUSTICE MARTIN J. SCHULMAN: NY R L QUEENS Schulman, Part 29.
JUSTICE BERNICE D. SIEGAL: NY R L QUEENS Siegal, Part 25G.
JUSTICE JANICE A. TAYLOR: NY R L QUEENS Taylor, Part 15.
JUSTICE CARMEN R. VELASQUEZ: NY R L QUEENS Velasquez, Part 38.
JUSTICE LOURDES M VENTURA: [NY R L QUEENS Ventura, Part 37, as amended by NY ORDER 20-0334].
JUSTICE WILLIAM A. VISCOVICH: NY R L QUEENS Viscovich, Part 63.
JUSTICE ALLAN B. WEISS: NY R L QUEENS Weiss, Part 2.
COMPLIANCE, SETTLEMENT AND CONFERENCE PART: NY R L QUEENS Doc 1.
PRELIMINARY CONFERENCE PART: [NY R L QUEENS Doc. 2, as amended by NY ORDER 20-0335].
MEDICAL MALPRACTICE CONFERENCE PART: [NY R L QUEENS Doc. 3, as amended by NY ORDER 20-0336].
TRIAL SCHEDULING PART: NY R L QUEENS Doc. 4.
SUMMARY JURY TRIAL PROGRAM: NY R L QUEENS Doc. 7.
RESIDENTIAL FORECLOSURE PART: NY R L QUEENS Doc. 9.
FORECLOSURE AUCTION RULES: NY R L QUEENS Doc. 10.
MATRIMONIAL PRELIMINARY CONFERENCE PART: NY R L QUEENS Doc. 11.
NON-CUSTODIAL CONTESTED MATRIMONIAL PART: NY R L QUEENS Doc. 12.

Motions, Oppositions and Replies
Motion for Leave to Reargue or Renew

Document Last Updated August 2020

A. Checklist

- (I) ❑ Matters to consider for moving party
  - (a) ❑ Required documents
    - (1) ❑ Notice of motion, order to show cause, or affidavit on ex parte motion
    - (2) ❑ Motion
    - (3) ❑ Request for judicial intervention
    - (4) ❑ Proof of service
    - (5) ❑ ALBANY COUNTY: Additional required documents
      - (i) ❑ Affirmation of good faith effort
  - (b) ❑ Supplemental documents
    - (1) ❑ Supporting evidence; Exhibits
    - (2) ❑ Brief
    - (3) ❑ Notice to produce papers not in possession of the court
    - (4) ❑ Filing fees
    - (5) ❑ Working copies
    - (6) ❑ ERIE COUNTY: Additional supplemental documents
      - (i) ❑ Notice of hard copy submission in e-filed case
    - (7) ❑ KINGS COUNTY: Additional supplemental documents
      - (i) ❑ Forms when filing in hard copy
    - (8) ❑ NEW YORK COUNTY: Additional supplemental documents
      - (i) ❑ Notice of hard copy submission

(ii) ❑ Unpublished opinions

(9) ❑ ONONDAGA COUNTY: Additional supplemental documents

(i) ❑ Notice of hard copy submission

(10) ❑ QUEENS COUNTY: Additional supplemental documents

(i) ❑ Notice of hard copy submission

(c) ❑ Timing

(1) ❑ A motion for leave to reargue shall be made within thirty (30) days after service of a copy of the order determining the prior motion and written notice of its entry

(2) ❑ A motion to renew is not subject to any specific time limitation

(3) ❑ The moving party shall serve copies of all affidavits and briefs upon all other parties at the time of service of the notice of motion

(4) ❑ A notice of motion and supporting affidavits shall be served at least eight (8) days before the time at which the motion is noticed to be heard

(5) ❑ It is also good practice to make motions returnable at least three (3) weeks away from the planned date of mailing and to always include a demand in the motion that the other side serve answering papers at least seven (7) days before the return day

(6) ❑ BRONX COUNTY: Additional timing

(i) ❑ A Notice of Motion must be served at least eight (8) days, by personal service, nine (9) days by overnight express and thirteen (13) days by mail before the return date

(7) ❑ NEW YORK COUNTY: Additional timing

(i) ❑ In an e-filed case, all of the moving papers shall be e-filed at least eight (8) business days prior to the return date

(8) ❑ ONONDAGA COUNTY: Additional timing

(i) ❑ Onondaga County local court rules require that any additional papers relating to motions must be e-filed at least two (2) business days prior to the return date, excluding the return date

(9) ❑ QUEENS COUNTY: Additional timing

(i) ❑ Motions must be in the possession of the Motion Support Office at least nine (9) days before the noticed return date of the motion

(II) ❑ Matters to consider for opposing party

(a) ❑ Required documents

(1) ❑ Opposition

(2) ❑ Proof of service

(b) ❑ Supplemental documents

(1) ❑ Supporting evidence; Exhibits

(2) ❑ Brief

(3) ❑ Filing fees

(4) ❑ Working copies

(5) ❑ ERIE COUNTY: Additional supplemental documents

(i) ❑ Notice of hard copy submission in e-filed case

(6) ❑ KINGS COUNTY: Additional supplemental documents

(i) ❑ Forms when filing in hard copy

(7) ❑ NEW YORK COUNTY: Additional supplemental documents

(i) ❑ Notice of hard copy submission

(ii) ❑ Unpublished opinions

(8) ❑ ONONDAGA COUNTY: Additional supplemental documents

(i) ❑ Notice of hard copy submission

(9) ❑ QUEENS COUNTY: Additional supplemental documents

(i) ❑ Notice of hard copy submission

(c) ❑ Timing

(1) ❑ Answering affidavits shall be served at least two (2) days before the time at which the motion is noticed to be heard

(2) ❑ Answering affidavits and any notice of cross-motion, with supporting papers, if any, shall be served at least seven (7) days before such time if a notice of motion served at least sixteen (16) days before such time so demands

B. Timing

1. *Time to bring motion for leave to reargue or renew*

a. *Motion for leave to reargue.* A motion for leave to reargue shall be made within thirty (30) days after service of a copy of the order determining the prior motion and written notice of its entry. NY CPLR Rule 2221(d)(3).

b. *Motion for leave to renew.* A motion to renew is not subject to any specific time limitation. NYPRAC-COMM § 31:68.

2. *Time to serve.* The moving party shall serve copies of all affidavits and briefs upon all other parties at the time of service of the notice of motion. NY R UNIF TRIAL CTS § 202.8(c). A notice of motion and supporting affidavits shall be served at least eight (8) days before the time at which the motion is noticed to be heard. NY CPLR Rule 2214(b).

a. *Return dates; Best practice.* It is also good practice to make motions returnable at least three (3) weeks away from the planned date of mailing and to always include a demand in the motion that the other side serve answering papers at least seven (7) days before the return day. This enables the motion to be served by mail, gives sufficient notice to support the seven (7) day demand, and leaves a few days for a delayed mailing if some snag prevents posting on the day planned. If speed is needed, the shorter eight (8) day notice period can be used, forfeiting the right to seven (7) day answering papers and a reply. If even eight (8) days notice is too much under the circumstances, the order to show cause is the remedy. SIEGEL-NYPRAC § 247.

i. *ALBANY COUNTY.* All motions, except for certain matters in Albany County as specified in NY R 3 JD SUP Doc. 1(E) and NY R 3 JD SUP Doc. 1(F), brought on by notice of motion or by order to show cause will be made returnable on any day, Monday through Friday, as chosen by the movant in compliance with the CPLR. Parties shall submit all papers in a timely fashion as required by the CPLR by delivering them or mailing them directly to the Supreme Court Clerk's Office[. . .]except that motions and other applications subject to a filing fee shall first be presented to the County Clerk's Office for payment of the requisite fee and then subsequently filed with the Supreme Court Clerk's Office. NY R 3 JD SUP Doc. 1(B).

ii. *BRONX COUNTY.* A Notice of Motion must be served at least eight (8) days, by personal service, nine (9) days by overnight express and thirteen (13) days by mail before the return date. NY R BRONX FIL R Doc. 3. All unassigned motions must be accompanied with a properly filled out RJI and shall be filed in the Motion Support Office, room 217, within five (5) days of service. All motions on actions already assigned to a Justice must be filed at least five (5) business days before the return date. NY R BRONX FIL R Doc. 3. All papers served must strictly comply with the time requirements of NY CPLR Rule 2101, NY CPLR Rule 2103 and NY CPLR Rule 2214(b). NY R BRONX FIL R Doc. 8.

iii. *KINGS COUNTY.* Motion papers, answering affidavits and reply affidavits must be served on adversaries in accordance with NY CPLR Rule 2214. NY R L KINGS Pt. C, Rule 1.

iv. *NEW YORK COUNTY.* In an e-filed case, all of the moving papers shall be e-filed at least eight (8) business days prior to the return date. The clerk will calendar the motion for the Motion Submission Part Courtroom (Room 130) for the return date selected. NY R NY CTY Procedure II(A); NY R NY CTY E FIL Doc. 2(D)(1).

v. *ONONDAGA COUNTY.* Onondaga County local court rules require that any additional papers relating to motions must be e-filed at least two (2) business days prior to the return date, excluding the return date. NY R ONDGA E FIL Protocol(B)(9)(e).

vi. *QUEENS COUNTY.* Motions must be in the possession of the Motion Support Office at least nine (9) days before the noticed return date of the motion. NY R L QUEENS MOT SUP Doc. 1; NY R L QUEENS E-FILE Doc. 1(H)(1).

b. *Order to show cause; Shorter time.* The court in a proper case may grant an order to show cause, to be served in lieu of a notice of motion, at a time and in a manner specified therein. NY CPLR Rule 2214(d). An ordinary notice of motion can't be brought on for hearing earlier than the eighth (8th) day after the motion papers are served. With an order to show cause, the hearing can be brought on at any time the court directs, which can be fewer than eight (8) days or as close as the very day on which it is signed. If the court is convinced there is a real emergency, it can schedule the hearing for a few hours later or, in the direst case, "forthwith" the service of the order to show cause. SIEGEL-NYPRAC § 248.

c. *Time to serve answering affidavits; Other answering papers.* Answering affidavits shall be served at least two (2) days before the time at which the motion is noticed to be heard. Answering affidavits and any notice of cross-motion, with supporting papers, if any, shall be served at least seven (7) days before such time if a notice of motion served at least sixteen (16) days before such time so demands; whereupon any reply or responding affidavits shall be served at least one (1) day before such time. NY CPLR Rule 2214(b); NY R UNIF TRIAL CTS § 202.8(c).

i. *BRONX COUNTY.* All answering papers must be submitted to the Clerk 's Office on the return date of the motion. Answering papers will not be accepted prior to the return date. NY R BRONX FIL R Doc. 8.

ii. *NEW YORK COUNTY.* Cross-motions, papers in opposition, and reply papers on motions/petitions on notice returnable in Room 130 in a hard-copy case shall be submitted to the Motion Submission Part Courtroom (Room 130) on the final return date of the motion/petition and will not be accepted until that date. Subsequent documents on motions/petitions in e-filed cases shall be e-filed in a timely manner. Working copies when required shall be submitted to Room 130 on the final return date. NY R NY CTY Procedure II(A).

d. *Time to serve cross-motion.* At least three (3) days prior to the time at which the motion is noticed to be heard, or seven (7) days prior to such time if demand is properly made pursuant to NY CPLR Rule 2214(b), a party may serve upon the moving party a notice of cross-motion demanding relief, with or without supporting papers; provided, however, that:

i. If such notice and any supporting papers are served by mailing, as provided in NY CPLR Rule 2103(b)(2), they shall be served three (3) days earlier than as prescribed in NY CPLR Rule 2215; and

ii. If served by overnight delivery, as provided in NY CPLR Rule 2103(b)(6), they shall be served one (1) day earlier than as prescribed in NY CPLR Rule 2215. Relief in the alternative or of several different types may be demanded; relief need not be responsive to that demanded by the moving party. NY CPLR Rule 2215(a); NY CPLR Rule 2215(b).

iii. *BRONX COUNTY.* Cross motions may be presented for approval on or before the return date, provided that there is a motion already calendared. NY R BRONX FIL R Doc. 8.

iv. *ERIE COUNTY.* Cross-motions must be filed at least two (2) days before the return date of the motion. NY R L KINGS Pt. A, Papers.

v. *KINGS COUNTY.* Hard copies are required to be filed for any motions, answering papers, stipulations, etc. for E-Filed cases returnable in [the Central Compliance Part] at least [two (2)] days before return date. . . .for cross motions. NY R L KINGS Pt. E, Rule 8.

vi. *QUEENS COUNTY.* Motion Support does not process or forward responsive papers, including cross-motions. They must be brought to the calendar call in the judge's part. NY R L QUEENS MOT SUP Doc. 1. E-filed cross motions: across motion must be noticed for the same return date as the main motion and have the confirmation of filing attached in the same manner as a motion. NY R L QUEENS E-FILE Doc. 1(H)(2)(e).

3. *Filing before return date.* All motions shall be returnable before the assigned judge, and all papers shall be filed with the court on or before the return date. NY R UNIF TRIAL CTS § 202.8(a).

a. *BRONX COUNTY: Time for filing*

i. *Unassigned motions.* Unassigned motions must be in the Clerk's Office within five (5) days of the date of service of the motion. NY R BRONX FIL R Doc. 8.

ii. *Assigned motions.* Assigned motions must be filed in the Clerk's Office not less than five (5) business days prior to the return date of the motion. NY R BRONX FIL R Doc. 8.

iii. *Motions returnable in room 217.* The moving documents must be e-filed no later than eight (8) days prior to the return date. NY R BRONX E FIL R Doc. 1(1).

b. *KINGS COUNTY: Time and place of filing.* Motion papers must be filed with the E-file/Motion Support Office located in Room 227. . . at 360 Adams Street at least five (5) business days before the return date of the motion. NY R L

KINGS Pt. A, Papers. Hard copies are required to be filed for any motions, answering papers, stipulations, etc. for E-Filed cases returnable in [the Central Compliance Part] at least five (5) days before return date for main motions. NY R L KINGS Pt. E, Rule 8. The moving documents must be e-filed no later than eight (8) days prior to the return date. NY R L KINGS E FIL Doc. 1(D).

4. *NEW YORK COUNTY: Briefing schedule.* Once a motion is made, counsel for all parties are strongly encouraged to agree upon a briefing schedule and submit a stipulation of adjournment reflecting that schedule using service or a clerk. Where a briefing schedule has not been agreed upon, the movant can avoid the need to attend simply to see if anyone will hand up opposing papers by demanding papers as provided by NY CPLR Rule 2214(b). To protect movants against the submission of late opposition papers or cross-motions, the General Clerk's Office will screen motions in which such papers are submitted without a response (reply or opposition respectively) to ensure that proper time to respond has been afforded and it will sua sponte adjourn for one (1) week cases in which such time has not been given. NY R NY CTY Procedure II(C).
5. *QUEENS COUNTY: Time to pay fees.* As motions and petitions are time sensitive, if opting to pay at the County Clerk's Office payment MUST be made, if filed with an RJI, a minimum of nine (9) business days prior to the application's return date and if filed post RJI, a minimum of nine (9) business days prior to the application's return date. NY R L QUEENS E-FILE Doc. 1(H)(1).
6. *Computation of time*
   a. *Units of time*
      i. *Day.* A calendar day includes the time from midnight to midnight. Sunday or any day of the week specifically mentioned means a calendar day. NY GEN CONSTR § 19.
      ii. *Month.* In a statute, contract or public or private instrument, unless otherwise provided in such contract or instrument or by law, the term month means a calendar month and not a lunar month. NY GEN CONSTR § 31.
      iii. *Year.* For information on the definition of a year, including the definitions of a half-year and quarter-year, refer to NY GEN CONSTR § 58 and NY GEN CONSTR § 50. For information on leap years, refer to NY GEN CONSTR § 57.
   b. *Periods of time*
      i. *Number of days.* A number of days specified as a period from a certain day within which or after or before which an act is authorized or required to be done means such number of calendar days exclusive of the calendar day from which the reckoning is made. NY GEN CONSTR § 20.
         - If such period is a period of two (2) days, Saturday, Sunday or a public holiday must be excluded from the reckoning if it is an intervening day between the day from which the reckoning is made and the last day of the period. NY GEN CONSTR § 20.
         - In computing any specified period of time from a specified event, the day upon which the event happens is deemed the day from which the reckoning is made. The day from which any specified period of time is reckoned shall be excluded in making the reckoning. NY GEN CONSTR § 20.
      ii. *Number of months.* A number of months after or before a certain day shall be computed by counting such number of calendar months from such day, exclusive of the calendar month in which such day occurs, and shall include the day of the month in the last month so counted having the same numerical order in days of the month as the day from which the computation is made, unless there be not so many days in the last month so counted, in which case the period computed shall expire with the last day of the month so counted. NY GEN CONSTR § 30.
      iii. *Publication of notice; Number of days.* The period of publication of a legal notice shall be computed by excluding the first day of publication and including the day on which the act or event of which notice is given is to take place or which completes the full period of publication. NY CPLR § 2402.
      iv. *Periods ending on Saturday, Sunday or public holiday.* When any period of time, computed from a certain day, within which or after which or before which an act is authorized or required to be done, ends on a Saturday, Sunday or a public holiday, such act may be done on the next succeeding business day and if the period ends at a specified hour, such act may be done at or before the same hour of such next succeeding business day, except that where a period of time specified by contract ends on a Saturday, Sunday or a public holiday, the extension of such period is governed by NY GEN CONSTR § 25. NY GEN CONSTR § 25-a(1).
         - For a list of public holidays, refer to NY GEN CONSTR § 24.

v. *Additional time after certain kinds of service*

- *Service by mail.* Where a period of time prescribed by law is measured from the service of a paper and service is by mail, five (5) days shall be added to the prescribed period. NY CPLR Rule 2103(b)(2).
- *Service by overnight delivery service.* Where a period of time prescribed by law is measured from the service of a paper and service is by overnight delivery, one (1) business day shall be added to the prescribed period. NY CPLR Rule 2103(b)(6).

vi. *Daylight saving time.* For information on New York's time zone and the effect of daylight saving time, refer to NY GEN CONSTR § 52.

c. *Hours of court.* Notwithstanding any provision of law or rule of court to the contrary, throughout the State of New York the sessions of the Supreme Court for the disposition of business before the court shall commence not later than 9:30 a.m. and conclude not earlier than 5 p.m. Where warranted, the Chief Administrator of the Courts may authorize variances in the opening and closing hours of the courts, but, in such event, daily sessions shall total not less than six (6) hours. NY R CHIEF J § 3.1.

d. *Time limits; Extension of time.* Any act required by or in pursuance of law to be performed at or within a prescribed time, shall be performed according to the standard time. NY GEN CONSTR § 53.

i. Except where otherwise expressly prescribed by law, the court may extend the time fixed by any statute, rule or order for doing any act, upon such terms as may be just and upon good cause shown, whether the application for extension is made before or after the expiration of the time fixed. NY CPLR § 2004. Refer to the New York KeyRules Motion for Continuance/Extension of Time document for more information.

C. General Requirements

1. *Motions, generally.* There shall be compliance with the procedures prescribed in the CPLR for the bringing of motions. NY R UNIF TRIAL CTS § 202.7(a).

a. *Motions on notice.* A notice of motion shall specify the time and place of the hearing on the motion, the supporting papers upon which the motion is based, the relief demanded and the grounds therefor. NY CPLR Rule 2214(a). A motion on notice in an action in the supreme court shall be noticed to be heard in the judicial district where the action is triable or in a county adjoining the county where the action is triable. Unless statute, civil practice rule or local court rule provides otherwise, the motion shall be noticed to be heard before a motion term or, upon order to show cause granted by a justice, before that justice out of court. NY CPLR § 2212(a). Except as provided in NY R UNIF TRIAL CTS § 202.7(d), no motion shall be filed with the court unless there have been served and filed with the motion papers a notice of motion. NY R UNIF TRIAL CTS § 202.7(a)(1).

b. *Ex parte motions.* A motion in an action in the supreme court that may be made without notice may be made at a motion term or to a justice out of court in any county in the state. NY CPLR § 2212(b).

i. *KINGS COUNTY.* For more information on submitting a motion ex parte, refer to NY R L KINGS E FIL Doc. 1(G).

ii. *NEW YORK COUNTY.* For more information on submitting matters ex parte, refer to NY R NY CTY Procedure III and NY R NY CTY E FIL Doc. 2(G).

iii. *QUEENS COUNTY.* For more information on submitting matters ex parte, refer to NY R L QUEENS EX PARTE Doc. 1.

c. *Alternative relief.* Relief in the alternative or of several different types may be demanded. NY CPLR Rule 2214(a). The types of relief need not be related. In one motion, for example, the defendant can seek to dismiss the plaintiff's claim for lack of jurisdiction, to get an extension of time to answer, to require the plaintiff to join X as a party, and to quash a disclosure subpoena served in behalf of the plaintiff on a nonparty witness. So doing, the movant must of course specify all of these items of relief in the notice of motion, and the grounds for them, and the supporting papers must contain the entire proof requisite to the items of relief sought. NY CPLR Rule 2214(Practice Commentary, C2214:4).

d. *General relief.* It is common practice to include at the end of the relief request in the notice of motion a so-called "general relief" clause. This is merely a few words to cover the possibility that the relief appropriate to what the movant proves was not specifically asked for, but is close enough to enable the court to grant it. After stating the specific relief desired, the lawyer will often add something like: and for such other, further, or different relief as this court may deem just and proper. NY CPLR Rule 2214(Practice Commentary, C2214:5).

e. *Motion in improper form.* If the court finds it appropriate in the interests of justice, it may convert a motion into a

special proceeding, or vice-versa, upon such terms as may be just, including the payment of fees and costs. NY CPLR § 103(c).

f. *Order to show cause.* An order to show cause is basically only a substitute for a notice of motion. An ordinary notice of motion merely notifies the recipient that a motion is being made for specified relief. The burden of proof is on the movant. Although in most cases it is just as innocent as an ordinary notice of motion, the order to show cause gets its name by directing the recipient to "show cause" why the particular relief being asked for should not be granted. It sounds as if the burden of proof is being shifted to the recipient. It isn't. It specifies the time and place of the hearing on the application but when the hearing comes on, the burden of proof is where it always is on a motion: on the movant. SIEGEL-NYPRAC § 248.

   i. The CPLR says nothing more about an order to show cause than that it may be used "in a proper case", which leaves it entirely to the judge's discretion to determine what a proper case is. Any fact suggesting a problem as to any of the items listed above would be sufficient to invoke judicial discretion and justify the show cause procedure, which is in fact liberally used. SIEGEL-NYPRAC § 248.

   ii. An order to show cause against a state body or officers must be served in addition to service upon the defendant or respondent state body or officers upon the attorney general by delivery to an assistant attorney general at an office of the attorney general in the county in which venue of the action is designated or if there is no office of the attorney general in such county, at the office of the attorney general nearest such county. NY CPLR Rule 2214(d).

   iii. *BRONX COUNTY.* For information on submitting an order to show cause, refer to NY R BRONX E FIL R Doc. 2 and NY R BRONX LEG SUP Doc. 1.

   iv. *ERIE COUNTY.* For information on submitting an order to show cause, refer to NY R ERIE E FIL Doc. 3(VI).

   v. *KINGS COUNTY.* For information on submitting an order to show cause, refer to NY R L KINGS E FIL Doc. 1(F).

   vi. *NEW YORK COUNTY.* For information on submitting an order to show cause, refer to NY R NY CTY E FIL Doc. 2(F).

   vii. *ONONDAGA COUNTY.* For information on submitting an order to show cause, refer to NY R ONDGA E FIL Protocol(B)(10) and NY R ONDGA E FIL Protocol(J).

g. *Motions before preliminary conference.* Motions in actions to which NY R UNIF TRIAL CTS § 202.12 is applicable made after the preliminary conference has been scheduled may be denied unless there is shown good cause why such relief is warranted before the preliminary conference is held. NY R UNIF TRIAL CTS § 202.12(h).

h. *ALBANY COUNTY: Good faith effort to resolve.* Prior to the submission of a notice of motion relating to disclosure or a bill of particulars, the parties must make a good faith effort to resolve the matter in question and submit an affirmation attesting to this good faith effort. NY R 3 JD SUP Doc. 1(B).

i. *NEW YORK COUNTY: Documents with motions.* Counsel must attach to motion papers copies of all pleadings and other documents as required by the CPLR and as necessary for an informed decision on the motion. Documents in a foreign language shall be properly translated. NY R NY CTY J RUL Rule 14(a).

j. *NEW YORK COUNTY: Motions in multiple cases made together.* On occasion, attorneys may wish to make a motion in more than one case on a single set of papers. In such cases, by definition consolidation will not have been directed since consolidation signifies the combination of more than one case into a single one with a single caption and index number and ending in a single judgment. NY R NY CTY Procedure II(B). For more information on motions made with the same papers, refer to NY R NY CTY Procedure II(A).

k. *QUEENS COUNTY: Motion sequence numbers.* A motion sequence number is required for all E-filed motions. After a motion is E-filed, please consult the e-courts website within twenty-four (24) to forty-eight (48) hours to obtain the sequence number. The Confirmation Notice of E-filing MUST indicate the sequence number of any motion submitted at the Centralized Motion Part calendar call. NY R L QUEENS E-FILE Doc. 1(H)(5).

2. *Motion for leave to reargue*

a. *Generally.* A motion to reargue is based on no new proof; it seeks to convince the court that it overlooked or misapprehended something on the first go around and ought to change its mind. SIEGEL-NYPRAC § 254.

   i. A motion for leave to reargue shall be identified specifically as such. NY CPLR Rule 2221(d)(1).

   ii. A motion for leave to reargue shall be based upon matters of fact or law allegedly overlooked or misapprehended by the court in determining the prior motion, but shall not include any matters of fact not offered on the prior motion. NY CPLR Rule 2221(d)(2).

iii. A motion for leave to reargue shall be made within thirty (30) days after service of a copy of the order determining the prior motion and written notice of its entry. NY CPLR Rule 2221 shall not apply to motions to reargue a decision made by the appellate division or the court of appeals. NY CPLR Rule 2221(d)(3).

- There are good policy reasons for retaining the old rule. Some lower court cases nevertheless held that it was displaced by the adoption of NY CPLR Rule 2221(d)(3) and that a motion to reargue is now strictly limited to thirty (30) days from the time of the service of the objectionable order notwithstanding the pendency of an appeal from it. The First Department rejected that construction, however, and held in favor of the older rule in Leist v. Goldstein, 305 A.D.2d 468, 468, 760 N.Y.S.2d 191, 192 (2003), and the Second Department did likewise in Itzkowitz v. King Kullen Grocery Co., 22 A.D.3d 636, 638, 804 N.Y.S.2d 350, 352 (2005). SIEGEL-NYPRAC § 254; Leist v. Goldstein, 305 A.D.2d 468, 469, 760 N.Y.S.2d 191, 192 (2003); Itzkowitz v. King Kullen Grocery Co., 22 A.D.3d 636, 638, 804 N.Y.S.2d 350, 352 (2005). Under these appellate decisions, the pendency of an appeal from the order continues to be a time period available for a motion to reargue, which is indeed the preferable construction. SIEGEL-NYPRAC § 254.

b. *On whom made.* A motion for leave to renew or to reargue a prior motion, for leave to appeal from, or to stay, vacate or modify, an order shall be made, on notice, to the judge who signed the order, unless he or she is for any reason unable to hear it, except that:

i. If the order was made upon a default such motion may be made, on notice, to any judge of the court; and

ii. If the order was made without notice such motion may be made, without notice, to the judge who signed it, or, on notice, to any other judge of the court. NY CPLR Rule 2221(a).

iii. A motion made to other than a proper judge under NY CPLR Rule 2221 shall be transferred to the proper judge. NY CPLR Rule 2221(c).

c. *Appeal.* An order on a motion to reargue is appealable only if it grants the motion. An order denying a motion to reargue is not appealable: it would amount to a extension of time in which to appeal the original order. SIEGEL-NYPRAC § 254. An order granting a motion to reargue is appealable even if, after the granting, the prior decision is adhered to. It has also been held that an order granting reargument supersedes the original order. SIEGEL-NYPRAC § 254; Dennis v. Stout, 24 A.D.2d 461, 260 N.Y.S.2d 325, 326 (1965).

d. *Rules of the chief administrator of the courts.* The chief administrator may by rule exclude motions within a department, district or county from the operation of NY CPLR Rule 2221(a). NY CPLR Rule 2221(b).

3. *Motion for leave to renew*

a. *Generally.* The motion to renew (or rehear) is based on new or additional proof not used the first time around. SIEGEL-NYPRAC § 254; NY CPLR Rule 2221(Practice Commentaries, C2221:9).

i. A motion for leave to renew shall be identified specifically as such. NY CPLR Rule 2221(e)(1).

ii. A motion for leave to renew shall be based upon new facts not offered on the prior motion that would change the prior determination or shall demonstrate that there has been a change in the law that would change the prior determination. NY CPLR Rule 2221(e)(2).

- While NY CPLR Rule 2221(e)(3) requires a party seeking renewal based on new facts to provide a reasonable justification for failing to present the facts on the prior motion, it does not require a similar justification when moving for renewal based on a change in the law. Nonetheless, a party seeking renewal based on a change in the law that would change the earlier determination should act expeditiously. SIEGEL-NYPRAC § 254; NY CPLR Rule 2221(e)(2); Glicksman v. Bd. of Educ./Cent. Sch. Bd. of Comsewogue Union Free Sch. Dist., 278 A.D.2d 364, 366, 717 N.Y.S.2d 373, 374 (2000).

iii. A motion for leave to renew shall contain reasonable justification for the failure to present such facts on the prior motion. NY CPLR Rule 2221(e)(3).

- Ideally, it should be shown that the proof being offered on the motion has been only recently discovered and that the movant is acting with reasonable dispatch in bringing it before the court. SIEGEL-NYPRAC § 254.

b. *On whom made.* A motion for leave to renew or to reargue a prior motion, for leave to appeal from, or to stay, vacate or modify, an order shall be made, on notice, to the judge who signed the order, unless he or she is for any reason unable to hear it, except that:

i. If the order was made upon a default such motion may be made, on notice, to any judge of the court; and

ii. If the order was made without notice such motion may be made, without notice, to the judge who signed it, or, on notice, to any other judge of the court. NY CPLR Rule 2221(a).

iii. A motion made to other than a proper judge under NY CPLR Rule 2221 shall be transferred to the proper judge. NY CPLR Rule 2221(c).

c. *Proof.* Ideally, it should be shown that the proof being offered on the motion has been only recently discovered and that the movant is acting with reasonable dispatch in bringing it before the court. SIEGEL-NYPRAC § 254.

d. *Appeal.* An order on a motion to renew is appealable whether it grants or denies the motion. SIEGEL-NYPRAC § 254.

4. *Combined motions.* A combined motion for leave to reargue and leave to renew shall identify separately and support separately each item of relief sought. The court, in determining a combined motion for leave to reargue and leave to renew, shall decide each part of the motion as if it were separately made. If a motion for leave to reargue or leave to renew is granted, the court may adhere to the determination on the original motion or may alter that determination. NY CPLR Rule 2221(f).

a. If a motion is based on new proof, but is erroneously termed a "reargument" motion, the mislabel will be ignored and the motion will be treated as one to renew. SIEGEL-NYPRAC § 254; Turkel v. I.M.I. Warp Knits, Inc., 50 A.D.2d 543, 543, 375 N.Y.S.2d 333, 335 (1975). And vice-versa. This is of course important on the question of appealability. SIEGEL-NYPRAC § 254; SIEGEL-NYPRAC § 532.

5. *Oppositions.* In the absence of statutory provision or court rule, a motion ordinarily does not require a written answer, although an adverse party may be permitted to file an answer in opposition to the showing made in the motion or its supporting affidavits. AMJUR MOTIONS § 26. When a party files a motion and the opposing party fails to respond, the court may construe such failure to respond as non-opposition to the motion or an admission that the motion was meritorious, may take the facts alleged in the motion as true, and may grant the motion if the relief requested appears to be justified. However, the severity of such a result demands that a court impose it only with great caution. AMJUR MOTIONS § 28.

6. *Governing law.* The civil practice law and rules (NY CPLR § 101, et seq.) shall govern the procedure in civil judicial proceedings in all courts of the state and before all judges, except where the procedure is regulated by inconsistent statute. The civil practice law and rules shall succeed the civil practice act and rules of civil practice and shall be deemed substituted therefor throughout the statutes and rules of the state. NY CPLR § 101. The civil practice law and rules shall be liberally construed to secure the just, speedy and inexpensive determination of every civil judicial proceeding. NY CPLR § 104.

a. *Uniform trial court rules.* The uniform civil rules for the Supreme Court and County Court (NY R UNIF TRIAL CTS § 202.1, et seq.) shall be applicable to civil actions and proceedings in the Supreme Court and the County Court. NY R UNIF TRIAL CTS § 202.1(a). The provisions of the uniform rules shall be construed consistent with the Civil Practice Law and Rules (CPLR), and matters not covered by the uniform rules shall be governed by the CPLR. NY R UNIF TRIAL CTS § 202.1(d).

b. *Local rules.* Local court rules, not inconsistent with law or with uniform civil rules for the Supreme Court and County Court (NY R UNIF TRIAL CTS § 202.1, et seq.), shall comply with Part 9 of the Rules of the Chief Judge (NY R CHIEF J § 9.1). NY R UNIF TRIAL CTS § 202.1(c).

c. *Official forms.* The state administrator shall have the power to adopt, amend and rescind an appendix of forms. Forms adopted pursuant to NY CPLR § 107 shall be sufficient under the civil practice law and rules and shall illustrate the simplicity and brevity of statement which the civil practice law and rules contemplate. NY CPLR § 107.

7. *Rules of the commercial division.* [Editor's note: certain types of civil cases or civil cases meeting certain monetary thresholds that are filed in the state of New York must be filed in the Commercial Division of the New York Supreme Courts. Rules governing practice in the commercial division are found in NY R UNIF TRIAL CTS § 202.70]. Cases which must be filed in the commercial division are listed below. For more information, refer to NY R UNIF TRIAL CTS § 202.70.

a. *Monetary thresholds.* Except as set forth in NY R UNIF TRIAL CTS § 202.70(b), the monetary thresholds of the Commercial Division, exclusive of punitive damages, interests, costs, disbursements and counsel fees claimed, are established as follows: (1) Albany County, fifty thousand dollars ($50,000); (2) Eighth Judicial District, one hundred thousand dollars ($100,000); (3) Kings County, one hundred fifty thousand dollars ($150,000); (4) Nassau County, two hundred thousand dollars ($200,000); (5) New York County, five hundred thousand dollars ($500,000); (6) Onondaga County, fifty thousand dollars ($50,000); (7) Queens County, one hundred thousand dollars ($100,000); (8) Seventh Judicial District, fifty thousand dollars ($50,000); (9) Suffolk County, one hundred thousand dollars

($100,000); and (10) Westchester County, one hundred thousand dollars ($100,000). NY R UNIF TRIAL CTS § 202.70(a).

i. *ALBANY COUNTY.* The Commercial Division of the Albany County Supreme Court exercises jurisdiction over selected business and commercial disputes in which the amount at issue generally involves damage claims in a minimum amount of fifty thousand dollars ($50,000) as well as claims for unspecified amounts where the value of the commercial asset(s) in dispute exceeds fifty thousand dollars ($50,000). A separate publication promulgating the rules and criteria relating to the filing and management of Commercial Court cases in this part may be obtained from the Albany County Supreme Court Clerk's Office. A section of the Uniform Civil Rules for the Supreme Court and County Court sets forth statewide rules. NY R 3 JD SUP Doc. 1(E).

ii. *BRONX COUNTY.* The monetary threshold for commercial cases in Bronx County will be seventy-five thousand dollars ($75,000). All other parameters including the type of matters that will be heard are contained within the Rules of the Commercial Division of the Supreme Court (NY R UNIF TRIAL CTS § 202.70). NY R BRONX FIL R Doc. 12.

iii. *NEW YORK COUNTY.* The monetary threshold in the New York County Commercial Division, which is generally applicable, is an amount in controversy of five hundred thousand dollars ($500,000) or more (exclusive of punitive damages, interest, costs, disbursements, and counsel fees). If the case is designated a commercial one and the Addendum is submitted, the clerk will review the pleadings to determine whether the amount in controversy in the case meets the monetary threshold or whether an exception to the threshold applies. NY R NY CTY Procedure IA(B). For more information on assigning a case to the commercial division in New York County, refer to NY R NY CTY Procedure IA(B).

b. *Commercial cases.* Actions in which the principal claims involve or consist of the following will be heard in the Commercial Division provided that the monetary threshold is met or equitable or declaratory relief is sought:

i. Breach of contract or fiduciary duty, fraud, misrepresentation, business tort (e.g., unfair competition), or statutory and/or common law violation where the breach or violation is alleged to arise out of business dealings (e.g., sales of assets or securities; corporate restructuring; partnership, shareholder, joint venture, and other business agreements; trade secrets; restrictive covenants; and employment agreements not including claims that principally involve alleged discriminatory practices);

ii. Transactions governed by the Uniform Commercial Code (exclusive of those concerning individual cooperative or condominium units);

iii. Transactions involving commercial real property, including Yellowstone injunctions and excluding actions for the payment of rent only;

iv. Shareholder derivative actions—without consideration of the monetary threshold;

v. Commercial class actions—without consideration of the monetary threshold;

vi. Business transactions involving or arising out of dealings with commercial banks and other financial institutions;

vii. Internal affairs of business organizations;

viii. Malpractice by accountants or actuaries, and legal malpractice arising out of representation in commercial matters;

ix. Environmental insurance coverage;

x. Commercial insurance coverage (e.g., directors and officers, errors and omissions, and business interruption coverage);

xi. Dissolution of corporations, partnerships, limited liability companies, limited liability partnerships and joint ventures—without consideration of the monetary threshold; and

xii. Applications to stay or compel arbitration and affirm or disaffirm arbitration awards and related injunctive relief pursuant to Article 75 of the New York Civil Practice Law and Rules (NY CPLR § 7501, et seq.) involving any of the foregoing enumerated commercial issues. Where the applicable arbitration agreement provides for the arbitration to be heard outside the United States, the monetary threshold set forth in NY R UNIF TRIAL CTS § 202.70(a) shall not apply. NY R UNIF TRIAL CTS § 202.70(b).

c. *Non-commercial cases.* The following will not be heard in the Commercial Division even if the monetary threshold is met:

i. Suits to collect professional fees;

ii. Cases seeking a declaratory judgment as to insurance coverage for personal injury or property damage;

iii. Residential real estate disputes, including landlord-tenant matters, and commercial real estate disputes involving the payment of rent only;

iv. Home improvement contracts involving residential properties consisting of one to four residential units or individual units in any residential building, including cooperative or condominium units;

v. Proceedings to enforce a judgment regardless of the nature of the underlying case;

vi. First-party insurance claims and actions by insurers to collect premiums or rescind non-commercial policies; and

vii. Attorney malpractice actions except as otherwise provided in NY R UNIF TRIAL CTS § 202.70(b)(8). NY R UNIF TRIAL CTS § 202.70(c).

d. For more information on the Commercial Division, refer to NY R UNIF TRIAL CTS § 202.70.

D. Documents

1. *Documents for moving party*

a. *Required documents*

i. *Notice of motion, order to show cause, or affidavit on ex parte motion.* The notice of motion shall be substantially in the form found in NY R UNIF TRIAL CTS § 202.7(b). NY R UNIF TRIAL CTS § 202.7(b). The supporting papers should be referred to in the notice of motion. SIEGEL-NYPRAC § 246. The court in a proper case may grant an order to show cause, to be served in lieu of a notice of motion. NY CPLR Rule 2214(d). An ex parte motion shall be accompanied by an affidavit stating the result of any prior motion for similar relief and specifying the new facts, if any, that were not previously shown. NY CPLR Rule 2217(b).

- *Request for oral argument.* A party requesting oral argument shall set forth such request in its notice of motion or in its order to show cause or on the first page of the answering papers, as the case may be. Where all parties to a motion request oral argument, oral argument shall be granted unless the court shall determine it to be unnecessary. Where a motion is brought on by order to show cause, the court may set forth in the order that oral argument is required on the return date of the motion. NY R UNIF TRIAL CTS § 202.8(d).

ii. *Motion.* Refer to the General Requirements section of this document for information on the notice of motion and motion.

iii. *Request for judicial intervention.* At any time after service of process, a party may file a request for judicial intervention. Except as provided in NY R UNIF TRIAL CTS § 202.6(b), in an action not yet assigned to a judge, the court shall not accept for filing a notice of motion, order to show cause, or application for ex parte order, unless such notice or application is accompanied by a request for judicial intervention. NY R UNIF TRIAL CTS § 202.6(a).

- *BRONX COUNTY.* Generally, the Request For Judicial Intervention, commonly referred to as an "RJI", is required to be filed in any action where the assignment of a Justice is required. The RJI sets forth the information which is entered into the court system's database. It must be completely and accurately filled out. The full caption, as stated on the Summons, must be set forth. Use of terms "et al." and "etc." are not permitted. Only one (1) RJI may be filed in each action. Either a self represented litigant or an attorney must sign the affirmation at the end of the form. Once completed, the RJI must be filed in duplicate. Except in the case of an ex-parte application, the RJI must also be served together with the accompanying application upon all parties. Proof of accuracy of the index number must accompany the RJI. Check the Fee Schedule[. . .]for any applicable filing fees. NY R BRONX FIL R Doc. 2.
- *KINGS COUNTY.* An RJI with the relevant required addendum in a NYSCEF case shall be submitted via NYSCEF. Once e-filed, the RJI and any accompanying document will be forwarded to the relevant support office for random assignment of the case and processing of the document. A filer or counsel need not appear (as to Proposed Orders to Show Cause, however, see below). A copy of the pleadings must be submitted only if the document has not previously been e-filed. If the RJI seeks intervention with regard to a document that is intended for review by a Justice, such as a motion, a working copy of the RJI must be submitted with the working copy of the motion and the NYSCEF Confirmation Notice. NY R L KINGS E FIL Doc. 1(C).
- *NEW YORK COUNTY.* To obtain the assignment of an IAS Justice to a case, a Request for Judicial Intervention (cost ninety-five dollars ($95)) must be filed, with NYSCEF in an e-filed case or in paper in an authorized hard-copy one. A no-fee RJI, which will generally result in the referral of an application to an Ex

Parte Justice, is also required with regard to certain kinds of applications for which, prior to 2011, no RJI was required. NY R NY CTY Procedure I(C). A "fillable" form RJI is available on-line. The form must be filed in duplicate in hard-copy cases. NY R NY CTY Procedure IA(A)(1). The filer of an RJI must check off a box identifying the type of case at issue. Where the RJI seeks judicial assignment, this designation will bring about a random assignment of the case by computer to a Justice handling cases of that type. NY R NY CTY Procedure IA(A)(1). The RJI and any addendum can be completed and submitted electronically in an e-filed case. NY R NY CTY Procedure II(A). The RJI shall be marked to reflect the existence of any "related case" as explained on the "Commencement of Cases" page under "Case Processing" on the court's website. NY R NY CTY Procedure II(A); NY R NY CTY E FIL Doc. 2(C).

- *ONONDAGA COUNTY.* The RJI will be submitted via the NYSCEF system along with any required RJI addendum forms. When the RJI is filed and the fee paid online, the Onondaga County Clerk's Office will electronically forward the RJI and any accompanying documents to the Onondaga Supreme Court Clerk's Office for assignment and processing. Counsel will receive notification of judge assignment via the NYSCEF system. NY R ONDGA E FIL Protocol(B)(3).
- *QUEENS COUNTY.* A Request for Judicial Intervention ("RJI") in an E-filed case shall be submitted via the E-filing System. When the RJI is approved, filed and paid for on-line, it will be forwarded to the relevant back office for random assignment of the case and processing of the document. In the case of RJIs seeking assignment to the Commercial Division, the filer must submit therewith, a Commercial Addendum as required by the standards for assignment of cases to the Commercial Division. NY R L QUEENS E-FILE Doc. 1(F).

iv. *Proof of service.* In addition to complying with the provisions of NY CPLR Rule 2101, every paper filed in court shall have annexed thereto appropriate proof of service on all parties where required. NY R UNIF TRIAL CTS § 202.5(a).

- *QUEENS COUNTY.* With regard to service of a motion/petition on notice in an E-filed action, NY CPLR Rule 2214(b) and NY R UNIF TRIAL CTS § 202.5-b(f) applies. Where required, proof of service shall be filed on-line as a separate document. NY R L QUEENS E-FILE Doc. 1(H)(3).

v. *ALBANY COUNTY: Additional required documents*

- *Affirmation of good faith effort.* The parties must[. . .]submit an affirmation attesting to [their good faith effort to resolve the matter]. The affirmation of good faith effort to resolve the issues raised by the motion shall indicate the time, place and nature of the consultation and the issues discussed and any resolutions, or shall indicate good cause why no such conferral with counsel for opposing parties was held. An assigned justice or judge may dismiss a motion for failure to demonstrate that such effort was made with leave to renew the motion after such effort has been demonstrated. NY R 3 JD SUP Doc. 1(B).

b. *Supplemental documents*

i. *Supporting evidence; Exhibits.* The main supporting papers on a motion are affidavits, but any relevant exhibits, documents, depositions, etc., are also includible. SIEGEL-NYPRAC § 246.

- *Affidavits accompanying motion.* Affidavits shall be for a statement of the relevant facts. NY R UNIF TRIAL CTS § 202.8(c).
- *Foreign language documents.* Where an affidavit or exhibit annexed to a paper served or filed is in a foreign language, it shall be accompanied by an English translation and an affidavit by the translator stating his qualifications and that the translation is accurate. NY CPLR Rule 2101(b).
- *Statement of attorney in lieu of affidavit.* The statement of an attorney admitted to practice in the courts of the state, or of a physician, osteopath or dentist, authorized by law to practice in the state, who is not a party to an action, when subscribed and affirmed by him to be true under the penalties of perjury, may be served or filed in the action in lieu of and with the same force and effect as an affidavit. NY CPLR Rule 2106.
- *NEW YORK COUNTY: Form of presented exhibits.* Exhibits should be tabbed and be legible; a typed version of any exhibit that is difficult to read should be submitted with the original. Exhibits printed on both sides of the page should be bound and tabbed on the side. NY R NY CTY J RUL Rule 14(a).
- *QUEENS COUNTY.* Attorneys submitting exhibits to the court on E-file cases shall make each exhibit a separate, labeled attachment to an affidavit/affirmation. NY R L QUEENS E-FILE Doc. 1(H)(4).

ii. *Brief.* Briefs shall be for a statement of the relevant law. NY R UNIF TRIAL CTS § 202.8(c).

iii. *Notice to produce papers not in possession of the court.* If a paper relied on by the movant is in the possession of the other side, it may be demanded of that side with a notice to produce it at the hearing. Where such papers are in the possession of an adverse party, they shall be produced by him at the hearing on notice served with the motion papers. NY CPLR Rule 2214(Practice Commentary, C2214:23).

iv. *Filing fees.* The County Clerk shall require the payment of any applicable statutory fees, or an order of the Court waiving payment of such fees, before accepting a paper for filing. NY R UNIF TRIAL CTS § 202.5(d)(1). For information on filing fees, if any, refer to NY CPLR § 8001, et seq.

- *ALBANY COUNTY.* In general, any filing subsequent to the commencement of an action which is designated as a motion or cross-motion requires the payment of a filing fee to the County Clerk's Office prior to submission to the Supreme Court Clerk's Office for referral to the assigned justice. The fee is assessed regardless of whether an application is made by notice of motion, order to show cause or ex parte. No fee will be charged upon the filing of a motion for poor person status in conjunction with an application which serves to commence an action or special proceeding. In the event a motion is received by the court unaccompanied by proof of payment to the County Clerk, the Supreme Court Clerk's Office will contact the submitting party to advise that the application will be held pending receipt of the filing fee only until the return date of the motion. If proof of payment is not submitted to the Supreme Court Clerk's Office by the return date (ex parte applications will be held ten (10) days), the papers will be returned by mail with a notification that the motion has been removed from the court's calendar and that it must be re-noticed and re-filed with the court along with the requisite filing fee. Inquiries concerning the applicability of the motion fee to a proposed filing may be directed to the Supreme Court Clerk's Office. NY R 3 JD SUP Doc. 1(B).
- *BRONX COUNTY.* In accordance with the new civil fee schedule set forth in Article 80 of the C.P.L.R. (NY CPLR § 8001, et seq.), effective July 14, 2003, all motions, and cross motions must be approved in Room 217 prior to payment of said fees in the County Clerk's Office, Room 118. NY R BRONX FIL R Doc. 8. The motion fee [must be] paid for via NYSCEF by credit/debit card. NY R BRONX E FIL R Doc. 1(1).
- *ERIE COUNTY.* Payment for fee-bearing NYSCEF documents must be made online via credit or debit card (American Express, MasterCard or Visa) at the time of submission. NY R ERIE E FIL Doc. 3(III)(E).
- *KINGS COUNTY.* The motion must be filed with NYSCEF and the motion fee paid. NY R L KINGS E FIL Doc. 1(D). Court fees in NYSCEF cases must be paid via NYSCEF by a credit or bank card (MasterCard, Visa, or American Express). Fees are no longer accepted in person in the Kings County Clerk's Office in NYSCEF cases. NY R L KINGS E FIL Doc. 1(B)(6).
- *NEW YORK COUNTY.* A motion fee must be paid on motions made in writing by notice of motion, order to show cause or ex parte after the commencement of an action. For this purpose, the term "action" shall mean any application to the court that requires the assignment of an index number, regardless of whether a formal pleading is filed. Applications or motions that commence an action and for which an index number fee must be paid require no motion fee. [A]ny motions made after the initial applications in these situations would require payment of the motion fee. A motion that is the initial application in a case commenced by the filing of a summons and complaint would require a motion fee since the filing of the summons and complaint rather than the application itself would require the purchase of an index number. NY R NY CTY Procedure II(A). In e-filed cases the motion fee must be paid when the documents are filed. Payment is made on-line by Visa, Mastercard, or American Express credit or bank card. NY R NY CTY Procedure II(A); NY R NY CTY E FIL Doc. 2(B)(5).
- *ONONDAGA COUNTY.* Court fees in e-filed cases must be paid online with the NYSCEF system using a credit card. The document is not considered to have been filed until payment of the fee has been tendered. NY R ONDGA E FIL Protocol(B)(2). Fees must be paid on all cross motions. NY R ONDGA E FIL Protocol(B)(9)(e).
- *QUEENS COUNTY.* The Motion Support Office does not receive, forward or process any fees or waiver of fees. All applications requiring payment of statutory fees or waiver of fees must be sent directly to the Queens County Clerk's office. NY R L QUEENS MOT SUP Doc. 1. Court fees (e.g., RJI fee, motion fee) in E-filed cases may be paid for on-line using a credit card. Papers may also be filed with the E-file system and the fee may be paid at the County Clerk's Office. In the latter case, the paper is not considered to have been filed until payment of the fee has been tendered. NY R L QUEENS E-FILE Doc. 1(E)(1). The motion/petition shall be filed on-line and the fee paid for either on-line by credit card or by the "Pay at the County Clerk's Office" option. NY R L QUEENS E-FILE Doc. 1(H)(1).

v. *Working copies.* The court may require the parties to provide working copies of documents filed electronically.

In such event, each working copy shall include, firmly affixed thereto, a copy of a confirmation notice in a form prescribed by the Chief Administrator. NY R UNIF TRIAL CTS § 202.5-b(d)(5).

- *BRONX COUNTY.* After papers on motions have been e-filed, working copies thereof, with Confirmation Notice firmly attached as the back page facing out, must be submitted. (Each document or group of documents that is separately bound shall bear a Confirmation Notice.) Working copies lacking the Notice will not be accepted. WORKING COPIES OF MOTION PAPERS MUST BE SUBMITTED NO LATER THAN 4:45 P.M. ON THE RETURN DATE IN THE MOTION SUPPORT OFFICE (ROOM 217) AS EXPLAINED in NY R BRONX E FIL R Doc. 1(4). If an attorney has failed to submit required working copies on or before the return date, the motion will be transmitted as is to the Justice for such action as the Justice finds appropriate. Attorneys may submit working copies on motions by mail or overnight delivery. Any such submission shall be sent in a timely manner to the Motion Support Office (Room 217) and be conspicuously marked on the outside "NYSCEF Matter"; lack of such marking may delay processing. NY R BRONX E FIL R Doc. 1(4)(a).
- *ERIE COUNTY.* Electronically filed documents subject to review and processing by the Part Clerk do not require a working copy unless otherwise directed or provided for in IAS Part Rules. NY R UNIF TRIAL CTS § 202.5-b(d)(4), any working copy submitted shall include, as a cover page firmly fastened thereto, a copy of the Confirmation Notice generated by the NYSCEF site at the time of filing. Please consult the individual Justice's Part Rules and/or consult with the Judge's chambers to determine whether and how working copies are to be provided. Working copies will not be printed or delivered by the Erie County Clerk or the Chief Clerk of the Courts or any of their personnel to chambers. The official record of a document in an electronically filed case is the document filed via the NYSCEF system. Working copies are intended only for use by the Justice. The Court will discard all working copies after the Justice has finished with them. Thus, in the event that counsel fails to file a document via the NYSCEF system, the document will not be part of the court record. NY R ERIE E FIL Doc. 3(III)(O); NY R ERIE E FIL Doc. 3(V)(E).
- *KINGS COUNTY.* No courtesy copies of motion papers are required by the Court, except as may be required for electronic filing or by the Judge's Part Rules. In tort cases against the City of New York, courtesy copies shall be supplied to the Corporation Counsel's office in Brooklyn. NY R L KINGS Pt. C, Rule 5. Unless otherwise directed by the Court or as described herein, and with the exceptions listed below, in all NYSCEF cases in which an RJI has been filed, working copies of e-filed documents that are intended for judicial review must be submitted to the court. Working copies are not required of documents that are only processed by a support office (e.g. preliminary conference request, note of issue). Working copies shall include exhibit tabs and backs; for motion papers, the motion sequence number and the return date and part. The confirmation notice with the motion sequence number on it should be the back page of the motion facing out. In addition, the filer of a working copy must firmly bind thereto, with the back page facing out, a copy of the Confirmation Notice that was generated by NYSCEF when that document was efiled. Working copies that are submitted without the related Confirmation Notice will not be accepted. NY R L KINGS E FIL Doc. 1(B)(7); NY R L KINGS E FIL Doc. 1(D). WORKING COPIES OF MOTION PAPERS MUST BE SUBMITTED IN THE MOTION SUPPORT OFFICE (ROOM 227) AS EXPLAINED HEREIN. THEY MUST NOT BE DELIVERED TO THE PART OR CHAMBERS, EXCEPT WHERE THE INDIVIDUAL JUSTICE'S PART RULES PROVIDE OTHERWISE; DOING SO WILL CAUSE ADMINISTRATIVE CONFUSION AND POSSIBLE MISPLACEMENT OF PAPERS. Any such submission shall be sent in a timely manner (kindly review individual Justice's rules) and be conspicuously marked on the outside "NYSCEF Matter;" lack of such marking may delay processing. NY R L KINGS E FIL Doc. 1(D).
- *NEW YORK COUNTY.* Some Justices require that working copies of e-filed motion papers be submitted. See the E-filing Protocol for information on the many Parts that do not require working copies. Where required, working copies of the moving documents and all other documents on the motion or application shall be submitted to the Motion Submission Part Courtroom (Room 130) on, but not before, the final return date. A Confirmation Notice from the NYSCEF system, which is generated when a document is e-filed, shall be firmly affixed, as the back page facing out, to each separate working copy or group of such copies. NY R NY CTY Procedure II(A) NY R NY CTY E FIL Doc. 2(B)(5)(a); NY R NY CTY J RUL Rule 14(a). For more information on working copies, including which parts don't require them, refer to NY R NY CTY E FIL Doc. 2(B)(6).
- *ONONDAGA COUNTY.* Any courtesy "working" copies, if required (see NY R ONDGA E FIL Protocol(B)(7)), must be provided directly to the assigned justice. NY R ONDGA E FIL Protocol(B)(9)(e).

For information as to whether or not an Onondaga Supreme Court Justice requires working (courtesy) copies of e-filed documents, please consult the Onondaga County Individual E-filing Rules. NY R ONDGA E FIL Protocol(B)(7)(a). The Supreme Court Clerk's Office and the Onondaga County Clerk's Office will NOT accept the working copies. Working copies must be sent directly to the assigned justice's chambers. NY R ONDGA E FIL Protocol(B)(7)(b). A copy of the Confirmation Notice, generated by the NYSCEF system at the time a document is e-filed, must be attached to every working copy provided to chambers. If the Confirmation Notice is missing, the copy will not be accepted. NY R ONDGA E FIL Protocol(B)(7)(c). Courtesy copies do not become part of the official court record as maintained by the Onondaga County Clerk's Office and will be destroyed by chambers at the disposition of the case. In the event that counsel fails to file a document via NYSCEF, the document will not be part of the court record. NY R ONDGA E FIL Protocol(B)(7)(d).

- *QUEENS COUNTY.* Working copies of E-Filed notices of motion/notices of petition are NOT to be sent to the Motion Support Office. They must be brought to the calendar call in the judge's part. NY R L QUEENS MOT SUP Doc. 1. Unless otherwise directed or authorized by the court, counsel should file papers with the E-file system first and thereafter deliver a working copy to at the calendar call of the Centralized Motion Part or Assigned Justice in accordance with individual Part Rules. NY R L QUEENS E-FILE Doc. 1(E)(4). On the return date of a motion that has been E-filed, the movant must provide the Centralized Motion Part (CMP) with a working copy of the entire motion including the notice of motion with sequence number and all of the attached exhibits. The motion must have the confirmation of filing firmly affixed to the back of the papers (facing outward). The confirmation of filing is a separate notice from the payment notice and will say confirmation clearly across the top of the page. NY R L QUEENS E-FILE Doc. 1(H)(2)(a). The motion or Order to Show Cause must have clearly written across its face the words "Working Copy," it must also have the assigned Judge's name, motion sequence number and calendar number—which may be obtained from the posted calendar outside courtroom on the return date of the motion. A confirmation of filing must attached thereto. Working copies of e-filed Orders to Show Cause must contain a copy of the signed order and all supporting papers. NY R L QUEENS E-FILE Doc. 1(H)(2)(c). The Confirmation Notice must be an updated version that indicates the sequence number of the motion being submitted at the CMP calendar call. WORKING COPIES WITHOUT A CONFIRMATION NOTICE WILL NOT BE ACCEPTED. NY R L QUEENS E-FILE Doc. 1(H)(7).

vi. *ERIE COUNTY: Additional supplemental documents*

- *Notice of hard copy submission in e-filed case.* In accordance with NY R UNIF TRIAL CTS § 202.5-b(d), the County Clerk shall refuse to accept for filing, hard copy papers filed to an action subject to electronic filing unless hard copy filing is permitted by the Uniform Rules or NY R ERIE E FIL Doc. 3 and the papers bear a completed Notice of Hard Copy Submission—E-Filed Case form. NY R ERIE E FIL Doc. 3(III)(D).

vii. *KINGS COUNTY: Additional supplemental documents*

- *Forms when filing in hard copy.* An attorney who certifies in good faith that he or she lacks the equipment or knowledge needed to e-file and have no staff member or employee under his or her direction who has such knowledge and equipment may opt out of participation in e-filing in a mandatory case by filing a "Notice of Opt-Out from Participation in Action Subject to Mandatory Electronic Filing" form EFM-2 with the Clerk. NY R L KINGS E FIL Doc. 1(A)(2). Where in accordance with the E-Filing Rules a party submits a document in hard copy in an e-filed case (principally, a document submitted by a nonparticipating party (e.g., an attorney) in a consensual case, an emergency filing made in accordance with the Mandatory E-Filing Rules, and any document filed with the court in hard copy by an attorney who has opted out of participation in mandatory e-filing, the document must bear the back page facing out, a "Notice of Hard Copy Submission—E-Filed Cases" form EFM-3. NY R L KINGS E FIL Doc. 1(B)(3).

viii. *NEW YORK COUNTY: Additional supplemental documents*

- *Notice of hard copy submission.* Where in accordance with the E-Filing Rules an attorney or an unrepresented litigant who is participating in e-filing submits a document in hard copy in an e-filed case, the document must bear, as the back page facing out, a Notice of Hard-Copy Submission—E-Filed Case (a form available in the "Forms" section on the NYSCEF website (Form EFM-3) and in the court's back offices). NY R NY CTY E FIL Doc. 2(B)(3). For more information refer to NY R NY CTY E FIL Doc. 2.
- *Unpublished decisions.* Whenever reliance is placed upon a decision or other authority not officially published or readily available to the New York County Supreme Court, a copy of the case or of pertinent portions of the authority shall be submitted with the motion papers. NY R NY CTY J RUL Rule 14(a).

ix. *ONONDAGA COUNTY: Additional supplemental documents*

- *Notice of hard copy submission.* Any papers to be filed with the court in an e-filed case must be filed online with the E-filing system except where a special exemption is granted (e.g., oversized maps, photographs). If such an exemption is granted, Form EFM-3, "Notice of Hard Copy Submission—E-Filed Case," must be attached to such documents forms which are not filed on line. Also, Form EFM-4 "Notice of Hard Copy Exhibit Filing" must be completed and uploaded to the action's e-file. Both of these forms may be found on the NYSCEF website. NY R ONDGA E FIL Protocol(B)(4).

x. *QUEENS COUNTY: Additional supplemental documents*

- *Notice of hard copy submission.* Any party opting out of the e-filing system must have a "Notice of Hard Copy Submission" firmly affixed to the back of the papers. NY R L QUEENS E-FILE Doc. 1(H)(2)(f).

2. *Documents for opposing party*

a. *Required documents*

i. *Opposition.* Refer to the General Requirements section of this document for information on the opposition.

- *Request for oral argument.* A party requesting oral argument shall set forth such request in its notice of motion or in its order to show cause or on the first page of the answering papers, as the case may be. Where all parties to a motion request oral argument, oral argument shall be granted unless the court shall determine it to be unnecessary. Where a motion is brought on by order to show cause, the court may set forth in the order that oral argument is required on the return date of the motion. NY R UNIF TRIAL CTS § 202.8(d).
- *QUEENS COUNTY: E-filing opposition papers.* E-filed opposition papers and/or reply papers must also be provided to the Centralized Motion Part in the same manner as the moving papers with the confirmation of filing firmly attached to the back of the papers. NY R L QUEENS E-FILE Doc. 1(H)(2)(d).

ii. *Proof of service.* In addition to complying with the provisions of NY CPLR Rule 2101, every paper filed in court shall have annexed thereto appropriate proof of service on all parties where required. NY R UNIF TRIAL CTS § 202.5(a).

b. *Supplemental documents*

i. *Supporting evidence; Exhibits.* The main supporting papers on a motion are affidavits, but any relevant exhibits, documents, depositions, etc., are also includible. SIEGEL-NYPRAC § 246.

- *Affidavits accompanying opposition.* Affidavits shall be for a statement of the relevant facts. NY R UNIF TRIAL CTS § 202.8(c).
- *Foreign language documents.* Where an affidavit or exhibit annexed to a paper served or filed is in a foreign language, it shall be accompanied by an English translation and an affidavit by the translator stating his qualifications and that the translation is accurate. NY CPLR Rule 2101(b).
- *Statement of attorney in lieu of affidavit.* The statement of an attorney admitted to practice in the courts of the state, or of a physician, osteopath or dentist, authorized by law to practice in the state, who is not a party to an action, when subscribed and affirmed by him to be true under the penalties of perjury, may be served or filed in the action in lieu of and with the same force and effect as an affidavit. NY CPLR Rule 2106.
- *NEW YORK COUNTY: Form of presented exhibits.* Exhibits should be tabbed and be legible; a typed version of any exhibit that is difficult to read should be submitted with the original. Exhibits printed on both sides of the page should be bound and tabbed on the side. NY R NY CTY J RUL Rule 14(a).
- *QUEENS COUNTY.* Attorneys submitting exhibits to the court on E-file cases shall make each exhibit a separate, labeled attachment to an affidavit/affirmation. NY R L QUEENS E-FILE Doc. 1(H)(4).

ii. *Brief.* Briefs shall be for a statement of the relevant law. NY R UNIF TRIAL CTS § 202.8(c).

iii. *Filing fees.* The County Clerk shall require the payment of any applicable statutory fees, or an order of the Court waiving payment of such fees, before accepting a paper for filing. NY R UNIF TRIAL CTS § 202.5(d)(1). For information on filing fees, if any, refer to NY CPLR § 8001, et seq.

- *ALBANY COUNTY.* In general, any filing subsequent to the commencement of an action which is designated as a motion or cross-motion requires the payment of a filing fee to the County Clerk's Office prior to submission to the Supreme Court Clerk's Office for referral to the assigned justice. The fee is assessed regardless of whether an application is made by notice of motion, order to show cause or ex parte. No fee will be charged upon the filing of a motion for poor person status in conjunction with an application which serves to commence an action or special proceeding. In the event a motion is received by the court unaccompanied by proof of payment to the County Clerk, the Supreme Court Clerk's Office will contact the submitting party to advise that the application will be held pending receipt of the filing fee only until the return date of the motion. If proof of payment is not submitted to the Supreme Court Clerk's Office by the return date (ex parte applications will be held ten (10) days), the papers will be returned by mail with a notification that the motion has been removed from the court's calendar and that it must be re-noticed and re-filed with the court along with the requisite filing fee. Inquiries concerning the applicability of the motion fee to a proposed filing may be directed to the Supreme Court Clerk's Office. NY R 3 JD SUP Doc. 1(B).

- *BRONX COUNTY.* In accordance with the new civil fee schedule set forth in Article 80 of the C.P.L.R. (NY CPLR § 8001, et seq.), effective July 14, 2003, all motions, and cross motions must be approved in Room 217 prior to payment of said fees in the County Clerk's Office, Room 118. NY R BRONX FIL R Doc. 8. The motion fee [must be] paid for via NYSCEF by credit/debit card. NY R BRONX E FIL R Doc. 1(1).
- *ERIE COUNTY.* Payment for fee-bearing NYSCEF documents must be made online via credit or debit card (American Express, MasterCard or Visa) at the time of submission. NY R ERIE E FIL Doc. 3(III)(E).
- *KINGS COUNTY.* The motion must be filed with NYSCEF and the motion fee paid. NY R L KINGS E FIL Doc. 1(D). Court fees in NYSCEF cases must be paid via NYSCEF by a credit or bank card (MasterCard, Visa, or American Express). Fees are no longer accepted in person in the Kings County Clerk's Office in NYSCEF cases. NY R L KINGS E FIL Doc. 1(B)(6).
- *NEW YORK COUNTY.* A motion fee must be paid on motions made in writing by notice of motion, order to show cause or ex parte after the commencement of an action. For this purpose, the term "action" shall mean any application to the court that requires the assignment of an index number, regardless of whether a formal pleading is filed. Applications or motions that commence an action and for which an index number fee must be paid require no motion fee. [A]ny motions made after the initial applications in these situations would require payment of the motion fee. A motion that is the initial application in a case commenced by the filing of a summons and complaint would require a motion fee since the filing of the summons and complaint rather than the application itself would require the purchase of an index number. NY R NY CTY Procedure II(A). In e-filed cases the motion fee must be paid when the documents are filed. Payment is made on-line by Visa, Mastercard, or American Express credit or bank card. NY R NY CTY Procedure II(A); NY R NY CTY E FIL Doc. 2(B)(5).
- *ONONDAGA COUNTY.* Court fees in e-filed cases must be paid online with the NYSCEF system using a credit card. The document is not considered to have been filed until payment of the fee has been tendered. NY R ONDGA E FIL Protocol(B)(2). Fees must be paid on all cross motions. NY R ONDGA E FIL Protocol(B)(9)(e).
- *QUEENS COUNTY.* The Motion Support Office does not receive, forward or process any fees or waiver of fees. All applications requiring payment of statutory fees or waiver of fees must be sent directly to the Queens County Clerk's office. NY R L QUEENS MOT SUP Doc. 1. Court fees (e.g., RJI fee, motion fee) in E-filed cases may be paid for on-line using a credit card. Papers may also be filed with the E-file system and the fee may be paid at the County Clerk's Office. In the latter case, the paper is not considered to have been filed until payment of the fee has been tendered. NY R L QUEENS E-FILE Doc. 1(E)(1). The motion/petition shall be filed on-line and the fee paid for either on-line by credit card or by the "Pay at the County Clerk's Office" option. NY R L QUEENS E-FILE Doc. 1(H)(1).

iv. *Working copies.* The court may require the parties to provide working copies of documents filed electronically. In such event, each working copy shall include, firmly affixed thereto, a copy of a confirmation notice in a form prescribed by the Chief Administrator. NY R UNIF TRIAL CTS § 202.5-b(d)(5).

- *BRONX COUNTY.* After papers on motions have been e-filed, working copies thereof, with Confirmation Notice firmly attached as the back page facing out, must be submitted. (Each document or group of documents that is separately bound shall bear a Confirmation Notice.) Working copies lacking the Notice will not be accepted. WORKING COPIES OF MOTION PAPERS MUST BE SUBMITTED NO LATER THAN 4:45 P.M. ON THE RETURN DATE IN THE MOTION SUPPORT OFFICE (ROOM 217) AS EXPLAINED in NY R BRONX E FIL R Doc. 1(4). If an attorney has failed to submit required working copies on or before the return date, the motion will be transmitted as is to the Justice for such action as the Justice finds appropriate. Attorneys may submit working copies on motions by mail or overnight delivery. Any such submission shall be sent in a timely manner to the Motion Support Office (Room 217) and be conspicuously marked on the outside "NYSCEF Matter"; lack of such marking may delay processing. NY R BRONX E FIL R Doc. 1(4)(a).

- *ERIE COUNTY.* Electronically filed documents subject to review and processing by the Part Clerk do not require a working copy unless otherwise directed or provided for in IAS Part Rules. NY R UNIF TRIAL CTS § 202.5-b(d)(4), any working copy submitted shall include, as a cover page firmly fastened thereto, a copy of the Confirmation Notice generated by the NYSCEF site at the time of filing. Please consult the individual Justice's Part Rules and/or consult with the Judge's chambers to determine whether and how working copies are to be provided. Working copies will not be printed or delivered by the Erie County Clerk or the Chief Clerk of the Courts or any of their personnel to chambers. The official record of a document in an electronically filed case is the document filed via the NYSCEF system. Working copies are intended only for use by the Justice. The Court will discard all working copies after the Justice has finished with them. Thus, in the event that counsel fails to file a document via the NYSCEF system, the document will not be part of the court record. NY R ERIE E FIL Doc. 3(III)(O); NY R ERIE E FIL Doc. 3(V)(E).
- *KINGS COUNTY.* No courtesy copies of motion papers are required by the Court, except as may be required for electronic filing or by the Judge's Part Rules. In tort cases against the City of New York, courtesy copies shall be supplied to the Corporation Counsel's office in Brooklyn. NY R L KINGS Pt. C, Rule 5. Unless otherwise directed by the Court or as described herein, and with the exceptions listed below, in all NYSCEF cases in which an RJI has been filed, working copies of e-filed documents that are intended for judicial review must be submitted to the court. Working copies are not required of documents that are only processed by a support office (e.g. preliminary conference request, note of issue). Working copies shall include exhibit tabs and backs; for motion papers, the motion sequence number and the return date and part. The confirmation notice with the motion sequence number on it should be the back page of the motion facing out. In addition, the filer of a working copy must firmly bind thereto, with the back page facing out, a copy of the Confirmation Notice that was generated by NYSCEF when that document was efiled. Working copies that are submitted without the related Confirmation Notice will not be accepted. NY R L KINGS E FIL Doc. 1(B)(7); NY R L KINGS E FIL Doc. 1(D). WORKING COPIES OF MOTION PAPERS MUST BE SUBMITTED IN THE MOTION SUPPORT OFFICE (ROOM 227) AS EXPLAINED HEREIN. THEY MUST NOT BE DELIVERED TO THE PART OR CHAMBERS, EXCEPT WHERE THE INDIVIDUAL JUSTICE'S PART RULES PROVIDE OTHERWISE; DOING SO WILL CAUSE ADMINISTRATIVE CONFUSION AND POSSIBLE MISPLACEMENT OF PAPERS. Any such submission shall be sent in a timely manner (kindly review individual Justice's rules) and be conspicuously marked on the outside "NYSCEF Matter;" lack of such marking may delay processing. NY R L KINGS E FIL Doc. 1(D).
- *NEW YORK COUNTY.* Some Justices require that working copies of e-filed motion papers be submitted. See the E-filing Protocol for information on the many Parts that do not require working copies. Where required, working copies of the moving documents and all other documents on the motion or application shall be submitted to the Motion Submission Part Courtroom (Room 130) on, but not before, the final return date. A Confirmation Notice from the NYSCEF system, which is generated when a document is e-filed, shall be firmly affixed, as the back page facing out, to each separate working copy or group of such copies. NY R NY CTY Procedure II(A) NY R NY CTY E FIL Doc. 2(B)(5)(a); NY R NY CTY J RUL Rule 14(a). For more information on working copies, including which parts don't require them, refer to NY R NY CTY E FIL Doc. 2(B)(6).
- *ONONDAGA COUNTY.* Any courtesy "working" copies, if required (see NY R ONDGA E FIL Protocol(B)(7)), must be provided directly to the assigned justice. NY R ONDGA E FIL Protocol(B)(9)(e). For information as to whether or not an Onondaga Supreme Court Justice requires working (courtesy) copies of e-filed documents, please consult the Onondaga County Individual E-filing Rules. NY R ONDGA E FIL Protocol(B)(7)(a). The Supreme Court Clerk's Office and the Onondaga County Clerk's Office will NOT accept the working copies. Working copies must be sent directly to the assigned justice's chambers. NY R ONDGA E FIL Protocol(B)(7)(b). A copy of the Confirmation Notice, generated by the NYSCEF system at the time a document is e-filed, must be attached to every working copy provided to chambers. If the Confirmation Notice is missing, the copy will not be accepted. NY R ONDGA E FIL Protocol(B)(7)(c). Courtesy copies do not become part of the official court record as maintained by the Onondaga County Clerk's Office and will be destroyed by chambers at the disposition of the case. In the event that counsel fails to file a document via NYSCEF, the document will not be part of the court record. NY R ONDGA E FIL Protocol(B)(7)(d).

- *QUEENS COUNTY.* Working copies of E-Filed notices of motion/notices of petition are NOT to be sent to the Motion Support Office. They must be brought to the calendar call in the judge's part. NY R L QUEENS MOT SUP Doc. 1. Unless otherwise directed or authorized by the court, counsel should file papers with the E-file system first and thereafter deliver a working copy to at the calendar call of the Centralized Motion Part or Assigned Justice in accordance with individual Part Rules. NY R L QUEENS E-FILE Doc. 1(E)(4). On the return date of a motion that has been E-filed, the movant must provide the Centralized Motion Part (CMP) with a working copy of the entire motion including the notice of motion with sequence number and all of the attached exhibits. The motion must have the confirmation of filing firmly affixed to the back of the papers (facing outward). The confirmation of filing is a separate notice from the payment notice and will say confirmation clearly across the top of the page. NY R L QUEENS E-FILE Doc. 1(H)(2)(a). The motion or Order to Show Cause must have clearly written across its face the words "Working Copy," it must also have the assigned Judge's name, motion sequence number and calendar number—which may be obtained from the posted calendar outside courtroom on the return date of the motion. A confirmation of filing must attached thereto. Working copies of e-filed Orders to Show Cause must contain a copy of the signed order and all supporting papers. NY R L QUEENS E-FILE Doc. 1(H)(2)(c). The Confirmation Notice must be an updated version that indicates the sequence number of the motion being submitted at the CMP calendar call. WORKING COPIES WITHOUT A CONFIRMATION NOTICE WILL NOT BE ACCEPTED. NY R L QUEENS E-FILE Doc. 1(H)(7).

v. *ERIE COUNTY: Additional supplemental documents*

- *Notice of hard copy submission in e-filed case.* In accordance with NY R UNIF TRIAL CTS § 202.5-b(d), the County Clerk shall refuse to accept for filing, hard copy papers filed to an action subject to electronic filing unless hard copy filing is permitted by the Uniform Rules or NY R ERIE E FIL Doc. 3 and the papers bear a completed Notice of Hard Copy Submission—E-Filed Case form. NY R ERIE E FIL Doc. 3(III)(D).

vi. *KINGS COUNTY: Additional supplemental documents*

- *Forms when filing in hard copy.* An attorney who certifies in good faith that he or she lacks the equipment or knowledge needed to e-file and have no staff member or employee under his or her direction who has such knowledge and equipment may opt out of participation in e-filing in a mandatory case by filing a "Notice of Opt-Out from Participation in Action Subject to Mandatory Electronic Filing" form EFM-2 with the Clerk. NY R L KINGS E FIL Doc. 1(A)(2). Where in accordance with the E-Filing Rules a party submits a document in hard copy in an e-filed case (principally, a document submitted by a nonparticipating party (e.g., an attorney) in a consensual case, an emergency filing made in accordance with the Mandatory E-Filing Rules, and any document filed with the court in hard copy by an attorney who has opted out of participation in mandatory e-filing, the document must bear the back page facing out, a "Notice of Hard Copy Submission—E-Filed Cases" form EFM-3. NY R L KINGS E FIL Doc. 1(B)(3).

vii. *NEW YORK COUNTY: Additional supplemental documents*

- *Notice of hard copy submission.* Where in accordance with the E-Filing Rules an attorney or an unrepresented litigant who is participating in e-filing submits a document in hard copy in an e-filed case, the document must bear, as the back page facing out, a Notice of Hard-Copy Submission—E-Filed Case (a form available in the "Forms" section on the NYSCEF website (Form EFM-3) and in the court's back offices). NY R NY CTY E FIL Doc. 2(B)(3). For more information refer to NY R NY CTY E FIL Doc. 2.
- *Unpublished decisions.* Whenever reliance is placed upon a decision or other authority not officially published or readily available to the New York County Supreme Court, a copy of the case or of pertinent portions of the authority shall be submitted with the motion papers. NY R NY CTY J RUL Rule 14(a).

viii. *ONONDAGA COUNTY: Additional supplemental documents*

- *Notice of hard copy submission.* Any papers to be filed with the court in an e-filed case must be filed online with the E-filing system except where a special exemption is granted (e.g., oversized maps, photographs). If such an exemption is granted, Form EFM-3, "Notice of Hard Copy Submission—E-Filed Case," must be attached to such documents forms which are not filed on line. Also, Form EFM-4 "Notice of Hard Copy Exhibit Filing" must be completed and uploaded to the action's e-file. Both of these forms may be found on the NYSCEF website. NY R ONDGA E FIL Protocol(B)(4).

ix. *QUEENS COUNTY: Additional supplemental documents*

- *Notice of hard copy submission.* Any party opting out of the e-filing system must have a "Notice of Hard Copy Submission" firmly affixed to the back of the papers. NY R L QUEENS E-FILE Doc. 1(H)(2)(f).

E. Format

1. *Form of documents*

   a. *Size and form of paper.* Each paper served or filed shall be durable, white and, except for summonses, subpoenas, notices of appearance, notes of issue, orders of protection, temporary orders of protection and exhibits, shall be eleven by eight and one-half (11 x 8-1/2) inches in size. NY CPLR Rule 2101(a).

   b. *Writing and language.* The writing shall be legible and in black ink. NY CPLR Rule 2101(a). Each paper served or filed shall be in the English language which, where practicable, shall be of ordinary usage. NY CPLR Rule 2101(b).

   c. *Caption.* Each paper served or filed shall begin with a caption setting forth the name of the court, the venue, the title of the action, the nature of the paper and the index number of the action if one has been assigned. In all papers other than a summons, a complaint or a judgment it shall be sufficient to state the name of the first named party on each side with an appropriate indication of any omissions. NY CPLR Rule 2101(c).

      i. *Further contents of first page.* After the first paper has been filed in each case the index number shall appear on the cover and first page to the right of the caption of every paper tendered for filing in the action. Each such cover and first page also shall contain an indication of the county of venue and a brief description of the nature of the paper and, where the case has been assigned to an individual judge, shall contain the name of the assigned judge to the right of the caption. NY R UNIF TRIAL CTS § 202.5(a); NY R UNIF TRIAL CTS § 202.5(b); NY R UNIF TRIAL CTS § 202.5(d)(1)(i).

      ii. *ALBANY COUNTY: Request for oral argument.* A party may request oral argument on a motion by indicating such request on the first page of the notice of motion, order to show cause, or answering papers in the area across from the caption of the action/proceeding. NY R 3 JD SUP Doc. 1(B).

      iii. *NEW YORK COUNTY: Request for oral argument.* Counsel who wish oral argument must so request conspicuously on the front of their papers. NY R NY CTY Procedure II(D).

   d. *Index number.* No paper in an action in the supreme or a county court, other than an order submitted for signature to a judge out of court, shall be submitted for any purpose to the supreme or county court or to a clerk thereof unless there is endorsed on such paper the index number of the action assigned by the clerk of the county. NY CPLR § 8018(c).

      i. *ALBANY COUNTY: Index number on all filed documents.* The index number, the request for judicial intervention number and the assigned justice's name shall appear on [all papers filed with the Court subsequent to the complaint]. NY R 3 JD SUP Doc. 1(A).

      ii. *ERIE COUNTY: Index number after initial filing.* Cases that are initially commenced by the filing of papers with the NYSCEF system are identified as e-filed cases by assignment of an Index Number that has "800-899" as the first three (3) digits of the index number (i.e. 802391/2012). NY R ERIE E FIL Doc. 3(II). [The] Index Number must be affixed to all document submissions, filings, and communications to the Erie County Clerk and the Court. Cases that are converted from paper to e-filing shall retain the original index number. NY R ERIE E FIL Doc. 3(II).

      iii. *KINGS COUNTY: Index number after initial filing.* In cases commenced electronically by the filing of initiating papers with the NYSCEF system and payment of the statutory fees, the Kings County Clerk will issue an NYSCEF designated index number and the filer shall be notified via the NYSCEF system of the index number assigned and filing date. Such index number must be affixed to all document submissions, filings and communications to the Kings County Clerk and Supreme Court. If counsel faces exigent circumstances that require accelerated assignment, counsel may contact Administration of the Kings County Clerk at kcco-efile@nycourts.gov, during normal business hours of the court. NY R L KINGS E FIL Doc. 1(B)(5).

      iv. *NEW YORK COUNTY: Index number on hard copy filings.* Papers subsequently presented for filing in hardcopy format will be filed in this jacket. NY R NY CTY Procedure I(B). Index numbers take the form of six digits followed by a slash and the four digits of the year the case began, e.g., 340705/2018. The first or first two integers of the index number identify the type of case. If a case is commenced electronically, the second integer will be a "5", except as indicated otherwise in the list below. There are many tax certiorari matters e-filed annually and the index numbers therefor will normally run over into those with a "6" as the second integer, and the same will occur with general cases if necessary. The principal types of cases and their index number categories are listed in NY R NY CTY Procedure I(B). NY R NY CTY Procedure I(B); NY R NY CTY Procedure XI(A).

      v. *ONONDAGA COUNTY: Index number.* The index number must be referenced on all e-filed documents and correspondence. All e-filed case index numbers will contain the letters "EF" between the year and the file number (for example, 2012EF9999). NY R ONDGA E FIL Protocol(B)(1).

vi. *QUEENS COUNTY: Index number on converted cases.* Cases originally commenced in hard-copy form but later converted to an E-file case, either by stipulation or order will bear a regular index number initially. The County Clerk will issue a new E-file index number. NY R L QUEENS E-FILE Doc. 1(B).

e. *Line spacing.* Every paper filed in court, if typewritten, shall have at least double space between each line, except for quotations and the names and addresses of attorneys appearing in the action. NY R UNIF TRIAL CTS § 202.5(a).

f. *Font size.* Each. . .paper printed or typed, served or filed, except for summonses. . .and exhibits, shall be in clear type of no less than ten (10) point in size. NY CPLR Rule 2101(a).

i. Whenever a requirement relating to size of type is stated in point size, the type size requirement shall be deemed met if the x-height of the type is a minimum of forty-five percent (45%) of the specified point size. Each point shall be measured as .351 millimeter. The x-height size shall be measured as it appears on the page. The x-height is the height of the lower case letters, exclusive of ascenders or descenders. NY CPLR § 105(t).

g. *Margins.* Every paper filed in court shall have at least one (1) inch margins. NY R UNIF TRIAL CTS § 202.5(a).

h. *Citations*

i. *Civil practice law and rules.* NY CPLR § 101, et seq. shall be known as the civil practice law and rules, and may be cited as "CPLR". Reference to a provision in the civil practice law and rules may, except when such provision is being enacted or amended, be made without indicating whether it is a rule or section. NY CPLR § 101.

i. *Indorsement by attorney.* Each paper served or filed shall be indorsed with the name, address and telephone number of the attorney for the party serving or filing the paper, or if the party does not appear by attorney, with the name, address and telephone number of the party. NY CPLR Rule 2101(d).

j. *One-sided printing.* In addition, every paper filed in court, other than an exhibit or printed form, shall contain writing on one side only, except that papers that are fastened on the side may contain writing on both sides. NY R UNIF TRIAL CTS § 202.5(a).

k. *Use of copies authorized.* Except where otherwise specifically prescribed, copies, rather than originals, of all papers, including orders, affidavits and exhibits may be served or filed. Where it is required that the original be served or filed and the original is lost or withheld, the court may authorize a copy to be served or filed. NY CPLR Rule 2101(e).

i. Where a certified copy of a paper is required by law, an attorney admitted to practice in the courts of the state may certify that it has been compared by him with the original and found to be a true and complete copy. Such a certificate, when subscribed by such attorney, has the same effect as if made by a clerk. NY CPLR § 2105.

l. *Recycled paper.* It is the policy of the Unified Court System that litigants, where practicable, should file or submit to the courts of the Unified Court System of the State of New York papers printed or reproduced on recycled paper. Paper is considered recycled if it contains a minimum content of thirty percent (30%) waste paper. NY R UNIF TRIAL CTS § 215.2. The signature page of every paper filed or submitted to the court on recycled paper should bear the legend: "Printed [Reproduced] on Recycled Paper." NY R UNIF TRIAL CTS § 215.3.

m. *Form of request for judicial intervention; Copies.* A request for judicial intervention must be submitted, in duplicate, on a form authorized by the Chief of the Courts, with proof of service on the other parties to the action (but proof of service is not required where the application is ex parte). NY R UNIF TRIAL CTS § 202.6(a).

n. *KINGS COUNTY: Tabs on filings.* Motions, orders and other filed papers shall be indexed with protruding tabs. Clerks are required to reject papers that do not have protruding exhibit tabs, except papers in matrimonial cases and papers filed by pro se litigants. NY R L KINGS Pt. A, Papers.

o. *NEW YORK COUNTY: Length of briefs.* Unless advance permission otherwise is granted by the court for good cause, memoranda of law shall not exceed thirty (30) pages each (exclusive of table of contents and table of authorities) and affidavits/affirmations shall not exceed twenty-five (25) pages each. NY R NY CTY J RUL Rule 14(b).

p. *QUEENS COUNTY: Form and size of motion filings.* All motions filed in Queens Supreme Court-Civil Term, must adhere to the Motion Support rules and the rules of the assigned judge. NY R L QUEENS MOT SUP Doc. 1. Due to space limitations, the Motion Support Office cannot accept notices of motion/notices of petition and accompanying exhibits which measure greater than eight (8) inches. If your documents measure greater than eight (8) inches you are directed to submit only the notice of motion/notice of petition to the Motion Support Office and bring all exhibits to the calendar call on your return date. NY R L QUEENS MOT SUP Doc. 1.

2. *Form of electronic documents.* Each paper served or filed by electronic means, as defined in NY CPLR Rule 2103(f), shall

be capable of being reproduced by the receiver so as to comply with the provisions of NY CPLR Rule 2101(a) through NY CPLR Rule 2101(d). NY CPLR Rule 2101(g).

a. *File format.* All e-filed documents shall comply with the technical requirements set forth at the NYSCEF site. NY R UNIF TRIAL CTS § 202.5-b(d)(1)(i).

b. *Heading of document.* The subject matter heading for each paper sent by electronic means must indicate that the matter being transmitted electronically is related to a court proceeding. NY CPLR Rule 2103(b)(7).

c. *E-filed documents identification*

i. *ERIE COUNTY.* E-filed cases must be readily identifiable and marked as such. If counsel presents papers to the Office of the Erie County Clerk or the Office of the Chief Clerk in a NYSCEF matter where authorized, counsel should alert the Clerk that the case is a NYSCEF matter. NY R ERIE E FIL Doc. 3(II).

ii. *KINGS COUNTY.* The Supreme Court's Civil Case Information System ("CCIS") will further identify e-filed cases by the addition of a suffix to the index number (e.g. 500136/2006E). This suffix should be used on all documents filed with the court in e-filed matters. NY R L KINGS E FIL Doc. 1(A)(1).

3. *Signature blocks.* Every pleading, written motion, and other paper, served on another party or filed or submitted to the court shall be signed by an attorney, or by a party if the party is not represented by an attorney, with the name of the attorney or party clearly printed or typed directly below the signature. NY R CHIEF ADMIN § 130-1.1-a(a); NY R UNIF TRIAL CTS § 202.5(d)(1)(iv).

a. *Printed name.* Beneath each signature shall be printed the name signed. NY CPLR Rule 2101(a).

b. *Failure to sign.* Absent good cause shown, the court shall strike any unsigned paper if the omission of the signature is not corrected promptly after being called to the attention of the attorney or party. NY R CHIEF ADMIN § 130-1.1-a(a).

c. *Signature as certification.* By signing a paper, an attorney or party certifies that, to the best of that person's knowledge, information and belief, formed after an inquiry reasonable under the circumstances the presentation of the paper or the contentions therein are not frivolous as defined in NY R CHIEF ADMIN § 130-1.1(c). NY R CHIEF ADMIN § 130-1.1-a(b)(1).

d. *Electronic signatures.* A document shall be considered to have been signed by an attorney or party in compliance with NY R CHIEF ADMIN § 130-1.1-a if it has been signed by such attorney or party as provided in NY R UNIF TRIAL CTS § 202.5-b(e)(1) and it bears the signatory's name. NY R UNIF TRIAL CTS § 202.5-b(e)(2). An electronically filed document shall be considered to have been signed by, and shall be binding upon, the person identified as a signatory, if:

i. It bears the physical signature of such person and is scanned into an electronic format that reproduces such signature; or

ii. The signatory has electronically affixed the digital image of his or her signature to the document; or

iii. It is electronically filed under the User ID and password of that person; or

iv. In a tax certiorari action in which the parties have stipulated to this procedure, it is an initiating document that is electronically filed without the signature of the signatory in a form provided above in NY R UNIF TRIAL CTS § 202.5-b(e)(iv), provided that, prior to filing, the document is signed in full in hard copy (which hard copy must be preserved until the conclusion of all proceedings, including appeals, in the case in which it is filed); or

v. In a small claims assessment review proceeding, it is a petition recorded by the NYSCEF site upon the filing of a text file as provided in NY R UNIF TRIAL CTS § 202.5-b(b)(1), provided that prior to filing, the document was signed in full in hard copy (which hard copy must be preserved until the conclusion of all proceedings in the matter, including article 78 (NY CPLR § 7801, et seq.) review and any appeals, and must be made available during the proceeding upon request of the respondent or the court); or

vi. It otherwise bears the electronic signature of the signatory in a format conforming to such standards and requirements as may hereafter be established by the Chief Administrator. NY R UNIF TRIAL CTS § 202.5-b(e).

4. *Confidentiality of personal information.* No person may file any document available for public inspection with any state agency, political subdivision, or in any court of this state that contains a Social Security account number of any other person, unless such other person is a dependent child, or has consented to such filing, except as required by federal or state law or regulation, or by court rule. NY GEN BUS § 399-ddd. Submissions pursuant to e-filing procedures shall have the same confidentiality rights as paper documents. NY R UNIF TRIAL CTS § 202.5-b(k)(1).

a. *Confidential personal information.* Except in the actions designated in NY R UNIF TRIAL CTS § 202.5(e)(1), or as

otherwise provided by rule or law or court order, and whether or not a sealing order is or has been sought, the parties shall omit or redact confidential personal information in papers submitted to the court for filing. For purposes of NY R UNIF TRIAL CTS § 202.5(e), confidential personal information ("CPI") means:

i. The taxpayer identification number of an individual or an entity, including a Social Security number, an employer identification number, and an individual taxpayer identification number, except the last four (4) digits thereof;

ii. The date of an individual's birth, except the year thereof;

iii. The full name of an individual known to be a minor, except the minor's initials;

iv. A financial account number, including a credit and/or debit card number, a bank account number, an investment account number, and/or an insurance account number, except the last four (4) digits or letters thereof; and

v. Any of the documents or testimony in a matrimonial action protected by NY DOM REL § 235 or evidence sealed by the court in such an action which are attached as exhibits or referenced in the papers filed in any other civil action. For purposes of NY R UNIF TRIAL CTS § 202.5, a matrimonial action shall mean: an action to annul a marriage or declare the nullity of a void marriage, an action or agreement for a separation, an action for a divorce, or an action or proceeding for custody, visitation, writ of habeus corpus, child support, maintenance or paternity. NY R UNIF TRIAL CTS § 202.5(e)(1).

vi. *ERIE COUNTY.* An attorney or unrepresented litigant filing a document via the NYSCEF system must comply with the requirements of NY R UNIF TRIAL CTS § 202.5(e) regarding the redaction of Confidential Personal Information and NY GEN BUS § 399-ddd(6) concerning the filing of documents containing Social Security Numbers. It is the sole responsibility of counsel or unrepresented litigant filing to be aware of and to comply with existing laws requiring non-disclosure of personal information contained in any document e-filed in NYSCEF. NY R ERIE E FIL Doc. 3(III)(G); NY R ERIE E FIL Doc. 3(III).

vii. *KINGS COUNTY.* An attorney or unrepresented litigant filing a document via the NYSCEF system must comply with the requirements of General Business Law § 399-dd(6), which often require redaction of any Social Security number that appear in the original document. The NYSCEF system automatically redacts portions of filed documents which apparently contain Social Security numbers pursuant to NY R UNIF TRIAL CTS § 202.5-b(k). In the event the filing party receives e-mail notice through NYSCEF that a Social Security number in a filed document has been redacted, and the filing party concludes such redaction is erroneous, the filer should click on the link provided in the e-mail to permit the County Clerk to revert the redaction. For Confidential Personal Information, see NY R UNIF TRIAL CTS § 202.5(e) and NY R L KINGS E FIL Doc. 1(B)(11). [Editor's note: the reference to General Business Law § 399-dd(6) is likely a reference to NY GEN BUS § 399-ddd(6)]. NY R L KINGS E FIL Doc. 1(B)(10); NY R L KINGS E FIL Doc. 1(K)(1).

viii. *NEW YORK COUNTY.* It is the responsibility of counsel and parties to comply with rules restricting disclosure of confidential personal information. Nevertheless, NYSCEF screens filings and endeavors to identify any that contain social security numbers. When such numbers are discovered through this process, NYSCEF will restrict portions of or all of such documents from public view. Where NYSCEF has redacted what it believes to be a social security number, it will transmit to the filer a notice advising of the action taken and requesting that the filer review the matter and provide notification as set forth in the notice if the redaction has been made in error. NY R NY CTY E FIL Doc. 2(K)(1); NY R NY CTY J RUL Rule A-1. Documents filed in the past in "secure status" under a procedure no longer in place will retain that status unless otherwise directed by the court. NY R NY CTY E FIL Doc. 2(K)(2).

b. *Submission of confidential personal information.* Where a person submitting a paper to a court for filing believes in good faith that the inclusion of the full confidential personal information described in NY R UNIF TRIAL CTS § 202.5(e)(1) is material and necessary to the adjudication of the action or proceeding before the court, he or she may apply to the court for leave to serve and file together with a paper in which such information has been set forth in abbreviated form a confidential affidavit or affirmation setting forth the same information in unabbreviated form, appropriately referenced to the page or pages of the paper at which the abbreviated form appears. NY R UNIF TRIAL CTS § 202.5(e)(3).

c. *Home addresses.* For information on when home addresses and other personal information must be redacted, refer to NY CPLR Rule 2103-a.

5. *Defective papers.* A defect in the form of a paper, if a substantial right of a party is not prejudiced, shall be disregarded by the court, and leave to correct shall be freely given. NY CPLR Rule 2101(f). Papers that are stapled or bound securely shall not be rejected for filing simply because they are not bound with a backer of any kind. NY R UNIF TRIAL CTS § 202.5(a).

A paper filed in accordance with the rules of the chief administrator or any local rule or practice established by the court shall be deemed filed. NY CPLR Rule 2102(b).

a. *Objection to defective papers.* The party on whom a paper is served shall be deemed to have waived objection to any defect in form unless, within fifteen (15) days after the receipt thereof, the party on whom the paper is served returns the paper to the party serving it with a statement of particular objections. NY CPLR Rule 2101(f).

F. Filing and Service Requirements

1. *Filing requirements.* Except where otherwise prescribed by law or order of court, papers required to be filed shall be filed with the clerk of the court in which the action is triable. In an action or proceeding in supreme or court, papers required to be filed shall be filed with the clerk of the county in which the proceeding is brought. NY CPLR Rule 2102(a).

a. *Furnishing papers to the court.* Each party shall furnish to the court all papers served by him. The moving party shall furnish at the hearing all other papers not already in the possession of the court necessary to the consideration of the questions involved. Where such papers are in the possession of an adverse party, they shall be produced by him at the hearing on notice served with the motion papers. Only papers served in accordance with the provisions of NY CPLR Rule 2214 shall be read in support of, or in opposition to, the motion, unless the court for good cause shall otherwise direct. NY CPLR Rule 2214(c).

i. *Submission to judge.* All papers for signature or consideration of the court shall be presented to the clerk of the trial court in the appropriate courtroom or clerk's office, except that where the clerk is unavailable or the judge so directs, papers may be submitted to the judge and a copy filed with the clerk at the first available opportunity. All papers for any judge that are filed in the clerk's office shall be promptly delivered to the judge by the clerk. The papers shall be clearly addressed to the judge for whom they are intended and prominently show the nature of the papers, the title and index number of the action in which they are filed, the judge's name and the name of the attorney or party submitting them. NY R UNIF TRIAL CTS § 202.5(b).

ii. *BRONX COUNTY: Approval of motions before filing.* All motion papers must be approved by the Motion Support Office, Supreme Court, Civil Term, room 217, before the motion papers are filed and the appropriate fee paid to the County Clerk. NY R BRONX FIL R Doc. 1.

iii. *ERIE COUNTY: Filing motions.* A motion on notice or a notice of petition in a NYSCEF case shall be filed through the NYSCEF system and must be accompanied by a Request for Judicial Intervention if the motion is being filed upon commencement of the action or if the matter has not yet been assigned to an IAS Justice. In addition, cross motions with the appropriate filing fees and opposition and reply papers must be submitted via the NYSCEF system. NY R ERIE E FIL Doc. 3(V)(A).

iv. *NEW YORK COUNTY: Filing hard copies.* Where in the narrow circumstances described by the e-filing rules a motion is made in hard-copy form or opposition papers are submitted in such form in an e-filed case, the hard-copy documents shall be submitted in the same way papers are submitted in non-e-filed cases, except that there shall be firmly affixed to each separate document or group of documents, as the back page facing out, a Notice of Hard Copy Submission—E-Filed Case. NY R NY CTY Procedure II(A). For more information on filing in hard copy cases, refer to NY R NY CTY Procedure II(A).

v. *ONONDAGA COUNTY: Submission of responsive papers and cross-motions.* Cross-motions, opposition and reply papers must be submitted online. NY R ONDGA E FIL Protocol(B)(9)(e). Motions and Orders to Show Cause are assigned a sequence number by the system. Counsel must be sure that cross motions and other filings correspond with the correct sequence number so that a cross motion will not be associated with the wrong original motion. NY R ONDGA E FIL Protocol(B)(9)(f).

b. *Electronic filing.* On consent, documents may be filed and served by electronic means in Supreme Court in such civil actions and in such counties as shall be authorized by order of the Chief Administrator of the Courts and only to the extent and in the manner provided in NY R UNIF TRIAL CTS § 202.5-b. NY R UNIF TRIAL CTS § 202.5-b(a)(1). For the definitions of terms used in electronic filing, refer to NY R UNIF TRIAL CTS § 202.5-b(a)(2).

i. *E-filing mandatory.* In any action subject to e-filing, all documents required to be filed with the court by an e-filing party shall be filed and served electronically, except as provided in NY R UNIF TRIAL CTS § 202.5-b. NY R UNIF TRIAL CTS § 202.5-b(d)(1)(i).

- *ERIE COUNTY.* Case types currently eligible and accepted for e-filing are listed at the NYSCEF website. Note that some actions or special proceedings, (i.e., name changes) which are otherwise subject to mandatory e-filing, if commenced by unrepresented litigants will NOT be maintained in the NYSCEF system; individual cases may be found either at NYSCEF or in the Erie County Clerk's online records system. NY R ERIE E FIL Doc. 3(I)(E).

- *KINGS COUNTY.* Cases that are commenced by filing of the initiating papers with NYSCEF are identified as e-filed cases by assignment of a special index number (i.e., Index Numbers beginning with 500,000). NY R L KINGS E FIL Doc. 1(A)(1). All cases required to be e-filed are listed in Uniform Rule 202.5-bb (Mandatory E-Filing Rules) and on the NYSCEF website. All such cases must be commenced by filing with the County Clerk electronically through NYSCEF and all subsequent documents in such cases must be e-filed. Any questions regarding mandatory e-filing in Kings County can be e-mailed to kcco-efile@nycourts.gov. NY R L KINGS E FIL Doc. 1(A)(2).
- *NEW YORK COUNTY.* Unless otherwise provided in the Rules or in NY R NY CTY E FIL Doc. 2 or where a special exemption is granted due to physical requirements (e.g., oversized maps; see NY R NY CTY E FIL Doc. 2(B)(10)), all documents to be filed with the court in a NYSCEF case, including all documents on motions and all letters to the court (where permitted), must be filed with the NYSCEF system. Documents that attorneys would not ordinarily file with the court in a hard-copy case need not be e-filed. Unless otherwise provided by the E-Filing Rules or this Protocol, in e-filed cases the County Clerk and the court will not accept documents filed in paper form. NY R NY CTY E FIL Doc. 2(B)(1). E-filing is mandatory in all types of cases (other than election law, matrimonial, Art. 78, and Mental Hygiene Law matters, and Art. 70 habeas corpus proceedings) that are commenced in this court on or after February 19, 2013. All such cases must be commenced by filing with the County Clerk electronically through NYSCEF and all subsequent documents in such cases must be e-filed. NY R NY CTY E FIL Doc. 2(A)(2)(a). For more information, including information on consensual e-filing and filing scanned hard copy documents, refer to NY R NY CTY E FIL Doc. 2(A)(2).
- *QUEENS COUNTY.* All authorized Torts, Commercial and Tax Certiorari cases may be commenced by E-Filing, however all parties must consent for the action to continue as an E-file case. NY R L QUEENS E-FILE Doc. 1(A). All papers to be filed with the court in an E-filed case shall be filed on-line with the E-file system except as directed by the court. Papers that attorneys would not ordinarily file with the court in a hard-copy case need not be filed in an E-filed matter. NY R L QUEENS E-FILE Doc. 1(E)(2).

ii. *Who may file.* Documents may be filed or served electronically only by a person who has registered as an authorized e-filing user or as otherwise provided in NY R UNIF TRIAL CTS § 202.5-b(c). NY R UNIF TRIAL CTS § 202.5-b(c)(1).

iii. *When filing made.* Documents may be transmitted at any time of the day or night to the NYSCEF site. A document other than an order or judgment is filed when its electronic transmission or, in the case of a petition that is e-filed by submission of a text file as provided in NY R UNIF TRIAL CTS § 202.5-b(b)(1), the electronic transmission of the text file is recorded at that site, provided, however, that where payment of a fee is required upon the filing of a document, the document is not filed until transmission of the document and the information or form or information as required in NY R UNIF TRIAL CTS § 202.5-b(d)(2)(i), NY R UNIF TRIAL CTS § 202.5-b(d)(2)(ii) or NY R UNIF TRIAL CTS § 202.5-b(d)(2)(iii) has been recorded at the NYSCEF site; or, if no transmission of that information or form or information is recorded, where permitted by the County Clerk, until payment is presented to the County Clerk. NY R UNIF TRIAL CTS § 202.5-b(d)(3)(i).

iv. *Notification of filing.* No later than the close of business on the business day following the electronic filing of a document, a notification, in a form prescribed by the Chief Administrator, shall be transmitted electronically by the NYSCEF site to the person filing such document and the e-mail service addresses of all other participating parties in such action. NY R UNIF TRIAL CTS § 202.5-b(d)(3)(ii).

v. *Removal of confidential information and other corrections.* If a document filed electronically is subsequently discovered to contain confidential data—including but not limited to trade secrets, information protected by confidentiality agreement, or personal confidential information as defined by statute or court rule—or otherwise to have been filed in error, the filer or another party or affected person may (1) notify the parties and any non-party filers in the action of the confidentiality issue or other error raised by the filing, and of his or her intention to seek judicial relief to correct the filing: (2) following such notification, request that the appropriate County Clerk, exercising his or her administrative discretion, place the document temporarily in "restricted" status on the NYSCEF site, to be made available for viewing by court staff and the parties but not the general public; and (3) file an application to correct the filing by order to show cause within five (5) business days of such notification (or such time as the court may direct), including a request for preliminary injunctive relief limiting interim disclosure of the document at issue. Unless otherwise directed by the court, any document placed in restricted status in response to such a request shall be returned to public view upon expiration of this five (5) day

period. The Chief Administrator of the Courts shall promulgate forms to implement this process. NY R UNIF TRIAL CTS § 202.5-b(d)(3)(iii).

- *KINGS COUNTY.* For information on what to do when a document was erroneously filed with confidential information, refer to NY R L KINGS E FIL Doc. 1(B)(11).
- *NEW YORK COUNTY.* For information on what to do when a document was erroneously filed with confidential information, refer to NY R NY CTY E FIL Doc. 2(B)(8).
- *QUEENS COUNTY.* For information on what to do when a document was erroneously filed with confidential information, refer to NY R L QUEENS E-FILE Doc. 1(E)(7).

vi. *Documents requiring judge's signature.* Except where the court directs otherwise, any document that requires a judge's signature shall be transmitted electronically and in hard copy to the court. NY R UNIF TRIAL CTS § 202.5-b(d)(6).

vii. *Documents which would be inconvenient to file electronically; Hard copies.* Notwithstanding any other provision of NY R UNIF TRIAL CTS § 202.5-b, and subject to such guidelines as may be established by the Chief Administrative Judge, the County Clerk or his or her designee may require or permit a party to file in hard copy, in accordance with procedures set by the County Clerk or designee, an exhibit or other document which it is impractical or inconvenient to file electronically. NY R UNIF TRIAL CTS § 202.5-b(d)(7).

- *ERIE COUNTY.* Please contact the Supervisor of Actions & Proceedings, Erie County Clerk's Office by calling (716) 858-6662 or the Deputy County Clerk—Legal at (716) 858-6348 for information. NY R ERIE E FIL Doc. 3(III)(F).
- *KINGS COUNTY.* With limited exceptions, as set forth in the Uniform Rules and herein, all documents to be filed with the court in a NYSCEF case shall be filed online via the NYSCEF system. However, should the size, consistency or context of a hard copy document preclude electronic filing, the user shall electronically file a "Notice of Hard Copy Submission—E-Filed Cases" form EFM-3. Any hard copy submitted pursuant to NY R L KINGS E FIL Doc. 1(B)(9) shall include, as a cover page firmly fastened thereto, a copy of the Confirmation Notice received from the NYSCEF site confirming receipt of the "Notice of Hard Copy Submission—E-Filed Cases". Any party may object to such hard copy filing. The Court, in response to such objection, may, following the hard copy filing, fashion such relief as it deems appropriate pursuant to and in furtherance of the Uniform Rules and NY R L KINGS E FIL Doc. 1, including, but not limited to, an Order directing the filing party to file such documents online via the NYSCEF system. When exhibits are impractical to file pursuant to NY R UNIF TRIAL CTS § 202.5-b(d)(7), an additional "Notice of Hard Copy Exhibit Filing" form EFM-4 is required to be submitted. NY R L KINGS E FIL Doc. 1(B)(9).
- *NEW YORK COUNTY.* If a filer needs to submit unusual exhibits in original form that cannot practically be e-filed, such as oversized maps or electronic recordings, the filer should consult with the County Clerk's E-File Department by telephone at 646-386-3737 (procedural questions only) or by e-mail at ccnyef@nycourts.gov, which will normally require that the filer retain custody of the original subject to possible future directives of the court. NY R NY CTY E FIL Doc. 2(B)(10). In such instances, the filing counsel shall file with NYSCEF a "placeholder" in the form of a Notice of Hard Copy Exhibit Filing (NYSCEF Form EF 21). The Notice should be uploaded to NYSCEF as document type "Exhibit" and the filer should indicate in the "Additional Document Information" field that the filer is retaining custody of the original. Failure to e-file the Notice may result in a gap in the official record of the court. NY R NY CTY E FIL Doc. 2(B)(10).

viii. *Documents containing sensitive or proprietary information.* In an action subject to e-filing, any person may apply for an order prohibiting or restricting the electronic filing in the action of specifically identified materials on the grounds that such materials are subject to copyright or other proprietary rights, or trade secret or other privacy interests, and that electronic filing in the action is likely to result in substantial prejudice to those rights or interests. NY R UNIF TRIAL CTS § 202.5-b(k)(2).

ix. *Refusal to accept paper filings.* In accordance with NY CPLR Rule 2102(c), a County Clerk and a chief clerk of the Supreme Court or County Court, as appropriate, shall refuse to accept for filing papers filed in actions and proceedings when the paper sought to be filed:

- Is in an action subject to electronic filing pursuant to Rules of the Chief Administrator,
- Is not being filed electronically, and

- Does not include the notice required by NY R UNIF TRIAL CTS § 202.5-b(d)(1). NY R UNIF TRIAL CTS § 202.5(d)(1)(v); NY R UNIF TRIAL CTS § 202.5-bb(d).

x. *Emergency filings; Hard copies.* For information on when an emergency filing may be filed and served in hard copy, refer to NY R UNIF TRIAL CTS § 202.5-b(d)(1)(ii), NY R UNIF TRIAL CTS § 202.5-b(d)(1)(iii) and NY R UNIF TRIAL CTS § 202.5-bb(c)(3).

- *KINGS COUNTY.* Under the rules, a participating emergency e-filer must electronically file the documents initially filed in hard copy form within three (3) business days of the emergency filing; the originals will be discarded after the documents have been processed and the failure to e-file as required will therefore lead to an incomplete record. NY R L KINGS E FIL Doc. 1(B)(3).
- *NEW YORK COUNTY.* Occasionally an emergency will arise requiring expedited entry of a document with the County Clerk (e.g., an order issued in the courtroom after a conference or argument of a critical matter), such as for purposes of an immediate appeal. Expedition can be achieved by the Part as follows: the document should be carried by a Court Officer or staff member to the General Clerk's Office to assure immediate and proper recordation in the computer and, as appropriate, the posting of the document to NYSCEF or the Supreme Court Records On-Line Library ("Scroll"). The court will accommodate counsel in emergencies. NY R NY CTY Procedure XI(A).
- *NEW YORK COUNTY.* For more information on how to bring emergency matters before the court, refer to NY R NY CTY Procedure IV.

xi. *Technical failures.* The NYSCEF site shall be considered to be subject to a technical failure on a given day if the site is unable to accept filings or provide access to filed documents continuously or intermittently over the course of any period of time greater than one (1) hour after 12:00 noon of that day. Notice of all such technical failures shall be provided on the site. NY R UNIF TRIAL CTS § 202.5-b(i).

- When e-filing is hindered by a technical failure, a party may file with the appropriate clerk and serve in hard copy. NY R UNIF TRIAL CTS § 202.5-b(i). In the event an attorney or party shall file and serve documents in hard copy pursuant to NY R UNIF TRIAL CTS § 202.5-b(i), each such document shall include the notice required by NY R UNIF TRIAL CTS § 202.5-b(d)(1), and the filer shall file those documents with the NYSCEF site within three (3) business days after restoration of normal operations at that site. NY R UNIF TRIAL CTS § 202.5-b(i).
- With the exception of deadlines that by law cannot be extended, the time for filing of any document that is delayed due to technical failure of the site shall be extended for one (1) day for each day on which such failure occurs, unless otherwise ordered by the court. NY R UNIF TRIAL CTS § 202.5-b(i).
- *ERIE COUNTY.* When filing by electronic means is hindered by a technical failure, please refer to the NY R UNIF TRIAL CTS § 202.5-b(i). NY R ERIE E FIL Doc. 3(III)(K).
- *KINGS COUNTY.* When filing by electronic means is hindered by a NYSCEF technical failure (as set forth in NY R UNIF TRIAL CTS § 202.5-b(i)), a party may file with the appropriate Clerk in hard copy. Except for deadlines that by law cannot be extended (e.g. Statute of limitations, Notice of Appeal), the time for filing of any document that is delayed due to technical failure of the NYSCEF system shall be extended for one day for each day on which such failure occurs, unless otherwise ordered by the court. NY R L KINGS E FIL Doc. 1(B)(13).
- *ONONDAGA COUNTY.* When filing by electronic means is hindered by a technical failure (as set forth in NY R UNIF TRIAL CTS § 202.5-b(h)(3)(i)), a party may file a hard copy with the County Clerk. With the exception of deadlines that by law cannot be extended (e.g., a statute of limitations or the deadline for filing a Notice of Appeal), the time for filing of any document that is delayed due to technical failure of the NYSCEF system will be extended for one day for each day on which such failure occurs, unless otherwise ordered by the court. A "Notice of Hard Copy Filing Submission—E-Filed Case' must accompany any documents not filed via NYSCEF. NY R ONDGA E FIL Protocol(B)(8).

xii. *Filing fees.* For information on what information must be provided to pay filing fees, refer to NY R UNIF TRIAL CTS § 202.5-b(d)(2).

xiii. *Exemption from e-filing.* For information on exemptions from e-filing, refer to NY R UNIF TRIAL CTS § 202.5-bb(e).

xiv. *Filing exhibits*

- *ERIE COUNTY.* In the NYSCEF system, each exhibit must be uploaded as a separate .pdf file. After

uploading a primary document, please choose the document type "Exhibit" and enter the appropriate number or letter and a brief description of the exhibit; each exhibit should bear a separate cover sheet clearly marked as "Exhibit A," "Exhibit B," etc. "Exhibit A" or "Exhibit B" is unacceptable as a brief description of the exhibit. Exhibits, where referenced in a signed Order as attached or affixed shall be uploaded with the signed Order as one .pdf document. NY R ERIE E FIL Doc. 3(III)(H); NY R ERIE E FIL Doc. 3(V)(D).

- *KINGS COUNTY.* In the NYSCEF system, each exhibit should be uploaded as a separate PDF file. After uploading a primary document, please choose the document type "Exhibit", enter the appropriate number or letter, and be sure to place a check mark to the right of "Attach to main document". Each exhibit shall bear a separate cover sheet clearly marked as Exhibit A, Exhibit B, etc. NY R L KINGS E FIL Doc. 1(B)(12). Whenever possible, attorneys submitting exhibits in NYSCEF cases should make each exhibit a separate attachment to an affidavit/affirmation in the system (i.e., multiple exhibits should not be filed as a single PDF). NY R L KINGS E FIL Doc. 1(D)(1).
- *NEW YORK COUNTY.* Attorneys submitting exhibits in NYSCEF cases should make each exhibit a separate attachment to an affidavit/affirmation in the system; i.e., exhibits should not be filed as a single PDF-A together with the affidavit/affirmation or grouped together as a single PDF-A attachment because either of these two formats makes it difficult for the Justice to locate particular exhibits as needed. Counsel must also include appropriate descriptive language in the "Additional Document Information" field in NYSCEF. NY R NY CTY E FIL Doc. 2(D)(6).
- *ONONDAGA COUNTY.* All exhibits in e-filed cases must be e-filed individually as separate attachments. NY R ONDGA E FIL Protocol(B)(9)(b).

xv. *Correcting documents*

- *ERIE COUNTY.* Submission of documents which, upon examination, require correction or addition will result in notification to the filer advising that the document has been returned for correction. The filer shall make the required corrections and/or additions as indicated in the e-mail transmission sent by the County Clerk or Part Clerk through the NYSCEF site. The corrected documents may be resubmitted using the "Re-file this document" link highlighted in the filer's document list for the respective case. Please note that in the case of multiple submissions, all related documents filed at the same time may be removed from the case record and returned until all documents are properly submitted. NY R ERIE E FIL Doc. 3(III)(J).
- *KINGS COUNTY.* Submission of documents which, upon examination, require correction or addition will result in notification to the filer advising that there is a problem with a document. The filer shall make the required corrections and/or additions and resubmit the corrected document using the "Refile this document" link. In the event a document is returned for correction, the original file date will be preserved. For corrections of documents filed with the Kings County Clerk which require a court order, refer to the procedure in NY R UNIF TRIAL CTS § 202.5-b(d)(3)(iii) and NY R L KINGS E FIL Doc. 1(B)(11). NY R L KINGS E FIL Doc. 1(B)(3).
- *ONONDAGA COUNTY.* If there is an error or an additional document is required, the system will notify the filing party, who will make the corrections/additions and resubmit them online. NY R ONDGA E FIL Protocol(B)(6).
- *QUEENS COUNTY.* Generally speaking, documents that have been E-filed will not thereafter be deleted by the County Clerk from NYCEF because the filer asserts that the filing contains an error or a significant omission. When the filer wishes to correct a perceived error or omission in a filed document, he or she should file an amended version of the document, with the original remaining on file, or else obtain a court order providing for deletion of the original. The County Clerk will only delete a document upon request of the filer or on the County Clerk's own initiative when it is obvious from the face of the document alone that the filer made a fundamental error and never intended to file the document that was filed (e.g., a completely unrelated non-litigation document, a different case, or a wrong county). The County Clerk will advise the filer when any such fundamental errors are detected. NY R L QUEENS E-FILE Doc. 1(E)(6).

c. *Facsimile filing.* In the Supreme Court, facsimile filing shall be limited to commercial claims and tax certiorari, conservatorship, and mental hygiene proceedings in Monroe, Westchester, New York and Suffolk Counties. NY R UNIF TRIAL CTS § 202.5-a(a)(1). Refer to NY R UNIF TRIAL CTS § 202.5-a for information on the procedures for facsimile filing.

i. *NEW YORK COUNTY.* Unless indicated otherwise by the court in a particular case or in NY R NY CTY J RUL Doc. 1, Justices do not accept papers by fax. NY R NY CTY J RUL Rule 4.

d. *ERIE COUNTY: Filing request for judicial intervention.* An RJI in a NYSCEF case shall be filed via the NYSCEF system and will be filed after all other documents have been uploaded. The filer may choose between filing a .pdf image of the prepared RJI and any Addendum or having the system prepare the RJI which shall conform to Uniform Rules. Addenda, such as the Commercial Division Addendum, if prepared by the filer must be filed simultaneously with and attached to an RJI and uploaded as one .pdf document with the RJI. If the RJI is prepared by the e-filing system, no separate Addendum is required. Whether or not the filer elects to allow NYSCEF to create the RJI or chooses to upload a prepared RJI, data in addition to the nature of the judicial intervention, including information that appears on any Addenda will be collected through completion of the fields presented. If the filing of the RJI is accomplished through a filing agent, a prepared RJI and Addendum must be filed in lieu of the creation of the RJI by the NYSCEF system, as the RJI must be signed by the attorney. NY R ERIE E FIL Doc. 3(IV). For information on RJIs in specific types of action, refer to NY R ERIE E FIL Doc. 3(IV).

2. *Service requirements*

a. *Who may serve.* Except where otherwise prescribed by law or order of court, papers may be served by any person not a party of the age of eighteen years or over. NY CPLR Rule 2103(a).

b. *Service upon attorney.* Except where otherwise prescribed by law or order of court, papers to be served upon a party in a pending action shall be served upon the party's attorney. Where the same attorney appears for two or more parties, only one (1) copy need be served upon the attorney. Such service upon an attorney shall be made:

i. By delivering the paper to the attorney personally. NY CPLR Rule 2103(b)(1).

ii. By mailing the paper to the attorney at the address designated by that attorney for that purpose or, if none is designated, at the attorney's last known address; service by mail shall be complete upon mailing. NY CPLR Rule 2103(b)(2).

- *BRONX COUNTY.* Service by mail must be within the state. NY R BRONX FIL R Doc. 3.

iii. If the attorney's office is open, by leaving the paper with a person in charge, or if no person is in charge, by leaving it in a conspicuous place; or if the attorney's office is not open, by depositing the paper, enclosed in a sealed wrapper directed to the attorney, in the attorney's office letter drop or box. NY CPLR Rule 2103(b)(3).

iv. By leaving it at the attorney's residence within the state with a person of suitable age and discretion. Service upon an attorney shall not be made at the attorney's residence unless service at the attorney's office cannot be made. NY CPLR Rule 2103(b)(4).

v. By transmitting the paper to the attorney by facsimile transmission, provided that a facsimile telephone number is designated by the attorney for that purpose. Service by facsimile transmission shall be complete upon the receipt by the sender of a signal from the equipment of the attorney served indicating that the transmission was received, and the mailing of a copy of the paper to that attorney. The designation of a facsimile telephone number in the address block subscribed on a paper served or filed in the course of an action or proceeding shall constitute consent to service by facsimile transmission in accordance with NY CPLR Rule 2103(b)(5). An attorney may change or rescind a facsimile telephone number by serving a notice on the other parties. NY CPLR Rule 2103(b)(5).

vi. By dispatching the paper to the attorney by overnight delivery service at the address designated by the attorney for that purpose or, if none is designated, at the attorney's last known address. Service by overnight delivery service shall be complete upon deposit of the paper enclosed in a properly addressed wrapper into the custody of the overnight delivery service for overnight delivery, prior to the latest time designated by the overnight delivery service for overnight delivery. "Overnight delivery service" means any delivery service which regularly accepts items for overnight delivery to any address in the state. NY CPLR Rule 2103(b)(6).

vii. By transmitting the paper to the attorney by electronic means where and in the manner authorized by the chief administrator of the courts by rule and, unless such rule shall otherwise provide, such transmission shall be upon the party's written consent. The subject matter heading for each paper sent by electronic means must indicate that the matter being transmitted electronically is related to a court proceeding. NY CPLR Rule 2103(b)(7).

- *KINGS COUNTY.* Pursuant to the E-Filing Rules, service of interlocutory documents is made by posting a document to the NYSCEF site, which automatically and immediately transmits an email notice of the filing, including a link to the document, to all participating counsel and unrepresented litigants on the case. The Rules also authorize service by other methods permitted by the CPLR. If service by such other method is made, proof of service must be filed with NYSCEF. NY R L KINGS E FIL Doc. 1(I).
- *NEW YORK COUNTY.* Service. . .will be made automatically through NYSCEF upon all participating

counsel and unrepresented parties in the case. There are limited exceptions to the requirement for e-filing in the covered kinds of cases. NY R NY CTY Procedure XI(A). Pursuant to the E-Filing Rules, service of interlocutory documents is made by posting a document to the NYSCEF site, which automatically and immediately transmits an e-mail notice of the filing, including a link to the document, to all participating counsel and unrepresented litigants on the case. The Rules also authorize service by other methods permitted by the CPLR. If service by such a method is made, proof of service must be filed with NYSCEF. NY R NY CTY E FIL Doc. 2(I).

- *QUEENS COUNTY.* Filing with the system permits counsel to serve the papers electronically pursuant to NY R UNIF TRIAL CTS § 202.5-b(f) once consent to E-Filing has been filed on-line. Consult NY R UNIF TRIAL CTS § 202.5-bb(c) for service in mandatory e-filing. Any required proof of service should be E-filed as a separate document. NY R L QUEENS E-FILE Doc. 1(E)(4).

c. *Electronic service mandatory; Consenting to electronic service; How electronic service may be made.* Except as otherwise provided in NY R UNIF TRIAL CTS § 202.5-bb, filing and service of all documents in an action that has been commenced electronically in accordance with NY R UNIF TRIAL CTS § 202.5-bb shall be by electronic means. NY R UNIF TRIAL CTS § 202.5-bb(c)(1).

i. *Party's consent required for certain e-filing.* After commencement of an action wherein e-filing is authorized, documents may be electronically filed and served, but only by, and electronic service shall be made only upon, a party or parties who have consented thereto. NY R UNIF TRIAL CTS § 202.5-b(b)(2)(i).

- A consent to e-filing in an action shall state that the party providing it agrees to the use of e-filing in the action and to be bound by the filing and service provisions in NY R UNIF TRIAL CTS § 202.5-b. NY R UNIF TRIAL CTS § 202.5-b(b)(2)(ii).

ii. *Address for service; Duty to notify as to changes.* The e-mail service address recorded at the time of registration is the e-mail address at which service of interlocutory documents on that party may be made through notification transmitted by the NYSCEF site. It is the responsibility of each filing user to monitor that address and promptly notify the Resource Center in the event of a change in his or her e-mail service address. NY R UNIF TRIAL CTS § 202.5-b(f)(2)(i).

iii. *How service made.* An e-filing party causes service of an interlocutory document to be made upon another party participating in e-filing by filing the document electronically. Upon receipt of an interlocutory document, the NYSCEF site shall automatically transmit electronic notification to all e-mail service addresses in such action. NY R UNIF TRIAL CTS § 202.5-b(f)(2)(ii).

- Except as provided otherwise in NY R UNIF TRIAL CTS § 202.5-b(h)(3), the electronic transmission of the notification shall constitute service of the document on the e-mail service addresses identified therein; however, such service will not be effective if the filing party learns that the notification did not reach the address of the person to be served. Proof of such service will be recorded on the NYSCEF site. A party may, however, utilize other service methods permitted by the CPLR provided that, if one of such other methods is used, proof of that service shall be filed electronically. NY R UNIF TRIAL CTS § 202.5-b(f)(2)(ii).

iv. *Signatures on hard copies; Proof of service filed electronically.* When an e-filing party serves a document in hard copy on a non-participating party, the document served shall bear full signatures of all signatories and proof of such service shall be filed electronically. NY R UNIF TRIAL CTS § 202.5-b(b)(2)(i).

- *ERIE COUNTY.* In the NYSCEF system, each Affidavit of Service must be uploaded as a separate .pdf file. After uploading the Affidavit, please choose the document type: "Affirmation/Affidavit of Service" and enter the name of the party served as Additional Document Information. NY R ERIE E FIL Doc. 3(III)(I); NY R ERIE E FIL Doc. 3(V)(F).

v. *Effect of failure to consent.* A party's failure to consent to participation in electronic filing and service shall not bar any other party to the action from filing documents electronically with the County Clerk and the court or serving documents upon any other party who has consented to participation. A party who has not consented to participation shall file documents with the court and the County Clerk, and serve and be served with documents, in hard copy. NY R UNIF TRIAL CTS § 202.5-b(b)(2)(i).

d. *Service upon party.* If a party has not appeared by an attorney or the party's attorney cannot be served, service shall be upon the party by a method specified in NY CPLR Rule 2103(b)(1), NY CPLR Rule 2103(b)(2), NY CPLR Rule 2103(b)(4), NY CPLR Rule 2103(b)(5) or NY CPLR Rule 2103(b)(6). NY CPLR Rule 2103(c).

e. *Service on all parties.* Each paper served on any party shall be served on every other party who has appeared, except

as otherwise may be provided by court order or as provided in NY CPLR § 3012 or in NY CPLR § 3215(f). Upon demand by a party, the plaintiff shall supply that party with a list of those who have appeared and the names and addresses of their attorneys. NY CPLR Rule 2103(e).

f. *Service by filing.* If a paper cannot be served by any of the methods specified in NY CPLR Rule 2103(b) and NY CPLR Rule 2103(c), service may be made by filing the paper as if it were a paper required to be filed. NY CPLR Rule 2103(d).

g. *Definitions.* For the purposes of NY CPLR Rule 2103:

i. "Mailing" means the deposit of a paper enclosed in a first class postpaid wrapper, addressed to the address designated by a person for that purpose or, if none is designated, at that person's last known address, in a post office or official depository under the exclusive care and custody of the United States Postal Service within the state;

ii. "Electronic means" means any method of transmission of information between computers or other machines designed for the purpose of sending and receiving such transmissions, and which allows the recipient to reproduce the information transmitted in a tangible medium of expression;

iii. "Facsimile transmission" means any method of transmission of documents to a facsimile machine at a remote location which can automatically produce a tangible copy of such documents. NY CPLR Rule 2103(f).

G. Hearings

1. *Oral argument.* Motion papers received by the clerk of the court on or before the return date shall be deemed submitted as of the return date. The assigned judge, in his or her discretion or at the request of a party, thereafter may determine that any motion be orally argued and may fix a time for oral argument. NY R UNIF TRIAL CTS § 202.8(d).

a. A party requesting oral argument shall set forth such request in its notice of motion or in its order to show cause or on the first page of the answering papers, as the case may be. Where all parties to a motion request oral argument, oral argument shall be granted unless the court shall determine it to be unnecessary. NY R UNIF TRIAL CTS § 202.8(d).

b. Where a motion is brought on by order to show cause, the court may set forth in the order that oral argument is required on the return date of the motion. NY R UNIF TRIAL CTS § 202.8(d).

i. *BRONX COUNTY.* All orders to show cause, with the exception of orders to show cause that are returnable in the City Part, the STP Part, the Matrimonial Part and the Preliminary/Compliance Conference Part (IA-11), submitted on or after August 25, 2003, will be returnable on a Monday in the assigned Justice's part and appear on his or her motion calendar. Appearances will be required on orders to show cause. NY R BRONX FIL R Doc. 8. A motion on notice or a notice of petition in a New York Supreme Court E-File (hereafter known as NYSCEF) case, as in others, shall be made returnable in the Motion Support Office (Room 217). NY R BRONX E FIL R Doc. 1(1).

- After a motion/petition and notice are filed with the NYSCEF system, the Motion Support Office will automatically place the motion/proceeding on the submit calendar in the Motion Support Office (Room 217) for the return date. No appearance or other action by the filing attorney is required in order for the motion to be calendared if the motion fee is paid for via NYSCEF. Motions in e-filed cases (other than tax certiorari cases) appear on the submit calendar in Room 217 on the return date. NY R BRONX E FIL R Doc. 1(2).

c. *KINGS COUNTY.* All motions require appearances and oral argument. NY R L KINGS Pt. C, Rule 3.

2. *Return date; Time for hearing.* A notice of motion shall specify the time and place of the hearing on the motion. NY CPLR Rule 2214(a). The moving party determines when a motion on notice shall be heard, but she has to consult the court's or judge's calendar practice first. The movant picks out a "return day" sufficiently far off to assure that the notice requirements of NY CPLR Rule 2214(b) can be met, and to assure as well that the day picked is a day on which the assigned judge hears motions. SIEGEL-NYPRAC § 247.

a. *Judge assigned to hear motion*

i. *Referral to judge supervising disclosure.* Unless the chief administrator of the courts has, by rule, provided otherwise, if a case has been assigned to a judge to supervise disclosure pursuant to NY CPLR § 3104, all motions preliminary to trial shall be referred to such judge whenever practicable. NY CPLR Rule 3214(a).

ii. *Referral to judge who decided prior motion.* Any motion may be referred to a judge who decided a prior motion in the action. NY CPLR Rule 2217(a).

iii. *Transfer when judge unable to hear motion.* If a motion is made to a judge who is or will be for any reason unable

to hear it, it may be transferred by order of such judge or by written stipulation of the parties to any other judge to whom it might originally have been made. NY CPLR Rule 2217(c).

iv. *Procedure for unassigned cases.* If a case has not been assigned to a judge, the motion shall be made returnable before the court, and a copy of the moving papers, together with a request for judicial intervention, shall be filed with the court, with proof of service upon all other parties, where required by NY R UNIF TRIAL CTS § 202.6, within five (5) days of service upon the other parties. The moving party shall give written notice of the index number to all other parties immediately after filing of the papers. NY R UNIF TRIAL CTS § 202.8(b).

- *Responding papers.* Copies of all responding papers shall be submitted to the court, with proof of service and with the index number set forth in the papers, on or before the return date. NY R UNIF TRIAL CTS § 202.8(b).
- *Assignment after request for judicial intervention.* The case shall be assigned to a judge as soon as practicable after the filing of the request for judicial intervention pursuant to NY R UNIF TRIAL CTS § 202.6, but in no event later than the return date. After assignment to the judge, the court shall provide for appropriate notice to the parties of the name of the assigned judge. NY R UNIF TRIAL CTS § 202.8(b).
- *Motions to be heard in another county.* Motion papers noticed to be heard in a county other than the county where the venue of the action has been placed by the plaintiff shall be assigned to a judge in accordance with procedures established by the Chief Administrator. NY R UNIF TRIAL CTS § 202.8(b).

v. *ALBANY COUNTY: Motions referred to IAS Justice.* All motions made after a case has been assigned a day certain shall be referred to the IAS Justice unless the motion is returnable during the term in which the matter has been assigned a day certain, in that event, the matter will be referred to the Part 1 Justice for that particular term who may entertain the motion or refer such motion to the IAS Justice. Under those circumstances, the Part I Justice shall decide whether or not to strike the note of issue or assign the matter a new day certain. NY R 3 JD SUP Doc. 1(H)(2). All motions shall be returnable before the assigned justice. NY R 3 JD SUP Doc. 1(B).

b. *Trial of issue raised by motion.* The court may order that an issue of fact raised on a motion shall be separately tried by the court or a referee. If the issue is triable of right by jury, the court shall give the parties an opportunity to demand a jury trial of such issue. Failure to make such demand within the time limited by the court, or, if no such time is limited, before trial begins, shall be deemed a waiver of the right to trial by jury. An order under NY CPLR § 2218 shall specify the issue to be tried. NY CPLR § 2218.

c. *Audio-visual coverage of trial court proceeding.* Audio-visual coverage of proceedings in the trial courts shall be permitted only in accordance with the provisions of Part 131 of the Rules of the Chief Administrator (NY R CHIEF ADMIN § 131.1, et seq.). NY R CHIEF J § 29.3.

d. *Adjournment of return date.* Stipulations of adjournment of the return date made by the parties shall be in writing and shall be submitted to the assigned judge. Such stipulation shall be effective unless the court otherwise directs. No more than three (3) stipulated adjournments for an aggregate period of sixty (60) days shall be submitted without prior permission of the court. NY R UNIF TRIAL CTS § 202.8(e)(1).

i. Absent agreement by the parties, a request by any party for an adjournment shall be submitted in writing, upon notice to the other party, to the assigned judge on or before the return date. The court will notify the requesting party whether the adjournment has been granted. NY R UNIF TRIAL CTS § 202.8(e)(2).

ii. *BRONX COUNTY.* Non-disclosure motions for IA5, IA7 and IA22 will be adjourned for oral argument to the Monday of the second week following the week of the return date of the motion. All other non-disclosure motions will be deemed submitted on the return date and forwarded to Chambers unless a stipulation of adjournment complying with the requirements of NY R UNIF TRIAL CTS § 202.8(e) is submitted, in which event, the motion will be adjourned for the requested date and kept in the Clerk's Office. If a non-stipulated request for adjournment or notice is submitted, the motion and request will be forwarded to Chambers for judicial approval or denial of the request. In either event, the attorney requesting the adjournment will be notified, via telephone, of the granting or denial of the request and instructed to notify his adversary. NY R BRONX FIL R Doc. 8.

iii. *BRONX COUNTY.* Motions that have been e-filed may be adjourned in Room 217 if an adjournment complies with the procedures of the Motion Support Office (explained in the "Filing Rules—Motion Procedure" section of the "Courthouse Procedures" link on the website of [the] court). An adjournment that so complies may be obtained by filing a stipulation of all parties with NYSCEF (designated in the filing menu as a "Stipulation to Adjourn Motion"). NY R BRONX E FIL R Doc. 1(3).

iv. *NEW YORK COUNTY.* The Courtroom also maintains a "APB (All Papers By)" Calendar, which is used when

a party seeks an adjournment but fails to comply with the Courtroom's procedures or there is a failure to comply with procedures that requires the clerk to adjourn the motion/application (e.g., failure to submit a Confirmation Notice in an e-filed case). The case may be put over for three days to allow compliance with those procedures, as described further below. NY R NY CTY Procedure II(C); NY R NY CTY E FIL Doc. 2(D)(2). E-filed applications may be adjourned in the Part if an adjournment complies with the Part's procedures (see the Uniform Rules of the Justices (Local Rules) on the court's website). An adjournment that so complies may be obtained by filing with NYSCEF a stipulation of all parties (designated in the filing menu as a Stipulation—Adjournment of Motion—Before Judge); the motion number and the current return date of the motion being adjourned shall be set forth in the "Additional Document Information" field in NYSCEF. Absent any problems, the Part will effectuate the adjournment without need for an appearance or any other action by the parties. NY R NY CTY E FIL Doc. 2(D)(4).

v. *QUEENS COUNTY.* The Motion Support Office is NOT authorized to grant adjournments. NY R L QUEENS MOT SUP Doc. 1.

e. *ALBANY COUNTY: Motion terms.* There shall be a. . . Motion Term on each Friday in the Supreme Court, Albany County. The Friday Motion Term shall include all Article 78 Proceedings involving New York State and proceedings commenced pursuant to Article 14 of the Civil Service Law (including applications for injunctive relief made pursuant to section 209-a of the Civil Service Law). NY R 3 JD SUP Doc. 1(F). Generally, parties will be granted only one adjournment for the Friday Motion Term. NY R 3 JD SUP Doc. 1(F).

f. *ALBANY COUNTY: Motion determined without hearing.* All motions are deemed "submitted" on the return date and no appearances are required by the parties. NY R 3 JD SUP Doc. 1(B). In the event oral argument is requested, the parties should not appear on the return date. At the discretion of the assigned Judge and upon the granting of a request for oral argument, the parties will be notified by Chambers of the scheduled time and place at which argument will be heard. Where a motion is brought on by order to show cause, the court may set forth in the order that appearances and/or oral argument are required on the return date of the motion. NY R 3 JD SUP Doc. 1(B).

g. *BRONX COUNTY: Return date.* All assigned and unassigned motions will be returnable five (5) days a week in the Civil Branch Clerk's Office, Room 217, at 9:30 a.m. NY R BRONX FIL R Doc. 8.

i. If on any submitted non-disclosure motion oral argument is requested and granted, or directed by the Court, the motion shall be adjourned for oral argument before the I.A. Judge on the second Monday following the week of the return date of the motion. Attorneys will be notified via telephone of the adjourned date. NY R BRONX FIL R Doc. 8.

h. *BRONX COUNTY: Oral argument.* Calendars of disclosure motions and other motions adjourned for oral argument will be published for the four (4) business days preceding the rescheduled appearance date and on the rescheduled date of the motion. These repetitive publications will serve as the notification of procedure of adjournment of all motions. In addition, two (2) days before the return date of unassigned motions a list of such motions indicating the assigned Justice and the adjourned date of the motion will be published. NY R BRONX FIL R Doc. 8.

i. *BRONX COUNTY: Resolution before return date.* Counsel/parties must advise the Court in writing on or before the return date of all motions that have been resolved by Counsel/parties themselves and all motions the movant(s) wish to be withdrawn. NY R BRONX FIL R Doc. 8.

j. *ERIE COUNTY: Calendaring of motions.* Refer to individual Justice's Part Rules. NY R ERIE E FIL Doc. 3(V)(B).

k. *KINGS COUNTY: Return date set by court.* Irrespective of the return date indicated in the notice of motion, motions will be rescheduled by the E-file/Motion Support Office to a date designated by the assigned Judge. NY R L KINGS Pt. C, Rule 2.

l. *KINGS COUNTY: Calendar calls.* There shall be two (2) calendar calls on motion days. The first calendar call shall be at 9:30 AM and the second calendar call shall be at 10:45 AM, unless the Judge's Part Rules provide otherwise. Defaults shall only be taken on second call. Attorneys with appearances elsewhere in the courthouse may advise the clerk of their whereabouts to avoid a default. Failure to so advise the clerk or appear at the default calendar call will result in a default order being entered or the motion being marked off the calendar. NY R L KINGS Pt. C, Rule 7.

m. *NEW YORK COUNTY: Return date and assigned courtroom.* Motions made by notice of motion and petitions and notices of petition in special proceedings are processed by the General Clerk's Office (Room 119) and are to be made returnable in the Motion Submission Part Courtroom (Room 130) on any business day of the week at 9:30 AM. There are some differences in electronically-filed cases. NY R NY CTY Procedure II; NY R NY CTY Procedure II(C); NY R NY CTY J RUL Rule 13(a).

i. For the convenience of counsel, between 9:00 A.M. and 9:30 A.M. each day, in advance of the "call," Room 130

accepts (1) written stipulations; (2) affidavits/affirmations reciting the required details as to an adjournment on consent; (3) stipulations, letters or other writings withdrawing motions; and (4) final papers or complete sets of papers on motions. For motions in which these items are handed in before the "call," no one need remain to answer the "call." Counsel/parties must advise the court, either between 9:00 A.M. and 9:30 A.M. or at the "call," of all motions or cases that have been resolved by counsel/parties themselves and all motions that the movant no longer wishes to pursue. If such resolution occurs subsequent to the "call", the assigned Justice must be advised as soon as possible, by written notice sent to the Part, so that the court does not do unnecessary work. NY R NY CTY Procedure II(C).

ii. Depending upon the assigned Part, contested motions submitted in the Motion Submission Part Courtroom are submitted without argument, or rescheduled for oral argument if so directed by the assigned Justice. For Justices who schedule argument on a case-by-case basis, notice of the argument date will be transmitted by the court. Counsel may ascertain how a motion submitted in Courtroom 130 was marked by consulting Scroll on the court's website, the e-Track application, or, on the two (2) days immediately following the submission date, the New York Law Journal. NY R NY CTY J RUL Rule 13(a).

n. *NEW YORK COUNTY: Motion call.* Each day in the Motion Submission Part Courtroom, commencing at 9:30 A.M., all motions returnable that day will be "called" for the submission of these papers, which must be handed up at this "call" or, as described below, immediately before. Because hundreds of motions appear on the Room 130 calendars every day, motion papers (other than part of the moving papers as described above) cannot be accepted on any day prior to the return date. Courtesy copies are not required nor accepted, but working copies are required by certain Justices in e-filed cases. NY R NY CTY Procedure II(C). If argument is directed, it will take place on an announced date shortly after the day of submission. NY R NY CTY Procedure II(C).

o. *NEW YORK COUNTY: Oral arguments.* Pursuant to request of some Justices, motions submitted in Room 130 will automatically be scheduled for a set argument date in the Part. Other Justices determine on a case-by-case basis after submission in Room 130 whether to accept a particular substantive motion on submission, to require oral argument, or to hold a conference. NY R NY CTY Procedure II(D). If argument is directed by the Justice automatically, notice of argument and the argument date will be given in Room 130. Any appearing party is expected to give notice to all parties and an announcement to this effect is made in Room 130. If the motion is submitted in Room 130 and the Justice, after examining the file, determines that argument should be directed, notice of the argument and the argument date will not be sent by the court. To obtain notification of the argument date and other developments, counsel should use e-Track. If argument notification is not given or transmitted as just described, counsel should understand that the motion has been taken on submission for decision on the papers. NY R NY CTY Procedure II(D).

i. Calendars of motions to be argued in the Parts are published on the morning of the argument date and on the day before in the New York Law Journal under each Part. Argument information is available on a case-by-case basis in Scroll, and e-mail notifications are sent by e-Track to participating attorneys whenever a motion is scheduled for argument in the court's computer system. NY R NY CTY J RUL Rule 15(a)

p. *NEW YORK COUNTY: Motion determined without hearing.* Given the purpose of the Room 130 procedure, the substance of motions will not be addressed at the submission "call." No Judge is present. To the extent possible, motions submitted in Room 130 will be decided "on the papers." Indeed, attorneys are encouraged to use service or clerks to deliver papers or working copies, or to agree among themselves to have one of them deliver papers for all parties by service or a clerk. Counsel for the movant need not appear to "take a default" on any motion or for any other reason. Motions will be submitted, not marked off, in the absence of the movant. Opposing counsel similarly need not appear in person in order to avoid suffering a default. Delivery of papers by service or a clerk will suffice. The court's goal is to be able to collect papers on motions in an orderly fashion but without any attorney having to make an appearance in Room 130 at any time. NY R NY CTY Procedure II(C).

q. *ONONDAGA COUNTY: Return date.* If the motion is the first filing in an action, the case will be assigned and counsel will be notified by the Supreme Court Clerk's Office via the NYSCEF system of the assigned justice and return date. NY R ONDGA E FIL Protocol(B)(7)(c). If the motion is on a previously assigned case, counsel may choose a return date from the assigned justice's motion term schedule. If the date in unavailable, the Supreme Court Clerk's Office will assign the motion to the next available motion term date and will notify counsel via e-mail. The change will also appear in the notification generated by the NYSCEF system. NY R ONDGA E FIL Protocol(B)(7)(d).

r. *QUEENS COUNTY: Return date.* Motions must be made returnable on the proper day/time based on the assigned judge. NY R L QUEENS MOT SUP Doc. 1. Failure to make a motion returnable on the proper day/time may result in the motion being administratively rescheduled or marked off. NY R L QUEENS MOT SUP Doc. 1.

s. *QUEENS COUNTY: Unassigned motions.* For RJI/Motions, due to the fact that the movant would not know who the

assigned judge will be, the notice of motion may be returnable any day of the week. RJI/Motions shall be made returnable in "Queens Supreme Court" with no address designated. The motion will be administratively rescheduled to the proper day of the week based on the judge (once a judge has been assigned). Within one (1) week of filing, the movant must check online to see who the assigned judge is (and therefore the location/date/time) that their motion is now returnable. Movant must then notify their adversary of this information prior to the return date. NY R L QUEENS MOT SUP Doc. 1.

3. *Entry of order after hearing.* An order determining a motion shall be entered and filed in the office of the clerk of the court where the action is triable, and all papers used on the motion and any opinion or memorandum in writing shall be filed with that clerk unless the order dispenses with such filing. When a statute or civil practice rule requires such filing and entry in a county other than that in which the order was made, the party prevailing on the motion shall file the order and the papers used on the motion with the proper clerk after receiving them. If a party fails to file any papers required to be filed under NY CPLR Rule 2220(a), the order may be vacated as irregular, with costs. NY CPLR Rule 2220(a). For more information on the entry of an order after a motion, refer to NY CPLR Rule 2219.
   a. *BRONX COUNTY: Settled orders.* A Judge's decision will often call for a Settled Order. The purpose of the settled order is to give effect to the decision by directing that some action be done and/or that a court official perform some task. NY R BRONX LEG SUP Doc. 2. A settled order consists of a notice of settlement informing all parties that the proposed order will be presented to the judge who made the decision on a date certain. Next comes the proposed order which will be presented to the judge. This order should conform to the judge's decision and should direct the relief granted in the decision. This should be followed by proof of service upon all parties who were noticed with the decision. It is also helpful if a copy of the judge's decision is included along with the other papers. A settled order should always be noticed before the judge who made the decision. NY R BRONX LEG SUP Doc. 2.
      i. Although an order is usually settled by the party who prevailed on the motion, any party may settle the order. It should be presented to the court within sixty (60) days of the decision. The other parties are entitled to ten (10) days notice where service of the settled order is done by mail, five (5) days if the notice is personally delivered. An attorney who is served with a notice of settlement which he believes does not accurately reflect the decision may settle a counter order. The counter order must be noticed for the same day and must be served not less than seven (7) days if by mail and two (2) days if personally delivered. NY R BRONX LEG SUP Doc. 2.
      ii. Settled orders are usually sent to the judge the day after they noticed for settlement. No appearance is necessary or even contemplated on a settled order. If the decision directs "submit order", then no notice is necessary, and the order will be sent to the judge as soon a practical after it is received. No fees are collected on settled orders. NY R BRONX LEG SUP Doc. 2.
   b. *ERIE COUNTY: Proposed orders.* Proposed orders shall be submitted through the NYSCEF system and a working copy provided to the IAS Justice for signature, if Part Rules so require. NY R ERIE E FIL Doc. 3(V)(G).
   c. *KINGS COUNTY: Long form orders.* If the Court directs that an order be settled or submitted on a motion in a NYSCEF case, the proposed order, with Notice of Settlement where required, and any proposed counter-order shall be filed with the Court via NYSCEF. The relevant clerk's office will process the documents in the customary manner. NY R L KINGS E FIL Doc. 1(E).
      i. WORKING COPIES OF PROPOSED ORDERS WITH NOTICE OF SETTLEMENT MUST BE SUBMITTED IN THE MOTION SUPPORT OFFICE (ROOM 227) AS EXPLAINED HEREIN. THEY MUST NOT BE DELIVERED TO THE PART OR CHAMBERS, EXCEPT WHERE THE INDIVIDUAL JUSTICE'S PART RULES PROVIDE OTHERWISE; DOING SO WILL CAUSE ADMINISTRATIVE CONFUSION AND POSSIBLE MISPLACEMENT OF PAPERS. Any such submission shall be sent in a timely manner (kindly review individual Justice's rules) and be conspicuously marked on the outside "NYSCEF Matter;" lack of such marking may delay processing. After an order/counter-order has been signed, it will be scanned, and the County Clerk will affix the entry stamp into the NYSCEF system, which will immediately transmit notice of this event via e-mail, including a link to the entered document, to all participating attorneys and unrepresented litigants in the case. Such transmittal does not constitute Notice of Entry. NY R L KINGS E FIL Doc. 1(E).
   d. *NEW YORK COUNTY: Long form orders.* Although the court strongly favors the use of short form orders and judgments, there are instances when settlement of an order or judgment is appropriate. When a Justice directs in a decision that a long form order or judgment be settled, that decision is recorded in the court's computer system by the General Clerk's Office and the motion file with decision is held in the Order Section of the Office in Room 119. The settlement process takes place there. NY R NY CTY Procedure II(D); NY R NY CTY E FIL Doc. 2(E).
      i. A proposed long form order or judgment in compliance NY R UNIF TRIAL CTS § 202.48 must be presented to

the relevant back office, together with a notice of settlement which bears a settlement date, the date on which the order is to be ready for formal presentation to the Justice. In an e-filed case the submission shall be made electronically. The proposed order or counter-order should be e-filed and it will be transmitted automatically by the NYSCEF system to the appropriate back office. The return date and time of the proposed order must be at 9:30 A.M. no sooner than either five (5) days from personal service of the proposed order or ten (10) days from service by mail. Proof of timely service on the other parties must accompany the proposed order in a hard copy case. If an order or judgment is submitted late (later than sixty (60) days from signing and filing of the decision) and the proponent can show good cause for this tardiness, an affidavit or affirmation justifying the delay should be annexed to the proposed order, together with proof of service thereof. If persuaded, the Justice will consider the proposed order despite its untimeliness. NY R NY CTY Procedure II(D); NY R NY CTY E FIL Doc. 2(E).

ii. Sometimes a decision will state "Submit Order." The submitting party should prepare a long form order and make it returnable without notice. Counsel should deliver the proposed order to the Order Section of the appropriate back office, except in an e-filed case, when it shall be submitted electronically. NY R NY CTY Procedure II(D). If the decision of the court directs that a proposed order be settled or submitted in the Part or in Chambers, that direction, should, of course, be followed without presentation of the proposal to the back office. NY R NY CTY Procedure II(D).

iii. For information on proposed counter-orders, refer to NY R NY CTY Procedure II(D) and NY R NY CTY J RUL Rule 16(b).

e. *QUEENS COUNTY: Proposed orders.* If the court directs that an order be settled or submitted on a motion in an E-file case, the proposed order and any proposed counter-order shall be filed with the court on-line with proof of service. (If a decision refers to a proceeding on the record, a copy of the transcript must be submitted.) Working copies of all proposed orders MUST be submitted to the Motion Support Office before an order can be reviewed. NY R L QUEENS E-FILE Doc. 1(I).

i. Counsel are advised to adhere to NY R UNIF TRIAL CTS § 202.48 regarding the submission or settlement of their proposed order or judgment. Persons who are submitting proposed orders/judgments pursuant to a previously issued memorandum decision must submit a copy of the memorandum decision with their proposed order/judgment. Upon E-Filing a proposed order/judgement, a working copy of the proposed order/judgement must be provided to the Motion Support Office. NY R L QUEENS MOT SUP Doc. 1.

H. Forms

1. Official Motion for Leave to Renew or Reargue Forms for New York

a. Request for judicial intervention. NY R UNIF TRIAL CTS § 202.6.

b. Notice of motion. NY R UNIF TRIAL CTS § 202.7(b).

2. New York Motion to Reargue or Renew Forms

a. Form; Notice of motion for leave to renew. NYPRAC-CIVAPP § 5:15.

b. Form; Affirmation in support of motion for leave to renew. NYPRAC-CIVAPP § 5:16.

c. Form; Notice of motion for reargument. NYPRAC-CIVAPP § 5:17.

d. Form; Affidavit in support of motion for reargument. NYPRAC-CIVAPP § 5:18.

e. Notice of motion for reargument. MCF CPLR § 5:56.

f. Affidavit in support of motion for reargument. MCF CPLR § 5:57.

g. Notice of motion for leave to renew prior motion for consolidation and joint trial. MCF CPLR § 5:61.

h. Affirmation in support of motion for leave to renew prior motion. MCF CPLR § 5:62.

i. Affidavit in support of motion for leave to renew prior motion. MCF CPLR § 5:63.

j. Affirmation in support of motion for leave to renew prior motion for consolidation and joint trial. MCF CPLR § 5:64.

k. Notice of cross-motion for reargument and renewal. MCF CPLR § 5:66.

l. Affidavit of merits in support of cross-motion for reargument and renewal. MCF CPLR § 5:67.

m. Affirmation in support of cross-motion for reargument and renewal. MCF CPLR § 5:68.

n. General form of affidavit of service of motion papers. MCF CPLR § 5:24.

I. Applicable Rules

1. *State rules*

   a. Short title; Application; Construction; Definitions. NY CPLR § 101; NY CPLR § 103; NY CPLR § 104; NY CPLR § 105.

   b. Appendix of official forms. NY CPLR § 107.

   c. Extensions of time generally. NY CPLR § 2004.

   d. Form of papers. NY CPLR Rule 2101; NY CPLR Rule 2102; NY CPLR § 2105; NY CPLR Rule 2106; NY GEN BUS § 399-ddd; NY R UNIF TRIAL CTS § 215.2; NY R UNIF TRIAL CTS § 215.3.

   e. Service of papers. NY CPLR Rule 2103.

   f. Where motion made; In supreme court action. NY CPLR § 2212.

   g. Motion papers; Service; Time. NY CPLR Rule 2214.

   h. Relief demanded by other than moving party. NY CPLR Rule 2215.

   i. Prior motion; Ex parte motion; Transfer of motion; Hearings; Orders. NY CPLR Rule 2217; NY CPLR § 2218; NY CPLR Rule 2220.

   j. Motion affecting prior order. NY CPLR Rule 2221.

   k. Computation of time. NY CPLR § 2402; NY GEN CONSTR § 19; NY GEN CONSTR § 20; NY GEN CONSTR § 25-a; NY GEN CONSTR § 30; NY GEN CONSTR § 31; NY GEN CONSTR § 53.

   l. Motions heard by judge supervising disclosure; Stay of disclosure. NY CPLR Rule 3214.

   m. Fees; Index number fees of county clerks. NY CPLR § 8018.

   n. Hours of court; Proceedings in court. NY R CHIEF J § 3.1; NY R CHIEF J § 29.3.

   o. Application of part; Waiver; Additional rules; Application of CPLR; Definitions. NY R UNIF TRIAL CTS § 202.1.

   p. Papers filed in court; Electronic filing in supreme court. NY R UNIF TRIAL CTS § 202.5; NY R UNIF TRIAL CTS § 202.5-a; NY R UNIF TRIAL CTS § 202.5-b; NY R UNIF TRIAL CTS § 202.5-bb.

   q. Request for judicial intervention. NY R UNIF TRIAL CTS § 202.6.

   r. Calendaring of motions; Uniform notice of motion form; Affirmation of good faith. NY R UNIF TRIAL CTS § 202.7.

   s. Motion procedure; Preliminary conferences. NY R UNIF TRIAL CTS § 202.8; NY R UNIF TRIAL CTS § 202.12.

   t. Rules of the commercial division of the Supreme Court. NY R UNIF TRIAL CTS § 202.70.

   u. Signing of papers. NY R CHIEF ADMIN § 130-1.1-a.

2. *Local rules*

   a. *Albany County*

      i. Third judicial district rules. NY R 3 JD SUP Doc. 1.

   b. *Bronx County*

      i. Filing of papers in supreme court. NY R BRONX FIL R Doc. 1.

      ii. Request for judicial intervention. NY R BRONX FIL R Doc. 2.

      iii. Motion procedure. NY R BRONX FIL R Doc. 8.

      iv. Commercial division. NY R BRONX FIL R Doc. 12.

      v. Motions on notice. NY R BRONX E FIL R Doc. 1.

      vi. Settled orders. NY R BRONX LEG SUP Doc. 2.

   c. *Erie County*

      i. Joint protocols for New York State Courts E-Filing (NYSCEF) cases filed in Supreme Court, Erie County. NY R ERIE E FIL Doc. 3.

   d. *Kings County*

      i. Papers. NY R L KINGS Pt. A, Papers.

      ii. Service of motion papers. NY R L KINGS Pt. C, Rule 1.

iii. Scheduling of motions. NY R L KINGS Pt. C, Rule 2.
iv. Appearance and argument. NY R L KINGS Pt. C, Rule 3.
v. Courtesy copies. NY R L KINGS Pt. C, Rule 5.
vi. Motion calendar calls. NY R L KINGS Pt. C, Rule 7.
vii. Protocol on courthouse and county clerk procedures for electronically filed cases. NY R L KINGS E FIL Doc. 1.

e. *New York County*

i. Commencement of cases. NY R NY CTY Procedure I.
ii. RJIs and assignments. NY R NY CTY Procedure IA.
iii. Motions and special proceedings by notice of motion/petition. NY R NY CTY Procedure II.
iv. County clerk litigation functions. NY R NY CTY Procedure XI.
v. Protocol on courthouse and county clerk procedures for electronically filed cases. NY R NY CTY E FIL Doc. 2.
vi. Redaction of information in documents filed with the county clerk and the court. NY R NY CTY J RUL Rule A-1.
vii. Papers by fax. NY R NY CTY J RUL Rule 4.
viii. Motions on notice; Orders to show cause. NY R NY CTY J RUL Rule 13.
ix. Motion papers. NY R NY CTY J RUL Rule 14.
x. Oral argument; Adjournments. NY R NY CTY J RUL Rule 15.

f. *Onondaga County*

i. Onondaga county protocol for case filings New York State Electronic Files (NYSCEF). NY R ONDGA E FIL Protocol.

g. *Queens County*

i. Motion support office. NY R L QUEENS MOT SUP Doc. 1.
ii. Queens county protocol on courthouse procedures for electronically filed cases. NY R L QUEENS E-FILE Doc. 1.

J. Miscellaneous

NOTE: Individual judges' rules may apply.

ALBANY COUNTY

JUSTICE LISA M. FISHER: NY R 3 JD FISHER Fisher; NY R 3 JD FISHER Fisher, PC Order.

JUSTICE RICHARD MOTT: NY R 3 JD MOTT Mott.

JUSTICE STEPHAN G. SCHICK: NY R 3 JD Schick.

FORECLOSURE SETTLEMENT PART: NY R 3 JD Foreclosure Settlement.

BRONX COUNTY

JUSTICE PAUL L. ALPERT: [NY R BRONX J Part IA-29, as amended by NY ORDER 20-0337].

JUSTICE BEN BARBATO: NY R BRONX J Part IA-21.

JUSTICE MARY ANNE BRIGANTTI: [NY R BRONX J Part IA-15, as amended by NY ORDER 20-0338].

JUSTICE JOSEPH E. CAPELLA: NY R BRONX J Part IA-23.

JUSTICE MITCHELL DANZIGER: NY R BRONX J Part IA-3/33 ; [NY R BRONX J Danziger, Part IA-3/33, as amended by NY ORDER 20-0339].

JUSTICE LAURA G. DOUGLAS: NY R BRONX J Part IA-11.

JUSTICE RUBEN FRANCO: NY R BRONX J Part IA-26.

JUSTICE DORIS M. GONZALEZ: NY R BRONX J Part IA-24.

JUSTICE WILMA GUZMAN: NY R BRONX J Part IA-7; [NY R BRONX J Guzman, Part IA-7 Virtual, as amended by NY ORDER 20-0340].

JUSTICE ROBERT T. JOHNSON: NY R BRONX J Part IA-12.

JUSTICE DONALD A. MILES: NY R BRONX J Part IA-8.

JUSTICE DONNA M. MILLS: NY R BRONX J Part IA-9.

JUSTICE JULIA I. RODRIGUEZ: NY R BRONX J Part IA-18; [NY R BRONX J Part IA-27, as amended by NY ORDER 20-0341].

JUSTICE LLINET M. ROSADO: [NY R BRONX J Part IA-25, as amended by NY ORDER 20-0342].

JUSTICE NORMA RUIZ: NY R BRONX J Part IA-22; [NY R BRONX J Ruiz, Part IA-22 Virtual, as amended by NY ORDER 20-0343].

JUSTICE HOWARD H. SHERMAN: NY R BRONX J Part IA-4.

JUSTICE FERNANDO TAPIA: NY R BRONX J Part IA-13.

JUSTICE ELIZABETH A. TAYLOR: NY R BRONX J Part IA-2.

JUSTICE ALISON Y. TRUITT: NY R BRONX J Part IA-5.

PART IDV: NY R BRONX J Doc. 1.

PRE-TRIAL PART RULES: NY R BRONX J Doc. 2.

PRE TRIAL WORKSHEET: NY R BRONX J Doc. 3.

FORECLOSURE SETTLEMENT PART RULES: NY R BRONX J Doc. 4.

GUARDIANSHIP PART RULES: NY R BRONX J Doc. 5.

LPM PART RULES: NY R BRONX J Doc. 6.

ERIE COUNTY

JUSTICE M. WILLIAM BOLLER: NY R 8 JD J Boller.

JUSTICE RALPH A. BONIELLO: NY R 8 JD J Boniello.

JUSTICE CHRISTOPHER J. BURN: NY R 8 JD J Burns.

JUSTICE RUSSELL P. BUSCAGLIA: NY R 8 JD J Buscaglia.

JUSTICE FRANK CARUSO: NY R 8 JD J Caruso.

JUSTICE STEPHEN W. CASS: NY R 8 JD J Cass.

JUSTICE DEBORAH A. CHIMES: NY R 8 JD J Chimes.

JUSTICE EMILIO COLAIACOVO: [NY R 8 JD J Colaiacovo, as amended by NY ORDER 20-0252].

JUSTICE DIANE Y. DEVLIN: NY R 8 JD J Devlin.

JUSTICE JAMES H. DILLON: NY R 8 JD J Dillon.

JUSTICE PAULA L. FEROLETO: NY R 8 JD J Feroleto.

JUSTICE DANIEL J. FURLONG: [NY R 8 JD J Furlong, as amended by NY ORDER 20-0253].

JUSTICE JOSEPH R. GLOWNIA: NY R 8 JD J Glownia.

JUSTICE MARK J. GRISANTI: NY R 8 JD J Grisanti.

JUSTICE DEBORAH A. HAENDIGES: NY R 8 JD J Haendiges.

JUSTICE LYNN W. KEANE: [NY R 8 JD J Keane, as amended by NY ORDER 20-0254].

JUSTICE RICHARD C. KLOCH, Sr.: NY R 8 JD J Kloch.

JUSTICE FREDERICK J. MARSHALL: [NY R 8 JD J Marshall, as amended by NY ORDER 20-0255.

JUSTICE JOHN L. MICHALSKI: NY R 8 JD J Michalski.

JUSTICE MARK A. MONTOUR: [NY R 8 JD J Montour, as amended by NY ORDER 20-0256].

JUSTICE HENRY NOWAK: NY R 8 JD J Nowak.

JUSTICE JOHN F. O'DONNELL: NY R 8 JD J O'Donnell.

JUSTICE JEANETTE OGDEN: NY R 8 JD J Ogden.

JUSTICE CATHERINE NUGENT-PANEPINTO: NY R 8 JD J Nugent-Panepinto.
JUSTICE FRANK A. SEDITA, III: [NY R 8 JD J Sedita, as amended by NY ORDER 20-0257].
JUSTICE SARA SHELDON: NY R 8 JD J Sheldon.
JUSTICE DONNA M. SIWEK: NY R 8 JD J Siwek.
JUSTICE MARY L. SLISZ: NY R 8 JD J Slisz.
JUSTICE TIMOTHY J. WALKER: [NY R 8 JD J Walker, as amended by NY ORDER 20-0258].
JUSTICE DENNIS E. WARD: NY R 8 JD J Ward.
JUSTICE PAUL B. WOJTASZEK: [NY R 8 JD J Wojtaszek, as amended by NY ORDER 20-0259].
JUSTICE CHARLES N. ZAMBITO: [NY R 8 JD J Zambito, as amended by NY ORDER 20-0260].
SUPREME COURT LEGAL STAFF: NY R 8 JD J Legal Staff.

KINGS COUNTY

JUSTICE RACHEL A. ADAMS: NY R KINGS J Part 5F.
JUSTICE LOREN BAILY-SCHIFFMAN: NY R KINGS J Part 65.
JUSTICE REGINALD A. BODDIE: NY R KINGS J Part 95.
JUSTICE THERESA M. CICCOTTO: NY R KINGS J Part 19; NY R KINGS J Part 5J.
JUSTICE LISSETTE COLON: NY R KINGS J Part Rules.
JUSTICE GENINE EDWARDS: NY R KINGS J Part 80.
JUSTICE PAMELA L. FISHER: [NY R KINGS J Part 94, as amended by NY ORDER 20-0208].
JUSTICE ROBIN GARSON: NY R KINGS J Part 75.
JUSTICE LARA J. GENOVISI: [NY R KINGS J Part 34, as amended by NY ORDER 20-0209].
JUSTICE BERNARD J. GRAHAM: NY R KINGS J Part 36.
JUSTICE DAWN JIMENEZ-SALTA: NY R KINGS J Part 88.
JUSTICE INGRID JOSEPH: [NY R KINGS J Part FRP3 and Part 83, as amended by NY ORDER 20-0210].
JUSTICE KATHY J. KING: NY R KINGS J Part 64, 76K.
JUSTICE LAWRENCE KNIPEL: NY R KINGS J Part 57.
JUSTICE DONALD KURTZ: NY R KINGS J Part 26.
JUSTICE CARL LANDICINO: [NY R KINGS J Part 81, as amended by NY ORDER 20-0211].
JUSTICE KATHERINE LEVINE: [NY R KINGS J Part 20, 25, 92, as amended by NY ORDER 20-0211].
JUSTICE LORNA MCALLISTER: [NY R KINGS J Part 10, as amended by NY ORDER 20-0211].
JUSTICE ROSEMARIE MONTALBANO: [NY R KINGS J Part 19, 71, and 22, as amended by NY ORDER 20-0211].
JUSTICE RICHARD J. MONTELIONE: [NY R KINGS J Part 99 and DJMP, as amended by NY ORDER 20-0215].
JUSTICE LISA S. OTTLEY: NY R KINGS J Part 24.
JUSTICE MARK I. PARTNOW: NY R KINGS J Part 43.
JUSTICE ERIC I. PRUS: NY R KINGS J Part 5A.
JUSTICE FRANCOIS RIVERA: NY R KINGS J Part 52.
JUSTICE KAREN B. ROTHENBERG: NY R KINGS J Part 35.
JUSTICE LEON RUCHELSMAN: NY R KINGS J Part 1.
JUSTICE WAYNE P. SAITTA: NY R KINGS J Part 29.
JUSTICE ROBIN K. SHEARES: NY R KINGS J Part 96.
JUSTICE KENNETH P. SHERMAN: NY R KINGS J Part 67 and 78.
JUSTICE DEBRA SILBER: NY R KINGS J Part 9 and 5K.
JUSTICE ELLEN M. SPODEK: NY R KINGS J Part 63.

JUSTICE MARSHA L. STEINHARDT: NY R KINGS J Part 15.

JUSTICE JEFFREY S. SUNSHINE: NY R KINGS J Part 5G.

JUSTICE PETER P. SWEENEY: [NY R KINGS J Part 35, as amended by NY ORDER 20-0218].

JUSTICE DELORES J. THOMAS: [NY R KINGS J Part 5T, as amended by NY ORDER 20-0221].

JUSTICE WAVNY TOUSSAINT: NY R KINGS J Part 70.

JUSTICE RICHARD VELASQUEZ: NY R KINGS J Part 66.

JUSTICE CAROLYN E. WADE: NY R KINGS J Part 84.

JUSTICE EDWARD G. WALKER: [NY R KINGS J Part 90, as amended by NY ORDER 20-0219].

JUSTICE LILLIAN WAN: [NY R KINGS J Part 17, as amended by NY ORDER 20-0220].

JUSTICE MICHELLE WESTON: NY R KINGS J Part 3.

MENTAL HYGIENE PART: NY R KINGS J Part 77.

MATRIMONIAL PARTS DURING COVID-19 EMERGENCY: JUSTICE KAREN B. ROTHENBERG: NY R KINGS J Doc. 1.

NASSAU COUNTY

JUSTICE ANNA R. ANZALONE: NY R NASSAU S J Anzalone, Part 26.

JUSTICE STACY D. BENNETT: NY R NASSAU S J Bennett; NY R NASSAU S J Bennett, Form 1.

JUSTICE ANTONIO BRANDVEEN: NY R NASSAU S J Brandveen, Part 31.

JUSTICE JEFFREY S. BROWN: [NY R NASSAU S J Brown, as amended by NY ORDER 20-0297].

JUSTICE STEPHEN A. BUCARIA: NY R NASSAU S J Bucaria.

JUSTICE JULIANNE T. CAPETOLA: NY R NASSAU S J Capetola, Part 28.

JUSTICE EDMUND M. DANE: NY R NASSAU S J Dane, Part 33.

JUSTICE VITO M. DESTEFANO: NY R NASSAU S J DeStefano, Part 13; NY R NASSAU S J DeStefano, Form 1.

JUSTICE ARTHUR M. DIAMOND: NY R NASSAU S J Diamond, Part 7.

JUSTICE THOMAS FEINMAN: NY R NASSAU S J Feinman, Part 5.

JUSTICE JOHN M. GALASSO: NY R NASSAU S J Galasso, Part 22.

JUSTICE SHARON M.J. GIANELLI: NY R NASSAU S J Gianelli, Part 22; NY R NASSAU S J Gianelli, Form 1.

JUSTICE JEFFREY A. GOODSTEIN: NY R NASSAU S J Goodstein, Part 33; NY R NASSAU S J Goodstein, Form 1.

JUSTICE DAVID J. GUGERTY: [NY R NASSAU S J Gugerty, Part 31, as amended by NY ORDER 20-0298].

JUSTICE HELENE F. GUGERTY: NY R NASSAU S J Gugerty, Part 47.

JUSTICE STEVEN M. JAEGER: NY R NASSAU S J Jaeger, Part 35; NY R NASSAU S J Jaeger, Form 1.

JUSTICE JACK L. LIBERT: NY R NASSAU S J Libert, Part 23.

JUSTICE JOSEPH H. LORINTZ: NY R NASSAU S J Lorintz, Part 26; NY R NASSAU S J Lorintz, Form 1.

JUSTICE ROY S. MAHON: NY R NASSAU S J Mahon, Part 3.

JUSTICE RANDY SUE MARBER: NY R NASSAU S J Marber, Part 8.

JUSTICE JAMES P. MCCORMACK: [NY R NASSAU S J McCormack, Part 18, as amended by NY ORDER, 20-0299].

JUSTICE DICCIA T. PINEDA-KIRWAN: [NY R NASSAU S J Pineda-Kirwan, as amended by NY ORDER 20-0300].

JUSTICE THOMAS RADEMAKER: [NY R NASSAU S J Rademaker, Part 28, as amended by NY ORDER 20-0301]; [NY R NASSAU S J Rademaker, Form 1, as amended by NY ORDER 20-0301].

JUSTICE DENISE L. SHER: NY R NASSAU S J Rademaker, Part 32.

JUSTICE LEONARD D. STEINMAN: [NY R NASSAU S J Steinman, Part 15, as amended by NY ORDER 20-0303]; NY R NASSAU S J Steinman, Form 1.

JUSTICE HOWARD E. STURIM: NY R NASSAU S J Sturim, Part 50; NY R NASSAU S J Sturim, Form 1.

JUSTICE HELEN VOUTSINAS: [NY R NASSAU S J Voutsinas, Part 25, as amended by NY ORDER 20-0304]; [NY R NASSAU S J Voutsinas, Form 1, as amended by NY ORDER 20-0305].

JUSTICE HOPE SCHWARTZ ZIMMERMAN: NY R NASSAU S J Zimmerman, Part 17.

NEW YORK COUNTY

JUDGE'S RULES; BASIC INFORMATION: [NY R NY CTY J RUL Doc. 1, as amended by NY ORDER 20-0202].

ONONDAGA COUNTY

JUSTICE ROBERT E. ANTONACCI II: [NY R ONDGA E FIL Doc. 1, as amended by 20-0239].

JUSTICE MICHAEL V. COCCOMI: NY R ONDGA E FIL Doc. 2.

JUSTICE GREGORY R. GILBERT: NY R 5 JD JUDGES Gilbert; NY R ONDGA E FIL Doc. 3.

JUSTICE DONALD A. GREENWOOD: NY R ONDGA E FIL Doc. 4.

JUSTICE DEBORAH H. KARALUNAS: NY R ONDGA E FIL Doc. 5.

JUSTICE JAMES MCCLUSKY: NY R 5 JD MCCLUSKY McClusky.

JUSTICE CHARLES C. MERRELL: NY R 5 JD MERRELL Merrell.

JUSTICE PATRICK F. MACRAE: NY R 5 JD MACRAE Doc. 1.

JUSTICE JAMES P. MURPHY: NY R ONDGA E FIL Doc. 7.

JUSTICE GERALD J. NERI: [NY R 5 JD JUDGES Neri, as amended by NY ORDER 20-0236]; [NY R ONDGA E FIL Doc. 8, as amended by NY ORDER 20-0241].

JUSTICE ANTHONY J. PARIS: NY R 5 JD JUDGES Paris; [NY R ONDGA E FIL Doc. 9, as amended by NY ORDER 20-0242].

JUSTICE NORMAN W. SEITER, JR.: NY R 5 JD JUDGES Seiter.

JUSTICE KEVIN G. YOUNG: [NY R ONDGA E FIL Doc. 10, as amended by NY ORDER 20-0243].

QUEENS COUNTY

JUSTICE PAM JACKMAN BROWN: [NY R L QUEENS Brown, Part 19, as amended by NY ORDER 20-0321].

JUSTICE CHEREE A. BUGGS: NY R L QUEENS Buggs, Part 30.

JUSTICE PAM JACKMAN BROWN: [NY R L QUEENS Brown, Part 19, as amended by NY ORDER 20-0321].

JUSTICE DENIS J. BUTLER: NY R L QUEENS Butler, Part 12.

JUSTICE ROBERT I. CALORAS: [NY R L QUEENS Caloras, Part 36, as amended by NY ORDER 20-0322].

JUSTICE ANNA CULLEY: NY R L QUEENS Culley, Part 53.

JUSTICE TIMOTHY DUFFICY: NY R L QUEENS Dufficy, Part 35.

JUSTICE DAVID ELLIOT: NY R L QUEENS Elliot, Part 14.

JUSTICE JOSEPH J. ESPOSITO: NY R L QUEENS Esposito, Part 6.

JUSTICE DARRELL L. GAVRIN: [NY R L QUEENS Gavrin, Part 27, as amended by NY ORDER 20-0323].

JUSTICE WYATT N. GIBBONS: [NY R L QUEENS Gibbons, Part 5, as amended by NY ORDER 20-0330.

JUSTICE DONNA-MARIE E. GOLIA: [NY R L QUEENS Golia, Part 21, as amended by NY ORDER 20-0331].

JUSTICE MARGUERITE A. GRAYS: [NY R L QUEENS Grays, Part 4, as amended by NY ORDER 20-0324].

JUSTICE RUDOLPH E. GRECO: [NY R L QUEENS Greco, Part 32, as amended by NY ORDER 20-0325].

JUSTICE MAUREEN HEALY: NY R L QUEENS Healy, Part 6.

JUSTICE PHILLIP HOM: [NY R L QUEENS Hom, Part 43, as amended by NY ORDER 20-0332].

JUSTICE KEVIN J. KERRIGAN: NY R L QUEENS Kerrigan, Part 10.

JUSTICE MOJGAN C. LANCMAN: NY R L QUEENS Lancman, Part 20.

JUSTICE RICHARD G. LATIN: NY R L QUEENS Latin, Part 40.

JUSTICE ULYSSES B. LEVERETT: [NY R L QUEENS Leverett, Part 6, as amended by NY ORDER 20-0326].

JUSTICE LEONARD LIVOTE: NY R L QUEENS Livote, Part 33.

JUSTICE LEE A. MAYERSOHN: NY R L QUEENS Mayersohn, Part 22; NY R L QUEENS Mayersohn, Part 22G; [NY R L QUEENS Mayersohn, Part 22G COVID, as amended by NY ORDER 20-0327].

JUSTICE ROBERT J. MCDONALD: NY R L QUEENS McDonald, Part 34.
JUSTICE MARGARET MCGOWAN: NY R L QUEENS McGowan, Part 52.
JUSTICE MAURICE E. MUIR: [NY R L QUEENS Muir, Part 42, as amended by NY ORDER 20-0333].
JUSTICE JODI ORLOW: NY R L QUEENS Orlow, Part 51.
JUSTICE LESLIE J. PURIFICCION: NY R L QUEENS Purificcion, Part 39.
JUSTICE JOSEPH RISI: [NY R L QUEENS Risi, Part 3, as amended by NY ORDER 20-0328].
JUSTICE FREDERICK D.R. SAMPSON: [NY R L QUEENS Sampson, Part 31, as amended by NY ORDER 20-0329].
JUSTICE MARTIN J. SCHULMAN: NY R L QUEENS Schulman, Part 29.
JUSTICE BERNICE D. SIEGAL: NY R L QUEENS Siegal, Part 25G.
JUSTICE JANICE A. TAYLOR: NY R L QUEENS Taylor, Part 15.
JUSTICE CARMEN R. VELASQUEZ: NY R L QUEENS Velasquez, Part 38.
JUSTICE LOURDES M VENTURA: [NY R L QUEENS Ventura, Part 37, as amended by NY ORDER 20-0334].
JUSTICE WILLIAM A. VISCOVICH: NY R L QUEENS Viscovich, Part 63.
JUSTICE ALLAN B. WEISS: NY R L QUEENS Weiss, Part 2.
COMPLIANCE, SETTLEMENT AND CONFERENCE PART: NY R L QUEENS Doc 1.
PRELIMINARY CONFERENCE PART: [NY R L QUEENS Doc. 2, as amended by NY ORDER 20-0335].
MEDICAL MALPRACTICE CONFERENCE PART: [NY R L QUEENS Doc. 3, as amended by NY ORDER 20-0336].
TRIAL SCHEDULING PART: NY R L QUEENS Doc. 4.
SUMMARY JURY TRIAL PROGRAM: NY R L QUEENS Doc. 7.
RESIDENTIAL FORECLOSURE PART: NY R L QUEENS Doc. 9.
FORECLOSURE AUCTION RULES: NY R L QUEENS Doc. 10.
MATRIMONIAL PRELIMINARY CONFERENCE PART: NY R L QUEENS Doc. 11.
NON-CUSTODIAL CONTESTED MATRIMONIAL PART: NY R L QUEENS Doc. 12.

Motions, Oppositions and Replies
Motion to Transfer Venue

Document Last Updated August 2020

A. Checklist

(I) ❑ Matters to consider for moving party
- (a) ❑ Required documents
  - (1) ❑ Notice of motion, order to show cause, or affidavit on ex parte motion
  - (2) ❑ Motion
  - (3) ❑ Request for judicial intervention
  - (4) ❑ Proof of service
  - (5) ❑ ALBANY COUNTY: Additional required documents
    - (i) ❑ Affirmation of good faith effort
- (b) ❑ Supplemental documents
  - (1) ❑ Supporting evidence; Exhibits
  - (2) ❑ Brief
  - (3) ❑ Affidavit in support of convenience of witnesses
  - (4) ❑ Notice to produce papers not in possession of the court

(5) ❑ Filing fees

(6) ❑ Working copies

(7) ❑ Statement of authorization in electronic filing cases

(8) ❑ ERIE COUNTY: Additional supplemental documents

(i) ❑ Notice of hard copy submission in e-filed case

(9) ❑ KINGS COUNTY: Additional supplemental documents

(i) ❑ Forms when filing in hard copy

(10) ❑ NEW YORK COUNTY: Additional supplemental documents

(i) ❑ Notice of hard copy submission

(ii) ❑ Unpublished opinions

(11) ❑ ONONDAGA COUNTY: Additional supplemental documents

(i) ❑ Notice of hard copy submission

(12) ❑ QUEENS COUNTY: Additional supplemental documents

(i) ❑ Notice of hard copy submission

(c) ❑ Timing

(1) ❑ A demand under NY CPLR Rule 511(b) for change of place of trial on the ground that the county designated for that purpose is not a proper county shall be served with the answer or before the answer is served

(2) ❑ A motion for change of place of trial on any other ground shall be made within a reasonable time after commencement of the action

(3) ❑ The moving party shall serve copies of all affidavits and briefs upon all other parties at the time of service of the notice of motion

(4) ❑ A notice of motion and supporting affidavits shall be served at least eight (8) days before the time at which the motion is noticed to be heard

(5) ❑ It is also good practice to make motions returnable at least three (3) weeks away from the planned date of mailing and to always include a demand in the motion that the other side serve answering papers at least seven (7) days before the return day

(6) ❑ BRONX COUNTY: Additional timing

(i) ❑ A Notice of Motion must be served at least eight (8) days, by personal service, nine (9) days by overnight express and thirteen (13) days by mail before the return date

(7) ❑ NEW YORK COUNTY: Additional timing

(i) ❑ In an e-filed case, all of the moving papers shall be e-filed at least eight (8) business days prior to the return date

(8) ❑ ONONDAGA COUNTY: Additional timing

(i) ❑ Onondaga County local court rules require that any additional papers relating to motions must be e-filed at least two (2) business days prior to the return date, excluding the return date

(9) ❑ QUEENS COUNTY: Additional timing

(i) ❑ Motions must be in the possession of the Motion Support Office at least nine (9) days before the noticed return date of the motion

(II) ❑ Matters to consider for opposing party

(a) ❑ Required documents

(1) ❑ Opposition

(2) ❑ Proof of service

(b) ❑ Supplemental documents

(1) ❑ Supporting evidence; Exhibits

(2) ❑ Brief

(3) ❑ Filing fees

(4) ❑ Working copies

(5) ❑ ERIE COUNTY: Additional supplemental documents

(i) ❑ Notice of hard copy submission in e-filed case

(6) ❑ KINGS COUNTY: Additional supplemental documents

(i) ❑ Forms when filing in hard copy

(7) ❑ NEW YORK COUNTY: Additional supplemental documents

(i) ❑ Notice of hard copy submission

(ii) ❑ Unpublished opinions

(8) ❑ ONONDAGA COUNTY: Additional supplemental documents

(i) ❑ Notice of hard copy submission

(9) ❑ QUEENS COUNTY: Additional supplemental documents

(i) ❑ Notice of hard copy submission

(c) ❑ Timing

(1) ❑ Answering affidavits shall be served at least two (2) days before the time at which the motion is noticed to be heard

(2) ❑ Answering affidavits and any notice of cross-motion, with supporting papers, if any, shall be served at least seven (7) days before such time if a notice of motion served at least sixteen (16) days before such time so demands

B. Timing

1. *Time to bring motion to transfer venue*

a. *Demand for change of place of trial upon ground of improper venue.* A demand under NY CPLR Rule 511(b) for change of place of trial on the ground that the county designated for that purpose is not a proper county shall be served with the answer or before the answer is served. NY CPLR Rule 511(a). Refer to the New York KeyRules Answer document for the timing requirements of the answer.

i. The defendant shall serve a written demand that the action be tried in a county he specifies as proper. Thereafter the defendant may move to change the place of trial within fifteen (15) days after service of the demand, unless within five (5) days after such service plaintiff serves a written consent to change the place of trial to that specified by the defendant. NY CPLR Rule 511(b).

ii. Defendant may notice such motion to be heard as if the action were pending in the county he specified, unless plaintiff within five (5) days after service of the demand serves an affidavit showing either that the county specified by the defendant is not proper or that the county designated by him is proper. NY CPLR Rule 511(b).

b. *Motion on other grounds.* A motion for change of place of trial on any other ground shall be made within a reasonable time after commencement of the action. NY CPLR Rule 511(a).

i. What's "reasonable" is of course sui generis. Five (5) months has been held reasonable when no prejudice traceable to the delay could be shown. SIEGEL-NYPRAC § 124; Ryan v. Great Atl. & Pac. Tea Co., 30 A.D.2d 549, 549, 290 N.Y.S.2d 849, 850 (1968).

2. *Time to serve.* The moving party shall serve copies of all affidavits and briefs upon all other parties at the time of service of the notice of motion. NY R UNIF TRIAL CTS § 202.8(c). A notice of motion and supporting affidavits shall be served at least eight (8) days before the time at which the motion is noticed to be heard. NY CPLR Rule 2214(b).

a. *Return dates; Best practice.* It is also good practice to make motions returnable at least three (3) weeks away from the planned date of mailing and to always include a demand in the motion that the other side serve answering papers at least seven (7) days before the return day. This enables the motion to be served by mail, gives sufficient notice to support the seven (7) day demand, and leaves a few days for a delayed mailing if some snag prevents posting on the day planned. If speed is needed, the shorter eight (8) day notice period can be used, forfeiting the right to seven (7) day answering papers and a reply. If even eight (8) days notice is too much under the circumstances, the order to show cause is the remedy. SIEGEL-NYPRAC § 247.

i. *ALBANY COUNTY.* All motions, except for certain matters in Albany County as specified in NY R 3 JD SUP

Doc. 1(E) and NY R 3 JD SUP Doc. 1(F), brought on by notice of motion or by order to show cause will be made returnable on any day, Monday through Friday, as chosen by the movant in compliance with the CPLR. Parties shall submit all papers in a timely fashion as required by the CPLR by delivering them or mailing them directly to the Supreme Court Clerk's Office[. . .]except that motions and other applications subject to a filing fee shall first be presented to the County Clerk's Office for payment of the requisite fee and then subsequently filed with the Supreme Court Clerk's Office. NY R 3 JD SUP Doc. 1(B).

ii. *BRONX COUNTY.* A Notice of Motion must be served at least eight (8) days, by personal service, nine (9) days by overnight express and thirteen (13) days by mail before the return date. NY R BRONX FIL R Doc. 3. All unassigned motions must be accompanied with a properly filled out RJI and shall be filed in the Motion Support Office, room 217, within five (5) days of service. All motions on actions already assigned to a Justice must be filed at least five (5) business days before the return date. NY R BRONX FIL R Doc. 3. All papers served must strictly comply with the time requirements of NY CPLR Rule 2101, NY CPLR Rule 2103 and NY CPLR Rule 2214(b). NY R BRONX FIL R Doc. 8.

iii. *KINGS COUNTY.* Motion papers, answering affidavits and reply affidavits must be served on adversaries in accordance with NY CPLR Rule 2214. NY R L KINGS Pt. C, Rule 1.

iv. *NEW YORK COUNTY.* In an e-filed case, all of the moving papers shall be e-filed at least eight (8) business days prior to the return date. The clerk will calendar the motion for the Motion Submission Part Courtroom (Room 130) for the return date selected. NY R NY CTY Procedure II(A); NY R NY CTY E FIL Doc. 2(D)(1).

v. *ONONDAGA COUNTY.* Onondaga County local court rules require that any additional papers relating to motions must be e-filed at least two (2) business days prior to the return date, excluding the return date. NY R ONDGA E FIL Protocol(B)(9)(e).

vi. *QUEENS COUNTY.* Motions must be in the possession of the Motion Support Office at least nine (9) days before the noticed return date of the motion. NY R L QUEENS MOT SUP Doc. 1; NY R L QUEENS E-FILE Doc. 1(H)(1).

b. *Order to show cause; Shorter time.* The court in a proper case may grant an order to show cause, to be served in lieu of a notice of motion, at a time and in a manner specified therein. NY CPLR Rule 2214(d). An ordinary notice of motion can't be brought on for hearing earlier than the eighth (8th) day after the motion papers are served. With an order to show cause, the hearing can be brought on at any time the court directs, which can be fewer than eight (8) days or as close as the very day on which it is signed. If the court is convinced there is a real emergency, it can schedule the hearing for a few hours later or, in the direst case, "forthwith" the service of the order to show cause. SIEGEL-NYPRAC § 248.

c. *Time to serve answering affidavits; Other answering papers.* Answering affidavits shall be served at least two (2) days before the time at which the motion is noticed to be heard. Answering affidavits and any notice of cross-motion, with supporting papers, if any, shall be served at least seven (7) days before such time if a notice of motion served at least sixteen (16) days before such time so demands; whereupon any reply or responding affidavits shall be served at least one (1) day before such time. NY CPLR Rule 2214(b); NY R UNIF TRIAL CTS § 202.8(c).

i. *BRONX COUNTY.* All answering papers must be submitted to the Clerk 's Office on the return date of the motion. Answering papers will not be accepted prior to the return date. NY R BRONX FIL R Doc. 8.

ii. *NEW YORK COUNTY.* Cross-motions, papers in opposition, and reply papers on motions/petitions on notice returnable in Room 130 in a hard-copy case shall be submitted to the Motion Submission Part Courtroom (Room 130) on the final return date of the motion/petition and will not be accepted until that date. Subsequent documents on motions/petitions in e-filed cases shall be e-filed in a timely manner. Working copies when required shall be submitted to Room 130 on the final return date. NY R NY CTY Procedure II(A).

d. *Time to serve cross-motion.* At least three (3) days prior to the time at which the motion is noticed to be heard, or seven (7) days prior to such time if demand is properly made pursuant to NY CPLR Rule 2214(b), a party may serve upon the moving party a notice of cross-motion demanding relief, with or without supporting papers; provided, however, that:

i. If such notice and any supporting papers are served by mailing, as provided in NY CPLR Rule 2103(b)(2), they shall be served three (3) days earlier than as prescribed in NY CPLR Rule 2215; and

ii. If served by overnight delivery, as provided in NY CPLR Rule 2103(b)(6), they shall be served one (1) day earlier than as prescribed in NY CPLR Rule 2215. Relief in the alternative or of several different types may be demanded; relief need not be responsive to that demanded by the moving party. NY CPLR Rule 2215(a); NY CPLR Rule 2215(b).

iii. *BRONX COUNTY.* Cross motions may be presented for approval on or before the return date, provided that there is a motion already calendared. NY R BRONX FIL R Doc. 8.

iv. *ERIE COUNTY.* Cross-motions must be filed at least two (2) days before the return date of the motion. NY R L KINGS Pt. A, Papers.

v. *KINGS COUNTY.* Hard copies are required to be filed for any motions, answering papers, stipulations, etc. for E-Filed cases returnable in [the Central Compliance Part] at least [two (2)] days before return date. . .for cross motions. NY R L KINGS Pt. E, Rule 8.

vi. *QUEENS COUNTY.* Motion Support does not process or forward responsive papers, including cross-motions. They must be brought to the calendar call in the judge's part. NY R L QUEENS MOT SUP Doc. 1. E-filed cross motions: across motion must be noticed for the same return date as the main motion and have the confirmation of filing attached in the same manner as a motion. NY R L QUEENS E-FILE Doc. 1(H)(2)(e).

3. *Filing before return date.* All motions shall be returnable before the assigned judge, and all papers shall be filed with the court on or before the return date. NY R UNIF TRIAL CTS § 202.8(a).

a. *BRONX COUNTY: Time for filing*

i. *Unassigned motions.* Unassigned motions must be in the Clerk's Office within five (5) days of the date of service of the motion. NY R BRONX FIL R Doc. 8.

ii. *Assigned motions.* Assigned motions must be filed in the Clerk's Office not less than five (5) business days prior to the return date of the motion. NY R BRONX FIL R Doc. 8.

iii. *Motions returnable in room 217.* The moving documents must be e-filed no later than eight (8) days prior to the return date. NY R BRONX E FIL R Doc. 1(1).

b. *KINGS COUNTY: Time and place of filing.* Motion papers must be filed with the E-file/Motion Support Office located in Room 227. . . at 360 Adams Street at least five (5) business days before the return date of the motion. NY R L KINGS Pt. A, Papers. Hard copies are required to be filed for any motions, answering papers, stipulations, etc. for E-Filed cases returnable in [the Central Compliance Part] at least five (5) days before return date for main motions. NY R L KINGS Pt. E, Rule 8. The moving documents must be e-filed no later than eight (8) days prior to the return date. NY R L KINGS E FIL Doc. 1(D).

4. *NEW YORK COUNTY: Briefing schedule.* Once a motion is made, counsel for all parties are strongly encouraged to agree upon a briefing schedule and submit a stipulation of adjournment reflecting that schedule using service or a clerk. Where a briefing schedule has not been agreed upon, the movant can avoid the need to attend simply to see if anyone will hand up opposing papers by demanding papers as provided by NY CPLR Rule 2214(b). To protect movants against the submission of late opposition papers or cross-motions, the General Clerk's Office will screen motions in which such papers are submitted without a response (reply or opposition respectively) to ensure that proper time to respond has been afforded and it will sua sponte adjourn for one (1) week cases in which such time has not been given. NY R NY CTY Procedure II(C).

5. *QUEENS COUNTY: Time to pay fees.* As motions and petitions are time sensitive, if opting to pay at the County Clerk's Office payment MUST be made, if filed with an RJI, a minimum of nine (9) business days prior to the application's return date and if filed post RJI, a minimum of nine (9) business days prior to the application's return date. NY R L QUEENS E-FILE Doc. 1(H)(1).

6. *Computation of time*

a. *Units of time*

i. *Day.* A calendar day includes the time from midnight to midnight. Sunday or any day of the week specifically mentioned means a calendar day. NY GEN CONSTR § 19.

ii. *Month.* In a statute, contract or public or private instrument, unless otherwise provided in such contract or instrument or by law, the term month means a calendar month and not a lunar month. NY GEN CONSTR § 31.

iii. *Year.* For information on the definition of a year, including the definitions of a half-year and quarter-year, refer to NY GEN CONSTR § 58 and NY GEN CONSTR § 50. For information on leap years, refer to NY GEN CONSTR § 57.

b. *Periods of time*

i. *Number of days.* A number of days specified as a period from a certain day within which or after or before which

an act is authorized or required to be done means such number of calendar days exclusive of the calendar day from which the reckoning is made. NY GEN CONSTR § 20.

- If such period is a period of two (2) days, Saturday, Sunday or a public holiday must be excluded from the reckoning if it is an intervening day between the day from which the reckoning is made and the last day of the period. NY GEN CONSTR § 20.
- In computing any specified period of time from a specified event, the day upon which the event happens is deemed the day from which the reckoning is made. The day from which any specified period of time is reckoned shall be excluded in making the reckoning. NY GEN CONSTR § 20.

ii. *Number of months.* A number of months after or before a certain day shall be computed by counting such number of calendar months from such day, exclusive of the calendar month in which such day occurs, and shall include the day of the month in the last month so counted having the same numerical order in days of the month as the day from which the computation is made, unless there be not so many days in the last month so counted, in which case the period computed shall expire with the last day of the month so counted. NY GEN CONSTR § 30.

iii. *Publication of notice; Number of days.* The period of publication of a legal notice shall be computed by excluding the first day of publication and including the day on which the act or event of which notice is given is to take place or which completes the full period of publication. NY CPLR § 2402.

iv. *Periods ending on Saturday, Sunday or public holiday.* When any period of time, computed from a certain day, within which or after which or before which an act is authorized or required to be done, ends on a Saturday, Sunday or a public holiday, such act may be done on the next succeeding business day and if the period ends at a specified hour, such act may be done at or before the same hour of such next succeeding business day, except that where a period of time specified by contract ends on a Saturday, Sunday or a public holiday, the extension of such period is governed by NY GEN CONSTR § 25. NY GEN CONSTR § 25-a(1).

- For a list of public holidays, refer to NY GEN CONSTR § 24.

v. *Additional time after certain kinds of service*

- *Service by mail.* Where a period of time prescribed by law is measured from the service of a paper and service is by mail, five (5) days shall be added to the prescribed period. NY CPLR Rule 2103(b)(2).
- *Service by overnight delivery service.* Where a period of time prescribed by law is measured from the service of a paper and service is by overnight delivery, one (1) business day shall be added to the prescribed period. NY CPLR Rule 2103(b)(6).

vi. *Daylight saving time.* For information on New York's time zone and the effect of daylight saving time, refer to NY GEN CONSTR § 52.

c. *Hours of court.* Notwithstanding any provision of law or rule of court to the contrary, throughout the State of New York the sessions of the Supreme Court for the disposition of business before the court shall commence not later than 9:30 a.m. and conclude not earlier than 5 p.m. Where warranted, the Chief Administrator of the Courts may authorize variances in the opening and closing hours of the courts, but, in such event, daily sessions shall total not less than six (6) hours. NY R CHIEF J § 3.1.

d. *Time limits; Extension of time.* Any act required by or in pursuance of law to be performed at or within a prescribed time, shall be performed according to the standard time. NY GEN CONSTR § 53.

i. Except where otherwise expressly prescribed by law, the court may extend the time fixed by any statute, rule or order for doing any act, upon such terms as may be just and upon good cause shown, whether the application for extension is made before or after the expiration of the time fixed. NY CPLR § 2004. Refer to the New York KeyRules Motion for Continuance/Extension of Time document for more information.

C. General Requirements

1. *Motions, generally.* There shall be compliance with the procedures prescribed in the CPLR for the bringing of motions. NY R UNIF TRIAL CTS § 202.7(a).

a. *Motions on notice.* A notice of motion shall specify the time and place of the hearing on the motion, the supporting papers upon which the motion is based, the relief demanded and the grounds therefor. NY CPLR Rule 2214(a). A motion on notice in an action in the supreme court shall be noticed to be heard in the judicial district where the action is triable or in a county adjoining the county where the action is triable. Unless statute, civil practice rule or local court rule provides otherwise, the motion shall be noticed to be heard before a motion term or, upon order to show cause granted by a justice, before that justice out of court. NY CPLR § 2212(a). Except as provided in NY R UNIF TRIAL

CTS § 202.7(d), no motion shall be filed with the court unless there have been served and filed with the motion papers a notice of motion. NY R UNIF TRIAL CTS § 202.7(a)(1).

b. *Ex parte motions.* A motion in an action in the supreme court that may be made without notice may be made at a motion term or to a justice out of court in any county in the state. NY CPLR § 2212(b).

   i. *KINGS COUNTY.* For more information on submitting a motion ex parte, refer to NY R L KINGS E FIL Doc. 1(G).

   ii. *NEW YORK COUNTY.* For more information on submitting matters ex parte, refer to NY R NY CTY Procedure III and NY R NY CTY E FIL Doc. 2(G).

   iii. *QUEENS COUNTY.* For more information on submitting matters ex parte, refer to NY R L QUEENS EX PARTE Doc. 1.

c. *Alternative relief.* Relief in the alternative or of several different types may be demanded. NY CPLR Rule 2214(a). The types of relief need not be related. In one motion, for example, the defendant can seek to dismiss the plaintiff's claim for lack of jurisdiction, to get an extension of time to answer, to require the plaintiff to join X as a party, and to quash a disclosure subpoena served in behalf of the plaintiff on a nonparty witness. So doing, the movant must of course specify all of these items of relief in the notice of motion, and the grounds for them, and the supporting papers must contain the entire proof requisite to the items of relief sought. NY CPLR Rule 2214(Practice Commentary, C2214:4).

d. *General relief.* It is common practice to include at the end of the relief request in the notice of motion a so-called "general relief" clause. This is merely a few words to cover the possibility that the relief appropriate to what the movant proves was not specifically asked for, but is close enough to enable the court to grant it. After stating the specific relief desired, the lawyer will often add something like: and for such other, further, or different relief as this court may deem just and proper. NY CPLR Rule 2214(Practice Commentary, C2214:5).

e. *Motion in improper form.* If the court finds it appropriate in the interests of justice, it may convert a motion into a special proceeding, or vice-versa, upon such terms as may be just, including the payment of fees and costs. NY CPLR § 103(c).

f. *Order to show cause.* An order to show cause is basically only a substitute for a notice of motion. An ordinary notice of motion merely notifies the recipient that a motion is being made for specified relief. The burden of proof is on the movant. Although in most cases it is just as innocent as an ordinary notice of motion, the order to show cause gets its name by directing the recipient to "show cause" why the particular relief being asked for should not be granted. It sounds as if the burden of proof is being shifted to the recipient. It isn't. It specifies the time and place of the hearing on the application but when the hearing comes on, the burden of proof is where it always is on a motion: on the movant. SIEGEL-NYPRAC § 248.

   i. The CPLR says nothing more about an order to show cause than that it may be used "in a proper case", which leaves it entirely to the judge's discretion to determine what a proper case is. Any fact suggesting a problem as to any of the items listed above would be sufficient to invoke judicial discretion and justify the show cause procedure, which is in fact liberally used. SIEGEL-NYPRAC § 248.

   ii. An order to show cause against a state body or officers must be served in addition to service upon the defendant or respondent state body or officers upon the attorney general by delivery to an assistant attorney general at an office of the attorney general in the county in which venue of the action is designated or if there is no office of the attorney general in such county, at the office of the attorney general nearest such county. NY CPLR Rule 2214(d).

   iii. *BRONX COUNTY.* For information on submitting an order to show cause, refer to NY R BRONX E FIL R Doc. 2 and NY R BRONX LEG SUP Doc. 1.

   iv. *ERIE COUNTY.* For information on submitting an order to show cause, refer to NY R ERIE E FIL Doc. 3(VI).

   v. *KINGS COUNTY.* For information on submitting an order to show cause, refer to NY R L KINGS E FIL Doc. 1(F).

   vi. *NEW YORK COUNTY.* For information on submitting an order to show cause, refer to NY R NY CTY E FIL Doc. 2(F).

   vii. *ONONDAGA COUNTY.* For information on submitting an order to show cause, refer to NY R ONDGA E FIL Protocol(B)(10) and NY R ONDGA E FIL Protocol(J).

g. *Motions before preliminary conference.* Motions in actions to which NY R UNIF TRIAL CTS § 202.12 is applicable made after the preliminary conference has been scheduled may be denied unless there is shown good cause why such relief is warranted before the preliminary conference is held. NY R UNIF TRIAL CTS § 202.12(h).

h. *ALBANY COUNTY: Good faith effort to resolve.* Prior to the submission of a notice of motion relating to disclosure or a bill of particulars, the parties must make a good faith effort to resolve the matter in question and submit an affirmation attesting to this good faith effort. NY R 3 JD SUP Doc. 1(B).

i. *NEW YORK COUNTY: Documents with motions.* Counsel must attach to motion papers copies of all pleadings and other documents as required by the CPLR and as necessary for an informed decision on the motion. Documents in a foreign language shall be properly translated. NY R NY CTY J RUL Rule 14(a).

j. *NEW YORK COUNTY: Motions in multiple cases made together.* On occasion, attorneys may wish to make a motion in more than one case on a single set of papers. In such cases, by definition consolidation will not have been directed since consolidation signifies the combination of more than one case into a single one with a single caption and index number and ending in a single judgment. NY R NY CTY Procedure II(B). For more information on motions made with the same papers, refer to NY R NY CTY Procedure II(A).

k. *QUEENS COUNTY: Motion sequence numbers.* A motion sequence number is required for all E-filed motions. After a motion is E-filed, please consult the e-courts website within twenty-four (24) to forty-eight (48) hours to obtain the sequence number. The Confirmation Notice of E-filing MUST indicate the sequence number of any motion submitted at the Centralized Motion Part calendar call. NY R L QUEENS E-FILE Doc. 1(H)(5).

2. *Motion to transfer venue*

a. *Motion/demand for change of place of trial.* When a defendant contends that plaintiff has laid venue in an improper county and the defendant seeks to change it to a proper county as a matter of right, the defendant must follow the special "demand" procedure of NY CPLR Rule 511(b). SIEGEL-NYPRAC § 123.

i. *Service of demand.* The defendant shall serve a written demand that the action be tried in a county he specifies as proper. Thereafter the defendant may move to change the place of trial within fifteen (15) days after service of the demand, unless within five (5) days after such service plaintiff serves a written consent to change the place of trial to that specified by the defendant. NY CPLR Rule 511(b).

- Plaintiff's failure to respond to the demand within the five (5) days does not automatically entitle defendant to the venue change; it merely gives the defendant a broader option on where to move for it. Nor does plaintiff, by omitting to respond, forfeit the right to resist the motion. Wherever defendant moves, the plaintiff may still oppose the motion and show that his chosen county is proper (or that defendant's is not). SIEGEL-NYPRAC § 123; McDermott v. McDermott, 267 A.D. 171, 172-73, 45 N.Y.S.2d 321, 322-23 (App. Div. 1943).
- If the defendant does not so move within the fifteen (15) days, she is no longer entitled to a change of venue as of right. The change does lie in the court's discretion, however, so the defendant may still make the motion at any time before trial, but because of its tardiness the defendant in that situation is not entitled to the change as a matter of right. If there is strong reason to prefer the proper county, such as where real property records are involved in what qualifies as a local action, the court's discretion is likely to favor the change, tardy as the motion may be. SIEGEL-NYPRAC § 123; Reichenbach v. Corn Exch. Bank Tr. Co., 249 A.D. 539, 540—41, 292 N.Y.S. 732, 734 (App. Div. 1937).

ii. *Notice of motion.* Defendant may notice such motion to be heard as if the action were pending in the county he specified, unless plaintiff within five (5) days after service of the demand serves an affidavit showing either that the county specified by the defendant is not proper or that the county designated by him is proper. NY CPLR Rule 511(b).

iii. *Stay of proceedings.* No order to stay proceedings for the purpose of changing the place of trial shall be granted unless it appears from the papers that the change is sought with due diligence. NY CPLR Rule 511(c).

iv. *Subsequent proceedings.* Subsequent proceedings shall be had in the county to which the change is made as if it had been designated originally as the place of trial, except as otherwise directed by the court. NY CPLR Rule 511(d).

v. *Appeal.* An appeal from an order changing the place of trial shall be taken in the department in which the motion for the order was heard and determined. NY CPLR Rule 511(d).

b. *Grounds for change of place of trial.* The court, upon motion, may change the place of trial of an action where: (1) the county designated for that purpose is not a proper county; or (2) there is reason to believe that an impartial trial cannot be had in the proper county; or (3) the convenience of material witnesses and the ends of justice will be promoted by the change. NY CPLR § 510.

i. Perhaps the most frequent ground for a discretionary change of venue is the convenience of witnesses. The witnesses whose convenience counts here are the "material" ones: those who can testify to the facts of the occurrence or transaction involved in the case. And the convenience of witnesses testifying on issues of liability is "entitled to greater weight" than that of witnesses testifying only on damages. SIEGEL-NYPRAC § 124; Katz v. Goodyear Tire & Rubber Co., 116 A.D.2d 506, 507, 497 N.Y.S.2d 376, 377-78 (1986).

ii. Plaintiff's choice of forum will not be disturbed unless there is a clear balance in favor of the defendant's witnesses. SIEGEL-NYPRAC § 124; Marzello v. Kiamesha Concord, Inc., 26 A.D.2d 986, 986, 274 N.Y.S.2d 1002, 1003 (1966). It has also been held that where, on a change of venue motion, the convenience of witnesses is fairly evenly balanced between sides, a "transitory action should be tried in the county where the cause of action arose." SIEGEL-NYPRAC § 124; Katz v. Goodyear Tire & Rubber Co., 116 A.D.2d 506, 497 N.Y.S.2d 376, 377 (1986); Strosberg v. Kiamesha Concord, Inc., 26 A.D.2d 723, 723, 271 N.Y.S.2d 767, 769 (1966).

iii. A motion for change of place of trial on any ground other than NY CPLR Rule 511(b) shall be made within a reasonable time after commencement of the action. NY CPLR Rule 511(a).

c. *Issue triable without a jury.* The place of trial of an action or any issue triable without a jury may be, in the discretion of the court, in any county within the judicial district in which the action is triable. After the trial, the decision and all other papers relating to the trial shall be filed and the judgment entered in the county where the action is pending. NY CPLR Rule 512.

d. *Misplacement of venue in consumer credit transaction.* In an action arising out of a consumer credit transaction, the clerk shall not accept a summons for filing when it appears upon its face that the proper venue is a county other than the county where such summons is offered for filing. NY CPLR § 513(a).

i. The clerk shall indicate upon the summons the date of the rejection and shall enter such date in a register maintained by him together with the name of the counties in which the summons may properly be filed. NY CPLR § 513(b).

ii. Notwithstanding NY CPLR § 308(1) and NY CPLR § 308(3), where a summons has been rejected for filing by virtue of NY CPLR § 513, service is complete ten (10) days after such summons is filed in the proper county with proof of service upon the defendant of the summons, together with proof of service upon the defendant by registered or certified mail of a notice setting forth the following:

- The proper county,
- The date of filing of the summons,
- The date within which the answer or notice of appearance is to be filed, and
- The address at which it is to be filed. NY CPLR § 513(c).

3. *Inconvenient forum*

a. *Inconvenient forum; Substantial justice.* When the court finds that in the interest of substantial justice the action should be heard in another forum, the court, on the motion of any party, may stay or dismiss the action in whole or in part on any conditions that may be just. The domicile or residence in this state of any party to the action shall not preclude the court from staying or dismissing the action. NY CPLR Rule 327(a). A motion for change of place of trial on any ground other than NY CPLR Rule 511(b) shall be made within a reasonable time after commencement of the action. NY CPLR Rule 511(a).

i. There is no stated time limit on when the motion can be made, but a defendant bent on avoiding inconvenience should make the motion before answering. If a defendant has subjected itself to the inconvenience of a trial, and lost on the merits, a court should not accept its inconvenience argument if saved until then. SIEGEL-NYPRAC § 28.

b. *Certain contract actions not subject to inconvenient forum.* Notwithstanding NY CPLR Rule 327(a), the court shall not stay or dismiss any action on the ground of inconvenient forum, where the action arises out of or relates to a contract, agreement or undertaking to which NY GEN OBLIG § 5-1402 applies, and the parties to the contract have agreed that the law of this state shall govern their rights or duties in whole or in part. NY CPLR Rule 327(b).

c. *Residence of parties as factor.* If the plaintiff is a New York resident, a conveniens dismissal, although permissible, is less likely than when the defendant is the New York resident. The obvious reason is that the New York courts are primarily for the use of New Yorkers. But a conveniens dismissal can visit even a case in which all parties are New

York residents, a result that should be rare, indeed, reserved solely for a case in which all of the other contacts—situs of the transaction, performance, witnesses, documents, physical evidence, etc.—are elsewhere. SIEGEL-NYPRAC § 28; Westwood Assocs. v. Deluxe Gen., Inc., 53 N.Y.2d 618, 420 N.E.2d 966, 966 (1981).

d. *Other factors.* The conveniens doctrine is one of judicial discretion "to be exercised by reviewing and evaluating all the pertinent competing considerations," which include among other things the burden on the court, the hardship to the defendant that an action in New York would entail, and the availability elsewhere of a reputable forum. SIEGEL-NYPRAC § 28; Varkonyi v. S. A. Empresa De Viacao Airea Rio Grandense (Varig), 22 N.Y.2d 333, 338, 239 N.E.2d 542, 544 (1968).

   i. If the "elsewhere" is a foreign country rather than a sister state, a conveniens dismissal is permissible but somewhat less likely. It depends on how much confidence we have in the jurisprudence of the foreign nation. SIEGEL-NYPRAC § 28; Islamic Republic of Iran v. Pahlavi, 62 N.Y.2d 474, 481, 467 N.E.2d 245, 249 (1984).

   ii. While no single factor is controlling, all relevant considerations raised by the parties must be weighed by the court. SIEGEL-NYPRAC § 28.

4. *Issue pending in another court.* Upon motion of any party, the supreme court may order that an issue of fact in an action pending in another court, except an action relating to real property pending in a county court, be tried in the supreme court in another county upon such terms as may be just. After the trial, the clerk of the county in which it has taken place shall certify the minutes thereof, which shall be filed with the clerk of the court in which the action is pending. Subsequent proceedings shall be the same as if the issue had been tried in the court in which the action is pending. NY CPLR § 604.

5. *Venue; Specific cases*

   a. *Contractual provisions fixing venue.* Subject to the provisions of NY CPLR § 510(2), written agreement fixing place of trial, made before an action is commenced, shall be enforced upon a motion for change of place of trial. NY CPLR § 501.

   b. *Conflicting venue provisions.* Where, because of joinder of claims or parties, there is a conflict of provisions under NY CPLR § 501, et seq., the court, upon motion, shall order as the place of trial one proper under NY CPLR § 501, et seq. as to at least one of the parties or claims. NY CPLR § 502.

   c. *Venue based on residence*

      i. *Generally.* Except where otherwise prescribed by law, the place of trial shall be in the county in which one of the parties resided when it was commenced; or, if none of the parties then resided in the state, in any county designated by the plaintiff. A party resident in more than one county shall be deemed a resident of each such county. NY CPLR § 503(a).

      ii. *Executor, administrator, trustee, committee, conservator, general or testamentary guardian, or receiver.* An executor, administrator, trustee, committee, conservator, general or testamentary guardian, or receiver shall be deemed a resident of the county of his appointment as well as the county in which he actually resides. NY CPLR § 503(b).

      iii. *Corporation.* A domestic corporation, or a foreign corporation authorized to transact business in the state, shall be deemed a resident of the county in which its principal office is located; except that such a corporation, if a railroad or other common carrier, shall also be deemed a resident of the county where the cause of action arose. NY CPLR § 503(c).

      iv. *Unincorporated association, partnership, or individually-owned business.* A president or treasurer of an unincorporated association, suing or being sued on behalf of the association, shall be deemed a resident of any county in which the association has its principal office, as well as the county in which he actually resides. A partnership or an individually-owned business shall be deemed a resident of any county in which it has its principal office, as well as the county in which the partner or individual owner suing or being sued actually resides. NY CPLR § 503(d).

      v. *Assignee.* In an action for a sum of money only, brought by an assignee other than an assignee for the benefit of creditors or a holder in due course of a negotiable instrument, the assignee's residence shall be deemed the same as that of the original assignor at the time of the original assignment. NY CPLR § 503(e).

      vi. *Consumer credit transaction.* In an action arising out of a consumer credit transaction where a purchaser, borrower or debtor is a defendant, the place of trial shall be the residence of a defendant, if one resides within the state or the county where such transaction took place, if it is within the state, or, in other cases, as set forth in NY CPLR § 503(a). NY CPLR § 503(f).

   d. *Actions against counties, cities, towns villages, school districts and district corporations.* Notwithstanding the provisions of any charter heretofore granted by the state and subject to the provisions of NY CPLR § 506(b), the place of trial of all actions against counties, cities, towns, villages, school districts and district corporations or any of their officers, boards or departments shall be, for:

i. A county, in such county;

ii. A city, except the city of New York, town, village, school district or district corporation, in the county in which such city, town, village, school district or district corporation is situated, or if such school district or district corporation is situated in more than one county, in either county; and

iii. The city of New York, in the county within the city in which the cause of action arose, or if it arose outside of the city, in the county of New York. NY CPLR § 504.

e. *Actions involving public authorities.* The place of trial of an action by or against a public authority constituted under the laws of the state shall be in the county in which the authority has its principal office or where it has facilities involved in the action. NY CPLR § 505(a).

i. *Special rule for actions against the New York City transit authority.* The place of trial of an action against the New York city transit authority shall be in the county within the city of New York in which the cause of action arose, or, if it arose outside of the city, in the county of New York. NY CPLR § 505(b).

f. *Real property actions.* The place of trial of an action in which the judgment demanded would affect the title to, or the possession, use or enjoyment of, real property shall be in the county in which any part of the subject of the action is situated. NY CPLR § 507.

g. *Actions to recover a chattel.* The place of trial of an action to recover a chattel may be in the county in which any part of the subject of the action is situated at the time of the commencement of the action. NY CPLR § 508.

h. *Venue in county designated.* Notwithstanding any provision of NY CPLR § 501, et seq., the place of trial of an action shall be in the county designated by the plaintiff, unless the place of trial is changed to another county by order upon motion, or by consent as provided in NY CPLR Rule 511(b). NY CPLR § 509.

6. *Oppositions.* In the absence of statutory provision or court rule, a motion ordinarily does not require a written answer, although an adverse party may be permitted to file an answer in opposition to the showing made in the motion or its supporting affidavits. AMJUR MOTIONS § 26. When a party files a motion and the opposing party fails to respond, the court may construe such failure to respond as non-opposition to the motion or an admission that the motion was meritorious, may take the facts alleged in the motion as true, and may grant the motion if the relief requested appears to be justified. However, the severity of such a result demands that a court impose it only with great caution. AMJUR MOTIONS § 28.

a. *Plaintiff's affidavit responding to motion to transfer venue.* Plaintiff's affidavit (responding to the demand) must at least purport to justify the plaintiff's choice, or to negate the defendant's. An affidavit that purports to do neither has been deemed no affidavit at all, thus permitting the defendant to move in the proposed transferee county. SIEGEL-NYPRAC § 123; Payne v. Civil Serv. Emp. Ass'n, 15 A.D.2d 265, 268, 222 N.Y.S.2d 725, 727—28 (1961).

i. If the plaintiff has several choices (such as counties X and Y) available, but lays venue in an improper county (Z), plaintiff's right of first choice will be forfeited to the defendant. Thus if the plaintiff, opposing the defendant's motion, urges that the change be to X, while the defendant wants Y, Y will be the county to which the venue is ordered changed. SIEGEL-NYPRAC § 123; Kelson v. Nedicks Stores, Inc., 104 A.D.2d 315, 316, 478 N.Y.S.2d 648, 649 (1984). The point is that plaintiff may lose first choice to the defendant by laying initial venue in an altogether improper county. SIEGEL-NYPRAC § 123.

7. *Governing law.* The civil practice law and rules (NY CPLR § 101, et seq.) shall govern the procedure in civil judicial proceedings in all courts of the state and before all judges, except where the procedure is regulated by inconsistent statute. The civil practice law and rules shall succeed the civil practice act and rules of civil practice and shall be deemed substituted therefor throughout the statutes and rules of the state. NY CPLR § 101. The civil practice law and rules shall be liberally construed to secure the just, speedy and inexpensive determination of every civil judicial proceeding. NY CPLR § 104.

a. *Uniform trial court rules.* The uniform civil rules for the Supreme Court and County Court (NY R UNIF TRIAL CTS § 202.1, et seq.) shall be applicable to civil actions and proceedings in the Supreme Court and the County Court. NY R UNIF TRIAL CTS § 202.1(a). The provisions of the uniform rules shall be construed consistent with the Civil Practice Law and Rules (CPLR), and matters not covered by the uniform rules shall be governed by the CPLR. NY R UNIF TRIAL CTS § 202.1(d).

b. *Local rules.* Local court rules, not inconsistent with law or with uniform civil rules for the Supreme Court and County

Court (NY R UNIF TRIAL CTS § 202.1, et seq.), shall comply with Part 9 of the Rules of the Chief Judge (NY R CHIEF J § 9.1). NY R UNIF TRIAL CTS § 202.1(c).

c. *Official forms.* The state administrator shall have the power to adopt, amend and rescind an appendix of forms. Forms adopted pursuant to NY CPLR § 107 shall be sufficient under the civil practice law and rules and shall illustrate the simplicity and brevity of statement which the civil practice law and rules contemplate. NY CPLR § 107.

8. *Rules of the commercial division.* [Editor's note: certain types of civil cases or civil cases meeting certain monetary thresholds that are filed in the state of New York must be filed in the Commercial Division of the New York Supreme Courts. Rules governing practice in the commercial division are found in NY R UNIF TRIAL CTS § 202.70]. Cases which must be filed in the commercial division are listed below. For more information, refer to NY R UNIF TRIAL CTS § 202.70.

a. *Monetary thresholds.* Except as set forth in NY R UNIF TRIAL CTS § 202.70(b), the monetary thresholds of the Commercial Division, exclusive of punitive damages, interests, costs, disbursements and counsel fees claimed, are established as follows: (1) Albany County, fifty thousand dollars ($50,000); (2) Eighth Judicial District, one hundred thousand dollars ($100,000); (3) Kings County, one hundred fifty thousand dollars ($150,000); (4) Nassau County, two hundred thousand dollars ($200,000); (5) New York County, five hundred thousand dollars ($500,000); (6) Onondaga County, fifty thousand dollars ($50,000); (7) Queens County, one hundred thousand dollars ($100,000); (8) Seventh Judicial District, fifty thousand dollars ($50,000); (9) Suffolk County, one hundred thousand dollars ($100,000); and (10) Westchester County, one hundred thousand dollars ($100,000). NY R UNIF TRIAL CTS § 202.70(a).

i. *ALBANY COUNTY.* The Commercial Division of the Albany County Supreme Court exercises jurisdiction over selected business and commercial disputes in which the amount at issue generally involves damage claims in a minimum amount of fifty thousand dollars ($50,000) as well as claims for unspecified amounts where the value of the commercial asset(s) in dispute exceeds fifty thousand dollars ($50,000). A separate publication promulgating the rules and criteria relating to the filing and management of Commercial Court cases in this part may be obtained from the Albany County Supreme Court Clerk's Office. A section of the Uniform Civil Rules for the Supreme Court and County Court sets forth statewide rules. NY R 3 JD SUP Doc. 1(E).

ii. *BRONX COUNTY.* The monetary threshold for commercial cases in Bronx County will be seventy-five thousand dollars ($75,000). All other parameters including the type of matters that will be heard are contained within the Rules of the Commercial Division of the Supreme Court (NY R UNIF TRIAL CTS § 202.70). NY R BRONX FIL R Doc. 12.

iii. *NEW YORK COUNTY.* The monetary threshold in the New York County Commercial Division, which is generally applicable, is an amount in controversy of five hundred thousand dollars ($500,000) or more (exclusive of punitive damages, interest, costs, disbursements, and counsel fees). If the case is designated a commercial one and the Addendum is submitted, the clerk will review the pleadings to determine whether the amount in controversy in the case meets the monetary threshold or whether an exception to the threshold applies. NY R NY CTY Procedure IA(B). For more information on assigning a case to the commercial division in New York County, refer to NY R NY CTY Procedure IA(B).

b. *Commercial cases.* Actions in which the principal claims involve or consist of the following will be heard in the Commercial Division provided that the monetary threshold is met or equitable or declaratory relief is sought:

i. Breach of contract or fiduciary duty, fraud, misrepresentation, business tort (e.g., unfair competition), or statutory and/or common law violation where the breach or violation is alleged to arise out of business dealings (e.g., sales of assets or securities; corporate restructuring; partnership, shareholder, joint venture, and other business agreements; trade secrets; restrictive covenants; and employment agreements not including claims that principally involve alleged discriminatory practices);

ii. Transactions governed by the Uniform Commercial Code (exclusive of those concerning individual cooperative or condominium units);

iii. Transactions involving commercial real property, including Yellowstone injunctions and excluding actions for the payment of rent only;

iv. Shareholder derivative actions—without consideration of the monetary threshold;

v. Commercial class actions—without consideration of the monetary threshold;

vi. Business transactions involving or arising out of dealings with commercial banks and other financial institutions;

vii. Internal affairs of business organizations;

viii. Malpractice by accountants or actuaries, and legal malpractice arising out of representation in commercial matters;

ix. Environmental insurance coverage;

x. Commercial insurance coverage (e.g., directors and officers, errors and omissions, and business interruption coverage);

xi. Dissolution of corporations, partnerships, limited liability companies, limited liability partnerships and joint ventures—without consideration of the monetary threshold; and

xii. Applications to stay or compel arbitration and affirm or disaffirm arbitration awards and related injunctive relief pursuant to Article 75 of the New York Civil Practice Law and Rules (NY CPLR § 7501, et seq.) involving any of the foregoing enumerated commercial issues. Where the applicable arbitration agreement provides for the arbitration to be heard outside the United States, the monetary threshold set forth in NY R UNIF TRIAL CTS § 202.70(a) shall not apply. NY R UNIF TRIAL CTS § 202.70(b).

c. *Non-commercial cases.* The following will not be heard in the Commercial Division even if the monetary threshold is met:

i. Suits to collect professional fees;

ii. Cases seeking a declaratory judgment as to insurance coverage for personal injury or property damage;

iii. Residential real estate disputes, including landlord-tenant matters, and commercial real estate disputes involving the payment of rent only;

iv. Home improvement contracts involving residential properties consisting of one to four residential units or individual units in any residential building, including cooperative or condominium units;

v. Proceedings to enforce a judgment regardless of the nature of the underlying case;

vi. First-party insurance claims and actions by insurers to collect premiums or rescind non-commercial policies; and

vii. Attorney malpractice actions except as otherwise provided in NY R UNIF TRIAL CTS § 202.70(b)(8). NY R UNIF TRIAL CTS § 202.70(c).

d. For more information on the Commercial Division, refer to NY R UNIF TRIAL CTS § 202.70.

D. Documents

1. *Documents for moving party*

a. *Required documents*

i. *Notice of motion, order to show cause, or affidavit on ex parte motion.* The notice of motion shall be substantially in the form found in NY R UNIF TRIAL CTS § 202.7(b). NY R UNIF TRIAL CTS § 202.7(b). The supporting papers should be referred to in the notice of motion. SIEGEL-NYPRAC § 246. The court in a proper case may grant an order to show cause, to be served in lieu of a notice of motion. NY CPLR Rule 2214(d). An ex parte motion shall be accompanied by an affidavit stating the result of any prior motion for similar relief and specifying the new facts, if any, that were not previously shown. NY CPLR Rule 2217(b).

- *Request for oral argument.* A party requesting oral argument shall set forth such request in its notice of motion or in its order to show cause or on the first page of the answering papers, as the case may be. Where all parties to a motion request oral argument, oral argument shall be granted unless the court shall determine it to be unnecessary. Where a motion is brought on by order to show cause, the court may set forth in the order that oral argument is required on the return date of the motion. NY R UNIF TRIAL CTS § 202.8(d).

ii. *Motion.* Refer to the General Requirements section of this document for information on the notice of motion and motion.

iii. *Request for judicial intervention.* At any time after service of process, a party may file a request for judicial intervention. Except as provided in NY R UNIF TRIAL CTS § 202.6(b), in an action not yet assigned to a judge, the court shall not accept for filing a notice of motion, order to show cause, or application for ex parte order, unless such notice or application is accompanied by a request for judicial intervention. NY R UNIF TRIAL CTS § 202.6(a).

- *BRONX COUNTY.* Generally, the Request For Judicial Intervention, commonly referred to as an "RJI", is required to be filed in any action where the assignment of a Justice is required. The RJI sets forth the information which is entered into the court system's database. It must be completely and accurately filled out. The full caption, as stated on the Summons, must be set forth. Use of terms "et al." and "etc." are not permitted. Only one (1) RJI may be filed in each action. Either a self represented litigant or an attorney must sign the affirmation at the end of the form. Once completed, the RJI must be filed in duplicate. Except in the case of an ex-parte application, the RJI must also be served together with the accompanying application upon all parties. Proof of accuracy of the index number must accompany the RJI. Check the Fee Schedule[. . .]for any applicable filing fees. NY R BRONX FIL R Doc. 2.

- *KINGS COUNTY.* An RJI with the relevant required addendum in a NYSCEF case shall be submitted via NYSCEF. Once e-filed, the RJI and any accompanying document will be forwarded to the relevant support office for random assignment of the case and processing of the document. A filer or counsel need not appear (as to Proposed Orders to Show Cause, however, see below). A copy of the pleadings must be submitted only if the document has not previously been e-filed. If the RJI seeks intervention with regard to a document that is intended for review by a Justice, such as a motion, a working copy of the RJI must be submitted with the working copy of the motion and the NYSCEF Confirmation Notice. NY R L KINGS E FIL Doc. 1(C).
- *NEW YORK COUNTY.* To obtain the assignment of an IAS Justice to a case, a Request for Judicial Intervention (cost ninety-five dollars ($95)) must be filed, with NYSCEF in an e-filed case or in paper in an authorized hard-copy one. A no-fee RJI, which will generally result in the referral of an application to an Ex Parte Justice, is also required with regard to certain kinds of applications for which, prior to 2011, no RJI was required. NY R NY CTY Procedure I(C). A "fillable" form RJI is available on-line. The form must be filed in duplicate in hard-copy cases. NY R NY CTY Procedure IA(A)(1). The filer of an RJI must check off a box identifying the type of case at issue. Where the RJI seeks judicial assignment, this designation will bring about a random assignment of the case by computer to a Justice handling cases of that type. NY R NY CTY Procedure IA(A)(1). The RJI and any addendum can be completed and submitted electronically in an e-filed case. NY R NY CTY Procedure II(A). The RJI shall be marked to reflect the existence of any "related case" as explained on the "Commencement of Cases" page under "Case Processing" on the court's website. NY R NY CTY Procedure II(A); NY R NY CTY E FIL Doc. 2(C).
- *ONONDAGA COUNTY.* The RJI will be submitted via the NYSCEF system along with any required RJI addendum forms. When the RJI is filed and the fee paid online, the Onondaga County Clerk's Office will electronically forward the RJI and any accompanying documents to the Onondaga Supreme Court Clerk's Office for assignment and processing. Counsel will receive notification of judge assignment via the NYSCEF system. NY R ONDGA E FIL Protocol(B)(3).
- *QUEENS COUNTY.* A Request for Judicial Intervention ("RJI") in an E-filed case shall be submitted via the E-filing System. When the RJI is approved, filed and paid for on-line, it will be forwarded to the relevant back office for random assignment of the case and processing of the document. In the case of RJIs seeking assignment to the Commercial Division, the filer must submit therewith, a Commercial Addendum as required by the standards for assignment of cases to the Commercial Division. NY R L QUEENS E-FILE Doc. 1(F).

iv. *Proof of service.* In addition to complying with the provisions of NY CPLR Rule 2101, every paper filed in court shall have annexed thereto appropriate proof of service on all parties where required. NY R UNIF TRIAL CTS § 202.5(a).

- *QUEENS COUNTY.* With regard to service of a motion/petition on notice in an E-filed action, NY CPLR Rule 2214(b) and NY R UNIF TRIAL CTS § 202.5-b(f) applies. Where required, proof of service shall be filed on-line as a separate document. NY R L QUEENS E-FILE Doc. 1(H)(3).

v. *ALBANY COUNTY: Additional required documents*

- *Affirmation of good faith effort.* The parties must[. . .]submit an affirmation attesting to [their good faith effort to resolve the matter]. The affirmation of good faith effort to resolve the issues raised by the motion shall indicate the time, place and nature of the consultation and the issues discussed and any resolutions, or shall indicate good cause why no such conferral with counsel for opposing parties was held. An assigned justice or judge may dismiss a motion for failure to demonstrate that such effort was made with leave to renew the motion after such effort has been demonstrated. NY R 3 JD SUP Doc. 1(B).

b. *Supplemental documents*

i. *Supporting evidence; Exhibits.* The main supporting papers on a motion are affidavits, but any relevant exhibits, documents, depositions, etc., are also includible. SIEGEL-NYPRAC § 246.

- *Affidavits accompanying motion.* Affidavits shall be for a statement of the relevant facts. NY R UNIF TRIAL CTS § 202.8(c).
- *Foreign language documents.* Where an affidavit or exhibit annexed to a paper served or filed is in a foreign language, it shall be accompanied by an English translation and an affidavit by the translator stating his qualifications and that the translation is accurate. NY CPLR Rule 2101(b).
- *Statement of attorney in lieu of affidavit.* The statement of an attorney admitted to practice in the courts of the state, or of a physician, osteopath or dentist, authorized by law to practice in the state, who is not a party to an action, when subscribed and affirmed by him to be true under the penalties of perjury, may be served or filed in the action in lieu of and with the same force and effect as an affidavit. NY CPLR Rule 2106.
- *NEW YORK COUNTY: Form of presented exhibits.* Exhibits should be tabbed and be legible; a typed version of any exhibit that is difficult to read should be submitted with the original. Exhibits printed on both sides of the page should be bound and tabbed on the side. NY R NY CTY J RUL Rule 14(a).
- *QUEENS COUNTY.* Attorneys submitting exhibits to the court on E-file cases shall make each exhibit a separate, labeled attachment to an affidavit/affirmation. NY R L QUEENS E-FILE Doc. 1(H)(4).

ii. *Brief.* Briefs shall be for a statement of the relevant law. NY R UNIF TRIAL CTS § 202.8(c).

iii. *Affidavit in support of convenience of witnesses.* The motion for a change of venue based on the convenience of witnesses requires a detailed affidavit from the moving party setting forth "what he expects to prove by the alleged witnesses, and that he cannot safely proceed to trial without the testimony of such witnesses, as he is advised by his counsel". SIEGEL-NYPRAC § 124; Dairymen's League Co-op. Ass'n v. Brundo, 131 Misc. 548, 549, 227 N.Y.S. 203, 206 (N.Y.Sup. 1927). Even more ideal, although not essential, are affidavits secured from the potential witnesses themselves. SIEGEL-NYPRAC § 124.

iv. *Notice to produce papers not in possession of the court.* If a paper relied on by the movant is in the possession of the other side, it may be demanded of that side with a notice to produce it at the hearing. Where such papers are in the possession of an adverse party, they shall be produced by him at the hearing on notice served with the motion papers. NY CPLR Rule 2214(Practice Commentary, C2214:23).

v. *Filing fees.* The County Clerk shall require the payment of any applicable statutory fees, or an order of the Court waiving payment of such fees, before accepting a paper for filing. NY R UNIF TRIAL CTS § 202.5(d)(1). For information on filing fees, if any, refer to NY CPLR § 8001, et seq.

- *ALBANY COUNTY.* In general, any filing subsequent to the commencement of an action which is designated as a motion or cross-motion requires the payment of a filing fee to the County Clerk's Office prior to submission to the Supreme Court Clerk's Office for referral to the assigned justice. The fee is assessed regardless of whether an application is made by notice of motion, order to show cause or ex parte. No fee will be charged upon the filing of a motion for poor person status in conjunction with an application which serves to commence an action or special proceeding. In the event a motion is received by the court unaccompanied by proof of payment to the County Clerk, the Supreme Court Clerk's Office will contact the submitting party to advise that the application will be held pending receipt of the filing fee only until the return date of the motion. If proof of payment is not submitted to the Supreme Court Clerk's Office by the return date (ex parte applications will be held ten (10) days), the papers will be returned by mail with a notification that the motion has been removed from the court's calendar and that it must be re-noticed and re-filed with the court along with the requisite filing fee. Inquiries concerning the applicability of the motion fee to a proposed filing may be directed to the Supreme Court Clerk's Office. NY R 3 JD SUP Doc. 1(B).
- *BRONX COUNTY.* In accordance with the new civil fee schedule set forth in Article 80 of the C.P.L.R. (NY CPLR § 8001, et seq.), effective July 14, 2003, all motions, and cross motions must be approved in Room 217 prior to payment of said fees in the County Clerk's Office, Room 118. NY R BRONX FIL R Doc. 8. The motion fee [must be] paid for via NYSCEF by credit/debit card. NY R BRONX E FIL R Doc. 1(1).
- *ERIE COUNTY.* Payment for fee-bearing NYSCEF documents must be made online via credit or debit card (American Express, MasterCard or Visa) at the time of submission. NY R ERIE E FIL Doc. 3(III)(E).
- *KINGS COUNTY.* The motion must be filed with NYSCEF and the motion fee paid. NY R L KINGS E FIL

Doc. 1(D). Court fees in NYSCEF cases must be paid via NYSCEF by a credit or bank card (MasterCard, Visa, or American Express). Fees are no longer accepted in person in the Kings County Clerk's Office in NYSCEF cases. NY R L KINGS E FIL Doc. 1(B)(6).

- *NEW YORK COUNTY.* A motion fee must be paid on motions made in writing by notice of motion, order to show cause or ex parte after the commencement of an action. For this purpose, the term "action" shall mean any application to the court that requires the assignment of an index number, regardless of whether a formal pleading is filed. Applications or motions that commence an action and for which an index number fee must be paid require no motion fee. [A]ny motions made after the initial applications in these situations would require payment of the motion fee. A motion that is the initial application in a case commenced by the filing of a summons and complaint would require a motion fee since the filing of the summons and complaint rather than the application itself would require the purchase of an index number. NY R NY CTY Procedure II(A). In e-filed cases the motion fee must be paid when the documents are filed. Payment is made on-line by Visa, Mastercard, or American Express credit or bank card. NY R NY CTY Procedure II(A); NY R NY CTY E FIL Doc. 2(B)(5).
- *ONONDAGA COUNTY.* Court fees in e-filed cases must be paid online with the NYSCEF system using a credit card. The document is not considered to have been filed until payment of the fee has been tendered. NY R ONDGA E FIL Protocol(B)(2). Fees must be paid on all cross motions. NY R ONDGA E FIL Protocol(B)(9)(e).
- *QUEENS COUNTY.* The Motion Support Office does not receive, forward or process any fees or waiver of fees. All applications requiring payment of statutory fees or waiver of fees must be sent directly to the Queens County Clerk's office. NY R L QUEENS MOT SUP Doc. 1. Court fees (e.g., RJI fee, motion fee) in E-filed cases may be paid for on-line using a credit card. Papers may also be filed with the E-file system and the fee may be paid at the County Clerk's Office. In the latter case, the paper is not considered to have been filed until payment of the fee has been tendered. NY R L QUEENS E-FILE Doc. 1(E)(1). The motion/petition shall be filed on-line and the fee paid for either on-line by credit card or by the "Pay at the County Clerk's Office" option. NY R L QUEENS E-FILE Doc. 1(H)(1).

vi. *Working copies.* The court may require the parties to provide working copies of documents filed electronically. In such event, each working copy shall include, firmly affixed thereto, a copy of a confirmation notice in a form prescribed by the Chief Administrator. NY R UNIF TRIAL CTS § 202.5-b(d)(5).

- *BRONX COUNTY.* After papers on motions have been e-filed, working copies thereof, with Confirmation Notice firmly attached as the back page facing out, must be submitted. (Each document or group of documents that is separately bound shall bear a Confirmation Notice.) Working copies lacking the Notice will not be accepted. WORKING COPIES OF MOTION PAPERS MUST BE SUBMITTED NO LATER THAN 4:45 P.M. ON THE RETURN DATE IN THE MOTION SUPPORT OFFICE (ROOM 217) AS EXPLAINED in NY R BRONX E FIL R Doc. 1(4). If an attorney has failed to submit required working copies on or before the return date, the motion will be transmitted as is to the Justice for such action as the Justice finds appropriate. Attorneys may submit working copies on motions by mail or overnight delivery. Any such submission shall be sent in a timely manner to the Motion Support Office (Room 217) and be conspicuously marked on the outside "NYSCEF Matter"; lack of such marking may delay processing. NY R BRONX E FIL R Doc. 1(4)(a).
- *ERIE COUNTY.* Electronically filed documents subject to review and processing by the Part Clerk do not require a working copy unless otherwise directed or provided for in IAS Part Rules. NY R UNIF TRIAL CTS § 202.5-b(d)(4), any working copy submitted shall include, as a cover page firmly fastened thereto, a copy of the Confirmation Notice generated by the NYSCEF site at the time of filing. Please consult the individual Justice's Part Rules and/or consult with the Judge's chambers to determine whether and how working copies are to be provided. Working copies will not be printed or delivered by the Erie County Clerk or the Chief Clerk of the Courts or any of their personnel to chambers. The official record of a document in an electronically filed case is the document filed via the NYSCEF system. Working copies are intended only for use by the Justice. The Court will discard all working copies after the Justice has finished with them. Thus, in the event that counsel fails to file a document via the NYSCEF system, the document will not be part of the court record. NY R ERIE E FIL Doc. 3(III)(O); NY R ERIE E FIL Doc. 3(V)(E).
- *KINGS COUNTY.* No courtesy copies of motion papers are required by the Court, except as may be required for electronic filing or by the Judge's Part Rules. In tort cases against the City of New York, courtesy copies shall be supplied to the Corporation Counsel's office in Brooklyn. NY R L KINGS Pt. C,

Rule 5. Unless otherwise directed by the Court or as described herein, and with the exceptions listed below, in all NYSCEF cases in which an RJI has been filed, working copies of e-filed documents that are intended for judicial review must be submitted to the court. Working copies are not required of documents that are only processed by a support office (e.g. preliminary conference request, note of issue). Working copies shall include exhibit tabs and backs; for motion papers, the motion sequence number and the return date and part. The confirmation notice with the motion sequence number on it should be the back page of the motion facing out. In addition, the filer of a working copy must firmly bind thereto, with the back page facing out, a copy of the Confirmation Notice that was generated by NYSCEF when that document was efiled. Working copies that are submitted without the related Confirmation Notice will not be accepted. NY R L KINGS E FIL Doc. 1(B)(7); NY R L KINGS E FIL Doc. 1(D). WORKING COPIES OF MOTION PAPERS MUST BE SUBMITTED IN THE MOTION SUPPORT OFFICE (ROOM 227) AS EXPLAINED HEREIN. THEY MUST NOT BE DELIVERED TO THE PART OR CHAMBERS, EXCEPT WHERE THE INDIVIDUAL JUSTICE'S PART RULES PROVIDE OTHERWISE; DOING SO WILL CAUSE ADMINISTRATIVE CONFUSION AND POSSIBLE MISPLACEMENT OF PAPERS. Any such submission shall be sent in a timely manner (kindly review individual Justice's rules) and be conspicuously marked on the outside "NYSCEF Matter;" lack of such marking may delay processing. NY R L KINGS E FIL Doc. 1(D).

- *NEW YORK COUNTY.* Some Justices require that working copies of e-filed motion papers be submitted. See the E-filing Protocol for information on the many Parts that do not require working copies. Where required, working copies of the moving documents and all other documents on the motion or application shall be submitted to the Motion Submission Part Courtroom (Room 130) on, but not before, the final return date. A Confirmation Notice from the NYSCEF system, which is generated when a document is e-filed, shall be firmly affixed, as the back page facing out, to each separate working copy or group of such copies. NY R NY CTY Procedure II(A) NY R NY CTY E FIL Doc. 2(B)(5)(a); NY R NY CTY J RUL Rule 14(a). For more information on working copies, including which parts don't require them, refer to NY R NY CTY E FIL Doc. 2(B)(6).
- *ONONDAGA COUNTY.* Any courtesy "working" copies, if required (see NY R ONDGA E FIL Protocol(B)(7)), must be provided directly to the assigned justice. NY R ONDGA E FIL Protocol(B)(9)(e). For information as to whether or not an Onondaga Supreme Court Justice requires working (courtesy) copies of e-filed documents, please consult the Onondaga County Individual E-filing Rules. NY R ONDGA E FIL Protocol(B)(7)(a). The Supreme Court Clerk's Office and the Onondaga County Clerk's Office will NOT accept the working copies. Working copies must be sent directly to the assigned justice's chambers. NY R ONDGA E FIL Protocol(B)(7)(b). A copy of the Confirmation Notice, generated by the NYSCEF system at the time a document is e-filed, must be attached to every working copy provided to chambers. If the Confirmation Notice is missing, the copy will not be accepted. NY R ONDGA E FIL Protocol(B)(7)(c). Courtesy copies do not become part of the official court record as maintained by the Onondaga County Clerk's Office and will be destroyed by chambers at the disposition of the case. In the event that counsel fails to file a document via NYSCEF, the document will not be part of the court record. NY R ONDGA E FIL Protocol(B)(7)(d).
- *QUEENS COUNTY.* Working copies of E-Filed notices of motion/notices of petition are NOT to be sent to the Motion Support Office. They must be brought to the calendar call in the judge's part. NY R L QUEENS MOT SUP Doc. 1. Unless otherwise directed or authorized by the court, counsel should file papers with the E-file system first and thereafter deliver a working copy to at the calendar call of the Centralized Motion Part or Assigned Justice in accordance with individual Part Rules. NY R L QUEENS E-FILE Doc. 1(E)(4). On the return date of a motion that has been E-filed, the movant must provide the Centralized Motion Part (CMP) with a working copy of the entire motion including the notice of motion with sequence number and all of the attached exhibits. The motion must have the confirmation of filing firmly affixed to the back of the papers (facing outward). The confirmation of filing is a separate notice from the payment notice and will say confirmation clearly across the top of the page. NY R L QUEENS E-FILE Doc. 1(H)(2)(a). The motion or Order to Show Cause must have clearly written across its face the words "Working Copy," it must also have the assigned Judge's name, motion sequence number and calendar number—which may be obtained from the posted calendar outside courtroom on the return date of the motion. A confirmation of filing must attached thereto. Working copies of e-filed Orders to Show Cause must contain a copy of the signed order and all supporting papers. NY R L QUEENS E-FILE Doc. 1(H)(2)(c). The Confirmation Notice must be an updated version that indicates the sequence number of the motion being submitted at the CMP calendar call. WORKING COPIES WITHOUT A CONFIRMATION NOTICE WILL NOT BE ACCEPTED. NY R L QUEENS E-FILE Doc. 1(H)(7).

vii. *Statement of authorization in electronic filing cases.* A filing agent (other than one employed by a governmental entity) shall e-file a statement of authorization from counsel of record in an action, in a form approved by the Chief Administrator, prior to or together with the first e-filing in that action by the agent on behalf of that counsel. NY R UNIF TRIAL CTS § 202.5-b(d)(1)(i).

viii. *ERIE COUNTY: Additional supplemental documents*

- *Notice of hard copy submission in e-filed case.* In accordance with NY R UNIF TRIAL CTS § 202.5-b(d), the County Clerk shall refuse to accept for filing, hard copy papers filed to an action subject to electronic filing unless hard copy filing is permitted by the Uniform Rules or NY R ERIE E FIL Doc. 3 and the papers bear a completed Notice of Hard Copy Submission—E-Filed Case form. NY R ERIE E FIL Doc. 3(III)(D).

ix. *KINGS COUNTY: Additional supplemental documents*

- *Forms when filing in hard copy.* An attorney who certifies in good faith that he or she lacks the equipment or knowledge needed to e-file and have no staff member or employee under his or her direction who has such knowledge and equipment may opt out of participation in e-filing in a mandatory case by filing a "Notice of Opt-Out from Participation in Action Subject to Mandatory Electronic Filing" form EFM-2 with the Clerk. NY R L KINGS E FIL Doc. 1(A)(2). Where in accordance with the E-Filing Rules a party submits a document in hard copy in an e-filed case (principally, a document submitted by a nonparticipating party (e.g., an attorney) in a consensual case, an emergency filing made in accordance with the Mandatory E-Filing Rules, and any document filed with the court in hard copy by an attorney who has opted out of participation in mandatory e-filing, the document must bear the back page facing out, a "Notice of Hard Copy Submission—E-Filed Cases" form EFM-3. NY R L KINGS E FIL Doc. 1(B)(3).

x. *NEW YORK COUNTY: Additional supplemental documents*

- *Notice of hard copy submission.* Where in accordance with the E-Filing Rules an attorney or an unrepresented litigant who is participating in e-filing submits a document in hard copy in an e-filed case, the document must bear, as the back page facing out, a Notice of Hard-Copy Submission—E-Filed Case (a form available in the "Forms" section on the NYSCEF website (Form EFM-3) and in the court's back offices). NY R NY CTY E FIL Doc. 2(B)(3). For more information refer to NY R NY CTY E FIL Doc. 2.
- *Unpublished decisions.* Whenever reliance is placed upon a decision or other authority not officially published or readily available to the New York County Supreme Court, a copy of the case or of pertinent portions of the authority shall be submitted with the motion papers. NY R NY CTY J RUL Rule 14(a).

xi. *ONONDAGA COUNTY: Additional supplemental documents*

- *Notice of hard copy submission.* Any papers to be filed with the court in an e-filed case must be filed online with the E-filing system except where a special exemption is granted (e.g., oversized maps, photographs). If such an exemption is granted, Form EFM-3, "Notice of Hard Copy Submission—E-Filed Case," must be attached to such documents forms which are not filed on line. Also, Form EFM-4 "Notice of Hard Copy Exhibit Filing" must be completed and uploaded to the action's e-file. Both of these forms may be found on the NYSCEF website. NY R ONDGA E FIL Protocol(B)(4).

xii. *QUEENS COUNTY: Additional supplemental documents*

- *Notice of hard copy submission.* Any party opting out of the e-filing system must have a "Notice of Hard Copy Submission" firmly affixed to the back of the papers. NY R L QUEENS E-FILE Doc. 1(H)(2)(f).

2. *Documents for opposing party*

a. *Required documents*

i. *Opposition.* Refer to the General Requirements section of this document for information on the opposition.

- *Request for oral argument.* A party requesting oral argument shall set forth such request in its notice of motion or in its order to show cause or on the first page of the answering papers, as the case may be. Where all parties to a motion request oral argument, oral argument shall be granted unless the court shall determine it to be unnecessary. Where a motion is brought on by order to show cause, the court may set forth in the order that oral argument is required on the return date of the motion. NY R UNIF TRIAL CTS § 202.8(d).
- *QUEENS COUNTY: E-filing opposition papers.* E-filed opposition papers and/or reply papers must also be provided to the Centralized Motion Part in the same manner as the moving papers with the confirmation of filing firmly attached to the back of the papers. NY R L QUEENS E-FILE Doc. 1(H)(2)(d).

ii. *Proof of service.* In addition to complying with the provisions of NY CPLR Rule 2101, every paper filed in court shall have annexed thereto appropriate proof of service on all parties where required. NY R UNIF TRIAL CTS § 202.5(a).

b. *Supplemental documents*

i. *Supporting evidence; Exhibits.* The main supporting papers on a motion are affidavits, but any relevant exhibits, documents, depositions, etc., are also includible. SIEGEL-NYPRAC § 246.

- *Affidavits accompanying opposition.* Affidavits shall be for a statement of the relevant facts. NY R UNIF TRIAL CTS § 202.8(c).
- *Foreign language documents.* Where an affidavit or exhibit annexed to a paper served or filed is in a foreign language, it shall be accompanied by an English translation and an affidavit by the translator stating his qualifications and that the translation is accurate. NY CPLR Rule 2101(b).
- *Statement of attorney in lieu of affidavit.* The statement of an attorney admitted to practice in the courts of the state, or of a physician, osteopath or dentist, authorized by law to practice in the state, who is not a party to an action, when subscribed and affirmed by him to be true under the penalties of perjury, may be served or filed in the action in lieu of and with the same force and effect as an affidavit. NY CPLR Rule 2106.
- *NEW YORK COUNTY: Form of presented exhibits.* Exhibits should be tabbed and be legible; a typed version of any exhibit that is difficult to read should be submitted with the original. Exhibits printed on both sides of the page should be bound and tabbed on the side. NY R NY CTY J RUL Rule 14(a).
- *QUEENS COUNTY.* Attorneys submitting exhibits to the court on E-file cases shall make each exhibit a separate, labeled attachment to an affidavit/affirmation. NY R L QUEENS E-FILE Doc. 1(H)(4).

ii. *Brief.* Briefs shall be for a statement of the relevant law. NY R UNIF TRIAL CTS § 202.8(c).

iii. *Filing fees.* The County Clerk shall require the payment of any applicable statutory fees, or an order of the Court waiving payment of such fees, before accepting a paper for filing. NY R UNIF TRIAL CTS § 202.5(d)(1). For information on filing fees, if any, refer to NY CPLR § 8001, et seq.

- *ALBANY COUNTY.* In general, any filing subsequent to the commencement of an action which is designated as a motion or cross-motion requires the payment of a filing fee to the County Clerk's Office prior to submission to the Supreme Court Clerk's Office for referral to the assigned justice. The fee is assessed regardless of whether an application is made by notice of motion, order to show cause or ex parte. No fee will be charged upon the filing of a motion for poor person status in conjunction with an application which serves to commence an action or special proceeding. In the event a motion is received by the court unaccompanied by proof of payment to the County Clerk, the Supreme Court Clerk's Office will contact the submitting party to advise that the application will be held pending receipt of the filing fee only until the return date of the motion. If proof of payment is not submitted to the Supreme Court Clerk's Office by the return date (ex parte applications will be held ten (10) days), the papers will be returned by mail with a notification that the motion has been removed from the court's calendar and that it must be re-noticed and re-filed with the court along with the requisite filing fee. Inquiries concerning the applicability of the motion fee to a proposed filing may be directed to the Supreme Court Clerk's Office. NY R 3 JD SUP Doc. 1(B).
- *BRONX COUNTY.* In accordance with the new civil fee schedule set forth in Article 80 of the C.P.L.R. (NY CPLR § 8001, et seq.), effective July 14, 2003, all motions, and cross motions must be approved in Room 217 prior to payment of said fees in the County Clerk's Office, Room 118. NY R BRONX FIL R Doc. 8. The motion fee [must be] paid for via NYSCEF by credit/debit card. NY R BRONX E FIL R Doc. 1(1).
- *ERIE COUNTY.* Payment for fee-bearing NYSCEF documents must be made online via credit or debit card (American Express, MasterCard or Visa) at the time of submission. NY R ERIE E FIL Doc. 3(III)(E).
- *KINGS COUNTY.* The motion must be filed with NYSCEF and the motion fee paid. NY R L KINGS E FIL Doc. 1(D). Court fees in NYSCEF cases must be paid via NYSCEF by a credit or bank card (MasterCard, Visa, or American Express). Fees are no longer accepted in person in the Kings County Clerk's Office in NYSCEF cases. NY R L KINGS E FIL Doc. 1(B)(6).
- *NEW YORK COUNTY.* A motion fee must be paid on motions made in writing by notice of motion, order to show cause or ex parte after the commencement of an action. For this purpose, the term "action" shall mean any application to the court that requires the assignment of an index number, regardless of whether a formal pleading is filed. Applications or motions that commence an action and for which an index number fee must be paid require no motion fee. [A]ny motions made after the initial applications in these situations

would require payment of the motion fee. A motion that is the initial application in a case commenced by the filing of a summons and complaint would require a motion fee since the filing of the summons and complaint rather than the application itself would require the purchase of an index number. NY R NY CTY Procedure II(A). In e-filed cases the motion fee must be paid when the documents are filed. Payment is made on-line by Visa, Mastercard, or American Express credit or bank card. NY R NY CTY Procedure II(A); NY R NY CTY E FIL Doc. 2(B)(5).

- *ONONDAGA COUNTY.* Court fees in e-filed cases must be paid online with the NYSCEF system using a credit card. The document is not considered to have been filed until payment of the fee has been tendered. NY R ONDGA E FIL Protocol(B)(2). Fees must be paid on all cross motions. NY R ONDGA E FIL Protocol(B)(9)(e).
- *QUEENS COUNTY.* The Motion Support Office does not receive, forward or process any fees or waiver of fees. All applications requiring payment of statutory fees or waiver of fees must be sent directly to the Queens County Clerk's office. NY R L QUEENS MOT SUP Doc. 1. Court fees (e.g., RJI fee, motion fee) in E-filed cases may be paid for on-line using a credit card. Papers may also be filed with the E-file system and the fee may be paid at the County Clerk's Office. In the latter case, the paper is not considered to have been filed until payment of the fee has been tendered. NY R L QUEENS E-FILE Doc. 1(E)(1). The motion/petition shall be filed on-line and the fee paid for either on-line by credit card or by the "Pay at the County Clerk's Office" option. NY R L QUEENS E-FILE Doc. 1(H)(1).

iv. *Working copies.* The court may require the parties to provide working copies of documents filed electronically. In such event, each working copy shall include, firmly affixed thereto, a copy of a confirmation notice in a form prescribed by the Chief Administrator. NY R UNIF TRIAL CTS § 202.5-b(d)(5).

- *BRONX COUNTY.* After papers on motions have been e-filed, working copies thereof, with Confirmation Notice firmly attached as the back page facing out, must be submitted. (Each document or group of documents that is separately bound shall bear a Confirmation Notice.) Working copies lacking the Notice will not be accepted. WORKING COPIES OF MOTION PAPERS MUST BE SUBMITTED NO LATER THAN 4:45 P.M. ON THE RETURN DATE IN THE MOTION SUPPORT OFFICE (ROOM 217) AS EXPLAINED in NY R BRONX E FIL R Doc. 1(4). If an attorney has failed to submit required working copies on or before the return date, the motion will be transmitted as is to the Justice for such action as the Justice finds appropriate. Attorneys may submit working copies on motions by mail or overnight delivery. Any such submission shall be sent in a timely manner to the Motion Support Office (Room 217) and be conspicuously marked on the outside "NYSCEF Matter"; lack of such marking may delay processing. NY R BRONX E FIL R Doc. 1(4)(a).
- *ERIE COUNTY.* Electronically filed documents subject to review and processing by the Part Clerk do not require a working copy unless otherwise directed or provided for in IAS Part Rules. NY R UNIF TRIAL CTS § 202.5-b(d)(4), any working copy submitted shall include, as a cover page firmly fastened thereto, a copy of the Confirmation Notice generated by the NYSCEF site at the time of filing. Please consult the individual Justice's Part Rules and/or consult with the Judge's chambers to determine whether and how working copies are to be provided. Working copies will not be printed or delivered by the Erie County Clerk or the Chief Clerk of the Courts or any of their personnel to chambers. The official record of a document in an electronically filed case is the document filed via the NYSCEF system. Working copies are intended only for use by the Justice. The Court will discard all working copies after the Justice has finished with them. Thus, in the event that counsel fails to file a document via the NYSCEF system, the document will not be part of the court record. NY R ERIE E FIL Doc. 3(III)(O); NY R ERIE E FIL Doc. 3(V)(E).
- *KINGS COUNTY.* No courtesy copies of motion papers are required by the Court, except as may be required for electronic filing or by the Judge's Part Rules. In tort cases against the City of New York, courtesy copies shall be supplied to the Corporation Counsel's office in Brooklyn. NY R L KINGS Pt. C, Rule 5. Unless otherwise directed by the Court or as described herein, and with the exceptions listed below, in all NYSCEF cases in which an RJI has been filed, working copies of e-filed documents that are intended for judicial review must be submitted to the court. Working copies are not required of documents that are only processed by a support office (e.g. preliminary conference request, note of issue). Working copies shall include exhibit tabs and backs; for motion papers, the motion sequence number and the return date and part. The confirmation notice with the motion sequence number on it should be the back page of the motion facing out. In addition, the filer of a working copy must firmly bind thereto, with the back page facing out, a copy of the Confirmation Notice that was generated by NYSCEF when that document was efiled.

Working copies that are submitted without the related Confirmation Notice will not be accepted. NY R L KINGS E FIL Doc. 1(B)(7); NY R L KINGS E FIL Doc. 1(D). WORKING COPIES OF MOTION PAPERS MUST BE SUBMITTED IN THE MOTION SUPPORT OFFICE (ROOM 227) AS EXPLAINED HEREIN. THEY MUST NOT BE DELIVERED TO THE PART OR CHAMBERS, EXCEPT WHERE THE INDIVIDUAL JUSTICE'S PART RULES PROVIDE OTHERWISE; DOING SO WILL CAUSE ADMINISTRATIVE CONFUSION AND POSSIBLE MISPLACEMENT OF PAPERS. Any such submission shall be sent in a timely manner (kindly review individual Justice's rules) and be conspicuously marked on the outside "NYSCEF Matter;" lack of such marking may delay processing. NY R L KINGS E FIL Doc. 1(D).

- *NEW YORK COUNTY.* Some Justices require that working copies of e-filed motion papers be submitted. See the E-filing Protocol for information on the many Parts that do not require working copies. Where required, working copies of the moving documents and all other documents on the motion or application shall be submitted to the Motion Submission Part Courtroom (Room 130) on, but not before, the final return date. A Confirmation Notice from the NYSCEF system, which is generated when a document is e-filed, shall be firmly affixed, as the back page facing out, to each separate working copy or group of such copies. NY R NY CTY Procedure II(A) NY R NY CTY E FIL Doc. 2(B)(5)(a); NY R NY CTY J RUL Rule 14(a). For more information on working copies, including which parts don't require them, refer to NY R NY CTY E FIL Doc. 2(B)(6).
- *ONONDAGA COUNTY.* Any courtesy "working" copies, if required (see NY R ONDGA E FIL Protocol(B)(7)), must be provided directly to the assigned justice. NY R ONDGA E FIL Protocol(B)(9)(e). For information as to whether or not an Onondaga Supreme Court Justice requires working (courtesy) copies of e-filed documents, please consult the Onondaga County Individual E-filing Rules. NY R ONDGA E FIL Protocol(B)(7)(a). The Supreme Court Clerk's Office and the Onondaga County Clerk's Office will NOT accept the working copies. Working copies must be sent directly to the assigned justice's chambers. NY R ONDGA E FIL Protocol(B)(7)(b). A copy of the Confirmation Notice, generated by the NYSCEF system at the time a document is e-filed, must be attached to every working copy provided to chambers. If the Confirmation Notice is missing, the copy will not be accepted. NY R ONDGA E FIL Protocol(B)(7)(c). Courtesy copies do not become part of the official court record as maintained by the Onondaga County Clerk's Office and will be destroyed by chambers at the disposition of the case. In the event that counsel fails to file a document via NYSCEF, the document will not be part of the court record. NY R ONDGA E FIL Protocol(B)(7)(d).
- *QUEENS COUNTY.* Working copies of E-Filed notices of motion/notices of petition are NOT to be sent to the Motion Support Office. They must be brought to the calendar call in the judge's part. NY R L QUEENS MOT SUP Doc. 1. Unless otherwise directed or authorized by the court, counsel should file papers with the E-file system first and thereafter deliver a working copy to at the calendar call of the Centralized Motion Part or Assigned Justice in accordance with individual Part Rules. NY R L QUEENS E-FILE Doc. 1(E)(4). On the return date of a motion that has been E-filed, the movant must provide the Centralized Motion Part (CMP) with a working copy of the entire motion including the notice of motion with sequence number and all of the attached exhibits. The motion must have the confirmation of filing firmly affixed to the back of the papers (facing outward). The confirmation of filing is a separate notice from the payment notice and will say confirmation clearly across the top of the page. NY R L QUEENS E-FILE Doc. 1(H)(2)(a). The motion or Order to Show Cause must have clearly written across its face the words "Working Copy," it must also have the assigned Judge's name, motion sequence number and calendar number—which may be obtained from the posted calendar outside courtroom on the return date of the motion. A confirmation of filing must attached thereto. Working copies of e-filed Orders to Show Cause must contain a copy of the signed order and all supporting papers. NY R L QUEENS E-FILE Doc. 1(H)(2)(c). The Confirmation Notice must be an updated version that indicates the sequence number of the motion being submitted at the CMP calendar call. WORKING COPIES WITHOUT A CONFIRMATION NOTICE WILL NOT BE ACCEPTED. NY R L QUEENS E-FILE Doc. 1(H)(7).

v. *ERIE COUNTY: Additional supplemental documents*

- *Notice of hard copy submission in e-filed case.* In accordance with NY R UNIF TRIAL CTS § 202.5-b(d), the County Clerk shall refuse to accept for filing, hard copy papers filed to an action subject to electronic filing unless hard copy filing is permitted by the Uniform Rules or NY R ERIE E FIL Doc. 3 and the papers bear a completed Notice of Hard Copy Submission—E-Filed Case form. NY R ERIE E FIL Doc. 3(III)(D).

vi. *KINGS COUNTY: Additional supplemental documents*

- *Forms when filing in hard copy.* An attorney who certifies in good faith that he or she lacks the equipment or knowledge needed to e-file and have no staff member or employee under his or her direction who has such knowledge and equipment may opt out of participation in e-filing in a mandatory case by filing a "Notice of Opt-Out from Participation in Action Subject to Mandatory Electronic Filing" form EFM-2 with the Clerk. NY R L KINGS E FIL Doc. 1(A)(2). Where in accordance with the E-Filing Rules a party submits a document in hard copy in an e-filed case (principally, a document submitted by a nonparticipating party (e.g., an attorney) in a consensual case, an emergency filing made in accordance with the Mandatory E-Filing Rules, and any document filed with the court in hard copy by an attorney who has opted out of participation in mandatory e-filing, the document must bear the back page facing out, a "Notice of Hard Copy Submission—E-Filed Cases" form EFM-3. NY R L KINGS E FIL Doc. 1(B)(3).

vii. *NEW YORK COUNTY: Additional supplemental documents*

- *Notice of hard copy submission.* Where in accordance with the E-Filing Rules an attorney or an unrepresented litigant who is participating in e-filing submits a document in hard copy in an e-filed case, the document must bear, as the back page facing out, a Notice of Hard-Copy Submission—E-Filed Case (a form available in the "Forms" section on the NYSCEF website (Form EFM-3) and in the court's back offices). NY R NY CTY E FIL Doc. 2(B)(3). For more information refer to NY R NY CTY E FIL Doc. 2.
- *Unpublished decisions.* Whenever reliance is placed upon a decision or other authority not officially published or readily available to the New York County Supreme Court, a copy of the case or of pertinent portions of the authority shall be submitted with the motion papers. NY R NY CTY J RUL Rule 14(a).

viii. *ONONDAGA COUNTY: Additional supplemental documents*

- *Notice of hard copy submission.* Any papers to be filed with the court in an e-filed case must be filed online with the E-filing system except where a special exemption is granted (e.g., oversized maps, photographs). If such an exemption is granted, Form EFM-3, "Notice of Hard Copy Submission—E-Filed Case," must be attached to such documents forms which are not filed on line. Also, Form EFM-4 "Notice of Hard Copy Exhibit Filing" must be completed and uploaded to the action's e-file. Both of these forms may be found on the NYSCEF website. NY R ONDGA E FIL Protocol(B)(4).

ix. *QUEENS COUNTY: Additional supplemental documents*

- *Notice of hard copy submission.* Any party opting out of the e-filing system must have a "Notice of Hard Copy Submission" firmly affixed to the back of the papers. NY R L QUEENS E-FILE Doc. 1(H)(2)(f).

E. Format

1. *Form of documents*

a. *Size and form of paper.* Each paper served or filed shall be durable, white and, except for summonses, subpoenas, notices of appearance, notes of issue, orders of protection, temporary orders of protection and exhibits, shall be eleven by eight and one-half (11 x 8-1/2) inches in size. NY CPLR Rule 2101(a).

b. *Writing and language.* The writing shall be legible and in black ink. NY CPLR Rule 2101(a). Each paper served or filed shall be in the English language which, where practicable, shall be of ordinary usage. NY CPLR Rule 2101(b).

c. *Caption.* Each paper served or filed shall begin with a caption setting forth the name of the court, the venue, the title of the action, the nature of the paper and the index number of the action if one has been assigned. In all papers other than a summons, a complaint or a judgment it shall be sufficient to state the name of the first named party on each side with an appropriate indication of any omissions. NY CPLR Rule 2101(c).

i. *Further contents of first page.* After the first paper has been filed in each case the index number shall appear on the cover and first page to the right of the caption of every paper tendered for filing in the action. Each such cover and first page also shall contain an indication of the county of venue and a brief description of the nature of the paper and, where the case has been assigned to an individual judge, shall contain the name of the assigned judge to the right of the caption. NY R UNIF TRIAL CTS § 202.5(a); NY R UNIF TRIAL CTS § 202.5(b); NY R UNIF TRIAL CTS § 202.5(d)(1)(i).

ii. *ALBANY COUNTY: Request for oral argument.* A party may request oral argument on a motion by indicating such request on the first page of the notice of motion, order to show cause, or answering papers in the area across from the caption of the action/proceeding. NY R 3 JD SUP Doc. 1(B).

iii. *NEW YORK COUNTY: Request for oral argument.* Counsel who wish oral argument must so request conspicuously on the front of their papers. NY R NY CTY Procedure II(D).

d. *Index number.* No paper in an action in the supreme or a county court, other than an order submitted for signature to

a judge out of court, shall be submitted for any purpose to the supreme or county court or to a clerk thereof unless there is endorsed on such paper the index number of the action assigned by the clerk of the county. NY CPLR § 8018(c).

i. *ALBANY COUNTY: Index number on all filed documents.* The index number, the request for judicial intervention number and the assigned justice's name shall appear on [all papers filed with the Court subsequent to the complaint]. NY R 3 JD SUP Doc. 1(A).

ii. *ERIE COUNTY: Index number after initial filing.* Cases that are initially commenced by the filing of papers with the NYSCEF system are identified as e-filed cases by assignment of an Index Number that has "800-899" as the first three (3) digits of the index number (i.e. 802391/2012). NY R ERIE E FIL Doc. 3(II). [The] Index Number must be affixed to all document submissions, filings, and communications to the Erie County Clerk and the Court. Cases that are converted from paper to e-filing shall retain the original index number. NY R ERIE E FIL Doc. 3(II).

iii. *KINGS COUNTY: Index number after initial filing.* In cases commenced electronically by the filing of initiating papers with the NYSCEF system and payment of the statutory fees, the Kings County Clerk will issue an NYSCEF designated index number and the filer shall be notified via the NYSCEF system of the index number assigned and filing date. Such index number must be affixed to all document submissions, filings and communications to the Kings County Clerk and Supreme Court. If counsel faces exigent circumstances that require accelerated assignment, counsel may contact Administration of the Kings County Clerk at kcco-efile@nycourts.gov, during normal business hours of the court. NY R L KINGS E FIL Doc. 1(B)(5).

iv. *NEW YORK COUNTY: Index number on hard copy filings.* Papers subsequently presented for filing in hardcopy format will be filed in this jacket. NY R NY CTY Procedure I(B). Index numbers take the form of six digits followed by a slash and the four digits of the year the case began, e.g., 340705/2018. The first or first two integers of the index number identify the type of case. If a case is commenced electronically, the second integer will be a "5", except as indicated otherwise in the list below. There are many tax certiorari matters e-filed annually and the index numbers therefor will normally run over into those with a "6" as the second integer, and the same will occur with general cases if necessary. The principal types of cases and their index number categories are listed in NY R NY CTY Procedure I(B). NY R NY CTY Procedure I(B); NY R NY CTY Procedure XI(A).

v. *ONONDAGA COUNTY: Index number.* The index number must be referenced on all e-filed documents and correspondence. All e-filed case index numbers will contain the letters "EF" between the year and the file number (for example, 2012EF9999). NY R ONDGA E FIL Protocol(B)(1).

vi. *QUEENS COUNTY: Index number on converted cases.* Cases originally commenced in hard-copy form but later converted to an E-file case, either by stipulation or order will bear a regular index number initially. The County Clerk will issue a new E-file index number. NY R L QUEENS E-FILE Doc. 1(B).

e. *Line spacing.* Every paper filed in court, if typewritten, shall have at least double space between each line, except for quotations and the names and addresses of attorneys appearing in the action. NY R UNIF TRIAL CTS § 202.5(a).

f. *Font size.* Each. . .paper printed or typed, served or filed, except for summonses. . .and exhibits, shall be in clear type of no less than ten (10) point in size. NY CPLR Rule 2101(a).

i. Whenever a requirement relating to size of type is stated in point size, the type size requirement shall be deemed met if the x-height of the type is a minimum of forty-five percent (45%) of the specified point size. Each point shall be measured as .351 millimeter. The x-height size shall be measured as it appears on the page. The x-height is the height of the lower case letters, exclusive of ascenders or descenders. NY CPLR § 105(t).

g. *Margins.* Every paper filed in court shall have at least one (1) inch margins. NY R UNIF TRIAL CTS § 202.5(a).

h. *Citations*

i. *Civil practice law and rules.* NY CPLR § 101, et seq. shall be known as the civil practice law and rules, and may be cited as "CPLR". Reference to a provision in the civil practice law and rules may, except when such provision is being enacted or amended, be made without indicating whether it is a rule or section. NY CPLR § 101.

i. *Indorsement by attorney.* Each paper served or filed shall be indorsed with the name, address and telephone number of the attorney for the party serving or filing the paper, or if the party does not appear by attorney, with the name, address and telephone number of the party. NY CPLR Rule 2101(d).

j. *One-sided printing.* In addition, every paper filed in court, other than an exhibit or printed form, shall contain writing on one side only, except that papers that are fastened on the side may contain writing on both sides. NY R UNIF TRIAL CTS § 202.5(a).

k. *Use of copies authorized.* Except where otherwise specifically prescribed, copies, rather than originals, of all papers,

including orders, affidavits and exhibits may be served or filed. Where it is required that the original be served or filed and the original is lost or withheld, the court may authorize a copy to be served or filed. NY CPLR Rule 2101(e).

i. Where a certified copy of a paper is required by law, an attorney admitted to practice in the courts of the state may certify that it has been compared by him with the original and found to be a true and complete copy. Such a certificate, when subscribed by such attorney, has the same effect as if made by a clerk. NY CPLR § 2105.

l. *Recycled paper.* It is the policy of the Unified Court System that litigants, where practicable, should file or submit to the courts of the Unified Court System of the State of New York papers printed or reproduced on recycled paper. Paper is considered recycled if it contains a minimum content of thirty percent (30%) waste paper. NY R UNIF TRIAL CTS § 215.2. The signature page of every paper filed or submitted to the court on recycled paper should bear the legend: "Printed [Reproduced] on Recycled Paper." NY R UNIF TRIAL CTS § 215.3.

m. *Form of request for judicial intervention; Copies.* A request for judicial intervention must be submitted, in duplicate, on a form authorized by the Chief of the Courts, with proof of service on the other parties to the action (but proof of service is not required where the application is ex parte). NY R UNIF TRIAL CTS § 202.6(a).

n. *KINGS COUNTY: Tabs on filings.* Motions, orders and other filed papers shall be indexed with protruding tabs. Clerks are required to reject papers that do not have protruding exhibit tabs, except papers in matrimonial cases and papers filed by pro se litigants. NY R L KINGS Pt. A, Papers.

o. *NEW YORK COUNTY: Length of briefs.* Unless advance permission otherwise is granted by the court for good cause, memoranda of law shall not exceed thirty (30) pages each (exclusive of table of contents and table of authorities) and affidavits/affirmations shall not exceed twenty-five (25) pages each. NY R NY CTY J RUL Rule 14(b).

p. *QUEENS COUNTY: Form and size of motion filings.* All motions filed in Queens Supreme Court-Civil Term, must adhere to the Motion Support rules and the rules of the assigned judge. NY R L QUEENS MOT SUP Doc. 1. Due to space limitations, the Motion Support Office cannot accept notices of motion/notices of petition and accompanying exhibits which measure greater than eight (8) inches. If your documents measure greater than eight (8) inches you are directed to submit only the notice of motion/notice of petition to the Motion Support Office and bring all exhibits to the calendar call on your return date. NY R L QUEENS MOT SUP Doc. 1.

2. *Form of electronic documents.* Each paper served or filed by electronic means, as defined in NY CPLR Rule 2103(f), shall be capable of being reproduced by the receiver so as to comply with the provisions of NY CPLR Rule 2101(a) through NY CPLR Rule 2101(d). NY CPLR Rule 2101(g).

a. *File format.* All e-filed documents shall comply with the technical requirements set forth at the NYSCEF site. NY R UNIF TRIAL CTS § 202.5-b(d)(1)(i).

b. *Heading of document.* The subject matter heading for each paper sent by electronic means must indicate that the matter being transmitted electronically is related to a court proceeding. NY CPLR Rule 2103(b)(7).

c. *E-filed documents identification*

i. *ERIE COUNTY.* E-filed cases must be readily identifiable and marked as such. If counsel presents papers to the Office of the Erie County Clerk or the Office of the Chief Clerk in a NYSCEF matter where authorized, counsel should alert the Clerk that the case is a NYSCEF matter. NY R ERIE E FIL Doc. 3(II).

ii. *KINGS COUNTY.* The Supreme Court's Civil Case Information System ("CCIS") will further identify e-filed cases by the addition of a suffix to the index number (e.g. 500136/2006E). This suffix should be used on all documents filed with the court in e-filed matters. NY R L KINGS E FIL Doc. 1(A)(1).

3. *Signature blocks.* Every pleading, written motion, and other paper, served on another party or filed or submitted to the court shall be signed by an attorney, or by a party if the party is not represented by an attorney, with the name of the attorney or party clearly printed or typed directly below the signature. NY R CHIEF ADMIN § 130-1.1-a(a); NY R UNIF TRIAL CTS § 202.5(d)(1)(iv).

a. *Printed name.* Beneath each signature shall be printed the name signed. NY CPLR Rule 2101(a).

b. *Failure to sign.* Absent good cause shown, the court shall strike any unsigned paper if the omission of the signature is not corrected promptly after being called to the attention of the attorney or party. NY R CHIEF ADMIN § 130-1.1-a(a).

c. *Signature as certification.* By signing a paper, an attorney or party certifies that, to the best of that person's knowledge, information and belief, formed after an inquiry reasonable under the circumstances the presentation of the paper or the contentions therein are not frivolous as defined in NY R CHIEF ADMIN § 130-1.1(c). NY R CHIEF ADMIN § 130-1.1-a(b)(1).

d. *Electronic signatures.* A document shall be considered to have been signed by an attorney or party in compliance with NY R CHIEF ADMIN § 130-1.1-a if it has been signed by such attorney or party as provided in NY R UNIF TRIAL CTS § 202.5-b(e)(1) and it bears the signatory's name. NY R UNIF TRIAL CTS § 202.5-b(e)(2). An electronically filed document shall be considered to have been signed by, and shall be binding upon, the person identified as a signatory, if:

   i. It bears the physical signature of such person and is scanned into an electronic format that reproduces such signature; or
   ii. The signatory has electronically affixed the digital image of his or her signature to the document; or
   iii. It is electronically filed under the User ID and password of that person; or
   iv. In a tax certiorari action in which the parties have stipulated to this procedure, it is an initiating document that is electronically filed without the signature of the signatory in a form provided above in NY R UNIF TRIAL CTS § 202.5-b(e)(iv), provided that, prior to filing, the document is signed in full in hard copy (which hard copy must be preserved until the conclusion of all proceedings, including appeals, in the case in which it is filed); or
   v. In a small claims assessment review proceeding, it is a petition recorded by the NYSCEF site upon the filing of a text file as provided in NY R UNIF TRIAL CTS § 202.5-b(b)(1), provided that prior to filing, the document was signed in full in hard copy (which hard copy must be preserved until the conclusion of all proceedings in the matter, including article 78 (NY CPLR § 7801, et seq.) review and any appeals, and must be made available during the proceeding upon request of the respondent or the court); or
   vi. It otherwise bears the electronic signature of the signatory in a format conforming to such standards and requirements as may hereafter be established by the Chief Administrator. NY R UNIF TRIAL CTS § 202.5-b(e).

4. *Confidentiality of personal information.* No person may file any document available for public inspection with any state agency, political subdivision, or in any court of this state that contains a Social Security account number of any other person, unless such other person is a dependent child, or has consented to such filing, except as required by federal or state law or regulation, or by court rule. NY GEN BUS § 399-ddd. Submissions pursuant to e-filing procedures shall have the same confidentiality rights as paper documents. NY R UNIF TRIAL CTS § 202.5-b(k)(1).

   a. *Confidential personal information.* Except in the actions designated in NY R UNIF TRIAL CTS § 202.5(e)(1), or as otherwise provided by rule or law or court order, and whether or not a sealing order is or has been sought, the parties shall omit or redact confidential personal information in papers submitted to the court for filing. For purposes of NY R UNIF TRIAL CTS § 202.5(e), confidential personal information ("CPI") means:

      i. The taxpayer identification number of an individual or an entity, including a Social Security number, an employer identification number, and an individual taxpayer identification number, except the last four (4) digits thereof;
      ii. The date of an individual's birth, except the year thereof;
      iii. The full name of an individual known to be a minor, except the minor's initials;
      iv. A financial account number, including a credit and/or debit card number, a bank account number, an investment account number, and/or an insurance account number, except the last four (4) digits or letters thereof; and
      v. Any of the documents or testimony in a matrimonial action protected by NY DOM REL § 235 or evidence sealed by the court in such an action which are attached as exhibits or referenced in the papers filed in any other civil action. For purposes of NY R UNIF TRIAL CTS § 202.5, a matrimonial action shall mean: an action to annul a marriage or declare the nullity of a void marriage, an action or agreement for a separation, an action for a divorce, or an action or proceeding for custody, visitation, writ of habeus corpus, child support, maintenance or paternity. NY R UNIF TRIAL CTS § 202.5(e)(1).
      vi. *ERIE COUNTY.* An attorney or unrepresented litigant filing a document via the NYSCEF system must comply with the requirements of NY R UNIF TRIAL CTS § 202.5(e) regarding the redaction of Confidential Personal Information and NY GEN BUS § 399-ddd(6) concerning the filing of documents containing Social Security Numbers. It is the sole responsibility of counsel or unrepresented litigant filing to be aware of and to comply with existing laws requiring non-disclosure of personal information contained in any document e-filed in NYSCEF. NY R ERIE E FIL Doc. 3(III)(G); NY R ERIE E FIL Doc. 3(III).
      vii. *KINGS COUNTY.* An attorney or unrepresented litigant filing a document via the NYSCEF system must comply with the requirements of General Business Law § 399-dd(6), which often require redaction of any Social Security number that appear in the original document. The NYSCEF system automatically redacts portions of

filed documents which apparently contain Social Security numbers pursuant to NY R UNIF TRIAL CTS § 202.5-b(k). In the event the filing party receives e-mail notice through NYSCEF that a Social Security number in a filed document has been redacted, and the filing party concludes such redaction is erroneous, the filer should click on the link provided in the e-mail to permit the County Clerk to revert the redaction. For Confidential Personal Information, see NY R UNIF TRIAL CTS § 202.5(e) and NY R L KINGS E FIL Doc. 1(B)(11). [Editor's note: the reference to General Business Law § 399-dd(6) is likely a reference to NY GEN BUS § 399-ddd(6)]. NY R L KINGS E FIL Doc. 1(B)(10); NY R L KINGS E FIL Doc. 1(K)(1).

viii. *NEW YORK COUNTY.* It is the responsibility of counsel and parties to comply with rules restricting disclosure of confidential personal information. Nevertheless, NYSCEF screens filings and endeavors to identify any that contain social security numbers. When such numbers are discovered through this process, NYSCEF will restrict portions of or all of such documents from public view. Where NYSCEF has redacted what it believes to be a social security number, it will transmit to the filer a notice advising of the action taken and requesting that the filer review the matter and provide notification as set forth in the notice if the redaction has been made in error. NY R NY CTY E FIL Doc. 2(K)(1); NY R NY CTY J RUL Rule A-1. Documents filed in the past in "secure status" under a procedure no longer in place will retain that status unless otherwise directed by the court. NY R NY CTY E FIL Doc. 2(K)(2).

b. *Submission of confidential personal information.* Where a person submitting a paper to a court for filing believes in good faith that the inclusion of the full confidential personal information described in NY R UNIF TRIAL CTS § 202.5(e)(1) is material and necessary to the adjudication of the action or proceeding before the court, he or she may apply to the court for leave to serve and file together with a paper in which such information has been set forth in abbreviated form a confidential affidavit or affirmation setting forth the same information in unabbreviated form, appropriately referenced to the page or pages of the paper at which the abbreviated form appears. NY R UNIF TRIAL CTS § 202.5(e)(3).

c. *Home addresses.* For information on when home addresses and other personal information must be redacted, refer to NY CPLR Rule 2103-a.

5. *Defective papers.* A defect in the form of a paper, if a substantial right of a party is not prejudiced, shall be disregarded by the court, and leave to correct shall be freely given. NY CPLR Rule 2101(f). Papers that are stapled or bound securely shall not be rejected for filing simply because they are not bound with a backer of any kind. NY R UNIF TRIAL CTS § 202.5(a). A paper filed in accordance with the rules of the chief administrator or any local rule or practice established by the court shall be deemed filed. NY CPLR Rule 2102(b).

a. *Objection to defective papers.* The party on whom a paper is served shall be deemed to have waived objection to any defect in form unless, within fifteen (15) days after the receipt thereof, the party on whom the paper is served returns the paper to the party serving it with a statement of particular objections. NY CPLR Rule 2101(f).

F. Filing and Service Requirements

1. *Filing requirements.* Except where otherwise prescribed by law or order of court, papers required to be filed shall be filed with the clerk of the court in which the action is triable. In an action or proceeding in supreme or court, papers required to be filed shall be filed with the clerk of the county in which the proceeding is brought. NY CPLR Rule 2102(a).

a. *Furnishing papers to the court.* Each party shall furnish to the court all papers served by him. The moving party shall furnish at the hearing all other papers not already in the possession of the court necessary to the consideration of the questions involved. Where such papers are in the possession of an adverse party, they shall be produced by him at the hearing on notice served with the motion papers. Only papers served in accordance with the provisions of NY CPLR Rule 2214 shall be read in support of, or in opposition to, the motion, unless the court for good cause shall otherwise direct. NY CPLR Rule 2214(c).

i. *Submission to judge.* All papers for signature or consideration of the court shall be presented to the clerk of the trial court in the appropriate courtroom or clerk's office, except that where the clerk is unavailable or the judge so directs, papers may be submitted to the judge and a copy filed with the clerk at the first available opportunity. All papers for any judge that are filed in the clerk's office shall be promptly delivered to the judge by the clerk. The papers shall be clearly addressed to the judge for whom they are intended and prominently show the nature of the papers, the title and index number of the action in which they are filed, the judge's name and the name of the attorney or party submitting them. NY R UNIF TRIAL CTS § 202.5(b).

ii. *BRONX COUNTY: Approval of motions before filing.* All motion papers must be approved by the Motion Support Office, Supreme Court, Civil Term, room 217, before the motion papers are filed and the appropriate fee paid to the County Clerk. NY R BRONX FIL R Doc. 1.

iii. *ERIE COUNTY: Filing motions.* A motion on notice or a notice of petition in a NYSCEF case shall be filed through the NYSCEF system and must be accompanied by a Request for Judicial Intervention if the motion is being filed upon commencement of the action or if the matter has not yet been assigned to an IAS Justice. In addition, cross motions with the appropriate filing fees and opposition and reply papers must be submitted via the NYSCEF system. NY R ERIE E FIL Doc. 3(V)(A).

iv. *NEW YORK COUNTY: Filing hard copies.* Where in the narrow circumstances described by the e-filing rules a motion is made in hard-copy form or opposition papers are submitted in such form in an e-filed case, the hard-copy documents shall be submitted in the same way papers are submitted in non-e-filed cases, except that there shall be firmly affixed to each separate document or group of documents, as the back page facing out, a Notice of Hard Copy Submission—E-Filed Case. NY R NY CTY Procedure II(A). For more information on filing in hard copy cases, refer to NY R NY CTY Procedure II(A).

v. *ONONDAGA COUNTY: Submission of responsive papers and cross-motions.* Cross-motions, opposition and reply papers must be submitted online. NY R ONDGA E FIL Protocol(B)(9)(e). Motions and Orders to Show Cause are assigned a sequence number by the system. Counsel must be sure that cross motions and other filings correspond with the correct sequence number so that a cross motion will not be associated with the wrong original motion. NY R ONDGA E FIL Protocol(B)(9)(f).

b. *Electronic filing.* On consent, documents may be filed and served by electronic means in Supreme Court in such civil actions and in such counties as shall be authorized by order of the Chief Administrator of the Courts and only to the extent and in the manner provided in NY R UNIF TRIAL CTS § 202.5-b. NY R UNIF TRIAL CTS § 202.5-b(a)(1). For the definitions of terms used in electronic filing, refer to NY R UNIF TRIAL CTS § 202.5-b(a)(2).

i. *E-filing mandatory.* In any action subject to e-filing, all documents required to be filed with the court by an e-filing party shall be filed and served electronically, except as provided in NY R UNIF TRIAL CTS § 202.5-b. NY R UNIF TRIAL CTS § 202.5-b(d)(1)(i).

- *ERIE COUNTY.* Case types currently eligible and accepted for e-filing are listed at the NYSCEF website. Note that some actions or special proceedings, (i.e., name changes) which are otherwise subject to mandatory e-filing, if commenced by unrepresented litigants will NOT be maintained in the NYSCEF system; individual cases may be found either at NYSCEF or in the Erie County Clerk's online records system. NY R ERIE E FIL Doc. 3(I)(E).
- *KINGS COUNTY.* Cases that are commenced by filing of the initiating papers with NYSCEF are identified as e-filed cases by assignment of a special index number (i.e., Index Numbers beginning with 500,000). NY R L KINGS E FIL Doc. 1(A)(1). All cases required to be e-filed are listed in Uniform Rule 202.5-bb (Mandatory E-Filing Rules) and on the NYSCEF website. All such cases must be commenced by filing with the County Clerk electronically through NYSCEF and all subsequent documents in such cases must be e-filed. Any questions regarding mandatory e-filing in Kings County can be e-mailed to kcco-efile@nycourts.gov. NY R L KINGS E FIL Doc. 1(A)(2).
- *NEW YORK COUNTY.* Unless otherwise provided in the Rules or in NY R NY CTY E FIL Doc. 2 or where a special exemption is granted due to physical requirements (e.g., oversized maps; see NY R NY CTY E FIL Doc. 2(B)(10)), all documents to be filed with the court in a NYSCEF case, including all documents on motions and all letters to the court (where permitted), must be filed with the NYSCEF system. Documents that attorneys would not ordinarily file with the court in a hard-copy case need not be e-filed. Unless otherwise provided by the E-Filing Rules or this Protocol, in e-filed cases the County Clerk and the court will not accept documents filed in paper form. NY R NY CTY E FIL Doc. 2(B)(1). E-filing is mandatory in all types of cases (other than election law, matrimonial, Art. 78, and Mental Hygiene Law matters, and Art. 70 habeas corpus proceedings) that are commenced in this court on or after February 19, 2013. All such cases must be commenced by filing with the County Clerk electronically through NYSCEF and all subsequent documents in such cases must be e-filed. NY R NY CTY E FIL Doc. 2(A)(2)(a). For more information, including information on consensual e-filing and filing scanned hard copy documents, refer to NY R NY CTY E FIL Doc. 2(A)(2).
- *QUEENS COUNTY.* All authorized Torts, Commercial and Tax Certiorari cases may be commenced by E-Filing, however all parties must consent for the action to continue as an E-file case. NY R L QUEENS E-FILE Doc. 1(A). All papers to be filed with the court in an E-filed case shall be filed on-line with the E-file system except as directed by the court. Papers that attorneys would not ordinarily file with the court in a hard-copy case need not be filed in an E-filed matter. NY R L QUEENS E-FILE Doc. 1(E)(2).

ii. *Who may file.* Documents may be filed or served electronically only by a person who has registered as an authorized e-filing user or as otherwise provided in NY R UNIF TRIAL CTS § 202.5-b(c). NY R UNIF TRIAL CTS § 202.5-b(c)(1).

iii. *When filing made.* Documents may be transmitted at any time of the day or night to the NYSCEF site. A document other than an order or judgment is filed when its electronic transmission or, in the case of a petition that is e-filed by submission of a text file as provided in NY R UNIF TRIAL CTS § 202.5-b(b)(1), the electronic transmission of the text file is recorded at that site, provided, however, that where payment of a fee is required upon the filing of a document, the document is not filed until transmission of the document and the information or form or information as required in NY R UNIF TRIAL CTS § 202.5-b(d)(2)(i), NY R UNIF TRIAL CTS § 202.5-b(d)(2)(ii) or NY R UNIF TRIAL CTS § 202.5-b(d)(2)(iii) has been recorded at the NYSCEF site; or, if no transmission of that information or form or information is recorded, where permitted by the County Clerk, until payment is presented to the County Clerk. NY R UNIF TRIAL CTS § 202.5-b(d)(3)(i).

iv. *Notification of filing.* No later than the close of business on the business day following the electronic filing of a document, a notification, in a form prescribed by the Chief Administrator, shall be transmitted electronically by the NYSCEF site to the person filing such document and the e-mail service addresses of all other participating parties in such action. NY R UNIF TRIAL CTS § 202.5-b(d)(3)(ii).

v. *Removal of confidential information and other corrections.* If a document filed electronically is subsequently discovered to contain confidential data—including but not limited to trade secrets, information protected by confidentiality agreement, or personal confidential information as defined by statute or court rule—or otherwise to have been filed in error, the filer or another party or affected person may (1) notify the parties and any non-party filers in the action of the confidentiality issue or other error raised by the filing, and of his or her intention to seek judicial relief to correct the filing: (2) following such notification, request that the appropriate County Clerk, exercising his or her administrative discretion, place the document temporarily in "restricted" status on the NYSCEF site, to be made available for viewing by court staff and the parties but not the general public; and (3) file an application to correct the filing by order to show cause within five (5) business days of such notification (or such time as the court may direct), including a request for preliminary injunctive relief limiting interim disclosure of the document at issue. Unless otherwise directed by the court, any document placed in restricted status in response to such a request shall be returned to public view upon expiration of this five (5) day period. The Chief Administrator of the Courts shall promulgate forms to implement this process. NY R UNIF TRIAL CTS § 202.5-b(d)(3)(iii).

- *KINGS COUNTY.* For information on what to do when a document was erroneously filed with confidential information, refer to NY R L KINGS E FIL Doc. 1(B)(11).
- *NEW YORK COUNTY.* For information on what to do when a document was erroneously filed with confidential information, refer to NY R NY CTY E FIL Doc. 2(B)(8).
- *QUEENS COUNTY.* For information on what to do when a document was erroneously filed with confidential information, refer to NY R L QUEENS E-FILE Doc. 1(E)(7).

vi. *Documents requiring judge's signature.* Except where the court directs otherwise, any document that requires a judge's signature shall be transmitted electronically and in hard copy to the court. NY R UNIF TRIAL CTS § 202.5-b(d)(6).

vii. *Documents which would be inconvenient to file electronically; Hard copies.* Notwithstanding any other provision of NY R UNIF TRIAL CTS § 202.5-b, and subject to such guidelines as may be established by the Chief Administrative Judge, the County Clerk or his or her designee may require or permit a party to file in hard copy, in accordance with procedures set by the County Clerk or designee, an exhibit or other document which it is impractical or inconvenient to file electronically. NY R UNIF TRIAL CTS § 202.5-b(d)(7).

- *ERIE COUNTY.* Please contact the Supervisor of Actions & Proceedings, Erie County Clerk's Office by calling (716) 858-6662 or the Deputy County Clerk—Legal at (716) 858-6348 for information. NY R ERIE E FIL Doc. 3(III)(F).
- *KINGS COUNTY.* With limited exceptions, as set forth in the Uniform Rules and herein, all documents to be filed with the court in a NYSCEF case shall be filed online via the NYSCEF system. However, should the size, consistency or context of a hard copy document preclude electronic filing, the user shall electronically file a "Notice of Hard Copy Submission—E-Filed Cases" form EFM-3. Any hard copy submitted pursuant to NY R L KINGS E FIL Doc. 1(B)(9) shall include, as a cover page firmly fastened thereto, a copy of the Confirmation Notice received from the NYSCEF site confirming receipt of the "Notice of Hard Copy Submission—E-Filed Cases". Any party may object to such hard copy filing. The

Court, in response to such objection, may, following the hard copy filing, fashion such relief as it deems appropriate pursuant to and in furtherance of the Uniform Rules and NY R L KINGS E FIL Doc. 1, including, but not limited to, an Order directing the filing party to file such documents online via the NYSCEF system. When exhibits are impractical to file pursuant to NY R UNIF TRIAL CTS § 202.5-b(d)(7), an additional "Notice of Hard Copy Exhibit Filing" form EFM-4 is required to be submitted. NY R L KINGS E FIL Doc. 1(B)(9).

- *NEW YORK COUNTY.* If a filer needs to submit unusual exhibits in original form that cannot practically be e-filed, such as oversized maps or electronic recordings, the filer should consult with the County Clerk's E-File Department by telephone at 646-386-3737 (procedural questions only) or by e-mail at ccnyef@nycourts.gov, which will normally require that the filer retain custody of the original subject to possible future directives of the court. NY R NY CTY E FIL Doc. 2(B)(10). In such instances, the filing counsel shall file with NYSCEF a "placeholder" in the form of a Notice of Hard Copy Exhibit Filing (NYSCEF Form EF 21). The Notice should be uploaded to NYSCEF as document type "Exhibit" and the filer should indicate in the "Additional Document Information" field that the filer is retaining custody of the original. Failure to e-file the Notice may result in a gap in the official record of the court. NY R NY CTY E FIL Doc. 2(B)(10).

viii. *Documents containing sensitive or proprietary information.* In an action subject to e-filing, any person may apply for an order prohibiting or restricting the electronic filing in the action of specifically identified materials on the grounds that such materials are subject to copyright or other proprietary rights, or trade secret or other privacy interests, and that electronic filing in the action is likely to result in substantial prejudice to those rights or interests. NY R UNIF TRIAL CTS § 202.5-b(k)(2).

ix. *Refusal to accept paper filings.* In accordance with NY CPLR Rule 2102(c), a County Clerk and a chief clerk of the Supreme Court or County Court, as appropriate, shall refuse to accept for filing papers filed in actions and proceedings when the paper sought to be filed:

- Is in an action subject to electronic filing pursuant to Rules of the Chief Administrator,
- Is not being filed electronically, and
- Does not include the notice required by NY R UNIF TRIAL CTS § 202.5-b(d)(1). NY R UNIF TRIAL CTS § 202.5(d)(1)(v); NY R UNIF TRIAL CTS § 202.5-bb(d).

x. *Emergency filings; Hard copies.* For information on when an emergency filing may be filed and served in hard copy, refer to NY R UNIF TRIAL CTS § 202.5-b(d)(1)(ii), NY R UNIF TRIAL CTS § 202.5-b(d)(1)(iii) and NY R UNIF TRIAL CTS § 202.5-bb(c)(3).

- *KINGS COUNTY.* Under the rules, a participating emergency e-filer must electronically file the documents initially filed in hard copy form within three (3) business days of the emergency filing; the originals will be discarded after the documents have been processed and the failure to e-file as required will therefore lead to an incomplete record. NY R L KINGS E FIL Doc. 1(B)(3).
- *NEW YORK COUNTY.* Occasionally an emergency will arise requiring expedited entry of a document with the County Clerk (e.g., an order issued in the courtroom after a conference or argument of a critical matter), such as for purposes of an immediate appeal. Expedition can be achieved by the Part as follows: the document should be carried by a Court Officer or staff member to the General Clerk's Office to assure immediate and proper recordation in the computer and, as appropriate, the posting of the document to NYSCEF or the Supreme Court Records On-Line Library ("Scroll"). The court will accommodate counsel in emergencies. NY R NY CTY Procedure XI(A).
- *NEW YORK COUNTY.* For more information on how to bring emergency matters before the court, refer to NY R NY CTY Procedure IV.

xi. *Technical failures.* The NYSCEF site shall be considered to be subject to a technical failure on a given day if the site is unable to accept filings or provide access to filed documents continuously or intermittently over the course of any period of time greater than one (1) hour after 12:00 noon of that day. Notice of all such technical failures shall be provided on the site. NY R UNIF TRIAL CTS § 202.5-b(i).

- When e-filing is hindered by a technical failure, a party may file with the appropriate clerk and serve in hard copy. NY R UNIF TRIAL CTS § 202.5-b(i). In the event an attorney or party shall file and serve documents in hard copy pursuant to NY R UNIF TRIAL CTS § 202.5-b(i), each such document shall include the notice required by NY R UNIF TRIAL CTS § 202.5-b(d)(1), and the filer shall file those documents with the

NYSCEF site within three (3) business days after restoration of normal operations at that site. NY R UNIF TRIAL CTS § 202.5-b(i).

- With the exception of deadlines that by law cannot be extended, the time for filing of any document that is delayed due to technical failure of the site shall be extended for one (1) day for each day on which such failure occurs, unless otherwise ordered by the court. NY R UNIF TRIAL CTS § 202.5-b(i).
- *ERIE COUNTY.* When filing by electronic means is hindered by a technical failure, please refer to the NY R UNIF TRIAL CTS § 202.5-b(i). NY R ERIE E FIL Doc. 3(III)(K).
- *KINGS COUNTY.* When filing by electronic means is hindered by a NYSCEF technical failure (as set forth in NY R UNIF TRIAL CTS § 202.5-b(i)), a party may file with the appropriate Clerk in hard copy. Except for deadlines that by law cannot be extended (e.g. Statute of limitations, Notice of Appeal), the time for filing of any document that is delayed due to technical failure of the NYSCEF system shall be extended for one day for each day on which such failure occurs, unless otherwise ordered by the court. NY R L KINGS E FIL Doc. 1(B)(13).
- *ONONDAGA COUNTY.* When filing by electronic means is hindered by a technical failure (as set forth in NY R UNIF TRIAL CTS § 202.5-b(h)(3)(i)), a party may file a hard copy with the County Clerk. With the exception of deadlines that by law cannot be extended (e.g., a statute of limitations or the deadline for filing a Notice of Appeal), the time for filing of any document that is delayed due to technical failure of the NYSCEF system will be extended for one day for each day on which such failure occurs, unless otherwise ordered by the court. A "Notice of Hard Copy Filing Submission—E-Filed Case' must accompany any documents not filed via NYSCEF. NY R ONDGA E FIL Protocol(B)(8).

xii. *Filing fees.* For information on what information must be provided to pay filing fees, refer to NY R UNIF TRIAL CTS § 202.5-b(d)(2).

xiii. *Exemption from e-filing.* For information on exemptions from e-filing, refer to NY R UNIF TRIAL CTS § 202.5-bb(e).

xiv. *Filing exhibits*

- *ERIE COUNTY.* In the NYSCEF system, each exhibit must be uploaded as a separate .pdf file. After uploading a primary document, please choose the document type "Exhibit" and enter the appropriate number or letter and a brief description of the exhibit; each exhibit should bear a separate cover sheet clearly marked as "Exhibit A," "Exhibit B," etc. "Exhibit A" or "Exhibit B" is unacceptable as a brief description of the exhibit. Exhibits, where referenced in a signed Order as attached or affixed shall be uploaded with the signed Order as one .pdf document. NY R ERIE E FIL Doc. 3(III)(H); NY R ERIE E FIL Doc. 3(V)(D).
- *KINGS COUNTY.* In the NYSCEF system, each exhibit should be uploaded as a separate PDF file. After uploading a primary document, please choose the document type "Exhibit", enter the appropriate number or letter, and be sure to place a check mark to the right of "Attach to main document". Each exhibit shall bear a separate cover sheet clearly marked as Exhibit A, Exhibit B, etc. NY R L KINGS E FIL Doc. 1(B)(12). Whenever possible, attorneys submitting exhibits in NYSCEF cases should make each exhibit a separate attachment to an affidavit/affirmation in the system (i.e., multiple exhibits should not be filed as a single PDF). NY R L KINGS E FIL Doc. 1(D)(1).
- *NEW YORK COUNTY.* Attorneys submitting exhibits in NYSCEF cases should make each exhibit a separate attachment to an affidavit/affirmation in the system; i.e., exhibits should not be filed as a single PDF-A together with the affidavit/affirmation or grouped together as a single PDF-A attachment because either of these two formats makes it difficult for the Justice to locate particular exhibits as needed. Counsel must also include appropriate descriptive language in the "Additional Document Information" field in NYSCEF. NY R NY CTY E FIL Doc. 2(D)(6).
- *ONONDAGA COUNTY.* All exhibits in e-filed cases must be e-filed individually as separate attachments. NY R ONDGA E FIL Protocol(B)(9)(b).

xv. *Correcting documents*

- *ERIE COUNTY.* Submission of documents which, upon examination, require correction or addition will result in notification to the filer advising that the document has been returned for correction. The filer shall make the required corrections and/or additions as indicated in the e-mail transmission sent by the County Clerk or Part Clerk through the NYSCEF site. The corrected documents may be resubmitted using the

"Re-file this document" link highlighted in the filer's document list for the respective case. Please note that in the case of multiple submissions, all related documents filed at the same time may be removed from the case record and returned until all documents are properly submitted. NY R ERIE E FIL Doc. 3(III)(J).

- *KINGS COUNTY.* Submission of documents which, upon examination, require correction or addition will result in notification to the filer advising that there is a problem with a document. The filer shall make the required corrections and/or additions and resubmit the corrected document using the "Refile this document" link. In the event a document is returned for correction, the original file date will be preserved. For corrections of documents filed with the Kings County Clerk which require a court order, refer to the procedure in NY R UNIF TRIAL CTS § 202.5-b(d)(3)(iii) and NY R L KINGS E FIL Doc. 1(B)(11). NY R L KINGS E FIL Doc. 1(B)(3).
- *ONONDAGA COUNTY.* If there is an error or an additional document is required, the system will notify the filing party, who will make the corrections/additions and resubmit them online. NY R ONDGA E FIL Protocol(B)(6).
- *QUEENS COUNTY.* Generally speaking, documents that have been E-filed will not thereafter be deleted by the County Clerk from NYCEF because the filer asserts that the filing contains an error or a significant omission. When the filer wishes to correct a perceived error or omission in a filed document, he or she should file an amended version of the document, with the original remaining on file, or else obtain a court order providing for deletion of the original. The County Clerk will only delete a document upon request of the filer or on the County Clerk's own initiative when it is obvious from the face of the document alone that the filer made a fundamental error and never intended to file the document that was filed (e.g., a completely unrelated non-litigation document, a different case, or a wrong county). The County Clerk will advise the filer when any such fundamental errors are detected. NY R L QUEENS E-FILE Doc. 1(E)(6).

c. *Facsimile filing.* In the Supreme Court, facsimile filing shall be limited to commercial claims and tax certiorari, conservatorship, and mental hygiene proceedings in Monroe, Westchester, New York and Suffolk Counties. NY R UNIF TRIAL CTS § 202.5-a(a)(1). Refer to NY R UNIF TRIAL CTS § 202.5-a for information on the procedures for facsimile filing.

   i. *NEW YORK COUNTY.* Unless indicated otherwise by the court in a particular case or in NY R NY CTY J RUL Doc. 1, Justices do not accept papers by fax. NY R NY CTY J RUL Rule 4.

d. *ERIE COUNTY: Filing request for judicial intervention.* An RJI in a NYSCEF case shall be filed via the NYSCEF system and will be filed after all other documents have been uploaded. The filer may choose between filing a .pdf image of the prepared RJI and any Addendum or having the system prepare the RJI which shall conform to Uniform Rules. Addenda, such as the Commercial Division Addendum, if prepared by the filer must be filed simultaneously with and attached to an RJI and uploaded as one .pdf document with the RJI. If the RJI is prepared by the e-filing system, no separate Addendum is required. Whether or not the filer elects to allow NYSCEF to create the RJI or chooses to upload a prepared RJI, data in addition to the nature of the judicial intervention, including information that appears on any Addenda will be collected through completion of the fields presented. If the filing of the RJI is accomplished through a filing agent, a prepared RJI and Addendum must be filed in lieu of the creation of the RJI by the NYSCEF system, as the RJI must be signed by the attorney. NY R ERIE E FIL Doc. 3(IV). For information on RJIs in specific types of action, refer to NY R ERIE E FIL Doc. 3(IV).

2. *Service requirements*

a. *Who may serve.* Except where otherwise prescribed by law or order of court, papers may be served by any person not a party of the age of eighteen years or over. NY CPLR Rule 2103(a).

b. *Service upon attorney.* Except where otherwise prescribed by law or order of court, papers to be served upon a party in a pending action shall be served upon the party's attorney. Where the same attorney appears for two or more parties, only one (1) copy need be served upon the attorney. Such service upon an attorney shall be made:

   i. By delivering the paper to the attorney personally. NY CPLR Rule 2103(b)(1).

   ii. By mailing the paper to the attorney at the address designated by that attorney for that purpose or, if none is designated, at the attorney's last known address; service by mail shall be complete upon mailing. NY CPLR Rule 2103(b)(2).

   - *BRONX COUNTY.* Service by mail must be within the state. NY R BRONX FIL R Doc. 3.

   iii. If the attorney's office is open, by leaving the paper with a person in charge, or if no person is in charge, by leaving it in a conspicuous place; or if the attorney's office is not open, by depositing the paper, enclosed in a sealed wrapper directed to the attorney, in the attorney's office letter drop or box. NY CPLR Rule 2103(b)(3).

iv. By leaving it at the attorney's residence within the state with a person of suitable age and discretion. Service upon an attorney shall not be made at the attorney's residence unless service at the attorney's office cannot be made. NY CPLR Rule 2103(b)(4).

v. By transmitting the paper to the attorney by facsimile transmission, provided that a facsimile telephone number is designated by the attorney for that purpose. Service by facsimile transmission shall be complete upon the receipt by the sender of a signal from the equipment of the attorney served indicating that the transmission was received, and the mailing of a copy of the paper to that attorney. The designation of a facsimile telephone number in the address block subscribed on a paper served or filed in the course of an action or proceeding shall constitute consent to service by facsimile transmission in accordance with NY CPLR Rule 2103(b)(5). An attorney may change or rescind a facsimile telephone number by serving a notice on the other parties. NY CPLR Rule 2103(b)(5).

vi. By dispatching the paper to the attorney by overnight delivery service at the address designated by the attorney for that purpose or, if none is designated, at the attorney's last known address. Service by overnight delivery service shall be complete upon deposit of the paper enclosed in a properly addressed wrapper into the custody of the overnight delivery service for overnight delivery, prior to the latest time designated by the overnight delivery service for overnight delivery. "Overnight delivery service" means any delivery service which regularly accepts items for overnight delivery to any address in the state. NY CPLR Rule 2103(b)(6).

vii. By transmitting the paper to the attorney by electronic means where and in the manner authorized by the chief administrator of the courts by rule and, unless such rule shall otherwise provide, such transmission shall be upon the party's written consent. The subject matter heading for each paper sent by electronic means must indicate that the matter being transmitted electronically is related to a court proceeding. NY CPLR Rule 2103(b)(7).

- *KINGS COUNTY.* Pursuant to the E-Filing Rules, service of interlocutory documents is made by posting a document to the NYSCEF site, which automatically and immediately transmits an email notice of the filing, including a link to the document, to all participating counsel and unrepresented litigants on the case. The Rules also authorize service by other methods permitted by the CPLR. If service by such other method is made, proof of service must be filed with NYSCEF. NY R L KINGS E FIL Doc. 1(I).
- *NEW YORK COUNTY.* Service. . .will be made automatically through NYSCEF upon all participating counsel and unrepresented parties in the case. There are limited exceptions to the requirement for e-filing in the covered kinds of cases. NY R NY CTY Procedure XI(A). Pursuant to the E-Filing Rules, service of interlocutory documents is made by posting a document to the NYSCEF site, which automatically and immediately transmits an e-mail notice of the filing, including a link to the document, to all participating counsel and unrepresented litigants on the case. The Rules also authorize service by other methods permitted by the CPLR. If service by such a method is made, proof of service must be filed with NYSCEF. NY R NY CTY E FIL Doc. 2(I).
- *QUEENS COUNTY.* Filing with the system permits counsel to serve the papers electronically pursuant to NY R UNIF TRIAL CTS § 202.5-b(f) once consent to E-Filing has been filed on-line. Consult NY R UNIF TRIAL CTS § 202.5-bb(c) for service in mandatory e-filing. Any required proof of service should be E-filed as a separate document. NY R L QUEENS E-FILE Doc. 1(E)(4).

c. *Electronic service mandatory; Consenting to electronic service; How electronic service may be made.* Except as otherwise provided in NY R UNIF TRIAL CTS § 202.5-bb, filing and service of all documents in an action that has been commenced electronically in accordance with NY R UNIF TRIAL CTS § 202.5-bb shall be by electronic means. NY R UNIF TRIAL CTS § 202.5-bb(c)(1).

i. *Party's consent required for certain e-filing.* After commencement of an action wherein e-filing is authorized, documents may be electronically filed and served, but only by, and electronic service shall be made only upon, a party or parties who have consented thereto. NY R UNIF TRIAL CTS § 202.5-b(b)(2)(i).

- A consent to e-filing in an action shall state that the party providing it agrees to the use of e-filing in the action and to be bound by the filing and service provisions in NY R UNIF TRIAL CTS § 202.5-b. NY R UNIF TRIAL CTS § 202.5-b(b)(2)(ii).

ii. *Address for service; Duty to notify as to changes.* The e-mail service address recorded at the time of registration is the e-mail address at which service of interlocutory documents on that party may be made through notification transmitted by the NYSCEF site. It is the responsibility of each filing user to monitor that address and promptly notify the Resource Center in the event of a change in his or her e-mail service address. NY R UNIF TRIAL CTS § 202.5-b(f)(2)(i).

iii. *How service made.* An e-filing party causes service of an interlocutory document to be made upon another party participating in e-filing by filing the document electronically. Upon receipt of an interlocutory document, the NYSCEF site shall automatically transmit electronic notification to all e-mail service addresses in such action. NY R UNIF TRIAL CTS § 202.5-b(f)(2)(ii).

- Except as provided otherwise in NY R UNIF TRIAL CTS § 202.5-b(h)(3), the electronic transmission of the notification shall constitute service of the document on the e-mail service addresses identified therein; however, such service will not be effective if the filing party learns that the notification did not reach the address of the person to be served. Proof of such service will be recorded on the NYSCEF site. A party may, however, utilize other service methods permitted by the CPLR provided that, if one of such other methods is used, proof of that service shall be filed electronically. NY R UNIF TRIAL CTS § 202.5-b(f)(2)(ii).

iv. *Signatures on hard copies; Proof of service filed electronically.* When an e-filing party serves a document in hard copy on a non-participating party, the document served shall bear full signatures of all signatories and proof of such service shall be filed electronically. NY R UNIF TRIAL CTS § 202.5-b(b)(2)(i).

- *ERIE COUNTY.* In the NYSCEF system, each Affidavit of Service must be uploaded as a separate .pdf file. After uploading the Affidavit, please choose the document type: "Affirmation/Affidavit of Service" and enter the name of the party served as Additional Document Information. NY R ERIE E FIL Doc. 3(III)(I); NY R ERIE E FIL Doc. 3(V)(F).

v. *Effect of failure to consent.* A party's failure to consent to participation in electronic filing and service shall not bar any other party to the action from filing documents electronically with the County Clerk and the court or serving documents upon any other party who has consented to participation. A party who has not consented to participation shall file documents with the court and the County Clerk, and serve and be served with documents, in hard copy. NY R UNIF TRIAL CTS § 202.5-b(b)(2)(i).

d. *Service upon party.* If a party has not appeared by an attorney or the party's attorney cannot be served, service shall be upon the party by a method specified in NY CPLR Rule 2103(b)(1), NY CPLR Rule 2103(b)(2), NY CPLR Rule 2103(b)(4), NY CPLR Rule 2103(b)(5) or NY CPLR Rule 2103(b)(6). NY CPLR Rule 2103(c).

e. *Service on all parties.* Each paper served on any party shall be served on every other party who has appeared, except as otherwise may be provided by court order or as provided in NY CPLR § 3012 or in NY CPLR § 3215(f). Upon demand by a party, the plaintiff shall supply that party with a list of those who have appeared and the names and addresses of their attorneys. NY CPLR Rule 2103(e).

f. *Service by filing.* If a paper cannot be served by any of the methods specified in NY CPLR Rule 2103(b) and NY CPLR Rule 2103(c), service may be made by filing the paper as if it were a paper required to be filed. NY CPLR Rule 2103(d).

g. *Definitions.* For the purposes of NY CPLR Rule 2103:

i. "Mailing" means the deposit of a paper enclosed in a first class postpaid wrapper, addressed to the address designated by a person for that purpose or, if none is designated, at that person's last known address, in a post office or official depository under the exclusive care and custody of the United States Postal Service within the state;

ii. "Electronic means" means any method of transmission of information between computers or other machines designed for the purpose of sending and receiving such transmissions, and which allows the recipient to reproduce the information transmitted in a tangible medium of expression;

iii. "Facsimile transmission" means any method of transmission of documents to a facsimile machine at a remote location which can automatically produce a tangible copy of such documents. NY CPLR Rule 2103(f).

G. Hearings

1. *Oral argument.* Motion papers received by the clerk of the court on or before the return date shall be deemed submitted as of the return date. The assigned judge, in his or her discretion or at the request of a party, thereafter may determine that any motion be orally argued and may fix a time for oral argument. NY R UNIF TRIAL CTS § 202.8(d).

a. A party requesting oral argument shall set forth such request in its notice of motion or in its order to show cause or on the first page of the answering papers, as the case may be. Where all parties to a motion request oral argument, oral argument shall be granted unless the court shall determine it to be unnecessary. NY R UNIF TRIAL CTS § 202.8(d).

b. Where a motion is brought on by order to show cause, the court may set forth in the order that oral argument is required on the return date of the motion. NY R UNIF TRIAL CTS § 202.8(d).

i. *BRONX COUNTY.* All orders to show cause, with the exception of orders to show cause that are returnable in the

City Part, the STP Part, the Matrimonial Part and the Preliminary/Compliance Conference Part (IA-11), submitted on or after August 25, 2003, will be returnable on a Monday in the assigned Justice's part and appear on his or her motion calendar. Appearances will be required on orders to show cause. NY R BRONX FIL R Doc. 8. A motion on notice or a notice of petition in a New York Supreme Court E-File (hereafter known as NYSCEF) case, as in others, shall be made returnable in the Motion Support Office (Room 217). NY R BRONX E FIL R Doc. 1(1).

- After a motion/petition and notice are filed with the NYSCEF system, the Motion Support Office will automatically place the motion/proceeding on the submit calendar in the Motion Support Office (Room 217) for the return date. No appearance or other action by the filing attorney is required in order for the motion to be calendared if the motion fee is paid for via NYSCEF. Motions in e-filed cases (other than tax certiorari cases) appear on the submit calendar in Room 217 on the return date. NY R BRONX E FIL R Doc. 1(2).

c. *KINGS COUNTY.* All motions require appearances and oral argument. NY R L KINGS Pt. C, Rule 3.

2. *Return date; Time for hearing.* A notice of motion shall specify the time and place of the hearing on the motion. NY CPLR Rule 2214(a). The moving party determines when a motion on notice shall be heard, but she has to consult the court's or judge's calendar practice first. The movant picks out a "return day" sufficiently far off to assure that the notice requirements of NY CPLR Rule 2214(b) can be met, and to assure as well that the day picked is a day on which the assigned judge hears motions. SIEGEL-NYPRAC § 247.

a. *Judge assigned to hear motion*

i. *Referral to judge supervising disclosure.* Unless the chief administrator of the courts has, by rule, provided otherwise, if a case has been assigned to a judge to supervise disclosure pursuant to NY CPLR § 3104, all motions preliminary to trial shall be referred to such judge whenever practicable. NY CPLR Rule 3214(a).

ii. *Referral to judge who decided prior motion.* Any motion may be referred to a judge who decided a prior motion in the action. NY CPLR Rule 2217(a).

iii. *Transfer when judge unable to hear motion.* If a motion is made to a judge who is or will be for any reason unable to hear it, it may be transferred by order of such judge or by written stipulation of the parties to any other judge to whom it might originally have been made. NY CPLR Rule 2217(c).

iv. *Procedure for unassigned cases.* If a case has not been assigned to a judge, the motion shall be made returnable before the court, and a copy of the moving papers, together with a request for judicial intervention, shall be filed with the court, with proof of service upon all other parties, where required by NY R UNIF TRIAL CTS § 202.6, within five (5) days of service upon the other parties. The moving party shall give written notice of the index number to all other parties immediately after filing of the papers. NY R UNIF TRIAL CTS § 202.8(b).

- *Responding papers.* Copies of all responding papers shall be submitted to the court, with proof of service and with the index number set forth in the papers, on or before the return date. NY R UNIF TRIAL CTS § 202.8(b).
- *Assignment after request for judicial intervention.* The case shall be assigned to a judge as soon as practicable after the filing of the request for judicial intervention pursuant to NY R UNIF TRIAL CTS § 202.6, but in no event later than the return date. After assignment to the judge, the court shall provide for appropriate notice to the parties of the name of the assigned judge. NY R UNIF TRIAL CTS § 202.8(b).
- *Motions to be heard in another county.* Motion papers noticed to be heard in a county other than the county where the venue of the action has been placed by the plaintiff shall be assigned to a judge in accordance with procedures established by the Chief Administrator. NY R UNIF TRIAL CTS § 202.8(b).

v. *ALBANY COUNTY: Motions referred to IAS Justice.* All motions made after a case has been assigned a day certain shall be referred to the IAS Justice unless the motion is returnable during the term in which the matter has been assigned a day certain; in that event, the matter will be referred to the Part 1 Justice for that particular term who may entertain the motion or refer such motion to the IAS Justice. Under those circumstances, the Part I Justice shall decide whether or not to strike the note of issue or assign the matter a new day certain. NY R 3 JD SUP Doc. 1(H)(2). All motions shall be returnable before the assigned justice. NY R 3 JD SUP Doc. 1(B).

b. *Trial of issue raised by motion.* The court may order that an issue of fact raised on a motion shall be separately tried by the court or a referee. If the issue is triable of right by jury, the court shall give the parties an opportunity to demand a jury trial of such issue. Failure to make such demand within the time limited by the court, or, if no such time is limited, before trial begins, shall be deemed a waiver of the right to trial by jury. An order under NY CPLR § 2218 shall specify the issue to be tried. NY CPLR § 2218.

c. *Audio-visual coverage of trial court proceeding.* Audio-visual coverage of proceedings in the trial courts shall be permitted only in accordance with the provisions of Part 131 of the Rules of the Chief Administrator (NY R CHIEF ADMIN § 131.1, et seq.). NY R CHIEF J § 29.3.

d. *Adjournment of return date.* Stipulations of adjournment of the return date made by the parties shall be in writing and shall be submitted to the assigned judge. Such stipulation shall be effective unless the court otherwise directs. No more than three (3) stipulated adjournments for an aggregate period of sixty (60) days shall be submitted without prior permission of the court. NY R UNIF TRIAL CTS § 202.8(e)(1).

   i. Absent agreement by the parties, a request by any party for an adjournment shall be submitted in writing, upon notice to the other party, to the assigned judge on or before the return date. The court will notify the requesting party whether the adjournment has been granted. NY R UNIF TRIAL CTS § 202.8(e)(2).

   ii. *BRONX COUNTY.* Non-disclosure motions for IA5, IA7 and IA22 will be adjourned for oral argument to the Monday of the second week following the week of the return date of the motion. All other non-disclosure motions will be deemed submitted on the return date and forwarded to Chambers unless a stipulation of adjournment complying with the requirements of NY R UNIF TRIAL CTS § 202.8(e) is submitted, in which event, the motion will be adjourned for the requested date and kept in the Clerk's Office. If a non-stipulated request for adjournment or notice is submitted, the motion and request will be forwarded to Chambers for judicial approval or denial of the request. In either event, the attorney requesting the adjournment will be notified, via telephone, of the granting or denial of the request and instructed to notify his adversary. NY R BRONX FIL R Doc. 8.

   iii. *BRONX COUNTY.* Motions that have been e-filed may be adjourned in Room 217 if an adjournment complies with the procedures of the Motion Support Office (explained in the "Filing Rules—Motion Procedure" section of the "Courthouse Procedures" link on the website of [the] court). An adjournment that so complies may be obtained by filing a stipulation of all parties with NYSCEF (designated in the filing menu as a "Stipulation to Adjourn Motion"). NY R BRONX E FIL R Doc. 1(3).

   iv. *NEW YORK COUNTY.* The Courtroom also maintains a "APB (All Papers By)" Calendar, which is used when a party seeks an adjournment but fails to comply with the Courtroom's procedures or there is a failure to comply with procedures that requires the clerk to adjourn the motion/application (e.g., failure to submit a Confirmation Notice in an e-filed case). The case may be put over for three days to allow compliance with those procedures, as described further below. NY R NY CTY Procedure II(C); NY R NY CTY E FIL Doc. 2(D)(2). E-filed applications may be adjourned in the Part if an adjournment complies with the Part's procedures (see the Uniform Rules of the Justices (Local Rules) on the court's website). An adjournment that so complies may be obtained by filing with NYSCEF a stipulation of all parties (designated in the filing menu as a Stipulation—Adjournment of Motion—Before Judge); the motion number and the current return date of the motion being adjourned shall be set forth in the "Additional Document Information" field in NYSCEF. Absent any problems, the Part will effectuate the adjournment without need for an appearance or any other action by the parties. NY R NY CTY E FIL Doc. 2(D)(4).

   v. *QUEENS COUNTY.* The Motion Support Office is NOT authorized to grant adjournments. NY R L QUEENS MOT SUP Doc. 1.

e. *ALBANY COUNTY: Motion terms.* There shall be a. . . Motion Term on each Friday in the Supreme Court, Albany County. The Friday Motion Term shall include all Article 78 Proceedings involving New York State and proceedings commenced pursuant to Article 14 of the Civil Service Law (including applications for injunctive relief made pursuant to section 209-a of the Civil Service Law). NY R 3 JD SUP Doc. 1(F). Generally, parties will be granted only one adjournment for the Friday Motion Term. NY R 3 JD SUP Doc. 1(F).

f. *ALBANY COUNTY: Motion determined without hearing.* All motions are deemed "submitted" on the return date and no appearances are required by the parties. NY R 3 JD SUP Doc. 1(B). In the event oral argument is requested, the parties should not appear on the return date. At the discretion of the assigned Judge and upon the granting of a request for oral argument, the parties will be notified by Chambers of the scheduled time and place at which argument will be heard. Where a motion is brought on by order to show cause, the court may set forth in the order that appearances and/or oral argument are required on the return date of the motion. NY R 3 JD SUP Doc. 1(B).

g. *BRONX COUNTY: Return date.* All assigned and unassigned motions will be returnable five (5) days a week in the Civil Branch Clerk's Office, Room 217, at 9:30 a.m. NY R BRONX FIL R Doc. 8.

   i. If on any submitted non-disclosure motion oral argument is requested and granted, or directed by the Court, the motion shall be adjourned for oral argument before the I.A. Judge on the second Monday following the week of the return date of the motion. Attorneys will be notified via telephone of the adjourned date. NY R BRONX FIL R Doc. 8.

h. *BRONX COUNTY: Oral argument.* Calendars of disclosure motions and other motions adjourned for oral argument will be published for the four (4) business days preceding the rescheduled appearance date and on the rescheduled date of the motion. These repetitive publications will serve as the notification of procedure of adjournment of all motions. In addition, two (2) days before the return date of unassigned motions a list of such motions indicating the assigned Justice and the adjourned date of the motion will be published. NY R BRONX FIL R Doc. 8.

i. *BRONX COUNTY: Resolution before return date.* Counsel/parties must advise the Court in writing on or before the return date of all motions that have been resolved by Counsel/parties themselves and all motions the movant(s) wish to be withdrawn. NY R BRONX FIL R Doc. 8.

j. *ERIE COUNTY: Calendaring of motions.* Refer to individual Justice's Part Rules. NY R ERIE E FIL Doc. 3(V)(B).

k. *KINGS COUNTY: Return date set by court.* Irrespective of the return date indicated in the notice of motion, motions will be rescheduled by the E-file/Motion Support Office to a date designated by the assigned Judge. NY R L KINGS Pt. C, Rule 2.

l. *KINGS COUNTY: Calendar calls.* There shall be two (2) calendar calls on motion days. The first calendar call shall be at 9:30 AM and the second calendar call shall be at 10:45 AM, unless the Judge's Part Rules provide otherwise. Defaults shall only be taken on second call. Attorneys with appearances elsewhere in the courthouse may advise the clerk of their whereabouts to avoid a default. Failure to so advise the clerk or appear at the default calendar call will result in a default order being entered or the motion being marked off the calendar. NY R L KINGS Pt. C, Rule 7.

m. *NEW YORK COUNTY: Return date and assigned courtroom.* Motions made by notice of motion and petitions and notices of petition in special proceedings are processed by the General Clerk's Office (Room 119) and are to be made returnable in the Motion Submission Part Courtroom (Room 130) on any business day of the week at 9:30 AM. There are some differences in electronically-filed cases. NY R NY CTY Procedure II; NY R NY CTY Procedure II(C); NY R NY CTY J RUL Rule 13(a).

   i. For the convenience of counsel, between 9:00 A.M. and 9:30 A.M. each day, in advance of the "call," Room 130 accepts (1) written stipulations; (2) affidavits/affirmations reciting the required details as to an adjournment on consent; (3) stipulations, letters or other writings withdrawing motions; and (4) final papers or complete sets of papers on motions. For motions in which these items are handed in before the "call," no one need remain to answer the "call." Counsel/parties must advise the court, either between 9:00 A.M. and 9:30 A.M. or at the "call," of all motions or cases that have been resolved by counsel/parties themselves and all motions that the movant no longer wishes to pursue. If such resolution occurs subsequent to the "call", the assigned Justice must be advised as soon as possible, by written notice sent to the Part, so that the court does not do unnecessary work. NY R NY CTY Procedure II(C).

   ii. Depending upon the assigned Part, contested motions submitted in the Motion Submission Part Courtroom are submitted without argument, or rescheduled for oral argument if so directed by the assigned Justice. For Justices who schedule argument on a case-by-case basis, notice of the argument date will be transmitted by the court. Counsel may ascertain how a motion submitted in Courtroom 130 was marked by consulting Scroll on the court's website, the e-Track application, or, on the two (2) days immediately following the submission date, the New York Law Journal. NY R NY CTY J RUL Rule 13(a).

n. *NEW YORK COUNTY: Motion call.* Each day in the Motion Submission Part Courtroom, commencing at 9:30 A.M., all motions returnable that day will be "called" for the submission of these papers, which must be handed up at this "call" or, as described below, immediately before. Because hundreds of motions appear on the Room 130 calendars every day, motion papers (other than part of the moving papers as described above) cannot be accepted on any day prior to the return date. Courtesy copies are not required nor accepted, but working copies are required by certain Justices in e-filed cases. NY R NY CTY Procedure II(C). If argument is directed, it will take place on an announced date shortly after the day of submission. NY R NY CTY Procedure II(C).

o. *NEW YORK COUNTY: Oral arguments.* Pursuant to request of some Justices, motions submitted in Room 130 will automatically be scheduled for a set argument date in the Part. Other Justices determine on a case-by-case basis after submission in Room 130 whether to accept a particular substantive motion on submission, to require oral argument, or to hold a conference. NY R NY CTY Procedure II(D). If argument is directed by the Justice automatically, notice of argument and the argument date will be given in Room 130. Any appearing party is expected to give notice to all parties and an announcement to this effect is made in Room 130. If the motion is submitted in Room 130 and the Justice, after examining the file, determines that argument should be directed, notice of the argument and the argument date will not be sent by the court. To obtain notification of the argument date and other developments, counsel should use e-Track. If argument notification is not given or transmitted as just described, counsel should understand that the motion has been taken on submission for decision on the papers. NY R NY CTY Procedure II(D).

i. Calendars of motions to be argued in the Parts are published on the morning of the argument date and on the day before in the New York Law Journal under each Part. Argument information is available on a case-by-case basis in Scroll, and e-mail notifications are sent by e-Track to participating attorneys whenever a motion is scheduled for argument in the court's computer system. NY R NY CTY J RUL Rule 15(a)

p. *NEW YORK COUNTY: Motion determined without hearing.* Given the purpose of the Room 130 procedure, the substance of motions will not be addressed at the submission "call." No Judge is present. To the extent possible, motions submitted in Room 130 will be decided "on the papers." Indeed, attorneys are encouraged to use service or clerks to deliver papers or working copies, or to agree among themselves to have one of them deliver papers for all parties by service or a clerk. Counsel for the movant need not appear to "take a default" on any motion or for any other reason. Motions will be submitted, not marked off, in the absence of the movant. Opposing counsel similarly need not appear in person in order to avoid suffering a default. Delivery of papers by service or a clerk will suffice. The court's goal is to be able to collect papers on motions in an orderly fashion but without any attorney having to make an appearance in Room 130 at any time. NY R NY CTY Procedure II(C).

q. *ONONDAGA COUNTY: Return date.* If the motion is the first filing in an action, the case will be assigned and counsel will be notified by the Supreme Court Clerk's Office via the NYSCEF system of the assigned justice and return date. NY R ONDGA E FIL Protocol(B)(7)(c). If the motion is on a previously assigned case, counsel may choose a return date from the assigned justice's motion term schedule. If the date in unavailable, the Supreme Court Clerk's Office will assign the motion to the next available motion term date and will notify counsel via e-mail. The change will also appear in the notification generated by the NYSCEF system. NY R ONDGA E FIL Protocol(B)(7)(d).

r. *QUEENS COUNTY: Return date.* Motions must be made returnable on the proper day/time based on the assigned judge. NY R L QUEENS MOT SUP Doc. 1. Failure to make a motion returnable on the proper day/time may result in the motion being administratively rescheduled or marked off. NY R L QUEENS MOT SUP Doc. 1.

s. *QUEENS COUNTY: Unassigned motions.* For RJI/Motions, due to the fact that the movant would not know who the assigned judge will be, the notice of motion may be returnable any day of the week. RJI/Motions shall be made returnable in "Queens Supreme Court" with no address designated. The motion will be administratively rescheduled to the proper day of the week based on the judge (once a judge has been assigned). Within one (1) week of filing, the movant must check online to see who the assigned judge is (and therefore the location/date/time) that their motion is now returnable. Movant must then notify their adversary of this information prior to the return date. NY R L QUEENS MOT SUP Doc. 1.

3. *Entry of order after hearing.* An order determining a motion shall be entered and filed in the office of the clerk of the court where the action is triable, and all papers used on the motion and any opinion or memorandum in writing shall be filed with that clerk unless the order dispenses with such filing. When a statute or civil practice rule requires such filing and entry in a county other than that in which the order was made, the party prevailing on the motion shall file the order and the papers used on the motion with the proper clerk after receiving them. If a party fails to file any papers required to be filed under NY CPLR Rule 2220(a), the order may be vacated as irregular, with costs. NY CPLR Rule 2220(a). For more information on the entry of an order after a motion, refer to NY CPLR Rule 2219.

a. *BRONX COUNTY: Settled orders.* A Judge's decision will often call for a Settled Order. The purpose of the settled order is to give effect to the decision by directing that some action be done and/or that a court official perform some task. NY R BRONX LEG SUP Doc. 2. A settled order consists of a notice of settlement informing all parties that the proposed order will be presented to the judge who made the decision on a date certain. Next comes the proposed order which will be presented to the judge. This order should conform to the judge's decision and should direct the relief granted in the decision. This should be followed by proof of service upon all parties who were noticed with the decision. It is also helpful if a copy of the judge's decision is included along with the other papers. A settled order should always be noticed before the judge who made the decision. NY R BRONX LEG SUP Doc. 2.

i. Although an order is usually settled by the party who prevailed on the motion, any party may settle the order. It should be presented to the court within sixty (60) days of the decision. The other parties are entitled to ten (10) days notice where service of the settled order is done by mail, five (5) days if the notice is personally delivered. An attorney who is served with a notice of settlement which he believes does not accurately reflect the decision may settle a counter order. The counter order must be noticed for the same day and must be served not less than seven (7) days if by mail and two (2) days if personally delivered. NY R BRONX LEG SUP Doc. 2.

ii. Settled orders are usually sent to the judge the day after they noticed for settlement. No appearance is necessary or even contemplated on a settled order. If the decision directs "submit order", then no notice is necessary, and the order will be sent to the judge as soon a practical after it is received. No fees are collected on settled orders. NY R BRONX LEG SUP Doc. 2.

b. *ERIE COUNTY: Proposed orders.* Proposed orders shall be submitted through the NYSCEF system and a working copy provided to the IAS Justice for signature, if Part Rules so require. NY R ERIE E FIL Doc. 3(V)(G).

c. *KINGS COUNTY: Long form orders.* If the Court directs that an order be settled or submitted on a motion in a NYSCEF case, the proposed order, with Notice of Settlement where required, and any proposed counter-order shall be filed with the Court via NYSCEF. The relevant clerk's office will process the documents in the customary manner. NY R L KINGS E FIL Doc. 1(E).

   i. WORKING COPIES OF PROPOSED ORDERS WITH NOTICE OF SETTLEMENT MUST BE SUBMITTED IN THE MOTION SUPPORT OFFICE (ROOM 227) AS EXPLAINED HEREIN. THEY MUST NOT BE DELIVERED TO THE PART OR CHAMBERS, EXCEPT WHERE THE INDIVIDUAL JUSTICE'S PART RULES PROVIDE OTHERWISE; DOING SO WILL CAUSE ADMINISTRATIVE CONFUSION AND POSSIBLE MISPLACEMENT OF PAPERS. Any such submission shall be sent in a timely manner (kindly review individual Justice's rules) and be conspicuously marked on the outside "NYSCEF Matter;" lack of such marking may delay processing. After an order/counter-order has been signed, it will be scanned, and the County Clerk will affix the entry stamp into the NYSCEF system, which will immediately transmit notice of this event via e-mail, including a link to the entered document, to all participating attorneys and unrepresented litigants in the case. Such transmittal does not constitute Notice of Entry. NY R L KINGS E FIL Doc. 1(E).

d. *NEW YORK COUNTY: Long form orders.* Although the court strongly favors the use of short form orders and judgments, there are instances when settlement of an order or judgment is appropriate. When a Justice directs in a decision that a long form order or judgment be settled, that decision is recorded in the court's computer system by the General Clerk's Office and the motion file with decision is held in the Order Section of the Office in Room 119. The settlement process takes place there. NY R NY CTY Procedure II(D); NY R NY CTY E FIL Doc. 2(E).

   i. A proposed long form order or judgment in compliance NY R UNIF TRIAL CTS § 202.48 must be presented to the relevant back office, together with a notice of settlement which bears a settlement date, the date on which the order is to be ready for formal presentation to the Justice. In an e-filed case the submission shall be made electronically. The proposed order or counter-order should be e-filed and it will be transmitted automatically by the NYSCEF system to the appropriate back office. The return date and time of the proposed order must be at 9:30 A.M. no sooner than either five (5) days from personal service of the proposed order or ten (10) days from service by mail. Proof of timely service on the other parties must accompany the proposed order in a hard copy case. If an order or judgment is submitted late (later than sixty (60) days from signing and filing of the decision) and the proponent can show good cause for this tardiness, an affidavit or affirmation justifying the delay should be annexed to the proposed order, together with proof of service thereof. If persuaded, the Justice will consider the proposed order despite its untimeliness. NY R NY CTY Procedure II(D); NY R NY CTY E FIL Doc. 2(E).

   ii. Sometimes a decision will state "Submit Order." The submitting party should prepare a long form order and make it returnable without notice. Counsel should deliver the proposed order to the Order Section of the appropriate back office, except in an e-filed case, when it shall be submitted electronically. NY R NY CTY Procedure II(D). If the decision of the court directs that a proposed order be settled or submitted in the Part or in Chambers, that direction, should, of course, be followed without presentation of the proposal to the back office. NY R NY CTY Procedure II(D).

   iii. For information on proposed counter-orders, refer to NY R NY CTY Procedure II(D) and NY R NY CTY J RUL Rule 16(b).

e. *QUEENS COUNTY: Proposed orders.* If the court directs that an order be settled or submitted on a motion in an E-file case, the proposed order and any proposed counter-order shall be filed with the court on-line with proof of service. (If a decision refers to a proceeding on the record, a copy of the transcript must be submitted.) Working copies of all proposed orders MUST be submitted to the Motion Support Office before an order can be reviewed. NY R L QUEENS E-FILE Doc. 1(I).

   i. Counsel are advised to adhere to NY R UNIF TRIAL CTS § 202.48 regarding the submission or settlement of their proposed order or judgment. Persons who are submitting proposed orders/judgments pursuant to a previously issued memorandum decision must submit a copy of the memorandum decision with their proposed order/judgment. Upon E-Filing a proposed order/judgement, a working copy of the proposed order/judgement must be provided to the Motion Support Office. NY R L QUEENS MOT SUP Doc. 1.

H. Forms

1. Official Motion to Transfer Venue Forms for New York

a. Request for judicial intervention. NY R UNIF TRIAL CTS § 202.6.

b. Notice of motion. NY R UNIF TRIAL CTS § 202.7(b).

2. New York Motion to Transfer Venue Forms

a. Demand for change of place of trial to proper county. MCF CPLR § 2:143.

b. Notice of motion to change place of trial to proper county. MCF CPLR § 2:147.

c. Affidavit of defendant in support of motion to change place of trial to proper county. MCF CPLR § 2:149.

d. Affidavit of attorney in support of motion to change place of trial to proper county. MCF CPLR § 2:150.

e. Notice of cross-motion for consolidation of actions and change of venue to county where first action initially commenced. MCF CPLR § 2:156.

f. Notice of cross-motion to retain venue in county in which action brought. MCF CPLR § 2:159.

g. Demand for change of place of trial to proper county; Action against county officer. MCF CPLR § 2:162.

h. Notice of cross-motion for change of place of trial to proper county; Action against county officer. MCF CPLR § 2:163.

i. Demand for change of place of trial to proper county; Action against subsidiary corporation of metropolitan transportation authority. MCF CPLR § 2:166.

j. Affidavit in support of motion to change place of trial to proper county; Action against subsidiary corporation of metropolitan transportation authority. MCF CPLR § 2:167.

k. Notice of motion to change place of trial to proper county; Personal injury action. MCF CPLR § 2:168.

l. Affidavit of attorney in support of motion to change place of trial to proper county; Personal injury action. MCF CPLR § 2:169.

m. Notice of motion to change place of trial for purpose of impartial trial. MCF CPLR § 2:171.

n. Affidavit in support of motion to change place of trial for purpose of impartial trial. MCF CPLR § 2:172.

o. Notice of motion to change place of trial on ground of convenience of witnesses. MCF CPLR § 2:174.

p. Affidavit in support of motion to change place of trial for convenience of witnesses. MCF CPLR § 2:175.

q. Notice of motion to change place of trial on ground of convenience of witnesses and to stay discovery. MCF CPLR § 2:179.

r. Affidavit in support of motion to change place of trial on ground of convenience of witnesses and to stay discovery. MCF CPLR § 2:180.

s. Notice to defendant of misplacement of venue in consumer credit transactions. MCF CPLR § 2:189.

t. Notice of motion to dismiss complaint on ground of forum non conveniens; Personal injury action. MCF CPLR § 2:192.

u. Affidavit in support of motion to dismiss complaint on ground of forum non conveniens. MCF CPLR § 2:195.

v. General form of affidavit of service of motion papers. MCF CPLR § 5:24.

I. Applicable Rules

1. *State rules*

a. Short title; Application; Construction; Definitions. NY CPLR § 101; NY CPLR § 103; NY CPLR § 104; NY CPLR § 105.

b. Appendix of official forms. NY CPLR § 107.

c. Inconvenient forum. NY CPLR Rule 327.

d. Grounds for change of place of trial. NY CPLR § 501; NY CPLR § 502; NY CPLR § 503; NY CPLR § 504; NY CPLR § 505; NY CPLR § 507; NY CPLR § 508; NY CPLR § 509; NY CPLR § 510; NY CPLR Rule 511; NY CPLR Rule 512; NY CPLR § 513; NY CPLR § 604.

e. Extensions of time generally. NY CPLR § 2004.

f. Form of papers. NY CPLR Rule 2101; NY CPLR Rule 2102; NY CPLR § 2105; NY CPLR Rule 2106; NY GEN BUS § 399-ddd; NY R UNIF TRIAL CTS § 215.2; NY R UNIF TRIAL CTS § 215.3.

g. Service of papers. NY CPLR Rule 2103.

h. Where motion made; In supreme court action. NY CPLR § 2212.

i. Motion papers; Service; Time. NY CPLR Rule 2214.

j. Relief demanded by other than moving party. NY CPLR Rule 2215.

k. Prior motion; Ex parte motion; Transfer of motion; Hearings; Orders. NY CPLR Rule 2217; NY CPLR § 2218; NY CPLR Rule 2220.

l. Computation of time. NY CPLR § 2402; NY GEN CONSTR § 19; NY GEN CONSTR § 20; NY GEN CONSTR § 25-a; NY GEN CONSTR § 30; NY GEN CONSTR § 31; NY GEN CONSTR § 53.

m. Motions heard by judge supervising disclosure; Stay of disclosure. NY CPLR Rule 3214.

n. Fees; Index number fees of county clerks. NY CPLR § 8018.

o. Hours of court; Proceedings in court. NY R CHIEF J § 3.1; NY R CHIEF J § 29.3.

p. Application of part; Waiver; Additional rules; Application of CPLR; Definitions. NY R UNIF TRIAL CTS § 202.1.

q. Papers filed in court; Electronic filing in supreme court. NY R UNIF TRIAL CTS § 202.5; NY R UNIF TRIAL CTS § 202.5-a; NY R UNIF TRIAL CTS § 202.5-b; NY R UNIF TRIAL CTS § 202.5-bb.

r. Request for judicial intervention. NY R UNIF TRIAL CTS § 202.6.

s. Calendaring of motions; Uniform notice of motion form; Affirmation of good faith. NY R UNIF TRIAL CTS § 202.7.

t. Motion procedure; Preliminary conferences. NY R UNIF TRIAL CTS § 202.8; NY R UNIF TRIAL CTS § 202.12.

u. Rules of the commercial division of the Supreme Court. NY R UNIF TRIAL CTS § 202.70.

v. Signing of papers. NY R CHIEF ADMIN § 130-1.1-a.

2. *Local rules*

a. *Albany County*

i. Third judicial district rules. NY R 3 JD SUP Doc. 1.

b. *Bronx County*

i. Filing of papers in supreme court. NY R BRONX FIL R Doc. 1.

ii. Request for judicial intervention. NY R BRONX FIL R Doc. 2.

iii. Motion procedure. NY R BRONX FIL R Doc. 8.

iv. Commercial division. NY R BRONX FIL R Doc. 12.

v. Motions on notice. NY R BRONX E FIL R Doc. 1.

vi. Settled orders. NY R BRONX LEG SUP Doc. 2.

c. *Erie County*

i. Joint protocols for New York State Courts E-Filing (NYSCEF) cases filed in Supreme Court, Erie County. NY R ERIE E FIL Doc. 3.

d. *Kings County*

i. Papers. NY R L KINGS Pt. A, Papers.

ii. Service of motion papers. NY R L KINGS Pt. C, Rule 1.

iii. Scheduling of motions. NY R L KINGS Pt. C, Rule 2.

iv. Appearance and argument. NY R L KINGS Pt. C, Rule 3.

v. Courtesy copies. NY R L KINGS Pt. C, Rule 5.

vi. Motion calendar calls. NY R L KINGS Pt. C, Rule 7.

vii. Protocol on courthouse and county clerk procedures for electronically filed cases. NY R L KINGS E FIL Doc. 1.

e. *New York County*

i. Commencement of cases. NY R NY CTY Procedure I.

ii. RJIs and assignments. NY R NY CTY Procedure IA.

iii. Motions and special proceedings by notice of motion/petition. NY R NY CTY Procedure II.

iv. County clerk litigation functions. NY R NY CTY Procedure XI.

v. Protocol on courthouse and county clerk procedures for electronically filed cases. NY R NY CTY E FIL Doc. 2.

vi. Redaction of information in documents filed with the county clerk and the court. NY R NY CTY J RUL Rule A-1.

vii. Papers by fax. NY R NY CTY J RUL Rule 4.

viii. Motions on notice; Orders to show cause. NY R NY CTY J RUL Rule 13.

ix. Motion papers. NY R NY CTY J RUL Rule 14.

x. Oral argument; Adjournments. NY R NY CTY J RUL Rule 15.

f. *Onondaga County*

i. Onondaga county protocol for case filings New York State Electronic Files (NYSCEF). NY R ONDGA E FIL Protocol.

g. *Queens County*

i. Motion support office. NY R L QUEENS MOT SUP Doc. 1.

ii. Queens county protocol on courthouse procedures for electronically filed cases. NY R L QUEENS E-FILE Doc. 1.

J. Miscellaneous

NOTE: Individual judges' rules may apply.

ALBANY COUNTY

JUSTICE LISA M. FISHER: NY R 3 JD FISHER Fisher; NY R 3 JD FISHER Fisher, PC Order.

JUSTICE RICHARD MOTT: NY R 3 JD MOTT Mott.

JUSTICE STEPHAN G. SCHICK: NY R 3 JD Schick.

FORECLOSURE SETTLEMENT PART: NY R 3 JD Foreclosure Settlement.

BRONX COUNTY

JUSTICE PAUL L. ALPERT: [NY R BRONX J Part IA-29, as amended by NY ORDER 20-0337].

JUSTICE BEN BARBATO: NY R BRONX J Part IA-21.

JUSTICE MARY ANNE BRIGANTTI: [NY R BRONX J Part IA-15, as amended by NY ORDER 20-0338].

JUSTICE JOSEPH E. CAPELLA: NY R BRONX J Part IA-23.

JUSTICE MITCHELL DANZIGER: NY R BRONX J Part IA-3/33 ; [NY R BRONX J Danziger, Part IA-3/33, as amended by NY ORDER 20-0339].

JUSTICE LAURA G. DOUGLAS: NY R BRONX J Part IA-11.

JUSTICE RUBEN FRANCO: NY R BRONX J Part IA-26.

JUSTICE DORIS M. GONZALEZ: NY R BRONX J Part IA-24.

JUSTICE WILMA GUZMAN: NY R BRONX J Part IA-7; [NY R BRONX J Guzman, Part IA-7 Virtual, as amended by NY ORDER 20-0340].

JUSTICE ROBERT T. JOHNSON: NY R BRONX J Part IA-12.

JUSTICE DONALD A. MILES: NY R BRONX J Part IA-8.

JUSTICE DONNA M. MILLS: NY R BRONX J Part IA-9.

JUSTICE JULIA I. RODRIGUEZ: NY R BRONX J Part IA-18; [NY R BRONX J Part IA-27, as amended by NY ORDER 20-0341].

JUSTICE LLINET M. ROSADO: [NY R BRONX J Part IA-25, as amended by NY ORDER 20-0342].

JUSTICE NORMA RUIZ: NY R BRONX J Part IA-22; [NY R BRONX J Ruiz, Part IA-22 Virtual, as amended by NY ORDER 20-0343].

JUSTICE HOWARD H. SHERMAN: NY R BRONX J Part IA-4.

JUSTICE FERNANDO TAPIA: NY R BRONX J Part IA-13.

JUSTICE ELIZABETH A. TAYLOR: NY R BRONX J Part IA-2.

JUSTICE ALISON Y. TRUITT: NY R BRONX J Part IA-5.

PART IDV: NY R BRONX J Doc. 1.

PRE-TRIAL PART RULES: NY R BRONX J Doc. 2.

PRE TRIAL WORKSHEET: NY R BRONX J Doc. 3.

FORECLOSURE SETTLEMENT PART RULES: NY R BRONX J Doc. 4.

GUARDIANSHIP PART RULES: NY R BRONX J Doc. 5.

LPM PART RULES: NY R BRONX J Doc. 6.

ERIE COUNTY

JUSTICE M. WILLIAM BOLLER: NY R 8 JD J Boller.

JUSTICE RALPH A. BONIELLO: NY R 8 JD J Boniello.

JUSTICE CHRISTOPHER J. BURN: NY R 8 JD J Burns.

JUSTICE RUSSELL P. BUSCAGLIA: NY R 8 JD J Buscaglia.

JUSTICE FRANK CARUSO: NY R 8 JD J Caruso.

JUSTICE STEPHEN W. CASS: NY R 8 JD J Cass.

JUSTICE DEBORAH A. CHIMES: NY R 8 JD J Chimes.

JUSTICE EMILIO COLAIACOVO: [NY R 8 JD J Colaiacovo, as amended by NY ORDER 20-0252].

JUSTICE DIANE Y. DEVLIN: NY R 8 JD J Devlin.

JUSTICE JAMES H. DILLON: NY R 8 JD J Dillon.

JUSTICE PAULA L. FEROLETO: NY R 8 JD J Feroleto.

JUSTICE DANIEL J. FURLONG: [NY R 8 JD J Furlong, as amended by NY ORDER 20-0253].

JUSTICE JOSEPH R. GLOWNIA: NY R 8 JD J Glownia.

JUSTICE MARK J. GRISANTI: NY R 8 JD J Grisanti.

JUSTICE DEBORAH A. HAENDIGES: NY R 8 JD J Haendiges.

JUSTICE LYNN W. KEANE: [NY R 8 JD J Keane, as amended by NY ORDER 20-0254].

JUSTICE RICHARD C. KLOCH, Sr.: NY R 8 JD J Kloch.

JUSTICE FREDERICK J. MARSHALL: [NY R 8 JD J Marshall, as amended by NY ORDER 20-0255.

JUSTICE JOHN L. MICHALSKI: NY R 8 JD J Michalski.

JUSTICE MARK A. MONTOUR: [NY R 8 JD J Montour, as amended by NY ORDER 20-0256].

JUSTICE HENRY NOWAK: NY R 8 JD J Nowak.

JUSTICE JOHN F. O'DONNELL: NY R 8 JD J O'Donnell.

JUSTICE JEANETTE OGDEN: NY R 8 JD J Ogden.

JUSTICE CATHERINE NUGENT-PANEPINTO: NY R 8 JD J Nugent-Panepinto.

JUSTICE FRANK A. SEDITA, III: [NY R 8 JD J Sedita, as amended by NY ORDER 20-0257].

JUSTICE SARA SHELDON: NY R 8 JD J Sheldon.

JUSTICE DONNA M. SIWEK: NY R 8 JD J Siwek.

JUSTICE MARY L. SLISZ: NY R 8 JD J Slisz.

JUSTICE TIMOTHY J. WALKER: [NY R 8 JD J Walker, as amended by NY ORDER 20-0258].

JUSTICE DENNIS E. WARD: NY R 8 JD J Ward.

JUSTICE PAUL B. WOJTASZEK: [NY R 8 JD J Wojtaszek, as amended by NY ORDER 20-0259].

JUSTICE CHARLES N. ZAMBITO: [NY R 8 JD J Zambito, as amended by NY ORDER 20-0260].

SUPREME COURT LEGAL STAFF: NY R 8 JD J Legal Staff.

KINGS COUNTY

JUSTICE RACHEL A. ADAMS: NY R KINGS J Part 5F.

JUSTICE LOREN BAILY-SCHIFFMAN: NY R KINGS J Part 65.

JUSTICE REGINALD A. BODDIE: NY R KINGS J Part 95.

JUSTICE THERESA M. CICCOTTO: NY R KINGS J Part 19; NY R KINGS J Part 5J.

JUSTICE LISSETTE COLON: NY R KINGS J Part Rules.

JUSTICE GENINE EDWARDS: NY R KINGS J Part 80.

JUSTICE PAMELA L. FISHER: [NY R KINGS J Part 94, as amended by NY ORDER 20-0208].

JUSTICE ROBIN GARSON: NY R KINGS J Part 75.

JUSTICE LARA J. GENOVISI: [NY R KINGS J Part 34, as amended by NY ORDER 20-0209].

JUSTICE BERNARD J. GRAHAM: NY R KINGS J Part 36.

JUSTICE DAWN JIMENEZ-SALTA: NY R KINGS J Part 88.

JUSTICE INGRID JOSEPH: [NY R KINGS J Part FRP3 and Part 83, as amended by NY ORDER 20-0210].

JUSTICE KATHY J. KING: NY R KINGS J Part 64, 76K.

JUSTICE LAWRENCE KNIPEL: NY R KINGS J Part 57.

JUSTICE DONALD KURTZ: NY R KINGS J Part 26.

JUSTICE CARL LANDICINO: [NY R KINGS J Part 81, as amended by NY ORDER 20-0211].

JUSTICE KATHERINE LEVINE: [NY R KINGS J Part 20, 25, 92, as amended by NY ORDER 20-0211].

JUSTICE LORNA MCALLISTER: [NY R KINGS J Part 10, as amended by NY ORDER 20-0211].

JUSTICE ROSEMARIE MONTALBANO: [NY R KINGS J Part 19, 71, and 22, as amended by NY ORDER 20-0211].

JUSTICE RICHARD J. MONTELIONE: [NY R KINGS J Part 99 and DJMP, as amended by NY ORDER 20-0215].

JUSTICE LISA S. OTTLEY: NY R KINGS J Part 24.

JUSTICE MARK I. PARTNOW: NY R KINGS J Part 43.

JUSTICE ERIC I. PRUS: NY R KINGS J Part 5A.

JUSTICE FRANCOIS RIVERA: NY R KINGS J Part 52.

JUSTICE KAREN B. ROTHENBERG: NY R KINGS J Part 35.

JUSTICE LEON RUCHELSMAN: NY R KINGS J Part 1.

JUSTICE WAYNE P. SAITTA: NY R KINGS J Part 29.

JUSTICE ROBIN K. SHEARES: NY R KINGS J Part 96.

JUSTICE KENNETH P. SHERMAN: NY R KINGS J Part 67 and 78.

JUSTICE DEBRA SILBER: NY R KINGS J Part 9 and 5K.

JUSTICE ELLEN M. SPODEK: NY R KINGS J Part 63.

JUSTICE MARSHA L. STEINHARDT: NY R KINGS J Part 15.

JUSTICE JEFFREY S. SUNSHINE: NY R KINGS J Part 5G.

JUSTICE PETER P. SWEENEY: [NY R KINGS J Part 35, as amended by NY ORDER 20-0218].

JUSTICE DELORES J. THOMAS: [NY R KINGS J Part 5T, as amended by NY ORDER 20-0221].

JUSTICE WAVNY TOUSSAINT: NY R KINGS J Part 70.

JUSTICE RICHARD VELASQUEZ: NY R KINGS J Part 66.

JUSTICE CAROLYN E. WADE: NY R KINGS J Part 84.

JUSTICE EDWARD G. WALKER: [NY R KINGS J Part 90, as amended by NY ORDER 20-0219].

JUSTICE LILLIAN WAN: [NY R KINGS J Part 17, as amended by NY ORDER 20-0220].

JUSTICE MICHELLE WESTON: NY R KINGS J Part 3.

MENTAL HYGIENE PART: NY R KINGS J Part 77.

MATRIMONIAL PARTS DURING COVID-19 EMERGENCY: JUSTICE KAREN B. ROTHENBERG: NY R KINGS J Doc. 1.

NASSAU COUNTY

JUSTICE ANNA R. ANZALONE: NY R NASSAU S J Anzalone, Part 26.

JUSTICE STACY D. BENNETT: NY R NASSAU S J Bennett; NY R NASSAU S J Bennett, Form 1.

JUSTICE ANTONIO BRANDVEEN: NY R NASSAU S J Brandveen, Part 31.

JUSTICE JEFFREY S. BROWN: [NY R NASSAU S J Brown, as amended by NY ORDER 20-0297].

JUSTICE STEPHEN A. BUCARIA: NY R NASSAU S J Bucaria.

JUSTICE JULIANNE T. CAPETOLA: NY R NASSAU S J Capetola, Part 28.

JUSTICE EDMUND M. DANE: NY R NASSAU S J Dane, Part 33.

JUSTICE VITO M. DESTEFANO: NY R NASSAU S J DeStefano, Part 13; NY R NASSAU S J DeStefano, Form 1.

JUSTICE ARTHUR M. DIAMOND: NY R NASSAU S J Diamond, Part 7.

JUSTICE THOMAS FEINMAN: NY R NASSAU S J Feinman, Part 5.

JUSTICE JOHN M. GALASSO: NY R NASSAU S J Galasso, Part 22.

JUSTICE SHARON M.J. GIANELLI: NY R NASSAU S J Gianelli, Part 22; NY R NASSAU S J Gianelli, Form 1.

JUSTICE JEFFREY A. GOODSTEIN: NY R NASSAU S J Goodstein, Part 33; NY R NASSAU S J Goodstein, Form 1.

JUSTICE DAVID J. GUGERTY: [NY R NASSAU S J Gugerty, Part 31, as amended by NY ORDER 20-0298].

JUSTICE HELENE F. GUGERTY: NY R NASSAU S J Gugerty, Part 47.

JUSTICE STEVEN M. JAEGER: NY R NASSAU S J Jaeger, Part 35; NY R NASSAU S J Jaeger, Form 1.

JUSTICE JACK L. LIBERT: NY R NASSAU S J Libert, Part 23.

JUSTICE JOSEPH H. LORINTZ: NY R NASSAU S J Lorintz, Part 26; NY R NASSAU S J Lorintz, Form 1.

JUSTICE ROY S. MAHON: NY R NASSAU S J Mahon, Part 3.

JUSTICE RANDY SUE MARBER: NY R NASSAU S J Marber, Part 8.

JUSTICE JAMES P. MCCORMACK: [NY R NASSAU S J McCormack, Part 18, as amended by NY ORDER, 20-0299].

JUSTICE DICCIA T. PINEDA-KIRWAN: [NY R NASSAU S J Pineda-Kirwan, as amended by NY ORDER 20-0300].

JUSTICE THOMAS RADEMAKER: [NY R NASSAU S J Rademaker, Part 28, as amended by NY ORDER 20-0301]; [NY R NASSAU S J Rademaker, Form 1, as amended by NY ORDER 20-0301].

JUSTICE DENISE L. SHER: NY R NASSAU S J Rademaker, Part 32.

JUSTICE LEONARD D. STEINMAN: [NY R NASSAU S J Steinman, Part 15, as amended by NY ORDER 20-0303]; NY R NASSAU S J Steinman, Form 1.

JUSTICE HOWARD E. STURIM: NY R NASSAU S J Sturim, Part 50; NY R NASSAU S J Sturim, Form 1.

JUSTICE HELEN VOUTSINAS: [NY R NASSAU S J Voutsinas, Part 25, as amended by NY ORDER 20-0304]; [NY R NASSAU S J Voutsinas, Form 1, as amended by NY ORDER 20-0305].

JUSTICE HOPE SCHWARTZ ZIMMERMAN: NY R NASSAU S J Zimmerman, Part 17.

NEW YORK COUNTY

JUDGE'S RULES; BASIC INFORMATION: [NY R NY CTY J RUL Doc. 1, as amended by NY ORDER 20-0202].

ONONDAGA COUNTY

JUSTICE ROBERT E. ANTONACCI II: [NY R ONDGA E FIL Doc. 1, as amended by 20-0239].

JUSTICE MICHAEL V. COCCOMI: NY R ONDGA E FIL Doc. 2.

JUSTICE GREGORY R. GILBERT: NY R 5 JD JUDGES Gilbert; NY R ONDGA E FIL Doc. 3.

JUSTICE DONALD A. GREENWOOD: NY R ONDGA E FIL Doc. 4.

JUSTICE DEBORAH H. KARALUNAS: NY R ONDGA E FIL Doc. 5.

JUSTICE JAMES MCCLUSKY: NY R 5 JD MCCLUSKY McClusky.

JUSTICE CHARLES C. MERRELL: NY R 5 JD MERRELL Merrell.

JUSTICE PATRICK F. MACRAE: NY R 5 JD MACRAE Doc. 1.

JUSTICE JAMES P. MURPHY: NY R ONDGA E FIL Doc. 7.

JUSTICE GERALD J. NERI: [NY R 5 JD JUDGES Neri, as amended by NY ORDER 20-0236]; [NY R ONDGA E FIL Doc. 8, as amended by NY ORDER 20-0241].

JUSTICE ANTHONY J. PARIS: NY R 5 JD JUDGES Paris; [NY R ONDGA E FIL Doc. 9, as amended by NY ORDER 20-0242].

JUSTICE NORMAN W. SEITER, JR.: NY R 5 JD JUDGES Seiter.

JUSTICE KEVIN G. YOUNG: [NY R ONDGA E FIL Doc. 10, as amended by NY ORDER 20-0243].

QUEENS COUNTY

JUSTICE PAM JACKMAN BROWN: [NY R L QUEENS Brown, Part 19, as amended by NY ORDER 20-0321].

JUSTICE CHEREE A. BUGGS: NY R L QUEENS Buggs, Part 30.

JUSTICE PAM JACKMAN BROWN: [NY R L QUEENS Brown, Part 19, as amended by NY ORDER 20-0321].

JUSTICE DENIS J. BUTLER: NY R L QUEENS Butler, Part 12.

JUSTICE ROBERT I. CALORAS: [NY R L QUEENS Caloras, Part 36, as amended by NY ORDER 20-0322].

JUSTICE ANNA CULLEY: NY R L QUEENS Culley, Part 53.

JUSTICE TIMOTHY DUFFICY: NY R L QUEENS Dufficy, Part 35.

JUSTICE DAVID ELLIOT: NY R L QUEENS Elliot, Part 14.

JUSTICE JOSEPH J. ESPOSITO: NY R L QUEENS Esposito, Part 6.

JUSTICE DARRELL L. GAVRIN: [NY R L QUEENS Gavrin, Part 27, as amended by NY ORDER 20-0323].

JUSTICE WYATT N. GIBBONS: [NY R L QUEENS Gibbons, Part 5, as amended by NY ORDER 20-0330.

JUSTICE DONNA-MARIE E. GOLIA: [NY R L QUEENS Golia, Part 21, as amended by NY ORDER 20-0331].

JUSTICE MARGUERITE A. GRAYS: [NY R L QUEENS Grays, Part 4, as amended by NY ORDER 20-0324].

JUSTICE RUDOLPH E. GRECO: [NY R L QUEENS Greco, Part 32, as amended by NY ORDER 20-0325].

JUSTICE MAUREEN HEALY: NY R L QUEENS Healy, Part 6.

JUSTICE PHILLIP HOM: [NY R L QUEENS Hom, Part 43, as amended by NY ORDER 20-0332].

JUSTICE KEVIN J. KERRIGAN: NY R L QUEENS Kerrigan, Part 10.

JUSTICE MOJGAN C. LANCMAN: NY R L QUEENS Lancman, Part 20.

JUSTICE RICHARD G. LATIN: NY R L QUEENS Latin, Part 40.

JUSTICE ULYSSES B. LEVERETT: [NY R L QUEENS Leverett, Part 6, as amended by NY ORDER 20-0326].

JUSTICE LEONARD LIVOTE: NY R L QUEENS Livote, Part 33.

JUSTICE LEE A. MAYERSOHN: NY R L QUEENS Mayersohn, Part 22; NY R L QUEENS Mayersohn, Part 22G; [NY R L QUEENS Mayersohn, Part 22G COVID, as amended by NY ORDER 20-0327].

JUSTICE ROBERT J. MCDONALD: NY R L QUEENS McDonald, Part 34.

JUSTICE MARGARET MCGOWAN: NY R L QUEENS McGowan, Part 52.

JUSTICE MAURICE E. MUIR: [NY R L QUEENS Muir, Part 42, as amended by NY ORDER 20-0333].

JUSTICE JODI ORLOW: NY R L QUEENS Orlow, Part 51.

JUSTICE LESLIE J. PURIFICCION: NY R L QUEENS Purificcion, Part 39.

JUSTICE JOSEPH RISI: [NY R L QUEENS Risi, Part 3, as amended by NY ORDER 20-0328].

JUSTICE FREDERICK D.R. SAMPSON: [NY R L QUEENS Sampson, Part 31, as amended by NY ORDER 20-0329].
JUSTICE MARTIN J. SCHULMAN: NY R L QUEENS Schulman, Part 29.
JUSTICE BERNICE D. SIEGAL: NY R L QUEENS Siegal, Part 25G.
JUSTICE JANICE A. TAYLOR: NY R L QUEENS Taylor, Part 15.
JUSTICE CARMEN R. VELASQUEZ: NY R L QUEENS Velasquez, Part 38.
JUSTICE LOURDES M VENTURA: [NY R L QUEENS Ventura, Part 37, as amended by NY ORDER 20-0334].
JUSTICE WILLIAM A. VISCOVICH: NY R L QUEENS Viscovich, Part 63.
JUSTICE ALLAN B. WEISS: NY R L QUEENS Weiss, Part 2.
COMPLIANCE, SETTLEMENT AND CONFERENCE PART: NY R L QUEENS Doc 1.
PRELIMINARY CONFERENCE PART: [NY R L QUEENS Doc. 2, as amended by NY ORDER 20-0335].
MEDICAL MALPRACTICE CONFERENCE PART: [NY R L QUEENS Doc. 3, as amended by NY ORDER 20-0336].
TRIAL SCHEDULING PART: NY R L QUEENS Doc. 4.
SUMMARY JURY TRIAL PROGRAM: NY R L QUEENS Doc. 7.
RESIDENTIAL FORECLOSURE PART: NY R L QUEENS Doc. 9.
FORECLOSURE AUCTION RULES: NY R L QUEENS Doc. 10.
MATRIMONIAL PRELIMINARY CONFERENCE PART: NY R L QUEENS Doc. 11.
NON-CUSTODIAL CONTESTED MATRIMONIAL PART: NY R L QUEENS Doc. 12.

Motions, Oppositions and Replies
Motion to Dismiss

Document Last Updated August 2020

A. Checklist

(I) ❑ Matters to consider for moving party
- (a) ❑ Required documents
  - (1) ❑ Notice of motion, order to show cause, or affidavit on ex parte motion
  - (2) ❑ Motion
  - (3) ❑ Request for judicial intervention
  - (4) ❑ Proof of service
  - (5) ❑ ALBANY COUNTY: Additional required documents
    - (i) ❑ Affirmation of good faith effort
- (b) ❑ Supplemental documents
  - (1) ❑ Supporting evidence; Exhibits
  - (2) ❑ Brief
  - (3) ❑ Notice to produce papers not in possession of the court
  - (4) ❑ Filing fees
  - (5) ❑ Working copies
  - (6) ❑ Statement of authorization in electronic filing cases
  - (7) ❑ ERIE COUNTY: Additional supplemental documents
    - (i) ❑ Notice of hard copy submission in e-filed case
  - (8) ❑ KINGS COUNTY: Additional supplemental documents
    - (i) ❑ Forms when filing in hard copy

- (9) ❑ NEW YORK COUNTY: Additional supplemental documents
  - (i) ❑ Notice of hard copy submission
  - (ii) ❑ Unpublished opinions
- (10) ❑ ONONDAGA COUNTY: Additional supplemental documents
  - (i) ❑ Notice of hard copy submission
- (11) ❑ QUEENS COUNTY: Additional supplemental documents
  - (i) ❑ Notice of hard copy submission

(c) ❑ Timing

- (1) ❑ At any time before service of the responsive pleading is required, a party may move on one or more of the grounds set forth in NY CPLR Rule 3211(a)
- (2) ❑ The moving party shall serve copies of all affidavits and briefs upon all other parties at the time of service of the notice of motion
- (3) ❑ A notice of motion and supporting affidavits shall be served at least eight (8) days before the time at which the motion is noticed to be heard
- (4) ❑ It is also good practice to make motions returnable at least three (3) weeks away from the planned date of mailing and to always include a demand in the motion that the other side serve answering papers at least seven (7) days before the return day
- (5) ❑ BRONX COUNTY: Additional timing
  - (i) ❑ A Notice of Motion must be served at least eight (8) days, by personal service, nine (9) days by overnight express and thirteen (13) days by mail before the return date
- (6) ❑ NEW YORK COUNTY: Additional timing
  - (i) ❑ In an e-filed case, all of the moving papers shall be e-filed at least eight (8) business days prior to the return date
- (7) ❑ ONONDAGA COUNTY: Additional timing
  - (i) ❑ Onondaga County local court rules require that any additional papers relating to motions must be e-filed at least two (2) business days prior to the return date, excluding the return date
- (8) ❑ QUEENS COUNTY: Additional timing
  - (i) ❑ Motions must be in the possession of the Motion Support Office at least nine (9) days before the noticed return date of the motion

(II) ❑ Matters to consider for opposing party

(a) ❑ Required documents

- (1) ❑ Opposition
- (2) ❑ Proof of service

(b) ❑ Supplemental documents

- (1) ❑ Supporting evidence; Exhibits
- (2) ❑ Brief
- (3) ❑ Filing fees
- (4) ❑ Working copies
- (5) ❑ ERIE COUNTY: Additional supplemental documents
  - (i) ❑ Notice of hard copy submission in e-filed case
- (6) ❑ KINGS COUNTY: Additional supplemental documents
  - (i) ❑ Forms when filing in hard copy
- (7) ❑ NEW YORK COUNTY: Additional supplemental documents
  - (i) ❑ Notice of hard copy submission

(ii) ❑ Unpublished opinions

(8) ❑ ONONDAGA COUNTY: Additional supplemental documents

(i) ❑ Notice of hard copy submission

(9) ❑ QUEENS COUNTY: Additional supplemental documents

(i) ❑ Notice of hard copy submission

(c) ❑ Timing

(1) ❑ Answering affidavits shall be served at least two (2) days before the time at which the motion is noticed to be heard

(2) ❑ Answering affidavits and any notice of cross-motion, with supporting papers, if any, shall be served at least seven (7) days before such time if a notice of motion served at least sixteen (16) days before such time so demands

B. Timing

1. *Time to bring motion to dismiss.* At any time before service of the responsive pleading is required, a party may move on one or more of the grounds set forth in NY CPLR Rule 3211(a), and no more than one such motion shall be permitted. NY CPLR Rule 3211(e).

   a. *Grounds which must be raised in or before responsive pleadings.* Any objection or defense based upon a ground set forth in NY CPLR Rule 3211(a)(1), NY CPLR Rule 3211(a)(3), NY CPLR Rule 3211(a)(4), NY CPLR Rule 3211(a)(5) and NY CPLR Rule 3211(a)(6) is waived unless raised either by such motion or in the responsive pleading. NY CPLR Rule 3211(e). An objection based upon a ground specified in NY CPLR Rule 3211(a)(8) or NY CPLR Rule 3211(a)(9) is waived if a party moves on any of the grounds set forth in NY CPLR Rule 3211(a) without raising such objection or if, having made no objection under NY CPLR Rule 3211(a), he or she does not raise such objection in the responsive pleading. NY CPLR Rule 3211(e).

   b. *Grounds which may be raised after responsive pleading.* A motion based upon a ground specified in NY CPLR Rule 3211(a)(2), NY CPLR Rule 3211(a)(7) or NY CPLR Rule 3211(a)(10) may be made at any subsequent time or in a later pleading, if one is permitted. NY CPLR Rule 3211(e).

   c. *Objection to service of initiating documents.* An objection that the summons and complaint, summons with notice, or notice of petition and petition was not properly served is waived if, having raised such an objection in a pleading, the objecting party does not move for judgment on that ground within sixty (60) days after serving the pleading, unless the court extends the time upon the ground of undue hardship. NY CPLR Rule 3211(e).

      i. The papers in opposition to a motion based on improper service shall contain a copy of the proof of service, whether or not previously filed. NY CPLR Rule 3211(e).

   d. *Time to serve responsive pleading.* Refer to the New York KeyRules Answer document for information on the time to serve responsive pleadings.

2. *Extension of time to plead.* Service of a notice of motion under NY CPLR Rule 3211(a) or NY CPLR Rule 3211(b) before service of a pleading responsive to the cause of action or defense sought to be dismissed extends the time to serve the pleading until ten (10) days after service of notice of entry of the order. NY CPLR Rule 3211(f).

3. *Time to serve.* The moving party shall serve copies of all affidavits and briefs upon all other parties at the time of service of the notice of motion. NY R UNIF TRIAL CTS § 202.8(c). A notice of motion and supporting affidavits shall be served at least eight (8) days before the time at which the motion is noticed to be heard. NY CPLR Rule 2214(b).

   a. *Return dates; Best practice.* It is also good practice to make motions returnable at least three (3) weeks away from the planned date of mailing and to always include a demand in the motion that the other side serve answering papers at least seven (7) days before the return day. This enables the motion to be served by mail, gives sufficient notice to support the seven (7) day demand, and leaves a few days for a delayed mailing if some snag prevents posting on the day planned. If speed is needed, the shorter eight (8) day notice period can be used, forfeiting the right to seven (7) day answering papers and a reply. If even eight (8) days notice is too much under the circumstances, the order to show cause is the remedy. SIEGEL-NYPRAC § 247.

      i. *ALBANY COUNTY.* All motions, except for certain matters in Albany County as specified in NY R 3 JD SUP Doc. 1(E) and NY R 3 JD SUP Doc. 1(F), brought on by notice of motion or by order to show cause will be made returnable on any day, Monday through Friday, as chosen by the movant in compliance with the CPLR. Parties shall submit all papers in a timely fashion as required by the CPLR by delivering them or mailing them directly to the Supreme Court Clerk's Office[. . .]except that motions and other applications subject to a filing fee shall first be presented to the County Clerk's Office for payment of the requisite fee and then subsequently filed with the Supreme Court Clerk's Office. NY R 3 JD SUP Doc. 1(B).

ii. *BRONX COUNTY.* A Notice of Motion must be served at least eight (8) days, by personal service, nine (9) days by overnight express and thirteen (13) days by mail before the return date. NY R BRONX FIL R Doc. 3. All unassigned motions must be accompanied with a properly filled out RJI and shall be filed in the Motion Support Office, room 217, within five (5) days of service. All motions on actions already assigned to a Justice must be filed at least five (5) business days before the return date. NY R BRONX FIL R Doc. 3. All papers served must strictly comply with the time requirements of NY CPLR Rule 2101, NY CPLR Rule 2103 and NY CPLR Rule 2214(b). NY R BRONX FIL R Doc. 8.

iii. *KINGS COUNTY.* Motion papers, answering affidavits and reply affidavits must be served on adversaries in accordance with NY CPLR Rule 2214. NY R L KINGS Pt. C, Rule 1.

iv. *NEW YORK COUNTY.* In an e-filed case, all of the moving papers shall be e-filed at least eight (8) business days prior to the return date. The clerk will calendar the motion for the Motion Submission Part Courtroom (Room 130) for the return date selected. NY R NY CTY Procedure II(A); NY R NY CTY E FIL Doc. 2(D)(1).

v. *ONONDAGA COUNTY.* Onondaga County local court rules require that any additional papers relating to motions must be e-filed at least two (2) business days prior to the return date, excluding the return date. NY R ONDGA E FIL Protocol(B)(9)(e).

vi. *QUEENS COUNTY.* Motions must be in the possession of the Motion Support Office at least nine (9) days before the noticed return date of the motion. NY R L QUEENS MOT SUP Doc. 1; NY R L QUEENS E-FILE Doc. 1(H)(1).

b. *Order to show cause; Shorter time.* The court in a proper case may grant an order to show cause, to be served in lieu of a notice of motion, at a time and in a manner specified therein. NY CPLR Rule 2214(d). An ordinary notice of motion can't be brought on for hearing earlier than the eighth (8th) day after the motion papers are served. With an order to show cause, the hearing can be brought on at any time the court directs, which can be fewer than eight (8) days or as close as the very day on which it is signed. If the court is convinced there is a real emergency, it can schedule the hearing for a few hours later or, in the direst case, "forthwith" the service of the order to show cause. SIEGEL-NYPRAC § 248.

c. *Time to serve answering affidavits; Other answering papers.* Answering affidavits shall be served at least two (2) days before the time at which the motion is noticed to be heard. Answering affidavits and any notice of cross-motion, with supporting papers, if any, shall be served at least seven (7) days before such time if a notice of motion served at least sixteen (16) days before such time so demands; whereupon any reply or responding affidavits shall be served at least one (1) day before such time. NY CPLR Rule 2214(b); NY R UNIF TRIAL CTS § 202.8(c).

i. *BRONX COUNTY.* All answering papers must be submitted to the Clerk 's Office on the return date of the motion. Answering papers will not be accepted prior to the return date. NY R BRONX FIL R Doc. 8.

ii. *NEW YORK COUNTY.* Cross-motions, papers in opposition, and reply papers on motions/petitions on notice returnable in Room 130 in a hard-copy case shall be submitted to the Motion Submission Part Courtroom (Room 130) on the final return date of the motion/petition and will not be accepted until that date. Subsequent documents on motions/petitions in e-filed cases shall be e-filed in a timely manner. Working copies when required shall be submitted to Room 130 on the final return date. NY R NY CTY Procedure II(A).

d. *Time to serve cross-motion.* At least three (3) days prior to the time at which the motion is noticed to be heard, or seven (7) days prior to such time if demand is properly made pursuant to NY CPLR Rule 2214(b), a party may serve upon the moving party a notice of cross-motion demanding relief, with or without supporting papers; provided, however, that:

i. If such notice and any supporting papers are served by mailing, as provided in NY CPLR Rule 2103(b)(2), they shall be served three (3) days earlier than as prescribed in NY CPLR Rule 2215; and

ii. If served by overnight delivery, as provided in NY CPLR Rule 2103(b)(6), they shall be served one (1) day earlier than as prescribed in NY CPLR Rule 2215. Relief in the alternative or of several different types may be demanded; relief need not be responsive to that demanded by the moving party. NY CPLR Rule 2215(a); NY CPLR Rule 2215(b).

iii. *BRONX COUNTY.* Cross motions may be presented for approval on or before the return date, provided that there is a motion already calendared. NY R BRONX FIL R Doc. 8.

iv. *ERIE COUNTY.* Cross-motions must be filed at least two (2) days before the return date of the motion. NY R L KINGS Pt. A, Papers.

v. *KINGS COUNTY.* Hard copies are required to be filed for any motions, answering papers, stipulations, etc. for E-Filed cases returnable in [the Central Compliance Part] at least [two (2)] days before return date. . .for cross motions. NY R L KINGS Pt. E, Rule 8.

vi. *QUEENS COUNTY.* Motion Support does not process or forward responsive papers, including cross-motions. They must be brought to the calendar call in the judge's part. NY R L QUEENS MOT SUP Doc. 1. E-filed cross motions: across motion must be noticed for the same return date as the main motion and have the confirmation of filing attached in the same manner as a motion. NY R L QUEENS E-FILE Doc. 1(H)(2)(e).

4. *Time for initial appearance.* The defendant appears by serving an answer or a notice of appearance, or by making a motion which has the effect of extending the time to answer. An appearance shall be made within twenty (20) days after service of the summons, except that if the summons was served on the defendant by delivering it to an official of the state authorized to receive service in his behalf or if it was served pursuant to NY CPLR § 303, NY CPLR § 308(2), NY CPLR § 308(3), NY CPLR § 308(4) or NY CPLR § 308(5), or NY CPLR § 313, NY CPLR § 314 or NY CPLR § 315, the appearance shall be made within thirty (30) days after service is complete. NY CPLR Rule 320(a).

a. *Extension of time when complaint not served with summons.* If the complaint is not served with the summons, the time to appear may be extended as provided in NY CPLR § 3012(b). NY CPLR Rule 320(a).

b. *Written demand for complaint; Effect on time to appear.* If the complaint is not served with the summons, the defendant may serve a written demand for the complaint within the time provided in NY CPLR Rule 320(a) for an appearance. Service of the demand shall extend the time to appear until twenty (20) days after service of the complaint. A demand or motion under NY CPLR § 3012(b) does not of itself constitute an appearance in the action. NY CPLR § 3012(b).

5. *Time to acknowledge service of initiating papers*

a. *Served by electronic means.* A party served by electronic means shall, within twenty-four (24) hours of service, provide the serving party or attorney with an electronic confirmation that the service has been effected. NY R UNIF TRIAL CTS § 202.5-b(f)(1); NY R UNIF TRIAL CTS § 202.5-bb(b)(3).

b. *Served by mail.* The defendant, an authorized employee of the defendant, defendant's attorney or an employee of the attorney must complete the acknowledgement of receipt and mail or deliver one (1) copy of it within thirty (30) days from the date of receipt. Service is complete on the date the signed acknowledgement of receipt is mailed or delivered to the sender. The signed acknowledgement of receipt shall constitute proof of service. NY CPLR § 312-a(b)(1).

i. *Acknowledgement to be sworn.* The acknowledgement of receipt of service shall be subscribed and affirmed as true under penalties of perjury and shall have the same force and effect as an affidavit. NY CPLR § 312-a(c).

ii. *Time for answer after acknowledgement.* Where a complaint or petition is served with the summons or notice of petition, the defendant shall serve an answer within twenty (20) days after the date the signed acknowledgement of receipt is mailed or delivered to the sender. NY CPLR § 312-a(b)(2).

6. *Filing before return date.* All motions shall be returnable before the assigned judge, and all papers shall be filed with the court on or before the return date. NY R UNIF TRIAL CTS § 202.8(a).

a. *BRONX COUNTY: Time for filing*

i. *Unassigned motions.* Unassigned motions must be in the Clerk's Office within five (5) days of the date of service of the motion. NY R BRONX FIL R Doc. 8.

ii. *Assigned motions.* Assigned motions must be filed in the Clerk's Office not less than five (5) business days prior to the return date of the motion. NY R BRONX FIL R Doc. 8.

iii. *Motions returnable in room 217.* The moving documents must be e-filed no later than eight (8) days prior to the return date. NY R BRONX E FIL R Doc. 1(1).

b. *KINGS COUNTY: Time and place of filing.* Motion papers must be filed with the E-file/Motion Support Office located in Room 227. . . at 360 Adams Street at least five (5) business days before the return date of the motion. NY R L KINGS Pt. A, Papers. Hard copies are required to be filed for any motions, answering papers, stipulations, etc. for E-Filed cases returnable in [the Central Compliance Part] at least five (5) days before return date for main motions. NY R L KINGS Pt. E, Rule 8. The moving documents must be e-filed no later than eight (8) days prior to the return date. NY R L KINGS E FIL Doc. 1(D).

7. *NEW YORK COUNTY: Briefing schedule.* Once a motion is made, counsel for all parties are strongly encouraged to agree

upon a briefing schedule and submit a stipulation of adjournment reflecting that schedule using service or a clerk. Where a briefing schedule has not been agreed upon, the movant can avoid the need to attend simply to see if anyone will hand up opposing papers by demanding papers as provided by NY CPLR Rule 2214(b). To protect movants against the submission of late opposition papers or cross-motions, the General Clerk's Office will screen motions in which such papers are submitted without a response (reply or opposition respectively) to ensure that proper time to respond has been afforded and it will sua sponte adjourn for one (1) week cases in which such time has not been given. NY R NY CTY Procedure II(C).

8. *QUEENS COUNTY: Time to pay fees.* As motions and petitions are time sensitive, if opting to pay at the County Clerk's Office payment MUST be made, if filed with an RJI, a minimum of nine (9) business days prior to the application's return date and if filed post RJI, a minimum of nine (9) business days prior to the application's return date. NY R L QUEENS E-FILE Doc. 1(H)(1).
9. *Computation of time*
   a. *Units of time*
      i. *Day.* A calendar day includes the time from midnight to midnight. Sunday or any day of the week specifically mentioned means a calendar day. NY GEN CONSTR § 19.
      ii. *Month.* In a statute, contract or public or private instrument, unless otherwise provided in such contract or instrument or by law, the term month means a calendar month and not a lunar month. NY GEN CONSTR § 31.
      iii. *Year.* For information on the definition of a year, including the definitions of a half-year and quarter-year, refer to NY GEN CONSTR § 58 and NY GEN CONSTR § 50. For information on leap years, refer to NY GEN CONSTR § 57.
   b. *Periods of time*
      i. *Number of days.* A number of days specified as a period from a certain day within which or after or before which an act is authorized or required to be done means such number of calendar days exclusive of the calendar day from which the reckoning is made. NY GEN CONSTR § 20.
         - If such period is a period of two (2) days, Saturday, Sunday or a public holiday must be excluded from the reckoning if it is an intervening day between the day from which the reckoning is made and the last day of the period. NY GEN CONSTR § 20.
         - In computing any specified period of time from a specified event, the day upon which the event happens is deemed the day from which the reckoning is made. The day from which any specified period of time is reckoned shall be excluded in making the reckoning. NY GEN CONSTR § 20.
      ii. *Number of months.* A number of months after or before a certain day shall be computed by counting such number of calendar months from such day, exclusive of the calendar month in which such day occurs, and shall include the day of the month in the last month so counted having the same numerical order in days of the month as the day from which the computation is made, unless there be not so many days in the last month so counted, in which case the period computed shall expire with the last day of the month so counted. NY GEN CONSTR § 30.
      iii. *Publication of notice; Number of days.* The period of publication of a legal notice shall be computed by excluding the first day of publication and including the day on which the act or event of which notice is given is to take place or which completes the full period of publication. NY CPLR § 2402.
      iv. *Periods ending on Saturday, Sunday or public holiday.* When any period of time, computed from a certain day, within which or after which or before which an act is authorized or required to be done, ends on a Saturday, Sunday or a public holiday, such act may be done on the next succeeding business day and if the period ends at a specified hour, such act may be done at or before the same hour of such next succeeding business day, except that where a period of time specified by contract ends on a Saturday, Sunday or a public holiday, the extension of such period is governed by NY GEN CONSTR § 25. NY GEN CONSTR § 25-a(1).
         - For a list of public holidays, refer to NY GEN CONSTR § 24.
      v. *Additional time after certain kinds of service*
         - *Service by mail.* Where a period of time prescribed by law is measured from the service of a paper and service is by mail, five (5) days shall be added to the prescribed period. NY CPLR Rule 2103(b)(2).
         - *Service by overnight delivery service.* Where a period of time prescribed by law is measured from the service of a paper and service is by overnight delivery, one (1) business day shall be added to the prescribed period. NY CPLR Rule 2103(b)(6).

vi. *Daylight saving time.* For information on New York's time zone and the effect of daylight saving time, refer to NY GEN CONSTR § 52.

c. *Hours of court.* Notwithstanding any provision of law or rule of court to the contrary, throughout the State of New York the sessions of the Supreme Court for the disposition of business before the court shall commence not later than 9:30 a.m. and conclude not earlier than 5 p.m. Where warranted, the Chief Administrator of the Courts may authorize variances in the opening and closing hours of the courts, but, in such event, daily sessions shall total not less than six (6) hours. NY R CHIEF J § 3.1.

d. *Time limits; Extension of time.* Any act required by or in pursuance of law to be performed at or within a prescribed time, shall be performed according to the standard time. NY GEN CONSTR § 53.

i. Except where otherwise expressly prescribed by law, the court may extend the time fixed by any statute, rule or order for doing any act, upon such terms as may be just and upon good cause shown, whether the application for extension is made before or after the expiration of the time fixed. NY CPLR § 2004. Refer to the New York KeyRules Motion for Continuance/Extension of Time document for more information.

C. General Requirements

1. *Motions, generally.* There shall be compliance with the procedures prescribed in the CPLR for the bringing of motions. NY R UNIF TRIAL CTS § 202.7(a).

a. *Motions on notice.* A notice of motion shall specify the time and place of the hearing on the motion, the supporting papers upon which the motion is based, the relief demanded and the grounds therefor. NY CPLR Rule 2214(a). A motion on notice in an action in the supreme court shall be noticed to be heard in the judicial district where the action is triable or in a county adjoining the county where the action is triable. Unless statute, civil practice rule or local court rule provides otherwise, the motion shall be noticed to be heard before a motion term or, upon order to show cause granted by a justice, before that justice out of court. NY CPLR § 2212(a). Except as provided in NY R UNIF TRIAL CTS § 202.7(d), no motion shall be filed with the court unless there have been served and filed with the motion papers a notice of motion. NY R UNIF TRIAL CTS § 202.7(a)(1).

b. *Ex parte motions.* A motion in an action in the supreme court that may be made without notice may be made at a motion term or to a justice out of court in any county in the state. NY CPLR § 2212(b).

i. *KINGS COUNTY.* For more information on submitting a motion ex parte, refer to NY R L KINGS E FIL Doc. 1(G).

ii. *NEW YORK COUNTY.* For more information on submitting matters ex parte, refer to NY R NY CTY Procedure III and NY R NY CTY E FIL Doc. 2(G).

iii. *QUEENS COUNTY.* For more information on submitting matters ex parte, refer to NY R L QUEENS EX PARTE Doc. 1.

c. *Alternative relief.* Relief in the alternative or of several different types may be demanded. NY CPLR Rule 2214(a). The types of relief need not be related. In one motion, for example, the defendant can seek to dismiss the plaintiff's claim for lack of jurisdiction, to get an extension of time to answer, to require the plaintiff to join X as a party, and to quash a disclosure subpoena served in behalf of the plaintiff on a nonparty witness. So doing, the movant must of course specify all of these items of relief in the notice of motion, and the grounds for them, and the supporting papers must contain the entire proof requisite to the items of relief sought. NY CPLR Rule 2214(Practice Commentary, C2214:4).

d. *General relief.* It is common practice to include at the end of the relief request in the notice of motion a so-called "general relief" clause. This is merely a few words to cover the possibility that the relief appropriate to what the movant proves was not specifically asked for, but is close enough to enable the court to grant it. After stating the specific relief desired, the lawyer will often add something like: and for such other, further, or different relief as this court may deem just and proper. NY CPLR Rule 2214(Practice Commentary, C2214:5).

e. *Motion in improper form.* If the court finds it appropriate in the interests of justice, it may convert a motion into a special proceeding, or vice-versa, upon such terms as may be just, including the payment of fees and costs. NY CPLR § 103(c).

f. *Order to show cause.* An order to show cause is basically only a substitute for a notice of motion. An ordinary notice of motion merely notifies the recipient that a motion is being made for specified relief. The burden of proof is on the movant. Although in most cases it is just as innocent as an ordinary notice of motion, the order to show cause gets its name by directing the recipient to "show cause" why the particular relief being asked for should not be granted. It sounds as if the burden of proof is being shifted to the recipient. It isn't. It specifies the time and place of the hearing on the application but when the hearing comes on, the burden of proof is where it always is on a motion: on the movant. SIEGEL-NYPRAC § 248.

i. The CPLR says nothing more about an order to show cause than that it may be used "in a proper case", which leaves it entirely to the judge's discretion to determine what a proper case is. Any fact suggesting a problem as to any of the items listed above would be sufficient to invoke judicial discretion and justify the show cause procedure, which is in fact liberally used. SIEGEL-NYPRAC § 248.

ii. An order to show cause against a state body or officers must be served in addition to service upon the defendant or respondent state body or officers upon the attorney general by delivery to an assistant attorney general at an office of the attorney general in the county in which venue of the action is designated or if there is no office of the attorney general in such county, at the office of the attorney general nearest such county. NY CPLR Rule 2214(d).

iii. *BRONX COUNTY.* For information on submitting an order to show cause, refer to NY R BRONX E FIL R Doc. 2 and NY R BRONX LEG SUP Doc. 1.

iv. *ERIE COUNTY.* For information on submitting an order to show cause, refer to NY R ERIE E FIL Doc. 3(VI).

v. *KINGS COUNTY.* For information on submitting an order to show cause, refer to NY R L KINGS E FIL Doc. 1(F).

vi. *NEW YORK COUNTY.* For information on submitting an order to show cause, refer to NY R NY CTY E FIL Doc. 2(F).

vii. *ONONDAGA COUNTY.* For information on submitting an order to show cause, refer to NY R ONDGA E FIL Protocol(B)(10) and NY R ONDGA E FIL Protocol(J).

g. *Motions before preliminary conference.* Motions in actions to which NY R UNIF TRIAL CTS § 202.12 is applicable made after the preliminary conference has been scheduled may be denied unless there is shown good cause why such relief is warranted before the preliminary conference is held. NY R UNIF TRIAL CTS § 202.12(h).

h. *ALBANY COUNTY: Good faith effort to resolve.* Prior to the submission of a notice of motion relating to disclosure or a bill of particulars, the parties must make a good faith effort to resolve the matter in question and submit an affirmation attesting to this good faith effort. NY R 3 JD SUP Doc. 1(B).

i. *NEW YORK COUNTY: Documents with motions.* Counsel must attach to motion papers copies of all pleadings and other documents as required by the CPLR and as necessary for an informed decision on the motion. Documents in a foreign language shall be properly translated. NY R NY CTY J RUL Rule 14(a).

j. *NEW YORK COUNTY: Motions in multiple cases made together.* On occasion, attorneys may wish to make a motion in more than one case on a single set of papers. In such cases, by definition consolidation will not have been directed since consolidation signifies the combination of more than one case into a single one with a single caption and index number and ending in a single judgment. NY R NY CTY Procedure II(B). For more information on motions made with the same papers, refer to NY R NY CTY Procedure II(A).

k. *QUEENS COUNTY: Motion sequence numbers.* A motion sequence number is required for all E-filed motions. After a motion is E-filed, please consult the e-courts website within twenty-four (24) to forty-eight (48) hours to obtain the sequence number. The Confirmation Notice of E-filing MUST indicate the sequence number of any motion submitted at the Centralized Motion Part calendar call. NY R L QUEENS E-FILE Doc. 1(H)(5).

2. *Motion to dismiss*

a. *Grounds for dismissing cause of action.* A party may move for judgment dismissing one or more causes of action asserted against him on the ground that:

i. A defense is founded upon documentary evidence. NY CPLR Rule 3211(a)(1).

ii. The court has not jurisdiction of the subject matter of the cause of action. NY CPLR Rule 3211(a)(2).

iii. The party asserting the cause of action has not legal capacity to sue. NY CPLR Rule 3211(a)(3).

iv. There is another action pending between the same parties for the same cause of action in a court of any state or the United States; the court need not dismiss upon this ground but may make such order as justice requires. NY CPLR Rule 3211(a)(4).

v. The cause of action may not be maintained because of arbitration and award, collateral estoppel, discharge in bankruptcy, infancy or other disability of the moving party, payment, release, res judicata, statute of limitations, or statute of frauds. NY CPLR Rule 3211(a)(5).

vi. With respect to a counterclaim, it may not properly be interposed in the action. NY CPLR Rule 3211(a)(6).

vii. The pleading fails to state a cause of action. NY CPLR Rule 3211(a)(7).

viii. The court has not jurisdiction of the person of the defendant. NY CPLR Rule 3211(a)(8).

ix. The court has not jurisdiction in an action where service was made under NY CPLR § 314 or NY CPLR § 315. NY CPLR Rule 3211(a)(9).

x. The court should not proceed in the absence of a person who should be a party. NY CPLR Rule 3211. NY CPLR Rule 3211(a)(10).

xi. The party is immune from liability pursuant to NY NOT PROF CORP § 720-a. NY CPLR Rule 3211(a)(11).

xii. If the wrong ground is designated on the motion, but some other NY CPLR Rule 3211(a) ground does apply, the court can treat the motion as having specified the right ground, as long as no prejudice can be claimed. SIEGEL-NYPRAC § 258.

b. *Grounds for dismissing defense.* A party may move for judgment dismissing one or more defenses, on the ground that a defense is not stated or has no merit. NY CPLR Rule 3211(b).

c. *Grounds raised together.* It is permissible to use NY CPLR Rule 3211(a) against all claims pleaded, or against one, or a selected few. Indeed, NY CPLR Rule 3211(a) may even be used to dismiss but part of a single cause of action if the part is severable without macerating the whole case. SIEGEL-NYPRAC § 258; Forse v. Turner, 55 Misc. 2d 810, 812, 286 N.Y.S.2d 538, 541 (Sup. Ct. 1968).

i. *Grounds raised in motion or answer.* If a defendant has available a number of the objections listed in NY CPLR Rule 3211(a), NY CPLR Rule 3211(e) allows him to raise them all by a dismissal motion or, instead, plead all of them as defenses in the answer. Or, a defendant may divide them up and take some by motion and—if the motion does not succeed—plead the rest by answer. It is of course preferable as a rule to take them all by motion since an answer will not be needed at all if the motion is granted. SIEGEL-NYPRAC § 274.

- *Certain jurisdictional defects to be raised in first responsive paper.* There is an important caveat to the above rule for the objections of personal or rem jurisdiction, the grounds listed in NY CPLR Rule 3211(a)(8) and NY CPLR Rule 3211(a)(9). These objections are deemed so fundamental that wasting the court's time on a NY CPLR Rule 3211(a) motion based on any other grounds without including the jurisdictional ones waives them. SIEGEL-NYPRAC § 274; NY CPLR Rule 3211(e); Competello v. Giordano, 51 N.Y.2d 904, 905, 415 N.E.2d 965, 965 (1980).
- *Objections raised in amended answer.* Objections listed in NY CPLR Rule 3211(a) may be added in an amended answer if omitted from the original one, but while this has been held to be automatically permissible for an amendment as of course under NY CPLR Rule 3025(a), it will be allowed in an amendment by leave under NY CPLR Rule 3025(b) only if there is no prejudice to the plaintiff. SIEGEL-NYPRAC § 237; NY CPLR Rule 3025(Practice Commentaries, C3025:7). It is up to the plaintiff to show prejudice in that situation. SIEGEL-NYPRAC § 237; Lermit Plastics Co. v. C. W. Lauman & Co., 40 A.D.2d 680, 680, 336 N.Y.S.2d 187, 188 (1972).

ii. *Wrong NY CPLR Rule 3211(a) ground designated in motion.* If the wrong ground is designated on the motion, but some other NY CPLR Rule 3211(a) ground does apply, the court can treat the motion as having specified the right ground, as long as no prejudice can be claimed. SIEGEL-NYPRAC § 258.

- In one case where defendant based his motion on NY CPLR Rule 3211(a)(1), NY CPLR Rule 3211(a)(2), and NY CPLR Rule 3211(a)(8), for example, the court granted it on NY CPLR Rule 3211(a)(3) and NY CPLR Rule 3211(a)(7) instead. The court based its decision on the general relief clause contained in the notice of motion—which all well-drawn motions include—and on the absence of prejudice to plaintiff. SIEGEL-NYPRAC § 258; Nehmadi v. Davis, 95 A.D.3d 1181, 1184, 945 N.Y.S.2d 122, 125 (2012).
- If the plaintiff did not have notice of the undesignated grounds from any appropriate source, or if the court is convinced that plaintiff's opposing proof would have differed if the intended grounds had been properly designated, the court can of course deny the motion, stay it for further affidavits, etc. SIEGEL-NYPRAC § 258.

d. *Effect of bringing motion; Stay of disclosure.* Service of a notice of motion under NY CPLR Rule 3211 stays disclosure until determination of the motion unless the court orders otherwise. If the motion is based solely on the defense that the summons and complaint, summons with notice, or notice of petition and petition was not properly served, disclosure shall not be stayed unless the court orders otherwise. NY CPLR Rule 3214(b).

e. *Evidence on motion to dismiss.* Upon the hearing of a motion made under NY CPLR Rule 3211(a) or NY CPLR Rule 3211(b), either party may submit any evidence that could properly be considered on a motion for summary judgment. Whether or not issue has been joined, the court, after adequate notice to the parties, may treat the motion as a motion for summary judgment. The court may, when appropriate for the expeditious disposition of the controversy, order immediate trial of the issues raised on the motion. NY CPLR Rule 3211(c).

i. *Evidence permitted.* Affidavits, depositions, documentary proof, admissions, letters, and any other papers or proof having an evidentiary impact in the particular situation may be considered on any NY CPLR Rule 3211 motion regardless of its ground. SIEGEL-NYPRAC § 257.

ii. *Immediate trial of fact issue*

- NY CPLR Rule 3211(c) allows the court, "when appropriate for the expeditious disposition of the controversy," to order an immediate trial of an issue of fact arising on a NY CPLR Rule 3211 motion. SIEGEL-NYPRAC § 271. The power is broad, but is exercised only when the immediate trial has some potential for ending the litigation. SIEGEL-NYPRAC § 271.
- If the claim itself would have been triable by jury and the grant of the motion would effectively put an end to the case on the merits, the disputed issue must be tried by jury if either party requests it. SIEGEL-NYPRAC § 271; Herzog v. Brown, 217 A.D. 402, 404, 216 N.Y.S. 134, 136 (App. Div.), aff'd, 243 N.Y. 599, 154 N.E. 622 (1926). But if a grant of the motion would not preclude a new action for the same relief, the fact issue would not be jury triable even though the main claim itself, were its merits reached, would be. SIEGEL-NYPRAC § 271; NY CPLR Rule 3211 (Practice Commentaries, C3211:48).

f. *Facts unavailable to opposing party.* Should it appear from affidavits submitted in opposition to a motion made under NY CPLR Rule 3211(a) or NY CPLR Rule 3211(b) that facts essential to justify opposition may exist but cannot then be stated, the court may deny the motion, allowing the moving party to assert the objection in his responsive pleading, if any, or may order a continuance to permit further affidavits to be obtained or disclosure to be had and may make such other order as may be just. NY CPLR Rule 3211(d).

g. *Second motion*

i. *Original motion premature.* A second motion may be permitted on any of the NY CPLR Rule 3211(a) grounds if the first motion was premature and it was only because of the prematurity that the motion was not considered on its merits. SIEGEL-NYPRAC § 273. Where, for example, an NY CPLR Rule 3211(a)(8) motion (lack of personal jurisdiction) was made before a complaint had been served, and it was necessary to consider the complaint because jurisdiction was based on NY CPLR § 302 and the claim's New York contacts had to be examined, the court denied the motion without prejudice to renewal after service of the complaint. SIEGEL-NYPRAC § 273; Fraley v. Desilu Prods., Inc., 23 A.D.2d 79, 83, 258 N.Y.S.2d 294, 297-98 (1965).

ii. *Motion aimed at new pleading.* It is also permissible for a party to make a second NY CPLR Rule 3211 motion if each aims at a different pleading. In one case, for example, where defendant moved to dismiss plaintiff's claim and then moved to dismiss a co-defendant's crossclaim, both motions were allowed. SIEGEL-NYPRAC § 273; Nassau Roofing & Sheet Metal Co. v. Celotex Corp., 74 A.D.2d 679, 680-81, 424 N.Y.S.2d 786, 788 (1980).

iii. *Subsequent motion for summary judgment.* If the NY CPLR Rule 3211 motion is used up, motion relief is not yet lost. As long as the NY CPLR Rule 3211(a) objection has been preserved by being included as a defense in the answer, it can be made the subject of a summary judgment motion under NY CPLR Rule 3212 after the answer has been served. SIEGEL-NYPRAC § 273; SIEGEL-NYPRAC § 283. If it is, and the second motion is labeled a NY CPLR Rule 3211 motion, the court may just treat it as if it were properly labeled a summary judgment motion and dispose of it on its merits. SIEGEL-NYPRAC § 273; Hertz Corp. v. Luken, 126 A.D.2d 446, 448, 510 N.Y.S.2d 590, 593 (1987).

h. *Motion to dismiss for lack of subject matter jurisdiction.* Whenever a court lacks jurisdiction of the subject matter of a case, the way to raise the objection is by motion to dismiss under NY CPLR Rule 3211(a)(2). As is true of all the objections listed in NY CPLR Rule 3211(a), so with this one: it may be taken as a defense in the answer instead of by motion, but the motion is usually the more expeditious route. There is no time limit for moving to dismiss on the ground of lack of subject matter jurisdiction. The defect is deemed to go to the root of the court's power. SIEGEL-NYPRAC § 260; SIEGEL-NYPRAC § 272.

i. *Motion treated as one for summary judgment.* Under NY CPLR Rule 3211(c), the court is empowered to treat any NY CPLR Rule 3211 motion as a summary judgment motion. The effect of doing this will ordinarily mean that the resulting judgment is to be deemed a judgment on the merits, invoking the doctrine of res judicata.

SIEGEL-NYPRAC § 270. Refer to the New York KeyRules Motion for Summary Judgment document for more information on summary judgment.

- Because of its res judicata impact, treating a NY CPLR Rule 3211 motion as one for summary judgment is drastic. Before it can be done, therefore, the court must clearly notify the parties of its intention to make the treatment so as to enable them to submit whatever additional proof they may have to buttress their positions. SIEGEL-NYPRAC § 270; Mareno v. Kibbe, 32 A.D.2d 825, 825, 302 N.Y.S.2d 324, 325 (1969).
- The nature of the ground on which the NY CPLR Rule 3211(a)(2) motion was made may not necessarily have elicited all the evidence that might be expected on an outright summary judgment application. This notice requirement therefore offers the parties an opportunity to submit everything they've got. SIEGEL-NYPRAC § 270; State Bd. of Equalization & Assessment v. Kerwick, 72 A.D.2d 292, 301, 425 N.Y.S.2d 640, 645 (1980), aff'd, 52 N.Y.2d 557, 421 N.E.2d 803 (1981).
- To implement it, the court notifies the parties that it is considering NY CPLR Rule 3211(c)'s treat-as-summary-judgment option, that they have until X date in which to submit further proof, and that a determination of the motion will be held in abeyance until then. SIEGEL-NYPRAC § 270; Lustig v. Congregation B'Nai Israel of Midwood, 62 Misc. 2d 216, 217, 308 N.Y.S.2d 480, 482-83 (Sup. Ct. 1970).
- No matter what ground the NY CPLR Rule 3211 motion was made on, any aggregate of proof before the court that arouses the court's suspicion that this is a one-sided situation on the merits with no genuine issue of fact is sufficient to invoke this treatment. Realistically speaking, the grounds most likely to produce a record thorough enough to give the court that kind of insight into the case are NY CPLR Rule 3211(a)(7), the motion to dismiss a claim for insufficiency, and NY CPLR Rule 3211(b), the motion to dismiss a defense. SIEGEL-NYPRAC § 270; Martin v. State Liquor Auth., 43 Misc. 2d 682, 690, 252 N.Y.S.2d 365, 374 (Sup. Ct. 1964), aff'd, 15 N.Y.2d 707, 204 N.E.2d 496 (1965).
- Technically, however, the court has the power to make the summary judgment treatment regardless of the specific ground on which the NY CPLR Rule 3211 motion was originally based. SIEGEL-NYPRAC § 270.

ii. *Motion not waived.* Omitting the insufficiency objection from an initial NY CPLR Rule 3211 motion will not waive it, in any event. It is just a matter of determining what mechanical device to use for interposing the NY CPLR Rule 3211(a)(2) objection after the defendant's NY CPLR Rule 3211 motion has been used up. If NY CPLR Rule 3211 is unavailable, the defendant can raise the objection just as well with a summary judgment motion under NY CPLR Rule 3212. It is usually best for the defendant to join the insufficiency ground on any NY CPLR Rule 3211 motion the defendant chooses to make on any ground, even though it's not obligatory. SIEGEL-NYPRAC § 273.

i. *Motion to dismiss for lack of personal jurisdiction.* The motion lies whatever the nature of the defect, as long as the defect goes to personal jurisdiction. It lies if the claim has a basis for extraterritorial jurisdiction, but service was improper, or where service was proper, but made beyond the state without an extraterritorial basis. It applies where the initiatory papers are sufficient, but were not properly filed or properly served, or where the service is good, but the papers are defective. SIEGEL-NYPRAC § 266; SIEGEL-NYPRAC § 629. It applies even when the initiatory papers are well drawn and served by a proper means within the state, but the enticement or immunity doctrine applies to bar personal jurisdiction. SIEGEL-NYPRAC § 266; SIEGEL-NYPRAC § 67; SIEGEL-NYPRAC § 68.

i. *Personal jurisdiction generally.* Personal jurisdiction has to do with the court's authority to bind a particular party to its judgment. A plaintiff submits to that authority by bringing an action in the court; the defendant is subjected to it when she is served with the court's process under circumstances that require her to defend the action—i.e., when a jurisdictional basis exists against her. SIEGEL-NYPRAC § 8.

ii. *Lack of personal jurisdiction raised in answer; Tactical considerations.* For tactical reasons, a defendant sometimes prefers to include an objection to personal jurisdiction as a defense in the answer instead of taking it by motion under NY CPLR Rule 3211(a). If the action was timely commenced, but just barely, postponing the adjudication of the objection can, if it prevails, bring on a dismissal of the action too late for the plaintiff to start over. The plaintiff had best be alert to this. SIEGEL-NYPRAC § 266; SIEGEL-NYPRAC § 269.

iii. *Lack of personal jurisdiction as to some claims.* If the lack of jurisdiction affects the whole complaint, as where the defendant maintains that he was never served with process, the motion seeks dismissal of the entire action. If it affects only a given claim, as where the defendant was served outside New York and one claim has a basis for extraterritorial service under NY CPLR § 302 and NY CPLR § 313, but another has not, the motion seeks to strike only the latter. SIEGEL-NYPRAC § 266.

iv. *Improper service.* With the objection of improper service a special rule governs: if the defendant takes the objection as a defense in the answer, the defendant must move for judgment on it within sixty (60) days or the objection is waived. SIEGEL-NYPRAC § 266; NY CPLR Rule 3211(e); SIEGEL-NYPRAC § 274. Note that this applies only to the objection of improper service, which is just one of several specific objections that fall under the category of "jurisdiction of the person." SIEGEL-NYPRAC § 266.

- The court may grant a discretionary extension, but only upon a showing of "undue hardship", a strict standard that has been held more demanding than the "good cause" showing that can earn time extensions in other contexts. SIEGEL-NYPRAC § 266; Abitol v. Schiff, 180 Misc. 2d 949, 951, 691 N.Y.S.2d 753, 755 (Sup. Ct. 1999), aff'd as modified, 276 A.D.2d 571, 714 N.Y.S.2d 880 (2000).

j. *Motion to dismiss for failure to state a cause of action.* One of the most important and frequently used dismissal grounds is the failure to state a cause of action of NY CPLR Rule 3211(a)(7). The motion of course lies if the pleading is defective on its face, and in that respect it's the equivalent of the old common law demurrer (presumably long since abandoned in New York), which conceded the truth of everything pleaded but contended that, even so, the pleading stated nothing actionable under the law. SIEGEL-NYPRAC § 265.

i. *Motion attacking perfectly plead claim.* More important under the Civil Practice Law and Rules is that the motion may be made even against a claim perfectly pleaded. SIEGEL-NYPRAC § 265; Kelly v. Bank of Buffalo, 32 A.D.2d 875, 875, 302 N.Y.S.2d 60, 60-61 (1969). At least the way the Civil Practice Law and Rules' drafters envisioned it, the motion may—upon affidavits and the same kind of other proof that might be used on any NY CPLR Rule 3211 motion—go behind the pleading and prove that the claim lacks merit. And since pleadings have been so successfully informalized by the Civil Practice Law and Rules, so that it does not take much to "state" a cause of action, the NY CPLR Rule 3211(a)(7) motion is used more often today to attack the merits of the claim than to attack its articulation. SIEGEL-NYPRAC § 265; Foley v. D'Agostino, 21 A.D.2d 60, 62, 248 N.Y.S.2d 121, 124-25 (1964).

- Of course, in order to succeed on the motion, the defendant must convince the court that nothing the plaintiff can reasonably be expected to prove would help; that the plaintiff just doesn't have a claim. The criterion for determining such a motion is akin to that used to decide a motion for summary judgment, for which reason the court may treat the motion as such if the court is so disposed and the proof warrants it. SIEGEL-NYPRAC § 265; SIEGEL-NYPRAC § 270; SIEGEL-NYPRAC § 272.

ii. *Plaintiff's burden.* As long as the complaint states a claim on its face, the plaintiff need not—in response to the defendant's NY CPLR Rule 3211(a)(7) objection—come forward with affidavits or other proof unless the court does in fact elect to treat the motion as one for summary judgment. SIEGEL-NYPRAC § 265; Rovello v. Orofino Realty Co., 40 N.Y.2d 633, 636, 357 N.E.2d 970, 972 (1976).

- This has resulted in holdings that the court cannot even consider the defendant's affidavits on a NY CPLR Rule 3211(a)(7) motion unless and until it has elected to exercise its treat-as-summary-judgment power. SIEGEL-NYPRAC § 265; Henbest & Morrisey Inc. v. W.H. Ins. Agency Inc., 259 A.D.2d 829, 829, 686 N.Y.S.2d 207, 208 (1999).
- This might in turn lead defendants to assume that they should not even bother submitting affidavits. Defendants should make no such assumption unless, of course, it is their intention to test only the face of the complaint. SIEGEL-NYPRAC § 265; SIEGEL-NYPRAC § 270; SIEGEL-NYPRAC § 275.

iii. *Allegations of pleading deemed true for purpose of motion.* For purposes of a NY CPLR Rule 3211(a)(7) motion, especially when it attacks the pleading on its face, the allegations of the pleading are deemed to be true. More than that, the pleading will be deemed to allege whatever may be implied from its statements by reasonable intendment. In sum, the pleader is entitled to every favorable inference that might be drawn. SIEGEL-NYPRAC § 265; Underpinning & Found. Constructors, Inc. v. Chase Manhattan Bank, N.A., 46 N.Y.2d 459, 462, 386 N.E.2d 1319, 1320 (1979); Natixis Real Estate Capital Tr. 2007-HE2 v. Natixis Real Estate Holdings, LLC, 149 A.D.3d 127, 50 N.Y.S.3d 13 (N.Y. App. Div. 2017).

iv. *When plead in answer.* While the general rule about the NY CPLR Rule 3211(a) objections is that any of them can at the defendant's option be used as a defense in the answer instead of being taken by motion under NY CPLR Rule 3211, there was some doubt about whether this was true of the NY CPLR Rule 3211(a)(7) objection of failure to state a cause of action. That objection is implicit in the very fact that there's a lawsuit, a tune imbedded in the vocal chords of just about every defendant. The Second Department had held that the objection cannot be stated in the answer and that the plaintiff may therefore move to strike such a defense under NY CPLR Rule 3211(b). The court reversed itself in Butler v. Catinella, 58 A.D.3d 145, 868 N.Y.S.2d 101 (2008), however, and adopted the First Department position, which is that the inclusion of the defense in the answer is surplusage at worst and that no motion by the plaintiff lies under NY CPLR Rule 3211(b) to strike the defense. Such a motion would, in effect, "amount[] to an endeavor by the plaintiff to test the sufficiency of his or her own claim." Furthermore, the objection is so fundamental that the defendant can raise it at any time during the action, whether pleaded as a defense in the answer or not. SIEGEL-NYPRAC § 265; Butler v. Catinella, 58 A.D.3d 145, 868 N.Y.S.2d 101 (2008).

v. *Motion to dismiss in cases involving licensed architects, engineers, land surveyors or landscape architects.* For information on special requirements for dismissal under NY CPLR Rule 3211(a)(7) of a case against professional architects, engineers, and surveyors, refer to NY CPLR Rule 3211(h).

k. *Motion to dismiss for failure to join indispensable parties.* The conclusion of whether a party's presence is necessary is reached only as a last resort today if it is reached at all. Considering the numerous alternatives available to the court, it is a rare case in which such a dismissal is warranted, and so the mission of NY CPLR Rule 3211(a)(10) is a curtailed one. SIEGEL-NYPRAC § 268; NY CPLR § 1001(b). But if the issue does arise, as it does from time to time, the defendant can raise the issue by a motion to dismiss under NY CPLR Rule 3211(a)(10). SIEGEL-NYPRAC § 268; Storrs v. Holcomb, 245 A.D.2d 943, 945, 666 N.Y.S.2d 835, 837 (1997).

i. *Nonjoinder; Misjoinder distinguished.* Nonjoinder of a party who should be joined under NY CPLR § 1001 is a ground for dismissal of an action without prejudice unless the court allows the action to proceed without that party under the provisions of that section. Misjoinder of parties is not a ground for dismissal of an action. Parties may be added at any stage of the action by leave of court or by stipulation of all parties who have appeared, or once without leave of court within twenty (20) days after service of the original summons or at anytime before the period for responding to that summons expires or within twenty (20) days after service of a pleading responding to it. NY CPLR § 1003.

ii. *Parties which need not be joined.* Except where otherwise prescribed by order of the court, an executor, administrator, guardian of the property of an infant, committee of the property of a judicially declared incompetent, conservator of the property of a conservatee, trustee of an express trust, insured person who has executed to his insurer either a loan or subrogation receipt, trust agreement, or other similar agreement, or person with whom or in whose name a contract has been made for the benefit of another, may sue or be sued without joining with him the person for or against whose interest the action is brought. NY CPLR § 1004.

l. *Motion to dismiss for inconvenient forum.* When the court finds that in the interest of substantial justice the action should be heard in another forum, the court, on the motion of any party, may stay or dismiss the action in whole or in part on any conditions that may be just. The domicile or residence in this state of any party to the action shall not preclude the court from staying or dismissing the action. NY CPLR Rule 327(a).

i. Notwithstanding the provisions of NY CPLR Rule 327(a), the court shall not stay or dismiss any action on the ground of inconvenient forum, where the action arises out of or relates to a contract, agreement or undertaking to which NY GEN OBLIG § 5-1402 applies, and the parties to the contract have agreed that the law of this state shall govern their rights or duties in whole or in part. NY CPLR Rule 327(b).

ii. Refer to the New York KeyRules Motion to Transfer Venue document for information on moving a case to a different venue.

m. *Grounds when motion based on rights to public petition and participation.* A motion to dismiss based on NY CPLR Rule 3211(a)(7), in which the moving party has demonstrated that the action, claim, cross claim or counterclaim subject to the motion is an action involving public petition and participation as defined in NY CIV RTS § 76-a(a), shall be granted unless the party responding to the motion demonstrates that the cause of action has a substantial basis in law or is supported by a substantial argument for an extension, modification or reversal of existing law. The court shall grant preference in the hearing of such motion. NY CPLR Rule 3211(g).

3. *Oppositions.* In the absence of statutory provision or court rule, a motion ordinarily does not require a written answer, although an adverse party may be permitted to file an answer in opposition to the showing made in the motion or its supporting affidavits. AMJUR MOTIONS § 26. When a party files a motion and the opposing party fails to respond, the court may construe such failure to respond as non-opposition to the motion or an admission that the motion was meritorious, may take the facts alleged in the motion as true, and may grant the motion if the relief requested appears to be justified. However, the severity of such a result demands that a court impose it only with great caution. AMJUR MOTIONS § 28.

4. *Effect of defendant's appearance.* Subject to the provisions of NY CPLR Rule 320(c), an appearance of the defendant is

equivalent to personal service of the summons upon him, unless an objection to jurisdiction under NY CPLR Rule 3211(a)(8) is asserted by motion or in the answer as provided in NY CPLR Rule 3211. NY CPLR Rule 320(b).

a. *Appearance not conferring jurisdiction; Limited appearance.* When the court's jurisdiction is not based upon personal service on the defendant, an appearance is not equivalent to personal service upon the defendant:

   i. In a case specified in NY CPLR § 314(3), if jurisdiction is based solely upon a levy on defendant's property within the state pursuant to an order of attachment; or

   ii. In any other case specified in NY CPLR § 314, if an objection to jurisdiction under NY CPLR Rule 3211(a)(8) or NY CPLR Rule 3211(a)(9), or both, is asserted by motion or in the answer as provided in NY CPLR Rule 3211, unless the defendant proceeds with the defense after asserting the objection to jurisdiction and the objection is not ultimately sustained. NY CPLR Rule 320(c).

b. *Effect on publication of summons.* Where the defendant appears during the period of publication of a summons against him, the service by publication shall be deemed completed by the appearance. NY CPLR Rule 320(d).

5. *Governing law.* The civil practice law and rules (NY CPLR § 101, et seq.) shall govern the procedure in civil judicial proceedings in all courts of the state and before all judges, except where the procedure is regulated by inconsistent statute. The civil practice law and rules shall succeed the civil practice act and rules of civil practice and shall be deemed substituted therefor throughout the statutes and rules of the state. NY CPLR § 101. The civil practice law and rules shall be liberally construed to secure the just, speedy and inexpensive determination of every civil judicial proceeding. NY CPLR § 104.

   a. *Uniform trial court rules.* The uniform civil rules for the Supreme Court and County Court (NY R UNIF TRIAL CTS § 202.1, et seq.) shall be applicable to civil actions and proceedings in the Supreme Court and the County Court. NY R UNIF TRIAL CTS § 202.1(a). The provisions of the uniform rules shall be construed consistent with the Civil Practice Law and Rules (CPLR), and matters not covered by the uniform rules shall be governed by the CPLR. NY R UNIF TRIAL CTS § 202.1(d).

   b. *Local rules.* Local court rules, not inconsistent with law or with uniform civil rules for the Supreme Court and County Court (NY R UNIF TRIAL CTS § 202.1, et seq.), shall comply with Part 9 of the Rules of the Chief Judge (NY R CHIEF J § 9.1). NY R UNIF TRIAL CTS § 202.1(c).

   c. *Official forms.* The state administrator shall have the power to adopt, amend and rescind an appendix of forms. Forms adopted pursuant to NY CPLR § 107 shall be sufficient under the civil practice law and rules and shall illustrate the simplicity and brevity of statement which the civil practice law and rules contemplate. NY CPLR § 107.

6. *Rules of the commercial division.* [Editor's note: certain types of civil cases or civil cases meeting certain monetary thresholds that are filed in the state of New York must be filed in the Commercial Division of the New York Supreme Courts. Rules governing practice in the commercial division are found in NY R UNIF TRIAL CTS § 202.70]. Cases which must be filed in the commercial division are listed below. For more information, refer to NY R UNIF TRIAL CTS § 202.70.

   a. *Monetary thresholds.* Except as set forth in NY R UNIF TRIAL CTS § 202.70(b), the monetary thresholds of the Commercial Division, exclusive of punitive damages, interests, costs, disbursements and counsel fees claimed, are established as follows: (1) Albany County, fifty thousand dollars ($50,000); (2) Eighth Judicial District, one hundred thousand dollars ($100,000); (3) Kings County, one hundred fifty thousand dollars ($150,000); (4) Nassau County, two hundred thousand dollars ($200,000); (5) New York County, five hundred thousand dollars ($500,000); (6) Onondaga County, fifty thousand dollars ($50,000); (7) Queens County, one hundred thousand dollars ($100,000); (8) Seventh Judicial District, fifty thousand dollars ($50,000); (9) Suffolk County, one hundred thousand dollars ($100,000); and (10) Westchester County, one hundred thousand dollars ($100,000). NY R UNIF TRIAL CTS § 202.70(a).

      i. *ALBANY COUNTY.* The Commercial Division of the Albany County Supreme Court exercises jurisdiction over selected business and commercial disputes in which the amount at issue generally involves damage claims in a minimum amount of fifty thousand dollars ($50,000) as well as claims for unspecified amounts where the value of the commercial asset(s) in dispute exceeds fifty thousand dollars ($50,000). A separate publication promulgating the rules and criteria relating to the filing and management of Commercial Court cases in this part may be obtained from the Albany County Supreme Court Clerk's Office. A section of the Uniform Civil Rules for the Supreme Court and County Court sets forth statewide rules. NY R 3 JD SUP Doc. 1(E).

      ii. *BRONX COUNTY.* The monetary threshold for commercial cases in Bronx County will be seventy-five thousand dollars ($75,000). All other parameters including the type of matters that will be heard are contained within the Rules of the Commercial Division of the Supreme Court (NY R UNIF TRIAL CTS § 202.70). NY R BRONX FIL R Doc. 12.

iii. *NEW YORK COUNTY.* The monetary threshold in the New York County Commercial Division, which is generally applicable, is an amount in controversy of five hundred thousand dollars ($500,000) or more (exclusive of punitive damages, interest, costs, disbursements, and counsel fees). If the case is designated a commercial one and the Addendum is submitted, the clerk will review the pleadings to determine whether the amount in controversy in the case meets the monetary threshold or whether an exception to the threshold applies. NY R NY CTY Procedure IA(B). For more information on assigning a case to the commercial division in New York County, refer to NY R NY CTY Procedure IA(B).

b. *Commercial cases.* Actions in which the principal claims involve or consist of the following will be heard in the Commercial Division provided that the monetary threshold is met or equitable or declaratory relief is sought:

i. Breach of contract or fiduciary duty, fraud, misrepresentation, business tort (e.g., unfair competition), or statutory and/or common law violation where the breach or violation is alleged to arise out of business dealings (e.g., sales of assets or securities; corporate restructuring; partnership, shareholder, joint venture, and other business agreements; trade secrets; restrictive covenants; and employment agreements not including claims that principally involve alleged discriminatory practices);

ii. Transactions governed by the Uniform Commercial Code (exclusive of those concerning individual cooperative or condominium units);

iii. Transactions involving commercial real property, including Yellowstone injunctions and excluding actions for the payment of rent only;

iv. Shareholder derivative actions—without consideration of the monetary threshold;

v. Commercial class actions—without consideration of the monetary threshold;

vi. Business transactions involving or arising out of dealings with commercial banks and other financial institutions;

vii. Internal affairs of business organizations;

viii. Malpractice by accountants or actuaries, and legal malpractice arising out of representation in commercial matters;

ix. Environmental insurance coverage;

x. Commercial insurance coverage (e.g., directors and officers, errors and omissions, and business interruption coverage);

xi. Dissolution of corporations, partnerships, limited liability companies, limited liability partnerships and joint ventures—without consideration of the monetary threshold; and

xii. Applications to stay or compel arbitration and affirm or disaffirm arbitration awards and related injunctive relief pursuant to Article 75 of the New York Civil Practice Law and Rules (NY CPLR § 7501, et seq.) involving any of the foregoing enumerated commercial issues. Where the applicable arbitration agreement provides for the arbitration to be heard outside the United States, the monetary threshold set forth in NY R UNIF TRIAL CTS § 202.70(a) shall not apply. NY R UNIF TRIAL CTS § 202.70(b).

c. *Non-commercial cases.* The following will not be heard in the Commercial Division even if the monetary threshold is met:

i. Suits to collect professional fees;

ii. Cases seeking a declaratory judgment as to insurance coverage for personal injury or property damage;

iii. Residential real estate disputes, including landlord-tenant matters, and commercial real estate disputes involving the payment of rent only;

iv. Home improvement contracts involving residential properties consisting of one to four residential units or individual units in any residential building, including cooperative or condominium units;

v. Proceedings to enforce a judgment regardless of the nature of the underlying case;

vi. First-party insurance claims and actions by insurers to collect premiums or rescind non-commercial policies; and

vii. Attorney malpractice actions except as otherwise provided in NY R UNIF TRIAL CTS § 202.70(b)(8). NY R UNIF TRIAL CTS § 202.70(c).

d. For more information on the Commercial Division, refer to NY R UNIF TRIAL CTS § 202.70.

D. Documents

1. *Documents for moving party*

a. *Required documents*

i. *Notice of motion, order to show cause, or affidavit on ex parte motion.* The notice of motion shall be substantially in the form found in NY R UNIF TRIAL CTS § 202.7(b). NY R UNIF TRIAL CTS § 202.7(b). The supporting papers should be referred to in the notice of motion. SIEGEL-NYPRAC § 246. The court in a proper case may grant an order to show cause, to be served in lieu of a notice of motion. NY CPLR Rule 2214(d). An ex parte motion shall be accompanied by an affidavit stating the result of any prior motion for similar relief and specifying the new facts, if any, that were not previously shown. NY CPLR Rule 2217(b).

- *Request for oral argument.* A party requesting oral argument shall set forth such request in its notice of motion or in its order to show cause or on the first page of the answering papers, as the case may be. Where all parties to a motion request oral argument, oral argument shall be granted unless the court shall determine it to be unnecessary. Where a motion is brought on by order to show cause, the court may set forth in the order that oral argument is required on the return date of the motion. NY R UNIF TRIAL CTS § 202.8(d).

ii. *Motion.* Refer to the General Requirements section of this document for information on the notice of motion and motion.

iii. *Request for judicial intervention.* At any time after service of process, a party may file a request for judicial intervention. Except as provided in NY R UNIF TRIAL CTS § 202.6(b), in an action not yet assigned to a judge, the court shall not accept for filing a notice of motion, order to show cause, or application for ex parte order, unless such notice or application is accompanied by a request for judicial intervention. NY R UNIF TRIAL CTS § 202.6(a).

- *BRONX COUNTY.* Generally, the Request For Judicial Intervention, commonly referred to as an "RJI", is required to be filed in any action where the assignment of a Justice is required. The RJI sets forth the information which is entered into the court system's database. It must be completely and accurately filled out. The full caption, as stated on the Summons, must be set forth. Use of terms "et al." and "etc." are not permitted. Only one (1) RJI may be filed in each action. Either a self represented litigant or an attorney must sign the affirmation at the end of the form. Once completed, the RJI must be filed in duplicate. Except in the case of an ex-parte application, the RJI must also be served together with the accompanying application upon all parties. Proof of accuracy of the index number must accompany the RJI. Check the Fee Schedule[. . .]for any applicable filing fees. NY R BRONX FIL R Doc. 2.
- *KINGS COUNTY.* An RJI with the relevant required addendum in a NYSCEF case shall be submitted via NYSCEF. Once e-filed, the RJI and any accompanying document will be forwarded to the relevant support office for random assignment of the case and processing of the document. A filer or counsel need not appear (as to Proposed Orders to Show Cause, however, see below). A copy of the pleadings must be submitted only if the document has not previously been e-filed. If the RJI seeks intervention with regard to a document that is intended for review by a Justice, such as a motion, a working copy of the RJI must be submitted with the working copy of the motion and the NYSCEF Confirmation Notice. NY R L KINGS E FIL Doc. 1(C).
- *NEW YORK COUNTY.* To obtain the assignment of an IAS Justice to a case, a Request for Judicial Intervention (cost ninety-five dollars ($95)) must be filed, with NYSCEF in an e-filed case or in paper in an authorized hard-copy one. A no-fee RJI, which will generally result in the referral of an application to an Ex Parte Justice, is also required with regard to certain kinds of applications for which, prior to 2011, no RJI was required. NY R NY CTY Procedure I(C). A "fillable" form RJI is available on-line. The form must be filed in duplicate in hard-copy cases. NY R NY CTY Procedure IA(A)(1). The filer of an RJI must check off a box identifying the type of case at issue. Where the RJI seeks judicial assignment, this designation will bring about a random assignment of the case by computer to a Justice handling cases of that type. NY R NY CTY Procedure IA(A)(1). The RJI and any addendum can be completed and submitted electronically in an e-filed case. NY R NY CTY Procedure II(A). The RJI shall be marked to reflect the existence of any "related case" as explained on the "Commencement of Cases" page under "Case Processing" on the court's website. NY R NY CTY Procedure II(A); NY R NY CTY E FIL Doc. 2(C).
- *ONONDAGA COUNTY.* The RJI will be submitted via the NYSCEF system along with any required RJI addendum forms. When the RJI is filed and the fee paid online, the Onondaga County Clerk's Office will electronically forward the RJI and any accompanying documents to the Onondaga Supreme Court Clerk's Office for assignment and processing. Counsel will receive notification of judge assignment via the NYSCEF system. NY R ONDGA E FIL Protocol(B)(3).

- *QUEENS COUNTY.* A Request for Judicial Intervention ("RJI") in an E-filed case shall be submitted via the E-filing System. When the RJI is approved, filed and paid for on-line, it will be forwarded to the relevant back office for random assignment of the case and processing of the document. In the case of RJIs seeking assignment to the Commercial Division, the filer must submit therewith, a Commercial Addendum as required by the standards for assignment of cases to the Commercial Division. NY R L QUEENS E-FILE Doc. 1(F).

iv. *Proof of service.* In addition to complying with the provisions of NY CPLR Rule 2101, every paper filed in court shall have annexed thereto appropriate proof of service on all parties where required. NY R UNIF TRIAL CTS § 202.5(a).

- *QUEENS COUNTY.* With regard to service of a motion/petition on notice in an E-filed action, NY CPLR Rule 2214(b) and NY R UNIF TRIAL CTS § 202.5-b(f) applies. Where required, proof of service shall be filed on-line as a separate document. NY R L QUEENS E-FILE Doc. 1(H)(3).

v. *ALBANY COUNTY: Additional required documents*

- *Affirmation of good faith effort.* The parties must[. . .]submit an affirmation attesting to [their good faith effort to resolve the matter]. The affirmation of good faith effort to resolve the issues raised by the motion shall indicate the time, place and nature of the consultation and the issues discussed and any resolutions, or shall indicate good cause why no such conferral with counsel for opposing parties was held. An assigned justice or judge may dismiss a motion for failure to demonstrate that such effort was made with leave to renew the motion after such effort has been demonstrated. NY R 3 JD SUP Doc. 1(B).

b. *Supplemental documents*

i. *Supporting evidence; Exhibits.* The main supporting papers on a motion are affidavits, but any relevant exhibits, documents, depositions, etc., are also includible. SIEGEL-NYPRAC § 246.

- *Affidavits accompanying motion.* Affidavits shall be for a statement of the relevant facts. NY R UNIF TRIAL CTS § 202.8(c).
- *Foreign language documents.* Where an affidavit or exhibit annexed to a paper served or filed is in a foreign language, it shall be accompanied by an English translation and an affidavit by the translator stating his qualifications and that the translation is accurate. NY CPLR Rule 2101(b).
- *Statement of attorney in lieu of affidavit.* The statement of an attorney admitted to practice in the courts of the state, or of a physician, osteopath or dentist, authorized by law to practice in the state, who is not a party to an action, when subscribed and affirmed by him to be true under the penalties of perjury, may be served or filed in the action in lieu of and with the same force and effect as an affidavit. NY CPLR Rule 2106.
- *NEW YORK COUNTY: Form of presented exhibits.* Exhibits should be tabbed and be legible; a typed version of any exhibit that is difficult to read should be submitted with the original. Exhibits printed on both sides of the page should be bound and tabbed on the side. NY R NY CTY J RUL Rule 14(a).
- *QUEENS COUNTY.* Attorneys submitting exhibits to the court on E-file cases shall make each exhibit a separate, labeled attachment to an affidavit/affirmation. NY R L QUEENS E-FILE Doc. 1(H)(4).

ii. *Brief.* Briefs shall be for a statement of the relevant law. NY R UNIF TRIAL CTS § 202.8(c).

iii. *Notice to produce papers not in possession of the court.* If a paper relied on by the movant is in the possession of the other side, it may be demanded of that side with a notice to produce it at the hearing. Where such papers are in the possession of an adverse party, they shall be produced by him at the hearing on notice served with the motion papers. NY CPLR Rule 2214(Practice Commentary, C2214:23).

iv. *Filing fees.* The County Clerk shall require the payment of any applicable statutory fees, or an order of the Court waiving payment of such fees, before accepting a paper for filing. NY R UNIF TRIAL CTS § 202.5(d)(1). For information on filing fees, if any, refer to NY CPLR § 8001, et seq.

- *ALBANY COUNTY.* In general, any filing subsequent to the commencement of an action which is designated as a motion or cross-motion requires the payment of a filing fee to the County Clerk's Office prior to submission to the Supreme Court Clerk's Office for referral to the assigned justice. The fee is assessed regardless of whether an application is made by notice of motion, order to show cause or ex parte. No fee will be charged upon the filing of a motion for poor person status in conjunction with an application which serves to commence an action or special proceeding. In the event a motion is received by the court unaccompanied by proof of payment to the County Clerk, the Supreme Court Clerk's Office will contact the submitting party to advise that the application will be held pending receipt of the filing fee only until the return date of the motion. If proof of payment is not submitted to the Supreme Court Clerk's Office by the return date (ex parte applications will be held ten (10) days), the papers will be returned by mail with a notification that the motion has been removed from the court's calendar and that it must be re-noticed and re-filed with the court along with the requisite filing fee. Inquiries concerning the applicability of the motion fee to a proposed filing may be directed to the Supreme Court Clerk's Office. NY R 3 JD SUP Doc. 1(B).

- *BRONX COUNTY.* In accordance with the new civil fee schedule set forth in Article 80 of the C.P.L.R. (NY CPLR § 8001, et seq.), effective July 14, 2003, all motions, and cross motions must be approved in Room 217 prior to payment of said fees in the County Clerk's Office, Room 118. NY R BRONX FIL R Doc. 8. The motion fee [must be] paid for via NYSCEF by credit/debit card. NY R BRONX E FIL R Doc. 1(1).
- *ERIE COUNTY.* Payment for fee-bearing NYSCEF documents must be made online via credit or debit card (American Express, MasterCard or Visa) at the time of submission. NY R ERIE E FIL Doc. 3(III)(E).
- *KINGS COUNTY.* The motion must be filed with NYSCEF and the motion fee paid. NY R L KINGS E FIL Doc. 1(D). Court fees in NYSCEF cases must be paid via NYSCEF by a credit or bank card (MasterCard, Visa, or American Express). Fees are no longer accepted in person in the Kings County Clerk's Office in NYSCEF cases. NY R L KINGS E FIL Doc. 1(B)(6).
- *NEW YORK COUNTY.* A motion fee must be paid on motions made in writing by notice of motion, order to show cause or ex parte after the commencement of an action. For this purpose, the term "action" shall mean any application to the court that requires the assignment of an index number, regardless of whether a formal pleading is filed. Applications or motions that commence an action and for which an index number fee must be paid require no motion fee. [A]ny motions made after the initial applications in these situations would require payment of the motion fee. A motion that is the initial application in a case commenced by the filing of a summons and complaint would require a motion fee since the filing of the summons and complaint rather than the application itself would require the purchase of an index number. NY R NY CTY Procedure II(A). In e-filed cases the motion fee must be paid when the documents are filed. Payment is made on-line by Visa, Mastercard, or American Express credit or bank card. NY R NY CTY Procedure II(A); NY R NY CTY E FIL Doc. 2(B)(5).
- *ONONDAGA COUNTY.* Court fees in e-filed cases must be paid online with the NYSCEF system using a credit card. The document is not considered to have been filed until payment of the fee has been tendered. NY R ONDGA E FIL Protocol(B)(2). Fees must be paid on all cross motions. NY R ONDGA E FIL Protocol(B)(9)(e).
- *QUEENS COUNTY.* The Motion Support Office does not receive, forward or process any fees or waiver of fees. All applications requiring payment of statutory fees or waiver of fees must be sent directly to the Queens County Clerk's office. NY R L QUEENS MOT SUP Doc. 1. Court fees (e.g., RJI fee, motion fee) in E-filed cases may be paid for on-line using a credit card. Papers may also be filed with the E-file system and the fee may be paid at the County Clerk's Office. In the latter case, the paper is not considered to have been filed until payment of the fee has been tendered. NY R L QUEENS E-FILE Doc. 1(E)(1). The motion/petition shall be filed on-line and the fee paid for either on-line by credit card or by the "Pay at the County Clerk's Office" option. NY R L QUEENS E-FILE Doc. 1(H)(1).

v. *Working copies.* The court may require the parties to provide working copies of documents filed electronically. In such event, each working copy shall include, firmly affixed thereto, a copy of a confirmation notice in a form prescribed by the Chief Administrator. NY R UNIF TRIAL CTS § 202.5-b(d)(5).

- *BRONX COUNTY.* After papers on motions have been e-filed, working copies thereof, with Confirmation Notice firmly attached as the back page facing out, must be submitted. (Each document or group of documents that is separately bound shall bear a Confirmation Notice.) Working copies lacking the Notice will not be accepted. WORKING COPIES OF MOTION PAPERS MUST BE SUBMITTED NO LATER THAN 4:45 P.M. ON THE RETURN DATE IN THE MOTION SUPPORT OFFICE (ROOM 217) AS EXPLAINED in NY R BRONX E FIL R Doc. 1(4). If an attorney has failed to submit required working copies on or before the return date, the motion will be transmitted as is to the Justice for such action as the Justice finds appropriate. Attorneys may submit working copies on motions by mail or overnight delivery. Any such submission shall be sent in a timely manner to the Motion Support Office (Room 217) and be conspicuously marked on the outside "NYSCEF Matter"; lack of such marking may delay processing. NY R BRONX E FIL R Doc. 1(4)(a).

- *ERIE COUNTY.* Electronically filed documents subject to review and processing by the Part Clerk do not require a working copy unless otherwise directed or provided for in IAS Part Rules. NY R UNIF TRIAL CTS § 202.5-b(d)(4), any working copy submitted shall include, as a cover page firmly fastened thereto, a copy of the Confirmation Notice generated by the NYSCEF site at the time of filing. Please consult the individual Justice's Part Rules and/or consult with the Judge's chambers to determine whether and how working copies are to be provided. Working copies will not be printed or delivered by the Erie County Clerk or the Chief Clerk of the Courts or any of their personnel to chambers. The official record of a document in an electronically filed case is the document filed via the NYSCEF system. Working copies are intended only for use by the Justice. The Court will discard all working copies after the Justice has finished with them. Thus, in the event that counsel fails to file a document via the NYSCEF system, the document will not be part of the court record. NY R ERIE E FIL Doc. 3(III)(O); NY R ERIE E FIL Doc. 3(V)(E).
- *KINGS COUNTY.* No courtesy copies of motion papers are required by the Court, except as may be required for electronic filing or by the Judge's Part Rules. In tort cases against the City of New York, courtesy copies shall be supplied to the Corporation Counsel's office in Brooklyn. NY R L KINGS Pt. C, Rule 5. Unless otherwise directed by the Court or as described herein, and with the exceptions listed below, in all NYSCEF cases in which an RJI has been filed, working copies of e-filed documents that are intended for judicial review must be submitted to the court. Working copies are not required of documents that are only processed by a support office (e.g. preliminary conference request, note of issue). Working copies shall include exhibit tabs and backs; for motion papers, the motion sequence number and the return date and part. The confirmation notice with the motion sequence number on it should be the back page of the motion facing out. In addition, the filer of a working copy must firmly bind thereto, with the back page facing out, a copy of the Confirmation Notice that was generated by NYSCEF when that document was efiled. Working copies that are submitted without the related Confirmation Notice will not be accepted. NY R L KINGS E FIL Doc. 1(B)(7); NY R L KINGS E FIL Doc. 1(D). WORKING COPIES OF MOTION PAPERS MUST BE SUBMITTED IN THE MOTION SUPPORT OFFICE (ROOM 227) AS EXPLAINED HEREIN. THEY MUST NOT BE DELIVERED TO THE PART OR CHAMBERS, EXCEPT WHERE THE INDIVIDUAL JUSTICE'S PART RULES PROVIDE OTHERWISE; DOING SO WILL CAUSE ADMINISTRATIVE CONFUSION AND POSSIBLE MISPLACEMENT OF PAPERS. Any such submission shall be sent in a timely manner (kindly review individual Justice's rules) and be conspicuously marked on the outside "NYSCEF Matter;" lack of such marking may delay processing. NY R L KINGS E FIL Doc. 1(D).
- *NEW YORK COUNTY.* Some Justices require that working copies of e-filed motion papers be submitted. See the E-filing Protocol for information on the many Parts that do not require working copies. Where required, working copies of the moving documents and all other documents on the motion or application shall be submitted to the Motion Submission Part Courtroom (Room 130) on, but not before, the final return date. A Confirmation Notice from the NYSCEF system, which is generated when a document is e-filed, shall be firmly affixed, as the back page facing out, to each separate working copy or group of such copies. NY R NY CTY Procedure II(A) NY R NY CTY E FIL Doc. 2(B)(5)(a); NY R NY CTY J RUL Rule 14(a). For more information on working copies, including which parts don't require them, refer to NY R NY CTY E FIL Doc. 2(B)(6).
- *ONONDAGA COUNTY.* Any courtesy "working" copies, if required (see NY R ONDGA E FIL Protocol(B)(7)), must be provided directly to the assigned justice. NY R ONDGA E FIL Protocol(B)(9)(e). For information as to whether or not an Onondaga Supreme Court Justice requires working (courtesy) copies of e-filed documents, please consult the Onondaga County Individual E-filing Rules. NY R ONDGA E FIL Protocol(B)(7)(a). The Supreme Court Clerk's Office and the Onondaga County Clerk's Office will NOT accept the working copies. Working copies must be sent directly to the assigned justice's chambers. NY R ONDGA E FIL Protocol(B)(7)(b). A copy of the Confirmation Notice, generated by the NYSCEF system at the time a document is e-filed, must be attached to every working copy provided to chambers. If the Confirmation Notice is missing, the copy will not be accepted. NY R ONDGA E FIL Protocol(B)(7)(c). Courtesy copies do not become part of the official court record as maintained by the Onondaga County Clerk's Office and will be destroyed by chambers at the disposition of the case. In the event that counsel fails to file a document via NYSCEF, the document will not be part of the court record. NY R ONDGA E FIL Protocol(B)(7)(d).
- *QUEENS COUNTY.* Working copies of E-Filed notices of motion/notices of petition are NOT to be sent to the Motion Support Office. They must be brought to the calendar call in the judge's part. NY R L QUEENS

MOT SUP Doc. 1. Unless otherwise directed or authorized by the court, counsel should file papers with the E-file system first and thereafter deliver a working copy to at the calendar call of the Centralized Motion Part or Assigned Justice in accordance with individual Part Rules. NY R L QUEENS E-FILE Doc. 1(E)(4). On the return date of a motion that has been E-filed, the movant must provide the Centralized Motion Part (CMP) with a working copy of the entire motion including the notice of motion with sequence number and all of the attached exhibits. The motion must have the confirmation of filing firmly affixed to the back of the papers (facing outward). The confirmation of filing is a separate notice from the payment notice and will say confirmation clearly across the top of the page. NY R L QUEENS E-FILE Doc. 1(H)(2)(a). The motion or Order to Show Cause must have clearly written across its face the words "Working Copy," it must also have the assigned Judge's name, motion sequence number and calendar number—which may be obtained from the posted calendar outside courtroom on the return date of the motion. A confirmation of filing must attached thereto. Working copies of e-filed Orders to Show Cause must contain a copy of the signed order and all supporting papers. NY R L QUEENS E-FILE Doc. 1(H)(2)(c). The Confirmation Notice must be an updated version that indicates the sequence number of the motion being submitted at the CMP calendar call. WORKING COPIES WITHOUT A CONFIRMATION NOTICE WILL NOT BE ACCEPTED. NY R L QUEENS E-FILE Doc. 1(H)(7).

vi. *Statement of authorization in electronic filing cases.* A filing agent (other than one employed by a governmental entity) shall e-file a statement of authorization from counsel of record in an action, in a form approved by the Chief Administrator, prior to or together with the first e-filing in that action by the agent on behalf of that counsel. NY R UNIF TRIAL CTS § 202.5-b(d)(1)(i).

vii. *ERIE COUNTY: Additional supplemental documents*

- *Notice of hard copy submission in e-filed case.* In accordance with NY R UNIF TRIAL CTS § 202.5-b(d), the County Clerk shall refuse to accept for filing, hard copy papers filed to an action subject to electronic filing unless hard copy filing is permitted by the Uniform Rules or NY R ERIE E FIL Doc. 3 and the papers bear a completed Notice of Hard Copy Submission—E-Filed Case form. NY R ERIE E FIL Doc. 3(III)(D).

viii. *KINGS COUNTY: Additional supplemental documents*

- *Forms when filing in hard copy.* An attorney who certifies in good faith that he or she lacks the equipment or knowledge needed to e-file and have no staff member or employee under his or her direction who has such knowledge and equipment may opt out of participation in e-filing in a mandatory case by filing a "Notice of Opt-Out from Participation in Action Subject to Mandatory Electronic Filing" form EFM-2 with the Clerk. NY R L KINGS E FIL Doc. 1(A)(2). Where in accordance with the E-Filing Rules a party submits a document in hard copy in an e-filed case (principally, a document submitted by a nonparticipating party (e.g., an attorney) in a consensual case, an emergency filing made in accordance with the Mandatory E-Filing Rules, and any document filed with the court in hard copy by an attorney who has opted out of participation in mandatory e-filing, the document must bear the back page facing out, a "Notice of Hard Copy Submission—E-Filed Cases" form EFM-3. NY R L KINGS E FIL Doc. 1(B)(3).

ix. *NEW YORK COUNTY: Additional supplemental documents*

- *Notice of hard copy submission.* Where in accordance with the E-Filing Rules an attorney or an unrepresented litigant who is participating in e-filing submits a document in hard copy in an e-filed case, the document must bear, as the back page facing out, a Notice of Hard-Copy Submission—E-Filed Case (a form available in the "Forms" section on the NYSCEF website (Form EFM-3) and in the court's back offices). NY R NY CTY E FIL Doc. 2(B)(3). For more information refer to NY R NY CTY E FIL Doc. 2.
- *Unpublished decisions.* Whenever reliance is placed upon a decision or other authority not officially published or readily available to the New York County Supreme Court, a copy of the case or of pertinent portions of the authority shall be submitted with the motion papers. NY R NY CTY J RUL Rule 14(a).

x. *ONONDAGA COUNTY: Additional supplemental documents*

- *Notice of hard copy submission.* Any papers to be filed with the court in an e-filed case must be filed online with the E-filing system except where a special exemption is granted (e.g., oversized maps, photographs). If such an exemption is granted, Form EFM-3, "Notice of Hard Copy Submission—E-Filed Case," must be attached to such documents forms which are not filed on line. Also, Form EFM-4 "Notice of Hard Copy Exhibit Filing" must be completed and uploaded to the action's e-file. Both of these forms may be found on the NYSCEF website. NY R ONDGA E FIL Protocol(B)(4).

xi. *QUEENS COUNTY: Additional supplemental documents*

- *Notice of hard copy submission.* Any party opting out of the e-filing system must have a "Notice of Hard Copy Submission" firmly affixed to the back of the papers. NY R L QUEENS E-FILE Doc. 1(H)(2)(f).

2. *Documents for opposing party*

a. *Required documents*

i. *Opposition.* Refer to the General Requirements section of this document for information on the opposition.

- *Request for oral argument.* A party requesting oral argument shall set forth such request in its notice of motion or in its order to show cause or on the first page of the answering papers, as the case may be. Where all parties to a motion request oral argument, oral argument shall be granted unless the court shall determine it to be unnecessary. Where a motion is brought on by order to show cause, the court may set forth in the order that oral argument is required on the return date of the motion. NY R UNIF TRIAL CTS § 202.8(d).
- *QUEENS COUNTY: E-filing opposition papers.* E-filed opposition papers and/or reply papers must also be provided to the Centralized Motion Part in the same manner as the moving papers with the confirmation of filing firmly attached to the back of the papers. NY R L QUEENS E-FILE Doc. 1(H)(2)(d).

ii. *Proof of service.* In addition to complying with the provisions of NY CPLR Rule 2101, every paper filed in court shall have annexed thereto appropriate proof of service on all parties where required. NY R UNIF TRIAL CTS § 202.5(a).

b. *Supplemental documents*

i. *Supporting evidence; Exhibits.* The main supporting papers on a motion are affidavits, but any relevant exhibits, documents, depositions, etc., are also includible. SIEGEL-NYPRAC § 246.

- *Affidavits accompanying opposition.* Affidavits shall be for a statement of the relevant facts. NY R UNIF TRIAL CTS § 202.8(c).
- *Foreign language documents.* Where an affidavit or exhibit annexed to a paper served or filed is in a foreign language, it shall be accompanied by an English translation and an affidavit by the translator stating his qualifications and that the translation is accurate. NY CPLR Rule 2101(b).
- *Statement of attorney in lieu of affidavit.* The statement of an attorney admitted to practice in the courts of the state, or of a physician, osteopath or dentist, authorized by law to practice in the state, who is not a party to an action, when subscribed and affirmed by him to be true under the penalties of perjury, may be served or filed in the action in lieu of and with the same force and effect as an affidavit. NY CPLR Rule 2106.
- *NEW YORK COUNTY: Form of presented exhibits.* Exhibits should be tabbed and be legible; a typed version of any exhibit that is difficult to read should be submitted with the original. Exhibits printed on both sides of the page should be bound and tabbed on the side. NY R NY CTY J RUL Rule 14(a).
- *QUEENS COUNTY.* Attorneys submitting exhibits to the court on E-file cases shall make each exhibit a separate, labeled attachment to an affidavit/affirmation. NY R L QUEENS E-FILE Doc. 1(H)(4).

ii. *Brief.* Briefs shall be for a statement of the relevant law. NY R UNIF TRIAL CTS § 202.8(c).

iii. *Filing fees.* The County Clerk shall require the payment of any applicable statutory fees, or an order of the Court waiving payment of such fees, before accepting a paper for filing. NY R UNIF TRIAL CTS § 202.5(d)(1). For information on filing fees, if any, refer to NY CPLR § 8001, et seq.

- *ALBANY COUNTY.* In general, any filing subsequent to the commencement of an action which is designated as a motion or cross-motion requires the payment of a filing fee to the County Clerk's Office prior to submission to the Supreme Court Clerk's Office for referral to the assigned justice. The fee is assessed regardless of whether an application is made by notice of motion, order to show cause or ex parte. No fee will be charged upon the filing of a motion for poor person status in conjunction with an application which serves to commence an action or special proceeding. In the event a motion is received by the court unaccompanied by proof of payment to the County Clerk, the Supreme Court Clerk's Office will contact the submitting party to advise that the application will be held pending receipt of the filing fee only until the return date of the motion. If proof of payment is not submitted to the Supreme Court Clerk's Office by the return date (ex parte applications will be held ten (10) days), the papers will be returned by mail with a notification that the motion has been removed from the court's calendar and that it must be re-noticed and re-filed with the court along with the requisite filing fee. Inquiries concerning the applicability of the motion fee to a proposed filing may be directed to the Supreme Court Clerk's Office. NY R 3 JD SUP Doc. 1(B).

- *BRONX COUNTY.* In accordance with the new civil fee schedule set forth in Article 80 of the C.P.L.R. (NY CPLR § 8001, et seq.), effective July 14, 2003, all motions, and cross motions must be approved in Room 217 prior to payment of said fees in the County Clerk's Office, Room 118. NY R BRONX FIL R Doc. 8. The motion fee [must be] paid for via NYSCEF by credit/debit card. NY R BRONX E FIL R Doc. 1(1).
- *ERIE COUNTY.* Payment for fee-bearing NYSCEF documents must be made online via credit or debit card (American Express, MasterCard or Visa) at the time of submission. NY R ERIE E FIL Doc. 3(III)(E).
- *KINGS COUNTY.* The motion must be filed with NYSCEF and the motion fee paid. NY R L KINGS E FIL Doc. 1(D). Court fees in NYSCEF cases must be paid via NYSCEF by a credit or bank card (MasterCard, Visa, or American Express). Fees are no longer accepted in person in the Kings County Clerk's Office in NYSCEF cases. NY R L KINGS E FIL Doc. 1(B)(6).
- *NEW YORK COUNTY.* A motion fee must be paid on motions made in writing by notice of motion, order to show cause or ex parte after the commencement of an action. For this purpose, the term "action" shall mean any application to the court that requires the assignment of an index number, regardless of whether a formal pleading is filed. Applications or motions that commence an action and for which an index number fee must be paid require no motion fee. [A]ny motions made after the initial applications in these situations would require payment of the motion fee. A motion that is the initial application in a case commenced by the filing of a summons and complaint would require a motion fee since the filing of the summons and complaint rather than the application itself would require the purchase of an index number. NY R NY CTY Procedure II(A). In e-filed cases the motion fee must be paid when the documents are filed. Payment is made on-line by Visa, Mastercard, or American Express credit or bank card. NY R NY CTY Procedure II(A); NY R NY CTY E FIL Doc. 2(B)(5).
- *ONONDAGA COUNTY.* Court fees in e-filed cases must be paid online with the NYSCEF system using a credit card. The document is not considered to have been filed until payment of the fee has been tendered. NY R ONDGA E FIL Protocol(B)(2). Fees must be paid on all cross motions. NY R ONDGA E FIL Protocol(B)(9)(e).
- *QUEENS COUNTY.* The Motion Support Office does not receive, forward or process any fees or waiver of fees. All applications requiring payment of statutory fees or waiver of fees must be sent directly to the Queens County Clerk's office. NY R L QUEENS MOT SUP Doc. 1. Court fees (e.g., RJI fee, motion fee) in E-filed cases may be paid for on-line using a credit card. Papers may also be filed with the E-file system and the fee may be paid at the County Clerk's Office. In the latter case, the paper is not considered to have been filed until payment of the fee has been tendered. NY R L QUEENS E-FILE Doc. 1(E)(1). The motion/petition shall be filed on-line and the fee paid for either on-line by credit card or by the "Pay at the County Clerk's Office" option. NY R L QUEENS E-FILE Doc. 1(H)(1).

iv. *Working copies.* The court may require the parties to provide working copies of documents filed electronically. In such event, each working copy shall include, firmly affixed thereto, a copy of a confirmation notice in a form prescribed by the Chief Administrator. NY R UNIF TRIAL CTS § 202.5-b(d)(5).

- *BRONX COUNTY.* After papers on motions have been e-filed, working copies thereof, with Confirmation Notice firmly attached as the back page facing out, must be submitted. (Each document or group of documents that is separately bound shall bear a Confirmation Notice.) Working copies lacking the Notice will not be accepted. WORKING COPIES OF MOTION PAPERS MUST BE SUBMITTED NO LATER THAN 4:45 P.M. ON THE RETURN DATE IN THE MOTION SUPPORT OFFICE (ROOM 217) AS EXPLAINED in NY R BRONX E FIL R Doc. 1(4). If an attorney has failed to submit required working copies on or before the return date, the motion will be transmitted as is to the Justice for such action as the Justice finds appropriate. Attorneys may submit working copies on motions by mail or overnight delivery. Any such submission shall be sent in a timely manner to the Motion Support Office (Room 217) and be conspicuously marked on the outside "NYSCEF Matter"; lack of such marking may delay processing. NY R BRONX E FIL R Doc. 1(4)(a).
- *ERIE COUNTY.* Electronically filed documents subject to review and processing by the Part Clerk do not require a working copy unless otherwise directed or provided for in IAS Part Rules. NY R UNIF TRIAL CTS § 202.5-b(d)(4), any working copy submitted shall include, as a cover page firmly fastened thereto, a copy of the Confirmation Notice generated by the NYSCEF site at the time of filing. Please consult the

individual Justice's Part Rules and/or consult with the Judge's chambers to determine whether and how working copies are to be provided. Working copies will not be printed or delivered by the Erie County Clerk or the Chief Clerk of the Courts or any of their personnel to chambers. The official record of a document in an electronically filed case is the document filed via the NYSCEF system. Working copies are intended only for use by the Justice. The Court will discard all working copies after the Justice has finished with them. Thus, in the event that counsel fails to file a document via the NYSCEF system, the document will not be part of the court record. NY R ERIE E FIL Doc. 3(III)(O); NY R ERIE E FIL Doc. 3(V)(E).

- *KINGS COUNTY.* No courtesy copies of motion papers are required by the Court, except as may be required for electronic filing or by the Judge's Part Rules. In tort cases against the City of New York, courtesy copies shall be supplied to the Corporation Counsel's office in Brooklyn. NY R L KINGS Pt. C, Rule 5. Unless otherwise directed by the Court or as described herein, and with the exceptions listed below, in all NYSCEF cases in which an RJI has been filed, working copies of e-filed documents that are intended for judicial review must be submitted to the court. Working copies are not required of documents that are only processed by a support office (e.g. preliminary conference request, note of issue). Working copies shall include exhibit tabs and backs; for motion papers, the motion sequence number and the return date and part. The confirmation notice with the motion sequence number on it should be the back page of the motion facing out. In addition, the filer of a working copy must firmly bind thereto, with the back page facing out, a copy of the Confirmation Notice that was generated by NYSCEF when that document was efiled. Working copies that are submitted without the related Confirmation Notice will not be accepted. NY R L KINGS E FIL Doc. 1(B)(7); NY R L KINGS E FIL Doc. 1(D). WORKING COPIES OF MOTION PAPERS MUST BE SUBMITTED IN THE MOTION SUPPORT OFFICE (ROOM 227) AS EXPLAINED HEREIN. THEY MUST NOT BE DELIVERED TO THE PART OR CHAMBERS, EXCEPT WHERE THE INDIVIDUAL JUSTICE'S PART RULES PROVIDE OTHERWISE; DOING SO WILL CAUSE ADMINISTRATIVE CONFUSION AND POSSIBLE MISPLACEMENT OF PAPERS. Any such submission shall be sent in a timely manner (kindly review individual Justice's rules) and be conspicuously marked on the outside "NYSCEF Matter;" lack of such marking may delay processing. NY R L KINGS E FIL Doc. 1(D).
- *NEW YORK COUNTY.* Some Justices require that working copies of e-filed motion papers be submitted. See the E-filing Protocol for information on the many Parts that do not require working copies. Where required, working copies of the moving documents and all other documents on the motion or application shall be submitted to the Motion Submission Part Courtroom (Room 130) on, but not before, the final return date. A Confirmation Notice from the NYSCEF system, which is generated when a document is e-filed, shall be firmly affixed, as the back page facing out, to each separate working copy or group of such copies. NY R NY CTY Procedure II(A) NY R NY CTY E FIL Doc. 2(B)(5)(a); NY R NY CTY J RUL Rule 14(a). For more information on working copies, including which parts don't require them, refer to NY R NY CTY E FIL Doc. 2(B)(6).
- *ONONDAGA COUNTY.* Any courtesy "working" copies, if required (see NY R ONDGA E FIL Protocol(B)(7)), must be provided directly to the assigned justice. NY R ONDGA E FIL Protocol(B)(9)(e). For information as to whether or not an Onondaga Supreme Court Justice requires working (courtesy) copies of e-filed documents, please consult the Onondaga County Individual E-filing Rules. NY R ONDGA E FIL Protocol(B)(7)(a). The Supreme Court Clerk's Office and the Onondaga County Clerk's Office will NOT accept the working copies. Working copies must be sent directly to the assigned justice's chambers. NY R ONDGA E FIL Protocol(B)(7)(b). A copy of the Confirmation Notice, generated by the NYSCEF system at the time a document is e-filed, must be attached to every working copy provided to chambers. If the Confirmation Notice is missing, the copy will not be accepted. NY R ONDGA E FIL Protocol(B)(7)(c). Courtesy copies do not become part of the official court record as maintained by the Onondaga County Clerk's Office and will be destroyed by chambers at the disposition of the case. In the event that counsel fails to file a document via NYSCEF, the document will not be part of the court record. NY R ONDGA E FIL Protocol(B)(7)(d).
- *QUEENS COUNTY.* Working copies of E-Filed notices of motion/notices of petition are NOT to be sent to the Motion Support Office. They must be brought to the calendar call in the judge's part. NY R L QUEENS MOT SUP Doc. 1. Unless otherwise directed or authorized by the court, counsel should file papers with the E-file system first and thereafter deliver a working copy to at the calendar call of the Centralized Motion Part or Assigned Justice in accordance with individual Part Rules. NY R L QUEENS E-FILE Doc. 1(E)(4). On the return date of a motion that has been E-filed, the movant must provide the Centralized Motion Part

(CMP) with a working copy of the entire motion including the notice of motion with sequence number and all of the attached exhibits. The motion must have the confirmation of filing firmly affixed to the back of the papers (facing outward). The confirmation of filing is a separate notice from the payment notice and will say confirmation clearly across the top of the page. NY R L QUEENS E-FILE Doc. 1(H)(2)(a). The motion or Order to Show Cause must have clearly written across its face the words "Working Copy," it must also have the assigned Judge's name, motion sequence number and calendar number—which may be obtained from the posted calendar outside courtroom on the return date of the motion. A confirmation of filing must attached thereto. Working copies of e-filed Orders to Show Cause must contain a copy of the signed order and all supporting papers. NY R L QUEENS E-FILE Doc. 1(H)(2)(c). The Confirmation Notice must be an updated version that indicates the sequence number of the motion being submitted at the CMP calendar call. WORKING COPIES WITHOUT A CONFIRMATION NOTICE WILL NOT BE ACCEPTED. NY R L QUEENS E-FILE Doc. 1(H)(7).

v. *ERIE COUNTY: Additional supplemental documents*

- *Notice of hard copy submission in e-filed case.* In accordance with NY R UNIF TRIAL CTS § 202.5-b(d), the County Clerk shall refuse to accept for filing, hard copy papers filed to an action subject to electronic filing unless hard copy filing is permitted by the Uniform Rules or NY R ERIE E FIL Doc. 3 and the papers bear a completed Notice of Hard Copy Submission—E-Filed Case form. NY R ERIE E FIL Doc. 3(III)(D).

vi. *KINGS COUNTY: Additional supplemental documents*

- *Forms when filing in hard copy.* An attorney who certifies in good faith that he or she lacks the equipment or knowledge needed to e-file and have no staff member or employee under his or her direction who has such knowledge and equipment may opt out of participation in e-filing in a mandatory case by filing a "Notice of Opt-Out from Participation in Action Subject to Mandatory Electronic Filing" form EFM-2 with the Clerk. NY R L KINGS E FIL Doc. 1(A)(2). Where in accordance with the E-Filing Rules a party submits a document in hard copy in an e-filed case (principally, a document submitted by a nonparticipating party (e.g., an attorney) in a consensual case, an emergency filing made in accordance with the Mandatory E-Filing Rules, and any document filed with the court in hard copy by an attorney who has opted out of participation in mandatory e-filing, the document must bear the back page facing out, a "Notice of Hard Copy Submission—E-Filed Cases" form EFM-3. NY R L KINGS E FIL Doc. 1(B)(3).

vii. *NEW YORK COUNTY: Additional supplemental documents*

- *Notice of hard copy submission.* Where in accordance with the E-Filing Rules an attorney or an unrepresented litigant who is participating in e-filing submits a document in hard copy in an e-filed case, the document must bear, as the back page facing out, a Notice of Hard-Copy Submission—E-Filed Case (a form available in the "Forms" section on the NYSCEF website (Form EFM-3) and in the court's back offices). NY R NY CTY E FIL Doc. 2(B)(3). For more information refer to NY R NY CTY E FIL Doc. 2.
- *Unpublished decisions.* Whenever reliance is placed upon a decision or other authority not officially published or readily available to the New York County Supreme Court, a copy of the case or of pertinent portions of the authority shall be submitted with the motion papers. NY R NY CTY J RUL Rule 14(a).

viii. *ONONDAGA COUNTY: Additional supplemental documents*

- *Notice of hard copy submission.* Any papers to be filed with the court in an e-filed case must be filed online with the E-filing system except where a special exemption is granted (e.g., oversized maps, photographs). If such an exemption is granted, Form EFM-3, "Notice of Hard Copy Submission—E-Filed Case," must be attached to such documents forms which are not filed on line. Also, Form EFM-4 "Notice of Hard Copy Exhibit Filing" must be completed and uploaded to the action's e-file. Both of these forms may be found on the NYSCEF website. NY R ONDGA E FIL Protocol(B)(4).

ix. *QUEENS COUNTY: Additional supplemental documents*

- *Notice of hard copy submission.* Any party opting out of the e-filing system must have a "Notice of Hard Copy Submission" firmly affixed to the back of the papers. NY R L QUEENS E-FILE Doc. 1(H)(2)(f).

E. Format

1. *Form of documents*

a. *Size and form of paper.* Each paper served or filed shall be durable, white and, except for summonses, subpoenas, notices of appearance, notes of issue, orders of protection, temporary orders of protection and exhibits, shall be eleven by eight and one-half (11 x 8-1/2) inches in size. NY CPLR Rule 2101(a).

b. *Writing and language.* The writing shall be legible and in black ink. NY CPLR Rule 2101(a). Each paper served or filed shall be in the English language which, where practicable, shall be of ordinary usage. NY CPLR Rule 2101(b).

c. *Caption.* Each paper served or filed shall begin with a caption setting forth the name of the court, the venue, the title of the action, the nature of the paper and the index number of the action if one has been assigned. In all papers other than a summons, a complaint or a judgment it shall be sufficient to state the name of the first named party on each side with an appropriate indication of any omissions. NY CPLR Rule 2101(c).

   i. *Further contents of first page.* After the first paper has been filed in each case the index number shall appear on the cover and first page to the right of the caption of every paper tendered for filing in the action. Each such cover and first page also shall contain an indication of the county of venue and a brief description of the nature of the paper and, where the case has been assigned to an individual judge, shall contain the name of the assigned judge to the right of the caption. NY R UNIF TRIAL CTS § 202.5(a); NY R UNIF TRIAL CTS § 202.5(b); NY R UNIF TRIAL CTS § 202.5(d)(1)(i).

   ii. *ALBANY COUNTY: Request for oral argument.* A party may request oral argument on a motion by indicating such request on the first page of the notice of motion, order to show cause, or answering papers in the area across from the caption of the action/proceeding. NY R 3 JD SUP Doc. 1(B).

   iii. *NEW YORK COUNTY: Request for oral argument.* Counsel who wish oral argument must so request conspicuously on the front of their papers. NY R NY CTY Procedure II(D).

d. *Index number.* No paper in an action in the supreme or a county court, other than an order submitted for signature to a judge out of court, shall be submitted for any purpose to the supreme or county court or to a clerk thereof unless there is endorsed on such paper the index number of the action assigned by the clerk of the county. NY CPLR § 8018(c).

   i. *ALBANY COUNTY: Index number on all filed documents.* The index number, the request for judicial intervention number and the assigned justice's name shall appear on [all papers filed with the Court subsequent to the complaint]. NY R 3 JD SUP Doc. 1(A).

   ii. *ERIE COUNTY: Index number after initial filing.* Cases that are initially commenced by the filing of papers with the NYSCEF system are identified as e-filed cases by assignment of an Index Number that has "800-899" as the first three (3) digits of the index number (i.e. 802391/2012). NY R ERIE E FIL Doc. 3(II). [The] Index Number must be affixed to all document submissions, filings, and communications to the Erie County Clerk and the Court. Cases that are converted from paper to e-filing shall retain the original index number. NY R ERIE E FIL Doc. 3(II).

   iii. *KINGS COUNTY: Index number after initial filing.* In cases commenced electronically by the filing of initiating papers with the NYSCEF system and payment of the statutory fees, the Kings County Clerk will issue an NYSCEF designated index number and the filer shall be notified via the NYSCEF system of the index number assigned and filing date. Such index number must be affixed to all document submissions, filings and communications to the Kings County Clerk and Supreme Court. If counsel faces exigent circumstances that require accelerated assignment, counsel may contact Administration of the Kings County Clerk at kcco-efile@nycourts.gov, during normal business hours of the court. NY R L KINGS E FIL Doc. 1(B)(5).

   iv. *NEW YORK COUNTY: Index number on hard copy filings.* Papers subsequently presented for filing in hardcopy format will be filed in this jacket. NY R NY CTY Procedure I(B). Index numbers take the form of six digits followed by a slash and the four digits of the year the case began, e.g., 340705/2018. The first or first two integers of the index number identify the type of case. If a case is commenced electronically, the second integer will be a "5", except as indicated otherwise in the list below. There are many tax certiorari matters e-filed annually and the index numbers therefor will normally run over into those with a "6" as the second integer, and the same will occur with general cases if necessary. The principal types of cases and their index number categories are listed in NY R NY CTY Procedure I(B). NY R NY CTY Procedure I(B); NY R NY CTY Procedure XI(A).

   v. *ONONDAGA COUNTY: Index number.* The index number must be referenced on all e-filed documents and correspondence. All e-filed case index numbers will contain the letters "EF" between the year and the file number (for example, 2012EF9999). NY R ONDGA E FIL Protocol(B)(1).

   vi. *QUEENS COUNTY: Index number on converted cases.* Cases originally commenced in hard-copy form but later converted to an E-file case, either by stipulation or order will bear a regular index number initially. The County Clerk will issue a new E-file index number. NY R L QUEENS E-FILE Doc. 1(B).

e. *Line spacing.* Every paper filed in court, if typewritten, shall have at least double space between each line, except for quotations and the names and addresses of attorneys appearing in the action. NY R UNIF TRIAL CTS § 202.5(a).

f. *Font size.* Each. . .paper printed or typed, served or filed, except for summonses. . .and exhibits, shall be in clear type of no less than ten (10) point in size. NY CPLR Rule 2101(a).

i. Whenever a requirement relating to size of type is stated in point size, the type size requirement shall be deemed met if the x-height of the type is a minimum of forty-five percent (45%) of the specified point size. Each point shall be measured as .351 millimeter. The x-height size shall be measured as it appears on the page. The x-height is the height of the lower case letters, exclusive of ascenders or descenders. NY CPLR § 105(t).

g. *Margins.* Every paper filed in court shall have at least one (1) inch margins. NY R UNIF TRIAL CTS § 202.5(a).

h. *Citations*

i. *Civil practice law and rules.* NY CPLR § 101, et seq. shall be known as the civil practice law and rules, and may be cited as "CPLR". Reference to a provision in the civil practice law and rules may, except when such provision is being enacted or amended, be made without indicating whether it is a rule or section. NY CPLR § 101.

i. *Indorsement by attorney.* Each paper served or filed shall be indorsed with the name, address and telephone number of the attorney for the party serving or filing the paper, or if the party does not appear by attorney, with the name, address and telephone number of the party. NY CPLR Rule 2101(d).

j. *One-sided printing.* In addition, every paper filed in court, other than an exhibit or printed form, shall contain writing on one side only, except that papers that are fastened on the side may contain writing on both sides. NY R UNIF TRIAL CTS § 202.5(a).

k. *Use of copies authorized.* Except where otherwise specifically prescribed, copies, rather than originals, of all papers, including orders, affidavits and exhibits may be served or filed. Where it is required that the original be served or filed and the original is lost or withheld, the court may authorize a copy to be served or filed. NY CPLR Rule 2101(e).

i. Where a certified copy of a paper is required by law, an attorney admitted to practice in the courts of the state may certify that it has been compared by him with the original and found to be a true and complete copy. Such a certificate, when subscribed by such attorney, has the same effect as if made by a clerk. NY CPLR § 2105.

l. *Recycled paper.* It is the policy of the Unified Court System that litigants, where practicable, should file or submit to the courts of the Unified Court System of the State of New York papers printed or reproduced on recycled paper. Paper is considered recycled if it contains a minimum content of thirty percent (30%) waste paper. NY R UNIF TRIAL CTS § 215.2. The signature page of every paper filed or submitted to the court on recycled paper should bear the legend: "Printed [Reproduced] on Recycled Paper." NY R UNIF TRIAL CTS § 215.3.

m. *Form of request for judicial intervention; Copies.* A request for judicial intervention must be submitted, in duplicate, on a form authorized by the Chief of the Courts, with proof of service on the other parties to the action (but proof of service is not required where the application is ex parte). NY R UNIF TRIAL CTS § 202.6(a).

n. *KINGS COUNTY: Tabs on filings.* Motions, orders and other filed papers shall be indexed with protruding tabs. Clerks are required to reject papers that do not have protruding exhibit tabs, except papers in matrimonial cases and papers filed by pro se litigants. NY R L KINGS Pt. A, Papers.

o. *NEW YORK COUNTY: Length of briefs.* Unless advance permission otherwise is granted by the court for good cause, memoranda of law shall not exceed thirty (30) pages each (exclusive of table of contents and table of authorities) and affidavits/affirmations shall not exceed twenty-five (25) pages each. NY R NY CTY J RUL Rule 14(b).

p. *QUEENS COUNTY: Form and size of motion filings.* All motions filed in Queens Supreme Court-Civil Term, must adhere to the Motion Support rules and the rules of the assigned judge. NY R L QUEENS MOT SUP Doc. 1. Due to space limitations, the Motion Support Office cannot accept notices of motion/notices of petition and accompanying exhibits which measure greater than eight (8) inches. If your documents measure greater than eight (8) inches you are directed to submit only the notice of motion/notice of petition to the Motion Support Office and bring all exhibits to the calendar call on your return date. NY R L QUEENS MOT SUP Doc. 1.

2. *Form of electronic documents.* Each paper served or filed by electronic means, as defined in NY CPLR Rule 2103(f), shall be capable of being reproduced by the receiver so as to comply with the provisions of NY CPLR Rule 2101(a) through NY CPLR Rule 2101(d). NY CPLR Rule 2101(g).

a. *File format.* All e-filed documents shall comply with the technical requirements set forth at the NYSCEF site. NY R UNIF TRIAL CTS § 202.5-b(d)(1)(i).

b. *Heading of document.* The subject matter heading for each paper sent by electronic means must indicate that the matter being transmitted electronically is related to a court proceeding. NY CPLR Rule 2103(b)(7).

c. *E-filed documents identification*

i. *ERIE COUNTY.* E-filed cases must be readily identifiable and marked as such. If counsel presents papers to the

Office of the Erie County Clerk or the Office of the Chief Clerk in a NYSCEF matter where authorized, counsel should alert the Clerk that the case is a NYSCEF matter. NY R ERIE E FIL Doc. 3(II).

ii. *KINGS COUNTY.* The Supreme Court's Civil Case Information System ("CCIS") will further identify e-filed cases by the addition of a suffix to the index number (e.g. 500136/2006E). This suffix should be used on all documents filed with the court in e-filed matters. NY R L KINGS E FIL Doc. 1(A)(1).

3. *Signature blocks.* Every pleading, written motion, and other paper, served on another party or filed or submitted to the court shall be signed by an attorney, or by a party if the party is not represented by an attorney, with the name of the attorney or party clearly printed or typed directly below the signature. NY R CHIEF ADMIN § 130-1.1-a(a); NY R UNIF TRIAL CTS § 202.5(d)(1)(iv).

a. *Printed name.* Beneath each signature shall be printed the name signed. NY CPLR Rule 2101(a).

b. *Failure to sign.* Absent good cause shown, the court shall strike any unsigned paper if the omission of the signature is not corrected promptly after being called to the attention of the attorney or party. NY R CHIEF ADMIN § 130-1.1-a(a).

c. *Signature as certification.* By signing a paper, an attorney or party certifies that, to the best of that person's knowledge, information and belief, formed after an inquiry reasonable under the circumstances the presentation of the paper or the contentions therein are not frivolous as defined in NY R CHIEF ADMIN § 130-1.1(c). NY R CHIEF ADMIN § 130-1.1-a(b)(1).

d. *Electronic signatures.* A document shall be considered to have been signed by an attorney or party in compliance with NY R CHIEF ADMIN § 130-1.1-a if it has been signed by such attorney or party as provided in NY R UNIF TRIAL CTS § 202.5-b(e)(1) and it bears the signatory's name. NY R UNIF TRIAL CTS § 202.5-b(e)(2). An electronically filed document shall be considered to have been signed by, and shall be binding upon, the person identified as a signatory, if:

i. It bears the physical signature of such person and is scanned into an electronic format that reproduces such signature; or

ii. The signatory has electronically affixed the digital image of his or her signature to the document; or

iii. It is electronically filed under the User ID and password of that person; or

iv. In a tax certiorari action in which the parties have stipulated to this procedure, it is an initiating document that is electronically filed without the signature of the signatory in a form provided above in NY R UNIF TRIAL CTS § 202.5-b(e)(iv), provided that, prior to filing, the document is signed in full in hard copy (which hard copy must be preserved until the conclusion of all proceedings, including appeals, in the case in which it is filed); or

v. In a small claims assessment review proceeding, it is a petition recorded by the NYSCEF site upon the filing of a text file as provided in NY R UNIF TRIAL CTS § 202.5-b(b)(1), provided that prior to filing, the document was signed in full in hard copy (which hard copy must be preserved until the conclusion of all proceedings in the matter, including article 78 (NY CPLR § 7801, et seq.) review and any appeals, and must be made available during the proceeding upon request of the respondent or the court); or

vi. It otherwise bears the electronic signature of the signatory in a format conforming to such standards and requirements as may hereafter be established by the Chief Administrator. NY R UNIF TRIAL CTS § 202.5-b(e).

4. *Confidentiality of personal information.* No person may file any document available for public inspection with any state agency, political subdivision, or in any court of this state that contains a Social Security account number of any other person, unless such other person is a dependent child, or has consented to such filing, except as required by federal or state law or regulation, or by court rule. NY GEN BUS § 399-ddd. Submissions pursuant to e-filing procedures shall have the same confidentiality rights as paper documents. NY R UNIF TRIAL CTS § 202.5-b(k)(1).

a. *Confidential personal information.* Except in the actions designated in NY R UNIF TRIAL CTS § 202.5(e)(1), or as otherwise provided by rule or law or court order, and whether or not a sealing order is or has been sought, the parties shall omit or redact confidential personal information in papers submitted to the court for filing. For purposes of NY R UNIF TRIAL CTS § 202.5(e), confidential personal information ("CPI") means:

i. The taxpayer identification number of an individual or an entity, including a Social Security number, an employer identification number, and an individual taxpayer identification number, except the last four (4) digits thereof;

ii. The date of an individual's birth, except the year thereof;

iii. The full name of an individual known to be a minor, except the minor's initials;

iv. A financial account number, including a credit and/or debit card number, a bank account number, an investment account number, and/or an insurance account number, except the last four (4) digits or letters thereof; and

v. Any of the documents or testimony in a matrimonial action protected by NY DOM REL § 235 or evidence sealed by the court in such an action which are attached as exhibits or referenced in the papers filed in any other civil action. For purposes of NY R UNIF TRIAL CTS § 202.5, a matrimonial action shall mean: an action to annul a marriage or declare the nullity of a void marriage, an action or agreement for a separation, an action for a divorce, or an action or proceeding for custody, visitation, writ of habeus corpus, child support, maintenance or paternity. NY R UNIF TRIAL CTS § 202.5(e)(1).

vi. *ERIE COUNTY.* An attorney or unrepresented litigant filing a document via the NYSCEF system must comply with the requirements of NY R UNIF TRIAL CTS § 202.5(e) regarding the redaction of Confidential Personal Information and NY GEN BUS § 399-ddd(6) concerning the filing of documents containing Social Security Numbers. It is the sole responsibility of counsel or unrepresented litigant filing to be aware of and to comply with existing laws requiring non-disclosure of personal information contained in any document e-filed in NYSCEF. NY R ERIE E FIL Doc. 3(III)(G); NY R ERIE E FIL Doc. 3(III).

vii. *KINGS COUNTY.* An attorney or unrepresented litigant filing a document via the NYSCEF system must comply with the requirements of General Business Law § 399-dd(6), which often require redaction of any Social Security number that appear in the original document. The NYSCEF system automatically redacts portions of filed documents which apparently contain Social Security numbers pursuant to NY R UNIF TRIAL CTS § 202.5-b(k). In the event the filing party receives e-mail notice through NYSCEF that a Social Security number in a filed document has been redacted, and the filing party concludes such redaction is erroneous, the filer should click on the link provided in the e-mail to permit the County Clerk to revert the redaction. For Confidential Personal Information, see NY R UNIF TRIAL CTS § 202.5(e) and NY R L KINGS E FIL Doc. 1(B)(11). [Editor's note: the reference to General Business Law § 399-dd(6) is likely a reference to NY GEN BUS § 399-ddd(6)]. NY R L KINGS E FIL Doc. 1(B)(10); NY R L KINGS E FIL Doc. 1(K)(1).

viii. *NEW YORK COUNTY.* It is the responsibility of counsel and parties to comply with rules restricting disclosure of confidential personal information. Nevertheless, NYSCEF screens filings and endeavors to identify any that contain social security numbers. When such numbers are discovered through this process, NYSCEF will restrict portions of or all of such documents from public view. Where NYSCEF has redacted what it believes to be a social security number, it will transmit to the filer a notice advising of the action taken and requesting that the filer review the matter and provide notification as set forth in the notice if the redaction has been made in error. NY R NY CTY E FIL Doc. 2(K)(1); NY R NY CTY J RUL Rule A-1. Documents filed in the past in "secure status" under a procedure no longer in place will retain that status unless otherwise directed by the court. NY R NY CTY E FIL Doc. 2(K)(2).

b. *Submission of confidential personal information.* Where a person submitting a paper to a court for filing believes in good faith that the inclusion of the full confidential personal information described in NY R UNIF TRIAL CTS § 202.5(e)(1) is material and necessary to the adjudication of the action or proceeding before the court, he or she may apply to the court for leave to serve and file together with a paper in which such information has been set forth in abbreviated form a confidential affidavit or affirmation setting forth the same information in unabbreviated form, appropriately referenced to the page or pages of the paper at which the abbreviated form appears. NY R UNIF TRIAL CTS § 202.5(e)(3).

c. *Home addresses.* For information on when home addresses and other personal information must be redacted, refer to NY CPLR Rule 2103-a.

5. *Defective papers.* A defect in the form of a paper, if a substantial right of a party is not prejudiced, shall be disregarded by the court, and leave to correct shall be freely given. NY CPLR Rule 2101(f). Papers that are stapled or bound securely shall not be rejected for filing simply because they are not bound with a backer of any kind. NY R UNIF TRIAL CTS § 202.5(a). A paper filed in accordance with the rules of the chief administrator or any local rule or practice established by the court shall be deemed filed. NY CPLR Rule 2102(b).

a. *Objection to defective papers.* The party on whom a paper is served shall be deemed to have waived objection to any defect in form unless, within fifteen (15) days after the receipt thereof, the party on whom the paper is served returns the paper to the party serving it with a statement of particular objections. NY CPLR Rule 2101(f).

F. Filing and Service Requirements

1. *Filing requirements.* Except where otherwise prescribed by law or order of court, papers required to be filed shall be filed

with the clerk of the court in which the action is triable. In an action or proceeding in supreme or court, papers required to be filed shall be filed with the clerk of the county in which the proceeding is brought. NY CPLR Rule 2102(a).

a. *Furnishing papers to the court.* Each party shall furnish to the court all papers served by him. The moving party shall furnish at the hearing all other papers not already in the possession of the court necessary to the consideration of the questions involved. Where such papers are in the possession of an adverse party, they shall be produced by him at the hearing on notice served with the motion papers. Only papers served in accordance with the provisions of NY CPLR Rule 2214 shall be read in support of, or in opposition to, the motion, unless the court for good cause shall otherwise direct. NY CPLR Rule 2214(c).

i. *Submission to judge.* All papers for signature or consideration of the court shall be presented to the clerk of the trial court in the appropriate courtroom or clerk's office, except that where the clerk is unavailable or the judge so directs, papers may be submitted to the judge and a copy filed with the clerk at the first available opportunity. All papers for any judge that are filed in the clerk's office shall be promptly delivered to the judge by the clerk. The papers shall be clearly addressed to the judge for whom they are intended and prominently show the nature of the papers, the title and index number of the action in which they are filed, the judge's name and the name of the attorney or party submitting them. NY R UNIF TRIAL CTS § 202.5(b).

ii. *BRONX COUNTY: Approval of motions before filing.* All motion papers must be approved by the Motion Support Office, Supreme Court, Civil Term, room 217, before the motion papers are filed and the appropriate fee paid to the County Clerk. NY R BRONX FIL R Doc. 1.

iii. *ERIE COUNTY: Filing motions.* A motion on notice or a notice of petition in a NYSCEF case shall be filed through the NYSCEF system and must be accompanied by a Request for Judicial Intervention if the motion is being filed upon commencement of the action or if the matter has not yet been assigned to an IAS Justice. In addition, cross motions with the appropriate filing fees and opposition and reply papers must be submitted via the NYSCEF system. NY R ERIE E FIL Doc. 3(V)(A).

iv. *NEW YORK COUNTY: Filing hard copies.* Where in the narrow circumstances described by the e-filing rules a motion is made in hard-copy form or opposition papers are submitted in such form in an e-filed case, the hard-copy documents shall be submitted in the same way papers are submitted in non-e-filed cases, except that there shall be firmly affixed to each separate document or group of documents, as the back page facing out, a Notice of Hard Copy Submission—E-Filed Case. NY R NY CTY Procedure II(A). For more information on filing in hard copy cases, refer to NY R NY CTY Procedure II(A).

v. *ONONDAGA COUNTY: Submission of responsive papers and cross-motions.* Cross-motions, opposition and reply papers must be submitted online. NY R ONDGA E FIL Protocol(B)(9)(e). Motions and Orders to Show Cause are assigned a sequence number by the system. Counsel must be sure that cross motions and other filings correspond with the correct sequence number so that a cross motion will not be associated with the wrong original motion. NY R ONDGA E FIL Protocol(B)(9)(f).

b. *Electronic filing.* On consent, documents may be filed and served by electronic means in Supreme Court in such civil actions and in such counties as shall be authorized by order of the Chief Administrator of the Courts and only to the extent and in the manner provided in NY R UNIF TRIAL CTS § 202.5-b. NY R UNIF TRIAL CTS § 202.5-b(a)(1). For the definitions of terms used in electronic filing, refer to NY R UNIF TRIAL CTS § 202.5-b(a)(2).

i. *E-filing mandatory.* In any action subject to e-filing, all documents required to be filed with the court by an e-filing party shall be filed and served electronically, except as provided in NY R UNIF TRIAL CTS § 202.5-b. NY R UNIF TRIAL CTS § 202.5-b(d)(1)(i).

- *ERIE COUNTY.* Case types currently eligible and accepted for e-filing are listed at the NYSCEF website. Note that some actions or special proceedings, (i.e., name changes) which are otherwise subject to mandatory e-filing, if commenced by unrepresented litigants will NOT be maintained in the NYSCEF system; individual cases may be found either at NYSCEF or in the Erie County Clerk's online records system. NY R ERIE E FIL Doc. 3(I)(E).
- *KINGS COUNTY.* Cases that are commenced by filing of the initiating papers with NYSCEF are identified as e-filed cases by assignment of a special index number (i.e., Index Numbers beginning with 500,000). NY R L KINGS E FIL Doc. 1(A)(1). All cases required to be e-filed are listed in Uniform Rule 202.5-bb (Mandatory E-Filing Rules) and on the NYSCEF website. All such cases must be commenced by filing with the County Clerk electronically through NYSCEF and all subsequent documents in such cases must be e-filed. Any questions regarding mandatory e-filing in Kings County can be e-mailed to kcco-efile@nycourts.gov. NY R L KINGS E FIL Doc. 1(A)(2).

- *NEW YORK COUNTY.* Unless otherwise provided in the Rules or in NY R NY CTY E FIL Doc. 2 or where a special exemption is granted due to physical requirements (e.g., oversized maps; see NY R NY CTY E FIL Doc. 2(B)(10)), all documents to be filed with the court in a NYSCEF case, including all documents on motions and all letters to the court (where permitted), must be filed with the NYSCEF system. Documents that attorneys would not ordinarily file with the court in a hard-copy case need not be e-filed. Unless otherwise provided by the E-Filing Rules or this Protocol, in e-filed cases the County Clerk and the court will not accept documents filed in paper form. NY R NY CTY E FIL Doc. 2(B)(1). E-filing is mandatory in all types of cases (other than election law, matrimonial, Art. 78, and Mental Hygiene Law matters, and Art. 70 habeas corpus proceedings) that are commenced in this court on or after February 19, 2013. All such cases must be commenced by filing with the County Clerk electronically through NYSCEF and all subsequent documents in such cases must be e-filed. NY R NY CTY E FIL Doc. 2(A)(2)(a). For more information, including information on consensual e-filing and filing scanned hard copy documents, refer to NY R NY CTY E FIL Doc. 2(A)(2).
- *QUEENS COUNTY.* All authorized Torts, Commercial and Tax Certiorari cases may be commenced by E-Filing, however all parties must consent for the action to continue as an E-file case. NY R L QUEENS E-FILE Doc. 1(A). All papers to be filed with the court in an E-filed case shall be filed on-line with the E-file system except as directed by the court. Papers that attorneys would not ordinarily file with the court in a hard-copy case need not be filed in an E-filed matter. NY R L QUEENS E-FILE Doc. 1(E)(2).

ii. *Who may file.* Documents may be filed or served electronically only by a person who has registered as an authorized e-filing user or as otherwise provided in NY R UNIF TRIAL CTS § 202.5-b(c). NY R UNIF TRIAL CTS § 202.5-b(c)(1).

iii. *When filing made.* Documents may be transmitted at any time of the day or night to the NYSCEF site. A document other than an order or judgment is filed when its electronic transmission or, in the case of a petition that is e-filed by submission of a text file as provided in NY R UNIF TRIAL CTS § 202.5-b(b)(1), the electronic transmission of the text file is recorded at that site, provided, however, that where payment of a fee is required upon the filing of a document, the document is not filed until transmission of the document and the information or form or information as required in NY R UNIF TRIAL CTS § 202.5-b(d)(2)(i), NY R UNIF TRIAL CTS § 202.5-b(d)(2)(ii) or NY R UNIF TRIAL CTS § 202.5-b(d)(2)(iii) has been recorded at the NYSCEF site; or, if no transmission of that information or form or information is recorded, where permitted by the County Clerk, until payment is presented to the County Clerk. NY R UNIF TRIAL CTS § 202.5-b(d)(3)(i).

iv. *Notification of filing.* No later than the close of business on the business day following the electronic filing of a document, a notification, in a form prescribed by the Chief Administrator, shall be transmitted electronically by the NYSCEF site to the person filing such document and the e-mail service addresses of all other participating parties in such action. NY R UNIF TRIAL CTS § 202.5-b(d)(3)(ii).

v. *Removal of confidential information and other corrections.* If a document filed electronically is subsequently discovered to contain confidential data—including but not limited to trade secrets, information protected by confidentiality agreement, or personal confidential information as defined by statute or court rule—or otherwise to have been filed in error, the filer or another party or affected person may (1) notify the parties and any non-party filers in the action of the confidentiality issue or other error raised by the filing, and of his or her intention to seek judicial relief to correct the filing: (2) following such notification, request that the appropriate County Clerk, exercising his or her administrative discretion, place the document temporarily in "restricted" status on the NYSCEF site, to be made available for viewing by court staff and the parties but not the general public; and (3) file an application to correct the filing by order to show cause within five (5) business days of such notification (or such time as the court may direct), including a request for preliminary injunctive relief limiting interim disclosure of the document at issue. Unless otherwise directed by the court, any document placed in restricted status in response to such a request shall be returned to public view upon expiration of this five (5) day period. The Chief Administrator of the Courts shall promulgate forms to implement this process. NY R UNIF TRIAL CTS § 202.5-b(d)(3)(iii).

- *KINGS COUNTY.* For information on what to do when a document was erroneously filed with confidential information, refer to NY R L KINGS E FIL Doc. 1(B)(11).
- *NEW YORK COUNTY.* For information on what to do when a document was erroneously filed with confidential information, refer to NY R NY CTY E FIL Doc. 2(B)(8).
- *QUEENS COUNTY.* For information on what to do when a document was erroneously filed with confidential information, refer to NY R L QUEENS E-FILE Doc. 1(E)(7).

vi. *Documents requiring judge's signature.* Except where the court directs otherwise, any document that requires a judge's signature shall be transmitted electronically and in hard copy to the court. NY R UNIF TRIAL CTS § 202.5-b(d)(6).

vii. *Documents which would be inconvenient to file electronically; Hard copies.* Notwithstanding any other provision of NY R UNIF TRIAL CTS § 202.5-b, and subject to such guidelines as may be established by the Chief Administrative Judge, the County Clerk or his or her designee may require or permit a party to file in hard copy, in accordance with procedures set by the County Clerk or designee, an exhibit or other document which it is impractical or inconvenient to file electronically. NY R UNIF TRIAL CTS § 202.5-b(d)(7).

- *ERIE COUNTY.* Please contact the Supervisor of Actions & Proceedings, Erie County Clerk's Office by calling (716) 858-6662 or the Deputy County Clerk—Legal at (716) 858-6348 for information. NY R ERIE E FIL Doc. 3(III)(F).
- *KINGS COUNTY.* With limited exceptions, as set forth in the Uniform Rules and herein, all documents to be filed with the court in a NYSCEF case shall be filed online via the NYSCEF system. However, should the size, consistency or context of a hard copy document preclude electronic filing, the user shall electronically file a "Notice of Hard Copy Submission—E-Filed Cases" form EFM-3. Any hard copy submitted pursuant to NY R L KINGS E FIL Doc. 1(B)(9) shall include, as a cover page firmly fastened thereto, a copy of the Confirmation Notice received from the NYSCEF site confirming receipt of the "Notice of Hard Copy Submission—E-Filed Cases". Any party may object to such hard copy filing. The Court, in response to such objection, may, following the hard copy filing, fashion such relief as it deems appropriate pursuant to and in furtherance of the Uniform Rules and NY R L KINGS E FIL Doc. 1, including, but not limited to, an Order directing the filing party to file such documents online via the NYSCEF system. When exhibits are impractical to file pursuant to NY R UNIF TRIAL CTS § 202.5-b(d)(7), an additional "Notice of Hard Copy Exhibit Filing" form EFM-4 is required to be submitted. NY R L KINGS E FIL Doc. 1(B)(9).
- *NEW YORK COUNTY.* If a filer needs to submit unusual exhibits in original form that cannot practically be e-filed, such as oversized maps or electronic recordings, the filer should consult with the County Clerk's E-File Department by telephone at 646-386-3737 (procedural questions only) or by e-mail at ccnyef@nycourts.gov, which will normally require that the filer retain custody of the original subject to possible future directives of the court. NY R NY CTY E FIL Doc. 2(B)(10). In such instances, the filing counsel shall file with NYSCEF a "placeholder" in the form of a Notice of Hard Copy Exhibit Filing (NYSCEF Form EF 21). The Notice should be uploaded to NYSCEF as document type "Exhibit" and the filer should indicate in the "Additional Document Information" field that the filer is retaining custody of the original. Failure to e-file the Notice may result in a gap in the official record of the court. NY R NY CTY E FIL Doc. 2(B)(10).

viii. *Documents containing sensitive or proprietary information.* In an action subject to e-filing, any person may apply for an order prohibiting or restricting the electronic filing in the action of specifically identified materials on the grounds that such materials are subject to copyright or other proprietary rights, or trade secret or other privacy interests, and that electronic filing in the action is likely to result in substantial prejudice to those rights or interests. NY R UNIF TRIAL CTS § 202.5-b(k)(2).

ix. *Refusal to accept paper filings.* In accordance with NY CPLR Rule 2102(c), a County Clerk and a chief clerk of the Supreme Court or County Court, as appropriate, shall refuse to accept for filing papers filed in actions and proceedings when the paper sought to be filed:

- Is in an action subject to electronic filing pursuant to Rules of the Chief Administrator,
- Is not being filed electronically, and
- Does not include the notice required by NY R UNIF TRIAL CTS § 202.5-b(d)(1). NY R UNIF TRIAL CTS § 202.5(d)(1)(v); NY R UNIF TRIAL CTS § 202.5-bb(d).

x. *Emergency filings; Hard copies.* For information on when an emergency filing may be filed and served in hard copy, refer to NY R UNIF TRIAL CTS § 202.5-b(d)(1)(ii), NY R UNIF TRIAL CTS § 202.5-b(d)(1)(iii) and NY R UNIF TRIAL CTS § 202.5-bb(c)(3).

- *KINGS COUNTY.* Under the rules, a participating emergency e-filer must electronically file the documents initially filed in hard copy form within three (3) business days of the emergency filing; the originals will be discarded after the documents have been processed and the failure to e-file as required will therefore lead to an incomplete record. NY R L KINGS E FIL Doc. 1(B)(3).

- *NEW YORK COUNTY.* Occasionally an emergency will arise requiring expedited entry of a document with the County Clerk (e.g., an order issued in the courtroom after a conference or argument of a critical matter), such as for purposes of an immediate appeal. Expedition can be achieved by the Part as follows: the document should be carried by a Court Officer or staff member to the General Clerk's Office to assure immediate and proper recordation in the computer and, as appropriate, the posting of the document to NYSCEF or the Supreme Court Records On-Line Library ("Scroll"). The court will accommodate counsel in emergencies. NY R NY CTY Procedure XI(A).
- *NEW YORK COUNTY.* For more information on how to bring emergency matters before the court, refer to NY R NY CTY Procedure IV.

xi. *Technical failures.* The NYSCEF site shall be considered to be subject to a technical failure on a given day if the site is unable to accept filings or provide access to filed documents continuously or intermittently over the course of any period of time greater than one (1) hour after 12:00 noon of that day. Notice of all such technical failures shall be provided on the site. NY R UNIF TRIAL CTS § 202.5-b(i).

- When e-filing is hindered by a technical failure, a party may file with the appropriate clerk and serve in hard copy. NY R UNIF TRIAL CTS § 202.5-b(i). In the event an attorney or party shall file and serve documents in hard copy pursuant to NY R UNIF TRIAL CTS § 202.5-b(i), each such document shall include the notice required by NY R UNIF TRIAL CTS § 202.5-b(d)(1), and the filer shall file those documents with the NYSCEF site within three (3) business days after restoration of normal operations at that site. NY R UNIF TRIAL CTS § 202.5-b(i).
- With the exception of deadlines that by law cannot be extended, the time for filing of any document that is delayed due to technical failure of the site shall be extended for one (1) day for each day on which such failure occurs, unless otherwise ordered by the court. NY R UNIF TRIAL CTS § 202.5-b(i).
- *ERIE COUNTY.* When filing by electronic means is hindered by a technical failure, please refer to the NY R UNIF TRIAL CTS § 202.5-b(i). NY R ERIE E FIL Doc. 3(III)(K).
- *KINGS COUNTY.* When filing by electronic means is hindered by a NYSCEF technical failure (as set forth in NY R UNIF TRIAL CTS § 202.5-b(i)), a party may file with the appropriate Clerk in hard copy. Except for deadlines that by law cannot be extended (e.g. Statute of limitations, Notice of Appeal), the time for filing of any document that is delayed due to technical failure of the NYSCEF system shall be extended for one day for each day on which such failure occurs, unless otherwise ordered by the court. NY R L KINGS E FIL Doc. 1(B)(13).
- *ONONDAGA COUNTY.* When filing by electronic means is hindered by a technical failure (as set forth in NY R UNIF TRIAL CTS § 202.5-b(h)(3)(i)), a party may file a hard copy with the County Clerk. With the exception of deadlines that by law cannot be extended (e.g., a statute of limitations or the deadline for filing a Notice of Appeal), the time for filing of any document that is delayed due to technical failure of the NYSCEF system will be extended for one day for each day on which such failure occurs, unless otherwise ordered by the court. A "Notice of Hard Copy Filing Submission—E-Filed Case' must accompany any documents not filed via NYSCEF. NY R ONDGA E FIL Protocol(B)(8).

xii. *Filing fees.* For information on what information must be provided to pay filing fees, refer to NY R UNIF TRIAL CTS § 202.5-b(d)(2).

xiii. *Exemption from e-filing.* For information on exemptions from e-filing, refer to NY R UNIF TRIAL CTS § 202.5-bb(e).

xiv. *Filing exhibits*

- *ERIE COUNTY.* In the NYSCEF system, each exhibit must be uploaded as a separate .pdf file. After uploading a primary document, please choose the document type "Exhibit" and enter the appropriate number or letter and a brief description of the exhibit; each exhibit should bear a separate cover sheet clearly marked as "Exhibit A," "Exhibit B," etc. "Exhibit A" or "Exhibit B" is unacceptable as a brief description of the exhibit. Exhibits, where referenced in a signed Order as attached or affixed shall be uploaded with the signed Order as one .pdf document. NY R ERIE E FIL Doc. 3(III)(H); NY R ERIE E FIL Doc. 3(V)(D).
- *KINGS COUNTY.* In the NYSCEF system, each exhibit should be uploaded as a separate PDF file. After uploading a primary document, please choose the document type "Exhibit", enter the appropriate number or letter, and be sure to place a check mark to the right of "Attach to main document". Each exhibit shall bear

a separate cover sheet clearly marked as Exhibit A, Exhibit B, etc. NY R L KINGS E FIL Doc. 1(B)(12). Whenever possible, attorneys submitting exhibits in NYSCEF cases should make each exhibit a separate attachment to an affidavit/affirmation in the system (i.e., multiple exhibits should not be filed as a single PDF). NY R L KINGS E FIL Doc. 1(D)(1).

- *NEW YORK COUNTY.* Attorneys submitting exhibits in NYSCEF cases should make each exhibit a separate attachment to an affidavit/affirmation in the system; i.e., exhibits should not be filed as a single PDF-A together with the affidavit/affirmation or grouped together as a single PDF-A attachment because either of these two formats makes it difficult for the Justice to locate particular exhibits as needed. Counsel must also include appropriate descriptive language in the "Additional Document Information" field in NYSCEF. NY R NY CTY E FIL Doc. 2(D)(6).
- *ONONDAGA COUNTY.* All exhibits in e-filed cases must be e-filed individually as separate attachments. NY R ONDGA E FIL Protocol(B)(9)(b).

xv. *Correcting documents*

- *ERIE COUNTY.* Submission of documents which, upon examination, require correction or addition will result in notification to the filer advising that the document has been returned for correction. The filer shall make the required corrections and/or additions as indicated in the e-mail transmission sent by the County Clerk or Part Clerk through the NYSCEF site. The corrected documents may be resubmitted using the "Re-file this document" link highlighted in the filer's document list for the respective case. Please note that in the case of multiple submissions, all related documents filed at the same time may be removed from the case record and returned until all documents are properly submitted. NY R ERIE E FIL Doc. 3(III)(J).
- *KINGS COUNTY.* Submission of documents which, upon examination, require correction or addition will result in notification to the filer advising that there is a problem with a document. The filer shall make the required corrections and/or additions and resubmit the corrected document using the "Refile this document" link. In the event a document is returned for correction, the original file date will be preserved. For corrections of documents filed with the Kings County Clerk which require a court order, refer to the procedure in NY R UNIF TRIAL CTS § 202.5-b(d)(3)(iii) and NY R L KINGS E FIL Doc. 1(B)(11). NY R L KINGS E FIL Doc. 1(B)(3).
- *ONONDAGA COUNTY.* If there is an error or an additional document is required, the system will notify the filing party, who will make the corrections/additions and resubmit them online. NY R ONDGA E FIL Protocol(B)(6).
- *QUEENS COUNTY.* Generally speaking, documents that have been E-filed will not thereafter be deleted by the County Clerk from NYCEF because the filer asserts that the filing contains an error or a significant omission. When the filer wishes to correct a perceived error or omission in a filed document, he or she should file an amended version of the document, with the original remaining on file, or else obtain a court order providing for deletion of the original. The County Clerk will only delete a document upon request of the filer or on the County Clerk's own initiative when it is obvious from the face of the document alone that the filer made a fundamental error and never intended to file the document that was filed (e.g., a completely unrelated non-litigation document, a different case, or a wrong county). The County Clerk will advise the filer when any such fundamental errors are detected. NY R L QUEENS E-FILE Doc. 1(E)(6).

c. *Facsimile filing.* In the Supreme Court, facsimile filing shall be limited to commercial claims and tax certiorari, conservatorship, and mental hygiene proceedings in Monroe, Westchester, New York and Suffolk Counties. NY R UNIF TRIAL CTS § 202.5-a(a)(1). Refer to NY R UNIF TRIAL CTS § 202.5-a for information on the procedures for facsimile filing.

i. *NEW YORK COUNTY.* Unless indicated otherwise by the court in a particular case or in NY R NY CTY J RUL Doc. 1, Justices do not accept papers by fax. NY R NY CTY J RUL Rule 4.

d. *ERIE COUNTY: Filing request for judicial intervention.* An RJI in a NYSCEF case shall be filed via the NYSCEF system and will be filed after all other documents have been uploaded. The filer may choose between filing a .pdf image of the prepared RJI and any Addendum or having the system prepare the RJI which shall conform to Uniform Rules. Addenda, such as the Commercial Division Addendum, if prepared by the filer must be filed simultaneously with and attached to an RJI and uploaded as one .pdf document with the RJI. If the RJI is prepared by the e-filing system, no separate Addendum is required. Whether or not the filer elects to allow NYSCEF to create the RJI or chooses to upload a prepared RJI, data in addition to the nature of the judicial intervention, including information that appears on any Addenda will be collected through completion of the fields presented. If the filing of the RJI is accomplished through a filing agent, a prepared RJI and Addendum must be filed in lieu of the creation of the RJI by the NYSCEF system, as the RJI must be signed by the attorney. NY R ERIE E FIL Doc. 3(IV). For information on RJIs in specific types of action, refer to NY R ERIE E FIL Doc. 3(IV).

2. *Service requirements*

a. *Who may serve.* Except where otherwise prescribed by law or order of court, papers may be served by any person not a party of the age of eighteen years or over. NY CPLR Rule 2103(a).

b. *Service upon attorney.* Except where otherwise prescribed by law or order of court, papers to be served upon a party in a pending action shall be served upon the party's attorney. Where the same attorney appears for two or more parties, only one (1) copy need be served upon the attorney. Such service upon an attorney shall be made:

i. By delivering the paper to the attorney personally. NY CPLR Rule 2103(b)(1).

ii. By mailing the paper to the attorney at the address designated by that attorney for that purpose or, if none is designated, at the attorney's last known address; service by mail shall be complete upon mailing. NY CPLR Rule 2103(b)(2).

- *BRONX COUNTY.* Service by mail must be within the state. NY R BRONX FIL R Doc. 3.

iii. If the attorney's office is open, by leaving the paper with a person in charge, or if no person is in charge, by leaving it in a conspicuous place; or if the attorney's office is not open, by depositing the paper, enclosed in a sealed wrapper directed to the attorney, in the attorney's office letter drop or box. NY CPLR Rule 2103(b)(3).

iv. By leaving it at the attorney's residence within the state with a person of suitable age and discretion. Service upon an attorney shall not be made at the attorney's residence unless service at the attorney's office cannot be made. NY CPLR Rule 2103(b)(4).

v. By transmitting the paper to the attorney by facsimile transmission, provided that a facsimile telephone number is designated by the attorney for that purpose. Service by facsimile transmission shall be complete upon the receipt by the sender of a signal from the equipment of the attorney served indicating that the transmission was received, and the mailing of a copy of the paper to that attorney. The designation of a facsimile telephone number in the address block subscribed on a paper served or filed in the course of an action or proceeding shall constitute consent to service by facsimile transmission in accordance with NY CPLR Rule 2103(b)(5). An attorney may change or rescind a facsimile telephone number by serving a notice on the other parties. NY CPLR Rule 2103(b)(5).

vi. By dispatching the paper to the attorney by overnight delivery service at the address designated by the attorney for that purpose or, if none is designated, at the attorney's last known address. Service by overnight delivery service shall be complete upon deposit of the paper enclosed in a properly addressed wrapper into the custody of the overnight delivery service for overnight delivery, prior to the latest time designated by the overnight delivery service for overnight delivery. "Overnight delivery service" means any delivery service which regularly accepts items for overnight delivery to any address in the state. NY CPLR Rule 2103(b)(6).

vii. By transmitting the paper to the attorney by electronic means where and in the manner authorized by the chief administrator of the courts by rule and, unless such rule shall otherwise provide, such transmission shall be upon the party's written consent. The subject matter heading for each paper sent by electronic means must indicate that the matter being transmitted electronically is related to a court proceeding. NY CPLR Rule 2103(b)(7).

- *KINGS COUNTY.* Pursuant to the E-Filing Rules, service of interlocutory documents is made by posting a document to the NYSCEF site, which automatically and immediately transmits an email notice of the filing, including a link to the document, to all participating counsel and unrepresented litigants on the case. The Rules also authorize service by other methods permitted by the CPLR. If service by such other method is made, proof of service must be filed with NYSCEF. NY R L KINGS E FIL Doc. 1(I).
- *NEW YORK COUNTY.* Service. . .will be made automatically through NYSCEF upon all participating counsel and unrepresented parties in the case. There are limited exceptions to the requirement for e-filing in the covered kinds of cases. NY R NY CTY Procedure XI(A). Pursuant to the E-Filing Rules, service of interlocutory documents is made by posting a document to the NYSCEF site, which automatically and immediately transmits an e-mail notice of the filing, including a link to the document, to all participating counsel and unrepresented litigants on the case. The Rules also authorize service by other methods permitted by the CPLR. If service by such a method is made, proof of service must be filed with NYSCEF. NY R NY CTY E FIL Doc. 2(I).
- *QUEENS COUNTY.* Filing with the system permits counsel to serve the papers electronically pursuant to

NY R UNIF TRIAL CTS § 202.5-b(f) once consent to E-Filing has been filed on-line. Consult NY R UNIF TRIAL CTS § 202.5-bb(c) for service in mandatory e-filing. Any required proof of service should be E-filed as a separate document. NY R L QUEENS E-FILE Doc. 1(E)(4).

c. *Electronic service mandatory; Consenting to electronic service; How electronic service may be made.* Except as otherwise provided in NY R UNIF TRIAL CTS § 202.5-bb, filing and service of all documents in an action that has been commenced electronically in accordance with NY R UNIF TRIAL CTS § 202.5-bb shall be by electronic means. NY R UNIF TRIAL CTS § 202.5-bb(c)(1).

   i. *Party's consent required for certain e-filing.* After commencement of an action wherein e-filing is authorized, documents may be electronically filed and served, but only by, and electronic service shall be made only upon, a party or parties who have consented thereto. NY R UNIF TRIAL CTS § 202.5-b(b)(2)(i).

   - A consent to e-filing in an action shall state that the party providing it agrees to the use of e-filing in the action and to be bound by the filing and service provisions in NY R UNIF TRIAL CTS § 202.5-b. NY R UNIF TRIAL CTS § 202.5-b(b)(2)(ii).

   ii. *Address for service; Duty to notify as to changes.* The e-mail service address recorded at the time of registration is the e-mail address at which service of interlocutory documents on that party may be made through notification transmitted by the NYSCEF site. It is the responsibility of each filing user to monitor that address and promptly notify the Resource Center in the event of a change in his or her e-mail service address. NY R UNIF TRIAL CTS § 202.5-b(f)(2)(i).

   iii. *How service made.* An e-filing party causes service of an interlocutory document to be made upon another party participating in e-filing by filing the document electronically. Upon receipt of an interlocutory document, the NYSCEF site shall automatically transmit electronic notification to all e-mail service addresses in such action. NY R UNIF TRIAL CTS § 202.5-b(f)(2)(ii).

   - Except as provided otherwise in NY R UNIF TRIAL CTS § 202.5-b(h)(3), the electronic transmission of the notification shall constitute service of the document on the e-mail service addresses identified therein; however, such service will not be effective if the filing party learns that the notification did not reach the address of the person to be served. Proof of such service will be recorded on the NYSCEF site. A party may, however, utilize other service methods permitted by the CPLR provided that, if one of such other methods is used, proof of that service shall be filed electronically. NY R UNIF TRIAL CTS § 202.5-b(f)(2)(ii).

   iv. *Signatures on hard copies; Proof of service filed electronically.* When an e-filing party serves a document in hard copy on a non-participating party, the document served shall bear full signatures of all signatories and proof of such service shall be filed electronically. NY R UNIF TRIAL CTS § 202.5-b(b)(2)(i).

   - *ERIE COUNTY.* In the NYSCEF system, each Affidavit of Service must be uploaded as a separate .pdf file. After uploading the Affidavit, please choose the document type: "Affirmation/Affidavit of Service" and enter the name of the party served as Additional Document Information. NY R ERIE E FIL Doc. 3(III)(I); NY R ERIE E FIL Doc. 3(V)(F).

   v. *Effect of failure to consent.* A party's failure to consent to participation in electronic filing and service shall not bar any other party to the action from filing documents electronically with the County Clerk and the court or serving documents upon any other party who has consented to participation. A party who has not consented to participation shall file documents with the court and the County Clerk, and serve and be served with documents, in hard copy. NY R UNIF TRIAL CTS § 202.5-b(b)(2)(i).

d. *Service upon party.* If a party has not appeared by an attorney or the party's attorney cannot be served, service shall be upon the party by a method specified in NY CPLR Rule 2103(b)(1), NY CPLR Rule 2103(b)(2), NY CPLR Rule 2103(b)(4), NY CPLR Rule 2103(b)(5) or NY CPLR Rule 2103(b)(6). NY CPLR Rule 2103(c).

e. *Service on all parties.* Each paper served on any party shall be served on every other party who has appeared, except as otherwise may be provided by court order or as provided in NY CPLR § 3012 or in NY CPLR § 3215(f). Upon demand by a party, the plaintiff shall supply that party with a list of those who have appeared and the names and addresses of their attorneys. NY CPLR Rule 2103(e).

f. *Service by filing.* If a paper cannot be served by any of the methods specified in NY CPLR Rule 2103(b) and NY CPLR Rule 2103(c), service may be made by filing the paper as if it were a paper required to be filed. NY CPLR Rule 2103(d).

g. *Definitions.* For the purposes of NY CPLR Rule 2103:

   i. "Mailing" means the deposit of a paper enclosed in a first class postpaid wrapper, addressed to the address designated by a person for that purpose or, if none is designated, at that person's last known address, in a post office or official depository under the exclusive care and custody of the United States Postal Service within the state;

ii. "Electronic means" means any method of transmission of information between computers or other machines designed for the purpose of sending and receiving such transmissions, and which allows the recipient to reproduce the information transmitted in a tangible medium of expression;

iii. "Facsimile transmission" means any method of transmission of documents to a facsimile machine at a remote location which can automatically produce a tangible copy of such documents. NY CPLR Rule 2103(f).

G. Hearings

1. *Oral argument.* Motion papers received by the clerk of the court on or before the return date shall be deemed submitted as of the return date. The assigned judge, in his or her discretion or at the request of a party, thereafter may determine that any motion be orally argued and may fix a time for oral argument. NY R UNIF TRIAL CTS § 202.8(d).

a. A party requesting oral argument shall set forth such request in its notice of motion or in its order to show cause or on the first page of the answering papers, as the case may be. Where all parties to a motion request oral argument, oral argument shall be granted unless the court shall determine it to be unnecessary. NY R UNIF TRIAL CTS § 202.8(d).

b. Where a motion is brought on by order to show cause, the court may set forth in the order that oral argument is required on the return date of the motion. NY R UNIF TRIAL CTS § 202.8(d).

i. *BRONX COUNTY.* All orders to show cause, with the exception of orders to show cause that are returnable in the City Part, the STP Part, the Matrimonial Part and the Preliminary/Compliance Conference Part (IA-11), submitted on or after August 25, 2003, will be returnable on a Monday in the assigned Justice's part and appear on his or her motion calendar. Appearances will be required on orders to show cause. NY R BRONX FIL R Doc. 8. A motion on notice or a notice of petition in a New York Supreme Court E-File (hereafter known as NYSCEF) case, as in others, shall be made returnable in the Motion Support Office (Room 217). NY R BRONX E FIL R Doc. 1(1).

- After a motion/petition and notice are filed with the NYSCEF system, the Motion Support Office will automatically place the motion/proceeding on the submit calendar in the Motion Support Office (Room 217) for the return date. No appearance or other action by the filing attorney is required in order for the motion to be calendared if the motion fee is paid for via NYSCEF. Motions in e-filed cases (other than tax certiorari cases) appear on the submit calendar in Room 217 on the return date. NY R BRONX E FIL R Doc. 1(2).

c. *KINGS COUNTY.* All motions require appearances and oral argument. NY R L KINGS Pt. C, Rule 3.

2. *Return date; Time for hearing.* A notice of motion shall specify the time and place of the hearing on the motion. NY CPLR Rule 2214(a). The moving party determines when a motion on notice shall be heard, but she has to consult the court's or judge's calendar practice first. The movant picks out a "return day" sufficiently far off to assure that the notice requirements of NY CPLR Rule 2214(b) can be met, and to assure as well that the day picked is a day on which the assigned judge hears motions. SIEGEL-NYPRAC § 247.

a. *Judge assigned to hear motion*

i. *Referral to judge supervising disclosure.* Unless the chief administrator of the courts has, by rule, provided otherwise, if a case has been assigned to a judge to supervise disclosure pursuant to NY CPLR § 3104, all motions preliminary to trial shall be referred to such judge whenever practicable. NY CPLR Rule 3214(a).

ii. *Referral to judge who decided prior motion.* Any motion may be referred to a judge who decided a prior motion in the action. NY CPLR Rule 2217(a).

iii. *Transfer when judge unable to hear motion.* If a motion is made to a judge who is or will be for any reason unable to hear it, it may be transferred by order of such judge or by written stipulation of the parties to any other judge to whom it might originally have been made. NY CPLR Rule 2217(c).

iv. *Procedure for unassigned cases.* If a case has not been assigned to a judge, the motion shall be made returnable before the court, and a copy of the moving papers, together with a request for judicial intervention, shall be filed with the court, with proof of service upon all other parties, where required by NY R UNIF TRIAL CTS § 202.6, within five (5) days of service upon the other parties. The moving party shall give written notice of the index number to all other parties immediately after filing of the papers. NY R UNIF TRIAL CTS § 202.8(b).

- *Responding papers.* Copies of all responding papers shall be submitted to the court, with proof of service and with the index number set forth in the papers, on or before the return date. NY R UNIF TRIAL CTS § 202.8(b).

- *Assignment after request for judicial intervention.* The case shall be assigned to a judge as soon as practicable after the filing of the request for judicial intervention pursuant to NY R UNIF TRIAL CTS § 202.6, but in no event later than the return date. After assignment to the judge, the court shall provide for appropriate notice to the parties of the name of the assigned judge. NY R UNIF TRIAL CTS § 202.8(b).
- *Motions to be heard in another county.* Motion papers noticed to be heard in a county other than the county where the venue of the action has been placed by the plaintiff shall be assigned to a judge in accordance with procedures established by the Chief Administrator. NY R UNIF TRIAL CTS § 202.8(b).

v. *ALBANY COUNTY: Motions referred to IAS Justice.* All motions made after a case has been assigned a day certain shall be referred to the IAS Justice unless the motion is returnable during the term in which the matter has been assigned a day certain, in that event, the matter will be referred to the Part 1 Justice for that particular term who may entertain the motion or refer such motion to the IAS Justice. Under those circumstances, the Part I Justice shall decide whether or not to strike the note of issue or assign the matter a new day certain. NY R 3 JD SUP Doc. 1(H)(2). All motions shall be returnable before the assigned justice. NY R 3 JD SUP Doc. 1(B).

b. *Trial of issue raised by motion.* The court may order that an issue of fact raised on a motion shall be separately tried by the court or a referee. If the issue is triable of right by jury, the court shall give the parties an opportunity to demand a jury trial of such issue. Failure to make such demand within the time limited by the court, or, if no such time is limited, before trial begins, shall be deemed a waiver of the right to trial by jury. An order under NY CPLR § 2218 shall specify the issue to be tried. NY CPLR § 2218.

c. *Audio-visual coverage of trial court proceeding.* Audio-visual coverage of proceedings in the trial courts shall be permitted only in accordance with the provisions of Part 131 of the Rules of the Chief Administrator (NY R CHIEF ADMIN § 131.1, et seq.). NY R CHIEF J § 29.3.

d. *Adjournment of return date.* Stipulations of adjournment of the return date made by the parties shall be in writing and shall be submitted to the assigned judge. Such stipulation shall be effective unless the court otherwise directs. No more than three (3) stipulated adjournments for an aggregate period of sixty (60) days shall be submitted without prior permission of the court. NY R UNIF TRIAL CTS § 202.8(e)(1).

i. Absent agreement by the parties, a request by any party for an adjournment shall be submitted in writing, upon notice to the other party, to the assigned judge on or before the return date. The court will notify the requesting party whether the adjournment has been granted. NY R UNIF TRIAL CTS § 202.8(e)(2).

ii. *BRONX COUNTY.* Non-disclosure motions for IA5, IA7 and IA22 will be adjourned for oral argument to the Monday of the second week following the week of the return date of the motion. All other non-disclosure motions will be deemed submitted on the return date and forwarded to Chambers unless a stipulation of adjournment complying with the requirements of NY R UNIF TRIAL CTS § 202.8(e) is submitted, in which event, the motion will be adjourned for the requested date and kept in the Clerk's Office. If a non-stipulated request for adjournment or notice is submitted, the motion and request will be forwarded to Chambers for judicial approval or denial of the request. In either event, the attorney requesting the adjournment will be notified, via telephone, of the granting or denial of the request and instructed to notify his adversary. NY R BRONX FIL R Doc. 8.

iii. *BRONX COUNTY.* Motions that have been e-filed may be adjourned in Room 217 if an adjournment complies with the procedures of the Motion Support Office (explained in the "Filing Rules—Motion Procedure" section of the "Courthouse Procedures" link on the website of [the] court). An adjournment that so complies may be obtained by filing a stipulation of all parties with NYSCEF (designated in the filing menu as a "Stipulation to Adjourn Motion"). NY R BRONX E FIL R Doc. 1(3).

iv. *NEW YORK COUNTY.* The Courtroom also maintains a "APB (All Papers By)" Calendar, which is used when a party seeks an adjournment but fails to comply with the Courtroom's procedures or there is a failure to comply with procedures that requires the clerk to adjourn the motion/application (e.g., failure to submit a Confirmation Notice in an e-filed case). The case may be put over for three days to allow compliance with those procedures, as described further below. NY R NY CTY Procedure II(C); NY R NY CTY E FIL Doc. 2(D)(2). E-filed applications may be adjourned in the Part if an adjournment complies with the Part's procedures (see the Uniform Rules of the Justices (Local Rules) on the court's website). An adjournment that so complies may be obtained by filing with NYSCEF a stipulation of all parties (designated in the filing menu as a Stipulation—Adjournment of Motion—Before Judge); the motion number and the current return date of the motion being adjourned shall be set forth in the "Additional Document Information" field in NYSCEF. Absent any problems, the Part will effectuate the adjournment without need for an appearance or any other action by the parties. NY R NY CTY E FIL Doc. 2(D)(4).

v. *QUEENS COUNTY.* The Motion Support Office is NOT authorized to grant adjournments. NY R L QUEENS MOT SUP Doc. 1.

e. *ALBANY COUNTY: Motion terms.* There shall be a. . . Motion Term on each Friday in the Supreme Court, Albany County. The Friday Motion Term shall include all Article 78 Proceedings involving New York State and proceedings commenced pursuant to Article 14 of the Civil Service Law (including applications for injunctive relief made pursuant to section 209-a of the Civil Service Law). NY R 3 JD SUP Doc. 1(F). Generally, parties will be granted only one adjournment for the Friday Motion Term. NY R 3 JD SUP Doc. 1(F).

f. *ALBANY COUNTY: Motion determined without hearing.* All motions are deemed "submitted" on the return date and no appearances are required by the parties. NY R 3 JD SUP Doc. 1(B). In the event oral argument is requested, the parties should not appear on the return date. At the discretion of the assigned Judge and upon the granting of a request for oral argument, the parties will be notified by Chambers of the scheduled time and place at which argument will be heard. Where a motion is brought on by order to show cause, the court may set forth in the order that appearances and/or oral argument are required on the return date of the motion. NY R 3 JD SUP Doc. 1(B).

g. *BRONX COUNTY: Return date.* All assigned and unassigned motions will be returnable five (5) days a week in the Civil Branch Clerk's Office, Room 217, at 9:30 a.m. NY R BRONX FIL R Doc. 8.

i. If on any submitted non-disclosure motion oral argument is requested and granted, or directed by the Court, the motion shall be adjourned for oral argument before the I.A. Judge on the second Monday following the week of the return date of the motion. Attorneys will be notified via telephone of the adjourned date. NY R BRONX FIL R Doc. 8.

h. *BRONX COUNTY: Oral argument.* Calendars of disclosure motions and other motions adjourned for oral argument will be published for the four (4) business days preceding the rescheduled appearance date and on the rescheduled date of the motion. These repetitive publications will serve as the notification of procedure of adjournment of all motions. In addition, two (2) days before the return date of unassigned motions a list of such motions indicating the assigned Justice and the adjourned date of the motion will be published. NY R BRONX FIL R Doc. 8.

i. *BRONX COUNTY: Resolution before return date.* Counsel/parties must advise the Court in writing on or before the return date of all motions that have been resolved by Counsel/parties themselves and all motions the movant(s) wish to be withdrawn. NY R BRONX FIL R Doc. 8.

j. *ERIE COUNTY: Calendaring of motions.* Refer to individual Justice's Part Rules. NY R ERIE E FIL Doc. 3(V)(B).

k. *KINGS COUNTY: Return date set by court.* Irrespective of the return date indicated in the notice of motion, motions will be rescheduled by the E-file/Motion Support Office to a date designated by the assigned Judge. NY R L KINGS Pt. C, Rule 2.

l. *KINGS COUNTY: Calendar calls.* There shall be two (2) calendar calls on motion days. The first calendar call shall be at 9:30 AM and the second calendar call shall be at 10:45 AM, unless the Judge's Part Rules provide otherwise. Defaults shall only be taken on second call. Attorneys with appearances elsewhere in the courthouse may advise the clerk of their whereabouts to avoid a default. Failure to so advise the clerk or appear at the default calendar call will result in a default order being entered or the motion being marked off the calendar. NY R L KINGS Pt. C, Rule 7.

m. *NEW YORK COUNTY: Return date and assigned courtroom.* Motions made by notice of motion and petitions and notices of petition in special proceedings are processed by the General Clerk's Office (Room 119) and are to be made returnable in the Motion Submission Part Courtroom (Room 130) on any business day of the week at 9:30 AM. There are some differences in electronically-filed cases. NY R NY CTY Procedure II; NY R NY CTY Procedure II(C); NY R NY CTY J RUL Rule 13(a).

i. For the convenience of counsel, between 9:00 A.M. and 9:30 A.M. each day, in advance of the "call," Room 130 accepts (1) written stipulations; (2) affidavits/affirmations reciting the required details as to an adjournment on consent; (3) stipulations, letters or other writings withdrawing motions; and (4) final papers or complete sets of papers on motions. For motions in which these items are handed in before the "call," no one need remain to answer the "call." Counsel/parties must advise the court, either between 9:00 A.M. and 9:30 A.M. or at the "call," of all motions or cases that have been resolved by counsel/parties themselves and all motions that the movant no longer wishes to pursue. If such resolution occurs subsequent to the "call", the assigned Justice must be advised as soon as possible, by written notice sent to the Part, so that the court does not do unnecessary work. NY R NY CTY Procedure II(C).

ii. Depending upon the assigned Part, contested motions submitted in the Motion Submission Part Courtroom are submitted without argument, or rescheduled for oral argument if so directed by the assigned Justice. For Justices who schedule argument on a case-by-case basis, notice of the argument date will be transmitted by the court. Counsel may ascertain how a motion submitted in Courtroom 130 was marked by consulting Scroll on the court's website, the e-Track application, or, on the two (2) days immediately following the submission date, the New York Law Journal. NY R NY CTY J RUL Rule 13(a).

n. *NEW YORK COUNTY: Motion call.* Each day in the Motion Submission Part Courtroom, commencing at 9:30 A.M., all motions returnable that day will be "called" for the submission of these papers, which must be handed up at this "call" or, as described below, immediately before. Because hundreds of motions appear on the Room 130 calendars every day, motion papers (other than part of the moving papers as described above) cannot be accepted on any day prior to the return date. Courtesy copies are not required nor accepted, but working copies are required by certain Justices in e-filed cases. NY R NY CTY Procedure II(C). If argument is directed, it will take place on an announced date shortly after the day of submission. NY R NY CTY Procedure II(C).

o. *NEW YORK COUNTY: Oral arguments.* Pursuant to request of some Justices, motions submitted in Room 130 will automatically be scheduled for a set argument date in the Part. Other Justices determine on a case-by-case basis after submission in Room 130 whether to accept a particular substantive motion on submission, to require oral argument, or to hold a conference. NY R NY CTY Procedure II(D). If argument is directed by the Justice automatically, notice of argument and the argument date will be given in Room 130. Any appearing party is expected to give notice to all parties and an announcement to this effect is made in Room 130. If the motion is submitted in Room 130 and the Justice, after examining the file, determines that argument should be directed, notice of the argument and the argument date will not be sent by the court. To obtain notification of the argument date and other developments, counsel should use e-Track. If argument notification is not given or transmitted as just described, counsel should understand that the motion has been taken on submission for decision on the papers. NY R NY CTY Procedure II(D).

i. Calendars of motions to be argued in the Parts are published on the morning of the argument date and on the day before in the New York Law Journal under each Part. Argument information is available on a case-by-case basis in Scroll, and e-mail notifications are sent by e-Track to participating attorneys whenever a motion is scheduled for argument in the court's computer system. NY R NY CTY J RUL Rule 15(a)

p. *NEW YORK COUNTY: Motion determined without hearing.* Given the purpose of the Room 130 procedure, the substance of motions will not be addressed at the submission "call." No Judge is present. To the extent possible, motions submitted in Room 130 will be decided "on the papers." Indeed, attorneys are encouraged to use service or clerks to deliver papers or working copies, or to agree among themselves to have one of them deliver papers for all parties by service or a clerk. Counsel for the movant need not appear to "take a default" on any motion or for any other reason. Motions will be submitted, not marked off, in the absence of the movant. Opposing counsel similarly need not appear in person in order to avoid suffering a default. Delivery of papers by service or a clerk will suffice. The court's goal is to be able to collect papers on motions in an orderly fashion but without any attorney having to make an appearance in Room 130 at any time. NY R NY CTY Procedure II(C).

q. *ONONDAGA COUNTY: Return date.* If the motion is the first filing in an action, the case will be assigned and counsel will be notified by the Supreme Court Clerk's Office via the NYSCEF system of the assigned justice and return date. NY R ONDGA E FIL Protocol(B)(7)(c). If the motion is on a previously assigned case, counsel may choose a return date from the assigned justice's motion term schedule. If the date in unavailable, the Supreme Court Clerk's Office will assign the motion to the next available motion term date and will notify counsel via e-mail. The change will also appear in the notification generated by the NYSCEF system. NY R ONDGA E FIL Protocol(B)(7)(d).

r. *QUEENS COUNTY: Return date.* Motions must be made returnable on the proper day/time based on the assigned judge. NY R L QUEENS MOT SUP Doc. 1. Failure to make a motion returnable on the proper day/time may result in the motion being administratively rescheduled or marked off. NY R L QUEENS MOT SUP Doc. 1.

s. *QUEENS COUNTY: Unassigned motions.* For RJI/Motions, due to the fact that the movant would not know who the assigned judge will be, the notice of motion may be returnable any day of the week. RJI/Motions shall be made returnable in "Queens Supreme Court" with no address designated. The motion will be administratively rescheduled to the proper day of the week based on the judge (once a judge has been assigned). Within one (1) week of filing, the movant must check online to see who the assigned judge is (and therefore the location/date/time) that their motion is now returnable. Movant must then notify their adversary of this information prior to the return date. NY R L QUEENS MOT SUP Doc. 1.

3. *Entry of order after hearing.* An order determining a motion shall be entered and filed in the office of the clerk of the court where the action is triable, and all papers used on the motion and any opinion or memorandum in writing shall be filed with

that clerk unless the order dispenses with such filing. When a statute or civil practice rule requires such filing and entry in a county other than that in which the order was made, the party prevailing on the motion shall file the order and the papers used on the motion with the proper clerk after receiving them. If a party fails to file any papers required to be filed under NY CPLR Rule 2220(a), the order may be vacated as irregular, with costs. NY CPLR Rule 2220(a). For more information on the entry of an order after a motion, refer to NY CPLR Rule 2219.

a. *BRONX COUNTY: Settled orders.* A Judge's decision will often call for a Settled Order. The purpose of the settled order is to give effect to the decision by directing that some action be done and/or that a court official perform some task. NY R BRONX LEG SUP Doc. 2. A settled order consists of a notice of settlement informing all parties that the proposed order will be presented to the judge who made the decision on a date certain. Next comes the proposed order which will be presented to the judge. This order should conform to the judge's decision and should direct the relief granted in the decision. This should be followed by proof of service upon all parties who were noticed with the decision. It is also helpful if a copy of the judge's decision is included along with the other papers. A settled order should always be noticed before the judge who made the decision. NY R BRONX LEG SUP Doc. 2.

   i. Although an order is usually settled by the party who prevailed on the motion, any party may settle the order. It should be presented to the court within sixty (60) days of the decision. The other parties are entitled to ten (10) days notice where service of the settled order is done by mail, five (5) days if the notice is personally delivered. An attorney who is served with a notice of settlement which he believes does not accurately reflect the decision may settle a counter order. The counter order must be noticed for the same day and must be served not less than seven (7) days if by mail and two (2) days if personally delivered. NY R BRONX LEG SUP Doc. 2.

   ii. Settled orders are usually sent to the judge the day after they noticed for settlement. No appearance is necessary or even contemplated on a settled order. If the decision directs "submit order", then no notice is necessary, and the order will be sent to the judge as soon a practical after it is received. No fees are collected on settled orders. NY R BRONX LEG SUP Doc. 2.

b. *ERIE COUNTY: Proposed orders.* Proposed orders shall be submitted through the NYSCEF system and a working copy provided to the IAS Justice for signature, if Part Rules so require. NY R ERIE E FIL Doc. 3(V)(G).

c. *KINGS COUNTY: Long form orders.* If the Court directs that an order be settled or submitted on a motion in a NYSCEF case, the proposed order, with Notice of Settlement where required, and any proposed counter-order shall be filed with the Court via NYSCEF. The relevant clerk's office will process the documents in the customary manner. NY R L KINGS E FIL Doc. 1(E).

   i. WORKING COPIES OF PROPOSED ORDERS WITH NOTICE OF SETTLEMENT MUST BE SUBMITTED IN THE MOTION SUPPORT OFFICE (ROOM 227) AS EXPLAINED HEREIN. THEY MUST NOT BE DELIVERED TO THE PART OR CHAMBERS, EXCEPT WHERE THE INDIVIDUAL JUSTICE'S PART RULES PROVIDE OTHERWISE; DOING SO WILL CAUSE ADMINISTRATIVE CONFUSION AND POSSIBLE MISPLACEMENT OF PAPERS. Any such submission shall be sent in a timely manner (kindly review individual Justice's rules) and be conspicuously marked on the outside "NYSCEF Matter;" lack of such marking may delay processing. After an order/counter-order has been signed, it will be scanned, and the County Clerk will affix the entry stamp into the NYSCEF system, which will immediately transmit notice of this event via e-mail, including a link to the entered document, to all participating attorneys and unrepresented litigants in the case. Such transmittal does not constitute Notice of Entry. NY R L KINGS E FIL Doc. 1(E).

d. *NEW YORK COUNTY: Long form orders.* Although the court strongly favors the use of short form orders and judgments, there are instances when settlement of an order or judgment is appropriate. When a Justice directs in a decision that a long form order or judgment be settled, that decision is recorded in the court's computer system by the General Clerk's Office and the motion file with decision is held in the Order Section of the Office in Room 119. The settlement process takes place there. NY R NY CTY Procedure II(D); NY R NY CTY E FIL Doc. 2(E).

   i. A proposed long form order or judgment in compliance NY R UNIF TRIAL CTS § 202.48 must be presented to the relevant back office, together with a notice of settlement which bears a settlement date, the date on which the order is to be ready for formal presentation to the Justice. In an e-filed case the submission shall be made electronically. The proposed order or counter-order should be e-filed and it will be transmitted automatically by the NYSCEF system to the appropriate back office. The return date and time of the proposed order must be at 9:30 A.M. no sooner than either five (5) days from personal service of the proposed order or ten (10) days from service by mail. Proof of timely service on the other parties must accompany the proposed order in a hard copy case. If an order or judgment is submitted late (later than sixty (60) days from signing and filing of the decision) and the proponent can show good cause for this tardiness, an affidavit or affirmation justifying the delay should be annexed to the proposed order, together with proof of service thereof. If persuaded, the Justice will consider the proposed order despite its untimeliness. NY R NY CTY Procedure II(D); NY R NY CTY E FIL Doc. 2(E).

ii. Sometimes a decision will state "Submit Order." The submitting party should prepare a long form order and make it returnable without notice. Counsel should deliver the proposed order to the Order Section of the appropriate back office, except in an e-filed case, when it shall be submitted electronically. NY R NY CTY Procedure II(D). If the decision of the court directs that a proposed order be settled or submitted in the Part or in Chambers, that direction, should, of course, be followed without presentation of the proposal to the back office. NY R NY CTY Procedure II(D).

iii. For information on proposed counter-orders, refer to NY R NY CTY Procedure II(D) and NY R NY CTY J RUL Rule 16(b).

e. *QUEENS COUNTY: Proposed orders.* If the court directs that an order be settled or submitted on a motion in an E-file case, the proposed order and any proposed counter-order shall be filed with the court on-line with proof of service. (If a decision refers to a proceeding on the record, a copy of the transcript must be submitted.) Working copies of all proposed orders MUST be submitted to the Motion Support Office before an order can be reviewed. NY R L QUEENS E-FILE Doc. 1(I).

i. Counsel are advised to adhere to NY R UNIF TRIAL CTS § 202.48 regarding the submission or settlement of their proposed order or judgment. Persons who are submitting proposed orders/judgments pursuant to a previously issued memorandum decision must submit a copy of the memorandum decision with their proposed order/judgment. Upon E-Filing a proposed order/judgement, a working copy of the proposed order/judgement must be provided to the Motion Support Office. NY R L QUEENS MOT SUP Doc. 1.

H. Forms

1. Official Motion to Dismiss Forms for New York

a. Request for judicial intervention. NY R UNIF TRIAL CTS § 202.6.

b. Notice of motion. NY R UNIF TRIAL CTS § 202.7(b).

2. New York Motion to Dismiss Forms

a. Notice of motion to dismiss complaint; General form. MCF CPLR § 5:71.

b. Notice of motion to dismiss complaint; Official form. MCF CPLR § 5:72.

c. Notice of motion to dismiss complaint; Proposed official form 27. MCF CPLR § 5:74.

d. Notice of motion to dismiss complaint or cause of action upon ground that court has no jurisdiction of subject matter. MCF CPLR § 5:80.

e. Notice of motion to dismiss complaint upon ground that court has no jurisdiction of subject matter or of person of defendant. MCF CPLR § 5:81.

f. Affidavit in support of motion to dismiss complaint or cause of action upon ground that court has no jurisdiction of subject matter. MCF CPLR § 5:82.

g. Affidavit in support of motion to dismiss complaint upon ground that court has no jurisdiction of subject matter or of person of defendant. MCF CPLR § 5:83.

h. Notice of motion to dismiss complaint or cause of action upon ground that complaint fails to state cause of action; Example 1. MCF CPLR § 5:131.

i. Notice of motion to dismiss complaint upon ground that complaint fails to state cause of action; Example 2. MCF CPLR § 5:132.

j. Affidavit in support of motion to dismiss complaint or cause of action upon ground that it fails to state cause of action. MCF CPLR § 5:133.

k. Affidavit in support of motion to dismiss complaint upon ground that it fails to state cause of action. MCF CPLR § 5:134.

l. Affidavit of defendant in support of motion to dismiss complaint upon ground that it fails to state cause of action. MCF CPLR § 5:135.

m. Affirmation in support of motion to dismiss complaint upon ground that it fails to state cause of action. MCF CPLR § 5:136.

n. Notice of motion to dismiss complaint or cause of action upon ground that court has no jurisdiction of person of defendant. MCF CPLR § 5:138.

o. Notice of motion to dismiss complaint upon grounds that complaint fails to state cause of action and lack of personal jurisdiction. MCF CPLR § 5:139.

p. Affidavit of defendant in support of motion to dismiss complaint upon ground of failure to state cause of action and lack of personal jurisdiction. MCF CPLR § 5:140.

q. Notice of motion to dismiss complaint upon ground that court has no jurisdiction of person of defendant; Example 1. MCF CPLR § 5:141.

r. Affidavit of attorney in support of motion to dismiss complaint or cause of action upon ground that court has no jurisdiction of person of defendant. MCF CPLR § 5:144.

s. Affidavit of defendant in support of motion to dismiss complaint upon ground that court has no jurisdiction of person of defendant; Example 1. MCF CPLR § 5:146.

t. Notice of motion to dismiss complaint or cause of action upon ground that court should not proceed in absence of person who should be a party. MCF CPLR § 5:157.

u. Affidavit in support of motion to dismiss complaint or cause of action upon ground that court should not proceed in absence of person who should be a party. MCF CPLR § 5:158.

v. General form of affidavit of service of motion papers. MCF CPLR § 5:24.

I. Applicable Rules

1. *State rules*

a. Short title; Application; Construction; Definitions. NY CPLR § 101; NY CPLR § 103; NY CPLR § 104; NY CPLR § 105.

b. Appendix of official forms. NY CPLR § 107.

c. Personal service by mail; Defendant's appearance; Inconvenient forum. NY CPLR § 312-a; NY CPLR Rule 320; NY CPLR Rule 327.

d. Joinder. NY CPLR § 1001; NY CPLR § 1003; NY CPLR § 1004.

e. Extensions of time generally. NY CPLR § 2004.

f. Form of papers. NY CPLR Rule 2101; NY CPLR Rule 2102; NY CPLR § 2105; NY CPLR Rule 2106; NY GEN BUS § 399-ddd; NY R UNIF TRIAL CTS § 215.2; NY R UNIF TRIAL CTS § 215.3.

g. Service of papers. NY CPLR Rule 2103.

h. Where motion made; In supreme court action. NY CPLR § 2212.

i. Motion papers; Service; Time. NY CPLR Rule 2214.

j. Relief demanded by other than moving party. NY CPLR Rule 2215.

k. Prior motion; Ex parte motion; Transfer of motion; Hearings; Orders. NY CPLR Rule 2217; NY CPLR § 2218; NY CPLR Rule 2220.

l. Computation of time. NY CPLR § 2402; NY GEN CONSTR § 19; NY GEN CONSTR § 20; NY GEN CONSTR § 25-a; NY GEN CONSTR § 30; NY GEN CONSTR § 31; NY GEN CONSTR § 53.

m. Service of pleadings and demand for complaint. NY CPLR § 3012.

n. Amended and supplemental pleadings. NY CPLR Rule 3025.

o. Motion to dismiss. NY CPLR Rule 3211.

p. Motions heard by judge supervising disclosure; Stay of disclosure. NY CPLR Rule 3214.

q. Fees; Index number fees of county clerks. NY CPLR § 8018.

r. Hours of court; Proceedings in court. NY R CHIEF J § 3.1; NY R CHIEF J § 29.3.

s. Application of part; Waiver; Additional rules; Application of CPLR; Definitions. NY R UNIF TRIAL CTS § 202.1.

t. Papers filed in court; Electronic filing in supreme court. NY R UNIF TRIAL CTS § 202.5; NY R UNIF TRIAL CTS § 202.5-a; NY R UNIF TRIAL CTS § 202.5-b; NY R UNIF TRIAL CTS § 202.5-bb.

u. Request for judicial intervention. NY R UNIF TRIAL CTS § 202.6.

v. Calendaring of motions; Uniform notice of motion form; Affirmation of good faith. NY R UNIF TRIAL CTS § 202.7.

w. Motion procedure; Preliminary conferences. NY R UNIF TRIAL CTS § 202.8; NY R UNIF TRIAL CTS § 202.12.

x. Rules of the commercial division of the Supreme Court. NY R UNIF TRIAL CTS § 202.70.

y. Signing of papers. NY R CHIEF ADMIN § 130-1.1-a.

2. *Local rules*

a. *Albany County*

i. Third judicial district rules. NY R 3 JD SUP Doc. 1.

b. *Bronx County*

i. Filing of papers in supreme court. NY R BRONX FIL R Doc. 1.

ii. Request for judicial intervention. NY R BRONX FIL R Doc. 2.

iii. Motion procedure. NY R BRONX FIL R Doc. 8.

iv. Commercial division. NY R BRONX FIL R Doc. 12.

v. Motions on notice. NY R BRONX E FIL R Doc. 1.

vi. Settled orders. NY R BRONX LEG SUP Doc. 2.

c. *Erie County*

i. Joint protocols for New York State Courts E-Filing (NYSCEF) cases filed in Supreme Court, Erie County. NY R ERIE E FIL Doc. 3.

d. *Kings County*

i. Papers. NY R L KINGS Pt. A, Papers.

ii. Service of motion papers. NY R L KINGS Pt. C, Rule 1.

iii. Scheduling of motions. NY R L KINGS Pt. C, Rule 2.

iv. Appearance and argument. NY R L KINGS Pt. C, Rule 3.

v. Courtesy copies. NY R L KINGS Pt. C, Rule 5.

vi. Motion calendar calls. NY R L KINGS Pt. C, Rule 7.

vii. Protocol on courthouse and county clerk procedures for electronically filed cases. NY R L KINGS E FIL Doc. 1.

e. *New York County*

i. Commencement of cases. NY R NY CTY Procedure I.

ii. RJIs and assignments. NY R NY CTY Procedure IA.

iii. Motions and special proceedings by notice of motion/petition. NY R NY CTY Procedure II.

iv. County clerk litigation functions. NY R NY CTY Procedure XI.

v. Protocol on courthouse and county clerk procedures for electronically filed cases. NY R NY CTY E FIL Doc. 2.

vi. Redaction of information in documents filed with the county clerk and the court. NY R NY CTY J RUL Rule A-1.

vii. Papers by fax. NY R NY CTY J RUL Rule 4.

viii. Motions on notice; Orders to show cause. NY R NY CTY J RUL Rule 13.

ix. Motion papers. NY R NY CTY J RUL Rule 14.

x. Oral argument; Adjournments. NY R NY CTY J RUL Rule 15.

f. *Onondaga County*

i. Onondaga county protocol for case filings New York State Electronic Files (NYSCEF). NY R ONDGA E FIL Protocol.

g. *Queens County*

i. Motion support office. NY R L QUEENS MOT SUP Doc. 1.

ii. Queens county protocol on courthouse procedures for electronically filed cases. NY R L QUEENS E-FILE Doc. 1.

J. Miscellaneous

NOTE: Individual judges' rules may apply.

ALBANY COUNTY

JUSTICE LISA M. FISHER: NY R 3 JD FISHER Fisher; NY R 3 JD FISHER Fisher, PC Order.

JUSTICE RICHARD MOTT: NY R 3 JD MOTT Mott.

JUSTICE STEPHAN G. SCHICK: NY R 3 JD Schick.

FORECLOSURE SETTLEMENT PART: NY R 3 JD Foreclosure Settlement.

BRONX COUNTY

JUSTICE PAUL L. ALPERT: [NY R BRONX J Part IA-29, as amended by NY ORDER 20-0337].

JUSTICE BEN BARBATO: NY R BRONX J Part IA-21.

JUSTICE MARY ANNE BRIGANTTI: [NY R BRONX J Part IA-15, as amended by NY ORDER 20-0338].

JUSTICE JOSEPH E. CAPELLA: NY R BRONX J Part IA-23.

JUSTICE MITCHELL DANZIGER: NY R BRONX J Part IA-3/33 ; [NY R BRONX J Danziger, Part IA-3/33, as amended by NY ORDER 20-0339].

JUSTICE LAURA G. DOUGLAS: NY R BRONX J Part IA-11.

JUSTICE RUBEN FRANCO: NY R BRONX J Part IA-26.

JUSTICE DORIS M. GONZALEZ: NY R BRONX J Part IA-24.

JUSTICE WILMA GUZMAN: NY R BRONX J Part IA-7; [NY R BRONX J Guzman, Part IA-7 Virtual, as amended by NY ORDER 20-0340].

JUSTICE ROBERT T. JOHNSON: NY R BRONX J Part IA-12.

JUSTICE DONALD A. MILES: NY R BRONX J Part IA-8.

JUSTICE DONNA M. MILLS: NY R BRONX J Part IA-9.

JUSTICE JULIA I. RODRIGUEZ: NY R BRONX J Part IA-18; [NY R BRONX J Part IA-27, as amended by NY ORDER 20-0341].

JUSTICE LLINET M. ROSADO: [NY R BRONX J Part IA-25, as amended by NY ORDER 20-0342].

JUSTICE NORMA RUIZ: NY R BRONX J Part IA-22; [NY R BRONX J Ruiz, Part IA-22 Virtual, as amended by NY ORDER 20-0343].

JUSTICE HOWARD H. SHERMAN: NY R BRONX J Part IA-4.

JUSTICE FERNANDO TAPIA: NY R BRONX J Part IA-13.

JUSTICE ELIZABETH A. TAYLOR: NY R BRONX J Part IA-2.

JUSTICE ALISON Y. TRUITT: NY R BRONX J Part IA-5.

PART IDV: NY R BRONX J Doc. 1.

PRE-TRIAL PART RULES: NY R BRONX J Doc. 2.

PRE TRIAL WORKSHEET: NY R BRONX J Doc. 3.

FORECLOSURE SETTLEMENT PART RULES: NY R BRONX J Doc. 4.

GUARDIANSHIP PART RULES: NY R BRONX J Doc. 5.

LPM PART RULES: NY R BRONX J Doc. 6.

ERIE COUNTY

JUSTICE M. WILLIAM BOLLER: NY R 8 JD J Boller.

JUSTICE RALPH A. BONIELLO: NY R 8 JD J Boniello.

JUSTICE CHRISTOPHER J. BURN: NY R 8 JD J Burns.

JUSTICE RUSSELL P. BUSCAGLIA: NY R 8 JD J Buscaglia.

JUSTICE FRANK CARUSO: NY R 8 JD J Caruso.

JUSTICE STEPHEN W. CASS: NY R 8 JD J Cass.

JUSTICE DEBORAH A. CHIMES: NY R 8 JD J Chimes.

JUSTICE EMILIO COLAIACOVO: [NY R 8 JD J Colaiacovo, as amended by NY ORDER 20-0252].

JUSTICE DIANE Y. DEVLIN: NY R 8 JD J Devlin.

JUSTICE JAMES H. DILLON: NY R 8 JD J Dillon.

JUSTICE PAULA L. FEROLETO: NY R 8 JD J Feroleto.

JUSTICE DANIEL J. FURLONG: [NY R 8 JD J Furlong, as amended by NY ORDER 20-0253].

JUSTICE JOSEPH R. GLOWNIA: NY R 8 JD J Glownia.

JUSTICE MARK J. GRISANTI: NY R 8 JD J Grisanti.

JUSTICE DEBORAH A. HAENDIGES: NY R 8 JD J Haendiges.

JUSTICE LYNN W. KEANE: [NY R 8 JD J Keane, as amended by NY ORDER 20-0254].

JUSTICE RICHARD C. KLOCH, Sr.: NY R 8 JD J Kloch.

JUSTICE FREDERICK J. MARSHALL: [NY R 8 JD J Marshall, as amended by NY ORDER 20-0255.

JUSTICE JOHN L. MICHALSKI: NY R 8 JD J Michalski.

JUSTICE MARK A. MONTOUR: [NY R 8 JD J Montour, as amended by NY ORDER 20-0256].

JUSTICE HENRY NOWAK: NY R 8 JD J Nowak.

JUSTICE JOHN F. O'DONNELL: NY R 8 JD J O'Donnell.

JUSTICE JEANETTE OGDEN: NY R 8 JD J Ogden.

JUSTICE CATHERINE NUGENT-PANEPINTO: NY R 8 JD J Nugent-Panepinto.

JUSTICE FRANK A. SEDITA, III: [NY R 8 JD J Sedita, as amended by NY ORDER 20-0257].

JUSTICE SARA SHELDON: NY R 8 JD J Sheldon.

JUSTICE DONNA M. SIWEK: NY R 8 JD J Siwek.

JUSTICE MARY L. SLISZ: NY R 8 JD J Slisz.

JUSTICE TIMOTHY J. WALKER: [NY R 8 JD J Walker, as amended by NY ORDER 20-0258].

JUSTICE DENNIS E. WARD: NY R 8 JD J Ward.

JUSTICE PAUL B. WOJTASZEK: [NY R 8 JD J Wojtaszek, as amended by NY ORDER 20-0259].

JUSTICE CHARLES N. ZAMBITO: [NY R 8 JD J Zambito, as amended by NY ORDER 20-0260].

SUPREME COURT LEGAL STAFF: NY R 8 JD J Legal Staff.

KINGS COUNTY

JUSTICE RACHEL A. ADAMS: NY R KINGS J Part 5F.

JUSTICE LOREN BAILY-SCHIFFMAN: NY R KINGS J Part 65.

JUSTICE REGINALD A. BODDIE: NY R KINGS J Part 95.

JUSTICE THERESA M. CICCOTTO: NY R KINGS J Part 19; NY R KINGS J Part 5J.

JUSTICE LISSETTE COLON: NY R KINGS J Part Rules.

JUSTICE GENINE EDWARDS: NY R KINGS J Part 80.

JUSTICE PAMELA L. FISHER: [NY R KINGS J Part 94, as amended by NY ORDER 20-0208].

JUSTICE ROBIN GARSON: NY R KINGS J Part 75.

JUSTICE LARA J. GENOVISI: [NY R KINGS J Part 34, as amended by NY ORDER 20-0209].

JUSTICE BERNARD J. GRAHAM: NY R KINGS J Part 36.

JUSTICE DAWN JIMENEZ-SALTA: NY R KINGS J Part 88.

JUSTICE INGRID JOSEPH: [NY R KINGS J Part FRP3 and Part 83, as amended by NY ORDER 20-0210].

JUSTICE KATHY J. KING: NY R KINGS J Part 64, 76K.

JUSTICE LAWRENCE KNIPEL: NY R KINGS J Part 57.
JUSTICE DONALD KURTZ: NY R KINGS J Part 26.
JUSTICE CARL LANDICINO: [NY R KINGS J Part 81, as amended by NY ORDER 20-0211].
JUSTICE KATHERINE LEVINE: [NY R KINGS J Part 20, 25, 92, as amended by NY ORDER 20-0211].
JUSTICE LORNA MCALLISTER: [NY R KINGS J Part 10, as amended by NY ORDER 20-0211].
JUSTICE ROSEMARIE MONTALBANO: [NY R KINGS J Part 19, 71, and 22, as amended by NY ORDER 20-0211].
JUSTICE RICHARD J. MONTELIONE: [NY R KINGS J Part 99 and DJMP, as amended by NY ORDER 20-0215].
JUSTICE LISA S. OTTLEY: NY R KINGS J Part 24.
JUSTICE MARK I. PARTNOW: NY R KINGS J Part 43.
JUSTICE ERIC I. PRUS: NY R KINGS J Part 5A.
JUSTICE FRANCOIS RIVERA: NY R KINGS J Part 52.
JUSTICE KAREN B. ROTHENBERG: NY R KINGS J Part 35.
JUSTICE LEON RUCHELSMAN: NY R KINGS J Part 1.
JUSTICE WAYNE P. SAITTA: NY R KINGS J Part 29.
JUSTICE ROBIN K. SHEARES: NY R KINGS J Part 96.
JUSTICE KENNETH P. SHERMAN: NY R KINGS J Part 67 and 78.
JUSTICE DEBRA SILBER: NY R KINGS J Part 9 and 5K.
JUSTICE ELLEN M. SPODEK: NY R KINGS J Part 63.
JUSTICE MARSHA L. STEINHARDT: NY R KINGS J Part 15.
JUSTICE JEFFREY S. SUNSHINE: NY R KINGS J Part 5G.
JUSTICE PETER P. SWEENEY: [NY R KINGS J Part 35, as amended by NY ORDER 20-0218].
JUSTICE DELORES J. THOMAS: [NY R KINGS J Part 5T, as amended by NY ORDER 20-0221].
JUSTICE WAVNY TOUSSAINT: NY R KINGS J Part 70.
JUSTICE RICHARD VELASQUEZ: NY R KINGS J Part 66.
JUSTICE CAROLYN E. WADE: NY R KINGS J Part 84.
JUSTICE EDWARD G. WALKER: [NY R KINGS J Part 90, as amended by NY ORDER 20-0219].
JUSTICE LILLIAN WAN: [NY R KINGS J Part 17, as amended by NY ORDER 20-0220].
JUSTICE MICHELLE WESTON: NY R KINGS J Part 3.
MENTAL HYGIENE PART: NY R KINGS J Part 77.
MATRIMONIAL PARTS DURING COVID-19 EMERGENCY: JUSTICE KAREN B. ROTHENBERG: NY R KINGS J Doc. 1.

NASSAU COUNTY

JUSTICE ANNA R. ANZALONE: NY R NASSAU S J Anzalone, Part 26.
JUSTICE STACY D. BENNETT: NY R NASSAU S J Bennett; NY R NASSAU S J Bennett, Form 1.
JUSTICE ANTONIO BRANDVEEN: NY R NASSAU S J Brandveen, Part 31.
JUSTICE JEFFREY S. BROWN: [NY R NASSAU S J Brown, as amended by NY ORDER 20-0297].
JUSTICE STEPHEN A. BUCARIA: NY R NASSAU S J Bucaria.
JUSTICE JULIANNE T. CAPETOLA: NY R NASSAU S J Capetola, Part 28.
JUSTICE EDMUND M. DANE: NY R NASSAU S J Dane, Part 33.
JUSTICE VITO M. DESTEFANO: NY R NASSAU S J DeStefano, Part 13; NY R NASSAU S J DeStefano, Form 1.
JUSTICE ARTHUR M. DIAMOND: NY R NASSAU S J Diamond, Part 7.
JUSTICE THOMAS FEINMAN: NY R NASSAU S J Feinman, Part 5.
JUSTICE JOHN M. GALASSO: NY R NASSAU S J Galasso, Part 22.

JUSTICE SHARON M.J. GIANELLI: NY R NASSAU S J Gianelli, Part 22; NY R NASSAU S J Gianelli, Form 1.

JUSTICE JEFFREY A. GOODSTEIN: NY R NASSAU S J Goodstein, Part 33; NY R NASSAU S J Goodstein, Form 1.

JUSTICE DAVID J. GUGERTY: [NY R NASSAU S J Gugerty, Part 31, as amended by NY ORDER 20-0298].

JUSTICE HELENE F. GUGERTY: NY R NASSAU S J Gugerty, Part 47.

JUSTICE STEVEN M. JAEGER: NY R NASSAU S J Jaeger, Part 35; NY R NASSAU S J Jaeger, Form 1.

JUSTICE JACK L. LIBERT: NY R NASSAU S J Libert, Part 23.

JUSTICE JOSEPH H. LORINTZ: NY R NASSAU S J Lorintz, Part 26; NY R NASSAU S J Lorintz, Form 1.

JUSTICE ROY S. MAHON: NY R NASSAU S J Mahon, Part 3.

JUSTICE RANDY SUE MARBER: NY R NASSAU S J Marber, Part 8.

JUSTICE JAMES P. MCCORMACK: [NY R NASSAU S J McCormack, Part 18, as amended by NY ORDER, 20-0299].

JUSTICE DICCIA T. PINEDA-KIRWAN: [NY R NASSAU S J Pineda-Kirwan, as amended by NY ORDER 20-0300].

JUSTICE THOMAS RADEMAKER: [NY R NASSAU S J Rademaker, Part 28, as amended by NY ORDER 20-0301]; [NY R NASSAU S J Rademaker, Form 1, as amended by NY ORDER 20-0301].

JUSTICE DENISE L. SHER: NY R NASSAU S J Rademaker, Part 32.

JUSTICE LEONARD D. STEINMAN: [NY R NASSAU S J Steinman, Part 15, as amended by NY ORDER 20-0303]; NY R NASSAU S J Steinman, Form 1.

JUSTICE HOWARD E. STURIM: NY R NASSAU S J Sturim, Part 50; NY R NASSAU S J Sturim, Form 1.

JUSTICE HELEN VOUTSINAS: [NY R NASSAU S J Voutsinas, Part 25, as amended by NY ORDER 20-0304]; [NY R NASSAU S J Voutsinas, Form 1, as amended by NY ORDER 20-0305].

JUSTICE HOPE SCHWARTZ ZIMMERMAN: NY R NASSAU S J Zimmerman, Part 17.

NEW YORK COUNTY

JUDGE'S RULES; BASIC INFORMATION: [NY R NY CTY J RUL Doc. 1, as amended by NY ORDER 20-0202].

ONONDAGA COUNTY

JUSTICE ROBERT E. ANTONACCI II: [NY R ONDGA E FIL Doc. 1, as amended by 20-0239].

JUSTICE MICHAEL V. COCCOMI: NY R ONDGA E FIL Doc. 2.

JUSTICE GREGORY R. GILBERT: NY R 5 JD JUDGES Gilbert; NY R ONDGA E FIL Doc. 3.

JUSTICE DONALD A. GREENWOOD: NY R ONDGA E FIL Doc. 4.

JUSTICE DEBORAH H. KARALUNAS: NY R ONDGA E FIL Doc. 5.

JUSTICE JAMES MCCLUSKY: NY R 5 JD MCCLUSKY McClusky.

JUSTICE CHARLES C. MERRELL: NY R 5 JD MERRELL Merrell.

JUSTICE PATRICK F. MACRAE: NY R 5 JD MACRAE Doc. 1.

JUSTICE JAMES P. MURPHY: NY R ONDGA E FIL Doc. 7.

JUSTICE GERALD J. NERI: [NY R 5 JD JUDGES Neri, as amended by NY ORDER 20-0236]; [NY R ONDGA E FIL Doc. 8, as amended by NY ORDER 20-0241].

JUSTICE ANTHONY J. PARIS: NY R 5 JD JUDGES Paris; [NY R ONDGA E FIL Doc. 9, as amended by NY ORDER 20-0242].

JUSTICE NORMAN W. SEITER, JR.: NY R 5 JD JUDGES Seiter.

JUSTICE KEVIN G. YOUNG: [NY R ONDGA E FIL Doc. 10, as amended by NY ORDER 20-0243].

QUEENS COUNTY

JUSTICE PAM JACKMAN BROWN: [NY R L QUEENS Brown, Part 19, as amended by NY ORDER 20-0321].

JUSTICE CHEREE A. BUGGS: NY R L QUEENS Buggs, Part 30.

JUSTICE PAM JACKMAN BROWN: [NY R L QUEENS Brown, Part 19, as amended by NY ORDER 20-0321].

JUSTICE DENIS J. BUTLER: NY R L QUEENS Butler, Part 12.

JUSTICE ROBERT I. CALORAS: [NY R L QUEENS Caloras, Part 36, as amended by NY ORDER 20-0322].

JUSTICE ANNA CULLEY: NY R L QUEENS Culley, Part 53.
JUSTICE TIMOTHY DUFFICY: NY R L QUEENS Dufficy, Part 35.
JUSTICE DAVID ELLIOT: NY R L QUEENS Elliot, Part 14.
JUSTICE JOSEPH J. ESPOSITO: NY R L QUEENS Esposito, Part 6.
JUSTICE DARRELL L. GAVRIN: [NY R L QUEENS Gavrin, Part 27, as amended by NY ORDER 20-0323].
JUSTICE WYATT N. GIBBONS: [NY R L QUEENS Gibbons, Part 5, as amended by NY ORDER 20-0330.
JUSTICE DONNA-MARIE E. GOLIA: [NY R L QUEENS Golia, Part 21, as amended by NY ORDER 20-0331].
JUSTICE MARGUERITE A. GRAYS: [NY R L QUEENS Grays, Part 4, as amended by NY ORDER 20-0324].
JUSTICE RUDOLPH E. GRECO: [NY R L QUEENS Greco, Part 32, as amended by NY ORDER 20-0325].
JUSTICE MAUREEN HEALY: NY R L QUEENS Healy, Part 6.
JUSTICE PHILLIP HOM: [NY R L QUEENS Hom, Part 43, as amended by NY ORDER 20-0332].
JUSTICE KEVIN J. KERRIGAN: NY R L QUEENS Kerrigan, Part 10.
JUSTICE MOJGAN C. LANCMAN: NY R L QUEENS Lancman, Part 20.
JUSTICE RICHARD G. LATIN: NY R L QUEENS Latin, Part 40.
JUSTICE ULYSSES B. LEVERETT: [NY R L QUEENS Leverett, Part 6, as amended by NY ORDER 20-0326].
JUSTICE LEONARD LIVOTE: NY R L QUEENS Livote, Part 33.
JUSTICE LEE A. MAYERSOHN: NY R L QUEENS Mayersohn, Part 22; NY R L QUEENS Mayersohn, Part 22G; [NY R L QUEENS Mayersohn, Part 22G COVID, as amended by NY ORDER 20-0327].
JUSTICE ROBERT J. MCDONALD: NY R L QUEENS McDonald, Part 34.
JUSTICE MARGARET MCGOWAN: NY R L QUEENS McGowan, Part 52.
JUSTICE MAURICE E. MUIR: [NY R L QUEENS Muir, Part 42, as amended by NY ORDER 20-0333].
JUSTICE JODI ORLOW: NY R L QUEENS Orlow, Part 51.
JUSTICE LESLIE J. PURIFICCION: NY R L QUEENS Purificcion, Part 39.
JUSTICE JOSEPH RISI: [NY R L QUEENS Risi, Part 3, as amended by NY ORDER 20-0328].
JUSTICE FREDERICK D.R. SAMPSON: [NY R L QUEENS Sampson, Part 31, as amended by NY ORDER 20-0329].
JUSTICE MARTIN J. SCHULMAN: NY R L QUEENS Schulman, Part 29.
JUSTICE BERNICE D. SIEGAL: NY R L QUEENS Siegal, Part 25G.
JUSTICE JANICE A. TAYLOR: NY R L QUEENS Taylor, Part 15.
JUSTICE CARMEN R. VELASQUEZ: NY R L QUEENS Velasquez, Part 38.
JUSTICE LOURDES M VENTURA: [NY R L QUEENS Ventura, Part 37, as amended by NY ORDER 20-0334].
JUSTICE WILLIAM A. VISCOVICH: NY R L QUEENS Viscovich, Part 63.
JUSTICE ALLAN B. WEISS: NY R L QUEENS Weiss, Part 2.
COMPLIANCE, SETTLEMENT AND CONFERENCE PART: NY R L QUEENS Doc 1.
PRELIMINARY CONFERENCE PART: [NY R L QUEENS Doc. 2, as amended by NY ORDER 20-0335].
MEDICAL MALPRACTICE CONFERENCE PART: [NY R L QUEENS Doc. 3, as amended by NY ORDER 20-0336].
TRIAL SCHEDULING PART: NY R L QUEENS Doc. 4.
SUMMARY JURY TRIAL PROGRAM: NY R L QUEENS Doc. 7.
RESIDENTIAL FORECLOSURE PART: NY R L QUEENS Doc. 9.
FORECLOSURE AUCTION RULES: NY R L QUEENS Doc. 10.
MATRIMONIAL PRELIMINARY CONFERENCE PART: NY R L QUEENS Doc. 11.
NON-CUSTODIAL CONTESTED MATRIMONIAL PART: NY R L QUEENS Doc. 12.

Requests, Notices and Applications
Interrogatories

Document Last Updated August 2020

A. Checklist

(I) ❑ Matters to be considered by requesting party
  (a) ❑ Required documents
    (1) ❑ Interrogatories
    (2) ❑ Proof of service
  (b) ❑ Supplemental documents
    (1) ❑ Working copies
  (c) ❑ Timing
    (1) ❑ After commencement of an action, any party may serve written interrogatories upon any other party

(II) ❑ Matters to be considered by responding party
  (a) ❑ Required documents
    (1) ❑ Responses to interrogatories
    (2) ❑ Proof of service
  (b) ❑ Supplemental documents
    (1) ❑ Working copies
  (c) ❑ Timing
    (1) ❑ Within twenty (20) days after service of interrogatories, the party upon whom they are served shall serve upon each of the parties a copy of the answer to each interrogatory, except one to which the party objects, in which event the reasons for the objection shall be stated with reasonable particularity

B. Timing

1. *Time to serve interrogatories.* After commencement of an action, any party may serve written interrogatories upon any other party. Interrogatories may not be served upon a defendant before that defendant's time for serving a responsive pleading has expired, except by leave of court granted with or without notice. NY CPLR Rule 3132.

2. *Motions staying disclosure.* Service of a notice of motion under NY CPLR Rule 3211, NY CPLR Rule 3212, or NY CPLR § 3213 stays disclosure until determination of the motion unless the court orders otherwise. If the motion is based solely on the defense that the summons and complaint, summons with notice, or notice of petition and petition was not properly served, disclosure shall not be stayed unless the court orders otherwise. NY CPLR Rule 3214(b).

   a. *Personal injury actions involving terminally ill patients.* Notwithstanding the provisions of NY CPLR Rule 3214(b), the service or pendency of a motion under NY CPLR Rule 3211, NY CPLR Rule 3212, or NY CPLR § 3213 shall not stay disclosure in an action where a preliminary conference order has been entered pursuant to NY CPLR Rule 3407. NY CPLR Rule 3407(b)(3).

3. *KINGS COUNTY: Discovery timing.* At [the Compliance Conference, the court will] schedule all outstanding discovery to be completed prior to date fixed for filing Note of Issue. NY R L KINGS Rule I(B).

   a. *Deadlines in orders.* Discovery scheduled in Compliance Conference orders shall be strictly adhered to and may not be extended without leave of the court. Unjustified failure to comply with the provisions of the CCP order will result in preclusion, the striking of a pleading or imposition of sanctions, as appropriate. NY R L KINGS Rule I(B)(2).

   b. *Cases with extensive discovery.* Where post Compliance Conference discovery is to be extensive, cases may be retracked from standard to complex, which will provide for three (3) additional months of post Compliance Conference discovery and extend the Note of Issue date by three (3) months. NY R L KINGS Rule I(B)(1).

   c. *Discovery not stayed.* Ordinarily the Court/JHO will not stay discovery during pendency of motions to withdraw, or during pendency of settlement, or during pendency of dispositive motions. NY R L KINGS Rule IV.

   d. *Expedited discovery in certain cases.* Discovery in third party and joint actions will be expedited. NY R L KINGS Pt. B, Rule 5.

e. For more information on discovery scheduling, refer to NY R L KINGS Flow Chart.

4. *NEW YORK COUNTY: Deadlines in orders.* Strict compliance with all discovery orders is required. Unexcused or unjustified failure to comply with deadlines fixed by the court, including those set out in Preliminary Conference Orders, may result in an award of costs, conditional or otherwise, or the imposition of another penalty authorized by NY CPLR § 3126. NY R NY CTY J RUL Rule 8.

5. *Computation of time*

   a. *Units of time*

      i. *Day.* A calendar day includes the time from midnight to midnight. Sunday or any day of the week specifically mentioned means a calendar day. NY GEN CONSTR § 19.

      ii. *Month.* In a statute, contract or public or private instrument, unless otherwise provided in such contract or instrument or by law, the term month means a calendar month and not a lunar month. NY GEN CONSTR § 31.

      iii. *Year.* For information on the definition of a year, including the definitions of a half-year and quarter-year, refer to NY GEN CONSTR § 58 and NY GEN CONSTR § 50. For information on leap years, refer to NY GEN CONSTR § 57.

   b. *Periods of time*

      i. *Number of days.* A number of days specified as a period from a certain day within which or after or before which an act is authorized or required to be done means such number of calendar days exclusive of the calendar day from which the reckoning is made. NY GEN CONSTR § 20.

         - If such period is a period of two (2) days, Saturday, Sunday or a public holiday must be excluded from the reckoning if it is an intervening day between the day from which the reckoning is made and the last day of the period. NY GEN CONSTR § 20.
         - In computing any specified period of time from a specified event, the day upon which the event happens is deemed the day from which the reckoning is made. The day from which any specified period of time is reckoned shall be excluded in making the reckoning. NY GEN CONSTR § 20.

      ii. *Number of months.* A number of months after or before a certain day shall be computed by counting such number of calendar months from such day, exclusive of the calendar month in which such day occurs, and shall include the day of the month in the last month so counted having the same numerical order in days of the month as the day from which the computation is made, unless there be not so many days in the last month so counted, in which case the period computed shall expire with the last day of the month so counted. NY GEN CONSTR § 30.

      iii. *Publication of notice; Number of days.* The period of publication of a legal notice shall be computed by excluding the first day of publication and including the day on which the act or event of which notice is given is to take place or which completes the full period of publication. NY CPLR § 2402.

      iv. *Periods ending on Saturday, Sunday or public holiday.* When any period of time, computed from a certain day, within which or after which or before which an act is authorized or required to be done, ends on a Saturday, Sunday or a public holiday, such act may be done on the next succeeding business day and if the period ends at a specified hour, such act may be done at or before the same hour of such next succeeding business day, except that where a period of time specified by contract ends on a Saturday, Sunday or a public holiday, the extension of such period is governed by NY GEN CONSTR § 25. NY GEN CONSTR § 25-a(1).

         - For a list of public holidays, refer to NY GEN CONSTR § 24.

      v. *Additional time after certain kinds of service*

         - *Service by mail.* Where a period of time prescribed by law is measured from the service of a paper and service is by mail, five (5) days shall be added to the prescribed period. NY CPLR Rule 2103(b)(2).
         - *Service by overnight delivery service.* Where a period of time prescribed by law is measured from the service of a paper and service is by overnight delivery, one (1) business day shall be added to the prescribed period. NY CPLR Rule 2103(b)(6).

      vi. *Daylight saving time.* For information on New York's time zone and the effect of daylight saving time, refer to NY GEN CONSTR § 52.

   c. *Hours of court.* Notwithstanding any provision of law or rule of court to the contrary, throughout the State of New York the sessions of the Supreme Court for the disposition of business before the court shall commence not later than 9:30 a.m. and conclude not earlier than 5 p.m. Where warranted, the Chief Administrator of the Courts may authorize variances in the opening and closing hours of the courts, but, in such event, daily sessions shall total not less than six (6) hours. NY R CHIEF J § 3.1.

d. *Time limits; Extension of time.* Any act required by or in pursuance of law to be performed at or within a prescribed time, shall be performed according to the standard time. NY GEN CONSTR § 53.

   i. Except where otherwise expressly prescribed by law, the court may extend the time fixed by any statute, rule or order for doing any act, upon such terms as may be just and upon good cause shown, whether the application for extension is made before or after the expiration of the time fixed. NY CPLR § 2004. Refer to the New York KeyRules Motion for Continuance/Extension of Time document for more information.

C. General Requirements

1. *Rules governing disclosure*

   a. *Generally.* There shall be full disclosure of all matter material and necessary in the prosecution or defense of an action, regardless of the burden of proof, by:

      i. A party, or the officer, director, member, agent or employee of a party;

      ii. A person who possessed a cause of action or defense asserted in the action;

      iii. A person about to depart from the state, or without the state, or residing at a greater distance from the place of trial than one hundred miles, or so sick or infirm as to afford reasonable grounds of belief that he or she will not be able to attend the trial, or a person authorized to practice medicine, dentistry or podiatry who has provided medical, dental or podiatric care or diagnosis to the party demanding disclosure, or who has been retained by such party as an expert witness; and

      iv. Any other person, upon notice stating the circumstances or reasons such disclosure is sought or required. NY CPLR § 3101(a).

      v. The statutory phrase "material and necessary", said the Court of Appeals, must be interpreted liberally to require disclosure upon request, of any facts bearing on the controversy which will assist preparation for trial by sharpening the issues and reducing delay and prolixity. The test is one of usefulness and reason. SIEGEL-NYPRAC § 344; Allen v. Crowell-Collier Pub. Co., 21 N.Y.2d 403, 235 N.E.2d 430 (1968).

      vi. Another potential problem that the original NY CPLR § 3101(a) posed was that it spoke of "evidence" that is material and necessary, which might have been construed to permit disclosure to elicit only that which would itself qualify as "evidence" admissible at trial. It was, however, construed more broadly than that. Well-considered caselaw specifically rejected this "evidence in chief" doctrine, stating that disclosure extends as well "to all relevant information calculated to lead to relevant evidence," a standard similar to that applicable in federal court. With an amendment that took effect on January 1, 1994, changing "evidence" to "matter" in NY CPLR § 3101(a), these generous interpretations of the statute were in effect approved by the legislature. SIEGEL-NYPRAC § 344.

      vii. If a party is a corporation, each of its officers, directors, members, agents, and employees is also deemed a "party" for disclosure purposes. A party who needs relevant data or material from a nonparty corporation can seek it through NY CPLR § 3101(a)(2), NY CPLR § 3101(a)(3) or NY CPLR § 3101(a)(4), under which the corporate entity is treated as a "person." These subdivisions should also apply to any entity, corporate or otherwise, from whom disclosure is sought through its agents. A corporate employee who has the requisite knowledge and information may respond to a disclosure request on behalf of the corporation. A party who can't single out the particular person in the corporation's employ to whom a disclosure request should be properly directed can direct it to the corporation as such and leave it to the corporation to designate the appropriate person to respond. Whenever disclosure is sought from a corporation through a deposition, whether as a party or as a nonparty witness, the choice in the first instance of who will be produced in the corporate behalf is with the corporation rather than the examining party. SIEGEL-NYPRAC § 345.

      viii. NY CPLR § 3101(a)(4) permits a party to obtain disclosure from a nonparty by merely serving a subpoena on the nonparty providing notice of "the circumstances or reasons such disclosure is sought or required." SIEGEL-NYPRAC § 345.

   b. *Methods of obtaining disclosure.* Information is obtainable by one or more of the following disclosure devices: depositions upon oral questions or without the state upon written questions, interrogatories, demands for addresses, discovery and inspection of documents or property, physical and mental examinations of persons, and requests for admission. NY CPLR § 3102(a).

      i. *Stipulation or notice.* Unless otherwise provided by the civil practice law and rules or by the court, disclosure shall be obtained by stipulation or on notice without leave of the court. NY CPLR § 3102(b).

ii. *Before action commenced; Court order required.* Before an action is commenced, disclosure to aid in bringing an action, to preserve information or to aid in arbitration, may be obtained, but only by court order. The court may appoint a referee to take testimony. NY CPLR § 3102(c).

iii. *During trial; Court order required.* Except as provided in NY CPLR § 5223, during and after trial, disclosure may be obtained only by order of the trial court on notice. NY CPLR § 3102(d).

iv. *Action pending in another jurisdiction.* Except as provided in NY CPLR § 3119, when under any mandate, writ or commission issued out of any court of record in any other state, territory, district or foreign jurisdiction, or whenever upon notice or agreement, it is required to take the testimony of a witness in the state, he or she may be compelled to appear and testify in the same manner and by the same process as may be employed for the purpose of taking testimony in actions pending in the state. The supreme court or a county court shall make any appropriate order in aid of taking such a deposition. NY CPLR § 3102(e).

v. *Actions to which state is a party.* In an action in which the state is properly a party, whether as plaintiff, defendant or otherwise, disclosure by the state shall be available as if the state were a private person. NY CPLR § 3102(f).

c. *Privileged matter.* Upon objection by a person entitled to assert the privilege, privileged matter shall not be obtainable. NY CPLR § 3101(b).

i. A determination of whether information is privileged is governed by the rules of evidence, which apply as they would at a trial. Whatever is privileged at the trial is privileged as well on pretrial disclosure. SIEGEL-NYPRAC § 346.

d. *Attorney's work product.* The work product of an attorney shall not be obtainable. NY CPLR § 3101(c).

i. NY CPLR § 3101(c) makes unobtainable the "work product of an attorney"—an ill-defined category whose potential for mischief has been avoided only because the judiciary has accorded it a very narrow scope. It is a category wholly distinct from the "materials . . . prepared in anticipation of litigation" of NY CPLR § 3101(d)(2). The fact that immunity is absolute under NY CPLR § 3101(c), while that of NY CPLR § 3101(d)(2) is only conditional, is the factor that requires as sharp a line as possible between the two categories. SIEGEL-NYPRAC § 347.

ii. The judiciary has cast precious little under the "work product" category of NY CPLR § 3101(c), preferring instead to fit doubtful items under the "materials . . . prepared in anticipation of litigation" banner of NY CPLR § 3101(d)(2), where the conditional immunity can be overcome and the matters ordered disclosed when stated conditions are met. SIEGEL-NYPRAC § 347.

e. *Trial preparation*

i. *Experts.* Upon request, each party shall identify each person whom the party expects to call as an expert witness at trial and shall disclose in reasonable detail the subject matter on which each expert is expected to testify, the substance of the facts and opinions on which each expert is expected to testify, the qualifications of each expert witness and a summary of the grounds for each expert's opinion. NY CPLR § 3101(d)(1)(i).

- However, where a party for good cause shown retains an expert an insufficient period of time before the commencement of trial to give appropriate notice thereof, the party shall not thereupon be precluded from introducing the expert's testimony at the trial solely on grounds of noncompliance with NY CPLR § 3101(d)(1). In that instance, upon motion of any party, made before or at trial, or on its own initiative, the court may make whatever order may be just. In an action for medical, dental or podiatric malpractice, a party, in responding to a request, may omit the names of medical, dental or podiatric experts but shall be required to disclose all other information concerning such experts otherwise required by NY CPLR § 3101(d)(1). NY CPLR § 3101(d)(1)(i).
- In an action for medical, dental or podiatric malpractice, any party may, by written offer made to and served upon all other parties and filed with the court, offer to disclose the name of, and to make available for examination upon oral deposition, any person the party making the offer expects to call as an expert witness at trial. Within twenty (20) days of service of the offer, a party shall accept or reject the offer by serving a written reply upon all parties and filing a copy thereof with the court. Failure to serve a reply within twenty (20) days of service of the offer shall be deemed a rejection of the offer. If all parties accept the offer, each party shall be required to produce his or her expert witness for examination upon oral deposition upon receipt of a notice to take oral deposition in accordance with NY CPLR Rule 3107. If any party, having made or accepted the offer, fails to make that party's expert available for oral deposition, that party shall be precluded from offering expert testimony at the trial of the action. NY CPLR § 3101(d)(1)(ii).

- Further disclosure concerning the expected testimony of any expert may be obtained only by court order upon a showing of special circumstances and subject to restrictions as to scope and provisions concerning fees and expenses as the court may deem appropriate. However, a party, without court order, may take the testimony of a person authorized to practice medicine, dentistry or podiatry who is the party's treating or retained expert, as described in NY CPLR § 3101(a)(3), in which event any other party shall be entitled to the full disclosure authorized by Article 31 of Chapter 8 of the Civil Practice Law and Rules (NY CPLR § 3101, et seq.) with respect to that expert without court order. NY CPLR § 3101(d)(1)(iii).

ii. *Materials.* Subject to the provisions of NY CPLR § 3101(d)(1), materials otherwise discoverable under NY CPLR § 3101(a) and prepared in anticipation of litigation or for trial by or for another party, or by or for that other party's representative (including an attorney, consultant, surety, indemnitor, insurer or agent), may be obtained only upon a showing that the party seeking discovery has substantial need of the materials in the preparation of the case and is unable without undue hardship to obtain the substantial equivalent of the materials by other means. In ordering discovery of the materials when the required showing has been made, the court shall protect against disclosure of the mental impressions, conclusions, opinions or legal theories of an attorney or other representative of a party concerning the litigation. NY CPLR § 3101(d)(2).

- In order to qualify as "litigation" material the item must have been prepared exclusively for litigation. Incidental potential use in litigation, the courts have observed, may also be a function of such reports, but they have at least an equal if not greater mission "to prevent future accidents, discipline careless employees, or, generally, to increase the economy and efficiency of the operation." SIEGEL-NYPRAC § 348.

f. *Party's statement.* A party may obtain a copy of his own statement. NY CPLR § 3101(e).

i. Moreover, NY CPLR § 3101(e) has been broadly interpreted to include photographs. Items such as photographs and videotapes are now independently subject to disclosure under NY CPLR § 3101(i). SIEGEL-NYPRAC § 348.

g. *Contents of insurance agreement.* A party may obtain discovery of the existence and contents of any insurance agreement under which any person carrying on an insurance business may be liable to satisfy part or all of a judgment which may be entered in the action or to indemnify or reimburse for payments made to satisfy the judgment. Information concerning the insurance agreement is not by reason of disclosure admissible in evidence at trial. For purpose of NY CPLR § 3101(f), an application for insurance shall not be treated as part of an insurance agreement. NY CPLR § 3101(f).

h. *Accident reports.* Except as is otherwise provided by law, in addition to any other matter which may be subject to disclosure, there shall be full disclosure of any written report of an accident prepared in the regular course of business operations or practices of any person, firm, corporation, association or other public or private entity, unless prepared by a police or peace officer for a criminal investigation or prosecution and disclosure would interfere with a criminal investigation or prosecution. NY CPLR § 3101(g).

i. *Amendment or supplementation of responses.* A party shall amend or supplement a response previously given to a request for disclosure promptly upon the party's thereafter obtaining information that the response was incorrect or incomplete when made, or that the response, though correct and complete when made, no longer is correct and complete, and the circumstances are such that a failure to amend or supplement the response would be materially misleading. NY CPLR § 3101(h).

i. Where a party obtains such information an insufficient period of time before the commencement of trial appropriately to amend or supplement the response, the party shall not thereupon be precluded from introducing evidence at the trial solely on grounds of noncompliance with NY CPLR § 3101(h). In that instance, upon motion of any party, made before or at trial, or on its own initiative, the court may make whatever order may be just. Further amendment or supplementation may be obtained by court order. NY CPLR § 3101(h).

j. *Other disclosures.* In addition to any other matter which may be subject to disclosure, there shall be full disclosure of any films, photographs, video tapes or audio tapes, including transcripts or memoranda thereof, involving a person referred to in NY CPLR § 3101(a)(1). There shall be disclosure of all portions of such material, including out-takes, rather than only those portions a party intends to use. The provisions of NY CPLR § 3101(i) shall not apply to materials compiled for law enforcement purposes which are exempt from disclosure under NY PUB OFF § 87. NY CPLR § 3101(i).

i. While NY CPLR § 3101(i) was enacted with the defendant's surreptitious tapes of the plaintiff in mind, its language is broad enough to embrace any films, photographs, and audio or video tapes of a party, even those made by the party from whom disclosure is sought. SIEGEL-NYPRAC § 348.

k. *Protective orders.* The court may at any time on its own initiative, or on motion of any party or of any person from whom discovery is sought, make a protective order denying, limiting, conditioning or regulating the use of any disclosure device. NY CPLR § 3103(a). Refer to the New York KeyRules Motion for Protective Order document for more information.

l. *Supervision of disclosure.* Upon the motion of any party or witness on notice to all parties or on its own initiative without notice, the court in which an action is pending may by one of its judges or a referee supervise all or part of any disclosure procedure. NY CPLR § 3104(a).

i. *Selection of referee.* A judicial hearing officer may be designated as a referee under NY CPLR § 3104, or the court may permit all of the parties in an action to stipulate that a named attorney may act as referee. In such latter event, the stipulation shall provide for payment of his fees which shall, unless otherwise agreed, be taxed as disbursements. NY CPLR § 3104(b).

ii. *Powers of referee; Motions referred to person supervising disclosure.* A referee under NY CPLR § 3104 shall have all the powers of the court under NY CPLR § 3101, et seq. except the power to relieve himself of his duties, to appoint a successor, or to adjudge any person guilty of contempt. All motions or applications made under Article 31 of Chapter 8 of the Civil Practice Law and Rules (NY CPLR § 3101, et seq.) shall be returnable before the judge or referee, designated under NY CPLR § 3104 and after disposition, if requested by any party, his order shall be filed in the office of the clerk. NY CPLR § 3104(c).

iii. *Review of order of referee.* Any party or witness may apply for review of an order made under NY CPLR § 3104 by a referee. The application shall be by motion made in the court in which the action is pending within five (5) days after the order is made. Service of a notice of motion for review shall suspend disclosure of the particular matter in dispute. If the question raised by the motion may affect the rights of a witness, notice shall be served on him personally or by mail at his last known address. It shall set forth succinctly the order complained of, the reason it is objectionable and the relief demanded. NY CPLR § 3104(d).

iv. *Payment of expenses of referee.* Except where a judicial hearing officer has been designated a referee hereunder, the court may make an appropriate order for the payment of the reasonable expenses of the referee. NY CPLR § 3104(e).

2. *Interrogatories.* Except as otherwise provided herein, after commencement of an action, any party may serve upon any other party written interrogatories. NY CPLR § 3130(1).

a. *Scope of interrogatories.* Interrogatories may relate to any matters embraced in the disclosure requirement of NY CPLR § 3101 and the answers may be used to the same extent as the depositions of a party. Interrogatories may require copies of such papers, documents or photographs as are relevant to the answers required, unless opportunity for this examination and copying be afforded. NY CPLR § 3131.

i. Interrogatories may also require the furnishing of copies of papers and documents relevant to the answers, but a party intent on securing such items will usually find the discovery device of NY CPLR Rule 3120 more effective for that purpose. SIEGEL-NYPRAC § 361.

ii. Interrogatories must not be overly broad, oppressive, or burdensome, or seek far more information than needed. CW2D § 42:427. Although the Civil Practice Law and Rules provides that copies of documents relevant to the answers may be requested, it does not authorize an all-inclusive demand for production of documents of any kind. CW2D § 42:427.

- Interrogatories that include blanket demands for production of "any document," without any attempt to identify the specific documents or categories of documents sought, are overly broad and burdensome and fail to satisfy the requisite standard of reasonable particularity required in designating documents to be produced. CW2D § 42:427.
- Similarly, an interrogatory that is unlimited in time and applies to every discussion or writing by the defendants relating to a vast range of topics is the kind of vague "blunderbuss" question not permitted by the discovery rules. CW2D § 42:427.

iii. Interrogatories may be found oppressive and improper due to their unreasonable length and complexity, and the undue breadth or questionable relevance of the information sought. CW2D § 42:427; Amherst Synagogue v. Schuele Paint Co., 30 A.D.3d 1055, 816 N.Y.S.2d 782 (2006) (defendants' interrogatories, consisting of over two hundred (200) questions that spanned twenty-one (21) pages as well as four (4) pages of instructions, were unduly burdensome and oppressive, and rose to the level of harassment).

iv. The best practice is to carefully craft each interrogatory to be proper in form and substance so as to avoid the delays and expenses associated with objections to the propriety of the question. NYDISC § 11:14.

v. Additional sets of interrogatories may be warranted where the responses to the prior interrogatories are insufficient, incomplete, or not meaningful. They are also warranted where they will further expedite the discovery process. Additional sets of interrogatories are not warranted where they are abusive, oppressive, unduly burdensome, repetitive, or the like. NYDISC § 11:16.50.

vi. The remedy for a party's failure to respond to interrogatories is a motion under NY CPLR Rule 3124 to compel a response, and the motion for a protective order under NY CPLR § 3103 is of course on standby to cure abuses. If the court finds in a given case that the interrogatories are "burdensome, oppressive and improper", it will vacate them in toto rather than prune them. When they are "burdensome, oppressive and improper", they are just as much so to the court as to the adverse party. SIEGEL-NYPRAC § 361.

b. *Use of interrogatories at trial*

i. Although NY CPLR § 3131 states the answers to interrogatories "may be used to the same extent as the depositions of a party," that may be misleading. It was held in Matter of New York City Asbestos Litig., 173 Misc. 2d 121, 660 N.Y.S.2d 803 (Sup. Ct. 1997), for example, that the answer to an interrogatory may be used against the answering party as an admission, but otherwise it is just hearsay. SIEGEL-NYPRAC § 361; Matter of New York City Asbestos Litig., 173 Misc. 2d 121, 660 N.Y.S.2d 803 (Sup. Ct. 1997).

ii. By making the admissibility of depositions the standard for admitting interrogatory answers as well, NY CPLR § 3131 invokes NY CPLR Rule 3117 and its conditions. NY CPLR Rule 3117 prevents a party from introducing his own answers unless a proper foundation is laid, while ordinarily allowing a party to use his adversary's answers without such a foundation. SIEGEL-NYPRAC § 361; NY CPLR Rule 3117(a).

c. *Demand for address of party or of person who possessed an assigned cause of action or defense.* A party may serve on any party a written notice demanding a verified statement setting forth the post office address and residence of the party, of any specified officer or member of the party and of any person who possessed a cause of action or defense asserted in the action which has been assigned. The demand shall be complied with within ten (10) days of its service. NY CPLR Rule 3118.

d. *When interrogatories may not be used*

i. *No interrogatories when bill of particulars demanded.* Except in a matrimonial action, a party may not serve written interrogatories on another party and also demand a bill of particulars of the same party pursuant to NY CPLR § 3041. NY CPLR § 3130(1). For information on procedure in a matrimonial action, refer to NY CPLR § 3130(2).

ii. *No interrogatories when deposition conducted in personal injury action.* In the case of an action to recover damages for personal injury, injury to property or wrongful death predicated solely on a cause or causes of action for negligence, a party shall not be permitted to serve interrogatories on and conduct a deposition of the same party pursuant to NY CPLR Rule 3107 without leave of court. NY CPLR § 3130(1).

- When something other than negligence, or in addition to negligence, is the ground, both devices are available as to all grounds and no choice is necessary. SIEGEL-NYPRAC § 361.
- Because the interrogatory tends to duplicate the function of the bill of particulars, another basic restriction in NY CPLR § 3130(1) is that a party can't use both devices against the same party. If defendant has demanded a bill of particulars of plaintiff, in other words, which many defendants' lawyers do automatically upon serving an answer, he may not afterwards serve interrogatories on plaintiff. The practitioner should consider carefully whether the bill of particulars or the interrogatory would better serve his case, lest a forfeiture of the choice result from the knee-jerk service of the bill of particulars demand. SIEGEL-NYPRAC § 361.

3. *Governing law.* The civil practice law and rules (NY CPLR § 101, et seq.) shall govern the procedure in civil judicial proceedings in all courts of the state and before all judges, except where the procedure is regulated by inconsistent statute. The civil practice law and rules shall succeed the civil practice act and rules of civil practice and shall be deemed substituted therefor throughout the statutes and rules of the state. NY CPLR § 101. The civil practice law and rules shall be liberally construed to secure the just, speedy and inexpensive determination of every civil judicial proceeding. NY CPLR § 104.

a. *Uniform trial court rules.* The uniform civil rules for the Supreme Court and County Court (NY R UNIF TRIAL CTS § 202.1, et seq.) shall be applicable to civil actions and proceedings in the Supreme Court and the County Court. NY R UNIF TRIAL CTS § 202.1(a). The provisions of the uniform rules shall be construed consistent with the Civil Practice Law and Rules (CPLR), and matters not covered by the uniform rules shall be governed by the CPLR. NY R UNIF TRIAL CTS § 202.1(d).

b. *Local rules.* Local court rules, not inconsistent with law or with uniform civil rules for the Supreme Court and County Court (NY R UNIF TRIAL CTS § 202.1, et seq.), shall comply with Part 9 of the Rules of the Chief Judge (NY R CHIEF J § 9.1). NY R UNIF TRIAL CTS § 202.1(c).

c. *Official forms.* The state administrator shall have the power to adopt, amend and rescind an appendix of forms. Forms adopted pursuant to NY CPLR § 107 shall be sufficient under the civil practice law and rules and shall illustrate the simplicity and brevity of statement which the civil practice law and rules contemplate. NY CPLR § 107.

4. *Rules of the commercial division.* [Editor's note: certain types of civil cases or civil cases meeting certain monetary thresholds that are filed in the state of New York must be filed in the Commercial Division of the New York Supreme Courts. Rules governing practice in the commercial division are found in NY R UNIF TRIAL CTS § 202.70]. Cases which must be filed in the commercial division are listed below. For more information, refer to NY R UNIF TRIAL CTS § 202.70.

a. *Monetary thresholds.* Except as set forth in NY R UNIF TRIAL CTS § 202.70(b), the monetary thresholds of the Commercial Division, exclusive of punitive damages, interests, costs, disbursements and counsel fees claimed, are established as follows: (1) Albany County, fifty thousand dollars ($50,000); (2) Eighth Judicial District, one hundred thousand dollars ($100,000); (3) Kings County, one hundred fifty thousand dollars ($150,000); (4) Nassau County, two hundred thousand dollars ($200,000); (5) New York County, five hundred thousand dollars ($500,000); (6) Onondaga County, fifty thousand dollars ($50,000); (7) Queens County, one hundred thousand dollars ($100,000); (8) Seventh Judicial District, fifty thousand dollars ($50,000); (9) Suffolk County, one hundred thousand dollars ($100,000); and (10) Westchester County, one hundred thousand dollars ($100,000). NY R UNIF TRIAL CTS § 202.70(a).

i. *ALBANY COUNTY.* The Commercial Division of the Albany County Supreme Court exercises jurisdiction over selected business and commercial disputes in which the amount at issue generally involves damage claims in a minimum amount of fifty thousand dollars ($50,000) as well as claims for unspecified amounts where the value of the commercial asset(s) in dispute exceeds fifty thousand dollars ($50,000). A separate publication promulgating the rules and criteria relating to the filing and management of Commercial Court cases in this part may be obtained from the Albany County Supreme Court Clerk's Office. A section of the Uniform Civil Rules for the Supreme Court and County Court sets forth statewide rules. NY R 3 JD SUP Doc. 1(E).

ii. *BRONX COUNTY.* The monetary threshold for commercial cases in Bronx County will be seventy-five thousand dollars ($75,000). All other parameters including the type of matters that will be heard are contained within the Rules of the Commercial Division of the Supreme Court (NY R UNIF TRIAL CTS § 202.70). NY R BRONX FIL R Doc. 12.

iii. *NEW YORK COUNTY.* The monetary threshold in the New York County Commercial Division, which is generally applicable, is an amount in controversy of five hundred thousand dollars ($500,000) or more (exclusive of punitive damages, interest, costs, disbursements, and counsel fees). If the case is designated a commercial one and the Addendum is submitted, the clerk will review the pleadings to determine whether the amount in controversy in the case meets the monetary threshold or whether an exception to the threshold applies. NY R NY CTY Procedure IA(B). For more information on assigning a case to the commercial division in New York County, refer to NY R NY CTY Procedure IA(B).

b. *Commercial cases.* Actions in which the principal claims involve or consist of the following will be heard in the Commercial Division provided that the monetary threshold is met or equitable or declaratory relief is sought:

i. Breach of contract or fiduciary duty, fraud, misrepresentation, business tort (e.g., unfair competition), or statutory and/or common law violation where the breach or violation is alleged to arise out of business dealings (e.g., sales of assets or securities; corporate restructuring; partnership, shareholder, joint venture, and other business agreements; trade secrets; restrictive covenants; and employment agreements not including claims that principally involve alleged discriminatory practices);

ii. Transactions governed by the Uniform Commercial Code (exclusive of those concerning individual cooperative or condominium units);

iii. Transactions involving commercial real property, including Yellowstone injunctions and excluding actions for the payment of rent only;

iv. Shareholder derivative actions—without consideration of the monetary threshold;

v. Commercial class actions—without consideration of the monetary threshold;

vi. Business transactions involving or arising out of dealings with commercial banks and other financial institutions;

vii. Internal affairs of business organizations;

viii. Malpractice by accountants or actuaries, and legal malpractice arising out of representation in commercial matters;

ix. Environmental insurance coverage;

x. Commercial insurance coverage (e.g., directors and officers, errors and omissions, and business interruption coverage);

xi. Dissolution of corporations, partnerships, limited liability companies, limited liability partnerships and joint ventures—without consideration of the monetary threshold; and

xii. Applications to stay or compel arbitration and affirm or disaffirm arbitration awards and related injunctive relief pursuant to Article 75 of the New York Civil Practice Law and Rules (NY CPLR § 7501, et seq.) involving any of the foregoing enumerated commercial issues. Where the applicable arbitration agreement provides for the arbitration to be heard outside the United States, the monetary threshold set forth in NY R UNIF TRIAL CTS § 202.70(a) shall not apply. NY R UNIF TRIAL CTS § 202.70(b).

c. *Non-commercial cases.* The following will not be heard in the Commercial Division even if the monetary threshold is met:

i. Suits to collect professional fees;

ii. Cases seeking a declaratory judgment as to insurance coverage for personal injury or property damage;

iii. Residential real estate disputes, including landlord-tenant matters, and commercial real estate disputes involving the payment of rent only;

iv. Home improvement contracts involving residential properties consisting of one to four residential units or individual units in any residential building, including cooperative or condominium units;

v. Proceedings to enforce a judgment regardless of the nature of the underlying case;

vi. First-party insurance claims and actions by insurers to collect premiums or rescind non-commercial policies; and

vii. Attorney malpractice actions except as otherwise provided in NY R UNIF TRIAL CTS § 202.70(b)(8). NY R UNIF TRIAL CTS § 202.70(c).

d. For more information on the Commercial Division, refer to NY R UNIF TRIAL CTS § 202.70.

D. Documents

1. *Required documents*

a. *Interrogatories.* A copy of the interrogatories and of any order made under NY CPLR Rule 3132 shall be served on each party. NY CPLR Rule 3132. Refer to the General Requirements section of this document for more information on interrogatories.

b. *Proof of service.* In addition to complying with the provisions of NY CPLR Rule 2101, every paper filed in court shall have annexed thereto appropriate proof of service on all parties where required. NY R UNIF TRIAL CTS § 202.5(a).

2. *Supplemental documents*

a. *Working copies.* The court may require the parties to provide working copies of documents filed electronically. In such event, each working copy shall include, firmly affixed thereto, a copy of a confirmation notice in a form prescribed by the Chief Administrator. NY R UNIF TRIAL CTS § 202.5-b(d)(5).

E. Format

1. *Form of documents*

a. *Size and form of paper.* Each paper served or filed shall be durable, white and, except for summonses, subpoenas, notices of appearance, notes of issue, orders of protection, temporary orders of protection and exhibits, shall be eleven by eight and one-half (11 x 8-1/2) inches in size. NY CPLR Rule 2101(a).

b. *Writing and language.* The writing shall be legible and in black ink. NY CPLR Rule 2101(a). Each paper served or filed shall be in the English language which, where practicable, shall be of ordinary usage. NY CPLR Rule 2101(b).

c. *Caption.* Each paper served or filed shall begin with a caption setting forth the name of the court, the venue, the title of the action, the nature of the paper and the index number of the action if one has been assigned. In all papers other

than a summons, a complaint or a judgment it shall be sufficient to state the name of the first named party on each side with an appropriate indication of any omissions. NY CPLR Rule 2101(c).

i. *Further contents of first page.* After the first paper has been filed in each case the index number shall appear on the cover and first page to the right of the caption of every paper tendered for filing in the action. Each such cover and first page also shall contain an indication of the county of venue and a brief description of the nature of the paper and, where the case has been assigned to an individual judge, shall contain the name of the assigned judge to the right of the caption. NY R UNIF TRIAL CTS § 202.5(a); NY R UNIF TRIAL CTS § 202.5(b); NY R UNIF TRIAL CTS § 202.5(d)(1)(i).

d. *Index number.* No paper in an action in the supreme or a county court, other than an order submitted for signature to a judge out of court, shall be submitted for any purpose to the supreme or county court or to a clerk thereof unless there is endorsed on such paper the index number of the action assigned by the clerk of the county. NY CPLR § 8018(c).

e. *Line spacing.* Every paper filed in court, if typewritten, shall have at least double space between each line, except for quotations and the names and addresses of attorneys appearing in the action. NY R UNIF TRIAL CTS § 202.5(a).

f. *Font size.* Each. . .paper printed or typed, served or filed, except for summonses. . .and exhibits, shall be in clear type of no less than ten (10) point in size. NY CPLR Rule 2101(a).

i. Whenever a requirement relating to size of type is stated in point size, the type size requirement shall be deemed met if the x-height of the type is a minimum of forty-five percent (45%) of the specified point size. Each point shall be measured as .351 millimeter. The x-height size shall be measured as it appears on the page. The x-height is the height of the lower case letters, exclusive of ascenders or descenders. NY CPLR § 105(t).

g. *Margins.* Every paper filed in court shall have at least one (1) inch margins. NY R UNIF TRIAL CTS § 202.5(a).

h. *Citations*

i. *Civil practice law and rules.* NY CPLR § 101, et seq. shall be known as the civil practice law and rules, and may be cited as "CPLR". Reference to a provision in the civil practice law and rules may, except when such provision is being enacted or amended, be made without indicating whether it is a rule or section. NY CPLR § 101.

i. *Indorsement by attorney.* Each paper served or filed shall be indorsed with the name, address and telephone number of the attorney for the party serving or filing the paper, or if the party does not appear by attorney, with the name, address and telephone number of the party. NY CPLR Rule 2101(d).

j. *One-sided printing.* In addition, every paper filed in court, other than an exhibit or printed form, shall contain writing on one side only, except that papers that are fastened on the side may contain writing on both sides. NY R UNIF TRIAL CTS § 202.5(a).

k. *Use of copies authorized.* Except where otherwise specifically prescribed, copies, rather than originals, of all papers, including orders, affidavits and exhibits may be served or filed. Where it is required that the original be served or filed and the original is lost or withheld, the court may authorize a copy to be served or filed. NY CPLR Rule 2101(e).

i. Where a certified copy of a paper is required by law, an attorney admitted to practice in the courts of the state may certify that it has been compared by him with the original and found to be a true and complete copy. Such a certificate, when subscribed by such attorney, has the same effect as if made by a clerk. NY CPLR § 2105.

l. *Recycled paper.* It is the policy of the Unified Court System that litigants, where practicable, should file or submit to the courts of the Unified Court System of the State of New York papers printed or reproduced on recycled paper. Paper is considered recycled if it contains a minimum content of thirty percent (30%) waste paper. NY R UNIF TRIAL CTS § 215.2. The signature page of every paper filed or submitted to the court on recycled paper should bear the legend: "Printed [Reproduced] on Recycled Paper." NY R UNIF TRIAL CTS § 215.3.

2. *Form of electronic documents.* Each paper served or filed by electronic means, as defined in NY CPLR Rule 2103(f), shall be capable of being reproduced by the receiver so as to comply with the provisions of NY CPLR Rule 2101(a) through NY CPLR Rule 2101(d). NY CPLR Rule 2101(g).

a. *File format.* All e-filed documents shall comply with the technical requirements set forth at the NYSCEF site. NY R UNIF TRIAL CTS § 202.5-b(d)(1)(i).

b. *Heading of document.* The subject matter heading for each paper sent by electronic means must indicate that the matter being transmitted electronically is related to a court proceeding. NY CPLR Rule 2103(b)(7).

3. *Signature blocks.* Every pleading, written motion, and other paper, served on another party or filed or submitted to the court shall be signed by an attorney, or by a party if the party is not represented by an attorney, with the name of the attorney or

party clearly printed or typed directly below the signature. NY R CHIEF ADMIN § 130-1.1-a(a); NY R UNIF TRIAL CTS § 202.5(d)(1)(iv).

a. *Printed name.* Beneath each signature shall be printed the name signed. NY CPLR Rule 2101(a).

b. *Failure to sign.* Absent good cause shown, the court shall strike any unsigned paper if the omission of the signature is not corrected promptly after being called to the attention of the attorney or party. NY R CHIEF ADMIN § 130-1.1-a(a).

c. *Signature as certification.* By signing a paper, an attorney or party certifies that, to the best of that person's knowledge, information and belief, formed after an inquiry reasonable under the circumstances the presentation of the paper or the contentions therein are not frivolous as defined in NY R CHIEF ADMIN § 130-1.1(c). NY R CHIEF ADMIN § 130-1.1-a(b)(1).

d. *Electronic signatures.* A document shall be considered to have been signed by an attorney or party in compliance with NY R CHIEF ADMIN § 130-1.1-a if it has been signed by such attorney or party as provided in NY R UNIF TRIAL CTS § 202.5-b(e)(1) and it bears the signatory's name. NY R UNIF TRIAL CTS § 202.5-b(e)(2). An electronically filed document shall be considered to have been signed by, and shall be binding upon, the person identified as a signatory, if:

i. It bears the physical signature of such person and is scanned into an electronic format that reproduces such signature; or

ii. The signatory has electronically affixed the digital image of his or her signature to the document; or

iii. It is electronically filed under the User ID and password of that person; or

iv. In a tax certiorari action in which the parties have stipulated to this procedure, it is an initiating document that is electronically filed without the signature of the signatory in a form provided above in NY R UNIF TRIAL CTS § 202.5-b(e)(iv), provided that, prior to filing, the document is signed in full in hard copy (which hard copy must be preserved until the conclusion of all proceedings, including appeals, in the case in which it is filed); or

v. In a small claims assessment review proceeding, it is a petition recorded by the NYSCEF site upon the filing of a text file as provided in NY R UNIF TRIAL CTS § 202.5-b(b)(1), provided that prior to filing, the document was signed in full in hard copy (which hard copy must be preserved until the conclusion of all proceedings in the matter, including article 78 (NY CPLR § 7801, et seq.) review and any appeals, and must be made available during the proceeding upon request of the respondent or the court); or

vi. It otherwise bears the electronic signature of the signatory in a format conforming to such standards and requirements as may hereafter be established by the Chief Administrator. NY R UNIF TRIAL CTS § 202.5-b(e).

4. *Confidentiality of personal information.* No person may file any document available for public inspection with any state agency, political subdivision, or in any court of this state that contains a Social Security account number of any other person, unless such other person is a dependent child, or has consented to such filing, except as required by federal or state law or regulation, or by court rule. NY GEN BUS § 399-ddd. Submissions pursuant to e-filing procedures shall have the same confidentiality rights as paper documents. NY R UNIF TRIAL CTS § 202.5-b(k)(1).

a. *Confidential personal information.* Except in the actions designated in NY R UNIF TRIAL CTS § 202.5(e)(1), or as otherwise provided by rule or law or court order, and whether or not a sealing order is or has been sought, the parties shall omit or redact confidential personal information in papers submitted to the court for filing. For purposes of NY R UNIF TRIAL CTS § 202.5(e), confidential personal information ("CPI") means:

i. The taxpayer identification number of an individual or an entity, including a Social Security number, an employer identification number, and an individual taxpayer identification number, except the last four (4) digits thereof;

ii. The date of an individual's birth, except the year thereof;

iii. The full name of an individual known to be a minor, except the minor's initials;

iv. A financial account number, including a credit and/or debit card number, a bank account number, an investment account number, and/or an insurance account number, except the last four (4) digits or letters thereof; and

v. Any of the documents or testimony in a matrimonial action protected by NY DOM REL § 235 or evidence sealed by the court in such an action which are attached as exhibits or referenced in the papers filed in any other civil action. For purposes of NY R UNIF TRIAL CTS § 202.5, a matrimonial action shall mean: an action to annul a marriage or declare the nullity of a void marriage, an action or agreement for a separation, an action for a divorce, or an action or proceeding for custody, visitation, writ of habeus corpus, child support, maintenance or paternity. NY R UNIF TRIAL CTS § 202.5(e)(1).

b. *Submission of confidential personal information.* Where a person submitting a paper to a court for filing believes in good faith that the inclusion of the full confidential personal information described in NY R UNIF TRIAL CTS § 202.5(e)(1) is material and necessary to the adjudication of the action or proceeding before the court, he or she may apply to the court for leave to serve and file together with a paper in which such information has been set forth in abbreviated form a confidential affidavit or affirmation setting forth the same information in unabbreviated form, appropriately referenced to the page or pages of the paper at which the abbreviated form appears. NY R UNIF TRIAL CTS § 202.5(e)(3).

c. *Home addresses.* For information on when home addresses and other personal information must be redacted, refer to NY CPLR Rule 2103-a.

5. *Defective papers.* A defect in the form of a paper, if a substantial right of a party is not prejudiced, shall be disregarded by the court, and leave to correct shall be freely given. NY CPLR Rule 2101(f). Papers that are stapled or bound securely shall not be rejected for filing simply because they are not bound with a backer of any kind. NY R UNIF TRIAL CTS § 202.5(a). A paper filed in accordance with the rules of the chief administrator or any local rule or practice established by the court shall be deemed filed. NY CPLR Rule 2102(b).

a. *Objection to defective papers.* The party on whom a paper is served shall be deemed to have waived objection to any defect in form unless, within fifteen (15) days after the receipt thereof, the party on whom the paper is served returns the paper to the party serving it with a statement of particular objections. NY CPLR Rule 2101(f).

F. Filing and Service Requirements

1. *Filing requirements.* Except where otherwise prescribed by law or order of court, papers required to be filed shall be filed with the clerk of the court in which the action is triable. In an action or proceeding in supreme or court, papers required to be filed shall be filed with the clerk of the county in which the proceeding is brought. NY CPLR Rule 2102(a).

a. *Electronic filing.* On consent, documents may be filed and served by electronic means in Supreme Court in such civil actions and in such counties as shall be authorized by order of the Chief Administrator of the Courts and only to the extent and in the manner provided in NY R UNIF TRIAL CTS § 202.5-b. NY R UNIF TRIAL CTS § 202.5-b(a)(1). For the definitions of terms used in electronic filing, refer to NY R UNIF TRIAL CTS § 202.5-b(a)(2).

i. *Electronic filing of discovery materials.* In any action subject to e-filing, parties and non-parties producing materials in response to discovery demands may enter into a stipulation, which shall be e-filed, authorizing the electronic filing of discovery responses and discovery materials to the degree and upon terms and conditions set forth in the stipulation. In the absence of such a stipulation, no party shall file electronically any such materials except in the form of excerpts, quotations, or selected exhibits from such materials as part of motion papers, pleadings or other filings with the court. NY R UNIF TRIAL CTS § 202.5-b(j).

ii. *E-filing mandatory.* In any action subject to e-filing, all documents required to be filed with the court by an e-filing party shall be filed and served electronically, except as provided in NY R UNIF TRIAL CTS § 202.5-b. NY R UNIF TRIAL CTS § 202.5-b(d)(1)(i).

iii. *Who may file.* Documents may be filed or served electronically only by a person who has registered as an authorized e-filing user or as otherwise provided in NY R UNIF TRIAL CTS § 202.5-b(c). NY R UNIF TRIAL CTS § 202.5-b(c)(1).

iv. *When filing made.* Documents may be transmitted at any time of the day or night to the NYSCEF site. A document other than an order or judgment is filed when its electronic transmission or, in the case of a petition that is e-filed by submission of a text file as provided in NY R UNIF TRIAL CTS § 202.5-b(b)(1), the electronic transmission of the text file is recorded at that site, provided, however, that where payment of a fee is required upon the filing of a document, the document is not filed until transmission of the document and the information or form or information as required in NY R UNIF TRIAL CTS § 202.5-b(d)(2)(i), NY R UNIF TRIAL CTS § 202.5-b(d)(2)(ii) or NY R UNIF TRIAL CTS § 202.5-b(d)(2)(iii) has been recorded at the NYSCEF site; or, if no transmission of that information or form or information is recorded, where permitted by the County Clerk, until payment is presented to the County Clerk. NY R UNIF TRIAL CTS § 202.5-b(d)(3)(i).

v. *Notification of filing.* No later than the close of business on the business day following the electronic filing of a document, a notification, in a form prescribed by the Chief Administrator, shall be transmitted electronically by the NYSCEF site to the person filing such document and the e-mail service addresses of all other participating parties in such action. NY R UNIF TRIAL CTS § 202.5-b(d)(3)(ii).

vi. *Removal of confidential information and other corrections.* If a document filed electronically is subsequently discovered to contain confidential data—including but not limited to trade secrets, information protected by confidentiality agreement, or personal confidential information as defined by statute or court rule—or otherwise to have been filed in error, the filer or another party or affected person may (1) notify the parties and any non-party filers in the action of the confidentiality issue or other error raised by the filing, and of his or her intention to seek judicial relief to correct the filing: (2) following such notification, request that the appropriate County Clerk, exercising his or her administrative discretion, place the document temporarily in "restricted" status on the NYSCEF site, to be made available for viewing by court staff and the parties but not the general public; and (3) file an application to correct the filing by order to show cause within five (5) business days of such notification (or such time as the court may direct), including a request for preliminary injunctive relief limiting interim disclosure of the document at issue. Unless otherwise directed by the court, any document placed in restricted status in response to such a request shall be returned to public view upon expiration of this five (5) day period. The Chief Administrator of the Courts shall promulgate forms to implement this process. NY R UNIF TRIAL CTS § 202.5-b(d)(3)(iii).

vii. *Documents requiring judge's signature.* Except where the court directs otherwise, any document that requires a judge's signature shall be transmitted electronically and in hard copy to the court. NY R UNIF TRIAL CTS § 202.5-b(d)(6).

viii. *Documents which would be inconvenient to file electronically; Hard copies.* Notwithstanding any other provision of NY R UNIF TRIAL CTS § 202.5-b, and subject to such guidelines as may be established by the Chief Administrative Judge, the County Clerk or his or her designee may require or permit a party to file in hard copy, in accordance with procedures set by the County Clerk or designee, an exhibit or other document which it is impractical or inconvenient to file electronically. NY R UNIF TRIAL CTS § 202.5-b(d)(7).

ix. *Documents containing sensitive or proprietary information.* In an action subject to e-filing, any person may apply for an order prohibiting or restricting the electronic filing in the action of specifically identified materials on the grounds that such materials are subject to copyright or other proprietary rights, or trade secret or other privacy interests, and that electronic filing in the action is likely to result in substantial prejudice to those rights or interests. NY R UNIF TRIAL CTS § 202.5-b(k)(2).

x. *Refusal to accept paper filings.* In accordance with NY CPLR Rule 2102(c), a County Clerk and a chief clerk of the Supreme Court or County Court, as appropriate, shall refuse to accept for filing papers filed in actions and proceedings when the paper sought to be filed:

- Is in an action subject to electronic filing pursuant to Rules of the Chief Administrator,
- Is not being filed electronically, and
- Does not include the notice required by NY R UNIF TRIAL CTS § 202.5-b(d)(1). NY R UNIF TRIAL CTS § 202.5(d)(1)(v); NY R UNIF TRIAL CTS § 202.5-bb(d).

xi. *Emergency filings; Hard copies.* For information on when an emergency filing may be filed and served in hard copy, refer to NY R UNIF TRIAL CTS § 202.5-b(d)(1)(ii), NY R UNIF TRIAL CTS § 202.5-b(d)(1)(iii) and NY R UNIF TRIAL CTS § 202.5-bb(c)(3).

xii. *Technical failures.* The NYSCEF site shall be considered to be subject to a technical failure on a given day if the site is unable to accept filings or provide access to filed documents continuously or intermittently over the course of any period of time greater than one (1) hour after 12:00 noon of that day. Notice of all such technical failures shall be provided on the site. NY R UNIF TRIAL CTS § 202.5-b(i).

- When e-filing is hindered by a technical failure, a party may file with the appropriate clerk and serve in hard copy. NY R UNIF TRIAL CTS § 202.5-b(i). In the event an attorney or party shall file and serve documents in hard copy pursuant to NY R UNIF TRIAL CTS § 202.5-b(i), each such document shall include the notice required by NY R UNIF TRIAL CTS § 202.5-b(d)(1), and the filer shall file those documents with the NYSCEF site within three (3) business days after restoration of normal operations at that site. NY R UNIF TRIAL CTS § 202.5-b(i).
- With the exception of deadlines that by law cannot be extended, the time for filing of any document that is delayed due to technical failure of the site shall be extended for one (1) day for each day on which such failure occurs, unless otherwise ordered by the court. NY R UNIF TRIAL CTS § 202.5-b(i).

xiii. *Filing fees.* For information on what information must be provided to pay filing fees, refer to NY R UNIF TRIAL CTS § 202.5-b(d)(2).

xiv. *Exemption from e-filing.* For information on exemptions from e-filing, refer to NY R UNIF TRIAL CTS § 202.5-bb(e).

b. *Facsimile filing.* In the Supreme Court, facsimile filing shall be limited to commercial claims and tax certiorari, conservatorship, and mental hygiene proceedings in Monroe, Westchester, New York and Suffolk Counties. NY R UNIF TRIAL CTS § 202.5-a(a)(1). Refer to NY R UNIF TRIAL CTS § 202.5-a for information on the procedures for facsimile filing.

2. *Service requirements*

a. *Who may serve.* Except where otherwise prescribed by law or order of court, papers may be served by any person not a party of the age of eighteen years or over. NY CPLR Rule 2103(a).

b. *Service upon attorney.* Except where otherwise prescribed by law or order of court, papers to be served upon a party in a pending action shall be served upon the party's attorney. Where the same attorney appears for two or more parties, only one (1) copy need be served upon the attorney. Such service upon an attorney shall be made:

i. By delivering the paper to the attorney personally. NY CPLR Rule 2103(b)(1).

ii. By mailing the paper to the attorney at the address designated by that attorney for that purpose or, if none is designated, at the attorney's last known address; service by mail shall be complete upon mailing. NY CPLR Rule 2103(b)(2).

iii. If the attorney's office is open, by leaving the paper with a person in charge, or if no person is in charge, by leaving it in a conspicuous place; or if the attorney's office is not open, by depositing the paper, enclosed in a sealed wrapper directed to the attorney, in the attorney's office letter drop or box. NY CPLR Rule 2103(b)(3).

iv. By leaving it at the attorney's residence within the state with a person of suitable age and discretion. Service upon an attorney shall not be made at the attorney's residence unless service at the attorney's office cannot be made. NY CPLR Rule 2103(b)(4).

v. By transmitting the paper to the attorney by facsimile transmission, provided that a facsimile telephone number is designated by the attorney for that purpose. Service by facsimile transmission shall be complete upon the receipt by the sender of a signal from the equipment of the attorney served indicating that the transmission was received, and the mailing of a copy of the paper to that attorney. The designation of a facsimile telephone number in the address block subscribed on a paper served or filed in the course of an action or proceeding shall constitute consent to service by facsimile transmission in accordance with NY CPLR Rule 2103(b)(5). An attorney may change or rescind a facsimile telephone number by serving a notice on the other parties. NY CPLR Rule 2103(b)(5).

vi. By dispatching the paper to the attorney by overnight delivery service at the address designated by the attorney for that purpose or, if none is designated, at the attorney's last known address. Service by overnight delivery service shall be complete upon deposit of the paper enclosed in a properly addressed wrapper into the custody of the overnight delivery service for overnight delivery, prior to the latest time designated by the overnight delivery service for overnight delivery. "Overnight delivery service" means any delivery service which regularly accepts items for overnight delivery to any address in the state. NY CPLR Rule 2103(b)(6).

vii. By transmitting the paper to the attorney by electronic means where and in the manner authorized by the chief administrator of the courts by rule and, unless such rule shall otherwise provide, such transmission shall be upon the party's written consent. The subject matter heading for each paper sent by electronic means must indicate that the matter being transmitted electronically is related to a court proceeding. NY CPLR Rule 2103(b)(7).

c. *Electronic service mandatory; Consenting to electronic service; How electronic service may be made.* Except as otherwise provided in NY R UNIF TRIAL CTS § 202.5-bb, filing and service of all documents in an action that has been commenced electronically in accordance with NY R UNIF TRIAL CTS § 202.5-bb shall be by electronic means. NY R UNIF TRIAL CTS § 202.5-bb(c)(1).

i. *Party's consent required for certain e-filing.* After commencement of an action wherein e-filing is authorized, documents may be electronically filed and served, but only by, and electronic service shall be made only upon, a party or parties who have consented thereto. NY R UNIF TRIAL CTS § 202.5-b(b)(2)(i).

- A consent to e-filing in an action shall state that the party providing it agrees to the use of e-filing in the action and to be bound by the filing and service provisions in NY R UNIF TRIAL CTS § 202.5-b. NY R UNIF TRIAL CTS § 202.5-b(b)(2)(ii).

ii. *Address for service; Duty to notify as to changes.* The e-mail service address recorded at the time of registration

is the e-mail address at which service of interlocutory documents on that party may be made through notification transmitted by the NYSCEF site. It is the responsibility of each filing user to monitor that address and promptly notify the Resource Center in the event of a change in his or her e-mail service address. NY R UNIF TRIAL CTS § 202.5-b(f)(2)(i).

iii. *How service made.* An e-filing party causes service of an interlocutory document to be made upon another party participating in e-filing by filing the document electronically. Upon receipt of an interlocutory document, the NYSCEF site shall automatically transmit electronic notification to all e-mail service addresses in such action. NY R UNIF TRIAL CTS § 202.5-b(f)(2)(ii).

- Except as provided otherwise in NY R UNIF TRIAL CTS § 202.5-b(h)(3), the electronic transmission of the notification shall constitute service of the document on the e-mail service addresses identified therein; however, such service will not be effective if the filing party learns that the notification did not reach the address of the person to be served. Proof of such service will be recorded on the NYSCEF site. A party may, however, utilize other service methods permitted by the CPLR provided that, if one of such other methods is used, proof of that service shall be filed electronically. NY R UNIF TRIAL CTS § 202.5-b(f)(2)(ii).

iv. *Signatures on hard copies; Proof of service filed electronically.* When an e-filing party serves a document in hard copy on a non-participating party, the document served shall bear full signatures of all signatories and proof of such service shall be filed electronically. NY R UNIF TRIAL CTS § 202.5-b(b)(2)(i).

v. *Effect of failure to consent.* A party's failure to consent to participation in electronic filing and service shall not bar any other party to the action from filing documents electronically with the County Clerk and the court or serving documents upon any other party who has consented to participation. A party who has not consented to participation shall file documents with the court and the County Clerk, and serve and be served with documents, in hard copy. NY R UNIF TRIAL CTS § 202.5-b(b)(2)(i).

d. *Service upon party.* If a party has not appeared by an attorney or the party's attorney cannot be served, service shall be upon the party by a method specified in NY CPLR Rule 2103(b)(1), NY CPLR Rule 2103(b)(2), NY CPLR Rule 2103(b)(4), NY CPLR Rule 2103(b)(5) or NY CPLR Rule 2103(b)(6). NY CPLR Rule 2103(c).

i. When a party is in default for failure to appear, he shall not be entitled to notice or service of any copy required under NY CPLR § 3101, et seq. NY CPLR Rule 3105.

e. *Service on all parties.* Each paper served on any party shall be served on every other party who has appeared, except as otherwise may be provided by court order or as provided in NY CPLR § 3012 or in NY CPLR § 3215(f). Upon demand by a party, the plaintiff shall supply that party with a list of those who have appeared and the names and addresses of their attorneys. NY CPLR Rule 2103(e).

f. *Service by filing.* If a paper cannot be served by any of the methods specified in NY CPLR Rule 2103(b) and NY CPLR Rule 2103(c), service may be made by filing the paper as if it were a paper required to be filed. NY CPLR Rule 2103(d).

g. *Definitions.* For the purposes of NY CPLR Rule 2103:

i. "Mailing" means the deposit of a paper enclosed in a first class postpaid wrapper, addressed to the address designated by a person for that purpose or, if none is designated, at that person's last known address, in a post office or official depository under the exclusive care and custody of the United States Postal Service within the state;

ii. "Electronic means" means any method of transmission of information between computers or other machines designed for the purpose of sending and receiving such transmissions, and which allows the recipient to reproduce the information transmitted in a tangible medium of expression;

iii. "Facsimile transmission" means any method of transmission of documents to a facsimile machine at a remote location which can automatically produce a tangible copy of such documents. NY CPLR Rule 2103(f).

G. Hearings

1. There is no hearing required or contemplated in the New York rules governing the interrogatories.

H. Forms

1. New York Interrogatories Forms

a. Form; Defendant's interrogatories to plaintiff in products-liability action; Injury to employee from allegedly defective equipment. CW2D § 42:424.

b. Form; Defendant's interrogatories to plaintiff in breach of contract action involving acquisition of business equipment, software, and programming. CW2D § 42:425.

c. Interrogatories. MCF CPLR § 6:200.

d. Affidavit in support of motion for leave to serve interrogatories within 20 days after service of summons and complaint. MCF CPLR § 6:208.

e. Order permitting service of interrogatories within 20 days after service of summons and complaint. MCF CPLR § 6:209.

I. Applicable Rules

1. *State rules*

a. Short title; Application; Construction; Definitions. NY CPLR § 101; NY CPLR § 104; NY CPLR § 105.

b. Appendix of official forms. NY CPLR § 107.

c. Extensions of time generally. NY CPLR § 2004.

d. Form of papers. NY CPLR Rule 2101; NY CPLR Rule 2102; NY CPLR § 2105; NY GEN BUS § 399-ddd; NY R UNIF TRIAL CTS § 215.2; NY R UNIF TRIAL CTS § 215.3.

e. Service of papers. NY CPLR Rule 2103.

f. Computation of time. NY CPLR § 2402; NY GEN CONSTR § 19; NY GEN CONSTR § 20; NY GEN CONSTR § 25-a; NY GEN CONSTR § 30; NY GEN CONSTR § 31; NY GEN CONSTR § 53.

g. Scope of disclosure. NY CPLR § 3101; NY CPLR § 3102; NY CPLR § 3103; NY CPLR § 3104; NY CPLR Rule 3105; NY CPLR Rule 3117; NY CPLR Rule 3118.

h. Interrogatories. NY CPLR § 3130; NY CPLR § 3131; NY CPLR Rule 3132.

i. Motions staying disclosure. NY CPLR Rule 3214; NY CPLR Rule 3407.

j. Index number fees of county clerks. NY CPLR § 8018.

k. Hours of court. NY R CHIEF J § 3.1.

l. Application of part; Waiver; Additional rules; Application of CPLR; Definitions. NY R UNIF TRIAL CTS § 202.1.

m. Papers filed in court; Electronic filing in supreme court. NY R UNIF TRIAL CTS § 202.5; NY R UNIF TRIAL CTS § 202.5-a; NY R UNIF TRIAL CTS § 202.5-b; NY R UNIF TRIAL CTS § 202.5-bb.

n. Rules of the commercial division of the Supreme Court. NY R UNIF TRIAL CTS § 202.70.

o. Signing of papers. NY R CHIEF ADMIN § 130-1.1-a.

2. *Local rules*

a. *Albany County*

i. Third judicial district rules. NY R 3 JD SUP Doc. 1.

b. *Bronx County*

i. Commercial division. NY R BRONX FIL R Doc. 12.

c. *Kings County*

i. Expedited discovery. NY R L KINGS Pt. B, Rule 5.

ii. Pre calendar procedures. NY R L KINGS Rule I.

iii. Both pre and post note procedures. NY R L KINGS Rule IV.

d. *New York County*

i. RJIs and assignments. NY R NY CTY Procedure IA.

ii. Discovery schedule. NY R NY CTY J RUL Rule 8.

J. Miscellaneous

NOTE: Individual judges' rules may apply.

ALBANY COUNTY

JUSTICE LISA M. FISHER: NY R 3 JD FISHER Fisher; NY R 3 JD FISHER Fisher, PC Order.

JUSTICE RICHARD MOTT: NY R 3 JD MOTT Mott.

JUSTICE STEPHAN G. SCHICK: NY R 3 JD Schick.

FORECLOSURE SETTLEMENT PART: NY R 3 JD Foreclosure Settlement.

BRONX COUNTY

JUSTICE PAUL L. ALPERT: [NY R BRONX J Part IA-29, as amended by NY ORDER 20-0337].

JUSTICE BEN BARBATO: NY R BRONX J Part IA-21.

JUSTICE MARY ANNE BRIGANTTI: [NY R BRONX J Part IA-15, as amended by NY ORDER 20-0338].

JUSTICE JOSEPH E. CAPELLA: NY R BRONX J Part IA-23.

JUSTICE MITCHELL DANZIGER: NY R BRONX J Part IA-3/33 ; [NY R BRONX J Danziger, Part IA-3/33, as amended by NY ORDER 20-0339].

JUSTICE LAURA G. DOUGLAS: NY R BRONX J Part IA-11.

JUSTICE RUBEN FRANCO: NY R BRONX J Part IA-26.

JUSTICE DORIS M. GONZALEZ: NY R BRONX J Part IA-24.

JUSTICE WILMA GUZMAN: NY R BRONX J Part IA-7; [NY R BRONX J Guzman, Part IA-7 Virtual, as amended by NY ORDER 20-0340].

JUSTICE ROBERT T. JOHNSON: NY R BRONX J Part IA-12.

JUSTICE DONALD A. MILES: NY R BRONX J Part IA-8.

JUSTICE DONNA M. MILLS: NY R BRONX J Part IA-9.

JUSTICE JULIA I. RODRIGUEZ: NY R BRONX J Part IA-18; [NY R BRONX J Part IA-27, as amended by NY ORDER 20-0341].

JUSTICE LLINET M. ROSADO: [NY R BRONX J Part IA-25, as amended by NY ORDER 20-0342].

JUSTICE NORMA RUIZ: NY R BRONX J Part IA-22; [NY R BRONX J Ruiz, Part IA-22 Virtual, as amended by NY ORDER 20-0343].

JUSTICE HOWARD H. SHERMAN: NY R BRONX J Part IA-4.

JUSTICE FERNANDO TAPIA: NY R BRONX J Part IA-13.

JUSTICE ELIZABETH A. TAYLOR: NY R BRONX J Part IA-2.

JUSTICE ALISON Y. TRUITT: NY R BRONX J Part IA-5.

PART IDV: NY R BRONX J Doc. 1.

PRE-TRIAL PART RULES: NY R BRONX J Doc. 2.

PRE TRIAL WORKSHEET: NY R BRONX J Doc. 3.

FORECLOSURE SETTLEMENT PART RULES: NY R BRONX J Doc. 4.

GUARDIANSHIP PART RULES: NY R BRONX J Doc. 5.

LPM PART RULES: NY R BRONX J Doc. 6.

ERIE COUNTY

JUSTICE M. WILLIAM BOLLER: NY R 8 JD J Boller.

JUSTICE RALPH A. BONIELLO: NY R 8 JD J Boniello.

JUSTICE CHRISTOPHER J. BURN: NY R 8 JD J Burns.

JUSTICE RUSSELL P. BUSCAGLIA: NY R 8 JD J Buscaglia.

JUSTICE FRANK CARUSO: NY R 8 JD J Caruso.

JUSTICE STEPHEN W. CASS: NY R 8 JD J Cass.

JUSTICE DEBORAH A. CHIMES: NY R 8 JD J Chimes.

JUSTICE EMILIO COLAIACOVO: [NY R 8 JD J Colaiacovo, as amended by NY ORDER 20-0252].

JUSTICE DIANE Y. DEVLIN: NY R 8 JD J Devlin.

JUSTICE JAMES H. DILLON: NY R 8 JD J Dillon.

JUSTICE PAULA L. FEROLETO: NY R 8 JD J Feroleto.

JUSTICE DANIEL J. FURLONG: [NY R 8 JD J Furlong, as amended by NY ORDER 20-0253].

JUSTICE JOSEPH R. GLOWNIA: NY R 8 JD J Glownia.

JUSTICE MARK J. GRISANTI: NY R 8 JD J Grisanti.

JUSTICE DEBORAH A. HAENDIGES: NY R 8 JD J Haendiges.

JUSTICE LYNN W. KEANE: [NY R 8 JD J Keane, as amended by NY ORDER 20-0254].

JUSTICE RICHARD C. KLOCH, Sr.: NY R 8 JD J Kloch.

JUSTICE FREDERICK J. MARSHALL: [NY R 8 JD J Marshall, as amended by NY ORDER 20-0255.

JUSTICE JOHN L. MICHALSKI: NY R 8 JD J Michalski.

JUSTICE MARK A. MONTOUR: [NY R 8 JD J Montour, as amended by NY ORDER 20-0256].

JUSTICE HENRY NOWAK: NY R 8 JD J Nowak.

JUSTICE JOHN F. O'DONNELL: NY R 8 JD J O'Donnell.

JUSTICE JEANETTE OGDEN: NY R 8 JD J Ogden.

JUSTICE CATHERINE NUGENT-PANEPINTO: NY R 8 JD J Nugent-Panepinto.

JUSTICE FRANK A. SEDITA, III: [NY R 8 JD J Sedita, as amended by NY ORDER 20-0257].

JUSTICE SARA SHELDON: NY R 8 JD J Sheldon.

JUSTICE DONNA M. SIWEK: NY R 8 JD J Siwek.

JUSTICE MARY L. SLISZ: NY R 8 JD J Slisz.

JUSTICE TIMOTHY J. WALKER: [NY R 8 JD J Walker, as amended by NY ORDER 20-0258].

JUSTICE DENNIS E. WARD: NY R 8 JD J Ward.

JUSTICE PAUL B. WOJTASZEK: [NY R 8 JD J Wojtaszek, as amended by NY ORDER 20-0259].

JUSTICE CHARLES N. ZAMBITO: [NY R 8 JD J Zambito, as amended by NY ORDER 20-0260].

SUPREME COURT LEGAL STAFF: NY R 8 JD J Legal Staff.

KINGS COUNTY

JUSTICE RACHEL A. ADAMS: NY R KINGS J Part 5F.

JUSTICE LOREN BAILY-SCHIFFMAN: NY R KINGS J Part 65.

JUSTICE REGINALD A. BODDIE: NY R KINGS J Part 95.

JUSTICE THERESA M. CICCOTTO: NY R KINGS J Part 19; NY R KINGS J Part 5J.

JUSTICE LISSETTE COLON: NY R KINGS J Part Rules.

JUSTICE GENINE EDWARDS: NY R KINGS J Part 80.

JUSTICE PAMELA L. FISHER: [NY R KINGS J Part 94, as amended by NY ORDER 20-0208].

JUSTICE ROBIN GARSON: NY R KINGS J Part 75.

JUSTICE LARA J. GENOVISI: [NY R KINGS J Part 34, as amended by NY ORDER 20-0209].

JUSTICE BERNARD J. GRAHAM: NY R KINGS J Part 36.

JUSTICE DAWN JIMENEZ-SALTA: NY R KINGS J Part 88.

JUSTICE INGRID JOSEPH: [NY R KINGS J Part FRP3 and Part 83, as amended by NY ORDER 20-0210].

JUSTICE KATHY J. KING: NY R KINGS J Part 64, 76K.

JUSTICE LAWRENCE KNIPEL: NY R KINGS J Part 57.

JUSTICE DONALD KURTZ: NY R KINGS J Part 26.

JUSTICE CARL LANDICINO: [NY R KINGS J Part 81, as amended by NY ORDER 20-0211].

JUSTICE KATHERINE LEVINE: [NY R KINGS J Part 20, 25, 92, as amended by NY ORDER 20-0211].

JUSTICE LORNA MCALLISTER: [NY R KINGS J Part 10, as amended by NY ORDER 20-0211].
JUSTICE ROSEMARIE MONTALBANO: [NY R KINGS J Part 19, 71, and 22, as amended by NY ORDER 20-0211].
JUSTICE RICHARD J. MONTELIONE: [NY R KINGS J Part 99 and DJMP, as amended by NY ORDER 20-0215].
JUSTICE LISA S. OTTLEY: NY R KINGS J Part 24.
JUSTICE MARK I. PARTNOW: NY R KINGS J Part 43.
JUSTICE ERIC I. PRUS: NY R KINGS J Part 5A.
JUSTICE FRANCOIS RIVERA: NY R KINGS J Part 52.
JUSTICE KAREN B. ROTHENBERG: NY R KINGS J Part 35.
JUSTICE LEON RUCHELSMAN: NY R KINGS J Part 1.
JUSTICE WAYNE P. SAITTA: NY R KINGS J Part 29.
JUSTICE ROBIN K. SHEARES: NY R KINGS J Part 96.
JUSTICE KENNETH P. SHERMAN: NY R KINGS J Part 67 and 78.
JUSTICE DEBRA SILBER: NY R KINGS J Part 9 and 5K.
JUSTICE ELLEN M. SPODEK: NY R KINGS J Part 63.
JUSTICE MARSHA L. STEINHARDT: NY R KINGS J Part 15.
JUSTICE JEFFREY S. SUNSHINE: NY R KINGS J Part 5G.
JUSTICE PETER P. SWEENEY: [NY R KINGS J Part 35, as amended by NY ORDER 20-0218].
JUSTICE DELORES J. THOMAS: [NY R KINGS J Part 5T, as amended by NY ORDER 20-0221].
JUSTICE WAVNY TOUSSAINT: NY R KINGS J Part 70.
JUSTICE RICHARD VELASQUEZ: NY R KINGS J Part 66.
JUSTICE CAROLYN E. WADE: NY R KINGS J Part 84.
JUSTICE EDWARD G. WALKER: [NY R KINGS J Part 90, as amended by NY ORDER 20-0219].
JUSTICE LILLIAN WAN: [NY R KINGS J Part 17, as amended by NY ORDER 20-0220].
JUSTICE MICHELLE WESTON: NY R KINGS J Part 3.
MENTAL HYGIENE PART: NY R KINGS J Part 77.
MATRIMONIAL PARTS DURING COVID-19 EMERGENCY: JUSTICE KAREN B. ROTHENBERG: NY R KINGS J Doc. 1.

NASSAU COUNTY

JUSTICE ANNA R. ANZALONE: NY R NASSAU S J Anzalone, Part 26.
JUSTICE STACY D. BENNETT: NY R NASSAU S J Bennett; NY R NASSAU S J Bennett, Form 1.
JUSTICE ANTONIO BRANDVEEN: NY R NASSAU S J Brandveen, Part 31.
JUSTICE JEFFREY S. BROWN: [NY R NASSAU S J Brown, as amended by NY ORDER 20-0297].
JUSTICE STEPHEN A. BUCARIA: NY R NASSAU S J Bucaria.
JUSTICE JULIANNE T. CAPETOLA: NY R NASSAU S J Capetola, Part 28.
JUSTICE EDMUND M. DANE: NY R NASSAU S J Dane, Part 33.
JUSTICE VITO M. DESTEFANO: NY R NASSAU S J DeStefano, Part 13; NY R NASSAU S J DeStefano, Form 1.
JUSTICE ARTHUR M. DIAMOND: NY R NASSAU S J Diamond, Part 7.
JUSTICE THOMAS FEINMAN: NY R NASSAU S J Feinman, Part 5.
JUSTICE JOHN M. GALASSO: NY R NASSAU S J Galasso, Part 22.
JUSTICE SHARON M.J. GIANELLI: NY R NASSAU S J Gianelli, Part 22; NY R NASSAU S J Gianelli, Form 1.
JUSTICE JEFFREY A. GOODSTEIN: NY R NASSAU S J Goodstein, Part 33; NY R NASSAU S J Goodstein, Form 1.
JUSTICE DAVID J. GUGERTY: [NY R NASSAU S J Gugerty, Part 31, as amended by NY ORDER 20-0298].
JUSTICE HELENE F. GUGERTY: NY R NASSAU S J Gugerty, Part 47.

JUSTICE STEVEN M. JAEGER: NY R NASSAU S J Jaeger, Part 35; NY R NASSAU S J Jaeger, Form 1.

JUSTICE JACK L. LIBERT: NY R NASSAU S J Libert, Part 23.

JUSTICE JOSEPH H. LORINTZ: NY R NASSAU S J Lorintz, Part 26; NY R NASSAU S J Lorintz, Form 1.

JUSTICE ROY S. MAHON: NY R NASSAU S J Mahon, Part 3.

JUSTICE RANDY SUE MARBER: NY R NASSAU S J Marber, Part 8.

JUSTICE JAMES P. MCCORMACK: [NY R NASSAU S J McCormack, Part 18, as amended by NY ORDER, 20-0299].

JUSTICE DICCIA T. PINEDA-KIRWAN: [NY R NASSAU S J Pineda-Kirwan, as amended by NY ORDER 20-0300].

JUSTICE THOMAS RADEMAKER: [NY R NASSAU S J Rademaker, Part 28, as amended by NY ORDER 20-0301]; [NY R NASSAU S J Rademaker, Form 1, as amended by NY ORDER 20-0301].

JUSTICE DENISE L. SHER: NY R NASSAU S J Rademaker, Part 32.

JUSTICE LEONARD D. STEINMAN: [NY R NASSAU S J Steinman, Part 15, as amended by NY ORDER 20-0303]; NY R NASSAU S J Steinman, Form 1.

JUSTICE HOWARD E. STURIM: NY R NASSAU S J Sturim, Part 50; NY R NASSAU S J Sturim, Form 1.

JUSTICE HELEN VOUTSINAS: [NY R NASSAU S J Voutsinas, Part 25, as amended by NY ORDER 20-0304]; [NY R NASSAU S J Voutsinas, Form 1, as amended by NY ORDER 20-0305].

JUSTICE HOPE SCHWARTZ ZIMMERMAN: NY R NASSAU S J Zimmerman, Part 17.

NEW YORK COUNTY

JUDGE'S RULES; BASIC INFORMATION: [NY R NY CTY J RUL Doc. 1, as amended by NY ORDER 20-0202].

ONONDAGA COUNTY

JUSTICE ROBERT E. ANTONACCI II: [NY R ONDGA E FIL Doc. 1, as amended by 20-0239].

JUSTICE MICHAEL V. COCCOMI: NY R ONDGA E FIL Doc. 2.

JUSTICE GREGORY R. GILBERT: NY R 5 JD JUDGES Gilbert; NY R ONDGA E FIL Doc. 3.

JUSTICE DONALD A. GREENWOOD: NY R ONDGA E FIL Doc. 4.

JUSTICE DEBORAH H. KARALUNAS: NY R ONDGA E FIL Doc. 5.

JUSTICE JAMES MCCLUSKY: NY R 5 JD MCCLUSKY McClusky.

JUSTICE CHARLES C. MERRELL: NY R 5 JD MERRELL Merrell.

JUSTICE PATRICK F. MACRAE: NY R 5 JD MACRAE Doc. 1.

JUSTICE JAMES P. MURPHY: NY R ONDGA E FIL Doc. 7.

JUSTICE GERALD J. NERI: [NY R 5 JD JUDGES Neri, as amended by NY ORDER 20-0236]; [NY R ONDGA E FIL Doc. 8, as amended by NY ORDER 20-0241].

JUSTICE ANTHONY J. PARIS: NY R 5 JD JUDGES Paris; [NY R ONDGA E FIL Doc. 9, as amended by NY ORDER 20-0242].

JUSTICE NORMAN W. SEITER, JR.: NY R 5 JD JUDGES Seiter.

JUSTICE KEVIN G. YOUNG: [NY R ONDGA E FIL Doc. 10, as amended by NY ORDER 20-0243].

QUEENS COUNTY

JUSTICE PAM JACKMAN BROWN: [NY R L QUEENS Brown, Part 19, as amended by NY ORDER 20-0321].

JUSTICE CHEREE A. BUGGS: NY R L QUEENS Buggs, Part 30.

JUSTICE PAM JACKMAN BROWN: [NY R L QUEENS Brown, Part 19, as amended by NY ORDER 20-0321].

JUSTICE DENIS J. BUTLER: NY R L QUEENS Butler, Part 12.

JUSTICE ROBERT I. CALORAS: [NY R L QUEENS Caloras, Part 36, as amended by NY ORDER 20-0322].

JUSTICE ANNA CULLEY: NY R L QUEENS Culley, Part 53.

JUSTICE TIMOTHY DUFFICY: NY R L QUEENS Dufficy, Part 35.

JUSTICE DAVID ELLIOT: NY R L QUEENS Elliot, Part 14.

JUSTICE JOSEPH J. ESPOSITO: NY R L QUEENS Esposito, Part 6.

JUSTICE DARRELL L. GAVRIN: [NY R L QUEENS Gavrin, Part 27, as amended by NY ORDER 20-0323].

JUSTICE WYATT N. GIBBONS: [NY R L QUEENS Gibbons, Part 5, as amended by NY ORDER 20-0330.

JUSTICE DONNA-MARIE E. GOLIA: [NY R L QUEENS Golia, Part 21, as amended by NY ORDER 20-0331].

JUSTICE MARGUERITE A. GRAYS: [NY R L QUEENS Grays, Part 4, as amended by NY ORDER 20-0324].

JUSTICE RUDOLPH E. GRECO: [NY R L QUEENS Greco, Part 32, as amended by NY ORDER 20-0325].

JUSTICE MAUREEN HEALY: NY R L QUEENS Healy, Part 6.

JUSTICE PHILLIP HOM: [NY R L QUEENS Hom, Part 43, as amended by NY ORDER 20-0332].

JUSTICE KEVIN J. KERRIGAN: NY R L QUEENS Kerrigan, Part 10.

JUSTICE MOJGAN C. LANCMAN: NY R L QUEENS Lancman, Part 20.

JUSTICE RICHARD G. LATIN: NY R L QUEENS Latin, Part 40.

JUSTICE ULYSSES B. LEVERETT: [NY R L QUEENS Leverett, Part 6, as amended by NY ORDER 20-0326].

JUSTICE LEONARD LIVOTE: NY R L QUEENS Livote, Part 33.

JUSTICE LEE A. MAYERSOHN: NY R L QUEENS Mayersohn, Part 22; NY R L QUEENS Mayersohn, Part 22G; [NY R L QUEENS Mayersohn, Part 22G COVID, as amended by NY ORDER 20-0327].

JUSTICE ROBERT J. MCDONALD: NY R L QUEENS McDonald, Part 34.

JUSTICE MARGARET MCGOWAN: NY R L QUEENS McGowan, Part 52.

JUSTICE MAURICE E. MUIR: [NY R L QUEENS Muir, Part 42, as amended by NY ORDER 20-0333].

JUSTICE JODI ORLOW: NY R L QUEENS Orlow, Part 51.

JUSTICE LESLIE J. PURIFICCION: NY R L QUEENS Purificcion, Part 39.

JUSTICE JOSEPH RISI: [NY R L QUEENS Risi, Part 3, as amended by NY ORDER 20-0328].

JUSTICE FREDERICK D.R. SAMPSON: [NY R L QUEENS Sampson, Part 31, as amended by NY ORDER 20-0329].

JUSTICE MARTIN J. SCHULMAN: NY R L QUEENS Schulman, Part 29.

JUSTICE BERNICE D. SIEGAL: NY R L QUEENS Siegal, Part 25G.

JUSTICE JANICE A. TAYLOR: NY R L QUEENS Taylor, Part 15.

JUSTICE CARMEN R. VELASQUEZ: NY R L QUEENS Velasquez, Part 38.

JUSTICE LOURDES M VENTURA: [NY R L QUEENS Ventura, Part 37, as amended by NY ORDER 20-0334].

JUSTICE WILLIAM A. VISCOVICH: NY R L QUEENS Viscovich, Part 63.

JUSTICE ALLAN B. WEISS: NY R L QUEENS Weiss, Part 2.

COMPLIANCE, SETTLEMENT AND CONFERENCE PART: NY R L QUEENS Doc 1.

PRELIMINARY CONFERENCE PART: [NY R L QUEENS Doc. 2, as amended by NY ORDER 20-0335].

MEDICAL MALPRACTICE CONFERENCE PART: [NY R L QUEENS Doc. 3, as amended by NY ORDER 20-0336].

TRIAL SCHEDULING PART: NY R L QUEENS Doc. 4.

SUMMARY JURY TRIAL PROGRAM: NY R L QUEENS Doc. 7.

RESIDENTIAL FORECLOSURE PART: NY R L QUEENS Doc. 9.

FORECLOSURE AUCTION RULES: NY R L QUEENS Doc. 10.

MATRIMONIAL PRELIMINARY CONFERENCE PART: NY R L QUEENS Doc. 11.

NON-CUSTODIAL CONTESTED MATRIMONIAL PART: NY R L QUEENS Doc. 12.

Requests, Notices and Applications
Response to Interrogatories

Document Last Updated August 2020

A. Checklist

(I) ❑ Matters to be considered by requesting party
- (a) ❑ Required documents
  - (1) ❑ Interrogatories
  - (2) ❑ Proof of service
- (b) ❑ Supplemental documents
  - (1) ❑ Working copies
- (c) ❑ Timing
  - (1) ❑ After commencement of an action, any party may serve written interrogatories upon any other party

(II) ❑ Matters to be considered by responding party
- (a) ❑ Required documents
  - (1) ❑ Responses to interrogatories
  - (2) ❑ Proof of service
- (b) ❑ Supplemental documents
  - (1) ❑ Working copies
- (c) ❑ Timing
  - (1) ❑ Within twenty (20) days after service of interrogatories, the party upon whom they are served shall serve upon each of the parties a copy of the answer to each interrogatory, except one to which the party objects, in which event the reasons for the objection shall be stated with reasonable particularity

B. Timing

1. *Time to respond to interrogatories.* Within twenty (20) days after service of interrogatories, the party upon whom they are served shall serve upon each of the parties a copy of the answer to each interrogatory, except one to which the party objects, in which event the reasons for the objection shall be stated with reasonable particularity. NY CPLR Rule 3133(a).
   a. *Time to respond to demand for address of party or of person who possessed an assigned cause of action or defense.* A party may serve on any party a written notice demanding a verified statement setting forth the post office address and residence of the party, of any specified officer or member of the party and of any person who possessed a cause of action or defense asserted in the action which has been assigned. The demand shall be complied with within ten (10) days of its service. NY CPLR Rule 3118.
2. *Motions staying disclosure.* Service of a notice of motion under NY CPLR Rule 3211, NY CPLR Rule 3212, or NY CPLR § 3213 stays disclosure until determination of the motion unless the court orders otherwise. If the motion is based solely on the defense that the summons and complaint, summons with notice, or notice of petition and petition was not properly served, disclosure shall not be stayed unless the court orders otherwise. NY CPLR Rule 3214(b).
   a. *Personal injury actions involving terminally ill patients.* Notwithstanding the provisions of NY CPLR Rule 3214(b), the service or pendency of a motion under NY CPLR Rule 3211, NY CPLR Rule 3212, or NY CPLR § 3213 shall not stay disclosure in an action where a preliminary conference order has been entered pursuant to NY CPLR Rule 3407. NY CPLR Rule 3407(b)(3).
3. *KINGS COUNTY: Discovery timing.* At [the Compliance Conference, the court will] schedule all outstanding discovery to be completed prior to date fixed for filing Note of Issue. NY R L KINGS Rule I(B).
   a. *Deadlines in orders.* Discovery scheduled in Compliance Conference orders shall be strictly adhered to and may not be extended without leave of the court. Unjustified failure to comply with the provisions of the CCP order will result in preclusion, the striking of a pleading or imposition of sanctions, as appropriate. NY R L KINGS Rule I(B)(2).
   b. *Cases with extensive discovery.* Where post Compliance Conference discovery is to be extensive, cases may be retracked from standard to complex, which will provide for three (3) additional months of post Compliance Conference discovery and extend the Note of Issue date by three (3) months. NY R L KINGS Rule I(B)(1).

c. *Discovery not stayed.* Ordinarily the Court/JHO will not stay discovery during pendency of motions to withdraw, or during pendency of settlement, or during pendency of dispositive motions. NY R L KINGS Rule IV.

d. *Expedited discovery in certain cases.* Discovery in third party and joint actions will be expedited. NY R L KINGS Pt. B, Rule 5.

e. For more information on discovery scheduling, refer to NY R L KINGS Flow Chart.

4. *NEW YORK COUNTY: Deadlines in orders.* Strict compliance with all discovery orders is required. Unexcused or unjustified failure to comply with deadlines fixed by the court, including those set out in Preliminary Conference Orders, may result in an award of costs, conditional or otherwise, or the imposition of another penalty authorized by NY CPLR § 3126. NY R NY CTY J RUL Rule 8.

5. *Computation of time*

a. *Units of time*

i. *Day.* A calendar day includes the time from midnight to midnight. Sunday or any day of the week specifically mentioned means a calendar day. NY GEN CONSTR § 19.

ii. *Month.* In a statute, contract or public or private instrument, unless otherwise provided in such contract or instrument or by law, the term month means a calendar month and not a lunar month. NY GEN CONSTR § 31.

iii. *Year.* For information on the definition of a year, including the definitions of a half-year and quarter-year, refer to NY GEN CONSTR § 58 and NY GEN CONSTR § 50. For information on leap years, refer to NY GEN CONSTR § 57.

b. *Periods of time*

i. *Number of days.* A number of days specified as a period from a certain day within which or after or before which an act is authorized or required to be done means such number of calendar days exclusive of the calendar day from which the reckoning is made. NY GEN CONSTR § 20.

- If such period is a period of two (2) days, Saturday, Sunday or a public holiday must be excluded from the reckoning if it is an intervening day between the day from which the reckoning is made and the last day of the period. NY GEN CONSTR § 20.
- In computing any specified period of time from a specified event, the day upon which the event happens is deemed the day from which the reckoning is made. The day from which any specified period of time is reckoned shall be excluded in making the reckoning. NY GEN CONSTR § 20.

ii. *Number of months.* A number of months after or before a certain day shall be computed by counting such number of calendar months from such day, exclusive of the calendar month in which such day occurs, and shall include the day of the month in the last month so counted having the same numerical order in days of the month as the day from which the computation is made, unless there be not so many days in the last month so counted, in which case the period computed shall expire with the last day of the month so counted. NY GEN CONSTR § 30.

iii. *Publication of notice; Number of days.* The period of publication of a legal notice shall be computed by excluding the first day of publication and including the day on which the act or event of which notice is given is to take place or which completes the full period of publication. NY CPLR § 2402.

iv. *Periods ending on Saturday, Sunday or public holiday.* When any period of time, computed from a certain day, within which or after which or before which an act is authorized or required to be done, ends on a Saturday, Sunday or a public holiday, such act may be done on the next succeeding business day and if the period ends at a specified hour, such act may be done at or before the same hour of such next succeeding business day, except that where a period of time specified by contract ends on a Saturday, Sunday or a public holiday, the extension of such period is governed by NY GEN CONSTR § 25. NY GEN CONSTR § 25-a(1).

- For a list of public holidays, refer to NY GEN CONSTR § 24.

v. *Additional time after certain kinds of service*

- *Service by mail.* Where a period of time prescribed by law is measured from the service of a paper and service is by mail, five (5) days shall be added to the prescribed period. NY CPLR Rule 2103(b)(2).
- *Service by overnight delivery service.* Where a period of time prescribed by law is measured from the service of a paper and service is by overnight delivery, one (1) business day shall be added to the prescribed period. NY CPLR Rule 2103(b)(6).

vi. *Daylight saving time.* For information on New York's time zone and the effect of daylight saving time, refer to NY GEN CONSTR § 52.

c. *Hours of court.* Notwithstanding any provision of law or rule of court to the contrary, throughout the State of New York the sessions of the Supreme Court for the disposition of business before the court shall commence not later than 9:30 a.m. and conclude not earlier than 5 p.m. Where warranted, the Chief Administrator of the Courts may authorize variances in the opening and closing hours of the courts, but, in such event, daily sessions shall total not less than six (6) hours. NY R CHIEF J § 3.1.

d. *Time limits; Extension of time.* Any act required by or in pursuance of law to be performed at or within a prescribed time, shall be performed according to the standard time. NY GEN CONSTR § 53.

i. Except where otherwise expressly prescribed by law, the court may extend the time fixed by any statute, rule or order for doing any act, upon such terms as may be just and upon good cause shown, whether the application for extension is made before or after the expiration of the time fixed. NY CPLR § 2004. Refer to the New York KeyRules Motion for Continuance/Extension of Time document for more information.

C. General Requirements

1. *Rules governing disclosure*

a. *Generally.* There shall be full disclosure of all matter material and necessary in the prosecution or defense of an action, regardless of the burden of proof, by:

i. A party, or the officer, director, member, agent or employee of a party;

ii. A person who possessed a cause of action or defense asserted in the action;

iii. A person about to depart from the state, or without the state, or residing at a greater distance from the place of trial than one hundred miles, or so sick or infirm as to afford reasonable grounds of belief that he or she will not be able to attend the trial, or a person authorized to practice medicine, dentistry or podiatry who has provided medical, dental or podiatric care or diagnosis to the party demanding disclosure, or who has been retained by such party as an expert witness; and

iv. Any other person, upon notice stating the circumstances or reasons such disclosure is sought or required. NY CPLR § 3101(a).

v. The statutory phrase "material and necessary", said the Court of Appeals, must be interpreted liberally to require disclosure upon request, of any facts bearing on the controversy which will assist preparation for trial by sharpening the issues and reducing delay and prolixity. The test is one of usefulness and reason. SIEGEL-NYPRAC § 344; Allen v. Crowell-Collier Pub. Co., 21 N.Y.2d 403, 235 N.E.2d 430 (1968).

vi. Another potential problem that the original NY CPLR § 3101(a) posed was that it spoke of "evidence" that is material and necessary, which might have been construed to permit disclosure to elicit only that which would itself qualify as "evidence" admissible at trial. It was, however, construed more broadly than that. Well-considered caselaw specifically rejected this "evidence in chief" doctrine, stating that disclosure extends as well "to all relevant information calculated to lead to relevant evidence," a standard similar to that applicable in federal court. With an amendment that took effect on January 1, 1994, changing "evidence" to "matter" in NY CPLR § 3101(a), these generous interpretations of the statute were in effect approved by the legislature. SIEGEL-NYPRAC § 344.

vii. If a party is a corporation, each of its officers, directors, members, agents, and employees is also deemed a "party" for disclosure purposes. A party who needs relevant data or material from a nonparty corporation can seek it through NY CPLR § 3101(a)(2), NY CPLR § 3101(a)(3) or NY CPLR § 3101(a)(4), under which the corporate entity is treated as a "person." These subdivisions should also apply to any entity, corporate or otherwise, from whom disclosure is sought through its agents. A corporate employee who has the requisite knowledge and information may respond to a disclosure request on behalf of the corporation. A party who can't single out the particular person in the corporation's employ to whom a disclosure request should be properly directed can direct it to the corporation as such and leave it to the corporation to designate the appropriate person to respond. Whenever disclosure is sought from a corporation through a deposition, whether as a party or as a nonparty witness, the choice in the first instance of who will be produced in the corporate behalf is with the corporation rather than the examining party. SIEGEL-NYPRAC § 345.

viii. NY CPLR § 3101(a)(4) permits a party to obtain disclosure from a nonparty by merely serving a subpoena on the nonparty providing notice of "the circumstances or reasons such disclosure is sought or required." SIEGEL-NYPRAC § 345.

b. *Methods of obtaining disclosure.* Information is obtainable by one or more of the following disclosure devices: depositions upon oral questions or without the state upon written questions, interrogatories, demands for addresses, discovery and inspection of documents or property, physical and mental examinations of persons, and requests for admission. NY CPLR § 3102(a).

i. *Stipulation or notice.* Unless otherwise provided by the civil practice law and rules or by the court, disclosure shall be obtained by stipulation or on notice without leave of the court. NY CPLR § 3102(b).

ii. *Before action commenced; Court order required.* Before an action is commenced, disclosure to aid in bringing an action, to preserve information or to aid in arbitration, may be obtained, but only by court order. The court may appoint a referee to take testimony. NY CPLR § 3102(c).

iii. *During trial; Court order required.* Except as provided in NY CPLR § 5223, during and after trial, disclosure may be obtained only by order of the trial court on notice. NY CPLR § 3102(d).

iv. *Action pending in another jurisdiction.* Except as provided in NY CPLR § 3119, when under any mandate, writ or commission issued out of any court of record in any other state, territory, district or foreign jurisdiction, or whenever upon notice or agreement, it is required to take the testimony of a witness in the state, he or she may be compelled to appear and testify in the same manner and by the same process as may be employed for the purpose of taking testimony in actions pending in the state. The supreme court or a county court shall make any appropriate order in aid of taking such a deposition. NY CPLR § 3102(e).

v. *Actions to which state is a party.* In an action in which the state is properly a party, whether as plaintiff, defendant or otherwise, disclosure by the state shall be available as if the state were a private person. NY CPLR § 3102(f).

c. *Privileged matter.* Upon objection by a person entitled to assert the privilege, privileged matter shall not be obtainable. NY CPLR § 3101(b).

i. A determination of whether information is privileged is governed by the rules of evidence, which apply as they would at a trial. Whatever is privileged at the trial is privileged as well on pretrial disclosure. SIEGEL-NYPRAC § 346.

d. *Attorney's work product.* The work product of an attorney shall not be obtainable. NY CPLR § 3101(c).

i. NY CPLR § 3101(c) makes unobtainable the "work product of an attorney"—an ill-defined category whose potential for mischief has been avoided only because the judiciary has accorded it a very narrow scope. It is a category wholly distinct from the "materials . . . prepared in anticipation of litigation" of NY CPLR § 3101(d)(2). The fact that immunity is absolute under NY CPLR § 3101(c), while that of NY CPLR § 3101(d)(2) is only conditional, is the factor that requires as sharp a line as possible between the two categories. SIEGEL-NYPRAC § 347.

ii. The judiciary has cast precious little under the "work product" category of NY CPLR § 3101(c), preferring instead to fit doubtful items under the "materials . . . prepared in anticipation of litigation" banner of NY CPLR § 3101(d)(2), where the conditional immunity can be overcome and the matters ordered disclosed when stated conditions are met. SIEGEL-NYPRAC § 347.

e. *Trial preparation*

i. *Experts.* Upon request, each party shall identify each person whom the party expects to call as an expert witness at trial and shall disclose in reasonable detail the subject matter on which each expert is expected to testify, the substance of the facts and opinions on which each expert is expected to testify, the qualifications of each expert witness and a summary of the grounds for each expert's opinion. NY CPLR § 3101(d)(1)(i).

- However, where a party for good cause shown retains an expert an insufficient period of time before the commencement of trial to give appropriate notice thereof, the party shall not thereupon be precluded from introducing the expert's testimony at the trial solely on grounds of noncompliance with NY CPLR § 3101(d)(1). In that instance, upon motion of any party, made before or at trial, or on its own initiative, the court may make whatever order may be just. In an action for medical, dental or podiatric malpractice, a party, in responding to a request, may omit the names of medical, dental or podiatric experts but shall be required to disclose all other information concerning such experts otherwise required by NY CPLR § 3101(d)(1). NY CPLR § 3101(d)(1)(i).
- In an action for medical, dental or podiatric malpractice, any party may, by written offer made to and served upon all other parties and filed with the court, offer to disclose the name of, and to make available for examination upon oral deposition, any person the party making the offer expects to call as an expert witness at trial. Within twenty (20) days of service of the offer, a party shall accept or reject the offer by serving a written reply upon all parties and filing a copy thereof with the court. Failure to serve a reply within twenty (20) days of service of the offer shall be deemed a rejection of the offer. If all parties accept the offer, each

party shall be required to produce his or her expert witness for examination upon oral deposition upon receipt of a notice to take oral deposition in accordance with NY CPLR Rule 3107. If any party, having made or accepted the offer, fails to make that party's expert available for oral deposition, that party shall be precluded from offering expert testimony at the trial of the action. NY CPLR § 3101(d)(1)(ii).

- Further disclosure concerning the expected testimony of any expert may be obtained only by court order upon a showing of special circumstances and subject to restrictions as to scope and provisions concerning fees and expenses as the court may deem appropriate. However, a party, without court order, may take the testimony of a person authorized to practice medicine, dentistry or podiatry who is the party's treating or retained expert, as described in NY CPLR § 3101(a)(3), in which event any other party shall be entitled to the full disclosure authorized by Article 31 of Chapter 8 of the Civil Practice Law and Rules (NY CPLR § 3101, et seq.) with respect to that expert without court order. NY CPLR § 3101(d)(1)(iii).

ii. *Materials.* Subject to the provisions of NY CPLR § 3101(d)(1), materials otherwise discoverable under NY CPLR § 3101(a) and prepared in anticipation of litigation or for trial by or for another party, or by or for that other party's representative (including an attorney, consultant, surety, indemnitor, insurer or agent), may be obtained only upon a showing that the party seeking discovery has substantial need of the materials in the preparation of the case and is unable without undue hardship to obtain the substantial equivalent of the materials by other means. In ordering discovery of the materials when the required showing has been made, the court shall protect against disclosure of the mental impressions, conclusions, opinions or legal theories of an attorney or other representative of a party concerning the litigation. NY CPLR § 3101(d)(2).

- In order to qualify as "litigation" material the item must have been prepared exclusively for litigation. Incidental potential use in litigation, the courts have observed, may also be a function of such reports, but they have at least an equal if not greater mission "to prevent future accidents, discipline careless employees, or, generally, to increase the economy and efficiency of the operation." SIEGEL-NYPRAC § 348.

f. *Party's statement.* A party may obtain a copy of his own statement. NY CPLR § 3101(e).

i. Moreover, NY CPLR § 3101(e) has been broadly interpreted to include photographs. Items such as photographs and videotapes are now independently subject to disclosure under NY CPLR § 3101(i). SIEGEL-NYPRAC § 348.

g. *Contents of insurance agreement.* A party may obtain discovery of the existence and contents of any insurance agreement under which any person carrying on an insurance business may be liable to satisfy part or all of a judgment which may be entered in the action or to indemnify or reimburse for payments made to satisfy the judgment. Information concerning the insurance agreement is not by reason of disclosure admissible in evidence at trial. For purpose of NY CPLR § 3101(f), an application for insurance shall not be treated as part of an insurance agreement. NY CPLR § 3101(f).

h. *Accident reports.* Except as is otherwise provided by law, in addition to any other matter which may be subject to disclosure, there shall be full disclosure of any written report of an accident prepared in the regular course of business operations or practices of any person, firm, corporation, association or other public or private entity, unless prepared by a police or peace officer for a criminal investigation or prosecution and disclosure would interfere with a criminal investigation or prosecution. NY CPLR § 3101(g).

i. *Amendment or supplementation of responses.* A party shall amend or supplement a response previously given to a request for disclosure promptly upon the party's thereafter obtaining information that the response was incorrect or incomplete when made, or that the response, though correct and complete when made, no longer is correct and complete, and the circumstances are such that a failure to amend or supplement the response would be materially misleading. NY CPLR § 3101(h).

i. Where a party obtains such information an insufficient period of time before the commencement of trial appropriately to amend or supplement the response, the party shall not thereupon be precluded from introducing evidence at the trial solely on grounds of noncompliance with NY CPLR § 3101(h). In that instance, upon motion of any party, made before or at trial, or on its own initiative, the court may make whatever order may be just. Further amendment or supplementation may be obtained by court order. NY CPLR § 3101(h).

j. *Other disclosures.* In addition to any other matter which may be subject to disclosure, there shall be full disclosure of any films, photographs, video tapes or audio tapes, including transcripts or memoranda thereof, involving a person referred to in NY CPLR § 3101(a)(1). There shall be disclosure of all portions of such material, including out-takes, rather than only those portions a party intends to use. The provisions of NY CPLR § 3101(i) shall not apply to materials compiled for law enforcement purposes which are exempt from disclosure under NY PUB OFF § 87. NY CPLR § 3101(i).

i. While NY CPLR § 3101(i) was enacted with the defendant's surreptitious tapes of the plaintiff in mind, its language is broad enough to embrace any films, photographs, and audio or video tapes of a party, even those made by the party from whom disclosure is sought. SIEGEL-NYPRAC § 348.

k. *Protective orders.* The court may at any time on its own initiative, or on motion of any party or of any person from whom discovery is sought, make a protective order denying, limiting, conditioning or regulating the use of any disclosure device. NY CPLR § 3103(a). Refer to the New York KeyRules Motion for Protective Order document for more information.

l. *Supervision of disclosure.* Upon the motion of any party or witness on notice to all parties or on its own initiative without notice, the court in which an action is pending may by one of its judges or a referee supervise all or part of any disclosure procedure. NY CPLR § 3104(a).

i. *Selection of referee.* A judicial hearing officer may be designated as a referee under NY CPLR § 3104, or the court may permit all of the parties in an action to stipulate that a named attorney may act as referee. In such latter event, the stipulation shall provide for payment of his fees which shall, unless otherwise agreed, be taxed as disbursements. NY CPLR § 3104(b).

ii. *Powers of referee; Motions referred to person supervising disclosure.* A referee under NY CPLR § 3104 shall have all the powers of the court under NY CPLR § 3101, et seq. except the power to relieve himself of his duties, to appoint a successor, or to adjudge any person guilty of contempt. All motions or applications made under Article 31 of Chapter 8 of the Civil Practice Law and Rules (NY CPLR § 3101, et seq.) shall be returnable before the judge or referee, designated under NY CPLR § 3104 and after disposition, if requested by any party, his order shall be filed in the office of the clerk. NY CPLR § 3104(c).

iii. *Review of order of referee.* Any party or witness may apply for review of an order made under NY CPLR § 3104 by a referee. The application shall be by motion made in the court in which the action is pending within five (5) days after the order is made. Service of a notice of motion for review shall suspend disclosure of the particular matter in dispute. If the question raised by the motion may affect the rights of a witness, notice shall be served on him personally or by mail at his last known address. It shall set forth succinctly the order complained of, the reason it is objectionable and the relief demanded. NY CPLR § 3104(d).

iv. *Payment of expenses of referee.* Except where a judicial hearing officer has been designated a referee hereunder, the court may make an appropriate order for the payment of the reasonable expenses of the referee. NY CPLR § 3104(e).

2. *Response to interrogatories.* Interrogatories shall be answered in writing under oath by the party served, if an individual, or, if the party served is a corporation, a partnership or a sole proprietorship, by an officer, director, member, agent or employee having the information. Each question shall be answered separately and fully, and each answer shall be preceded by the question to which it responds. NY CPLR Rule 3133(b).

a. *Answers.* Answers must be under oath. If the party is a business entity of some kind, the answers must be furnished by an employee or agent having the requisite knowledge or data. SIEGEL-NYPRAC § 361.

b. *Nature of objections.* Objections range from simple defects in form to substantive objections such as immunity from disclosure generally. NYDISC § 11:19. Grounds that have been raised successfully include objections that the interrogatories were:

i. Patently burdensome, oppressive and improper, including objections based on the length and number of interrogatories posed,

ii. Vague,

iii. Duplicative of other interrogatories,

iv. Overly broad,

v. Inappropriate to use of the device, for example, where the interrogatories seek voluminous documentary disclosure,

vi. Involved information subject to immunity or privilege from disclosure,

vii. Irrelevant or immaterial,

viii. Excessive as to the time period covered,

ix. Require the respondent-party to express an opinion or a conclusion of law,

x. Require respondent to hire an expert to issue an opinion that the party requesting the interrogatory answer will undoubtedly dispute at trial. NYDISC § 11:19.

xi. It is not a valid ground for objection that the material sought is inadmissible at trial. NYDISC § 11:19.

c. *Outrageous requests; Motion for protective order.* It has been held that when the demand is itself "outrageous" in its excessiveness and in the irrelevance of many of its items, the recipient may still, instead of responding to the demand at all, seek to strike it altogether with a motion for a protective order. SIEGEL-NYPRAC § 361.

d. *Amendment and supplementation of responses.* Except with respect to amendment or supplementation of responses pursuant to NY CPLR § 3101(h), answers to interrogatories may be amended or supplemented only by order of the court upon motion. NY CPLR Rule 3133(c).

i. Because each answer to an interrogatory is carefully formulated under the guidance of counsel before being sent to the adverse party, an amendment is seldom needed, in contrast with the more frequent need of a deponent to correct her deposition. SIEGEL-NYPRAC § 361.

3. *Governing law.* The civil practice law and rules (NY CPLR § 101, et seq.) shall govern the procedure in civil judicial proceedings in all courts of the state and before all judges, except where the procedure is regulated by inconsistent statute. The civil practice law and rules shall succeed the civil practice act and rules of civil practice and shall be deemed substituted therefor throughout the statutes and rules of the state. NY CPLR § 101. The civil practice law and rules shall be liberally construed to secure the just, speedy and inexpensive determination of every civil judicial proceeding. NY CPLR § 104.

a. *Uniform trial court rules.* The uniform civil rules for the Supreme Court and County Court (NY R UNIF TRIAL CTS § 202.1, et seq.) shall be applicable to civil actions and proceedings in the Supreme Court and the County Court. NY R UNIF TRIAL CTS § 202.1(a). The provisions of the uniform rules shall be construed consistent with the Civil Practice Law and Rules (CPLR), and matters not covered by the uniform rules shall be governed by the CPLR. NY R UNIF TRIAL CTS § 202.1(d).

b. *Local rules.* Local court rules, not inconsistent with law or with uniform civil rules for the Supreme Court and County Court (NY R UNIF TRIAL CTS § 202.1, et seq.), shall comply with Part 9 of the Rules of the Chief Judge (NY R CHIEF J § 9.1). NY R UNIF TRIAL CTS § 202.1(c).

c. *Official forms.* The state administrator shall have the power to adopt, amend and rescind an appendix of forms. Forms adopted pursuant to NY CPLR § 107 shall be sufficient under the civil practice law and rules and shall illustrate the simplicity and brevity of statement which the civil practice law and rules contemplate. NY CPLR § 107.

4. *Rules of the commercial division.* [Editor's note: certain types of civil cases or civil cases meeting certain monetary thresholds that are filed in the state of New York must be filed in the Commercial Division of the New York Supreme Courts. Rules governing practice in the commercial division are found in NY R UNIF TRIAL CTS § 202.70]. Cases which must be filed in the commercial division are listed below. For more information, refer to NY R UNIF TRIAL CTS § 202.70.

a. *Monetary thresholds.* Except as set forth in NY R UNIF TRIAL CTS § 202.70(b), the monetary thresholds of the Commercial Division, exclusive of punitive damages, interests, costs, disbursements and counsel fees claimed, are established as follows: (1) Albany County, fifty thousand dollars ($50,000); (2) Eighth Judicial District, one hundred thousand dollars ($100,000); (3) Kings County, one hundred fifty thousand dollars ($150,000); (4) Nassau County, two hundred thousand dollars ($200,000); (5) New York County, five hundred thousand dollars ($500,000); (6) Onondaga County, fifty thousand dollars ($50,000); (7) Queens County, one hundred thousand dollars ($100,000); (8) Seventh Judicial District, fifty thousand dollars ($50,000); (9) Suffolk County, one hundred thousand dollars ($100,000); and (10) Westchester County, one hundred thousand dollars ($100,000). NY R UNIF TRIAL CTS § 202.70(a).

i. *ALBANY COUNTY.* The Commercial Division of the Albany County Supreme Court exercises jurisdiction over selected business and commercial disputes in which the amount at issue generally involves damage claims in a minimum amount of fifty thousand dollars ($50,000) as well as claims for unspecified amounts where the value of the commercial asset(s) in dispute exceeds fifty thousand dollars ($50,000). A separate publication promulgating the rules and criteria relating to the filing and management of Commercial Court cases in this part may be obtained from the Albany County Supreme Court Clerk's Office. A section of the Uniform Civil Rules for the Supreme Court and County Court sets forth statewide rules. NY R 3 JD SUP Doc. 1(E).

ii. *BRONX COUNTY.* The monetary threshold for commercial cases in Bronx County will be seventy-five thousand dollars ($75,000). All other parameters including the type of matters that will be heard are contained within the

Rules of the Commercial Division of the Supreme Court (NY R UNIF TRIAL CTS § 202.70). NY R BRONX FIL R Doc. 12.

iii. *NEW YORK COUNTY.* The monetary threshold in the New York County Commercial Division, which is generally applicable, is an amount in controversy of five hundred thousand dollars ($500,000) or more (exclusive of punitive damages, interest, costs, disbursements, and counsel fees). If the case is designated a commercial one and the Addendum is submitted, the clerk will review the pleadings to determine whether the amount in controversy in the case meets the monetary threshold or whether an exception to the threshold applies. NY R NY CTY Procedure IA(B). For more information on assigning a case to the commercial division in New York County, refer to NY R NY CTY Procedure IA(B).

b. *Commercial cases.* Actions in which the principal claims involve or consist of the following will be heard in the Commercial Division provided that the monetary threshold is met or equitable or declaratory relief is sought:

   i. Breach of contract or fiduciary duty, fraud, misrepresentation, business tort (e.g., unfair competition), or statutory and/or common law violation where the breach or violation is alleged to arise out of business dealings (e.g., sales of assets or securities; corporate restructuring; partnership, shareholder, joint venture, and other business agreements; trade secrets; restrictive covenants; and employment agreements not including claims that principally involve alleged discriminatory practices);

   ii. Transactions governed by the Uniform Commercial Code (exclusive of those concerning individual cooperative or condominium units);

   iii. Transactions involving commercial real property, including Yellowstone injunctions and excluding actions for the payment of rent only;

   iv. Shareholder derivative actions—without consideration of the monetary threshold;

   v. Commercial class actions—without consideration of the monetary threshold;

   vi. Business transactions involving or arising out of dealings with commercial banks and other financial institutions;

   vii. Internal affairs of business organizations;

   viii. Malpractice by accountants or actuaries, and legal malpractice arising out of representation in commercial matters;

   ix. Environmental insurance coverage;

   x. Commercial insurance coverage (e.g., directors and officers, errors and omissions, and business interruption coverage);

   xi. Dissolution of corporations, partnerships, limited liability companies, limited liability partnerships and joint ventures—without consideration of the monetary threshold; and

   xii. Applications to stay or compel arbitration and affirm or disaffirm arbitration awards and related injunctive relief pursuant to Article 75 of the New York Civil Practice Law and Rules (NY CPLR § 7501, et seq.) involving any of the foregoing enumerated commercial issues. Where the applicable arbitration agreement provides for the arbitration to be heard outside the United States, the monetary threshold set forth in NY R UNIF TRIAL CTS § 202.70(a) shall not apply. NY R UNIF TRIAL CTS § 202.70(b).

c. *Non-commercial cases.* The following will not be heard in the Commercial Division even if the monetary threshold is met:

   i. Suits to collect professional fees;

   ii. Cases seeking a declaratory judgment as to insurance coverage for personal injury or property damage;

   iii. Residential real estate disputes, including landlord-tenant matters, and commercial real estate disputes involving the payment of rent only;

   iv. Home improvement contracts involving residential properties consisting of one to four residential units or individual units in any residential building, including cooperative or condominium units;

   v. Proceedings to enforce a judgment regardless of the nature of the underlying case;

   vi. First-party insurance claims and actions by insurers to collect premiums or rescind non-commercial policies; and

   vii. Attorney malpractice actions except as otherwise provided in NY R UNIF TRIAL CTS § 202.70(b)(8). NY R UNIF TRIAL CTS § 202.70(c).

d. For more information on the Commercial Division, refer to NY R UNIF TRIAL CTS § 202.70.

D. Documents

1. *Required documents*

a. *Responses to interrogatories.* Refer to the General Requirements section of this document for information on the responses to interrogatories.

b. *Proof of service.* In addition to complying with the provisions of NY CPLR Rule 2101, every paper filed in court shall have annexed thereto appropriate proof of service on all parties where required. NY R UNIF TRIAL CTS § 202.5(a).

2. *Supplemental documents*

a. *Working copies.* The court may require the parties to provide working copies of documents filed electronically. In such event, each working copy shall include, firmly affixed thereto, a copy of a confirmation notice in a form prescribed by the Chief Administrator. NY R UNIF TRIAL CTS § 202.5-b(d)(5).

E. Format

1. *Form of documents*

a. *Size and form of paper.* Each paper served or filed shall be durable, white and, except for summonses, subpoenas, notices of appearance, notes of issue, orders of protection, temporary orders of protection and exhibits, shall be eleven by eight and one-half (11 x 8-1/2) inches in size. NY CPLR Rule 2101(a).

b. *Writing and language.* The writing shall be legible and in black ink. NY CPLR Rule 2101(a). Each paper served or filed shall be in the English language which, where practicable, shall be of ordinary usage. NY CPLR Rule 2101(b).

c. *Caption.* Each paper served or filed shall begin with a caption setting forth the name of the court, the venue, the title of the action, the nature of the paper and the index number of the action if one has been assigned. In all papers other than a summons, a complaint or a judgment it shall be sufficient to state the name of the first named party on each side with an appropriate indication of any omissions. NY CPLR Rule 2101(c).

i. *Further contents of first page.* After the first paper has been filed in each case the index number shall appear on the cover and first page to the right of the caption of every paper tendered for filing in the action. Each such cover and first page also shall contain an indication of the county of venue and a brief description of the nature of the paper and, where the case has been assigned to an individual judge, shall contain the name of the assigned judge to the right of the caption. NY R UNIF TRIAL CTS § 202.5(a); NY R UNIF TRIAL CTS § 202.5(b); NY R UNIF TRIAL CTS § 202.5(d)(1)(i).

d. *Index number.* No paper in an action in the supreme or a county court, other than an order submitted for signature to a judge out of court, shall be submitted for any purpose to the supreme or county court or to a clerk thereof unless there is endorsed on such paper the index number of the action assigned by the clerk of the county. NY CPLR § 8018(c).

e. *Line spacing.* Every paper filed in court, if typewritten, shall have at least double space between each line, except for quotations and the names and addresses of attorneys appearing in the action. NY R UNIF TRIAL CTS § 202.5(a).

f. *Font size.* Each. . .paper printed or typed, served or filed, except for summonses. . .and exhibits, shall be in clear type of no less than ten (10) point in size. NY CPLR Rule 2101(a).

i. Whenever a requirement relating to size of type is stated in point size, the type size requirement shall be deemed met if the x-height of the type is a minimum of forty-five percent (45%) of the specified point size. Each point shall be measured as .351 millimeter. The x-height size shall be measured as it appears on the page. The x-height is the height of the lower case letters, exclusive of ascenders or descenders. NY CPLR § 105(t).

g. *Margins.* Every paper filed in court shall have at least one (1) inch margins. NY R UNIF TRIAL CTS § 202.5(a).

h. *Citations*

i. *Civil practice law and rules.* NY CPLR § 101, et seq. shall be known as the civil practice law and rules, and may be cited as "CPLR". Reference to a provision in the civil practice law and rules may, except when such provision is being enacted or amended, be made without indicating whether it is a rule or section. NY CPLR § 101.

i. *Indorsement by attorney.* Each paper served or filed shall be indorsed with the name, address and telephone number of the attorney for the party serving or filing the paper, or if the party does not appear by attorney, with the name, address and telephone number of the party. NY CPLR Rule 2101(d).

j. *One-sided printing.* In addition, every paper filed in court, other than an exhibit or printed form, shall contain writing on one side only, except that papers that are fastened on the side may contain writing on both sides. NY R UNIF TRIAL CTS § 202.5(a).

k. *Use of copies authorized.* Except where otherwise specifically prescribed, copies, rather than originals, of all papers, including orders, affidavits and exhibits may be served or filed. Where it is required that the original be served or filed and the original is lost or withheld, the court may authorize a copy to be served or filed. NY CPLR Rule 2101(e).

i. Where a certified copy of a paper is required by law, an attorney admitted to practice in the courts of the state may certify that it has been compared by him with the original and found to be a true and complete copy. Such a certificate, when subscribed by such attorney, has the same effect as if made by a clerk. NY CPLR § 2105.

l. *Recycled paper.* It is the policy of the Unified Court System that litigants, where practicable, should file or submit to the courts of the Unified Court System of the State of New York papers printed or reproduced on recycled paper. Paper is considered recycled if it contains a minimum content of thirty percent (30%) waste paper. NY R UNIF TRIAL CTS § 215.2. The signature page of every paper filed or submitted to the court on recycled paper should bear the legend: "Printed [Reproduced] on Recycled Paper." NY R UNIF TRIAL CTS § 215.3.

2. *Form of electronic documents.* Each paper served or filed by electronic means, as defined in NY CPLR Rule 2103(f), shall be capable of being reproduced by the receiver so as to comply with the provisions of NY CPLR Rule 2101(a) through NY CPLR Rule 2101(d). NY CPLR Rule 2101(g).

a. *File format.* All e-filed documents shall comply with the technical requirements set forth at the NYSCEF site. NY R UNIF TRIAL CTS § 202.5-b(d)(1)(i).

b. *Heading of document.* The subject matter heading for each paper sent by electronic means must indicate that the matter being transmitted electronically is related to a court proceeding. NY CPLR Rule 2103(b)(7).

3. *Signature blocks.* Every pleading, written motion, and other paper, served on another party or filed or submitted to the court shall be signed by an attorney, or by a party if the party is not represented by an attorney, with the name of the attorney or party clearly printed or typed directly below the signature. NY R CHIEF ADMIN § 130-1.1-a(a); NY R UNIF TRIAL CTS § 202.5(d)(1)(iv).

a. *Printed name.* Beneath each signature shall be printed the name signed. NY CPLR Rule 2101(a).

b. *Failure to sign.* Absent good cause shown, the court shall strike any unsigned paper if the omission of the signature is not corrected promptly after being called to the attention of the attorney or party. NY R CHIEF ADMIN § 130-1.1-a(a).

c. *Signature as certification.* By signing a paper, an attorney or party certifies that, to the best of that person's knowledge, information and belief, formed after an inquiry reasonable under the circumstances the presentation of the paper or the contentions therein are not frivolous as defined in NY R CHIEF ADMIN § 130-1.1(c). NY R CHIEF ADMIN § 130-1.1-a(b)(1).

d. *Electronic signatures.* A document shall be considered to have been signed by an attorney or party in compliance with NY R CHIEF ADMIN § 130-1.1-a if it has been signed by such attorney or party as provided in NY R UNIF TRIAL CTS § 202.5-b(e)(1) and it bears the signatory's name. NY R UNIF TRIAL CTS § 202.5-b(e)(2). An electronically filed document shall be considered to have been signed by, and shall be binding upon, the person identified as a signatory, if:

i. It bears the physical signature of such person and is scanned into an electronic format that reproduces such signature; or

ii. The signatory has electronically affixed the digital image of his or her signature to the document; or

iii. It is electronically filed under the User ID and password of that person; or

iv. In a tax certiorari action in which the parties have stipulated to this procedure, it is an initiating document that is electronically filed without the signature of the signatory in a form provided above in NY R UNIF TRIAL CTS § 202.5-b(e)(iv), provided that, prior to filing, the document is signed in full in hard copy (which hard copy must be preserved until the conclusion of all proceedings, including appeals, in the case in which it is filed); or

v. In a small claims assessment review proceeding, it is a petition recorded by the NYSCEF site upon the filing of a text file as provided in NY R UNIF TRIAL CTS § 202.5-b(b)(1), provided that prior to filing, the document was signed in full in hard copy (which hard copy must be preserved until the conclusion of all proceedings in the matter, including article 78 (NY CPLR § 7801, et seq.) review and any appeals, and must be made available during the proceeding upon request of the respondent or the court); or

vi. It otherwise bears the electronic signature of the signatory in a format conforming to such standards and requirements as may hereafter be established by the Chief Administrator. NY R UNIF TRIAL CTS § 202.5-b(e).

4. *Confidentiality of personal information.* No person may file any document available for public inspection with any state

agency, political subdivision, or in any court of this state that contains a Social Security account number of any other person, unless such other person is a dependent child, or has consented to such filing, except as required by federal or state law or regulation, or by court rule. NY GEN BUS § 399-ddd. Submissions pursuant to e-filing procedures shall have the same confidentiality rights as paper documents. NY R UNIF TRIAL CTS § 202.5-b(k)(1).

a. *Confidential personal information.* Except in the actions designated in NY R UNIF TRIAL CTS § 202.5(e)(1), or as otherwise provided by rule or law or court order, and whether or not a sealing order is or has been sought, the parties shall omit or redact confidential personal information in papers submitted to the court for filing. For purposes of NY R UNIF TRIAL CTS § 202.5(e), confidential personal information ("CPI") means:

   i. The taxpayer identification number of an individual or an entity, including a Social Security number, an employer identification number, and an individual taxpayer identification number, except the last four (4) digits thereof;

   ii. The date of an individual's birth, except the year thereof;

   iii. The full name of an individual known to be a minor, except the minor's initials;

   iv. A financial account number, including a credit and/or debit card number, a bank account number, an investment account number, and/or an insurance account number, except the last four (4) digits or letters thereof; and

   v. Any of the documents or testimony in a matrimonial action protected by NY DOM REL § 235 or evidence sealed by the court in such an action which are attached as exhibits or referenced in the papers filed in any other civil action. For purposes of NY R UNIF TRIAL CTS § 202.5, a matrimonial action shall mean: an action to annul a marriage or declare the nullity of a void marriage, an action or agreement for a separation, an action for a divorce, or an action or proceeding for custody, visitation, writ of habeus corpus, child support, maintenance or paternity. NY R UNIF TRIAL CTS § 202.5(e)(1).

b. *Submission of confidential personal information.* Where a person submitting a paper to a court for filing believes in good faith that the inclusion of the full confidential personal information described in NY R UNIF TRIAL CTS § 202.5(e)(1) is material and necessary to the adjudication of the action or proceeding before the court, he or she may apply to the court for leave to serve and file together with a paper in which such information has been set forth in abbreviated form a confidential affidavit or affirmation setting forth the same information in unabbreviated form, appropriately referenced to the page or pages of the paper at which the abbreviated form appears. NY R UNIF TRIAL CTS § 202.5(e)(3).

c. *Home addresses.* For information on when home addresses and other personal information must be redacted, refer to NY CPLR Rule 2103-a.

5. *Defective papers.* A defect in the form of a paper, if a substantial right of a party is not prejudiced, shall be disregarded by the court, and leave to correct shall be freely given. NY CPLR Rule 2101(f). Papers that are stapled or bound securely shall not be rejected for filing simply because they are not bound with a backer of any kind. NY R UNIF TRIAL CTS § 202.5(a). A paper filed in accordance with the rules of the chief administrator or any local rule or practice established by the court shall be deemed filed. NY CPLR Rule 2102(b).

   a. *Objection to defective papers.* The party on whom a paper is served shall be deemed to have waived objection to any defect in form unless, within fifteen (15) days after the receipt thereof, the party on whom the paper is served returns the paper to the party serving it with a statement of particular objections. NY CPLR Rule 2101(f).

F. Filing and Service Requirements

1. *Filing requirements.* Except where otherwise prescribed by law or order of court, papers required to be filed shall be filed with the clerk of the court in which the action is triable. In an action or proceeding in supreme or court, papers required to be filed shall be filed with the clerk of the county in which the proceeding is brought. NY CPLR Rule 2102(a).

   a. *Electronic filing.* On consent, documents may be filed and served by electronic means in Supreme Court in such civil actions and in such counties as shall be authorized by order of the Chief Administrator of the Courts and only to the extent and in the manner provided in NY R UNIF TRIAL CTS § 202.5-b. NY R UNIF TRIAL CTS § 202.5-b(a)(1). For the definitions of terms used in electronic filing, refer to NY R UNIF TRIAL CTS § 202.5-b(a)(2).

      i. *Electronic filing of discovery materials.* In any action subject to e-filing, parties and non-parties producing materials in response to discovery demands may enter into a stipulation, which shall be e-filed, authorizing the electronic filing of discovery responses and discovery materials to the degree and upon terms and conditions set forth in the stipulation. In the absence of such a stipulation, no party shall file electronically any such materials except in the form of excerpts, quotations, or selected exhibits from such materials as part of motion papers, pleadings or other filings with the court. NY R UNIF TRIAL CTS § 202.5-b(j).

ii. *E-filing mandatory.* In any action subject to e-filing, all documents required to be filed with the court by an e-filing party shall be filed and served electronically, except as provided in NY R UNIF TRIAL CTS § 202.5-b. NY R UNIF TRIAL CTS § 202.5-b(d)(1)(i).

iii. *Who may file.* Documents may be filed or served electronically only by a person who has registered as an authorized e-filing user or as otherwise provided in NY R UNIF TRIAL CTS § 202.5-b(c). NY R UNIF TRIAL CTS § 202.5-b(c)(1).

iv. *When filing made.* Documents may be transmitted at any time of the day or night to the NYSCEF site. A document other than an order or judgment is filed when its electronic transmission or, in the case of a petition that is e-filed by submission of a text file as provided in NY R UNIF TRIAL CTS § 202.5-b(b)(1), the electronic transmission of the text file is recorded at that site, provided, however, that where payment of a fee is required upon the filing of a document, the document is not filed until transmission of the document and the information or form or information as required in NY R UNIF TRIAL CTS § 202.5-b(d)(2)(i), NY R UNIF TRIAL CTS § 202.5-b(d)(2)(ii) or NY R UNIF TRIAL CTS § 202.5-b(d)(2)(iii) has been recorded at the NYSCEF site; or, if no transmission of that information or form or information is recorded, where permitted by the County Clerk, until payment is presented to the County Clerk. NY R UNIF TRIAL CTS § 202.5-b(d)(3)(i).

v. *Notification of filing.* No later than the close of business on the business day following the electronic filing of a document, a notification, in a form prescribed by the Chief Administrator, shall be transmitted electronically by the NYSCEF site to the person filing such document and the e-mail service addresses of all other participating parties in such action. NY R UNIF TRIAL CTS § 202.5-b(d)(3)(ii).

vi. *Removal of confidential information and other corrections.* If a document filed electronically is subsequently discovered to contain confidential data—including but not limited to trade secrets, information protected by confidentiality agreement, or personal confidential information as defined by statute or court rule—or otherwise to have been filed in error, the filer or another party or affected person may (1) notify the parties and any non-party filers in the action of the confidentiality issue or other error raised by the filing, and of his or her intention to seek judicial relief to correct the filing: (2) following such notification, request that the appropriate County Clerk, exercising his or her administrative discretion, place the document temporarily in "restricted" status on the NYSCEF site, to be made available for viewing by court staff and the parties but not the general public; and (3) file an application to correct the filing by order to show cause within five (5) business days of such notification (or such time as the court may direct), including a request for preliminary injunctive relief limiting interim disclosure of the document at issue. Unless otherwise directed by the court, any document placed in restricted status in response to such a request shall be returned to public view upon expiration of this five (5) day period. The Chief Administrator of the Courts shall promulgate forms to implement this process. NY R UNIF TRIAL CTS § 202.5-b(d)(3)(iii).

vii. *Documents requiring judge's signature.* Except where the court directs otherwise, any document that requires a judge's signature shall be transmitted electronically and in hard copy to the court. NY R UNIF TRIAL CTS § 202.5-b(d)(6).

viii. *Documents which would be inconvenient to file electronically; Hard copies.* Notwithstanding any other provision of NY R UNIF TRIAL CTS § 202.5-b, and subject to such guidelines as may be established by the Chief Administrative Judge, the County Clerk or his or her designee may require or permit a party to file in hard copy, in accordance with procedures set by the County Clerk or designee, an exhibit or other document which it is impractical or inconvenient to file electronically. NY R UNIF TRIAL CTS § 202.5-b(d)(7).

ix. *Documents containing sensitive or proprietary information.* In an action subject to e-filing, any person may apply for an order prohibiting or restricting the electronic filing in the action of specifically identified materials on the grounds that such materials are subject to copyright or other proprietary rights, or trade secret or other privacy interests, and that electronic filing in the action is likely to result in substantial prejudice to those rights or interests. NY R UNIF TRIAL CTS § 202.5-b(k)(2).

x. *Refusal to accept paper filings.* In accordance with NY CPLR Rule 2102(c), a County Clerk and a chief clerk of the Supreme Court or County Court, as appropriate, shall refuse to accept for filing papers filed in actions and proceedings when the paper sought to be filed:

- Is in an action subject to electronic filing pursuant to Rules of the Chief Administrator,
- Is not being filed electronically, and
- Does not include the notice required by NY R UNIF TRIAL CTS § 202.5-b(d)(1). NY R UNIF TRIAL CTS § 202.5(d)(1)(v); NY R UNIF TRIAL CTS § 202.5-bb(d).

xi. *Emergency filings; Hard copies.* For information on when an emergency filing may be filed and served in hard copy, refer to NY R UNIF TRIAL CTS § 202.5-b(d)(1)(ii), NY R UNIF TRIAL CTS § 202.5-b(d)(1)(iii) and NY R UNIF TRIAL CTS § 202.5-bb(c)(3).

xii. *Technical failures.* The NYSCEF site shall be considered to be subject to a technical failure on a given day if the site is unable to accept filings or provide access to filed documents continuously or intermittently over the course of any period of time greater than one (1) hour after 12:00 noon of that day. Notice of all such technical failures shall be provided on the site. NY R UNIF TRIAL CTS § 202.5-b(i).

- When e-filing is hindered by a technical failure, a party may file with the appropriate clerk and serve in hard copy. NY R UNIF TRIAL CTS § 202.5-b(i). In the event an attorney or party shall file and serve documents in hard copy pursuant to NY R UNIF TRIAL CTS § 202.5-b(i), each such document shall include the notice required by NY R UNIF TRIAL CTS § 202.5-b(d)(1), and the filer shall file those documents with the NYSCEF site within three (3) business days after restoration of normal operations at that site. NY R UNIF TRIAL CTS § 202.5-b(i).
- With the exception of deadlines that by law cannot be extended, the time for filing of any document that is delayed due to technical failure of the site shall be extended for one (1) day for each day on which such failure occurs, unless otherwise ordered by the court. NY R UNIF TRIAL CTS § 202.5-b(i).

xiii. *Filing fees.* For information on what information must be provided to pay filing fees, refer to NY R UNIF TRIAL CTS § 202.5-b(d)(2).

xiv. *Exemption from e-filing.* For information on exemptions from e-filing, refer to NY R UNIF TRIAL CTS § 202.5-bb(e).

b. *Facsimile filing.* In the Supreme Court, facsimile filing shall be limited to commercial claims and tax certiorari, conservatorship, and mental hygiene proceedings in Monroe, Westchester, New York and Suffolk Counties. NY R UNIF TRIAL CTS § 202.5-a(a)(1). Refer to NY R UNIF TRIAL CTS § 202.5-a for information on the procedures for facsimile filing.

2. *Service requirements*

a. *Who may serve.* Except where otherwise prescribed by law or order of court, papers may be served by any person not a party of the age of eighteen years or over. NY CPLR Rule 2103(a).

b. *Service upon attorney.* Except where otherwise prescribed by law or order of court, papers to be served upon a party in a pending action shall be served upon the party's attorney. Where the same attorney appears for two or more parties, only one (1) copy need be served upon the attorney. Such service upon an attorney shall be made:

i. By delivering the paper to the attorney personally. NY CPLR Rule 2103(b)(1).

ii. By mailing the paper to the attorney at the address designated by that attorney for that purpose or, if none is designated, at the attorney's last known address; service by mail shall be complete upon mailing. NY CPLR Rule 2103(b)(2).

iii. If the attorney's office is open, by leaving the paper with a person in charge, or if no person is in charge, by leaving it in a conspicuous place; or if the attorney's office is not open, by depositing the paper, enclosed in a sealed wrapper directed to the attorney, in the attorney's office letter drop or box. NY CPLR Rule 2103(b)(3).

iv. By leaving it at the attorney's residence within the state with a person of suitable age and discretion. Service upon an attorney shall not be made at the attorney's residence unless service at the attorney's office cannot be made. NY CPLR Rule 2103(b)(4).

v. By transmitting the paper to the attorney by facsimile transmission, provided that a facsimile telephone number is designated by the attorney for that purpose. Service by facsimile transmission shall be complete upon the receipt by the sender of a signal from the equipment of the attorney served indicating that the transmission was received, and the mailing of a copy of the paper to that attorney. The designation of a facsimile telephone number in the address block subscribed on a paper served or filed in the course of an action or proceeding shall constitute consent to service by facsimile transmission in accordance with NY CPLR Rule 2103(b)(5). An attorney may change or rescind a facsimile telephone number by serving a notice on the other parties. NY CPLR Rule 2103(b)(5).

vi. By dispatching the paper to the attorney by overnight delivery service at the address designated by the attorney for that purpose or, if none is designated, at the attorney's last known address. Service by overnight delivery service shall be complete upon deposit of the paper enclosed in a properly addressed wrapper into the custody of the overnight delivery service for overnight delivery, prior to the latest time designated by the overnight delivery service for overnight delivery. "Overnight delivery service" means any delivery service which regularly accepts items for overnight delivery to any address in the state. NY CPLR Rule 2103(b)(6).

vii. By transmitting the paper to the attorney by electronic means where and in the manner authorized by the chief administrator of the courts by rule and, unless such rule shall otherwise provide, such transmission shall be upon the party's written consent. The subject matter heading for each paper sent by electronic means must indicate that the matter being transmitted electronically is related to a court proceeding. NY CPLR Rule 2103(b)(7).

c. *Electronic service mandatory; Consenting to electronic service; How electronic service may be made.* Except as otherwise provided in NY R UNIF TRIAL CTS § 202.5-bb, filing and service of all documents in an action that has been commenced electronically in accordance with NY R UNIF TRIAL CTS § 202.5-bb shall be by electronic means. NY R UNIF TRIAL CTS § 202.5-bb(c)(1).

i. *Party's consent required for certain e-filing.* After commencement of an action wherein e-filing is authorized, documents may be electronically filed and served, but only by, and electronic service shall be made only upon, a party or parties who have consented thereto. NY R UNIF TRIAL CTS § 202.5-b(b)(2)(i).

- A consent to e-filing in an action shall state that the party providing it agrees to the use of e-filing in the action and to be bound by the filing and service provisions in NY R UNIF TRIAL CTS § 202.5-b. NY R UNIF TRIAL CTS § 202.5-b(b)(2)(ii).

ii. *Address for service; Duty to notify as to changes.* The e-mail service address recorded at the time of registration is the e-mail address at which service of interlocutory documents on that party may be made through notification transmitted by the NYSCEF site. It is the responsibility of each filing user to monitor that address and promptly notify the Resource Center in the event of a change in his or her e-mail service address. NY R UNIF TRIAL CTS § 202.5-b(f)(2)(i).

iii. *How service made.* An e-filing party causes service of an interlocutory document to be made upon another party participating in e-filing by filing the document electronically. Upon receipt of an interlocutory document, the NYSCEF site shall automatically transmit electronic notification to all e-mail service addresses in such action. NY R UNIF TRIAL CTS § 202.5-b(f)(2)(ii).

- Except as provided otherwise in NY R UNIF TRIAL CTS § 202.5-b(h)(3), the electronic transmission of the notification shall constitute service of the document on the e-mail service addresses identified therein; however, such service will not be effective if the filing party learns that the notification did not reach the address of the person to be served. Proof of such service will be recorded on the NYSCEF site. A party may, however, utilize other service methods permitted by the CPLR provided that, if one of such other methods is used, proof of that service shall be filed electronically. NY R UNIF TRIAL CTS § 202.5-b(f)(2)(ii).

iv. *Signatures on hard copies; Proof of service filed electronically.* When an e-filing party serves a document in hard copy on a non-participating party, the document served shall bear full signatures of all signatories and proof of such service shall be filed electronically. NY R UNIF TRIAL CTS § 202.5-b(b)(2)(i).

v. *Effect of failure to consent.* A party's failure to consent to participation in electronic filing and service shall not bar any other party to the action from filing documents electronically with the County Clerk and the court or serving documents upon any other party who has consented to participation. A party who has not consented to participation shall file documents with the court and the County Clerk, and serve and be served with documents, in hard copy. NY R UNIF TRIAL CTS § 202.5-b(b)(2)(i).

d. *Service upon party.* If a party has not appeared by an attorney or the party's attorney cannot be served, service shall be upon the party by a method specified in NY CPLR Rule 2103(b)(1), NY CPLR Rule 2103(b)(2), NY CPLR Rule 2103(b)(4), NY CPLR Rule 2103(b)(5) or NY CPLR Rule 2103(b)(6). NY CPLR Rule 2103(c).

i. When a party is in default for failure to appear, he shall not be entitled to notice or service of any copy required under NY CPLR § 3101, et seq. NY CPLR Rule 3105.

e. *Service on all parties.* Each paper served on any party shall be served on every other party who has appeared, except as otherwise may be provided by court order or as provided in NY CPLR § 3012 or in NY CPLR § 3215(f). Upon demand by a party, the plaintiff shall supply that party with a list of those who have appeared and the names and addresses of their attorneys. NY CPLR Rule 2103(e).

f. *Service by filing.* If a paper cannot be served by any of the methods specified in NY CPLR Rule 2103(b) and NY CPLR Rule 2103(c), service may be made by filing the paper as if it were a paper required to be filed. NY CPLR Rule 2103(d).

g. *Definitions.* For the purposes of NY CPLR Rule 2103:

   i. "Mailing" means the deposit of a paper enclosed in a first class postpaid wrapper, addressed to the address designated by a person for that purpose or, if none is designated, at that person's last known address, in a post office or official depository under the exclusive care and custody of the United States Postal Service within the state;

   ii. "Electronic means" means any method of transmission of information between computers or other machines designed for the purpose of sending and receiving such transmissions, and which allows the recipient to reproduce the information transmitted in a tangible medium of expression;

   iii. "Facsimile transmission" means any method of transmission of documents to a facsimile machine at a remote location which can automatically produce a tangible copy of such documents. NY CPLR Rule 2103(f).

G. Hearings

1. There is no hearing required or contemplated in the New York rules governing the response to interrogatories.

H. Forms

1. New York Response to Interrogatories Forms

a. Notice of motion to amend answer to interrogatories. MCF CPLR § 6:217.

b. Affidavit in support of motion to amend answer to interrogatories. MCF CPLR § 6:218.

c. Order permitting amendment of answer to interrogatories. MCF CPLR § 6:219.

I. Applicable Rules

1. *State rules*

   a. Short title; Application; Construction; Definitions. NY CPLR § 101; NY CPLR § 104; NY CPLR § 105.

   b. Appendix of official forms. NY CPLR § 107.

   c. Extensions of time generally. NY CPLR § 2004.

   d. Form of papers. NY CPLR Rule 2101; NY CPLR Rule 2102; NY CPLR § 2105; NY GEN BUS § 399-ddd; NY R UNIF TRIAL CTS § 215.2; NY R UNIF TRIAL CTS § 215.3.

   e. Service of papers. NY CPLR Rule 2103.

   f. Computation of time. NY CPLR § 2402; NY GEN CONSTR § 19; NY GEN CONSTR § 20; NY GEN CONSTR § 25-a; NY GEN CONSTR § 30; NY GEN CONSTR § 31; NY GEN CONSTR § 53.

   g. Scope of disclosure. NY CPLR § 3101; NY CPLR § 3102; NY CPLR § 3103; NY CPLR § 3104; NY CPLR Rule 3105; NY CPLR Rule 3118.

   h. Service of answers or objections to interrogatories. NY CPLR Rule 3133.

   i. Motions staying disclosure. NY CPLR Rule 3214; NY CPLR Rule 3407.

   j. Index number fees of county clerks. NY CPLR § 8018.

   k. Hours of court. NY R CHIEF J § 3.1.

   l. Application of part; Waiver; Additional rules; Application of CPLR; Definitions. NY R UNIF TRIAL CTS § 202.1.

   m. Papers filed in court; Electronic filing in supreme court. NY R UNIF TRIAL CTS § 202.5; NY R UNIF TRIAL CTS § 202.5-a; NY R UNIF TRIAL CTS § 202.5-b; NY R UNIF TRIAL CTS § 202.5-bb.

   n. Rules of the commercial division of the Supreme Court. NY R UNIF TRIAL CTS § 202.70.

   o. Signing of papers. NY R CHIEF ADMIN § 130-1.1-a.

2. *Local rules*

   a. *Albany County*

      i. Third judicial district rules. NY R 3 JD SUP Doc. 1.

   b. *Bronx County*

      i. Commercial division. NY R BRONX FIL R Doc. 12.

   c. *Kings County*

      i. Expedited discovery. NY R L KINGS Pt. B, Rule 5.

ii. Pre calendar procedures. NY R L KINGS Rule I.

iii. Both pre and post note procedures. NY R L KINGS Rule IV.

d. *New York County*

i. RJIs and assignments. NY R NY CTY Procedure IA.

ii. Discovery schedule. NY R NY CTY J RUL Rule 8.

J. Miscellaneous

NOTE: Individual judges' rules may apply.

ALBANY COUNTY

JUSTICE LISA M. FISHER: NY R 3 JD FISHER Fisher; NY R 3 JD FISHER Fisher, PC Order.

JUSTICE RICHARD MOTT: NY R 3 JD MOTT Mott.

JUSTICE STEPHAN G. SCHICK: NY R 3 JD Schick.

FORECLOSURE SETTLEMENT PART: NY R 3 JD Foreclosure Settlement.

BRONX COUNTY

JUSTICE PAUL L. ALPERT: [NY R BRONX J Part IA-29, as amended by NY ORDER 20-0337].

JUSTICE BEN BARBATO: NY R BRONX J Part IA-21.

JUSTICE MARY ANNE BRIGANTTI: [NY R BRONX J Part IA-15, as amended by NY ORDER 20-0338].

JUSTICE JOSEPH E. CAPELLA: NY R BRONX J Part IA-23.

JUSTICE MITCHELL DANZIGER: NY R BRONX J Part IA-3/33 ; [NY R BRONX J Danziger, Part IA-3/33, as amended by NY ORDER 20-0339].

JUSTICE LAURA G. DOUGLAS: NY R BRONX J Part IA-11.

JUSTICE RUBEN FRANCO: NY R BRONX J Part IA-26.

JUSTICE DORIS M. GONZALEZ: NY R BRONX J Part IA-24.

JUSTICE WILMA GUZMAN: NY R BRONX J Part IA-7; [NY R BRONX J Guzman, Part IA-7 Virtual, as amended by NY ORDER 20-0340].

JUSTICE ROBERT T. JOHNSON: NY R BRONX J Part IA-12.

JUSTICE DONALD A. MILES: NY R BRONX J Part IA-8.

JUSTICE DONNA M. MILLS: NY R BRONX J Part IA-9.

JUSTICE JULIA I. RODRIGUEZ: NY R BRONX J Part IA-18; [NY R BRONX J Part IA-27, as amended by NY ORDER 20-0341].

JUSTICE LLINET M. ROSADO: [NY R BRONX J Part IA-25, as amended by NY ORDER 20-0342].

JUSTICE NORMA RUIZ: NY R BRONX J Part IA-22; [NY R BRONX J Ruiz, Part IA-22 Virtual, as amended by NY ORDER 20-0343].

JUSTICE HOWARD H. SHERMAN: NY R BRONX J Part IA-4.

JUSTICE FERNANDO TAPIA: NY R BRONX J Part IA-13.

JUSTICE ELIZABETH A. TAYLOR: NY R BRONX J Part IA-2.

JUSTICE ALISON Y. TRUITT: NY R BRONX J Part IA-5.

PART IDV: NY R BRONX J Doc. 1.

PRE-TRIAL PART RULES: NY R BRONX J Doc. 2.

PRE TRIAL WORKSHEET: NY R BRONX J Doc. 3.

FORECLOSURE SETTLEMENT PART RULES: NY R BRONX J Doc. 4.

GUARDIANSHIP PART RULES: NY R BRONX J Doc. 5.

LPM PART RULES: NY R BRONX J Doc. 6.

ERIE COUNTY

JUSTICE M. WILLIAM BOLLER: NY R 8 JD J Boller.
JUSTICE RALPH A. BONIELLO: NY R 8 JD J Boniello.
JUSTICE CHRISTOPHER J. BURN: NY R 8 JD J Burns.
JUSTICE RUSSELL P. BUSCAGLIA: NY R 8 JD J Buscaglia.
JUSTICE FRANK CARUSO: NY R 8 JD J Caruso.
JUSTICE STEPHEN W. CASS: NY R 8 JD J Cass.
JUSTICE DEBORAH A. CHIMES: NY R 8 JD J Chimes.
JUSTICE EMILIO COLAIACOVO: [NY R 8 JD J Colaiacovo, as amended by NY ORDER 20-0252].
JUSTICE DIANE Y. DEVLIN: NY R 8 JD J Devlin.
JUSTICE JAMES H. DILLON: NY R 8 JD J Dillon.
JUSTICE PAULA L. FEROLETO: NY R 8 JD J Feroleto.
JUSTICE DANIEL J. FURLONG: [NY R 8 JD J Furlong, as amended by NY ORDER 20-0253].
JUSTICE JOSEPH R. GLOWNIA: NY R 8 JD J Glownia.
JUSTICE MARK J. GRISANTI: NY R 8 JD J Grisanti.
JUSTICE DEBORAH A. HAENDIGES: NY R 8 JD J Haendiges.
JUSTICE LYNN W. KEANE: [NY R 8 JD J Keane, as amended by NY ORDER 20-0254].
JUSTICE RICHARD C. KLOCH, Sr.: NY R 8 JD J Kloch.
JUSTICE FREDERICK J. MARSHALL: [NY R 8 JD J Marshall, as amended by NY ORDER 20-0255.
JUSTICE JOHN L. MICHALSKI: NY R 8 JD J Michalski.
JUSTICE MARK A. MONTOUR: [NY R 8 JD J Montour, as amended by NY ORDER 20-0256].
JUSTICE HENRY NOWAK: NY R 8 JD J Nowak.
JUSTICE JOHN F. O'DONNELL: NY R 8 JD J O'Donnell.
JUSTICE JEANETTE OGDEN: NY R 8 JD J Ogden.
JUSTICE CATHERINE NUGENT-PANEPINTO: NY R 8 JD J Nugent-Panepinto.
JUSTICE FRANK A. SEDITA, III: [NY R 8 JD J Sedita, as amended by NY ORDER 20-0257].
JUSTICE SARA SHELDON: NY R 8 JD J Sheldon.
JUSTICE DONNA M. SIWEK: NY R 8 JD J Siwek.
JUSTICE MARY L. SLISZ: NY R 8 JD J Slisz.
JUSTICE TIMOTHY J. WALKER: [NY R 8 JD J Walker, as amended by NY ORDER 20-0258].
JUSTICE DENNIS E. WARD: NY R 8 JD J Ward.
JUSTICE PAUL B. WOJTASZEK: [NY R 8 JD J Wojtaszek, as amended by NY ORDER 20-0259].
JUSTICE CHARLES N. ZAMBITO: [NY R 8 JD J Zambito, as amended by NY ORDER 20-0260].
SUPREME COURT LEGAL STAFF: NY R 8 JD J Legal Staff.

KINGS COUNTY

JUSTICE RACHEL A. ADAMS: NY R KINGS J Part 5F.
JUSTICE LOREN BAILY-SCHIFFMAN: NY R KINGS J Part 65.
JUSTICE REGINALD A. BODDIE: NY R KINGS J Part 95.
JUSTICE THERESA M. CICCOTTO: NY R KINGS J Part 19; NY R KINGS J Part 5J.
JUSTICE LISSETTE COLON: NY R KINGS J Part Rules.
JUSTICE GENINE EDWARDS: NY R KINGS J Part 80.
JUSTICE PAMELA L. FISHER: [NY R KINGS J Part 94, as amended by NY ORDER 20-0208].
JUSTICE ROBIN GARSON: NY R KINGS J Part 75.

JUSTICE LARA J. GENOVISI: [NY R KINGS J Part 34, as amended by NY ORDER 20-0209].
JUSTICE BERNARD J. GRAHAM: NY R KINGS J Part 36.
JUSTICE DAWN JIMENEZ-SALTA: NY R KINGS J Part 88.
JUSTICE INGRID JOSEPH: [NY R KINGS J Part FRP3 and Part 83, as amended by NY ORDER 20-0210].
JUSTICE KATHY J. KING: NY R KINGS J Part 64, 76K.
JUSTICE LAWRENCE KNIPEL: NY R KINGS J Part 57.
JUSTICE DONALD KURTZ: NY R KINGS J Part 26.
JUSTICE CARL LANDICINO: [NY R KINGS J Part 81, as amended by NY ORDER 20-0211].
JUSTICE KATHERINE LEVINE: [NY R KINGS J Part 20, 25, 92, as amended by NY ORDER 20-0211].
JUSTICE LORNA MCALLISTER: [NY R KINGS J Part 10, as amended by NY ORDER 20-0211].
JUSTICE ROSEMARIE MONTALBANO: [NY R KINGS J Part 19, 71, and 22, as amended by NY ORDER 20-0211].
JUSTICE RICHARD J. MONTELIONE: [NY R KINGS J Part 99 and DJMP, as amended by NY ORDER 20-0215].
JUSTICE LISA S. OTTLEY: NY R KINGS J Part 24.
JUSTICE MARK I. PARTNOW: NY R KINGS J Part 43.
JUSTICE ERIC I. PRUS: NY R KINGS J Part 5A.
JUSTICE FRANCOIS RIVERA: NY R KINGS J Part 52.
JUSTICE KAREN B. ROTHENBERG: NY R KINGS J Part 35.
JUSTICE LEON RUCHELSMAN: NY R KINGS J Part 1.
JUSTICE WAYNE P. SAITTA: NY R KINGS J Part 29.
JUSTICE ROBIN K. SHEARES: NY R KINGS J Part 96.
JUSTICE KENNETH P. SHERMAN: NY R KINGS J Part 67 and 78.
JUSTICE DEBRA SILBER: NY R KINGS J Part 9 and 5K.
JUSTICE ELLEN M. SPODEK: NY R KINGS J Part 63.
JUSTICE MARSHA L. STEINHARDT: NY R KINGS J Part 15.
JUSTICE JEFFREY S. SUNSHINE: NY R KINGS J Part 5G.
JUSTICE PETER P. SWEENEY: [NY R KINGS J Part 35, as amended by NY ORDER 20-0218].
JUSTICE DELORES J. THOMAS: [NY R KINGS J Part 5T, as amended by NY ORDER 20-0221].
JUSTICE WAVNY TOUSSAINT: NY R KINGS J Part 70.
JUSTICE RICHARD VELASQUEZ: NY R KINGS J Part 66.
JUSTICE CAROLYN E. WADE: NY R KINGS J Part 84.
JUSTICE EDWARD G. WALKER: [NY R KINGS J Part 90, as amended by NY ORDER 20-0219].
JUSTICE LILLIAN WAN: [NY R KINGS J Part 17, as amended by NY ORDER 20-0220].
JUSTICE MICHELLE WESTON: NY R KINGS J Part 3.
MENTAL HYGIENE PART: NY R KINGS J Part 77.
MATRIMONIAL PARTS DURING COVID-19 EMERGENCY: JUSTICE KAREN B. ROTHENBERG: NY R KINGS J Doc. 1.

NASSAU COUNTY

JUSTICE ANNA R. ANZALONE: NY R NASSAU S J Anzalone, Part 26.
JUSTICE STACY D. BENNETT: NY R NASSAU S J Bennett; NY R NASSAU S J Bennett, Form 1.
JUSTICE ANTONIO BRANDVEEN: NY R NASSAU S J Brandveen, Part 31.
JUSTICE JEFFREY S. BROWN: [NY R NASSAU S J Brown, as amended by NY ORDER 20-0297].
JUSTICE STEPHEN A. BUCARIA: NY R NASSAU S J Bucaria.
JUSTICE JULIANNE T. CAPETOLA: NY R NASSAU S J Capetola, Part 28.

JUSTICE EDMUND M. DANE: NY R NASSAU S J Dane, Part 33.

JUSTICE VITO M. DESTEFANO: NY R NASSAU S J DeStefano, Part 13; NY R NASSAU S J DeStefano, Form 1.

JUSTICE ARTHUR M. DIAMOND: NY R NASSAU S J Diamond, Part 7.

JUSTICE THOMAS FEINMAN: NY R NASSAU S J Feinman, Part 5.

JUSTICE JOHN M. GALASSO: NY R NASSAU S J Galasso, Part 22.

JUSTICE SHARON M.J. GIANELLI: NY R NASSAU S J Gianelli, Part 22; NY R NASSAU S J Gianelli, Form 1.

JUSTICE JEFFREY A. GOODSTEIN: NY R NASSAU S J Goodstein, Part 33; NY R NASSAU S J Goodstein, Form 1.

JUSTICE DAVID J. GUGERTY: [NY R NASSAU S J Gugerty, Part 31, as amended by NY ORDER 20-0298].

JUSTICE HELENE F. GUGERTY: NY R NASSAU S J Gugerty, Part 47.

JUSTICE STEVEN M. JAEGER: NY R NASSAU S J Jaeger, Part 35; NY R NASSAU S J Jaeger, Form 1.

JUSTICE JACK L. LIBERT: NY R NASSAU S J Libert, Part 23.

JUSTICE JOSEPH H. LORINTZ: NY R NASSAU S J Lorintz, Part 26; NY R NASSAU S J Lorintz, Form 1.

JUSTICE ROY S. MAHON: NY R NASSAU S J Mahon, Part 3.

JUSTICE RANDY SUE MARBER: NY R NASSAU S J Marber, Part 8.

JUSTICE JAMES P. MCCORMACK: [NY R NASSAU S J McCormack, Part 18, as amended by NY ORDER, 20-0299].

JUSTICE DICCIA T. PINEDA-KIRWAN: [NY R NASSAU S J Pineda-Kirwan, as amended by NY ORDER 20-0300].

JUSTICE THOMAS RADEMAKER: [NY R NASSAU S J Rademaker, Part 28, as amended by NY ORDER 20-0301]; [NY R NASSAU S J Rademaker, Form 1, as amended by NY ORDER 20-0301].

JUSTICE DENISE L. SHER: NY R NASSAU S J Rademaker, Part 32.

JUSTICE LEONARD D. STEINMAN: [NY R NASSAU S J Steinman, Part 15, as amended by NY ORDER 20-0303]; NY R NASSAU S J Steinman, Form 1.

JUSTICE HOWARD E. STURIM: NY R NASSAU S J Sturim, Part 50; NY R NASSAU S J Sturim, Form 1.

JUSTICE HELEN VOUTSINAS: [NY R NASSAU S J Voutsinas, Part 25, as amended by NY ORDER 20-0304]; [NY R NASSAU S J Voutsinas, Form 1, as amended by NY ORDER 20-0305].

JUSTICE HOPE SCHWARTZ ZIMMERMAN: NY R NASSAU S J Zimmerman, Part 17.

NEW YORK COUNTY

JUDGE'S RULES; BASIC INFORMATION: [NY R NY CTY J RUL Doc. 1, as amended by NY ORDER 20-0202].

ONONDAGA COUNTY

JUSTICE ROBERT E. ANTONACCI II: [NY R ONDGA E FIL Doc. 1, as amended by 20-0239].

JUSTICE MICHAEL V. COCCOMI: NY R ONDGA E FIL Doc. 2.

JUSTICE GREGORY R. GILBERT: NY R 5 JD JUDGES Gilbert; NY R ONDGA E FIL Doc. 3.

JUSTICE DONALD A. GREENWOOD: NY R ONDGA E FIL Doc. 4.

JUSTICE DEBORAH H. KARALUNAS: NY R ONDGA E FIL Doc. 5.

JUSTICE JAMES MCCLUSKY: NY R 5 JD MCCLUSKY McClusky.

JUSTICE CHARLES C. MERRELL: NY R 5 JD MERRELL Merrell.

JUSTICE PATRICK F. MACRAE: NY R 5 JD MACRAE Doc. 1.

JUSTICE JAMES P. MURPHY: NY R ONDGA E FIL Doc. 7.

JUSTICE GERALD J. NERI: [NY R 5 JD JUDGES Neri, as amended by NY ORDER 20-0236]; [NY R ONDGA E FIL Doc. 8, as amended by NY ORDER 20-0241].

JUSTICE ANTHONY J. PARIS: NY R 5 JD JUDGES Paris; [NY R ONDGA E FIL Doc. 9, as amended by NY ORDER 20-0242].

JUSTICE NORMAN W. SEITER, JR.: NY R 5 JD JUDGES Seiter.

JUSTICE KEVIN G. YOUNG: [NY R ONDGA E FIL Doc. 10, as amended by NY ORDER 20-0243].

QUEENS COUNTY

JUSTICE PAM JACKMAN BROWN: [NY R L QUEENS Brown, Part 19, as amended by NY ORDER 20-0321].

JUSTICE CHEREE A. BUGGS: NY R L QUEENS Buggs, Part 30.

JUSTICE PAM JACKMAN BROWN: [NY R L QUEENS Brown, Part 19, as amended by NY ORDER 20-0321].

JUSTICE DENIS J. BUTLER: NY R L QUEENS Butler, Part 12.

JUSTICE ROBERT I. CALORAS: [NY R L QUEENS Caloras, Part 36, as amended by NY ORDER 20-0322].

JUSTICE ANNA CULLEY: NY R L QUEENS Culley, Part 53.

JUSTICE TIMOTHY DUFFICY: NY R L QUEENS Dufficy, Part 35.

JUSTICE DAVID ELLIOT: NY R L QUEENS Elliot, Part 14.

JUSTICE JOSEPH J. ESPOSITO: NY R L QUEENS Esposito, Part 6.

JUSTICE DARRELL L. GAVRIN: [NY R L QUEENS Gavrin, Part 27, as amended by NY ORDER 20-0323].

JUSTICE WYATT N. GIBBONS: [NY R L QUEENS Gibbons, Part 5, as amended by NY ORDER 20-0330.

JUSTICE DONNA-MARIE E. GOLIA: [NY R L QUEENS Golia, Part 21, as amended by NY ORDER 20-0331].

JUSTICE MARGUERITE A. GRAYS: [NY R L QUEENS Grays, Part 4, as amended by NY ORDER 20-0324].

JUSTICE RUDOLPH E. GRECO: [NY R L QUEENS Greco, Part 32, as amended by NY ORDER 20-0325].

JUSTICE MAUREEN HEALY: NY R L QUEENS Healy, Part 6.

JUSTICE PHILLIP HOM: [NY R L QUEENS Hom, Part 43, as amended by NY ORDER 20-0332].

JUSTICE KEVIN J. KERRIGAN: NY R L QUEENS Kerrigan, Part 10.

JUSTICE MOJGAN C. LANCMAN: NY R L QUEENS Lancman, Part 20.

JUSTICE RICHARD G. LATIN: NY R L QUEENS Latin, Part 40.

JUSTICE ULYSSES B. LEVERETT: [NY R L QUEENS Leverett, Part 6, as amended by NY ORDER 20-0326].

JUSTICE LEONARD LIVOTE: NY R L QUEENS Livote, Part 33.

JUSTICE LEE A. MAYERSOHN: NY R L QUEENS Mayersohn, Part 22; NY R L QUEENS Mayersohn, Part 22G; [NY R L QUEENS Mayersohn, Part 22G COVID, as amended by NY ORDER 20-0327].

JUSTICE ROBERT J. MCDONALD: NY R L QUEENS McDonald, Part 34.

JUSTICE MARGARET MCGOWAN: NY R L QUEENS McGowan, Part 52.

JUSTICE MAURICE E. MUIR: [NY R L QUEENS Muir, Part 42, as amended by NY ORDER 20-0333].

JUSTICE JODI ORLOW: NY R L QUEENS Orlow, Part 51.

JUSTICE LESLIE J. PURIFICCION: NY R L QUEENS Purificcion, Part 39.

JUSTICE JOSEPH RISI: [NY R L QUEENS Risi, Part 3, as amended by NY ORDER 20-0328].

JUSTICE FREDERICK D.R. SAMPSON: [NY R L QUEENS Sampson, Part 31, as amended by NY ORDER 20-0329].

JUSTICE MARTIN J. SCHULMAN: NY R L QUEENS Schulman, Part 29.

JUSTICE BERNICE D. SIEGAL: NY R L QUEENS Siegal, Part 25G.

JUSTICE JANICE A. TAYLOR: NY R L QUEENS Taylor, Part 15.

JUSTICE CARMEN R. VELASQUEZ: NY R L QUEENS Velasquez, Part 38.

JUSTICE LOURDES M VENTURA: [NY R L QUEENS Ventura, Part 37, as amended by NY ORDER 20-0334].

JUSTICE WILLIAM A. VISCOVICH: NY R L QUEENS Viscovich, Part 63.

JUSTICE ALLAN B. WEISS: NY R L QUEENS Weiss, Part 2.

COMPLIANCE, SETTLEMENT AND CONFERENCE PART: NY R L QUEENS Doc 1.

PRELIMINARY CONFERENCE PART: [NY R L QUEENS Doc. 2, as amended by NY ORDER 20-0335].

MEDICAL MALPRACTICE CONFERENCE PART: [NY R L QUEENS Doc. 3, as amended by NY ORDER 20-0336].

TRIAL SCHEDULING PART: NY R L QUEENS Doc. 4.

SUMMARY JURY TRIAL PROGRAM: NY R L QUEENS Doc. 7.

RESIDENTIAL FORECLOSURE PART: NY R L QUEENS Doc. 9.
FORECLOSURE AUCTION RULES: NY R L QUEENS Doc. 10.
MATRIMONIAL PRELIMINARY CONFERENCE PART: NY R L QUEENS Doc. 11.
NON-CUSTODIAL CONTESTED MATRIMONIAL PART: NY R L QUEENS Doc. 12.

Requests, Notices and Applications
Request for Production of Documents

Document Last Updated August 2020

A. Checklist

(I) ❑ Matters to be considered by requesting party

- (a) ❑ Required documents
  - (1) ❑ Request for production of documents
  - (2) ❑ Proof of service
- (b) ❑ Supplemental documents
  - (1) ❑ Written authorization of patient
  - (2) ❑ Working copies
- (c) ❑ Timing
  - (1) ❑ After commencement of an action, any party may serve on any other party a notice or on any other person a subpoena duces tecum

(II) ❑ Matters to be considered by responding party

- (a) ❑ Required documents
  - (1) ❑ Response to request for production of documents
  - (2) ❑ Proof of service
- (b) ❑ Supplemental documents
  - (1) ❑ Certification of business records
  - (2) ❑ Working copies
- (c) ❑ Timing
  - (1) ❑ The notice or subpoena duces tecum shall specify the time, which shall be not less than twenty (20) days after service of the notice or subpoena, of making the inspection, copy, test or photograph, or of the entry upon the land or other property
  - (2) ❑ Within twenty (20) days of service of a notice or subpoena duces tecum under NY CPLR Rule 3120, the party or person to whom the notice or subpoena duces tecum is directed, if that party or person objects to the disclosure, inspection or examination, shall serve a response which shall state with reasonable particularity the reasons for each objection

B. Timing

1. *Time for request for production of documents.* After commencement of an action, any party may serve on any other party a notice or on any other person a subpoena duces tecum:
   - a. To produce and permit the party seeking discovery, or someone acting on his or her behalf, to inspect, copy, test or photograph any designated documents or any things which are in the possession, custody or control of the party or person served; or
   - b. To permit entry upon designated land or other property in the possession, custody or control of the party or person served for the purpose of inspecting, measuring, surveying, sampling, testing, photographing or recording by motion pictures or otherwise the property or any specifically designated object or operation thereon. NY CPLR Rule 3120(1).
   - c. The party issuing a subpoena duces tecum as provided hereinabove shall at the same time serve a copy of the

subpoena upon all other parties and, within five (5) days of compliance therewith, in whole or in part, give to each party notice that the items produced in response thereto are available for inspection and copying, specifying the time and place thereof. NY CPLR Rule 3120(3).

2. *Motions staying disclosure.* Service of a notice of motion under NY CPLR Rule 3211, NY CPLR Rule 3212, or NY CPLR § 3213 stays disclosure until determination of the motion unless the court orders otherwise. If the motion is based solely on the defense that the summons and complaint, summons with notice, or notice of petition and petition was not properly served, disclosure shall not be stayed unless the court orders otherwise. NY CPLR Rule 3214(b).

   a. *Personal injury actions involving terminally ill patients.* Notwithstanding the provisions of NY CPLR Rule 3214(b), the service or pendency of a motion under NY CPLR Rule 3211, NY CPLR Rule 3212, or NY CPLR § 3213 shall not stay disclosure in an action where a preliminary conference order has been entered pursuant to NY CPLR Rule 3407. NY CPLR Rule 3407(b)(3).

3. *KINGS COUNTY: Discovery timing.* At [the Compliance Conference, the court will] schedule all outstanding discovery to be completed prior to date fixed for filing Note of Issue. NY R L KINGS Rule I(B).

   a. *Deadlines in orders.* Discovery scheduled in Compliance Conference orders shall be strictly adhered to and may not be extended without leave of the court. Unjustified failure to comply with the provisions of the CCP order will result in preclusion, the striking of a pleading or imposition of sanctions, as appropriate. NY R L KINGS Rule I(B)(2).

   b. *Cases with extensive discovery.* Where post Compliance Conference discovery is to be extensive, cases may be retracked from standard to complex, which will provide for three (3) additional months of post Compliance Conference discovery and extend the Note of Issue date by three (3) months. NY R L KINGS Rule I(B)(1).

   c. *Discovery not stayed.* Ordinarily the Court/JHO will not stay discovery during pendency of motions to withdraw, or during pendency of settlement, or during pendency of dispositive motions. NY R L KINGS Rule IV.

   d. *Expedited discovery in certain cases.* Discovery in third party and joint actions will be expedited. NY R L KINGS Pt. B, Rule 5.

   e. For more information on discovery scheduling, refer to NY R L KINGS Flow Chart.

4. *NEW YORK COUNTY: Deadlines in orders.* Strict compliance with all discovery orders is required. Unexcused or unjustified failure to comply with deadlines fixed by the court, including those set out in Preliminary Conference Orders, may result in an award of costs, conditional or otherwise, or the imposition of another penalty authorized by NY CPLR § 3126. NY R NY CTY J RUL Rule 8.

5. *Computation of time*

   a. *Units of time*

      i. *Day.* A calendar day includes the time from midnight to midnight. Sunday or any day of the week specifically mentioned means a calendar day. NY GEN CONSTR § 19.

      ii. *Month.* In a statute, contract or public or private instrument, unless otherwise provided in such contract or instrument or by law, the term month means a calendar month and not a lunar month. NY GEN CONSTR § 31.

      iii. *Year.* For information on the definition of a year, including the definitions of a half-year and quarter-year, refer to NY GEN CONSTR § 58 and NY GEN CONSTR § 50. For information on leap years, refer to NY GEN CONSTR § 57.

   b. *Periods of time*

      i. *Number of days.* A number of days specified as a period from a certain day within which or after or before which an act is authorized or required to be done means such number of calendar days exclusive of the calendar day from which the reckoning is made. NY GEN CONSTR § 20.

         - If such period is a period of two (2) days, Saturday, Sunday or a public holiday must be excluded from the reckoning if it is an intervening day between the day from which the reckoning is made and the last day of the period. NY GEN CONSTR § 20.
         - In computing any specified period of time from a specified event, the day upon which the event happens is deemed the day from which the reckoning is made. The day from which any specified period of time is reckoned shall be excluded in making the reckoning. NY GEN CONSTR § 20.

      ii. *Number of months.* A number of months after or before a certain day shall be computed by counting such number of calendar months from such day, exclusive of the calendar month in which such day occurs, and shall include the day of the month in the last month so counted having the same numerical order in days of the month as the day from which the computation is made, unless there be not so many days in the last month so counted, in which case the period computed shall expire with the last day of the month so counted. NY GEN CONSTR § 30.

iii. *Publication of notice; Number of days.* The period of publication of a legal notice shall be computed by excluding the first day of publication and including the day on which the act or event of which notice is given is to take place or which completes the full period of publication. NY CPLR § 2402.

iv. *Periods ending on Saturday, Sunday or public holiday.* When any period of time, computed from a certain day, within which or after which or before which an act is authorized or required to be done, ends on a Saturday, Sunday or a public holiday, such act may be done on the next succeeding business day and if the period ends at a specified hour, such act may be done at or before the same hour of such next succeeding business day, except that where a period of time specified by contract ends on a Saturday, Sunday or a public holiday, the extension of such period is governed by NY GEN CONSTR § 25. NY GEN CONSTR § 25-a(1).

- For a list of public holidays, refer to NY GEN CONSTR § 24.

v. *Additional time after certain kinds of service*

- *Service by mail.* Where a period of time prescribed by law is measured from the service of a paper and service is by mail, five (5) days shall be added to the prescribed period. NY CPLR Rule 2103(b)(2).
- *Service by overnight delivery service.* Where a period of time prescribed by law is measured from the service of a paper and service is by overnight delivery, one (1) business day shall be added to the prescribed period. NY CPLR Rule 2103(b)(6).

vi. *Daylight saving time.* For information on New York's time zone and the effect of daylight saving time, refer to NY GEN CONSTR § 52.

c. *Hours of court.* Notwithstanding any provision of law or rule of court to the contrary, throughout the State of New York the sessions of the Supreme Court for the disposition of business before the court shall commence not later than 9:30 a.m. and conclude not earlier than 5 p.m. Where warranted, the Chief Administrator of the Courts may authorize variances in the opening and closing hours of the courts, but, in such event, daily sessions shall total not less than six (6) hours. NY R CHIEF J § 3.1.

d. *Time limits; Extension of time.* Any act required by or in pursuance of law to be performed at or within a prescribed time, shall be performed according to the standard time. NY GEN CONSTR § 53.

i. Except where otherwise expressly prescribed by law, the court may extend the time fixed by any statute, rule or order for doing any act, upon such terms as may be just and upon good cause shown, whether the application for extension is made before or after the expiration of the time fixed. NY CPLR § 2004. Refer to the New York KeyRules Motion for Continuance/Extension of Time document for more information.

C. General Requirements

1. *Rules governing disclosure*

a. *Generally.* There shall be full disclosure of all matter material and necessary in the prosecution or defense of an action, regardless of the burden of proof, by:

i. A party, or the officer, director, member, agent or employee of a party;

ii. A person who possessed a cause of action or defense asserted in the action;

iii. A person about to depart from the state, or without the state, or residing at a greater distance from the place of trial than one hundred miles, or so sick or infirm as to afford reasonable grounds of belief that he or she will not be able to attend the trial, or a person authorized to practice medicine, dentistry or podiatry who has provided medical, dental or podiatric care or diagnosis to the party demanding disclosure, or who has been retained by such party as an expert witness; and

iv. Any other person, upon notice stating the circumstances or reasons such disclosure is sought or required. NY CPLR § 3101(a).

v. The statutory phrase "material and necessary", said the Court of Appeals, must be interpreted liberally to require disclosure upon request, of any facts bearing on the controversy which will assist preparation for trial by sharpening the issues and reducing delay and prolixity. The test is one of usefulness and reason. SIEGEL-NYPRAC § 344; Allen v. Crowell-Collier Pub. Co., 21 N.Y.2d 403, 235 N.E.2d 430 (1968).

vi. Another potential problem that the original NY CPLR § 3101(a) posed was that it spoke of "evidence" that is material and necessary, which might have been construed to permit disclosure to elicit only that which would itself qualify as "evidence" admissible at trial. It was, however, construed more broadly than that. Well-considered caselaw specifically rejected this "evidence in chief" doctrine, stating that disclosure extends as well "to all relevant information calculated to lead to relevant evidence," a standard similar to that applicable in federal court. With an amendment that took effect on January 1, 1994, changing "evidence" to "matter" in NY CPLR § 3101(a), these generous interpretations of the statute were in effect approved by the legislature. SIEGEL-NYPRAC § 344.

vii. If a party is a corporation, each of its officers, directors, members, agents, and employees is also deemed a "party" for disclosure purposes. A party who needs relevant data or material from a nonparty corporation can seek it through NY CPLR § 3101(a)(2), NY CPLR § 3101(a)(3) or NY CPLR § 3101(a)(4), under which the corporate entity is treated as a "person." These subdivisions should also apply to any entity, corporate or otherwise, from whom disclosure is sought through its agents. A corporate employee who has the requisite knowledge and information may respond to a disclosure request on behalf of the corporation. A party who can't single out the particular person in the corporation's employ to whom a disclosure request should be properly directed can direct it to the corporation as such and leave it to the corporation to designate the appropriate person to respond. Whenever disclosure is sought from a corporation through a deposition, whether as a party or as a nonparty witness, the choice in the first instance of who will be produced in the corporate behalf is with the corporation rather than the examining party. SIEGEL-NYPRAC § 345.

viii. NY CPLR § 3101(a)(4) permits a party to obtain disclosure from a nonparty by merely serving a subpoena on the nonparty providing notice of "the circumstances or reasons such disclosure is sought or required." SIEGEL-NYPRAC § 345.

b. *Methods of obtaining disclosure.* Information is obtainable by one or more of the following disclosure devices: depositions upon oral questions or without the state upon written questions, interrogatories, demands for addresses, discovery and inspection of documents or property, physical and mental examinations of persons, and requests for admission. NY CPLR § 3102(a).

i. *Stipulation or notice.* Unless otherwise provided by the civil practice law and rules or by the court, disclosure shall be obtained by stipulation or on notice without leave of the court. NY CPLR § 3102(b).

ii. *Before action commenced; Court order required.* Before an action is commenced, disclosure to aid in bringing an action, to preserve information or to aid in arbitration, may be obtained, but only by court order. The court may appoint a referee to take testimony. NY CPLR § 3102(c).

iii. *During trial; Court order required.* Except as provided in NY CPLR § 5223, during and after trial, disclosure may be obtained only by order of the trial court on notice. NY CPLR § 3102(d).

iv. *Action pending in another jurisdiction.* Except as provided in NY CPLR § 3119, when under any mandate, writ or commission issued out of any court of record in any other state, territory, district or foreign jurisdiction, or whenever upon notice or agreement, it is required to take the testimony of a witness in the state, he or she may be compelled to appear and testify in the same manner and by the same process as may be employed for the purpose of taking testimony in actions pending in the state. The supreme court or a county court shall make any appropriate order in aid of taking such a deposition. NY CPLR § 3102(e).

v. *Actions to which state is a party.* In an action in which the state is properly a party, whether as plaintiff, defendant or otherwise, disclosure by the state shall be available as if the state were a private person. NY CPLR § 3102(f).

c. *Privileged matter.* Upon objection by a person entitled to assert the privilege, privileged matter shall not be obtainable. NY CPLR § 3101(b).

i. A determination of whether information is privileged is governed by the rules of evidence, which apply as they would at a trial. Whatever is privileged at the trial is privileged as well on pretrial disclosure. SIEGEL-NYPRAC § 346.

d. *Attorney's work product.* The work product of an attorney shall not be obtainable. NY CPLR § 3101(c).

i. NY CPLR § 3101(c) makes unobtainable the "work product of an attorney"—an ill-defined category whose potential for mischief has been avoided only because the judiciary has accorded it a very narrow scope. It is a category wholly distinct from the "materials . . . prepared in anticipation of litigation" of NY CPLR § 3101(d)(2). The fact that immunity is absolute under NY CPLR § 3101(c), while that of NY CPLR § 3101(d)(2) is only conditional, is the factor that requires as sharp a line as possible between the two categories. SIEGEL-NYPRAC § 347.

ii. The judiciary has cast precious little under the "work product" category of NY CPLR § 3101(c), preferring instead to fit doubtful items under the "materials . . . prepared in anticipation of litigation" banner of NY CPLR § 3101(d)(2), where the conditional immunity can be overcome and the matters ordered disclosed when stated conditions are met. SIEGEL-NYPRAC § 347.

e. *Trial preparation*

i. *Experts.* Upon request, each party shall identify each person whom the party expects to call as an expert witness at trial and shall disclose in reasonable detail the subject matter on which each expert is expected to testify, the substance of the facts and opinions on which each expert is expected to testify, the qualifications of each expert witness and a summary of the grounds for each expert's opinion. NY CPLR § 3101(d)(1)(i).

- However, where a party for good cause shown retains an expert an insufficient period of time before the commencement of trial to give appropriate notice thereof, the party shall not thereupon be precluded from introducing the expert's testimony at the trial solely on grounds of noncompliance with NY CPLR § 3101(d)(1). In that instance, upon motion of any party, made before or at trial, or on its own initiative, the court may make whatever order may be just. In an action for medical, dental or podiatric malpractice, a party, in responding to a request, may omit the names of medical, dental or podiatric experts but shall be required to disclose all other information concerning such experts otherwise required by NY CPLR § 3101(d)(1). NY CPLR § 3101(d)(1)(i).
- In an action for medical, dental or podiatric malpractice, any party may, by written offer made to and served upon all other parties and filed with the court, offer to disclose the name of, and to make available for examination upon oral deposition, any person the party making the offer expects to call as an expert witness at trial. Within twenty (20) days of service of the offer, a party shall accept or reject the offer by serving a written reply upon all parties and filing a copy thereof with the court. Failure to serve a reply within twenty (20) days of service of the offer shall be deemed a rejection of the offer. If all parties accept the offer, each party shall be required to produce his or her expert witness for examination upon oral deposition upon receipt of a notice to take oral deposition in accordance with NY CPLR Rule 3107. If any party, having made or accepted the offer, fails to make that party's expert available for oral deposition, that party shall be precluded from offering expert testimony at the trial of the action. NY CPLR § 3101(d)(1)(ii).
- Further disclosure concerning the expected testimony of any expert may be obtained only by court order upon a showing of special circumstances and subject to restrictions as to scope and provisions concerning fees and expenses as the court may deem appropriate. However, a party, without court order, may take the testimony of a person authorized to practice medicine, dentistry or podiatry who is the party's treating or retained expert, as described in NY CPLR § 3101(a)(3), in which event any other party shall be entitled to the full disclosure authorized by Article 31 of Chapter 8 of the Civil Practice Law and Rules (NY CPLR § 3101, et seq.) with respect to that expert without court order. NY CPLR § 3101(d)(1)(iii).

ii. *Materials.* Subject to the provisions of NY CPLR § 3101(d)(1), materials otherwise discoverable under NY CPLR § 3101(a) and prepared in anticipation of litigation or for trial by or for another party, or by or for that other party's representative (including an attorney, consultant, surety, indemnitor, insurer or agent), may be obtained only upon a showing that the party seeking discovery has substantial need of the materials in the preparation of the case and is unable without undue hardship to obtain the substantial equivalent of the materials by other means. In ordering discovery of the materials when the required showing has been made, the court shall protect against disclosure of the mental impressions, conclusions, opinions or legal theories of an attorney or other representative of a party concerning the litigation. NY CPLR § 3101(d)(2).

- In order to qualify as "litigation" material the item must have been prepared exclusively for litigation. Incidental potential use in litigation, the courts have observed, may also be a function of such reports, but they have at least an equal if not greater mission "to prevent future accidents, discipline careless employees, or, generally, to increase the economy and efficiency of the operation." SIEGEL-NYPRAC § 348.

f. *Party's statement.* A party may obtain a copy of his own statement. NY CPLR § 3101(e).

i. Moreover, NY CPLR § 3101(e) has been broadly interpreted to include photographs. Items such as photographs and videotapes are now independently subject to disclosure under NY CPLR § 3101(i). SIEGEL-NYPRAC § 348.

g. *Contents of insurance agreement.* A party may obtain discovery of the existence and contents of any insurance agreement under which any person carrying on an insurance business may be liable to satisfy part or all of a judgment which may be entered in the action or to indemnify or reimburse for payments made to satisfy the judgment. Information concerning the insurance agreement is not by reason of disclosure admissible in evidence at trial. For purpose of NY CPLR § 3101(f), an application for insurance shall not be treated as part of an insurance agreement. NY CPLR § 3101(f).

h. *Accident reports.* Except as is otherwise provided by law, in addition to any other matter which may be subject to disclosure, there shall be full disclosure of any written report of an accident prepared in the regular course of business operations or practices of any person, firm, corporation, association or other public or private entity, unless prepared by a police or peace officer for a criminal investigation or prosecution and disclosure would interfere with a criminal investigation or prosecution. NY CPLR § 3101(g).

i. *Amendment or supplementation of responses.* A party shall amend or supplement a response previously given to a request for disclosure promptly upon the party's thereafter obtaining information that the response was incorrect or incomplete when made, or that the response, though correct and complete when made, no longer is correct and complete, and the circumstances are such that a failure to amend or supplement the response would be materially misleading. NY CPLR § 3101(h).

   i. Where a party obtains such information an insufficient period of time before the commencement of trial appropriately to amend or supplement the response, the party shall not thereupon be precluded from introducing evidence at the trial solely on grounds of noncompliance with NY CPLR § 3101(h). In that instance, upon motion of any party, made before or at trial, or on its own initiative, the court may make whatever order may be just. Further amendment or supplementation may be obtained by court order. NY CPLR § 3101(h).

j. *Other disclosures.* In addition to any other matter which may be subject to disclosure, there shall be full disclosure of any films, photographs, video tapes or audio tapes, including transcripts or memoranda thereof, involving a person referred to in NY CPLR § 3101(a)(1). There shall be disclosure of all portions of such material, including out-takes, rather than only those portions a party intends to use. The provisions of NY CPLR § 3101(i) shall not apply to materials compiled for law enforcement purposes which are exempt from disclosure under NY PUB OFF § 87. NY CPLR § 3101(i).

   i. While NY CPLR § 3101(i) was enacted with the defendant's surreptitious tapes of the plaintiff in mind, its language is broad enough to embrace any films, photographs, and audio or video tapes of a party, even those made by the party from whom disclosure is sought. SIEGEL-NYPRAC § 348.

k. *Protective orders.* The court may at any time on its own initiative, or on motion of any party or of any person from whom discovery is sought, make a protective order denying, limiting, conditioning or regulating the use of any disclosure device. NY CPLR § 3103(a). Refer to the New York KeyRules Motion for Protective Order document for more information.

l. *Supervision of disclosure.* Upon the motion of any party or witness on notice to all parties or on its own initiative without notice, the court in which an action is pending may by one of its judges or a referee supervise all or part of any disclosure procedure. NY CPLR § 3104(a).

   i. *Selection of referee.* A judicial hearing officer may be designated as a referee under NY CPLR § 3104, or the court may permit all of the parties in an action to stipulate that a named attorney may act as referee. In such latter event, the stipulation shall provide for payment of his fees which shall, unless otherwise agreed, be taxed as disbursements. NY CPLR § 3104(b).

   ii. *Powers of referee; Motions referred to person supervising disclosure.* A referee under NY CPLR § 3104 shall have all the powers of the court under NY CPLR § 3101, et seq. except the power to relieve himself of his duties, to appoint a successor, or to adjudge any person guilty of contempt. All motions or applications made under Article 31 of Chapter 8 of the Civil Practice Law and Rules (NY CPLR § 3101, et seq.) shall be returnable before the judge or referee, designated under NY CPLR § 3104 and after disposition, if requested by any party, his order shall be filed in the office of the clerk. NY CPLR § 3104(c).

   iii. *Review of order of referee.* Any party or witness may apply for review of an order made under NY CPLR § 3104 by a referee. The application shall be by motion made in the court in which the action is pending within five (5) days after the order is made. Service of a notice of motion for review shall suspend disclosure of the particular matter in dispute. If the question raised by the motion may affect the rights of a witness, notice shall be served on him personally or by mail at his last known address. It shall set forth succinctly the order complained of, the reason it is objectionable and the relief demanded. NY CPLR § 3104(d).

   iv. *Payment of expenses of referee.* Except where a judicial hearing officer has been designated a referee hereunder, the court may make an appropriate order for the payment of the reasonable expenses of the referee. NY CPLR § 3104(e).

2. *Request for production of documents*
   a. *In general.* After commencement of an action, any party may serve on any other party a notice or on any other person a subpoena duces tecum:
      i. To produce and permit the party seeking discovery, or someone acting on his or her behalf, to inspect, copy, test or photograph any designated documents or any things which are in the possession, custody or control of the party or person served; or
      ii. To permit entry upon designated land or other property in the possession, custody or control of the party or person served for the purpose of inspecting, measuring, surveying, sampling, testing, photographing or recording by motion pictures or otherwise the property or any specifically designated object or operation thereon. NY CPLR Rule 3120(1).
   b. *Contents of request.* The notice or subpoena duces tecum shall specify the time, which shall be not less than twenty (20) days after service of the notice or subpoena, and the place and manner of making the inspection, copy, test or photograph, or of the entry upon the land or other property and, in the case of an inspection, copying, testing or photographing, shall set forth the items to be inspected, copied, tested or photographed by individual item or by category, and shall describe each item and category with reasonable particularity. NY CPLR Rule 3120(2).
      i. Unless the subpoena duces tecum directs the production of original documents for inspection and copying at the place where such items are usually maintained, it shall be sufficient for the custodian or other qualified person to deliver complete and accurate copies of the items to be produced. NY CPLR Rule 3122(d).
      ii. The reasonable production expenses of a non-party witness shall be defrayed by the party seeking discovery. NY CPLR Rule 3122(d).
   c. *Use with other discovery devices.* The discovery and inspection device is generally not affected by priority rules, although it is often typical practice to conduct a deposition prior to demanding the production of items, and to utilize the deposition to identify particular items or documents that will be the subject of a proper discovery and inspection request. Nevertheless, it is clear that a discovery and inspection request cannot be utilized to circumvent proper use of other discovery and disclosure devices. NYDISC § 12:3.
   d. *Limits of device.* A party may be required to produce only preexisting and tangible items that are in the possession, custody, or control of the party served; it is not the function of the statute to require the party to create new documents. CW2D § 42:437.
      i. If the seeking party doesn't know who has the paper or thing sought, but an adverse party does, the latter must reveal that person's name. SIEGEL-NYPRAC § 362; Major Chevrolet, Inc. v. Charles Pisacano, Inc., 58 Misc.2d 374, 295 N.Y.S.2d 363 (N.Y.C.Civ.Ct. 1968).
   e. *Subpoena to library, bureau, or office of municipal corporation.* Nothing contained in NY CPLR Rule 3120 shall be construed to change the requirement of NY CPLR § 2307 that a subpoena duces tecum to be served upon a library or a department or bureau of a municipal corporation, or of the state, or an officer thereof, requires a motion made on notice to the library, department, bureau or officer, and the adverse party, to a justice of the supreme court or a judge of the court in which the action is triable. NY CPLR Rule 3120(4).
   f. *Remedy for failure to respond.* The party seeking disclosure under NY CPLR Rule 3120 may move for an order under NY CPLR Rule 3124 or NY CPLR § 2308 with respect to any objection to, or other failure to respond to or permit inspection as requested by, the notice or subpoena duces tecum, respectively, or any part thereof. NY CPLR Rule 3122(a)(1).
   g. *Subpoenas, generally.* Refer to the New York KeyRules Subpoena document for more information on subpoenas.
3. *Governing law.* The civil practice law and rules (NY CPLR § 101, et seq.) shall govern the procedure in civil judicial proceedings in all courts of the state and before all judges, except where the procedure is regulated by inconsistent statute. The civil practice law and rules shall succeed the civil practice act and rules of civil practice and shall be deemed substituted therefor throughout the statutes and rules of the state. NY CPLR § 101. The civil practice law and rules shall be liberally construed to secure the just, speedy and inexpensive determination of every civil judicial proceeding. NY CPLR § 104.
   a. *Uniform trial court rules.* The uniform civil rules for the Supreme Court and County Court (NY R UNIF TRIAL CTS § 202.1, et seq.) shall be applicable to civil actions and proceedings in the Supreme Court and the County Court. NY R UNIF TRIAL CTS § 202.1(a). The provisions of the uniform rules shall be construed consistent with the Civil Practice Law and Rules (CPLR), and matters not covered by the uniform rules shall be governed by the CPLR. NY R UNIF TRIAL CTS § 202.1(d).

b. *Local rules.* Local court rules, not inconsistent with law or with uniform civil rules for the Supreme Court and County Court (NY R UNIF TRIAL CTS § 202.1, et seq.), shall comply with Part 9 of the Rules of the Chief Judge (NY R CHIEF J § 9.1). NY R UNIF TRIAL CTS § 202.1(c).

c. *Official forms.* The state administrator shall have the power to adopt, amend and rescind an appendix of forms. Forms adopted pursuant to NY CPLR § 107 shall be sufficient under the civil practice law and rules and shall illustrate the simplicity and brevity of statement which the civil practice law and rules contemplate. NY CPLR § 107.

4. *Rules of the commercial division.* [Editor's note: certain types of civil cases or civil cases meeting certain monetary thresholds that are filed in the state of New York must be filed in the Commercial Division of the New York Supreme Courts. Rules governing practice in the commercial division are found in NY R UNIF TRIAL CTS § 202.70]. Cases which must be filed in the commercial division are listed below. For more information, refer to NY R UNIF TRIAL CTS § 202.70.

a. *Monetary thresholds.* Except as set forth in NY R UNIF TRIAL CTS § 202.70(b), the monetary thresholds of the Commercial Division, exclusive of punitive damages, interests, costs, disbursements and counsel fees claimed, are established as follows: (1) Albany County, fifty thousand dollars ($50,000); (2) Eighth Judicial District, one hundred thousand dollars ($100,000); (3) Kings County, one hundred fifty thousand dollars ($150,000); (4) Nassau County, two hundred thousand dollars ($200,000); (5) New York County, five hundred thousand dollars ($500,000); (6) Onondaga County, fifty thousand dollars ($50,000); (7) Queens County, one hundred thousand dollars ($100,000); (8) Seventh Judicial District, fifty thousand dollars ($50,000); (9) Suffolk County, one hundred thousand dollars ($100,000); and (10) Westchester County, one hundred thousand dollars ($100,000). NY R UNIF TRIAL CTS § 202.70(a).

i. *ALBANY COUNTY.* The Commercial Division of the Albany County Supreme Court exercises jurisdiction over selected business and commercial disputes in which the amount at issue generally involves damage claims in a minimum amount of fifty thousand dollars ($50,000) as well as claims for unspecified amounts where the value of the commercial asset(s) in dispute exceeds fifty thousand dollars ($50,000). A separate publication promulgating the rules and criteria relating to the filing and management of Commercial Court cases in this part may be obtained from the Albany County Supreme Court Clerk's Office. A section of the Uniform Civil Rules for the Supreme Court and County Court sets forth statewide rules. NY R 3 JD SUP Doc. 1(E).

ii. *BRONX COUNTY.* The monetary threshold for commercial cases in Bronx County will be seventy-five thousand dollars ($75,000). All other parameters including the type of matters that will be heard are contained within the Rules of the Commercial Division of the Supreme Court (NY R UNIF TRIAL CTS § 202.70). NY R BRONX FIL R Doc. 12.

iii. *NEW YORK COUNTY.* The monetary threshold in the New York County Commercial Division, which is generally applicable, is an amount in controversy of five hundred thousand dollars ($500,000) or more (exclusive of punitive damages, interest, costs, disbursements, and counsel fees). If the case is designated a commercial one and the Addendum is submitted, the clerk will review the pleadings to determine whether the amount in controversy in the case meets the monetary threshold or whether an exception to the threshold applies. NY R NY CTY Procedure IA(B). For more information on assigning a case to the commercial division in New York County, refer to NY R NY CTY Procedure IA(B).

b. *Commercial cases.* Actions in which the principal claims involve or consist of the following will be heard in the Commercial Division provided that the monetary threshold is met or equitable or declaratory relief is sought:

i. Breach of contract or fiduciary duty, fraud, misrepresentation, business tort (e.g., unfair competition), or statutory and/or common law violation where the breach or violation is alleged to arise out of business dealings (e.g., sales of assets or securities; corporate restructuring; partnership, shareholder, joint venture, and other business agreements; trade secrets; restrictive covenants; and employment agreements not including claims that principally involve alleged discriminatory practices);

ii. Transactions governed by the Uniform Commercial Code (exclusive of those concerning individual cooperative or condominium units);

iii. Transactions involving commercial real property, including Yellowstone injunctions and excluding actions for the payment of rent only;

iv. Shareholder derivative actions—without consideration of the monetary threshold;

v. Commercial class actions—without consideration of the monetary threshold;

vi. Business transactions involving or arising out of dealings with commercial banks and other financial institutions;

vii. Internal affairs of business organizations;

viii. Malpractice by accountants or actuaries, and legal malpractice arising out of representation in commercial matters;

ix. Environmental insurance coverage;

x. Commercial insurance coverage (e.g., directors and officers, errors and omissions, and business interruption coverage);

xi. Dissolution of corporations, partnerships, limited liability companies, limited liability partnerships and joint ventures—without consideration of the monetary threshold; and

xii. Applications to stay or compel arbitration and affirm or disaffirm arbitration awards and related injunctive relief pursuant to Article 75 of the New York Civil Practice Law and Rules (NY CPLR § 7501, et seq.) involving any of the foregoing enumerated commercial issues. Where the applicable arbitration agreement provides for the arbitration to be heard outside the United States, the monetary threshold set forth in NY R UNIF TRIAL CTS § 202.70(a) shall not apply. NY R UNIF TRIAL CTS § 202.70(b).

c. *Non-commercial cases.* The following will not be heard in the Commercial Division even if the monetary threshold is met:

i. Suits to collect professional fees;

ii. Cases seeking a declaratory judgment as to insurance coverage for personal injury or property damage;

iii. Residential real estate disputes, including landlord-tenant matters, and commercial real estate disputes involving the payment of rent only;

iv. Home improvement contracts involving residential properties consisting of one to four residential units or individual units in any residential building, including cooperative or condominium units;

v. Proceedings to enforce a judgment regardless of the nature of the underlying case;

vi. First-party insurance claims and actions by insurers to collect premiums or rescind non-commercial policies; and

vii. Attorney malpractice actions except as otherwise provided in NY R UNIF TRIAL CTS § 202.70(b)(8). NY R UNIF TRIAL CTS § 202.70(c).

d. For more information on the Commercial Division, refer to NY R UNIF TRIAL CTS § 202.70.

D. Documents

1. *Required documents*

a. *Request for production of documents.* Refer to the General Requirements section of this document for information on the request for production of documents.

b. *Proof of service.* In addition to complying with the provisions of NY CPLR Rule 2101, every paper filed in court shall have annexed thereto appropriate proof of service on all parties where required. NY R UNIF TRIAL CTS § 202.5(a).

2. *Supplemental documents*

a. *Written authorization of patient.* Any subpoena served upon a medical provider requesting the medical records of a patient shall state in conspicuous boldfaced type that the records shall not be provided unless the subpoena is accompanied by a written authorization by the patient, or the court has issued the subpoena or otherwise directed the production of the documents. NY CPLR Rule 3122(a)(2).

b. *Working copies.* The court may require the parties to provide working copies of documents filed electronically. In such event, each working copy shall include, firmly affixed thereto, a copy of a confirmation notice in a form prescribed by the Chief Administrator. NY R UNIF TRIAL CTS § 202.5-b(d)(5).

E. Format

1. *Form of documents*

a. *Size and form of paper.* Each paper served or filed shall be durable, white and, except for summonses, subpoenas, notices of appearance, notes of issue, orders of protection, temporary orders of protection and exhibits, shall be eleven by eight and one-half (11 x 8-1/2) inches in size. NY CPLR Rule 2101(a).

b. *Writing and language.* The writing shall be legible and in black ink. NY CPLR Rule 2101(a). Each paper served or filed shall be in the English language which, where practicable, shall be of ordinary usage. NY CPLR Rule 2101(b).

c. *Caption.* Each paper served or filed shall begin with a caption setting forth the name of the court, the venue, the title of the action, the nature of the paper and the index number of the action if one has been assigned. In all papers other than a summons, a complaint or a judgment it shall be sufficient to state the name of the first named party on each side with an appropriate indication of any omissions. NY CPLR Rule 2101(c).

   i. *Further contents of first page.* After the first paper has been filed in each case the index number shall appear on the cover and first page to the right of the caption of every paper tendered for filing in the action. Each such cover and first page also shall contain an indication of the county of venue and a brief description of the nature of the paper and, where the case has been assigned to an individual judge, shall contain the name of the assigned judge to the right of the caption. NY R UNIF TRIAL CTS § 202.5(a); NY R UNIF TRIAL CTS § 202.5(b); NY R UNIF TRIAL CTS § 202.5(d)(1)(i).

d. *Index number.* No paper in an action in the supreme or a county court, other than an order submitted for signature to a judge out of court, shall be submitted for any purpose to the supreme or county court or to a clerk thereof unless there is endorsed on such paper the index number of the action assigned by the clerk of the county. NY CPLR § 8018(c).

e. *Line spacing.* Every paper filed in court, if typewritten, shall have at least double space between each line, except for quotations and the names and addresses of attorneys appearing in the action. NY R UNIF TRIAL CTS § 202.5(a).

f. *Font size.* Each. . .paper printed or typed, served or filed, except for summonses. . .and exhibits, shall be in clear type of no less than ten (10) point in size. NY CPLR Rule 2101(a).

   i. Whenever a requirement relating to size of type is stated in point size, the type size requirement shall be deemed met if the x-height of the type is a minimum of forty-five percent (45%) of the specified point size. Each point shall be measured as .351 millimeter. The x-height size shall be measured as it appears on the page. The x-height is the height of the lower case letters, exclusive of ascenders or descenders. NY CPLR § 105(t).

g. *Margins.* Every paper filed in court shall have at least one (1) inch margins. NY R UNIF TRIAL CTS § 202.5(a).

h. *Citations*

   i. *Civil practice law and rules.* NY CPLR § 101, et seq. shall be known as the civil practice law and rules, and may be cited as "CPLR". Reference to a provision in the civil practice law and rules may, except when such provision is being enacted or amended, be made without indicating whether it is a rule or section. NY CPLR § 101.

i. *Indorsement by attorney.* Each paper served or filed shall be indorsed with the name, address and telephone number of the attorney for the party serving or filing the paper, or if the party does not appear by attorney, with the name, address and telephone number of the party. NY CPLR Rule 2101(d).

j. *One-sided printing.* In addition, every paper filed in court, other than an exhibit or printed form, shall contain writing on one side only, except that papers that are fastened on the side may contain writing on both sides. NY R UNIF TRIAL CTS § 202.5(a).

k. *Use of copies authorized.* Except where otherwise specifically prescribed, copies, rather than originals, of all papers, including orders, affidavits and exhibits may be served or filed. Where it is required that the original be served or filed and the original is lost or withheld, the court may authorize a copy to be served or filed. NY CPLR Rule 2101(e).

   i. Where a certified copy of a paper is required by law, an attorney admitted to practice in the courts of the state may certify that it has been compared by him with the original and found to be a true and complete copy. Such a certificate, when subscribed by such attorney, has the same effect as if made by a clerk. NY CPLR § 2105.

l. *Recycled paper.* It is the policy of the Unified Court System that litigants, where practicable, should file or submit to the courts of the Unified Court System of the State of New York papers printed or reproduced on recycled paper. Paper is considered recycled if it contains a minimum content of thirty percent (30%) waste paper. NY R UNIF TRIAL CTS § 215.2. The signature page of every paper filed or submitted to the court on recycled paper should bear the legend: "Printed [Reproduced] on Recycled Paper." NY R UNIF TRIAL CTS § 215.3.

2. *Form of electronic documents.* Each paper served or filed by electronic means, as defined in NY CPLR Rule 2103(f), shall be capable of being reproduced by the receiver so as to comply with the provisions of NY CPLR Rule 2101(a) through NY CPLR Rule 2101(d). NY CPLR Rule 2101(g).

   a. *File format.* All e-filed documents shall comply with the technical requirements set forth at the NYSCEF site. NY R UNIF TRIAL CTS § 202.5-b(d)(1)(i).

   b. *Heading of document.* The subject matter heading for each paper sent by electronic means must indicate that the matter being transmitted electronically is related to a court proceeding. NY CPLR Rule 2103(b)(7).

3. *Signature blocks.* Every pleading, written motion, and other paper, served on another party or filed or submitted to the court

shall be signed by an attorney, or by a party if the party is not represented by an attorney, with the name of the attorney or party clearly printed or typed directly below the signature. NY R CHIEF ADMIN § 130-1.1-a(a); NY R UNIF TRIAL CTS § 202.5(d)(1)(iv).

a. *Printed name.* Beneath each signature shall be printed the name signed. NY CPLR Rule 2101(a).

b. *Failure to sign.* Absent good cause shown, the court shall strike any unsigned paper if the omission of the signature is not corrected promptly after being called to the attention of the attorney or party. NY R CHIEF ADMIN § 130-1.1-a(a).

c. *Signature as certification.* By signing a paper, an attorney or party certifies that, to the best of that person's knowledge, information and belief, formed after an inquiry reasonable under the circumstances the presentation of the paper or the contentions therein are not frivolous as defined in NY R CHIEF ADMIN § 130-1.1(c). NY R CHIEF ADMIN § 130-1.1-a(b)(1).

d. *Electronic signatures.* A document shall be considered to have been signed by an attorney or party in compliance with NY R CHIEF ADMIN § 130-1.1-a if it has been signed by such attorney or party as provided in NY R UNIF TRIAL CTS § 202.5-b(e)(1) and it bears the signatory's name. NY R UNIF TRIAL CTS § 202.5-b(e)(2). An electronically filed document shall be considered to have been signed by, and shall be binding upon, the person identified as a signatory, if:

i. It bears the physical signature of such person and is scanned into an electronic format that reproduces such signature; or

ii. The signatory has electronically affixed the digital image of his or her signature to the document; or

iii. It is electronically filed under the User ID and password of that person; or

iv. In a tax certiorari action in which the parties have stipulated to this procedure, it is an initiating document that is electronically filed without the signature of the signatory in a form provided above in NY R UNIF TRIAL CTS § 202.5-b(e)(iv), provided that, prior to filing, the document is signed in full in hard copy (which hard copy must be preserved until the conclusion of all proceedings, including appeals, in the case in which it is filed); or

v. In a small claims assessment review proceeding, it is a petition recorded by the NYSCEF site upon the filing of a text file as provided in NY R UNIF TRIAL CTS § 202.5-b(b)(1), provided that prior to filing, the document was signed in full in hard copy (which hard copy must be preserved until the conclusion of all proceedings in the matter, including article 78 (NY CPLR § 7801, et seq.) review and any appeals, and must be made available during the proceeding upon request of the respondent or the court); or

vi. It otherwise bears the electronic signature of the signatory in a format conforming to such standards and requirements as may hereafter be established by the Chief Administrator. NY R UNIF TRIAL CTS § 202.5-b(e).

4. *Confidentiality of personal information.* No person may file any document available for public inspection with any state agency, political subdivision, or in any court of this state that contains a Social Security account number of any other person, unless such other person is a dependent child, or has consented to such filing, except as required by federal or state law or regulation, or by court rule. NY GEN BUS § 399-ddd. Submissions pursuant to e-filing procedures shall have the same confidentiality rights as paper documents. NY R UNIF TRIAL CTS § 202.5-b(k)(1).

a. *Confidential personal information.* Except in the actions designated in NY R UNIF TRIAL CTS § 202.5(e)(1), or as otherwise provided by rule or law or court order, and whether or not a sealing order is or has been sought, the parties shall omit or redact confidential personal information in papers submitted to the court for filing. For purposes of NY R UNIF TRIAL CTS § 202.5(e), confidential personal information ("CPI") means:

i. The taxpayer identification number of an individual or an entity, including a Social Security number, an employer identification number, and an individual taxpayer identification number, except the last four (4) digits thereof;

ii. The date of an individual's birth, except the year thereof;

iii. The full name of an individual known to be a minor, except the minor's initials;

iv. A financial account number, including a credit and/or debit card number, a bank account number, an investment account number, and/or an insurance account number, except the last four (4) digits or letters thereof; and

v. Any of the documents or testimony in a matrimonial action protected by NY DOM REL § 235 or evidence sealed by the court in such an action which are attached as exhibits or referenced in the papers filed in any other civil action. For purposes of NY R UNIF TRIAL CTS § 202.5, a matrimonial action shall mean: an action to annul a marriage or declare the nullity of a void marriage, an action or agreement for a separation, an action for a divorce, or an action or proceeding for custody, visitation, writ of habeus corpus, child support, maintenance or paternity. NY R UNIF TRIAL CTS § 202.5(e)(1).

b. *Submission of confidential personal information.* Where a person submitting a paper to a court for filing believes in good faith that the inclusion of the full confidential personal information described in NY R UNIF TRIAL CTS § 202.5(e)(1) is material and necessary to the adjudication of the action or proceeding before the court, he or she may apply to the court for leave to serve and file together with a paper in which such information has been set forth in abbreviated form a confidential affidavit or affirmation setting forth the same information in unabbreviated form, appropriately referenced to the page or pages of the paper at which the abbreviated form appears. NY R UNIF TRIAL CTS § 202.5(e)(3).

c. *Home addresses.* For information on when home addresses and other personal information must be redacted, refer to NY CPLR Rule 2103-a.

5. *Defective papers.* A defect in the form of a paper, if a substantial right of a party is not prejudiced, shall be disregarded by the court, and leave to correct shall be freely given. NY CPLR Rule 2101(f). Papers that are stapled or bound securely shall not be rejected for filing simply because they are not bound with a backer of any kind. NY R UNIF TRIAL CTS § 202.5(a). A paper filed in accordance with the rules of the chief administrator or any local rule or practice established by the court shall be deemed filed. NY CPLR Rule 2102(b).

a. *Objection to defective papers.* The party on whom a paper is served shall be deemed to have waived objection to any defect in form unless, within fifteen (15) days after the receipt thereof, the party on whom the paper is served returns the paper to the party serving it with a statement of particular objections. NY CPLR Rule 2101(f).

F. Filing and Service Requirements

1. *Filing requirements.* Except where otherwise prescribed by law or order of court, papers required to be filed shall be filed with the clerk of the court in which the action is triable. In an action or proceeding in supreme or court, papers required to be filed shall be filed with the clerk of the county in which the proceeding is brought. NY CPLR Rule 2102(a).

a. *Electronic filing.* On consent, documents may be filed and served by electronic means in Supreme Court in such civil actions and in such counties as shall be authorized by order of the Chief Administrator of the Courts and only to the extent and in the manner provided in NY R UNIF TRIAL CTS § 202.5-b. NY R UNIF TRIAL CTS § 202.5-b(a)(1). For the definitions of terms used in electronic filing, refer to NY R UNIF TRIAL CTS § 202.5-b(a)(2).

i. *Electronic filing of discovery materials.* In any action subject to e-filing, parties and non-parties producing materials in response to discovery demands may enter into a stipulation, which shall be e-filed, authorizing the electronic filing of discovery responses and discovery materials to the degree and upon terms and conditions set forth in the stipulation. In the absence of such a stipulation, no party shall file electronically any such materials except in the form of excerpts, quotations, or selected exhibits from such materials as part of motion papers, pleadings or other filings with the court. NY R UNIF TRIAL CTS § 202.5-b(j).

ii. *E-filing mandatory.* In any action subject to e-filing, all documents required to be filed with the court by an e-filing party shall be filed and served electronically, except as provided in NY R UNIF TRIAL CTS § 202.5-b. NY R UNIF TRIAL CTS § 202.5-b(d)(1)(i).

iii. *Who may file.* Documents may be filed or served electronically only by a person who has registered as an authorized e-filing user or as otherwise provided in NY R UNIF TRIAL CTS § 202.5-b(c). NY R UNIF TRIAL CTS § 202.5-b(c)(1).

iv. *When filing made.* Documents may be transmitted at any time of the day or night to the NYSCEF site. A document other than an order or judgment is filed when its electronic transmission or, in the case of a petition that is e-filed by submission of a text file as provided in NY R UNIF TRIAL CTS § 202.5-b(b)(1), the electronic transmission of the text file is recorded at that site, provided, however, that where payment of a fee is required upon the filing of a document, the document is not filed until transmission of the document and the information or form or information as required in NY R UNIF TRIAL CTS § 202.5-b(d)(2)(i), NY R UNIF TRIAL CTS § 202.5-b(d)(2)(ii) or NY R UNIF TRIAL CTS § 202.5-b(d)(2)(iii) has been recorded at the NYSCEF site; or, if no transmission of that information or form or information is recorded, where permitted by the County Clerk, until payment is presented to the County Clerk. NY R UNIF TRIAL CTS § 202.5-b(d)(3)(i).

v. *Notification of filing.* No later than the close of business on the business day following the electronic filing of a document, a notification, in a form prescribed by the Chief Administrator, shall be transmitted electronically by the NYSCEF site to the person filing such document and the e-mail service addresses of all other participating parties in such action. NY R UNIF TRIAL CTS § 202.5-b(d)(3)(ii).

vi. *Removal of confidential information and other corrections.* If a document filed electronically is subsequently discovered to contain confidential data—including but not limited to trade secrets, information protected by confidentiality agreement, or personal confidential information as defined by statute or court rule—or otherwise to have been filed in error, the filer or another party or affected person may (1) notify the parties and any non-party filers in the action of the confidentiality issue or other error raised by the filing, and of his or her intention to seek judicial relief to correct the filing: (2) following such notification, request that the appropriate County Clerk, exercising his or her administrative discretion, place the document temporarily in "restricted" status on the NYSCEF site, to be made available for viewing by court staff and the parties but not the general public; and (3) file an application to correct the filing by order to show cause within five (5) business days of such notification (or such time as the court may direct), including a request for preliminary injunctive relief limiting interim disclosure of the document at issue. Unless otherwise directed by the court, any document placed in restricted status in response to such a request shall be returned to public view upon expiration of this five (5) day period. The Chief Administrator of the Courts shall promulgate forms to implement this process. NY R UNIF TRIAL CTS § 202.5-b(d)(3)(iii).

vii. *Documents requiring judge's signature.* Except where the court directs otherwise, any document that requires a judge's signature shall be transmitted electronically and in hard copy to the court. NY R UNIF TRIAL CTS § 202.5-b(d)(6).

viii. *Documents which would be inconvenient to file electronically; Hard copies.* Notwithstanding any other provision of NY R UNIF TRIAL CTS § 202.5-b, and subject to such guidelines as may be established by the Chief Administrative Judge, the County Clerk or his or her designee may require or permit a party to file in hard copy, in accordance with procedures set by the County Clerk or designee, an exhibit or other document which it is impractical or inconvenient to file electronically. NY R UNIF TRIAL CTS § 202.5-b(d)(7).

ix. *Documents containing sensitive or proprietary information.* In an action subject to e-filing, any person may apply for an order prohibiting or restricting the electronic filing in the action of specifically identified materials on the grounds that such materials are subject to copyright or other proprietary rights, or trade secret or other privacy interests, and that electronic filing in the action is likely to result in substantial prejudice to those rights or interests. NY R UNIF TRIAL CTS § 202.5-b(k)(2).

x. *Refusal to accept paper filings.* In accordance with NY CPLR Rule 2102(c), a County Clerk and a chief clerk of the Supreme Court or County Court, as appropriate, shall refuse to accept for filing papers filed in actions and proceedings when the paper sought to be filed:

- Is in an action subject to electronic filing pursuant to Rules of the Chief Administrator,
- Is not being filed electronically, and
- Does not include the notice required by NY R UNIF TRIAL CTS § 202.5-b(d)(1). NY R UNIF TRIAL CTS § 202.5(d)(1)(v); NY R UNIF TRIAL CTS § 202.5-bb(d).

xi. *Emergency filings; Hard copies.* For information on when an emergency filing may be filed and served in hard copy, refer to NY R UNIF TRIAL CTS § 202.5-b(d)(1)(ii), NY R UNIF TRIAL CTS § 202.5-b(d)(1)(iii) and NY R UNIF TRIAL CTS § 202.5-bb(c)(3).

xii. *Technical failures.* The NYSCEF site shall be considered to be subject to a technical failure on a given day if the site is unable to accept filings or provide access to filed documents continuously or intermittently over the course of any period of time greater than one (1) hour after 12:00 noon of that day. Notice of all such technical failures shall be provided on the site. NY R UNIF TRIAL CTS § 202.5-b(i).

- When e-filing is hindered by a technical failure, a party may file with the appropriate clerk and serve in hard copy. NY R UNIF TRIAL CTS § 202.5-b(i). In the event an attorney or party shall file and serve documents in hard copy pursuant to NY R UNIF TRIAL CTS § 202.5-b(i), each such document shall include the notice required by NY R UNIF TRIAL CTS § 202.5-b(d)(1), and the filer shall file those documents with the NYSCEF site within three (3) business days after restoration of normal operations at that site. NY R UNIF TRIAL CTS § 202.5-b(i).
- With the exception of deadlines that by law cannot be extended, the time for filing of any document that is delayed due to technical failure of the site shall be extended for one (1) day for each day on which such failure occurs, unless otherwise ordered by the court. NY R UNIF TRIAL CTS § 202.5-b(i).

xiii. *Filing fees.* For information on what information must be provided to pay filing fees, refer to NY R UNIF TRIAL CTS § 202.5-b(d)(2).

xiv. *Exemption from e-filing.* For information on exemptions from e-filing, refer to NY R UNIF TRIAL CTS § 202.5-bb(e).

b. *Facsimile filing.* In the Supreme Court, facsimile filing shall be limited to commercial claims and tax certiorari, conservatorship, and mental hygiene proceedings in Monroe, Westchester, New York and Suffolk Counties. NY R UNIF TRIAL CTS § 202.5-a(a)(1). Refer to NY R UNIF TRIAL CTS § 202.5-a for information on the procedures for facsimile filing.

2. *Service requirements*

a. *Who may serve.* Except where otherwise prescribed by law or order of court, papers may be served by any person not a party of the age of eighteen years or over. NY CPLR Rule 2103(a).

b. *Service upon attorney.* Except where otherwise prescribed by law or order of court, papers to be served upon a party in a pending action shall be served upon the party's attorney. Where the same attorney appears for two or more parties, only one (1) copy need be served upon the attorney. Such service upon an attorney shall be made:

i. By delivering the paper to the attorney personally. NY CPLR Rule 2103(b)(1).

ii. By mailing the paper to the attorney at the address designated by that attorney for that purpose or, if none is designated, at the attorney's last known address; service by mail shall be complete upon mailing. NY CPLR Rule 2103(b)(2).

iii. If the attorney's office is open, by leaving the paper with a person in charge, or if no person is in charge, by leaving it in a conspicuous place; or if the attorney's office is not open, by depositing the paper, enclosed in a sealed wrapper directed to the attorney, in the attorney's office letter drop or box. NY CPLR Rule 2103(b)(3).

iv. By leaving it at the attorney's residence within the state with a person of suitable age and discretion. Service upon an attorney shall not be made at the attorney's residence unless service at the attorney's office cannot be made. NY CPLR Rule 2103(b)(4).

v. By transmitting the paper to the attorney by facsimile transmission, provided that a facsimile telephone number is designated by the attorney for that purpose. Service by facsimile transmission shall be complete upon the receipt by the sender of a signal from the equipment of the attorney served indicating that the transmission was received, and the mailing of a copy of the paper to that attorney. The designation of a facsimile telephone number in the address block subscribed on a paper served or filed in the course of an action or proceeding shall constitute consent to service by facsimile transmission in accordance with NY CPLR Rule 2103(b)(5). An attorney may change or rescind a facsimile telephone number by serving a notice on the other parties. NY CPLR Rule 2103(b)(5).

vi. By dispatching the paper to the attorney by overnight delivery service at the address designated by the attorney for that purpose or, if none is designated, at the attorney's last known address. Service by overnight delivery service shall be complete upon deposit of the paper enclosed in a properly addressed wrapper into the custody of the overnight delivery service for overnight delivery, prior to the latest time designated by the overnight delivery service for overnight delivery. "Overnight delivery service" means any delivery service which regularly accepts items for overnight delivery to any address in the state. NY CPLR Rule 2103(b)(6).

vii. By transmitting the paper to the attorney by electronic means where and in the manner authorized by the chief administrator of the courts by rule and, unless such rule shall otherwise provide, such transmission shall be upon the party's written consent. The subject matter heading for each paper sent by electronic means must indicate that the matter being transmitted electronically is related to a court proceeding. NY CPLR Rule 2103(b)(7).

c. *Electronic service mandatory; Consenting to electronic service; How electronic service may be made.* Except as otherwise provided in NY R UNIF TRIAL CTS § 202.5-bb, filing and service of all documents in an action that has been commenced electronically in accordance with NY R UNIF TRIAL CTS § 202.5-bb shall be by electronic means. NY R UNIF TRIAL CTS § 202.5-bb(c)(1).

i. *Party's consent required for certain e-filing.* After commencement of an action wherein e-filing is authorized, documents may be electronically filed and served, but only by, and electronic service shall be made only upon, a party or parties who have consented thereto. NY R UNIF TRIAL CTS § 202.5-b(b)(2)(i).

- A consent to e-filing in an action shall state that the party providing it agrees to the use of e-filing in the action and to be bound by the filing and service provisions in NY R UNIF TRIAL CTS § 202.5-b. NY R UNIF TRIAL CTS § 202.5-b(b)(2)(ii).

ii. *Address for service; Duty to notify as to changes.* The e-mail service address recorded at the time of registration

is the e-mail address at which service of interlocutory documents on that party may be made through notification transmitted by the NYSCEF site. It is the responsibility of each filing user to monitor that address and promptly notify the Resource Center in the event of a change in his or her e-mail service address. NY R UNIF TRIAL CTS § 202.5-b(f)(2)(i).

iii. *How service made.* An e-filing party causes service of an interlocutory document to be made upon another party participating in e-filing by filing the document electronically. Upon receipt of an interlocutory document, the NYSCEF site shall automatically transmit electronic notification to all e-mail service addresses in such action. NY R UNIF TRIAL CTS § 202.5-b(f)(2)(ii).

- Except as provided otherwise in NY R UNIF TRIAL CTS § 202.5-b(h)(3), the electronic transmission of the notification shall constitute service of the document on the e-mail service addresses identified therein; however, such service will not be effective if the filing party learns that the notification did not reach the address of the person to be served. Proof of such service will be recorded on the NYSCEF site. A party may, however, utilize other service methods permitted by the CPLR provided that, if one of such other methods is used, proof of that service shall be filed electronically. NY R UNIF TRIAL CTS § 202.5-b(f)(2)(ii).

iv. *Signatures on hard copies; Proof of service filed electronically.* When an e-filing party serves a document in hard copy on a non-participating party, the document served shall bear full signatures of all signatories and proof of such service shall be filed electronically. NY R UNIF TRIAL CTS § 202.5-b(b)(2)(i).

v. *Effect of failure to consent.* A party's failure to consent to participation in electronic filing and service shall not bar any other party to the action from filing documents electronically with the County Clerk and the court or serving documents upon any other party who has consented to participation. A party who has not consented to participation shall file documents with the court and the County Clerk, and serve and be served with documents, in hard copy. NY R UNIF TRIAL CTS § 202.5-b(b)(2)(i).

d. *Service upon party.* If a party has not appeared by an attorney or the party's attorney cannot be served, service shall be upon the party by a method specified in NY CPLR Rule 2103(b)(1), NY CPLR Rule 2103(b)(2), NY CPLR Rule 2103(b)(4), NY CPLR Rule 2103(b)(5) or NY CPLR Rule 2103(b)(6). NY CPLR Rule 2103(c).

i. When a party is in default for failure to appear, he shall not be entitled to notice or service of any copy required under NY CPLR § 3101, et seq. NY CPLR Rule 3105.

e. *Service on all parties.* Each paper served on any party shall be served on every other party who has appeared, except as otherwise may be provided by court order or as provided in NY CPLR § 3012 or in NY CPLR § 3215(f). Upon demand by a party, the plaintiff shall supply that party with a list of those who have appeared and the names and addresses of their attorneys. NY CPLR Rule 2103(e).

f. *Service by filing.* If a paper cannot be served by any of the methods specified in NY CPLR Rule 2103(b) and NY CPLR Rule 2103(c), service may be made by filing the paper as if it were a paper required to be filed. NY CPLR Rule 2103(d).

g. *Definitions.* For the purposes of NY CPLR Rule 2103:

i. "Mailing" means the deposit of a paper enclosed in a first class postpaid wrapper, addressed to the address designated by a person for that purpose or, if none is designated, at that person's last known address, in a post office or official depository under the exclusive care and custody of the United States Postal Service within the state;

ii. "Electronic means" means any method of transmission of information between computers or other machines designed for the purpose of sending and receiving such transmissions, and which allows the recipient to reproduce the information transmitted in a tangible medium of expression;

iii. "Facsimile transmission" means any method of transmission of documents to a facsimile machine at a remote location which can automatically produce a tangible copy of such documents. NY CPLR Rule 2103(f).

G. Hearings

1. There is no hearing required or contemplated in the New York rules governing the request for production of documents.

H. Forms

1. New York Request for Production of Documents Forms

a. Notice for discovery and inspection. MCF CPLR § 6:148.

b. Notice of demand for production of documents for discovery and inspection. MCF CPLR § 6:149.

I. Applicable Rules

1. *State rules*
   a. Short title; Application; Construction; Definitions. NY CPLR § 101; NY CPLR § 104; NY CPLR § 105.
   b. Appendix of official forms. NY CPLR § 107.
   c. Extensions of time generally. NY CPLR § 2004.
   d. Form of papers. NY CPLR Rule 2101; NY CPLR Rule 2102; NY CPLR § 2105; NY GEN BUS § 399-ddd; NY R UNIF TRIAL CTS § 215.2; NY R UNIF TRIAL CTS § 215.3.
   e. Service of papers. NY CPLR Rule 2103.
   f. Computation of time. NY CPLR § 2402; NY GEN CONSTR § 19; NY GEN CONSTR § 20; NY GEN CONSTR § 25-a; NY GEN CONSTR § 30; NY GEN CONSTR § 31; NY GEN CONSTR § 53.
   g. Scope of disclosure. NY CPLR § 3101; NY CPLR § 3102; NY CPLR § 3103; NY CPLR § 3104; NY CPLR Rule 3105; NY CPLR Rule 3122.
   h. Discovery and production of documents and things for inspection, testing, copying or photographing. NY CPLR Rule 3120.
   i. Motions staying disclosure. NY CPLR Rule 3214; NY CPLR Rule 3407.
   j. Index number fees of county clerks. NY CPLR § 8018.
   k. Hours of court. NY R CHIEF J § 3.1.
   l. Application of part; Waiver; Additional rules; Application of CPLR; Definitions. NY R UNIF TRIAL CTS § 202.1.
   m. Papers filed in court; Electronic filing in supreme court. NY R UNIF TRIAL CTS § 202.5; NY R UNIF TRIAL CTS § 202.5-a; NY R UNIF TRIAL CTS § 202.5-b; NY R UNIF TRIAL CTS § 202.5-bb.
   n. Rules of the commercial division of the Supreme Court. NY R UNIF TRIAL CTS § 202.70.
   o. Signing of papers. NY R CHIEF ADMIN § 130-1.1-a.
2. *Local rules*
   a. *Albany County*
      i. Third judicial district rules. NY R 3 JD SUP Doc. 1.
   b. *Bronx County*
      i. Commercial division. NY R BRONX FIL R Doc. 12.
   c. *Kings County*
      i. Expedited discovery. NY R L KINGS Pt. B, Rule 5.
      ii. Pre calendar procedures. NY R L KINGS Rule I.
      iii. Both pre and post note procedures. NY R L KINGS Rule IV.
   d. *New York County*
      i. RJIs and assignments. NY R NY CTY Procedure IA.
      ii. Discovery schedule. NY R NY CTY J RUL Rule 8.

J. Miscellaneous

NOTE: Individual judges' rules may apply.

ALBANY COUNTY

JUSTICE LISA M. FISHER: NY R 3 JD FISHER Fisher; NY R 3 JD FISHER Fisher, PC Order.

JUSTICE RICHARD MOTT: NY R 3 JD MOTT Mott.

JUSTICE STEPHAN G. SCHICK: NY R 3 JD Schick.

FORECLOSURE SETTLEMENT PART: NY R 3 JD Foreclosure Settlement.

BRONX COUNTY

JUSTICE PAUL L. ALPERT: [NY R BRONX J Part IA-29, as amended by NY ORDER 20-0337].

JUSTICE BEN BARBATO: NY R BRONX J Part IA-21.

JUSTICE MARY ANNE BRIGANTTI: [NY R BRONX J Part IA-15, as amended by NY ORDER 20-0338].

JUSTICE JOSEPH E. CAPELLA: NY R BRONX J Part IA-23.

JUSTICE MITCHELL DANZIGER: NY R BRONX J Part IA-3/33 ; [NY R BRONX J Danziger, Part IA-3/33, as amended by NY ORDER 20-0339].

JUSTICE LAURA G. DOUGLAS: NY R BRONX J Part IA-11.

JUSTICE RUBEN FRANCO: NY R BRONX J Part IA-26.

JUSTICE DORIS M. GONZALEZ: NY R BRONX J Part IA-24.

JUSTICE WILMA GUZMAN: NY R BRONX J Part IA-7; [NY R BRONX J Guzman, Part IA-7 Virtual, as amended by NY ORDER 20-0340].

JUSTICE ROBERT T. JOHNSON: NY R BRONX J Part IA-12.

JUSTICE DONALD A. MILES: NY R BRONX J Part IA-8.

JUSTICE DONNA M. MILLS: NY R BRONX J Part IA-9.

JUSTICE JULIA I. RODRIGUEZ: NY R BRONX J Part IA-18; [NY R BRONX J Part IA-27, as amended by NY ORDER 20-0341].

JUSTICE LLINET M. ROSADO: [NY R BRONX J Part IA-25, as amended by NY ORDER 20-0342].

JUSTICE NORMA RUIZ: NY R BRONX J Part IA-22; [NY R BRONX J Ruiz, Part IA-22 Virtual, as amended by NY ORDER 20-0343].

JUSTICE HOWARD H. SHERMAN: NY R BRONX J Part IA-4.

JUSTICE FERNANDO TAPIA: NY R BRONX J Part IA-13.

JUSTICE ELIZABETH A. TAYLOR: NY R BRONX J Part IA-2.

JUSTICE ALISON Y. TRUITT: NY R BRONX J Part IA-5.

PART IDV: NY R BRONX J Doc. 1.

PRE-TRIAL PART RULES: NY R BRONX J Doc. 2.

PRE TRIAL WORKSHEET: NY R BRONX J Doc. 3.

FORECLOSURE SETTLEMENT PART RULES: NY R BRONX J Doc. 4.

GUARDIANSHIP PART RULES: NY R BRONX J Doc. 5.

LPM PART RULES: NY R BRONX J Doc. 6.

ERIE COUNTY

JUSTICE M. WILLIAM BOLLER: NY R 8 JD J Boller.

JUSTICE RALPH A. BONIELLO: NY R 8 JD J Boniello.

JUSTICE CHRISTOPHER J. BURN: NY R 8 JD J Burns.

JUSTICE RUSSELL P. BUSCAGLIA: NY R 8 JD J Buscaglia.

JUSTICE FRANK CARUSO: NY R 8 JD J Caruso.

JUSTICE STEPHEN W. CASS: NY R 8 JD J Cass.

JUSTICE DEBORAH A. CHIMES: NY R 8 JD J Chimes.

JUSTICE EMILIO COLAIACOVO: [NY R 8 JD J Colaiacovo, as amended by NY ORDER 20-0252].

JUSTICE DIANE Y. DEVLIN: NY R 8 JD J Devlin.

JUSTICE JAMES H. DILLON: NY R 8 JD J Dillon.

JUSTICE PAULA L. FEROLETO: NY R 8 JD J Feroleto.

JUSTICE DANIEL J. FURLONG: [NY R 8 JD J Furlong, as amended by NY ORDER 20-0253].

JUSTICE JOSEPH R. GLOWNIA: NY R 8 JD J Glownia.

JUSTICE MARK J. GRISANTI: NY R 8 JD J Grisanti.

JUSTICE DEBORAH A. HAENDIGES: NY R 8 JD J Haendiges.
JUSTICE LYNN W. KEANE: [NY R 8 JD J Keane, as amended by NY ORDER 20-0254].
JUSTICE RICHARD C. KLOCH, Sr.: NY R 8 JD J Kloch.
JUSTICE FREDERICK J. MARSHALL: [NY R 8 JD J Marshall, as amended by NY ORDER 20-0255.
JUSTICE JOHN L. MICHALSKI: NY R 8 JD J Michalski.
JUSTICE MARK A. MONTOUR: [NY R 8 JD J Montour, as amended by NY ORDER 20-0256].
JUSTICE HENRY NOWAK: NY R 8 JD J Nowak.
JUSTICE JOHN F. O'DONNELL: NY R 8 JD J O'Donnell.
JUSTICE JEANETTE OGDEN: NY R 8 JD J Ogden.
JUSTICE CATHERINE NUGENT-PANEPINTO: NY R 8 JD J Nugent-Panepinto.
JUSTICE FRANK A. SEDITA, III: [NY R 8 JD J Sedita, as amended by NY ORDER 20-0257].
JUSTICE SARA SHELDON: NY R 8 JD J Sheldon.
JUSTICE DONNA M. SIWEK: NY R 8 JD J Siwek.
JUSTICE MARY L. SLISZ: NY R 8 JD J Slisz.
JUSTICE TIMOTHY J. WALKER: [NY R 8 JD J Walker, as amended by NY ORDER 20-0258].
JUSTICE DENNIS E. WARD: NY R 8 JD J Ward.
JUSTICE PAUL B. WOJTASZEK: [NY R 8 JD J Wojtaszek, as amended by NY ORDER 20-0259].
JUSTICE CHARLES N. ZAMBITO: [NY R 8 JD J Zambito, as amended by NY ORDER 20-0260].
SUPREME COURT LEGAL STAFF: NY R 8 JD J Legal Staff.

KINGS COUNTY

JUSTICE RACHEL A. ADAMS: NY R KINGS J Part 5F.
JUSTICE LOREN BAILY-SCHIFFMAN: NY R KINGS J Part 65.
JUSTICE REGINALD A. BODDIE: NY R KINGS J Part 95.
JUSTICE THERESA M. CICCOTTO: NY R KINGS J Part 19; NY R KINGS J Part 5J.
JUSTICE LISSETTE COLON: NY R KINGS J Part Rules.
JUSTICE GENINE EDWARDS: NY R KINGS J Part 80.
JUSTICE PAMELA L. FISHER: [NY R KINGS J Part 94, as amended by NY ORDER 20-0208].
JUSTICE ROBIN GARSON: NY R KINGS J Part 75.
JUSTICE LARA J. GENOVISI: [NY R KINGS J Part 34, as amended by NY ORDER 20-0209].
JUSTICE BERNARD J. GRAHAM: NY R KINGS J Part 36.
JUSTICE DAWN JIMENEZ-SALTA: NY R KINGS J Part 88.
JUSTICE INGRID JOSEPH: [NY R KINGS J Part FRP3 and Part 83, as amended by NY ORDER 20-0210].
JUSTICE KATHY J. KING: NY R KINGS J Part 64, 76K.
JUSTICE LAWRENCE KNIPEL: NY R KINGS J Part 57.
JUSTICE DONALD KURTZ: NY R KINGS J Part 26.
JUSTICE CARL LANDICINO: [NY R KINGS J Part 81, as amended by NY ORDER 20-0211].
JUSTICE KATHERINE LEVINE: [NY R KINGS J Part 20, 25, 92, as amended by NY ORDER 20-0211].
JUSTICE LORNA MCALLISTER: [NY R KINGS J Part 10, as amended by NY ORDER 20-0211].
JUSTICE ROSEMARIE MONTALBANO: [NY R KINGS J Part 19, 71, and 22, as amended by NY ORDER 20-0211].
JUSTICE RICHARD J. MONTELIONE: [NY R KINGS J Part 99 and DJMP, as amended by NY ORDER 20-0215].
JUSTICE LISA S. OTTLEY: NY R KINGS J Part 24.
JUSTICE MARK I. PARTNOW: NY R KINGS J Part 43.

JUSTICE ERIC I. PRUS: NY R KINGS J Part 5A.
JUSTICE FRANCOIS RIVERA: NY R KINGS J Part 52.
JUSTICE KAREN B. ROTHENBERG: NY R KINGS J Part 35.
JUSTICE LEON RUCHELSMAN: NY R KINGS J Part 1.
JUSTICE WAYNE P. SAITTA: NY R KINGS J Part 29.
JUSTICE ROBIN K. SHEARES: NY R KINGS J Part 96.
JUSTICE KENNETH P. SHERMAN: NY R KINGS J Part 67 and 78.
JUSTICE DEBRA SILBER: NY R KINGS J Part 9 and 5K.
JUSTICE ELLEN M. SPODEK: NY R KINGS J Part 63.
JUSTICE MARSHA L. STEINHARDT: NY R KINGS J Part 15.
JUSTICE JEFFREY S. SUNSHINE: NY R KINGS J Part 5G.
JUSTICE PETER P. SWEENEY: [NY R KINGS J Part 35, as amended by NY ORDER 20-0218].
JUSTICE DELORES J. THOMAS: [NY R KINGS J Part 5T, as amended by NY ORDER 20-0221].
JUSTICE WAVNY TOUSSAINT: NY R KINGS J Part 70.
JUSTICE RICHARD VELASQUEZ: NY R KINGS J Part 66.
JUSTICE CAROLYN E. WADE: NY R KINGS J Part 84.
JUSTICE EDWARD G. WALKER: [NY R KINGS J Part 90, as amended by NY ORDER 20-0219].
JUSTICE LILLIAN WAN: [NY R KINGS J Part 17, as amended by NY ORDER 20-0220].
JUSTICE MICHELLE WESTON: NY R KINGS J Part 3.
MENTAL HYGIENE PART: NY R KINGS J Part 77.
MATRIMONIAL PARTS DURING COVID-19 EMERGENCY: JUSTICE KAREN B. ROTHENBERG: NY R KINGS J Doc. 1.

NASSAU COUNTY

JUSTICE ANNA R. ANZALONE: NY R NASSAU S J Anzalone, Part 26.
JUSTICE STACY D. BENNETT: NY R NASSAU S J Bennett; NY R NASSAU S J Bennett, Form 1.
JUSTICE ANTONIO BRANDVEEN: NY R NASSAU S J Brandveen, Part 31.
JUSTICE JEFFREY S. BROWN: [NY R NASSAU S J Brown, as amended by NY ORDER 20-0297].
JUSTICE STEPHEN A. BUCARIA: NY R NASSAU S J Bucaria.
JUSTICE JULIANNE T. CAPETOLA: NY R NASSAU S J Capetola, Part 28.
JUSTICE EDMUND M. DANE: NY R NASSAU S J Dane, Part 33.
JUSTICE VITO M. DESTEFANO: NY R NASSAU S J DeStefano, Part 13; NY R NASSAU S J DeStefano, Form 1.
JUSTICE ARTHUR M. DIAMOND: NY R NASSAU S J Diamond, Part 7.
JUSTICE THOMAS FEINMAN: NY R NASSAU S J Feinman, Part 5.
JUSTICE JOHN M. GALASSO: NY R NASSAU S J Galasso, Part 22.
JUSTICE SHARON M.J. GIANELLI: NY R NASSAU S J Gianelli, Part 22; NY R NASSAU S J Gianelli, Form 1.
JUSTICE JEFFREY A. GOODSTEIN: NY R NASSAU S J Goodstein, Part 33; NY R NASSAU S J Goodstein, Form 1.
JUSTICE DAVID J. GUGERTY: [NY R NASSAU S J Gugerty, Part 31, as amended by NY ORDER 20-0298].
JUSTICE HELENE F. GUGERTY: NY R NASSAU S J Gugerty, Part 47.
JUSTICE STEVEN M. JAEGER: NY R NASSAU S J Jaeger, Part 35; NY R NASSAU S J Jaeger, Form 1.
JUSTICE JACK L. LIBERT: NY R NASSAU S J Libert, Part 23.
JUSTICE JOSEPH H. LORINTZ: NY R NASSAU S J Lorintz, Part 26; NY R NASSAU S J Lorintz, Form 1.
JUSTICE ROY S. MAHON: NY R NASSAU S J Mahon, Part 3.
JUSTICE RANDY SUE MARBER: NY R NASSAU S J Marber, Part 8.

JUSTICE JAMES P. MCCORMACK: [NY R NASSAU S J McCormack, Part 18, as amended by NY ORDER, 20-0299].

JUSTICE DICCIA T. PINEDA-KIRWAN: [NY R NASSAU S J Pineda-Kirwan, as amended by NY ORDER 20-0300].

JUSTICE THOMAS RADEMAKER: [NY R NASSAU S J Rademaker, Part 28, as amended by NY ORDER 20-0301]; [NY R NASSAU S J Rademaker, Form 1, as amended by NY ORDER 20-0301].

JUSTICE DENISE L. SHER: NY R NASSAU S J Rademaker, Part 32.

JUSTICE LEONARD D. STEINMAN: [NY R NASSAU S J Steinman, Part 15, as amended by NY ORDER 20-0303]; NY R NASSAU S J Steinman, Form 1.

JUSTICE HOWARD E. STURIM: NY R NASSAU S J Sturim, Part 50; NY R NASSAU S J Sturim, Form 1.

JUSTICE HELEN VOUTSINAS: [NY R NASSAU S J Voutsinas, Part 25, as amended by NY ORDER 20-0304]; [NY R NASSAU S J Voutsinas, Form 1, as amended by NY ORDER 20-0305].

JUSTICE HOPE SCHWARTZ ZIMMERMAN: NY R NASSAU S J Zimmerman, Part 17.

NEW YORK COUNTY

JUDGE'S RULES; BASIC INFORMATION: [NY R NY CTY J RUL Doc. 1, as amended by NY ORDER 20-0202].

ONONDAGA COUNTY

JUSTICE ROBERT E. ANTONACCI II: [NY R ONDGA E FIL Doc. 1, as amended by 20-0239].

JUSTICE MICHAEL V. COCCOMI: NY R ONDGA E FIL Doc. 2.

JUSTICE GREGORY R. GILBERT: NY R 5 JD JUDGES Gilbert; NY R ONDGA E FIL Doc. 3.

JUSTICE DONALD A. GREENWOOD: NY R ONDGA E FIL Doc. 4.

JUSTICE DEBORAH H. KARALUNAS: NY R ONDGA E FIL Doc. 5.

JUSTICE JAMES MCCLUSKY: NY R 5 JD MCCLUSKY McClusky.

JUSTICE CHARLES C. MERRELL: NY R 5 JD MERRELL Merrell.

JUSTICE PATRICK F. MACRAE: NY R 5 JD MACRAE Doc. 1.

JUSTICE JAMES P. MURPHY: NY R ONDGA E FIL Doc. 7.

JUSTICE GERALD J. NERI: [NY R 5 JD JUDGES Neri, as amended by NY ORDER 20-0236]; [NY R ONDGA E FIL Doc. 8, as amended by NY ORDER 20-0241].

JUSTICE ANTHONY J. PARIS: NY R 5 JD JUDGES Paris; [NY R ONDGA E FIL Doc. 9, as amended by NY ORDER 20-0242].

JUSTICE NORMAN W. SEITER, JR.: NY R 5 JD JUDGES Seiter.

JUSTICE KEVIN G. YOUNG: [NY R ONDGA E FIL Doc. 10, as amended by NY ORDER 20-0243].

QUEENS COUNTY

JUSTICE PAM JACKMAN BROWN: [NY R L QUEENS Brown, Part 19, as amended by NY ORDER 20-0321].

JUSTICE CHEREE A. BUGGS: NY R L QUEENS Buggs, Part 30.

JUSTICE PAM JACKMAN BROWN: [NY R L QUEENS Brown, Part 19, as amended by NY ORDER 20-0321].

JUSTICE DENIS J. BUTLER: NY R L QUEENS Butler, Part 12.

JUSTICE ROBERT I. CALORAS: [NY R L QUEENS Caloras, Part 36, as amended by NY ORDER 20-0322].

JUSTICE ANNA CULLEY: NY R L QUEENS Culley, Part 53.

JUSTICE TIMOTHY DUFFICY: NY R L QUEENS Dufficy, Part 35.

JUSTICE DAVID ELLIOT: NY R L QUEENS Elliot, Part 14.

JUSTICE JOSEPH J. ESPOSITO: NY R L QUEENS Esposito, Part 6.

JUSTICE DARRELL L. GAVRIN: [NY R L QUEENS Gavrin, Part 27, as amended by NY ORDER 20-0323].

JUSTICE WYATT N. GIBBONS: [NY R L QUEENS Gibbons, Part 5, as amended by NY ORDER 20-0330.

JUSTICE DONNA-MARIE E. GOLIA: [NY R L QUEENS Golia, Part 21, as amended by NY ORDER 20-0331].

JUSTICE MARGUERITE A. GRAYS: [NY R L QUEENS Grays, Part 4, as amended by NY ORDER 20-0324].

JUSTICE RUDOLPH E. GRECO: [NY R L QUEENS Greco, Part 32, as amended by NY ORDER 20-0325].

JUSTICE MAUREEN HEALY: NY R L QUEENS Healy, Part 6.

JUSTICE PHILLIP HOM: [NY R L QUEENS Hom, Part 43, as amended by NY ORDER 20-0332].

JUSTICE KEVIN J. KERRIGAN: NY R L QUEENS Kerrigan, Part 10.

JUSTICE MOJGAN C. LANCMAN: NY R L QUEENS Lancman, Part 20.

JUSTICE RICHARD G. LATIN: NY R L QUEENS Latin, Part 40.

JUSTICE ULYSSES B. LEVERETT: [NY R L QUEENS Leverett, Part 6, as amended by NY ORDER 20-0326].

JUSTICE LEONARD LIVOTE: NY R L QUEENS Livote, Part 33.

JUSTICE LEE A. MAYERSOHN: NY R L QUEENS Mayersohn, Part 22; NY R L QUEENS Mayersohn, Part 22G; [NY R L QUEENS Mayersohn, Part 22G COVID, as amended by NY ORDER 20-0327].

JUSTICE ROBERT J. MCDONALD: NY R L QUEENS McDonald, Part 34.

JUSTICE MARGARET MCGOWAN: NY R L QUEENS McGowan, Part 52.

JUSTICE MAURICE E. MUIR: [NY R L QUEENS Muir, Part 42, as amended by NY ORDER 20-0333].

JUSTICE JODI ORLOW: NY R L QUEENS Orlow, Part 51.

JUSTICE LESLIE J. PURIFICCION: NY R L QUEENS Purificcion, Part 39.

JUSTICE JOSEPH RISI: [NY R L QUEENS Risi, Part 3, as amended by NY ORDER 20-0328].

JUSTICE FREDERICK D.R. SAMPSON: [NY R L QUEENS Sampson, Part 31, as amended by NY ORDER 20-0329].

JUSTICE MARTIN J. SCHULMAN: NY R L QUEENS Schulman, Part 29.

JUSTICE BERNICE D. SIEGAL: NY R L QUEENS Siegal, Part 25G.

JUSTICE JANICE A. TAYLOR: NY R L QUEENS Taylor, Part 15.

JUSTICE CARMEN R. VELASQUEZ: NY R L QUEENS Velasquez, Part 38.

JUSTICE LOURDES M VENTURA: [NY R L QUEENS Ventura, Part 37, as amended by NY ORDER 20-0334].

JUSTICE WILLIAM A. VISCOVICH: NY R L QUEENS Viscovich, Part 63.

JUSTICE ALLAN B. WEISS: NY R L QUEENS Weiss, Part 2.

COMPLIANCE, SETTLEMENT AND CONFERENCE PART: NY R L QUEENS Doc 1.

PRELIMINARY CONFERENCE PART: [NY R L QUEENS Doc. 2, as amended by NY ORDER 20-0335].

MEDICAL MALPRACTICE CONFERENCE PART: [NY R L QUEENS Doc. 3, as amended by NY ORDER 20-0336].

TRIAL SCHEDULING PART: NY R L QUEENS Doc. 4.

SUMMARY JURY TRIAL PROGRAM: NY R L QUEENS Doc. 7.

RESIDENTIAL FORECLOSURE PART: NY R L QUEENS Doc. 9.

FORECLOSURE AUCTION RULES: NY R L QUEENS Doc. 10.

MATRIMONIAL PRELIMINARY CONFERENCE PART: NY R L QUEENS Doc. 11.

NON-CUSTODIAL CONTESTED MATRIMONIAL PART: NY R L QUEENS Doc. 12.

Requests, Notices and Applications
Response to Request for Production of Documents

Document Last Updated August 2020

A. Checklist

(I) ❑ Matters to be considered by requesting party

- (a) ❑ Required documents
  - (1) ❑ Request for production of documents
  - (2) ❑ Proof of service

- (b) ❑ Supplemental documents
  - (1) ❑ Written authorization of patient
  - (2) ❑ Working copies
- (c) ❑ Timing
  - (1) ❑ After commencement of an action, any party may serve on any other party a notice or on any other person a subpoena duces tecum

(II) ❑ Matters to be considered by responding party

- (a) ❑ Required documents
  - (1) ❑ Response to request for production of documents
  - (2) ❑ Proof of service
- (b) ❑ Supplemental documents
  - (1) ❑ Certification of business records
  - (2) ❑ Working copies
- (c) ❑ Timing
  - (1) ❑ The notice or subpoena duces tecum shall specify the time, which shall be not less than twenty (20) days after service of the notice or subpoena, of making the inspection, copy, test or photograph, or of the entry upon the land or other property
  - (2) ❑ Within twenty (20) days of service of a notice or subpoena duces tecum under NY CPLR Rule 3120, the party or person to whom the notice or subpoena duces tecum is directed, if that party or person objects to the disclosure, inspection or examination, shall serve a response which shall state with reasonable particularity the reasons for each objection

B. Timing

1. *Time to respond to request for production of documents.* After commencement of an action, any party may serve on any other party a notice or on any other person a subpoena duces tecum. NY CPLR Rule 3120(1). The notice or subpoena duces tecum shall specify the time, which shall be not less than twenty (20) days after service of the notice or subpoena, and the place and manner of making the inspection, copy, test or photograph, or of the entry upon the land or other property and, in the case of an inspection, copying, testing or photographing, shall set forth the items to be inspected, copied, tested or photographed by individual item or by category, and shall describe each item and category with reasonable particularity. NY CPLR Rule 3120(2).
   a. *Time to object.* Within twenty (20) days of service of a notice or subpoena duces tecum under NY CPLR Rule 3120. NY CPLR Rule 3122(a)(1).
2. *Motions staying disclosure.* Service of a notice of motion under NY CPLR Rule 3211, NY CPLR Rule 3212, or NY CPLR § 3213 stays disclosure until determination of the motion unless the court orders otherwise. If the motion is based solely on the defense that the summons and complaint, summons with notice, or notice of petition and petition was not properly served, disclosure shall not be stayed unless the court orders otherwise. NY CPLR Rule 3214(b).
   a. *Personal injury actions involving terminally ill patients.* Notwithstanding the provisions of NY CPLR Rule 3214(b), the service or pendency of a motion under NY CPLR Rule 3211, NY CPLR Rule 3212, or NY CPLR § 3213 shall not stay disclosure in an action where a preliminary conference order has been entered pursuant to NY CPLR Rule 3407. NY CPLR Rule 3407(b)(3).
3. *KINGS COUNTY: Discovery timing.* At [the Compliance Conference, the court will] schedule all outstanding discovery to be completed prior to date fixed for filing Note of Issue. NY R L KINGS Rule I(B).
   a. *Deadlines in orders.* Discovery scheduled in Compliance Conference orders shall be strictly adhered to and may not be extended without leave of the court. Unjustified failure to comply with the provisions of the CCP order will result in preclusion, the striking of a pleading or imposition of sanctions, as appropriate. NY R L KINGS Rule I(B)(2).
   b. *Cases with extensive discovery.* Where post Compliance Conference discovery is to be extensive, cases may be retracked from standard to complex, which will provide for three (3) additional months of post Compliance Conference discovery and extend the Note of Issue date by three (3) months. NY R L KINGS Rule I(B)(1).
   c. *Discovery not stayed.* Ordinarily the Court/JHO will not stay discovery during pendency of motions to withdraw, or during pendency of settlement, or during pendency of dispositive motions. NY R L KINGS Rule IV.

d. *Expedited discovery in certain cases.* Discovery in third party and joint actions will be expedited. NY R L KINGS Pt. B, Rule 5.

e. For more information on discovery scheduling, refer to NY R L KINGS Flow Chart.

4. *NEW YORK COUNTY: Deadlines in orders.* Strict compliance with all discovery orders is required. Unexcused or unjustified failure to comply with deadlines fixed by the court, including those set out in Preliminary Conference Orders, may result in an award of costs, conditional or otherwise, or the imposition of another penalty authorized by NY CPLR § 3126. NY R NY CTY J RUL Rule 8.

5. *Computation of time*

a. *Units of time*

i. *Day.* A calendar day includes the time from midnight to midnight. Sunday or any day of the week specifically mentioned means a calendar day. NY GEN CONSTR § 19.

ii. *Month.* In a statute, contract or public or private instrument, unless otherwise provided in such contract or instrument or by law, the term month means a calendar month and not a lunar month. NY GEN CONSTR § 31.

iii. *Year.* For information on the definition of a year, including the definitions of a half-year and quarter-year, refer to NY GEN CONSTR § 58 and NY GEN CONSTR § 50. For information on leap years, refer to NY GEN CONSTR § 57.

b. *Periods of time*

i. *Number of days.* A number of days specified as a period from a certain day within which or after or before which an act is authorized or required to be done means such number of calendar days exclusive of the calendar day from which the reckoning is made. NY GEN CONSTR § 20.

- If such period is a period of two (2) days, Saturday, Sunday or a public holiday must be excluded from the reckoning if it is an intervening day between the day from which the reckoning is made and the last day of the period. NY GEN CONSTR § 20.
- In computing any specified period of time from a specified event, the day upon which the event happens is deemed the day from which the reckoning is made. The day from which any specified period of time is reckoned shall be excluded in making the reckoning. NY GEN CONSTR § 20.

ii. *Number of months.* A number of months after or before a certain day shall be computed by counting such number of calendar months from such day, exclusive of the calendar month in which such day occurs, and shall include the day of the month in the last month so counted having the same numerical order in days of the month as the day from which the computation is made, unless there be not so many days in the last month so counted, in which case the period computed shall expire with the last day of the month so counted. NY GEN CONSTR § 30.

iii. *Publication of notice; Number of days.* The period of publication of a legal notice shall be computed by excluding the first day of publication and including the day on which the act or event of which notice is given is to take place or which completes the full period of publication. NY CPLR § 2402.

iv. *Periods ending on Saturday, Sunday or public holiday.* When any period of time, computed from a certain day, within which or after which or before which an act is authorized or required to be done, ends on a Saturday, Sunday or a public holiday, such act may be done on the next succeeding business day and if the period ends at a specified hour, such act may be done at or before the same hour of such next succeeding business day, except that where a period of time specified by contract ends on a Saturday, Sunday or a public holiday, the extension of such period is governed by NY GEN CONSTR § 25. NY GEN CONSTR § 25-a(1).

- For a list of public holidays, refer to NY GEN CONSTR § 24.

v. *Additional time after certain kinds of service*

- *Service by mail.* Where a period of time prescribed by law is measured from the service of a paper and service is by mail, five (5) days shall be added to the prescribed period. NY CPLR Rule 2103(b)(2).
- *Service by overnight delivery service.* Where a period of time prescribed by law is measured from the service of a paper and service is by overnight delivery, one (1) business day shall be added to the prescribed period. NY CPLR Rule 2103(b)(6).

vi. *Daylight saving time.* For information on New York's time zone and the effect of daylight saving time, refer to NY GEN CONSTR § 52.

c. *Hours of court.* Notwithstanding any provision of law or rule of court to the contrary, throughout the State of New

York the sessions of the Supreme Court for the disposition of business before the court shall commence not later than 9:30 a.m. and conclude not earlier than 5 p.m. Where warranted, the Chief Administrator of the Courts may authorize variances in the opening and closing hours of the courts, but, in such event, daily sessions shall total not less than six (6) hours. NY R CHIEF J § 3.1.

d. *Time limits; Extension of time.* Any act required by or in pursuance of law to be performed at or within a prescribed time, shall be performed according to the standard time. NY GEN CONSTR § 53.

   i. Except where otherwise expressly prescribed by law, the court may extend the time fixed by any statute, rule or order for doing any act, upon such terms as may be just and upon good cause shown, whether the application for extension is made before or after the expiration of the time fixed. NY CPLR § 2004. Refer to the New York KeyRules Motion for Continuance/Extension of Time document for more information.

C. General Requirements

1. *Rules governing disclosure*

   a. *Generally.* There shall be full disclosure of all matter material and necessary in the prosecution or defense of an action, regardless of the burden of proof, by:

      i. A party, or the officer, director, member, agent or employee of a party;

      ii. A person who possessed a cause of action or defense asserted in the action;

      iii. A person about to depart from the state, or without the state, or residing at a greater distance from the place of trial than one hundred miles, or so sick or infirm as to afford reasonable grounds of belief that he or she will not be able to attend the trial, or a person authorized to practice medicine, dentistry or podiatry who has provided medical, dental or podiatric care or diagnosis to the party demanding disclosure, or who has been retained by such party as an expert witness; and

      iv. Any other person, upon notice stating the circumstances or reasons such disclosure is sought or required. NY CPLR § 3101(a).

      v. The statutory phrase "material and necessary", said the Court of Appeals, must be interpreted liberally to require disclosure upon request, of any facts bearing on the controversy which will assist preparation for trial by sharpening the issues and reducing delay and prolixity. The test is one of usefulness and reason. SIEGEL-NYPRAC § 344; Allen v. Crowell-Collier Pub. Co., 21 N.Y.2d 403, 235 N.E.2d 430 (1968).

      vi. Another potential problem that the original NY CPLR § 3101(a) posed was that it spoke of "evidence" that is material and necessary, which might have been construed to permit disclosure to elicit only that which would itself qualify as "evidence" admissible at trial. It was, however, construed more broadly than that. Well-considered caselaw specifically rejected this "evidence in chief" doctrine, stating that disclosure extends as well "to all relevant information calculated to lead to relevant evidence," a standard similar to that applicable in federal court. With an amendment that took effect on January 1, 1994, changing "evidence" to "matter" in NY CPLR § 3101(a), these generous interpretations of the statute were in effect approved by the legislature. SIEGEL-NYPRAC § 344.

      vii. If a party is a corporation, each of its officers, directors, members, agents, and employees is also deemed a "party" for disclosure purposes. A party who needs relevant data or material from a nonparty corporation can seek it through NY CPLR § 3101(a)(2), NY CPLR § 3101(a)(3) or NY CPLR § 3101(a)(4), under which the corporate entity is treated as a "person." These subdivisions should also apply to any entity, corporate or otherwise, from whom disclosure is sought through its agents. A corporate employee who has the requisite knowledge and information may respond to a disclosure request on behalf of the corporation. A party who can't single out the particular person in the corporation's employ to whom a disclosure request should be properly directed can direct it to the corporation as such and leave it to the corporation to designate the appropriate person to respond. Whenever disclosure is sought from a corporation through a deposition, whether as a party or as a nonparty witness, the choice in the first instance of who will be produced in the corporate behalf is with the corporation rather than the examining party. SIEGEL-NYPRAC § 345.

      viii. NY CPLR § 3101(a)(4) permits a party to obtain disclosure from a nonparty by merely serving a subpoena on the nonparty providing notice of "the circumstances or reasons such disclosure is sought or required." SIEGEL-NYPRAC § 345.

   b. *Methods of obtaining disclosure.* Information is obtainable by one or more of the following disclosure devices: depositions upon oral questions or without the state upon written questions, interrogatories, demands for addresses, discovery and inspection of documents or property, physical and mental examinations of persons, and requests for admission. NY CPLR § 3102(a).

i. *Stipulation or notice.* Unless otherwise provided by the civil practice law and rules or by the court, disclosure shall be obtained by stipulation or on notice without leave of the court. NY CPLR § 3102(b).

ii. *Before action commenced; Court order required.* Before an action is commenced, disclosure to aid in bringing an action, to preserve information or to aid in arbitration, may be obtained, but only by court order. The court may appoint a referee to take testimony. NY CPLR § 3102(c).

iii. *During trial; Court order required.* Except as provided in NY CPLR § 5223, during and after trial, disclosure may be obtained only by order of the trial court on notice. NY CPLR § 3102(d).

iv. *Action pending in another jurisdiction.* Except as provided in NY CPLR § 3119, when under any mandate, writ or commission issued out of any court of record in any other state, territory, district or foreign jurisdiction, or whenever upon notice or agreement, it is required to take the testimony of a witness in the state, he or she may be compelled to appear and testify in the same manner and by the same process as may be employed for the purpose of taking testimony in actions pending in the state. The supreme court or a county court shall make any appropriate order in aid of taking such a deposition. NY CPLR § 3102(e).

v. *Actions to which state is a party.* In an action in which the state is properly a party, whether as plaintiff, defendant or otherwise, disclosure by the state shall be available as if the state were a private person. NY CPLR § 3102(f).

c. *Privileged matter.* Upon objection by a person entitled to assert the privilege, privileged matter shall not be obtainable. NY CPLR § 3101(b).

i. A determination of whether information is privileged is governed by the rules of evidence, which apply as they would at a trial. Whatever is privileged at the trial is privileged as well on pretrial disclosure. SIEGEL-NYPRAC § 346.

d. *Attorney's work product.* The work product of an attorney shall not be obtainable. NY CPLR § 3101(c).

i. NY CPLR § 3101(c) makes unobtainable the "work product of an attorney"—an ill-defined category whose potential for mischief has been avoided only because the judiciary has accorded it a very narrow scope. It is a category wholly distinct from the "materials . . . prepared in anticipation of litigation" of NY CPLR § 3101(d)(2). The fact that immunity is absolute under NY CPLR § 3101(c), while that of NY CPLR § 3101(d)(2) is only conditional, is the factor that requires as sharp a line as possible between the two categories. SIEGEL-NYPRAC § 347.

ii. The judiciary has cast precious little under the "work product" category of NY CPLR § 3101(c), preferring instead to fit doubtful items under the "materials . . . prepared in anticipation of litigation" banner of NY CPLR § 3101(d)(2), where the conditional immunity can be overcome and the matters ordered disclosed when stated conditions are met. SIEGEL-NYPRAC § 347.

e. *Trial preparation*

i. *Experts.* Upon request, each party shall identify each person whom the party expects to call as an expert witness at trial and shall disclose in reasonable detail the subject matter on which each expert is expected to testify, the substance of the facts and opinions on which each expert is expected to testify, the qualifications of each expert witness and a summary of the grounds for each expert's opinion. NY CPLR § 3101(d)(1)(i).

- However, where a party for good cause shown retains an expert an insufficient period of time before the commencement of trial to give appropriate notice thereof, the party shall not thereupon be precluded from introducing the expert's testimony at the trial solely on grounds of noncompliance with NY CPLR § 3101(d)(1). In that instance, upon motion of any party, made before or at trial, or on its own initiative, the court may make whatever order may be just. In an action for medical, dental or podiatric malpractice, a party, in responding to a request, may omit the names of medical, dental or podiatric experts but shall be required to disclose all other information concerning such experts otherwise required by NY CPLR § 3101(d)(1). NY CPLR § 3101(d)(1)(i).
- In an action for medical, dental or podiatric malpractice, any party may, by written offer made to and served upon all other parties and filed with the court, offer to disclose the name of, and to make available for examination upon oral deposition, any person the party making the offer expects to call as an expert witness at trial. Within twenty (20) days of service of the offer, a party shall accept or reject the offer by serving a written reply upon all parties and filing a copy thereof with the court. Failure to serve a reply within twenty (20) days of service of the offer shall be deemed a rejection of the offer. If all parties accept the offer, each

party shall be required to produce his or her expert witness for examination upon oral deposition upon receipt of a notice to take oral deposition in accordance with NY CPLR Rule 3107. If any party, having made or accepted the offer, fails to make that party's expert available for oral deposition, that party shall be precluded from offering expert testimony at the trial of the action. NY CPLR § 3101(d)(1)(ii).

- Further disclosure concerning the expected testimony of any expert may be obtained only by court order upon a showing of special circumstances and subject to restrictions as to scope and provisions concerning fees and expenses as the court may deem appropriate. However, a party, without court order, may take the testimony of a person authorized to practice medicine, dentistry or podiatry who is the party's treating or retained expert, as described in NY CPLR § 3101(a)(3), in which event any other party shall be entitled to the full disclosure authorized by Article 31 of Chapter 8 of the Civil Practice Law and Rules (NY CPLR § 3101, et seq.) with respect to that expert without court order. NY CPLR § 3101(d)(1)(iii).

ii. *Materials.* Subject to the provisions of NY CPLR § 3101(d)(1), materials otherwise discoverable under NY CPLR § 3101(a) and prepared in anticipation of litigation or for trial by or for another party, or by or for that other party's representative (including an attorney, consultant, surety, indemnitor, insurer or agent), may be obtained only upon a showing that the party seeking discovery has substantial need of the materials in the preparation of the case and is unable without undue hardship to obtain the substantial equivalent of the materials by other means. In ordering discovery of the materials when the required showing has been made, the court shall protect against disclosure of the mental impressions, conclusions, opinions or legal theories of an attorney or other representative of a party concerning the litigation. NY CPLR § 3101(d)(2).

- In order to qualify as "litigation" material the item must have been prepared exclusively for litigation. Incidental potential use in litigation, the courts have observed, may also be a function of such reports, but they have at least an equal if not greater mission "to prevent future accidents, discipline careless employees, or, generally, to increase the economy and efficiency of the operation." SIEGEL-NYPRAC § 348.

f. *Party's statement.* A party may obtain a copy of his own statement. NY CPLR § 3101(e).

i. Moreover, NY CPLR § 3101(e) has been broadly interpreted to include photographs. Items such as photographs and videotapes are now independently subject to disclosure under NY CPLR § 3101(i). SIEGEL-NYPRAC § 348.

g. *Contents of insurance agreement.* A party may obtain discovery of the existence and contents of any insurance agreement under which any person carrying on an insurance business may be liable to satisfy part or all of a judgment which may be entered in the action or to indemnify or reimburse for payments made to satisfy the judgment. Information concerning the insurance agreement is not by reason of disclosure admissible in evidence at trial. For purpose of NY CPLR § 3101(f), an application for insurance shall not be treated as part of an insurance agreement. NY CPLR § 3101(f).

h. *Accident reports.* Except as is otherwise provided by law, in addition to any other matter which may be subject to disclosure, there shall be full disclosure of any written report of an accident prepared in the regular course of business operations or practices of any person, firm, corporation, association or other public or private entity, unless prepared by a police or peace officer for a criminal investigation or prosecution and disclosure would interfere with a criminal investigation or prosecution. NY CPLR § 3101(g).

i. *Amendment or supplementation of responses.* A party shall amend or supplement a response previously given to a request for disclosure promptly upon the party's thereafter obtaining information that the response was incorrect or incomplete when made, or that the response, though correct and complete when made, no longer is correct and complete, and the circumstances are such that a failure to amend or supplement the response would be materially misleading. NY CPLR § 3101(h).

i. Where a party obtains such information an insufficient period of time before the commencement of trial appropriately to amend or supplement the response, the party shall not thereupon be precluded from introducing evidence at the trial solely on grounds of noncompliance with NY CPLR § 3101(h). In that instance, upon motion of any party, made before or at trial, or on its own initiative, the court may make whatever order may be just. Further amendment or supplementation may be obtained by court order. NY CPLR § 3101(h).

j. *Other disclosures.* In addition to any other matter which may be subject to disclosure, there shall be full disclosure of any films, photographs, video tapes or audio tapes, including transcripts or memoranda thereof, involving a person referred to in NY CPLR § 3101(a)(1). There shall be disclosure of all portions of such material, including out-takes, rather than only those portions a party intends to use. The provisions of NY CPLR § 3101(i) shall not apply to materials compiled for law enforcement purposes which are exempt from disclosure under NY PUB OFF § 87. NY CPLR § 3101(i).

i. While NY CPLR § 3101(i) was enacted with the defendant's surreptitious tapes of the plaintiff in mind, its language is broad enough to embrace any films, photographs, and audio or video tapes of a party, even those made by the party from whom disclosure is sought. SIEGEL-NYPRAC § 348.

k. *Protective orders.* The court may at any time on its own initiative, or on motion of any party or of any person from whom discovery is sought, make a protective order denying, limiting, conditioning or regulating the use of any disclosure device. NY CPLR § 3103(a). Refer to the New York KeyRules Motion for Protective Order document for more information.

l. *Supervision of disclosure.* Upon the motion of any party or witness on notice to all parties or on its own initiative without notice, the court in which an action is pending may by one of its judges or a referee supervise all or part of any disclosure procedure. NY CPLR § 3104(a).

i. *Selection of referee.* A judicial hearing officer may be designated as a referee under NY CPLR § 3104, or the court may permit all of the parties in an action to stipulate that a named attorney may act as referee. In such latter event, the stipulation shall provide for payment of his fees which shall, unless otherwise agreed, be taxed as disbursements. NY CPLR § 3104(b).

ii. *Powers of referee; Motions referred to person supervising disclosure.* A referee under NY CPLR § 3104 shall have all the powers of the court under NY CPLR § 3101, et seq. except the power to relieve himself of his duties, to appoint a successor, or to adjudge any person guilty of contempt. All motions or applications made under Article 31 of Chapter 8 of the Civil Practice Law and Rules (NY CPLR § 3101, et seq.) shall be returnable before the judge or referee, designated under NY CPLR § 3104 and after disposition, if requested by any party, his order shall be filed in the office of the clerk. NY CPLR § 3104(c).

iii. *Review of order of referee.* Any party or witness may apply for review of an order made under NY CPLR § 3104 by a referee. The application shall be by motion made in the court in which the action is pending within five (5) days after the order is made. Service of a notice of motion for review shall suspend disclosure of the particular matter in dispute. If the question raised by the motion may affect the rights of a witness, notice shall be served on him personally or by mail at his last known address. It shall set forth succinctly the order complained of, the reason it is objectionable and the relief demanded. NY CPLR § 3104(d).

iv. *Payment of expenses of referee.* Except where a judicial hearing officer has been designated a referee hereunder, the court may make an appropriate order for the payment of the reasonable expenses of the referee. NY CPLR § 3104(e).

2. *Response to request for production of documents*

a. *Contents of response.* The notice or subpoena duces tecum shall specify the time, which shall be not less than twenty (20) days after service of the notice or subpoena, and the place and manner of making the inspection, copy, test or photograph, or of the entry upon the land or other property and, in the case of an inspection, copying, testing or photographing, shall set forth the items to be inspected, copied, tested or photographed by individual item or by category, and shall describe each item and category with reasonable particularity. NY CPLR Rule 3120(2).

i. *Manner in which documents produced.* Whenever a person is required pursuant to such notice or order to produce documents for inspection, that person shall produce them as they are kept in the regular course of business or shall organize and label them to correspond to the categories in the request. NY CPLR Rule 3122(c). Thus, the option of choosing the method of production lies with the responding party regardless of whether the production is sought by individual item or category. The responding party is likely to favor producing the documents "as they are kept in the regular course of business," which may perpetuate the kind of overbroad response NY CPLR Rule 3122(c) was designed to discourage. SIEGEL-NYPRAC § 362.

- Unless the subpoena duces tecum directs the production of original documents for inspection and copying at the place where such items are usually maintained, it shall be sufficient for the custodian or other qualified person to deliver complete and accurate copies of the items to be produced. NY CPLR Rule 3122(d).
- The reasonable production expenses of a non-party witness shall be defrayed by the party seeking discovery. NY CPLR Rule 3122(d).

ii. *Medical provider served with subpoena.* A medical provider served with a subpoena duces tecum, other than a trial subpoena issued by a court, requesting the production of a patient's medical records pursuant to NY CPLR

Rule 3122 need not respond or object to the subpoena if the subpoena is not accompanied by a written authorization by the patient. NY CPLR Rule 3122(a)(2).

iii. *Documents withheld.* Whenever a person is required pursuant to such a notice, subpoena duces tecum or order to produce documents for inspection, and where such person withholds one or more documents that appear to be within the category of the documents required by the notice, subpoena duces tecum or order to be produced, such person shall give notice to the party seeking the production and inspection of the documents that one or more such documents are being withheld. This notice shall indicate the legal ground for withholding each such document, and shall provide the following information as to each such document, unless the party withholding the document states that divulgence of such information would cause disclosure of the allegedly privileged information:

- The type of document;
- The general subject matter of the document;
- The date of the document; and
- Such other information as is sufficient to identify the document for a subpoena duces tecum. NY CPLR Rule 3122(b).

b. *Time to object.* Within twenty (20) days of service of a notice or subpoena duces tecum under NY CPLR Rule 3120, the party or person to whom the notice or subpoena duces tecum is directed, if that party or person objects to the disclosure, inspection or examination, shall serve a response which shall state with reasonable particularity the reasons for each objection. If objection is made to part of an item or category, the part shall be specified. The party seeking disclosure under NY CPLR Rule 3120 may move for an order under NY CPLR Rule 3124 or NY CPLR § 2308 with respect to any objection to, or other failure to respond to or permit inspection as requested by, the notice or subpoena duces tecum, respectively, or any part thereof. NY CPLR Rule 3122(a)(1).

c. *Production of business records.* Business records produced pursuant to a subpoena duces tecum under NY CPLR Rule 3120 shall be accompanied by a certification, sworn in the form of an affidavit and subscribed by the custodian or other qualified witness charged with responsibility of maintaining the records, stating in substance each of the following:

i. The affiant is the duly authorized custodian or other qualified witness and has authority to make the certification;

ii. To the best of the affiant's knowledge, after reasonable inquiry, the records or copies thereof are accurate versions of the documents described in the subpoena duces tecum that are in the possession, custody, or control of the person receiving the subpoena;

iii. To the best of the affiant's knowledge, after reasonable inquiry, the records or copies produced represent all the documents described in the subpoena duces tecum, or if they do not represent a complete set of the documents subpoenaed, an explanation of which documents are missing and a reason for their absence is provided; and

iv. The records or copies produced were made by the personnel or staff of the business, or persons acting under their control, in the regular course of business, at the time of the act, transaction, occurrence or event recorded therein, or within a reasonable time thereafter, and that it was the regular course of business to make such records. NY CPLR Rule 3122-a(a).

v. A certification made in compliance with NY CPLR Rule 3122-a(a) is admissible as to the matters set forth therein and as to such matters shall be presumed true. When more than one person has knowledge of the facts, more than one certification may be made. NY CPLR Rule 3122-a(b).

3. *Governing law.* The civil practice law and rules (NY CPLR § 101, et seq.) shall govern the procedure in civil judicial proceedings in all courts of the state and before all judges, except where the procedure is regulated by inconsistent statute. The civil practice law and rules shall succeed the civil practice act and rules of civil practice and shall be deemed substituted therefor throughout the statutes and rules of the state. NY CPLR § 101. The civil practice law and rules shall be liberally construed to secure the just, speedy and inexpensive determination of every civil judicial proceeding. NY CPLR § 104.

a. *Uniform trial court rules.* The uniform civil rules for the Supreme Court and County Court (NY R UNIF TRIAL CTS § 202.1, et seq.) shall be applicable to civil actions and proceedings in the Supreme Court and the County Court. NY R UNIF TRIAL CTS § 202.1(a). The provisions of the uniform rules shall be construed consistent with the Civil Practice Law and Rules (CPLR), and matters not covered by the uniform rules shall be governed by the CPLR. NY R UNIF TRIAL CTS § 202.1(d).

b. *Local rules.* Local court rules, not inconsistent with law or with uniform civil rules for the Supreme Court and County

Court (NY R UNIF TRIAL CTS § 202.1, et seq.), shall comply with Part 9 of the Rules of the Chief Judge (NY R CHIEF J § 9.1). NY R UNIF TRIAL CTS § 202.1(c).

c. *Official forms.* The state administrator shall have the power to adopt, amend and rescind an appendix of forms. Forms adopted pursuant to NY CPLR § 107 shall be sufficient under the civil practice law and rules and shall illustrate the simplicity and brevity of statement which the civil practice law and rules contemplate. NY CPLR § 107.

4. *Rules of the commercial division.* [Editor's note: certain types of civil cases or civil cases meeting certain monetary thresholds that are filed in the state of New York must be filed in the Commercial Division of the New York Supreme Courts. Rules governing practice in the commercial division are found in NY R UNIF TRIAL CTS § 202.70]. Cases which must be filed in the commercial division are listed below. For more information, refer to NY R UNIF TRIAL CTS § 202.70.

a. *Monetary thresholds.* Except as set forth in NY R UNIF TRIAL CTS § 202.70(b), the monetary thresholds of the Commercial Division, exclusive of punitive damages, interests, costs, disbursements and counsel fees claimed, are established as follows: (1) Albany County, fifty thousand dollars ($50,000); (2) Eighth Judicial District, one hundred thousand dollars ($100,000); (3) Kings County, one hundred fifty thousand dollars ($150,000); (4) Nassau County, two hundred thousand dollars ($200,000); (5) New York County, five hundred thousand dollars ($500,000); (6) Onondaga County, fifty thousand dollars ($50,000); (7) Queens County, one hundred thousand dollars ($100,000); (8) Seventh Judicial District, fifty thousand dollars ($50,000); (9) Suffolk County, one hundred thousand dollars ($100,000); and (10) Westchester County, one hundred thousand dollars ($100,000). NY R UNIF TRIAL CTS § 202.70(a).

i. *ALBANY COUNTY.* The Commercial Division of the Albany County Supreme Court exercises jurisdiction over selected business and commercial disputes in which the amount at issue generally involves damage claims in a minimum amount of fifty thousand dollars ($50,000) as well as claims for unspecified amounts where the value of the commercial asset(s) in dispute exceeds fifty thousand dollars ($50,000). A separate publication promulgating the rules and criteria relating to the filing and management of Commercial Court cases in this part may be obtained from the Albany County Supreme Court Clerk's Office. A section of the Uniform Civil Rules for the Supreme Court and County Court sets forth statewide rules. NY R 3 JD SUP Doc. 1(E).

ii. *BRONX COUNTY.* The monetary threshold for commercial cases in Bronx County will be seventy-five thousand dollars ($75,000). All other parameters including the type of matters that will be heard are contained within the Rules of the Commercial Division of the Supreme Court (NY R UNIF TRIAL CTS § 202.70). NY R BRONX FIL R Doc. 12.

iii. *NEW YORK COUNTY.* The monetary threshold in the New York County Commercial Division, which is generally applicable, is an amount in controversy of five hundred thousand dollars ($500,000) or more (exclusive of punitive damages, interest, costs, disbursements, and counsel fees). If the case is designated a commercial one and the Addendum is submitted, the clerk will review the pleadings to determine whether the amount in controversy in the case meets the monetary threshold or whether an exception to the threshold applies. NY R NY CTY Procedure IA(B). For more information on assigning a case to the commercial division in New York County, refer to NY R NY CTY Procedure IA(B).

b. *Commercial cases.* Actions in which the principal claims involve or consist of the following will be heard in the Commercial Division provided that the monetary threshold is met or equitable or declaratory relief is sought:

i. Breach of contract or fiduciary duty, fraud, misrepresentation, business tort (e.g., unfair competition), or statutory and/or common law violation where the breach or violation is alleged to arise out of business dealings (e.g., sales of assets or securities; corporate restructuring; partnership, shareholder, joint venture, and other business agreements; trade secrets; restrictive covenants; and employment agreements not including claims that principally involve alleged discriminatory practices);

ii. Transactions governed by the Uniform Commercial Code (exclusive of those concerning individual cooperative or condominium units);

iii. Transactions involving commercial real property, including Yellowstone injunctions and excluding actions for the payment of rent only;

iv. Shareholder derivative actions—without consideration of the monetary threshold;

v. Commercial class actions—without consideration of the monetary threshold;

vi. Business transactions involving or arising out of dealings with commercial banks and other financial institutions;

vii. Internal affairs of business organizations;

viii. Malpractice by accountants or actuaries, and legal malpractice arising out of representation in commercial matters;

ix. Environmental insurance coverage;

x. Commercial insurance coverage (e.g., directors and officers, errors and omissions, and business interruption coverage);

xi. Dissolution of corporations, partnerships, limited liability companies, limited liability partnerships and joint ventures—without consideration of the monetary threshold; and

xii. Applications to stay or compel arbitration and affirm or disaffirm arbitration awards and related injunctive relief pursuant to Article 75 of the New York Civil Practice Law and Rules (NY CPLR § 7501, et seq.) involving any of the foregoing enumerated commercial issues. Where the applicable arbitration agreement provides for the arbitration to be heard outside the United States, the monetary threshold set forth in NY R UNIF TRIAL CTS § 202.70(a) shall not apply. NY R UNIF TRIAL CTS § 202.70(b).

c. *Non-commercial cases.* The following will not be heard in the Commercial Division even if the monetary threshold is met:

i. Suits to collect professional fees;

ii. Cases seeking a declaratory judgment as to insurance coverage for personal injury or property damage;

iii. Residential real estate disputes, including landlord-tenant matters, and commercial real estate disputes involving the payment of rent only;

iv. Home improvement contracts involving residential properties consisting of one to four residential units or individual units in any residential building, including cooperative or condominium units;

v. Proceedings to enforce a judgment regardless of the nature of the underlying case;

vi. First-party insurance claims and actions by insurers to collect premiums or rescind non-commercial policies; and

vii. Attorney malpractice actions except as otherwise provided in NY R UNIF TRIAL CTS § 202.70(b)(8). NY R UNIF TRIAL CTS § 202.70(c).

d. For more information on the Commercial Division, refer to NY R UNIF TRIAL CTS § 202.70.

D. Documents

1. *Required documents*

a. *Response to request for production of documents.* Refer to the General Requirements section of this document for information regarding the response to request for production of documents.

b. *Proof of service.* In addition to complying with the provisions of NY CPLR Rule 2101, every paper filed in court shall have annexed thereto appropriate proof of service on all parties where required. NY R UNIF TRIAL CTS § 202.5(a).

2. *Supplemental documents*

a. *Certification of business records.* Refer to the General Requirements section of this document for information on the requirement to certify business records when responding to a request for production of documents.

b. *Working copies.* The court may require the parties to provide working copies of documents filed electronically. In such event, each working copy shall include, firmly affixed thereto, a copy of a confirmation notice in a form prescribed by the Chief Administrator. NY R UNIF TRIAL CTS § 202.5-b(d)(5).

E. Format

1. *Form of documents*

a. *Size and form of paper.* Each paper served or filed shall be durable, white and, except for summonses, subpoenas, notices of appearance, notes of issue, orders of protection, temporary orders of protection and exhibits, shall be eleven by eight and one-half (11 x 8-1/2) inches in size. NY CPLR Rule 2101(a).

b. *Writing and language.* The writing shall be legible and in black ink. NY CPLR Rule 2101(a). Each paper served or filed shall be in the English language which, where practicable, shall be of ordinary usage. NY CPLR Rule 2101(b).

c. *Caption.* Each paper served or filed shall begin with a caption setting forth the name of the court, the venue, the title of the action, the nature of the paper and the index number of the action if one has been assigned. In all papers other

than a summons, a complaint or a judgment it shall be sufficient to state the name of the first named party on each side with an appropriate indication of any omissions. NY CPLR Rule 2101(c).

i. *Further contents of first page.* After the first paper has been filed in each case the index number shall appear on the cover and first page to the right of the caption of every paper tendered for filing in the action. Each such cover and first page also shall contain an indication of the county of venue and a brief description of the nature of the paper and, where the case has been assigned to an individual judge, shall contain the name of the assigned judge to the right of the caption. NY R UNIF TRIAL CTS § 202.5(a); NY R UNIF TRIAL CTS § 202.5(b); NY R UNIF TRIAL CTS § 202.5(d)(1)(i).

d. *Index number.* No paper in an action in the supreme or a county court, other than an order submitted for signature to a judge out of court, shall be submitted for any purpose to the supreme or county court or to a clerk thereof unless there is endorsed on such paper the index number of the action assigned by the clerk of the county. NY CPLR § 8018(c).

e. *Line spacing.* Every paper filed in court, if typewritten, shall have at least double space between each line, except for quotations and the names and addresses of attorneys appearing in the action. NY R UNIF TRIAL CTS § 202.5(a).

f. *Font size.* Each. . .paper printed or typed, served or filed, except for summonses. . .and exhibits, shall be in clear type of no less than ten (10) point in size. NY CPLR Rule 2101(a).

i. Whenever a requirement relating to size of type is stated in point size, the type size requirement shall be deemed met if the x-height of the type is a minimum of forty-five percent (45%) of the specified point size. Each point shall be measured as .351 millimeter. The x-height size shall be measured as it appears on the page. The x-height is the height of the lower case letters, exclusive of ascenders or descenders. NY CPLR § 105(t).

g. *Margins.* Every paper filed in court shall have at least one (1) inch margins. NY R UNIF TRIAL CTS § 202.5(a).

h. *Citations*

i. *Civil practice law and rules.* NY CPLR § 101, et seq. shall be known as the civil practice law and rules, and may be cited as "CPLR". Reference to a provision in the civil practice law and rules may, except when such provision is being enacted or amended, be made without indicating whether it is a rule or section. NY CPLR § 101.

i. *Indorsement by attorney.* Each paper served or filed shall be indorsed with the name, address and telephone number of the attorney for the party serving or filing the paper, or if the party does not appear by attorney, with the name, address and telephone number of the party. NY CPLR Rule 2101(d).

j. *One-sided printing.* In addition, every paper filed in court, other than an exhibit or printed form, shall contain writing on one side only, except that papers that are fastened on the side may contain writing on both sides. NY R UNIF TRIAL CTS § 202.5(a).

k. *Use of copies authorized.* Except where otherwise specifically prescribed, copies, rather than originals, of all papers, including orders, affidavits and exhibits may be served or filed. Where it is required that the original be served or filed and the original is lost or withheld, the court may authorize a copy to be served or filed. NY CPLR Rule 2101(e).

i. Where a certified copy of a paper is required by law, an attorney admitted to practice in the courts of the state may certify that it has been compared by him with the original and found to be a true and complete copy. Such a certificate, when subscribed by such attorney, has the same effect as if made by a clerk. NY CPLR § 2105.

l. *Recycled paper.* It is the policy of the Unified Court System that litigants, where practicable, should file or submit to the courts of the Unified Court System of the State of New York papers printed or reproduced on recycled paper. Paper is considered recycled if it contains a minimum content of thirty percent (30%) waste paper. NY R UNIF TRIAL CTS § 215.2. The signature page of every paper filed or submitted to the court on recycled paper should bear the legend: "Printed [Reproduced] on Recycled Paper." NY R UNIF TRIAL CTS § 215.3.

2. *Form of electronic documents.* Each paper served or filed by electronic means, as defined in NY CPLR Rule 2103(f), shall be capable of being reproduced by the receiver so as to comply with the provisions of NY CPLR Rule 2101(a) through NY CPLR Rule 2101(d). NY CPLR Rule 2101(g).

a. *File format.* All e-filed documents shall comply with the technical requirements set forth at the NYSCEF site. NY R UNIF TRIAL CTS § 202.5-b(d)(1)(i).

b. *Heading of document.* The subject matter heading for each paper sent by electronic means must indicate that the matter being transmitted electronically is related to a court proceeding. NY CPLR Rule 2103(b)(7).

3. *Signature blocks.* Every pleading, written motion, and other paper, served on another party or filed or submitted to the court shall be signed by an attorney, or by a party if the party is not represented by an attorney, with the name of the attorney or

party clearly printed or typed directly below the signature. NY R CHIEF ADMIN § 130-1.1-a(a); NY R UNIF TRIAL CTS § 202.5(d)(1)(iv).

a. *Printed name.* Beneath each signature shall be printed the name signed. NY CPLR Rule 2101(a).

b. *Failure to sign.* Absent good cause shown, the court shall strike any unsigned paper if the omission of the signature is not corrected promptly after being called to the attention of the attorney or party. NY R CHIEF ADMIN § 130-1.1-a(a).

c. *Signature as certification.* By signing a paper, an attorney or party certifies that, to the best of that person's knowledge, information and belief, formed after an inquiry reasonable under the circumstances the presentation of the paper or the contentions therein are not frivolous as defined in NY R CHIEF ADMIN § 130-1.1(c). NY R CHIEF ADMIN § 130-1.1-a(b)(1).

d. *Electronic signatures.* A document shall be considered to have been signed by an attorney or party in compliance with NY R CHIEF ADMIN § 130-1.1-a if it has been signed by such attorney or party as provided in NY R UNIF TRIAL CTS § 202.5-b(e)(1) and it bears the signatory's name. NY R UNIF TRIAL CTS § 202.5-b(e)(2). An electronically filed document shall be considered to have been signed by, and shall be binding upon, the person identified as a signatory, if:

i. It bears the physical signature of such person and is scanned into an electronic format that reproduces such signature; or

ii. The signatory has electronically affixed the digital image of his or her signature to the document; or

iii. It is electronically filed under the User ID and password of that person; or

iv. In a tax certiorari action in which the parties have stipulated to this procedure, it is an initiating document that is electronically filed without the signature of the signatory in a form provided above in NY R UNIF TRIAL CTS § 202.5-b(e)(iv), provided that, prior to filing, the document is signed in full in hard copy (which hard copy must be preserved until the conclusion of all proceedings, including appeals, in the case in which it is filed); or

v. In a small claims assessment review proceeding, it is a petition recorded by the NYSCEF site upon the filing of a text file as provided in NY R UNIF TRIAL CTS § 202.5-b(b)(1), provided that prior to filing, the document was signed in full in hard copy (which hard copy must be preserved until the conclusion of all proceedings in the matter, including article 78 (NY CPLR § 7801, et seq.) review and any appeals, and must be made available during the proceeding upon request of the respondent or the court); or

vi. It otherwise bears the electronic signature of the signatory in a format conforming to such standards and requirements as may hereafter be established by the Chief Administrator. NY R UNIF TRIAL CTS § 202.5-b(e).

4. *Confidentiality of personal information.* No person may file any document available for public inspection with any state agency, political subdivision, or in any court of this state that contains a Social Security account number of any other person, unless such other person is a dependent child, or has consented to such filing, except as required by federal or state law or regulation, or by court rule. NY GEN BUS § 399-ddd. Submissions pursuant to e-filing procedures shall have the same confidentiality rights as paper documents. NY R UNIF TRIAL CTS § 202.5-b(k)(1).

a. *Confidential personal information.* Except in the actions designated in NY R UNIF TRIAL CTS § 202.5(e)(1), or as otherwise provided by rule or law or court order, and whether or not a sealing order is or has been sought, the parties shall omit or redact confidential personal information in papers submitted to the court for filing. For purposes of NY R UNIF TRIAL CTS § 202.5(e), confidential personal information ("CPI") means:

i. The taxpayer identification number of an individual or an entity, including a Social Security number, an employer identification number, and an individual taxpayer identification number, except the last four (4) digits thereof;

ii. The date of an individual's birth, except the year thereof;

iii. The full name of an individual known to be a minor, except the minor's initials;

iv. A financial account number, including a credit and/or debit card number, a bank account number, an investment account number, and/or an insurance account number, except the last four (4) digits or letters thereof; and

v. Any of the documents or testimony in a matrimonial action protected by NY DOM REL § 235 or evidence sealed by the court in such an action which are attached as exhibits or referenced in the papers filed in any other civil action. For purposes of NY R UNIF TRIAL CTS § 202.5, a matrimonial action shall mean: an action to annul a marriage or declare the nullity of a void marriage, an action or agreement for a separation, an action for a divorce, or an action or proceeding for custody, visitation, writ of habeus corpus, child support, maintenance or paternity. NY R UNIF TRIAL CTS § 202.5(e)(1).

b. *Submission of confidential personal information.* Where a person submitting a paper to a court for filing believes in good faith that the inclusion of the full confidential personal information described in NY R UNIF TRIAL CTS § 202.5(e)(1) is material and necessary to the adjudication of the action or proceeding before the court, he or she may apply to the court for leave to serve and file together with a paper in which such information has been set forth in abbreviated form a confidential affidavit or affirmation setting forth the same information in unabbreviated form, appropriately referenced to the page or pages of the paper at which the abbreviated form appears. NY R UNIF TRIAL CTS § 202.5(e)(3).

c. *Home addresses.* For information on when home addresses and other personal information must be redacted, refer to NY CPLR Rule 2103-a.

5. *Defective papers.* A defect in the form of a paper, if a substantial right of a party is not prejudiced, shall be disregarded by the court, and leave to correct shall be freely given. NY CPLR Rule 2101(f). Papers that are stapled or bound securely shall not be rejected for filing simply because they are not bound with a backer of any kind. NY R UNIF TRIAL CTS § 202.5(a). A paper filed in accordance with the rules of the chief administrator or any local rule or practice established by the court shall be deemed filed. NY CPLR Rule 2102(b).

a. *Objection to defective papers.* The party on whom a paper is served shall be deemed to have waived objection to any defect in form unless, within fifteen (15) days after the receipt thereof, the party on whom the paper is served returns the paper to the party serving it with a statement of particular objections. NY CPLR Rule 2101(f).

F. Filing and Service Requirements

1. *Filing requirements.* Except where otherwise prescribed by law or order of court, papers required to be filed shall be filed with the clerk of the court in which the action is triable. In an action or proceeding in supreme or court, papers required to be filed shall be filed with the clerk of the county in which the proceeding is brought. NY CPLR Rule 2102(a).

a. *Electronic filing.* On consent, documents may be filed and served by electronic means in Supreme Court in such civil actions and in such counties as shall be authorized by order of the Chief Administrator of the Courts and only to the extent and in the manner provided in NY R UNIF TRIAL CTS § 202.5-b. NY R UNIF TRIAL CTS § 202.5-b(a)(1). For the definitions of terms used in electronic filing, refer to NY R UNIF TRIAL CTS § 202.5-b(a)(2).

i. *Electronic filing of discovery materials.* In any action subject to e-filing, parties and non-parties producing materials in response to discovery demands may enter into a stipulation, which shall be e-filed, authorizing the electronic filing of discovery responses and discovery materials to the degree and upon terms and conditions set forth in the stipulation. In the absence of such a stipulation, no party shall file electronically any such materials except in the form of excerpts, quotations, or selected exhibits from such materials as part of motion papers, pleadings or other filings with the court. NY R UNIF TRIAL CTS § 202.5-b(j).

ii. *E-filing mandatory.* In any action subject to e-filing, all documents required to be filed with the court by an e-filing party shall be filed and served electronically, except as provided in NY R UNIF TRIAL CTS § 202.5-b. NY R UNIF TRIAL CTS § 202.5-b(d)(1)(i).

iii. *Who may file.* Documents may be filed or served electronically only by a person who has registered as an authorized e-filing user or as otherwise provided in NY R UNIF TRIAL CTS § 202.5-b(c). NY R UNIF TRIAL CTS § 202.5-b(c)(1).

iv. *When filing made.* Documents may be transmitted at any time of the day or night to the NYSCEF site. A document other than an order or judgment is filed when its electronic transmission or, in the case of a petition that is e-filed by submission of a text file as provided in NY R UNIF TRIAL CTS § 202.5-b(b)(1), the electronic transmission of the text file is recorded at that site, provided, however, that where payment of a fee is required upon the filing of a document, the document is not filed until transmission of the document and the information or form or information as required in NY R UNIF TRIAL CTS § 202.5-b(d)(2)(i), NY R UNIF TRIAL CTS § 202.5-b(d)(2)(ii) or NY R UNIF TRIAL CTS § 202.5-b(d)(2)(iii) has been recorded at the NYSCEF site; or, if no transmission of that information or form or information is recorded, where permitted by the County Clerk, until payment is presented to the County Clerk. NY R UNIF TRIAL CTS § 202.5-b(d)(3)(i).

v. *Notification of filing.* No later than the close of business on the business day following the electronic filing of a document, a notification, in a form prescribed by the Chief Administrator, shall be transmitted electronically by the NYSCEF site to the person filing such document and the e-mail service addresses of all other participating parties in such action. NY R UNIF TRIAL CTS § 202.5-b(d)(3)(ii).

vi. *Removal of confidential information and other corrections.* If a document filed electronically is subsequently discovered to contain confidential data—including but not limited to trade secrets, information protected by confidentiality agreement, or personal confidential information as defined by statute or court rule—or otherwise to have been filed in error, the filer or another party or affected person may (1) notify the parties and any non-party filers in the action of the confidentiality issue or other error raised by the filing, and of his or her intention to seek judicial relief to correct the filing: (2) following such notification, request that the appropriate County Clerk, exercising his or her administrative discretion, place the document temporarily in "restricted" status on the NYSCEF site, to be made available for viewing by court staff and the parties but not the general public; and (3) file an application to correct the filing by order to show cause within five (5) business days of such notification (or such time as the court may direct), including a request for preliminary injunctive relief limiting interim disclosure of the document at issue. Unless otherwise directed by the court, any document placed in restricted status in response to such a request shall be returned to public view upon expiration of this five (5) day period. The Chief Administrator of the Courts shall promulgate forms to implement this process. NY R UNIF TRIAL CTS § 202.5-b(d)(3)(iii).

vii. *Documents requiring judge's signature.* Except where the court directs otherwise, any document that requires a judge's signature shall be transmitted electronically and in hard copy to the court. NY R UNIF TRIAL CTS § 202.5-b(d)(6).

viii. *Documents which would be inconvenient to file electronically; Hard copies.* Notwithstanding any other provision of NY R UNIF TRIAL CTS § 202.5-b, and subject to such guidelines as may be established by the Chief Administrative Judge, the County Clerk or his or her designee may require or permit a party to file in hard copy, in accordance with procedures set by the County Clerk or designee, an exhibit or other document which it is impractical or inconvenient to file electronically. NY R UNIF TRIAL CTS § 202.5-b(d)(7).

ix. *Documents containing sensitive or proprietary information.* In an action subject to e-filing, any person may apply for an order prohibiting or restricting the electronic filing in the action of specifically identified materials on the grounds that such materials are subject to copyright or other proprietary rights, or trade secret or other privacy interests, and that electronic filing in the action is likely to result in substantial prejudice to those rights or interests. NY R UNIF TRIAL CTS § 202.5-b(k)(2).

x. *Refusal to accept paper filings.* In accordance with NY CPLR Rule 2102(c), a County Clerk and a chief clerk of the Supreme Court or County Court, as appropriate, shall refuse to accept for filing papers filed in actions and proceedings when the paper sought to be filed:

- Is in an action subject to electronic filing pursuant to Rules of the Chief Administrator,
- Is not being filed electronically, and
- Does not include the notice required by NY R UNIF TRIAL CTS § 202.5-b(d)(1). NY R UNIF TRIAL CTS § 202.5(d)(1)(v); NY R UNIF TRIAL CTS § 202.5-bb(d).

xi. *Emergency filings; Hard copies.* For information on when an emergency filing may be filed and served in hard copy, refer to NY R UNIF TRIAL CTS § 202.5-b(d)(1)(ii), NY R UNIF TRIAL CTS § 202.5-b(d)(1)(iii) and NY R UNIF TRIAL CTS § 202.5-bb(c)(3).

xii. *Technical failures.* The NYSCEF site shall be considered to be subject to a technical failure on a given day if the site is unable to accept filings or provide access to filed documents continuously or intermittently over the course of any period of time greater than one (1) hour after 12:00 noon of that day. Notice of all such technical failures shall be provided on the site. NY R UNIF TRIAL CTS § 202.5-b(i).

- When e-filing is hindered by a technical failure, a party may file with the appropriate clerk and serve in hard copy. NY R UNIF TRIAL CTS § 202.5-b(i). In the event an attorney or party shall file and serve documents in hard copy pursuant to NY R UNIF TRIAL CTS § 202.5-b(i), each such document shall include the notice required by NY R UNIF TRIAL CTS § 202.5-b(d)(1), and the filer shall file those documents with the NYSCEF site within three (3) business days after restoration of normal operations at that site. NY R UNIF TRIAL CTS § 202.5-b(i).
- With the exception of deadlines that by law cannot be extended, the time for filing of any document that is delayed due to technical failure of the site shall be extended for one (1) day for each day on which such failure occurs, unless otherwise ordered by the court. NY R UNIF TRIAL CTS § 202.5-b(i).

xiii. *Filing fees.* For information on what information must be provided to pay filing fees, refer to NY R UNIF TRIAL CTS § 202.5-b(d)(2).

xiv. *Exemption from e-filing.* For information on exemptions from e-filing, refer to NY R UNIF TRIAL CTS § 202.5-bb(e).

b. *Facsimile filing.* In the Supreme Court, facsimile filing shall be limited to commercial claims and tax certiorari, conservatorship, and mental hygiene proceedings in Monroe, Westchester, New York and Suffolk Counties. NY R UNIF TRIAL CTS § 202.5-a(a)(1). Refer to NY R UNIF TRIAL CTS § 202.5-a for information on the procedures for facsimile filing.

2. *Service requirements*

a. *Who may serve.* Except where otherwise prescribed by law or order of court, papers may be served by any person not a party of the age of eighteen years or over. NY CPLR Rule 2103(a).

b. *Service upon attorney.* Except where otherwise prescribed by law or order of court, papers to be served upon a party in a pending action shall be served upon the party's attorney. Where the same attorney appears for two or more parties, only one (1) copy need be served upon the attorney. Such service upon an attorney shall be made:

i. By delivering the paper to the attorney personally. NY CPLR Rule 2103(b)(1).

ii. By mailing the paper to the attorney at the address designated by that attorney for that purpose or, if none is designated, at the attorney's last known address; service by mail shall be complete upon mailing. NY CPLR Rule 2103(b)(2).

iii. If the attorney's office is open, by leaving the paper with a person in charge, or if no person is in charge, by leaving it in a conspicuous place; or if the attorney's office is not open, by depositing the paper, enclosed in a sealed wrapper directed to the attorney, in the attorney's office letter drop or box. NY CPLR Rule 2103(b)(3).

iv. By leaving it at the attorney's residence within the state with a person of suitable age and discretion. Service upon an attorney shall not be made at the attorney's residence unless service at the attorney's office cannot be made. NY CPLR Rule 2103(b)(4).

v. By transmitting the paper to the attorney by facsimile transmission, provided that a facsimile telephone number is designated by the attorney for that purpose. Service by facsimile transmission shall be complete upon the receipt by the sender of a signal from the equipment of the attorney served indicating that the transmission was received, and the mailing of a copy of the paper to that attorney. The designation of a facsimile telephone number in the address block subscribed on a paper served or filed in the course of an action or proceeding shall constitute consent to service by facsimile transmission in accordance with NY CPLR Rule 2103(b)(5). An attorney may change or rescind a facsimile telephone number by serving a notice on the other parties. NY CPLR Rule 2103(b)(5).

vi. By dispatching the paper to the attorney by overnight delivery service at the address designated by the attorney for that purpose or, if none is designated, at the attorney's last known address. Service by overnight delivery service shall be complete upon deposit of the paper enclosed in a properly addressed wrapper into the custody of the overnight delivery service for overnight delivery, prior to the latest time designated by the overnight delivery service for overnight delivery. "Overnight delivery service" means any delivery service which regularly accepts items for overnight delivery to any address in the state. NY CPLR Rule 2103(b)(6).

vii. By transmitting the paper to the attorney by electronic means where and in the manner authorized by the chief administrator of the courts by rule and, unless such rule shall otherwise provide, such transmission shall be upon the party's written consent. The subject matter heading for each paper sent by electronic means must indicate that the matter being transmitted electronically is related to a court proceeding. NY CPLR Rule 2103(b)(7).

c. *Electronic service mandatory; Consenting to electronic service; How electronic service may be made.* Except as otherwise provided in NY R UNIF TRIAL CTS § 202.5-bb, filing and service of all documents in an action that has been commenced electronically in accordance with NY R UNIF TRIAL CTS § 202.5-bb shall be by electronic means. NY R UNIF TRIAL CTS § 202.5-bb(c)(1).

i. *Party's consent required for certain e-filing.* After commencement of an action wherein e-filing is authorized, documents may be electronically filed and served, but only by, and electronic service shall be made only upon, a party or parties who have consented thereto. NY R UNIF TRIAL CTS § 202.5-b(b)(2)(i).

- A consent to e-filing in an action shall state that the party providing it agrees to the use of e-filing in the action and to be bound by the filing and service provisions in NY R UNIF TRIAL CTS § 202.5-b. NY R UNIF TRIAL CTS § 202.5-b(b)(2)(ii).

ii. *Address for service; Duty to notify as to changes.* The e-mail service address recorded at the time of registration

is the e-mail address at which service of interlocutory documents on that party may be made through notification transmitted by the NYSCEF site. It is the responsibility of each filing user to monitor that address and promptly notify the Resource Center in the event of a change in his or her e-mail service address. NY R UNIF TRIAL CTS § 202.5-b(f)(2)(i).

iii. *How service made.* An e-filing party causes service of an interlocutory document to be made upon another party participating in e-filing by filing the document electronically. Upon receipt of an interlocutory document, the NYSCEF site shall automatically transmit electronic notification to all e-mail service addresses in such action. NY R UNIF TRIAL CTS § 202.5-b(f)(2)(ii).

- Except as provided otherwise in NY R UNIF TRIAL CTS § 202.5-b(h)(3), the electronic transmission of the notification shall constitute service of the document on the e-mail service addresses identified therein; however, such service will not be effective if the filing party learns that the notification did not reach the address of the person to be served. Proof of such service will be recorded on the NYSCEF site. A party may, however, utilize other service methods permitted by the CPLR provided that, if one of such other methods is used, proof of that service shall be filed electronically. NY R UNIF TRIAL CTS § 202.5-b(f)(2)(ii).

iv. *Signatures on hard copies; Proof of service filed electronically.* When an e-filing party serves a document in hard copy on a non-participating party, the document served shall bear full signatures of all signatories and proof of such service shall be filed electronically. NY R UNIF TRIAL CTS § 202.5-b(b)(2)(i).

v. *Effect of failure to consent.* A party's failure to consent to participation in electronic filing and service shall not bar any other party to the action from filing documents electronically with the County Clerk and the court or serving documents upon any other party who has consented to participation. A party who has not consented to participation shall file documents with the court and the County Clerk, and serve and be served with documents, in hard copy. NY R UNIF TRIAL CTS § 202.5-b(b)(2)(i).

d. *Service upon party.* If a party has not appeared by an attorney or the party's attorney cannot be served, service shall be upon the party by a method specified in NY CPLR Rule 2103(b)(1), NY CPLR Rule 2103(b)(2), NY CPLR Rule 2103(b)(4), NY CPLR Rule 2103(b)(5) or NY CPLR Rule 2103(b)(6). NY CPLR Rule 2103(c).

i. When a party is in default for failure to appear, he shall not be entitled to notice or service of any copy required under NY CPLR § 3101, et seq. NY CPLR Rule 3105.

e. *Service on all parties.* Each paper served on any party shall be served on every other party who has appeared, except as otherwise may be provided by court order or as provided in NY CPLR § 3012 or in NY CPLR § 3215(f). Upon demand by a party, the plaintiff shall supply that party with a list of those who have appeared and the names and addresses of their attorneys. NY CPLR Rule 2103(e).

f. *Service by filing.* If a paper cannot be served by any of the methods specified in NY CPLR Rule 2103(b) and NY CPLR Rule 2103(c), service may be made by filing the paper as if it were a paper required to be filed. NY CPLR Rule 2103(d).

g. *Definitions.* For the purposes of NY CPLR Rule 2103:

i. "Mailing" means the deposit of a paper enclosed in a first class postpaid wrapper, addressed to the address designated by a person for that purpose or, if none is designated, at that person's last known address, in a post office or official depository under the exclusive care and custody of the United States Postal Service within the state;

ii. "Electronic means" means any method of transmission of information between computers or other machines designed for the purpose of sending and receiving such transmissions, and which allows the recipient to reproduce the information transmitted in a tangible medium of expression;

iii. "Facsimile transmission" means any method of transmission of documents to a facsimile machine at a remote location which can automatically produce a tangible copy of such documents. NY CPLR Rule 2103(f).

G. Hearings

1. There is no hearing required or contemplated in the New York rules governing the response to request for production of documents.

H. Forms

1. New York Response to Request for Production of Documents Forms

a. Notice for discovery and inspection. MCF CPLR § 6:148.

b. Notice of demand for production of documents for discovery and inspection. MCF CPLR § 6:149.

I. Applicable Rules

1. *State rules*
   a. Short title; Application; Construction; Definitions. NY CPLR § 101; NY CPLR § 104; NY CPLR § 105.
   b. Appendix of official forms. NY CPLR § 107.
   c. Extensions of time generally. NY CPLR § 2004.
   d. Form of papers. NY CPLR Rule 2101; NY CPLR Rule 2102; NY CPLR § 2105; NY GEN BUS § 399-ddd; NY R UNIF TRIAL CTS § 215.2; NY R UNIF TRIAL CTS § 215.3.
   e. Service of papers. NY CPLR Rule 2103.
   f. Computation of time. NY CPLR § 2402; NY GEN CONSTR § 19; NY GEN CONSTR § 20; NY GEN CONSTR § 25-a; NY GEN CONSTR § 30; NY GEN CONSTR § 31; NY GEN CONSTR § 53.
   g. Scope of disclosure. NY CPLR § 3101; NY CPLR § 3102; NY CPLR § 3103; NY CPLR § 3104; NY CPLR Rule 3105.
   h. Discovery and production of documents and things for inspection, testing, copying or photographing. NY CPLR Rule 3120.
   i. Objection to disclosure, inspection or examination; Compliance. NY CPLR Rule 3122.
   j. Certification of business records. NY CPLR Rule 3122-a.
   k. Motions staying disclosure. NY CPLR Rule 3214; NY CPLR Rule 3407.
   l. Index number fees of county clerks. NY CPLR § 8018.
   m. Hours of court. NY R CHIEF J § 3.1.
   n. Application of part; Waiver; Additional rules; Application of CPLR; Definitions. NY R UNIF TRIAL CTS § 202.1.
   o. Papers filed in court; Electronic filing in supreme court. NY R UNIF TRIAL CTS § 202.5; NY R UNIF TRIAL CTS § 202.5-a; NY R UNIF TRIAL CTS § 202.5-b; NY R UNIF TRIAL CTS § 202.5-bb.
   p. Rules of the commercial division of the Supreme Court. NY R UNIF TRIAL CTS § 202.70.
   q. Signing of papers. NY R CHIEF ADMIN § 130-1.1-a.
2. *Local rules*
   a. *Albany County*
      i. Third judicial district rules. NY R 3 JD SUP Doc. 1.
   b. *Bronx County*
      i. Commercial division. NY R BRONX FIL R Doc. 12.
   c. *Kings County*
      i. Expedited discovery. NY R L KINGS Pt. B, Rule 5.
      ii. Pre calendar procedures. NY R L KINGS Rule I.
      iii. Both pre and post note procedures. NY R L KINGS Rule IV.
   d. *New York County*
      i. RJIs and assignments. NY R NY CTY Procedure IA.
      ii. Discovery schedule. NY R NY CTY J RUL Rule 8.

J. Miscellaneous

NOTE: Individual judges' rules may apply.

ALBANY COUNTY

JUSTICE LISA M. FISHER: NY R 3 JD FISHER Fisher; NY R 3 JD FISHER Fisher, PC Order.

JUSTICE RICHARD MOTT: NY R 3 JD MOTT Mott.

JUSTICE STEPHAN G. SCHICK: NY R 3 JD Schick.

FORECLOSURE SETTLEMENT PART: NY R 3 JD Foreclosure Settlement.

BRONX COUNTY

JUSTICE PAUL L. ALPERT: [NY R BRONX J Part IA-29, as amended by NY ORDER 20-0337].

JUSTICE BEN BARBATO: NY R BRONX J Part IA-21.

JUSTICE MARY ANNE BRIGANTTI: [NY R BRONX J Part IA-15, as amended by NY ORDER 20-0338].

JUSTICE JOSEPH E. CAPELLA: NY R BRONX J Part IA-23.

JUSTICE MITCHELL DANZIGER: NY R BRONX J Part IA-3/33 ; [NY R BRONX J Danziger, Part IA-3/33, as amended by NY ORDER 20-0339].

JUSTICE LAURA G. DOUGLAS: NY R BRONX J Part IA-11.

JUSTICE RUBEN FRANCO: NY R BRONX J Part IA-26.

JUSTICE DORIS M. GONZALEZ: NY R BRONX J Part IA-24.

JUSTICE WILMA GUZMAN: NY R BRONX J Part IA-7; [NY R BRONX J Guzman, Part IA-7 Virtual, as amended by NY ORDER 20-0340].

JUSTICE ROBERT T. JOHNSON: NY R BRONX J Part IA-12.

JUSTICE DONALD A. MILES: NY R BRONX J Part IA-8.

JUSTICE DONNA M. MILLS: NY R BRONX J Part IA-9.

JUSTICE JULIA I. RODRIGUEZ: NY R BRONX J Part IA-18; [NY R BRONX J Part IA-27, as amended by NY ORDER 20-0341].

JUSTICE LLINET M. ROSADO: [NY R BRONX J Part IA-25, as amended by NY ORDER 20-0342].

JUSTICE NORMA RUIZ: NY R BRONX J Part IA-22; [NY R BRONX J Ruiz, Part IA-22 Virtual, as amended by NY ORDER 20-0343].

JUSTICE HOWARD H. SHERMAN: NY R BRONX J Part IA-4.

JUSTICE FERNANDO TAPIA: NY R BRONX J Part IA-13.

JUSTICE ELIZABETH A. TAYLOR: NY R BRONX J Part IA-2.

JUSTICE ALISON Y. TRUITT: NY R BRONX J Part IA-5.

PART IDV: NY R BRONX J Doc. 1.

PRE-TRIAL PART RULES: NY R BRONX J Doc. 2.

PRE TRIAL WORKSHEET: NY R BRONX J Doc. 3.

FORECLOSURE SETTLEMENT PART RULES: NY R BRONX J Doc. 4.

GUARDIANSHIP PART RULES: NY R BRONX J Doc. 5.

LPM PART RULES: NY R BRONX J Doc. 6.

ERIE COUNTY

JUSTICE M. WILLIAM BOLLER: NY R 8 JD J Boller.

JUSTICE RALPH A. BONIELLO: NY R 8 JD J Boniello.

JUSTICE CHRISTOPHER J. BURN: NY R 8 JD J Burns.

JUSTICE RUSSELL P. BUSCAGLIA: NY R 8 JD J Buscaglia.

JUSTICE FRANK CARUSO: NY R 8 JD J Caruso.

JUSTICE STEPHEN W. CASS: NY R 8 JD J Cass.

JUSTICE DEBORAH A. CHIMES: NY R 8 JD J Chimes.

JUSTICE EMILIO COLAIACOVO: [NY R 8 JD J Colaiacovo, as amended by NY ORDER 20-0252].

JUSTICE DIANE Y. DEVLIN: NY R 8 JD J Devlin.

JUSTICE JAMES H. DILLON: NY R 8 JD J Dillon.

JUSTICE PAULA L. FEROLETO: NY R 8 JD J Feroleto.

JUSTICE DANIEL J. FURLONG: [NY R 8 JD J Furlong, as amended by NY ORDER 20-0253].
JUSTICE JOSEPH R. GLOWNIA: NY R 8 JD J Glownia.
JUSTICE MARK J. GRISANTI: NY R 8 JD J Grisanti.
JUSTICE DEBORAH A. HAENDIGES: NY R 8 JD J Haendiges.
JUSTICE LYNN W. KEANE: [NY R 8 JD J Keane, as amended by NY ORDER 20-0254].
JUSTICE RICHARD C. KLOCH, Sr.: NY R 8 JD J Kloch.
JUSTICE FREDERICK J. MARSHALL: [NY R 8 JD J Marshall, as amended by NY ORDER 20-0255.
JUSTICE JOHN L. MICHALSKI: NY R 8 JD J Michalski.
JUSTICE MARK A. MONTOUR: [NY R 8 JD J Montour, as amended by NY ORDER 20-0256].
JUSTICE HENRY NOWAK: NY R 8 JD J Nowak.
JUSTICE JOHN F. O'DONNELL: NY R 8 JD J O'Donnell.
JUSTICE JEANETTE OGDEN: NY R 8 JD J Ogden.
JUSTICE CATHERINE NUGENT-PANEPINTO: NY R 8 JD J Nugent-Panepinto.
JUSTICE FRANK A. SEDITA, III: [NY R 8 JD J Sedita, as amended by NY ORDER 20-0257].
JUSTICE SARA SHELDON: NY R 8 JD J Sheldon.
JUSTICE DONNA M. SIWEK: NY R 8 JD J Siwek.
JUSTICE MARY L. SLISZ: NY R 8 JD J Slisz.
JUSTICE TIMOTHY J. WALKER: [NY R 8 JD J Walker, as amended by NY ORDER 20-0258].
JUSTICE DENNIS E. WARD: NY R 8 JD J Ward.
JUSTICE PAUL B. WOJTASZEK: [NY R 8 JD J Wojtaszek, as amended by NY ORDER 20-0259].
JUSTICE CHARLES N. ZAMBITO: [NY R 8 JD J Zambito, as amended by NY ORDER 20-0260].
SUPREME COURT LEGAL STAFF: NY R 8 JD J Legal Staff.

KINGS COUNTY

JUSTICE RACHEL A. ADAMS: NY R KINGS J Part 5F.
JUSTICE LOREN BAILY-SCHIFFMAN: NY R KINGS J Part 65.
JUSTICE REGINALD A. BODDIE: NY R KINGS J Part 95.
JUSTICE THERESA M. CICCOTTO: NY R KINGS J Part 19; NY R KINGS J Part 5J.
JUSTICE LISSETTE COLON: NY R KINGS J Part Rules.
JUSTICE GENINE EDWARDS: NY R KINGS J Part 80.
JUSTICE PAMELA L. FISHER: [NY R KINGS J Part 94, as amended by NY ORDER 20-0208].
JUSTICE ROBIN GARSON: NY R KINGS J Part 75.
JUSTICE LARA J. GENOVISI: [NY R KINGS J Part 34, as amended by NY ORDER 20-0209].
JUSTICE BERNARD J. GRAHAM: NY R KINGS J Part 36.
JUSTICE DAWN JIMENEZ-SALTA: NY R KINGS J Part 88.
JUSTICE INGRID JOSEPH: [NY R KINGS J Part FRP3 and Part 83, as amended by NY ORDER 20-0210].
JUSTICE KATHY J. KING: NY R KINGS J Part 64, 76K.
JUSTICE LAWRENCE KNIPEL: NY R KINGS J Part 57.
JUSTICE DONALD KURTZ: NY R KINGS J Part 26.
JUSTICE CARL LANDICINO: [NY R KINGS J Part 81, as amended by NY ORDER 20-0211].
JUSTICE KATHERINE LEVINE: [NY R KINGS J Part 20, 25, 92, as amended by NY ORDER 20-0211].
JUSTICE LORNA MCALLISTER: [NY R KINGS J Part 10, as amended by NY ORDER 20-0211].
JUSTICE ROSEMARIE MONTALBANO: [NY R KINGS J Part 19, 71, and 22, as amended by NY ORDER 20-0211].

JUSTICE RICHARD J. MONTELIONE: [NY R KINGS J Part 99 and DJMP, as amended by NY ORDER 20-0215].
JUSTICE LISA S. OTTLEY: NY R KINGS J Part 24.
JUSTICE MARK I. PARTNOW: NY R KINGS J Part 43.
JUSTICE ERIC I. PRUS: NY R KINGS J Part 5A.
JUSTICE FRANCOIS RIVERA: NY R KINGS J Part 52.
JUSTICE KAREN B. ROTHENBERG: NY R KINGS J Part 35.
JUSTICE LEON RUCHELSMAN: NY R KINGS J Part 1.
JUSTICE WAYNE P. SAITTA: NY R KINGS J Part 29.
JUSTICE ROBIN K. SHEARES: NY R KINGS J Part 96.
JUSTICE KENNETH P. SHERMAN: NY R KINGS J Part 67 and 78.
JUSTICE DEBRA SILBER: NY R KINGS J Part 9 and 5K.
JUSTICE ELLEN M. SPODEK: NY R KINGS J Part 63.
JUSTICE MARSHA L. STEINHARDT: NY R KINGS J Part 15.
JUSTICE JEFFREY S. SUNSHINE: NY R KINGS J Part 5G.
JUSTICE PETER P. SWEENEY: [NY R KINGS J Part 35, as amended by NY ORDER 20-0218].
JUSTICE DELORES J. THOMAS: [NY R KINGS J Part 5T, as amended by NY ORDER 20-0221].
JUSTICE WAVNY TOUSSAINT: NY R KINGS J Part 70.
JUSTICE RICHARD VELASQUEZ: NY R KINGS J Part 66.
JUSTICE CAROLYN E. WADE: NY R KINGS J Part 84.
JUSTICE EDWARD G. WALKER: [NY R KINGS J Part 90, as amended by NY ORDER 20-0219].
JUSTICE LILLIAN WAN: [NY R KINGS J Part 17, as amended by NY ORDER 20-0220].
JUSTICE MICHELLE WESTON: NY R KINGS J Part 3.
MENTAL HYGIENE PART: NY R KINGS J Part 77.
MATRIMONIAL PARTS DURING COVID-19 EMERGENCY: JUSTICE KAREN B. ROTHENBERG: NY R KINGS J Doc. 1.

NASSAU COUNTY

JUSTICE ANNA R. ANZALONE: NY R NASSAU S J Anzalone, Part 26.
JUSTICE STACY D. BENNETT: NY R NASSAU S J Bennett; NY R NASSAU S J Bennett, Form 1.
JUSTICE ANTONIO BRANDVEEN: NY R NASSAU S J Brandveen, Part 31.
JUSTICE JEFFREY S. BROWN: [NY R NASSAU S J Brown, as amended by NY ORDER 20-0297].
JUSTICE STEPHEN A. BUCARIA: NY R NASSAU S J Bucaria.
JUSTICE JULIANNE T. CAPETOLA: NY R NASSAU S J Capetola, Part 28.
JUSTICE EDMUND M. DANE: NY R NASSAU S J Dane, Part 33.
JUSTICE VITO M. DESTEFANO: NY R NASSAU S J DeStefano, Part 13; NY R NASSAU S J DeStefano, Form 1.
JUSTICE ARTHUR M. DIAMOND: NY R NASSAU S J Diamond, Part 7.
JUSTICE THOMAS FEINMAN: NY R NASSAU S J Feinman, Part 5.
JUSTICE JOHN M. GALASSO: NY R NASSAU S J Galasso, Part 22.
JUSTICE SHARON M.J. GIANELLI: NY R NASSAU S J Gianelli, Part 22; NY R NASSAU S J Gianelli, Form 1.
JUSTICE JEFFREY A. GOODSTEIN: NY R NASSAU S J Goodstein, Part 33; NY R NASSAU S J Goodstein, Form 1.
JUSTICE DAVID J. GUGERTY: [NY R NASSAU S J Gugerty, Part 31, as amended by NY ORDER 20-0298].
JUSTICE HELENE F. GUGERTY: NY R NASSAU S J Gugerty, Part 47.
JUSTICE STEVEN M. JAEGER: NY R NASSAU S J Jaeger, Part 35; NY R NASSAU S J Jaeger, Form 1.
JUSTICE JACK L. LIBERT: NY R NASSAU S J Libert, Part 23.

JUSTICE JOSEPH H. LORINTZ: NY R NASSAU S J Lorintz, Part 26; NY R NASSAU S J Lorintz, Form 1.

JUSTICE ROY S. MAHON: NY R NASSAU S J Mahon, Part 3.

JUSTICE RANDY SUE MARBER: NY R NASSAU S J Marber, Part 8.

JUSTICE JAMES P. MCCORMACK: [NY R NASSAU S J McCormack, Part 18, as amended by NY ORDER, 20-0299].

JUSTICE DICCIA T. PINEDA-KIRWAN: [NY R NASSAU S J Pineda-Kirwan, as amended by NY ORDER 20-0300].

JUSTICE THOMAS RADEMAKER: [NY R NASSAU S J Rademaker, Part 28, as amended by NY ORDER 20-0301]; [NY R NASSAU S J Rademaker, Form 1, as amended by NY ORDER 20-0301].

JUSTICE DENISE L. SHER: NY R NASSAU S J Rademaker, Part 32.

JUSTICE LEONARD D. STEINMAN: [NY R NASSAU S J Steinman, Part 15, as amended by NY ORDER 20-0303]; NY R NASSAU S J Steinman, Form 1.

JUSTICE HOWARD E. STURIM: NY R NASSAU S J Sturim, Part 50; NY R NASSAU S J Sturim, Form 1.

JUSTICE HELEN VOUTSINAS: [NY R NASSAU S J Voutsinas, Part 25, as amended by NY ORDER 20-0304]; [NY R NASSAU S J Voutsinas, Form 1, as amended by NY ORDER 20-0305].

JUSTICE HOPE SCHWARTZ ZIMMERMAN: NY R NASSAU S J Zimmerman, Part 17.

NEW YORK COUNTY

JUDGE'S RULES; BASIC INFORMATION: [NY R NY CTY J RUL Doc. 1, as amended by NY ORDER 20-0202].

ONONDAGA COUNTY

JUSTICE ROBERT E. ANTONACCI II: [NY R ONDGA E FIL Doc. 1, as amended by 20-0239].

JUSTICE MICHAEL V. COCCOMI: NY R ONDGA E FIL Doc. 2.

JUSTICE GREGORY R. GILBERT: NY R 5 JD JUDGES Gilbert; NY R ONDGA E FIL Doc. 3.

JUSTICE DONALD A. GREENWOOD: NY R ONDGA E FIL Doc. 4.

JUSTICE DEBORAH H. KARALUNAS: NY R ONDGA E FIL Doc. 5.

JUSTICE JAMES MCCLUSKY: NY R 5 JD MCCLUSKY McClusky.

JUSTICE CHARLES C. MERRELL: NY R 5 JD MERRELL Merrell.

JUSTICE PATRICK F. MACRAE: NY R 5 JD MACRAE Doc. 1.

JUSTICE JAMES P. MURPHY: NY R ONDGA E FIL Doc. 7.

JUSTICE GERALD J. NERI: [NY R 5 JD JUDGES Neri, as amended by NY ORDER 20-0236]; [NY R ONDGA E FIL Doc. 8, as amended by NY ORDER 20-0241].

JUSTICE ANTHONY J. PARIS: NY R 5 JD JUDGES Paris; [NY R ONDGA E FIL Doc. 9, as amended by NY ORDER 20-0242].

JUSTICE NORMAN W. SEITER, JR.: NY R 5 JD JUDGES Seiter.

JUSTICE KEVIN G. YOUNG: [NY R ONDGA E FIL Doc. 10, as amended by NY ORDER 20-0243].

QUEENS COUNTY

JUSTICE PAM JACKMAN BROWN: [NY R L QUEENS Brown, Part 19, as amended by NY ORDER 20-0321].

JUSTICE CHEREE A. BUGGS: NY R L QUEENS Buggs, Part 30.

JUSTICE PAM JACKMAN BROWN: [NY R L QUEENS Brown, Part 19, as amended by NY ORDER 20-0321].

JUSTICE DENIS J. BUTLER: NY R L QUEENS Butler, Part 12.

JUSTICE ROBERT I. CALORAS: [NY R L QUEENS Caloras, Part 36, as amended by NY ORDER 20-0322].

JUSTICE ANNA CULLEY: NY R L QUEENS Culley, Part 53.

JUSTICE TIMOTHY DUFFICY: NY R L QUEENS Dufficy, Part 35.

JUSTICE DAVID ELLIOT: NY R L QUEENS Elliot, Part 14.

JUSTICE JOSEPH J. ESPOSITO: NY R L QUEENS Esposito, Part 6.

JUSTICE DARRELL L. GAVRIN: [NY R L QUEENS Gavrin, Part 27, as amended by NY ORDER 20-0323].

JUSTICE WYATT N. GIBBONS: [NY R L QUEENS Gibbons, Part 5, as amended by NY ORDER 20-0330.

JUSTICE DONNA-MARIE E. GOLIA: [NY R L QUEENS Golia, Part 21, as amended by NY ORDER 20-0331].

JUSTICE MARGUERITE A. GRAYS: [NY R L QUEENS Grays, Part 4, as amended by NY ORDER 20-0324].

JUSTICE RUDOLPH E. GRECO: [NY R L QUEENS Greco, Part 32, as amended by NY ORDER 20-0325].

JUSTICE MAUREEN HEALY: NY R L QUEENS Healy, Part 6.

JUSTICE PHILLIP HOM: [NY R L QUEENS Hom, Part 43, as amended by NY ORDER 20-0332].

JUSTICE KEVIN J. KERRIGAN: NY R L QUEENS Kerrigan, Part 10.

JUSTICE MOJGAN C. LANCMAN: NY R L QUEENS Lancman, Part 20.

JUSTICE RICHARD G. LATIN: NY R L QUEENS Latin, Part 40.

JUSTICE ULYSSES B. LEVERETT: [NY R L QUEENS Leverett, Part 6, as amended by NY ORDER 20-0326].

JUSTICE LEONARD LIVOTE: NY R L QUEENS Livote, Part 33.

JUSTICE LEE A. MAYERSOHN: NY R L QUEENS Mayersohn, Part 22; NY R L QUEENS Mayersohn, Part 22G; [NY R L QUEENS Mayersohn, Part 22G COVID, as amended by NY ORDER 20-0327].

JUSTICE ROBERT J. MCDONALD: NY R L QUEENS McDonald, Part 34.

JUSTICE MARGARET MCGOWAN: NY R L QUEENS McGowan, Part 52.

JUSTICE MAURICE E. MUIR: [NY R L QUEENS Muir, Part 42, as amended by NY ORDER 20-0333].

JUSTICE JODI ORLOW: NY R L QUEENS Orlow, Part 51.

JUSTICE LESLIE J. PURIFICCION: NY R L QUEENS Purificcion, Part 39.

JUSTICE JOSEPH RISI: [NY R L QUEENS Risi, Part 3, as amended by NY ORDER 20-0328].

JUSTICE FREDERICK D.R. SAMPSON: [NY R L QUEENS Sampson, Part 31, as amended by NY ORDER 20-0329].

JUSTICE MARTIN J. SCHULMAN: NY R L QUEENS Schulman, Part 29.

JUSTICE BERNICE D. SIEGAL: NY R L QUEENS Siegal, Part 25G.

JUSTICE JANICE A. TAYLOR: NY R L QUEENS Taylor, Part 15.

JUSTICE CARMEN R. VELASQUEZ: NY R L QUEENS Velasquez, Part 38.

JUSTICE LOURDES M VENTURA: [NY R L QUEENS Ventura, Part 37, as amended by NY ORDER 20-0334].

JUSTICE WILLIAM A. VISCOVICH: NY R L QUEENS Viscovich, Part 63.

JUSTICE ALLAN B. WEISS: NY R L QUEENS Weiss, Part 2.

COMPLIANCE, SETTLEMENT AND CONFERENCE PART: NY R L QUEENS Doc 1.

PRELIMINARY CONFERENCE PART: [NY R L QUEENS Doc. 2, as amended by NY ORDER 20-0335].

MEDICAL MALPRACTICE CONFERENCE PART: [NY R L QUEENS Doc. 3, as amended by NY ORDER 20-0336].

TRIAL SCHEDULING PART: NY R L QUEENS Doc. 4.

SUMMARY JURY TRIAL PROGRAM: NY R L QUEENS Doc. 7.

RESIDENTIAL FORECLOSURE PART: NY R L QUEENS Doc. 9.

FORECLOSURE AUCTION RULES: NY R L QUEENS Doc. 10.

MATRIMONIAL PRELIMINARY CONFERENCE PART: NY R L QUEENS Doc. 11.

NON-CUSTODIAL CONTESTED MATRIMONIAL PART: NY R L QUEENS Doc. 12.

Requests, Notices and Applications
Request for Admissions

Document Last Updated August 2020

A. Checklist

(I) ❑ Matters to consider for requesting party
  (a) ❑ Required documents
    (1) ❑ Request for admissions
    (2) ❑ Proof of service
  (b) ❑ Supplemental documents
    (1) ❑ Copies of document referred to in the request
    (2) ❑ Working copies
  (c) ❑ Timing
    (1) ❑ At any time after service of the answer or after the expiration of twenty (20) days from service of the summons, whichever is sooner, and not later than twenty (20) days before the trial, a party may serve upon any other party a written request for admission by the latter

(II) ❑ Matters to consider for responding party
  (a) ❑ Required documents
    (1) ❑ Response to request for admissions
    (2) ❑ Proof of service
  (b) ❑ Supplemental documents
    (1) ❑ Working copies
  (c) ❑ Timing
    (1) ❑ Each of the matters of which an admission is requested shall be deemed admitted unless within twenty (20) days after service thereof or within such further time as the court may allow, the party to whom the request is directed serves upon the party requesting the admission a sworn statement either denying specifically the matters of which an admission is requested or setting forth in detail the reasons why he cannot truthfully either admit or deny those matters

B. Timing

1. *Time to request admissions.* At any time after service of the answer or after the expiration of twenty (20) days from service of the summons, whichever is sooner, and not later than twenty (20) days before the trial, a party may serve upon any other party a written request for admission by the latter of the genuineness of any papers or documents, or the correctness or fairness of representation of any photographs, described in and served with the request, or of the truth of any matters of fact set forth in the request, as to which the party requesting the admission reasonably believes there can be no substantial dispute at the trial and which are within the knowledge of such other party or can be ascertained by him upon reasonable inquiry. NY CPLR § 3123(a).

   a. *Usual time to request admissions.* The usual time for serving the notice to admit is after the joinder of issue, but before the filing of the note of issue, which is also the usual time frame for pretrial disclosure. NY CPLR § 3123(a) also permits the device to be used twenty (20) days after the service of the summons and any time up to twenty (20) days before the trial. SIEGEL-NYPRAC § 364.

2. *Motions staying disclosure.* Service of a notice of motion under NY CPLR Rule 3211, NY CPLR Rule 3212, or NY CPLR § 3213 stays disclosure until determination of the motion unless the court orders otherwise. If the motion is based solely on the defense that the summons and complaint, summons with notice, or notice of petition and petition was not properly served, disclosure shall not be stayed unless the court orders otherwise. NY CPLR Rule 3214(b).

   a. *Personal injury actions involving terminally ill patients.* Notwithstanding the provisions of NY CPLR Rule 3214(b), the service or pendency of a motion under NY CPLR Rule 3211, NY CPLR Rule 3212, or NY CPLR § 3213 shall not stay disclosure in an action where a preliminary conference order has been entered pursuant to NY CPLR Rule 3407. NY CPLR Rule 3407(b)(3).

3. *KINGS COUNTY: Discovery timing.* At [the Compliance Conference, the court will] schedule all outstanding discovery to be completed prior to date fixed for filing Note of Issue. NY R L KINGS Rule I(B).
   a. *Deadlines in orders.* Discovery scheduled in Compliance Conference orders shall be strictly adhered to and may not be extended without leave of the court. Unjustified failure to comply with the provisions of the CCP order will result in preclusion, the striking of a pleading or imposition of sanctions, as appropriate. NY R L KINGS Rule I(B)(2).
   b. *Cases with extensive discovery.* Where post Compliance Conference discovery is to be extensive, cases may be retracked from standard to complex, which will provide for three (3) additional months of post Compliance Conference discovery and extend the Note of Issue date by three (3) months. NY R L KINGS Rule I(B)(1).
   c. *Discovery not stayed.* Ordinarily the Court/JHO will not stay discovery during pendency of motions to withdraw, or during pendency of settlement, or during pendency of dispositive motions. NY R L KINGS Rule IV.
   d. *Expedited discovery in certain cases.* Discovery in third party and joint actions will be expedited. NY R L KINGS Pt. B, Rule 5.
   e. For more information on discovery scheduling, refer to NY R L KINGS Flow Chart.
4. *NEW YORK COUNTY: Deadlines in orders.* Strict compliance with all discovery orders is required. Unexcused or unjustified failure to comply with deadlines fixed by the court, including those set out in Preliminary Conference Orders, may result in an award of costs, conditional or otherwise, or the imposition of another penalty authorized by NY CPLR § 3126. NY R NY CTY J RUL Rule 8.
5. *Computation of time*
   a. *Units of time*
      i. *Day.* A calendar day includes the time from midnight to midnight. Sunday or any day of the week specifically mentioned means a calendar day. NY GEN CONSTR § 19.
      ii. *Month.* In a statute, contract or public or private instrument, unless otherwise provided in such contract or instrument or by law, the term month means a calendar month and not a lunar month. NY GEN CONSTR § 31.
      iii. *Year.* For information on the definition of a year, including the definitions of a half-year and quarter-year, refer to NY GEN CONSTR § 58 and NY GEN CONSTR § 50. For information on leap years, refer to NY GEN CONSTR § 57.
   b. *Periods of time*
      i. *Number of days.* A number of days specified as a period from a certain day within which or after or before which an act is authorized or required to be done means such number of calendar days exclusive of the calendar day from which the reckoning is made. NY GEN CONSTR § 20.
         - If such period is a period of two (2) days, Saturday, Sunday or a public holiday must be excluded from the reckoning if it is an intervening day between the day from which the reckoning is made and the last day of the period. NY GEN CONSTR § 20.
         - In computing any specified period of time from a specified event, the day upon which the event happens is deemed the day from which the reckoning is made. The day from which any specified period of time is reckoned shall be excluded in making the reckoning. NY GEN CONSTR § 20.
      ii. *Number of months.* A number of months after or before a certain day shall be computed by counting such number of calendar months from such day, exclusive of the calendar month in which such day occurs, and shall include the day of the month in the last month so counted having the same numerical order in days of the month as the day from which the computation is made, unless there be not so many days in the last month so counted, in which case the period computed shall expire with the last day of the month so counted. NY GEN CONSTR § 30.
      iii. *Publication of notice; Number of days.* The period of publication of a legal notice shall be computed by excluding the first day of publication and including the day on which the act or event of which notice is given is to take place or which completes the full period of publication. NY CPLR § 2402.
      iv. *Periods ending on Saturday, Sunday or public holiday.* When any period of time, computed from a certain day, within which or after which or before which an act is authorized or required to be done, ends on a Saturday, Sunday or a public holiday, such act may be done on the next succeeding business day and if the period ends at a specified hour, such act may be done at or before the same hour of such next succeeding business day, except that where a period of time specified by contract ends on a Saturday, Sunday or a public holiday, the extension of such period is governed by NY GEN CONSTR § 25. NY GEN CONSTR § 25-a(1).
         - For a list of public holidays, refer to NY GEN CONSTR § 24.

v. *Additional time after certain kinds of service*

- *Service by mail.* Where a period of time prescribed by law is measured from the service of a paper and service is by mail, five (5) days shall be added to the prescribed period. NY CPLR Rule 2103(b)(2).
- *Service by overnight delivery service.* Where a period of time prescribed by law is measured from the service of a paper and service is by overnight delivery, one (1) business day shall be added to the prescribed period. NY CPLR Rule 2103(b)(6).

vi. *Daylight saving time.* For information on New York's time zone and the effect of daylight saving time, refer to NY GEN CONSTR § 52.

c. *Hours of court.* Notwithstanding any provision of law or rule of court to the contrary, throughout the State of New York the sessions of the Supreme Court for the disposition of business before the court shall commence not later than 9:30 a.m. and conclude not earlier than 5 p.m. Where warranted, the Chief Administrator of the Courts may authorize variances in the opening and closing hours of the courts, but, in such event, daily sessions shall total not less than six (6) hours. NY R CHIEF J § 3.1.

d. *Time limits; Extension of time.* Any act required by or in pursuance of law to be performed at or within a prescribed time, shall be performed according to the standard time. NY GEN CONSTR § 53.

i. Except where otherwise expressly prescribed by law, the court may extend the time fixed by any statute, rule or order for doing any act, upon such terms as may be just and upon good cause shown, whether the application for extension is made before or after the expiration of the time fixed. NY CPLR § 2004. Refer to the New York KeyRules Motion for Continuance/Extension of Time document for more information.

C. General Requirements

1. *Rules governing disclosure*

a. *Generally.* There shall be full disclosure of all matter material and necessary in the prosecution or defense of an action, regardless of the burden of proof, by:

i. A party, or the officer, director, member, agent or employee of a party;

ii. A person who possessed a cause of action or defense asserted in the action;

iii. A person about to depart from the state, or without the state, or residing at a greater distance from the place of trial than one hundred miles, or so sick or infirm as to afford reasonable grounds of belief that he or she will not be able to attend the trial, or a person authorized to practice medicine, dentistry or podiatry who has provided medical, dental or podiatric care or diagnosis to the party demanding disclosure, or who has been retained by such party as an expert witness; and

iv. Any other person, upon notice stating the circumstances or reasons such disclosure is sought or required. NY CPLR § 3101(a).

v. The statutory phrase "material and necessary", said the Court of Appeals, must be interpreted liberally to require disclosure upon request, of any facts bearing on the controversy which will assist preparation for trial by sharpening the issues and reducing delay and prolixity. The test is one of usefulness and reason. SIEGEL-NYPRAC § 344; Allen v. Crowell-Collier Pub. Co., 21 N.Y.2d 403, 235 N.E.2d 430 (1968).

vi. Another potential problem that the original NY CPLR § 3101(a) posed was that it spoke of "evidence" that is material and necessary, which might have been construed to permit disclosure to elicit only that which would itself qualify as "evidence" admissible at trial. It was, however, construed more broadly than that. Well-considered caselaw specifically rejected this "evidence in chief" doctrine, stating that disclosure extends as well "to all relevant information calculated to lead to relevant evidence," a standard similar to that applicable in federal court. With an amendment that took effect on January 1, 1994, changing "evidence" to "matter" in NY CPLR § 3101(a), these generous interpretations of the statute were in effect approved by the legislature. SIEGEL-NYPRAC § 344.

vii. If a party is a corporation, each of its officers, directors, members, agents, and employees is also deemed a "party" for disclosure purposes. A party who needs relevant data or material from a nonparty corporation can seek it through NY CPLR § 3101(a)(2), NY CPLR § 3101(a)(3) or NY CPLR § 3101(a)(4), under which the corporate entity is treated as a "person." These subdivisions should also apply to any entity, corporate or otherwise, from whom disclosure is sought through its agents. A corporate employee who has the requisite knowledge and information may respond to a disclosure request on behalf of the corporation. A party who can't single out the particular person in the corporation's employ to whom a disclosure request should be properly directed can direct it to the corporation as such and leave it to the corporation to designate the appropriate person to respond. Whenever disclosure is sought from a corporation through a deposition, whether as a party or as a nonparty witness, the choice in the first instance of who will be produced in the corporate behalf is with the corporation rather than the examining party. SIEGEL-NYPRAC § 345.

viii. NY CPLR § 3101(a)(4) permits a party to obtain disclosure from a nonparty by merely serving a subpoena on the nonparty providing notice of "the circumstances or reasons such disclosure is sought or required." SIEGEL-NYPRAC § 345.

b. *Methods of obtaining disclosure.* Information is obtainable by one or more of the following disclosure devices: depositions upon oral questions or without the state upon written questions, interrogatories, demands for addresses, discovery and inspection of documents or property, physical and mental examinations of persons, and requests for admission. NY CPLR § 3102(a).

i. *Stipulation or notice.* Unless otherwise provided by the civil practice law and rules or by the court, disclosure shall be obtained by stipulation or on notice without leave of the court. NY CPLR § 3102(b).

ii. *Before action commenced; Court order required.* Before an action is commenced, disclosure to aid in bringing an action, to preserve information or to aid in arbitration, may be obtained, but only by court order. The court may appoint a referee to take testimony. NY CPLR § 3102(c).

iii. *During trial; Court order required.* Except as provided in NY CPLR § 5223, during and after trial, disclosure may be obtained only by order of the trial court on notice. NY CPLR § 3102(d).

iv. *Action pending in another jurisdiction.* Except as provided in NY CPLR § 3119, when under any mandate, writ or commission issued out of any court of record in any other state, territory, district or foreign jurisdiction, or whenever upon notice or agreement, it is required to take the testimony of a witness in the state, he or she may be compelled to appear and testify in the same manner and by the same process as may be employed for the purpose of taking testimony in actions pending in the state. The supreme court or a county court shall make any appropriate order in aid of taking such a deposition. NY CPLR § 3102(e).

v. *Actions to which state is a party.* In an action in which the state is properly a party, whether as plaintiff, defendant or otherwise, disclosure by the state shall be available as if the state were a private person. NY CPLR § 3102(f).

c. *Privileged matter.* Upon objection by a person entitled to assert the privilege, privileged matter shall not be obtainable. NY CPLR § 3101(b).

i. A determination of whether information is privileged is governed by the rules of evidence, which apply as they would at a trial. Whatever is privileged at the trial is privileged as well on pretrial disclosure. SIEGEL-NYPRAC § 346.

d. *Attorney's work product.* The work product of an attorney shall not be obtainable. NY CPLR § 3101(c).

i. NY CPLR § 3101(c) makes unobtainable the "work product of an attorney"—an ill-defined category whose potential for mischief has been avoided only because the judiciary has accorded it a very narrow scope. It is a category wholly distinct from the "materials . . . prepared in anticipation of litigation" of NY CPLR § 3101(d)(2). The fact that immunity is absolute under NY CPLR § 3101(c), while that of NY CPLR § 3101(d)(2) is only conditional, is the factor that requires as sharp a line as possible between the two categories. SIEGEL-NYPRAC § 347.

ii. The judiciary has cast precious little under the "work product" category of NY CPLR § 3101(c), preferring instead to fit doubtful items under the "materials . . . prepared in anticipation of litigation" banner of NY CPLR § 3101(d)(2), where the conditional immunity can be overcome and the matters ordered disclosed when stated conditions are met. SIEGEL-NYPRAC § 347.

e. *Trial preparation*

i. *Experts.* Upon request, each party shall identify each person whom the party expects to call as an expert witness at trial and shall disclose in reasonable detail the subject matter on which each expert is expected to testify, the substance of the facts and opinions on which each expert is expected to testify, the qualifications of each expert witness and a summary of the grounds for each expert's opinion. NY CPLR § 3101(d)(1)(i).

- However, where a party for good cause shown retains an expert an insufficient period of time before the commencement of trial to give appropriate notice thereof, the party shall not thereupon be precluded from introducing the expert's testimony at the trial solely on grounds of noncompliance with NY CPLR § 3101(d)(1). In that instance, upon motion of any party, made before or at trial, or on its own initiative, the court may make whatever order may be just. In an action for medical, dental or podiatric malpractice, a party, in responding to a request, may omit the names of medical, dental or podiatric experts but shall be required to disclose all other information concerning such experts otherwise required by NY CPLR § 3101(d)(1). NY CPLR § 3101(d)(1)(i).

- In an action for medical, dental or podiatric malpractice, any party may, by written offer made to and served upon all other parties and filed with the court, offer to disclose the name of, and to make available for examination upon oral deposition, any person the party making the offer expects to call as an expert witness at trial. Within twenty (20) days of service of the offer, a party shall accept or reject the offer by serving a written reply upon all parties and filing a copy thereof with the court. Failure to serve a reply within twenty (20) days of service of the offer shall be deemed a rejection of the offer. If all parties accept the offer, each party shall be required to produce his or her expert witness for examination upon oral deposition upon receipt of a notice to take oral deposition in accordance with NY CPLR Rule 3107. If any party, having made or accepted the offer, fails to make that party's expert available for oral deposition, that party shall be precluded from offering expert testimony at the trial of the action. NY CPLR § 3101(d)(1)(ii).
- Further disclosure concerning the expected testimony of any expert may be obtained only by court order upon a showing of special circumstances and subject to restrictions as to scope and provisions concerning fees and expenses as the court may deem appropriate. However, a party, without court order, may take the testimony of a person authorized to practice medicine, dentistry or podiatry who is the party's treating or retained expert, as described in NY CPLR § 3101(a)(3), in which event any other party shall be entitled to the full disclosure authorized by Article 31 of Chapter 8 of the Civil Practice Law and Rules (NY CPLR § 3101, et seq.) with respect to that expert without court order. NY CPLR § 3101(d)(1)(iii).

ii. *Materials.* Subject to the provisions of NY CPLR § 3101(d)(1), materials otherwise discoverable under NY CPLR § 3101(a) and prepared in anticipation of litigation or for trial by or for another party, or by or for that other party's representative (including an attorney, consultant, surety, indemnitor, insurer or agent), may be obtained only upon a showing that the party seeking discovery has substantial need of the materials in the preparation of the case and is unable without undue hardship to obtain the substantial equivalent of the materials by other means. In ordering discovery of the materials when the required showing has been made, the court shall protect against disclosure of the mental impressions, conclusions, opinions or legal theories of an attorney or other representative of a party concerning the litigation. NY CPLR § 3101(d)(2).

- In order to qualify as "litigation" material the item must have been prepared exclusively for litigation. Incidental potential use in litigation, the courts have observed, may also be a function of such reports, but they have at least an equal if not greater mission "to prevent future accidents, discipline careless employees, or, generally, to increase the economy and efficiency of the operation." SIEGEL-NYPRAC § 348.

f. *Party's statement.* A party may obtain a copy of his own statement. NY CPLR § 3101(e).

i. Moreover, NY CPLR § 3101(e) has been broadly interpreted to include photographs. Items such as photographs and videotapes are now independently subject to disclosure under NY CPLR § 3101(i). SIEGEL-NYPRAC § 348.

g. *Contents of insurance agreement.* A party may obtain discovery of the existence and contents of any insurance agreement under which any person carrying on an insurance business may be liable to satisfy part or all of a judgment which may be entered in the action or to indemnify or reimburse for payments made to satisfy the judgment. Information concerning the insurance agreement is not by reason of disclosure admissible in evidence at trial. For purpose of NY CPLR § 3101(f), an application for insurance shall not be treated as part of an insurance agreement. NY CPLR § 3101(f).

h. *Accident reports.* Except as is otherwise provided by law, in addition to any other matter which may be subject to disclosure, there shall be full disclosure of any written report of an accident prepared in the regular course of business operations or practices of any person, firm, corporation, association or other public or private entity, unless prepared by a police or peace officer for a criminal investigation or prosecution and disclosure would interfere with a criminal investigation or prosecution. NY CPLR § 3101(g).

i. *Amendment or supplementation of responses.* A party shall amend or supplement a response previously given to a request for disclosure promptly upon the party's thereafter obtaining information that the response was incorrect or incomplete when made, or that the response, though correct and complete when made, no longer is correct and complete, and the circumstances are such that a failure to amend or supplement the response would be materially misleading. NY CPLR § 3101(h).

i. Where a party obtains such information an insufficient period of time before the commencement of trial appropriately to amend or supplement the response, the party shall not thereupon be precluded from introducing evidence at the trial solely on grounds of noncompliance with NY CPLR § 3101(h). In that instance, upon motion of any party, made before or at trial, or on its own initiative, the court may make whatever order may be just. Further amendment or supplementation may be obtained by court order. NY CPLR § 3101(h).

j. *Other disclosures.* In addition to any other matter which may be subject to disclosure, there shall be full disclosure of any films, photographs, video tapes or audio tapes, including transcripts or memoranda thereof, involving a person referred to in NY CPLR § 3101(a)(1). There shall be disclosure of all portions of such material, including out-takes, rather than only those portions a party intends to use. The provisions of NY CPLR § 3101(i) shall not apply to materials compiled for law enforcement purposes which are exempt from disclosure under NY PUB OFF § 87. NY CPLR § 3101(i).

   i. While NY CPLR § 3101(i) was enacted with the defendant's surreptitious tapes of the plaintiff in mind, its language is broad enough to embrace any films, photographs, and audio or video tapes of a party, even those made by the party from whom disclosure is sought. SIEGEL-NYPRAC § 348.

k. *Protective orders.* The court may at any time on its own initiative, or on motion of any party or of any person from whom discovery is sought, make a protective order denying, limiting, conditioning or regulating the use of any disclosure device. NY CPLR § 3103(a). Refer to the New York KeyRules Motion for Protective Order document for more information.

l. *Supervision of disclosure.* Upon the motion of any party or witness on notice to all parties or on its own initiative without notice, the court in which an action is pending may by one of its judges or a referee supervise all or part of any disclosure procedure. NY CPLR § 3104(a).

   i. *Selection of referee.* A judicial hearing officer may be designated as a referee under NY CPLR § 3104, or the court may permit all of the parties in an action to stipulate that a named attorney may act as referee. In such latter event, the stipulation shall provide for payment of his fees which shall, unless otherwise agreed, be taxed as disbursements. NY CPLR § 3104(b).

   ii. *Powers of referee; Motions referred to person supervising disclosure.* A referee under NY CPLR § 3104 shall have all the powers of the court under NY CPLR § 3101, et seq. except the power to relieve himself of his duties, to appoint a successor, or to adjudge any person guilty of contempt. All motions or applications made under Article 31 of Chapter 8 of the Civil Practice Law and Rules (NY CPLR § 3101, et seq.) shall be returnable before the judge or referee, designated under NY CPLR § 3104 and after disposition, if requested by any party, his order shall be filed in the office of the clerk. NY CPLR § 3104(c).

   iii. *Review of order of referee.* Any party or witness may apply for review of an order made under NY CPLR § 3104 by a referee. The application shall be by motion made in the court in which the action is pending within five (5) days after the order is made. Service of a notice of motion for review shall suspend disclosure of the particular matter in dispute. If the question raised by the motion may affect the rights of a witness, notice shall be served on him personally or by mail at his last known address. It shall set forth succinctly the order complained of, the reason it is objectionable and the relief demanded. NY CPLR § 3104(d).

   iv. *Payment of expenses of referee.* Except where a judicial hearing officer has been designated a referee hereunder, the court may make an appropriate order for the payment of the reasonable expenses of the referee. NY CPLR § 3104(e).

2. *Request for admissions*

   a. *Generally.* At any time after service of the answer or after the expiration of twenty (20) days from service of the summons, whichever is sooner, and not later than twenty (20) days before the trial, a party may serve upon any other party a written request for admission by the latter of:

      i. The genuineness of any papers or documents, or

      ii. The correctness or fairness of representation of any photographs, described in and served with the request, or

      iii. Of the truth of any matters of fact set forth in the request, as to which the party requesting the admission reasonably believes there can be no substantial dispute at the trial and which are within the knowledge of such other party or can be ascertained by him upon reasonable inquiry. NY CPLR § 3123(a).

   b. *Form and content.* Requests for admissions should be simple and direct. They should only include "clear-cut" matters of fact. A notice to admit that is unnecessarily protracted and appears patently burdensome to answer will be vacated. A plaintiff need not make a motion to preclude relating to a notice to admit, since a proper notice to admit is self-executing. CW2D § 53:5.

c. *Purpose and use.* The purpose of the device is to save a party the trouble and expense of proving a readily admittable fact. SIEGEL-NYPRAC § 364. Because of its inherent limitations, the notice to admit is under-used. It is also true that the matters to which it lends itself are often admitted by opposing parties in the course of the pleadings or depositions or other disclosure devices, or preliminary conferences, or are so easily and inexpensively proved that a party feels no need to avoid the proof by securing the admission. SIEGEL-NYPRAC § 364.

i. The device may be used only when the seeking party "reasonably believes there can be no substantial dispute" about the matter at the trial and when it is within the knowledge of the other party or ascertainable by him "upon reasonable inquiry." SIEGEL-NYPRAC § 364. The notice is not truly a disclosure device, but just a procedure designed to "crystallize issues." SIEGEL-NYPRAC § 364.

ii. It may not be used, in other words, "to cover ultimate conclusions, which can only be made after a full and complete trial." SIEGEL-NYPRAC § 364; DeSilva by DeSilva v. Rosenberg, 236 A.D.2d 508, 654 N.Y.S.2d 30 (1997). Nor may it be used for technical or scientific information such as is ordinarily elicited from an expert. SIEGEL-NYPRAC § 364; Berg v. Flower Fifth Ave. Hosp., 102 A.D.2d 760, 476 N.Y.S.2d 895 (1984); Johantgen v. Hobart Mfg. Co., 64 A.D.2d 858, 407 N.Y.S.2d 355 (1978).

iii. The notice to admit may not be used to make one party admit what some other party knows. SIEGEL-NYPRAC § 364. A separate notice to admit should be drawn for each party so as not to elicit from one something suitable for admission only by another. SIEGEL-NYPRAC § 364.

d. *Effect of admission.* Any admission made, or deemed to be made, by a party pursuant to a request made under NY CPLR § 3123 is for the purpose of the pending action only and does not constitute an admission by him for any other purpose nor may it be used against him in any other proceeding; and the court, at any time, may allow a party to amend or withdraw any admission on such terms as may be just. Any admission shall be subject to all pertinent objections to admissibility which may be interposed at the trial. NY CPLR § 3123(b).

e. *Copies.* Copies of the papers, documents or photographs shall be served with the request unless copies have already been furnished. NY CPLR § 3123(a).

3. *Governing law.* The civil practice law and rules (NY CPLR § 101, et seq.) shall govern the procedure in civil judicial proceedings in all courts of the state and before all judges, except where the procedure is regulated by inconsistent statute. The civil practice law and rules shall succeed the civil practice act and rules of civil practice and shall be deemed substituted therefor throughout the statutes and rules of the state. NY CPLR § 101. The civil practice law and rules shall be liberally construed to secure the just, speedy and inexpensive determination of every civil judicial proceeding. NY CPLR § 104.

a. *Uniform trial court rules.* The uniform civil rules for the Supreme Court and County Court (NY R UNIF TRIAL CTS § 202.1, et seq.) shall be applicable to civil actions and proceedings in the Supreme Court and the County Court. NY R UNIF TRIAL CTS § 202.1(a). The provisions of the uniform rules shall be construed consistent with the Civil Practice Law and Rules (CPLR), and matters not covered by the uniform rules shall be governed by the CPLR. NY R UNIF TRIAL CTS § 202.1(d).

b. *Local rules.* Local court rules, not inconsistent with law or with uniform civil rules for the Supreme Court and County Court (NY R UNIF TRIAL CTS § 202.1, et seq.), shall comply with Part 9 of the Rules of the Chief Judge (NY R CHIEF J § 9.1). NY R UNIF TRIAL CTS § 202.1(c).

c. *Official forms.* The state administrator shall have the power to adopt, amend and rescind an appendix of forms. Forms adopted pursuant to NY CPLR § 107 shall be sufficient under the civil practice law and rules and shall illustrate the simplicity and brevity of statement which the civil practice law and rules contemplate. NY CPLR § 107.

4. *Rules of the commercial division.* [Editor's note: certain types of civil cases or civil cases meeting certain monetary thresholds that are filed in the state of New York must be filed in the Commercial Division of the New York Supreme Courts. Rules governing practice in the commercial division are found in NY R UNIF TRIAL CTS § 202.70]. Cases which must be filed in the commercial division are listed below. For more information, refer to NY R UNIF TRIAL CTS § 202.70.

a. *Monetary thresholds.* Except as set forth in NY R UNIF TRIAL CTS § 202.70(b), the monetary thresholds of the Commercial Division, exclusive of punitive damages, interests, costs, disbursements and counsel fees claimed, are established as follows: (1) Albany County, fifty thousand dollars ($50,000); (2) Eighth Judicial District, one hundred thousand dollars ($100,000); (3) Kings County, one hundred fifty thousand dollars ($150,000); (4) Nassau County, two hundred thousand dollars ($200,000); (5) New York County, five hundred thousand dollars ($500,000); (6) Onondaga County, fifty thousand dollars ($50,000); (7) Queens County, one hundred thousand dollars ($100,000); (8) Seventh Judicial District, fifty thousand dollars ($50,000); (9) Suffolk County, one hundred thousand dollars

($100,000); and (10) Westchester County, one hundred thousand dollars ($100,000). NY R UNIF TRIAL CTS § 202.70(a).

i. *ALBANY COUNTY.* The Commercial Division of the Albany County Supreme Court exercises jurisdiction over selected business and commercial disputes in which the amount at issue generally involves damage claims in a minimum amount of fifty thousand dollars ($50,000) as well as claims for unspecified amounts where the value of the commercial asset(s) in dispute exceeds fifty thousand dollars ($50,000). A separate publication promulgating the rules and criteria relating to the filing and management of Commercial Court cases in this part may be obtained from the Albany County Supreme Court Clerk's Office. A section of the Uniform Civil Rules for the Supreme Court and County Court sets forth statewide rules. NY R 3 JD SUP Doc. 1(E).

ii. *BRONX COUNTY.* The monetary threshold for commercial cases in Bronx County will be seventy-five thousand dollars ($75,000). All other parameters including the type of matters that will be heard are contained within the Rules of the Commercial Division of the Supreme Court (NY R UNIF TRIAL CTS § 202.70). NY R BRONX FIL R Doc. 12.

iii. *NEW YORK COUNTY.* The monetary threshold in the New York County Commercial Division, which is generally applicable, is an amount in controversy of five hundred thousand dollars ($500,000) or more (exclusive of punitive damages, interest, costs, disbursements, and counsel fees). If the case is designated a commercial one and the Addendum is submitted, the clerk will review the pleadings to determine whether the amount in controversy in the case meets the monetary threshold or whether an exception to the threshold applies. NY R NY CTY Procedure IA(B). For more information on assigning a case to the commercial division in New York County, refer to NY R NY CTY Procedure IA(B).

b. *Commercial cases.* Actions in which the principal claims involve or consist of the following will be heard in the Commercial Division provided that the monetary threshold is met or equitable or declaratory relief is sought:

i. Breach of contract or fiduciary duty, fraud, misrepresentation, business tort (e.g., unfair competition), or statutory and/or common law violation where the breach or violation is alleged to arise out of business dealings (e.g., sales of assets or securities; corporate restructuring; partnership, shareholder, joint venture, and other business agreements; trade secrets; restrictive covenants; and employment agreements not including claims that principally involve alleged discriminatory practices);

ii. Transactions governed by the Uniform Commercial Code (exclusive of those concerning individual cooperative or condominium units);

iii. Transactions involving commercial real property, including Yellowstone injunctions and excluding actions for the payment of rent only;

iv. Shareholder derivative actions—without consideration of the monetary threshold;

v. Commercial class actions—without consideration of the monetary threshold;

vi. Business transactions involving or arising out of dealings with commercial banks and other financial institutions;

vii. Internal affairs of business organizations;

viii. Malpractice by accountants or actuaries, and legal malpractice arising out of representation in commercial matters;

ix. Environmental insurance coverage;

x. Commercial insurance coverage (e.g., directors and officers, errors and omissions, and business interruption coverage);

xi. Dissolution of corporations, partnerships, limited liability companies, limited liability partnerships and joint ventures—without consideration of the monetary threshold; and

xii. Applications to stay or compel arbitration and affirm or disaffirm arbitration awards and related injunctive relief pursuant to Article 75 of the New York Civil Practice Law and Rules (NY CPLR § 7501, et seq.) involving any of the foregoing enumerated commercial issues. Where the applicable arbitration agreement provides for the arbitration to be heard outside the United States, the monetary threshold set forth in NY R UNIF TRIAL CTS § 202.70(a) shall not apply. NY R UNIF TRIAL CTS § 202.70(b).

c. *Non-commercial cases.* The following will not be heard in the Commercial Division even if the monetary threshold is met:

i. Suits to collect professional fees;

ii. Cases seeking a declaratory judgment as to insurance coverage for personal injury or property damage;

iii. Residential real estate disputes, including landlord-tenant matters, and commercial real estate disputes involving the payment of rent only;

iv. Home improvement contracts involving residential properties consisting of one to four residential units or individual units in any residential building, including cooperative or condominium units;

v. Proceedings to enforce a judgment regardless of the nature of the underlying case;

vi. First-party insurance claims and actions by insurers to collect premiums or rescind non-commercial policies; and

vii. Attorney malpractice actions except as otherwise provided in NY R UNIF TRIAL CTS § 202.70(b)(8). NY R UNIF TRIAL CTS § 202.70(c).

d. For more information on the Commercial Division, refer to NY R UNIF TRIAL CTS § 202.70.

D. Documents

1. *Required documents*

a. *Request for admissions.* Refer to the General Requirements section of this document for information on the request for admissions.

b. *Proof of service.* In addition to complying with the provisions of NY CPLR Rule 2101, every paper filed in court shall have annexed thereto appropriate proof of service on all parties where required. NY R UNIF TRIAL CTS § 202.5(a).

2. *Supplemental documents*

a. *Copies of documents referred to in the request.* Copies of the papers, documents or photographs whose genuineness is requested to be admitted shall be served with the request unless copies have already been furnished. NY CPLR § 3123(a).

b. *Working copies.* The court may require the parties to provide working copies of documents filed electronically. In such event, each working copy shall include, firmly affixed thereto, a copy of a confirmation notice in a form prescribed by the Chief Administrator. NY R UNIF TRIAL CTS § 202.5-b(d)(5).

E. Format

1. *Form of documents*

a. *Size and form of paper.* Each paper served or filed shall be durable, white and, except for summonses, subpoenas, notices of appearance, notes of issue, orders of protection, temporary orders of protection and exhibits, shall be eleven by eight and one-half (11 x 8-1/2) inches in size. NY CPLR Rule 2101(a).

b. *Writing and language.* The writing shall be legible and in black ink. NY CPLR Rule 2101(a). Each paper served or filed shall be in the English language which, where practicable, shall be of ordinary usage. NY CPLR Rule 2101(b).

c. *Caption.* Each paper served or filed shall begin with a caption setting forth the name of the court, the venue, the title of the action, the nature of the paper and the index number of the action if one has been assigned. In all papers other than a summons, a complaint or a judgment it shall be sufficient to state the name of the first named party on each side with an appropriate indication of any omissions. NY CPLR Rule 2101(c).

i. *Further contents of first page.* After the first paper has been filed in each case the index number shall appear on the cover and first page to the right of the caption of every paper tendered for filing in the action. Each such cover and first page also shall contain an indication of the county of venue and a brief description of the nature of the paper and, where the case has been assigned to an individual judge, shall contain the name of the assigned judge to the right of the caption. NY R UNIF TRIAL CTS § 202.5(a); NY R UNIF TRIAL CTS § 202.5(b); NY R UNIF TRIAL CTS § 202.5(d)(1)(i).

d. *Index number.* No paper in an action in the supreme or a county court, other than an order submitted for signature to a judge out of court, shall be submitted for any purpose to the supreme or county court or to a clerk thereof unless there is endorsed on such paper the index number of the action assigned by the clerk of the county. NY CPLR § 8018(c).

e. *Line spacing.* Every paper filed in court, if typewritten, shall have at least double space between each line, except for quotations and the names and addresses of attorneys appearing in the action. NY R UNIF TRIAL CTS § 202.5(a).

f. *Font size.* Each. . .paper printed or typed, served or filed, except for summonses. . .and exhibits, shall be in clear type of no less than ten (10) point in size. NY CPLR Rule 2101(a).

i. Whenever a requirement relating to size of type is stated in point size, the type size requirement shall be deemed met if the x-height of the type is a minimum of forty-five percent (45%) of the specified point size. Each point shall be measured as .351 millimeter. The x-height size shall be measured as it appears on the page. The x-height is the height of the lower case letters, exclusive of ascenders or descenders. NY CPLR § 105(t).

g. *Margins.* Every paper filed in court shall have at least one (1) inch margins. NY R UNIF TRIAL CTS § 202.5(a).

h. *Citations*

   i. *Civil practice law and rules.* NY CPLR § 101, et seq. shall be known as the civil practice law and rules, and may be cited as "CPLR". Reference to a provision in the civil practice law and rules may, except when such provision is being enacted or amended, be made without indicating whether it is a rule or section. NY CPLR § 101.

i. *Indorsement by attorney.* Each paper served or filed shall be indorsed with the name, address and telephone number of the attorney for the party serving or filing the paper, or if the party does not appear by attorney, with the name, address and telephone number of the party. NY CPLR Rule 2101(d).

j. *One-sided printing.* In addition, every paper filed in court, other than an exhibit or printed form, shall contain writing on one side only, except that papers that are fastened on the side may contain writing on both sides. NY R UNIF TRIAL CTS § 202.5(a).

k. *Use of copies authorized.* Except where otherwise specifically prescribed, copies, rather than originals, of all papers, including orders, affidavits and exhibits may be served or filed. Where it is required that the original be served or filed and the original is lost or withheld, the court may authorize a copy to be served or filed. NY CPLR Rule 2101(e).

   i. Where a certified copy of a paper is required by law, an attorney admitted to practice in the courts of the state may certify that it has been compared by him with the original and found to be a true and complete copy. Such a certificate, when subscribed by such attorney, has the same effect as if made by a clerk. NY CPLR § 2105.

l. *Recycled paper.* It is the policy of the Unified Court System that litigants, where practicable, should file or submit to the courts of the Unified Court System of the State of New York papers printed or reproduced on recycled paper. Paper is considered recycled if it contains a minimum content of thirty percent (30%) waste paper. NY R UNIF TRIAL CTS § 215.2. The signature page of every paper filed or submitted to the court on recycled paper should bear the legend: "Printed [Reproduced] on Recycled Paper." NY R UNIF TRIAL CTS § 215.3.

2. *Form of electronic documents.* Each paper served or filed by electronic means, as defined in NY CPLR Rule 2103(f), shall be capable of being reproduced by the receiver so as to comply with the provisions of NY CPLR Rule 2101(a) through NY CPLR Rule 2101(d). NY CPLR Rule 2101(g).

   a. *File format.* All e-filed documents shall comply with the technical requirements set forth at the NYSCEF site. NY R UNIF TRIAL CTS § 202.5-b(d)(1)(i).

   b. *Heading of document.* The subject matter heading for each paper sent by electronic means must indicate that the matter being transmitted electronically is related to a court proceeding. NY CPLR Rule 2103(b)(7).

3. *Signature blocks.* Every pleading, written motion, and other paper, served on another party or filed or submitted to the court shall be signed by an attorney, or by a party if the party is not represented by an attorney, with the name of the attorney or party clearly printed or typed directly below the signature. NY R CHIEF ADMIN § 130-1.1-a(a); NY R UNIF TRIAL CTS § 202.5(d)(1)(iv).

   a. *Printed name.* Beneath each signature shall be printed the name signed. NY CPLR Rule 2101(a).

   b. *Failure to sign.* Absent good cause shown, the court shall strike any unsigned paper if the omission of the signature is not corrected promptly after being called to the attention of the attorney or party. NY R CHIEF ADMIN § 130-1.1-a(a).

   c. *Signature as certification.* By signing a paper, an attorney or party certifies that, to the best of that person's knowledge, information and belief, formed after an inquiry reasonable under the circumstances the presentation of the paper or the contentions therein are not frivolous as defined in NY R CHIEF ADMIN § 130-1.1(c). NY R CHIEF ADMIN § 130-1.1-a(b)(1).

   d. *Electronic signatures.* A document shall be considered to have been signed by an attorney or party in compliance with NY R CHIEF ADMIN § 130-1.1-a if it has been signed by such attorney or party as provided in NY R UNIF TRIAL CTS § 202.5-b(e)(1) and it bears the signatory's name. NY R UNIF TRIAL CTS § 202.5-b(e)(2). An electronically filed document shall be considered to have been signed by, and shall be binding upon, the person identified as a signatory, if:

      i. It bears the physical signature of such person and is scanned into an electronic format that reproduces such signature; or

ii. The signatory has electronically affixed the digital image of his or her signature to the document; or

iii. It is electronically filed under the User ID and password of that person; or

iv. In a tax certiorari action in which the parties have stipulated to this procedure, it is an initiating document that is electronically filed without the signature of the signatory in a form provided above in NY R UNIF TRIAL CTS § 202.5-b(e)(iv), provided that, prior to filing, the document is signed in full in hard copy (which hard copy must be preserved until the conclusion of all proceedings, including appeals, in the case in which it is filed); or

v. In a small claims assessment review proceeding, it is a petition recorded by the NYSCEF site upon the filing of a text file as provided in NY R UNIF TRIAL CTS § 202.5-b(b)(1), provided that prior to filing, the document was signed in full in hard copy (which hard copy must be preserved until the conclusion of all proceedings in the matter, including article 78 (NY CPLR § 7801, et seq.) review and any appeals, and must be made available during the proceeding upon request of the respondent or the court); or

vi. It otherwise bears the electronic signature of the signatory in a format conforming to such standards and requirements as may hereafter be established by the Chief Administrator. NY R UNIF TRIAL CTS § 202.5-b(e).

4. *Confidentiality of personal information.* No person may file any document available for public inspection with any state agency, political subdivision, or in any court of this state that contains a Social Security account number of any other person, unless such other person is a dependent child, or has consented to such filing, except as required by federal or state law or regulation, or by court rule. NY GEN BUS § 399-ddd. Submissions pursuant to e-filing procedures shall have the same confidentiality rights as paper documents. NY R UNIF TRIAL CTS § 202.5-b(k)(1).

a. *Confidential personal information.* Except in the actions designated in NY R UNIF TRIAL CTS § 202.5(e)(1), or as otherwise provided by rule or law or court order, and whether or not a sealing order is or has been sought, the parties shall omit or redact confidential personal information in papers submitted to the court for filing. For purposes of NY R UNIF TRIAL CTS § 202.5(e), confidential personal information ("CPI") means:

i. The taxpayer identification number of an individual or an entity, including a Social Security number, an employer identification number, and an individual taxpayer identification number, except the last four (4) digits thereof;

ii. The date of an individual's birth, except the year thereof;

iii. The full name of an individual known to be a minor, except the minor's initials;

iv. A financial account number, including a credit and/or debit card number, a bank account number, an investment account number, and/or an insurance account number, except the last four (4) digits or letters thereof; and

v. Any of the documents or testimony in a matrimonial action protected by NY DOM REL § 235 or evidence sealed by the court in such an action which are attached as exhibits or referenced in the papers filed in any other civil action. For purposes of NY R UNIF TRIAL CTS § 202.5, a matrimonial action shall mean: an action to annul a marriage or declare the nullity of a void marriage, an action or agreement for a separation, an action for a divorce, or an action or proceeding for custody, visitation, writ of habeus corpus, child support, maintenance or paternity. NY R UNIF TRIAL CTS § 202.5(e)(1).

b. *Submission of confidential personal information.* Where a person submitting a paper to a court for filing believes in good faith that the inclusion of the full confidential personal information described in NY R UNIF TRIAL CTS § 202.5(e)(1) is material and necessary to the adjudication of the action or proceeding before the court, he or she may apply to the court for leave to serve and file together with a paper in which such information has been set forth in abbreviated form a confidential affidavit or affirmation setting forth the same information in unabbreviated form, appropriately referenced to the page or pages of the paper at which the abbreviated form appears. NY R UNIF TRIAL CTS § 202.5(e)(3).

c. *Home addresses.* For information on when home addresses and other personal information must be redacted, refer to NY CPLR Rule 2103-a.

5. *Defective papers.* A defect in the form of a paper, if a substantial right of a party is not prejudiced, shall be disregarded by the court, and leave to correct shall be freely given. NY CPLR Rule 2101(f). Papers that are stapled or bound securely shall not be rejected for filing simply because they are not bound with a backer of any kind. NY R UNIF TRIAL CTS § 202.5(a). A paper filed in accordance with the rules of the chief administrator or any local rule or practice established by the court shall be deemed filed. NY CPLR Rule 2102(b).

a. *Objection to defective papers.* The party on whom a paper is served shall be deemed to have waived objection to any defect in form unless, within fifteen (15) days after the receipt thereof, the party on whom the paper is served returns the paper to the party serving it with a statement of particular objections. NY CPLR Rule 2101(f).

F. Filing and Service Requirements

1. *Filing requirements.* Except where otherwise prescribed by law or order of court, papers required to be filed shall be filed with the clerk of the court in which the action is triable. In an action or proceeding in supreme or court, papers required to be filed shall be filed with the clerk of the county in which the proceeding is brought. NY CPLR Rule 2102(a).

   a. *Electronic filing.* On consent, documents may be filed and served by electronic means in Supreme Court in such civil actions and in such counties as shall be authorized by order of the Chief Administrator of the Courts and only to the extent and in the manner provided in NY R UNIF TRIAL CTS § 202.5-b. NY R UNIF TRIAL CTS § 202.5-b(a)(1). For the definitions of terms used in electronic filing, refer to NY R UNIF TRIAL CTS § 202.5-b(a)(2).

      i. *Electronic filing of discovery materials.* In any action subject to e-filing, parties and non-parties producing materials in response to discovery demands may enter into a stipulation, which shall be e-filed, authorizing the electronic filing of discovery responses and discovery materials to the degree and upon terms and conditions set forth in the stipulation. In the absence of such a stipulation, no party shall file electronically any such materials except in the form of excerpts, quotations, or selected exhibits from such materials as part of motion papers, pleadings or other filings with the court. NY R UNIF TRIAL CTS § 202.5-b(j).

      ii. *E-filing mandatory.* In any action subject to e-filing, all documents required to be filed with the court by an e-filing party shall be filed and served electronically, except as provided in NY R UNIF TRIAL CTS § 202.5-b. NY R UNIF TRIAL CTS § 202.5-b(d)(1)(i).

      iii. *Who may file.* Documents may be filed or served electronically only by a person who has registered as an authorized e-filing user or as otherwise provided in NY R UNIF TRIAL CTS § 202.5-b(c). NY R UNIF TRIAL CTS § 202.5-b(c)(1).

      iv. *When filing made.* Documents may be transmitted at any time of the day or night to the NYSCEF site. A document other than an order or judgment is filed when its electronic transmission or, in the case of a petition that is e-filed by submission of a text file as provided in NY R UNIF TRIAL CTS § 202.5-b(b)(1), the electronic transmission of the text file is recorded at that site, provided, however, that where payment of a fee is required upon the filing of a document, the document is not filed until transmission of the document and the information or form or information as required in NY R UNIF TRIAL CTS § 202.5-b(d)(2)(i), NY R UNIF TRIAL CTS § 202.5-b(d)(2)(ii) or NY R UNIF TRIAL CTS § 202.5-b(d)(2)(iii) has been recorded at the NYSCEF site; or, if no transmission of that information or form or information is recorded, where permitted by the County Clerk, until payment is presented to the County Clerk. NY R UNIF TRIAL CTS § 202.5-b(d)(3)(i).

      v. *Notification of filing.* No later than the close of business on the business day following the electronic filing of a document, a notification, in a form prescribed by the Chief Administrator, shall be transmitted electronically by the NYSCEF site to the person filing such document and the e-mail service addresses of all other participating parties in such action. NY R UNIF TRIAL CTS § 202.5-b(d)(3)(ii).

      vi. *Removal of confidential information and other corrections.* If a document filed electronically is subsequently discovered to contain confidential data—including but not limited to trade secrets, information protected by confidentiality agreement, or personal confidential information as defined by statute or court rule—or otherwise to have been filed in error, the filer or another party or affected person may (1) notify the parties and any non-party filers in the action of the confidentiality issue or other error raised by the filing, and of his or her intention to seek judicial relief to correct the filing: (2) following such notification, request that the appropriate County Clerk, exercising his or her administrative discretion, place the document temporarily in "restricted" status on the NYSCEF site, to be made available for viewing by court staff and the parties but not the general public; and (3) file an application to correct the filing by order to show cause within five (5) business days of such notification (or such time as the court may direct), including a request for preliminary injunctive relief limiting interim disclosure of the document at issue. Unless otherwise directed by the court, any document placed in restricted status in response to such a request shall be returned to public view upon expiration of this five (5) day period. The Chief Administrator of the Courts shall promulgate forms to implement this process. NY R UNIF TRIAL CTS § 202.5-b(d)(3)(iii).

      vii. *Documents requiring judge's signature.* Except where the court directs otherwise, any document that requires a judge's signature shall be transmitted electronically and in hard copy to the court. NY R UNIF TRIAL CTS § 202.5-b(d)(6).

      viii. *Documents which would be inconvenient to file electronically; Hard copies.* Notwithstanding any other provision of NY R UNIF TRIAL CTS § 202.5-b, and subject to such guidelines as may be established by the Chief Administrative Judge, the County Clerk or his or her designee may require or permit a party to file in hard copy, in accordance with procedures set by the County Clerk or designee, an exhibit or other document which it is impractical or inconvenient to file electronically. NY R UNIF TRIAL CTS § 202.5-b(d)(7).

ix. *Documents containing sensitive or proprietary information.* In an action subject to e-filing, any person may apply for an order prohibiting or restricting the electronic filing in the action of specifically identified materials on the grounds that such materials are subject to copyright or other proprietary rights, or trade secret or other privacy interests, and that electronic filing in the action is likely to result in substantial prejudice to those rights or interests. NY R UNIF TRIAL CTS § 202.5-b(k)(2).

x. *Refusal to accept paper filings.* In accordance with NY CPLR Rule 2102(c), a County Clerk and a chief clerk of the Supreme Court or County Court, as appropriate, shall refuse to accept for filing papers filed in actions and proceedings when the paper sought to be filed:

- Is in an action subject to electronic filing pursuant to Rules of the Chief Administrator,
- Is not being filed electronically, and
- Does not include the notice required by NY R UNIF TRIAL CTS § 202.5-b(d)(1). NY R UNIF TRIAL CTS § 202.5(d)(1)(v); NY R UNIF TRIAL CTS § 202.5-bb(d).

xi. *Emergency filings; Hard copies.* For information on when an emergency filing may be filed and served in hard copy, refer to NY R UNIF TRIAL CTS § 202.5-b(d)(1)(ii), NY R UNIF TRIAL CTS § 202.5-b(d)(1)(iii) and NY R UNIF TRIAL CTS § 202.5-bb(c)(3).

xii. *Technical failures.* The NYSCEF site shall be considered to be subject to a technical failure on a given day if the site is unable to accept filings or provide access to filed documents continuously or intermittently over the course of any period of time greater than one (1) hour after 12:00 noon of that day. Notice of all such technical failures shall be provided on the site. NY R UNIF TRIAL CTS § 202.5-b(i).

- When e-filing is hindered by a technical failure, a party may file with the appropriate clerk and serve in hard copy. NY R UNIF TRIAL CTS § 202.5-b(i). In the event an attorney or party shall file and serve documents in hard copy pursuant to NY R UNIF TRIAL CTS § 202.5-b(i), each such document shall include the notice required by NY R UNIF TRIAL CTS § 202.5-b(d)(1), and the filer shall file those documents with the NYSCEF site within three (3) business days after restoration of normal operations at that site. NY R UNIF TRIAL CTS § 202.5-b(i).
- With the exception of deadlines that by law cannot be extended, the time for filing of any document that is delayed due to technical failure of the site shall be extended for one (1) day for each day on which such failure occurs, unless otherwise ordered by the court. NY R UNIF TRIAL CTS § 202.5-b(i).

xiii. *Filing fees.* For information on what information must be provided to pay filing fees, refer to NY R UNIF TRIAL CTS § 202.5-b(d)(2).

xiv. *Exemption from e-filing.* For information on exemptions from e-filing, refer to NY R UNIF TRIAL CTS § 202.5-bb(e).

b. *Facsimile filing.* In the Supreme Court, facsimile filing shall be limited to commercial claims and tax certiorari, conservatorship, and mental hygiene proceedings in Monroe, Westchester, New York and Suffolk Counties. NY R UNIF TRIAL CTS § 202.5-a(a)(1). Refer to NY R UNIF TRIAL CTS § 202.5-a for information on the procedures for facsimile filing.

2. *Service requirements*

a. *Who may serve.* Except where otherwise prescribed by law or order of court, papers may be served by any person not a party of the age of eighteen years or over. NY CPLR Rule 2103(a).

b. *Service upon attorney.* Except where otherwise prescribed by law or order of court, papers to be served upon a party in a pending action shall be served upon the party's attorney. Where the same attorney appears for two or more parties, only one (1) copy need be served upon the attorney. Such service upon an attorney shall be made:

i. By delivering the paper to the attorney personally. NY CPLR Rule 2103(b)(1).

ii. By mailing the paper to the attorney at the address designated by that attorney for that purpose or, if none is designated, at the attorney's last known address; service by mail shall be complete upon mailing. NY CPLR Rule 2103(b)(2).

iii. If the attorney's office is open, by leaving the paper with a person in charge, or if no person is in charge, by leaving it in a conspicuous place; or if the attorney's office is not open, by depositing the paper, enclosed in a sealed wrapper directed to the attorney, in the attorney's office letter drop or box. NY CPLR Rule 2103(b)(3).

iv. By leaving it at the attorney's residence within the state with a person of suitable age and discretion. Service upon an attorney shall not be made at the attorney's residence unless service at the attorney's office cannot be made. NY CPLR Rule 2103(b)(4).

v. By transmitting the paper to the attorney by facsimile transmission, provided that a facsimile telephone number is designated by the attorney for that purpose. Service by facsimile transmission shall be complete upon the receipt by the sender of a signal from the equipment of the attorney served indicating that the transmission was received, and the mailing of a copy of the paper to that attorney. The designation of a facsimile telephone number in the address block subscribed on a paper served or filed in the course of an action or proceeding shall constitute consent to service by facsimile transmission in accordance with NY CPLR Rule 2103(b)(5). An attorney may change or rescind a facsimile telephone number by serving a notice on the other parties. NY CPLR Rule 2103(b)(5).

vi. By dispatching the paper to the attorney by overnight delivery service at the address designated by the attorney for that purpose or, if none is designated, at the attorney's last known address. Service by overnight delivery service shall be complete upon deposit of the paper enclosed in a properly addressed wrapper into the custody of the overnight delivery service for overnight delivery, prior to the latest time designated by the overnight delivery service for overnight delivery. "Overnight delivery service" means any delivery service which regularly accepts items for overnight delivery to any address in the state. NY CPLR Rule 2103(b)(6).

vii. By transmitting the paper to the attorney by electronic means where and in the manner authorized by the chief administrator of the courts by rule and, unless such rule shall otherwise provide, such transmission shall be upon the party's written consent. The subject matter heading for each paper sent by electronic means must indicate that the matter being transmitted electronically is related to a court proceeding. NY CPLR Rule 2103(b)(7).

c. *Electronic service mandatory; Consenting to electronic service; How electronic service may be made.* Except as otherwise provided in NY R UNIF TRIAL CTS § 202.5-bb, filing and service of all documents in an action that has been commenced electronically in accordance with NY R UNIF TRIAL CTS § 202.5-bb shall be by electronic means. NY R UNIF TRIAL CTS § 202.5-bb(c)(1).

i. *Party's consent required for certain e-filing.* After commencement of an action wherein e-filing is authorized, documents may be electronically filed and served, but only by, and electronic service shall be made only upon, a party or parties who have consented thereto. NY R UNIF TRIAL CTS § 202.5-b(b)(2)(i).

- A consent to e-filing in an action shall state that the party providing it agrees to the use of e-filing in the action and to be bound by the filing and service provisions in NY R UNIF TRIAL CTS § 202.5-b. NY R UNIF TRIAL CTS § 202.5-b(b)(2)(ii).

ii. *Address for service; Duty to notify as to changes.* The e-mail service address recorded at the time of registration is the e-mail address at which service of interlocutory documents on that party may be made through notification transmitted by the NYSCEF site. It is the responsibility of each filing user to monitor that address and promptly notify the Resource Center in the event of a change in his or her e-mail service address. NY R UNIF TRIAL CTS § 202.5-b(f)(2)(i).

iii. *How service made.* An e-filing party causes service of an interlocutory document to be made upon another party participating in e-filing by filing the document electronically. Upon receipt of an interlocutory document, the NYSCEF site shall automatically transmit electronic notification to all e-mail service addresses in such action. NY R UNIF TRIAL CTS § 202.5-b(f)(2)(ii).

- Except as provided otherwise in NY R UNIF TRIAL CTS § 202.5-b(h)(3), the electronic transmission of the notification shall constitute service of the document on the e-mail service addresses identified therein; however, such service will not be effective if the filing party learns that the notification did not reach the address of the person to be served. Proof of such service will be recorded on the NYSCEF site. A party may, however, utilize other service methods permitted by the CPLR provided that, if one of such other methods is used, proof of that service shall be filed electronically. NY R UNIF TRIAL CTS § 202.5-b(f)(2)(ii).

iv. *Signatures on hard copies; Proof of service filed electronically.* When an e-filing party serves a document in hard copy on a non-participating party, the document served shall bear full signatures of all signatories and proof of such service shall be filed electronically. NY R UNIF TRIAL CTS § 202.5-b(b)(2)(i).

v. *Effect of failure to consent.* A party's failure to consent to participation in electronic filing and service shall not bar any other party to the action from filing documents electronically with the County Clerk and the court or serving documents upon any other party who has consented to participation. A party who has not consented to participation shall file documents with the court and the County Clerk, and serve and be served with documents, in hard copy. NY R UNIF TRIAL CTS § 202.5-b(b)(2)(i).

d. *Service upon party.* If a party has not appeared by an attorney or the party's attorney cannot be served, service shall be upon the party by a method specified in NY CPLR Rule 2103(b)(1), NY CPLR Rule 2103(b)(2), NY CPLR Rule 2103(b)(4), NY CPLR Rule 2103(b)(5) or NY CPLR Rule 2103(b)(6). NY CPLR Rule 2103(c).

   i. When a party is in default for failure to appear, he shall not be entitled to notice or service of any copy required under NY CPLR § 3101, et seq. NY CPLR Rule 3105.

e. *Service on all parties.* Each paper served on any party shall be served on every other party who has appeared, except as otherwise may be provided by court order or as provided in NY CPLR § 3012 or in NY CPLR § 3215(f). Upon demand by a party, the plaintiff shall supply that party with a list of those who have appeared and the names and addresses of their attorneys. NY CPLR Rule 2103(e).

f. *Service by filing.* If a paper cannot be served by any of the methods specified in NY CPLR Rule 2103(b) and NY CPLR Rule 2103(c), service may be made by filing the paper as if it were a paper required to be filed. NY CPLR Rule 2103(d).

g. *Definitions.* For the purposes of NY CPLR Rule 2103:

   i. "Mailing" means the deposit of a paper enclosed in a first class postpaid wrapper, addressed to the address designated by a person for that purpose or, if none is designated, at that person's last known address, in a post office or official depository under the exclusive care and custody of the United States Postal Service within the state;

   ii. "Electronic means" means any method of transmission of information between computers or other machines designed for the purpose of sending and receiving such transmissions, and which allows the recipient to reproduce the information transmitted in a tangible medium of expression;

   iii. "Facsimile transmission" means any method of transmission of documents to a facsimile machine at a remote location which can automatically produce a tangible copy of such documents. NY CPLR Rule 2103(f).

G. Hearings

1. There is no hearing required or contemplated in the New York rules governing the request for admissions.

H. Forms

1. New York Request for Admissions Forms

a. Form; Notice to admit; Facts regarding premises. CW2D § 53:8.

b. Form; Notice to admit; Facts regarding subway line that was site of accident. CW2D § 53:9.

c. Form; Notice to admit; Truth of facts or genuineness of papers or documents; Contract for sale of real property. CW2D § 53:10.

d. Form; Notice of motion to strike notice to admit and quash subpoena; Admission of ultimate issues and privileged communications between attorney and client. CW2D § 53:11.

e. Form; Notice of motion to strike notice to admit and for order prohibiting plaintiff from seeking same information by any other disclosure device; Youthful offender records. CW2D § 53:13.

f. General form. NYDISC § 39:2.

g. General form; Injury to invitee. NYDISC § 39:3.

h. General form; Criminal charges. NYDISC § 39:4.

I. Applicable Rules

1. *State rules*

a. Short title; Application; Construction; Definitions. NY CPLR § 101; NY CPLR § 104; NY CPLR § 105.

b. Appendix of official forms. NY CPLR § 107.

c. Extensions of time generally. NY CPLR § 2004.

d. Form of papers. NY CPLR Rule 2101; NY CPLR Rule 2102; NY CPLR § 2105; NY GEN BUS § 399-ddd; NY R UNIF TRIAL CTS § 215.2; NY R UNIF TRIAL CTS § 215.3.

e. Service of papers. NY CPLR Rule 2103.

f. Computation of time. NY CPLR § 2402; NY GEN CONSTR § 19; NY GEN CONSTR § 20; NY GEN CONSTR § 25-a; NY GEN CONSTR § 30; NY GEN CONSTR § 31; NY GEN CONSTR § 53.

g. Scope of disclosure. NY CPLR § 3101; NY CPLR § 3102; NY CPLR § 3103; NY CPLR § 3104; NY CPLR Rule 3105.

h. Admissions as to matters of fact, papers, documents and photographs. NY CPLR § 3123.

i. Motions staying disclosure. NY CPLR Rule 3214; NY CPLR Rule 3407.

j. Index number fees of county clerks. NY CPLR § 8018.

k. Hours of court. NY R CHIEF J § 3.1.

l. Application of part; Waiver; Additional rules; Application of CPLR; Definitions. NY R UNIF TRIAL CTS § 202.1.

m. Papers filed in court; Electronic filing in supreme court. NY R UNIF TRIAL CTS § 202.5; NY R UNIF TRIAL CTS § 202.5-a; NY R UNIF TRIAL CTS § 202.5-b; NY R UNIF TRIAL CTS § 202.5-bb.

n. Rules of the commercial division of the Supreme Court. NY R UNIF TRIAL CTS § 202.70.

o. Signing of papers. NY R CHIEF ADMIN § 130-1.1-a.

2. *Local rules*

a. *Albany County*

i. Third judicial district rules. NY R 3 JD SUP Doc. 1.

b. *Bronx County*

i. Commercial division. NY R BRONX FIL R Doc. 12.

c. *Kings County*

i. Expedited discovery. NY R L KINGS Pt. B, Rule 5.

ii. Pre calendar procedures. NY R L KINGS Rule I.

iii. Both pre and post note procedures. NY R L KINGS Rule IV.

d. *New York County*

i. RJIs and assignments. NY R NY CTY Procedure IA.

ii. Discovery schedule. NY R NY CTY J RUL Rule 8.

J. Miscellaneous

NOTE: Individual judges' rules may apply.

ALBANY COUNTY

JUSTICE LISA M. FISHER: NY R 3 JD FISHER Fisher; NY R 3 JD FISHER Fisher, PC Order.

JUSTICE RICHARD MOTT: NY R 3 JD MOTT Mott.

JUSTICE STEPHAN G. SCHICK: NY R 3 JD Schick.

FORECLOSURE SETTLEMENT PART: NY R 3 JD Foreclosure Settlement.

BRONX COUNTY

JUSTICE PAUL L. ALPERT: [NY R BRONX J Part IA-29, as amended by NY ORDER 20-0337].

JUSTICE BEN BARBATO: NY R BRONX J Part IA-21.

JUSTICE MARY ANNE BRIGANTTI: [NY R BRONX J Part IA-15, as amended by NY ORDER 20-0338].

JUSTICE JOSEPH E. CAPELLA: NY R BRONX J Part IA-23.

JUSTICE MITCHELL DANZIGER: NY R BRONX J Part IA-3/33 ; [NY R BRONX J Danziger, Part IA-3/33, as amended by NY ORDER 20-0339].

JUSTICE LAURA G. DOUGLAS: NY R BRONX J Part IA-11.

JUSTICE RUBEN FRANCO: NY R BRONX J Part IA-26.

JUSTICE DORIS M. GONZALEZ: NY R BRONX J Part IA-24.

JUSTICE WILMA GUZMAN: NY R BRONX J Part IA-7; [NY R BRONX J Guzman, Part IA-7 Virtual, as amended by NY ORDER 20-0340].

JUSTICE ROBERT T. JOHNSON: NY R BRONX J Part IA-12.

JUSTICE DONALD A. MILES: NY R BRONX J Part IA-8.

JUSTICE DONNA M. MILLS: NY R BRONX J Part IA-9.

JUSTICE JULIA I. RODRIGUEZ: NY R BRONX J Part IA-18; [NY R BRONX J Part IA-27, as amended by NY ORDER 20-0341].

JUSTICE LLINET M. ROSADO: [NY R BRONX J Part IA-25, as amended by NY ORDER 20-0342].

JUSTICE NORMA RUIZ: NY R BRONX J Part IA-22; [NY R BRONX J Ruiz, Part IA-22 Virtual, as amended by NY ORDER 20-0343].

JUSTICE HOWARD H. SHERMAN: NY R BRONX J Part IA-4.

JUSTICE FERNANDO TAPIA: NY R BRONX J Part IA-13.

JUSTICE ELIZABETH A. TAYLOR: NY R BRONX J Part IA-2.

JUSTICE ALISON Y. TRUITT: NY R BRONX J Part IA-5.

PART IDV: NY R BRONX J Doc. 1.

PRE-TRIAL PART RULES: NY R BRONX J Doc. 2.

PRE TRIAL WORKSHEET: NY R BRONX J Doc. 3.

FORECLOSURE SETTLEMENT PART RULES: NY R BRONX J Doc. 4.

GUARDIANSHIP PART RULES: NY R BRONX J Doc. 5.

LPM PART RULES: NY R BRONX J Doc. 6.

ERIE COUNTY

JUSTICE M. WILLIAM BOLLER: NY R 8 JD J Boller.

JUSTICE RALPH A. BONIELLO: NY R 8 JD J Boniello.

JUSTICE CHRISTOPHER J. BURN: NY R 8 JD J Burns.

JUSTICE RUSSELL P. BUSCAGLIA: NY R 8 JD J Buscaglia.

JUSTICE FRANK CARUSO: NY R 8 JD J Caruso.

JUSTICE STEPHEN W. CASS: NY R 8 JD J Cass.

JUSTICE DEBORAH A. CHIMES: NY R 8 JD J Chimes.

JUSTICE EMILIO COLAIACOVO: [NY R 8 JD J Colaiacovo, as amended by NY ORDER 20-0252].

JUSTICE DIANE Y. DEVLIN: NY R 8 JD J Devlin.

JUSTICE JAMES H. DILLON: NY R 8 JD J Dillon.

JUSTICE PAULA L. FEROLETO: NY R 8 JD J Feroleto.

JUSTICE DANIEL J. FURLONG: [NY R 8 JD J Furlong, as amended by NY ORDER 20-0253].

JUSTICE JOSEPH R. GLOWNIA: NY R 8 JD J Glownia.

JUSTICE MARK J. GRISANTI: NY R 8 JD J Grisanti.

JUSTICE DEBORAH A. HAENDIGES: NY R 8 JD J Haendiges.

JUSTICE LYNN W. KEANE: [NY R 8 JD J Keane, as amended by NY ORDER 20-0254].

JUSTICE RICHARD C. KLOCH, Sr.: NY R 8 JD J Kloch.

JUSTICE FREDERICK J. MARSHALL: [NY R 8 JD J Marshall, as amended by NY ORDER 20-0255.

JUSTICE JOHN L. MICHALSKI: NY R 8 JD J Michalski.

JUSTICE MARK A. MONTOUR: [NY R 8 JD J Montour, as amended by NY ORDER 20-0256].

JUSTICE HENRY NOWAK: NY R 8 JD J Nowak.

JUSTICE JOHN F. O'DONNELL: NY R 8 JD J O'Donnell.

JUSTICE JEANETTE OGDEN: NY R 8 JD J Ogden.

JUSTICE CATHERINE NUGENT-PANEPINTO: NY R 8 JD J Nugent-Panepinto.

JUSTICE FRANK A. SEDITA, III: [NY R 8 JD J Sedita, as amended by NY ORDER 20-0257].

JUSTICE SARA SHELDON: NY R 8 JD J Sheldon.

JUSTICE DONNA M. SIWEK: NY R 8 JD J Siwek.

JUSTICE MARY L. SLISZ: NY R 8 JD J Slisz.

JUSTICE TIMOTHY J. WALKER: [NY R 8 JD J Walker, as amended by NY ORDER 20-0258].

JUSTICE DENNIS E. WARD: NY R 8 JD J Ward.

JUSTICE PAUL B. WOJTASZEK: [NY R 8 JD J Wojtaszek, as amended by NY ORDER 20-0259].

JUSTICE CHARLES N. ZAMBITO: [NY R 8 JD J Zambito, as amended by NY ORDER 20-0260].

SUPREME COURT LEGAL STAFF: NY R 8 JD J Legal Staff.

KINGS COUNTY

JUSTICE RACHEL A. ADAMS: NY R KINGS J Part 5F.

JUSTICE LOREN BAILY-SCHIFFMAN: NY R KINGS J Part 65.

JUSTICE REGINALD A. BODDIE: NY R KINGS J Part 95.

JUSTICE THERESA M. CICCOTTO: NY R KINGS J Part 19; NY R KINGS J Part 5J.

JUSTICE LISSETTE COLON: NY R KINGS J Part Rules.

JUSTICE GENINE EDWARDS: NY R KINGS J Part 80.

JUSTICE PAMELA L. FISHER: [NY R KINGS J Part 94, as amended by NY ORDER 20-0208].

JUSTICE ROBIN GARSON: NY R KINGS J Part 75.

JUSTICE LARA J. GENOVISI: [NY R KINGS J Part 34, as amended by NY ORDER 20-0209].

JUSTICE BERNARD J. GRAHAM: NY R KINGS J Part 36.

JUSTICE DAWN JIMENEZ-SALTA: NY R KINGS J Part 88.

JUSTICE INGRID JOSEPH: [NY R KINGS J Part FRP3 and Part 83, as amended by NY ORDER 20-0210].

JUSTICE KATHY J. KING: NY R KINGS J Part 64, 76K.

JUSTICE LAWRENCE KNIPEL: NY R KINGS J Part 57.

JUSTICE DONALD KURTZ: NY R KINGS J Part 26.

JUSTICE CARL LANDICINO: [NY R KINGS J Part 81, as amended by NY ORDER 20-0211].

JUSTICE KATHERINE LEVINE: [NY R KINGS J Part 20, 25, 92, as amended by NY ORDER 20-0211].

JUSTICE LORNA MCALLISTER: [NY R KINGS J Part 10, as amended by NY ORDER 20-0211].

JUSTICE ROSEMARIE MONTALBANO: [NY R KINGS J Part 19, 71, and 22, as amended by NY ORDER 20-0211].

JUSTICE RICHARD J. MONTELIONE: [NY R KINGS J Part 99 and DJMP, as amended by NY ORDER 20-0215].

JUSTICE LISA S. OTTLEY: NY R KINGS J Part 24.

JUSTICE MARK I. PARTNOW: NY R KINGS J Part 43.

JUSTICE ERIC I. PRUS: NY R KINGS J Part 5A.

JUSTICE FRANCOIS RIVERA: NY R KINGS J Part 52.

JUSTICE KAREN B. ROTHENBERG: NY R KINGS J Part 35.

JUSTICE LEON RUCHELSMAN: NY R KINGS J Part 1.

JUSTICE WAYNE P. SAITTA: NY R KINGS J Part 29.

JUSTICE ROBIN K. SHEARES: NY R KINGS J Part 96.

JUSTICE KENNETH P. SHERMAN: NY R KINGS J Part 67 and 78.

JUSTICE DEBRA SILBER: NY R KINGS J Part 9 and 5K.

JUSTICE ELLEN M. SPODEK: NY R KINGS J Part 63.

JUSTICE MARSHA L. STEINHARDT: NY R KINGS J Part 15.

JUSTICE JEFFREY S. SUNSHINE: NY R KINGS J Part 5G.

JUSTICE PETER P. SWEENEY: [NY R KINGS J Part 35, as amended by NY ORDER 20-0218].

JUSTICE DELORES J. THOMAS: [NY R KINGS J Part 5T, as amended by NY ORDER 20-0221].

JUSTICE WAVNY TOUSSAINT: NY R KINGS J Part 70.

JUSTICE RICHARD VELASQUEZ: NY R KINGS J Part 66.

JUSTICE CAROLYN E. WADE: NY R KINGS J Part 84.

JUSTICE EDWARD G. WALKER: [NY R KINGS J Part 90, as amended by NY ORDER 20-0219].

JUSTICE LILLIAN WAN: [NY R KINGS J Part 17, as amended by NY ORDER 20-0220].

JUSTICE MICHELLE WESTON: NY R KINGS J Part 3.

MENTAL HYGIENE PART: NY R KINGS J Part 77.

MATRIMONIAL PARTS DURING COVID-19 EMERGENCY: JUSTICE KAREN B. ROTHENBERG: NY R KINGS J Doc. 1.

NASSAU COUNTY

JUSTICE ANNA R. ANZALONE: NY R NASSAU S J Anzalone, Part 26.

JUSTICE STACY D. BENNETT: NY R NASSAU S J Bennett; NY R NASSAU S J Bennett, Form 1.

JUSTICE ANTONIO BRANDVEEN: NY R NASSAU S J Brandveen, Part 31.

JUSTICE JEFFREY S. BROWN: [NY R NASSAU S J Brown, as amended by NY ORDER 20-0297].

JUSTICE STEPHEN A. BUCARIA: NY R NASSAU S J Bucaria.

JUSTICE JULIANNE T. CAPETOLA: NY R NASSAU S J Capetola, Part 28.

JUSTICE EDMUND M. DANE: NY R NASSAU S J Dane, Part 33.

JUSTICE VITO M. DESTEFANO: NY R NASSAU S J DeStefano, Part 13; NY R NASSAU S J DeStefano, Form 1.

JUSTICE ARTHUR M. DIAMOND: NY R NASSAU S J Diamond, Part 7.

JUSTICE THOMAS FEINMAN: NY R NASSAU S J Feinman, Part 5.

JUSTICE JOHN M. GALASSO: NY R NASSAU S J Galasso, Part 22.

JUSTICE SHARON M.J. GIANELLI: NY R NASSAU S J Gianelli, Part 22; NY R NASSAU S J Gianelli, Form 1.

JUSTICE JEFFREY A. GOODSTEIN: NY R NASSAU S J Goodstein, Part 33; NY R NASSAU S J Goodstein, Form 1.

JUSTICE DAVID J. GUGERTY: [NY R NASSAU S J Gugerty, Part 31, as amended by NY ORDER 20-0298].

JUSTICE HELENE F. GUGERTY: NY R NASSAU S J Gugerty, Part 47.

JUSTICE STEVEN M. JAEGER: NY R NASSAU S J Jaeger, Part 35; NY R NASSAU S J Jaeger, Form 1.

JUSTICE JACK L. LIBERT: NY R NASSAU S J Libert, Part 23.

JUSTICE JOSEPH H. LORINTZ: NY R NASSAU S J Lorintz, Part 26; NY R NASSAU S J Lorintz, Form 1.

JUSTICE ROY S. MAHON: NY R NASSAU S J Mahon, Part 3.

JUSTICE RANDY SUE MARBER: NY R NASSAU S J Marber, Part 8.

JUSTICE JAMES P. MCCORMACK: [NY R NASSAU S J McCormack, Part 18, as amended by NY ORDER, 20-0299].

JUSTICE DICCIA T. PINEDA-KIRWAN: [NY R NASSAU S J Pineda-Kirwan, as amended by NY ORDER 20-0300].

JUSTICE THOMAS RADEMAKER: [NY R NASSAU S J Rademaker, Part 28, as amended by NY ORDER 20-0301]; [NY R NASSAU S J Rademaker, Form 1, as amended by NY ORDER 20-0301].

JUSTICE DENISE L. SHER: NY R NASSAU S J Rademaker, Part 32.

JUSTICE LEONARD D. STEINMAN: [NY R NASSAU S J Steinman, Part 15, as amended by NY ORDER 20-0303]; NY R NASSAU S J Steinman, Form 1.

JUSTICE HOWARD E. STURIM: NY R NASSAU S J Sturim, Part 50; NY R NASSAU S J Sturim, Form 1.

JUSTICE HELEN VOUTSINAS: [NY R NASSAU S J Voutsinas, Part 25, as amended by NY ORDER 20-0304]; [NY R NASSAU S J Voutsinas, Form 1, as amended by NY ORDER 20-0305].

JUSTICE HOPE SCHWARTZ ZIMMERMAN: NY R NASSAU S J Zimmerman, Part 17.

NEW YORK COUNTY

JUDGE'S RULES; BASIC INFORMATION: [NY R NY CTY J RUL Doc. 1, as amended by NY ORDER 20-0202].

ONONDAGA COUNTY

JUSTICE ROBERT E. ANTONACCI II: [NY R ONDGA E FIL Doc. 1, as amended by 20-0239].

JUSTICE MICHAEL V. COCCOMI: NY R ONDGA E FIL Doc. 2.

JUSTICE GREGORY R. GILBERT: NY R 5 JD JUDGES Gilbert; NY R ONDGA E FIL Doc. 3.

JUSTICE DONALD A. GREENWOOD: NY R ONDGA E FIL Doc. 4.

JUSTICE DEBORAH H. KARALUNAS: NY R ONDGA E FIL Doc. 5.

JUSTICE JAMES MCCLUSKY: NY R 5 JD MCCLUSKY McClusky.

JUSTICE CHARLES C. MERRELL: NY R 5 JD MERRELL Merrell.

JUSTICE PATRICK F. MACRAE: NY R 5 JD MACRAE Doc. 1.

JUSTICE JAMES P. MURPHY: NY R ONDGA E FIL Doc. 7.

JUSTICE GERALD J. NERI: [NY R 5 JD JUDGES Neri, as amended by NY ORDER 20-0236]; [NY R ONDGA E FIL Doc. 8, as amended by NY ORDER 20-0241].

JUSTICE ANTHONY J. PARIS: NY R 5 JD JUDGES Paris; [NY R ONDGA E FIL Doc. 9, as amended by NY ORDER 20-0242].

JUSTICE NORMAN W. SEITER, JR.: NY R 5 JD JUDGES Seiter.

JUSTICE KEVIN G. YOUNG: [NY R ONDGA E FIL Doc. 10, as amended by NY ORDER 20-0243].

QUEENS COUNTY

JUSTICE PAM JACKMAN BROWN: [NY R L QUEENS Brown, Part 19, as amended by NY ORDER 20-0321].

JUSTICE CHEREE A. BUGGS: NY R L QUEENS Buggs, Part 30.

JUSTICE PAM JACKMAN BROWN: [NY R L QUEENS Brown, Part 19, as amended by NY ORDER 20-0321].

JUSTICE DENIS J. BUTLER: NY R L QUEENS Butler, Part 12.

JUSTICE ROBERT I. CALORAS: [NY R L QUEENS Caloras, Part 36, as amended by NY ORDER 20-0322].

JUSTICE ANNA CULLEY: NY R L QUEENS Culley, Part 53.

JUSTICE TIMOTHY DUFFICY: NY R L QUEENS Dufficy, Part 35.

JUSTICE DAVID ELLIOT: NY R L QUEENS Elliot, Part 14.

JUSTICE JOSEPH J. ESPOSITO: NY R L QUEENS Esposito, Part 6.

JUSTICE DARRELL L. GAVRIN: [NY R L QUEENS Gavrin, Part 27, as amended by NY ORDER 20-0323].

JUSTICE WYATT N. GIBBONS: [NY R L QUEENS Gibbons, Part 5, as amended by NY ORDER 20-0330.

JUSTICE DONNA-MARIE E. GOLIA: [NY R L QUEENS Golia, Part 21, as amended by NY ORDER 20-0331].

JUSTICE MARGUERITE A. GRAYS: [NY R L QUEENS Grays, Part 4, as amended by NY ORDER 20-0324].

JUSTICE RUDOLPH E. GRECO: [NY R L QUEENS Greco, Part 32, as amended by NY ORDER 20-0325].

JUSTICE MAUREEN HEALY: NY R L QUEENS Healy, Part 6.

JUSTICE PHILLIP HOM: [NY R L QUEENS Hom, Part 43, as amended by NY ORDER 20-0332].

JUSTICE KEVIN J. KERRIGAN: NY R L QUEENS Kerrigan, Part 10.

JUSTICE MOJGAN C. LANCMAN: NY R L QUEENS Lancman, Part 20.

JUSTICE RICHARD G. LATIN: NY R L QUEENS Latin, Part 40.

JUSTICE ULYSSES B. LEVERETT: [NY R L QUEENS Leverett, Part 6, as amended by NY ORDER 20-0326].

JUSTICE LEONARD LIVOTE: NY R L QUEENS Livote, Part 33.

JUSTICE LEE A. MAYERSOHN: NY R L QUEENS Mayersohn, Part 22; NY R L QUEENS Mayersohn, Part 22G; [NY R L QUEENS Mayersohn, Part 22G COVID, as amended by NY ORDER 20-0327].

JUSTICE ROBERT J. MCDONALD: NY R L QUEENS McDonald, Part 34.

JUSTICE MARGARET MCGOWAN: NY R L QUEENS McGowan, Part 52.

JUSTICE MAURICE E. MUIR: [NY R L QUEENS Muir, Part 42, as amended by NY ORDER 20-0333].

JUSTICE JODI ORLOW: NY R L QUEENS Orlow, Part 51.

JUSTICE LESLIE J. PURIFICCION: NY R L QUEENS Purificcion, Part 39.

JUSTICE JOSEPH RISI: [NY R L QUEENS Risi, Part 3, as amended by NY ORDER 20-0328].

JUSTICE FREDERICK D.R. SAMPSON: [NY R L QUEENS Sampson, Part 31, as amended by NY ORDER 20-0329].

JUSTICE MARTIN J. SCHULMAN: NY R L QUEENS Schulman, Part 29.

JUSTICE BERNICE D. SIEGAL: NY R L QUEENS Siegal, Part 25G.

JUSTICE JANICE A. TAYLOR: NY R L QUEENS Taylor, Part 15.

JUSTICE CARMEN R. VELASQUEZ: NY R L QUEENS Velasquez, Part 38.

JUSTICE LOURDES M VENTURA: [NY R L QUEENS Ventura, Part 37, as amended by NY ORDER 20-0334].

JUSTICE WILLIAM A. VISCOVICH: NY R L QUEENS Viscovich, Part 63.

JUSTICE ALLAN B. WEISS: NY R L QUEENS Weiss, Part 2.

COMPLIANCE, SETTLEMENT AND CONFERENCE PART: NY R L QUEENS Doc 1.

PRELIMINARY CONFERENCE PART: [NY R L QUEENS Doc. 2, as amended by NY ORDER 20-0335].

MEDICAL MALPRACTICE CONFERENCE PART: [NY R L QUEENS Doc. 3, as amended by NY ORDER 20-0336].

TRIAL SCHEDULING PART: NY R L QUEENS Doc. 4.

SUMMARY JURY TRIAL PROGRAM: NY R L QUEENS Doc. 7.

RESIDENTIAL FORECLOSURE PART: NY R L QUEENS Doc. 9.

FORECLOSURE AUCTION RULES: NY R L QUEENS Doc. 10.

MATRIMONIAL PRELIMINARY CONFERENCE PART: NY R L QUEENS Doc. 11.

NON-CUSTODIAL CONTESTED MATRIMONIAL PART: NY R L QUEENS Doc. 12.

Requests, Notices and Applications
Response to Request for Admissions

Document Last Updated August 2020

A. Checklist

(I) ❑ Matters to consider for requesting party

- (a) ❑ Required documents
  - (1) ❑ Request for admissions
  - (2) ❑ Proof of service
- (b) ❑ Supplemental documents
  - (1) ❑ Copies of document referred to in the request
  - (2) ❑ Working copies
- (c) ❑ Timing
  - (1) ❑ At any time after service of the answer or after the expiration of twenty (20) days from service of the summons, whichever is sooner, and not later than twenty (20) days before the trial, a party may serve upon any other party a written request for admission by the latter

(II) ❑ Matters to consider for responding party

- (a) ❑ Required documents
  - (1) ❑ Response to request for admissions
  - (2) ❑ Proof of service

(b) ❑ Supplemental documents

(1) ❑ Working copies

(c) ❑ Timing

(1) ❑ Each of the matters of which an admission is requested shall be deemed admitted unless within twenty (20) days after service thereof or within such further time as the court may allow, the party to whom the request is directed serves upon the party requesting the admission a sworn statement either denying specifically the matters of which an admission is requested or setting forth in detail the reasons why he cannot truthfully either admit or deny those matters

B. Timing

1. *Response to request for admissions.* Each of the matters of which an admission is requested shall be deemed admitted unless within twenty (20) days after service thereof or within such further time as the court may allow, the party to whom the request is directed serves upon the party requesting the admission a sworn statement either denying specifically the matters of which an admission is requested or setting forth in detail the reasons why he cannot truthfully either admit or deny those matters. NY CPLR § 3123(a).
2. *Motions staying disclosure.* Service of a notice of motion under NY CPLR Rule 3211, NY CPLR Rule 3212, or NY CPLR § 3213 stays disclosure until determination of the motion unless the court orders otherwise. If the motion is based solely on the defense that the summons and complaint, summons with notice, or notice of petition and petition was not properly served, disclosure shall not be stayed unless the court orders otherwise. NY CPLR Rule 3214(b).
   a. *Personal injury actions involving terminally ill patients.* Notwithstanding the provisions of NY CPLR Rule 3214(b), the service or pendency of a motion under NY CPLR Rule 3211, NY CPLR Rule 3212, or NY CPLR § 3213 shall not stay disclosure in an action where a preliminary conference order has been entered pursuant to NY CPLR Rule 3407. NY CPLR Rule 3407(b)(3).
3. *KINGS COUNTY: Discovery timing.* At [the Compliance Conference, the court will] schedule all outstanding discovery to be completed prior to date fixed for filing Note of Issue. NY R L KINGS Rule I(B).
   a. *Deadlines in orders.* Discovery scheduled in Compliance Conference orders shall be strictly adhered to and may not be extended without leave of the court. Unjustified failure to comply with the provisions of the CCP order will result in preclusion, the striking of a pleading or imposition of sanctions, as appropriate. NY R L KINGS Rule I(B)(2).
   b. *Cases with extensive discovery.* Where post Compliance Conference discovery is to be extensive, cases may be retracked from standard to complex, which will provide for three (3) additional months of post Compliance Conference discovery and extend the Note of Issue date by three (3) months. NY R L KINGS Rule I(B)(1).
   c. *Discovery not stayed.* Ordinarily the Court/JHO will not stay discovery during pendency of motions to withdraw, or during pendency of settlement, or during pendency of dispositive motions. NY R L KINGS Rule IV.
   d. *Expedited discovery in certain cases.* Discovery in third party and joint actions will be expedited. NY R L KINGS Pt. B, Rule 5.
   e. For more information on discovery scheduling, refer to NY R L KINGS Flow Chart.
4. *NEW YORK COUNTY: Deadlines in orders.* Strict compliance with all discovery orders is required. Unexcused or unjustified failure to comply with deadlines fixed by the court, including those set out in Preliminary Conference Orders, may result in an award of costs, conditional or otherwise, or the imposition of another penalty authorized by NY CPLR § 3126. NY R NY CTY J RUL Rule 8.
5. *Computation of time*
   a. *Units of time*
      i. *Day.* A calendar day includes the time from midnight to midnight. Sunday or any day of the week specifically mentioned means a calendar day. NY GEN CONSTR § 19.
      ii. *Month.* In a statute, contract or public or private instrument, unless otherwise provided in such contract or instrument or by law, the term month means a calendar month and not a lunar month. NY GEN CONSTR § 31.
      iii. *Year.* For information on the definition of a year, including the definitions of a half-year and quarter-year, refer to NY GEN CONSTR § 58 and NY GEN CONSTR § 50. For information on leap years, refer to NY GEN CONSTR § 57.
   b. *Periods of time*
      i. *Number of days.* A number of days specified as a period from a certain day within which or after or before which

an act is authorized or required to be done means such number of calendar days exclusive of the calendar day from which the reckoning is made. NY GEN CONSTR § 20.

- If such period is a period of two (2) days, Saturday, Sunday or a public holiday must be excluded from the reckoning if it is an intervening day between the day from which the reckoning is made and the last day of the period. NY GEN CONSTR § 20.
- In computing any specified period of time from a specified event, the day upon which the event happens is deemed the day from which the reckoning is made. The day from which any specified period of time is reckoned shall be excluded in making the reckoning. NY GEN CONSTR § 20.

ii. *Number of months.* A number of months after or before a certain day shall be computed by counting such number of calendar months from such day, exclusive of the calendar month in which such day occurs, and shall include the day of the month in the last month so counted having the same numerical order in days of the month as the day from which the computation is made, unless there be not so many days in the last month so counted, in which case the period computed shall expire with the last day of the month so counted. NY GEN CONSTR § 30.

iii. *Publication of notice; Number of days.* The period of publication of a legal notice shall be computed by excluding the first day of publication and including the day on which the act or event of which notice is given is to take place or which completes the full period of publication. NY CPLR § 2402.

iv. *Periods ending on Saturday, Sunday or public holiday.* When any period of time, computed from a certain day, within which or after which or before which an act is authorized or required to be done, ends on a Saturday, Sunday or a public holiday, such act may be done on the next succeeding business day and if the period ends at a specified hour, such act may be done at or before the same hour of such next succeeding business day, except that where a period of time specified by contract ends on a Saturday, Sunday or a public holiday, the extension of such period is governed by NY GEN CONSTR § 25. NY GEN CONSTR § 25-a(1).

- For a list of public holidays, refer to NY GEN CONSTR § 24.

v. *Additional time after certain kinds of service*

- *Service by mail.* Where a period of time prescribed by law is measured from the service of a paper and service is by mail, five (5) days shall be added to the prescribed period. NY CPLR Rule 2103(b)(2).
- *Service by overnight delivery service.* Where a period of time prescribed by law is measured from the service of a paper and service is by overnight delivery, one (1) business day shall be added to the prescribed period. NY CPLR Rule 2103(b)(6).

vi. *Daylight saving time.* For information on New York's time zone and the effect of daylight saving time, refer to NY GEN CONSTR § 52.

c. *Hours of court.* Notwithstanding any provision of law or rule of court to the contrary, throughout the State of New York the sessions of the Supreme Court for the disposition of business before the court shall commence not later than 9:30 a.m. and conclude not earlier than 5 p.m. Where warranted, the Chief Administrator of the Courts may authorize variances in the opening and closing hours of the courts, but, in such event, daily sessions shall total not less than six (6) hours. NY R CHIEF J § 3.1.

d. *Time limits; Extension of time.* Any act required by or in pursuance of law to be performed at or within a prescribed time, shall be performed according to the standard time. NY GEN CONSTR § 53.

i. Except where otherwise expressly prescribed by law, the court may extend the time fixed by any statute, rule or order for doing any act, upon such terms as may be just and upon good cause shown, whether the application for extension is made before or after the expiration of the time fixed. NY CPLR § 2004. Refer to the New York KeyRules Motion for Continuance/Extension of Time document for more information.

C. General Requirements

1. *Rules governing disclosure*

a. *Generally.* There shall be full disclosure of all matter material and necessary in the prosecution or defense of an action, regardless of the burden of proof, by:

i. A party, or the officer, director, member, agent or employee of a party;

ii. A person who possessed a cause of action or defense asserted in the action;

iii. A person about to depart from the state, or without the state, or residing at a greater distance from the place of trial than one hundred miles, or so sick or infirm as to afford reasonable grounds of belief that he or she will not be able to attend the trial, or a person authorized to practice medicine, dentistry or podiatry who has provided medical, dental or podiatric care or diagnosis to the party demanding disclosure, or who has been retained by such party as an expert witness; and

iv. Any other person, upon notice stating the circumstances or reasons such disclosure is sought or required. NY CPLR § 3101(a).

v. The statutory phrase "material and necessary", said the Court of Appeals, must be interpreted liberally to require disclosure upon request, of any facts bearing on the controversy which will assist preparation for trial by sharpening the issues and reducing delay and prolixity. The test is one of usefulness and reason. SIEGEL-NYPRAC § 344; Allen v. Crowell-Collier Pub. Co., 21 N.Y.2d 403, 235 N.E.2d 430 (1968).

vi. Another potential problem that the original NY CPLR § 3101(a) posed was that it spoke of "evidence" that is material and necessary, which might have been construed to permit disclosure to elicit only that which would itself qualify as "evidence" admissible at trial. It was, however, construed more broadly than that. Well-considered caselaw specifically rejected this "evidence in chief" doctrine, stating that disclosure extends as well "to all relevant information calculated to lead to relevant evidence," a standard similar to that applicable in federal court. With an amendment that took effect on January 1, 1994, changing "evidence" to "matter" in NY CPLR § 3101(a), these generous interpretations of the statute were in effect approved by the legislature. SIEGEL-NYPRAC § 344.

vii. If a party is a corporation, each of its officers, directors, members, agents, and employees is also deemed a "party" for disclosure purposes. A party who needs relevant data or material from a nonparty corporation can seek it through NY CPLR § 3101(a)(2), NY CPLR § 3101(a)(3) or NY CPLR § 3101(a)(4), under which the corporate entity is treated as a "person." These subdivisions should also apply to any entity, corporate or otherwise, from whom disclosure is sought through its agents. A corporate employee who has the requisite knowledge and information may respond to a disclosure request on behalf of the corporation. A party who can't single out the particular person in the corporation's employ to whom a disclosure request should be properly directed can direct it to the corporation as such and leave it to the corporation to designate the appropriate person to respond. Whenever disclosure is sought from a corporation through a deposition, whether as a party or as a nonparty witness, the choice in the first instance of who will be produced in the corporate behalf is with the corporation rather than the examining party. SIEGEL-NYPRAC § 345.

viii. NY CPLR § 3101(a)(4) permits a party to obtain disclosure from a nonparty by merely serving a subpoena on the nonparty providing notice of "the circumstances or reasons such disclosure is sought or required." SIEGEL-NYPRAC § 345.

b. *Methods of obtaining disclosure.* Information is obtainable by one or more of the following disclosure devices: depositions upon oral questions or without the state upon written questions, interrogatories, demands for addresses, discovery and inspection of documents or property, physical and mental examinations of persons, and requests for admission. NY CPLR § 3102(a).

i. *Stipulation or notice.* Unless otherwise provided by the civil practice law and rules or by the court, disclosure shall be obtained by stipulation or on notice without leave of the court. NY CPLR § 3102(b).

ii. *Before action commenced; Court order required.* Before an action is commenced, disclosure to aid in bringing an action, to preserve information or to aid in arbitration, may be obtained, but only by court order. The court may appoint a referee to take testimony. NY CPLR § 3102(c).

iii. *During trial; Court order required.* Except as provided in NY CPLR § 5223, during and after trial, disclosure may be obtained only by order of the trial court on notice. NY CPLR § 3102(d).

iv. *Action pending in another jurisdiction.* Except as provided in NY CPLR § 3119, when under any mandate, writ or commission issued out of any court of record in any other state, territory, district or foreign jurisdiction, or whenever upon notice or agreement, it is required to take the testimony of a witness in the state, he or she may be compelled to appear and testify in the same manner and by the same process as may be employed for the purpose of taking testimony in actions pending in the state. The supreme court or a county court shall make any appropriate order in aid of taking such a deposition. NY CPLR § 3102(e).

v. *Actions to which state is a party.* In an action in which the state is properly a party, whether as plaintiff, defendant or otherwise, disclosure by the state shall be available as if the state were a private person. NY CPLR § 3102(f).

c. *Privileged matter.* Upon objection by a person entitled to assert the privilege, privileged matter shall not be obtainable. NY CPLR § 3101(b).

i. A determination of whether information is privileged is governed by the rules of evidence, which apply as they would at a trial. Whatever is privileged at the trial is privileged as well on pretrial disclosure. SIEGEL-NYPRAC § 346.

d. *Attorney's work product.* The work product of an attorney shall not be obtainable. NY CPLR § 3101(c).

i. NY CPLR § 3101(c) makes unobtainable the "work product of an attorney"—an ill-defined category whose potential for mischief has been avoided only because the judiciary has accorded it a very narrow scope. It is a category wholly distinct from the "materials . . . prepared in anticipation of litigation" of NY CPLR § 3101(d)(2). The fact that immunity is absolute under NY CPLR § 3101(c), while that of NY CPLR § 3101(d)(2) is only conditional, is the factor that requires as sharp a line as possible between the two categories. SIEGEL-NYPRAC § 347.

ii. The judiciary has cast precious little under the "work product" category of NY CPLR § 3101(c), preferring instead to fit doubtful items under the "materials . . . prepared in anticipation of litigation" banner of NY CPLR § 3101(d)(2), where the conditional immunity can be overcome and the matters ordered disclosed when stated conditions are met. SIEGEL-NYPRAC § 347.

e. *Trial preparation*

i. *Experts.* Upon request, each party shall identify each person whom the party expects to call as an expert witness at trial and shall disclose in reasonable detail the subject matter on which each expert is expected to testify, the substance of the facts and opinions on which each expert is expected to testify, the qualifications of each expert witness and a summary of the grounds for each expert's opinion. NY CPLR § 3101(d)(1)(i).

- However, where a party for good cause shown retains an expert an insufficient period of time before the commencement of trial to give appropriate notice thereof, the party shall not thereupon be precluded from introducing the expert's testimony at the trial solely on grounds of noncompliance with NY CPLR § 3101(d)(1). In that instance, upon motion of any party, made before or at trial, or on its own initiative, the court may make whatever order may be just. In an action for medical, dental or podiatric malpractice, a party, in responding to a request, may omit the names of medical, dental or podiatric experts but shall be required to disclose all other information concerning such experts otherwise required by NY CPLR § 3101(d)(1). NY CPLR § 3101(d)(1)(i).
- In an action for medical, dental or podiatric malpractice, any party may, by written offer made to and served upon all other parties and filed with the court, offer to disclose the name of, and to make available for examination upon oral deposition, any person the party making the offer expects to call as an expert witness at trial. Within twenty (20) days of service of the offer, a party shall accept or reject the offer by serving a written reply upon all parties and filing a copy thereof with the court. Failure to serve a reply within twenty (20) days of service of the offer shall be deemed a rejection of the offer. If all parties accept the offer, each party shall be required to produce his or her expert witness for examination upon oral deposition upon receipt of a notice to take oral deposition in accordance with NY CPLR Rule 3107. If any party, having made or accepted the offer, fails to make that party's expert available for oral deposition, that party shall be precluded from offering expert testimony at the trial of the action. NY CPLR § 3101(d)(1)(ii).
- Further disclosure concerning the expected testimony of any expert may be obtained only by court order upon a showing of special circumstances and subject to restrictions as to scope and provisions concerning fees and expenses as the court may deem appropriate. However, a party, without court order, may take the testimony of a person authorized to practice medicine, dentistry or podiatry who is the party's treating or retained expert, as described in NY CPLR § 3101(a)(3), in which event any other party shall be entitled to the full disclosure authorized by Article 31 of Chapter 8 of the Civil Practice Law and Rules (NY CPLR § 3101, et seq.) with respect to that expert without court order. NY CPLR § 3101(d)(1)(iii).

ii. *Materials.* Subject to the provisions of NY CPLR § 3101(d)(1), materials otherwise discoverable under NY CPLR § 3101(a) and prepared in anticipation of litigation or for trial by or for another party, or by or for that other party's representative (including an attorney, consultant, surety, indemnitor, insurer or agent), may be obtained only upon a showing that the party seeking discovery has substantial need of the materials in the preparation of the case and is unable without undue hardship to obtain the substantial equivalent of the materials by other means. In ordering discovery of the materials when the required showing has been made, the court shall protect against disclosure of the mental impressions, conclusions, opinions or legal theories of an attorney or other representative of a party concerning the litigation. NY CPLR § 3101(d)(2).

- In order to qualify as "litigation" material the item must have been prepared exclusively for litigation. Incidental potential use in litigation, the courts have observed, may also be a function of such reports, but they have at least an equal if not greater mission "to prevent future accidents, discipline careless employees, or, generally, to increase the economy and efficiency of the operation." SIEGEL-NYPRAC § 348.

f. *Party's statement.* A party may obtain a copy of his own statement. NY CPLR § 3101(e).

   i. Moreover, NY CPLR § 3101(e) has been broadly interpreted to include photographs. Items such as photographs and videotapes are now independently subject to disclosure under NY CPLR § 3101(i). SIEGEL-NYPRAC § 348.

g. *Contents of insurance agreement.* A party may obtain discovery of the existence and contents of any insurance agreement under which any person carrying on an insurance business may be liable to satisfy part or all of a judgment which may be entered in the action or to indemnify or reimburse for payments made to satisfy the judgment. Information concerning the insurance agreement is not by reason of disclosure admissible in evidence at trial. For purpose of NY CPLR § 3101(f), an application for insurance shall not be treated as part of an insurance agreement. NY CPLR § 3101(f).

h. *Accident reports.* Except as is otherwise provided by law, in addition to any other matter which may be subject to disclosure, there shall be full disclosure of any written report of an accident prepared in the regular course of business operations or practices of any person, firm, corporation, association or other public or private entity, unless prepared by a police or peace officer for a criminal investigation or prosecution and disclosure would interfere with a criminal investigation or prosecution. NY CPLR § 3101(g).

i. *Amendment or supplementation of responses.* A party shall amend or supplement a response previously given to a request for disclosure promptly upon the party's thereafter obtaining information that the response was incorrect or incomplete when made, or that the response, though correct and complete when made, no longer is correct and complete, and the circumstances are such that a failure to amend or supplement the response would be materially misleading. NY CPLR § 3101(h).

   i. Where a party obtains such information an insufficient period of time before the commencement of trial appropriately to amend or supplement the response, the party shall not thereupon be precluded from introducing evidence at the trial solely on grounds of noncompliance with NY CPLR § 3101(h). In that instance, upon motion of any party, made before or at trial, or on its own initiative, the court may make whatever order may be just. Further amendment or supplementation may be obtained by court order. NY CPLR § 3101(h).

j. *Other disclosures.* In addition to any other matter which may be subject to disclosure, there shall be full disclosure of any films, photographs, video tapes or audio tapes, including transcripts or memoranda thereof, involving a person referred to in NY CPLR § 3101(a)(1). There shall be disclosure of all portions of such material, including out-takes, rather than only those portions a party intends to use. The provisions of NY CPLR § 3101(i) shall not apply to materials compiled for law enforcement purposes which are exempt from disclosure under NY PUB OFF § 87. NY CPLR § 3101(i).

   i. While NY CPLR § 3101(i) was enacted with the defendant's surreptitious tapes of the plaintiff in mind, its language is broad enough to embrace any films, photographs, and audio or video tapes of a party, even those made by the party from whom disclosure is sought. SIEGEL-NYPRAC § 348.

k. *Protective orders.* The court may at any time on its own initiative, or on motion of any party or of any person from whom discovery is sought, make a protective order denying, limiting, conditioning or regulating the use of any disclosure device. NY CPLR § 3103(a). Refer to the New York KeyRules Motion for Protective Order document for more information.

l. *Supervision of disclosure.* Upon the motion of any party or witness on notice to all parties or on its own initiative without notice, the court in which an action is pending may by one of its judges or a referee supervise all or part of any disclosure procedure. NY CPLR § 3104(a).

   i. *Selection of referee.* A judicial hearing officer may be designated as a referee under NY CPLR § 3104, or the court may permit all of the parties in an action to stipulate that a named attorney may act as referee. In such latter event, the stipulation shall provide for payment of his fees which shall, unless otherwise agreed, be taxed as disbursements. NY CPLR § 3104(b).

   ii. *Powers of referee; Motions referred to person supervising disclosure.* A referee under NY CPLR § 3104 shall have all the powers of the court under NY CPLR § 3101, et seq. except the power to relieve himself of his duties, to appoint a successor, or to adjudge any person guilty of contempt. All motions or applications made under Article 31 of Chapter 8 of the Civil Practice Law and Rules (NY CPLR § 3101, et seq.) shall be returnable before the judge or referee, designated under NY CPLR § 3104 and after disposition, if requested by any party, his order shall be filed in the office of the clerk. NY CPLR § 3104(c).

iii. *Review of order of referee.* Any party or witness may apply for review of an order made under NY CPLR § 3104 by a referee. The application shall be by motion made in the court in which the action is pending within five (5) days after the order is made. Service of a notice of motion for review shall suspend disclosure of the particular matter in dispute. If the question raised by the motion may affect the rights of a witness, notice shall be served on him personally or by mail at his last known address. It shall set forth succinctly the order complained of, the reason it is objectionable and the relief demanded. NY CPLR § 3104(d).

iv. *Payment of expenses of referee.* Except where a judicial hearing officer has been designated a referee hereunder, the court may make an appropriate order for the payment of the reasonable expenses of the referee. NY CPLR § 3104(e).

2. *Response to request for admissions*

a. *Request for admissions, generally.* A party may serve upon any other party a written request for admission by the latter of the genuineness of any papers or documents, or the correctness or fairness of representation of any photographs, described in and served with the request, or of the truth of any matters of fact set forth in the request, as to which the party requesting the admission reasonably believes there can be no substantial dispute at the trial and which are within the knowledge of such other party or can be ascertained by him upon reasonable inquiry. NY CPLR § 3123(a).

i. *Form and content.* Requests for admissions should be simple and direct. They should only include "clear-cut" matters of fact. A notice to admit that is unnecessarily protracted and appears patently burdensome to answer will be vacated. A plaintiff need not make a motion to preclude relating to a notice to admit, since a proper notice to admit is self-executing. CW2D § 53:5.

ii. *Purpose and use.* The purpose of the device is to save a party the trouble and expense of proving a readily admittable fact. SIEGEL-NYPRAC § 364. Because of its inherent limitations, the notice to admit is under-used. It is also true that the matters to which it lends itself are often admitted by opposing parties in the course of the pleadings or depositions or other disclosure devices, or preliminary conferences, or are so easily and inexpensively proved that a party feels no need to avoid the proof by securing the admission. SIEGEL-NYPRAC § 364.

- The device may be used only when the seeking party "reasonably believes there can be no substantial dispute" about the matter at the trial and when it is within the knowledge of the other party or ascertainable by him "upon reasonable inquiry." SIEGEL-NYPRAC § 364. The notice is not truly a disclosure device, but just a procedure designed to "crystallize issues." SIEGEL-NYPRAC § 364.
- It may not be used, in other words, "to cover ultimate conclusions, which can only be made after a full and complete trial." SIEGEL-NYPRAC § 364; DeSilva by DeSilva v. Rosenberg, 236 A.D.2d 508, 654 N.Y.S.2d 30 (1997). Nor may it be used for technical or scientific information such as is ordinarily elicited from an expert. SIEGEL-NYPRAC § 364; Berg v. Flower Fifth Ave. Hosp., 102 A.D.2d 760, 476 N.Y.S.2d 895 (1984); Johantgen v. Hobart Mfg. Co., 64 A.D.2d 858, 407 N.Y.S.2d 355 (1978).
- The notice to admit may not be used to make one party admit what some other party knows. SIEGEL-NYPRAC § 364. A separate notice to admit should be drawn for each party so as not to elicit from one something suitable for admission only by another. SIEGEL-NYPRAC § 364.

b. *Response to request; Qualification of admission.* If the matters of which an admission is requested cannot be fairly admitted without some material qualification or explanation, or if the matters constitute a trade secret or such party would be privileged or disqualified from testifying as a witness concerning them, such party may, in lieu of a denial or statement, serve a sworn statement setting forth in detail his claim and, if the claim is that the matters cannot be fairly admitted without some material qualification or explanation, admitting the matters with such qualification or explanation. NY CPLR § 3123(a).

c. *Effect of admission.* Any admission made, or deemed to be made, by a party pursuant to a request made under NY CPLR § 3123 is for the purpose of the pending action only and does not constitute an admission by him for any other purpose nor may it be used against him in any other proceeding; and the court, at any time, may allow a party to amend or withdraw any admission on such terms as may be just. Any admission shall be subject to all pertinent objections to admissibility which may be interposed at the trial. NY CPLR § 3123(b).

d. *Penalty for unreasonable denial.* If a party, after being served with a request under NY CPLR § 3123(a) does not admit and if the party requesting the admission thereafter proves the genuineness of any such paper or document, or the correctness or fairness of representation of any such photograph, or the truth of any such matter of fact, he may move at or immediately following the trial for an order requiring the other party to pay him the reasonable expenses incurred in making such proof, including reasonable attorney's fees. Unless the court finds that there were good reasons for the denial or the refusal otherwise to admit or that the admissions sought were of no substantial importance, the order shall be made irrespective of the result of the action. Upon a trial by jury, the motion for such an order shall be determined by the court outside the presence of the jury. NY CPLR § 3123(c).

3. *Governing law.* The civil practice law and rules (NY CPLR § 101, et seq.) shall govern the procedure in civil judicial proceedings in all courts of the state and before all judges, except where the procedure is regulated by inconsistent statute. The civil practice law and rules shall succeed the civil practice act and rules of civil practice and shall be deemed substituted therefor throughout the statutes and rules of the state. NY CPLR § 101. The civil practice law and rules shall be liberally construed to secure the just, speedy and inexpensive determination of every civil judicial proceeding. NY CPLR § 104.

   a. *Uniform trial court rules.* The uniform civil rules for the Supreme Court and County Court (NY R UNIF TRIAL CTS § 202.1, et seq.) shall be applicable to civil actions and proceedings in the Supreme Court and the County Court. NY R UNIF TRIAL CTS § 202.1(a). The provisions of the uniform rules shall be construed consistent with the Civil Practice Law and Rules (CPLR), and matters not covered by the uniform rules shall be governed by the CPLR. NY R UNIF TRIAL CTS § 202.1(d).

   b. *Local rules.* Local court rules, not inconsistent with law or with uniform civil rules for the Supreme Court and County Court (NY R UNIF TRIAL CTS § 202.1, et seq.), shall comply with Part 9 of the Rules of the Chief Judge (NY R CHIEF J § 9.1). NY R UNIF TRIAL CTS § 202.1(c).

   c. *Official forms.* The state administrator shall have the power to adopt, amend and rescind an appendix of forms. Forms adopted pursuant to NY CPLR § 107 shall be sufficient under the civil practice law and rules and shall illustrate the simplicity and brevity of statement which the civil practice law and rules contemplate. NY CPLR § 107.

4. *Rules of the commercial division.* [Editor's note: certain types of civil cases or civil cases meeting certain monetary thresholds that are filed in the state of New York must be filed in the Commercial Division of the New York Supreme Courts. Rules governing practice in the commercial division are found in NY R UNIF TRIAL CTS § 202.70]. Cases which must be filed in the commercial division are listed below. For more information, refer to NY R UNIF TRIAL CTS § 202.70.

   a. *Monetary thresholds.* Except as set forth in NY R UNIF TRIAL CTS § 202.70(b), the monetary thresholds of the Commercial Division, exclusive of punitive damages, interests, costs, disbursements and counsel fees claimed, are established as follows: (1) Albany County, fifty thousand dollars ($50,000); (2) Eighth Judicial District, one hundred thousand dollars ($100,000); (3) Kings County, one hundred fifty thousand dollars ($150,000); (4) Nassau County, two hundred thousand dollars ($200,000); (5) New York County, five hundred thousand dollars ($500,000); (6) Onondaga County, fifty thousand dollars ($50,000); (7) Queens County, one hundred thousand dollars ($100,000); (8) Seventh Judicial District, fifty thousand dollars ($50,000); (9) Suffolk County, one hundred thousand dollars ($100,000); and (10) Westchester County, one hundred thousand dollars ($100,000). NY R UNIF TRIAL CTS § 202.70(a).

      i. *ALBANY COUNTY.* The Commercial Division of the Albany County Supreme Court exercises jurisdiction over selected business and commercial disputes in which the amount at issue generally involves damage claims in a minimum amount of fifty thousand dollars ($50,000) as well as claims for unspecified amounts where the value of the commercial asset(s) in dispute exceeds fifty thousand dollars ($50,000). A separate publication promulgating the rules and criteria relating to the filing and management of Commercial Court cases in this part may be obtained from the Albany County Supreme Court Clerk's Office. A section of the Uniform Civil Rules for the Supreme Court and County Court sets forth statewide rules. NY R 3 JD SUP Doc. 1(E).

      ii. *BRONX COUNTY.* The monetary threshold for commercial cases in Bronx County will be seventy-five thousand dollars ($75,000). All other parameters including the type of matters that will be heard are contained within the Rules of the Commercial Division of the Supreme Court (NY R UNIF TRIAL CTS § 202.70). NY R BRONX FIL R Doc. 12.

      iii. *NEW YORK COUNTY.* The monetary threshold in the New York County Commercial Division, which is generally applicable, is an amount in controversy of five hundred thousand dollars ($500,000) or more (exclusive of punitive damages, interest, costs, disbursements, and counsel fees). If the case is designated a commercial one and the Addendum is submitted, the clerk will review the pleadings to determine whether the amount in controversy in the case meets the monetary threshold or whether an exception to the threshold applies. NY R NY CTY Procedure IA(B). For more information on assigning a case to the commercial division in New York County, refer to NY R NY CTY Procedure IA(B).

   b. *Commercial cases.* Actions in which the principal claims involve or consist of the following will be heard in the Commercial Division provided that the monetary threshold is met or equitable or declaratory relief is sought:

      i. Breach of contract or fiduciary duty, fraud, misrepresentation, business tort (e.g., unfair competition), or statutory and/or common law violation where the breach or violation is alleged to arise out of business dealings (e.g., sales of assets or securities; corporate restructuring; partnership, shareholder, joint venture, and other business agreements; trade secrets; restrictive covenants; and employment agreements not including claims that principally involve alleged discriminatory practices);

ii. Transactions governed by the Uniform Commercial Code (exclusive of those concerning individual cooperative or condominium units);

iii. Transactions involving commercial real property, including Yellowstone injunctions and excluding actions for the payment of rent only;

iv. Shareholder derivative actions—without consideration of the monetary threshold;

v. Commercial class actions—without consideration of the monetary threshold;

vi. Business transactions involving or arising out of dealings with commercial banks and other financial institutions;

vii. Internal affairs of business organizations;

viii. Malpractice by accountants or actuaries, and legal malpractice arising out of representation in commercial matters;

ix. Environmental insurance coverage;

x. Commercial insurance coverage (e.g., directors and officers, errors and omissions, and business interruption coverage);

xi. Dissolution of corporations, partnerships, limited liability companies, limited liability partnerships and joint ventures—without consideration of the monetary threshold; and

xii. Applications to stay or compel arbitration and affirm or disaffirm arbitration awards and related injunctive relief pursuant to Article 75 of the New York Civil Practice Law and Rules (NY CPLR § 7501, et seq.) involving any of the foregoing enumerated commercial issues. Where the applicable arbitration agreement provides for the arbitration to be heard outside the United States, the monetary threshold set forth in NY R UNIF TRIAL CTS § 202.70(a) shall not apply. NY R UNIF TRIAL CTS § 202.70(b).

c. *Non-commercial cases.* The following will not be heard in the Commercial Division even if the monetary threshold is met:

i. Suits to collect professional fees;

ii. Cases seeking a declaratory judgment as to insurance coverage for personal injury or property damage;

iii. Residential real estate disputes, including landlord-tenant matters, and commercial real estate disputes involving the payment of rent only;

iv. Home improvement contracts involving residential properties consisting of one to four residential units or individual units in any residential building, including cooperative or condominium units;

v. Proceedings to enforce a judgment regardless of the nature of the underlying case;

vi. First-party insurance claims and actions by insurers to collect premiums or rescind non-commercial policies; and

vii. Attorney malpractice actions except as otherwise provided in NY R UNIF TRIAL CTS § 202.70(b)(8). NY R UNIF TRIAL CTS § 202.70(c).

d. For more information on the Commercial Division, refer to NY R UNIF TRIAL CTS § 202.70.

D. Documents

1. *Required documents*

a. *Response to request for admissions.* Refer to the General Requirements section of this document for information on the response to request for admissions.

b. *Proof of service.* In addition to complying with the provisions of NY CPLR Rule 2101, every paper filed in court shall have annexed thereto appropriate proof of service on all parties where required. NY R UNIF TRIAL CTS § 202.5(a).

2. *Supplemental documents*

a. *Working copies.* The court may require the parties to provide working copies of documents filed electronically. In such event, each working copy shall include, firmly affixed thereto, a copy of a confirmation notice in a form prescribed by the Chief Administrator. NY R UNIF TRIAL CTS § 202.5-b(d)(5).

E. Format

1. *Form of documents*

   a. *Size and form of paper.* Each paper served or filed shall be durable, white and, except for summonses, subpoenas, notices of appearance, notes of issue, orders of protection, temporary orders of protection and exhibits, shall be eleven by eight and one-half (11 x 8-1/2) inches in size. NY CPLR Rule 2101(a).

   b. *Writing and language.* The writing shall be legible and in black ink. NY CPLR Rule 2101(a). Each paper served or filed shall be in the English language which, where practicable, shall be of ordinary usage. NY CPLR Rule 2101(b).

   c. *Caption.* Each paper served or filed shall begin with a caption setting forth the name of the court, the venue, the title of the action, the nature of the paper and the index number of the action if one has been assigned. In all papers other than a summons, a complaint or a judgment it shall be sufficient to state the name of the first named party on each side with an appropriate indication of any omissions. NY CPLR Rule 2101(c).

      i. *Further contents of first page.* After the first paper has been filed in each case the index number shall appear on the cover and first page to the right of the caption of every paper tendered for filing in the action. Each such cover and first page also shall contain an indication of the county of venue and a brief description of the nature of the paper and, where the case has been assigned to an individual judge, shall contain the name of the assigned judge to the right of the caption. NY R UNIF TRIAL CTS § 202.5(a); NY R UNIF TRIAL CTS § 202.5(b); NY R UNIF TRIAL CTS § 202.5(d)(1)(i).

   d. *Index number.* No paper in an action in the supreme or a county court, other than an order submitted for signature to a judge out of court, shall be submitted for any purpose to the supreme or county court or to a clerk thereof unless there is endorsed on such paper the index number of the action assigned by the clerk of the county. NY CPLR § 8018(c).

   e. *Line spacing.* Every paper filed in court, if typewritten, shall have at least double space between each line, except for quotations and the names and addresses of attorneys appearing in the action. NY R UNIF TRIAL CTS § 202.5(a).

   f. *Font size.* Each. . .paper printed or typed, served or filed, except for summonses. . .and exhibits, shall be in clear type of no less than ten (10) point in size. NY CPLR Rule 2101(a).

      i. Whenever a requirement relating to size of type is stated in point size, the type size requirement shall be deemed met if the x-height of the type is a minimum of forty-five percent (45%) of the specified point size. Each point shall be measured as .351 millimeter. The x-height size shall be measured as it appears on the page. The x-height is the height of the lower case letters, exclusive of ascenders or descenders. NY CPLR § 105(t).

   g. *Margins.* Every paper filed in court shall have at least one (1) inch margins. NY R UNIF TRIAL CTS § 202.5(a).

   h. *Citations*

      i. *Civil practice law and rules.* NY CPLR § 101, et seq. shall be known as the civil practice law and rules, and may be cited as "CPLR". Reference to a provision in the civil practice law and rules may, except when such provision is being enacted or amended, be made without indicating whether it is a rule or section. NY CPLR § 101.

   i. *Indorsement by attorney.* Each paper served or filed shall be indorsed with the name, address and telephone number of the attorney for the party serving or filing the paper, or if the party does not appear by attorney, with the name, address and telephone number of the party. NY CPLR Rule 2101(d).

   j. *One-sided printing.* In addition, every paper filed in court, other than an exhibit or printed form, shall contain writing on one side only, except that papers that are fastened on the side may contain writing on both sides. NY R UNIF TRIAL CTS § 202.5(a).

   k. *Use of copies authorized.* Except where otherwise specifically prescribed, copies, rather than originals, of all papers, including orders, affidavits and exhibits may be served or filed. Where it is required that the original be served or filed and the original is lost or withheld, the court may authorize a copy to be served or filed. NY CPLR Rule 2101(e).

      i. Where a certified copy of a paper is required by law, an attorney admitted to practice in the courts of the state may certify that it has been compared by him with the original and found to be a true and complete copy. Such a certificate, when subscribed by such attorney, has the same effect as if made by a clerk. NY CPLR § 2105.

   l. *Recycled paper.* It is the policy of the Unified Court System that litigants, where practicable, should file or submit to the courts of the Unified Court System of the State of New York papers printed or reproduced on recycled paper. Paper is considered recycled if it contains a minimum content of thirty percent (30%) waste paper. NY R UNIF TRIAL CTS

§ 215.2. The signature page of every paper filed or submitted to the court on recycled paper should bear the legend: "Printed [Reproduced] on Recycled Paper." NY R UNIF TRIAL CTS § 215.3.

2. *Form of electronic documents.* Each paper served or filed by electronic means, as defined in NY CPLR Rule 2103(f), shall be capable of being reproduced by the receiver so as to comply with the provisions of NY CPLR Rule 2101(a) through NY CPLR Rule 2101(d). NY CPLR Rule 2101(g).

   a. *File format.* All e-filed documents shall comply with the technical requirements set forth at the NYSCEF site. NY R UNIF TRIAL CTS § 202.5-b(d)(1)(i).

   b. *Heading of document.* The subject matter heading for each paper sent by electronic means must indicate that the matter being transmitted electronically is related to a court proceeding. NY CPLR Rule 2103(b)(7).

3. *Signature blocks.* Every pleading, written motion, and other paper, served on another party or filed or submitted to the court shall be signed by an attorney, or by a party if the party is not represented by an attorney, with the name of the attorney or party clearly printed or typed directly below the signature. NY R CHIEF ADMIN § 130-1.1-a(a); NY R UNIF TRIAL CTS § 202.5(d)(1)(iv).

   a. *Printed name.* Beneath each signature shall be printed the name signed. NY CPLR Rule 2101(a).

   b. *Failure to sign.* Absent good cause shown, the court shall strike any unsigned paper if the omission of the signature is not corrected promptly after being called to the attention of the attorney or party. NY R CHIEF ADMIN § 130-1.1-a(a).

   c. *Signature as certification.* By signing a paper, an attorney or party certifies that, to the best of that person's knowledge, information and belief, formed after an inquiry reasonable under the circumstances the presentation of the paper or the contentions therein are not frivolous as defined in NY R CHIEF ADMIN § 130-1.1(c). NY R CHIEF ADMIN § 130-1.1-a(b)(1).

   d. *Electronic signatures.* A document shall be considered to have been signed by an attorney or party in compliance with NY R CHIEF ADMIN § 130-1.1-a if it has been signed by such attorney or party as provided in NY R UNIF TRIAL CTS § 202.5-b(e)(1) and it bears the signatory's name. NY R UNIF TRIAL CTS § 202.5-b(e)(2). An electronically filed document shall be considered to have been signed by, and shall be binding upon, the person identified as a signatory, if:

      i. It bears the physical signature of such person and is scanned into an electronic format that reproduces such signature; or

      ii. The signatory has electronically affixed the digital image of his or her signature to the document; or

      iii. It is electronically filed under the User ID and password of that person; or

      iv. In a tax certiorari action in which the parties have stipulated to this procedure, it is an initiating document that is electronically filed without the signature of the signatory in a form provided above in NY R UNIF TRIAL CTS § 202.5-b(e)(iv), provided that, prior to filing, the document is signed in full in hard copy (which hard copy must be preserved until the conclusion of all proceedings, including appeals, in the case in which it is filed); or

      v. In a small claims assessment review proceeding, it is a petition recorded by the NYSCEF site upon the filing of a text file as provided in NY R UNIF TRIAL CTS § 202.5-b(b)(1), provided that prior to filing, the document was signed in full in hard copy (which hard copy must be preserved until the conclusion of all proceedings in the matter, including article 78 (NY CPLR § 7801, et seq.) review and any appeals, and must be made available during the proceeding upon request of the respondent or the court); or

      vi. It otherwise bears the electronic signature of the signatory in a format conforming to such standards and requirements as may hereafter be established by the Chief Administrator. NY R UNIF TRIAL CTS § 202.5-b(e).

4. *Confidentiality of personal information.* No person may file any document available for public inspection with any state agency, political subdivision, or in any court of this state that contains a Social Security account number of any other person, unless such other person is a dependent child, or has consented to such filing, except as required by federal or state law or regulation, or by court rule. NY GEN BUS § 399-ddd. Submissions pursuant to e-filing procedures shall have the same confidentiality rights as paper documents. NY R UNIF TRIAL CTS § 202.5-b(k)(1).

   a. *Confidential personal information.* Except in the actions designated in NY R UNIF TRIAL CTS § 202.5(e)(1), or as otherwise provided by rule or law or court order, and whether or not a sealing order is or has been sought, the parties shall omit or redact confidential personal information in papers submitted to the court for filing. For purposes of NY R UNIF TRIAL CTS § 202.5(e), confidential personal information ("CPI") means:

      i. The taxpayer identification number of an individual or an entity, including a Social Security number, an employer identification number, and an individual taxpayer identification number, except the last four (4) digits thereof;

ii. The date of an individual's birth, except the year thereof;

iii. The full name of an individual known to be a minor, except the minor's initials;

iv. A financial account number, including a credit and/or debit card number, a bank account number, an investment account number, and/or an insurance account number, except the last four (4) digits or letters thereof; and

v. Any of the documents or testimony in a matrimonial action protected by NY DOM REL § 235 or evidence sealed by the court in such an action which are attached as exhibits or referenced in the papers filed in any other civil action. For purposes of NY R UNIF TRIAL CTS § 202.5, a matrimonial action shall mean: an action to annul a marriage or declare the nullity of a void marriage, an action or agreement for a separation, an action for a divorce, or an action or proceeding for custody, visitation, writ of habeus corpus, child support, maintenance or paternity. NY R UNIF TRIAL CTS § 202.5(e)(1).

b. *Submission of confidential personal information.* Where a person submitting a paper to a court for filing believes in good faith that the inclusion of the full confidential personal information described in NY R UNIF TRIAL CTS § 202.5(e)(1) is material and necessary to the adjudication of the action or proceeding before the court, he or she may apply to the court for leave to serve and file together with a paper in which such information has been set forth in abbreviated form a confidential affidavit or affirmation setting forth the same information in unabbreviated form, appropriately referenced to the page or pages of the paper at which the abbreviated form appears. NY R UNIF TRIAL CTS § 202.5(e)(3).

c. *Home addresses.* For information on when home addresses and other personal information must be redacted, refer to NY CPLR Rule 2103-a.

5. *Defective papers.* A defect in the form of a paper, if a substantial right of a party is not prejudiced, shall be disregarded by the court, and leave to correct shall be freely given. NY CPLR Rule 2101(f). Papers that are stapled or bound securely shall not be rejected for filing simply because they are not bound with a backer of any kind. NY R UNIF TRIAL CTS § 202.5(a). A paper filed in accordance with the rules of the chief administrator or any local rule or practice established by the court shall be deemed filed. NY CPLR Rule 2102(b).

a. *Objection to defective papers.* The party on whom a paper is served shall be deemed to have waived objection to any defect in form unless, within fifteen (15) days after the receipt thereof, the party on whom the paper is served returns the paper to the party serving it with a statement of particular objections. NY CPLR Rule 2101(f).

F. Filing and Service Requirements

1. *Filing requirements.* Except where otherwise prescribed by law or order of court, papers required to be filed shall be filed with the clerk of the court in which the action is triable. In an action or proceeding in supreme or court, papers required to be filed shall be filed with the clerk of the county in which the proceeding is brought. NY CPLR Rule 2102(a).

a. *Electronic filing.* On consent, documents may be filed and served by electronic means in Supreme Court in such civil actions and in such counties as shall be authorized by order of the Chief Administrator of the Courts and only to the extent and in the manner provided in NY R UNIF TRIAL CTS § 202.5-b. NY R UNIF TRIAL CTS § 202.5-b(a)(1). For the definitions of terms used in electronic filing, refer to NY R UNIF TRIAL CTS § 202.5-b(a)(2).

i. *Electronic filing of discovery materials.* In any action subject to e-filing, parties and non-parties producing materials in response to discovery demands may enter into a stipulation, which shall be e-filed, authorizing the electronic filing of discovery responses and discovery materials to the degree and upon terms and conditions set forth in the stipulation. In the absence of such a stipulation, no party shall file electronically any such materials except in the form of excerpts, quotations, or selected exhibits from such materials as part of motion papers, pleadings or other filings with the court. NY R UNIF TRIAL CTS § 202.5-b(j).

ii. *E-filing mandatory.* In any action subject to e-filing, all documents required to be filed with the court by an e-filing party shall be filed and served electronically, except as provided in NY R UNIF TRIAL CTS § 202.5-b. NY R UNIF TRIAL CTS § 202.5-b(d)(1)(i).

iii. *Who may file.* Documents may be filed or served electronically only by a person who has registered as an authorized e-filing user or as otherwise provided in NY R UNIF TRIAL CTS § 202.5-b(c). NY R UNIF TRIAL CTS § 202.5-b(c)(1).

iv. *When filing made.* Documents may be transmitted at any time of the day or night to the NYSCEF site. A document other than an order or judgment is filed when its electronic transmission or, in the case of a petition that is e-filed by submission of a text file as provided in NY R UNIF TRIAL CTS § 202.5-b(b)(1), the electronic transmission of the text file is recorded at that site, provided, however, that where payment of a fee is required upon the filing of a document, the document is not filed until transmission of the document and the information or form or information as required in NY R UNIF TRIAL CTS § 202.5-b(d)(2)(i), NY R UNIF TRIAL CTS § 202.5-b(d)(2)(ii) or NY R UNIF TRIAL CTS § 202.5-b(d)(2)(iii) has been recorded at the NYSCEF site; or, if no transmission of that information or form or information is recorded, where permitted by the County Clerk, until payment is presented to the County Clerk. NY R UNIF TRIAL CTS § 202.5-b(d)(3)(i).

v. *Notification of filing.* No later than the close of business on the business day following the electronic filing of a document, a notification, in a form prescribed by the Chief Administrator, shall be transmitted electronically by the NYSCEF site to the person filing such document and the e-mail service addresses of all other participating parties in such action. NY R UNIF TRIAL CTS § 202.5-b(d)(3)(ii).

vi. *Removal of confidential information and other corrections.* If a document filed electronically is subsequently discovered to contain confidential data—including but not limited to trade secrets, information protected by confidentiality agreement, or personal confidential information as defined by statute or court rule—or otherwise to have been filed in error, the filer or another party or affected person may (1) notify the parties and any non-party filers in the action of the confidentiality issue or other error raised by the filing, and of his or her intention to seek judicial relief to correct the filing: (2) following such notification, request that the appropriate County Clerk, exercising his or her administrative discretion, place the document temporarily in "restricted" status on the NYSCEF site, to be made available for viewing by court staff and the parties but not the general public; and (3) file an application to correct the filing by order to show cause within five (5) business days of such notification (or such time as the court may direct), including a request for preliminary injunctive relief limiting interim disclosure of the document at issue. Unless otherwise directed by the court, any document placed in restricted status in response to such a request shall be returned to public view upon expiration of this five (5) day period. The Chief Administrator of the Courts shall promulgate forms to implement this process. NY R UNIF TRIAL CTS § 202.5-b(d)(3)(iii).

vii. *Documents requiring judge's signature.* Except where the court directs otherwise, any document that requires a judge's signature shall be transmitted electronically and in hard copy to the court. NY R UNIF TRIAL CTS § 202.5-b(d)(6).

viii. *Documents which would be inconvenient to file electronically; Hard copies.* Notwithstanding any other provision of NY R UNIF TRIAL CTS § 202.5-b, and subject to such guidelines as may be established by the Chief Administrative Judge, the County Clerk or his or her designee may require or permit a party to file in hard copy, in accordance with procedures set by the County Clerk or designee, an exhibit or other document which it is impractical or inconvenient to file electronically. NY R UNIF TRIAL CTS § 202.5-b(d)(7).

ix. *Documents containing sensitive or proprietary information.* In an action subject to e-filing, any person may apply for an order prohibiting or restricting the electronic filing in the action of specifically identified materials on the grounds that such materials are subject to copyright or other proprietary rights, or trade secret or other privacy interests, and that electronic filing in the action is likely to result in substantial prejudice to those rights or interests. NY R UNIF TRIAL CTS § 202.5-b(k)(2).

x. *Refusal to accept paper filings.* In accordance with NY CPLR Rule 2102(c), a County Clerk and a chief clerk of the Supreme Court or County Court, as appropriate, shall refuse to accept for filing papers filed in actions and proceedings when the paper sought to be filed:

- Is in an action subject to electronic filing pursuant to Rules of the Chief Administrator,
- Is not being filed electronically, and
- Does not include the notice required by NY R UNIF TRIAL CTS § 202.5-b(d)(1). NY R UNIF TRIAL CTS § 202.5(d)(1)(v); NY R UNIF TRIAL CTS § 202.5-bb(d).

xi. *Emergency filings; Hard copies.* For information on when an emergency filing may be filed and served in hard copy, refer to NY R UNIF TRIAL CTS § 202.5-b(d)(1)(ii), NY R UNIF TRIAL CTS § 202.5-b(d)(1)(iii) and NY R UNIF TRIAL CTS § 202.5-bb(c)(3).

xii. *Technical failures.* The NYSCEF site shall be considered to be subject to a technical failure on a given day if the site is unable to accept filings or provide access to filed documents continuously or intermittently over the course of any period of time greater than one (1) hour after 12:00 noon of that day. Notice of all such technical failures shall be provided on the site. NY R UNIF TRIAL CTS § 202.5-b(i).

- When e-filing is hindered by a technical failure, a party may file with the appropriate clerk and serve in hard copy. NY R UNIF TRIAL CTS § 202.5-b(i). In the event an attorney or party shall file and serve documents in hard copy pursuant to NY R UNIF TRIAL CTS § 202.5-b(i), each such document shall include the notice required by NY R UNIF TRIAL CTS § 202.5-b(d)(1), and the filer shall file those documents with the NYSCEF site within three (3) business days after restoration of normal operations at that site. NY R UNIF TRIAL CTS § 202.5-b(i).

- With the exception of deadlines that by law cannot be extended, the time for filing of any document that is delayed due to technical failure of the site shall be extended for one (1) day for each day on which such failure occurs, unless otherwise ordered by the court. NY R UNIF TRIAL CTS § 202.5-b(i).

xiii. *Filing fees.* For information on what information must be provided to pay filing fees, refer to NY R UNIF TRIAL CTS § 202.5-b(d)(2).

xiv. *Exemption from e-filing.* For information on exemptions from e-filing, refer to NY R UNIF TRIAL CTS § 202.5-bb(e).

b. *Facsimile filing.* In the Supreme Court, facsimile filing shall be limited to commercial claims and tax certiorari, conservatorship, and mental hygiene proceedings in Monroe, Westchester, New York and Suffolk Counties. NY R UNIF TRIAL CTS § 202.5-a(a)(1). Refer to NY R UNIF TRIAL CTS § 202.5-a for information on the procedures for facsimile filing.

2. *Service requirements*

a. *Who may serve.* Except where otherwise prescribed by law or order of court, papers may be served by any person not a party of the age of eighteen years or over. NY CPLR Rule 2103(a).

b. *Service upon attorney.* Except where otherwise prescribed by law or order of court, papers to be served upon a party in a pending action shall be served upon the party's attorney. Where the same attorney appears for two or more parties, only one (1) copy need be served upon the attorney. Such service upon an attorney shall be made:

i. By delivering the paper to the attorney personally. NY CPLR Rule 2103(b)(1).

ii. By mailing the paper to the attorney at the address designated by that attorney for that purpose or, if none is designated, at the attorney's last known address; service by mail shall be complete upon mailing. NY CPLR Rule 2103(b)(2).

iii. If the attorney's office is open, by leaving the paper with a person in charge, or if no person is in charge, by leaving it in a conspicuous place; or if the attorney's office is not open, by depositing the paper, enclosed in a sealed wrapper directed to the attorney, in the attorney's office letter drop or box. NY CPLR Rule 2103(b)(3).

iv. By leaving it at the attorney's residence within the state with a person of suitable age and discretion. Service upon an attorney shall not be made at the attorney's residence unless service at the attorney's office cannot be made. NY CPLR Rule 2103(b)(4).

v. By transmitting the paper to the attorney by facsimile transmission, provided that a facsimile telephone number is designated by the attorney for that purpose. Service by facsimile transmission shall be complete upon the receipt by the sender of a signal from the equipment of the attorney served indicating that the transmission was received, and the mailing of a copy of the paper to that attorney. The designation of a facsimile telephone number in the address block subscribed on a paper served or filed in the course of an action or proceeding shall constitute consent to service by facsimile transmission in accordance with NY CPLR Rule 2103(b)(5). An attorney may change or rescind a facsimile telephone number by serving a notice on the other parties. NY CPLR Rule 2103(b)(5).

vi. By dispatching the paper to the attorney by overnight delivery service at the address designated by the attorney for that purpose or, if none is designated, at the attorney's last known address. Service by overnight delivery service shall be complete upon deposit of the paper enclosed in a properly addressed wrapper into the custody of the overnight delivery service for overnight delivery, prior to the latest time designated by the overnight delivery service for overnight delivery. "Overnight delivery service" means any delivery service which regularly accepts items for overnight delivery to any address in the state. NY CPLR Rule 2103(b)(6).

vii. By transmitting the paper to the attorney by electronic means where and in the manner authorized by the chief administrator of the courts by rule and, unless such rule shall otherwise provide, such transmission shall be upon the party's written consent. The subject matter heading for each paper sent by electronic means must indicate that the matter being transmitted electronically is related to a court proceeding. NY CPLR Rule 2103(b)(7).

c. *Electronic service mandatory; Consenting to electronic service; How electronic service may be made.* Except as otherwise provided in NY R UNIF TRIAL CTS § 202.5-bb, filing and service of all documents in an action that has been commenced electronically in accordance with NY R UNIF TRIAL CTS § 202.5-bb shall be by electronic means. NY R UNIF TRIAL CTS § 202.5-bb(c)(1).

i. *Party's consent required for certain e-filing.* After commencement of an action wherein e-filing is authorized, documents may be electronically filed and served, but only by, and electronic service shall be made only upon, a party or parties who have consented thereto. NY R UNIF TRIAL CTS § 202.5-b(b)(2)(i).

- A consent to e-filing in an action shall state that the party providing it agrees to the use of e-filing in the action and to be bound by the filing and service provisions in NY R UNIF TRIAL CTS § 202.5-b. NY R UNIF TRIAL CTS § 202.5-b(b)(2)(ii).

ii. *Address for service; Duty to notify as to changes.* The e-mail service address recorded at the time of registration is the e-mail address at which service of interlocutory documents on that party may be made through notification transmitted by the NYSCEF site. It is the responsibility of each filing user to monitor that address and promptly notify the Resource Center in the event of a change in his or her e-mail service address. NY R UNIF TRIAL CTS § 202.5-b(f)(2)(i).

iii. *How service made.* An e-filing party causes service of an interlocutory document to be made upon another party participating in e-filing by filing the document electronically. Upon receipt of an interlocutory document, the NYSCEF site shall automatically transmit electronic notification to all e-mail service addresses in such action. NY R UNIF TRIAL CTS § 202.5-b(f)(2)(ii).

- Except as provided otherwise in NY R UNIF TRIAL CTS § 202.5-b(h)(3), the electronic transmission of the notification shall constitute service of the document on the e-mail service addresses identified therein; however, such service will not be effective if the filing party learns that the notification did not reach the address of the person to be served. Proof of such service will be recorded on the NYSCEF site. A party may, however, utilize other service methods permitted by the CPLR provided that, if one of such other methods is used, proof of that service shall be filed electronically. NY R UNIF TRIAL CTS § 202.5-b(f)(2)(ii).

iv. *Signatures on hard copies; Proof of service filed electronically.* When an e-filing party serves a document in hard copy on a non-participating party, the document served shall bear full signatures of all signatories and proof of such service shall be filed electronically. NY R UNIF TRIAL CTS § 202.5-b(b)(2)(i).

v. *Effect of failure to consent.* A party's failure to consent to participation in electronic filing and service shall not bar any other party to the action from filing documents electronically with the County Clerk and the court or serving documents upon any other party who has consented to participation. A party who has not consented to participation shall file documents with the court and the County Clerk, and serve and be served with documents, in hard copy. NY R UNIF TRIAL CTS § 202.5-b(b)(2)(i).

d. *Service upon party.* If a party has not appeared by an attorney or the party's attorney cannot be served, service shall be upon the party by a method specified in NY CPLR Rule 2103(b)(1), NY CPLR Rule 2103(b)(2), NY CPLR Rule 2103(b)(4), NY CPLR Rule 2103(b)(5) or NY CPLR Rule 2103(b)(6). NY CPLR Rule 2103(c).

i. When a party is in default for failure to appear, he shall not be entitled to notice or service of any copy required under NY CPLR § 3101, et seq. NY CPLR Rule 3105.

e. *Service on all parties.* Each paper served on any party shall be served on every other party who has appeared, except as otherwise may be provided by court order or as provided in NY CPLR § 3012 or in NY CPLR § 3215(f). Upon demand by a party, the plaintiff shall supply that party with a list of those who have appeared and the names and addresses of their attorneys. NY CPLR Rule 2103(e).

f. *Service by filing.* If a paper cannot be served by any of the methods specified in NY CPLR Rule 2103(b) and NY CPLR Rule 2103(c), service may be made by filing the paper as if it were a paper required to be filed. NY CPLR Rule 2103(d).

g. *Definitions.* For the purposes of NY CPLR Rule 2103:

i. "Mailing" means the deposit of a paper enclosed in a first class postpaid wrapper, addressed to the address designated by a person for that purpose or, if none is designated, at that person's last known address, in a post office or official depository under the exclusive care and custody of the United States Postal Service within the state;

ii. "Electronic means" means any method of transmission of information between computers or other machines designed for the purpose of sending and receiving such transmissions, and which allows the recipient to reproduce the information transmitted in a tangible medium of expression;

iii. "Facsimile transmission" means any method of transmission of documents to a facsimile machine at a remote location which can automatically produce a tangible copy of such documents. NY CPLR Rule 2103(f).

G. Hearings

1. There is no hearing required or contemplated in the New York rules governing the response to request for admissions.

H. Forms

1. New York Response to Request for Admissions Forms

a. Form; Notice of motion to extend time to respond to notice to admit. CW2D § 53:22.

b. Form; Affirmation of plaintiff's attorney in support of motion to extend time to respond to notice to admit. CW2D § 53:23.

c. Form; Notice of motion to strike notice to admit and quash subpoena; Admission of ultimate issues and privileged communications between attorney and client. CW2D § 53:11.

d. Form; Notice of motion to strike notice to admit and for order prohibiting plaintiff from seeking same information by any other disclosure device; Youthful offender records. CW2D § 53:13.

I. Applicable Rules

1. *State rules*

a. Short title; Application; Construction; Definitions. NY CPLR § 101; NY CPLR § 104; NY CPLR § 105.

b. Appendix of official forms. NY CPLR § 107.

c. Extensions of time generally. NY CPLR § 2004.

d. Form of papers. NY CPLR Rule 2101; NY CPLR Rule 2102; NY CPLR § 2105; NY GEN BUS § 399-ddd; NY R UNIF TRIAL CTS § 215.2; NY R UNIF TRIAL CTS § 215.3.

e. Service of papers. NY CPLR Rule 2103.

f. Computation of time. NY CPLR § 2402; NY GEN CONSTR § 19; NY GEN CONSTR § 20; NY GEN CONSTR § 25-a; NY GEN CONSTR § 30; NY GEN CONSTR § 31; NY GEN CONSTR § 53.

g. Scope of disclosure. NY CPLR § 3101; NY CPLR § 3102; NY CPLR § 3103; NY CPLR § 3104; NY CPLR Rule 3105.

h. Admissions as to matters of fact, papers, documents and photographs. NY CPLR § 3123.

i. Motions staying disclosure. NY CPLR Rule 3214; NY CPLR Rule 3407.

j. Index number fees of county clerks. NY CPLR § 8018.

k. Hours of court. NY R CHIEF J § 3.1.

l. Application of part; Waiver; Additional rules; Application of CPLR; Definitions. NY R UNIF TRIAL CTS § 202.1.

m. Papers filed in court; Electronic filing in supreme court. NY R UNIF TRIAL CTS § 202.5; NY R UNIF TRIAL CTS § 202.5-a; NY R UNIF TRIAL CTS § 202.5-b; NY R UNIF TRIAL CTS § 202.5-bb.

n. Rules of the commercial division of the Supreme Court. NY R UNIF TRIAL CTS § 202.70.

o. Signing of papers. NY R CHIEF ADMIN § 130-1.1-a.

2. *Local rules*

a. *Albany County*

i. Third judicial district rules. NY R 3 JD SUP Doc. 1.

b. *Bronx County*

i. Commercial division. NY R BRONX FIL R Doc. 12.

c. *Kings County*

i. Expedited discovery. NY R L KINGS Pt. B, Rule 5.

ii. Pre calendar procedures. NY R L KINGS Rule I.

iii. Both pre and post note procedures. NY R L KINGS Rule IV.

d. *New York County*

i. RJIs and assignments. NY R NY CTY Procedure IA.

ii. Discovery schedule. NY R NY CTY J RUL Rule 8.

J. Miscellaneous

NOTE: Individual judges' rules may apply.

ALBANY COUNTY

JUSTICE LISA M. FISHER: NY R 3 JD FISHER Fisher; NY R 3 JD FISHER Fisher, PC Order.

JUSTICE RICHARD MOTT: NY R 3 JD MOTT Mott.

JUSTICE STEPHAN G. SCHICK: NY R 3 JD Schick.

FORECLOSURE SETTLEMENT PART: NY R 3 JD Foreclosure Settlement.

BRONX COUNTY

JUSTICE PAUL L. ALPERT: [NY R BRONX J Part IA-29, as amended by NY ORDER 20-0337].

JUSTICE BEN BARBATO: NY R BRONX J Part IA-21.

JUSTICE MARY ANNE BRIGANTTI: [NY R BRONX J Part IA-15, as amended by NY ORDER 20-0338].

JUSTICE JOSEPH E. CAPELLA: NY R BRONX J Part IA-23.

JUSTICE MITCHELL DANZIGER: NY R BRONX J Part IA-3/33 ; [NY R BRONX J Danziger, Part IA-3/33, as amended by NY ORDER 20-0339].

JUSTICE LAURA G. DOUGLAS: NY R BRONX J Part IA-11.

JUSTICE RUBEN FRANCO: NY R BRONX J Part IA-26.

JUSTICE DORIS M. GONZALEZ: NY R BRONX J Part IA-24.

JUSTICE WILMA GUZMAN: NY R BRONX J Part IA-7; [NY R BRONX J Guzman, Part IA-7 Virtual, as amended by NY ORDER 20-0340].

JUSTICE ROBERT T. JOHNSON: NY R BRONX J Part IA-12.

JUSTICE DONALD A. MILES: NY R BRONX J Part IA-8.

JUSTICE DONNA M. MILLS: NY R BRONX J Part IA-9.

JUSTICE JULIA I. RODRIGUEZ: NY R BRONX J Part IA-18; [NY R BRONX J Part IA-27, as amended by NY ORDER 20-0341].

JUSTICE LLINET M. ROSADO: [NY R BRONX J Part IA-25, as amended by NY ORDER 20-0342].

JUSTICE NORMA RUIZ: NY R BRONX J Part IA-22; [NY R BRONX J Ruiz, Part IA-22 Virtual, as amended by NY ORDER 20-0343].

JUSTICE HOWARD H. SHERMAN: NY R BRONX J Part IA-4.

JUSTICE FERNANDO TAPIA: NY R BRONX J Part IA-13.

JUSTICE ELIZABETH A. TAYLOR: NY R BRONX J Part IA-2.

JUSTICE ALISON Y. TRUITT: NY R BRONX J Part IA-5.

PART IDV: NY R BRONX J Doc. 1.

PRE-TRIAL PART RULES: NY R BRONX J Doc. 2.

PRE TRIAL WORKSHEET: NY R BRONX J Doc. 3.

FORECLOSURE SETTLEMENT PART RULES: NY R BRONX J Doc. 4.

GUARDIANSHIP PART RULES: NY R BRONX J Doc. 5.

LPM PART RULES: NY R BRONX J Doc. 6.

ERIE COUNTY

JUSTICE M. WILLIAM BOLLER: NY R 8 JD J Boller.

JUSTICE RALPH A. BONIELLO: NY R 8 JD J Boniello.

JUSTICE CHRISTOPHER J. BURN: NY R 8 JD J Burns.

JUSTICE RUSSELL P. BUSCAGLIA: NY R 8 JD J Buscaglia.

JUSTICE FRANK CARUSO: NY R 8 JD J Caruso.
JUSTICE STEPHEN W. CASS: NY R 8 JD J Cass.
JUSTICE DEBORAH A. CHIMES: NY R 8 JD J Chimes.
JUSTICE EMILIO COLAIACOVO: [NY R 8 JD J Colaiacovo, as amended by NY ORDER 20-0252].
JUSTICE DIANE Y. DEVLIN: NY R 8 JD J Devlin.
JUSTICE JAMES H. DILLON: NY R 8 JD J Dillon.
JUSTICE PAULA L. FEROLETO: NY R 8 JD J Feroleto.
JUSTICE DANIEL J. FURLONG: [NY R 8 JD J Furlong, as amended by NY ORDER 20-0253].
JUSTICE JOSEPH R. GLOWNIA: NY R 8 JD J Glownia.
JUSTICE MARK J. GRISANTI: NY R 8 JD J Grisanti.
JUSTICE DEBORAH A. HAENDIGES: NY R 8 JD J Haendiges.
JUSTICE LYNN W. KEANE: [NY R 8 JD J Keane, as amended by NY ORDER 20-0254].
JUSTICE RICHARD C. KLOCH, Sr.: NY R 8 JD J Kloch.
JUSTICE FREDERICK J. MARSHALL: [NY R 8 JD J Marshall, as amended by NY ORDER 20-0255.
JUSTICE JOHN L. MICHALSKI: NY R 8 JD J Michalski.
JUSTICE MARK A. MONTOUR: [NY R 8 JD J Montour, as amended by NY ORDER 20-0256].
JUSTICE HENRY NOWAK: NY R 8 JD J Nowak.
JUSTICE JOHN F. O'DONNELL: NY R 8 JD J O'Donnell.
JUSTICE JEANETTE OGDEN: NY R 8 JD J Ogden.
JUSTICE CATHERINE NUGENT-PANEPINTO: NY R 8 JD J Nugent-Panepinto.
JUSTICE FRANK A. SEDITA, III: [NY R 8 JD J Sedita, as amended by NY ORDER 20-0257].
JUSTICE SARA SHELDON: NY R 8 JD J Sheldon.
JUSTICE DONNA M. SIWEK: NY R 8 JD J Siwek.
JUSTICE MARY L. SLISZ: NY R 8 JD J Slisz.
JUSTICE TIMOTHY J. WALKER: [NY R 8 JD J Walker, as amended by NY ORDER 20-0258].
JUSTICE DENNIS E. WARD: NY R 8 JD J Ward.
JUSTICE PAUL B. WOJTASZEK: [NY R 8 JD J Wojtaszek, as amended by NY ORDER 20-0259].
JUSTICE CHARLES N. ZAMBITO: [NY R 8 JD J Zambito, as amended by NY ORDER 20-0260].
SUPREME COURT LEGAL STAFF: NY R 8 JD J Legal Staff.

KINGS COUNTY

JUSTICE RACHEL A. ADAMS: NY R KINGS J Part 5F.
JUSTICE LOREN BAILY-SCHIFFMAN: NY R KINGS J Part 65.
JUSTICE REGINALD A. BODDIE: NY R KINGS J Part 95.
JUSTICE THERESA M. CICCOTTO: NY R KINGS J Part 19; NY R KINGS J Part 5J.
JUSTICE LISSETTE COLON: NY R KINGS J Part Rules.
JUSTICE GENINE EDWARDS: NY R KINGS J Part 80.
JUSTICE PAMELA L. FISHER: [NY R KINGS J Part 94, as amended by NY ORDER 20-0208].
JUSTICE ROBIN GARSON: NY R KINGS J Part 75.
JUSTICE LARA J. GENOVISI: [NY R KINGS J Part 34, as amended by NY ORDER 20-0209].
JUSTICE BERNARD J. GRAHAM: NY R KINGS J Part 36.
JUSTICE DAWN JIMENEZ-SALTA: NY R KINGS J Part 88.
JUSTICE INGRID JOSEPH: [NY R KINGS J Part FRP3 and Part 83, as amended by NY ORDER 20-0210].

JUSTICE KATHY J. KING: NY R KINGS J Part 64, 76K.
JUSTICE LAWRENCE KNIPEL: NY R KINGS J Part 57.
JUSTICE DONALD KURTZ: NY R KINGS J Part 26.
JUSTICE CARL LANDICINO: [NY R KINGS J Part 81, as amended by NY ORDER 20-0211].
JUSTICE KATHERINE LEVINE: [NY R KINGS J Part 20, 25, 92, as amended by NY ORDER 20-0211].
JUSTICE LORNA MCALLISTER: [NY R KINGS J Part 10, as amended by NY ORDER 20-0211].
JUSTICE ROSEMARIE MONTALBANO: [NY R KINGS J Part 19, 71, and 22, as amended by NY ORDER 20-0211].
JUSTICE RICHARD J. MONTELIONE: [NY R KINGS J Part 99 and DJMP, as amended by NY ORDER 20-0215].
JUSTICE LISA S. OTTLEY: NY R KINGS J Part 24.
JUSTICE MARK I. PARTNOW: NY R KINGS J Part 43.
JUSTICE ERIC I. PRUS: NY R KINGS J Part 5A.
JUSTICE FRANCOIS RIVERA: NY R KINGS J Part 52.
JUSTICE KAREN B. ROTHENBERG: NY R KINGS J Part 35.
JUSTICE LEON RUCHELSMAN: NY R KINGS J Part 1.
JUSTICE WAYNE P. SAITTA: NY R KINGS J Part 29.
JUSTICE ROBIN K. SHEARES: NY R KINGS J Part 96.
JUSTICE KENNETH P. SHERMAN: NY R KINGS J Part 67 and 78.
JUSTICE DEBRA SILBER: NY R KINGS J Part 9 and 5K.
JUSTICE ELLEN M. SPODEK: NY R KINGS J Part 63.
JUSTICE MARSHA L. STEINHARDT: NY R KINGS J Part 15.
JUSTICE JEFFREY S. SUNSHINE: NY R KINGS J Part 5G.
JUSTICE PETER P. SWEENEY: [NY R KINGS J Part 35, as amended by NY ORDER 20-0218].
JUSTICE DELORES J. THOMAS: [NY R KINGS J Part 5T, as amended by NY ORDER 20-0221].
JUSTICE WAVNY TOUSSAINT: NY R KINGS J Part 70.
JUSTICE RICHARD VELASQUEZ: NY R KINGS J Part 66.
JUSTICE CAROLYN E. WADE: NY R KINGS J Part 84.
JUSTICE EDWARD G. WALKER: [NY R KINGS J Part 90, as amended by NY ORDER 20-0219].
JUSTICE LILLIAN WAN: [NY R KINGS J Part 17, as amended by NY ORDER 20-0220].
JUSTICE MICHELLE WESTON: NY R KINGS J Part 3.
MENTAL HYGIENE PART: NY R KINGS J Part 77.
MATRIMONIAL PARTS DURING COVID-19 EMERGENCY: JUSTICE KAREN B. ROTHENBERG: NY R KINGS J Doc. 1.

NASSAU COUNTY

JUSTICE ANNA R. ANZALONE: NY R NASSAU S J Anzalone, Part 26.
JUSTICE STACY D. BENNETT: NY R NASSAU S J Bennett; NY R NASSAU S J Bennett, Form 1.
JUSTICE ANTONIO BRANDVEEN: NY R NASSAU S J Brandveen, Part 31.
JUSTICE JEFFREY S. BROWN: [NY R NASSAU S J Brown, as amended by NY ORDER 20-0297].
JUSTICE STEPHEN A. BUCARIA: NY R NASSAU S J Bucaria.
JUSTICE JULIANNE T. CAPETOLA: NY R NASSAU S J Capetola, Part 28.
JUSTICE EDMUND M. DANE: NY R NASSAU S J Dane, Part 33.
JUSTICE VITO M. DESTEFANO: NY R NASSAU S J DeStefano, Part 13; NY R NASSAU S J DeStefano, Form 1.
JUSTICE ARTHUR M. DIAMOND: NY R NASSAU S J Diamond, Part 7.
JUSTICE THOMAS FEINMAN: NY R NASSAU S J Feinman, Part 5.

JUSTICE JOHN M. GALASSO: NY R NASSAU S J Galasso, Part 22.

JUSTICE SHARON M.J. GIANELLI: NY R NASSAU S J Gianelli, Part 22; NY R NASSAU S J Gianelli, Form 1.

JUSTICE JEFFREY A. GOODSTEIN: NY R NASSAU S J Goodstein, Part 33; NY R NASSAU S J Goodstein, Form 1.

JUSTICE DAVID J. GUGERTY: [NY R NASSAU S J Gugerty, Part 31, as amended by NY ORDER 20-0298].

JUSTICE HELENE F. GUGERTY: NY R NASSAU S J Gugerty, Part 47.

JUSTICE STEVEN M. JAEGER: NY R NASSAU S J Jaeger, Part 35; NY R NASSAU S J Jaeger, Form 1.

JUSTICE JACK L. LIBERT: NY R NASSAU S J Libert, Part 23.

JUSTICE JOSEPH H. LORINTZ: NY R NASSAU S J Lorintz, Part 26; NY R NASSAU S J Lorintz, Form 1.

JUSTICE ROY S. MAHON: NY R NASSAU S J Mahon, Part 3.

JUSTICE RANDY SUE MARBER: NY R NASSAU S J Marber, Part 8.

JUSTICE JAMES P. MCCORMACK: [NY R NASSAU S J McCormack, Part 18, as amended by NY ORDER, 20-0299].

JUSTICE DICCIA T. PINEDA-KIRWAN: [NY R NASSAU S J Pineda-Kirwan, as amended by NY ORDER 20-0300].

JUSTICE THOMAS RADEMAKER: [NY R NASSAU S J Rademaker, Part 28, as amended by NY ORDER 20-0301]; [NY R NASSAU S J Rademaker, Form 1, as amended by NY ORDER 20-0301].

JUSTICE DENISE L. SHER: NY R NASSAU S J Rademaker, Part 32.

JUSTICE LEONARD D. STEINMAN: [NY R NASSAU S J Steinman, Part 15, as amended by NY ORDER 20-0303]; NY R NASSAU S J Steinman, Form 1.

JUSTICE HOWARD E. STURIM: NY R NASSAU S J Sturim, Part 50; NY R NASSAU S J Sturim, Form 1.

JUSTICE HELEN VOUTSINAS: [NY R NASSAU S J Voutsinas, Part 25, as amended by NY ORDER 20-0304]; [NY R NASSAU S J Voutsinas, Form 1, as amended by NY ORDER 20-0305].

JUSTICE HOPE SCHWARTZ ZIMMERMAN: NY R NASSAU S J Zimmerman, Part 17.

NEW YORK COUNTY

JUDGE'S RULES; BASIC INFORMATION: [NY R NY CTY J RUL Doc. 1, as amended by NY ORDER 20-0202].

ONONDAGA COUNTY

JUSTICE ROBERT E. ANTONACCI II: [NY R ONDGA E FIL Doc. 1, as amended by 20-0239].

JUSTICE MICHAEL V. COCCOMI: NY R ONDGA E FIL Doc. 2.

JUSTICE GREGORY R. GILBERT: NY R 5 JD JUDGES Gilbert; NY R ONDGA E FIL Doc. 3.

JUSTICE DONALD A. GREENWOOD: NY R ONDGA E FIL Doc. 4.

JUSTICE DEBORAH H. KARALUNAS: NY R ONDGA E FIL Doc. 5.

JUSTICE JAMES MCCLUSKY: NY R 5 JD MCCLUSKY McClusky.

JUSTICE CHARLES C. MERRELL: NY R 5 JD MERRELL Merrell.

JUSTICE PATRICK F. MACRAE: NY R 5 JD MACRAE Doc. 1.

JUSTICE JAMES P. MURPHY: NY R ONDGA E FIL Doc. 7.

JUSTICE GERALD J. NERI: [NY R 5 JD JUDGES Neri, as amended by NY ORDER 20-0236]; [NY R ONDGA E FIL Doc. 8, as amended by NY ORDER 20-0241].

JUSTICE ANTHONY J. PARIS: NY R 5 JD JUDGES Paris; [NY R ONDGA E FIL Doc. 9, as amended by NY ORDER 20-0242].

JUSTICE NORMAN W. SEITER, JR.: NY R 5 JD JUDGES Seiter.

JUSTICE KEVIN G. YOUNG: [NY R ONDGA E FIL Doc. 10, as amended by NY ORDER 20-0243].

QUEENS COUNTY

JUSTICE PAM JACKMAN BROWN: [NY R L QUEENS Brown, Part 19, as amended by NY ORDER 20-0321].

JUSTICE CHEREE A. BUGGS: NY R L QUEENS Buggs, Part 30.

JUSTICE PAM JACKMAN BROWN: [NY R L QUEENS Brown, Part 19, as amended by NY ORDER 20-0321].

JUSTICE DENIS J. BUTLER: NY R L QUEENS Butler, Part 12.

JUSTICE ROBERT I. CALORAS: [NY R L QUEENS Caloras, Part 36, as amended by NY ORDER 20-0322].
JUSTICE ANNA CULLEY: NY R L QUEENS Culley, Part 53.
JUSTICE TIMOTHY DUFFICY: NY R L QUEENS Dufficy, Part 35.
JUSTICE DAVID ELLIOT: NY R L QUEENS Elliot, Part 14.
JUSTICE JOSEPH J. ESPOSITO: NY R L QUEENS Esposito, Part 6.
JUSTICE DARRELL L. GAVRIN: [NY R L QUEENS Gavrin, Part 27, as amended by NY ORDER 20-0323].
JUSTICE WYATT N. GIBBONS: [NY R L QUEENS Gibbons, Part 5, as amended by NY ORDER 20-0330.
JUSTICE DONNA-MARIE E. GOLIA: [NY R L QUEENS Golia, Part 21, as amended by NY ORDER 20-0331].
JUSTICE MARGUERITE A. GRAYS: [NY R L QUEENS Grays, Part 4, as amended by NY ORDER 20-0324].
JUSTICE RUDOLPH E. GRECO: [NY R L QUEENS Greco, Part 32, as amended by NY ORDER 20-0325].
JUSTICE MAUREEN HEALY: NY R L QUEENS Healy, Part 6.
JUSTICE PHILLIP HOM: [NY R L QUEENS Hom, Part 43, as amended by NY ORDER 20-0332].
JUSTICE KEVIN J. KERRIGAN: NY R L QUEENS Kerrigan, Part 10.
JUSTICE MOJGAN C. LANCMAN: NY R L QUEENS Lancman, Part 20.
JUSTICE RICHARD G. LATIN: NY R L QUEENS Latin, Part 40.
JUSTICE ULYSSES B. LEVERETT: [NY R L QUEENS Leverett, Part 6, as amended by NY ORDER 20-0326].
JUSTICE LEONARD LIVOTE: NY R L QUEENS Livote, Part 33.
JUSTICE LEE A. MAYERSOHN: NY R L QUEENS Mayersohn, Part 22; NY R L QUEENS Mayersohn, Part 22G; [NY R L QUEENS Mayersohn, Part 22G COVID, as amended by NY ORDER 20-0327].
JUSTICE ROBERT J. MCDONALD: NY R L QUEENS McDonald, Part 34.
JUSTICE MARGARET MCGOWAN: NY R L QUEENS McGowan, Part 52.
JUSTICE MAURICE E. MUIR: [NY R L QUEENS Muir, Part 42, as amended by NY ORDER 20-0333].
JUSTICE JODI ORLOW: NY R L QUEENS Orlow, Part 51.
JUSTICE LESLIE J. PURIFICCION: NY R L QUEENS Purificcion, Part 39.
JUSTICE JOSEPH RISI: [NY R L QUEENS Risi, Part 3, as amended by NY ORDER 20-0328].
JUSTICE FREDERICK D.R. SAMPSON: [NY R L QUEENS Sampson, Part 31, as amended by NY ORDER 20-0329].
JUSTICE MARTIN J. SCHULMAN: NY R L QUEENS Schulman, Part 29.
JUSTICE BERNICE D. SIEGAL: NY R L QUEENS Siegal, Part 25G.
JUSTICE JANICE A. TAYLOR: NY R L QUEENS Taylor, Part 15.
JUSTICE CARMEN R. VELASQUEZ: NY R L QUEENS Velasquez, Part 38.
JUSTICE LOURDES M VENTURA: [NY R L QUEENS Ventura, Part 37, as amended by NY ORDER 20-0334].
JUSTICE WILLIAM A. VISCOVICH: NY R L QUEENS Viscovich, Part 63.
JUSTICE ALLAN B. WEISS: NY R L QUEENS Weiss, Part 2.
COMPLIANCE, SETTLEMENT AND CONFERENCE PART: NY R L QUEENS Doc 1.
PRELIMINARY CONFERENCE PART: [NY R L QUEENS Doc. 2, as amended by NY ORDER 20-0335].
MEDICAL MALPRACTICE CONFERENCE PART: [NY R L QUEENS Doc. 3, as amended by NY ORDER 20-0336].
TRIAL SCHEDULING PART: NY R L QUEENS Doc. 4.
SUMMARY JURY TRIAL PROGRAM: NY R L QUEENS Doc. 7.
RESIDENTIAL FORECLOSURE PART: NY R L QUEENS Doc. 9.
FORECLOSURE AUCTION RULES: NY R L QUEENS Doc. 10.
MATRIMONIAL PRELIMINARY CONFERENCE PART: NY R L QUEENS Doc. 11.
NON-CUSTODIAL CONTESTED MATRIMONIAL PART: NY R L QUEENS Doc. 12.

Requests, Notices and Applications
Notice of Deposition

Document Last Updated August 2020

A. Checklist

(I) ❑ Matters to consider for party noticing deposition on oral examination

- (a) ❑ Required documents
  - (1) ❑ Notice of deposition
  - (2) ❑ Proof of service
- (b) ❑ Supplemental documents
  - (1) ❑ Working copies
  - (2) ❑ Subpoena
- (c) ❑ Timing
  - (1) ❑ A party desiring to take the deposition of any person upon oral examination shall give to each party twenty (20) days' notice, unless the court orders otherwise
  - (2) ❑ A party to be examined pursuant to notice served by another party may serve notice of at least ten (10) days for the examination of any other party

(II) ❑ Matters to consider for party noticing deposition on written questions

- (a) ❑ Required documents
  - (1) ❑ Notice of deposition
  - (2) ❑ Written questions
  - (3) ❑ Proof of service
- (b) ❑ Supplemental documents
  - (1) ❑ Working copies
  - (2) ❑ Subpoena
- (c) ❑ Timing
  - (1) ❑ There are no specific timing requirements for serving a notice of deposition on written questions

B. Timing

1. *Notice of deposition on oral examination.* A party desiring to take the deposition of any person upon oral examination shall give to each party twenty (20) days' notice, unless the court orders otherwise. NY CPLR Rule 3107. Leave of the court, granted on motion, shall be obtained if notice of the taking of the deposition of a party is served by the plaintiff before that party's time for serving a responsive pleading has expired. NY CPLR Rule 3106(a).
   a. *Party to be examined; Noticing successive deposition.* A party to be examined pursuant to notice served by another party may serve notice of at least ten (10) days for the examination of any other party, his agent or employee, such examination to be noticed for and to follow at the same time and place. NY CPLR Rule 3107.
   b. *Scheduling deposition.* The party noticing the deposition will ordinarily want to confirm that the deponent will be able to attend the deposition at the appointed place and time. Without that consultation, usually with the deponent's attorney, the court is less likely to visit any penalty for a nonappearance. SIEGEL-NYPRAC § 354.
2. *Notice of deposition on written questions.* There are no specific timing requirements for serving a notice of deposition on written questions. A party desiring to take the deposition of any person upon written questions shall serve such questions upon each party together with a notice stating the name and address of the person to be examined, if known, and, if the name is not known, a general description sufficient to identify him or the particular class or group to which he belongs, and the name or descriptive title and address of the officer before whom the deposition is to be taken. NY CPLR Rule 3109(a). Leave of the court, granted on motion, shall be obtained if notice of the taking of the deposition of a party is served by the plaintiff before that party's time for serving a responsive pleading has expired. NY CPLR Rule 3106(a).
   a. *Cross-questions.* Within fifteen (15) days thereafter a party so served may serve written cross-questions upon each party. NY CPLR Rule 3109(a).

b. *Redirect questions.* Within seven (7) days thereafter the original party may serve written redirect questions upon each party. NY CPLR Rule 3109(a).

c. *Recross-questions.* Within five (5) days after being served with written redirect questions, a party may serve written recross-questions upon each party. NY CPLR Rule 3109(a).

d. *Objections to written questions.* Objections to the form of written questions are waived unless served in writing upon the party propounding the questions within the time allowed for serving succeeding questions or within three (3) days after service. NY CPLR Rule 3115(e).

3. *When subpoena required; Timing.* Where the person to be examined is not a party or a person who at the time of taking the deposition is an officer, director, member or employee of a party, he shall be served with a subpoena. Unless the court orders otherwise, on motion with or without notice, such subpoena shall be served at least twenty (20) days before the examination. Where a motion for a protective order against such an examination is made, the witness shall be notified by the moving party that the examination is stayed. NY CPLR Rule 3106(b).

4. *Time to object to error in notice.* All errors and irregularities in the notice for taking a deposition are waived unless at least three (3) days before the time for taking the deposition written objection is served upon the party giving the notice. NY CPLR Rule 3112.

5. *Motions staying disclosure.* Service of a notice of motion under NY CPLR Rule 3211, NY CPLR Rule 3212, or NY CPLR § 3213 stays disclosure until determination of the motion unless the court orders otherwise. If the motion is based solely on the defense that the summons and complaint, summons with notice, or notice of petition and petition was not properly served, disclosure shall not be stayed unless the court orders otherwise. NY CPLR Rule 3214(b).

a. *Personal injury actions involving terminally ill patients.* Notwithstanding the provisions of NY CPLR Rule 3214(b), the service or pendency of a motion under NY CPLR Rule 3211, NY CPLR Rule 3212, or NY CPLR § 3213 shall not stay disclosure in an action where a preliminary conference order has been entered pursuant to NY CPLR Rule 3407. NY CPLR Rule 3407(b)(3).

6. *KINGS COUNTY: Discovery timing.* At [the Compliance Conference, the court will] schedule all outstanding discovery to be completed prior to date fixed for filing Note of Issue. NY R L KINGS Rule I(B).

a. *Deadlines in orders.* Discovery scheduled in Compliance Conference orders shall be strictly adhered to and may not be extended without leave of the court. Unjustified failure to comply with the provisions of the CCP order will result in preclusion, the striking of a pleading or imposition of sanctions, as appropriate. NY R L KINGS Rule I(B)(2).

b. *Cases with extensive discovery.* Where post Compliance Conference discovery is to be extensive, cases may be retracked from standard to complex, which will provide for three (3) additional months of post Compliance Conference discovery and extend the Note of Issue date by three (3) months. NY R L KINGS Rule I(B)(1).

c. *Discovery not stayed.* Ordinarily the Court/JHO will not stay discovery during pendency of motions to withdraw, or during pendency of settlement, or during pendency of dispositive motions. NY R L KINGS Rule IV.

d. *Expedited discovery in certain cases.* Discovery in third party and joint actions will be expedited. NY R L KINGS Pt. B, Rule 5.

e. For more information on discovery scheduling, refer to NY R L KINGS Flow Chart.

7. *NEW YORK COUNTY: Deadlines in orders.* Strict compliance with all discovery orders is required. Unexcused or unjustified failure to comply with deadlines fixed by the court, including those set out in Preliminary Conference Orders, may result in an award of costs, conditional or otherwise, or the imposition of another penalty authorized by NY CPLR § 3126. NY R NY CTY J RUL Rule 8.

8. *Computation of time*

a. *Units of time*

i. *Day.* A calendar day includes the time from midnight to midnight. Sunday or any day of the week specifically mentioned means a calendar day. NY GEN CONSTR § 19.

ii. *Month.* In a statute, contract or public or private instrument, unless otherwise provided in such contract or instrument or by law, the term month means a calendar month and not a lunar month. NY GEN CONSTR § 31.

iii. *Year.* For information on the definition of a year, including the definitions of a half-year and quarter-year, refer to NY GEN CONSTR § 58 and NY GEN CONSTR § 50. For information on leap years, refer to NY GEN CONSTR § 57.

b. *Periods of time*

i. *Number of days.* A number of days specified as a period from a certain day within which or after or before which

an act is authorized or required to be done means such number of calendar days exclusive of the calendar day from which the reckoning is made. NY GEN CONSTR § 20.

- If such period is a period of two (2) days, Saturday, Sunday or a public holiday must be excluded from the reckoning if it is an intervening day between the day from which the reckoning is made and the last day of the period. NY GEN CONSTR § 20.
- In computing any specified period of time from a specified event, the day upon which the event happens is deemed the day from which the reckoning is made. The day from which any specified period of time is reckoned shall be excluded in making the reckoning. NY GEN CONSTR § 20.

ii. *Number of months.* A number of months after or before a certain day shall be computed by counting such number of calendar months from such day, exclusive of the calendar month in which such day occurs, and shall include the day of the month in the last month so counted having the same numerical order in days of the month as the day from which the computation is made, unless there be not so many days in the last month so counted, in which case the period computed shall expire with the last day of the month so counted. NY GEN CONSTR § 30.

iii. *Publication of notice; Number of days.* The period of publication of a legal notice shall be computed by excluding the first day of publication and including the day on which the act or event of which notice is given is to take place or which completes the full period of publication. NY CPLR § 2402.

iv. *Periods ending on Saturday, Sunday or public holiday.* When any period of time, computed from a certain day, within which or after which or before which an act is authorized or required to be done, ends on a Saturday, Sunday or a public holiday, such act may be done on the next succeeding business day and if the period ends at a specified hour, such act may be done at or before the same hour of such next succeeding business day, except that where a period of time specified by contract ends on a Saturday, Sunday or a public holiday, the extension of such period is governed by NY GEN CONSTR § 25. NY GEN CONSTR § 25-a(1).

- For a list of public holidays, refer to NY GEN CONSTR § 24.

v. *Additional time after certain kinds of service*

- *Service by mail.* Where a period of time prescribed by law is measured from the service of a paper and service is by mail, five (5) days shall be added to the prescribed period. NY CPLR Rule 2103(b)(2).
- *Service by overnight delivery service.* Where a period of time prescribed by law is measured from the service of a paper and service is by overnight delivery, one (1) business day shall be added to the prescribed period. NY CPLR Rule 2103(b)(6).

vi. *Daylight saving time.* For information on New York's time zone and the effect of daylight saving time, refer to NY GEN CONSTR § 52.

c. *Hours of court.* Notwithstanding any provision of law or rule of court to the contrary, throughout the State of New York the sessions of the Supreme Court for the disposition of business before the court shall commence not later than 9:30 a.m. and conclude not earlier than 5 p.m. Where warranted, the Chief Administrator of the Courts may authorize variances in the opening and closing hours of the courts, but, in such event, daily sessions shall total not less than six (6) hours. NY R CHIEF J § 3.1.

d. *Time limits; Extension of time.* Any act required by or in pursuance of law to be performed at or within a prescribed time, shall be performed according to the standard time. NY GEN CONSTR § 53.

i. Except where otherwise expressly prescribed by law, the court may extend the time fixed by any statute, rule or order for doing any act, upon such terms as may be just and upon good cause shown, whether the application for extension is made before or after the expiration of the time fixed. NY CPLR § 2004. Refer to the New York KeyRules Motion for Continuance/Extension of Time document for more information.

C. General Requirements

1. *Rules governing disclosure*

a. *Generally.* There shall be full disclosure of all matter material and necessary in the prosecution or defense of an action, regardless of the burden of proof, by:

i. A party, or the officer, director, member, agent or employee of a party;

ii. A person who possessed a cause of action or defense asserted in the action;

iii. A person about to depart from the state, or without the state, or residing at a greater distance from the place of trial than one hundred miles, or so sick or infirm as to afford reasonable grounds of belief that he or she will not be able to attend the trial, or a person authorized to practice medicine, dentistry or podiatry who has provided medical, dental or podiatric care or diagnosis to the party demanding disclosure, or who has been retained by such party as an expert witness; and

iv. Any other person, upon notice stating the circumstances or reasons such disclosure is sought or required. NY CPLR § 3101(a).

v. The statutory phrase "material and necessary", said the Court of Appeals, must be interpreted liberally to require disclosure upon request, of any facts bearing on the controversy which will assist preparation for trial by sharpening the issues and reducing delay and prolixity. The test is one of usefulness and reason. SIEGEL-NYPRAC § 344; Allen v. Crowell-Collier Pub. Co., 21 N.Y.2d 403, 235 N.E.2d 430 (1968).

vi. Another potential problem that the original NY CPLR § 3101(a) posed was that it spoke of "evidence" that is material and necessary, which might have been construed to permit disclosure to elicit only that which would itself qualify as "evidence" admissible at trial. It was, however, construed more broadly than that. Well-considered caselaw specifically rejected this "evidence in chief" doctrine, stating that disclosure extends as well "to all relevant information calculated to lead to relevant evidence," a standard similar to that applicable in federal court. With an amendment that took effect on January 1, 1994, changing "evidence" to "matter" in NY CPLR § 3101(a), these generous interpretations of the statute were in effect approved by the legislature. SIEGEL-NYPRAC § 344.

vii. If a party is a corporation, each of its officers, directors, members, agents, and employees is also deemed a "party" for disclosure purposes. A party who needs relevant data or material from a nonparty corporation can seek it through NY CPLR § 3101(a)(2), NY CPLR § 3101(a)(3) or NY CPLR § 3101(a)(4), under which the corporate entity is treated as a "person." These subdivisions should also apply to any entity, corporate or otherwise, from whom disclosure is sought through its agents. A corporate employee who has the requisite knowledge and information may respond to a disclosure request on behalf of the corporation. A party who can't single out the particular person in the corporation's employ to whom a disclosure request should be properly directed can direct it to the corporation as such and leave it to the corporation to designate the appropriate person to respond. Whenever disclosure is sought from a corporation through a deposition, whether as a party or as a nonparty witness, the choice in the first instance of who will be produced in the corporate behalf is with the corporation rather than the examining party. SIEGEL-NYPRAC § 345.

viii. NY CPLR § 3101(a)(4) permits a party to obtain disclosure from a nonparty by merely serving a subpoena on the nonparty providing notice of "the circumstances or reasons such disclosure is sought or required." SIEGEL-NYPRAC § 345.

b. *Methods of obtaining disclosure.* Information is obtainable by one or more of the following disclosure devices: depositions upon oral questions or without the state upon written questions, interrogatories, demands for addresses, discovery and inspection of documents or property, physical and mental examinations of persons, and requests for admission. NY CPLR § 3102(a).

i. *Stipulation or notice.* Unless otherwise provided by the civil practice law and rules or by the court, disclosure shall be obtained by stipulation or on notice without leave of the court. NY CPLR § 3102(b).

ii. *Before action commenced; Court order required.* Before an action is commenced, disclosure to aid in bringing an action, to preserve information or to aid in arbitration, may be obtained, but only by court order. The court may appoint a referee to take testimony. NY CPLR § 3102(c).

iii. *During trial; Court order required.* Except as provided in NY CPLR § 5223, during and after trial, disclosure may be obtained only by order of the trial court on notice. NY CPLR § 3102(d).

iv. *Action pending in another jurisdiction.* Except as provided in NY CPLR § 3119, when under any mandate, writ or commission issued out of any court of record in any other state, territory, district or foreign jurisdiction, or whenever upon notice or agreement, it is required to take the testimony of a witness in the state, he or she may be compelled to appear and testify in the same manner and by the same process as may be employed for the purpose of taking testimony in actions pending in the state. The supreme court or a county court shall make any appropriate order in aid of taking such a deposition. NY CPLR § 3102(e).

v. *Actions to which state is a party.* In an action in which the state is properly a party, whether as plaintiff, defendant or otherwise, disclosure by the state shall be available as if the state were a private person. NY CPLR § 3102(f).

c. *Privileged matter.* Upon objection by a person entitled to assert the privilege, privileged matter shall not be obtainable. NY CPLR § 3101(b).

i. A determination of whether information is privileged is governed by the rules of evidence, which apply as they would at a trial. Whatever is privileged at the trial is privileged as well on pretrial disclosure. SIEGEL-NYPRAC § 346.

d. *Attorney's work product.* The work product of an attorney shall not be obtainable. NY CPLR § 3101(c).

i. NY CPLR § 3101(c) makes unobtainable the "work product of an attorney"—an ill-defined category whose potential for mischief has been avoided only because the judiciary has accorded it a very narrow scope. It is a category wholly distinct from the "materials . . . prepared in anticipation of litigation" of NY CPLR § 3101(d)(2). The fact that immunity is absolute under NY CPLR § 3101(c), while that of NY CPLR § 3101(d)(2) is only conditional, is the factor that requires as sharp a line as possible between the two categories. SIEGEL-NYPRAC § 347.

ii. The judiciary has cast precious little under the "work product" category of NY CPLR § 3101(c), preferring instead to fit doubtful items under the "materials . . . prepared in anticipation of litigation" banner of NY CPLR § 3101(d)(2), where the conditional immunity can be overcome and the matters ordered disclosed when stated conditions are met. SIEGEL-NYPRAC § 347.

e. *Trial preparation*

i. *Experts.* Upon request, each party shall identify each person whom the party expects to call as an expert witness at trial and shall disclose in reasonable detail the subject matter on which each expert is expected to testify, the substance of the facts and opinions on which each expert is expected to testify, the qualifications of each expert witness and a summary of the grounds for each expert's opinion. NY CPLR § 3101(d)(1)(i).

- However, where a party for good cause shown retains an expert an insufficient period of time before the commencement of trial to give appropriate notice thereof, the party shall not thereupon be precluded from introducing the expert's testimony at the trial solely on grounds of noncompliance with NY CPLR § 3101(d)(1). In that instance, upon motion of any party, made before or at trial, or on its own initiative, the court may make whatever order may be just. In an action for medical, dental or podiatric malpractice, a party, in responding to a request, may omit the names of medical, dental or podiatric experts but shall be required to disclose all other information concerning such experts otherwise required by NY CPLR § 3101(d)(1). NY CPLR § 3101(d)(1)(i).
- In an action for medical, dental or podiatric malpractice, any party may, by written offer made to and served upon all other parties and filed with the court, offer to disclose the name of, and to make available for examination upon oral deposition, any person the party making the offer expects to call as an expert witness at trial. Within twenty (20) days of service of the offer, a party shall accept or reject the offer by serving a written reply upon all parties and filing a copy thereof with the court. Failure to serve a reply within twenty (20) days of service of the offer shall be deemed a rejection of the offer. If all parties accept the offer, each party shall be required to produce his or her expert witness for examination upon oral deposition upon receipt of a notice to take oral deposition in accordance with NY CPLR Rule 3107. If any party, having made or accepted the offer, fails to make that party's expert available for oral deposition, that party shall be precluded from offering expert testimony at the trial of the action. NY CPLR § 3101(d)(1)(ii).
- Further disclosure concerning the expected testimony of any expert may be obtained only by court order upon a showing of special circumstances and subject to restrictions as to scope and provisions concerning fees and expenses as the court may deem appropriate. However, a party, without court order, may take the testimony of a person authorized to practice medicine, dentistry or podiatry who is the party's treating or retained expert, as described in NY CPLR § 3101(a)(3), in which event any other party shall be entitled to the full disclosure authorized by Article 31 of Chapter 8 of the Civil Practice Law and Rules (NY CPLR § 3101, et seq.) with respect to that expert without court order. NY CPLR § 3101(d)(1)(iii).

ii. *Materials.* Subject to the provisions of NY CPLR § 3101(d)(1), materials otherwise discoverable under NY CPLR § 3101(a) and prepared in anticipation of litigation or for trial by or for another party, or by or for that other party's representative (including an attorney, consultant, surety, indemnitor, insurer or agent), may be obtained only upon a showing that the party seeking discovery has substantial need of the materials in the preparation of the case and is unable without undue hardship to obtain the substantial equivalent of the materials by other means. In ordering discovery of the materials when the required showing has been made, the court shall protect against disclosure of the mental impressions, conclusions, opinions or legal theories of an attorney or other representative of a party concerning the litigation. NY CPLR § 3101(d)(2).

- In order to qualify as "litigation" material the item must have been prepared exclusively for litigation. Incidental potential use in litigation, the courts have observed, may also be a function of such reports, but they have at least an equal if not greater mission "to prevent future accidents, discipline careless employees, or, generally, to increase the economy and efficiency of the operation." SIEGEL-NYPRAC § 348.

f. *Party's statement.* A party may obtain a copy of his own statement. NY CPLR § 3101(e).

i. Moreover, NY CPLR § 3101(e) has been broadly interpreted to include photographs. Items such as photographs and videotapes are now independently subject to disclosure under NY CPLR § 3101(i). SIEGEL-NYPRAC § 348.

g. *Contents of insurance agreement.* A party may obtain discovery of the existence and contents of any insurance agreement under which any person carrying on an insurance business may be liable to satisfy part or all of a judgment which may be entered in the action or to indemnify or reimburse for payments made to satisfy the judgment. Information concerning the insurance agreement is not by reason of disclosure admissible in evidence at trial. For purpose of NY CPLR § 3101(f), an application for insurance shall not be treated as part of an insurance agreement. NY CPLR § 3101(f).

h. *Accident reports.* Except as is otherwise provided by law, in addition to any other matter which may be subject to disclosure, there shall be full disclosure of any written report of an accident prepared in the regular course of business operations or practices of any person, firm, corporation, association or other public or private entity, unless prepared by a police or peace officer for a criminal investigation or prosecution and disclosure would interfere with a criminal investigation or prosecution. NY CPLR § 3101(g).

i. *Amendment or supplementation of responses.* A party shall amend or supplement a response previously given to a request for disclosure promptly upon the party's thereafter obtaining information that the response was incorrect or incomplete when made, or that the response, though correct and complete when made, no longer is correct and complete, and the circumstances are such that a failure to amend or supplement the response would be materially misleading. NY CPLR § 3101(h).

i. Where a party obtains such information an insufficient period of time before the commencement of trial appropriately to amend or supplement the response, the party shall not thereupon be precluded from introducing evidence at the trial solely on grounds of noncompliance with NY CPLR § 3101(h). In that instance, upon motion of any party, made before or at trial, or on its own initiative, the court may make whatever order may be just. Further amendment or supplementation may be obtained by court order. NY CPLR § 3101(h).

j. *Other disclosures.* In addition to any other matter which may be subject to disclosure, there shall be full disclosure of any films, photographs, video tapes or audio tapes, including transcripts or memoranda thereof, involving a person referred to in NY CPLR § 3101(a)(1). There shall be disclosure of all portions of such material, including out-takes, rather than only those portions a party intends to use. The provisions of NY CPLR § 3101(i) shall not apply to materials compiled for law enforcement purposes which are exempt from disclosure under NY PUB OFF § 87. NY CPLR § 3101(i).

i. While NY CPLR § 3101(i) was enacted with the defendant's surreptitious tapes of the plaintiff in mind, its language is broad enough to embrace any films, photographs, and audio or video tapes of a party, even those made by the party from whom disclosure is sought. SIEGEL-NYPRAC § 348.

k. *Protective orders.* The court may at any time on its own initiative, or on motion of any party or of any person from whom discovery is sought, make a protective order denying, limiting, conditioning or regulating the use of any disclosure device. NY CPLR § 3103(a). Refer to the New York KeyRules Motion for Protective Order document for more information.

l. *Supervision of disclosure.* Upon the motion of any party or witness on notice to all parties or on its own initiative without notice, the court in which an action is pending may by one of its judges or a referee supervise all or part of any disclosure procedure. NY CPLR § 3104(a).

i. *Selection of referee.* A judicial hearing officer may be designated as a referee under NY CPLR § 3104, or the court may permit all of the parties in an action to stipulate that a named attorney may act as referee. In such latter event, the stipulation shall provide for payment of his fees which shall, unless otherwise agreed, be taxed as disbursements. NY CPLR § 3104(b).

ii. *Powers of referee; Motions referred to person supervising disclosure.* A referee under NY CPLR § 3104 shall have all the powers of the court under NY CPLR § 3101, et seq. except the power to relieve himself of his duties, to appoint a successor, or to adjudge any person guilty of contempt. All motions or applications made under Article 31 of Chapter 8 of the Civil Practice Law and Rules (NY CPLR § 3101, et seq.) shall be returnable before the judge or referee, designated under NY CPLR § 3104 and after disposition, if requested by any party, his order shall be filed in the office of the clerk. NY CPLR § 3104(c).

iii. *Review of order of referee.* Any party or witness may apply for review of an order made under NY CPLR § 3104 by a referee. The application shall be by motion made in the court in which the action is pending within five (5) days after the order is made. Service of a notice of motion for review shall suspend disclosure of the particular matter in dispute. If the question raised by the motion may affect the rights of a witness, notice shall be served on him personally or by mail at his last known address. It shall set forth succinctly the order complained of, the reason it is objectionable and the relief demanded. NY CPLR § 3104(d).

iv. *Payment of expenses of referee.* Except where a judicial hearing officer has been designated a referee hereunder, the court may make an appropriate order for the payment of the reasonable expenses of the referee. NY CPLR § 3104(e).

2. *Notice of deposition; In general.* After an action is commenced, any party may take the testimony of any person by deposition upon oral or written questions. NY CPLR Rule 3106(a).

a. *Specific deponents*

i. *Witnesses.* Where the person to be examined is not a party or a person who at the time of taking the deposition is an officer, director, member or employee of a party, he shall be served with a subpoena. NY CPLR Rule 3106(b).

ii. *Prisoners.* The deposition of a person confined under legal process may be taken only by leave of the court. NY CPLR Rule 3106(c).

iii. *Designation of deponent.* A party desiring to take the deposition of a particular officer, director, member or employee of a person shall include in the notice or subpoena served upon such person the identity, description or title of such individual. Such person shall produce the individual so designated unless they shall have, no later than ten (10) days prior to the scheduled deposition, notified the requesting party that another individual would instead be produced and the identity, description or title of such individual is specified. If timely notification has been so given, such other individual shall instead be produced. NY CPLR Rule 3106(d).

b. *Location of deposition.* A deposition within the state on notice shall be taken:

i. When the person to be examined is a party or an officer, director, member or employee of a party, within the county in which he resides or has an office for the regular transaction of business in person or where the action is pending; or

ii. When any other person to be examined is a resident, within the county in which he resides, is regularly employed or has an office for the regular transaction of business in person, or if he is not a resident, within the county in which he is served, is regularly employed or has an office for the regular transaction of business in person; or

iii. When the party to be examined is a public corporation or any officer, agent or employee thereof, within the county in which the action is pending; the place of such examination shall be the office of any of the attorneys for such a public corporation or any officer, agent or authorized employee thereof unless the parties stipulate otherwise. NY CPLR Rule 3110.

iv. For the purpose of NY CPLR Rule 3110 New York city shall be considered one county. NY CPLR Rule 3110.

v. A deposition may be taken on written questions when the examining party and the deponent so stipulate or when the testimony is to be taken without the state. A commission or letters rogatory may be issued where necessary or convenient for the taking of a deposition outside of the state. NY CPLR Rule 3108.

3. *Notice of deposition; On oral examination*

a. *Contents of notice.* The notice shall be in writing, stating the time and place for taking the deposition, the name and address of each person to be examined, if known, and, if any name is not known, a general description sufficient to identify him or the particular class or group to which he belongs. NY CPLR Rule 3107.

i. The notice need not enumerate the matters upon which the person is to be examined. NY CPLR Rule 3107.

4. *Notice of deposition; On written questions*

a. *Contents of notice.* A party desiring to take the deposition of any person upon written questions shall serve such questions upon each party together with a notice stating the name and address of the person to be examined, if known, and, if the name is not known, a general description sufficient to identify him or the particular class or group to which he belongs, and the name or descriptive title and address of the officer before whom the deposition is to be taken. NY CPLR Rule 3109(a).

i. *Procedure regarding officer.* A copy of the notice and copies of all written questions served shall be delivered by the party taking the deposition to the officer designated in the notice. The officer shall proceed promptly to take the testimony of the witness in response to the written questions and to prepare the deposition. NY CPLR Rule 3109(b).

5. *Conduct of deposition*

a. *Persons before whom depositions may be taken.* Depositions may be taken before any of the following persons except an attorney, or employee of an attorney, for a party or prospective party and except a person who would be disqualified to act as a juror because of interest in the event or consanguinity or affinity to a party:

i. Within the state, a person authorized by the laws of the state to administer oaths;

ii. Without the state but within the United States or within a territory or possession subject to the jurisdiction of the United States, a person authorized to take acknowledgments of deeds outside of the state by the real property law of the state or to administer oaths by the laws of the United States or of the place where the deposition is taken; and

iii. In a foreign country, any diplomatic or consular agent or representative of the United States, appointed or accredited to, and residing within, the country, or a person appointed by commission or under letters rogatory, or an officer of the armed forces authorized to take the acknowledgment of deeds. NY CPLR Rule 3113(a).

iv. Officers may be designated in notices or commissions either by name or descriptive title and letters rogatory may be addressed "To the Appropriate Authority in (here name the state or country)." NY CPLR Rule 3113(a).

b. *Oath of witness; Recording of testimony; Objections; Continuous examination; Written questions read by examining officer*

i. The officer before whom the deposition is to be taken shall put the witness on oath and shall personally, or by someone acting under his direction, record the testimony. The testimony shall be recorded by stenographic or other means, subject to such rules as may be adopted by the appellate division in the department where the action is pending. NY CPLR Rule 3113(b).

ii. All objections made at the time of the examination to the qualifications of the officer taking the deposition or the person recording it, or to the manner of taking it, or to the testimony presented, or to the conduct of any person, and any other objection to the proceedings, shall be noted by the officer upon the deposition and the deposition shall proceed subject to the right of a person to apply for a protective order. NY CPLR Rule 3113(b).

iii. The deposition shall be taken continuously and without unreasonable adjournment, unless the court otherwise orders or the witness and parties present otherwise agree. NY CPLR Rule 3113(b).

iv. In lieu of participating in an oral examination, any party served with notice of taking a deposition may transmit written questions to the officer, who shall propound them to the witness and record the answers. NY CPLR Rule 3113(b).

c. *Examination and cross-examination.* Examination and cross-examination of deponents shall proceed as permitted in the trial of actions in open court, except that a non-party deponent's counsel may participate in the deposition and make objections on behalf of his or her client in the same manner as counsel for a party. When the deposition of a party is taken at the instance of an adverse party, the deponent may be cross-examined by his or her own attorney. Cross-examination need not be limited to the subject matter of the examination in chief. NY CPLR Rule 3113(c).

d. *Production of documents at deposition.* The notice or subpoena may require the production of books, papers and other things in the possession, custody or control of the person to be examined to be marked as exhibits, and used on the examination. The reasonable production expenses of a non-party witness shall be defrayed by the party seeking discovery. NY CPLR Rule 3111.

i. *Exhibits annexed to deposition.* Documentary evidence exhibited before the officer or exhibits marked for identification during the examination of the witness shall be annexed to and returned with the deposition. However, if requested by the party producing documentary evidence or on exhibit, the officer shall mark it for identification as an exhibit in the case, give each party an opportunity to copy or inspect it, and return it to the party offering it, and it may then be used in the same manner as if annexed to and returned with the deposition. NY CPLR Rule 3116(c).

e. *Objections to conduct of deposition.* Errors and irregularities occurring at the oral examination in the manner of taking the deposition, in the form of the questions or answers, in the oath or affirmation, or in the conduct of persons, and errors of any kind which might be obviated or removed if objection were promptly presented, are waived unless reasonable objection thereto is made at the taking of the deposition. NY CPLR Rule 3115(b). For more information on objections to the conduct of the deposition, refer to NY CPLR Rule 3115.

f. *Signing of deposition by witness.* The deposition shall be submitted to the witness for examination and shall be read to or by him or her, and any changes in form or substance which the witness desires to make shall be entered at the end of the deposition with a statement of the reasons given by the witness for making them. The deposition shall then be signed by the witness before any officer authorized to administer an oath. If the witness fails to sign and return the deposition within sixty (60) days, it may be used as fully as though signed. No changes to the transcript may be made by the witness more than sixty (60) days after submission to the witness for examination. NY CPLR Rule 3116(a).

   i. *Errors in transcription.* Errors and irregularities of the officer or the person transcribing the deposition are waived unless a motion to suppress the deposition or some part thereof is made with reasonable promptness after such defect is, or with due diligence might have been, ascertained. NY CPLR Rule 3116(e).

g. *Deposition by telephone or other remote means.* The parties may stipulate that a deposition be taken by telephone or other remote electronic means and that a party may participate electronically. The stipulation shall designate reasonable provisions to ensure that an accurate record of the deposition is generated, shall specify, if appropriate, reasonable provisions for the use of exhibits at the deposition; shall specify who must and who may physically be present at the deposition; and shall provide for any other provisions appropriate under the circumstances. Unless otherwise stipulated to by the parties, the officer administering the oath shall be physically present at the place of the deposition and the additional costs of conducting the deposition by telephonic or other remote electronic means, such as telephone charges, shall be borne by the party requesting that the deposition be conducted by such means. NY CPLR Rule 3113(d).

h. *Witnesses who do not speak English.* If the witness to be examined does not understand the English language, the examining party must, at his own expense, provide a translation of all questions and answers. Where the court settles questions, it may settle them in the foreign language and in English. It may use the services of one or more experts whose compensation shall be paid by the party seeking the examination and may be taxed as a disbursement. NY CPLR Rule 3114.

i. *Expense of deposition.* Unless the court orders otherwise, the party taking the deposition shall bear the expense thereof. NY CPLR Rule 3116(d).

j. *Video recording of depositions; Further considerations on conduct at depositions.* For information on videotape recording of depositions, refer to NY R UNIF TRIAL CTS § 202.15. For more information on conduct of depositions, refer to NY R UNIF TRIAL CTS § 221.1, et seq.

6. *Governing law.* The civil practice law and rules (NY CPLR § 101, et seq.) shall govern the procedure in civil judicial proceedings in all courts of the state and before all judges, except where the procedure is regulated by inconsistent statute. The civil practice law and rules shall succeed the civil practice act and rules of civil practice and shall be deemed substituted therefor throughout the statutes and rules of the state. NY CPLR § 101. The civil practice law and rules shall be liberally construed to secure the just, speedy and inexpensive determination of every civil judicial proceeding. NY CPLR § 104.

   a. *Uniform trial court rules.* The uniform civil rules for the Supreme Court and County Court (NY R UNIF TRIAL CTS § 202.1, et seq.) shall be applicable to civil actions and proceedings in the Supreme Court and the County Court. NY R UNIF TRIAL CTS § 202.1(a). The provisions of the uniform rules shall be construed consistent with the Civil Practice Law and Rules (CPLR), and matters not covered by the uniform rules shall be governed by the CPLR. NY R UNIF TRIAL CTS § 202.1(d).

   b. *Local rules.* Local court rules, not inconsistent with law or with uniform civil rules for the Supreme Court and County Court (NY R UNIF TRIAL CTS § 202.1, et seq.), shall comply with Part 9 of the Rules of the Chief Judge (NY R CHIEF J § 9.1). NY R UNIF TRIAL CTS § 202.1(c).

   c. *Official forms.* The state administrator shall have the power to adopt, amend and rescind an appendix of forms. Forms adopted pursuant to NY CPLR § 107 shall be sufficient under the civil practice law and rules and shall illustrate the simplicity and brevity of statement which the civil practice law and rules contemplate. NY CPLR § 107.

7. *Rules of the commercial division.* [Editor's note: certain types of civil cases or civil cases meeting certain monetary thresholds that are filed in the state of New York must be filed in the Commercial Division of the New York Supreme Courts. Rules governing practice in the commercial division are found in NY R UNIF TRIAL CTS § 202.70]. Cases which must be filed in the commercial division are listed below. For more information, refer to NY R UNIF TRIAL CTS § 202.70.

   a. *Monetary thresholds.* Except as set forth in NY R UNIF TRIAL CTS § 202.70(b), the monetary thresholds of the Commercial Division, exclusive of punitive damages, interests, costs, disbursements and counsel fees claimed, are established as follows: (1) Albany County, fifty thousand dollars ($50,000); (2) Eighth Judicial District, one hundred thousand dollars ($100,000); (3) Kings County, one hundred fifty thousand dollars ($150,000); (4) Nassau County, two hundred thousand dollars ($200,000); (5) New York County, five hundred thousand dollars ($500,000); (6) Onondaga County, fifty thousand dollars ($50,000); (7) Queens County, one hundred thousand dollars ($100,000); (8) Seventh Judicial District, fifty thousand dollars ($50,000); (9) Suffolk County, one hundred thousand dollars ($100,000); and (10) Westchester County, one hundred thousand dollars ($100,000). NY R UNIF TRIAL CTS § 202.70(a).

i. *ALBANY COUNTY.* The Commercial Division of the Albany County Supreme Court exercises jurisdiction over selected business and commercial disputes in which the amount at issue generally involves damage claims in a minimum amount of fifty thousand dollars ($50,000) as well as claims for unspecified amounts where the value of the commercial asset(s) in dispute exceeds fifty thousand dollars ($50,000). A separate publication promulgating the rules and criteria relating to the filing and management of Commercial Court cases in this part may be obtained from the Albany County Supreme Court Clerk's Office. A section of the Uniform Civil Rules for the Supreme Court and County Court sets forth statewide rules. NY R 3 JD SUP Doc. 1(E).

ii. *BRONX COUNTY.* The monetary threshold for commercial cases in Bronx County will be seventy-five thousand dollars ($75,000). All other parameters including the type of matters that will be heard are contained within the Rules of the Commercial Division of the Supreme Court (NY R UNIF TRIAL CTS § 202.70). NY R BRONX FIL R Doc. 12.

iii. *NEW YORK COUNTY.* The monetary threshold in the New York County Commercial Division, which is generally applicable, is an amount in controversy of five hundred thousand dollars ($500,000) or more (exclusive of punitive damages, interest, costs, disbursements, and counsel fees). If the case is designated a commercial one and the Addendum is submitted, the clerk will review the pleadings to determine whether the amount in controversy in the case meets the monetary threshold or whether an exception to the threshold applies. NY R NY CTY Procedure IA(B). For more information on assigning a case to the commercial division in New York County, refer to NY R NY CTY Procedure IA(B).

b. *Commercial cases.* Actions in which the principal claims involve or consist of the following will be heard in the Commercial Division provided that the monetary threshold is met or equitable or declaratory relief is sought:

i. Breach of contract or fiduciary duty, fraud, misrepresentation, business tort (e.g., unfair competition), or statutory and/or common law violation where the breach or violation is alleged to arise out of business dealings (e.g., sales of assets or securities; corporate restructuring; partnership, shareholder, joint venture, and other business agreements; trade secrets; restrictive covenants; and employment agreements not including claims that principally involve alleged discriminatory practices);

ii. Transactions governed by the Uniform Commercial Code (exclusive of those concerning individual cooperative or condominium units);

iii. Transactions involving commercial real property, including Yellowstone injunctions and excluding actions for the payment of rent only;

iv. Shareholder derivative actions—without consideration of the monetary threshold;

v. Commercial class actions—without consideration of the monetary threshold;

vi. Business transactions involving or arising out of dealings with commercial banks and other financial institutions;

vii. Internal affairs of business organizations;

viii. Malpractice by accountants or actuaries, and legal malpractice arising out of representation in commercial matters;

ix. Environmental insurance coverage;

x. Commercial insurance coverage (e.g., directors and officers, errors and omissions, and business interruption coverage);

xi. Dissolution of corporations, partnerships, limited liability companies, limited liability partnerships and joint ventures—without consideration of the monetary threshold; and

xii. Applications to stay or compel arbitration and affirm or disaffirm arbitration awards and related injunctive relief pursuant to Article 75 of the New York Civil Practice Law and Rules (NY CPLR § 7501, et seq.) involving any of the foregoing enumerated commercial issues. Where the applicable arbitration agreement provides for the arbitration to be heard outside the United States, the monetary threshold set forth in NY R UNIF TRIAL CTS § 202.70(a) shall not apply. NY R UNIF TRIAL CTS § 202.70(b).

c. *Non-commercial cases.* The following will not be heard in the Commercial Division even if the monetary threshold is met:

i. Suits to collect professional fees;

ii. Cases seeking a declaratory judgment as to insurance coverage for personal injury or property damage;

iii. Residential real estate disputes, including landlord-tenant matters, and commercial real estate disputes involving the payment of rent only;

iv. Home improvement contracts involving residential properties consisting of one to four residential units or individual units in any residential building, including cooperative or condominium units;

v. Proceedings to enforce a judgment regardless of the nature of the underlying case;

vi. First-party insurance claims and actions by insurers to collect premiums or rescind non-commercial policies; and

vii. Attorney malpractice actions except as otherwise provided in NY R UNIF TRIAL CTS § 202.70(b)(8). NY R UNIF TRIAL CTS § 202.70(c).

d. For more information on the Commercial Division, refer to NY R UNIF TRIAL CTS § 202.70.

D. Documents

1. *Deposition on oral examination*

a. *Required documents*

i. *Notice of deposition.* Refer to the General Requirements section of this document for information on the notice of deposition.

ii. *Proof of service.* In addition to complying with the provisions of NY CPLR Rule 2101, every paper filed in court shall have annexed thereto appropriate proof of service on all parties where required. NY R UNIF TRIAL CTS § 202.5(a).

b. *Supplemental documents*

i. *Working copies.* The court may require the parties to provide working copies of documents filed electronically. In such event, each working copy shall include, firmly affixed thereto, a copy of a confirmation notice in a form prescribed by the Chief Administrator. NY R UNIF TRIAL CTS § 202.5-b(d)(5).

ii. *Subpoena.* Refer to the New York KeyRules Subpoena document for information on preparing a subpoena.

2. *Deposition on written questions*

a. *Required documents*

i. *Notice of deposition.* Refer to the General Requirements section of this document for information on the notice of deposition.

ii. *Written questions.* A party desiring to take the deposition of any person upon written questions shall serve such questions upon each party. NY CPLR Rule 3109(a).

iii. *Proof of service.* In addition to complying with the provisions of NY CPLR Rule 2101, every paper filed in court shall have annexed thereto appropriate proof of service on all parties where required. NY R UNIF TRIAL CTS § 202.5(a).

b. *Supplemental documents*

i. *Working copies.* The court may require the parties to provide working copies of documents filed electronically. In such event, each working copy shall include, firmly affixed thereto, a copy of a confirmation notice in a form prescribed by the Chief Administrator. NY R UNIF TRIAL CTS § 202.5-b(d)(5).

ii. *Subpoena.* Refer to the New York KeyRules Subpoena document for information on preparing a subpoena.

E. Format

1. *Form of documents*

a. *Size and form of paper.* Each paper served or filed shall be durable, white and, except for summonses, subpoenas, notices of appearance, notes of issue, orders of protection, temporary orders of protection and exhibits, shall be eleven by eight and one-half (11 x 8-1/2) inches in size. NY CPLR Rule 2101(a).

b. *Writing and language.* The writing shall be legible and in black ink. NY CPLR Rule 2101(a). Each paper served or filed shall be in the English language which, where practicable, shall be of ordinary usage. NY CPLR Rule 2101(b).

c. *Caption.* Each paper served or filed shall begin with a caption setting forth the name of the court, the venue, the title of the action, the nature of the paper and the index number of the action if one has been assigned. In all papers other than a summons, a complaint or a judgment it shall be sufficient to state the name of the first named party on each side with an appropriate indication of any omissions. NY CPLR Rule 2101(c).

   i. *Further contents of first page.* After the first paper has been filed in each case the index number shall appear on the cover and first page to the right of the caption of every paper tendered for filing in the action. Each such cover and first page also shall contain an indication of the county of venue and a brief description of the nature of the paper and, where the case has been assigned to an individual judge, shall contain the name of the assigned judge to the right of the caption. NY R UNIF TRIAL CTS § 202.5(a); NY R UNIF TRIAL CTS § 202.5(b); NY R UNIF TRIAL CTS § 202.5(d)(1)(i).

d. *Index number.* No paper in an action in the supreme or a county court, other than an order submitted for signature to a judge out of court, shall be submitted for any purpose to the supreme or county court or to a clerk thereof unless there is endorsed on such paper the index number of the action assigned by the clerk of the county. NY CPLR § 8018(c).

e. *Line spacing.* Every paper filed in court, if typewritten, shall have at least double space between each line, except for quotations and the names and addresses of attorneys appearing in the action. NY R UNIF TRIAL CTS § 202.5(a).

f. *Font size.* Each. . .paper printed or typed, served or filed, except for summonses. . .and exhibits, shall be in clear type of no less than ten (10) point in size. NY CPLR Rule 2101(a).

   i. Whenever a requirement relating to size of type is stated in point size, the type size requirement shall be deemed met if the x-height of the type is a minimum of forty-five percent (45%) of the specified point size. Each point shall be measured as .351 millimeter. The x-height size shall be measured as it appears on the page. The x-height is the height of the lower case letters, exclusive of ascenders or descenders. NY CPLR § 105(t).

g. *Margins.* Every paper filed in court shall have at least one (1) inch margins. NY R UNIF TRIAL CTS § 202.5(a).

h. *Citations*

   i. *Civil practice law and rules.* NY CPLR § 101, et seq. shall be known as the civil practice law and rules, and may be cited as "CPLR". Reference to a provision in the civil practice law and rules may, except when such provision is being enacted or amended, be made without indicating whether it is a rule or section. NY CPLR § 101.

i. *Indorsement by attorney.* Each paper served or filed shall be indorsed with the name, address and telephone number of the attorney for the party serving or filing the paper, or if the party does not appear by attorney, with the name, address and telephone number of the party. NY CPLR Rule 2101(d).

j. *One-sided printing.* In addition, every paper filed in court, other than an exhibit or printed form, shall contain writing on one side only, except that papers that are fastened on the side may contain writing on both sides. NY R UNIF TRIAL CTS § 202.5(a).

k. *Use of copies authorized.* Except where otherwise specifically prescribed, copies, rather than originals, of all papers, including orders, affidavits and exhibits may be served or filed. Where it is required that the original be served or filed and the original is lost or withheld, the court may authorize a copy to be served or filed. NY CPLR Rule 2101(e).

   i. Where a certified copy of a paper is required by law, an attorney admitted to practice in the courts of the state may certify that it has been compared by him with the original and found to be a true and complete copy. Such a certificate, when subscribed by such attorney, has the same effect as if made by a clerk. NY CPLR § 2105.

l. *Recycled paper.* It is the policy of the Unified Court System that litigants, where practicable, should file or submit to the courts of the Unified Court System of the State of New York papers printed or reproduced on recycled paper. Paper is considered recycled if it contains a minimum content of thirty percent (30%) waste paper. NY R UNIF TRIAL CTS § 215.2. The signature page of every paper filed or submitted to the court on recycled paper should bear the legend: "Printed [Reproduced] on Recycled Paper." NY R UNIF TRIAL CTS § 215.3.

2. *Form of electronic documents.* Each paper served or filed by electronic means, as defined in NY CPLR Rule 2103(f), shall be capable of being reproduced by the receiver so as to comply with the provisions of NY CPLR Rule 2101(a) through NY CPLR Rule 2101(d). NY CPLR Rule 2101(g).

   a. *File format.* All e-filed documents shall comply with the technical requirements set forth at the NYSCEF site. NY R UNIF TRIAL CTS § 202.5-b(d)(1)(i).

   b. *Heading of document.* The subject matter heading for each paper sent by electronic means must indicate that the matter being transmitted electronically is related to a court proceeding. NY CPLR Rule 2103(b)(7).

3. *Signature blocks.* Every pleading, written motion, and other paper, served on another party or filed or submitted to the court

shall be signed by an attorney, or by a party if the party is not represented by an attorney, with the name of the attorney or party clearly printed or typed directly below the signature. NY R CHIEF ADMIN § 130-1.1-a(a); NY R UNIF TRIAL CTS § 202.5(d)(1)(iv).

a. *Printed name.* Beneath each signature shall be printed the name signed. NY CPLR Rule 2101(a).

b. *Failure to sign.* Absent good cause shown, the court shall strike any unsigned paper if the omission of the signature is not corrected promptly after being called to the attention of the attorney or party. NY R CHIEF ADMIN § 130-1.1-a(a).

c. *Signature as certification.* By signing a paper, an attorney or party certifies that, to the best of that person's knowledge, information and belief, formed after an inquiry reasonable under the circumstances the presentation of the paper or the contentions therein are not frivolous as defined in NY R CHIEF ADMIN § 130-1.1(c). NY R CHIEF ADMIN § 130-1.1-a(b)(1).

d. *Electronic signatures.* A document shall be considered to have been signed by an attorney or party in compliance with NY R CHIEF ADMIN § 130-1.1-a if it has been signed by such attorney or party as provided in NY R UNIF TRIAL CTS § 202.5-b(e)(1) and it bears the signatory's name. NY R UNIF TRIAL CTS § 202.5-b(e)(2). An electronically filed document shall be considered to have been signed by, and shall be binding upon, the person identified as a signatory, if:

i. It bears the physical signature of such person and is scanned into an electronic format that reproduces such signature; or

ii. The signatory has electronically affixed the digital image of his or her signature to the document; or

iii. It is electronically filed under the User ID and password of that person; or

iv. In a tax certiorari action in which the parties have stipulated to this procedure, it is an initiating document that is electronically filed without the signature of the signatory in a form provided above in NY R UNIF TRIAL CTS § 202.5-b(e)(iv), provided that, prior to filing, the document is signed in full in hard copy (which hard copy must be preserved until the conclusion of all proceedings, including appeals, in the case in which it is filed); or

v. In a small claims assessment review proceeding, it is a petition recorded by the NYSCEF site upon the filing of a text file as provided in NY R UNIF TRIAL CTS § 202.5-b(b)(1), provided that prior to filing, the document was signed in full in hard copy (which hard copy must be preserved until the conclusion of all proceedings in the matter, including article 78 (NY CPLR § 7801, et seq.) review and any appeals, and must be made available during the proceeding upon request of the respondent or the court); or

vi. It otherwise bears the electronic signature of the signatory in a format conforming to such standards and requirements as may hereafter be established by the Chief Administrator. NY R UNIF TRIAL CTS § 202.5-b(e).

4. *Confidentiality of personal information.* No person may file any document available for public inspection with any state agency, political subdivision, or in any court of this state that contains a Social Security account number of any other person, unless such other person is a dependent child, or has consented to such filing, except as required by federal or state law or regulation, or by court rule. NY GEN BUS § 399-ddd. Submissions pursuant to e-filing procedures shall have the same confidentiality rights as paper documents. NY R UNIF TRIAL CTS § 202.5-b(k)(1).

a. *Confidential personal information.* Except in the actions designated in NY R UNIF TRIAL CTS § 202.5(e)(1), or as otherwise provided by rule or law or court order, and whether or not a sealing order is or has been sought, the parties shall omit or redact confidential personal information in papers submitted to the court for filing. For purposes of NY R UNIF TRIAL CTS § 202.5(e), confidential personal information ("CPI") means:

i. The taxpayer identification number of an individual or an entity, including a Social Security number, an employer identification number, and an individual taxpayer identification number, except the last four (4) digits thereof;

ii. The date of an individual's birth, except the year thereof;

iii. The full name of an individual known to be a minor, except the minor's initials;

iv. A financial account number, including a credit and/or debit card number, a bank account number, an investment account number, and/or an insurance account number, except the last four (4) digits or letters thereof; and

v. Any of the documents or testimony in a matrimonial action protected by NY DOM REL § 235 or evidence sealed by the court in such an action which are attached as exhibits or referenced in the papers filed in any other civil action. For purposes of NY R UNIF TRIAL CTS § 202.5, a matrimonial action shall mean: an action to annul a marriage or declare the nullity of a void marriage, an action or agreement for a separation, an action for a divorce, or an action or proceeding for custody, visitation, writ of habeus corpus, child support, maintenance or paternity. NY R UNIF TRIAL CTS § 202.5(e)(1).

b. *Submission of confidential personal information.* Where a person submitting a paper to a court for filing believes in good faith that the inclusion of the full confidential personal information described in NY R UNIF TRIAL CTS § 202.5(e)(1) is material and necessary to the adjudication of the action or proceeding before the court, he or she may apply to the court for leave to serve and file together with a paper in which such information has been set forth in abbreviated form a confidential affidavit or affirmation setting forth the same information in unabbreviated form, appropriately referenced to the page or pages of the paper at which the abbreviated form appears. NY R UNIF TRIAL CTS § 202.5(e)(3).

c. *Home addresses.* For information on when home addresses and other personal information must be redacted, refer to NY CPLR Rule 2103-a.

5. *Defective papers.* A defect in the form of a paper, if a substantial right of a party is not prejudiced, shall be disregarded by the court, and leave to correct shall be freely given. NY CPLR Rule 2101(f). Papers that are stapled or bound securely shall not be rejected for filing simply because they are not bound with a backer of any kind. NY R UNIF TRIAL CTS § 202.5(a). A paper filed in accordance with the rules of the chief administrator or any local rule or practice established by the court shall be deemed filed. NY CPLR Rule 2102(b).

a. *Objection to defective papers.* The party on whom a paper is served shall be deemed to have waived objection to any defect in form unless, within fifteen (15) days after the receipt thereof, the party on whom the paper is served returns the paper to the party serving it with a statement of particular objections. NY CPLR Rule 2101(f).

F. Filing and Service Requirements

1. *Filing requirements.* Except where otherwise prescribed by law or order of court, papers required to be filed shall be filed with the clerk of the court in which the action is triable. In an action or proceeding in supreme or court, papers required to be filed shall be filed with the clerk of the county in which the proceeding is brought. NY CPLR Rule 2102(a).

a. *Electronic filing.* On consent, documents may be filed and served by electronic means in Supreme Court in such civil actions and in such counties as shall be authorized by order of the Chief Administrator of the Courts and only to the extent and in the manner provided in NY R UNIF TRIAL CTS § 202.5-b. NY R UNIF TRIAL CTS § 202.5-b(a)(1). For the definitions of terms used in electronic filing, refer to NY R UNIF TRIAL CTS § 202.5-b(a)(2).

i. *Electronic filing of discovery materials.* In any action subject to e-filing, parties and non-parties producing materials in response to discovery demands may enter into a stipulation, which shall be e-filed, authorizing the electronic filing of discovery responses and discovery materials to the degree and upon terms and conditions set forth in the stipulation. In the absence of such a stipulation, no party shall file electronically any such materials except in the form of excerpts, quotations, or selected exhibits from such materials as part of motion papers, pleadings or other filings with the court. NY R UNIF TRIAL CTS § 202.5-b(j).

ii. *E-filing mandatory.* In any action subject to e-filing, all documents required to be filed with the court by an e-filing party shall be filed and served electronically, except as provided in NY R UNIF TRIAL CTS § 202.5-b. NY R UNIF TRIAL CTS § 202.5-b(d)(1)(i).

iii. *Who may file.* Documents may be filed or served electronically only by a person who has registered as an authorized e-filing user or as otherwise provided in NY R UNIF TRIAL CTS § 202.5-b(c). NY R UNIF TRIAL CTS § 202.5-b(c)(1).

iv. *When filing made.* Documents may be transmitted at any time of the day or night to the NYSCEF site. A document other than an order or judgment is filed when its electronic transmission or, in the case of a petition that is e-filed by submission of a text file as provided in NY R UNIF TRIAL CTS § 202.5-b(b)(1), the electronic transmission of the text file is recorded at that site, provided, however, that where payment of a fee is required upon the filing of a document, the document is not filed until transmission of the document and the information or form or information as required in NY R UNIF TRIAL CTS § 202.5-b(d)(2)(i), NY R UNIF TRIAL CTS § 202.5-b(d)(2)(ii) or NY R UNIF TRIAL CTS § 202.5-b(d)(2)(iii) has been recorded at the NYSCEF site; or, if no transmission of that information or form or information is recorded, where permitted by the County Clerk, until payment is presented to the County Clerk. NY R UNIF TRIAL CTS § 202.5-b(d)(3)(i).

v. *Notification of filing.* No later than the close of business on the business day following the electronic filing of a document, a notification, in a form prescribed by the Chief Administrator, shall be transmitted electronically by the NYSCEF site to the person filing such document and the e-mail service addresses of all other participating parties in such action. NY R UNIF TRIAL CTS § 202.5-b(d)(3)(ii).

vi. *Removal of confidential information and other corrections.* If a document filed electronically is subsequently discovered to contain confidential data—including but not limited to trade secrets, information protected by confidentiality agreement, or personal confidential information as defined by statute or court rule—or otherwise to have been filed in error, the filer or another party or affected person may (1) notify the parties and any non-party filers in the action of the confidentiality issue or other error raised by the filing, and of his or her intention to seek judicial relief to correct the filing: (2) following such notification, request that the appropriate County Clerk, exercising his or her administrative discretion, place the document temporarily in "restricted" status on the NYSCEF site, to be made available for viewing by court staff and the parties but not the general public; and (3) file an application to correct the filing by order to show cause within five (5) business days of such notification (or such time as the court may direct), including a request for preliminary injunctive relief limiting interim disclosure of the document at issue. Unless otherwise directed by the court, any document placed in restricted status in response to such a request shall be returned to public view upon expiration of this five (5) day period. The Chief Administrator of the Courts shall promulgate forms to implement this process. NY R UNIF TRIAL CTS § 202.5-b(d)(3)(iii).

vii. *Documents requiring judge's signature.* Except where the court directs otherwise, any document that requires a judge's signature shall be transmitted electronically and in hard copy to the court. NY R UNIF TRIAL CTS § 202.5-b(d)(6).

viii. *Documents which would be inconvenient to file electronically; Hard copies.* Notwithstanding any other provision of NY R UNIF TRIAL CTS § 202.5-b, and subject to such guidelines as may be established by the Chief Administrative Judge, the County Clerk or his or her designee may require or permit a party to file in hard copy, in accordance with procedures set by the County Clerk or designee, an exhibit or other document which it is impractical or inconvenient to file electronically. NY R UNIF TRIAL CTS § 202.5-b(d)(7).

ix. *Documents containing sensitive or proprietary information.* In an action subject to e-filing, any person may apply for an order prohibiting or restricting the electronic filing in the action of specifically identified materials on the grounds that such materials are subject to copyright or other proprietary rights, or trade secret or other privacy interests, and that electronic filing in the action is likely to result in substantial prejudice to those rights or interests. NY R UNIF TRIAL CTS § 202.5-b(k)(2).

x. *Refusal to accept paper filings.* In accordance with NY CPLR Rule 2102(c), a County Clerk and a chief clerk of the Supreme Court or County Court, as appropriate, shall refuse to accept for filing papers filed in actions and proceedings when the paper sought to be filed:

- Is in an action subject to electronic filing pursuant to Rules of the Chief Administrator,
- Is not being filed electronically, and
- Does not include the notice required by NY R UNIF TRIAL CTS § 202.5-b(d)(1). NY R UNIF TRIAL CTS § 202.5(d)(1)(v); NY R UNIF TRIAL CTS § 202.5-bb(d).

xi. *Emergency filings; Hard copies.* For information on when an emergency filing may be filed and served in hard copy, refer to NY R UNIF TRIAL CTS § 202.5-b(d)(1)(ii), NY R UNIF TRIAL CTS § 202.5-b(d)(1)(iii) and NY R UNIF TRIAL CTS § 202.5-bb(c)(3).

xii. *Technical failures.* The NYSCEF site shall be considered to be subject to a technical failure on a given day if the site is unable to accept filings or provide access to filed documents continuously or intermittently over the course of any period of time greater than one (1) hour after 12:00 noon of that day. Notice of all such technical failures shall be provided on the site. NY R UNIF TRIAL CTS § 202.5-b(i).

- When e-filing is hindered by a technical failure, a party may file with the appropriate clerk and serve in hard copy. NY R UNIF TRIAL CTS § 202.5-b(i). In the event an attorney or party shall file and serve documents in hard copy pursuant to NY R UNIF TRIAL CTS § 202.5-b(i), each such document shall include the notice required by NY R UNIF TRIAL CTS § 202.5-b(d)(1), and the filer shall file those documents with the NYSCEF site within three (3) business days after restoration of normal operations at that site. NY R UNIF TRIAL CTS § 202.5-b(i).
- With the exception of deadlines that by law cannot be extended, the time for filing of any document that is delayed due to technical failure of the site shall be extended for one (1) day for each day on which such failure occurs, unless otherwise ordered by the court. NY R UNIF TRIAL CTS § 202.5-b(i).

xiii. *Filing fees.* For information on what information must be provided to pay filing fees, refer to NY R UNIF TRIAL CTS § 202.5-b(d)(2).

xiv. *Exemption from e-filing.* For information on exemptions from e-filing, refer to NY R UNIF TRIAL CTS § 202.5-bb(e).

b. *Facsimile filing.* In the Supreme Court, facsimile filing shall be limited to commercial claims and tax certiorari, conservatorship, and mental hygiene proceedings in Monroe, Westchester, New York and Suffolk Counties. NY R UNIF TRIAL CTS § 202.5-a(a)(1). Refer to NY R UNIF TRIAL CTS § 202.5-a for information on the procedures for facsimile filing.

2. *Service requirements*

a. *Who may serve.* Except where otherwise prescribed by law or order of court, papers may be served by any person not a party of the age of eighteen years or over. NY CPLR Rule 2103(a).

b. *Service upon attorney.* Except where otherwise prescribed by law or order of court, papers to be served upon a party in a pending action shall be served upon the party's attorney. Where the same attorney appears for two or more parties, only one (1) copy need be served upon the attorney. Such service upon an attorney shall be made:

i. By delivering the paper to the attorney personally. NY CPLR Rule 2103(b)(1).

ii. By mailing the paper to the attorney at the address designated by that attorney for that purpose or, if none is designated, at the attorney's last known address; service by mail shall be complete upon mailing. NY CPLR Rule 2103(b)(2).

iii. If the attorney's office is open, by leaving the paper with a person in charge, or if no person is in charge, by leaving it in a conspicuous place; or if the attorney's office is not open, by depositing the paper, enclosed in a sealed wrapper directed to the attorney, in the attorney's office letter drop or box. NY CPLR Rule 2103(b)(3).

iv. By leaving it at the attorney's residence within the state with a person of suitable age and discretion. Service upon an attorney shall not be made at the attorney's residence unless service at the attorney's office cannot be made. NY CPLR Rule 2103(b)(4).

v. By transmitting the paper to the attorney by facsimile transmission, provided that a facsimile telephone number is designated by the attorney for that purpose. Service by facsimile transmission shall be complete upon the receipt by the sender of a signal from the equipment of the attorney served indicating that the transmission was received, and the mailing of a copy of the paper to that attorney. The designation of a facsimile telephone number in the address block subscribed on a paper served or filed in the course of an action or proceeding shall constitute consent to service by facsimile transmission in accordance with NY CPLR Rule 2103(b)(5). An attorney may change or rescind a facsimile telephone number by serving a notice on the other parties. NY CPLR Rule 2103(b)(5).

vi. By dispatching the paper to the attorney by overnight delivery service at the address designated by the attorney for that purpose or, if none is designated, at the attorney's last known address. Service by overnight delivery service shall be complete upon deposit of the paper enclosed in a properly addressed wrapper into the custody of the overnight delivery service for overnight delivery, prior to the latest time designated by the overnight delivery service for overnight delivery. "Overnight delivery service" means any delivery service which regularly accepts items for overnight delivery to any address in the state. NY CPLR Rule 2103(b)(6).

vii. By transmitting the paper to the attorney by electronic means where and in the manner authorized by the chief administrator of the courts by rule and, unless such rule shall otherwise provide, such transmission shall be upon the party's written consent. The subject matter heading for each paper sent by electronic means must indicate that the matter being transmitted electronically is related to a court proceeding. NY CPLR Rule 2103(b)(7).

c. *Electronic service mandatory; Consenting to electronic service; How electronic service may be made.* Except as otherwise provided in NY R UNIF TRIAL CTS § 202.5-bb, filing and service of all documents in an action that has been commenced electronically in accordance with NY R UNIF TRIAL CTS § 202.5-bb shall be by electronic means. NY R UNIF TRIAL CTS § 202.5-bb(c)(1).

i. *Party's consent required for certain e-filing.* After commencement of an action wherein e-filing is authorized, documents may be electronically filed and served, but only by, and electronic service shall be made only upon, a party or parties who have consented thereto. NY R UNIF TRIAL CTS § 202.5-b(b)(2)(i).

- A consent to e-filing in an action shall state that the party providing it agrees to the use of e-filing in the action and to be bound by the filing and service provisions in NY R UNIF TRIAL CTS § 202.5-b. NY R UNIF TRIAL CTS § 202.5-b(b)(2)(ii).

ii. *Address for service; Duty to notify as to changes.* The e-mail service address recorded at the time of registration

is the e-mail address at which service of interlocutory documents on that party may be made through notification transmitted by the NYSCEF site. It is the responsibility of each filing user to monitor that address and promptly notify the Resource Center in the event of a change in his or her e-mail service address. NY R UNIF TRIAL CTS § 202.5-b(f)(2)(i).

iii. *How service made.* An e-filing party causes service of an interlocutory document to be made upon another party participating in e-filing by filing the document electronically. Upon receipt of an interlocutory document, the NYSCEF site shall automatically transmit electronic notification to all e-mail service addresses in such action. NY R UNIF TRIAL CTS § 202.5-b(f)(2)(ii).

- Except as provided otherwise in NY R UNIF TRIAL CTS § 202.5-b(h)(3), the electronic transmission of the notification shall constitute service of the document on the e-mail service addresses identified therein; however, such service will not be effective if the filing party learns that the notification did not reach the address of the person to be served. Proof of such service will be recorded on the NYSCEF site. A party may, however, utilize other service methods permitted by the CPLR provided that, if one of such other methods is used, proof of that service shall be filed electronically. NY R UNIF TRIAL CTS § 202.5-b(f)(2)(ii).

iv. *Signatures on hard copies; Proof of service filed electronically.* When an e-filing party serves a document in hard copy on a non-participating party, the document served shall bear full signatures of all signatories and proof of such service shall be filed electronically. NY R UNIF TRIAL CTS § 202.5-b(b)(2)(i).

v. *Effect of failure to consent.* A party's failure to consent to participation in electronic filing and service shall not bar any other party to the action from filing documents electronically with the County Clerk and the court or serving documents upon any other party who has consented to participation. A party who has not consented to participation shall file documents with the court and the County Clerk, and serve and be served with documents, in hard copy. NY R UNIF TRIAL CTS § 202.5-b(b)(2)(i).

d. *Service upon party.* If a party has not appeared by an attorney or the party's attorney cannot be served, service shall be upon the party by a method specified in NY CPLR Rule 2103(b)(1), NY CPLR Rule 2103(b)(2), NY CPLR Rule 2103(b)(4), NY CPLR Rule 2103(b)(5) or NY CPLR Rule 2103(b)(6). NY CPLR Rule 2103(c).

i. When a party is in default for failure to appear, he shall not be entitled to notice or service of any copy required under NY CPLR § 3101, et seq. NY CPLR Rule 3105.

e. *Service on all parties.* Each paper served on any party shall be served on every other party who has appeared, except as otherwise may be provided by court order or as provided in NY CPLR § 3012 or in NY CPLR § 3215(f). Upon demand by a party, the plaintiff shall supply that party with a list of those who have appeared and the names and addresses of their attorneys. NY CPLR Rule 2103(e).

f. *Service by filing.* If a paper cannot be served by any of the methods specified in NY CPLR Rule 2103(b) and NY CPLR Rule 2103(c), service may be made by filing the paper as if it were a paper required to be filed. NY CPLR Rule 2103(d).

g. *Definitions.* For the purposes of NY CPLR Rule 2103:

i. "Mailing" means the deposit of a paper enclosed in a first class postpaid wrapper, addressed to the address designated by a person for that purpose or, if none is designated, at that person's last known address, in a post office or official depository under the exclusive care and custody of the United States Postal Service within the state;

ii. "Electronic means" means any method of transmission of information between computers or other machines designed for the purpose of sending and receiving such transmissions, and which allows the recipient to reproduce the information transmitted in a tangible medium of expression;

iii. "Facsimile transmission" means any method of transmission of documents to a facsimile machine at a remote location which can automatically produce a tangible copy of such documents. NY CPLR Rule 2103(f).

G. Hearings

1. There is no hearing required or contemplated in the New York rules governing the notice of deposition.

H. Forms

1. New York Notice of Deposition Forms

a. Notice of deposition; General form. NYDISC § 34:2.

b. Notice of deposition; To depose corporation. NYDISC § 34:3.

c. Notice of deposition; By videotaping. NYDISC § 34:4.
d. Demand to sign deposition. NYDISC § 34:5.
e. Corrections. NYDISC § 34:6.
f. Form; Notice to take deposition of party upon oral questions. CW2D § 42:349.
g. Form; Notice to take oral deposition of nonparty witness. CW2D § 42:350.
h. Form; Notice to take oral deposition of nonparty witness; With subpoena. CW2D § 42:351.
i. Form; Notice of taking deposition on written questions. CW2D § 42:356.
j. Form; Notice of motion by defendant to issue commission to take deposition outside New York on written questions. CW2D § 42:360.
k. Form; Notice of motion for letters rogatory; Personal injury action. CW2D § 42:365.
l. Affidavit on application to examine witness in this state under commission issued in action pending in another jurisdiction. MCF CPLR § 6:47.
m. Order directing examination of witness in this state under commission issued in action pending in another jurisdiction. MCF CPLR § 6:48.

I. Applicable Rules

1. *State rules*
    a. Short title; Application; Construction; Definitions. NY CPLR § 101; NY CPLR § 104; NY CPLR § 105.
    b. Appendix of official forms. NY CPLR § 107.
    c. Extensions of time generally. NY CPLR § 2004.
    d. Form of papers. NY CPLR Rule 2101; NY CPLR Rule 2102; NY CPLR § 2105; NY GEN BUS § 399-ddd; NY R UNIF TRIAL CTS § 215.2; NY R UNIF TRIAL CTS § 215.3.
    e. Service of papers. NY CPLR Rule 2103.
    f. Computation of time. NY CPLR § 2402; NY GEN CONSTR § 19; NY GEN CONSTR § 20; NY GEN CONSTR § 25-a; NY GEN CONSTR § 30; NY GEN CONSTR § 31; NY GEN CONSTR § 53.
    g. Scope of disclosure. NY CPLR § 3101; NY CPLR § 3102; NY CPLR § 3103; NY CPLR § 3104; NY CPLR Rule 3105.
    h. Depositions. NY CPLR Rule 3106; NY CPLR Rule 3107; NY CPLR Rule 3108; NY CPLR Rule 3109; NY CPLR Rule 3110; NY CPLR Rule 3111; NY CPLR Rule 3112; NY CPLR Rule 3113; NY CPLR Rule 3114; NY CPLR Rule 3115; NY CPLR Rule 3116.
    i. Motions staying disclosure. NY CPLR Rule 3214; NY CPLR Rule 3407.
    j. Index number fees of county clerks. NY CPLR § 8018.
    k. Hours of court. NY R CHIEF J § 3.1.
    l. Application of part; Waiver; Additional rules; Application of CPLR; Definitions. NY R UNIF TRIAL CTS § 202.1.
    m. Papers filed in court; Electronic filing in supreme court. NY R UNIF TRIAL CTS § 202.5; NY R UNIF TRIAL CTS § 202.5-a; NY R UNIF TRIAL CTS § 202.5-b; NY R UNIF TRIAL CTS § 202.5-bb.
    n. Rules of the commercial division of the Supreme Court. NY R UNIF TRIAL CTS § 202.70.
    o. Signing of papers. NY R CHIEF ADMIN § 130-1.1-a.
2. *Local rules*
    a. *Albany County*
        i. Third judicial district rules. NY R 3 JD SUP Doc. 1.
    b. *Bronx County*
        i. Commercial division. NY R BRONX FIL R Doc. 12.
    c. *Kings County*
        i. Expedited discovery. NY R L KINGS Pt. B, Rule 5.

ii. Pre calendar procedures. NY R L KINGS Rule I.

iii. Both pre and post note procedures. NY R L KINGS Rule IV.

d. *New York County*

i. RJIs and assignments. NY R NY CTY Procedure IA.

ii. Discovery schedule. NY R NY CTY J RUL Rule 8.

J. Miscellaneous

NOTE: Individual judges' rules may apply.

ALBANY COUNTY

JUSTICE LISA M. FISHER: NY R 3 JD FISHER Fisher; NY R 3 JD FISHER Fisher, PC Order.

JUSTICE RICHARD MOTT: NY R 3 JD MOTT Mott.

JUSTICE STEPHAN G. SCHICK: NY R 3 JD Schick.

FORECLOSURE SETTLEMENT PART: NY R 3 JD Foreclosure Settlement.

BRONX COUNTY

JUSTICE PAUL L. ALPERT: [NY R BRONX J Part IA-29, as amended by NY ORDER 20-0337].

JUSTICE BEN BARBATO: NY R BRONX J Part IA-21.

JUSTICE MARY ANNE BRIGANTTI: [NY R BRONX J Part IA-15, as amended by NY ORDER 20-0338].

JUSTICE JOSEPH E. CAPELLA: NY R BRONX J Part IA-23.

JUSTICE MITCHELL DANZIGER: NY R BRONX J Part IA-3/33 ; [NY R BRONX J Danziger, Part IA-3/33, as amended by NY ORDER 20-0339].

JUSTICE LAURA G. DOUGLAS: NY R BRONX J Part IA-11.

JUSTICE RUBEN FRANCO: NY R BRONX J Part IA-26.

JUSTICE DORIS M. GONZALEZ: NY R BRONX J Part IA-24.

JUSTICE WILMA GUZMAN: NY R BRONX J Part IA-7; [NY R BRONX J Guzman, Part IA-7 Virtual, as amended by NY ORDER 20-0340].

JUSTICE ROBERT T. JOHNSON: NY R BRONX J Part IA-12.

JUSTICE DONALD A. MILES: NY R BRONX J Part IA-8.

JUSTICE DONNA M. MILLS: NY R BRONX J Part IA-9.

JUSTICE JULIA I. RODRIGUEZ: NY R BRONX J Part IA-18; [NY R BRONX J Part IA-27, as amended by NY ORDER 20-0341].

JUSTICE LLINET M. ROSADO: [NY R BRONX J Part IA-25, as amended by NY ORDER 20-0342].

JUSTICE NORMA RUIZ: NY R BRONX J Part IA-22; [NY R BRONX J Ruiz, Part IA-22 Virtual, as amended by NY ORDER 20-0343].

JUSTICE HOWARD H. SHERMAN: NY R BRONX J Part IA-4.

JUSTICE FERNANDO TAPIA: NY R BRONX J Part IA-13.

JUSTICE ELIZABETH A. TAYLOR: NY R BRONX J Part IA-2.

JUSTICE ALISON Y. TRUITT: NY R BRONX J Part IA-5.

PART IDV: NY R BRONX J Doc. 1.

PRE-TRIAL PART RULES: NY R BRONX J Doc. 2.

PRE TRIAL WORKSHEET: NY R BRONX J Doc. 3.

FORECLOSURE SETTLEMENT PART RULES: NY R BRONX J Doc. 4.

GUARDIANSHIP PART RULES: NY R BRONX J Doc. 5.

LPM PART RULES: NY R BRONX J Doc. 6.

ERIE COUNTY

JUSTICE M. WILLIAM BOLLER: NY R 8 JD J Boller.
JUSTICE RALPH A. BONIELLO: NY R 8 JD J Boniello.
JUSTICE CHRISTOPHER J. BURN: NY R 8 JD J Burns.
JUSTICE RUSSELL P. BUSCAGLIA: NY R 8 JD J Buscaglia.
JUSTICE FRANK CARUSO: NY R 8 JD J Caruso.
JUSTICE STEPHEN W. CASS: NY R 8 JD J Cass.
JUSTICE DEBORAH A. CHIMES: NY R 8 JD J Chimes.
JUSTICE EMILIO COLAIACOVO: [NY R 8 JD J Colaiacovo, as amended by NY ORDER 20-0252].
JUSTICE DIANE Y. DEVLIN: NY R 8 JD J Devlin.
JUSTICE JAMES H. DILLON: NY R 8 JD J Dillon.
JUSTICE PAULA L. FEROLETO: NY R 8 JD J Feroleto.
JUSTICE DANIEL J. FURLONG: [NY R 8 JD J Furlong, as amended by NY ORDER 20-0253].
JUSTICE JOSEPH R. GLOWNIA: NY R 8 JD J Glownia.
JUSTICE MARK J. GRISANTI: NY R 8 JD J Grisanti.
JUSTICE DEBORAH A. HAENDIGES: NY R 8 JD J Haendiges.
JUSTICE LYNN W. KEANE: [NY R 8 JD J Keane, as amended by NY ORDER 20-0254].
JUSTICE RICHARD C. KLOCH, Sr.: NY R 8 JD J Kloch.
JUSTICE FREDERICK J. MARSHALL: [NY R 8 JD J Marshall, as amended by NY ORDER 20-0255.
JUSTICE JOHN L. MICHALSKI: NY R 8 JD J Michalski.
JUSTICE MARK A. MONTOUR: [NY R 8 JD J Montour, as amended by NY ORDER 20-0256].
JUSTICE HENRY NOWAK: NY R 8 JD J Nowak.
JUSTICE JOHN F. O'DONNELL: NY R 8 JD J O'Donnell.
JUSTICE JEANETTE OGDEN: NY R 8 JD J Ogden.
JUSTICE CATHERINE NUGENT-PANEPINTO: NY R 8 JD J Nugent-Panepinto.
JUSTICE FRANK A. SEDITA, III: [NY R 8 JD J Sedita, as amended by NY ORDER 20-0257].
JUSTICE SARA SHELDON: NY R 8 JD J Sheldon.
JUSTICE DONNA M. SIWEK: NY R 8 JD J Siwek.
JUSTICE MARY L. SLISZ: NY R 8 JD J Slisz.
JUSTICE TIMOTHY J. WALKER: [NY R 8 JD J Walker, as amended by NY ORDER 20-0258].
JUSTICE DENNIS E. WARD: NY R 8 JD J Ward.
JUSTICE PAUL B. WOJTASZEK: [NY R 8 JD J Wojtaszek, as amended by NY ORDER 20-0259].
JUSTICE CHARLES N. ZAMBITO: [NY R 8 JD J Zambito, as amended by NY ORDER 20-0260].
SUPREME COURT LEGAL STAFF: NY R 8 JD J Legal Staff.

KINGS COUNTY

JUSTICE RACHEL A. ADAMS: NY R KINGS J Part 5F.
JUSTICE LOREN BAILY-SCHIFFMAN: NY R KINGS J Part 65.
JUSTICE REGINALD A. BODDIE: NY R KINGS J Part 95.
JUSTICE THERESA M. CICCOTTO: NY R KINGS J Part 19; NY R KINGS J Part 5J.
JUSTICE LISSETTE COLON: NY R KINGS J Part Rules.
JUSTICE GENINE EDWARDS: NY R KINGS J Part 80.
JUSTICE PAMELA L. FISHER: [NY R KINGS J Part 94, as amended by NY ORDER 20-0208].
JUSTICE ROBIN GARSON: NY R KINGS J Part 75.

JUSTICE LARA J. GENOVISI: [NY R KINGS J Part 34, as amended by NY ORDER 20-0209].
JUSTICE BERNARD J. GRAHAM: NY R KINGS J Part 36.
JUSTICE DAWN JIMENEZ-SALTA: NY R KINGS J Part 88.
JUSTICE INGRID JOSEPH: [NY R KINGS J Part FRP3 and Part 83, as amended by NY ORDER 20-0210].
JUSTICE KATHY J. KING: NY R KINGS J Part 64, 76K.
JUSTICE LAWRENCE KNIPEL: NY R KINGS J Part 57.
JUSTICE DONALD KURTZ: NY R KINGS J Part 26.
JUSTICE CARL LANDICINO: [NY R KINGS J Part 81, as amended by NY ORDER 20-0211].
JUSTICE KATHERINE LEVINE: [NY R KINGS J Part 20, 25, 92, as amended by NY ORDER 20-0211].
JUSTICE LORNA MCALLISTER: [NY R KINGS J Part 10, as amended by NY ORDER 20-0211].
JUSTICE ROSEMARIE MONTALBANO: [NY R KINGS J Part 19, 71, and 22, as amended by NY ORDER 20-0211].
JUSTICE RICHARD J. MONTELIONE: [NY R KINGS J Part 99 and DJMP, as amended by NY ORDER 20-0215].
JUSTICE LISA S. OTTLEY: NY R KINGS J Part 24.
JUSTICE MARK I. PARTNOW: NY R KINGS J Part 43.
JUSTICE ERIC I. PRUS: NY R KINGS J Part 5A.
JUSTICE FRANCOIS RIVERA: NY R KINGS J Part 52.
JUSTICE KAREN B. ROTHENBERG: NY R KINGS J Part 35.
JUSTICE LEON RUCHELSMAN: NY R KINGS J Part 1.
JUSTICE WAYNE P. SAITTA: NY R KINGS J Part 29.
JUSTICE ROBIN K. SHEARES: NY R KINGS J Part 96.
JUSTICE KENNETH P. SHERMAN: NY R KINGS J Part 67 and 78.
JUSTICE DEBRA SILBER: NY R KINGS J Part 9 and 5K.
JUSTICE ELLEN M. SPODEK: NY R KINGS J Part 63.
JUSTICE MARSHA L. STEINHARDT: NY R KINGS J Part 15.
JUSTICE JEFFREY S. SUNSHINE: NY R KINGS J Part 5G.
JUSTICE PETER P. SWEENEY: [NY R KINGS J Part 35, as amended by NY ORDER 20-0218].
JUSTICE DELORES J. THOMAS: [NY R KINGS J Part 5T, as amended by NY ORDER 20-0221].
JUSTICE WAVNY TOUSSAINT: NY R KINGS J Part 70.
JUSTICE RICHARD VELASQUEZ: NY R KINGS J Part 66.
JUSTICE CAROLYN E. WADE: NY R KINGS J Part 84.
JUSTICE EDWARD G. WALKER: [NY R KINGS J Part 90, as amended by NY ORDER 20-0219].
JUSTICE LILLIAN WAN: [NY R KINGS J Part 17, as amended by NY ORDER 20-0220].
JUSTICE MICHELLE WESTON: NY R KINGS J Part 3.
MENTAL HYGIENE PART: NY R KINGS J Part 77.
MATRIMONIAL PARTS DURING COVID-19 EMERGENCY: JUSTICE KAREN B. ROTHENBERG: NY R KINGS J Doc. 1.

NASSAU COUNTY

JUSTICE ANNA R. ANZALONE: NY R NASSAU S J Anzalone, Part 26.
JUSTICE STACY D. BENNETT: NY R NASSAU S J Bennett; NY R NASSAU S J Bennett, Form 1.
JUSTICE ANTONIO BRANDVEEN: NY R NASSAU S J Brandveen, Part 31.
JUSTICE JEFFREY S. BROWN: [NY R NASSAU S J Brown, as amended by NY ORDER 20-0297].
JUSTICE STEPHEN A. BUCARIA: NY R NASSAU S J Bucaria.
JUSTICE JULIANNE T. CAPETOLA: NY R NASSAU S J Capetola, Part 28.

JUSTICE EDMUND M. DANE: NY R NASSAU S J Dane, Part 33.

JUSTICE VITO M. DESTEFANO: NY R NASSAU S J DeStefano, Part 13; NY R NASSAU S J DeStefano, Form 1.

JUSTICE ARTHUR M. DIAMOND: NY R NASSAU S J Diamond, Part 7.

JUSTICE THOMAS FEINMAN: NY R NASSAU S J Feinman, Part 5.

JUSTICE JOHN M. GALASSO: NY R NASSAU S J Galasso, Part 22.

JUSTICE SHARON M.J. GIANELLI: NY R NASSAU S J Gianelli, Part 22; NY R NASSAU S J Gianelli, Form 1.

JUSTICE JEFFREY A. GOODSTEIN: NY R NASSAU S J Goodstein, Part 33; NY R NASSAU S J Goodstein, Form 1.

JUSTICE DAVID J. GUGERTY: [NY R NASSAU S J Gugerty, Part 31, as amended by NY ORDER 20-0298].

JUSTICE HELENE F. GUGERTY: NY R NASSAU S J Gugerty, Part 47.

JUSTICE STEVEN M. JAEGER: NY R NASSAU S J Jaeger, Part 35; NY R NASSAU S J Jaeger, Form 1.

JUSTICE JACK L. LIBERT: NY R NASSAU S J Libert, Part 23.

JUSTICE JOSEPH H. LORINTZ: NY R NASSAU S J Lorintz, Part 26; NY R NASSAU S J Lorintz, Form 1.

JUSTICE ROY S. MAHON: NY R NASSAU S J Mahon, Part 3.

JUSTICE RANDY SUE MARBER: NY R NASSAU S J Marber, Part 8.

JUSTICE JAMES P. MCCORMACK: [NY R NASSAU S J McCormack, Part 18, as amended by NY ORDER, 20-0299].

JUSTICE DICCIA T. PINEDA-KIRWAN: [NY R NASSAU S J Pineda-Kirwan, as amended by NY ORDER 20-0300].

JUSTICE THOMAS RADEMAKER: [NY R NASSAU S J Rademaker, Part 28, as amended by NY ORDER 20-0301]; [NY R NASSAU S J Rademaker, Form 1, as amended by NY ORDER 20-0301].

JUSTICE DENISE L. SHER: NY R NASSAU S J Rademaker, Part 32.

JUSTICE LEONARD D. STEINMAN: [NY R NASSAU S J Steinman, Part 15, as amended by NY ORDER 20-0303]; NY R NASSAU S J Steinman, Form 1.

JUSTICE HOWARD E. STURIM: NY R NASSAU S J Sturim, Part 50; NY R NASSAU S J Sturim, Form 1.

JUSTICE HELEN VOUTSINAS: [NY R NASSAU S J Voutsinas, Part 25, as amended by NY ORDER 20-0304]; [NY R NASSAU S J Voutsinas, Form 1, as amended by NY ORDER 20-0305].

JUSTICE HOPE SCHWARTZ ZIMMERMAN: NY R NASSAU S J Zimmerman, Part 17.

NEW YORK COUNTY

JUDGE'S RULES; BASIC INFORMATION: [NY R NY CTY J RUL Doc. 1, as amended by NY ORDER 20-0202].

ONONDAGA COUNTY

JUSTICE ROBERT E. ANTONACCI II: [NY R ONDGA E FIL Doc. 1, as amended by 20-0239].

JUSTICE MICHAEL V. COCCOMI: NY R ONDGA E FIL Doc. 2.

JUSTICE GREGORY R. GILBERT: NY R 5 JD JUDGES Gilbert; NY R ONDGA E FIL Doc. 3.

JUSTICE DONALD A. GREENWOOD: NY R ONDGA E FIL Doc. 4.

JUSTICE DEBORAH H. KARALUNAS: NY R ONDGA E FIL Doc. 5.

JUSTICE JAMES MCCLUSKY: NY R 5 JD MCCLUSKY McClusky.

JUSTICE CHARLES C. MERRELL: NY R 5 JD MERRELL Merrell.

JUSTICE PATRICK F. MACRAE: NY R 5 JD MACRAE Doc. 1.

JUSTICE JAMES P. MURPHY: NY R ONDGA E FIL Doc. 7.

JUSTICE GERALD J. NERI: [NY R 5 JD JUDGES Neri, as amended by NY ORDER 20-0236]; [NY R ONDGA E FIL Doc. 8, as amended by NY ORDER 20-0241].

JUSTICE ANTHONY J. PARIS: NY R 5 JD JUDGES Paris; [NY R ONDGA E FIL Doc. 9, as amended by NY ORDER 20-0242].

JUSTICE NORMAN W. SEITER, JR.: NY R 5 JD JUDGES Seiter.

JUSTICE KEVIN G. YOUNG: [NY R ONDGA E FIL Doc. 10, as amended by NY ORDER 20-0243].

QUEENS COUNTY

JUSTICE PAM JACKMAN BROWN: [NY R L QUEENS Brown, Part 19, as amended by NY ORDER 20-0321].

JUSTICE CHEREE A. BUGGS: NY R L QUEENS Buggs, Part 30.

JUSTICE PAM JACKMAN BROWN: [NY R L QUEENS Brown, Part 19, as amended by NY ORDER 20-0321].

JUSTICE DENIS J. BUTLER: NY R L QUEENS Butler, Part 12.

JUSTICE ROBERT I. CALORAS: [NY R L QUEENS Caloras, Part 36, as amended by NY ORDER 20-0322].

JUSTICE ANNA CULLEY: NY R L QUEENS Culley, Part 53.

JUSTICE TIMOTHY DUFFICY: NY R L QUEENS Dufficy, Part 35.

JUSTICE DAVID ELLIOT: NY R L QUEENS Elliot, Part 14.

JUSTICE JOSEPH J. ESPOSITO: NY R L QUEENS Esposito, Part 6.

JUSTICE DARRELL L. GAVRIN: [NY R L QUEENS Gavrin, Part 27, as amended by NY ORDER 20-0323].

JUSTICE WYATT N. GIBBONS: [NY R L QUEENS Gibbons, Part 5, as amended by NY ORDER 20-0330.

JUSTICE DONNA-MARIE E. GOLIA: [NY R L QUEENS Golia, Part 21, as amended by NY ORDER 20-0331].

JUSTICE MARGUERITE A. GRAYS: [NY R L QUEENS Grays, Part 4, as amended by NY ORDER 20-0324].

JUSTICE RUDOLPH E. GRECO: [NY R L QUEENS Greco, Part 32, as amended by NY ORDER 20-0325].

JUSTICE MAUREEN HEALY: NY R L QUEENS Healy, Part 6.

JUSTICE PHILLIP HOM: [NY R L QUEENS Hom, Part 43, as amended by NY ORDER 20-0332].

JUSTICE KEVIN J. KERRIGAN: NY R L QUEENS Kerrigan, Part 10.

JUSTICE MOJGAN C. LANCMAN: NY R L QUEENS Lancman, Part 20.

JUSTICE RICHARD G. LATIN: NY R L QUEENS Latin, Part 40.

JUSTICE ULYSSES B. LEVERETT: [NY R L QUEENS Leverett, Part 6, as amended by NY ORDER 20-0326].

JUSTICE LEONARD LIVOTE: NY R L QUEENS Livote, Part 33.

JUSTICE LEE A. MAYERSOHN: NY R L QUEENS Mayersohn, Part 22; NY R L QUEENS Mayersohn, Part 22G; [NY R L QUEENS Mayersohn, Part 22G COVID, as amended by NY ORDER 20-0327].

JUSTICE ROBERT J. MCDONALD: NY R L QUEENS McDonald, Part 34.

JUSTICE MARGARET MCGOWAN: NY R L QUEENS McGowan, Part 52.

JUSTICE MAURICE E. MUIR: [NY R L QUEENS Muir, Part 42, as amended by NY ORDER 20-0333].

JUSTICE JODI ORLOW: NY R L QUEENS Orlow, Part 51.

JUSTICE LESLIE J. PURIFICCION: NY R L QUEENS Purificcion, Part 39.

JUSTICE JOSEPH RISI: [NY R L QUEENS Risi, Part 3, as amended by NY ORDER 20-0328].

JUSTICE FREDERICK D.R. SAMPSON: [NY R L QUEENS Sampson, Part 31, as amended by NY ORDER 20-0329].

JUSTICE MARTIN J. SCHULMAN: NY R L QUEENS Schulman, Part 29.

JUSTICE BERNICE D. SIEGAL: NY R L QUEENS Siegal, Part 25G.

JUSTICE JANICE A. TAYLOR: NY R L QUEENS Taylor, Part 15.

JUSTICE CARMEN R. VELASQUEZ: NY R L QUEENS Velasquez, Part 38.

JUSTICE LOURDES M VENTURA: [NY R L QUEENS Ventura, Part 37, as amended by NY ORDER 20-0334].

JUSTICE WILLIAM A. VISCOVICH: NY R L QUEENS Viscovich, Part 63.

JUSTICE ALLAN B. WEISS: NY R L QUEENS Weiss, Part 2.

COMPLIANCE, SETTLEMENT AND CONFERENCE PART: NY R L QUEENS Doc 1.

PRELIMINARY CONFERENCE PART: [NY R L QUEENS Doc. 2, as amended by NY ORDER 20-0335].

MEDICAL MALPRACTICE CONFERENCE PART: [NY R L QUEENS Doc. 3, as amended by NY ORDER 20-0336].

TRIAL SCHEDULING PART: NY R L QUEENS Doc. 4.

SUMMARY JURY TRIAL PROGRAM: NY R L QUEENS Doc. 7.

RESIDENTIAL FORECLOSURE PART: NY R L QUEENS Doc. 9.

FORECLOSURE AUCTION RULES: NY R L QUEENS Doc. 10.

MATRIMONIAL PRELIMINARY CONFERENCE PART: NY R L QUEENS Doc. 11.

NON-CUSTODIAL CONTESTED MATRIMONIAL PART: NY R L QUEENS Doc. 12.

Requests, Notices and Applications
Pretrial Conferences, Scheduling, Management

Document Last Updated August 2020

A. Checklist

(I) ❑ Matters to consider for preliminary conference

(a) ❑ Documents to consider

(1) ❑ Request for preliminary conference

(2) ❑ Request for judicial intervention

(3) ❑ Physician's affidavit

(4) ❑ Working copies

(5) ❑ ERIE COUNTY: Additional documents to consider

(i) ❑ Notice of hard copy submission in e-filed case

(6) ❑ KINGS COUNTY: Additional documents to consider

(i) ❑ Forms when filing in hard copy

(7) ❑ NEW YORK COUNTY: Additional documents to consider

(i) ❑ Notice of hard copy submission

(8) ❑ ONONDAGA COUNTY: Additional documents to consider

(i) ❑ Notice of hard copy submission

(9) ❑ QUEENS COUNTY: Additional documents to consider

(i) ❑ Notice of hard copy submission

(b) ❑ Timing

(1) ❑ A party may request a preliminary conference at any time after service of process

(2) ❑ The court shall notify all parties of the scheduled conference date, which shall be not more than forty-five (45) days from the date the request for judicial intervention is filed unless the court orders otherwise

(3) ❑ BRONX COUNTY: Additional timing

(i) ❑ All cases eligible under the CCJP are scheduled so a Preliminary Conference (PC) can be held within forty-five (45) days of filing an RJI

(4) ❑ KINGS COUNTY: Additional timing

(i) ❑ The filing/purchasing of an RJI will automatically prompt the scheduling of a preliminary conference

(5) ❑ NEW YORK COUNTY: Additional timing

(i) ❑ A preliminary conference must be held within forty-five (45) days after the RJI is filed

(ii) ❑ The Rule is interpreted to mean that if the RJI accompanies a non-discovery motion, the conference shall be held within forty-five (45) days after the decision on the motion, assuming that the decision does not dispose of the case

(iii) ❑ If the RJI accompanies a disclosure motion, the preliminary conference shall be held within forty-five (45) days

(II) ❑ Matters to consider for pretrial conference

(a) ❑ Documents to consider

(1) ❑ Pleadings

(2) ❑ Proof of injuries

(3) ❑ Trial documents

(4) ❑ Working copies

(5) ❑ ERIE COUNTY: Additional documents to consider

(i) ❑ Notice of hard copy submission in e-filed case

(6) ❑ KINGS COUNTY: Additional documents to consider

(i) ❑ Forms when filing in hard copy

(7) ❑ NEW YORK COUNTY: Additional documents to consider

(i) ❑ Notice of hard copy submission

(8) ❑ ONONDAGA COUNTY: Additional documents to consider

(i) ❑ Notice of hard copy submission

(9) ❑ QUEENS COUNTY: Additional documents to consider

(i) ❑ Notice of hard copy submission

(b) ❑ Timing

(1) ❑ A pretrial conference shall be held within one hundred-eighty (180) days of the filing of the note of issue

(2) ❑ To the extent practicable, pretrial conferences shall be held not less than fifteen (15) nor more than forty-five (45) days before trial is anticipated

B. Timing

1. *Time for preliminary conference.* A party may request a preliminary conference at any time after service of process. If the action has not been assigned to a judge, the party shall file a request for judicial intervention together with the request for a preliminary conference. NY R UNIF TRIAL CTS § 202.12(a). In all actions and proceedings to which Part 202 of the Uniform Civil Rules for the Supreme Court (NY R UNIF TRIAL CTS § 202.1, et seq.) is applicable, a preliminary conference shall be ordered by the court to be held within forty-five (45) days after the request for judicial intervention is filed. NY R UNIF TRIAL CTS § 202.19(b)(1). The court shall notify all parties of the scheduled conference date, which shall be not more than forty-five (45) days from the date the request for judicial intervention is filed unless the court orders otherwise. NY R UNIF TRIAL CTS § 202.12(b).

a. *Advancing date of conference.* A party may move to advance the date of a preliminary conference upon a showing of special circumstances. NY R UNIF TRIAL CTS § 202.12(g).

b. *BRONX COUNTY: Time after filing a request for judicial intervention.* All cases eligible under the CCJP are scheduled so a Preliminary Conference (PC) can be held within forty-five (45) days of filing an RJI. NY R BRONX DCM Doc. 1.

c. *KINGS COUNTY: Scheduled after filing request for judicial intervention.* The filing/purchasing of an RJI will automatically prompt the scheduling of a preliminary conference. NY R L KINGS Pt. B, Rule 1.

i. PC Conference is not to be adjourned, even on consent, unless good cause is shown for the adjournment. Mere failure to serve B/P is insufficient reason to adjourn PC Conference. A PC Order will be entered on default of any non appearing party. If no party appears, the case should be dismissed for non appearance, either side. Irrespective of service of BP, copies of medical records and authorizations shall be served upon all parties, where practicable, at least twenty (20) days before the PC Conference. NY R L KINGS Rule I(A)(1).

d. *NEW YORK COUNTY: Time for conference after RJI.* Pursuant to NY R UNIF TRIAL CTS § 202.19(b)(1), a preliminary conference must be held within forty-five (45) days after the RJI is filed. The Rule is interpreted to mean that if the RJI accompanies a non-discovery motion, the conference shall be held within forty-five (45) days after the decision on the motion, assuming that the decision does not dispose of the case. If the RJI accompanies a disclosure motion, the preliminary conference shall be held within forty-five (45) days. The DCM clock is not tolled when a motion is filed with the RJI. At the preliminary conference, the court will consider requests by a party to modify the

DCM track assigned upon filing of the RJI. NY R NY CTY Procedure V(A). The preliminary conference. . .shall take place at the Justice's regularly scheduled conference time. NY R NY CTY Procedure V(B).

i. Preliminary conferences sought by parties pursuant to NY R UNIF TRIAL CTS § 202.12 are scheduled upon filing with the General Clerk's Office (Room 119) of a request for a preliminary conference with proof of service. If the case has not yet been assigned to a Justice, the party must also submit, in a paper case, an original and one copy of an RJI and RJI Addendum (go to the "Forms" page on the Unified Court System website (www.nycourts.gov)), if required, with proof of service and proof of purchase of the index number for the main action, if applicable, and of payment of filing fees for all third-party actions. In an e-filed case, the request and RJI and Addendum, if required, shall be filed with NYSCEF as provided therein and the RJI fee paid via NYSCEF. NY R NY CTY Procedure V(B).

ii. A preliminary conference will be held or, in Motor Vehicle cases and most tort cases against the City of New York, an automated Differentiated Case Management ("DCM") scheduling order issued (i) within forty-five (45) days of assignment of a case to a Justice, unless impracticable for unusual reasons; or (ii) where a Request for Judicial Intervention is accompanied by a dispositive motion, within forty-five (45) days following disposition of such motion (if the case is not mooted by that disposition). NY R NY CTY J RUL Rule 5(a).

2. *Preliminary conference in response to disclosure related motion.* Where a motion relates to disclosure or to a bill of particulars, and a preliminary conference has not been held, the court shall notify all parties of a scheduled date to appear for a preliminary conference, which shall be not more than forty-five (45) days from the return date of the motion unless the court orders otherwise. NY R UNIF TRIAL CTS § 202.8(f).

a. *NEW YORK COUNTY.* If the RJI accompanies a disclosure motion, the preliminary conference shall be held within forty-five (45) days. NY R NY CTY Procedure V(A).

3. *Compliance conference.* No later than sixty (60) days before the date fixed for completion of discovery, a compliance conference shall be held to monitor the progress of discovery, explore potential settlement, and set a deadline for the filing of the Note of Issue. NY R UNIF TRIAL CTS § 202.19(b)(3).

a. *BRONX COUNTY: Preliminary conference order.* Attorneys and pro se litigants are required to check the final "Preliminary Conference Order" for the date of the compliance conference, if any, and for any additional directives ordered by the Court. NY R BRONX FIL R Doc. 9. The PC Order outlines a schedule for discovery and provides a date to return for a Compliance Conference (CC) appearance, which is held approximately ninety (90) days before the discovery deadline date. NY R BRONX DCM Doc. 1. If, at any time prior to reassignment to the Special Trial Part (STP) a party to an action feels that Discovery Orders are not being complied with by another party, they may request a further status conference through the DCM Department by E Mail, fax or letter. NY R BRONX DCM Doc. 1.

b. *KINGS COUNTY: Preliminary conference order.* Strict compliance with the PC order shall be enforced by the imposition of costs and sanctions when appropriate. NY R L KINGS Pt. B, Rule 4.

i. *Time when court will schedule compliance conference.* Schedule a Compliance Conference for a date no later than five (5) months after date of PC Conference. However, if PC Conference is held more than forty-five (45) days after RJI, then schedule the Compliance Conference to a date no later than six and a half (6-1/2) months after the RJI. NY R L KINGS Rule I(A)(3).

ii. *Purpose of conference.* The purpose of the compliance conference is to monitor the progress of discovery, set a deadline for filing a Note of Issue and resolve any outstanding discovery issues. Consequently, parties attending the compliance conference must be fully familiar with the case, the status of any disclosure proceedings, and any settlement negotiations. NY R L KINGS Pt. E, Rule 1. Appearance at the compliance conference is not necessary if a Note of issue has been served and filed with the court prior to the compliance conference date. In such cases, a copy of the Note of Issue may be presented to the part clerk on or before the date of the conference or a party may notify the clerk prior thereto. NY R L KINGS Pt. E, Rule 2.

iii. *Final compliance conference.* At CCP Conference, Final Compliance Conference to be scheduled three (3) months thereafter (or, if retracked at CCP, to a date six (6) weeks prior to new Note of Issue file date). Whether complex or standard tracked, the Final Compliance Conference will be six (6) weeks prior to expiration of Pre Note S&G. NY R L KINGS Rule I(B)(3).

c. *NEW YORK COUNTY: Preliminary conference order.* The preliminary conference order will normally contain a date for a compliance conference. The PC order may also contain a date by which a note of issue must be filed, or such a date will be specified at a later point. Compliance and pretrial conferences may also be fixed by the Justice in a compliance conference order or in a decision on a motion. NY R NY CTY Procedure V(B).

i. Notifications of. . .post-PC conferences are not sent by the court by mail. Since these dates are fixed in orders or decisions of the court, counsel will be aware of them immediately or promptly after they are set. In addition, attorneys who use E-Track will obtain notification by e-mail when such a date is recorded in the court's computer and whenever a scheduled such date is adjourned. E-Track can also transmit e-mail reminders prior to scheduled appearances. Scroll will show the dates set for scheduled conferences. NY R NY CTY Procedure V(B).

4. *Pretrial conference.* A pretrial conference shall be held within one hundred-eighty (180) days of the filing of the Note of Issue. NY R UNIF TRIAL CTS § 202.19(c)(1).
    a. To the extent practicable, pretrial conferences shall be held not less than fifteen (15) nor more than forty-five (45) days before trial is anticipated. NY R UNIF TRIAL CTS § 202.26(b).
5. *NEW YORK COUNTY: Settlement conference in medical malpractice cases.* The court shall hold a settlement conference in medical, dental, and podiatric malpractice actions within forty-five (45) days after the filing of the note of issue and certificate of readiness or, if a party moves to vacate the note of issue and certificate of readiness and that motion is denied, within forty-five (45) days after denial of the motion. NY R NY CTY Procedure V(B).
6. *Computation of time*
    a. *Units of time*
        i. *Day.* A calendar day includes the time from midnight to midnight. Sunday or any day of the week specifically mentioned means a calendar day. NY GEN CONSTR § 19.
        ii. *Month.* In a statute, contract or public or private instrument, unless otherwise provided in such contract or instrument or by law, the term month means a calendar month and not a lunar month. NY GEN CONSTR § 31.
        iii. *Year.* For information on the definition of a year, including the definitions of a half-year and quarter-year, refer to NY GEN CONSTR § 58 and NY GEN CONSTR § 50. For information on leap years, refer to NY GEN CONSTR § 57.
    b. *Periods of time*
        i. *Number of days.* A number of days specified as a period from a certain day within which or after or before which an act is authorized or required to be done means such number of calendar days exclusive of the calendar day from which the reckoning is made. NY GEN CONSTR § 20.
            - If such period is a period of two (2) days, Saturday, Sunday or a public holiday must be excluded from the reckoning if it is an intervening day between the day from which the reckoning is made and the last day of the period. NY GEN CONSTR § 20.
            - In computing any specified period of time from a specified event, the day upon which the event happens is deemed the day from which the reckoning is made. The day from which any specified period of time is reckoned shall be excluded in making the reckoning. NY GEN CONSTR § 20.
        ii. *Number of months.* A number of months after or before a certain day shall be computed by counting such number of calendar months from such day, exclusive of the calendar month in which such day occurs, and shall include the day of the month in the last month so counted having the same numerical order in days of the month as the day from which the computation is made, unless there be not so many days in the last month so counted, in which case the period computed shall expire with the last day of the month so counted. NY GEN CONSTR § 30.
        iii. *Publication of notice; Number of days.* The period of publication of a legal notice shall be computed by excluding the first day of publication and including the day on which the act or event of which notice is given is to take place or which completes the full period of publication. NY CPLR § 2402.
        iv. *Periods ending on Saturday, Sunday or public holiday.* When any period of time, computed from a certain day, within which or after which or before which an act is authorized or required to be done, ends on a Saturday, Sunday or a public holiday, such act may be done on the next succeeding business day and if the period ends at a specified hour, such act may be done at or before the same hour of such next succeeding business day, except that where a period of time specified by contract ends on a Saturday, Sunday or a public holiday, the extension of such period is governed by NY GEN CONSTR § 25. NY GEN CONSTR § 25-a(1).
            - For a list of public holidays, refer to NY GEN CONSTR § 24.
        v. *Additional time after certain kinds of service*
            - *Service by mail.* Where a period of time prescribed by law is measured from the service of a paper and service is by mail, five (5) days shall be added to the prescribed period. NY CPLR Rule 2103(b)(2).
            - *Service by overnight delivery service.* Where a period of time prescribed by law is measured from the

service of a paper and service is by overnight delivery, one (1) business day shall be added to the prescribed period. NY CPLR Rule 2103(b)(6).

vi. *Daylight saving time.* For information on New York's time zone and the effect of daylight saving time, refer to NY GEN CONSTR § 52.

c. *Hours of court.* Notwithstanding any provision of law or rule of court to the contrary, throughout the State of New York the sessions of the Supreme Court for the disposition of business before the court shall commence not later than 9:30 a.m. and conclude not earlier than 5 p.m. Where warranted, the Chief Administrator of the Courts may authorize variances in the opening and closing hours of the courts, but, in such event, daily sessions shall total not less than six (6) hours. NY R CHIEF J § 3.1.

d. *Time limits; Extension of time.* Any act required by or in pursuance of law to be performed at or within a prescribed time, shall be performed according to the standard time. NY GEN CONSTR § 53.

i. Except where otherwise expressly prescribed by law, the court may extend the time fixed by any statute, rule or order for doing any act, upon such terms as may be just and upon good cause shown, whether the application for extension is made before or after the expiration of the time fixed. NY CPLR § 2004. Refer to the New York KeyRules Motion for Continuance/Extension of Time document for more information.

C. General Requirements

1. *Preliminary conference.* Officially, the preliminary conference is an early meeting between the lawyers and judge designed to (1) simplify the issues, (2) establish a timetable for using and completing the disclosure devices, including any electronic discovery, (3) add other parties, if necessary, and (4) discuss settlement and other issues the court deems appropriate. SIEGEL-NYPRAC § 77D; NY R UNIF TRIAL CTS § 202.12(c). Despite the uniformity at which the conference rule aims, however, what the conference turns out to be depends in large measure on the individual judge. It thus behooves each lawyer, whatever she may cull from the specific instruction of the applicable rule, to determine the practice and propensities of the assigned judge. SIEGEL-NYPRAC § 77D.

a. *Request for preliminary conference.* A party may request a preliminary conference at any time after service of process. The request shall state the title of the action; index number; names, addresses and telephone numbers of all attorneys appearing in the action; and the nature of the action. If the action has not been assigned to a judge, the party shall file a request for judicial intervention together with the request for a preliminary conference. The request shall be served on all other parties and filed with the clerk for transmittal to the assigned judge. The court shall order a preliminary conference in any action upon compliance with the requirements of NY R UNIF TRIAL CTS § 202.12(a). NY R UNIF TRIAL CTS § 202.12(a).

i. *BRONX COUNTY: Request for preliminary conference.* A party may request a preliminary conference at any time after service of process. The request shall state the title of the action, index number, names, addresses and telephone numbers of all attorneys appearing in the action, and the nature of the action. If the action has not been assigned to a judge, the party shall file a request for judicial intervention (RJI) together with the request for preliminary conference. The request shall be served on all other parties and be filed with the clerk for transmittal to the assigned judge. NY R BRONX FIL R Doc. 4. For information on requesting a preliminary conference in malpractice actions, refer to NY R BRONX FIL R Doc. 4.

b. *Preliminary conference; Form stipulation and timetable.* The court shall notify all parties of the scheduled conference date, and a form of a stipulation and order, prescribed by the Chief Administrator of the Courts, shall be made available which the parties may sign, agreeing to a timetable which shall provide for completion of disclosure within twelve (12) months of the filing of the request for judicial intervention for a standard case, or within fifteen (15) months of such filing for a complex case. NY R UNIF TRIAL CTS § 202.12(b); NY R UNIF TRIAL CTS § 202.8(f).

i. *Cancellation of conference due to agreement of the parties.* If all parties sign the form and return it to the court before the scheduled preliminary conference, such form shall be "so ordered" by the court, and, unless the court orders otherwise, the scheduled preliminary conference shall be cancelled. NY R UNIF TRIAL CTS § 202.12(b); NY R UNIF TRIAL CTS § 202.8(f). Where a motion relates to disclosure or to a bill of particulars, and a preliminary conference has not been held, if all parties sign the form and return it to the court before the return date of the motion the motion shall be deemed withdrawn. NY R UNIF TRIAL CTS § 202.8(f).

- *NEW YORK COUNTY.* If counsel submit, prior to the scheduled conference date, a completed preliminary conference stipulation and order form, which can be done via NYSCEF in an e-filed case, and if the court finds no problems with the completed form, counsel need not appear and the court will remove the case from the conference calendar and make an entry in the court computer or mark the calendar. The stipulated form should show a date for the filing of the note of issue that will assure compliance with the applicable

DCM target deadline. If the stipulation and order form is not submitted, the preliminary conference shall take place as scheduled. NY R NY CTY Procedure V(B).

ii. *Appearance at conference; Attorney's appearance; Requirements in cases likely to involve discovery of electronically stored information.* If such stipulation is not returned signed by all parties, the parties shall appear at the conference. Except where a party appears in the action pro se, an attorney thoroughly familiar with the action and authorized to act on behalf of the party shall appear at the conference. Where a case is reasonably likely to include electronic discovery, counsel for all parties who appear at the preliminary conference must be sufficiently versed in matters relating to their clients' technological systems to discuss competently all issues relating to electronic discovery; counsel may bring a client representative or outside expert to assist in such e-discovery discussions. NY R UNIF TRIAL CTS § 202.12(b); NY R UNIF TRIAL CTS § 202.8(f). Where a motion relates to disclosure or to a bill of particulars, and a preliminary conference has not been held, issues raised by the motion and not resolved at the conference shall be determined by the court. NY R UNIF TRIAL CTS § 202.8(f). A non-exhaustive list of considerations for determining whether a case is reasonably likely to include electronic discovery is:

- Does potentially relevant electronically stored information ("ESI") exist;
- Do any of the parties intend to seek or rely upon ESI;
- Are there less costly or less burdensome alternatives to secure the necessary information without recourse to discovery of ESI;
- Are the cost and burden of preserving and producing ESI proportionate to the amount in controversy; and
- What is the likelihood that discovery of ESI will aid in the resolution of the dispute. NY R UNIF TRIAL CTS § 202.12(b)(1).
- *BRONX COUNTY.* Pursuant to NY R UNIF TRIAL CTS § 202.8 and NY R UNIF TRIAL CTS § 202.12 regarding first disclosure motions or preliminary conferences, appearances will not be required if before the rescheduled date of the motion or the scheduled date of the preliminary conference a "Preliminary Conference Order" in the prescribed form is filed with the Civil Branch Clerk's Office, Room 217. Forms are available in the Clerk's Office and in the DCM Part, Room 707 and most importantly on the Web. NY R BRONX FIL R Doc. 9.
- *NEW YORK COUNTY.* Counsel who appear at preliminary conferences must have sufficient familiarity with the case and authority to be able to discuss a discovery schedule in a meaningful way and to enter into agreements with regard thereto. Counsel who appear at other conferences and at the argument of motions must be familiar with the entire case in regard to which they appear and fully authorized to enter into agreements, both substantive and procedural, on behalf of their clients. NY R NY CTY J RUL Rule 1.

c. *Matters to be considered at preliminary conference.* The matters to be considered at the preliminary conference shall include:

i. Simplification and limitation of factual and legal issues, where appropriate;

ii. Establishment of a timetable for the completion of all disclosure proceedings, provided that all such procedures must be completed within the timeframes set forth in NY R UNIF TRIAL CTS § 202.12(b), unless otherwise shortened or extended by the court depending upon the circumstances of the case;

iii. Where the court deems appropriate, it may establish the method and scope of any electronic discovery. In establishing the method and scope of electronic discovery, the court may consider the following non-exhaustive list, including but not limited to:

- Identification of potentially relevant types or categories of ESI and the relevant time frame;
- Disclosure of the applications and manner in which the ESI is maintained;
- Identification of potentially relevant sources of ESI and whether the ESI is reasonably accessible;
- Implementation of a preservation plan for potentially relevant ESI;
- Identification of the individual(s) responsible for preservation of ESI;
- The scope, extent, order, and form of production;
- Identification, redaction, labeling, and logging of privileged or confidential ESI;
- Claw-back or other provisions for privileged or protected ESI;

- The scope or method for searching and reviewing ESI; and
- The anticipated cost and burden of data recovery and proposed initial allocation of such cost.

iv. Addition of other necessary parties;

v. Settlement of the action;

vi. Removal to a lower court pursuant to NY CPLR § 325, where appropriate; and

vii. Any other matters that the court may deem relevant. NY R UNIF TRIAL CTS § 202.12(c).

d. *Differentiated case management.* NY R UNIF TRIAL CTS § 202.19 shall apply to such categories of cases designated by the Chief Administrator of the Courts as being subject to differentiated case management, and shall be implemented in such counties, courts or parts of courts as designated by the Chief Administrator. The provisions of NY R UNIF TRIAL CTS § 202.12, relating to the preliminary conference, and NY R UNIF TRIAL CTS § 202.26, relating to the pretrial conference, shall apply to the extent not inconsistent with NY R UNIF TRIAL CTS § 202.19. NY R UNIF TRIAL CTS § 202.19(a). At the preliminary conference, the court shall designate the track to which the case shall be assigned in accordance with the following:

i. Expedited—discovery to be completed within eight (8) months. NY R UNIF TRIAL CTS § 202.19(b)(2)(i).

ii. Standard—discovery to be completed within twelve (12) months. NY R UNIF TRIAL CTS § 202.19(b)(2)(ii).

iii. Complex—discovery to be completed within fifteen (15) months. NY R UNIF TRIAL CTS § 202.19(b)(2)(iii).

iv. The timeframes must be complied with unless otherwise shortened or extended by the court depending upon the circumstances of the case. NY R UNIF TRIAL CTS § 202.19(b)(2).

v. *NEW YORK COUNTY.* Upon the filing of the RJI, each case will be assigned to a Differentiated Case Management ("DCM") track which represents a time frame for completion of pre-note-of-issue proceedings (NY R UNIF TRIAL CTS § 202.19). The assignment will be made by the clerk in accordance with a protocol issued by the court, as indicated in NY R NY CTY Procedure IA. NY R NY CTY Procedure IA(C); NY R NY CTY Procedure V(A). Each Part is expected to schedule pre-note proceedings in accordance with the applicable DCM target, and particularly to ensure that the note of issue is filed within the DCM target deadline therefor, although the Justice does have discretion to extend DCM deadlines in an individual case when there is good reason for doing so; thus, the scheduling orders of the Justice will govern the parties in each case. NY R NY CTY Procedure V(A).

- Although the Justice does have the discretion indicated, the DCM track deadlines serve also as what are commonly referred to as "pre-note standards and goals," which are internal standards for measuring the productivity and efficiency of individual Parts and the court as a whole. Considered as "standards and goals," the DCM deadlines are inflexible. DCM is applicable to all, or virtually all, types of cases in New York County Supreme Court. NY R NY CTY Procedure V(A).
- At a preliminary conference the court will, at the request of a party or on its own, confirm or modify the DCM track to which the case was assigned when the RJI was filed, and will establish a schedule for discovery and other pre-trial proceedings within the applicable DCM note-of-issue target deadline. NY R NY CTY Procedure V(B).
- The court will afford all parties an opportunity to raise objections to the track assignment or any DCM scheduling order issued without a conference. NY R NY CTY J RUL Rule 5(a).
- For information on what cases are assigned to complex or nonstandard case tracks, refer to NY R NY CTY Procedure V(A).

e. *Written order after conference.* At the conclusion of the conference the court shall make a written order including its directions to the parties as well as stipulations of counsel. Alternatively, in the court's discretion, all directions of the court and stipulations of counsel may be recorded by a reporter. Where the latter procedure is followed, the parties shall procure and share equally the cost of a transcript thereof unless the court in its discretion otherwise provides. The transcript, corrected if necessary on motion or by stipulation of the parties approved by the court, shall have the force and effect of an order of the court. The transcript shall be filed by the plaintiff with the clerk of the court. NY R UNIF TRIAL CTS § 202.12(d).

i. *Failure to comply with order; Sanctions.* In the discretion of the court, failure by a party to comply with the order or transcript resulting from the preliminary conference, or with the so-ordered stipulation provided for in NY R UNIF TRIAL CTS § 202.12(b), or the making of unnecessary or frivolous motions by a party, shall result in the imposition upon such party of the costs or such other sanctions as are authorized by law. NY R UNIF TRIAL CTS § 202.12(f).

- *NEW YORK COUNTY.* Failure to comply with the terms of a preliminary conference order, and making frivolous motions, shall, in the discretion of the court, result in the imposition of costs or other sanctions on the offending party. NY R NY CTY Procedure V(B).

ii. *Failure to comply with order; Effect on readiness for trial.* No action or proceeding to which NY R UNIF TRIAL CTS § 202.12 is applicable shall be deemed ready for trial unless there is compliance with the provisions of NY R UNIF TRIAL CTS § 202.12 and any order issued pursuant thereto. NY R UNIF TRIAL CTS § 202.12(i).

- *NEW YORK COUNTY.* Particular attention is drawn to deadlines for adding parties, depositions, completing all discovery, and filing a note of issue, as these dates are important to efficient case management. NY R NY CTY Procedure V(B).

f. *Duties when filing note of issue.* The granting or continuation of a special preference shall be conditional upon full compliance by the party who has requested any such preference with the foregoing order or transcript. When a note of issue and certificate of readiness are filed pursuant to NY R UNIF TRIAL CTS § 202.21, in an action to which NY R UNIF TRIAL CTS § 202.12 is applicable, the filing party, in addition to complying with all other applicable rules of the court, shall file with the note of issue and certificate of readiness an affirmation or affidavit, with proof of service on all parties who have appeared, showing specific compliance with the preliminary conference order or transcript. NY R UNIF TRIAL CTS § 202.12(e).

i. *KINGS COUNTY.* At PC Conference, fix Note of Issue file date to a date four (4) weeks prior to expiration of Pre Note S&G. NY R L KINGS Rule I(A)(2). The filing requirement for Notes of Issue in Kings County is an original and two (2) copies. NY R L KINGS Pt. D, Rule 1.

g. *Motions before preliminary conference.* Motions in actions to which NY R UNIF TRIAL CTS § 202.12 is applicable made after the preliminary conference has been scheduled may be denied unless there is shown good cause why such relief is warranted before the preliminary conference is held. NY R UNIF TRIAL CTS § 202.12(h).

h. *Application of NY R UNIF TRIAL CTS § 202.12 to matrimonial and separation actions.* The provisions of NY R UNIF TRIAL CTS § 202.12 shall apply to preliminary conferences required in matrimonial actions and actions based upon a separation agreement, in medical malpractice actions, and in real property tax assessment review proceedings within the City of New York, only to the extent that these provisions are not inconsistent with the provisions of NY R UNIF TRIAL CTS § 202.16, NY R UNIF TRIAL CTS § 202.56 and NY R UNIF TRIAL CTS § 202.60, respectively. NY R UNIF TRIAL CTS § 202.12(k).

i. *Application of NY R UNIF TRIAL CTS § 202.12 to actions involving a terminally ill party.* The provisions of NY R UNIF TRIAL CTS § 202.12 shall apply where a request is filed for a preliminary conference in an action involving a terminally ill party governed by NY CPLR Rule 3407 only to the extent that the provisions of NY R UNIF TRIAL CTS § 202.12 are not inconsistent with the provisions of NY CPLR Rule 3407. In an action governed by NY CPLR Rule 3407 the request for a preliminary conference may be filed at any time after commencement of the action, and shall be accompanied by the physician's affidavit required by NY CPLR Rule 3407. NY R UNIF TRIAL CTS § 202.12(l).

j. *Further conferences.* The court, in its discretion, at any time may order such conferences as the court may deem helpful or necessary in any matter before the court. NY R UNIF TRIAL CTS § 202.12(j).

k. *KINGS COUNTY: Preparation for conference.* The parties must be prepared with bills of particulars, medical reports and insurance coverage. NY R L KINGS Pt. B, Rule 3.

l. *NEW YORK COUNTY: Preliminary conference in city and motor vehicle cases.* For information on differentiated case management and preliminary conferences in city and motor vehicle cases, refer to NY R NY CTY Procedure V.

m. *NEW YORK COUNTY: Consultation before conference.* Prior to a preliminary or compliance conference, counsel for all parties shall consult one another about, and shall make a good faith effort to reach agreement on, (i) resolution of the case, in whole or in part, and (ii) discovery and any other issues to be discussed at the conference. NY R NY CTY J RUL Rule 7.

2. *Pretrial conference.* After the filing of a note of issue and certificate of readiness in any action, the judge shall order a pretrial conference, unless the judge dispenses with such a conference in any particular case. NY R UNIF TRIAL CTS § 202.26(a).

a. *Attendance of attorneys at conference.* Where parties are represented by counsel, only attorneys fully familiar with the action and authorized to make binding stipulations, or accompanied by a person empowered to act on behalf of the party represented, will be permitted to appear at a pretrial conference. Where appropriate, the court may order parties, representatives of parties, representatives of insurance carriers or persons having an interest in any settlement, including those holding liens on any settlement or verdict, to also attend in person or telephonically at the settlement conference. NY R UNIF TRIAL CTS § 202.26(e). Failure to comply with NY R UNIF TRIAL CTS § 202.26(e) may be deemed a default. Absence of an attorney's file shall not be an acceptable excuse for failing to comply with NY R UNIF TRIAL CTS § 202.26(e). NY R UNIF TRIAL CTS § 202.26(e).

b. *Matters to be considered at pretrial conference.* The judge shall consider at the conference with the parties or their counsel the following:
   i. Simplification and limitation of the issues;
   ii. Obtaining admission of fact and of documents to avoid unnecessary proof;
   iii. Disposition of the action including scheduling the action for trial;
   iv. Amendment of pleadings or bill of particulars;
   v. Limitation of number of expert witnesses; and
   vi. Insurance coverage where relevant. NY R UNIF TRIAL CTS § 202.26(c).
   vii. The judge also may consider with the parties any other matters deemed relevant. NY R UNIF TRIAL CTS § 202.26(c).
   viii. In actions brought under the simplified procedure sections of the CPLR, the court shall address those matters referred to in NY CPLR Rule 3036(5). NY R UNIF TRIAL CTS § 202.26(d). At a pre-trial conference, or at any other time on motion of any party or on its own motion, on notice to the parties, and upon such terms and conditions as in its discretion may seem proper, the court may:
      - Order or allow any party to serve an additional or amended statement of facts;
      - Direct pre-trial disclosure of evidence and discovery and inspection of books, records and documents;
      - Permit the taking of depositions for use at the hearing;
      - Limit or restrict the number of experts to be heard as witnesses;
      - Clarify and define the issues to be tried;
      - Stay or transfer and consolidate with the action any other civil action or proceeding pending in any court between parties to the action;
      - Grant summary judgment in favor of any party as in NY CPLR Rule 3212 provided. NY CPLR Rule 3036(g).
   ix. *NEW YORK COUNTY.* The court will also address, to the extent appropriate, limitation of issues, addition of parties, ADR, and settlement. NY R NY CTY Procedure V(B).

c. *Settlement at pretrial conference.* If any action is settled or discontinued by stipulation at a pretrial conference, complete minutes of such stipulation shall be made at the direction of the court. Such transcribed stipulation shall be enforceable as though made in open court. NY R UNIF TRIAL CTS § 202.26(f).

d. *Fixing time for trial.* At the pretrial conference, the court shall fix a date for the commencement of trial, which shall be no later than eight (8) weeks after the date of the conference. NY R UNIF TRIAL CTS § 202.19(c)(2).

e. *Identification of trial counsel.* Unless the court otherwise provides, where the attorney of record for any party arranges for another attorney to conduct the trial, the trial counsel must be identified in writing to the court and all parties no later than fifteen (15) days after the pretrial conference or, if there is no pretrial conference, at least ten (10) days before trial. The notice must be signed by both the attorney of record and the trial counsel. NY R UNIF TRIAL CTS § 202.31.

f. *Transfer to lower court at pretrial conference.* At the pretrial conference, if it appears that the action falls within the monetary jurisdiction of a court of limited jurisdiction, there is nothing to justify its being retained in the court in which it is then pending, and it would be reached for trial more quickly in a lower court, the judge shall order the case transferred to the appropriate lower court, specifying the paragraph of NY CPLR § 325 under which the action is taken. NY R UNIF TRIAL CTS § 202.26(g)(1).
   i. With respect to transfers to the New York City Civil Court pursuant to NY CPLR § 325, if, at the pretrial conference, the conditions in NY R UNIF TRIAL CTS § 202.26(g)(1) are met except that the case will not be reached for trial more quickly in the lower court, the judge, in his or her discretion, may order the case so

transferred if it will be reached for trial in the lower court within thirty (30) days of the conference. In determining whether the action will be reached for trial in the lower court within thirty (30) days, the judge shall consult with the administrative judge of his or her court, who shall advise, after due inquiry, whether calendar conditions and clerical considerations will permit the trial of actions in the lower court within the thirty (30) day timeframe. If the action is not transferred to a lower court, it shall be tried in the superior court in its proper calendar progression. NY R UNIF TRIAL CTS § 202.26(g)(2).

3. *Special conferences for specific actions*
   a. *Mandatory pre-calendar conference in dental, podiatric and medical malpractice actions.* The chief administrator of the courts, in accordance with such standards and administrative policies as may be promulgated pursuant to NY CONST Art. 6, § 28, shall adopt special calendar control rules for actions to recover damages for dental, podiatric or medical malpractice. Such rules shall require a pre-calendar conference in such an action, the purpose of which shall include, but not be limited to, encouraging settlement, simplifying or limiting issues and establishing a timetable for disclosure, establishing a timetable for offers and depositions pursuant to NY CPLR § 3101(d)(1)(ii), future conferences, and trial. The timetable for disclosure shall provide for the completion of disclosure not later than twelve months after the notice of dental, podiatric or medical malpractice is filed and shall require that all parties be ready for the trial of the case not later than eighteen months after such notice is filed. The initial pre-calendar conference shall be held after issue is joined in a case but before a note of issue is filed. To the extent feasible, the justice convening the pre-calendar conference shall hear and decide all subsequent pre-trial motions in the case and shall be assigned the trial of the case. The chief administrator of the courts also shall provide for the imposition of costs or other sanctions, including imposition of reasonable attorney's fees, dismissal of an action, claim, cross-claim, counterclaim or defense, or rendering a judgment by default for failure of a party or a party's attorney to comply with these special calendar control rules or any order of a court made thereunder. The chief administrator of the courts, in the exercise of discretion, may provide for exemption from the requirement of a pre-calendar conference in any judicial district or a county where there exists no demonstrated need for such conferences. NY CPLR Rule 3406(b). For more information on preliminary conferences in dental, podiatric, and medical malpractice actions, refer to NY CPLR Rule 3409 and NY R UNIF TRIAL CTS § 202.56.
   b. *Preliminary conference in personal injury actions involving terminally ill patients.* At any time, a party to an action who is terminally ill, and who asserts in a pleading in such action that such terminal illness is the result of the culpable conduct of another party to such action, may request an expedited preliminary conference in such action. Such request shall be filed in writing with the clerk of the court, and shall be accompanied by a physician's affidavit stating that the party is terminally ill, the nature of the terminal illness, and the duration of life expectancy of such party, if known. The court shall hold a preliminary conference in such action within twenty (20) days after the filing of such a request. NY CPLR Rule 3407(a). For more information on preliminary conferences in cases involving terminally ill patients, refer to NY CPLR Rule 3407.
   c. *Mandatory settlement conference in residential foreclosure actions.* For information on the mandatory settlement conference in residential foreclosure actions, refer to NY CPLR Rule 3407 and NY R UNIF TRIAL CTS § 202.12-a.
4. *NEW YORK COUNTY: Status conferences.* The court may, from time to time, schedule status conferences in the Part. The court, at the request of a Justice, will provide notice to the attorneys in each of the cases in an inventory that have been selected to undergo this procedure. The notice will announce that counsel must appear for the conference on a given date pursuant to a directive of the presiding Justice. Failure to respond will result in appropriate judicial action. When counsel appear, the Justice will make whatever order is required to insure future progress in the case. NY R NY CTY Procedure V(B).
5. *NEW YORK COUNTY: Early settlement conference and judicial mediation conference.* Counsel will be notified when a case is first scheduled for an Early Settlement Conference appearance through E-Track, the court system's e-mail notification service. NY R NY CTY Procedure VIII(C)(1). Only counsel fully familiar with and authorized to settle shall appear at these conferences. NY R NY CTY Procedure VIII(C)(1). Cases that are not resolved in the Early Settlement Conference Parts will be referred to the Judicial Mediation Part (Part J-Med), where they will undergo an intensive settlement effort. Conferences in the Judicial Mediation Part will be conducted in Room 422 at 60 Centre Street (646-386-3722). Attorneys will be notified of the first appearance in a case in Part J-Med at the last Early Settlement Conference and/or through E-Track. NY R NY CTY Procedure VIII(C)(1). All counsel attending Judicial Mediation conferences must have familiarity with all aspects of the case. Further, counsel attending the conferences must either (i) have full authority to discuss settlement and enter into settlement agreements, or (ii) ensure that the client is present at the conference or is immediately available by telephone. A demand, if not already provided, must be provided to the defendant(s) in advance of this conference so as to facilitate discussion at the conference. NY R NY CTY Procedure VIII(C)(1). For more information refer to NY R NY CTY Procedure VIII(C)(1).

6. *NEW YORK COUNTY: Final pretrial conference.* In cases to be tried in IAS Parts (i.e., not including cases scheduled for trial through the Administrative Coordinating Part (Part 40 or Part 40 City)), the court will conduct a pretrial conference at which settlement will be explored and a trial date will be confirmed or a firm date set. Prior to the pretrial conference, counsel shall confer in a good faith effort to identify issues not in contention, resolve all disputed questions without need for court intervention, and settle the case. Unless otherwise directed by the court, each party must be represented at the pretrial conference by counsel having full knowledge of the case and specific authority to settle or the ability immediately to contact by telephone a person with such authority. To permit the fixing of a trial date, counsel must, prior to the conference, consult their own schedules and those of their witnesses and be prepared to furnish a realistic estimate of the trial's length and discuss a suitable trial date unless previously fixed. NY R NY CTY J RUL Rule 19.
7. *ONONDAGA COUNTY: Final pretrial conference*
    a. *In jury cases.* The IAS Justice will hold a final pre-trial conference in chambers at 9:30 a.m. on the trial date. Counsel must be prepared to discuss settlement, witness and exhibit lists, scheduling of witnesses, identity of expert witnesses, voir dire, proposed jury charges, special verdict sheet, motions in limine, EBT transcripts, videotaped testimony, stipulations and courtroom assignment. If an attorney does not have settlement authority, then his/her client and/or insurance adjuster must be personally present at the pre-trial conference. NY R ONDGA JURY TRIAL Rule 1. Be prepared to discuss possible stipulations at the final pre-trial conference. NY R ONDGA JURY TRIAL Rule 8.
    b. *In non-jury cases.* The IAS Justice will hold a final pre-trial conference in chambers at 9:30 A.M. on the trial date. Counsel must be prepared to discuss settlement, witness and exhibit lists, scheduling of witnesses, identity of expert witnesses, motions in limine, EBT transcripts, videotaped testimony, proposed findings of fact and conclusions of law and stipulations. If an attorney does not have settlement authority, then his/her client and/or insurance adjuster must be personally present at the pre-trial conference. NY R ONDGA NON JURY TRIAL Rule 1. Be prepared to discuss possible stipulations at the pre-trial conference. NY R ONDGA NON JURY TRIAL Rule 8.
8. *Governing law.* The civil practice law and rules (NY CPLR § 101, et seq.) shall govern the procedure in civil judicial proceedings in all courts of the state and before all judges, except where the procedure is regulated by inconsistent statute. The civil practice law and rules shall succeed the civil practice act and rules of civil practice and shall be deemed substituted therefor throughout the statutes and rules of the state. NY CPLR § 101. The civil practice law and rules shall be liberally construed to secure the just, speedy and inexpensive determination of every civil judicial proceeding. NY CPLR § 104.
    a. *Uniform trial court rules.* The uniform civil rules for the Supreme Court and County Court (NY R UNIF TRIAL CTS § 202.1, et seq.) shall be applicable to civil actions and proceedings in the Supreme Court and the County Court. NY R UNIF TRIAL CTS § 202.1(a). The provisions of the uniform rules shall be construed consistent with the Civil Practice Law and Rules (CPLR), and matters not covered by the uniform rules shall be governed by the CPLR. NY R UNIF TRIAL CTS § 202.1(d).
    b. *Local rules.* Local court rules, not inconsistent with law or with uniform civil rules for the Supreme Court and County Court (NY R UNIF TRIAL CTS § 202.1, et seq.), shall comply with Part 9 of the Rules of the Chief Judge (NY R CHIEF J § 9.1). NY R UNIF TRIAL CTS § 202.1(c).
    c. *Official forms.* The state administrator shall have the power to adopt, amend and rescind an appendix of forms. Forms adopted pursuant to NY CPLR § 107 shall be sufficient under the civil practice law and rules and shall illustrate the simplicity and brevity of statement which the civil practice law and rules contemplate. NY CPLR § 107.
9. *Rules of the commercial division.* [Editor's note: certain types of civil cases or civil cases meeting certain monetary thresholds that are filed in the state of New York must be filed in the Commercial Division of the New York Supreme Courts. Rules governing practice in the commercial division are found in NY R UNIF TRIAL CTS § 202.70]. Cases which must be filed in the commercial division are listed below. For more information, refer to NY R UNIF TRIAL CTS § 202.70.
    a. *Monetary thresholds.* Except as set forth in NY R UNIF TRIAL CTS § 202.70(b), the monetary thresholds of the Commercial Division, exclusive of punitive damages, interests, costs, disbursements and counsel fees claimed, are established as follows: (1) Albany County, fifty thousand dollars ($50,000); (2) Eighth Judicial District, one hundred thousand dollars ($100,000); (3) Kings County, one hundred fifty thousand dollars ($150,000); (4) Nassau County, two hundred thousand dollars ($200,000); (5) New York County, five hundred thousand dollars ($500,000); (6) Onondaga County, fifty thousand dollars ($50,000); (7) Queens County, one hundred thousand dollars ($100,000); (8) Seventh Judicial District, fifty thousand dollars ($50,000); (9) Suffolk County, one hundred thousand dollars ($100,000); and (10) Westchester County, one hundred thousand dollars ($100,000). NY R UNIF TRIAL CTS § 202.70(a).
        i. *ALBANY COUNTY.* The Commercial Division of the Albany County Supreme Court exercises jurisdiction over

selected business and commercial disputes in which the amount at issue generally involves damage claims in a minimum amount of fifty thousand dollars ($50,000) as well as claims for unspecified amounts where the value of the commercial asset(s) in dispute exceeds fifty thousand dollars ($50,000). A separate publication promulgating the rules and criteria relating to the filing and management of Commercial Court cases in this part may be obtained from the Albany County Supreme Court Clerk's Office. A section of the Uniform Civil Rules for the Supreme Court and County Court sets forth statewide rules. NY R 3 JD SUP Doc. 1(E).

ii. *BRONX COUNTY.* The monetary threshold for commercial cases in Bronx County will be seventy-five thousand dollars ($75,000). All other parameters including the type of matters that will be heard are contained within the Rules of the Commercial Division of the Supreme Court (NY R UNIF TRIAL CTS § 202.70). NY R BRONX FIL R Doc. 12.

iii. *NEW YORK COUNTY.* The monetary threshold in the New York County Commercial Division, which is generally applicable, is an amount in controversy of five hundred thousand dollars ($500,000) or more (exclusive of punitive damages, interest, costs, disbursements, and counsel fees). If the case is designated a commercial one and the Addendum is submitted, the clerk will review the pleadings to determine whether the amount in controversy in the case meets the monetary threshold or whether an exception to the threshold applies. NY R NY CTY Procedure IA(B). For more information on assigning a case to the commercial division in New York County, refer to NY R NY CTY Procedure IA(B).

b. *Commercial cases.* Actions in which the principal claims involve or consist of the following will be heard in the Commercial Division provided that the monetary threshold is met or equitable or declaratory relief is sought:

i. Breach of contract or fiduciary duty, fraud, misrepresentation, business tort (e.g., unfair competition), or statutory and/or common law violation where the breach or violation is alleged to arise out of business dealings (e.g., sales of assets or securities; corporate restructuring; partnership, shareholder, joint venture, and other business agreements; trade secrets; restrictive covenants; and employment agreements not including claims that principally involve alleged discriminatory practices);

ii. Transactions governed by the Uniform Commercial Code (exclusive of those concerning individual cooperative or condominium units);

iii. Transactions involving commercial real property, including Yellowstone injunctions and excluding actions for the payment of rent only;

iv. Shareholder derivative actions—without consideration of the monetary threshold;

v. Commercial class actions—without consideration of the monetary threshold;

vi. Business transactions involving or arising out of dealings with commercial banks and other financial institutions;

vii. Internal affairs of business organizations;

viii. Malpractice by accountants or actuaries, and legal malpractice arising out of representation in commercial matters;

ix. Environmental insurance coverage;

x. Commercial insurance coverage (e.g., directors and officers, errors and omissions, and business interruption coverage);

xi. Dissolution of corporations, partnerships, limited liability companies, limited liability partnerships and joint ventures—without consideration of the monetary threshold; and

xii. Applications to stay or compel arbitration and affirm or disaffirm arbitration awards and related injunctive relief pursuant to Article 75 of the New York Civil Practice Law and Rules (NY CPLR § 7501, et seq.) involving any of the foregoing enumerated commercial issues. Where the applicable arbitration agreement provides for the arbitration to be heard outside the United States, the monetary threshold set forth in NY R UNIF TRIAL CTS § 202.70(a) shall not apply. NY R UNIF TRIAL CTS § 202.70(b).

c. *Non-commercial cases.* The following will not be heard in the Commercial Division even if the monetary threshold is met:

i. Suits to collect professional fees;

ii. Cases seeking a declaratory judgment as to insurance coverage for personal injury or property damage;

iii. Residential real estate disputes, including landlord-tenant matters, and commercial real estate disputes involving the payment of rent only;

iv. Home improvement contracts involving residential properties consisting of one to four residential units or individual units in any residential building, including cooperative or condominium units;

v. Proceedings to enforce a judgment regardless of the nature of the underlying case;

vi. First-party insurance claims and actions by insurers to collect premiums or rescind non-commercial policies; and

vii. Attorney malpractice actions except as otherwise provided in NY R UNIF TRIAL CTS § 202.70(b)(8). NY R UNIF TRIAL CTS § 202.70(c).

d. For more information on the Commercial Division, refer to NY R UNIF TRIAL CTS § 202.70.

D. Documents

1. *Documents to consider for preliminary conference*

a. *Request for preliminary conference.* Refer to the General Requirements section of this document for information on the request for a preliminary conference.

b. *Request for judicial intervention.* At any time after service of process, a party may file a request for judicial intervention. Except as provided in NY R UNIF TRIAL CTS § 202.6(b), in an action not yet assigned to a judge, the court shall not accept for filing a notice of motion, order to show cause, or application for ex parte order, unless such notice or application is accompanied by a request for judicial intervention. NY R UNIF TRIAL CTS § 202.6(a).

i. *BRONX COUNTY.* Generally, the Request For Judicial Intervention, commonly referred to as an "RJI", is required to be filed in any action where the assignment of a Justice is required. The RJI sets forth the information which is entered into the court system's database. It must be completely and accurately filled out. The full caption, as stated on the Summons, must be set forth. Use of terms "et al." and "etc." are not permitted. Only one RJI may be filed in each action. Either a self represented litigant or an attorney must sign the affirmation at the end of the form. Once completed, the RJI must be filed in duplicate. Except in the case of an ex-parte application, the RJI must also be served together with the accompanying application upon all parties. Proof of accuracy of the index number must accompany the RJI. NY R BRONX FIL R Doc. 2.

ii. *KINGS COUNTY.* An RJI with the relevant required addendum in a NYSCEF case shall be submitted via NYSCEF. Once e-filed, the RJI and any accompanying document will be forwarded to the relevant support office for random assignment of the case and processing of the document. A filer or counsel need not appear (as to Proposed Orders to Show Cause, however, see below). A copy of the pleadings must be submitted only if the document has not previously been e-filed. If the RJI seeks intervention with regard to a document that is intended for review by a Justice, such as a motion, a working copy of the RJI must be submitted with the working copy of the motion and the NYSCEF Confirmation Notice. NY R L KINGS E FIL Doc. 1(C).

iii. *NEW YORK COUNTY.* To obtain the assignment of an IAS Justice to a case, a Request for Judicial Intervention (cost ninety-five dollars ($95)) must be filed, with NYSCEF in an e-filed case or in paper in an authorized hard-copy one. A no-fee RJI, which will generally result in the referral of an application to an Ex Parte Justice, is also required with regard to certain kinds of applications for which, prior to 2011, no RJI was required. NY R NY CTY Procedure I(C). A "fillable" form RJI is available on-line. The form must be filed in duplicate in hard-copy cases. NY R NY CTY Procedure IA(A)(1). The filer of an RJI must check off a box identifying the type of case at issue. Where the RJI seeks judicial assignment, this designation will bring about a random assignment of the case by computer to a Justice handling cases of that type. NY R NY CTY Procedure IA(A)(1). The RJI and any addendum can be completed and submitted electronically in an e-filed case. NY R NY CTY Procedure II(A). The RJI shall be marked to reflect the existence of any "related case" as explained on the "Commencement of Cases" page under "Case Processing" on the court's website. NY R NY CTY Procedure II(A); NY R NY CTY E FIL Doc. 2(C). Requests for preliminary conferences in unassigned cases should be filed with an RJI in the General Clerk's Office (Room 119). In assigned cases, if the court itself does not direct a conference in a decision nor issue an order scheduling pretrial proceedings, counsel should contact the Part Clerk. NY R NY CTY J RUL Rule 5(a).

iv. *ONONDAGA COUNTY.* The RJI will be submitted via the NYSCEF system along with any required RJI addendum forms. When the RJI is filed and the fee paid online, the Onondaga County Clerk's Office will electronically forward the RJI and any accompanying documents to the Onondaga Supreme Court Clerk's Office for assignment and processing. Counsel will receive notification of judge assignment via the NYSCEF system. NY R ONDGA E FIL Protocol(B)(3).

c. *Physician's affidavit.* Where a request is filed for a preliminary conference in an action involving a terminally ill party governed by NY CPLR Rule 3407, the request shall be accompanied by the physician's affidavit required by that provision. NY R UNIF TRIAL CTS § 202.12(l).

d. *Working copies.* The court may require the parties to provide working copies of documents filed electronically. In such event, each working copy shall include, firmly affixed thereto, a copy of a confirmation notice in a form prescribed by the Chief Administrator. NY R UNIF TRIAL CTS § 202.5-b(d)(5).

e. *ERIE COUNTY: Additional documents to consider*

i. *Notice of hard copy submission in e-filed case.* In accordance with NY R UNIF TRIAL CTS § 202.5-b(d), the County Clerk shall refuse to accept for filing, hard copy papers filed to an action subject to electronic filing unless hard copy filing is permitted by the Uniform Rules or NY R ERIE E FIL Doc. 3 and the papers bear a completed Notice of Hard Copy Submission—E-Filed Case form. NY R ERIE E FIL Doc. 3(III)(D).

f. *KINGS COUNTY: Additional documents to consider*

i. *Forms when filing in hard copy.* An attorney who certifies in good faith that he or she lacks the equipment or knowledge needed to e-file and have no staff member or employee under his or her direction who has such knowledge and equipment may opt out of participation in e-filing in a mandatory case by filing a "Notice of Opt-Out from Participation in Action Subject to Mandatory Electronic Filing" form EFM-2 with the Clerk. NY R L KINGS E FIL Doc. 1(A)(2). Where in accordance with the E-Filing Rules a party submits a document in hard copy in an e-filed case (principally, a document submitted by a nonparticipating party (e.g., an attorney) in a consensual case, an emergency filing made in accordance with the Mandatory E-Filing Rules, and any document filed with the court in hard copy by an attorney who has opted out of participation in mandatory e-filing, the document must bear the back page facing out, a "Notice of Hard Copy Submission—E-Filed Cases" form EFM-3. NY R L KINGS E FIL Doc. 1(B)(3).

g. *NEW YORK COUNTY: Additional documents to consider*

i. *Notice of hard copy submission.* Where in accordance with the E-Filing Rules an attorney or an unrepresented litigant who is participating in e-filing submits a document in hard copy in an e-filed case, the document must bear, as the back page facing out, a Notice of Hard-Copy Submission—E-Filed Case (a form available in the "Forms" section on the NYSCEF website (Form EFM-3) and in the court's back offices). NY R NY CTY E FIL Doc. 2(B)(3). For more information refer to NY R NY CTY E FIL Doc. 2.

h. *ONONDAGA COUNTY: Additional documents to consider*

i. *Notice of hard copy submission.* Any papers to be filed with the court in an e-filed case must be filed online with the E-filing system except where a special exemption is granted (e.g., oversized maps, photographs). If such an exemption is granted, Form EFM-3, "Notice of Hard Copy Submission—E-Filed Case," must be attached to such documents forms which are not filed on line. Also, Form EFM-4 "Notice of Hard Copy Exhibit Filing" must be completed and uploaded to the action's e-file. Both of these forms may be found on the NYSCEF website. NY R ONDGA E FIL Protocol(B)(4).

i. *QUEENS COUNTY: Additional documents to consider*

i. *Notice of hard copy submission.* Any party opting out of the e-filing system must have a "Notice of Hard Copy Submission" firmly affixed to the back of the papers. NY R L QUEENS E-FILE Doc. 1(H)(2)(f).

2. *Documents to consider for pretrial conference*

a. *Pleadings.* Plaintiff shall submit marked copies of the pleadings. NY R UNIF TRIAL CTS § 202.26(e).

b. *Proof of injuries.* A verified bill of particulars and a doctor's report or hospital record, or both, as to the nature and extent of injuries claimed, if any, shall be submitted by the plaintiff and by any defendant who counterclaims. The judge may require additional data, or may waive any requirement for submission of documents on suitable alternate proof of damages. NY R UNIF TRIAL CTS § 202.26(e).

c. *Trial documents*

i. *Pleadings for trial.* Upon the trial of an action, the following papers, if not yet submitted, shall be submitted to the court by the party who has filed the note of issue:

- Copies of all pleadings marked as required by NY CPLR Rule 4012; and
- A copy of the bill of particulars, if any. NY R UNIF TRIAL CTS § 202.35(a).

ii. *Statutory provisions relied upon.* Upon the trial of an action, a copy of any statutory provision in effect at the time the cause of action arose shall be submitted to the court by the party who intends to rely upon such statute. NY R UNIF TRIAL CTS § 202.35(b).

iii. *Trial memorandum.* If so ordered, the parties shall submit to the court, before the commencement of trial, trial memoranda which shall be exchanged among counsel. NY R UNIF TRIAL CTS § 202.35(c).

d. *Working copies.* The court may require the parties to provide working copies of documents filed electronically. In such event, each working copy shall include, firmly affixed thereto, a copy of a confirmation notice in a form prescribed by the Chief Administrator. NY R UNIF TRIAL CTS § 202.5-b(d)(5).

e. *ERIE COUNTY: Additional documents to consider*

i. *Notice of hard copy submission in e-filed case.* In accordance with NY R UNIF TRIAL CTS § 202.5-b(d), the County Clerk shall refuse to accept for filing, hard copy papers filed to an action subject to electronic filing unless hard copy filing is permitted by the Uniform Rules or NY R ERIE E FIL Doc. 3 and the papers bear a completed Notice of Hard Copy Submission—E-Filed Case form. NY R ERIE E FIL Doc. 3(III)(D).

f. *KINGS COUNTY: Additional documents to consider*

i. *Forms when filing in hard copy.* An attorney who certifies in good faith that he or she lacks the equipment or knowledge needed to e-file and have no staff member or employee under his or her direction who has such knowledge and equipment may opt out of participation in e-filing in a mandatory case by filing a "Notice of Opt-Out from Participation in Action Subject to Mandatory Electronic Filing" form EFM-2 with the Clerk. NY R L KINGS E FIL Doc. 1(A)(2). Where in accordance with the E-Filing Rules a party submits a document in hard copy in an e-filed case (principally, a document submitted by a nonparticipating party (e.g., an attorney) in a consensual case, an emergency filing made in accordance with the Mandatory E-Filing Rules, and any document filed with the court in hard copy by an attorney who has opted out of participation in mandatory e-filing, the document must bear the back page facing out, a "Notice of Hard Copy Submission—E-Filed Cases" form EFM-3. NY R L KINGS E FIL Doc. 1(B)(3).

g. *NEW YORK COUNTY: Additional documents to consider*

i. *Notice of hard copy submission.* Where in accordance with the E-Filing Rules an attorney or an unrepresented litigant who is participating in e-filing submits a document in hard copy in an e-filed case, the document must bear, as the back page facing out, a Notice of Hard-Copy Submission—E-Filed Case (a form available in the "Forms" section on the NYSCEF website (Form EFM-3) and in the court's back offices). NY R NY CTY E FIL Doc. 2(B)(3). For more information refer to NY R NY CTY E FIL Doc. 2.

h. *ONONDAGA COUNTY: Additional documents to consider*

i. *Notice of hard copy submission.* Any papers to be filed with the court in an e-filed case must be filed online with the E-filing system except where a special exemption is granted (e.g., oversized maps, photographs). If such an exemption is granted, Form EFM-3, "Notice of Hard Copy Submission—E-Filed Case," must be attached to such documents forms which are not filed on line. Also, Form EFM-4 "Notice of Hard Copy Exhibit Filing" must be completed and uploaded to the action's e-file. Both of these forms may be found on the NYSCEF website. NY R ONDGA E FIL Protocol(B)(4).

i. *QUEENS COUNTY: Additional documents to consider*

i. *Notice of hard copy submission.* Any party opting out of the e-filing system must have a "Notice of Hard Copy Submission" firmly affixed to the back of the papers. NY R L QUEENS E-FILE Doc. 1(H)(2)(f).

E. Format

1. *Form of documents*

a. *Size and form of paper.* Each paper served or filed shall be durable, white and, except for summonses, subpoenas, notices of appearance, notes of issue, orders of protection, temporary orders of protection and exhibits, shall be eleven by eight and one-half (11 x 8-1/2) inches in size. NY CPLR Rule 2101(a).

b. *Writing and language.* The writing shall be legible and in black ink. NY CPLR Rule 2101(a). Each paper served or filed shall be in the English language which, where practicable, shall be of ordinary usage. NY CPLR Rule 2101(b).

c. *Caption.* Each paper served or filed shall begin with a caption setting forth the name of the court, the venue, the title of the action, the nature of the paper and the index number of the action if one has been assigned. In all papers other than a summons, a complaint or a judgment it shall be sufficient to state the name of the first named party on each side with an appropriate indication of any omissions. NY CPLR Rule 2101(c).

i. *Further contents of first page.* After the first paper has been filed in each case the index number shall appear on the cover and first page to the right of the caption of every paper tendered for filing in the action. Each such cover and first page also shall contain an indication of the county of venue and a brief description of the nature of the paper and, where the case has been assigned to an individual judge, shall contain the name of the assigned judge to the right of the caption. NY R UNIF TRIAL CTS § 202.5(a); NY R UNIF TRIAL CTS § 202.5(b); NY R UNIF TRIAL CTS § 202.5(d)(1)(i).

d. *Index number.* No paper in an action in the supreme or a county court, other than an order submitted for signature to a judge out of court, shall be submitted for any purpose to the supreme or county court or to a clerk thereof unless there is endorsed on such paper the index number of the action assigned by the clerk of the county. NY CPLR § 8018(c).

   i. *ALBANY COUNTY: Index number on all filed documents.* The index number, the request for judicial intervention number and the assigned justice's name shall appear on [all papers filed with the Court subsequent to the complaint]. NY R 3 JD SUP Doc. 1(A).

   ii. *ERIE COUNTY: Index number after initial filing.* Cases that are initially commenced by the filing of papers with the NYSCEF system are identified as e-filed cases by assignment of an Index Number that has "800-899" as the first three (3) digits of the index number (i.e. 802391/2012). NY R ERIE E FIL Doc. 3(II). [The] Index Number must be affixed to all document submissions, filings, and communications to the Erie County Clerk and the Court. Cases that are converted from paper to e-filing shall retain the original index number. NY R ERIE E FIL Doc. 3(II).

   iii. *KINGS COUNTY: Index number after initial filing.* In cases commenced electronically by the filing of initiating papers with the NYSCEF system and payment of the statutory fees, the Kings County Clerk will issue an NYSCEF designated index number and the filer shall be notified via the NYSCEF system of the index number assigned and filing date. Such index number must be affixed to all document submissions, filings and communications to the Kings County Clerk and Supreme Court. If counsel faces exigent circumstances that require accelerated assignment, counsel may contact Administration of the Kings County Clerk at kcco-efile@nycourts.gov, during normal business hours of the court. NY R L KINGS E FIL Doc. 1(B)(5).

   iv. *NEW YORK COUNTY: Index number on hard copy filings.* Papers subsequently presented for filing in hardcopy format will be filed in this jacket. NY R NY CTY Procedure I(B). Index numbers take the form of six digits followed by a slash and the four digits of the year the case began, e.g., 340705/2018. The first or first two integers of the index number identify the type of case. If a case is commenced electronically, the second integer will be a "5", except as indicated otherwise in the list below. There are many tax certiorari matters e-filed annually and the index numbers therefor will normally run over into those with a "6" as the second integer, and the same will occur with general cases if necessary. The principal types of cases and their index number categories are listed in NY R NY CTY Procedure I(B). NY R NY CTY Procedure I(B); NY R NY CTY Procedure XI(A).

   v. *ONONDAGA COUNTY: Index number.* The index number must be referenced on all e-filed documents and correspondence. All e-filed case index numbers will contain the letters "EF" between the year and the file number (for example, 2012EF9999). NY R ONDGA E FIL Protocol(B)(1).

   vi. *QUEENS COUNTY: Index number on converted cases.* Cases originally commenced in hard-copy form but later converted to an E-file case, either by stipulation or order will bear a regular index number initially. The County Clerk will issue a new E-file index number. NY R L QUEENS E-FILE Doc. 1(B).

e. *Line spacing.* Every paper filed in court, if typewritten, shall have at least double space between each line, except for quotations and the names and addresses of attorneys appearing in the action. NY R UNIF TRIAL CTS § 202.5(a).

f. *Font size.* Each. . .paper printed or typed, served or filed, except for summonses. . .and exhibits, shall be in clear type of no less than ten (10) point in size. NY CPLR Rule 2101(a).

   i. Whenever a requirement relating to size of type is stated in point size, the type size requirement shall be deemed met if the x-height of the type is a minimum of forty-five percent (45%) of the specified point size. Each point shall be measured as .351 millimeter. The x-height size shall be measured as it appears on the page. The x-height is the height of the lower case letters, exclusive of ascenders or descenders. NY CPLR § 105(t).

g. *Margins.* Every paper filed in court shall have at least one (1) inch margins. NY R UNIF TRIAL CTS § 202.5(a).

h. *Citations*

   i. *Civil practice law and rules.* NY CPLR § 101, et seq. shall be known as the civil practice law and rules, and may be cited as "CPLR". Reference to a provision in the civil practice law and rules may, except when such provision is being enacted or amended, be made without indicating whether it is a rule or section. NY CPLR § 101.

i. *Indorsement by attorney.* Each paper served or filed shall be indorsed with the name, address and telephone number of the attorney for the party serving or filing the paper, or if the party does not appear by attorney, with the name, address and telephone number of the party. NY CPLR Rule 2101(d).

j. *One-sided printing.* In addition, every paper filed in court, other than an exhibit or printed form, shall contain writing on one side only, except that papers that are fastened on the side may contain writing on both sides. NY R UNIF TRIAL CTS § 202.5(a).

k. *Use of copies authorized.* Except where otherwise specifically prescribed, copies, rather than originals, of all papers, including orders, affidavits and exhibits may be served or filed. Where it is required that the original be served or filed and the original is lost or withheld, the court may authorize a copy to be served or filed. NY CPLR Rule 2101(e).

i. Where a certified copy of a paper is required by law, an attorney admitted to practice in the courts of the state may certify that it has been compared by him with the original and found to be a true and complete copy. Such a certificate, when subscribed by such attorney, has the same effect as if made by a clerk. NY CPLR § 2105.

l. *Recycled paper.* It is the policy of the Unified Court System that litigants, where practicable, should file or submit to the courts of the Unified Court System of the State of New York papers printed or reproduced on recycled paper. Paper is considered recycled if it contains a minimum content of thirty percent (30%) waste paper. NY R UNIF TRIAL CTS § 215.2. The signature page of every paper filed or submitted to the court on recycled paper should bear the legend: "Printed [Reproduced] on Recycled Paper." NY R UNIF TRIAL CTS § 215.3.

m. *Form of request for judicial intervention; Copies.* A request for judicial intervention must be submitted, in duplicate, on a form authorized by the Chief of the Courts, with proof of service on the other parties to the action (but proof of service is not required where the application is ex parte). NY R UNIF TRIAL CTS § 202.6(a).

n. *KINGS COUNTY: Tabs on filings.* Motions, orders and other filed papers shall be indexed with protruding tabs. Clerks are required to reject papers that do not have protruding exhibit tabs, except papers in matrimonial cases and papers filed by pro se litigants. NY R L KINGS Pt. A, Papers.

2. *Form of electronic documents.* Each paper served or filed by electronic means, as defined in NY CPLR Rule 2103(f), shall be capable of being reproduced by the receiver so as to comply with the provisions of NY CPLR Rule 2101(a) through NY CPLR Rule 2101(d). NY CPLR Rule 2101(g).

a. *File format.* All e-filed documents shall comply with the technical requirements set forth at the NYSCEF site. NY R UNIF TRIAL CTS § 202.5-b(d)(1)(i).

b. *Heading of document.* The subject matter heading for each paper sent by electronic means must indicate that the matter being transmitted electronically is related to a court proceeding. NY CPLR Rule 2103(b)(7).

c. *E-filed documents identification*

i. *ERIE COUNTY.* E-filed cases must be readily identifiable and marked as such. If counsel presents papers to the Office of the Erie County Clerk or the Office of the Chief Clerk in a NYSCEF matter where authorized, counsel should alert the Clerk that the case is a NYSCEF matter. NY R ERIE E FIL Doc. 3(II).

ii. *KINGS COUNTY.* The Supreme Court's Civil Case Information System ("CCIS") will further identify e-filed cases by the addition of a suffix to the index number (e.g. 500136/2006E). This suffix should be used on all documents filed with the court in e-filed matters. NY R L KINGS E FIL Doc. 1(A)(1).

3. *Signature blocks.* Every pleading, written motion, and other paper, served on another party or filed or submitted to the court shall be signed by an attorney, or by a party if the party is not represented by an attorney, with the name of the attorney or party clearly printed or typed directly below the signature. NY R CHIEF ADMIN § 130-1.1-a(a); NY R UNIF TRIAL CTS § 202.5(d)(1)(iv).

a. *Printed name.* Beneath each signature shall be printed the name signed. NY CPLR Rule 2101(a).

b. *Failure to sign.* Absent good cause shown, the court shall strike any unsigned paper if the omission of the signature is not corrected promptly after being called to the attention of the attorney or party. NY R CHIEF ADMIN § 130-1.1-a(a).

c. *Signature as certification.* By signing a paper, an attorney or party certifies that, to the best of that person's knowledge, information and belief, formed after an inquiry reasonable under the circumstances the presentation of the paper or the contentions therein are not frivolous as defined in NY R CHIEF ADMIN § 130-1.1(c). NY R CHIEF ADMIN § 130-1.1-a(b)(1).

d. *Electronic signatures.* A document shall be considered to have been signed by an attorney or party in compliance with NY R CHIEF ADMIN § 130-1.1-a if it has been signed by such attorney or party as provided in NY R UNIF TRIAL CTS § 202.5-b(e)(1) and it bears the signatory's name. NY R UNIF TRIAL CTS § 202.5-b(e)(2). An electronically filed document shall be considered to have been signed by, and shall be binding upon, the person identified as a signatory, if:

i. It bears the physical signature of such person and is scanned into an electronic format that reproduces such signature; or

ii. The signatory has electronically affixed the digital image of his or her signature to the document; or

iii. It is electronically filed under the User ID and password of that person; or

iv. In a tax certiorari action in which the parties have stipulated to this procedure, it is an initiating document that is electronically filed without the signature of the signatory in a form provided above in NY R UNIF TRIAL CTS § 202.5-b(e)(iv), provided that, prior to filing, the document is signed in full in hard copy (which hard copy must be preserved until the conclusion of all proceedings, including appeals, in the case in which it is filed); or

v. In a small claims assessment review proceeding, it is a petition recorded by the NYSCEF site upon the filing of a text file as provided in NY R UNIF TRIAL CTS § 202.5-b(b)(1), provided that prior to filing, the document was signed in full in hard copy (which hard copy must be preserved until the conclusion of all proceedings in the matter, including article 78 (NY CPLR § 7801, et seq.) review and any appeals, and must be made available during the proceeding upon request of the respondent or the court); or

vi. It otherwise bears the electronic signature of the signatory in a format conforming to such standards and requirements as may hereafter be established by the Chief Administrator. NY R UNIF TRIAL CTS § 202.5-b(e).

4. *Confidentiality of personal information.* No person may file any document available for public inspection with any state agency, political subdivision, or in any court of this state that contains a Social Security account number of any other person, unless such other person is a dependent child, or has consented to such filing, except as required by federal or state law or regulation, or by court rule. NY GEN BUS § 399-ddd. Submissions pursuant to e-filing procedures shall have the same confidentiality rights as paper documents. NY R UNIF TRIAL CTS § 202.5-b(k)(1).

a. *Confidential personal information.* Except in the actions designated in NY R UNIF TRIAL CTS § 202.5(e)(1), or as otherwise provided by rule or law or court order, and whether or not a sealing order is or has been sought, the parties shall omit or redact confidential personal information in papers submitted to the court for filing. For purposes of NY R UNIF TRIAL CTS § 202.5(e), confidential personal information ("CPI") means:

i. The taxpayer identification number of an individual or an entity, including a Social Security number, an employer identification number, and an individual taxpayer identification number, except the last four (4) digits thereof;

ii. The date of an individual's birth, except the year thereof;

iii. The full name of an individual known to be a minor, except the minor's initials;

iv. A financial account number, including a credit and/or debit card number, a bank account number, an investment account number, and/or an insurance account number, except the last four (4) digits or letters thereof; and

v. Any of the documents or testimony in a matrimonial action protected by NY DOM REL § 235 or evidence sealed by the court in such an action which are attached as exhibits or referenced in the papers filed in any other civil action. For purposes of NY R UNIF TRIAL CTS § 202.5, a matrimonial action shall mean: an action to annul a marriage or declare the nullity of a void marriage, an action or agreement for a separation, an action for a divorce, or an action or proceeding for custody, visitation, writ of habeus corpus, child support, maintenance or paternity. NY R UNIF TRIAL CTS § 202.5(e)(1).

vi. *ERIE COUNTY.* An attorney or unrepresented litigant filing a document via the NYSCEF system must comply with the requirements of NY R UNIF TRIAL CTS § 202.5(e) regarding the redaction of Confidential Personal Information and NY GEN BUS § 399-ddd(6) concerning the filing of documents containing Social Security Numbers. It is the sole responsibility of counsel or unrepresented litigant filing to be aware of and to comply with existing laws requiring non-disclosure of personal information contained in any document e-filed in NYSCEF. NY R ERIE E FIL Doc. 3(III)(G); NY R ERIE E FIL Doc. 3(III).

vii. *KINGS COUNTY.* An attorney or unrepresented litigant filing a document via the NYSCEF system must comply with the requirements of General Business Law § 399-dd(6), which often require redaction of any Social Security number that appear in the original document. The NYSCEF system automatically redacts portions of filed documents which apparently contain Social Security numbers pursuant to NY R UNIF TRIAL CTS § 202.5-b(k). In the event the filing party receives e-mail notice through NYSCEF that a Social Security number in a filed document has been redacted, and the filing party concludes such redaction is erroneous, the filer should click on the link provided in the e-mail to permit the County Clerk to revert the redaction. For Confidential Personal Information, see NY R UNIF TRIAL CTS § 202.5(e) and NY R L KINGS E FIL Doc. 1(B)(11). [Editor's note: the reference to General Business Law § 399-dd(6) is likely a reference to NY GEN BUS § 399-ddd(6)]. NY R L KINGS E FIL Doc. 1(B)(10); NY R L KINGS E FIL Doc. 1(K)(1).

viii. *NEW YORK COUNTY.* It is the responsibility of counsel and parties to comply with rules restricting disclosure of confidential personal information. Nevertheless, NYSCEF screens filings and endeavors to identify any that contain social security numbers. When such numbers are discovered through this process, NYSCEF will restrict portions of or all of such documents from public view. Where NYSCEF has redacted what it believes to be a social security number, it will transmit to the filer a notice advising of the action taken and requesting that the filer review the matter and provide notification as set forth in the notice if the redaction has been made in error. NY R NY CTY E FIL Doc. 2(K)(1); NY R NY CTY J RUL Rule A-1. Documents filed in the past in "secure status" under a procedure no longer in place will retain that status unless otherwise directed by the court. NY R NY CTY E FIL Doc. 2(K)(2).

b. *Submission of confidential personal information.* Where a person submitting a paper to a court for filing believes in good faith that the inclusion of the full confidential personal information described in NY R UNIF TRIAL CTS § 202.5(e)(1) is material and necessary to the adjudication of the action or proceeding before the court, he or she may apply to the court for leave to serve and file together with a paper in which such information has been set forth in abbreviated form a confidential affidavit or affirmation setting forth the same information in unabbreviated form, appropriately referenced to the page or pages of the paper at which the abbreviated form appears. NY R UNIF TRIAL CTS § 202.5(e)(3).

c. *Home addresses.* For information on when home addresses and other personal information must be redacted, refer to NY CPLR Rule 2103-a.

5. *Defective papers.* A defect in the form of a paper, if a substantial right of a party is not prejudiced, shall be disregarded by the court, and leave to correct shall be freely given. NY CPLR Rule 2101(f). Papers that are stapled or bound securely shall not be rejected for filing simply because they are not bound with a backer of any kind. NY R UNIF TRIAL CTS § 202.5(a). A paper filed in accordance with the rules of the chief administrator or any local rule or practice established by the court shall be deemed filed. NY CPLR Rule 2102(b).

a. *Objection to defective papers.* The party on whom a paper is served shall be deemed to have waived objection to any defect in form unless, within fifteen (15) days after the receipt thereof, the party on whom the paper is served returns the paper to the party serving it with a statement of particular objections. NY CPLR Rule 2101(f).

F. Filing and Service Requirements

1. *Filing requirements.* Except where otherwise prescribed by law or order of court, papers required to be filed shall be filed with the clerk of the court in which the action is triable. In an action or proceeding in supreme or court, papers required to be filed shall be filed with the clerk of the county in which the proceeding is brought. NY CPLR Rule 2102(a).

a. *Electronic filing.* On consent, documents may be filed and served by electronic means in Supreme Court in such civil actions and in such counties as shall be authorized by order of the Chief Administrator of the Courts and only to the extent and in the manner provided in NY R UNIF TRIAL CTS § 202.5-b. NY R UNIF TRIAL CTS § 202.5-b(a)(1). For the definitions of terms used in electronic filing, refer to NY R UNIF TRIAL CTS § 202.5-b(a)(2).

i. *E-filing mandatory.* In any action subject to e-filing, all documents required to be filed with the court by an e-filing party shall be filed and served electronically, except as provided in NY R UNIF TRIAL CTS § 202.5-b. NY R UNIF TRIAL CTS § 202.5-b(d)(1)(i).

- *ERIE COUNTY.* Case types currently eligible and accepted for e-filing are listed at the NYSCEF website. Note that some actions or special proceedings, (i.e., name changes) which are otherwise subject to mandatory e-filing, if commenced by unrepresented litigants will NOT be maintained in the NYSCEF system; individual cases may be found either at NYSCEF or in the Erie County Clerk's online records system. NY R ERIE E FIL Doc. 3(I)(E).
- *KINGS COUNTY.* Cases that are commenced by filing of the initiating papers with NYSCEF are identified as e-filed cases by assignment of a special index number (i.e., Index Numbers beginning with 500,000). NY R L KINGS E FIL Doc. 1(A)(1). All cases required to be e-filed are listed in Uniform Rule 202.5-bb (Mandatory E-Filing Rules) and on the NYSCEF website. All such cases must be commenced by filing with the County Clerk electronically through NYSCEF and all subsequent documents in such cases must be e-filed. Any questions regarding mandatory e-filing in Kings County can be e-mailed to kcco-efile@nycourts.gov. NY R L KINGS E FIL Doc. 1(A)(2).

- *NEW YORK COUNTY.* Unless otherwise provided in the Rules or in NY R NY CTY E FIL Doc. 2 or where a special exemption is granted due to physical requirements (e.g., oversized maps; see NY R NY CTY E FIL Doc. 2(B)(10)), all documents to be filed with the court in a NYSCEF case, including all documents on motions and all letters to the court (where permitted), must be filed with the NYSCEF system. Documents that attorneys would not ordinarily file with the court in a hard-copy case need not be e-filed. Unless otherwise provided by the E-Filing Rules or this Protocol, in e-filed cases the County Clerk and the court will not accept documents filed in paper form. NY R NY CTY E FIL Doc. 2(B)(1). E-filing is mandatory in all types of cases (other than election law, matrimonial, Art. 78, and Mental Hygiene Law matters, and Art. 70 habeas corpus proceedings) that are commenced in this court on or after February 19, 2013. All such cases must be commenced by filing with the County Clerk electronically through NYSCEF and all subsequent documents in such cases must be e-filed. NY R NY CTY E FIL Doc. 2(A)(2)(a). For more information, including information on consensual e-filing and filing scanned hard copy documents, refer to NY R NY CTY E FIL Doc. 2(A)(2).
- *QUEENS COUNTY.* All authorized Torts, Commercial and Tax Certiorari cases may be commenced by E-Filing, however all parties must consent for the action to continue as an E-file case. NY R L QUEENS E-FILE Doc. 1(A). All papers to be filed with the court in an E-filed case shall be filed on-line with the E-file system except as directed by the court. Papers that attorneys would not ordinarily file with the court in a hard-copy case need not be filed in an E-filed matter. NY R L QUEENS E-FILE Doc. 1(E)(2).

ii. *Who may file.* Documents may be filed or served electronically only by a person who has registered as an authorized e-filing user or as otherwise provided in NY R UNIF TRIAL CTS § 202.5-b(c). NY R UNIF TRIAL CTS § 202.5-b(c)(1).

iii. *When filing made.* Documents may be transmitted at any time of the day or night to the NYSCEF site. A document other than an order or judgment is filed when its electronic transmission or, in the case of a petition that is e-filed by submission of a text file as provided in NY R UNIF TRIAL CTS § 202.5-b(b)(1), the electronic transmission of the text file is recorded at that site, provided, however, that where payment of a fee is required upon the filing of a document, the document is not filed until transmission of the document and the information or form or information as required in NY R UNIF TRIAL CTS § 202.5-b(d)(2)(i), NY R UNIF TRIAL CTS § 202.5-b(d)(2)(ii) or NY R UNIF TRIAL CTS § 202.5-b(d)(2)(iii) has been recorded at the NYSCEF site; or, if no transmission of that information or form or information is recorded, where permitted by the County Clerk, until payment is presented to the County Clerk. NY R UNIF TRIAL CTS § 202.5-b(d)(3)(i).

iv. *Notification of filing.* No later than the close of business on the business day following the electronic filing of a document, a notification, in a form prescribed by the Chief Administrator, shall be transmitted electronically by the NYSCEF site to the person filing such document and the e-mail service addresses of all other participating parties in such action. NY R UNIF TRIAL CTS § 202.5-b(d)(3)(ii).

v. *Removal of confidential information and other corrections.* If a document filed electronically is subsequently discovered to contain confidential data—including but not limited to trade secrets, information protected by confidentiality agreement, or personal confidential information as defined by statute or court rule—or otherwise to have been filed in error, the filer or another party or affected person may (1) notify the parties and any non-party filers in the action of the confidentiality issue or other error raised by the filing, and of his or her intention to seek judicial relief to correct the filing: (2) following such notification, request that the appropriate County Clerk, exercising his or her administrative discretion, place the document temporarily in "restricted" status on the NYSCEF site, to be made available for viewing by court staff and the parties but not the general public; and (3) file an application to correct the filing by order to show cause within five (5) business days of such notification (or such time as the court may direct), including a request for preliminary injunctive relief limiting interim disclosure of the document at issue. Unless otherwise directed by the court, any document placed in restricted status in response to such a request shall be returned to public view upon expiration of this five (5) day period. The Chief Administrator of the Courts shall promulgate forms to implement this process. NY R UNIF TRIAL CTS § 202.5-b(d)(3)(iii).

- *KINGS COUNTY.* For information on what to do when a document was erroneously filed with confidential information, refer to NY R L KINGS E FIL Doc. 1(B)(11).
- *NEW YORK COUNTY.* For information on what to do when a document was erroneously filed with confidential information, refer to NY R NY CTY E FIL Doc. 2(B)(8).
- *QUEENS COUNTY.* For information on what to do when a document was erroneously filed with confidential information, refer to NY R L QUEENS E-FILE Doc. 1(E)(7).

vi. *Documents requiring judge's signature.* Except where the court directs otherwise, any document that requires a judge's signature shall be transmitted electronically and in hard copy to the court. NY R UNIF TRIAL CTS § 202.5-b(d)(6).

vii. *Documents which would be inconvenient to file electronically; Hard copies.* Notwithstanding any other provision of NY R UNIF TRIAL CTS § 202.5-b, and subject to such guidelines as may be established by the Chief Administrative Judge, the County Clerk or his or her designee may require or permit a party to file in hard copy, in accordance with procedures set by the County Clerk or designee, an exhibit or other document which it is impractical or inconvenient to file electronically. NY R UNIF TRIAL CTS § 202.5-b(d)(7).

- *ERIE COUNTY.* Please contact the Supervisor of Actions & Proceedings, Erie County Clerk's Office by calling (716) 858-6662 or the Deputy County Clerk—Legal at (716) 858-6348 for information. NY R ERIE E FIL Doc. 3(III)(F).
- *KINGS COUNTY.* With limited exceptions, as set forth in the Uniform Rules and herein, all documents to be filed with the court in a NYSCEF case shall be filed online via the NYSCEF system. However, should the size, consistency or context of a hard copy document preclude electronic filing, the user shall electronically file a "Notice of Hard Copy Submission—E-Filed Cases" form EFM-3. Any hard copy submitted pursuant to NY R L KINGS E FIL Doc. 1(B)(9) shall include, as a cover page firmly fastened thereto, a copy of the Confirmation Notice received from the NYSCEF site confirming receipt of the "Notice of Hard Copy Submission—E-Filed Cases". Any party may object to such hard copy filing. The Court, in response to such objection, may, following the hard copy filing, fashion such relief as it deems appropriate pursuant to and in furtherance of the Uniform Rules and NY R L KINGS E FIL Doc. 1, including, but not limited to, an Order directing the filing party to file such documents online via the NYSCEF system. When exhibits are impractical to file pursuant to NY R UNIF TRIAL CTS § 202.5-b(d)(7), an additional "Notice of Hard Copy Exhibit Filing" form EFM-4 is required to be submitted. NY R L KINGS E FIL Doc. 1(B)(9).
- *NEW YORK COUNTY.* If a filer needs to submit unusual exhibits in original form that cannot practically be e-filed, such as oversized maps or electronic recordings, the filer should consult with the County Clerk's E-File Department by telephone at 646-386-3737 (procedural questions only) or by e-mail at ccnyef@nycourts.gov, which will normally require that the filer retain custody of the original subject to possible future directives of the court. NY R NY CTY E FIL Doc. 2(B)(10). In such instances, the filing counsel shall file with NYSCEF a "placeholder" in the form of a Notice of Hard Copy Exhibit Filing (NYSCEF Form EF 21). The Notice should be uploaded to NYSCEF as document type "Exhibit" and the filer should indicate in the "Additional Document Information" field that the filer is retaining custody of the original. Failure to e-file the Notice may result in a gap in the official record of the court. NY R NY CTY E FIL Doc. 2(B)(10).

viii. *Documents containing sensitive or proprietary information.* In an action subject to e-filing, any person may apply for an order prohibiting or restricting the electronic filing in the action of specifically identified materials on the grounds that such materials are subject to copyright or other proprietary rights, or trade secret or other privacy interests, and that electronic filing in the action is likely to result in substantial prejudice to those rights or interests. NY R UNIF TRIAL CTS § 202.5-b(k)(2).

ix. *Refusal to accept paper filings.* In accordance with NY CPLR Rule 2102(c), a County Clerk and a chief clerk of the Supreme Court or County Court, as appropriate, shall refuse to accept for filing papers filed in actions and proceedings when the paper sought to be filed:

- Is in an action subject to electronic filing pursuant to Rules of the Chief Administrator,
- Is not being filed electronically, and
- Does not include the notice required by NY R UNIF TRIAL CTS § 202.5-b(d)(1). NY R UNIF TRIAL CTS § 202.5(d)(1)(v); NY R UNIF TRIAL CTS § 202.5-bb(d).

x. *Emergency filings; Hard copies.* For information on when an emergency filing may be filed and served in hard copy, refer to NY R UNIF TRIAL CTS § 202.5-b(d)(1)(ii), NY R UNIF TRIAL CTS § 202.5-b(d)(1)(iii) and NY R UNIF TRIAL CTS § 202.5-bb(c)(3).

- *KINGS COUNTY.* Under the rules, a participating emergency e-filer must electronically file the documents initially filed in hard copy form within three (3) business days of the emergency filing; the originals will be discarded after the documents have been processed and the failure to e-file as required will therefore lead to an incomplete record. NY R L KINGS E FIL Doc. 1(B)(3).

- *NEW YORK COUNTY.* Occasionally an emergency will arise requiring expedited entry of a document with the County Clerk (e.g., an order issued in the courtroom after a conference or argument of a critical matter), such as for purposes of an immediate appeal. Expedition can be achieved by the Part as follows: the document should be carried by a Court Officer or staff member to the General Clerk's Office to assure immediate and proper recordation in the computer and, as appropriate, the posting of the document to NYSCEF or the Supreme Court Records On-Line Library ("Scroll"). The court will accommodate counsel in emergencies. NY R NY CTY Procedure XI(A).

xi. *Technical failures.* The NYSCEF site shall be considered to be subject to a technical failure on a given day if the site is unable to accept filings or provide access to filed documents continuously or intermittently over the course of any period of time greater than one (1) hour after 12:00 noon of that day. Notice of all such technical failures shall be provided on the site. NY R UNIF TRIAL CTS § 202.5-b(i).

- When e-filing is hindered by a technical failure, a party may file with the appropriate clerk and serve in hard copy. NY R UNIF TRIAL CTS § 202.5-b(i). In the event an attorney or party shall file and serve documents in hard copy pursuant to NY R UNIF TRIAL CTS § 202.5-b(i), each such document shall include the notice required by NY R UNIF TRIAL CTS § 202.5-b(d)(1), and the filer shall file those documents with the NYSCEF site within three (3) business days after restoration of normal operations at that site. NY R UNIF TRIAL CTS § 202.5-b(i).
- With the exception of deadlines that by law cannot be extended, the time for filing of any document that is delayed due to technical failure of the site shall be extended for one (1) day for each day on which such failure occurs, unless otherwise ordered by the court. NY R UNIF TRIAL CTS § 202.5-b(i).
- *ERIE COUNTY.* When filing by electronic means is hindered by a technical failure, please refer to the NY R UNIF TRIAL CTS § 202.5-b(i). NY R ERIE E FIL Doc. 3(III)(K).
- *KINGS COUNTY.* When filing by electronic means is hindered by a NYSCEF technical failure (as set forth in NY R UNIF TRIAL CTS § 202.5-b(i)), a party may file with the appropriate Clerk in hard copy. Except for deadlines that by law cannot be extended (e.g. Statute of limitations, Notice of Appeal), the time for filing of any document that is delayed due to technical failure of the NYSCEF system shall be extended for one day for each day on which such failure occurs, unless otherwise ordered by the court. NY R L KINGS E FIL Doc. 1(B)(13).
- *ONONDAGA COUNTY.* When filing by electronic means is hindered by a technical failure (as set forth in NY R UNIF TRIAL CTS § 202.5-b(h)(3)(i)), a party may file a hard copy with the County Clerk. With the exception of deadlines that by law cannot be extended (e.g., a statute of limitations or the deadline for filing a Notice of Appeal), the time for filing of any document that is delayed due to technical failure of the NYSCEF system will be extended for one day for each day on which such failure occurs, unless otherwise ordered by the court. A "Notice of Hard Copy Filing Submission—E-Filed Case' must accompany any documents not filed via NYSCEF. NY R ONDGA E FIL Protocol(B)(8).

xii. *Filing fees.* For information on what information must be provided to pay filing fees, refer to NY R UNIF TRIAL CTS § 202.5-b(d)(2).

xiii. *Exemption from e-filing.* For information on exemptions from e-filing, refer to NY R UNIF TRIAL CTS § 202.5-bb(e).

xiv. *Filing exhibits*

- *ERIE COUNTY.* In the NYSCEF system, each exhibit must be uploaded as a separate .pdf file. After uploading a primary document, please choose the document type "Exhibit" and enter the appropriate number or letter and a brief description of the exhibit; each exhibit should bear a separate cover sheet clearly marked as "Exhibit A," "Exhibit B," etc. "Exhibit A" or "Exhibit B" is unacceptable as a brief description of the exhibit. Exhibits, where referenced in a signed Order as attached or affixed shall be uploaded with the signed Order as one .pdf document. NY R ERIE E FIL Doc. 3(III)(H).
- *KINGS COUNTY.* In the NYSCEF system, each exhibit should be uploaded as a separate PDF file. After uploading a primary document, please choose the document type "Exhibit", enter the appropriate number or letter, and be sure to place a check mark to the right of "Attach to main document". Each exhibit shall bear a separate cover sheet clearly marked as Exhibit A, Exhibit B, etc. NY R L KINGS E FIL Doc. 1(B)(12).
- *NEW YORK COUNTY.* Attorneys submitting exhibits in NYSCEF cases should make each exhibit a separate attachment to an affidavit/affirmation in the system; i.e., exhibits should not be filed as a single

PDF-A together with the affidavit/affirmation or grouped together as a single PDF-A attachment because either of these two formats makes it difficult for the Justice to locate particular exhibits as needed. Counsel must also include appropriate descriptive language in the "Additional Document Information" field in NYSCEF. NY R NY CTY E FIL Doc. 2(D)(6).

- *ONONDAGA COUNTY.* All exhibits in e-filed cases must be e-filed individually as separate attachments. NY R ONDGA E FIL Protocol(B)(9)(b).

xv. *Correcting documents*

- *ERIE COUNTY.* Submission of documents which, upon examination, require correction or addition will result in notification to the filer advising that the document has been returned for correction. The filer shall make the required corrections and/or additions as indicated in the e-mail transmission sent by the County Clerk or Part Clerk through the NYSCEF site. The corrected documents may be resubmitted using the "Re-file this document" link highlighted in the filer's document list for the respective case. Please note that in the case of multiple submissions, all related documents filed at the same time may be removed from the case record and returned until all documents are properly submitted. NY R ERIE E FIL Doc. 3(III)(J).
- *KINGS COUNTY.* Submission of documents which, upon examination, require correction or addition will result in notification to the filer advising that there is a problem with a document. The filer shall make the required corrections and/or additions and resubmit the corrected document using the "Refile this document" link. In the event a document is returned for correction, the original file date will be preserved. For corrections of documents filed with the Kings County Clerk which require a court order, refer to the procedure in NY R UNIF TRIAL CTS § 202.5-b(d)(3)(iii) and NY R L KINGS E FIL Doc. 1(B)(11). NY R L KINGS E FIL Doc. 1(B)(3).
- *ONONDAGA COUNTY.* If there is an error or an additional document is required, the system will notify the filing party, who will make the corrections/additions and resubmit them online. NY R ONDGA E FIL Protocol(B)(6).
- *QUEENS COUNTY.* Generally speaking, documents that have been E-filed will not thereafter be deleted by the County Clerk from NYCEF because the filer asserts that the filing contains an error or a significant omission. When the filer wishes to correct a perceived error or omission in a filed document, he or she should file an amended version of the document, with the original remaining on file, or else obtain a court order providing for deletion of the original. The County Clerk will only delete a document upon request of the filer or on the County Clerk's own initiative when it is obvious from the face of the document alone that the filer made a fundamental error and never intended to file the document that was filed (e.g., a completely unrelated non-litigation document, a different case, or a wrong county). The County Clerk will advise the filer when any such fundamental errors are detected. NY R L QUEENS E-FILE Doc. 1(E)(6).

b. *Facsimile filing.* In the Supreme Court, facsimile filing shall be limited to commercial claims and tax certiorari, conservatorship, and mental hygiene proceedings in Monroe, Westchester, New York and Suffolk Counties. NY R UNIF TRIAL CTS § 202.5-a(a)(1). Refer to NY R UNIF TRIAL CTS § 202.5-a for information on the procedures for facsimile filing.

i. *NEW YORK COUNTY.* Unless indicated otherwise by the court in a particular case or in NY R NY CTY J RUL Doc. 1, Justices do not accept papers by fax. NY R NY CTY J RUL Rule 4.

c. *ERIE COUNTY. Filing request for judicial intervention.* An RJI in a NYSCEF case shall be filed via the NYSCEF system and will be filed after all other documents have been uploaded. The filer may choose between filing a .pdf image of the prepared RJI and any Addendum or having the system prepare the RJI which shall conform to Uniform Rules. Addenda, such as the Commercial Division Addendum, if prepared by the filer must be filed simultaneously with and attached to an RJI and uploaded as one .pdf document with the RJI. If the RJI is prepared by the e-filing system, no separate Addendum is required. Whether or not the filer elects to allow NYSCEF to create the RJI or chooses to upload a prepared RJI, data in addition to the nature of the judicial intervention, including information that appears on any Addenda will be collected through completion of the fields presented. If the filing of the RJI is accomplished through a filing agent, a prepared RJI and Addendum must be filed in lieu of the creation of the RJI by the NYSCEF system, as the RJI must be signed by the attorney. NY R ERIE E FIL Doc. 3(IV). For information on RJIs in specific types of action, refer to NY R ERIE E FIL Doc. 3(IV).

2. *Service requirements*

a. *Who may serve.* Except where otherwise prescribed by law or order of court, papers may be served by any person not a party of the age of eighteen years or over. NY CPLR Rule 2103(a).

b. *Service upon attorney.* Except where otherwise prescribed by law or order of court, papers to be served upon a party in a pending action shall be served upon the party's attorney. Where the same attorney appears for two or more parties, only one (1) copy need be served upon the attorney. Such service upon an attorney shall be made:

i. By delivering the paper to the attorney personally. NY CPLR Rule 2103(b)(1).

ii. By mailing the paper to the attorney at the address designated by that attorney for that purpose or, if none is designated, at the attorney's last known address; service by mail shall be complete upon mailing. NY CPLR Rule 2103(b)(2).

iii. If the attorney's office is open, by leaving the paper with a person in charge, or if no person is in charge, by leaving it in a conspicuous place; or if the attorney's office is not open, by depositing the paper, enclosed in a sealed wrapper directed to the attorney, in the attorney's office letter drop or box. NY CPLR Rule 2103(b)(3).

iv. By leaving it at the attorney's residence within the state with a person of suitable age and discretion. Service upon an attorney shall not be made at the attorney's residence unless service at the attorney's office cannot be made. NY CPLR Rule 2103(b)(4).

v. By transmitting the paper to the attorney by facsimile transmission, provided that a facsimile telephone number is designated by the attorney for that purpose. Service by facsimile transmission shall be complete upon the receipt by the sender of a signal from the equipment of the attorney served indicating that the transmission was received, and the mailing of a copy of the paper to that attorney. The designation of a facsimile telephone number in the address block subscribed on a paper served or filed in the course of an action or proceeding shall constitute consent to service by facsimile transmission in accordance with NY CPLR Rule 2103(b)(5). An attorney may change or rescind a facsimile telephone number by serving a notice on the other parties. NY CPLR Rule 2103(b)(5).

vi. By dispatching the paper to the attorney by overnight delivery service at the address designated by the attorney for that purpose or, if none is designated, at the attorney's last known address. Service by overnight delivery service shall be complete upon deposit of the paper enclosed in a properly addressed wrapper into the custody of the overnight delivery service for overnight delivery, prior to the latest time designated by the overnight delivery service for overnight delivery. "Overnight delivery service" means any delivery service which regularly accepts items for overnight delivery to any address in the state. NY CPLR Rule 2103(b)(6).

vii. By transmitting the paper to the attorney by electronic means where and in the manner authorized by the chief administrator of the courts by rule and, unless such rule shall otherwise provide, such transmission shall be upon the party's written consent. The subject matter heading for each paper sent by electronic means must indicate that the matter being transmitted electronically is related to a court proceeding. NY CPLR Rule 2103(b)(7).

- *KINGS COUNTY.* Pursuant to the E-Filing Rules, service of interlocutory documents is made by posting a document to the NYSCEF site, which automatically and immediately transmits an email notice of the filing, including a link to the document, to all participating counsel and unrepresented litigants on the case. The Rules also authorize service by other methods permitted by the CPLR. If service by such other method is made, proof of service must be filed with NYSCEF. NY R L KINGS E FIL Doc. 1(I).
- *NEW YORK COUNTY.* Service. . .will be made automatically through NYSCEF upon all participating counsel and unrepresented parties in the case. There are limited exceptions to the requirement for e-filing in the covered kinds of cases. NY R NY CTY Procedure XI(A). Pursuant to the E-Filing Rules, service of interlocutory documents is made by posting a document to the NYSCEF site, which automatically and immediately transmits an e-mail notice of the filing, including a link to the document, to all participating counsel and unrepresented litigants on the case. The Rules also authorize service by other methods permitted by the CPLR. If service by such a method is made, proof of service must be filed with NYSCEF. NY R NY CTY E FIL Doc. 2(I).
- *QUEENS COUNTY.* Filing with the system permits counsel to serve the papers electronically pursuant to NY R UNIF TRIAL CTS § 202.5-b(f) once consent to E-Filing has been filed on-line. Consult NY R UNIF TRIAL CTS § 202.5-bb(c) for service in mandatory e-filing. Any required proof of service should be E-filed as a separate document. NY R L QUEENS E-FILE Doc. 1(E)(4).

c. *Electronic service mandatory; Consenting to electronic service; How electronic service may be made.* Except as otherwise provided in NY R UNIF TRIAL CTS § 202.5-bb, filing and service of all documents in an action that has been commenced electronically in accordance with NY R UNIF TRIAL CTS § 202.5-bb shall be by electronic means. NY R UNIF TRIAL CTS § 202.5-bb(c)(1).

i. *Party's consent required for certain e-filing.* After commencement of an action wherein e-filing is authorized, documents may be electronically filed and served, but only by, and electronic service shall be made only upon, a party or parties who have consented thereto. NY R UNIF TRIAL CTS § 202.5-b(b)(2)(i).

- A consent to e-filing in an action shall state that the party providing it agrees to the use of e-filing in the action and to be bound by the filing and service provisions in NY R UNIF TRIAL CTS § 202.5-b. NY R UNIF TRIAL CTS § 202.5-b(b)(2)(ii).

ii. *Address for service; Duty to notify as to changes.* The e-mail service address recorded at the time of registration is the e-mail address at which service of interlocutory documents on that party may be made through notification transmitted by the NYSCEF site. It is the responsibility of each filing user to monitor that address and promptly notify the Resource Center in the event of a change in his or her e-mail service address. NY R UNIF TRIAL CTS § 202.5-b(f)(2)(i).

iii. *How service made.* An e-filing party causes service of an interlocutory document to be made upon another party participating in e-filing by filing the document electronically. Upon receipt of an interlocutory document, the NYSCEF site shall automatically transmit electronic notification to all e-mail service addresses in such action. NY R UNIF TRIAL CTS § 202.5-b(f)(2)(ii).

- Except as provided otherwise in NY R UNIF TRIAL CTS § 202.5-b(h)(3), the electronic transmission of the notification shall constitute service of the document on the e-mail service addresses identified therein; however, such service will not be effective if the filing party learns that the notification did not reach the address of the person to be served. Proof of such service will be recorded on the NYSCEF site. A party may, however, utilize other service methods permitted by the CPLR provided that, if one of such other methods is used, proof of that service shall be filed electronically. NY R UNIF TRIAL CTS § 202.5-b(f)(2)(ii).

iv. *Signatures on hard copies; Proof of service filed electronically.* When an e-filing party serves a document in hard copy on a non-participating party, the document served shall bear full signatures of all signatories and proof of such service shall be filed electronically. NY R UNIF TRIAL CTS § 202.5-b(b)(2)(i).

- *ERIE COUNTY.* In the NYSCEF system, each Affidavit of Service must be uploaded as a separate .pdf file. After uploading the Affidavit, please choose the document type: "Affirmation/Affidavit of Service" and enter the name of the party served as Additional Document Information. NY R ERIE E FIL Doc. 3(III)(I).

v. *Effect of failure to consent.* A party's failure to consent to participation in electronic filing and service shall not bar any other party to the action from filing documents electronically with the County Clerk and the court or serving documents upon any other party who has consented to participation. A party who has not consented to participation shall file documents with the court and the County Clerk, and serve and be served with documents, in hard copy. NY R UNIF TRIAL CTS § 202.5-b(b)(2)(i).

d. *Service upon party.* If a party has not appeared by an attorney or the party's attorney cannot be served, service shall be upon the party by a method specified in NY CPLR Rule 2103(b)(1), NY CPLR Rule 2103(b)(2), NY CPLR Rule 2103(b)(4), NY CPLR Rule 2103(b)(5) or NY CPLR Rule 2103(b)(6). NY CPLR Rule 2103(c).

e. *Service on all parties.* Each paper served on any party shall be served on every other party who has appeared, except as otherwise may be provided by court order or as provided in NY CPLR § 3012 or in NY CPLR § 3215(f). Upon demand by a party, the plaintiff shall supply that party with a list of those who have appeared and the names and addresses of their attorneys. NY CPLR Rule 2103(e).

f. *Service by filing.* If a paper cannot be served by any of the methods specified in NY CPLR Rule 2103(b) and NY CPLR Rule 2103(c), service may be made by filing the paper as if it were a paper required to be filed. NY CPLR Rule 2103(d).

g. *Definitions.* For the purposes of NY CPLR Rule 2103:

i. "Mailing" means the deposit of a paper enclosed in a first class postpaid wrapper, addressed to the address designated by a person for that purpose or, if none is designated, at that person's last known address, in a post office or official depository under the exclusive care and custody of the United States Postal Service within the state;

ii. "Electronic means" means any method of transmission of information between computers or other machines designed for the purpose of sending and receiving such transmissions, and which allows the recipient to reproduce the information transmitted in a tangible medium of expression;

iii. "Facsimile transmission" means any method of transmission of documents to a facsimile machine at a remote location which can automatically produce a tangible copy of such documents. NY CPLR Rule 2103(f).

G. Hearings

1. There is no hearing required or contemplated in the New York rules governing the pretrial conferences.

H. Forms

1. Official Pretrial Conferences, Scheduling, Management Forms for New York

a. Request for judicial intervention. NY R UNIF TRIAL CTS § 202.6.

b. Note of issue. NY R UNIF TRIAL CTS § 202.21(b).

c. Certificate of readiness for trial. NY R UNIF TRIAL CTS § 202.21(b).

d. Notice of medical, dental or podiatric malpractice action. NY R UNIF TRIAL CTS § 202.56.

e. Preliminary conference stipulation and order. NY R UNIF TRIAL CTS App. D(1).

f. Preliminary conference stipulation and order for commercial cases. NY R UNIF TRIAL CTS App. D(2).

2. New York Pretrial Conferences, Scheduling, Management Forms

a. Request for preliminary conference. MCF CPLR § 7:4.

b. Preliminary conference stipulation and order for supreme and county courts; Noncommercial cases; Official form. MCF CPLR § 7:5.

c. Preliminary conference stipulation and order for supreme court; Commercial cases; Official form. MCF CPLR § 7:6.

d. Physician's affidavit in support of request for expedited preliminary conference in personal injury action involving terminally ill party. MCF CPLR § 7:14.

I. Applicable Rules

1. *State rules*

a. Short title; Application; Construction; Definitions. NY CPLR § 101; NY CPLR § 104; NY CPLR § 105.

b. Appendix of official forms. NY CPLR § 107.

c. Extensions of time generally. NY CPLR § 2004.

d. Form of papers. NY CPLR Rule 2101; NY CPLR Rule 2102; NY CPLR § 2105; NY GEN BUS § 399-ddd; NY R UNIF TRIAL CTS § 215.2; NY R UNIF TRIAL CTS § 215.3.

e. Service of papers. NY CPLR Rule 2103.

f. Computation of time. NY CPLR § 2402; NY GEN CONSTR § 19; NY GEN CONSTR § 20; NY GEN CONSTR § 25-a; NY GEN CONSTR § 30; NY GEN CONSTR § 31; NY GEN CONSTR § 53.

g. Court determination. NY CPLR Rule 3036.

h. Preliminary conferences in specific actions. NY CPLR Rule 3406; NY CPLR Rule 3407; NY R UNIF TRIAL CTS § 202.12-a.

i. Index number fees of county clerks. NY CPLR § 8018.

j. Hours of court. NY R CHIEF J § 3.1.

k. Application of part; Waiver; Additional rules; Application of CPLR; Definitions. NY R UNIF TRIAL CTS § 202.1.

l. Papers filed in court; Electronic filing in supreme court. NY R UNIF TRIAL CTS § 202.5; NY R UNIF TRIAL CTS § 202.5-a; NY R UNIF TRIAL CTS § 202.5-b; NY R UNIF TRIAL CTS § 202.5-bb.

m. Request for judicial intervention. NY R UNIF TRIAL CTS § 202.6.

n. Motion procedure. NY R UNIF TRIAL CTS § 202.8.

o. Preliminary conference. NY R UNIF TRIAL CTS § 202.12.

p. Differentiated case management. NY R UNIF TRIAL CTS § 202.19.

q. Pretrial conference. NY R UNIF TRIAL CTS § 202.26; NY R UNIF TRIAL CTS § 202.31; NY R UNIF TRIAL CTS § 202.35.

r. Rules of the commercial division of the Supreme Court. NY R UNIF TRIAL CTS § 202.70.

s. Signing of papers. NY R CHIEF ADMIN § 130-1.1-a.

2. *Local rules*
   a. *Albany County*
      i. Third judicial district rules. NY R 3 JD SUP Doc. 1.
   b. *Bronx County*
      i. Commercial division. NY R BRONX FIL R Doc. 12.
   c. *Erie County*
      i. Request for judicial intervention. NY R BRONX FIL R Doc. 2.
      ii. Requests for preliminary conference. NY R BRONX FIL R Doc. 4.
      iii. Preliminary conferences. NY R BRONX FIL R Doc. 9.
      iv. Joint protocols for New York State Courts E-Filing (NYSCEF) cases filed in Supreme Court, Erie County. NY R ERIE E FIL Doc. 3.
      v. Differentiated case management. NY R BRONX DCM Doc. 1.
   d. *Kings County*
      i. Papers. NY R L KINGS Pt. A, Papers.
      ii. Scheduling of preliminary conference. NY R L KINGS Pt. B, Rule 1.
      iii. Preparation for preliminary conference. NY R L KINGS Pt. B, Rule 3.
      iv. Enforcement of orders. NY R L KINGS Pt. B, Rule 4.
      v. Filing of note of issue. NY R L KINGS Pt. D, Rule 1.
      vi. Purpose of compliance conference. NY R L KINGS Pt. E, Rule 1.
      vii. Appearance at compliance conference. NY R L KINGS Pt. E, Rule 2.
      viii. Pre calendar procedures. NY R L KINGS Rule I.
      ix. Protocol on courthouse and county clerk procedures for electronically filed cases. NY R L KINGS E FIL Doc. 1.
   e. *New York County*
      i. Commencement of cases. NY R NY CTY Procedure I.
      ii. RJIs and assignments. NY R NY CTY Procedure IA.
      iii. Motions and special proceedings by notice of motion/petition. NY R NY CTY Procedure II.
      iv. Conferences & case management. NY R NY CTY Procedure V.
      v. County clerk litigation functions. NY R NY CTY Procedure XI.
      vi. Protocol on courthouse and county clerk procedures for electronically filed cases. NY R NY CTY E FIL Doc. 2.
      vii. Redaction of information in documents filed with the county clerk and the court. NY R NY CTY J RUL Rule A-1.
      viii. Appearances by counsel; Knowledge and authority. NY R NY CTY J RUL Rule 1.
      ix. Papers by fax. NY R NY CTY J RUL Rule 4.
      x. Preliminary conferences; Requests. NY R NY CTY J RUL Rule 5.
      xi. Consultation prior to preliminary and compliance conferences. NY R NY CTY J RUL Rule 7.
      xii. Pretrial conference. NY R NY CTY J RUL Rule 19.
   f. *Onondaga County*
      i. Onondaga county protocol for case filings New York State Electronic Files (NYSCEF). NY R ONDGA E FIL Protocol.
   g. *Queens County*
      i. Final pre-trial conference. NY R ONDGA JURY TRIAL Rule 1.
      ii. Stipulations. NY R ONDGA JURY TRIAL Rule 8.

iii. Final pre-trial conference. NY R ONDGA NON JURY TRIAL Rule 1.

iv. Stipulations. NY R ONDGA NON JURY TRIAL Rule 8.

v. Queens county protocol on courthouse procedures for electronically filed cases. NY R L QUEENS E-FILE Doc. 1.

J. Miscellaneous

NOTE: Individual judges' rules may apply.

ALBANY COUNTY

JUSTICE LISA M. FISHER: NY R 3 JD FISHER Fisher; NY R 3 JD FISHER Fisher, PC Order.

JUSTICE RICHARD MOTT: NY R 3 JD MOTT Mott.

JUSTICE STEPHAN G. SCHICK: NY R 3 JD Schick.

FORECLOSURE SETTLEMENT PART: NY R 3 JD Foreclosure Settlement.

BRONX COUNTY

JUSTICE PAUL L. ALPERT: [NY R BRONX J Part IA-29, as amended by NY ORDER 20-0337].

JUSTICE BEN BARBATO: NY R BRONX J Part IA-21.

JUSTICE MARY ANNE BRIGANTTI: [NY R BRONX J Part IA-15, as amended by NY ORDER 20-0338].

JUSTICE JOSEPH E. CAPELLA: NY R BRONX J Part IA-23.

JUSTICE MITCHELL DANZIGER: NY R BRONX J Part IA-3/33 ; [NY R BRONX J Danziger, Part IA-3/33, as amended by NY ORDER 20-0339].

JUSTICE LAURA G. DOUGLAS: NY R BRONX J Part IA-11.

JUSTICE RUBEN FRANCO: NY R BRONX J Part IA-26.

JUSTICE DORIS M. GONZALEZ: NY R BRONX J Part IA-24.

JUSTICE WILMA GUZMAN: NY R BRONX J Part IA-7; [NY R BRONX J Guzman, Part IA-7 Virtual, as amended by NY ORDER 20-0340].

JUSTICE ROBERT T. JOHNSON: NY R BRONX J Part IA-12.

JUSTICE DONALD A. MILES: NY R BRONX J Part IA-8.

JUSTICE DONNA M. MILLS: NY R BRONX J Part IA-9.

JUSTICE JULIA I. RODRIGUEZ: NY R BRONX J Part IA-18; [NY R BRONX J Part IA-27, as amended by NY ORDER 20-0341].

JUSTICE LLINET M. ROSADO: [NY R BRONX J Part IA-25, as amended by NY ORDER 20-0342].

JUSTICE NORMA RUIZ: NY R BRONX J Part IA-22; [NY R BRONX J Ruiz, Part IA-22 Virtual, as amended by NY ORDER 20-0343].

JUSTICE HOWARD H. SHERMAN: NY R BRONX J Part IA-4.

JUSTICE FERNANDO TAPIA: NY R BRONX J Part IA-13.

JUSTICE ELIZABETH A. TAYLOR: NY R BRONX J Part IA-2.

JUSTICE ALISON Y. TRUITT: NY R BRONX J Part IA-5.

PART IDV: NY R BRONX J Doc. 1.

PRE-TRIAL PART RULES: NY R BRONX J Doc. 2.

PRE TRIAL WORKSHEET: NY R BRONX J Doc. 3.

FORECLOSURE SETTLEMENT PART RULES: NY R BRONX J Doc. 4.

GUARDIANSHIP PART RULES: NY R BRONX J Doc. 5.

LPM PART RULES: NY R BRONX J Doc. 6.

ERIE COUNTY

JUSTICE M. WILLIAM BOLLER: NY R 8 JD J Boller.

JUSTICE RALPH A. BONIELLO: NY R 8 JD J Boniello.
JUSTICE CHRISTOPHER J. BURN: NY R 8 JD J Burns.
JUSTICE RUSSELL P. BUSCAGLIA: NY R 8 JD J Buscaglia.
JUSTICE FRANK CARUSO: NY R 8 JD J Caruso.
JUSTICE STEPHEN W. CASS: NY R 8 JD J Cass.
JUSTICE DEBORAH A. CHIMES: NY R 8 JD J Chimes.
JUSTICE EMILIO COLAIACOVO: [NY R 8 JD J Colaiacovo, as amended by NY ORDER 20-0252].
JUSTICE DIANE Y. DEVLIN: NY R 8 JD J Devlin.
JUSTICE JAMES H. DILLON: NY R 8 JD J Dillon.
JUSTICE PAULA L. FEROLETO: NY R 8 JD J Feroleto.
JUSTICE DANIEL J. FURLONG: [NY R 8 JD J Furlong, as amended by NY ORDER 20-0253].
JUSTICE JOSEPH R. GLOWNIA: NY R 8 JD J Glownia.
JUSTICE MARK J. GRISANTI: NY R 8 JD J Grisanti.
JUSTICE DEBORAH A. HAENDIGES: NY R 8 JD J Haendiges.
JUSTICE LYNN W. KEANE: [NY R 8 JD J Keane, as amended by NY ORDER 20-0254].
JUSTICE RICHARD C. KLOCH, Sr.: NY R 8 JD J Kloch.
JUSTICE FREDERICK J. MARSHALL: [NY R 8 JD J Marshall, as amended by NY ORDER 20-0255.
JUSTICE JOHN L. MICHALSKI: NY R 8 JD J Michalski.
JUSTICE MARK A. MONTOUR: [NY R 8 JD J Montour, as amended by NY ORDER 20-0256].
JUSTICE HENRY NOWAK: NY R 8 JD J Nowak.
JUSTICE JOHN F. O'DONNELL: NY R 8 JD J O'Donnell.
JUSTICE JEANETTE OGDEN: NY R 8 JD J Ogden.
JUSTICE CATHERINE NUGENT-PANEPINTO: NY R 8 JD J Nugent-Panepinto.
JUSTICE FRANK A. SEDITA, III: [NY R 8 JD J Sedita, as amended by NY ORDER 20-0257].
JUSTICE SARA SHELDON: NY R 8 JD J Sheldon.
JUSTICE DONNA M. SIWEK: NY R 8 JD J Siwek.
JUSTICE MARY L. SLISZ: NY R 8 JD J Slisz.
JUSTICE TIMOTHY J. WALKER: [NY R 8 JD J Walker, as amended by NY ORDER 20-0258].
JUSTICE DENNIS E. WARD: NY R 8 JD J Ward.
JUSTICE PAUL B. WOJTASZEK: [NY R 8 JD J Wojtaszek, as amended by NY ORDER 20-0259].
JUSTICE CHARLES N. ZAMBITO: [NY R 8 JD J Zambito, as amended by NY ORDER 20-0260].
SUPREME COURT LEGAL STAFF: NY R 8 JD J Legal Staff.

KINGS COUNTY

JUSTICE RACHEL A. ADAMS: NY R KINGS J Part 5F.
JUSTICE LOREN BAILY-SCHIFFMAN: NY R KINGS J Part 65.
JUSTICE REGINALD A. BODDIE: NY R KINGS J Part 95.
JUSTICE THERESA M. CICCOTTO: NY R KINGS J Part 19; NY R KINGS J Part 5J.
JUSTICE LISSETTE COLON: NY R KINGS J Part Rules.
JUSTICE GENINE EDWARDS: NY R KINGS J Part 80.
JUSTICE PAMELA L. FISHER: [NY R KINGS J Part 94, as amended by NY ORDER 20-0208].
JUSTICE ROBIN GARSON: NY R KINGS J Part 75.
JUSTICE LARA J. GENOVISI: [NY R KINGS J Part 34, as amended by NY ORDER 20-0209].

JUSTICE BERNARD J. GRAHAM: NY R KINGS J Part 36.
JUSTICE DAWN JIMENEZ-SALTA: NY R KINGS J Part 88.
JUSTICE INGRID JOSEPH: [NY R KINGS J Part FRP3 and Part 83, as amended by NY ORDER 20-0210].
JUSTICE KATHY J. KING: NY R KINGS J Part 64, 76K.
JUSTICE LAWRENCE KNIPEL: NY R KINGS J Part 57.
JUSTICE DONALD KURTZ: NY R KINGS J Part 26.
JUSTICE CARL LANDICINO: [NY R KINGS J Part 81, as amended by NY ORDER 20-0211].
JUSTICE KATHERINE LEVINE: [NY R KINGS J Part 20, 25, 92, as amended by NY ORDER 20-0211].
JUSTICE LORNA MCALLISTER: [NY R KINGS J Part 10, as amended by NY ORDER 20-0211].
JUSTICE ROSEMARIE MONTALBANO: [NY R KINGS J Part 19, 71, and 22, as amended by NY ORDER 20-0211].
JUSTICE RICHARD J. MONTELIONE: [NY R KINGS J Part 99 and DJMP, as amended by NY ORDER 20-0215].
JUSTICE LISA S. OTTLEY: NY R KINGS J Part 24.
JUSTICE MARK I. PARTNOW: NY R KINGS J Part 43.
JUSTICE ERIC I. PRUS: NY R KINGS J Part 5A.
JUSTICE FRANCOIS RIVERA: NY R KINGS J Part 52.
JUSTICE KAREN B. ROTHENBERG: NY R KINGS J Part 35.
JUSTICE LEON RUCHELSMAN: NY R KINGS J Part 1.
JUSTICE WAYNE P. SAITTA: NY R KINGS J Part 29.
JUSTICE ROBIN K. SHEARES: NY R KINGS J Part 96.
JUSTICE KENNETH P. SHERMAN: NY R KINGS J Part 67 and 78.
JUSTICE DEBRA SILBER: NY R KINGS J Part 9 and 5K.
JUSTICE ELLEN M. SPODEK: NY R KINGS J Part 63.
JUSTICE MARSHA L. STEINHARDT: NY R KINGS J Part 15.
JUSTICE JEFFREY S. SUNSHINE: NY R KINGS J Part 5G.
JUSTICE PETER P. SWEENEY: [NY R KINGS J Part 35, as amended by NY ORDER 20-0218].
JUSTICE DELORES J. THOMAS: [NY R KINGS J Part 5T, as amended by NY ORDER 20-0221].
JUSTICE WAVNY TOUSSAINT: NY R KINGS J Part 70.
JUSTICE RICHARD VELASQUEZ: NY R KINGS J Part 66.
JUSTICE CAROLYN E. WADE: NY R KINGS J Part 84.
JUSTICE EDWARD G. WALKER: [NY R KINGS J Part 90, as amended by NY ORDER 20-0219].
JUSTICE LILLIAN WAN: [NY R KINGS J Part 17, as amended by NY ORDER 20-0220].
JUSTICE MICHELLE WESTON: NY R KINGS J Part 3.
MENTAL HYGIENE PART: NY R KINGS J Part 77.
MATRIMONIAL PARTS DURING COVID-19 EMERGENCY: JUSTICE KAREN B. ROTHENBERG: NY R KINGS J Doc. 1.

NASSAU COUNTY

JUSTICE ANNA R. ANZALONE: NY R NASSAU S J Anzalone, Part 26.
JUSTICE STACY D. BENNETT: NY R NASSAU S J Bennett; NY R NASSAU S J Bennett, Form 1.
JUSTICE ANTONIO BRANDVEEN: NY R NASSAU S J Brandveen, Part 31.
JUSTICE JEFFREY S. BROWN: [NY R NASSAU S J Brown, as amended by NY ORDER 20-0297].
JUSTICE STEPHEN A. BUCARIA: NY R NASSAU S J Bucaria.
JUSTICE JULIANNE T. CAPETOLA: NY R NASSAU S J Capetola, Part 28.
JUSTICE EDMUND M. DANE: NY R NASSAU S J Dane, Part 33.

JUSTICE VITO M. DESTEFANO: NY R NASSAU S J DeStefano, Part 13; NY R NASSAU S J DeStefano, Form 1.

JUSTICE ARTHUR M. DIAMOND: NY R NASSAU S J Diamond, Part 7.

JUSTICE THOMAS FEINMAN: NY R NASSAU S J Feinman, Part 5.

JUSTICE JOHN M. GALASSO: NY R NASSAU S J Galasso, Part 22.

JUSTICE SHARON M.J. GIANELLI: NY R NASSAU S J Gianelli, Part 22; NY R NASSAU S J Gianelli, Form 1.

JUSTICE JEFFREY A. GOODSTEIN: NY R NASSAU S J Goodstein, Part 33; NY R NASSAU S J Goodstein, Form 1.

JUSTICE DAVID J. GUGERTY: [NY R NASSAU S J Gugerty, Part 31, as amended by NY ORDER 20-0298].

JUSTICE HELENE F. GUGERTY: NY R NASSAU S J Gugerty, Part 47.

JUSTICE STEVEN M. JAEGER: NY R NASSAU S J Jaeger, Part 35; NY R NASSAU S J Jaeger, Form 1.

JUSTICE JACK L. LIBERT: NY R NASSAU S J Libert, Part 23.

JUSTICE JOSEPH H. LORINTZ: NY R NASSAU S J Lorintz, Part 26; NY R NASSAU S J Lorintz, Form 1.

JUSTICE ROY S. MAHON: NY R NASSAU S J Mahon, Part 3.

JUSTICE RANDY SUE MARBER: NY R NASSAU S J Marber, Part 8.

JUSTICE JAMES P. MCCORMACK: [NY R NASSAU S J McCormack, Part 18, as amended by NY ORDER, 20-0299].

JUSTICE DICCIA T. PINEDA-KIRWAN: [NY R NASSAU S J Pineda-Kirwan, as amended by NY ORDER 20-0300].

JUSTICE THOMAS RADEMAKER: [NY R NASSAU S J Rademaker, Part 28, as amended by NY ORDER 20-0301]; [NY R NASSAU S J Rademaker, Form 1, as amended by NY ORDER 20-0301].

JUSTICE DENISE L. SHER: NY R NASSAU S J Rademaker, Part 32.

JUSTICE LEONARD D. STEINMAN: [NY R NASSAU S J Steinman, Part 15, as amended by NY ORDER 20-0303]; NY R NASSAU S J Steinman, Form 1.

JUSTICE HOWARD E. STURIM: NY R NASSAU S J Sturim, Part 50; NY R NASSAU S J Sturim, Form 1.

JUSTICE HELEN VOUTSINAS: [NY R NASSAU S J Voutsinas, Part 25, as amended by NY ORDER 20-0304]; [NY R NASSAU S J Voutsinas, Form 1, as amended by NY ORDER 20-0305].

JUSTICE HOPE SCHWARTZ ZIMMERMAN: NY R NASSAU S J Zimmerman, Part 17.

NEW YORK COUNTY

JUDGE'S RULES; BASIC INFORMATION: [NY R NY CTY J RUL Doc. 1, as amended by NY ORDER 20-0202].

ONONDAGA COUNTY

JUSTICE ROBERT E. ANTONACCI II: [NY R ONDGA E FIL Doc. 1, as amended by 20-0239].

JUSTICE MICHAEL V. COCCOMI: NY R ONDGA E FIL Doc. 2.

JUSTICE GREGORY R. GILBERT: NY R 5 JD JUDGES Gilbert; NY R ONDGA E FIL Doc. 3.

JUSTICE DONALD A. GREENWOOD: NY R ONDGA E FIL Doc. 4.

JUSTICE DEBORAH H. KARALUNAS: NY R ONDGA E FIL Doc. 5.

JUSTICE JAMES MCCLUSKY: NY R 5 JD MCCLUSKY McClusky.

JUSTICE CHARLES C. MERRELL: NY R 5 JD MERRELL Merrell.

JUSTICE PATRICK F. MACRAE: NY R 5 JD MACRAE Doc. 1.

JUSTICE JAMES P. MURPHY: NY R ONDGA E FIL Doc. 7.

JUSTICE GERALD J. NERI: [NY R 5 JD JUDGES Neri, as amended by NY ORDER 20-0236]; [NY R ONDGA E FIL Doc. 8, as amended by NY ORDER 20-0241].

JUSTICE ANTHONY J. PARIS: NY R 5 JD JUDGES Paris; [NY R ONDGA E FIL Doc. 9, as amended by NY ORDER 20-0242].

JUSTICE NORMAN W. SEITER, JR.: NY R 5 JD JUDGES Seiter.

JUSTICE KEVIN G. YOUNG: [NY R ONDGA E FIL Doc. 10, as amended by NY ORDER 20-0243].

QUEENS COUNTY

JUSTICE PAM JACKMAN BROWN: [NY R L QUEENS Brown, Part 19, as amended by NY ORDER 20-0321].

JUSTICE CHEREE A. BUGGS: NY R L QUEENS Buggs, Part 30.

JUSTICE PAM JACKMAN BROWN: [NY R L QUEENS Brown, Part 19, as amended by NY ORDER 20-0321].

JUSTICE DENIS J. BUTLER: NY R L QUEENS Butler, Part 12.

JUSTICE ROBERT I. CALORAS: [NY R L QUEENS Caloras, Part 36, as amended by NY ORDER 20-0322].

JUSTICE ANNA CULLEY: NY R L QUEENS Culley, Part 53.

JUSTICE TIMOTHY DUFFICY: NY R L QUEENS Dufficy, Part 35.

JUSTICE DAVID ELLIOT: NY R L QUEENS Elliot, Part 14.

JUSTICE JOSEPH J. ESPOSITO: NY R L QUEENS Esposito, Part 6.

JUSTICE DARRELL L. GAVRIN: [NY R L QUEENS Gavrin, Part 27, as amended by NY ORDER 20-0323].

JUSTICE WYATT N. GIBBONS: [NY R L QUEENS Gibbons, Part 5, as amended by NY ORDER 20-0330.

JUSTICE DONNA-MARIE E. GOLIA: [NY R L QUEENS Golia, Part 21, as amended by NY ORDER 20-0331].

JUSTICE MARGUERITE A. GRAYS: [NY R L QUEENS Grays, Part 4, as amended by NY ORDER 20-0324].

JUSTICE RUDOLPH E. GRECO: [NY R L QUEENS Greco, Part 32, as amended by NY ORDER 20-0325].

JUSTICE MAUREEN HEALY: NY R L QUEENS Healy, Part 6.

JUSTICE PHILLIP HOM: [NY R L QUEENS Hom, Part 43, as amended by NY ORDER 20-0332].

JUSTICE KEVIN J. KERRIGAN: NY R L QUEENS Kerrigan, Part 10.

JUSTICE MOJGAN C. LANCMAN: NY R L QUEENS Lancman, Part 20.

JUSTICE RICHARD G. LATIN: NY R L QUEENS Latin, Part 40.

JUSTICE ULYSSES B. LEVERETT: [NY R L QUEENS Leverett, Part 6, as amended by NY ORDER 20-0326].

JUSTICE LEONARD LIVOTE: NY R L QUEENS Livote, Part 33.

JUSTICE LEE A. MAYERSOHN: NY R L QUEENS Mayersohn, Part 22; NY R L QUEENS Mayersohn, Part 22G; [NY R L QUEENS Mayersohn, Part 22G COVID, as amended by NY ORDER 20-0327].

JUSTICE ROBERT J. MCDONALD: NY R L QUEENS McDonald, Part 34.

JUSTICE MARGARET MCGOWAN: NY R L QUEENS McGowan, Part 52.

JUSTICE MAURICE E. MUIR: [NY R L QUEENS Muir, Part 42, as amended by NY ORDER 20-0333].

JUSTICE JODI ORLOW: NY R L QUEENS Orlow, Part 51.

JUSTICE LESLIE J. PURIFICCION: NY R L QUEENS Purificcion, Part 39.

JUSTICE JOSEPH RISI: [NY R L QUEENS Risi, Part 3, as amended by NY ORDER 20-0328].

JUSTICE FREDERICK D.R. SAMPSON: [NY R L QUEENS Sampson, Part 31, as amended by NY ORDER 20-0329].

JUSTICE MARTIN J. SCHULMAN: NY R L QUEENS Schulman, Part 29.

JUSTICE BERNICE D. SIEGAL: NY R L QUEENS Siegal, Part 25G.

JUSTICE JANICE A. TAYLOR: NY R L QUEENS Taylor, Part 15.

JUSTICE CARMEN R. VELASQUEZ: NY R L QUEENS Velasquez, Part 38.

JUSTICE LOURDES M VENTURA: [NY R L QUEENS Ventura, Part 37, as amended by NY ORDER 20-0334].

JUSTICE WILLIAM A. VISCOVICH: NY R L QUEENS Viscovich, Part 63.

JUSTICE ALLAN B. WEISS: NY R L QUEENS Weiss, Part 2.

COMPLIANCE, SETTLEMENT AND CONFERENCE PART: NY R L QUEENS Doc 1.

PRELIMINARY CONFERENCE PART: [NY R L QUEENS Doc. 2, as amended by NY ORDER 20-0335].

MEDICAL MALPRACTICE CONFERENCE PART: [NY R L QUEENS Doc. 3, as amended by NY ORDER 20-0336].

TRIAL SCHEDULING PART: NY R L QUEENS Doc. 4.

SUMMARY JURY TRIAL PROGRAM: NY R L QUEENS Doc. 7.

RESIDENTIAL FORECLOSURE PART: NY R L QUEENS Doc. 9.

FORECLOSURE AUCTION RULES: NY R L QUEENS Doc. 10.
MATRIMONIAL PRELIMINARY CONFERENCE PART: NY R L QUEENS Doc. 11.
NON-CUSTODIAL CONTESTED MATRIMONIAL PART: NY R L QUEENS Doc. 12.

Requests, Notices and Applications
Request for a Mental or Physical Examination of Witness

Document Last Updated August 2020

A. Checklist

(I) ❑ Matters to be considered by requesting party
- (a) ❑ Required documents
  - (1) ❑ Request for a mental or physical examination
  - (2) ❑ Proof of service
- (b) ❑ Supplemental documents
  - (1) ❑ Working copies
- (c) ❑ Timing
  - (1) ❑ After commencement of an action in which the mental or physical condition or the blood relationship of a party, or of an agent, employee or person in the custody or under the legal control of a party, is in controversy, any party may serve notice on another party to submit to a physical, mental or blood examination by a designated physician, or to produce for such examination his agent, employee or the person in his custody or under his legal control
  - (2) ❑ The notice shall specify the time, which shall be not less than twenty (20) days after service of the notice

B. Timing

1. *Request for a mental or physical examination of witness.* After commencement of an action in which the mental or physical condition or the blood relationship of a party, or of an agent, employee or person in the custody or under the legal control of a party, is in controversy, any party may serve notice on another party to submit to a physical, mental or blood examination by a designated physician, or to produce for such examination his agent, employee or the person in his custody or under his legal control. NY CPLR § 3121(a).
   a. *Time for examination.* The notice shall specify the time, which shall be not less than twenty (20) days after service of the notice, and the conditions and scope of the examination. NY CPLR § 3121(a).
   b. *Objection to examination.* Within twenty (20) days of service of a notice or subpoena duces tecum under NY CPLR Rule 3120 or NY CPLR § 3121, the party or person to whom the notice or subpoena duces tecum is directed, if that party or person objects to the disclosure, inspection or examination, shall serve a response which shall state with reasonable particularity the reasons for each objection. NY CPLR Rule 3122(a)(1).
2. *Examination in personal injury and wrongful death actions.* At any time after joinder of issue and service of a bill of particulars, the party to be examined or any other party may serve on all other parties a notice fixing the time and place of examination. Unless otherwise stipulated, the examination shall be held not less than thirty (30) nor more than sixty (60) days after service of the notice. If served by any party other than the party to be examined, the notice shall name the examining medical provider or providers. If the notice is served by the party to be examined, the examining parties shall, within five (5) days of receipt thereof, submit to the party to be examined the name of the medical providers who will conduct the examination. Any party may move to modify or vacate the notice fixing the time and place of examination or the notice naming the examining medical providers, within ten (10) days of the receipt thereof, on the grounds that the time or place fixed or the medical provider named is objectionable, or that the nature of the action is such that the interests of justice will not be served by an examination, exchange of medical reports or delivery of authorizations. NY R UNIF TRIAL CTS § 202.17(a).
3. *Motions staying disclosure.* Service of a notice of motion under NY CPLR Rule 3211, NY CPLR Rule 3212, or NY CPLR § 3213 stays disclosure until determination of the motion unless the court orders otherwise. If the motion is based solely on the defense that the summons and complaint, summons with notice, or notice of petition and petition was not properly served, disclosure shall not be stayed unless the court orders otherwise. NY CPLR Rule 3214(b).
   a. *Personal injury actions involving terminally ill patients.* Notwithstanding the provisions of NY CPLR Rule 3214(b),

the service or pendency of a motion under NY CPLR Rule 3211, NY CPLR Rule 3212, or NY CPLR § 3213 shall not stay disclosure in an action where a preliminary conference order has been entered pursuant to NY CPLR Rule 3407. NY CPLR Rule 3407(b)(3).

4. *KINGS COUNTY: Discovery timing.* At [the Compliance Conference, the court will] schedule all outstanding discovery to be completed prior to date fixed for filing Note of Issue. NY R L KINGS Rule I(B).
   a. *Deadlines in orders.* Discovery scheduled in Compliance Conference orders shall be strictly adhered to and may not be extended without leave of the court. Unjustified failure to comply with the provisions of the CCP order will result in preclusion, the striking of a pleading or imposition of sanctions, as appropriate. NY R L KINGS Rule I(B)(2).
   b. *Cases with extensive discovery.* Where post Compliance Conference discovery is to be extensive, cases may be retracked from standard to complex, which will provide for three (3) additional months of post Compliance Conference discovery and extend the Note of Issue date by three (3) months. NY R L KINGS Rule I(B)(1).
   c. *Discovery not stayed.* Ordinarily the Court/JHO will not stay discovery during pendency of motions to withdraw, or during pendency of settlement, or during pendency of dispositive motions. NY R L KINGS Rule IV.
   d. *Expedited discovery in certain cases.* Discovery in third party and joint actions will be expedited. NY R L KINGS Pt. B, Rule 5.
   e. For more information on discovery scheduling, refer to NY R L KINGS Flow Chart.

5. *NEW YORK COUNTY: Deadlines in orders.* Strict compliance with all discovery orders is required. Unexcused or unjustified failure to comply with deadlines fixed by the court, including those set out in Preliminary Conference Orders, may result in an award of costs, conditional or otherwise, or the imposition of another penalty authorized by NY CPLR § 3126. NY R NY CTY J RUL Rule 8.

6. *Computation of time*
   a. *Units of time*
      i. *Day.* A calendar day includes the time from midnight to midnight. Sunday or any day of the week specifically mentioned means a calendar day. NY GEN CONSTR § 19.
      ii. *Month.* In a statute, contract or public or private instrument, unless otherwise provided in such contract or instrument or by law, the term month means a calendar month and not a lunar month. NY GEN CONSTR § 31.
      iii. *Year.* For information on the definition of a year, including the definitions of a half-year and quarter-year, refer to NY GEN CONSTR § 58 and NY GEN CONSTR § 50. For information on leap years, refer to NY GEN CONSTR § 57.
   b. *Periods of time*
      i. *Number of days.* A number of days specified as a period from a certain day within which or after or before which an act is authorized or required to be done means such number of calendar days exclusive of the calendar day from which the reckoning is made. NY GEN CONSTR § 20.
         - If such period is a period of two (2) days, Saturday, Sunday or a public holiday must be excluded from the reckoning if it is an intervening day between the day from which the reckoning is made and the last day of the period. NY GEN CONSTR § 20.
         - In computing any specified period of time from a specified event, the day upon which the event happens is deemed the day from which the reckoning is made. The day from which any specified period of time is reckoned shall be excluded in making the reckoning. NY GEN CONSTR § 20.
      ii. *Number of months.* A number of months after or before a certain day shall be computed by counting such number of calendar months from such day, exclusive of the calendar month in which such day occurs, and shall include the day of the month in the last month so counted having the same numerical order in days of the month as the day from which the computation is made, unless there be not so many days in the last month so counted, in which case the period computed shall expire with the last day of the month so counted. NY GEN CONSTR § 30.
      iii. *Publication of notice; Number of days.* The period of publication of a legal notice shall be computed by excluding the first day of publication and including the day on which the act or event of which notice is given is to take place or which completes the full period of publication. NY CPLR § 2402.
      iv. *Periods ending on Saturday, Sunday or public holiday.* When any period of time, computed from a certain day, within which or after which or before which an act is authorized or required to be done, ends on a Saturday, Sunday or a public holiday, such act may be done on the next succeeding business day and if the period ends at

a specified hour, such act may be done at or before the same hour of such next succeeding business day, except that where a period of time specified by contract ends on a Saturday, Sunday or a public holiday, the extension of such period is governed by NY GEN CONSTR § 25. NY GEN CONSTR § 25-a(1).

- For a list of public holidays, refer to NY GEN CONSTR § 24.

v. *Additional time after certain kinds of service*

- *Service by mail.* Where a period of time prescribed by law is measured from the service of a paper and service is by mail, five (5) days shall be added to the prescribed period. NY CPLR Rule 2103(b)(2).
- *Service by overnight delivery service.* Where a period of time prescribed by law is measured from the service of a paper and service is by overnight delivery, one (1) business day shall be added to the prescribed period. NY CPLR Rule 2103(b)(6).

vi. *Daylight saving time.* For information on New York's time zone and the effect of daylight saving time, refer to NY GEN CONSTR § 52.

c. *Hours of court.* Notwithstanding any provision of law or rule of court to the contrary, throughout the State of New York the sessions of the Supreme Court for the disposition of business before the court shall commence not later than 9:30 a.m. and conclude not earlier than 5 p.m. Where warranted, the Chief Administrator of the Courts may authorize variances in the opening and closing hours of the courts, but, in such event, daily sessions shall total not less than six (6) hours. NY R CHIEF J § 3.1.

d. *Time limits; Extension of time.* Any act required by or in pursuance of law to be performed at or within a prescribed time, shall be performed according to the standard time. NY GEN CONSTR § 53.

i. Except where otherwise expressly prescribed by law, the court may extend the time fixed by any statute, rule or order for doing any act, upon such terms as may be just and upon good cause shown, whether the application for extension is made before or after the expiration of the time fixed. NY CPLR § 2004. Refer to the New York KeyRules Motion for Continuance/Extension of Time document for more information.

C. General Requirements

1. *Rules governing disclosure*

a. *Generally.* There shall be full disclosure of all matter material and necessary in the prosecution or defense of an action, regardless of the burden of proof, by:

i. A party, or the officer, director, member, agent or employee of a party;

ii. A person who possessed a cause of action or defense asserted in the action;

iii. A person about to depart from the state, or without the state, or residing at a greater distance from the place of trial than one hundred miles, or so sick or infirm as to afford reasonable grounds of belief that he or she will not be able to attend the trial, or a person authorized to practice medicine, dentistry or podiatry who has provided medical, dental or podiatric care or diagnosis to the party demanding disclosure, or who has been retained by such party as an expert witness; and

iv. Any other person, upon notice stating the circumstances or reasons such disclosure is sought or required. NY CPLR § 3101(a).

v. The statutory phrase "material and necessary", said the Court of Appeals, must be interpreted liberally to require disclosure upon request, of any facts bearing on the controversy which will assist preparation for trial by sharpening the issues and reducing delay and prolixity. The test is one of usefulness and reason. SIEGEL-NYPRAC § 344; Allen v. Crowell-Collier Pub. Co., 21 N.Y.2d 403, 235 N.E.2d 430 (1968).

vi. Another potential problem that the original NY CPLR § 3101(a) posed was that it spoke of "evidence" that is material and necessary, which might have been construed to permit disclosure to elicit only that which would itself qualify as "evidence" admissible at trial. It was, however, construed more broadly than that. Well-considered caselaw specifically rejected this "evidence in chief" doctrine, stating that disclosure extends as well "to all relevant information calculated to lead to relevant evidence," a standard similar to that applicable in federal court. With an amendment that took effect on January 1, 1994, changing "evidence" to "matter" in NY CPLR § 3101(a), these generous interpretations of the statute were in effect approved by the legislature. SIEGEL-NYPRAC § 344.

vii. If a party is a corporation, each of its officers, directors, members, agents, and employees is also deemed a "party" for disclosure purposes. A party who needs relevant data or material from a nonparty corporation can seek it through NY CPLR § 3101(a)(2), NY CPLR § 3101(a)(3) or NY CPLR § 3101(a)(4), under which the corporate entity is treated as a "person." These subdivisions should also apply to any entity, corporate or otherwise, from whom disclosure is sought through its agents. A corporate employee who has the requisite knowledge and information may respond to a disclosure request on behalf of the corporation. A party who can't single out the particular person in the corporation's employ to whom a disclosure request should be properly directed can direct it to the corporation as such and leave it to the corporation to designate the appropriate person to respond. Whenever disclosure is sought from a corporation through a deposition, whether as a party or as a nonparty witness, the choice in the first instance of who will be produced in the corporate behalf is with the corporation rather than the examining party. SIEGEL-NYPRAC § 345.

viii. NY CPLR § 3101(a)(4) permits a party to obtain disclosure from a nonparty by merely serving a subpoena on the nonparty providing notice of "the circumstances or reasons such disclosure is sought or required." SIEGEL-NYPRAC § 345.

b. *Methods of obtaining disclosure.* Information is obtainable by one or more of the following disclosure devices: depositions upon oral questions or without the state upon written questions, interrogatories, demands for addresses, discovery and inspection of documents or property, physical and mental examinations of persons, and requests for admission. NY CPLR § 3102(a).

i. *Stipulation or notice.* Unless otherwise provided by the civil practice law and rules or by the court, disclosure shall be obtained by stipulation or on notice without leave of the court. NY CPLR § 3102(b).

ii. *Before action commenced; Court order required.* Before an action is commenced, disclosure to aid in bringing an action, to preserve information or to aid in arbitration, may be obtained, but only by court order. The court may appoint a referee to take testimony. NY CPLR § 3102(c).

iii. *During trial; Court order required.* Except as provided in NY CPLR § 5223, during and after trial, disclosure may be obtained only by order of the trial court on notice. NY CPLR § 3102(d).

iv. *Action pending in another jurisdiction.* Except as provided in NY CPLR § 3119, when under any mandate, writ or commission issued out of any court of record in any other state, territory, district or foreign jurisdiction, or whenever upon notice or agreement, it is required to take the testimony of a witness in the state, he or she may be compelled to appear and testify in the same manner and by the same process as may be employed for the purpose of taking testimony in actions pending in the state. The supreme court or a county court shall make any appropriate order in aid of taking such a deposition. NY CPLR § 3102(e).

v. *Actions to which state is a party.* In an action in which the state is properly a party, whether as plaintiff, defendant or otherwise, disclosure by the state shall be available as if the state were a private person. NY CPLR § 3102(f).

c. *Privileged matter.* Upon objection by a person entitled to assert the privilege, privileged matter shall not be obtainable. NY CPLR § 3101(b).

i. A determination of whether information is privileged is governed by the rules of evidence, which apply as they would at a trial. Whatever is privileged at the trial is privileged as well on pretrial disclosure. SIEGEL-NYPRAC § 346.

d. *Attorney's work product.* The work product of an attorney shall not be obtainable. NY CPLR § 3101(c).

i. NY CPLR § 3101(c) makes unobtainable the "work product of an attorney"—an ill-defined category whose potential for mischief has been avoided only because the judiciary has accorded it a very narrow scope. It is a category wholly distinct from the "materials . . . prepared in anticipation of litigation" of NY CPLR § 3101(d)(2). The fact that immunity is absolute under NY CPLR § 3101(c), while that of NY CPLR § 3101(d)(2) is only conditional, is the factor that requires as sharp a line as possible between the two categories. SIEGEL-NYPRAC § 347.

ii. The judiciary has cast precious little under the "work product" category of NY CPLR § 3101(c), preferring instead to fit doubtful items under the "materials . . . prepared in anticipation of litigation" banner of NY CPLR § 3101(d)(2), where the conditional immunity can be overcome and the matters ordered disclosed when stated conditions are met. SIEGEL-NYPRAC § 347.

e. *Trial preparation*

i. *Experts.* Upon request, each party shall identify each person whom the party expects to call as an expert witness at trial and shall disclose in reasonable detail the subject matter on which each expert is expected to testify, the substance of the facts and opinions on which each expert is expected to testify, the qualifications of each expert witness and a summary of the grounds for each expert's opinion. NY CPLR § 3101(d)(1)(i).

- However, where a party for good cause shown retains an expert an insufficient period of time before the commencement of trial to give appropriate notice thereof, the party shall not thereupon be precluded from introducing the expert's testimony at the trial solely on grounds of noncompliance with NY CPLR § 3101(d)(1). In that instance, upon motion of any party, made before or at trial, or on its own initiative, the court may make whatever order may be just. In an action for medical, dental or podiatric malpractice, a party, in responding to a request, may omit the names of medical, dental or podiatric experts but shall be required to disclose all other information concerning such experts otherwise required by NY CPLR § 3101(d)(1). NY CPLR § 3101(d)(1)(i).

- In an action for medical, dental or podiatric malpractice, any party may, by written offer made to and served upon all other parties and filed with the court, offer to disclose the name of, and to make available for examination upon oral deposition, any person the party making the offer expects to call as an expert witness at trial. Within twenty (20) days of service of the offer, a party shall accept or reject the offer by serving a written reply upon all parties and filing a copy thereof with the court. Failure to serve a reply within twenty (20) days of service of the offer shall be deemed a rejection of the offer. If all parties accept the offer, each party shall be required to produce his or her expert witness for examination upon oral deposition upon receipt of a notice to take oral deposition in accordance with NY CPLR Rule 3107. If any party, having made or accepted the offer, fails to make that party's expert available for oral deposition, that party shall be precluded from offering expert testimony at the trial of the action. NY CPLR § 3101(d)(1)(ii).
- Further disclosure concerning the expected testimony of any expert may be obtained only by court order upon a showing of special circumstances and subject to restrictions as to scope and provisions concerning fees and expenses as the court may deem appropriate. However, a party, without court order, may take the testimony of a person authorized to practice medicine, dentistry or podiatry who is the party's treating or retained expert, as described in NY CPLR § 3101(a)(3), in which event any other party shall be entitled to the full disclosure authorized by Article 31 of Chapter 8 of the Civil Practice Law and Rules (NY CPLR § 3101, et seq.) with respect to that expert without court order. NY CPLR § 3101(d)(1)(iii).

ii. *Materials.* Subject to the provisions of NY CPLR § 3101(d)(1), materials otherwise discoverable under NY CPLR § 3101(a) and prepared in anticipation of litigation or for trial by or for another party, or by or for that other party's representative (including an attorney, consultant, surety, indemnitor, insurer or agent), may be obtained only upon a showing that the party seeking discovery has substantial need of the materials in the preparation of the case and is unable without undue hardship to obtain the substantial equivalent of the materials by other means. In ordering discovery of the materials when the required showing has been made, the court shall protect against disclosure of the mental impressions, conclusions, opinions or legal theories of an attorney or other representative of a party concerning the litigation. NY CPLR § 3101(d)(2).

- In order to qualify as "litigation" material the item must have been prepared exclusively for litigation. Incidental potential use in litigation, the courts have observed, may also be a function of such reports, but they have at least an equal if not greater mission "to prevent future accidents, discipline careless employees, or, generally, to increase the economy and efficiency of the operation." SIEGEL-NYPRAC § 348.

f. *Party's statement.* A party may obtain a copy of his own statement. NY CPLR § 3101(e).

i. Moreover, NY CPLR § 3101(e) has been broadly interpreted to include photographs. Items such as photographs and videotapes are now independently subject to disclosure under NY CPLR § 3101(i). SIEGEL-NYPRAC § 348.

g. *Contents of insurance agreement.* A party may obtain discovery of the existence and contents of any insurance agreement under which any person carrying on an insurance business may be liable to satisfy part or all of a judgment which may be entered in the action or to indemnify or reimburse for payments made to satisfy the judgment. Information concerning the insurance agreement is not by reason of disclosure admissible in evidence at trial. For purpose of NY CPLR § 3101(f), an application for insurance shall not be treated as part of an insurance agreement. NY CPLR § 3101(f).

h. *Accident reports.* Except as is otherwise provided by law, in addition to any other matter which may be subject to disclosure, there shall be full disclosure of any written report of an accident prepared in the regular course of business operations or practices of any person, firm, corporation, association or other public or private entity, unless prepared by a police or peace officer for a criminal investigation or prosecution and disclosure would interfere with a criminal investigation or prosecution. NY CPLR § 3101(g).

i. *Amendment or supplementation of responses.* A party shall amend or supplement a response previously given to a request for disclosure promptly upon the party's thereafter obtaining information that the response was incorrect or incomplete when made, or that the response, though correct and complete when made, no longer is correct and complete, and the circumstances are such that a failure to amend or supplement the response would be materially misleading. NY CPLR § 3101(h).

i. Where a party obtains such information an insufficient period of time before the commencement of trial appropriately to amend or supplement the response, the party shall not thereupon be precluded from introducing evidence at the trial solely on grounds of noncompliance with NY CPLR § 3101(h). In that instance, upon motion of any party, made before or at trial, or on its own initiative, the court may make whatever order may be just. Further amendment or supplementation may be obtained by court order. NY CPLR § 3101(h).

j. *Other disclosures.* In addition to any other matter which may be subject to disclosure, there shall be full disclosure of any films, photographs, video tapes or audio tapes, including transcripts or memoranda thereof, involving a person referred to in NY CPLR § 3101(a)(1). There shall be disclosure of all portions of such material, including out-takes, rather than only those portions a party intends to use. The provisions of NY CPLR § 3101(i) shall not apply to materials compiled for law enforcement purposes which are exempt from disclosure under NY PUB OFF § 87. NY CPLR § 3101(i).

i. While NY CPLR § 3101(i) was enacted with the defendant's surreptitious tapes of the plaintiff in mind, its language is broad enough to embrace any films, photographs, and audio or video tapes of a party, even those made by the party from whom disclosure is sought. SIEGEL-NYPRAC § 348.

k. *Protective orders.* The court may at any time on its own initiative, or on motion of any party or of any person from whom discovery is sought, make a protective order denying, limiting, conditioning or regulating the use of any disclosure device. NY CPLR § 3103(a). Refer to the New York KeyRules Motion for Protective Order document for more information.

l. *Supervision of disclosure.* Upon the motion of any party or witness on notice to all parties or on its own initiative without notice, the court in which an action is pending may by one of its judges or a referee supervise all or part of any disclosure procedure. NY CPLR § 3104(a).

i. *Selection of referee.* A judicial hearing officer may be designated as a referee under NY CPLR § 3104, or the court may permit all of the parties in an action to stipulate that a named attorney may act as referee. In such latter event, the stipulation shall provide for payment of his fees which shall, unless otherwise agreed, be taxed as disbursements. NY CPLR § 3104(b).

ii. *Powers of referee; Motions referred to person supervising disclosure.* A referee under NY CPLR § 3104 shall have all the powers of the court under NY CPLR § 3101, et seq. except the power to relieve himself of his duties, to appoint a successor, or to adjudge any person guilty of contempt. All motions or applications made under Article 31 of Chapter 8 of the Civil Practice Law and Rules (NY CPLR § 3101, et seq.) shall be returnable before the judge or referee, designated under NY CPLR § 3104 and after disposition, if requested by any party, his order shall be filed in the office of the clerk. NY CPLR § 3104(c).

iii. *Review of order of referee.* Any party or witness may apply for review of an order made under NY CPLR § 3104 by a referee. The application shall be by motion made in the court in which the action is pending within five (5) days after the order is made. Service of a notice of motion for review shall suspend disclosure of the particular matter in dispute. If the question raised by the motion may affect the rights of a witness, notice shall be served on him personally or by mail at his last known address. It shall set forth succinctly the order complained of, the reason it is objectionable and the relief demanded. NY CPLR § 3104(d).

iv. *Payment of expenses of referee.* Except where a judicial hearing officer has been designated a referee hereunder, the court may make an appropriate order for the payment of the reasonable expenses of the referee. NY CPLR § 3104(e).

2. *Request for a mental or physical examination of a witness*

a. *Generally.* NY CPLR § 3121(a) requires that a party whose physical or mental condition, or blood relationship to someone, is "in controversy," must, at the behest of another party, submit to an examination by "a designated physician." Agents, employees, and others under the party's control confront this examination, too, if their condition is in controversy, but it is mainly the party proper, notably the plaintiff in the ubiquitous personal injury case, who makes the caselaw on this device. SIEGEL-NYPRAC § 363.

i. When dispute arises as to whether a party's condition is in controversy, the burden of showing that it is on the party seeking the examination. SIEGEL-NYPRAC § 363; Koump v. Smith, 25 N.Y.2d 287, 295, 250 N.E.2d 857, 861 (1969).

ii. The tendency of the courts is to allow an examination—physical, mental, or blood—if it can be shown to have some practical value in the case. SIEGEL-NYPRAC § 363; Carpinelli v. Manhattan Bottling Corp., 21 A.D.2d 792, 793, 250 N.Y.S.2d 756, 757 (1964). If the examination "presents the possibility of danger to [the] life or health" of the person, it can be dispensed with. SIEGEL-NYPRAC § 363; Lefkowitz v. Nassau Cty. Med. Ctr., 94 A.D.2d 18, 21, 462 N.Y.S.2d 903, 906 (1983).

iii. The reference in NY CPLR § 3121(a) is to a "physician." The Court of Appeals has held that while this may bar examinations by other professionals under NY CPLR § 3121, non-physician professionals can conduct examinations under the general and broader terms of NY CPLR § 3101(a) whenever relevant. SIEGEL-NYPRAC § 363; Kavanagh v. Ogden Allied Maint. Corp., 92 N.Y.2d 952, 953, 705 N.E.2d 1197, 1198 (1998).

b. *Notice of examination*

i. After commencement of an action in which the mental or physical condition or the blood relationship of a party, or of an agent, employee or person in the custody or under the legal control of a party, is in controversy, any party may serve notice on another party to submit to a physical, mental or blood examination by a designated physician, or to produce for such examination his agent, employee or the person in his custody or under his legal control. NY CPLR § 3121(a).

ii. The notice may require duly executed and acknowledged written authorizations permitting all parties to obtain, and make copies of, the records of specified hospitals relating to such mental or physical condition or blood relationship; where a party obtains a copy of a hospital record as a result of the authorization of another party, he shall deliver a duplicate of the copy to such party. A copy of the notice shall be served on the person to be examined. NY CPLR § 3121(a).

c. *Objection to notice.* If objection is made to part of an item or category, the part shall be specified. The party seeking disclosure under NY CPLR Rule 3120 or NY CPLR § 3121 may move for an order under NY CPLR Rule 3124 or NY CPLR § 2308 with respect to any objection to, or other failure to respond to or permit inspection as requested by, the notice or subpoena duces tecum, respectively, or any part thereof. NY CPLR Rule 3122(a)(1).

d. *Copy of report.* A copy of a detailed written report of the examining physician setting out his findings and conclusions shall be delivered by the party seeking the examination to any party requesting to exchange therefore a copy of each report in his control of an examination made with respect to the mental or physical condition in controversy. NY CPLR § 3121(b).

i. While NY CPLR § 3121(b) is addressed to the exchange of medical reports in general, it applies only to the report of a nontreating physician, i.e., one whose report is made after an examination conducted pursuant to NY CPLR § 3121(a), or otherwise made solely for litigation. The Court said that the report of a treating physician is not in that category and may therefore be discovered under the basic relevance standard in NY CPLR § 3101(a). It is not material prepared exclusively for litigation under NY CPLR § 3101(d)(2), in other words, and thus faces no discovery impediment from that statute. Nor may it be deemed the product of an examination conducted pursuant to NY CPLR § 3121(a) and, therefore, is not subject to the exchange requirement of NY CPLR § 3121(b). SIEGEL-NYPRAC § 363; Hoenig v. Westphal, 52 N.Y.2d 605, 608, 422 N.E.2d 491, 492 (1981).

ii. It has been held that when a physician bases his report solely on hospital records and not on a personal examination of the party, the report is not subject to the exchange directed by NY CPLR § 3121(b). SIEGEL-NYPRAC § 363; Edelman v. Holmes Private Ambulances, Inc., 32 A.D.2d 563, 563, 300 N.Y.S.2d 372, 373 (1969).

3. *Exchange of medical reports in personal injury and wrongful death actions.* Except where the court otherwise directs, in all actions in which recovery is sought for personal injuries, disability or death, physical examinations and the exchange of medical information shall be governed by the provisions set forth in NY R UNIF TRIAL CTS § 202.17. NY R UNIF TRIAL CTS § 202.17.

a. *Preparation for examination; Information to be delivered to medical provider.* At least twenty (20) days before the date of such examination, or on such other date as the court may direct, the party to be examined shall serve upon and deliver to all other parties the following, which may be used by the examining medical provider:

i. Copies of the medical reports of those medical providers who have previously treated or examined the party seeking recovery. These shall include a recital of the injuries and conditions as to which testimony will be offered at the trial, referring to and identifying those x-ray and technicians' reports which will be offered at the trial, including a description of the injuries, a diagnosis and a prognosis. Medical reports may consist of completed medical provider, workers' compensation, or insurance forms that provide the information required by NY R UNIF TRIAL CTS § 202.17(b)(1). NY R UNIF TRIAL CTS § 202.17(b)(1).

ii. Duly executed and acknowledged written authorizations permitting all parties to obtain and make copies of all hospital records and such other records, including x-ray and technicians' reports, as may be referred to and identified in the reports of those medical providers who have treated or examined the party seeking recovery. NY R UNIF TRIAL CTS § 202.17(b)(2).

b. *Copies of reports to all parties.* Copies of the reports of the medical providers making examinations pursuant to NY R UNIF TRIAL CTS § 202.17 shall be served on all other parties within forty-five (45) days after completion of the examination. These shall comply with the requirements of NY R UNIF TRIAL CTS § 202.17(b)(1). NY R UNIF TRIAL CTS § 202.17(c).

c. *Hospital records in lieu of other reports.* Parties relying solely on hospital records may so certify in lieu of serving medical providers' reports. NY R UNIF TRIAL CTS § 202.17(e).

d. *Compliance with rules on exchange of medical reports.* No case otherwise eligible to be noticed for trial may be noticed unless there has been compliance with NY R UNIF TRIAL CTS § 202.17, or an order dispensing with compliance or extending the time therefor has been obtained; or, where the party to be examined was served a notice as provided in NY R UNIF TRIAL CTS § 202.17(a), and the party so served has not responded thereto. NY R UNIF TRIAL CTS § 202.17(f).

e. *Examinations performed before action.* Where an examination is conducted on consent prior to the institution of an action, the party to be examined shall deliver the documents specified in NY R UNIF TRIAL CTS § 202.17(b)(1) and NY R UNIF TRIAL CTS § 202.17(b)(2), and the report of the examining medical provider shall be delivered as provided in NY R UNIF TRIAL CTS § 202.17(c). In that event, examination after institution of the action may be waived. The waiver, which shall recite that medical reports have been exchanged and that all parties waive further physical examination, shall be filed with the note of issue. This shall not be a bar, however, to proceeding under NY R UNIF TRIAL CTS § 202.17(g) in a proper case. NY R UNIF TRIAL CTS § 202.17(k).

f. For more information on exchanging medical records during discovery in personal injury and wrongful death cases, refer to NY R UNIF TRIAL CTS § 202.17.

4. *Governing law.* The civil practice law and rules (NY CPLR § 101, et seq.) shall govern the procedure in civil judicial proceedings in all courts of the state and before all judges, except where the procedure is regulated by inconsistent statute. The civil practice law and rules shall succeed the civil practice act and rules of civil practice and shall be deemed substituted therefor throughout the statutes and rules of the state. NY CPLR § 101. The civil practice law and rules shall be liberally construed to secure the just, speedy and inexpensive determination of every civil judicial proceeding. NY CPLR § 104.

a. *Uniform trial court rules.* The uniform civil rules for the Supreme Court and County Court (NY R UNIF TRIAL CTS § 202.1, et seq.) shall be applicable to civil actions and proceedings in the Supreme Court and the County Court. NY R UNIF TRIAL CTS § 202.1(a). The provisions of the uniform rules shall be construed consistent with the Civil Practice Law and Rules (CPLR), and matters not covered by the uniform rules shall be governed by the CPLR. NY R UNIF TRIAL CTS § 202.1(d).

b. *Local rules.* Local court rules, not inconsistent with law or with uniform civil rules for the Supreme Court and County Court (NY R UNIF TRIAL CTS § 202.1, et seq.), shall comply with Part 9 of the Rules of the Chief Judge (NY R CHIEF J § 9.1). NY R UNIF TRIAL CTS § 202.1(c).

c. *Official forms.* The state administrator shall have the power to adopt, amend and rescind an appendix of forms. Forms adopted pursuant to NY CPLR § 107 shall be sufficient under the civil practice law and rules and shall illustrate the simplicity and brevity of statement which the civil practice law and rules contemplate. NY CPLR § 107.

5. *Rules of the commercial division.* [Editor's note: certain types of civil cases or civil cases meeting certain monetary thresholds that are filed in the state of New York must be filed in the Commercial Division of the New York Supreme Courts. Rules governing practice in the commercial division are found in NY R UNIF TRIAL CTS § 202.70]. Cases which must be filed in the commercial division are listed below. For more information, refer to NY R UNIF TRIAL CTS § 202.70.

a. *Monetary thresholds.* Except as set forth in NY R UNIF TRIAL CTS § 202.70(b), the monetary thresholds of the Commercial Division, exclusive of punitive damages, interests, costs, disbursements and counsel fees claimed, are established as follows: (1) Albany County, fifty thousand dollars ($50,000); (2) Eighth Judicial District, one hundred thousand dollars ($100,000); (3) Kings County, one hundred fifty thousand dollars ($150,000); (4) Nassau County, two hundred thousand dollars ($200,000); (5) New York County, five hundred thousand dollars ($500,000); (6) Onondaga County, fifty thousand dollars ($50,000); (7) Queens County, one hundred thousand dollars ($100,000); (8) Seventh Judicial District, fifty thousand dollars ($50,000); (9) Suffolk County, one hundred thousand dollars

($100,000); and (10) Westchester County, one hundred thousand dollars ($100,000). NY R UNIF TRIAL CTS § 202.70(a).

i. *ALBANY COUNTY.* The Commercial Division of the Albany County Supreme Court exercises jurisdiction over selected business and commercial disputes in which the amount at issue generally involves damage claims in a minimum amount of fifty thousand dollars ($50,000) as well as claims for unspecified amounts where the value of the commercial asset(s) in dispute exceeds fifty thousand dollars ($50,000). A separate publication promulgating the rules and criteria relating to the filing and management of Commercial Court cases in this part may be obtained from the Albany County Supreme Court Clerk's Office. A section of the Uniform Civil Rules for the Supreme Court and County Court sets forth statewide rules. NY R 3 JD SUP Doc. 1(E).

ii. *BRONX COUNTY.* The monetary threshold for commercial cases in Bronx County will be seventy-five thousand dollars ($75,000). All other parameters including the type of matters that will be heard are contained within the Rules of the Commercial Division of the Supreme Court (NY R UNIF TRIAL CTS § 202.70). NY R BRONX FIL R Doc. 12.

iii. *NEW YORK COUNTY.* The monetary threshold in the New York County Commercial Division, which is generally applicable, is an amount in controversy of five hundred thousand dollars ($500,000) or more (exclusive of punitive damages, interest, costs, disbursements, and counsel fees). If the case is designated a commercial one and the Addendum is submitted, the clerk will review the pleadings to determine whether the amount in controversy in the case meets the monetary threshold or whether an exception to the threshold applies. NY R NY CTY Procedure IA(B). For more information on assigning a case to the commercial division in New York County, refer to NY R NY CTY Procedure IA(B).

b. *Commercial cases.* Actions in which the principal claims involve or consist of the following will be heard in the Commercial Division provided that the monetary threshold is met or equitable or declaratory relief is sought:

i. Breach of contract or fiduciary duty, fraud, misrepresentation, business tort (e.g., unfair competition), or statutory and/or common law violation where the breach or violation is alleged to arise out of business dealings (e.g., sales of assets or securities; corporate restructuring; partnership, shareholder, joint venture, and other business agreements; trade secrets; restrictive covenants; and employment agreements not including claims that principally involve alleged discriminatory practices);

ii. Transactions governed by the Uniform Commercial Code (exclusive of those concerning individual cooperative or condominium units);

iii. Transactions involving commercial real property, including Yellowstone injunctions and excluding actions for the payment of rent only;

iv. Shareholder derivative actions—without consideration of the monetary threshold;

v. Commercial class actions—without consideration of the monetary threshold;

vi. Business transactions involving or arising out of dealings with commercial banks and other financial institutions;

vii. Internal affairs of business organizations;

viii. Malpractice by accountants or actuaries, and legal malpractice arising out of representation in commercial matters;

ix. Environmental insurance coverage;

x. Commercial insurance coverage (e.g., directors and officers, errors and omissions, and business interruption coverage);

xi. Dissolution of corporations, partnerships, limited liability companies, limited liability partnerships and joint ventures—without consideration of the monetary threshold; and

xii. Applications to stay or compel arbitration and affirm or disaffirm arbitration awards and related injunctive relief pursuant to Article 75 of the New York Civil Practice Law and Rules (NY CPLR § 7501, et seq.) involving any of the foregoing enumerated commercial issues. Where the applicable arbitration agreement provides for the arbitration to be heard outside the United States, the monetary threshold set forth in NY R UNIF TRIAL CTS § 202.70(a) shall not apply. NY R UNIF TRIAL CTS § 202.70(b).

c. *Non-commercial cases.* The following will not be heard in the Commercial Division even if the monetary threshold is met:

i. Suits to collect professional fees;

ii. Cases seeking a declaratory judgment as to insurance coverage for personal injury or property damage;

iii. Residential real estate disputes, including landlord-tenant matters, and commercial real estate disputes involving the payment of rent only;

iv. Home improvement contracts involving residential properties consisting of one to four residential units or individual units in any residential building, including cooperative or condominium units;

v. Proceedings to enforce a judgment regardless of the nature of the underlying case;

vi. First-party insurance claims and actions by insurers to collect premiums or rescind non-commercial policies; and

vii. Attorney malpractice actions except as otherwise provided in NY R UNIF TRIAL CTS § 202.70(b)(8). NY R UNIF TRIAL CTS § 202.70(c).

d. For more information on the Commercial Division, refer to NY R UNIF TRIAL CTS § 202.70.

D. Documents

1. *Required documents*

a. *Request for a mental or physical examination.* Refer to the General Requirements section of this document for information on the request for a mental or physical examination.

b. *Proof of service.* In addition to complying with the provisions of NY CPLR Rule 2101, every paper filed in court shall have annexed thereto appropriate proof of service on all parties where required. NY R UNIF TRIAL CTS § 202.5(a).

2. *Supplemental documents*

a. *Working copies.* The court may require the parties to provide working copies of documents filed electronically. In such event, each working copy shall include, firmly affixed thereto, a copy of a confirmation notice in a form prescribed by the Chief Administrator. NY R UNIF TRIAL CTS § 202.5-b(d)(5).

E. Format

1. *Form of documents*

a. *Size and form of paper.* Each paper served or filed shall be durable, white and, except for summonses, subpoenas, notices of appearance, notes of issue, orders of protection, temporary orders of protection and exhibits, shall be eleven by eight and one-half (11 x 8-1/2) inches in size. NY CPLR Rule 2101(a).

b. *Writing and language.* The writing shall be legible and in black ink. NY CPLR Rule 2101(a). Each paper served or filed shall be in the English language which, where practicable, shall be of ordinary usage. NY CPLR Rule 2101(b).

c. *Caption.* Each paper served or filed shall begin with a caption setting forth the name of the court, the venue, the title of the action, the nature of the paper and the index number of the action if one has been assigned. In all papers other than a summons, a complaint or a judgment it shall be sufficient to state the name of the first named party on each side with an appropriate indication of any omissions. NY CPLR Rule 2101(c).

i. *Further contents of first page.* After the first paper has been filed in each case the index number shall appear on the cover and first page to the right of the caption of every paper tendered for filing in the action. Each such cover and first page also shall contain an indication of the county of venue and a brief description of the nature of the paper and, where the case has been assigned to an individual judge, shall contain the name of the assigned judge to the right of the caption. NY R UNIF TRIAL CTS § 202.5(a); NY R UNIF TRIAL CTS § 202.5(b); NY R UNIF TRIAL CTS § 202.5(d)(1)(i).

d. *Index number.* No paper in an action in the supreme or a county court, other than an order submitted for signature to a judge out of court, shall be submitted for any purpose to the supreme or county court or to a clerk thereof unless there is endorsed on such paper the index number of the action assigned by the clerk of the county. NY CPLR § 8018(c).

e. *Line spacing.* Every paper filed in court, if typewritten, shall have at least double space between each line, except for quotations and the names and addresses of attorneys appearing in the action. NY R UNIF TRIAL CTS § 202.5(a).

f. *Font size.* Each. . .paper printed or typed, served or filed, except for summonses. . .and exhibits, shall be in clear type of no less than ten (10) point in size. NY CPLR Rule 2101(a).

i. Whenever a requirement relating to size of type is stated in point size, the type size requirement shall be deemed met if the x-height of the type is a minimum of forty-five percent (45%) of the specified point size. Each point shall be measured as .351 millimeter. The x-height size shall be measured as it appears on the page. The x-height is the height of the lower case letters, exclusive of ascenders or descenders. NY CPLR § 105(t).

g. *Margins.* Every paper filed in court shall have at least one (1) inch margins. NY R UNIF TRIAL CTS § 202.5(a).

h. *Citations*

 i. *Civil practice law and rules.* NY CPLR § 101, et seq. shall be known as the civil practice law and rules, and may be cited as "CPLR". Reference to a provision in the civil practice law and rules may, except when such provision is being enacted or amended, be made without indicating whether it is a rule or section. NY CPLR § 101.

i. *Indorsement by attorney.* Each paper served or filed shall be indorsed with the name, address and telephone number of the attorney for the party serving or filing the paper, or if the party does not appear by attorney, with the name, address and telephone number of the party. NY CPLR Rule 2101(d).

j. *One-sided printing.* In addition, every paper filed in court, other than an exhibit or printed form, shall contain writing on one side only, except that papers that are fastened on the side may contain writing on both sides. NY R UNIF TRIAL CTS § 202.5(a).

k. *Use of copies authorized.* Except where otherwise specifically prescribed, copies, rather than originals, of all papers, including orders, affidavits and exhibits may be served or filed. Where it is required that the original be served or filed and the original is lost or withheld, the court may authorize a copy to be served or filed. NY CPLR Rule 2101(e).

 i. Where a certified copy of a paper is required by law, an attorney admitted to practice in the courts of the state may certify that it has been compared by him with the original and found to be a true and complete copy. Such a certificate, when subscribed by such attorney, has the same effect as if made by a clerk. NY CPLR § 2105.

l. *Recycled paper.* It is the policy of the Unified Court System that litigants, where practicable, should file or submit to the courts of the Unified Court System of the State of New York papers printed or reproduced on recycled paper. Paper is considered recycled if it contains a minimum content of thirty percent (30%) waste paper. NY R UNIF TRIAL CTS § 215.2. The signature page of every paper filed or submitted to the court on recycled paper should bear the legend: "Printed [Reproduced] on Recycled Paper." NY R UNIF TRIAL CTS § 215.3.

2. *Form of electronic documents.* Each paper served or filed by electronic means, as defined in NY CPLR Rule 2103(f), shall be capable of being reproduced by the receiver so as to comply with the provisions of NY CPLR Rule 2101(a) through NY CPLR Rule 2101(d). NY CPLR Rule 2101(g).

 a. *File format.* All e-filed documents shall comply with the technical requirements set forth at the NYSCEF site. NY R UNIF TRIAL CTS § 202.5-b(d)(1)(i).

 b. *Heading of document.* The subject matter heading for each paper sent by electronic means must indicate that the matter being transmitted electronically is related to a court proceeding. NY CPLR Rule 2103(b)(7).

3. *Signature blocks.* Every pleading, written motion, and other paper, served on another party or filed or submitted to the court shall be signed by an attorney, or by a party if the party is not represented by an attorney, with the name of the attorney or party clearly printed or typed directly below the signature. NY R CHIEF ADMIN § 130-1.1-a(a); NY R UNIF TRIAL CTS § 202.5(d)(1)(iv).

 a. *Printed name.* Beneath each signature shall be printed the name signed. NY CPLR Rule 2101(a).

 b. *Failure to sign.* Absent good cause shown, the court shall strike any unsigned paper if the omission of the signature is not corrected promptly after being called to the attention of the attorney or party. NY R CHIEF ADMIN § 130-1.1-a(a).

 c. *Signature as certification.* By signing a paper, an attorney or party certifies that, to the best of that person's knowledge, information and belief, formed after an inquiry reasonable under the circumstances the presentation of the paper or the contentions therein are not frivolous as defined in NY R CHIEF ADMIN § 130-1.1(c). NY R CHIEF ADMIN § 130-1.1-a(b)(1).

 d. *Electronic signatures.* A document shall be considered to have been signed by an attorney or party in compliance with NY R CHIEF ADMIN § 130-1.1-a if it has been signed by such attorney or party as provided in NY R UNIF TRIAL CTS § 202.5-b(e)(1) and it bears the signatory's name. NY R UNIF TRIAL CTS § 202.5-b(e)(2). An electronically filed document shall be considered to have been signed by, and shall be binding upon, the person identified as a signatory, if:

  i. It bears the physical signature of such person and is scanned into an electronic format that reproduces such signature; or

  ii. The signatory has electronically affixed the digital image of his or her signature to the document; or

  iii. It is electronically filed under the User ID and password of that person; or

iv. In a tax certiorari action in which the parties have stipulated to this procedure, it is an initiating document that is electronically filed without the signature of the signatory in a form provided above in NY R UNIF TRIAL CTS § 202.5-b(e)(iv), provided that, prior to filing, the document is signed in full in hard copy (which hard copy must be preserved until the conclusion of all proceedings, including appeals, in the case in which it is filed); or

v. In a small claims assessment review proceeding, it is a petition recorded by the NYSCEF site upon the filing of a text file as provided in NY R UNIF TRIAL CTS § 202.5-b(b)(1), provided that prior to filing, the document was signed in full in hard copy (which hard copy must be preserved until the conclusion of all proceedings in the matter, including article 78 (NY CPLR § 7801, et seq.) review and any appeals, and must be made available during the proceeding upon request of the respondent or the court); or

vi. It otherwise bears the electronic signature of the signatory in a format conforming to such standards and requirements as may hereafter be established by the Chief Administrator. NY R UNIF TRIAL CTS § 202.5-b(e).

4. *Confidentiality of personal information.* No person may file any document available for public inspection with any state agency, political subdivision, or in any court of this state that contains a Social Security account number of any other person, unless such other person is a dependent child, or has consented to such filing, except as required by federal or state law or regulation, or by court rule. NY GEN BUS § 399-ddd. Submissions pursuant to e-filing procedures shall have the same confidentiality rights as paper documents. NY R UNIF TRIAL CTS § 202.5-b(k)(1).

a. *Confidential personal information.* Except in the actions designated in NY R UNIF TRIAL CTS § 202.5(e)(1), or as otherwise provided by rule or law or court order, and whether or not a sealing order is or has been sought, the parties shall omit or redact confidential personal information in papers submitted to the court for filing. For purposes of NY R UNIF TRIAL CTS § 202.5(e), confidential personal information ("CPI") means:

i. The taxpayer identification number of an individual or an entity, including a Social Security number, an employer identification number, and an individual taxpayer identification number, except the last four (4) digits thereof;

ii. The date of an individual's birth, except the year thereof;

iii. The full name of an individual known to be a minor, except the minor's initials;

iv. A financial account number, including a credit and/or debit card number, a bank account number, an investment account number, and/or an insurance account number, except the last four (4) digits or letters thereof; and

v. Any of the documents or testimony in a matrimonial action protected by NY DOM REL § 235 or evidence sealed by the court in such an action which are attached as exhibits or referenced in the papers filed in any other civil action. For purposes of NY R UNIF TRIAL CTS § 202.5, a matrimonial action shall mean: an action to annul a marriage or declare the nullity of a void marriage, an action or agreement for a separation, an action for a divorce, or an action or proceeding for custody, visitation, writ of habeus corpus, child support, maintenance or paternity. NY R UNIF TRIAL CTS § 202.5(e)(1).

b. *Submission of confidential personal information.* Where a person submitting a paper to a court for filing believes in good faith that the inclusion of the full confidential personal information described in NY R UNIF TRIAL CTS § 202.5(e)(1) is material and necessary to the adjudication of the action or proceeding before the court, he or she may apply to the court for leave to serve and file together with a paper in which such information has been set forth in abbreviated form a confidential affidavit or affirmation setting forth the same information in unabbreviated form, appropriately referenced to the page or pages of the paper at which the abbreviated form appears. NY R UNIF TRIAL CTS § 202.5(e)(3).

c. *Home addresses.* For information on when home addresses and other personal information must be redacted, refer to NY CPLR Rule 2103-a.

5. *Defective papers.* A defect in the form of a paper, if a substantial right of a party is not prejudiced, shall be disregarded by the court, and leave to correct shall be freely given. NY CPLR Rule 2101(f). Papers that are stapled or bound securely shall not be rejected for filing simply because they are not bound with a backer of any kind. NY R UNIF TRIAL CTS § 202.5(a). A paper filed in accordance with the rules of the chief administrator or any local rule or practice established by the court shall be deemed filed. NY CPLR Rule 2102(b).

a. *Objection to defective papers.* The party on whom a paper is served shall be deemed to have waived objection to any defect in form unless, within fifteen (15) days after the receipt thereof, the party on whom the paper is served returns the paper to the party serving it with a statement of particular objections. NY CPLR Rule 2101(f).

F. Filing and Service Requirements

1. *Filing requirements.* Except where otherwise prescribed by law or order of court, papers required to be filed shall be filed

with the clerk of the court in which the action is triable. In an action or proceeding in supreme or court, papers required to be filed shall be filed with the clerk of the county in which the proceeding is brought. NY CPLR Rule 2102(a).

a. *Electronic filing.* On consent, documents may be filed and served by electronic means in Supreme Court in such civil actions and in such counties as shall be authorized by order of the Chief Administrator of the Courts and only to the extent and in the manner provided in NY R UNIF TRIAL CTS § 202.5-b. NY R UNIF TRIAL CTS § 202.5-b(a)(1). For the definitions of terms used in electronic filing, refer to NY R UNIF TRIAL CTS § 202.5-b(a)(2).

   i. *Electronic filing of discovery materials.* In any action subject to e-filing, parties and non-parties producing materials in response to discovery demands may enter into a stipulation, which shall be e-filed, authorizing the electronic filing of discovery responses and discovery materials to the degree and upon terms and conditions set forth in the stipulation. In the absence of such a stipulation, no party shall file electronically any such materials except in the form of excerpts, quotations, or selected exhibits from such materials as part of motion papers, pleadings or other filings with the court. NY R UNIF TRIAL CTS § 202.5-b(j).

   ii. *E-filing mandatory.* In any action subject to e-filing, all documents required to be filed with the court by an e-filing party shall be filed and served electronically, except as provided in NY R UNIF TRIAL CTS § 202.5-b. NY R UNIF TRIAL CTS § 202.5-b(d)(1)(i).

   iii. *Who may file.* Documents may be filed or served electronically only by a person who has registered as an authorized e-filing user or as otherwise provided in NY R UNIF TRIAL CTS § 202.5-b(c). NY R UNIF TRIAL CTS § 202.5-b(c)(1).

   iv. *When filing made.* Documents may be transmitted at any time of the day or night to the NYSCEF site. A document other than an order or judgment is filed when its electronic transmission or, in the case of a petition that is e-filed by submission of a text file as provided in NY R UNIF TRIAL CTS § 202.5-b(b)(1), the electronic transmission of the text file is recorded at that site, provided, however, that where payment of a fee is required upon the filing of a document, the document is not filed until transmission of the document and the information or form or information as required in NY R UNIF TRIAL CTS § 202.5-b(d)(2)(i), NY R UNIF TRIAL CTS § 202.5-b(d)(2)(ii) or NY R UNIF TRIAL CTS § 202.5-b(d)(2)(iii) has been recorded at the NYSCEF site; or, if no transmission of that information or form or information is recorded, where permitted by the County Clerk, until payment is presented to the County Clerk. NY R UNIF TRIAL CTS § 202.5-b(d)(3)(i).

   v. *Notification of filing.* No later than the close of business on the business day following the electronic filing of a document, a notification, in a form prescribed by the Chief Administrator, shall be transmitted electronically by the NYSCEF site to the person filing such document and the e-mail service addresses of all other participating parties in such action. NY R UNIF TRIAL CTS § 202.5-b(d)(3)(ii).

   vi. *Removal of confidential information and other corrections.* If a document filed electronically is subsequently discovered to contain confidential data—including but not limited to trade secrets, information protected by confidentiality agreement, or personal confidential information as defined by statute or court rule—or otherwise to have been filed in error, the filer or another party or affected person may (1) notify the parties and any non-party filers in the action of the confidentiality issue or other error raised by the filing, and of his or her intention to seek judicial relief to correct the filing: (2) following such notification, request that the appropriate County Clerk, exercising his or her administrative discretion, place the document temporarily in "restricted" status on the NYSCEF site, to be made available for viewing by court staff and the parties but not the general public; and (3) file an application to correct the filing by order to show cause within five (5) business days of such notification (or such time as the court may direct), including a request for preliminary injunctive relief limiting interim disclosure of the document at issue. Unless otherwise directed by the court, any document placed in restricted status in response to such a request shall be returned to public view upon expiration of this five (5) day period. The Chief Administrator of the Courts shall promulgate forms to implement this process. NY R UNIF TRIAL CTS § 202.5-b(d)(3)(iii).

   vii. *Documents requiring judge's signature.* Except where the court directs otherwise, any document that requires a judge's signature shall be transmitted electronically and in hard copy to the court. NY R UNIF TRIAL CTS § 202.5-b(d)(6).

   viii. *Documents which would be inconvenient to file electronically; Hard copies.* Notwithstanding any other provision of NY R UNIF TRIAL CTS § 202.5-b, and subject to such guidelines as may be established by the Chief Administrative Judge, the County Clerk or his or her designee may require or permit a party to file in hard copy, in accordance with procedures set by the County Clerk or designee, an exhibit or other document which it is impractical or inconvenient to file electronically. NY R UNIF TRIAL CTS § 202.5-b(d)(7).

ix. *Documents containing sensitive or proprietary information.* In an action subject to e-filing, any person may apply for an order prohibiting or restricting the electronic filing in the action of specifically identified materials on the grounds that such materials are subject to copyright or other proprietary rights, or trade secret or other privacy interests, and that electronic filing in the action is likely to result in substantial prejudice to those rights or interests. NY R UNIF TRIAL CTS § 202.5-b(k)(2).

x. *Refusal to accept paper filings.* In accordance with NY CPLR Rule 2102(c), a County Clerk and a chief clerk of the Supreme Court or County Court, as appropriate, shall refuse to accept for filing papers filed in actions and proceedings when the paper sought to be filed:

- Is in an action subject to electronic filing pursuant to Rules of the Chief Administrator,
- Is not being filed electronically, and
- Does not include the notice required by NY R UNIF TRIAL CTS § 202.5-b(d)(1). NY R UNIF TRIAL CTS § 202.5(d)(1)(v); NY R UNIF TRIAL CTS § 202.5-bb(d).

xi. *Emergency filings; Hard copies.* For information on when an emergency filing may be filed and served in hard copy, refer to NY R UNIF TRIAL CTS § 202.5-b(d)(1)(ii), NY R UNIF TRIAL CTS § 202.5-b(d)(1)(iii) and NY R UNIF TRIAL CTS § 202.5-bb(c)(3).

xii. *Technical failures.* The NYSCEF site shall be considered to be subject to a technical failure on a given day if the site is unable to accept filings or provide access to filed documents continuously or intermittently over the course of any period of time greater than one (1) hour after 12:00 noon of that day. Notice of all such technical failures shall be provided on the site. NY R UNIF TRIAL CTS § 202.5-b(i).

- When e-filing is hindered by a technical failure, a party may file with the appropriate clerk and serve in hard copy. NY R UNIF TRIAL CTS § 202.5-b(i). In the event an attorney or party shall file and serve documents in hard copy pursuant to NY R UNIF TRIAL CTS § 202.5-b(i), each such document shall include the notice required by NY R UNIF TRIAL CTS § 202.5-b(d)(1), and the filer shall file those documents with the NYSCEF site within three (3) business days after restoration of normal operations at that site. NY R UNIF TRIAL CTS § 202.5-b(i).
- With the exception of deadlines that by law cannot be extended, the time for filing of any document that is delayed due to technical failure of the site shall be extended for one (1) day for each day on which such failure occurs, unless otherwise ordered by the court. NY R UNIF TRIAL CTS § 202.5-b(i).

xiii. *Filing fees.* For information on what information must be provided to pay filing fees, refer to NY R UNIF TRIAL CTS § 202.5-b(d)(2).

xiv. *Exemption from e-filing.* For information on exemptions from e-filing, refer to NY R UNIF TRIAL CTS § 202.5-bb(e).

b. *Facsimile filing.* In the Supreme Court, facsimile filing shall be limited to commercial claims and tax certiorari, conservatorship, and mental hygiene proceedings in Monroe, Westchester, New York and Suffolk Counties. NY R UNIF TRIAL CTS § 202.5-a(a)(1). Refer to NY R UNIF TRIAL CTS § 202.5-a for information on the procedures for facsimile filing.

2. *Service requirements*

a. *Who may serve.* Except where otherwise prescribed by law or order of court, papers may be served by any person not a party of the age of eighteen years or over. NY CPLR Rule 2103(a).

b. *Service upon attorney.* Except where otherwise prescribed by law or order of court, papers to be served upon a party in a pending action shall be served upon the party's attorney. Where the same attorney appears for two or more parties, only one (1) copy need be served upon the attorney. Such service upon an attorney shall be made:

i. By delivering the paper to the attorney personally. NY CPLR Rule 2103(b)(1).

ii. By mailing the paper to the attorney at the address designated by that attorney for that purpose or, if none is designated, at the attorney's last known address; service by mail shall be complete upon mailing. NY CPLR Rule 2103(b)(2).

iii. If the attorney's office is open, by leaving the paper with a person in charge, or if no person is in charge, by leaving it in a conspicuous place; or if the attorney's office is not open, by depositing the paper, enclosed in a sealed wrapper directed to the attorney, in the attorney's office letter drop or box. NY CPLR Rule 2103(b)(3).

iv. By leaving it at the attorney's residence within the state with a person of suitable age and discretion. Service upon an attorney shall not be made at the attorney's residence unless service at the attorney's office cannot be made. NY CPLR Rule 2103(b)(4).

v. By transmitting the paper to the attorney by facsimile transmission, provided that a facsimile telephone number is designated by the attorney for that purpose. Service by facsimile transmission shall be complete upon the receipt by the sender of a signal from the equipment of the attorney served indicating that the transmission was received, and the mailing of a copy of the paper to that attorney. The designation of a facsimile telephone number in the address block subscribed on a paper served or filed in the course of an action or proceeding shall constitute consent to service by facsimile transmission in accordance with NY CPLR Rule 2103(b)(5). An attorney may change or rescind a facsimile telephone number by serving a notice on the other parties. NY CPLR Rule 2103(b)(5).

vi. By dispatching the paper to the attorney by overnight delivery service at the address designated by the attorney for that purpose or, if none is designated, at the attorney's last known address. Service by overnight delivery service shall be complete upon deposit of the paper enclosed in a properly addressed wrapper into the custody of the overnight delivery service for overnight delivery, prior to the latest time designated by the overnight delivery service for overnight delivery. "Overnight delivery service" means any delivery service which regularly accepts items for overnight delivery to any address in the state. NY CPLR Rule 2103(b)(6).

vii. By transmitting the paper to the attorney by electronic means where and in the manner authorized by the chief administrator of the courts by rule and, unless such rule shall otherwise provide, such transmission shall be upon the party's written consent. The subject matter heading for each paper sent by electronic means must indicate that the matter being transmitted electronically is related to a court proceeding. NY CPLR Rule 2103(b)(7).

c. *Electronic service mandatory; Consenting to electronic service; How electronic service may be made.* Except as otherwise provided in NY R UNIF TRIAL CTS § 202.5-bb, filing and service of all documents in an action that has been commenced electronically in accordance with NY R UNIF TRIAL CTS § 202.5-bb shall be by electronic means. NY R UNIF TRIAL CTS § 202.5-bb(c)(1).

i. *Party's consent required for certain e-filing.* After commencement of an action wherein e-filing is authorized, documents may be electronically filed and served, but only by, and electronic service shall be made only upon, a party or parties who have consented thereto. NY R UNIF TRIAL CTS § 202.5-b(b)(2)(i).

- A consent to e-filing in an action shall state that the party providing it agrees to the use of e-filing in the action and to be bound by the filing and service provisions in NY R UNIF TRIAL CTS § 202.5-b. NY R UNIF TRIAL CTS § 202.5-b(b)(2)(ii).

ii. *Address for service; Duty to notify as to changes.* The e-mail service address recorded at the time of registration is the e-mail address at which service of interlocutory documents on that party may be made through notification transmitted by the NYSCEF site. It is the responsibility of each filing user to monitor that address and promptly notify the Resource Center in the event of a change in his or her e-mail service address. NY R UNIF TRIAL CTS § 202.5-b(f)(2)(i).

iii. *How service made.* An e-filing party causes service of an interlocutory document to be made upon another party participating in e-filing by filing the document electronically. Upon receipt of an interlocutory document, the NYSCEF site shall automatically transmit electronic notification to all e-mail service addresses in such action. NY R UNIF TRIAL CTS § 202.5-b(f)(2)(ii).

- Except as provided otherwise in NY R UNIF TRIAL CTS § 202.5-b(h)(3), the electronic transmission of the notification shall constitute service of the document on the e-mail service addresses identified therein; however, such service will not be effective if the filing party learns that the notification did not reach the address of the person to be served. Proof of such service will be recorded on the NYSCEF site. A party may, however, utilize other service methods permitted by the CPLR provided that, if one of such other methods is used, proof of that service shall be filed electronically. NY R UNIF TRIAL CTS § 202.5-b(f)(2)(ii).

iv. *Signatures on hard copies; Proof of service filed electronically.* When an e-filing party serves a document in hard copy on a non-participating party, the document served shall bear full signatures of all signatories and proof of such service shall be filed electronically. NY R UNIF TRIAL CTS § 202.5-b(b)(2)(i).

v. *Effect of failure to consent.* A party's failure to consent to participation in electronic filing and service shall not bar any other party to the action from filing documents electronically with the County Clerk and the court or serving documents upon any other party who has consented to participation. A party who has not consented to participation shall file documents with the court and the County Clerk, and serve and be served with documents, in hard copy. NY R UNIF TRIAL CTS § 202.5-b(b)(2)(i).

d. *Service upon party.* If a party has not appeared by an attorney or the party's attorney cannot be served, service shall be upon the party by a method specified in NY CPLR Rule 2103(b)(1), NY CPLR Rule 2103(b)(2), NY CPLR Rule 2103(b)(4), NY CPLR Rule 2103(b)(5) or NY CPLR Rule 2103(b)(6). NY CPLR Rule 2103(c).

   i. When a party is in default for failure to appear, he shall not be entitled to notice or service of any copy required under NY CPLR § 3101, et seq. NY CPLR Rule 3105.

e. *Service on all parties.* Each paper served on any party shall be served on every other party who has appeared, except as otherwise may be provided by court order or as provided in NY CPLR § 3012 or in NY CPLR § 3215(f). Upon demand by a party, the plaintiff shall supply that party with a list of those who have appeared and the names and addresses of their attorneys. NY CPLR Rule 2103(e).

f. *Service by filing.* If a paper cannot be served by any of the methods specified in NY CPLR Rule 2103(b) and NY CPLR Rule 2103(c), service may be made by filing the paper as if it were a paper required to be filed. NY CPLR Rule 2103(d).

g. *Definitions.* For the purposes of NY CPLR Rule 2103:

   i. "Mailing" means the deposit of a paper enclosed in a first class postpaid wrapper, addressed to the address designated by a person for that purpose or, if none is designated, at that person's last known address, in a post office or official depository under the exclusive care and custody of the United States Postal Service within the state;

   ii. "Electronic means" means any method of transmission of information between computers or other machines designed for the purpose of sending and receiving such transmissions, and which allows the recipient to reproduce the information transmitted in a tangible medium of expression;

   iii. "Facsimile transmission" means any method of transmission of documents to a facsimile machine at a remote location which can automatically produce a tangible copy of such documents. NY CPLR Rule 2103(f).

G. Hearings

1. There is no hearing required or contemplated in the New York rules governing the request for a mental or physical examination.

H. Forms

1. New York Request for a Mental or Physical Examination of Witness Forms

a. Notice to submit to physical examination. MCF CPLR § 6:165.

b. Notice to submit to eye examination. MCF CPLR § 6:166.

c. Notice of motion to require plaintiff to submit to physical examination. MCF CPLR § 6:167.

d. Notice of motion to require plaintiff to submit to physical examination; Based in part on affidavit of physician. MCF CPLR § 6:168.

e. Affirmation of attorney in support of motion to require plaintiff to submit to physical examination. MCF CPLR § 6:169.

f. Affirmation of attorney in support of motion to require plaintiff to submit to physical examination; Defendant as corporation. MCF CPLR § 6:170.

g. Affidavit of doctor in support of motion to require plaintiff to submit to physical examination. MCF CPLR § 6:171.

h. Notice of motion to require plaintiff to submit to the taking of x-rays. MCF CPLR § 6:173.

i. Affidavit in support of motion to require plaintiff to submit to the taking of x-rays. MCF CPLR § 6:174.

j. Notice of motion (short form) for order directing that physical examination of plaintiff be conducted without presence of stenographer. MCF CPLR § 6:175.

k. Affidavit in support of motion for order directing that physical examination of plaintiff be conducted without presence of stenographer. MCF CPLR § 6:176.

l. Notice of cross-motion (short form) for protective order to allow plaintiff to have attorney, medical representative, and stenographer present at physical examination of plaintiff. MCF CPLR § 6:177.

m. Reply affidavit in support of motion of defendants for order directing that physical examination of plaintiff be conducted without presence of stenographer and in opposition to cross-motion of plaintiffs for protective order to allow plaintiffs to have attorney, medical representative, and court stenographer present. MCF CPLR § 6:179.

n. Notice of motion for protective order on notice to submit to physical examination. MCF CPLR § 6:181.
o. Affidavit in support of motion for protective order on notice to submit to physical examination. MCF CPLR § 6:182.
p. Request for exchange of reports of examining physicians. MCF CPLR § 6:184.

I. Applicable Rules

1. *State rules*
   a. Short title; Application; Construction; Definitions. NY CPLR § 101; NY CPLR § 104; NY CPLR § 105.
   b. Appendix of official forms. NY CPLR § 107.
   c. Extensions of time generally. NY CPLR § 2004.
   d. Form of papers. NY CPLR Rule 2101; NY CPLR Rule 2102; NY CPLR § 2105; NY GEN BUS § 399-ddd; NY R UNIF TRIAL CTS § 215.2; NY R UNIF TRIAL CTS § 215.3.
   e. Service of papers. NY CPLR Rule 2103.
   f. Computation of time. NY CPLR § 2402; NY GEN CONSTR § 19; NY GEN CONSTR § 20; NY GEN CONSTR § 25-a; NY GEN CONSTR § 30; NY GEN CONSTR § 31; NY GEN CONSTR § 53.
   g. Scope of disclosure. NY CPLR § 3101; NY CPLR § 3102; NY CPLR § 3103; NY CPLR § 3104; NY CPLR Rule 3105.
   h. Physical or mental examination. NY CPLR § 3121.
   i. Objection to disclosure, inspection or examination; Compliance. NY CPLR Rule 3122.
   j. Motions staying disclosure. NY CPLR Rule 3214; NY CPLR Rule 3407.
   k. Index number fees of county clerks. NY CPLR § 8018.
   l. Hours of court. NY R CHIEF J § 3.1.
   m. Application of part; Waiver; Additional rules; Application of CPLR; Definitions. NY R UNIF TRIAL CTS § 202.1.
   n. Papers filed in court; Electronic filing in supreme court. NY R UNIF TRIAL CTS § 202.5; NY R UNIF TRIAL CTS § 202.5-a; NY R UNIF TRIAL CTS § 202.5-b; NY R UNIF TRIAL CTS § 202.5-bb.
   o. Exchange of medical reports in personal injury and wrongful death actions. NY R UNIF TRIAL CTS § 202.17.
   p. Rules of the commercial division of the Supreme Court. NY R UNIF TRIAL CTS § 202.70.
   q. Signing of papers. NY R CHIEF ADMIN § 130-1.1-a.
2. *Local rules*
   a. *Albany County*
      i. Third judicial district rules. NY R 3 JD SUP Doc. 1.
   b. *Bronx County*
      i. Commercial division. NY R BRONX FIL R Doc. 12.
   c. *Kings County*
      i. Expedited discovery. NY R L KINGS Pt. B, Rule 5.
      ii. Pre calendar procedures. NY R L KINGS Rule I.
      iii. Both pre and post note procedures. NY R L KINGS Rule IV.
   d. *New York County*
      i. RJIs and assignments. NY R NY CTY Procedure IA.
      ii. Discovery schedule. NY R NY CTY J RUL Rule 8.

J. Miscellaneous

NOTE: Individual judges' rules may apply.

ALBANY COUNTY

JUSTICE LISA M. FISHER: NY R 3 JD FISHER Fisher; NY R 3 JD FISHER Fisher, PC Order.

JUSTICE RICHARD MOTT: NY R 3 JD MOTT Mott.

JUSTICE STEPHAN G. SCHICK: NY R 3 JD Schick.

FORECLOSURE SETTLEMENT PART: NY R 3 JD Foreclosure Settlement.

BRONX COUNTY

JUSTICE PAUL L. ALPERT: [NY R BRONX J Part IA-29, as amended by NY ORDER 20-0337].

JUSTICE BEN BARBATO: NY R BRONX J Part IA-21.

JUSTICE MARY ANNE BRIGANTTI: [NY R BRONX J Part IA-15, as amended by NY ORDER 20-0338].

JUSTICE JOSEPH E. CAPELLA: NY R BRONX J Part IA-23.

JUSTICE MITCHELL DANZIGER: NY R BRONX J Part IA-3/33 ; [NY R BRONX J Danziger, Part IA-3/33, as amended by NY ORDER 20-0339].

JUSTICE LAURA G. DOUGLAS: NY R BRONX J Part IA-11.

JUSTICE RUBEN FRANCO: NY R BRONX J Part IA-26.

JUSTICE DORIS M. GONZALEZ: NY R BRONX J Part IA-24.

JUSTICE WILMA GUZMAN: NY R BRONX J Part IA-7; [NY R BRONX J Guzman, Part IA-7 Virtual, as amended by NY ORDER 20-0340].

JUSTICE ROBERT T. JOHNSON: NY R BRONX J Part IA-12.

JUSTICE DONALD A. MILES: NY R BRONX J Part IA-8.

JUSTICE DONNA M. MILLS: NY R BRONX J Part IA-9.

JUSTICE JULIA I. RODRIGUEZ: NY R BRONX J Part IA-18; [NY R BRONX J Part IA-27, as amended by NY ORDER 20-0341].

JUSTICE LLINET M. ROSADO: [NY R BRONX J Part IA-25, as amended by NY ORDER 20-0342].

JUSTICE NORMA RUIZ: NY R BRONX J Part IA-22; [NY R BRONX J Ruiz, Part IA-22 Virtual, as amended by NY ORDER 20-0343].

JUSTICE HOWARD H. SHERMAN: NY R BRONX J Part IA-4.

JUSTICE FERNANDO TAPIA: NY R BRONX J Part IA-13.

JUSTICE ELIZABETH A. TAYLOR: NY R BRONX J Part IA-2.

JUSTICE ALISON Y. TRUITT: NY R BRONX J Part IA-5.

PART IDV: NY R BRONX J Doc. 1.

PRE-TRIAL PART RULES: NY R BRONX J Doc. 2.

PRE TRIAL WORKSHEET: NY R BRONX J Doc. 3.

FORECLOSURE SETTLEMENT PART RULES: NY R BRONX J Doc. 4.

GUARDIANSHIP PART RULES: NY R BRONX J Doc. 5.

LPM PART RULES: NY R BRONX J Doc. 6.

ERIE COUNTY

JUSTICE M. WILLIAM BOLLER: NY R 8 JD J Boller.

JUSTICE RALPH A. BONIELLO: NY R 8 JD J Boniello.

JUSTICE CHRISTOPHER J. BURN: NY R 8 JD J Burns.

JUSTICE RUSSELL P. BUSCAGLIA: NY R 8 JD J Buscaglia.

JUSTICE FRANK CARUSO: NY R 8 JD J Caruso.

JUSTICE STEPHEN W. CASS: NY R 8 JD J Cass.

JUSTICE DEBORAH A. CHIMES: NY R 8 JD J Chimes.

JUSTICE EMILIO COLAIACOVO: [NY R 8 JD J Colaiacovo, as amended by NY ORDER 20-0252].

JUSTICE DIANE Y. DEVLIN: NY R 8 JD J Devlin.

JUSTICE JAMES H. DILLON: NY R 8 JD J Dillon.

JUSTICE PAULA L. FEROLETO: NY R 8 JD J Feroleto.

JUSTICE DANIEL J. FURLONG: [NY R 8 JD J Furlong, as amended by NY ORDER 20-0253].

JUSTICE JOSEPH R. GLOWNIA: NY R 8 JD J Glownia.

JUSTICE MARK J. GRISANTI: NY R 8 JD J Grisanti.

JUSTICE DEBORAH A. HAENDIGES: NY R 8 JD J Haendiges.

JUSTICE LYNN W. KEANE: [NY R 8 JD J Keane, as amended by NY ORDER 20-0254].

JUSTICE RICHARD C. KLOCH, Sr.: NY R 8 JD J Kloch.

JUSTICE FREDERICK J. MARSHALL: [NY R 8 JD J Marshall, as amended by NY ORDER 20-0255.

JUSTICE JOHN L. MICHALSKI: NY R 8 JD J Michalski.

JUSTICE MARK A. MONTOUR: [NY R 8 JD J Montour, as amended by NY ORDER 20-0256].

JUSTICE HENRY NOWAK: NY R 8 JD J Nowak.

JUSTICE JOHN F. O'DONNELL: NY R 8 JD J O'Donnell.

JUSTICE JEANETTE OGDEN: NY R 8 JD J Ogden.

JUSTICE CATHERINE NUGENT-PANEPINTO: NY R 8 JD J Nugent-Panepinto.

JUSTICE FRANK A. SEDITA, III: [NY R 8 JD J Sedita, as amended by NY ORDER 20-0257].

JUSTICE SARA SHELDON: NY R 8 JD J Sheldon.

JUSTICE DONNA M. SIWEK: NY R 8 JD J Siwek.

JUSTICE MARY L. SLISZ: NY R 8 JD J Slisz.

JUSTICE TIMOTHY J. WALKER: [NY R 8 JD J Walker, as amended by NY ORDER 20-0258].

JUSTICE DENNIS E. WARD: NY R 8 JD J Ward.

JUSTICE PAUL B. WOJTASZEK: [NY R 8 JD J Wojtaszek, as amended by NY ORDER 20-0259].

JUSTICE CHARLES N. ZAMBITO: [NY R 8 JD J Zambito, as amended by NY ORDER 20-0260].

SUPREME COURT LEGAL STAFF: NY R 8 JD J Legal Staff.

KINGS COUNTY

JUSTICE RACHEL A. ADAMS: NY R KINGS J Part 5F.

JUSTICE LOREN BAILY-SCHIFFMAN: NY R KINGS J Part 65.

JUSTICE REGINALD A. BODDIE: NY R KINGS J Part 95.

JUSTICE THERESA M. CICCOTTO: NY R KINGS J Part 19; NY R KINGS J Part 5J.

JUSTICE LISSETTE COLON: NY R KINGS J Part Rules.

JUSTICE GENINE EDWARDS: NY R KINGS J Part 80.

JUSTICE PAMELA L. FISHER: [NY R KINGS J Part 94, as amended by NY ORDER 20-0208].

JUSTICE ROBIN GARSON: NY R KINGS J Part 75.

JUSTICE LARA J. GENOVISI: [NY R KINGS J Part 34, as amended by NY ORDER 20-0209].

JUSTICE BERNARD J. GRAHAM: NY R KINGS J Part 36.

JUSTICE DAWN JIMENEZ-SALTA: NY R KINGS J Part 88.

JUSTICE INGRID JOSEPH: [NY R KINGS J Part FRP3 and Part 83, as amended by NY ORDER 20-0210].

JUSTICE KATHY J. KING: NY R KINGS J Part 64, 76K.

JUSTICE LAWRENCE KNIPEL: NY R KINGS J Part 57.

JUSTICE DONALD KURTZ: NY R KINGS J Part 26.

JUSTICE CARL LANDICINO: [NY R KINGS J Part 81, as amended by NY ORDER 20-0211].

JUSTICE KATHERINE LEVINE: [NY R KINGS J Part 20, 25, 92, as amended by NY ORDER 20-0211].

JUSTICE LORNA MCALLISTER: [NY R KINGS J Part 10, as amended by NY ORDER 20-0211].

JUSTICE ROSEMARIE MONTALBANO: [NY R KINGS J Part 19, 71, and 22, as amended by NY ORDER 20-0211].
JUSTICE RICHARD J. MONTELIONE: [NY R KINGS J Part 99 and DJMP, as amended by NY ORDER 20-0215].
JUSTICE LISA S. OTTLEY: NY R KINGS J Part 24.
JUSTICE MARK I. PARTNOW: NY R KINGS J Part 43.
JUSTICE ERIC I. PRUS: NY R KINGS J Part 5A.
JUSTICE FRANCOIS RIVERA: NY R KINGS J Part 52.
JUSTICE KAREN B. ROTHENBERG: NY R KINGS J Part 35.
JUSTICE LEON RUCHELSMAN: NY R KINGS J Part 1.
JUSTICE WAYNE P. SAITTA: NY R KINGS J Part 29.
JUSTICE ROBIN K. SHEARES: NY R KINGS J Part 96.
JUSTICE KENNETH P. SHERMAN: NY R KINGS J Part 67 and 78.
JUSTICE DEBRA SILBER: NY R KINGS J Part 9 and 5K.
JUSTICE ELLEN M. SPODEK: NY R KINGS J Part 63.
JUSTICE MARSHA L. STEINHARDT: NY R KINGS J Part 15.
JUSTICE JEFFREY S. SUNSHINE: NY R KINGS J Part 5G.
JUSTICE PETER P. SWEENEY: [NY R KINGS J Part 35, as amended by NY ORDER 20-0218].
JUSTICE DELORES J. THOMAS: [NY R KINGS J Part 5T, as amended by NY ORDER 20-0221].
JUSTICE WAVNY TOUSSAINT: NY R KINGS J Part 70.
JUSTICE RICHARD VELASQUEZ: NY R KINGS J Part 66.
JUSTICE CAROLYN E. WADE: NY R KINGS J Part 84.
JUSTICE EDWARD G. WALKER: [NY R KINGS J Part 90, as amended by NY ORDER 20-0219].
JUSTICE LILLIAN WAN: [NY R KINGS J Part 17, as amended by NY ORDER 20-0220].
JUSTICE MICHELLE WESTON: NY R KINGS J Part 3.
MENTAL HYGIENE PART: NY R KINGS J Part 77.
MATRIMONIAL PARTS DURING COVID-19 EMERGENCY: JUSTICE KAREN B. ROTHENBERG: NY R KINGS J Doc. 1.

NASSAU COUNTY

JUSTICE ANNA R. ANZALONE: NY R NASSAU S J Anzalone, Part 26.
JUSTICE STACY D. BENNETT: NY R NASSAU S J Bennett; NY R NASSAU S J Bennett, Form 1.
JUSTICE ANTONIO BRANDVEEN: NY R NASSAU S J Brandveen, Part 31.
JUSTICE JEFFREY S. BROWN: [NY R NASSAU S J Brown, as amended by NY ORDER 20-0297].
JUSTICE STEPHEN A. BUCARIA: NY R NASSAU S J Bucaria.
JUSTICE JULIANNE T. CAPETOLA: NY R NASSAU S J Capetola, Part 28.
JUSTICE EDMUND M. DANE: NY R NASSAU S J Dane, Part 33.
JUSTICE VITO M. DESTEFANO: NY R NASSAU S J DeStefano, Part 13; NY R NASSAU S J DeStefano, Form 1.
JUSTICE ARTHUR M. DIAMOND: NY R NASSAU S J Diamond, Part 7.
JUSTICE THOMAS FEINMAN: NY R NASSAU S J Feinman, Part 5.
JUSTICE JOHN M. GALASSO: NY R NASSAU S J Galasso, Part 22.
JUSTICE SHARON M.J. GIANELLI: NY R NASSAU S J Gianelli, Part 22; NY R NASSAU S J Gianelli, Form 1.
JUSTICE JEFFREY A. GOODSTEIN: NY R NASSAU S J Goodstein, Part 33; NY R NASSAU S J Goodstein, Form 1.
JUSTICE DAVID J. GUGERTY: [NY R NASSAU S J Gugerty, Part 31, as amended by NY ORDER 20-0298].
JUSTICE HELENE F. GUGERTY: NY R NASSAU S J Gugerty, Part 47.
JUSTICE STEVEN M. JAEGER: NY R NASSAU S J Jaeger, Part 35; NY R NASSAU S J Jaeger, Form 1.

JUSTICE JACK L. LIBERT: NY R NASSAU S J Libert, Part 23.

JUSTICE JOSEPH H. LORINTZ: NY R NASSAU S J Lorintz, Part 26; NY R NASSAU S J Lorintz, Form 1.

JUSTICE ROY S. MAHON: NY R NASSAU S J Mahon, Part 3.

JUSTICE RANDY SUE MARBER: NY R NASSAU S J Marber, Part 8.

JUSTICE JAMES P. MCCORMACK: [NY R NASSAU S J McCormack, Part 18, as amended by NY ORDER, 20-0299].

JUSTICE DICCIA T. PINEDA-KIRWAN: [NY R NASSAU S J Pineda-Kirwan, as amended by NY ORDER 20-0300].

JUSTICE THOMAS RADEMAKER: [NY R NASSAU S J Rademaker, Part 28, as amended by NY ORDER 20-0301]; [NY R NASSAU S J Rademaker, Form 1, as amended by NY ORDER 20-0301].

JUSTICE DENISE L. SHER: NY R NASSAU S J Rademaker, Part 32.

JUSTICE LEONARD D. STEINMAN: [NY R NASSAU S J Steinman, Part 15, as amended by NY ORDER 20-0303]; NY R NASSAU S J Steinman, Form 1.

JUSTICE HOWARD E. STURIM: NY R NASSAU S J Sturim, Part 50; NY R NASSAU S J Sturim, Form 1.

JUSTICE HELEN VOUTSINAS: [NY R NASSAU S J Voutsinas, Part 25, as amended by NY ORDER 20-0304]; [NY R NASSAU S J Voutsinas, Form 1, as amended by NY ORDER 20-0305].

JUSTICE HOPE SCHWARTZ ZIMMERMAN: NY R NASSAU S J Zimmerman, Part 17.

NEW YORK COUNTY

JUDGE'S RULES; BASIC INFORMATION: [NY R NY CTY J RUL Doc. 1, as amended by NY ORDER 20-0202].

ONONDAGA COUNTY

JUSTICE ROBERT E. ANTONACCI II: [NY R ONDGA E FIL Doc. 1, as amended by 20-0239].

JUSTICE MICHAEL V. COCCOMI: NY R ONDGA E FIL Doc. 2.

JUSTICE GREGORY R. GILBERT: NY R 5 JD JUDGES Gilbert; NY R ONDGA E FIL Doc. 3.

JUSTICE DONALD A. GREENWOOD: NY R ONDGA E FIL Doc. 4.

JUSTICE DEBORAH H. KARALUNAS: NY R ONDGA E FIL Doc. 5.

JUSTICE JAMES MCCLUSKY: NY R 5 JD MCCLUSKY McClusky.

JUSTICE CHARLES C. MERRELL: NY R 5 JD MERRELL Merrell.

JUSTICE PATRICK F. MACRAE: NY R 5 JD MACRAE Doc. 1.

JUSTICE JAMES P. MURPHY: NY R ONDGA E FIL Doc. 7.

JUSTICE GERALD J. NERI: [NY R 5 JD JUDGES Neri, as amended by NY ORDER 20-0236]; [NY R ONDGA E FIL Doc. 8, as amended by NY ORDER 20-0241].

JUSTICE ANTHONY J. PARIS: NY R 5 JD JUDGES Paris; [NY R ONDGA E FIL Doc. 9, as amended by NY ORDER 20-0242].

JUSTICE NORMAN W. SEITER, JR.: NY R 5 JD JUDGES Seiter.

JUSTICE KEVIN G. YOUNG: [NY R ONDGA E FIL Doc. 10, as amended by NY ORDER 20-0243].

QUEENS COUNTY

JUSTICE PAM JACKMAN BROWN: [NY R L QUEENS Brown, Part 19, as amended by NY ORDER 20-0321].

JUSTICE CHEREE A. BUGGS: NY R L QUEENS Buggs, Part 30.

JUSTICE PAM JACKMAN BROWN: [NY R L QUEENS Brown, Part 19, as amended by NY ORDER 20-0321].

JUSTICE DENIS J. BUTLER: NY R L QUEENS Butler, Part 12.

JUSTICE ROBERT I. CALORAS: [NY R L QUEENS Caloras, Part 36, as amended by NY ORDER 20-0322].

JUSTICE ANNA CULLEY: NY R L QUEENS Culley, Part 53.

JUSTICE TIMOTHY DUFFICY: NY R L QUEENS Dufficy, Part 35.

JUSTICE DAVID ELLIOT: NY R L QUEENS Elliot, Part 14.

JUSTICE JOSEPH J. ESPOSITO: NY R L QUEENS Esposito, Part 6.

JUSTICE DARRELL L. GAVRIN: [NY R L QUEENS Gavrin, Part 27, as amended by NY ORDER 20-0323].

JUSTICE WYATT N. GIBBONS: [NY R L QUEENS Gibbons, Part 5, as amended by NY ORDER 20-0330.

JUSTICE DONNA-MARIE E. GOLIA: [NY R L QUEENS Golia, Part 21, as amended by NY ORDER 20-0331].

JUSTICE MARGUERITE A. GRAYS: [NY R L QUEENS Grays, Part 4, as amended by NY ORDER 20-0324].

JUSTICE RUDOLPH E. GRECO: [NY R L QUEENS Greco, Part 32, as amended by NY ORDER 20-0325].

JUSTICE MAUREEN HEALY: NY R L QUEENS Healy, Part 6.

JUSTICE PHILLIP HOM: [NY R L QUEENS Hom, Part 43, as amended by NY ORDER 20-0332].

JUSTICE KEVIN J. KERRIGAN: NY R L QUEENS Kerrigan, Part 10.

JUSTICE MOJGAN C. LANCMAN: NY R L QUEENS Lancman, Part 20.

JUSTICE RICHARD G. LATIN: NY R L QUEENS Latin, Part 40.

JUSTICE ULYSSES B. LEVERETT: [NY R L QUEENS Leverett, Part 6, as amended by NY ORDER 20-0326].

JUSTICE LEONARD LIVOTE: NY R L QUEENS Livote, Part 33.

JUSTICE LEE A. MAYERSOHN: NY R L QUEENS Mayersohn, Part 22; NY R L QUEENS Mayersohn, Part 22G; [NY R L QUEENS Mayersohn, Part 22G COVID, as amended by NY ORDER 20-0327].

JUSTICE ROBERT J. MCDONALD: NY R L QUEENS McDonald, Part 34.

JUSTICE MARGARET MCGOWAN: NY R L QUEENS McGowan, Part 52.

JUSTICE MAURICE E. MUIR: [NY R L QUEENS Muir, Part 42, as amended by NY ORDER 20-0333].

JUSTICE JODI ORLOW: NY R L QUEENS Orlow, Part 51.

JUSTICE LESLIE J. PURIFICCION: NY R L QUEENS Purificcion, Part 39.

JUSTICE JOSEPH RISI: [NY R L QUEENS Risi, Part 3, as amended by NY ORDER 20-0328].

JUSTICE FREDERICK D.R. SAMPSON: [NY R L QUEENS Sampson, Part 31, as amended by NY ORDER 20-0329].

JUSTICE MARTIN J. SCHULMAN: NY R L QUEENS Schulman, Part 29.

JUSTICE BERNICE D. SIEGAL: NY R L QUEENS Siegal, Part 25G.

JUSTICE JANICE A. TAYLOR: NY R L QUEENS Taylor, Part 15.

JUSTICE CARMEN R. VELASQUEZ: NY R L QUEENS Velasquez, Part 38.

JUSTICE LOURDES M VENTURA: [NY R L QUEENS Ventura, Part 37, as amended by NY ORDER 20-0334].

JUSTICE WILLIAM A. VISCOVICH: NY R L QUEENS Viscovich, Part 63.

JUSTICE ALLAN B. WEISS: NY R L QUEENS Weiss, Part 2.

COMPLIANCE, SETTLEMENT AND CONFERENCE PART: NY R L QUEENS Doc 1.

PRELIMINARY CONFERENCE PART: [NY R L QUEENS Doc. 2, as amended by NY ORDER 20-0335].

MEDICAL MALPRACTICE CONFERENCE PART: [NY R L QUEENS Doc. 3, as amended by NY ORDER 20-0336].

TRIAL SCHEDULING PART: NY R L QUEENS Doc. 4.

SUMMARY JURY TRIAL PROGRAM: NY R L QUEENS Doc. 7.

RESIDENTIAL FORECLOSURE PART: NY R L QUEENS Doc. 9.

FORECLOSURE AUCTION RULES: NY R L QUEENS Doc. 10.

MATRIMONIAL PRELIMINARY CONFERENCE PART: NY R L QUEENS Doc. 11.

NON-CUSTODIAL CONTESTED MATRIMONIAL PART: NY R L QUEENS Doc. 12.

Requests, Notices and Applications
Subpoena

Document Last Updated August 2020

A. Checklist

(I) ❑ Matters to consider for party serving subpoena

(a) ❑ Required documents

(1) ❑ Subpoena

(2) ❑ Witness fees

(3) ❑ Proof of service

(b) ❑ Timing

(1) ❑ There are no timing requirements for the subpoena

(2) ❑ Where a subpoena duces tecum is served upon a hospital, or upon a department or bureau of a municipal corporation or of the state, or an officer thereof, requiring the production of records relating to the condition or treatment of a patient, such a subpoena shall be served at least three (3) days before the time fixed for the production of the records unless otherwise ordered by a court

(3) ❑ A subpoena duces tecum to be served upon a library, or a department or bureau of a municipal corporation or of the state must be served upon such library, or such department or bureau of such municipal corporation or of the state or an officer having custody of the book, document or other thing and the adverse party at least twenty-four (24) hours before the time fixed for the production of such records

B. Timing

1. *Time for subpoena.* There are no timing requirements for the subpoena.

a. *Special rule for medical records.* Where a subpoena duces tecum is served upon a hospital, or upon a department or bureau of a municipal corporation or of the state, or an officer thereof, requiring the production of records relating to the condition or treatment of a patient, such a subpoena shall be served at least three (3) days before the time fixed for the production of the records unless otherwise ordered by a court. NY CPLR § 2306(a).

b. *Special rule for government library, department or bureau.* A subpoena duces tecum to be served upon a library, or a department or bureau of a municipal corporation or of the state, or an officer thereof, requiring the production of any books, papers or other things, shall be issued by a justice of the supreme court in the district in which the book, paper or other thing is located or by a judge of the court in which an action for which it is required is triable. Such subpoena must be served upon such library, or such department or bureau of such municipal corporation or of the state or an officer having custody of the book, document or other thing and the adverse party at least twenty-four (24) hours before the time fixed for the production of such records unless in the case of an emergency the court shall by order dispense with such notice otherwise required. NY CPLR § 2307.

2. *Time to bring motion for subpoena.* A subpoena to compel production of an original record or document where a certified transcript or copy is admissible in evidence, or to compel attendance of any person confined in a penitentiary or jail, shall be issued by the court. Unless the court orders otherwise, a motion for such subpoena shall be made on at least one (1) day's notice to the person having custody of the record, document or person confined. NY CPLR § 2302(b).

a. *Time to bring motion against government library, department or bureau.* A subpoena duces tecum to be served upon a library, or a department or bureau of a municipal corporation or of the state, or an officer thereof, requiring the production of any books, papers or other things, shall be issued by a justice of the supreme court in the district in which the book, paper or other thing is located or by a judge of the court in which an action for which it is required is triable. Unless the court orders otherwise, a motion for such subpoena shall be made on at least one (1) day's notice to the library, department, bureau or officer having custody of the book, document or other thing and the adverse party. NY CPLR § 2307.

3. *KINGS COUNTY: Discovery timing.* At [the Compliance Conference, the court will] schedule all outstanding discovery to be completed prior to date fixed for filing Note of Issue. NY R L KINGS Rule I(B).

a. *Deadlines in orders.* Discovery scheduled in Compliance Conference orders shall be strictly adhered to and may not be extended without leave of the court. Unjustified failure to comply with the provisions of the CCP order will result in preclusion, the striking of a pleading or imposition of sanctions, as appropriate. NY R L KINGS Rule I(B)(2).

b. *Cases with extensive discovery.* Where post Compliance Conference discovery is to be extensive, cases may be retracked from standard to complex, which will provide for three (3) additional months of post Compliance Conference discovery and extend the Note of Issue date by three (3) months. NY R L KINGS Rule I(B)(1).

c. *Discovery not stayed.* Ordinarily the Court/JHO will not stay discovery during pendency of motions to withdraw, or during pendency of settlement, or during pendency of dispositive motions. NY R L KINGS Rule IV.

d. *Expedited discovery in certain cases.* Discovery in third party and joint actions will be expedited. NY R L KINGS Pt. B, Rule 5.

e. For more information on discovery scheduling, refer to NY R L KINGS Flow Chart.

4. *NEW YORK COUNTY: Deadlines in orders.* Strict compliance with all discovery orders is required. Unexcused or unjustified failure to comply with deadlines fixed by the court, including those set out in Preliminary Conference Orders, may result in an award of costs, conditional or otherwise, or the imposition of another penalty authorized by NY CPLR § 3126. NY R NY CTY J RUL Rule 8.

5. *Computation of time*

a. *Units of time*

i. *Day.* A calendar day includes the time from midnight to midnight. Sunday or any day of the week specifically mentioned means a calendar day. NY GEN CONSTR § 19.

ii. *Month.* In a statute, contract or public or private instrument, unless otherwise provided in such contract or instrument or by law, the term month means a calendar month and not a lunar month. NY GEN CONSTR § 31.

iii. *Year.* For information on the definition of a year, including the definitions of a half-year and quarter-year, refer to NY GEN CONSTR § 58 and NY GEN CONSTR § 50. For information on leap years, refer to NY GEN CONSTR § 57.

b. *Periods of time*

i. *Number of days.* A number of days specified as a period from a certain day within which or after or before which an act is authorized or required to be done means such number of calendar days exclusive of the calendar day from which the reckoning is made. NY GEN CONSTR § 20.

- If such period is a period of two (2) days, Saturday, Sunday or a public holiday must be excluded from the reckoning if it is an intervening day between the day from which the reckoning is made and the last day of the period. NY GEN CONSTR § 20.
- In computing any specified period of time from a specified event, the day upon which the event happens is deemed the day from which the reckoning is made. The day from which any specified period of time is reckoned shall be excluded in making the reckoning. NY GEN CONSTR § 20.

ii. *Number of months.* A number of months after or before a certain day shall be computed by counting such number of calendar months from such day, exclusive of the calendar month in which such day occurs, and shall include the day of the month in the last month so counted having the same numerical order in days of the month as the day from which the computation is made, unless there be not so many days in the last month so counted, in which case the period computed shall expire with the last day of the month so counted. NY GEN CONSTR § 30.

iii. *Publication of notice; Number of days.* The period of publication of a legal notice shall be computed by excluding the first day of publication and including the day on which the act or event of which notice is given is to take place or which completes the full period of publication. NY CPLR § 2402.

iv. *Periods ending on Saturday, Sunday or public holiday.* When any period of time, computed from a certain day, within which or after which or before which an act is authorized or required to be done, ends on a Saturday, Sunday or a public holiday, such act may be done on the next succeeding business day and if the period ends at a specified hour, such act may be done at or before the same hour of such next succeeding business day, except that where a period of time specified by contract ends on a Saturday, Sunday or a public holiday, the extension of such period is governed by NY GEN CONSTR § 25. NY GEN CONSTR § 25-a(1).

- For a list of public holidays, refer to NY GEN CONSTR § 24.

v. *Additional time after certain kinds of service*

- *Service by mail.* Where a period of time prescribed by law is measured from the service of a paper and service is by mail, five (5) days shall be added to the prescribed period. NY CPLR Rule 2103(b)(2).
- *Service by overnight delivery service.* Where a period of time prescribed by law is measured from the

service of a paper and service is by overnight delivery, one (1) business day shall be added to the prescribed period. NY CPLR Rule 2103(b)(6).

vi. *Daylight saving time.* For information on New York's time zone and the effect of daylight saving time, refer to NY GEN CONSTR § 52.

c. *Hours of court.* Notwithstanding any provision of law or rule of court to the contrary, throughout the State of New York the sessions of the Supreme Court for the disposition of business before the court shall commence not later than 9:30 a.m. and conclude not earlier than 5 p.m. Where warranted, the Chief Administrator of the Courts may authorize variances in the opening and closing hours of the courts, but, in such event, daily sessions shall total not less than six (6) hours. NY R CHIEF J § 3.1.

d. *Time limits; Extension of time.* Any act required by or in pursuance of law to be performed at or within a prescribed time, shall be performed according to the standard time. NY GEN CONSTR § 53.

i. Except where otherwise expressly prescribed by law, the court may extend the time fixed by any statute, rule or order for doing any act, upon such terms as may be just and upon good cause shown, whether the application for extension is made before or after the expiration of the time fixed. NY CPLR § 2004. Refer to the New York KeyRules Motion for Continuance/Extension of Time document for more information.

C. General Requirements

1. *Subpoena*

a. *Definitions.* A subpoena requires the attendance of a person to give testimony. A subpoena duces tecum requires production of books, papers and other things. A child support subpoena is a subpoena issued pursuant to NY SOC SERV § 111-p by the office of temporary and disability assistance or a local social services district, or its authorized representative, or another state's child support enforcement agency governed by 42 U.S.C.A. § 651, et seq. A trial subpoena duces tecum shall state on its face that all papers or other items delivered to the court pursuant to such subpoena shall be accompanied by a copy of such subpoena. NY CPLR § 2301.

b. *Subpoena; Issuance; By attorney of record in action.* Subpoenas may be issued without a court order by the clerk of the court, a judge where there is no clerk, the attorney general, an attorney of record for a party to an action, an administrative proceeding or an arbitration, an arbitrator, a referee, or any member of a board, commission or committee authorized by law to hear, try or determine a matter or to do any other act, in an official capacity, in relation to which proof may be taken or the attendance of a person as a witness may be required. NY CPLR § 2302(a).

i. *Subpoena for clinical records; Court order required.* A subpoena to compel production of a patient's clinical record maintained pursuant to the provisions of NY MENT HYG § 33.13 shall be accompanied by a court order. NY CPLR § 2302(a).

ii. *Child support subpoena; Issued by department.* A child support subpoena may be issued by the department, or the child support enforcement unit coordinator or support collection unit supervisor of a social services district, or his or her designee, or another state's child support enforcement agency governed by 42 U.S.C.A. § 651, et seq. NY CPLR § 2302(a).

iii. *Subpoena to compel production of original document; Issued by court.* A subpoena to compel production of an original record or document where a certified transcript or copy is admissible in evidence, or to compel attendance of any person confined in a penitentiary or jail, shall be issued by the court. NY CPLR § 2302(b).

- A subpoena to produce a prisoner so confined shall be issued by a judge to whom a petition for habeas corpus could be made under NY CPLR § 7002(b) or a judge of the court of claims, if the matter is pending before the court of claims, or a judge of the surrogate's court, if the matter is pending before the surrogate's court, or a judge or support magistrate of the family court, if the matter is pending before the family court, or a judge of the New York city civil court, if the matter is pending before the New York city civil court and it has been removed thereto from the supreme court pursuant to NY CPLR § 325(d). In the absence of an authorization by a patient, a trial subpoena duces tecum for the patient's medical records may only be issued by a court. NY CPLR § 2302(b).

c. *Subpoena to attend.* A subpoena may provide that the person subpoenaed shall appear on the date stated and any recessed or adjourned date of the trial, hearing or examination. If he is given reasonable notice of such recess or adjournment, no further process shall be required to compel his attendance on the adjourned date. At the end of each day's attendance, the person subpoenaed may demand his fee for the next day on which he is to attend. If the fee is not then paid, he shall be deemed discharged. NY CPLR § 2305(a).

d. *Subpoena duces tecum.* A subpoena duces tecum may be joined with a subpoena to testify at a trial, hearing or examination or may be issued separately. NY CPLR § 2305(b)(1).

i. *Attendance by person familiar with books or records.* Any person may comply with a subpoena duces tecum for a trial, hearing or examination by having the requisite books, documents or things produced by a person able to identify them and testify respecting their origin, purpose and custody. NY CPLR § 2305(b)(2).

ii. *Subpoena for medical records.* Where a subpoena duces tecum is served upon a hospital, or upon a department or bureau of a municipal corporation or of the state, or an officer thereof, requiring the production of records relating to the condition or treatment of a patient, a transcript or a full-sized legible reproduction, certified as correct by the superintendent or head of the hospital, department or bureau or his assistant, or the officer, may be produced unless otherwise ordered by a court. NY CPLR § 2306(a).

- Where a court has designated a clerk to receive records described in NY CPLR § 2306(a), delivery may be made to him at or before the time fixed for their production. The clerk shall give a receipt for the records and notify the person subpoenaed when they are no longer required. The records shall be delivered in a sealed envelope indicating the title of the action, the date fixed for production and the name and address of the attorney appearing on the subpoena. They shall be available for inspection pursuant to the rules or order of the court. NY CPLR § 2306(b).

iii. *Subpoena to government library, department, or bureau.* A subpoena duces tecum to be served upon a library, or a department or bureau of a municipal corporation or of the state, or an officer thereof, requiring the production of any books, papers or other things, shall be issued by a justice of the supreme court in the district in which the book, paper or other thing is located or by a judge of the court in which an action for which it is required is triable. NY CPLR § 2307.

- Compliance with a subpoena duces tecum may be made by producing a full-sized legible reproduction of the item or items required to be produced certified as complete and accurate by the person in charge of such library, department or bureau, or a designee of such person, and no personal appearance to certify such item or items shall be required of such person or designee, unless the court shall order otherwise pursuant to NY CPLR Rule 2214(d). Where a stipulation would serve the same purpose as production of the book, document or other thing and the subpoena is required because the parties will not stipulate, the judge may impose terms on any party, including the cost of production of the book or document, and require such cost to be paid as an additional fee to the library, department or officer. NY CPLR § 2307.

2. *Disobedience of a subpoena*

a. *Judicial*

i. Failure to comply with a subpoena issued by a judge, clerk or officer of the court shall be punishable as a contempt of court. If the witness is a party the court may also strike his or her pleadings. A subpoenaed person shall also be liable to the person on whose behalf the subpoena was issued for a penalty not exceeding one hundred fifty dollars ($150) and damages sustained by reason of the failure to comply. A court may issue a warrant directing a sheriff to bring the witness into court. NY CPLR § 2308(a).

ii. If a person so subpoenaed attends or is brought into court, but refuses without reasonable cause to be examined, or to answer a legal and pertinent question, or to produce a book, paper or other thing which he or she was directed to produce by the subpoena, or to subscribe his or her deposition after it has been correctly reduced to writing, the court may forthwith issue a warrant directed to the sheriff of the county where the person is, committing him or her to jail, there to remain until he or she submits to do the act which he or she was so required to do or is discharged according to law. Such a warrant of commitment shall specify particularly the cause of the commitment and, if the witness is committed for refusing to answer a question, the question shall be inserted in the warrant. NY CPLR § 2308(a).

b. *Non-judicial*

i. Unless otherwise provided, if a person fails to comply with a subpoena which is not returnable in a court, the issuer or the person on whose behalf the subpoena was issued may move in the supreme court to compel compliance. If the court finds that the subpoena was authorized, it shall order compliance and may impose costs not exceeding fifty dollars ($50). A subpoenaed person shall also be liable to the person on whose behalf the subpoena was issued for a penalty not exceeding fifty dollars ($50) and damages sustained by reason of the failure to comply. A court may issue a warrant directing a sheriff to bring the witness before the person or body requiring his appearance. NY CPLR § 2308(b)(1).

ii. If a person so subpoenaed attends or is brought before such person or body, but refuses without reasonable cause to be examined, or to answer a legal and pertinent question, or to produce a book, paper or other thing which he was directed to produce by the subpoena, or to subscribe his deposition after it has been correctly reduced to writing, the court, upon proof by affidavit, may issue a warrant directed to the sheriff of the county where the person is, committing him to jail, there to remain until he submits to do the act which he was so required to do or is discharged according to law. Such a warrant of commitment shall specify particularly the cause of the commitment and, if the witness is committed for refusing to answer a question, the question shall be inserted in the warrant. NY CPLR § 2308(b)(1).

iii. Notwithstanding the provisions of NY CPLR § 2308(b)(1), if a person fails to comply with a subpoena issued pursuant to NY SOC SERV § 111-p by the office of temporary and disability assistance or a social services district, or its authorized representative, or another state's child support enforcement agency governed by Title IV-D of the Social Security act (42 U.S.C.A. § 651, et seq.), such office or district is authorized to impose a penalty against the subpoenaed person. The amount of the penalty shall be determined by the commissioner of the office of temporary and disability assistance and set forth in regulation, and shall not exceed fifty dollars ($50). Payment of the penalty shall not be required, however, if in response to notification of the imposition of the penalty the subpoenaed person complies immediately with the subpoena. NY CPLR § 2308(b)(2).

c. *Review of proceedings*

i. Within ninety days (90) after the offender shall have been committed to jail he shall, if not then discharged by law, be brought, by the sheriff, or other officer, as a matter of course personally before the court issuing the warrant of commitment and a review of the proceedings shall then be held to determine whether the offender shall be discharged from commitment. At periodic intervals of not more than ninety (90) days following such review, the offender, if not then discharged by law from such commitment, shall be brought, by the sheriff, or other officer, personally before the court issuing the warrant of commitment and further reviews of the proceedings shall then be held to determine whether he shall be discharged from commitment. NY CPLR § 2308(c).

ii. The clerk of the court before which such review of the proceedings shall be held, or the judge or justice of such court in case there be no clerk, shall give reasonable notice in writing of the date, time and place of each such review to each party or his attorney who shall have appeared of record in the proceeding resulting in the issuance of the warrant of commitment, at their last known address. NY CPLR § 2308(c).

3. *Attendance fees*

a. *Persons subpoenaed.* Any person whose attendance is compelled by a subpoena, whether or not actual testimony is taken, shall receive for each day's attendance fifteen dollars ($15) for attendance fees and twenty-three cents (¢23) as travel expenses for each mile to the place of attendance from the place where he or she was served, and return. There shall be no mileage fee for travel wholly within a city. NY CPLR § 8001(a).

b. *Persons subpoenaed upon an examination before trial.* If a witness who is not a party, or agent or employee of a party, is subpoenaed to give testimony, or produce books, papers and other things at an examination before trial, he shall receive an additional three dollars ($3) for each day's attendance. NY CPLR § 8001(b).

c. *Transcripts of records.* Wherever the preparation of a transcript of records is required in order to comply with a subpoena, the person subpoenaed shall receive an additional fee of ten cents (¢10) per folio upon demand. NY CPLR § 8001(c).

4. *Governing law.* The civil practice law and rules (NY CPLR § 101, et seq.) shall govern the procedure in civil judicial proceedings in all courts of the state and before all judges, except where the procedure is regulated by inconsistent statute. The civil practice law and rules shall succeed the civil practice act and rules of civil practice and shall be deemed substituted therefor throughout the statutes and rules of the state. NY CPLR § 101. The civil practice law and rules shall be liberally construed to secure the just, speedy and inexpensive determination of every civil judicial proceeding. NY CPLR § 104.

a. *Uniform trial court rules.* The uniform civil rules for the Supreme Court and County Court (NY R UNIF TRIAL CTS § 202.1, et seq.) shall be applicable to civil actions and proceedings in the Supreme Court and the County Court. NY R UNIF TRIAL CTS § 202.1(a). The provisions of the uniform rules shall be construed consistent with the Civil Practice Law and Rules (CPLR), and matters not covered by the uniform rules shall be governed by the CPLR. NY R UNIF TRIAL CTS § 202.1(d).

b. *Local rules.* Local court rules, not inconsistent with law or with uniform civil rules for the Supreme Court and County Court (NY R UNIF TRIAL CTS § 202.1, et seq.), shall comply with Part 9 of the Rules of the Chief Judge (NY R CHIEF J § 9.1). NY R UNIF TRIAL CTS § 202.1(c).

c. *Official forms.* The state administrator shall have the power to adopt, amend and rescind an appendix of forms. Forms adopted pursuant to NY CPLR § 107 shall be sufficient under the civil practice law and rules and shall illustrate the simplicity and brevity of statement which the civil practice law and rules contemplate. NY CPLR § 107.

5. *Rules of the commercial division.* [Editor's note: certain types of civil cases or civil cases meeting certain monetary thresholds that are filed in the state of New York must be filed in the Commercial Division of the New York Supreme Courts. Rules governing practice in the commercial division are found in NY R UNIF TRIAL CTS § 202.70]. Cases which must be filed in the commercial division are listed below. For more information, refer to NY R UNIF TRIAL CTS § 202.70.

a. *Monetary thresholds.* Except as set forth in NY R UNIF TRIAL CTS § 202.70(b), the monetary thresholds of the Commercial Division, exclusive of punitive damages, interests, costs, disbursements and counsel fees claimed, are established as follows: (1) Albany County, fifty thousand dollars ($50,000); (2) Eighth Judicial District, one hundred thousand dollars ($100,000); (3) Kings County, one hundred fifty thousand dollars ($150,000); (4) Nassau County, two hundred thousand dollars ($200,000); (5) New York County, five hundred thousand dollars ($500,000); (6) Onondaga County, fifty thousand dollars ($50,000); (7) Queens County, one hundred thousand dollars ($100,000); (8) Seventh Judicial District, fifty thousand dollars ($50,000); (9) Suffolk County, one hundred thousand dollars ($100,000); and (10) Westchester County, one hundred thousand dollars ($100,000). NY R UNIF TRIAL CTS § 202.70(a).

i. *ALBANY COUNTY.* The Commercial Division of the Albany County Supreme Court exercises jurisdiction over selected business and commercial disputes in which the amount at issue generally involves damage claims in a minimum amount of fifty thousand dollars ($50,000) as well as claims for unspecified amounts where the value of the commercial asset(s) in dispute exceeds fifty thousand dollars ($50,000). A separate publication promulgating the rules and criteria relating to the filing and management of Commercial Court cases in this part may be obtained from the Albany County Supreme Court Clerk's Office. A section of the Uniform Civil Rules for the Supreme Court and County Court sets forth statewide rules. NY R 3 JD SUP Doc. 1(E).

ii. *BRONX COUNTY.* The monetary threshold for commercial cases in Bronx County will be seventy-five thousand dollars ($75,000). All other parameters including the type of matters that will be heard are contained within the Rules of the Commercial Division of the Supreme Court (NY R UNIF TRIAL CTS § 202.70). NY R BRONX FIL R Doc. 12.

iii. *NEW YORK COUNTY.* The monetary threshold in the New York County Commercial Division, which is generally applicable, is an amount in controversy of five hundred thousand dollars ($500,000) or more (exclusive of punitive damages, interest, costs, disbursements, and counsel fees). If the case is designated a commercial one and the Addendum is submitted, the clerk will review the pleadings to determine whether the amount in controversy in the case meets the monetary threshold or whether an exception to the threshold applies. NY R NY CTY Procedure IA(B). For more information on assigning a case to the commercial division in New York County, refer to NY R NY CTY Procedure IA(B).

b. *Commercial cases.* Actions in which the principal claims involve or consist of the following will be heard in the Commercial Division provided that the monetary threshold is met or equitable or declaratory relief is sought:

i. Breach of contract or fiduciary duty, fraud, misrepresentation, business tort (e.g., unfair competition), or statutory and/or common law violation where the breach or violation is alleged to arise out of business dealings (e.g., sales of assets or securities; corporate restructuring; partnership, shareholder, joint venture, and other business agreements; trade secrets; restrictive covenants; and employment agreements not including claims that principally involve alleged discriminatory practices);

ii. Transactions governed by the Uniform Commercial Code (exclusive of those concerning individual cooperative or condominium units);

iii. Transactions involving commercial real property, including Yellowstone injunctions and excluding actions for the payment of rent only;

iv. Shareholder derivative actions—without consideration of the monetary threshold;

v. Commercial class actions—without consideration of the monetary threshold;

vi. Business transactions involving or arising out of dealings with commercial banks and other financial institutions;

vii. Internal affairs of business organizations;

viii. Malpractice by accountants or actuaries, and legal malpractice arising out of representation in commercial matters;

ix. Environmental insurance coverage;

x. Commercial insurance coverage (e.g., directors and officers, errors and omissions, and business interruption coverage);

xi. Dissolution of corporations, partnerships, limited liability companies, limited liability partnerships and joint ventures—without consideration of the monetary threshold; and

xii. Applications to stay or compel arbitration and affirm or disaffirm arbitration awards and related injunctive relief pursuant to Article 75 of the New York Civil Practice Law and Rules (NY CPLR § 7501, et seq.) involving any of the foregoing enumerated commercial issues. Where the applicable arbitration agreement provides for the arbitration to be heard outside the United States, the monetary threshold set forth in NY R UNIF TRIAL CTS § 202.70(a) shall not apply. NY R UNIF TRIAL CTS § 202.70(b).

c. *Non-commercial cases.* The following will not be heard in the Commercial Division even if the monetary threshold is met:

i. Suits to collect professional fees;

ii. Cases seeking a declaratory judgment as to insurance coverage for personal injury or property damage;

iii. Residential real estate disputes, including landlord-tenant matters, and commercial real estate disputes involving the payment of rent only;

iv. Home improvement contracts involving residential properties consisting of one to four residential units or individual units in any residential building, including cooperative or condominium units;

v. Proceedings to enforce a judgment regardless of the nature of the underlying case;

vi. First-party insurance claims and actions by insurers to collect premiums or rescind non-commercial policies; and

vii. Attorney malpractice actions except as otherwise provided in NY R UNIF TRIAL CTS § 202.70(b)(8). NY R UNIF TRIAL CTS § 202.70(c).

d. For more information on the Commercial Division, refer to NY R UNIF TRIAL CTS § 202.70.

D. Documents

1. *Required documents*

a. *Subpoena.* Refer to the General Requirements section of this document for information on the subpoena.

b. *Witness fees.* Any person subpoenaed shall be paid or tendered in advance authorized traveling expenses and one (1) day's witness fee. NY CPLR § 2303(a).

c. *Proof of service.* In addition to complying with the provisions of NY CPLR Rule 2101, every paper filed in court shall have annexed thereto appropriate proof of service on all parties where required. NY R UNIF TRIAL CTS § 202.5(a).

E. Format

1. *Form of documents*

a. *Size and form of paper.* Each paper served or filed shall be durable, white and, except for summonses, subpoenas, notices of appearance, notes of issue, orders of protection, temporary orders of protection and exhibits, shall be eleven by eight and one-half (11 x 8-1/2) inches in size. NY CPLR Rule 2101(a).

b. *Writing and language.* The writing shall be legible and in black ink. NY CPLR Rule 2101(a). Each paper served or filed shall be in the English language which, where practicable, shall be of ordinary usage. NY CPLR Rule 2101(b).

c. *Caption.* Each paper served or filed shall begin with a caption setting forth the name of the court, the venue, the title of the action, the nature of the paper and the index number of the action if one has been assigned. In all papers other than a summons, a complaint or a judgment it shall be sufficient to state the name of the first named party on each side with an appropriate indication of any omissions. NY CPLR Rule 2101(c).

i. *Further contents of first page.* After the first paper has been filed in each case the index number shall appear on the cover and first page to the right of the caption of every paper tendered for filing in the action. Each such cover and first page also shall contain an indication of the county of venue and a brief description of the nature of the paper and, where the case has been assigned to an individual judge, shall contain the name of the assigned judge to the right of the caption. NY R UNIF TRIAL CTS § 202.5(a); NY R UNIF TRIAL CTS § 202.5(b); NY R UNIF TRIAL CTS § 202.5(d)(1)(i).

d. *Index number.* No paper in an action in the supreme or a county court, other than an order submitted for signature to a judge out of court, shall be submitted for any purpose to the supreme or county court or to a clerk thereof unless there is endorsed on such paper the index number of the action assigned by the clerk of the county. NY CPLR § 8018(c).

e. *Line spacing.* Every paper filed in court, if typewritten, shall have at least double space between each line, except for quotations and the names and addresses of attorneys appearing in the action. NY R UNIF TRIAL CTS § 202.5(a).

f. *Font size.* Each. . .paper printed or typed, served or filed, except for summonses. . .and exhibits, shall be in clear type of no less than ten (10) point in size. NY CPLR Rule 2101(a).

   i. Whenever a requirement relating to size of type is stated in point size, the type size requirement shall be deemed met if the x-height of the type is a minimum of forty-five percent (45%) of the specified point size. Each point shall be measured as .351 millimeter. The x-height size shall be measured as it appears on the page. The x-height is the height of the lower case letters, exclusive of ascenders or descenders. NY CPLR § 105(t).

g. *Margins.* Every paper filed in court shall have at least one (1) inch margins. NY R UNIF TRIAL CTS § 202.5(a).

h. *Citations*

   i. *Civil practice law and rules.* NY CPLR § 101, et seq. shall be known as the civil practice law and rules, and may be cited as "CPLR". Reference to a provision in the civil practice law and rules may, except when such provision is being enacted or amended, be made without indicating whether it is a rule or section. NY CPLR § 101.

i. *Indorsement by attorney.* Each paper served or filed shall be indorsed with the name, address and telephone number of the attorney for the party serving or filing the paper, or if the party does not appear by attorney, with the name, address and telephone number of the party. NY CPLR Rule 2101(d).

j. *One-sided printing.* In addition, every paper filed in court, other than an exhibit or printed form, shall contain writing on one side only, except that papers that are fastened on the side may contain writing on both sides. NY R UNIF TRIAL CTS § 202.5(a).

k. *Use of copies authorized.* Except where otherwise specifically prescribed, copies, rather than originals, of all papers, including orders, affidavits and exhibits may be served or filed. Where it is required that the original be served or filed and the original is lost or withheld, the court may authorize a copy to be served or filed. NY CPLR Rule 2101(e).

   i. Where a certified copy of a paper is required by law, an attorney admitted to practice in the courts of the state may certify that it has been compared by him with the original and found to be a true and complete copy. Such a certificate, when subscribed by such attorney, has the same effect as if made by a clerk. NY CPLR § 2105.

l. *Recycled paper.* It is the policy of the Unified Court System that litigants, where practicable, should file or submit to the courts of the Unified Court System of the State of New York papers printed or reproduced on recycled paper. Paper is considered recycled if it contains a minimum content of thirty percent (30%) waste paper. NY R UNIF TRIAL CTS § 215.2. The signature page of every paper filed or submitted to the court on recycled paper should bear the legend: "Printed [Reproduced] on Recycled Paper." NY R UNIF TRIAL CTS § 215.3.

2. *Form of electronic documents.* Each paper served or filed by electronic means, as defined in NY CPLR Rule 2103(f), shall be capable of being reproduced by the receiver so as to comply with the provisions of NY CPLR Rule 2101(a) through NY CPLR Rule 2101(d). NY CPLR Rule 2101(g).

   a. *File format.* All e-filed documents shall comply with the technical requirements set forth at the NYSCEF site. NY R UNIF TRIAL CTS § 202.5-b(d)(1)(i).

   b. *Heading of document.* The subject matter heading for each paper sent by electronic means must indicate that the matter being transmitted electronically is related to a court proceeding. NY CPLR Rule 2103(b)(7).

3. *Signature blocks.* Every pleading, written motion, and other paper, served on another party or filed or submitted to the court shall be signed by an attorney, or by a party if the party is not represented by an attorney, with the name of the attorney or party clearly printed or typed directly below the signature. NY R CHIEF ADMIN § 130-1.1-a(a); NY R UNIF TRIAL CTS § 202.5(d)(1)(iv).

   a. *Printed name.* Beneath each signature shall be printed the name signed. NY CPLR Rule 2101(a).

   b. *Failure to sign.* Absent good cause shown, the court shall strike any unsigned paper if the omission of the signature is not corrected promptly after being called to the attention of the attorney or party. NY R CHIEF ADMIN § 130-1.1-a(a).

   c. *Signature as certification.* By signing a paper, an attorney or party certifies that, to the best of that person's knowledge, information and belief, formed after an inquiry reasonable under the circumstances the presentation of the paper or the contentions therein are not frivolous as defined in NY R CHIEF ADMIN § 130-1.1(c). NY R CHIEF ADMIN § 130-1.1-a(b)(1).

d. *Electronic signatures.* A document shall be considered to have been signed by an attorney or party in compliance with NY R CHIEF ADMIN § 130-1.1-a if it has been signed by such attorney or party as provided in NY R UNIF TRIAL CTS § 202.5-b(e)(1) and it bears the signatory's name. NY R UNIF TRIAL CTS § 202.5-b(e)(2). An electronically filed document shall be considered to have been signed by, and shall be binding upon, the person identified as a signatory, if:

i. It bears the physical signature of such person and is scanned into an electronic format that reproduces such signature; or

ii. The signatory has electronically affixed the digital image of his or her signature to the document; or

iii. It is electronically filed under the User ID and password of that person; or

iv. In a tax certiorari action in which the parties have stipulated to this procedure, it is an initiating document that is electronically filed without the signature of the signatory in a form provided above in NY R UNIF TRIAL CTS § 202.5-b(e)(iv), provided that, prior to filing, the document is signed in full in hard copy (which hard copy must be preserved until the conclusion of all proceedings, including appeals, in the case in which it is filed); or

v. In a small claims assessment review proceeding, it is a petition recorded by the NYSCEF site upon the filing of a text file as provided in NY R UNIF TRIAL CTS § 202.5-b(b)(1), provided that prior to filing, the document was signed in full in hard copy (which hard copy must be preserved until the conclusion of all proceedings in the matter, including article 78 (NY CPLR § 7801, et seq.) review and any appeals, and must be made available during the proceeding upon request of the respondent or the court); or

vi. It otherwise bears the electronic signature of the signatory in a format conforming to such standards and requirements as may hereafter be established by the Chief Administrator. NY R UNIF TRIAL CTS § 202.5-b(e).

4. *Confidentiality of personal information.* No person may file any document available for public inspection with any state agency, political subdivision, or in any court of this state that contains a Social Security account number of any other person, unless such other person is a dependent child, or has consented to such filing, except as required by federal or state law or regulation, or by court rule. NY GEN BUS § 399-ddd. Submissions pursuant to e-filing procedures shall have the same confidentiality rights as paper documents. NY R UNIF TRIAL CTS § 202.5-b(k)(1).

a. *Confidential personal information.* Except in the actions designated in NY R UNIF TRIAL CTS § 202.5(e)(1), or as otherwise provided by rule or law or court order, and whether or not a sealing order is or has been sought, the parties shall omit or redact confidential personal information in papers submitted to the court for filing. For purposes of NY R UNIF TRIAL CTS § 202.5(e), confidential personal information ("CPI") means:

i. The taxpayer identification number of an individual or an entity, including a Social Security number, an employer identification number, and an individual taxpayer identification number, except the last four (4) digits thereof;

ii. The date of an individual's birth, except the year thereof;

iii. The full name of an individual known to be a minor, except the minor's initials;

iv. A financial account number, including a credit and/or debit card number, a bank account number, an investment account number, and/or an insurance account number, except the last four (4) digits or letters thereof; and

v. Any of the documents or testimony in a matrimonial action protected by NY DOM REL § 235 or evidence sealed by the court in such an action which are attached as exhibits or referenced in the papers filed in any other civil action. For purposes of NY R UNIF TRIAL CTS § 202.5, a matrimonial action shall mean: an action to annul a marriage or declare the nullity of a void marriage, an action or agreement for a separation, an action for a divorce, or an action or proceeding for custody, visitation, writ of habeus corpus, child support, maintenance or paternity. NY R UNIF TRIAL CTS § 202.5(e)(1).

b. *Submission of confidential personal information.* Where a person submitting a paper to a court for filing believes in good faith that the inclusion of the full confidential personal information described in NY R UNIF TRIAL CTS § 202.5(e)(1) is material and necessary to the adjudication of the action or proceeding before the court, he or she may apply to the court for leave to serve and file together with a paper in which such information has been set forth in abbreviated form a confidential affidavit or affirmation setting forth the same information in unabbreviated form, appropriately referenced to the page or pages of the paper at which the abbreviated form appears. NY R UNIF TRIAL CTS § 202.5(e)(3).

c. *Home addresses.* For information on when home addresses and other personal information must be redacted, refer to NY CPLR Rule 2103-a.

5. *Defective papers.* A defect in the form of a paper, if a substantial right of a party is not prejudiced, shall be disregarded by the court, and leave to correct shall be freely given. NY CPLR Rule 2101(f). Papers that are stapled or bound securely shall not be rejected for filing simply because they are not bound with a backer of any kind. NY R UNIF TRIAL CTS § 202.5(a). A paper filed in accordance with the rules of the chief administrator or any local rule or practice established by the court shall be deemed filed. NY CPLR Rule 2102(b).

   a. *Objection to defective papers.* The party on whom a paper is served shall be deemed to have waived objection to any defect in form unless, within fifteen (15) days after the receipt thereof, the party on whom the paper is served returns the paper to the party serving it with a statement of particular objections. NY CPLR Rule 2101(f).

F. Filing and Service Requirements

1. *Filing requirements.* Except where otherwise prescribed by law or order of court, papers required to be filed shall be filed with the clerk of the court in which the action is triable. In an action or proceeding in supreme or court, papers required to be filed shall be filed with the clerk of the county in which the proceeding is brought. NY CPLR Rule 2102(a).

   a. *Electronic filing.* On consent, documents may be filed and served by electronic means in Supreme Court in such civil actions and in such counties as shall be authorized by order of the Chief Administrator of the Courts and only to the extent and in the manner provided in NY R UNIF TRIAL CTS § 202.5-b. NY R UNIF TRIAL CTS § 202.5-b(a)(1). For the definitions of terms used in electronic filing, refer to NY R UNIF TRIAL CTS § 202.5-b(a)(2).

      i. *E-filing mandatory.* In any action subject to e-filing, all documents required to be filed with the court by an e-filing party shall be filed and served electronically, except as provided in NY R UNIF TRIAL CTS § 202.5-b. NY R UNIF TRIAL CTS § 202.5-b(d)(1)(i).

      ii. *Who may file.* Documents may be filed or served electronically only by a person who has registered as an authorized e-filing user or as otherwise provided in NY R UNIF TRIAL CTS § 202.5-b(c). NY R UNIF TRIAL CTS § 202.5-b(c)(1).

      iii. *When filing made.* Documents may be transmitted at any time of the day or night to the NYSCEF site. A document other than an order or judgment is filed when its electronic transmission or, in the case of a petition that is e-filed by submission of a text file as provided in NY R UNIF TRIAL CTS § 202.5-b(b)(1), the electronic transmission of the text file is recorded at that site, provided, however, that where payment of a fee is required upon the filing of a document, the document is not filed until transmission of the document and the information or form or information as required in NY R UNIF TRIAL CTS § 202.5-b(d)(2)(i), NY R UNIF TRIAL CTS § 202.5-b(d)(2)(ii) or NY R UNIF TRIAL CTS § 202.5-b(d)(2)(iii) has been recorded at the NYSCEF site; or, if no transmission of that information or form or information is recorded, where permitted by the County Clerk, until payment is presented to the County Clerk. NY R UNIF TRIAL CTS § 202.5-b(d)(3)(i).

      iv. *Notification of filing.* No later than the close of business on the business day following the electronic filing of a document, a notification, in a form prescribed by the Chief Administrator, shall be transmitted electronically by the NYSCEF site to the person filing such document and the e-mail service addresses of all other participating parties in such action. NY R UNIF TRIAL CTS § 202.5-b(d)(3)(ii).

      v. *Removal of confidential information and other corrections.* If a document filed electronically is subsequently discovered to contain confidential data—including but not limited to trade secrets, information protected by confidentiality agreement, or personal confidential information as defined by statute or court rule—or otherwise to have been filed in error, the filer or another party or affected person may (1) notify the parties and any non-party filers in the action of the confidentiality issue or other error raised by the filing, and of his or her intention to seek judicial relief to correct the filing: (2) following such notification, request that the appropriate County Clerk, exercising his or her administrative discretion, place the document temporarily in "restricted" status on the NYSCEF site, to be made available for viewing by court staff and the parties but not the general public; and (3) file an application to correct the filing by order to show cause within five (5) business days of such notification (or such time as the court may direct), including a request for preliminary injunctive relief limiting interim disclosure of the document at issue. Unless otherwise directed by the court, any document placed in restricted status in response to such a request shall be returned to public view upon expiration of this five (5) day period. The Chief Administrator of the Courts shall promulgate forms to implement this process. NY R UNIF TRIAL CTS § 202.5-b(d)(3)(iii).

      vi. *Documents requiring judge's signature.* Except where the court directs otherwise, any document that requires a judge's signature shall be transmitted electronically and in hard copy to the court. NY R UNIF TRIAL CTS § 202.5-b(d)(6).

vii. *Documents which would be inconvenient to file electronically; Hard copies.* Notwithstanding any other provision of NY R UNIF TRIAL CTS § 202.5-b, and subject to such guidelines as may be established by the Chief Administrative Judge, the County Clerk or his or her designee may require or permit a party to file in hard copy, in accordance with procedures set by the County Clerk or designee, an exhibit or other document which it is impractical or inconvenient to file electronically. NY R UNIF TRIAL CTS § 202.5-b(d)(7).

viii. *Documents containing sensitive or proprietary information.* In an action subject to e-filing, any person may apply for an order prohibiting or restricting the electronic filing in the action of specifically identified materials on the grounds that such materials are subject to copyright or other proprietary rights, or trade secret or other privacy interests, and that electronic filing in the action is likely to result in substantial prejudice to those rights or interests. NY R UNIF TRIAL CTS § 202.5-b(k)(2).

ix. *Refusal to accept paper filings.* In accordance with NY CPLR Rule 2102(c), a County Clerk and a chief clerk of the Supreme Court or County Court, as appropriate, shall refuse to accept for filing papers filed in actions and proceedings when the paper sought to be filed:

- Is in an action subject to electronic filing pursuant to Rules of the Chief Administrator,
- Is not being filed electronically, and
- Does not include the notice required by NY R UNIF TRIAL CTS § 202.5-b(d)(1). NY R UNIF TRIAL CTS § 202.5(d)(1)(v); NY R UNIF TRIAL CTS § 202.5-bb(d).

x. *Emergency filings; Hard copies.* For information on when an emergency filing may be filed and served in hard copy, refer to NY R UNIF TRIAL CTS § 202.5-b(d)(1)(ii), NY R UNIF TRIAL CTS § 202.5-b(d)(1)(iii) and NY R UNIF TRIAL CTS § 202.5-bb(c)(3).

xi. *Technical failures.* The NYSCEF site shall be considered to be subject to a technical failure on a given day if the site is unable to accept filings or provide access to filed documents continuously or intermittently over the course of any period of time greater than one (1) hour after 12:00 noon of that day. Notice of all such technical failures shall be provided on the site. NY R UNIF TRIAL CTS § 202.5-b(i).

- When e-filing is hindered by a technical failure, a party may file with the appropriate clerk and serve in hard copy. NY R UNIF TRIAL CTS § 202.5-b(i). In the event an attorney or party shall file and serve documents in hard copy pursuant to NY R UNIF TRIAL CTS § 202.5-b(i), each such document shall include the notice required by NY R UNIF TRIAL CTS § 202.5-b(d)(1), and the filer shall file those documents with the NYSCEF site within three (3) business days after restoration of normal operations at that site. NY R UNIF TRIAL CTS § 202.5-b(i).
- With the exception of deadlines that by law cannot be extended, the time for filing of any document that is delayed due to technical failure of the site shall be extended for one (1) day for each day on which such failure occurs, unless otherwise ordered by the court. NY R UNIF TRIAL CTS § 202.5-b(i).

xii. *Filing fees.* For information on what information must be provided to pay filing fees, refer to NY R UNIF TRIAL CTS § 202.5-b(d)(2).

xiii. *Exemption from e-filing.* For information on exemptions from e-filing, refer to NY R UNIF TRIAL CTS § 202.5-bb(e).

b. *Facsimile filing.* In the Supreme Court, facsimile filing shall be limited to commercial claims and tax certiorari, conservatorship, and mental hygiene proceedings in Monroe, Westchester, New York and Suffolk Counties. NY R UNIF TRIAL CTS § 202.5-a(a)(1). Refer to NY R UNIF TRIAL CTS § 202.5-a for information on the procedures for facsimile filing.

2. *Service requirements; Subpoenaed party*

a. *Served in same manner as summons.* A subpoena requiring attendance or a subpoena duces tecum shall be served in the same manner as a summons, except that where service of such a subpoena is made pursuant to NY CPLR § 308(2) or NY CPLR § 308(4), the filing of proof of service shall not be required and service shall be deemed complete upon the later of the delivering or mailing of the subpoena, if made pursuant to NY CPLR § 308(2), or upon the later of the affixing or mailing of the subpoena, if made pursuant to NY CPLR § 308(4). NY CPLR § 2303(a).

i. *Certain child support subpoenas.* A child support subpoena issued pursuant to NY SOC SERV § 111-p to public utility companies and corporations, including but not limited to cable television, gas, electric, steam, and telephone companies and corporations, as defined in NY PUB SERV § 2, may be served by regular mail, or through an automated process where information sought is maintained in an automated data base. All other child support subpoenas issued pursuant to NY SOC SERV § 111-p shall be served in accordance with the provisions of NY CPLR § 2303(a). NY CPLR § 2303(b).

b. *NY CPLR Rule 2103 inapplicable.* NY CPLR Rule 2103 generally applies to the service of "interlocutory" papers—the myriad litigation documents served and filed after jurisdiction has been obtained, and the action is pending. Initiatory papers, usually the summons and complaint (or an order to show cause or notice of petition and petition), are governed by the rigid service rules under Article 3 of the CPLR (NY CPLR § 301, et seq.) and various other statutes that apply to the acquisition of personal jurisdiction. NY CPLR Rule 2103(Practice Commentary, C:2103:1).

c. *Service of process.* The complaint may be served with the summons. NY CPLR § 3012(a). When the complaint is served together with the summons, the rules of summons service in NY CPLR § 308 ("Personal service upon a natural person") and NY CPLR § 312-a ("Personal service by mail") generally govern. NY CPLR § 3012(Practice Commentaries, C3012:5).

   i. *Sheriff to serve.* Upon written request by the issuer thereof, the sheriff shall serve all civil process regardless of whether it has been issued by the court. NY COUNTY § 650(2).

   ii. *Service on Sunday prohibited.* All service or execution of legal process, of any kind whatever, on the first day of the week is prohibited, except in criminal proceedings or where service or execution is specially authorized by statute. Service or execution of any process upon said day except as herein permitted is absolutely void for any and every purpose whatsoever. NY GEN BUS § 11.

   - *Persons who keep Saturday as holy time.* Whoever maliciously procures any process in a civil action to be served on Saturday, upon any person who keeps Saturday as holy time, and does not labor on that day, or serves upon him any process returnable on that day, or maliciously procures any civil action to which such person is a party to be adjourned to that day for trial, is guilty of a misdemeanor. NY GEN BUS § 13.
   - *Service invalid if maliciously served on Saturday.* Service on a Saturday is a misdemeanor if made "maliciously" on one who actually celebrates Saturday as the Sabbath, and caselaw permits the service to be invalidated on motion if that showing is made. SIEGEL-NYPRAC § 63; Jewish Center of Baldwin v. Winer, 216 N.Y.S.2d 153, 154 (N.Y.Sup. 1961).

   iii. *Service of complaint after service of summons.* If the complaint is not served with the summons, the defendant may serve a written demand for the complaint within the time provided in NY CPLR Rule 320(a) for an appearance. NY CPLR § 3012(b). Refer to the Timing section of this document for more information.

d. *Forms of service*

   i. *Personal service on an individual.* Personal service upon a natural person shall be made by any of the following methods:

   - By delivering the summons within the state to the person to be served. NY CPLR § 308(1).
   - By delivering the summons within the state to a person of suitable age and discretion at the actual place of business, dwelling place or usual place of abode of the person to be served and by either mailing the summons to the person to be served at his or her last known residence or by mailing the summons by first class mail to the person to be served at his or her actual place of business in an envelope bearing the legend "personal and confidential" and not indicating on the outside thereof, by return address or otherwise, that the communication is from an attorney or concerns an action against the person to be served, such delivery and mailing to be effected within twenty (20) days of each other; proof of such service shall be filed with the clerk of the court designated in the summons within twenty (20) days of either such delivery or mailing, whichever is effected later; service shall be complete ten (10) days after such filing; proof of service shall identify such person of suitable age and discretion and state the date, time and place of service, except in matrimonial actions where service hereunder may be made pursuant to an order made in accordance with the provisions of NY DOM REL § 232(a). NY CPLR § 308(2).
   - By delivering the summons within the state to the agent for service of the person to be served as designated under NY CPLR Rule 318, except in matrimonial actions where service hereunder may be made pursuant to an order made in accordance with the provisions of NY DOM REL § 232(a). NY CPLR § 308(3).
   - Where service under NY CPLR § 308(1) and NY CPLR § 308(2) cannot be made with due diligence, by affixing the summons to the door of either the actual place of business, dwelling place or usual place of abode within the state of the person to be served and by either mailing the summons to such person at his or her last known residence or by mailing the summons by first class mail to the person to be served at his

or her actual place of business in an envelope bearing the legend "personal and confidential" and not indicating on the outside thereof, by return address or otherwise, that the communication is from an attorney or concerns an action against the person to be served, such affixing and mailing to be effected within twenty (20) days of each other; proof of such service shall be filed with the clerk of the court designated in the summons within twenty (20) days of either such affixing or mailing, whichever is effected later; service shall be complete ten (10) days after such filing, except in matrimonial actions where service hereunder may be made pursuant to an order made in accordance with the provisions of NY DOM REL § 232(a). NY CPLR § 308(4).

- In such manner as the court, upon motion without notice, directs, if service is impracticable under NY CPLR § 308(1), NY CPLR § 308(2) and NY CPLR § 308(4). NY CPLR § 308(5).
- For purposes of NY CPLR § 308, "actual place of business" shall include any location that the defendant, through regular solicitation or advertisement, has held out as its place of business. NY CPLR § 308(6).

ii. *Service on designated agent.* A person may be designated by a natural person, corporation or partnership as an agent for service in a writing, executed and acknowledged in the same manner as a deed, with the consent of the agent endorsed thereon. The writing shall be filed in the office of the clerk of the county in which the principal to be served resides or has its principal office. The designation shall remain in effect for three (3) years from such filing unless it has been revoked by the filing of a revocation, or by the death, judicial declaration of incompetency or legal termination of the agent or principal. NY CPLR Rule 318.

iii. *Service by mail.* As an alternative to the methods of personal service authorized by NY CPLR § 307, NY CPLR § 308, NY CPLR § 310, NY CPLR § 311 or NY CPLR § 312, a summons and complaint, or summons and notice, or notice of petition and petition may be served by the plaintiff or any other person by mailing to the person or entity to be served, by first class mail, postage prepaid, a copy of the summons and complaint, or summons and notice or notice of petition and petition, together with two (2) copies of a statement of service by mail and acknowledgement of receipt in the form set forth in NY CPLR § 312-a(d), with a return envelope, postage prepaid, addressed to the sender. NY CPLR § 312-a(a).

- The defendant, an authorized employee of the defendant, defendant's attorney or an employee of the attorney must complete the acknowledgement of receipt and mail or deliver one (1) copy of it within thirty (30) days from the date of receipt. Service is complete on the date the signed acknowledgement of receipt is mailed or delivered to the sender. The signed acknowledgement of receipt shall constitute proof of service. NY CPLR § 312-a(b)(1).
- Where a duly executed acknowledgement is not returned, upon the subsequent service of process in another manner permitted by law, the summons or notice of petition or paper served with the summons or notice of petition shall indicate that an attempt previously was made to effect service pursuant to NY CPLR § 312-a. NY CPLR § 312-a(e).
- The statement of service by mail and the acknowledgement of receipt of such service shall be in substantially the form found in NY CPLR § 312-a(d). NY CPLR § 312-a(d).

iv. *Electronic service.* Initiating documents may be served in hard copy pursuant to Article 3 of the CPLR (NY CPLR § 301, et seq.) and shall bear full signatures as required thereby, or by electronic means if the party served agrees to accept such service. NY R UNIF TRIAL CTS § 202.5-b(f)(1); NY R UNIF TRIAL CTS § 202.5-bb(b)(3).

v. *Service by publication.* The court, upon motion without notice, shall order service of a summons by publication in an action described in NY CPLR § 314 if service cannot be made by another prescribed method with due diligence. NY CPLR § 315. For information on the contents of an order for service by publication, refer to NY CPLR Rule 316.

- The first publication of the summons shall be made within thirty (30) days after the order is granted. Service by publication is complete on the twenty-eighth (28th) day after the day of first publication, except that in a matrimonial action it is complete on the twenty-first (21st) day after the day of first publication. NY CPLR Rule 316(c).
- Where because of circumstances beyond the control of a party required to publish, publication required by any statute, rule or court order cannot be made or completed in the specified place or newspaper in the required manner, the court may by order require such other publication as will not unduly prejudice any other party. NY CPLR § 2401(1).
- Notwithstanding the provisions of NY CPLR § 2401(1), if publication required by any statute, rule or court

order has been commenced and cannot be completed because of the suspension or termination of publication by a newspaper, publication may be completed in any other newspaper which complies with the statute, rule, or order without further court order. NY CPLR § 2401(2).

- For the definition of a "newspaper" for the purposes of publication, refer to NY GEN CONSTR § 60.

e. *Effect of service outside the state.* A person domiciled in the state or subject to the jurisdiction of the courts of the state under NY CPLR § 301 or NY CPLR § 302, or his executor or administrator, may be served with the summons without the state, in the same manner as service is made within the state, by any person authorized to make service within the state who is a resident of the state or by any person authorized to make service by the laws of the state, territory, possession or country in which service is made or by any duly qualified attorney, solicitor, barrister, or equivalent in such jurisdiction. NY CPLR § 313. For information on cases where service outside the state does not confer personal jurisdiction, refer to NY CPLR § 314.

f. *Service of process; Dependent on entities to be served*

i. *Personal service upon a corporation.* Personal service upon a corporation shall be made by delivering the summons, upon any domestic or foreign corporation, to an officer, director, managing or general agent, or cashier or assistant cashier or to any other agent authorized by appointment or by law to receive service. A business corporation may also be served pursuant to NY BUS CORP § 306 or NY BUS CORP § 307. A not-for-profit corporation may also be served pursuant to NY NOT PROF CORP § 306 or NY NOT PROF CORP § 307. NY CPLR § 311(a)(1).

- If service upon a domestic or foreign corporation within the one hundred twenty (120) days allowed by NY CPLR § 306-b is impracticable under NY CPLR § 311(a)(1) or any other law, service upon the corporation may be made in such manner, and proof of service may take such form, as the court, upon motion without notice, directs. NY CPLR § 311(b).

ii. *Personal service upon a limited liability company.* Service of process on any domestic or foreign limited liability company shall be made by delivering a copy personally to:

- Any member of the limited liability company in this state, if the management of the limited liability company is vested in its members;
- Any manager of the limited liability company in this state, if the management of the limited liability company is vested in one or more managers;
- To any other agent authorized by appointment to receive process; or
- To any other person designated by the limited liability company to receive process, in the manner provided by law for service of a summons as if such person was a defendant. NY CPLR § 311-a(a).
- Service of process upon a limited liability company may also be made pursuant to article three of the limited liability company law (NY Limit Liab Co § 101, et seq.). NY CPLR § 311-a(a).
- If service is impracticable under NY CPLR § 311-a(a), it may be made in such manner as the court, upon motion without notice, directs. NY CPLR § 311-a(b).

iii. *Personal service upon a partnership.* Personal service upon persons conducting a business as a partnership may be made by personally serving the summons upon any one of them. NY CPLR § 310(a).

- Personal service upon said partnership may also be made within the state by delivering the summons to the managing or general agent of the partnership or the person in charge of the office of the partnership within the state at such office and by either mailing the summons to the partner thereof intended to be served by first class mail to his last known residence or to the place of business of the partnership. Proof of such service shall be filed within twenty (20) days with the clerk of the court designated in the summons; service shall be complete ten (10) days after such filing; proof of service shall identify the person to whom the summons was so delivered and state the date, time of day and place of service. NY CPLR § 310(b).
- Where service under NY CPLR § 310(a) and NY CPLR § 310(b) cannot be made with due diligence, it may be made by affixing a copy of the summons to the door of the actual place of business of the partnership within the state and by either mailing the summons by first class mail to the partner intended to be so served to such person to his last known residence or to said person at the office of said partnership within the state. Proof of such service shall be filed within twenty (20) days thereafter with the clerk of the court designated in the summons; service shall be complete ten (10) days after filing. NY CPLR § 310(c).
- Personal service on such partnership may also be made by delivering the summons to any other agent or

employee of the partnership authorized by appointment to receive service; or to any other person designated by the partnership to receive process in writing, filed in the office of the clerk of the county wherein such partnership is located. NY CPLR § 310(d).

- If service is impracticable under NY CPLR § 310(a), NY CPLR § 310(b) and NY CPLR § 310(c), it may be made in such manner as the court, upon motion without notice directs. NY CPLR § 310(e).

iv. *Personal service upon a limited partnership.* Personal service upon any domestic or foreign limited partnership shall be made by delivering a copy personally to any managing or general agent or general partner of the limited partnership in this state, to any other agent or employee of the limited partnership authorized by appointment to receive service or to any other person designated by the limited partnership to receive process, in the manner provided by law for service of summons, as if such person was the defendant. Personal service upon a limited partnership subject to the NY PARTNER § 121-101, et seq. may also be made pursuant to NY PARTNER § 121-109. NY CPLR § 310-a(a).

- If service is impracticable under NY CPLR § 310-a(a), it may be made in such manner as the court, upon motion without notice, directs. NY CPLR § 310-a(b).
- A limited liability partnership may also be served pursuant to NY PARTNER § 121-1505. NY CPLR § 310-a(c).

v. *Personal service upon the state.* Personal service upon the state shall be made by delivering the summons to an assistant attorney-general at an office of the attorney-general or to the attorney-general within the state. NY CPLR § 307(1).

vi. *Personal service upon a state officer.* Personal service on a state officer sued solely in an official capacity or state agency, which shall be required to obtain personal jurisdiction over such an officer or agency, shall be made by (1) delivering the summons to such officer or to the chief executive officer of such agency or to a person designated by such chief executive officer to receive service, or (2) by mailing the summons by certified mail, return receipt requested, to such officer or to the chief executive officer of such agency, and by personal service upon the state in the manner provided by NY CPLR § 307(1). Service by certified mail shall not be complete until the summons is received in a principal office of the agency and until personal service upon the state in the manner provided by NY CPLR § 307(1) is completed. For purposes of NY CPLR § 307(2), the term "principal office of the agency" shall mean the location at which the office of the chief executive officer of the agency is generally located. Service by certified mail shall not be effective unless the front of the envelope bears the legend "URGENT LEGAL MAIL" in capital letters. The chief executive officer of every such agency shall designate at least one person, in addition to himself or herself, to accept personal service on behalf of the agency. For purposes of NY CPLR § 307(2) the term state agency shall be deemed to refer to any agency, board, bureau, commission, division, tribunal or other entity which constitutes the state for purposes of service under NY CPLR § 307(1). NY CPLR § 307(2).

vii. *Personal service upon a governmental subdivision.* Personal service upon a governmental subdivision shall be made by delivering the summons as follows:

- Upon the city of New York, to the corporation counsel or to any person designated to reċeive process in a writing filed in the office of the clerk of New York county. NY CPLR § 311(a)(2).
- Upon any other city, to the mayor, comptroller, treasurer, counsel or clerk; or, if the city lacks such officers, to an officer performing a corresponding function under another name. NY CPLR § 311(a)(3).
- Upon a county, to the chair or clerk of the board of supervisors, clerk, attorney or treasurer. NY CPLR § 311(a)(4).
- Upon a town, to the supervisor or the clerk. NY CPLR § 311(a)(5).
- Upon a village, to the mayor, clerk, or any trustee. NY CPLR § 311(a)(6).
- Upon a school district, to a school officer, as defined in the education law. NY CPLR § 311(a)(7).
- Upon a park, sewage or other district, to the clerk, any trustee or any member of the board. NY CPLR § 311(a)(8).

viii. *Personal service upon a court, board or commission.* Personal service upon a court consisting of three or more judges may be made by delivering the summons to any one of them. Personal service upon a board or commission having a chairman or other presiding officer, secretary or clerk, by whatever official title he is called, may be made by delivering the summons to him. Personal service upon a board or commission of a town or village may also be made by delivering the summons to the clerk of the town or village. Personal service upon any other board or commission shall be made by delivering the summons to any one of the members. NY CPLR § 312.

ix. *Personal service upon an infant, incompetent, or conservatee*

- *Upon an infant.* Personal service upon an infant shall be made by personally serving the summons within the state upon a parent or any guardian or any person having legal custody or, if the infant is married, upon an adult spouse with whom the infant resides, or, if none are within the state, upon any other person with whom he resides, or by whom he is employed. If the infant is of the age of fourteen (14) years or over, the summons shall also be personally served upon him within the state. NY CPLR § 309(a).
- *Upon a person judicially declared to be incompetent.* Personal service upon a person judicially declared to be incompetent to manage his affairs and for whom a committee has been appointed shall be made by personally serving the summons within the state upon the committee and upon the incompetent, but the court may dispense with service upon the incompetent. NY CPLR § 309(b).
- *Upon a conservatee.* Personal service on a person for whom a conservator has been appointed shall be made by personally serving the summons within the state upon the conservator and upon the conservatee, but the court may dispense with service upon the conservatee. NY CPLR § 309(c).

x. *Other specialized entities.* [Editor's note: New York has numerous rules related to service on specific regulated entities, for example, NY INS § 1212 relates to insurers, NY Limit Liab Co § 304 relates to unauthorized limited liability companies, and NY EXEC § 172-c relates to non-resident charitable organizations. For more information, refer to the chapter of New York law relating to the entity in question].

3. *Service requirements; Other parties to action.* A copy of any subpoena duces tecum served in a pending civil judicial proceeding shall also be served, in the manner set forth in NY CPLR Rule 2103, on each party who has appeared in the civil judicial proceeding so that it is received by such parties promptly after service on the witness and before the production of books, papers or other things. NY CPLR § 2303(a). Where the attendance at trial of a party or person within the party's control can be compelled by a trial subpoena, that subpoena may be served by delivery in accordance with NY CPLR Rule 2103(b) to the party's attorney of record. NY CPLR § 2303-a.

a. *Who may serve.* Except where otherwise prescribed by law or order of court, papers may be served by any person not a party of the age of eighteen years or over. NY CPLR Rule 2103(a).

b. *Service upon attorney.* Except where otherwise prescribed by law or order of court, papers to be served upon a party in a pending action shall be served upon the party's attorney. Where the same attorney appears for two or more parties, only one (1) copy need be served upon the attorney. Such service upon an attorney shall be made:

i. By delivering the paper to the attorney personally. NY CPLR Rule 2103(b)(1).

ii. By mailing the paper to the attorney at the address designated by that attorney for that purpose or, if none is designated, at the attorney's last known address; service by mail shall be complete upon mailing. NY CPLR Rule 2103(b)(2).

iii. If the attorney's office is open, by leaving the paper with a person in charge, or if no person is in charge, by leaving it in a conspicuous place; or if the attorney's office is not open, by depositing the paper, enclosed in a sealed wrapper directed to the attorney, in the attorney's office letter drop or box. NY CPLR Rule 2103(b)(3).

iv. By leaving it at the attorney's residence within the state with a person of suitable age and discretion. Service upon an attorney shall not be made at the attorney's residence unless service at the attorney's office cannot be made. NY CPLR Rule 2103(b)(4).

v. By transmitting the paper to the attorney by facsimile transmission, provided that a facsimile telephone number is designated by the attorney for that purpose. Service by facsimile transmission shall be complete upon the receipt by the sender of a signal from the equipment of the attorney served indicating that the transmission was received, and the mailing of a copy of the paper to that attorney. The designation of a facsimile telephone number in the address block subscribed on a paper served or filed in the course of an action or proceeding shall constitute consent to service by facsimile transmission in accordance with NY CPLR Rule 2103(b)(5). An attorney may change or rescind a facsimile telephone number by serving a notice on the other parties. NY CPLR Rule 2103(b)(5).

vi. By dispatching the paper to the attorney by overnight delivery service at the address designated by the attorney for that purpose or, if none is designated, at the attorney's last known address. Service by overnight delivery service shall be complete upon deposit of the paper enclosed in a properly addressed wrapper into the custody of the overnight delivery service for overnight delivery, prior to the latest time designated by the overnight delivery service for overnight delivery. "Overnight delivery service" means any delivery service which regularly accepts items for overnight delivery to any address in the state. NY CPLR Rule 2103(b)(6).

vii. By transmitting the paper to the attorney by electronic means where and in the manner authorized by the chief administrator of the courts by rule and, unless such rule shall otherwise provide, such transmission shall be upon the party's written consent. The subject matter heading for each paper sent by electronic means must indicate that the matter being transmitted electronically is related to a court proceeding. NY CPLR Rule 2103(b)(7).

c. *Electronic service mandatory; Consenting to electronic service; How electronic service may be made.* Except as otherwise provided in NY R UNIF TRIAL CTS § 202.5-bb, filing and service of all documents in an action that has been commenced electronically in accordance with NY R UNIF TRIAL CTS § 202.5-bb shall be by electronic means. NY R UNIF TRIAL CTS § 202.5-bb(c)(1).

i. *Party's consent required for certain e-filing.* After commencement of an action wherein e-filing is authorized, documents may be electronically filed and served, but only by, and electronic service shall be made only upon, a party or parties who have consented thereto. NY R UNIF TRIAL CTS § 202.5-b(b)(2)(i).

- A consent to e-filing in an action shall state that the party providing it agrees to the use of e-filing in the action and to be bound by the filing and service provisions in NY R UNIF TRIAL CTS § 202.5-b. NY R UNIF TRIAL CTS § 202.5-b(b)(2)(ii).

ii. *Address for service; Duty to notify as to changes.* The e-mail service address recorded at the time of registration is the e-mail address at which service of interlocutory documents on that party may be made through notification transmitted by the NYSCEF site. It is the responsibility of each filing user to monitor that address and promptly notify the Resource Center in the event of a change in his or her e-mail service address. NY R UNIF TRIAL CTS § 202.5-b(f)(2)(i).

iii. *How service made.* An e-filing party causes service of an interlocutory document to be made upon another party participating in e-filing by filing the document electronically. Upon receipt of an interlocutory document, the NYSCEF site shall automatically transmit electronic notification to all e-mail service addresses in such action. NY R UNIF TRIAL CTS § 202.5-b(f)(2)(ii).

- Except as provided otherwise in NY R UNIF TRIAL CTS § 202.5-b(h)(3), the electronic transmission of the notification shall constitute service of the document on the e-mail service addresses identified therein; however, such service will not be effective if the filing party learns that the notification did not reach the address of the person to be served. Proof of such service will be recorded on the NYSCEF site. A party may, however, utilize other service methods permitted by the CPLR provided that, if one of such other methods is used, proof of that service shall be filed electronically. NY R UNIF TRIAL CTS § 202.5-b(f)(2)(ii).

iv. *Signatures on hard copies; Proof of service filed electronically.* When an e-filing party serves a document in hard copy on a non-participating party, the document served shall bear full signatures of all signatories and proof of such service shall be filed electronically. NY R UNIF TRIAL CTS § 202.5-b(b)(2)(i).

v. *Effect of failure to consent.* A party's failure to consent to participation in electronic filing and service shall not bar any other party to the action from filing documents electronically with the County Clerk and the court or serving documents upon any other party who has consented to participation. A party who has not consented to participation shall file documents with the court and the County Clerk, and serve and be served with documents, in hard copy. NY R UNIF TRIAL CTS § 202.5-b(b)(2)(i).

d. *Service upon party.* If a party has not appeared by an attorney or the party's attorney cannot be served, service shall be upon the party by a method specified in NY CPLR Rule 2103(b)(1), NY CPLR Rule 2103(b)(2), NY CPLR Rule 2103(b)(4), NY CPLR Rule 2103(b)(5) or NY CPLR Rule 2103(b)(6). NY CPLR Rule 2103(c).

e. *Service on all parties.* Each paper served on any party shall be served on every other party who has appeared, except as otherwise may be provided by court order or as provided in NY CPLR § 3012 or in NY CPLR § 3215(f). Upon demand by a party, the plaintiff shall supply that party with a list of those who have appeared and the names and addresses of their attorneys. NY CPLR Rule 2103(e).

f. *Service by filing.* If a paper cannot be served by any of the methods specified in NY CPLR Rule 2103(b) and NY CPLR Rule 2103(c), service may be made by filing the paper as if it were a paper required to be filed. NY CPLR Rule 2103(d).

g. *Definitions.* For the purposes of NY CPLR Rule 2103:

i. "Mailing" means the deposit of a paper enclosed in a first class postpaid wrapper, addressed to the address designated by a person for that purpose or, if none is designated, at that person's last known address, in a post office or official depository under the exclusive care and custody of the United States Postal Service within the state;

ii. "Electronic means" means any method of transmission of information between computers or other machines designed for the purpose of sending and receiving such transmissions, and which allows the recipient to reproduce the information transmitted in a tangible medium of expression;

iii. "Facsimile transmission" means any method of transmission of documents to a facsimile machine at a remote location which can automatically produce a tangible copy of such documents. NY CPLR Rule 2103(f).

G. Hearings

1. There is no hearing required or contemplated in the New York rules governing the subpoena.

H. Forms

1. New York Subpoena Forms

a. Form of subpoena. SIEGEL-NYPRAC § 386.

b. Form; Subpoena duces tecum. NYPRAC-FAMCT § 2:116.

c. Information subpoena with restraining order. NYPRAC-COLL § 8:349.

d. Subpoena and subpoena duces tecum for examination under commission issued in action pending in another jurisdiction. MCF CPLR § 6:49.

e. Affirmation on application for an order to examine witness in this state under subpoena issued in action pending in another jurisdiction. MCF CPLR § 6:50.

f. Subpoena requiring witness to attend examination before trial. MCF CPLR § 6:98.

g. Affidavit in support of motion for permission to serve subpoena on witness less than 20 days before examination. MCF CPLR § 6:99.

h. Traditional form of subpoena. MCF CPLR § 12:68.

i. Subpoena requiring attendance at examination before trial. MCF CPLR § 12:70.

j. Subpoena duces tecum upon examination before trial. MCF CPLR § 12:71.

k. Subpoena requiring attendance before legislative committee. MCF CPLR § 12:72.

l. Subpoena requiring attendance of witness at trial. MCF CPLR § 12:73.

m. Subpoena duces tecum upon trial of action. MCF CPLR § 12:74.

n. Notice of motion for subpoena to compel production of original record. MCF CPLR § 12:79.

o. Affidavit in support of motion for subpoena to compel production of original record. MCF CPLR § 12:80.

p. Subpoena duces tecum for production of original record. MCF CPLR § 12:82.

q. Notice of motion for subpoena to compel attendance of prisoner at trial of action. MCF CPLR § 12:83.

r. Affidavit in support of motion for subpoena to compel attendance of prisoner at trial of action. MCF CPLR § 12:84.

s. Subpoena compelling attendance of prisoner at trial of action. MCF CPLR § 12:86.

t. Affidavit of personal service of subpoena. MCF CPLR § 12:88.

u. Notice of motion for subpoena duces tecum requiring production of original hospital records. MCF CPLR § 12:113.

v. Affidavit in support of motion for subpoena duces tecum requiring production of original hospital records. MCF CPLR § 12:114.

w. Subpoena duces tecum requiring production of original hospital records. MCF CPLR § 12:116.

I. Applicable Rules

1. *State rules*

a. Short title; Application; Construction; Definitions. NY CPLR § 101; NY CPLR § 104; NY CPLR § 105.

b. Appendix of official forms. NY CPLR § 107.

c. Service of process. NY CPLR § 307; NY CPLR § 308; NY CPLR § 309; NY CPLR § 310; NY CPLR § 310-a; NY

CPLR § 311; NY CPLR § 311-a; NY CPLR § 312; NY CPLR § 312-a; NY CPLR § 313; NY CPLR § 315; NY CPLR Rule 316; NY CPLR Rule 318; NY CPLR § 2401; NY COUNTY § 650; NY GEN BUS § 11; NY GEN BUS § 13.

d. Extensions of time generally. NY CPLR § 2004.
e. Form of papers. NY CPLR Rule 2101; NY CPLR Rule 2102; NY CPLR § 2105; NY GEN BUS § 399-ddd; NY R UNIF TRIAL CTS § 215.2; NY R UNIF TRIAL CTS § 215.3.
f. Service of papers. NY CPLR Rule 2103.
g. Scope of subpoena. NY CPLR § 2301.
h. Authority to issue. NY CPLR § 2302.
i. Service of subpoena; Payment of fees in advance. NY CPLR § 2303.
j. Service of a trial subpoena. NY CPLR § 2303-a.
k. Attendance required pursuant to subpoena; Possession of books, records, documents or papers. NY CPLR § 2305.
l. Hospital records; Medical records of department or bureau of a municipal corporation or of the state. NY CPLR § 2306.
m. Books, papers and other things of a library, department or bureau of a municipal corporation or of the state. NY CPLR § 2307.
n. Disobedience of subpoena. NY CPLR § 2308.
o. Computation of time. NY CPLR § 2402; NY GEN CONSTR § 19; NY GEN CONSTR § 20; NY GEN CONSTR § 25-a; NY GEN CONSTR § 30; NY GEN CONSTR § 31; NY GEN CONSTR § 53.
p. Service of pleadings and demand for complaint. NY CPLR § 3012.
q. Persons subpoenaed; Examination before trial; Transcripts of records. NY CPLR § 8001.
r. Index number fees of county clerks. NY CPLR § 8018.
s. Hours of court. NY R CHIEF J § 3.1.
t. Application of part; Waiver; Additional rules; Application of CPLR; Definitions. NY R UNIF TRIAL CTS § 202.1.
u. Papers filed in court; Electronic filing in supreme court. NY R UNIF TRIAL CTS § 202.5; NY R UNIF TRIAL CTS § 202.5-a; NY R UNIF TRIAL CTS § 202.5-b; NY R UNIF TRIAL CTS § 202.5-bb.
v. Rules of the commercial division of the Supreme Court. NY R UNIF TRIAL CTS § 202.70.
w. Signing of papers. NY R CHIEF ADMIN § 130-1.1-a.

2. *Local rules*
   a. *Albany County*
      i. Third judicial district rules. NY R 3 JD SUP Doc. 1.
   b. *Bronx County*
      i. Commercial division. NY R BRONX FIL R Doc. 12.
   c. *Kings County*
      i. Expedited discovery. NY R L KINGS Pt. B, Rule 5.
      ii. Pre calendar procedures. NY R L KINGS Rule I.
      iii. Both pre and post note procedures. NY R L KINGS Rule IV.
   d. *New York County*
      i. RJIs and assignments. NY R NY CTY Procedure IA.
      ii. Discovery schedule. NY R NY CTY J RUL Rule 8.

J. Miscellaneous

NOTE: Individual judges' rules may apply.

ALBANY COUNTY

JUSTICE LISA M. FISHER: NY R 3 JD FISHER Fisher; NY R 3 JD FISHER Fisher, PC Order.

JUSTICE RICHARD MOTT: NY R 3 JD MOTT Mott.

JUSTICE STEPHAN G. SCHICK: NY R 3 JD Schick.

FORECLOSURE SETTLEMENT PART: NY R 3 JD Foreclosure Settlement.

BRONX COUNTY

JUSTICE PAUL L. ALPERT: [NY R BRONX J Part IA-29, as amended by NY ORDER 20-0337].

JUSTICE BEN BARBATO: NY R BRONX J Part IA-21.

JUSTICE MARY ANNE BRIGANTTI: [NY R BRONX J Part IA-15, as amended by NY ORDER 20-0338].

JUSTICE JOSEPH E. CAPELLA: NY R BRONX J Part IA-23.

JUSTICE MITCHELL DANZIGER: NY R BRONX J Part IA-3/33 ; [NY R BRONX J Danziger, Part IA-3/33, as amended by NY ORDER 20-0339].

JUSTICE LAURA G. DOUGLAS: NY R BRONX J Part IA-11.

JUSTICE RUBEN FRANCO: NY R BRONX J Part IA-26.

JUSTICE DORIS M. GONZALEZ: NY R BRONX J Part IA-24.

JUSTICE WILMA GUZMAN: NY R BRONX J Part IA-7; [NY R BRONX J Guzman, Part IA-7 Virtual, as amended by NY ORDER 20-0340].

JUSTICE ROBERT T. JOHNSON: NY R BRONX J Part IA-12.

JUSTICE DONALD A. MILES: NY R BRONX J Part IA-8.

JUSTICE DONNA M. MILLS: NY R BRONX J Part IA-9.

JUSTICE JULIA I. RODRIGUEZ: NY R BRONX J Part IA-18; [NY R BRONX J Part IA-27, as amended by NY ORDER 20-0341].

JUSTICE LLINET M. ROSADO: [NY R BRONX J Part IA-25, as amended by NY ORDER 20-0342].

JUSTICE NORMA RUIZ: NY R BRONX J Part IA-22; [NY R BRONX J Ruiz, Part IA-22 Virtual, as amended by NY ORDER 20-0343].

JUSTICE HOWARD H. SHERMAN: NY R BRONX J Part IA-4.

JUSTICE FERNANDO TAPIA: NY R BRONX J Part IA-13.

JUSTICE ELIZABETH A. TAYLOR: NY R BRONX J Part IA-2.

JUSTICE ALISON Y. TRUITT: NY R BRONX J Part IA-5.

PART IDV: NY R BRONX J Doc. 1.

PRE-TRIAL PART RULES: NY R BRONX J Doc. 2.

PRE TRIAL WORKSHEET: NY R BRONX J Doc. 3.

FORECLOSURE SETTLEMENT PART RULES: NY R BRONX J Doc. 4.

GUARDIANSHIP PART RULES: NY R BRONX J Doc. 5.

LPM PART RULES: NY R BRONX J Doc. 6.

ERIE COUNTY

JUSTICE M. WILLIAM BOLLER: NY R 8 JD J Boller.

JUSTICE RALPH A. BONIELLO: NY R 8 JD J Boniello.

JUSTICE CHRISTOPHER J. BURN: NY R 8 JD J Burns.

JUSTICE RUSSELL P. BUSCAGLIA: NY R 8 JD J Buscaglia.

JUSTICE FRANK CARUSO: NY R 8 JD J Caruso.

JUSTICE STEPHEN W. CASS: NY R 8 JD J Cass.

JUSTICE DEBORAH A. CHIMES: NY R 8 JD J Chimes.

JUSTICE EMILIO COLAIACOVO: [NY R 8 JD J Colaiacovo, as amended by NY ORDER 20-0252].

JUSTICE DIANE Y. DEVLIN: NY R 8 JD J Devlin.

JUSTICE JAMES H. DILLON: NY R 8 JD J Dillon.

JUSTICE PAULA L. FEROLETO: NY R 8 JD J Feroleto.
JUSTICE DANIEL J. FURLONG: [NY R 8 JD J Furlong, as amended by NY ORDER 20-0253].
JUSTICE JOSEPH R. GLOWNIA: NY R 8 JD J Glownia.
JUSTICE MARK J. GRISANTI: NY R 8 JD J Grisanti.
JUSTICE DEBORAH A. HAENDIGES: NY R 8 JD J Haendiges.
JUSTICE LYNN W. KEANE: [NY R 8 JD J Keane, as amended by NY ORDER 20-0254].
JUSTICE RICHARD C. KLOCH, Sr.: NY R 8 JD J Kloch.
JUSTICE FREDERICK J. MARSHALL: [NY R 8 JD J Marshall, as amended by NY ORDER 20-0255.
JUSTICE JOHN L. MICHALSKI: NY R 8 JD J Michalski.
JUSTICE MARK A. MONTOUR: [NY R 8 JD J Montour, as amended by NY ORDER 20-0256].
JUSTICE HENRY NOWAK: NY R 8 JD J Nowak.
JUSTICE JOHN F. O'DONNELL: NY R 8 JD J O'Donnell.
JUSTICE JEANETTE OGDEN: NY R 8 JD J Ogden.
JUSTICE CATHERINE NUGENT-PANEPINTO: NY R 8 JD J Nugent-Panepinto.
JUSTICE FRANK A. SEDITA, III: [NY R 8 JD J Sedita, as amended by NY ORDER 20-0257].
JUSTICE SARA SHELDON: NY R 8 JD J Sheldon.
JUSTICE DONNA M. SIWEK: NY R 8 JD J Siwek.
JUSTICE MARY L. SLISZ: NY R 8 JD J Slisz.
JUSTICE TIMOTHY J. WALKER: [NY R 8 JD J Walker, as amended by NY ORDER 20-0258].
JUSTICE DENNIS E. WARD: NY R 8 JD J Ward.
JUSTICE PAUL B. WOJTASZEK: [NY R 8 JD J Wojtaszek, as amended by NY ORDER 20-0259].
JUSTICE CHARLES N. ZAMBITO: [NY R 8 JD J Zambito, as amended by NY ORDER 20-0260].
SUPREME COURT LEGAL STAFF: NY R 8 JD J Legal Staff.

KINGS COUNTY

JUSTICE RACHEL A. ADAMS: NY R KINGS J Part 5F.
JUSTICE LOREN BAILY-SCHIFFMAN: NY R KINGS J Part 65.
JUSTICE REGINALD A. BODDIE: NY R KINGS J Part 95.
JUSTICE THERESA M. CICCOTTO: NY R KINGS J Part 19; NY R KINGS J Part 5J.
JUSTICE LISSETTE COLON: NY R KINGS J Part Rules.
JUSTICE GENINE EDWARDS: NY R KINGS J Part 80.
JUSTICE PAMELA L. FISHER: [NY R KINGS J Part 94, as amended by NY ORDER 20-0208].
JUSTICE ROBIN GARSON: NY R KINGS J Part 75.
JUSTICE LARA J. GENOVISI: [NY R KINGS J Part 34, as amended by NY ORDER 20-0209].
JUSTICE BERNARD J. GRAHAM: NY R KINGS J Part 36.
JUSTICE DAWN JIMENEZ-SALTA: NY R KINGS J Part 88.
JUSTICE INGRID JOSEPH: [NY R KINGS J Part FRP3 and Part 83, as amended by NY ORDER 20-0210].
JUSTICE KATHY J. KING: NY R KINGS J Part 64, 76K.
JUSTICE LAWRENCE KNIPEL: NY R KINGS J Part 57.
JUSTICE DONALD KURTZ: NY R KINGS J Part 26.
JUSTICE CARL LANDICINO: [NY R KINGS J Part 81, as amended by NY ORDER 20-0211].
JUSTICE KATHERINE LEVINE: [NY R KINGS J Part 20, 25, 92, as amended by NY ORDER 20-0211].
JUSTICE LORNA MCALLISTER: [NY R KINGS J Part 10, as amended by NY ORDER 20-0211].

JUSTICE ROSEMARIE MONTALBANO: [NY R KINGS J Part 19, 71, and 22, as amended by NY ORDER 20-0211].
JUSTICE RICHARD J. MONTELIONE: [NY R KINGS J Part 99 and DJMP, as amended by NY ORDER 20-0215].
JUSTICE LISA S. OTTLEY: NY R KINGS J Part 24.
JUSTICE MARK I. PARTNOW: NY R KINGS J Part 43.
JUSTICE ERIC I. PRUS: NY R KINGS J Part 5A.
JUSTICE FRANCOIS RIVERA: NY R KINGS J Part 52.
JUSTICE KAREN B. ROTHENBERG: NY R KINGS J Part 35.
JUSTICE LEON RUCHELSMAN: NY R KINGS J Part 1.
JUSTICE WAYNE P. SAITTA: NY R KINGS J Part 29.
JUSTICE ROBIN K. SHEARES: NY R KINGS J Part 96.
JUSTICE KENNETH P. SHERMAN: NY R KINGS J Part 67 and 78.
JUSTICE DEBRA SILBER: NY R KINGS J Part 9 and 5K.
JUSTICE ELLEN M. SPODEK: NY R KINGS J Part 63.
JUSTICE MARSHA L. STEINHARDT: NY R KINGS J Part 15.
JUSTICE JEFFREY S. SUNSHINE: NY R KINGS J Part 5G.
JUSTICE PETER P. SWEENEY: [NY R KINGS J Part 35, as amended by NY ORDER 20-0218].
JUSTICE DELORES J. THOMAS: [NY R KINGS J Part 5T, as amended by NY ORDER 20-0221].
JUSTICE WAVNY TOUSSAINT: NY R KINGS J Part 70.
JUSTICE RICHARD VELASQUEZ: NY R KINGS J Part 66.
JUSTICE CAROLYN E. WADE: NY R KINGS J Part 84.
JUSTICE EDWARD G. WALKER: [NY R KINGS J Part 90, as amended by NY ORDER 20-0219].
JUSTICE LILLIAN WAN: [NY R KINGS J Part 17, as amended by NY ORDER 20-0220].
JUSTICE MICHELLE WESTON: NY R KINGS J Part 3.
MENTAL HYGIENE PART: NY R KINGS J Part 77.
MATRIMONIAL PARTS DURING COVID-19 EMERGENCY: JUSTICE KAREN B. ROTHENBERG: NY R KINGS J Doc. 1.

NASSAU COUNTY

JUSTICE ANNA R. ANZALONE: NY R NASSAU S J Anzalone, Part 26.
JUSTICE STACY D. BENNETT: NY R NASSAU S J Bennett; NY R NASSAU S J Bennett, Form 1.
JUSTICE ANTONIO BRANDVEEN: NY R NASSAU S J Brandveen, Part 31.
JUSTICE JEFFREY S. BROWN: [NY R NASSAU S J Brown, as amended by NY ORDER 20-0297].
JUSTICE STEPHEN A. BUCARIA: NY R NASSAU S J Bucaria.
JUSTICE JULIANNE T. CAPETOLA: NY R NASSAU S J Capetola, Part 28.
JUSTICE EDMUND M. DANE: NY R NASSAU S J Dane, Part 33.
JUSTICE VITO M. DESTEFANO: NY R NASSAU S J DeStefano, Part 13; NY R NASSAU S J DeStefano, Form 1.
JUSTICE ARTHUR M. DIAMOND: NY R NASSAU S J Diamond, Part 7.
JUSTICE THOMAS FEINMAN: NY R NASSAU S J Feinman, Part 5.
JUSTICE JOHN M. GALASSO: NY R NASSAU S J Galasso, Part 22.
JUSTICE SHARON M.J. GIANELLI: NY R NASSAU S J Gianelli, Part 22; NY R NASSAU S J Gianelli, Form 1.
JUSTICE JEFFREY A. GOODSTEIN: NY R NASSAU S J Goodstein, Part 33; NY R NASSAU S J Goodstein, Form 1.
JUSTICE DAVID J. GUGERTY: [NY R NASSAU S J Gugerty, Part 31, as amended by NY ORDER 20-0298].
JUSTICE HELENE F. GUGERTY: NY R NASSAU S J Gugerty, Part 47.
JUSTICE STEVEN M. JAEGER: NY R NASSAU S J Jaeger, Part 35; NY R NASSAU S J Jaeger, Form 1.

JUSTICE JACK L. LIBERT: NY R NASSAU S J Libert, Part 23.

JUSTICE JOSEPH H. LORINTZ: NY R NASSAU S J Lorintz, Part 26; NY R NASSAU S J Lorintz, Form 1.

JUSTICE ROY S. MAHON: NY R NASSAU S J Mahon, Part 3.

JUSTICE RANDY SUE MARBER: NY R NASSAU S J Marber, Part 8.

JUSTICE JAMES P. MCCORMACK: [NY R NASSAU S J McCormack, Part 18, as amended by NY ORDER, 20-0299].

JUSTICE DICCIA T. PINEDA-KIRWAN: [NY R NASSAU S J Pineda-Kirwan, as amended by NY ORDER 20-0300].

JUSTICE THOMAS RADEMAKER: [NY R NASSAU S J Rademaker, Part 28, as amended by NY ORDER 20-0301]; [NY R NASSAU S J Rademaker, Form 1, as amended by NY ORDER 20-0301].

JUSTICE DENISE L. SHER: NY R NASSAU S J Rademaker, Part 32.

JUSTICE LEONARD D. STEINMAN: [NY R NASSAU S J Steinman, Part 15, as amended by NY ORDER 20-0303]; NY R NASSAU S J Steinman, Form 1.

JUSTICE HOWARD E. STURIM: NY R NASSAU S J Sturim, Part 50; NY R NASSAU S J Sturim, Form 1.

JUSTICE HELEN VOUTSINAS: [NY R NASSAU S J Voutsinas, Part 25, as amended by NY ORDER 20-0304]; [NY R NASSAU S J Voutsinas, Form 1, as amended by NY ORDER 20-0305].

JUSTICE HOPE SCHWARTZ ZIMMERMAN: NY R NASSAU S J Zimmerman, Part 17.

NEW YORK COUNTY

JUDGE'S RULES; BASIC INFORMATION: [NY R NY CTY J RUL Doc. 1, as amended by NY ORDER 20-0202].

ONONDAGA COUNTY

JUSTICE ROBERT E. ANTONACCI II: [NY R ONDGA E FIL Doc. 1, as amended by 20-0239].

JUSTICE MICHAEL V. COCCOMI: NY R ONDGA E FIL Doc. 2.

JUSTICE GREGORY R. GILBERT: NY R 5 JD JUDGES Gilbert; NY R ONDGA E FIL Doc. 3.

JUSTICE DONALD A. GREENWOOD: NY R ONDGA E FIL Doc. 4.

JUSTICE DEBORAH H. KARALUNAS: NY R ONDGA E FIL Doc. 5.

JUSTICE JAMES MCCLUSKY: NY R 5 JD MCCLUSKY McClusky.

JUSTICE CHARLES C. MERRELL: NY R 5 JD MERRELL Merrell.

JUSTICE PATRICK F. MACRAE: NY R 5 JD MACRAE Doc. 1.

JUSTICE JAMES P. MURPHY: NY R ONDGA E FIL Doc. 7.

JUSTICE GERALD J. NERI: [NY R 5 JD JUDGES Neri, as amended by NY ORDER 20-0236]; [NY R ONDGA E FIL Doc. 8, as amended by NY ORDER 20-0241].

JUSTICE ANTHONY J. PARIS: NY R 5 JD JUDGES Paris; [NY R ONDGA E FIL Doc. 9, as amended by NY ORDER 20-0242].

JUSTICE NORMAN W. SEITER, JR.: NY R 5 JD JUDGES Seiter.

JUSTICE KEVIN G. YOUNG: [NY R ONDGA E FIL Doc. 10, as amended by NY ORDER 20-0243].

QUEENS COUNTY

JUSTICE PAM JACKMAN BROWN: [NY R L QUEENS Brown, Part 19, as amended by NY ORDER 20-0321].

JUSTICE CHEREE A. BUGGS: NY R L QUEENS Buggs, Part 30.

JUSTICE PAM JACKMAN BROWN: [NY R L QUEENS Brown, Part 19, as amended by NY ORDER 20-0321].

JUSTICE DENIS J. BUTLER: NY R L QUEENS Butler, Part 12.

JUSTICE ROBERT I. CALORAS: [NY R L QUEENS Caloras, Part 36, as amended by NY ORDER 20-0322].

JUSTICE ANNA CULLEY: NY R L QUEENS Culley, Part 53.

JUSTICE TIMOTHY DUFFICY: NY R L QUEENS Dufficy, Part 35.

JUSTICE DAVID ELLIOT: NY R L QUEENS Elliot, Part 14.

JUSTICE JOSEPH J. ESPOSITO: NY R L QUEENS Esposito, Part 6.

JUSTICE DARRELL L. GAVRIN: [NY R L QUEENS Gavrin, Part 27, as amended by NY ORDER 20-0323].

JUSTICE WYATT N. GIBBONS: [NY R L QUEENS Gibbons, Part 5, as amended by NY ORDER 20-0330.

JUSTICE DONNA-MARIE E. GOLIA: [NY R L QUEENS Golia, Part 21, as amended by NY ORDER 20-0331].

JUSTICE MARGUERITE A. GRAYS: [NY R L QUEENS Grays, Part 4, as amended by NY ORDER 20-0324].

JUSTICE RUDOLPH E. GRECO: [NY R L QUEENS Greco, Part 32, as amended by NY ORDER 20-0325].

JUSTICE MAUREEN HEALY: NY R L QUEENS Healy, Part 6.

JUSTICE PHILLIP HOM: [NY R L QUEENS Hom, Part 43, as amended by NY ORDER 20-0332].

JUSTICE KEVIN J. KERRIGAN: NY R L QUEENS Kerrigan, Part 10.

JUSTICE MOJGAN C. LANCMAN: NY R L QUEENS Lancman, Part 20.

JUSTICE RICHARD G. LATIN: NY R L QUEENS Latin, Part 40.

JUSTICE ULYSSES B. LEVERETT: [NY R L QUEENS Leverett, Part 6, as amended by NY ORDER 20-0326].

JUSTICE LEONARD LIVOTE: NY R L QUEENS Livote, Part 33.

JUSTICE LEE A. MAYERSOHN: NY R L QUEENS Mayersohn, Part 22; NY R L QUEENS Mayersohn, Part 22G; [NY R L QUEENS Mayersohn, Part 22G COVID, as amended by NY ORDER 20-0327].

JUSTICE ROBERT J. MCDONALD: NY R L QUEENS McDonald, Part 34.

JUSTICE MARGARET MCGOWAN: NY R L QUEENS McGowan, Part 52.

JUSTICE MAURICE E. MUIR: [NY R L QUEENS Muir, Part 42, as amended by NY ORDER 20-0333].

JUSTICE JODI ORLOW: NY R L QUEENS Orlow, Part 51.

JUSTICE LESLIE J. PURIFICCION: NY R L QUEENS Purificcion, Part 39.

JUSTICE JOSEPH RISI: [NY R L QUEENS Risi, Part 3, as amended by NY ORDER 20-0328].

JUSTICE FREDERICK D.R. SAMPSON: [NY R L QUEENS Sampson, Part 31, as amended by NY ORDER 20-0329].

JUSTICE MARTIN J. SCHULMAN: NY R L QUEENS Schulman, Part 29.

JUSTICE BERNICE D. SIEGAL: NY R L QUEENS Siegal, Part 25G.

JUSTICE JANICE A. TAYLOR: NY R L QUEENS Taylor, Part 15.

JUSTICE CARMEN R. VELASQUEZ: NY R L QUEENS Velasquez, Part 38.

JUSTICE LOURDES M VENTURA: [NY R L QUEENS Ventura, Part 37, as amended by NY ORDER 20-0334].

JUSTICE WILLIAM A. VISCOVICH: NY R L QUEENS Viscovich, Part 63.

JUSTICE ALLAN B. WEISS: NY R L QUEENS Weiss, Part 2.

COMPLIANCE, SETTLEMENT AND CONFERENCE PART: NY R L QUEENS Doc 1.

PRELIMINARY CONFERENCE PART: [NY R L QUEENS Doc. 2, as amended by NY ORDER 20-0335].

MEDICAL MALPRACTICE CONFERENCE PART: [NY R L QUEENS Doc. 3, as amended by NY ORDER 20-0336].

TRIAL SCHEDULING PART: NY R L QUEENS Doc. 4.

SUMMARY JURY TRIAL PROGRAM: NY R L QUEENS Doc. 7.

RESIDENTIAL FORECLOSURE PART: NY R L QUEENS Doc. 9.

FORECLOSURE AUCTION RULES: NY R L QUEENS Doc. 10.

MATRIMONIAL PRELIMINARY CONFERENCE PART: NY R L QUEENS Doc. 11.

NON-CUSTODIAL CONTESTED MATRIMONIAL PART: NY R L QUEENS Doc. 12.

Appendix - Related Court Documents

Complaint

2019 WL 1751501 (N.Y.Sup.)

Westlaw Query>>

To find more Complaint filings on Westlaw: access New York Civil Trial Court Documents (from the Home page, click Trial Court Documents, then New York), click the Advanced Search link, select Complaint, and click Search. Use the Jurisdiction filter on the left to narrow results to New York Trial Ct.

Supreme Court of New York,

Nassau County.

Nancy L. KELLY, Plaintiff,

v.

BIRCHWOOD COURT OWNERS, INC. And Con-Kel Landscapiing Inc., Defendants.

No. 601465/2014.

2019.

Verified Complaint

Timothy Kilgannon, Kilgannon & Kilgannon, LLP, 1551 Kellum Place, Mineola, New York 11501, (516) 746-5530, for plaintiff.

Plaintiff, by her attorney, KILGANNON & KILGANNON, LLP, complaining of the defendants, respectfully shows to this Court and alleges:

FIRST: That at all times hereinafter mentioned the plaintiff was and still is a resident of the County of Nassau, State of New York.

SECOND: That upon information and belief, at all times hereinafter mentioned, the defendant, BIRCHWOOD COURT OWNERS, INC., owned premises located at 3 Birchwood Court, Mineola, New York.

THIRD: Upon information and belief, at all times hereinafter mentioned, the defendant, BIRCHWOOD COURT OWNERS, INC., was and still is a corporation duly organized and existing under the laws of the State of New York.

FOURTH: Upon information and belief, at all times hereinafter mentioned, the defendant, CON-KEL LANDSCAPING INC., was and still is a corporation duly organized and existing under the laws of the State of New York.

FIFTH: That upon information and belief, at all times hereinafter mentioned, the defendant, CON-KEL LANDSCAPING INC., had a contract to clear parking lot of premises and keep it clear of snow and ice.

SIXTH: That upon information and belief, the sidewalks, walkways and parking lots on the property described herein were much traveled ways in common use by the residents of the apartments located thereat.

SEVENTH: That Plaintiff on December 17, 2013 at or about 9:15 a.m., was lawfully walking in the parking lot behind the premises and at or near spot 307 of the above described premises on crevices and uneven pavement that had accumulated ice in the crevices which caused plaintiff to fall causing serious personal injuries.

EIGHTH: Said accident, fall and injuries resulting therefrom were caused solely by the negligence of the defendants, their agents, employees and/or assigns, without any negligence on the part of the plaintiff contributing thereto.

NINTH: That the negligence of the defendant which caused plaintiff to fall consisted of the defendant's failure to properly maintain said parking area safe for walking travel; failure to keep area; failure to keep area free of crevices accumulating ice; permitting the parking area to accumulate water and ice which becomes frozen thus creating a nuisance and trap; failure to clear parking area of accumulated ice and water; failure to maintain the parking lot and sidewalks in a safe condition; failure to properly level, repair and maintain the parking lot so as to remain in a cracked, unlevel and unsafe condition for extended length of time.

TENTH: That the condition of the location herein stated was allowed to exist for an unnecessary lengthy period of time and/or was created by the negligence of the defendants.

ELEVENTH: Defendants knew of or should have known of the dangerous condition that existed in the parking lot, in particular behind parking spot 307.

WHEREFORE, Plaintiff demand judgment against defendants in an amount to be determined upon the trial of this action but which amount exceeds the jurisdiction of all lower courts, together with the costs and disbursements of this action.

KILGANNON & KILGANNON, LLP

Timothy Kilgannon

Attorneys for Plaintiff

1551 Kellum Place

Mineola, New York 11501

(516) 746-5530

Answer

2020 WL 4730707 (N.Y.Sup.)

Supreme Court of New York,

New York County.

Paul KIM,

v.

Jonathan FRANCIS, et al.

No. 650481/2018.

February 5, 2020.

Verified Answer of David Arabov to Amended Complaint and Cross-Claim Against Defendant Jonathon Francis a/k/a Jonathon Francis San Pedro, a/k/a Jonathon F. San Pedro

Alan A. Heller, Esq., Kara M. Steger, Esq., Foster Garvey, P.C., 100 Wall Street, 20th Floor, New York, New York 10005, (212) 965-4526, (212) 965-4536, alan.heller@foster.com, kara.steger@foster.com, for defendant David Arabov.

Defendant, David Arabov ("Defendant"), as and for his Verified Answer to the Verified Amended Complaint of Plaintiff, and his Cross-Claim against defendant Jonathan Francis a/k/a Jonathon Francis San Pedro a/k/a Jonathon F. San Pedro, alleges as follows:

1. Denies the allegations of Paragraph 1 of the Verified Amended Complaint.

2. Denies the allegations of Paragraph 2 of the Verified Amended Complaint.

3. Denies the allegations of Paragraph 3 of the Verified Amended Complaint.

4. Denies the allegations of Paragraph 4 of the Verified Amended Complaint.

5. Denies the allegations of Paragraph 5 of the Verified Amended Complaint.

6. Denies the allegations of Paragraph 6 of the Verified Amended Complaint.

7. Denies the allegations of Paragraph 7 of the Verified Amended Complaint.

8. Denies knowledge or information sufficient to form a belief as to the allegations of Paragraph 8 of the Verified Amended Complaint.

9. Denies knowledge or information sufficient to form a belief as to the allegations of Paragraph 9 of the Verified Amended Complaint.

10. Denies the allegations of Paragraph 10 of the Complaint.

11. Denies knowledge or information sufficient to form a belief as to the allegations of Paragraph 11 of the Verified Amended Complaint.

12. Denies knowledge or information sufficient to form a belief as to the allegations of Paragraph 12 of the Verified Amended Complaint.

13. Denies knowledge or information sufficient to form a belief as to the allegations of Paragraph 13 of the Verified Amended Complaint.

14. Denies knowledge or information sufficient to form a belief as to the allegations of Paragraph 14 of the Verified Amended Complaint.

15. Denies knowledge or information sufficient to form a belief as to the allegations of Paragraph 15 of the Verified Amended Complaint.

16. Denies the allegations of Paragraph 16 of the Verified Amended Complaint.

17. Denies knowledge or information sufficient to form a belief as to the allegations of Paragraph 17 of the Verified Amended Complaint and refer all questions of law to the Court.

18. Denies the allegations of Paragraph 18 of the Verified Amended Complaint.

19. Denies the allegations of Paragraph 19 of the Verified Amended Complaint.

20. Denies the allegations of Paragraph 20 of the Verified Amended Complaint.

21. Denies the allegations of Paragraph 21 of the Verified Amended Complaint except refers the court to the alleged e-mail which document speaks for itself.

22. Denies knowledge or information sufficient to form a belief as to the allegations of Paragraph 22 of the Verified Amended Complaint.

23. Denies knowledge or information sufficient to form a belief as to the allegations of Paragraph 23 of the Verified Amended Complaint.

24. Denies the allegations of Paragraph 24 of the Verified Amended Complaint except refers the court to the alleged e-mail which document speaks for itself and denies that San Pedro had the authority to bind Arabov or the other Defendants to the alleged agreement.

25. Denies the allegations of Paragraph 25 of the Verified Amended Complaint.

26. Denies the allegations of Paragraph 26 of the Verified Amended Complaint.

27. Denies knowledge or information sufficient to form a belief as to the allegations of Paragraph 27 of the Verified Amended Complaint.

28. Denies the allegations of Paragraph 28 of the Verified Amended Complaint.

29. Denies knowledge or information sufficient to form a belief as to the allegations of Paragraph 29 of the Verified Amended Complaint except refers the court to the alleged e-mail which document speaks for itself.

30. Denies knowledge or information sufficient to form a belief as to the allegations of Paragraph 30 of the Verified Amended Complaint.

31. Denies the allegations of Paragraph 31 of the Verified Amended Complaint and refers the court to the alleged e-mail which document speaks for itself.

32. Denies the allegations of Paragraph 32 of the Verified Amended Complaint and refers the court to the trademark registration which registration speaks for itself.

33. Denies knowledge or information sufficient to form a belief as to the allegations of Paragraph 33 of the Verified Amended Complaint except refers the court to the alleged e-mails.

34. Denies the allegations of Paragraph 34 of the Verified Amended Complaint except refers the court to the alleged e-mails.

35. Denies the allegations of Paragraph 35 of the Verified Amended Complaint except refers the court to the alleged e-mail which document speaks for itself.

36. Denies the allegations of Paragraph 36 of the Verified Amended Complaint except refers the court to the alleged e-mail which document speaks for itself.

37. Denies knowledge or information sufficient to form a belief as to the allegations of Paragraph 37 of the Verified Amended Complaint except admit that Elite Daily was sold.

38. Denies knowledge or information sufficient to form a belief as to the allegations of Paragraph 38 of the Verified Amended Complaint.

39. Denies knowledge or information sufficient to form a belief as to the allegations of Paragraph 39 of the Verified Amended Complaint.

40. Denies knowledge or information sufficient to form a belief as to the allegations of Paragraph 40 of the Verified Amended Complaint.

41. Denies knowledge or information sufficient to form a belief as to the allegations of Paragraph 41 of the Verified Amended Complaint.

42. Denies knowledge or information sufficient to form a belief as to the allegations of Paragraph 42 of the Verified Amended Complaint.

43. Denies knowledge or information sufficient to form a belief as to the allegations of Paragraph 43 of the Verified Amended Complaint.

44. Denies knowledge or information sufficient to form a belief as to the allegations of Paragraph 44 of the Verified Amended Complaint.

45. Denies allegations of Paragraph 45 of the Verified Amended Complaint except admits that DMG Media purchased Elite Daily in or about 2015.

AS AND FOR A RESPONSE TO PLAINTIFF'S FIRST CAUSE OF ACTION
BREACH OF CONTRACT

46. Repeats and realleges paragraphs 1 through 45 above in answer to Paragraph 46 of the Verified Amended Complaint.

47. Denies the allegations of Paragraph 47 of the Verified Amended Complaint.

48. Denies the allegations of Paragraph 48 of the Verified Amended Complaint.

49. Denies the allegations of Paragraph 49 of the Verified Amended Complaint.

50. Denies the allegations of Paragraph 50 of the Verified Amended Complaint.

51. Denies the allegations of Paragraph 51 of the Verified Amended Complaint.

52. Denies the allegations of Paragraph 52 of the Verified Amended Complaint.

53. Denies the allegations of Paragraph 53 of the Verified Amended Complaint.

AS AND FOR A RESPONSE TO PLAINTIFF'S SECOND CAUSE OF ACTION
FRAUD

54. Paragraph 54 is part of Plaintiff's Second Cause of Action, which was dismissed by order of the court dated January 16, 2020.

55. Paragraph 55 is part of Plaintiff's Second Cause of Action, which was dismissed by order of the court dated January 16, 2020.

56. Paragraph 56 is part of Plaintiff's Second Cause of Action, which was dismissed by order of the court dated January 16, 2020.

57. Paragraph 57 is part of Plaintiff's Second Cause of Action, which was dismissed by order of the court dated January 16, 2020.

58. Paragraph 58 is part of Plaintiff's Second Cause of Action, which was dismissed by order of the court dated January 16, 2020.

59. Paragraph 59 is part of Plaintiff's Second Cause of Action, which was dismissed by order of the court dated January 16, 2020.

60. Paragraph 60 is part of Plaintiff's Second Cause of Action, which was dismissed by order of the court dated January 16, 2020.

AS AND FOR A RESPONSE TO PLAINTIFF'S THIRD CAUSE OF ACTION
FRAUD IN THE INDUCEMENT

61. Paragraph 61 is part of Plaintiffs Third Cause of Action, which was dismissed by order of the court dated January 16, 2020.

62. Paragraph 62 is part of Plaintiffs Third Cause of Action, which was dismissed by order of the court dated January 16, 2020.

63. Paragraph 63 is part of Plaintiffs Third Cause of Action, which was dismissed by order of the court dated January 16, 2020.

64. Paragraph 64 is part of Plaintiffs Third Cause of Action, which was dismissed by order of the court dated January 16, 2020.

65. Paragraph 65 is part of Plaintiffs Third Cause of Action, which was dismissed by order of the court dated January 16, 2020.

66. Paragraph 66 is part of Plaintiffs Third Cause of Action, which was dismissed by order of the court dated January 16, 2020.

AS AND FOR A RESPONSE TO PLAINTIFF'S FOURTH CAUSE OF ACTION
CIVIL CONSPIRACY

67. Paragraph 67 is part of Plaintiffs Fourth Cause of Action, which was dismissed by order of the court dated January 16, 2020.

68. Paragraph 68 is part of Plaintiffs Fourth Cause of Action, which was dismissed by order of the court dated January 16, 2020.

69. Paragraph 69 is part of Plaintiffs Fourth Cause of Action, which was dismissed by order of the court dated January 16, 2020.

70. Paragraph 70 is part of Plaintiffs Fourth Cause of Action, which was dismissed by order of the court dated January 16, 2020.

AS AND FOR A RESPONSE TO LAINTIFF'S FIFTH CAUSE OF ACTION
UNFAIR COMPETITION

71. Paragraph 71 is part of Plaintiffs Fifth Cause of Action, which was dismissed by order of the court dated January 16, 2020.

72. Paragraph 72 is part of Plaintiffs Fifth Cause of Action, which was dismissed by order of the court dated January 16, 2020.

73. Paragraph 73 is part of Plaintiffs Fifth Cause of Action, which was dismissed by order of the court dated January 16, 2020.

AS AND FOR A RESPONSE TO PLAINTIFF'S SIXTH CAUSE OF ACTION
CONVERSION

74. Paragraph 74 is part of Plaintiffs Sixth Cause of Action, which was dismissed by order of the court dated January 16, 2020.

75. Paragraph 75 is part of Plaintiffs Sixth Cause of Action, which was dismissed by order of the court dated January 16, 2020.

76. Paragraph 76 is part of Plaintiffs Sixth Cause of Action, which was dismissed by order of the court dated January 16, 2020.

AS AND FOR A RESPONSE TO PLAINTIFF'S SEVENTH CAUSE OF ACTION
BREACH OF IMPLIED COVENANT OF GOOD FAITH AND FAIR DEALING

77. Paragraph 77 is part of Plaintiffs Seventh Cause of Action, which was dismissed by order of the court dated January 16, 2020.

78. Paragraph 78 is part of Plaintiffs Seventh Cause of Action, which was dismissed by order of the court dated January 16, 2020.

79. Paragraph 79 is part of Plaintiffs Seventh Cause of Action, which was dismissed by order of the court dated January 16, 2020.

80. Paragraph 80 is part of Plaintiffs Seventh Cause of Action, which was dismissed by order of the court dated January 16, 2020.

AS AND FOR A RESPONSE TO PLAINTIFF'S EIGHTH CAUSE OF ACTION
ACCOUNT STATED AGAINST DEFENDANTS

81. Paragraph 81 is part of Plaintiffs Eighth Cause of Action, which was dismissed by order of court dated January 16, 2020.

82. Paragraph 82 is part of Plaintiffs Eighth Cause of Action, which was dismissed by court dated January 16, 2020.

83. Paragraph 83 is part of Plaintiffs Eighth Cause of Action, which was dismissed by court dated January 16, 2020.

84. Paragraph 84 is part of Plaintiffs Eighth Cause of Action, which was dismissed by court dated January 16, 2020.

85. Paragraph 85 is part of Plaintiffs Eighth Cause of Action, which was dismissed by court dated January 16, 2020.

86. Paragraph 86 is part of Plaintiffs Eighth Cause of Action, which was dismissed by order of the court dated January 16, 2020.

AS AND FOR A RESPONSE TO PLAINTIFF'S NINTH CAUSE OF ACTION
VIOLATION OF NEW YORK GENERAL BUSINESS LAWSECTION 349

87. Paragraph 87 is part of Plaintiffs Ninth Cause of Action, which was dismissed by order of the court dated January 16, 2020.

88. Paragraph 88 is part of Plaintiffs Ninth Cause of Action, which was dismissed by order of the court dated January 16, 2020.

89. Paragraph 89 is part of Plaintiffs Ninth Cause of Action, which was dismissed by order of the court dated January 16, 2020.

90. Paragraph 90 is part of Plaintiffs Ninth Cause of Action, which was dismissed by order of the court dated January 16, 2020.

91. Paragraph 91 is part of Plaintiffs Ninth Cause of Action, which was dismissed by order of the court dated January 16, 2020.

AS AND FOR A RESPONSE TO PLAINTIFF'S TENTH CAUSE OF ACTION
BREACH OF FIDUCIARY DUTY

92. Paragraph 92 is part of Plaintiffs Tenth Cause of Action, which was dismissed by order of the court dated January 16, 2020.

93. Paragraph 93 is part of Plaintiffs Tenth Cause of Action, which was dismissed by order of the court dated January 16, 2020.

94. Paragraph 94 is part of Plaintiffs Tenth Cause of Action, which was dismissed by order of the court dated January 16, 2020.

95. Paragraph 95 is part of Plaintiffs Tenth Cause of Action, which was dismissed by order of the court dated January 16, 2020.

96. Paragraph 96 is part of Plaintiffs Tenth Cause of Action, which was dismissed by order of the court dated January 16, 2020.

AS AND FOR A RESPONSE TO PLAINTIFF'S ELEVENTH CAUSE OF ACTION
PROMISSORY ESTOPPEL

97. Repeats and realleges Paragraphs 1 through 96 above in answer to paragraph 97 of the Verified Amended Complaint.

98. Denies the allegations of Paragraph 98 of the Verified Amended Complaint.

99. Denies the allegations of Paragraph 99 of the Verified Amended Complaint.

100. Denies the allegations of Paragraph 100 of the Verified Amended Complaint.

101. Denies the allegations of Paragraph 101 of the Verified Amended Complaint.

102. Denies the allegations of Paragraph 102 of the Verified Amended Complaint.

103. Denies the allegations of Paragraph 103 of the Verified Amended Complaint.

104. Denies the allegations of Paragraph 104 of the Verified Amended Complaint.

105. Denies the allegations of Paragraph 105 of the Verified Amended Complaint.

AS AND FOR A RESPONSE TO PLAINTIFF'S TWELFTH CAUSE OF ACTION
UNJUST ENRICHMENT

106. Repeats and realleges Paragraphs 1 through 105 above in answer to paragraph 106 of the Verified Amended Complaint.

107. Denies the allegations of Paragraph 107 of the Verified Amended Complaint.

108. Denies the allegations of Paragraph 108 of the Verified Amended Complaint.

109. Denies the allegations of Paragraph 109 of the Verified Amended Complaint.

110. Denies the allegations of Paragraph 110 of the Verified Amended Complaint.

111. Denies the allegations of Paragraph 111 of the Verified Amended Complaint.

112. Denies the allegations of Paragraph 112 of the Verified Amended Complaint.

113. Denies the allegations of Paragraph 113 of the Verified Amended Complaint.

AS AND FOR A FIRST AFFIRMATIVE DEFENSE

114. Plaintiffs Verified Amended Complaint fails to state a cause of action upon which relief can be granted.

AS AND FOR A SECOND AFFIRMATIVE DEFENSE

115. The Verified Amended Complaint is barred in whole or in part by the statute of limitations.

AS AND FOR A THIRD AFFIRMATIVE DEFENSE

116. The Verified Amended Complaint is barred in whole or in part by the doctrine of laches.

AS AND FOR A FOURTH AFFIRMATIVE DEFENSE

117. The Verified Amended Complaint is barred in whole or in part by the doctrine of waiver.

AS AND FOR A FIFTH AFFIRMATIVE DEFENSE

118. The Verified Amended Complaint is barred in whole or in part by the doctrine of estoppel.

AS AND FOR A SIXTH AFFIRMATIVE DEFENSE

119. Plaintiff failed to take reasonable steps to mitigate, alter, reduce or otherwise diminish his alleged damages, and accordingly, is barred from recovery of any damages that might have been prevented by such mitigation.

AS AND FOR A SEVENTH AFFIRMATIVE DEFENSE

120. Plaintiffs claims are barred by the doctrine of accord and satisfaction.

AS AND FOR AN EIGHTH AFFIRMATIVE DEFENSE

121. Plaintiffs damages are improperly calculated.

AS AND FOR AN NINTH AFFIRMATIVE DEFENSE

122. Plaintiffs claims are barred by the Statute of Frauds.

AS AND FOR AN TENTH AFFIRMATIVE DEFENSE

123. Arabov did not enter into, consent to or authorize the alleged agreement with Plaintiff.

AS AND FOR A FIRST CROSS-CLAIM AGAINST DEFENDANT JONATHON FRANCIS A/K/A JONATHON FRANCIS SAN PEDRO, A/K/A JONATHON F. SAN PEDRO

(Indemnification)

124. Repeats and reallges each and every allegation contained in paragraphs "1" through "123" of the Answer and Affirmative Defenses with the same force and effect as if fully set forth herein.

125. Although Defendant Arabov has denied the allegations of wrongdoing asserted against him and the other individual defendants in the Complaint, Arabov claims that if his is found to be liable to Plaintiff, his liability results solely from secondary, imputed, vicarious or passive, negligence or other liability, and that is liability is secondary and vicarious to that of the defendant Jonathon Francis a/k/a Jonathon Francis San Pedro, a/k/a Jonathon F. San Pedro ("San Pedro") whose liability is primary, and that, accordingly, any damages which may ultimately be determined to be the responsibility of Arabov are properly chargeable to San Pedro.

AS AND FOR A SECOND CROSS-CLAIM AGAINST DEFENDANT SAN PEDRO

(Contribution)

126. Repeats and realiges each and every allegation contained in paragraphs "1" through "125" of the Answer and Affirmative Defenses with the same force and effect as if fully set forth herein.

127. Although Arabov has denied the allegations of wrongdoing asserted against him and the other individual defendants in the Complaint, nevertheless, should Arabov be found to be liable to Plaintiff, then Arabov is entitled to an apportionment of fault against defendant San Pedro in proportion to the relative degrees of fault or wrongdoing among the parties to this action.

128. By reason of the foregoing, to the extent that Arabov is found to be liable to Plaintiff for any amount, Arabov is entitled to a judgment of contribution from San Pedro in accordance with the relative degrees of fault or wrongdoing of the parties to this action.

Dated: New York, New York February 5, 2020

FOSTER GARVEY, P.C.

By: */s/ Alan A. Heller*

Alan A. Heller, Esq.

Kara M. Steger, Esq.

Attorneys for Defendant David Arabov

100 Wall Street, 20th Floor

New York, New York 10005

(212) 965-4526

alan.heller@foster.com

(212) 965-4536

kara.steger@foster.com

Motion for Summary Judgment

2020 WL 3887865 (N.Y.Sup.)

> **Westlaw Query>>**
>
> To find more Motion for Summary Judgment filings on Westlaw: access New York Civil Trial Court Documents (from the Home page, click Trial Court Documents, then New York), click the Advanced Search link, select Motion for Summary Judgment, and click Search. Use the Jurisdiction filter on the left to narrow results to New York Trial Ct.

Supreme Court of New York,

New York County.

AVEMAR 2318 CORP., Plaintiff,

v.

PRODIGY NETWORK, LLC and Prodigy Shorewood Domestic Feeder Rep Fund, LLC, Defendants.

No. 655357/2019.

June 17, 2020.

Defendants' Reply Memorandum of Law in Support of Motion for Summary Judgment

Winston & Strawn LLP, 200 Park Avenue, New York, New York 10166, (212) 294-6700, for defendants Prodigy Network, LLC and Prodigy Shorewood Domestic Feeder Rep Fund, LLC.

Justice Jennifer G. Schecter.

MOTION SEQUENCE NO. 004

TABLE OF AUTHORITIES

Cases

Black Bull Contracting, LLC v. Indian Harbor Ins. Co., 135 A.D.3d 401 (1st Dep't 2016) 4, 6

In re Lipper Holdings, LLC, 1 A.D.3d 170, 766 N.Y.S.2d 561 (1st Dep't 2003) 8

Muzak Corp. v. Hotel Taft Corp., 1 N.Y.2d 42 (1956) 6

Solow Mgt. Corp. v. Hochman, 191 A.D.2d 250 (1st Dep't 1993) 5

W.W.W. Assoc., Inc. v. Giancontieri, 77 NY2d 157 (1990) 4

Defendants Prodigy Network, LLC ("Prodigy Network") and Prodigy Shorewood Domestic Feeder Rep Fund, LLC ("Prodigy Shorewood," and collectively with Prodigy Network, "Prodigy" or "Defendants") respectfully submit this Reply Memorandum of Law in support of their Motion for Summary Judgment. Capitalized terms not otherwise defined herein shall have the meanings ascribed to them in Prodigy's opening Memorandum of Law (NYSCEF No. 38).

PRELIMINARY STATEMENT

In its pleadings and Opposition to Prodigy's Motion for Summary Judgment, Avemar either explicitly concedes or does not dispute three propositions, which together compel summary judgment for Prodigy.

First, Avemar admits that Prodigy Network has the unilateral right to suspend "dealings," which the parties agree includes redemption of an investment, if Prodigy Network believes that such dealings are "not practicable or would be prejudicial to non-redeeming investors."[1]

Second, it is undisputed that Prodigy Network has held that belief since August 2019, and that Prodigy Network told Avemar and other investors *at that time* that it was suspending its payment of redemption requests as a result.[2]

Third, Avemar admits that, once Prodigy Network has suspended dealings, it has no obligation to redeem any investments, Avemar's included.[3]

These undisputed facts are themselves enough to end the inquiry. Indeed, they should have been enough to convince Avemar not to bring this case in the first instance. But Avemar's desperation to get out of the deal it struck (and its willingness to jeopardize the entire project and harm its fellow investors in the process) leads it to ignore the Offering Memorandum's clear and unambiguous language as well as its own admissions. Instead, it contends that Prodigy Network—despite its explicit statements to investors that their "redemption requests would have to wait"—somehow never suspended Avemar's redemption request *at all*. *See* Avemar Opp.[4] at 4 n.2.

Avemar advances this counterintuitive and counterfactual argument in two ways. First, it contends that, in order to suspend *any* dealings (such as the payment of redemption requests), Prodigy Network is required by the language of the Offering Memorandum to suspend *all* dealings. Second, Avemar suggests that in order to suspend dealings, Prodigy Network must first provide notification of such suspension in an appropriate publication. Put differently, Avemar has identified what it calls two "conditions precedent" for the suspension of Avemar's redemption request: first, the complete suspension of *all* of Prodigy Network's business activities; and second, notification of same "in an appropriate publication." According to Avemar, it is *only* if Prodigy Network takes these two steps that it may refuse to redeem Avemar's investment.

As Prodigy Network explained in its opening brief as well as its Memorandum of Law in Opposition to Avemar's Motion for Summary Judgment (the "Prodigy Opposition"), there are three separate but equally fatal flaws in Avemar's argument. First, it contradicts the express language of the Offering Memorandum. Second, it writes out of that agreement a number of critical provisions, thus violating the bedrock principle that a contract must be construed to give effect to all its terms. And third, it results in an arrangement that on its face is commercially unreasonable and completely absurd—one which would effectively end any chance that the Standard Hotel in Chicago would actually be built before the first cornerstone was even laid.

ARGUMENT

Given the amount of ink spilled by the parties to date, it may make sense to begin with the actual language of Section XIV of the Offering Memorandum, reproduced here in its entirety:

> "**[Prodigy Network] may suspend dealings**, or suspend the valuation of the Fund (i) during any period in which circumstances exist as a result of which, in the opinion of [Prodigy Network], it is not reasonably practicable to fairly determine the Net Asset Value of the Fund or it is not reasonably practicable for the Fund to realize or dispose of investments held for the Fund; (ii) during any breakdown in the means of communication between the Fund or [Prodigy Network] or in any system or infrastructure of the Fund or [Prodigy Network] to such extent that the Net Asset Value of the Fund cannot be accurately calculated; (iii) during any other breakdown in the means normally employed by [Prodigy Network] in assessing the value of investments; (iv) during any period in which the transfer of funds involved in the realization or acquisition of any investments by the Fund cannot be effected at normal rates of exchange; (v) **when there exists in the opinion of [Prodigy Network] a state of affairs where disposal of the Fund's assets**, or the determination of the Net Asset Value of the Fund, **would not be reasonably practicable or would be seriously prejudicial to the non-redeeming Investors**; and, (vi) **for any period during which the redemption of Interests would cause a breach or default under any covenant** in any agreement entered into by the Fund for borrowing or cash management purposes.

---

1. Section XIV(v), Offering Memorandum at 52-53; *see* Avemar Opp. at 3 (conceding same).

2. Andresen Aff. ¶¶ 7-8; Am. Compl. ¶ 19 ("[Prodigy Network] informed investors, including Plaintiff, that the Fund did not have sufficient capital to meet financial obligations relating to the Project, including payment of the pending redemption requests."); Compl. ¶ 28 ("Defendants . . . represent[ed] to Plaintiff that unless Prodigy Network can successfully raise additional capital through a large investor, redemption requests will have to wait.").

3. Avemar Opp. at 4 n.2. ("Avemar agrees with Defendants as to the effect of a suspension of dealings").

4. Plaintiff's Memorandum of Law in Opposition to Defendants Prodigy Network LLC and Prodigy Shorewood Domestic Feeder Rep Fund, LLC's Motion for Summary Judgment, NYSCEF No. 47 (herein, the "Avemar Opposition").

Any suspension of dealings or the valuation of the Fund, as the case may be, **shall take effect at such time as [Prodigy Network] shall declare** and, thereafter, there will be no dealings or valuation of the Fund, as the case may be, until [Prodigy Network] shall declare any such suspension to be at an end or the condition giving rise to the suspension having ceased to exist.

Notification of any suspension of dealings or valuation of the Fund or of any reinstatement following a suspension thereof will be made in an appropriate publication and **reasonable steps will be taken to bring any suspension to an end as soon as possible**."

Offering Memorandum at 52-53 (emphasis added).

As an initial matter, the above language easily disposes of Avemar's "notification" argument. Nothing in Section XIV states—or even implies—that "notification . . . in an appropriate publication" is a "condition precedent" for a suspension of dealings.[5] To the contrary, Section XIV explicitly enumerates six different substantive scenarios under which Prodigy Network may suspend dealings (the existence of at least one of which is thus a "condition precedent" to such suspension), and then states that "[a]ny suspension of dealings . . . *shall take effect* at such time as [Prodigy Network] shall declare " *Id.* (emphasis added). In other words, as long as one of the conditions in Section XIV(i)-(vi) is satisfied, and Prodigy Network then "declares" that it is suspending certain dealings, those dealings are suspended. *W.W.W. Assoc., Inc. v. Giancontieri*, 77 NY2d 157, 162 (1990) ("[W]hen parties set down their agreement in a clear, complete document, their writing should as a rule be enforced according to its terms.").

Here, Avemar does not dispute that "there exist[ed] in the opinion of [Prodigy Network] a state of affairs where disposal of the Fund's assets . . . would not be reasonably practicable or would be seriously prejudicial to the non-redeeming Investors," an actual condition precedent that gave Prodigy Network the authority to suspend payment of redemption requests. Offering Memorandum at 52-53; Andresen Aff. ¶¶ 7-8. And it explicitly concedes that Prodigy Network expressly "declared" to Avemar and other investors that it was exercising that authority.[6] Under the express terms of Section XIV, nothing more was required to make that suspension "effective," and Prodigy Network thus was under no obligation to redeem Avemar's investment. Avemar Opp. at 4 n.2 ("Avemar agrees with Defendants as to the effect of a suspension of dealings "); *Solow Mgt. Corp. v. Hochman*, 191 A.D.2d 250, 251 (1st Dep't 1993) ("Where, as here, the case turns upon an unambiguous written agreement and notice, and the material facts of the case are not in dispute, summary judgment [is] properly granted.").

Moreover, and as argued in greater detail in the Prodigy Opposition, that same "declaration" also constituted an actual "publication" and "notification" to Avemar that Prodigy Network was suspending payment of its redemption request within the meaning of the agreement. *See* Prodigy Opposition, NYSCEF No. 49 at 12-14; *see also* Compl ¶ 28; Am. Compl. ¶ 19. But even if the announcement did not qualify as such, that would not operate to nullify Avemar's right to suspend redemptions (or retroactively void such a suspension); it would simply give rise to a different cause of action for breach of the notification provision— one which would be doomed to fail for lack of damages given Avemar's repeated admissions that it received actual notice of same.

Avemar's second attempt to retroactively nullify the suspension by claiming that Prodigy Network did not suspend *enough* dealings is similarly untenable.

First, and as discussed above, Section XIV gives Prodigy Network the right to suspend "dealings" when one of six circumstances are met, and states that "*any* suspension of dealings shall take effect" upon Prodigy Network's declaration of same. Nothing in that language suggests that, before suspending *any* dealings, Prodigy Network must first suspend *all* dealings.

Second, even if Avemar were correct that, upon suspending any dealings, such as payment of redemption requests, Prodigy Network had a further obligation to suspend *all* dealings (a nonsensical reading of Section XIV, as discussed below), it simply would not follow that Prodigy Network's partial suspension of dealings *never happened*, as Avemar effectively suggests. To the contrary, the

---

5. Plaintiffs' citation of *Black Bull* does not lend any support for its argument that these portions of the contract are conditions precedent. 135 A.D.3d 401 (1st Dep't 2016). In fact, nowhere in *Black Bull* does the court even reference conditions precedent. Rather, as discussed below, *Black Bull* stands for the axiomatic principle that no provision of a contract can be left without force or effect—a principle violated by Avemar's interpretation of the contract.

6. *See* Plaintiff's Memorandum of Law in Support of Its Motion for Summary Judgment, NYSCEF No. 19 at 4 ("Defendants informed Project investors that . . . the Fund lacked sufficient capital to meet the Project's financial obligations—including the payment of pending redemption requests, such as Avemar's."); Am. Compl. ¶ 19 ("[Prodigy Network] informed investors, including Plaintiff, that the Fund did not have sufficient capital to meet financial obligations relating to the Project, including payment of the pending redemptions requests."); Compl. ¶ 28 ("Defendants . . . represent[ed] to Plaintiff that unless Prodigy Network can successfully raise additional capital through a large investor, redemption requests will have to wait."). In light of these admissions, it is difficult to understand how Mr. Volcovich-Mustri could swear in his affidavit that Prodigy Network did not "announce[]" its suspension. NYSCEF No. 23 ¶ 17 ("At no time have the Defendants announced or published that they have suspended dealings.").

suspension of redemptions would remain in effect (as Prodigy Network would have satisfied the only conditions precedent laid out by Section XIV(v)), but Avemar might have a *separate* breach of contract claim for Prodigy Network's failure to suspend all *other* dealings. Under that scenario, nothing would stop Avemar from filing suit and seeking damages and/or injunctive relief. But that is not the scenario with which we are dealing, and that is not the breach of contract claim Avemar filed.

Third, and as explained in greater detail in Prodigy Network's opening brief as well as the Prodigy Opposition, Avemar's suggested reading would neuter a number of the Offering Memorandum's provisions, which is impermissible under the black-letter law of this Court. *See* NYSCEF No. 38 at 13-14; Prodigy Opposition, NYSCEF No. 49 at 7-9; *see also Black Bull Contracting, LLC v. Indian Harbor Ins. Co.*, 135 A.D.3d 401, 406 (1st Dep't 2016) ("The rules of construction of contracts require us to adopt an interpretation which gives meaning to every provision of a contract or, in the negative, no provision of a contract should be left without force and effect." (quoting *Muzak Corp. v. Hotel Taft Corp.*, 1 N.Y.2d 42, 46 (1956)). For instance, Section XIV(vi), which allows Prodigy Network to "suspend dealings . . . for any period during which the redemption of Interests would cause a breach or default under any covenant in any agreement entered into by the Fund for borrowing or cash management purposes," necessarily implies that, while the suspension of dealings is in effect, Prodigy Network is permitted to meet its obligations under certain other agreements, such as paying interest or principal on loans. Indeed, permitting it to meet those obligations is the *entire purpose* of Subsection (vi). But, according to Avemar, "dealings" encompasses "all business activities," meaning that Avemar's suggested reading would actually *bar* Prodigy Network from doing so. *See* Avemar Opp. at 5-6. That cannot be right.

Similarly, if a suspension of dealings truly meant a suspension of *all* dealings, it would also make it impossible for Prodigy Network to comply with Section XIV's explicit directive that it take "reasonable steps . . . to bring any suspension to an end as soon as possible." Offering Memorandum at 53. Forcing Prodigy Network to suspend all dealings would mean that it could not hire contractors or architects, obtain permits, purchase the property, make payments under past contractual agreements (including those for borrowing or cash management purposes), or even pay its own employees—all "reasonable steps" towards advancing the project and thus putting itself in a position where it could redeem investments. Indeed, it would even be barred from working to solicit *new* investments so that it could pay such redemptions in the near term (which is presumably Avemar's goal).

In other words, any "suspension" of redemption requests would by necessity become permanent, which is at odds with both the plain meaning of the word "suspension" (*i.e.*, a "temporary prevention" of something) as well as the explicit language of Section XIV, which explicitly contemplates that the "conditions giving rise to a suspension" will at one point "cease[] to exist." Offering Memorandum at 53. Moreover, and perhaps most critically, such permanent suspension of dealings—effectively, cancellation of the project—would by definition be "severely prejudicial to the non-redeeming investors," thus defeating the *entire purpose* of the right to suspend dealings laid out in Section XIV(v) and exercised by Prodigy Network here.

Fourth, and finally, Avemar's reading of the parties' agreement makes no commercial sense. As discussed in more detail in the Prodigy Opposition, it is undisputed that Avemar signed up for a project which estimated a *maximum* 14-18% return over at least five (and possibly as long as eleven) years. *See* Prodigy Opposition, NYSCEF No. 49 at 10-11; Supplement at 8; NYSCEF No. 51 (Investor Fact Sheet). Yet, Avemar's position is that every investor with a redemption right is guaranteed to collect that same 18% return—compounded, no less—after just *one* year. That by itself would be unreasonable enough, but the alternative is even more absurd: should Prodigy Network exercise its explicit right not to redeem such a request, Avemar's interpretation of the agreement would effectively allow that same investor to kill off the entire $100 million project *in its entirety*. No rational actor—on either side of the transaction—could have ever intended such a result. *In re Lipper Holdings, LLC*, 1 A.D.3d 170, 171, 766 N.Y.S.2d 561, 562 (1st Dep't 2003) ("A contract should not be interpreted to produce a result that is absurd, commercially unreasonable, or contrary to the reasonable expectations of the parties." (citations omitted)).

CONCLUSION

For the foregoing reasons, Defendants respectfully request that this Court grant their Motion for Summary Judgment.

Dated: New York, New York

June 17, 2020

Respectfully submitted,

By: *s/ George E. Mastoris*

George E. Mastoris

Adam P. Moskowitz

WINSTON & STRAWN LLP

200 Park Avenue

New York, New York 10166

Telephone: (212) 294-6700
Facsimile: (212) 294-4700
gmastoris@winston.com
apmoskowitz@winston.com
Counsel for Defendants Prodigy Network, LLC and Prodigy Shorewood Domestic Feeder Rep Fund, LLC

Motion to Compel Disclosure

2020 WL 5100123 (N.Y.Sup.)

> **Westlaw Query>>**
> To find more Motion to Compel Disclosure filings on Westlaw: access New York Civil Trial Court Documents (from the Home page, click Trial Court Documents, then New York), click the Advanced Search link, select Motion to Compel, and click Search. Use the Jurisdiction filter on the left to narrow results to New York Trial Ct.

Supreme Court of New York,

New York County.

Ketevan SANCHEZ, individually and on behalf of all other persons similarly situated who were employed by Mj-Mc Home Health Care Agency, Inc., along with other entities affiliated or controlled by Mj-Mc Home Health Care Agency, Inc., Plaintiffs,

v.

MJ-MC HOME HEALTH CARE AGENCY, INC. and/or any other related entities, Defendant.

No. 160461/2018.

July 24, 2020.

Memorandum of Law in Support of Plaintiffs' Motion to Compel Discovery

Ladonna M. Lusher, Esq., Michele A. Moreno, Esq., Joel L. Goldenberg, Esq., Virginia & Ambinder, LLP, 40 Broad Street, 7th Floor, New York, New York 10004, for plaintiffs.

PRELIMINARY STATEMENT

Named Plaintiffs Ketevan Sanchez and Gulchehra Abdujamilova[1], individually and on behalf of other members of the putative class (collectively "Plaintiffs"), through their counsel, submit this memorandum of law in support of Plaintiffs' motion seeking to: (1) compel, pursuant to CPLR § 3124, Defendant MJ-MC Home Health Care Agency, Inc. (hereinafter "Defendant") to provide responses to Plaintiffs' First Pre-Class Certification Set of Interrogatory Demands and Plaintiffs' First Pre-Class Certification Demand for the Production of Documents and Things, (collectively referred as "Plaintiffs' Pre-Class Certification Discovery Demands"), so that Plaintiffs may adduce evidence to meet their burden of demonstrating they meet the statutory prerequisites of class certification pursuant to CPLR § § 901 and 902; (2) extend the deadlines for pre-class certification discovery, discovery, time to move for class certification, and the note of issue; and (3) grant such other relief as this Court deems necessary or proper. For the reasons set forth below, and in the accompanying affirmation, Plaintiffs' motion should be granted in its entirety.

STATEMENT OF FACTUAL AND PROCEDURAL HISTORY

The relevant facts and procedural history are set forth in the Good Faith Affirmation of LaDonna M. Lusher dated July 24, 2020 ("Lusher Aff.") and the exhibits annexed thereto.

---

1. *Abdujamilova v. MJ-MC Home Health Care Agency, Inc.*, Kings County Supreme Court Index No. 522586/2016, was consolidated with the instant action on March 6, 2020. [Dkt. No. 27].

ARGUMENT

A. Plaintiffs' Request to Compel Defendant to Produce Pre-Certification Discovery Should be Granted Because the Discovery is Necessary for Plaintiffs to Fulfill the Prerequisites of Class Certification.

The CPLR directs that there shall be "full disclosure of all evidence, material and necessary in the prosecution or defense of an action." CPLR § 3101(a). This statute "embodies the policy determination that liberal discovery encourages fair and effective resolution of disputes on the merits, minimizing the possibility for ambush and unfair surprise." *Penchas v. Hilton Hotels Corp.,* 590 N.Y.S.2d 669, 672 (Sup. Ct. N.Y. Co. 1992) (citing *Spectrum Systems Int'l Corp. v. Chemical,* 78 N.Y.2d 371, 376 (1991)). Accordingly, CPLR § 3124 provides that "if a person fails to respond to or comply with any request, notice, interrogatory, demand, question or order under this article, except a notice to admit under section 3123, the party seeking disclosure may move to compel compliance or a response."

In the instant matter, Plaintiffs seek to compel disclosure from Defendant who has failed to provide any documents whatsoever related to putative class members. Specifically, Plaintiffs have demanded discovery regarding the putative class to gather evidence and demonstrate Plaintiffs meet the requirements of class certification set forth in CPLR § § 901 and 902. However, Defendant has failed to provide responses to Plaintiffs' Pre-Class Certification Discovery Demands regarding any information pertaining the putative class. Defendant has not provided any justification whatsoever for its failure to produce these simple pre-class certification discovery responses.

It is well established that plaintiffs who are seeking to establish the necessary facts to satisfy the prerequisites for class action certification are entitled to obtain disclosure. *Dabrowski v. ABAX Incorporated,* Index No. 106778/07, 2009 N.Y. Misc. LEXIS 5640 (Sup. Ct. N.Y. Co., April 21, 2009) (granting plaintiffs' motion to compel pre-class certification discovery and reasoning that "plaintiffs are entitled to limited pre-certification discovery to establish the prerequisites for class certification."); *see also Citipostal, Inc. v. Unistar Leasing,* 283 A.D.2d 916, 920 (4th Dept. 2001) (time for plaintiffs to move for class certification extended because "plaintiffs are entitled to discovery to adduce evidence to meet their burden of showing that the statutory pre-requisites for certification" are met); Casey v. Prudential Secs. Inc., 268 A.D.2d 833, 834 (3d Dept. 2000); *Meraner v. Albany Med. Ctr.,* 199 A.D.2d 740 (3d Dept. 1993); *Scott v. Prudential Ins. Co. of Amer.,* 112 A.D.2d 714 (4th Dept. 1985) (plaintiff entitled to insurance agents' debit sheets in order that plaintiff could define her proposed class); Berger v. Nationwide Leisure Corp., 1979 N.Y. Misc. LEXIS 2868 (Sup. Ct. N.Y. Co., Special Term, 1979) (defendant ordered to produce charter flight manifests so plaintiff could establish nature of the class sought and number and identity of members).

Courts allow this pre-certification discovery because the party seeking class certification bears the burden of showing that each of the requirements have been met, i.e., numerosity, commonality, typicality, adequate representation, and superiority. See Andry-eyeva v. N.Y. Health Care, Inc., 994 N.Y.S. 2d 278, 281 (Sup. Ct. N.Y. Co. 2014) (referring to a previous order that "ruled that limited discovery must be conducted in order to determine whether the requirements of CPLR 901 have been met and to assess the considerations listed in CPLR 902."); Dabrowski, 2009 N.Y. Misc. LEXIS 5640 at *7-10 (same); Ring v. AXA Fin., Inc., 2009 N.Y. Misc. LEXIS 5840 *6 (Sup. Ct. N.Y. Co. 2009) ("It is undisputed that plaintiffs are entitled to limited pre-certification discovery to establish the pre-requisites for class certification."); Citipostal, 283 A.D.2d at 920 (holding that "plaintiffs are entitled to discovery to adduce evidence to meet their burden of showing that the statutory pre-requisites for certification" are met.); Casey, 268 A.D.2d at 834 (plaintiff entitled to obtain information needed to demonstrate the statutory pre-requisites for certification are met, particularly with respect to numerosity); Katz v. NVF, Co., 100 A.D. 2d 470, 474 (1st Dept. 1984) ("A further development of the facts is necessary to determine whether each of the prerequisites contained in CPLR 901 have been met").

Indeed, a court is likely to expect parties to conduct pre-certification discovery in order to develop a sufficient record, so that the court need not defer or deny a motion for class certification in order to allow the parties to conduct discovery. See Andyeyeva, 994 N.Y.S. 2d 2782; see also Dabrowski, 2009 N.Y. Misc. LEXIS 5640 at *3 ("Before a motion for class certification is brought, plaintiffs are entitled to limited pre-certification discovery to establish the pre-requisites for class certification"); Ring, 2009 N.Y. Misc. LEXIS 5840 at * 6; Katz, 100 A.D. 2d 470, 474 (directing the parties to conduct discovery relevant to each of the NY CPLR § 901 prerequisites because "the record at this point is a blunderbuss approach"); Simon v. Cunard Line Ltd., 75 A.D.2d 283, 290 (1st Dept. 1980) ("Discovery proceedings are necessary to determine the nature and size of the class").

Indeed, on plaintiffs' second motion for class certification in Andryeyeva, another class action brought by home attendants and almost identical to the instant matter, the court noted that:

> In [the court's previous] decision and order this court denied plaintiffs' class certification motion without prejudice and ruled that limited discovery must be conducted in order to determine whether the requirements of CPLR 901 have been met and to assess the considerations listed in CPLR 902.

994 N.Y.S. 2d at 281. The Andyeyeva court then granted plaintiff's second motion for class certification based on the record developed from the previously necessary and compelled precertification discovery production that included payroll records

covering the proposed class for the propose period and which allowed plaintiffs to identify 1,063 home attendants who worked 24-hour shifts. Likewise, in *Kodirov v. Cmty. Home Care Referral Serv., Inc.,* 2012 N.Y. misc. LEXIS 2126 (Sup. Ct. Kings Co. 2012) (Demarest, J.), another similar class action brought on behalf of home health attendants, the court found that the "[p]laintiffs must be allowed to assemble evidence to meet their burden of showing that the statutory prerequisites to certification of a class are met." *Id.* at *5. There, the Court dismissed the defendants' objections that the class was "fatally overbroad," and the court ordered the defendants to produce class-wide discovery. *Id.* at *7-8.

A similarly situated defendant-employer was ordered by the Honorable Gerald Lebovits J.S.C. to produce the same pre-class certification discovery as requested here in a nearly identical class action involving home health attendants. *See Troshin v. Stella Orton Home Care Agency, Inc.,* 2018 N.Y. Misc. LEXIS 1814, Index No. 159312/2016, (Sup. Ct. N.Y. Co. May 11, 2018) (Lebovits, J). Judge Lebovits found that the plaintiffs demonstrated that the information sought was material and necessary to establish the commonality of the class claims and that the named plaintiff's claims were typical of all the putative class members. *Id.* He further noted that "class certification has routinely been granted in similar actions. In *Andryeyeva* (153 A.D.3d at 1217), plaintiffs could establish the prerequisites to class certification for 'a class of approximately 1,063 home attendants who had worked 24-hour shifts between December 28, 2007 and March 8, 2013.' In response, defendant has failed to establish how the requests are overbroad or unduly burdensome."

Additionally, in an almost identical matter brought by home health attendants alleging the same claims as the Plaintiffs allege here, the Honorable Frank P. Nervo, J.S.C. ordered the defendant-agency to produce pre-class certification discovery identical to the discovery requested in this action. *See Wallace v. Tri-Med Home Care Servs., Inc.,* 2019 N.Y. Misc. LEXIS 2844, Index No. 157235 (Sup. Ct. N.Y. Co. May 28, 2019) (Nervo, J.). The Tri-Med court concluded that the "material sought by plaintiff is necessary to determine whether the requirements of CPLR § § 901 and 902 can be met by the putative class. *Id.,* at *4.

In the instant matter, like the cases cited above, Plaintiffs need the information requested to demonstrate they meet the statutory prerequisites of class certification under CPLR § § 901 and 902. Plaintiffs have the burden of establishing numerosity, commonality, typicality, adequate representation and superiority of their claims and the claims of the putative class. Defendant's refusal to disclose the requested documents and information precludes Plaintiffs of their opportunity to adduce evidence to demonstrate they meet those requirements.

In addition, Plaintiffs have granted Defendant multiple extensions of time to respond to Plaintiffs' Demands. [*See* Lusher Aff. Ex. E, May 14, 2020 Deficiency Letter to Defendant (giving Defendant until May 28, 2020 to respond); Lusher Aff. Ex. F, Stipulation (extending the deadline to respond to pre-class certification discovery to June 26, 2020); Lusher Aff. Ex. G Stipulation (extending the deadline to respond to pre-class certification discovery to July 24, 2020)]. Each one of these extensions was granted by Plaintiffs in good faith, with the goal of allowing Defendant more time to collect and produce documents in response to Plaintiffs' demands. Plaintiffs also hoped to avoid the costly and timely detractions of motion practice. Defendant has nevertheless not provided any discovery related to putative class members whatsoever. Defendant has not offered any reasonable justification why it failed to do so. Further, this Court has already held that "[w]hile one named plaintiff is classified as an hourly employee and another as a 24-hour employee and another as a 24-hour employee, this would only go to the quantum of damages, which is insufficient to defeat class certification." [Lusher Aff. Ex. C].

As evidenced by the case law cited above, Defendant must produce the discovery related to the putative class. Accordingly, Plaintiffs' motion should be granted.

B. THE DEADLINES FOR PRE-CLASS CERTIFICATION DISCOVERY, TIME TO MOVE FOR CLASS CERTIFICATION, AND NOTE OF ISSUE SHOULD BE EXTENDED

Plaintiffs should not be prejudiced as a result of Defendant's refusal to comply with rudimentary discovery obligations. It would be highly prejudicial for Plaintiffs to be forced to make a motion for class certification without the benefit of pre-class certification discovery. As such, Plaintiffs respectfully request that the Court not only compel Defendant to produce the discovery, but also allow enough time for Plaintiffs to review it and conduct pre-class certification depositions thereafter. To do so, Plaintiffs request that the Court set a reasonable deadline for preclass certification discovery and for Plaintiffs' filing of the Note of Issue and Certificate of Readiness.

CONCLUSION

For the reasons set forth above, it is respectfully requested that this Court grant Plaintiffs' motion to: (1) compel Defendant, MJ-MC Home Health Care, Inc., to respond to Plaintiffs' Pre-Class Certification Discovery Demands pursuant to CPLR § 3124; (2) extend the deadlines for pre-class certification discovery, discovery, time to move for class certification, and the note of issue; and (3) grant such other relief as this Court deems necessary or proper.

Dated: July 24, 2020 New York, New York

VIRGINIA & AMBINDER, LLP
By: */s/La Donna M. Lusher, Esq.*
La Donna M. Lusher, Esq.
Michele A. Moreno, Esq.
Joel L. Goldenberg, Esq.
40 Broad Street, 7th Floor
New York, New York 10004
Tel: (212) 943-9080
Fax: (212) 943-9082
Email: llusher@vandallp.com
Counsel for the Plaintiffs and the Putative Class

Motion for Protective Order

2018 WL 2473395 (N.Y.Sup.)

Supreme Court of New York,

New York County.

Marvin SANDLER, Mimi Berman Sandler, and Mimarv, Inc. f/k/a Independent Living Aids, Inc., Plaintiffs,

v.

INDEPENDENT LIVING AIDS, LLC (a New York LLC), Independent Living Aids LLC (a Delaware LLC), Rss Adventure Capital, LLC, the Chow/Speach Trust, Economic Solutions, Inc., Matthew Sheppard, Prince John Radziwill and Irwin Schneidmill, Defendants.

No. 652154/2013.

April 6, 2018.

Motion Sequence No. 6

Memorandum of Law in Support of Motion for a Protective Order Made By Defendants Independent Living Aids, LLC (a Delaware LLC), Independent Living Aids, LLC (a New York LLC), Rss Adventure Capital, LLC, the Chow/Speach Trust, Economic Solutions, Inc., Matthew Sheppard, Prince John Radziwill and Irwin Schneidmill

Reisman, Rubeo & McClure & Altman, LLP, (A Delaware LLC), Independent Living Aids, LLC (a New York LLC), RSS Adventure Capital, LLC, The Chow/Speach Trust, Economic Solutions, Inc., Matthew Sheppard, Prince John Radziwill, and Irwin Schneidmill, 151 Broadway, Hawthorne, New York 10532, (914) 495-3050, for defendants Independent Living Aids, LLC.

TABLE OF CONTENTS

TABLE OF AUTHORITIES

Statutes

Cases

Rules

PRELIMINARY STATEMENT

This Memorandum of Law is submitted by Defendants Independent Living Aids, LLC (A Delaware LLC), Independent Living Aids, LLC (A New York LLC), RSS Adventure Capital, LLC, The Chow/Speach Trust, Economic Solutions, Inc., Matthew Sheppard, John Radziwill and Irwin Schneidmill (collectively, "Defendants"), in support of their motion for a protective order, pursuant to C.P.L.R. § 3103, shielding from disclosure certain items in the file of Defendants' expert, Raiche, Ende, Malter & Co. LLP / Mitchell Sorkin, CPA ("Defendants' Expert") which would otherwise be subject to production pursuant to this Court's Order dated March 22, 2018 ("the Conference Order"). The Conference Order directs Defendants' Expert to turn over "his file, hard copy and electronically, kept in this matter, to Plaintiff, by April 6, 2018." This motion is made by order to show cause pursuant to the Rules of IAS Part 48 and pursuant to the Conference Order issued by Hon. Andrea Masley, J.S.C.

PROCEDURAL HISTORY

The relevant procedural history of this matter is set forth at length in the Affirmation of Mark I. Reisman, Esq., dated April 5, 2018, submitted in support of this motion.

DISCUSSION

POINT I

DEFENDANTS ARE ENTITLED TO A PROTECTIVE ORDER WITH RESPECT TO EMAILS TO AND FROM DEFENDANTS' EXPERT AND COUNSEL FOR DEFENDANT

This motion seeks to protect production of two broad categories of emails between Mitchell Sorkin, C.P.A., (Defendants' Expert) and counsel for Defendants. Pursuant to N.Y. C.P.L.R. 3101(d) and applicable case law concerning an expert who is expected testify at trial, a party is obligated to not only identify the expert but to "disclose in reasonable detail the subject matter on which each expert is expected to testify, the substance of the facts and opinions on which expert is expected to testify, the qualifications of each expert and a summary of the grounds for each expert's opinion." Rule 13 of the Rules of the Commercial Division further describes the contents of required expert disclosure and allows for depositions of testifying experts. 22 N.Y.C.R.R. § 202.70.

However, materials prepared in anticipation of litigation or prepared by a representative of a party "may only be obtained upon a showing that the party seeking discovery has substantial need of the materials in the preparation of the case[i]n ordering the discovery, the court shall protect against disclosure of the mental impressions, conclusions, opinions or legal theories of an attorney or other representative of a party concerning the litigation." CPLR. 3101(d)(2); Carafiello v. Massachusetts Life Ins. Co., 266 A.D.2d 117 (1st Dep't 1999); MBIA Ins. Co. v. Countrywide Home Loans, Inc., 35 Misc.3d. 1205(A) *6 (Sup. Ct. N.Y. Co. 2011), aff'd, 93 A.D.3d 574 (1st Dept. 2012) ("The proper test for whether documents are to be accorded protection is not a didactic test as to whether the documents are created solely for purposes of litigation, but whether the documents were created primarily for the purposes of litigation."); Straus v. Ambinder, 61 A.D.3d 672 (2d Dept. 2009) (documents subpoenaed from plaintiff's accountant protected by attorney-client privilege and also as material prepared in anticipation of litigation); Oakwood Realty Corp. v. HRH Construction Corp., 51 A.D.3d 747 (2d Dept. 2008) (consultant's report prepared in anticipation of litigation protected from disclosure under attorney-client privilege and as attorney work product).

Moreover, on at least one prior occasion, correspondence exchanged between an attorney for a party and that party's expert witness at trial has been considered by an appellate court to be attorney work product and therefore not subject to disclosure. See, Holmes v. Weissman, 251 A.D. 2d 1078 (4th Dept., 1998) (internal citations omitted) (letter written by attorney to medical expert).

Emails, if any, between Mr. Sorkin and Defendants' attorneys prior to Mr. Sorkin's engagement as an expert witness on September 15, 2016 should be protected from disclosure inasmuch as neither Mr. Sorkin nor his firm were, as of that time, engaged to be a testifying expert in this matter (see August 31, 2016 Engagement Letter, fully executed on September 15, 2016, annexed to Reisman Affirmation as Exhibit C). Mr. Sorkin's communications with counsel prior to his being hired as the testifying expert were that of a consultant to Defendants' counsel, and thus are afforded a blanket protection from disclosure. See Santariga v. McCann, 161 A.D.2d 320, 321 (1st Dept. 1990) (experts hired solely as consultants are generally seen as an adjunct to the lawyer's strategic thought processes, thus qualifying for complete exemption from disclosure under subdivision; even the actual reports of such experts are immune from disclosure). See also, Hudson Insurance Co. v. Oppenheim, 72 A.D.3d 489 (1st Dept. 2010) ("Such [attorney work product] privilege extends to experts retained as consultants to assist in analyzing or preparing the case, 'as adjunct to the lawyer's strategic thought processes, thus qualifying for complete exemption from disclosure.'"). In Delta Financial Corp. v. Morrison, 14 Misc. 3d 428, (Sup. Ct. Nassau Co. 2006) the Court recognized just such a "cut-off date prior to which a consultant is not deemed a "testifying" expert. The Court in Delta goes on to clarify that, once retained, while there will be a greater duty of disclosure as to such a testifying expert, such disclosure would not include certain documents as to which privilege was claimed. Id. at 434 (court found various documents were indeed subject to protection inasmuch as "the Court finds that there is no exception to the privilege afforded to the disputed documents.").

The second category of emails Defendants seek to protect are emails to and from Defendants' counsel after September 15, 2016, the date that Defendants retained Mr. Sorkin as an expert witness. We respectfully submit that as with the draft reports discussed above, emails from Defendants' counsel to Mr. Sorkin, containing the actual words and thoughts of Defendants' counsel, contain or may give insight into mental impressions of Defendants' counsel which should be protected from disclosure. Email responses from Mr. Sorkin in reply to Defendants' counsel should similarly be protected as such responses emails would necessarily reveal, in addressing a matter raised by counsel, the mental impressions of Defendants' counsel contained in the original communication. See Holmes, supra. As is discussed above relating to drafts of the expert's report, absent a true showing of "need," which we submit cannot be successfully argued by the Plaintiffs, these should be protected from disclosure so as to guard against revealing the mental impressions of counsel.

New York courts have protected such communications. In Bernard v. Brookfield Properties Corp., No. 107211/08, 2012 WL 2502775 (Sup. Ct. N.Y. Co, June 14, 2012), after the plaintiff had obtained various factual documents from the defendant's witness, a former employee of the defendant, the plaintiff sought, at the former employee's deposition, to question the witness as to the contents of conversations he had conducted with the defendant's attorney. Noting that the defendant had not objected to any questions relating to facts that might be in the former employee's possession, the Court deemed the communications with defendant's counsel to be protected from disclosure inasmuch as "the responses to such broad questions, if provided, likely would have given Plaintiff an inappropriate glimpse into the strategy of opposing counsel. Such questions plainly fall under the rubric of the work product privilege." Id.

Similarly, in Beller v. William Penn Life Ins. Co., 15 Misc.3d 350 (Sup. Ct. Nassau Co. 2007), the Court addressed an expert witness's verbal communications with counsel. The Court found that the defendant had established that the attorney's conversations with the expert would "fall under the umbrella of CPLR 3101(d)(2) as material prepared for litigation in preparation for trial." The Court then shifted the burden to the Plaintiff: "to convince the court that there is a 'substantial need of the materials in the preparation of the case and [he] is unable without undue hardship to obtain the substantial equivalent of the materials by other means.' CPLR 3101(d)(2)." Id. at 356. Notwithstanding a finding of "need," the court in Beller nonetheless held that communications between counsel and the expert might qualify for protection as "work product" or "material prepared for trial." Ultimately, the court in Beller ruled that while inquiries to the expert would be allowed to proceed, the mental impressions of the attorney were to be protected. In reaching this decision, the Beller court noted that while prevailing federal practice may well require the disclosure of attorney communications with a testifying expert, there is no comparable requirement in state practice. Id. at 358, footnote 1.

Here, Plaintiffs have shown no compelling need for correspondence between Mr. Sorkin and Defendants' counsel sufficient to overcome the statutory protection of attorney work product of material prepared for trial. C.P.L.R. § 3101(d)(2). As such, these emails, which may reveal the mental impressions of counsel, should be protected from disclosure.

Ironically, at the February 27, 2018 deposition of Plaintiffs' expert, Henry Dubrow, Plaintiffs' counsel argued that communications between himself and Mr. Dubrow were "privileged" and directed the witness not to answer such questions. At one point during his deposition, Mr. Dubrow testified in substance that, in reaching a particular conclusion, he had relied upon certain information received from Plaintiffs' counsel. When Defendants' counsel followed up with a question regarding the content of that conversation with Plaintiffs' counsel, Plaintiffs' counsel objected to this line of inquiry based on privilege and did not allow Mr. Dubrow to answer the question:

Q. Okay. So are you telling me you never read Irwin Schneidmills deposition testimony with respect to this Dunkin' Donuts account?

A. No.

Q. You did not read it?

A. I did read it.

Q. Okay. Did you see his explanation of the Dunkin' Donuts account in the deposition transcript?

A. Yes.

Q. Okay. So did you review Irwin Schneidmill's testimony to come to the conclusion that, for accounting purposes, that entry had no legitimate purpose, or did you rely on the statements made to you by the lawyers?

A. I relied on plaintiffs' counsel.

Q. Okay. Did plaintiffs' counsel explain to you, in words or substance, why they, in words or substance, --

MR. HUBELL: Objection.

MR. COZIER: Objection.

MR. REISMAN: Why?

MR. COZIER: It's privileged.

MR. REISMAN: Are you saying you don't want him to answer?

MR. COZIER: Yeah.

See relevant portions of Transcript of Deposition of Henry Dubrow, February 27, 2018, pp. 139-140 (emphasis supplied), annexed to Reisman Affirmation as Exhibit F.

Given that Plaintiffs' counsel has declared communications between counsel and their expert to be privileged, Plaintiffs should be estopped from seeking the exact communications, albeit written ones, between Defendants' expert and Defendants' counsel. To the extent the Court finds otherwise, then any order issued by the Court should clarify that no such privilege attaches to Plaintiffs' expert either, and that his communications with Plaintiffs' counsel are subject to disclosure to the same extent as are those between Defendants' expert and Defendants' counsel.

POINT II
DEFENDANTS ARE ENTITLED TO A PROTECTIVE ORDER RELATING TO PRIOR DRAFTS OF THE EXPERT REPORT

Defendants also seek a protective order with respect to a prior draft of the report of Defendants' Expert. That draft, dated February 28, 2017, was revised by Defendants' Expert several weeks after that date. Because the edits could reflect the mental impressions of Defendants' counsel, the prior draft should be protected from disclosure under C.P.L.R. § 3101(d). Moreover, Plaintiffs can show no pressing "need" for the first draft.

In his March 20, 2018 letter to the Court explaining why he sought disclosure of Defendant's Expert's file, counsel for Plaintiff failed to identify any basis whatsoever for "needing" the prior draft of Mr. Sorkin's report (See Hubell letter, annexed to Reisman Affirmation as Exhibit E). In the absence of any showing of true "need," it is respectfully submitted that the presumption that attorneys' mental impressions should be protected from disclosure should take precedence.

Furthermore, any argument Plaintiffs have made or will make as to "need" should be considered in the context of the fact that Plaintiffs' own identified expert, Henry Dubrow, has no significant disagreement with the report of Defendants' Expert report other than two discrete items.[1] Defendants' expert report addresses a single critical issue in this case - namely, the financial condition of ILA Delaware just prior to the sale of its assets and the transfer of its liabilities to ILA New York. Plaintiffs' expert's concession that he had no disagreement with anything in Mr. Sorkin's report, other than the minor one-day discrepancy in the valuation date and the treatment of good will, the validity of all of the Defendants' expert's numbers and conclusions, underscores how Plaintiffs have absolutely need of Mr. Sorkin's draft report.

Mr. Dubrow also questioned Defendants' Experts failure to include the value of goodwill as an element of its financial condition as of May 30, 2012. Notwithstanding this question, Mr. Dubrow did not calculate or ascribe any specific goodwill value for the company as of May 31, 2012. Rather, Mr. Dubrow stated that he had a "question" as to the treatment of goodwill in the report. (See Dubrow deposition transcript of February 27, 2018, annexed to Reisman Affirmation as Exhibit F, pp. 163-167).

Q. With respect to, is there anything else in this report with which you disagree in any way?

A. Other than the date, to me, I did not understand the date.

Q. All right. Anything else?

A. No.

Reisman Affirmation, Exhibit F, p. 141 (emphasis supplied).

In light of the fact that Plaintiffs' expert has endorsed every valuation in the Defendants' expert's report other than the single line item as to goodwill, Plaintiffs will be hard pressed to demonstrate a compelling need for the prior draft of Mr. Sorkin's report. As set forth above, the release of the earlier draft would constitute disclosure of Defendants' counsel's mental impressions, which are covered by the provisions of C.P.L.R. § 3101(d). As such, the mental impressions of Defendants' counsel should not be subject to production and should be protected from production via the requested protective order.

POINT III
AT THE VERY LEAST, THE COURT SHOULD CONDUCT AN IN CAMERA INSPECTION OF THE EXPERT'S DRAFT REPORT AND CORRESPONDENCE TO DETERMINE IF THEY ARE SUBJECT TO DISCLOSURE

If, despite the above arguments, the Court determines that Plaintiffs have demonstrated a need for Mr. Sorkin's draft and correspondence with counsel that is so compelling as to warrant disclosure, it is respectfully requested that the Court first conduct an in camera inspection of Mr. Sorkin's file, to determine the proper extent of disclosure. See, e.g., In re New York City Asbestos Litigation, 109 A.D.3d 7, (1st Dept. 2013).

CONCLUSION

For the reasons set forth herein and in the accompanying Affirmation of Mark I. Reisman, it is respectfully requested that the Court grant Defendants' motion for a protective order relating to any prior drafts of Defendants' expert's report, and emails between Defendants' expert and Defendants' counsel, pursuant to C.P.L.R. § 3103, along with such additional relief as the Court deems just and proper.

Dated: Hawthorne, New York April 5, 2018

REISMAN, RUBEO, McCLURE & ALTMAN, LLP

By:

MARK I. REISMAN, ESQ.

Attorneys for Defendants

151 Broadway

Hawthorne, New York 10532

(914) 495-3050

---

1. Mr. Dubrow questioned why Defendants' expert had chosen to provide a valuation of ILA Delaware "as of May 30, 2012, rather than May 31, 2012, the last day of ILA Delaware's operations before the sale of its assets and the assignment of its liabilities as of June 1, 2012, the sale date as reflected in the sale documents. This concern was easily explained by Defendants' Expert who stated in substance that the records of the company as of May 31, 2012 were not materially different from those in existence as of May 30, 2012 so that the financial condition of the company as of May 31, 2012 was not materially different from the prior day. Mr. Dubrow's first concern about Defendants' expert's report was, therefore, of no consequence.

Motion for Preliminary Injunction

2020 WL 4194510 (N.Y.Sup.)

> **Westlaw Query>>**
>
> To find more Motion for Preliminary Injunction filings on Westlaw: access New York Civil Trial Court Documents (from the Home page, click Trial Court Documents, then New York), click the Advanced Search link, select Motion for Preliminary Injunction, and click Search. Use the Jurisdiction filter on the left to narrow results to New York Trial Ct.

Supreme Court of New York,

New York County.

MEIDU ENERGY CORPORATION and MeiDu America, Inc., Plaintiffs,

v.

MC CREDIT FUND I LP, MC Credit I a LP, MC Credit II Fund LP, MC Credit Fund III, MC Credit Fund III-U, MC Credit Fund III, Tao Talents LLC, TPG Specialty Lending Inc., Arena Limited SPV LLC, Prudential Legacy, Insurance Company of New Jersey, the Prudential Insurance Company of America, Robert Warshauer, and Donald Ritter, Defendants,

MD AMERICA ENERGY HOLDINGS, INC., MD America Intermediate Holdings, LLC, MD America Holdings, LLC, MD America Energy, LLC, MD America Pipeline, LLC, and MD America Finance Corporation, Nominal Defendants.

No. 652519/2020.

June 24, 2020.

Plaintiff's Memorandum of Law in Support of Motion for Preliminary Injunction

Becker & Poliakoff, LLP, James J. Mahon, Paul H. Shur, Vincenzo Mogavero, Oliver Edwards VII, Samantha A. Lesser, 45 Broadway, 17th Floor, New York, New York 10006, (212) 599-3322, jmahon@beckerlawyers.com, for plaintiffs.

PRELIMINARY STATEMENT

Plaintiffs MeiDu Energy Corporation ("MeiDu China") and MeiDu America Inc. ("MeiDu America") (together, "Plaintiffs") respectfully submit this memorandum of law in support of their motion, by way of Order to Show Cause, for an Order:

(a) temporarily and preliminarily enjoining and restraining defendants MC Credit Fund I LP, MC Credit I A (Cayman Master) LP, MC Credit Fund II LP, MC Credit Fund III (Delaware) LP, MC Credit Fund III-U (Delaware) LP, MC Credit Fund III (Cayman Islands) LP, Tao Talents LLC, TPG Specialty Lending Inc., Arena Limited SPV LLC, Prudential Legacy Insurance Company of New Jersey, The Prudential Insurance Company of America (collectively, the "Lenders" and "Lender Entities"), Robert Warshauer and Donald Ritter (the "Lenders' Board") (together with the Lender Entities, "Defendants"), their agents and employees, and all other persons acting in concert with Defendants from taking any action, whether informal or formal, written or oral, in the place of a director, manager, shareholder, and/or member of any of the following entities: MD America Energy Holdings, Inc., MD America Intermediate Holdings, LLC, MD America Holdings, LLC, MD America Energy, LLC, MD America Pipeline, LLC, and MD America Finance Corporation (collectively, "MeiDu Subs" or "Nominal Defendants"); and,

(b) temporarily and preliminarily enjoining and restraining the Lenders' Board from taking any action as a purported manager or director of any of the MeiDu Subs, and in particular, pending the determination of this action, from selling, canceling, dissipating, transferring, encumbering, borrowing from or against, gifting and/or otherwise disposing of or destroying any property of the MeiDu Subs; and

(c) granting Plaintiffs such other and further relief as the Court deems appropriate.

This motion is critical to halting the Lender Entities' attempts to wrest control of the MeiDu Subs from MeiDu, their owner, and to prevent the irreparable harm inflicted by Lender Entities' irresponsible gutting of the MeiDu Subs, refusal to engage in reasonable negotiations for alternate financing, and active attacks on the value of MeiDu, as well as the Lenders' Board's continuing dereliction of their duties to the MeiDu Subs in favor of actions which would instead benefit the Lenders. Having engineered a technical default by manipulating pricing standards in the First Amendment to the Credit Agreement, the Lenders took advantage of the unprecedented hardships imposed on MeiDu by the COVID-19 epidemic to assert control of the MeiDu Subs in violation of Article 9 of the Uniform Commercial Code ("UCC"). Absent the Court's intervention, the Lenders and the Lenders' Board will accelerate the divestment of the MeiDu Subs operations, the personnel necessary to maintain their value as an ongoing oil-drilling concern, while simultaneously (on information and belief) acting to drain the capital of the MeiDu Subs.

STATEMENT OF FACTS

In the interest of judicial economy, the facts relevant to this motion are detailed in the accompanying Verified Complaint, and the supporting June 16, 2020 Affidavit of Haixiao Shao ("Shao Aff") and the emergency affidavit of James J. Mahon ("JJM Aff'). Unless otherwise indicated, all capitalized terms used herein shall have the meanings assigned to them in the Verified Complaint, Shao Aff, and JJM Aff.

ARGUMENT

CPLR § 6301 provides in relevant part, that

> A preliminary injunction may be granted in any action where it appears that defendant threatens or is about to do, or is doing or procuring or suffering to be done, an act in violation of plaintiff's rights respecting the subject of the action, and tending to render the judgment ineffectual, or in any action where the plaintiff has demanded and would be entitled to a judgment restraining the defendant from the commission or continuance of an act, which, if committed or continued during the pendency of the action, would produce injury to the plaintiff.

Under New York law, a preliminary injunction will be granted if the moving party demonstrates that: (1) it is likely to ultimately succeed on the merits of its claims; (2) it will suffer irreparable harm if the injunction is not granted; and (3) the equities, on balance, favor relief. *See Four Time Sq. Assoc., LLC v. Cigna Invs., Inc.*, 306 A.D.2d 4, 5 (1st Dep't 2003).

The principal objective of preliminary relief is to maintain the status quo pending the outcome of litigation between the parties. *See McLaughlin, Piven, Vogel, Inc. v. W.J. Nolan and Co.*, 114 A.D.2d 165 (2d Dep't 1986); Schlosser v. United Presbyt. *Home of Syosset, Inc.*, 56 A.D.2d 615 (2d Dep't 1977). Here, as explained below, any further usurpation of the management of the MeiDu Subs during the pendency of this action will disrupt the status quo.

Moreover, "[a] temporary restraining order may be granted where it appears that immediate and irreparable injury, loss or damage will result unless the defendant is restrained before the hearing can be had." CPLR § 6301. Plaintiff easily satisfies these standards.

I. *Plaintiff is Likely to Succeed on the Merits*

It is well settled that on a motion for preliminary injunctive relief, a plaintiff need only make a *prima facie* showing of a likelihood of success on the merits, and need not demonstrate certainty of success. *Parkmed Co. v. Pro-Life Counselling, Inc.*, 91 A.D.2d 551, 553 (1st Dep't 1982); *see also Terrell v. Terrell*, 279 A.D.2d 301, 303 (1st Dep't 2001) (evidence showing likelihood of success on the merits need not be conclusive); *Demartini v. Chatham Green, Inc.*, 169 A.D.2d 689 (1st Dep't 1991) (same). Here, Plaintiffs are likely to prevail on their claims for declaratory relief, conversion, a permanent injunction, breach of fiduciary duty, and set-off.

a. *Lenders Violated Article 9, Invalidating Their Attempt to Assume Control*

Succinctly put, Lenders' attempt to take over control of the Meidu Subs is violative of Article 9 of the UCC and the salutary goals it espouses.

It is well settled that under the UCC, any agreement that purports to waive debtor protections is invalid and violative of Article 9. UCC § 9-602. For example, in the case of *Haraway v. Burnett*, the parties entered into a purchase/security agreement where Haraway agreed to purchase from Burnett 1,000 shares of stock in Redwing Technical Systems, Inc. representing 100% of the stock issued by Redwing Technical in addition to patents for a total price of $35,000. *Haraway v. Burnett*, No. 02A01-9508-CH-00179, 1997 WL 563224 (Tenn. Ct. App. Sept. 8, 1997). As security, Haraway granted Burnett a security interest in the stock and patents and executed an irrevocable stock power, which in the event of default, assigned all of Haraway's interest in stock to Burnett. *Id.*

The *Haraway* court found that "a stock pledge agreement which purports to vest the stock in the secured creditor upon the debtor's default is invalid; such an agreement neither waives the debtor's rights under Article 9 nor terminates the debtor's rights of ownership in the stock." *Id.* Therefore, the stock power did not entitle Burnett to assume control of Redwing.

Similarly, courts have generally held that pre-default waiver of the right to redeem collateral is invalid. If there is no default at the time of the purported waiver, it is not binding on the debtor. *Data Sec., Inc. v. Plessman*, 1 Neb.App. 659 (1993). In the case of *Trimble*, the court found that a stock pledge agreement purportedly vesting the stock in the seller upon the buyer's default was prohibited under the common law and the Tennessee UCC because it was entered into before the default occurred. *Trimble v. Sonitrol of Memphis, Inc.*, 723 S.W.2d 633, 638-39 (Tenn. App. 1986); *see also Kellos v. Parker-Sharpe, Inc.*, 245 Ga. 130, 263 S.E.2d 138 (1980).

Here, just as in *Haraway* and *Trimble*, the MeiDu Subs entered into pledge agreements secured by 100% ownership interests in all the stock they owned; because of the vertical, sole-owner structure of the MeiDu Subs, they effectively pledged all stock in themselves. *See* Verified Complaint's Ex. B Pledge Agreement. However, the Pledge Agreement entitled the lender to exercise control as the outright owner in the event of default. *Id.* at § 7. Therefore, just as in *Haraway*, the Lenders' stock pledge agreement is invalid because it waives the debtor's rights under Article 9 and terminates their rights in ownership well before the default has occurred.

b. *The Lenders' Board Has Violated Their Fiduciary Duties*

To the extent, therefore, that the Lenders' Board exercised their purported authority, they breached their fiduciary duties to the shareholders of the MeiDu Subs by operating in the best interest of the Lenders and not in the best interest of Plaintiffs and the MeiDu Subs.

Under New York law, a director "is required to perform his or her dutiesin good faith with a degree of care which an ordinarily prudent person in a like position would use under similar circumstances." N.Y. Bus. Corp. Law § 717(a); *RSL Communications PLC v. Bildrici*, 649 F.Supp.2d 184, 209 (S.D.N.Y. 2009). This duty "carries with it certain fundamental fiduciary obligations to the corporation and its shareholders." *In Re Bear Sterns Litig.*, 23 Misc. 3d. 447, 870 N.Y.S. 2d 709, 739 (Sup.Ct.N.Y.Cnty. 2008); *see also Cohen v. Cocoline Products, Inc.*, 179 N.Y.s.2D 262 (N.Y. Special Term 1958); *Aronson v. Lewis*, 473 A.2d 805, 811 (Del. 1984). The core fiduciary duties are those of loyalty and due care, which "operate to benefit the corporation's owners, who stand to gain from the firm's success and also bear the risk of its potential financial failure." *RSL Communications*, 649 F.Supp.2d 184; *see In Re Bear Sterns Litig.*, 23 Misc. 3d 447. A lack of due care is evidenced by bad faith, which "may be shownwhere a fiduciary intentionally acts with a purpose other than that of advancing the best interests of the corporation." *In re Walt Disney Co. Derivative Litig.*, 906 A.2d 27 at 67 (Del. 2006).

Here, the Lenders' Board has violated their fiduciary duty of due care to the MeiDu Subs. Not only has the new board greatly reduced the MeiDu Subs' work force, but it also plans to further reduce its workforce in the next coming days. While it is in the best interest of the Lenders to cut costs, it is not in the best interest of the MeiDu Subs because when they begin to start operating at their usual capacity after COVID-19, they will be hampered by an extreme loss in human capital that will impair the operational ability moving forward. Further, because the auditors were not able to obtain the necessary information from the Lenders' Board, which has closed off all access to critical business records, MeiDu America's auditors had to issue a qualified opinion. Lastly, press releases in China triggered by the purported takeover of the Lenders' Board have caused the stock price to crater, which has put Meidu China at risk for being de-listed from the Shanghai Stock Exchange. As may be seen, the Lenders' Board has breached their fiduciary duty to Plaintiffs by acting in the best interest of the MeiDu Subs' creditors instead of their shareholders.

c. *Plaintiffs Are Entitled To A Permanent Injunction*

Even if the Lenders' Board had acted properly, the fact that they have retained the collateral, assumed management of the businesses, and have not made either (i) a commercially reasonable disposition under § 9-610 or (ii) opted for strict foreclosure under § 9-620, reflect a violation under UCC § 9-625, that has resulted and will continue to result in irreparably injury to MeiDu America. Therefore, an injunction is the proper remedy.

Article 9 of the UCC governs the enforcement of a creditor's security interest. After default, a secured party may either dispose of its collateral in a commercially reasonable manner or strictly foreclose on the collateral in satisfaction of the obligation. *See* UCC § 9-610; UCC § 9-620. A party's failure to comply with Article 9 will result in a panoply of remedies including money damages and judicial orders. UCC § 9-625.

i. *Strict Foreclosure*

As respects strict foreclosure, the debtor may consent to full satisfaction of its debt, but the remedy is only available if the debtor consents after it has defaulted. UCC § 9-620. After notification of the intent to strictly foreclose, the debtor has twenty days to object to the proposal. UCC 9-620(c)(2)(C); *In re CBGG Holdings*, LLC, 439 B.R. 551 (Bankr. S.D.N.Y. 2010). Here, the Creditor did not evidence any intent to strictly foreclose on the collateral before or after the default. Therefore, no attempts were made to strictly foreclose on the collateral in full or partial satisfaction of the obligation.

ii. *Disposition of Collateral*

If the creditor chooses to dispose of the collateral, "every aspect of the disposition, including the method, manner, time, place and other terms, must be commercially reasonable." UCC § 9-610(b). The determination whether the disposition is commercially reasonable is a case-by-case inquiry. *United States Fin. Servs. v. Young's Funeral* Home, Inc., 2010 Del. C.P. LEXIS 32, 2010 WL 3002063. Generally, courts have found that a delay in disposition that decreases the value of the collateral is not commercially reasonable. *Id.*

Here, just as in *Financial Services*, the Lenders have taken possession of the stock certificates as collateral and have failed to proceed to dispose of the collateral—conduct that is, by any measure, commercially unreasonable. Like a vehicle languishing in a junkyard, the company is being held hostage by the new board of directors and is being damaged by its reduction in work force and the pending delisting of its' parent from the Shanghai Stock Exchange. While the company is seeking to cut costs, the loss of human capital will cause the company substantial hardships in the long-term. Moreover, press releases have caused a precipitous decline in stock value. Therefore, the Lenders' failure to comply with the procedures of UCC has rendered its conduct commercially unreasonable.

iii. *Remedies—Injunctive Relief*

If a party fails to comply with Article 9 of the UCC, there are various remedies that may be pursued, such as a judicial order or monetary damages. UCC § 9-625; *see Rapillo v. CitiMortgage, Inc.*, 2018 WL 1175127, *8 2018 U S. Dist. LEXIS 35491 (E.D.N.Y. March 5, 2018); *Atlas MF Mezzanine Borrower, LLC v. Macquarie Tex. Loan Holder LLC*, 174 A.D.3d 150, 105 N.Y.S.3d 59 (1st Dept. 2019). In particular, "if it is established that a secured party is not proceeding in accordance with [Article 9], a court may order or restrain collection, enforcement, or disposition of collateral on appropriate terms and conditions." UCC § 9-625(a).

However, the availability of injunctive relief is dependent upon the status of the collateral at issue. *Atlas MF Mezzanine Borrower, LLC*, 105 N.Y.S.3d 59. Where, as here, the collateral has not yet been sold, the debtor may seek injunctive relief in addition to monetary damages at law. Id., see also *In re Enron Corp.*, 2005 WL 3873890, *10, 2005 Bankr. LEXIS 3469 (Bankr. S.D.N.Y. June 16, 2005) (finding that UCC § 9-625(a) is not applicable where the secured party has already disposed of the collateral). If the disposition of collateral has already occurred, the party may only pursue a remedy for money damages, "as the offending party is liable for damages in the amount of any loss caused by failure to comply with [Article 9]." UCC § 625(b); *See Atlas MF Mezzanine Borrower, LLC*, 105 N.Y.S.3d 59.

Here, a disposition of collateral has not occurred. Generally, "a secured creditor's transfer of collateral, such as stock, to the creditor's own name does not constitute a disposition under UCC § 9-504." *Haraway v. Burnett*, No. 02A01-9508-CH-00179, 1997 WL 563224 (Tenn. Ct. App., Sept. 8, 1997); *see Fletcher v. Cobuzzi*, 499 F.Supp. 694 (W.D.Pa. 1980). Since the collateral has not been sold, MeiDu is entitled to injunctive relief pursuant to UCC § 9-625(a).

II. *Plaintiff Will Suffer Immediate and Irrenarahle Harm Absent a Restraint*

Plaintiff will suffer irreparable harm if this Court declines to grant injunctive relief. Irreparable harm has been defined as "that which cannot be repaired, restored or adequately compensated in money, or where the compensation cannot be safely measured." *McLaughlin, Pive, Vogel v. Nolan & Co.*, 114 A.D.2d 165 (2nd Dep't 1986). "[A]n injunction should be granted if the activity complained of will cause irreparable injury to the party seeking such relief before a trial can be held to resolve the underlying controversy. In this context, irreparable injury means a continuing harm resulting in substantial prejudice caused by the acts sought to be restrained if permitted to continue ." *Chrysler Corp. v. Fedders Corp.*, 63 A.D.2d 567, 569 (1st Dep't 1978). As the Court of Appeals has explained, "where the injury is permanent in character, and the damages resulting therefrom continuous in their natures, and especially where, from the nature of and the act and the injury suffered, it is impossible, or difficult, to ascertain or determine the extent of the injury which may flow from a continuance of the wrong, an injunction is the proper remedy." *Poughkeepsie Gas Co. v. Citizens' Gas Co.*, 89 N.Y. 493, 497-498 (1882).

It is well-established that in struggles for control of closely held corporations, damages alone cannot compensate a Plaintiff for loss of the opportunity to derive a livelihood from their investment. *See generally, Street v. Vitti*, 685 F. Supp. 379, 384 (S.D.N.Y. 1988) [holding that monetary compensation would be inadequate to compensate plaintiffs for a violation of a shareholder's agreement which destroyed their voice in management]; *International Banknote Co. v. Muller*, 713 F. Supp. 612, 623 (S.D.N.Y. 1989) [in action seeking to enjoin enforcement of corporate bylaw limiting time period in which slates of proposed directors must be filed, the court held that frustrating shareholders in an attempt to obtain representation on board of directors constituted irreparable harm]; *see also, Davisv. Rondina*, 741 F. Supp.1115, 1125 (S.D.N.Y.1990).

The denial of bargained-for rights, without more has been held to constitute irreparable harm for purposes of obtaining preliminary injunctive relief where such rights are central to preserving an agreed-upon balance in corporate management. *See, Wisdom Imp. Sales Co., L.L.C. v. Labatt Brewing Co.*, 339 F.3d 101 (2d Cir. 2003); *United Acquisition Corp. v. Banque Paribas*, 631 F. Supp. 797, 805 (S.D.N.Y. 1985). Thus, Defendants actions easily satisfy the irreparable-harm standard.

III. *The Balancing of the Equities Tips Sharply in Plaintiffs Favor*

The balance of the equities favors injunctive relief where "it is apparent that if relief is granted, defendant will suffer no prejudice or inconvenience, while denial of such relief will cause plaintiff substantial and irreparable harm." *Konishi v. Por Kung Lin*, 88 A.D.2d 905 (2d Dep't 1982). That is the case here. Therefore, due to the Defendants failure to provide complete financial records for Plaintiffs to prepare their financial reports, the direct violations of Article 9 of the Uniform Commercial Code by wrongfully appointing an illegal board of directors and rebuffing attempts to refinance by ZG group in bad faith—there has been irreparable harm to Plaintiffs for which this Court, sitting in equity, may supply a remedy.

CONCLUSION

For all of these reasons, Plaintiffs respectfully requests that the temporary and preliminary injunctive relief requested be granted, together with such other and further relief as this Court deems just and proper.

Dated: New York, New York

June 16, 2020

BECKER & POLIAKOFF, LLP

Attorneys for Plaintiffs

By: */s/ James J. Mahon*

James J. Mahon

Paul H. Shur

Vincenzo Mogavero

Oliver Edwards VII

Samantha A. Lesser

45 Broadway, 17th Floor

New York, New York 10006

(212) 599-3322

imahon@beckerlawvers.com

Motion to Dismiss

2019 WL 3388815 (N.Y.Sup.)

Supreme Court of New York,

Kings County.

Joycelyn TAYLOR, Plaintiff,

v.

CHRISTIAN CULTURAL CENTER, INC. and Christian Cultural Center Community Development Corp., Defendants.

No. 514710/17.

July 16, 2019.

Memorandum in Support of Defendant's Motion to Dismiss

Jeffrey Samel & Partners, Trial Counsel to Claudia Lovas, Esq., Christian Cultural Center, Inc, 150 Broadway, Suite 1600, New York, New York 10038, (212) 587-9690, File No.: 55-0069, for defendant.

PLAINTIFF HAS NOT PROVED NOTICE

It is axiomatic that notice must be proved when suing in a "foreign substance" case. Here, the foreign substance was water and/or "wetness" on the floor. Plaintiff has offered no evidence of notice of the wet condition which caused her to fall.

Plaintiff testified that as she was exiting the Macedonia Room she slipped on a wet floor. She gave no description of the "wetness." She did not testify as to the amount or extent of the "wetness." She did not testify as to the area it covered. She only testified that she was caused to fall due to the combination of the plastic runner and the water.

Plaintiff alleges that the presence of water was foreseeable, as the Church was conducting Baptisms, and the Church was acutely aware that water could spill onto the floor. In fact, Defendant admitted that it was aware of the situation and made efforts to police the area. Nonetheless, there is no testimony as to how long the particular "wetness" that caused Plaintiff to fall existed. It may have been there for a second, a moment or an hour.

NOTICE MUST BE PROVED EVEN IN *SITUATIONS WHERE SPILLS ARE ANTICIPATED*

The mere expectation that water might spill on the floor does not vitiate the need to prove notice of the specific defect that caused the fall. The lead case, *Piacquadio v. Racine,* 84 NY2d 967, is directed on point. Its progeny is prodigious. It is indistinguishable from the case sub justice.

In *Piacquadio,* Plaintiff slipped on a spilled drink at a catering hall event. Knowing that spills were common, the Catering Hall had placed "non-skid" treading on the stairway, but had failed to maintain them. At the time of the accident. the steps were smooth.

The Appellate Division ruled in favor of Plaintiff, finding the Defendant catering hall negligent for failing to have non-skid treading on the steps, despite the fact that there was no proof that they had notice of the particular liquid which caused Plaintiff to fall.

The Court of Appeals reversed and dismissed the case. The holding now stands for the ubiquitous proposition that "a general awareness that a dangerous condition may be present is legally insufficient to constitute notice of the particular condition that caused plaintiff to fall," *Gordon v. Museum of Natural History,* 76 NY2d 836 general knowledge of debris piling up on the steps did not obviate the need to prove notice of the specific defect, *Wasserman v. New York City Transit Authority,* 267 AD2d 36, fact that surface flooring was slippery and became more slippery when wet did not obviate the need to prove notice of the specific defect that caused her to fall, *Madrid v. City of New York,* 42 NY2d 1039, *Bogart v. Woolworth Company,* 24 NY2d 936.

Moreover, as in the case herein, Plaintiff in *Piacquadio* argued that the material used in the flooring was inadequate. Plaintiff herein argues that the plastic runner with the striated groves was similarly inappropriate, and in combination with the water, caused the accident. The Court of Appeals in *Piacquadio* held that *even in the presence of inappropriate flooring materials,* notice of the specific defect must still be proved. Absent the water, Plaintiff would not have fallen.

Accordingly, based upon Plaintiffs failure to establish notice, the Complaint should be dismissed, see *Gloria v. MGM Emerald Enterprises,* 298 AD2d 355, patron slipped on dance floor known to be wet. Employment of "runner" to police the floor did not obviate need to prove notice of the specific spill that caused injury, citing *Piacquadio,* supra. *Gordon* supra, general awareness of garbage strewn in front of building not sufficient to prove notice, *Winecki v. West Seneca,* Post 8113, 227 AD2d 978, Plaintiff must prove notice of specific defect despite "negligent configuration of banquet room requiring patrons to carry drinks unreasonably far, *Monje v. Legman,* 192 AD2d 1133, *Anderson v. Klein Foods,* 139 AD2d 904, configuration of aisle partially blocking patron's view did not obviate the need to prove notice of the produce that had fallen on the floor, citing *Piacquadio* with approval.

Dated: New York, New York

June 21, 2019

Yours, etc.,

JEFFREY SAME & PARTNERS

By: <<signature>>

ROBERT G. SPEVACK, ESQ.

Trial Counsel to Claudia Lovas, Esq.

Attorneys for DEFENDANT

CHRISTIAN CULTURAL CENTER, INC

150 Broadway, Suite 1600

New York, New York 10038

(212) 587-9690

File No.: 55-0069

Table of Laws and Rules

McKINNEY'S CONSOLIDATED LAWS OF NEW YORK ANNOTATED—CIVIL PRACTICE LAW AND RULES—Continued

McKINNEY'S CONSOLIDATED LAWS OF NEW YORK ANNOTATED—CIVIL PRACTICE LAW AND RULES—Continued

McKINNEY'S CONSOLIDATED LAWS OF NEW YORK ANNOTATED—CIVIL PRACTICE LAW AND RULES—Continued

McKINNEY'S CONSOLIDATED LAWS OF NEW YORK ANNOTATED—CIVIL PRACTICE LAW AND RULES—Continued

McKINNEY'S CONSOLIDATED LAWS OF NEW YORK ANNOTATED—CIVIL PRACTICE LAW AND RULES—Continued

McKINNEY'S CONSOLIDATED LAWS OF NEW YORK ANNOTATED—CIVIL PRACTICE LAW AND RULES—Continued

McKINNEY'S CONSOLIDATED LAWS OF NEW YORK ANNOTATED—CIVIL PRACTICE LAW AND RULES—Continued

McKINNEY'S CONSOLIDATED LAWS OF NEW YORK ANNOTATED—CIVIL PRACTICE LAW AND RULES—Continued

McKINNEY'S CONSOLIDATED LAWS OF NEW YORK ANNOTATED—CIVIL RIGHTS LAW

McKINNEY'S CONSOLIDATED LAWS OF NEW YORK ANNOTATED—CORRECTION LAW

McKINNEY'S CONSOLIDATED LAWS OF NEW YORK ANNOTATED—COUNTY LAW

McKINNEY'S CONSOLIDATED LAWS OF NEW YORK ANNOTATED—DOMESTIC RELATIONS LAW

McKINNEY'S CONSOLIDATED LAWS OF NEW YORK ANNOTATED—EDUCATION LAW

McKINNEY'S CONSOLIDATED LAWS OF NEW YORK ANNOTATED—EXECUTIVE LAW

McKINNEY'S CONSOLIDATED LAWS OF NEW YORK ANNOTATED—GENERAL ASSOCIATIONS LAW

McKINNEY'S CONSOLIDATED LAWS OF NEW YORK ANNOTATED—GENERAL BUSINESS LAW

McKINNEY'S CONSOLIDATED LAWS OF NEW YORK ANNOTATED—GENERAL CONSTRUCTION LAW

McKINNEY'S CONSOLIDATED LAWS OF NEW YORK ANNOTATED—GENERAL CONSTRUCTION LAW—Continued

McKINNEY'S CONSOLIDATED LAWS OF NEW YORK ANNOTATED—GENERAL OBLIGATIONS LAW

McKINNEY'S CONSOLIDATED LAWS OF NEW YORK ANNOTATED—INSURANCE LAW

McKINNEY'S CONSOLIDATED LAWS OF NEW YORK ANNOTATED—JUDICIARY LAW

RULES OF PROFESSIONAL CONDUCT

McKINNEY'S CONSOLIDATED LAWS OF NEW YORK ANNOTATED—LABOR LAW

McKINNEY'S CONSOLIDATED LAWS OF NEW YORK ANNOTATED—LIMITED LIABILITY COMPANY LAW

McKINNEY'S CONSOLIDATED LAWS OF NEW YORK ANNOTATED—NOT-FOR-PROFIT CORPORATION LAW

McKINNEY'S CONSOLIDATED LAWS OF NEW YORK ANNOTATED—PARTNERSHIP LAW

McKINNEY'S CONSOLIDATED LAWS OF NEW YORK ANNOTATED—PUBLIC OFFICERS LAW

McKINNEY'S CONSOLIDATED LAWS OF NEW YORK ANNOTATED—REAL PROPERTY ACTIONS AND PROCEEDINGS LAW

McKINNEY'S CONSOLIDATED LAWS OF NEW YORK ANNOTATED—SOCIAL SERVICES LAW

McKINNEY'S NEW YORK RULES OF COURT—RULES OF THE CHIEF JUDGE

McKINNEY'S NEW YORK RULES OF COURT—RULES OF THE CHIEF ADMINISTRATOR OF THE COURTS

McKINNEY'S NEW YORK RULES OF COURT—RULES OF THE CHIEF ADMINISTRATOR OF THE COURTS—Continued

McKINNEY'S NEW YORK RULES OF COURT—UNIFORM RULES FOR THE NEW YORK STATE TRIAL COURTS

McKINNEY'S NEW YORK RULES OF COURT—UNIFORM RULES FOR THE NEW YORK STATE TRIAL COURTS—Continued

McKINNEY'S NEW YORK RULES OF COURT—UNIFORM RULES FOR THE NEW YORK STATE TRIAL COURTS—Continued

McKINNEY'S NEW YORK RULES OF COURT—UNIFORM RULES FOR THE NEW YORK STATE TRIAL COURTS—Continued

McKINNEY'S NEW YORK RULES OF COURT—UNIFORM RULES FOR THE NEW YORK STATE TRIAL COURTS—Continued

McKINNEY'S NEW YORK RULES OF COURT—FIRST JUDICIAL DISTRICT—NEW YORK COUNTY

McKINNEY'S NEW YORK RULES OF COURT—FIRST JUDICIAL DISTRICT—NEW YORK COUNTY—Continued

McKINNEY'S NEW YORK RULES OF COURT—SECOND JUDICIAL DISTRICT—KINGS COUNTY

McKINNEY'S NEW YORK RULES OF COURT—SECOND JUDICIAL DISTRICT—KINGS COUNTY—Continued

McKINNEY'S NEW YORK RULES OF COURT—ELEVENTH JUDICIAL DISTRICT—QUEENS COUNTY

McKINNEY'S NEW YORK RULES OF COURT—ELEVENTH JUDICIAL DISTRICT—QUEENS COUNTY—Continued

McKINNEY'S NEW YORK RULES OF COURT—TWELFTH JUDICIAL DISTRICT—BRONX COUNTY

McKINNEY'S NEW YORK RULES OF COURT—TWELFTH JUDICIAL DISTRICT—BRONX COUNTY—Continued

NEW YORK COURT ORDERS

NEW YORK COURT ORDERS—Continued

Table of Cases

A

B

C

D